THE

CYCLOPEDIC LAW DICTIONARY

COMPRISING

THE TERMS AND PHRASES OF AMERICAN JURISPRUDENCE, INCLUDING ANCIENT AND MODERN COMMON LAW, INTERNATIONAL LAW, AND NUMEROUS SELECT TITLES FROM THE CIVIL LAW, THE FRENCH AND THE SPANISH LAW, ETC., ETC.

WITH

AN EXHAUSTIVE COLLECTION OF LEGAL MAXIMS

By WALTER A. SHUMAKER

AND

GEORGE FOSTER LONGSDORF

SECOND EDITION

By JAMES C. CAHILL

THE LAWBOOK EXCHANGE, LTD.
Clark, New Jersey

ISBN 978-1-886363-85-4

Lawbook Exchange edition 2001, 2026

The quality of this reprint is equivalent to the quality of the original work.

THE LAWBOOK EXCHANGE, LTD.
33 Terminal Avenue
Clark, New Jersey 07066-1321

Please see our website for a selection of our other publications and fine facsimile reprints of classic works of legal history:
www.lawbookexchange.com

Library of Congress Cataloging-in-Publication Data

Shumaker, Walter A.
The cyclopedic law dictionary : comprising the terms and phrases of American jurisprudence, including ancient and modern common law, international law, and numerous select titles from the civil law... : with an exhaustive collection of legal maxims / by Walter A. Shumaker and George Foster Longsdorf.
p. cm.
Originally published: 2nd ed. / by James C. Cahill. Chicago : Callaghan and Co. 1922.
ISBN 1-886363-85-4 (cloth : acid-free paper)
1. Laws--United States--Dictionaries. 2. Legal maxims--United States. 3. Law--Dictionaries. 4. Legal maxims. I. Longsdorf, George Foster. II. Cahill, James Christopher, 1885- .
III. Title.
KF156.S54 1999 (IN PROCESS)
340'03--dc21 99-11404
CIP

Printed in the United States of America on acid-free paper

THE

CYCLOPEDIC LAW DICTIONARY

COMPRISING

THE TERMS AND PHRASES OF AMERICAN JURISPRUDENCE, INCLUDING ANCIENT AND MODERN COMMON LAW, INTERNATIONAL LAW, AND NUMEROUS SELECT TITLES FROM THE CIVIL LAW, THE FRENCH AND THE SPANISH LAW, ETC., ETC.

WITH

AN EXHAUSTIVE COLLECTION OF LEGAL MAXIMS

By WALTER A. SHUMAKER

AND

GEORGE FOSTER LONGSDORF

SECOND EDITION

By JAMES C. CAHILL

CHICAGO
CALLAGHAN AND COMPANY
1922

Preface to Second Edition

The present edition of the Cyclopedic Law Dictionary is necessitated by causes seldom occurring in legal publications. The popularity of the work has been such that the innumerable reprints required to supply the demand literally wore out the plates of the first edition. No greater tribute to the merit of the work is possible.

In this edition the earlier edition has been carefully revised and approximately two thousand additional words and definitions have been incorporated.

The selection of this additional material involved the careful examination of every source, including unpublished manuscripts, every effort being directed toward making the work as complete as possible and to increase its value not only to the student, but to the general practitioner as well.

A complete table of abbreviations of standard legal works of reference will be found in the appendix.

An expression of grateful appreciation is due to Mr. Basil Jones for his suggestions and assistance.

JAMES C. CAHILL.

Chicago: July, 1922.

Preface to First Edition

The purpose of this dictionary is to present, within one volume of convenient size, every legal definition or other appropriate matter which is requisite to any probable need of the student or the practitioner. It is believed that, on the one hand, both convenience and economy require that a work designed to be primarily a dictionary of the law should not exceed a single volume. On the other hand, no law dictionary is complete if it fails to define every word or phrase, ancient or modern, which the searcher may reasonably expect to find therein. Moreover, while a mere general definition is ordinarily sufficient as to foreign and obsolete terms, yet in respect to those terms of jurisprudence which in themselves describe recognized topics of the law, or are of present interest, or are in a formative state, a bare definition is of no particular value.

These topical terms the authors have endeavored to treat encyclopedically, avoiding the comprehensiveness of a treatise or commentary, but exhibiting all the elements of a subject in a complete and logical manner. They realize that only by those having legislative authority can definitions of such terms be framed which will be in every particular correct, and, like all writers dealing with modern law, they can do no more than present the result of a critical examination of the adjudged cases. In addition to this, it has been the aim to make the work exhaustive as a glossary, covering all matters within the research, not only of the practitioner and the student of the law, but of the lay student of ancient laws and history. The principal terms of the Saxon, Norman, and Old Scotch law, and of International and Feudal law, with many titles from other foreign systems, and the great variety of entire and fragmentary phrases in various languages to be met with in old law books and records, are defined and explained. Particular attention has been given to the Civil law, long explanatory articles being devoted to the more important Roman customs and institutions.

There has been considerable discussion in the past as to the propriety of including in a law dictionary terms and phrases no longer in current use. To the authors it seems that a dictionary which does not include such terms fulfills but a small part of its essential purpose. The law of the present day is rooted in the antiquities of the English common law, and that, in its turn, is inextricably interwoven with the law of the civilians. No question of law can be exhaustively investigated without bringing the searcher in contact with a multitude of legal terms and phrases now regarded as obsolete. The authors are unwilling to believe that the modern tendency toward codification and superficial case-learning has progressed so far that there is no longer a demand for the definitions and explanations which will enable the student to trace the doctrines of the law to their head-waters, and the practitioner to investigate particular questions with equal thoroughness.

A considerable collection of the terms of Spanish law has been inserted, in the belief that the annexation and close political relation to the United States of countries lately under Spanish rule will make a definition of such terms desirable to the practitioner.

The collection of maxims of the law is believed to be the most complete ever given in a single work. These maxims are placed throughout the book in their proper alphabetical order.

While it has been the effort to make the treatment as nearly exhaustive as possible within the realm of the terms of jurisprudence, this very exhaustiveness precludes any excursion beyond the scope of a law dictionary proper. The so-called "adjudged words and phrases," that is to say, the judicial interpretation of words having no distinctive legal meaning, but interpreted solely in the light of their context or use in particular connections, have been omitted, as have the ordinary terms of our language having no technical significance. The technical terms of commerce and of the stock exchange form a well-defined exception, and it is thought that the collection of these is the most extensive ever attempted in a work of this character.

The known and settled habits of the profession in associating particular principles with certain terms have been regarded, and therefore the definititons have, wherever practicable, been given under the specific words deemed most likely to suggest themselves to the searcher, instead of being grouped under some broad generic head. In the interest of space, some few exceptions to this rule have been made: (1) Where a word has several forms, it is defined under that best known or most correct, and from the others a cross-reference made to such definition. (2) Where the treatment of a general head necessarily includes the statement and definition of a number of terms included therein as elements or classes, cross-references are usually made to such general head for such definition, though in many cases a brief definition is given under the specific title, and a reference to the general title for further discussion.

As to the sources from which the matter herein contained was obtained, the basis of the work was the edition of 1867 of Bouvier's Law Dictionary, the original work of Mr. Bouvier, so far as it was consistent with the scope of the present dictionary, being so far classic as to be incapable of improvement, and presenting an element of authority which no new production could assume. To this, however, matter was added, more than doubling the number of terms defined, and developing, in the light of modern authorities, the discussion and definition of modern terms, which have been largely reformulated by the authors. The English dictionaries of Sweet, Wharton and Stroud have been principally resorted to for the explanation of distinctively English terms and institutions, while for the terms of ancient law, free use has been made of the dictionaries of Cowell, Spelman, and Jacob, and the treatises of Bracton, Britton, Viner, Coke, Littleton, Bacon, Blackstone, Chitty, Stephen, and Maine, as well as the American classics of Story, Greenleaf and Kent.

The terms of the civil law are mainly derived from the Novels, Digest, Institutes and Code of Justinian, the Lexicon of Calvin and the treatises of Mackeldey, Heineccius, and Pothier. The scholarly work of Mr. Burrill has been of great assistance. In formulating the definitions of modern terms, reference has always been had to the standard text book dealing with the subject, and the number of these is too great for enumeration, due credit being given in the body of the work for all definitions derived from such sources.

The more modern dictionaries of Anderson, Abbott, Black, and Rapalje & Lawrence have been used for reference and comparison.

The materials collected would have made two volumes of the size of the present work, but by diligent revision and condensation, it is believed that all that was useful and within its scope has been preserved.

WALTER A. SHUMAKER.
GEORGE FOSTER LONGSDORF.

St. Paul, Minn., November 25, 1901.

ABBREVIATIONS

OF THE

Less-Known and Ancient Books Referred to in This Work

A complete table of abbreviations of legal reference works will be found in the appendix.

Abbott. Abbott's Law Dictionary (1879).
Adams, Rom. Ant. Adams' Roman Antiquities.
Ainsworth, Lex. Ainsworth's Lat.-Eng. Dictionary (1837).
Arg. Fr. Merc. Law. Argyle's French Mercantile Law.
Artic. Cleri. Articuli Cleri.
Artic. sup. Chart. Articuli super Chartas.
Assis. de Jerus. Assises de Jerusalem.
Aul. Gell. Noct. Att. Auli Gellii Noctes Atticae.
Ayliffe, Pand. Ayliffe's Pandect.
Ayliffe, Par. Ayliffe's Parergon.
Azuni, Mar. Law. Azuni's Maritime Law.

Bac. Abr. Bacon's Abridgment.
Bac. Max. Bacon's Maxims.
Bac. Read. Uses. Bacon's Reading on the Statute of Uses.
Barr. Obs. St. Barrington's Observations on the Statutes.
Beames, Glanv. Beames' Glanville.
Beawes, Lex Merc. Beawes' Lex Mercatoria.
Bell, Comm. Bell's Commentaries on the Law of Scotland.
Bell, Dict. Bell's Dictionary of the Law of Scotland.
Ben. Adm. Prac. Benedict's Admiralty Practice.
Benl. Benloe's Reports.
Benth. Jud. Ev. Bentham's Rationale of Judicial Evidence.
Biret, Vocab. Biret's Vocabulaire des Cinq Codes (1862).
Bl. Comm. Blackstone's Commentaries.
Blount. Blount's Nomo Lexicon.
Bohun, Curs. Canc. Bohun's Cursus Cancellariae.
Bohun, Inst. Leg. Bohun's Institutio Legalis.
Bonnetti, Ital. Dict. Bonnetti's Italian Dictionary.
Bonnier, E. des Preuves. Bonnier's E. Traite des Preuves (1852).
Boote, Hist. Boote's Historical Treatise of a Suit at Law.
Bouch. Inst. Boucher's Institutes au Droit Maritime.
Boul. P. Dr. Com. Boulay-Paty Droit Commun.
Bouv. Inst. Bouvier's Institutes of American Law.
Bracton. Bracton, de Legibus et Consuetudinibus Angliae.
Branch, Princ. Branch's Principia Legis et Aequitatis.
Brande. Brande's Dictionary of Science, etc.
Brissonius. Brissonius de Verborum Significatione.
Britt. Noveau Dictionaire Civil et Canonique de Droit et de Pratique.
Brooke, Abr. Brooke's Abridgment.
Broom, Leg. Max. Broom's Legal Maxims.
Brown. Brown's Law Dictionary and Institute (1874).
Burge, Col. & For. Law. Burge on Colonial and Foreign Law.
Burn, Ecc. Law. Burn's Ecclesiastical Law.
Burr. Sett. Cas. Burrow's Settlement Cases.
Butler, Co. Litt. Butler's Notes to Coke on Littleton.
Butler, Hor. Jur. Butler's Horae Juridicae.
Bynk. Obs. Jur. Rom. Bynkershoek's Observationum Juris Roman Libri.
Bynk. Quaest. Jur. Pub. Bynkershoek's Quaestiones Juris Publici.

Calv. Lex. Calvini Lexicon Juridicum.
Cas. temp. Hardw. Cases tempore Hardwicke.
Cas. temp. Lee. Cases tempore Lee (Eng. Ecc.).
Cas. temp. Talb. Cases tempore Talbot.
Cassiod. Var. Cassiodori Variarum.
Chart. Foresta. Charta de Foresta.
Clerke, Prax. Clerke's Praxis Curiae Admiralitatis.
Co. Entr. Coke's Entries.
Co. Litt. Coke on Littleton.
Code. Codex Justiniani.
Code Civ. Code Civil.
Code Theodos. Codex Theodosianus.
Colq. Civ. Law. Colquhoun on Roman Civil Law.
Comyn. Comyn's Reports.
Comyn, Dig. Comyn's Digest.
Conf. Chart. Confirmatio Chartarum.
Consol. del Mare. Consolato del Mare.
Cooper, Just. Inst. Cooper's Justinian's Institutes.
Corp. Jur. Can. Corpus Juris Canonici.
Corp. Jur. Civ. Corpus Juris Civilis.
Corp. Jus. Canon. Corpus Juris Canonique.
Cowell. Cowell's Interpreter.
Cruise, Dig. Cruise's Digest.

Dalloz. Dalloz, Dictionaire General et Raisonne de Legislation (1835).
Dane, Abr. Dane's Abridgment.
Decret. Childeb. ad L. Salic. Decreta Childeberti ad Legem Salicam.

Dial. de Scacc. Dialogus de Scaccario.
Dig. Digestum or Digesta. The Digest or Digests of Justinian.
Diss. ad Flet. Selden's Dissertatio ad Fletam.
Doct. and Stud. Doctor and Student.
Doct. Plac. Doctrina Placitandi.
Domat, Civ. Law. Domat's Civil Law.
Domat, Dr. Pub. Domat's Droit Publique.
Domat, Liv. Prel. Domat's Livres du Droit Public.
Dufresne. Dufresne's Glossary.
Dugd. Orig. Jur. Dugdale's Origines Juridiciales.
Durand. Spec. Jur. Durandi Speculum Juris.

Emerig. Tr. des Assur. Emerigon Traite des Assurances.
Ersk. Princ. Erskine's Principles of the Law of Scotland.
Esp. N. P. Espinasse's Nisi Prius Reports.
Esprit des Lois. Montesquieu's Spirit of Laws.

Ferriere, Dict. de Jur. Ferriere's Dictionary of Jurisprudence.
Feud. Lib. Feudorum Libri or Liber.
Fitzh. Nat. Brev. Fitzherbert's Natura Brevium.
Fleta. Fleta, seu Commentarius Juris Anglici.
Fleury, Hist. Fleury's History of the Origin of French Laws (1724).
Flor. Wigorn. Florentius Wigornensis, Florence of Worcester.
Foelix, Droit Int. Princ. Foelix, Droit International Prive.
Formul. Solen. Formulae Solemnes.
Fortesc. de L. L. Angl. Fortescue de Laudibus Legum Angliae.
Francis, Max. Francis' Maxims.

Gaius, Inst. Gaius' Institutes.
Gibb. Rom. Emp. Gibbon's Decline and Fall of the Roman Empire.
Gibs. Code. Gibson's Codex.
Gilb. For. Rom. Gilbert's Forum Romanum.
Glanv. Glanville, de Legibus et Consuetudinibus Regni Angliae.
Godolph. Ecc. Law. Godolphin's Ecclesiastical Law.
Godolph. Orph. Leg. Godolphin's Orphan's Legacy.
Grand Coust. Norm. Grand Coustumier of Normandy.
Greg. Turon. Gregory of Tours.
Grot. de Aequit. Grotius de Aequitate.
Grotius de Jure Belli. Grotius de Jure Belli ac Pacis.
Guyot. Inst. Feod. Guyot's Institutes Feodales.

Halifax, Anal. Halifax' Analysis of the Roman Civil Law.
Halk. Tech. Terms. Halkerston's Technical Terms of the Law.
Hargr. Co. Litt. Hargrave's Notes to Coke on Littleton.
Heath, Max. Heath's Maxims.
Heinec. Elem. Jur. Camb. Heineccii Elementa Juris Cambialis.
Heinec. Elem. Jur. Civ. Heineccii Elementa Juris Civilis.
Hincmar. Epist. Hincmari Epistolae.
Holthouse. Holthouse's Law Dictionary.
Hotom. in Verb. Feud. Hotomannus de Verbis Feudalibus.
Houard, Ang. Sax. Laws. Houard's Anglo-Saxon Laws.
Hov. Ann. Hoveden's Annals.
How. St. Tr. Howell's State Trials.
Hub. Prael. Jur. Civ. Huberi Praelectiones Juris Civilis.
Hugo, Hist. Dr. Rom. Hugo's History Druit Romain.

Ingulph. Hist. Croyl. Ingulphi Historia Croylandiae.
Inst. Institutes of Justinian.
Inst. Institutes of Lord Coke.
Inst. Cler. Instructor Clericalis.
Irving, Civ. Law. Irving's Civil Law.

Jacob. Jacob's Law Dictionary.
Jornand. de Reb. Get. Jornandes de Rebus Geticis.
Jul. Frontin. Julius Frontinus.

Kaufm. Mackeld. Civ. Law. Kaufmann's Edition of Mackeldey's Civil Law.
Kelham. Kelham's Norman Dictionary.
Kennett. Kennett's Glossary.
Kennett, Par. Ant. Kennett's Parochial Antiquities.
Kitch. Cts. Kitchin on Courts.
Kluber, Dr. des Gens. Kluber's Droit des Gens.

L. Alem. Law of the Alemanni.
L. Baiwar. or *Boior.* Law of the Bavarians.
L. Ripuar. Law of the Ripuarians.
L. Salic. Salic Law.
Law Fr. Dict. Law French Dictionary.
Law Lat. Dict. Law Latin Dictionary.
LL. Aluredi. Laws of Alfred.
LL. Athelst. Laws of Athelstan.
LL. Burgund. Laws of the Burgundians.
LL. Canuti R. Laws of King Canute.
LL. Edw. Conf. Laws of Edward the Confessor.
LL. Gul. Conq. Laws of William the Conqueror.
LL. Hen. I. Laws of Henry I.
LL. Inae. Laws of Ina.
LL. Longobard. Laws of the Lombards.
LL. Malcolm. R. Scott. Laws of Malcolm, King of Scotland.
LL. Neapolit. Laws of Naples.
LL. Wisegotho. Laws of the Visigoths.
LL. Wm. Noth. Laws of William the Bastard.
Lamb. Archaion. Lambard's Archaionomia.
Lamb. Eiren. Lambard's Eirenarcha.
Lamb. Explic. Lambard's Explication.
Las Partidas. Las Siete Partidas.
Lec. Elm. Lecon's Elementaires du Droit Civile.
Lib. Feud. Libri Feudorum; the Books of Feuds.
Lib. Nig. Scacc. Liber Niger Scaccarii; Black Book of the Exchequer.
Lib. Rames. Liber Ramesiensis; Book of Ramsey.

Lib. Rub. Scacc. Liber Ruber Scaccarii; Red Book of the Exchequer.
Lieber, Civ. Lib. Lieber's Civil Liberty.
Litt. Littleton's Tenures; Littleton's Reports.
Locc. de Jur. Mar. Loccenius de Jure Maritimo.
Lyndw. Prov. Lyndwode's Provinciale.

Mackeld. Civ. Law. Mackeldey's Civil Law.
Mad. Form. Angl. Madox' Formulare Anglicanum.
Mad. Hist. Exch. Madox' History of the Exchequer.
Magna Chart. or Cart. Magna Charta, or Carta.
Magna Rot. Pip. Magnus Rotulus Pipae; Great Roll of the Pipe.
Manw. For. Law. Manwood's Forest Law.
Mascard. de Prob. Mascardus de Probationibus.
Merlin, Quest. de Droit. Merlin's Questions de Droit qui se Presentent le Plus Frequemment Dans les Tribunaux (1819).
Merlin, Repert. Merlin's Repertoire.
Meyer, des Inst. Judiciares. Meyer, des Institutiones Judiciares.
Mirr. Mirror of Justices.
Molloy de Jur. Mar. Molloy de Jure Maritimo.
Mon. Angl. Monasticon Anglicanum.
Mozley & W. Mozley & Whitely's Law Dictionary (Eng.).
Murat. Antiq. Med. Aevi. Muratori's Antiquitates Medii Aevi.

Nov. Novellae, Novels.
Nov. Recop. Novisima Recopilacion.
Noy, Max. Noy's Maxims.

Old Nat. Brev. Old Natura Brevium.
Onuphr. de Interp. Voc. Eccles. Onuphrius de Interpretatione Vocum Ecclesiae.
Ord. Mar. Ordonnance de la Marine.
Ort. Hist. Ortolan's History of the Roman Law.
Ort. Inst. Ortolan's Institute de Justinian.
Ought. Oughton's Ordo Judiciorum.

Paillet, Dr. Pub. Paillet's Manuel de Droit Francais.
Palg. Rise, etc. Palgrave's Rise and Progress of the English Commonwealth.
Par. Ant. Parochial Antiquities.
Pardessus, Dr. Com. Pardessus' Cours de Droit Commercial.
Petron. Satyric. Petronius' (Titus) Arbiter, Satyricon, etc.
Pitc. Cr. Tr. Pitcairn's (Scotch) Criminal Trials.
Pitisc. Lex. Pitisci's Lexicon.
Plac. Abbrev. Placitorum Abbreviatio.
Plowd. Plowden's Commentaries and Reports.
Poth. Pothier (De Change, De Rente, Obligationes, De la Procedure Civil, De la Procedure Criminelle, Des Fiefs, De Pandectae).
Puffendorf. Puffendorf's Law of Nature.

Quon. Attach. Quoniam Attachiamenta.

Rapalje & L. Rapalje & Lawrence's Law Dictionary.
Reeve, Hist. Eng. Law. Reeve's History of the English Law.
Reg. Brev. Registrum Brevium.
Reg. Jud. Registrum Judiciale.
Reg. Maj. Regiam Majestatem.
Reg. Orig. Registrum Originale.
Rocc. de Nav. et Nau. Roccus de Navibus et Naulo.
Rog. Hov. Roger de Hovenden, Chronica.
Rolle. Abr. Rolle's Abridgment.
Rot. Claus. Rotuli Clausi; Close Rolls.
Rot. Parl. Rotuli Parliamenti; Parliament Rolls.
Rot. Pat. Rotuli Patentes; Patent Rolls.

Santerna de Ass. Santerna de Assecurationibus et Sponsionibus Mercatorum.
Savigny, Hist. Rom. Law. Savigny's History of the Roman Law.
Savigny, System. Savigny's System des Leutigen Romischen Rechts.
Schmidt, Civ. Law. Schmidt's Civil Law of Spain and Mexico.
Seld. Mare Claus. Selden's Mare Clausum.
Seld. Tit. Hon. Selden's Titles of Honor.
Shep. Touch. Sheppard's Touchstone.
Skene de Verb. Sign. Skene de Verborum Significatione.
Spelman. Spelman's Glossary.
St. Gloc. Statute of Glocester.
St. Marlb. Statute of Marlbridge.
St. Mert. Statute of Merton.
St. Mod. Lev. Fin. Statute Modus Levandi Fines.
Staundf. Pl. Cor. Staundford's Placita Coronae.
Staundf. Prerog. Staundford's Exposition of the King's Prerogative.
Style, Pr. Reg. Style's Practical Register.

Termes de la Ley. Termes de la Ley (1685).
Tomlins. Tomlins' Law Dictionary.
Trye, Jus Filiz. Trye's Jus Filizarii.

Vicat. Vicat's Vocabularium Juris Utriusque ex Variis Ante Editis.
Viner, Abr. Viner's Abridgment.
Vinn. ad Inst. or *Vinnius.* Vinnius' Commentary on the Institutes of Justinian.

West, Symb. West's Symboleography.
Wharton. Wharton's Law Lexicon.
Whishaw. Whishaw's Law Dictionary.
Wooddesson, Lect. Wooddesson's Lecture.

Y. B. Year Book.

Cyclopedic Law Dictionary

A

A.

——**In Latin Phrases.** A preposition, denoting from, by, in, on, of, at.

——**In French Phrases.** A preposition, denoting of, at, to, for, in, with.

——**In Citation of Reported Decisions.** Used for *adversus* (*versus*) in some law reports. See Abb. Prac. (N. Y.; O. S.)

——**In Notes.** May be regarded as synonymous with "at." Belford v. Beatty, 145 Ill. 418.

——**In Roman Criminal Law.** The judges were furnished with small tables covered with wax, and each one inscribed on it the initial letter of his vote,—"A." (the initial letter of *absolvo*) when he voted to absolve the party on trial; "C." (the initial letter of *condemno*) when he was for condemnation; and "N. L." (the initial letters of *non liquet*) when the matter did not appear clearly, and he desired a new argument.

——**In Roman Elections.** It was used in elections as the initial letter of *antiquo* (for the old law), being a vote against the proposed law; an affirmative vote being indicated by "U. R." (*ut rogas*, as you propose).

——**Among the Puritans.** An "A" of red cloth was hung upon the dress of a convicted adulteress.

A CANCELLIS (Law Lat.) A chancellor. See "Chancellor."

A COELO USQUE AD CENTRUM (Lat.) From the heavens to the center of the earth.

A COMMUNI OBSERVANTIA NON EST recedendum. There should be no departure from common observance (or usage). Co. Litt. 186; Wingate, Max. 203; 2 Coke, 74.

A CONSILIIS (Lat. *consilium*, advice). A counsellor. The term is used in the civil law by some writers instead of *a responsis.* Spelman, voc. "Apocrisiarius."

A DATU, or **A DATO** (Law Lat.) From the date. 2 Salk. 413; Cro. Jac. 135.

——**A Die Datus.** From the day of the date. 2 Salk. 413; 2 Crabb. Real Prop. p. 248, § 1301; 1 Ld. Raym. 84, 480; 2 Ld. Raym. 1242.

A DIGNIORI FIERI DEBET DENOMINatio et resolutio. The denomination and explanation of a person or thing ought to be derived from the more worthy. Wingate, Max. 265; Fleta, lib. 4, c. 10, § 12.

A FORFAIT ET SANS GARANTIE (Fr.) A phrase used in the indorsement of negotiable instruments; substantially the same as "without recourse."

A FORTIORI. By (or from) the stronger reason. Applied to the argument that, because of the concession or establishment of a given proposition, another included in it is by the greater reason true.

A GRATIA. By grace; not of right. Also written *ex gratia.*

A LATERE (Lat. *latus*, side).

——**In Respect to Property Rights.** (1) Collateral. Used in this sense in speaking of the succession to property. Bracton, 20b, 62b. (2) Without right. Bracton, 42b.

——**In Ecclesiastical Law.** Apostolic. A legate *a latere* is one having full powers to represent the pope as if he were present. Du Cange; 4 Bl. Comm. 306.

A LIBELLIS (Law Lat.) An officer who had charge of the *libelli* or petitions addressed to the sovereign. Calv. Lex.

A name sometimes given to a chancellor (*cancellarius*) in the early history of that office. Spelman, voc. "Cancellarius." See "Chancellor."

A L'IMPOSSIBLE NUL N'EST TENU. No one is bound to do what is impossible.

A MANIBUS (Law Lat.) An officer who wrote for the emperor; one whose hand (*manus*) was used for writing; an amanuensis. Calv. Lex.

A ME (Lat. *ego*, I). A term denoting, in the feudal law, direct tenure of the superior lord. 2 Bell, H. L. Sc. 133.

To withhold *a me* (from me) is to obtain possession of my property unjustly. Calv. Lex.

To pay *a me*, is to pay from my money.

A MENSA ET THORO. See "Divorce."

A NON POSSE AD NON ESSE SEQUITUR argumentum necessarie negative licet non affirmative. From impossibility to nonexistence, the inference follows necessarily in the negative, though not in the affirmative. Hob. 336b.

A PIRATIS AUT LATRONIBUS CAPTI liberi permanent. Those captured by pirates or robbers remain free. Dig. 49. 15. 19. 2; Grotius de Jure Belli, lib. 3, c. 3. § 1.

A PIRATIS ET LATRONIBUS CAPTA dominium non mutant. Things captured by pirates and robbers do not change ownership. 1 Kent, Comm. 108, 184; 2 Wooddeson, Lect. 258, 259.

A POSTERIORI (Lat. by the later reason). In logic. An argument proceeding from effects to causes.

A PRENDRE (Fr. to take, to seize). Rightfully taken from the soil. 5 Adol. & E. 764; Nev. & P. 172; 4 Pick. (Mass.) 145. See "Profit a Prendre."

A PRIORI (Lat. by the prior reason). In logic. An argument proceding from causes to effects.

A QUO (Lat.) From which.

——**Terminus a Quo.** The point from which distance is reckoned.

——**Court a Quo.** The court from which a cause is removed.

——**Judge a Quo.** The judge of such court.

——**Ad Quem.** To which; the correlative.

A RENDRE (Fr. to render, to yield). Which are to be paid or yielded. *Profits a rendre* comprehend rents and services. Hammond, N. P. 192.

A RESCRIPTIS VALET ARGUMENTUM. An argument from rescripts (*i. e.*, original writs in the register) is valid.

A RESPONSIS (Law Lat.) In ecclesiastical law. One whose office it was to give or convey answers; otherwise termed *responsalis* and *apocrisiarius*. One who, being consulted on ecclesiastical matters gave answers, counsel, or advice; otherwise termed *a consiliis*. Spelman, voc. "Apocrisiarius."

A RETRO (Lat.) In arrear. Fleta, lib. 2, c. 55, § 2.

A RUBRO AD NIGRUM (Lat. from red to black). As a rule of interpretation, to refer from the (red) title or rubric to the (black) body of the statute. It was anciently the custom to print statutes in this manner. Ersk. Inst. 1. 1. 49.

A SUMMO REMEDIO AD INFERIOREM actionem non habetur regressus neque auxilium. From the highest remedy to an inferior action there is no return or assistance. Fleta. lib. 6, c. 1; Bracton, 104a, 112b; 3 Sharswood, Bl. Comm. 193, 194.

A TEMPORE CUJUS CONTRARII MEmoria non existet. From time of which memory to the contrary does not exist.

A TERME (Law Fr.) For a term.

——**A Terme de sa Vie.** For the term of his life. Y. B. T. 1 Edw. II. 16; Y. B. M. 3 Edw. II. 55, 57.

——**A Terme Que Passe Est.** For a term which is past. Y. B. M. 4 Edw. III. 59.

A TORT (Law Fr.) Of or by wrong; wrongfully. *De ses avers a tort pris*, of his beasts wrongfully taken. Y. B. M. 3 Hen. VI. 20.

A TOUT LA COMMUNE D'ENGLEterre. To all the people of England. St. Articuli sup. Chartas, c. 1.

A VERBIS LEGIS NON EST RECEDENdum. From the words of the law there should be no departure. Broom, Leg. Max. (3d London Ed.) 555; Wingate, Max. 25; 5 Coke, 119.

A VINCULO MATRIMONII. See "Divorce."

AB. In Latin phrases. A preposition having the same significance as "A" (*q. v.*) "A" is used before words beginning with consonants, and "Ab" before those beginning with vowels.

AB ABUSU AD USUM NON VALET consequentia. A conclusion as to the use of a thing from its abuse is invalid. Broom, Leg. Max. 17.

AB ACTIS (Lat. *actus*, an act). A notary; one who takes down words as they are spoken; a name anciently applied to the chancellor. Du Cange, "Acta"; Spelman, voc. "Cancellarius." See "Chancellor."

A reporter who took down the decisions or *acta* of the court as they were given.

AB AGENDO. Disabled; unable to act.

AB ANTE (Lat. *ante*, before). In advance.

AB ANTECEDENTE (Lat. *antecedens*). Beforehand. 5 Maule & S. 110.

AB ANTIQUO (Lat.) Of old.

AB ASSUETIS NON FIT INJURIA. No injury is done by things long acquiesced in. Jenk. Cent. Cas. Introd. viii.

AB EPISTOLIS (Lat.) An officer having charge of the correspondence (*epistolae*) of his superior or sovereign; a secretary. Calv. Lex.

AB EXTRA (Lat. *extra*, beyond, without). From without. 14 Mass. 151.

AB INCONVENIENTI (Lat. *inconveniens*). From hardship; from what is inconvenient. An argument *ab inconvenienti* is an argument drawn from the hardship of the case.

AB INITIO (Lat. *initium*, beginning). From the beginning; entirely; as to all the acts done; in the inception. An estate may be said to be good, an agreement to be void, an act to be unlawful, a trespass to have existed, *ab initio.* Plowd. 6a; 11 East, 395; 10 Johns. (N. Y.) 253, 369; 1 Bl. Comm. 440.

Before. Contrasted in this sense with *ex post facto* (2 Bl. Comm. 308), or with *postea* (Calv. Lex. voc. "Initium").

AB INITIO MUNDI (Lat.) From the beginning of the world.

AB INTESTAT. Intestate. 2 Lower Can. 219.

AB INTESTATO (Lat. *testatus*, having made a will). From an intestate. Used both in the common and civil law to denote an inheritance derived from an ancestor who died without making a will. 2 Bl. Comm. 490; Story, Confl. Laws, 480.

AB INVITO (Lat. *invitum*). Unwillingly See "In Invitum."

AB IRATO (Lat. *iratus*, **an angry man**). By one who is angry. A devise or gift made by a man adversely to the interests of his heirs, on account of anger or hatred against them, is said to be made *ab irato*. A suit to set aside such a will is called an action *ab irato*. Merlin, Repert.

AB OLIM (Law Lat.) Of old. 3 Bl. Comm. 96.

ABACTOR (Lat. *ab* and *agere*, to lead away). One who stole cattle in herds. Jacob. *Abigeus* (*q. v.*) was the term more commonly used to denote such an offender.

ABADENGO. In Spanish law. Lands, towns, and villages belonging to an abbot, and under his jurisdiction. All lands belonging to ecclesiastical corporations, and as such exempt from taxation. Escriche, Dic. Raz. Lands of this kind were usually held in mortmain, and hence a law was enacted declaring that no land liable to taxation could be given to ecclesiastical institutions "*ningun realengo non pase a abadengo*," which is repeatedly insisted on.

ABALIENATIO (Lat. *alienatio*). The most complete method of transferring lands, used among the Romans. It could take place only between Roman citizens. Calv. Lex.

ABANDONEE. A party to whom a right or property is abandoned or relinquished by another. Applied to the insurers of vessels and cargoes. Lord Ellenborough, C. J., 5 Maule & S. 82; Abbott, J., Id. 87; Holroyd, J., Id. 89.

ABANDONMENT. Relinquishment; surrender; desertion; waiver.

——**Of Property.** The relinquishment of property or right with intent not to reclaim the same. It implies a relinquishment to the public generally, or to the next comer; a surrender to a particular person not being an abandonment. 11 Cal. 363. To constitute an abandonment there must be (1) an intent to abandon (21 Cal. 291; 49 Minn. 148; 49 N. Y. 346), and (2) an unequivocal act of abandonment (77 N. C. 186; 42 Conn. 377; 116 Mo. 123). Mere nonuser is not sufficient (61 Mo. 178; 15 N. H. 412); but abandonment may be presumed from long-continued nonuser (43 Pa. St. 427; 34 Me. 394).

——**Of Invention.** Either a relinquishing of a contemplated invention before it is perfected, or a permitting of the use of an invention by the public, constitutes an abandonment of the invention to the public, and prevents the inventor from enforcing any exclusive claim to the same. 4 Fish. Pat. Cas. (U. S.) 300.

——**Of Duties.** The willful and unauthorized desertion or forsaking of a duty, as a contract or a service, or of a person as to whom the abandoner is charged with a duty, as of a child by its parents, or of a wife by her husband. In case of abandonment of domestic relations, an intent to cause a permanent separation is necessary. See "Desertion."

In connection with statutes punishing abandonment of wife or family it is synonymous with "desert." Virtue v. People, 122 Ill. App. 224.

——**To Underwriters.** The right of an insured, who has suffered a loss, to relinquish the residue to the underwriters, and claim for a total loss, though the insured property is capable of recovery and repair. This right is confined to marine insurance, unless specially given by the policy. May, Ins. § 421.

——**For Torts.** The ancient right of the owner of an animal or of a slave which had committed an injury for which the owner was civilly liable to surrender it to the injured person in satisfaction. The doctrine has been applied to vessels, and authorizes the owner to surrender the vessel in satisfaction of a debt contracted by the master. By Rev. St. U. S. § 4285, the right to surrender a vessel and exonerate the owner from personal liability was extended to damages by collision.

ABANDUN, or ABANDUM. Anything sequestered, proscribed, or abandoned. Abandon, *i. e.*, *in bannum res missa*, a thing banned or denounced as forfeited or lost; whence to abandon, desert, or forsake, as lost and gone. Cowell. Pasquier thinks it a coalition of *a ban donner*, to give up to a prescription, in which sense it signifies the ban of the empire. Wharton.

ABARNARE (Lat.) To discover and disclose to a magistrate any secret crime. Leges Canuti, c. 1.

ABATAMENTUM (Lat. *abatare*). An entry by interposition. Co. Litt. 277. An abatement. Yelv. 151.

ABATARE. To abate. Yelv. 151.

ABATEMENT (Fr. *abattre*, Law Fr. *abater*, signifying to throw down).

——**In Practice.** A suspension of all proceedings in a suit, from the want of proper parties capable of proceding therein, as on the death of a party pending the suit. 2 Paige (N. Y.) 211.

In modern practice the term signifies generally the suspension of a suit by any matter arising after its commencement.

Abatement in chancery differs from an abatement at law in this: That in the latter the action is entirely dead, and cannot be revived in the absence of statute (3 Bl. Comm. 168), but in the former the right to proceed is merely suspended, and may be revived by a supplemental bill in the nature of a bill of revivor (21 N. H. 246; Story, Eq. Pl. § 354; Mitf. Eq. Pl. [by Jeremy] 57.

——**In Pleading.** The overthrow of an action caused by the defendant pleading some matter of fact tending to impeach the correctness of the writ or declaration, and which defeats the action for the present, but does not debar the plaintiff from recommencing it in a better way. Steph. Pl. 47; 3 Bl. Comm. 168; 1 Chit. Pl. (6th London Ed.) 446; Gould, Pl. c. 5, § 65.

It has been applied rather inappropriately as a generic term to all pleas of a dilatory nature; whereas the word "dilatory" would seem to be the more proper generic term, and the word "abatement" applicable to a certain portion of dilatory pleas. Comyn, Dig. "Abatement" (B); 1 Chit. Pl. (6th London Ed.) 440; Gould, Pl. c. 5, § 65. In this general sense it has been used to include pleas to the jurisdiction of the court.

——**In Contracts.** A reduction made by the creditor for the prompt payment of a debt due by the payer or debtor. Weskett, Ins. 7.

——**Of Customs Duties.** The deduction from, or the refunding of, duties sometimes made at the custom house, on account of damages received by goods during importation or while in store. See Act Cong. March 2, 1799, § 52; 1 Story, U. S. Laws, 617; Andrews, Rev. Laws, §§ 113, 162.

——**Of Legacies.** The reduction of a legacy, general or specific, on account of the insufficiency of the estate of the testator to pay his debts and legacies. When the estate of a testator is insufficient to pay both debts and legacies, it is the rule that the general legacies must abate proportionably to an amount sufficient to pay the debts. See "Ademption."

——**Of Nuisances.** The prostration or removal of a nuisance, whether by action, or summarily by an individual. 3 Bl. Comm. 5. See "Nuisance."

——**Of Taxes.** A diminution or decrease in the amount of tax imposed upon any person. The provisions for securing this abatement are entirely matters of statute regulation (5 Gray [Mass.] 365; 4 R. I. 313; 30 Pa. St. 227; 18 Ark. 380; 18 Ill. 312), and vary in the different states.

ABATEMENT OF FREEHOLD. A wrongful entry by a stranger on lands of a decedent before the heir or devisee has taken possession. 3 Bl. Comm. 167. See, also, "Amotion;' "Intrusion;" "Disseisin."

ABATOR. One who abates or destroys a nuisance.

One who, having no right of entry, gets possession of the freehold to the prejudice of an heir or devisee, after the time when the ancestor died, and before the heir or devisee enters. Litt. § 397; Perk. § 383; 2 Prest. Abstr. 296, 300. See Adams, Ej. 43; I Washb. Real Prop. 225.

ABATUDA. Anything diminished; as, *moneta abatuda*, which is money clipped or diminished in value. Cowell.

ABBACY. The government of a religious house, and the revenues thereof, subject to an abbot, as a bishopric is to a bishop. Cowell.

ABBREVIATE. In Scotch law. An abstract. Ersk. Inst. bk. 2, tit. 12, § 43.

ABBREVIATE OF ADJUDICATION. In Scotch law. The recorded abstract of an adjudication (*q. v.*)

ABBREVIATIO PLACITORUM. An abstract of ancient judicial records, prior to the Year Books. See Steph. Pl. (7th Ed.) 410.

ABBREVIATION. A shortened form of a word obtained by the omission of one or more letters or syllables from the middle or end of the word.

The abbreviations in common use in modern times consist of the initial letter or letters, syllable or syllables, of the word. Anciently, also, contracted forms of words, obtained by the omission of letters intermediate between the initial and final letters, were much in use. These latter forms are now more commonly designated by the term "contraction." Abbreviations are of frequent use in referring to text books, reports, etc., and in indicating dates, but should be very sparingly employed, if at all, in formal and important legal documents. See 4 Car. & P. 51; 9 Coke, 48. No part of an indictment should contain any abbreviations except in cases where a *fac simile* of a written instrument is necessary to be set out. 1 East, 180, note. The variety and number of abbreviations is as nearly illimitable as the ingenuity of man can make them, and the advantages arising from their use are, to a great extent, counterbalanced by the ambiguity and uncertainty resulting from the usually inconsiderate selection which is made.

Abbreviations in judicial records do not conform to requirements that proceedings shall be conducted in the English language unless they are so well known or so commonly used that they may be said to constitute part of the language. Stein v. Meyers, 253 Ill. 199.

As to abbreviations by which standard textbooks, reports, etc., are cited, see table in Appendix.

Abbreviations of ancient and less-known authorities cited herein, see pp. v-viii, ante.

ABBREVIATIONUM ILLE NUMERUS ET sensus accipiendus est, ut concessio non sit inanis. Such a number and sense is to be given to abbreviations that the grant may not fail. 9 Coke, 48.

ABBREVIATORS. In ecclesiastical law. Officers whose duty it is to assist in drawing up the pope's briefs, and reducing petitions into proper form, to be converted into papal bulls.

ABBROCHMENT. In old English law. The forestalling of a market or fair.

ABDICATION. A renunciation; a putting away; a renunciation of the sovereignty by an incumbent thereof.

James II. of England, Charles V. of Germany, and Christiana, Queen of Sweden, are said to have abdicated. When James II. of England left the the kingdom, the commons voted that he had abdicated the government, and that thereby the throne had become vacant. The house of lords preferred the word "deserted," but the commons thought it not comprehensive enough, for then the king might have the liberty of returning.

Also applied to the renunciation or surrender of any office, and in this sense it has been distinguished from "resignation," the latter being the giving up of an office to the appointing power from whom it was received, or who has the power to fill the vacancy, while abdication is the renunciation of an office which was conferred by act of law. See, however, 26 Barb. (N. Y.) 487.

ABDUCTION.

——**In England.** By St. 3 Hen. VII c. 2, the taking of any woman having property, or being heir apparent thereto, to be married or defiled.

Under a later statute (24 & 25 Vict. c. 100), the taking of any woman, having certain property or expectancies, to be married or defiled; the taking of such a woman, being under the age of twenty-one years, out of the possession of the person having lawful charge of her; the taking of any woman of any age by force, with intent to cause her to be married or defiled; the taking of any unmarried girl, under the age of sixteen years, out of possession of the person having lawful possession of her; or the taking of any child, under the age of fourteen years, with intent to deprive its lawful guardian of its custody.

——**In the United States.** In most, if not all, of the United States, the crime is regulated by statute; but allowing for statutory variations, the elements may be stated as: (1) The taking, which must be by some affirmative act of force or persuasion. 6 Park. Cr. R. 129, 86 N. Y. 369. (2) From the custody of a parent or guardian; but a mere enticing for the forbidden purpose to a place near her home, to which she is shortly permitted to return, is sufficient. 90 Ill. 274. In some states this is not essential. (3) For the purpose of making the female a prostitute or concubine, or of procuring her to be forcibly married or defiled. The purposes inhibited vary with the statutes, some of the above being omitted, and in some states that of fornication being added. The purpose need not be accomplished. 4 N. Y. Cr. R. 306; 5 N. Y. Cr. R. 61. (4) In some states, the female is required to have been of previous chaste character, or to be below a given age. Where these elements actually exist, defendant's ignorance of them is no defense. 115 Mo. 480.

ABEARANCE. Behavior; as, a recognizance to be of good abearance signifies to be of good behavior. 4 Bl. Comm. 251, 256.

ABEREMURDER. In old English law. An apparent, plain, or downright murder. It was used to distinguish a willful murder from chance-medley, or manslaughter. Spelman; Cowell; Blount. See "Homicide."

ABESSE (Lat.) In the civil law. To be absent; to be away from a place. Said of a person who was *extra continentia urbis*, beyond the suburbs of the city.

ABET. In criminal law. To encourage or set another on to commit a crime. This word is always applied to aiding the commission of a crime. To abet another to commit a murder is to command, procure, or counsel him to commit it. Old Nat. Brev. 21; Co. Litt. 475. See "Accessary."

ABETMENT (Law Lat. *abettum, abbettum;* Law Fr. *abette*). In old criminal law. An encouraging or instigation. Staund. P. C. 10r; Cowell; Blount.

ABETTATOR. See "Abettor."

ABETTOR. An instigator, or setter on; one that promotes, procures, or assists in, the commission of a crime; a principal in the second degree.

The distinction between abettors and accessaries is the presence or absence at the commission of the crime. Co. Litt. 475; 81 Ill. 333; 44 Iowa, 104. Presence and participation are necessary to constitute a person an abettor. 4 Sharswood, Bl. Comm. 33; 1 Hall (N. Y.) 446; Russ. & R. 99; 9 Bing. N. C. 440; 13 Mo. 382; 1 Wis. 159; 10 Pick. (Mass.) 477.

ABEYANCE (Fr. *abbayer*, to expect). In expectation, remembrance, and contemplation of law; the condition of a freehold when there is no person in being in whom it is vested.

In such cases, the freehold has been said to be *in nubibus* (in the clouds), and *in gremio legis* (in the bosom of the law). It has been denied by some that there is such a thing as an estate in abeyance. Fearne, Cont. Rem. 513. See, also, the note to 2 Sharswood, Bl. Comm. 107.

ABIDE THE EVENT. A stipulation that succeeding cases shall "abide the event" of a named case means that such cases shall abide the final outcome and end of the litigation, and that the parties finally successful in that case should be successful in all. 35 Ill. App. 660.

ABIDING BY. In Scotch law. A judicial declaration that the party abides by the deed on which he founds, in an action where the deed or writing is attacked as forged. Unless this is done, a decree that the deed is false will be pronounced. Paterson, Comp. It has the effect of pledging the party to stand the consequences of founding on a forged deed. Bell, Dict.

ABIGEAT. A particular kind of larceny, which is committed not by taking and carrying away the property from one place to another, but by driving a living thing away with an intention of feloniously appropriating the same.

ABIGEATUS (Lat.) In the civil law. The offense of stealing or driving away cattle. Dig. 47, 14, 2. See "Abigeus."

ABIGEUS (Lat. *abigere*). One who steals cattle in numbers.

This is the common word used to denote a stealer of cattle in large numbers, which latter circumstance distinguishes the *abigeus* from the *fur*, who was simply a thief. He who steals a single animal may be called *fur;* he who steals a flock or herd is an *abigeus*. The word is derived from *abigere*, to lead or drive away, and is the same in signification as *abactor, abigeatores, abigatores, abigei.* Du Cange; Guyot, Rep. Univ.; 4 Bl. Comm. 239.

A distinction is also taken by some writers depending upon the place whence the cattle are taken; thus, one who takes cattle from a stable is called *fur.* Calv. Lex, "Abigei."

ABILITY. In divorce law. Power of husband to provide, as element of wife's right to alimony. It is sometimes called "faculty."

ABISHERSING. Quit of amercements. It originally signified a forfeiture or amercement, and is more properly *mishering, mishersing*, or *miskering*, according to Spelman. It has since been termed a liberty of freedom, because, wherever this word is used in a grant, the persons to whom the grant is made have the forfeitures and amercements of all others, and are themselves free from the control of any within their fee.

ABJUDICATIO (Lat. *abjudicare*). A removal from court. Calv. Lex. It has the same signification as *foris judicatio*, both in the civil and canon law. Co. Litt. 100b; Calv. Lex.

ABJURATION (Lat. *abjuratio*, from *abjurare*, to abjure, to forswear or renounce on oath). A renunciation of allegiance, upon oath. Sometimes loosely used in the sense of "abandonment."

ABLE BODIED. Ability to perform work usually performed by able-bodied men. The existence of a slight disability not resulting in impairment is immaterial. 29 Ill. App. 382.

ABLEGATI. Papal ambassadors of the second rank, who are sent with a less extensive commission to a court where there are no nuncios. This title is equivalent to "Envoy" (*q. v.*)

ABLOCATIO, or **ABLOCATION.** A letting out to hire for money. Wharton.

ABODE. Dwelling place. See "Residence."

ABOLITION (Lat. *abolitio*, from *abolere*, to utterly destroy). The extinguishment, abrogation, or annihilation of a thing.

In the civil, French, and German law, abolition is used nearly synonymously with pardon, remission, grace. Dig. 39. 4. 3. 3. There is, however, this difference: Grace is the generic term; pardon, according to those laws, is the clemency which the prince extends to a man who has participated in a crime, without being a principal or accomplice; remission is made in cases of involuntary homicides and self-defense. Abolition is different,—it is used when the crime cannot be remitted. The prince then may, by letters of abolition, remit the punishment, but the infamy remains, unless letters of abolition have been obtained before sentence. Enc. D'Alembert.

ABONDANCE (Law Fr.) In old practice. Surplusage. Y. B. P. 7 Hen. VI. 12.

ABORDAGE (Fr.) The collision of vessels.

ABORTION. The expulsion of the foetus at a period of utero gestation so early that it has not acquired the power of sustaining an independent life.

It may be either innocent, as when accidental, or criminal. Criminal abortion is the willful production of the miscarriage of a pregnant woman, whether by the administration of drugs, or the use of instruments, or other means, the same not being necessary to save her life. At common law, the woman must have been quick with child (78 Ky. 204; 63 Mich. 229), but this is no longer necessary (49 Iowa, 260; 33 Me. 48; 83 N. C. 360; 45 Ark. 333). It is an aggravation of the offense, and in some states constitutes manslaughter, if the death of the woman is produced.

ABORTIVE TRIAL. A term descriptive of the result when a case has gone off, and no verdict has been pronounced, without the fault, contrivance, or management of the parties. Jebb & B. 51.

ABORTUS. The fruit of an abortion; the child born before its time, incapable of life.

ABOUT. In contiguity or proximity to; not far from; in connection with; nigh; near; in concern with; engaged in; dealing with; occupied upon (155 Ill. 228); nearly; in close correspondence to; in the immediate neighborhood of (118 Ill. App. 190).

The word gives a margin for a moderate excess in or diminution of the quantity mentioned and negatives the idea that exact precision is intended. 198 Ill. 325.

ABOUTISSEMENT (Fr.) An abuttal or abutment. See Guyot, Rep. Univ. "Aboutissans."

ABOVE. Higher; superior; as, court above; bail above.

ABRIDGE. In practice. To shorten a declaration or count by taking away or severing some of the substance of it. Brooke, Abr. "Abridgment;" Comyn, Dig. "Abridgment;" 1 Viner, Abr. 109.

To abridge a plaint is to strike out a part of the demand, and pray that the tenant answer to the rest. This was allowable generally in real actions where the writ was *de libero tenemento*, as assize, dower, etc., where the demandant claims land of which the tenant was not seized. See 1 Wm. Saund. 207, note 2; 2 Wm. Saund. 24, 330; Brooke, Abr. "Abridgment;" 1 Pet. (U. S.) 74; Stearns, Real Actions, 204.

To abridge damage is to reduce the same after the rendition of the verdict.

ABRIDGMENT. An epitome or compendium of another and larger work, wherein the principal ideas of the larger work are summarily contained.

ABROGATION. The destruction of or annulling a former law by an act of the legislative power, or by usage.

It is a total annulment, as distinguished from derogation, which is a repeal of part. Abrogation may be express or implied.

——**Express Abrogation.** That literally pronounced by the new law either in general terms, as when a final clause abrogates or repeals all laws contrary to the provisions of the new one, or in particular terms, as where it abrogates certain preceding laws, which are named.

——**Implied Abrogation.** That which takes place when the new law contains provisions which are positively contrary to the former laws, without expressly abrogating such laws; for it is a maxim, *Posteriora derogant prioribus* (10 Mart. [La.] 172, 560); and also when the order of things for which the law had been made no longer exists, and hence the motives which had caused its enactment have ceased to operate, *Ratione legis omnino cessante cessat lex.* Toullier, Dr. Civ. tit. prel. § 11, note 151; Merlin, Repert.

ABSCOND. To go in a clandestine manner out of the jurisdiction of the courts, or to lie concealed, in order to avoid their process.

ABSCONDING DEBTOR. One who absconds from his creditors.

The statutes of the various states, and the decisions upon them, have determined who shall be treated in those states, respectively, as absconding debtors, and liable to be proceeded against as such. A person who has been in a state only transiently, or has come into it without any intention of settling therein, cannot be treated as an absconding debtor (2 Caines [N. Y.] 318; 15 Johns. [N. Y.] 196; 4 Watts [Pa.] 422); nor can one who openly changes his residence (3 Yerg. [Tenn.] 414; 5 Conn. 117). For the rule in Vermont, see 2 Vt. 489; 6 Vt. 614. It is not necessary that the debtor should actually leave the state. 7 Md. 209.

ABSENCE. The state of being away from one's domicile or usual place of residence.

In its specific applications, particular qualifications are usually added. Thus, to toll the statute of limitations, the absence must generally be from the jurisdiction. To raise a presumption of death, the whereabouts of the absent person must be unknown, and the absence must continue a certain time,—usually seven years.

The word "absent" conveys the idea of a temporary condition, and the probability of return. 35 Ill. App. 124.

——**In Scotch Law.** Default of appearance.

ABSENTE (Lat. ablative of *absens*). Being absent. A common term in the old reports. "The three justices, *absente* North, C. J., were clear of opinion." 2 Mod. 14.

ABSENTEE. One who absents himself from a state, from his residence, or from an office or place where official duty is to be performed. Applied to a landlord who resides in a country other than that from which he draws his rents. McCulloch, Polit. Econ.

——**In Louisiana Practice.** Either a nonresident or a resident who has departed from the state, leaving no one to represent him. 14 La. 447; 15 La. 81; 16 La. Ann. 390.

A resident temporarily absent, but retaining his domicile, so that service may be made on him there, is not an absentee. 16 La. Ann. 390; 18 La. Ann. 695.

A *curator ad hoc (q. v.)* may be appointed for an absentee.

ABSENTEES, or DES ABSENTEES. The name of a parliament held at Dublin, 10th May, 8 Hen. VIII.

ABSENTEM ACCIPERE DEBEMUS EUM qui non est eo loci in quo petitur. We must call him absent who is not in that place in which he is sought. Dig. 50. 16. 199.

ABSENTIO EJUS QUI REIPUBLICAE cause abest, neque ei neque alii damnosa esse debet. The absence of him who is employed in the service of the state ought not to be prejudicial to him nor to others. Dig. 50. 17. 140.

ABSOILE. To pardon; to deliver from excommunication. Stamford, P. C. 72; Kelham. Sometimes spelled *assoile (q. v.)*

ABSOLUTA SENTENTIA EXPOSITORE non indiget. An absolute, unqualified sentence (or proposition) needs no expositor. 2 Inst. 533.

ABSOLUTE (Lat. *absolvere*). Complete; perfect; final; without any condition or incumbrance; as an absolute bond *(simplex obligatio)*, in distinction from a conditional bond.

——**Absolute Estate.** One that is free from all manner of condition or incumbrance. See "Condition."

——**Absolute Rule.** One which, on the hearing, has been confirmed and made final.

——**Absolute Conveyance.** One conveying unconditional title, as distinguished from a mortgage or other conditional conveyance. 1 Powell, Mortg. 125.

——**Absolute Rights.** Such as appertain and belong to particular persons merely as individuals or single persons, as distinguished from relative rights, which are incident to them as members of society. 1 Sharswood, Bl. Comm. 123; 1 Chit. Pl. 364; 1 Chit. Prac. 32.

——**Absolute Property.** Where a man hath solely and exclusively the right and also the occupation of movable chattels; distinguished from a qualified property, as that of a bailee. 2 Sharswood, Bl. Comm. 388; 2 Kent, Comm. 347. It includes not only the property, but the right to an immediate and unqualified possession. 7 Barb. (N. Y.) 590.

——**Absolute Covenant.** One which is unconditional or unqualified.

——**Absolute Interest.** One which is so completely vested in the individual that he can by no contingency be deprived of it without his own consent.

However, the use of the word "absolute" in a deed may be so limited by the context that it may be used in connection with an interest in property without being regarded as the equivalent of "unqualifiedly." 196 Ill. 87.

——**Absolute Law.** The law of nature, which alone is immutable in theory. 1 Steph. Comm. 21 et seq.

——**Absolute Warrandice.** In Scotch law. A warranty against all incumbrançes whatever. 1 Kames, Eq. 290, 293.

ABSOLUTION.

——**In Civil Law.** A sentence whereby a party accused is declared innocent of the crime laid to his charge.

——**In Canon Law.** A juridical act, whereby the clergy declare that the sins of such as are penitent are remitted. The formula of absolution in the Roman Church is absolute; in the Greek Church it is deprecatory; in the Reformed Churches, declaratory. Among Protestants it is chiefly used for a sentence by which a person who stands excommunicated is released or freed from that punishment. Enc. Brit.

——**In French Law.** The dismissal of an accusation.

The term "acquitment" is employed when the accused is declared not guilty, and "absolution" when he is recognized as guilty, but the act is not punishable by law, or he is exonerated by some defect of intention or will.

ABSOLUTISM. That government in which public power is vested in some person or persons, unchecked and uncontrolled by any law or institution.

The word was first used at the beginning of this century, in Spain, where he who was in favor of the absolute power of the king, and opposed to the constitutional system introduced by the Cortes during the struggle with the French, was called *absolutista.*

ABSQUE. In Latin phrases. A preposition denoting without, or except for.

ABSQUE ALIQUO INDE REDDENDO (Lat. without reserving any rent therefrom). A term used of a free grant by the crown. 2 Rolle, Abr. 502.

ABSQUE CONSIDERATIONE CURIAE (Lat.) In old practice. Without the consideration of the court; without judgment. St. Marlb., cited in Fleta, lib. 2, c. 47, § 13.

ABSQUE HOC (Lat.) Without this. See "Traverse."

ABSQUE IMPETITIONE VASTI (Lat. without impeachment of waste). A term indicating freedom from any liability on the part of the tenant or lessee to answer in damages for the waste he may commit. See "Waste."

ABSQUE TALI CAUSA (Lat. without such cause). In pleading. A form of replication in an action *ex delicto*, which works a general denial of the whole matter of the defendant's plea of *de injuria.* Gould, Pl. c. 7, § 10.

ABSTENTION. In French Law. The tacit renunciation of a succession by an heir. Merlin, Repert.

ABSTRACT. An abridgment or synopsis. In appellate practice. A condensed statement of the evidence or record.

——**Of a Fine.** An abstract of the writ of covenant and the concord; naming the parties, the parcel of land, and the agreement. 2 Bl. Comm. 351.

——**Of a Title.** A brief account of all the deeds upon which the title rests. A synopsis of the distinctive portions of the various instruments which constitute the muniments of title. See Prest. Abstr.; Wharton.

ABUNDANS CAUTELA NON NOCET. Abundant caution does no harm. 11 Coke, 6; Fleta, lib. 1, c. 28, § 1.

ABUSE. Everything which is contrary to good order established by usage. Merlin, Repert.

Among the civilians, abuse has another signification, which is the destruction of the substance of a thing in using it. For example, the borrower of wine or grain abuses the article lent by using it, because he cannot enjoy it without consuming it.

——**Of Distress.** The using an animal or chattel distrained, which makes the distrainer liable as for a conversion.

——**Of Female Child.** Carnal knowledge. See "Rape."

——**Of Process.** There is an abuse of process when an adversary, through the malicious and unfounded use of some regular legal proceeding, obtains some advantage over his opponent. Wharton. See 63 How. Pr. (N. Y.) 326; 15 App. Div. (N. Y.) 205.

Process is abused when employed to accomplish some purpose which the process was not intended by law to effect, or where used in the mode and manner designed by law, but with an ulterior purpose to effect some unlawful collateral end, the legal use of it being but ostensible, while the real design was to pervert its force and efficiency to the success of the unlawful collateral design. 52 Ill. App. 38.

ABUT. To reach; to touch. In old law, the ends were said to abut, the sides to adjoin. Cro. Jac. 184.

To take a new direction; as where a bounding line changes its course. Spelman, voc. "Abuttare." In the modern law, to bound upon. 2 Chit. Pl. 660.

ABUTTALS (Fr.) The buttings or boundings of lands, showing to what other lands, highways, or places they belong or are abutting. Termes de la Ley.

ABUTTER. The owner of land abutting on a public street, in the bed of which the owner has no title or private right except such as are incident to a lot so situated. 122 N. Y. 1; 130 N. Y. 14.

An abutter has two distinct kinds of rights in a highway,—those which he enjoys in common with all citizens, and those which arise from his ownership of contiguous property. 130 N. Y. 618.

He may or may not own the fee in the street, and his rights of the second class vary according to this fact. 131 N. Y. 293.

AC ETIAM. (Lat. and also.) The introduction to the statement of the real cause of action, used in those cases where it was necessary to allege a fictitious cause of action to give the court jurisdiction, and also the real cause in compliance with the statutes. It was first used in the king's bench, and was afterwards adopted by Lord C. J. North in addition to the *clausum fregit* writs of his court upon which writs of *capias* might issue. He balanced a while whether he should not use the words *nec non* instead of *ac etiam*. See Burgess, Ins. 149-157; 3 Sharswood, Bl. Comm. 288.

AC ETIAM BILLAE (Law Lat. and also to a bill). The initial words of a clause inserted in a writ of *capias ad respondendum*, where bail is required, in order to express the true cause of action; the writ requiring the defendant "to answer the plaintiff of a plea of trespass, and also to a bill of the plaintiff" against the defendant, for whatever the real cause of action may be. 3 Bl. Comm. 288; Id. Append. No. 3, § 3. See "Capias ad Respondendum." This clause is now dispensed with in the process of the English courts. St. 2 Wm. IV. c. 39. See "Bill."

AC SI (Lat.) As if. Towns. Pl. 23, 27. There words frequently occur in old English statutes. Lord Bacon expounds their meaning in the statute of uses: "The statute gives entry, not *simpliciter*, but with an *ac si*." Bac. Read. Uses, Works, iv. 195.

ACAPTE. In French feudal law. A species of relief; a seignorial right due on every change of a tenant. A feudal right which formerly prevailed in Languedoc and Guyenne, being attached to that species of heritable estates which were granted on the contract of *emphyteusis*. Guyot, Inst. Feud. c. 5, § 12.

ACCAPITARE, ACAPITARE, or ACAPtare (Law Lat.) From *caput*, head, or chief.

(1) To pay homage to a chief lord, on becoming his vassal. Bracton, fol. 78n; Fleta, lib. 3, c. 16, § 6.

(2) To acknowledge the sovereignty of a chief lord in special cases, as against a mesne; to attorn *(acapitare et se atturnare)*. Bracton, fol. 389a; Fleta, lib. 3, c. 16, § 38; Id. lib. 6, c. 28, § 1.

(3) To attorn to another person than the chief lord, and in derogation of his rights. Fleta, lib. 2, c. 50, § 16.

ACCEDAS AD CURIAM (Lat. that you go to court). In English law. An original writ issuing out of chancery and directed to the sheriff, for the purpose of removing a replevin suit from the hundred court or court baron before one of the superior courts of law. It directs the sheriff to go to the lower court, and there cause the plaint to be recorded, and to return, etc. See Fitzh. Nat. Brev. 18; Dyer, 169.

ACCEDAS AD VICE COMITEM (Lat. that you go to the sheriff). In English law. A writ directed to the coroner, commanding him to deliver a writ to the sheriff, who suppresses a pone which has been delivered to him, which commands the latter officer to return the pone.

ACCELERATION. An estate is said to be accelerated when it is reduced to possession by the extinguishment of the precedent estate sooner than it would have been in the due course of events.

Thus a remainder is said to be "accelerated" when the first taker is incapable of taking or refuses to take.

ACCEPTANCE (Lat. *accipere*).

——**Of Property.** The receipt of a thing offered by another with an intention to retain it, indicated by some act sufficient for the purpose. 2 Pars. Cont. 221.

The element of receipt must enter into every acceptance, though receipt does not necessarily mean, in this sense, actual manual taking. To this element there must be added an intention to retain. This retention may exist at the time of the receipt, or subsequently; it may be indicated by words, or acts, or any medium understood by the parties; and an acceptance of goods will be implied from mere detention, in many instances.

An acceptance involves very generally the idea of a receipt in consequence of a previous undertaking, on the part of the person offering, to deliver such a thing as the party accepting is in some manner bound to receive. It is through this meaning that the term "acceptance," as used in reference to bills of exchange, has a relation to the more general use of the term. As distinguished from "assent," acceptance would denote receipt of something in compliance and satisfactory fulfillment of a contract to which assent has been previously given. See "Assent."

——**Of Bills of Exchange.** An engagement to pay the bill in money when due. 4 East, 72; 19 Law J. 297.

Acceptances of bills of exchange are:

(1) Absolute, being a positive engagement to pay the bill according to its tenor.

(2) Conditional, being an undertaking to pay the bill on a contingency.

(3) Partial, being one varying from the tenor of the bill.

(4) Qualified, being either conditional or partial.

(5) Supra protest, being the acceptance of the bill after protest for nonacceptance by the drawee, for the honor of the drawer, or a particular indorser.

They are also either:

(6) Express, being an undertaking in direct and express terms to pay the bill.

(7) Implied, being an undertaking to pay the bill inferred from acts of a character fairly to warrant such an inference.

ACCEPTANCE AU BESOIN. In French law. Acceptance in case of need. See "Au Besoin."

ACCEPTARE (Lat.)

——**In Old Pleading.** To accept. *Acceptavit,* he accepted. 2 Strange, 817. *Non acceptavit,* he did not accept. 4 Man. & G. 7.

——**In the Civil Law.** To accept; to assent; to assent to a promise made by another. Grotius de Jure Belli, lib. 2, c. 11, § 14.

ACCEPTILATION. In civil law. A release made by a creditor to his debtor of his debt, without receiving any consideration. Ayliffe, Pand. tit. 26, p. 570. It is a species of donation, but not subject to the forms of the latter, and is valid unless in fraud of creditors. Merlin, Repert.

ACCEPTOR. The party who accepts a bill of exchange. 3 Kent, Comm. 75.

The party who undertakes to pay a bill of exchange in the first instance.

ACCEPTOR SUPRA PROTEST. A party who accepts a bill which has been protested, for the honor of the drawer or any one of the indorsers.

ACCESS. Approach, or the means or power of approaching. The right of the occupant of land to pass from his premises to a highway.

Sometimes by access is understood sexual intercourse; at other times, the opportunity of communicating together, so that sexual intercourse may have taken place, is also called access. In this sense, a man who can readily be in company with his wife is said to have access to her, and in that case her issue are presumed to be his issue; but this presumption may be rebutted by positive evidence that no sexual intercourse took place. 1 Turn. & R. 141.

ACCESSARY. In criminal law. He who is not the chief actor in the perpetration of the offense, nor present at its performance, but is some way concerned therein, either before or after the fact committed.

——**Before the Fact.** One who, being absent at the time of the crime committed, yet procures, counsels, or commands another to commit it. 1 Hale, P. C. 615.

The essentials are:

(1) Absence from the scene of the crime. 9 Pick. (Mass.) 496.

(2) Actual procurement, counsel, or command; bare permission (1 Hale, P. C. 616) or failure to disclose a known intent to commit crime (7 Tex. App. 549) not being enough.

(3) A criminal intent. 157 Pa. St. 13.

——**After the Fact.** One who, knowing a felony to have been committed, receives, relieves, comforts, or assists the felon. 4 Bl. Comm. 37. The essentials are:

(1) The commission of a crime by the principal. 39 Miss. 702.

(2) Knowledge thereof by the alleged accessary. 42 Ga. 22.

(3) Assistance rendered to the principal personally. 26 Grat. (Va.) 952.

ACCESSARY TO ADULTERY. In divorce law. A spouse who directly commands or procures the commission of adultery by the other. It is a stronger term than "conniver," which implies mere acquiescence, but is practically unused in America, "connivance" being used to denote all noncollusive participation.

ACCESSIO (Lat. an accession). An increase or addition; that which lies next to a thing, and is supplementary and necessary to the principal thing; that which arises or is produced from the principal thing. Calv. Lex.

A manner of acquiring the property in a thing which becomes united with that which a person already possesses.

The doctrine of property arising from accessions is grounded on the rights of occupancy. It is said to be of six kinds in the Roman law:

(1) That which assigns to the owner of a thing its products, as the fruit of trees, the young of animals.

(2) That which makes a man the owner of a thing which is made of another's property, upon payment of the value of the material taken. See, also, Civ. Code La. art. 491. As where wine, bread, or oil is made of another man's grapes, olives, or wheat. 2 Sharswood, Bl. Comm. 404; 10 Johns. (N. Y.) 288.

(3) That which gives the owner of land new land formed by gradual deposit. See "Alluvion."

(4) That which gives the owner of a thing the property in what is added to it by way of adorning or completing it; as, if a tailor should use the cloth of B. in repairing A.'s coat, all would belong to A., but B. would have an action against both A. and the tailor for the cloth so used. This doctrine holds in the common law. Moore, 20; Poph. 38; Brooke, Abr. "Propertiae," 23.

(5) That which gives islands formed in a stream to the owner of the adjacent lands on either side.

(6) That which gives a person the property in things added to his own so that they cannot be separated without damage. Guyot, Rep. Univ.

An accessary obligation, and sometimes also the person who enters into an obligation as surety in which another is principal. Calv. Lex.

ACCESSION.

——**To Property.** The right to all which one's own property produces, whether that property be movable or immovable, including the increase of animals, and the right to that which is so united to it, either naturally or artificially, as not to be readily separable. See 45 Vt. 4; 2 Kent, Comm. 360; 2 Bl. Comm. 404. See "Confusion of Goods."

It is sometimes used in a narrower sense, as including only the acquirement by the owner of property of that which is added to or incorporated with it, as by the erection of additions to a building, the setting out of trees, etc., and in this sense is to be distinguished from "specification," which is the transformation of property into another species by the labor of another, as by the sawing of trees into lumber. See 2 Bl. Comm. 404.

Distinction between "accession" and "confusion," see "Confusion of Goods."

——**In International Law.** The absolute or conditional acceptance, by one or several states, of a treaty already concluded between other sovereignties. Merlin, Repert.

ACCESSION, DEED OF. In Scotch law. A deed executed by the creditors of a bankrupt or insolvent debtor, by which they approve of a trust given by their debtor for the general behoof, and bind themselves to concur in the plans proposed for extricating his affairs. Bell, Dict.

ACCESSORIUM NON DUCIT SED SEQUItur suum principale. The principal draws after it the accessory, not the accessory the principal. Co. Litt. 152a, 389a; 5 El. Bl. 772; Broom, Leg. Max. (3d London Ed.) 433. Literally, the accessory does not draw, but follows, its principal.

ACCESSORIUS SEQUITUR NATURAM sui principalis. An accessory follows the nature of his principal. Coke, 3d Inst. 139; 4 Sharswood, Bl. Comm. 36; Broom, Leg. Max. (3d London Ed.) 440.

ACCESSORY. Anything which is joined to another thing as an ornament, or to render it more perfect. For example, the halter of a horse, the frame of a picture, the keys of a house, and the like, each belong to the principal thing. The sale of the materials of a newspaper establishment will carry with it, as an accessory, the subscription list (2 Watts [Pa.] 111); but a bequest of a house would not carry the furniture in it, as accessory to it (Domat, Civ. Law, p. 2, liv. 4, tit. 2, § 4, note 1). *Accessorium non ducit, sed sequitur principale.* Co. Litt. 152a.

Used, also, in the same sense as "Accessary" *(q. v.)*

ACCESSORY ACTIONS. In Scotch law. Those which are in some degree subservient to others. Bell, Dict.

ACCESSORY CONTRACTS. Those made for assuring the performance of a prior contract, either by the same parties or by others; such as suretyship, mortgages, and pledges.

ACCESSORY OBLIGATIONS. In Scotch law. Obligations to antecedent or primary obligations, such as obligations to pay interest, etc. Ersk. Inst. lib. 3, tit. 3, § 60.

ACCIDENT (Lat. *accidere,—ad,* to, and *cadere,* to fall). An event which, under the circumstances, is unusual and unexpected by the person to whom it happens.

The happening of an event without the concurrence of the will of the person by whose agency it was caused; or the happening of an event without any human agency. 32 Conn. 85. See "Inevitable Accident."

——**In Equity Practice.** Such an unforeseen event, misfortune, loss, act, or omission as is not the result of any negligence or misconduct in the party. Story, Eq. Jur. § 78; 35 Conn. 198.

An occurrence in relation to a contract which was not anticipated by the parties when the same was entered into, and which gives an undue advantage to one of them over the other in a court of law. Jeremy, Eq. 358. This definition is objected to, because, as accidents may arise in relation to other things besides contracts, it is inaccurate in confining accidents to contracts; besides, it does not exclude cases of unanticipated occurrences resulting from the negligence or misconduct of the party seeking relief. See, also, 1 Spence, Eq. Jur. 628.

An unforeseen or unexpected event occurring external to the party affected by it, and of which his own agency is not the proximate cause, whereby, contrary to his own intention and wish, he loses some right which it would be a violation of good conscience for the person obtaining to retain. 2 Pom. Eq. Jur. § 823.

It differs from "mistake" in that the latter is based on a voluntary action of the person affected under a mistaken impression.

ACCION, or ACCYOUN (Law Fr.) An action. Kelham. *Accion sur le cas,* an action on the case.

ACCIPERE QUID UT JUSTITIAM FAcias, non est tam accipere quam extorquere. To accept anything as a reward for doing justice is rather extorting than accepting. Lofft, 72.

ACCIPITARE. To pay relief to lords of manors. *Capitali domino accipitare, i. e.,* to pay a relief, homage, or obedience to the chief lord on becoming his vassal. Fleta, lib. 2, c. 50.

ACCO (Law Lat.) An abbreviation of *actio.* Towns. Pl. 26.

ACCOLA.

——**In the Civil Law.** One who inhabits or occupies land near a place, as one who dwells by a river, or on the bank of a river. Dig. 43. 13. 3. 6.

——**In Feudal Law.** A husbandman; an agricultural tenant; a tenant of a manor. Spelman. A name given to a class of villeins in Italy. Barr. Obs. St. 302.

ACCOMENDA. A contract which takes place when an individual intrusts personal property with the master of a vessel, to be sold for their joint account. In such case, two contracts take place,—the contract called *mandatum,* by which the owner of the property gives the master power to dispose of it, and the contract of partnership, in virtue of which the profits are to be divided between them. One party runs the risk of losing his capital; the other his labor. If the sale produces no more than first cost, the owner takes all the proceeds; it is only the profits which are to be divided. Emerig. Mar. Loans, § 5.

ACCOMMODATION. A contract or obligation made or assumed as a favor, and not on a consideration.

ACCOMMODATION LANDS. A name given in England to lands obtained or improved for the purpose of augmenting the value of other lands.

ACCOMMODATION PAPER. A negotiable instrument made or indorsed without consideration for the benefit of another.

ACCOMMODATION PARTY. One who has signed the instrument as maker, drawer, acceptor, or indorser without receiving value therefor, and for the purpose of lending his name to some other person. Neg. Inst. Law N. Y. § 55.

ACCOMMODATION ROAD. One constructed to give access to a particular tract of land.

ACCOMMODATION WORKS. The name given to the facilities, such as gates and culverts, which a railroad company in England, which has acquired property by eminent domain, is required by section 68 of the act of 1845 to construct for the benefit of the adjoining owners.

ACCOMPLICE (Lat. *ad* and *complicare,—con,* with, together; *plicare,* to fold, to wrap, —to fold together).

——**In Criminal Law.** One who is in some way concerned in the commission of a crime, though not as a principal.

The term in its fullness includes in its meaning all persons who have been concerned in the commission of a crime, all *participes criminis,* whether they are considered in strict legal propriety as principals in the first or second degree, or merely as accessaries before or after the fact. 1 Russ. Crimes, 21; 4 Bl. Comm. 331; 1 Phil. Ev. 28.

ACCORD. Abbreviation of the French "accordant," and English "accordingly;"

frequently used in the books, especially in the reports, to denote the accordance or agreement between one adjudged case and another, in establishing or confirming the same doctrine, and sometimes the accordance of judges in opinion in the same case. See "Accordant." The disagreement or opposition of cases is denoted by "contra."

——**In Contracts.** A satisfaction agreed on between the party injuring and the party injured, which, when performed, is a bar to all actions upon his account. Generally used in the phrase "accord and satisfaction," satisfaction being the performance of the accord. 2 Greenl. Ev. 28; 3 Bl. Comm. 16; 4 Denio (N. Y.) 418; 83 Va. 397; 78 Wis. 682; 5 Md. 170.

Something of legal value, to which the creditor before had no right, agreed on in full satisfaction of the debt, without regard to the magnitude of the satisfaction. 43 Conn. 462.

The substitution of an agreement in lieu of a right of action between the parties.

A part payment is not a good accord and satisfaction, though received in full. 20 Conn. 559; 99 Mich. 247; 64 Barb. (N. Y.) 215; 8 R. I. 381; 23 Wis. 471; 79 N. C. 585.

ACCORDANT (Fr. and Eng.) Agreeing; concurring. "Baron Parker, accordant," Hardr. 93; "Holt, C. J., accordant," 6 Mod. 298, 299; "Powys, J., accord.," "Powell, J., accord.," Id.

ACCOUCHEMENT. The act of giving birth to a child.

ACCOUNT. A detailed statement of mutual demands in the nature of debt and credit between the parties, arising out of contract or some fiduciary relation. 45 Mo. 573.

A written statement of pecuniary transactions. Abbott.

It is to be distinguished from "balance," which is but the conclusion or result of the account. 45 Mo. 574.

——**Stated Account.** One which has been approved by the parties, and the balance shown by it agreed to either (1) expressly, or (2) impliedly, as by retaining an account rendered without objection.

——**Open Account.** One which has not been closed or stated.

——**Current Account.** One kept open in expectation of further dealings.

——**Book Accounts.** Those evidenced by entries in books of account.

——**Account Rendered.** An account presented by the creditor to the debtor.

ACCOUNT, ACTION OF (sometimes called "Account," or "Account Render"). An action or writ which lay against one who was required, by his official or fiduciary position, to render an account.

ACCOUNT BOOK. A book kept by a merchant, trader, mechanic, or other person, in which are entered from time to time the transactions of his trade or business. Such books, when regularly kept, may be admitted in evidence. Greenl. Ev. §§ 115-118.

ACCOUNT IN BANK. See "Bank Account."

ACCOUNT STATED. See "Account."

ACCOUNTABLE RECEIPT. An acknowledgment of the receipt of money to be accounted for by the person receiving it, as distinguished from a receipt for money paid in discharge of a debt. 1 Exch. 138.

ACCOUNTANT. One who is versed in accounts. A person or officer appointed to keep the accounts of a public company. A certified public accountant is one who is certified by proper authority to be competent to examine and report on accounts.

He who renders to another or to a court a just and detailed statement of the property which he holds as trustee, executor, administrator, or guardian. See 16 Viner, Abr. 155.

ACCOUNTANT GENERAL, or ACCOMPTANT GENERAL. An officer of the English court of chancery, by whom the moneys paid into court are received, deposited in bank, and disbursed. The office appears to have been established by an order of May 26, 1725, and 12 Geo. I. c. 32, before which time the effects of the suitors were locked up in the vaults of the Bank of England, under the care of the masters and two of the six clerks. 1 Smith, Ch. Prac. 22. It is now abolished. 35 & 36 Vict. 44.

ACCOUNTING. The making and rendering of an account. Usually, but not necessarily, applied to accountings under order of court.

ACCOUPLE. To marry; married.

ACCREDIT. In international law. To acknowledge. Used of the act by which a diplomatic agent is acknowledged by the government near which he is sent, which makes his public character known, and becomes his protection, and also of the act by which his sovereign commissions him.

ACCREDITULARE, or ACCREDULITARE (Lat.) To purge one's self of an offense by oath. Whishaw; Blount.

ACCRESCERE (Lat. to be added to). The term is used is speaking of islands which are formed in rivers by deposit. Calv. Lex.; 3 Kent, Comm. 428.

——**In Scotch Law.** To pass to any one. Bell, Dict.

It is used in a related sense in the common-law phrase *jus accrescendi*, the right of survivorship. 1 Washb. Real Prop. 426.

——**In Pleading.** To commence; to arise; to accrue. *Quod actio non accrevit infra* *sex annos*, that the action did not accrue within six years. 3 Chit. Pl. 914.

ACCRETION (Lat. *accrescere*, to grow to). The increase of real estate by the addition of portions of soil, by gradual deposition through the operation of natural causes, to that already in possession of the owner. 2 Washb. Real Prop. 451. It is immaterial whether the stream be navigable or not, or whether artificial causes contribute. 64 Ill. 56.

"Alluvion" comprises both soil and other things, such as seaweed, etc. Tiedeman, Real Prop. § 686; 2 Johns. (N. Y.) 313.

The term "alluvion" is applied to the deposit itself, while "accretion" rather denotes the act.

Sometimes, however, alluvion is used to denote the act of increase also, and accretion as a generic term including, also, reliction and avulsion *(q. v.)*

ACCROACH. To attempt to exercise royal power. 4 Bl. Comm. 76.

A knight who forcibly assaulted and detained one of the king's subjects till he paid him a sum of money was held to have committed treason on the ground of accroachment. 1 Hale, P. C. 80.

——**In French Law.** To delay. Whishaw.

ACCRUE. To grow to; to be added to, as the interest accrues on the principal. Accruing costs are those which become due and are created after judgment; as the costs of an execution.

To arise, to happen, to come to pass; as the statute of limitation does not commence running until the cause of action has accrued. 1 Bouv. Inst. note 861; 2 Rawle (Pa.) 277; 10 Watts (Pa.) 363; Bac. Abr. "Limitation of Actions" (D 3); 59 Hun (N. Y.) 145; 159 Pa. St. 556.

ACCRUER, CLAUSE OF. See "Survivorship, Clause of."

ACCUMULATIONS.

(1) The income of a trust fund, when reinvested as a new capital by the trustee.

(2) The suspension of absolute ownership in the rents and profits of personalty, which is, in many states, limited by statute. See 1 Rev. St. N. Y. p. 773, §§ 2-4.

ACCUMULATIVE JUDGMENT (or **SENtence**). See "Cumulative Sentence."

ACCUMULATIVE LEGACY. A double or additional legacy; a legacy given in addition to another given by the same instrument, or by another instrument. 4 Ves. 90; 1 P. Wms. 424.

ACCUSARE NEMO DEBET SE, NISI coram deo. No one is obliged to accuse himself unless before God. Hardr. 139.

ACCUSATION. In criminal law. A charge made to a competent officer against one who has committed a crime, so that he may be brought to justice and punishment.

ACCUSATOR POST RATIONABILE tempus non est audiendus, nisi se bene de omissione excusaverit. An accuser is not to be heard after a reasonable time, unless he excuse himself satisfactorily for the omission. Moore, 817.

ACCUSED. One who is charged with a crime.

ACCUSER. One who makes an accusation.

ACEPHALI (Graeco-Lat.) Persons without a head or superior.

——**In Civil Law.** A sect of religious persons enumerated among the heretics. Otherwise called *acephalitae*. So termed, according to Calvin, because their head or founder was unknown, and they acknowledged no religious superiors. Calv. Lex.

——**In Feudal Law.** Persons without a feudal superior; who held of no one as their lord. *Baronorum homines et acephalos*. LL. Hen. I. c. 22. This is thought by Burrill to be the passage referred to in Cowell as descriptive of a class of levelers who acknowledged no head or superior.

ACHATE, ACHAT, ACHATA, or **ACHET** (Law Fr.) In old English law. Purchase; a purchase, contract, or bargain. *Per colour de achate*, by color of purchase. St. Westminster I. c. 1. Bought. *Achate arere*, bought back. Dyer (Fr. Ed.) 35b.

ACHEREST. An ancient English measure of grain, supposed to be the same with their quarter, or eight bushels.

ACKNOWLEDGMENT. The act of one who has executed a deed, in going before some competent officer or court, and declaring it to be his act or deed.

The acknowledgment is certified by the officer or court; and the term "acknowledgment" is sometimes used to designate the certificate.

Sometimes loosely used for "admission" *(q. v.)*

ACKNOWLEDGMENT MONEY. In English law. A sum paid by tenants of copyhold in some parts of England, as a recognition of their superior lords. Cowell; Blount. Called a fine by Blackstone. 2 Bl. Comm. 98.

ACOLYTE. An inferior church servant, who, next under the deacon, followed and waited upon the priest and deacons, and performed the meaner offices of lighting the candles, carrying the bread and wine, and paying other servile attendance.

ACQUEST. An estate acquired by purchase.

ACQUETS. In civil law. Property which has been acquired by purchase, gift, or otherwise than by succession.

Immovable property which has been acquired otherwise than by succession. Merlin, Repert.

The profits of all the effects of which the husband has the administration and enjoyment, either of right or in fact, of the produce of the reciprocal industry and labor of both husband and wife, and of the estates which they may acquire during the marriage, either by donations, made jointly to them both, or by purchase, or in any other similar way, even although the purchase be only in the name of one of the two, and not of both. Civ. Code La. art. 2371.

ACQUIESCENCE. A silent appearance of consent. Worcester.

It is to be distinguished from avowed consent, on the one hand, and from open discontent or opposition, on the other. It amounts to a consent which is impliedly given by one or both parties to a proposition, a clause, a condition, a judgment, or to any act whatever.

It imports an assent which, though implied, is to some extent active, and is to be distinguished from *laches*, which is mere passive neglect. 69 Cal. 255.

ACQUIETANDIS PLEGIIS. A writ of justices, formerly lying for the surety against a creditor who refuses to acquit him after the debt has been satisfied. Reg. Writs, 158; Cowell; Blount.

ACQUIRE (Lat. *ad*, for, and *quaerere*, to seek). To make property one's own.

It is regularly applied to a permanent acquisition. A man is said to obtain or procure a mere temporary acquisition.

ACQUISITION. The act by which a person procures the property of a thing.

The thing the property in which is secured.

Original acquisition is that by which a man secures a property in a thing which is not at the time he acquires it, and in its then existing condition, the property of any other individual. It may result from occupancy (1 Bouv. Inst. note 490; 2 Kent, Comm. 289), accession (1 Bouv. Inst. note 499; 2 Kent, Comm. 293), intellectual labor, —namely, for inventions, which are secured by patent rights,—and for the authorship of books, maps, and charts, which is protected by copyrights (1 Bouv. Inst. note 508).

Derivative acquisition is that by which property is procured from others, either by act of law or by act of the parties. Goods and chattels may change owners by act of law in the cases of forfeiture, succession, marriage, judgment, insolvency, and intestacy, or by act of the parties, as by gift, will, or sale.

An acquisition may result from the act of the party himself, or those who are in his power acting for him, as his children while minors. 1 N. H. 28. See Dig. 41. 1. 53; Inst. 2. 9. 3.

ACQUITTAL.

——**In Contracts.** A release or discharge from an obligation or engagement. 26 Wend. (N. Y.) 283.

According to Lord Coke, there are three kinds of acquittal, namely, by deed, when the party releases the obligation; by prescription; by tenure. Co. Litt. 100a.

——**In Criminal Practice.** The absolution of a party charged with a crime or misdemeanor.

The absolution of a party accused on a trial before a traverse jury. 1 Nott & McC. (S. C.) 36; 3 McCord (S. C.) 461.

Acquittals in fact are those which take place when the jury, upon trial, finds a verdict of not guilty.

Acquittals in law are those which take place by mere operation of law; as where a man has been charged merely as an accessary, and the principal has been acquitted. 2 Inst. 364.

Effect on subsequent prosecution, see "Jeopardy."

ACQUITTANCE. In contracts. An agreement in writing to discharge a party from an engagement to pay a sum of money. It is evidence of payment, and differs from a release in this, that the latter must be under seal, while an acquittance need not be under seal. Poth. Obl. note 781. See 3 Salk. 298; Co. Litt. 212a, 273a; 1 Rawle (Pa.) 391.

ACRE (Ger. *aker;* perhaps Lat. *ager*, a field). A quantity of land containing one hundred and sixty square rods of land, in whatever shape. Sergeant, Land Laws Pa. 185; Cro. Eliz. 476, 665; 6 Coke, 67; Poph. 55; Co. Litt. 5b. The word formerly signified an open field; whence acre-fight, a contest in an open field. Jacob.

The measure seems to have been variable in amount in its earliest use, but was fixed by statute at a remote period. As originally used, it was applicable especially to meadow lands. Cowell.

ACT (Lat. *agere*, to do; *actus*, done). Something done or established.

In its general legal sense, the word may denote something done by an individual, as a private citizen, or as an officer; or by a body of men, as a legislature, a council, or a court of justice; including not merely physical acts, but also decrees, edicts, laws, judgments, resolves, awards, and determinations. Some general laws made by the congress of the United States are styled "joint resolutions," and these have the same force and effect as those styled "acts."

An instrument in writing to verify facts. Webster. It is used in this sense to signify published acts of assembly, congress, etc. In a sense approaching this, it has been held in trials for treason that letters and other written documents were acts. 1 Fost. C. C. 198; 2 Starkie, 116.

——**In Civil Law.** A writing which states in a legal form that a thing has been done, said, or agreed. Merlin, Repert.

Private acts are those made by private persons as registers in relation to their receipts and expenditures, schedules, acquittances, and the like. Code, 7. 32. 6; Id. 4. 21; Dig. 22. 4; Civ. Code La. arts. 2231-2254; 8 Toullier, Dr. Civ. 94.

Acts under private signature are those which have been made by private individuals, under their hands. An act of this kind does not acquire the force of an authentic act by being registered in the office of a notary (11 Mart. [La.]243; 5 Mart. [La.; N. S.] 693; 8 Mart. [La.] 568; 3 Mart. [La.; N. S.] 396; 3 La. Ann. 419), unless it has been properly acknowledged before the officer by the parties to it (5 Mart. [La.; N. S.] 196).

Public acts are those which have a public authority, and which have been made before public officers, are authorized by a public seal, have been made public by the authority of a magistrate, or which have been extracted and been properly authenticated from public records.

——**In Legislation.** A statute or law made by a legislative body.

General or public acts are those which bind the whole community. Of these the courts take judicial cognizance.

Private or special acts are those which operate only upon particular persons and private concerns.

——**In Scotch Practice.** As a noun, an abbreviation of *actor* (proctor or advocate, especially for a plaintiff or pursuer), used in records. "*Act.* A. *Alt.* B." an abbreviation of *Actor*, A. *Alter*, B.; that is, for the pursuer or plaintiff, A., for the defender, B. 1 Brown, 336, note; 2 Brown, 144, note; Id. 507, note.

As a verb, to do or perform judicially; to enter of record. Surety "acted in the books of adjournal." 1 Brown, 4.

ACT BOOK. In Scotch practice. The minute book of a court. 1 Swinb. 81.

ACT IN PAIS. An act performed out of court, and which is not a matter of record.

A deed or an assurance transacted between two or more private persons in the country, that is, according to the old common law, upon the very spot to be transferred, is matter *in pais*. 2 Bl. Comm. 294. See "In Pais."

ACT OF ATTAINDER. See "Bill of Attainder."

ACT OF BANKRUPTCY. An act which subjects a person to be proceeded against as a bankrupt.

The acts of bankruptcy enumerated in the bankruptcy act of 1898, § 3, are (1) concealment, transfer, or removal of property with intent to hinder, delay, or defraud creditors; (2) transfer of property while insolvent, with intent to give a preference; (3) permitting, while insolvent, a creditor to obtain a preference by legal proceedings, and not vacating such preference within five days; (4) making a general assignment for the benefit of creditors; (5) admitting, in writing, inability to pay debts, and willingness to be adjudged a bankrupt.

ACT OF CURATORY. In Scotch practice. The act extracted by the clerk, upon any one's acceptance of being curator. Forbes, Inst. pt. 1, bk. 1, c. 2, tit. 2; 2 Kames, Eq. 291. Corresponding with the order for the appointment of a guardian, in English and American practice.

ACT OF GOD. A natural cause which operate without interference or aid from man. 1 Pars. Cont. 635.

That which proceeds from the violence of nature; by that kind of force of the elements which human ability could not have foreseen or prevented. 6 Grat. (Va.) 189.

The term is sometimes defined as equivalent to inevitable accident, but incorrectly, as there is a distinction between the two, although Sir William Jones proposed the use of "inevitable accident" instead of "act of God." Jones, Bailm. 104. See Story, Bailm, § 25; 2 Sharswood, Bl. Comm. 122; 2 Crabb, Real Prop. § 2176; 4 Doug. 287; 21 Wend. (N. Y.) 190; 2 Ga. 349; 10 Miss. 572; 5 Blackf. (Ind.) 222.

All acts of God are inevitable accidents, but not all inevitable accidents are the act of God, *i. e.*, caused by the forces of nature. 29 N. Y. 115.

See, also, "Vis Major."

ACT OF GRACE. In Scotch law. A statute by which the incarcerating creditor is bound to aliment his debtor in prison, if such debtor has no means of support, under penalty of a liberation of his debtor if such aliment be not provided. Paterson, Comp.

ACT OF HONOR. An instrument drawn up by a notary public, after protest of a bill of exchange, when a third party is desirous of paying or accepting the bill for the honor of any or all of the parties to it.

ACT OF INSOLVENCY. An act indicating insolvency, and subjecting the party to insolvency proceedings. See "Insolvency."

ACT OF LAW. A result, like the devolution of a title, produced by operation of law without the design of the parties concerned.

ACT OF SETTLEMENT. The statute of 12 & 13 Wm. III. c. 2, limiting the English crown to the Princess Sophia, of Hanover, and the heirs of her body being Protestants

ACT OF STATE. An act done by the sovereign power of a country, or by its delegate, within the limits of the power vested in him. An act of state cannot be questioned or made the subject of legal proceedings in a court of law.

ACT OF SUPREMACY. The statute of 1 Eliz. c. 1, declaring the supremacy of the crown over the ecclesiastical authorities.

ACT OF UNIFORMITY. The statute of 13 & 14 Car. II. c. 4, enacting that the book of common prayer, as then recently revised, should be used in every parish church and other place of public worship, and otherwise ordaining a uniformity in religious services, etc. 3 Steph. Comm. 104.

ACT OF UNION. The statute of 5 Anne, c. 8, by which the articles of union between the two kingdoms of England and Scotland were ratified and confirmed. 1 Bl. Comm. 97.

ACT ON PETITION. A form of summary proceeding formerly in use in the high court of admiralty, in England, in which the parties stated their respective cases briefly, and supported their statements by affidavit. 2 Dods. Adm. 174, 184; 1 Hagg. Adm. 1, note.

ACTA DIURNA (Lat.) A formula often used in signing, in the sense of "done on this day." Du Cange.

Daily transactions, chronicles, journals, registers. "I do not find the thing published in the *acta diurna* (daily records of affairs)." Tacitus, Ann. 3, 3; Ainsworth, Lex.; Smith, Lex.

ACTA EXTERIORA INDICANT INTERIora secreta. Outward acts indicate the inward intent. Broom, Leg. Max. (3d London Ed.) 270; 1 Smith, Lead. Cas. (4th Am. Ed.) 115; 8 Coke, 291; 13 Johns. (N. Y.) 414; 15 Johns. (N. Y.) 401.

ACTA IN UNO JUDICIO NON PROBANT in alio nisi inter easdem personas. Things done in one action cannot be taken as evidence in another, unless it be between the same parties. Tray. Lat. Max. 11.

ACTA PUBLICA (Lat.) Things of general knowledge and concern; matters transacted before certain public officers. Calv. Lex.

ACTE. In French law. Denotes a document, or formal, solemn writing, embodying a legal attestation that something has been done, corresponding to one sense or use of the English word "act." Thus, *actes de naissance* are the certificates of birth, and must contain the day, hour, and place of birth, together with the sex and intended Christian name of the child, and the names of the parents and of the witnesses. *Actes de mariage* are the marriage certificates, and contain names, professions, ages, and places of birth and domicile of the two persons marrying, and of their parents; also the consent of these latter, and the mutual agreements of the intended husband and wife to take each other for better and worse, together with the usual attestations. *Actes de deces* are the certificates of death, which are required to be drawn up before any one may be buried. *Les actes de l'etat civil* are public documents. Brown.

ACTIO. In civil law. A specific mode of enforcing a right before the courts of law, *e. g., legis actio; actio sacramenti.* In this sense we speak of actions in our law, *e. g.,* the action of debt. The right to a remedy, thus: *Ex nudo pacto non oritur actio,* no right of action can arise upon a naked pact. In this sense we rarely use the word "action." 3 Ortolan, Inst. § 1830; 5 Savigny, System, 10; Mackeld. Civ. Law (13th Ed.) § 193.

The first sense here given is the older one. Justinian, following Celsus, gives the well-known definition: *Actio nihil aliud est, quam jus persequendi in judicio, quod sibi debetur,* which may be thus rendered: An action is simply the right to enforce one's demand in a court of law. Inst. 4. 6, "De Actionibus." See "Action."

Divisions:

——**According to Nature.** In the sense of a specific form of remedy, there are various divisions of *actiones*. *Actiones civiles* are those forms of remedies which were established under the rigid and inflexible system of the civil law, the *jus civile*. *Actiones honorariae* are those which were gradually introduced by the praetors and aediles, by virtue of their equitable powers, in order to prevent the failure of justice which too often resulted from the employment of the *actiones civiles*. These were found so beneficial in practice that they eventually supplanted the old remedies, of which, in the time of Justinian, hardly a trace remained. Mackeld. Civ. Law, § 194; 5 Savigny, System. *Directae actiones*, as a class, were forms of remedies for cases clearly defined and recognized as actionable by the law. *Utiles actiones* were remedies granted by the magistrate in cases to which no *actio directa* was applicable. They were framed for the special occasion, by analogy to the existing form, and were generally fictitious; that is, they proceeded upon the assumption that a state of things existed which would have entitled the party to an *actio directa*, and the cause was tried upon this assumption, which the other party was not allowed to dispute. 5 Savigny, System, § 215.

——**According to Subject-Matter.** Again there are *actiones in personam* and *actiones in rem.* The former class includes all remedies for the breach of an obligation, and are considered to be directed against the person of the wrongdoer. The second class comprehends all remedies devised for the recovery of property, or the enforcement of a right not founded upon a contract between the parties, and are therefore considered as rather aimed at the thing in dispute than at the person of the defendant. Mackeld. Civ. Law, § 195; 5 Savigny, System, §§ 206-209; 3 Ortolan, Inst. § 1952 et seq.

——**According to Object.** In respect to their object, actions are either (a) *actiones rei persequendae causa comparatae*, for the recovery of property or damages, to which class belong all *actiones in rem*, and those of the *actiones in personam*, which were directed merely to the recovery of the value of a thing, or compensation for an injury; or (b) *actiones poenales* (called, also, *actiones ex delicto*), in which a penalty was recovered of the delinquent; or (c) *actiones mixtae*, in which were recovered both the actual damages and a penalty in addition. *Actiones poenales* and *actiones mixtae* comprehended cases of injuries for which the civil law permitted redress by private action, but which modern civilization universally regards as crimes; that is, offenses against society at large, and punished by proceedings in the name of the state alone. Thus, theft, receiving stolen goods, robbery, malicious mischief, and the murder or negligent homicide of a slave (in which case an injury to property was involved), gave rise to private actions for damages against the delinquent. Inst. 4. 1. *De obligationibus quae ex delicto nascuntur.* Id. 2. *De bonis vi raptis.* Id. 3. *De lege aquilia.* And see Mackeld. Civ. Law, § 196, 5 Savigny, System, §§ 210-212.

——**According to Procedure.** In respect to the mode of procedure, *actiones in personam* are divided into *stricti juris*, and *bonae fidei actiones*. In the former, the court was confined to the strict letter of the law, in the latter, something was left to the discretion of the judge, who was governed in his decision by considerations of what ought to be expected from an honest man under circumstances similar to those of the plaintiff or defendant. Mackeld. Civ. Law, § 197a.

Besides this classification, the different actions had specific names, the principal of which follow.

ACTIO AD EXHIBENDUM. In civil law. An action instituted for the purpose of compelling the person against whom it was brought to exhibit some thing or title in his power.

It was always preparatory to another action, which lay for the recovery of a thing movable or immovable. 1 Merlin, Quest. de Droit, 84.

ACTIO ARBITRARIA. In the civil law. An arbitrary action; one depending upon the discretion of the judge (*ex arbitrio judicis pendens*); or in which the judge was allowed to determine, according to equity and the circumstances of the particular case, how satisfaction should be made to the plaintiff (*permittitur judici ex bono et aequo, secundum cujusque rei de qua actum est naturam, aestimare quemadmodum actori satisfieri oporteat*). If the defendant refused to conform to the decision of the judge, he might be condemned at discretion (*nisi arbitrio judicis actori satisfaciat,—condemnari debeat*). Inst. 4. 6. 31.

ACTIO BONAE FIDEI. See "Actio" (4).

ACTIO CALUMNIAE. In the civil law. An action to restrain the defendant from prosecuting a groundless proceeding or trumped-up charge against the plaintiff. Hunter, Rom. Law, 859.

ACTIO CIVILIS. See "Actio" (1).

ACTIO COMMODATI CONTRARIA. In civil law. An action by the borrower against the lender, to compel the execution of the contract. Poth. Pret. a Usage, note 75.

ACTIO COMMODATI DIRECTA. In civil law. An action by a lender against a borrower, the principal object of which is to obtain a restitution of the thing lent. Poth. Pret. a Usage, notes 65, 68.

ACTIO COMMUNI DIVIDUNDO. In civil law. An action for a division of the property held in common. Story, Partn. (Bennett Ed.) § 352.

ACTIO COMMUNIS. A common action. A term applied by Bracton to an action where the thing demanded was common, and not several. Bracton, fol. 103.

ACTIO CONDICTIO INDEBITATI. In civil law. An action by which the plaintiff recovers the amount of a sum of money or other thing he paid by mistake. Poth. Promutuum, note 140.

ACTIO CONFESSORIA. In the civil law. An affirmative action; an action founded upon the affirmative allegation of some right in the plaintiff in another's land, as a right of way, etc., and not upon the denial of the right of another in his land. Inst. 4. 6. 2. *Confessoria dicitur, quia constituta est verbis affirmativis.* Bracton, fol. 103. See "Actio Negatoria."

ACTIO CONTRARIA. In the civil law. A contrary or cross action, as distinguished from *actio directa.* Heinec. Elem. Jur. Civ. lib. 3, tit. 15, §§ 805, 816, 826; Bracton, fol. 103.

ACTIO CRIMINALIS. In the common law. A criminal action. Bracton, fol. 102b.

ACTIO DE DOLO MALO. In the civil law. An action of fraud; an action which lay for a defrauded person against the defrauder and his heirs, who had been enriched by the fraud, to obtain the restitution of the thing of which he had been fraudulently deprived, with all its accessions (*cum omni causa*); or, where this was not practicable, for compensation in damages. 1 Mackeld. Civ. Law, p. 221, § 217; Heinec. Elem. Jur. Civ. lib. 4, tit. 6, § 1152; Dig. 4. 3; Code, 2. 21; Bracton, fol. 103b.

ACTIO DE IN REM VERSO. In the civil law. An action concerning a thing converted to the profit of another; an action granted to one who had contract with a son or slave, in order to recover whatever the father or master, by means of such contract, had converted to their own advantage. Inst. 4. 7. 4; Dig. 15. 3; Code, 4. 26; Heinec. Elem. Jur. Civ. lib. 4, tit. 7, § 1222; Halifax, Anal. bk. 3, c. 2, note 7.

ACTIO DE PECULIO. In the civil law. An action concerning or against the peculium, patrimony, or separate estate. Inst. action to which fathers and masters were liable on the contracts of their children and servants, to the extent of the latter's peculium, patrimony, or separate estate. Inst. 4. 6. 10; Id. 4. 7. 4; Dig. 15. 1; Code, 4. 26; Heinec. Elem. Jur. Civ. lib. 4, tit. 7, § 1219.

ACTIO DE PECUNIA CONSTITUTA. In the civil law. An action for money engaged to be paid; an action which lay against any person who had engaged to pay money for himself, or for another, without any formal stipulation (*nulla stipulatione interposita*). Inst. 4. 6. 9; Dig. 13. 5; Code, 4. 18.

ACTIO DEPOSITI CONTRARIA. In civil law. An action which the depositary has against the depositor, to compel him to fulfill his engagement toward him. Poth. du Depot, note 69.

ACTIO DEPOSITI DIRECTA. In civil law. An action which is brought by the depositor against the depositary, in order to get back the thing deposited. Poth. du Depot, note 60.

ACTIO DIRECTA. See "Actio" (1).

ACTIO EMPTI. See "Actio ex Empto."

ACTIO EX CONDUCTO. In civil law. An action which the bailor of a thing for hire may bring against the bailee, in order to compel him to redeliver the thing hired. Poth. du Contr. de Louage, note 59.

ACTIO EX CONTRACTU. See "Action."

ACTIO EX DELICTO. See "Action."

ACTIO EX EMPTO. In the civil law. An action of purchase, or upon purchase; an action which a buyer is entitled to maintain against a seller, in order to cause him to deliver possession of the thing sold, with its titles and fruits, and everything dependent upon it. Poth. Cont. pt. 2, c. 1, art. 5; Inst. 4. 6. 28. Otherwise called *actio empti*, or *emti*. Dig. 19. 1; Code, 4. 49; Heinec. Elem. Jur. Civ. lib. 3, tit. 24, § 912.

ACTIO EX LOCATO. In the civil law. An action upon letting; an action which the person (locator) who let a thing for hire to another might have against the hirer (conductor). Dig. 19. 2; Code, 4. 65. See "Actio Locati."

ACTIO EX STIPULATU. In the civil law. An action to enforce a stipulation.

ACTIO EX VENDITO. In the civil law. An action upon sale; an action which a seller is entitled to maintain against a buyer to recover the price of a thing sold and delivered. Inst. 4. 6. 28; Heinec. Elem. Jur. Civ. lib. 3, tit. 24, § 915. Called *actio venditi*. Id.; Dig. 19. 1; Code, 4. 49.

ACTIO EXERCITORIA. In the civil law. An action against the *exercitor* or employer of a vessel. See "Exercitoria Actio."

ACTIO FAMILIAE ERCISCUNDAE. In civil law. An action for the division of an inheritance. Inst. 4. 6. 20; Bracton, 100b.

ACTIO FINIUM REGUNDORUM. In the civil law. An action for the determination of boundaries between adjoining lands. Inst. 4. 17. 6; Id. 4. 6. 20. Enumerated by Bracton and Fleta among mixed actions. Bracton, fol. 444; Fleta, lib. 5, c. 9, § 3. See "Finium Regundorum Actio."

ACTIO FURTI. In the civil law. An action of theft; an action founded upon theft. Inst. 4. 1. 13-17; Bracton, fol. 444. This could only be brought for the penalty attached to the offense (*tantum ad poenoe persecutionem pertinet*), and not to recover the thing stolen itself, for which other actions were provided. Inst. 4. 1. 19.

ACTIO HONORARIA. See "Actio" (1).

ACTIO IN FACTUM. In civil law. An action adapted to the particular case which had an analogy to some *actio in jus*, which was founded on some subsisting acknowledged law. Spence, Eq. Jur. 212. The origin of these actions is strikingly similar to that of actions on the case at common law. See "Case."

ACTIO IN PERSONAM (Lat.) an action against the person. See "Actio" (2).

A personal action.

This is the term in use in the civil law to denote the actions which in the common law are called "personal." In modern usage it is applied in English and American law to those suits in admiralty which are directed against the person of the defendant, as distinguished from those *in rem*, which are directed against the specific thing from which (or rather the proceeds of the sale of which) the complainant expects and claims a right to derive satisfaction for the injury done to him.

ACTIO IN QUADRUPLUM. In the civil law. An action for the quadruple value of a thing. Inst. 4. 6. 21; Bracton, fol. 103a.

ACTIO IN REM. An action against the thing. See "Actio" (2).

ACTIO IN SIMPLUM. In the civil law. An action for the single value of a thing. Inst. 4. 6. 21. 22; Bracton, fol. 103a.

ACTIO IN TRIPLUM. In the civil law. An action for the triple value of a thing. Inst. 4. 6. 21. 24; Bracton, fol. 103a.

ACTIO INDIRECTA. An indirect action. A species of action mentioned by Bracton, probably the reverse of the *actio directa.* Bracton, fol. 103a.

ACTIO INJURIARUM, or **DAMNI INJURia.** In the civil law. An action for injuries done by beating, wounding, slanderous language, libel, and the like. Inst. 4. 4. pr. 1, 12; Bracton, fol. 103b.

ACTIO JUDICATI. In civil law. An action instituted, after four months had elapsed after the rendition of judgment, in which the judge issued his warrant to seize, first, the movables, which were sold within eight days afterwards, and then the immovables, which were delivered in pledge to the creditors, or put under the care of a curator, and if, at the end of two months, the debt was not paid, the land was sold. Dig. 42. 1; Code, 8. 34.

According to some authorities, if the defendant then utterly denied the rendition of the former judgment, the plaintiff was driven to a new action, conducted like any other action, which was called *actio judicati,* and which had for its object the determination of the question whether such a judgment had been rendered. The exact meaning of the term is by no means clear. See Savigny, System, 305, 411; 3 Ortolan, Just. § 2033.

ACTIO LEGIS. In the Roman law. A legal or lawful action; an action of or at law. Dig. 1. 2. 2. 6.

One of the sources of the unwritten law of Rome. Butler, Hor. Jur. 47. So called, according to Gaius, either because they were expressly given by the laws, or because they were expressed in the words of the laws. Gaius, Inst. iv. § 11.

ACTIO LEGIS AQUILLE. In the civil law. An action under the Aquilian law; an action to recover damages for maliciously or injuriously killing or wounding the slave or beast of another, or injuring in any way a thing belonging to another. Otherwise called *damni injuriae actio.* Inst. 4. 3; Heinec. Elem. Jur. Civ. lib. 4, tit. 3; Halifax, Anal. bk. 2, c. 24; Bracton, fol. 103b.

ACTIO LOCATI. In the civil law. An action which lay for the letter (locator) of a thing against the hirer, where the terms of the contract were not complied with by the latter. Inst. 3. 25. pr.; Dig. 19. 2; Heinec. Elem. Jur. Civ. lib. 3, tit. 25, § 928. See "Actio ex Locato."

ACTIO MANDATI. In civil law. An action founded upon a mandate.

ACTIO MIXTA (or **MISTA**). See "Actio" (3).

An action in which each party is actor, or plaintiff; such as the actions *finium regundorum, familiae erciscundae, communi dividundo,* and others. Dig. 47. 7. 37. 1.

ACTIO NEGATORIA, (or **NEGATIVA**). In the civil law. A negatory or negative action; an action founded on the denial (*negatio*) of another's right; as where a right of way or other servitude in a particular estate is denied. Inst. 4. 6. 2; Bracton, fol. 103a; Heinec. Elem. Jur. Civ. lib. 4, tit. 6, § 1136; Halifax, Anal. bk. 3, c. 1, note 8. See "Actio Confessoria."

ACTIO NEGOTIORUM GESTORUM. In the civil law. An action upon, or on account of, business done. An action given in cases where a person transacted the business of another during his absence (*cum quis negotia absentis gesserit*), or without a commission or authority (*sine mandato*). Inst. 3. 28. This was of two kinds—a direct action, which lay for the person whose business had been transacted, against him who had transacted it (*domino rei gestae adversus eum qui gessit*), and a cross action, which lay for the *negotiorum gestor,* as he was called against the other. Id.; Heinec. Elem. Jur. Civ. lib. 3, tit. 28, §§ 973, 974. See "Negotiorum Gestio."

This action is enumerated by Bracton and Fleta among actions arising *quasi ex contractu,* or *ex quasi contractu.* Bracton, fol. 100b; Fleta, lib. 2, c. 60, § 1.

ACTIO NOMINATAE (Lat. a named action). In English law. A writ for which there was a precedent in the English chancery prior to St. 13 Edw. 1. (Westminster II.) c. 34.

The clerks would make no writs except in such actions prior to this statute, according to some accounts. 17 Serg. & R. (Pa.) 195. See "Action;" "Case."

ACTIO NON. In pleading. The declaration in a special plea "that the said plaintiff ought not to have or maintain his aforesaid action thereof against" the defendant (in Latin, *actio non habere debet*).

It follows immediately after the statement of appearance and defense. 1 Chit. Pl. 531; 2 Chit. Pl. 421; Steph. Pl. 394.

ACTIO NON ACCREVIT INFRA SEX ANNOS (Lat.) The action did not accrue within six years.

——**In Pleading.** A plea of the statute of limitations, by which the defendant insists that the plaintiff's action has not accrued within six years. It differs from *non assumpsit* in this: *Non assumpsit* is the proper plea to an action on a simple contract, when the action accrues on the promise; but when it does not accrue on the promise, but subsequently to it, the proper plea is *actio non accrevit*, etc. Lawes, Pl. 733; 5 Bin. (Pa.) 200, 203; 2 Salk. 422; 1 Saund. 33, note 2; 2 Saund. 63b.

ACTIO NON DATUR NON DAMNIFICO. An action is not given to one who is not injured. Jenk. Cent. Cas. 69.

ACTIO NON FACIT REUM, NISI MENS sit rea. An action does not make one guilty unless the intention be bad. Lofft, 37.

ACTIO NON ULTERIUS (Lat.) In English pleading. A name given to the distinctive clause in the plea to the further maintenance of the action, introduced in place of the plea *puis darrein continuance;* the averment being that the plaintiff ought not further (*ulterius*) to have or maintain his action. Steph. Pl. 64, 65, 401.

ACTIO NOXALIS. In the civil law. A noxal action; an action which lay against a master for a crime committed or injury done by his slave, and in which the master had the alternative either to pay for the damage done or to deliver up the slave to the complaining party. Inst. 4. 8. pr.; Heinec. Elem. Jur. Civ. lib. 4, tit. 8; Halifax, Anal. bk. 3, c. 2. So called from *noxa*, the slave or offending person or *noxia*, the offense or injury itself. Inst. 4. 8. 1.

ACTIO PERPETUA. In the civil law. A perpetual or unlimited action; one not limited to any particular period within which it should be brought. Inst. 4. 12. pr. The opposite of the *actio temporalis (q. v.)*

ACTIO PERSONALIS. A personal action. The proper term in the civil law is *actio in personam.*

ACTIO PERSONALIS MORITUR CUM persona (Lat.) A personal action dies with the person.

——**In Practice.** A maxim which formerly expressed the law in regard to the surviving of personal actions.

ACTIO PIGNORATICIA. In the civil law. An action of pledge; an action founded on the contract of pledge (*pignus*). Dig. 13. 7; Code, 4. 24.

ACTIO POENAE PERSECUTORIA. In the civil law. An action prosecuted for a penalty only, and not for a specific thing. Inst. 4. 6. 16. 18.

ACTIO POENALIS. In the civil law. A penal action; an action brought to enforce the payment of a private penalty. 1 Mackeld. Civ. Law, p. 193, § 196.

ACTIO POENALIS IN HAEREDEM NON datur, nisi forte ex damno locupletior haeres factus sit. A penal action is not given against an heir, unless, indeed, such heir is benefited by the wrong.

ACTIO PRAEJUDICIALIS. In the civil law. A preliminary or preparatory action; an action brought for the determination of some point or question arising in another or principal action, and so called from its being determined before (*prius*, or *prae judicari*) the principal action could proceed. Bracton, 104a; Cowell. Of this nature were actions for determining a man's civil state or condition, as whether he was a freeman or a slave, legitimate or illegitimate. Inst. 4. 6. 13; Heinec. Elem. Jur. Civ. lib. 4, tit. 6, § 1142; Halifax, Anal. bk. 3, c. 1, note 14.

ACTIO PRAESCRIPTIS VERBIS. In civil law. A form of action which derived its force from continued usage or the *responsa prudentium*, and was founded on the unwritten law. 1 Spence, Eq. Jur. 212.

The distinction between this action and an *actio in factum* is said to be that the latter was founded, not on usage or the unwritten law, but by analogy to or on the equity of some subsisting law. 1 Spence, Eq. Jur. 212.

ACTIO PRAETORIA. In the civil law. A praetorian action; one introduced by the praetor, as distinguished from the more ancient *actio civilis*. Inst. 4. 6. 3; 1 Mackeld. Civ. Law, p. 189, § 194.

ACTIO PRO SOCIO. In the civil law. An action for a copartner; an action which one copartner (*socius*) might have against another. Dig. 17. 2; Code, 4. 37.

ACTIO PROPRIA. An action brought for the recovery of a several thing (*res propria*), as distinguished from a thing held in common. Bracton, fol. 103a.

ACTIO PUBLICIANA. In the civil law. An action which lay for one who had lost a thing of which he had *bona fide* obtained possession before he had gained a property (*dominium*) in it, in order to have it restored, under color that he had obtained a property in it by prescription. Inst. 4. 6. 4; Dig. 6. 2; Heinec. Elem. Jur. Civ. lib. 4, tit. 6, § 1131; Halifax, Anal. bk. 3, c. 1, note 9. It was an honorary action, and derived its name from the praetor Publicius, by whose edict it was first given. Inst. 4. 6. 4.

ACTIO QUAELIBET IT SUA VIA. Every action proceeds in its own course. Jenk. Cent. Cas. 77.

ACTIO QUANTI MINORIS. In the civil law. An action given to a purchaser who had paid more for a thing than it was intrinsically worth, to recover back so much of the price as the thing was of less value (*quanti minoris*), or fell short in value, by reason of the defect. Poth. Cont. pt. 2, c. 1, § 4, art. 5; 1 Kames, Eq. 271.

ACTIO QUOD JUSSU. In the civil law. An action given against a master, founded on some business done by his slave, acting under his order (*jussu*). Inst. 4. 7. 1; Dig. 15. 4; Code, 4. 26.

ACTIO QUOD METUS CAUSA. In the civil law. An action granted by unlawful force, or fear (*metus causa*) that was not groundless (*metus probabilis* or *justus*), to deliver, sell, or promise a thing to another. Bracton, fol. 103b; 1 Mackeld. Civ. Law, p. 120, § 216.

ACTIO (or INTERDICTUM) QUOD VI aut clam. In the civil law. An action which lay where one forcibly or clandestinely (*vi aut clam*) erected or demolished a building on his own or another's ground, and thereby unlawfully injured another; its object being to get everything restored to its former condition, and to obtain damages. Dig. 43. 24. 1. Bracton gives this action a place in his system of remedies, defining it as one which lay against him who had erected or prostrated a building on another's land, and concealed himself in order to avoid being prevented from doing it (*et se occultavit, ne sibi prohiberetur*), and observes that the offender might by this action be compelled to restore everything to its former state, at his own expense. Bracton, fols. 103b, 104a.

ACTIO REALIS (Lat.) A real action. The proper term in the civil law was *rei vindicatio.*

ACTIO REDHIBITORIA. In civil law. An action to compel a vendor to take back the thing sold, and return the price paid.

ACTIO REI PERSECUTORIA. In the civil law. An action for the recovery of a specific thing (*rei presequendae causa comparata*) or damages; as distinguished from the *actio poenae persecutoria,* and the *actio mixta.* Inst. 4. 6. 16. 17; 1 Mackeld. Civ. Law, p. 192, § 196.

ACTIO RERUM AMOTARUM. In the civil law. An action for things removed; an action which, in cases of divorce, lay for a husband against a wife, to recover things carried away by the latter, in contemplation of such divorce (*divortii consilio*). Dig. 25. 2; Id. 25. 2. 25. 30. It also lay for the wife against the husband in such cases. Id. 25. 2. 7. 11; Code, 5, 21.

ACTIO RESCISSORIA. In civil law. An action for rescinding a title acquired by prescription in a case where the party bringing the action was entitled to exemption from the operation of the prescription.

ACTIO SEPULCHRI VIOLATI. In the civil law. An action for violating a grave. Dig. 47. 12; Code, 9. 19.

ACTIO SERVIANA. In the civil law. An action which lay for the lessor of a farm, or rural estate, to recover the goods of the lessee or farmer, which were pledged or bound for the rent. Inst. 4. 6. 7; Heinec. Elem. Jur. Civ. lib. 4, tit. 6, § 1139; Halifax, Anal. bk. 3, c. 1, note 12.

ACTIO SPECIALIS. In the civil law. A special action; an action brought to enforce the delivery of one of several single things. 1 Mackeld. Civ. Law, p. 193, § 196; Dig. 6. 1. 1.

ACTIO STRICTI JURIS (Lat. an action of strict right). An action in which the judge followed the formula that was sent to him closely, administered such relief only as that warranted, and admitted such claims as were distinctly set forth by the pleadings of the parties. 1 Spence, Eq. Jur. 218.

ACTIO TEMPORALIS. In the civil law. A temporary action; an action limited to a certain time, within which it was to be instituted, on pain of losing it; the opposite of *actio perpetua (q. v.)* Inst. 4. 12.

ACTIO TRIBUTORIA. In the civil law. An action for distribution (Lat. *tribuere,* to distribute); an action which lay for the creditor of a son or slave, who had traded upon his *peculium,* with the knowledge of his father or master, to obtain from the latter a distributive or proportionate share of the goods traded in (*peculiares merces*), or their proceeds. Inst. 4. 7. 3; Heinec. Elem. Jur. Civ. lib. 4, tit. 7, § 1217; Halifax, Anal. bk. 3, c. 2, note 6.

ACTIO TUTELAE. In the civil law. An action of tutelage.

ACTIO (or INTERDICTUM) UNDE VI. In the civil law. An action or interdict which lay to recover possession of an immovable thing, as land, of which one had been deprived by force. So called from the formal words in it,—*unde tu illum vi dejecisti,* from which you have ejected him by force. Gaius, Inst. iv. 154; Inst. 4. 15. 6; Dig. 43. 16. It resembled the modern action of ejectment, and is adopted by Bracton in his system of actions. Bracton, fol. 103b.

ACTIO UTILIS. An action for the benefit of those who had the beneficial use of property, but not the legal title; an equitable action. 1 Spence, Eq. Jur. 214.

It was subsequently extended to include many other instances where a party was equitably entitled to relief, although he did not come within the strict letter of the law and the *formulae* appropriate thereto.

ACTIO VENDITI. See "Actio ex Vendito."

ACTIO VI BONORUM RAPTORUM. In the civil law. An action for goods taken by force; a species of mixed action, which lay for a party whose goods or movables (*bona*) had been taken from him by force (*vi*), to recover the things so taken, together with a penalty of triple the value. Inst. 4. 2; Id. 4. 6. 19. Bracton describes it as lying *de rebus mobilibus vi ablatis sive robbatis*, for movable things taken away by force, or robbed. Bracton, fol. 103b.

ACTIO VULGARIS. In civil law. A legal action; a common action.

ACTION (Lat. *agere*, to do; to lead; to conduct). A doing of something; something done.

The term is, in legal usage, confined to practice, having no technical meaning, in the substantive law, except in the French law, in which it denotes shares in a company, or stock in a corporation.

It signifies the formal demand of one's right from another person or party made and insisted on in a court of justice.

In Justinian's Institute, "action" was defined as the right of pursuing in a court of justice what was due one's self. Inst. 4. In the Digest, however, it was defined as the right of pursuing, the pursuit itself, or exercise of this right, or the form of proceedings by which it was exercised. Dig. 50. 16. 16; Id. 1. 2. 10. This definition is adopted by Mr. Taylor (Tayl. Civ. Law, p. 50). In modern usage, the signification of the right of pursuing has been generally dropped, though it is recognized by Bracton (98b), Coke (2d Inst. 40), and Blackstone (3 Comm. 116), while the two latter senses, of the exercise of the right, and the means or method of its exercise, are in general use.

The vital idea of an action is a proceeding on the part of one person as actor against another, for the infringement of some right of the first, before a court of justice, in the manner prescribed by the court or the law. Subordinate to this is now connected in a quite common use the idea of the answer of the defendant or person proceeded against; the adducing evidence by each party to sustain his position; the adjudication of the court upon the right of the plaintiff; and the means taken to enforce the right, or recompense the wrong done, in case the right is established and shown to have been injuriously affected. 3 How. Pr. (N. Y.) 318.

All proceedings in the court up to the final termination of the litigation, whether instituted by a party, by a third person, or by the court of its own motion, are part of the action, if incidental; the principal remedy constituting the action, and founded on its existence. Even when regulated by special statute, such proceedings are considered proceedings in the action, and not special proceedings, except where the statutes otherwise declare, or the papers are so entitled as to forbid their being so treated.

As distinguished from "suit," the word "action" is generally applied to proceedings at law, and "suit" to proceedings in equity. 9 Barb. (N. Y.) 300. See "Suit."

Actions are to be distinguished from those proceedings, such as writ of error, *scire facias*, *mandamus*, and the like, where, under the form of proceedings, the court, and not the plaintiff, appears to be the actor. 6 Bin. (Pa.) 9.

Actions are classified as (1) in the civil law, or (2) in the common law.

——(1a) **Civil Actions in the Civil Law.** Those personal actions which are instituted to compel payments, or do some other thing purely civil. Poth. Introd. Gen. aux Coutumes, 110.

——(1b) **Criminal Actions in the Civil Law.** Those personal actions in which the plaintiff asks reparation for the commission of some tort or injury which he or those who belong to him have sustained.

——(1c) **Mixed Actions in the Civil Law.** Those which partake of the nature of both real and personal actions; as actions of partition; actions to recover property and damages. Inst. 4. 6. 18-20; Domat. Supp. Civ. Law, liv. 4, tit. 1, note 4.

——(1d) **Mixed Personal Actions in the Civil Law.** Those which partake of both a civil and a criminal character.

——(1e) **Personal Actions in the Civil Law.** Those in which one person (*actor*) sues another as defendant (*reus*) in respect of some obligation which he is under to the actor, either *ex contractu* or *ex delicto*, to perform some act or make some compensation.

——(1f) **Real Actions in the Civil Law.** Those by which a person seeks to recover his property, which is in the possession of another.

——(2a) **Civil Actions in the Common Law.** Those actions which have for their object the recovery of private or civil rights, or of compensation for their infraction.

——(2b) **Criminal Actions in the Common Law.** Those actions prosecuted in a court of justice, in the name of the government, against one or more individuals accused of a crime. See 1 Chit. Crim. Law.

——(2c) **Local Actions in the Common Law.** Those civil actions the cause of which could have arisen in some particular place or county only. See "Local Action."

——(2d) **Mixed Actions in the Common Law.** Those which partake of the nature of both real and personal actions. See "Mixed Action."

——(2e) **Personal Actions in the Common Law.** Those civil actions which are brought for the recovery of personal property, for the enforcement of some contract, or to recover damages for the commission of an injury to the person or property. See "Personal Action."

——(2f) **Real Actions in the Common Law.** Those brought for the specific recovery of lands, tenements, or hereditaments. Steph. Pl. 3. See "Real Action."

——(2g) **Transitory Actions in the Common Law.** Those civil actions the cause of which might have arisen in one place or county as well as another.

ACTION FOR POINDING OF THE ground. See "Poinding."

ACTION IN PERSONAM. See "Actio in Personam."

ACTION IN REM. See "Actio in Rem."

ACTION OF A WRIT. A phrase used when a defendant pleads some matter by which he shows that the plaintiff had no cause to have the writ sued upon, although it may be that he is entitled to another writ or action for the same matter. Cowell.

ACTION OF ABSTRACTED MULTURES. In Scotch law. An action for multures or tolls against those who are thirled to a mill, *i. e.*, bound to grind their corn at a certain mill, and fail to do so. Bell, Dict.

ACTION OF ADHERENCE. In Scotch law. An action competent to a husband or wife, to compel either party to adhere in case of desertion. It is analogous to the English suit for restitution of conjugal rights. Wharton.

ACTION OF BOOK DEBT. A form of action resorted to in the states of Connecticut and Vermont for the recovery of claims, such as usually evidenced by a book account. 1 Day (Conn.) 105; 4 Day (Conn.) 105; 2 Vt. 366. See 1 Conn. 75; 11 Conn. 205.

ACTION ON THE CASE. See "Case."

ACTION ORDINARY. In Scotch law. All actions which are not rescissory.

ACTION REDHIBITORY. See "Redhibitory Action."

ACTION RESCISSORY. See "Rescissory Actions."

ACTIONABLE. For which an action will lie 3 Bl. Comm. 23.

ACTIONARY. A commercial term used in Europe to denote a proprietor of shares or *actions* in a joint-stock company.

ACTIONES. Actions. Plural of *actio* (*q. v.*), and is used in combination in the same manner.

ACTIONUM GENERA MAXIME SUNT servanda. The kinds of actions are especially to be preserved. Lofft, 460.

ACTIVE. That which requires action. Thus, an active trust is one requiring action by the trustee to execute the donor's will.

ACTON BURNELL. An ancient English statute, so called because enacted by a parliament held at the village of Acton Burnell. It is otherwise known as *statutum mercatorum* or *de mercatoribus*, the statute of the merchants. It was a statute for the collection of debts, the earliest of its class, being enacted in 1283.

A further statute for the same object, and known as *De Mercatoribus*, was enacted 13 Edw. I. c. 3. See "Statute Merchant."

ACTOR (Lat. *agere*). In civil law.

(1) A patron, pleader, or advocate. Du Cange; Cowell; Spelman.

Actor ecclesiae was an advocate for a church; one who protects the temporal interests of a church. *Actor villae* was the steward or head bailiff of a town or village. Cowell.

(2) One who takes care of his lord's lands. Du Cange.

(3) A guardian or tutor; one who transacts the business of his lord or principal; nearly synonymous with "agent," which comes from the same word.

The word has a variety of closely related meanings, very nearly corresponding with "manager." Thus, *actor dominae*, manager of his master's farms; *actor ecclesiae*, manager of church property; *actores provinciarum*, tax gatherers, treasurers, and managers of the public debt.

(4) A plaintiff; contrasted with *reus*, the defendant. *Actores regis*, those who claimed money of the king. Du Cange; Spelman; Cowell.

ACTOR QUI CONTRA REGULAM QUID adduxit non est audrindus. A pleader ought not to be heard who advances a proposition contrary to the rules of law.

ACTOR SEQUITUR FORUM REI. The plaintiff must follow the forum of the thing in dispute. Kames, Law Tr. 232; Story, Confl. Laws, § 325k; 2 Kent, Comm. 462.

ACTORE NON PROBANTE REUS AB solvitur. If the plaintiff does not prove his case, the defendant is absolved. Hob. 103.

ACTORI INCUMBIT ONUS PROBANDI. The burden of proof lies on the plaintiff. Hob. 103.

ACTORNAY. In old Scotch law. Attorney; an attorney. Skene de Verb. Sign. voc. "Actornatus."

ACTRIX (Lat.) A female actor; a female plaintiff. Calv. Lex.

ACTS OF COURT. Legal memoranda made in the admiralty courts in England, in the nature of pleas. For example, the English court of admiralty disregards all tenders except those formally made by acts of court. Abb. Shipp. 403; Dunlop, Adm. Prac. 104, 105; 4 C. Rob. Adm. 103; 1 Hagg. Adm. 157.

ACTS OF SEDERUNT. In Scotch law. Ordinances for regulating the forms of proceeding, before the court of session, in the administration of justice, made by the judges, who have the power by virtue of a Scotch act of parliament passed in 1540. Ersk. Princ. bk. 1, tit. 1, § 14.

ACTUAL CASH VALUE. The fair and reasonable cash price for which property can be sold in the market. It is synonymous with "fair cash value." 193 Ill. 474.

ACTUAL DAMAGES. See "Damages."

ACTUAL DELIVERY. See "Delivery."

ACTUAL EVICTION. An eviction coupled with a physical expulsion. 167 Ill. 98.

ACTUAL FRAUD. Deception practiced in order to induce another to part with property or to surrender some legal right, and which accomplishes the end designated. 156 Ill. 55.

ACTUAL NOTICE. See "Notice."

ACTUAL OCCUPATION. See "Occupation."

ACTUAL OUSTER. See "Ouster."

ACTUAL POSSESSION. See "Possession."

ACTUAL TOTAL LOSS. In marine insurance the complete destruction of the insured vessel, so that it cannot be recovered or repaired, as distinguished from constructive total, which authorizes an abandonment to the underwriters. 25 Ohio St. 64. See "Abandonment."

ACTUARIUS (Lat.) One who drew the acts or statutes; one who wrote in brief the public acts.

An officer who had charge of the public baths; an officer who received the money for the soldiers, and distributed it among them; a sotary.

An actor *(q. v.)* Du Cagne.

ACTUARY. The manager of a joint-stock company, particularly an insurance company. Penny, Cyc.

A clerk, in some corporations vested with various powers.

——**In Ecclesiastical Law.** A clerk who registers the acts and constitutions of the convocation.

ACTUM (Lat. *agere*). A deed; something done.

Datum relates to the time of the delivery of the instrument; *actum*, the time of making it; *factum*, the thing made. *Gestum* denotes a thing done without writing; *actum*, a thing done in writing. Du Cagne, "Actus."

ACTUS (Lat. *agere*, to do; *actus*, done).

——**In Civil Law.** A thing done. See "Actum."

——**In Roman Law.** A servitude which carried the right of driving animals and vehicles across the lands of another.

It included also the *iter*, or right of passing across on foot or on horseback.

——**In English Law.** An act of parliament. 8 Coke, 40.

A foot and horse way. Co. Litt. 56a.

ACTUS CURIAE NEMINEM GRAVABIT. An act of the court shall prejudice no man. Jenk. Cent. Cas. 118; Broom, Leg. Max. (3d London Ed.) 115; 1 Strange, 126; 1 Smith, Lead. Cas. 245-255; 12 C. B. 415.

ACTUS DEI NEMINEM FACIT INJURIam. The act of God does wrong to no one,—that is, no one is responsible in damages for inevitable accidents. 2 Bl. Comm. 122; 1 Coke, 97b; 5 Coke, 87; Co. Litt. 206a; 4 Taunt. 309; 1 Term R. 33. See "Act of God."

ACTUS INCEPTUS CUJUS PERFECTIO pendet ex voluntate partium, revocari potest; si autem pendet ex voluntate tertiae personae, vel ex contingenti, revocari non potest. An act already begun, whose completion depends upon the will of the parties, may be recalled; but if it depend on the consent of a third person, or on a contingency, it cannot be recalled. Bac. Max. reg. 20. See Story, Ag. § 424.

ACTUS JUDICIARIUS CORAM NON JUdice irritus habetur; de ministerili autem a quocunque provenit ratum esto. A judicial act before one not a judge is void; as to a ministerial act, from whomsoever it proceeds, let it be valid. Lofft, 458.

ACTUS LEGIS NEMINI EST DAMNOSUS. The act of the law is hurtful to no one; an act in law shall prejudice no man. 2 Inst. 287.

ACTUS LEGIS NEMINI FACIT INJURIam. The act of the law does no one wrong. 5 Coke, 116; 2 Sarswood, Bl. Comm. 123.

ACTUS LEGITIMI NON RECIPIUNT MOdum. Acts required by law admit of no qualification. Hob. 153; Branch, Princ.

ACTUS ME INVITO FACTUS, NON EST meus actus. An act done by me against my will is not my act. Bracton, 101b.

ACTUS NON REUM FACIT NISI MENS rea. The act does not make a person guilty unless the intention be guilty also. This maxim applies only in criminal cases; in civil matters it is otherwise. Broom, Leg. Max. (3d London Ed.) 270, 275, 329; 7 Term R. 514; 3 Bing. N. C. 34, 468; 5 Man. & G. 639; 3 C. B. 229; 5 C. B. 380; 9 Clark & F. 531; 4 N. Y. 159, 163, 195; 2 Bouv. Inst. note 2211.

ACTUS REPUGNUM NON POTEST IN esse produci. A repugnant act cannot be brought into being, *i. e.*, cannot be made effectual. Plowd. 355.

ACTUS SERVI IN IIS QUIBUS OPERA ejus communiter adhibita est, actus domini habetur. The act of a servant in those things in which he is usually employed is considered the act of his master. Lofft, 227.

AD. In Latin phrases. A preposition denoting at, by, for, near, on account of, to, until, upon.

AD ABUNDANTIOREM CAUTELAM (Lat.) For greater caution.

AD ADMITTENDUM CLERICUM. For the admitting of the clerk. A writ commanding the bishop to admit his clerk, upon the success of the latter in a *quare impedit*.

AD ALIUD EXAMEN (Lat.) To another tribunal. Calv. Lex.

AD ALIUM DIEM. At another day. A common phrase in the old reports. Y. B. P. 7 Hen. VI. 13.

AD ASSISAS CAPIENDAS. To take assizes; to take or hold the assizes. Bracton, fol. 110a; 3 Bl. Comm. 185. *Ad assisam capiendam*, to take an assize. Bracton, fol. 110b.

AD AUDIENDUM ET TERMINANDUM. To hear and determine.

AD BARRAM (Lat.) To the bar; at the bar. 3 How. St. Tr. 112.

AD CAMPI PARTEM. For a share of the field or land (*ut particeps fiat*) for champert. Fleta, lib. 2, c. 36, § 4.

AD CAPTUM VULGI. Adapted to the common understanding.

AD COLLIGENDUM BONA DEFUNCTI. To collect the goods of the deceased. Special letters of administration granted to one or more persons, authorizing them to collect and preserve the goods of the deceased, are so called. 2 Bl. Comm. 505; 2 Steph. Comm. 241. These are otherwise termed "letters *ad colligendum*," and the party to whom they are granted, a "collector." 2 Rev. St. N. Y. p. 19, §§ 38, 39.

AD COMMUNEM LEGEM. At common law. The name of a species of writ of entry, now obsolete.

Formerly, when tenants for life in dower or by the curtesy aliened the land which they held, the reversioner might, after their death, have the writ to recover possession. 3 Bl. Comm. 183, note (z); 1 Rosc. Real Actions, 93, 94.

AD COMPARENDUM. To appear. Reg. Orig. 60a. *Ad comparendum, et ad standum juri*, to appear and to stand to the law, or abide the judgment of the court. Cro. Jac. 67.

AD COMPUTUM REDDENDUM. To render an account.

AD CURIAM. At or to court.

AD CUSTUM, or AD CUSTAGIA. At the cost. 1 Sharswood, Bl. Comm. 314; Toullier, Dr. Civ., Cowell; Whishaw.

AD DAMNUM (Lat. *damnae*). To the damage.

—**In Pleading.** The technical name of that part of the writ which contains a statement of the amount of the plaintiff's injury.

The plaintiff cannot recover greater damages than he has laid in the *ad damnum*. 2 Greenl. Ev. § 260.

AD DEFENDENDUM (Lat.) to defend. 1 Bl. Comm. 227.

AD DIEM (Lat.) At a (or the) day.

AD EA QUAE FREQUENTIM ACCIDUNT jura adaptantur. The laws are adapted to those cases which occur more frequently. Coke, 2d Inst. 137; Wingate, Max. 216; Dig. 1. 3. 3; 19 How. St. Tr. 1061; 3 Barn. & C. 178, 183; 2 Cromp. & J. 108; 7 Mees. & W. 599, 600; Vaughan, 373; 5 Coke, 38, 128; 6 Coke, 77; 11 Exch. 476; 12 How. (U. S.) 312; Broom, Leg. Max. (3d London Ed.) 41.

AD EXCAMBIUM (Lat.) For exchange; for compensation.

AD EXHAEREDITATIONEM. To the disherison, or disinheriting.

The writ of waste calls upon the tenant to appear and show cause why he hath committed waste and destruction in the place named *ad exhaereditationem*, etc. 3 Bl. Comm. 228; Fitzh. Nat. Brev. 55.

AD EXITUM (Lat.) At the end of the pleadings; at issue. Steph. Pl. 24.

AD FACTUM PRAESTANDUM. In Scotch law. The name given to a class of obligations of great strictness.

A debtor *ad fac. praes.* is denied the benefit of the act of grace, the privilege of sanctuary, and the *cessio bonorum*. Ersk. Inst. lib. 3, tit. 3, § 62; Kames, Eq. 216.

AD FIDEM. In allegiance. 2 Kent, Comm. 56. Subjects born in allegiance are said to be born *ad fidem*.

AD FILUM AQUAE. To the thread of the stream; to the middle of the stream. 2 Cush. (Mass.) 207; 4 Hill (N. Y.) 369; 2 N. H. 369; 2 Washb. Real Prop. 632, 633; 3 Kent, Comm. 423 et seq.

A former meaning seems to have been, to a stream of water. Cowell; Blount. *Ad medium filum aquae* would be etymologically more exact (2 Eden. Inj. 260), and is often used; but the common use of *ad filum aquae* is undoubtedly to the thread of the stream (3 Sumn. [U. S.] 170; 1 McCord [S. C.] 580; 3 Kent, Comm. 431; 20 Wend. [N. Y.] 149; 4 Pick. [Mass.] 272).

AD FILUM VIAE (Lat.) To the middle of the way. 8 Metc. (Mass.) 260.

AD FINEM (Lat., abbreviated *ad fin.*) To the end.

AD FIRMAM. To farm.

Derived from an old Saxon word denoting rent, according to Blackstone, occurring in the phrase, *dedi concessi et ad firmam tradidi,* I have given, granted, and to farm let. 2 Sharswood, Bl. Comm. 317. *Ad firmam noctis* was a fine or penalty equal in amount to the estimated cost of entertaining the king for one night. Cowell. *Ad feodi firmam,* to fee farm. Spelman; Cowell.

AD GAOLAS DELIBERANDAS (Lat.) To deliver the gaols; to empty the gaols. Bracton, fol. 109b.

AD GRAVAMEN (Lat.) To the injury.

AD HUNC DIEM (Lat.) At this day.

AD IDEM (Lat.) To the same point or effect.

AD INDE (Lat.) Thereunto.

AD INFINITUM (Lat.) Indefinitely; without limit.

AD INQUIRENDUM (Lat. for inquiry.) In practice. A judicial writ, commanding inquiry to be made of anything relating to a cause depending in court.

AD INSTANTIAM (Lat.) At the instance.

AD INTERIM (Lat.) In the meantime.

An officer is sometimes appointed *ad interim,* when the principal officer is absent, or for some cause incapable of acting for the time.

AD JUDICIUM. To judgment; to court.

AD JUNGENDUM AUXILIUM. To joining in aid; to join in aid. See "Aid Prayer."

AD JURA REGIS. To the rights of the king; a writ which was brought by the king's clerk; presented to a living, against those who endeavored to eject him, to the prejudice of the king's title. Reg. Writs, 61.

AD LARGUM. At large; as, title at large; assize at large. See Dane, Abr. c. 144, art. 16, § 7.

AD LITEM (Lat. *lites*). For the suit.

Every court has the power to appoint a guardian *ad litem.* 2 Kent, Comm. 229; 2 Sharswood, Bl. Comm. 427.

AD LUCRANDUM VEL PERDENDUM. For gain or loss.

AD MAJOREM CAUTELAM (Lat.) For greater caution.

AD MANUM. Ready at hand.

AD MEDIUM FILUM AQUAE. To the middle thread of the stream.

AD MEDIUM FILUM VIAE. To the middle thread of the way.

AD MELIUS INQUIRENDUM. A writ directing a coroner to hold a second or further inquest

AD MORDENDUM ASSUETUS. Accustomed to bite. A term applied to ferocious animals.

AD NOCUMENTUM. To the nuisance. Formal words in the assize of nuisance. 3 Bl. Comm. 221.

AD OFFICIUM JUSTI CIARIORUM SPECtat, unicuique coram eis placitanti justitiam exhibere. It is the duty of justices to administer justice to every one pleading before them. Coke, 2d Inst. 451.

AD OSTENDENDUM (Lat. to show). Formal words in old writs. Fleta, lib. 4, c. 65, § 12.

AD OSTIUM ECCLESIAE (Lat.) At the church door.

One of the five species of dower formerly recognized at the common law. 1 Washb. Real Prop. 149; 2 Bl. Comm. 132. See "Dower."

AD PROXIMUM ANTECEDENS FIAT relatio, nisi impediatur sententia. A relative is to be referred to the next antecedent, unless the sense would be thereby impaired. Noy, Max. (9th Ed.) 4; 2 Exch. 479; 17 Q. B. 833; 2 Hurl. & N. 625; 3 Bing. N. C. 217; 9 Coke, 13; 13 How. (U. S.) 142.

AD QUAERIMONIAM. On complaint of.

AD QUAESTIONEM FACTI NON REspondent judices; ad quaestionem legis non respondent juratores. Judges do not answer to a question of fact; jurors do not answer to a question of law. Co. Litt. 295b; 8 Coke, 308 (155). Or, as the converse is sometimes affirmatively stated. *Ad quaestionem juris respondent judices; ad quaestionem facti respondent juratores,* judges answer to a question of law; jurors, to a question of fact; or *ad quaestiones legis judices, et non juratores respondent,* judges, and not jurors, respond to questions of law. 7 Mass. 279.

AD QUEM. (Lat.) To which.

The correlative term to *a quo (q. v.),* used in the computation of time, definition of a risk, etc., denoting the end of the period or journey.

The *terminus a quo* is the point of beginning or departure; the *terminus ad quem,* the end of the period, or point of arrival.

AD QUOD CURIA CONCORDAVIT. To which the court agreed.

AD QUOD DAMNUM (Lat.) What injury. A writ issuing out of and returnable into chancery, directed to the sheriff, commanding him to inquire by a jury what damage it will be to the king, or any other, to grant a liberty, fair, market, highway, or the like.

The name is derived from the characteristic words denoting the nature of the writ, to inquire how great an injury it will be to the king to grant the favor asked. Whishaw; Fitzh. Nat. Brev. 221; Termes de la Ley.

AD QUOD NON FUIT RESPONSUM (Law Lat.) To which there was no answer. A phrase used in the reports, where a point advanced in argument by one party was not denied by the other; or where a point or argument of counsel was not met or noticed by the court; or where an objection was met by the court, and not replied to by the counsel who raised it. 3 Coke, 9; 4 Coke, 40.

AD RATIONEM PONERE. To cite a person to appear.

AD RECOGNOSCENDUM. To recognize. Fleta, lib. 2, c. 65, § 12. Formal words in old writs.

AD RECTE DOCENDUM OPORTET, primum inquirere nomina, quia rerum cognitio a nominibus rerum dependet. In order rightly to comprehend a thing, inquire first into the names, for a right knowledge of things depends upon their names. Co. Litt. 68.

AD REPARATIONEM ET SUSTENTAtionem. For repairing and keeping in suitable condition.

AD RESPONDENDUM. See "Capias ad Respondendum;" "Habeas Corpus."

AD SATISFACIENDUM. See "Capias ad Satisfaciendum."

AD SECTAM. At the suit of.

It is commonly abbreviated. It is used where it is desirable to put the name of the defendant first, as in some cases where the defendant is filing his papers; thus, Roe *ads.* Doe, where Doe is plaintiff and Roe defendant. It is found in the indexes to cases decided in some of our older American books of reports, but has become pretty much disused.

AD STUDENDUM ET ORANDUM. For studying and praying; for the promotion of learning and religion. A phrase applied to colleges and universities. 1 Bl. Comm. 467; T. Raym. 101.

AD TERMINUM ANNORUM. For a term of years.

AD TERMINUM QUI PRAETERIT. A writ of entry which formerly lay for the lessor or his heirs, when a lease had been made of lands and tenements, for term of life or years, and, after the term had expired, the lands were withheld from the lessor by the tenant, or other person possessing the same. Fitzh. Nat. Brev. 201.

The remedy now applied for holding over is by ejectment, or under local regulations, by summary proceedings.

AD TRISTEM PARTEM STRENUA EST suspicio. Suspicion lies heavy on the unfortunate side.

AD TUNC ET IBIDEM. In pleading. The technical name of that part of an indictment containing the statement of the subject-matter's "then and there being found." Bac. Abr. "Indictment" (G 4); 1 N. C. 93.

AD ULTIMAM VIM TERMINORUM. To the utmost import of the terms.

AD USUM ET COMMODUM. To the use and benefit.

AD VALENTIAM. See "Ad Valorem."

AD VALOREM (Lat.) According to the valuation.

Duties may be specific or *ad valorem. Ad valorem* duties are always estimated at a certain per cent. on the valuation of the property. 3 U. S. St. at Large, 732; 24 Miss. 501.

AD VENTREM INSPICIENDUM. To inspect the womb. A writ for the summoning of a jury of matrons to determine the question of pregnancy.

AD VIM MAJOREM VEL AD CASUS fortuitos non tenetur quis, nisi sua culpa intervenerit. No one is held to answer for the effects of a superior force, or of an accident, unless his own fault has contributed. Fleta, lib. 2, c. 72, § 16.

AD VITAM. For life.

AD VITAM AUT CULPAM. For life, or until misbehavior.

Words descriptive of a tenure of office "for life or good behavior," equivalent to *quamdiu bene se gesserit.*

AD VOLUNTATEM. At will.

AD WARACTUM. See "Waractum."

ADCORDABILIS DENARII. Money paid by a vassal to his lord upon the selling or exchanging of a feud. Enc. Lond.

ADDICERE (Lat.) In civil law. To condemn. Calv. Lex.

Addictio denotes a transfer of the goods of a deceased debtor to one who assumes his liabilities. Calv. Lex. The giving up to a creditor of his debtor's person by a magistrate; also the transfer of the debtor's goods to one who assumes his liabilities.

Also used of an assignment of the person of the debtor to the successful party in a suit.

ADDITIO PROBAT MINORITATEM. An addition proves inferiority. Coke, 4th Inst. 80; Wingate, Max. 211, max. 60; Litt. § 293; Co. Litt. 189a.

ADDITION (Lat. *additio*, an adding to). Whatever is added to a man's name by way of title or description, as additions of mystery, place, or degree. Cowell; Termes de la Ley; 10 Wentw. Pl. 371; Salk. 5; 2 Ld. Raym. 988; 1 Wils. 244.

Additions are:

(1) Additions of estate, as "esquire," "gentleman," and the like. These titles can, however, be claimed by none, and may be assumed by any one. In Nash v. Battersby, 2 Ld. Raym. 986, 6 Mod. 80, the plaintiff declared with the addition of gentleman. The defendant pleaded in abatement that the plaintiff was no gentleman. The plaintiff demurred, and it was held ill; for, said the court, it amounts to a confession that the plaintiff is no gentleman, and then not the person named in the count. He should have replied that he is a gentleman.

(2) Additions of mystery, as scrivener, painter, printer, manufacturer, etc.

(3) Additions of places, descriptions by the place of residence, as "A. B., of Philadelphia," and the like. See Bac. Abr.; Doct. Plac. 71; 2 Viner, Abr. 77; 1 Lilly, Reg. 39; 1 Metc. (Mass.) 151.

——**In French Law.** A supplementary process to obtain additional information. Guyot, Rep. Univ.

ADDITIONALES. Additional terms or propositions to be added to a former agreement.

ADDONE, or ADDONNE (Law Fr.) Given to. Kelham.

ADDRESS.

——**In Equity Pleading.** That part of a bill which contains the appropriate and technical description of the court where the plaintiff seeks his remedy. Coop. Eq. Pl. 8; Bart. Suit in Eq. 26; Story, Eq. Pl. § 26; Van Heythuysen, Eq. Draft. 2.

——**In Legislation.** A formal request addressed to the executive by one or both branches of the legislative body, requesting him to perform some act.

ADDUCE. To offer, present, allege, advance, cite, mention. 40 Ill. App. 559.

ADEEM. To recall or revoke. See "Ademption."

ADELANTADO. In Spanish law. The military and political governor of a frontier province. His powers were equivalent to those of the president of a Roman province. He commanded the army of the territory which he governed, and, assisted by persons learned in the law, took cognizance of the civil and criminal suits that arose in his province. This office has long since been abolished.

ADELING, or ATHELING. Noble; excellent. A title of honor among the Saxons, gives to the king's children and heirs to the crown. Clito; Spelman.

ADEMPTION. The extinction of a specific legacy by the testator's parting with the subject thereof during his life. Also applied to the payment of the testator during his life of a general legacy; but this is more properly known as "satisfaction." 9 Barb. (N. Y.) 35; 3 Duer (N. Y.) 477.

The term is not applied to devises. 108 N. Y. 535.

ADEO (Lat.) So; as. *Adeo plene et integre*, as fully and entirely. 10 Coke, 65.

ADEQUATE CONSIDERATION. One which is a fair equivalent in value for the benefit obtained.

ADEQUATE REMEDY. A legal remedy, to be "adequate," so as to exclude the jurisdiction of equity, must be "as practical and efficient to the ends of justice and its prompt administration as the remedy in equity." 3 Pet. (U. S.) 210. See 134 U. S. 338.

ADESSE. In the civil law. To be present; the opposite of *abesse*. Calv. Lex.

To advocate, to undertake the management of a cause. Calv. Lex.; Brissonius.

ADEU. See "Adieu."

ADFERRUMINATIO. In the civil law. The welding together of iron; a species of *adjunction (q. v.)* Called also *ferruminatio*. Mackeld. Civ. Law, § 268.

ADHERENCE. In Scotch law. The name of a form of action by which the mutual obligation of marriage may be enforced by either party. Bell, Dict.

ADHERING (Lat. *adhaerere*, to cling to). Cleaving to, or joining; as, adhering to the enemies of the United States.

The constitution of the United States, (article 3, § 3) defines treason against the United States to consist only in levying war against them, or in adhering to their enemies, giving them aid and comfort.

A citizen's cruising in an enemy's ship, with a design to capture or destroy American ships, would be adhering to the enemies of the United States. 4 How. St. Tr. 328; Salk. 634; 2 Gilb. Ev. (Lofft Ed.) 798.

ADHIBERE (Lat.) In the civil law. To apply; to employ; to exercise; to use. *Adhibere diligentiam*, to use care. *Adhibere vim*, to employ force. Dig. 4. 2. 12. 2.

ADIATION. A term used in the laws of Holland for the application of property by an executor. Wharton.

ADIEU. (Law Fr. without day). A common term in the Year Books, implying final dismissal from court. Literally, "to God." Frequently written "Adeu." Y. B. T. 5 Edw. II. 173.

ADIRATUS. Lost; strayed; a price or value set upon things stolen or lost, as a recompense to the owner. Cowell.

ADIT. Approach or access. As used in mining law, a horizontal opening by which a mine is entered, or by which water and ores are carried away. Also called "drift."

ADITUS (Lat. *adire*). An approach; a way; a public way. Co. Litt. 56a.

ADJACENT. To lie near; close or contiguous; in the neighborhood or vicinity of. 239 Ill. 209.

Two of three lots of land might be described as adjacent to the first, while only the second could be said to be adjoining. 1 Cooke (Tenn.) 128.

ADJECTIVE LAW. That which regulates procedure; so called from its function to aid the substantive. Holland, Jur. 78.

The law of pleading, practice, evidence, remedies and procedure, designed merely to secure and enforce in an orderly manner the substantive law. 253 Ill. 171.

ADJOINING. Touching or contiguous, as distinguished from lying near or adjacent. Y.) 54. See "Postponement."

ADJOURN. In strictness, to put off to a day specified. Also to suspend business for a time; to defer or delay. 14 How. Pr. (N. Y.) 54. See "Postponement."

ADJOURNAL. In Scotch practice. A term applied to the records of criminal courts. Books of Adjournal (old Scotch, "Bukis of Adiornale") were the original records of criminal trials, most of which are now lost. 1 Pitc. Crim. Tr. pt. 2, p. 225. An act of adjournal is an order of the court of justiciary, entered on its minutes. Shaw, Rep., Appendix.

ADJOURNAMENTUM EST AD DIEM dicere seu diem dare. An adjournment is to appoint a day or give a day. 4 Inst. 27. Hence the formula "*eat sine die.*"

ADJOURNATUR (Law Lat. from *adjournare*, to adjourn). It is adjourned. A word with which the old reports very frequently conclude a case. 1 Ld. Raym. 602; 1 Show. 7; 1 Leon. 88.

ADJOURNED SUMMONS. In English practice. A summons or citation issued in chambers, and adjourned into court for argument.

ADJOURNED TERM. A continuation of a previous or regular term. 4 Ohio St. 473; 22 Ala. (N. S.) 27. Gen. St. Mass. c. 112, § 26, provides for holding an adjourned law term from time to time.

ADJOURNMENT. The dismissal by some court, legislative assembly, or properly authorized officer, of the business before them, either finally, which, as popularly used, is called an adjournment *sine die*, without day, or to meet again at another time appointed, which is called a temporary adjournment. See "Postponement."

——**In Civil Law.** A calling into court; a summoning at an appointed time. Du Cange.

ADJOURNMENT DAY. In English practice. A day appointed by the judges at the regular sittings for the trial of causes at *nisi prius*.

ADJOURNMENT DAY IN ERROR. In English practice. A day appointed some days before the end of the term, at which matters left undone on the affirmance day are finished. 2 Tidd, Pr. 1224.

ADJOURNMENT IN EYRE. The appointment of a day when the justices in eyre mean to sit again. Cowell; Spelman; Sharswood, Bl. Comm. 186.

ADJUDICATAIRE. In Canadian law. A purchaser at a sheriff's sale. See 1 Low. (U. S.) 241; 10 Low. (U. S.) 325.

ADJUDICATION.

——**In Practice.** A judgment; giving or pronouncing judgment in a case. See "Former Adjudication."

The application of the law to the facts and an authoritative declaration of result. 113 Ill. 312.

——**In Scotch Law.** A process for transferring the estate of a debtor to his creditor. Ersk. Inst. lib. 2, tit. 12, §§ 39-55; Bell, Dict. (Shaw Ed.) 944.

It may be raised not only on a decree of court, but also where the debt is for a liquidated sum. The execution of a summons and notice to the opposite party prevents any transfer of the estate. Every creditor who obtains a decree within a year and a day is entitled to share with the first creditor, and, after ten years' possession under his adjudication, the title of the creditor is complete. Paterson, Comp. 1137, note. The matter is regulated by St. Feb. 26, 1684, p. 1672, c. 19. See Ersk. Inst. lib. 2, c. 12, §§ 15, 16.

ADJUDICATION CONTRA HAEREDITAtem jacentem. In Scotch law. Adjudication against a renouncing heir. Brought by the ancestor's creditor to establish his debt against the realty when the heir apparent renounces his rigrht of inheritance.

ADJUDICATION IN IMPLEMENT. In Scotch law. An action to enforce a contract to convey.

ADJUNCTION (Lat. *adjungere,* to join to). In civil law. The attachment or union permanently of a thing belonging to one person to that belonging to another. This union may be caused by inclusion, as if one man's diamond be set in another's ring; by soldering, as if one's guard be soldered on another's sword; by sewing, as by employing the silk of one to make the coat of another; by construction, as by building on another's land; by writing, as when one writes on another's parchment; or by painting, as when one paints a picture on another's canvas. Inst. 2. 1. 34; Dig. 41. 1. 9. 2. See 2 Bl. Comm. 404; 1 Bouv. Inst. note 499.

ADJUNCTS. Additional judges sometimes appointed in the high court of delegates. See Shelf. Lun. 310.

ADJUNCTUM ACCESSORIUM. An accessory or appurtenance.

ADJURATION. A swearing or binding upon oath.

ADJUSTMENT. In insurance. The determining of the amount of a loss by fire or marine disaster. 2 Phil. Ins. §§ 1814, 1815.

ADJUVARI QUIPPE NOS, NON DECIPI, beneficio oportet. We ought to be favored, not injured, by that which is intended for our benefit. The species of bailment called "loan" must be to the advantage of the borrower, not to his detriment. Story, Bailm. § 275. See 8 El. & Bl. 1051.

ADLEGIARE. To purge one's self of a crime by oath.

ADMANUENSIS. A person who swore by laying his hands on the Book.

ADMEASUREMENT OF DOWER. A remedy which lay for the heir, on reaching his majority, to rectify an assignment of dower made during his minority, by which the doweress had received more than she was legally entitled to. 2 Bl. Comm. 136; Gilb. Uses, 379.

The remedy is still subsisting, though of rare occurrence. See 1 Washb. Real Prop. 225, 226; 1 Pick. (Mass.) 314; 2 Ind. 336.

In some of the states, the special proceeding which is given by statute to enable the widow to compel an assignment of dower is termed an "admeasurement of dower."

ADMEASUREMENT OF PASTURE. A remedy which lay in certain cases for surcharge of common of pasture.

It lay where a common of pasture appurtenant or in gross was certain as to number; or where one had common appendant or appurtenant, the quantity of which had never been ascertained. The sheriff proceeded, with the assistance of a jury of twelve men, to admeasure and apportion the common as well of those who had surcharged as those who had not, and, when the writ was fully executed, returned it to the superior court. Termes de la Ley.

The remedy is now abolished in England (3 Sharswood, Bl. Comm. 239, note) ; and in the United States (3 Kent, Comm. 419).

ADMEZATORES. (from Ital. *mezzatura,* middle). In old Italian law. Persons chosen by the consent of contending parties to decide questions between them. Literally, mediators. Spelman.

ADMINICLE.

——**In Scotch Law.** Any writing or deed introduced for the purpose of proof of the tenor of a lost deed to which it refers. Ersk. Inst. lib. 4, tit. 1, § 55; Stair, Inst. lib. 4, tit. 32, §§ 6, 7.

——**In English Law.** Aid; support. St. 1 Edw. IV. c. 1.

——**In Civil Law.** Imperfect proof. Merlin, Repert.

ADMINICULAR (from *adminiculum, q. v.*) Auxiliary to. "The murder would be adminicular to the robbery," *i. e.,* committed to accomplish it. Story, J., 3 Mason (U. S.) 121.

ADMINICULAR EVIDENCE. In ecclesiastical law. Evidence brought in to explain and complete other evidence. 2 Lee, Ecc. 595.

ADMINICULATE. To give adminicular evidence.

ADMINICULATOR. An officer in the Romish church, who administered to the wants of widows, orphans, and afflicted persons. Spelman.

ADMINICULUM (Lat.) In the civil and old English law. Aid or support; sometimes rendered *adminicle (q. v.) Juris adminiculum,* the support of the law. Dig. 26. 7. 39. 9. *Cum juris adminiculo concurrente,* with the support of right concurring. Bracton, fol. 38b.

Cumulative or corroborative testimony.

That which belongs to a thing as accessory. 1 Mackeld. Civ. Law, 347, note (d).

Whatever pertains to judicial proceedings, writs, records, etc. Fleta, lib. 2, c. 3, § 4.

ADMINISTRATION (Lat. *administrare,* to assist in). Management or control.

——**Of Government.** The management of the executive department of the government. Those charged with the management of the executive department of the government.

——**Of Estates.** The management of the estate of an intestate, or of a testator who has no executor. 2 Bl. Comm. 494. The term is applied broadly to denote the management of an estate by an executor, and also the management of estates of minors, lunatics, insolvents, etc., in those cases where trustees have been appointed by authority of law to take charge of such estate in place of the legal owners.

The species of administration are:

——**Ad Colligendum.** That which is granted for collecting and preserving goods about to perish (*bona peritura*). The only power over these goods is under the form prescribed by statute.

——**Ancillary.** That which is subordinate to the principal administration, for collecting the assets of foreigners. It is taken out in the country where the assets are locally situate. Kent, Comm. 43 et seq; 1 Williams, Ex'rs, Am. Notes; 14 Ala. 329.

——***Cum Testamento Annexo.*** That which is granted where no executor is named in the will, or where the one named dies, or is incompetent or unwilling to act. Such an administrator must follow the statute rules of distribution, except when otherwise directed by the will. Williams, Ex'rs; 2 Bradf. Sur. (N. Y.) 22. The residuary legatee is appointed such administrator, rather than the next of kin. 1 Vent. 217; 4 Leigh (Va.) 152; 2 Add. (Pa.) 352.

——**De Bonis non.** That which is granted when the first administrator dies before having fully administered. The person so appointed has in general the powers of a common administrator. Bac. Abr. "Executors" (B 1); Rolle, Abr. 907; 22 Miss. 47; 27 Ala. 273; 9 Ind. 342; 4 Sneed (Tenn.) 411; 31 Miss. 519; 29 Vt. 170; 11 Md. 412.

——**De Bonis non cum Testamento Annexo.** That which is granted when an executor dies leaving a part of the estate unadministered. Comyn, Dig. "Administrators" (B 1).

——***Durante Absentia.*** That which subsists during the absence of the executor, and until he has proved the will. It is generally granted when the next of kin is beyond sea, lest the goods perish, or the debts be lost. In England, it is not determined by the executor's dying abroad. 4 Hagg. Ecc. 360; 3 Bos. & P. 26.

——**Durante Minori Aetate.** That which is granted when the executor is a minor. It continues until the minor attains his lawful age to act, which, at common law, is seventeen years. Godolph. Orph. Leg. 102; 5 Coke, 29.

——**Pendente Lite.** That which is granted pending the controversy respecting an alleged will or the right of appointment. An officer of the court is appointed to take care of the estate only till the suit terminates. 2 P. Wms. 589; 2 Atk. 286; 2 Cas. temp. Lee, 258; 1 Hagg. Ecc. 313; 26 N. H. 533; 9 Tex. 13; 16 Ga. 13. He may maintain suits, but cannot distribute the assets. 1 Ves. Sr. 325; 2 Ves. & B. 97; 1 Ball & B. 192; 7 Md. 282.

——**Public.** That which the public administrator performs. This happens in many of the states by statute in those cases where persons die intestate, not leaving any who are entitled to apply for letters of administration. 3 Bradf. Sur. (N. Y.) 151; 4 Bradf. Sur. (N. Y.) 252.

——***Special.*** That which is limited either in time or in power. Such administration does not come under the statutes of 31 Edw. III. c. 11, and 21 Hen. VIII. c. 5, on which the modern English and American laws are founded.

——**Domestic.** That had at the residence of the decedent.

——**Foreign.** An administration under the sanction and jurisdiction of a different state or nation. It may be domiciliary or ancillary.

ADMINISTRATION SUIT. In English practice. A suit usually by a creditor for the administration of the insolvent estate of a decedent.

ADMINISTRATIVE LAW. That branch of the criminal law which regulates the manner in which the different agencies of the governing body are set in motion to punish crime, as opposed to the penal law, which describes offenses, and prescribes punishments.

ADMINISTRATOR. A person authorized to manage and distribute the estate of an intestate, or of a testator, who has no executor. See "Administration."

In English law, administrators are the officers of the ordinary appointed by him in pursuance of the statute, and their title and authority are derived exclusively from the ecclesiastical judge, by grants called "letters of administration." Williams, Ex'rs, 331. At first the ordinary was appointed administrator under the statute of Westminster II. Next, St. 31 Edw. III. c. 11, required the ordinary to appoint the next of kin and the relations by blood of the deceased. Next, under 21 Hen. VIII., he could appoint the widow, or next of kin, or both, at his discretion.

ADMIRALTY.

——**In England.** A court which has a very extensive jurisdiction of maritime causes, civil and criminal.

A court of admiralty exists in Ireland, but the Scotch court was abolished by 1 Wm. IV. c. 69. See "Vice Admiralty Courts."

——**In American Law.** A tribunal exercising jurisdiction over all maritime contracts, torts, injuries, or offenses. 2 Pars. Mar. Law, 508.

The court of original admiralty jurisdiction in the United States is the United States district court. From this court causes may be removed, in certain cases, to the circuit, and ultimately to the supreme court.

ADMISSION (Lat. *ad*, to; *mittere*, to send).

——**In Evidence.** Concession or voluntary acknowledgment made by a party of the existence or truth of certain facts.

As distinguished from a confession, the term is applied to civil transactions, and to matters of fact in criminal cases where there is no criminal intent. See "Confession."

As distinguished from consent, an admission may be said to be evidence furnished by the party's own act of his consent at a previous period.

Direct, called also "express," admissions, are those which are made in direct terms.

Implied admissions are those which result from some act or failure to act of the party.

Incidental admissions are those made in some other connection, or involved in the admission of some other fact. See 1 Greenl. Ev. § 194.

——**In Pleading.** The acknowledgment or recognition by one party of the truth of some matter alleged by the opposite party.

Partial admissions are those which are delivered in terms of uncertainty, mixed up with explanatory or qualifying circumstances.

Plenary admissions are those which admit the truth of the matter without qualification, whether it be asserted as from information and belief, or as from actual knowledge.

——**At Law.** In all pleading in confession, an admission of the truth of the opposite party's pleading is made. Express admissions may be made of matters of fact only.

——**Of Attorneys.** The act by which attorneys and counsellors become recognized as officers of the court, and are allowed to practice. The qualifications required vary widely in the different states.

——**In Corporations or Companies.** The act of a corporation or company by which an individual acquires the rights of a member of such corporation or company.

In trading and joint-stock corporations, no vote of admission is requisite; for any person who owns stock therein, either by original subscription or by conveyance, is in general entitled to, and cannot be refused, the rights and privileges of a member. 3 Mass. 364; Doug. 524; 1 Man. & R. 529.

ADMISSIONALIS. In European law. An usher. Spelman.

ADMITTANCE. In English law. The act of giving possession of a copyhold estate. It is of three kinds, namely, upon a voluntary grant by the lord, upon a surrender by the former tenant, and upon descent.

ADMITTENDO IN SOCIUM. In English law. A writ associating certain persons to justices of assize.

ADMONISH. To caution or advise, 267 Ill. 48.

ADMONITIO TRINA. The third warning given to one standing mute, before the infliction of the *peine forte et dure.* 4 Bl. Comm. 325.

ADMONITION. A reprimand from a judge to a person accused, on being discharged, warning him of the consequences of his conduct, and intimating to him that, should he be guilty of the same fault for which he has been admonished, he will be punished with greater severity. Merlin, Repert. The admonition was authorized as a species of punishment for slight misdemeanors.

A caution by the court to jurors as to the rules for their conduct while hearing or deliberating on a case.

ADMORTIZATION. The reduction of property of lands or tenements to mortmain, in the feudal customs.

ADNICHILED. Annulled; cancelled; made void.

ADNIHILARE (Law Lat. from *ad*, to, and *nihil*, nothing). In old English law. To reduce to nothing; to treat as nothing; to hold as or for nought; to avoid. Fleta, lib. 2, c. 63, § 1.

Adnichile is used in St. 28 Hen. VIII. c. 7, and *adnichilate* by old English writers. Rich. Dict.

ADNOTATIO (Lat. *notare*). A subscription or signing.

In the civil law, casual homicide was excused by the indulgence of the emperor, signed with his own sign manual, called *adnotatio.* Code, 9. 16. 5; 4 Sharswood, Bl. Comm. 187.

ADOLESCENCE. That age which follows puberty, and precedes the age of majority. It commences for males at fourteen, and for females at twelve years completed, and continues till twenty-one years complete.

ADOLESCENTIA (Lat. from *adolescere*, to grow). In the civil law. Adolescence (*q. v.*).

ADOPTION. The act by which a person takes the child of another into his family, and treats him as his own.

A juridical act creating between two persons certain relations, purely civil, or paternity and filiation. 6 Demolombe Code Nap. § 1.

As used in the law the word has a strict significance and implies some form of legal procedure. 201 Ill. 116.

ADOPTIVUS (Lat. from *adoptare*, to adopt). In the civil law. Adoptive. Applied both to the parent adopting, and the child adopted. Inst. 2. 13. 4; Id. 3. 1. 10-14.

AD-PROMISSOR. (Lat. *promittere*). One who binds himself for another; a surety; a peculiar species of *fidejussor*. Calv. Lex.

The term is used in the same sense in the Scotch law. The cautionary engagement was undertaken by a separate act; hence, one entering into it was called adpromissor (promissor in addition to). Ersk. Inst. 3. 3. 1.

ADQUIETO. Payment. Blount.

ADRECTARE. To do right, satisfy, or make amends.

ADRHAMIRE (Law. Lat. from old Fr. *arrimir*). In old European law. To undertake, declare, or promise solemnly; to pledge; to pledge one's self to make oath. Also written *arhamire, arramire,* and *arramare.* Spelman.

ADROGATION. In civil law. The adoption of one who was *impubes,*—that is, if a male, under fourteen years of age; if a female, under twelve. Dig. 1. 7. 17. 1.

ADS. See "Ad Sectam."

ADSCENDENTS (Lat.) In the civil law. Ascendants. Dig. 23. 2. 68; Code, 5. 5. 6.

ADSCRIPTI (Lat. *scribere*). Joined to by writing; ascribed; set apart; assigned to; annexed to.

ADSCRIPTITI (Lat.) A species of slaves.

Those persons who were enrolled and liable to be drafted as legionary soldiers. Calv. Lex.

ADSCRIPTITII (or **ADSCRIPTITI**) **GLEbae** (Lat.) In old English law. Annexed, bound, or adstricted to the soil; employed in cultivating it, and in performing other rural services for the owner. Harg. Co. Litt. note 1 to lib. 2. "Ascriptitious to the soil." Bl. Law Tr. 96-98. A term applied to tenants by *villein socage,* and commonly supposed to denote a condition approaching nearer to that of slaves than of freemen. Harg. Co. Litt. ubi supra. But, according to Bracton, they were so called because, so long as they did the appointed services, they had the privilege not to be removed from the soil (*gaudent privilegio quod a gleba amoveri non poterunt*), and were in fact freemen. Bracton, fols. 7a, 209a; Id. fol. 4b. See Fleta, lib. 1, c. 8, § 3. The term is also used in old Scotch law. Skene de Verb. Sign. voc. "Bondagium."

ADSCRIPTITIUS, ADSCRIPTICIUS, or **adscriptitius** (Lat. from *adscriptus*). In the civil law. United, annexed, or bound to. *Adscriptitii* (*q. v.*) were a class of cultivators who were annexed to the land, without the power of leaving it, and whose earnings or *peculium* belonged to their owners or masters. Code, 11. 47. 19. There was very little difference between them and slaves. See Code, 11. 47. 21. And see further, as to their condition, Id. 23, 24; Nov. Inst. 54; Const. Imp. Just. 2.

ADSESSORES (Lat. *sedere*). Side judges. Those who were joined to the regular magistrates as assistants or advisors; those who were appointed to supply the place of the regular magistrates in certain cases. Calv. Lex.

ADSTIPULATOR. In Roman law. An accessory party to a promise, who received the same promise as his principal did, and could equally receive and exact payment; or he only stipulated for a part of that for which the principal stipulated, and then his rights were coextensive with the amount of his own stipulation. Sandars, Just. Inst. (5th Ed.) 348.

ADULT.

——**In Civil Law.** A male infant who has attained the age of fourteen; a female infant who has attained the age of twelve. To be distinguished from full age in the civil law, which was twenty-five years. See "Age." Domat, Civ. Law, tit. 2, § 2, note 8.

——**In Common Law.** One of the full age of twenty-one. Swanst. Ch. 553.

ADULTER (Lat.) One who corrupts; one who corrupts another man's wife.

Adulter solidorum, a corrupter of metals; a counterfeiter. Calv. Lex.

ADULTERA (Lat.) A woman who commits adultery. Calv. Lex.

ADULTERATION. The act of corrupting or debasing; the act of mixing something impure or spurious with something pure or genuine, or an inferior article with a superior one of the same kind.

ADULTERATOR (Lat.) A corrupter; a counterfeiter.

Adulterator monetae, a forger. Du Cange.

ADULTERINE. The issue of adulterous intercourse.

ADULTERINE GUILDS. Companies of traders acting as corporations, without charters, and paying a fine annually for the privilege of exercising their usurped privileges. Smith, Wealth of Nations, bk. 1, c. 10; Wharton.

ADULTERIUM. A fine imposed for the commission of adultery. Barr. Obs. St. 62, note.

ADULTERY. The voluntary sexual intercourse of a married person with a person other than the offender's husband or wife. Bish. Mar. & Div. § 415; 6 Metc. (Mass.) 243; 36 Me. 261; 11 Ga. 56; 2 Strobh. Eq. (S. C.) 174.

The voluntary sexual intercourse of a married woman with a man other than her husband.

Unlawful voluntary sexual intercourse between two persons, one of whom at least is married, is the essence of the crime in all cases. In general, it is sufficient if either party is married; and the crime of the married party will be adultery, while that of the unmarried party will be fornication. 1 Yeates (Pa.) 6; 2 Dall. (Pa.) 124; 5 Jones (N. C.) 416; 27 Ala. (N. S.) 23; 35 Me. 205; 7 Grat. (Va.) 591; 6 Grat. (Va.) 673; 1 Pin. (Wis.) 91. In some of the states, if the woman be married, though the man be unmarried, he is guilty of adultery. 21 Pick. (Mass.) 509; 2 Blackf. (Ind.) 318; 18 Ga. 264; 9 N. H. 515. And see 1 Harr. (N. J.) 380; 29 Ala. 313. In other states, it seems that to constitute the offense of adultery it is necessary that the woman should be married; that if the man only is married, it is not the crime of adultery at common law or under the statute, so that an indictment for adultery could be sustained against either party; though, within the meaning of the law respecting divorces, it is adultery in the man. 56 Ind. 263; 9 N. H. 55; 4 Minn. 335; Tappan (Ohio) 90.

ADVANCE. As a noun means something that precedes, such as a payment of money made before it is due. 169 Ill. App. 341.

ADVANCEMENT. A gift by anticipation from a parent to a child of the whole or a part of what it is supposed such child would inherit on the death of the parent. 6 Watts (Pa.) 87; 4 Serg. & R. (Pa.) 333; 17 Mass. 358; 11 Johns. (N. Y.) 91; Wright (Ohio) 339.

An advancement can be made only by a parent to a child (5 Miss. 356; 2 Jones [N. C.] 137); or in some states, by statute, to a grandchild (4 Kent, Comm. 419; 4 Watts [Pa.] 82; 4 Ves. 437).

The intention of the parent is to decide whether a gift is intended as an advancement. 23 Pa. St. 85; 11 Johns. (N. Y.) 91; 2 McCord (S. C.) 103. See 26 Vt. 665.

——**Ademption, distinguished.**

An advancement, unlike an ademption has to do with intestate estates only.

——**Debt, distinguished.**

An advancement differs from a debt in that there is no liability on the part of the child to repay during the lifetime of the donor, nor after his death except by way of suffering a deduction from his portion of the estate.

——**Gift, distinguished.**

An advancement differs from a gift in that it is charged against the child.

——**Loan, distinguished.**

An advancement is not the equivalent of a loan, as one making an advancement cannot require its return. 223 Ill. 288.

ADVANCES. Payments made on account of moneys to become due. It is applied to a number of specific transactions, as payments made to the owner of goods by a factor or agent, who has or is to have possession of the goods for the purpose of selling them, payments by a guardian to the ward out of the latter's funds, etc.

ADVANTAGIUM. In old pleading. An advantage. Co. Entr. 484; Towns. Pl. 50.

ADVENA (Lat. *venire*). In Roman law. One of foreign birth, who has left his own country and settled elsewhere, and who has not acquired citizenship in his new locality; often called *albanus*. Du Cange.

ADVENT. The period commencing on Sunday falling on St. Andrew's day (30th of November), or the first Sunday after, and continuing till Christmas.

It took its name from the fact that it immediately preceded the day set apart to commemorate the birth or coming (advent) of Christ. Cowell; Termes de la Ley.

Formerly, during this period, "all contentions at law were omitted." But, by statute 13 Edw. 1. (Westminster II.) c. 48, certain actions were allowed.

ADVENTITIOUS (Lat. *adventitius*). That which comes incidentally, or out of the regular course.

Adventitia bona are goods which fall to a man otherwise than by inheritance.

Adventitia dos is a dowry or portion given by some friend other than the parent.

ADVENTURA (Lat. an adventure). Flotsam, jetsam, and ligan are styled *adventurae maris*, adventures of the sea. Hale de Jur. Mar. pt. 1, c. 7.

ADVENTURE. Sending goods abroad under charge of a supercargo or other agent, which are to be disposed of to the best advantage for the benefit of the owners.

The goods themselves so sent.

——**In Marine Insurance.** The risk or peril insured against. See 14 Fed. 233.

ADVERSE ENJOYMENT. The possession or exercise of an easement or privilege under a claim of right against the owner of the land out of which the easement is derived. 2 Washb. Real Prop. 42.

ADVERSE POSSESSION. The enjoyment of land, or such estate as lies in grant, under such circumstances as indicate that such enjoyment has been commenced and continued under an assertion or color of right on the part of the possessor. 3 East, 394; 1 Pick. (Mass.) 466; 2 Serg. & R. (Pa.) 527; 3 Pa. St. 132; 8 Conn. 440; 2 Aik. (Vt.) 364; 9 Johns. (N. Y.) 174; 18 Johns. (N. Y.) 40, 355; 5 Pet. (U. S.) 402; 4 Bibb (Ky.) 550.

There must be actual possession. 45 Ill. 388; 36 Minn. 525; 78 N. C. 354; 1 Grat. (Va.) 211. But what constitutes such possession varies with the nature and situation of the premises. 11 Grat. (Va.) 420; 8 Barb. (N. Y.) 253. Cultivation, improvement, or inclosure always constitutes occupation, and, if the occupant holds under a paper title, a use for supply of fuel, etc., or a use as subservient to land actually occupied, will constitute an occupation. Code Civ. Proc. N. Y. §§ 370, 371.

The possession must be open and notorious (42 Mass. 95; 16 Wis. 594), distinct and exclusive (150 U. S. 597; 6 Md. 201), hostile (15 Ill. 271; 13 Ohio St. 42; 89 Wis. 551), and continuous in the occupant or those claiming under him for the period prescribed by statute (47 U. S. 550; 5 Md. 256; 36 W. Va. 445).

ADVERSE WITNESS. A witness who manifests a bias against the party calling him. A party may be allowed to propound leading questions to such a witness.

ADVERSUS (Lat.) Against.

ADVERTISE. To publish notice of; to publish a written or printed account of. 39 Ill. App. 401.

ADVERTISEMENT (Lat. *advertere*, to turn to).

Information or knowledge communicated to individuals or the public in a manner designed to attract general attention.

A notice published either in handbills or in a newspaper. A posting of notice on a signboard is an advertisement within a statute making the advertising of lottery tickets penal. 5 Pick. (Mass.) 42. And see 8 Watts & S. (Pa.) 373; 16 Pa. St. 68; 38 Ill. App. 400.

ADVERTISEMENTS OF QUEEN ELIZAbeth. Certain articles or ordinances drawn up by Archbishop Parker and some of the bishops in 1564, at the request of Queen Elizabeth, the object of which was to enforce decency and uniformity in the ritual of the church. The queen subsequently refused to give her official sanction to these advertisements, and left them to be enforced by the bishops under their general powers. Phil. Ecc. Law, 910; 2 Prob. Div. 276; Id. 354.

ADVICE. Information given by letter by one merchant or banker to another in regard to some business transaction which concerns him.

ADVICE OF COUNSEL. The opinion of an attorney at law on facts stated to him. If given on a full and fair statement of the facts, it relieves the client of any imputation of malice in acting in it, and hence is a defense in all actions to which malice is essential.

ADVISARE, or ADVISARI (Lat.) To advise; to consider; to be advised; to consult.

Occurring often in the phrase *curia advisari vult* (usually abbreviated *cur. adv. vult*), the court wishes to consider of the matter.

ADVISEMENT. Consideration; deliberation; consultation.

ADVISORY. By way of counsel. The verdict on a feigned issue is said to be advisory because the chancellor may, in his discretion, disregard it.

ADVOCASSIE (Law Fr.) The office of an advocate; advocacy. Kelham.

ADVOCATA. In old English law. A patroness; a woman who had the right of presenting to a church. Liber Ramesiens, § 140, cited in Spelman, voc. "Advocatus."

ADVOCATE. An assistant; adviser; a pleader of causes.

Derived from *advocare*, to summon to one's assistance. *Advocatus* originally signified an assistant or helper of any kind, even an accomplice in the commission of a crime. Cicero, pro Caecina, c. 8; Livy, lib. ii. 55; iii. 47; Tertullian de Idolatr. c. 23; Petron. Satyric, c. 25. Secondarily, it was applied to one called in to assist a party in the conduct of a suit. Inst. 1. 11; Dig. 50. 13. Hence, a pleader, which is its present signification.

——**In Civil and Ecclesiastical Law.** An officer of the court, learned in the law, who is engaged by a suitor to maintain or defend his cause. Advocates, like counsellors, have the exclusive privilege of addressing the court either orally or in written pleadings; and, in general, in regard to duties, liabilities, and privileges, the same rules apply *mutatis mutandis* to advocates as to counsellors. See "Counsellor."

Lord advocate was an officer in Scotland appointed by the crown, during pleasure, to take care of the king's interest before the courts of session, judiciary, and exchequer. All actions that concern the king's interest, civil or criminal, must be carried on with concourse of the lord advocate. He also discharges the duties of public prosecutor, either in person or by one of his four deputies, who are called *advocates depute*. Indictments for crimes must be in his name as accuser. He supervises the proceedings in important criminal cases, and has the right to appear in all such cases. He is, in fact, secretary of state for Scotland, and the principal duties are connected directly with the administration of the government.

Inferior courts have a *procurator fiscal*, who supplies before them the place of the lord advocate in criminal cases. See 2 Bankt. Inst. 492.

College or faculty of advocates was a corporate body in Scotland, consisting of the members of the bar in Edinburgh. A large portion of its members are not active practitioners, however. 2 Bankt. Inst. 486.

Church or ecclesiastical advocates were pleaders appointed by the church to maintain its rights.

——**In Ecclesiastical Law.** A patron of a living; one who has the advowson, *advocatio*. Tech. Dict.; Ayliffe, Par. 53; Dane, Abr. c. 31, § 20; Ersk. Inst. 79. 9.

ADVOCATE, QUEEN'S (or **KING'S**). See "Queen's Advocate."

ADVOCATI (Lat.) In Roman law. Patrons; pleaders; speakers.

Anciently, any one who lent his aid to a friend, and who was supposed to be able in any way to influence a judge, was called *advocatus.*

Causidicus denoted a speaker or pleader merely; *advocatus* resembled more nearly a counsellor; or, still more exactly, *causidicus* must be rendered "barrister," and *advocatus* "attorney," though the duties of an *advocatus* were much more extended than those of a modern attorney. Du Cange; Calv. Lex.

A witness.

ADVOCATI ECCLESIAE. Advocates of the church.

These were of two sorts; those retained as pleaders to argue the cases of the church and attend to its law matters, and advocates, or patrons of the advowson. Cowell; Spelman.

ADVOCATI FISCI. In civil law. Those chosen by the emperor to argue his cause whenever a question arose affecting his revenues. Calv. Lex.; 3 Sharswood, Bl. Comm. 27.

ADVOCATIA. In civil law. The function, duty, or privilege of an advocate. Du Cange.

ADVOCATION. In Scotch law. The removal of a cause from an inferior to a superior court by virtue of a writ or warrant issuing from the superior court. See "Bill of Advocation;" "Letter of Advocation."

ADVOCATOR.

——**In Old Practice.** One who called on or vouched another to warrant a title; a voucher. *Advocatus,* the person called on, or vouched; a vouchee. Spelman; Towns. Pl. 45.

——**In Scotch Practice.** An appellant. 1 Brown, 67.

ADVOCATUS. A pleader; a narrator. Bracton, fols. 372b, 412a.

ADVOCATUS DIABOLI. The devil's advocate; a person designated to present to the college of cardinals matter in opposition to a canonization.

ADVOCATUS EST, AD QUEM PERTINENT jus advocationis alicujus ecclesiae, ut ad ecclesiam, nomine proprio, non alieno, possit praesentare. A patron is he to whom appertains the right of presentation to a church, in such a manner that he may present to such a church in his own name, and not in the name of another. Co. Litt. 119.

ADVOWEE. In English ecclesiastical law. A patron; one who has a right to present to a benefice. Cowell; Britt. c. 95.

ADVOWEE PARAMOUNT. The sovereign, who was the highest advowee.

ADVOWSON. A right of presentation to a church or benefice.

He who possesses this right is called the "patron" or "advocate." When there is no patron, or he neglects to exercise his right within six months, it is called a "lapse," and a title is given to the ordinary to collate to a church. When a presentation is made by one who has no right, it is called a "usurpation."

Advowsons are of different kinds:

——**Advowson Appendant.** When it depends upon a manor, etc.

——**Advowson in Gross.** When it belongs to a person and not to a manor.

——**Advowson Presentative.** Where the patron presents to the bishop.

——**Advowson Donative.** Where the king or patron puts the clerk into possession without presentation.

——**Advowson Collative.** Where the bishop himself is patron.

——**Advowson of the Moiety of the Church.** Where there are two several patrons and two incumbents in the same church.

——**A Moiety of Advowson.** Where two must join the presentation of one incumbent.

——**Advowson of Religious Houses.** That which is vested in the person who founded such a house.

See 2 Bl. Comm. 21; Mireh. Advow. "Advowson;" Comyn, Dig. "Advowson, Quare Impedit;" Bac. Abr. "Simony;" Burns, Ecc. Law.

ADVOWTRY, or ADVOUTRY. In English law. The crime committed by a woman who, having committed adultery, continued to live with the adulterer. Cowell; Termes de la Ley.

AEDES (Lat.) In civil law. A dwelling; a house; a temple.

In the country everything upon the surface of the soil passed under the term *aedes.* Du Cange; Calv. Lex.

AEDIFICARE (Lat. from *aedes,* a house, and *facere,* to build). In civil and old English law. To make or build a house; to erect a building. Dig. 45. 1. 75. 7. Sometimes applied to other objects, as a ship. Dig. 49. 14. 46. 2.

AEDIFICARE IN TUO PROPRIO SOLO non licet quod alteri noceat. It is not lawful to build upon one's own land what may be injurious to another. Coke, 3d Inst. 201; Broom, Leg. Max. (3d London Ed.) 331.

AEDIFICATUM SOLO, SOLO CEDIT. That which is built upon the land goes with the land. Co. Litt. 4a; Broom, Leg. Max. (3d London Ed.) 349, 355; Inst. 2. 1. 29; Dig. 47. 3. 1.

AEDIFICIA SOLO CEDUNT. Buildings pass by a grant of the land. Fleta, lib. 3, c. 2, § 12.

AEDILE (Lat.) In Roman law. An officer who attended to the repairs of the temples and other public buildings; the repairs and cleanliness of the streets; the care of the weights and measures; the providing for funerals and games; and regulating the prices of provisions. Ainsworth; Smith; Du Cange.

AEDILITIUM EDICTUM (Lat.) In Roman law. That provision by which the buyer of a diseased or imperfect slave, horse, or other animal was relieved at the expense of the vendor who had sold him as sound, knowing him to be imperfect. Calv. Lex.

AEFESN. In old English law. The remuneration to the proprietor of a domain for the privilege of feeding swine under the oaks and beeches of his woods.

AEGROTO (Lat. ablative of *aegrotus*, sick). Being sick or indisposed. A term used in some of the older reports. "Holt, *aegroto*." 11 Mod. 179.

AEL (Law Fr.) A grandfather. Britt. c. 89, fol. 221. Also spelled *aieul* and *ayle*.

AEQUIOR EST DISPOSITIO LEGIS quam hominis. The disposition of the law is more impartial than that of man. 8 Coke, 152; Bracton, fol. 3a.

AEQUITAS. Equity.

AEQUITAS AGIT IN PERSONAM. Equity acts upon the person. 4 Bouv. Inst. note 3733.

AEQUITAS SEQUITUR LEGEM. Equity follows the law. 1 Story, Eq. Jur. § 64; 3 Wooddeson, Lect. 479, 482; Branch, Max. 8; 2 Sharswood, Bl. Comm. 330; Gilb. 136; 2 Eden, 316; 10 Mod. 3; 15 How. (U. S.) 299.

AEQUUM ET BONUM, EST LEX LEGUM. What is just and right is the law of laws. Hob. 224.

AERARIUM (Lat. from *aes*, money). In the Roman law. The treasury (*fiscus*). Calv. Lex.

AES (Lat.) In the Roman law. Money (literally, brass); metallic money in general, including gold. Dig. 9. 2. 2. pr.; Id. 9. 2. 27. 5; Id. 50. 16. 159.

AES ALIENUM (Lat.) In civil law. A debt.

Literally translated, the property or money of another; the civil law considering borrowed money as the property of another, as distinguished from *aes suum*, one's own.

AESNECIA. In old English law. Esnecy; the right or privilege of the eldest born. Spelman; Glanv. lib. 7, c. 3; Fleta, lib. 2, c. 66, §§ 5, 6. The privilege allowed the eldest daughter of drawing first in the partition of lands by lot. Called, also, *pars enecia*, *enetia*, or *eneia*. Bracton, fol. 75.

AESTIMATIO CAPITIS (Lat. the value of a head). The price to be paid for taking the life of a human being.

King Athelstan declared, in an assembly held at Exeter, that mulcts were to be paid *per aestimatio capitis*. For a king's head (or life), 30,000 thuringae; for an archbishop's or prince's, 15,000; for a priest's or thane's, 2,000. Leg. Hen. I.

AESTIMATIO PRAETERITI DELICTI ex postremo facto nunquam crescit. The estimation of a crime committed never increases from a subsequent fact. Bac. Max. reg. 8; Dig. 50. 17. 139; Broom, Leg. Max. (3d London Ed.) 17.

AETAS. In the Roman law. Age. See "Age."

AETATE PROBANDA. See "De Aetate Probande."

AFFECT. To act upon. 219 Ill. 15.

AFFECTIO TUA NOMEN IMPONIT operi tuo. Your motive gives a name to your act. Bracton, fols. 2b, 101b.

AFFECTION. The making over, pawning, or mortgaging a thing to assure the payment of a sum of money, or the discharge of some other duty or service. Tech. Dict.

AFFECTUS (Lat.) Movement of the mind; disposition; intention.

One of the causes for a challenge of a juror is *propter affectum*, on account of a suspicion of bias or favor. 3 Bl. Comm. 363; Co. Litt. 156.

AFFECTUS PUNITUR LICET NON SEquitur effectus. The intention is punished, although the consequence do not follow. 9 Coke, 56.

AFFEERIE. In English law. To fix in amount; to liquidate.

To affeer an amercement is to establish the amount which one amerced in a court-leet should pay.

To affeer an account is to confirm it on oath in the exchequer.

AFFEERORS. In old English law. Those appointed by a court-leet to mulct those punishable, not by a fixed fine, but by an arbitrary sum, called "amercement." Termes de la Ley.

AFFIANCE (Lat. *affidare, ad, fidem, dare*, to pledge to).

A plighting of troth between man and woman. Litt. § 39.

An agreement by which a man and woman promise each other that they will marry together. Poth. du Mar. note 24.

Marriage. Co. Litt. 34a. See Dig. 23. 1. 1; Code, 5. 1. 4.

AFFIANT. One who makes an affidavit (*q. v.*)

AFFIDARE.

——**In Canon Law.** To betroth; to plight one's faith generally. Bracton, fol. 29a; Co. Litt. 34a.

——**In Feudal Law.** To swear fealty, as a tenant to his lord. Spelman.

——**In Old Practice.** To make oath.

AFFIDATIO. In canon and feudal law. A plighting or pledging of faith; a giving or swearing of fealty. Spelman.

AFFIDATIO DOMINORUM. An oath taken by the lords in parliament.

AFFIDATUS. One who is not a vassal, but who, for the sake of protection, has connected himself with one more powerful. Spelman; 2 Sharswood, Bl. Comm. 46.

AFFIDAVIT (Lat.) In practice. A statement or declaration reduced to writing, and sworn or affirmed to before some officer who has authority to administer an oath. 80 Ill. 307; 59 Mo. App. 188; 1 Mich. N. P. 189.

It differs from a deposition in this, that in the latter the opposite party has an opportunity to cross-examine the witness, whereas an affidavit is always taken *ex parte*. 3 Blatchf. (U. S.) 456; 4 Kan. 124.

It is not synonymous with "oath" (76 Ky. 417), but includes the oath (2 Chand. [Wis.] 29-32, note).

It is not a pleading. 7 Kan. 359.

AFFIDAVIT OF DEFENSE.

——**In Practice.** A statement made in proper form that the defendant has a good ground of defense to the plaintiff's action upon the merits. The statements required in such an affidavit vary considerably in the different states where they are required. In some, it must state a ground of defense; in others, a simple statement of belief that it exists is sufficient. Called, also, an "affidavit of merits."

——**In Pennsylvania Practice.** A statement of the facts constituting the defense required to accompany a general plea. Thus, with a plea of *nil debet* must be filed an affidavit of defense showing the facts by reason of which defendant claims not to be indebted.

AFFIDAVIT TO HOLD TO BAIL. In practice. An affidavit which is required in many cases before a person can be arrested in a civil action.

AFFILARE. To put on record; to file. 8 Coke, 319; 2 Maule & S. 202.

AFFILE. To put on file. Now written "file."

AFFILIATION. The fixing upon one the paternity of a bastard.

——**In French Law.** A species of adoption which exists by custom in some parts of France.

The person affiliated succeeded equally with other heirs to the property acquired by the deceased to whom he had been affiliated, but not to that which he inherited.

——**In Ecclesiastical Law.** A condition which prevented the superior from removing the person affiliated to another convent. Guyot, Rep. Univ.

AFFINAGE. Refining metal; hence "fine" and "refined." Blount.

AFFINES (Lat. *finis*). In civil law. Connections by marriage, whether of the persons or their relatives. Calv. Lex.

From this word we have affinity, denoting relationship by marriage. 1 Bl. Comm. 434.

The singular, *affinis*, is used in a variety of related significations,—a boundary (Du Cange; a partaker or sharer, *affinis culpae* (an aider or one who has knowledge of a crime (Calv. Lex.).

AFFINIS MEI AFFINIS NON EST MIHI affinis. A connection (*i. e.*, by marriage) of my connection is not a connection of mine. Shelf. Mar. & Div. 174.

AFFINITAS. In civil law. Affinity.

AFFINITAS AFFINITATIS. That connection between parties arising from marriage which is neither consanguinity nor affinity.

This term intends the connection between the kinsmen of the two persons married, as, for example, the husband's brother and the wife's sister. Ersk. Inst. 1. 6. 8.

AFFINITY. The connection existing, in consequence of marriage, between each of the married persons and the kindred of the other. The relation contracted on marriage between a husband and his wife's kindred, and between the wife and her husband's kindred, as distinguished from consanguinity or relationship by blood. 1 Denio (N. Y.) 25.

The relations of the wife, her brothers, her sisters, her uncles, are allied to the husband by affinity; and his brothers, sisters, etc., are allied in the same way to the wife. 1 Denio (N. Y.) 186. But the brother and the sister of the wife are not allied by the ties of affinity. 2 Barb. Ch. (N. Y.) 331.

AFFIRM (Lat. *affirmare*, to make firm; to establish).

To ratify or confirm a former law or judgment. Cowell.

Especially used of confirmations of the judgments of an inferior by an appellate tribunal.

To ratify or confirm a voidable act of the party.

To make a solemn religious asseveration in the nature of an oath. See "Affirmation."

AFFIRMANCE. The confirmation of a voidable act by the party acting, who is to be bound thereby.

The term is in accuracy to be distinguished from "ratification," which is a recognition of the validity or binding force, as against the party ratifying, or some act performed by another person, and from "confirmation," which would seem to apply more properly to cases where a doubtful authority has been exercised by another in behalf of the person ratifying; but these distinctions are not generally observed with much care. 1 Pars. Cont. 243.

Express affirmance takes place where the party declares his determination of fulfilling the contract. Dud. (Ga.) 203.

Implied affirmance arises from the acts of the party without any express declaration. 15 Mass. 220. See 10 N. H. 194; 11 Serg. & R. (Pa.) 305; 1 Pars. Cont. 243; 1 Sharswood, Bl. Comm. 466, note 10.

——**In Appellate Practice.** The approval by an appellate court of the judgment or order under review.

AFFIRMANCE-DAY-GENERAL. In the English court of exchequer. A day appointed by the judges of the common pleas, and barons of the exchequer, to be held a few days after the beginning of every term for the general affirmance or reversal of judgments. 2 Tidd, Prac. 1091.

AFFIRMANT. In practice. One who makes affirmation instead of making oath that the evidence which he is about to give shall be the truth, as if he had been sworn.

AFFIRMANTI, NON NEGANTI, INCUMbit probatio. The proof lies upon him who affirms, not on him who denies. See Phil. Ev. 493.

AFFIRMANTIS EST PROBATIO. He who affirms must prove. 9 Cush. (Mass.) 535.

AFFIRMATION. In practice. A solemn religious asseveration in the nature of an oath. 1 Greenl. Ev. § 371.

AFFIRMATIVE. That which establishes; that which asserts a thing to be true.

AFFIRMATIVE PREGNANT. In pleading. An affirmative allegation implying some negative in favor of the adverse party. For example, if to an action of *assumpsit*, which is barred by the act of limitations in six years, the defendant pleads that he did not undertake, etc., within ten years, a replication that he did undertake, etc., within ten years would be an affirmative pregnant, since it would impliedly admit that the defendant had not promised within six years. Such a plea should be demurred to. Gould, Pl. c. 6, §§ 29, 37; Steph. Pl. 381; Lawes, Civ. Pl. 113; Bac. Abr. "Pleas" (note 6). See "Negative Pregnant."

AFFIRMATIVE STATUTE. See "Statute."

AFFIRMATIVE WARRANTY. In insurance law. A warranty as to existing facts, as distinguished from promissory warranties relating to future conduct.

AFFIXUS. Affixed.

AFFORATUS. Appraised, assessed, or valued. Blount.

AFFORCE. To increase or strengthen.

AFFORCE THE ASSIZE. To compel unanimity among the jurors who disagree.

It was done either by confining them without meat and drink, or, more anciently, by adding other jurors to the panel to a limited extent, securing the concurrence of twelve in a verdict. See Bracton, fols. 185b, 292a; Fleta, bk. 4, c. 9, § 2.

The practice is now discontinued.

AFFORER, or **AFFORARE.** To estimate, assess, or tax. Kelham; Blount.

AFFOREST. To convert land into a "forest," in the legal sense of the word.

AFFRANCHIR (Law Fr.) To set free. Kelham.

AFFRANCHISE. To make free.

AFFRAY. In criminal law. The fighting of two or more persons in some public place to the terror of the people. 53 Ala. 640; 15 Ark. 204; 57 Mo. App. 502.

It differs from a riot in not being premeditated; for if any persons meet together upon any lawful or innocent occasion, and happen on a sudden to engage in fighting, they are not guilty of a riot, but an affray only; and in that case none are guilty except those actually engaged in it. Hawk. P. C. bk. 1, c. 65; § 3; 4 Bl. Comm. 146; 1 Russ. Crimes, 271.

Fighting in a private place is only an assault. 1 Cromp., M. & R. 757; 1 Cox, C. C. 177; 22 Ala. 15; 29 Ind. 206.

AFFRECTAMENTUM (Fr. *fret*). *Affreightment.*

The word *fret* means tons, according to Cowell.

Affreightamentum was sometimes used. Du Cange.

AFFREIGHTMENT. The contract by which a vessel, or the use of it, is let out to hire.

AFFRI. In old English law. Plow cattle, bullocks, or plow horses. *Affri*, or *afri* *carucae*, beasts of the plow. Reg. Orig. 150a; St. Westminster II. c. 18; Spelman. *Affri carectae*, beasts of the cart. Fleta, lib. 2, c. 85.

AFORESAID. Before mentioned; already spoken of or described. See 20 Mo. 411; 20 Ala. 35.

AFORETHOUGHT. In criminal law. Premeditation; prepense. See "Malice Aforethought."

AFTERMATH. The second crop of grass. A right to have the last crop of grass or pasturage. 1 Chit. Prac. 181.

AGAINST THE FORM OF THE STATute. Technical words which must be used in framing an indictment for a breach of the statute prohibiting the act complained of.

The Latin phrase is *contra formam statuti.*

AGAINST THE PEACE. See "Contra Pacem."

AGAINST THE WILL. Technical words which must be used in framing an indictment for robbery from the person. 1 Chit. Cr. Law, 244.

In the statute of 13 Edw. I. (Westminster II.) c. 34, the offense of rape is described to be ravishing a woman "where she did not consent," and not ravishing against her will. Per Tindal, C. J., and Parke, B., in the addenda to 1 Den. C. C. 1. And in a later case this statute definition was adopted by all the judges. Bell, C. C. 63, 71.

AGALMA. An impression or image of anything on a seal. Cowell.

AGARD. An award.

AGARDER (Law Fr.) To award, adjudge, or determine; to sentence, or condemn.

AGE. Years of life; that period of life at which the law allows persons to do acts or discharge functions which, for want of years, they were prohibited from doing or undertaking before.

——**At Common Law.** Males, before fourteen, are said not to be of discretion; at that age they may consent to marriage, and choose a guardian. Twenty-one years is full age for all private purposes, and they may then exercise their rights as citizens by voting for public officers, and are eligible to all offices, unless otherwise provided for in the constitution.

Females, at twelve, arrive at years of discretion, and may consent to marriage; at fourteen, they may choose a guardian; and twenty-one as in males is full age, when they may exercise all the rights which belong to their sex. The age of puberty for both sexes is fourteen.

——**In French Law.** A person must have attained the age of forty to be a member of the legislative body; twenty-five, to be a judge of a tribunal *de premiere instance;* twenty-seven to be its president, or to be judge or clerk of a *cour royale;* thirty, to be its president or *procureur-general;* twenty-five, to be a justice of the peace; thirty, to be a judge of a tribunal of commerce, and thirty-five to be its president; twenty-five to be a notary public; twenty-one, to be a testamentary witness; thirty, to be a juror. At sixteen, a minor may devise one-half of his property as if he were a major. A male cannot contract marriage till after the eighteenth year, nor a female before full fifteen years. At twenty-one, both males and females are capable to perform all the acts of civil life. Toullier, Dr. Civ. liv. 1, Introd. note 188.

——**In Roman Law.** Infancy (*infantia*) extended to the age of seven; the period of childhood (*pueritia*), which extended from seven to fourteen, was divided into two periods,—the first, extending from seven to ten and a half, was called the period nearest childhood (*aetas infantiae proxima*); the other from ten and a half to fourteen, the period nearest puberty (*aetas pubertati proxima*); puberty (*pubertas*) extended from fourteen to eighteen; full puberty extended from eighteen to twenty-five; at twenty-five, the person was of legal age (*aetas legitima*), sometimes expressed as full age (*aetas perfecta*). See Tayl. Civ. Law, 254; Lec. Elem. Civ. 22.

AGE PRAYER. A statement made in a real action, to which an infant is a party, of the fact of infancy, and a request that the proceedings may be stayed until the infant becomes of age.

It is now abolished. St. 11 Geo. IV.; 1 Wm. IV. c. 37, § 10; 1 Lilly, Reg. 54; 3 Bl. Comm. 300.

AGENCY. A relation between two or more persons, by which one party, usually called the "agent" or "attorney," is authorized to do certain acts for, or in relation to the rights or property of, the other, who is denominated the "principal," "constituent," or "employer." Prof. Joel Parker, MSS. Lect. 1851. See "Agent."

AGENCY, DEED OF. A revocable and voluntary trust for payment of debts. Wharton.

AGENFRIDA (Saxon). The true lord or owner of a thing. Spelman.

AGENHINE, AGENHINA, or **AWNHINE.** In Saxon law. A domestic or inmate. One who stayed three nights in an inn was counted an *agenhine.* Laws Edw. Conf. c. 17.

AGENS (Lat. *agere*, to do; to conduct). A conductor or manager of affairs. Distinguished from *factor*, a workman.

A plaintiff. Fleta, lib. 4, c. 15, § 8.

AGENT (Lat. *agens*, from *agere*, to do). One who undertakes to transact some business, or to manage some affair, for another, by the authority and on account of the latter, and to render an account of it. 1 Livermore, Ag. 67; 2 Bouv. Inst. 3.

The term is one of a very wide application, and includes a great many classes of persons to which distinctive appellations are given; as, factors, brokers, attorneys, cashiers of banks, auctioneers, clerks, supercargoes, consignees, ships' husbands, masters of ships, and the like. The terms "agent" and "attorney" are often used synonymously. Thus, a letter or power of attorney is constantly spoken of as the formal instrument by which an agency is created. Paley, Ag. (Dunl. Ed.) 1, note.

Agents are "general" or "special;" a general agent being one authorized to represent his principal in all matters, in which case he is sometimes called a "universal agent" (*q. v.*), or in all matters of a particular class; a special agent, one authorized to act only on one occasion, or in one transaction.

The distinction between an "agent" and a "servant" is that the former acts as a substitute for his principal, *i. e.*, represents him in some transaction with third persons, while the latter merely performs the master's work.

——**In International Law.** The agents of a state in international affairs are (a) the persons to whom are delegated the management of the foreign affairs of the state by the constitution, and (b) all persons directly subordinate to them, the latter being generally designated as "diplomatic agents." Glenn, Int. Law, 105.

——**In English Parliamentary Practice.** Persons acting as solicitors in appealed cases in the privy council and house of lords are known as "agents," or "law agents." Macph. Privy Council, 65.

AGENT AND PATIENT. A phrase indicating the state of a person who is required to do a thing, and is at the same time the person to whom it is done; as, when a man is indebted to another, and he appoints him his executor, the latter is required to pay the debt in his capacity of executor, and entitled to receive it in his own right; he is then *agent and patient.* Termes de la Ley.

AGENTES ET CONSENTIENTES PARI poena plectentur. Acting and consenting parties are liable to the same punishment. 5 Coke, 80.

AGER (Lat.) In civil law. A field; land generally.

A portion of land enclosed by definite boundaries.

Used like the word *acre* in the old English law, denoting a measure of undetermined and variable value. Spelman; Du Cange; 3 Kent, Comm. 441.

AGGER (Lat.) In the civil law. A dam, bank, or mound. Code, 9. 38; Towns. Pl. 48.

AGGRAVATED ASSAULT. An assault attended by circumstances of aggravation, as the use of a weapon, or disparity of age or sex between the assailant and person assaulted.

AGGRAVATION (Lat. *ad*, to, and *gravis*, heavy; *aggravare*, to make heavy), that which increases the enormity of a crime or the injury of a wrong.

——**In Criminal Law.** One of the rules respecting variances is that cumulative allegations, or such as merely operate in aggravation, are immaterial, provided that sufficient is proved to establish some right, offense, or justification included in the claim, charge or defense specified on the record. This rule runs through the whole criminal law, that it is invariably enough to prove so much of the indictment as shows that the defendant has committed a substantive crime therein specified. Per Lord Ellenborough. 2 Campb. 583; 4 Barn. & C. 329; 21 Pick. (Mass.) 525; 4 Gray (Mass.) 18; 7 Gray (Mass.) 49, 331; 1 Tayl. Ev. § 215. Thus, on an indictment for murder, the prisoner may be convicted of manslaughter, for the averment of malice aforethought is merely matter of aggravation. Co. Litt. 282a.

——**In Pleading.** The introduction of matter into the declaration which tends to increase the amount of damages, but does not affect the right of action itself. Steph. Pl. 257; 12 Mod. 597. See 3 Am. Jur. 287-313.

An example of this is found in the case where a plaintiff declares in trespass for entering his house, and breaking his close, and tossing his goods about. The entry of the house is the principal ground and foundation of the action, and the rest is only stated by way of aggravation (3 Wils. 294), and this matter need not be proved by the plaintiff, or answered by the defendant.

AGGREGATE. A collection of particular persons or items, formed into one body. See "Corporation."

AGGREGATIO MENTIUM. A meeting of minds. See "Agreement."

AGGRESSOR. He who begins a quarrel or dispute, either by threatening or striking another. No man may strike another because he has been threatened, or in consequence of the use of any words.

AGGRIEVED. Injuriously affected.

AGILD. In Saxon law. Free from penalty (*sine mulcta vel compensatione*), not subject to the payment of *gild*, or *weregild;* that is, the customary fine or pecuniary compensation for an offense. Spelman; Cowell.

AGILER. In Saxon law. An observer or informer.

AGILLARIUS (Law Lat.) In old English law. A hayward, herdward, or keeper of the herd of cattle in a common field. Cowell.

AGIO. A term used in commercial transactions to denote the difference of price between the value of bank notes or other nominal money and the coin of the country. 5 Mees. & W. 535.

AGIOTAGE. From *agis.* Speculation in public securities.

AGISTER. See "Agistment."

AGISTMENT. The taking of another person's cattle into one's own ground to be fed, for a consideration to be paid by the owner. The person so taking cattle to pasture is called an "agister." Schouler, Bailm. § 96; Story, Bailm. § 443; 68 Cal. 290.

——**In Old English Law.** The taking of the cattle of strangers to pasture on the king's land, and collecting fees therefor to the use of the king. Spelman.

AGNATES. In Scotch law. Relations on the father's side.

AGNATI. In civil law. The members of a Roman family who traced their origin and name to a common deceased ancestor through the male line, under whose paternal power they would be if he were living.

They were called *adgnati,—adcnati,* from the words *ad eum nati.* Ulpianus says: "*Adgnati autem sunt cognati virilis sexus ab eodem orti; nam post suos et consaguineos statim mihi proximus est consanguinei mei filius, et ego ei; patris quoque frater qui patruus appellatur; deinceps ceteri, si qui sunt, hinc orti in infinitum.*" Dig. 38. 16; De Suis 2, § 1. Thus, although the grandfather and father be dead, the children become *sui juris,* and the males may become the founders of new families, still they all continue to be *agnates;* and the *agnatio* spreads and is perpetuated not only in the direct, but also in the collateral, line. Marriage, adoption, and adrogation also create the relationship of the *agnatio.* In the Sentences of Paulus, the order of inheritance is stated as follows: *Intestatorum hereditas, lege Duodecim Tabularum primum suis heredibus, de inde adgnatis et aliquando quoque gentibus deferebatur.*

They are distinguished from the *cognati,* those related through females. See "Cognati."

AGNATIC. Derived from or through males. 2 Bl. Comm. 236.

AGNATIO (Lat.) In civil law. A relationship through males; the male children. Especially spoken of the children of a free father and slave mother. The rule in such cases was *agnatio sequitur ventrem.* Du Cange.

AGNATION. Relationship on the father's side. See "Agnates."

AGNOMEN (Lat.) A name or title which a man gets by some action or peculiarity; the last of the four names sometimes given a Roman. Thus, Scipio Africanus (the African), from his African victories. Ainsworth; Calv. Lex. See "Nomen."

AGRARIAN LAWS. In Roman law. Those laws by which the commonwealth disposed of its public land, or regulated the possession thereof by individuals, were termed "Agrarian Laws."

The greater part of the public lands acquired by conquest were laid open to the possession of any citizen, but the state reserved the title and the right to resume possession. The object of many of the agrarian laws was to limit the area of public land of which any one person might take possession. The law of Cassius, B. C. 486, is the most noted of these laws.

Until a comparatively recent period, it has been assumed that these laws were framed to reach private property, as well as to restrict possession of the public domain, and hence the term "agrarian" is, in legal and political literature, to a great degree fixed with the meaning of a confiscatory law, intended to reduce large estates, and increase the number of landholders. Harrington, in his "Oceana," and the philosophers of the French Revolution, have advocated agrarian laws in this sense. The researches of Heyne (Op. 4, 351), Niehbuhr (Hist. vol. 2, trans.), and Savigny (Das Recht des Besitzes), have redeemed the Roman word from the burden of this meaning.

AGRARIUM. A tax upon or tribute payable out of land.

AGREAMENTUM. Agreement.

Spelman says that it is equivalent in meaning to *aggregatio mentium,* though not derived therefrom.

AGREEMENT (from Lat. *aggregatio mentium*). A coming together of parties in opinion or determination; the union of two or more minds in a thing done or to be done; a mutual assent to do a thing. Comyn, Dig. "Agreement" (A. 1); Plowd, 5a, 6a.

The consent of two or more persons concurring, the one in parting with, the other in receiving, some property, right, or benefit. Bac. Abr.

A mutual contract in consideration between two or more parties. 5 East, 10; 4 Gill & J. (Md.) 1; 12 How. (U. S.) 126.

Agreement is seldom applied to specialties; contract is generally confined to simple contracts; and promise refers to the engagement of a party without reference to the reasons or considerations for it, or the duties of other parties. Pars. Cont. 6.

An agreement ceases to be such by being put in writing under seal, but not when put in writing for a memorandum. Dane, Abr. c. 11.

A promise or undertaking. This is a loose and inaccurate use of the word. 3 Conn. 335.

The writing or instrument which is evidence of an agreement. This is a loose and evidently inaccurate use of the term. The agreement may be valid, and yet the written evidence thereof insufficient.

Agreements are:

(1) Conditional, being those which are to have full effect only in case of the happening of certain events, or the existence of a given state of things.

(2) Absolute, being dependent on no contingency.

They are also:

(3) Executed, being those where nothing further remains to be done by the parties, or

(4) Executory, being such as rest on articles, memorandums, parol promises or undertakings, and the like, to be performed in the future, or which are entered into preparatory to more solemn and formal alienations of property. Powell, Cont. An executed agreement always conveys a chose in possession, while an executory one conveys a chose in action only.

They are also:

(5) Express, being those in which the terms are openly uttered and avowed by the parties at the time of making, or

(6) Implied, being those which the law supposes the parties to have made, although the terms were not openly expressed.

AGREEMENT FOR INSURANCE. An agreement often made in short terms preliminary to the filling out and delivery of a policy with the specific stipulations.

Such an agreement, specifying the rate of premium, the subject and risk, and amount to be insured, in general terms, and being assented to by the parties, is binding. 1 Phil. Ins. c. 1, § 3; 2 Curt. C. C. (U. S.) 277; 19 N. Y. 305.

AGREER, or AGGREER (Law Fr.)

——**In Old Practice.** To agree.

——**In French Marine Law.** To rig or equip a vessel. Ord. Mar. liv. 1, tit. 2, art. 1.

AGREES. The word "agrees" used in a contract *ex vi termini*, means that it is the agreement of both parties, both concurring on the point, whether both sign or not. 27 Ill. App. 231.

AGREZ (Fr.) In French marine law. The rigging or tackle of a vessel. Ord. Mar. liv. 1, tit. 2, art. 1; Id. tit. 11, art. 2; Id. liv. 3, tit. 1, art. 11.

AGRI. Arable lands in common fields.

AGRI LIMITATI. In Roman law. Lands belonging to the state by right of conquest, and granted or sold in plots. Sandars, Just. Inst. (5th Ed.) 98.

AHTEID.

——**In Old European Law.** A kind of oath among the Bavarians. Spelman.

——**In Saxon Law.** One bound by oath, (*q. v.*); "oath-tied." From *ath*, oath, and *tied*. Spelman.

AID AND COMFORT. Help; support; assistance; counsel; encouragement.

The constitution of the United States (article 3, § 3) declares that adhering to the enemies of the United States, giving them aid and comfort, shall be treason. These words, as they are to be understood in the constitution, have not received a full judicial construction. They import, however, help, support, assistance, countenance, encouragement. The word "aid," which occurs in St. Westminster I. c. 14, is explained by Lord Coke (2 Inst. 182) as comprehending all persons counseling, abetting, plotting, assenting, consenting, and encouraging to do the act (and he adds, what is not applicable to the crime of treason), who are not present when the act is done. See, also, 1 Burn, Just. 5, 6; 4 Bl. Comm. 37, 38.

AID BONDS. Public (usually municipal or county) bonds issued in aid of a private enterprise operating for the benefit of the community generally.

AID OF THE KING. Intervention prayed by the king's tenant when another questioned his tenure, or demanded rent of him.

AID PRAYER. In English law. A petition to the court calling in help from another person who has an interest in the matter in dispute. For example, a tenant for life, by the curtesy, or for years, being impleaded, may pray aid of him in reversion; that is, desire the court that he may be called by writ, to allege what he thinks proper for the maintenance of the right of the person calling him, and of his own. Fitzh. Nat. Brev. 50; Cowell.

AIDER BY VERDICT. In pleading. The presumption which arises after verdict, whether in a civil or criminal case, that those facts, without proof of which the verdict could not have been found, were proved, though they are not distinctly alleged in the record; provided it contains terms sufficiently general to comprehend them in reasonable intendment.

AIDING AND ABETTING. In criminal law. The offense committed by those persons, who, although not the direct perpetrators of a crime, are yet present at its commission, doing some act to render aid to the actual perpetrator thereof. 4 Sharswood, Bl. Comm. 34; Russ. & R. 363, 421; 9 Ired. (N. C.) 440; 1 Woodb. & M. 221; 10 Pick. (Mass.) 477; 12 Whart. (Pa.) 460; 26 Miss. 299.

A principal in the second degree is he who is present aiding and abetting the fact to be done. 1 Hale, P. C. 615. See "Principal."

AIDS. In English law. A species of tax payable by the tenant of lands to his superior lord on the happening of certain events.

They were originally mere benevolences granted to the lord in certain times of danger and distress, but soon came to be claimed as a right. They were originally given in three cases only, and were of uncertain amount. For a period they were demanded in additional cases, but this abuse was corrected by *Magna Charta* (of John) and St. 25 Edw. I. (*confirmatio chartarum*), and they were made payable only,—to ransom the lord's person, when taken prisoner; to make the lord's eldest son a knight; to marry the lord's eldest daughter, by giving her a suitable portion. The first of these remained uncertain; the other two were fixed by act of parliament (25 Edw. III. c. 11) at twenty shillings each, being the supposed twentieth part of a knight's fee. 2 Bl. Comm. 64. They were abolished by 12 Car. II. c. 24. 2 Sharswood, Bl. Comm. 77, note.

AIR. That fluid transparent substance which surrounds our globe. See "Easement."

AIRE. In old Scotch law. The court of the justices itinerant, corresponding to the English *eyre*. Skene de Verb. Sign. voc. "Iter."

Heir. "His *airis* and *assignais*." Pitc. Crim. Tr. pt. 2, p. 342.

AISMENTUM, AISIAMENTUM, or **ESAmentum.** An easement. Spelman.

AISNE, or **EIGNE.** In old English law. Eldest or first born. *Aisne* is the opposite of *puisne*. Spelman, "Aesnecia."

AJUAR. In Spanish law. The jewels and furniture which a wife bring in marriage.

AJUTAGE, or **ADJUTAGE.** A conical tube used in drawing water through an aperture, by the use of which the quantity of water drawn is much increased.

When a privilege to draw water from a canal, through the forebay or tunnel, by means of an aperture, has been granted, it is not lawful to add an *ajutage*, unless such was the intention of the parties. 2 Whart. (Pa.) 477.

AKIN. In old English law. Of kin. "Next-a-kin." 7 Mod. 140.

AL (Law Fr.) At; to. *Al huis d'esglise*, at the church door. Litt. § 38. *Al contrary*, to the contrary. Dyer, 5b.

ALAE ECCLESIAE. The wings or side aisles of a church. Blount.

ALANERARIUS. A manager and keeper of dogs for the sport of hawking; from *alanus*, a dog known to the ancients. A falconer. Blount.

ALBA FIRMA. White rents; rents reserved payable in silver, or white money. They were so called to distinguish them from *reditus nigri* which were rents reserved payable in work, grain, and the like. 2 Inst. 19.

ALBANAGIUM. In old French law. The state of alienage; of being a foreigner or alien.

ALBANUS. See "Advena."

ALBINATUS (Law Lat.) In old French law. The state or condition of an alien or foreigner.

ALBINATUS JUS. In old French law. The right of albanage. A right formerly existing in France, entitling the king, on the death of an alien, to all his property, unless he had a peculiar exemption. Spelman; Bl. Comm. 372; 2 Kent, Comm. 69.

ALBUM BREVE. A blank writ; a writ with a blank or omission in it, as, where it is returned with the sheriff's surname omitted. Hob. 113b; Yelv. 110.

ALBUS LIBER. An ancient book containing a compilation of the law and customs of the city of London. Wharton.

ALCABALA (Spanish). A duty of a certain per cent. paid to the treasury on the sale or exchange of property. Schmidt, Civ. Law, 81, note 1.

ALCALDE. In Spanish law. A judicial officer in Spain, and in those countries which have received the body of their laws from those of Spain. His powers and duties are similar to those of a justice of the peace.

ALDERMAN (equivalent to "senator" or "senior").

——**In English Law.** An associate to the chief civil magistrate of a corporate town or city.

The word was formerly of very extended signification. Spelman enumerates eleven classes of aldermen. Their duties among the Saxons embraced both magisterial and executive power, but would seem to have been rather an appellation of honor, originally, than a distinguishing mark of office.

Aldermannus civitatis, burgi seu castellae (alderman of a city, borough, or castle). 1 Sharswood, Bl. Comm. 475, note.

Aldermannus comitatus (alderman of the county), who is thought by Spelman to have held an intermediate place between an earl and sheriff; by others, held the same as the earl. 1 Sharswood, Bl. Comm. 116.

Aldermannus hundredi seu wapentachii (alderman of a hundred or wapentake). Spelman.

Aldermannus regis (alderman of the king) was so called, either because he was appointed by the king, or because he gave the judgment of the king in the premises allotted to him.

Aldermannus totius Angliae (alderman of all England). An officer of high rank, whose duties cannot be precisely determined. See Spelman.

The aldermen of the city of London were probably originally the chiefs of guilds. See 1 Spence, Eq. Jur. 54, 56.

——**In American Cities.** The aldermen are generally a legislative body, having limited judicial powers as a body, as in matters of internal police regulation, laying out and repairing streets, constructing sewers, and the like; though in many cities they hold separate courts, and have magisterial powers to a considerable extent. Consult Spelman; Cowell; 1 Sharswood, Bl. Comm. 116; Reeve, Hist. Eng. Law; Spence, Eq. Jur.; McQuillin Mun. Corp.

ALE CONNER (also called "ale taster"). An officer appointed by the court leet, sworn to look to the assize and goodness of ale and beer within the precincts of the leet. Kitch. Cts. 46; Whishaw. An officer appointed in every court leet, and sworn to look to the assize of bread, ale, or beer, within the precincts of that lordship. Cowell. This officer is still continued in name, though the duties are changed or given up. 1 Crabb, Real Prop. 501.

ALEATOR (Lat. *alea*, dice). A dice player; a gambler.

ALEATORY CONTRACT. In civil law. A mutual agreement, of which the effects, with respect both to the advantages and losses, whether to all the parties or to some of them, depend on an uncertain event. Civ. Code La. art. 2951.

The term includes contracts, such as insurance, annuities, and the like.

ALER A DIEU (Law Fr.) In old practice. To be dismissed from court; to go quit. Literally, "to go to God." Y. B. H. 2 Edw. III. 6; Y. B. T. 5 Edw. II. 173; Y. B. H. 3 Edw. II. 75.

ALLER SANS JOUR (Fr. *aller sans jour*, to go without day). In practice. A phrase formerly used to indicate the final dismissal of a case from court. The defendant was then at liberty to go, without any day appointed for his subsequent appearance. Kitch. Cts. 146.

ALEU (Fr.) In French feudal law. An allodial estate, as distinguished from a feudal estate or benefice. Guyot, Inst. Feud. c. 28, § 2.

ALFET. The vessel in which hot water was put, for the purpose of dipping a criminal's arm in it up to the elbow in the ordeal by water. Cowell.

ALGARUM MARIS. Probably a corruption of *laganum maris; lagan* being a right, in the middle ages, like *jetsam* and *flotsam*, by which goods thrown from a vessel in distress became the property of the king, or the lord on whose shores they were stranded. Spelman; Jacob; Du Cange.

ALIA ENORMIA (Lat. other wrongs). In pleading. A general allegation, at the end of a declaration, of wrongful acts committed by the defendant to the damage of the plaintiff. In form it is, "and other wrongs then and there did against the peace," etc. Under this allegation, damages and matters which naturally arise from the act complained of may be given in evidence (2 Greenl. Ev. § 678), including battery of servants, etc., in a declaration for breaking into and entering a house (6 Mod. 127; 2 Term R. 166; 7 Har. & J. [Md.] 68), and all matters in general which go in aggravation of damages merely, but would not of themselves be ground for an action (Buller, N. P. 89; 3 Mass. 222; 6 Munf. [Va.] 308). But matters in aggravation may be stated specially (15 Mass. 194; Gilm. [Va.] 227), and matters which of themselves would constitute a ground of action must be so stated (1 Chit. Pl. 348; 17 Pick. [Mass.] 284). See, generally, 1 Chit. Pl. 648; Buller, N. P. 89; 2 Greenl. Ev. §§ 268, 273, 278; 2 Salk. 643; Peake, Ev. 505.

ALIAS (Lat. *alius*, another). In practice. Before; at another time.

An *alias* writ is a writ issued where one of the same kind has been issued before in the same cause. The second writ runs, in such case, "We command you, as we have before commanded you" (*sicut alias*), and the Latin word *alias* is used to denote both the writ and the clause in which it or its corresponding English word is found. It is used of all species of writs.

ALIAS DICTUS (Lat. otherwise called). A description of the defendant by adding to his real name that by which he is known in some writing on which he is to be charged, or by which he is known. 4 Johns. (N. Y.) 118; 2 Caines (N. Y.) 362; 3 Caines (N. Y.) 219.

ALIBI (Lat. elsewhere). Presence in another place than that described.

When a person, charged with a crime, proves (*se eadem die fuisse alibi*) that he was, at the time alleged, in a different place from that in which it was committed, he is said to prove an *alibi*, the effect of which is to lay a foundation for the necessary inference that he could not have committed it. See Bracton, 140.

ALIEN (Lat. *alienus*, belonging to another; foreign). A foreigner; one of foreign birth.

——**In England.** One born out of the allegiance of the king.

——**In the United States.** One born out of the jurisdiction of the United States, and who has not been naturalized under their constitution and laws. 2 Kent, Comm. 50. The children of ambassadors and ministers at foreign courts, however, are not aliens. And see 10 U. S. St. at Large, 604.

ALIEN AMY. An alien friend; *i. e.*, a subject of a friendly nation.

ALIEN ENEMY. One who owes allegiance to the adverse belligerent. 1 Kent, Comm. 73.

He who owes a temporary, but not a permanent, allegiance, is an alien enemy in respect to acts done during such temporary allegiance only, and when his allegiance terminates, his hostile character terminates also. 1 Bos. & P. 163.

ALIENABLE. Subject of alienation.

ALIENAGE. The condition or state of an alien.

ALIENATE. To convey; to transfer. Co. Litt. 118b. "Alien" is very commonly used in the same sense. 1 Washb. Real Prop. 53. See "Alienation."

ALIENATIO LICET PROHIBEATUR, consensu tamen omnium, in quorum favorem prohibita est, potest fieri, et quilibet potest renunciare juri pro se introducto. Although alienation be prohibited, yet, by the consent of all in whose favor it is prohibited, it may take place, for it is in the power of any man to renounce a right introduced for his own benefit. Co. Litt. 98; 9 N. Y. 291.

ALIENATIO REI PRAEFERTUR JURI accrescendi. Alienation is favored by the law, rather than accumulation. Co. Litt. 185a, 381a, note; Broom, Leg. Max. (3d London Ed.) 393, 409; Wright, Ten. 154 et. seq.; 1 Cruise, Dig. (4th Ed.) 77, 78.

ALIENATION.

——**Of Property.** The transfer of property and possession of lands, tenements, or other things from one person to another. Termes de la Ley. It is particularly applied to absolute conveyances of real property. A transfer of less than the whole title is not, in the United States, an alienation. 11 Barb. (N. Y.) 624.

Alienation is either by deed, or by matter of record.

(1) Alienations by deed are:

(a) Original or primary alienations are those by which a benefit or estate is created or first arises. They are feoffment, gift, grant, lease, exchange, and partition.

(b) Derivative or secondary alienations are those by which the benefit or estate originally created is enlarged, restrained, transferred or extinguished; or they may be made by conveyances under the statute of uses. They are release, confirmation, surrender, assignment, and defeasance. Those deriving their force from the statute of uses are covenant to stand seized, bargain and sale, lease and release, deeds to declare the uses of other more direct conveyances, and deeds of revocation of uses.

(2) Alienation by matter of record may be by private act of the legislature, by patents and other public grants, by fine, by common recovery.

——**In Medical Jurisprudence.** A generic term, denoting the different kinds of aberration of the human understanding. 1 Beck, Med. Jur. 535.

ALIENATION OFFICE. In English law. An office to which all writs of covenants and entries were carried for the recovery of fines levied thereon.

ALIENEE. One to whom an alienation is made.

ALIENI GENERIS (Lat.) Of another kind.

ALIENI JURIS (Lat.) Subject to the authority of another. An infant who is under the authority of his father or guardian, and a wife under the power of her husband, are said to be *alieni juris*. See "Sui Juris."

ALIENIGENA (Lat.) One of foreign birth; an alien. 7 Coke, 31.

ALIENOR. He who makes a grant or alienation.

ALIENUS (Lat.) That which belongs to another.

ALIMENT.

——**In Scotch Law.** To support; to provide with necessaries. Paterson, Comp. §§ 845, 850.

Maintenance; support; an allowance from the husband's estate for the support of the wife. Paterson, Comp. § 893.

——**In Civil Law.** Food and other things necessary to the support of life; money allowed for the purpose of procuring these. Dig. 50. 16. 43.

——**In Common Law.** To supply with necessaries. 3 Edw. Ch. (N. Y.) 194.

ALIMENTA (Lat.) In the civil law. Aliments; means of support, including food (*cibaria*), clothing (*vestitus*), and habitation (*habitatio*). Dig. 34. 1. 6.

ALIMONY. Money paid for aliment or support.

The allowance which a husband, by order of court, pays to his wife, living separate from him, for her maintenance. Bish. Mar. & Div. § 549.

The term is sometimes restricted to an allowance for a wife's support, made either pending an action for divorce, or after a decree of divorce.

Alimony *pendente lite* is that ordered during the pendency of a suit.

Permanent alimony is that ordered for the use of the wife after the termination of the suit, during their joint lives, or until the further order of the court.

ALIO INTUITU (Lat.) Under a different aspect. See "Diverso Intuitu."

ALIQUID CONCEDITUR NE INJURIA remaneat impunita, quod alias non concederetur. Something is conceded lest a wrong should remain unpunished which otherwise would not be conceded. Co. Litt. 197.

ALIQUID POSSESSIONIS ET NIHIL juris (Law Lat.) Somewhat of possession, and nothing of right (but no right). A phrase used by Bracton to describe that kind of possession which a person might have of a thing as a guardian, creditor, or the like, and also that kind of possession which was granted for a term of years, where nothing could be demanded but the usufruct. Bracton, fols. 39a, 160a.

ALIQUIS NON DEBET ESSE JUDEX IN propria causa, quia non potest esse judex et pars. A person ought not to be judge in his own cause, because he cannot act both as judge and party. Co. Litt. 141a; Broom, Leg. Max. (3d London Ed.) 112; Litt. § 212; 13 Q. B. 327; 17 Q. B. 1; 15 C. B. 769; 1 C. B. (N. S.) 329.

ALITER (Lat.) Otherwise; otherwise held or decided.

ALIUD EST CELARE; ALIUD TACERE. To conceal is one thing; to be silent another. 3 Burrows, 1910. See 2 Wheat. (U. S.) 176; 9 Wheat. (U. S.) 631; 3 Bing. 77; 4 Taunt. 851; 2 Car. & P. 341; Broom, Leg. Max. (3d London Ed.) 701.

ALIUD EST DISTINCTIO; ALIUD SEPAratio. Distinction is one thing; separation another. Bacon's arg. Case of Postnati of Scotland, Works, iv. 351.

ALIUD EST POSSIDERE; ALIUD ESSE in possessione. It is one thing to possess; it is another to be in possession. Hob. 163; Bracton, 206.

ALIUD EST VENDERE; ALIUD VENdenti consentire. To sell is one thing; to give consent to him who sells, another. Dig. 50. 17. 160.

ALIUD EXAMEN (Lat.) A different or foreign mode of trial. 1 Hale, Hist. Com. Laws, 38 (30).

ALIUNDE (Lat.) From another place. Evidence *aliunde* (*i. e.*, from without the will) may be received to explain an ambiguity in a will. 1 Greenl. Ev. § 291.

ALL FOURS. A metaphorical expression, signifying that a case agrees in all its circumstances with another.

ALL THE ESTATE. The name given in England to the short clause in a conveyance or other assurance which purports to convey "all the estate, right, title, interest, claim, and demand" of the grantor, lessor, etc., in the property dealt with. Dav. Prec. Conv. 93.

ALLEGANS CONTRARIA NON EST audiendus. One making contradictory allegations is not to be heard. Jenk. Cent. Cas. 16; Broom, Leg. Max. (3d London Ed.) 160, 268; 4 Term R. 211; 3 Exch. 446, 527, 678; 4 Exch. 187; 11 Exch. 493; 3 El. & Bl. 363; 5 El. & Bl. 502; 5 C. B. 195, 886; 10 Mass. 163; Coke, 4th Inst. 279.

ALLEGANS SUAM TURPITUDINEM non est audiendus. One alleging his own infamy is not to be heard. Coke, 4th Inst. 299; 2 Johns. Ch. (N. Y.) 339, 350.

ALLEGARI NON DEBUIT QUOD PRObatum non relevat. That ought not to be alleged which, if proved, is not relevant. 1 Ch. Cas. 45.

ALLEGATA. A word which the emperors formerly signed at the bottom of their rescripts and constitutions; under other instruments they usually wrote *signata* or *testata*. Enc. Lond.

ALLEGATA ET PROBATA (Lat. things alleged and proved). The allegations made by a party to a suit, and the proof adduced in their support.

ALLEGATIO CONTRA FACTUM NON est admittenda. An allegation contrary to the deed (or fact) is not admissible.

ALLEGATION. The assertion, declaration, or statement of a party of what he can prove.

——**In Ecclesiastical Law.** The statement of the facts intended to be relied on in support of the contested suit. It is applied either to the libel, or to the answer of the respondent, setting forth new facts, the latter being, however, generally called the defensive allegation. See 1 Browne, Civ. Law, 472, 473, note.

ALLEGATION OF FACULTIES. A statement made by the wife of the property of her husband, in order to her obtaining alimony. 11 Ala. (N. S.) 763; 3 Tex. 168.

ALLEGIANCE. The tie which binds the citizen to the government, in return for the protection which the government affords him.

——**Natural Allegiance.** That which results from the birth of a person within the territory, and under the obedience of the government. 2 Kent, Comm. 42.

——**Acquired Allegiance.** That binding a citizen who was born an alien, but has been naturalized.

——**Local Allegiance.** That which is due from an alien while resident in a country, in return for the protection afforded by the government. 16 Wall. (U. S.) 154.

ALLEGIARE. To defend and clear one's self; to wage one's own law.

ALLEGING DIMINUTION. The allegation in an appellate court of some error in a subordinate part of the record below.

ALLEVIARE (Law Lat.) In old records. To levy or pay an accustomed fine or composition. Cowell. To redeem by such payment. Burrill.

ALLIANCE (Lat. *ad,* to, *ligare,* to bind). The union or connection of two persons or families by marriage; affinity.

——**In International Law.** A contract, treaty, or league between two sovereigns or states, made to insure their safety and common defense.

Alliances are defensive, or offensive.

(1) Defensive alliances are those in which a nation agrees to defend her ally in case she is attacked.

(2) Offensive alliances are those in which nations unite for the purpose of making an attack, or jointly waging the war against another nation. Alliances may be at the same time offensive and defensive; and most offensive alliances are of this character. Vattel, bk. 3, c. 6, § 79; 2 Dall. (Pa.) 15.

ALLISON. Running one vessel against another. To be distinguished from collision, which denotes the running of two vessels against each other. The distinction is not very carefully observed, but collision is used to denote cases strictly of allision.

ALLOCATION. An allowance upon an account in the English exchequer. Cowell. Placing or adding to a thing. Enc. Lond.

ALLOCATIONE FACIENDA. In English law. A writ directed to the lord treasurer and barons of the exchequer, commanding that an allowance be made to an accountant for such moneys as he has lawfully expended in his office.

ALLOCATO COMITATU. In old English practice. In proceedings in outlawry, when there were but two county courts holden between the delivery of the writ of *exigi facias* to the sheriff and its return, a special *exigi facias,* with an *allocato comitatu* issued to the sheriff in order to complete the proceedings. Bac. Abr. "Outlawry."

ALLOCATUR (Lat. it is allowed). A Latin word formerly used to denote that a writ or order was allowed.

A word denoting the allowance by a master or prothonotary of a bill referred for his consideration, whether touching costs, damages, or matter of account. Lee, Dict.

ALLOCATUR EXIGENT. A writ of exigent which issued in a process of outlawry, upon the sheriff's making return to the original exigent that there were not five county courts held between the *teste* of the original writ and the return day. 1 Tidd, Prac. 128.

ALLOCUTUS. In criminal procedure When a prisoner is convicted on a trial for treason or felony, the court is bound to demand of him what he has to say as to why the court should not proceed to judgment against him. This demand is called the "*allocutus,*" and is entered on the record. Archb. Crim. Pl. 173.

ALLODARII. Those who own allodial lands.

Those who have as large an estate as a subject can have. Co. Litt. 1; Bac. Abr. "Tenure" (A).

ALLODIUM (Sax. *a,* privative, and *lode* or *leude,* a vassal; that is, without vassalage). An estate held by absolute ownership, without recognizing any superior to whom any duty is due on account thereof. 1 Washb. Real Prop. 16; 9 Cow. (N. Y.) 513.

It is used in opposition to *feodum* or *fief,* which means property the use of which was bestowed upon another by the proprietor, on condition that the grantee should perform certain services for the grantor, and upon the failure of which the property should revert to the original possessor.

ALLOGRAPH. A document not written by any of the parties thereto; opposed to autograph.

ALLONGE (Fr.) A piece of paper annexed to a bill of exchange or promissory note, on which to write indorsements for which there is no room on the instrument itself. Pardessus, note 343; Story, Prom. Notes, §§ 121, 151.

ALLOTMENT NOTE. In English law. An assignment by a seaman of future wages. Such assignments are regulated by law as to form and amount, and as to the persons to whom they may be made. Mozley & W.

ALLOTMENT SYSTEM. A system in force in England, by which the borough sanitary authorities are required to obtain, by condemnation, if necessary, lots of land, and to allot them among the laboring classes at a rent charged not to exceed what is necessary to protect the public from loss.

ALLOTMENT WARDEN. By the English general inclosure act of 1845 (section 108), when an allotment for the laboring poor of a district has been made on an inclosure under the act, the land so allotted is to be under the management of the incumbent and church warden of the parish, and two other persons elected by the parish, and they are to be styled "the allotment wardens" of the parish. Sweet.

ALLOTTEE. One to whom an allotment is made.

ALLOY, or ALLAY. An inferior metal used with gold and silver in making coin. The amount of alloy to be used is determined by law, and is subject to changes from time to time.

ALLOYNOUR (Law Fr.) One who conceals, steals, or carries off a thing privately. Britt. c. 17.

ALLUVIO MARIS (Lat.) Soil formed by the washing up of earth from the sea. Schultes, Aq. Rights, 138.

ALLUVION. That increase of the earth on a shore or bank of a river by the force of the water, as by a current or by waves, which is so gradual that no one can judge how much is added at each moment of time. Inst. 1. 2, tit. 1, § 20; 3 Barn. & C. 91; Code Civil Annote, note 556. See "Accretion;" "Reliction."

ALLY. A nation which has entered into an alliance with another nation. 1 Kent, Comm. 69.

A citizen or subject of one of two or more allied nations. 4 C. Rob. Adm. 251; 6 C. Rob. Adm. 205; 2 Dall. (Pa.) 15; Dane, Abr., Index.

ALMESFEOH. In Saxon law. Alms fee; alms money. Otherwise called "Peterpence." Cowell.

ALMOIGN (Law Fr.) Alms; a tenure of lands by divine service. See "Frankalmoigne."

ALMOXARIFAZGO. In Spanish law. A general term, signifying both export and import duties, as well as excise. Derived from the Arabic, and said to signify the same as *portorium* in Latin. Schmidt, Civ. Law, 81, note 2.

ALMS. Any species of relief bestowed upon the poor.

That which is given by public authority for the relief of the poor. Shelf. Mortm. 802, note x; Hayw. Elect. 263; 1 Doug. Elect. 370; 2 Doug. Elect. 107.

ALNAGER, or ULNAGER. A public sworn officer of the king, who, by himself or his deputy, looks to the assize of woolen cloth made throughout the land, and to the putting on the seals for that purpose ordained. St. 17 Rich. II. c. 2; Cowell; Blount; Termes de la Ley.

ALNETUM. A place where alder trees grow. Domesday Book; Cowell; Blount.

ALODE, ALODES, or ALODIS (Law Lat.) In feudal law. Old forms of *alodium* or *allodium* (*q. v.*) Spelman.

ALONG. By the length of, as distinguished from across. 119 Ill. 225.

ALSO. Likewise; in like manner; in addition to. 22 Ill. 375; 189 Ill. 280; 197 Ill. 565.

ALT (Law Fr.) In Scotch practice. An abbreviation of *alter;* the other; the opposite party; the defender. 1 Brown, 336, note.

High. Kelham.

ALTA PRODITIO. High treason.

ALTA VIA. The highway.

ALTARAGE. In ecclesiastical law. Offerings made on the altar; all profits which accrue to the priest by means of the altar. Ayliffe, Par. 61; 2 Croke, 516.

ALTERATION. A change in the terms of a contract, made by the agreement of the parties thereto.

An act done upon an instrument in writting by a party entitled under it, without the consent of the other party, by which its meaning or language is changed.

The term is properly applied to the change in the language of instruments, and is not used of changes in the contract itself; and it is in strictness to be distinguished from the act of a stranger in changing the form or language of the instrument, which is called a "spoliation." This latter distinction is not always observed in practice, however.

ALTERIUS CIRCUMVENTIO ALII NON praebet actionem. Dig. 50. 17. 49. A deception practiced upon one person does not give a cause of action to another.

ALTERNAT. A usage among diplomatist by which the rank and places of different powers, who have the same right and pretentions to precedence, are changed from time to time, either in a certain regular order, or one determined by lot. In drawing up treaties and conventions, for example, it is the usage of certain powers to alternate, both in the preamble and the signatures, so that each power occupies, in the copy intended to be delivered to it, the first place. Wheat. Int. Law, pt. 2, c. 3, § 4.

ALTERNATIM (Law Lat.) Interchangeably. Litt. § 371; Towns. Pl. 37.

ALTERNATIVA PETITIO NON EST audienda. An alternative petition is not to be heard. 5 Coke, 40.

ALTERNATIVE. Allowing a choice between two or more things or acts to be done.

In contracts, a party has often the choice which of several things to perform. A writ is in the alternative which commands the defendant to do the thing required, or show the reason wherefore he has not done it. Finch, 257; 3 Bl. Comm. 273. The first *mandamus* is an alternative writ. 3 Bl. Comm. 111. See "Nisi."

ALTERNATIVE REMEDY. One of several remedies between which one must elect. See "Cumulative Remedy."

ALTERNATIVE WRIT. A writ commanding the person against whom it is issued to do a specified thing, or show cause to the court why he should not be compelled to do it.

ALTERNIS VICIBUS (Law Lat.) By alternate turns; at alternate times; alternately. Co. Litt. 4a; Shep. Touch. 206.

ALTERUM NON LAEDERE. Not to injure another. One of Justinian's three principles, basis of all law. Inst. 1. 1. See "Honeste Vivere," and "Suam Cuique Tribuere."

ALTIUS NON TOLLENDI. In civil law. A servitude by which the owner of a house is restrained from building beyond a certain height.

ALTIUS TOLLENDI. In civil law. A servitude which consists in the right, to him who is entitled to it, to build his house as high as he may think proper. In general, every one enjoys this privilege, unless he is restrained by some contrary title.

ALTO ET BASSO. High and low. This phrase is applied to an agreement made between two contending parties to submit all matters in dispute, *alto et basso*, to arbitration. Cowell.

ALTUM MARE. The high sea.

ALUMNUS. A foster child.

ALVEUS (Lat.) The bed or channel through which the stream flows when it runs within its ordinary channel. Calv. Lex.

Alveus derelictus, a deserted channel. 1 Mackeld. Civ. Law, 280.

AMALPHITAN TABLE. A code of sea laws compiled for the free and trading republic of Amalphi toward the end of the eleventh century. 3 Kent, Comm. 9. It consists of the laws on maritime subjects which were or had been in force in countries bordering on the Mediterranean, and, on account of its being collected into one regular system, it was for a long time received as authority in those countries. 1 Azuni, Mar. Law, 376.

AMBACTUS (Lat. *ambire*, to go about). A servant sent about; one whose services his master hired out. Spelman.

AMBASCIATOR. A person sent about in the service of another; a person sent on a service. A word of frequent occurrence in the writers of the middle ages. Spelman.

AMBASSADOR. In international law. A public minister sent abroad by some sovereign state or prince, with a legal commission and authority to transact business on behalf of his country with the government to which he is sent.

Ambassadors extraordinary are those employed on particular or extraordinary occasions, or residing at a foreign court for an indeterminate period. Vattel, lib. 4, c. 6, §§ 70-79.

Ambassadors ordinary are those sent on permanent missions.

An ambassador is a minister of the highest rank.

The United States were formerly represented by ministers plenipotentiary, sending no person of the rank of an ambassador, in the diplomatic sense. 1 Kent, Comm. 39, note. Ambassadors are now sent by the United States to Japan and the principal nations of Europe and South America.

AMBIDEXTER (Lat.) Skillful with both hands.

Applied anciently to an attorney who took pay from both sides, and subsequently to a juror guilty of the same offense. Cowell.

AMBIGUA RESPONSIO CONTRA PROferentem est accipienda. An ambiguous answer is to be taken against the party who offers it. 10 Coke, 58.

AMBIGUIS CASIBUS SEMPER PRAEsumitur pro rege. In doubtful cases the presumption is always in favor of the king. Lofft, 248.

AMBIGUITAS VERBORUM LATENS verificatione suppletur; nam quod ex facto oritur ambiguum verificatione facti tollitur. A latent ambiguity may be supplied by evidence, for an ambiguity which arises out of a fact may be removed by proof of the fact. Bac. Max. reg. 23; 8 Bing. 247. See 1 Powell, Dev. 477; 2 Kent, Comm. 557; Broom, Leg. Max. (3d London Ed.) 541; 13 Pet. (U. S.) 97; 8 Johns. (N. Y.) 90; 3 Halst. (N. J.) 71.

AMBIGUITAS VERBORUM PATENS nulla verificatione excluditur. A patent ambiguity is never holpen by averment. Lofft, 249; Bac. Max. 25; Cowen, J., 21 Wend. (N. Y.) 651, 659; 23 Wend. (N. Y.) 71, 78;

Story, J., 1 Mason (U. S.) 11; Lipscomb, J., 1 Tex. 377, 383.

AMBIGUITY (Lat. *ambiguitas*, indistinctness; duplicity). Duplicity, indistinctness, or uncertainty of meaning of an expression used in a written instrument.

The term does not include mere inaccuracy, or such uncertainty as arises from the use of peculiar words, or of common words in a peculiar sense (Wigram, Wills, 174; 3 Sim. 24; 3 Man. & G. 452; 8 Metc. [Mass.] 576; 13 Vt. 36. See 21 Wend. [N. Y.] 651), and intends such expressions as would be found of uncertain meaning by persons of competent skill and information (1 Greenl. Ev. § 298).

It has also been confined to duplicity of meaning, and thus distinguished from general uncertainty. 2 Pars. Cont. 557, note.

Latent ambiguity is that which arises from some collateral circumstance or extrinsic matter in cases where the instrument itself is sufficiently certain and intelligible. 1 Gray (Mass.) 134.

Patent ambiguity is that which appears on the face of the instrument; that which occurs when the expression of an instrument is so defective that a court of law which is obliged to put a construction upon it, placing itself in the situation of the parties, cannot ascertain therefrom the parties' intention. 4 Mass. 205; 4 Cranch (U. S.) 167; 1 Greenl. Ev. § 292-300.

AMBIGUUM PLACITUM INTERPRETARI debet contra proferentem. An ambiguous plea ought to be interpreted against the party pleading it. Co. Litt. 303b; Broom, Leg. Max. (3d London Ed.) 535; Steph. Pl. (5th Ed.) 415; Bac. Max. reg. 3; 2 H. Bl. 531; 2 Mees. & W. 444.

AMBIT. A boundary line.

AMBITUS (Lat.) A space beside a building, two and a half feet in width, and of the same length as the building; a space two and a half feet in width between two adjacent buildings; the circuit, or distance around. Calv. Lex.

AMBRA. In Saxon law. A vessel or measure, the capacity of which is now unknown. Spelman.

AMBULATORIA EST VOLUNTAS DEfuncti usque ad vitae supremum exitum. The will of a deceased person is ambulatory until the last moment of life. Dig. 34. 4. 4; Broom, Leg. Max. (3d London Ed.) 445; 2 Bl. Comm. 502; Co. Litt. 322b; 1 Vict. c. 26, § 24; 3 El. & Bl. 572; 1 Jarm. Wills (2d Ed.) 11; 1 Mylne & K. 485; 2 Mylne & K. 73.

AMBULATORY (Lat. *ambulare*, to walk about). Movable; changeable; that which is not fixed.

Ambulatoria voluntas (a changeable will) denotes the power which a testator possesses of altering his will during his lifetime.

AMELIORATIONS. Betterments. 6 Low. (U. S.) 294; 9 Low. (U. S.) 503.

AMENABLE. Responsible; subject to answer in a court of justice; liable to punishment.

AMENDE HONORABLE.

——**In English Law.** A penalty imposed upon a person by way of disgrace or infamy, as a punishment for any offense, or for the purpose of making reparation for any injury done to another, as the walking into church in a white sheet, with a rope about the neck and a torch in the hand, and begging the pardon of God, or the king, or any private individual, for some delinquency.

——**In French Law.** A punishment somewhat similar to this, and which bore the same name, was common in France. It was abolished by the law of the 25th of September, 1791. Merlin, Repert.

AMENDMENT.

——**In Practice.** The correction, by allowance of the court, of an error committed in the progress of a cause, whether in process, pleading, proceedings, or judgment. It has been held not to include the substitution of a new pleading. 31 How. Pr. (N. Y.) 164; but see 4 Daly (N. Y.) 494.

——**In Legislation.** An alteration or change of something proposed in a bill or established as law.

AMENDS. A satisfaction given by a wrongdoer to the party injured for a wrong committed. 1 Lilly, Reg. 81.

By St. 24 Geo. II. c. 44, in England, and by similar statutes in some of the United States, justices of the peace, upon being notified of an intended suit against them, may tender amends for the wrong alleged or done by them in their official character, and, if found sufficient, the tender debars the action. 5 Serg. & R. (Pa.) 209, 517; 4 Bin. (Pa.) 20; 6 Bin. (Pa.) 83.

AMENTIA. Insanity; idiocy.

AMERALIUS (Law Lat.) A naval commander, under the eastern Roman empire, but not of the highest rank; the origin, according to Spelman, of the modern title and office of admiral. Spelman.

AMERCEMENT. In practice. A pecuniary penalty imposed upon an offender by a judicial tribunal.

The judgment of the court is that the party be at the mercy of the court (*sit in misericordia*), upon which the *affeerors*—or, in the superior courts, the coroner—liquidate the penalty. As distinguished from a fine, at the old law an amercement was for a lesser offense, might be imposed by a court not of record, and was for an uncertain amount until it had been affeered, while the amount of a fine was regulated by statute. Either party to a suit who failed was to be amerced *pro clamore falso* (for his false claim), but these amercements have been long since disused. 4 Bl. Comm. 379; Bac. Abr. "Fines and Amercements."

The officers of the court, and any person who committed a contempt of court, was also liable to be amerced.

AMESUREMENT (Law Fr.) In old English law. Admeasurement. Britt. c. 58; Reg. Orig. 155, "Regula."

AMI, or **AMY** (Fr.) A friend. See "Prochein Ami."

AMICABLE ACTION. In practice. An action entered by agreement of parties on the dockets of the courts.

AMICABLE COMPOUNDERS. "There are two sorts of arbitrators,—the arbitrators properly so called, and the amicable compounders. The arbitrators ought to determine as judges, agreeably to the strictness of law. Amicable compounders are authorized to abate something of the strictness of the law in favor of natural equity. Amicable compounders are in other respects subject to the same rules which are provided for the arbitrators by the present title." Civ. Code La. arts. 3109, 3110.

AMICUS CURIAE (Lat. a friend of the court). One who, for the assistance of the court, gives information of some matter of law in regard to which the court is doubtful or mistaken. Coke, 2d Inst. 178; 2 Viner, Abr. 475. The information may extend to any matter of which the court takes judicial cognizance. 8 Coke, 15.

AMITTERE CURIAM (Lat. to lose court). To be excluded from the right to attend court. St. Westminster II. c. 44.

AMITTERE LIBERAM LEGEM. Lose all rights under the law.

AMNESTY. An act of oblivion of past offenses, granted by the government to those who have been guilty of any neglect or crime, usually upon condition that they return to their duty within a certain period.

Express amnesty is one granted in direct terms.

Implied amnesty is one which results when a treaty of peace is made between contending parties. Vattel, lib. 4, c. 2, §§ 20-22.

Amnesty and pardon are very different. The former is an act of the sovereign power, the object of which is to efface and to cause to be forgotten a crime or misdemeaner; the latter is an act of the same authority, which exempts the individual on whom it is bestowed from the punishment the law inflicts for the crime he has committed. 7 Pet. (U. S.) 160. Amnesty is the abolition and forgetfulness of the offense; pardon is forgiveness. A pardon is given to one who is certainly guilty, or has been convicted; amnesty, to those who may have been so.

Their effects are also different. That of pardon is the remission of the whole or a part of the punishment awarded by the law,—the conviction remaining unaffected when only a partial pardon is granted. An amnesty, on the contrary, has the effect of destroying the criminal act, so that it is as if it had not been committed, as far as the public interests are concerned.

Their application also differs. Pardon is always given to individuals, and properly only after judgment or conviction. Amnesty may be granted either before judgment or afterwards, and it is in general given to whole classes of criminals, or supposed criminals, for the purpose of restoring tranquility in the state; but sometimes amnesties are limited, and certain classes are excluded from their operation. See Phil. (N. C.) 247.

AMORTISE. To alien lands in mortmain.

AMORTIZATION. An alienation of lands or tenements in mortmain.

The reduction of the property of lands or tenements to mortmain.

As to financial matters, the extinguishment of an obligation or liability, generally by means of a sinking fund.

AMOTION. (Lat. *amovere*, to remove; to take away). An unlawful taking of personal chattels out of the possession of the owner, or of one who has a special authority in them.

A turning out the proprietor of an estate in realty before the termination of his estate. 3 Bl. Comm. 198, 199.

——**In Corporations.** A removal of an official agent of a corporation from the station assigned to him before the expiration of the term for which he was appointed. 6 Conn. 532.

The term is distinguished from disfranchisement, which deprives a member of all rights as a corporator. The term seems in strictness not to apply properly to cases where officers are appointed merely during the will of the corporation, and are superseded by the choice of a successor, but as commonly used includes such cases. 4 Abb. Pr. (N. S.; N. Y.) 192.

AMOUNT. As applied to money the word amount is synonymous with "sum." 156 Ill. 337.

AMOUNT COVERED. In insurance. The amount that is insured, and for which underwriters are liable for loss under a policy of insurance.

AMOUNT OF LOSS. In insurance. The diminution, destruction, or defeat to the insured of the value of, or of the charge upon, the insured object, by the direct consequence of the operation of the risk insured against, according to its value in the policy, or in contribution for loss, so far as its value is covered by the insurance. 2 Phil. Ins. cc. 25-27; 2 Pars. Mar. Law, c. 10, § 1, cc. 11, 12; 9 Cush. (Mass.) 415; 1 Gray (Mass.) 371; 26 N. H. 389; 31 N. H. 238; 5 Duer (N. Y.) 1; 1 Dutch. (N. J.) 506; 6 Ohio St. 200; 5 R. I. 426; 2 Md. 217; 7 El. & Bl. 172.

AMOVEAS MANUS (Lat. that you remove your hands). After office found, the king was entitled to the things forfeited, either lands or personal property. The remedy for a person aggrieved was by "petition," or "*monstrans de droit,*" or "*traverses,*" to establish his superior right. Thereupon a writ issued, *quod manus domini regis amoveantur.* 3 Sharswood, Bl. Comm. 260.

AMPARO (Spanish). A document protecting the claimant of land till properly authorized papers can be issued. 1 Tex. 790.

AMPLIATION.

——**In Civil Law.** A deferring of judgment until the cause is further examined. In this case, the judges pronounced the word *amplius,* or by writing the letters N. L. for *non liquet,* signifying that the cause was not clear. It is very similar to the common-law practice of entering *cur. adv. vult* in similar cases.

——**In French Law.** A duplicate of an acquittance or other instrument.

A notary's copy of acts passed before him, delivered to the parties.

AMPLIUS (Lat.) In the Roman law. More; further; more time. A word which the praetor pronounced in cases where there was any obscurity in a cause, and the *judices* were uncertain whether to condemn or acquit, by which the case was deferred to a day named. Adam, Rom. Ant. 287.

AMY (Fr.) Friend. See "Prochein Ami."

AN, JOUR, ET WASTE. See "Year, Day, and Waste."

ANACRISIS. In the civil law. An investigation of truth, interrogation of witnesses, and inquiry made into any fact, especially by torture.

ANAGRAPH. A register, or inventory.

ANALOGY. The similitude of relations which exist between things compared.

ANARCHIST. An anarch; one who excites revolt or promotes disorder in a state.

ANARCHY. The absence of all political government; by extension, confusion in government.

A state of society where there is no law or supreme power. 122 Ill. 253.

ANATHEMA. In ecclesiastical law. A punishment by which a person is separated from the body of the church, and forbidden all intercourse with the faithful. It differs from excommunication, which simply forbids the person excommunicated from going into the church and communicating with the faithful.

ANATOCISM. In civil law. Taking interest on interest; receiving compound interest.

ANCESTOR. One who has preceded another in a direct line of descent; an ascendant.

A former possessor; the person last seised. Termes de la Ley; 2 Sharswood, Bl. Comm. 201.

In the common law, the word is understood as well of the immediate parents as of those that are higher; as may appear by St. 25 Edw. III., *De natis ultra mare,* and by St. 6 Rich. II. c. 6, and by many others. But the civilians' relations in the ascending line, up to the great-grandfather's parents, and those above them, they term *majores,* which common lawyers aptly expound *antecessors,* or ancestors, for in the descendants of like degree they are called *posteriores.* Cary, Litt. 45. The term "ancestor" is applied to natural persons. The words "predecessors" and "successors" are used in respect to the persons composing a body corporate. See 2 Bl. Comm. 209; Bac. Abr.; Ayliffe, Pand. 58; Reeve, Descents.

ANCESTRAL. What relates to or has been done by one's ancestors; as homage ancestral, and the like.

That which belonged to one's ancestors.

Ancestral estates are such as come to the possessor by descent. 2 Washb. Real Prop. 411, 412.

ANCHOR, or ANKER. A measure containing ten gallons.

ANCHOR WATCH. The lookout required to be kept on the deck of a vessel riding at anchor. See 102 U. S. 200; 29 Fed. 601.

ANCHORAGE. A toll paid for every anchor cast from a ship in a port.

ANCIENT DEED. A deed which, by reason of its age, is presumed to be authentic, and hence admissible in evidence without direct proof of its execution.

It must be at least thirty years old, be found in proper custody and possession under it must be shown or some other corroborative evidence, freeing it from all just grounds of suspicion. 117 U. S. 255.

ANCIENT DEMESNE. Manors which, in the time of William the Conqueror, were in the hands of the crown, and are so recorded in the Domesday Book. Fitzh. Nat. Brev. 14, 56.

Tenure in ancient demesne may be pleaded in abatement to an action of ejectment. 2 Burrows, 1046.

Tenants of this class had many privileges. 2 Sharswood, Bl. Comm. 99.

ANCIENT HOUSE. One which has stood long enough to acquire an easement of support. 3 Kent, Comm. 437; 2 Washb. Real Prop. 74, 76. See "Eastment."

ANCIENT LIGHTS. Windows or openings which have remained in the same place and condition twenty years or more. 5 Har. & J. (Md.) 477; 12 Mass. 157, 220.

——**In England.** A right to unobstructed light and air through such openings is secured by mere user.

——**In the United States.** Such right is not acquired without an express grant, in most of the states. 2 Washb. Real Prop. 62, 63; 3 Kent, Comm. 446, note. See 11 Md. 1. See "Air."

ANCIENT READINGS. Essays on the early English statutes. Co. Litt. 280.

ANCIENT RENT. The rent reserved at the time the lease was made, if the building was not then under lease. 2 Vern. 542.

ANCIENT SERJEANT. In English law. The eldest of the queen's serjeants.

Serjeants were distinguished as ancient and *puisne*.

ANCIENT WRITINGS. Deeds, wills, and other writings, more than thirty years old.

ANCIENTS. Gentlemen in the Inns of Courts who are of a certain standing.

In the Middle Temple, all who have passed their readings are termed "ancients." In Gray's Inn, the ancients are the oldest barristers; besides which, the society consists of benchers, barristers, and students. In the Inns of Chancery, it consists of ancients and students or clerks.

ANCIENTRY. Eldership; seniority. Used in St. Ir. 14 Hen. VIII. Cowell.

ANCILLARY (Lat. *ancilla*, a handmaid). Auxiliary; subordinate.

ANCILLARY ADMINISTRATION. See "Administration."

ANCIPITIS USUS (Lat.) Useful for various purposes.

As it is impossible to ascertain the final use of an article *ancipitis usus*, it is not an injurious rule which deduces the final use from its immediate destination. 1 Kent, Comm. 140.

AND. While a copulative conjunction signifying a continuation of what has gone before or in addition to, it may, in a statute, be construed as "or" where necessary to effectuate the plain intent of the legislature or where the context requires it.

ANDROCHIA. In old English law. A dairy woman. Fleta, lib. 2, c. 87.

ANDROGYNOUS. Hermaphroditical.

ANDROGYNUS, or **ANDROGYNE.** An hermaphrodite. Johnson.

ANDROLEPSY. The taking by one nation of the citizens or subjects of another, in order to compel the latter to do justice to the former. Wolff. Inst. § 1164; Molloy de Jur. Mar. 26.

ANECIUS, AESNECIUS, ENTITIUS, AENeas, or eneyus (Lat.) The eldest born; the first born; senior, as contrasted with the *puisne* (younger). Spelman, "Aesnecia."

ANGARIA.

——**In Roman Law.** A service or punishment exacted by government. They were of six kinds, viz., maintaining a post station where horses are changed; furnishing horses or carts; burdens imposed on lands or persons; disturbance, injury, anxiety of mind; the three or four day periods of fasting observed during the year; saddles or yokes borne by criminals from county to county, as a disgraceful mode of punishment among the Germans or Franks. Du Cange.

——**In Feudal Law.** Any troublesome or vexatious personal service paid by the tenant to his lord. Spelman.

ANGEL. An ancient English coin, of the value of ten shillings sterling. Jacob.

ANGILD, ANGYLDE, or **ANGELD** (Sax. from an, one, and gild, a payment or satisfaction). The single value of a man or other thing; the compensation for a thing according to its single value or estimation." See "Trigild;" Spelman. The rate fixed by law at which injuries to person or property were to be paid for. Also the fixed price at which cattle and other goods were received as currency. Wharton.

ANGLESCHERIA. In old English law. Englishery; the fact of being an Englishman. Fleta, lib. 1, c. 30; Bracton uses "Englesheria" (fol. 135).

Under Canute and William the Conquerer, for the protection of their subjects from assassination, a heavier fine was imposed on the vill or hundred for the killing of a Dane or Norman than for the killing of a native. It was an object, therefore, for the hundred to prove *Anglescheria* to relieve itself from the added penalty. *Anglescheria* was abolished by St. 14 Edw. III. c. 4. 4 Bl. Comm. 195.

ANGLIAE JURA IN OMNI CASU LIBERtati dant favorem. The laws of England are favorable in every case to liberty. Halk. Max. 12.

ANGLICE. In English. A term formerly used in pleading when a thing is described both in Latin and English, inserted immediately after the Latin, and as an introduction of the English translation.

ANGYLDE. See "Angild."

ANHLOTE (Saxon). The sense is that every one should pay, according to the custom of the country, his respective part and share. Spelman.

ANIENS, or ANIENT. Void; of no force. Fitzh. Nat. Brev. 214.

ANIMAL. Any animate being which is not human, endowed with the power of voluntary motion.

Domitae are those which have been tamed by man; domestic.

Ferae naturae are those which still retain their wild nature.

Mansuetae naturae, those which are tame by nature.

ANIMALIA FERA, SI FACTA SINT mansueta et ex consuetudine eunt et redeunt, volant et revolant, ut cervi, cygni, etc., eo usque nostra sunt, et ita intelliguntur quamdiu habuerunt animum revertendi. Wild animals, if they be made tame, and are accustomed to go out and return, fly away and fly back, as stags, swans, etc., are considered to belong to us so long as they have the intention of returning to us. 7 Coke, 16.

ANIMALS OF A BASE NATURE. Those animals which, though they may be reclaimed, are not such that at common law a larceny may be committed of them, by reason of the baseness of their nature. Some animals which are now usually tamed come within this class, as dogs and cats; and others which, though wild by nature, and often reclaimed by art and industry, clearly fall within the same rule, as bears, foxes, apes, monkeys, ferrets, and the like. Coke, 3d Inst. 109; 1 Hale, P. C. 511, 512; 1 Hawk. P. C. 33, § 36; 4 Bl. Comm. 236; 2 East, P. C. 614. See 1 Wm. Saund. 84, note 2.

ANIMO (Lat.) With intention.

Animo is used in combination in the same manner as *animus* (*q. v.*) Thus, *animo furandi*, with intent to steal, etc.

ANIMO ET CORPORE (Lat.) By the mind and by the body; by intent and act.

ANIMUS (Lat. mind). The intention with which an act is done.

——**Animus Cancellandi.** An intention to destroy or cancel. See "Cancellation."

——**Animus Capiendi.** The intention to take. 4 C. Rob. Adm. 126, 155.

——**Animus Dedicandi.** The intention of donating or dedicating.

——**Animus Defamandi.** The intention of defaming.

——**Animus Derelinquendi.** The intention of abandoning. 4 C. Rob. Adm. 216.

——**Animus Differendi.** The intention of delaying.

——**Animus Donandi.** The intention of giving.

——**Animus Felonico.** Felonious intent.

——**Animus Furandi.** The intention to steal.

In order to constitute larceny, the thief must take the property *animo furandi;* but this is expressed in the definition of larceny by the word "felonious." 3 Inst. 107; Hale, P. C. 503; 4 Bl. Comm. 229. See 2 Russ. Crimes, 96; 2 Tyl. Comm. 272. When the taking of property is lawful, although it may afterwards be converted *animo furandi* to the taker's use, it is not larceny. Bac. Abr. "Felony" (C); 14 Johns. (N. Y.) 294; Ryan & M. 137, 160; Principles of Penal Law, c. 22, § 3, pp. 279, 281.

——**Animus Lucandi.** The intent to gain a profit. 3 Kent, Comm. 357.

——**Animus Manendi.** The intention of remaining.

To acquire a domicile, the party must have his abode in one place, with the intention of remaining there; for, without such intention, no new domicile can be gained, and the old will not be lost. See "Domicile."

——**Animus Morandi.** The intention to remain, or to delay.

——**Animus Possidendi.** The intention of possessing.

——**Animus Quo.** The intent with which.

——**Animus Recipiendi.** The intention of receiving.

A man will acquire no title to a thing unless he possesses it with an intention of receiving it for himself: as, if a thing be bailed to a man, he acquires no title.

——**Animus Recuperandi.** The intention of recovering. Locc. de Jur. Mar. lib. 2, c. 4, § 10.

——**Animus Republicandi.** The intention to republish.

——**Animus Restituendi.** The intention of restoring.

——**Animus Revertendi.** The intention of returning.

A man retains his domicile if he leaves it *animo revertendi.* 3 Rawle (Pa.) 312; 4 Bl. Comm. 225; 2 Russ. Crimes, 18; Poph. 42, 52; 4 Coke, 40. See "Domicile."

——**Animus Testandi.** An intention to make a testament or will.

This is required to make a valid will; for, whatever form may have been adopted, if there was no *animus testandi*, there can be no will. An idiot, for example, can make no will, because he can have no intention.

ANIMUS AD SE OMNE JUS DICIT. It is to the intention that all law applies.

ANIMUS HOMINIS EST ANIMA SCRIPti. The intention of the party is the soul of the instrument. 3 Bulst. 67; Pitman, Prin. & Sur. 26.

ANN, or ANNAT. In Scotch Law. Half a year's stipend, over and above what is owing for the incumbency, due to a minister's relict, or child, or next of kin, after his decease. Whishaw; Bell, Dict. See Ersk. Inst. bk. 2, tit. 10, §§ 65-67.

ANNALES (Lat.) Annuals; a title formerly given to the Year Books. 9 London, Leg. Obs. 323.

——**In Old Records.** Yearlings; cattle of the first year. Cowell.

ANNALY. In Scotch law. To alienate; to convey.

ANNATES. In ecclesiastical law. First fruits paid out of spiritual benefices to the pope, being the value of one year's profit.

ANNEXATION (Lat. *ad*, to, *nexare*, to bind). The union of one thing to another.

It conveys the idea, properly, of fastening a smaller thing to a larger; an incident to a principal. It has been applied to denote the union of Texas to the United States.

Actual annexation includes every movement by which a chattel can be joined or united to the freehold.

Constructive annexation is the union of such things as have been holden parcel of the realty, but which are not actually annexed, fixed, or fastened to the freehold. Shep. Touch. 469; Amos & F. Fixt. 2. See "Fixtures."

ANNI ET TEMPORA (Lat.) Years and terms. An old title of the Year Books. 9 London, Leg. Obs. 323.

ANNI NUBILES. (Lat. marriageable years). The age at which a girl becomes by law fit for marriage; the age of twelve.

ANNICULUS (Lat.) A child a year old. Calv. Lex.

ANNICULUS TRECENTESIMO SEXAgesimo quinto die dicitur, incipiente plane non exacto die, quia annum civiliter non ad momenta temporum sed ad dies numeramur. We call a child a year old on the three hundred and sixty-fifth day, when the day is fairly begun, but not ended, because we calculate the civil year not by moments, but by days. Dig. 50. 16. 134; Id. 132; Calv. Lex.

ANNIENTED (Fr. *aneantir*). Abrogated, or made null. Litt. § 741.

ANNO DOMINI (Lat. the year of our Lord; abbreviated A. D.) The computation of time from the incarnation of Jesus Christ.

The Jews began their computation of time from the creation; the Romans, from the building of Rome; the Mohammedans, from the Hegira, or flight of the prophet; the Greeks reckoned by Olympiads; but Christians everywhere reckon from the birth of Jesus Christ.

In a complaint, the year of the alleged offense may be stated by means of the letters "A. D.," followed by words expressing the year. 4 Cush. (Mass.) 596. But an indictment or complaint which states the year of the commission of the offense in figures only, without prefixing the letters "A. D.," is insufficient. 5 Gray (Mass.) 91. The letters "A. D.," followed by figures expressing the year, have been held sufficient in several states. 3 Vt. 481; 1 G. Greene (Iowa) 418; 35 Me. 489; 1 Bennett & H. Lead. Cr. Cas. 512.

ANNONA (Lat.) Barley; corn; grain; a yearly contribution of food, of various kinds, for support.

Annona porcum, acorns; *annona frumentum hordeo admixtum*, corn and barley mixed; *annona panis*, bread, without reference to the amount. Du Cange; Spelman; Cowell.

The term is used in the old English law, and also in the civil law quite generally, to denote anything contributed by one person towards the support of another; as, *si quis mancipio annonam dederit*, if any shall have given food to a slave. Du Cange; Spelman.

ANNONAE CIVILES. Yearly rents issuing out of certain lands, and payable to monasteries.

ANNOTATION. In civil law.

(1) The answers of the prince to questions put to him by private persons respecting some doubtful point of law. See "Rescript."

(2) Summoning an absentee. Dig. 1. 5.

(3) The designation of a place of deportation. Dig. 32. 1. 3.

ANNOUNCEMENT. The act of announcing or giving public notice; that which announces; proclamation; publication. 170 Ill. 634.

ANNUA NEC DEBITUM JUDEX NON separat ipse. Even the judge divides not annuities or debt. 8 Coke, 52. See Story, Eq. Jur. §§ 480, 517; 1 Salk. 36, 65.

ANNUA PENSIONE. See "De Annua Pensione."

ANNUAL ASSAY. An annual trial of the gold and silver coin of the United States, to ascertain whether the standard fineness and weight of the coinage is maintained.

ANNUAL PENSION. In Scotch law. Annual rent or profit.

ANNUAL RENT. In Scotch law. Interest.

To avoid the law against taking interest, a yearly rent was purchased, hence the term came to signify interest. Bell, Dict.; Paterson, Comp. §§ 19, 265.

ANNUITIES OF TIENDS. In Scotch law. Annuities of tithes.

The yearly tax or allowance to the crown on tithes not set apart for pious uses.

ANNUITY (Lat. *annuus*, yearly). A yearly sum stipulated to be paid to another in fee, or for life, or years, and chargeable only on the person of the grantor. Co. Litt. 144b; 2 Bl. Comm. 40; Lumley, Ann. 1; 5 Mart. (La.) 312; Dav. Ir. 14.

An annuity is different from a rent charge, with which it is sometimes confounded,—the annuity being chargeable on the person merely, and so far personalty, while a rent charge is something reserved out of realty, or fixed as a burden upon the estate in land. 2 Sharswood, Bl. Comm. 40; Rolle, Abr. 226; 10 Watts (Pa.) 127. An annuity in fee is said to be a personal fee; for, though transmissible, as is real estate of inheritance (Amb. 782), liable to forfeiture as a hereditament (7 Coke, 34a), and not constituting assets in the hands of an executor, it lacks some other characteristics of realty. The husband is not entitled to curtesy, nor the wife to dower, in an annuity. Co. Litt. 32a. It cannot be conveyed by way of use (2 Wils. 224), is not within the statute of frauds, and may be bequeathed and assigned as personal estate (2 Ves. Sr. 70; 4 Barn. & A. 59; Roscoe, Real Actions, 35, 68; 3 Kent, Comm. 460).

ANNUITY TAX. An impost levied annually in Scotland for the maintenance of the ministers of religion. Abolished 33 & 34 Vict. c. 87.

ANNULUS (Lat.) In old English law. A ring; the ring of a door. *Per haspam vel annulum hostii exterioris*, by the hasp or ring of the outer door. Fleta, lib. 3, c. 15, § 5.

ANNULUS ET BACULUS (Lat. ring and staff). The investiture of a bishop was *per annulum et baculum*, by the prince's delivering to the prelate a ring and pastoral staff, or crozier. 1 Sharswood, Bl. Comm. 378; Spelman.

ANNUM, DIEM, ET VASTUM. See "Year. Day, and Waste."

ANNUS (Lat.) In civil law and old English law. A year; the period of three hundred and sixty-five days. Dig. 40. 7. 4. 5; Bracton, fol. 359. See "Year."

ANNUS DELIBERANDI (Lat.) In Scotch law. A year of deliberating; a year to deliberate. The year allowed by law to the heir to deliberate whether he will enter and represent his ancestor. It commences on the death of the ancestor, unless in the case of a posthumous heir, when the year runs from his birth. Bell, Dict.

ANNUS, DIES ET VASTUM. See "Year, Day, and Waste."

ANNUS EST MORA MOTUS QUO SUUM planeta pervolat circulum. A year is the duration of the motion by which a planet revolves through its orbit. Dig. 40. 7. 4. 5; Calv. Lex.; Bracton, 359b.

ANNUS LUCTUS (Lat.) The year of mourning. Code, 5. 9. 2.

It was a rule among the Romans, and also the Danes and Saxons, that the widows should not marry *infra annum luctus* (within the year of mourning). 1 Sharswood, Bl. Comm. 457.

ANNUS UTILIS. A year made up of available or serviceable days. Brissonius; Calv. Lex.

ANNUUS REDITUS (or REDDITUS). A yearly rent; annuity. 2 Sharswood, Bl. Comm. 41; Reg. Orig. 158b.

ANONYMOUS. Without name. Books published without the name of the author are said to be anonymous. Cases in the reports of which the names of the parties are not given are said to be anonymous.

ANSEL, ANSUL, or AUNCEL. In old English law. An ancient mode of weighing by hanging scales or hooks at either end of a beam or staff, which, being lifted with one's finger or hand by the middle, showed the equality or difference between the weight at one end and the thing weighed at the other. Termes de la Ley, 66.

ANSWER.

——**In Equity Pleading.** A defense in writing, made by a defendant to the charges contained in a bill or information filed by the plaintiff against him in a court of equity.

——**In Code Pleading.** The defendant's pleading in any civil action.

——**In Practice.** The statement of a witness in response to a question.

ANTAPOCHA (Lat.) An instrument by which the debtor acknowledges the debt due the creditor, and binds himself. A copy of the *apocha*, signed by the debtor, and delivered to the creditor. Calv. Lex.

ANTE EXHIBITIONEM BILLAE. Before the exhibition of the bill; before suit begun.

ANTE FACTUM, or ANTE GESTUM. Done before. A Roman law term for a previous act, or thing done before.

ANTE JURAMENTUM, or JURAMENtum calumniae (Lat.) The oath formerly required of the parties previous to a suit,—of the plaintiff that he would prosecute and of the defendant that he was innocent. Jacob; Whishaw.

ANTE LITEM MOTAM. Before suit brought.

ANTECESSOR. An ancestor (*q. v.*)

ANTEDATE. To put a date to an instrument of a time before the time it was written.

ANTENATI (Lat. born before). Those born in a country before a change in its political condition such as to affect their allegiance.

The correlative term is *postnati.*

——**In the United States.** It ordinarily denotes those born in this country prior to the Declaration of Independence. See 7 Wheat. (U. S.) 535.

——**In England.** It ordinarily denotes those born before the union with Scotland.

ANTENUPTIAL. Before marriage; before marriage, with a view to entering into marriage.

ANTI MANIFESTO. The declaration of the reasons which one of the belligerents publishes, to show that the war as to him is defensive. Wolffius, § 1187.

ANTICHRESIS (Lat.) In civil law. An agreement by which the debtor gives to the creditor the income from the property which he has pledged, in lieu of the interest on his debt. Guyot, Rep. Univ.

It is analogous to the Welsh mortgage of the common law. In the French law, if the income was more than the interest, the debtor was entitled to demand an account of the income, and might claim any excess. Civ. Code La. art. 2085. See Dig. 20. 1. 11; Id. 13. 7. 1; Code, 8. 28, 1; 11 Pet. (U. S.) 351; 1 Kent, Comm. 137.

ANTICIPATION (Lat. *ante*, before, *capere*, to take). The act of doing or taking a thing before its proper time.

In deeds of trust there is frequently a provision that the income of the estate shall be paid by the trustee as it shall accrue, and not by way of anticipation. A payment made contrary to such provision would not be considered as a discharge of the trustee.

ANTIGRAPH. A copy.

ANTIGRAPHUS. In the Roman law. An officer whose duty it was to keep an eye over the money which the tax gatherers collected for the use of the state.

A controller or supervisor of public moneys.

ANTINOMIA. In Roman law. A real or apparent contradiction or inconsistency in the laws. Merlin, Repert.

It is sometimes used as an English word, and spelled "Antinomy."

ANTIQUA CUSTUMA (Law Lat. ancient custom). The duty due upon wool, woolfells, and leather, under St. 3 Edw. I.

The distinction between *antiqua* and *nova custuma* arose upon the imposition of a new and increased duty upon the same articles, by the king, in the twenty-second year of his reign. Bac. Abr. "Smuggling" (C 1).

ANTIQUA STATUTA. English statutes from the time of Richard I. to Edward III.

ANTIQUARE. In the Roman law. To restore a former law or practice; to reject or vote against a new law; to prefer the old law. Those who voted against a proposed law wrote on their ballots the letter "A," the initial of *antiquo*, I am for the old law. Calv. Lex.

ANTIQUUM DOMINICUM. In old English law. Ancient demesne, contrasted with *novum perquisitum*, new purchase or acquest. Fleta, lib. 2, c. 71, § 15.

ANTITHETARIUS. In old English law. A man who endeavors to discharge himself of the crime of which he is accused, by retorting the charge on the accuser. He differs from an approver in this, that the latter does not charge the accuser, but others. Jacob.

ANTRUSTIO, or **AMTRUSTIO.** In early feudal law. A confidential vassal. A term applied to the followers of the ancient German chiefs, and of the kings and counts of the Franks. Spelman.

ANUELS LIVRES (Law Fr.) The Year Books (*q. v.*) Kelham.

ANY. Same; an indefinite number or quantity. 134 Ill. 179. It may be used as synonymous with "all" or "every." 187 Ill. 134.

APANGE. In French law. A portion set apart for the use and support of the younger ones, upon condition, however, that it should revert, upon failure of male issue, to his original donor and his heirs. Spelman.

APARTMENT. A part of a house occupied by a person, while the rest is occupied by another, or others. 7 Man. & G. 95; 6 Mod. 214; Woodfall, Landl. & Ten. 178. As to what is not an apartment, see 10 Pick. (Mass.) 293.

APATISATIO. An agreement or compart. Du Cange.

APERTA BREVIA. Open, unsealed writs.

APERTUM FACTUM. An overt act.

APERTURA TESTAMENTI. A form of proving a will, in the civil law, by the witnesses acknowledging before a magistrate their having sealed it. 1 Williams, Ex'rs, 329.

APEX JURIS (Lat. the summit of the law). A rule of law of extreme refinement. A term used to denote a stricter application of the rules of law than is indicated by the phrase *summum jus*. 2 Caines (N. Y.) 117; 2 Story (U. S.) 143; 5 Conn. 334; 2 Pars. Notes & Bills, c. 25, § 11. See, also, Co. Litt. 3046; Wingate, Max. 19.

APICES JURIS NON SUNT JURA. Legal niceties are not laws. Co. Litt. 304; 3 Scott, 773; 10 Coke, 126; Broom, Leg. Max. 142. See "Apex Juris."

APICES LITIGANDI (Lat.) Subtleties of law; extreme technicalities.

APOCAE (Lat.) A writing acknowledging payments; acquittance.

It differs from "acceptilation" in this, that acceptilation imports a complete discharge of the former obligation, whether payment be made or not; *apocha*, discharge only upon payment being made. Calv. Lex.

APOCHAE ONERATORIAE (Law Lat.) In old commercial law. Bills of lading Casaregis, disc. 1, note 111; Id. disc. 10, note 25; Id. disc. 25, note 5.

APOCRISARIUS (Lat.) In civil law. A messenger; an ambassador.

Applied to legates or messengers, as they carried the messages of their principals. They performed several duties distinct in character, but generally pertaining to ecclesiastical affairs.

A messenger sent to transact ecelesiastical business, and report to his superior; an officer who had charge of the treasury of a monastic edifice; an officer who took charge of opening and closing the doors. Du Cange; Spelman; Calv. Lex.

Apocrisarius cancellarius, an officer who took charge of the royal seal, and signed royal despatches.

Called, also, *secretarius consiliarius* (from his giving advice); *referendarius; a consiliis* (from his acting as counsellor); *a responsis*, or *responsalis*.

APOGRAPHA. In civil law. An examination and enumeration of things possessed; an inventory. Calv. Lex.

APOSTASY. The total renunciation of Christianity, by embracing either a false religion, or no religion at all. This offense can only take place in such as have once professed Christianity. 4 Bl. Comm. 43.

APOSTATA. In civil and old English law. An apostate. Code, 1. 7; Reg. Orig. 71b.

APOSTATA CAPIENDO. An obsolete English writ which issued against an apostate, or one who had violated the rules of his religious order. It was addressed to the sheriff, and commanded him to deliver the defendant into the custody of the abbot or prior. Reg. Orig. 71, 267; Jacob; Wharton.

APOSTILLE, or **APPOSTILLE** (Law Fr.) An addition; note or observation. Kelham. A marginal note. Rich. Dict.

APOSTLES. Brief letters of dismissal granted to a party who takes an appeal from the decision of an English court of admiralty, stating the case, and declaring that the record will be transmitted. 2 Brown, Civ. & Adm. Law, 438; Dig. 49. 6.

This term was used in the civil law. It is derived from *apostolis*, a Greek word, which signifies "one sent," because the judge from whose sentence an appeal was made sent to the superior judge these letters of dismission, or apostles. Merlin, Repert, mot "Apotres;" 1 Pars. Mar. Law, 745; 1 Blatchf. (U. S.) 663.

APOSTOLI. In civil law. Certificates of the inferior judge from whom a cause is removed, directed to the superior. Dig. 49. 6. See "Apostles."

Those sent as messengers. Spelman.

APOSTOLUS. A messenger; an ambassador, legate, or nuncio. Spelman.

APOTHECA. In the civil law. A repository; a place of deposit, as of wine, oil, books, etc. Calv. Lex.

APPARATOR (Law Lat.) One who furnishes or provides. A sheriff was formerly styled in England *apparator comitatus*, as having charge of certain county arrangements and expenditures. Cowell.

APPARENT DANGER. That degree of peril of death or great bodily harm which will justify the killing of an assailant in self-defense. The danger need not be real, but must be sufficient to cause a reasonably prudent and courageous man to believe himself in imminent peril.

APPARENT DEFECTS. In a thing sold, those which can be discovered by simple inspection. Code La. art. 2497.

APPARENT (or **CONTINUOUS**) **EASEment.** One depending on some artificial structure or natural formation permanent in character and obvious. One which is at all times known to the owner of the subservient tenement by apparent signs. 18 N. J. Eq. 262; 1 Hurl. & N. 916.

APPARENT HEIR. One whose right of inheritance is indefeasible, provided he outlive the ancestor. 2 Bl. Comm. 208.

——**In Scotch Law.** One who is entitled to enter heir to a deceased ancestor, before actual entry. Ersk. Inst. bk. 3, tit. 8, § 54.

APPARENT MATURITY. Of a negotiable instrument. The time when, by its face, it will fall due.

APPARITIO. An appearance.

APPARITOR (Lat.). An officer or messenger employed to serve the process of the spiritual courts in England, and summon offenders. Cowell.

APPARLEMENT. In old English law. Resemblance; likelihood, as apparlement of war. St. 2 Rich. II. St. 1, c. 6; Cowell.

APPARURA (Lat.) In old English law. Furniture or implements.

Carucariae apparura, plough tackle. Cowell; Jacob.

APPEAL (Fr. *appeler,* to call).

——**In Practice.** The removal of a cause from a court of inferior to one of superior jurisdiction, for the purpose of obtaining a review and retrial. Ellsworth, C. J., 3 Dall. (U. S.) 321; 7 Cranch (U. S.) 110; 10 Pet. (U. S.) 205; 14 Mass. 414; 1 Serg. & R. (Pa.) 78; 1 Bin. (Pa.) 219; 3 Bin. (Pa.) 48.

It is sometimes used as meaning generally the removal of a cause to a higher court (4 N. J. Eq. 137), and in this sense it includes writ of error (1 Ill. 334).

It is a civil-law proceeding in its origin, and differs from a writ of error in this, that it subjects both the law and the facts to a review and a retrial, while a writ of error is a common-law process which removes matter of law only for re-examination. 7 Cranch (U. S.) 111.

On an appeal, the whole case is examined and tried, as if it had not been tried before; while on a writ of error, the matters of law merely are examined, and judgment reversed if any errors have been committed. Dane, Abr. "Appeal." The word is used in the sense here given both in chancery and in common-law practice (16 Md. 282; 20 How. [U. S.] 198), and in criminal as well as in civil law (9 Ind. 569; 6 Fla. 679); and in many states the writ of error has been abolished, and appeal established as the ordinary method of review in all cases, the scope of the reviewing varying in the different states.

——**In Old Criminal Practice.** A formal accusation made by one private person against another of having committed some heinous crime. 4 Bl. Comm. 312.

——**In Legislation.** The act by which a member of a legislative body who questions the correctness of a decision of the presiding officer, or "chair," procures a vote of the body upon the decision.

APPEARANCE. In practice. A coming into court as party to a suit, whether as plaintiff or defendant.

The formal proceeding by which a defendant submits himself to the jurisdiction of the court.

"'Appearance' in the law has several significations, and the word must always be understood in reference to the particular business or subject-matter to which it relates. In some cases it means to appear in person; in others, by attorney. Sometimes an obligation to appear can only be satisfied by actually coming into court, while in others it will be sufficient to put in special bail, or enter an appearance in the common rule book. In one case it may be necessary for the party to appear on the specified day, while in another it will be sufficient if done within ten or twenty days thereafter. The purpose or end to be answered by the appearance is also important. In most, if not all, cases where a party is bound to a personal appearance in court to answer any charge or action against him, he must not only appear, but must remain in court until discharged by due course of law, and how long he must attend depends on the nature of the proceedings and the course and practice of the court. 19 Wend. (N. Y.) 459.

It may be of the following kinds:

(1) Compulsory. That which takes place in consequence of the service of process.

(2) Voluntary. That which is made in answer to a subpoena or summons, without process. 1 Barb. Ch. (N. Y.) 77.

(3) General. A simple and absolute submission to the jurisdiction of the court.

(4) Special. That which is made for certain purposes only, and does not extend to all the purposes of the suit.

(5) Conditional. One which is coupled with conditions as to its becoming general.

(6) *De bene esse.* One which is to remain an appearance, except in a certain event. See "De Bene Esse."

(7) Gratis. One made before the party has been legally notified to appear.

(8) Optional. One made where the party is not under any obligation to appear, but does so to save his rights. It occurs in chancery practice, especially in England.

(9) Subsequent. An appearance by the defendant after one has already been entered for him by the plaintiff. See Daniell, Ch. Pr.

APPEARANCE DAY. The day on which an appearance is required.

APPEARAND HEIR. An apparent heir (*q. v.*)

APPEL (Law Fr.; Law Lat. *appellum*). In old English law. An appeal. Britt. c. 22. See "Appeal."

APPELLANT. In practice. He who makes an appeal from one jurisdiction to another.

APPELLATE. In practice. Pertaining to appeals; having cognizance of appeals.

APPELLATE JURISDICTION. In practice. The jurisdiction which a superior court has to rehear causes which have been tried in inferior courts. See "Jurisdiction."

APPELLATIO (Lat.) An appeal.

APPELLE (Law Fr.) In old practice. The party accused by the process of appeal. Britt. c. 23. See "Appeal."

APPELLEE. In practice. The party in a cause against whom an appeal has been taken.

APPELLO (Lat.) In the civil law. I appeal. The form of making an appeal *apud acta.* Dig. 49. 1. 2.

APPELLOR. A criminal who accuses his accomplices; one who challenges a jury.

APPELLOUR (Law Fr.) In old practice. The party who brought an appeal; the plaintiff in an appeal. Britt. c. 22.

APPENDANT (Lat. *ad,* to, *pendere,* to hang). Annexed or belonging to something superior; an incorporeal inheritance belonging to another inheritance.

Appendant in deeds includes nothing which is substantial corporeal property, capable of passing by feoffment and livery of seisin. Co. Litt. 121; 4 Coke, 86; 8 Barn. & C. 150; 6 Bing. 150. A matter appendant must arise by prescription, while a matter appurtenant may be created at any time. 2 Viner, Abr. 594; 3 Kent, Comm. 404.

APPENDITIA (Lat. *appendere,* to hang at or on). The appendages or pertinances of an estate; the appurtenances to a dwelling, etc.; thus, penthouses are the *appenditia domus.*

APPENSURA. Payment of money by weight instead of by count. Cowell.

APPERTINANCES. An old form of appurtenances (*q. v.*) Cowell.

APPLICARE (Lat.) In old English law. To fasten to; to moor (a vessel).

Anciently rendered, "to apply." Hale de Jure Mar. par. 2, c. 3. This sense of the word seems to have been derived from the civil law. Dig. 1. 8. 5.

APPLICATIO EST VITA REGULAE. Application is the life of a rule. 2 Bulst. 79.

APPLICATION (Lat. *applicare*). The act of making a request for something.

A written request.

The use or disposition made of a thing.

——**In Insurance.** The preliminary statement made by a party applying for an insurance on life, or against fire.

——**Of Purchase Money.** The use or disposition made of the funds received by a trustee on a sale of real estate held under the trust.

——**Of Payment.** See "Appropriation."

APPOINTEE. A person who is appointed or selected for a particular purpose; as the appointee under a power is the person who is to receive the benefit of the trust of power.

APPOINTMENT. The designation of a person, by the person or persons having authority therefor, to discharge the duties of some office or trust.

As distinguished from an election, it seems that an appointment is generally made by one person, or a limited number acting with delegated powers, while an election is made by all of a class.

The word is sometimes used in a sense quite akin to this, and apparently derived from it as denoting the right or privilege conferred by an appointment. Thus, the act of authorizing a man to print the laws of the United States by authority, and the right thereby conveyed, are considered such an appointment, but the right is not an office. 17 Serg. & R. (Pa.) 29, 233. And see 3 Serg. & R. (Pa.) 157; Cooper, Just. 599, 604.

The exercise of a right to designate the person or persons who are to take the use of real estate. 2 Washb. Real Prop. 302.

APPOINTOR. One authorized by the donor, under the statute of uses, to execute a power. 2 Bouv. Inst. note 1923. Also called "donee."

APPORT (Law Fr.) In old English law. Tax; tallage; tribute; imposition; payment; charge; expenses. Kelham.

APPORTIONMENT. The division or distribution of a subject-matter in proportionate parts. Co. Litt. 147; 1 Swanst. 37, note; 1 Story, Eq. Jur. 475a.

——**Of Contracts.** The allowance, in case of the partial performance of a contract, of a proportionate part of what the party would have received as a recompense for the entire performance of the contract.

——**Of Incumbrances.** Determining the amounts which each of several parties interested in an estate shall pay towards the removal or in support of the burden of an incumbrance.

——**Of Rent.** The allotment of their shares in a rent to each of several parties owning it.

The determination of the amount of rent to be paid when the tenancy is terminated at some period other than one of the regular intervals for the payment of rent.

——**Of Corporate Shares.** The distribution *pro rata* among the shareholders when there has been an oversubscription.

——**Of an Annuity.** *Pro rata* allowance for part of a year; not allowed at common law, but allowed as to some classes by 11 Geo. II.

——**Of Representatives.** The fixing of the number of representatives in congress allowed to each state, made on the basis of population as shown by each United States census. Const. U. S. art. 1, § 2.

APPORTUM. In old English law. The revenue, profit, or emolument which a thing brings to the owner. Commonly applied to a corody or pension. Blount.

APPOSAL OF SHERIFFS. In English law. The charging them with money received upon account of the exchequer. 22 & 23 Car. II.; Cowell.

APPOSER. In English law. An officer of the exchequer, whose duty it was to examine the sheriffs in regard to their accounts handed in to the exchequer. He was also called the "foreign apposer."

APPOSTILLE. In French law. An addition or annotation made in the margin of a writing. Merlin, Repert.

APPRAISEMENT. A just valuation of property.

A valuation under public authority as of the goods of a decedent, or of property taken for public use.

Appraisal for taxation is called "assessment" (*q. v.*)

While sometimes used interchangeably, there is a clear distinction between an appraisement and an arbitration, the purpose of the former being to prevent the arising of differences, while the latter presupposes a controversy. 254 Ill. 446.

APPRAISER. In practice. A person appointed by competent authority to appraise or value goods or real estate.

APPREHENSIO (Lat.) In the civil and old English law. A taking hold of a person or thing; apprehension; the seizure or capture of a person. Calv. Lex.

One of the varieties or subordinate forms of *occupatio*, or the mode of acquiring title to things not belonging to any one. Fleta applies it to the finding of things on the seashore. Fleta, lib. 3, c. 2, § 5.

APPREHENSION.

——In Practice. The capture or arrest of a person on a criminal charge.

The term "apprehension" is applied to criminal cases, and "arrest" to civil cases; as, one having authority may arrest on civil process, and apprehend on a criminal warrant. See "Arrest."

——In the Civil Law. A physical or corporal act (*corpus*) on the part of one who intends to acquire possession of a thing, by which he brings himself into such a relation to the thing that he may subject it to his exclusive control, or by which he obtains the physical ability to exercise his power over the thing whenever he pleases. One of the requisites to the acquisition of judicial possession, and by which, when accompanied by intention (*animus*), possession is acquired. Mackeld. Civ. Law, §§ 248-250.

APPRENDRE. See "A Prendre."

APPRENTICE. A person bound in due form of law to a master, to learn from him his art, trade, or business, and to serve him during the time of his apprenticeship. 1 Bl. Comm. 426; 2 Kent, Comm. 211; 3 Rawle (Pa.) 307; 61 N. Y. 274. A mere agreement by a father that his son should work for three years for wages to be paid the father, and should be taught the employer's trade, does not constitute the son an apprentice. 3 N. J. Law, 413. See 90 N. Y. 213.

APPRENTICE EN LA LEY. An accident name for students at law, and afterwards applied to counsellors, *apprentici ad barras*, from which comes the more modern word "barrister."

APPRENTICESHIP. A contract by which one person who understands some art, trade, or business, and called the "master," undertakes to teach the same to another person, commonly a minor, and called the "apprentice," who, on his part, is bound to serve the master, during a definite period of time, in such art, trade, or business.

The term during which an apprentice is to serve. Pardessus, Dr. Com. note 34.

APPRENTICIUS AD LEGEM. An apprentice to the law; a law student; a counsellor below the degree of serjeant; a barrister. See "Apprentice en la Ley."

APPRIZING. In Scotch law. A form of process by which a creditor formerly took possession of the estates of the debtor in payment of the debt due.

It is now superseded by "adjudication."

APPROACH. The right of visit or visitation to determine the national character of the ship approached for that purpose only. 1 Kent, Comm. 153.

APPROBATE AND REPROBATE. In Scotch law. To approve and reject.

The doctrine of approbate and reprobate is the English doctrine of election. A party cannot both approbate and reprobate the same deed. 4 Wils. & S. H. L. 460; 1 Ross, Lead. Cas. 617; Paterson, Comp. 710; 1 Bell, Comm. 146.

APPROPRIATION.

——Of Payments. The application of a payment made to a creditor by his debtor, to one or more of several debts. In the absence of an agreement, the application is presumed to be that most favorable to the debtor.

——In Ecclesiastical Law. The perpetual annexation of an ecclesiastical benefice which is the general property of the church to the use of some spiritual corporation, either sole or aggregate. It corresponds with "impropriation," which is setting apart a benefice to the use of a lay corporation. The name came from the custom of monks in England to retain the churches in their gift, and all the profits of them *in proprio usus* to their own immediate benefit. 1 Burn, Ecc. Law, 71.

——**Of Government Money.** No money can be drawn from the treasury of the United States but in consequence of appropriations made by law. Const. art. 1, § 9. Under this clause of the constitution it is necessary for congress to appropriate money for the support of the federal government, and in payment of claims against it, and this is done annually by acts of appropriation, some of which are for the general purposes of government, and others special and private in their nature.

APPROVE. To increase the profits upon a thing. Used of common or waste lands which were inclosed and devoted to husbandry. 3 Kent, Comm. 406; Old Nat. Brev. 79.

While confessing crime one's self, to accuse another of the same crime. It is so called because the accuser must prove what he asserts. Staundf. P. C. 142; Cromp. Jus. Peace, 250.

To vouch; to appropriate; to improve. Kelham.

APPROVED ENDORSED NOTES. Notes endorsed by another person than the maker, for additional security. See 20 Wend. (N. Y.) 431.

APPROVEMENT. By the common law, approvement is said to be a species of confession, and incident to the arraignment of a prisoner indicted for treason or felony, who confesses the fact before plea pleaded, and appeals or accuses others, his accomplices, in the same crime, in order to obtain his own pardon.

APPROVER. In English criminal law One confessing himself guilty of felony, and accusing others of the same crime to save himself. Comp. Inst. 250; 3 Inst. 129. Such an one was obliged to maintain the truth of his charge, by the old law. Cowell. The approvement must have taken place before plea pleaded. 4 Bl. Comm. 330.

Certain men sent into the several counties to increase the farms (rents) of hundreds and *wapentakes*, which formerly were let at a certain value to the sheriffs. Cowell.

Sheriffs are called the "king's approvers." Termes de la Ley.

Approvers in the Marches were those who had license to sell and purchase beasts there.

APPRUARE (Law Lat.) To improve land; to obtain a profit by improvement. St. Westminster II. c. 46.

APPULSUS (Lat.) In the civil law. A driving to, as of cattle to water. Dig. 8. 3. 1. 1.

APPURTENANCES. Things belonging to another thing as principal, and which pass as incidents to such principal thing. 10 Pet. (U. S.) 25; 1 Serg. & R. (Pa.) 169; 117 Mo. 61; 61 N. Y. 390; 53 N. H. 508.

Appurtenances must be of an inferior nature to the principal (16 Conn. 260), and must not only be appendant in utility, but there must be unity of right to both in the same person (29 Ohio St. 649).

Appurtenances are distinguished from appendages in that the latter are those appendant things which become so by prescription, while the latter are those otherwise acquired. 1 Johns. Cas. (N. Y.) 291; 11 Johns. (N. Y.) 498.

APPURTENANT. Pertaining to. See "Appurtenances."

APT WORDS. Correct technical words, requiring no latitude of construction to give them the meaning intended.

APTA VIRO A marriageable woman; sometimes used to denote that she is of legal age, and discovert, but oftener with respect to physical capacity.

APUD ACTA (Lat.) Among the recorded acts. This was one of the verbal appeals (so called by the French commentators), and was obtained by simply saying, *appello.*

AQUA (Lat.) Water. It is a rule that water belongs to the land which it covers when it is stationary. *Aqua cedit solo*, water follows the soil. 2 Bl. Comm. 18; Co. Litt. 4.

AQUA AESTIVA. Water that was drawn in summer only.

AQUA CEDIT SOLO. The water yields or accompanies the soil. The grant of the soil or land carries the water. Hale, de Jur. Mar. pt. 1, c. 1; 2 Bl. Comm. 18.

AQUA COOPERTA. Covered with water. 2 P. Wms. 128.

AQUA CURRENS. Running water. Fleta, lib. 4, c. 6, § 3.

AQUA CURRIT ET DEBET CURRERE ut currere solebat. Water runs and ought to run as it has used to run. 3 Rawle (Pa.) 84, 88; 26 Pa. St. 413; 3 Kent, Comm. 439; Angell, Watercourses, 413; Gale & W. Easem. 182.

AQUA FONTANEA. Spring water. Fleta, lib. 4, c. 27, § 8.

AQUA PLUVIA. Rain water. Dig. 39. 3. 1. pr.

AQUA PROFLUENS. Flowing or running water. Dig. 1. 8. 2.

AQUA QUOTIDIANA. Water which might be drawn at all times of the year.

AQUA SALSA. Salt water. Reg. Orig. 97.

AQUA TRESTORNATA. A stream turned out of its course.

AQUAE DUCTUS. In civil law. A servitude which consists in the right to carry water by means of pipes or conduits over or through the estate of another. Dig. 8. 3. 1; Inst. 2. 3; Lalaure des Serv. c. 5, p. 23.

AQUAE HAUSTUS. In civil law. A servitude which consists in the right to draw water from the fountain, pool, or spring of another. Inst. 2. 3. 2; Dig. 8. 3. 1. 1.

AQUAE IMMITTENDAE. In civil law A servitude which frequently occurs among neighbors.

It is the right which the owner of a house, built in such a manner as to be surrounded with other buildings, so that it has no outlet for its waters, has to cast water out of his windows on his neighbor's roof, court, or soil. Lalaure des Serv. 23. It is recognized in the common law as an easement of drip. 15 Barb. (N. Y.) 96; Gale & W. Easem. See "Easement."

AQUAGIUM (Lat.) A watercourse. Cowell. Canals or ditches through marshes. Spelman. A signal placed in the *aquagium* to indicate the height of water therein. Spelman.

AQUATIC RIGHTS. Rights which individuals have to the use of water, and to lands under water. Includes rights of fishing, navigation, etc.

ARABANT (Lat.) They ploughed. Applied to vassals who were bound to plough and harrow the lands of the lord within his manor. Spelman.

ARAHO. In feudal law. To make oath in the church or some other holy place. Cowell; Spelman.

ARAHUM (Law Lat. from Saxon *ar*, reverence). A consecrated place.

ARALIA (Lat. *arare*). Land fit for the plough. Denoting the character of land, rather than its condition. Spelman. Kindred in meaning, *arare*, to plough; *arator*, a ploughman; *aratrum terrae*, as much land as could be cultivated by a single *arator; araturia,* land fit for cultivation.

ARATURA TERRAE. The plowing of land by the tenant, or vassal, in the service of his lord. Whishaw.

ARATURIA. Land suitable for the plow; arable land. Spelman.

ARBITER. A person bound to decide according to the rules of law and equity, as distinguished from an arbitrator, who may proceed wholly at his own discretion, so that it be according to the judgment of a sound man. Cowell. This distinction between arbiters and arbitrators is not observed in modern law. Russ. Arb. 112. See "Arbitrator."

One appointed by the praetor to decide by the equity of the case, as distinguished from the *judex,* who followed the law. Calv. Lex.

One chosen by the parties to decide the dispute; an arbitrator. Bell, Dict.

ARBITRAMENT AND AWARD. A plea to an action brought for the same cause which had been submitted to arbitration, and on which an award had been made. Watson, Arb. 256.

ARBITRARY PUNISHMENT. In practice. That punishment which is left to the decision of the judge, in distinction from those defined by statute.

ARBITRATION (Lat. *arbitratio*). In practice. The investigation and determination of a matter or matters of difference between contending parties, by one or more unofficial persons, chosen by the parties, and called "arbitrators," or "referees." Worcester; 3 Bl. Comm. 16; 17 How. (U. S.) 344.

It is either:

(1) Compulsory arbitration, being that which takes place when the consent of one of the parties is enforced by statutory provisions; or

(2) Voluntary arbitration, being that which takes place by mutual and free consent of the parties. It usually takes place in pursuance of an agreement (commonly in writing) between the parties, termed a "submission," and the determination of the arbitrators or referee is called an "award."

At common law it was also either

(3) *In pais,* that is, by simple agreement of the parties; or

(4) By rule of court, that is by the intervention of a court of law or equity. 3 Bl. Comm. 16.

ARBITRATION OF EXCHANGE. Where a merchant pays his debts in one country by a bill of exchange upon another. 2 Mill. Pol. Econ. 168.

ARBITRATOR. In practice. A private extraordinary judge, to whose decision matters in controversy are referred by consent of the parties. Worcester.

"Reference" is of frequent modern use as a synonym of "arbitrator," but is in its origin of broader signification, and less accurate than arbitrator.

ARBITRIMENTUM AEQUUM TRIBUIT cuique suum. A just arbitration renders to every one his own. Noy, Max. 248.

ARBITRIUM (Lat.) Decision; award; judgment.

For some cases the law does not prescribe an exact rule, but leaves them to the judgment of sound men. 1 Sharswood, Bl. Comm. 61. The decision of an arbiter is *arbitrium*, as the etymology indicates, and the word denotes, in the passage cited, the decision of a man of good judgment who is not controlled by technical rules of law, but is at liberty to adapt the general principles of justice to the peculiar circumstances of the case.

ARBITRIUM EST JUDICIUM. An award is a judgment. Jenk. Cent. Cas. 137; 3 Bulst. 64.

ARBITRIUM EST JUDICIUM BONI VIRI, secundum aequum et bonum. An award is the judgment of a good man, according to justice. 3 Bulst. 64.

ARBOR (Lat.) A tree; a plant; something larger than an herb; a general term including vines, osiers, and even reeds. The mast of a ship. Brissonius; Ainsworth; Calv. Lex.

Arbor civilis. A genealogical tree. Co. Inst.

A common form of showing genealogies is by means of a tree representing the different branches of the family. Many of the terms in the law of descent are figurative, and derived hence. Such a tree is called, also, *arbor consanguinitatis.*

ARBOR DUM CRESCIT; LIGNUM DUM crescere nescit. A tree while it is growing; wood when it cannot grow. Cro. Jac. 166; 12 Johns. (N. Y.) 239, 241.

ARBOR FINALIS. In old English law. A boundary tree; a tree used for making a boundary line. Bracton, fols. 167, 207b.

ARCANA IMPERII. State secrets. 1 Bl. Comm. 337.

ARCARIUS (Lat. *arca*). A treasurer; one who keeps the public money. Spelman.

ARCHAIONOMIA. The name of a collection of Saxon laws published during the reign of the English Queen Elizabeth, in the Saxon language, with a Latin version, by Mr. Lambard. Dr. Wilkins enlarged this collection in his work entitled "*Leges Anglo-Saxonicae,*" containing all the Saxon laws extant, together with those ascribed to Edward the Confessor, in Latin; those of William the Conqueror, in Norman and Latin; and of Henry I., Stephen, and Henry II., in Latin.

ARCHBISHOP. In ecclesiastical law. The chief of the clergy of a whole province. He has the inspection of the bishops of that province, as well as of the inferior clergy, and may deprive them on notorious cause. The archbishop has also his own diocese, in which he exercises episcopal jurisdiction, as in his province he exercises archiepiscopal authority. 1 Bl. Comm. 380; 1 Ld. Raym. 541.

ARCHDEACON. In ecclesiastical law. A ministerial officer subordinate to the bishop.

In the primitive church, the archdeacons were employed by the bishop in the more servile duties of collecting and distributing alms and offerings. Afterwards they became, in effect, "eyes to the overseers of the church." Cowell. His jurisdiction is ecclesiastical, and immediately subordinate to that of the bishop, throughout the whole or a part of the diocese. He is a ministerial officer. 1 Sharswood, Bl. Comm. 383.

ARCHDEACON'S COURT. In English law. The lowest court of ecclesiastical jurisdiction in England. It is held before a person appointed by the archdeacon, called his "official." Its jurisdiction is limited to ecclesiastical causes arising within the archdeaconry. It had until recently, also, jurisdiction of matters of probate and granting administrations. In ordinary cases, its jurisdiction is concurrent with that of the bishop's court, but in some instances cases must be commenced in this court. In all cases, an appeal lies to the bishop's court. 24 Hen. VIII. c. 12; 3 Bl. Comm. 64.

ARCHERY. A service of keeping a bow for the lord's use in the defense of his castle. Co. Litt. 157.

ARCHES' COURT. See "Court of Arches."

ARCHETYPE. The original copy.

ARCHICAPELLANUS (Law Lat.) In old European law. A chief or high chancellor (*summus cancellarius*). Spelman.

ARCHITECT. One who makes it his occupation to form or devise plans and designs and to draw up specifications for buildings or structures and to superintend their construction.

ARCHIVES (Lat. *archivum, arcibum*). The rolls; any place where ancient records, charters, and evidences are kept. In libraries, the private depositary. Cowell; Spelman. The records need not be ancient to constitute the place of keeping them the "archives."

ARCHIVIST. One to whose care the archives have been confided.

ARCTA ET SALVA CUSTODIA (Lat.) In safe and close custody or keeping.

When a defendant is arrested on a *capias ad satisfaciendum (ca. sa.)* he is to be kept *arcta et salva custodia.* 3 Sharswood, Bl. Comm. 415.

ARDOUR. In old English law. An incendiary; a house burner.

ARE. A French measure of surface. This is a square the sides of which are of the length of ten metres. The *are* is equal to 1076.441 square feet.

AREA. An inclosed yard or opening in a house; an open place adjoining to a house. 1 Chit. Prac. 176.

ARENALES. In Spanish law. Sandy beaches.

ARENIFODINA (from *arena,* sand, and *fodire,* to dig). In the civil law. A sand pit. Dig. 7. 1. 13. 5.

ARENTARE (Lat.) To rent; to let out at a certain rent. Cowell.

Arentatio, a renting.

AREOPAGITE. In ancient Greek law. A lawyer or chief judge of the Areopagus in capital matters in Athens; a tribunal so called after a hill or slight eminence, in a street of that city dedicated to Mars, where the court was held in which those judges were wont to sit. Wharton.

ARETRO. See "A Retro."

ARG. An abbreviation of *arguendo,* much used in the reports.

ARGENT. In heraldry. Silver.

ARGENTARII (Lat. *argentum*). Money-lenders. Called, also, *nummularii* (from *nummus,* coin) *mensarii* (lenders by the month). They were so called, whether living in Rome or in the country towns, and had their shops or tables in the forum. *Argentarius* is the singular. *Argentarium* denotes the instrument of the loan, approaching in sense to our note or bond.

Argentarius miles was the servant or porter who carried the money from the lower to the upper treasury to be tested. Spelman.

ARGENTEUS (Law Lat.) An old French coin, answering nearly to the English shilling. Spelman.

ARGENTUM. Silver; silver plate. 1 Ld. Raym. 20.

Uncoined silver; money paid by weight. Spelman.

Money paid by tale or counted (*pecunia numerata.*) Spelman.

Goods generally. Spelman.

ARGENTUM ALBUM (Lat.) Unstamped silver; bullion. Spelman; Cowell.

ARGENTUM DEI (Lat.) God's money; God's penny; money given as earnest in making a bargain. Cowell.

ARGUMENT AB INCONVENIENTI. See "Ab Inconvenienti."

ARGUMENTATIVE. By way of reasoning.

A plea must be (among other things) direct and positive, and not argumentative. 3 Sharswood, Bl. Comm. 308.

ARGUMENTUM A COMMUNITER ACcidentibus in jure frequens est. An argument drawn from things commonly happening is frequent in law. Broom, Leg. Max. 44.

ARGUMENTUM A DIVISIONE EST fortissimum in jure. An argument arising from a division is most powerful in law. 6 Coke, 60; Co. Litt. 213b.

ARGUMENTUM A MAJORI AD MINUS negative non valet; valet e converso. An argument from the greater to the less is of no force negatively; conversely it is. Jenk. Cent. Cas. 281.

ARGUMENTUM A SIMILI VALET IN lege. An argument drawn from a similar case, or analogy, avails in law. Co. Litt. 191.

ARGUMENTUM AB AUCTORITATE est fortissimum in lege. An argument drawn from authority is the strongest in law. Co. Litt. 254.

ARGUMENTUM AB IMPOSSIBILI PLUrimum valet in lege. An argument deduced from impossibility greatly avails in law. Co. Litt. 92.

ARGUMENTUM AB INCONVENIENTI est validum in lege; quia lex non permittit aliquod inconveniens. An argument drawn from what is inconvenient is good in law, because the law will not permit any inconvenience. Co. Litt. 66a, 258; 7 Taunt. 527; 3 Barn. & C. 131; 6 Clark & F. 671.

ARGUMENTUM AB INCONVENIENTI plurimum vale (est validum) in lege. An argument drawn from inconvenience is of the greatest weight (is forcible) in law. Co. Litt. 66a, 97a, 152b, 258b; Broom, Leg. Max. 184. If there be in any deed or instrument equivocal expressions, and great inconvenience must necessarily follow from one construction, it is strong to show that such construction is not according to the true intention of the grantor; but where there is no equivocal expression in the instrument, and the words used admit only of one meaning, arguments of inconvenience prove only want of foresight in the grantor. 3 Madd. 540; 7 Taunt. 496.

ARGYLDE. Not compensated for.

ARIBANNUM, or ARRIBANNUM (Law Lat.) In old European law. A fine for not joining the army, when called out by public summons. Spelman.

The summons or proclamation itself. Spelman. Spelman thinks the proper form of this word was *heribannum,* unless it be considered a contraction of *arrieribannum* (*q. v.*) See "Herebannum."

ARIMANNI (Lat.) The possessors of lands holden or derived from their lords.

Clients joined to some lord for protection. By some, said to be soldiers holding lands from the lord; but the term is also applied to women and slaves. Spelman.

ARISTOCRACY. A government in which a class of men rules supreme.

ARISTODEMOCRACY. A form of government where the power is divided between the great men of the nation and the people.

ARLES. Earnest. Used in Yorkshire in the phrase arles-penny. Cowell. In Scotland it has the same signification. Bell, Dict.

ARM OF THE SEA. A portion of the sea projecting inland, in which the tide ebbs and flows.

It includes bays, roads, creeks, coves ports, and rivers where the water flows and reflows. An arm of the sea is considered as extending as far into the interior of a country as the water of fresh rivers is propelled backward by the ingress and pressure of the tide. Angell, Tide Waters (2d Ed.) 73; 7 Pet. (U. S.) 324; 2 Conn. 484; 8 N. Y. 199; Olc. Adm. 21.

"But it does not follow that every creek or rivulet in which the tide ebbs and flows, and which may be used as certain tides by small boats for individual convenience, is to be dignified by the appellation of an 'arm of the sea.'" 10 N. J. Eq. 223.

ARMA (Lat.) Arms; weapons, offensive and defensive. Co. Litt. 161b, 162a.

——**In the Civil Law.** It included not only arms of warfare, but any weapon, as a club or a stone.

Armor, arms, or cognizances of families. Spelman.

ARMA DARE. To dub or make a knight. Cowell. *Arma capere* or *suscipere*, to take upon one the order of knighthood. 2 Reeves, Hist. Eng. Law, 288.

ARMA IN ARMATOS SUMERE JURA sinunt. The laws permit the taking up of arms against armed persons. 2 Inst. 574.

ARMA MOLUTA (Lat.) Sharp weapons; weapons which cut, as distinguished from those which bruise. Cowell; Blount.

ARMATA VIS (Lat.) In the civil law. Armed force. Dig. 43. 16. 3; Fleta, lib. 4. c. 4.

ARMIGER (Lat.) An armor bearer; an esquire; a title of dignity belonging to gentlemen authorized to bear arms. Kennett, Par. Ant.; Cowell.

In its earlier meaning, a servant who carried the arms of a knight. Spelman.

A tenant by scutage; a servant or valet; applied, also, to the higher servants in convents. Spelman; Whishaw.

ARMISCARA. An ancient mode of punishment, which was to carry a saddle at the back as a token of subjection. Spelman.

A kind of fine. Spelman.

ARMISTICE. A cessation of hostilities between belligerent nations for a considerable time.

It is either partial and local, or general. It differs from a mere suspension of arms, which takes place to enable the two armies to bury their dead, their chiefs to hold conferences or pourparlers, and the like. Vattel, Droit des Gens, lib. 3, c. 16, § 233. The terms "truce" and "armistice" are sometimes used in the same sense. See "Truce."

ARMORUM APPELLATIONE, NON SOlum scuta et gladii et galeae, sed et fustes et lapides continentur. Under the name of "arms" are included not only shields and swords and helmets, but also clubs and stones. Co. Litt. 162.

ARMS. Anything that a man wears for his defense, or takes in his hands, or uses in his anger, to cast at or strike at another. Co. Litt. 161b, 162a; Cromp. Jus. Peace, 65; Cunningham. Every description of weapon, offensive and defensive. 4 Ark. 21.

The constitution of the United States (Amend. art. 2) declares that, "a well-regulated militia being necessary to the security of a free state, the right of the people to keep and bear arms shall not be infringed." This has been held to mean only such arms as are adapted to military purposes. 3 Heisk. (Tenn.) 179; 35 Tex. 476.

Signs of arms, or drawings, painted on shields, banners, and the like. The arms of the United States are described in the resolution of congress of June 20, 1782.

ARMY. The military forces of a nation intended for service on land. It does not include the marine corps. 2 Sawy. (U. S.) 200; 21 N. Y. Supp. 104. Contra, 7 Rob. (N. Y.) 635.

As used in the United States constitution and laws it does not include the state militia. 16 Grat. (Va.) 475.

AROMATARIUS. In old pleadings. A grocer. But see 1 Vent. 142.

ARPENNUS. A measure of land, of uncertain amount. It was called "arpent," also. Spelman; Cowell.

——**In French Law.** A measure of different amount in each of the sixty-four provinces. Guyot, Rep. Univ. "Arpenteur."

The measure was adopted in Louisiana. 6 Pet. (U. S.) 763.

ARPENT, or ARPEN. A quantity of land containing a French acre. 4 Hall, Law I. 518.

ARPENTATOR. A measurer or surveyor of land.

ARRA. In civil law. Earnest; evidence of a completed bargain. Used of a contract of marriage, as well as any other. Spelled, also, *arrha, arrae.* Calv. Lex.

ARRAGE (Law Fr.) Mad or insane. *Home arrage,* a madman or lunatic. Britt. c. 26.

ARRAIGN. To call a prisoner to the bar of the court to answer the matter charged in the indictment. 2 Hale, P. C. 216. To set in order. An assize may be arraigned. Litt. § 242; 3 Mod. 273; Termes de la Ley; Cowell.

ARRAIGNMENT. In criminal practice. Calling the defendant to the bar of the court, to answer the accusation contained in the indictment.

The first step in the proceeding consists in calling the defendant to the bar by his name, and commanding him to hold up his hand. This is done for the purpose of completely identifying the prisoner as the person named in the indictment. The holding up his hand is not, however, indispensable, for, if the prisoner should refuse to do so, he may be identified by any admission that he is the person intended. 1 W. Bl. 33. See Archb. Crim. Pl. (1859 Ed.) 128.

The second step is the reading the indictment to the accused person. This is done to enable him fully to understand the charge to be produced against him. The mode in which it is read is, after saying, "A. B. hold up your hand," to proceed, "You stand indicted by the name of A. B., late of, etc., for that you, on," etc., and then go through the whole of the indictment.

The third step is to ask the prisoner: "How say you [A. B.], are you guilty, or not guilty?" Upon this, if the prisoner confesses the charge, and it appears to the satisfaction of the judge that he rightly comprehends the effect of his plea, the confession is recorded, and nothing further is done till judgment. If, on the contrary, he answers, "Not guilty," that plea is entered for him, and the clerk or attorney general replies that he is guilty; when an issue is formed. 1 Mass. 95.

If the defendant, when called upon, makes no answer, and it is a matter of doubt whether or not he is mute of malice, the court may direct a jury to be forthwith impaneled and sworn, to try whether the prisoner is mute of malice or *ex visitatione Dei;* and such jury may consist of any twelve men who may happen to be present. If a person is found to be mute *ex visitatione Dei,* the court, in its discretion, will use such means as may be sufficient to enable the defendant to understand the charge and make his answer; and if this is found impracticable, a plea of not guilty will be entered, and the trial proceed. But if the jury return a verdict that he is mute fraudulently and willfully, the court will pass sentence as upon a conviction. 1 Mass. 103; 13 Mass. 299; 9 Mass. 402; 10 Metc. (Mass.) 222; Archb. Crim. Pl. (14th London Ed.) 129; Car. Crim. Law, 57; 3 Car. & K. 121; Roscoe, Crim. Ev. (4th London Ed.) 215. See the case of a deaf person who could not be induced to plead (1 Leach, C. C. [4th Ed.] 451); of a person deaf and dumb (1 Leach, C. C. [4th Ed.] 102; 14 Mass. 207; 7 Car. & P. 303; 6 Cox, C. C. 386; 3 Car. & K. 328). See "Peine et Forte Dure."

ARRAIGNS, CLERK OF. An assistant to the clerk of assise.

ARRAMEUR. An ancient officer of a port, whose business was to load and unload vessels.

ARRAS. In Spanish law. The donation which the husband makes to his wife, by reason or on account of marriage, and in consideration of the *dote,* or portion, which he receives, from her. Aso & M. Inst. bk. 1, tit. 7, c. 3.

The property contributed by the husband *ad sustinenda onera matrimonii* (for bearing the expenses).

The husband is under no obligation to give *arras,* but it is a donation purely voluntary. He is not permitted to give in *arras* more than a tenth of his property. The *arras* is the exclusive property of the wife, subject to the husband's usufruct during his life. Burge, Confl. Laws, 417.

ARRAY. In practice. The whole body of jurors summoned to attend a court, as they are arrayed or arranged on the panel. See "Challenge;" Dane, Abr. Index; 1 Chit. Crim. Law, 536; Comyn, Dig. "Challenge" (B).

ARREARAGES. Arrears.

ARREARS (Fr.) The remainder of an account or sum of money in the hands of an accountant. Any money due and unpaid at a given time. Cowell; Spelman.

ARRECT. To accuse. *Arrectati,* those accused or suspected.

ARRENDAMIENTO (Spanish). In Spanish law. The contract of letting and hiring an estate or land (*heredad*). White, New Recop. bk. 2, tit. 14. c. 1.

ARREST (Fr. *arreter,* to stay, to stop, to detain). To deprive a person of his liberty by legal authority. The seizing a person and detaining him in the custody of the law.

As ordinarily used, the terms "arrest" and "attachment" coincide in meaning to some extent; though in strictness, as a distinction, an arrest may be said to be the act resulting from the service of an attachment. And in the more extended sense which is sometimes given to attachment, including the act of taking, it would seem to differ from arrest in that it is more peculiarly applicable to a taking of property, while arrest is more commonly used in speaking of persons. The terms are, however, often interchanged when speaking of the taking a man by virtue of legal authority. Arrest is also applied in some instances to a seizure and detention of personal chattels, especially of ships and vessels, but this use of the term is not common in modern law.

——**In Civil Practice.** The apprehension of a person by virtue of a lawful authority to answer the demand against him in a civil action.

——**In Criminal Practice.** The apprehending of a person to answer for an alleged or suspected crime. The word "arrest" is said to be more properly used in civil cases, and "apprehension" in criminal.

——**In Admiralty Practice.** The seizure of a vessel on process in an action *in rem.*

ARREST OF INQUEST. Pleading in arrest of taking the inquest on a former issue, and showing cause why an inquest should not be taken. Wharton.

ARRESTANDIS BONIS NE DISSIPENtur. In English law. A writ for him whose cattle or goods, being taken during a controversy, are likely to be wasted and consumed.

ARRESTANDO IPSUM QUI PECUNIAM recepit. In old English law. A writ which issued for apprehending a person who had taken the king's prest money to serve in the wars, and then hid himself in order to avoid going. Reg. Orig. 24.

ARRESTEE. In Scotch law. He in whose hands a debt, or property in his possession, has been arrested by a regular arrestment.

If, in contempt of the arrestment, he make payment of the sum or deliver the goods arrested to the common debtor, he is not only liable criminally for breach of the arrestment, but he must pay the debt again to the arrestor. Ersk. Inst. 3. 6. 6.

ARRESTER. In Scotch law. One who sues out and obtains an arrestment of his debtor's goods or movable obligations. Ersk. Inst. 3. 6. 1.

ARRESTMENT. In Scotch law. Securing a criminal's person till trial, or that of a debtor till he gives security *judicio sisti.* The order of a judge, by which he who is debtor in a movable obligation to the arrester's debtor is prohibited to make payment or delivery till the debt due to the arrester be paid or secured. Ersk. Inst. 3. 6. 1. Id. 1. 2. 12.

Where arrestment proceeds on a depending action, it may be loosed by the common debtor's giving security to the arrester for his debt, in the event it shall be found due. Ersk. Inst. 3. 6. 7.

ARRESTMENT JURISDICTIONIS FUNdandae causa. In Scotch law. A process to bring a foreigner within the jurisdiction of the courts of Scotland. The warrant attaches a foreigner's goods within the jurisdiction, and these will not be released unless caution or security be given. Wharton.

ARRESTO FACTO SUPER BONIS MERcatorum alienigenorum. A writ against the goods of aliens found within this kingdom, in recompense of goods taken from a denizen in a foreign country, after denial of restitution. Reg. Orig. 129. The ancient civilians called it *"clarigatio,"* but by the moderns it is termed *"reprisalia."* Wharton.

ARRET (Fr.) A judgment, sentence, or decree of a court of competent jurisdiction.

The term is derived from the French law, and is used in Canada and Louisiana.

Saisie arret is an attachment of property in the hands of a third person. Code Prac. La. art. 209; 2 Low. (U. S.) 77; 5 Low. (U. S.) 198, 218.

ARRETTED (*arrectatus, i. e., ad rectum vocatus*). Convened before a judge and charged with a crime.

Ad rectum malefactorem is, according to Bracton, to have a malefactor forthcoming to be put on his trial.

Imputed, or laid to one's charge; as, no folly may be *arretted* to any one under age. Bracton, lib. 3, tr. 2, c. 10; Cunningham.

ARRHABO (Lat.) In the civil law. Earnest; money given to bind a bargain. Calv. Lex; Brissonius, voc. "Arra."

ARRHAE. In the civil law. Money or other valuable things given by the buyer to the seller, for the purpose of evidencing the contract; earnest.

There are two kinds of *arrhae:* One kind given when a contract has only been proposed; the other when a sale has actually taken place. Those which are given when a bargain has been merely proposed, before it has been concluded, form the matter of the contract, by which he who gives the *arrhae* consents and agrees to lose them, and to transfer the title to them in the opposite party, in case he should refuse to complete the proposed bargain; and the receiver of *arrhae* is obliged on his part to return double the amount to the giver of them in case he should fail to complete his part of the contract. Poth. Vente, note 498. After the contract of sale has been completed, the purchaser usually gives *arrhae* as evidence that the contract has been perfected. *Arrhae* are therefore defined *quod ante pretium datur, et fidem fecit contractus, facti totiusque pecuniae solvendae.* Id. note 506; Code, 4. 45. 2.

ARRIAGE AND CARRIAGE. Services of an indefinite amount formerly exacted from tenants under the Scotch law. Bell, Dict.

ARRIER BAN. A second summons to join the lord, addressed to those who had neglected the first. A summons of the inferiors or vassals of the lord. Spelman.

To be distinguished from *aribannum.*

ARRIERE FIEF (Fr.) An inferior fee granted out of a superior.

ARRIERE VASSAL. In feudal law. The vassal of a vassal. One who held of a vassal of the crown.

ARRIVE. To come to a particular place; to reach a particular or certain place. See 1 Brock. (U. S.) 411; 2 Cush. (Mass.) 439; 8 Barn. & C. 119.

ARROGATION. The adoption of a person *sui juris.* 1 Brown, Civ. Law, 119, Dig. 1. 7. 5; Inst. 1. 11. 3.

ARRONDISSEMENT. One of the subdivisions of a department (*q. v.*) in France.

ARSAE ET PENSATAE (Law Lat.) Burnt and weighed. A term formerly applied to money melted and then weighed to test its purity.

ARSENALS. Storehouses of arms and other military supplies.

ARSER IN LE MAIN. Burning in the hand. The punishment inflicted on those who received the benefit of clergy. Termes de la Ley.

ARSON (Lat. *ardere,* to burn). At common law. The malicious burning of the house of another. Coke, 3d Inst. 66; Bish. Crim. Law, § 415; 4 Bl. Comm. 220; 2 Pick. (Mass.) 320; 10 Cush. (Mass.) 479; 7 Grat. (Va.) 619; 9 Ala. 175; 7 Blackf. (Ind.) 168; 1 Leach, C. C. (4th Ed.) 218. By statute in most, if not all, the states, the house need not be that of another.

The house, or some part of it, however small, must be consumed by fire. 9 Car. & P. 45; 16 Mass. 105; 110 Mass. 403; 5 Ired. (N. C.) 350; 25 Ired. (N. C.) 570; 62 N. Y. 117.

At common law, the building must have been a dwelling house, but this included all buildings within the curtilage. By statute the offense has been extended to other buildings.

ARSURA. The trial of money by heating it after it was coined. Now obsolete.

ART. A principle put in practice, and applied to some art, machine, manufacture, or composition of matter. 4 Mason (U. S.) 1. See Act Cong. July 4, 1836, § 6.

Copper-plate printing on the back of a banknote is an art for which a patent may be granted. 4 Wash. C. C. (U. S.) 9.

ART AND PART. In Scotch law. The offense committed by one who aids and assists the commission of a crime, but who is not the principal or chief actor in its actual commission. An accessary; a principal in the second degree. Paterson, Comp.

ART, WORDS OF. Words used in their technical sense; sometimes words which bear such a sense, without regard to the correctness of their use.

ARTHEL (properly **ARDDELW,** or **ARDdel**). In Welsh and old English law. To avouch. Cowell.

Used, also, as a substantive. Thus, in the laws of Hoel Dha it was provided that if a man were taken with stolen goods, he must be allowed a lawful *arddelw* (vouchee) to clear him of his felony. This was abolished by St. 26 Hen. VIII. c. 6. Blount.

ARTICLE. A distinct part of an instrument, consisting of two or more particulars. Hence systems of rules and instruments composed of various particulars, or arranged in several divisions, are called "articles." The term was anciently applied to statutes drawn in this form.

——**In French Law.** A point.

——**In English Ecclesiastical Law.** A charge or libel. The introductory part of such a pleading is: "We article and object," etc.

——**In Scotch Practice.** A subject or matter. "Article of dittay." 1 Brown, 62.

ARTICLED CLERK. One who binds himself by articles to serve in the office of a solicitor, in consideration of receiving instruction.

ARTICLES APPROBATORY. In Scotch law. That part of the proceedings which corresponds to the answer to the charge in an English bill in chancery. Paterson, Comp.

ARTICLES IMPROBATORY. In Scotch law. Articulate averments setting forth the facts relied upon. Bell, Dict.

That part of the proceedings which corresponds to the charge in our English bill in chancery to set aside a deed. Paterson, Comp. The answer is called "articles approbatory."

ARTICLES, LORDS OF. A committee of the Scotch parliament, which, in the mode of its election, and by the nature of its powers, was calculated to increase the influence of the crown, and to confer upon it a power equivalent to that of a negative before debate. This system appeared inconsistent with the freedom of parliament, and at the revolution the convention of estates declared it a grievance, and accordingly it was suppressed by Act 1690, c. 3. Wharton.

ARTICLES OF AGREEMENT. A written memorandum of the terms of an agreement.

ARTICLES OF CONFEDERATION. The title of the compact which was made by the thirteen original states of the United States of America.

ARTICLES OF FAITH. See "Articles of Religion."

ARTICLES OF IMPEACHMENT. A written allegation of the causes for impeachment.

They are called by Blackstone a kind of bill of indictment, and perform the same office which an indictment does in a common criminal case. They do not usually pursue the strict form and accuracy of an indictment, but are sometimes quite general in the form of the allegations. Wooddeson, Lect. 605; Comyn, Dig. "Parliament" (L 21); Story, Const. § 806.

ARTICLES OF INCORPORATION. The papers drawn up by or on behalf of the incorporators of a proposed corporation to be presented for approval to some officer or court.

ARTICLES OF PARTNERSHIP. A written agreement by which the parties enter into a partnership upon the conditions therein mentioned. These are to be distinguished from agreements to enter into a partnership at a future time.

ARTICLES OF RELIGION. The "Thirty-Nine Articles" of religious dogma drawn up in the reign of James I, and approved by him.

ARTICLES OF ROUP. In Scotch law. The conditions under which property is offered for sale at auction. Peterson, Comp.

ARTICLES OF SET. In Scotch law. An agreement for a lease. Paterson, Comp.

ARTICLES OF THE CLERGY. See "Articuli Cleri."

ARTICLES OF THE NAVY. A system of rules for the government of the navy.

ARTICLES OF THE PEACE. A complaint made before a court of competent jurisdiction by one who has just cause to fear that an injury to his person or property is about to be committed or caused by the party complained of, alleging the causes of his belief, and asking the protection of the court.

The object of articles is to compel the party complained of to find sureties of the peace.

ARTICLES OF UNION. Articles, twenty-five in number, adopted by the parliaments of England and Scotland in 1707, and taking effect May 1st of that year, for the union of the two countries. 1 Bl. Comm. 96.

ARTICLES OF WAR. The code of laws established for the government of the army.

The term is used in this sense both in England and the United States. The term also includes the code established for the government of the navy. See Acts April 23, 1800, and April 10, 1806, and 22 Geo. II. c. 33; 19 Geo. III. c. 17; 37 Geo. III. cc. 70, 71; 47 Geo. III. c. 71. See "Martial Law."

ARTICULATE ADJUDICATION. In Scotch law. Separate adjudication for each of several claims of a creditor. It is so made in order that a mistake in accumulating one debt need not affect the proceedings on other claims which are correctly accumulated.

ARTICULI (Lat.) Articles; items or heads. A term applied to some old English statutes, and occasionally to treatises.

ARTICULI CLERI. Articles of the clergy; the title of a statute passed in the ninth year of Edw. II. to adjust questions of cognizance between the ecclesiastical and temporal courts. 2 Reeve, Hist. Eng. Law, 291; 2 Inst. 599.

ARTICULI DE MONETA. Articles concerning money, or the currency. The title of a statute passed in the twentieth year of Edward I. 2 Reeve, Hist. Eng. Law, 228; Crabb, Hist. Eng. Law (Am. Ed.) 167.

ARTICULI MAGNAE CHARTAE. The preliminary articles, forty-nine in number, upon which the *Magna Charta* was founded.

ARTICULI SUPER CHARTAS. St. 28 Edward I. st. 3, confirming and enlarging *Magna Charta*, and the *Charta de Foresta*. 2 Reeve, Hist. Eng. Law, 103, 233.

ARTICULO MORTIS. See "In Articulo Mortis."

ARTIFICER. One by whom something is made. 4 Strobh. (S. C.) 365.

A skilled workman. 13 Q. B. Div. 832.

ARTIFICIAL. Having its existence in the given manner by virtue of or in consideration only of the law.

An artificial person is a body, company, or corporation considered in law as an individual.

ARTIFICIAL PRESUMPTIONS. In the law of evidence. Presumptions (otherwise termed "legal") which derive from the law a technical or artificial operation and effect beyond their mere natural tendency to produce belief. 3 Starkie, Ev. 1235.

ARURA. Days' work at ploughing.

AS (Lat.) A pound. It was composed of twelve ounces. The parts were reckoned, as may be seen in the law, *servum de haeredibus* (Inst. lib. 13, Pandect) as follows: *Uncia*, 1 ounce; *sextans*, 2 ounces; *triens*, 3 ounces; *quadrans*, 4 ounces; *quincunx*, 5 ounces; *semis*, 6 ounces; *septunx*, 7 ounces; *bes*, 8 ounces; *dodrans*, 9 ounces; *dextans*, 10 ounces; *deunx*, 11 ounces.

The whole of a thing, *solidum quid*. Thus, *as* signified the whole of an inheritance, so that an heir *ex asse* was an heir of the whole inheritance. An heir *ex triente*, *ex semisse*, *ex besse*, or *ex deunce* was an heir of one-third, one-half, two-thirds, or eleven-twelfths.

AS NEAR AS MAY BE. A statute providing that procedure in a named case shall conform "as near as may be" to those in another named case does not mean "as near as may be possible," or "as near as may be practicable," or require a strict compliance with the requirements of the latter named act, but is merely directory and advisory, and to be construed as contemplating some variation from the prescribed course, leaving it to the discretion of the court to reject such of the provisions of the act referred to as are not strictly applicable to the character of the proceedings involved. 173 Ill. 600; 149 Ill. App. 498.

AS THEIR INTEREST MAY APPEAR. The expression "as their interest may appear," used in a fire insurance policy relating to the interest of a mortgagee, has relation to and contemplates an insurable interest in the mortgagee which exists at the time the contract was made, and has no application to any new interest not then in existence, such as a simple contract indebtedness incurred by the mortgagor to the mortgagee and not secured by the mortgage. 94 Ill. App. 499.

ASCENDANTS (Lat. *ascendere*, to ascend, to go up to, to climb up to). Those from whom a person is descended, or from whom he derives his birth, however remote they may be.

Every one has two ascendants at the first degree, his father and mother; four at the second degree, his paternal grandfather and grandmother, and his maternal grandfather and grandmother; eight at the third. Thus, in going up we ascend by various lines, which fork at every generation. By this progress, sixteen ascendants are found at the fourth degree; thirty-two at the fifth; sixty-four, at the sixth; one hundred and twenty-eight, at the seventh; and so on. By this progressive increase, a person has at the twenty-fifth generation thirty-three million five hundred and fifty-four thousand four hundred and thirty-two ascendants. But, as many of the ascendants of a person have descended from the same ancestor, the lines which were forked reunite to the first common ancestor, from whom the other descends; and this multiplication, thus frequently interrupted by the common ancestors, may be reduced to a few persons.

ASCENDIENTES. In Spanish law. Ascendants; ascending heirs; heirs in the ascending line. White, New Recop. bk. 1, tit. 7, c. 3, note; Schmidt, Civ. Law, 259.

ASCERTAIN. To make certain to the mind; to free from obscurity, doubt or chance; to make sure of; fix; to determine. 246 Ill. 229.

To make sure or certain; fix; to establish; to determine; to settle. 95 Ill. 550.

ASCRIPTITIUS. One enrolled; foreigners who have been enrolled. Among the Romans, *ascriptitii* were foreigners who had been naturalized, and who had in general the same rights as natives. Nov. 22, c. 17; Code, 11. 47. *Ascriptitii* is the plural. See "Adscriptitii."

ASPECT. View of possibility. A pleading "with a double aspect" is one based on alternative hypotheses of fact.

ASPHYXIA. In medical jurisprudence. A temporary suspension of the motion of the heart and arteries; swooning; fainting.

ASPORTATION. Carrying away. A common-law ingredient of larceny. "There must be such a caption that the accused acquires dominion over the property, followed by such an asportation or carrying away as to supersede the possession of the owner for an appreciable period of time." 94 Ala. 535.

Thus it has been held not larceny to merely set a package of goods on end, with intent to steal it in the future (1 Leg. C. C. 237), or to touch a pocketbook in another's pocket without removing it (99 Mass. 431), or to attempt to carry away property which is attached by a chain to the person of the owner (1 Leg. C. C. 321). On the other hand, the slightest asportation is sufficient, and it has been held larceny to remove a package from one end of a wagon to the other (1 Leg. C. C. 236), or to partly lift money from a pocket, though it was dropped before being entirely removed (1 Moody, C. C. 78; 20 Ohio St. 508).

The asportation need not be by the hand of the trespasser; a carrying away by an innocent agent (125 Mass. 390), or by mechanical means, as by fraudulently connecting a private pipe with gas mains (1 Cox, C. C. 213), being sufficient.

ASPORTAVIT. He carried away. See "Asportation."

ASSACH, or ASSATH. In old Welsh law. An oath made by compurgators. Applied in St. 1 Hen. V. c. 6, to the Welsh custom of clearing one accused of homicide by the oaths of three hundred persons.

The origin and exact meaning of the term is uncertain, and Mr. Barrington could only collect its meaning from the above statute. Barr. Obs. St. 382.

ASSART, or ESSART. In English forest and ecclesiastical law. The offense of pulling up by the roots the woods that are thickets and coverts for the deer, and making them clear as arable land. Manw. For. Law, p. 2, c. 9, note 1; Cowell; 1 Crabb, Real Prop. pp. 486, 487, § 627.

Written, in the law Latin, *assartum,* in Bracton and Fleta, and *essartum,* in the *Charta de Foresta* and the Black Book of the Exchequer.

ASSASSINATION. Murder committed for hire, without provocation or cause of resentment given to the murderer by the person upon whom the crime is committed. Ersk. Inst. bk. 4, tit. 4, note 45.

A murder committed treacherously, with advantage of time, place, or other circumstances.

In modern usage, at least, it is not a technical term of the law of homicide.

ASSATH, or ASSAITH. See "Assach."

ASSAULT. An unlawful offer or attempt with force or violence to do a corporal hurt to another. It may consist of any act tending to such injury, and accompanied by such circumstances as denote an intention and a present ability of personal violence. 1 Hill (N. Y.) 351.

Force unlawfully directed or applied to the person of another under such circumstances as to cause a well-founded apprehension of immediate peril.

Aggravated assault is one committed with the intention of committing some additional crime, or under circumstances of peculiar turpitude.

Simple assault is one committed with no intention to do any other injury.

Assault is generally coupled with battery, and for the excellent practical reason that they generally go together; but the assault is rather the initiation or offer to commit the act of which the battery is the consummation. An assault is included in every battery. 1 Hawk. P. C. c. 62, § 1.

Mere words do not constitute an assault (59 Ind. 300), but some overt act is required (55 Hun [N. Y.] 214).

ASSAY. The proof or trial of the purity or fineness of metals, particularly the precious metals, gold and silver.

ASSAY OFFICE. An establishment, or department, in which the manipulations attending the assay of bullion and coins are conducted. See "Assay."

ASSAYER OF THE KING. An officer of the royal mint, appointed by St. 2 Hen. VI. c. 12, who received and tested the bullion taken in for coining. Also called *assayator regis.* Cowell; Termes de la Ley.

ASSECURARE (Lat.) To assure; to make secure by pledges, or any solemn interposition of faith. Spelman; Cowell.

ASSECURATION. In European law. Assurance; insurance of a vessel, freight, or cargo. Opposition to the decree of Grenoble. Ferriere.

ASSECURATOR. An insurer.

ASSEDATION. In Scotch law. An old term, used indiscriminately to signify a lease or feu-right. Bell, Dict.; Ersk. Inst. lib. 2, tit. 6, § 20.

ASSEMBLY. The meeting of a number of persons in the same place.

——**Political Assemblies.** Those required by the constitution and laws. For example, the general assembly, which includes the senate and house of representatives. The meeting of the electors of the president and vice-president of the United States may also be called an assembly.

——**Popular Assemblies.** Those where the people meet to deliberate upon their rights. These are guaranteed by the constitution. Const. U. S. Amend. art. 1.

——**Unlawful Assembly.** The meeting of three or more persons to do an unlawful act, although they may not carry their purpose into execution. It differs from a riot or rout because in each of the latter cases there is some act done besides the simple meeting. See 1 Ired. (N. C.) 30; 9 Car. & P. 91, 431; 5 Car. & P. 154; 1 Bish. Crim. Law, § 395; 2 Bish. Crim. Law, §§ 1039, 1040.

ASSEMBLY GENERAL. The supreme ecclesiastical court in Scotland.

ASSENT. Approval of something done. An undertaking to do something in compliance with a request.

In strictness, "assent" is to be distinguished from "consent," which denotes a willingness that something about to be done be done; "acceptance," compliance with, or receipt of, something offered; "ratification," rendering valid something done without authority; and "approval," an expression of satisfaction with some act done for the benefit of another besides the party approving. But in practice the term is often used in the sense of acceptance and approval. Thus, an offer is said to be assented to, although properly an offer and acceptance complete an agreement. It is apprehended that this confusion has arisen from the fact that a request, assent, and concurrence of the party requesting complete a contract as fully as an offer and acceptance. Thus, it is said there must be a request on one side, and assent on the other, in every contract (5 Bing. N. C. 75), and this assent becomes a promise enforceable by the party requesting, when he has done anything to entitle him to the right. Assent thus becomes in reality (so far as it is assent merely, and not acceptance) an offer made in response to a request. Assent and approval as applied to acts of parliament and of congress, have become confounded, from the fact that the bills of parliament were originally requests from parliament to the king. See 1 Bl. Comm. 183.

Express assent is that which is openly declared.

Implied assent is that which is presumed by law.

ASSERTORY COVENANT. One which asserts or warrants the existence of a particular state of facts.

ASSESS. To rate or fix the proportion which every person has to pay of any particular tax.

To tax.

To adjust the shares of a contribution by several towards a common beneficial object, according to the benefit received.

To fix the value of; to fix the amount of.

ASSESSMENT. Determining the value of a man's property or occupation for the purpose of levying a tax.

Determining the share of a tax to be paid by each individual.

Laying a tax.

Adjusting the shares of a contribution by several towards a common beneficial object, according to the benefit received. The term is used in this latter sense in New York, distinguishing some kinds of local taxation, whereby a peculiar benefit arises to the parties, from general taxation. 11 Johns. (N. Y.) 77; 3 Wend. (N. Y.) 263; 4 Hill (N. Y.) 76; 4 N. Y. 419.

——**Of Damages.** Fixing the amount of damages to which the prevailing party in a suit is entitled. It may be done by the court through its proper officer, the clerk or prothonotary, where the assessment is a mere matter of calculation, but must be by a jury in other cases. See "Damages."

——**In Insurance.** An apportionment made in general average upon the various articles and interests at risk, according to their value at the time and place of being in safety, for contribution for damage and sacrifices purposely made, and expenses incurred for escape from impending common peril. 2 Phil. Ins. c. 25.

ASSESSORS. Those appointed to make assessments.

——**In Civil and Scotch Law.** Persons skilled in law, selected to advise the judges of the inferior courts. Bell, Dict.; Dig. 1. 22; Code, 1. 51.

ASSETS (Fr. *assez,* enough). All the stock in trade, cash, and all available property belonging to a merchant or company. Equivalent to "property." 2 Sandf. (N. Y.) 202.

The property in the hands of an heir, executor, administrator, or trustee, which is legally or equitably chargeable with the obligations which such heir, executor, administrator, or other trustee is, as such, required to discharge.

——**Equitable Assets.** Such as can be reached only by the aid of a court of equity, and which are to be divided, *pari passu,* among all the creditors. 2 Fonbl. Eq. 401 et seq.; Willis, Trustees, 118.

——**Legal Assets.** Such as constitute the fund for the payment of debts according to their legal priority.

——**Assets per Descent.** That portion of the ancestor's estate which descends to the heir, and which is sufficient to charge him, as far as it goes, with the specialty debts of his ancestors. 2 Williams, Ex'rs, 1011.

——**Personal Assets.** Goods and personal chattels to which the executor or administrator is entitled.

——**Real Assets.** Such as descend to the heir, as, an estate in fee simple.

ASSETS ENTRE MAINS (Law Fr.) Assets in hand; assets in the hands of executors or administrators, applicable for the payment of debts. Termes de la Ley; 2 Bl. Comm. 510; 1 Crabb, Real Prop. p. 23, § 31. Called, in modern law, "personal assets."

ASSEVERATION. The proof which a man gives of the truth of what he says, by appealing to his conscience as a witness. It differs from an oath in this, that by the latter he appeals to God as a witness of the truth of what he says, and invokes him, as the avenger of falsehood and perfidy, to punish him if he speaks not the truth. See "Affirmation;" "Oath."

ASSEWIARE (Law Lat.) In old records. To draw or drain out water from marshy grounds. Cowell; Blount.

ASSIGN. To make or set over to another. Cowell; 2 Bl. Comm. 326; 5 Johns. (N. Y.) 391.

To appoint; to select; to allot. 3 Bl. Comm. 58.

To set forth; to point out; as, to assign errors. Fitzh. Nat. Brev. 19.

ASSIGNATION. In Scotch law. Assignment. (*q. v.*)

ASSIGNATUS UTITUR JURE AUCTORis. An assigner is clothed with the rights of his principal. Halk. Max. 14; Broom, Leg. Max. (3d London Ed.) 415, 416, 423, 425; Wingate, Max. p. 56; 1 Exch. 32; 18 Q. B. 878.

ASSIGNAY, or ASSIGNEY. In Scotch law. An assignee. "*Airis* and *Assignais,*" 1 Pitc. Crim. Tr. p. 342; "*Aires* or *Assigneys,*" 5 Bell, App. Cas. 83. "*Assignay*" (Law Fr.) occurs in Y. B. M. 7 Edw. III. 5,

ASSIGNEE. One to whom an assignment has been made.

Assignee in fact is one to whom an assignment has been made in fact by the party having the right.

Assignee in law is one in whom the law vests the right; as, an executor or administrator. See "Assignment."

ASSIGNMENT (Law Lat. *assignatio*, from *assigno,—ad* and *signum,*—to mark for; to appoint to one; to appropriate to). At common law. "The transferring and setting over to another of some right, title, or interest in things in which a third party, not a party to the assignment, has a concern and interest." 1 Bac. Abr. 329; 1 Iowa, 582.

It is more loosely used to indicate any transfer or making over to another of the whole of any property, real or personal, in possession or in action, or of any estate or right therein. 35 Fed. 436; 78 Iowa, 101; 3 Minn. 389 (Gil. 282); 16 Barb. (N. Y.) 580.

ASSIGNMENT FOR BENEFIT OF CREDitors. An assignment by an insolvent debtor of his property, in trust for the distribution of such property among the assignor's creditors.

ASSIGNMENT OF DOWER. The act by which the share of a widow in her deceased husband's real estate is ascertained and set apart to her.

The assignment may be made *in pais* by the heir or his guardian, or the devisee or other persons seised of the lands subject to dower (19 N. H. 240; 23 Pick. [Mass.] 80, 88; 4 Ala. [N. S.] 160; 4 Me. 67; 2 Ind. 388; White & T. Lead. Cas. 51), or it may be made after a course of judicial proceedings, where a voluntary assignment is refused. In this case, the assignment will be made by the sheriff, who will set off her share by metes and bounds. 2 Bl. Comm. 136; 1 Washb. Real Prop. 229. The assignment should be made within forty days after the death of the husband, during which time the widow shall remain in her husband's capital mansion house.

ASSIGNMENT OF ERRORS. In practice. The statement of the case of the plaintiff in error on a writ of error setting forth the errors complained of. It corresponds with the declaration in an ordinary action. 2 Tidd, Prac. 1168; 3 Steph. Comm. 644.

In those states in which the remedy by appeal is extended to actions at law and criminal prosecutions, the assignment of errors is a schedule of the errors complained of, filed by appellant, and usually prefixed to his brief.

ASSIGNOR. One who makes an assignment; one who transfers property to another.

ASSIGNS. Assignees; those to whom property shall have been transferred. Now seldom used except in the phrase, in deeds, "heirs, administrators, and assigns."

As used in a covenant to convey land it is not confined to assignees of the contract, but includes grantees. (156 Ill. 210), and as used in a deed it includes tenants for years. (118 Ill. App. 57).

ASSISA (Lat. *assidere*). A kind of jury or inquest. *Assisa vertitur in juratum,* the assize has been turned into a jury. See "Assize."

A writ, as, an assize of *novel disseisin,* assize of common pasture.

An ordinance, as *assisa panis.* Spelman; Litt. § 234; 3 Sharswood, Bl. Comm. 402.

A fixed specific time, sum, or quantity; a tribute; tax fixed by law; a fine. Spelman.

ASSISA ARMORUM. A statute ordering the keeping arms.

ASSISA CADERE. To be nonsuited. Cowell; 3 Bl. Comm. 402.

ASSISA CONTINUANDA. A writ for the continuation of the assize to allow the production of papers. Reg. Orig. 217.

ASSISA DE CLARENDON. The statute of Clarendon, passed 10 Hen. II., allowing an additional time for preparation to persons compelled to abjure the realm. See "Abjuration."

ASSISA DE FORESTA. Assize of the forest (*q. v.*)

ASSISA DE MENSURIS (Law Lat.) Assize of measures. A common rule for weights and measures, established throughout England by Richard I., in the eighth year of his reign. Hale, Hist. Com. Law, c. 7.

ASSISA DE NOCUMENTO. Assize of nuisance. In old English practice, a writ which lay to remove a nuisance, and recover damages. 3 Bl. Comm. 221, 222; Reg. Orig. 197b. Now abolished with the other real actions.

ASSISA DE UTRUM (assize of Utrum). In old English practice. An assize, otherwise called a writ of *juris utrum,* which lay for a parson or prebendary at common law, and for a vicar by St. 14 Edw. III. c. 17, to recover lands and tenements belonging to the church, which were alienated by the predecessor, or of which he was disseised, or which were recovered against him by verdict, confession, or default, without praying in aid of the patron and ordinary, or on which any person had intruded since the predecessor's death. 3 Bl. Comm. 253; Roscoe, Real Actions, 74; Bracton, lib. 4, tr. 5; Fleta, lib. 5, c. 20. It derived its name from the emphatic word in the writ by which the jury were required to determine "whether" (*utrum*) the tenements in question were frankalmoign belonging to the church of the demandant, or the lay fee of the defendant. Bracton, fol. 286; Reg. Orig. 32b. The writ has long been obsolete, principally because of the restraining statute of 13 Eliz. c. 10. 3 Bl. Comm. 253.

ASSISA FRISCAE FORTIAE. Assize of fresh force (*q. v.*)

ASSISA MORTIS ANTECESSORIS (Law Lat.) *Assise of mort d'ancestor (q. v.)* Bracton, lib. 4, tr. 3; Fleta, lib. 4, c. 1; Id. lib. 5, c. 1. Called, also, *assisa de morte antecessoris.*

ASSISA MORTIS D'ANCESTORIS. Assize of *mort d'ancestor (q. v.)*

ASSISA NOVAE DISSEYSINAE. Assize of novel disseisin (*q. v.*)

ASSISA PANIS ET CEREVISLAE (Law Lat.) Assize of bread and ale, or beer. The name of a statute passed in the fifty-first year of Henry III., containing regulations for the sale of bread and ale; sometimes called the "statute of bread and ale." Co. Litt. 159b; 2 Reeve, Hist. Eng. Law, 56; Cowell; Bracton, fol. 155; Barr. Obs. St. 52. The particular provisions of this statute, which are very minute, may be found in Britton and Fleta. Britt. c. 30; Fleta, lib. 2, cc. 9, 11. Spelman considers the statutes passing under the names of *assisa panis, assisa vini et cervisiae,* etc., to belong to an earlier period.

The power or privilege of assising or adjusting the weights and measures of bread and beer. Cowell.

ASSISA PROROGANDA. A writ to stay proceedings where one of the parties is engaged in a suit of the king. Reg. Orig. 208.

ASSISA ULTIMAE PRAESENTATIONIS. Assize of *darrein presentment.*

ASSISA VENALIUM. Statutes regulating the sale of certain articles. Spelman.

ASSISORS. In Scotch law. Jurors.

ASSISTANCE. See "Writ of Assistance."

ASSISUS (Lat. from *assidere,* to fix or settle). In old English law. Fixed or certain. *Assisus reditus,* a fixed, certain, or pending rent. Kennett, Par. Ant. 314, 335. Called "rent of assize." 2 Bl. Comm. 42. *Terra assisa,* land let or farmed out for a certain assessed rent. Cowell.

ASSITHMENT. Compensation by a pecuniary mulct. Cowell.

ASSIZE (Lat. *assidere,* to sit by or near, through the Fr. *assisa,* a session).

——**In English Law.** A writ directed to the sheriff for the recovery of immovable property, corporeal or incorporeal. Cowell; Litt. § 234.

The action or proceedings in court based upon such a writ. Magna Charta, c. 12; St. 13 Edw. I. (Westminster II.) c. 25; 3 Bl. Comm. 57, 252; Sellon, Prac. Introd. xii.

Such actions were to be tried by special courts, of which the judicial officers were justices of assize. See "Courts of Assize and Nisi Prius." This form of remedy is said to have been introduced by the parliament of Northampton (or Nottingham, A. D. 1176), for the purpose of trying titles to land in a more certain and expeditious manner before commissioners appointed by the crown than before the suitors in the county court or the king's justiciars in the *aula regis.* The action is properly a mixed action, whereby the plaintiff recovers his land and damages for the injury sustained by the disseisin. The value of the action as a means for the recovery of land led to its general adoption for that purpose; those who had suffered injury not really amounting to a disseisin alleging a disseisin to entitle themselves to the remedy. The scope of the remedy was also extended so as to allow the recovery of incorporeal hereditaments, as franchises, estovers, etc. It gave place to the action of ejectment, and is now abolished, having been previously almost, if not quite, entirely disused. St. 3 & 4 Wm. IV. c. 27, § 36. Stearns, Real Actions, 187.

A jury summoned by virtue of a writ of assize.

The verdict or judgment of the jurors or recognitors of assize. 3 Bl. Comm. 57, 59.

A court composed of an assembly of knights and other substantial men, with the baron or justice, in a certain place, at an appointed time. Grand Coutum, cc. 24, 25.

An ordinance or statute. Litt. § 234; Reg. Orig. 239. Anything reduced to a certainty in respect to number, quantity, quality, weight, measure, etc. 2 Sharswood, Bl. Comm. 42; Cowell; Spelman, "Assisa." See the articles immediately following.

——**In Scotch Law.** The jury, consisting of fifteen men, in criminal cases tried in the court of judiciary. Paterson, Comp.; Bell, Dict.

ASSIZE OF DARREIN PRESENTMENT. A writ of assize which formerly lay for a person who had himself, or whose ancestors had upon the last preceding avoidance, presented a clerk to a benefice where a stranger presented a clerk for the purpose of obtaining a writ commanding the bishop to institute the patron's clerk, and to obtain damages for the interference. 3 Sharswood, Bl. Comm. 245; St. 13 Edw. I. (Westminster II.) c. 5. It has given way to the remedy by *quare impedit.*

ASSIZE OF FRESH FORCE. A writ of assize which lay where the disseisin had been committed within forty days. Fitzh. Nat. Brev. 7.

ASSIZE OF MORT D'ANCESTOR. A writ of assize which lay to recover possession of lands against an abator or his alienee. It lay where the ancestor from whom the claimant derived title died seised. Cowell; Spelman; 3 Sharswood, Bl. Comm. 185.

ASSIZE OF NOVEL DISSEISIN. A writ of assize which lay where the claimant had been lately disseised. The action must have been brought subsequent to the next preceding session of the eyre or circuit of justices which took place once in seven years. Co. Litt. 153; Booth, Real Actions, 210.

ASSIZE OF NUISANCE. A writ of assize which lay where a nuisance had been committed to the complainant's freehold.

The complainant alleged some particular fact done which worked an injury to his freehold (*ad nocumentum liberi tenementi sui*), and, if successful, recovered judgment for the abatement of the nuisance, and also for damages. Fitzh. Nat. Brev. 183; 3 Sharswood, Bl. Comm. 221; 9 Coke, 55.

ASSIZE OF THE FOREST. A statute or ordinance concerning the royal forests passed in the thirty-third year of Edw. I. Otherwise called *Ordinatio Forestae*. Another statute of the same title was passed in the thirty-fourth year of Edw. I. 2 Reeve, Hist. Eng. Law, 104, 106; Co. Litt. 159b.

ASSIZE OF UTRUM. A writ of assize which lay for a parson to recover lands which his predecessor had improperly allowed the church to be deprived of. 3 Bl. Comm. 257. See "Assisa De Utrum."

ASSIZE RENT. The fixed or established rent of the freeholders and ancient copyholders of a manor, which cannot be departed from or varied. 2 Bl. Comm. 42.

ASSIZES. Sessions of the justices or commissioners of assize. These assizes are held twice in each year in each of the various shires of England, with some exceptions, by virtue of several commissions, for the trial of matters of fact in issue in both civil and criminal cases. They still retain the ancient name in popular language, though the commission of assize is no longer issued. 3 Steph. Comm. 424, note. See "Assize;" "Nisi Prius;" "Courts of Assize and Nisi Prius."

ASSIZES DE JERUSALEM. A code or feudal law prepared at a general assembly of lords after the conquest of Jerusalem. It was compiled principally from the laws and customs of France. It was reduced to form by Jean d'Iblin, Comte de Japhe et Ascalon, about the year 1290. 1 Fournel, Hist. des Av. 49; 2 Dupin, Prof. des Av. 674-680; Steph. Pl. Append. xi.

ASSOCIATED PRESS. A corporation organized under the laws of the state of Illinois in 1892, whose object is to buy, gather and accumulate information and news to vend, supply, distribute and publish the same; to purchase, erect, lease, operate and sell telegraph and telephone lines and other means of transmitting news to public periodicals; to make and deal in periodicals and other goods, wares and merchandise. 184 Ill. 442.

ASSOCIATION. The act of a number of persons in uniting for some purpose, whether social, business or benevolent.

The persons so joining, or the organization by them formed.

Though the term covers any united action, however temporary, it is generally applied to a formal union under an associate name, and by an agreement known as "articles of association." The organization resembles a corporation, but the powers and liabilities of its members and representatives are more nearly related to those of a partnership, from which they differ in having no *delectus personarum*, and in the fact that the authority as to the public is in officers, and not in the members generally. See "Joint-Stock Company."

——**In English Law.** A writ directing certain persons (usually the clerk and his subordinate officers) to associate themselves with the justices and sergeants for the purpose of taking the assizes. 3 Sharswood, Bl. Comm. 59.

ASSOIL, ASSOILE, or **ASSOILYIE.** To set free; to deliver from excommunication. St. 1 Hen. IV. c. 7; Cowell.

ASSOILZIE. In Scotch law. To acquit.

ASSOYL. (Law. Fr.) To forgive; to pardon; to absolve. *Que Dieu assoyl*, whom God assoil; on whom God have mercy. Kelham.

ASSUME. To take on; to undertake. 90 Cal. 147. To take in appearance. See 75 Cal. 73.

The word "assume," used in deeds with reference to incumbrances on the property conveyed, has the same meaning as if the words "to pay" followed it, and amounts to a personal covenant to pay. 243 Ill. 557; 194 Ill. 224.

The definition of the word "assume," in law, is "to take upon one's self." 194 Ill. 222; 93 Ill. App. 263.

ASSUMED RISKS. Risks which the law implies the servant to have assumed as part of his contract of employment, and for injuries to the servant arising out of which the master is not liable.

ASSUMPSIT (Lat. *assumere,* to assume, to undertake; *assumpsit,* he has undertaken).

——**In Contracts.** An undertaking, either express or implied, to perform a parol agreement. 1 Lilly, Reg. 132.

Express *assumpsit* is an undertaking made orally by writing not under seal, or by matter of record, to perform an act, or to pay a sum of money to another.

Implied *assumpsit* is an undertaking presumed in law to have been made by a party, from his conduct, although he has not made any express promise.

——**In Practice.** A form of action which lies for the recovery of damages for the nonperformance of a parol or simple contract. 7 Term R. 351; 3 Johns. Cas. (N. Y.) 60.

It differs from debt, since the amount claimed need not be liquidated (see "Debt"), and from covenant, since it does not require a contract under seal to support it (see "Covenant"). See 4 Coke, 91; 4 Burrows, 1008; 14 Pick. (Mass.) 428; 2 Metc. (Mass.) 181. *Assumpsit* is one of the class of actions called "actions upon the case," and in the older books is called "action upon the case upon *assumpsit.*" Comyn, Dig.

Special *assumpsit* is an action of *assumpsit* brought upon an express contract or promise.

General *assumpsit,* sometimes called *indebitatus assumpsit,* is an action of *assumpsit* brought upon the promise or contract implied by law in certain cases. See 2 Smith, Lead. Cas. (5th Am. Ed.) 14.

See "Common Counts."

ASSUMPTION. The agreement of the transferee of property to pay obligations of the transferer which are chargeable on it. 194 Ill. 222.

ASSUMPTION OF RISK. A term of the contract of employment, either express or implied from the circumstances of the employment, by which the servant agrees that dangers obviously incident to the discharge of his duty shall be at the servant's risk.

Assumption of risk is to be distinguished from contributory negligence in that the first rests on the law of contracts, while the latter rests on the law of torts.

ASSURANCE.

——**In Conveyancing.** Any instrument which confirms the title to an estate.

Legal evidence of the transfer of property. 2 Bl. Comm. 294.

The term "assurances" includes, in an enlarged sense, all instruments which dispose of property, whether they be the grants of private persons, or not; such are fines and recoveries, and private acts of the legislature. Eunom. Dial. 2, § 5.

——**In Commercial Law.** A term formerly used in English maritime law, in the sense of the modern term "insurance," and still retained in policies, but otherwise obsolete. Molloy de Jur. Mar. 287. Latterly, however, its use has been revived in its application to contracts of indemnity against life contingencies, which are now frequently termed "assurances upon lives," by way of distinction from indemnity against losses by fire or at sea, etc., to which the term "insurance" is particularly appropriated. 3 Kent, Comm. 365. The word "assured" has always been retained in its ancient sense. See "Assure." "Assurance" is the term used in French law. Ord. Mar. liv. 3, tit. 6; Emerig. Tr. des Assur.

ASSURE (Fr. *assurer;* law Lat. *assecurare, assurare*). To make sure, or secure; to confirm or establish; to insure. The party in whose favor a contract or policy of insurance has been executed is still called the "assured;" the other party being termed the "insurer." 2 Steph. Comm. 172.

To convey. "If one be obliged to assure twenty acres of land," etc. Cro. Eliz. 665. See "Assurance."

ASSURED. A person who has been insured by some insurance company or underwriter against losses or perils mentioned in the policy of insurance.

ASSURER. An insurer; an underwriter.

ASSYTHEMENT. In Scotch law. Damages awarded to the relative of a murdered person from the guilty party, who has not been convicted and punished. Paterson, Comp.

The action to recover it lies for the personal representatives (26 Scott. Jur. Sc. 156), and may be brought by collateral relations (27 Scott. Jur. Sc. 450).

ASTIPULATION. A mutual agreement.

ASTITRARIUS HAERES. An heir apparent who hath been, by conveyance of his ancestors, placed in a dwelling house in the ancestor's lifetime. Co. Litt. 8.

ASTITUTION. Arraignment (*q. v.*)

ASTRARIUS (from *astre,* a hearth). A householder.

ASTRER. In old English law. A householder, or occupant of a house or hearth. Britt. 59.

ASTRICT. In Scotch law. To assign to a particular mill

Used of land, the occupants of which were bound to grind at a certain mill. Bell, Dict.; Paterson, Comp. note 290; Ersk. Inst. 2. 9. 18. 32.

ASTRIHILTET. In Saxon law. A penalty for a wrong done by one in the king's peace. The offender was to replace the damage twofold. Spelman.

ASTRUM. A house, or place of habitation. Bracton, fol. 367b; Cowell.

ASYLUM. An institution for the protection or relief of the unfortunate, as an asylum for the poor, for the deaf and dumb, or for the insane. Webster.

——**In International Law.** Refuge to a fugitive from justice.

——**In old English Law.** A sanctuary (*q. v.*)

AT. The word "at" is generally used as a word of limitation, but its meaning is governed by the context, which determines whether it is to be used in an inclusive or exclusive sense.

As applied to place, it means a relation of proximity to; nearness; near; about. 70 Ill. App. 242.

In its customary acceptation, the word "at," used as descriptive of time, is generally understood to mean "at the time of," —not before or after. 154 Ill. 247.

AT ARM'S LENGTH. As applied to dealings, formality and vigilance on both sides; absence of confidence or personal influence.

AT BAR. Before the court; under consideration; as the case at bar.

AT ISSUE. Whenever the parties come to a point in the pleadings which is affirmed on one side and denied on the other, they are said to be "at issue." 215 Ill. 154; 136 Ill. 52.

AT LARGE.

(1) Not limited to any particular question or matter.

(2) Free; unrestrained; not under corporal control; as a ferocious animal so free from restraint as to be liable to do mischief.

(3) Representing no particular place or district; as delegate at large.

(4) *In extenso.*

AT LAW. According to the course of the common law; in the law.

AT SEA. Outside of port. In opposition to being "in port;" not in opposition to being "at home." 3 Hill (N. Y.) 118.

ATHA, ATTA, ATHE, or ATTE. In Saxon law. An oath. Cowell; Spelman.

Athes, or *athaa*, a power or privilege of exacting and administering an oath in certain cases. Cowell; Blount.

ATHEIST. One who does not believe in the existence of a God.

ATIA. See "De Odio et Atia."

ATILIUM (Lat.) Tackle; the rigging of a ship; plough tackle. Spelman.

ATTACH. See "Apprehension."

ATTACHE. One attached to the suite of an ambassador; one attached to a foreign legation.

ATTACHIAMENTA DE SPINIS ET boscis. A privilege granted to the officers of a forest to take to their own use thorns, brush, and windfalls, within their precincts. Kennett, Par. Ant. 209.

ATTACHIAMENTUM. In old English law. An attachment. *Attachiamenta bonorum*, attachment of goods. Spelman; Reg. Orig. 18. *Solemnitas attachiamentorum*, the formality of attachments; the practice of issuing them one after another in a regular series. Bracton, fol. 437.

ATTACHMENT. Taking into the custody of the law the person or property of one already before the court, or of one whom it is sought to bring before it.

A writ for the accomplishment of this purpose. This is the more common sense of the word.

——**Of Persons.** A writ issued by a court of record, commanding the sheriff to bring before it a person who has been guilty of contempt of court.

——**Of Property.** A writ issued at the institution or during the progress of an action, commanding the sheriff or other proper officer to attach the property, rights, credits, or effects of the defendant to satisfy the demands of the plaintiff.

The original design of this writ was to secure the appearance of one who had disregarded the original summons, by taking possession of his property as a pledge. 3 Bl. Comm. 280.

By an extension of this principle, in the New England states, properly attached remains in the custody of the law after an appearance, until final judgment in the suit. See 7 Mass. 127.

In some states, attachments are distinguished as foreign and domestic,—the former issued against a nonresident of the state, the latter against a resident. Where this distinction is preserved, the foreign attachment inures solely to the benefit of the party suing it out; while the avails of the domestic attachment may be shared by other creditors, who come into court and present their claims for that purpose.

ATTACHMENT OF PRIVILEGE. In English law. A process by which a man, by virtue of his privilege, calls another to litigate in that court to which he himself belongs, and who has the privilege to answer there.

A writ issued to apprehend a person in a privileged place. Termes de la Ley.

ATTACHMENT OF THE FOREST. One of the three courts formerly held in forests. The highest court was called "justice in eyre's seat;" the middle, the "swainmote;" and the lowest, the "attachment." Manw. For. Law, 90, 99.

ATTAINDER. That extinction of civil rights and capacities which takes place whenever a person who has committed treason or felony receives sentence of death for his crime. 1 Steph. Comm. 408; 1 Bish. Crim. Law, § 641.

Attainder by confession is either by pleading guilty at the bar before the judges, and not putting one's self on one's trial by a jury, or before the coroner in sanctuary, when, in ancient times, the offender was obliged to abjure the realm.

Attainder by verdict is when the prisoner at the bar pleads not guilty to the indictment, and is pronounced guilty by the verdict of the jury.

Attainder by process or outlawry is when the party flies, and is subsequently outlawed. Co. Litt. 391.

The effect of attainder upon a felon is, in general terms, that all his estate, real and personal, is forfeited; that his blood is corrupted, and so nothing passes by inheritance to, from, or through him (1 Wm. Saund. 361, note; 6 Coke, 63a, 68b; 2 Rob. Ecc. 547; 24 Eng. Law & Eq. 598); that he cannot sue in a court of justice (Co. Litt. 130a). See 2 Gibbett, Crim. Law; 1 Bish. Crim. Law, § 641.

ATTAINDER, BILL OF. See "Bill of Attainder."

ATTAINT. Attainted, stained, or blackened.

A writ which lies to inquire whether a jury of twelve men gave a false verdict. Bracton, lib. 4, tr. 1, c. 134; Fleta, lib. 5, c. 22, § 8.

This latter was a trial by jury of twenty-four men impanelled to try the goodness of a former verdict. 3 Bl. Comm. 351; 3 Gilb. Ev. (Lofft Ed.) 1146. See "Assize."

ATTAINT D'UNE CAUSE. In French law. The gain of a suit. *Estre attaint en uncan cas*, to be overcome in any case. Cowell.

ATTEMPT. In criminal law. An endeavor to accomplish a crime carried beyond mere preparation for it, but falling short of the ultimate design. 5 Cush. (Mass.) 367. The elements are (1) intent to commit a crime; (2) an affirmative act in pursuance of that intent, but falling short of the crime intended 1 Bish. Crim. Law, § 510. Such act need not be "the last proximate act to the consummation of the crime in contemplation, but it is sufficient if it be an act apparently adapted to produce the result intended. It must be more than mere preparation." 86 Va. 382.

ATTENDANT. One who owes a duty or service to another, or in some sort depends upon him. Termes de la Ley.

ATTENDANT TERMS. Long leases or mortgages so arranged as to protect the title of the owner. Thus, to raise a portion for younger children, it was quite common to make a mortgage to trustees. The powers of these trustees were generally to take possession of the estate, or to sell a part of the term if the portions were not duly paid. If the deed did not become *ipso facto* void, upon payment of the portion, a release was necessary from the trustees to discharge the mortgage. If this was not given, the term became an outstanding satisfied term. The purchaser from the heir then procured an assignment of the term to trustees for his benefit, which then became a satisfied term to attend the inheritance, or an attendant term. These terms were held attendant by the courts, also, without any assignment, and operated to defeat intermediate alienations to some extent. There were other ways of creating outstanding terms besides the method by mortgage, but the effect and general operation of all these were essentially the same. 1 Washb. Real Prop. 311; 4 Kent, Comm. 86-93.

ATTENTAT. In the civil and canon law. Anything whatsoever wrongfully innovated or attempted in the suit by the judge *a quo*, pending an appeal. 1 Add. Ecc. 22, note; Ayliffe, Par. 100.

ATTERMINARE (Lat.) To put off to a succeeding term; to prolong the time of payment of a debt. St. Westminster II. c. 4; Cowell; Blount.

ATTERMINING. The granting a time or term for the payment of a debt.

ATTERMOIEMENT. In canon law. A making terms; a composition, as with creditors. 7 Low. (U. S.) 272, 306.

ATTESTATION (Lat. *ad*, to, *testari*, to witness). The act of witnessing an instrument in writing, at the request of the party making the same, and subscribing it as a witness. 3 P. Wms. 254; 2 Ves. Jr. 454; 1 Ves. & B. 362; 3 A. K. Marsh. (Ky.) 146; 17 Pick. (Mass.) 373.

ATTESTATION CLAUSE. That clause wherein the witnesses certify that the instrument has been executed before them, and the manner of the execution of the same.

ATTESTING WITNESS. One who, upon being required by the parties to an instrument, signs his name to it to prove it, and for the purpose of identification. 3 Campb. 232.

ATTESTOR OF A CAUTIONER. In Scotch practice. A person who attests the sufficiency of a cautioner, and agrees to become *subsidiarie* liable for the debt. Bell, Dict.

ATTILE. In old English law. Rigging; tackle. Cowell.

ATTORN. To turn over; to transfer to another money or goods; to assign to some particular use or service. Kennett, Par. Ant. 283.

——**In Feudal Law.** Used of a lord's transferring the homage and service of his tenant to a new lord. Bracton, 81, 82; 1 Sullivan, Lect. 227.

——**In Modern Law.** For the tenant of one to acknowledge or agree that the fee is in another, or that such other is his landlord. 3 A. K. Marsh. (Ky.) 611.

A valid attornment may be made to one in privity with the landlord, as to the vendee on sale of the premises, but an attornment to a stranger is void.

ATTORNARE. In the feudal law. To attorn.

ATTORNARE REM. To attorn or turn over a thing, as money and goods, *i. e.*, to assign or appropriate them to some particular use and service. Kennett, Par. Ant. 283; Cowell.

ATTORNATO FACIENDO VEL RECIPIendo. An obsolete writ, which commanded a sheriff or steward of a county court or hundred court to receive and admit an attorney to appear for the person who owed suit of court. Fitzh. Nat. Brev. 156.

ATTORNE (Law Fr.) In old English law. An attorney. Britt. c. 126.

ATTORNEY. One put in the place, turn, or stead of another, to manage his affairs; one who manages the affairs of another by direction of his principal. Spelman; Termes de la Ley.

One who acts for another by virtue of an appointment by the latter.

——**Attorney in Fact.** A person to whom the authority of another, who is called the "constituent," is by him lawfully delegated.

——**Attorney at Law.** A person licensed to manage causes in court for the parties thereto.

In England, attorneys at law are divided into barristers or counsel, who are advocates admitted to plead at the bar, and solicitors or attorneys who engage in the drawing of pleadings, preparation of evidence, etc. These latter are called "attorneys" in courts of law, "solicitors" in courts of equity, and "proctors" in admiralty. The distinction between barristers and attorneys or solicitors obtained for a time in some of the United States, but is now obsolete.

ATTORNEY GENERAL.

——**In English Law.** A great officer, under the king, made by letters patent, whose office is to exhibit informations, and prosecute for the crown in matters criminal; to file bills in the exchequer in any matter concerning the king's revenue. Others may bring bills against the kings' attorney. 3 Sharswood, Bl. Comm. 27; Termes de la Ley.

——**In American Law.** In each state there is an attorney general, or similar officer, who appears for the people, as in England he appears for the crown.

ATTORNEY GENERAL OF THE UNITed States. A member of the president's cabinet. His duties are to prosecute and conduct all suits in the supreme court in which the United States shall be concerned, and give his advice upon questions of law when required by the president, or when requested by the heads of any of the departments, touching matters that may concern their departments. Act Sept. 24, 1789.

ATTORNEY OF THE WARDS AND liveries. The third officer of the Duchy court. Bac. Abr. tit. "Attorney."

ATTORNEY'S CERTIFICATE. In English law. A certificate of the commissioners of stamps that the attorney therein named has paid the annual duty. This must be renewed yearly, and the penalty for practicing without such certificate is fifty pounds. St. 37 Geo. III. c. 90, §§ 26, 28, 30. See, also, 7 & 8 Vict. c. 73, §§ 21-26; 16 & 17 Vict. c. 63.

ATTORNMENT. See "Attorn."

ATTRACTIVE NUISANCE. A machine or other dangerous thing or place which is especially attractive to children, who, in obedience to their childish instincts, are likely to be drawn to it, but which is dangerous to them. 256 Ill. 406.

Attractive nuisances fall into two classes:

First—Where the injury results from some dangerous element a part of, or inseparably connected with, the alluring thing or device, as in the turn-table cases.

Second—Where the attractive device or thing is so located or situated that in yielding to its allurement the child, without such intervention of another element as breaks the relation or cause and effect, is brought directly in contact with danger from some independent source which occasions the injury. 224 Ill. 585.

AU BESOIN (Fr. in case of need). "*Au besoin chez Messieurs* —— *a* ——," "In case of need, apply to Messrs. —— at ——."

A phrase used in the direction of a bill of exchange, pointing out the person to whom application may be made for payment in case of failure or refusal of the drawee to pay. Story, Bills, § 65.

AUBAINE. See "Droit d'Aubaine."

AUCTION. A public sale of property to the highest bidder.

The manner of conducting an auction is immaterial, whether it be by public outcry, or by any other manner. The essential part is the selection of a purchaser from a number of bidders. In a case where a woman continued silent during the whole time of the sale, but whenever any one bid she gave him a glass of brandy, and, when the sale broke up, the person who received the last glass of brandy was taken into a private room and he was declared to be the purchaser, this was adjudged to be an auction. 1 Dowl. Bailm. 115.

AUCTIONARIUS (Lat.) A seller; a regrator; a retailer; one who bought and sold; an auctioneer, in the modern sense. Spelman. One who buys poor, old, worn-out things to sell again at a greater price. Du Cange.

AUCTIONEER. A person authorized by law to sell the goods of others at public sale; one who conducts a public sale or auction.

AUCTOR.

—**In Roman Law.** An auctioneer.

In auction sales, a spear was fixed upright in the forum, besides which the seller took his stand; hence goods thus sold were said to be sold *sub hasta* under the spear. The catalogue of goods was on tablets called *auctionariae.*

—**In Old French Law.** A plaintiff. See "Actor."

AUCTORITAS.

—**In Civil Law.** Authority. Brissonius.

—**In old European law.** A diploma, or royal charter. A word frequently used by Gregory of Tours and later writers. Spelman.

AUCTORITATES PHILOSOPHORUM, medicorum et poetarum, sunt in causis allegandae et tenendae. The opinions of philosophers, physicians, and poets are to be alleged and received in causes. Co. Litt. 264.

AUCUPIA VERBORUM SUNT JUDICE indigna. Catching at words is unworthy of a judge. Hob. 343.

AUDI ALTERAM PARTEM. Hear the other side; hear both sides. No man should be condemned unheard. Broom, Leg. Max. 113. See L. R. 2 P. C. 106.

AUDIENCE (Lat. *audire,* to hear). A hearing or interview.

It is usual for the executive of a country to whom a minister has been sent to give such minister an audience; and after a minister has been recalled, an audience of leave usually takes place.

AUDIENCE COURT. In English law. A court belonging to the archbishop of Canterbury, and held by him in his palace for the transaction of matters of form only, as the confirmation of bishops, elections, consecrations, and the like. This court has the same authority with the court of arches, but is of inferior dignity and antiquity. The dean of the arches is the official auditor of the audience. The archbishop of York has also his audience court. Termes de la Ley.

AUDIENDO ET TERMINANDO. A writ or commission to certain persons to appease and punish any insurrection or great riot. Fitzh. Nat. Brev. 110.

AUDIT. To examine, adjust, settle, etc., an account, and then allow it. 3 Denio (N. Y.) 381; 5 Daly (N. Y.) 200; 24 Hun (N. Y.) 419.

AUDITA QUERELA (Lat.) A form of action which lies for a defendant to recall or prevent an execution, on account of some matter occurring after judgment amounting to a discharge, and which could not have been, and cannot be, taken advantage of otherwise. 12 Mass. 270.

It is a regular suit, in which the parties appear and plead (17 Johns. [N. Y.] 484; 12 Vt. 56, 435; 30 Vt. 420; 8 Miss. 103), and in which damages may be recovered if execution was issued improperly (Brooke, Abr. "Damages," 38), but the writ must be allowed in open court, and is not of itself a *supersedeas* (2 Johns. [N. Y.] 227).

It is a remedial process, equitable in its nature, based upon facts, and not upon the erroneous judgments or acts of the court. 2 Wm. Saund. 148, note; 10 Mass. 103; 14 Mass. 448; 17 Mass. 159; 1 Aik. (Vt.) 363; 24 Vt. 211; 2 Johns. Cas. (N. Y.) 227; 1 Overt. (Tenn.) 425. And see 7 Gray (Mass.) 206.

In modern practice, the same relief is usually granted on motion, and the writ is dismissed.

The original purpose of this writ is said to have been relieving a party from the wrongful acts of his adversary and permitting him to show any matter of discharge which may have occurred since the rendition of the judgment.

AUDITOR (Lat. *audire,* to hear). An officer of the government, whose duty it is to examine the accounts of officers who have received and disbursed public moneys by lawful authority. Acts Cong. April 3, 1817, and Feb. 24, 1819; 3 Story, U. S. Laws, 1630, 1722; 4 Inst. 107; 46 Geo. III. c. 1.

—**In Practice.** An officer (or officers) of the court, assigned to state the items of debit and credit between the parties in a suit where accounts are in question, and exhibit the balance. 1 Metc. (Mass.) 218.

They may be appointed by courts either of law or equity. They are appointed at common law in actions of account (Bac. Abr. "Accompt" [F]), and in many of the states in other actions, under statute regulations (6 Pick. [Mass.] 193; 14 N. H. 427; 3 R. I. 60).

AUDITORS OF THE IMPREST. Officers in the English exchequer, who formerly had the charge of auditing the accounts of the customs, naval and military expenses, etc., now performed by the commissioners for auditing public accounts. Wharton.

AUGMENTATION. The increase arising to the crown's revenues from the suppression of monasteries and religious houses, and the appropriation of their lands and revenues.

A court erected by Henry VIII., which was invested with the power of determining suits and controversies relating to monasteries and abbey lands. The court was dissolved in the reign of Mary; but the office of augmentations remained long after. Cowell.

A share of the great tithes temporarily granted to the vicars by the appropriators, and made perpetual by St. 29 Car. II. c. 8. The word is used in used in a similar sense in the Canadian law.

AUGUSTA LEGIBUS SOLUTA NON est. The empress or queen is not privileged or exempted from subjection to the laws. 1 Bl. Comm. 219; Dig. 1. 3. 31.

AULA, HAULA, or **HALLA.** In old English law. A hall, or court; the court of a baron, or manor; a court baron; a hall or chief mansion house; the usual appanage of a manor. Whitshaw; Spelman.

AULA REGIA, or **AULA REGIS.** In English law. The king's hall or palace. A court established in England by William the Conqueror in his own hall.

AULNAGE, or **ALNAGE.** A duty collected on the putting on of the seals on the assise of woolen cloth. The officer charged with such duty was called "aulnage," "alnager," or "ulnager."

AUMONE, SERVICE IN. Where lands are given in alms to a church or religious house, upon condition that masses, service, or prayers shall be offered at certain times for the repose of the donor's soul. Britt. 164.

AUNCEL WEIGHT. An ancient manner of weighing by means of a beam held in the hand. Termes de la Ley; Cowell.

AURES. In Saxon law. The punishment of cutting off the ears.

AURUM REGINAE. (Queen's gold (*q. v.*) 1 Bl. Comm. 219, 220.

AUTER (Law Fr.) Another. This word is frequently used in composition, as *auter droit, auter vie, auter action,* etc.

AUTER ACTION PENDANT (Law Fr. another action pending). In pleading. A plea that another action is already pending. This plea may be made either at law or in equity. 1 Chit. Pl. 393; Story, Eq. Pl. § 736.

AUTER DROIT. Another right; in another's right. See "En Auter Droit."

AUTHENTIC ACT. In civil law. An act which has been executed before a notary or other public officer authorized to execute such functions, or which is testified by a public seal, or has been rendered public by the authority of a competent magistrate, or which is certified as being a copy of a public register. Nov. 73, c. 2; Code, 7. 52; Id. 6. 4. 21; Dig. 22. 4.

An act which has been executed before a notary public or other officer authorized to execute such functions, in presence of two witnesses, free, male, and aged at least fourteen years; or of three witnesses, if the party be blind. Civ. Code La. art. 2231. If the party does not know how to sign, the notary must cause him to affix his mark to the instrument. Id. art. 2231. The authentic act is full proof of the agreement contained in it, against the contracting parties and their heirs or assigns, unless it be declared and proved to be a forgery. Id. art. 2233. See Merlin, Repert.

AUTHENTICATION. In practice. A proper or legal attestation.

Acts done with a view of causing an instrument to be known and identified.

Under the constitution of the United States, congress has power to provide a method of authenticating copies of the records of a state with a view to their production as evidence in other states. For the various statutes on the subject, see "Foreign Judgment;" "Record."

AUTHENTICS. A collection of the Novels of Justinian, made by an unknown person. They are entire, and are distinguished by their name from the epitome made by Julian. See 1 Mackeld. Civ. Law, § 72.

A collection of extracts made from the Novels by a lawyer named Irnier, and which he inserted in the Code at the places to which they refer. These extracts have the reputation of not being correct. Merlin Repert. "Authentique."

AUTHENTICUM (Lat.) In the civil law. An original instrument or writing; the original of a will or other instrument, as distinguished from a copy. Dig. 22. 4. 2; Id. 29. 3. 12.

AUTHORITIES. Enactments and opinions relied upon as establishing or declaring the rule of law which is to be applied in any case.

The opinion of a court, or of counsel, or of a text writer upon any question, is usually fortified by a citation of authorities.

AUTHORITY. Power.

——**In Contracts.** The power lawfully delegated to a person by another.

Authority coupled with an interest is an authority given to an agent for a valuable consideration, or which forms part of a security.

Express authority is that given explicitly, either in writing or verbally.

General authority is that which authorizes the agent to do everything connected with a particular business. Story, Ag. § 17. It empowers him to bind his employer by all acts within the scope of his employment, and it cannot be limited by any private order or direction not known to the party dealing with him. Paley, Ag. 199-201.

Limited authority is that where the agent is bound by precise instructions.

Special authority is that which is confined to an individual transaction. Story, Ag. § 19; 15 East, 400, 408; 6 Cow. (N. Y.) 354. Such an authority does not bind the employer, unless it is strictly pursued, for it is the business of the party dealing with the agent to examine his authority, and therefore, if there be any qualification or express restriction annexed to it, it must be observed; otherwise, the principal is discharged. Paley, Ag. 202.

Naked authority is that where the principal delegates the power to the agent wholly for the benefit of the former. A naked authority may be revoked; an authority coupled with an interest is irrevocable.

Unlimited authority is that where the agent is left to pursue his own discretion.

——**In Governmental Law.** The right and power which an officer has, in the exercise of a public function, to compel obedience to his lawful commands. A judge, for example, has authority to enforce obedience to his lawful orders.

AUTO ACORDADO. In Spanish colonial law. An order emanating from some superior tribunal, promulgated in the name and by the authority of the sovereign. Schmidt, Civ. Law, 93.

AUTOCRACY. A government where the power of the monarch is unlimited by law.

AUTONOMY. The state of independence. The *autonomos* was he who lived according to his own laws,—who was free. The term was chiefly used of communities or states, and meant those which were independent of others. It was introduced into the English language by the divines of the seventeenth century, when it and its translation—self-government—were chiefly used in a theological sense. Gradually its translation received a political meaning, in which it is now employed almost exclusively. Of late the word "autonomy" has been revived in diplomatic language in Europe, meaning "independence," the negation of a state of political influence from without or foreign powers. See Lieber, Civ. Lib.

AUTOPSY. Dissection of a dead body for the purpose of ascertaining the cause, seat, or nature of a disease; a *post mortem* examination.

AUTRE, AUTRY, AUTRI, or **AUTER** (Law Fr.) Other; another. Britt. c. 54; Kelham.

AUTRE (or **AUTER**) **VIE** (Law Fr. another's life). A person holding an estate for oı during the life of another is called a tenant *"pur autre vie,"* or *"pur terme d'autre vie."* Litt. § 56; 2 Bl. Comm. 120.

AUTREFOIS. Formerly; heretofore.

AUTREFOIS ACQUIT (Fr. formerly acquitted). A plea made by a defendant indicted for a crime, that he has formerly been tried and acquitted of the same offense. See "Jeopardy."

AUTREFOIS ATTAINT (Fr. formerly attainted). In criminal pleading. A plea that the defendant has been attainted for one felony, and cannot, therefore, be criminally prosecuted for another. 4 Bl. Comm. 336. Now obsolete.

AUTREFOIS CONVICT (Fr. formerly convicted). In criminal pleading. A plea made by a defendant indicted for a crime or misdemeanor, that he has formerly been tried and convicted of the same. This plea is substantially the same in form as the plea of *autrefois acquit,* and is grounded on the same principle, viz., that no man's life or liberty shall be twice put in jeopardy for the same offense. 1 Bish. Crim. Law, §§ 651-680; 1 Green (N J.) 362; 1 McLean (U. S.) 429; 7 Ala. 610; 2 Swan (Tenn.) 493.

A plea of *autrefois convict* which shows that the judgment on the former indictment has been reversed for an error in the judgment, is not a good bar to another indictment for the same offense. 3 Car. & K. 190. But a prior conviction by judgment before a justice of the peace, and a performance of the sentence pursuant to the judgment, constitute a bar to an indictment for the same offense, although the complaint on which the justice proceeded was so defective that his judgment might have been reversed for error. 3 Metc. (Mass.) 328; 8 Metc. (Mass.) 532. See "Jeopardy."

AUXILIA AD FILIUM MILITEM FAciendum vel ad filiam maritandam. Aids to make the lord's son a knight, or to marry his daughter. See "Aids." Bracton, fol. 36b.

AUXILIUM (Lat.) An aid; tribute or services paid by the tenant to his lord.

AUXILIUM CURIAE. An order of the court summoning one party, at the suit and request of another, to appear and warrant something. Kennett, Par. Ant. 477.

AUXILIUM REGIS. A subsidy paid to the king. Spelman.

AUXILIUM VICE COMITI. An ancient duty paid to sheriffs. Cowell; Whishaw.

AVAIL OF MARRIAGE.

——**In Scotch Law.** A certain sum due by the heir of a deceased ward vassal, when the heir became of marriageable age. Ersk. Inst. lib. 2, tit. 5, § 18.

——**In Feudal Law.** The right of a guardian in chivalry to dispose of the hand of his ward in marriage. 2 Bl. Comm. 88.

AVAILS. In wills, the net proceeds of the estate; that which remains after paying debts. See 3 N. Y. 276.

AVAL. In Canadian law. An act of suretyship or guaranty on a promissory note. 1 Low. (U. S.) 221; 9 Low. (U. S.) 360.

AVANTURE (Law Fr.) Chance; hazard; mischance. Kelham.

AVARIA, or **AVARIE.** Average; the loss and damage suffered in the course of a navigation. Poth. du Contr. de Louage, 105.

AVENGE (Law Lat.) In old English law. A certain quantity of oats paid to a landlord in lieu of some other duties, or as a rent from the tenant. Cowell. A rent paid in oats.

AVENTURE, or **ADVENTURE.** A mischance causing the death of a man, as by drowning, or being killed suddenly without felony. Co. Litt. 391; Whishaw.

AVER. To assert. See "Averment."

To make or prove true; to verify. The defendant will offer to aver. Cowell; Co. Litt. 362b.

Cattle of any kind. Cowell; Kelham.

AVER CORN. A rent reserved to religious houses, to be paid in corn; corn drawn by the tenant's cattle. Cowell.

AVER ET TENIR (or **TENER**). To have and to hold. See "Habendum."

AVER LAND. Land ploughed by the tenant for the proper use of the lord of the soil. Blount.

AVER PENNY. Money paid to the king's averages to be free therefrom. Termes de la Ley.

AVER SILVER. A rent formerly so called. Cowell.

AVERAGE. In marine insurance. Loss or damage to a part of the vessel or cargo insured.

The contribution due from one owner to another, on a partial loss.

——**General Average.** General (also called "gross") average consists of expense purposely incurred, sacrifice made, or damage sustained for the common safety of the vessel, freight, and cargo, or the two of them, at risk, and is to be contributed for by the several interests in the proportion of their respective values exposed to the common danger, and ultimately surviving, including the amount of expense, sacrifice or damage so incurred in the contributory value. 2 Phil. Ins. § 1269 et seq.; and see 2 Curt. C. C. (U. S.) 59; 9 Cush. (Mass.) 415; 93 Ky. 102; 5 Ohio, 307; 3 Wall. (U. S.) 370; 3 Kent, Comm. 232.

——**Particular Average.** Particular average (also called "partial loss") is an accidental loss on the ship, cargo, or freight, to be borne by the owner of the subject on which it happens, and is so called in distinction from general average, and, if not total, it is also called a partial loss. 2 Phil. Ins. c. 16; 3 Bosw. (N. Y.) 395; 4 B. Mon. (Ky.) 164.

AVERIA (Lat.) Cattle; working cattle. *Averia carucae* (draft cattle) are exempt from distress. 3 Bl. Comm. 9; 4 Term R. 566.

AVERIA CARUCAE. Beasts of the plow, which, at common law, were privileged over other cattle.

AVERIA OTIOSA. Idle beasts; as distinguished from *averia carucae*, beasts of the plow.

AVERIIS CAPTIS IN WITHERNAM. In English law. A writ which lies in favor of a man whose cattle have been unlawfully taken by another, and driven out of the county where they were taken, so that they cannot be replevied.

It issues against the wrongdoer to take his cattle for the plaintiff's use. Reg. Brev. 82.

AVERMENT. In pleading. A positive statement of facts, as opposed to an argumentative or inferential one. Cowp. 683; Bac. Abr. "Pleas" (B).

Averments must contain not only matter, but form.

In old pleading, the conclusion of a plea, whereby the pleader alleged his readiness to verify the foregoing.

Averments were formerly said to be general and particular; but only particular averments are found in modern pleading. 1 Chit. Pl. 277.

——**Particular Averments.** The assertions of particular facts. There must be an averment of every substantive material fact on which the party relies, so that it may be replied to by the opposite party.

——**Negative Averments.** Those in which a negative is asserted. Generally, under the rules of pleading, the party asserting the affirmative must prove it; but an averment of illegitimacy (2 Selw. N. P. 709), or criminal neglect of duty, must be proven (2 Gall. [U. S.] 498; 19 Johns. [N. Y.] 345; 1 Mass. 54; 10 East, 211; 3 Campb. 10; 3 Bos. & P. 302; 1 Greenl. Ev. § 80; 3 Bouv. Inst. note 3089).

——**Immaterial and Impertinent Averments.** Those which need not be made, and, if made, need not be proved. They are synonymous. 5 Dowl. & R. 209. The allegation of deceit in the seller of goods in action on the warranty is such an averment. (2 East, 446; 17 Johns. [N. Y.] 92).

——**Unnecessary Averments.** Statements of matters which need not be alleged, but which, if alleged must be proved. Carth. 200.

AVERRARE, or AVERARE. In feudal law. To carry goods upon loaded horses or in a wagon; a duty formerly required of some customary tenants. Spelman. To drive cattle (*averia*) to some fair or market. Cowell.

AVERSIO (Lat.) An averting; a turning away; a sale in gross or in bulk.

Letting a house altogether, instead of in chambers. 4 Kent, Comm. 517.

AVERSIO PERICULI. An averting or turning away of peril. A name given to the contract of insurance (marine) because one of the parties undertakes to avert from the other the peril of the sea. According to Emerigon, the words signify that the insurer charges himself with, and takes upon himself, the peril which the things insured run upon the sea. Tr. des Assur. c. 1, pr. See 3 Kent, Comm. 263; Locc. de Jur. Mar. lib. 2, c. 5, § 1.

AVERUM (Lat.) Goods; property; a beast of burden. Spelman.

AVET. In Scotch law. To abet or assist. Tomlin.

AVIZANDUM. In Scotch law. To make *avizandum* with a process is to take it from the public court to the private consideration of the judge. Bell, Dict.

AVOCAT (Fr.) Advocate; an advocate. Ord. Mar. liv. 1, tit. 3.

AVOIDANCE. A making void, useless, or empty.

——**In Ecclesiastical Law.** It exists when a benefice becomes vacant for want of an incumbent.

——**In Pleading.** Repelling or excluding the conclusions or implications arising from the admission of the truth of the allegations of the opposite party. See "Confession and Avoidance."

AVOIRDUPOIS. The name of a weight. This kind of weight is so named, in distinction from the Troy weight. One pound avordupois contains seven thousand grains Troy; that is, fourteen ounces, eleven pennyweights and sixteen grains Troy; a pound avoirdupois contains sixteen ounces; and an ounce, sixteen drachms. Thirty-two cubic feet of pure spring water, at the temperature of fifty-six degrees of Fahrenheit's thermometer, make a ton of two thousand pounds avoirdupois, or two thousand two hundred and forty pounds net weight. Dane, Abr. c. 211, art 12, § 6. The avoirdupois ounce is less than the Troy ounce in the proportior of 72 to 79, though the pound is greater. Enc. Amer. "Avoirdupois." For the derivation of this phrase, see Barr. Obs. St. 206. See the Report of Secretary of State of the United States to the Senate, February 22, 1821, pp. 44, 72, 76, 79, 81, 87, for a learned exposition of the whole subject.

AVOUCHER. See "Voucher."

AVOUE.

——**In Old French Law.** A feudal chief who acted as protector of a church or monastery; the suzerain of the fief.

——**In Modern French Law.** A barrister; advocate; attorney. Duverger.

AVOW. To acknowledge the commission of an act, and claim that it was done with right. 3 Bl. Comm. 150.

To make an avowry. For example, when replevin is brought for a thing distrained, and the party taking claims that he had a right to make the distress, he is said to avow. See Fleta, lib. 1, c. 4, § 4; Cunningham. See "Avowry;" "Justification."

AVOWANT. One who makes an avowry.

AVOWEE, or AVOWE. See "Advowee."

AVOWRY. In pleading. The answer of the defendant in an action of replevin brought to recover property taken in distress, in which he acknowledges the taking, and, setting forth the cause thereof, claims a right in himself or his wife to do so. 4 Bouv. Inst. note 3571; 3 Bl. Comm. 149.

A justification is made where the defendant shows that the plaintiff had no property, by showing either that it was the defendant's or some third person's, or where he shows that he took it by a right which was sufficient at the time of taking, though not subsisting at the time of answer. The avowry admits the property to have been the plaintiff's, and shows a right which had then accrued, and still subsists, to make such caption. See Gilb. Distr. 176-178; 2 W. Jones, 25.

AVOWTERER. In English law. An adulterer with whom a married woman continues in adultery. Termes de la Ley.

AVOWTRY. In English law. The crime of adultery.

AVULSION (Lat. *avellere,* to tear away). The removal of a considerable quantity of soil from the land of one man, and its deposit upon or annexation to the land of another, suddenly and by the perceptible action of water. 2 Washb. Real Prop. 452. In such case, the property belongs to the first owner. Bracton, 221; Hargrave, Tract. de Jure Mar.; Schultes, Aq. Rights, 115-138. The perceptible character of the deposit distinguishes it from accretion (*q. v.*) See also, "Reliction."

AWAIT. To lay in wait; to waylay.

AWARD (Law. Lat. *awarda, awardum;* old French, *agarda,* from *a garder*). To keep, preserve; to be guarded, or kept. So called because it is imposed on the parties to be observed or kept by them. Spelman.

The judgment or decision of arbitrators or referees on a matter submitted to them. The writing containing such judgment. Cowell; Termes de la Ley; 3 Bouv. Inst. note 2402.

AWAY-GOING CROP. A crop sown before the expiration of a tenancy, which cannot ripen until after its expiration, to which, however, the tenant is entitled. Broom, Leg. Max. 306. See "Emblements."

AWM, or **AUME.** An ancient measure used in measuring Rhenish wines. Termes de la Ley. Its value varied in the different cities. Cowell.

AYANT CAUSE. In French law. This term, which is used in Louisiana, signifies one to whom a right has been assigned, either by will, gift, sale, exchange, or the like; an assignee. An *ayant cause* differs from an heir who acquires the right by inheritance. 8 Toullier, Dr. Civ. note 245.

AYRE In old Scotch law. Eyre; a circuit, eyre, or iter. Bell, Dict. voc. "Justice Ayres."

AYUNTAMIENTO. In Spanish law. A congress of persons; the municipal council of a city or town. 1 White, New Coll. 416; 12 Pet. (U. S.) 442, note.

B

B. F. *Bonum factum,* a good deed. A form of approval among the civilians.

BACEREND, or **BACKBEREND.** An old English law term for a thief caught with the stolen goods in his possession (upon his back). Spelman; Bracton, 150b.

BACHELERIA. Commonalty or yeomanry, in contradistinction to baronage. Wharton.

BACHELOR.

(1) The holder of the first or lowest degree conferred by a college or university, *e. g.,* a bachelor of arts, bachelor of law, etc.

(2) A kind of inferior knight; an esquire.

(3) A man who has never been married.

BACK BOND. A bond of indemnification given to a surety.

——**In Scotch Law.** A declaration of trust; a defeasance; a bond given by one who is apparently absolute owner, so as to reduce his right to that of a trustee or holder of a bond and disposition in security. Paterson, Comp.

BACK WATER. That water in a stream which, in consequence of some obstruction below, is detained or checked in its course, or reflows.

The term is usually employed to designate the water which is turned back, by a dam erected in the stream below, upon the wheel of a mill above, so as to retard its revolution.

BACKADATION, or **BACKWARDATION.** A consideration given to keep back the delivery of stock when the price is lower for time than for ready money. Wharton.

BACKBEAR. In forest law. Carrying on the back. One of the cases in which an offender against vert and venison might be arrested, as being taken with the mainour, or manner, or found carrying a deer off on his back. Manw. For. Law; Cowell.

BACKBEREND (Saxon). See "Bacerend."

BACKING. Indorsement; indorsement by a magistrate.

Backing a warrant becomes necessary when it is desired to serve it in a county other than that in which it was first issued. In such a case the indorsement of a magistrate of the new county authorizes its service there as fully as if first issued in that county. The custom prevails in England, Scotland, and some of the United States.

BACKSIDE. A yard at the back part of or behind a house, and belonging thereto.

The term was formerly much used both in conveyances and in pleading, but is now of infrequent occurrence, except in conveyances which repeat an ancient description. Chit. Prac. 177; 2 Ld. Raym. 1399.

BACULUS (Lat.) In old English practice. A staff, rod, or wand, anciently used in the ceremony of making livery of seisin, where there was no building on the land. *Fiat seysina per fustim et per baculum,* seisin should be made by rod and staff. Bracton, fol. 40; Fleta, lib. 3, c. 15, § 5. *Baculus nuntiatorius,* a warning or summoning stick. A white stick or wand, by erecting which on the grounds of a defendant in real actions he was anciently warned or summoned to appear in court at the return of the original writ. 8 Bl. Comm. 379.

A baton, such as combatants fought with in the *duellum. Frangitur eorum baculus,* their baton is broken.

A term anciently applied to persons convicted of a felony on their own confession, signifying that they could not bring an appeal against any one. Bracton, fol. 152. See Fleta, lib. 1, c. 38, § 16; 2 Reeve, Hist. Eng. Law, 43. See "Baston."

BADGE OF FRAUD. A circumstance attending a transaction tending to throw upon it suspicion of fraud, though not in itself constituting fraud. 64 N. C. 374.

An act which, from the common experience of mankind, is regarded as ground of suspicion.

BADGER (Fr.) Baggage, a bundle, and thence is derived *bagagier,* a carrier of goods.

One who buys corn or vituals in one place, and carries them to another to sell and make profit by them. And such a one is exempted in St. 5 & 6 Edw. VI. c. 14, from the punishment of an ingrosser within that statute. But by 5 Eliz. c. 12, badgers are to be licensed by the justices of the peace in the sessions, whose licenses will be in force for one year, and no longer, and the persons to whom granted must enter into a recognizance that they will not, by color of their licenses, forstall, or do anything contrary to the statutes made against forestallers, ingrossers, and regrators. If any person shall act as a badger without license, he is to forfeit £5, one moiety to the king, and the other to the prosecutor, leviable by warrant from justices of the peace, etc. Jacob.

BAGA (Law Lat.) In old English law. Bag; a bag. *Et d'denvers eux unam bagam, ove C. 1. in ead' baga content.* Y. B. M. 18 Hen. VI. 5. See "Petty Bag Office."

BAGGAGE. Whatever, connected with the objects of the journey, and not exceeding the limits of reason and custom, a traveller takes with him for his personal use, whether during actual travel, or in intervals between trips, or upon the termination of the journey. Bish. Non-Cont. Law, § 1156.

It does not include samples of merchandise (98 Mass. 83), money not necessary for travelling (22 Ill. 278), jewelry intended for presents (17 N. Y. Super. Ct. 225).

It includes weapons (22 Ill. 278), books (121 Ind. 226), tools (14 Pa. St. 129), opera glasses (33 Ind. 379), bedding for use on the trip (1 Whit. & W. Civ. Cas. Ct. App. [Tex.] § 1253).

BAHADUM. A chest or coffer. Fleta, lib. 2, c. 21.

BAIL (Fr. *bailler*, to deliver). Those persons who become sureties for the appearance of the defendant in court.

The delivery of the defendant to persons who, in the manner prescribed by law, become security for his appearance in court.

The word is used both as a substantive and a verb, though more frequently as a substantive, and in civil cases, at least, in the first sense given above. In its more ancient signification, the word includes the delivery of property, real or personal, by one person to another.

——**Bail Above.** Sureties who bind themselves either to satisfy the plaintiff his debt and costs, or to surrender the defendant into custody, provided judgment be against him in the action, and he fail to do so. Sellon, Prac. 137.

——**Bail to the Action.** Bail above.

——**Bail Below.** Sureties who bind themselves to the sheriff to secure the defendant's appearance, or his putting in bail to the action on the return day of the writ. It may be demanded by the sheriff whenever he has arrested a defendant on a bailable process, as a prerequisite to releasing the defendant.

——**Bail to the Sheriff.** Bail below.

——**Civil Bail.** That taken in civil actions.

——**Common Bail.** Fictitious sureties formally entered in the proper office of the court. It is a kind of bail above, similar in form to special bail, but having fictitious persons, John Doe and Richard Doe, as sureties. Filing common bail is tantamount to entering an appearance.

——**Special Bail.** Responsible sureties who undertake as bail above.

——**Bail in Error.** The bond given to secure a stay of proceedings on writ of error.

——**In Canadian Law.** A lease. See Merlin, Repert. "Bail." *Bail emphyteotique*, a lease for years, with a right to prolong indefinitely. 5 Low (U. S.) 381. It is equivalent to an alienation. 6 Low. (U. S.) 58.

BAIL BOND. In practice. A specialty by which the defendant and other persons become bound to the sheriff in a penal sum proportioned to the damages claimed in the action, and which is conditioned for the due appearance of such defendant to answer to the legal process therein described, and by which the sheriff has been commanded to arrest him.

BAIL PIECE. A certificate given by a judge or the clerk of a court, or other person authorized to keep the record, in which it is certified that the bail became bail for the defendant in a certain sum, and in a particular case.

BAILABLE ACTION. An action in which the defendant is entitled to be discharged from arrest only upon giving bond to answer.

BAILABLE PROCESS. Process under which the sheriff is directed to arrest the defendant, and is required by law to discharge him upon his tendering suitable bail as security for his appearance. A *capias ad respondendum* is bailable; not so a *capias ad satisfaciendum.*

BAILEE. Contracts. One to whom goods are bailed. See "Bailment."

BAILIE. In Scotch law. An officer appointed to give infeftment.

In certain cases it is the duty of the sheriff, as king's bailie, to act. Generally, any one may be made bailie by filling in his name in the praecept of sasine.

A magistrate possessing a limited criminal and civil jurisdiction. Bell, Dict.

BAILIFF. A person to whom some authority, care, guardianship, or jurisdiction is delivered, committed, or intrusted. Spelman.

A sheriff's officer or deputy. 1 Bl. Comm. 344.

A magistrate, who formerly administered justice in the parliaments or courts of France, answering to the English sheriffs as mentioned by Bracton.

There are still bailiffs of particular towns in England; as, the bailiff of Dover Castle, etc.; otherwise, bailiffs are now only officers or stewards, etc.; as bailiffs of liberties, appointed by every lord within his liberty, to serve writs, etc.; bailiffs errant or itinerant, appointed to go about the country for the same purpose; sheriff's bailiffs, sheriff's officers to execute writs; these are also called "bound bailiffs," because they are usually bound in a bond to the sheriff for the due execution of their office; bailiffs of court baron, to summon the court, etc.; bailiffs of husbandry, appointed by private persons to collect their rents and manage their estates; water bailiffs, officers in port towns for searching ships, gathering tolls, etc. Bac. Abr.

——**In Account Render.** A person who has by delivery the custody and administration of lands or goods for the benefit of the owner or bailor, and is liable to render an account thereof. Co. Litt. 271; 2 Leon. 245; Story, Eq. Jur. § 446.

BAILIFF ERRANT. A deputy bailiff.

BAILIFFS OF FRANCHISES. In English law. Officers who perform the duties of sheriffs within liberties or privileged jurisdictions, in which formerly the king's writ could not be executed by the sheriff. Spelman, voc. "Balivus."

BAILIFFS OF HUNDREDS. In English law. Officers appointed over hundreds, by the sheriffs to collect fines therein, and summon juries; to attend the judges and justices at the assizes and quarter sessions; and also to execute writs and process in the several hundreds. 1 Bl. Comm. 345; 3 Steph. Comm. 29; Bracton, fol. 116.

BAILIFFS OF MANORS. In English law. Stewards or agents appointed by the lord (generally by an authority under seal) to superintend the manor, collect fines and quitrents, inspect the buildings, order repairs, cut down trees, impound cattle trespassing, take an account of wastes, spoils and misdemeanors in the woods and demesne lands, and do other acts for the lord's interest. Cowell; Fleta, lib. 2, cc. 72, 73.

BAILIVIA. A bailiwick (*q. v.*) Wharton.

BAILIWICK. The jurisdiction of a sheriff or bailiff. 1 Bl. Comm. 344.

A liberty or exclusive jurisdiction which was exempted from the sheriff of the county, and over which the lord appointed a bailiff, with such powers within his precinct as the under sheriff exercised under the sheriff of the county. Wishaw.

BAILLEW DE FONDS. In Canadian law. The unpaid vendor of real estate.

BAILLI. In old French law. A person to whom judicial authority and jurisdiction were assigned or delivered by a superior.

BAILMENT (Fr. *bailler*, to put into the hands of; to deliver). A delivery of something of a personal nature by one party to another, to be held according to the purpose or object of the delivery, and to be returned or delivered over when that purpose is accomplished. Prof. Joel Parker, MSS. Lect. Dane Law School, Harvard Coll. 1851.

The right to hold may terminate, and a duty of restoration may arise, before the accomplishment of the purpose, but that does not necessarily enter into the definition, because such duty of restoration was not the original purpose of the delivery, but arises upon a subsequent contingency. The party delivering the thing is called the "bailor;" the party receiving it, the "bailee." It is distinguished from a sale by the fact that in bailment only the right of possession, and not the title, is transferred. Benj. Sales, §§ 1, 2.

Various attempts have been made to give a precise definition of this term, upon some of which there have been elaborate criticisms. See Story, Bailm. (4th Ed.) § 2, note 1, exemplifying the maxim, *Omnis definitio in lege periculosa est.*

Some of these definitions are here given as illustrating more completely than is possible in any other way the elements considered necessary to a bailment by the different authors cited.

A delivery of a thing in trust for some special object or purpose, and upon a contract, express or implied, to conform to the object or purpose of the trust. Story, Bailm. § 2. See Merlin, Repert. "Bail."

A delivery of goods in trust upon a contract, either expressed or implied, that the trust shall be faithfully executed on the part of the bailee. 2 Bl. Comm. 451. See Id. 395.

A delivery of goods in trust on a contract, tract, expressed or implied, that the trust shall be duly executed, and the goods restored by the bailee as soon as the purposes of the bailment shall be answered. 2 Kent, Comm. 559.

A delivery of goods on a condition, express or implied, that they shall be restored by the bailee to the bailor, or according to his directions, as soon as the purpose for which they are bailed shall be answered. Jones, Bailm. 1.

A delivery of goods in trust on a contract, either expressed or implied, that the trust shall be duly executed, and the goods redelivered as soon as the time or use for which they were bailed shall have elapsed or be performed. Jones, Bailm. 117.

According to Story, the contract does not necessarily imply an undertaking to redeliver the goods; and the first definition of Jones here given would seem to allow of a similar conclusion. On the other hand, Blackstone, although his definition does not include the return, speaks of it in all his examples of bailments as a duty of the bailee; and Kent says that the application of the term to cases in which no return or delivery or redelivery to the owner or his agent is contemplated, is extending the definition of the term beyond its ordinary acceptation in the English law. A consignment to a factor would be a bailment for sale, according to Story, while according to

Kent it would not be included under the term "bailment."

Sir William Jones has divided bailments into five sorts, namely, *depositum*, or deposit; *mandatum*, or commission without recompense; *commodatum*, or loan for use without pay; *pignori acceptum*, or pawn; *locatum*, or hiring, which is always with reward. This last is subdivided into *locatio rei*, or hiring, by which the hirer gains a temporary use of the thing; *locatio operis faciendi*, when something is to be done to the thing delivered; *locatio operis mercium vehendarum*, when the thing is merely to be carried from one place to another. Jones, Bailm. 36.

Lord Holt divides them into six classes: *Depositum*, or deposit for keeping for the benefit of the bailor; *commodatum*, or gratuitous loan; *locatio rei*, or letting for hire; *vadium*, pledge or pawn; *locatio operis faciendi*, or delivery that something may be done upon the chattels by the bailee for hire; *mandatum*, or mandate, a delivery that something may be done upon the chattels by the bailee gratuitously. 2 Ld. Raym. 909.

A better general division, however, for practical purposes, suggested, but not adopted, by Story (Bailm. §§ 4-8), and first adopted by Schouler (Bailm. § 14), is into three kinds: First, those bailments which are for the benefit of the bailor, or for some person whom he represents; second, those for the benefit of the bailee, or some person represented by him; third, those which are for the benefit of both parties.

BAILOR. He who bails a thing to another. See "Bailment."

BAIR-MAN. In Scotch law. A poor debtor.

BAIRNS. In Scotch law. A known term, used to denote one's whole issue. Ersk. Inst. 3. 8. 48. But it is sometimes used in a more limited sense. Bell, Dict.

BAIRNS' PART. In Scotch law. Children's part; a third part of the defunct's free movables, debts deducted, if the wife survive, and a half if there be no relict.

BALAENA. A large fish, called by Blackstone a "whale." Of this the king had the head and the queen the tail as a perquisite whenever one was taken on the coast of England. Prynne, Ann. Reg. 127; 1 Bl. Comm. 221.

BALANCE. The amount which remains due by one of two persons, who have been dealing together, to the other, after the settlement of their accounts.

"There is a broad distinction between an account and the mere balance of an account, resembling the distinction in logic between the premises of an argument and the conclusions drawn therefrom. A balance is but the conclusion or result of the debit and credit sides of an account. It implies mutual dealings and the existence of debit and credit, without which there could be no balance." 45 Mo. 573.

The word is sometimes used in the sense of "residue."

BALANCE SHEET. A statement made by merchants and others to show the true state of a particular business. A balance sheet should exhibit all the balances of debits and credits, also the value of merchandise, and the result of the whole.

BALCANIFER, or **BALDAKINIFER.** The standard bearer of the Knights Templar. Wharton.

BALDIO. In Spanish law. Vacant land having no particular owner, and usually abandoned to the public for the purposes of pasture. The word is supposed to be derived from the Arabic *balt*, signifying a thing of little value. For the legislation on this subject, see Escriche, Dic. Raz.

BALIUS. In civil law. A teacher; one who has the care of youth; a tutor; a guardian. Du Cange, "Bajultis;" Spelman.

BALIVA, or **BALLIVA.** Equivalent to *balivatus*. *Balivia*, a bailiwick; the jurisdiction of a sheriff; the whole district within which the trust of the sheriff was to be executed. Cowell. Occurring in the return of the sheriff, *non est inventus in balliva mea*, he has not been found in my bailiwick; afterwards abbreviated to the simple *non est inventus*. 3 Bl. Comm. 283.

BALIVO AMOVENDO (Law Lat. for removing a bailiff). A writ to remove a bailiff out of his office.

BALLAST. Heavy substance carried in the hold of a ship to trim her, and bring her to a safe and proper draft. It differs from "dunnage" (*q. v.*) 13 Wall. (U. S.) 674.

Rock, gravel or other material placed on the roadbed of a railway to support and retain the ties and track.

BALLASTAGE. A toll paid for the privilege of taking up ballast from the bottom of the port. This arises from the property in the soil. 2 Chit. Com. Law, 16.

BALLOT. A paper bearing the names of candidates for designated offices, and delivered by electors to the election officers in expressing their choice for such offices. It is usually printed, and is in various prescribed forms, especially in states which have adopted the Australian ballot system, or modifications of it.

BALNEARII (Lat.) Those who stole the clothes of bathers in the public baths. 4 Bl. Comm. 239; Calv. Lex.

BAN.

——In Old English and Civil Law. A proclamation; a public notice; the announcement of an intended marriage. Cowell. An excommunication; a curse, publicly pronounced; proclamation of silence made by a crier in court before the meeting of champions in combat. Cowell. A statute, edict, or command; a fine, or penalty.

An open field; the outskirts of a village; a territory endowed with certain privileges. A summons, as, *arriere ban.* Spelman.

——In French Law. The right of announcing the time of mowing, reaping, and gathering the vintage, exercised by certain seignorial lords. Guyot, Rep. Univ.

BANAL, or **BANNAL** (Fr.) In old French and Canadian law. Having qualities derived from a ban or privileged space; privileged. A banal mill is one to which the seignior or lord may require his tenant to carry his grain to be ground. Dunkin's Address, 89.

BANALITY. In Canadian law. The right by virtue of which a lord subjects his vassals to grind at his mill, bake at his oven, etc. Used also of the region within which this right applied. Guyot, Rep. Univ. It prevents the erection of a mill within the seignorial limits (1 Low. [U. S.] 31), whether steam or water (3 Low. [U. S.] 1).

BANC (Fr. bench). The seat of judgment; as, *banc le roy,* the king's bench; *bance le common pleas,* the bench of common pleas; the full bench.

BANCI NARRATORES. In old English law. Advocates; countors; serjeants. Applied to advocates in the common pleas courts. 1 Bl. Comm. 24; Cowell.

BANCUS (Lat.) A bench; the seat or bench of justice; a stall or table on which goods are exposed for sale. Often used for the court itself.

A full bench, when all the judges are present. Cowell; Spelman.

The English court of common pleas was formerly called "*bancus.*" Viner, Abr. "Courts." See "Bench;" "Common Bench."

BANCUS REGINAE (Law Lat.) The queen's bench.

BANCUS REGIS (Lat.) The king's bench; the supreme tribunal of the king after parliament. 3 Sharswood, Bl. Comm. 41.

In banco regis, in or before the court of king's bench.

The king has several times sat in his own person on the bench in this court, and all the proceedings are said to be *coram rege ipso,* before the king himself. Still, James I. was not allowed to deliver an opinion, although sitting *in banco regis.* Viner, Abr. "Courts" (H. L.); 3 Bl. Comm. 41; Co. Litt. 71 (C).

BANCUS SUPERIOR (Lat.) Abbreviated *banc. sup.* The upper bench; the king's bench was so called during the Protectorate.

BAND. In old Scotch law. A proclamation calling out a military force. 1 Pitc. Crim. Tr. pt. 1, p. 205.

BANDIT. A man outlawed; one under ban.

BANE. A malefactor. Bracton, lib. 1, tit. 8, c. 1.

BANI. Forfeited goods; deodand (*q. v.*)

BANISHMENT. A punishment inflicted upon criminals, by compelling them to quit a city, place, or country for a specified period of time, or for life. See 4 Dall. (Pa.) 14. It is to be distinguished from "transportation," which implies a confinement in some place beyond the realm.

BANK (Anglicised form of *bancus,* a bench). The bench of justice.

A session in bank is one held by more than one judge of the court to determine matters of law.

Distinguished from *nisi prius* sittings to determine facts. 3 Sharswood, Bl. Comm. 28, note.

Bank le roy, the king's bench. Finch, Law, 198.

——In Commercial Law. A place for the deposit of money.

An institution, generally incorporated, authorized to receive deposits of money, to lend money, and to issue promissory notes. —usually known by the name of "bank notes,"—or to perform some one or more of these functions.

Banks are said to be of three kinds, viz., of deposit, of discount, and of circulation. They generally perform all these operations, but an institution performing but one is a bank. 17 Wall. (U. S.) 118; but see 52 Cal. 196. A corporation loaning its own funds on note and mortgage is not a bank. 5 Sawy. (U. S.) 32.

It was the custom of the early money changers to transact their business in public places, at the doors of churches, at markets, and, among the Jews, in the temple (Mark xi. 15). They used tables or benches for their convenience in counting and assorting their coins. The table so used was called *banche,* and the traders themselves, "bankers," or ""benchers." In times still more ancient, their benches were called *cambii,* and they themselves were called *cambiators.* Du Cange, "Cambii."

BANK ACCOUNT. A fund deposited by a customer of a bank into its common cash, to be drawn out by checks from time to time, as the depositor may require.

The statement of the amount deposited and drawn, which is kept in duplicate, one in the depositor's bank book, and the other in the books of the bank.

BANK BILLS. Demand notes of a bank, designed to circulate as money. See 3 Scam. (Ill.) 328.

BANK NOTE. A promissory note, payable on demand to the bearer, and intended to circulate as money, made and issued by a person or persons acting as bankers, and authorized by law to issue such notes.

BANKABLE. Bank notes, checks and other securities for money which will be received as cash by the banks in the place where the word is used.

BANKER. A dealer in capital,—an intermediate party between the borrower and the lender,—who borrows of one party and lends to another; and the business of banking is, among other things, the establishing of a common fund for lending money. 163 Ill. 65.

BANKEROUT. Old English. Bankrupt.

BANKER'S NOTE. A promissory note given by a private banker or banking institution not incorporate, but resembling a bank note in all other respects. 6 Mod. 29; 3 Chit. Com. Law, 590; 1 Leigh, N. P. 338.

BANKRUPT. (See "Banque.") A person against whom an involuntary petition or an application to set a composition aside has been filed, or who has filed a voluntary petition, or who has been adjudged a bankrupt. U. S. Bankrupt Act 1898, § 1. Loosely used for "insolvent." (*q. v.*)

BANKRUPTCY. The state or condition of a bankrupt. See "Insolvency." (*q. v.*)

BANLEUCA. A certain space surrounding towns or cities, distinguished by peculiar privileges. Spelman. It is the same as the French *banlieue.*

BANLIEU. In Canadian law. See "Banleuca."

BANNERET, or BANERET. One knighted on the field. So called, according to Wharton, from the formula of cutting off the point of his standard, so as to make it a banner.

BANNI NUPTIARUM (Law Lat.) In old English law. The bans of matrimony. Spelman; Cowell. Bracton uses the singular, *bannum.* Bracton, fol. 307b. Fleta uses *bannus.* Fleta, lib. 5, c. 30, § 3. See "Bannum;" "Bannus."

BANNIRE AD PLACITA, AD MOLENdinum. To summon tenants to serve at the lord's courts, to bring corn to be ground at his mill.

BANNITUS. One outlawed or banished. Calv. Lex.

BANNUM. A ban. (*q. v.*)

BANNUS. In old English law. A proclamation. *Banuus regis*, the king's proclamation, made by the voice of a herald, forbidding all present at the trial by combat to interfere, either by motion or word, whatever they might see or hear. Bracton, fol. 142; Fleta, lib. 1, c. 34, § 1.

The bans of marriage. Fleta, lib. 5, c. 30, § 3.

BANQUE. A bench; the table or counter of a trader, merchant, or banker. *Banque route,* a broken bench or counter; bankrupt, or, in old English, *bankerout.*

BANS OF MATRIMONY. Public notice or proclamation of a matrimonial contract, and the intended celebration of the marriage of the parties in pursuance of such contract, to the end that persons objecting to the same may have an opportunity to declare such objections before the marriage is solemnized. Poth. du Mariage, p. 2, c. 2.

BAR.

(1) A particular part of the court room. As thus applied, and secondarily in various ways, it takes its name from the actual bar, or inclosing rail, which originally divided the bench from the rest of the room, as well as from that bar, or rail, which then divided, and now divides, the space including the bench, and the place which lawyers occupy in attending on and conducting trials, from the body of the court room. Those who, as advocates or counsellors, appeared as speakers in court, were said to be "called to the bar," that is, called to appear in presence of the court, as barristers, or persons who stay or attend at the bar of court. Rich. Dict. "Barrister." By a natural transition, a secondary use of the word was applied to the persons who were so called, and the advocates were, as a class, called "the bar." And in this country, since attorneys, as well as counsellors, appear in court to conduct causes, the members of the legal profession, generally, are called the "bar."

(2) The court, in its strictest sense, sitting in full term.

Thus, a civil case of great consequence was not left to be tried at *nisi prius*, but was tried at the "bar of the court itself," at Westminster. 3 Bl. Comm. 352. So a criminal trial for a capital offense was had "at bar" (4 Bl. Comm. 351), and in this sense the term "at bar" is still used. It is also used in this sense, with a shade of difference (as not distinguishing *nisi prius* from full term, but as applied to any term of the court), when a person indicted for crime is called "the prisoner at the bar," or is said to stand at the bar to plead to the indictment. See Merlin, Repert. "Barreau;" 1 Dupin, Prof. d'Av. 451.

(3) An obstacle or opposition. Thus, relationship within the prohibited degrees, or the fact that a person is already married, is a bar to marriage.

(4) A perpetual destruction of the action of the plaintiff. 1 Ore. 47.

(5) Bar in the old books is sometimes used for "plea in bar." Co. Litt. 303b.

BAR FEE. In English law. A fee taken by the sheriff, time out of mind, for every prisoner who is acquitted. Bac. Abr. "Extortion."

BARAGARIA (Spanish). A concubine.

BARATRIAM COMMITTIT QUI PROPTER pecuniam justitiam baractat. He is guilty of barratry who for money sells justice. Bell, Dict. Barratry at common law has a different signification. See "Barratry."

BARBANUS. In old Lombardic law. An uncle (*patruus*). Spelman.

BARBICANAGE. Money paid to support a barbican or watch tower.

BARE TRUSTEE. See "Trustee."

BARET (Law Fr.) A wrangling suit. Britt. c. 92; Co. Litt. 368b.

BARGAIN. An agreement between parties concerning the sale of property; or a contract, by which one party binds himself to transfer the right to some property for a consideration, and the other party binds himself to receive the property and pay the consideration, an agreement or stipulation of any kind. 209 Ill. 477.

BARGAIN AND SALE. A contract or bargain by the owner of land, in consideration of money or its equivalent paid, to sell land to another person, called the "bargainee," whereupon a use arises in favor of the latter, to whom the seisin is transferred by force of the statute of uses. 2 Washb. Real Prop. 128.

A real contract, whereby a person bargains and sells his lands to another for a pecuniary consideration, in consequence of which a use arises to the bargainee, and by the statute of uses the legal estate and actual possessions are immediately transferred to the *cestui que use* without any entry or other act on his part, thus dispensing with livery of seisin. Devl. Deeds, § 23.

BARGAINEE. The grantee of an estate in a deed of bargain and sale; the person to whom property is tendered in a bargain.

BARGAINOR. The person who makes a bargain; he who is to deliver the property and receive the consideration.

BARLEYCORN. The third of an inch. Wharton.

BARMOTE COURTS. Courts held in certain mining districts belonging to the Duchy of Lancaster, for regulation of the mines, and for deciding questions of title and other matters relating thereto. 3 Steph. Comm. 347, note (b); St. 14 & 15 Vict. c. 94.

BARNARD'S INN. An inn of chancery. See "Inns of Chancery."

BARO. A man, whether slave or free.

Si quis homicidium perpetraverit in barone libro seu servo, if any one shall have perpetrated a murder upon any man, slave or free. A freeman or freedman; a strong man; a hired soldier; a vassal; a feudal client.

Those who held of the king immediately were called "barons of the king."

A man of dignity and rank; a knight.

A magnate in the church.

A judge in the exchequer (*baro scaccarii*).

The first-born child.

A husband.

The word is said by Spelman to have been used more frequently in its latter sense.

It is quite easy to trace the history of *baro,* from meaning simply "man," to its various derived significations. Denoting a man, one who possessed the manly qualities of courage and strength would be desirable as a soldier, or might misuse them as a robber. One who possessed them in an eminent degree would be "the" man; and hence *baro,* in its sense of a title of dignity or honor, particularly applicable in a warlike age to the best soldier. See, generally, Bac. Abr.; Comyn, Dig.; Spelman.

BARON. A general title of nobility (1 Bl. Comm. 398); a particular title of nobility, next to that of viscount; a judge of the exchequer (Cowell; 1 Bl. Comm. 44).

A husband. In this sense it occurs in the phrase *baron et feme,* husband and wife (1 Bl. Comm. 432), and this is the only sense in which it is used in the American law, and even in this sense it is now but seldom found.

A freeman. Especially applied to the inhabitants of the Cinque Ports,—Romney, Sandwich, Hastings, Rotherhithe, and Dover, and the two latterly constituted ports of Winchelsea and Rye.

It has essentially the same meanings as *bara* (*q. v.*)

BARON ET FEME. Man and woman; husband and wife. It is doubtful if the words had originally in this phrase more meaning than man and woman. The vulgar use of man and woman for husband and wife suggest the change of meaning which might naturally occur from man and woman to husband and wife. Spelman; 1 Bl. Comm. 442.

BARONAGE. The nobility generally; the collective body of barons.

BARONET. An English title of dignity. It is an hereditary dignity, descendible, but not a title of nobility. It is of very early use. Spelman; 1 Bl. Comm. 403.

BARONS OF THE CINQUE PORTS. Members of parliament from these ports; freemen resident in these ports, viz., Sandwich, Romney, Hastings, Hithe and Dover, Winchelsea and Rye.

BARONS OF THE EXCHEQUER. The judges of the exchequer. See "Exchequer."

BARONY OF LAND. A quantity of land amounting to fifteen acres. In Ireland, a subdivision of a county.

BARONY. The dignity of a baron; a species of tenure; the territory or lands held by a baron. Spelman.

BARRA, or **BARRE.** In old practice. A plea in bar. Dyer, 56. The bar of the court; a barrister. Co. Litt. 372a; 1 Ld. Raym. 595.

BARRATOR. One who commits barratry.

BARRATRY (Fr. *barat, baraterie*, robbery, deceit, fraud).

——**In Criminal Law.** Common barratry is the offense of frequently exciting and stirring up quarrels and suits, either at law or otherwise. 4 Bl. Comm. 134; Co. Litt. 368. Sometimes called "barretry."

An attorney is not liable to indictment for maintaining another in a groundless action. 1 Bailey (S. C.) 379. See 1 Bish. Crim. Law, §§ 401, 645, 646; 2 Bish. Crim. Law, §§ 57-61; Bac. Abr.; 8 Coke, 36b; 9 Cow. (N. Y.) 587; 15 Mass. 229; 11 Pick. (Mass.) 432; 13 Pick. (Mass.) 362.

——**In Maritime Law and Insurance.** An unlawful or fraudulent act, or very gross and culpable negligence, of the master or mariners of a vessel, in violation of their duty as such, and directly prejudicial to the owner, and without his consent. 1 Phil. Ins. c. 13; Abb. Shipp. 167, note; 2 Caines (N. Y.) 67, 222; 3 Caines (N. Y.) 1; 1 Johns. (N. Y.) 229; 11 Johns. (N. Y.) 40, 13 Johns. (N. Y.) 451; 2 Bin. (Pa.) 274; 8 Cranch (U. S.) 139; 5 Day (Conn.) 1; 3 Wheat. (U. S.) 163; 4 Dall. (U. S.) 294.

——**In Scotch Law.** The crime of a judge who receives a bribe for his judgment. Skene de Verb. Sign.

BARREN MONEY. A debt which bears no interest.

BARRENNESS. Sterility in a female; the incapacity to produce a child.

BARRISTER. In English law. A counsellor admitted to plead at the bar.

——**Inner Barrister.** A serjeant or king's counsel who pleads within the bar.

——**Ouster Barrister.** One who pleads ouster, or without the bar.

——**Vacation Barrister.** A counsellor newly called to the bar, who is to attend for several long vacations the exercise of the house.

Barristers are called apprentices, *apprentitii ad legem*, being looked upon as learners, and not qualified until they obtain the degree of serjeant. Edmund Plowden, the author of the Commentaries, a volume of elaborate reports in the reigns of Edward VI., Mary, Philip and Mary, and Elizabeth, describes himself as an apprentice of the common law. See "Attorney."

BARTER. A contract by which parties exchange goods for goods. It differs from a sale in that a barter is always of goods for goods; a sale is of goods for money, or for money and goods. In a sale there is a fixed price; in a barter there is not.

There must be a delivery of goods to complete the contract.

BARTON. In old English law. The demesne land of a manor; a farm distinct from the mansion.

BAS CHEVALIERS. Knights by tenure of a base military fee, as distinguished from bannerets, who were the chief or superior knights. Kennett, Par. Ant.; Blount.

BASE COURT. In English law. Any inferior court that is not of record, as a court baron, etc. Kitch. Cts. 95, 96; Cowell.

BASE ESTATE. The estate which "base tenants" (*q. v.*) have in their land. Cowell.

BASE FEE. A fee which has a qualification annexed to it, and which must be determined whenever the annexed qualification requires.

A grant to A. and his heirs, tenants of Dale, continues only while they are such tenants. 2 Bl. Comm. 109.

The proprietor of such a fee has all the rights of the owner of a fee simple until his estate is determined. Plowd. 557; 1 Washb. Real Prop. 62; 1 Prest. Est. 431; Co. Litt. 1b.

One of the peculiarities of a base or determinable fee is that it may become a fee simple absolute on the happening of any event which renders impossible the event or combination of events upon which such an estate is to end.

It is the uncertainty of the event, and the possibility that the fee may not last forever, that renders a base or determinable estate a fee, and not merely a freehold.

BASE INFEFTMENT (Scotch). A disposition of land by a vassal, to be held of himself.

BASE RIGHT. In Scotch law. A subordinate right; the right of a subvassal in the lands held by him. Bell, Dict.

BASE SERVICES. Such services as were unworthy to be performed by the nobler men, and were performed by the peasants and those of servile rank. 2 Bl. Comm. 62; 1 Washb. Real Prop. 25.

BASE TENANTS.
(1) Tenants who held their lands at the will of their superior lord, as distinguished from "frank tenants" (*q. v.*), who were freeholders.
(2) Tenants who rendered to their lords services in villeinage. Cowell.

BASE TENURE. A tenure by villeinage, or other customary service, as distinguished from tenure by military service, or from tenure by free service. Cowell.

BASILEUS. The title of the Emperor Justinian in Novs. 2. 3. 4. 6. et seq., and sometimes applied to the king of England, in charters prior to the Norman conquest. 1 Bl. Comm. 242.

BASILICA. An abridgment of the Corpus Juris Civilis of Justinian, translated into Greek, and first published in the ninth century.

BASILS (Lat. basilli). In old English law. A kind of money or coin abolished by Henry II. Spelman; Cowell.

BASKET TENURE. Lands held by the service of making the king's baskets.

BASSE JUSTICE. In feudal law. Low justice; the right of a feudal lord to try persons accused of petty offenses or trespasses.

BASTARD (*bas* or *bast*, abject, low, base; *aerd*, nature).
One born of an illicit connection. It includes children begotten and born out of lawful wedlock, whose parents do not subsequently marry, and children born in wedlock, but begotten of an adulterous intercourse.
A child begotten out of wedlock, but whose parents marry before its birth, is legitimate (62 Iowa, 343; 43 Ohio St. 473; 75 Pa. St. 433), and, by the weight of authority, a marriage after the birth renders the child legitimate (9 Ala. 965; 85 Ind. 357; 38 Ky. 170; 20 Tex. 731).
The child of a voidable marriage is legitimate (13 Iowa, 198), but, at common law, the issue of a void marriage is a bastard (22 Md. 468; 1 N. J. Eq. 96); but by statute in many states, such issue is made legitimate if the marriage was in good faith.

BASTARD EIGNE. Bastard elder.
By the old English law, when a man had a bastard son, and he afterwards married the mother, and by her had a legitimate son, the first was called a *bastard eigne*, or, as it is now spelled, *aine*, and the second son was called *puisne*, or since born, or sometimes he was called *mulier puisne*. See 2 Bl. Comm. 248.

BASTARDA. A female bastard. Calv. Lex.

BASTARDUS NON POTEST HABERE haeredem nisi de corpore suo legitime procreatum. A bastard can have no heir unless it be one lawfully begotten of his own body. Tray, Lat. Max. 51.

BASTARDUS NULLIUS EST FILIUS, aut filius populi. A bastard is nobody's son, or the son of the people.

BASTARDY. The offense of begetting a bastard child; the condition of a bastard.

BASTARDY PROCESS (or **PROCEEDings**). The statutory mode of proceeding against the putative father of a bastard to secure a proper maintenance for the bastard.

BASTON. In old English law. A staff or club.
In some old English statutes, the servants or officers of the wardens of the fleet are so called, because they attended the king's courts with a red staff.

BATABLE GROUND. Land that is in controversy, or about the possession of which there is a dispute, as the lands which were situated between England and Scotland before the union. Skene de Verb. Sign.

BATAILLE. In old English law. Battel; the trial by combat or *duellum*. Brit. c. 25; Y. B. M. 4 Edw. III. 12.

BATH, KNIGHTS OF THE. In English law. A military order of knighthood, instituted by Richard II. The order was newly regulated by notifications in the London Gazette of 25th May, 1847, and 16th August, 1850. Wharton.

BATIMENT. In French marine law. A vessel. Ord. Mar. liv. 1, tit. 14, art. 2.

BATTEL. Trial by combat.
It was called also "wager of battel" or "battaile," and could be claimed in appeals of felony. It was of frequent use in affairs of chivalry and honor, and in civil cases upon certain issues. Co. Litt. § 294. It was not abolished in England till the enactment of St. 59 Geo. III. c. 46. See 1 Barn. & Ald. 405; 3 Sharswood, Bl. Comm. 339; 4 Sharswood, Bl. Comm. 347. See "Appeal." This mode of trial was not peculiar to England. The emperor Otho, A. D. 983, held a diet at Verona, at which several sovereigns and great lords of Italy, Germany, and France were present. In order

to put a stop to the frequent perjuries in judicial trials, this diet substituted in all cases, even in those which followed the course of the Roman law, proof by combat for proof by oath. Henrion de Pansey, Auth. Judic. Introd. c. 3. And for a detailed account of this mode of trial, see Herbert, Inns of Court, 119-145.

BATTERY. Any unlawful beating, or other wrongful physical violence or constraint, inflicted on a human being without his consent. 2 Bish. Crim. Law, § 62; 17 Ala. 540; 9 N. H. 491. It includes every touching of another in a rude, angry, or hostile manner. 65 Ala. 520; 53 Ill. 111; 67 Ind. 304.

BATTURE (Fr. shoals, shallows). An elevation of the bed of a river under the surface of the water; but it is sometimes used to signify the same elevation when it has risen above the surface. 6 Mart. (La.) 19, 216.

The term "battures" is applied principally to certain portions of the bed of the river Mississippi, which are left dry when the water is low, and are covered again, either in whole or in part, by the annual swells.

BAWD. A procurer; one who procures for other persons opportunities for illicit cohabitation. 4 Mo. 216.

BAWDY HOUSE. A house of ill fame, kept for the resort and unlawful commerce of lewd people of both sexes.

BAY. An inclosure, or other contrivance, to keep in the water for the supply of a mill, so that the water may be able to drive the wheels of such mill. St. 27 Eliz. c. 19.

An inlet of the sea.

BAYLEY. In old English law. Bailiff. This term is used in the laws of the colony of New Plymouth, Mass. A. D. 1670, 1671.

BAYOU. A stream which is the outlet of a swamp near the sea. Applied to the creeks in the lowlands lying on the Gulf of Mexico.

BEACONAGE. Money paid for the maintenance of a beacon. Comyn, Dig. "Navigation" (H).

BEADLE (Saxon, *beodan*, to bid). A church servant chosen by the vestry, whose business it is to attend the vestry, to give notice of its meetings, to execute its orders, to attend upon inquests, and to assist the constables.

BEARER. One who bears or carries a thing.

If a bill or note be made payable to bearer, it will pass by delivery only, without indorsement, and whoever fairly acquires a right to it may maintain an action against the drawer or acceptor.

BEARERS. Such as bear down or oppress others; maintainers.

BEARING DATE. Words frequently used in pleading and conveyancing to introduce the date which has been put upon an instrument.

When, in a declaration, the plaintiff alleges that the defendant made his promissory note on such a day, he will not be considered as having alleged that it bore date on that day, so as to cause a variance between the declaration and the note produced bearing a different date. 2 Greenl. Ev. § 160; 2 Dowl. & L. 759.

BEASTGATE. In Suffolk, England, imports land and common for one beast. 2 Strange, 1084; Rosc. Real Actions, 485.

BEASTS. Four-footed animals. They were anciently divided into "beasts of the plow,"—those used in husbandry; "beasts of the chase,"—the buck, doe, fox, marten, and roe; "beasts of the forest,"—the hart, hind, hare, boar, and wolf; and "beasts of the warren,"—the hare and coney. 2 Bl. Comm. 39; Co. Litt. 233.

BEAT. See "Assault."

BEAUPLEADER (Law Fr. fair pleading). A writ of prohibition directed to the sheriff or other, directing him not to take a fine for beaupleader.

There was anciently a fine imposed called a "fine for beaupleader," which is explained by Coke to have been originally imposed for bad pleading. Coke, 2d Inst. 123. It was set at the will of the judge of the court, and reduced to certainty by consent, and annually paid. Comyn, Dig. "Prerogative" (D 52). St. Marlebridge (52 Hen. III.) c. 11, enacts that neither in the circuit of justices, nor in counties, hundreds, or courts baron, any fines shall be taken for fair pleading, namely, for not pleading fairly or aptly to the purpose. Upon this statute, this writ was ordained, directed to the sheriff, bailiff, or him who shall demand the fine, and it is a prohibition or command not to do it. New Nat. Brev. 596; Fitzh. Nat. Brev. 270a; Hall. Hist. Com. Law, c. 7. Mr. Reeve explains it as a fine paid for the privilege of a fair hearing. 2 Reeve, Hist. Eng. Law, 70. This latter view would perhaps derive some confirmation from the connection in point of time of this statute with *Magna Charta*, and the resemblance which the custom bore to the other customs against which the clause in the charter of *nulli vendemus*, etc., was directed. See Comyn, Dig. "Prerogative"

(D 51, 52); Cowell; 2 Inst. 122, 123; Crabb, Hist. Eng. Law, 150.

BED OF JUSTICE (Fr.) The seat or throne upon which the king sat when personally present in parliament; hence it signified the parliament itself.

BED OF THE RIVER. That portion of the river which is alternately covered and left bare, as there may be an increase or diminution in the supply of water, and which is adequate to contain it at its average and mean stage during the entire year, without reference to the extraordinary freshets of the winter or spring, or the extreme droughts of the summer or autumn. 224 Ill. 54.

That part between the banks worn by the regular flow of the water. 239 Ill. 233.

BEDEL. In English law. A crier or messenger of court, who summons men to appear and answer therein. Cowell. An inferior officer in a parish or liberty. See "Beadle."

BEDELARY. The jurisdiction of a bedel, as a bailiwick is the jurisdiction of a bailiff. Co. Litt. 234b; Cowell.

BEDEREPE. A service which certain tenants were anciently bound to perform, as to reap their landlord's corn at harvest. Said by Whishaw to be still in existence in some parts of England. Blount; Cowell; Whishaw.

BEER. A fermented liquor, made from any malted grain, with hops and other bitter flavoring matters. A fermented extract of the roots and other parts of various plants, as, spruce, ginger, sassafras, etc. 120 Ill. 24.

The word "beer," when employed in connection with sales in a place where intoxicating liquors are usually sold, means an intoxicating drink. 134 Ill. App. 560.

BEGGAR. One who obtains his livelihood by asking alms. The laws of several of the states punish begging as an offense.

Words of solicitation are not necessary, but the solicitation may be by attitude or gesture. 3 Abb. N. C. (N. Y.) 65.

BEHAVIOR. Manner of having, holding, or keeping one's self; carriage of one's self, with respect to propriety, morals, and the requirements of law. Surety to be of good behavior is a larger requrement than surety to keep the peace. Dalton, c. 122; 4 Burns, Just. 355; 240 Ill. 564.

A "breach of good behavior," for which an official can be removed, is not confined to misbehavior in office. 2 Mart. (La.; N. S.) 700.

BEHETRIA (Arabic, without nobility or lordship). In Spanish law. Lands situated in districts and manors in which the inhabitants had the right to select their own lords.

Behetrias were of two kinds: *Behetrias de entre parientes*, when the choice was restricted to a relation of the deceased lord, and *behetrias de mar a mar*, when the choice was unrestricted.

The lord, when elected, enjoyed various privileges, called *yantor, conducho, martiniego, marzadga, infurcion*, etc. These contributions were intended for his maintenance, the construction of his dwelling, the support of his family and his followers, etc. Escriche, Dic. Raz.; Sempere y Guarinos, Vinculos y Mayarazgos, p. 67, note. See, also, on this subject, Fuero Viejo de Castilla, bk. 1, tit. 8; Las Partidas, tit. 25, p. 4; El Ordenamiento de Acala in different laws in title 32. See, likewise, book 6, tit. 1, of the Novisima Recopilacion.

BEHOFF (Saxon). Use; service; profit; advantage. It occurs in conveyances.

BELIEF. Conviction of the mind, arising not from actual perception or knowledge, but by way of inference, or from evidence received or information derived from others. It differs from "knowledge" only in degree. 9 Gray (Mass.) 274. It is said to be a stronger word than "imagination." (4 Ga. 37), or "suspicion" (5 Cush. [Mass.] 374), but has been held to be substantially synonymous with "supposition" (102 Ill. 277).

Belief may evidently be stronger or weaker, according to the weight of evidence adduced in favor of the proposition to which belief is granted or refused, and so "firm belief" in a statute means more than "belief." 4 Serg. & R. (Pa.) 137; 1 Greenl. Ev. §§ 7-13. See 1 Starkie, Ev. 41; 2 W. Bl. 881; 8 Watts (Pa.) 406.

BELLIGERENT. Actually at war. Applied to nations. Wheat. Int. Law, 380 et seq.; 1 Kent, Comm. 89. The subject of a hostile power.

BELLO PARTA CEDUNT REIPUBLIcae. Things acquired in war go to the state. Cited 2 Russ. & M. 56; 1 Kent, Comm. 101; 5 C. Rob. Adm. 155, 163; 1 Gall. (U. S.) 558.

BELONG. To be the property of. 248 Ill. 610.

BELOW. Inferior; preliminary. The court below is the court from which a cause has been removed. See "Bail."

BENCH. A tribunal for the administration of justice.

The judges taken collectively, as distinguished from counsellors and advocates, who are called the "bar."

The term, indicating originally the seat of the judges, came to denote the body of judges taken collectively, and also the tribunal itself. The *jus banci*, says Spelman, properly belongs to the king's judges, who administer justice in the last resort. The judges of the inferior courts, as of the barons, are deemed to judge *plano pede*, and are such as are called in the civil law *pedanei judices*. The Romans used the words *sellae* and *tribunalia* to designate the seats of their higher judges, and *subsellia* to designate those of the lower. See Spelman, "Bancus;" 1 Reeve, Hist. Eng. Law (4th Ed.) 40.

"The court of common pleas in England was formerly called *bancus*, the bench, as distinguished from *bancus regis*, the king's bench. It was also called *communis bancus*, the common bench; and this title is still retained by the reporters of the decisions in the court of common pleas. Mention is made in the *Magna Charta 'de justiciariis nostris de banco,'* which all men know to be the justices of the court of common pleas, commonly called the common bench, or the bench." Viner, Abr. "Courts," note 2.

BENCH WARRANT. An order issued by or from a bench, for the attachment or arrest of a person. It may issue either in case of a contempt, or where an indictment has been found. It is so called because issued by order of a court or bench, as distinguished from warrant issued by a magistrate.

BENCHER. A senior in the Inns of Court, intrusted with their government or direction.

The benchers have the absolute and irresponsible power of punishing a barrister guilty of misconduct, by either admonishing or rebuking him, by prohibiting him from dining in the hall, or even by expelling him from the bar, called "disbarring." They might also refuse admission to a student, or reject his call to the bar. Wharton.

BENE (Lat.) In old English law. Well; sufficiently; in due form; safely. *Bene et in pace*, well and in peace, Magna Cart. Johan. c. 63. See "Biens."

BENEDICTA EST EXPOSITIO QUANDO res redimitur a destructione. Blessed is the exposition when the thing is saved from destruction. 4 Coke, 26.

BENEFICE. An ecclesiastical preferment. In its more extended sense, it includes any such preferment; in a more limited sense, it applies to rectories and vicarages only. See "Beneficium."

BENEFICE DE DISCUSSION. Benefit of discussion (*q. v.*)

BENEFICE DE DIVISION. In French law. The right of contribution between sureties.

BENEFICE D'INVENTAIRE. This, in French, corresponds to the *beneficium inventarii* of Roman law, and substantially to the English-law doctrine that the executor properly accounting is only liable to the extent of the assets received by him. Brown.

BENEFICIAL ENJOYMENT. The enjoyment of an estate in one's own right, and for his own benefit, and not as trustee for another. 3 Hurl. & C. 1030.

BENEFICIAL INTEREST. Profit, benefit, or advantage resulting from a contract, or the ownership of an estate, as distinct from the legal ownership or control.

A *cestui que trust* has the beneficial interest in a trust estate, while the trustee has the legal estate. If A. makes a contract with B. to pay C. a sum of money, C. has the beneficial interest in the contract.

A beneficial interest, when considered as a designation of the character of an estate, is such an interest as a devisee takes solely for his own use or benefit and not as a mere holder of the title for the use of another. 266 Ill. 340; 208 Ill. 442.

BENEFICIAL POWER. "A power is beneficial when no person other than the grantee has, by the terms of its creation, any interest in its execution." Rev. St. N. Y. § 79.

A power is beneficial if, by the terms of its creation, no interest in its execution is given to a person other than the grantee, though no such interest is especially given to the grantee. 73 N. Y. 234.

BENEFICIARY. A term suggested by Judge Story as a substitute for *cestui que trust (q. v.)* (1 Story, Eq. Jur. § 321), and now quite largely adopted.

BENEFICIO PRIMO (more fully, *beneficio primo ecclesiastico habendo*). A writ directed from the king to the chancellor commanding him to bestow the benefice which shall first fall in the king's gift, above or under a certain value, upon a particular and certain person. Reg. Orig. 307.

BENEFICIUM (Lat. *beneficere*). A portion of land or other immovable thing granted by a lord to his followers for their stipend or maintenance.

A general term applied to ecclesiastical livings. 4 Bl. Comm. 107; Cowell.

In the early feudal times, grants were made to continue only during the pleasure of the grantor, which were called *munera*, but soon afterwards these grants were made for life, and then they assumed the name of *beneficia*. Dalr. Feud. Prop. 199. Pomponius Laetus, as cited by Hotoman (De Feudis, c. 2), says "that it was an ancient custom, revived by the Emperor Constantine, to give lands and villas to those generals, prefects, and tribunes who had grown old in enlarging the empire, to supply their necessities as long as they lived, which they called 'parochial,'—parishes, etc. But between fiefs or feuds (*feuda*) and parishes (*parochias*) there was this difference, that the latter were given to old men, veterans, etc., who, as they deserved well of the republic, were sustained the rest of their life (*publico beneficio*) by the public benefaction; or, if any war afterwards arose, they were called out not so much as soldiers as leaders (*magistri militum*). Feuds (*feuda*), on the other hand, were usually given to robust young men who could sustain the labors of war. In later times, the word *parochia* was appropriated exclusively to ecclesiastical persons, while the word *beneficium (militare)* continued to be used in reference to military fiefs or fees."

——**In Civil Law.** Any favor or privilege.

BENEFICIUM ABSTINENDI. In Roman law. The power of an heir to abstain from accepting the inheritance. Sandars, Just. Inst. (5th Ed.) 214; Cum. Com. Law, 156.

BENEFICIUM CEDENDARUM ACTIONUM. The privilege by which a surety could, before paying the creditor, compel him to make over to him the actions which belonged to the stipulator, so as to avail himself of them. Sandars, Just. Inst. (5th Ed.) 332, 351.

BENEFICIUM CLERICALE. Benefit of clergy (*q. v.*)

BENEFICIUM COMPETENTIAE.

——**In Scotch Law.** The privilege of retaining a competence belonging to the obligor in a gratuitous obligation. Such a claim constitutes a good defense in part to an action on the bond. Paterson, Comp.

——**In Civil Law.** The right which an insolvent debtor had, among the Romans, on making cession of his property for the benefit of his creditors, to retain what was required for him to live honestly according to his condition. 7 Toullier, Dr. Civ. note 258.

BENEFICIUM DIVISIONS. In Scotch and civil law. A privilege whereby a co-surety may insist upon paying only his share of the debt along with the other sureties. In Scotch law this is lost if the cautioners (sureties) bind themselves "conjunctly and severally." Ersk. Inst. lib. 3, tit. 3, § 63.

BENEFICIUM INVENTARI. Benefit of inventory (*q. v.*)

BENEFICIUM NON DATUM NISI PROPTER OFFICIUM. A remuneration not given unless an account of a duty performed. Hob. 148.

BENEFICIUM ORDINIS. In Scotch and civil law. The privilege of the surety allowing him to require that the creditor shall take complete legal proceedings against the debtor to exhaust him before he calls upon the surety. 1 Bell, Comm. 347.

BENEFICIUM SEPARATIONIS. In the civil law. The right to have the goods of an heir separated from those of the testator in favor of creditors.

BENEFIT OF CESSION. In civil law. The release of a debtor from future imprisonment for his debts, which the law operates in his favor upon the surrender of his property for the benefit of his creditors. Pothier, Proced. Civ. 5eme part, c. 2, § 1. This was something like a discharge under the insolvent laws, which releases the person of the debtor, but not the goods he may acquire afterwards. See "Bankrupt;" "Cessio Bonorum;" "Insolvent."

BENEFIT OF CLERGY. In English law. An exemption of the punishment of death, which the laws impose on the commission of certain crimes, on the culprit demanding it. By modern statutes, benefit of clergy was rather a substitution of more mild punishment for the punishment of death.

A clergyman was exempt from capital punishment *toties quoties*, as often as, from acquired habit, or otherwise, he repeated the same species of offense. The laity, provided they could read, were exempted only for a first offense; for a second, though of an entirely different nature, they were hanged. Among the laity, however, there was this distinction: Peers and peeresses were discharged for their first fault without reading, or any punishment at all; commoners, if of the male sex, and readers, were branded in the hand. Women commoners had no benefit of clergy.

Benefit of clergy was latterly granted, not only to the clergy, as was formerly the case, but to all persons. The benefit of clergy seems never to have been extended to the crime of high treason, nor to have embraced misdemeanors inferior to felony. See 1 Chit. Crim. Law, 667, 668; 4 Bl. Comm. c. 28; 1 Bish. Crim. Law, §§ 622-624. But this privilege, improperly given to the clergy, because they had more learning than others, was abolished by St. 7 Geo. IV. c. 28, § 6.

By the act of congress of April 30, 1790, it is provided (section 30) that the benefit of clergy shall not be used or allowed upon conviction of any crime for which, by any statute of the United States, the punishment is, or shall be declared to be, death.

In some early state decisions, the right was recognized in the United States (1 Murph. [N. C.] 147; 4 Strobh. [S. C.] 372), while in others it is held to be obsolete (1 Blackf. [Ind.] 66; 3 Minn. 246).

BENEFIT OF DISCUSSION. In civil law. The right which a surety has to cause the property of the principal debtor to be applied in satisfaction of the obligation in the first instance. Civ. Code La. arts. 3014-3020.

BENEFIT OF DIVISION. In civil law. The right of one of several joint sureties, when sued alone, to have the whole obligation apportioned amongst the solvent sureties, so that he need pay but his share. Civ. Code La. arts. 3014-3020. See 2 Bouv. Inst. note 1414.

BENEFIT OF INVENTORY. In civil law. The privilege which the heir obtains of being liable for the charges and debts of the succession, only to the value of the effects of the succession, by causing an inventory of these effects within the time and manner prescribed by law. Civ. Code La. art. 1025; Poth. des Success. c. 3, § 3a. 2. See, also, Paterson, Comp., as to the Scotch law upon this subject.

BENERTH. A feudal service rendered by the tenant to his lord with plow and cart. Cowell; Spelman.

BENEVOLENCE. Good will; kindness; humanity. It is a broader word than "charity." 19 N. J. Eq. 307; 44 Conn. 60; 11 Mass. 267.

——**In Old English Law.** A voluntary gratuity given by the subjects to the king. Cowell. Benevolences were first granted to Edward IV.; but under subsequent monarchs they became anything but voluntary gifts, and in the Petition of Rights (3 Car. I.) it is made an article that no benevolence shall be extorted without the consent of parliament. The illegal claim and collection of these benevolences was one of the prominently alleged causes of the rebellion of 1640. 1 Bl. Comm. 140; 4 Bl. Comm. 436; Cowell.

BENEVOLENT. A term of wider and more indefinite meaning than "charitable," and generally held too indefinite to uphold a bequest for such purposes. 19 N. J. Eq., 307; 5 Beav. 300; 107 U. S. 184.

BENIGNAE FACIENDAE SUNT INTERpretationes chartarum, ut res magis valeat quam pereat. Constructions of documents are to be made favorably, that the instrument may rather avail than perish.

BENIGNE FACIENDAE SUNT INTERpretationes chartarum, ut res magis valeat quam pereat, et quaelibet concessio fortissime contra donatorem interpretanda est. Liberal interpretations are to be made of deeds, so that more may stand than fall, and every grant is to be taken most strongly against the grantor. 4 Mass. 134; 1 Sandf. Ch. (N. Y.) 258, 268; compare 275, 277.

BENIGNE FACIENDAE SUNT INTERpretationes propter simplicitatem laicorum, ut res magis valtae quam pereat; et verba intentione, non e contra, debent inservire. Constructions should be liberal, on account of the ignorance of the laity, or nonprofessional persons, so that the subject-matter may avail rather than perish; and words must be subject to the intention, not the intention to the words. Co. Litt. 36a; Broom, Leg. Max. (3d London Ed.) 481, 504; 11 Q. B. 852, 856, 868, 870; 4 H. L. Cas. 556; 1 Bulst. 175; Hob. 304.

BENIGNIOR SENTENTIA, IN VERBIS generalibus seu dubiis, est preferanda. The more favorable construction is to be placed on general or doubtful expressions. 4 Coke, 15; Dig. 50. 17. 192. 1; 2 Kent, Comm. 557.

BENIGNIUS LEGES INTERPRETANdae sunt quo voluntas earum conservetur. Laws are to be more favorably interpreted, that their intent may be preserved. Dig. 1. 3. 16.

BEQUEATH. To give personal property by will to another. 13 Barb. (N. Y.) 106. The word may be construed "devise," so as to pass real estate. 36 Me. 216; 119 Mass. 525.

BEQUEST. A gift by will of personal property. It is synonymous with "legacy" (*q. v.*)

BERCARIA. A sheep fold; a tan house or heath house, where barks or rinds of trees are laid to tan. Domesday Book; Co. Litt. 56.

BERCARIUS, or BERCATOR. A shepherd.

BEREWICA, BEREWICHA, BEREWICHus, berewita, or berwita (Law Lat.) In old English law. A manor, or rather a part of a manor, separated from the main body; a smaller manor, belonging to a larger one (*manerium minus ad majus pertinens*). Spelman.

A hamlet, or small village, appurtenant to some town or manor (*villula, manerii vicus*). Spelman; Blount, voc. "Berwica." A word of frequent occurrence in Domesday Book. Id. According to Lord Coke, it signifies a town. Co. Litt. 116a.

A corn farm. Spelman.

BERGHMAYSTER (from Saxon *berg*, a mountain. An officer having charge of a mine. A bailiff or chief officer among the Derbyshire miners, who, in addition to his other duties, executes the office of coroner among them. Blount; Cowell.

BERGHMOTE, or BERGMOTH. In old English law. A court for deciding controversies among the Derbyshire miners. Blount; Cowell.

BERLINSKI TEST. A test used by neurologists consisting in the application of a test tube containing hot water, a test tube containing cold water, a piece of metal which feels cold when applied to a person's skin in its normal sensitiveness, a piece of wood and a piece of cloth.

BERM SIDE. The side opposite the tow path of a canal.

BERME. A horizontal ledge or shelf at the bottom or part way up a bank or slope. People v. Klehm, 238 Ill. 92.

BERNET. In Saxon law. Burning; the crime of house burning, now called "arson." Cowell; Blount.

BERRA (Law Lat.) In old law. A plain; open heath. Cowell; Spelman.

BERRY, or BURY (from Saxon *beorg*, a hill or castle). A villa or seat of habitation of a nobleman; a dwelling or mansion house; a sanctuary.

BERTON. A large farm; the barnyard of a large farm.

BES (Lat.; pl. *besses*). In the Roman law. A division of the *as*, or pound, consisting of eight *unciae*, or duodecimal parts, and amounting to two-thirds of the *as*. 2 Bl. Comm. 462, note (m).

Two-thirds of an inheritance. Inst. 2. 14. 5.

Eight per cent. interest. 2 Bl. Comm. ubi supra.

BESAYLE, BESAYEL, BESAILE, or BESAIEL (Law Fr). In old English law. A great-grandfather. 1 Bl. Comm. 186.

A writ (law Lat. *brev. de proavo*) which lay where a great-grandfather died seised of lands and tenements in fee simple, and on the day of his death a stranger abated, or entered and kept out the heir. Reg. Orig. 226; Fitzh. Nat. Brev. 221 (D); 3 Bl. Comm. 186. Now abolished with other real actions.

BEST EVIDENCE. The best evidence of which the nature of the case admits, not the highest or strongest evidence which the nature of the thing to be proved admits of; *e. g.*, a copy of a deed is not the best evidence; the deed itself is better. Gilb. Ev. 15; Starkie, Ev. 437; 2 Campb. 605; 3 Campb. 236; 1 Esp. 127; 1 Pet. (U. S.) 591; 6 Pet. (U. S.) 352; 7 Pet. (U. S.) 100. The term is confined to cases where the law has divided evidence into primary and secondary. 33 Mich. 53. The rule requiring the best evidence does not exclude a witness on the ground that another is more credible, but merely excludes such evidence as is substitutionary in its character, if the original evidence can be had. 65 Me. 467.

BESTIALITY. Carnal connection between a human being and a beast. 10 Ind. 356. See "Buggery."

BET. An agreement that some valuable thing or sum of money, in contributing which all the parties take part, shall become the property of some one or more of them on the happening of some event which is at present uncertain. 81 N. Y. 539. See, also, 7 Port. (Ala.) 465. "If one of the parties may gain, but cannot lose, and the other may lose, but cannot gain, and there must be either a gain by the one, or a loss by the other, according to the happening of the contingency, it is as much a bet or wager as if the parties had shared equally the chances of gain or loss." 15 Grat. (Va.) 661.

The words "bet" and "wager" are synonymous. 11 Ind. 16.

BETROTHMENT, or BETROTHAL. A contract between a man and a woman that at a future time they will intermarry.

BETTER EQUITY. The right which, in a court of equity, a second incumbrancer has who has taken securities against subsequent dealings to his prejudice, which a prior incumbrancer neglected to take, although he had an opportunity. 1 Chanc. Prec. 470, note; 4 Rawle (Pa.) 144. See 3 Bouv. Inst. note 2462.

BETTERMENTS. Improvements made to an estate. It signifies such improvements as have been made to the estate which render it better than mere repairs. 11 Me. 482; 23 Me. 110; 24 Me. 192; 13 Ohio, 308; 10 Yerg. (Tenn.) 477; 13 Vt. 533; 17 Vt. 109. The term is also applied to denote the additional value which an estate acquires in consequence of some public improvement, as laying out or widening a street, etc.

BETWEEN. A grant of land lying between two named lots would not embrace either of the named lots. 14 Ill. 333.

When the word "between" is used with reference to a period of time bounded by two other specified periods of time, such as between two days named, the days or other periods of time named as boundaries are excluded. 14 Ill. 333; 87 Ill. App. 298; 76 Ill. App. 318.

The word "between," when used in reference to two named boundaries of space, excludes both the boundaries named. 87 Ill. App. 298

BEWARED (Old English). Expended. Before the Britons and Saxons had introduced the general use of money, they traded chiefly by exchange of wares. Wharton.

BEYOND SEA. Out of the kingdom of England; out of the state; out of the United States.

——**In England.** By St. 3 & 4 Wm. IV. c. 27, no island under the English dominion, and lying adjacent to the United Kingdom, is to be regarded as "beyond the seas."

——**In the United States.** It is commonly held to mean outside the state in whose statute it is used (13 N. H. 86; 1 Har. & J. [Md.] 353; 26 Ga. 182; 8 Blackf. [Ind.] 515; 23 Ala. 486; 14 Pet. [U. S.] 145); but it has been held to mean outside the limits of the United States (71 N. C. 176; 24 Ill. 159; 14 Mo. 433; 9 Serg. & R. [Pa.] 291).

BI-SCOT. In old English law. A fine imposed for not repairing banks, ditches, and causeways. Blount; Whishaw.

BIAS. A particular influential power which sways the judgment; the inclination or propensity of the mind towards a particular object. "Bias is not synonymous with 'prejudice.' A man cannot be prejudiced against another without being biased, but he may be biased without being prejudiced." 12 Ga. 444.

BID.

(1) An offer to pay a specified price for an article about to be sold at auction.

(2) An offer to do work or furnish materials at a specified price.

BIDALE, or **BIDALL.** An invitation of friends to drink ale at the house of some poor man, who thereby hopes charitable contribution for his relief. Something like this seems to be what we call "house-warming," when persons are invited in this manner on their first beginning housekeeping. Jacob.

BIDDER. One who offers to purchase an article offered for sale at a public auction (11 Ill. 254), or to furnish materials or services at a price submitted.

BIELBRIEF (Ger.)

——**In European Maritime Law.** A document furnished by the builder of a vessel, containing a register of her admeasurement, particularizing the length, breadth, and dimensions of every part of the ship. It sometimes also contains the terms of agreement between the parties for whose account the ship is built, and the shipbuilder. It has been termed in English the "grand bill of sale;" in French, "*contrat de construction ou de la vente d'un vaisseau,*" and corresponds in a great degree with the English, French, and American "register" (*q. v.*), being an equally essential document to the lawful ownership of vessels. Jac. Sea Laws, 12, 13, and note.

——**In the Danish Law.** Used to denote the contract of bottomry.

BIENS (Fr. goods). Property of every description, except estates of freehold and inheritance. Sugd. Vend. 495; Co. Litt. 118b; Dane, Abr.

——**In French Law.** This term includes all kinds of property, real and personal. *Biens* are divided into *biens meubles*, movable property, and *biens immeubles*, immovable property. This distinction between movable and immovable property is recognized by them, and gives rise, in the civil as well as in the common law, to many important distinctions as to rights and remedies. Story, Confl. Laws, § 13, note 1. 168 Ill. 636.

BIGA, or **BIGATA.** A cart or chariot drawn with two horses, coupled side by side; but it is said to be properly a cart with two wheels sometimes drawn by one horse, and in the ancient records it is used for any cart, wain, or wagon. Jacob.

BIGAMUS. In civil law. One who had been twice married, whether both wives were alive at the same time or not; one who had married a widow.

Especially used in ecclesiastical matters as a reason for denying benefit of the clergy. Termes de la Ley.

BIGAMY.

——**At Common Law.** The willfully contracting a second marriage when the contracting party knows that the first is still subsisting.

The state of a man who has two wives, or of a woman who has two husbands, living at the same time.

When the man has more than two wives, or the woman more than two husbands, living at the same time, then the party is said to have committed polygamy; but the name of "bigamy" is more frequently given to this offense in legal proceedings. 1 Russ. Crimes, 187; Clark & Marshall. Crimes, 1103. "But as the substance of the offense is marrying a second time while having a lawful husband or wife living, without regard to the number of marriages that may have taken place, 'bigamy' seems not an inappropriate term. The objection to its use urged by Blackstone (4 Bl. Comm. 163) seems to be founded not so much upon considerations of the etymology of the word, as upon the propriety of distinguishing the ecclesiastical offense, termed 'bigamy' in the canon law, and defined below, from the offense known as 'bigamy' in the modern criminal law. The same distinction is carefully made by Lord Coke, 4 Inst 88. But the ecclesiastical offense being now obsolete, this reason ceases to have weight." Abbott.

——**In the Canon Law.** According to canonists, bigamy is threefold, viz., *vera, interpretativa, et similitudinaria*, real, interpretative, and similitudinary. The first consisted in marrying two wives successively (virgins they may be), or in once marrying a widow; the second consisted, not in a repeated marriage, but in marrying (*e. g., meretricem vel ab alio corruptam*) a harlot; the third arose from two marriages, indeed, but the one metaphorical or spiritual, the other carnal. This last was confined to persons initiated in sacred orders, or under the vow of continence. Deferriere's Tract. Juris Canon. tit. 21. See, also, Bac. Abr. "Marriage."

BILAGINES (Lat.) By-laws of towns; municipal laws.

BILAN. A book in which bankers, merchants, and traders write a statement of all they owe and all that is due to them. A balance sheet. 3 Mart. (La.; N. S.) 446.

The term is used in Louisiana, and is derived from the French. 5 Mart. (La.; N. S.) 158.

BILANCIIS DEFERENDIS. In English law. A writ addressed to a corporation for the carrying of weights to such a haven, there to weigh the wool that persons, by our ancient laws, were licensed to transport. Reg. Orig. 270.

BILATERAL CONTRACT. A contract in which both the contracting parties are bound to fulfill obligations reciprocally towards each other. Lec. Elm. § 781. See "Contract."

BILINE. Collateral.

BILINGUIS. Using two languages. A term formerly applied to juries half of one nation and half of another. Plowd. 2.

BILL (Lat. *billa*). A formal written statement, account, or declaration.

The principal legal significations of the term are:

——**In Old English Practice.** The original petition by which an action in the court of king's bench was begun. 3 Bl. Comm. 43.

——**In Chancery Practice.** A complaint in writing, addressed to the chancellor, containing the names of the parties to the suit, both complainant and defendant, a statement of the facts on which the complainant relies, and the allegations which he makes, with an averment that the acts complained of are contrary to equity, and a prayer for relief and proper process.

——**In Legislation.** A special act passed by the legislature in the exercise of a *quasi* judicial power. Thus, bills of attainder, bills of pains and penalties, are spoken of.

The draft of a law submitted to the consideration of a legislative body for its adoption. 26 Pa. St. 450. After a bill has been adopted, it is properly known as an "act."

——**In Mercantile Law.** The creditor's written statement of his claim, specifying the items. It differs from an account stated in this, that a bill is the creditor's statement, and an account stated is a statement which has been assented to by both parties.

The term is also sometimes used for "bill of exchange," "bill of exceptions," "bill of costs," etc. (*q. v.*)

BILL CHAMBER. In Scotch law. A department of the court of sessions, in which petitions for suspension, interdict, etc., are entertained. It is equivalent to sittings in chambers in the English and American practice. Paterson, Comp.

BILL FOR A NEW TRIAL. In equity practice. One filed in a court of equity praying for an injunction after a judgment at law when there is any fact which renders it against conscience to execute such judgment, and of which the injured party could not avail himself in a court of law, or, if he could, was prevented by fraud or accident, unmixed with any fault or negligence of himself or his agents. Mitf. Eq. Pl. (Jeremy Ed.) 131; 2 Story, Eq. Jur. § 887. Of late years, bills of this description are not countenanced. 1 Johns. Ch. (N. Y.) 432; 6 Johns. Ch. (N. Y.) 479.

BILL FOR FORECLOSURE. In equity practice. One which is filed by a mortgagee against the mortgagor, for the purpose of having the estate sold, thereby to obtain the sum mortgaged on the premises, with interest and costs. 1 Madd. Ch. Pr. 528. See "Foreclosure."

BILL IMPEACHING A DECREE FOR fraud. In equity practice. This must be an original bill, which may be filed without leave of court. 1 Schoales & L. 355; 2 Schoales & L. 576; 1 Ves. Jr. 120; 3 Brown, 74; 1 Turn. & R. 178.

BILL IN NATURE OF A BILL IN REview. One which is brought by a person not bound by a decree, praying that the same may be examined and reversed; as where a decree is made against a person who has no interest at all in the matter in dispute, or had not an interest sufficient to render the decree against him binding upon some person claiming after him.

The term is used in two senses: (1) A bill brought by one not a party to a decree, to obtain the reversal thereof. Adam, Eq. 419. (2) A bill to set aside a decree on the ground of fraud. 48 Mich. 375.

BILL IN NATURE OF A BILL OF REVIVOR. One which is filed when the death of a party, whose interest is not determined by his death, is attended with such a transmission of his interest that the title to it, as well as the person entitled, may be litigated in the court of chancery; as, in the case of a devise of real estate, the suit is not permitted to be continued by bill of revivor. In such cases, an original bill, upon which the title may be litigated, must be filed, and this bill will have so far the effect of a bill of revivor that, if the title of the representative by the act of the deceased party is established, the same benefit may be had of the proceedings upon the former bill as if the suit had been continued by bill of revivor. Story, Eq. Pl. §§ 378-380; 2 Paige (N. Y.) 358; 3 Atk. 217.

BILL IN NATURE OF A SUPPLEMENTAL BILL. One which is filed when the interest of the plaintiff or defendant, suing or defending, wholly determines, and the same property becomes vested in another person not claiming under him. The principal difference between this and a supplemental bill seems to be that a supplemental bill is applicable to such cases only where the same parties or the same interests remain before the court; whereas an original bill in the nature of a supplemental bill is properly applicable where new parties, with new interests, arising from events occurring since the institution of the suit, are brought before the court. Story, Eq. Pl. § 345.

BILL OBLIGATORY. A bond absolute for the payment of money. It is called, also, a single bill, and differs from a promissory note only in having a seal. 2 Serg. & R. (Pa.) 115. See Read, Pl. 236; West, Symb.

BILL OF ADVENTURE. A writing signed by a merchant, ship owner, or master to testify that goods shipped on board a certain vessel are at the venture of another person, he himself being answerable only for the produce.

BILL OF ADVOCATION. In Scotch law. A petition in writing, by which a party to a cause applies to the supreme court to call the action out of the inferior court to itself.

BILL OF APPEAL. An abolished, criminal prosecution. Wharton. See "Battel."

BILL OF ATTAINDER. A special act of the legislature pronouncing judgment of treason or felony on one who has not been tried in the courts, and passing sentence of death and attainder upon him. If the act inflicts a less punishment than death, it is called a "bill of pains and penalties."

BILL OF CERTIORARI. A bill praying for a writ of certiorari. See "Certiorari."

BILL OF CONFORMITY. In equity practice. One filed by an executor or administrator, who finds the affairs of the deceased so much involved that he cannot safely administer the estate except under the direction of a court of chancery. This bill is filed against the creditors generally, for the purpose of having all their claims adjusted, and procuring a final decree settling the order of payment of the assets. 1 Story, Eq. Jur. 440.

BILL OF COSTS. A statement of the items which form the total amount of the costs of a suit or action. See "Costs."

BILL OF CREDIT.

—**In Constitutional Law.** Paper issued by the authority of a state on the faith of the state, and designed to circulate as money. 11 Pet. (U. S.) 257.

Promissory notes or bills issued by a state government, exclusively, on the credit of the state, and intended to circulate through the community for its ordinary purposes as money, redeemable at a future day, and for the payment of which the faith of the state is pledged. 4 Kent, Comm. 408.

The constitution of the United States provides that no state shall emit bills of credit, or make anything but gold and silver coin a tender in payment of debts. Article 1, § 10. This prohibition, it seems, does not apply to bills issued by a bank owned by the state, but having a specific capital set apart (11 Pet. [U. S.] 257; 13 How. [U. S.] 12; but see 4 Pet. [U. S.] 410) nor does it apply to notes issued by corporations or individuals which are not made legal tender (4 Kent, Comm. 408, and note).

—**In Mercantile Law.** A letter desiring the addressee to give credit to the bearer for goods or money. More commonly called "letter of credit." Comyn, Dig. "Merchant" (F 3); 3 Burrows, 1667; 13 Miss. 491; 4 Ark. 44; R. M. Charlt. (Ga.) 151.

BILL OF DEBT. An ancient term, including promissory notes and bonds for the payment of money. Comyn, Dig. "Merchant." (F 2).

BILL OF DISCOVERY. In equity practice. One which prays for the discovery of facts resting within the knowledge of the person against whom the bill is exhibited, or of deeds, writings, or other things in his custody or power. It does not seek for relief in consequence of the discovery (and this constitutes its characteristic feature), though it may ask for a stay of proceedings till discovery is made (2 Story, Eq. Jur. § 1483), and such relief as does not require a hearing before the court, it is said, may be part of the prayer (2 Daniell, Ch. Pr. 1557; 1 Pom. Eq. Jur. § 191). See "Discovery."

BILL OF ENTRY. A statement required by the revenue laws of the consignor, consignee, origin, destination, and character of goods entered at the custom house for export or import.

BILL OF EXCEPTIONS. A written statement of objections to the decision of the court upon a point of law, made by a party to the cause, and properly certified by the judge or court who made the decision. Powell, App. Proc. 211. It contains only the facts on which the adjudication complained of is founded. 10 Mo. 660. But where the sufficiency of the evidence is questioned, all the evidence must be set out. 13 Ind. 412.

BILL OF EXCHANGE. A written order from one person to another, directing the person to whom it is addressed to pay to a third person a certain sum of money therein named. Byles, Bills, 1.

An unconditional order in writing addressed by one person to another, signed by the person giving it, and requiring the person to whom it is addressed to pay on demand, or at a fixed or determinable future time, a sum certain in money to order or to bearer. N. Y. Neg. Inst. Law, § 210.

A bill of exchange may be negotiable or nonnegotiable. If negotiable, it may be transferred either before or after acceptance.

The person making the bill, called the drawer, is said to draw upon the person to whom it is directed, and undertakes impliedly to pay the amount with certain costs if he refuse to comply with the command. The drawee is not liable on the bill till after acceptance, and then becomes liable as principal to the extent of the terms of the acceptance; while the drawer becomes liable to the payee and indorsee conditionally upon the failure of the acceptor to pay. The liabilities between indorsers and indorsees are subject to the same rules as those of indorsers and indorsees on promissory notes. Regularly, the drawee is the person to become acceptor; but other parties may accept, under special circumstances.

BILL OF GROSS ADVENTURE. In French maritime law. Any written instrument which contains a contract of bottomry, *respondentia*, or any other kind of maritime loan. There is no corresponding English term. Hall, Mar. Loans, 182, note. See "Bottomry;" "Gross Adventure;" "Respondentia."

BILL OF HEALTH.

——In Commercial Law. A certificate, properly authenticated, that a certain ship or vessel therein named comes from a place where no contagious distempers prevail, and that none of the crew at the time of her departure were infected with any such distemper. It is generally found on board ships coming from the Levant, or from the coasts of Barbary, where the plague prevails (1 Marsh. Ins. 408), and is necessary whenever a ship sails from a suspected port, or where it is required at the port of destination (Holt, 167; 1 Bell; Comm. [5th Ed.] 553).

——In Scotch Law. An application of a person in custody to be discharged on account of ill health. Where the health of a prisoner requires it, he may be indulged, under proper regulations, with such a degree of liberty as may be necessary to restore him. 2 Bell, Comm. (5th Ed.) 549; Paterson, Comp. § 1129.

BILL OF INDEMNITY. An act of parliament frequently passed in England for the relief of officers who have not properly qualified, as by failure to take the oath of office, etc. Abbott; Wharton.

BILL OF INDICTMENT. In practice. A written accusation of one or more persons of a crime or misdemeanor, lawfully presented to a grand jury. See "Indictment."

BILL OF INFORMATION. In equity practice. One which is instituted by the attorney general or other proper officer in behalf of the state, or of those whose rights are the objects of its care and protection. If the suit immediately concerns the right of the state, the information is generally exhibited without a relator. If it does not immediately concern those rights, it is conducted at the instance and under the immediate direction of some person whose name is inserted in the information, and is termed the "relator." In case a relator is concerned, the officers of the state are not further concerned than as they are instructed and advised by those whose rights the state is called upon to protect and establish. 3 Bl. Comm. 261; Story, Eq. Pl. 5.

BILL OF INTERPLEADER. One in which the person exhibiting it claims no right in opposition to the rights claimed by the person against whom the bill is exhibited, but prays the decree of the court touching the rights of those persons, for the safety of the person exhibiting the bill. 24 Barb. (N. Y.) 154; 19 Ga. 513.

A bill exhibited by one who, not knowing to whom he ought of right to render a debt or duty, fears he may be hurt by some of the claimants, and therefore prays he may interplead, so that the court may judge to whom the thing belongs, and he is thereby safe on the payment. 2 Paige, Ch. (N. Y.) 199, 570; 6 Johns. Ch. (N. Y.) 445; 3 Jones (N. C.) 83.

BILL OF LADING. The written evidence of a contract for the carriage and delivery of goods sent by sea for a certain freight. Loughborough, J., 1 H. Bl. 359.

"A formal acknowledgment of the receipt of goods, and an engagement to deliver them to the consignee." 1 Rawle (Pa.) 203.

"A written acknowledgment, signed by the master, that he has received the goods therein described from the shipper, to be transported on the terms therein expressed to the prescribed destination, and there to be delivered to the consignee or parties therein designated." 14 Wall. (U. S.) 579.

The term is commonly applied, as well, to similar acknowledgments by carriers by land.

A bill of lading partakes of the nature of both a receipt and a contract. 30 Ala. 608; 13 Ind. 519. So much of it as is a mere receipt for goods may be contradicted or varied by parol (34 Me. 554; 74 Mass. 281), but so much of it as is a contract is governed by the rules applying to other contracts in writing (26 Ala. 487; 4 Ohio, 334; 61 Mo. App. 204).

BILL OF MIDDLESEX. An old form of process similar to a *capias*, issued out of the court of king's bench in personal actions, directed to the sheriff of the county of Middlesex (hence the name), and commanding him to take the defendant and have him before the king at Westminster on a day named, to answer the plaintiff's complaint.

Once, when the court sat at Oxford, it was termed a "Bill of Oxfordshire." 3 Steph. Comm. 404, note (1). It was abolished by St. 2 Wm. IV. c. 39.

BILL OF MORTALITY. A written statement or account of the number of deaths which have occurred in a certain district during a given time, usually spoken of in the plural. In some places, as in London, births, as well as deaths, are included.

BILL OF OXFORDSHIRE. See "Bill of Middlesex."

BILL OF PAINS AND PENALTIES. A special act of the legislature which inflicts a punishment less than death upon persons supposed to be guilty of high offenses, such as treason and felony, without any conviction in the ordinary course of judicial proceedings. 2 Wooddeson, Lect. 625. It differs from a bill of attainder in this, that the punishment inflicted by the latter is death. It has been thought by some that the clause in the constitution prohibiting bills of attainder includes bills of pains and penalties. 6 Cranch (U. S.) 138; Story, Const. § 1338.

BILL OF PARCELS. An account containing in detail the names of the items which compose a parcel or package of goods. It is usually transmitted with the goods to the purchaser, in order that, if any mistake have been made, it may be corrected.

BILL OF PARTICULARS. In practice. A detailed informal statement of a plaintiff's cause of action, or of the defendant's set-off, furnished by one party to the other in compliance with a statute, rule or special order of court. It may be required in actions of tort, as well as on contract.

BILL OF PEACE. One brought to restrain repeated attempts to litigate the same right. Bispham, Eq. § 415; Daniell, Ch. Pr. 1532.

BILL OF PRIVILEGE. In English law. The form of proceeding against an attorney of the court, who is not liable to arrest. Brooke, Abr. "Bille;" 12 Mod. 163; 3 Bl. Comm. 289.

BILL OF PROOF. In English practice. The claim made by a third person to the subject-matter in dispute between the parties to a suit in the court of the mayor of London. 2 Chit. Prac. 492; 1 Marsh. 233.

BILL OF REVIEW. One which is brought to have a decree in equity of the court reviewed, altered, or reversed. The object of the bill is to reverse the decree as far as it is erroneous, and to retry the cause. 69 Ala. 65.

BILL OF REVIVOR. A bill in equity brought to continue a suit which has abated before its final consummation, as, for example, by death, or marriage of a female plaintiff. Story, Eq. Pl. § 20.

BILL OF REVIVOR AND SUPPLEMENT. In equity practice. One which is a compound of a supplemental bill and bill of revivor, and not only continues the suit, which has abated by the death of the plaintiff, or the like, but supplies any defects in the original bill arising from subsequent events, so as to entitle the party to relief on the whole merits of his case. 5 Johns. Ch. (N. Y.) 334; Mitf. Eq. Pl. 32, 74.

BILL OF RIGHTS. In constitutional law. A formal and public declaration or assertion, in writing, of popular rights and liberties, usually expressed in the form of a statute, or promulgated on occasions of revolution, or the establishment of new forms of government, or new constitutions. The English statute of 1 Wm. & Mary, st. 2, c. 2, is denominated the "Bill of Rights." 1 Bl. Comm. 128. Several of the United States have incorporated formal bills of rights into their constitutions. See 2 Kent, Comm. 1-11.

BILL OF SALE. A written agreement, often under seal, by which one person transfers his right to or interest in goods and personal chattels to another, but a seal is not essential. 14 Wall. (U. S.) 244. It is in frequent use in the transfer of personal property, especially that of which immediate possession is not or cannot be given.

In England, a bill of sale of a ship at sea or out of the country in called a "grand bill of sale," but no distinction is recognized in this country between grand and ordinary bills of sale. 4 Mass. 661. The effect of a bill of sale is to transfer the property in the thing sold.

BILL OF SIGHT. A written description of goods, supposed to be inaccurate, but made as nearly exact as possible, furnished by an importer or his agent to the proper officer of the customs, to procure a landing and inspection of the goods. It is allowed by an English statute where the merchant is ignorant of the real quantity and quality of goods consigned to him, so as to be unable to make a proper entry of them. The entry must be perfected within three days after landing the goods. St. 3 & 4 Wm. IV. c. 52, § 24.

BILL OF STORE. In English law. A kind of license granted at the custom house to merchants to carry such stores and provisions as are necessary for their voyage, custom free. Jacob.

BILL OF SUFFERANCE. In English law. A license granted to a merchant, permitting him to trade from one English port to another without paying customs.

BILL PAYABLE. In mercantile law. A bill of exchange accepted, or a promissory note made, by a merchant, whereby he has engaged to pay money. It is so called as being payable by him. An account is usually kept of such bills in a book with that title, and also in the ledger. See Pars. Notes & Bills.

BILL PENAL. In contracts. A written obligation, by which a debtor acknowledges himself indebted in a certain sum, and binds himself for the payment thereof in a larger sum.

Bonds with conditions have superseded such bills in modern practice. Steph. Pl. 265, note. They are sometimes called "bills obligatory," and are properly so called, but every bill obligatory is not a bill penal. Comyn, Dig. "Obligations" (D); Cro. Car. 515. See 2 Vent. 106, 198.

BILL QUIA TIMET. In equity practice. A remedy by bill in equity to protect rights against possible future injuries or impairment. One which is filed when a person is entitled to property of a personal nature after another's death, and has reason to apprehend it may be destroyed by the present possessor; or when he is apprehensive of being subjected to a future inconvenience, probable or even possible, to happen or be occasioned by the neglect, inadvertence, or culpability of another.

Upon a proper case being made out, the court will, in one case, secure the property for the use of the party (which is the object of the bill), by compelling the person in possession of it to give a proper security against any subsequent disposition or willful destruction, and, in the other case, they will quiet the party's apprehension of future inconvenience by removing the causes which may lead to it. 1 Madd. Ch. Pr. 218; Blake, Ch. Pr. 37, 47; 2 Story, Eq. Jur. §§ 825, 851. See 9 Grat. (Va.) 398; 11 Ga. 570; 8 Tex. 337; 2 Md. Ch. Dec. 157, 442; 4 Edw. Ch. (N. Y.) 228; Bouv. Inst.

BILL RECEIVABLE. In mercantile law. A promissory note, bill of exchange, or other written security for money payable at a future day, which a merchant holds. So called because the amounts for which they are given are receivable by the merchant. They are entered in a book so called, and are charged to an account in the ledger under the same title, to which account the cash, when received, is credited. See Pars. Notes & Bills.

BILL RENDERED. See "Account."

BILL, SINGLE. In contracts. A written unconditional promise by one or more persons to pay to another person or other persons, therein named, a sum of money at a time therein specified. It is usually under seal, and may then be called a "bill obligatory." 2 Serg. & R. (Pa.) 115. It has no condition attached, and is not given in a penal sum. Comyn, Dig. "Obligation" (C).

BILL TO CARRY A DECREE INTO EXECUTION. In equity practice. One which is filed when, from the neglect of parties, or some other cause, it may become impossible to carry a decree into execution without the further decree of the court. Hinde, Ch. Pr. 68.

BILL TO MARSHAL ASSETS. See "Marshalling Assets."

BILL TO MARSHAL SECURITIES. See "Marshalling Securities."

BILL TO PERPETUATE TESTIMONY. In equity practice. One which is brought to secure the testimony of witnesses with reference to some matter which is not in litigation, but is liable to become so. It differs from a bill to take testimony *de bene esse*, inasmuch as the latter is sustainable only when there is a suit already depending. It is demurrable if it contain a prayer for relief. 1 Dickens, 98; 2 P. Wms. 162; 2 Ves. Jr. 497; 2 Madd. Ch. 37. And see 1 Schoales & L. 316.

BILL TO SUSPEND A DECREE. In equity practice. One brought to avoid or suspend a decree under special circumstances. See 1 Ch. Cas. 3, 61; 2 Ch. Cas. 8; Mitf. Eq. Pl. 85, 86.

BILL TO TAKE TESTIMONY DE BENE esse. In equity practice. One which is brought to take the testimony of witnesses to a fact material to the prosecution of a suit at law which is actually commenced, where there is good cause to fear that the testimony may otherwise be lost before the time of trial. See 1 Sim. & S. 83; 2 Story, Eq. Jur. § 1813, note.

It lies, in general, where witnesses are aged or infirm (Coop. Eq. Pl. 57; Ambl. 65; 13 Ves. 56, 261), propose to leave the country (3 Dickens, 454; Story, Eq. Pl. § 308), or there is but a single witness to a fact (1 P. Wms. 97; 2 Dickens, 648).

BILLA CASSETUR (Lat. that the bill be quashed or made void). A plea in abatement concluded, when the pleadings were in Latin, *quod billa cassetur*, that the bill be quashed. 3 Bl. Comm. 303; Graham, Prac. 611.

BILLA EXCAMBII (or **ESCAMBII**). A bill of exchange.

BILLA EXONERATIONIS. A bill of lading.

BILLA VERA (Lat. a true bill). The form of words indorsed on a bill of indictment, when proceedings were conducted in Latin, to indicate the opinion of the grand jury that the person therein accused ought to be tried.

BILLET (Law Lat.) In old English law. A bill or petition exhibited in parliament. Cowell.

BILLET DE CHANGE. In French law. A contract to furnish a bill of exchange; a contract to pay the value of a bill of exchange already furnished. Guyot, Rep. Univ.

Where a person intends to furnish a bill of exchange (*lettre de change*), and is not quite prepared to do so, he gives a *billet de change*, which is a contract to furnish a *lettre de change* at a future time. Guyot, Rep. Univ.; Story, Bills, § 2.

BILLETING SOLDIERS. Quartering them in the houses of citizens.

BIND OUT. To engage as an apprentice.

BIND OVER. The order of a magistrate in requiring one to give bail to appear for hearing in a higher court, or to keep the peace.

BINDING OUT. A term applied to the contract of apprenticeship.

BINDING OVER. The act by which a magistrate or court hold to bail a party accused of a crime or misdemeanor. The binding over may be to appear at a court having jurisdiction of the offense charged, to answer, or to be of good behavior, or to keep the peace.

BIPARTITE. Of two parts. This term is used in conveyancing; as, this indenture bipartite, between A., of the one part, and B., of the other part.

BIRRETUM, or BIRRETUS. A cap or coif used formerly in England by judges and sergeants at law. Spelman; Cunningham.

BIRTH. The act of being wholly brought into the world.

The conditions of live birth are not satisfied when a part only of the body is born. The whole body must be brought into the world, and detached from that of the mother, and after this event the child must be alive. 5 Car. & P. 329; 7 Car. & P. 814. The circulating system must also be changed, and the child must have an independent circulation. 5 Car. & P. 539; 9 Car. & P. 154. But it is not necessary that there should have been a separation of the umbilical cord. That may still connect the child with its mother, and yet the killing of it will constitute murder. 7 Car. & P. 814; 9 Car. & P. 25. See 1 Beck, Med. Jur. 478; 1 Chit. Med. Jur. 438.

BIS. (Lat.) Twice.

BIS DAT QUI CITO DAT. He gives twice who gives quickly.

BIS IDEM EXIGI BONA FIDES NON PAtitur, et in satisfactionibus, non permittitur amplius fieri quam semel factum est. Good faith does not suffer the same thing to be exacted twice, and, in making satisfaction, it is not permitted that more should be done after satisfaction is once made. 9 Coke, 53; Dig. 50. 17. 57.

BISANTIUM, BESANTINE, or BEZANT. An ancient coin, first issued at Constantinople. It was of two sorts,—gold, equivalent to a ducat, valued at 9s. 6d., and silver, computed at 2s. They were both current in England. Wharton.

BISHOP. An ecclesiastical officer, who is the chief of the clergy of his diocese, and is the archbishop's assistant. No such officer is recognized by law in the United States.

BISHOPRIC. In ecclesiastical law. The extent of country over which a bishop has jurisdiction; a see; a diocese.

BISHOP'S COURT. In English law. An ecclesiastical court held in the cathedral of each diocese, the judge of which is the bishop's chancellor.

BISSEXTILE. The day which is added every fourth year to the month of February, in order to make the year agree with the course of the sun.

It was called "bissextile" because in the Roman calendar it was fixed on the sixth day before the calends of March (which answers to the twenty-fourth day of February), and this day was counted twice,

The first was called *bissextus prior*, and the other *bissextus posterior*, but the latter was properly called "bissextile" or "intercalary" day.

BLACK ACRE and WHITE ACRE. Terms used by the old writers to distinguish one parcel of land from another, to avoid ambiguity, as well as the inconvenience of a full description.

They are mere names of convenience, adopted, as "A." and "B." are, to distinguish persons or things under similar circumstances.

BLACK ACT. In English law. The act of parliament 9 Geo. II. c. 22. This act was passed for the punishment of certain marauders, who committed great outrages disguised and with faces blackened. It was repealed by 7 & 8 Geo. IV. c. 11. See 4 Bl. Comm. 245.

BLACK ACTS. Old Scotch statutes passed in the reigns of the Stuarts and down to the year 1586 or 1587. So called because printed in black letter. Bell, Dict.; Wharton.

BLACK BOOK OF HEREFORD. In English law. An old record frequently referred to by Cowell and other early writers.

BLACK BOOK OF THE ADMIRALTY. An ancient book compiled in the reign of Edward III. It has always been deemed of the highest authority in matters concerning the admiralty. It contains the laws of Oleron, at large, a view of the crimes and offenses cognizable in the admiralty, ordinances and commentaries on matters of prize and maritime torts, injuries, and contracts. 2 Gall. (U. S.) 404. It is said by Selden to be not more ancient than the reign of Henry VI. Selden, de Laud. Leg. Ang. c. 32. By other writers it is said to have been composed earlier.

BLACK BOOK OF THE EXCHEQUER. The name of a book kept in the English exchequer, containing a collection of treaties, conventions, charters, etc.

BLACK CAP. It is a vulgar error that the headdress worn by the judge in pronouncing the sentence of death is assumed as an emblem of the sentence. It is part of the judicial full dress, and is worn by the judges on occasions of especial state. Wharton.

BLACK GAME. Heath fowl, in contradistinction to red game, as grouse..

BLACK MAIL. Rents reserved, payable in work, grain, and the like. Such rents were called "black mail" (*reditus nigri*), in distinction from white rents (*blanche firmes*), which were rents paid in silver.

A yearly payment made for security and protection to those bands of marauders who infested the borders of England and Scotland about the middle of the sixteenth century, and laid the inhabitants under contribution. Hume, Hist. Eng. vol. 1, p. 473; Id. vol. 2, App. No. 8; Cowell.

In common usage the term signifies the obtaining of money by a demand accompanied by threats of prosecution, exposure or injury in case of nonpayment The corrup. taking under color of office is "extortion." (*q. v.*)

BLACK RENTS. Rents reserved in work, grain, or baser money than silver. Whishaw.

BLACK ROD, GENTLEMAN USHER OF. A chief officer of the king, deriving his name from the black rod of office, on the top of which reposes a golden lion, which he carries. During the session of parliament he attends on the peers, and to his custody all peers impeached for crime or contempt are first committed.

BLACK WARD. A subvassal, who held ward of the king's vassal.

BLADA. Growing crops of grain. Spelman. Any annual crop. Cowell. Used of crops, either growing or gathered. Reg. Orig. 94b; Coke, 2d Inst. 81.

BLADARIUS. In old English law. A corn monger; meal man or corn chandler; a bladier, or engrosser of corn or grain. Blount; 2 Inst. 81.

BLANC SEIGN. *Carte blanche (q. v.)* See 6 Mart. (La.) 718.

BLANCH HOLDING. In Scotch law. A tènure by which land is held. The duty is generally a trifling one, as a peppercorn. It may happen, however, that the duty is of greater value, and then the distinction received in practice is founded on the nature of the duty. Stair, Inst. sec. iii. lib. 3, § 33. See Paterson, Comp. 15; 2 Sharswood, Bl. Comm. 42.

BLANCHE FIRME. A rent reserved, payable in silver.

BLANCUS (Law Lat.) In old law and practice. White, as paper or parchment is when there is no writing or other mark upon it; otherwise called *albus*. See "Album Breve." Hence the modern term "blank."

Plain or smooth, as silver money that has no impression, or from which the impression has been worn.

BLANK. A space left in writing, to be filled up with one or more words to complete sense.

A skeleton document, in which the formal words are printed, and blanks left for the insertion of words necessary to adapt the same to the particular case.

BLANK ACCEPTANCE. An acceptance written on the paper before the bill is made, and delivered by the acceptor. In England it will charge the acceptor to the extent warranted by the stamp.

BLANK BAR. See "Common Bar."

BLANK BONDS. Scotch securities, in which the creditor's name was left blank, and which passed by mere delivery, the bearer being at liberty to put in his name, and sue for payment. Declared void by Act 1696, c. 25.

BLANK INDORSEMENT. An indorsement which does not mention the name of the person in whose favor it is made. Such an indorsement is generally effected by writing the indorser's name merely on the back of the bill. Chit. Bills, 170.

BLANKET POLICY. A fire insurance policy not on particular goods, but on whatever there may be at a certain time, of a varying quantity, as on a stock of goods subject to sale and replenishing. See 93 U. S. 541.

BLANKS. A kind of white money (value 8d). coined by Henry V. in those parts of France which were then subject to England; forbidden to be current in that realm by 2 Hen. VI. c. 9. Wharton.

BLASARIUS. An incendiary. Blount.

BLASPHEMY. In criminal law. To attribute to God that which is contrary to his nature, and does not belong to him, and to deny what does. A false reflection uttered with a malicious design of reviling God. Emlyn's Pref. to 8 St. Tr.

To willfully revile the Deity or sacred things.

Malicious reproach of God, his name, attributes, or religion. 2 Bish. Crim. Law, § 76.

In general, blashphemy may be described as consisting in speaking evil of the Deity with an impious purpose to derogate from the divine majesty, and to alienate the minds of others from the love and reverence of God. It is purposely using words concerning God calculated and designed to impair and destroy the reverence, respect, and confidence due to him as the intelligent creator, governor, and judge of the world. It embraces the idea of detraction, when used towards the Supreme Being; as "calumny" usually carries the same idea when applied to an individual. It is a willful and malicious attempt to lessen men's reverence of God by denying his existence, or his attributes as an intelligent creator, governor, and judge of men, and to prevent their having confidence in him as such. 20 Pick. (Mass.) 211, 212, per Shaw, C. J.

BLENCH, or BLENCH HOLDING. See "Blanch Holding."

BLENDED FUND. In England, where a testator directs his real and personal estate to be sold, and disposes of the proceeds as forming one aggregate, this is called a "blended fund." The expression is chiefly used in cases where part of the testator's disposition fails, by lapse or otherwise, so that it becomes a question whether so much of the undisposed-of portion as consists of or arises from land goes to the testator's heir at law or next of kin. 1 Brown, 503; 1 White & T. Lead. Cas. 783; 1 Mylne & K. 665.

BLINKS. In old English law. Boughs broken down from trees and thrown in a way where deer are likely to pass. Jacob.

BLOCKADE. Blockade is where a belligerent power maintains such a naval force near the shore or ports of the other belligent as to prevent access to them, or, as it is sometimes put, the vessels must be so disposed that there is an evident danger in entering the port, or approaching the shore, notwithstanding that the blockading squadron may be accidentally absent for a time, *e. g.*, from being blown off by the wind. Under the Declaration of Paris (*q. v.*), a blockade is not effective unless maintained by an adequate force.

A blockade *de facto* is where the blockade has not been notified (as is usually done) by the belligerent to neutral governments, so that every approaching vessel has to be warned off by the squadron. Vessels attempting to pass a blockade are liable to confiscation.

It is not necessary that the place should be invested by land as well as by sea; but a blockade by sea does not impair the right of neutrals to carry on a trade by land. 1 Kent, Comm. 147.

A *pacific* blockade is the interruption of commercial intercourse with certain ports or coasts of a state to secure redress for an international wrong. Davis Int. L. 67.

BLOOD. Relationship; stock; family. 1 Rop. Leg. 103; 1 Belt, Supp. Ves. 365. Kindred. Bac. Max. reg. 18.

Brothers and sisters are said to be of the whole blood if they have the same father and mother, and of the half-blood if they have only one parent in common. 5 Whart. (Pa.) 477.

BLOOD MONEY. Money paid to the relatives of one killed by another.

Money paid as a reward for the conviction of one charged with a capital offense.

BLOODWIT. An amercement for bloodshed. Cowell. The privilege of taking such amercements. Skene de Verb. Sign. A privilege or exemption from paying a fine or amercement assessed for bloodshed. Cowell; Kennett, Par. Ant.; Termes de la Ley.

BLOODY HAND. In forest law. The having the hands or other parts bloody, which, in a person caught trespassing in the forest against venison, was one of the four kinds of circumstantial evidence of his having killed deer, although he was not found in the act of chasing or hunting. Manw. For. Law; Cowell. See "Backbear." Corresponds to the Scotch "Red Hand." Blount.

BLUE LAWS. A name applied to certain laws of extreme rigor, supposed to have been anciently in force in Connecticut. Rigorous puritanical laws, generally.

BOARD. The governing body of officers of a corporation or municipality. The members are usually called directors, trustees, aldermen, or supervisors.

Also, the body or commission invested with control or supervision of particular functions, and matters of government, as public health, charities, or improvements.

BOARD OF HEALTH. An executive or administrative body organized as part of the government or of its local divisions, like cities, to regulate and supervise matters affecting the public health or sanitation.

BOARD OF SUPERVISORS. A county board, under a system existing in some of the states, to whom the fiscal affairs of the county are intrusted, composed of delegates representing the several organized towns or townships of the county. This system originated in the state of New York, and has been adopted in others. The board, when convened, forms a deliberative body, usually acting under parliamentary rules.

BOARD OF TRADE. See "Chamber of Commerce."

BOARD OF WORKS. The name of a board of officers appointed for the better local management of the English metropolis. They have the care and management of all grounds and gardens dedicated to the use of the inhabitants in the metropolis; also the superintendence of the drainage; also the regulation of the street traffic, and generally, of the buildings of the metropolis. Brown.

BOARDER. One who, by a special contract, obtains food, with or without lodging, in the house of another. To be distinguished from a guest (*q. v.*) Story, Bailm. § 477; 26 Vt. 343; 26 Ala. (N. S.) 371; 7 Cush. (Mass.) 417.

BOARDING HOUSE. A *quasi* public house where boarders are habitually kept, and which is held out and known as a place of entertainment of that kind. 1 Lans. (N. Y.) 484, 486; 3 Abb. Pr. (N. S.; N. Y.) 26. The characteristic of a boarding house is that accommodation is furnished for a definite period. 24 How. Pr. (N. Y.) 62.

BOC (Saxon). A writing; a book. Used of the *land bocs*, or evidences of title among the Saxons, corresponding to modern deeds. These *bocs* were destroyed by William the Conqueror. 1 Spence, Eq. Jur. 22; 1 Washb. Real Prop. 17, 21.

BOC HORDE. A place where books, evidences, or writings are kept. Cowell. These were generally in monasteries. 1 Spence, Eq. Jur. 22.

BOC LAND. Allodial lands held by written evidence of title. Such lands might be granted upon such terms as the owner should see fit, by greater or less estate, to take effect presently, or at a future time, or on the happening of any event. In this respect they differed essentially from feuds. 1 Washb. Real Prop. 17; 4 Kent, Comm. 441.

BOCERAS (Saxon). A scribe, notary, or chancellor among the Saxons. Crabb, Hist. Eng. Law, 28; Barr. Obs. St. 404, note (1).

BODILY HEIRS. The expression "bodily heirs," when used in a conveyance or devise of real estate, has no other or different meaning than the words "heirs of his body." Turner v. Hause, 199 Ill. 470.

BODMERIE, BODEMERIE, or **BODDEmerey** (Belg. and Ger.) Bottomry (*q. v.*) Locc. de Jur. Mar. lib. 2, c. 6, § 1.

BODY. A person. Used of a natural body, or of an artificial one created by law, as a corporation.

The main part or frame of anything, as distinguished from its subordinate parts. 22 N. Y. 147; 5 Mason (U. S.) 300.

A collection of individuals united for a common purpose. See 23 Wend. (N. Y.) 141.

BODY CORPORATE. A corporation. This is an early and undoubtedly correct term to apply to a corporation. Co. Litt. 250a; 23 Wend. (N. Y.) 141; 81 Pa. St. 389.

BODY OF A COUNTY. A county at large, as distinguished from any particular place within it. See 25 Wis. 364.

Under the common law, in both civil and criminal cases, the jury were to be taken from the visne or neighborhood,—from among the neighbors and equals of the litigants or the accused,—and by long usage this came to mean from the body of the county. 232 Ill. 114.

BODY OF AN INSTRUMENT. The main and operative part; the substantive provisions, as distinguished from the recitals, title, jurat, etc. Wharton.

BODY POLITIC (or **POLITIQUE**). The old term for a corporation. Statute of Uses, § 1; Co. Litt. 95a, 250a.

Applied generally to the state or nation.

BOILARY. Water rising from a salt well belonging to a person who is not the owner of the soil.

BOIS, BOYS, or **BOYES** (Law F.; Lat. *boscus*), Wood; *haut bois*, high timber; *sub bois*, underwood. Cowell.

BOLHAGIUM, or **BOLDAGIUM**. A little house or cottage. Blount.

BOLTING. In English practice. A term formerly used in the English inns of court, but more particularly at Gray's Inn, signifying the private arguing of cases, as distinguished from mooting, which was a more formal and public mode of argument. Cowell; Tomlin; Holthouse.

The deserting by one or more persons from the political party to which they belong, or the permanent withdrawal of a portion of the delegates in a political convention.

BON (Fr.)

——**In Old French Law.** A royal order or check on the treasury, invented by Francis I. *Bon pour mille livres*, good for a thousand livres. Steph. Lect. 387.

——**In Modern Law.** The name of a clause (*bon pour* ——, good for so much) added to a cedule or promise, where it is not in the handwriting of the signer, containing the amount of the sum which he obliges himself to pay. Poth. Obl. pt. 4, c. 1, art. 2, § 1.

BONA (Lat. *bonus*). Goods; personal property; chattels, real or personal; real property.

Bona et catalla (goods and chattels) includes all kinds of property which a man may possess. In the Roman law it signified every kind of property, real, personal, and mixed; but chiefly it was applied to real estate, chattels being distinguished by the words "effects," "movables," etc. *Bona* were, however, divided into *bona mobilia* and *bona immobilia*. It is taken in the civil law in nearly the sense of *biens* in the French law.

BONA CONFISCATA. Goods confiscated or forfeited to the imperial *fisc* or treasury. 1 Sharswood, Bl. Comm. 299.

BONA ET CATALLA. Goods and chattels; movable property of every description. See 16 Mees. & W. 68.

BONA FELONUM (Lat.) In English law. Goods of felons; the goods of one convicted of felony. 5 Coke, 110.

BONA FIDE POSSESSOR FACIT FRUCtus consumptos suos. By good faith, a possessor makes the fruits consumed his own. Tray. Lat. Max. 57.

BONA FIDE PURCHASER. One who buys property without notice, actual or constructive, that some third person has a right to or interest in it, and pays a full and fair price for it at the time of such purchase, or before he has notice of the claim or interest of such third person. 65 Barb. (N. Y.) 227. If he has paid but a part of the consideration, he is a *bona fide* purchaser *pro tanto* only. 3 Barb. Ch. (N. Y.) 498.

There must be (a) absence of notice or of suspicious circumstances tending to put a reasonably cautious man on inquiry (12 Barb. [N. Y.] 605), and (b) a present valuable consideration, a good consideration (49 N. Y. 286), or one that is past (52 N. Y. 138) or executory (14 Mich. 514), being insufficient. The term implies an actual reliance in good faith on the apparent right of the seller. 28 Ga. 170.

BONA FIDES. Good faith, honesty, as distinguished from *mala fides*, bad faith.

Bona fide, in good faith.

BONA FIDES EXIGIT UT QUOD CONvenit fiat. Good faith demands that what is agreed upon shall be done. Dig. 19. 20. 21; Id. 19. 1. 50; Id. 50. 8. 2. 13.

BONA FIDES NON PATITUR, UT BIS idem exigatur. Good faith does not allow us to demand twice the payment of the same thing. Dig. 50. 17. 57.

BONA FORISFACTA. Forfeited goods. 1 Bl. Comm. 299.

BONA FUGITIVORUM (Lat.) In English law. Goods of fugitives; the proper goods of him who flies for felony. 5 Coke, 109b.

BONA GESTURA. Good behavior.

BONA GRATIA. Voluntarily; by mutual consent. Used of a divorce obtained by the agreement of both parties.

BONA MEMORIA. Good memory. Used chiefly in respect to testamentary capacity. Abbott.

BONA MOBILIA. In civil law. Movables. Those things which move themselves or can be transported from one place to another; which are not intended to make a permanent part of a farm, heritage, or building.

BONA NOTABILIA. Chattels or goods of sufficient value to be accounted for.

Where a decedent leaves goods of sufficient amount (*bona notabilia*) in different dioceses, administration is granted by the metropolitan, to prevent the confusion arising from the appointment of many different administrators. 2 Bl. Comm. 509; Rolle, Abr. 908; Williams, Ex'rs, Index. The value necessary to constitute property *bona notabilia* has varied at different periods, but was finally established at £5, in 1603.

BONA PATRIA. In Scotch law. An assize or jury of countrymen or good neighbors. Bell, Dict.

BONA PERITURA. Perishable goods.

An executor, administrator, or trustee is bound to use due diligence in disposing of perishable goods, such as fattened cattle, grain, fruit, or any other article which may be worse for keeping. Bac. Abr. "Executors;" 1 Rolle, Abr. 910; 5 Coke, 9; Cro. Eliz. 518, 3 Munf. (Va.) 288; 1 Beatty, 5, 14; Dane, Abr. Index.

BONA UTLAGATORUM. In English law. Goods of outlaws. Hale, Anal. § VIII.

BONA VACANTIA. Goods to which no one claims a property, as shipwrecks, treasure trove, etc.; vacant goods. These *bona vacantia* belonged, under the common law, to the finder, except in certain instances, when they were the property of the king. 1 Sharswood, Bl. Comm. 298, note.

BONA WAVIATA. Goods waived or thrown away by a thief in his fright for fear of being apprehended. Such goods belong to the sovereign. 1 Bl. Comm. 296.

BONAE FIDEI (Lat.) In good faith.

BONAE FIDEI EMPTOR. A *bona fide* purchaser (*q. v.*)

BONAE FIDEI POSSESSOR IN ID TANtum quod ad se pervenerit tenetur. A *bona fide* possessor is bound for that only which has come to him. Coke, 2d Inst. 285; Grotius, de Jure Belli, lib. 2, c. 10, § 3 et seq.

BOND. A sealed obligation to pay money, either absolutely or conditionally. 2 Serg. & R. (Pa.) 502; 11 Ala. 19; 1 Harp. (S. C.) 434; 1 Blackf. (Ind.) 241; 6 Vt. 40; 1 Baldw. (U. S.) 129; 110 Mass. 454.

It may be single,—*simplex obligatio,*—as where the obligor obliges himself, his heirs, executors, and administrators, to pay a certain sum of money to another at a day named, or it may be conditional (which is the kind more generally used), that if the obligor does some particular act, the obligation shall be void, or else shall remain in full force, as payment of rent, performance of covenants in a deed, or repayment of a principal sum of money borrowed of the obligee, with interest, which principal sum is usually one-half of the penal sum specified in the bond. The term is usually applied only to the latter class. 3 Redf. Sur. (N. Y.) 459.

Certificates of indebtedness issued by corporations and municipal and governmental bodies, are also known as "bonds."

BOND FOR A DEED. An agreement to make title in the future. National, etc., Co. v. Three States, etc., Co. 217 Ill. 122; Langlois v. Stewart, 156 Ill. 612.

BOND TENANTS. In English law. Copyholders and customary tenants are sometimes so called. 2 Bl. Comm. 148.

BONDAGE. Is a term which has not obtained a juridical use distinct from the vernacular, in which it is either taken as a synonym with "slavery," or as applicable to any kind of personal servitude which is involuntary in its continuation.

BONDSMAN. A surety on a bond.

BONES GENTS. In old English law. Good men.

BONI HOMINES (Law Lat.) In old European law. Good men; a name given, in early European jurisprudence, to the tenants of the lord, who judged each other in the lord's courts. 3 Bl. Comm. 349. Blackstone, speaking of the origin of juries, says that all the nations which adopted the feudal system, as Germany, France, and Italy, had a tribunal composed of twelve good men and true (*boni homines*), usually the vassals or tenants of the lord, being the equals or peers of the parties litigant. Esprit des Lois, liv. 30, c. 18. This term has survived in the courts to the present day.

BONI JUDICIS EST AMPLIARE JURISdictionem; justitiam in. It is the part of a good judge to enlarge his jurisdiction; that is, his remedial authority. 1 Burrows, 304; Chanc. Prec. 329; 1 Wils. 284; 9 Mees. & W. 818; 1 C. B. (N. S.) 255; 4 Bing. N. C. 233; 4 Scott, N. R. 229; 17 Mass. 310.

BONI JUDICIS EST CAUSAS LITIUM dirimere. It is the duty of a good judge to remove causes of litigation. 2 Inst. 306.

BONI JUDICIS EST JUDICIUM SINE dilatione mandare executioni. It is the duty of a good judge to cause execution to issue on a judgment without delay. Co. Litt. 289.

BONI JUDICIS EST LITES DIRIMERE, ne lis ex lite oritur, et interest reipublicae ut sint fines litium. It is the duty of a good judge to prevent litigations, that suit may not grow out of suit, and it concerns the welfare of a state that an end be put to litigation. 4 Coke, 15; 5 Coke, 31a.

BONIS CEDERE (Lat.) In the civil law. To make a transfer or surrender of property, as a debtor did to his creditors. Code, 7. 71.

BONIS NON-AMOVENDIS. A writ addressed to the sheriff, when a writ of error has been brought, commanding that the person against whom judgment has been obtained be not suffered to remove his goods till the error be tried and determined. Reg. Orig. 131.

BONITARIAN. In the Roman law. Right of possession. Hence *bonitarian* ownership was an equitable title or special property, as distinguished from quiritarian ownership, that in accordance with the strict forms of law.

BONO ET MALO. A special writ of jail delivery, which formerly issued of course for each particular prisoner. 4 Bl. Comm. 270.

BONORUM POSSESSIO EDICTALIS. Lat. Possession of goods or property by edict. Inst. 3, 5, 8, 9, 10; Digs. 3, 28, 37, 38, 43.

BONUM DEFENDENTIS EX INTEGRA causa; malum ex quolibet defectu. The good of a defendant arises from a perfect case; his harm from some defect. 11 Coke, 68.

BONUM NECESSARIUM EXTRA TERminos necessitatis non est bonum. A thing good from necessity is not good beyond the limits of the necessity. Hob. 144.

BONUS. Something over and above, something additional, by way of compensation for something done or omitted; something not a gratuity, but beyond what is regularly due. 16 Wal. 471; 24 Conn. 154.

A premium paid to a grantor or vendor or donated sum beyond strict legal right.

A consideration given for what is received. Extraordinary profit accruing in the operations of a stock company or private corporation. 10 Ves. 185; 7 Sim. 634; 2 Spence, Eq. Jur. 569.

An additional premium paid for the use of money beyond the legal interest. 2 Pars. Cont. 391.

In its original sense of "good," the word was formerly much used. Thus, a jury was to be composed of twelve good men (*boni homines*) (3 Bl. Comm. 349), *bonus judex* (a good judge) (Co. Litt. 246).

An extra or donated sum beyond strict legal right.

BONUS JUDEX SECUNDUM AEQUUM et bonum judicat, et aequitatem stricto juri praefert. A good judge decides according to justice and right, and prefers equity to strict law. Co. Litt. 24; 4 Term R. 344; 2 Q. B. 837; Broom, Leg. Max. (3d London Ed.) 77.

BOOK. A general name given to every literary composition which is printed, but appropriately to a printed composition bound in a volume. A book may consist of but one page, and need not be bound. 2 Campb. 30, 32.

BOOK DEBT. A statutory remedy existing in several states for the collection of a debt evidenced by entries in books of account.

BOOK LAND. In English law. Land, also called charter land, which was held by deed under certain rents and fee services, and differed in nothing from free socage land. 2 Bl. Comm. 90. See 2 Spelman, English Works, 233, tit. "Of Ancient Deeds and Charters;" "Boc. Land."

BOOK OF ACTS. The records of a surrogate's court.

BOOK OF ADJOURNAL. In Scotch law. The records of the court of judiciary.

BOOK OF RATES. An account or enumeration of the duties or tariffs authorized by parliament. 1 Sharswood, Bl. Comm. 316; Jacob.

BOOK OF RESPONSES. In Scotch law. An account which the director of the chancery keeps particularly to note a seizure when he gives an order to the sheriff in that part to give it to an heir whose service has been returned to him. Wharton.

BOOKS OF SCIENCE. In evidence. Medical books, even of received authority, are not admissible in evidence. 12 Cush. (Mass.) 193; 1 Gray (Mass.) 337; 5 Car. & P. 74. See 2 Ind. 617; 1 Jones (N. C.) 386; 1 Chand. (Wis.) 178; 1 Cox, C. C. 94; 1 Towns. St. Tr. 357, 358.

BOON DAYS. Certain days in the year on which copyhold tenants were bound to perform certain services for the lord. Called, also, "due days." Whishaw.

BOOT, or BOTE. An old Saxon word, equivalent to "estovers." Brownl. & G. 170.

BOOTING (or BOTING) CORN. Certain rent corn, anciently so called. Cowell; Blount.

BOOTY. Personal property captured by a public enemy on land, in contradistinction to "prize," which is such property captured by such an enemy on the sea.

After booty has been in complete possession of the enemy for twenty-four hours, it becomes absolutely his, without any right of postliminy in favor of the original owner, particularly when it has passed *bona fide* into the hands of a neutral. 1 Kent, Comm. 110. The right to the booty, Pothier says, belongs to the sovereign; but sometimes the right of the sovereign, or of the public, is transferred to the soldiers, to encourage them. Poth. Dr. de Propriete, p. 1, c. 2, a. 1, § 2; 2 Burlam. Nat. Law, pt. 4, c. 7, note 12.

BORD. An old Saxon word, signifying a cottage; a house; a table.

BORD-HALFPENNY. A customary small toll paid to the lord of a town for setting up boards, tables, booths, etc., in fairs or markets.

BORD LANDS. Lands held in bordage.

The demesnes which the lords keep in their hands for the maintenance of their *bord* or table. Cowell.

BORDAGE. A species of base tenure by which *bord* lands were held. The tenants were called *bordarii (q. v.)*

BORDARII, or BORDIMANNI. In old English law. Tenants of a less servile condition than the *villani,* who had a *bord* or cottage, with a small parcel of land, allowed to them, on condition they should supply the lord with poultry and eggs, and other small provisions for his board or entertainment. Spelman.

BORDBRIGCH, BORGHBRECH, or **burghbrech.** In Saxon law. Breach or violation of pledge (*fide jussionis violatio*); pledge-breach (*plegii fractio*). Spelman. The offense of violating the *borg*, or pledge given by the inhabitants of a tithing. See "Borg."

BORDER WARRANT. A process granted by a judge ordinary, on either side of the border between England and Scotland, for arresting the person or effects of a person living on the opposite side, until he find security, *judicio sisti.* Bell, Dict.

BORDLODE. The rent or quantity of food which the *bordarii* paid for their lands. Cowell.

BORDSERVICE. A tenure of *bord* lands.

BOREL FOLK. Country people; derived from the French *bourre* (Lat. *floccus*), a lock of wool, because they covered their heads with such stuff. Blount.

BORG (Saxon). Suretyship.

Borgbriche (violation of a pledge of suretyship) was a fine imposed on the *borg* for property stolen within its limits.

A tithing in which each one became a surety for the others for their good behavior. Spelman; Cowell; 1 Bl. Comm. 115.

BORGESMON (Saxon). The land of each family composing a tithing.

BORGH OF HAMHALD. In old Scotch law. A pledge or surety given by the seller of goods to the buyer, to make the goods forthcoming as his own proper goods, and to warrant the same to him. Skene de Verb. Sign.

BOROUGH. In the old sense of the word, borough is "an ancient towne, holden of the king or any other lord, which sendeth burgesses to the parliament." Litt. § 164; Co. Litt. 109a. Many of these boroughs, however, having been disfranchised in modern times, are now only boroughs to this extent, that the land within them is held by tenure in burgage or subject to the custom of borough English (*q. v.*) At the present day, "borough" almost always means either a borough corporate, or municipal borough, or a parliamentary borough (see 1 Bl. Comm. 115; 1 Steph. Comm. 125), most, if not all, municipal boroughs being also parliamentary.

A parliamentary borough is a town which returns one or more members to parliament. See Parliamentary and Municipal Registration Act 1878, § 4. Some of these towns are ancient boroughs; others are towns on which the right of returning members has been conferred by statute. St. 2 Wm. IV. c. 45; 30 & 31 Vict. c. 102.

——In Scotch Law. A corporation organized under a royal charter. Bell, Dict.

——In American Law. The word is little used. In Pennsylvania and Connecticut, however, it is in common use, and denotes an incorporated town or village. Bright. Purd. Dig. 115; 23 Conn. 128.

Borough, synonymous with "town." 1 Bl. Comm. 114. Borough, synonymous with "village." 18 Ohio St. 496.

BOROUGH COURTS. In English law. Private courts of limited jurisdiction held in particular districts by prescription, charter, or act of parliament, for the prosecution of petty suits. 19 Geo. III. c. 70; 3 Wm. IV. c. 74; 3 Bl. Comm. 80.

BOROUGH ENGLISH. A custom prevalent in some parts of England, by which the younger son inherits the estate in preference to his older brothers. 1 Bl. Comm. 75.

The custom is said by Blacktone to have been derived from the Saxons, and to have been so called in distinction from the Norman rule of descent. 2 Bl. Comm. 83. A reason for the custom is found in the fact that the elder children were usually provided for during the life of the parent as they grew up, and removed, while the younger son usually remained. See, also, Bac. Abr.; Comyn. Dig.; Termes de la Ley; Cowell. The custom applies to socage lands. 2 Bl. Comm. 83.

BOROUGH-HEAD, or BOROW-HEAD. The chief man or head of a borough. Cowell. See "Headborow."

BOROUGH-REEVE. The chief municipal officer in towns unincorporated before the municipal corporations act (5 & 6 Wm. IV. c. 76).

BOROUGH SESSIONS. Courts established in boroughs under the municipal corporations act (5 & 6 Wm. IV. c. 76, amended by 6 & 7 Wm. IV. c. 105, and 6 & 7 Vict. c. 89). They are held by the recorders of the respective boroughs once a quarter, or oftener if they think fit, and at times to be fixed by them. The jurisdiction is over such offenses as are cognizable by the country sessions, whose powers extend to all boroughs which may not have petitioned for a separate court by virtue of section 103 of the municipal corporations act. Wharton.

BORROW. To obtain the use of the property of another, with an agreement to return the same, ordinarily in specie, but where, as in case of money, the nature of the case does not admit of it, to return in kind. See 14 Neb. 381.

BORROWE. In old Scotch law. A pledge. Skene de Verb. Sign. voc. "Forensis."

BORROWER. He to whom a thing is lent at his request.

As used in usury laws, it includes any person who is a party to the original contract, or in any way liable to pay the loan. 64 N. Y. 247; 65 N. Y. 432; 11 Wend. (N.

Y.) 329; 7 Hill (N. Y.) 391; 75 N. Y. 516, 523, 31 Am. Rep. 484, reversing 10 Hun, 468.

In general, he has the right to use the thing borrowed, himself, during the time and for the purpose intended between the parties. He is bound to take extraordinary care of the thing borrowed; to use it according to the intention of the lender; to restore it in proper condition at the proper time. See "Bailment;" Story, Bailm. § 268; 2 Kent, Comm. 446-449; 1 Bouv. Inst. 1078-1090.

BORSHOLDER. A corruption of *borhesalder*, another form of *borhealder*. Spelman.

——**In Saxon Law.** The borough's ealder, or head borough, supposed to be the most discreet man in the borough, town, or tithing. 1 Bl. Comm. 114, 355.

BOSCAGE. That food which wood and trees yield to cattle.

To be quit of boscage is to be discharged of paying any duty of wind-fall wood in forest. Whishaw; Manw. For. Law.

BOSCARIA (from Lat. *bos*). Wood-houses, or ox-houses.

BOSCUS. Wood growing; wood; both high wood or trees, and underwood or coppice. The high wood is properly called *saltus*. Cowell; Spelman; Co. Litt. 5a.

BOTE. A recompense or compensation. The common word "boot" comes from this word. Cowell. The term is applied as well to making repairs in houses, bridges, etc., as to making a recompense for slaying a man or stealing property. House bote, materials which may be taken to repair a house; hedge bote, to repair hedges; brig bote, to repair bridges; man bote, compensation to be paid by a murderer. Bote is known to the English law also under the name of "estover." 1 Washb. Real Prop. 99; 2 Bl. Comm. 35.

BOTELESS. In old English law. Without amends; without the privilege of making satisfaction for a crime by a pecuniary payment; without relief or remedy. Cowell; Blount. The word (written "bootless") is still retained in the sense of "vain" or "useless." Cowell.

BOTH. The one and the other; the two; the pair or couple; without exception of either. 143 Ill. 104.

The term is never used as inclusive of or as referring to three or more, and can apply only to two of the matters or subjects previously mentioned. 143 Ill. 103.

BOTHA. In old English law. A booth, stall, or tent to stand in, in fairs or markets. Cowell; Blount.

BOTHAGIUM, or BOOTHAGE. Customary dues paid to the lord of a manor or soil for the pitching or standing of booths in fairs or markets.

BOTHNA, BUTHNA, or BOTHENA. In old Scotch law. A park where cattle are inclosed and fed. Bothna also signifies a barony, lordship, etc. Skene de Verb. Sign.

BOTTOMAGE (Law Fr.) Bottomry. Latch. 252.

BOTTOMRY. A contract in the nature of a mortgage, by which the owner of a ship, or the master, as his agent, borrows money for the use of the ship, and for a specified voyage, or for a definite period, pledges the ship (or the keel or bottom of the ship, *pars pro toto*) as a security for its payment, with maritime or extraordinary interest on account of the marine risks to be borne by the lender; it being stipulated that if the ship be lost in the course of the specified voyage, or during the limited time, by any of the perils enumerated in the contract, the lender shall also lose his money. 2 Hagg. Adm. 48. 53; 2 Sumn. (U. S.) 157; Abb. Shipp. 117-131. Where the loan is made on the credit of the cargo alone, the contract is called *respondentia (q. v.)*

BOUCHE (Fr. mouth). *Ne gist en le bouche*, it does not lie in the mouth, *i. e.*, it is not for one to say. Litt. § 58. A phrase still used. *En bouch del lay gents*, in the mouth of the common people. Cro. Jac. 700. *Il port meate en son bouche*, it supports itself. Dyer, 28 (Fr. Ed.). Said of a deed.

An allowance of provision. *Avoir bouche a court*, to have an allowance at court; to be in ordinary at court; to have meat and drink scot-free there. Blount; Cowell, "Munitions de Bouche;" Ord. Mar. liv. 3, tit. 8, art. 11.

BOUCHE OF COURT, or BUDGE OF court. A certain allowance of provision from the king to his knights and servants that attended him in any military expedition. The French *avoir bouche a court*, is to have an allowance at court of meat and drink. From *bouche*, a mouth. But sometimes it extended only to bread, beer, and wine, and this was anciently in use as well in the houses of noblemen as in the king's court. Jacob.

BOUGH OF A TREE. A symbol which gave seisin of land, to hold of the donor *in capite*.

BOUGHT NOTE. A written memorandum of a sale, delivered by the broker who effects the sale, to the vendee. Story, Ag. § 28; 11 Adol. & E. 589; 8 Mees. & W. 834.

Bought and sold notes are made out usually at the same time, the former being delivered to the vendee, the latter to the vendor.

BOULEVARD. A public drive, adapted and set aside for purposes of ornament, exercise, and amusement. It is not technically a street, avenue, or highway, though a carriage way over it be a chief feature. 52 How. Pr. (N. Y.) 440.

Originally "boulevard" was a bulwark or rampart of a fortification or fortified town; hence, a public walk or street occupying the site of demolished fortifications, the name being now sometimes extended to any street or walk encircling a town, and also to a street which is of especial width, is given a park-like appearance by reserving spaces at the sides or center for shade trees, flowers, seats, and the like, and is not used for heavy teaming. 171 Ill. 160.

BOUND BAILIFF. A sheriff's officer, who serves writs and makes arrests. He is so called because bound to the sheriff for the due execution of his office. 1 Bl. Comm. 345.

BOUNDARY. Any separation, natural or artificial, which marks the confines or line of two contiguous estates. Hunt, Boundaries.

The term is applied to include the objects placed or existing at the angles of the bounding lines, as well as those which extend along the lines of separation.

A natural boundary is a natural object remaining where it was placed by nature.

An artificial boundary is one erected by man.

BOUNDED TREE. A tree marking or standing at the corner of a field or estate.

BOUNDERS. Visible marks or objects at the ends of the lines drawn in surveys of land, showing the courses and distances.

BOUNTY. An additional benefit conferred upon, or a compensation paid to, a class of persons. It differs from a reward, which is usually applied to a sum paid for the performance of some specific act to some person or persons. It may or may not be part of a contract. Thus, the bounty offered a soldier would seem to be part of the consideration for his services. The bounty paid to fishermen is not a consideration for any contract, however.

BOUNTY LANDS. Lands given away by the government by way of bounty.

BOUNTY OF QUEEN ANNE. A royal charter confirmed by St. 2 Anne, c. 11, providing for the forming a perpetual fund for the augmentation of poor ecclesiastical livings. Wharton.

BOURG (Fr.) In old French law. An assemblage of houses surrounded with walls; a fortified town or village. Steph. Lect. 118.

Originally, any aggregation of houses. Id.

A corporate town. Id.

BOURGEOIS. In old French law. The inhabitant of a *bourg (q. v.)* Steph. Lect. 118.

A person entitled to the privileges of a municipal corporation; a burgess. Id.

BOURSE DE COMMERCE. In the French law. An aggregation, sanctioned by government, of merchants, captains of vessels, exchange agents, and courtiers, the two latter being nominated by the government, in each city which has a *bourse.* Brown.

BOUWERYE, or **BOUWERIE** (Dutch). A farm.

BOUWMEESTER, or **BOUWMASTER** (Dutch). A farmer.

BOVATA TERRAE. As much land as one ox can cultivate. Said by some to be thirteen, by others eighteen, acres in extent. Skene de Verb. Sign.; Spelman; Co. Litt. 5a.

BOW-BEARER. An under officer of the forest, whose duty it is to oversee and true inquisition make, as well of sworn men as unsworn, in every bailiwick of the forest, and of all manner of trespasses done, either to vert or venison, and cause them to be presented, without any concealment, in the next court of attachment, etc. Cromp. Jur. 201.

BOWYERS. Manufacturers of bows and shafts. An ancient company of the city of London. 12 Edw. IV. c. 2; 33 Hen. VIII. c. 6.

BOYCOTT. A conspiracy to injure the business of any person by inducing others to abstain from business relations with him. The methods are so diverse as not to be comprehended by any definition. For illustrations, see 84 Va. 927; 45 Fed. 135; 55 Conn. 79.

If force or intimidation is resorted to, such combinations are unlawful. As to their legality in the absence of such measures, see 15 Q. B. Div. 476.

BOZERO. In Spanish law. An advocate; one who pleads the causes of others, either suing or defending. Las Partidas, pt. 3, tit. 1, 1-6.

Called, also, *abogadas.* Amongst other classes of persons excluded from this office are minors under seventeen, the deaf, the dumb, friars, women and infamous persons. White, New Recop. 274.

BRANCH. A portion of the descendants of a person, who trace their descent to some common ancestor, who is himself a descendant of such person.

The whole of a genealogy is often called the "genealogical tree," and sometimes it is made to take the form of a tree, which is in the first place divided into as many branches as there are children, afterwards into as many branches as there are grandchildren, then great-grandchildren, etc. If, for example, it be desired to form the genealogical tree of Peter's family, Peter will be made the trunk of the tree; if he has had two children, John and James, their names will be written on the first two branches, which will themselves shoot out into as many smaller branches as John and James have children; from these others proceed, till the whole family is represented on the tree. Thus the origin, the application, and the use of the word "branch" in genealogy will be at once perceived. See "Line."

BRANDING. An ancient mode of punishment by inflicting a mark on an offender with a hot iron. It is generally disused in civil law, but is a recognized punishment for some military offenses.

BRANKS. An instrument of punishment formerly made use of in some parts of England for the correction of scolds, which it was said to do so effectually and so very safely that it was looked upon by Dr. Plotts, in his History of Staffordshire (page 389), "as much to be preferred to the ducking-stool, which not only endangered the health of the party, but also gives the tongue liberty 'twixt every dip, to neither of which is this liable. It brings such a bridle for the tongue as not only quite deprives them of speech, but brings shame for the transgression and humiliation thereupon before it is taken off."

BRASS KNUCKLES (or KNUCKS). A weapon consisting of metal covering part of the hand, and used to strike with. It was originally made of brass, and the name is now used as that of the weapon, without regard to the metal used. 3 Lea (Tenn.) 575; 3 S. W. 477.

BRAWL. Tumult; loud, angry contention. See 42 N. H. 464.

Originally used in connection with disturbances in churches or churchyards. 4 Bl. Comm. 146; Steph. Cr. Dig. 102.

BREACH.

——**In Contracts.** The violation of an obligation, engagement, or duty.

Breach may be either by renunciation,—that is, by the declaration of the party that he does not intend to perform (32 Iowa, 409; 61 N. Y. 362; 52 Wis. 240), by such acts as will render performance impossible (82 N. Y. 108; 22 Fed. 522; 16 Mass. 161),—or by actually failing to perform any or all the terms of the contract; the two first mentioned being constructive breaches, and the last, actual breach.

A continuing breach is one where the condition of things constituting a breach continues during a period of time, or where the acts constituting a breach are repeated at brief intervals. F. Moore, 242; 1 Leon. 62; 1 Salk. 141; Holt, 178; 2 Ld. Raym. 1125.

——**In Pleading.** That part of the declaration in which the violation of the defendant's contract is stated.

BREACH OF CLOSE. Every unwarrantable entry upon the soil of another is a breach of his close. 3 Bl. Comm. 209.

BREACH OF COVENANT. A violation of, or a failure to perform the conditions of, a bond of covenant. The remedy is in some cases by a writ of covenant; in others, by an action of debt. 3 Bl. Comm. 156.

BREACH OF POUND. See "Pound Breach."

BREACH OF PRISON. An unlawful breaking out of prison. This is of itself a misdemeanor. 1 Russ. Crimes, 378; 4 Bl. Comm. 129; 2 Hawk. P. C. c. 18, § 1; 7 Conn. 752. The remedy for this offense is by indictment. The climbing of a wall is not a breaking out, but if loose bricks be thrown from the wall it is. Russ. & R. 458. See "Escape."

BREACH OF PRIVILEGE. An act in violation of the privilege of a legislative body.

BREACH OF THE PEACE. A violation of public order; the offense of disturbing the public peace. 6 Coldw. (Tenn.) 283. An act of public indecorum is also a breach of the peace.

BREACH OF TRUST.

(1) The willful misappropriation, by a trustee, of a thing which had been lawfully delivered to him in confidence.

The distinction between larceny and a breach of trust is to be found chiefly in the terms or way in which the thing was taken originally into the party's possession; and the rule seems to be that whenever the article is obtained upon a fair contract not for a mere temporary purpose, or by one who is in the employment of the deliverer, then the subsequent misappropriation is to be considered as an act of breach of trust.

(2) Any wrongful act of a trustee in violation of his duty as such, though not amounting to a crime.

BREAKING. Parting or dividing by force and violence, a solid substance, or piercing, penetrating, or bursting through the same.

In cases of burglary and housebreaking, the removal of any part of the house, or of the fastenings provided to secure it, with violence and a felonious intent, is a breaking, as the raising of a closed window (107 N. C. 905), or the opening of a closed door (68 Ill. 271; 20 Iowa, 413), but an entry by an open door or window (85 Pa. St. 66; 25 Neb. 780) is not, though an entry through a chimney is a breaking into the house, for that is as much closed as the nature of things will permit (52 Ala. 376; 13 Ired. [N. C.] 244).

A constructive breaking is the procuring of an entry for felonious purpose by fraud or covin, as by pretending to have business with the owner (9 Ired. [N. C.] 463), or by collusion with an inmate (98 N. C. 629).

BREAKING OF ARRESTMENT. The contempt of the law committed by an arrestee who disregards the arrestment used in his hands, and pays the sum or delivers the goods arrested to the debtor. The breaker is liable to the arrester in damages. See "Arrestment."

BREAST OF THE COURT. The judgment or conscience of the court. A record is in the breast of the court, subject to correction, until the term is closed, after which it imports verity.

BREATH. In medical jurisprudence. The air expelled from the chest at each expiration.

BREDWITE. In Saxon and old English law. A fine, penalty, or amercement imposed for defaults in the assize of bread. Kennett, Par. Ant. 114; Cowell.

BREHON LAW. The ancient system of Irish law; so named from the judges, called "Brehons," or "Breitheamhuin." Its existence has been traced from the earliest period of Irish history down to the time of the Anglo-Norman invasion. It is still a subject of antiquarian research. An outline of the system will be found in Knight's English Cyclopaedia.

BRENAGIUM. A payment in bran, which tenants anciently made to feed their lord's hounds. Blount.

BREPHOTROPHI. In civil law. Persons appointed to take care of houses destined to receive foundlings. Clef des Lois Rom. "Administrateurs."

BRETHWALDA, or BRETTWALDA. The leader of the Saxon heptarchy. Steph. Lect. 696.

BRETTS and SCOTTS, LAWS OF THE. A code or system of laws in use among the Celtic tribes of Scotland down to the beginning of the fourteenth century, and then abolished by Edward I. of England. A fragment only is now extant. See Acts Parl. Scotland, vol. 1, pp. 299-301, Edin. 1844. It is interesting, like the Brehon laws of Ireland, in a historical point of view.

BREVA INNOMINATA. See "Breve Innominatum."

BREVE (Law Lat.) In old English law. A writ; properly an original writ (*breve originale*), by which all actions in the superior courts of England were once required to be commenced. *Non potest quis sine brevi agere*, no man can sue without a writ. Bracton, fols. 413b, 112; Fleta, lib. 2, c. 13, § 4; Steph. Pl. 5, 6; 3 Bl. Comm. 272, 273.

BREVE DE RECTO. A writ of right. The writ of right patent is of the highest nature of any in the law. Cowell; Fitzh. Nat. Brev.

BREVE INNOMINATUM. A writ containing a general statement only of the cause of action.

BREVE ITA DICITUR, QUIA REM DE qua agitur, et intentionem petentis, paucis verbis breviter enarrat. A writ is so called because it briefly states, in few words, the matter in dispute, and the object of the party seeking relief. 2 Inst. 39.

BREVE JUDICIALE DEBET SEQUI suum originale, et accessorium suum principale. A judicial writ ought to follow its original, and an accessory its principal. Jenk. Cent. Cas. 292.

BREVE JUDICIALE NON CADIT PRO defectu firmae. A judicial writ fails not through defect of form. Jenk. Cent. Cas. 43.

BREVE NOMINATUM. A writ containing a statement of the circumstances of the action.

BREVE ORIGINALE. An original writ.

BREVE PERQUIRERE. To purchase a writ or license of trial, in the king's courts, by the plaintiff, *qui breve perquisivit;* whence the usage of paying 6s. 8d fine to the crown where the debt is £40, and of 10s. where the debt is £100, etc., in suits and trials for money due upon bond, etc. Wharton.

BREVE TESTATUM. A written memorandum introduced to perpetuate the tenor of the conveyance and investiture of lands. 2 Bl. Comm. 307. It was prepared after the transaction, and depended for its validity upon the testimony of witnesses, as it was not sealed. Spelman.

——**In Scotch Law.** A similar memorandum made out at the time of the transfer, attested by the *pares curiae*, and by the seal of the superior. Bell, Dict.

BREVET.

——**In French Law.** A warrant granted by government to authorize an individual to do something for his own benefit.

Brevet d'invention. A patent.

——**In American Law.** A commission conferring on a military officer a degree of rank specified in the commission, without, however, conveying a right to receive corresponding pay.

BREVIA (Lat.) Writs. The plural of *breve (q. v.)*

BREVIA ADVERSARIA. Adversary writs; those brought adversely to recover land.

BREVIA AMICABILIA. Amicable or friendly writs; writs brought by agreement or consent of the parties.

BREVIA ANTICIPANTIA. Anticipating writs; writs of prevention. See Termes de la Ley.

BREVIA DE CURSU. Formal writs issuing as of course. See "Brevia Formata."

BREVIA FORMATA (Lat.) Certain writs of approved and established form which were granted of course in actions to which they were applicable, and which could not be changed but by consent of the great council of the realm. Bracton, 413b.

BREVIA INNOMINATA. See "Breve Innominatum."

BREVIA JUDICIALIA (Lat.) Judicial writs. Subsidiary writs issued from the court during the progress of an action, or in execution of the judgment.

BREVIA MAGISTRALIA. Writs framed and issued by masters in chancery, not following any established form, but varying in accordance with the peculiarities of the particular case. Bracton, 413b.

BREVIA NOMINATA. See "Breve Nominatum."

BREVIA SELECTA. Choice or selected writs or processes. Often abbreviated to *brev. sel.*

BREVIA, TAM ORIGINALIA QUAM JUDICIALIA, patiuntur Anglica nomina. Writs, as well original as judicial, bear English names. 10 Coke, 132.

BREVIA TESTATA. See "Breve Testatum."

BREVIARIUM ALARICIANUM (or **ANIANI**) (Lat.) A code of law compiled by order of Alaric II., king of the Visigoths, for the use of the Romans, living in his empire, published A. D. 506. It was collected by a committee of sixteen Roman lawyers, from the Codex Gregorianus, Hermogenianus, and Theodosianus, some of the later novels, and the writings of Gaius, Paulus, and Papinianus. In the middle ages, it is commonly referred to, under the titles Corpus Theodosianum, Lex Theodosiana, Liber Legum, or Lex Romana. 1 Mackeld. Civ. Law, p. 49, § 59.

BREVIATE. An abstract or epitome of a writing. Holthouse.

BREVIBUS ET ROTULIS LIBERANDIS. A writ or mandate directed to a sheriff, commanding him to deliver to his successor the county and the appurtenances, with all the briefs, rolls, remembrances, and other things belonging to his office.

BRIBE. The gift or promise, which is accepted, of some advantage as the inducement for some illegal act or omission; or of some illegal emolument, as a consideration for preferring one person to another, in the performance of a legal act.

BRIBERY. At common law. The receiving or offering any undue reward by or to any person whomsoever, whose ordinary profession or business relates to the administration of public justice, in order to influence his behavior in office, and to incline him to act contrary to his duty and the known rules of honesty and integrity. Coke, 3d Inst. 149; 1 Hawk. P. C. c. 67, § 2; 4 Bl. Comm. 139; 1 Russ. Crimes, 156.

The term "bribery" now extends further, and includes the offense of giving a bribe to many other officers. The offense of the giver and of the receiver of the bribe has the same name. For the sake of distinction, that of the former—viz., the briber—might be properly denominated "active bribery;" while that of the latter—viz., the person bribed—might be called "passive bribery."

"The voluntary giving or receiving of anything of value in corrupt payment for an official act done or to be done." 2 Bish. Crim. Law, § 85.

BRIBOUR. One that pilfers other men's goods; a thief. See St. 28 Edw. II. c. 1.

BRICOLIS. An engine by which walls were beaten down. Blount.

BRIDEWELL. A house of correction in England.

BRIDGE. A structure erected over a river, creek, stream, ditch, ravine, or other place, to facilitate the passage thereof; including, by the term, both arches and abutments. 3 Har. (N. J.) 108; 15 Vt. 438.

The common-law definition, *flumen vel cursus aquae*, etc., has a more enlarged significance in modern usage, and the term "bridge" in statutes signifies also crossings over public ways on land. 37 Me. 451.

Bridges are either public or private. Public bridges are such as form a part of the highway, common, according to their character, as foot, horse, or carriage bridges, to the public generally, with or without toll (2 East, 342); though their use may be limited to particular occasions, as to seasons of flood or frost (2 Maule & S. 262; 4 Campb. 189).

BRIDGE MASTERS. Persons chosen by the citizens to have the care and supervision of bridges, and having certain fees and profits belonging to their office, as in the case of London Bridge. Lex. Lond. 283.

BRIEF (Lat. *brevis;* Law Fr. *briefe,* short). A short or condensed statement.

——**In Ecclesiastical Law.** A papal rescript sealed with wax. See "Bull."

——**In Old Practice.** A writ. It is found in this sense in the ancient law authors. 2 Co. Litt. 73b.

——**In English Practice.** A statement by a solicitor to counsel, containing the facts and issues, the names of the witnesses, etc., to obtain the advice of counsel on a point of law, or to enable him to prepare for trial.

——**In American Practice.** The written or printed points, authorities, and argument furnished to the court by counsel. It must contain some statement of the case and argument therein; a mere copy of part of the assignments of error being insufficient. 12 Ind. 654. And see 43 Ind. 356.

BRIEF A L'EVESQUE. A writ to the bishop which, in *quare impedit*, shall go to remove an incumbent, unless he recover or be presented *pendente lite.* 1 Keb. 386.

BRIEF OF TITLE. An abstract of title (*q. v.*)

BRIEF (or BRIEVE) OUT OF THE chancery. A writ issued in Scotland in the name of the sovereign in the election of tutors to minors, the cognoscing of lunatics or of idiots, and the ascertaining the widow's terce; and sometimes in dividing the property belonging to heirs-portioners. In these cases, only brieves are now in use. Bell, Dict.

BRIEF, PAPAL. The pope's letter upon matters of discipline.

BRIEVE (from *breve, q. v.*) In Scotch law. A writ. 1 Kames, Eq. 146; 1 Forbes, Inst. pt. 4 bk. 2, c. 1, tit. 2, § 1.

BRIGA (Law Lat.) In old European law. Strife; contention; litigation; controversy. Spelman; Cowell; Blount.

BRIGANDINE. A coat of mail or ancient armor, consisting of numerous jointed scale-like plates, very pliant and easy for the body.

BRIGBOTE (Saxon). A contribution to repair a bridge.

BRINGING MONEY INTO COURT. The act of depositing money in the hands of the proper officer of the court for the purpose of satisfying a debt or duty, or of an interpleader. See "Payment into Court."

BRIS. In French maritime law. Literally, breaking; wreck. Distinguished from *naufrage (q. v.)* Ord. Mar. liv. 2, tit. 9.

BRISTOL BARGAIN. A contract by which A. lends B. £1,000 on good security, and it is agreed that £500, together with interest, shall be paid at a time stated, and, as to the other £500, that B., in consideration thereof, shall pay to A. £100 *per annum* for seven years. Wharton.

BROCAGE. See "Brokerage."

BROCARIUS, or BROCATOR. A broker; a middle-man between buyer and seller; the agent of both transacting parties. Used in the old Scotch and English law. Bell, Dict.; Cowell.

BROCELLA. A thicket, or covert, of bushes and brushwood. "Browse" is said to be derived hence. Cowell.

BROKERAGE, or BROCAGE. The trade or occupation of a broker; the commissions paid to a broker for his services.

BROKERS. Those who are engaged for others in the negotiation of contracts relative to property, with the custody of which they have no concern. Paley, Ag. 13. See 16 Gray (Mass.) 436; 45 Ill. 79; 16 How. Pr. (N. Y.) 440.

One who receives a commission for making a bargain for another. 6 Bing. 702.

A salaried agent is not a broker. 1 Ore. 218.

A broker differs from a factor in that he has no possession of the property he sells. 47 Cal. 213; 41 N. Y. 235; 104 Mass. 259.

A person employed by merchants English and merchants strangers in contriving, making and concluding bargains and contracts between them concerning their wares and merchandise, and the moneys to be taken up by exchange between such merchants and tradesmen. Banta v. Chicago, 172 Ill. 213.

——**Bill and Note Brokers.** Those who negotiate the purchase and sale of bills of exchange and promissory notes.

——**Exchange Brokers.** Those who negotiate bills of exchange drawn on foreign countries, or on other places in this country.

——**Insurance Brokers.** Those who procure insurance, and negotiate between insurers and insured.

——**Merchandise Brokers.** Those who negotiate the sale of merchandise without having possession or control of it, as factors have.

——**Pawnbrokers.** Those who lend money in small sums, on the security of personal property, at usurious rates of interest. They are licensed by the authorities, and excepted from the operation of the usury laws.

——**Real-Estate Brokers.** Those who negotiate the sale or purchase of real property. They are a numerous class, and, in addition to the above duty, sometimes procure loans on mortgage security, collect rents, and attend to the letting and leasing of houses and lands.

——**Ship Brokers.** Those who negotiate the purchase and sale of ships, and the business of freighting vessels. Like other brokers, they receive a commission from the seller only.

——**Stock Brokers.** Those employed to buy and sell shares of stock in incorporated companies, and the indebtedness of governments. These brokers have possession of the certificates and other written evidences of title.

BROSSUS. Bruised, or injured with blows, wounds or other casualty. Cowell.

BROTHEL. A bawdy house; a common habitation of prostitutes.

BROTHER. He who is born from the same father and mother with another, or from one of them only.

Brothers are of the whole blood when they are born of the same father and mother, and of the half-blood when they are the issue of one of them only. In the civil law, when they are the children of the same father and mother, they are called "brothers germain;" when they descend from the same father, but not the same mother, they are "consanguine brothers;" when they are the issue of the same mother, but not the same father, they are "uterine brothers." A "half-brother" is one who is born of the same father or mother, but not of both; one born of the same parents before they were married, a "left-sided brother;" and a bastard born of the same father or mother is called a "natural brother." See "Blood;" "Half-Blood;" "Line;" Merlin, Repert. Frere; Dict. de Jurisp. Frere; Code, 3. 28. 27; Nov. 84; praef.; Dane, Abr. Index.

BROTHER-IN-LAW. The brother of a wife, or the husband of a sister.

There is no relationship, in the former case, between the husband and the brother-in-law, nor in the latter, between the brother and the husband of the sister; there is only affinity between them. See Vaughan, 302, 329.

BRUARIUM, BRUERA, BRUERIA, or **bruerum.** In old English law. A heath ground; ground where heath grows. Spelman; Fleta, lib. 2, c. 71, § 7; Id. lib. 2, c. 41, § 2; Id. lib. 4, c. 27, § 16. Bracton, fol. 229b, 231; Co. Litt. 4b; Reg. Orig. 1b, 2.

BRUGBOTE. See "Brigbote."

BRUILLUS. A wood or grove; a thicket or clump of trees in a park or forest. Jacob.

BRUISE. In medical jurisprudence. An injury done with violence to the person, without breaking the skin. It is nearly synonymous with "contusion" (*q. v.*) 1 Chanc. Prac. 38. See 4 Car. & P. 381, 487, 558, 565.

BRUKBARN. In old Swedish law. The child of a woman conceiving after a rape, which was made legitimate. Literally, the child of a struggle. Barr. Obs. St.

BRUTUM FULMEN. An empty noise; an empty threat.

BUBBLE ACT. The name given to the statute 6 Geo. I. c. 18, which was passed in 1719, and was intended "for restraining several extravagant and unwarrantable practices therein mentioned." See 2 P. Wms. 219.

BUCKSTALL. A toil to take deer. 4 Inst. 306.

BUGGERY. Includes both "bestiality," or carnal connection between a human being and a beast, and "sodomy," or carnal connection between human beings against the order of nature. 3 Inst. 58.

BUILDING. An edifice erected by art and fixed upon or over the soil, composed of stone, brick, marble, wood, or other proper substance, connected together, and designed for use in the position in which it is so fixed.

Taken in its broadest sense, it can mean only an erection intended for use and occupation as a habitation, or for some purpose of trade, ornament, or use. 13 Gray (Mass.) 312.

A bridge (11 Wis. 119), a floating dock (2 Vroom [N. J.] 477), seats or platforms in a park (55 Cal. 159; 39 Conn. 41) have been held not to be buildings, while an unfinished house (L. R. 1 C. C. 338), a stable (94 Ill. 456), a church (10 Pa. 413) are buildings.

BUILDING AND LOAN ASSOCIATION. An organization created for the purpose of accumulating a fund by the monthly subscriptions or savings of its members, to assist them in building or purchasing for themselves dwellings or real estate, by loaning to them the requisite money from the funds of the society upon good security. 173 Ill. 629.

The purpose of a building and loan association is to enable a number of associates to combine and invest their savings to mutual advantage, so that any individual among them may receive out of the accumulations a sum by way of loan, wherewith to buy or build a house, mortgaging it to the association as security for the money borrowed, and ultimately making it his own by paying off the encumbrance out of his subscription. 173 Ill. 629.

BUILDING LEASE. A lease of the soil for the purpose of erecting buildings thereon, usually for a long term. See "Ground Rent."

BULK. Merchandise which is neither counted, weighed, nor measured.

A sale by bulk is a sale of a quantity of goods such as they are, without measuring, counting, or weighing. Civ. Code La. art. 3522, note 6.

BULL. A letter from the pope of Rome. written on parchment, to which is attached a leaden seal impressed with the images of Saint Peter and Saint Paul.

There are three kinds of apostolical rescripts,—the "brief," the "signature," and the "bull," which last is most commonly used in legal matters. Bulls may be compared to the edicts and letters patent of secular princes. When the bull grants a favor, the seal is attached by means of silken strings; and when to direct execution to be performed, with flax cords. Bulls are written in Latin, in a round and Gothic hand. Ayliffe, Par. 132; Ayliffe, Pand. 21; Merlin, Repert.

BULLA (Lat.) A seal used by the Roman emperors during the lower empire, and which was of four kinds,—gold, silver, wax, and lead. These are described by Spelman in detail.

A letter, brief, or charter, sealed with such a seal (*literae bullatae*). Spelman.

A brief, mandate, or bull of the pope, having usually a leaden, but sometimes a golden, seal. Spelman; Blount; Cowell; Burrill.

BULLETIN. An official account of public transactions on matters of importance. In France, it is the registry of the laws.

BULLION. The term "bullion" is commonly applied to uncoined gold and silver, in the mass or lump.

BULLION FUND. A deposit of public money at the mint and its branches. The object of this fund is to enable the mint to make returns of coins to private depositors of bullion without waiting until such bullion is actually coined. If the bullion fund is sufficiently large, depositors are paid as soon as their bullion is melted and assayed, and the value ascertained. It thus enables the mint to have a stock of coin on hand to pay depositors in advance. Such bullion becomes the property of the government, and, being subsequently coined, is available as a means of prompt payment to other depositors. Act May 23, 1850 (9 U. S. St. at Large, 436).

BUM-BAILIFF. A person employed to dun one for a debt; the bailiff employed to arrest a debtor. Black thinks it a vulgar corruption of "bound-bailiff" (*q. v.*) Hall says that, from the notion of a humming or droning noise, the word "bum" was applied to dunning for a debt.

BUNDA, BONDA, or **BONNA.** In old English law. A bound, boundary, border, or limit (*terminus, limes*). Spelman, voc. "Bannum;" "Bonna." 4 Inst. 318; Bracton, fol. 166b; 2 Crabb, Real Prop. 146; Reg. Orig. 263b.

BUOY. A piece of wood, or an empty barrel, or other thing, moored at a particular place, and floating on the water, to show the place where it is shallow, to mark the channel, or to indicate the danger there is to navigation.

BURDEN OF PROOF. The duty of proving the facts in dispute on an issue raised between the parties in a cause. See 16 N. Y. 66; 1 Gray (Mass.) 500; 6 Wheat. (U. S.) 481.

Burden of proof is to be distinguished from *prima facie* evidence or a *prima facie* case. Generally, when the latter is shown, the duty imposed upon the party having the burden will be satisfied, but it is not necessarily so. 6 Cush. (Mass.) 364; 11 Metc. (Mass.) 460; 22 Ala. 20; 7 Blackf. (Ind.) 427; 1 Gray (Mass.) 61; 7 Boston Law Rep. 439.

BUREAU. The word "bureau," as applied to a division of an administrative department, implies not only a division where business is to be conducted under certain rules and regulations, but includes the operating force as well. People v. Coffin, 202 Ill. App. 100.

BUREAUCRACY. A government by departments, each under a chief; a word to describe the system used in an invidious sense. Wharton.

BURG, or **BURGH.** A term anciently applied to a castle or fortified place; a borough (*q. v.*) Spelman.

BURGAGE. A species of tenure, described by old law writers as but tenure in socage, where the king or other person was lord of an ancient borough, in which the tenements were held by a rent certain.

Such boroughs had, and still have, certain peculiar customs connected with the tenure, which distinguished it from the ordinary socage tenure. These customs are known by the name of "Borough English" (*q. v*), and they alter the law in respect of descent, as well as of dower, and the power of devising. By it the youngest son inherits the lands of which his father died seised. A widow, in some boroughs, has dower in respect to all the tenements which were her husband's; in others, she has a moiety of her husband's lands so long as she remains unmarried; and with respect to devises, in some places, such lands only can be devised as were acquired by purchase; in others, estates can only be devised for life. 2 Bl. Comm. 82; Glanv. bk. 7, c. 3; Litt. § 162; Cro. Car. 411; 1 Salk. 243; 2 Ld. Raym. 1024; 1 P. Wms. 63; Fitzh. Nat. Brev. 150; Cro. Eliz. 415.

BURGAGE HOLDING. A tenure by which lands in royal boroughs in Scotland were held of the sovereign. The service was watching and warding, and was done by the burgesses within the territory of the borough, whether expressed in the charter or not. See 31 & 32 Vict. c. 101.

BURGAGE TENURE. In English law. A tenure by which houses, or lands which were formerly the site of houses, in ancient boroughs, are held of the king, or other lord of the borough, at a certain yearly rent. Glanv. lib. 7, c. 3; Litt. §§ 162, 163; Co. Litt. 108b; 2 Bl. Comm. 82; Blount; 1 Steph. Comm. 198; 1 Crabb, Real Prop. p. 593, § 749.

BURGATOR. One who breaks into houses or inclosed places, as distinguished from one who committed robbery in the open country. Spelman, voc. "Burglaria."

BURGBOTE. A term applied, in the old English law, to a contribution towards the repair of castles or walls of defense, or of a borough.

BURGENSES. In old English law. The inhabitants of a borough.

BURGERISTH. A word used in Domesday, signifying a breach of the peace in a town. Jacob.

BURGESS. A magistrate of a borough. Blount. An officer who discharges the same duties for a borough that a mayor does for a city. The word is used in this sense in Pennsylvania.

An inhabitant of a town; a freeman; one legally admitted as a member of a corporation. Spelman. A qualified voter. 3 Steph. Comm. 192. A representative in parliament of a town or borough. 1 Bl. Comm. 174.

BURGESS ROLL. A list of those entitled to new rights under the act of 5 & 6 Wm. IV. c. 74; 3 Steph. Comm. 192 et seq.

BURGH ENGLISH. See "Borough English."

BURGH ENGLOYS. Borough English (*q. v.*) Y. B. P. 1 Edw. III. 38.

BURGHBRECH, or **BURGHBRECHE.** A fine imposed on the community of a town for a breach of the peace, etc.

BURGHMAILS. Yearly payments to the crown of Scotland, introduced by Malcolm III., and resembling the English fee-farm rents. Enc. Lond.

BURGHMOTE. In Saxon law. A court of justice held twice a year, or oftener, in a burg. All the thanes and free owners above the rank of ceorls were bound to attend without summons. The bishop or lord held the court. Spence, Eq. Jur.

BURGLAR. One who commits burglary (*q. v.*)

BURGLARIOUSLY. In pleading. A technical word which must be introduced into an indictment for burglary at common law. No other word at common law will answer the purpose, nor will any circumlocution be sufficient. 4 Coke, 39; 5 Coke, 121; Cro. Eliz. 920; Bac. Abr. "Indictment" (G, C). But there is this distinction: When a statute punishes an offense, by its legal designation, without enumerating the acts which constitute it, then it is necessary to use the terms which technically charge the offense named, at common law. But this is not necessary when the statute describes the whole offense, and the indictment charges the crime in the words of the statute. Thus, an indictment which charges the statute crime of burglary is sufficient, without averring that the crime was committed "burglariously." 4 Metc. (Mass.) 357.

BURGLARITER. In old criminal pleading. Burglariously.

BURGLARY. At common law, the breaking and entering the house of another in the nighttime, with intent to commit a felony therein, whether the felony be actually committed or not. Coke, 3d Inst. 63; 1 Hale, P. C. 549; 1 Hawk. P. C. c. 38, § 1; 4 Bl. Comm. 224; 2 East, P. C. c. 15, § 1, p. 484; 2 Russ. Crimes, 2; Rosc. Crim. Ev. 252; 1 Coxe (N. J.) 441; 7 Mass. 247.

The elements of the offense are:

(1) The breaking (105 Mass. 588); but a constructive breaking is sufficient (9 Ired. [N. C.] 463). See "Breaking."

(2) The entry. 111 Mass. 395.

(3) The building broken and entered must be the dwelling house of another (43 Ala. 17); but an outstanding building within the curtilage is regarded as part of the dwelling (26 Ala. 45).

(4) Both breaking and entry must be in the nighttime. 10 N. H. 105.

(5) And both must be with intent to commit a felony in the house (12 N. H. 42); but the felony need not have been committed (29 Ind. 80).

The offense has been enlarged by statute both as to the buildings broken into, and as to the time of the breaking and entry.

BURGOMASTER. In Germany, this is the title of an officer who performs the duties of a mayor.

BURGWHAR. A burgess (*q. v.*)

BURIAL. The act of interring the dead.

No burial is lawful unless made in conformity with the local regulations; and when a dead body has been found, it cannot be lawfully buried until the coroner has held an inquest over it. In England it is the practice for coroners to issue warrants to bury, after a view. The leaving unburied the corpse of a person for whom the defendant is bound to provide Christian burial, as a wife or child, is an indictable misdemeanor, if he is shown to have been of ability to provide such burial. 2 Den. C. C. 325.

BURKING, or **BURKISM.** Committing murder in order to sell the body for dissection. So called from the first perpetrator. See 4 Redf. Sur. (N. Y.) 540.

BURLAW (BYRLAW, or BIRLAW) courts. In Scotch law. Assemblages of neighbors to elect burlaw men, or those who were to act as rustic judges in determining disputes in their neighborhood. Skene de Verb. Sign.; Bell, Dict.

BURLAWS, BIRLAWS, or BYRLAWS. In Scotch law. Laws made by neighbors elected by common consent in the birlaw courts. Skene de Verb. Sign.

Laws made by husbandmen, etc., concerning neighborhood (*rusticorum leges*). Spelman, voc. "Bellagines," considers this word essentially the same with "by-laws" (*q. v.*)

BURNING. See "Accident;" "Fire."

BURNING IN THE HAND. When a layman was admitted to benefit of the clergy he was burned in the hand, "in the brawn of the left thumb," in order that he might not claim the benefit twice. This practice was finally abolished by St. 19 Geo. III. c. 74, though before that time the burning was often done with a cold iron. 12 Mod. 448; 4 Bl. Comm. 267 et seq.

BURROCHIUM. A burroch, dam, or small wear over a river, where fish traps are laid. Cowell.

BURROWMEALIS. A term in the Scotch law, used to designate the rents paid into the king's private treasury by the burgesses or inhabitants of a borough.

BURSA, or BURSE. A purse. Spelman; Bracton, fol. 84; Britt, c. 29.

BURSARIA. The bursery or exchequer of collegiate and conventual bodies; or the place of receiving and paying and accounting by the bursarii, or bursers. A. D. 1277. But the word "bursarii" did not only signify the bursers of a convent or college, but formerly stipendiary scholars were called by the name of "bursarii," as they lived on the burse or fund, or public stock of the university. At Paris, and among the Cistercian monks, they were particularly termed by this name. Jacob.

BURYING ALIVE. In English law. The ancient punishment of sodomites, and those who contracted with Jews. Fleta, lib. 1, c. 27, § 3.

BURYING GROUND. A place appropriated for depositing the dead; a cemetery. In Massachusetts, burying grounds cannot be appropriated to roads without the consent to the owners. Gen. St. Mass. 244.

BUSCARL, or BUTSECARL. In Saxon and old English law. Seamen or marines; *milites nautici.* Spelman.

BUSHEL. The Winchester bushel, established by 13 Wm. III. c. 5 (1701), was made the standard of grain. A cylindrical vessel, eighteen and a half inches in diameter, and eight inches deep inside, contains a bushel. The capacity is 2,145.42 cubic inches. The bushel established by 5 & 6 Geo. IV. c. 74, is to contain 2,218.192 cubic inches. This measure has been adopted in many of the United States. In New York the heaped bushel is allowed, containing 2,815 cubic inches. The exceptions, as far as known, are Connecticut, where the bushel holds 2,198 cubic inches; Kentucky, 2,150.66; Indiana, Ohio, Mississippi, and Missouri, where it contains 2,150.4 cubic inches. Dane, Abr. c. 211, a. 12, § 4. See the whole subject discussed in Report of the Secretary of State of the United States to the Senate, Feb. 22, 1821.

In accordance with a joint resolution of congress, adopted in June, 1836, a uniform scale of weights and measures has been adopted in many states, by which the bushel shall contain 2,150 cubic inches. See Dom. Commerce Act N. Y. § 2.

It is further provided that, where any commodity is sold by the bushel, and no special agreement is made as to the mode of measuring, the bushel shall consist of 70 pounds of lime; 60 pounds of wheat, peas, potatoes, clover seed, or beans; 57 pounds of onions; 56 pounds of Indian corn or rye; 55 pounds of flaxseed; 54 pounds of sweet potatoes; 50 pounds of corn meal, rye meal, or carrots; 48 pounds of barley, apples, or buckwheat; 45 pounds of beard grass, timothy seed, or rice; 33 pounds of dried peaches; 32 pounds of oats; 25 pounds dried apples; 20 pounds bran or shorts. Id. § 8.

BUSINESS. Occupation or employment. 178 Ill. App. 176.

The employment which occupies the time, attention and labor. 37 Ill. App. 503.

BUSINESS CORPORATION. A stock corporation other than insurance, banking, and transportation corporations. Gen. Corp. Law N. Y. § 2.

BUSINESS HOURS. The time of the day during which business is transacted. In respect to the time of presentment and demand of bills and notes, business hours generally range through the whole day down to the hours of rest in the evening, except when the paper is payable at a bank, or by a banker. 2 Hill (N. Y.) 835. See 15 Me. 67; 17 Me. 230.

BUSONES. A word found only in Bracton (folio 115b). From the context, it means the principal persons of the county, and is thought to have been synonymous with "barons." 2 Reeve. Hist. Eng. Law, 2, note; Crabb, Hist. Eng. Law, 161.

BUSSA, or BUSCIA. In old English law. A ship of large size and clumsy construction. Spelman.

BUT. Except; unless; save; yet; still; however; nevertheless. 251 Ill. 218.

The word "but," whether used as a conjunction or a preposition, indicates exception. 251 Ill. 218.

As a conjunction, the word "but" is used as a connective of sentences more or less exceptive or adversative, marking opposition in passing from one thought to another. 251 Ill. 218.

BUTLERAGE. A certain portion of every cask of wine imported by an alien, which the king's butler was allowed to take.

Called also "prisage." 2 Bulst. 254. Anciently, it might be taken also of wine imported by a subject. 1 Bl. Comm. 315; Termes de la Ley; Cowell.

BUTLER'S ORDINANCE. In English law. A law for the heir to punish waste in the life of the ancestor. "Though it be on record in the parliament book of Edward I., yet it never was a statute, nor ever so received; but only some constitution of the king's council, or lords in parliament, which never obtained the strength or force of an act of parliament." Hale, Hist. Com. Law, 18.

BUTT. A measure of capacity, equal to one hundred and eight gallons. See "Measure."

BUTTALS. The bounding lines of land at the end; abuttals.

BUTTED AND BOUNDED. A phrase sometimes used in conveyancing, to denote the boundaries of lands. See "Butts and Bounds."

BUTTS. The ends or short pieces of arable lands left in ploughing. Cowell.

Butt also denotes a measure of land (Jacob; Cowell), and a measure of quantity, equal to one hundred and eight gallons. See "Measure."

BUTTS AND BOUNDS. The lines bounding an estate; the angles or points where these lines change their direction. Cowell; Spelman.

BUTTY. A local term in the north of England, for the associate or deputy of another; also of things used in common.

BUYING TITLES. The purchase of the rights of a disseisee to lands of which a third person has the possession.

BY, or **BYE.** A habitation. Co. Litt.; 18 App. Div. (N. Y.) 142.

BY-BIDDING. Bidding on property offered for sale at auction, by or in behalf of the owner, for the mere purpose of raising the price, or inducing others to bid higher. Sometimes called "puffing." By-bidding by the owner, or caused by the owner, or ratified by him, has often been held to be a fraud, and avoids the sale. 8 How. (U. S.) 153.

BY BILL, or **BY BILL WITHOUT WRIT.** These terms were anciently applied to actions commenced by original bill, instead of by original writ. 1 Archb. Pr. pp. 2, 337; 5 Hill (N. Y.) 213. They were later used to denote actions commenced by *capias.*

BY ESTIMATION. A term used in conveyances. In sales of land it not unfrequently occurs that the property is said to contain a certain number of acres "by estimation," or so many acres, "more or less." When these expressions are used, if the land fall short by a small quantity, the purchaser will receive no relief. In one case of this kind, the land fell short two-fifths, and the purchaser received no relief. 2 Freem. 106. See 1 Call. (Va.) 301; 4 Hen. & M. (Va.) 184; 6 Bin. (Pa.) 106; 1 Serg. & R. (Pa.) 166; 2 Johns. (N. Y.) 37; 5 Johns. (N. Y.) 508; 15 Johns. (N. Y.) 471; 3 Mass. 380; 5 Mass. 355; 1 Root (Conn.) 528. The meaning of these words has never been precisely ascertained by judicial decision. See Sugd. Vend. 231-236; Wolff, Inst. § 658; and the cases cited under the articles "Constitution;" "More or Less;" "Subdivision."

BY GOD AND MY COUNTRY. In old English criminal practice. The established formula of reply by a prisoner, when arraigned at the bar, to the question, "Culprit, how wilt thou be tried?" Mr. Barrington thinks the correct formula must originally have been, "By God or my country," *i. e.*, by ordeal (the *judicium Dei*), or by jury, for the reason that the question asked supposes an option in the prisoner, and the answer is meant to assert his innocence by declining neither sort of trial. Barr. Obs. St. 84 note (i). But it is clear that, in answering the question, the prisoner was expected to select one particular mode of trial, which the alternative expression contended for would not amount to. That the expression "By God" did not necessarily and exclusively import the ordeal appears from the form of issue in cases of trial by the grand assize, which always was that the party put himself "on God and on the grand assize." See Britt. c. 48; Y. B. T. 20 Hen. VI. 4. That every word of this formula was deemed essential appears from several cases on record, in which the prisoner's replies, "By God and my good country," "By God and honest men," were severally rejected, and he was compelled to use the precise words of the form. 1 How. St. Tr. 1143; 3 How. St. Tr. 520; 6 How. St. Tr. 75; 7 How. St. Tr. 831. On the trial of John James for high treason (13 Car. II. 1661), and the prisoner requesting an explanation of the form, the judge said that "By God" meant "by the law of God," and "by the country," twelve Middlesex men of truth, that would judge impartially between the king and him. 6 How. St. Tr. 75.

BY-LAW MEN. In an ancient deed, certain parties are described as "yeomen and by-law men for this present year in Easinguold." 6 Q. B. 60. They appear to have been men appointed for some purpose of limited authority by the other inhabitants, as the name would suggest, under by-laws of the corporation appointing.

BY-LAWS.

——**In Old English Law.** The ordinances of a town or village. See "By."

——**In Modern Usage.** Rules and ordinances made by a corporation for its own government. See 18 App. Div. (N. Y.) 142. Distinguished from resolution, see "Resolution."

BY-ROAD. "There are three kinds of roads known to our law: (1) Public roads; (2) private roads; (3) by-roads. All these differ from a mere right of way. A by-road is, as its name imports, an obscure or neighborhood road in its earlier existence, not used to any great extent by the public, yet so far a public road that the public have of right free access to it at all times." 34 N. J. Law, 89; 46 N. J. Law, 509.

BY THE BYE. In practice. Without process. A declaration is said to be filed by the bye when it is filed against a party already in the custody of the court under process in another suit. This might have been done, formerly, where the party was under arrest, and technically in the custody of the court; and even giving common bail was a sufficient custody in the king's bench. 1 Sellon, Prac. 228; 1 Tidd. Prac. 419. It is no longer allowed. Archb. New Prac. 293.

C

C. The third letter of the alphabet. It was used on the ballots of Roman jurors to denote condemnation, being the initial letter of *condemno*. See "A."

"C" is sometimes used for "t" in old records, as "tercia" for "tertia," and "tocius" for "totius." Mag. Cart. 9 Hen. III. c. 7.

C. A. V. An abbreviation for *curia advisari vult* (*q. v.*)

C. I. F. (Cost, insurance and freight.) An expression which indicates that the price fixed covers the cost of the goods and insurance and freight on them to the place of destination. Under such a contract, the seller must ship the goods, arrange the contract of affreightment to the place of destination, pay its cost and allow it from the purchase price, and procure insurance for the buyer's benefit for the safe arrival of the goods and pay therefor. When the seller has done this, and forwarded the papers to the buyer, he has fulfilled his contract, and delivery is complete. 273 Fed. 475.

C. O. D. Collect on delivery. The abbreviation has acquired an established meaning (39 Ill. 312), but judicial notice will not be taken thereof (55 N. Y. 200).

C. P. A. A certified public accountant.

C. T. A. *Cum testamento annexo.* A species of administration (*q. v.*)

CABAL (Hebrew, *cabala*, tradition; or Fr. *cabale*, intrigue).

(1) A hidden or imaginary art practiced by the Jews. 1 Hall. Lit. Hist. 205. The Jews believed that Moses received in Sinai not only the law, but also certain unwritten principles of interpretation, called "*cabala*" or "tradition," which were handed down from father to son, and in which mysterious and magical powers were supposed to reside.

(2) A junto or private meeting of small parties. This name was given to that ministry in the reign of Charles II., formed by Clifford, Ashley, Buckingham, Arlington, and Lauderdale, who concerted for the restoration of Catholicism.

CABALLERIA. In Spanish law. A portion of spoils taken or lands conquered in a war, granted to a horse soldier. Dict. Span. Acad.; 12 Pet. (U. S.) 444, note.

A quantity of land, varying in extent in different provinces. In those parts of the United States which formerly belonged to Spain, it is a lot of one hundred feet front, two hundred feet depth, and equivalent to five peonias. 2 White, New Recop. 49; 12 Pet. (U. S.) 444, note; Escriche, Dic. Raz.

CABALLERO (Spanish; from Latin *caballus*, a horse). In Spanish law. A knight. So called on account of its being more honorable to go on horseback (*a caballo*) than on any other beast. White, New Recop. bk. 1, tit. 5, c. 3, § 3; Id. bk. 1, tit. 5, c. 1; Id. bk. 4, tit. 10, c. 1, § 6.

CABINET. Certain officers who, taken collectively, form a council or advisory board; as the cabinet of the president of the United States, which is composed of the secretary of state, the secretary of the treasury, the secretary of the interior, the secretary of war, the secretary of the navy, the secretary of agriculture, the attorney general, the secretary of commerce, the secretary of labor, and the postmaster general.

CABINET COUNCIL. A private and confidential assembly of the most considerable ministers of state, to concert measures for the administration of public affairs; first established by Charles I. Wharton.

CABLISH. In forest law. Brush-wood. According to Spelman, windfallen wood. Spelman, voc. "Cablicia."

CACHEPOLUS, or CACHERELLAS. An inferior bailiff, or catchpoll. Jacob.

CACICAZGOS. In Spanish law. Lands held in entail by the *caciques* in Indian villages in Spanish America.

CADASTRE. In Spanish law. The official statement of the quantity and value of real property in any district, made for the purpose of justly apportioning the taxes payable on such property. 12 Pet. (U. S.) 428, note; 3 Am. St. Papers, 679.

CADASTU. In French law. Same as *cadastre* (*q. v.*)

CADERE (Lat.) To fall; to fail; to end; to terminate.

The word was generally used to denote the termination or failure of a writ, action, complaint, or attempt; as, *cadit actio*, the action fails, *cadit assisa*, the assise abates, *cadere causa*, or *a causa*, to lose a cause. Abate will translate *cadere* as often as any other word; the general signification being, as stated, to fail or cease. *Cadere ab actione* (literally, to fall from an action), to fail in an action; *cadere in partem*, to become subject to a division.

To become; to be changed to; *cadit assisa in juratum*, the assize has become a jury. Calv. Lex.; Smith.

CADI. A Turkish civil magistrate.

CADUCA. (Lat. *cadere*, to fall). In civil law. An inheritance; an escheat; everything which falls to the legal heir by descent.

By some writers, *bona caduca* are said to be those to which no heir succeeds, equivalent to escheats. Du Cange.

CAEDUA (Lat. from *caedere*, to cut). In the civil and old common law. Kept for cutting; intended or used to be cut. A term applied to wood. *Silva caedua est quae in hoc habetur ut caederetur, sylva caedua* is that kind of wood which is kept for the purpose of being cut. Dig. 50. 16. 30. According to Servius, it was that kind which, when cut down, grew up again from the trunks or roots. Id. See Dig. 7. 1. 10. 11; Id. 43. 24. 18.

CAETERIS PARIBUS. Other things being equal.

CAETERIS TACENTIBUS (Lat.) The others being silent; the other judges expressing no opinion. Comb. 186. A phrase in the old reports.

CAETERORUM (Lat.) Of the rest.

Administration granted as to the residue of an estate, which cannot be administered under the limited power already granted. 1 Williams, Ex'rs, 357; 2 Hagg. Ecc. 62; 4 Hagg. Ecc. 382, 386; 4 Man. & G. 398; 1 Curt. Ecc. 286.

It differs from administration *de bonis non* in this, that in *caeterorum* the full power granted is exercised and exhausted, while in the other the power is, for some cause, not fully exercised. See "Administration."

CAHIER (Fr.) In old French law. A list of grievances prepared for deputies in the states general. Steph. Lect. 254. A petition for the redress of grievances enumerated. Id. 257.

CAIRNS' ACT. So call from the solicitor general by whom it was introduced. Act 21 & 22 Vict. c. 27, enabling the court of chancery to award damages in addition to, or in substitution for, an injunction or decree for specific performance. Per Jessel, M. R., in 7 Ch. Div. 551.

CALCETUM (Law Lat.) In old English law. A causeway. Reg. Orig. 154; Fleta, lib. 2, c. 52, § 33.

CALE (Fr.) In old French law. A species of punishment inflicted upon sailors, by plunging into the water, and drawing up again. Ord. Mar. liv. 2, tit. 1, art. 22. The modern keel hauling.

CALEFAGIUM. A right to take fuel yearly. Blount.

CALENDAR. An almanac.

Julius Caesar ordained that the Roman year should consist of three hundred and sixty-five days, except every fourth year, which should contain three hundred and sixty-six,—the additional day to be reckoned by counting the 24th day of February (which was the 6th of the calends of March) twice. See "Bissextile." This period of time exceeds the solar year by eleven minutes, or thereabouts, which amounts to the error of a day in about one hundred and thirty-one years. In 1582 the error amounted to eleven days or more, which was corrected by Pope Gregory. Out of this correction grew the distinction between Old and New Style. The Gregorian or New Style was introduced into England in 1752; the 2d day of September (O. S.) of that year being reckoned as the 14th day of September (N. S.)

——**In Criminal Law.** A list of prisoners, containing their names, the time when they were committed, and by whom, and the cause of their commitments. 4 Bl. Comm. 403.

——**In Practice.** A list of cases arranged for trial or argument in court.

CALENDAR MONTH. A month as measured by the calendar, as distinguished from a business month (thirty days), or a lunar month (twenty-eight days).

CALENDS. Among the Romans, the first day of every month, being spoken of by itself, or the very day of the new moon, which usually happen together. And if *pridie*, the day before, be added to it, then it is the last day of the foregoing month, as *pridie calend. Septemb.* is the last day of August. If any number be placed with it, it signifies that day in the former month which comes so much before the month named, as the tenth calends of October is the 20th day of September; for if one reckons backwards, beginning at October, that 20th day of September makes the 10th day before October. In March, May, July, and October, the calends begin at the sixteenth day, but in other months at the fourteenth; which calends must ever bear the name of the month following, and be numbered backwards from the first day of the said following months. Jacob. See "Ides" for table of calends, nones, and ides.

CALL. An official declaration by the proper corporate authorities that the whole or a specified part of the subscriptions to the capital stock is required to be paid. 156 Ill. App. 519.

A call is an offer to sell property for some stated delivery, which, in consideration of a certain amount of money paid, is left open a certain length of time. 126 Ill. App. 186.

The word "call," as used by those dealing in commodities for future delivery, is the privilege of calling for or not calling for the thing bought. 160 Ill. 97.

——**In Conveyancing.** The designation in a survey of landmarks, courses, or distances is denominated a "call."

——**In Corporation Law.** A demand or assessment by the corporation on the stockholders due on their stock for the purposes of the corporation.

——**In the Parlance of Stock and Grain Exchanges.** An option to purchase stock or grain from another on a certain day at a given price. The opposite transaction to a "put" (*q. v.*)

CALLING THE JURY. The calling in court of the names on the jury list when a jury is to be selected and impanelled.

CALLING THE PLAINTIFF. A formal method of causing a nonsuit to be entered, the plaintiff absenting himself from the courtroom, and the case being dismissed for his nonappearance after he has been called by the crier.

CALLING TO THE BAR. Conferring the degree or dignity of barrister upon a member of the Inns of Court. Holthouse.

CALPE, or CAUPE. In old Scotch law. A gift of a horse, or other thing, made by a man in his lifetime and *liege poustie* (lawful power), to the chief of his clan or other superior, for his maintenance and protection, and which was delivered immediately after his decease. Skene de Verb. Sign. voc. "Caupes." A species of *heregeld* (*q. v.*)

CALUMNIA (Lat.) In the civil law. Calumny, malice, or ill design; a false accusation; a malicious prosecution. Inst. 4. 16. 1, Cooper's Notes; Dig. 3. 6; Code, 9. 46.

CALUMNIA, or CALUMPNIA (Law Lat.)

——**In Old English Law and Practice.** A claim or demand (*vindicatio*; law Lat. *clameus*). Spelman. The demand of a right in anything (*juris in re aliqua postulatio*). Id.

A challenge. Spelman; Reg. Orig. 223, 224; Co. Litt. 155b; Crabb, Hist. Eng. Law, 299.

——**In Feudal Law.** An objection. Feud. lib. 2, tit. 1.

CALUMNIAE JURAMENTUM. See "Calumniae Jusjurandum."

CALUMNIAE JUSJURANDUM (Lat.) The oath against calumny.

Both parties at the beginning of a suit, in certain cases, were obliged to take an oath that the suit was commenced in good faith, and in a firm belief that they had a good cause. Bell, Dict. The object was to prevent vexatious and unnecessary suits. It was especially used in divorce cases, though of little practical utility. Bish. Mar. & Div. § 353. A somewhat similar provision is to be found in the requirement made in some states that the defendant shall file an affidavit of merits.

CALUMNIATORS. In civil law. Persons who accuse others, whom they know to be innocent, of having committed crimes.

CALUMNY. Defamation. In old practice. The unjust prosecution or defense of a suit. See 30 Ohio St. 117.

CAMARA. In Spanish law. A treasury. Las Partidas, pt. 6, tit. 3, lib. 2.

The exchequer. White, New Recop. bk. 3, tit. 8, c. 1.

CAMBELLANUS, or CAMBELLARIUS (Lat.) In old law. A chamberlain. Spelman.

CAMBIATOR. In old English law. An exchanger. *Cambiatores monetae*, exchangers of money; money changers. Fleta, lib. 1, c. 22, § 7.

CAMBIO. Exchange.

CAMBIPARTIA. Champerty.

CAMBIPARTICEPS. A champertor.

CAMBIST. A person skilled in exchange; one who deals or trades in promissory notes or bills of exchange; a broker.

CAMBIUM. Change; exchange. Applied in the civil law to exchange of lands, as well as of money or debts. Du Cange.

Cambium reale or *manuale* was the term generally used to denote the technical common-law exchange of lands; *cambium locale, mercantile*, or *trajectitium* was used to designate the modern mercantile contract of exchange, whereby a man agrees, in consideration of a sum of money paid him in one place, to pay a like sum in another place. Poth. de Change, note 12; Story, Bills, § 2 et seq.

CAMERA (Law Lat.; Lat. *camera*, a vault or arched roof; an upper gallery; Spanish, *camara*).

——**In Old European Law.** A chamber; an apartment in a dwelling house.

A treasure chamber, or treasury; a chamber with a vaulted roof, for the keeping of the public treasure.

A private treasury; a place for keeping private funds or moneys; a coffer; personal funds, as distinguished from land.

——**In Old English Practice.** A judge's chamber. Dyer, 59b. (Fr. Ed.); Id. 140b.

CAMERA REGIS (Lat. the chambers of the king). A term formerly applied especially to harbors, and generally to all the harbors or ports of the kingdom. Cowell.

CAMERA SCACCARII. The exchequer chamber. Spelman.

CAMERA STELLATA. The star chamber.

CAMERALISTICS. The science of finance or public revenue, comprehending the means of raising and disposing of it. Wharton.

CAMERARIUS. A chamberlain; a keeper of the pubic money; a treasurer. Spelman, voc. "Cambellarius;" 1 Per. & D. 243.

CAMINO. In Spanish law. A road or highway. Las Partidas, pt. 3, tit. 2, lib. 6.

CAMPANA. In old European law. A bell. Spelman.

CAMPANA BAJULA. A small hand bell used in the ceremonies of the Roman Catholic church, and, among Protestants, by sextons, parish clerks, and criers. Cowell.

CAMPANARIUM, or CAMPANILE. A belfry, bell tower or steeple; a place where bells are hung. Spelman; Towns. Pl. 191, 213.

CAMPARTUM. A part or portion of a larger field or ground, which would otherwise be in gross or in common; champerty.

CAMPBELL'S ACT. The popular name for Act 9 & 10 Vict. c. 93, by which (as amended by St. 27 & 28 Vict. c. 115) an action for damages is given for the benefit of the wife, husband, parent, grandparent, stepparent, child, grandchild and stepchild of a person whose death has been caused by a wrongful act, neglect, or default for which he himself could, if death had not ensued, have recovered damages from the wrongdoer. Underh. Torts, 143; Campb. Neg. 20. Similar statutes of recent enactment exist in nearly all of the states, some of which permit the personal representatives of the person killed to sue.

CAMPERS, or CAMPIPARS (Law Lat.; Fr. *champert*). In old English statutes. A share or division of land, or other thing; champerty.

CAMPERTUM. A cornfield; a field of grain. Cowell; Whishaw.

CAMPFIGHT. In old English law. The fighting of two champions or combatants in the field (*campus*); the judicial combat, or *duellum*. 3 Inst. 221.

CAMPUS (Lat. a field). A share or division of land; a division of that which would otherwise be in gross; champerty. Blount; Cowell.

CAMPUS MAII (Law Lat.) The field of May. An anniversary assembly of the Saxons, held on May Day, when they confederated for the defense of the kingdom against all its enemies. Wharton.

CAMPUS MARTII (Law Lat.) The field of March. A national assemblage of the Franks held in that month.

CANAL. An artificial cut or trench in the earth, for conducting and confining water to be used for transportation.

CANCELLARIO. Chancery; the court of chancery. *Curia cancellaria* is also used in the same sense. See 4 Bl. Comm. 46; Cowell.

CANCELLARIUS (Law Lat.) A chancellor anciently so called from the *cancelli* (lattices, or latticed inclosure) within which he performed his office. Cassiodorus Variar. lib. 11, form 6; Spelman, voc. "Cancellarius."

A janitor, or one who stood at the door of the court, and was accustomed to carry out the commands of the judges; so called from his position as keeper of the gate or lattice. A scribe; a notary. Du Cange.

CANCELLATION. The act of crossing out a writing; the manual operation of tearing or destroying a written instrument. 1 Eq. Cas. Abr. 409; Roberts, Wills, 367, note.

Revocation or annulment of an instrument in any manner. See 58 Pa. St. 238.

CANCELLATURA. In old English law. A cancelling. Bracton, 398b; Fleta, lib. 6, c. 34, § 5.

CANCELLI. The rails or balusters inclosing the bar of a court of justice or the communion table; also the lines drawn on the face of a will or other writing, with the intention of revoking or annuling it. Wharton.

CANDIDATE (Lat. *candidus*, white). Said to be from the custom of Roman candidates to clothe themselves in a white tunic.

One who offers himself for an office. One must offer himself either directly, or by consenting to the presentation of his name by others to be a candidate. 2 Maule & S. 212.

It has been held to include persons seeking a nomination for office. 112 Pa. St. 624.

CANDLEMAS DAY. A festival appointed by the church to be observed on the second day of February in every year, in honor of the purification of the Virgin Mary, being forty days after her miraculous delivery. Candles are consecrated on this day for the service of the ensuing year. It is the fourth of the four cross quarter days of the year. Wharton.

CANFARA. A trial by hot iron, formerly in use in England. Jacob.

CANON.

(1) A prebendary, or member of a chapter of the Church of England. All members of chapters except deans are now to be entitled "canons," in England. 3 Steph. Comm. 67, note; 1 Bl. Comm. 382.

(2) A rule, maxim, or precept of law, as the "canons of construction," or the "'canons of descent." Most commonly a rule of ecclesiastical law. See "Canon Law."

(3) In Spanish law. The annual charge or rent paid on recognition of the *dominium utile* by holder thereof. 15 Cal. 556.

CANON LAW. A body of ecclesiastical law, which originated in the church of Rome, relating to matters of which that church has or claims jurisdiction.

A canon is a rule of doctrine or of discipline, and is the term generally applied to designate the ordinances of councils and decrees of popes. The position which the canon law obtains beyond the papal dominions depends on the extent to which it is sanctioned or permitted by the government of each country; and hence the system of canon law as it is administered in different countries varies somewhat.

Though this system of law is of primary importance in Catholic countries alone, it still maintains great influence and transmits many of its peculiar regulations down through the jurisprudence of Protestant countries which were formerly Catholic. Thus, the canon law has been a distinct branch of the profession in the ecclesiastical courts of England for several centuries; but the recent modifications of the jurisdiction of those courts have done much to reduce its independent importance.

The *Corpus Juris Canonici* is drawn from various sources,—the opinions of the ancient fathers of the church, the decrees of councils, and the decretal epistles and bulls of the holy see, together with the maxims of the civil law and the teachings of the Scriptures. These sources were first drawn upon for a regular ecclesiastical system about the time of Pope Alexander III., in the middle of the twelfth century, when one Gratian, an Italian monk, animated by the discovery of Justinian's Pandects, collected the ecclesiastical constitutions also into some method in three books, which he entitled *Concordia Discordantium Canonum.* These are generally known as *Decretum Gratiani.*

The subsequent papal decrees to the time of the pontificate of Gregory IX. were collected in much the same method, under the auspices of that pope, about the year 1230, in five books, entitled *Decretalia Gregorii Noni.* A sixth book was added by Boniface VIII., about the year 1298, which is called *Sextus Decretalium.* The Clementine Constitution, or decrees of Clement V., were in like manner authenticated in 1317 by his successor, John XXII., who also published twenty constitutions of his own, called the *Extravangantes Joannis,* so called because they were in addition to, or beyond the boundary of, the former collections, as the additions to the civil law were called Novels. To these have since been added some decrees of later popes, down to the time of Sixtus IV., in five books, called *Extravangantes Communes.* And all these together—Gratian's Decrees, Gregory's Decretals, the Sixth Decretals, the Clementine Constitutions, and the Extravagants of John and his successors—form the *Corpus Juris Canonici,* or body of the Roman law. 1 Bl. Comm. 82; Encyclopedie, Dr. Canon. Dr. Pub. Ecc.; Dict. de Jur. Dr. Canon.; Ersk. Inst. bk. 1, tit. 1, § 10.

CANON RELIGIOSORUM (Lat.) In ecclesiastical records. A book wherein the religious of every greater convent had a fair transcript of the rules of their order, frequently read among them as their local statutes. Kennett; Cowell.

CANONICUS (Law Lat.) A canon.

CANONRY. An ecclesiastical benefice attaching to the office of canon. Holthouse.

CANONS OF INHERITANCE, or CANONS of descent. The legal rules by which inheritances are regulated, and according to which estates are transmitted by descent from the ancestor to the heir. 2 Bl. Comm. 208; 1 Steph. Comm. 359.

CANT. In the civil law. A judicial sale at the request of tenants in common for the purpose of dividing the property. See 9 Mart. (La.) 87.

CANTEL (Law Lat. *cantellum velut quantillum*). In old English law. That which is added above measure; heaped measure. Spelman; Blount.

CANTRED. A hundred; a district containing a hundred villages. Used in Wales in the same sense as "hundred" in England. Cowell; Termes de la Ley.

CANUM (Law Lat. from Celt. *can, chan,* or *kain,* a head). In old Scotch law. A tribute or duty paid by the tenant of land to the lord, especially to ecclesiastical superiors. According to Skene, it was payable either in the produce of the land, or in money. Skene de Verb. Sign. But it seems to have been generally paid in produce, such as wheat, oats, poultry, etc. . The Scotch word was *cane* or *kain;* and the expressions "*cane* fowls," "*cane* cheese," "*cane* oats" are frequently made use of. See "Kain."

CANVASS. The act of examining the returns of votes for a public officer.

CAP OF MAINTENANCE. One of the regalia or ornaments of state belonging to the sovereigns of England, before whom it is carried at the coronation and other great solemnities. Caps of maintenance are also carried before the mayors of several cities in England. Enc. Lond.

CAPACITY. Ability, power, qualification, or competency of persons, natural or artificial. 2 Comyn. Dig. 294; Dane, Abr.

(1) Natural power or competency to perform an act, as capacity to contract, capacity to commit crime.

(2) Official, or representative power or character. As to when one is acting in an official, and not a personal capacity, see 3 Story (U. S.) 87; 6 Robt. (N. Y.) 502.

The word "capacity" does not include "experience." 234 Ill. 623; 227 Ill. 442.

CAPAX DOLI (Lat. capable of committing crime). The condition of one who has sufficient mind and understanding to be made responsible for his actions.

CAPAX NEGOTII. Capacity to contract.

CAPE. A judicial writ touching a plea of lands and tenements. The writs which bear this name are of two kinds, namely, *cape magnum,* or grand cape, and *cape parvum,* or petit cape. The petit cape is so called, not so much on account of the smallness of the writ as of the letter. Fleta, lib. 6, c. 55, § 40. For the difference between the form and the use of these writs, see 2 Wm. Saund. 45c, 45d; Fleta, lib. 6, c. 55, § 40.

A neck or narrow point of land extending some distance into a body of water.

In certain localities in the northern part of England, the word "cape" means the coping of a wall, and also ears of corn broken off in threshing.

The word "cape" is sometimes employed as descriptive of a kind of wine made at the Cape of Good Hope.

A garment or part of a garment used for covering the shoulders of the wearer. 175 Ill. 222.

CAPE AD VALENTIAM. A species of *cape magnum.* See "Cape."

CAPELLA.

——**In Old Records.** A box, cabinet, or repository in which were preserved the relics of martyrs. Spelman. A small building in which relics were preserved; an oratory or chapel. Id.

——**In Old English Law.** A chapel. Fleta, lib. 5, c. 12, § 1; Spelman; Cowell.

CAPERS. Vessels of war owned by private persons, and different from ordinary privateers only in size, being smaller. Beawes, Lex. Merc. 230.

CAPIAS (Lat. *capere* to take; *capias,* that you take). A writ directing the sheriff to take the person of the defendant into custody.

It is a judicial writ, and issued originally only to enforce compliance with the summons of an original writ, or with some judgment or decree of the court. It was originally issuable as a part of the original process in a suit only in case of injuries committed by force or with fraud, but was much extended by statutes. Being the first word of distinctive significance in the writ, when writs were framed in Latin, it came to denote the whole class of writs by which a defendant's person was to be arrested. It was issuable either by the court of common pleas or king's bench, and bore the seal of the court.

CAPIAS AD AUDIENDUM JUDICIUM. A writ issued, in a case of misdemeanor, after the defendant has appeared and is found guilty, to bring him to judgment if he is not present when called. 4 Sharswood, Bl. Comm. 368.

CAPIAS AD COMPUTANDUM. A writ which issued in the action of account render upon the judgment *quod computet,* when the defendant refused to appear in his proper person before the auditors and enter into his account.

According to the ancient practice, the defendant might, after arrest upon this process, be delivered on mainprize, or, in default of finding mainpernors, was committed to the Fleet prison, where the auditors attended upon him to hear and receive his account. The writ is now disused.

CAPIAS AD RESPONDENDUM. A writ commanding the sheriff to take the body of the defendant, if he may be found in his bailiwick or county, and him safely keep, so that he may have him in court on the day of the return to answer to the plaintiff of a plea of debt, trespass, etc., as the case may be. 97 Ill. 236.

This is the writ of *capias* which is generally intended by the use of the word *capias*, and was formerly a writ of great importance. For some account of its use and value, see "Arrest;" "Bail."

According to the course of the practice at common law, the writ bears *teste*, in the name of the chief justice, or presiding judge of the court, on some day in term time, when the judge is suppósed to be present, not being Sunday, and is made returnable on a regular return day.

If the writ has been served, and the defendant does not give bail, but remains in custody, it is returned C. C. (*cepi corpus*); if he have given bail, it is returned C. C. B. B. (*cepi corpus*, bail bond); if the defendant's appearance has been accepted, the return is, "C. C., and defendant's appearance accepted." See 1 Archb. Prac. 67.

CAPIAS AD SATISFACIENDUM. A judicial writ of execution, which issues out on the record of a judgment by which the sheriff is commanded to take the body of the defendant in execution, and him safely to keep, so that he have his body in court at the return of the writ to satisfy the plaintiff his debt and damages. 97 Ill. 236.

It is a writ of execution issued after judgment, and might have been issued against a plaintiff against whom judgment was obtained for costs, as well as against the defendant in a personal action. As a rule at common law, it lay in all cases where a *capias ad respondendum* lay as a part of the mesne process. Some classes of persons were, however, exempt from arrest on mesne process who were liable to it on final. It was a very common form of execution until within a few years, in many of the states, but its efficiency has been destroyed by statutes facilitating the discharge of the debtor in some states, and by statutes prohibiting its issue in others, except in specified cases. See "Arrest;" "Privilege." It is commonly known by the abbreviation *ca. sa.*

CAPIAS EXTENDI FACIAS. A writ of execution issuable in England against a debtor to the crown, which commands the sheriff to "take" or arrest the body, and "cause to be extended" the lands and goods of the debtor. Man. Exch. Prac. 5. It seems to be practically obsolete.

CAPIAS IN WITHERNAM. A writ directing the sheriff to take other goods of a distrainor equal in value to a distress which he has formerly taken and still withholds from the owner beyond the reach of process.

When chattels taken by distress were decided to have been wrongfully taken, and were by the distrainor *eloigned*, that is, carried out of the county or concealed, the sheriff made such a return. Thereupon this writ issued, thus putting distress against distress.

Goods taken *in withernam* are irrepleviable till the original distress be forthcoming. 3 Bl. Comm. 148.

CAPIAS PRO FINE. A writ which issued against a defendant who had been fined, and did not discharge the fine according to the judgment.

The object of the writ was to arrest a defendant against whom a plaintiff had obtained judgment, and detain him until he paid to the king the fine for the public misdemeanor, coupled with the remedy for the private injury sustained, in all cases of forcible torts (11 Coke, 43; 5 Mod. 285), falsehood in denying one's own deed (Co. Litt. 131; 8 Coke, 60), unjustly claiming property in replevin, or contempt by disobeying the command of the king's writ, or the express prohibition of any statute (8 Coke, 60). It is now abolished. 2 Sharswood, Bl. Comm. 398.

CAPIAS UTLIGATUM. A writ directing the arrest of an outlaw.

If general, it directs the sheriff to arrest the outlaw, and bring him before the court on a general return day.

If special, it directs the sheriff, in addition, to take possession of the goods and chattels of the outlaw, summoning a jury to determine their value.

It was a part of the process subsequent to the *capias*, and was issued to compel an appearance where the defendant had absconded, and a *capias* could not be served upon him. The outlawry was readily reversed upon any plausible pretext, upon appearance of a party in person or by attorney, as the object of the writ was then satisfied. The writ issued after an outlawry in a criminal as well as in a civil case. See 3 Sharswood, Bl. Comm. 284; 4 Bl. Comm. 320.

CAPIATUR PRO FINE. Let him be taken for the fine. In English practice. A clause inserted at the end of old judgment records in actions of debt, where the defendant denied his deed, and it was found against him upon his false plea, and the jury were troubled with the trial of it. Cro. Jac. 64.

CAPITA (Lat.) By heads. An expression of frequent occurrence in laws regulating the distribution of the estates of persons dying intestate. When all the persons entitled to shares in the distribution are of the same degree of kindred to the deceased person (*e. g.*, when all are grandchildren), and claim directly from him in their own right, and not through an intermediate relation, they take *per capita*, that is, equal shares, or share and share alike. But when they are of different degrees of kindred (*e. g.*, some the children, others the grandchildren or the great-grandchildren, of the deceased), those more remote take *per stirpem*, or *per stirpes*, that is, they take respectively the shares their parents (or other relation standing in the same degree with them of the surviving kindred entitled, who are in the nearest degree of kindred to the intestate) would have taken had they respectively survived the intestate. Reeve, Descent, Introd. xxvii. Also, 1 Rop. Leg. 126, 130. See "Per Capita;" "Per Stirpes;" "Stirpes."

CAPITAL.

(1) The amount of money invested in a business; the fund dedicated to a business to support its credit, to provide for contingencies, to suffer diminution from losses, and to derive accretion from gains and profits. 30 Fed. 410.

As used in the revenue act it does not include money temporarily borrowed. 21 Wall. (U. S.) 284.

(2) "The actual estate, whether in money or property, which is owned by an individual or a corporation. In reference to a corporation it is the aggregate of the sum subscribed and paid in by the shareholders, with the addition of all gains or profits realized in the use or investment of those sums." 23 N. Y. 219.

(3) Affecting human life. See "Capital Crime;" "Capital Punishment."

CAPITAL CRIME. One for which the punishment of death is inflicted.

CAPITAL PUNISHMENT. The punishment of death.

CAPITAL STOCK. The sum, divided into shares, which is raised by mutual subscription of the members of a corporation. It is said to be the sum upon which calls may be made upon the stockholders, and dividends are to be paid. 1 Sandf. Ch. (N. Y.) 280; Walford, Rys. 252; 4 Zab. (N. J.) 195; Angell & A. Corp. §§ 151, 556.

"The sums due by virtue of the subscriptions or collected from the subscribers, and invested for the benefit of the corporation." 30 Conn. 290.

It is never used to indicate the value of the property of the corporation. 3 Zab. (N. J.) 195.

The phrase is used as synonymous with "Capital." 23 N. Y. 222.

It is to be distinguished from "stock," which is the shareholder's individual interest in the capital stock. 9 Yerg. (Tenn.) 490.

CAPITALE. A thing which is stolen, or the value of it. Blount.

A beast or other animal considered as property; hence, according to Spelman, the term "chattel."

CAPITALE VIVENS. Live cattle. Blount.

CAPITALIS. In old English law. Chief, principal; at the head. A term applied to persons, places, judicial proceedings, and some kinds of property.

CAPITALIS BARO. In old English law. Chief baron. *Capitalis baro scaccarii domini regis*, chief baron of the exchequer. Towns. Pl. 211.

CAPITALIS CUSTOS. Chief warden or magistrate; mayor. Fleta, lib. 2, c. 64, § 2.

CAPITALIS DEBITOR. The chief or principal debtor, as distinguished from a surety (*plegius*). Called *principalis*. Fleta, lib. 2, c. 63, § 5.

CAPITALIS DOMINUS. Chief lord. Fleta, lib. 1, c. 12, § 4; Id. c. 28, § 5.

CAPITALIS JUSTICIARIUS. The chief justiciary; the principal minister of state, and guardian of the realm in the king's absence.

This office originated under William the Conqueror, but its power was greatly diminished by *Magna Charta*, and finally distributed among several courts by Edward I. Spelman; 8 Bl. Comm. 38.

CAPITALIS JUSTICIARIUS AD PLACIta coram rege tenenda. Chief justice for holding pleas before the king. The title or the chief justice of the king's bench, first assumed in the latter part of the reign of Henry III. 2 Reeve, Hist. Eng. Law, 91, 285.

CAPITALIS JUSTICIARIUS BANCI (or **de banco**). Chief justice of the brench. The title of the chief justice of the (now) court of common pleas, first mentioned in the first year of Edward I. 2 Reeve, Hist. Eng. Law, 48. Crabb, Hist. Eng. Law, 146.

CAPITALIS JUSTICIARIUS TOTIUS ANgliae. Chief justice of all England. The title of the presiding justice in the court of *aula regis*. 3 Bl. Comm. 38; 1 Reeve, Hist. Eng. Law, 48.

CAPITALIS PLEGIUS. A chief pledge; a head borough. Fleta, lib. 2, c. 52, & 5.

CAPITALIS REDDITUS. A chief rent (*q. v.*)

CAPITALIS TERRA. A headland; a piece of land lying at the head of other land.

CAPITANEUS. He who held his land or title directly from the king himself.

A commander or ruler over others, either in civil, military, or ecclesiastical matters.

A naval commander. This latter use began A. D. 1264. Spelman, voc. "Capitaneus;" "Admiralius."

CAPITARE. In old law and surveys. To head, front, or abut; to touch at the head, or end. Cowell, voc. "Laterare."

CAPITAS DEMINUTIO (or **DIMINUTIO**) (Lat.) In the civil law. The loss of a *status* or civil qualification; the change of a man's former condition (*prioris status* *mutatio*). Inst. 1. 16. pr. 1; Mackeld. Civ. Law, p. 131, § 121. Sometimes called *capitis minutio*. Dig. 4. 5. 1. This was of three kinds. See "Caput;" "Status."

CAPITATIM (Lat.) By the head; to each individual. 4 Maule & S. 206.

CAPITATION (Lat. *caput*, head). A poll-tax. An imposition yearly laid upon each person.

The constitution of the United States provides that "no capitation or other direct tax shall be laid, unless in proportion to the census, or enumeration, thereinbefore directed to be taken." Article 1, § 9, note 4. See 3 Dall. (Pa.) 171; 5 Wheat. (U. S.) 317.

CAPITE. See "Capita."

CAPITE MINUTUS. In the civil law. One who had suffered the *capitis diminutio*. Dig. 4. 5.

CAPITIS DIMINUTIO MAXIMA. The highest or most comprehensive loss of *status*. This occurred when a man's condition was changed from one of freedom to one of bondage, when he became a slave. It swept away with it all rights of citizenship, and all family rights.

CAPITIS DIMINUTIO MEDIA. A lesser or medium loss of *status*. This occurred where a man lost his rights of citizenship, but without losing his liberty. It carried away also the family rights.

CAPITIS DIMINUTIO MINIMA. The lowest or least comprehensive degree of loss of *status*. This occurred where a man's family relations alone were changed. It happened upon the arrogation of a person who had been his own master (*sui juris*), or upon the emancipation of one who had been under the *patria potestas*. It left the rights of liberty and citizenship unaltered. See Inst. 1. 16. pr.; Id. 1. 2. 3; Dig. 4. 5. 11; Mackeld. Civ. Law, § 144.

CAPITITIUM. A covering for the head, mentioned in St. 1 Hen. IV., and other old statutes, which prescribed what dresses shall be worn by all degrees of persons. Jacob.

CAPITULA. Collections of laws and ordinances drawn up under heads or divisions. Spelman.

The term is used in the civil and old English law, and applies to ecclesiastical law also. Du Cange.

CAPITULA CORONIS. Specific and minute schedules, or *capitula itineris*.

CAPITULA DE JUDAEIS. A register of mortgages made to the Jews. 2 Bl. Comm. 343; Crabb, Hist. Eng. Law, 130 et seq.

CAPITULA ITINERIS. Schedules of inquiry delivered to the justices in eyre before setting out on their circuits, and which were intended to embrace all possible crimes.

CAPITULA RURALIA. Assemblies or chapters, held by rural deans and parochial clergy, within the precinct of every deanery, which at first were every three weeks, afterwards once a month, and more solemnly once a quarter. Cowell.

CAPITULARY.

——**In French Law.** A collection of laws and ordinances orderly arranged by divisions. The term is especially applied to the collections of laws made and published by the early French emperors. The execution of these capitularies was intrusted to the bishops, courts, and *missi regis*, and many copies were made. The best edition of the Capitularies is said by Butler to be that of Baluze, 1677. Co. Litt. 191a, Butler's note 77.

——**In Ecclesiastical Law.** A collection of laws and ordinances, arranged by divisions. A book containing the beginning and end of each Gospel which is to be read every day in the ceremony of saying mass. Du Cange.

CAPITULATION.

(1) The treaty which determines the conditions under which a fortified place is abandoned to the commanding officer of the army which besieges it.

(2) In civil law. An agreement by which the prince and the people, or those who have the right of the people, regulate the manner in which the government is to be administered. Wolffius, § 989.

CAPITULI AGRI. Head fields; lands lying at the head or upper end of furrows, etc..

CAPITULUM EST CLERICORUM CONgregatio sub uno decano in ecclesia cathedrali. A chapter is a congregation of clergy under one dean in a cathedral church. Co. Litt. 98.

CAPITUR PRO FINE. See "Capias pro Fine."

CAPPA. In old records. A cap. *Cappa honoris*, the cap of honor. One of the solemnities or ceremonies of creating an earl or marquis. Bacon's Works, v. 474.

CAPTAIN (Lat. *capitaneus;* from *caput*, head). The commander of a company of soldiers. The term is also used of officers in the municipal police in a somewhat similar sense; as, captain of police; captain of the watch.

The master or commander of a merchant vessel, or a vessel of war.

A subordinate officer having charge of a certain part of a vessel of war.

In the United States, the commander of a merchant vessel is, in statutes and legal proceedings and language, more generally termed "master (*q. v.*) In foreign laws and languages he is frequently styled "patron."

The rank of captain in the United States navy is next above that of commander, and captains are generally appointed from this rank in the order of seniority. The president has the appointing power, subject to the approval and consent of the senate.

CAPTATION. In French law. Undue influence; the act of one who succeeds in controlling the will of another, so as to become master of it. It is generally taken in a bad sense.

Captation takes place by those demonstrations of attachment and friendship, by those assiduous attentions, by those services and officious little presents, which are usual among friends, and by all those means which ordinarily render us agreeable to others.

CAPTATOR. A person who obtains a gift or legacy through artifice. Rapalje & L.

CAPTIO (Lat. from *capere,* to take). In old English law and practice. A taking or seizure of a thing, as an animal. Bracton, fol. 156. *Est omnis captio justa vel injusta.* Fleta, lib. 2, c. 44, § 1. *Bene cognoscit captionem,* (he) well avows the taking. 1 Salk. 3.

A taking or seizure of land. *Dies captionis indorsari debet in tergo brevis,* the day of the taking ought to be indorsed on the back of the writ. Bracton, fol. 365b.

A taking or arrest of a person. Reg. Orig. 278b; Bracton, fol. 145b. *Injusta captio et injusta detentio.* Fleta, lib. 1, c. 42, § 1.

A taking or holding of a court. *Captio assisae,* the taking of the assize. Bracton, fol. 111, 202b.

A taking or receiving. *Homagii captio,* taking of homage. Bracton, fol. 16.

CAPTION.

(1) A taking, or seizing; an arrest. The word is no longer used in this sense.

(2) The heading of a legal instrument, in which is shown when, where, and by what authority it was taken, found, or executed. Principally used in respect to indictments. See, as to requisites, 3 Gray (Mass.) 454; 1 South. (N. J.) 46. This meaning, now the general one, is not justified by the derivation, which is from *capere,* to take, and not from *caput,* a head.

In the English practice, when an inferior court, in obedience to the writ of *certiorari,* returns an indictment into the king's bench, it is annexed to the caption, then called a "schedule," and the caption concludes with stating that "it is presented in manner and form as appears in a certain indictment thereto annexed," and the caption and indictment are returned on separate parchments. 1 Wm. Saund. 309, note 2.

CAPTIVE. A prisoner of war.

CAPTOR. One who has taken property from an enemy. This term is also employed to designate one who has taken an enemy.

CAPTURE. The taking of property by one belligerent from another. See 6 Allen (Mass.) 373. It is a taking by the military power, as distinguished from a taking by the civil power, which is known as "seizure." 35 Ga. 344. It originally included only a taking by one belligerent from another, but has been enlarged in usage to include taking by pirates, or the taking by a belligerent of neutral goods. 6 Allen (Mass.) 373; 6 Wall. (U. S.) 10.

CAPUT.

——**In Civil Law.** *Status;* a person's civil condition.

According to the Roman law, three elements concurred to form the *status or caput* of the citizen, namely, liberty, *libertas,* citizenship, *civitas,* and family, *familia.*

——**At Common Law.** A head. Chiefly used in phrases, thus: *Caput comitatis,* the head of the county; the sheriff; the king. Spelman. *Caput anni,* the beginning of the year. Cowell. *Caput legis,* a head of the law; *caput villae,* the chief man of a town; *caput feudi vel terrae,* the head or chief lord of lands held by feudal tenure; *caput baroniae,* the castle, manor house, or chief seat of a baron. Bracton, fol. 76b.

CAPUT LUPINUM (Lat.) Having a wolf's head.

Outlaws were anciently said to have *caput lupinum,* and might be killed by any one who met them. 4 Bl. Comm. 320. In the reign of Edward III. this power was restricted to the sheriff when armed with lawful process, and this power, even, has long since disappeared, the process of outlawry being resorted to merely as a means of compelling an appearance. Co. Litt. 128b; 3 Bl. Comm. 284.

CAPUT MORTUUM. A dead head; a thing void for all purposes. See 96 U. S. 195.

CAPUT PORTUS. In old English law. The head of a port. The town to which a port belongs, and which gives the denomination to the port, and is the head of it. Hale, de Jure Mar. pt. 2, c. 2; 4 Taunt. 660.

CAPUT, PRINCIPIUM, ET FINIS. The head, beginning, and end. A term applied in English law to the king, as head of parliament. 4 Inst. 3; 1 Bl. Comm. 188.

CAPUTAGIUM. Head money; the payment of head money. Spelman; Cowell.

CAPUTIUM. In old English law. A head of land; a headland. Cowell, voc. "Buttum."

CARABUS. In old English law. A kind of raft or boat. Spelman.

CARAT. A weight equal to three and one-sixth grains, in diamonds and the like. Jacob.

CARCAN. In French law. An instrument of punishment, somewhat resembling a pillory. It sometimes signifies the punishment itself. Biret, Vocab.

CARCANNUM. In old English law. A prison or workhouse.

CARCARE. In old English law. To load; to load a vessel (*in navibus carcare*). Reg. Orig. 279.

CARCATA. Loaded; freighted. Flet, lib. 1, c. 25, § 9.

CARCELAGE. Prison fees.

CARCER. A prison or gaol. Strictly, a place of detention and safe-keeping, and not of punishment. Burrill.

CARCER AD HOMINES CUSTODIENdos, non ad puniendos, dari debet. A prison ought to be given to the custody, not the punishment of persons. Co. Litt. 260. See Dig. 48. 19. 8. 9.

CARCER NON SUPPLICII CAUSA SED custodiae constitutus. A prison is ordained not for the sake of punishment, but of detention and guarding. Lofft, 119.

CARDINAL. In ecclesiastical law. The title given to one of the highest dignitaries of the court of Rome.

Cardinals are next to the pope in dignity, and he is elected by them. There are cardinal bishops, cardinal priests, and cardinal deacons. See Fleury, Hist. Eccles. liv. 25, note 17; note 19; Thomassin, pt. 2, liv. 1, c. 53; Id. pt. 4, liv. 1, cc. 79, 80; Loiseau, Traite des Ordres, c. 3, note 31; Andre, Droit Canon.

CARDS. In criminal law. Small rectangular pasteboards, generally of a fine quality, on which are painted figures of various colors, and used for playing certain games. See 4 Pick. (Mass.) 251.

CARE. Charge or oversight; diligence. See "Negligence."

The word "care," used in a statute defining embezzlement, is equivalent to "custody," and may mean "charge," "safekeeping," or "security." 110 Ill. 649.

CARE OF. The words "care of" written on a box delivered to a carrier for transportation merely mean that if the consignee named could not be found the goods might be delivered into the care of the person named. 48 Ill. 427.

CARENA, CARINA, or CARRENA (Law Lat.; from Fr. *quarante*, forty). In old ecclesiastical law. A period of forty days. Of the same meaning as *quarentena*. (Fr. *quarantaine*), quarantine. Spelman. See "Quarantine."

CARETA, CARRETA, or CARECTA. A cart; a cartload.

In *Magna Charta* (9 Hen. III. c. 21) it is ordained that no sheriff shall take horses or carts (*careta*) without paying the ancient livery therefor.

CARGA. In Spanish law. An incumbrance; a charge. White, New Recop. bk. 2, tit. 13, c. 2, § 2.

CARGARE. In old English law. To charge. Spelman.

CARGO. In martime law. The entire load of a ship or other vessel. 1 Mason (U. S.) 142. "Not the property on board belonging exclusively to the shipowner, but all the property constituting the ship's lading; all the property on which freight and profits were to accrue. 4 Mason (U. S.) 264.

The products of a whaling voyage are "cargo," but the implements used in whaling are not. 11 Pick. (Mass.) 230.

As used in policies of marine insurance, the term has a restricted meaning, derived from usage, which does not include deck load or live stock. 4 Pick. (Mass.) 433; 2 Gill & J. (Md.) 136.

The term is usually applied to goods only, but in a more extensive and less technical sense it includes persons. See 7 Man. & G. 729, 744.

CARISTIA. Dearth or scarcity.

CARLISLE TABLES. Tables of life expectancy, compiled in about 1780, at Carlisle, England. They are admissible in evidence on questions of expectancy.

CARMACK AMENDMENT. The purpose of the Carmack amendment to the Hepburn Act was to do away with the difficulties shippers had encountered in seeking to recover damages to property carried over more than one line of railroad, by giving the shipper the right to institute his action against the carrier receiving the property for interstate shipment, for damages occurring anywhere in the course of the transportation, leaving it to such carrier to recover from the carrier on whose line the damage occurred. 271 Ill. 541.

CARMEN. In the Roman law. Literally, a verse or song; a formula or form of words used on various occasions, as of divorce. Tayl. Civ. Law, 349.

CARNAL KNOWLEDGE. Sexual connection. The term is generally, if not exclusively, applied to the act of the male.

The term is a technical one, and has been always held adequate to express the idea of sexual bodily connection. 22 Ohio St. 541; 97 Mass. 61.

CARNALITER. In old criminal law. Carnally. *Carnaliter cognovit*, carnally knew.

Technical words in indictments for rape, and held essential. 1 Hale, P. C. 637-639; 3 Inst. 60.

CARNALLY KNEW. A technical phrase essential in an indictment to charge the defendant with the crime of rape. No other words nor circumlocution will answer. 1 Hale, P. C. 632; 1 Chit. Crim. Law, 243; Co. Litt. 137.

CARNO. An immunity or privilege. Cowell.

CARRICLE, or CARRACLE. A ship of great burden.

CARRIER. One who undertakes to transport goods from one place to another. 1 Pars. Cont. 632.

They are either "common" or "private." Private carriers incur the responsibility of the exercise of ordinary diligence only, like other bailees for hire. Story, Bailm. § 495; 13 Barb. (N. Y.) 481; 1 Wend. (N. Y.) 272; 1 Hayw. (N. C.) 14; 2 Dana (Ky.) 430; 4 Taunt. 787; 6 Taunt. 577; 2 Bos. & P. 417; 2 C. B. 877. See "Common Carriers."

CARRYING AWAY. See "Asportation."

CARRYING COSTS. A verdict or decision "carrying costs" is one entitling the party in whose favor it is made to tax costs thereon.

CART. A carriage for luggage or burden, with two wheels, as distinguished from a wagon, which has four wheels. Worcester.

The term has been held to include four-wheeled vehicles, to carry out the intent of a statute. 22 Ala. (N. S.) 621.

CART BOTE. An allowance to the tenant of wood sufficient for carts and other instruments of husbandry. 2 Bl. Comm. 35.

CARTA. A charter (*q. v.*) Any written instrument.

——**In Spanish Law.** A letter; a deed; a power of attorney. Las Partidas, pt. 3, tit. 18, lib. 30.

CARTA DE FORESTA. See "Charta de Foresta."

CARTE. In French marine law. A chart. Ord. Mar. liv. 1, tit. 8, arts. 2, 3.

CARTE BLANCHE. A white card signed at the bottom with a person's name, and sometimes sealed, giving another person power to superscribe what conditions he pleases. Applied, generally, in the sense of unlimited authority being granted. Wharton.

CARTEL. An agreement between two belligerent powers for the delivery of prisoners or deserters, and also a written challenge to a duel.

Cartel ship is a ship commissioned in time of war to exchange prisoners, or to carry any proposals between hostile powers. She must carry no cargo, ammunition, or implements of war, except a single gun for signals.

CARTMEN. Persons who carry goods and merchandise in carts, either for great or short distances, for hire.

CARUCAGE. A taxation of land by the *caruca* or *carue.*

The *caruca* was as much land as a man could cultivate in a year and a day with a single plough (*caruca*). *Carucage, carugage,* or *caruage* was the tribute paid for each *caruca* by the *carucarius,* or tenant. Spelman; Cowell.

CARUCATA. A certain quantity of land, used as the basis for taxation. As much, land as may be tilled by a single plough in a year and a day. Skene de Verb. Sign. A team of cattle; a cartload.

It may include houses, meadow, woods, etc. It is said by Littleton to be the same as *soca,* but has a much more extended signification. Spelman; Blount; Cowell.

CAS FORTUIT (Fr.) In the law of insurance. A fortuitous event; an inevitable accident. 3 Kent, Comm. 300; 120 U. S. 727.

Same as the Latin *casus fortuitus (q. v.)*

CASATA, or CASSATA. In old European law. A house with land sufficient for the support of one family. Otherwise called "*hida,*" a hide of land, and by Bede, "*Familia.*" Spelman, voc. "Casa."

CASATUS. In old European law. A vassal or feudal tenant possessing a *casata (q. v.),* that is, having a house, household, and property of his own. The *cassati* embraced both bond and free tenants. Spelman.

CASE. A question before a court of justice. 88 Ill. App. 199.

Any state of facts which furnishes occasion for the exercise of the jurisdication of a court of justice or any question contested before such a court. 257 Ill. 55.

A subject on which the judicial power is capable of acting and which has been submitted to it by a party in the form required by law. 88 Ill. App. 199.

A question contested before a court of justice; an action or suit at law or in equity. 1 Wheat. (U. S.) 352; 4 Iowa, 152.

A case arising under a treaty (Const. U. S. art. 3, § 2) is a suit where is drawn in question the construction of a treaty, and the decision is against the title set up by either party under such treaty. Story, J., 1 Wheat. (U. S.) 356. And see, also, 6 Cranch (U. S.) 286; 9 Wheat. (U. S.) 819; 11 How. (U. S.) 529; 12 How. (U. S.) 111.

A form of action which lies to recover damages for injuries for which the more ancient forms of action will not lie. Steph. Pl. 15.

"Case," or, more fully, "action upon the case," or "trespass on the case," includes in its widest sense *assumpsit* and *trover*, and distinguishes a class of actions in which the writ is framed according to the special circumstances of the case, from the ancient actions, the writs in which, called *brevia formata*, are collected in the Registrum Brevium.

Sometimes used for "case stated" (*q. v.*)

CASE AGREED ON. A statement of facts agreed upon by the parties, and submitted to the court, in order to obtain a decision upon the points of law involved, without going through the forms of a regular trial. 3 Whart. (Pa.) 143.

CASE FOR MOTION. In English divorce and probate practice, when a party desires to make a motion, he must file, among other papers, a case for motion, containing an abstract of the proceedings in the suit or action, a statement of the circumstances on which the motion is founded, and the prayer, or nature of the decree or order desired. Browne, Div. 251; Browne, Prob. Prac. 295.

CASE LAW. The law evidenced by or derived from the reported decisions. The law established by the force of such decisions as precedents, as distinguished from the reasons or philosophy of the law.

CASE ON APPEAL.

——**In American Practice.** Especially in states having reformed Codes of Procedure, a printed document prepared by an appellant, containing the substance of the evidence and proceedings on the trial in the court below.

——**In English Practice.** In the house of lords and privy council: (1) A statement prepared and printed by each party to an appeal, showing the facts on which he relies, and containing references to the evidence contained in the appendix. (2) A written statement by an inferior court or judge, raising a question of law for the opinion of a superior court.

CASE RESERVED. A statement in writing of the facts proved on the trial of a cause, drawn up and settled by the attorneys and counsel for the respective parties under the supervision of the judge, for the purpose of having certain points of law, which arose at the trial, and could not then be satisfactorily decided, determined upon full argument before the court *in banc.* This is otherwise called a "special case;" and it is usual for the parties, where the law of the case is doubtful, to agree that the jury shall find a general verdict for the plaintiff, subject to the opinion of the court upon such a case to be made, instead of obtaining from the jury a special verdict. Burrill.

CASE STATED. In practice. A statement of all the facts of a case, with the names of the witnesses, and a detail of the documents which are to support them; a brief.

An agreement in writing, between a plaintiff and defendant, that the facts in dispute between them are as there agreed upon and mentioned. 3 Whart. (Pa.) 143.

CASE TO MOVE FOR NEW TRIAL. In practice. A case prepared by the party against whom a verdict has been given, upon which to move the court to set aside the verdict, and grant a new trial. Graham, Prac. 330; 1 Burrill, Prac. 469.

CASH. That which circulates as money. It is generally held to include bank notes. 9 Johns. (N. Y.) 120; 10 Wheat. (U. S.) 347. But see 3 Halst. (N. J.) 172. Treasury notes (3 Conn. 534) and gold dust (1 Cal. 49) have been held not to be cash. See, also, 6 Md. 37; 44 Ala. 402.

Money at command; ready money. 28 Grat. (Va.) 175.

A sale for cash is a sale for money in hand (24 N. J. Law, 101), but a local custom may give the phrase another meaning (3 Mo. App. 149).

CASH BOOK. A book in which a merchant enters an account of all the cash he receives or pays. An entry of the same thing ought to be made, under the proper dates, in the journal. The object of the cash book is to afford a constant facility to ascertain the true state of a man's cash. Pardessus, note 87.

CASH SALE. In the language of the commercial world, the term "cash sale" is used to designate sales where the purchaser is to have a short credit, as for example, ten days, or even thirty days. 213 Ill. 586; 157 Ill. 515.

The strict legal signification of the term cash sale is one where delivery and payments are to be concurrent acts and be performed at the same instant of time. 213 Ill. 587; 157 Ill. 515.

CASHIER. An officer of a moneyed institution, or of a private person or firm, who is entitled by his office to take care of the cash or money of such institution, persons, or firm.

——**In Military Law.** To deprive a military officer of his office. See Articles of War, art. 14.

——**Of a Bank.** An executive officer, by whom its debts are received and paid, and its securities taken and transferred, whose ordinary duties are to keep all the funds of the bank, its notes, bills and other choses in action, to be used from time to time for the ordinary and extraordinary exigencies of the bank, and usually receiving directly, or through the subordinate officers of the bank, all the money and notes of the ank, delivering up all discounted notes nd other securities when they have been aid, drawing checks to withdraw the funds f the band when they have been deposited, nd, as the executive officer of the bank, ransacting most of its business. 22 Ill. ɩpp. 251.

CASSARE. To quash; to render void; to reak.

CASSATION. In French law. A decision manating from the sovereign authority, by which a decree or judgment in the court of ast resort is broken or annulled. See Cour de Cassation."

CASSETUR BILLA, or **QUOD BILLA** ɩassetur (Lat. that the bill be quashed). In ɩractice. The form of the judgment for the lefendant on a plea in abatement, where he action was commenced by bill (*billa*). ; Bl. Comm. 303; Steph. Pl. 128, 131. The orm of an entry made by a plaintiff on the ecord, after a plea in abatement, where ie found that the plea could not be conessed and avoided, nor traversed, nor denurred to; amounting in fact to a discon;inuance of the action. 2 Archb. Prac. K. B. }, 236; 1 Tidd. Prac. 683.

CASSETUR BREVE (Lat. that the writ ɔe quashed) In practice. A judgment some;imes entered against a plaintiff, at his request, when, in consequence of allegations of the defendant, he can no longer prosecute his suit with effect. The effect of such entry is to stop proceedings, and exonerate the plaintiff from liability for future costs, leaving him free to sue out new process. 3 Bl. Comm. 340. See Gould Pl. c. 5, § 139; 3 Bouv. Inst. notes 2913, 2914; 5 Term R. 634.

CAST (Law Fr. *jecter*, getter; Lat. *projicere*). In old English practice. To allege, offer, or present; to put forward. To cast an essoign was to allege an excuse for the failure of a party to appear in court, on the return of the original writ. 3 Steph. Comm. 659; 3 Bl. Comm. 278; Roscoe, Real Actions, 156. To cast a protection was to present or allege it as an excuse. Co. Litt. 128a. 130, 131; 3 Reeve, Hist. Eng. Law, 406.

This word is now used as a popular, rather than a technical, term, in the sense of to overcome, overthrow, or defeat in a civil action at law. Webster.

CASTELLAIN, or **CASTELLANUS.** The keeper or captain of a fortified castle; the constable of a castle. Spelman; Termes de la Ley; Blount.

CASTELLARIUM, or **CASTELLATUS.** In old English law. The precinct or jurisdiction of a castle. Blount.

CASTELLORUM OPERATIO. In old English law. Service or labor done by inferior tenants for the building and upholding of castles and public places of defense. Towards this some gave their personal service, and others, a contribution of money or goods. This was one branch of the *trinoda necessitas* (1 Bl. Comm. 263), from which no lands could be exempted under the Saxons, though immunity was sometimes allowed after the conquest. Kennett, Par. Ant. 114; Cowell.

CASTIGATORY. An engine used to punish women who have been convicted of being common scolds. It is sometimes called the trebucket, tumbrel, ducking-stool or cucking-stool. This barbarous punishment has perhaps never been inflicted in the United States. 12 Serg. & R. (Pa.) 225.

CASTING. In old English practice. Offering, alleging; thus, casting an essoign was alleging an excuse for nonappearance.

CASTING VOTE. The deciding vote in a deliberative or parliamentary body, cast by the presiding officer in the event of a tie. It sometimes signifies only such a vote, and sometimes the double vote of one who first votes as a member, and afterwards votes to cast off the tie, if one results. 1 Bl. Comm. 181, note; Jacob, "Parliament" (7).

CASTLEGUARD, CASTLEGARD, or **CASTLEWARD** (Law Lat. *castelgardum, castelli guardia, wardum castri, custodia castri*). In feudal and old English law. The defense or guard of a castle; otherwise called "watch" and "ward." A species of feudal service or tenure; a kind of tenure by knight's service. Spelman, voc. "Castelgardum;" Termes de la Ley; Litt. § 111; Co. Litt. 82b. The service was sometimes changed into an annual rent, and then the tenure became a tenure in socage. 4 Coke, 88. See 3 How. St. Tr. 866.

An imposition anciently laid upon such persons as lived within a certain distance of any castle, towards the maintenance of such as watched and warded the castle. Magna Charta, c. 20; St. 32 Hen. VIII. c. 48; Cowell.

The circuit itself, inhabited by such as were subject to this service. Cowell; Blount; Termes de lay Ley.

CASTRATION. In criminal law. The act of gelding. When this act is maliciously performed upon a man, it is a mayhem, and punishable as such, although the sufferer consented to it. 2 Bish. Crim. Law, §§ 842, 847.

CASU CONSIMILI. See "Consimili Casu.

CASU PROVISO (Lat. in the case provided for). In practice. A writ of entry framed under the provisions of the statute of Gloucester (6 Edw. I.) c. 7, which lay for the benefit of the reversioner when a tenant in dower aliened in fee or for life. It seems to have received this name to distinguish it from a similar writ framed under the provisions of St. Westminster II. (13 Edw. I.) c. 24, where a tenant by curtesy had alienated as above, and which was known emphatically as the writ *in consimili casu.*

The writ is now practically obsolete. Fitzh. Nat. Brev. 205; Dane, Abr. Index.

CASUAL EJECTOR. In practice. The person supposed to perform the fictitious ouster of the tenant of the demandant in an action of ejectment. See "Ejectment."

CASUAL EMPLOYMENT. Occasional, irregular or incidental employment in contradistinction from stated or regular. 277 Ill. 142.

CASUAL EVIDENCE. A phrase used to denote (in contradistinction to "preappointed evidence") all such evidence as happens to be adducible of a fact or event, but which was not prescribed by statute or otherwise arranged beforehand to be the evidence of the fact or event. Brown.

CASUAL PAUPER. A poor person who, in England, applies for relief in a parish other than that of his settlement. The ward in the workhouse to which they are admitted is called the "casual ward." Rapalje & L.

CASUALTIES OF SUPERIORITY. In Scotch law. Certain emoluments arising to the superior lord in regard to the tenacy.

They resemble the "incidents" to the feudal tenure at common law. They take precedence of a creditor's claim on the tenant's land, and constitute a personal claim also against the vassal. Bell, Dict. They have very generally disappeared. Paterson, Comp. 29.

CASUALTY. Inevitable accident. Unforeseen circumstances not to be guarded against by human agency, and in which man takes no part. Story, Bailm. § 240; 1 Pars. Cont. 543-547.

CASUS BELLI. An occurrence giving rise to or justifying war.

CASUS FOEDERIS (Lat.) In international law. A case within the stipulations of a treaty.

The question whether, in case of a treaty of alliance, a nation is bound to assist its ally in war against a third nation, is determined in a great measure by the justice or injustice of the war. If manifestly unjust on the part of the ally, it cannot be considered as *casus foederis.* Grotius de Jure Belli, bk. 2, c. 25; Vattel, bk. 2, c. 12, § 168. See 1 Kent, Comm. 49.

CASUS FORTUITUS (Lat.) An inevitable accident; a loss happening in spite of all human effort and sagacity. 3 Kent, Comm. 217, 300.

It includes such perils of the sea as strokes of lightning, etc. A loss happening through the agency of rats was held an unforeseen, but not an inevitable, accident. 1 Curt. C. C. (U. S.) 148. The happening of a *casus fortuitus* excuses ship owners from liability for goods conveyed. 3 Kent, Comm. 216.

CASUS FORTUITUS NON EST SPERANdus, et nemo tenetur divinare. A fortuitous event is not to be foreseen, and no person is held bound to divine it. 4 Coke, 66.

CASUS FORTUITUS NON EST SUPponendus. A fortuitous event is not to be presumed. Hardr. 82, arg.

CASUS MAJOR (Lat.) An unusual accident. Story, Bailm. § 240.

CASUS OMISSUS (Lat.) A case which is not provided for. When such cases arise in statutes which are intended to provide for all cases of a given character which may arise, the common law governs. 5 Coke, 38; 11 East, 1; 2 Bin. (Pa.) 279; 2 Sharswood, Bl. Comm. 260; Brown, Max. 37. A *casus omissus* may occur in a contract as well as in a statute. 2 Sharswood, Bl. Comm. 260.

CASUS OMISSUS ET OBLIVIONI DATUS dispositioni communis juris relinquitur. A case omitted and forgotten is left to the disposal of the common law. 5 Coke, 37; Broom, Leg. Max. (3d London Ed.) 45; 1 Exch. 476.

CATALLA (Law Lat.) In old English law. Chattels, or *catals,* as anciently written. A term including all property movable and immovable, except fees and freeholds.

This word is considered by Spelman as derived, by contraction, from *capitalia.* The singular, *catallum (q. v.),* rarely occurs, although Bracton uses it in several places. *Catalla,* according to the same writer, had nearly or quite the sense of *averia* (beasts or cattle), being demandable under that name. Bracton, fol. 159b. See "Averia." It seems to have been, from a very early period, united with the word *bona,* in the phrase *bona et catalla,* of which the familiar modern phrase "goods and chattels" is a translation. Bracton, fol. 60b; Reg. Orig. 140, 141.

CATALLA JUSTE POSSESSA AMITTI non possunt. Chattels justly possessed cannot be lost. Jenk. Cent. Cas. 28.

CATALLA OTIOSA (Lat.) Dead goods, and animals other than beasts of the plough, *averia carucae,* and sheep. 3 Sharswood, Bl. Comm. 9; Bracton, 217b.

CATALLA REPUTANTUR INTER MINima in lege. Chattels are considered in law among the minor things. Jenk. Cent. Cas. 52.

CATALLIS CAPTIS NOMINE DISTINCtionis. A writ which lay for rent of a house in a borough, and authorized distress of windows, doors, etc.

CATALLUM. A chattel. See "Catalla." The word is used more frequently in the plural, *catalla*, but has then the same signification, denoting all goods, movable or immovable, except such as are in the nature of fees and freeholds. Cowell; Du Cange.

CATALS. Goods and chattels. See "Catalla." Rapalje & L.

CATANEUS. A tenant *in capite;* a tenant holding immediately of the crown. Spelman.

CATCHING BARGAIN. An agreement made with an heir expectant for the purchase of his expectancy at an inadequate price. Any agreement, whether by sale, mortgage, or *post obit* bond, on insufficient consideration, to be performed by the heir on the vesting of his expectancy. 47 Mich. 94; 7 Mass. 112; 63 Pa. St. 448; 34 Me. 447.

CATCHLAND. Land in Norfolk, so called because it is not known to what parish it belongs, and the minister who first seizes the tithes of it, by right of preoccupation, enjoys them for that year. Cowell.

CATCHPOLE, or **CATCHPOLL.** A name formerly given to a sheriff's deputy, or to a constable, or other officer whose duty it is to arrest persons. He was a sort of sergeant. The word is not now in use as an official designation. Minshew.

CATER COUSIN. A very distant relation. Bl. Law Tracts, 6.

CATHEDRAL. In ecclesiastical law. A tract set apart for the service of the church.

The church of the bishop; so called from the fact that his *cathedra* or official chair is therein located.

CATHOLIC CREDITOR. In Scotch law. A creditor whose debt is secured on several parts or all of his debtor's property. Such a creditor is bound to take his payment with reference to the rights of the secondary creditors, or, if he disregards their rights, must assign over to them his claims. This rule applies where he collects his debts of a cautioner (surety). Bell, Dict.

CATHOLIC EMANCIPATION ACT. Act 10 Geo. IV. c. 7. This act relieves from disabilities and restores all civil rights to Catholics, except that of holding ecclesiastical offices and certain high state offices. 3 Steph. Comm. 109.

CATONIANA REGULA. In Roman law. The rule which is commonly expressed in the maxim, *Quod ab initio non valet tractu temporis non convalebit*, meaning that what is at the beginning void by reason of some technical (or other) legal defect will not become valid merely by length of time. The rule applied to the institution of *haeredes*, the bequest of legacies, and such like. The rule is not without its application also in English law; *e. g.*, a married woman's will (being void when made) is not made valid merely because she lives to become a widow. Brown.

CATTLE. From law Latin *capitalia.* Beasts subject of ownership at common law; domestic animals, useful as food or for labor.

The term "cattle" includes horses and asses as well as domesticated horned animals. 47 Ill. 463.

CATTLE GATE. A customary proportionate right of pasture enjoyed in common with others. The right is measured not by the number of cattle to be pastured, but by reference to the rights of others and the whole amount of pasture. 34 Eng. Law & Eq. 511; 1 Term R. 137.

CAUDA TERRAE. A land's end, or the bottom of a ridge in arable land. Cowell.

CAULCEIS (Law Fr.) A word used in old statutes (6 Hen. VI. c. 5) to signify causeways, or causeys. From the latin *calcetum* (*q. v.*) Cowell; Blount.

CAUPO (pl. *caupones*). In the civil law. An inkeeper. Dig. 4. 9. 4. 5; Story, Ag. § 458.

CAUPONA. In the civil law. An inn or tavern. Inst. 4. 5. 3; Dig. 4. 9. 1. 5.

CAURSINES. Italian merchants who came into England in the reign of Henry III., where they established themselves as money lenders, but were soon expelled for their usury and extortion. Cowell; Blount; Spelman. They seem to have been Lombards, deriving their name from a town in Lombardy.

CAUSA (Lat.) A cause; a reason.

A condition; a consideration. Used of contracts, and found in this sense in the Scotch law also. Bell, Dict.

A suit; an action pending. Used in this sense in the old English law.

Property. Used thus in the civil law in the sense of *res* (a thing). *Non porcellum. non agnellum, nec aliam causam*, not a hog, not a lamb, nor other thing. Du Cange.

By reason of. *Causa proxima*, the immediate cause. *Causa remota*, a cause operating indirectly by the intervention of other causes. In its general sense, *causa* denotes anything operating to produce an effect. 4 Gray (Mass.) 398; 4 Campb. 284.

CAUSA CAUSAE EST CAUSA CAUSATI. The cause of a cause is the cause of the effect. Freem. 329; 12 Mod. 637.

CAUSA CAUSANS. The immediate cause; the last link in the chain of causation. Rapalje & L.

CAUSA DATA ET NON SECUTA. In the civil law. Consideration given and not followed, that is, by the event upon which it was given. The name of an action by which a thing given in the view of a certain event was reclaimed if that event did not take place. Dig. 12. 4; Code, 4. 6.

CAUSA ECCLESIAE PUBLICIS AEQUIparatur; et summa est ratio quae pro religione facit. The cause of the church is equal to public cause; and paramount is the reason which makes for religion. Co. Litt. 341.

CAUSA ET ORIGO EST MATERIA NEgotii. Cause and origin is the material of business. 1 Coke, 99; Wingate, Max. 41, max. 21.

CAUSA HOSPITANDI. For the purpose of being entertained as a guest. 4 Maule & S. 310.

CAUSA JACTITATIONIS MARITAGII (Lat.) A form of action which anciently lay against a party who boasted or gave out that he or she was married to the plaintiff, whereby a common reputation of their marriage might ensue. 3 Bl. Comm. 93.

CAUSA MATRIMONII PRAELOCUTI (Lat.) A writ lying where a woman has given lands to a man in fee simple, with the intention that he shall marry her, and he refuses so to do within a reasonable time, upon suitable request. Cowell. Now obsolete. 3 Bl. Comm. 183, note.

CAUSA MORTIS. In anticipation of death. See "Donatio Causa Mortis."

CAUSA PATET. The reason is open, obvious, plain, clear, or manifest. A common expression in old writers. Perk. c. 1, §§ 11, 14, 97. *Causa patet ex praemissis,* the reason is plain from the premises. Id. c. 3, § 226.

CAUSA PROXIMA NON REMOTA SPECtatur (Lat.) The direct and not the remote cause is considered. See "Proximate Cause."

CAUSA REI (Lat.) In civil law. Things accessory or appurtenant. All those things which a man would have had if the thing had not been withheld. Du Cange. 1 Mackeld. Civ. Law, 55.

CAUSA REMOTA. A remote cause.

CAUSA SCIENTIAE PATET. The reason of the knowledge is evident. A technical phrase in Scotch practice, used in depositions of witnesses.

CAUSA SINE QUA NON. A necessary case; one without which the effect would not have been produced.

CAUSA TURPIS. An immoral cause.

CAUSA VAGA ET INCERTA NON EST causa rationabilis. A vague and uncertain cause is not a reasonable cause. 5 Coke, 57.

CAUSAE DOTIS, VITAE, LIBERTATIS, fisci sunt inter favorabilia in lege. Causes of dower, life, liberty, revenue are among the things favored in law. Co. Litt. 341.

CAUSAM NOBIS SIGNIFICES QUARE. You signify to us the reason. In old English practice. A writ addressed to a mayor of a town, etc., who was by the king's writ commanded to give seisin of lands to the king's grantee, on his delaying to do it, requiring him to show cause why he so delayed the performance of his duty. Blount; Cowell.

CAUSARE (Lat. to cause). To be engaged in a suit; to litigate; to conduct a cause. Used in the old English and in the civil law.

CAUSATOR (Lat.) A litigant; one who takes the part of the plaintiff or defendant in a suit.

CAUSE (Lat. *causa*). That which supplies the motive, or constitutes the reason, for any act. See "Probable Cause."

——**In Civil Law.** The consideration or motive for making a contract. Dig. 2. 14. 7; Toullier, Dr. Civ. liv. 3, tit. 3, c. 2, § 4.

——**In Pleading.** Reason; motive.

In a replication *de injuria,* for example, the plaintiff alleges that the defendant of his own wrong and without the cause by him, etc., where the word "cause" comprehends all the facts alleged as an excuse or reason for doing the act. 1 Chit. Pl. 585.

——**In Practice.** A suit or action; any question, civil or criminal, contested before a court of justice. Wood, Civ. Law, 301. It does not include a *quo warranto* proceeding (5 El. & Bl.), but includes a criminal prosecution (3 Q. B. 901).

CAUSE BOOKS. Books kept in the central office of the English supreme court, in which are entered all writs of summons issued in the office. Rules of Court, v. 8.

CAUSE LIST. An official list of actions, demurrers, petitions, appeals, etc., set down for trial or argument in open court. Similar to the American "calendar" or "docket" (*q. v.*)

CAUSE OF ACTION. The thing done or omitted to be done which confers the right upon the other to sue,—that is, the wrong against the plaintiffs which caused a grievance for which the law gives a remedy. 272 Ill. 156.

Matter for which an action may be brought; the right to maintain an action. 28 Barb. (N. Y.) 231.

A cause of action is said to accrue to any person when that person first comes to a right to bring an action. There is, however, an obvious distinction between a cause of action and a right, though a cause of action generally confers a right. Thus, statutes of limitation do not affect the cause of action, but take away the right. It is synonymous with "right of action" (26 How. Pr. [N. Y.] 108), but not with "chose in action" (10 How. Pr. [N. Y.] 1).

CAUSIDICUS. In the civil law. A pleader; one who argued a cause *ore tenus.* Code, 2. 6. 6. There was a distinction between *causidicus* and *advocatus (q. v.)*

CAUTELA (Lat.) Care; precaution vigilance.

CAUTI JURATORIA. Security given by the oath of the party. Inst. 4. 11. 2; 1 Mackeld. Civ. Law, p. 176, § 184; T. Raym. 226, arg.

CAUTIO, or **CAUTION.**

——**In Civil Law.** Security given for the performance of anything. A bond whereby the debtor acknowledges the receipt of money, and promises to pay it at a future day.

——**In French Law.** The person entering into an obligation as a surety.

——**In Scotch Law.** A pledge, bond, or other security for the performance of an obligation, or completion of the satisfaction to be obtained by a judicial process. Bell, Dict.

CAUTIO FIDEJUSSORIA. Security by means of bonds or pledges entered into by third parties. Du Cange.

CAUTIO PIGNORATITIA. A pledge by deposit of goods.

CAUTIO PRO EXPENSIS. Security for costs or expenses.

This term is used among the civilians (Nov. 112, c. 2), and generally on the continent of Europe. In nearly all the countries of Europe, a foreign plaintiff, whether resident there or not, is required to give caution *pro expensis*, that is, security for costs. In some states this requisition is modified, and when such plaintiff has real estate or a commercial or manufacturing establishment within the state, he is not required to give such caution. Foelix, Droit Int. Prive, note 106.

CAUTIO USUFRUCTUARIA. Security, which tenants for life give, to preserve the property rented free from waste and injury. Ersk. Inst. bk. 2, tit. 9, § 59.

CAUTION JURATORY. Security given by oath; that which a suspender swears is the best he can afford in order to obtain a suspension. Ersk. Prac. 4. 3. 6. Paterson, Comp.

CAUTIONARY. In Scotch law. The obligation by which a party becomes surety for another, answering to the English guarantee. It is defined by Stair: "The promise or contract of a man, not for himself, but another." Brande. See Ersk. Inst. bk. 3, tit. 7, § 22. See "Cautionary."

CAUTIONE ADMITTENDA. In English ecclesiastical law. A writ that lies against a bishop who holds an excommunicated person in prison for contempt, notwithstanding he offers sufficient caution or security to obey the orders and commandment of the church for the future. Reg. Orig. 66; Cowell.

CAUTIONER. A surety; a bondsman. One who binds himself in a bond with the principal for greater security. He is still a cautioner, whether the bond be to pay a debt, or whether he undertake to produce the person of the party for whom he is bound. Bell, Dict.

CAUTIONNEMENT. In French law. The same as becoming surety in English law.

CAUTIONRY. In Scotch law. Suretyship. The obligation of suretyship.

CAVEAT (Lat. let him beware).

——**In Practice.** A notice not to do an act, given to some officer, ministerial or judicial, by a party having an interest in the matter.

It is a formal caution or warning not to do the act mentioned, and is addressed frequently to prevent the admission to probate of wills, the granting letters of administration, etc. 1 Bouv. Inst. 71, 534; 3 Bl. Comm. 246; 2 Chit. Prac. 502, note b; 3 Bin (Pa.) 314; 3 Halst. (N. J.) 139.

It is also used to prevent the issuance of a patent for lands. See 9 Grat. (Va.) 508.

——**In Patent Law.** A legal notice not to issue a patent of a particular description to any other person without allowing caveator an opportunity to establish his priority of invention.

It is filed in the patent office under statutory regulations. This principal object of filing it is to obtain for an inventor time to perfect his invention without the risk of having a patent granted to another person for the same thing. Rev. St. U. S. § 4902.

CAVEAT EMPTOR (Lat. let the buyer beware). A maxim employed in the law to signify that a purchaser, whether of realty or personalty, is not only bound to discover obvious defects for himself, but is confined to the warranties which he has required, and cannot, in the absence of fraud, rely on the statements of the seller. Benj. Sales, 611; 17 Pick. (Mass.) 475; 10 Ga. 311; 9 N. Y. 36; 10 Wall. (U. S.) 383; 53 N. Y. 515.

As an exception to the rule, there is, however, an implied warranty of title. 88 Ga. 629.

CAVEAT EMPTOR; QUI IGNORARE non debuit quod jus alienum emit. Let a purchaser beware; who ought not to be ignorant that he is purchasing the rights of another. Hob. 99; Broom, Leg. Max. (3d London Ed.) 690; Co. Litt. 102a; 3 Taunt. 439; 1 Bouv. Inst. 383; Sugd. Vend. (13th Ed.) 272 et seq.; 1 Story, Eq. Jur. (6th Ed.) c. 6.

CAVEAT VENDITOR. Let the seller beware. Lofft, 328; 18 Wend. (N. Y.) 449, 453; 23 Wend. (N. Y.) 353; 2 Barb. (N. Y.) 323; 5 N. Y. 73, 82.

CAVEATOR. One who files a *caveat.*

CAVENDUM EST A FRAGMENTIS. Beware of fragments. Bac. Aph. 26.

CAVERE (Lat.) In the civil and common law. To take care; to exercise caution. See "Caveat Emptor."

To take care or provide for; to prove by law. *Cavetur,* provision is made, a remedy is given. Inst. 4. 3. 13. *Cautum est,* it is provided or enacted. Inst. 3. 8. 2; Id. 4. 3. pr.

To provide against; to forbid by law. Inst. 1. 25. 13.

To give security. *Nisi caveant tutores et curatores,* etc. Inst. 1. 24. 3. *Cautum,* secured. Dig. 50. 16. 188. 1.

To give caution or security on arrest. Clerke, Prax. tit. 4.

CAVERS. Offenders with respect to the mines in Derbyshire, who are punishable in the Berghmote or miners' court. Jacob.

CAYA. In old English law. A quay, kay, key, or wharf. Cowel.

CAYAGIUM. A toll or duty paid the king for landing goods at some quay or wharf. The barons of the Cinque Ports were free from this duty. Cowell.

CEAP. A bargain; anything for sale; a chattel; also cattle, as being the usual medium of barter. Sometimes used instead of *ceapgild* (*q. v.*)

CEAPGILD. Payment of an animal. An ancient species of forfeiture. Cowell; Spelman.

CEDE. To assign; to transfer. Applied to the act by which one state or nation transfers territory to another.

CEDENT. An assignor; the assignor of a chose in action. Kames, Eq. 43.

CEDULA. In Spanish law. A written obligation, under private signature, by which a party acknowledges himself indebted to another in a certain sum, which he promises to pay on demand or on some fixed day.

In order to obtain judgment on such an instrument, it is necessary that the party executing it should acknowledge it in open court, or that it be proved by two witnesses who saw its execution.

The citation affixed to the door of an absconding offender, requiring him to appear before the tribunal where the accusation is pending.

CEDULE. (Fr.) In French law. A note in writing. Poth. Obl. pt. 4, c. 1, art. 2, § 1.

CELATION. In medical jurisprudence. Concealment of pregnancy or delivery. Dungl. Med. Dict.

CELEBRATION OF MARRIAGE. The solemn act by which a man and woman take each other for husband and wife, conformably to the rules prescribed by law.

CELLERARIUS. A butler in a monastery; sometimes in universities called "manciple" or "caterer."

CEMETERY. A place or ground set apart for the burial of the dead. 121 Ill. 210.

CENDULAE. Small pieces of wood laid in the form of tiles to cover the roof of a house; shingles. Cowell.

CENEGILD. In Saxon law. A pecuniary mulct or fine paid to the relations of a murdered person by the murderer or his relations. Spelman.

CENELLAE. In old records. Acorns.

CENNINGA. A notice given by a buyer to a seller that the things which had been sold were claimed by another, in order that he might appear and justify the sale. Blount; Whishaw.

The exact significance of this term is somewhat doubtful. If probably denoted "notice," as defined above. The finder of stray cattle was not always entitled to it; for Spelman says: "As to strange (or stray) cattle, no one shall have them but with the consent of the hundred of tithingmen; unless he have one of these, we cannot allow him any *cenninga* (I think notice)." Spelman.

CENS. In Canadian law. An annual payment or due reserved to a seignior or lord, and imposed merely in recognition of his superiority. Guyot, Inst. c. 9.

The land or estate so held is called a *censive;* the tenant is a *censitaire.* It was originally a tribute of considerable amount, but became reduced in time to a nominal sum. It is distinct from the *rentes.* The *cens* varies in amount and in mode of payment. Payment is usually in kind, but may be in silver. 2 Low. (U. S.) 40.

CENSARIA. A farm, or house and land, let at a standing rent. Cowell.

CENSARII. In old English law. Farmers, or such persons as were liable to pay a census (tax). Blount; Cowell.

CENSERE. In the Roman law. To ordain; to decree. Dig. 50. 16. 111.

CENSITAIRE. See "Cens."

CENSIVE. See "Cens."

CENSO. In Spanish and Mexican law. An annuity; a ground rent; the right which a person acquires to receive a certain annual pension, for the delivery which he makes to another of a determined sum of money or of an immovable thing. Civ. Code Mex. art. 3206. See Schmidt, Civ. Law, 149, 309; White, New Recop. bk. 2, c. 7, § 4; 13 Tex. 655.

CENSO CONSIGNATIVO. In Spanish and Mexican law. A *censo* (*q. v.*) is called "*consignativo*" when he who receives the money assigns for the payment of the pension (annuity) the estate the fee in which he reserves. Civ. Code Mex. art. 3207.

CENSO ENFITEUTICO. In Spanish and Mexican law. An emphyteutic annuity. That species of *censo* (annuity) which exists where there is a right to require of another a certain canon or pension annually, on account of having transferred to that person forever certain real estate, but reserving the fee in the land. The owner who thus transfers the land is called the "*censualisto*," and the person who pays the annuity is called the "*censatario*." Hall, Mex. Law, § 756.

CENSUALES. In old European law. A species of *oblati* or voluntary slaves of churches or monasteries; those who, to procure the protection of the church, bound themselves to pay an annual tax or quit-rent only of their estates to a church or monastery.

CENSUERE. In Roman law. They have decreed. The term of art, or technical term for the judgment, resolution, or decree of the senate. Tayl. Civ. Law, 566.

CENSUMETHIDUS, or **CENSUMORTHIdus.** A dead rent, like that which is called "mortmain." Blount; Cowell.

CENSUS (Lat. *censere*, to reckon). An official reckoning or enumeration of the inhabitants and wealth of a country.

The census of the United States is taken every tenth year, in accordance with the provisions of the constitution, and many of the states have made provisions for a similar decennial reckoning at intervening periods. Const. U. S. art. 1, § 2; 1 Story, U. S. Laws, 73, 722, 751; 2 Story, U. S. Laws, 1134, 1139, 1169, 1194; 3 Story, U. S. Laws, 1776; 4 Sharswood, U. S. Laws, 2179.

——**In Old European Law.** A tax or tribute. Montesq. liv. 30, c. 14.

CENSUS REGALIS. In English law. The royal revenue. 1 Bl. Comm. 306.

CENT (Lat. *centum*, one hundred). A coin of the United States, weighing seventy-two grains, and composed of eighty-eight per centum of copper and twelve of nickel. Act Feb. 21, 1857, § 4. See 11 U. S. St. at Large, 163, 164.

CENTENA. (Law Lat. from *centum*, a hundred). A hundred; a district or division containing originally a hundred freemen, established among the Goths, Germans, Franks, and Lombards, for military and civil purposes, and answering to the Saxon hundred. Spelman; 1 Bl. Comm. 115; Esprit des Lois, liv. 30, c. 17. The Saxon division is also sometimes called *centena*, but is more commonly rendered in law Latin, *hundredum*, or *hundredus*. Spelman. See "Hundred;" "Centenarius;" "Centeni."

——**In Old Records and Pleadings.** A hundred weight. *Centena pisctium*, a hundred weight of fish. Pryn. 303. *Centena cerae zucarii, piperis, cumini, etc., continet tredecim petras et dimidium*, the hundred weight of wax, sugar, pepper, cummin, etc., contains thirteen stone and a half. Fleta, lib. 2, c. 12. 4. See Cro. Eliz. 754.

CENTENARIUS (Law Lat.; Fr. *centenier*, from *centena*, *q. v.*) In old European law. One of a *centena*, or hundred; the head or chief of a *centena* (*praefectus centenae*), among the Goths, Germans, Franks, and Lombards; an inferior judge.

CENTENI (Lat. from *centum*, a hundred). A hundred men; the number of men enrolled for military service from each district, among the ancient Germans, and which afterwards became their distinctive name.

CENTESIMA (Lat. *centum*). In Roman law. The hundredth part.

Usuriae centesimae. Twelve *per cent. per annum*, that is, a hundredth part of the principal, was due each month, the month being the unit of time from which the Romans reckoned interest. 2 Bl. Comm. 462, note.

CENTRAL CRIMINAL COURT. In English law. A court which has jurisdiction of all cases of treason, murder, felony, or misdemeanor committed within the city of London and county of Middlesex, and certain parts of the counties of Essex, Kent, and Surrey, and also of all serious offenses within the former jurisdiction of the admiralty court.

The court consists of the lord mayor, the lord chancellor, the judges of the three superior courts at Westminster, the judges in bankruptcy, the judges of the admiralty, the dean of the arches, the aldermen, recorder, and common serjeant of London, and the judges of the sheriff's court.

CENTRAL OFFICE. The central office of the supreme court of judicature in England is the office established in pursuance of the recommendation of the legal department's commission (2d Rep. 23, 47) in order to consolidate the offices of the masters and associates of the common-law divisions, the crown office of the queen's bench division, the record and writ clerk's report, and enrollment offices of the chancery division, and a few others. Judicature Act 1879, § 4 et seq. The central office is divided into the following departments, and the business and staff of the office are distributed accordingly (Rules of Court Dec. 1879, April, 1880): (1) Writ, appearance, and judgment; (2) summons and order, for the common-law divisions only; (3) filing and record, including the old chancery report office; (4) taxing, for the common-law divisions only; (5) enrollment; (6) judgments, for the registry of judgments, executions, etc.; (7) bills of sale; (8) married women's acknowledgments; (9) queen's remembrancer; (10) crown office; and (11) associates.

CENTUMVIRI (Lat. one hundred men). The name of a body of Roman judges. Their exact number was one hundred and five, there being selected three from each of the thirty-five tribes comprising all the citizens of Rome. They constituted, for ordinary purposes, four tribunals, but some cases (called *centumvirales causas*) required the judgment of all the judges. 3 Bl. Comm. 515.

CENTURY. One hundred; one hundred years.

One hundred men. The Romans were divided in "centuries," as the English were formerly divided into "hundreds."

CEORL. A tenant at will of free condition, who held land of the thane on condition of paying rent or services.

A freeman of inferior rank occupied in husbandry. Spelman.

Those who tilled the outlands paid rent; those who occupied or tilled the inlands, or demesne, rendered services. Under the Norman rule, this term, as did others which denoted workmen, especially those which applied to the conquered race, became a term of reproach, as is indicated by the popular signification of churl. Cowell; Spelman.

CEPI (Lat. I have taken). It was of frequent use in the returns of sheriffs when they were made in Latin; as, for example, *cepi corpus et* B. B., I have taken the body, and discharged him on bail bond; *cepi corpus et est in custodia,* I have taken the body, and it is in custody; *cepi corpus et est languidus,* I have taken the body, and he is sick.

CEPI CORPUS (Law Lat. I have taken the body). In practice. The technical name of the return made by a sheriff to a *capias,* that he has taken the body of the party. Fitzh. Nat. Brev. 26; 3 Bl. Comm. 288; 1 Tidd, Prac. 308-310. See "Capias." It is derived from the two emphatic words of the return which was anciently indorsed in law Latin on the writ.

Cepi corpus properly is the return where the defendant is out on bail. Where he is in actual custody, the return is *cepi corpus in custodia.* 1 Tidd, Prac. 308, 309. Sewell, Sheriffs, 387. *Cepi corpus et paratum habeo,* I have taken the body, and have it ready, is another form of this return, which anciently implied that the party was in actual custody, but is now the proper return where the defendant has been arrested and discharged on bail. Id.; 1 Tidd, Prac, ubi supra.

CEPIT (Lat. *capere,* to take; *cepit,* he took, or has taken).

——**In Civil Practice.** A form of replevin which is brought for carrying away goods merely. 3 Hill (N. Y.) 282. *Non detinet* is not the proper answer to such a charge. 17 Ark. 85. And see 3 Wis. 399. Success upon a *non cepit* does not entitle the defendant to a return of the property. 5 Wis. 85. A plea of *non cepit* is not inconsistent with a plea showing property in a third person. 8 Gill (Md.) 133.

——**In Criminal Practice.** Took. A technical word necessary in an indictment for larceny. The charge must be that the defendant took the thing stolen with a felonious design. Bac. Abr. "Indictment" (G 1).

CEPIT ET ABDUXIT (Lat. he took and led away). Applicable in a declaration in trespass or indictment for larceny, where the defendant has taken away a living chattel.

CEPIT ET ASPORTAVIT (Lat. he took and carried away). Applicable in a declaration in trespass or an indictment for larceny, where the defendant has carried away goods without right. 4 Bl. Comm. 231.

CEPIT IN ALIO LOCO (Lat. he took in another place). In pleading. A plea in replevin, by which the defendant alleges that he took the thing replevied in another place than that mentioned in the declaration. 1 Chit. Pl. 490; 2 Chit. Pl. 558; Rast. Entr. 554, 555; Willes, 475. It is the usual plea where the defendant intends to avow or justify the taking to entitle himself to a return. 4 Bouv. Inst. note 3569.

CEPPAGIUM. In old English law. The stumps or roots of trees which remain in the ground after the trees are felled. Fleta, lib. 2, c. 41, § 24.

CERA, or CERE. In old English law. Wax; a seal of wax. St. Westminster II. c. 10.

CERAGRUM. In old English law. A payment to provide candles in the church. Blount.

CEREVISIA. Ale or beer. Rapalje & L.

CERT MONEY. The head money given by the tenants of several manors yearly to the lords, for the purpose of keeping up certain inferior courts. Called in the ancient records *certum letae* (leet money). Cowell.

CERTA DEBET ESSE INTENTIO, ET narratio et certum fundamentum, et certa res quae deducitur in judicium. The intention, count, foundation, and thing, brought to judgment, ought to be certain. Co. Litt. 303a.

CERTA RES. In old English law. A certain thing. Fleta, lib. 2, c. 60, §§ 24, 25.

CERTAIN SERVICES. In feudal and old English law. Such services as were stinted (limited or defined) in quantity, and could not be exceeded on any pretense; as to pay a stated annual rent, or to plow such a field for three days. 2 Bl. Comm. 61.

CERTAINTY.

——**In Contracts.** Distinctness and accuracy of statement.

A thing is certain when its essence, quality, and quantity are described, distinctly set forth, etc. Dig. 12. 1. 6. It is uncertain when the description is not that of an individual object, but designates only the kind. Civ. Code La. art. 3522, No. 8; 5 Coke, 121.

——**In Pleading.** Such clearness and distinctness of statement of the facts which constitute the cause of action or ground of defense that they may be understood by the party who is to answer them, by the jury who are to ascertain the truth of the allegations, and by the court who are to give the judgment. 1 Chit. Pl. 257; Cowp. 682; Hob. 295; 13 East, 107; 2 Bos. & P. 267; Co. Litt. 303; Comyn, Dig. "Pleader," c. 17.

Certainty is said to be of three sorts:

(1) "Certainty to a common intent," which is attained by a form of statement in which words are used in their ordinary meaning, though by argument or inference they may be made to bear a different one. See 2 H. Bl. 530.

(2) "Certainty to a certain intent in general," which is attained when the meaning of the statute may be understood upon a fair and reasonable construction, without recurrence to possible facts which do not appear. 1 Wm. Saund. 49; 9 Johns. (N. Y.) 317; 5 Conn. 423.

(3) "Certainty to a certain intent in particular," which is attained by that technical accuracy of statement which precludes all argument, inference, and presumption against the party pleading. When this certainty is required, the party must not only state the facts of his case in the most precise way, but add to them such a show that they are not to be controverted, and, as it were, anticipate the case of his adversary. 1 Chit. Pl. 258; Lawes, Pl. 54, 55.

CERTIFICATE. In practice. A writing made in any court, and properly authenticated, to give notice to another court of any thing done therein.

A written statement, by a person having an official or public *status*, concerning some matter within his knowledge or authority. 3 Pet. (U. S.) 29; 6 Serg. & R. (Pa.) 324.

CERTIFICATE INTO CHANCERY. In English practice. The certificate by the common-law judges of their opinion of a question referred to them by the chancellor.

CERTIFICATE OF ASSIZE. A writ granted for the re-examination or retrial of a matter passed by assizes before justices. Fitzh. Nat. Brev. 181. It is now entirely obsolete. 3 Sharswood, Bl. Comm. 389. Consult, also, Comyn, Dig. "Assize" (B 27, 28).

CERTIFICATE OF COSTS. See "Judge's Certificate."

CERTIFICATE OF DEPOSIT. A certificate issued by a bank that the person named has a specified sum on deposit to his order in the bank.

CERTIFICATE OF EVIDENCE. The sole office or function of a certificate of evidence in chancery causes, as its very name implies, is to truly set forth the evidence offered, rejected, received and considered on the hearing. 123 Ill. 533.

CERTIFICATE OF REGISTRY. A certificate that a ship has been registered as the law requires. 3 Kent, Comm. 149. Under the United States statutes, "every alteration in the property of a ship must be indorsed on the certificate of registry, and must itself be registered." Unless this is done, the ship or vessel loses its national privileges as an American vessel. 1 Pars. Mar. Law, 48. The English statute makes such a transfer void. St. 3 & 4 Wm. IV. c. 54.

CERTIFICATE OF STOCK. A certificate that a person named is the owner of a specified number of shares of stock in a corporation.

CERTIFICATE, TRIAL BY. This is a mode of trial now little in use. It is resorted to in cases where the fact in issue lies out of the cognizance of the court, and the judges, in order to determine the question, are obliged to rely upon the solemn averment or information of persons in such a station as affords them the clearest and most competent knowledge of the truth. Steph. Pl. 112, 113; Co. Litt. 74; Brown.

CERTIFICATION. In Scotch law. A notice to a party in a suit that, if he fail to do something, certain consequences will follow. Paterson, Comp.

CERTIFIED CHECK. A check which has been recognized by the proper officer as a valid appropriation of the amount of money therein specified to the person therein named, and which bears upon itself the evidence of such recognition.

Certification of a check is usually accomplished by writing the name of the officer authorized to bind the bank in that manner across the face of the check. See "Check." Sewell, Bank.

CERTIFY. To testify to in writing; to make known or establish as a fact. 200 Ill. 243.

CERTIORARI. In practice. A writ issued by a superior to an inferior court of record, requiring the latter to send in to the former some proceeding therein pending, or the records and proceedings in some cause already terminated in cases where the procedure is not according to the course of the common law. 112 Mass. 206.

The office of the writs of *certiorari* and *mandamus* is often much the same. It is the practice of the United States supreme court, upon a suggestion of any defect in the transcript of the record sent up into that court upon a writ of error, to allow a special *certiorari*, requiring the court below to certify more fully. 3 Dall. (U. S.) 411; 7 Cranch (U. S.) 288; 3 How. (U. S.) 553. The same result might also be effected by a writ of *mandamus*. The two remedies are, when addressed to an inferior court of record, from a superior court, requiring the return of a record, much the same. But where diminution of the record is suggested in the inferior court, and the purpose is to obtain a more perfect record, and not merely a more perfect copy or transcript, it is believed that the writ of *mandamus* is the appropriate remedy.

In many of the states, the writ produces the same result in proceedings given by statute, such as the proceedings for obtaining damages under the mill acts, highway acts, pauper laws, etc., as the writ of error does when the proceedings are according to the course of the common law. Where the lower court is to be required to proceed in a cause, a writ of *procedendo* or *mandamus* is the proper remedy.

CERTUM EST QUOD CERTUM REDDI potest. That is sufficiently certain which can be made certain. Noy, Max. 481; Co. Litt. 45b, 96a, 142a; 2 Sharswood, Bl. Comm. 143; 2 Maule & S. 50; Broom, Leg. Max. (3d London Ed.) 555-558; 3 Term R. 463; 4 Cruise, Dig. (4th Ed.) 269; 3 Mylne & K. Ch. 353; 11 Cush. (Mass.) 380.

CERVISARII (*cervisia*, ale). Among the Saxons, tenants who were bound to supply drink for their lord's table. Cowell; Domesday Book.

CERVISIA. Ale. *Cervisarius*, an ale-brewer; an ale-house keeper. Cowell; Blount.

CERVUS (Lat.) A stag or deer.

CESIONARIO. In Spanish law. An assignee. White, New Recop. 304.

CESS. An assessment or tax. In Ireland, it was anciently applied to an exaction of victuals, at a certain rate, for soldiers in garrison. Wharton.

——**In Old English Law.** To cease. Hale, Anal. § 38c.

CESSA REGNARE, SI NON VIS JUDIcare. Cease to reign if you wish not to adjudicate. Hob. 155.

CESSANTE CAUSA CESSAT EFFECtus. The cause ceasing, the effect must cease. 1 Exch. 430; Broom, Leg. Max. (3d London Ed.) 151.

CESSANTE RATIONE LEGIS CESSAT, et ipsa lex. Reason is the soul of the law, and when the reason of any particular law ceases, so does the law itself. 4 Coke, 38; 7 Coke, 69; Co. Litt. 70b, 122a; Broom, Leg. Max. (3d London Ed.) 151, 152; 4 Rep. 38; 13 East, 348; 4 Bing. N. C. 388.

CESSANTE STATU PRIMITIVO, CESsat derivativus. The primary state ceasing, the derivative ceases. 8 Rep. 34; Broom, Leg. Max. (3d London Ed.) p. 438; 4 Kent, Comm. 32.

CESSAVIT PER BIENNIUM (Lat. he has ceased for two years). In practice. An obsolete writ, which could formerly have been sued out when the defendant had for two years ceased to perform such service or to pay such rent as he was bound to do by his tenure, and had not upon his lands sufficient goods or chattels to be distrained. Fitzh. Nat. Brev. 208. It also lay where a religious house held lands on condition of performing certain spiritual services, which it failed to do. 3 Bl. Comm. 232.

CESSE. An assessment or tax; a tenant of land was said to *cesse* when he neglected or ceased to perform the services due to the lord. Co. Litt. 373a, 380b.

CESSER, or CESSURE. Neglect; a ceasing from, or omission to do, a thing. 3 Bl. Comm. 232. "A substantial dismission and cesser." 6 Mod. 232.

The determination of an estate. 1 Coke, 84; 4 Kent, Comm. 33, 90, 105, 295.

CESSET EXECUTIO (Lat. let execution stay). In practice. The formal order for a stay of execution, when proceedings in court were conducted in Latin. See "Execution."

CESSET PROCESSUS (Lat. let process stay). In practice. The formal order for a stay of process or proceedings, when the proceedings in court were conducted in Latin. See 2 Doug. 627.

CESSIO BONORUM (Lat. a transfer of property). In civil law. An assignment of his property by a debtor for the benefit of his creditors. Such an assignment discharged the debtor to the extent of the property ceded only, but exempted him from imprisonment. Dig. 2. 4. 25; Id. 48. 19. 1; Nov. 4. 3. And see Civ. Code La. art. 2166; 2 Mart. (La.) 112; 2 La. 354; 11 La. 531; 2 Mart. (La.; N. S.) 108; 5 Mart. (La.; N. S.) 299; 4 Wheat. (U. S.) 122.

CESSIO IN JURE. In Roman law. A fictitious suit, in which the person who was to acquire the thing claimed (*vindicabat*) the thing as his own, the person who was to transfer it acknowledged the justice of the claim, and the magistrate pronounced it to be the property (*addicebat*) of the claimant. Sandars, Just. Inst. (5th Ed.) 89, 122.

CESSION (Lat. *cessio*, a yielding).

——**In Civil Law.** An assignment. The act by which a party transfers property to another.

——**In Ecclesiastical Law.** A surrender. When an ecclesiastic is created bishop, or when a parson takes another benefice, without dispensation, the first benefice becomes void by a legal cession or surrender. Cowell.

——**In Governmental Law.** The transfer of land by one government to another.

CESSION DES BIENS. In French law. The surrender which a debtor makes of all his goods to his creditors when he finds himself in insolvent circumstances. It is of two kinds,—either voluntary or compulsory (*judiciaire*), corresponding very nearly to liquidation by arrangement and bankruptcy in English and American law.

CESSIONARY. In Scotch law. An assignee. Bell, Dict.

CESSIONARY BANKRUPT. One who gives up his estate to be divided amongst his creditors. Wharton.

CESSMENT. An assessment.

CESSOR. One who ceases or neglects so long to perform a duty that he thereby incurs the danger of the law. Old Nat. Brev. 136.

CESSURE (Law Fr.) A receiver; a bailiff. Kelham.

C'EST ASCAVOIR (Law Fr.) That is to say, or to wit. Generally written as one word, *cestascavoir*, *cestascavoire*.

Another form was *cest asaver*, and in one word, *cestasaver*.

C'EST LE CRIME QUI FAIT LA HONTE, et non pas l'echafaud. It is the crime which causes the shame, and not the scaffold.

CESTUI, or **CESTUY** (Law Fr.) He.

CESTUI QUE TRUST. He for whose benefit another person is seized of lands or tenements, or is possessed of personal property.

He who has a right to a beneficial interest in and out of an estate the legal title to which is vested in another. 2 Washb. Real Prop. 163.

Judge Story suggests (1 Eq. Jur. § 321) that the word "beneficiary" be substituted for *cestui que trust*, and this term has come into very general use as such a substitute.

CESTUI QUE USE. He for whose benefit land is held by another person.

He who has a right to take the profits of lands of which another has the legal title and possession, together with the duty of defending the same, and to direct the making estates thereof. White & T. Lead. Cas. 252; 2 Bl. Comm. 330. See 2 Washb. Real Prop. 95. See "Use."

CESTUI QUE VIE. He whose life is the measure of the duration of an estate. 1 Washb. Real Prop. 88.

CESTUY QUE DOIT INHERITER AL pere doit inheriter al fils. He who would have been heir to the father of the deceased shall also be heir of the son. Fitzh. Abr. "Descent" (2); 2 Bl. Comm. 239, 250.

CF. Abbreviation of *conferee*, *compare*.

CHACE (Law Fr.) A chase or hunting ground. *Chacra*, a chase or hunting.

CHACEA. A station for game, more extended than a park, less so than a forest; the liberty of hunting within such limits. Cowell.

The driving or hunting animals; the way along which animals are driven. Spelman.

CHACEA EST AD COMMUNEM LEGEM. A chace is by common law. Reg. Brev. 806.

CHACEABLE (Law Fr.) That which may be chased or hunted.

CHAFEWAX. An officer in chancery who fits the wax for sealing to the writs, commissions, and other instruments there made to be issued out. He is probably so called because he warms (*chaufe*) the wax.

CHAFFERS. Anciently signified wares and merchandise. Hence the word *chaffering*, which is yet used for buying and selling, or beating down the price of an article. The word is used in St. 3 Edw. III. c. 4.

CHAFFERY Traffic; the practice of buying and selling. Rapalje & L.

CHAIRMAN. (1) The presiding officer of a deliberative body, legislative or otherwise; *e. g.* the speaker of a house of assembly, or of the house of representatives, or the presiding member of a board of directors of a corporation or association. (2) The president or senior member of a committee.

CHAIRMAN OF COMMITTEES OF THE whole house. In the English house of commons, this officer, always a member, is elected by the house on the assembling of every new parliament. When the house is in committee on bills introduced by the government, or in committee of ways and means, or supply, or in committee to consider preliminary resolutions, it is his duty to preside. He sits, not in the speaker's chair, but at the table in the seat of the clerk of the house. On divisions, when the numbers happen to be equal, he gives the casting vote (*q. v.*), but in committees he never otherwise votes. In August, 1853, it was, by resolution of the house, decided that, during the unavoidable absence of the speaker, this officer should preside in his stead, being only so appointed, however, from day to day. See 18 & 19 Vict. c. 84. In the house of lords the chairman of committees of the whole house is elected by the house every session. He usually holds in addition the office of deputy speaker of the house of lords. Dod. Parl. Comp.

In American legislative assemblies, the practice is to select a member as presiding officer for the particular session of the committee on resolving to go into committee of the whole.

CHALDRON. A measure of capacity, equal to fifty-eight and two-thirds cubic feet, nearly.

CHALLENGE. An objection to the capacity or right of a person.

——**In Practice.** An exception to the jurors who have been arrayed to pass upon a cause on its trial.

An exception to those who have been returned as jurors. Co. Litt. 155b.

The most satisfactory derivation of the word is that adopted by Webster and Crabb, from "call," challenge implying a calling off. The word is also used to denote exceptions taken to a judge's capacity on account of interest (2 Bin. [Pa.] 454; 4 Bin. [Pa.] 349), and to the sheriff for favor as well as affinity (Co. Litt. 158a; 10 Serg. & R. [Pa.] 336; 11 Serg. & R. [Pa.] 303).

Challenges are of the following classes:

(1) To the array. Those which apply to all the jurors as arrayed or set in order by the officer upon the panel. Such a challenge is, in general, founded upon some error or manifest partiality committed in obtaining the panel, and which, from its nature, applies to all the jurors so obtained. These are not allowed in the United States generally (Colby, Prac. 235; 2 Blatchf. [U. S.] 435), the same end being attained by a motion addressed to the court, but are in some states (33 Pa. St. 338; 12 Tex. 252; 24 Miss. 445; 1 Mann. [Mich.] 451; 20 Conn. 510; 1 Zab. [N. J.] 656).

(2) To the poll. Those made separately to each juror to whom they apply.

Challenges to the poll are either:

(a) For cause,—those for which some reason sanctioned by law is assigned.

(b) Peremptory,—those made without assigning any cause, and which must be allowed as of course. The number of these is variously limited by statute.

A challenge for cause lies also to the array. Challenge for cause was anciently divided into challenges:

(i) For principal cause,—being for such cause as, if substantiated, was sufficient to show bias or disqualification. The grounds of principal challenge were *propter defectum,* for disability, as infancy or mental unsoundness; *propter affectum,* for partiality, as where the juror was of kin to the party, or bore some confidential relation to him; *propter delictum,* on account of crime committed by the juror, whereby he was disqualified. 3 Bl. Comm. 361. To these was sometimes added *propter honoris respectum,* from respect to a party's rank or nobility.

(ii) To the favor,—those which are founded on reasonable ground to suspect that the jury is partial, though the cause be not so evident as to warrant a principal challenge.

Challenges for principal cause were tried by the court; those to the favor by triors.

The distinction between challenges to the favor and for principal cause is now obsolete.

Several other divisions of challenges for cause have been suggested by American statute or text writers, as that into challenge grounded on general disqualification, and challenges grounded on disqualification in respect of the particular case (Thomp. Trials, § 40), or that into challenges for actual bias, being for actual partiality as to the cause or the parties; and for implied bias, being such relationship towards a party or the cause as will, in contemplation of law, necessarily give rise to an implication of partiality, such as consanguinity to a party; confidential relation with a party; service on a previous jury in the cause, etc. Gen. St. Minn. 1878, c. 116, §§ 18, 19.

——**In Election Law.** Formal objection to the right of a person to vote at a particular election, or in a particular precinct. Generally made at the time the vote is offered.

——**In Criminal Law.** A request by one person to another to fight a duel. It may be oral or written.

CHAMBER OF ACCOUNTS. In French law. A sovereign court, of great antiquity in France, which took cognizance of and registered the accounts of the king's revenue. Nearly the same as the English court of exchequer. Enc. Brit.

CHAMBER OF COMMERCE. A society of the principal merchants and traders of a city, who meet to promote the general trade and commerce of the place. Similar societies exist in all the large commercial cities, and are known by various names, as, "board of trade," etc.

CHAMBERDEKINS, or **CHAMBER DEACONS.** In old English law. Certain poor Irish scholars, clothed in mean habit, and living under no rule; also beggars banished from England. 1 Hen. V. cc. 7, 8; Wharton.

CHAMBERLAIN (Law Lat. *camerarius, cambellarius, cambalarius, chamberlanus, chamberlingus;* from Fr. *chambellan*). Keeper of the chamber. Originally the chamberlain was the keeper of the treasure chamber (*camera*) of the prince or state; otherwise called "treasurer." Cowell, voc. "Chamberlain." See "Camerarius." Sir William Cavendish was treasurer of the chamber in the 24th year of Edward III. 3 Coke, 12; Spelman; Cowell.

The receiver of the rents and revenues of a city. Cowell; Blount. This is the modern meaning of the word in various cities of England and America.

The name of several high officers of state in England, as the lord great chamberlain of England, lord chamberlain of the household, chamberlain of the exchequer. See Cowell; Blount; Holthouse; Wharton. In modern times, the court officer styled "chamberlain" has the charge of the private apartments of the sovereign or noble to whom he is attached. Brande.

CHAMBERLARIA. Chamberlainship; the office of a chamberlain. Cowell.

CHAMBERS. Rooms or apartments.

The private room of the judge. Any hearing before a judge which does not take place during a term of court, or while the judge is sitting in court, or an order issued under such circumstances, is said to be "in chambers." The act may be an official one, and the hearing may be in the court room; but if the court is not in session, it is still said to be done "in chambers."

——**In England.** The office of a barrister.

An association of persons habitually meeting together, as a chamber of commerce.

CHAMBERS, WIDOW'S. A portion of the effects of a deceased person, reserved for the use of his widow, and consisting of her apparel and the furniture of her bed chamber, is called in London the "widow's chamber." 2 Bl. Comm. 518.

CHAMBIUM. In old English law. Change, or exchange. Bracton, fols. 117, 118.

Thought by Burrill to be another form of *cambium.*

CHAMP DE MAI. See "Campus Maii."

CHAMP DE MARS. See "Campus Martii."

CHAMPART. In French law. The grant of a piece of land by the owner to another, on condition that the latter would deliver to him a portion of the crops. 18 Toullier, Dr. Civ. note 182.

CHAMPERTOR. In criminal law. One who makes pleas or suits, or causes them to be moved, either directly or indirectly, and sues them at his proper costs, upon condition of having a part of the gain. St. 33 Edw. I. st. 2.

CHAMPERTY. A bargain with a plaintiff or defendant *campum partire* to divide the land or other matter sued for, between them, if they prevail at law, whereupon the champerter is to carry on the parties' own suit at his own expense. 112 Ill. 475.

A bargain with a plaintiff or defendant, in a suit for a portion of the land or other matter sued for, in case of a successful termination of the suit which the champertor undertakes to carry on at his own expense. 4 Bl. Comm. 435.

"The unlawful maintenance of a suit in consideration of part of the debt or other thing in dispute." Hawk. P. C. c. 84, § 1.

The gist of the offense consists in the mode of compensation, irrespective of the particular manner in which the suit is to be maintained. 4 Kern. (N. Y.) 289; 1 Hawk. P. C. 455, §§ 5-11.

There must be an actual assistance, and not merely an offer to assist. 1 Hempst. 300.

On the other hand, it has been held, following the definition of Blackstone, that a promise to pay the expenses or costs is essential. 57 Ga. 263; 13 Ohio, 167.

It is not essential that there be a suit commenced at the time of making the agreement. 14 Ky. 412.

Champerty differs from maintenance chiefly in this, that in champerty the compensation to be given for the service rendered is a part of the matter in suit, or some profit growing out of it (16 Ala. 488; 24 Ala. [N. S.] 472; 9 Metc. [Mass.] 489; 1 Jones, Eq. [N. C.] 100; 5 Johns. Ch. [N. Y.] 44; 4 Litt. [Ky.] 117), while in simple maintenance the question of compensation does not enter into the account (2 Bish. Crim. Law, § 111). See 4 Bl. Comm. 134, note.

CHAMPION. In old English law. He who fights for another, or takes his place in a quarrel; one who fights his own battles. Bracton, lib. 4, tit. 2, c. 12.

CHAMPION OF THE KING OR QUEEN. An ancient officer, whose duty it was to ride armed *cap-a-pie,* into Westminster Hall at the coronation, while the king was at dinner, and, by the proclamation of a herald, make a challenge "that, if any man shall deny the king's title to the crown, he is there ready to defend it in single combat." The king drank to him, and sent him a gilt cup covered, full of wine, which the champion drank, retaining the cup for his fee. The ceremony has been discontinued. Wharton.

CHANCE. "Pure chance consists in the absence of all means of calculating results." Morris (Iowa) 169. It is to be distinguished from "accident," which is "the unusual prevention of an effect naturally resulting from the means employed." Id.

Chance is always undeterminable; it neither forms nor designs; intention is never attributed to it; its events are uncertain. 59 Ill. 165.

CHANCE-MEDLEY. In criminal law. A sudden affray. This word is sometimes applied to any kind of homicide by misadventure, but in strictness it is applicable to such killing only as happens in defending one's self. 4 Bl. Comm. 184.

CHANCELLOR.

——**In the United States.** The presiding judge of a court of chancery.

——**In England.** A judicial officer of the king; a bishop or other high dignitary. See "Chancellor of the Exchequer," etc.

CHANCELLOR OF A CATHEDRAL. One of the *quattuor personae*, or four chief dignitaries of the cathedrals of the old foundation. The duties assigned to the office by the statutes of the different chapters vary, but they are chiefly of an educational character, with a special reference to the cultivation of theology. Rapalje & L.

CHANCELLOR OF DIOCESE. A judicial officer who acts as the delegate of the bishop in hearing ecclesiastical causes, etc. The office generally includes in it two other offices,—that of official principal, and that of vicar general (*q. v.;* and see "Court of Arches"). Phillim. Ecc. Law, 1208; 1 Bl. Comm. 382.

CHANCELLOR OF THE DUCHY OF Lancaster. In English law. An officer before whom, or his deputy, the court of the duchy chamber of Lancaster is held. This is a special jurisdiction concerning all manner of equity relating to lands holden of the king in right of the duchy of Lancaster. Hob. 77; 3 Bl. Comm. 78.

CHANCELLOR OF THE EXCHEQUER. A minister of state who presides in the exchequer, and takes care of the interests of the crown, in addition to his other parliamentary duties. With the lord treasurer, he leases the crown lands, and the two offices are often granted to the same person. Wharton. In addition to his duties in reference to the treasury of the king, the chancellor also sat as one of the judges in the equity court. 3 Bl. Comm. 45.

CHANCELLOR, THE LORD HIGH. The lord high chancellor of Great Britain is "created by the mere delivery of the king's great seal into his custody, whereby he becomes, without writ or patent, an officer of the greatest weight and power of any now subsisting in the kingdom, and superior in point of precedency to every temporal lord. He is a privy councillor by his office, and, according to Lord Chancellor Ellesmere, prolocutor (or speaker) of the house of lords by prescription. To him (under the crown) belongs the appointment of all justices of the peace throughout the kingdom. Being formerly usually an ecclesiastic (for none else was then capable of an office so conversant in writings), and presiding over the royal chapel, he became keeper of the king's conscience, visitor (in right of the king) of all hospitals and colleges of the king's foundation, and patron of all the king's livings under the value of twenty marks per annum in the king's books. Twelve canonries and 650 livings are now in the gift of the lord chancellor. Second Rep. Leg. Dep. Comm. 34. He is the general guardian of all infants, idiots, and lunatics, and has the general superintendence of all charitable uses in the kingdom." 3 Bl. Comm. 47. See Butler's note to Co. Litt. 290b. He was formerly the principal judge of the court of chancery, and is now president of the court of appeal, of the high court of justice, and of the chancery division of the high court, and acts as president of the house of lords when sitting as a court of appeal. He is therefore, of course, a barrister, and, as a rule, has previously either been attorney or solicitor general, or held some judicial office. He is also a cabinet minister, and has charge in the house of lords, of all legal measures brought forward by the government. See "Chancery;" "Vice Chancellor."

CHANCELLORS' COURTS IN THE TWO universities. In English law. Courts of local jurisdiction in and for the two universities of Oxford and Cambridge in England. These courts have jurisdiction of all civil actions or suits, except those in which a right of freehold is involved, and of all criminal offenses and misdemeanors, under the degree of treason, felony, or mayhem, at Oxford when a scholar or privileged person is one of the parties, and at Cambridge when both parties are scholars or privileged persons, and the cause of action arose within the town of Cambridge or its suburbs. 3 Sharswood, Bl. Comm. 83, note; St. 19 & 20 Vict. c. 17, § 18; Id. c. 88; Rep. temp. Hardw. 241; 2 Wils. 406; 12 East, 12; 13 East, 635; 15 East, 634.

CHANCERY. See "Court of Chancery."

CHANGE. As applied to money, the verb "change" means to convey it to some one who would give what in popular language is denominated "change," in exchange for it. 104 Ill. 535.

As applied to money, the noun "change" means bills, or gold or silver coins, or some of each, of lesser denominations, in amount of equal value. 104 Ill. 535.

CHANGER. Now obsolete. An officer of the English mint, whose duty was to exchange coin for bullion.

CHANNEL. The entire body of a stream from bank to bank, rather than the deep or navigable thread of it (55 Iowa, 558), the latter being more accurately the "main channel."

CHANTRY. A church or chapel endowed with lands for the maintenance of priests to say mass daily for the souls of the donors. Termes de la Ley; Cowell.

CHAPEL OF EASE. One which is used only for the ease of the parishioners in prayers and preaching, while the sacraments and burial are received and performed at the mother church. The curate of such a chapel is generally removable at the pleasure of the parochial minister.

CHAPELRY. The precinct of a chapel; the same thing for a chapel that a parish is for a church. Termes de la Ley; Cowell.

CHAPELS. Places of worship. They may be either "private" chapels, such as are built and maintained by a private person for his own use and at his own expense, or "free" chapels, so called from their freedom or exemption from all ordinary jurisdiction, or chapels "of ease," which are built by the mother church for the ease and convenience of its parishioners, and remain under its jurisdiction and control.

CHAPERON. A hood or bonnet anciently worn by the Knights of the Garter, as part of the habit of that order. Also a little escutcheon fixed in the forehead of horses drawing a hearse at a funeral. Wharton.

CHAPITRE. A summary of matters to be inquired of or presented before justices in eyre, justices of assize, or of the peace, in their sessions. Also articles delivered by the justice in his charge to the inquest. Britt. c. iii.

CHAPLAIN.

(1) An ecclesiastic who performs divine service in a chapel; but it more commonly means one who attends upon a king, prince, or other person of quality, for the performance of clerical duties in a private chapel. 4 Coke, 90; Wharton.

(2) A clergyman officially attached to a ship of war, to an army or regiment, or to some public institution, for the purpose of performing divine service. Webster.

CHAPMAN (said to be from German *copeman*). A trader who trades from place to place. Ryder, C. J., construing St. 5 Anne, c. 14.

CHAPTER. In ecclesiastical law. A congregation of clergymen. Such an assembly is termed *capitulum*, which signifies a little head; it being a kind of head, not only to govern the diocese in the vacation of the bishopric, but also for other purposes. Co. Litt. 103.

CHARACTER. In evidence. The opinion generally entertained of a person derived from the common report of the people who are acquainted with him. 3 Serg. & R. (Pa.) 336; 3 Mass. 192; 3 Esp. 236; 40 Neb. 810.

In its technical use, the word has lost its ordinary significance, and in such use is synonymous with "repute."

The moral character and conduct of a person in society may be used in proof before a jury in three classes of cases: First, to afford a presumption that a particular party has not been guilty of a criminal act (17 Mich. 9; 14 Mo. 502); second, to affect the damages in particular cases, where their amount depends on the character and conduct of any individual (30 N. Y. 285; 8 Iowa, 29; 4 Cush. [Mass.] 217); and, third, to impeach or confirm the veracity of a witness (16 Ohio St. 218; 7 N. Y. 378).

CHARGE. A duty or obligation imposed upon some person; a lien, incumbrance, or claim which is to be satisfied out of the specific thing or proceeds thereof to which it applies.

To impose such an obligation; to create such a claim.

To accuse.

The distinctive significance of the term rests in the idea of obligation directly bearing upon the individual thing or person to be affected, and binding him or it to the discharge of the duty or satisfaction of the claim imposed. Thus, charging an estate with the payment of a debt is appropriating a definite portion to the particular purpose; charging a person with the commission of a crime is pointing out the individual who is bound to answer for the wrong committed; charging a jury is stating the precise principles of law applicable to the case immediately in question. In this view, a charge will, in general terms, denote a responsibility peculiar to the person or thing affected and authoritatively imposed, or the act fixing such responsibility.

——**In Contracts.** An obligation, binding upon him who enters into it, which may be removed or taken away by a discharge. Termes de la Ley.

An undertaking to keep the custody of another person's goods.

An obligation entered into by the owner of an estate, which binds the estate for its performance. Comyn, Dig. "Rent," c. 6; 2 Ball & B. 223.

——**In Devises.** A duty imposed upon a devisee, either personally, or with respect to the estate devised.

——**In Equity Pleading.** An allegation in the bill of matters which disprove or avoid a defense which it is alleged the defendant is supposed to pretend or intend to set up. Story, Eq. Pl. § 31.

——**In Practice.** The instructions given by the court to the grand jury or inquest of the county, at the commencement of their session, in regard to their duty.

The exposition by the court to the petit jury of those principles of the law which the latter are bound to apply in order to render such a verdict as will, in the state of facts proved at the trial to exist, establish the rights of the parties to the suit.

CHARGE AND DISCHARGE. In equity practice. The mode or form of accounting before a master. Where a decree or order of the court directs an account to be taken and examined before a master, in such case the plaintiff delivers in an account before the master, in the form of a charge (*q. v.*) against the defendant, which being examined and gone through, the defendant or adverse party must bring in his discharge (*q. v.*) against such charge, which being likewise examined and gone through, the master will exercise his judgment upon the evidence, and allow or disallow the charge, or any part of it, as he thinks proper; and so, *e contra*, as to the discharge, after which the report is made. Cunningham; Whishaw; 2 Daniell, Ch. Pr. 1420-1422; Hoffman, Master in Chancery, 36-39.

CHARGE DES AFFAIRES, or **CHARGE d'affaires.** In international law. The title of a diplomatic representative or minister of an inferior grade, to whose care are confided the affairs of his nation.

He has not the title of minister, and is generally introduced and admitted through a verbal presentation of the minister at his departure or through letters of credence addressed to the minister of state of the court to which he is sent. He has the essential rights of a minister. 1 Kent, Comm. 39, note; 4 Dall. (Pa.) 321; 2 Story, U. S. Laws, 1171.

CHARGE TO ENTER HEIR. In Scotch law. A writ commanding a person to enter heir to his predecessor within forty days; otherwise, an action to be raised against him as if he had entered.

The heir might appear and renounce the succession, whereupon a decree *cognitionis causa* passed, ascertaining the creditor's debt. If the heir did not appear, he then became personally liable to the creditor. A charge was either general, or special, or general special. Charges are now abolished, by 10 & 11 Vict. c. 48, § 16, and a summons of constitution against the unentered heir substituted.

CHARGEANT. Weighty; heavy; penal; expensive. Kelham.

CHARGES. The expenses which have been incurred in relation either to a transaction or to a suit. It is a larger term than "costs."

CHARGING ORDER. By 1 & 2 Vict. c. 110, §§ 14-16, and 3 & 4 Vict. c. 82, when judgment has been recovered in an action, a judge at chambers may make an order that any government stock, funds, or annuities, or any stock or shares in a public company in England, standing in the name of the judgment debtor in his own right, or in the name of any person as trustee for him, shall stand charged with the payment of the judgment debt. Smith, Actions, 211; Rules of Court, xlvi, 1. The effect is to prevent the transfer of the stock, and to give the judgment creditor all the remedies which he would have been entitled to if the charge had been made in his favor by the judgment debtor, but he cannot enforce it until six months from the date of the order. 1 & 2 Vict. c. 110, § 14; Fish. Mortg. 113 et seq.

CHARITABLE USES, or **CHARITIES.** Gifts to general public uses, which may extend to the rich as well as the poor. Ambl. 651; 2 Sneed (Tenn.) 305.

Gifts to such purposes as are enumerated in Act 43 Eliz. c. 4, or which, by analogy, are deemed within its spirit or intendment. Boyle, Charity, 17.

"Whatever is given for the love of God, or for the love of your neighbor, in the catholic or universal sense, free from the stain or taint of every consideration that is personal, private or selfish," is a gift for charitable uses. 2 How. (U. S.) 127. The essentials are (1) that the gift be for the benefit of an indefinite number of persons (14 Allen [Mass.] 556; 107 U. S. 182); (2) that it be free from contractual obligation in or consideration to the donor (33 Pa. St. 419); (3) that the purpose be humanitarian in the broadest sense, whether it be religious (12 Mass. 537), educational (35 N. H. 445; 34 N. J. Eq. 101), benevolent (91 Mass. 442; 54 Ind. 549), or public (163 Mass. 509; 5 Del. Ch. 51).

CHARITY. The word "charity" in its widest sense, denotes all the good affection which men ought to bear towards each other, and in this sense it embraces all that is usually understood by the word benevolence, philanthropy and good will. In its more restricted sense it means merely relief or alms to the poor. In neither of these senses is it employed by the courts when used as descriptive of those uses and trusts which will be upheld as charitable. The words charity and charitable uses, at least in a state, where the statute of 43 Elizabeth, chap. 4, commonly known as the Statute of Charitable Uses, is held to be in force, must be determined with reference to the provisions of that statute. Among the results accomplished by the statute of Elizabeth was the establishment of an enumeration or kind of definition, standard or test, to which all gifts and grants in trust could be brought in order to determine whether they were charitable. Accordingly, since the statute, no bequests are deemed within the authority of chancery and capable of being established and regulated thereby, except bequests for those purposes which the statute enumerates as charitable, or which, by analogy, are deemed to be within its spirit or intendment. Perry on Trusts, pars. 696, 697; 2 Story's Eq. Juris, par. 1155. It is true many purposes not enumerated in the statute have been held to be charitable on the ground that though not within its letter, they are within its spirit, intention and principle. On the other hand, many objects of a general nature, though laudable and beneficent in their character, and of general utility, are held not to be included within the legal definition of charity. See 2 Ill. App. 377.

Whatever is given for the love of God or the love of one's neighbor, in the catholic and universal sense—given from these motives and to these ends—free from the stain or taint of every consideration that is personal, private or selfish. 75 Ill. App. 411.

A gift, to be applied consistently with existing laws, for the benefit of an indefinite number of persons, either by bringing their hearts under the influence of education or religion, by relieving their bodies from disease, suffering or constraint, by assisting them to establish themselves for life, or by erecting or maintaining public buildings or works or otherwise lessening the burthens of government, it being immaterial whether the purpose is called charitable in the gift itself, if it is so described as to show that it is charitable in its nature. 242 Ill. 27.

CHARIVARI. A mock serenade of discordant noises made with kettles, tin horns, etc., designed to annoy and insult; a vile or noisy music made with tin horns, bells, kettles, pans, etc., in derision of some person or event; a mock serenade. 198 Ill. 137.

CHARRE, or **CHARRUS.** A weight of lead, consisting of thirty pigs at seventy pounds each. Cowell.

CHARTA. A charter or deed in writing; any signal or token by which an estate was held.

——**Charta Chyrographata.** An indenture. The two parts were written on the same sheet, and the word "chyrograph" written between them in such a manner as to divide the word in the separation of the two parts of the indenture.

——**Charta Communis.** An indenture.

——**Charta Partita.** A charter party.

——**Charta de Una Parte.** A deed poll; a deed of one part.

Formerly this phrase was used to distinguish a deed poll—which is an agreement made by one party only; that is, only one of the parties does any act which is binding upon him—from a deed *inter partes.* Co. Litt. 229. See "Deed Poll."

CHARTA DE FORESTA. A collection of the laws of the forest, made in 9 Hen. III., and said to have been originally a part of *Magna Charta.*

CHARTA DE NON ENTE NON VALET. A charter or deed of a thing not in being is not valid. Co. Litt. 36.

CHARTAE LIBERTATUM. *Magna Charta* and *Charta de Foresta* (*q. v.*)

CHARTARUM SUPER FIDEM, MORTUIS testibus, ad patriam de necessitudine, recurrendum est. The witnesses being dead, the truth of charters must, of necessity, be referred to the country. Co. Litt. 36.

CHARTE PARTIE (Fr.) In French marine law. A charter party. Ord. Mar. liv. 3, tit. 1.

CHARTEL. A challenge to single combat. Used at the period when trial by single combat existed. Cowell.

CHARTER. A grant made by the sovereign, either to the whole people, or to a portion of them, securing to them the enjoyment of certain rights. 1 Story, Const. § 161; 1 Bl. Comm. 108.

Formerly included all deeds relating to hereditaments, especially deeds of feoffment (Co. Litt. 7a, 9b), but in this sense the term is now obsolete, and is now confined to grants by the government, the principal ones being grants of power to form corporations, either municipal or private.

CHARTER HOUSE. Formerly a convent of Carthusian monks in London; now a college founded and endowed by Thomas Sutton. The governors of the charter house are a corporation aggregate without a head, president, or superior, all the members being of equal authority. 3 Steph. Comm. (7th Ed.) 14, 97.

CHARTER LAND. In English law. Land formerly held by deed under certain rents and free services. It differed in nothing from free socage land; and it was also called "bookland." 2 Bl. Comm. 90.

CHARTER OF PARDON (Law Lat. *charta,* or *carta perdonationis*). In English criminal law. A charter or instrument under the great seal, by which a man is forgiven a felony, or other offense committed against the king's crown and dignity. Brown, Abr. "Charter of Pardon;" Dyer, 34 Cowell; 4 Bl. Comm. 400, 402. See the old form, Reg. Orig. 288, 308. And see 2 Reeve, Hist. Eng. Law, 437.

CHARTER PARTY. A contract of affreightment, by which the owner of a ship or other vessel lets the whole or a part of her to a merchant or other person for the conveyance of goods, on a particular voyage, in consideration of the payment of freight. 3 Kent, Comm. 201.

The term is derived from the fact that the contract which bears this name was formerly written on a card, and afterwards the card was cut into two parts from top to bottom, and one part was delivered to each of the parties, which was produced when required, and by this means counterfeits were prevented; the card so cut being called *charta partita*.

CHARTER ROLLS (Law Lat. *rotuli cartarum*). Rolls preserved amongst the ancient English records, containing the royal charters from the year 1199 to 1516. They comprise grants of privileges to cities, towns, bodies corporate, and private trading companies; grants of markets, fairs, and free warrens, of creations of nobility, of privileges to religious houses, etc. Hubback, Ev. Success. 616, and notes.

CHARTERER. One who engages a ship for a voyage.

CHARTIS REDDENDIS (Lat. for returning charters). A writ which lay against one who had charters of feoffment intrusted to his keeping which he refused to deliver. Reg. Orig. 159. It is now obsolete.

CHARTOPHYLAX. In old European law. A keeper of records or public instruments; a chartulary; a registrar. Spelman.

CHARUE. In old English law. A plow. *Bestes des charues*, beasts of the plow. Artic. Sup. Chart. c. 12; Britt. c. 21.

CHASE. The liberty or franchise of hunting one's self and keeping protected against all other persons beasts of the chase within a specified district, without regard to the ownership of the land. 2 Bl. Comm. 414-416.

The district within which such privilege is to be exercised.

A chase is a franchise granted to a subject, and hence is not subject to the forest laws. 2 Bl. Comm. 38. It differs from a park, because it may be another's ground, and is not inclosed. It is said by some to be smaller than a forest, and larger than a park. Termes de la Ley. But this seems to be a customary incident, and not an essential quality.

The act of acquiring possession of animals *ferae naturae* by force, cunning, or address.

CHASTITY. That virtue which prevents the unlawful commerce of the sexes. Content without lawful venery is continence; without unlawful is chastity. Webster.

CHATTEL (Norman Fr.) Goods of any kind; every species of property, movable or immovable, which is less than a freehold.

In the grand coustumier of Normandy it is described as a mere movable, but is set in opposition to a fief or feud; so that not only goods, but whatever was not a feud or fee, were accounted chattels, and it is in this latter sense that our law adopts it. 2 Bl. Comm. 385.

Blackstone says that the word "chattels" is derived from the Latin word "catalla," which in a secondary sense was applied to all movables in general. 19 Ill. 584.

The word "chattels" is a more comprehensive term than "goods," and includes animate as well as inanimate property, such as slaves, horses, cattle, while "goods" does not include such property. 19 Ill. 584.

Real chattels are interests which are annexed to or concern real estate, as, a lease for years of land; and the duration of the lease is immaterial, whether it be for one or a thousand years, provided there be a certainty about it, and a reversion or remainder in some other person. A lease to continue until a certain sum of money can be raised out of the rents is of the same description; and so in fact will be found to be any other interest in real estate whose duration is limited to a time certain beyond which it cannot subsist, and which is, therefore, something less than a freehold.

Personal chattels are properly things movable, which may be carried about by the owner, such as animals, household stuff, money, jewels, corn, garments, and everything else that can be put in motion, and transferred from one place to another, and the incorporeal hereditaments that grow out of movables. 2 Kent, Comm. 340; Co. Litt. 48a; 4 Coke, 6; 5 Mass. 419; 1 N. H. 350; Story, Eq. Jur. §§ 1021, 1040. See "Personal Property."

CHATTEL INTEREST. An interest in corporeal hereditaments less than a freehold. 2 Kent, Comm. 342.

There may be a chattel interest in real property, as in case of a lease. Stearns, Real Actions, 115. A term for years, no matter of how long duration, is but a chattel interest, unless declared otherwise by statute. See the subject fully treated in 1 Washb. Real Prop. 310 et seq.

CHATTEL MORTGAGE. At common law, a sale of a chattel on a condition subsequent, upon performance of which the title revests in the mortgagor, and upon breach of which the mortgagee's title becomes absolute.

It differs from a pledge, in that the title to the property, rather than the possession thereof, constitutes the security. 87 N. Y. 209; 37 Mich. 484.

It differs from a vendor's lien in that a lienor has no title to the property. 23 Ohio St. 114; 40 Me. 412.

It differs from a sale wherein the title is retained by the seller until the performance of some condition, in that no title passes from the debtor to the creditor, but the creditor simply retains a title which the debtor never had. 88 Ill. 447; 16 Ind. 380.

It differs from a sale with a right of repurchase in that the latter transaction is not a security for an obligation.

It differs from an assignment for the benefit of creditors, which is not a security, but implies an absolute appropriation of the property to the payment of the indebtedness. Hammon, Chat. Mortg. §§ 1-7.

CHAUD-MEDLEY (Fr. *chaud*). The killing of a person in the heat of an affray.

It is distinguished by Blackstone from chance-medley, an accidental homicide. 3 Bl. Comm. 184. The distinction is said to be, however, of no great importance. 1 Russ. Crimes, *660. Chance-medley is said to be the killing in self-defense, such as happens on a sudden reencounter, as distinguished from an accidental homicide. Id.

CHAUNTRY RENTS. Money paid to the crown by the servants or purchasers of chauntry or chantry lands. 22 Car. II. c. 6. See "Chantry."

CHEAT. "Deceitful practices in defrauding or endeavoring to defraud another of his known right, by some willful device, contrary to the plain rules of common honesty." Hawk. P. C. bk. 2, c. 23, § 1. "The fraudulent obtaining the property of another by any deceitful and illegal practice or token (short of felony) which affects or may affect the public." It did not include mere false pretenses. East, 818.

In order to constitute a cheat or indictable fraud, there must be a use of false tokens, false weights, or such other devices, or a prejudice received, and such injury must affect the public welfare, or have a tendency so to do. 2 East, P. C. 817; 1 Gabbett, Crim. Law, 199; 1 Deac. Crim. Law, 225.

CHEATERS, or ESCHEATORS. Officers appointed to look after the king's escheats, a duty which gave them great opportunities of fraud and oppression, and in consequence many complaints were made of their misconduct. Hence it seems that a "cheater" came to signify a fraudulent person, and thence the verb to "cheat" was derived. Rapalje & L.

CHECK. Contracts. A written order or request, addressed to a bank or persons carrying on the business of banking, by a party having money in their hands, on deposit, desiring them to pay, on presentment, to a person therein named, or bearer, or to such person, or order, a named sum of money.

The chief differences between checks and bills of exchange are: First, a check is not due until presented, and, consequently, it can be negotiated any time before presentment, and yet not subject the holder to any equities existing between the previous parties. 3 Johns. Cas. (N. Y.) 5, 9; 9 Barn. & C. 388; Chit. Bills (8th Ed.) 546. Secondly, the drawer of a check is not discharged for want of immediate presentment with due diligence, while the drawer of a bill of exchange is. The drawer of a check is only discharged by such neglect when he sustains actual damage by it, and then only *pro tanto*. 6 Cow. (N. Y.) 484; Kent, Comm. lect. 44 (5th Ed.) p. 104, note; 3 Johns. Cas. (N. Y.) 5, 259; 10 Wend. (N. Y.) 306; 2 Hill (N. Y.) 425. Thirdly, the death of the drawer of a check rescinds the authority of the banker to pay it, while the death of the drawer of a bill of exchange does not alter the relations of the parties. 3 Man. & G. 571-573. Fourthly, checks, unlike bills of exchange, are always payable without grace. 25 Wend. (N. Y.) 672; 6 Hill (N. Y.) 174.

CHECK BOOK. A book containing blanks for checks.

CHECK ROLL. A list or book, containing the names of such as are attendants on, or in the pay of, the queen or other great personages, as their household servants. 19 Car. II. c. 1. Rapalje & L.

CHECKER. The old Scotch form of exchequer. Skene de Verb. Sign.

CHEFE. In Anglo-Norman law. Were or weregild; the price of the head or person (*capitis pretium*). Laws Gul. Conq. 11.

CHEMERAGE. In old French law. The privilege or prerogative of the eldest. See "Chemier."

CHEMIER (Fr.) In old French law. The eldest born. A term used in Poitou and other places. Guyot, Inst. Feud. c. 18, § 4.

CHEMIN (Fr.) The road wherein every man goes; the king's highway. Called in law Latin *via regia*. Often spelled *chimin*. Termes de la Ley; Cowell; Spelman.

CHEMIS. In old Scotch law. A mansion house.

CHEVAGE. A sum of money paid by villeins to their lords in acknowledgment of their villeinage. It was paid to the lord in token of his being chief or head. It was exacted for permission to marry, and also for permission to remain without the dominion of the lord. When paid to the king, it was called "subjection." Termes de la Ley; Co. Litt. 140a; Spelman.

CHEVANTIA. A loan, or advance of money on credit. See "Chevisance."

CHEVISANCE (Fr. agreement). A bargain or contract; an unlawful bargain or contract.

CHEVITIAE (Lat.) In old records. Pieces of ground, or heads at the end of plowed lands. 2 Mon. Angl. 116; Cowell; Blount.

CHEZE. A homestead or homesfall which is accessory to a house. Rapalje & L.

CHICANE. The use of tricks and artifice.

CHIEF. One who is put above the rest; principal; the best of a number of things.
——**Declaration in Chief.** A declaration for the principal cause of action. 1 Tidd, Prac. 419.
——**Examination in Chief.** The first examination of a witness by the party who produces him. 1 Greenl. Ev. § 445.
——**Tenant in Chief.** One who held directly of the king. 1 Washb. Real Prop. 19.

CHIEF BARON. The title of the chief justice of the English court of exchequer. 3 Bl. Comm. 44.

CHIEF JUSTICE. The presiding or principal judge of a court.

CHIEF JUSTICIAR. Under the early Norman kings, the highest officer in the kingdom next to the king.

He was guardian of the realm in the king's absence. His power was diminished under the reign of successive kings, and, finally, completely distributed amongst various courts in the reign of Edward I. 3 Bl. Comm. 28. The same as *capitalis justiciarius*.

CHIEF LORD. The immediate lord of the fee. Burton, Real Prop. 317.

CHIEF PLEDGE. The borsholder or chief of the borough. Spelman.

CHIEF RENTS (Law Lat. *reditus capitales*). In English law. Rents of the freeholders of a manor. 2 Bl. Comm. 42. Called also "quit rents" (*quieti reditus*), because thereby the tenant goes quit and free of all other services. Id.

CHIEFRIE. A small rent paid to the lord paramount.

CHILD. The immediate progeny of human parents; offspring born to such parents. 262 Ill. 183; 200 Ill. 401.

The son or daughter, in relation to the father or mother; the correlative of "parent."

A young person of either sex. The age limit of childhood is undefined. 5 Har. & J. (Md.) 392.

It is not synonymous with "minor." 7 Tex. App. 298. And in a classification of females subject of rape, "child" has been held to mean one not arrived at puberty. 22 Ohio St. 102.

The word "child," in its popular signification, means a son or daughter; a descendant in the first degree (Webster's Int. Dict.); and the legal meaning of the word is the same as the popular one and does not include a grandchild. The word "children" is never extended to include grandchildren, in the absence of something in the instrument in which the word is employed showing the intention to use it with such an extended meaning or where it is necessary to render the instrument effective. 173 Ill. 239; 253 Ill. 402. See "Sons."

CHILDNIT (Saxon). A power to take a fine from a bondwoman gotten with child without the lord's consent.

By custom in Essex county, England, every reputed father of a bastard child was obliged to pay a small fine to the lord. This custom is known as childnit. Cowell.

CHILDREN. (See "Sons.") Legitimate offspring. L. R. 7 H. L. 568; 23 Hun (N. Y). 260; 14 N. J. Eq. 159. But see 42 Conn. 491. It includes only the first generation, and does not embrace grandchildren (21 N. J. Eq. 84; 19 Ohio St. 30; 104 Mass. 193), but it has been given that meaning in instruments where the context or the necessity of effectuating the instrument required it (15 N. J. Eq. 174; 37 N. Y. 42; 88 Pa. St. 478). It does not include stepchildren (8 Paige [N. Y.] 375), nor adopted children (54 Pa. St. 304. But see 115 Mass. 262).

CHILTERN HUNDREDS. A range of hills in England, formerly much infested by robbers.

To exterminate the robbers, a steward of the chiltern hundreds was appointed. The office long since became a sinecure, and is now used to enable a member of parliament to resign, which he can do only by the acceptance of some office within the gift of the chancellor. 2 Steph. Comm. 403; Wharton.

CHIMIN. See "Chemin."

CHIMINAGE. A toll for passing on a way through a forest; called in the civil law *pedagium*. Cowell. See Co. Litt. 56a; Spelman; Termes de la Ley.

CHIMINUS. The way by which the king and all his subjects and all under his protection have a right to pass, though the property of the soil of each side where the way lieth may belong to a private man. Cowell.

CHIMNEY MONEY, or HEARTH MONEY. A tax upon chimneys or hearths; an ancient tax or duty upon houses in England, now repealed. Cowell.

CHIPPINGAVEL. A toll for buying and selling; a tax imposed on goods brought for sale. Whishaw; Blount.

CHIRGEMOTE, CHIRCHGEMOTE, CIRCgemote, or kirkmote. (Saxon, *circgemote*, from *circ*, *ciric*, or *cyric*, a church, and *gemot*, a meeting or assembly). In Saxon law. An ecclesiastical court or assembly (*forum ecclesiasticum*); a synod; a meeting in a church or vestry. Blount; Spelman; LL. Hen. I. cc. 4. 8; 4 Inst. 321; Cunningham.

CHIROGRAPH.

——**In Old Conveyancing.** A deed or public instrument in writing.

Chirographs were anciently attested by the subscription and crosses of witnesses. Afterwards, to prevent frauds and concealments, deeds of mutual covenant were made in a script and rescript, or in a part and counterpart, and in the middle, between the two copies, they drew the capital letters of the alphabet, and then tallied, or cut asunder in an indented manner, the sheet or skin of parchment, one of which parts, being delivered to each of the parties, were proved authentic by matching with the answering to one another. Deeds thus made were denominated "syngrapha" by the canonists, because that word, instead of the letters of the alphabet or the word "chirographum," was used. 2 Bl. Comm. 296.

The last part of a fine of land.

It is called, more commonly, the foot of the fine. It is an instrument of writing, beginning with these words: "This is the final agreement," etc. It concludes the whole matter, reciting the parties, day, year, and place, and before whom the fine was acknowledged and levied. Cruise, Dig. tit. 35, c. 2, § 52.

——**In Civil and Canon Law.** An instrument written out and subscribed by the hands of the king or prince. An instrument written out by the parties, and signed by them. Du Cange; Cowell.

——**In Scotch Law.** A written voucher for a debt. Bell, Dict. The possession of this instrument by the debtor raises a presumption of payment by him. Bell, Dict.; Ersk. Inst. lib. 2, tit. 4, § 5.

CHIROGRAPHER OF FINES (Law Lat. *chirographus*, or *chirographarius finium et concordiarum*). In old English law. An officer of the court of common pleas, who engrossed the fines acknowledged in that court after they were examined, and fully passed by other officers, and who wrote and delivered the indentures of them to the parties. 2 Bl. Comm. 351; 2 Inst. 468; Cowell; Blount. See "Fine."

CHIROGRAPHUM. In Roman law. A handwriting; that which was written with a person's own hand; an obligation which a person wrote or subscribed with his own hand; an acknowledgment of debt, as of money received, with a promise to repay. For forms of such acknowledgments, see Dig. 22, 1. 41. 2; Id. 2. 14. 47. 1.

An evidence or voucher of debt; a security for debt. Dig. 26. 7. 57. pr.

A right of action for debt. Dig. 32. 59. And see Id. 34. 3. 31. 3; Id. 46. 3. 89. pr.; Code, 4. 2. 17.

CHIROGRAPHUM APUD DEBITOREM repertum presumitur solutum. An evidence of debt found in possession of the debtor is presumed to be paid. Halk. Max. 30. See 14 Mees. & W. 379.

CHIROGRAPHUM NON EXTANS PREsumitur solutum. An evidence of debt not existing is presumed to have been discharged. Tray. Lat. Max. 73.

CHIVALRY. In feudal law. Knight service. Tenure in chivalry was the same as tenure by knight service. 2 Bl. Comm. 61, 62. See "Tenure."

CHIVALRY, COURT OF. This court was anciently held as a court of honor merely, before the earl marshal, and as a criminal court before the lord high constable, jointly with the earl marshal. It had jurisdiction as to contracts and other matters touching deeds of arms or war, as well as pleas of life or member. It also corrected encroachments in matters of coat armor, precedency and other distinctions of families. It is now grown entirely out of use, on account of the feebleness of its jurisdiction and want of power to enforce its judgments, as it could neither fine nor imprison, not being a court of record. 3 Bl. Comm. 68; 4 Broom & H. Comm. 360, note; Wharton.

CHIVALRY, TENURE BY. Tenure by knight service. Co. Litt.

CHOP-CHURCH. A word mentioned in a statute of 9 Hen. VI., by the sense of which it was in those days a kind of trade, and by the judges declared to be lawful. But Brooke, in his Abridgment, says it was only permissible by law. It was, without doubt, a nickname given to those who used to change benefices, as to "chop and change" is a common expression. 9 Hen. VI. c. 65; Jacob.

CHORAL. In ancient times, a person admitted to sit and worship in the choir; a chorister.

CHOREPISCOPI. Bishops of the country in the early times of the church.

CHOSE (Fr.) thing. Personal property.

——**Choses in Possession.** Personal things of which one has possession.

——**Choses in Action.** Personal things of which the owner has not the possession, but merely a right of action for their possession. 2 Bl. Comm. 389, 397; 1 Chit. Plac. 99.

A right to receive or recover a debt, or money, or damages for breach of contract, or for a tort connected with contract, but which cannot be enforced without action. Comyn, Dig. "Biens;" Chit. Eq. Dig.

In modern usage, the phrase is broader and includes rights of action for tort (4 Ala. 350; 12 N. Y. 622), and rights enforceable only in equity (Wms. 6).

——**Chose Local.** A local thing; a thing annexed to a place, as a mill. Kitch. Cts. fol. 18; Cowell; Blount. Answering probably to the *res immobilis* of the civil law.

——**Chose Transitory.** A thing which is movable, and may be taken away or carried from place to place. Cowell; Blount.

CHOSEN FREEHOLDERS. In New Jersey. A board of county officers, having charge of the finances of the county, and composed of persons chosen by and representing the several towns or townships of the county. In some states, similar officers are called "county commissioners" (*q. v.*), and in others, the "board of supervisors" (*q. v.*)

CHRENECRUDA (Law Lat.) A singular ceremony among the Salians, by which a poor person applied to a rich relative to pay his debt or fine. It consisted (after certain preliminaries) in throwing green herbs upon the party, the effect of which was to bind him to pay the whole demand. L. Salic. tit. 61. Spelman, who describes it, finds the elements of the word in the Belgian *groen*, green, and *cruid*, herb.

CHRISTIANITATIS CURIA (Law Lat.) The court of Christianity; the court Christian, or ecclesiastical judicature, as opposed to the civil court, or lay tribunal. Cowell. See "Courts Christian."

CHURCH. A society of persons who profess the Christian religion. 7 Halst. (N. J.) 206, 214; 10 Pick. (Mass.) 193; 3 Pa. St. 282; 31 Pa. St. 9; 9 Barb. (N. Y.) 95.

The place where such persons regularly assemble for worship. 3 Tex. 288; 9 Barb. (N. Y.) 95; 160 Ill. 579.

CHURCH BUILDING ACTS. Statutes passed in England in and since the year 1818, with the object of extending the accommodation afforded by the national church, so as to make it more commensurate with the wants of the people. 3 Steph. Comm. 152-164.

CHURCH DISCIPLINE ACT. St. 3 & 4 Vict. c. 86, containing regulations for trying clerks in holy orders charged with offenses against ecclesiastical law, and for enforcing sentences pronounced in such cases. Phillim. Ecc. Law, 1314.

CHURCH RATE. A tribute by which the expenses of the church are to be defrayed. They are to be laid by the parishoners, in England, and may be recovered before two justices, or in the ecclesiastical court. Wharton.

CHURCH REEVE. A church warden.

CHURCH SCOT. Customary obligations paid to the parish priest; from which duties the religious sometimes purchased an exemption for themselves and their tenants. Wharton.

CHURCH WARDEN. An officer whose duty it is to take care of or guard the church.

They are taken to be a kind of corporation in favor of the church for some purposes. They may have, in that name, property in goods and chattels, and bring actions for them for the use and benefit of the church, but may not waste the church property, and are liable to be called to account. 3 Steph. Comm. 90; 1 Bl. Comm. 394; Cowell.

CHURCHESSET, CHURCHSET, CIRSET, kirkset, or **chirset.** In old English law. A certain portion or measure of wheat, anciently paid to the church on St. Martin's day, and which, according to Fleta, was paid as well in the time of the Britons as of the English. Fleta, lib. 1, c. 47, § 28. An annual tribute paid to the church in grain or other product, *census vel tributum ecclesiae, frumenti tributum.* Spelman. voc. "Cirset;" Lindenbrog; Domesday Book. Sometimes written *chirchsed,* and translated "churchseed," *semen ecclesiae.* Fleta, ubi supra; Co. Litt. 88b. But the proper spelling, according to Spelman, is *ciricset,* or *ciricsceat.*

CHURL. See "Ceorl."

CI, CY, or **SI** (Law Fr.) So. *Pur ceo que fine est ci hault barre, et de ci graund force, et de ci puissant nature,* because a fine is so high a bar, and of so great force, and of so powerful a nature. St. Modus Lev. Fin.; 2 Inst. 510.

CIBARIA (Lat. pl. of *cibarium,* from *cibes,* food). In the civil law. Food; victuals. Dig. 34. 1.

CINQUE PORTS. The five ports of England which lie towards France.

These ports, on account of their importance as defenses to the kingdom, early had certain privileges granted them, and in recompense were bound to furnish a certain number of ships and men to serve on the king's summons once in each year. "The service that the barons of the Cinque Ports acknowledge to owe, upon the king's summons, if it shall happen, to attend with their ships fifteen days at their own cost and charges, and so long as the king pleases, at his own charge." Cowell, "Quinque Portus," The Cinque Ports are Dover, Sandwich, Hastings, Hithe, and Romney. Winchelsea and Rye are reckoned parts of Sandwich;

and the other of the Cinque Ports have ports appended to them in like manner. The Cinque Ports have a lord warden, who had a peculiar jurisdiction, sending out writs in his own name, and who is also constable of Dover Castle. The jurisdiction was abolished by 18 & 19 Vict. c. 48; 20 & 21 Vict. c. 1. The representatives in parliament and the inhabitants of the Cinque Ports are each termed "barons." Brande; Cowell; Termes de la Ley.

CIPPI. The stocks. Reg. Orig. 96b. Bracton and Fleta used in *cippo*. Bracton fol. 145b; Fleta, lib. 1, c. 42, §§ 1, 2.

CIRC BRYCE. A violation of ecclesiastical privilege.

CIRC SCEAT. Church scot; an ecclesiastical due.

CIRCADA. In old English law. A tribute anciently paid to the bishop or archbishop for visiting the churches. Du Fresne; Whishaw.

CIRCUIT. A division of the country, appointed for a particular judge to visit for the trial of causes, or for the administration of justice. See 3 Bl. Comm. 58; 3 Bouv. Inst. note 2532.

In England the term is oftener applied, perhaps, to the periodical journeys of the judges through their various circuits. The judges, or, in England, commissioners of assize and *nisi prius*, are said "to make their circuit." 3 Bl. Comm. 57.

In England there are eight judicial circuits, viz., the North and South Wales, northern, northeastern, southeastern, western, Midland and Oxford. See 3 Bl. Comm. 58; 3 Steph. Comm. 221.

For the purposes of federal jurisdiction, the United States is divided into nine circuits, designated by number. Rev. St. U. S. 1878, § 604. See "Circuit Courts."

CIRCUIT COURT OF APPEALS. A federal court created in 1891 in each circuit (*q. v.*), consisting of three judges, and having final appellate jurisdiction of cases from the circuit and district courts except in certain cases. The court was designed to relieve the supreme court of the United States. See Act Cong. March 3, 1891.

CIRCUIT COURTS. In American law. Courts whose jurisdiction extends over several counties or districts, and of which terms are held in the various counties or districts to which their jurisdiction extends.

The term is applied in several states to courts of general original jurisdiction, terms of which are held in the various counties or districts of the state. It is unknown in the classification of English courts, and conveys a different idea in the various states in which it is adopted.

In the federal jurisprudence of the United States, the circuit courts were a system of federal courts, holding terms in several places in each of the several judicial circuits. See "Circuit."

They had original jurisdiction of substantially all civil cases which, by reason of the citizenship of the parties, or the nature of the subject-matter, were of federal cognizance. See "District Courts." 1 Kent, Comm. 301-303; Rev. St. U. S. 1878, § 605 et seq. They were abolished by the Act of March 3, 1911, 36 Stat. 1167.

CIRCUITUS EST EVITANDUS. Circuity is to be avoided. Co. Litt. 384a; Smith, Lead. Cas. (4th Am. Ed.) 20; Wingate, Max. 179; Broom, Leg. Max. (3d London Ed.) 309; 5 Coke, 34; 15 Mees. & W. 208; 5 Exch. 829.

CIRCUITUS EST EVITANDUS; ET BONI judices est lites dirimere, ne lis ex lite oriatur. Circuity is to be avoided; and it is the duty of a good judge to determine litigations, lest one lawsuit arise out of another. 5 Coke, 31.

CIRCUITY OF ACTION. Indirectly obtaining, by means of a subsequent action, a result which may be reached in an action already pending.

This is particularly obnoxious to the law, as tending to multiply suits. 1 Term R. 441; 4 Cow. (N. Y.) 682.

CIRCULAR NOTES. Similar instruments to "letters of credit." They are drawn by resident bankers upon their foreign correspondents, in favor of persons traveling abroad. The correspondents must be satisfied of the identity of the applicant before payment, and the requisite proof of such identity is usually furnished, upon the applicant's producing a letter with his signature, by a comparison of the signatures. Brown.

CIRCULATING MEDIUM. This term is more comprehensive than the term "money," as it is the medium of exchanges, or purchases and sales, whether it be gold or silver coin, or any other article. Rapalje & L.

CIRCUMDUCTION. In Scotch law. A closing of the period for lodging papers, or doing any other act required in a cause. Paterson, Comp.

——**Circumduction of the Term.** The sentence of a judge, declaring the time elapsed within which a proof ought to have been led, and precluding the party from bringing forward any further evidence. Bell, Dict.

CIRCUMSPECTE AGATIS. Act circumspectly. The title of a statute passed 13 Edw. I. A. D. 1285, and so called from the initial words of it, the object of which was to ascertain the boundaries of ecclesiastical jurisdiction in some particulars, or, in other words, to regulate the jurisdiction of the ecclesiastical and temporal courts. 2 Reeve, Hist. Eng. Law, 215.

CIRCUMSTANCES. The particulars which accompany an act; the surroundings at the commission of an act.

Though sometimes used in the sense of "fact," a circumstance is a "relative" fact, as distinguished from the "principal" fact, which it may corroborate or disprove.

CIRCUMSTANTIAL EVIDENCE. The proof of certain facts and circumstances in a given case from which the jury may infer other connected facts which uusally and reasonably follow according to the common experience of mankind. 272 Ill. 179.

That which is applied to the principal fact indirectly, or through the medium of other facts, by establishing certain circumstances or minor facts from which the principal fact is gathered by a process of inference. See 3 Benth. Jud. Ev. 2, 5.

The process by which a fact not directly known is inferred from known facts or circumstances. 1 Starkie, Ev. 18.

The terms "circumstantial" and "presumptive" are often used interchangeably to denote the same kind of evidence, but in strictness this is not correct. Presumptive evidence is a species of circumstantial evidence, though so large a species as to be almost coextensive with its genus.

Evidence may be circumstantial without being presumptive, either because it fails to raise a presumption, or because the inference to which it gives rise is stronger than mere presumption. Burrill, Circ. Ev. 76.

Circumstantial evidence is of two kinds, namely: certain, or that from which the conclusion in question necessarily follows; and uncertain, or that from which the conclusion does not necessarily follow, but is probable only, and is obtained by process of reasoning. 127 Ill. 520.

CIRCUMSTANTIBUS. See "Tales."

CIRCUMVENTION. In Scotch law. Any act of fraud whereby a person is reduced to a deed by decreet. Tech. Dict. It has the same sense in the civil law. Dig. 50. 17. 49. 155; Id. 12. 6. 6. 2; Id. 41. 2. 34.

CIRLISCUS. A *ceorl* (*q. v.*) Spelman.

CITACION. In Spanish law. The order of a legal tribunal directing an individual against whom a suit has been instituted to appear and defend it within a given time. It is synonymous with the term *emplazamiento* in the old Spanish law, and the *in jus vocatio* of the Roman law.

CITATIO. A citation or summons to court. Skene de Verb. Sign. voc. "Adjurnatus."

CITATIO AD REASSUMENDAM CAUSam. In civil law. The name of a citation, which issued when a party died pending a suit, against the heir of the defendant, or, when the plaintiff died, for the heir of the plaintiff. Our bill of revivor is probably borrowed from this proceeding.

CITATIO EST DE JURI NATURALI. A summons is by natural right. Cases in Banco Regis Wm. III. 453.

CITATION (Lat. *citare*, to call, to summon).

——**In Practice.** A writ issued out of a court of competent jurisdiction, commanding a person therein named to appear on a day named, and do something therein mentioned, or show cause why he should not. Proctor, Prac.

The act by which a person is so summoned or cited.

It is applied particularly to process from probate and ecclesiastical courts, and to notices issued in special proceedings in some states.

It is usually the original process in any proceeding, and is in that respect analogous to the writ of *capias* or summons at law, and the *subpoena* in chancery.

In the ecclesiastical law, the citation is the beginning and foundation of the whole cause, and is said to have six requisites, namely, the insertion of the name of the judge, of the promovert, of the impugnant, of the cause of suit, of the place, and of the time of appearance; to which may be added the affixing the seal of the court, and the name of the register or his deputy. 1 Brown, Civ. Law, 453, 454; 3 Bl. Comm. 100.

——**In Scotch Practice.** The calling of a party to an action done by an officer of the court under a proper warrant.

The service of a writ or bill of summons. Paterson, Comp.

——**Of Authorities.** The production of or reference to the text of acts of legislatures, treatises, or cases of similar nature decided by the courts, in order to support propositions advanced.

CITATIONES NON CONCEDANTUR PRIusquam exprimatur super qua re fieri debet citatio. Citations should not be granted before it is stated about what matter the citation is to be made. (A maxim of ecclesiastical law.) 12 Coke, 44.

CITIZEN. A citizen, in the popular and appropriate sense of the term, is one who by birth, naturalization or otherwise is a member of an independent political society called a state, kingdom or empire, and as such is subject to its laws and entitled to its protection in all his rights incident to that relation. 177 Ill. 258; 113 Ill. 64.

——**In English Law.** An inhabitant of a city. 1 Rolle, Abr. 138. The representative of a city, in parliament. 1 Bl. Comm. 174.

——**In American Law.** One who, under the constitution and laws of the United States, has a right to vote for public officers, and who is qualified to fill offices in the gift of the people.

One of the sovereign people; a constituent member of the sovereignty, synonymous with the people. 19 How. (U. S.) 404.

"All persons born or naturalized in the United States, and subject to the jurisdiction thereof, are citizens of the United States and of the state wherein they reside." Const. U. S. Amend. XIV.

CITY.

——**In England.** An incorporated town or borough which is or has been the see of a bishop. Co. Litt. 108; 1 Bl. Comm. 114; Cowell.

A large town incorporated with certain privileges; the inhabitants of a city; the citizens. Worcester.

Although the first definition here given is sanctioned by high authority, it is questionable if it is essential to its character as a city, even in England, that it has been at any time a see; and it certainly retains its character of a city after it has lost its ecclesiastical character (1 Steph. Comm. 115; 1 Bl. Comm. 114), and in the United States it is clearly unnecessary that it should ever have possessed this character. Originally, this word did not signify a town, but a portion of mankind who lived under the same government,—what the Romans called *civitas,* and the Greeks *polis;* whence the word *politeia, civitas seu reipublicae status et administratio.* Toullier, Dr. Civ. Fr. lib. 1, tit. 1, note 202; Henrion de Pansey, Pouvoir Municipal, pp. 36, 37.

——**In the United States.** The highest class of municipal corporation, having extensive municipal powers, required by the presence of a large population.

A body politic and corporate established by law, not only to regulate and administer local affairs, but to assist in the civil government of the country. 133 Ill. 440.

CITY OF LONDON COURT. A court having a local jurisdiction within the city of London. It is to all intents and purposes a county court, having the same jurisdiction and procedure. St. 30 & 31 Vict. c. 142, § 35. It has exclusive jurisdiction in admiralty matters within the city. Rosc. Adm. 75; St. 31 & 32 Vict. c. 71. See "Mayor's Court."

CIVIL.

Pertaining to a citizen, as civil rights (*q. v.*)

In contradistinction to "barbarous" or "savage," indicates a state of society reduced to order and regular government. Thus, we speak of civil life, civil society, civil government and civil liberty.

In contradistinction to "criminal," to indicate the private rights and remedies of men, as members of the community, in contrast to those which are public and relate to the government. Thus, we speak of civil process and criminal process, civil jurisdiction and criminal jurisdiction.

It is also used in contradistinction to "military" or "ecclesiastical," to "natural" or "foreign." Thus, we speak of a civil station, as opposed to a military or an ecclesiastical station; a civil death, as opposed to a natural death; a civil war, as opposed to a foreign war. Story, Const. § 789; 1 Bl. Comm. 6, 125, 251; Montesquieu, Sp. Laws, bk. 1, c. 3; Rutherforth, Inst. bk. 2, c. 2; Id. c. 3; Id. c. 8, p. 359; Heinec. Elem. Jur. Civ. b. 2, c. 6.

CIVIL ACTION.

——**In Civil Law.** A personal action which is instituted to compel payment, or the doing some other thing which is purely civil. Poth. Introd. Gen. aux Cont. 110.

——**At Common Law.** An action which has for its object the recovery of private or civil rights or compensation for their infraction.

All actions which are not criminal are said to be civil.

In states where there has been partial codification, it is generally enacted in effect that the distinction between actions at law and suits in equity is abolished, and that there shall be but one form of action for the enforcement of private rights, and the redress of private wrongs, which shall be known as the "civil action." Code Civ. Proc. N. Y. § 69; Gen. St. Minn. 1878, c. 66, § 1. See "Action."

CIVIL BILL COURT. A tribunal in Ireland with a jurisdiction analogous to that of the county courts in England. The judge of it is also chairman of quarter sessions (where the jurisdiction is more extensive than in England), and performs the duty of revising barrister. The procedure of the civil bill courts is regulated by 27 & 28 Vict. c. 99; 28 & 29 Vict. c. 1; and 37 & 38 Vict. c. 66. Wharton.

CIVIL COMMOTION. An insurrection of the people for general purposes, though it may not amount to rebellion where there is an usurped power. 2 Marsh. Ins. 793.

CIVIL CORPORATIONS. One of the two classes into which lay corporations are divided; the other division embracing what are termed "eleemosynary" corporations. 3 Steph. Comm. 170. Municipal corporations (as counties, cities, towns and villages), incorporated manufacturing, banking, insurance, and trading companies, and the like, are examples of civil corporations. Id.; 2 Kent, Comm. 275. "Eleemosynary Corporations."

CIVIL DAMAGE ACTS. A name given to statutes rendering the seller of intoxicating liquors civilly liable to the wife or family of a purchaser of liquor for damage sustained by them by reason of the sale to him.

CIVIL DEATH. That change of state of a person which is considered in the law as equivalent to death. See "Death."

CIVIL INJURY. An infringement or privation of some civil right, and which is a subject for civil redress or compensation, as distinguished from a crime, which is a subject for punishment. 3 Steph. Comm. 556. See "Civil Rights."

CIVIL LAW. This term is generally used to designate the Roman jurisprudence, *jus civile Romanorum.*

In its most extensive sense, the term "Roman law" comprises all those legal rules and principles which were in force among the Romans, without reference to the time when they were adopted. But in a more restricted sense we understand by it the law compiled under the auspices of the Emperor Justinian, and which are still in force in many of the states of modern Europe, and to which all refer as authority or written reason.

The ancient *leges curiatae* are said to have been collected in the time of Tarquin, the last of the kings, by a *pontifex maximus* of the name of *Sextus* or *Publius Papirius.* This collection is known under the title of *Jus Civile Papirianum;* its existing fragments are few, and those of an apocryphal character. Mackeld. Civ. Law, § 21.

After a fierce and uninterrupted struggle between the patricians and plebeians, the latter extorted from the former the celebrated law of the Twelve Tables, in the year 300 of Rome. This law, framed by the decemvirs, and adopted in the *comitia centuriata,* acquired great authority, and constituted the foundation of all the public and private laws of the Romans, subsequently, until the time of Justinian. It is called *Lex Decemviralis.* Mackeld. Civ. Law,· § 21. From this period, the sources of the *jus scriptum* consisted in the *leges,* the *plebiscita,* the *senatusconsulta,* and the constitutions of the emperors, *constitutiones principum;* and the *jus non scriptum* was found partly in the *mores majorum,* the *consuetudo,* and the *res judicata,* or *auctoritas rerum perpetua similiter judicatorum.* The edicts of the magistrates, or *jus honorarium,* also formed a part of the unwritten law; but by far the most prolific source of the *jus non scriptum* consisted in the opinions and writings of the lawyers,—*responsa prudentium.*

The few fragments of the Twelve Tables that have come down to us are stamped with the harsh features of their aristocratic origin. But the *jus honorarium* established by the praetors and other magistrates, as well as that part of the customary law which was built up by the opinions and writings of the *prudentes,* are founded essentially on principles of natural justice.

Many collections of the imperial constitutions had been made before the advent of Justinian to the throne. He was the first after Theodosius who ordered a new compilation to be made. For this purpose he appointed a committee of ten lawyers, with very extensive powers. At their head was the *exquaestor sacri palatii,* Johannes, and among them the afterwards well-known Tribonian. His instructions were to select, in the most laconic form, all that was still of value in the existing collections, as well as in the later constitutions; to omit all obsolete matter; to introduce such alterations as were required by the times; and to divide the whole into appropriate titles. Within fourteen months, the committee had finished their labors. Justinian confirmed this new code, which consisted of twelve books, by a special ordinance and prohibited the use of the older collections of rescripts and edicts. This Code of Justinian, which is now called *Codex Vetus,* has been entirely lost.

After the completion of this code, Justinian ordered Tribonian, in 530, who was now invested with the dignity of *quaestor sacri palatii,* and sixteen other jurists, to select all the most valuable passages from the writings of the old jurists which were regarded as authoritative, and to arrange them, according to their subjects, under suitable heads. These commissioners also enjoyed very extensive powers. They had the privilege, at their discretion, to abbreviate, to add, and to make such other alterations as they might consider adapted to the times; and they were especially ordered to remove all the contradictions of the old jurists, to avoid all repetitions, and to omit all that had become entirely obsolete. The natural consequence of this was that the extracts did not always truly represent the originals, but were often interpolated and amended in conformity with the existing law. Alterations, modifications, and additions of this kind are now usually called *Emblemata Triboniani.* This great work is called the "Pandects," or "Digest," and was completed by the commissioners in three years. Within that short space of time, they had extracted from the writings of no less than thirty-nine jurists all that they considered valuable for the purpose of this compilation. It was divided into fifty books, and was entitled *Digesta sive Pandectae Juris Enucleati ex Omni Vetere Jure Collecti.* The Pandects were published on the 16th December, 533, but they did not go into operation until the 30th of that month. In confirming the Pandects, Justinian prohibited further reference to the old jurists; and, in order to prevent legal science from becoming so diffuse, indefinite, and uncertain as it had previously been, he forbade the writing of commentaries upon the new compilation, and permitted only the making of literal translations into Greek.

In preparing the Pandects, the compilers met very frequently with controversies in the writings of the jurists. Such questions, to the number of thirty-four, had been already determined by Justinian before the commencement of the collection of the Pandects, and before its completion the decisions of this kind were increased to fifty, and were known as the "fifty decisions of Justinian." These decisions were at first collected separately, and afterwards embodied in the new code.

For the purpose of facilitating the study of the law, Justinian ordered Tribonian, with the assistance of Theophilus and Dorotheus, to prepare a brief system of law under the title of "Institutes," which should contain the elements of legal science. This work was founded on, and to a great extent copied from, the commentaries of Gaius, which, after having been lost for many centuries, were discovered by the great historian Niebuhr, in 1816, in a palimpsest, or rewritten manuscript of some of the homilies of St. Jerome, in the Chapter Library of Verona. What had become obsolete in the commentaries was omitted in the Institutes, and references were made to the new constitutions of Justinian so far as they had been issued at the time. Justinian published his Institutes on the 21st November, 533, and they obtained the force of law at the same time with the Pandects, December 30, 533. Theophilus, one of the editors, delivered lectures on the Institutes in the Greek language, and from these lectures originated the valuable commentaries known under the Latin title, *Theophili Antecessoris Paraphrasis Graeca Institutionum Caesarearum.* The Institutes consist of four books, each of which contains several titles.

After the publication of the Pandects and the Institutes, Justinian ordered a revision of the Code, which had been promulgated in the year 529. This became necessary on account of the great number of new constitutions which he had issued, and of the fifty decisions not included in the old Code, and by which the law had been altered, amended, or modified. He therefore directed Tribonian, with the assistance of Dorotheus, Menna, Constantinus, and Johannes, to revise the old Code, and to incorporate the new constitutions into it. This revision was completed in the same year; and the new edition of the Code, *Codex Repetitae Praelectionis,* was confirmed on the 16th November, 534, and the old Code abolished. The Code contains twelve books, subdivided into appropriate titles.

During the interval between the publication of the *Codex Repetitae Praelectionis,* in 535, to the end of his reign, in 565, Justinian issued, at different times, a great number of new constitutions, by which the law on many subjects was entirely changed. The greater part of these constitutions were written in Greek, in obscure and pompous language, and published under the name of *Novellae Constitutiones,* which are known to us as the "Novels of Justinian." Soon after his death, a collection of one hundred and sixty-eight Novels was made, one hundred and fifty-four of which had been issued by Justinian, and the others by his successors.

Justinian's collections were, in ancient times, always copied separately, and afterwards they were printed in the same way. When taken together, they were indeed called, at an early period, the *Corpus Juris Civilis;* but this was not introduced as the regular title comprehending the whole body. Each volume had its own title until Dionysius Gothofredus gave this general title in the second edition of his glossed *Corpus Juris Civilis,* in 1604. Since that time this title has been used in all the editions of Justinian's collections

It is generally believed that the laws of Justinian were entirely lost and forgotten in the Western Empire from the middle of the eighth century until the alleged discovery of a copy of the Pandects at the storming and pilage of Amalfi, in 1135. This is one of those popular errors which had been handed down from generation to generation without question or inquiry, but which has now been completely exploded by the learned discussion, supported by conclusive evidence, of Savigny, in his History of the Roman Law during the Middle Ages. Indeed, several years before the sack of Amalfi, the celebrated Irnerius delivered lectures on the Pandects in the University of Bologna. The pretended discovery of a copy of the Digest at Amalfi, and its being given by Lothaire II. to his allies, the Pisans, as a reward for their services, is an absurd fable. No doubt, during the five or six centuries when the human intellect was in a complete state of torpor, the study of the Roman law, like that of every other branch of knowledge, was neglected; but on the first dawn of the revival of learning, the science of Roman jurisprudence was one of the first to attract the attention of mankind; and it was taught with such brilliant success as to immortalize the name of Irnerius, its great professor.

Even at the present time the Roman law exercises dominion in every state in Europe except England. The countrymen of Lycurgus and Solon are governed by it, and in the vast empire of Russia it furnished until the revolution, the rule of civil conduct. In America, it is the foundation of the law of Louisiana, Canada, Mexico, and all the republics of South America. Its influence in the formation of the common law of England cannot be denied by the impartial inquirer. It was publicly taught in England, by Roger Vacarius, as early as 1149; and all admit that the whole equity jurisprudence prevailing in England and the United States is mainly based on the civil law. See "Code;" "Digest;" "Institute;" "Novels."

CIVIL LIABILITY. Amenability to a civil action, as distinguished from amenability to criminal prosecution.

CIVIL LIBERTY. The liberty of a member of society, being a man's natural liberty, so far restrained by human laws (and no further) as is necessary and expedient for the general advantage of the public. 1 Bl. Comm. 125; 2 Steph. Comm. 487. The power of doing whatever the laws permit. 1 Bl. Comm. 6; Inst. 1. 3. 1.

Blackstone's definition is substantially that of the civilians; that of Justinian being: "The natural power of doing whatever one pleases, except what is prohibited by force or law." Inst. 1. 3. 1. This is adopted by Bracton almost in terms. Bracton, fol. 46b. Blackstone's amendment, as will be seen, consists in the elimination of the idea of restraint by force.

CIVIL LIST. An annual sum granted by the English parliament at the commencement of each reign, for the expenses of the royal household and establishment, as distinguished from the general exigencies of the state. It is the provision for the crown made out of the taxes in lieu of its proper patrimony, and in consideration of the assignment of that patrimony to the public use. Wharton.

CIVIL OBLIGATION. One which binds in law, and which may be enforced in a court of justice. Poth. Obl. 173, 191.

CIVIL OFFICER. Any officer of the United States who holds his appointment under the national government, whether his duties are executive or judicial, in the highest or lowest departments of the government, with the exception of officers of the army and navy. Rawle, Const. 213; 2 Story, Const. § 790.

The term occurs in the constitution of the United States (article 2, § 4), which provides that the president, vice president, and civil officers of the United States shall be removed from office on impeachment for, and conviction of, treason, bribery, or other high crimes and misdemeanors. It has been decided that a senator of the United States is not a civil officer, within the meaning of this clause in the constitution. Senate Journal, 10th Jan. 1799; 4 Tucker, Bl. Comm. Append. 57, 58; Rawle, Const. 213; Serg. Const. Law, 376; Story, Const. § 791.

CIVIL REMEDY. In practice. The remedy which the party injured by the commission of a tortious act has by action against the party committing it, as distinguished from the proceeding by indictment, by which the wrongdoer is made to expiate the injury done to society.

CIVIL RESPONSIBILITY. See "Civil Liability."

CIVIL RIGHTS. The rights of a citizen; the rights of an individual as a citizen; the rights due from one citizen to another, the privation of which is a civil wrong, for which redress may be sought in a civil action.

Also sometimes applied to the rights secured by the thirteenth and fourteenth amendments to the United States constitution and the statutes pursuant thereto.

CIVIL SERVICE. Governmental service other than military or naval; administrative functions. More commonly used to signify those offices in the federal, state or municipal governments which are filled by appointment of persons competitively examined and passed for merit and ability, irrespective of partisan affiliations.

CIVIL SIDE. Civil proceedings in a court having both civil and criminal jurisdiction are said to be on the "civil side" of the court, whether heard by the same judge as tries the criminal cases or not.

CIVIL WAR. An internecine war in which the opposing forces both belong to the same country or nation, *e. g.* the Revolutionary War prior to the Declaration of Independence, or the late Rebellion prior to the president's proclamation of August 16, 1861.

CIVILIAN. A doctor, professor, or student of the civil law.

CIVILIS (Lat. from *civis*, a citizen). Civil, as distinguished from criminal. *Civilis actio*, a civil action. Bracton, fols. 101b, 102. *Civilis causa*, a civil cause. Id. *Placita civilia*, civil pleas. Fleta, lib. 2, c. 1, § 25. *Injuriae civiles*, civil injuries. Id. § 5.

Civil, belonging to a *civitas* or state; *jus civile*, civil law, the particular law of a state, as distinguished from *jus gentium*, the common law of nations. Inst. 1. 2. 1. 2.

CIVILISTA. In old English law. A civil lawyer, or civilian. Dyer, 267.

CIVILITER. Civilly; opposed to *criminaliter*, or criminally.

When a person does an unlawful act injurious to another, whether with or without an intention to commit a tort, he is responsible *civiliter*. In order to make him liable *criminaliter*, he must have intended to do the wrong; for it is a maxim, *actus non facit reum nisi mens sit rea*. 2 East, 104.

CIVILITER MORTUUS. Civilly dead; in a state of civil death.

CIVIS (Lat.) In the Roman law. A citizen; as distinguished from *incola* (an inhabitant); origin or birth constituting the former, domicile the latter. Code, 10. 40. 7.

CIVITAS (Lat.) In the Roman law. Any body of people living under the same laws; a state. *Jus civitatis*, the law of a state;

civil law. Inst. 1. 2. 1. 2. *Civitates foederatae*, towns in alliance with Rome, and considered to be free. Butler, Hor. Jur. 29.

Citizenship; one of the three *status*, conditions, or qualifications of persons. Mackeld. Civ. Law, § 131.

CIVITAS ET URBS IN HOC DIFFERunt, quod incolae dicuntur civitas, urbs vero complectitur aedificia. A city and a town differ in this, that the inhabitants are called the "city," but "town" includes the buildings. Co. Litt. 409.

CLAIM. A challenge of the ownership of a thing which is wrongfully withheld from the possession of the claimant. Plowd. 359. See 1 Dall. (Pa.) 444; 12 Serg. & R. (Pa.) 179.

The owner of property proceeded against in admiralty by a suit *in rem* must present a claim to such property, verified by oath or affirmation, stating that the claimant by whom or on whose behalf the claim is made, and no other person, is the true and *bona fide* owner thereof, as a necessary preliminary to his making defense. 2 Conkl. Adm. 201-210.

A demand entered of record of a mechanic or materialman for work done or material furnished in the erection of a building, in certain counties in Pennsylvania.

The assertion of a liability to the party making it to do some service or pay a sum of money. See 16 Pet. (U. S.) 539.

The possession of a settler upon the wild lands of the government of the United States; the lands which such a settler holds possession of.

CLAIM OF CONUSANCE. In practice. An intervention by a third person demanding jurisdiction of a cause which the plaintiff has commenced out of the claimant's court. Now obsolete. 2 Wils. 409; 3 Bl. Comm. 298.

CLAIM OF LIBERTY. A suit or petition to the crown, in the court of exchequer, to have liberties and franchises confirmed there by the attorney general. Wharton.

CLAIM, VI, AUT PRECARIO. By force, stealth, or importunity.

CLAIMANT.

——**In Admiralty Practice.** A person authorized and admitted to defend a libel brought *in rem* against property; thus, for example, thirty hogsheads of sugar. 9 Cranch (U. S.) 191.

——**In Old English Law.** The plaintiff in ejectment.

CLAM. In the civil law. Covertly; secretly.

CLAM DELINQUENTES MAGIS PUNIuntur quam palam. Those sinning secretly are punished more severely than those sinning openly. 8 Coke, 127.

CLAMEA ADMITTENDA IN ITINERE per attornatum. An ancient writ, by which the king commanded the justices in eyre to admit the claim by attorney of a person who was in the royal service, and could not appear in person. Reg. Orig. 19.

CLAMOR (Lat.) A suit or demand; a complaint. Du Cange; Spelman.

——**In Civil Law.** A claimant; a debt; anything claimed from another; a proclamation; an accusation. Du Cange.

CLARE CONSTAT (Lat.) It is clearly evident.

——**In Scotch Law.** A deed given by a mesne lord (subject superior) for the purpose of completing the title of the vassal's heir to the lands held by the deceased vassal under the grantor. Bell, Dict.

CLAREMETHEN. In old Scotch law. The warranty of stolen cattle or goods; the law regulating such warranty. Skene de Verb. Sign.

CLARENDON, CONSTITUTIONS OF. The constitutions of Clarendon were certain statutes made in the reign of Henry II., of England, at a parliament held at Clarendon, by which the king checked the power of the pope and his clergy, and greatly narrowed the exemption they claimed from secular jurisdiction.

Previous to this time, there had been an entire separation between the clergy and laity, as members of the same commonwealth. The clergy, having emancipated themselves from the laws as administered by the courts of law, had assumed powers and exemptions quite inconsistent with the good government of the country.

CLARIFICATIO (Lat.) In old Scotch law. A making clear; the purging or clearing (clenging) of an assize. Skene de Verb. Sign. *Clarificatio debiti*, the clearness of a debt which is sufficiently proved and verified.

CLASS. A number of persons or things ranked together for some common purpose, or as possessing some attribute in common.

The term is used of legatees (3 McCord [S. C.] 440), of obligees in a bond (3 Dev. [N. C.] 284; 4 Dev. [N. C.] 382), and of other collections of persons (17 Wend. [N. Y.] 52; 16 Pick. [Mass.] 132).

CLASSIARIUS. A seaman or soldier serving at sea.

CLASSICI. In the Roman law. Persons employed in servile duties on board of vessels. Code, 11. 12.

CLASSIFICATION. In English practice. In the English chancery division, where there are several parties to an administration action, including those who have been served with notice of the decree or judgment, and it appears to the judge (or chief clerk) that any of them form a class having the same interests (*e. g.* residuary legatees), he may require them to be represented by one solicitor, in order to prevent the expense of each of them attending by separate solicitors. This is termed "classifying the interests of the parties attending," or, shortly, "classifying" or "classification." In practice, the term is also applied to the directions given by the chief clerk as to which of the parties are to attend on each of the accounts and inquiries directed by the judgment. Consol. Orders, 20; Daniell, Ch. Pr. 1088. See, also, Rules of Court, xvi. 12b (April, 1880). Special regulations on this head are in force in the master of the roll's chambers.

CLAUSE. A part of a treaty; of a legislative act; of a deed; of a will, or other written instrument; a part of a sentence.

As used in a statute relating to wills, a clause is "some collocation of words in a will which, when removed out of the will, will leave the rest intelligible." The clause need not "be capable of being read as a document by itself, if taken alone." L. R. 4 App. Cas. 77.

CLAUSE IRRITANT. By this clause, in a deed or settlement, the acts or deeds of a tenant for life or other proprietor, contrary to the conditions of his right, become null and void, and, by the "resolutive" clause, such right becomes resolved and extinguished. Bell, Dict.

CLAUSE ROLLS. Contain all such matters of record as were committed to close writs. These rolls are preserved in the Tower. Rapalje & L.

CLAUSULA. A clause; a sentence or part of a sentence in a written instrument or law. So called as inclosing or including certain words.

CLAUSULA GENERALIS DE RESIDUO non ea complectitur quae non ejusdem sint generis cum iis quae speciatim dicta fuerant. A general clause of remainder does not embrace those things which are not of the same kind with those which had been specially mentioned. Lofft, 419.

CLAUSULA GENERALIS NON REFERtur ad expressa. A general clause does not refer to things expressed. 8 Coke, 154.

CLAUSULA QUAE ABROGATIONEM EXcludit ab initio non valet. A clause in a law which precludes its abrogation is invalid from the beginning. Bac. Max. reg. 19, p. 89; 2 Dwar. St. 673; Broom, Leg. Max. (3d London Ed.) 27

CLAUSULA VEL DISPOSITIO INUTILIS per praesumptionem remotam vel causam, ex post facto non fulcitur. A useless clause or disposition, *i. e.*, one which the law would have implied, is not supported by a remote presumption, or by a cause arising afterwards. Bac. Max. reg. 21; Broom, Leg. Max. (3d London Ed.) 599.

CLAUSULAE INCONSUETAE SEMPER inducunt suspicionem. Unusual clauses always excite a suspicion. 3 Coke, 81; Broom, Leg. Max. (3d London Ed.) 264.

CLAUSUM. Close; closed.

A writ was either *clausum* (close) or *apertum* (open). Grants were said to be by *literae patentae* (open grant) or *literae clausae* (close grant). 2 Bl. Comm. 346.

A close; an inclosure.

CLAUSUM FREGIT. See "Quare Clausum Fregit."

CLAUSURA. An inclosure.

CLAVES CURIAE. The keys of the court. A figurative term applied in Scotch law to the officers of court.

CLAVIA. A mace.

CLEAR DAYS. A specified number of clear days is to be reckoned, exclusive of both the first and last days. 1 Dowl. (N. S.) 767.

CLEARANCE. A certificate given by the collector of a port, in which it is stated that the master or commander (naming him) of a ship or vessel named and described, bound for a port named, and having on board goods described, in case the master requires the particulars of his cargo to be stated in such clearance, has entered and cleared his ship or vessel according to law.

CLEARING HOUSE. In commercial law. an office where bankers settle daily with each other the balances of their accounts. Morse, Banks, 450.

CLEMENTINES. In ecclesiastical law. The collection of decretals or constitutions of Pope Clement V., which was published, by order of John XXII., his successor, in 1317.

CLERGY. The name applicable to ecclesiastical ministers as a class.

CLERGYABLE. In English law. Allowing of, or entitled to, the benefit of clergy (*privilegium clericale*). Used of persons or crimes. 4 Bl. Comm. 371 et seq.

CLERICAL ERROR. An error made by a clerk in transcribing or otherwise. A mistake in writing or copying any document.

CLERICALE PRIVILEGIUM. Benefit of clergy (*q. v.*)

CLERICI DE CANCELLARIA. Clerks of chancery. See "Six Clerks in Chancery."

CLERICI PRAENOTARII. The six clerks in chancery. 2 Reeve, Hist. Eng. Law, 251. Fleta calls them *sex clerici praenotarii.*

CLERICO ADMITTENDO. See "De Clerico, etc."

CLERICO CAPTO PER STATUTUM mercatorum. See "De Clerico, etc."

CLERICO CONVICTO COMMISSO GAOlae in defectu ordinarii deliberando. See "De Clerico, etc."

CLERICO INFRA SACROS ORDINES constituto, non eligendo in officium. See "De Clerico, etc."

CLERICUS (Lat.)

——**In Civil Law.** Any one who has taken orders in church, of whatever rank; monks. A general term including bishops, subdeacons, readers, and cantors. Du Cange. Used, also, of those who were given up to the pursuit of letters, and who were learned therein. Also of the amanuenses of the judges or courts of the king. Du Cange.

——**In English Law.** A secular priest, in opposition to a regular one. Kennett, Par. Ant. 171. A clergyman or priest; one in orders. *Nullus clericus nisi causidicus,* no clerk but what is a pleader. 1 Bl. Comm. 17. A freeman, generally. One who was charged with various duties in the king's household. Du Cange.

CLERICUS ET AGRICOLA ET MERCAtor, tempore belli, ut oret, colat, et commutet, pace fruuntur. Clergymen, husbandmen, and merchants, in order that they may preach, cultivate, and trade, enjoy peace in time of war. 2 Inst. 58.

CLERICUS MERCATI. In old English law. Clerk of the market. Fleta, lib. 2, c. 8; 2 Inst. 543.

CLERICUS NON CONNUMERETUR IN duobus ecclesiis. A clergyman should not be appointed to two churches.

CLERICUS PAROCHIALIS. In old English law. A parish clerk. Towns. Pl. 213. Otherwise called *clericus sacerdotis.* Cowell.

CLERIGOS. In Spanish law. Clergy; men chosen for the service of God. White, New Recop. bk. 1, tit. 5, c. 4.

CLERK.

——**In Commercial Law.** A person in the employ of a merchant, who attends only to a part of his business, while the merchant himself superintends the whole. He differs from a factor in this, that the latter wholly supplies the place of his principal in respect to the property consigned to him. Pardessus, Dr. Com. note 38; 1 Chit. Prac. 80; 2 Bouv. Inst. note 1287.

A general name for salesmen, bookkeepers, amanuenses, and other employees of that class.

A person employed in an office, public or private, for keeping records or accounts.

——**In Ecclesiastical Law.** An individual who is attached to the ecclesiastical state, and has submitted to the tonsure. One who has been ordained. 1 Bl. Comm. 388. A clergyman. 4 Bl. Comm. 367.

CLERK OF ARRAIGNS. Officers attached to the central criminal court in England, and to each circuit. The clerk of arraigns "has to discharge, for the judge sitting on the crown side (*i. e.* in criminal cases), the duties which are discharged for him by a master on the civil side. Taxation of costs, allowance to witnesses, the business connected with jurors, their excuses and fines, the custody of documents, the duty of recording verdicts and making out warrants after sentence are, in addition to advising the court upon points of criminal procedure, among the duties of the clerk of arraigns." Second Rep. Leg. Dep. Comm. (1874) 22.

CLERK OF ASSIZE. The officer who is responsible for the due performance of the administrative duties of the courts of assizes on each circuit. He performs the same duties on circuit which the associate formerly performed, and which the masters now perform at the sittings of *nisi prius* at London and Middlesex.

CLERK OF COURT. An officer of a court of justice, having the custody of its records and seals, and whose duty it is, among other things, to certify to the correctness of transcripts from such record.

CLERK OF ENROLLMENTS. In English law. The former chief officer of the English enrollment office. He formed part of the staff of the central office (*q. v.*), but the office is now abolished.

CLERKS OF INDICTMENTS. Officers attached to the central criminal court in England, and to each circuit. They prepare and settle indictments against offenders, and assist the clerk of arraigns.

CLERK OF THE CROWN IN CHANcery. See "Crown Office in Chancery."

CLERK OF THE HOUSE OF COMMONS. One of the chief officers of the lower house of the English parliament. He is appointed by the crown as under clerk of the parliaments, to attend upon the commons. He makes a declaration, on entering upon his office, to make true entries, remembrances, and journals of the things done and passed in the house. He signs all orders of the house, indorses the bills sent or returned to the lords, and reads whatever is required to be read in the house. He has the custody of all records and other documents. May, Parl. Prac. 289.

CLERK OF THE PEACE. An officer appointed by the *custos rotulorum* (*q. v.*) to assist the justices of the peace in quarter sessions in drawing indictments, entering judgments, issuing process, etc. Pritch. Quar. Sess. 49.

CLERK OF THE PETTY BAG. See "Petty Bag Office."

CLERK OF THE PRIVY SEAL. There are four of these officers, who attend the lord privy seal, or, in the absence of the lord privy seal, the principal secretary of state. Their duty is to write and make out all things that are sent by warrant from the signet to the privy seal, and which are to be passed to the great seal, and also to make out "privy seals," as they are termed, upon any special occasion of his majesty's affairs, as for the loan of money, and such like purposes. 27 Hen. VIII. c. 11. Cowell.

CLERK OF THE SIGNET. An officer in England, whose duty it is to attend on the king's principal secretary, who always has the custody of the privy signet, as well for the purpose of sealing his majesty's private letters, as also grants which pass his majesty's hand by bill signed. There are four of these officers. 27 Hen. VIII. c. 11, Cowell.

CLERKS OF RECORDS AND WRITS. Officers formerly attached to the English court of chancery, whose duties consisted principally in sealing bills of complaint and writs of execution, filing affidavits, keeping a record of suits, and certifying office copies of pleadings and affidavits. They were three in number, and the business was distributed among them according to the letters of the alphabet. Second Rep. Leg. Dep. Comm. 43. By the judicature acts of 1873, 1875, they were transferred to the chancery division of the high court. Now, by the judicature (officers') act of 1879, they have been transferred to the central office of the supreme court, under the title of "Masters of the Supreme Court," and the office of clerk of records and writs has been abolished.

CLERKS OF SEATS. In the principal registry of the probate division of the English high court, clerks of seats discharge the duty of preparing and passing the grants of probate and letters of administration, under the supervision of the registrars. There are six seats, the business of which is regulated by an alphabetical arrangement, and each set has four clerks. They have to take bonds from administrators, and to receive caveats against a grant being made in a case where a will is contested. They also draw the "acts," *i. e.*, a short summary of each grant made, containing the name of the deceased, amount of assets, and other particulars. Second Rep. Leg. Dep. Comm. 79.

CLERKSHIP. The period which must be spent by a law student in the office of a practicing attorney before admission to the bar. 1 Tidd, Prac. 61 et seq.

CLIENT. One who employs and retains an attorney or counsellor to manage or defend a suit or action to which he is a party, or to advise him about some legal matters. See "Attorney at Law."

CLIENTELA. In old English law. The state of a client; clientship; protection; patronage; guardianship. Applied to the relation of a church to its patron. 2 Bl. Comm. 21.

CLIFFORD'S INN. An inn of chancery. See "Inns of Chancery."

CLITO. In Saxon law. The son of a king or emperor; the next heir to the throne; the Saxon adeling. Spelman.

CLOERE. A prison or dungeon.

CLOSE. An interest in the soil (Doctor & Stud. 30; 6 East, 154; 7 East, 207; 1 Burrows, 133), or in trees or growing crops (4 Mass. 266; 9 Johns. [N. Y.] 113).

An inclosed tract of land. 3 Bl. Comm. 209.

In every case where one has a right to exclude another from his land, the law encircles it, if not actually inclosed, with an imaginary fence, and entitles him to a compensation in damages for the injury he sustains by the act of another passing through his boundary, denominating such land a "close." Hammond, N. P. 151; Doctor & Stud. dial. 1, c. 8, p. 30; 2 Whart. (Pa.) 430.

CLOSE COPIES. Copies which might be written with any number of words on a sheet. Office copies were to contain only a prescribed number of words on each sheet.

CLOSE ROLLS. Rolls containing the record of the close writs (*literae clausae*) and grants of the king, kept with the public records. 2 Bl. Comm. 346.

CLOSE WRITS. Writs directed to the sheriff instead of to the lord. 3 Reeve, Hist. Eng. Law, 45. Writs containing grants from the crown to particular persons, and for particular purposes, which, not being intended for public inspection, are closed up and sealed on the outside, instead of being open and having the seal appended by a strip of parchment. 2 Bl. Comm. 346; Sewell, Sheriffs, 372.

CLOUD ON TITLE. A proceeding or instrument, such as a deed or mortgage, or a tax or assessment, judgment or decree, which, if valid, would apparently, and on its face, impair the title of a person to land, but which is in fact invalid, such invalidity being demonstrable by proof of extrinsic facts. Equity has jurisdiction of actions brought to remove clouds on title by cancellation of instruments creating them.

CLOUGH. A valley. An allowance of two pounds in every hundred weight for the turn of the scale, on buying goods wholesale by weight.

CLUB. The term "club" imports a deadly weapon. 178 Ill. App. 238; 32 Ill. App. 62.

CLUBS. A name applied loosely to voluntary organizations of persons for a common purpose, usually either social, recreative, political, or educative. The form of the organization is not essential, and, though usually unincorporated, a club may be incorporated. See "Association."

CLYPEUS, or **CLIPEUS.** In old English law. A shield; metaphorically one of a noble family. *Clypei prostrati,* noble families extinct. Mat. Paris, 463.

COADJUTOR. The assistant of a bishop; an assistant.

CO-ADMINISTRATOR. One who is administrator with one or more others. See "Administrator."

COADUNATIO. A conspiracy. 9 Coke, 56.

COAL NOTE. In English law. A species of promissory note authorized by St. 3 Geo. II. c. 26, §§ 7, 8, which, having these words expressed therein, namely, "value received in coals," are to be protected and noted as inland bills of exchange.

COALITION. In French law. An unlawful agreement among several persons not to do a thing except on some conditions agreed upon; a conspiracy.

COASSIGNEE. One who is assignee with one or more others. See "Assignment."

COAST. The margin of a country bounded by the sea. This term includes the natural appendages of the territory which rise out of the water, although they are not of sufficient firmness to be inhabited or fortified. Shoals perpetually covered with water are not, however, comprehended under the name of "coast." 5 C. Rob. Adm. 385c.

COASTING TRADE. Domestic trade between port and port in the United States, as distinguished from foreign trade between a port in the United States and a port in a foreign country. 1 Wend. (N. Y.) 557; 10 Cal. 504. It is said to include a trade between places in the same district on a navigable river (3 Cow. [N. Y.] 713), but not to the mere crossing of a river (1 Newb. 24).

COCKET. A seal appertaining to the king's custom house. Reg. Orig. 192.

A scroll or parchment sealed and delivered by the officers of the custom house to merchants, as an evidence that their wares are customed. Cowell; Spelman. See 7 Low. (U. S.) 116.

The entry office in the custom house itself.

A kind of bread said by Cowell to be hard-baked; sea biscuit.

COCKPIT. A name which used to be given to the judicial committee of the privy council, the council room being built on the old cockpit of Whitehall Place. Wharton.

CODE. A body of law established by the legislative authority of the state, and designed to regulate completely, so far as a statute may, the subjects to which it relates.

The idea of a code involves that of the exercise of the legislative power in its promulgation; but the name has been loosely applied also to private compilations of statutes. The subject of codes and the kindred topics of legal reform have received great attention from the jurists and statesmen of the present century. When it is considered how rapidly statutes accumulate as time passes, it is obvious that great convenience will be found in having the statute law in a systematic body, arranged according to subject-matter, instead of leaving it unorganized, scattered through the volumes in which it was from year to year promulgated. But when the transposition of the statutes from a chronological to a scientific order is undertaken, more radical changes immediately propose themselves. These are of two classes: First, amendments for the purpose of harmonizing the inconsistencies which such an arrangement brings to notice, and supplying defects; second, the introduction into the system of all other rules which are recognized as the unwritten or common law of the state. The object of the latter class of changes is to embody in one systematic enactment all that is thenceforth to be regarded as the law of the land. It is this attempt which is usually intended by the distinctive term "codification."

The first two of the questions thus indicated may be deemed as settled, by general concurrence, in favor of the expediency of such changes; and the process of the collection of the statute law in one general code, or in a number of partial codes or systematic statutes, accompanied by the amendments which such a revision invites, is a process which for some years has been renovating the laws of England and the United States. Although at the same time something has been done, especially in this country, towards embodying in these statutes principles which before rested in the common or report law, yet the feasibility of doing this completely, or even to any great extent, must be deemed an open question. It has been discussed with great ability by Bentham, Savigny, Thibaut, and others. It is undeniable that, however successfully a code might be supposed to embody all existing and declared law, so as to supersede previous sources, it cannot be expected to provide prospectively for all the innumerable cases which the diversity of affairs rapidly engenders, and there must soon come a time when it must be studied in the light of numerous explanatory decisions.

These discussions have called attention to a subject formerly little considered, but which is of fundamental importance to the successful preparation of a code,—the matter of statutory expression. There is no species of composition which demands more care and precision than that of drafting a statute. The writer needs not only to make his language intelligible, he must make it incapable of misconstruction. When it has passed to a law, it is no longer his intent that is to be considered, but the intent of the words which he has used; and that intent is to be ascertained under the strong pressure of an attempt of the advocate to win whatever possible construction may be most favorable to his cause. The true safeguard is found not in the old method of accumulating synonyms, and by an enumeration of particulars, but rather—as is shown by those American codes of which the Revised Statutes of New York and the revision of Massachusetts are admirable specimens—by concise but complete statement of the full principle in the fewest possible words, and the elimination of description and paraphrase by the separate statement of necessary definitions. One of the rules to which the New York revisors generally adhered, and which they found of very great importance, was to confine each section to a single proposition. In this way, the intricacy and obscurity of the old statutes were largely avoided. The reader who wishes to pursue this interesting subject will find much that is admirable in Coode's treatise on Legislative Expression (London, 1845). The larger work of Gael (Legal Composition, London, 1840) is more especially adapted to the wants of the English profession.

——**Austrian.** The Civil Code was promulgated in 1811,—the code of Joseph II. (1780) having been found wholly unsuited to the purpose and by his successor abrogated. It is founded in a great degree upon the Prussian. The Penal Code (1852) is said to adopt to some extent the characteristics of the French Penal Code.

——**Burgundian.** *Lex Romana,* otherwise known in modern times as the *Papiniani Responsorum.* Promuigated A. D. 517.

It was founded on the Roman law, and its chief interest is the indication which, in common with the other Barbaric codes, it affords of the modifications of jurisprudence under the changes of society amidst which it arose.

——**Consolato del Mare.** A code of maritime law of high antiquity and great celebrity.

Its origin is not certainly known. It has been ascribed to the authority of the ancient kings of Arragon; but there is some reason for maintaining the theory that it was gradually collected and handed down as a digest of all the principal rules and usages established among the maritime nations of Europe from the twelfth to the fourteenth century. Since it was first printed at Barcelona in the fourteenth century, it has been enlarged from time to time by the addition of various commercial regulations. Its doctrines are founded to a large extent on the Greek and Roman law. It seems to have been originally written in the dialect of Catalonia; but it has been translated into every language of Europe, except English. It is referred to at the present day as an authority in respect to the ownership of vessels, the rights and obligations thereto, to the rights and responsibilities of master and seamen, to the law of freight, of equipment and supply, of jettison and average, of salvage, of ransom and of prize. The edition of Pardessus, in his *Collection de Lois Maritimes* (volume 2), is deemed the best.

——**French Codes.** The chief French codes of the present day are five in number, sometimes known as *Les Cinq Codes.* They were in great part the work of Napoleon, and the first in order bears his name. They are all frequently printed in one duodecimo volume. These codes do not embody the whole French law, but minor codes and a number of scattered statutes must also be resorted to upon special subjects.

(1) *Code Civil,* or *Code Napoleon,* is composed of thirty-six laws, the first of which was passed in 1803, and the last in 1804, which united them all in one body, under the name of *Code Civil des Francais.*

The first steps towards its preparation were taken in 1793, but it was not prepared till some years subsequently, and was finally thoroughly discussed in all its details by the court of Cassation, of which Napoleon was president, and in the discussions of which he took an active part throughout. In 1807 a new edition was promulgated, the title *Code Napoleon* being substituted. In the third edition (1816) the old title was restored; but in 1852 it was again displaced by that of Napoleon.

Under Napoleon's reign, it became the law of Holland, of the Confederation of the Rhine, Westphalia, Bavaria, Italy, Naples, Spain, etc. It has undergone great amendment by laws enacted since it was established. It is divided into three books: Book 1, "Of Persons and the Enjoyment and Privation of Civil Rights." Book 2, "Property and Its Different Modifications." Book 3, "Different Ways of Acquiring Property."

Prefixed to it is a preliminary title, "Of the Publication, Effects, and Application of Laws in General."

One of the most perspicuous and able commentators on this code is Toullier, frequently cited in this work.

(2) *Code de Procedure Civil.* That part of the code which regulates civil proceedings.

It is divided into two parts: Part 1 consists of five books, the first of which treats of justices of the peace; the second, of inferior tribunals; the third, of royal (or appellate) courts; the fourth, of extraordinary means of proceeding; the fifth, of the execution of judgments. Part 2 is divided into three books, treating of various matters and proceedings special in their nature.

(3) *Code de Commerce.* The code for the regulation of commerce.

This code was enacted in 1807. Book 1 is entitled, "Of Commerce in General." Book 2, "Maritime Commerce." The whole law of this subject is not embodied in this book. Book 3, "Failures and Bankruptcy." This book was very largely amended by the law of 28th May, 1838. Book 4, "Of Commercial Jurisdiction,"—the organization, jurisdiction, and proceedings of commercial tribunals. This code is, in one sense, a supplement to the *Code Napoleon,* applying the principles of the latter to the various subjects of commercial law. The two contain much that is valuable upon commercial subjects. Pardessus is one of the most able of its expositors.

(4) *Code d'Instruction Criminelle.* The code regulating procedure in criminal cases, taking that phrase in a broad sense.

Book 1 treats of the police; book 2, of the administration of criminal justice. It was enacted in 1808 to take effect with the Penal Code in 1811.

(5) *Code Penal.* The penal or criminal code.

Enacted in 1810. Book 1 treats of penalties in criminal and correctional cases, and their effects; book 2, of crimes and misdemeanors, and their punishment; book 3, offenses against the police regulations, and their punishment. Important amendments of this code have been made by subsequent legislation.

(6) There is also a *Code Forestier;* and the name "code" has been inaptly given to some private compilations on other subjects.

——**Gregorian.** An unofficial compilation of the rescripts of the Roman emperors. It was made in the fourth century, and is not now extant.

The Theodosian Code, which was promulgated nearly a century afterwards, was a continuation of this, and of the collection of Hermogenes. The chief interest of all of these collections is in their relation to their great successor, the Justinian Code.

——**Hanse Towns, Laws of the.** A code of maritime law established by the Hanseatic towns.

It was first published in German, at Lubec, in 1597. In an assembly of deputies from the several towns, held at Lubec, May 23, 1614, it was revised and enlarged. The text, with a Latin translation, was published with a commentary by Kuricke; and a French translation has been given by Cleirac in *Us et Coutumes de la Mer.* It is not infrequently referred to on subjects of maritime law.

——**Henri** (French). The best-known of several collections of ordinances made during the sixteenth, seventeenth, and eighteenth centuries, the number of which in part both formed the necessity and furnished the material for the Code Napoleon.

——**Henri** (Haytien). A very judicious adaptation from the *Code Napoleon* for the Haytiens. It was promulgated in 1812 by Christophe (Henri I).

——**Hermogenian.** An unofficial compilation, made in the fourth century, supplementary to the Code of Gregorius. It is not now extant.

——**Institutes of Menu.** A code of Hindu law, of great antiquity, which still forms the basis of Hindu jurisprudence (Elphinstone's History of India, p. 83), and is said also to be the basis of the laws of the Burmese and of the Laos (Buckle, History of Civilization, vol. 1, p. 54, note 70).

The Institutes of Menu are ascribed to about the ninth century B. C. A translation will be found in the third volume of Sir William Jones' Works. See "Hindu Law."

——**Justinian Code.** A collection of imperial ordinances compiled by order of the emperor Justinian.

All the judicial wisdom of the Roman civilization which is of importance to the American lawyer is embodied in the compilations to which Justinian gave his name, and from which that name has received its lustre. Of these, first in contemporary importance, if not first in magnitude and present interest, was the Code. In the first year of his reign, he commanded Tribonian, a statesman of his court, to revise the imperial ordinances. The first result, now known as the *Codex Vetus,* is not extant. It was superseded a few years after its promulgation by a new and more complete edition. Although it is this alone which is now known as the Code of Justinian, yet the Pandects and the Institutes which followed it are a part of the same system, declared by the same authority; and the three together form one codification of the law of the Empire. The first of these works occupied Tribonian and nine associates fourteen months. It is comprised in twelve divisions or books, and embodies all that was deemed worthy of preservation of the imperial statutes from the time of Hadrian down. The Institutes is an elementary treatise prepared by Tribonian and two associates upon the basis of a similar work by Gaius, a lawyer of the second century.

The Pandects, which were made public about a month after the Institutes, were an abridgment of the treaties and the commentaries of the lawyers. They were presented in fifty books. Tribonian and the sixteen associates who aided him in this part of his labors accomplished this abridgment in three years. It has been judged to bear obvious marks of the haste with which it was compiled; but it is the chief embodiment of the Roman law, though not the most convenient resort for the modern student of that law.

Tribonian found the law, which for fourteen centuries had been accumulating, comprised in two thousand books, or—stated according to the Roman method of computation—in three million sentences. It is probable that this matter, if printed in law volumes such as are now used, would fill from three to five hundred volumes,—a library perhaps as large as that which would be composed by a collection of the Federal statutes and reports. The comparison, to be more exact, should take into account treatises and digests, which would add to the bulk of the collection more than to the substance of the material. The commissioners were instructed to extract a series of plain and concise laws, in which there should be no two laws contradictory or alike. In revising the imperial ordinances, they were empowered to amend in substance as well as in form.

The codification being completed, the emperor decreed that no resort should be had to the earlier writings, nor any comparison be made with them. Commentators were forbidden to disfigure the new with explanations, and lawyers were forbidden to cite the old. The imperial authority was sufficient to sink into oblivion nearly all the previously existing sources of law; but the new statutes which the emperor himself found it necessary to establish in order to explain, complete, and amend the law, rapidly accumulated throughout his long reign. These are known as the "Novels." The Code, the Institutes, the Pandects, and the Novels, with some subsequent additions, constitute the *Corpus Juris Civilis*. Though the Code has lost its sanction, and the Pandects are of secondary value to the present age, the Institutes stand an undisturbed monument of the science. The masterly arrangement of the outline of the law there adopted is to this day a model for digests and commentaries. The familiar classification employed by Blackstone is based on this. So far as translation and modern illustration go, it is through the Institutes that the civil law is most accessible to the student.

Among English translations of the Institutes are that by Cooper (Phila. 1812; N. Y. 1841),—which is regarded as a very good one,—and that by Sanders (Lond. 1853), which contains the original text also, and copious references to the Digests and Code. Among the French commentators are Ortolan and Pasquiere.

——**Livingston's Code.** Mr. Edward Livingston, one of the commissioners who prepared the Louisiana Code, prepared and presented to congress a draft of a penal code for the United States, which, though it was never adopted, is not infrequently referred to in the books as stating principles of criminal law.

——**Khammurabi.** A code promulgated by Khammurabi, the first king of the Babylonians. It was discovered at Susa, Persia, in December, 1901, and is the oldest code known to history.

——**Mosaic Code.** The code proclaimed by Moses for the government of the Jews, B. C. 1491.

One of the peculiar characteristics of this code is the fact that whilst all that has ever been successfully attempted in other cases has been to change details without reversing or ignoring the general principles which form the basis of the previous law, that which was chiefly done here was the assertion of great and fundamental principles in part contrary and in part perhaps entirely new to the customs and usages of the people. These principles, thus divinely revealed and sanctioned, have given the Mosaic Code vast influence in the subsequent legislation of other nations than the Hebrews. The topics on which it is most frequently referred to as an authority in our law are those of marriage and divorce, and questions of affinity, and of the punishment of murder and seduction. The commentaries of Michaelis and of Wines are valuable aids to its study.

——**Ordonnance de la Marine.** A code of maritime law enacted in the reign of Louis XIV.

It was promulgated in 1681, and with great completeness embodied all existing rules of maritime law, including insurance. Kent pronounces it a monument of the wisdom of the reign of Louis, "far more durable and more glorious than all the military trophies won by the valor of his armies." Its compilers are unknown. An English translation is contained in the appendix to Peters' Admiralty Reports, vol. 1. The ordinance has been at once illustrated and eclipsed by Valin's commentaries upon it.

——**Oleron, Laws of.** A code of maritime law, which takes its name from the island of Oleron.

Both the French and the English claim the honor of having originated this code,—the former attributing its compilation to the command of Queen Eleanor, Duchess of Guienne, near which province the island of Oleron lies; the latter ascribing its promulgation to her son, Richard I. The latter monarch, without doubt, caused it to be improved, if he did not originate it, and he introduced it into England. Some additions were made to it by King John. It was promulgated anew in the reign of Henry III., and again confirmed in the reign of Edward III. It is most accessible to the American profession in the translation contained in the appendix to the first volume of Peters' Admiralty Reports. The French version, with Cleirac's commentary, is contained in *Us et Coutumes de la Mer*. The subjects upon which it is now valuable are much the same as those of the Consolato del Mare.

——**Ostrogothic.** The code promulgated by Theodoric, king of the Ostrogoths, at Rome, A. D. 500. It was founded on the Roman law.

——**Prussian.** *Allgemeines Landrecht.* The former code of 1751 was not successful; but the attempt to establish one was resumed in 1780, under Frederic II.; and, after long and thorough discussion, the present code was finally promulgated in 1794. It is known also as the "Code Frederic."

——**Rhodian Laws.** A maritime code adopted by the people of Rhodes, and in force among the nations upon the Mediterranean nine or ten centuries before Christ. There is reason to suppose that the collection under this title in Vinnius is spurious, and, if so, the code is not extant. See Marsh. Ins. bk. 1, c. 4, p. 15.

——**Theodosian.** A code compiled by a commission of eight, under the direction of Theodosian the Younger.

It comprises the edicts and rescripts of sixteen emperors, embracing a period of one hundred and twenty-six years. It was promulgated in the Eastern empire in 438, and quickly adopted, also, in the Western empire. The great modern expounder of this code is Gothofredus (Godefroi). The results of modern researches regarding this code are well stated in the Foreign Quarterly Review (volume 9, p. 374).

——**Twelve Tables.** Laws of ancient Rome, compiled on the basis of those of Solon and other Greek legislators.

They first appeared in the year of Rome 303, inscribed on ten plates of brass. In the following year, two others were added, and the entire code bore the name of the "Laws of the Twelve Tables." The principles they contained were the germ of the body of the Roman law, and enter largely into the modern jurisprudence of Europe. See a fragment of the law of the Twelve Tables, in Cooper's Justinian, 656; Gibbon's Rome, c. 44.

——**Visigothic.** The *Lex Romani;* now known as *Breviarum Alaricianum.* Ordained by Alaric II. for his Roman subjects, A. D. 506.

——**Wisbuy, Laws of.** A concise but comprehensive code of maritime law, established by the "merchants and masters of the magnificent city of Wisbuy."

The port of Wisbuy, now in ruins, was situated on the northwestern coast of Gottland, in the Baltic sea. It was the capital of the island, and the seat of an extensive commerce, of which the chief relic and the most significant record is this code. It is a mooted point whether this code was derived from the Laws of Oleron, or that from this; but the similarity of the two leaves no doubt that one was the offspring of the other. It was of great authority in the northern parts of Europe. *"Lex Rhodia navalis,"* says Grotius, *"pro jure gentium in illo mare Mediterraneo vigebat; sicut apud Gallium leges Oleronis, et apud omnes transrhenanos, legis Wisbueneses."* De Jure Belli, lib. 2, c. 3. It is still referred to on subjects of maritime law. An English translation will be found in the appendix to the first volume of Peters' Admiralty Reports.

CODEX (Lat.) A volume or roll. The Code of Justinian.

CODICIL. Some addition to, or qualification of, a last will and testament. 1 Redf. Wills, 287.

This term is derived from the Latin *codicillus,* which is a diminutive of *codex,* and in strictness imports a little code or writing,—a little will. In the Roman civil law, codicil was defined as an act which contains dispositions of property in prospect of death, without the institution of an heir or executor. Domat, Civ. Law, pt. ii. bk. iv. tit. i. § 1; Just. de Codic. art. i. § 2. So, also, the early English writers upon wills define a codicil in much the same way. "A codicil is a just sentence of our will touching that which any would have done after their death, without the appointing of an executor." Swinb. Wills, pt. i. § v. pl. 2.

COEMPTIO (Lat.) In civil law. The ceremony of celebrating marriage by solemnities.

The parties met and gave each other a small sum of money. They then questioned each other in turn. The man asked the woman if she wished to be his *mater-familias.* She replied that she so wished. The woman then asked the man if he wished to be her *pater-familias.* He replied that he so wished. They then joined hands; and these were called nuptials by *coemptio.* Boethius, Coemptio; Calv. Lex.; Taylor.

COEMPTION. The act of purchasing the whole quantity of any commodity. Wharton.

COERCION. Constraint; compulsion; force.

Direct or positive coercion takes place when a man is by physical force compelled to do an act contrary to his will. For example, when a man falls into the hands of the enemies of his country, and they compel him, by a just fear of death, to fight against it.

Implied coercion exists where a person is legally under subjection to another, and is induced, in consequence of such subjection, to do an act contrary to his will. See "Duress."

COEXECUTOR. One who is executor with one or more others. See "Executor."

COFFERER OF THE QUEEN'S (or **king's) household.** In English law. A principal officer of the royal establishment, next under the controller, who, in the counting-house, and elsewhere, had a special charge and oversight of the other officers, whose wages he paid. Wharton.

COFRADIA. The congregation or brotherhood entered into by several persons for the purpose of performing pious works. No society of this kind can be lawfully formed without license from the king and the bishop of the diocese.

COGITATIONIS POENAM NEMO PATItur. No one is punished for his thoughts. Broom, Leg. Max. (3d London Ed.) 279.

COGNATES. In civil and Scotch law. Relations through females. 1 Mackeld. Civ. Law, 137; Bell, Dict.

COGNATI. In civil law. Collateral heirs through females; relations in the line of the mother. 2 Bl. Comm. 235.

The term is not used in the civil law as it now prevails in France. In the common law it has no technical sense; but as a word of discourse in English it signifies, generally, allied by blood, related in origin, of the same family.

COGNATION. In civil law. Signifies generally the kindred which exists between two persons who are united by ties of blood or family, or both.

Civil cognation is that which proceeds alone from the ties of families, as the kindred between the adopted father and the adopted child.

Mixed cognation is that which unites at the same time the ties of blood and family, as that which exists between brothers the issue of the same lawful marriage. Inst. 3. 6; Dig. 38. 10.

Natural cognation is that which is alone formed by ties of blood. Such is the kindred of those who owe their origin to an illicit connection, either in relation to their ascendants or collaterals.

COGNISANCE. See "Cognizance."

COGNITIO.

——**In Old English Law.** The acknowledgment of a fine; the certificate of such acknowledgment.

Cognizance or jurisdiction. Bracton, fol. 302b.

——**In the Roman Law.** The judicial examination or hearing of a cause. Plin. Epist. vii. 33.

COGNITIONIBUS MITTENDIS. An obsolete writ requiring a justice or other qualified person, who has taken a fine and neglects to certify it in the court of common pleas, to do so.

COGNITIONIS CAUSAE (Lat.) For the purpose of ascertaining. In Scotch practice. A name given to a judgment or decree pronounced by a court, ascertaining the amount of a debt against the estate of a deceased landed proprietor, on cause shown, or after due investigation. Bell, Dict.

COGNITOR.

——**In Old English Law.** One who acknowledges.

——**In Roman Law.** An advocate or defender in a private cause; one who defended the cause of a person who was present. Brissonius; Calv. Lex.

COGNIZANCE, CONUSANCE, or **COGNIsance** (Lat. *cognitio,* recognition, knowledge). Acknowledgment; recognition, jurisdiction; judicial power; hearing a matter judicially.

——**In Pleading.** The answer of the defendant in an action of replevin who is not entitled to the distress of goods which are the subject of the action, acknowledging the taking, and justifying it as having been done by the command of one who is so entitled. Lawes, Pl. 35, 36; 4 Bouv. Inst. note 3571. An acknowledgment made by the deforciant, in levying a fine, that the lands in question are the right of the complainant. 2 Sharswood, Bl. Comm. 350.

——**Cognizance of Pleas.** Jurisdiction of causes. A privilege granted by the king to a city or town to hold pleas within the same. Termes de la Ley. It is in frequent use among the older writers on English law in this latter sense, but is seldom used, if at all, in America, except in its more general meaning. The universities of Cambridge and Oxford possess this franchise Willes, 233; 1 Sid. 103; 11 East, 543; 1 W. Bl. 454; 10 Mod. 126; 3 Sharswood, Bl. Comm. 298.

——**Claim of Cognizance** (or **Conusance**). An intervention by a third person, demanding judicature in the cause against the plaintiff, who has chosen to commence his action out of claimant's court. 2 Wils. 409; 2 Sharswood, Bl. Comm. 350, note.

It is a question of jurisdiction between the two courts (Fortesque, 157; 5 Viner, Abr. 588), and not between the plaintiff and defendant, as in the case of plea to the jurisdiction, and must be demanded by the party entitled to conusance, or by his representative, and not by the defendant or his attorney (1 Chit. Pl. 403).

There are three sorts of conusance: *tenere placita,* which does not oust another court of its jurisdiction, but only creates a concurrent one. *Cognitio placitorum,* when the plea is commenced in one court, of which conusance belongs to another. A conusance of exclusive jurisdiction; as, that no other court shall hold plea, etc. Hardr. 509; Bac. Abr. "Courts" (D).

COGNIZEE. The party to whom a fine was levied. 2 Bl. Comm. 351.

COGNIZOR. In old conveyancing. The party levying a fine. 2 Bl. Comm. 350, 351.

COGNOMEN (Lat.) A family name.

The *praenomen* among the Romans distinguished the person, the *nomen* the gens, or all the kindred descended from a remote common stock through males, while the *cognomen* denoted the particular family. The *agnomen* was added on account of some barticular event, as a further distinction. Thus, in the designation Publius Cornelius Scipio Africanus, Publius is the *praenomen*, Cornelius is the *nomen*, Scipio the *cognomen*, and Africanus the *agnomen*. Vicat. These several terms occur frequently in the Roman laws. See Cas. temp. Hardw. 286; 6 Coke, 65; 1 Tayl. (N. C.) 148.

COGNOVI ACTIONEM (Lat.) He has confessed the action. *Cognovit* alone is in common use with the same significance.

——**In Pleading.** A written confession of an action by the defendant, subscribed, but not sealed, and authorizing the plaintiff to sign judgment and issue execution, usually for a sum named.

It is given after the action is brought, to save expense, and differs from a warrant of attorney, which is given before the commencement of any action, and is under seal. 3 Chanc. Prac. 664; 3 Bouv. Inst. 3229.

COHABIT. (Lat. *con* and *habere.*) To live together in the same house, claiming to be married. The word does not include in its signification, necessarily, the occupying the same bed (1 Hagg. Consist. 144; 4 Paige, Ch. [N. Y.] 425; 116 U. S. 55), though the word is popularly, and sometimes in statutes, used in this latter sense (20 Mo. 210; Bish. Mar. & Div. § 506, note). It does not include mere sexual intercourse, without a habitual dwelling together. 36 Ark. 84; 10 Mass. 153.

To live together in the same house. Used without reference to the relation of the parties to each other as husband and wife, or otherwise. Used of sisters or other members of the same family, or of persons not members of the same family, occupying the same house. 2 Vern. 323; Bish. Mar. & Div. 506, note.

COHAEREDES, or **COHAERES.** Coheirs; a term applies to coparceners who constitute, as it were, but one heir or body. Bracton, fols. 76b, 67b.

COHAEREDES UNA PERSONA CENSENTUR, propter unitatem juris quod habent. Coheirs are deemed as one person, on account of the unity of right which they possess. Co. Litt. 163.

COHUAGIUM. A tribute made by those who meet promiscuously in a market or fair. Du Cange.

COIF. A headdress.

In England there are certain serjeants at law who are called serjeants of the coif, from the lawn coif they wear on their heads under their thin caps when they are admitted to that order. It was anciently worn as a distinguishing badge. Spelman.

COJUDICES (Lat.) In old English law. Associate judges having equality of power with others.

COLD-WATER ORDEAL. The trial which was anciently used for the common sort of people, who, having a cord tied about them under their arms, were cast into a river. If they sank to the bottom until they were drawn up, which was in a very short time, then were they held guiltless; but such as did remain upon the water were held culpable, being, as they said, of the water rejected. Wharton.

COLIBERTUS. One who, holding in free socage, was obliged to do certain services for the lord. A middle class of tenants between servile and free, who held their freedom of tenure on condition of performing certain services. Said to be the same as the *conditionales*. Cowell.

COLLATERAL (Lat. *con*, with, *latus*, the side). That which is by the side, and not the direct line; that which is additional to or beyond a thing.

COLLATERAL ACT. In old practice. The name "collateral act" was given to any act (except the payment of money) for the performance of which a bond, recognizance, etc., was given as security.

COLLATERAL ANCESTORS. A phrase sometimes used to designate uncles and aunts, and other ascending collateral relatives, who are not strictly ancestors.

COLLATERAL ASSURANCE. That which is made over and above the deed itself.

COLLATERAL CONSANGUINITY. That relationship which subsists between persons who have the same ancestors, but not the same descendants; who do not descend one from the other. 2 Bl. Comm. 203.

The essential fact of consanguinity (common ancestral blood) is the same in lineal and collateral consanguinity, but the relationship is aside from the direct line. Thus, father, son, and grandson are lineally related; uncle and nephew, collaterally.

COLLATERAL DESCENT. Descent in a transverse or zigzag line, *i. e.*, up through the common ancestor, and then down from him; descent to collaterals.

COLLATERAL ESTOPPEL. The collateral determination of a question by a court having general jurisdiction of the subject. See 26 Vt. 209.

COLLATERAL FACTS. Facts not directly connected with the issue or matter in dispute. Such as afford no reasonable inference as to the principal fact. Greenl. Ev. § 52.

COLLATERAL IMPEACHMENT. A term frequently used in respect of the conclusiveness of judgments, the general rule being that a judgment of a court of record cannot be collaterally impeached, *i. e.*, in an action other than that in which it was rendered, except upon proof of fraud or want of jurisdiction.

COLLATERAL ISSUE. An issue taken upon some matter aside from the general issue in the case. Thus, for example, a plea by the criminal that he is not the person attainted, when an interval exists between attainder and execution, a plea in abatement, and other such pleas, each raise a collateral issue. 4 Bl. Comm. 396. And see 4 Bl. Comm. 338.

COLLATERAL KINSMEN. Those who descend from one and the same common ancestor, but not from one another. Thus, brothers and sisters are collateral to each other; the uncle and nephew are collateral kinsmen, and cousins are the same. All kinsmen are either "lineal" or "collateral."

COLLATERAL LIMITATION. A limitation in the conveyance of an estate, giving an interest for a specified period, but making the right of enjoyment depend upon some collateral event, as, an estate to A. till B. shall go to Rome. Park, Dower, 163; 4 Kent, Comm. 128; 1 Washb. Real Prop. 215.

COLLATERAL PROMISE. A promise is collateral if another is the primary or principal debtor, and the relations of debtor and creditor remain unchanged both as to the right and the remedy, and no trust is created by the transaction. 17 Ill. 507; 82 Ill. App. 308.

COLLATERAL SECURITY. A separate obligation attached to another contract to guaranty its performance. The transfer of property or of other contracts to insure the performance of a principal engagement. 38 Ga. 292; 9 Iowa 331.

The property or securities thus conveyed are also called collateral securities. 1 Powell, Mortg. 393; 2 Powell, Mortg. 666, note 871; 3 Powell, Mortg. 944, 1001.

COLLATERAL UNDERTAKING. A contract based upon a pre-existing debt, or other liability, and including a promise to pay, made by a third person having immediate respect to and founded upon such debt or liability, without any new consideration moving to him. 82 Ill. App. 308.

COLLATERAL WARRANTY. Warranty as to an estate made by one who was ancestor to the heir thereof, either actually or by implication of law, in respect to other property, but who could not have been so in respect to the estate in question.

Warranty made where the heir's title to the land neither was nor could have been derived from the warranting ancestor. Termes de la Ley; 2 Bl. Comm. 301; 4 Kent, Comm. 469.

COLLATERALES ET SOCII. The former title of masters in chancery.

COLLATIO BONORUM. A collation of goods. See "Collation."

COLLATIO SIGNORUM. The ancient mode of testing the genuineness of a seal, by comparing it with another known to be genuine. Bracton, fols. 389b, 398b; Fleta, lib. 6, c. 34, § 5.

COLLATION.

——In Civil Law. The bringing together of property into a common fund; hotchpot. 2 Bl. Comm. 517. Particularly applied to the supposed or real return to the mass of the succession, which an heir makes of the property he received in advance of his share, or otherwise, in order that such property may be divided together with the other effects of the succession. Civ. Code La. art. 1305.

——In Ecclesiastical Law. The act by which the bishop who has the bestowing of a benefice gives it to an incumbent.

——In Practice. The comparison of a copy with its original, in order to ascertain its correctness and conformity. The report of the officer who made the comparison is also called a collation.

COLLATION OF SEALS. When, upon the same label, one seal was set on the back or reverse of the other. Wharton.

COLLATION TO A BENEFICE (Law Lat. *collatio beneficii.*) In English ecclesiastical law. The conferring or bestowing of a benefice by the bishop, where he has himself the advowson, or right of patronage, and which single act of collation effects all that is done in common case by the acts of presentation and institution. 2 Bl. Comm. 22. Or, in other words, the presentation and institution are one and the same act, and, taken together, are called a "collation." 1 Bl. Comm. 391; 1 Wooddeson, Lect. 193. The advowson, in such cases, is termed an "advowson collative." 2 Bl. Comm. 22.

COLLATIONE FACTA UNI POST MORtem alterius. A writ directed to justices of the common pleas, commanding them to issue their writ to the bishop, for the admission of a clerk in the place of another presented by the crown, where there had been a demise of the crown during a suit; for judgment once passed for the king's clerk, and, he dying before admittance, the king may bestow his presentation on another. Reg. Orig. 31.

COLLATIONE HEREMITAGII. In old English law. A writ whereby the king conferred the keeping of an hermitage upon a clerk. Reg. Orig. 303, 308.

COLLECTOR. One appointed to receive taxes or other impositions, as collector of taxes, collector of militia fines, etc. A person appointed by a private person to collect the credits due him.

COLLECTOR OF THE CUSTOMS. An officer of the United States, appointed for the term of four years, but removable at the pleasure of the president. Act May 15, 1820, § 1; 3 Story, U. S. Laws, 1790.

The duties of a collector of the customs are to receive the entries of all ships or vessels, and of the goods, wares, and merchandise imported in them, estimate the amount of duties payable thereupon, and receive all moneys paid for duties. Act March 2, 1779, § 21; 1 Story, U. S. Laws, 590.

COLLEGA. In the civil law. A colleague; an associate; one having the same power with another, *qui sunt ejusdem potestatis.* Dig. 50. 16. 173.

COLLEGATARIUS. (Lat.; Eng. colegatory). In the civil law. A colegatee. Inst. 2. 20. 8.

COLLEGE. An organized collection or assemblage of persons; a civil corporation, society, or company, having, in general, some literary object.

The assemblage of the cardinals at Rome is called a "college." The body of presidential electors is called the "electoral college," although the whole body never come together.

An educational institution of the highest class.

COLLEGIA. The guild of a trade.

COLLEGIALITER. In a corporate capacity. 2 Kent, Comm. 296.

COLLEGIATE CHURCH. In English ecclesiastical law. A church built and endowed for a society or body corporate of a dean or other president, and secular priests, as canons or prebendaries in the said church, such as the churches of Westminster, Windsor, and others. Cowell.

COLLEGIUM (Lat. *colligere*, to collect). In civil law. A society or assemblage of those of the same rank or honor; an army; a company, in popular phrase; the whole order of bishops. Du Cange.

Collegium illicitum is one which abused its right, or assembled for any other purpose than that expressed in its charter.

Collegium licitum is an assemblage or society of men united for some useful purpose or business, with power to act like a single individual.

All *collegia* were *illicita* which were not ordained by a decree of the senate or of the emperor. 2 Kent, Comm. 269.

COLLEGIUM ADMIRALITATIS. The college or society of the admiralty. See a description in Locc. de Jur. Mar. lib. 1, c. 2.

COLLEGIUM EST SOCIETAS PLURIUM corporum simul habitantium. A college is a society of several persons dwelling together. Jenk. Cent. Cas. 229.

COLLIGENDUM BONA DEFUNCTI. See "Ad Colligendum, etc."

COLLISION. In maritime law. The act of ships or vessels striking together, or of one vessel running against or foul of another.

As ordinarily used, it includes "allision" (*q. v.*)

COLLISTRIGIUM. The pillory.

COLLITIGANT. A litigant.

COLLOBIUM. A hood or covering for the shoulders, formerly worn by serjeants at law. Spelman.

COLLOCATION. In French law. The act by which the creditors of an estate are arranged in the order in which they are to be paid according to law.

The order in which the creditors are placed is also called collocation. 2 Low. (U. S.) 9, 139.

COLLOQUIUM. In actions for libel or slander, the averment that the language in question was published or uttered of and concerning the plaintiff. It is, however, frequently used in practice to denote both the inducement (*q. v.*), and the colloquim proper. Towns. Libel & Slander, § 323.

It is to be distinguished from "innuendo," which is an explanation by reference to that which has been already sufficiently explained, and cannot extend the meaning of words unless there be something before averred, to which the innuendo may refer. 5 Johns. (N. Y.) 220.

COLLUSION. An agreement between two or more persons to defraud a person of his rights by the forms of law, or to obtain an object forbidden by law.

The act of married persons in procuring a divorce by mutual consent, whether by the preconcerted commission, by one, of a matrimonial offense, or by failure, in pursuance of agreement, to defend divorce proceedings. It is distinguished from "connivance," which is the abetting by a spouse of a matrimonial offense in order to procure a divorce therefor, but without previous agreement as to its commission. Nelson, Div. & Sep. § 500.

COLLYBISTA. In the civil law. A money changer.

COLLYBUM. In the civil law. Exchange, *cambium.* Grotius de Jure Belli, lib. 2, c. 12, § 3, par. 4.

COLNE, or CONE. In Saxon and old English law. An account or calculation. 1 Reeve, Hist. Eng. Law, 284, note.

COLONIAL LAWS. The laws of a colony.

——**In the United States.** The term is used to designate the body of law in force in the colonies of America at the time of the commencement of our independence, which was, in general, the common law of England, with such modifications as the colonial experience had introduced. The colonial law is thus a transition state, through which our present law is derived from the English common law.

——**In England.** The term "Colonial law" is used with reference to the present colonies of that realm.

COLONUS (Lat.) In civil law. A freeman of inferior rank, corresponding with the Saxon ceorl, and the German rural slaves.

COLONY. A union of citizens or subjects who have left their country to people another, and remain subject to the mother-country. 3 Wash. C. C. (U. S.) 287.

The country occupied by the colonists.

A colony differs from a possession or a dependency.

COLOR. In pleading. An apparent but legally insufficient ground of action admitted to subsist in the opposite party by the pleading of one of the parties to an action. 3 Sharswood, Bl. Comm. 309; 4 Barn. & C. 547; 1 Moore & P. 307. To give color is to give the plaintiff credit for having an apparent or *prima facie* right of action, independent of the matter introduced to destroy it, in order to introduce new matter in avoidance of the declaration. It was necessary that all pleadings in confession and avoidance should give color. See 3 Sharswood, Bl. Comm. 309, note; 1 Chit. Pl. 531.

Express color is a feigned matter, pleaded by the defendant, from which the plaintiff seems to have a good cause, whereas he has in truth only an appearance or color of cause. Bac. Abr. "Trespass" (I 4); 1 Chit. Pl. 530. It was not allowed in the plaintiff to traverse the colorable right thus given, and it thus became necessary to answer the plea on which the defendant intended to rely.

Implied color is that which arises from the nature of the defense, as where the defense consists of matter of law, the facts being admitted, but their legal sufficiency denied, by matters alleged in the plea. 1 Chit. Pl. 528; Steph. Pl. 206.

By giving color, the defendant could remove the decision of the case from before a jury, and introduce matter in a special plea, which would otherwise oblige him to plead the general issue. 3 Bl. Comm. 309.

The colorable right must be plausible, or afford a supposititious right, such as might induce an unlearned person to imagine it sufficient, and yet it must be in legal strictness inadequate to defeat the defendant's title as shown in the plea. Comyn, Dig. "Pleading;" Keilw. 1036; 1 Chit. Pl. 531; 4 Dane, Abr. 552; Archb. Pl. 211.

COLOR OF AUTHORITY. Authority derived by an election or appointment, however irregular or informal, so that the incumbent is not a mere volunteer. 248 Ill. 229.

COLOR OF OFFICE (Lat. *colore officii*). A pretense of official right to do an act made by one who has no such right. 9 East, 364. It implies an illegal claim of authority to do an act by virtue of one's office (23 Wend. [N. Y.] 606; 1 N. Y. 365; 16 N. Y. 439, 442), and is distinguished from by "virtue of office," implying lawful power (4 N. Y. 173).

COLOR OF TITLE. That which in appearance is title but which in reality is no title. 248 Ill. 229; 18 How. (U. S.) 50; 56 Mich. 337.

Anything in writing connected with the title which serves to define the extent of the claim. 70 Ga. 809.

A deed void on its face is not color of title. 27 Minn. 449; 2 Pet. (U. S.) 241; 7 Wend. (N. Y.) 152. But see, contra, 94 Ala. 135; 68 Iowa, 507. But defects in the execution (112 N. C. 223; 27 Ill. 224), or lack of title in the grantor (53 N. Y. 287; 71 Ill. 38), will not impair the effect of a deed to give color of title.

COLORABLE ALTERATION. An alteration made only for the purpose of evading the law,—of copyright, for instance.

COLORABLE IMITATION. As applied to trademark *(q. v.)*, colorable imitation is such a close or ingenious imitation as to be calculated to deceive ordinary persons. L. R. 5 H. L., at page 519.

COLORABLE PLEADING. The practice of giving color in pleading. 3 Reeve, Hist. Eng. Law, 438.

COLORE OFFICII. Color of office.

COLPINDACH. In old Scotch law. A young beast or cow, of the age of one or two years; in later times called a "cowdach," or "quoyach."

Skene says it is an Irish word, and properly signifies "foot follower."

COMBARONES. In old English law. Fellow barons; fellow citizens. The citizens or freemen of the Cinque Ports, being anciently called "barons"; the term "combarones" is used in this sense in a grant of Henry III. to the barons of the port of Fevresham. Cowell.

COMBAT. The form of a forcible encounter between two or more persons or bodies of men; an engagement or battle; a duel.

COMBATERRAE. A valley or piece of low ground between two hills. Kennett, Par. Ant.

COMBINATION.

——**In Criminal Law.** A union of men for the purpose of violating the law; a conspiracy *(q. v.)*

——**In Patent Law.** A union of different elements. A patent may be taken out for a new combination of existing machines. 2 Mason (U. S.) 112.

COMBINATION COVERAGE. An expression used in insurance meaning the covering of all employees against the Workmen's Compensation Act or any common-law liability prior to the Compensation Act. 195 Ill. App. 268.

COMBUSTIO. In old English law. The punishment of burning.

COMBUSTIO DOMORUM. Arson. 4 Bl. Comm. 272.

COMBUSTIO PECUNIAE (Law Lat.) In old English law. The burning (that is, melting) of money; the old way of trying mixed and corrupt money, by melting it down upon payments into the exchequer. Cowell.

COMES (Lat. *comes,* a companion). An earl; a companion, attendant, or follower.

COMINUS. Hand-to-hand; in personal contact.

COMITAS (Lat.) Courtesy; comity; an indulgence or favor granted another nation, as a mere matter of indulgence, without any claim of right made.

COMITATU COMMISSO. A writ or commission, whereby a sheriff is authorized to enter upon the charges of a county. Reg. Orig. 295.

COMITATU ET CASTRO COMMISSO. A writ by which the charge of a county, together with the keeping of a castle, is committed to the sheriff.

COMITATUS (Lat. from *comes*). A county; a shire; the portion of the country under the government of a *comes* or count. 1 Bl. Comm. 116.

An earldom. Earls and counts were originally the same as the *comitates.* 1 Ld. Raym. 13.

The county court, of great dignity among the Saxons. 1 Spence, Eq. Jur. 42, 66.

COMITES. Persons who are attached to a public minister. As to their privileges, see 1 Dall. (Pa.) 117; Baldw. (U. S.) 240. See "Ambassador."

COMITES PALEYS. Counts or earls palatine; those who had the government of a county palatine. Bracton, fol. 122b. Other copies of Bracton have it *comites palentynes.*

COMITIA (Lat.) The public assemblies of the Roman people, at which all the most important business of the state was transacted, including, in some cases, even the trial of persons charged with the commission of crime. Anthon, Rom. Ant. 51. The votes of all citizens were equal in the *comitiae.* 1 Kent, Comm. 518.

——**Comitia Calata.** A session of the *comitia curiata* for the purposes of adrogation, the confirmation of wills, and the adoption by an heir of the sacred rites which followed the inheritance.

——**Comitia Centuria,** or **Comitia Majora.** An assemblage of the people voting by centuries. The people acting in this form elected their own officers, and exercised an extensive jurisdiction for the trial of crimes. Anthon, Rom. Ant. 52.

——**Comitia Curiata.** An assemblage of the *populus* (the original burgesses) by tribes. In these assemblies no one of the *plebs* could vote. They were held for the purpose of confirming matters acted on by the senate, for electing certain high officers, and for carrying out certain religious observances.

——**Comitia Tributa.** Assemblies to create certain inferior magistrates, elect priests, make laws, and hold trials. Their power was increased very materially subsequently to their first creation, and the range of subjects acted on became much more extensive than at first. Anthon, Rom. Ant. 62; 1 Kent, Comm. 518.

COMITISSA. In old English law. A countess; an earl's wife. Towns. Pl. 149.

COMITIVA (Law Lat. from *comes, q. v.*) In old English law. The dignity and office of a *comes* (count or earl); the same with what was afterwards called *comitatus.* Spelman.

Used in the Register, in the sense of *comitatus,* a train, suite, following, attendance, or household. Reg. Orig. 23, 24.

COMITY. Courtesy; a disposition to accommodate.

Courts of justice in one state will, out of comity, enforce the laws of another state, when by such enforcement they will not violate their own laws, or inflict an injury on some one of their own citizens; as, for example, the discharge of a debtor under the insolvent laws of one state will be respected in another state, where there is a reciprocity in this respect.

COMMANDERY, or **COMMANDRY** (Lat. *praeceptoria.*) In English law. An establishment belonging to the priory of St. John of Jerusalem, consisting usually of a manor, or chief messuage, with lands and tenements appertaining thereto, under the government of an officer called a "commander," who received a part of the income thence arising for his own use, and accounted for the rest. Cowell; Termes de la Ley.

COMMANDITAIRES. Special partners; partners *en commandite.* See "Commandite."

COMMANDITE. In French law. A partnership in which some furnish money, and others furnish their skill and labor in place of capital. A special or limited partnership.

Those who embark capital in such a partnership are bound only to the extent of the capital so invested. Guyot, Rep. Univ.

COMMANDMENT.

——**In Practice.** An act of authority, as of a magistrate or judge, in committing a person to prison. Cowell.

——**In Old Criminal Law.** The act or offense of one who commands another to transgress the law, or do anything contrary to law, as theft, murder, or the like. Bracton, fols. 138, 139; Termes de la Ley; St. Westminster I. c. 14. Particularly applied to the act of an accessory before the fact, in inciting, procuring, setting on, or stirring up another to do the fact or act. 2 Inst. 128.

COMMARCHIO. A boundary, or border; a common boundary.

COMMENDA.

——**In French Law.** The delivery of a benefice to one who cannot hold the legal title, to keep and manage it for a time limited, and render an account of the proceeds. Guyot. Rep. Univ.

——**In Mercantile Law.** An association in which the management of the property was intrusted to individuals. Troubat, Lim. Partn. c. 3, § 27.

COMMENDA EST FACULTAS RECIPIendi et retinendi beneficium contra jus positivum a suprema potestate. A commendam is the power of receiving and retaining a benefice contrary to positive law, by supreme authority. Moore, 905.

COMMENDAM.

——**In Ecclesiastical Law.** The appointment of a suitable clerk to hold a void or vacant benefice or church living until a regular pastor be appointed. Hob. 144; Latch, 236.

——**In Louisiana.** A species of limited partnership.

It is formed by a contract, by which one person or partnership agrees to furnish another person or partnership a certain amount, either in property or money, to be employed by the person or partnership to whom it is furnished, in his or their own name or firm, on condition of receiving a share in the profits in the proportion determined by the contract, and of being liable to losses and expenses to the amount furnished, and no more. Civ. Code La. art. 2810. A similar partnership exists in France. Code de Comm. 26, 33; Sirey, 12, pt. 2, p. 25. He who makes this contract is called, in respect to those to whom he makes the advance of capital, a partner *in commendam.* Civ. Code La. art. 2811.

COMMENDATIO. In the civil law. Commendation; praise; that recommendation of his wares by a seller which does not bind him as a warranty.

COMMENDATION. In feudal law. Commendation was where an owner of land placed himself and his land under the protection of a lord, so as to constitute himself his vassal or feudal tenant. Commendation, and the grant of *beneficia* or feuds, were the two principal modes by which the feudal system was established. See 1 Stubbs, Const. Hist. 153.

COMMENDATORS. In ecclesiastical law. Secular persons upon whom ecclesiastical benefices are bestowed. So called because they are commended and intrusted to their oversight. They are merely trustees.

COMMENDATORY. He who holds a church living or preferment in *commendam.* Rapalje & L.

COMMENDATORY LETTERS. Letters written by one bishop to another on behalf of any of the clergy, or others of his diocese traveling thither, that they may be received among the faithful, or that the clerk may be promoted, or necessaries administered to others, etc. Wharton.

COMMENDATUS. In feudal law. One who, by voluntary homage, put himself under the protection of a superior lord. Cowell; Spelman.

COMMERCE. The exchange of property, including the usual agencies of communication and transportation to effect the exchange, and extending to the means employed to move the property involved and the persons making the contract. 223 Ill. 590.

The various agreements which have for their object facilitating the exchange of the products of the earth or the industry of man, with an intent to realize a profit. Pardessus, Dr. Com. note 1. Any reciprocal agreements between two persons, by which one delivers to the other a thing, which the latter accepts, and for which he pays a consideration. If the consideration be money, it is called a "sale;" if any other thing than money, it is called "exchange" or "barter." Domat, Dr. Pub. liv. 1, tit. 7, § 1, note 2.

Congress has power, by the constitution, to regulate commerce with foreign nations and among the several states, and with the

Indian tribes. 1 Kent, Comm. 431; Story, Const. § 1052 et seq. The sense in which the word "commerce" is used in the constitution seems not only to include traffic, but intercourse and navigation (Story, Const. § 1057; 9 Wheat. [U. S.] 190, 191, 215, 229; 12 Wheat. [U. S.] 419; 102 U. S. 691; 4 Biss. [U. S.] 156; 31 Iowa, 187), but only such intercourse as consists in trade or traffic (1 Stew. & P. [Ala.] 327).

COMMERCIA BELLI. Compacts entered into by belligerent nations to secure a temporary and limited peace. 1 Kent, Comm. 159.

Contracts made between citizens of hostile nations in time of war. 1 Kent, Comm. 104.

COMMERCIAL LAW. A phrase employed to denote those branches of the law which relate to the rights of property and relations of persons engaged in commerce.

This term denotes more than the phrase "maritime law," which is sometimes used as synonymous, but which more strictly relates to shipping and its incidents. See "Law Merchant."

COMMERCIAL PAPER. Bills, notes, checks, etc.; negotiable instruments.

COMMERCIAL RAILROADS. Commercial railroads embrace all railroads for general freight and passenger traffic between one town and another. 263 Ill. 206; 227 Ill. 496; 216 Ill. 528.

COMMERCIUM (Lat.) In the civil law. Commerce; business; trade; dealings in the way of purchase and sale; a contract. Dig. 49. 15. 16.

The right to purchase or sell. Inst. 3. 20 2.

COMMERCIUM JURE GENTIUM COMmune esse debet, et non in monopolium et privatum paucorum quaestum convertendum. Commerce, by the law of nations, ought to be common, and not to be converted into a monopoly and the private gain of a few. Coke, 3d Inst. *181, in marg.

COMMINALTY (Law Fr.) The commonalty or the people. St. Westminster I. 1, pr.

COMMINATORIUM (from *commonari*, to threaten). In old practice. A clause sometimes added at the end of writs, admonishing the sheriff to be faithful in executing them. Bracton, fol. 398.

COMMISE. In old French law. Forfeiture; the forfeiture of a fief; the penalty attached to the ingratitude of a vassal. Guyot, Inst. Feud. c. 12.

COMMISSARIA LEX. A principle of the Roman law relative to the forfeiture of contracts. It was not unusual to restrict a sale upon credit, by a clause in the agreement that if the buyer should fail to make due payment the seller might rescind the sale. In the meantime, however, the property was the buyer's, and at his risk. A debtor and his pledgee might also agree that, if the debtor did not pay at the day fixed, the pledge should become the absolute property of the creditor. 2 Kent, Comm. 583. This was abolished by law of Constantine. Code, 8. 35. 3.

COMMISSARY.

——**In Military Law.** An officer whose principal duties are to supply an army, or some portion thereof, with provisions.

——**In English Ecclesiastical Law.** A title formerly applied to an officer who exercised spiritual jurisdiction in distant places of the bishop's diocese; being specially ordained for the purpose of supplying the bishop's jurisdiction and office in the outplaces of his diocese, or else in such places as were peculiar to the bishop, and exempted from the jurisdiction of the archdeacon. Termes de la Ley; Cowell; Lyndewode, Prov. c. 1.

COMMISSARY COURT. In Scotch law. A court of general ecclesiastical jurisdiction. It was held before four commissioners, appointed by the crown from among the faculty of advocates. It had a double jurisdiction: First, that exercised within a certain district; second, another, universal, by which it reviewed the sentences of inferior commissioners, and confirmed the testaments of those dying abroad, or dying in the country without having an established domicile. Bell, Dict. It has been abrogated, its jurisdiction in matters of confirmation being given to the sheriff, and the jurisdiction as to marriage and divorce to the court of session. Paterson, Comp. See 4 Geo. IV. c. 47; 1 Wm. IV. c. 69; 6 & 7 Wm. IV. c. 41; 13 & 14 Vict. c. 36.

COMMISSION (Lat. *commissio;* from *committere,* to intrust to).

An undertaking without reward to do something for another, with respect to a thing bailed. Rutherforth, Inst. 105.

A body of persons authorized to act in a certain matter. 5 Barn. & C. 850.

The act of perpetrating an offense. An instrument issued by a court of justice, or other competent tribunal, to authorize a person to take depositions, or do any other act by authority of such court or tribunal, is called a "commission." For a form of a commission to take depositions, see Gresl. Eq. Ev. 72.

Letters patent granted by the government, under the public seal, to a person appointed to an office, giving him authority to perform the duties of his office. The commission is not the appointment, but only evidence of it, and, as soon as it is signed and sealed, vests the office in the appointee. 1 Cranch (U. S.) 137; 2 Nott & McC. (S. C.) 357; 1 McCord (S. C.) 233, 238. See 1 Pet. (U. S.) 194; 2 Sumn. (U. S.) 299; 8 Conn. 109; 1 Pa. St. 297; 2 Const. (S. C.) 696; 2 Tyler (Vt.) 235.

——**In Common Law.** A sum allowed, usually a certain per cent upon the value of the property involved, as compensation to a servant or agent for services performed. See "Commissions."

——**Of Array.** This commission issued to send into every county officers to muster or set in military order the inhabitants. The introduction of commissions of lieutenancy, which contained, in substance, the same powers as these commissions, superseded them. 2 Steph. Comm. (7th Ed.) 582.

——**Of Assize.** In English practice. A commission which formerly issued from the king, appointing certain persons as commissioners or judges of assize to hold the assizes in association with discreet knights during those years in which the justices in eyre did not come.

Other commissions were added to this, which has finally fallen into complete disuse. See "Courts of Assize and Nisi Prius."

——**Of Bankrupt.** A commission or authority formerly granted by the lord chancellor to such discreet persons as he should think proper, to examine the bankrupt in all matters relating to his trade and effects, and to perform various other important duties connected with bankruptcy matters. These persons were thence called "commissioners of bankruptcy," and had in most respects the powers and privileges of judges in their own courts; but regularly constituted courts and judges in bankruptcy have now superseded such commissions and commissioners. Brown.

——**Of Charitable Uses.** This commission issues out of chancery to the bishop and others, where lands given to charitable uses are misemployed, or there is any fraud or dispute concerning them, to inquire of and redress the same, etc. 43 Eliz. c. 4. Wharton.

——**Of Delegates.** When any sentence was given in any ecclesiastical cause by the archbishop, this commission, under the great seal, was directed to certain persons, usually lords, bishops, and judges of the law, to sit and hear an appeal of the same to the king, in the court of chancery; but latterly the judicial committee of the privy council has supplied the place of this commission. Brown.

——**Of Lunacy.** A writ issued out of chancery, or such court as may have jurisdiction of the case, directed to a proper officer, to inquire whether a person named therein is a lunatic or not. 1 Bouv. Inst. Note 382 et seq.

——**Of Partition.** Formerly a partition was fected in England by issuing a commission to commissioners, to divide the property, and, on their return coming in, the parties were ordered to execute mutual conveyances to carry out the division. Haynes, Eq. 153. Similar commissions are still issued in some of the states. See "Partition."

——**Of Rebellion.** In English law. A writ formerly issued out of chancery to compel an attendance. It was abolished by the order of August 8, 1841.

——**Of Review.** In English ecclesiastical law. A commission formerly sometimes granted in extraordinary cases, to revise the sentence of the court of delegates. 3 Bl. Comm. 67. Now out of use; the privy council being substituted for the court of delegates, as the great court of appeal in all ecclesiastical causes. 3 Steph. Comm. 432.

——**Of the Peace.** In English law. A commission from the crown, appointing certain persons therein named, jointly and severally, to keep the peace, etc. Justices of the peace are always appointed by special commission under the great seal, the form of which was settled by all the judges, A. D. 1590, and continues with little alteration to this day. 1 Bl. Comm. 351; 3 Steph. Comm. 39, 40.

——**Of Treaty with Foreign Princes.** Leagues and arrangements made between states and kingdoms, by their ambassadors and ministers, for the mutual advantage of the kingdoms in alliance. Wharton.

——**Of Unlivery.** In an action in the English admiralty division, where it is necessary to have the cargo in a ship unladen in order to have it appraised, a commission of unlivery is issued and executed by the marshal. Williams & B. Adm. Jur. 233.

——**To Take Answers in Equity.** When a defendant in a suit lived more than twenty miles from London, there might have been a commission granted to take his answer in the country, where the commissioners administered to him the usual oath, and then the answer being sealed up, either one of the commissioners carried it up to court or it was sent by a messenger, who swore that he received it from one of the commissioners, and that the same had not been opened or altered since he received it. But latterly such an answer might be sworn in the country before any solicitor of the court who has been appointed a commissioner to administer oaths in chancery. The present answer in chancery, and at common law, is a mere affidavit, and is not a pleading. It is sworn anywhere before a solicitor who is a commissioner to administer oaths. Brown.

COMMISSION DAY. In English practice. The opening day of the assizes. Wharton.

COMMISSION DEL CREDERE. See "Del Credere Commission."

COMMISSION MERCHANT. A factor (*q. v.*).

COMMISSIONER OF PATENTS. The title given by law to the head of the patent office bureau.

COMMISSIONERS OF BAIL. Officers appointed by some courts to take recognizances of bail in civil cases.

COMMISSIONERS OF BANKRUPT. In English law. Commissioners appointed under the great seal, and whose duties are to take proof of the petitioning creditor's debt, the trading and act of bankruptcy, to examine the bankrupt in all matters relating to his trade and effects, assign his property to assignees, and to perform various other important duties connected with bankruptcy matters. 1 Bl. Comm. 480-486; Eden, Bankr. Law, 79, et passim.

These commissioners now compose permanent courts of bankruptcy. St. 1 & 2 Wm. IV. c. 56; 5 & 6 Wm. IV. c. 29, § 21; 5 & 6 Vict. c. 122; 2 Steph. Comm. 199, 200; 3 Steph. Comm. 425, 426.

COMMISSIONERS OF HIGHWAYS. Officers having certain powers and duties concerning the highways within the limits of their jurisdiction. They are usually three in number. In some of the states they are county officers, and their jurisdiction is co-extensive with the county. In others, as in New York, Michigan, Illinois, and Wisconsin, they are town or township officers. They have power to establish, alter, and vacate highways, and it is their duty to cause them to be kept in repair.

COMMISSIONERS OF SEWERS.

——In English Law. A court of record of special jurisdiction in England.

It is a temporary tribunal, erected by virtue of a commission under the great seal, which formerly was granted *pro re nata* at the pleasure of the crown, but now at the discretion and nomination of the lord chancellor, lord treasurer, and chief justices, pursuant to the statute of sewers. 23 Hen. VIII. c. 5. Its jurisdiction is to overlook the repairs of the banks and walls of the seacoast and navigable rivers and the streams communicating therewith, and is confined to such county or particular district as the commission shall expressly name. The commissioners may take order for the removal of any annoyances, or the safeguard and conservation of the sewers within their commission, either according to the laws and customs of Romney Marsh, or otherwise, at their own discretion. They are also to assess and collect taxes for such repairs and for the expenses of the commission. They may proceed with the aid of a jury or upon their own view. Consult 7 Anne, c. 10; 4 & 5 Vict. c. 45; 11 & 12 Vict. c. 50; 18 & 19 Vict. c. 120; 3 & 4 Wm. IV. cc. 10, 19-22; 3 Bl. Comm. 73, 74; Crabb, Hist. Eng. Law. 469.

——In American Law. Commissioners have been appointed for the purpose of regulating the flow of water in streams. Their duties are discharged in the different states by county courts, county commissioners, etc.

COMMISSIONS. In practice. Compensation allowed to agents, factors, executors, trustees, receivers, and other persons who manage the affairs of others, in recompense for their services.

COMMITMENT. In practice. The warrant or order by which a court or magistrate directs a ministerial officer to take a person to prison. See 1 Metc. (Mass.) 504.

The act of sending a person to prison by means of such a warrant or order. 9 N. H. 204; 203 Ill. 262.

COMMITTEE. A person or body of persons to whom a matter is committed for superintendence, action, or recommendation.

——In Legislation. One or more members of a legislative body, to whom is specially referred some matter before that body, in order that they may investigate and examine into it, and report to those who delegated this authority to them.

——In Practice. A guardian appointed to take charge of the person or estate of one who has been found to be *non compos*.

COMMITTITUR PIECE. In English law. An instrument in writing, on paper or parchment, which charges a person already in prison, in execution at the suit of the person who arrested him.

COMMIXTION. In civil law. A term used to signify the act by which goods are mixed together.

The commixtion of liquids is called "confusion" (*q. v.*), and that of solids a "mixture." Lec. Elm. §§ 370, 371; Story, Bailm. § 40; 1 Bouv. Inst. note 506.

COMMODATE. In Scotch law. A loan for use. Ersk. Inst. bk. 3, tit. 1, § 20; 1 Bell, Comm. 225.

COMMODATI ACTIO (Lat.) See "Actio Commodatio," etc.

COMMODATO. In Spanish law. A contract by which one person lends gratuitously to another some object not consumable, to be restored to him in kind at a given period.

COMMODATUM. A species of bailment, by which one of the parties binds himself to return to the other certain personal chattels which the latter delivers to him to be used by him without reward; loan for use. Story, Bailm. § 221. See "Bailment."

COMMODITY. Due measure, just proportion (fr. *commodus* that has due measure, fr. *com-modus* measure). 1. The quality of being suitable, convenient, commodious. In this sense no longer used. 2. That which affords convenience, benefit, advantage; a thing that is suitable, convenient, commodious. That which affords advantage or profit. 102 Ia. 608; 162 Mass. 113.

In this sense the word is most commonly applied to things movable, the subjects of trade, merchandise.

The word includes all the movables which are the object of commerce. 29 How. Pr. 492.

"The word 'commodity' * * * is ordinarily used in the commercial sense of any movable and tangible thing that is ordinarily produced or used as the subject of barter or sale." 86 Tex. 265.

But the sense is wide and may be extended to include the privilege or convenience of carrying on a particular business, and thus to include a franchise.

"Commodity" (as in a constitution giving power to tax goods, wares, merchandise and commodities) is a general term, and includes the privilege and convenience of transacting a particular business. 123 Mass. 495; 162 Mass. 121.

COMMODUM EX INJURIA SUA NON habere debet. No man ought to derive any benefit of his own wrong. Jenk. Cent. Cas. 161; Finch, Law, bk. 1, c. 3, note 62.

COMMON. As an adjective,—owned by several; usual; habitual. As a noun,—an incorporeal hereditament, which consists in a profit which one man has in connection with one or more others in the land of another. 12 Serg. & R. (Pa.) 32; 10 Wend. (N. Y.) 647; 11 Johns. (N. Y.) 498; 16 Johns. (N. Y.) 14, 30; 10 Pick. (Mass.) 364; 3 Kent, Comm. 403.

——**Common of Estovers.** The liberty of taking necessary wood, for the use of furniture of a house or farm, from another man's estate. This right is inseparably attached to the house or farm, and is not apportionable. If, therefore, a farm entitled to estovers be divided by the act of the party among several tenants, neither of them can take estovers, and the right is extinguished. 2 Bl. Comm. 34; Plowd. 381; 10 Wend. (N. Y.) 639; 1 Barb. (N. Y.) 592. It is to be distinguished from the right to estovers which a tenant for life has in the estate which he occupies. See "Estovers."

——**Common of Pasture.** The right of feeding one's beasts on another's land. It is either appendant, appurtenant because of vicinage, or in gross.

——**Common of Piscary.** The liberty of fishing in another man's water. 2 Bl. Comm. 34. See "Fishery."

——**Common of Shack.** The right of persons occupying lands lying together in the same common field to turn out their cattle after harvest to feed promiscuously in that field. Wharton; 2 Steph. Comm. 6; 1 Barn. & Ald. 710.

——**Common of Turbary.** The liberty of digging turf in another man's ground. Common of turbary can only be appendant or appurtenant to a house, not to lands, because turves are to be spent in the house. 4 Coke, 37; 3 Atk. 189; Nov. 145; 7 East, 127.

——**Common Appendant.** A right annexed to the possession of land, by which the owner thereof is entitled to feed his beasts on the wastes of the manor. It can only be claimed by prescription, so that it cannot be pleaded by way of custom. 1 Rolle, Abr. 396; 6 Coke, 59.

——**Common Appurtenant.** This differs from common appendant in the following particulars, viz.: It may be claimed by grant or prescription, whereas common appendant can only arise from prescription; it does not arise from any connection of tenure, nor is it confined to arable land, but may be claimed as annexed to any kind of land; it may be not only for beasts usually commonable, such as horses, oxen, and sheep, but likewise for goats, swine, etc.; it may be severed from the land to which it is appurtenant; it may be commenced by grant; and an uninterrupted usage for twenty years is evidence of a grant. In most other respects, commons appendant and appurtenant agree. 2 Greenl. Cruise, Dig. 5; Bouv. Inst. note 1650; 30 Eng. Law & Eq. 176; 15 East, 108.

——**Common Because of Vicinage.** The right which the inhabitants of two or more contiguous townships or villas have of inter-commoning with each other. It ought to be claimed by prescription, and can only be used by cattle *levant* and *couchant* upon the lands to which the right is annexed, and cannot exist except between adjoining townships, where there is no intermediate land. Co. Litt. 122a; 4 Coke, 38a; 7 Coke, 5; 10 Q. B. 581, 589, 604; 19 Q. B. 620; 18 Barb. (N. Y.) 523.

It is, indeed, only a permissive right, intended to excuse what, in strictness, is a trespass in both, and to prevent a multiplicity of suits, and therefore either township may inclose and bar out the other, though they have intercommoned time out of mind. 2 Bl. Comm. 33; Co. Litt. 12a; Bracton, fol. 222.

Dr. Wooddeson observes that Blackstone's account of common *pur cause de vicinage* is not properly a definition, but rather a descriptive example or illustration, there being other occasions when the excuse for trespass may be used. 2 Wooddeson, Lect. 50.

——**Common in Gross.** A right of common which must be claimed by deed or prescription. It has no relation to land, but is annexed to a man's person, and may be for a certain or an indefinite number of cattle. It cannot be aliened so as to give the entire right to several persons to be enjoyed by each in severalty. And where it comes to several persons by operation of law, as by descents, it is incapable of division among them, and must be enjoyed jointly. Common appurtenant for a limited number of cattle may be granted over, and by such grant becomes common in gross. Co. Litt. 122a, 164a; 5 Taunt. 244; 16 Johns. (N. Y.) 30; 2 Bl. Comm. 34.

See, generally, Viner, Abr.; Bac. Abr.; Comyn, Dig.; 2 Sharswood, Bl. Comm. 34 et seq.; 2 Washb. Real Prop. 4.

COMMON ANCESTOR. The person from whom several others are directly descended.

COMMON ASSURANCES. Deeds which make safe or assure to a man the title to his estate, whether they are deeds of conveyance, or to charge or discharge.

COMMON BAIL. Fictitious sureties entered in the proper office of the court. See "Bail."

COMMON BAR. In pleading. A plea to compel the plaintiff to assign the particular place where the trespass has been committed. Steph. Pl. 256. It is sometimes called a "blank bar."

COMMON BARRATOR. In criminal law. One who frequently excites and stirs up suits and quarrels, either at law or otherwise. See "Barratry."

COMMON BARRATRY. See "Barratry."

COMMON BAWDY-HOUSE. This is a term sometimes used in English law to mean what is sometimes otherwise called "house of ill-fame," or simply "bawdy-house," or more commonly "brothel." Primarily it means *vi ex termini*, a house, but in the law it means also a room or set of rooms in a house, kept for purposes of prostitution. Rex v. Pierson (1700); Salk. 382; Singleton v. Ellison (1895); 1 Q. B. 607. Such a place so kept comes within the definition, whatever the outside appearance, whether indecent or disorderly or not. (Steph. Dig. Crim. Law.)

COMMON BENCH. The ancient name for the court of common pleas.

COMMON CARRIERS. Such as carry goods for hire indifferently for all persons.

The definition includes carriers by land and water.

One who plies between certain *termini*, and openly professes to carry for hire the goods of all such persons as may choose to employ him. Redf. Carr. 1.

One undertaking to carry for hire the goods of all persons indifferently. 3 Wend. (N. Y.) 161; 22 N. J. Law, 372.

"The test [of whether one is a common carrier] is not whether he is carrying as a public employment, or whether he carries to a fixed place, but whether he holds out, either expressly or by a course of conduct, that he will carry for hire, so long as he has room, the goods of all persons, indifferently, who send him goods to be carried." L. R. 1 C. P. 19, 423.

——**Common Carriers of Passengers.** Such as carry persons for hire, and are bound to carry all who offer. 19 Wend. (N. Y.) 239; 10 N. H. 486; 15 Ill. 472; 2 Sumn. (U. S.) 221; 3 Brod. & B. 54; 9 Price, 408.

COMMON CHASE. (Law. Fr. *Comon chace.*) In old English law. A place where the right of hunting wild animals (*touts beasts chaceables*) was common to all (*a toutzgents*). Y. B. P. 10 Edw. III. 28.

COMMON COUNCIL. The more numerous house of the municipal legislative assembly in some American cities.

The English parliament is the common council of the whole realm.

COMMON COUNTS. Certain general counts, not founded on any special contract, which are introduced in a declaration for the purpose of preventing a defeat of a just right by the accidental variance of the evidence.

These are, in an action of *assumpsit*, counts founded on express or implied promises to pay money in consideration of a precedent debt, and are of four descriptions, —the *indebitatus assumpsit*, the *quantum meruit*, the *quantum valebant*, and the account stated.

COMMON DAY (Law Lat. *dies communis*). In old English practice. An ordinary day in court (St. 13 Rich. II. st. 1, c. 17), such as *octabis Michaelis* (the octave of St. Michael), *quindena Paschae* (the quinzime of Easter), etc. (St. 51 Hen. III. sts. 2, 3; Cowell; Termes de la Ley).

COMMON DEBTOR. In Scotch law. A debtor whose effects have been arrested by several creditors. In regard to these creditors, he is their common debtor, and by this term is distinguished in the proceedings that take place in the competition. Bell, Dict.

COMMON DRUNKARD. See "Drunkard."

COMMON EMPLOYMENT. This is a phrase used in the law of master and servant to express the relation between servants of a common master which relieves the master from liability for injury received by one through the fault of the other.

Common employment is service of such kind that, in the exercise of ordinary sagacity, all who engage in it may be able to foresee, when accepting it, that through the negligence of fellow-servants, it may probably expose them to injury. 39 N. J. Law, 119.

The phrase in some, perhaps in most, jurisdictions, is used to mean co-operation by the servants concerned, the usual performance by them of duties, the performance of which brings them into habitual consociation promotive of the exercise of a cautionary and corrective influence by each over the other. (134 Ill. 209; s. c. 146 Ill. 603). It came into the law as a consequence of the doctrine laid down in *Priestly v. Fowler* (1838), 3 M. & W. 1, followed by *Hutchinson v. York, etc. R. Co.* (1850), 5 Exch. 343; *Wigmore v. Jay* (1850), 5 Exch. 354; *Lovell v. Howell* (1876), (C. P. D. 161) and finally confirmed by the case of *Bartonshill Coal Co. v. Reid* (1860, 3 Macq. Ap. Cas. 266). This doctrine was that the general maxim *qui facit per alium*, etc. (*q. v.*) had no application to the principal in this relation and with later delimitations stating more precisely what constituted common employment, denied to the injured workman a right to damages from his employer in many cases where, however it might be in logic, not merely humanity but social and commercial expediency required that he be compensated. The ultimate consequence, in England, was the employer's liability law (*q. v.*), by which in all such cases the refinements of the doctrine of contributory negligence were put out of the way. The application of the doctrine of common employment is a matter of almost infinite detail for which there is here no room. It is, however, in substance the same as the question who are fellow-servants. The Workmen's Compensation Acts now in force in nearly all states have greatly reduced the importance of the fellow-servant doctrine.

COMMON ERROR (Lat. *communis error*). An error for which there are many precedents. "'Common error goeth for a law." Finch, Law, bk. 1, c. 3, No. 54.

COMMON FIELD. 1. The arable land of an ancient village community which though divided into parcels, long narrow strips, separated by balks of turf perhaps a yard wide, and allotted to ownership in severalty, lay otherwise in common, were to some extent used in common, and were cultivated, or at any rate ploughed, in co-operation. In this sense usually in the plural. See Pool. & M. Hist. Eng. Law, I, 364.

2. In those parts of the southern states which were of French settlement, a field divided into lots from one to three arpents in width (front) by forty in length (depth) for cultivation by the inhabitants of a village, the whole enclosed by a common fence.

The term common field is of American invention, and adopted by congress to designate small tracts of ground of a peculiar shape, usually from one to three arpents in front by forty in depth, used by the occupants of the French villages for the purposes of cultivation, and protected from the inroads of cattle by a common fence. The peculiar shape of the lot, its contiguity to others of similar shape, and the purposes to which it was applied, constituted it a common-field lot. 1 Black. (U. S.) 600.

COMMON FINE (Law Lat. *finis communis*). In old English law. A certain sum of money which the residents in a leet paid to the lord of the leet, otherwise called head silver, cert money (*q. v.*), or *certum letae*. Termes de la Ley; Cowell. A sum of money paid by the inhabitants of a manor to their lord, towards the charge of holding a court leet. Bailey. See "Leet."

A fine or amercement imposed upon a county at large. Bracton, fol. 36b; St. Westminster I. c. 18; Fleta, lib. 3, c. 14, § 9; 2 Inst. 197.

COMMON FISHERY. A fishery to which all persons have a right, such as the cod fisheries off Newfoundland. A "common fishery" is different from a "common of fishery," which is the right to fish in another's pond, pool, or river. See "Fishery."

COMMON FORM. Proof of a will in "common form," according to the English practice, was made by taking the will before the judge of the proper court of probate and proving it by attesting witnesses without citing or giving notice to the parties interested. 247 Ill. 256; 122 Ill. 563.

COMMON HALL. A court in the city of London, at which all the citizens, or such as are free of the city, have a right to attend. Wharton.

COMMON HIGHWAY. By this term is meant a road to be used by the community at large for any purpose of transit or traffic. Hammond, N. P. 239. See "Highway."

COMMON INFORMER. One who, without being specially required by law or by virtue of his office, gives information of crimes, offenses, or misdemeanors which have been committed, in order to prosecute the offender; a prosecutor.

COMMON INTENT. The natural sense given to words.

It is the rule that when words are used which will bear a natural sense and an artificial one, or one to be made out by argument and inference, the natural sense shall prevail. It is simply a rule of construction, and not of addition. Common intent cannot add to a sentence words which have been omitted. 2 H. Bl. 530. In pleading, certainty is required; but certainty to a common intent is sufficient,—that is, what, upon a reasonable construction, may be called certain, without recurring to possible facts. Co. Litt. 203a; Doug. 163. See "'Certainty."

COMMON JURY. An ordinary petit jury, as distinguished from a special or struck jury.

COMMON LABOR. This is a term used in some of the states in statutes intended to secure abstention from ordinary week-day affairs on the Sabbath—statutes commonly called Sunday observance laws. The more usual phrases, such as "labor, business, or work," "secular labor, business, or employment," are more comprehensive and leave the citizen legally at liberty with respect to few of the ordinary acts of life, save acts of necessity or charity, of which the statutes generally make express exception. The general question and, these wider phrases are elsewhere noticed (see Labor, Business, etc.; Secular Labor, etc.; Sunday Observance). But as to the phrase "common labor," which is here in question, this has been held to mean, of course, ordinary manual labor as contradistinguished from merely intellectual. 2 Ohio St. 403. It is, however, of wider import, and is held to comprehend acts of ordinary secular business, such as buying, selling, bartering, etc. 15 Ohio 241. The making of ordinary contracts, the executing of promissory notes, penal bonds, etc. 7 Blackf. 480; 4 Ind. 620; 127 Ind. 44; but it does not extend to the acts of a public officer in the performance of official duty. 42 Ohio St. 591.

COMMON LAND. A more extended term for what is sometimes more shortly called simply common; land, *i. e.* in which there is right of common (see Common), land which there is right to use in common, for pasturing, etc. The term is also used rather popularly and loosely than legally to mean land owned in severalty but used in common.

COMMON LAW. That system of law or form of the science of jurisprudence which has prevailed in England and in the United States of America, in contradistinction to other great systems, such as the Roman or civil law.

As distinguished from statute law, those principles, usages, and rules of action applicable to the government and security of persons and of property, which do not rest for their authority upon any express and positive declaration of the will of the legislature. 1 Kent, Comm. 492.

The body of rules and remedies administered by courts of law, technically so called, in contradistinction to those of equity, and to the canon law. 3 Pet. (U. S.) 446.

The law of any country, to denote that which is common to the whole country, in contradistinction to laws and customs of local application.

As used in the United States, it includes both the unwritten law of England and the statutes passed before the settlement of the United States. 5 Pet. (U. S.) 124; 18 Wis. 147.

The common law is not fixed in its scope, but develops new principles by analogy as new conditions arise. 42 Ala. 597.

COMMON-LAW DEDICATION. The difference between a statutory and a common-law dedication is that one vests the legal title to the ground set apart for public uses in the municipal corporation in trust for the public, while the other leaves the legal title in the owner, charged with the same rights and interests in the public which it would have if the fee were in the corporation. 269 Ill. 415; 79 Ill. 32.

COMMON-LAW MARRIAGE. A marriage based upon agreement by which the parties agree *per verba de presenti* to become husband and wife, followed by sexual consummation.

To constitute a marriage legal, at common law, the contract and consent must be *per verba de presenti,* or if made *per verba de futuro cum copula,* the *copula* is presumed to have been allowed on the faith of the marriage promise, and that so the parties, at the time of the *copula,* accepted of each other as man and wife. 204 Ill. 28.

COMMON-LAW PROCEDURE ACTS. Three acts of parliament, passed in the years 1852, 1854, and 1860, respectively, for the amendment of the procedure in the common-law courts. The common-law procedure act of 1852 is St. 15 & 16 Vict. c. 76, that of 1854, St. 17 & 18 Vict. c. 125, and that of 1860, St. 23 & 24 Vict. c. 126. Mozley & W.

COMMON LAWYER. A lawyer learned in the common law.

COMMON LEARNING. Familiar law or doctrine. Dyer, 27b, 33.

COMMON NUISANCE. Hawkins, in his Pleas of the Crown, defines a common nuisance as an offense against the public, by doing anything injurious to all the King's subjects, or by omitting to do that which the common good requires. 71 Ill. 194.

One that affects the public at large and is a violation of a public right, either by a direct encroachment upon public property, or by doing some act which tends to the common injury, or by omitting to do, in the discharge of a legal duty, that which the common good requires. 214 Ill. 635.

One which affects the public in general, and not merely some particular person. 1 Hawk. P. C. 197. See "Nuisance."

COMMON OPINION IS GOOD AUTHORity in law. Co. Litt. 186a; 3 Barb. Ch. (N. Y.) 528, 577.

COMMON PLEAS. The name of a court having jurisdiction generally of civil actions.

Such pleas or actions as are brought by private persons against private persons, or by the government, when the cause of action is of a civil nature. In England, whence we derived this phrase, common pleas are so called to distinguish them from pleas of the crown.

COMMON RECOVERY. A judgment recovered in a fictitious suit, brought against the tenant of the freehold, in consequence of a default made by the person who is last vouched to warranty in the suit, which recovery, being a supposed adjudication of the right, binds all persons, and vests a free and absolute fee simple in the recoveror.

A common recovery is a kind of conveyance, and is resorted to when the object is to create an absolute bar of estates tail, and of the remainders and reversions expectant on the determination of such estates. 2 Bl. Comm. 357. Though it has been used in some of the states, this form of conveyance is nearly obsolete, easier and less expensive modes of making conveyances, which have the same effect, having been substituted. 2 Bouv. Inst. notes 2092, 2096, 7 N. H. 9: 9 Serg. & R. (Pa.) 390; 2 Rawle (Pa.) 168; 4 Yeates (Pa.) 413; 1 Whart. (Pa.) 151; 6 Mass. 328.

COMMON SANS NOMBRE. Common without number, that is, without limit as to the number of cattle which may be turned on; otherwise called "common without stint." Bracton, fols. 53b, 222b; 2 Steph. Comm. 6, 7; 2 Bl. Comm. 34; 3 Bl. Comm. 238; 1 Crabb, Real Prop. 269.

COMMON SCHOOLS. Schools for general elementary instruction, free to all the public. 2 Kent, Comm. 195-202.

A school that begins with the rudimental elements of an education, whatever else it may embrace, as contradistinguished from academies or universities devoted exclusively to teaching advanced pupils in the classics, and in all the higher branches of study usually included in the curriculum of the colleges. 97 Ill. 378.

COMMON SCOLD. One who, by the practice of frequent scolding, disturbs the neighborhood. Bish. Crim. Law, § 147.

The offense of being a common scold is cognizable at common law. It is a particular form of nuisance, and was punishable by the ducking stool at common law, in place of which punishment fine and imprisonment are substituted in the United States. 12 Serg. & R. (Pa.) 220; 3 Cranch, C. C. (U. S.) 620. See 1 Term R. 748; 6 Mod. 11; 4 Rog. (N. Y.) 90; 1 Russ. Crimes, 302; Rosc. Crim. Ev. 665.

COMMON SEAL. The seal of a corporation.

It was an ancient and technical rule of the common law that a corporation could not manifest its intentions by any personal act or oral discourse, and that it spoke and acted only by its common seal. 4 Kent, Comm. 288. This is said to be no longer law in the United States. 7 Cranch (U. S.) 299; 9 Paige, Ch. (N. Y.) 188; 21 Vt. 343; 21 Miss. 408; 1 Smith (Ind.) 98; 6 Ga. 166; 2 Kent, Comm. 289.

COMMON SERJEANT. A judicial officer of the city of London, who aids the recorder in disposing of the criminal business of the Old Bailey Sessions. Holthouse.

COMMON, TENANTS IN. See "Tenant."

COMMON TRAVERSE. See "Traverse."

COMMON VOUCHEE. In common recoveries, the person who is vouched to warranty. In this fictitious proceeding, the crier of the court usually performs the office of a common vouchee. 2 Bl. Comm. 358; 2 Bouv. Inst. note 2093.

COMMON WEAL (fr. common (q. v.) and *weal*, fr. As *wela*, wealth, prosperity; cp. Commonwealth.) 1. The common wellbeing; the common good; the public welfare. "The law favoreth things for the common weal. A man may justify the doing of a wrong in things that sound for the common weal. As, in time of war, to make bulwarks in another man's soil, without license; to raze one's house on fire, in safeguard of the neighbours' house," etc. (Finch, Law, b. 1, c. 3, 53.)

2. The whole body of the people; the body politic. In this sense equivalent to commonwealth (*q. v.*).

COMMONABLE. Entitled to common. Commonable beasts are either beasts of the plow, as horses and oxen, or such as manure the land, as kine and sheep. Beasts not commonable are swine, goats, and the like. Co. Litt. 122a; 2 Bl. Comm. 33.

COMMONAGE. In old conveyancing. The right of common. See "Common."

COMMONALTY. The common people of England, as distinguished from the king and nobles.

The body of a society or corporation, as distinguished from the officers. 1 Per. & D. 243. Charters of incorporation of the various tradesmen's societies, etc., in England are usually granted to the master, wardens, and commonalty of such corporation.

COMMONANCE, or COMMUNANCE. The commoners, or tenants and inhabitants, who have the right of common or commoning in open field. Cowell.

COMMONER. One possessing a right of common.

COMMONS. Those subjects of the English nation who are not noblemen. They are represented in parliament by the house of commons.

COMMONTY. In Scotch law. Land possessed in common by different proprietors, or by those having acquired rights of servitude. Bell, Dict.; 36 Eng. Law & Eq. 20.

COMMONWEALTH. A free state or republic having a republican form of government.

The English nation during the time of Cromwell was called a commonwealth. It is the legal title of the states of Kentucky, Massachusetts, Pennsylvania, and Virginia.

Used sometimes as denoting the public; the common welfare of the people.

COMMORANCY. The dwelling in any place as an inhabitant, which consists in usually lying there. 4 Bl. Comm. 273. In American law it is used to denote a mere temporary residence. 19 Pick. (Mass.) 247, 248.

COMMORANT. One residing in a particular town, city, or district. Barnes 162.

COMMORIENTES. Those who perish at the same time in consequence of the same calamity.

COMMORTH, or COMORTH. A contribution which was gathered at marriages, and when young priests said or sung the first masses. Prohibited by 26 Hen. VIII. c. 6. Cowell.

COMMOTE (Law Lat. *commotum*, from Brit. *cymbod; cym*, together, *bod*, being or dwelling; or from *cwmmwd*, a province). Half a cantred or hundred in Wales, containing, properly, fifty villages. St. Walliae, 12 Edw. I. 21 Hen. VIII. c. 26. Spelman, voc. "Commotum." The fourth part of a hundred, according to Mr. Barrington who cites Girald. Camb. c. 2. Barr. Obs. St. 125, note (h).

A great seigniory or lordship, including one or more manors. Co. Litt. 5a. Part of a seigniory. Thel. Dig. lib. 8, c. 2, § 18.

COMMUNE. A self-governing town or village. The name given to the committee of the people in the French revolution of 1793; and again, in the revolutionary uprising of 1871, it signified the attempt to establish absolute self-government in Paris, or the mass of those concerned in the attempt. In old French law, it signified any municipal corporation; and in old English law, the commonalty or common people.

COMMUNE CONCILIUM REGNI. The common council of the realm. One of the names of the English parliament.

COMMUNE FORUM. The common place of justice; the seat of the principal courts, especially those that are fixed. 7 Bell, App. Cas. 169.

COMMUNE PLACITUM. In old English law. A common plea or civil action, such as an action of debt. Fleta, lib. 2, c. 61, § 18.

COMMUNE VINCULUM. A common or mutual bond. Applied to the common stock of consanguinity, and to the feodal bond of fealty, as the common bond of union between lord and tenant. 2 Bl. Comm. 250; 3 Bl. Comm. 230.

COMMUNI CUSTODIA. An obsolete writ which anciently lay for the lord, whose tenant, holding by knight's service, died, and left his eldest son under age, against a stranger that entered the land, and obtained the ward of the body. Reg. Orig. 161.

COMMUNI DIVIDENDO. In civil law. An action which lies for those who have property in common, to procure a division. It lies where parties hold land in common, but not in partnership. Calv. Lex.

COMMUNIA. In old English law. Common. Bracton, fol. 222.

Common things (*res communes*), such as running water, the air, the sea, etc., Id. 7b.

COMMUNIA, or COMMUNIAE (Lat.) In old European law. Communities. Towns enfranchised by the crown, in most of the feudal kingdoms of Europe, about the twelfth century, and formed into free corporations, by what were termed "charters of community." 1 Robertson, Hist. Charles V. 24-29, and notes in Appendix.

COMMUNIA PLACITA. Actions between citizens, as distinguished from *placita coronae*, pleas of the crown, or criminal prosecutions.

COMMUNIA PLACITA NON TENENDA In scaccario. An ancient writ directed to the treasurer and barons of the exchequer, forbidding them to hold pleas between common persons (*i. e.*, not debtors to the king, who alone originally sued and were sued there) in that court, where neither of the parties belonged to the same. Reg. Orig. 187. Since superseded by 2 & 3 Wm. IV. c. 39.

COMMUNIA PLACITUM. In old English law. A common plea or action, such as an action of debt.

COMMUNIBUS ANNIS. In ordinary years; on the annual average. 2 Bl. Comm. 322.

COMMUNICATION. Information; consultation; conference. A letter is a communication. 49 N. J. Law, 256. But see 4 Metc. (Mass.) 459.

——**In French Law.** Discovery and inspection of books and papers. Arg. Fr. Merc. Law, 552.

COMMUNINGS. In Scotch law. The negotiations preliminary to a contract.

COMMUNIO BONORUM (Lat.) In civil law. A community of goods.

COMMUNION OF GOODS. In Scotch law. The right enjoyed by married persons in the movable goods belonging to them. Bell, Dict.

COMMUNIS ERROR FACIT JUS. A common error makes law. What was at first illegal, being repeated many times, is presumed to have acquired the force of usage; and then it would be wrong to depart from it. Hilliard, Real Prop. 268; 1 Ld. Raym. 42; 6 Clark & F. 172; 3 Maule & S. 396; 4 N. H. 458; 2 Mass. 357. The converse of this maxim is *communis error non facit jus*, a common error does not make law. Coke, 4th Inst. 242; 3 Term R. 725; 6 Term R. 564.

COMMUNIS OPINIO. Common opinion; general professional opinion. Co. Litt. 186a.

COMMUNIS PARIES. In the civil law. A common or party wall. Dig. 8. 2. 8. 13.

COMMUNIS RIXATRIX. In old English law. A common scold (*q. v.*). 4 Bl. Comm. 168.

COMMUNIS SCRIPTURA. In old English law. A common writing; a writing common to both parties; a chirograph. Glanv. lib. 8, c. 1.

COMMUNIS STIPES (Lat.) In old English law. A common stock; the common or root stock of descent; a common ancestor. Bl. Law Tr. 6.

COMMUNITAS REGNI ANGLIAE (Lat.) The general assembly of the kingdom of England. One of the ancient names of the English parliament. 1 Bl. Comm. 148. According to Cowell, it signified the barons and tenants in *capite* of the kingdom. But in St. Cart. Conf. 49 Hen. III., it is used in the sense of "commonalty," as distinguished from the prelates, earls, and barons (*prelatorum, comitum, baronum et communitatis regni*).

COMMUNITY (Lat. *communis*, common). ——**In Civil Law.** A corporation or body politic. Dig. 3. 4.

——**In French Law.** A species of partnership which a man and woman contract when they are lawfully married to each other.

Conventional community is that which is formed by express agreement in the contract of marriage. By this contract, the legal community which would otherwise subsist may be modified as to the proportions which each shall take, and as to the things which shall compose it. Civ. Code La. 2393.

Legal community is that which takes place by virtue of the contract of marriage itself.

COMMUNITY PROPERTY. Property acquired during the existence of the matrimonial relation, which in some states (Louisiana, Texas, New Mexico, Arizona, California, Idaho, and Washington) belongs equally to the spouses. The doctrine is of Spanish origin. See Schmidt, Civ. Law, p. 28; White, New Recop. p. 60.

The husband, as head of the community (*q. v.*), has control of the property during the existence of the marriage relation (101 Cal. 563; 3 Wash. 592); but on dissolution of the community by death or divorce, it is divided equally between the parties (63 Cal. 77); the testamentary power of the deceased spouse being limited to the testator's moiety. 18 Cal. 291.

COMMUTATION. The change of a punishment to which a person has been condemned into a less severe one. This can be granted only by the executive authority in which the pardoning power resides.

Not a conditional pardon, but "the substitution of one punishment known to the law for another and different punishment, also known to the law." 1 Nev. 321.

The substitution of a punishment of a lower degree for one of a higher degree. 257 Ill. 566.

COMMUTATION OF TAX. The term is used where there is a substitution of one form of payment for another for taxes levied. Laws regulating the commutation of taxes may be enacted by the legislature. (31 Ala. 91), provided there is no violation of the constitution, and the privilege to commute is extended to all classes alike, fairly and impartially (21 N. J. 557; 31 Ala. 91; 76 Ill. 11).

COMMUTATIVE CONTRACT. In civil law. One in which each of the contracting parties gives and receives an equivalent. The contract of sale is of this kind. The seller gives the thing sold, and receives the price, which is the equivalent. The buyer gives the price, and receives the thing sold, which is the equivalent. Such contracts are usually distributed into four classes, namely: *Do ut des*, I give that you may give; *facio ut facias*, I do that you may do; *facio ut des*, I do that you may give; *do ut facias*, I give that you may do. Poth. Obl. note 13. See Civ. Code La. art. 1761.

COMMUTATIVE JUSTICE. See "Justice."

COMPACT. Closely and firmly united, as the parts or particles of solid bodies having the parts or particles packed together; close; solid; dense. 270 Ill. 534; 261 Ill. 99; 155 Ill. 478.

An agreement; a contract between parties, which creates obligations and rights capable of being enforced, and contemplated as such between the parties, in their distinct and independent characters. Story, Const. bk. 3, c. 3; Rutherforth, Inst. bk. 2, c. 6, § 1.

The parties may be nations, states, or individuals, but it is commonly applied to the former, and in this sense is a broader term than "treaty." 14 Pet. (U. S.) 572.

As applied to individuals, it is synonymous with "contract." 8 Wheat. (U. S.) 92.

COMPANAGE. In old English Law any meat or other edibles to be eaten with bread; a relish with bread, as butter, cheese, meat, fish, fruit, etc.

"Any meat, or other edibles to be eat with bread." (Cowell, Interp.: cp. Spelman, Gloss.)

"Every two workmen had three Boon-loaves with companage allowed them." (Blount, Anc. Ten., 3).

COMPANION OF THE GARTER. A knight of the Order of the Garter. See "Knights of the Garter."

COMPANIONS. In French law. A general term, comprehending all persons who compose the crew of a ship or vessel. Poth. Mar. Cont. note 163.

COMPANY. An association of a number of individuals for the purpose of carrying on some legitimate business.

This term is not synonymous with "partnership," though every such unincorporated company is a partnership. Usage has reserved the term to associations whose members are in greater number, their capital more considerable, and their enterprises greater, either on account of their risk or importance.

When these companies are authorized by the government, they are known by the name of "corporations."

Sometimes the word is used to represent those members of a partnership whose names do not appear in the name of the firm. See 12 Toullier, Dr. Civ. 97.

COMPARATIO LITERARUM (Lat.) In the civil law. Comparison of writings, or handwritings. A mode of proof allowed in certain cases. Code, 4. 21. 20; Nov. 49, c. 2; Bell, Dict.

COMPARATIVE NEGLIGENCE. A doctrine whereby negligence is classified as "slight," "ordinary," or "gross." In such case, if the negligence of a defendant be gross, there may be a recovery, notwithstanding slight contributory negligence (96 Ill. 47); but not where the negligence of the parties is of the same class, or the defendant's "ordinary," and the plaintiff's "slight" (72 Ill. 351).

The doctrine is now abandoned in the only state where it prevailed as a common-law doctrine. 153 Ill. 165.

However, employer's liability acts in some states have modified the common law in a manner nearly akin to the old rule of comparative negligence. Under the Federal Employer's Liability Act of 1908, the negligence is compared in determining the damages, recovery being reduced proportionately to the extent that plaintiff's negligence has contributed to the accident. It varies from the old rule, however, in that no matter how gross the contributory negligence of the plaintiff may be when compared with the negligence of the defendant, it may be considered only in diminution of recovery and not in bar.

COMPARISON OF HANDWRITING. A mode of deducing evidence of the authenticity of a written instrument, by showing the likeness of the handwriting to that of another instrument proved to be that of the party whom it is sought to establish as the author of the instrument in question. 1 Greenl. Ev. § 578.

"This is as distinct and separate a thing from that comparison which a witness called to testify to handwriting makes between the writing in question and the exemplar in his mind as an external, visible, and tangible object is distinct from a mental impression or memory." 43 Pa. St. 12.

COMPASCUUM. Belonging to commonage. *Jus compascuum*, the right of common of pasture.

COMPASSING. Imagining or contriving.

COMPATERNITAS (Eng. compaternity). In the canon law. A kind of spiritual relationship (*cognatio spiritualis*) contracted by baptism. It was a ground of divorce. Bracton, fol. 298b.

COMPATIBILITY. Capability of harmony or accord.

——**Of Offices.** Such harmony between the duties of two offices that they may be discharged by one person.

——**In Divorce Law.** Incompatibility of temper is a ground of divorce in one or two states.

COMPEAR, or COMPEIR. In Scotch law. To appear. 1 Forbes, Inst. pt. 4, bk. 2, c. 2, tit. 2.

COMPEARANCE, or COMPEIRANCE. In Scotch practice. Appearance; an appearance made for a defendant; an appearance by counsel. Bell, Dict.

COMPELLATIVUM. In old records. An adversary or accuser. Whishaw.

COMPENDIA SUNT DISPENDIA. Abridgments are hindrances. Co. Litt. 305.

COMPENSACION. In Spanish law. The extinction of a debt by another debt of equal dignity between persons who have mutual claims on each other.

COMPENSATIO. In the civil law. Compensation, or set-off. A proceeding resembling a set-off in the common law, being a claim on the part of the defendant to have an amount due to him from the plaintiff deducted from his demand. Dig. 16. 2; Inst. 4. 6. 30. 39; 3 Bl. Comm. 305; 1 Kames, Eq. 395.

COMPENSATIO CRIMINIS. The compensation or set-off of one crime against another. For example, in questions of divorce, where one party claims the divorce on the ground of adultery of his or her companion, the latter may show that the complainant has been guilty of the same offense, and, having himself violated the contract, cannot complain of its violation on the other side. This principle is incorporated in the codes of most civilized nations. See 1 Hagg. Consist. 144; 1 Hagg. Ecc. 714; 2 Paige Ch. (N. Y.) 108; 2 Dev. & B. (N. C.) 64; Bish. Mar. & Div. §§ 393, 394.

COMPENSATION (Lat. *compendere*, to balance). Indemnification; recompense. Something to be done for or paid to another of equal value with something of which he has been deprived by the act or negligence of the party so doing or paying.

That which constitutes or is regarded as an equivalent. 161 Ill. 251; 154 Ill. 662.

As compared with "consideration" and "damages," "compensation," in its most careful use, seems to be between them. Consideration is amends for something given by consent, or by the owner's choice. Damages is amends exacted from a wrongdoer for a tort. Compensation is amends for something which was taken without the owner's choice, yet without commission of a tort. Thus, one should say, consideration for land sold; compensation for land taken for a railway; damages for a trespass. But such distinctions are not uniform. "Land damages" is a common expression for compensation for lands taken for public use. Abbott.

In a statute providing for compensation for property taken for public use, compensation means an equivalent for the value of the land. 17 N. J. Law, 47.

It is applied to the remuneration of officers, fiduciaries, etc., but is not synonymous with "salary." 76 Ill. 548.

——**In Civil Law.** A reciprocal liberation between two persons who are both creditors and debtors of each other. *Est debiti et crediti inter se contributio.* Dig. 16. 2. 1.

It resembles in many respects the common-law set-off. The principal difference is that a set-off must be pleaded to be effectual; whereas compensation is effectual without any such plea. See 2 Bouv. Inst. note 1407.

It may be legal, by way of exception, or by reconvention. 8 La. 158; Dig. 16. 2; Code, 4. 31; Inst. 4. 6. 30; Burge, Sur. bk. 2, c. 6, p. 181.

It takes place by mere operation of law, and extinguishes reciprocally the two debts as soon as they exist simultaneously, to the amount of their respective sums. It takes place only between two debts having equally for their object a sum of money, or a certain quantity of consumable things of one and the same kind, and which are equally liquidated and demandable. It takes place, whatever be the cause of the debts, except in case, first, of a demand of restitution of a thing of which the owner has been unjustly deprived; second, of a demand of restitution of a deposit and a loan for use; third, of a debt which has for its cause aliments declared not liable to seizure. Civ. Code La. arts. 2203-2208.

——**In Old Criminal Law.** Recrimination (*q. v.*)

COMPENSATORY DAMAGES. Damages in amount legally sufficient to indemnify the injured person for the loss sustained.

The term is sometimes taken to be equivalent to actual damages.

The term "compensatory damages" is, like "actual damages," very generally said to mean something different from "punitive damages" or "exemplary damages." Damages is intended not merely to compensate the injured person but to punish the wrongdoer.

COMPERENDINATIO. In the Roman law. The adjournment of a cause, in order to hear the parties or their advocates a second time; a second hearing of the parties to a cause. Calv. Lex.; Brissonius.

COMPERTORIUM. In the civil law. A judicial inquest made by delegates or commissioners to find out and relate the truth of a cause. Cowell.

COMPERUIT AD DIEM (Lat. he appeared at the day). In pleading. A plea in bar to an action of debt on a bail bond. The usual replication to this plea is *nul tiel record*, that there is not any such record of appearance of the said ———. For forms of this plea, see 5 Wentw. 470; Lilly, Entr. 114; 2 Chit. Pl. 527.

COMPETENCY. Qualification to act; capacity.

——**In the Law of Evidence.** The legal fitness or ability of a witness to be heard on the trial of a cause; that quality of written or other evidence which renders it proper to be given on the trial of a cause, if it be relevant to the issues therein. See "Relevancy."

There is a difference between competency and credibility. A witness may be competent, and, on examination, his story may be so contradictory and improbable that he may not be believed; on the contrary, he may be incompetent, and yet be perfectly credible if he were examined.

——**In French Law.** The right in a court to exercise jurisdiction in a particular case, as where the law gives jurisdiction to the court when a thousand francs shall be in dispute, the court is competent if the sum demanded is a thousand francs or upwards, although the plaintiff may ultimately recover less.

COMPETENT. Fit; qualified; lawful. Thus, "competent authority" is held to mean lawful authority (8 Pet. [U. S.] 449).

A "competent court," one having jurisdiction. 1 C. P. Div. 176.

COMPETENT AND OMITTED. In Scotch practice. A term applied to a plea which might have been urged by a party during the dependence of a cause, but which had been omitted. Bell, Dict.

COMPETENT PERSON. The expression "competent person" means ordinarily a person free from legal disqualification, and does not refer to the ability or experience of such person. 245 Ill. 50.

COMPETENT WITNESS. One who is legally qualified to be heard to testify in a cause.

COMPETITION. In Scotch practice. The contest among creditors claiming on their respective diligences, or creditors claiming on their securities. Bell, Dict.

The act of seeking or endeavoring to gain at the same time; common strife for the same object. 121 Ill. 317.

Not every conflict of temporal interest can be regarded as competition. Scott and Farmer, JJ., dissenting opinion. Barnes v. Typographical Union, 232 Ill. 439.

COMPILATION. A literary production, composed of the works of others, and arranged in a methodical manner.

When a compilation requires in its execution taste, learning, discrimination, and intellectual labor, it is an object of copyright: as, for example, Bacon's Abridgment. Curtis, Copyright, 186.

COMPLAINANT. One who makes a complaint. A plaintiff in a suit in chancery is so called.

The actor in a chancery suit.

COMPLAINT.

——**In Criminal Law.** The allegation made to a proper officer that some person, whether known or unknown, has been guilty of a designated offense, with an offer to prove the fact, and a request that the offender may be punished. It is a technical term, descriptive of proceedings before a magistrate. 11 Pick. (Mass.) 436.

——**In Code Pleading.** The plaintiff's first pleading in a civil action.

COMPLETE. Old forms; *Complet, compleet, compleate, compleat* (adap. Lat. *completus*, pa. pple. of *complere* to fill up, finish: cp. Fr. *complet*). 1. Wanting no part, member, or element; entire, perfect full. The word applied in this sense to title to land, in general means the right of property as well as possession and right of possession. A complete title to land, according to Blackstone, consists of *juris et sesinae conjunctio*; the possession, the right of possession and the right of property. (60 Miss. 1054; 6 Hill. 539.)

2. Perfect in nature, kind, or quality; consummate; thorough.

3. Finished; completed; ended. The premises were sold, in consideration of machinery to be furnished, complete, in the mill. This includes, not only the cost of the machinery, but the labor and material necessary to place it in proper position for operation. (58 Ill. 339.)

4. To add or supply what is wanting to; to finish, perfect, make complete.

5. To accomplish; to fulfill; to consummate, execute, achieve, realize. (28 N. Y. Supp. 445.)

COMPLETE PURCHASER. This is a term sometimes applied to the subsequent purchaser of land who, though subsequent, will, under certain circumstances, be protected as against prior purchasers where he has procured the evidence of his purchase to be recorded in accordance with the statute. In order to be a complete purchaser within the meaning of the term as thus employed, the purchaser, it appears to be uniformly held, must have paid the purchase money, not merely have given security for payment. 1 Whart. 410; 18 Ill. 343; 6 Bush. 192; 79 Va. 147. Whether he must also have received a conveyance, not a mere agreement to convey, is a point upon which the authorities are not agreed, but the later decisions are to the effect that it is enough that he has a full right to a conveyance.

COMPLETED. (Pa. pple. of *Complete, q. v.*) The word is used in the various senses of the verb, and may thus mean finished, perfected, etc. But it may be restricted by a context to a finishing, perfecting, accomplishing or fulfilling less entire than the word ordinarily imports.

COMPLETION. (Adap. Lat. *completio* of action of *complere* to complete, *q. v.*) The act of completing in various senses parallel with those of the verb. The word "completion [means] * * * the finishing or accomplishing in full of something which has already been commenced]." 121 N. C. 401. In its narrowest signification the meaning of the word is to carry out something already begun; to fill out something already outlined. 89 Fed. 266.

COMPLICE. An accomplice.

COMPOS MENTIS. See "Non Compos Mentis."

COMPOS SUI (Lat.) Having power of one's self; having the use of one's limbs, or the power of bodily motion. *Si fuit ita compos sui quod itinerare potuit de loco in locum*, if he had so far the use of his limbs as to be able to travel from place to place. Bracton, fol. 14b.

COMPOSITIO MENSURARUM. The ordinance of measures; the title of an ancient ordinance, not printed, mentioned in St. 23 Hen. VIII. c. 4, establishing a standard of measures. 1 Bl. Comm. 275.

COMPOSITIO ULNARUM ET PERTICArum. The statute of ells and perches. The title of an English statute establishing a standard of measures. 1 Bl. Comm. 275.

COMPOSITION. An agreement, made upon a sufficient consideration, between a debtor and creditor, by which the creditor accepts part of the debt due to him in satisfaction of the whole.

Generally applied to agreements between a debtor and several or all of his creditors.

——**In Ancient Law.** Compensation for crime; weregild.

COMPOSITION IN BANKRUPTCY. An agreement by the creditors of a bankrupt to receive a certain percentum of their claims in full satisfaction.

The national bankrupt act provides for such compositions, requiring a formal offer of composition by the bankrupt, a creditors' meeting to consider the same, and, if accepted by a majority both in number and amount of claims, an application for confirmation by the court. Loveland, Bankr. §§ 241-253.

COMPOSITION OF TITHES. Sometimes called "real composition." An agreement by a landowner with the incumbent, whereby the land is discharged from liability for tithes in consideration of some land or other real recompense given in lieu thereof. 2 Steph. Comm. 727.

COMPOTARIUS. In old English law. A party accounting. Fleta, lib. 2, c. 71, § 17.

COMPOUND INTEREST. A compensation for the use of money due as interest but not paid, generally called interest upon interest. Interest computed upon interest after maturity is compound interest. 23 Ill. 323; 32 Ill. App. 362.

COMPOUNDING A FELONY. The act of a party immediately aggrieved, who agrees with a thief or other felon that he will not prosecute him, on condition that he return to him the goods stolen, or who takes a reward not to prosecute.

It is not necessary that the person with whom the composition was made should be guilty of the alleged felony (42 Ohio St. 405; 13 Wend. [N. Y.] 592), nor that the consideration for the compounding was received for the benefit of another (58 Iowa, 151).

Though, at common law, the offense was restricted to the composition of felonies, *the composition of misdemeanors is made* penal in most of the United States.

COMPRA Y VENTA (Spanish). Buying and selling. The laws of contracts arising from purchase and sale are given very fully in Las Partidas, pt. 3, tit. xviii. 11. 56 et seq.

COMPRINT. The surreptitious printing of the copy of another to the intent to make a gain thereby. Strictly, it signifies to print together. There are several old statutes prohibiting this act. Jacob; Cowell.

COMPRIRIGUI (Lat.) Step-brothers or step-sisters; children who have one parent, and only one, in common. Calv. Lex.

COMPRIVIGNI. In the civil law. Children by a former marriage (individually called *"privigni,"* or *"privignae"*), considered relatively to each other. Thus, the son of a husband by a former wife, and the daughter of a wife by a former husband, are the *comprivigni* of each other. Inst. 1. 10. 8.

COMPROMISARIUS. In civil law. An arbitrator.

COMPROMISE. An agreement made between two or more parties as a settlement of matters in dispute between them.

——*In Civil Law.* An agreement between two or more persons, who, wishing to settle their disputes, refer the matter in controversy to arbitrators, who are so called because those who choose them give them full powers to arbitrate and decide what shall appear just and reasonable, to put an end to the differences of which they are made the judges. 1 Domat, Civ. Law, liv. 1, tit. 14.

COMPROMISSARII SUNT JUDICES. Arbitrators are judges. Jenk. Cent. Cas. 128.

COMPROMISSARIUS. In the civil law. An arbitrator. Dig. 4. 9. 41.

COMPROMISSUM. *In the civil law.* A submission to arbitration. Dig. 4. 8; 4 Reeves, Hist. Eng. Law, 13.

COMPROMISSUM AD SIMILITUDINEM judiciorum redigitur. A compromise is brought into affinity with judgments. 9 Cush. (Mass.) 571.

COMPTER. In Scotch law. An accounting party. Skene de Verb. Sign.

The name of a prison in London.

COMPTROLLER. An officer of a state, or of the United States, who has certain duties to perform in the regulation and management of the fiscal matters of the government under which he holds office.

COMPULSION. Forcible inducement to the commission of an act.

COMPULSORY. In ecclesiastical procedure. A compulsory is a kind of writ to compel the attendance of a witnes, to undergo examination. Phillim. Ecc. Law, 1258.

In order to render a payment compulsory, such a pressure must be exerted on the payor as to interfere with the free enjoyment of his rights of person or property, in the sense of depriving him of the exercise of his free will, and the compulsion must furnish the motive for the payment. 234 Ill. 543.

COMPURGATOR. One of several neighbors of a person accused of a crime, or charged as a defendant in a civil action, who appeared and swore that they believed *him on his oath.* 3 Bl. Comm. 341.

COMPUTUS (Lat. *computare,* to account). A writ to compel a guardian, bailiff, receiver, or accountant to yield up his accounts. It is founded on St. Westminster II. c. 12; Reg. Orig. 135.

COMTE (Fr.; Lat. *comes*). Count. A title of office in the ancient law of France, denoting a governor of a particular territory or district, who united the characters of a military leader and a judge. As a judge, he had an equal jurisdiction with the *missus dominicus,* or king's commissary. Esprit des Lois, liv. 28, c. 28; Id. liv. 30, c. 18. As a military officer, he commanded the freemen, and led them to the field. Id. liv. 30, cc. 17, 18. Montesquieu says he was at the head of all the freemen of the monarchy. Id. liv. 31, c. 23. See, also, Id. liv. 30, c. 18; Id. liv. 31, c. 1. The *comte* was subordinate to the *duc* (duke). Guyot, Inst. Feud. c. 1, § 8. See "Comes"; "Count."

In later times, a title of nobility. Boulainvilliers Etat de la France, iii. 56; Barr. Obs. St. 31.

CON BUENA FE. In Spanish law. With good faith; in good faith; *bona fide.* White, New Recop. bk. 2, tit. 2, c. 8.

CONACRE. In Irish practice. The payment of wages in land, the rent being worked out in labor at a money valuation. Wharton.

CONATUS QUID SIT, NON DEFINITUR in jure. What an attempt is, is not defined in law. 2 Bulst. 277.

CONCEALERS. Such as find out concealed lands; that is, lands privily kept from the king by common persons having nothing to show for them. They are called "a troublesome, disturbant sort of men; turbulent persons." Cowell.

CONCEALMENT. The improper suppression of any fact or circumstance by one of the parties to a contract from the other, which in justice ought to be known.

The omission by an applicant for insurance preliminarily to state facts known to him, or which he is bound to know, material to the risk proposed to be insured against, or omission to state truly the facts expressly inquired about by the underwriters to whom application for insurance is made, whether the same are or are not material to the risk. See 12 Cush. (Mass.) 416.

CONCEALMENT OF BIRTH. The concealing or endeavoring to conceal the birth of a child is very commonly made a criminal offense. It is in England by statute a misdemeanor punishable by two years' imprisonment with hard labor to conceal or endeavor to conceal the birth of a child by secret disposition of its dead body. (24 and 25 Vict. c. 100, § 60: cp. Steph. Dig. Crim. Law, 155; Russ. Crimes, 1.) And similar statutes having a similar purpose have been enacted in various of the states. The purpose of course is to protect the lives of bastard children, whom the parents might incline to put out of the way. The word "concealment" is used here, it would seem, in no peculiar sense, except by force of some peculiar context. The word is given point and limitation by the further phrase "by secret disposition of its dead body." This shuts out the idea of concealment by mere false representation. But in any case the statutory context should be considered.

CONCEPTUM. In the civil law. A theft (*furtum*) was called "*conceptum*" when the thing stolen was searched for, and found upon some person in the presence of witnesses. Inst. 4. 1. 4.

CONCERN. 1. That which relates or pertains to one; matter of concernment; affair; business.

2. An establishment for the carrying on of a business, as a buying and selling or manufacturing firm or company.

CONCERNED IN. This is a phrase often employed in statutes, contracts, etc., in the sense of having to do with, having part or share in, being engaged in or with, etc. "'Being concerned in' is * * * a colloquial expression, equivalent to 'being engaged in,' or 'taking part in'." 74 Fed. 217.

It is sometimes provided in policies of insurance that in case of loss the assured must produce a certificate of the fact from a magistrate not "concerned in" it as a creditor. The phrase has been held to mean a magistrate who has not a personal interest such as to tempt him to state what is not true, not a creditor in a trifling sum not affecting such an interest. 131 Mass. 44.

It is sometimes provided by statute that particular public officers shall not be "concerned in" the purchase of lands sold for taxes. The inhibition has been held to forbid an interest to the extent of a commission as agent for a purchaser. 70 Ia. 290.

CONCERT. Agreement in a design or plan; union formed by mutual communication of opinions and views. 192 Ill. 196.

CONCESSI (Lat. I have granted). A term formerly used in deeds.

It is a word of general extent, and is said to amount to a grant, feoffment, lease, release, and the like. 2 Saund. 96; Co. Litt. 301, 302; Dane, Abr. Index; 5 Whart. (Pa.) 278.

It has been held in a feoffment or fine to imply no warranty. Co. Litt. 384; 4 Coke, 80; Vaughan's Argument in Vaughan, 126; Butler's Note, Co. Litt. 384. But see 1 Freem. 339, 414.

CONCESSIMUS (Lat. we have granted). A term used in conveyances. It created a joint covenant on the part of the grantors. 5 Coke, 16; 3 Keb. 617; Bac. Abr. "Covenant."

CONCESSIO. In old English law. A grant; one of the old common assurances, or forms of conveyance, being properly of things incorporeal which cannot pass by deed. 2 Bl. Comm. 317.

CONCESSIO PER REGEM FIERI DEBET de certitudine. A grant by the king ought to be a grant of a certainty. 9 Coke, 46.

CONCESSIO VERSUS CONCEDENTEM latam interpretationem habere debet. A grant ought to have a liberal interpretation against the grantor. Jenk. Cent. Cas. 279.

CONCESSION. A grant. The word is frequently used in this sense when applied to grants made by the French and Spanish governments in Louisiana.

CONCESSIT SOLVERE. A form of action of debt on simple contract which lies by custom in the mayor's courts of London and Bristol. The declaration is to the effect that the defendant on a fictitious date, in consideration of divers fictitious sums of money before that time due and owing from him to the plaintiff, and then in arrear and unpaid, granted and agreed to pay (*concessit solvere*) to the plaintiff the sum sued for, but has not done so.

CONCESSOR. A grantor.

CONCESSUS. A grantee.

CONCILIABULUM. A council house. Towns. Pl. 184.

CONCILIUM. A council.

——**Concilium Ordinarium.** In Anglo-Norman times, an executive and residuary judicial committee of the *aula regis* (*q. v.*)

——**Concilium Regis.** A tribunal which existed in England during the times of Edward I. and Edward II., composed of the judges and sages of the law. To them were referred cases of great difficulty. Co. Litt. 304.

CONCLUSION (Lat. *con claudere*, to shut together). The close; the end.

——**In Pleading.** In declarations, that part which follows the statement of the cause of action. In personal or mixed actions, where the object is to recover damages, the conclusion is, properly, to the damage of the plaintiff, etc. Comyn, Dig. "Pleader," c. 84; 10 Coke, 1156.

The form was anciently, in the king's bench, "To the damage of the said A. B., and thereupon he brings suit;" in the exchequer, "To the damage," etc., "whereby he is the less able to satisfy our said lord the king the debts which he owes his said majesty at his exchequer, and therefore he brings his suit." 1 Chit. Pl. 356-358.

In pleas, the conclusion is either to the country,—which must be the case when an issue is tendered, that is, whenever the plaintiff's material statements are contradicted,—or by verification, which must be the case when new matter is introduced. Every plea in bar, it is said, must have its proper conclusion. All the formal parts of pleadings have been much modified by statute in the various states and in England within the last few years.

——**In Practice.** Making the last argument or address to the court or jury. The party on whom the *onus probandi* is cast, in general, has the conclusion.

——**In Remedies.** An estoppel; a bar; the act of a man by which he has confessed a matter or thing which he can no longer deny. For example, the sheriff is concluded by his return to a writ, and therefore, if upon a *capias* he return *cepi corpus*, he cannot afterwards show that he did not arrest the defendant, but is concluded by his return. See Plowd. 276b; 3 Thomas, Co. Litt. 600.

CONCLUSION TO THE COUNTRY. In pleading. The tender of an issue for trial by a jury. When the issue is tendered by the defendant, it is as follows: "And of this the said C. D. puts himself upon the country." When tendered by the plaintiff, the formula is, "And this the said A. B. prays may be inquired of by the country." It is held, however, that there is no material difference between these two modes of expression, and that if the one be substituted for the other the mistake is unimportant. 10 Mod. 166.

CONCLUSIVE EVIDENCE. That which cannot be controlled or contradicted by any other evidence.

CONCLUSIVE PRESUMPTION. A rule of law determining the quantity of evidence requisite for the support of a particular averment which is not permitted to be overcome by any proof that the fact is otherwise. 1 Greenl. Ev. § 15. Thus, for example, the possession of land under claim of title for a certain period of time raises a conclusive presumption of a grant.

In the civil law, such presumptions are said to be *juris et de jure*.

CONCORD. An agreement, or supposed agreement, between the parties in levying a fine of lands, in which the deforciant (or he who keeps the other out of possession) acknowledges that the lands in question are the right of the complainant, and from the acknowledgment or admission of right thus made, the party who levies the fine is called the "cognizor," and the person to whom it is levied, the "cognizee." 2 Bl. Comm. 350; Cruise, Dig. tit. 35, c. 2, § 33; Comyn, Dig. "Fine" (E 9).

CONCORDARE LEGES LEGIBUS EST optimus interpretandi modus. To make laws agree with laws is the best mode of interpreting them. Halk. Max. 70.

CONCORDAT. A convention; a pact; an agreement. The term is generally confined to the agreements made between independent governments, and most usually applied to those between the pope and some prince.

CONCORDIA (Lat.) In old English law. An agreement, or concord. Fleta, lib. 5, c. 3, § 5. The agreement or unanimity of a jury, *compellere ad concordiam.* Fleta, lib. 4, c. 9, § 2.

CONCORDIA DISCORDANTIUM CANOnum. The harmony of the discordant canons. A collection of ecclesiastical constitutions made by Gratian, an Italian monk, A. D. 1151; more commonly known by the name of *Decretum Gratiani.* 1 Bl. Comm. 82.

CONCORDIA PARVAE RES CRESCUNT et opulentia lites. Small means increase by concord, and litigations by opulence. Coke, 4th Inst. 74.

CONCUBARIA. A fold, pen, or place where cattle lie. Cowell.

CONCUBEANT. Lying together.

CONCUBINAGE. A species of marriage which took place among the ancients, and which is yet in use in some countries. See "Concubinatus."

The act or practice of cohabiting, in sexual commerce, without the authority of law or a legal marriage. See 1 Brown, Civ. Law, 80; Merlin, Repert.; Dig. 32. 49. 4; Id. 7. 1. 1; Code, 5. 27. 12.

CONCUBINATUS. A natural marriage, as contradistinguished from the *justae nuptiae*, or *justum matrimonium*, the civil marriage. The *concubinatus* was the only marriage which those who did not enjoy the *jus connubii* could contract. Although this natural marriage was authorized and regulated by law, yet it produced none of those important rights which flowed from the civil marriage, such as the paternal power, etc.; nor was the wife entitled to the honorable appellation of *mater-familias*, but was designated by the name of *concubina*. After the exclusive and aristocratic rules relative to the *connubium* had been relaxed, the *concubinatus* fell into disrepute and the law permitting it was repealed by a constitution of the Emperor Leo, the Philosopher, in the year 886 of the Christian era. See "Pater-Familias."

CONCUBINE. A woman who cohabits with a man as his wife without being married.

When a single woman consents unlawfully to cohabit with a man generally, as though the marriage relation existed between them, without any limit as to the duration of such illicit intercourse, .and actually commences cohabiting with him in pursuance of that understanding, she becomes his concubine. 124 Ill. 616.

CONCUR. In Louisiana. To claim a part of the estate of an insolvent along with other claimants (6 Mart. [La.; N. S.] 460): as "the wife concurs with her husband's creditors, and claims a privilege over them."

CONCURRENCE. In French law. The equality of rights, or privilege which several persons have over the same thing; as, for example, the right which two judgment creditors, whose judgments were rendered at the same time, have to be paid out of the proceeds of real estate bound by them. Dict. de Jur.

CONCURRENT. Running together; having the same authority. Thus, we say, a concurrent consideration occurs in the case of mutual promises; such and such courts have concurrent jurisdiction,—that is, each has the same jurisdiction.

CONCURRENT JURISDICTION. That which is possessed over the same parties or subject matter at the same time by two or more separate tribunals. 120 Ill. 81.

That jurisdiction exercised by different courts at the same time over the same subject matter and within the same territory, and wherein litigants may, in the first instance, resort to either court indifferently. 141 Ill. 498.

CONCURRENT SENTENCES. Such as, being passed on a conviction for several crimes, are computed as beginning simultaneously and running concurrently. See "Cumulative Sentences."

CONCURRENT WRIT. In English practice. A copy of the original writ of summons issued in an action, the very date being the same, the seal bears the word "concurrent" on it, and shows the date when the concurrent seal was impressed, *i. e.*, issued. A concurrent writ is frequently issued for service out of the jurisdiction. Brown.

CONCURSUS (Lat. from *concurrere*). In the civil law. A running together; a meeting or concurrence. *Concursus creditorum*, the conflict or conflicting rights of creditors, in relation to their liens, privileges, and priorities, in cases of insolvency and other cases. Story, Confl. Laws, 325c, 433a.

CONCUSS. In Scotch law. To coerce. Shaw, 322.

CONCUSSIO. In civil law. The offense of extortion by threats of violence. Dig. 47. 13.

CONCUSSION. In civil law. The unlawful forcing of another by threats of violence to give something of value. It differs from robbery in this, that in robbery the thing is taken by force, while in concussion it is obtained by threatened violence. Heinec. Lec. Elm. § 1071.

CONDEDIT. In ecclesiastical law. The name of a plea entered by a party to a libel filed in the ecclesiastical court, in which it is pleaded that the deceased made the will which is the subject of the suit, and that he was of sound mind. 2 Ecc. 438; 6 Ecc. 431.

CONDEMN. To sentence; to adjudge. 3 Bl. Comm. 291.

To declare a vessel a prize; to declare a vessel unfit for service. 1 Kent, Comm. 102; 5 Esp. 65.

To take by exercise of the power of eminent domain.

CONDEMNATION.

Sometimes used to indicate proceedings for taking property by right of eminent domain.

——**In Admiralty.** The sentence of a competent tribunal which declares a ship unfit for service. This sentence may be re-examined and litigated by the parties interested in disputing it. 5 Esp. 65; Abb. Shipp. 4.

The judgment, sentence or decree by which property seized and subject to forfeiture for an infraction of revenue, navigation, or other laws is condemned or forfeited to the government. See "Captor."

The sentence or judgment of a court of competent jurisdiction, that a ship or vessel taken as a prize on the high seas was liable to capture, and was properly and legally captured and held as prize.

——**In Civil Law.** A sentence or judgment which condemns some one to do, to give, or to pay something, or which declares that his claim or pretensions are unfounded.

——**In Criminal Law.** The word is used in this sense by common-law lawyers also, though it is more usual to say "conviction." 3 Bl. Comm. 291. It is a maxim that no man ought to be condemned unheard, and without the opportunity of being heard.

CONDEMNATION MONEY. In practice. The damages which the party failing in an action is adjudged or condemned to pay; sometimes simply called the "condemnation." 3 Bl. Comm. 291. It answers to the *judicatum* of the civil law. Id. 291, 292.

CONDESCENDENCE. In the Scotch law. A part of the proceedings in a cause, setting forth the facts of the case on the part of the pursuer or plaintiff.

CONDICTIO (Lat. from *condicere.*) In civil law. An assignment; a summons.

A personal action; an action arising from an obligation to do or give some certain, precise, and defined thing. Inst. 3. 15. pr.

Condictio is a general name given to personal actions, or actions arising from obligations, and is distinguished from *vindicatio* (real action), an action to regain possession of a thing belonging to the actor, and from mixed actions (*actiones mixtae*). *Condictio* is also distinguished from an action *ex stipulatu*, which is a personal action which lies where the thing to be done or given is uncertain in amount or identity. See Calv. Lex.; Halifax, Anal. 117.

——**Condictio Certi.** An action which lies upon a promise to do a thing, where such promise or stipulation is certain, *si certa sit stipulatio.* Inst. 3. 16. pr.; Id. 3. 15. pr.; Dig. 12. 1; Bracton, fol. 103b; Fleta, lib. 2, c. 60, § 23.

——**Condictio ex Lege.** An action arising where the law gave a remedy, but provided no appropriate form of action. Calv. Lex.

——**Condictio Indebitati.** An action which lies to recover that which the plaintiff has paid to the defendant, by mistake, and which he was not bound to pay, either in fact or in law.

This action does not lie if the money was due *ex aequitate,* or by a natural obligation, or if he who made the payment knew that nothing was due; for *qui consulto dat, quod non debet, praesumitur donare.* Bell, Dict.; Calv. Lex.; 1 Kames, Eq. 307.

——**Condictio Rei Furtivae.** An action against the thief or his heir to recover the thing stolen.

——**Condictio Sine Causa.** An action by which anything which has been parted with without consideration may be recovered. It also lay in case of failure of consideration, under certain circumstances. Calv. Lex.

CONDITIO (Lat.) A condition. Bracton, fols. 19, 47.

CONDITIO BENEFICIALIS, QUAE STATUM construit, benigne, secundum verborum intentionem est interpretanda; odiosa autem, quae statum destruit, stricte, secundum verborum proprietatem, accipienda. A beneficial condition, which creates an estate, ought to be construed favorably, according to the intention of the words; but an odious condition, which destroys an estate, ought to be construed strictly, according to the letter of the words. 8 Coke, 90; Shep. Touch. 134.

CONDITIO DICITUR, CUM QUID IN casum incertum qui potest tendere ad esse aut non esse, confertur. It is called a condition when something is given on an uncertain event, which may or may not come into existence. Co. Litt. 201.

CONDITIO ILLICITA HABETUR PRO non adjicta. An unlawful condition is deemed as not annexed.

CONDITIO PRAECEDENS ADIMPLERI debet priusquam sequatur effectus. A condition precedent must be fulfilled before the effect can follow. Co. Litt. 201.

CONDITION.

——**In Civil Law.** The situation of every person in some one of the different orders of persons which compose the general order of society, and allot to each person therein a distinct, separate rank. Domat, Civ. Law, tom. ii. lib. 1, tit. 9, § i, art. viii.

A paction or agreement which regulates that which the contractors have a mind should be done if a case which they foresee should come to pass. Domat Civ. Law, tom. i. lib. 1, tit. 1, § 4.

Domat says conditions are of three sorts. The first tend to accomplish the covenants to which they are annexed. The second dissolve covenants. The third neither accomplish nor avoid, but create, some change. When a condition of the first sort comes to pass, the covenant is thereby made effectual. In case of conditions of the second sort, all things remain in the condition they were in by the covenant, and the effect of the condition is in suspense until the condition comes to pass and the covenant is void. Domat, Civ. Law, lib. i. tit. 1, § 4, art. 6 et seq. See Poth Obl. pt. 1, c. 2, art. 1, § 1; Id. pt. ii. c. 3, art. 2.

(1) Casual conditions are such as depend upon accident, and are in no wise in the power of the person in whose favor the obligation is entered into.

(2) Mixed conditions are such as depend upon the joint wills of the person in whose favor the obligation is contracted, and of a third person; as, "If you marry my cousin, I will give," etc. Poth. Obl.

(3) Potestative conditions are those which are in the power of the person in whose favor the obligation was contracted; as, if I contract to give my neighbor a sum of money, in case he cuts down a tree.

(4) Resolutory conditions are those which are added not to suspend the obligation till their accomplishment, but to make it cease when they are accomplished.

(5) Suspensive obligations are those which suspend the obligation until the performance of the condition. They are casual, mixed, or potestative.

——**In Common Law.** The *status* or relative situation of a person in the state arising from the regulations of society. Thus, a person under twenty-one is an infant, with certain privileges and disabilities. Every person is bound to know the condition of the person with whom he deals.

A qualification, restriction, or limitation modifying or destroying the original act with which it is connected.

A clause in a contract or agreement intended to suspend, rescind, or modify the principal obligation, or, in case of a will, to suspend, revoke, or modify the devise or bequest. 1 Bouv. Inst. note 730.

A *modus* or quality annexed by him that hath an estate, or interest or right to the same, whereby an estate, etc., may either be defeated, enlarged, or created upon an uncertain event. Co. Litt. 201a.

A qualification or restriction annexed to a conveyance of lands, whereby it is provided that in case a particular event does or does not happen, or in case the grantor or grantee does or omits to do a particular act, an estate shall commence, be enlarged, or be defeated. Greenl. Cruise, Dig. tit. xiii. c. i. § 1.

A future uncertain event, on the happening or the nonhappening of which the accomplishment, modification, or rescission of a testamentary disposition is made to depend.

(1) Affirmative conditions are positive conditions. Affirmative conditions implying a negative are spoken of by the older writers, but no such class is now recognized. Shep. Touch. 117.

(2) Collateral conditions are those which require the doing of a collateral act. Shep. Touch. 117.

(3) Compulsory conditions are such as expressly require a thing to be done.

(4) Repugnant or insensible conditions are those inconsistent with the original act.

(5) Consistent conditions are those which agree with the other parts of the transaction.

(6) Copulative conditions are those which are composed of distinct parts or separate conditions, all of which must be performed. They are generally conditions precedent, but may be subsequent. Powell, Dev. c. 15.

(7) Disjunctive conditions are those which require the doing of one of several things. If a condition become impossible in the copulative, it may be taken in the disjunctive. Viner, Abr. "Condition" (S b) (Y b 2).

(8) Single conditions are those which require the doing of a single act only.

(9) Restrictive conditions are such as contain a restraint, as that a lessee shall not alien.

(10) Lawful conditions are those which the law allows to be made.

(11) Unlawful conditions are those which the law forbids.

(12) Independent conditions are those, each of which must be performed without regard to the performance of the others.

(13) Dependent conditions are those the failure of performance of one of which excuses performance of the others.

(14) Express conditions are those which are created by express words. Co. Litt. 328. Express conditions are also known as "conditions in deed."

(15) Implied conditions are those which the law supposes the parties to have had in mind at the time the transaction was entered into, though no condition was expressed. Implied conditions are also known as "covert conditions," or "conditions in law," but the latter term is little used by modern writers. 2 Bl. Comm. 155.

(16) Impossible conditions are those which cannot be performed in the course of nature.

(17) Possible conditions are those which may be performed.

(18) Inherent conditions are such as are annexed to the rent reserved out of the land whereof the estate is made. Shep. Touch. 118.

(19) Precedent conditions are those which are to be performed before the estate or the obligation commences, or the bequest takes effect. Powell, Dev. c. 15. A bond to convey land on the payment of the purchase money furnishes a common example of a condition precedent. 9 Cush. (Mass.) 95. They are distinguished from conditions subsequent.

If the language of the particular clause or the whole instrument shows that the act upon which the estate depends must be performed before the estate vests, the condition is precedent, but if the act does not necessarily precede the vesting of the estate but may accompany or follow it, the condition is subsequent. 267 Ill. 107.

(20) Subsequent conditions are those whose effect is not produced until after the vesting of the estate or bequest, or the commencement of the obligation.

One by which an interest already vested may be divested, or a contingent interest defeated before vested. 190 Ill. 207.

"Where a condition must be performed before the estate can commence, it is called a 'condition precedent'; but when the effect of the condition is to enlarge or defeat the estate already created, it is then called a 'condition subsequent.'" 12 Barb. (N. Y.) 440.

A condition subsequent determines an estate after breach upon entry or claim by the proper person; as, limitation marks the period which *ipso facto* determines an estate. 3 Gray (Mass.) 143.

CONDITIONAL FEE. A fee which, at the common law, was restrained to some particular heirs, exclusive of others. It was called a conditional fee by reason of the condition, expressed or implied in the donation of it, that, if the donee died without such particular heirs, the land should revert to the donor. For this was a condition annexed by law to all grants whatsoever, that, on failure of the heirs specified in the grant, the grant should be at an end, and the land return to its ancient proprietor. 2 Bl. Comm. 110.

CONDITIONAL LEGACY. A bequest whose existence depends upon the happening or not happening of some uncertain event, by which it is either to take place or to be defeated. 1 Rop. Leg. (3d Ed.) 645.

CONDITIONAL LIMITATION. A condition followed by a limitation over to a third person in case the condition be not fulfilled, or there be a breach of it.

A condition determines an estate after breach, upon entry or claim by the proper person. A limitation marks the period which determines an estate without any act on the part of him who has the next expectant interest. A conditional limitation is therefore of a mixed nature, partaking of that of a condition and a limitation. Bigelow, J., 3 Gray (Mass.) 143. The limitation over need not be to a stranger. 2 Bl. Comm. 155; 11 Metc. (Mass.) 102; Watk. Conv. 204.

It is distinguished from an estate on condition subsequent by the fact that, on breach of a conditional limitation, the estate terminates *ipso facto*. 1 Steph. Comm. 310.

CONDITIONAL OBLIGATION. An obligation subject to a condition.

——**In Louisiana.** An implied obligation. See 2 La. Ann. 989, 991.

CONDITIONAL STIPULATION. A stipulation on condition.

CONDITIONES QUAELIBET ODIOSAE; maxime autem contra matrimonium et commercium. Any conditions are odious, but especially those against matrimony and commerce. Lofft, 644.

CONDITIONS OF SALE. The terms upon which the vendor of property by auction proposes to sell it.

The instrument containing these terms, when reduced to writing or printing.

CONDOMINIA. In civil law. Co-ownerships or limited ownerships, such as *emphyteusis, superficies, pignus, hypotheca, ususfructus, usus* and *habitatio*. These were more than mere *jura in re aliena*, being portion of the *dominium* itself, although they are commonly distinguished from the *dominium* strictly so called. Brown.

CONDONACION. A Spanish law term, signifying the remission of a debt.

CONDONATION. The conditional forgiveness or remission, by a husband or wife, of a matrimonial offense which the other has committed.

Condonation is the remission by one of the named parties of an offense which he knows the other has committed, on the condition, implied where it is not expressed, of being continually afterwards treated by the other with conjugal kindness. 2 Bish. Mar., Div. & Sep. § 269.

Condonation may be either express or implied (27 Ind. 186), as by continued matrimonial cohabitation after knowledge of the offense (13 N. J. Eq. 81).

Conditional forgiveness, whereby one party forgives the other's wrong on the implied promise that there shall be no further violation of the marriage vows. 59 Ill. App. 571.

CONDUCT MONEY. In English practice. Money paid to a witness who has been subpoenaed on a trial, sufficient to defray the reasonable expenses of going to, staying at, and returning from the place of trial. Lush, Com. Law Prac. 460; Archb. New Prac. 639.

CONDUCTI ACTIO. See "Actio ex Conducto."

CONDUCTIO (Lat.) A hiring; a bailment for hire.

It is the correlative of *locatio*, a letting for hire. *Conducti actio*, in the civil law, is an action which the hirer of a thing or his heir had against the latter or his heir to be allowed to use the thing hired. *Conducere*, to hire a thing. *Conductor*, a hirer, a carrier; one who undertakes to perform labor on another's property for a specified sum. *Conductus*, the thing hired. Calv. Lex.; Du Cange; 2 Kent, Comm. 586.

CONDUCTOR. One who conducts or escorts. In the law and usage of railways, a trainman who directs the movements of the train and is responsible for the execution of orders in respect to the same, and, where passengers are carried, collects fares, etc.; one who performs like duties on street cars and other like cars.

CONDUIT. A method or means of conveying; a channel for passage or transmission, especially of water or other fluid.

"Conduit" is a general word which applies to any channel or structure by which flowing water can be conducted from one point to another. It includes a ditch, flume, pipe, or any kind of aqueduct. 103 Cal. 673.

CONE. See "Coine."

CONE AND KEY. A woman at fourteen or fifteen years of age may take charge of her house, and receive cone and key,—that is, keep the accounts and keys. Cowell. Said by Lord Coke to be "cover and keye," meaning that at that age a woman knew what in her house should be kept under lock and key. Coke, 2d Inst. 203.

CONFARREATIO. In Roman law. A sacrificial rite resorted to by marrying persons of high patrician or priestly degree, for the purpose of clothing the husband with the *manus* over his wife; the civil modes of effecting the same thing being *coemptio* (formal), and *usus mulieris* (informal). Brown.

CONFECTIO (Lat. from *conficere*). The making and completion of a written instrument. 5 Coke, 1.

CONFEDERACY.

——**In Criminal Law.** An agreement between two or more persons to do an unlawful act, or an act which, though not unlawful in itself, becomes so by the confederacy.

The technical term usually employed to signify this offense is "conspiracy."

——**In Equity Pleading.** An improper combination alleged to have been entered into between the defendants to a bill in equity.

A general charge of confederacy is made a part of a bill in chancery, and is the fourth part, in order, of the bill, but it has become merely formal, except in cases where the complainant intends to show that such a combination actually exists or existed, in which case a special charge of such confederacy must be made. Story, Eq. Pl. §§ 29, 30; Mitf. Eq. Pl. (Jeremy Ed.) 41; Cooper, Eq. Pl. 9.

——**In International Law.** An agreement between two or more states or nations, by which they unite for their mutual protection and good. This term is applied to such an agreement made between two independent nations, but it is also used to signify the union of different states of the same nation, as, the confederacy of the states.

CONFEDERATION. The name given to that form of government which the American colonies during the Revolution devised for their mutual safety and government.

CONFERENCE.

——**In French Law.** A similarity between two laws or two systems of laws.

——**In International Law.** Verbal explanations between the representatives of at least two nations, for the purpose of accelerating matters by avoiding the delays and other difficulties necessarily attending written communications.

——**In Legislation.** Mutual consultations by two committees appointed, one by each house of a legislature, in cases where the houses cannot agree in their action.

CONFESSIO FACTA IN JUDICIO OMNI probatione major est. A confession made in court is of greater effect than any proof. Jenk. Cent. Cas. 102.

CONFESSION. In criminal law. The voluntary declaration, made by a person who has committed a crime or misdemeanor, to another, of the agency or participation which he had in the same.

An admission or acknowledgment by a prisoner, when arraigned for an offense, that he committed the crime with which he is charged.

A confession is an admission of the criminal act, and is to be distinguished from "admissions" or "declarations" by the defendant of facts from which guilt may be inferred. 53 Iowa, 69; 17 Ill. 427.

Judicial confessions are those made before a magistrate or in court in the due course of legal proceedings.

Extrajudicial confessions are those made by the party elsewhere than before a magistrate or in open court. 1 Greenl. Ev. § 216.

The term "confession" is limited to the criminal act, and does not include statements, declarations, or admissions of facts incriminating in their nature or tending to prove guilt. 208 Ill. 607.

CONFESSION AND AVOIDANCE. In pleading. The admission in a pleading of the truth of the facts as stated in the pleading to which it is an answer, and the allegation of new and related matter of fact which destroys the legal effect of the facts so admitted. The plea and any of the subsequent pleadings may be by way of confession and avoidance, or, which is the same thing, "in" confession and avoidance. Pleadings in confession and avoidance must give color. See "Color"; 1 East, 212. They must admit the material facts of the opponent's pleading, either expressly in terms (Dyer, 171b), or in effect. They must conclude with a verification. 1 Saund. 103, note. For the form of statement, see Steph. Pl. 72, 79.

Pleas in confession and avoidance are either in justification and excuse, which go to show that the plaintiff never had any right of action, as, for example, *son assault demesne*, or in discharge, which go to show that his right has been released by some matter subsequent.

CONFESSOR. A priest of some Christian sect, who receives an account of the sins of his people, and undertakes to give them absolution of their sins. The common law does not recognize any such relation, at least so as to exempt or prevent the confessor from disclosing such communications as are made to him in this capacity, when he is called upon as a witness in a court of justice.

CONFESSORIA ACTIO. See "Actio Confessoria."

CONFESSUS IN JUDICIO PRO JUDIcato habetur et quodammodo sua sententia damnatur. A person who has confessed in court is deemed as having had judgment passed upon him, and, in a manner, is condemned by his own sentence. 11 Coke, 30. See Dig. 42, 2. 1.

CONFIDENCE GAME. A method of swindling. 265 Ill. 283.

Any swindling operation in which advantage is taken of the confidence reposed by the victim in the swindler. 261 Ill. 322.

CONFIDENTIAL COMMUNICATIONS. Those statements with regard to any transaction made by one person to another during the continuance of some relation between them which calls for or warrants such communications.

At law, certain classes of such communications are held not to be proper subjects of inquiry in courts of justice, and the persons receiving them are excluded from disclosing them when called upon as witnesses, upon grounds of public policy; as communications between husband and wife, between attorney and client, or between priest and penitent.

CONFIRM. To make firm, or more firm; to give more strength to. The word is held not to impart a warranty in a conveyance of real estate.

Used in a conveyance of real estate "confirm" does not impart a warranty. 9 N. Y. 541.

To make sure or certain; to give added assurance of truth to; to verify.

The word "confirm" sometimes means merely "verify": it is commonly used in that sense at the meetings of public bodies, who confirm the minutes of their last meeting, not meaning thereby that they give them force, but merely that they declare them accurate (Lord Campbell, C. J., *Reg. v. York* [1853], 1 E. & B. 594).

To make valid or binding by some formal act; to consummate; to ratify.

"You can only 'confirm' that which has been already 'entertained' or 'accepted' for you." (Lord Esher, M. R., *Ex parte Kearsley*, 18 Q. B. D. 173).

CONFIRMARE EST ID QUOD PRIUS INfirmum fuit simul firmare. To confirm is to make firm what was before infirm. Co. Litt. 295.

CONFIRMARE NEMO POTEST PRIUS quam jus ei acciderit. No one can confirm before the right accrues to him. 10 Coke, 48.

CONFIRMAT USUM QUI TOLLIT ABUSum. He confirms a use who removes an abuse. F. Moore, 764.

CONFIRMATIO (Lat. *confirmare*). The conveyance of an estate, or the communication of a right that one hath in or unto lands or tenements, to another that hath the possession thereof, or some other estate therein, whereby a voidable estate is made sure and unavoidable, or whereby a particular estate is increased or enlarged. Shep. Touch. 311; 2 Bl. Comm. 325.

Confirmatio crescens tends and serves to increase or enlarge a rightful estate, and so to pass an interest.

Confirmatio diminuens tends or serves to diminish and abridge the services whereby the tenant holds.

Confirmatio perficiens tends and serves to confirm and make good a wrongful and defeasible estate, by adding the right to the possession or defeasible seisin, or to make a conditional estate absolute, by discharging the condition.

CONFIRMATIO CHARTARUM (Lat. confirmation of the charters). A statute passed in 25 Edw. I., whereby the Great Charter is declared to be allowed as the common law; all judgments contrary to it are declared void; copies of it are ordered to be sent to all cathedral churches, and read twice a year to the people; and sentence of excommunication is directed to be as constantly denounced against all those that, by word or deed or counsel, act contrary thereto, or in any degree infringe it. 1 Bl. Comm. 128.

CONFIRMATIO EST NULLA, UBI DONum praecedens est invalidum. A confirmation is null where the preceding gift is invalid. Co. Litt. 295; F. Moore, 764.

CONFIRMATIO OMNES SUPPLET DEfectus, licet id quod actum est ab initio non valuit. Confirmation supplies all defects, though that which has been done was not valid at the beginning. Co. Litt. 295b.

CONFIRMATIO PERFICIENS (Law Lat.) In old English law. A perfecting confirmation; a confirmation which tends and serves to confirm and make good a wrongful and defeasible estate, by adding the right to the possession, or defeasible seisin, or to make a conditional estate absolute, by discharging the condition. Shep. Touch. (by Preston) 311.

CONFIRMATION. A contract by which that which was voidable is made firm and unavoidable.

A conveyance, whereby a voidable estate previously granted is made firm.

Ratification of an official act by a person or body having a supervisory jurisdiction; as confirmation of a referee's report by the court; confirmation of a sheriff's sale; confirmation by the legislative body of an appointment by the executive.

——**In Ecclesiastical Law.** Ratification by the archbishop of the election of a bishop by the dean and chapter. Wharton.

CONFIRMAVI (Lat.) I have confirmed. Used in ancient deeds of confirmation.

CONFIRMEE. He to whom a confirmation is made.

CONFIRMOR. He who makes a confirmation to another.

CONFISCARE. To confiscate.

CONFISCATE. To appropriate to the use of the state. Especially used of the goods and property of alien enemies found in a state in time of war. 1 Kent, Comm. 52 et seq. *Bona confiscata* and *forisfacta* are said to be the same (1 Bl. Comm. 299), and the result to the individual is the same whether the property be forfeited or confiscated; but, as distinguished, an individual forfeits, a state confiscates, goods or other property. Used also as an adjective,—forfeited. 1 Bl. Comm. 299.

Confiscation is to be distinguished from a proceeding in prize. "Confiscation is the act of the sovereign against a rebellious subject; condemnation as prize is the act of a belligerent against another belligerent." 14 Ct. Cl. Rep. 48.

CONFISK. An old form of confiscate. Finch, Law, bk. 3, c. 17.

CONFITENS REUS. An accused person who admits his guilt.

CONFLICT OF LAWS. A contrariety or opposition in the laws of states in those cases where, from their relations to each other, or to the subject-matter in dispute, the rights of the parties are liable to be affected by the laws of both jurisdictions.

An opposition or inconsistency of domestic laws upon the same subject.

As a term of art, it also includes the deciding which law is in such cases to have superiority. It also includes many cases where there is no opposition between two systems of law, but where the question is how much force may be allowed to a foreign law with reference to which an act has been done, either directly or by legal implication, in the absence of any domestic law exclusively applicable to the case.

CONFLICT OF PRESUMPTIONS. In this conflict, certain rules are applicable, viz.: (1) Special take procedence of general presumptions; (2) constant of casual ones; (3) presume in favor of innocence; (4) of legality; (5) of validity; and, when these rules fail, the matter is said to be "at large." Brown.

CONFORMITY. In English ecclesiastical law. Adherence to the doctrines and usages of the Church of England.

CONFORMITY, BILL OF. See "Bill of Conformity."

CONFRAIRIE (Fr.) A fraternity, brotherhood, or society. Cowell.

CONFRONTATION. In practice. The act by which a witness is brought into the presence of the accused, so that the latter may object to him, if he can, and the former may know and identify the accused, and maintain the truth in his presence. No man can be a witness unless confronted with the accused, except by consent.

CONFUSIO (Lat. *confundere*). In civil law. A pouring together of liquids; a melting of metals; a blending together of an inseparable compound.

It is distinguished from *commixtis* by the fact that in the latter case a separation may be made, while in a case of *confusio* there cannot be. Bowyer, Comm. 88; 2 Bl. Comm. 405.

CONFUSION.

——**In Common Law.** The intermixture of the goods of two persons, so that the several portions can be no longer distinguished. 2 Bl. Comm. 405. The term, and, in a great degree, the doctrine, are borrowed from the *confusio* of the civil law. The meaning of the former, however, has been so far modified as to include not only the intermixture or interfusion of liquids and metals (the *confusio* proper of the civil law), but also that of dry articles (properly expressed in the same law by the term *commixtio*). The doctrines, also, of the two systems so far differ that, while the civil law allows a party who wilfully intermixes his property with that of another, without his approbation or consent, a satisfaction for what he has so improvidently lost, the common law allows him nothing, but gives the entire property to the other party. 2 Bl. Comm. 405; Inst. 2. 1. 28; 2 Steph. Comm. 85; 2 Kent, Comm. 364; U. S. Dig. It is the admixture of goods of the same kind, as distinguished from "accession," which is the union of materials of different kinds.

——**In Civil Law.** The blending or union of the characters of debtor and creditor in the same person; the union of the obligation of the debtor with the right of the creditor, which dissolves or extinguishes the former. Heinec. Elem. Jur. Civ. bk. 3, tit. 30, § 1006; Ersk. Inst. lib. e, tit. 4, § 23. Thus, where a woman obligee marries the obligor, the debt is extinguished. 1 Salk. 306.

CONFUSION OF RIGHTS. A union of the qualities of debtor and creditor in the same person. The effect of such a union is generally to extinguish the debt. 1 Salk. 306; Cro. Car. 551; 1 Ld. Raym. 515. See 5 Term R. 281; Comyn, Dig. "Baron et Feme" (D).

CONGE. In French law. A clearance; a species of passport or permission to navigate.

CONGE D'ACCORDER (Fr. leave to accord). A phrase used in the process of levying a fine. Upon the delivery of the original writ, one of the parties immediately asked for a *conge d'accorder*, or leave to agree with the plaintiff. Termes de la Ley; Cowell. See "Licentia Concordandi"; 2 Bl. Comm. 350.

CONGE D'EMPARLER (Fr. leave to imparl). The privilege of an imparlance (*licentia loquendi*). 3 Sharswood, Bl. Comm. 299.

CONGE D'ESLIRE (Fr.) The king's permission royal to a dean and chapter in time of vacation to choose a bishop, or to an abbey or priory of his own foundation to choose the abbot or prior.

Originally, the king had free appointment of all ecclesiastical dignities whensoever they chanced to be void. Afterwards he made the election over to others, under certain forms and conditions, as, that at every vacation they should ask of the king *conge d'eslire*. Cowell; Termes de la Ley; 1 Bl. Comm. 379, 382.

CONGEABLE (Fr. *conge*, permission, leave). Lawful, or lawfully done, or done with permission; as, entry *congeable*, and the like. Litt. § 279.

CONGILDONES. In Saxon law. Fellow members of a guild. Spelman, voc. "Geldum."

CONGIUS. An ancient measure containing about a gallon and a pint. Cowell; Blount.

CONGREGATION. A society of a number of persons who compose an ecclesiastical body.

In the ecclesiastical law, this term is used to designate certain bureaus at Rome, where ecclesiastical matters are attended to.

In the United States, by congregation is meant the members of a particular church who meet in one place to worship. See 2 Russ. 120.

It is a broader term than "communicants," including all who habitually meet together for worship. 11 N. Y. 243.

CONGRESS. An assembly of deputies convened from different governments to treat of peace or of other international affairs.

The name of the legislative body of the United States, composed of the senate and house of representatives. U. S. Const. art. 1, § 1.

CONJECTIO. In the civil law of evidence. A throwing together; presumption; the putting of things together, with the inference drawn therefrom. Matt. Pr. c. 1, note 43.

CONJECTIO CAUSAE. In civil law. A statement of the case; a brief synopsis of the case given by the advocate to the judge in opening the trial. Calv. Lex.

CONJECTURE. A slight degree of credence, arising from evidence too weak or too remote to cause belief. 1 Mascardus de Prob. quaest. 14, note 14.

An idea or notion founded on a probability, without any demonstration of its truth.

CONJOINTS. Persons married to each other. Story, Confl. Laws, § 71. Wolff. Dr. Nat. § 858.

CONJUGAL RIGHTS. Rights arising from the relation of husband and wife.

In England, a writ lies for restitution to conjugal rights in case of intentional desertion, including, perhaps, a refusal to consummate marriage, under some circumstances, but this remedy has never been adopted in the United States. Bish. Mar. & Div. § 503 et seq.; 3 Bl. Comm. 94.

CONJUGIUM. One of the names of marriage, among the Romans. Tayl. Civ. Law, 284.

CONJUNCT. In Scotch law. Joint, as applied to rights. Ersk. Inst. bk. 3, tit. 8, § 34; Bell, Dict.

Connected, as applied to persons. Bell, Dict.

CONJUNCTA. In civil law. Things joined together or united; as distinguished from *disjuncta*; things disjoined or separated. Dig. 50. 16. 53.

CONJUNCTIM (Lat.) In old English law. Jointly. Inst. 2. 20. 8; Bracton, fol. 19.

CONJUNCTIM ET DIVISIM (Law Lat.)

——**In Old English Law.** Jointly and severally. Bracton, fol. 19.

——**In the Civil Law.** *Conjunctim et disjunctim* and *conjunctim et separatim* were used.

CONJUNCTIO. In civil law. Conjunction; connection of words in a sentence. See Dig. 50. 16. 29. 142.

CONJUNCTIO MARITI ET FEMINAE est de jure naturae. The union of a man and a woman is of the law of nature.

CONJUNCTIVE. Connecting in a manner denoting union.

CONJURATIO.

——**In Old English Law.** A swearing together; an oath administered to several together; a combination or confederacy under oath. Cowell; Blount; Tomlin.

——**In Old European Law.** A compact of the inhabitants of a commune, or municipality, confirmed by their oaths to each other, and which was the basis of the commune. Steph. Lect. 119.

CONJURATION (Lat. a swearing together). A plot, bargain, or compact, made by a number of persons under oath, to do some public harm.

Personal conference with the devil or some evil spirit, to know any secret or effect any purpose.

CONJURATOR. In old English law. One who swears or is sworn with others; one bound by oath with others; a compurgator; a conspirator. Britt. 27, 120; Fleta, lib. 2, c. 47, § 6.

CONNIVANCE. An agreement or consent, indirectly given, that something unlawful shall be done by another.

A married party's corrupt consenting to evil conduct, of which afterwards he complains. 2 Bish. Mar. & Div. § 203.

Connivance differs from condonation, though the same legal consequences may attend it. Connivance necessarily involves criminality on the part of the individual who connives; condonation may take place without imputing the slightest blame to the party who forgives the injury. Connivance must be the act of the mind before the offense has been committed; condonation is the result of a determination to forgive an injury which was not known until after it was inflicted. 3 Hagg. Ecc. 350.

An error of judgment not involving a willingness to have the delinquency committed is not connivance. 10 Jur. 829. Nor is a watching of the guilty parties, without interference. 109 Mass. 408.

CONNOISSEMENT. In French law. An instrument, signed by the master of a ship or his agent, containing a description of the goods loaded on a ship, the persons who have sent them, the persons to whom they were sent, and the undertaking to transport them. A bill of lading. Guyot, Rep. Univ.; Ord. de la Mar. lib. 3, tit. 2, art. 1.

CONNUBIUM (Lat.) A lawful marriage.

CONOCIAMENTO. In Spanish law. A recognizance. White, New Recop. bk. 3, tit. 7, c. 5, § 3.

CONOCIMIENTO. In Spanish law. A bill of lading. In the Mediterranean ports it is called *poliza de cargamiento*. For the requisites of this instrument, see Code Comm. Spain, arts. 799-811.

CONPOSSESSIO. In modern civil law. A joint possession. Mackeld. Civ. Law, § 245.

CONQUEREUR. In Norman and old English law. The first purchaser of an estate; he who first brought an estate into his family. 2 Bl. Comm. 243.

CONQUEROR. In old English and Scotch law. Same as "conquereur."

CONQUEST (Lat. *conquiro*, to seek for).

——**In Feudal Law.** Purchase; any means of obtaining an estate out of the usual course of inheritance.

The estate itself so acquired.

According to Blackstone and Sir Henry Spelman, the word in its original meaning was entirely dissociated from any connection with the modern idea of military subjugation, but was used solely in the sense of purchase.

——**In International Law.** The acquisition of the sovereignty of a country by force of arms, exercised by an independent power which reduces the vanquished to the submission of its empire.

CONQUETS. In French law. The name given to every acquisition which the husband and wife, jointly or severally, make during the conjugal community. Thus, whatever is acquired by the husband and wife, either by his or her industry or good fortune, inures to the extent of one-half for the benefit of the other. Merlin, Repert; Merlin, Quest. In Louisiana, these gains are called *aquets*. Civ. Code La. art. 2369. The *conquets* by a former marriage may not be settled on a second wife to prejudice the heirs. 2 Low. (U. S.) 175.

CONQUISITIO. In feudal and old English law. Acquisition. Spelman, voc. "Conquestus"; 2 Bl. Comm. 242.

CONQUISITOR. In feudal law. A purchaser, acquirer, or conqueror. 2 Bl. Comm. 242, 243.

CONSANGUINEOUS FRATER. A brother who has the same father. 2 Bl. Comm. 231.

CONSANGUINEUS. One within the degrees of consanguinity.

CONSANGUINEUS EST QUASI EODEM sanguine natus. A person related by consanguinity is, as it were, sprung from the same blood. Co. Litt. 157.

CONSANGUINITY (Lat. *consanguis*, blood together). The relation subsisting among all the different persons descending from the same stock or common ancestor.

——**Collateral Consanguinity.** The relation subsisting among persons who descend from the same common ancestor, but not one from the other. It is essential, to constitute this relation, that they spring from the same common root or stock, but in different branches.

The mode of computing degrees of collateral consanguinity at the common and by the canon law is to discover the common ancestor, to begin with him to reckon downwards, and the degree the two persons, or the more remote of them, is distant from the ancestor, is the degree of kindred subsisting between them. For instance, two brothers are related to each other in the first degree, because from the father to each of them is one degree. An uncle and a nephew are related to each other in the second degree, because the nephew is two degrees distant from the common ancestor; and the rule of computation is extended to the remotest degrees of collateral relationship.

The method of computing by the civil law is to begin at either of the persons in question, and count up to the common ancestor, and then downwards to the other person, calling it a degree for each person, both ascending and descending, and the degrees they stand from each other is the degree in which they stand related. Thus, from a nephew to his father is one degree; to the grandfather, two degrees; and then to the uncle, three; which points out the relationship.

The mode of the civil law is preferable for it points out the actual degree of kindred in all cases. By the mode adopted by the common law, different relations may stand in the same degree. The uncle and nephew stand related in the second degree by the common law, and so are two first cousins, or two sons of two brothers; but by the civil law the uncle and nephew are in the third degree, and the cousins are in the fourth. The mode of computation, however, is immaterial, for both will establish the same person to be the heir. 2 Bl. Comm. 202. See "Descent"; "Line."

——**Lineal Consanguinity.** That relation which exists among persons where one is descended from the other, as between the son and the father, or the grandfather, and so upwards in a direct ascending line, and between the father and the son, or the grandson, and so downwards in a direct descending line.

In computing the degree of lineal consanguinity existing between two persons, every generation in the direct course of relationship between the two parties makes a degree, and the rule is the same by the canon, civil, and common law.

CONSCIENCE. Internal or self knowledge or judgment of right or wrong. It is not identical with "principle." An "objection on principle" to the death penalty is not the same as a conscientious scruple. 7 Cal. 140.

CONSCIENCE, COURTS OF. Courts, not of record, constituted by act of parliament in the city of London, and other towns, for the recovery of small debts; otherwise and more commonly called "Courts of Requests." 3 Steph. Comm. 451.

CONSCIENTIA DICITUR A CON ET scio, quasi scire cum Deo. Conscience is called from *con* and *scio*, to know, as it were, with God. 1 Coke, 100.

CONSECRATIO EST PERIODUS ELECtionis; electio est praeambula consecrationis. Consecration is the termination of election; election is the preamble of consecration. 2 Rolle, Abr. 102.

CONSEIL DE FAMILLE. A council of the family. In French law, certain acts require the sanction of this body. For example, a guardian can neither accept nor reject an inheritance to which the minor has succeeded without his authority (Code Nap. 461); nor can he accept for the child a gift *inter vivos* without the like authority (Id. 463). So, also, in bringing or compromising a suit on behalf of the child, or generally in compounding claims, and in numerous personal relations, *e. g.*, consent to marriages of orphans, the authority of this body is necessary.

CONSEIL JUDICIAIRE. In French law. When a person has been subjected to an interdiction on the ground of his insane extravagance, but the interdiction is not absolute, but limited only, the court of first instance, which grants the interdiction, appoints a counsel, called by this name, with whose assistance the party may bring or defend actions, or compromise the same, alienate his estate, make or incur loans, and the like. Brown.

CONSENSUAL CONTRACT. In civil law. A contract completed by the consent of the parties merely, without any further act.

The contract of sale, among the civilians, is an example of a consensual contract, because the moment there is an agreement between the seller and the buyer as to the thing and the price, the vendor and the purchaser have reciprocal actions. On the contrary, on a loan, there is no action by the lender or borrower, although there may have been consent, until the thing is delivered, or the money counted. Poth. Obl. pt. 1, c. 1, § 1, art. 2; 1 Bell, Comm. (5th Ed.) 435.

CONSENSUS EST VOLUNTAS PLUrium ad quos res pertinet, simul juncta. Consent is the conjoint will of several persons to whom the thing belongs. Lofft, 514.

CONSENSUS FACIT LEGEM. Consent makes the law. A contract is law between the parties having received their consent. Branch, Princ.

CONSENSUS, NON CONCUBITUS, FACIT matrimonium. Consent, not coition, constitutes marriage. Co. Litt. 33a; Dig. 50. 17. 30. See 10 Clark & F. 534; 1 Bouv. Inst. 103; Broom, Leg. Max. (3d London Ed.) 129.

CONSENSUS, NON CONCUBITUS, FAcit nuptias vel matrimonium, et consentire non possunt ante annos nubiles. Consent, and not cohabitation, constitutes nuptials or marriage, and persons cannot consent before marriageable years. 6 Coke, 22; 1 Bl. Comm. 434.

CONSENSUS TOLLIT ERROREM. Consent removes or obviates a mistake. Co. Litt. 126; Coke, 2d Inst. 123; Broom, Leg. Max. (3d London Ed.) 129; 1 Bing. N. C. 68; 6 El. & Bl. 338; 7 Johns. (N. Y.) 611.

CONSENSUS VOLUNTAS MULTORUM ad quos res pertinet, simul juncta. Consent is the united will of several interested in one subject-matter. Dav. 48; Branch, Princ.

CONSENT (Lat. *con*, with, together, *sentire*, to feel). A concurrence of wills.

Express consent is that directly given, either *viva voce* or in writing.

Implied consent is that manifested by signs, actions, or facts, or by inaction or silence, which raise a presumption that the consent has been given.

Consent supposes a physical power to act, a moral power of acting, and a serious, determined, and free use of these powers. Fonbl. Eq. bk. 1, c. 2, § 1. See "Agreement"; "Contract."

CONSENT DECREE. A decree based upon the consent or agreement of the parties, which may supersede both pleading and evidence and even go to the length of pointing out and limiting the relief to be granted. 253 Ill. 491.

"A consent degree is not, in a strict legal sense 'a judicial sentence,' but it is in the nature of a solemn contract and which cannot be amended or in any way varied, without the like consent, or reheard in the court that rendered it, appealed from, or reversed upon a writ of error or bill for review." 120 Ill. App. 645; 174 Ill. 154.

CONSENT RULE. An entry of record by the defendant, confessing the lease, entry, and ouster by the plaintiff, in an action of ejectment. This was, until recently, used in England and in those of the United States in which the action of ejectment is still retained as a means of acquiring possession of land.

CONSENTIENTES ET AGENTES PARI poena plectentur. Those consenting and those perpetrating shall receive the same punishment. 5 Coke, 80.

CONSENTIRE MATRIMONIO NON POSsunt infra annos nubiles. Persons cannot consent to marriage before marriageable years. 5 Coke, 80; 6 Coke, 22.

CONSEQUENCE. That which follows something on which it depends; that which is produced by a cause; connection of cause and effect; that which follows from, or grows out of any act, cause or series of actions; an event or effect produced by some preceding influence, action, act or cause. 162 Ill. App. 113.

CONSEQUENTIAE NON EST CONSEquentia. A consequence ought not to be drawn from another consequence. Bac. Aph. 16.

CONSEQUENTIAL CONTEMPT. Contempts which without gross insolence or direct opposition plainly tend to create a universal disregard of the authority of the courts. 72 Ill. App. 176.

CONSEQUENTIAL DAMAGES. Those damages or those losses which arise not from the immediate act of the party, but in consequence of such act. Those produced naturally, but not directly.

CONSERVATOR (Lat. *conservare,* to preserve). A preserver; one whose business it is to attend to the enforcement of certain statutes.

A delegated umpire or standing arbitrator, chosen to compose and adjust difficulties arising between two parties. Cowell.

A guardian. So used in Connecticut. 3 Day (Conn.) 472; 5 Conn. 280; 3 Conn. 228; 12 Conn. 376.

CONSERVATOR OF THE PEACE. He who hath an especial charge, by virtue of his office, to see that the king's peace be kept.

Before the reign of Edward III., who created justices of the peace, there were sundry persons interested to keep the peace, of whom there were two classes; one of which had the power annexed to the office which they held; the other had it merely by itself, and were hence called "wardens" or "conservators of the peace." Lambard, Eiren. lib. 1, c. 3. This latter sort are superseded by the modern justices of the peace. 1 Bl. Comm. 349.

The judges and other similar officers of the various states, and also of the United States, are conservators of the public peace, being entitled "to hold to the security of the peace and during good behavior." 1 Sharswood, Bl. Comm. 349.

CONSERVATOR TRUCIS (Lat.) An officer whose duty it was to inquire into all offenses against the king's truces and safe-conducts upon the main seas out of the liberties of the Cinque Ports.

Under St. 2 Hen. V. st. 1, c. 6, such offenses are declared to be treason, and such officers are appointed in every port, to hear and determine such cases, "according to the ancient maritime law then practised in the admiral's court, as may arise upon the high seas, and with two associates to determine those arising upon land." 4 Bl. Comm. 69, 70.

CONSERVATORS OF RIVERS. In English law. Commissioners who are, by act of Parliament, given the control of a certain river.

CONSIDERATIO CURIAE. The consideration of the court; that is, the judgment of the court implying consideration or study.

CONSIDERATION (Law Lat. *consideratio*). The material cause which moves a contracting party to enter into a contract. 2 Bl. Comm. 443.

The price, motive, or matter of inducement to a contract,—whether it be the compensation which is paid, or the inconvenience which is suffered by the party from whom it proceeds. A compensation or equivalent. A cause or occasion meritorious, requiring mutual recompense in deed or in law. Viner, Abr. "Consideration" (A).

The *quid pro quo,* that which the party to whom a promise is made does or agrees to do in exchange therefor. 120 U. S. 197.

Mutuality of obligation, as to each party, is the obligation imposed by the contract on the other party.

As applied to contracts, "consideration" and "obligation" are really convertible terms, though frequently used as correlatives. The essence of every contract is its mutuality, and, in necessary consequence, the obligation of each party is the consideration running to the other, while the entire obligation of the contract is the mutual considerations.

"The motive for entering into a contract, and the consideration of the contract, are not the same. Nothing is consideration that is not regarded as such by both parties. It is the price voluntarily paid for the promisor's undertaking. Expectation of results will not constitute a consideration." Beach, Cont., § 147.

Consideration is the very life and essence of a contract, and a contract or promise for which there is no consideration cannot be enforced at law. Such a promise is called a *nudum pactum* (*ex nudo pacto non oritur actio*), or *nude pact,* because a gratuitous promise to do or pay anything on the one side, without any compensation on the other, could only be enforced, in the Roman law, when made (or clothed) with proper words or formalities,—*pactum verbis prescriptis vestitum.* 7 Watts & S. (Pa.) 317; Plowd. 308; Smith, Lead. Cas. 456; Doctor & Stud. 2, c. 24; 3 Call (Va.) 439; 7 Conn. 57; 1 Stew. (Ala.) 51; 5 Mass. 301; 4 Johns. (N. Y.) 235; 6 Yerg. (Tenn.) 418; Cooke (Tenn.) 467; 6 Halst. (N. J.) 174; 4 Munf. (Va.) 95; 11 Md. 281; 25 Miss. 66; 30 Me. 412.

Considerations, according to their general nature, are:

(1) Valuable, being one which confers some benefit on the party at whose instance it is made, or upon a third party, at his request, or some detriment sustained at the instance of the party promising by the party to whom the promise is made.

(2) Good, being one of blood, natural affection, or the like. Beach, Cont. § 148; Chit. Cont. 7; Doctor & Stud. 179; 1 Selw. N. P. 39, 40; 2 Pet. (U. S.) 182; 5 Cranch (U. S.) 142, 150; 1 Litt. (Ky.) 183; 3 Johns. (N. Y.) 100; 14 Johns. (N. Y.) 466; 8 N. Y. 207; 6 Mass. 58; 2 Bibb (Ky.) 30; 2 J. J. Marsh. (Ky.) 222; 2 N. H. 97; Wright (Ohio) 660; 5 Watts & S. (Pa.) 427; 13 Serg. & R. (Pa.) 29; 12 Ga. 52; 24 Miss. 9; 4 Ill. 33; 5 Humph. (Tenn.) 19; 4 Blackf. (Ind.) 388; 3 C. B. 321; 4 East, 55.

Valuable considerations are divided by the civilians into four classes, which are given, with literal translations: *Do ut des*, I give that you may give, *facio ut facias*, I do that you may do, *facio ut des*, I do that you may give, *do ut facias*, I give that you may do.

They are also:

(3) Executed or past, being those done or received before the obligor made the promise.

(4) Executory, being those by which it is undertaken to do something in the future. 95 U. S. 683; 6 Colo. 318.

They are also:

(5) Concurrent, being those which arise at the same time, or where the promises are simultaneous.

(6) Continuing, being those which are executed only in part.

(7) Equitable, being moral considerations.

(8) Moral, being such as, though not valuable, are of moral obligation, and are sufficient to support an executed contract. 18 S. E. 421.

(9) Gratuitous, being those which are not founded on such a deprivation or injury to the promisee as to make the consideration valid at law. 2 Mich. 381.

(10) Illegal, being agreements to do things in contravention of the common or of statute law.

(11) Impossible, being those which cannot be performed.

Considerations have been further classified as "express" or "implied," accordingly as they are stated in the contract, or left to be inferred by law, but the distinction is based rather on the manner of contracting than on the nature of the consideration. See "Contract."

CONSIDERATUM EST PER CURIAM (Lat. it is considered by the court). A formula used in giving judgments.

A judgment is the decision or sentence of the law, given by a court of justice, as the result of proceedings, instituted therein for the redress of an injury. The language of the judgment is not, therefore, that "it is decreed," or "resolved," by the court, but that "it is considered by the court," *consideratum est per curiam*, that the plaintiff recover his debt, etc. 3 Bouv. Inst. note 3298.

CONSIDERATUR (Law Lat. it is considered). Held to mean the same with *consideratum est*. 2 Strange, 874.

CONSIGN. To send goods to a factor or agent.

To deposit with another to be sold, disposed of or cared for, as merchandise or movable property; to send goods to an agent, commission merchant, correspondent or factor, to be sold, stored, etc. 82 Ill. App. 687.

——**In Civil Law.** To deposit in the custody of a third person a thing belonging to the debtor, for the benefit of the creditor, under the authority of a court of justice. Poth. Obl. pt. 3, c. 1, art. 8.

The term "to consign," or "consignation," is derived from the Latin *consignare*, which signifies to seal; for it was formerly the practice to seal up the money thus received in a bag or box. Aso & M. Inst. bk. 2, tit. 11, c. 1, § 5.

Generally, the consignation is made with a public officer. It is very similar to our practice of paying money into court.

CONSIGNATIO. See "Consign."

CONSIGNATION. From *consignare*, to seal up.

——**In Scotch Law.** The payment of money into the hands of a third party, when the creditor refuses to accept of it. The person to whom the money is given is termed the "consignatory." Bell, Dict.

——**In French Law.** A deposit which a debtor makes of the thing that he owes into the hands of a third person, and under the authority of a court of justice.

It is not properly a payment, but it is equivalent to a payment, and extinguishes the debt no less than if an actual payment had been made. Code, 8. 43. 9; Poth. Obl. pt. 3, c. 1, art. 8.

CONSIGNEE. One to whom a consignment is made.

CONSIGNMENT. The goods or property sent by means of a common carrier by one or more persons, called the "consignors," in one place, to one or more persons, called the "consignees," who are in another. The goods sent by one person to another, to be sold or disposed of by the latter for and on account of the former. The act of consigning goods.

——**In French Law.** "A deposit which the debtor makes of the thing that he owes into the hands of a third person, and under the authority of a court of justice." 1 Poth. Obl. 376.

CONSIGNOR. One who makes a consignment.

CONSILIA MULTORUM REQUIRUNTUR in magnis. The advice of many persons is requisite in great affairs. Coke, 4th Inst. 1.

CONSILIARIUS (Lat. *consiliare*, to advise). In the civil law. A counsellor, as distinguished from a pleader or advocate; an assistant judge; one who participates in the decisions. Du Cange.

CONSILIUM, or DIES CONSILII. A day appointed to hear the counsel of both parties. A case set down for argument.

It is commonly used for the day appointed for the argument of a demurrer, or errors assigned. 1 Tidd, Prac. 438; 2 Tidd, Prac. 684, 1122; 1 Sellon, Prac. 336; 2 Sellon, Prac. 385; 1 Archb. Prac. 191, 246.

CONSIMILI CASU (Lat. in like case). In practice. A writ of entry, framed under the provisions of St. Westminster II. (13 Edw. I.) c. 24, which lay for the benefit of the reversioner, where a tenant by the curtesy aliened in fee or for life.

Many other new writs were framed under the provisions of this statute, but this particular writ was known emphatically by the title here defined. The writ is now practically obsolete. See "Case"; "Assumpsit"; 3 Sharswood, Bl. Comm. 51; 3 Bouv. Inst. note 3482.

CONSISTORIUM. The state council of the Roman emperors. Mackeld. Civ. Law, § 58.

CONSISTORY. In ecclesiastical law. An assembly of cardinals convoked by the pope.

The consistory is either public or secret. It is public when the pope receives princes or gives audience to ambassadors; secret when he fills vacant sees, proceeds to the canonization of saints, or judges and settles certain contestations submitted to him.

CONSISTORY COURT. In English law. The courts of diocesan bishops held in their several cathedrals before the bishops' chancellor, or commissary, who is the judge, for the trial of all ecclesiastical causes arising within their respective dioceses, and also for granting probates and administrations. From the sentence of these courts an appeal lies to the archbishop of each province respectively. 2 Steph. Comm. 230, 237; 3 Steph. Comm. 430, 431; 3 Bl. Comm. 641; 1 Wooddeson, Lect. 145; Halifax, Anal. bk. 3, c. 10, note 12.

CONSOLATO DEL MARE. A code of sea laws, compiled by order of the ancient kings of Arragon. It comprised the ancient ordinances of the Greek and Roman emperors, and of the kings of France and Spain, and the laws of the Mediterranean islands and of Venice and Genoa. See "Admiralty." It was originally written in the dialect of Catalonia, as its title indicates, and it has been translated into every language of Europe. This code has been reprinted in the second volume of the Collection de Lois Maritimes Anterieures au XVIII Siecle, par J. M. Pardessus, Paris, 1831,—a collection of sea laws which is very complete. See, also, Riddu's Hist. Mar. Comm. 171; Marvin, Leg. Bibl.

CONSOLIDATED FUND. In England. Usually abbreviated to consols. A fund for the payment of the public debt.

CONSOLIDATED ORDERS. The orders regulating the practice of the English court of chancery, which were issued, in 1860, in substitution for the various orders which had previously been promulgated from time to time. Some of the consolidated orders have been abrogated by the judicature act, but others are still in force.

CONSOLIDATION.

——**In Civil Law.** The union of the usufruct with the estate out of which it issues, in the same person, which happens when the usufructuary acquires the estate, or *vice versa*. In either case the usufruct is extinct. Lec. Elm. 424.

It may take place in two ways: First, by the usufructuary surrendering his right to the proprietor, which in the common law is called a "surrender"; secondly, by the release by the proprietor of his rights to the usufructuary, which in our law is called a "release."

——**In Ecclesiastical Law.** The union of two or more benefices in one. Cowell.

——**In Practice.** The union of two or more pending actions in the same court between the same parties, and involving the same issues.

——**Of Corporations.** The merger of the franchises, rights, and effects of two or more corporations into one, whether the single corporation, known as the "consolidated company," be a new one then created, or one of the original companies continuing in existence with only larger rights, capacities, and property. 64 Ala. 656.

CONSOLIDATION RULE. In practice. An order of the court requiring the plaintiff to join in one suit several causes of action against the same defendant which may be so joined consistently with the rules of pleading, but upon which he has brought distinct suits. 1 Dall. (Pa.) 147; 1 Yeates (Pa.) 5; 4 Yeates (Pa.) 128; 3 Serg. & R. (Pa.) 264; 2 Arch. Prac. 180. The matter is regulated by statute in many of the states.

CONSOLS. Funds formed by the consolidation (of which word it is an abbreviation) of different annuities, which had been severally formed into a capital. See "Consolidated Fund."

CONSORTIO MALORUM ME QUOQUE malum facit. The company of wicked men makes me also wicked. Moore, 817.

CONSORTIUM. Under the term "consortium," as applied to the relations of husband and wife, are included the person's affections, society and aid. 186 Ill. 539.

——**In Civil Law.** A union of fortunes; one of the names of lawful marriage among the Romans. Tayl. Civ. Law, 284.

A union of several persons as parties in one action. 1 Mackeld. Civ. Law, 197.

——**In Old English Law.** Company; society. It occurs in this last sense in the phrase *per quod consortium amisit*, by which he has lost the companionship, used when the plaintiff declares for any bodily injury done to his wife by a third person. 3 Bl. Comm. 140.

——**In Pleading.** The company or society of a wife.

CONSPIRACY (Lat. *con*, together, *spiro*, to breathe). In criminal law. A combination of two or more persons by some concerted action to accomplish some criminal or unlawful purpose, or to accomplish some purpose, not in itself criminal or unlawful, by criminal or unlawful means. 2 Mass. 337, 538; 4 Metc. (Mass.) 111; 4 Wend. (N. Y.) 229; 15 N. H. 396; 5 Har. & J. (Md.) 317; 3 Serg. & R. (Pa.) 220; 12 Conn. 101; 11 Clark & F. 155; 4 Mich. 414.

CONSPIRATIONE. An ancient writ that lay against conspirators. Reg. Orig. 134; Fitzh. Nat. Brev. 114.

CONSPIRATORS. Persons guilty of a conspiracy.

CONSTABLE. An officer whose duty it is to keep the peace in the district which is assigned to him.

The most satisfactory derivation of the term and history of the origin of this office is that which deduces it from the French *comestable* (Lat. *comes-stabuli*), who was an officer second only to the king. He might take charge of the army, wherever it was, if the king were not present, and had the general control of everything relating to military matters, as the marching troops, their encampment, provisioning, etc. Guyot, Rep. Univ.

The same extensive duties pertained to the constable of Scotland. Bell, Dict.

The duties of this officer in England seem to have been first fully defined by St. Westminster (13 Edw. I.), and question has been frequently made whether the office existed in England before that time. 1 Bl. Comm. 356. It seems, however, to be pretty certain that the office in England is of Norman origin, being introduced by William, and that subsequently the duties of the Saxon tithing men, borsholders, etc., were added to its other functions. See Cowell; Willcock, Const.; 1 Bl. Comm. 356.

High constables were first ordained, according to Blackstone, by the statute of Westminster, though they were known as efficient public officers long before that time. 1 Sharswood, Bl. Comm. 356. They are to be appointed for each franchise or hundred by the leet, or, in default of such appointment, by the justices at quarter sessions. Their first duty is that of keeping the king's peace. In addition, they are to serve warrants, return lists of jurors, and perform various other services enumerated in Coke, 4th Inst. 267; 3 Steph. Comm. 47; Jacob, Law Dict. In some cities and towns in the United States there are officers called "high constables," who are the principal police officers in their jurisdiction.

Petty constables are inferior officers in every town or parish, subordinate to the high constable. They perform the duties of head borough, tithing man, or borsholder and in addition, their more modern duties appertaining to the keeping the peace within their town, village, or tithing.

In England, however, their duties have been much restricted by Act 5 & 6, Vict. c. 109, which deprives them of their power as conservators of the peace. 3 Steph. Comm. 47.

In the United States, generally, petty constables only are retained, their duties being generally the same as those of constables in England prior to 5 & 6 Vict. c. 109, including a limited judicial power as conservators of the peace, a ministerial power for the service of writs, etc., and some other duties not strictly referable to either of these heads.

CONSTABLE OF A CASTLE. The warden or keeper of a castle; the castellan. St. Westminster I. c. 7 (3 Edw. I.); Spelman.

The constable of Dover Castle was also warden of the Cinque Ports. There was besides a constable of the Tower, as well as other constables of castles of less note. Cowell; Lambard, Const.

CONSTABLE OF ENGLAND (called, also, "Marshal"). His office consisted in the care of the common peace of the realm in deeds of arms and matters of war. Lambard, Const. 4. He was to regulate all matters of chivalry, tournaments, and feats of arms which were performed on horseback. 3 Steph. Comm. 47. He held the court of chivalry, besides sitting in the *aula regis*. 4 Bl. Comm. 92.

The office is disused in England, except on coronation days and other such occasions of state, and was last held by Stafford, duke of Buckingham, under Henry VIII. His title is Lord High Constable of England. 3 Steph. Comm. 47; 1 Bl. Comm. 355.

CONSTABLE OF SCOTLAND. An officer who was formerly entitled to command all the king's armies, in the absence of the king, and to take cognizance of all crimes committed within four miles of the king's person or of parliament, the privy council, or any general convention of the states of the kingdom. The office was hereditary in the family of Errol, and was abolished by 20 Geo. III. c. 43. Bell, Dict.; Ersk. Inst. 1. 3. 37.

CONSTABLE OF THE EXCHEQUER. An officer spoken of in 51 Hen. III. st. 5, cited by Cowell.

CONSTABLEWICK. The territorial jurisdiction of a constable. 5 Nev. & M. 261.

CONSTABULARIUS (Lat.) An officer of horse; an officer having charge of foot or horse; a naval commander; an officer having charge of military affairs generally. Spelman.

The titles were very numerous, all derived, however, from *comes-stabuli,* and the duties were quite similar in all the countries where the civil law prevailed. His powers were second only to those of the king in all matters relating to the armies of the kingdom.

In England his power was early diminished and restricted to those duties which related to the preservation of the king's peace. The office is now abolished in England, except as a matter of ceremony, and in France. Guyot, Rep. Univ.; Cowell.

CONSTABULARY. A police force of a county, state or country.

CONSTAT (Lat. it appears). A certificate by an officer that certain matters therein stated appear of record. See 1 Hayw. (N. C.) 410.

An exemplification under the great seal of the enrollment of letters patent. Co. Litt. 225.

A certificate which the clerk of the pipe and auditors of the exchequer make at the request of any person who intends to plead or move in the court for the discharge of any thing, and the effect of it is the certifying what *constat* (appears) upon record touching the matter in question.

CONSTATE. To constitute or establish. "Constating instruments" is used to denote the charter, etc., of a corporation. See 37 N. J. Eq. 363.

CONSTITUENT (Lat. *constituo,* to appoint). He who gives authority to another to act for him. The constituent is bound by the acts of his attorney, and the attorney is responsible to his constituent.

CONSTITUERE. In old English law. To establish; to appoint; to ordain.

Used in letters of attorney, and translated "constitute." Applied generally, also, to denote "appointment." Reg. Orig. 172; Du Cange.

CONSTITUTED AUTHORITIES. The officers properly appointed under the constitution for the government of the people. Those powers which the constitution of each people has established to govern them, to cause their rights to be respected, and to maintain those of each of its members.

They are called "constituted," to distinguish them from the "constituting" authority which has created or organized them, or has delegated to an authority, which it has itself created, the right of establishing or regulating their movements.

CONSTITUTIO.

——**In Civil Law.** An establishment or settlement. Used of controversies settled by the parties without a trial. Calv. Lex.

A sum paid according to agreement. Du Cange.

An ordinance or decree having its force from the will of the emperor. Dig. 1. 4. 1, Cooper's notes.

——**In Old English Law.** An ordinance or statute; a provision of a statute.

CONSTITUTIO DOTIS. Establishment of dower.

CONSTITUTION. The form of government instituted by the people in their sovereign capacity, in which first principles and fundamental law are established. The supreme, permanent and fixed will of the people in their original, unlimited and sovereign capacity, and in it are determined the condition, rights and duties of every individual of the community. 1 Ill. 271.

The fundamental law of a free country, which characterizes the organism of the country, and secures the rights of the citizen, and determines his main duties as a freeman. 3 Barb. (N. Y.) 198.

The written instrument defining the powers, limitations, and functions of the United States of America.

It has been said to be a tripartite instrument, the parties being the state, the people, and the United States. 3 Wis. 96.

——**In Old English Law.** A statute.

CONSTITUTIONAL. That which is consonant to, and agrees with, the constitution.

CONSTITUTIONES. Laws promulgated, *i. e.,* enacted, by the Roman emperor. They were of the following kinds: (1) *Edicta;* (2) *decreta;* (3) *rescripta,* called, also, "*epistolae.*" Sometimes they were general, and intended to form a precedent for other like cases. At other times they were special, particular, or individual (*personales*), and not intended to form a precedent. The emperor had this power of irresponsible enactment by virtue of a certain *lex regia,* whereby he was made the fountain of justice and of mercy. Brown.

CONSTITUTIONES TEMPORE POSTERIORES POTIORES SUNT HIS QUAE IPSAS PRAECESSERUNT. Later laws prevail over those which preceded them. Dig. 1. 4. 4.

CONSTITUTIONS OF CLARENDON. See "Clarendon, Constitutions of."

CONSTITUTOR. In civil law. He who promised by a simple pact to pay the debt of another; and this is always a principal obligation. Inst. 4. 6. 9.

CONSTITUTUM (Lat.) An agreement to pay a subsisting debt which exists without any stipulation, whether of the promisor or another party. It differs from a stipulation in that it must be for an existing debt. Du Cange.

A day appointed for any purpose; a form of appeal. Calv. Lex.

CONSTITUTUM ESSE EAM DOMUM unicuique nostrum debere existimari, ubi quisque sedes et tabulas haberet, suarumque rerum constitutionem fecisset. It is settled that that is to be considered the home of each one of us where he may have his habitation and account books, and where he may have made an establishment of his business. Dig. 50. 16. 203.

CONSTRAINT. In Scotch law. Duress. It is a general rule that when one is compelled into a contract there is no effectual consent, though, ostensibly, there is the form of it. In such case, the contract will be declared void. The constraint requisite thus to annul a contract must be a *vis aut metus qui cadet in constantem virum,* such as would shake a man of firmness and resolution. Ersk. Inst. 3. 1. 16; Id. 4. 1. 26; 1 Bell, Comm. bk. 3, pt. 1, c. 1, § 1, art. 1, p. 295.

CONSTRUCTIO LEGIS NON FACIT INjuriam. The construction of law does not work an injury. Co. Litt. 183; Broom, Leg. Max. (3d London Ed.) 537.

CONSTRUCTION (Lat. *construere,* to put together). In practice. Determining the meaning and application as to the case in question of the provisions of a constitution, statute, will, or other instrument, or of an oral agreement.

Drawing conclusions respecting subjects that lie beyond the direct expressions of the term. Lieber, Leg. & Pol. Herm. 20.

"Interpretation," if an exact synonym, is a preferable term, since it has but a single significance; while "construction" is used also in a mechanical sense, but see "Interpretation" for an attempted distinction.

Some writers have distinguished between construction and interpretation, holding that interpretation is ascertaining the true sense of the language of the writing by limiting the inquiry to a consideration and comparison of the words themselves, while construction is the drawing of conclusions respecting subjects that lie beyond the direct expression of the text, from elements known from and given in the text—conclusions which are in the spirit, though not within the letter of the text. 9 Ill. App. 486.

The legitimate purpose of all construction of a contract or other instrument in writing, is, to ascertain the intention of the party or parties in making the same, and when this is determined, effect will be given thereto, unless to do so would violate some established rule of property. 122 Ill. 326.

CONSTRUCTION CONTRACTS. Contracts for works of permanent improvement to realty, whether by the erection of buildings, filling, excavating, digging wells, etc.

CONSTRUCTION, COURT OF. A court of equity or of common law, as the case may be, is called the "court of construction" with regard to wills, as opposed to the "court of probate," whose duty is to decide whether an instrument be a will at all. Now, the court of probate may decide that a given instrument is a will, and yet the court of construction may decide that it has no operation, by reason of perpetuities, illegality, uncertainty, etc. Wharton.

CONSTRUCTIVE. That which amounts, in the view of the law, to an act, although the act itself is not really performed. For words under this head, such as "constructive fraud," etc., see the various titles, "Fraud," etc.

CONSUETUDINARIUS (Lat.) In old English law. A ritual or book containing the rites and forms of divine offices, or the customs of abbeys and monasteries.

A record of the *consuetudines* (customs). Blount; Wishaw.

CONSUETUDINARY LAW. Customary or traditional law.

CONSUETUDINES FEUDORUM (Lat. feudal customs). A compilation of the law of feuds or fiefs in Lombardy, made A. D. 1170.

It is called, also, the "Book of Fiefs," and is of great and generally received authority. The compilation is said to have been ordered by Frederic Barbarossa (Ersk. Inst. 2. 3. 5), and to have been made by two Milanese lawyers (Spelman), but this is uncertain. It is commonly annexed to the *Corpus Juris Civilis,* and is easily accessible. See 3 Kent, Comm. (10th Ed.) 665, note; Spelman.

CONSUETUDO (Lat.) A custom; an established usage, or practice. Co. Litt. 58. Tolls; duties; taxes. Id. 58b. This use of *consuetudo* is not correct. *Custuma* is the proper word to denote duties, etc. 1 Sharswood, Bl. Comm. 313, note. An action formerly lay for the recovery of customs due, which was commenced by a writ *de consuetudinibus et servitiis,* of customs and services. This is said by Blount to be "a writ of right close which lies against the tenant that deforceth the lord of the rent and services due him." Blount; Old Nat. Brev. 77; Fitzh. Nat. Brev. 151.

There were various customs; as, *consuetudo Anglicana,* custom of England (as distinguished from *lex,* the Roman or civil law), *consuetudo curiae,* practice of a court, *consuetudo mercatorum,* custom of merchants. See "Custom."

CONSUETUDO CONTRA RATIONEM INtroducta, potius usurpatio quam consuetudo appellari debet. A custom introduced against reason ought rather to be called an usurpation than a custom. Co. Litt. 113.

CONSUETUDO CURIAE. The custom or practice of a court. Hardr. 141.

CONSUETUDO DEBET ESSE CERTA. A custom ought to be certain. Dav. 33.

CONSUETUDO EST ALTERA LEX. Custom is another law. 4 Coke, 21.

CONSUETUDO EST OPTIMUS INTERpres legum. Custom is the best expounder of the law. Coke, 2d Inst. 18; Dig. 1. 3. 37; Jenks. Cent. Cas. 273.

CONSUETUDO ET COMMUNIS ASSUREtudo vincit legem non scriptam, si sit specialis, et interpretatur legem scriptam, si lex sit generalis. Custom and common usage overcome the unwritten law, if it be special, and interpret the written law, if the law be general. Jenk. Cent. Cas. 273.

CONSUETUDO EX CERTA CAUSA RAtionabili usitata privat communem legem. Custom observed by reason of a certain and reasonable cause supersedes the common laws. Litt. § 169; Co. Litt. 33b. See 5 Bing. 293; Broom, Leg. Max. (3d London Ed.) p. 825.

CONSUETUDO, LICET SIT MAGNAE auctoritatis, nunquam tamen praejudicat manifestae veritati. A custom though it be of great authority, should never, however, be prejudicial to manifest truth. 4 Coke, 18.

CONSUETUDO LOCI OBSERVANDA EST. The custom of the place is to be observed. 4 Coke, 28b; 6 Coke, 67; 10 Coke, 139; 4 C. B. 48.

CONSUETUDO MANERII ET LOCI OBservanda est. A custom of a manor and place is to be observed. 6 Coke, 67.

CONSUETUDO MERCATORUM (Lat.) The custom of merchants; the same with *lex mercatoria* (*q. v.*)

CONSUETUDO NEQUE INJURIA ORITI, neque tolli potest. A custom can neither arise nor be abolished by a wrong. Lofft, 340.

CONSUETUDO NON HABITUR IN CONsequentiam. Custom is not to be drawn into a precedent. 3 Keb. 499.

CONSUETUDO NON TRAHITUR IN CONsequentiam. Custom is not drawn into consequence. 3 Keb. 499; 4 Jur. (N. S.) 139.

CONSUETUDO PRAESCRIPTA ET LEgitima vincit legem. A prescriptive and legitimate custom overcomes the law. Co. Litt. 113.

CONSUETUDO REGNI ANGLIAE EST lex Angliae. The custom of the kingdom of England is the law of England. Jenk. Cent. Cas. 119.

CONSUETUDO SEMEL REPROBATA non potest amplius induci. Custom once disallowed cannot again be produced. Dav. 33; Grounds and Rudiments of Law, 53.

CONSUETUDO TOLLIT COMMUNEM legem. Custom takes away the common law. Co. Litt. 33b.

CONSUETUDO VINCIT COMMUNEM legem. Custom overrules common law. 1 Roper, Husb. & Wife, 351; Co. Litt. 33b.

CONSUETUDO VOLENTES DUCIT; LEX nolentes trahit. Custom leads the willing; law compels or draws the unwilling. Jenk. Cent. Cas. 274.

CONSUL. A commercial agent of a country residing in a foreign seaport, whose duty is to promote the commerce of the state commissioning him. 83 Tex. 88. He is not a diplomatic agent, and has no authority to represent his country in diplomatic negotiations. 1 Kent, Comm. 43.

CONSULAR COURTS. Courts wherein, pursuant to treaty, the consul exercises judicial powers in cases involving the rights of citizens of the country by which he is commissioned. 1 Kent, Comm. 42.

CONSULTA ECCLESIA. In ecclesiastical law. A church full or provided for. Cowell.

CONSULTARY RESPONSE. The opinion of a court of law on a special case. Wharton.

CONSULTATION. The name of a writ whereby a cause, being formerly removed by prohibition out of an inferior court into some of the king's courts in Westminster, is returned thither again; for, if the judges of the superior court, comparing the proceedings with the suggestion of the party, find the suggestion false or not proved, and that, therefore, the cause was wrongfully called from the inferior court, then, upon consultation and deliberation, they decree it to be returned, whereupon this writ issues. Termes de la Ley; 2 Bl. Comm. 114.

——**In French Law.** The opinion of counsel upon a point of law submitted to them.

CONSUMMATE. Complete; finished; entire.

A marriage is said to be consummate. A right of dower is inchoate when coverture and seisin concur, consummate upon the husband's death. 1 Washb. Real Prop. 250, 251. A tenancy by the curtesy is initiate upon the birth of issue and consummate upon the death of the wife. 1 Washb. Real Prop. 140; 13 Conn. 83; 2 Me. 400; 2 Bl. Comm. 128.

A contract is said to be consummated when everything to be done in relation to it has been accomplished. It is frequently of great importance to know when a contract has been consummated, in order to ascertain the rights of the parties, particularly in the contract of sale. See "Delivery," where the subject is more fully examined. It is also sometimes of consequence to ascertain where the consummation of the contract took place, in order to decide by what law it is to be governed. See "Conflict of Laws;" "Lex Loci."

CONTANGO. In English law. The commission received for carrying over or putting off the time of execution of a contract to deliver stocks or pay for them at a certain time. Wharton.

CONTEK (Law Fr.) A contest; dispute; disturbance; opposition. Britt. c. 42; Kelham. *Conteckours*; brawlers; disturbers of the peace. Britt. c. 29.

CONTEMNER. A person guilty of contempt of court.

CONTEMPLATION OF BANKRUPTCY. As applied to transfers of property by an insolvent. In contemplation of committing an act in bankruptcy (*q. v.*), or of applying for the benefits of the bankrupt law. 13 How. (U. S.) 167; Fed. Cas. No. 3,317.

CONTEMPORANEA EXPOSITIO (Lat.) Contemporaneous exposition, or construction; a construction drawn from the time when, and the circumstances under which, the subject-matter to be construed, as a statute or custom, originated.

CONTEMPORANEA EXPOSITIO EST OPtima et fortissima in lege. A contemporaneous exposition is the best and most powerful in the law. Coke, 2d Inst. 11; 3 Coke, 7; Broom, Leg. Max. (3d London Ed.) 608.

CONTEMPT. A willful disregard or disobedience of a public authority, whether judicial or legislative.

Contempts are either (1) civil or (2) criminal.

(1) Civil contempts are those *quasi* contempts which consist in failing to do something which the contemnor is ordered to do for the benefit of another party to a proceeding before the court; while

(2) Criminal contempts are all acts in disrespect of the court or of its process obstructing the administration of justice generally, and tending to bring the court into disrepute. Rapalje, Contempt, § 21; 11 Fla. 184; 4 Keyes (N. Y.) 46.

Contempts are also classified as

(3) Direct contempts, being those committed in the presence of the court or so near as to disturb its proceedings; and

(4) Constructive contempts, being those arising from matters not transpiring in court. Rapalje, Contempt, § 23.

CONTEMPTIBILITER. Contemptuously.

CONTENEMENTUM (Law Lat. from *con*, together, and *tenementum*, a tenement, or thing holden). Countenance; appearance; credit or reputation.

CONTENTIOUS JURISDICTION. In ecclesiastical law. That which exists in cases where there is an action or judicial process, and matter in dispute is to be heard and determined between party and party. It is to be distinguished from voluntary jurisdiction, which exists in cases of taking probate of wills, granting letters of administration, and the like. 3 Sharswood, Bl. Comm. 66.

CONTERMINOUS. Adjacent or adjoining; having common boundaries. Hale, Hist. Com. Law, 98.

CONTEST. Struggle for superiority in legal usage, a litigation.

The word "contest," in constitutions and statutes, is a word of art. It means a litigation. It implies a plaintiff and a defendant, and a thing in controversy. When it is decided, it is, or should be, decided upon evidence, and the decision is a judgment. 112 Ky. 23.

CONTESTATIO LITIS.

——**In Civil Law.** The statement and answer of the plaintiff and defendant, thus bringing the case before the judge, conducted usually in the presence of witnesses. Calv. Lex.

This sense is retained in the canon law. 1 Kaufm. Mackeld. Civ. Law, 205. A cause is said to be *contestata* when the judge begins to hear the cause after an account of the claims, given not through the pleadings, but by statement of the plaintiff and answer of the defendant. Calv. Lex.

——**In Old English Law.** Coming to an issue; the issue so produced. Steph. Pl. 39; Crabb, Hist. Eng. Law, 216.

CONTESTATIO LITIS EGET TERMINOS contradictarios. An issue requires terms of contradiction; that is, there can be no issue without an affirmative on one side and a negative on the other. Jenk. Cent. Cas. 117.

CONTESTATION OF SUIT. In an ecclesiastical cause, that stage of the suit which is reached when the defendant has answered the libel by giving in an allegation (*q. v.*) If he confesses the libel, he is said to contest the suit affirmatively; if he denies it, he is said to contest the suit negatively; or he may give a qualified affirmative or negative by confessing the whole or part of the libel, and adding other facts. Phillim. Ecc. Law, 1255; Rog. Ecc. Law, 720. See "Confession and Avoidance." The term is a translation of *contestatio litis*, and is taken from the Roman law.

CONTEXT (Lat. *contextum*,—*con*, with, *tigere*, to weave,—that which is interwoven.) Those parts of a writing which precede and follow a phrase or passage in question; the connection.

CONTIGUOUS. In close proximity. 69 N. Y. 191, 25 Am. Rep. 168; affirming 7 Hun. (N. Y.) 455.

United or joined together. 261 Ill. 99.

Adjacent; in actual contact; touching; near. 143 Ill. App. 171.

In actual contact; touching; meeting or adjoining at the surface or border. 248 Ill. 166.

CONTINENCIA. In Spanish law. Continency or unity of the proceedings in a cause. White, New Recop. bk. 3, tit. 6, c. 1.

CONTINENS. In the Roman law. Continuing; holding together; joined together. Applied to buildings in the suburbs of Rome. Dig. 50. 16. 2.

CONTINENTIA. In old English practice. Continuance or connection. Applied to the proceedings in a cause. Bracton, fol. 362b. Countenance. Fleta, lib. 1, c. 48, § 2.

CONTINGENCY. An event which may or may not occur; that which is possible or probable; a fortuitous event; a chance. 82 Ill. App. 526.

A contingency has the element of uncertainty and doubt, and is defined as an event which is possible but which may or may not occur, in the nature of a casualty, accident, or chance, and results from an agency the operation of which is uncertain; dependent upon a possibility and on causes which are undetermined or unknown. 231 Ill. 127.

CONTINGENCY WITH DOUBLE ASpect. If there are remainders so limited that the second is a substitute for the first in case it should fail and not in derogation of it, the remainder is said to be in a contingency with double aspect. Fearne, Cont. Rem. 373.

CONTINGENT DAMAGES. Those given where the issues upon counts to which no demurrer has been filed are tried before demurrer to one or more counts in the same declaration has been decided. 1 Strange, 431.

CONTINGENT ESTATE. A contingent estate depends for its effect upon an event which may or may not happen; as, an estate limited to a person not *in esse*, or not yet born. Crabb, Real Prop. § 946. Distinguished from vested, see "Vested in Interest."

CONTINGENT LEGACY. A legacy made dependent upon some uncertain event. 1 Rop. Leg. 506.

A legacy which has not vested. Williams, Ex'rs.

CONTINGENT REMAINDER. An estate in remainder which is limited to take effect either to a dubious and uncertain person, or upon a dubious and uncertain event, by which no present or particular interest passes to the remainderman, so that the particular estate may chance to be determined, and the remainder never take effect. 2 Bl. Comm. 169.

A remainder limited so as to depend upon an event or condition which may never happen or be performed, or which may not happen or be performed till after the determination of the preceding estate. Fearne, Cont. Rem. 3; 1 Washb. Real Prop. 155. See "Remainder."

CONTINGENT USE. A use limited in a deed or conveyance of land which may or may not happen to vest, according to the contingency expressed in the limitation of such use.

Such a use as by possibility may happen in possession, reversion, or remainder. 1 Coke, 121; Comyn, Dig. "Uses" (K 6). A use limited to take effect upon the happening of some future contingent event; as where lands are conveyed to the use of A. and B. after a marriage had between them. 2 Sharswood, Bl. Comm. 234.

A contingent remainder limited by way of uses. Sugd. Uses, 175. See, also, 4 Kent, Comm. 237 et seq.

CONTINUAL CLAIM. In old English law. A formal claim made by a party entitled to enter upon any lands or tenements, but deterred from such entry by menaces, or bodily fear, for the purpose of preserving or keeping alive his right. It was called "continual," because it was required to be repeated once in the space of every year and day. It had to be made as near to the land as the party could approach with safety, and, when made in due form, had the same effect with, and in all respects amounted to, a legal entry. Litt. §§ 419-423; Co. Litt. 250a; 3 Bl. Comm. 175.

Lord Coke calls it an "entry in law," and says that it is as strong as an "entry in deed" (fact). Co. Litt. 256b.

It is now abolished. St. 3 & 4 Wm. IV. c. 27, § 11.

CONTINUANCE (Lat. *continuere*, to continue). In practice. The adjournment of a cause from one day to another of the same or a subsequent term.

The postponement of the trial of a cause.

CONTINUANDO (Lat. *continuare*, to continue; *continuando*, continuing). In pleading. An averment that a trespass has been continued during a number of days. 3 Sharswood, Bl. Comm. 212. It was allowed to prevent a multiplicity of actions (2 Rolle, Abr. 545) only where the injury was such as could, from its nature, be continued (1 Wm. Saund. 24, note 1).

The form is now disused, and the same end secured by alleging divers trespasses to have been committed between certain days. 1 Saund. 24, note 1. See, generally, Gould, Pl. c. 3, § 86; Hammond, N. P. 90, 91; Bacon, Abr. "Trespass" (I 2, note 2).

CONTINUING CONSIDERATION. See "Consideration."

CONTINUING DAMAGES. See "Damages."

CONTINUING GUARANTY. A guaranty limited as to amount but not limited as to time will in general be construed as a continuing guaranty unless the circumstances of the transaction show a different intention. 116 Ill. App. 645.

A guaranty which merely limits the amount of the guarantor's liability, without limiting the amount of credit which may be extended to the principal under the guaranty is a continuing guaranty. 145 Ill. 496.

CONTINUING INJURY. The expression "continuing injury," as applied to the right to maintain successive actions, means no more than that the case involves a transient injury, where the cause of such injury has been wrongfully allowed to continue. 112 Ill. App. 427.

CONTINUING NUISANCE. The failure of a levee and sanitary district to provide sufficient outlet for surface water from adjoining land outside the district, so that a tenant of such adjoining land may have as sufficient an outlet for the drainage of surface waters due to extraordinary floods as existed before the erection of the levee, constitutes a continuing nuisance for which successive suits may be maintained. 194 Ill. App. 266.

CONTINUOUS EASEMENT. See "Easement."

CONTRA (Lat.) Over; against; opposite; *per contra,* in opposition.

CONTRA BONOS MORES. Against sound morals.

Contracts which are incentive to crime, or of which the consideration is an obligation or engagement improperly prejudicial to the feelings of a third party, offensive to decency or morality, or which have a tendency to mischievous or pernicious consequences, are void, as being *contra bonos mores.* 2 Wils. 447; Cowp. 729; 4 Campb. 152; 1 Barn. & Ald. 683; 16 East, 150.

CONTRA FORMA COLLATIONIS. In old English law. A writ that issued where lands given in perpetual alms to lay houses of religion, or to an abbot and convent, or to the warden or master of an hospital and his convent, to find certain poor men with necessaries, and do divine service, etc., were alienated, to the disherison of the house and church. By means of this writ the donor or his heirs could recover the lands. Reg. Orig. 238; Fitzh. Nat. Brev. 210.

CONTRA FORMAM DONI. Against the form of the grant. See "Formedon."

CONTRA FORMAM FEOFFAMENTI. A writ that lay for the heir of a tenant, enfeoffed of certain lands or tenements, by charter of feoffment from a lord to make certain services and suits to his court, who was afterwards distrained for more services than were mentioned in the charter. Reg. Orig. 176; Old Nat. Brev. 162.

CONTRA FORMAM STATUTI (Lat. against the form of the statute). In pleading. The formal manner of alleging that the offense described in an indictment is one forbidden by statute.

CONTRA JUS BELLI (Lat.) Against the law of war. Grotius, de Jure Belli, lib. 3, c. 11, § 15; 1 Kent, Comm. 6.

CONTRA JUS COMMUNE. Against common right or law; contrary to the rule of the common law. Bracton, fol. 48b.

CONTRA LEGEM FACIT QUI ID FACIT quod lex prohibet; in fraudem vero qui, salvis verbis legis, sententiam ejus circumvenit. He does contrary to the law who does what the law prohibits; he acts in fraud of the law who, the letter of the law being inviolate, uses the law contrary to its intention. Dig. 1. 3. 29.

CONTRA LEGEM TERRAE. Against the law of the land. Mag. Ch. Johan. c. 55.

CONTRA NEGANTEM PRINCIPIA NON est disputandum. There is no disputing against one who denies principles. Co. Litt. 43; Grounds & Rudiments of Law, 57.

CONTRA NON VALENTEM AGERE nulla currit praescriptio. No prescription runs against a person unable to act. Broom, Leg. Max. (3d London Ed.) 810; Evans, Poth. 451.

CONTRA OMNES GENTES. Against all people; formal words in old covenants of warranty. Fleta, lib. 3, c. 14, § 11.

CONTRA PACEM (Lat. against the peace). In pleading. An allegation in an action of trespass or ejectment that the actions therein complained of were against the peace of the king. Such an allegation was formerly necessary, but has become a mere matter of form, and not traversable. 4 Term R. 503; 1 Chit. Pl. 375; Archb. Civ. Pl. 169. See "Trespass."

CONTRA TABULAS. In civil law. Against the will (testament). Dig. 37. 4.

CONTRA VADIUM ET PLEGIUM. In old English law. Against gage and pledge. Bracton, fol. 15b; Fleta, lib. 1, c. 42, § 2.

CONTRA VERITATEM LEX NUNQUAM aliquid permittit. The law never suffers anything contrary to truth. Coke, 2d Inst. 252. But sometimes it allows a conclusive presumption in opposition to truth. See 3 Bouv. Inst. note 3061.

CONTRABAND OF WAR. In international law. Goods which neutrals may not carry in time of war to either of the belligerent nations without subjecting themselves to the loss of the goods, and formerly the owners, also, to the loss of the ship and other cargo, if intercepted. 1 Kent, Comm. 138, 143.

"The classification of goods as contraband has much perplexed text writers and jurists. A strictly accurate and satisfactory classification is perhaps impracticable; but that which is best supported by American and English decisions may be said to divide all merchandise into three classes:

(1) Articles manufactured and primarily or ordinarily used for military purposes in time of war; (2) articles which may be, and are, used for purposes of war or peace, according to circumstances; (3) articles exclusively used for peaceful purposes. Merchandise of the first class destined to a belligerent country or place occupied by the army or navy of belligerent is always contraband. Merchandise of the second class is contraband only when destined to the military or naval use of the belligerent, while merchandise of a third class is not contraband at all, though liable to seizure and condemnation for violation of blockade or siege." 5 Wall. 58.

CONTRACAUSATOR. A criminal; one prosecuted for a crime.

CONTRACT (Lat. *contractus*, from *con*, with, and *traho*, to draw). An agreement between two or more parties to do or not do a particular thing. Marshall, C. J., 4 Pet. (U. S.) 420, 572. An agreement in which a party undertakes to do or not to do a particular thing. Marshall, C. J. 4 Wheat. (U. S.) 197. An agreement between two or more parties for the doing or not doing of some specified thing. 1 Pars. Cont. 5.

It has been variously defined as follows:

A compact between two or more parties. 6 Cranch (U. S.) 87, 136.

An agreement or covenant between two or more persons, in which each party binds himself to do or forbear some act, and each acquires a right to what the other promises. Enc. Amer.; Webster.

A contract or agreement is where a promise is made on one side and assented to on the other; or where two or more persons enter into an engagement with each other by a promise on either side. 2 Steph. Comm. 108, 109.

An agreement upon sufficient consideration to do or not to do a particular thing. 2 Bl. Comm. 446; 2 Kent, Comm. 449.

A covenant or agreement between two parties with a lawful consideration or cause. West. Symb. lib. 1, § 10; Cowell; Blount.

A deliberate engagement between competent parties upon a legal consideration to do or to abstain from doing some act. Story, Cont. § 1.

A mutual promise upon lawful consideration or cause which binds the parties to a performance.

The writing which contains the agreement of parties with the terms and conditions, and which serves as a proof of the obligation. The last is a distinct signification. 2 Hill (N. Y.) 551.

We have not included "consideration" in our definition of contract, because it does not seem to be essential to a contract, although it is necessary to its enforcement. See "Consideration." Mr. Stephen, whose definition of contract is given above, thus criticizes the definition of Blackstone, which has been adopted by Chancellor Kent and other high authorities: First, that the word "agreement" itself requires definition as much as "contract;" second, that the existence of a consideration, though essential to the validity of a parol contract, forms properly no part of the idea; third, that the definition takes no sufficient notice of the mutuality which properly distinguishes a contract from a promise. 2 Steph. Comm. 109.

The use of the word "agreement" (*aggregatio mentium*) seems to have the authority of the best writers in ancient and modern times (see above) as a part of the definition of contract. It is probably a translation of the civil law *conventio* (*con* and *venio*), a coming together, to which (being derived from *ad* and *grego*) it seems nearly equivalent. We do not think the objection that it is a synonym (or nearly so) a valid one. Some word of the kind is necessary as a basis of the definition. No two synonyms convey precisely the same idea. "Most of them have minute distinctions," says Reid. If two are entirely equivalent, it will soon be determined by accident which shall remain in use, and which become obsolete. To one who has no knowledge of a language, it is impossible to define any abstract idea; but to one who understands a language, an abstraction is defined by a synonym properly qualified. By pointing out distinctions and the mutual relations between synonyms, the object of definition is answered. Hence we do not thing Blackstone's definition open to the first objection.

As to the idea of consideration, Mr. Stephens seems correct, and to have the authority of some of the first legal minds of modern times. Consideration, however, may be necessary to enforce a contract, though not essential to the idea. Even in that class of contracts (by specialty) in which no consideration is in fact required, one is always presumed by law; the form of the instrument being held to import a consideration. 2 Kent, Comm. 450, note.

A contract without consideration is called a *nudum pactum* (nude pact), but it is still a *pactum*, and this implies that consideration is not an essential. The third objection of Mr. Stephen to the definition of Blackstone does not seem one to which it is fairly obnoxious.

There is an idea of mutuality in *con* and *traho*, to draw together, but we think that mutuality is implied in agreement as well. An *aggregatio mentium* seems impossible without mutuality. Blackstone, in his analysis, appears to have regarded agreement as implying mutuality; for he defines it (2 Bl. Comm. 442): "A mutual bargain or convention." In our definition, however, all ambiguity is avoided by the use of the words "between two or more parties" following agreement.

In its widest sense, "contract" includes records and specialties; but this use as a general term for all sorts of obligations, though of too great authority to be now doubted, seems to be an undue extension of the proper meaning of the term, which is much more nearly equivalent to "agreement," which is never applied to specialties. Mutuality is of the very essence of both,—not only mutuality of assent, but of act. As expressed by Lord Coke, *actus contra actum*. 2 Coke, 15; 7 Man. & G. 998, argument, and note.

This is illustrated in contracts of sale, bailment, hire, as well as partnership and marriage; and no other engagements but those with this kind of mutuality would seem properly to come under the head of contracts. In a bond there is none of this mutuality, no act to be done by the obligee to make the instrument binding. In a judgment there is no mutuality either of act or of assent. It is *judicium redditum in invitum*. It may properly be denied to be a contract, though Blackstone insists that one is implied. Per Mansfield, 3 Burrows, 1545; 1 Cow. (N. Y.) 316; per Story, J., 1 Mason (U. S.) 288. Mr. Chitty uses "obligation" as an alternative word of description when speaking of bonds and judgments. Chit. Cont. 2, 4. An act of legislature may be a contract. So may a legislative grant with exemption from taxes. 5 Ohio St. 361. So a charter is a contract between a state and a corporation, within the meaning of the constitution of the United States (article 1, § 10, cl. 1). 27 Miss. 417. See "Obligation of Contracts."

(1) Accessory contracts are those made for assuring the performance of a prior contract, either by the same parties or by others, such as suretyship, mortgage, and pledges. Civ. Code La. art. 1764; Poth. Obl. pt. 1, c. 1, § 1; art. 2, note 14.

(2) Contracts of beneficence are those by which only one of the contracting parties is benefited; as loans, deposit, and mandate. Civ. Code La. art. 1767.

(3) Certain contracts are those in which the thing to be done is supposed to depend on the will of the party, or when, in the usual course of events, it must happen in the manner stipulated.

(4) Commutative contracts are those in which what is done, given, or promised by one party is considered as an equivalent to or in consideration of what is done, given, or promised by the other. Civ. Code La. art. 1761.

(5) Gratuitous contracts are those of which the object is the benefit of the person with whom it is made, without any profit or advantage received or promised as a consideration for it. It is not, however, the less gratuitous if it proceed either from gratitude for a benefit before received, or from the hope of receiving one hereafter, although such benefit be of a pecuniary nature. Civ. Code La. § 1766.

(6) Hazardous contracts are those in which the performance of that which is one of its objects depends on an uncertain event. Civ. Code La. art. 1769.

(7) Consensual contracts are those which are formed by mere consent of the parties, such as all contracts of hiring and mandate.

(8) Executed contracts are those in which nothing remains to be done by either party, and where the transaction has been completed, or was completed at the time the contract or agreement was made; as where an article is sold and delivered, and payment therefor is made on the spot.

(9) Executory contracts are those in which some act remains to be done; as when an agreement is made to build a house in six months, to do an act before some future day, to lend money upon a certain interest payable at a future time.

A contract "executed" (which differs in nothing from a grant) conveys a chose in possession; a contract "executory" conveys a chose in action. 2 Bl. Comm. 443. As to the importance of grants considered as contracts, see "Obligation of Contracts."

(10) Express contracts are those in which the terms of the contract or agreement are openly and fully uttered and avowed at the time of making; as, to pay a stated price for certain specified goods; to deliver an ox, etc. 2 Bl. Comm. 443.

(11) Implied contracts are such as reason and justice dictate, and which, therefore, the law presumes that every man undertakes to perform. Thus, if I employ a person to do any business for me or perform any work, or take up wares with a tradesman, the law implies that I understood or contracted to pay the real value of the services or wares. 2 Bl. Comm. 443. These contracts form the web and woof of actual life. 1 Pars. Cont. 4.

There is one species of implied contract which runs through and is annexed to all other contracts, conditions, and covenants, viz., that if I fail in my part of the agreement, I shall pay the other party such damages as he has sustained by my neglect or refusal. See "Quantum Meruit;" "Quantum Valebat;" "Assumpsit;" Comyn, Dig. "Action upon the Case upon Assumpsit" (A 1); "Agreement."

(12) Independent contracts are those in which the mutual acts or promises have no relation to each other either as equivalents or as considerations. Civ. Code La. art. 1762.

(13) Mixed contracts are those by which one of the parties confers a benefit on the other, receiving something of inferior value in return, such as a donation subject to a charge.

(14) Contracts of mutual interest are such as are entered into for the reciprocal interest and utility of each of the parties; as sales, exchange, partnership, and the like.

(15) Entire contracts are those whose consideration is entire; divisible if the consideration is apportioned, or if an apportionment may be implied by law as to each item to be performed. 40 Cal. 251.

(16) Severable (or separable) contracts are those the considerations of which are by

their terms susceptible of apportionment or division on either side, so as to correspond to the several parts or portions of the consideration on the other side.

A contract to pay a person the worth of his services as long as he will do certain work, or so much per week as long as he shall work, or to give a certain price per bushel for every bushel of so much corn as corresponds to a sample, would be a severable contract. If the part to be performed by one party consists of several distinct and separate items, and the price to be paid by the other is apportioned to each item to be performed, or is left to be implied by law, such a contract will generally be held to be severable. So when the price to be paid is clearly and distinctly apportioned to different parts of what is to be performed, although the latter is in its nature single and entire. But the mere fact of sale by weight or measure—*i. e.*, so much per pound or bushel—does not make a contract severable.

(17) Simple contracts are those not of specialty or record. They are the lowest class of express contracts, and answer most nearly to our general definition of contract.

To constitute a sufficient parol agreement to be binding in law, there must be that reciprocal and mutual assent which is necessary to all contracts. They are by parol, which includes both oral and written. The only distinction between oral and written contracts is in their mode of proof. And it is inaccurate to distinguish verbal from written; for contracts are equally verbal whether the words are written or spoken,—the meaning of "verbal" being, "expressed in words." See 3 Burrows, 1670; 7 Term R. 350, note; 11 Mass. 27, 30; 5 Mass. 299, 301; 7 Conn. 57; 1 Caines (N. Y.) 386.

(18) Specialties are those which are under seal, as deeds and bonds.

Specialties are sometimes said to include also contracts of record (1 Pars. Cont. 7), in which case there would be but two classes at common law, viz., specialties and simple contracts. The term "specialty" is always used substantively.

They are the second kind of express contracts, under the ordinary common-law division. They are not merely written, but signed, sealed, and delivered by the party bound. The solemnities connected with these acts, and the formalities of witnessing, gave in early times an importance and character to this class of contracts which implied so much caution and deliberation (consideration) that it was unnecessary to prove the consideration even in a court of equity. Plowd. 305; 7 Term R. 477; 4 Barn. & Adol. 652; 3 Bing. 111; 1 Fonbl. Eq. 342, note. Though little of the real solemnity now remains, except witnessing, and a scroll is substituted in most of the states for the seal, the distinction with regard to specialties has still been preserved intact. See "Consideration."

When a contract by specialty is changed by a parol agreement, the whole contract becomes parol. 2 Watts (Pa.) 451; 9 Pick. (Mass.) 298; 13 Wend. (N. Y.) 71.

(19) Unilateral contracts are those in which the party to whom the engagement is made makes no express agreement on his part. They are so called even in cases where the law attaches certain obligations to his acceptance. Civ. Code La. art. 1758. A loan for use and a loan of money are of this kind. Poth. Obl. pt. 1, c. 1, § 1, art. 2.

(20) Onerous contracts are those in which something is given or promised as a consideration for the engagement or gift, or some service, interest, or condition is imposed on what is given or promised, although unequal to it in value.

(21) Principal contracts are those entered into by both parties on their own accounts, or in the several qualities or characters they assume.

(22) Real contracts are those in which it is necessary that there should be something more than mere consent, such as a loan of money, deposit, or pledge, which, from their nature, require a delivery of the thing (*res*).

(23) Reciprocal contracts are those by which the parties expressly enter into mutual engagements, such as sale, hire, and the like.

(24) Contracts of record are those which are evidenced by matter of record, such as judgments, recognizances, and statutes staple. These are the highest class of contracts. Statutes merchant and staple, and other securities of the like nature, are confined to England. They are contracts entered into by the intervention of some public authority, and are witnessed by the highest kind of evidence, *viz.*, matter of record. 4 Bl. Comm. 465.

(25) Verbal contracts are simple contracts.

(26) Written contracts are those evidenced by writing.

——**In the Civil Law.** Pothier's treatise on Obligations, taken in connection with the Civil Code of Louisiana, gives an idea of the divisions of the civil law. Poth. Obl. pt. 1, c. 1, § 1, art. 2, makes the five following classes: Reciprocal and unilateral; consensual and real; those of mutual interest, of beneficence and mixed: principal and accessory; those which are subjected by the civil law to certain rules and forms, and those which are regulated by mere natural justice.

It is true that almost all the rights of personal property do in great measure depend upon contracts of one kind or other, or at least might be reduced under some of them, which is the method taken by the civil law. It has referred the greatest part of the duties and rights of which it treats to the head of obligations *ex contractu* or *quasi ex contractu*. Inst. 3. 14. 2; 2 Bl. Comm. 443.

CONTRACTION (Lat. *con*, together, *traho*, to draw). A form of a word abbreviated by the omission of one or more letters. This was formerly much practiced, but in modern times has fallen into general disuse. Much information in regard to the rules for contraction is to be found in the Instructor Clericalis.

CONTRACTOR. One who enters into a contract. Those who undertake to do public work, or the work for a company or corporation on a large scale, at a certain fixed price, or to furnish goods to another at a fixed or ascertained price. 2 Pardessus, note 300. See 5 Whart. (Pa.) 366.

CONTRACTUS BONAE FIDEI. In Roman law, those contracts (*e. g., emptio venditio*) which admitted of equitable defenses and other equitable consideration. They were opposed to contracts *stricti juris* (*e. g., stipulatio*), which admitted no such equitable defenses or considerations, at least until their original character was compelled by statute to admit them. All the praetorian contracts were *contractus bonae fidei*, but some of the *civiles contractus* were also *bonae fidei*.

CONTRACTUS CIVILES. In Roman law. Those contracts (*e. g., venditio*) which were actionable either in virtue of the old common law, or by virtue of any particular statute. They were opposed to the *contractus praetorii* which were actionable only through the aid of the praetor, who, for that purpose, had to adopt the existing legal forms of actions.

CONTRACTUS EST QUASI ACTUS CONtra actum. A contract is, as it were, act against act. 2 Coke, 15.

CONTRACTUS EX TURPI CAUSA, VEL contra bonos mores nullus est. A contract founded on a base and unlawful consideration, or against good morals, is null. Hob. 167; Dig. 2, 14. 27. 4.

CONTRACTUS LEGEM EX CONVENtione accipiunt. The agreement of the parties makes the law of the contract. Dig. 16. 3. 1. 6.

CONTRADICT. In practice. To prove a fact contrary to what has been asserted by a witness.

CONTRADICTION IN TERMS. Express, patent, inconsistency between parts of a clause or of an instrument.

CONTRAESCRITURA. In Spanish law. Counter letter. An instrument, usually executed in secret, for the purpose of showing that an act of sale, or some other public instrument, has a different purpose from that imported on its face. Acts of this kind, though binding on the parties, have no effect as to third persons.

CONTRAFACTIO (Lat.) Counterfeiting; as, *contrafactio sigilli regis*, counterfeiting the king's seal. Cowell; Reg. Orig. 42. See "Counterfeit."

CONTRAINTE PAR CORPS. In French law. The civil process of arrest of the person, which is imposed upon vendors falsely representing their property to be unincumbered, or upon persons mortgaging property which they are aware does not belong to them, and in other cases of moral heinousness. Brown.

CONTRALIGATIO. In old English law. Counter obligation. Literally, counter binding. *Est enim obligatio quasi contraligatio.* Fleta, lib. 2, c. 56, § 1.

CONTRAMANDATIO. A countermanding. *Contramandatio placiti*, in old English law, was the respiting of a defendant, or giving him further time to answer, by countermanding the day fixed for him to plead, and appointing a new day; a sort of imparlance. Cowell.

CONTRAMANDATUM. A lawful excuse, which a defendant in a suit by attorney alleges for himself to show that the plaintiff has no cause of complaint. Blount.

CONTRAPLACITUM. In old English law. A counter plea. Towns. Pl. 61.

CONTRAPOSITIO. In old English law. A plea or answer. Blount. A counter position.

CONTRARIENTS. This word was used in the time of Edw. II. to signify those who were opposed to the government, but were neither rebels nor traitors. Jacob.

CONTRARIORUM CONTRARIA EST RAtio. The reason of contrary things is contrary. Hob. 344.

CONTRAROTULATOR (Fr. *contrerouleur*, a controller). One whose business it was to observe the money which the collectors had gathered for the use of the king or the people. Cowell.

CONTRAROTULATOR PIPAE. An officer of the exchequer that writeth out summons twice every year to the sheriffs to levy the farms (rents) and debts of the pipe. Blount.

CONTRAT. In French law. Contracts. Contracts are of the following varieties:

(1) *Bilateral*, or *synallagmatique*, where each party is bound to the other to do what is just and proper.

(2) *Unilateral*, where the one side only is bound.

(3) *Commutatif*, where one does to the other something which is supposed to be an equivalent for what the other does to him.

(4) *Aleatoire*, where the consideration for the act of the one is a mere chance.

(5) *Contrat de bienfaisance*, where the one party procures to the other a purely gratuitous benefit.

(6) *Contrat a titre onereux*, where each party is bound under some duty to the other. Brown.

CONTRATALLIA. In old English law. A counter tally. A term used in the exchequer. Mem. in Scacc. M. 26 Edw. I.

CONTRATENERE. To hold against; to withhold. Whishaw.

CONTRAVENTION. In French law. An act which violates the law, a treaty, or an agreement which the party has made. That infraction of the law punished by a fine which does not exceed fifteen francs, and by an imprisonment not exceeding three days.

CONTRE MAITRE. In French law. The second officer in command of a ship; the officer next in command to the master, and under him. His business is said to relate to providing fit things for the navigation of the vessel before the voyage,—ropes, sails, anchors, etc.; to attending to its condition through the voyage, reporting each day to the master, and attending to the anchoring and security of the vessel at the end of the voyage. Ord. de la Marine de 1681, liv. 2. He is always to execute, day or night, the commands of the master, and represents the master in his sickness or absence. Guyot, Rep. Univ.

CONTRECTARE (Lat.)

——**In Civil Law.** To handle; to take hold of; to meddle with.

——**In Old English Law.** To treat. *Vel male contrectet*, or shall ill treat. Fleta, lib. 1, c. 17, § 4.

CONTRECTATIO. In civil law. The removal of a thing from its place, amounting to a theft. The offense is purged by a restoration of the thing taken. Bowyer, Comm. 268.

CONTRECTATIO REI ALIENAE ANIMO furandi, est furtum. The touching or removing of another's property, with an intention of stealing, is theft. Jenk. Cent. Cas. 132.

CONTREFACON. In French law. The offense of those who print or cause to be printed, without lawful authority, a book of which the author or his assigns have a copyright. Merlin, Repert.

CONTRIBUTION.

——**At Common Law.** The payment by each or any one of several parties who are liable, in company with others, of his proportionate part of the whole liability or loss, to one or more of the parties so liable upon whom the whole loss has fallen, or who has been compelled to discharge the whole liability. 1 Bibb (Ky.) 562; 4 Johns. Ch. (N. Y.) 545; 4 Bouv. Inst. note 3935.

——**In Civil Law.** A partition by which the creditors of an insolvent debtor divide among themselves the proceeds of his property proportionably to the amount of their respective credits. Civ. Code La. art. 2522, note 10. It is a division *pro rata*. Merlin, Repert.

——**In Maritime Law.** Average (*q. v.*)

CONTRIBUTORY NEGLIGENCE. Failure of one injured by the negligence of another to use ordinary care, which failure is a concurrent cause with that of such other person in producing the injury.

CONTROLLER. A comptroller (*q. v.*)

CONTROLMENT. In old English law. The controlling or checking of another officer's account; the keeping of a counter roll. Sometimes called "contra rollment."

CONTROVER. One who invents false news. Coke, 2d Inst. 227.

CONTROVERSY. A dispute arising between two or more persons. It differs from case, which includes all suits, criminal as well as civil; whereas controversy is a civil, and not a criminal, proceeding. 2 Dall. (U. S.) 419, 431, 432; 1 Tucker, Bl. Comm. App. 420, 421; Story, Const. § 1668.

CONTUBERNIUM. In civil law. A marriage between persons of whom one or both were slaves. Poth. Cont. pt. 1, c. 2, § 4.

CONTUMACY (Lat. *contumacia*, disobedience). The refusal or neglect of a party accused to appear or answer to a charge preferred against him in a court of justice. Chiefly used in ecclesiastical courts; "contempt" being used in the civil courts.

Actual contumacy is the refusal of a party actually before the court to obey some order of the court.

Presumed contumacy is the act of refusing or declining to appear upon being cited. 3 Curt. Ecc. 1.

CONTUMAX. One accused of a crime who refuses to appear and answer to the charge; an outlaw.

CONTUSION. In medical jurisprudence. An injury or lesion, arising from the shock of a body with a large surface, which presents no loss of substance, and no apparent wound. If the skin be divided, the injury takes the name of a contused wound. See 1 Chanc. Prac. 38; 4 Car. & P. 381, 487, 558, 565; 6 Car. & P. 684; 2 Beck, Med. Jur. 178.

CONTUTOR (Lat.) In civil law. A cotutor, or co-guardian. Inst. 1. 24. 1.

CONUSANCE, CLAIM OF. See "Cognizance."

CONUSANT. One who knows; as, if a party knowing of an agreement in which he has an interest makes no objection to it, he is said to be conusant. Co. Litt. 157.

CONUSOR. A cognizor.

CONVENABLE. In old English law. Suitable; agreeable; convenient; fitting. Litt. § 103; Cowell.

CONVENE. In civil law. To bring an action.

CONVENT. The fraternity of a religious house, as of an abbey or priory. The word though in common usage restricted to companies of women, properly embraces companies of either men or women living together in the discipline of a religious order, either monks or nuns.

The house occupied by such a community, a monastery or nunnery; an abbey (*q. v.*)

CONVENTICLE. A private assembly of a few folks under pretense of exercise of religion. The name was first given to the meetings of Wickliffe, but afterwards applied to the meetings of the nonconformists. Cowell. The meetings were made illegal by 16 Car. II. c. 4, and the term, in its later signification, came to denote an unlawful religious assembly.

CONVENTIO (Lat. a coming together).

——In Canon Law. The act of summoning or calling together the parties by summoning the defendant. When the defendant was brought to answer, he was said to be convened, which the canonists called *conventio*, because the plaintiff and defendant met to contest. Story, Eq. Pl. 402; 4 Bouv. Inst. note 4117.

——In Contracts. An agreement; a covenant. Cowell. Often used in the maxim *conventio vincit legem*, the express agreement of the parties supersedes the law. Story, Ag. § 368. But this maxim does not apply, it is said, to prevent the application of the general rule of law. Broom, Leg. Max. 308.

CONVENTIO PRIVATORUM NON POtest publico juri derogare. An agreement of private persons cannot derogate from public right. Wingate, Max. p. 746, max. 201; Co. Litt. 166a; Dig. 50. 17. 45. 1.

CONVENTIO VINCIT LEGEM. The agreement of the parties overcomes or prevails against the law. Story, Ag. § 368; 6 Taunt. 430. See Dig. 16. 3. 1. 6.

CONVENTION.

——In Civil Law. A general term which comprehends all kinds of contracts, treaties, pacts, or agreements. The consent of two or more persons to form with each other an engagement, or to dissolve or change one which they had previously formed. Domat, Civ. Law; Dig. 2. 14. 1. 1; Bouv. Inst. note 100.

——In Legislation. This term is applied to a meeting of the delegates elected by the people for other purposes than usual legislation. It is mostly used to denote an assembly to make or amend the constitution of a state; but it sometimes indicates an assembly of the delegates of the people to nominate officers to be supported at an election.

CONVENTIONAL. Arising from, and dependent upon, the act of the parties, as distinguished from "legal," which is something arising from act of law. 2 Bl. Comm. 120.

CONVENTIONAL ESTATES. Those estates for life which are expressly created by the act of the parties, as distinguished from legal estates, or those which are created by operation of law. 2 Bl. Comm. 120.

CONVENTIONE. The name of a writ for the breach of any covenant in writing, whether real or personal. Reg. Orig. 115; Fitzh. Nat. Brev. 145.

CONVENTUAL CHURCH. In ecclesiastical law. That which consists of regular clerks, professing some order or religion; or of dean and chapter; or other societies of spiritual men.

CONVENTUALS. Religious men united in a convent or religious house. Cowell.

CONVENTUS (Lat. *convenire*). An assembly; *conventus magnatum vel procerum*, an assemblage of the chief men or nobility; a name of the English parliament. 1 Sharswood, Bl. Comm. 148.

——In Civil Law. A contract made between two or more parties.

A multitude of men, of all classes, gathered together.

A standing in a place to attract a crowd.

A collection of the people by the magistrate to give judgment. Calv. Lex.

CONVENTUS JURISDICUS. A Roman provincial court for the determination of civil causes.

CONVERSANT. One who is in the habit of being in a particular place is said to be conversant there. Barnes, 162.

Acquainted; familiar.

CONVERSANTES. In old English law. Conversant or dwelling; commorant. 2 Inst. 122.

CONVERSION (Lat. *con*, with, together, *vertere*, to turn; *conversio*, a turning to, with, together).

——In Equity. The exchange of one species of property for another, which takes place under some circumstances in the consideration of the law, although no such change has actually taken place.

Land is held to be converted into money, in equity, when the owner has contracted to sell; and if he die before making a conveyance, his executors will be entitled to the money, and not his heirs. 2 Vern. 52; 1 W. Bl. 129.

Money may be held to be converted into land under various circumstances; as where, for example, a man dies before a conveyance is made to him of land which he has bought. 10 Pet. (U. S.) 563; Bouv. Inst. Index.

——At Law. An unauthorized assumption and exercise of the right of ownership over goods or personal chattels belonging to another, to the alteration of their condition, or the exclusion of the owner's rights. 44 Me. 197; 36 N. H. 311.

A constructive conversion takes place when a person does such acts in reference to the goods or personal chattels of another as amount, in view of the law, to appropriation of the property to himself. 1 Kelly (Ga.) 381.

A direct conversion takes place when a person actually appropriates the property of another to his own beneficial use and enjoyment, or to that of a third person, or destroys it, or alters its nature. 27 Mich. 454.

CONVERTIBLE COUPON BONDS. "Convertible coupon bonds" have been defined as coupon bonds which expressly provide that they may, at the option of the holder, be converted into registered bonds. However, bonds are often referred to as "convertible" bonds where what is meant is that they provide that they may be converted into stock of the corporation, under certain conditions. 2 Fletcher Cyclopedia Corporations 1919.

CONVEY. The use of the word "convey" is equivalent to a grant at common law, and passes the title, importing a transfer of title from one person to another. 153 Ill. 510.

CONVEYANCE. The transfer of the title of land from one person or class of persons to another.

The instrument for effecting such transfer.

It is a general term, and comprehends the several modes of passing title to real estate. 54 Miss. 90.

Every instrument in writing by which any estate or interest in land is created, aliened, or mortgaged, or by which the title to land may be affected at law or in equity, except lost wills and testaments, leases for not to exceed three years, and executory contracts for the purchase or sale of land. 1 Rev. St. N. Y. p. 762, § 38.

CONVEYANCE OF VESSELS. The transfer of the title to vessels.

CONVEYANCER. One who makes it his business to draw deeds of conveyance of lands for others. 1 Bouv. Inst. note 2422. They frequently act as brokers for the sale of estates and obtaining loans on mortgage.

CONVEYANCING. A term including both the science and act of transferring titles to real estate from one man to another. It includes the examination of the title of the alienor, and also the preparation of the instruments of transfer. It is, in England and Scotland, and, to a greatly inferior extent, in the United States, a highly artificial system of law with a distinct class of practitioners. A profound and elaborate treatise on the English law of conveyancing is Mr. Preston's. Geldart and Thornton's works are important works; and an interesting and useful summation of the American law is given in Washburn on Real Property.

CONVEYANCING COUNSEL. By Act 15 & 16 Vict. c. 80, § 41, the lord chancellor is empowered to appoint not less than six barristers, who have practiced as conveyancing counsel for ten years at least, to be conveyancing counsel of the court of chancery, and the opinion of any of them may be received and acted on by the court or by a judge at chambers in the investigation of the title to an estate, or in the settlement of a draft, conveyance, mortgage, etc. Daniell, Ch. Pr. 1046. By the judicature act of 1873 (section 77) they were transferred to the supreme court.

CONVICIA SI IRASCARIS TUA DIVULgas; spreta exolescunt. If you be moved to anger by insults, you publish them; if despised, they are forgotten. 3 Inst. 198.

CONVICIUM. In civil law. The name of a species of slander or injury uttered in public, and which charged some one with some act *contra bonos mores*. Vicat; Bac. Abr. "Slander."

CONVICT. One who has been condemned by a competent court; one who has been convicted of a crime or misdemeanor.

To condemn; to find guilty of a crime or misdemeanor. 4 Bl. Comm. 362.

CONVICTED. A statute relative to the disqualification of those "convicted" of certain crimes, refers to the judgment of the court in a criminal case on the verdict of guilty, and not merely to the verdict. 51 Ill. 314.

CONVICTION (Lat. *convictio;* from *con*, with, and *vincere*, to bind). In practice. That legal proceeding of record which ascertains the guilt of the party, and upon which the sentence or judgment is founded. 7 Man. & G. 504.

Finding a person guilty by verdict of a jury. 1 Bish. Crim. Law, § 223.

A record of the summary proceedings upon any penal statute before one or more justices of the peace or other persons duly authorized, in a case where the offender has been convicted and sentenced. Holthouse.

The first of the definitions here given undoubtedly represents the accurate meaning of the term, and includes an ascertainment of the guilt of the party by an authorized magistrate in a summary way, or by confession of the party himself, as well as by verdict of a jury. The word is also used in each of the other senses given. It is said to be sometimes used to denote final judgment. Dwarr. St. (2d Ed.) 683. And a final judgment is usually held essential to conviction. 69 N. Y. 107; 99 Mass. 420.

Summary conviction is one which takes place before an authorized magistrate or inferior court, without the intervention of a common-law jury, or not according to the course of a common-law prosecution.

CONVINCING. Overcoming by reason, argument, evidence; causing to believe.

When one is convinced he cannot be more convinced. If evidence is convincing, it is sufficient in any case, and to say it ought to be more convincing in one case than another, is giving to the word degrees of comparison when the word itself is superlative. 57 Wis. 626.

"*Convincing proof*" may be said to mean that degree of certainty required to sustain a given postulate. 89 Me. 442.

CONVIVIUM. A lay tenure, whereby a tenant is bound to provide meat and drink for his lord once or oftener in the year. The same as *procuratio* with the clergy. Blount.

CONVOCATION (Lat. *con*, together, *voco*, to call). In ecclesiastical law. The general assembly of the clergy to consult upon ecclesiastical matters.

The clergy were always summoned at the commencement of each parliament. They themselves constituted a parliament, with a higher and lower house of convocation; the higher including the bishops and archbishops; the lower, the rest of the clergy. It is still summoned before each parliament *pro forma*, preserving the ancient custom, but adjourns without transacting any business. 2 Steph. Comm. 542; 2 Burn, Ecc. Law, 18 et seq.

CONVOY. A naval force, under the command of an officer appointed by government, for the protection of merchant ships and others, during the whole voyage, or such part of it as is known to require such protection. Marsh. Ins. bk. 1, c. 9, § 5; Park, Ins. 388.

Warranties are sometimes inserted in policies of insurance that the ship shall sail with convoy. To comply with this warranty, five things are essential: First, the ship must sail with the regular convoy appointed by the government; secondly, she must sail from the place of rendezvous appointed by the government; thirdly, the convoy must be for the voyage; fourthly, the ship insured must have sailing instructions; fifthly, she must depart and continue with the convoy till the end of the voyage, unless separated from it by necessity. Marsh. Ins. bk. 1, c. 9. § 5.

CO-OBLIGOR. One who is bound together with one or more others to fulfill an obligation. As to suing co-obligors, see "Parties;" "Joinder, etc."

COOL AND SWEET OATS. A name given in the grain markets and among grain dealers to a certain grade of oats for which it was required only that the grain be sound and arrive at its destination "cool and sweet," regardless of whether it is damp, unclean, or light in weight, or even whether it is so defective and faulty that it will not fill the requirements of any grade. 52 Ill. App. 217.

COOL BLOOD. Tranquillity, or calmness; the condition of one who has the calm and undisturbed use of his reason. In cases of homicide, it frequently becomes necessary to ascertain whether the act of the person killing was done in cool blood or not, in order to ascertain the degree of his guilt.

COOLING TIME. In criminal law. Time for passion to subside and reason to interpose. Cooling time destroys the effect of provocation, leaving homicide murder, the same as if no provocation had been given. 1 Russ. Crimes, 525; Whart. Hom. 179; 3 Grat. (Va.) 594.

CO-OPERATION. The act of working together to a common end or for a certain purpose. The word is used in this sense in the law of maritime capture.

"Co-operation," which will give a title to booty, must directly tend to produce the capture in question. 35 L. J. Adm. 17.

And it is used in the like sense in the law of patents to express the working together of the parts of a machine, etc., not (of necessity) simultaneously, but unitedly.

"The courts do not mean merely acting together or simultaneously, but unitedly, to a common end,—a unitary result. Each and every part must have its subfunction to perform, and each must have a certain relation to or dependence upon the other." 82 Fed. 444.

It is used also in the same general sense in the law of master and servant as another expression of what is meant by habitual association or consociation.

"Whether the co-operation is in a particular business in the same line of employment, or there is habitual association in the performance of duties, in either case the situation of the parties must be such that they may exercise a mutual influence upon each other promotive of proper caution." 182 Ill. 548.

CO-OPERTIO (Law Lat. from *co-operire*, to cover). In old English law. A covering, or exterior coat, as the bark of a tree. Cowell. *Quercus discooperta*, an oak stripped of its bark, or debarked. Id.

CO-OPERTUM, or CO-OPERTURA (Law Lat. from *co-operire*, to cover). In forest law. A covert; a thicket (*dumetum*) or shelter for wild beasts in a forest. Cart. de Foresta, c. 12; Reg. Orig. 258; Spelman. *Extra co-opertum forestae*, without the covert of the forest. Fleta, lib. 2, c. 41, § 2.

COPARCENARY, ESTATES IN. Estates of which two or more persons form one heir. 1 Washb. Real Prop. 414.

The title to such an estate is always by descent. The shares of the tenants need not be equal. The estate is rare in America, but sometimes exists. 3 Ind. 360; 4 Grat. (Va.) 16; 17 Mo. 13; 3 Md. 190. See Watkins, Conv. (Coventry Ed.) 145.

COPARCENERS. Persons to whom an estate of inheritance descends jointly, and by whom it is held as an entire estate. 2 Bl. Comm. 187.

In the old English and the American sense, the term includes males as well as females, but in the modern English use is limited to females. 4 Kent, Comm. 462; 2 Bouv. Inst. note 1781.

COPARTICEPS. In old English law. A coparcener. Co. Entr. 377, 711.

COPARTNER. One who is a partner with one or more other persons; a member of a partnership (*q. v.*)

COPARTNERSHIP. A partnership (*q. v.*)

COPARTNERY. In Scotch law. The contract of copartnership; a contract by which the several partners agree concerning the communication (sharing) of loss or gain, arising from the subject of the contract. Bell, Dict.

COPE, or **COPPE** (Saxon). A hill. Co. Litt. 4b.

The top or summit of a thing, as of a house. Cowell.

A tribute paid out of lead mines in England. Blount.

COPEMAN, or **COPESMAN.** A chapman (*q. v.*)

COPESMATE. A merchant; a partner in merchandise.

COPIA (Lat.) In civil and old English law. Opportunity or means of access.

COPIA VERA. In Scotch practice. A true copy; words written at the top of copies of instruments. 3 How. St. Tr. 427, 430, 432.

COPPA. In English law. A crop or cock of grass, hay, or corn, divided into titheable portions, that it may be more fairly and justly tithed. Wharton.

COPPICE, or **COPSE.** A small wood, consisting of underwood, which may be cut at twelve or fifteen years' growth for fuel.

COPULA. Sexual intercourse; the consummation of marriage.

COPULATIO VERBORUM INDICAT ACceptationem in eodem sensu. Coupling words together shows that they ought to be understood in the same sense. Bac. Max. reg. 3; Broom, Leg. Max. (3d London Ed.) 523.

COPULATIVE TERM. One which is placed between two or more others to join them together.

COPY. A true transcript of an original writing.

Exemplifications are copies verified by the great seal or by the seal of a court. 1 Gilb. Ev. 19.

Examined copies are those which have been compared with the original, or with an official record thereof.

Office copies are those made by officers intrusted with the originals, and authorized for that purpose.

COPYHOLD. A tenure by copy of court-roll; any species of holding by particular custom of the manor; the estate so held.

COPYHOLDER. A tenant by copyhold tenure (by copy of court roll). 2 Bl. Comm. 95.

COPYRIGHT. The exclusive privilege, secured according to certain legal forms, of printing, publishing, and vending copies of writings or drawings. 14 How. (U. S.) 530.

Literally the word "copyright" means the right to copy a work or the right to the copy. 238 Ill. 442.

CORAAGIUM. Measures of corn. An unusual and extraordinary tribute, arising only on special occasions. They are thus distinguished from services. Mentioned in connection with hidage and carvage. Blount.

CORAM IPSO REGE (Lat.) Before the king himself. Proceedings in the court of king's bench are said to be *coram rege ipso.* 3 Bl. Comm. 41.

CORAM JUDICE. A cause is "coram judice" whenever a case is presented which brings into action the power of jurisdiction. 139 Ill. 516.

CORAM NOBIS. A writ of error on a judgment in the king's bench is called a *coram nobis*, before us. So called because the record and proceedings were stated in the writ to remain "before us." 1 Archb. Prac. 234.

——**In Modern Practice.** A writ of error for a review before the same court which is alleged to have committed the error.

The writ of *error coram nobis* has been quite largely supplanted, under statutes, in most states, errors of fact being now reviewable on motion.

CORAM NON JUDICE. Acts done by a court which has no jurisdiction either over the person, the cause, or the process, are said to be *coram non judice.* 1 Conn. 40. Such acts have no validity. If an act is required to be done before a particular person, it would not be considered as done before him if he were asleep or *non compos mentis.* 5 Har. & J. (Md.) 42; 8 Cranch (U. S.) 9; Paine (U. S.) 55; 1 Prest. Conv. 266.

CORAM PARIBUS. Before the peers or freeholders. The attestation of deeds, like all other solemn transactions, was originally done only *coram paribus.* 2 Bl. Comm. 307. *Coram paribus de vicineto,* before the peers or freeholders of the neighborhood. Id. 315.

CORAM SECTATORIBUS. Before the suitors. Cro. Jac. 582.

CORAM VOBIS. A writ of error on judgments of other courts than the king's bench. 2 Tidd, Prac. 1056, 1137. So called because the record was stated to remain "before you," *i. e.*, before the justices of king's bench.

——**In Modern Practice.** A writ of error for a review in a higher court than that alleged to have committed error.

CO-RESPONDENT. In England, where a husband brings a suit against his wife charging her with adultery, the alleged adulterer must, as a rule, be made a party to the petition as a co-respondent. If the adultery is proved, the court may order him to pay damages to the husband. The term is sometimes applied in the United States to the alleged adulterer, though the practice of joining him does not obtain. Browne, Div. 143, 204; 20 & 21 Vict. c. 85, §§ 28, 33. See "Adultery;" "Dissolution."

CORIUM FORFISFACERE. To forfeit one's skin; applied to a person condemned to be whipped; the ancient punishment of a servant.

CORN LAWS. Laws regulating the trade in breadstuffs.

The object of corn laws is to secure a regular and steady supply of the great staples of food; and for this object the means adopted in different countries and at different times widely vary, sometimes involving restriction or prohibition upon the export, and sometimes, in order to stimulate production, offering a bounty upon the export. Of the former character was the famous system of corn laws of England, initiated in 1773 by Mr. Burke, and repealed in 1846 under Sir Robert Peel.

CORN RENTS. Rents reserved in corn,—that is, in wheat or malt. Proportions of rents on college leases (being one-third), directed by St. 18 Eliz. c. 6, to be reserved in wheat or malt. 3 Steph. Comm. 141, 142; 2 Bl. Comm. 322.

CORNAGE. A species of tenure in England, by which the tenant was bound to blow a horn for the sake of alarming the country on the approach of an enemy. Bac. Abr. "Tenure" (N).

CORNER. A term used in the stock market, meaning cases where a purchaser succeeds in buying for future delivery more property of a given kind than is possible for the seller to deliver before the day of maturity of the contract. 168 Ill. 91; 130 Ill. 84.

CORNET. A commissioned officer in a regiment of calvary.

CORODIUM. In old English law. A corody.

CORODY. An allowance of meat, drink, money, clothing, lodging, and such like necessaries for sustenance. 1 Bl. Comm. 282; 1 Chit. Prac. 225. An allowance from an abbey or house of religion, to one of the king's servants who dwells therein, of meat and other sustenance. Fitzh. Nat. Brev. 230.

An assize law for a corody. Cowell. Corodies are now obsolete. Coke, 2d Inst. 630; 2 Sharswood, Bl. Comm. 40.

CORONA MALA. In old English law. The clergy who abuse their character were so called. Blount.

CORONARE. In old records. To give the tonsure, which was done on the crown, or in the form of a crown; to make a man a priest. Cowell.

CORONARE FILIUM. To make one's son a priest. *Homo coronatus* was one who had received the first tonsure, as preparatory to superior orders, and the tonsure was in form of a corona, or crown of thorns. Cowell.

CORONATOR (Lat.) A coroner (*q. v.*) Spelman.

CORONER. An officer whose principal duty it is to hold an inquisition, with the assistance of a jury, over the body of any person who may have come to a violent death, or who has died in prison.

It is his duty also, in case of the death of the sheriff, or his incapacity, or when a vacancy occurs in that office, to serve all the writs and processes which the sheriff is usually bound to serve. 20 Ga. 336; 11 Tex. 284; 14 Ala. (N. S.) 326; 10 Humph. (Tenn.) 346; 1 Sharswood, Bl. Comm. 349.

The chief justice of the king's bench is the sovereign or chief coroner of all England, though it is not to be understood that he performs the active duties of that office in any one county. 4 Coke, 57b; Bac. Abr.; 3 Comyn, Dig. 242; 5 Comyn, Dig. 212.

It is also his duty to inquire concerning shipwreck, and to find who has possession of the goods; concerning treasure trove, who are the finders, and where the property is. 1 Sharswood, Bl. Comm. 349.

The office has lost much of the honor which formerly appertained to it, but the duties are of great consequence to society, both for bringing murderers to punishment, and protecting innocent persons from accusation. It may often happen that the imperfections of the early examination enable one who is undoubtedly a criminal to escape. It is proper, in most cases of homicide, to procure the examination to be made by a physician, and in many cases it is his duty. 4 Car. & P. 571.

CORPORAL (Lat. *corpus*, body). Bodily; relating to the body; as, corporal punishment.

A noncommissioned officer of the lowest grade in an infantry company.

——**Corporal Oath.** An oath which the party takes, laying his hand on the Gospels. Cowell. It is now held to mean solemn oath. 1 Ind. 184.

——**Corporal Touch.** Actual, bodily contact with the hand.

It was once held that, before a seller of personal property could be said to have stopped it *in transitu,* so as to regain the possession of it, it was necessary that it should come to his corporal touch, but the contrary is now settled. These words were used merely as a figurative expression. 3 Term R. 464; 5 East, 184.

CORPORALE SACRAMENTUM. In old English law. A corporal oath.

CORPORALIS INJURIA NON RECIPIT aestimationem de futuro. A personal injury does not receive satisfaction from a future course of proceeding. Bac. Max. reg. 6; 3 How. St. Tr. 71; Broom, Leg. Max. (3d London Ed.) 254.

CORPORATION (Lat. *corpus,* a body). A franchise possessed by one or more individuals, who subsist as a body politic under a special denomination, and are vested, by the policy of the law, with the capacity of perpetual succession, and of acting in several respects, however numerous the association may be, as a single individual. 2 Kent, Comm. 267.

"A corporation is a body, or artificial person, consisting of one or more individuals, or sometimes of individuals and other corporations created by law, and invested by the law with certain legal capacities, as the capacity of succession, and the capacity to sue and be sued, to make contracts, to take, hold, and convey property, to commit torts and crimes, and to do other acts, however numerous its members may be, like a single individual." Clark & Marshall, Corp. 2.

A body, consisting of one or more natural persons, established by law, usually for some specific purpose, and continued by a succession of members.

It is this last characteristic of a corporation, sometimes called its immortality, prolonging its existence beyond the term of natural life, and thereby enabling a long-continued effort and concentration of means to the end which it was designed to answer, that constitutes its principal utility. A corporation is modelled upon a state or nation, and is to this day called a body politic, as well as corporate, thereby indicating its origin and derivation. Its earliest form was, probably, the municipality or city, which necessity exacted for the control or local police of the marts and crowded places of the state or empire. The combination of the commonalty in this form for local government became the earliest bulwark against despotic power, and a late philosophical historian traces to the remains and remembrance of the Roman *municipia* the formation of those elective governments of towns and cities in modern Europe, which, after the fall of the Roman empire, contributed so largely to the preservation of order, and to the protection of the rights of life and property as to become the foundation of modern liberty. McIntosh, Hist. Eng. pp. 31, 32.

An association of persons united in one body, having perpetual succession, vested with political rights conferred upon it by the authority creating it. 155 Ill. 179; 199 Ill. 635.

——**Aggregate Corporations.** Those which are composed of two or more members at the same time.

An aggregate corporation is a corporation consisting of more than one member, and has been defined as "an artificial body of men, composed of divers individuals, the ligaments of which body are the franchises and liberties bestowed upon it, which bind and unite all into one, and in which consists the whole frame and essence of the corporation." 1 Fletcher Cyclopedia Corporations, 79.

——**Business.** A corporation organized for the purpose of conducting financial dealings, buying and selling, traffic in general and mercantile transactions is a business corporation. Usually the term applies to any banking, manufacturing and trading corporation, and insurance companies, whether fire, life or marine, have been held to be business corporations. Fletcher Cyclopedia Corporations, 131.

——**Civil Corporations.** Those which are created to facilitate the transaction of business.

——**Ecclesiastical Corporations.** Those which are created to secure the public worship of God.

——**Eleemosynary Corporations.** Those which are created for the purpose of charities, such as schools, hospitals, and the like.

——**Estoppel.** While as against the state a corporation cannot be created by the mere agreement or other act or omission of private persons, yet as between private litigants they may, by their agreements, admissions, or conduct, place themselves where they would not be permitted to deny the fact of the existence of the corporation. The corporation, under such circumstances, is often designated a corporation by estoppel. 1 Fletcher Cyclopedia Corporations, 660.

——**Lay Corporations.** Those which exist for secular purposes.

——**Pecuniary Profit.** Under the statutes of some states, separate provisions are made for the incorporation of corporations for "pecuniary profit" as distinguished from corporations "not for pecuniary profit." Within the meaning of such a provision, a corporation "for pecuniary profit" has been defined to be a corporation organized for the pecuniary profit of its stockholders or members. Fletcher Cyclopedia Corporations, 132.

——**Private Corporations.** Those which are created wholly or in part for purposes of private emolument. 4 Wheat. (U. S.) 668; 9 Wheat. (U. S.) 907.

——**Public Corporations.** Those which are exclusively instruments of the public interest.

——**Sole Corporations.** Those which by law consist of but one member at any one time.

——**State or Nation.** The word "corporation" in its extensive signification applies to a nation or state, and thus used, the United States, and the several states, or commonwealths, composing the Union may be termed "corporations." Accordingly, there are many decisions holding that the United States is a corporation or a body corporate, and it may, like other corporations, enter into contracts, take hold, and convey property and sue or be sued, if it consents. In a like manner, the various states have been held to be corporations, and the same rule applies to territories. 1 Fletcher Cyclopedia Corporations, 110.

——**Stock.** A stock corporation or joint stock corporation is a corporation having a capital stock divided into shares, and which is authorized by law to distribute to the holders thereof dividends or shares of the surplus of the corporation. 1 Fletcher Cyclopedia Corporations, 112.

CORPORATOR. A member of a corporation.

CORPORE ET ANIMO. See "Animo et Corpore."

CORPOREAL HEREDITAMENTS. Substantial, permanent objects which may be inherited. The term "land" will include all such. 2 Sharswood, Bl. Comm. 17.

CORPOREAL PROPERTY.

——**In Civil Law.** That which consists of such subjects as are palpable.

——**In Common Law.** The term to signify the same thing is "property in possession." It differs from incorporeal property, which consists of choses in action and easements, as a right of way, and the like.

CORPS DIPLOMATIQUE. The body of ambassadors and diplomatic persons. Wharton.

CORPSE. The dead body of a human being. 1 Russ. & R. 366, note; 2 Term R. 733; 1 Leach, C. C. 497; 8 Pick. (Mass.) 370; Dig. 47. 12. 3. 7; Id. 11. 7. 38; Code, 3. 44. 1.

CORPUS (Lat. a body). The substance. Used of a human body, a corporation, a collection of laws, etc.

CORPUS COMITATUS. In old English law. The body of a county. Cro. Jac. 514; 5 How. (U. S.) 453; 5 Mason (U. S.) 290. The county at large, as distinguished from any particular locality within it.

CORPUS CORPORATUM. A corporation; a corporate body, other than municipal. Burr. Sett. Cas. 143.

CORPUS CUM CAUSA. See "Habeas Corpus."

CORPUS DELICTI. The body of the offense. The offense itself, as distinguished from the participation of any person therein. Thus, the *corpus delicti* of homicide is that a person has died by violence, not merely that he has died (43 Miss. 472), though the weight of authority is that the mere fact that a building has been burned is the *corpus delicti* of arson (29 Ga. 105; 33 Miss. 347. Contra, 76 Ala. 42).

The proof of a charge in criminal cases involves the proof of two distinct propositions: First, that the act itself was done; and second, that it was done by the person or persons charged, and by none other—in other words, proof of a corpus delicti, and the identity of the person or persons. 158 Ill. 589; 150 Ill. 186.

CORPUS HUMANUM NON RECIPIT aestimationem. A human body is not susceptible of appraisement. Hob. 59.

CORPUS JURIS CANONICI (Lat. the body of the canon law). The name given to the collections of the decrees and canons of the Roman church. See "Canon Law."

CORPUS JURIS CIVILIS (Lat. the body of the civil law). The collection comprising the Institutes, the Pandects or Digest, the Code and the Novels of Justinian See those several titles, and also "Civil Law," for fuller information. The name is said to have been first applied to this collection early in the seventeenth century.

CORPUS PRO CORPORE (Lat.) In old records. Body for body. A phrase expressing the liability of manucaptors. 3 How. St. Tr. 110.

CORRECTION, HOUSE OF. A reformatory.

CORREGIDOR. In Spanish law. A magistrate who took cognizance of various misdemeanors, and of civil matters. 2 White, New Recop. 53.

CORREI. In civil law. Two or more bound or secured by the same obligation.

Correi credendi are creditors secured by the same obligation.

Correi debendi are two or more persons bound as principal debtors to pay or perform. Ersk. Inst. 3. 3. 74; Calv. Lex.; Bell, Dict.

CORRESPONDENCE. The letters written by one person to another, and the answer thereto. See "Letter."

CORROBORATE. In evidence. To sustain by the introduction of other evidence to the same mact Corroborative evidence is "such evidence as tends in some degree of its own strength, and independently to prove some allegation or issue." 6 N. M. 250.

CORRUPTIO OPTIMI EST PESSIMA. Corruption of the best is worst.

CORRUPTION. An act done with an intent to give some advantage inconsistent with official duty and the rights of others.

It includes bribery, but is more comprehensive, because an act may be corruptly done, though the advantage to be derived from it be not offered by another. Merlin, Repert.

Something against law; as a contract by which the borrower agreed to pay the lender usurious interest. It is said, in such case, that it was corruptly agreed, etc.

CORRUPTION OF BLOOD. The incapacity to inherit, or pass an inheritance, in consequence of an attainder to which the party has been subject.

CORRUPTLY. A witness who falsely testifies "wilfully and for the purpose of concealing the truth" brings himself within the meaning of "corruptly" testifying. 192 Ill. 516 (aff. 94 Ill. App. 324).

CORSE-PRESENT. In old English law, A gift of the second-best beast belonging to a man at his death, taken along with the corpse, and presented to the priest. St. 21 Hen. VIII. c. 6; Cowell; 2 Bl. Comm. 425.

CORSNED. In old English law. A piece of barley bread, which, after the pronunciation of certain imprecations, a person accused of crime was compelled to swallow.

A piece of cheese or bread of about an ounce weight was consecrated, with an exorcism desiring of the Almighty that it might cause convulsions and paleness, and find no passage, if the man was really guilty, but might turn to health and nourishment if he was innocent. Spelman. It was then given to the suspected person, who at the same time received the sacrament. If he swallowed it easily, he was esteemed innocent. If it choked him, he was esteemed guilty. See 4 Sharswood, Bl. Comm. 345.

CORTES. The name of the legislative assemblies of Spain and Portugal.

CORTEX. The bark of a tree; the outer covering of anything.

The letter of an instrument, as distinguished from its spirit.

CORTIS. In old records. A court or hall. Spelman.

CORTULARIUM, or CORTARIUM. In old records. A yard or court adjoining a country farm. Spelman.

CORVEE. In French law. Gratuitous labor exacted from the villages or communities, especially for repairing roads, constructing bridges, etc.

Corvee seigneuriale are services due the lord of the manor. Guyot, Rep. Univ.; 3 Low. (U. S.) 1.

COSA JUZGADA. In Spanish law. A cause or matter adjudged (*res adjudicata*). White, New Recop. bk. 3, tit. 8, note.

COSBERING. In feudal law. A prerogative or seignorial right of a lord, as to lie and feast himself and his followers at his tenants' houses. Cowell.

COSDUNA. In feudal law. A custom or tribute.

COSEN, or COZEN. In old English law. To cheat. "A cosening knave." 3 Leon. 171.

COSENING. In old English law. An offense whereby anything is done deceitfully whether in or out of contracts, which cannot be fitly termed by an especial name. Called in the civil law *stellionatus*. West, Symb. pt. 2, "Indictment," § 68; Blount; 4 Bl. Comm. 158.

COSHERING. In old English law. A feudal prerogative or custom for lords to lie and feast themselves at their tenants' houses. Cowell.

COSINAGE, COUSINAGE, or COSENAGE. A writ which lay where the father of the great-grandfather of the demandant had been disseised, and the heir brought his writ to recover possession. Fitzh. Nat. Brev. 221.

Relationship; affinity. St. 4 Hen. III. c. 8; 3 Bl. Comm. 186; Co. Litt. 160a.

COST. The price actually paid for goods. 18 N. Y. 337.

COSTIPULATOR. A joint promisor.

COSTS. A pecuniary allowance made by positive law to the successful party to a suit, or to some distinct proceeding in a suit in consideration of, and to reimburse, his probable expense. Abbott. See 4 N. M. 356.

At common law, there were no costs by name, but when the plaintiff failed, he was amerced for presenting a false claim, and, when judgment was rendered against defendant, he was fined for resisting the just claim of plaintiff.

Costs as allowed by statute in modern practice are the amount allowed the prevailing party in lieu of the common-law fines. The term is to be distinguished from "disbursements," which includes the amounts paid out by the prevailing party for certain purposes incident to the suit, and allowed to him as part of his recovery. 23 Orc. 451. See "Double Costs.

COSTS DE INCREMENTO. Increased costs; costs of increase; costs adjudged by the court in addition to those assessed by the jury. 13 How. (U. S.) 372.

The cost of the suit, etc., recovered originally under the statute of Gloucester, is said to be the origin of costs *de incremento*. Buller, N. P. 328a. Where the statute requires costs to be doubled in case of an unsuccessful appeal, costs *de incremento* stand on the same footing as jury costs. 2 Strange, 1048. Costs were enrolled in England in the time of Blackstone as "increase" of damages. 3 Bl. Comm. 299.

COSTS OF THE DAY (or **TERM**). Costs incurred in preparing for trial on a particular day or term. Adams, Eq. 343.

COSTUMBRE. In Spanish law. Custom! an unwritten law established by usage, during a long space of time. Las Partidas, pt. 1, tit. 2, lib. 4.

COSURETIES. Joint sureties; two or more sureties to the same obligation.

COTARIUS. In old English law. A cottager. Spelman.

COTERELLI. Anciently, a kind of peasantry who were outlaws; robbers. Blount.

COTERELLUS. A cottager.

Coterellus was distinguished from *cotarius* in this, that the *cotarius* held by socage tenure, but the *coterellus* held in mere villenage, and his person, issue, and goods were held at the will of the lord. Cowell.

COTESWOLD. A place where there is no wood.

COTLAND. Land held by a cottager, whether in socage or villenage. Cowell; Blount.

COTSETHLAND. In old English law. The seat of a cottage, including any land belonging to it.

COTSETUS. In old English law. A cottager or cottage holder who, by servile tenure, was bound to work for the lord. Cowell.

COTTAGE, COTA, or **COTTAGIUM.** In old English law. A small house without any land belonging to it, whereof mention is made in St. 4 Edw. I. But, by St. 31 Eliz. c. 7, no man may build such cottage for habitation unless he lay unto it four acres of freehold land, except in market towns, cities, or within a mile of the sea, or for the habitation of laborers in mines, shepherds, foresters, sailors, etc. Termes de la Ley. Twenty years' possession of cottage gives good title as against the lord. Buller, N. P. 103a, 104. By a grant of a cottage the curtilage will pass. 4 Viner, Abr. 582.

COTUCHANS. Boors; husbandmen. Domesday Book.

COTUCHANS. Boors; husbandmen. said to have been levant and couchant when they have been upon another person's land, damage feasant, one night at least. 3 Bl. Comm. 9.

COUCHER, or **COURCHER.** A factor who continues abroad for traffic (37 Edw. III. c. 16); also the general book wherein any corporation, etc., register their acts (3 & 4 Edw. VI. c. 10).

COUNCIL (Lat. *concilium*, an assembly). The legislative body in the government of cities or boroughs; an advisory body selected to aid the executive. See 14 Mass. 470; 3 Pick. (Mass.) 517; 4 Pick. (Mass.) 25.

A governor's council is still retained in some of the states of the United States. It is analogous in many respects to the privy council of the king of Great Britain, and of the governors of the British colonies, though of a much more limited range of duties. See "Privy Council."

COUNCIL OF CONCILIATION. By Act 30 & 31 Vict. c. 105, power is given for the crown to grant licenses for the formation of councils of conciliation and arbitration, consisting of a certain number of masters and workmen in any trade or employment, having power to hear and determine all questions between masters and workmen which may be submitted to them by both parties, arising out of or with respect to the particular trade or manufacture, and incapable of being otherwise settled. They have power to apply to a justice to enforce the performance of their award. The members are elected by persons engaged in the trade. Davis, Bldg. Soc. 232; Sweet.

COUNCIL OF JUDGES. Under the English judicature act of 1873 (section 75) an annual council of the judges of the supreme court is to be held, for the purpose of considering the operation of the new practice, offices, etc., introduced by the act, and of reporting to a secretary of state as to any alterations which they consider should be made in the law for the administration of justice. An extraordinary council may also be convened at any time by the lord chancellor. Sweet.

COUNCIL OF THE NORTH. A court instituted by Henry VIII. in 1537, to administer justice in Yorkshire and the four other northern counties. Under the presidency of Stratford, the court showed great rigor, bordering, it is alleged, on harshness. It was abolished by 16 Car. I., the same act which abolished the star chamber. Brown.

COUNSEL. The counsellors who are associated in the management of a particular cause, or who act as legal advisers in reference to any matter requiring legal knowledge and judgment.

The term is used both as a singular and plural noun, to denote one or more, though it is perhaps more common, when speaking of one of several counsellors concerned in the management of a case in court, to say that he is "of counsel."

Knowledge. A grand jury is sworn to keep secret "the commonwealth's counsel, their fellows' and their own."

COUNSELLOR AT LAW. See "Counsel;" "Attorney at Law."

COUNSEL'S SIGNATURE. In equity pleading. The signature of counsel required to be appended to a bill to denote to the court that he had perused the draft of it, or been informed of the contents thereof in such manner as would satisfy him that he might certify that it stated a case entitling the complainant to the relief prayed, and that it set the same forth with such regard to the essential rules of pleading, and with such a prayer as would entitle the bill to the consideration of the chancellor. 19 N. J. Eq. 180. Though the drawing of a bill is properly the duty of the solicitor, yet in practice it is usually both drawn and signed by counsel. Daniell, Ch. Pr. 311.

COUNT (Fr. *comte,* from the Latin *comes*). An earl. It gave way as a distinct title to the Saxon earl, but was retained in countess, viscount, and as the basis of county. Termes de la Ley; 1 Bl. Comm. 398. See "Comes."

——**In Pleading.** The plaintiff's statement of his cause of action. This word, derived from the French *conte,* a narrative, is in our old law books used synonymously with "declaration;" but practice has introduced the following distinction: When the plaintiff's complaint embraces only a single cause of action, and he makes only one statement of it, that statement is called, indifferently, a "declaration" or "count," though the former is the more usual term; but when the suit embraces two or more causes of action, each of which, of course, requires a different statement, or when the plaintiff makes two or more different statements of one and the same cause of action, each several statement is called a "count," and all of them collectively, constitute the "declaration." In all cases, however, in which there are two or more counts, whether there is actually but one cause of action or several, each count purports, upon the face of it, to disclose a distinct right of action, unconnected with that stated in any of the other counts.

COUNTEE. An earl. Litt. 61, 181, 335.

COUNTER, or **COMPTER.** The name of two prisons formerly standing in London, but now demolished. They were the Poultry Counter and Wood Street Counter. Cowell; Whishaw; Coke, 4th Inst. 248.

COUNTER AFFIDAVIT. An affidavit made in opposition to one already made. This is allowed in the preliminary examination of some cases.

COUNTER BOND. A bond to indemnify 2 Leon. 90.

COUNTER FEASANCE. The act of forging.

COUNTER LETTER. An agreement to recovery where property has been passed by absolute deed with the intention that it shall serve as security only. A defeasance by a separate instrument. 11 Pet. (U. S.) 351.

COUNTER ROLL (Law Fr. *contreroule, conterrolle;* Law Lat. *contra rotulus*). In old English law and practice. A roll kept by an officer as a check upon another officer's roll. Sheriffs and coroners were anciently required to keep rolls or records of what was done before them. Bracton, fols. 121b, 140b; Britt. c. 1. *Le vicont eit counterrolles ove les coroners, auxybien des appeals come des enquests,* etc., the sheriff shall have counter rolls with the coroners, as well of appeals as of inquests, etc. St. Westminster I. c. 10.

COUNTER SECURITY. Security given to one who has become security for another, the condition of which is, that if the one who first became surety shall be damnified, the one who gives the counter security will indemnify him.

COUNTERCLAIM. See "Set-Off."

COUNTERFEIT. In criminal law. To make something false in the semblance of that which is true. It always implies a fraudulent intent. Generally applied to the imitation of coin of the realm.

COUNTERMAND. A change or recalling of orders previously given.

Express countermand takes place when contrary orders are given, and a revocation of the prior order is made.

Implied countermand takes place when a new order is given which is inconsistent with the former order.

COUNTERPART. Formerly, each party to an indenture executed a separate deed; that part which was executed by the grantor was called the "original," and the rest the "counterparts." It is now usual for all the parties to execute every part, and this makes them all originals. 2 Bl. Comm. 29.

COUNTERPLEA. In pleading. A plea to some matter incidental to the main object of the suit, and out of the direct line of pleadings. 2 Wm. Saund. 45h.

Thus, counterplea of oyer is the defendant's allegations why oyer of an instrument should not be granted.

Counterplea of aid prayer is the demandant's allegation why the vouchee of the tenant in a real action, or a stranger who asks to come in to defend his right, should not be admitted.

Counterplea of voucher is the allegation of the vouchee in avoidance of the warranty after admission to plead.

Counterpleas are of rare occurrence. Termes de la Ley; Doct. Plac. 300; Comyn, Dig. "Voucher" (B 1, 2); Dane, Abr.

COUNTERSIGN. To sign what has already been signed by a superior; to authenticate by an additional signature. 40 Ill. 167.

COUNTEZ (Law Fr. count, or reckon). In old practice. A direction formerly given by the clerk of a court to the crier, after a jury was sworn, to number them, and which

Blackstone says was given in his time, in good English, "count these." 4 Bl. Comm. 340, note (u).

COUNTOR, COUNTER, or COUNTOUR (Law. Fr. *contour*, from *counter* or *conter*, to relate, recite, or state orally; Law Lat. *narrator*). In old English practice. An advocate or professional pleader; one who counted for his client, that is, related his case, recited his count, or orally pleaded his cause.

COUNTY. One of the civil divisions of a country for judicial and political purposes. 1 Bl. Comm. 113. Etymologically, it denotes that portion of the country under the immediate government of a count. Id. 116.

The United States are generally divided into counties. Counties are, in many of the states, divided into townships or towns. In the New England states, however, towns are the basis of all civil divisions, and the counties are rather to be considered as aggregates of towns, so far as their origin is concerned. In Pennsylvania, the state was originally divided into three counties by William Penn. See Proud, Hist. vol. 1, p. 234; Id. vol. 2, p. 258.

In the English law, this word signifies the same as "shire,"—county being derived from the French, and shire from the Saxon. Both these words signify a circuit or portion of the realm into which the whole land is divided, for the better government thereof, and the more easy administration of justice. There is no part of England that is not within some county; and the shire-reeve (sheriff) was the governor of the province under the *comes*, earl or count.

COUNTY COMMISSIONERS. Certain officers generally intrusted with the superintendence of the collection of the county taxes, and the disbursements made for the county. They are invested by the local laws with various powers.

COUNTY CORPORATE. A city or town, with more or less territory annexed, constituting a county by itself. 1 Bl. Comm. 120. Something similar to this exists in this country in regard to Philadelphia, New York, and Boston. They differ in no material points from other counties.

COUNTY COURT.

——**In English Law.** Tribunals of limited jurisdiction, originally established under St. 9 & 10 Vict. c. 95. They had, at their institution, jurisdiction of actions for the recovery of debts, damages, and demands, legacies, and balances of partnership accounts, where the sum sued for did not exceed twenty pounds. It has since been much extended, especially in cases where the parties give assent in writing. They are chiefly regulated by St. 9 & 10 Vict. c. 95; 12 & 13 Vict. c. 101; 13 & 14 Vict. c. 61; 15 & 16 Vict. c. 54; 19 & 20 Vict. c. 108; 21 & 22 Vict. c. 74. See 3 Sharswood, Bl. Comm. 76.

Tribunals of limited jurisdiction in the county of Middlesex, established under St. 22 Geo. II. c. 33.

These courts are held once a month at least in every hundred in the county of Middlesex, by the county clerk and a jury of twelve suitors, or freeholders, summoned for that purpose. They examine the parties under oath, and make such order in the case as they shall judge agreeable to conscience. 3 Steph. Comm. 452; 3 Bl. Comm. 83.

The county court was a court of great antiquity, and originally of much splendor and importance. It was a court of limited jurisdiction incident to the jurisdiction of the sheriff, in which, however, the suitors were really the judges, while the sheriff was a ministerial officer. It had jurisdiction of personal actions for the recovery of small debts, and of many real actions prior to their abolition. By virtue of a *justicies*, it might entertain jurisdiction of personal actions to any amount. At this court, all proclamations of laws, outlawries, etc., were made, and the elections of such officers as sheriffs, coroners, and others took place. In the time of Edward I. it was held by the earl and bishop, and was of great dignity. It was superseded by the courts of requests to a great degree; and these, in turn, gave way to the new county courts, as they are sometimes called distinctively.

——**In American Law.** Courts in many of the states of the United States, and in Canada, of widely varying powers, in some states being courts of general original jurisdiction, and in others courts of probate or limited jurisdiction.

COUNTY PALATINE. A county possessing certain peculiar privileges. The owners of such counties have kingly powers within their jurisdictions, as the pardoning crimes, issuing writs, etc. These counties have either passed into the hands of the crown, or have lost their peculiar privileges to a great degree. 1 Bl. Comm. 117; 4 Bl. Comm. 431. The name is derived from *palatium* (palace), and was applied because the earls anciently had palaces, and maintained regal state. Cowell; Spelman; 1 Bl. Comm. 117.

COUNTY RATE. An imposition levied on the occupiers of lands in England, and applied to many miscellaneous purposes, among which the most important are those of defraying the expenses connected with prisons, reimbursing to private parties the costs they have incurred in prosecuting public offenders, and defraying the expenses of the county police. Wharton.

COUNTY SESSIONS. In England. The general quarter sessions of the peace for each county, which are held four times a year. Wharton; Warren, Law Stud. 367.

COUPON BONDS. "Coupon bonds" are the ordinary form of corporate bond in this country. They are payable to bearer and are provided with interest warrants, called "coupons," for each installment of interest, also payable to bearer, which, when actually detached, are negotiable, and payable to bearer. 2 Fletcher Cyclopedia Corporations, 1919.

COUPONS. Those parts of a commercial instrument which are to be cut, and which are evidence of something connected with the contract mentioned in the instrument. They are generally attached to certificates of loan, where the interest is payable at particular periods, and, when the interest is paid, they are cut off and delivered to the payor.

COUR DE CASSATION. In French law. The supreme judicial tribunal and court of final resort. It is composed of forty-nine counsellors and judges, including a first president and three presidents of chamber, an attorney general and six advocates general, one head registrar and four deputy registrars appointed by the head registrar, and a certain number of ushers. Jones, Fr. Bar, 22; Guyot, Rep. Univ.

The jurisdiction of the court is only on error shown in the proceedings of the lower courts in matters of law, taking the facts as found by the lower courts.

COURSE. The direction of a line with reference to a meridian.

Where there are no monuments, the land must be bounded by the courses and distances mentioned in the patent or deed. 4 Wheat. (U. S.) 444; 3 Pet. (U. S.) 96; 3 Murph. (N. C.) 82; 2 Har. & J. (Md.) 267; 5 Har. & J. (Md.) 254. When the lines are actually marked, they must be adhered to, though they vary from the course mentioned in the deeds. 2 Overt. (Tenn.) 304; 7 Wheat. (U. S.) 7. See 3 Call (Va.) 239; 7 T. B. Mon. (Ky.) 333. See "Boundary."

COURSE OF EMPLOYMENT.

——**Agent.** Within the meaning of the rule as to the liability of a principal for the acts of an agent, such acts are within the "course of his employment" when the agent is endeavoring to promote his principal's business within the scope of the actual or apparent authority conferred upon him for that purpose. 190 Ill. App. 65; 177 Ill. App. 239.

——**Workmen's Compensation Act.** An injury occurs in the course of the employment, within the Workmen's Compensation Act, when it occurs within the period of employment, at a place where the employee may reasonably be, and while he is reasonably fulfilling the duties of employment or engaged in something incidental to it. 279 Ill. 11; 282 Ill. 489.

COURSE OF THE VOYAGE. By this term is understood the regular and customary track, if such there be, which a ship takes in going from one port to another, and the shortest way. Marsh. Ins. 185.

COURSE OF TRADE. What is usually done in the management of trade or business.

Men are presumed to act for their own interest, and to pursue the way usually adopted by men generally; hence it is presumed in law that men in their actions will pursue the usual course of trade.

COURT (Lat. *cohors*, an inclosure). A body in the government to which the public administration of justice is delegated.

A tribunal established for the administration of justice. 18 Mo. 570.

The presence of a sufficient number of the members of a judicial body regularly convened in an authorized place at an appointed time, engaged in the performance of its functions. It is to be observed, however, that a court does not come into being when it convenes, or pass out of existence when it adjourns.

The idea of place in the Latin word from which the term is derived is given too great prominence in some definitions, notably in that of Blackstone, that a court is "a place where justice is judicially administered" (3 Bl. Comm. 23); a court being a tribunal rather than a place.

The term is also used to signify the judge or judges themselves when duly convened, in contradistinction from the jury, and also in contradistinction from the judge or judges when not convened as a court.

It has been said that in every court there must be three constituent parts,—the plaintiff, the defendant, and the judicial power (*actor*, *reus*, and *judex*) (3 Bl. Comm. 25); but it is manifestly not essential to the idea of a court that it have a cause pending before it. See 1 Abb. Mich. Prac. § 2.

——**Classification.** Courts are divided into courts of record and courts not of record; a court of record being one whose acts and judicial proceedings are enrolled or recorded, and courts not of record being those inferior courts whose proceedings are not formally recorded or enrolled.

Courts are also divided, as to the extent of their jurisdiction, into courts of general jurisdiction, and courts of limited or special jurisdiction; the former being those courts whose jurisdiction extends to all cases comprised within a class or classes, especially to cases of a civil nature (109 U. S. 278), and the latter being those courts which are limited either as to the value or the nature of the pleas which they may entertain, or as to the territory over which their jurisdiction extends.

According to the nature of their jurisdiction, and the principles upon which it is exercised, courts are said to be of original jurisdiction, intermediate or appellate; civil or criminal; ecclesiastical; of law or of equity; of admiralty; courts martial.

COURT BARON. A domestic court, incident to every manor, to be held by the steward within the manor, for redressing misdemeanors and nuisances therein, and for settling disputes among the tenants relating to property. It is not a court of record.

Customary court baron is one appertaining entirely to copyholders. See "Customary Court Baron."

Freeholders' court baron is one held before the freeholders who owe suit and service to the manor. It is the court baron proper. These courts have now fallen into great disuse in England, and provision is made by St. 9 & 10 Vict. c. 95, § 14, enabling the lord of any manor which has a court in which debts or demands are recoverable to surrender to the crown the right of holding such court, and, upon such surrender, the court is discontinued, and the right of holding it ceases. In the state of New York, such courts were held while the state was a province. See charters in Bolton's History of New Chester. The court has derived its name from the fact that it was the court of the baron or lord of the manor (3 Sharswood, Bl. Comm. 33, note. See Fleta, lib. 2, c. 53), though it is explained by some as being the court of the freeholders, who were in some instances called barons (Co. Litt. 58a).

COURT FOR CROWN CASES RESERVed. The court created by St. 11 & 12 Vict. c. 78, for the decision of questions of law arising on the trial of a person convicted of treason, felony, or misdemeanor (*e. g.*, at the central criminal court, the assizes, or quarter sessions), and reserved by the judge or justices at the trial, for the consideration of the court. For this purpose, the judge or justices state and sign a case setting forth the question and the facts out of which it arises. Archb. Crim. Pl. 191. The jurisdiction is now exercised by the judges of the high court of justice, or five of them, at the least. Their decision is final. Judicature Act 1873, §§ 47, 100.

COURT FOR DIVORCE AND MATRIMOnial causes. In English law. A court which has the jurisdiction formerly exercised by the ecclesiastical courts in respect of divorces *a mensa et thoro*, suits of nullity of marriage, suits of jactitation of marriage, suits for restitution of conjugal rights, and all suits, causes, and matters matrimonial. It consists of the lord chancellor and the justices of the queen's bench, the common pleas, the exchequer, and the judge of the court of probate, who is entitled "Judge ordinary." The judge ordinary exercises all the powers of the court, except petitions for dissolving or annulling marriages, and applications for new trials of matters of fact, bills of exception, special verdict and special cases, for hearing which excepted cases he must be joined by two of the other judges. Provision is made for his absence by authorizing the lord chancellor to appoint one of certain judicial persons to act in such absence. Juries may be summoned to try matters of fact, and such trials are conducted in the same manner as jury trials at common law. See St. 20 & 21 Vict. c. 85; St. 21 & 22 Vict. c. 108; St. 22 & 23 Vict. c. 61.

COURT FOR THE RELIEF OF INSOLvent debtors in England. In English law. A local court which has its sittings in London only, which receives the petitions of insolvent debtors, and decides upon the question of granting a discharge. It is held by the commissioners of bankruptcy, and its decisions, if in favor of a discharge, are not reversible by any other tribunal. See 3 Steph. Comm. 426; 4 Steph. Comm. 287, 288.

COURT FOR THE TRIAL OF IMPEACHments. A tribunal for determining the guilt or innocence of any person properly impeached. In England, the house of lords, and in this country, generally, the more select branch of the legislative assembly, constitutes a court for the trial of impeachments. See "Impeachment."

COURT HAND. In old English practice. The peculiar hand in which the records of courts were written from the earliest period down to the reign of George II. Its characteristics were great strength, compactness, and undeviating uniformity, and its use undoubtedly gave to the ancient record its acknowledged superiority over the modern, in the important quality of durability. Sir James Burrows, speaking of St. 4 Geo. II. c. 26, thus forcibly contrasts this style of writing with that by which it was superseded: "A statute now took place for converting them [common-law pleadings] from a fixed dead language to a fluctuating, living one, and for altering the strong, solid, compact hand, calculated to last for ages, wherein they were used to be written, into a species of handwriting so weak, flimsy and diffuse that many a modern record will hardly outlive its writer, and few perhaps will survive much above a century." 1 Burrows, pref. iv. Sir William Blackstone mentions another disadvantage attending the disuse of the old hand, "whereby the reading of any record that is fifty years old is now become the object of science, and calls for the help of an antiquarian." 3 Bl. Comm. 323.

The writing of this hand, with its peculiar abbreviations and contractions, constituted, while it was in use, an art of no little importance, being an indispensable part of the profession of clerkship, as it was called. Two sizes of it were employed —a large and a small hand; the former, called "great court hand," being used for initial words or clauses, the placita of records, etc. Towns. Pl. passim; Instr. Cler. passim. See "Record."

COURT HOUSE. A building used for the holding of sessions of court, whether such use be permanent or temporary. 65 Ga. 165.

COURT LANDS. Domains or lands kept in the lord's hands to serve his family.

COURT LEET (Law Lat. *curia letae*, the court of the leet). A court of record in England, held once or twice in every year within a particular hundred, lordship, or manor, before the steward of the leet, for the preservation of the peace, and the punishment of all trivial misdemeanors. Kitch. Cts. Its original intent was to view the frank pledges,—that is, the freemen of the liberty who anciently were all mutually pledges for the good behavior of each other, —and hence it was called, by the Anglo-Normans, the "view of frank pledge," *visus franci plegii.* 4 Bl. Comm. 273; Spelman, voc. "Leta;" 4 Inst. 261; Mirr. c. 1, § 10; 2 Hawk. P. C. 72; 1 Crabb, Real Prop. 495, § 637 et seq.; Tomlin. It has, however, latterly fallen into almost total desuetude; its business having, for the most part, gradually devolved upon the quarter sessions. 4 Steph. Comm. 340. See "Leet;" "Frank Pledge;" "View of Frank Pledge."

COURT-MARTIAL. A military or naval tribunal, which has jurisdiction of offenses against the law of the service, military or naval, in which the offender is engaged.

The original tribunal, for which courts-martial are a partial substitute, was the court of chivalry (*q. v.*) These courts exist and have their jurisdiction by virtue of the military law, the court being constituted and empowered to act in each instance by authority from a commanding officer. The general principles applicable to courts-martial in the army and navy are essentially the same, and, for consideration of the exact distinctions between them, reference must be had to the works of writers upon these subjects. Courts-martial for the regulation of the militia are held in the various states under local statutes, which resemble in their main features those provided for in the army of the United States; and when in actual service, the militia, like the regular troops, are subject to courts-martial, composed, however, of militia officers.

As to their constitution and jurisdiction, these courts may belong to one of the following classes:

(1) General, which have jurisdiction over every species of offense of which courts-martial have jurisdiction. They are to be composed in the United States of not less than five nor more than thirteen commissioned officers of suitable rank, according to the exigencies of the service, and in England of not less than thirteen commissioned officers, except in special cases, and usually do consist of more than that number.

(2) Regimental, which have jurisdiction of some minor offenses occurring in a regiment or corps. They consist in the United States of not less than three commissioned officers; in England, of not less than five commissioned officers, when that number can be assembled without detriment to the service, and of not less than three, in any event. The jurisdiction of this class of courts-martial extends only to offenses less than capital committed by those below the rank of commissioned officers, and their decision is subject to revision by the commanding officer of the division, regiment, or detachment, by the officer who appointed them, or by certain superior officers.

(3) Garrison, which have jurisdiction of some minor offenses occurring in a garrison, fort, or barracks. They are of the same constitution as to number and qualifications of members as regimental courts-martial. Their limits of jurisdiction in degree are the same, and their decisions are in a similar manner subject to revision.

(4) Summary, of limited jurisdiction, for the trial of minor offenses.

COURT OF ADMIRALTY. See "Admiralty."

COURT OF ANCIENT DEMESNE. In English law. A court of peculiar constitution, held by a bailiff appointed by the king, in which alone the tenants of the king's demesne could be impleaded. 2 Burrows, 1046; 1 Spence, Eq. Jur. 100; 2 Sharswood, Bl. Comm. 99; 1 Report Eng. Real Prop. Comm. 28, 29; 3 Steph. Comm. 211, 212.

COURT OF APPEALS. In American law. An appellate tribunal, which, in some states, as Kentucky, Maryland, and New York, is the court of last resort, and in others, as Illinois, is an intermediate appellate court.

COURT OF ARBITRATION OF THE chamber of commerce. A court of arbitraors, created for the convenience of merchants in the city of New York, by act of the legislature of New York. Laws 1874, c. 278; Laws 1875, c. 495. It decides disputes between members and outside merchants who voluntarily submit themselves to the jurisdiction of the court.

COURT OF ARCHES (Law Lat. *curia de arcubus*). In English ecclesiastical law. A court of appeal, and of original jurisdiction.

The most ancient consistory court belonging to the archbishop of Canterbury for the trial of spiritual causes, the judge of which is called the "dean of the arches," because he anciently held his court in the church of St. Mary le Bow (*Sancta Maria de Arcubus*, —literally, "St. Mary of Arches"), so named from the style of its steeple. which is raised upon pillars built archwise, like so many bent bows. Termes de la Ley. It is now held, as are also the other spiritual courts, in the hall belonging to the College of Civilians, commonly called "Doctors' Commons."

Its proper jurisdiction is only over the thirteen peculiar parishes belonging to the archbishop in London; but, the office of dean of the arches having been for a long time united with that of the archbishop's principal official, the judge of the arches, in right of such added office, receives and determines appeals from the sentences of all inferior ecclesiastical courts within the province. 3 Bl. Comm. 64; 3 Steph. Comm. 431; Wharton, "Arches Court."

COURT OF ATTACHMENTS. The lowest of the three courts held in the forests. The highest court is called "Justice in Eyre's Seat;" the middle, the "Sweinmote;" and the lowest, the "Attachment." Sharswood, For. Laws, 90, 99; Wharton, "Attachment of the Forests."

The court of attachments is to be held before the verderors of the forest once in every forty days, to inquire of all offenders against vert and venison, by receiving from the foresters or keepers their attachments or presentments *de viridi et venatione*, enrolling them, and certifying them under their seals to the court of justice seat, or sweinmote; for this court can only inquire of offenders; it cannot convict them. 3 Bl. Comm. 439; Carta de Foresta, 9 Hen. III. c. 8; Termes de la Ley. But see "Forest Courts."

COURT OF AUDIENCE. Ecclesiastical courts, in which the primates once exercised in person a considerable part of their jurisdiction. They seem to be now obsolete, or at least to be only used on the rare occurrence of the trial of a bishop. Phillim. Ecc. Law, 1201, 1204.

COURT OF AUGMENTATION. A court established by 27 Hen. VIII. c. 27, for managing the revenues and possessions of all monasteries whose income was under two hundred pounds a year (which by an act of parliament of the same session had been given to the king), and for determining suits relating thereto. It was called the "Court of the Augmentations of the Revenues of the King's Crown," from the augmentation of the revenues of the crown derived from the suppression of the monasteries, and was a court of record, with one great seal and one privy seal; the officers being a chancellor, who had the great seal, a treasurer, a king's attorney and solicitor, ten auditors, seventeen receivers, with clerk, usher, etc.

COURT OF BANKRUPTCY. A court of record, in England, with jurisdiction in bankruptcy, primary and appellate, and which is declared a court of law and equity for that purpose. The nature of its constitution may be learned from the early sections of the bankrupt law consolidation act of 1849.

COURT OF CHANCERY, or CHANCERY. A court existing in England and several of the United States, which possesses an extensive equity jurisdiction.

The name is said by some to be derived from that of the chief judge, who is called a "chancellor." Others derive both names directly from the *cancelli* (bars), which in this court anciently separated the press of people from the officers. 3 Sharswood, Bl. Comm. 46, note. See "Cancellarius."

——**In American Law.** A court of general equity jurisdiction.

The terms "equity" and "chancery," "court of equity" and "court of chancery," are constantly used as synonymous in the United States. It is presumed that this custom arises from the circumstance that the equity jurisdiction which is exercised by the courts of the various states is assimilated to that possessed by the English courts of chancery. Indeed, in some of the states it is made identical therewith by statute, so far as comformable to our institutions.

Separate courts of chancery or equity exist in a few of the states; in others, the courts of law sit also as courts of equity; in others, equitable relief is administered under the forms of the common law; and in others, the distinction between law and equity has been formally abolished, or never existed. The federal courts exercise an equity jurisdiction, whether the state courts in the district are courts of equity or not. 2 McLean (U. S.) 568; 15 Pet. (U. S.) 9; 11 How. (U. S.) 669; 13 How. (U. S.) 268, 519.

——**In English Law.** The highest court of judicature next to parliament.

The superior court of chancery, called, distinctively, the "High Court of Chancery," consists of six separate tribunals, viz.: The court of the lord high chancellor of Great Britain; the court of the master of the rolls, or keeper of the records in chancery; the court of appeal in chancery (*q. v.*); the three separate courts of the vice chancellors.

COURT OF CHIVALRY. In English law, An ancient military court, possessing both civil and criminal jurisdiction touching matters of arms and deeds of war.

As a court of civil jurisdiction, it was held by the lord high constable of England while that office was filled, and the earl marshal, jointly, and subsequently to the attainder of Stafford, duke of Buckingham, in the time of Henry VIII., by the earl marshal alone. It had cognizance, by St. 13 Rich. II. c. 2, "of contracts and other matters touching deeds of arms and war, as well out of the realm as within it." This jurisdiction was of importance while the English kings held territories in France.

As a court of criminal jurisdiction, it could be held only by the lord high constable and earl marshal jointly. It had jurisdiction over "pleas of life and member arising in matters of arms and deeds of war, as well out of the realm as within it."

It was not a court of record, could neither fine nor imprison (7 Mod. 127), and has fallen entirely into disuse (3 Sharswood, Bl. Comm. 68; 4 Sharswood, Bl. Comm. 268).

COURT OF CLAIMS. This court, as originally created by the statute of February 24,

1855 (10 St. at Large, 12), consisted of three judges, with jurisdiction to hear and determine all claims founded upon any law of congress, or regulation of an executive department, or upon any contract, express or implied, with the government of the United States, and of all claims which might be referred to it by either house of congress.

The court had no power to render a judgment which it could execute, but reported to congress the cases upon which it had finally acted, the material facts it found established by the evidence, with its opinion in the case, and reasons therefor, or what was equivalent to an opinion in the nature of a judgment as to the rights of the parties upon the facts proved or admitted in the case. Bright. Dig. 198-200.

By an amendatory act of March 3, 1863, two judges were added. In addition to the jurisdiction previously conferred upon the court, it is now authorized to take jurisdiction of all set-offs, counterclaims, claims for damages, liquidated or unliquidated, or other demands whatsoever on the part of the government against any person making claim against the government in said court. If the judgment of the court shall be in favor of the government, it shall be filed in the office of the clerk of the proper district or circuit court of the United States, and shall *ipso facto* become and be a judgment of such district or circuit court, and shall be enforced in like manner as other judgments are. If the judgment shall be in favor of the claimant, the sum thereby found due to the claimant shall be paid out of any general appropriation made by law for the payment of private claims, on presentation to the secretary of the treasury of a duly-certified copy of said judgment.

Proceedings in the court of claims originate by petition filed; and testimony used in the hearing and determination of claims is taken by commissioners who are appointed by the court for the purpose.

In some of the states statutes provide for courts to hear and determine claims against the state, the jurisdiction and procedure being fixed by statute.

COURT OF COMMISSIONERS OF SEWERS. See "Commissioners of Sewers."

COURT OF COMMON PLEAS.

——**In American Law.** A court of original and general jurisdiction for the trial of issues of fact and law according to the principles of the common law.

Courts of this name still exist in some of the states of the United States, and frequently have a criminal as well as civil jurisdiction. They are, in general, courts of record, being expressly made so by statute in Pennsylvania. 3 Serg. & R. (Pa.) 246. In Pennsylvania they exercise an equity jurisdiction, also, as well as that at common law. Courts of substantially similar powers to those indicated in the definition exist in all the states, under various names; and for peculiarities in their constitution reference is made to the articles on the states in regard to which the question may arise.

——**In English Law.** One of the three superior courts of common law at Westminster.

This court, which is sometimes called, also, *bancus communis, bancus,* and common bench, is a branch of the *aula regis,* and was at its institution ambulatory, following the household of the king. In the eleventh clause of *Magna Charta,* A. D. 1214, it is provided that it shall be held at some fixed place, which is Westminster. The establishment of this court at Westminster, and the consequent construction of the Inns of Court, and gathering together of the common-law lawyers, enabled the law itself to withstand the attacks of the canonists and civilians. It derived its name from the fact that the causes of common people were heard there. It had exclusive jurisdiction of real actions as long as those actions were in use, and had also an extensive, and, for a long time, exclusive, jurisdiction of all actions between subjects. This latter jurisdiction, however, was gradually encroached upon by the king's bench and exchequer, with which it now has a concurrent jurisdiction in many matters. Formerly none but serjeants at law were admitted to practice before this court *in banc* (6 Bing. [N. C.] 235), but by St. 6 & 7 Vict. c. 18, § 61, and St. 9 & 10 Vict. c. 54, all barristers at law have the right of "practice, pleading and audience."

It consists of one chief and four puisne or associate justices.

It has a civil, common-law jurisdiction, concurrent with the king's bench and exchequer, of personal actions and actions of ejectment, and a peculiar or exclusive jurisdiction of real actions, actions under the railway and canal traffic act (17 & 18 Vict. c. 31), the registration of judgments, annuities, etc. (1 & 2 Vict. c. 110; 2 & 3 Vict. c. 11; 3 & 4 Vict. c. 82; 18 Vict. c. 15); respecting fees for conveyances under 3 & 4 Wm. IV. c. 74; the examination of married women concerning their conveyances (11 & 12 Vict. c. 70; 17 & 18 Vict. c. 75; 19 & 20 Vict. c. 108, § 73); and of appeals from the revising barristers' court (6 & 7 Vict. c. 18). Wharton.

Appeals formerly lay from this court to the king's bench; but, by the statutes of 11 Geo. IV. and 1 Wm. IV. c. 70, appeals for errors in law are now taken to the judges of the king's bench and barons of exchequer in the exchequer chambers, from whose judgment an appeal lies only to the house of lords. 3 Sharswood, Bl. Comm. 40.

COURT OF CONVOCATION. In English ecclesiastical law. A convocation or ecclesiastical synod, which is in the nature of an ecclesiastical parliament.

There is one for each province. They are composed, respectively, of the archbishop, all the bishops, deans, and archdeacons of their province, with one proctor, or representative, from each chapter, and, in the province of Canterbury, two proctors for the beneficed parochial clergy in each diocese, while in the province of York there are two proctors for each archdeaconry. In York the convocation consists of only one house; but in Canterbury there are two houses, of which the archbishop and bishops form the upper house, and the lower consists of the remaining members of the convocation. In this house a prolocutor, performing the duty of president, is elected. These assemblies meet at the time appointed in the queen's writ. The convocation has long been summoned *pro forma* only, but is still, in fact, summoned before the meeting of every new parliament, and adjourns immediately afterwards, without proceeding to the dispatch of any business.

The purpose of the convocation is stated to be the enactment of canon law, subject to the license and authority of the sovereign, and consulting on ecclesiastical matters.

In their judicial capacity, their jurisdiction extends to matters of heresy, schisms, and other mere spiritual or ecclesiastical causes; an appeal lying from their judicial proceedings to the queen in council, by St. 2 & 3 Wm. IV. c. 92. Cowell; Terms de la Ley; Bac. Abr. "Ecclesiastical Courts" (A 1); 1 Sharswood, Bl. Comm. 279.

COURT OF EQUITY. A court which administers justice according to the principles of equity.

As to the constitution and jurisdiction of such courts, see "Court of Chancery."

COURT OF EXCHEQUER.

——**In English Law.** A superior court of record, administering justice in questions of law and revenue.

It is the lowest in rank of the three superior common-law courts of record, and had jurisdiction originally only of cases of injury to the revenue by withholding or nonpayment. The privilege of suing and being sued in this court in personal actions was extended to the king's accountants, and then, by a fiction that the plaintiff was a debtor of the king, to all personal actions. It had formerly an equity jurisdiction, and there was then an equity court; but, by St. 5 Vict. c. 5, this jurisdiction was transferred to the court of chancery.

It consists of one chief and four puisne judges or barons.

As a court of revenue, its proceedings are regulated by 22 & 23 Vict. c. 1, § 9.

As a court of common law, it administers redress between subject and subject in all actions whatever, except real actions.

The appellate jurisdiction from this court is to the judges of the king's bench and common pleas sitting as the court of exchequer chamber, and from this latter court to the house of lords. 3 Steph. Comm. 400-402; 3 Sharswood, Bl. Comm. 44-46.

——**In Scotch Law.** A court which formerly had jurisdiction of matters of revenue, and a limited jurisdiction over cases between the crown and its vassals, where no questions of title were involved.

This court was established by St. 6 Anne, c. 26, and its processes resembled those in the English court of exchequer. It is now merged in the court of sessions; but the name is still applied to this branch of the latter court, which is held by two of the judges acting in rotation. Paterson, Comp. 1055, note. The proceedings are regulated by St. 19 & 20 Vict. c. 56.

COURT OF EXCHEQUER CHAMBER. In English law. A court for the correction and prevention of errors of law in the three superior common-law courts of the kingdom.

A court of exchequer chamber was first erected by St. 31 Edw. III. c. 12, to determine causes upon writs of error from the common-law side of the exchequer court. It consisted of the lord chancellor, lord treasurer, and the justices of the king's bench and common pleas. A second court of exchequer chamber was instituted by St. 27 Eliz. c. 8, consisting of the justices of the common pleas and the exchequer, which had jurisdiction in error of cases commenced in the king's bench. By the statutes of 11 Geo. IV. and 1 Wm. IV. c. 70, these courts were abolished, and the present court of exchequer chamber substituted in their place.

As a court of debate, it is composed of the judges of the three superior courts of law, to whom is sometimes added the lord chancellor. To this court, questions of unusual difficulty or moment are referred before judgment from either of the three courts.

As a court of appeals, it consists of the judges of two of the three superior courts of law (common bench, king's bench, and exchequer) sitting to decide questions appealed from the others. 3 Sharswood, Bl. Comm. 55. From the decisions of this court a writ of error lies to the house of lords.

COURT OF FACULTIES. In ecclesiastical law. A tribunal, in England, belonging to the archbishop.

It does not hold pleas in any suits, but creates rights to pews, monuments, and other mortuary matters. It has also various other powers under 25 Hen. VIII. c. 21, in granting licenses, faculties, dispensations, etc., of different descriptions; as, a license to marry, a faculty to erect an organ in a parish church, to level a church yard, to remove bodies previously buried; and it may also grant dispensations to eat flesh on days prohibited, or to ordain a deacon under age, and the like. The archbishop's office in this tribunal is called *magister ad faculates.* Coke, 4th Inst. 337; 2 Chit. Gen. Prac. 507.

COURT OF GENERAL QUARTER SESsions of the peace.

——**In American Law.** A court of criminal jurisdiction.

——**In English Law.** A court of criminal jurisdiction, in England, held in each county once in every quarter of a year. It is held before two or more justices of the peace, one of whom must be a justice of the quorum.

The stated times of holding sessions are fixed by St. 11 Geo. IV. and 1 Wm. IV. c. 70, § 35. When held at other times than quarterly, the sessions are called "general sessions of the peace."

As to the jurisdiction of the various sessions, see 5 & 6 Vict. c. 38; 7 & 8 Vict. c. 71; 9 & 10 Vict. c. 25; 4 Sharswood, Bl. Comm. 271.

COURT OF HUSTINGS.

——**In English Law.** The county court in the city of London. It is held nominally before the lord mayor, recorder, and aldermen, but the recorder is practically the sole judge. It has an appellate jurisdiction of causes in the sheriff's court of London. A writ of error lies from the decisions of this court to certain commissioners, usually five of the judges of the superior courts of law, from whose judgment a writ of error lies to the house of lords. No merely personal actions can be brought in this court. See 3 Bl. Comm. 80, note; 3 Steph. Comm. 449, note; Maddox, Hist. Exch. c. 20; Coke, 2d Inst. 327; Calth. 131.

——**In American Law.** A local court in some parts of the state of Virginia. 6 Grat. (Va.) 696.

COURT OF INQUIRY.

——**In English Law.** A court sometimes appointed by the crown to ascertain the propriety of resorting to ulterior proceedings against a party charged before a court-martial. See 2 Steph. Comm. 600, note (z); 1 Coleridge, Bl. Comm. 418, note; 2 Brod. & B. 130.

——**In American Law.** A court constituted by authority of the articles of war, invested with the power to examine into the nature of any transaction, accusation, or imputation against any officer or soldier. The said court shall consist of one or more officers, not exceeding three, and a judge advocate, or other suitable person, as a recorder, to reduce the proceedings and evidence to writing; all of whom shall be sworn to the performance of their duty. Rev. St. U. S. §§ 1342, 1624.

COURT OF JUSTICE SEAT. In English law. The principal of the forest courts.

It was held before the chief justice in eyre, or his deputy, to hear and determine all trespasses within the forest, and all claims of franchises, liberties, privileges, and all pleas and causes whatsoever, therein arising. It might also try presentments in the inferior courts of the forests, and give judgment upon conviction of the sweinmote. After presentment made or indictment found, the chief justice might issue his warrant to the officers of the forest to apprehend the offenders. It might be held every third year, and forty days' notice was to be given of its sitting.

COURT OF JUSTICIARY. In Scotch law. A court of general criminal and limited civil jurisdiction.

It consists of the lord justice general, the lord justice clerk, and five other members of the court of sessions. The kingdom is divided into three circuits, in each of which two sessions, of not less than three days each, are to be held annually. Any two of the justices, or the lord justice general alone, or, in Glasgow, a simple justice, may hold a term, except in Edinburgh, where three justices constitute a quorum, and four generally sit in important cases.

Its criminal jurisdiction extends to all crimes committed in any part of the kingdom; and it has the power of reviewing the sentences of all inferior criminal courts, unless excluded by statute. Alison, Prac. 25.

Its civil jurisdiction on circuits is appellate and final in cases involving not more than twelve pounds sterling. See Paterson, Comp. § 940, note, et seq.; Bell, Dict.; Alison, Prac. 25; 20 Geo. II. c. 43; 23 Geo. III. c. 45; 30 Geo. III. c. 17; 1 Wm. IV. c. 69, § 19; 11 & 12 Vict. c. 79, § 8.

COURT OF KING'S BENCH. In English law. The supreme court of common law in the kingdom.

It is one of the successors of the *aula regis*, and received its name, it is said, because the king formerly sat in it in person, the style of the court being *coram rege ipso*, before the king himself. During the reign of a queen it is called the "queen's bench," and during Cromwell's protectorate it was called the "upper bench." Its jurisdiction was originally confined to the correction of crimes and misdemeanors which amounted to a breach of the peace, including those trespasses which were committed with force (*vi et armis*), and in the commission of which there was, therefore, a breach of the peace. By aid of a fiction of the law, the number of actions which might be alleged to be so committed was gradually increased until the jurisdiction extended to all actions of the case, of debt upon statutes or where fraud was alleged, and, finally, included all personal actions whatever, and the action of ejectment. See "Assumpsit;" "Arrest;" "Attachment." It is, from its constitution, ambulatory, and liable to follow the king's person, all process in this court being returnable *"ubicunque fuerimus in Anglia,"* wherever in England we, the sovereign, may be, but has for some centuries been held at Westminster.

It consists of a lord chief justice and four puisne or associate justices, who are, by virtue of their office, conservators of the peace and supreme coroners of the land.

It has general criminal jurisdiction, and also a considerable civil jurisdiction.

COURT OF MAGISTRATES AND FREEholders. In American law. The name of a court existing in South Carolina, before the abolition of slavery, for the trial of slaves and free persons of color for criminal offenses.

COURT OF NISI PRIUS. In American law. A court of original civil jurisdiction in the city and county of Philadelphia, held by one of the judges of the supreme court of the state. See, also, "Courts of Assize and Nisi Prius;" "Nisi Prius."

COURT OF ORDINARY. In American law. A court which has jurisdiction of the probate of wills, and the regulation of the management of decedents' estates. Such courts exist in Georgia, New Jersey, South Carolina, and Texas. See 2 Kent, Comm. 409; "Ordinary."

COURT OF ORPHANS. In English law. The court of the lord mayor and aldermen of London, which has the care of those orphans whose parent died in London, and was free of the city.

By the custom of London, this court is entitled to the possession of the person, lands, and chattels of every infant whose parent was free of the city at the time of his death, and who died in the city. The executor or administrator of such deceased parent is obliged to exhibit inventories of the estate of the deceased, and give security to the chamberlain for the orphan's part or share. 2 Steph. Comm. 343.

COURT OF OYER AND TERMINER. In American law. The name of courts of criminal jurisdiction in several of the states of the American Union, as in Georgia, New Jersey, and New York.

COURT OF PASSAGE. An inferior court, possessing a very ancient jurisdiction over causes of action arising within the borough of Liverpool. It appears to have been also called the "borough court of Liverpool." It has the same jurisdiction in admiralty matters as the Lancashire county court. Rosc. Adm. 75.

COURT OF PECULIARS. In English law. A branch of the court of arches, to which it is annexed.

It has jurisdiction of all ecclesiastical causes arising in the peculiars of Canterbury or other dioceses which are exempt from the ordinary's jurisdiction, and subject to that of the metropolitan only. The court of arches has an appellate jurisdiction of causes tried in this court. 3 Bl. Comm. 65; 3 Steph. Comm. 431, 432. See "Peculiar."

COURT OF PIEPOUDRE (Fr. *pied*, foot, and *poudre*, dust, or *puldreaux*, old Fr. pedlar). In English law. A court of special jurisdiction incident to every fair or market.

The word *piepoudre*, spelled also *piedpoudre* and *pypowder*, has been considered as signifying dusty feet, pointing to the general condition of the feet of the suitors therein (Cowell; Blount); or as indicating the rapidity with which justice is administered,—as rapidly as dust can fall from the foot (Coke, 4th Inst. 472); or pedlar's feet as being the court of such chapmen or petty traders as resorted to fairs. It was not confined to fairs or markets, but might exist, by custom, in cities, boroughs, or vills for the collection of debts and the like. Cro. Jac. 313; Cro. Car. 46; 2 Salk. 604. It was held before the steward of him who was entitled to the tolls from the market. It has fallen into disuse.

The civil jurisdiction extended to all matters of contract arising within the precinct of the fair or market during the continuance of the particular fair or market at which the court was held, the plaintiff being obliged to make oath as to the time and place.

The criminal jurisdiction embraced all offenses committed at the particular fair or market at which the court was held. An appeal lay to the courts at Westminster. See Barr. Obs. St. 337; 3 Bl. Comm. 32; Skene de Verb. Sign. "Pede Pulverosus;" Bracton, 334.

COURT OF PLEAS. A court of the county palatine of Durham, having a local common-law jurisdiction. It was abolished by the judicature act, which transferred its jurisdiction to the high court. Judicature Act 1873, § 16; 3 Bl. Comm. 79.

COURT OF POLICIES OF INSURANCE. A court of special jurisdiction which took cognizance of cases involving claims made by those insured upon policies in the city of London.

COURT OF PROBATE.

——**In American Law.** A court which has jurisdiction of the probate of wills, and the regulation of the management and settlement of decedents' estates, as well as a more or less extensive control of the estates of minors and other persons who are under the especial protection of the law.

——**In English Law.** A court in England having exclusive jurisdiction of testamentary causes or proceedings relating to the validity of wills and the succession to the property of persons deceased intestate. See St. 20 & 21 Vict. c. 77; St. 21 & 22 Vict. c. 95.

COURT OF QUARTER SESSIONS OF the peace. In American law. A court of criminal jurisdiction in the state of Pennsylvania. There is one such court in each county of the state. Its sessions are, in general, held at the same time and by the same judges as the court of oyer and terminer and general jail delivery. See Purd. Dig. Pa. Laws (Stroud. & B. Ed.) 692.

COURT OF QUEEN'S BENCH. See "Court of King's Bench."

COURT OF RECORD. A judicial, organized tribunal having attributes and exercising functions independently of the person of the magistrate designated generally to hold it, and proceeding according to the course of the common law.

A court where the acts and proceedings are enrolled in parchment for a perpetual memorial and testimony. 3 Bl. Comm. 24.

A court which has jurisdiction to fine and imprison, or one having jurisdiction of civil causes above forty shillings, and proceeding according to the course of the common law. 37 Me. 29.

All courts are either "of record," or "not of record." The possession of the right to fine and imprison for contempt was formerly considered as furnishing decisive evidence that a court was a court of record (Co. Litt. 117b, 260a; 1 Salk. 144; 12 Mod. 388; 2 Wm. Saund. 101a; Viner, Abr. "Courts"), and it is said that the erection of a new tribunal with this power renders it by that very fact a court of record (1 Salk. 200; 12 Mod. 388; 1 Wooddeson, Lect. 98; 3 Bl. Comm. 24, 25); but every court of record does not possess this power (1 Sid. 145; 3 Sharswood, Bl. Comm. 25, note). The mere fact that a permanent record is kept does not, in modern law, stamp the character of the court, since many courts, as probate courts, and others of limited or special jurisdiction, are obliged to keep records, and yet are held to be courts not of record. See 11 Mass. 510; 22 Pick. (Mass.) 430; 1 Cow. (N. Y.) 212; 3 Wend. (N. Y.) 268; 10 Pa. St. 158; 5 Ohio, 545; 7 Ala. 351; 25 Ala. 540. The definition first given above is taken from the opinion of Shaw, C. J., in 8 Metc. (Mass.) 171, with an additional element not required in that case for purposes of distinction, and is believed to contain all the distinctive qualities which can be said to belong to all courts technically of record at modern law.

COURT OF REGARD. In English law. One of the forest courts, in England, held every third year, for the lawing or expeditation of dogs, to prevent them from running after deer. 3 Steph. Comm. 440; 3 Bl. Comm. 71, 72.

COURT OF REVIEW. A court instituted for the purpose of correcting errors committed by trial courts. 195 Ill. App. 523.

COURT OF SESSION.

——**In Scotch Law.** The supreme court of civil jurisdiction in Scotland.

The full title of the court is "council and session." It was established in 1425. In 1469 its jurisdiction was transferred to the king's council, which in 1503 was ordered to sit in Edinburgh. In 1532 the jurisdiction of both courts and the joint title were transferred to the present court. The regular number of judges was fifteen; but an additional number of justices might be appointed by the crown to an unlimited extent. This privilege was renounced by 10 Geo. I. c. 19.

It consists of fifteen judges, and is divided into an inner and an outer house.

The inner house is composed of two branches or chambers, of co-ordinate jurisdiction, each consisting of four judges, and called, respectively, the "first division" and the "second division." The first division is presided over by the lord president or lord justice general, the second by the lord justice clerk. The outer house is composed of five separate courts, each presided over by a single judge, called a "lord ordinary."

All causes commence before a lord ordinary, in general, and the party may select the one before whom he will bring his action, subject to a removal by the lord president in case of too great an accumulation before any one or more lords ordinary. See Bell, Dict.; Paterson, Comp. § 1055, note, et seq.

——**In American Law.** A court of criminal jurisdiction existing in some of the states of the United States. Courts of this name exist in California, New York, and, perhaps, other states.

COURT OF STAR CHAMBER. In English law. A court which was formerly held by divers lords, spiritual and temporal, who were members of the privy council, together with two judges of the courts of common law.

It was of very ancient origin, was new modelled by 3 Hen. VII. c. 1, and 21 Hen. VIII. c. 20, and was finally abolished, after having become very odious to the people, by 16 Car. I. c. 10. The name "star chamber" is of uncertain origin. It has been thought to be from the Saxon "steoran," to govern, alluding to the jurisdiction of the court over the crime of cosenage, and has been thought to have been given because the hall in which the court was held was full of windows (Lambard, Eiren. 148); or because the roof was originally studded with gilded stars (Coke, 4th Inst. 66); or, according to Blackstone, because the Jewish covenants (called *starrs* or *stars*, and which, by a statute of Richard I., were to be enrolled in three places, one of which was near the exchequer) were originally kept there. 4 Bl. Comm. 266, note. The derivation of Blackstone receives confirmation from the fact that this location (near the exchequer) is assigned to the star chamber the first time it is mentioned. The word "star" acquired at some time the recognized signification of inventory or schedule. St. Acad. Cont. 32; 4 Sharswood, Bl. Comm. 266, note.

The legal jurisdiction of this court extended originally to riots, perjuries, misbehavior of sheriffs, and other notorious misdemeanors. It acted without the assistance of a jury, and its proceedings were in secret, by reason of which it fell into popular disrepute. See Hudson, Court of Star Chamber (printed at the beginning of the second volume of the *Collectanea Juridica*); 4 Sharswood, Bl. Comm. 266, and notes.

COURT OF SWEINMOTE, SWAINMOTE, or **swaingemote** (Saxon *swang*, an attendant, a freeholder, and *mote* or *gemote*, a meeting). In English law. One of the forest courts, held before the verderors, as judges, by the steward, thrice in every year, —the sweins or freeholders within the forest composing the jury.

This court had jurisdiction to inquire into grievances and oppressions committed by the officers of the forest, and also to receive and try presentments certified from the court of attachments, certifying the cause, in turn, under the seals of the jury, in case of conviction, to the court of justice seat for the rendition of judgment. Cowell; 3 Bl. Comm. 71, 72; 3 Steph. Comm. 439.

COURT OF THE CLERK OF THE MARKET. In English law. A tribunal incident to every fair and market in the kingdom, to punish misdemeanors therein.

This is the most inferior court of criminal jurisdiction in the kingdom. The object of its jurisdiction is principally the recognizance of weights and measures, to try whether they are according to the true standard thereof, which standard was anciently committed to the custody of the bishop, who appointed some clerk under him to inspect the abuse of them more narrowly; and hence this officer, though usually a layman, is called the "clerk" of the market.

The jurisdiction over weights and measures formerly exercised by the clerk of the market has been taken from him by St. 5 & 6 Wm. IV. c. 63.

COURT OF THE CORONER. In English law. A court of record, to inquire, when any one dies in prison, or comes to a violent or sudden death, by what manner he came to his end. 4 Steph. Comm. 341; 4 Sharswood, Bl. Comm. 274. See "Coroner."

COURT OF THE DUCHY OF LANCASTER. In English law. A court of special jurisdiction, which has jurisdiction of all matters of equity relating to lands holden of the king in right of the duchy of Lancaster.

It is held by the chancellor or his deputy, is a court of equity jurisdiction, and not of record. It is to be distinguished from the court of the county palatine of Lancaster. 3 Bl. Comm. 78.

COURT OF THE LORD HIGH STEWARD. In English law. A court instituted for the trial of peers indicted for treason, felony, or misprision of either.

This court can be held only during a recess of parliament, since the trial of a peer for either of the above offenses can take place, during a session of that body, only before the high court of parliament. It consists of a lord high steward (appointed, in modern times, *pro hac vice* merely), and as many of the temporal lords as may desire to take the proper oath and act; and all the peers qualified to sit and vote in parliament are to be summoned at least twenty days before the trial. St. 7 Wm. III. c. 3.

COURT OF THE LORD HIGH STEWARD of the universities. In English law. A court constituted for the trial of scholars or privileged persons connected with the university at Oxford or Cambridge who are indicted for treason, felony, or mayhem.

COURT OF THE MARSHALSEA. In English law. A court which had jurisdiction of causes to which the domestic servants were parties.

It was held by the steward of the king's household, as judge, and the marshal was the ministerial officer, and held pleas of trespasses committed within twelve miles of the sovereign's residence (called the "verge of the court"), where one of the parties was a servant of the king's household, and of all debts, contracts, and covenants where both parties were servants as above. Where one of the parties only was of the king's household, a jury of the country was summoned; in the other case, the inquest was composed of men of the household only. This court was merged, in the time of Charles I., in the palace court, and abolished by 12 & 13 Vict. c. 101, § 13. See "Palace Court."

COURT OF THE STEWARD AND MARSHAL. See "Court of the Marshalsea."

COURT OF THE STEWARD OF THE king's household. In English law. A court which had jurisdiction of all cases of treason, misprision of treason, murder, manslaughter, bloodshed, and other malicious strikings whereby blood is shed, occurring in or within the limits of any of the palaces or houses of the king, or any other house where the royal person is abiding.

It was created by St. 33 Hen. VIII. c. 12, but long since fell into disuse. 4 Sharswood, Bl. Comm. 276, 277, and notes.

COURT OF WARDS AND LIVERIES. In English law. A court of record in England, which had the supervision and regulation of inquiries concerning the profits which arose to the crown from the fruits of tenure, and to grant to heirs the delivery of their lands from the possession of their guardians.

The court of the king's wards was instituted by St. 32 Hen. VIII. c. 46, to take the place of the ancient *inquisitio post mortem*, and the jurisdiction of the restoration of lands to heirs on their becoming of age (livery) was added by St. 33 Hen. VIII. c. 22, when it became the court of wards and liveries. It was abolished by St. 12 Car. II. c. 24.

The jurisdiction extended to the superintendence of lunatics and idiots in the king's custody, granting licenses to the king's widows to marry, and imposing fines for marrying without license. 4 Reeve, Hist. Eng. Law, 259; Crabb, Hist. Eng. Law, 468; 1 Steph. Comm. 183, 192; 4

Steph. Comm. 40; 2 Sharswood, Bl. Comm. 68, 77; 3 Sharswood, Bl. Comm. 258.

COURTESY. See "Curtesy."

COURTS CHRISTIAN. Ecclesiastical courts (*q. v.*)

COURTS OF ASSIZE AND NISI PRIUS. In English law. Courts composed of two or more commissioners, called "judges of assize" (or of assize and *nisi prius*), who are twice in every year sent by the queen's (or king's) commission on circuits all round the kingdom, to try, by a jury of the respective counties, the truth of such matters of fact as are then under dispute in the courts of Westminster Hall; there being, however, as to London and Middlesex, this exception: That, instead of their being comprised within any circuit, courts of *nisi prius* are held there for the same purpose, in and after every term, before the chief or other judge of the superior court, at what are called the London and Westminster sittings.

These judges of assize came into use in the room of the ancient justices in eyre (*justiciarii in itinere*), who were regularly established, if not first appointed, by the parliament of Northampton, A. D. 1176 (22 Hen. II.), with a delegated power from the king's great court, or *aula regis*, being looked upon as members thereof; though the present justices of assize and *nisi prius* are more immediately derived from St. Westminster II. (13 Edw. I. c. 30), and consist principally of the judges of the superior courts of common law, being assigned by that statute out of the king's sworn justices, associating to themselves one or two discreet knights of each county. By St. 27 Edw. I. c. 4 (explained by 12 Edw. II. c. 3), assizes and inquests are allowed to be taken before any one justice of the court in which the plea is brought, associating with him one knight or other approved man of the county. By St. 14 Edw. III. c. 16, inquests of *nisi prius* may be taken before any justice of either bench (though the plea be not depending in his own court), or before the chief baron of the exchequer, if he be a man of the law, or, otherwise, before the justices of assize, so that one of such justices be a judge of the king's bench or common pleas, or the king's sergeant sworn. And, finally, by 2 & 3 Vict. c. 22, all justices of assize may, on their respective circuits, try causes pending in the court of exchequer, without issuing (as it had till then been considered necessary to do) a separate commission from the exchequer for that purpose. 3 Steph. Comm. 421-423; 3 Bl. Comm. 57, 58.

COURTS OF CONSCIENCE. See "Courts of Requests."

COURTS OF OYER AND TERMINER and general gaol delivery.

——**In English Law.** Tribunals for the examination and trial of criminals.

They are held before commissioners selected by the queen, among whom are usually two justices of the superior courts at Westminster, twice in every year in all the counties of England except the four northern, where they are held once only, and Middlesex and parts of other counties, over which the central criminal court has jurisdiction.

Under the commission of oyer and terminer, the justices try indictments previously found at the same assizes for treason, felony, or misdemeanors. Under the commission of general gaol delivery, they may try and deliver every prisoner who is in gaol when the judges arrive at the circuit town, whenever or before whomsoever indicted, or for whatsoever crime committed. These commissions are joined with those of assize and *nisi prius* and the commission of the peace. See "Courts of Assize and Nisi Prius."

——**In American Law.** Courts of criminal jurisdiction in the state of Pennsylvania.

They are held at the same time with the court of quarter sessions, as a general rule, and by the same judges. See Purd. Dig. Pa. Laws (Stroud & B. Ed.) pp. 694, 1377.

COURTS OF PRINCIPALITY OF Wales. A species of private courts, of a limited though extensive jurisdiction, which, upon the thorough reduction of that principality, and the settling of its policy in the reign of Henry VIII., were erected all over the country. These courts, however, have been abolished by 1 Wm. IV. c. 70; the principality being now divided into two circuits, which the judges visit in the same manner as they do the circuits in England, for the purpose of disposing of those causes which are ready for trial. Brown.

COURTS OF REQUESTS, or **COURTS of conscience.** In English law. Courts of special jurisdiction, constituted by act of parliament in the city of London and other towns, for the recovery of small debts.

They were courts not of record, and proceeded in a summary way to examine upon oath the parties and other witnesses, without the aid of a jury, and made such order as is consonant to equity and good conscience.

They had jurisdiction of causes of debt generally to the amount of forty shillings, but in many instances to the amount of five pounds sterling.

The courts of requests in London consisted of two aldermen and four common councilmen, and was formerly a court of considerable importance, but was abolished, as well as all other courts of requests, by the small debts act (9 & 10 Vict. c. 95), and the order in council of May 9, 1847, and their jurisdiction transferred to the county courts.

The court of requests before the king in person was virtually abolished by 16 Car. I. c. 10, 3 Steph. Comm. 449, and note (j);

Bac. Abr. "Courts in London." See "County Court."

COURTS OF SURVEY. Courts for the hearing of appeals by owners or masters of ships, from orders for the detention of unsafe ships, made by the English board of trade under the merchant shipping act of 1876 (section 6), consisting of a judge summoned by the registrar from a list of wreck commissioners (*q. v.*), stipendiary magistrates, etc., which is provided for the purpose, and of two assessors; one appointed by the board of trade, and the other summonsed by the registrar out of a list of persons provided for the purpose (Id. § 7). Rules of Court of Survey 1876.

COURTS OF THE CINQUE PORTS. In English law. Courts of limited local jurisdiction, formerly held before the mayor and jurats (aldermen) of the Cinque Ports.

A writ of error lay to the lord warden in his court of Shepway, and from this court to the queen's bench. By 18 & 19 Vict. c. 48, and 20 & 21 Vict. c. 1, the jurisdiction and authority of the lord warden of the Cinque Ports and constable of Dover Castle, in or in relation to the administration of justice in actions, suits, or other civil proceedings, at law or in equity, are abolished. 3 Sharswood. Bl. Comm. 79; 3 Steph. Comm. 447, 448. See "Cinque Ports."

COURTS OF THE COUNTIES PALATINE. In English law. A species of private court which formerly appertained to the counties palatine of Lancaster and Durham.

They were local courts, which had exclusive jurisdiction in law and equity of all cases arising within the limits of the respective counties. The judges who held these courts sat by special commission from the owners of the several franchises, and under their seal, and all process was taken in the name of the owner of the franchise, though subsequently to 27 Hen. VIII. c. 24, it ran in the king's name. See "County Palatine."

COURTS OF THE TWO UNIVERSITIES. In English law. See "Chancellors' Courts in the Two Universities."

COURTS OF WESTMINSTER HALL. The superior courts, both of law and equity, were for centuries fixed at Westminster, an ancient palace of the monarchs of England. Formerly, all the superior courts were held before the king's capital justiciary of England, in the *aula regis*, or such of his palaces wherein his royal person resided, and removed with his household from one end of the kingdom to another. This was found to occasion great inconvenience to the suitors, to remedy which it was made an article of the great charter of liberties, both of King John and King Henry III., that "common pleas should no longer follow the king's court, but be held in some certain place," in consequence of which they have ever since been held (a few necessary removals in times of the plague excepted) in the palace of Westminster only. The courts of equity also sit at Westminster, nominally, during term time, although, actually only during the first day of term, for they generally sit in courts provided for the purpose in, or in the neighborhood of, Lincoln's Inn. Brown.

COUSIN. The son or daughter of the brother or sister of one's father or mother.

The issue, respectively, of two brothers or two sisters, or of a brother and a sister.

Those whc descend from the brother or sister of the father of the person spoken of are called "paternal cousins." "Maternal cousins" are those who are descended from the brothers or sisters of the mother. See 2 Brown, Ch. 125; 1 Sim. & S. 301; 3 Russ. 140; 9 Sim. 386, 457.

COUSINAGE. See "Cosinage."

COUSTUM (Fr.) Custom; duty; toll. 1 Sharswood, Bl. Comm. 314.

COUSTUMIER (Fr.) A collection of customs and usages in the old Norman law.

COUTHUTLAUGH. He that willingly receives an outlaw, and cherishes or conceals him. In ancient times he was subject to the same punishment as the outlaw. Blount.

COVENANT (Lat. *convenire*, to come together; *conventio*, a coming together). It is equivalent to the *factum conventum* of the civil law.

——**In Contracts.** An agreement between two or more persons, entered into by deed, whereby one of the parties promises the performance or nonperformance of certain acts, or that a given state of things does or shall, or does not or shall not, exist. It differs from an express *assumpsit* in that it must be by deed.

Covenants are classified on several lines of division, the principal ones being:

Affirmative or negative.

(1) Affirmative covenants are those in which the covenantor declares that something has been already done, or shall be done in the future. Such covenants do not operate to deprive covenantees of rights enjoyed independently of the covenants. Dyer, 19b; 1 Leon. 251.

(2) Negative covenants are those in which the party obligates himself not to do or perform some act. Courts are unwilling to construe a negative covenant a condition precedent, inasmuch as it cannot be said to be performed till a breach becomes impossible. 2 Wm. Saund. 156; 1 Mod. 64; 2 Keb. 674; 1 Sid. 87.

Inherent or collateral.

(3) Inherent covenants are those which relate directly to the land itself, or matter granted. Shep. Touch. 161. Distinguished from collateral covenants.

If real, they run with the land. Platt, Cov. 66.

(4) Collateral covenants are those which are entered into in connection with the grant of something, but which do not relate immediately to the thing granted; as, to pay a sum of money in gross, that the lessor shall distrain for rent on some other land than that which is demised, to build a house on the land of some third person, or the like. Platt, Cov. 69; Shep. Touch. 161; 4 Burrows, 2439; 3 Term R. 393; 2 J. B. Moore, 164; 5 Barn. & Ald. 7; 2 Wils. 27; 1 Ves. Jr. 56.

Dependent, concurrent, and independent.

(5) Dependent covenants are those in which the obligation to perform one is made to depend upon the performance of the other. Covenants may be so connected that the right to insist upon the performance of one of them depends upon a prior performance on the part of the party seeking enforcement. Platt, Cov. 71; 2 Selw. N. P. 443; Steph. N. P. 1071; 1 C. B. (N. S.) 646; 6 Cow. (N. Y.) 296; 2 Johns. (N. Y.) 209; 2 Watts & S. (Pa.) 227; 8 Serg. & R. (Pa.) 268; 4 Conn. 3; 24 Conn. 624; 11 Vt. 549; 17 Me. 232; 3 Ark. 581; 1 Blackf. (Ind.) 175; 6 Ala. 60; 3 Ala. (N. S.) 330.

(6) Concurrent covenants are those which are to be performed at the same time. When one party is ready and offers to perform his part, and the other refuses or neglects to perform his, he who is ready and offers has fulfilled his engagement, and may maintain an action for the default of the other, though it is not certain that either is obliged to do the first act. Platt, Cov. 71; 2 Selw. N. P. 443; Doug. 698; 18 Eng. Law & Eq. 81; 4 Wash. C. C. (U. S.) 714; 16 Mo. 450.

(7) Independent covenants are those the necessity of whose performance is determined entirely by the requirements of the covenant itself, without regard to other covenants between the parties relative to the same subject-matter or transactions or series of transactions.

Covenants are generally construed to be independent (Platt, Cov. 71; 2 Johns. [N. Y.] 145; 10 Johns. [N. Y.] 204; 21 Pick. [Mass.] 438; 1 Ld. Raym. 666; 3 Bing. [N. S.] 355); unless the undertaking on one side is in terms a condition to the stipulation of the other, and then only consistently with the intention of the parties (3 Maule & S. 308; 10 East, 295, 530); or unless dependency results from the nature of the acts to be done, and the order in which they must necessarily precede and follow each other in the progress of performance (Willes, 496); or unless the nonperformance on one side goes to the entire substance of the contract, and to the whole consideration (1 Seld. [N. Y.] 247). If once independent, they remain so. 19 Barb. (N. Y.) 416.

Executed or executory.

(8) Executed covenants are those which relate to acts already performed. Shep. Touch. 161.

(9) Executory covenants are those whose performance is to be future. Shep. Touch. 161.

Express or implied.

(10) Express covenants are those which are created by the express words of the parties to the deed declaratory of their intention. Platt, Cov. 25. The formal word "covenant" is not indispensably requisite for the creation of an express covenant. 2 Mod. 268; 3 Keb. 848; 1 Leon. 324; 1 Bing. 433; 8 J. B. Moore, 546; 12 East, 182, note; 16 East, 352; 1 Bibb (Ky.) 379; 2 Bibb (Ky.) 614; 3 Johns. (N. Y.) 44; 5 Cow. (N. Y.) 170; 4 Conn. 508; 1 Har. (Del.) 233. The words "I oblige," "I agree" (1 Ves. Jr. 516; 2 Mod. 266), "I bind myself" (Hardr. 178; 3 Leon. 119), have been held to be words of covenant, as are the words of a bond (1 Chanc. Cas. 194). Any words showing the intent of the parties to do or not to do a certain thing raise an express covenant (13 N. H. 513); but words importing merely an order or direction that other persons should pay a sum of money are not a covenant (6 J. B. Moore, 202, note [a]).

(11) Implied covenants are those which arise by intendment and construction of law from the use of certain words in some kinds of contracts. Bac. Abr. "Covenant" (B); Rawle, Cov. 364; 1 C. B. 402. Thus, in a conveyance of lands in fee, the words "grant, bargain, and sell" imply certain covenants (see 4 Kent, Comm. 473), and the word "give" implies a covenant of warranty during the life of the feoffor (10 Cush. [Mass.] 134; 4 Gray [Mass.] 468; 2 Caines [N. Y.] 193; 9 N. H. 222; 7 Ohio, pt. 2, p. 63); and in a lease the use of the words "grant and demise" (Co. Litt. 384; 4 Wend. [N. Y.] 502; 8 Cow. [N. Y.] 36), "grant" (Freem. Ch. 367; Cro. Eliz. 214; 4 Taunt. 609; 1 Per. & D. 360), "demise" (4 Coke, 80; 10 Mod. 162; Hob. 12; 9 N. H. 222; 15 N. Y. 327), "demisement" (1 Show. 79; 1 Salk. 137), raises an implied covenant on the part of the lessor, as do "yielding and paying" (9 Vt. 151) on the part of the lessee. In regard to the covenants arising to each grantee by implication on sale of an estate with conditions, in parcels to several grantees, see 23 Barb. (N. Y.) 153.

Obligatory or declaratory.

(12) Obligatory covenants are those which are binding on the party himself. 1 Sid. 27; 1 Keb. 337.

(13) Declaratory covenants are those which serve to limit or direct uses. 1 Sid. 27; 1 Hob. 224.

Principal or auxiliary.

(14) Principal covenants are those which relate directly to the principal matter of the contract entered into between the parties. They are distinguished from auxiliary.

(15) Auxiliary covenants are those which do not relate directly to the principal matter of contract between the parties, but to

something connected with it. Those the scope of whose operation is in aid or support of the principal covenant. If the principal covenant is void, the auxiliary is discharged. Anstr. 256; Prec. Chanc. 475.

Transitive or intransitive.

(16) Transitive covenants are those personal covenants the duty of performing which passes over to the representatives of the covenantor.

(17) Intransitive covenants are those the duty of performing which is limited to the covenantee himself, and does not pass over to his representative.

(18) Disjunctive or alternative covenants are those which are for the performance of one or more of several things, at the election of the covenantor or covenantee, as the case may be. Platt, Cov. 21; 1 Duer (N. Y.) 209.

(19) Covenants in deeds are express covenants.

(20) Covenants in gross are such as do not run with the land.

(21) Covenants in law are implied covenants.

(22) Illegal covenants are those which are expressly or impliedly forbidden by law. Covenants are absolutely void when entered into in violation of the express provisions of statutes (5 Har. & J. [Md.] 193; 5 N. H. 96; 6 N. H. 225; 1 Bin. [Pa.] 118; 6 Bin. [Pa.] 321; 4 Serg. & R. [Pa.] 159; 4 Halst. [N. J.] 252), or if they are of an immoral nature (3 Burrows, 1568; 1 Esp. 13; 1 Bos. & P. 340; 3 T. B. Mon. [Ky.] 35), against public policy (4 Mass. 370; 5 Mass. 385; 7 Me. 113; 5 Halst. [N. J.] 87; 3 Day [Conn.] 145; 7 Watts [Pa.] 152; 5 Watts & S. [Pa.] 315; 6 Miss. 769; 2 McLean [U. S.] 464; 4 Wash. C. C. [U. S.] 297; 11 Wheat. [U. S.] 258), in general restraint of trade (21 Wend. [N. Y.] 166; 7 Cow. [N. Y.] 307; 6 Pick. [Mass.] 206; 19 Pick. [Mass.] 51), or fraudulent between the parties (4 Serg. & R. [Pa.] 483; 7 Watts & S. [Pa.] 111; 5 Mass. 16), or third persons (3 Day [Conn.] 450; 14 Serg. & R. [Pa.] 214; 3 Caines [N. Y.] 213; 2 Johns. [N. Y.] 286; 12 Johns. [N. Y.] 306; 15 Pick. [Mass.] 49).

Covenants are also classified generally in the same manner as simple contracts. See "Contract."

The difference between covenants of seizin, right to convey, and against encumbrances, and those of warranty, quiet enjoyment, and further assurance, is that the former are in the present tense, relating to something being or existing at the time the covenant is made, while the latter relate to something future, and are to guard against the consequence of some future act, or for the performance of some future act which the condition of the title to the estate may require. Newman v. Sevier, 134 Ill. App. 548.

It is frequently difficult to determine whether a certain provision annexed to a grant is a condition, covenant, restriction, limitation or trust imposed on the property, but if it is doubtful whether the clause is a condition or a covenant it will be construed to be a covenant. 267 Ill. 622; 232 Ill. 597.

——**In Practice.** A form of action which lies to recover damages for breach of a contract under seal. It is one of the *brevia formata* of the register, is sometimes a concurrent remedy with debt, though never with *assumpsit,* and is the only proper remedy where the damages are unliquidated in nature, and the contract is under seal. Fitzh. Nat. Brev. 340; Chit. Pl. 112, 113; Steph. N. P. 1058.

COVENANT AGAINST INCUMBRANCES. One which has for its object security against those rights to, or interests in, the land granted which may subsist in third persons to the diminution of the value of the estate, though consistently with the passing of the fee by the deed of conveyance. For what constitutes an incumbrance, see "Incumbrance."

COVENANT COLLATERAL. A covenant which is conversant about some collateral thing that doth nothing at all, or not so immediately concern the thing granted; as to pay a sum of money in gross, etc. Shep. Touch. 161.

COVENANT FOR FURTHER ASSURANCE. One by which the covenantor undertakes to do such reasonable acts in addition to those already performed as may be necessary for the completion of the transfer made, or intended to be made, at the requirement of the covenantee. It relates both to the title of the vendor and to the instrument of conveyance to the vendee, and operates as well to secure the performance of all acts for supplying any defect in the former, as to remove all objections to the sufficiency and security of the latter. Platt, Cov. 341.

COVENANT FOR QUIET ENJOYMENT. An assurance against the consequences of a defective title, and of any disturbances thereupon. Platt, Cov. 312. By it, when general in its terms, the covenantor stipulates at all events (11 East, 642; 1 Mod. 101) to indemnify the covenantee against all acts committed by virtue of a paramount title (Platt, Cov. 313; 1 Lev. 83; 8 Lev. 305; Hob. 34; 4 Coke, 80b; Cro. Car. 5; 3 Term R. 584; 6 Term R. 66; 3 Duer [N. Y.] 464; 2 Jones [N. C.] 203; Busb. [N. C.] 384; 3 N. J. 260), not including the acts of a mob (19 Miss. 87; 2 Strobh. [S. C.] 366), nor a mere trespass by the lessor (10 N. Y. 151). It most generally occurs in leases.

COVENANT IN DEED (called, also, "covenant in fact," French, *covenant en fait,* and "covenant expressed"). A covenant expressed in words, or inserted in a deed in specific terms. Termes de la Ley; Shep. Touch. 160. There is no set form of words necessary to constitute a covenant. The usual form is that the covenantor, "for himself, his heirs, executors, and administrators, covenants, promises, and agrees to and with (the covenantee), his heirs, executors, administrators, and assigns, that," etc. 1 Archb. N. P. 250; U. S. Dig. "Covenant." The formal word "covenant" itself is not absolutely essential for this purpose. Bouvier, voc. "Covenant," pl. 10, and cases there cited; Hilliard, Real Prop. 364.

COVENANT INHERENT. A covenant which is conversant about the land, and knit to the estate in the land; as that the thing demised shall be quietly enjoyed, shall be kept in reparation, shall not be aliened, etc. Shep. Touch. 161.

COVENANT NOT TO SUE. One entered into by a party who has a cause of action at the time of making it, by which he agrees not to sue the party liable to such action.

A perpetual covenant not to sue is one by which the covenantor agrees not to sue the covenantee at any time. Such a covenant operates as a release to the covenantee, and may be pleaded as such. Cro. Eliz. 623; 1 Term R. 446; 8 Term R. 486; 2 Salk. 375; 3 Salk. 298; 12 Mod. 415; 7 Mass. 153; 16 Mass. 24; 17 Mass. 623; 3 Ind. 473. And see 11 Serg. & R. (Pa.) 149.

A limited covenant not to sue, by which the covenantor agrees not to sue for a limited time, does not operate a release; and a breach must be taken advantage of by action. Carth. 63; 1 Show. 46; 2 Salk. 573; 6 Wend. (N. Y.) 471; 5 Cal. 501. See 29 Ala. (N. S.) 322, as to requisite consideration.

A covenant never to sue is regarded as an absolute release, but a covenant not to sue within a limited time cannot be pleaded in bar of an action brought before the time has expired. 13 Ill. 8.

COVENANT OF RIGHT TO CONVEY. An assurance by the covenantor that the grantor has sufficient capacity and title to convey the estate which he by his deed undertakes to convey.

COVENANT OF SEISIN. An assurance to the grantee that the grantor has the very estate, both in quantity and quality, which he professes to convey. Platt, Cov. 306. 134 Ill. App. 548. It has given place in English conveyancing to the covenant of right to convey, but is in use in several states of the United States. 2 Washb. Real Prop. 648.

COVENANT OF WARRANTY. An assurance by the grantor of an estate that the grantee shall enjoy the same without interruption by virtue of paramount title. 2 Jones (N. C.) 203; 3 Duer (N. Y.) 464.

It is not in use in English conveyances, but is in general use in the United States (2 Washb. Real Prop. 659), and in several states is the only covenant in general use (Rawle, Cov. 203, note; 4 Ga. 593; 8 Grat. [Va.] 353; 6 Ala. 60).

The covenant of warranty originated at common law from the feudal system from the fact that as that system imposed on the grantee the duties of tenure, it also bound the lord to a reciprocal obligation, either to protect his tenant in his fief, or to give him another, and this liability descended to the heir as long as he had lands of his ancestor to answer it. 58 Ill. 68.

A covenant of warranty is in effect the same as a covenant for quiet enjoyment, its true meaning being that the grantee, his heirs and assigns, shall not be deprived of possession by a paramount title. 25 Ill. 180; 134 Ill. App. 548.

COVENANT REAL. A covenant in a deed binding the heirs of the covenantor, and passing to assignees, or to the purchaser. 2 Bl. Comm. 304; 4 Kent, Comm. 471, 472. A covenant which so runs with the land that he that hath the one hath or is subject to the other. Shep. Touch. 161. It is thus distinguished from a personal covenant, which affects only the covenantor, and the assets in the hands of his representatives after his death. 4 Kent, Comm. 470. The covenants in a deed that the grantor is lawfully seised, and has good right to convey, and that the land is free from incumbrance, are personal covenants, not running with the land; the covenant for quiet enjoyment, and the covenant of warranty, are in the nature of real covenants. Id. 471. But see Id. 472, and notes; 1 Sumn. (U. S.) 263.

In the old books, a covenant real is also defined to be a covenant by which a man binds himself to pass a thing real, as lands or tenements. Termes de la Ley; 3 Bl. Comm. 156.

COVENANT RUNNING WITH LAND. A covenant which goes with the land (conveyed by the deed in which it is expressed), as being annexed to the estate, and which cannot be separated from the land, and transferred without it. 4 Kent, Comm. 472, note. A covenant is said to run with the land when not only the original parties to the deed of conveyance, or their representatives, but each successive owner of the land, will be entitled to its benefit, or be liable, as the case may be, to its obligation. 1 Steph. Comm. 455, and note (r); Burton, Real Prop. 157. Or, in other words, it is so called when either the liability to perform it, or the right to take advantage of it, passes to the assignee of the land. 1 Smith, Lead. Cas. 27, note; 5 Coke, 16a; 4 Kent, Comm. 470-473. See 17 Wend. (N. Y.) 136; U. S. Dig. "Covenant."

A covenant to pay rent, to produce title deeds, or for renewal, are covenants which run with the land. All covenants concerning title run with the land, with the exception of those that are broken, if at all, before the land passes. 4 Kent, Comm. 473.

Whether a covenant will run with the

land depends not so much on whether it is to be performed on the land itself, as whether it tends directly or necessarily to enhance its value, or render it more beneficial and convenient to those by whom it is owned or occupied. 174 Ill. 453.

COVENANT TO CONVEY. A covenant by which the covenantor undertakes to convey to the covenantee the estate described in the covenant, under certain circumstances.

This form of conditional alienation of lands is in frequent use in several of the United States. 14 Pa. St. 308; 19 Barb. (N. Y.) 639; 4 Md. 498; 11 Ill. 194; 19 Ohio, 347. Substantially the same effect is secured as by a conveyance and a mortgage back for the purchase money, with the important difference, however, that the title of course remains in the covenantor till he actually executes the conveyance.

The remedy for breach may be by action on the covenant (29 Pa. St. 264), but the better remedy is said to be in equity for specific performance (1 Grant Cas. [Pa.] 230).

It is satisfied only by a perfect conveyance of the kind bargained for (19 Barb. [N. Y.] 639); otherwise where an imperfect conveyance has been accepted (4 Md. 498).

COVENANT TO STAND SEISED TO uses. A covenant by means of which, under the statute of uses, a conveyance of an estate may be effected. Burton, Real Prop. §§ 136, 145.

Such a covenant cannot furnish the ground for an action of covenant broken, and in this respect resembles the ancient real covenants.

The consideration for such a covenant must be relationship either by blood or marriage. 2 Washb. Real Prop. 129, 130. See 2 Seld. (N. Y.) 342.

As a mode of conveyance it has fallen into disuse; though the doctrine is often resorted to by courts in order to give effect to the intention of the parties who have undertaken to convey lands by deeds which are insufficient for the purpose, under the rules required in other forms of conveyance. 2 Washb. Real Prop. 155, 156; 2 Sanders, Uses, 79, 83; 4 Mass. 136; 18 Pick. (Mass.) 397; 22 Pick. (Mass.) 376; 5 Me. 232; 11 Johns. (N. Y.) 351; 20 Johns. (N. Y.) 85; 5 Yerg. (Tenn.) 249.

COVENANTEE. One in whose favor a covenant is made.

COVENANTOR. One who becomes bound to perform a covenant.

COVENANTS APPURTENANT. Those which run with the land.

COVENANTS FOR TITLE. Those in aid of the title to property, usually land, conveyed or sold. They are "covenant of seisin," "covenant against incumbrances," "covenant for further assurance," "covenant for quiet enjoyment," "covenant of warranty," and "covenant of right to convey" (*q. v.*)

COVENANTS PERFORMED. In pleading. A plea to an action of covenant, allowed in the state of Pennsylvania, whereby the defendant, upon informal notice to the plaintiff, may give anything in evidence which he might have pleaded. 4 Dall. (Pa.) 439; 2 Yeates (Pa.) 107; 15 Serg. & R. (Pa.) 105. And this evidence, it seems, may be given in the circuit court without notice, unless called for. 2 Wash. C. C. (U. S.) 456.

COVENTION IN UNUM. The agreement between the two parties to a contract upon the sense of the contract proposed. It is an essential part of the contract, following the pollicitation or proposal emanating from the one, and followed by the consension or agreement of the other. If the second party does not assent to the proposal in the sense in which it is made, he is not bound by his assent unless his mistake is unreasonable.

COVENTRY ACT. The common name for St. 22 & 23 Car. II. c. 1, against maiming by lying in wait, it having been enacted in consequence of an assault on Sir John Coventry in the street, and slitting his nose, in revenge, as was supposed, for some obnoxious words uttered by him in parliament.

COVERT. Covered; protected; sheltered. A *pound covert* is one that is close or covered over, as distinguished from *pound overt*, which is open overhead. Co. Litt. 47b; 3 Bl. Comm. 12. A *feme covert* is so called, as being under the wing, protection, or cover of her husband. 1 Bl. Comm. 442.

In the colony laws of New Plymouth, children are said to be "under the covert" of their parents.

COVERT BARON. A wife. So called from being under the protection of her husband, baron, or lord.

COVERTURE. The condition or state of a married woman.

During coverture, the civil existence of the wife is, for many purposes, merged in that of her husband. See "Abatement;" "Parties."

COVIN. A secret contrivance between two or more persons to defraud and prejudice another of his rights. Co. Litt. 357b; Comyn, Dig. "Covin" (A); 1 Viner, Abr. 473. See "Collusion;" "Fraud."

COWARDICE. Pusillanimity; fear; misbehavior through fear in relation to some duty to be performed before an enemy. O'Brien, Court-Martial, 142.

By both the army and navy regulations of the United States, this is an offense punishable in officers or privates with death, or such other punishment as may be inflicted by a court-martial. 1 Story, U. S. Laws, 761; Act Cong. April 10, 1806, art. 52.

CRANAGE. A toll paid for drawing merchandise out of vessels to the wharf. So called because the instrument used for the purpose is called a "crane." 8 Coke, 46.

CRASSA. Gross. *Crassa negligentia*, gross negligence; *crassa ignorantia*, gross ignorance.

CRASTINUM, or CRASTINO (Lat. tomorrow). On the day after. The return day of writs is made the second day of the term; the first day being some saint's day, which gives its name to the term. In the law Latin, *crastino* (the morning, the day after) would then denote the return day. 2 Reeve, Hist. Eng. Law, 56, 57.

CRATES. An iron gate before a prison. 1 Vent. 304.

CRAVE. To ask; to demand.

This word is frequently used in pleading; as, to crave oyer of a bond on which the suit is brought; and in the settlement of accounts the accountant general craves a credit or an allowance. 1 Chit. Prac. 520. See "Oyer."

CRAVEN, CRAVENT, or CRAVANT (from Saxon *crafan*, to crave, beg, or implore). In old English law. A word of obloquy and disgrace, in the ancient trial by battel, on the uttering of which by either champion, he was considered as yielding the victory to his opponent, and was condemned, as a recreant, *amittere liberam legem*, to lose his frank law, that is, to become infamous, and not to be accounted a free and lawful man, *liber et legalis homo*, being supposed by the court to be proved forsworn, and therefore never to be put on a jury or admitted as a witness in any cause. 3 Bl. Comm. 340; 4 Bl. Comm. 348; 4 Steph. Comm. 415. Called *verbum recreantisae*, the word of recreancy. Fleta, lib. 1, c. 38, § 18. The word is still popularly used in the same dishonorable sense. See "Battel;" "Champion;" "Recreant."

CREAMER. A foreign merchant; but generally taken for one who has a stall in a fair or market. Blount.

CREAMUS. We create. One of the words by which a corporation in England was formerly created by the king. 1 Bl. Comm. 473.

CREANCE (Law Fr. from *creier*, to believe). Belief; persuasion; trust; credit; faith. Law Fr. Dict.

A claim; a debt. 1 Bouv. Inst. note 1040.

CREANCER, or CREANSOR. One who trusts or gives credit; a creditor. Old Nat. Brev. 66; Britt. cc. 28, 78.

CREDENTIALS. Papers which give a title or claim to confidence.

——**In International Law.** The instruments which authorize and establish a public minister in his character with the state or prince to whom they are addressed. If the state or prince receive the minister, he can be received only in the quality attributed to him in his credentials. They are, as it were, his letter of attorney, his mandate patent, *mandatum manifestum*. Vattel, liv. 4, c. 6, § 76.

CREDIBILITY. In a witness. Worthiness of belief, as distinguished from competency or capacity to testify.

CREDIBLE EVIDENCE. Within the meaning of the rule that where a witness has wilfully or corruptly sworn falsely the jury may disregard his testimony unless corroborated by "credible evidence," the quoted expression means evidence worthy of belief—that is, worthy to be considered by the jury, and not evidence which is necessarily true. 210 Ill. 452.

CREDIBLE WITNESS. One who, being competent to give evidence, is worthy of belief. 5 Mass. 219; 17 Pick. (Mass.) 154; 2 Curt. Ecc. 336.

CREDIT. The word "credit" is derived from the Latin word "credere." 75 Ill. App. 665.

(1) The confidence reposed in the ability and intention of a purchaser or borrower to make payment at some future time, either specified or indefinite. 75 Ill. App. 665. The ability to borrow, on the opinion conceived by the lender that he will be repaid.

(2) A debt due in consequence of a contract of hire or borrowing of money.

(3) The time allowed by the creditor for the payment of goods sold by him to the debtor.

(4) That which is due to a merchant, as distinguished from "debit," that which is due by him.

(5) That influence connected with certain social positions. 20 Toullier, Dr. Civ. note 19.

CREDITOR. A person to whom a debt is owing by another person. 43 Ill. App. 426.

He who has a right to require the fulfillment of an obligation or contract. 122 Ill. 404; 80 Ill. App. 219.

One to whom a sum of money is due for any cause. 80 Ill. 219.

CREDITORS' BILL. A bill in equity, filed by one or more creditors, by and in behalf of him or themselves, and all other creditors who shall come in under the decree, for an account of the assets and a due settlement of the estate of a decedent.

The usual decree against the executor or administrator is *quod computet;* that is to say, it directs the master to take the accounts between the deceased and all his creditors, and to cause the creditors, upon due public notice, to come before him to prove their debts at a certain place, and within a limited time; and it also directs the master to take an account of all the personal estate of the deceased in the hands of the executor or administrator, and the same to be applied in payment of the debts and other charges in a due course of administration. 1 Story, Eq. Jur. 442.

CREDITORUM APPELLATIONE NON hi tantum accipiuntur qui pecuniam crediderunt, sed omnes quibus ex qualibet causa debetur. Under the head of creditors are included not alone those who have lent money, but all to whom, from any cause, a debt is owing. Dig. 50. 16. 11.

CREEK. In maritime law. Such little inlets of the sea, whether within, the precinct or extent of a port or without, which are narrow passages, and have shore on either side of them. Callis, Sew. 56; 5 Taunt. 705.

Such inlets that, though possibly for their extent and situation they might be ports, yet they are either members of or dependent upon other ports.

The term imports a recess, cove, bay, or inlet in the shore of a river, and not a separate or independent stream, though sometimes used in the latter meaning. 38 N. Y. 103.

In England the name arose thus: The king could not conveniently have a customer and comptroller in every port or haven; but such custom officers were fixed at some eminent port, and the smaller adjacent ports became by that means creeks, or appendants of that port where these custom officers were placed. 1 Chit. Com. Law, 726; Hale, de Port. Mar. pt. 2, c. 1, vol. 1, p. 46; Comyn, Dig. "Navigation" (C); Callis, Sew. 34.

CREMENTUM COMITATUS. The increase of the county. The increase of the king's rents above the old vicontial rents, for which the sheriffs were to account. Wharton.

CREPARE OCULUM. In Saxon law. To put out an eye; which had a pecuniary punishment of fifty shillings annexed to it. Wharton.

CREPUSCULUM. Daylight; twilight. The light which immediately precedes or follows the rising or setting of the sun. 4 Bl. Comm. 224. Housebreaking during the period in which there is sunlight enough to discern a person's face (*crepusculum*) is not burglary. Coke, 3d Inst. 63; 1 Russ. Crimes, 820; 3 Greenl. Ev. § 75.

CRESCENTE MALITIA CRESCERE DEbet et poena. Vice increasing, punishment ought also to increase. Coke, 2d Inst. 479.

CRETIO. Time for deliberation allowed an heir to decide whether he would or would not take an inheritance. Calv. Lex.; Taylor.

CREW. A ship's complement of men and officers. "In its general and popular sense, it is equivalent to 'company.' In the laws of the United States on maritime subjects, it is sometimes used to comprehend all persons composing the ship's company, including the master; sometimes to comprehend the officers as common seamen, excluding the master; and sometimes to include the common seamen only, excluding the master and officers. But in the last two classes it will be found that the context contains language which explains and limits the general to the particular use." 3 Sumn. (U. S.) 209.

CRIER. A bailiff or other attendant in court, whose duty is to make proclamations in court.

CRIEZ LA PEEZ. Rehearse the concord, or peace. A phrase used in the ancient proceedings for levying fines. It was the form of words by which the justice before whom the parties appeared directed the serjeant or countor in attendance to recite or read aloud the concord or agreement between the parties, as to the lands intended to be conveyed. 2 Reeve Hist. Eng. Law, 224, 225; Crabb, Hist. Eng. Law, 179.

CRIM. CON. An abbreviation for criminal conversation, of very frequent use, denoting adultery; unlawful sexual intercourse with a married woman. Buller, N. P. 27; Bac. Abr. "Marriage" (E 2); 4 Blackf. (Ind.) 157.

CRIME. Any act or omission prohibited by public law for the protection of the public, and made punishable by the state in a judicial proceeding in its own name. It is a public wrong, as distinguished from a mere private wrong or injury to an individual. 1 Clark & Marshall, Crimes, § 1.

A wrong which the government deems injurious to the public at large, and punishes through a judicial proceeding in its own name. 1 Bish. New Crim. Law, § 32.

An act committed or omitted in violation of a public law either forbidding or commanding it. 4 Bl. Comm. 15. This definition has frequently been quoted with approval, but it is inaccurate. In the first place, it is not the "act omitted" that constitutes a crime, but the omission to act. In the second place, the term "public law" is too broad, for it includes many other laws besides those which define and punish crimes. An act is not necessarily a crime because it is prohibited by a public law. To constitute a crime, it must be punished to protect the public, and must be punished by the state or other sovereign. Clark & Marshall, Crimes, § 1.

Violations of municipal ordinances are generally held not to be crimes, for the reason that such ordinances are not public laws, and the punishment for their violation is imposed by a less authority than the state. 29 Minn. 445; 36 Ala. 261; 47 Ohio St. 481; 55 Wis. 487. Contra, see 75 Mich. 611; 27 Tex. App. 342.

"Crime" is a generic term, including treason, felonies, and misdemeanors (31 Wis. 383; 75 Mich. 611; 60 Ill. 168; 42 Minn.

258; 48 Ind. 123), though some earlier writers use the term as excluding misdemeanors (4 Bl. Comm. 5).

CRIME AGAINST NATURE. Sodomy.

CRIMEN (Lat.) A crime.

In the civil law. A charge of crime.

——**Crimen Falsi.** In civil law. A fraudulent alteration, or forgery, to conceal or alter the truth, to the prejudice of another. This crime may be committed in three ways, namely: by forgery; by false declarations or false oath,—perjury; by acts, as by dealing with false weights and measures, by altering the current coin, by making false keys and the like. See Dig. 48. 10. 22; Id. 34. 8. 2; Code, 9. 22; Id. 2. 5. 9. 11. 16. 17. 23. 24; Merlin, Repert.; 1 Brown, Civ. Law, 426; 1 Phil. Ev. 26; 2 Starkie, Ev. 715.

At common law. Any crime which may injuriously affect the administration of justice, by the introduction of falsehood and fraud. 1 Greenl. Ev. § 373.

The meaning of this term at common law is not well defined. It has been held to include forgery (5 Mod. 74), perjury, subornation of perjury (Co. Litt. 6b; Comyn, Dig. "Testmoigne" [A 5]), suppression of testimony by bribery or conspiracy to procure the absence of a witness (Ryan & M. 434), conspiracy to accuse of crime (2 Hale, P. C. 277; 2 Leach, C. C. 496; 3 Starkie, 21; 2 Dods. Adm. 191), barratry (2 Salk. 690). The effect of a conviction for a crime of this class is infamy, and incompetency to testify. Statutes sometimes provide what shall be such crimes.

——**Crimen Furti.** The offense of theft.

——**Crimen Incendii.** In old criminal law. The crime of burning, which included not only the modern crime of arson, or burning of a house, but also the burning of a man, beast, or other chattel. Britt. c. 9; Crabb, Hist. Eng. Law, 308.

——**Crimen Innominatum.** The nameless crime; sodomy.

——**Crimen Laesae-Majestatis.** Injuring or violating the majesty of the king's person; any crime affecting the king's person. 4 Bl. Comm. 75.

——**Crimen Raptus.** Rape.

——**Crimen Roberiae.** Robbery.

——**Crimen Trahit Personam.** The crime carries the person; *i. e.*, the commission of a crime gives the courts of the place where it is committed jurisdiction over the person of the offender. 3 Denio (N. Y.) 190, 210.

CRIMEN FALSI DICITUR, CUM QUIS ILlicitur, cui non fuerit ad haec data auctoritas, de sigillo regis rapto vel invento brevia, cartasve consignaverit. The *crimen falsi* (crime of falsifying) is when any one illicitly, to whom power has not been given for such purposes, has signed writs or charters with the king's seal, which he has either stolen or found. Fleta, lib. 1, c. 23.

CRIMEN LAESAE MAJESTATIS OMNIA alia crimina excedit quoad poenam. The crime of treason exceeds all other crimes as far as its punishment is concerned. Coke, 3d Inst. 210.

CRIMEN OMNIA EX SE NATA VITIAT. Crime vitiates everything which springs from it. 5 Hill (N. Y.) 523, 531.

CRIMINA MORTE EXTINGUUNTUR Crimes are extinguished by death.

CRIMINAL. As a noun, one who has been guilty of a crime.

As an adjective, violative of the criminal law; pertaining to crime, or to penal jurisprudence.

CRIMINAL ACT. A crime. Sometimes applied to the act of crime, as severed from the criminal intent.

CRIMINAL ATTEMPT. Whenever one intending to commit a particular crime does an act toward it, but is interrupted, or some accident intervenes, so that he fails to accomplish what he meant, he is said to have been guilty of a criminal attempt. 181 Ill. 488.

CRIMINAL CONTEMPT. Acts in disrespect of the court or its process, or tending to bring it into disrepute, or obstruct the administration of justice. 153 Ill. 647.

A criminal contempt embraces all acts committed against the majesty of the law or the dignity of the court. 114 Ill. App. 326.

CRIMINAL CONVERSATION. See "Crim. Con."

CRIMINAL INFORMATION. A criminal suit brought, without the interposition of a grand jury, by the proper officer of the king or state. Cole, Crim. Inf.; 4 Bl. Comm. 398.

CRIMINAL INTENT. See "Intent."

CRIMINAL LAW. That branch of jurisprudence which treats of crimes and offenses.

CRIMINAL LAW CONSOLIDATION Acts. The English acts (24 & 25 Vict. cc. 94-100) whereby the criminal law of the country was practically codified.

CRIMINAL LETTERS. In Scotch law. A summons issued by the lord advocate or his deputies as the means of commencing a criminal process. It differs from an indictment, and is like a criminal information at common law.

CRIMINAL PROCEDURE. The course or system of proceedings established by law, whereby persons accused of crime are apprehended, tried, and their punishment fixed.

CRIMINALITER. Criminally; or criminal process.

CRIMINATE. To exhibit evidence of the commission of a criminal offense.

To charge with crime, or implicate in a charge of crime.

CRITICISM. The art of judging skillfully of the merits or beauties, defects or faults, of a literary or scientific performance, or of a production of art. When the criticism is reduced to writing, the writing itself is called a criticism.

CRO, CROO, or CROY. In old Scotch law. A composition, satisfaction, or assythment for the slaughter of a man. Same as weregild. Spelman.

CROCKARDS, or CROCARDS. A foreign coin of base metal, prohibited by St. 27 Edw. I. st. 3, from being brought into the realm. 4 Bl. Comm. 98; Crabb, Hist. Eng. Law, 176.

CROFT. A little close adjoining a dwelling house, and inclosed for pasture and tillage, or any particular use. Jacob, Law Dict. A small space fenced off, in which to keep farm cattle. Spelman. The word is now entirely obsolete.

CROISES. Pilgrims; so called, as wearing the sign of the cross on their upper garments. Britt. c. 122. The knights of the order of St. John of Jerusalem, created for the defense of the pilgrims. Cowell; Blount.

CROITEIR. A crofter; one holding a croft.

CROPPER. One who, having no interest in the land, works it in consideration of receiving a portion of the crop for his labor. 2 Rawle (Pa.) 12.

CROPS. Grain or other cultivated plants or fruits; the product of the harvest thereof.

CROSS ACTION. An action by a defendant in an action, against the plaintiff in the same action, upon the same contract, or for the same tort. Thus, if Peter bring an action of trespass against Paul, and Paul bring another action of trespass against Peter, the subject of the dispute being an assault and battery, it is evident that Paul could not set off the assault committed upon him by Peter, in the action which Peter had brought against him; therefore a cross action becomes necessary.

CROSS APPEAL. Where both parties appeal, the appeals are sometimes called "cross appeals."

CROSS BILL. A bill by a defendant to a bill in equity against the plaintiff or a co-defendant for further relief in respect to the matters embraced in the suit.

It is an auxiliary suit or dependency on the original suit. 35 N. H. 251.

CROSS DEMANDS. Mutual demands; claim and counterclaim.

CROSS ERRORS. Errors being assigned by the respondent in a writ of error, the errors assigned on both sides are called "cross errors."

CROSS EXAMINATION. In practice. The examination of a witness by the party opposed to the party who called him, and who examined or was entitled to examine him in chief.

CROSS REMAINDER. Where a particular estate is conveyed to several persons in common, and, upon the termination of the interest of either of them, his share is to remain over to the rest, and the reversioner or remainder man is not to take till the termination of all the estates, the parties take as tenants in common, with cross remainders between them. 4 Cruise, Dig. 249; 1 Hilliard, Real Prop. 650. It is not an essential quality of cross remainders that the original estates should be held in common. 1 Prest. Est. 94; 2 Washb. Real Prop. Index.

CROSS RULES. These were rules where each of the opposite litigants obtained a rule *nisi*, as the plaintiff to increase the damages, and the defendant to enter a nonsuit. Wharton.

CROWN CASES. In English law. Criminal prosecutions.

CROWN CASES RESERVED. Questions of law reserved on the trial of criminal cases at assize for consideration of the court of criminal appeal.

CROWN LAW. Criminal law; the crown being the prosecutor.

CROWN OFFICE. The criminal side of the court of king's bench. The king's attorney in this court is called "master of the crown office." 4 Bl. Comm. 308.

CROWN OFFICE IN CHANCERY. One of the offices of the English high court of chancery, now transferred to the high court of justice. The principal official, the clerk of the crown, is an officer of parliament, and of the lord chancellor, in his nonjudicial capacity, rather than an officer of the courts of law. Second Rep. Leg. Dep. Comm. 39. His principal duties are to make out and issue writs of summons and election for both houses of parliament, and to keep the custody of poll books and ballot papers. Nearly all patents passing the great seal, except those for inventions (Great Seal Act, 1880), are made out in his office, and he makes out the warrants for almost all letters patent under the great seal. See "Patent." He also does the duties formerly performed by the clerk of the Hanaper. They chiefly consisted in collecting fees, but have now ceased almost entirely. He is registrar of the lord high steward's court. Second Rep. Leg. Dep. Comm. 39; Rep. Comm. on Fees, 5; 2 & 3 Wm. IV. c. 3; 3 & 4 Wm. IV. c. 84; 15 & 16 Vict. c. 87; 37 & 38 Vict. c. 81.

CROWN PAPER. A paper containing the list of criminal cases which await the hearing or decision of the court, and particularly of the court of queen's bench; and it then includes all cases arising from informations *quo warranto*, criminal informations, criminal cases brought up from inferior courts by writ of *certiorari*, and cases from the sessions. Brown.

CROWN SIDE. The criminal side of the court of king's bench. Distinguished from the pleas side, which transacts the civil business. 4 Bl. Comm. 265.

CROWN SOLICITOR. In England, the solicitor to the treasury acts, in state prosecutions, as solicitor for the crown in preparing the prosecution. In Ireland there are officers called "crown solicitors" attached to each circuit, whose duty it is to get up every case for the crown in criminal prosecutions. They are paid by salaries. There is no such system in England, where prosecutions are conducted by solicitors appointed by the parish, or other persons bound over to prosecute by the magistrates on each committal; but in Scotland the still better plan exists of a crown prosecutor (called the "procurator-fiscal," and being a subordinate of the lord-advocate) in every county, who prepares every criminal prosecution. Wharton.

CROWNER, or CROUNER. In old Scotch law. Coroner; a coroner. Skene de Verb. Sign.

CROY. In old English law. Marsh land. Blount.

CRUCE SIGNATI. In old English law. Signed or marked with a cross. Pilgrims to the holy land, or crusaders. So called because they wore the sign of the cross upon their garments. Spelman, voc. "Crucifen."

CRUEL. Implies a merciless and savage disposition, taking pleasure in suffering, and without pity. The evil and malicious will must be present to constitute an act cruel. 15 Pa. Co. Ct. 515.

CRUEL AND ABUSIVE TREATMENT. To constitute grounds for divorce under the statutory provision, must be such as results in actual injury or creates reasonable apprehension of danger of such injury. 175 Mass. 7.

Actual personal violence or the reasonable apprehension of it, or such a course of treatment as endangers life or health and renders cohabitation unsafe. 48 Penn. St. 238.

CRUEL TREATMENT. Within the meaning of the civil code is the wilful infliction of pain, bodily or mental, upon another, such as reasonably justifies an apprehension of danger to life, limb, or health. 129 Ga. 247.

CRUELTY. Legal cruelty is such conduct on the part of one spouse as will endanger the life, limb, or health of the other, or create a reasonable apprehension of bodily harm. 36 Ga. 317. And may consist of duress or threats tending to injury to health, 39 L. J. P. & M. 28; 21 L. T. 564; or terrifying a wife into immorality, 35 L. J. P. & M. 37; publicly outraging a wife's feelings by insulting language and assaulting her, even though no personal injury be inflicted, 31 L. J. P. & M. 159; a violently intended, but futile, assault, or spitting on a wife, 1 Hagg. Ecc. Supp. 776; habitual insult and violence of temper, inducing quarrels and producing physical suffering, 34 L. J. P. & M. 112; knowingly or recklessly imparting a venereal disease, L. R. 1 P. & D. 233; Id. 46; 35 L. J. P. & M. 13; as to cutaneous disease, 1 Sp. Ecc. & Ad. 205; unreasonable denial of usual necessaries and comforts so as to affect health, 3 N. C. 340; 2 Add. 382; cruelty to children in the mother's presence, in order to wound her feelings, and to such an extent as probably to be injurious to her health, 28 L. J. P. & M. 46; 42 L. J. P. & M. 23; but such acts as drunkenness, 29 L. J. P. & M. 64; debauching household servants, 34 L. J. P. & M. 139; debarring a wife from intercourse with her family, 4 Hagg. Ecc. 269; sleeping in a separate bed, 1 Hagg. Ecc. Supp. 776, are not.

Cruelty is not excused by drunkenness or *delirium tremens*, 28 L. J. P. & M. 13; 1 Sw. & Tr. 312; 7 W. R. 129; or ungovernable passion, 27 L. J. P. & M. 73; 1 Sw. & Tr. 192; but insanity excuses, 33 L. J. P. & M. 65; 3 Sw. & Tr. 349; 1 Sw. & Tr. 591.

——Extreme and Repeated. Wilful misconduct which endangers the life or health of the other spouse, or exposes her to bodily hazard and intolerable hardship and renders cohabitation unsafe. Many acts are not necessary, but there must be more than one act of violence. 138 Ill. 445.

When charged to the wife, slight acts of violence are insufficient so long as it may be reasonably presumed that the husband will be able to protect himself. 140 Ill. 329.

——To Animals. Cruelly beating, ill-treating, over-driving, or inflicting unnecessary pain. Incensing cocks to fight, 32 L. J. M. C. 95; cutting cock's comb for exhibition purposes, 46 L. J. M. C. 211, is such cruelty; and so it may be such cruelty to turn an animal which is already suffering into a field to graze, when it can only do so by giving itself additional pain, 26 W. R. 332; 42 J. P. 248; 38 L. T. 360. But the mere omission to kill a suffering animal is not such cruelty Id.); nor the merely unlawful killing of an animal, or shooting it intending to kill it but leaving it to die in pain, 26 W. R. 721; nor the sending parrots a ten-hours' railway journey without water, 50 L. J. M. C. 67; 29 W. R. 538; 45 J. P. 522; 44 L. T. 424; nor a painful operation *bona fide* believed to be proper, *e. g.*,—spaying sows, to improve the flesh as human food, 56 L. J. M. C. 45.

CRUISE. A voyage or expedition in quest of vessels or fleets of the enemy which may be expected to sail in any particular track at a certain season of the year. The region in which these cruises are performed is usually termed the "rendezvous," or "cruising-latitude." When the ships employed for this purpose, which are accordingly called "cruisers," have arrived at the destined station, they traverse the sea backwards and forwards, under an easy sail, and within a limited space, conjectured to be in the track of their expected adversaries. Weskett, Ins.; Lex Merc. Rediv. 271, 284; Doug. 509; Park, Ins. 58; Marsh. Ins. 196, 199, 520; 2 Gall. (U. S.) 268.

CRY DE PAYS, or **CRY DE PAIS.** A hue and cry raised by the country. This was allowable, in the absence of the constable, when a felony had been committed.

CRYER. See "Crier."

CUCKING STOOL. An engine or machine for the punishment of scolds and unquiet women. Called, also, a "trebucket," "tumbrill," and "castigatory." Bakers and brewers were formerly also liable to the same punishment. Being fastened in the machine, they were immersed over head and ears in some pool. Blount; Coke, 3d Inst. 219; 4 Bl. Comm. 168.

CUI ANTE DIVORTIUM (Law Lat.) The full phrase was, *cui ipsa ante divortium contradicere non potuit,* whom she before the divorce could not gainsay.

——**In Practice.** A writ which anciently lay in favor of a woman who had been divorced from her husband to recover lands and tenements which she had in fee simple, fee tail, or for life, from him to whom her husband had aliened them during the marriage, when she could not gainsay it. Fitzh. Nat. Brev. 240; 3 Sharswood, Bl. Comm. 183, note; Stearns, Real Actions, 143; Booth, Real Actions, 188.

CUI IN VITA (Law Lat.) The full phrase was, *cui in vita sua, ipsa contradicere non potuit,* whom in his lifetime she could not gainsay.

——**In Practice.** A writ of entry which lay for a widow against a person to whom her husband had in his lifetime aliened her lands. Fitzh. Nat. Brev. 193. The object of the writ was to avoid a judgment obtained against the husband by confession or default. It is now of no use in England, by force of the provisions of St. 32 Hen. VIII. c. 28, § 6. See 6 Coke, 8, 9; Booth, Real Actions, 186. As to its use in Pennsylvania, see 3 Bin. (Pa.); Rep. Comm. Pa. Civ. Code 1835, 90, 91.

CUI JURISDICTIO DATA EST, EA QUOque concessa esse videntur sine quibus jurisdictio explicari non potest. To whom jurisdiction is given, to him those things also are held to be granted without which the jurisdiction cannot be exercised. Dig. 2. 1. 2; 1 Wooddeson, Lect. introd. lxxi; 1 Kent, Comm. 339.

CUI JUS EST DONANDI, EIDEM ET vendendi et concedendi jus est. He who has a right to give has also a right to sell and to grant. Dig 50. 17. 163.

CUI LICET QUOD MAJUS NON DEBET quod minus est non licere. He who has authority to do the more important act shall not be debarred from doing that of less importance. 4 Rep. 23; Co. Litt. 355b; 2 Inst. 307; Noy, Max. 26; Finch, Law, 22; 3 Mod. 382, 392; Broom, Leg. Max. (3d London Ed.) 165; Dig. 50. 70. 21.

CUI PATER EST POPULUS NON HAbet ille patrem. He to whom the people is father has not a father. Co. Litt. 123.

CUICUNQUE ALIQUIS QUID CONCEDIT concedere videtur et id, sine quo res ipsa esse non potuit. Whoever grants a thing is supposed also tacitly to grant that without which the grant itself would be of no effect. 11 Coke, 52; Broom, Leg. Max. (3d London Ed.) 426; Hob. 234; Vaughan, 109; 11 Exch. 775; Shep. Touch. 89; Co. Litt. 56a.

CUILIBET IN ARTE SUA PERITO EST credendum. Credence should be given to one skilled in his peculiar art. Co. Litt. 125; 1 Sharswood, Bl. Comm. 75; Phil. Ev. (Cow. & H. notes), pt. 1, p. 759; 11 Clark & F. 85.

CUILIBET LICET JURI PRO SE INTROducto renunciare. Any one may waive or renounce the benefit of a principle or rule of law that exists only for his protection.

CUIQUE IN SUA ARTE CREDENDUM est. Every one is to be believed in his own art. 9 Mass. 227.

CUJUS EST COMMODUM EJUS DEBET esse incommodum. He who receives the benefit should also bear the disadvantage. 1 Kames, Eq. 289; Broom, Leg. Max. (3d London Ed.) 837.

CUJUS EST DARE EJUS EST DISPOnere. He who has a right to give has the right to dispose of the gift. Wingate, Max. 53; Broom, Leg. Max. (3d London Ed.) 440; 2 Coke, 71.

CUJUS EST DIVISIO ALTERIUS EST electio. Whichever of two parties has the division, the other has the choice. Co. Litt. 166.

CUJUS EST DOMINIUM EJUS EST PERiculum. The risk lies upon the owner of the subject. Tray. Lat. Max. 114.

CUJUS EST INSTITUERE EJUS EST abrogare. Whose it is to institute, his it is also to abrogate. Sydney, Gov. 15; Broom, Leg. Max. (3d London Ed.) 785.

CUJUS EST SOLUM EJUS EST USQUE ad coelum. He who owns the soil owns it up to the sky. Broom, Leg. Max. (3d London Ed.) 309; Shep. Touch. 90; 2 Bouv. Inst. notes 15, 70; 2 Sharswood, Bl. Comm. 18; 9 Coke, 54; 4 Campb. 219; 11 Exch. 822; 6 El. & Bl. 76.

CUJUS JURIS (i. e., JURISDICTIONIS) est principale, ejusdem juris erit accessorium. He who has jurisdiction of the principal has also of the accessory. Coke, 2d Inst. 493; Bracton, 481.

CUJUS PER ERROREM DATI REPETITIO est, ejus consulto dati, donatio est. That which, when given through mistake, can be recovered back, when given with knowledge of the facts, is a gift. Dig. 50. 17. 53.

CUJUSQUE REI POTISSIMA PARS principium est. The principal part of everything is the beginning. Dig. 1. 2. 1; 10 Coke, 49.

CUL DE SAC (Fr. the bottom of a sack). A blind alley; a street which is open at one end only.

CULAGIUM. The laying up a ship in a dock for repair. Cowell; Blount.

CULPA. A fault; negligence. Jones, Bailm. 8.

Culpa is to be distinguished from *dolus*, the latter being a trick for the purpose of deception, the former merely negligence. There are three degrees of *culpa: Lata culpa*, gross fault or neglect; *levis culpa*, ordinary fault or neglect; *levissima culpa*, slight fault or neglect; and the definitions of these degrees are precisely the same as those in our law. Story, Bailm. § 18.

CULPA CARET, QUI SCIT, SED PROHIBere non potest. He is clear of blame who knows, but cannot prevent Dig. 50. 17. 50.

CULPA EST IMMISCERE SE REI AD SE non pertinenti. It is a fault to meddle with what does not belong to or does not concern you. Dig. 50. 17. 36; Coke, 2d Inst. 208.

CULPA LATA DOLO AEQUIPARATUR. Gross neglect is equivalent to fraud. Dig. 11. 6. 1.

CULPA TENET SUOS AUCTORES. A fault binds its own authors. Ersk. Inst. bk. 4, tit. 1, § 14; 6 Bell, App. Cas. 539.

CULPABILIS (Lat.) Guilty.

CULPAE POENA PAR ESTO. Let the punishment be proportioned to the crime. Branch, Princ.

CULPRIT. A person who is guilty, or supposed to be guilty, of a crime.

When a prisoner is arraigned, and he pleads not guilty, in English practice, the clerk, who arraigns him on behalf of the crown, replies that the prisoner is guilty, and that he is ready to prove the accusation. This is done by writing two monosyllabic abbreviations,—*cul. prit.* 4 Bl. Comm. 339; 1 Chit. Crim. Law, 416. See Christian's note to Bl. Comm. cited. The technical meaning has disappeared, and the compound is used in the popular sense as above given.

CULRACH. In old Scotch law. A species of pledge or cautioner (Scottice, *back borgh*), used in cases of the replevin of persons from one man's court to another's. Skene de Verb. Sign.

CULTURA. A parcel of arable land. Blount. Called a "wrong."

CULVERTAGE. A base kind of slavery; the confiscation or forfeiture, which takes place when a lord seizes his tenant's estate. Blount; Du Cange.

CUM ACTIO FUERIT MERE CRIMINALis, institui poterit ab initio criminaliter vel civiliter. When an action is merely criminal, it can be instituted from the beginning, either criminally or civilly. Bracton, 102.

CUM ADSUNT TESTIMONIA RERUM, quid opus est verbis? When the proofs of facts are present, what need is there of words? 2 Bulst. 53.

CUM ALIQUIS RENUNCIAVERIT SOCIetati, solvitur societas. When any partner renounces the partnership, the partnership is dissolved. Tray, Lat. Max. 118.

CUM CONFITENTE SPONTE MITIUS est agendum. One making a voluntary confession is to be dealt with more mercifully. Coke, 4th Inst. 66; Branch, Princ.

CUM DE LUCRO DUORUM QUAERItur mellior est causa possidentis. When the question of gain lies between two, the cause of the possessor is the better. Dig. 50. 17. 126.

CUM DUO INTER SE PUGNANTIA REperiuntur in testamento, ultimum ratum est. When two things repugnant to each other are found in a will, the last is to be confirmed. Co. Litt. 112; Shep. Touch. 451; Broom, Leg. Max. (3d London Ed.) 518; 1 Jarm. Wills (2d Ed.) 394; 16 Johns. (N. Y.) 146; 1 Phil. 536.

CUM DUO JURA CONCURRUNT IN una persona aequum est ac si essent in duobus. When two rights meet in one person, it is the same as if they were in two persons.

CUM IN CORPORE DISSENTITUR, APparet nullam esse acceptionem. When there is a disagreement in the substance, it appears that there is no acceptance. 12 Allen (Mass.) 44.

CUM IN TESTAMENTO AMBIGUE AUT etiam perperum scriptum, est benigne interpretari, et secundum id quod credibile est cogitatum credendum est. When an ambiguous or even an erroneous expression occurs in a will, it should be construed liberally, and in accordance with the testator's probable meaning. Dig. 34. 5. 24; Broom, Leg. Max. (3d London Ed.) 506; 3 Poth. ad Pand. (Ed. 1819) 46.

CUM LEGITIMAE NUPTIAE FACTAE sunt, patrem liberi sequuntur. Children born under a legitimate marriage follow the condition of the father.

CUM ONERE (Lat.) With the burden; subject to the incumbrance; subject to the charge. A purchaser with knowledge of an incumbrance takes the property *cum onere.* Co. Litt. 231a; 7 East, 164; Paley, Ag. 175.

CUM PAR DELICTUM EST DUORUM, semper oneratur petitor, et melior habetur possessoris causa. Where two parties are equally in fault, the claimant always is at a disadvantage, and the party in possession has the better cause. Dig. 50. 17. 154; Broom, Leg. Max. (3d London Ed.) 644.

CUM QUOD AGO NON VALET UT AGO, valeat quantum valere potest. When that which I do is of no effect as I do it, it shall have as much effect as it can, *i. e.*, in some other way. 4 Kent, Comm. 493.

CUM TESTAMENTO ANNEXO (Law Lat.) With the will annexed. A term applied to administration granted where a testator makes an incomplete will, without naming any executors, or where he names incapable persons, or where the executors named refuse to act. 2 Bl. Comm. 503, 504.

CUMULATIVE EVIDENCE. That which goes to prove what has already been established by other evidence.

CUMULATIVE LEGACY. See "Legacy."

CUMULATIVE REMEDY. A second or additional mode of procedure in addition to one already available, as opposed to alternative remedy. Wharton.

CUMULATIVE SENTENCES. Sentences on a trial and conviction of several crimes, each sentence being in addition to the others, and not for the same fine or concurrent terms of imprisonment. See "Concurrent Sentences."

CUMULATIVE VOTING. That by which the voter concentrates his ballots on one or more candidates, instead of voting for the full number to be elected. Thus, a stockholder holding fifty shares may, under such a system, if five directors are to be chosen, cast two hundred and fifty votes for one, or one hundred and twenty-five for each of two, instead of voting fifty votes for each of five.

CUNEATOR. A coiner. Du Cange. *Cuneare,* to coin; *cuneus,* the die with which to coin; *cuneata,* coined. Du Cange; Spelman.

CUR. A common abbreviation of *curia.* 1 Inst. Cler. 9.

CURA (Lat.) Care; charge; oversight; guardianship.

——**In the Civil Law.** A species of guardianship which commenced at the age of puberty, when the guardianship called "*tutela*" expired, and continued to the completion of the twenty-fifth year. Inst. 1. 23. pr.; Id. 1. 25. pr.; Halifax, Civ. Law, bk. 1, c. 9.

CURAGULOS. One who takes care of a thing.

CURATE. One who represents the incumbent of a church, parson, or vicar, and takes care of the church, and performs divine services in his stead. An officiating temporary minister in the English church, who represents the proper incumbent. Burn, Ecc. Law; 1 Bl. Comm. 393.

CURATIO (Lat.) In civil law. The power or duty of managing the property of him who, either on account of infancy or some defect of mind or body, cannot manage his own affairs; the duty of a curator or guardian. Calv. Lex.

CURATOR. One who has been legally appointed to take care of the interests of one who, on account of his youth, or defect of his understanding, or for some other cause, is unable to attend to them himself; a guardian.

There are curators *ad bona* (of property), who administer the estate of a minor, take care of his person, and intervene in all his contracts; curators *ad litem* (of suits), who assist the minor in courts of justice, and act as curators *ad bona* in cases where the interests of the curator are opposed to the interests of the minor. Civ. Code La. arts. 357-366. There are also curators of insane persons (Id. art. 31), and of vacant successions and absent heirs (Id. arts. 1105, 1125).

CURATOR AD HOC. A guardian for this special purpose; as one appointed to represent an absentee.

CURATOR AD LITEM (Lat.) Guardian for the suit. In English law, the corresponding phrase is "guardian *ad litem.*"

CURATOR BONIS (Lat.)

——**In Civil Law.** A guardian to take care of the property. Calv. Lex.

——**In Scotch Law.** A guardian for minors, lunatics, etc. Halk. Tech. Terms; Bell, Dict.

CURATORSHIP. The office of a curator.

Curatorship differs from tutorship (*q. v.*) in this, that the latter is instituted for the protection of property in the first place, and, secondly, of the person; while the former is intended to protect, first, the person, and, secondly, the property. 1 Lec. Elm. 241.

CURATRIX. A woman who has been appointed to the office of curator.

CURATUS NON HABET TITULUM. A curate has no title (to tithes). 3 Bulst. 310.

CURE OF SOULS. The ordinary duties of an officiating clergyman.

"Curate" more properly denotes the incumbent in general who hath the cure of souls, but more frequently it is understood to signify a clerk not instituted to the cure of souls, but exercising the spiritual office in a parish under the rector or vicar. 2 Burn, Ecc. Law, 54; 1 H. Bl. 424.

CURED BY VERDICT. The expression "cured by verdict" signifies that the court will, after a verdict, presume or intend that the particular thing which appears to be defectively or imperfectly stated or omitted in the pleadings, was duly proved at the trial, the intendment arising not merely from the verdict but from the united effect of the verdict and the issue on which it was given, but the particular thing presumed must always be such as may be implied from the allegations by a fair and reasonable intendment. 240 Ill. 265.

CURFEW (French, *couvre*, to cover, and *feu*, fire). This is generally supposed to be an institution of William the Conqueror, who required, by ringing of the bell at eight o'clock in the evening, that all lights and fires in dwellings should then be extinguished. But the custom is evidently older than the Norman; for we find an order of King Alfred that the inhabitants of Oxford should, at the ringing of that bell, cover up their fires and go to bed. And there is evidence that the same practice prevailed at this period in France, Normandy, Spain, and probably in most of the other countries of Europe. Henry, Hist. Brit. vol. 3, 567. It was doubtless intended, as a precaution against fires, which were very frequent and destructive when most houses were built of wood.

That it was not intended as a badge of infamy is evident from the fact that the law was of equal obligation upon the nobles of the court and upon the native-born serfs. And yet we find the name "curfew law" employed as a by-word denoting the most odious tyranny.

It appears to have met with so much opposition that in 1103 we find Henry I. repealing the enactment of his father on the subject; and Blackstone says that, though it is mentioned a century afterwards, it is rather spoken of as a time of night, than as a still subsisting custom. Shakespeare frequently refers to it in the same sense. This practice is still pursued in many parts of England and in this country, as a very convenient mode of apprising people of the time of night.

CURIA.

——**In Roman Law.** One of the divisions of the Roman people. The Roman people were divided by Romulus into three tribes and thirty *curiae*. The members of each *curia* were united by the tie of common religious rites, and also by certain common political and civil powers. Dion. Hal. lib. 2, p. 82; Liv. lib. 1, c. 13; Plut. in Romulo, p. 30; Festus Brisson, in Verb.

In later times the word signified the senate or aristocratic body of the provincial cities of the empire. Festus Brisson, in Verb.; Ort. Histoire, No. 25, 408; Ort. Inst. No. 125.

The senate house at Rome; the senate house of a provincial city. Code, 10. 31. 2; Spelman.

——**In English Law.** The king's court; the palace; the royal household. The residence of a noble; a manor or chief manse; the hall of a manor. Spelman.

A court of justice, whether of general or special jurisdiction. Fleta, lib. 2, l. 72, § 1; Spelman; Cowell; 3 Bl. Comm. c. iv. See "Court."

A courtyard or inclosed piece of ground; a close. St. Edw. Conf. 1, 6; Brac. 76, 222b, 335b, 356b, 358; Spelman. See "Curia Claudenda."

The civil or secular power, as distinguished from the church. Spelman.

CURIA ADVISARE VULT (Lat.) The court wishes to consider the matter.

——**In Practice.** The entry formerly made upon the record to vindicate the continuance of a cause until a final judgment should be rendered.

It is commonly abbreviated thus: *Cur. adv. vult.* Thus, from amongst many examples, in 2 Barn. & C. 172, after the report of the argument, we find *"cur. adv. vult.,"* then, "on a subsequent day judgment was delivered, etc."

CURIA BARONIS (or **BARONUM**). In old English law. A court baron. Fleta, lib. 2, c. 53.

CURIA CANCELLARIAE OFFICINA JUSTITIAE. The court of chancery is the workshop of justice. 2 Inst. 552.

CURIA CHRISTIANITATIS. A court Christian.

CURIA CLAUDENDA (Lat.) In practice. A writ which anciently lay to compel a party to inclose his land. Fitzh. Nat. Brev. 297.

CURIA COMITATUS (Law Lat.) In old English law. The court of the county; the county court, or court of the shire (Saxon, *scyregemot*), in the Saxon times. See "County Court."

CURIA CURSUS AQUAE. A court held by the lord of the manor of Gravesend for the better management of barges and boats plying on the river Thames between Gravesend and Windsor, and also at Gravesend bridge, etc. 2 Geo. II. c. 26.

CURIA DOMINI. In old English law The lord's court, house, or hall, where all the tenants met at the time of keeping court. Cowell.

CURIA LEGITIME AFFIRMATA (Law Lat.) In old Scotch practice. Court lawfully opened, or opened in due form. A formal phrase used in the captions of records. 3 How. St. Tr. 654; 1 Pitc. Crim. Tr. pt. 1, p. 143.

CURIA MAGNA. In old English law. The great court; one of the ancient names of parliament. 1 Bl. Comm. 148.

The king's court, or *aula regis*. Crabb, Hist. Eng. Law, 144.

CURIA MAJORIS. In old English law. The mayor's court. Calth. 144.

CURIA MILITUM. A court so called, anciently held at Carisbrook Castle, in the Isle of Wight. Cowell.

CURIA PALATII. In English law. The palace court.

CURIA PARLIAMENTI SUIS PROPRIIS legibus subsistit. The court of parliament is governed by its own peculiar laws. Coke, 4th Inst. 50; Broom, Leg. Max. (3d London Ed.) 82; 12 C. B. 413, 414.

CURIA PEDIS PULVERIZATI. In old English law. The court of *piedpoudre* or *piepoudres* (*q. v.*) 3 Bl. Comm. 32.

CURIA PENTICIARUM. A court held by the sheriff of Chester. In a place there called the "Pendice." Cowell.

CURIA PERSONAE. In old records. A parsonage house, or manse. Kennett, Par. Ant. 205; Cowell.

CURIA REGIS (Lat. the king's court). A term applied to the *aula regis*, the *bancus* or *communis bancus*, and the *iter* or *eyre*, as being courts of the king, but especially to the *aula regis* (*q. v.*)

CURIALTY. In Scotch law. Curtesy.

CURIOSA ET CAPTIOSA INTERPRETAtio in lege reprobatur. A curious and captious interpretation in the law is to be reproved. 1 Bulst. 6.

CURNOCK. In old English law. A measure containing four bushels or half a quarter of corn. Cowell; Blount.

CURRENCY. Coin, or such bank notes as pass freely in commercial transactions and regarded nearly equivalent to coin. 35 Ill. 163. "Currency," in its broad and comprehensive meaning, may be properly used with reference to things of different values, when applied to the medium of exchange of property, but so used does not necessarily mean cash, but is equally applicable to anything which is used as a circulating medium, and is generally accepted in trade as a representative of values of property. 27 Ill. 506. Currency is the value of cash, and excludes the idea of depreciated paper money. 30 Ill. 403. Current money (*q. v.*)

CURRENT. Present; now in progress or transit.

CURRENT ACCOUNT. An account which can be added to or drawn upon at any time without notice to the banker. 81 Ill. App. 218.

CURRENT MONEY. Lawful money; whatever passes current for money, whether coin or paper money. 27 Ill. 501; 9 Mo. 701; 8 Minn. 329.

In commercial use, "currency" is confined to paper money, as distinguished from "specie" or coin money. 14 Mich. 379; 12 Wall. (U. S.) 657.

CURRIT QUATUOR PEDIBUS (Law Lat. it runs upon four feet; or, as sometimes expressed, it runs upon all fours). A phrase used in arguments to signify the entire and exact application of a case quoted. "It does not follow that they run *quatuor pedibus*." 1 W. Bl. 145.

CURRIT TEMPUS CONTRA DESIDES et sui juris contemptores. Time runs against the slothful and those who neglect their rights. Bracton, fols. 100b, 101; Fleta, lib. 4, c. 5, § 12.

CURSITOR. A junior clerk in the court of chancery, whose business it formerly was to write out from the register those forms of writs which issued of course. Such writs were called writs *de cursu* (of course). whence the name, which had been acquired as early as the reign of Edward III. The body of cursitors constituted a corporation, each clerk having a certain number of counties assigned to him. Coke, 2d Inst. 670; 1 Spence, Eq. Jur. 238.

CURSITOR BARON. An officer of the court of exchequer, who is appointed by patent under the great seal to be one of the barons of the exchequer. The office is abolished by St. 19 & 20 Vict. c. 86. Wharton.

CURSOR. An inferior officer of the papal court.

CURSUS CURIAE EST LEX CURIAE. The practice of the court is the law of the court. 3 Burst. 53; Broom, Leg. Max. (3d London Ed.) 126; 12 C. B. 414; 17 Q. B. 86; 8 Exch. 199; 2 Maule & S. 25; 15 East, 226; 12 Mees. & W. 7; 4 Mylne & C. 635; 3 Scott, N. R. 599.

CURTESY. The estate to which, by common law, a man is entitled, on the death of his wife, in the lands or tenements of which she was seised in possession in fee simple or in tail during her coverture, provided they have had lawful issue born alive which might have been capable of inheriting the estate.

It is a freehold estate for the term of his natural life. 1 Washb. Real Prop. 127. In the common law, the word is used in the phrases "tenant by curtesy," or "estate by curtesy," but seldom alone; while in Scotland of itself it denotes the estate. See "Estates."

Some considerable question has been made as to the derivation both of the custom and its name. It seems pretty clear, however, that the term is derived from *curtis*, a court, and that the custom, in England at least, is of English origin, though a similar custom existed in Normandy, and still exists in Scotland. 1 Washb. Real Prop. 128, note; Wright, Ten. 192; Co. Litt. 30a; 2 Bl. Comm 126; Ersk. Inst. 380; Grand Cout. de Normandie, c. 119.

CURTILAGE. The inclosed space immediately surrounding a dwelling house, contained within the same inclosure.

It is defined by Blount as a yard, backside, or piece of ground near a dwelling house, in which they sow beans, etc., yet distinct from the garden. Blount; Spelman. By others it is said to be a waste piece of ground so situated. Cowell.

It has recently been defined as "a fence or inclosure of a small piece of land around a dwelling house, usually including the buildings occupied in connection with the dwelling house, the inclosure consisting either of a separate fence, or partly of a fence and partly of the exterior of buildings so within this inclosure." 10 Cush. (Mass.) 480.

The term is used in determining whether the offense of breaking into a barn or warehouse is burglary. See 4 Bl. Comm. 224; 1 Hale, P. C. 558; 2 Russ. Crimes, 13; 1 Russ. Crimes, 790; Russ. & R. 289; 1 Car. & K. 84; 10 Cush. (Mass.) 480.

In Michigan the meaning of curtilage has been extended to include more than an inclosure near the house. 2 Mich. 250.

CURTILES TERRAE. In old English law. Court lands. Cowell. See "Court Lands."

CURTILLUM. The area or space within the inclosure of a dwelling house. Spelman.

CURTIS. The area about a building; a garden; a hut or farmer's house; a farmers house with the land enrolled with it.

A village or a walled town containing a small number of houses.

The residence of a nobleman; a hall or palace.

A court; a tribunal of justice. 1 Washb. Real Prop. 120; Spelman; 3 Bl. Comm. 320.

The similarity of the derivative meaning of this word and of *aula* is quite noticeable, both coming to denote the court itself, from denoting the place where the court was held.

CUSTA, or **CUSTANTIA.** Costs.

CUSTODES. Keepers; guardians; conservators.

Custodes pacis, guardians of the peace. 1 Bl. Comm. 349.

Custodes libertatis Angliae auctoritate parliamenti, guardians of the liberty of England by authority of parliament. The style in which writs and all judicial process ran during the grand rebellion, from the death of Charles I. till Cromwell was declared protector. Jacob.

CUSTODIA LEGIS. In custody of the law.

CUSTODIAM LEASE. In English law. A grant from the crown under the exchequer seal, by which the custody of lands, etc., seized in the king's hands, is demised or committed to some person as custodee or lessee thereof. Wharton.

CUSTODY. The detainer of a person by virtue of a lawful authority. 3 Chit. Prac. 355.

The care and possession of a thing.

CUSTOM. Such a usage as by common consent and uniform practice has become the law of the place, or of the subject-matter, to which it relates.

It differs from prescription, which is personal, and is annexed to the person of the owner of a particular estate; while the other is local, and relates to a particular district. An instance of the latter occurs where the question is upon the manner of conducting a particular branch of trade at a certain place; of the former, where a certain person and his ancestors, or those whose estates he has, have been entitled to a certain advantage or privilege, as to have common of pasture in a certain close, or the like. 2 Bl. Comm. 263.

General customs are such as constitute a part of the common law, and extend to the whole country. Particular customs are those which are confined to a particular district.

CUSTOM HOUSE. A place appointed by law, in ports of entry, where importers of goods, wares, and merchandise are bound to enter the same, in order to pay or secure the duties or customs due to the government.

CUSTOM OF MERCHANTS. A system of customs acknowledged and taken notice of by all nations, and which are therefore a part of the general law of the land. See "Law Merchant"; 1 Chit. Bl. Comm. 76, note 9.

CUSTOMARY COURT BARON. A court baron, at which copyholders might transfer their estates, and where other matters relating to their tenures were transacted. 3 Bl. Comm. 33.

This court was held on the manor, the lord or his steward sitting as judge. 1 Crabb, Real Prop. § 633. It might be held anywhere in the manor, at the pleasure of the judge, unless there was a custom to the contrary. It might exist at the same time with a court baron proper, or even where there were no freeholders in the manor.

CUSTOMARY ESTATES. Estates which owe their origin and existence to the custom of the manor in which they are held. 2 Bl. Comm. 149.

CUSTOMARY FREEHOLD. A class of freeholds held according to the custom of the manor, derived from the ancient tenure in villein socage. Holders of such an estate have a freehold interest, though it is not held by a freehold tenure. 2 Bl. Comm. 149.

CUSTOMARY SERVICE. A service due by ancient custom or prescription only. Such is, for example, the service of doing suit at another's mill, where the persons resident in a particular place, by usage, time out of mind have been accustomed to grind corn at a particular mill. 3 Bl. Comm. 234.

CUSTOMARY TENANTS (Law Lat. *custumarii tenentes*). In English law. Such tenants as hold by the custom of the manor, as their special evidence. Termes de la Ley. Copyholders belong to this class. 2 Bl. Comm. 147, 148. See "Copyholder."

CUSTOMARY USE. The use of anything for the purpose and in the manner such thing is usually and ordinarily used. 256 Ill. 487.

CUSTOME SERRA PRISE STRICTE. Custom must be taken strictly. Jenk. Cent. Cas. 83.

CUSTOMERS. Persons who have dealings with one who is engaged in an occupation or employment. 178 Ill. App. 176.

CUSTOMS. This term is usually applied to those taxes which are payable upon goods and merchandise imported or exported. Story, Const. § 949; Bac. Abr. "Smuggling."

The duties, toll, tribute, or tariff payable upon merchandise exported or imported. These are called customs from having been paid from time immemorial. Expressed in law Latin by *custuma*, as distinguished from *consuetudines*, which are usages merely. 1 Sharswood, Bl. Comm. 314.

CUSTOMS AND SERVICES (Law Lat. *consuetudines et servitia*). In old English law. Services which the tenants of lands, under the feudal law, owed to their lords, and which, if withheld, the lord might resort to the writ of customs and services (*breve de consuetudinibus et servitiis*) to compel. Tomlin. See "De Consuetudinibus et Servitiis."

CUSTOMS CONSOLIDATION ACT. St. 16 & 17 Vict. c. 107, which has been frequently amended. See 2 Steph. Comm. 563.

CUSTOMS OF LONDON. Particular regulations in force within the city of London, in regard to trade, apprentices, widows and orphans, etc., which are recognized as forming part of the English common law. 1 Bl. Comm. 75.

CUSTOS. A custodian, guard, keeper, or warden; a magistrate.

CUSTOS BREVIUM (Lat.) Keeper of writs. An officer of the court of common pleas, whose duty it is to receive and keep all the writs returnable to that court, and put them upon file, and also to receive of the prothonotaries all records of *nisi prius*, called *posteas*. Blount. An officer in the king's bench, having similar duties. Cowell; Termes de la Ley. The office is now abolished.

CUSTOS FERARUM. A gamekeeper. Towns. Pl. 265.

CUSTOS HORREI REGII. Protector of the royal granary. 2 Bl. Comm. 394.

CUSTOS MARIS (Lat.) Warden or guardian of the seas. Among the Saxons, an admiral. Spelman, "Admiralius."

CUSTOS MORUM. The guardian of morals. The court of queen's bench has been so styled. 4 Steph. Comm. 377.

CUSTOS PLACITORUM CORONAE (Lat.) Keeper of the pleas of the crown (the criminal records). Said by Blount and Cowell to be the same as the *custos rotulorum.*

CUSTOS ROTULORUM (Lat.) Keeper of the rolls. The principal justice of the peace of a county, who is the keeper of the records of the county. 1 Bl. Comm. 349. He is always a justice of the peace and *quorum*, is the chief civil officer of the king in the county, and is nominated under the king's sign manual. He is rather to be considered a minister or officer than a judge. Blount; Cowell; Lambard, Eiren. lib. 4, c. 3, p. 373; 4 Bl. Comm. 272; 3 Steph. Comm. 37.

CUSTOS SPIRITUALIUM. In English ecclesiastical law. Keeper of the spiritualities; he who exercises the spiritual jurisdiction of a diocese during the vacancy of the see. Cowell.

CUSTOS STATUM HAEREDIS IN CUSTODIA EXISTENTIS MELIOREM NON DETERIOREM, FACERE POTEST. A guardian can make the estate of an heir living under his guardianship better, not worse. 7 Coke, 7.

CUSTOS TEMPORALIUM (Law Lat.) In English ecclesiastical law. Keeper of the temporalities. He to whose custody a vacant see or abbey was committed by the king, as supreme lord; who, as a steward of the goods and profits, was to give account to the escheator, and he into the exchequer. Cowell.

CUSTOS TERRAE. In old English law. Guardian, warden, or keeper of the land. Mag. Chart. c. 4.

CUSTUMA ANTIQUA SIVE MAGNA (Lat. ancient or great duties). The duties on wool, sheepskin, or wool pelts and leather exported were so called, and were payable by every merchant stranger as well as native, with the exception that merchant strangers paid one-half as much again as natives. 1 Sharswood, Bl. Comm. 314.

CUSTUMA PARVA ET NOVA (Lat.) An impost of three pence in the pound sterling on all commodities exported or imported by merchant strangers. Called at first the "Alien's duty," and first granted by St. 31 Edw. I. Maddox, Hist. Exch. 526, 532; 1 Sharswood, Bl. Comm. 314.

CUTH, or **COUTH** (Saxon). Known; knowing. *Uncuth,* unknown. See "Couthutlaugh"; "Uncuth."

CUTHRED. A knowing or skillful counsellor.

CUTPURSE (Law Lat. *bursarum scissor;* Law Fr. *cynsour de burse*). In old criminal law. An offender answering to the modern pickpocket. Fleta, lib. 1, c. 36, § 11.

CUTTER OF THE TALLIES. In old English law. An officer in the exchequer, to whom it belonged to provide wood for the tallies, and to cut the sum paid upon them, etc.

CY PRES (Law Fr. as near as). The rule of construction applied to a will, but not to a deed, by which, where the testator evinces a particular and a general intention, and the particular intention cannot take effect, the words shall be so construed as to give effect to the general intention. 3 Hare, 12; 2 Term R. 254; 2 Bligh, 49; Sugd. Powers, 60; 1 Spence, Eq. Jur. 532.

The principle is applied to sustain wills in which perpetuities are attempted to be created, so that, if it can possible be done, the devise is not regarded as utterly void, but is expounded in such a manner as to carry the testator's intention into effect as far as the law respecting perpetuities will allow. This is called a construction *cy pres.* Its rules are vague, and depend chiefly upon judicial discretion applied to the particular case. Sedgw. Const. Law, 265; Story, Eq. Jur. § 1169 et seq.

It is also applied to sustain devises and bequests for charity. Where there is a definite charitable purpose which cannot take place, the courts will not substitute another, as they once did; but if charity be the general substantial intention, though the mode provided for its execution fails, the English chancery will find some means of effectuating it, even by applying the fund to a different purpose from that contemplated by the testator, provided only it be charitable. Boyle, Char. 147, 155; Shelf. Mortm. 601; 3 Brown, Ch. 379; 4 Ves. 14; 7 Ves. 69, 82.

The doctrine is denied in Alabama (19 Ala. 814), Connecticut (22 Conn. 31), Delaware (2 Har. 18), Indiana (35 Ind. 198), Iowa (2 Iowa, 315), Maryland (5 Har. & J. 392), New York (23 N. Y. 298), North Carolina (37 N. C. 255), and Wisconsin (40 Wis. 276, 75 Wis. 431); but is in force in California (58 Cal. 457), Illinois (16 Ill. 225), Massachusetts (96 Mass. 539), Missouri (94 Mo. 459), Pennsylvania (51 Pa. St. 196), and Rhode Island (14 R. I. 412).

CYNEBOTE (Saxon, from *cyn,* kin, or relationship, and *bot,* a satisfaction). In Saxon law. A pecuniary composition for killing a relative; the same with *cenegild* (*q. v.*) Spelman, voc. "Cenegild."

CYPHONISM. A punishment used by the ancients, which some suppose to have been the smearing of the body with honey, and exposing the person to flies, wasps, etc. But the author of the notes on Hesychius says it is derived from the Greek, to bend or stoop, and signifies that kind of punishment still used by the Chinese, called by Sir George Staunton, "the wooden collar," by which the neck of the malefactor is bent or weighed down. Enc. Lond.; Wharton.

CYRCE (Saxon). A church.

CYRICBRYCE. In Saxon law. A breaking into a church. Blount.

CYROGRAPHARIUS. In old English law. A cyrographer; an officer of the common pleas court.

CYROGRAPHUM. A cirograph.

D

D. B. E. *De bene esse (q. v.)*.

D. B. N. *De bonis non*, a species of administration.

D. E. R. I. C. *De ea re ita consuere*, concerning this matter have decreed. A phrase used in the record of decrees of the Roman senate.

D. S. B. *Debitum sans* (or *sine*) *breve*.

DA TUA DUM TUA SUNT, POST MORtem tunc tua non sunt. Give the things which are yours whilst they are yours; after death then they are not yours. 3 Bulst. 18.

DABIS? DABO (Lat. will you give? I will give). In the Roman law. One of the forms of making a verbal stipulation. Inst. 3. 15. 1; Bracton, fol. 15b.

DACION. In Spanish law. The real and effective delivery of an object in the execution of a contract.

DAILY. Every day. A newspaper published six days in each week, whether Sunday or Monday be the day omitted, is held to be a "daily newspaper." 45 Minn. 27.

DAKER, or DIKER. Ten hides. Blount.

DALE and SALE. Fictitious names of places, used in the English books as examples. Perk. c. 2, § 152. "The manor of *Dale* and the manor of *Sale*, lying both in Vale." Bac. Abr. "Case of Revocation of Uses"; Perk. c. 3, § 230.

DALUS, DAILUS, or DAILIA. A certain measure of land; such narrow slips of pasture as are left between the plowed furrows in arable land. Cowell.

DAM. A construction of wood, stone, or other materials, made across a stream of water for the purpose of confining it; a mole.

DAMAGE. The loss caused by one person to another, or to his property, either with the design of injuring him, or with negligence and carelessness, or by inevitable accident. See "Damages."

DAMAGE CLEER. The tenth part in the common pleas, and the twentieth part in the king's bench and exchequer courts, of all damages beyond a certain sum, which was to be paid the prothonotary or chief officer of the court in which they were recovered before execution could be taken out. At first it was a gratuity, and of uncertain proportions. Abolished by St. 17 Car. II. c. 6. Cowell; Termes de la Ley.

DAMAGE FEASANT (Fr. *faisant dommage*, doing damage). A term usually applied to the injury which animals belonging to one person do upon the land of another by feeding there, and treading down his grass, corn, or other production of the earth. 3 Bl. Comm. 6; Co. Litt. 142, 161.

DAMAGED GOODS. In maritime law. Goods, subject to duties, which have received some injury either in the voyage home, or while bonded in warehouse.

DAMAGES. The indemnity recoverable by a person who has sustained an injury, either in his person, property, or relative rights, through the act or default of another.

The sum claimed as such indemnity by a plaintiff in his declaration.

The injury or loss for which compensation is sought.

The sums allowed by law for tortious injury or losses from breach of contract. 1 Suth. Dam. 3.

——**In Modern Law.** The term is not used in a legal sense to include the costs of suit, though it was formerly so used. Co. Litt. 267a; Doug. 751.

Damages are either direct or consequential.

(1) Direct are those which result immediately from the act complained of.

(2) Consequential are more remote consequences of such act. See "Consequential Damages."

Compensatory or exemplary; the latter being also called "punitive" or "vindictive."

(3) Compensatory damages are those allowed as recompense for the injury suffered.

(4) Exemplary damages are those allowed as a punishment for torts committed with fraud or actual malice. See "Exemplary Damages."

General or special.

(5) General damages are those necessarily and by implication of law resulting from the act or default complained of.

(6) Special damages are those arising directly, but not necessarily or by implication of law.

Liquidated or unliquidated.

(7) Liquidated damages are those whose amount has been determined by anticipatory agreement between the parties.

(8) Unliquidated damages are those not so fixed, but determined after they have resulted.

Substantial or nominal.

(9) Substantial damages are those allowed as actual compensation.

(10) Nominal damages are a trifling sum allowed where an infraction of a right is shown, but no resultant damage is proved. See "Nominal Damages."

DAMAIOUSE. In old English law. Causing damage or loss, as distinguished from *torcenouse*, wrongful. Britt. c. 61.

DAMNA (Lat. *damnum*). Damages, both inclusive and exclusive of costs.

DAMNI INJURIAE ACTIO (Lat.) In civil law. An action for the damage done by one who intentionally injured the beast of another. Calv. Lex.

DAMNOSA HAEREDITAS. A name given by Lord Kenyon to that species of property of a bankrupt which, so far from being valuable, would be a charge to the creditors; for example, a term of years, where the rent would exceed the revenue.

The assignees are not bound to take such property; but they must make their election, and, having once entered into possession, they cannot afterwards abandon the property. 7 East, 342; 3 Campb. 340.

DAMNUM ABSQUE INJURIA (Lat. injury without wrong). A wrong done to a man for which the law provides no remedy. Broom, Leg. Max. 1.

Damage sustained without the infraction of a legal right. 25 Conn. 265; 103 Ind. 314.

Injuria is here to be taken in the sense of "legal injury"; and, where no malice exists, there are many cases of wrong or suffering inflicted upon a man for which the law gives no remedy. 2 Ld. Raym. 595; 11 Mees. & W. 755; 11 Pick. (Mass.) 527; 10 Metc. (Mass.) 371. Thus, if the owner of property, in the prudent exercise of his own right of dominion, does acts which cause loss to another, it is *damnum absque injuria.* 2 Barb. (N. Y.) 168; 5 Barb. (N. Y.) 79; 10 Metc. (Mass.) 371; 10 Mees. & W. 109. See "Nominal Damages."

DAMNUM FATALE. In civil law. Damages caused by a fortuitous event, or inevitable accident; damages arising from the act of God. Among these were included losses by shipwreck, lightning, or other casualty; also losses by pirates, or by *vis major*, by fire, robbery, and burglary; but theft was not numbered among these casualties. In general, bailees are not liable for such damages. Story, Bailm. 471.

DAMNUM INFECTUM. In Roman law. Damage not yet committed, but threatened or impending. A preventive interdict might be obtained to prevent such damage from happening; and it was treated as a *quasi-delict*, because of the imminence of the danger.

DAMNUM REI AMISSAE. A loss arising from a payment made by a party in consequence of an error of law.

DAMNUM SINE INJURIA ESSE POTEST. There may be damage or injury inflicted without any act of injustice. Lofft, 112.

DAN. Anciently the better sort of men in England had this title; so the Spanish *Don.* The old term of honor for men, as we now say Master or Mister. Wharton.

DANEGELT. A tax or tribute imposed upon the English when the Danes got a footing in their island.

DANELAGE. The laws of the Danes which obtained in the eastern counties and part of the midland counties of England in the eleventh century. 1 Bl. Comm. 65.

DANGERIA. A money payment made by forest tenants, that they might have liberty to plow and sow in time of pannage, or mast feeding. Mann.

DANGEROUS WEAPON. A weapon calculated to cause death or great bodily harm. Guns, swords, knives, and the like, are dangerous weapons, as a matter of law. 110 N. C. 497; 1 Baldw. (U. S.) 78. Others are dangerous or not, according to their capability of causing great bodily harm in the manner in which they are used. Thus, a champagne bottle (33 Ga. 207), a chair (3 Tex. App. 13), a club (104 N. C. 786), a stone (10 Minn. 407) or a shovel (17 S. C. 55) may be a dangerous weapon.

DANGERS OF THE SEA. See "Perils of the Sea."

DANISM. The act of lending money on usury.

DANO. In Spanish law. Damage; the deterioration, injury, or destruction which a man suffers with respect to his person or his property by the fault (*culpa*) of another. White, New Recop. bk. 2, tit. 19, c. 3, § 1; Id. bk. 2, tit. 10, c. 12.

DANS ET RETINENS, NIHIL DAT. One who gives and yet retains does not give effectually. Tray. Lat. Max. 129. Or, one who gives yet retains [possession] gives nothing.

DAPIFER. A steward either of a king or lord. Spelman.

DARE. In the civil law. To transfer property. When this transfer is made in order to discharge a debt, it is *datio solvendi animo*; when in order to receive an equivalent, to create an obligation, it is *datio contrahendi animo;* lastly, when made *donandi animo*, from mere liberality, it is a gift, *dono datio.*

DARE AD REMANENTIAM. To give away in fee, or forever.

DARRAIGN. To clear a legal account; to answer an accusation; to settle a controversy.

DARREIN (Fr. *dernier*). Last. *Darrein continuance,* last continuance.

DARREIN PRESENTMENT (Law Fr.) In old English law. The last presentment. See "Assize of Darrein Presentment."

DARREIN SEISIN (Law Fr. last seisin). A plea which lay in some cases for the tenant in a writ of right. 3 Metc. (Mass.) 184; Jackson, Real Actions, 285. See 1 Roscoe, Real Actions, 206; 2 Prest. Abstr. 345.

DATA (from Lat. *dare*, to give). In old practice and conveyancing. The date of a deed; the time when it was given; that is, executed. Bl. Comm. Append. 1.

The date of a writ; the time when it was issued. Bracton, fol. 176.

DATE. The designation or indication in an instrument of writing of the time and place when and where it was made.

When the place is mentioned in the date of a deed, the law intends, unless the contrary appears, that it was executed at the place of the date. Plowd. 7b. The word is derived from the Latin *datum*, given; because, when instruments were in Latin, the form ran *datum*, etc., given the —— day of, etc.

The date of an instrument is that stated therein as that of its execution, rather than the actual time of execution. 32 N. J. Law, 515.

DATE CERTAINE. In French law. A fixed date; one made certain by the registration of the instrument.

DATIO. In civil law. A giving, or act of giving. *Datio in solutum*, a giving in payment; a species of accord and satisfaction. Called, in modern law, "dation."

Appointment or assignment. *Datio judicis*, the appointment of a judge to hear and determine a cause.

DATION. In civil law. The act of giving something. It differs from donation, which is a gift; dation, on the contrary, is giving something without any liberality; as, the giving of an office.

DATION EN PAIEMENT. In civil law. A giving by the debtor and receipt by the creditor of something in payment of a debt instead of a sum of money.

It is somewhat like the accord and satisfaction of the common law. 16 Toullier, Dr. Civ. note 45; Poth. Vente, note 601. *Dation en paiement* resembles in some respects the contract of sale; *dare in solutum est quasi vendere*. There is, however, a very marked difference between a sale and a *dation en paiement*. First, the contract of sale is complete by the mere agreement of the parties; the *dation en paiement* requires a delivery of the thing given. Second, when the debtor pays a certain sum which he supposed he was owing, and he discovers he did not owe so much, he may recover back the excess; not so when property other than money has been given in payment. Third, he who has in good faith sold a thing of which he believed himself to be the owner is not precisely required to transfer the property of it to the buyer; and, while he is not troubled in the possession of the thing, he cannot pretend that the seller has not fulfilled his obligations. On the contrary, the *dation en paiement* is good only when the debtor transfers to the creditor the property in the thing which he has agreed to take in payment; and if the thing thus delivered be the property of another, it will not operate as a payment. Poth. Vente, notes 602-604. See 1 Low. (U. S.) 53.

DATIVE.

——**In Old English Law.** In one's gift; that may be given and disposed of at will and pleasure. Applied to an officer in the sense of "removable," as distinguished from "perpetual." St. 9 Rich. II. c. 4; St. 45 Edw. III. cc. 9, 10; Cowell.

——**In Civil Law.** That which is given by the magistrate, as distinguished from that which is cast upon a party by the law or by a testator. Bouvier. A dative executor answers to the administrator of the common law. Code Louis, arts. 1671, 1672.

DATUM. A thing given.

DATUR DIGNIORI. It is given to the more worthy. 2 Vent. 268.

DAUGHTER. An immediate female descendant. See "Sons."

DAY. The space of time which elapses while the earth makes a complete revolution on its axis.

A portion of such space of time which, by usage or law, has come to be considered as the whole for some particular purpose.

The space of time which elapses between two successive midnights. 2 Bl. Comm. 141.

That portion of such space of time during which the sun is shining.

Generally, in legal signification, the term includes the time elapsing from one midnight to the succeeding one (2 Bl. Comm. 141), but it is also used to denote those hours during which business is ordinarily transacted, frequently called a "business" day (5 Hill [N. Y.] 437), as well as that portion of time during which the sun is above the horizon, called, sometimes, a "solar" day, and, in addition, that part of the morning or evening during which sufficient of his light is above for the features of a man to be reasonably discerned. Coke, 3d Inst. 63.

By custom, the word "day" may be understood to include working days only (3 Esp. 121), and, in a similar manner only, a certain number of hours less than the number during which the work actually continued each day (5 Hill [N. Y.] 437).

A day is generally, but not always, regarded in law as a point of time, and fractions will not be recognized. 15 Ves. 257; 2 Barn. & Ald. 586. And see 9 East, 154; 4 Campb. 397; 11 Conn. 17.

There is no indivisible unity about a day which prevents considering its component hours, in legal proceedings where it becomes important to the ends of justice, the rule that the law knows no divisions of a day being purely one of convenience, which must give way whenever the rights of parties require it. 37 Ill. 241.

DAY BOOK. In mercantile law. An account book in which merchants and others make entries of their daily transactions. This is generally a book of original entries, and, as such, may be given in evidence to prove the sale and delivery of merchandise, or of work done.

DAY RULE, or **DAY WRIT.** A rule or order of the court by which a prisoner on civil process, and not committed, is enabled, in term time, to go out of the prison and its rule or bounds. Tidd, Prac. 961. Abolished by 5 & 6 Vict. c. 22, § 12.

DAYBREAK. The dawn or first appearance of light in the morning. 167 Ill. App. 159.

DAYLIGHT. The daytime; between sunrise and sunset. 4 Bl. Comm. 224. Sufficient light, of day, to distinguish a man's features. 11 Car. & P. 297; 11 E. C. L. 398.

An insurance policy requiring lamps to be filled by daylight was held to mean not that they must be filled in the daytime, but that they must not be filled by artificial light. 134 U. S. 110.

DAYS IN BANK. In English practice. Days of appearance in the court of common pleas, usually called *bancum.* They are at the distance of about a week from each other, and are regulated by some festival of the church.

DAYS OF GRACE. In mercantile law. Certain days (generally three) allowed to the acceptor of a bill or the maker of a note in which to make payment, in addition to the time contracted for by the bill or note itself.

DAYSMAN. An arbitrator, umpire, or elected judge. Cowell.

DAYTIME. See "Daylight."

DAYWERE. As much arable land as could be ploughed in one day's work. Cowell.

DE. Of; about; concerning; respecting.

DE ACQUIRENDO RERUM DOMINIO. Of (about) acquiring the ownership of things. Dig. 11. 1; Bracton, lib. 2, fol. 8b.

DE ADMENSURATIONE. Of admeasurement.

Used of the writ of admeasurement of dower, which lies where the widow has had more dower assigned to her than she is entitled to. It is said by some to lie where either an infant heir or his guardian made such assignment, at suit of the infant heir whose rights are thus prejudiced. 2 Bl. Comm. 136; Fitzh. Nat. Brev. 348. It seems, however, that an assignment by a guardian binds the infant heir, and that, after such assignment, the heir cannot have his writ of admeasurement. 2 Ind. 388; 1 Pick. (Mass.) 314; 37 Me. 509; 1 Washb. Real Prop. 226.

Used also of the writ of admeasurement of pasture, which lies where the quantity of common due each one of several having rights thereto has not been ascertained. 3 Bl. Comm. 38. See "Admeasurement of Dower."

DE ADVISAMENTO CONSILII NOSTRI (Law Lat. with or by the advice of our council). A phrase used in the old writs of summons to parliament. Reg. Jud. Append. 7. 8; Crabb, Hist. Eng. Law, 240.

DE AEQUITATE. In equity. *De jure stricto, nihil possum vendicare, de aequitate tamen, nullo modo hoc obtinet,* in strict law, I can claim nothing, but in equity this by no means obtains. Fleta, lib. 3, c. 2, § 10.

DE AESTIMATO. In Roman law. One of the innominate contracts, and, in effect, a sale of land or goods at a price fixed (*aestimato*) and guaranteed by some third party, who undertook to find a purchaser.

DE AETATE PROBANDA (Law Lat.) Writ of (about) proving age. An old writ which lay to the escheator or sheriff of a county to summon a jury to inquire whether the heir of a tenant *in capite,* claiming his estate on the ground of full age, was, in fact, of age or not. Reg. Orig. 294; Fitzh. Nat. Brev. 257.

DE ALEATORIBUS. About gamesters. Dig. 11. 5.

DE ALLOCATIONE FACIENDA (Lat. for making allowance). A writ to allow the collectors of customs, and other such officers having charge of the king's money, for sums disbursed by them.

It was directed to the treasurer and barons of the exchequer.

DE ALTO ET BASSO. Of high and low. A phrase anciently used to denote the absolute submission of all differences to arbitration. Cowell; 2 Reeve, Hist. Eng. Law, 90.

DE AMBITU (Lat. concerning bribery). *Ambitus* (bribery) was the subject of several of the Roman laws; as, the *Lex Aufidia,* the *Lex Pompeia,* the *Lex Tullia,* and others. See "Ambitus."

DE ANNO BISSEXTILI. Of the bissextile or leap year. The title of a statute passed in the twenty-first year of Henry III., which in fact, however, is nothing more than a sort of writ or direction to the justices of the bench, instructing them how the extraordinary day in the leap year was to be reckoned in cases where persons had a day to appear at the distance of a year, as on the essoin *de malo lecti,* and the like. It was thereby directed that the additional day should, together with that which went before, be reckoned only as one, and so, of course, within the preceding year. 1 Reeve, Hist. Eng. Law, 266.

DE ANNUA PENSIONE (Lat. of annual pension). A writ by which the king, having due unto him an annual pension from any abbot or prior for any of his chaplains which he will name who is not provided with a competent living, demands it of the said abbot or prior for the one that is named in the writ. Fitzh. Nat. Brev. 231; Termes de la Ley.

DE ANNUO REDITU (Lat. for a yearly rent). A writ to recover an annuity, no matter how payable. 2 Reeve, Hist. Eng. Law, 258.

DE APOSTATA CAPIENDO (Lat. for taking an apostate). A writ directed to the sheriff for the taking the body of one who, having entered into and professed some order of religion, leaves his order and departs from his house and wanders in the country. Fitzh. Nat. Brev. 233; Termes de la Ley.

DE ARBITRATIONE FACTA (Lat. of arbitration had). A writ formerly used when an action was brought for a cause which had been settled by arbitration. Watson Arb. 256.

DE ARRESTANDIS BONIS NE DISSIpentur. An old writ which lay to seize goods in the hands of a party during the pendency of a suit, to prevent their being made away with. Reg. Orig. 126b.

DE ARRESTANDO IPSUM QUI PECUniam recepit. A writ which lay for the arrest of one who had taken the king's money to serve in the war, and hid himself to escape going. Reg. Orig. 24b; Blount.

DE ARTE ET PARTE. Of art and part. A phrase in old Scotch law. 1 Pitcairn, pt. 2, p. 55. See "Art and Part."

DE ASPORTATIS RELIGIOSORUM. Concerning the property of religious persons carried away. The title of St. 35 Edw. I. passed to check the abuses of clerical possessions, one of which was the waste they suffered by being drained into foreign countries. 2 Reeve, Hist. Eng. Law, 157; 2 Inst. 580.

DE ASSISA PROROGANDA (Lat. for proroguing assize). A writ to put off an assize issuing to the justices, where one of the parties is engaged in the service of the king.

DE ATTORNATO RECIPIENDO (Lat. for receiving an attorney). A writ to compel the judges to receive an attorney and admit him for the party. Fitzh. Nat. Brev. 156b.

DE AUDIENDO ET TERMINANDO. For hearing and determining; to hear and determine.

The name of a writ or commission granted to certain justices to hear and determine cases of heinous misdemeanor, trespass, riotous breach of the peace, etc. Reg. Orig. 123 et seq.; Fitzh. Nat. Brev. 110 (B). See "Oyer and Terminer."

DE AVERIIS CAPTIS IN WITHERNAM (Lat. for cattle taken in withernam). A writ which lies to take other cattle of the defendant where he has taken and carried away cattle of the plaintiff out of the country, so that they cannot be reached by replevin. Termes de la Ley; 3 Sharswood, Bl. Comm. 149.

DE AVERIIS REPLEGIANDIS (Lat.) A writ to replevy beasts. 3 Bl. Comm. 149.

DE AVERIIS RETORNANDIS (Lat. for returning cattle). Used of the pledges in the old action of replevin. 2 Reeve, Hist. Eng. Law, 177.

DE BENE ESSE (Lat. formally; conditionally; provisionally). A technical phrase applied to certain acts deemed for the time to be well done, or until an exception or other avoidance. It is equivalent to "provisionally," with which meaning the phrase is commonly employed. For example, a declaration is filed or delivered, special bail is put in, a witness is examined, etc., *de bene esse*, or provisionally.

DE BIEN ET DE MAL. See "De Bono et Malo."

DE BIENS LE MORT (Law Fr.). Of the goods of the deceased. Dyer, 32.

DE BIGAMIS. Concerning men twice married. The title of St. 4 Edw. I. st. 3; so-called from the initial words of the fifth chapter. 2 Inst. 272; 2 Reeve, Hist. Eng Law, 142.

DE BONE MEMORIE (Law Fr.) Of good memory; of sound mind. St. Mod. Lev. Fines; 2 Inst. 510.

DE BONIS ASPORTATIS (Lat. for goods carried away). The name of the action for trespass to personal property is trespass *de bonis asportatis.* Buller, N. P. 836; 1 Tidd, Prac. 5.

DE BONIS NON. See "Administration."

DE BONIS NON ADMINISTRATIS (Law Lat. of the goods not administered). Where the administration of the estate of an intestate is left unfinished, in consequence of the death, removal, etc., of the administrator, and a new administrator is appointed, the latter is termed an administrator *de bonis non; i. e.*, of the goods of the deceased not administered by the former administrator. 2 Steph. Comm. 243. An administrator of this kind is also sometimes appointed to succeed an executor. Id.

DE BONIS NON AMOVENDIS (Law Lat.) Writ for not removing goods. A writ anciently directed to the sheriffs of London. commanding them, in cases where a writ of error was brought by a defendant against whom a judgment was recovered, to see that his goods and chattels were safely kept without being removed, while the error remained undetermined, so that execution might be had of them, etc. Reg. Orig. 131b; Termes de la Ley. This seems to have been a local writ.

DE BONIS PROPRIIS (Lat. of his own goods). A judgment against an executor or administrator which is to be satisfied from his own property.

When an executor or administrator has been guilty of a *devastavit*, he is responsible for the loss which the estate has sustained *de bonis propriis*. He may also subject himself to the payment of a debt of the deceased *de bonis propriis* by his false plea when sued in a representative capacity; as, if he plead *plene administravit*, and it be found against him, or a release to him when false. In this latter case the judgment is *de bonis testatoris si, et si non de bonis propriis*. 1 Wm. Saund. 336b, note 10; Bac. Abr. "Executor" (B 3).

DE BONIS TESTATORIS (Lat. of the goods of the testator). A judgment rendered against an executor which is to be satisfied out of the goods or property of the testator. Distinguished from a judgment *de bonis propriis*.

DE BONIS TESTATORIS AC SI (Lat.) From the goods of the testator, if he has any, and, if not, from those of the executor. A judgment rendered where an executor falsely pleads any matter as a release, or, generally, in any case where he is to be charged in case his testator's estate is insufficient. 1 Wm. Saund. 366b; Bac. Abr. "Executor" (B 3); 2 Archb. Prac. 148.

DE BONO ET MALO (Lat. for good or ill). A person accused of crime was said to put himself upon his country *de bono et malo*. The French phrase *de bien et de mal* has the same meaning.

A special writ of gaol delivery, one being issued for each prisoner; now superseded by the general commission of gaol delivery. 4 Bl. Comm. 270.

DE BONO GESTU. For good behavior.

DE CAETERO, or **DE CETERO**. Henceforth; henceforward; hereafter; in the future.

DE CALCETO REPARENDO (Lat.) A writ for repairing a highway, directed to the sheriff, commanding him to distrain the inhabitants of a place to repair the highway. Reg. Orig. 154; Blount.

DE CAPITALIBUS DOMINIS FEODI. Of the chief lords of the fee.

A phrase in ancient charters, denoting the tenure by which the estate was granted to be held. 2 Bl. Comm. 298, 299.

DE CAPITE MINUTIS. Of those who have lost their status, or civil condition. Dig. 4. 5. See "Capitas Deminutio."

DE CARTIS REDDENDIS (Lat. for restoring charters). A writ to secure the delivery of charters; a writ of detinue. Reg. Orig. 159b.

DE CATALLIS REDDENDIS (Law Lat.) Writ for rendering chattels. A writ to compel the specific delivery of chattels detained from the owner. Reg. Orig. 139b; Old Nat. Brev. 63. A writ of detinue. Fitzh. Nat. Brev. 138; Cowell.

DE CAUTIONE ADMITTENDA (Lat. for admitting bail). A writ directed to a bishop who refused to allow a prisoner to go at large on giving sufficient bail, requiring him to admit him to bail. Fitzh. Nat. Brev. 63c

DE CERTIFICANDO. A writ requiring a thing to be certified; a kind of *certiorari*. Reg. Orig. 151, 152b.

DE CERTIORANDO. A writ for certifying. A writ directed to the sheriff, requiring him to certify to a particular fact. Reg. Orig. 24.

DE CHAMPERTIA. Writ of champerty. A writ directed to the justices of the bench, commanding the enforcement of the statute of *champertors*. Reg. Orig. 193; Fitzh. Nat. Brev. 172. See "Champerty."

DE CHAR ET DE SANK (Law Fr. of flesh and blood). *Affaire rechat de char et de sank*. Words used in claiming a person to be a villein, in the time of Edward II. Y. B. P. 1 Edw. II. p. 4.

DE CHIMINO. A writ for the enforcement of a right of way; a species of *quo permittat*. Reg. Orig. 155.

DE CIBARIIS UTENDIS. Of victuals to be used. The title of a sumptuary statute passed 10 Edw. III. st. 3, to restrain the expense of entertainments. Barr. Obs. St. 240.

DE CLAMIA ADMITTENDA IN ITINERE per attornatum (Law Lat.) An ancient writ, by which the king commanded the justices in eyre to admit a person's claim by attorney, who was employed in the king's service, and could not come in his own person. Reg. Orig. 19b.

DE CLARO DIE. By daylight. Fleta, lib. 2, c. 76, § 8.

DE CLAUSO FRACTO. Of close broken; of breach of close. See "Clausum Fregit."

DE CLERICO CAPTO PER STATUTUM mercatorium deliberando. Writ for delivering a clerk arrested on a statute merchant. A writ for the delivery of a clerk out of prison, who had been taken and imprisoned upon the breach of a statute merchant. Reg. Orig. 147b.

DE CLERO (Law Lat.) Concerning the clergy. The title of St. 25 Edw. III. st. 3; containing a variety of provisions on the subject of presentations, indictments of spiritual persons, and the like. 2 Reeve, Hist. Eng. Law, 378; Crabb, Hist. Eng. Law, 270.

DE COMBUSTIONE DOMORUM. Of house burning. One of the kinds of appeal formerly in use in England. Bracton, fol. 146b; 2 Reeve, Hist. Eng. Law, 38.

DE COMMUNI DIVIDENDO. In civil law. A writ of partition of common property. See "Communi Dividendo."

DE COMON DROIT (Law Fr.) Of common right; that is, by the common law. Co. Litt. 142a.

DE COMPUTO. Writ of account. A writ commanding a defendant to render a reasonable account to the plaintiff, or show cause to the contrary. Reg. Orig. 135-138; Fitzh. Nat. Brev. 117 (E). The foundation of the modern action of account.

DE CONCILIO CURIAE. See "De Consilio Curiae."

DE CONFLICTU LEGUM. Concerning the conflict of laws. The title of several works written on that subject. 2 Kent, Comm. 455.

DE CONJUNCTIM FEOFFATIS. Concerning persons jointly enfeoffed, or seised. The title of St. 34 Edw. I., which was passed to prevent the delay occasioned by tenants in novel disseisin, and other writs, pleading that some one else was seised jointly with them. 2 Reeve, Hist. Eng. Law, 243.

DE CONSANGUINEO. Writ of cosinage (*q. v.*) Reg. Orig. 226; Co. Litt. 160a.

DE CONSILIO. In old criminal law. Of counsel; concerning counsel or advice to commit a crime. Fleta, lib. 1, c. 31, § 8.

DE CONSILIO CURIAE. By the advice or direction of the court. Bracton, fol. 345b.

DE CONSUETUDINIBUS ET SERVICIIS (Law Lat.) Writ of customs and services. A writ which lay for a lord against his tenant, who withheld from him or deforced him of the rents and services due by custom or tenure for his land. Reg. Orig. 159; Fitzh. Nat. Brev. 151; Bracton, fol. 83; 3 Bl. Comm. 232; Roscoe, Rea. Actions, 32. See "Custom."

DE CONTINUANDO ASSISAM. Writ to continue an assize. Reg. Orig. 217b.

DE CONTRIBUTIONE FACIENDA (Law Lat.). Writ for making contribution. A writ, founded on the statute of Marlbridge (chapter 9), to compel coparceners, or tenants in common, to aid the eldest in performing the services due by him, or to make contribution, where the services had been already performed. Reg. Orig. 176b; Fitzh. Nat. Brev. 162 (B), (C); 2 Reeve, Hist. Eng. Law, 327; 3 Reeve, Hist. Eng. Law, 55; Crabb, Hist. Eng. Law, 212.

DE CONTUMACE CAPIENDO (Law Lat.) Writ for taking a contumacious person. A writ which issues out of the English court of chancery in cases where a person has been pronounced by an ecclesiastical court to be contumacious, and in contempt. Shelf. Mar. & Div. 494-496, and notes. It is a commitment for contempt. Id. 504, 505; 5 Adol. & E. (N. S.) 335.

DE COPIA LIBELLI DELIBERANDA (Law Lat.) Writ for delivering the copy of a libel. An ancient writ directed to the judge of a spiritual court, commanding him to deliver to a defendant a copy of the libel filed against him in such court. Reg. Orig. 58. The writ in the register is directed to the dean of Arches, and his commissary. Id. See "Copia."

DE CORONATORE ELIGENDO (Law Lat.) Writ for electing a coroner. A writ issued to the sheriff in England, commanding him to proceed to the election of a coroner, which is done in full county court (*in pleno comitatu*), the freeholders being the electors. Reg. Orig. 177; Reg. Jud. Appendix, 19; 1 Bl. Comm. 347; 3 Steph. Comm. 31; Sewell, Sheriffs, 372. A writ of this kind was issued as late as May, 1852. See 35 Eng. Law & Eq. 136.

DE CORONATORE EXONERANDO (Law Lat.) Writ for discharging or removing a coroner. A writ by which a coroner in England may be removed from office for some cause therein assigned. Fitzh. Nat. Brev. 163, 164; 1 Bl. Comm. 348; Sewell, Sheriffs, 373.

DE CORPORE COMITATUS. From the body of the county at large, as distinguished from a particular neighborhood (*de vicineto*). 3 Bl. Comm. 360.

DE CORRODIO HABENDO. Writ for having a corody. A writ to exact a corody from a religious house. Reg. Orig. 264; Fitzh. Nat. Brev. 230. See "Corody."

DE CURIA CLAUDENDA (Lat. of inclosing a court). An obsolete writ, to require a defendant to fence in his court or land about his house, where it was left open to the injury of his neighbor's freehold. 1 Crabb, Real Prop. 314; 6 Mass. 90.

DE CURSU. Of course. Reg. Orig. 29b. The formal proceedings in an action, as distinguished from those incidental proceedings that may be taken in summons, petition, or motion, all of which latter are called "summary proceedings."

DE CUSTODE ADMITTENDO. Writ for admitting a guardian. Reg. Orig. 93b, 198.

DE CUSTODE AMOVENDO. Writ for removing a guardian. Reg. Orig. 198.

DE CUSTODIA TERRAE ET HAEREDIS. Writ of ward, or writ of right of ward. A writ which lay for a guardian in knight's service or in socage, to recover the possession and custody of the infant, or the wardship of the land and heir. Reg. Orig. 161b; Fitzh. Nat. Brev. 139 (B); 3 Bl. Comm. 141.

DE DEBITO. Writ of debt. Reg. Orig. 139. Fitzh. Nat. Brev. 119 (C), 121.

DE DEBITORE IN PARTES SECANDO. Of cutting a debtor in pieces. This was the name of a law contained in the Twelve Tables, the meaning of which has occasioned much controversy. Some commentators have concluded that it was literally the privilege of the creditors of an insolvent debtor (all other means failing) to cut his body into pieces and distribute it among them. Others contend that the language of this law must be taken figuratively, denoting a cutting up and apportionment of the debtor's estate.

The latter view has been adopted by Montesquieu, Bynkershoek, Heineccius, and Taylor. Esprit des Lois, liv. 29, c. 2; Bynk. Obs. Jur. Rom. lib. 1, c. 1; Heinec. Ant. Rom. lib. 3, tit. 30, § 4; Tayl. Comm. Leg. Dec. The literal meaning, on the other hand, is advocated by Aulus Gellius and other writers of antiquity, and receives support from an expression (*semoto omni cruciatu*) in the Roman code itself. Aul. Gel. Noctes Atticae, lib. 20, c. 1; Code, 7. 7. 8. This is also the opinion of Gibbon, Gravina, Pothire, Hugo, and Niehbuhr. 3 Gib. Rom. Emp. (Am. Ed.) p. 183; Grav. de Jur. Nat. Gent. et XII. Tab. § 72; Poth. Introd. ad Pand.; Hugo, Hist. du Droit Rom. tom. i. p. 233, § 149; 2 Niehb. Hist. Rom. p. 597; 1 Kent, Comm. 523, note.

DE DECEPTIONE. A writ of deceit which lay against one who acted in the name of another, whereby the latter was damnified and deceived. Reg. Orig. 112; Fitzh. Nat. Brev. 95 (E); Reg. Jud. 9b. 10.

DE DEONERANDA PRO RATA PORtionis. A writ that lay where one was distrained for rent that ought to be paid by others proportionately with him. Fitzh. Nat. Brev. 234; Termes de la Ley.

DE DIE IN DIEM. From day to day. Bracton, fol. 205b; Holt, C. J., 6 Mod. 252.

DE DIVERSIS REGULIS JURIS ANtiqui. Of diverse rules of the ancient law. A celebrated title of the Digests, and the last in that collection. It consists of two hundred and eleven rules or maxims. Dig. 50. 17.

DE DOLO MALO. Of or founded upon fraud. Dig. 4. 3. See "Actio de Dolo Malo."

DE DOMO REPARANDA (Lat.) The name of an ancient common-law writ, by which one tenant in common might compel his cotenant to concur in the expense of repairing the property held in common. 8 Barn. & C. 269; 1 Thomas, Co. Litt. 216, note 17, and page 787.

DE DONIS. See "Estates."

DE DONIS, THE STATUTE (more fully, *de bonis conditionalibus*, concerning conditional gifts). St. Edw. I. c. 1.

The object of the statute was to prevent the alienation of estates by those who held only a part of the estate in such a manner as to defeat the estate of those who were to take subsequently. By introducing perpetuities, it built up great estates, and strengthened the power of the barons. See Bac. Abr. "Estates Tail"; 1 Cruise, Dig. 70; 1 Washb. Real Prop. 271.

DE DOTE ASSIGNANDA (Lat. for assigning dower). A writ commanding the king's escheator to assign dower to the widow of a tenant *in capite*. Fitzh. Nat. Brev. 263c.

DE DOTE UNDE NIHIL HABET (Lat. of dower in that whereof she has none). A writ of dower which lay for a widow where no part of her dower had been assigned to her. It is now much disused; but a form closely resembling it is still much used in the United States. 4 Kent, Comm. 63; Stearns, Real Actions, 302; 1 Washb. Real Prop. 230.

DE EJECTIONE CUSTODIAE (Law Lat.; Law Fr. *ejectment de gard*). Writ of ejectment of ward. A writ which lay where a guardian had been forcibly ejected from his wardship. Reg. Orig. 162.

DE EJECTIONE FIRMAE. A writ which lay at the suit of the tenant for years against the lessor, reversioner, remainderman, or stranger who had himself deprived the tenant of the occupation of the land during his term. 3 Bl. Comm. 199. Originally lying to recover damages only, it came to be used to recover the rest of the term, and then generally the possession of lands. Involving, in the question of who should have possession, the further question of who had the title, it gave rise to the modern action of ejectment. Brooke, Abr.; Adams, Ej.; 3 Sharswood, Bl. Comm. 199 et seq.

DE ESCAETA. A writ of escheat which lay for the lord to recover the land where the tenant died without an heir. Reg. Orig. 194.

DE ESCAMBIO MONETAE. A writ of exchange of money. An ancient writ to authorize a merchant to make a bill of exchange *literas cambitorias facere*. Reg. Orig. 194.

DE ESSE IN PEREGRINATIONE. Of being on a journey. A species of essoin. 1 Reeve, Hist. Eng. Law, 119.

DE ESSENDO QUIETUM DE THEOlonio (or **tolonio**) (Law Lat.) Writ of being quit of toll. A writ which lay for citizens and burgesses of any city or borough, and other persons, who, by charter or prescription, were exempted from toll, to enforce such exemption. Reg. Orig. 258b-261; Fitzh. Nat. Brev. 226 (I). An action was brought on such a writ as late as 29 Geo. III. 1 H. Bl. 206.

DE ESSONIO DE MALO LECTI. Writ of essoin of *malum lecti.* A writ which issued upon an essoin of *malum lecti* being cast, to examine whether the party was in fact sick or not. Reg. Orig. 8b. See "De Malo Lecti."

DE ESTOVERIIS HABENDIS (Lat. to obtain estovers). A writ which lay for a woman divorced *a mensa et thoro* to recover her alimony or estovers. 1 Bl. Comm. 441.

DE ESTREPAMENTO (Law Lat.) Writ of estrepement. A writ to prevent or stop the commission of waste in lands by a tenant during the pendency of a suit against him for their recovery. Reg. Orig. 76b; Fitzh. Nat. Brev. 60; 3 Bl. Comm. 225, 226. Abolished by St. 3 & 4 Wm. IV. c. 27. See "Estrepement."

DE EU ET TRENE (Law Fr.) Of water and whip of three cords. A term applied to a neife, that is, a bond woman or female villein, as employed in servile work, and subject to corporal punishment. Co. Litt. 25b.

DE EVE ET DE TREVE (Law Fr.; Lat. *de avo et de tritavo*). From grandfather and great-grandfather's, great-grandfather. A phrase used in year books in cases where a party was claimed by another as his villein, as descriptive of the ancestral rights of lords in such cases.

DE EXCOMMUNICATO CAPIENDO (Lat. for taking one who is excommunicated). A writ commanding the sheriff to arrest one who was excommunicated, and imprison him till he should become reconciled to the church. 3 Bl. Comm. 102.

DE EXCOMMUNICATO DELIBERANDO (Lat. for freeing one excommunicated). A writ to deliver an excommunicated person, who has made satisfaction to the church, from prison. 3 Bl. Comm. 102.

DE EXCOMMUNICATO RECAPIENDO (Law Lat.) Writ for retaking an excommunicated person, where he has been liberated from prison, without making satisfaction to the church, or giving security for that purpose. Reg. Orig. 67.

DE EXCUSATIONIBUS (Lat. of excuses). The first title of the twenty-seventh book of the Digests is so denominated, as treating of the circumstances which would excuse persons from serving in the offices of tutor or curator. It is made up, in a great degree, of extracts from the Greek work of Herennius Modestinus on the subject.

DE EXECUTIONE FACIENDA IN WITHernamium (Law Lat.) Writ for making execution in withernam. Reg. Orig. 82b. A species of *capias in withernam.*

DE EXECUTIONE JUDICII (Law Lat.) Writ of execution of judgment. A writ directed to a sheriff or bailiff, commanding him to do execution upon a judgment. Reg. Orig. 18; Fitzh. Nat. Brev. 20; 3 Reeve, Hist. Eng. Law, 56.

DE EXEMPLIFICATIONE. Writ of exemplification. A writ granted for the exemplification of an original. Reg. Orig. 290b.

DE EXONERATIONE SECTAE. A writ to free the king's ward from suit in any court lower than the court of common pleas during the time of such wardship.

DE EXPENSIS CIVIUM ET BURGENsium. An obsolete writ addressed to the sheriff to levy the expenses of every citizen and burgess of parliament. 4 Inst. 46.

DE EXPENSIS MILITUM NON LEVANdis (Law Lat.) Writ for levying the expenses of knights. A writ directed to the sheriff for levying the allowance for knights of the shire in parliament. Reg. Orig. 191b.

DE FACTO. Actually; in fact; in deed. A term used to denote a thing actually done.

An officer *de facto* is one who performs the duties of an office with apparent right, and under claim and color of an appointment, but without being actually qualified in law so to act. 37 Me. 423. See "Officer."

An officer in the actual exercise of executive power would be an officer *de facto,* and as such distinguished from one who, being legally entitled to such power, is deprived of it; such a one being an officer *de jure* only. An officer holding without strict legal authority. 2 Kent, Comm. 295. An officer *de facto* is frequently considered an officer *de jure,* and legal validity allowed his official acts. 10 Serg. & R. (Pa.) 250; 11 Serg. & R. (Pa.) 411; 1 Coxe (N. J.) 318; 10 Mass. 290; 15 Mass. 180; 5 Pick. (Mass.) 487; 25 Conn. 278; 5 Wis. 308; 24 Barb. (N. Y.) 587; 37 Me. 423; 19 N. H. 115; 2 Jones (N. C.) 124; 2 Swan (Tenn.) 87.

An officer *de facto* is *prima facie* one *de jure.* 21 Ga. 217.

A wife *de facto* only is one whose marriage is voidable by decree. 4 Kent, Comm. 36.

Blockade *de facto* is one actually maintained. 1 Kent, Comm. 44 et seq.

A corporation is a *de facto* corporation where there is a law authorizing such a corporation, and where the company has made an effort to organize under law and is transacting business in a corporate name. 238 Ill. 108.

DE FALSO JUDICIO. Writ of false judgment. Reg. Orig. 15; Fitzh. Nat. Brev. 18. See "False Judgment."

DE FALSO MONETA. Of false money. The title of St. 27 Edw. I., ordaining that persons importing certain coins, called "pollards," and "crokards," should forfeit their lives and goods, and everything they could forfeit. 2 Reeve, Hist. Eng. Law, 228, 229.

DE FEODO. This phrase is applied, in old statutes to officers who have their offices in fee.

De feodo suo; of his fee; belonging to his fee. Fleta, lib. 2, c. 47, § 15. *Forestarius de feodo;* forester of fee. Cart. de Forest. c. 14. *Marescallus de feodo;* marshal of fee. Stat. Westm. 2, c. 42. *In dominco. In demesne.* (*q. v.*)

DE FIDE ET OFFICIO JUDICIS NON recipitur quaestio, sed de scientia sive sit error juris sive facti. The *bona fides* and honesty of purpose of a judge cannot be questioned, but his decision may be impugned for error either of law or of fact. Bac. Max. reg. 17; 5 Johns. (N. Y.) 291; 9 Johns. (N. Y.) 396; 1 N. Y. 45; Broom, Leg. Max. (3d London Ed.) 82.

DE FIDEI LAESIONE. Of breach of faith or fidelity. 4 Reeve, Hist. Eng. Law, 99.

DE FINE CAPIENDO PRO TERRIS (Law Lat.) A writ which lay for a juror who had been attained for giving a false verdict, to obtain the release of his person, lands, and goods, on payment of a certain fine to the king. Reg. Orig. 232. See "Attaint."

DE FINE FORCE (Law. Fr.) Of necessity; of pure necessity. Dyer, 41. See "Fine Force."

DE FINE NON CAPIENDO PRO PULchre placitando (Law Lat.) A writ prohibiting the taking of fines for beaupleader. Reg. Orig. 179. See "Beaupleader."

DE FINE PRO REDISSEISINA CApiendo (Law Lat.) A writ which lay for the release of one imprisoned for a redisseisin, on payment of a reasonable fine. Reg. Orig. 222b.

DE FINIBUS LEVATIS. Concerning fines levied. The title of St. 27 Edw. I., requiring fines thereafter to be levied, to be read openly and solemnly in court. 2 Inst. 521; Barr. Obs. St. 176.

DE FORISFACTURE MARITAGII. A writ of forfeiture of marriage. Reg. Orig. 163, 164.

DE FRANGENTIBUS PRISONAM. Concerning those that break prison. The title of St. 1 Edw. II., ordaining that none from thenceforth who broke prison should have judgment of life or limb for breaking prison only, unless the cause for which he was taken and imprisoned required such a judgment if he was lawfully convicted thereof. 2 Reeve, Hist. Eng. Law, 290; 2 Inst. 589.

DE FURTO. Of theft. One of the kinds of criminal appeal formerly in use in England. 2 Reeve, Hist. Eng. Law, 40.

DE GESTU ET FAMA. Of behavior and reputation. An old writ which lay in cases where a person's conduct and reputation were impeached. Lambard, Eiren. lib. 4, c. 14.

DE GRATIA. Of grace or favor; by favor. Fleta, lib. 2, c. 57, § 11. *De speciali gratia,* of special grace or favor. Id.

DE GRATIA SPECIALI CERTA SCIENtia et mero motu, talis clausula non valet in his in quibus praesumitur principem esse ignorantem. The clause "of our special grace, certain knowledge, and mere motion," is of no avail in those things in which it is presumed that the prince was ignorant. 1 Coke, 53.

DE GROSSIS ARBORIBUS DECIMAE non dabuntur sed de sylvia caedua decimae dabuntur. Of whole trees, tithes are not given; but of wood cut to be used, tithes are given.

DE HAEREDE DELIBERANDO ALTERI qui habet custodiam terrae. An ancient writ, directed to the sheriff, to require one that had the body of an heir, being in ward, to deliver him to the person whose ward he was by reason of his land. Reg. Orig. 161.

DE HAEREDE DELIBERANDO ILLI QUI habet custodiam terrae. Writ for delivering an heir to him who has wardship of the land. A writ directed to the sheriff, to require one that had the body of him that was ward to another to deliver him to the person whose ward he was by reason of his land. Reg. Orig. 161.

DE HAEREDE RAPTO ET ABDUCTO. Writ concerning an heir ravished and carried away. A writ which anciently lay for a lord who, having by right the wardship of his tenant under age, could not obtain his body, the same being carried away by another person. Reg. Orig. 163; Old Nat. Brev. 93.

DE HAERETICO COMBURENDO (Lat. for burning a heretic). A writ which lay where a heretic had been convicted of heresy, had abjured, and had relapsed into heresy. Said to be very ancient. 4 Bl. Comm. 46.

DE HOMAGIO RESPECTUANDO. A writ for respiting or postponing homage. Fitzh. Nat. Brev. 269 (A).

DE HOMINE CAPTO IN WITHERNAM (Lat. for taking a man in withernam). A writ to take a man who had carried away a bondman or bondwoman into another country beyond the reach of a writ of replevin. 3 Bl. Comm. 129.

DE HOMINE REPLEGIANDO (Lat. for replevying a man). A writ which lies to replevy a man out of prison, or out of the custody of a private person, upon giving security to the sheriff that the man shall be forthcoming to answer any charge against him. Fitzh. Nat. Brev. 66; 3 Bl. Comm. 129. The statute—which had gone nearly out of use, having been superseded by the writ of *habeas corpus*—has been revived within a few years in some of the United States in an amended and more effectual form. 1 Kent. Comm. 404, note; Gen. St. Mass. c. 144, § 42 et seq.

DE IDENTITATE NOMINIS. A writ which lay for one arrested in a personal action, and committed to prison under a mistake as to his identity, the proper defendant bearing the same name. Reg. Orig. 194.

DE IDIOTA INQUIRENDO (Law Lat.) A writ to inquire whether a man be an idiot or not. Reg. Orig. 266; Fitzh. Nat. Brev. 232 (A); 1 Bl. Comm. 303.

DE IIS QUI PONENDI SUNT IN ASSISIS. Of those who are to be put on assizes. The title of a statute passed 21 Edw. I., defining the qualifications of jurors. Crabb, Hist. Eng. Law, 167, 189; 2 Reeve, Hist. Eng. Law, 184.

DE INCREMENTO (Lat. of increase). Costs *de incremento*, costs of increase,—that is, which the court assesses in addition to the damages established by the jury. See "Costs de Incremento."

DE INFIRMITATE. Of infirmity. The principal essoin in the time of Glanville; afterwards called "*de malo*." 1 Reeve, Hist. Eng. Law, 115. See "De Malo"; Essoin."

DE INGRESSU. A writ of entry. Bracton, fols. 318, 319. Reg. Orig. 227b, 231, 235-237; Cowell.

DE INJURIA (Lat.) The full form is *de injuria sua propria absque tali causa*, of his own wrong without such cause; or, where part of the plea is admitted, *absque residuo causae*, without the rest of the cause.

——**In Pleading.** The replication by which in an action of tort the plaintiff denies the effect of excuse or justification offered by the defendant.

It can only be used where the defendant pleads matter merely in excuse and not in justification of his act. It is confined to those instances in which the plea neither denies the original existence of the right which the defendant is charged with having violated, nor alleges that it has been released or extinguished, but sets up some new matter as a sufficient excuse or cause for that which would otherwise and in its own nature be wrongful. It cannot, therefore, be properly used when the defendant's plea alleges any matter in the nature of title, interest, authority, or matter of record. 8 Coke, 66; 1 Bos. & P. 76; 4 Johns. (N. Y.) 159, note; 5 Johns. (N. Y.) 112; 12 Johns (N. Y.) 491; 1 Wend. (N. Y.) 126; 8 Wend. (N. Y.) 129; 25 Vt. 328; Steph. Pl. 276.

DE INOFFICIOSO TESTAMENTO. Concerning an inofficious or undutiful will. A title of the civil law. Dig. 5, 2; Inst. 2, 18.

DE INTEGRO. Anew; a second time. 1 Vern. 223, 232.

As it was before. 5 Maule & S. 222.

DE INTRUSIONE. A writ of intrusion; where a stranger entered after the death of the tenant, to the injury of the revisioner. Reg. Orig. 233b.

DE JACTURA EVITANDA. For avoiding a loss. A phrase applied to a defendant, as *de lucro captando* is to a plaintiff. 1 Litt. (Ky.) 51.

DE JUDAISMO, STATUTUM. The name of a statute passed in the reign of Edward I., which enacted severe penalties against the Jews. Barr. Obs. St. 197.

DE JUDICATO SOLVENDO. For payment of the amount adjudged. A term applied in the Scotch law to bail to the action, or special bail. Clerke, Prax. tit. 11.

DE JUDICIIS. Of judicial proceedings. The title of the second part of the Digests or Pandects, including the fifth, sixth, seventh, eighth, ninth, tenth, and eleventh books. See Dig. proem. § 3.

DE JUDICIO SISTI. For appearing in court. A term applied in the Scotch and admiralty law to bail for a defendant's appearance. Clerke, Prax. tit. 11.

DE JURE. Rightfully; of right; lawfully; by legal title. Contrasted with *de facto* (*q. v.*) 4 Bl. Comm. 77.

Of right; distinguished from *de gratia*, by favor. By law, distinguished from *de aequitate*, by equity.

DE JURE DECIMARUM, ORIGINEM ducens de jure patronatus, tunc cognitio spectat at legem civilem, i. e., communem. With regard to the right of tithes, deducing its origin from the right of the patron, then the cognizance of them belongs to the civil law,—that is, the common law. Godb. 63.

DE JURE JUDICES, DE FACTO JURAtores, respondent. The judges answer concerning the law, the jury concerning the facts. See Co. Litt. 295; Broom, Leg. Max. (3d London Ed.) 99.

DE LA PLUS BELLE (Fr. of the fairest). A kind of dower. So called because assigned from the best part of the husband's estate. It was connected with the military tenures, and was abolished, with them. by

St. 12 Car. II. c. 24. Litt. § 48; 2 Bl. Comm. 132, 135; 1 Washb. Real Prop. 149, note.

DE LATERE. From the side; on the side; collaterally; of collaterals. Code, 5. 5. 6.

DE LEGATIS ET FIDEI COMMISSIS. Of legacies and trusts. Dig. 30.

DE LEPROSO AMOVENDO. Writ for removing a leper. A writ to remove a leper who thrust himself into the company of his neighbors in any parish, in public or private places, to their annoyance. Reg. Orig. 267; Fitzh. Nat. Brev. 234 (E); New Nat. Brev. 521.

DE LIBERA FALDA. Writ of free fold. A species of *quod permittat.* Reg. Orig. 155.

DE LIBERA PISCARIA. Writ of free fishery. A species of *quod permittat.* Reg. Orig. 155.

DE LIBERO PASSAGIO. Writ of free passage. A species of *quod permittat.* Reg. Orig. 155.

DE LIBERTATE PROBANDA. Writ for proving liberty. A writ which lay for such as, being demanded for villeins or niefs, offered to prove themselves free. Reg. Orig. 87b; Fitzh. Nat. Brev. 77 (F).

DE LIBERTATIBUS ALLOCANDIS (Lat. for allowing liberties). A writ, of various forms, to enable a citizen to recover the liberties to which he was entitled. Fitzh. Nat. Brev. 229; Reg. Orig. 262.

DE LICENTIA TRANSFRETANDI. Writ of permission to cross the sea. An old writ directed to the wardens of the port of Dover, or other seaport in England, commanding them to permit the persons named in the writ to cross the sea from such port, on certain conditions. Reg. Orig. 193b.

DE LUNATICO INQUIRENDO (Lat.) The name of a writ directed to the sheriff, directing him to inquire by good and lawful men whether the party charged is a lunatic or not. See 4 Rawle (Pa.) 234; 1 Whart. (Pa.) 52; 5 Halst. (N. J.) 217; 6 Wend. (N. Y.) 497.

DE MAGNA ASSISA ELIGENDA (Law Lat.) Writ of or for choosing the grand assize. A writ directed to the sheriff to summon four lawful knights, before the justices of assize, there upon their oaths, to choose twelve knights of the vicinage to be joined with them, which sixteen knights constituted the grand assize, or great jury, which was to try the matter of right in a writ of right. Reg. Orig. 8; Fitzh. Nat. Brev. 4 (F); 3 Bl. Comm. 351. Abolished by St. 3 & 4 Wm. IV. c. 27. See "Grand Assize."

DE MAJORI ET MINORI NON VARIANT jura. Concerning major and minor, laws do not vary. 2 Vern. 552.

DE MALO. Of illness. See "De Malo Lecti."

DE MALO LECTI (Law Lat.; Law Fr. *de mal de lyt*). Of infirmity or illness of (in) bed. Closely rendered, in old Scotch law, bed-evil (*bedde-evill*). A species of essoin or excuse for nonappearance in court, formerly allowed a defendant in England, and more anciently called *de infirmitate de reseantisa;* the excuse being that the defendant was confined to his house in bed (*lectus*) by infirmity or indisposition (*malum*). Glanv. lib. 1, c. 18, 19; Bracton, fol. 337, 344b; Britt. cc. 122, 123; Fleta, lib. 6, c. 10; 1 Reeve, Hist. Eng. Law, 115, 412; Skene de Verb. Sign. voc. "Reseantisa." This essoin commonly followed immediately upon that *de malo veniendi* (infra); for where a person, having been detained on the road by sickness, and having cast the essoin *de malo veniendi,* had found himself obliged to return home, the order of essoins, conformably with what was likely to be the real fact, led to the essoin *de malo lecti.* 1 Reeve, Hist. Eng. Law, 412; Bracton, fol. 344b.

DE MANUCAPTIARE (Lat. of mainprize). A writ directed to the sheriff, commanding him to take sureties for the prisoner's appearance,—usually called mainpernors,—and to set him at large. Fitzh. Nat. Brev. 250; 1 Hale, P. C. 141; Coke, "Bail & Mainprize," c. 10; Reg. Orig. 268b.

DE MANUTENENDO. Writ of maintenance. A writ which lay against a person for the offense of maintenance. Reg. Orig. 182b, 189.

DE MEDIETATE LINGUAE. See "Medietas Linguae."

DE MEDIO (Lat. of the *mesne*). A writ in the nature of a writ of right, which lies where, upon a subinfeudation, the *mesne* (or middle) lord suffers his under tenant or tenant *paravail* to be distrained upon by the lord paramount for the rent due him from the *mesne* lord. Booth, Real Actions, 136; Fitzh. Nat. Brev. 135; 3 Sharswood, Bl. Comm. 234; Co. Litt. 100a.

DE MELIORIBUS DAMNIS (Lat.) Of the better damages. When a plaintiff has sued several defendants, and the damages have been assessed severally against each, he has the choice of selecting the best, as he cannot recover the whole. This is done by making an election *de melioribus damnis.*

DE MERCATORIBUS, THE STATUTE. The statute of Acton Burnell. See "Acton Burnell."

DE MINIMIS NON CURAT LEX. The law does not notice (or care for) trifling matters. Broom, Leg. Max. (3d London Ed.) 134; Hob. 88; 5 Hill (N. Y.) 170.

DE MINIS. Writ of threats. A writ which lay where a person was threatened with personal violence, or the destruction of his property, to compel the offender to keep the peace. Reg. Orig. 88b, 89; Fitzh. Nat. Brev. 79 (G), 80.

DE MITTENDO TENOREM RECORDI. A writ to send the tenor of a record, or to exemplify it under the great seal. Reg. Orig. 220b.

DE MODERATA MISERICORDIA CApienda. Writ for taking a moderate amercement. A writ, founded on *Magna Charta* (c. 14), which lay for one who was excessively amerced in a court not of record, directed to the lord of the court, or his bailiff, commanding him to take a moderate amercement of the party. Reg. Orig. 86b; Fitzh. Nat. Brev. 75, 76.

DE MODO DECIMANDI (Lat. of a manner of taking tithes). A prescriptive manner of taking tithes, different from the general law of taking tithes in kind. It is usually by a compensation either in work or labor, and is generally called a *modus*. 1 Keb. 162; 1 Rolle, Abr. 649; 1 Lev. 179; Cro. Eliz. 446; Salk. 657; 2 P. Wms. 462; 2 Russ. & M. 102; 4 Younge & C. 269, 283; 12 East, 35; 2 Sharswood, Bl. Comm. 29 et seq.; 3 Steph. Comm. 130.

DE MOLENDINO DE NOVO ERECTO non jacet prohibitio. A prohibition lies not against a new-erected mill. Cro. Jac. 429.

DE MORTE HOMINIS NULLA EST cunctatio longa. When the death of a human being may be concerned, no delay is long. Co. Litt. 134. When the question is concerning the life or death of a man, no delay is too long to admit of inquiring into facts.

DE NATIVO HABENDO (Law Lat.; Law Fr. *briefe de naife*). Writ for having one's villein. A writ which lay for a lord whose villein had fled from him (*fugitivo*), directed to the sheriff, commanding him to apprehend the villein, and restore him, with all his chattels, to the lord. Reg. Orig. 87; Fitzh. Nat. Brev. 77; Roscoe, Real Actions, 34.

DE NOMINE PROPRIO NON EST CUrandum cum in substantia non erretur; quia nomina mutabilia sunt, res autem immobiles. As to the proper name, it is not to be regarded when one errs not in substance; because names are changeable, but things are immutable. 6 Coke, 66.

DE NON APPARENTIBUS ET NON EXistentibus eadem est lex. The law is the same respecting things which do not appear and those which do not exist. 6 Ired. (N. C.) 61; 12 How. (U. S.) 253; 5 Coke, 6; 6 Bing. N. C. 453; 7 Clark & F. 872; 5 C. B. 53; 8 C. B. 286; 1 Term R. 404; Broom, Leg. Max. (3d London Ed.) 150.

DE NON DECIMANDO (Lat. of not taking tithes). An exemption by custom from paying tithes is said to be a prescription *de non decimando*. A claim to be entirely discharged of the payment of tithes, and to pay no compensation in lieu of them. Cro. Eliz. 511; 3 Sharswood, Bl. Comm. 31.

DE NON PROCEDENDO AD ASSISAM. Writ for not proceeding to take an issue. A writ, directed to the justices assigned to hold assizes, commanding them not to proceed to take an assize in a particular case. Reg. Orig. 221.

DE NON RESIDENTIA CLERICI REGIS. An ancient writ where a parson was employed in the royal service, etc., to excuse and discharge him of nonresidence. 2 Inst. 264.

DE NON SANE MEMORIE (Law Fr.) Of unsound memory or mind; a phrase synonymous with *non compos mentis*. Litt. § 405; Plowd. 368. Stock, Non Compos Mentis, 1.

DE NOVI OPERIS NUNCIATIONE (Lat.) In civil law. A form of injunction or interdict which lies in some cases for the party aggrieved, where a thing is intended to be done against his right. Thus, where one builds a house contrary to the usual and received form of building, to the injury of his neighbor, there lies such an injunction, which, being served, the offender is either to desist from his work, or to put in sureties that he shall pull it down if he does not in a short time avow, *i. e.*, show, the lawfulness thereof. Ridley, Civ. & Ecc. Law, pt. 1, c. 1, § 8.

DE NOVO (Lat.) Anew; afresh. When a judgment upon an issue in part is reversed on error for some mistake made by the court in the course of the trial, a *venire de novo* is awarded, in order that the case may again be submitted to a jury.

DE NULLO, QUO EST SUA NATURA indivisible, et divisionem non patitur, nullam partem habebit vidua, sed satisfaciat ei ad valentiam. A widow shall have no part from that which in its own nature is indivisible, and is not susceptible of division, but let the heir satisfy her with an equivalent. Co. Litt. 32.

DE NULLO TENEMENTO, QUOD TENEtur ad terminum, fit homagii, fit tamen inde fidelitatis sacramentum. In no tenement which is held for a term of years is there an avail of homage; but there is the oath of fealty. Co. Litt. 67b.

DE ODIO ET ATIA (Lat. of hatred and ill will). A writ directed to the sheriff, commanding him to inquire whether a person charged with murder was committed upon just cause of suspicion, or merely *propter odium et atiam*, through hatred and ill will; and if, upon the inquisition, due cause of suspicion did not appear, then there issued another writ for the sheriff to admit him to bail. 3 Sharswood, Bl. Comm. 128.

DE OFFICE (Law Fr.) Of office; in virtue of office; officially; in the discharge of ordinary duty. *Le court d'office est tenu*, the court is bound in virtue of its office. Y. B. H. 4 Hen. VI. 16.

The phrase corresponds to the Latin *virtute officii.*

DE ONERANDO PRO RATA PORTIONE. Writ for charging according to a ratable proportion. A writ which lay for a joint tenant, or tenant in common, who was distrained for more rent than his proportion of the land came to. Reg. Orig. 182; Fitzh. Nat. Brev. 234 (H).

DE PACE ET LEGALITATE TUENDA (Law Lat.) For keeping the peace, and for good behavior. *Tradat fidejussores de pace et legalitate tuenda*, he shall deliver or find sureties for keeping the peace and good behavior. LL. Edw. Conf. c. 18; 4 Bl. Comm. 252, 254; Spelman, voc. "Legalitas."

DE PACE ET PLAGIS. Of peace (breach of peace), and wounds. One of the kinds of criminal appeal formerly in use in England, and which lay in cases of assault, wounding, and breach of the peace. Bracton, fol. 144; 2 Reeve, Hist. Eng. Law, 33.

DE PACE ET ROBERIA. Of peace (breach of peace) and robbery. One of the kinds of criminal appeal formerly in use in England, and which lay in cases of robbery and breach of the peace. Bracton, fol. 146; 2 Reeve, Hist. Eng. Law, 37.

DE PALABRA (Spanish). By word; by parol. White, New Recop. bk. 2, tit. 19, c. 3, § 2.

DE PARCO FRACTO (Lat. of pound breach). A writ which lay where cattle taken in distress were rescued by their owner after being actually impounded. Fitzh. Nat. Brev. 100; 3 Bl. Comm. 146; Reg. Orig. 116b; Co. Litt. 47b.

DE PARTITIONE FACIENDA (Lat. for making partition). The ancient writ for the partition of lands held by tenants in common.

DE PERAMBULATIONE FACIENDA (Lat. for making a perambulation). A writ which lay where there was a dispute as to the boundaries of two adjacent lordships or towns, directed to the sheriff, commanding him to take with him twelve discreet and lawful knights of his county, and make the perambulation, and set the bounds and limits in certainty. Fitzh. Nat. Brev.

DE PIGNORE SURREPTO FURTI, ACtio. In civil law. An action to recover a pledge stolen. Inst. 4. 1. 14.

DE PIPA VINI CARIANDA. A writ of trespass for carrying a pipe of wine so carelessly that it was stove, and the contents lost. Reg. Orig. 110. Alluded to by Sir William Jones in his remarks on the case of Coggs v. Barnard, 2 Ld. Raym. 909. Jones, Bailm. 59.

DE PLACITO (Law Lat. of a plea; of or in an action). Formal words used in declarations and other proceedings, as descriptive of the particular action brought. *De placito debiti*, of a plea of debt; *de placito conventionis fractae*, of a plea of breach of covenant; *de placito transgressionis*, of a plea of trespass; *de placito transgressionis super casum*, of a plea of trespass on the case. Towns. Pl. 162-165. See the older forms in Fleta, lib. 2, c. 65, § 12. See "Placitum."

DE PLAGIS ET MAHEMIO. Of wounds and mayhem. The name of a criminal appeal formerly in use in England in cases of wounding and maiming. Bracton, fol. 144b; 2 Reeve, Hist. Eng. Law, 34. See "Appeal."

DE PLANO (Lat.)

—**In Civil Law.** Without form; in a summary manner. The praetor was said to administer justice in this way (*de plano cognoscere*) when he did so standing on the ground, or on the same level with the suitors, instead of occupying a tribunal (*pro tribunali*) elevated seat, or "bench," as it was termed in the English law. See "Bench." The French *de plain* is derived from this.

—**In Common Law.** Clearly; manifestly. The phrase is used in this classical sense in the statute De Bigamis (4 Edw. I.).

By covin or collusion. St. Westminster II. c. 4. This did not mean by default. Id.; 2 Inst. 349. See 2 Reeve, Hist. Eng. Law, 191; 4 Reeve, Hist. Eng. Law, 23. 34. 36.

—**In Scotch Practice.** Forthwith. 2 Alison, Prac. 650.

DE PLEGIIS ACQUIETANDIS (Lat. for clearing pledges). A writ which lay where one had become surety for another to pay a sum of money at a specified day, and the principal failed to pay it. If the surety was obliged to pay, he was entitled to this writ against his principal. Fitzh. Nat. Brev. 37 (C); 3 Reeve, Hist. Eng. Law, 65.

DE PONENDO SIGILLUM AD EXCEPtionem. Writ for putting a seal to an exception. A writ by which justices were formerly commanded to put their seals to exceptions taken by a party in a suit. Reg. Orig. 182.

DE POST DISSEISINA. Writ of post disseisin. A writ which lay for him who, having recovered lands or tenements by *praecipe quod reddat*, on default, or reddition, was again disseised by the former disseisor. Reg. Orig. 208; Fitzh. Nat. Brev. 190.

DE PRAEROGATIVA REGIS (Law Lat. of the king's prerogative). The title of St. 17 Edw. II. st. 1, defining the prerogatives of the crown on certain subjects, partly of a feudal and partly of a political or general nature. Crabb, Hist. Eng. Law, 204 et seq.;

Barr. Obs. St. 202; Hale, Hist. Com. Law, c. 8.

DE PRAESENTI. Of the present; in the present tense. See "Per Verba de Praesenti."

DE PROPRIETATE PROBANDA (Lat. for proving property). A writ which issues in a case of replevin, when the defendant claims property in the chattels replevied, and the sheriff makes a return accordingly. The writ directs the sheriff to summon an inquest to determine on the validity of the claim; and, if they find for the defendant, the sheriff merely returns their finding. The plaintiff is not concluded by such finding. He may come into the court above and traverse it. Hammond, N. P. 456.

DE QUIBUS SUR DISSEISIN. An ancient writ of entry.

DE QUO, or **DE QUIBUS.** Of which. Formal words in the simple writ of entry, from which it was called a writ of entry "in the *quo*," or "in the *quibus*." 3 Reeve, Hist. Eng. Law, 33.

DE QUOTA LITIS (Lat.) In civil law. A contract by which one who has a claim difficult to recover agrees with another to give a part, for the purpose of obtaining his services to recover the rest. 1 Duv. note 201. See "Champerty."

DE RAPTU VIRGINUM. Of the ravishment of maids. The name of an appeal formerly in use in England in cases of rape. Bracton, fol. 147; 2 Reeve, Hist. Eng. Law, 38.

DE RATIONABILI PARTE BONORUM (Lat. of a reasonable part of the goods). A writ to enable the widow and children of a decedent to recover their proper shares of the inheritance. 2 Bl. Comm. 492. The writ is said to be founded on the customs of the counties, and not on the common-law allowance. Fitzh. Nat. Brev. 122 (L).

DE RATIONALIBUS DIVISIS (Lat. for reasonable boundaries). A writ which lies to determine the boundaries between the lands of two proprietors, which lie in different towns. The writ is to be brought by one against the other. Fitzh. Nat. Brev. 128 (M); 3 Reeve, Hist. Eng. Law, 48.

DE REBUS. Of things. The title of the third part of the Digests or Pandects, comprising the twelfth, thirteenth, fourteenth, fifteenth, sixteenth, seventeenth, eighteenth, and nineteenth books.

DE REBUS DUBIIS. Of doubtful things or matters. Dig. 34. 5.

DE RECORDO ET PROCESSU MITTENdis. Writ to send the record and process of a cause to a superior court; a species of writ of error. Reg. Orig. 209.

DE RECTO. Writ of right. Reg. Orig. 1, 2; Bracton, fol. 327b.

DE RECTO DE ADVOCATIONE (Lat. of right of advowson; called, also, *de droit de advocatione*). A writ which lay to restore the right of presentation to a benefice, for him who had an advowson, to himself and heirs in fee simple, if he was disturbed in the presentation. Y. B. 39 Hen. VI. 20a; Fitzh. Nat. Brev. 30 (B).

DE RECTO DE RATIONABILI PARTE. Writ of right of reasonable part. A writ which lay between privies in blood, as between brothers in gavelkind, or between sisters or other coparceners for lands in fee simple, where one was deprived of his or her share by another. Reg. Orig. 3b; Fitzh. Nat. Brev. 9 (B). Abolished by St. 3 & 4 Wm. IV. c. 27.

DE RECTO PATENS. Writ of right patent. Reg. Orig. 1.

DE REDISSEISINA. Writ of redisseisin. A writ which lay where a man recovered, by assize of novel disseisin, land, rent, or common, and the like, and was put in possession thereof by verdict, and afterwards was disseised of the same land, rent, or common by him by whom he was disseised before. Reg. Orig. 206b; Fitzh. Nat. Brev. 188 (B).

DE REPARATIONE FACIENDA (Lat.) The name of a writ which lies by one tenant in common against the other, to cause him to aid in repairing the common property. 8 Barn. & C. 269.

DE RESCUSSU. Writ of rescue. A writ which lay where cattle distrained, or persons arrested, were rescued from those taking them. Reg. Orig. 117, 118; Fitzh. Nat. Brev. 101 (C), (G).

DE RETORNO HABENDO (Lat.) The name of a writ issued after a judgment has been given in replevin that the defendant should have a return of the goods replevied. See 3 Bouv. Inst. note 3376.

DE RIEN CULPABLE (Law Fr.) Guilty of nothing; not guilty. Y. B. H. 7 Edw. II. 224; Keilw. 3b.

DE SA VIE (Law Fr.) Of his or her life; of his own life; as distinguished from *pur autre vie*, for another's life Litt. §§ 35, 36; Crabb, Hist. Eng. Law, 383.

DE SALVA GUARDIA (Lat. of safeguard). A writ to protect the persons of strangers seeking their rights in English courts. Reg. Orig. 26.

DE SALVO CONDUCTU. A writ of safeconduct. Reg. Orig. 25b, 26.

DE SCACCARIO. Of or concerning the exchequer. The title of a statute passed in the fifty-first year of Henry III. 2 Reeve, Hist. Eng. Law, 61.

DE SCUTAGIO HABENDO (Lat. of having scutage). A writ which lay in case a man held lands of the king by knight's service, to which homage, fealty, and escuage were appendant, to recover the services or fee due in case the knight failed to accompany the king to the war. It lay also for the tenant *in capite*, who had paid his fee, against his tenants. Fitzh. Nat. Brev. 83 (C).

DE SE BENE GERENDO. For behaving himself well; for his good behavior. Yelv. 90, 154.

DE SECTA AD MOLENDINUM (Lat. of suit to a mill). A writ which lies to compel one to continue his custom of grinding at a mill. 3 Bl. Comm. 235; Fitzh. Nat. Brev. 122 (M); 3 Reeve, Hist. Eng. Law, 55.

DE SIMILIBUS AD SIMILIA EADEM ratione procedendum est. From similars to similars we are to proceed by the same rule. Branch, Princ.

DE SIMILIBUS IDEM EST JUDICIUM. Concerning similars the judgment is the same. 7 Coke, 18.

DE SON TORT (Fr.) Of his own wrong. This term is usually applied to a person who, having no right to meddle with the affairs or estate of a deceased person, yet undertakes to do so by acting as executor of the deceased. See "Executor."

DE STATUTO MERCATORIO (Law Lat.) Writ of statute merchant. A writ which lay for imprisoning him who had forfeited a statute-merchant bond until the debt was satisfied. Reg. Orig. 146b. There are several writs under this head. Id. 148; Reg. Jud. 8. See "Statute Merchant."

DE STATUTO STAPULAE (Law Lat.) Writ of statute staple. A writ that lay to take the body to prison, and seize upon the lands and goods of one who had forfeited the bond called "statute staple." Reg. Orig. 151. See "Statute Staple."

DE SUPERONERATIONE PASTURAE (Lat. of surcharge of pasture). A writ lying where one who had been previously impleaded in the county court was again impleaded in the same court for surcharging common of pasture, and the cause was removed to Westminster Hall. Reg. Jur. 36b.

DE TABULIS EXHIBENDIS. Of showing the tablets of a will. Dig. 43. 5.

DE TALLAGIO NON CONCEDENDO (Lat. of not allowing talliage). The name given to St. 34 Edw. I., restricting the power of the king to grant talliage. Coke, 2d Inst. 532; 2 Reeve, Hist. Eng. Law, 104.

DE TEMPORE CUJUS CONTRARIUM memoria hominum non existat (Law Lat.) From time whereof the memory of man does not exist to the contrary. Litt. § 170.

DE TEMPORE IN TEMPUS, ET AD OMnia tempora. From time to time, and at all times. Towns, Pl. 17.

DE TEMPS DONT MEMORIE NE COURT (Law Fr.) From time whereof memory runneth not; time out of memory of man. Litt. §§ 143, 145, 170; Dyer, 70.

DE TESTAMENTIS. Of testaments. The title of the fifth part of the Digests or Pandects; comprising the twenty-eighth to the thirty-sixth books, both inclusive.

DE THEOLONIO. A writ which lay for a person who was prevented from taking toll. Reg. Orig. 103.

DE TRANSGRESSIONE. A writ of trespass. Reg. Orig. 92.

DE TRANSGRESSIONE, AD AUDIENdum et terminandum. A writ or commission for the hearing and determining any outrage or misdemeanor. 2 Reeve, Hist. Eng. Law, 170.

DE UNA PARTE (Lat.) A deed *de una parte* is one where only one party grants, gives, or binds himself to do a thing to another. It differs from a deed *inter partes* (*q. v.*) 2 Bouv. Inst. note 2001.

DE UXORE RAPTA ET ABDUCTA (Lat. of a wife ravished and carried away). A kind of writ of trespass. Fitzh. Nat. Brev. 89 (O); 3 Sharswood, Bl. Comm. 139.

DE VASTO. Writ of waste. A writ which might be brought by him who had the immediate estate of inheritance in reversion or remainder, against the tenant for life, in dower, by curtesy, or for years, where the latter had committed waste in lands; calling upon the tenant to appear and show cause why he committed waste and destruction in the place named, to the disinherison (*ad exhaeredationem*) of the plaintiff. Reg. Orig. 72-75; Reg. Jud. 17b; Fitzh. Nat. Brev. 55 (C); 3 Bl. Comm. 227, 228. Abolished by St. 3 & 4 Wm. IV. c. 27; 3 Steph. Comm. 506.

DE VENTRE INSPICIENDO (Lat. of inspecting the belly). A writ to inspect the body, where a woman feigns to be pregnant, to see whether she is with child. It lies for the heir presumptive to examine a widow suspected to be feigning pregnancy in order to enable a supposititious heir to obtain the estate. 1 Bl. Comm. 456; 2 Steph. Comm. 308; Cro. Eliz. 556; Cro. Jac. 685; 2 P. Wms. 593; 21 Viner, Abr. 547.

It lay also where a woman sentenced to death pleaded pregnancy. 4 Bl. Comm. 495. This writ has been recognized in America. 2 Chand. Am. Crim. Tr. 381.

DE VERBO IN VERBUM. Word for word. Bracton, fol. 138b. Literally, from word to word. Fleta uses *de verbo ad verbum*. Lib. 1, c. 21, § 3.

DE VERBORUM SIGNIFICATIONE. Of the signification of words. An important title of the Digests or Pandects (Dig. 50. 16), consisting entirely of definitions of words and phrases used in the Roman law, compiled from the writings of the best jurists, such as Ulpian, Paulus, Pomponius, Gaius, Scaevola, Javolenus, Celsus, Alfenus, Florentinus, Callistratus, and others.

DE VI LAICA AMOVENDA. Writ of (or for) removing lay force. A writ which lay where two parsons contended for a church, and one of them entered into it with a great number of laymen, and held out the other *vi et armis;* then he that was holden out had this writ directed to the sheriff, that he remove the force. Reg. Orig. 59; Fitzh. Nat. Brev. 54 (D).

DE VICINETO (Lat. from the neighborhood). The sheriff was anciently directed in some cases to summon a jury *de vicineto.* 3 Bl. Comm. 360.

DE WARRANTIA CHARTAE (Lat. of warranty of charter). This writ lieth properly where a man doth enfeoff another by deed, and bindeth himself and heirs to warranty. Now, if the defendant be impleaded in an assize, or in a writ of entry in the nature of an assize, in which actions he cannot vouch, then he shall have the writ against the feoffor or his heirs who made such warranty. Fitzh. Nat. Brev. 134 (D); Cowell; Termes de la Ley; Blount; 3 Reeve, Hist. Eng. Law, 55.

DE WARRANTIA DIEI. A writ which lay for a party in the service of the king who was required to appear in person on a certain day, commanding the justices not to record his default, the king certifying to the fact of such service. Fitzh. Nat. Brev. 36.

DEACON. In ecclesiastical law. A minister or servant in the church, whose office in some churches is to assist the priest in divine service, and in the distribution of the sacrament.

DEAD BODY. A corpse.

DEAD BORN. A dead-born child is to be considered as if it had never been conceived or born; in other words, it is presumed it never had life, it being a maxim of the common law that *mortuus exitus non est exitus.* Co. Litt. 29b. See 2 Paige, Ch. (N. Y.) 35; Domat, liv. prel. tit. 2, § 1, notes 4, 6; 4 Ves. 334.

This is also the doctrine of the civil law. Dig. 50. 16. 120. *Non nasci, et natum mori, pari sunt,* not to be born, and to be born dead, are equivalent. *Mortuus exitus non est exitus,* a dead birth is no birth. Civ. Code La. art. 28.

DEAD FREIGHT. The amount paid by a charterer for that part of the vessel's capacity which he does not occupy, although he has contracted for it.

When the charterer of a vessel has shipped part of the goods on board, and is not ready to ship the remainder, the master, unless restrained by his special contract, may take other goods on board, and the amount which is not supplied, required to complete the cargo, is considered dead freight. The dead freight is to be calculated according to the actual capacity of the vessel. 3 Chit. Com. Law, 399; 2 Starkie, 450.

DEAD LETTERS. Letters transmitted through the mails according to direction, and remaining for a specified time uncalled for by the persons addressed, are called "dead letters."

DEAD MAN'S PART. That portion of the personal estate of a person deceased which, by the custom of London, became the administrator's.

If the decedent left wife and children, this was one-third of the residue after deducting the widow's chamber. If only a widow, or only children, it was one-half. 1 P. Wms. 341; Salk. 246. If neither widow nor children, it was the whole. 2 Show, 175. This provision was repealed by St. 1 Jac. II. c. 17, and the same made subject to the statute of distributions. 2 Sharswood, Bl. Comm. 5. 8.

DEAD PLEDGE. A mortgage.

DEAD RENT. A rent payable on a mining lease in addition to a royalty. So called because it is payable, although the mine may not be worked. Wharton.

DEAD USE. A future use.

DEADHEAD. A term applied to persons other than the officers or employes of a railroad company who are permitted by the railroad to travel without payment of fare. Phil. Law (61 N. C.) 22.

DEADLY FEUD (Lat. *faida mortalis,* or *mortifera*). A profession of irreconcilable hatred against an enemy, until revenge were obtained even by his death. This was allowed by the ancient Saxon laws, where a man had been killed, and no pecuniary satisfaction had been made to his kindred. Spelman, voc. "Faida." The term was also applied to the predatory warfare carried on in the northern borders of England. St. 43 Eliz. c. 13; 4 Bl. Comm. 244. See "Faida."

DEADLY WEAPON. A dangerous weapon (*q. v.*)

DEAD'S PART. In Scotch law. The part remaining over beyond the shares secured to the widow and children by law. Of this the testator had the unqualified disposal. Stair, Inst. lib. iii. tit. 4, § 24; Bell, Dict.; Paterson, Comp. §§ 674, 848, 902.

DEAFFOREST. In old English law. To discharge from being forest; to free from forest laws.

DEALER. One who buys to sell again. 27 Pa. St. 495.

DEALINGS. Transactions in the course of business. Two sales of goods by one to a firm constitute "dealings" with it, so as to entitle one to notice of dissolution. 2 Barb. (N. Y.) 549.

DEAN. In ecclesiastical law. An ecclesiastical officer, who derives his name from the fact that he presides over ten canons, or prebendaries, at least.

There are several kinds of deans, namely, deans of chapters; deans of peculiars; rural deans; deans in the colleges; honorary deans; deans of provinces.

DEAN AND CHAPTER. In ecclesiastical law. The council of a bishop, to assist him with their advice in the religious and also in the temporal affairs of the see. 3 Coke, 75; 1 Bl. Comm. 382; Co. Litt. 103, 300; Termes de la Ley; 2 Burn, Ecc. Law, 120.

DEAN OF THE ARCHES. The presiding judge of the court of arches. He is also an assistant judge in the court of admiralty. 1 Kent, Comm. 371; 3 Steph. Comm. 727.

DEATH. The cessation of life; the ceasing to exist.

Civil death is the state of a person who, though possessing natural life, has lost all his civil rights, and as to them is considered as dead.

A person convicted and attainted of felony, and sentenced to the state prison for life, is, in the state of New York, in consequence of the act of March 29, 1799, and by virtue of the conviction and sentence of imprisonment for life, to be considered as civilly dead. 6 Johns. Ch. (N. Y.) 118; 4 Johns. Ch. (N. Y.) 228, 260; Laws N. Y. Sess. 24, c. 49, §§ 29, 30, 31. This is also true in a number of other states. And a similar doctrine anciently prevailed in other cases at common law in England. See Co. Litt. 133; 1 Sharswood, Bl. Comm. 132, note.

Natural death is the cessation of life. It is also used to denote a death which occurs by the unassisted operation of natural causes, as distinguished from a violent death, or one caused or accelerated by the interference of human agency.

DEATH BY ACCIDENT. Death from any unexpected event which happens as by chance, or which does not take place according to the usual course of things. 186 Ill. App. 503.

DEATH WITHOUT ISSUE. Where a will devised a particular estate preceding a gift over, the expression "death without issue" means death before the death of the life tenant, unless the will shows an intention to refer to a later date than the termination of the life estate. 266 Ill. 16.

DEATH-BED DEED. A deed made by one who was at the time sick of a disease from which he afterwards died. Bell, Dict.

DEATH'S PART. See "Dead's Part"; "Dead Man's Part."

DEATHSMAN. The executioner; hangman; he who executes the extreme penalty of the law.

DEBATUM. (Law Lat. from Fr. *debatre*). In old European law. A dispute or controversy. Spelman.

DEBAUCH. To entice or lead away. In modern usage it implies carnal knowledge. 97 Mo. 668. It has been held synonymous with "seduce." 8 Abb. Pr. (N. Y.) 384, 389. In early use it signified merely to draw away from duty, being derived from French *de* (from) and *bauche* (shop).

DEBENTURE (Lat. *debentur*, they [moneys] are due). The word with which certain obsolete bonds given by the exchequer began. Blount.

——**In English Law.** An instrument issued by a company or public body as security for a loan of money. It contains, either expressly or impliedly, a promise to pay the amount mentioned in it, and almost invariably creates a charge on the whole or part of the property of the company or public body. A debenture generally forms part of a series or issue of similar instruments, with a provision that they shall all rank *pari passu* in proportion to their amounts. As to debentures generally, see Cav. § 267 et seq.

——**In American Law.** A custom-house certificate given by the collector of the port to the exporter or importer of goods, entitling him, under certain circumstances, to a drawback of duties paid on exported or imported goods. See "Drawback."

In corporation law the term is applied to obligations of corporations, in some instances where secured by specific assets, in others, where not so secured. Fletcher Cyc. Corp. § 963.

DEBENTURE STOCK. A stock or fund representing money borrowed by a company or public body, in England, and charged on the whole or part of its property. It differs from debentures chiefly in these respects: The title of each original holder appears in a register, instead of being represented by an instrument complete in itself; and the stock is capable of being transferred in any amounts, unless the regulations of the company, etc., forbid the transfer of amounts or fractions less than £10, or the like. Provision is sometimes made for issuing to each holder a certificate representing the amount of his stock, transferable by delivery, so as to entitle the bearer for the time being to the stock in question. Such certificates generally have coupons for interest attached to them, and, while they are outstanding, the stock ceases to be transferable on the register. Perpetual debenture stock is stock which cannot be paid off. The principal statutes relating to debenture stock are the company clauses acts of 1845 and 1863, the commissioners clauses act of 1847, and the local loans act of 1875. Debenture stock issued under these acts is not within the mortmain or charitable uses act. 9 Ch. Div. 337.

DEBET ESSE FINIS LITIUM. There ought to be an end of lawsuits. Jenk. Cent. Cas. 61.

DEBET ET DETINET (Lat. he owes and withholds). In pleading. An action of debt is said to be in the *debet et detinet* when it is alleged that the defendant owes and unjustly withholds or detains the debt or thing in question.

The action is so brought between the contracting parties. See "Detinet."

DEBET ET SOLET (Lat. he owes and is used to). Where a man sues in a writ of right, or to recover any right of which he is for the first time disseised, as of a suit at a mill, or in case of a writ of *quod permittat,* he brings his writ in the *debet et solet.* Reg. Orig. 144a; Termes de la Ley; Fitzh. Nat. Brev. 122 (M).

DEBET QUIS JURI SUBJACERE UBI delinquit. Every one ought to be subject to the law of the place where he offends. 3 Inst. 34; Bracton, fol. 154b; Finch, Law, 14, 36; Wingate, Max. 113, 114; 3 Coke, 231; 8 Scott, N. R. 567.

DEBET SUA CUIQUE DOMUS ESSE perfugium tutissimum. Every man's house should be a perfectly safe refuge. 12 Johns. (N. Y.) 31, 54.

DEBILE FUNDAMENTUM, FALLIT opus. Where there is a weak foundation, the work falls. 2 Bouv. Inst. note 2068; Broom, Leg. Max. (3d London Ed.) 169, 171.

DEBITA FUNDI (Lat.) In Scotch law. Debts secured on land. Bell, Dict.

DEBITA LAICORUM (Lat.) Debts of the laity; those which may be recovered in civil courts.

DEBITA SEQUUNTUR PERSONAM debitoris. Debts follow the person of the debtor. Story, Confl. Laws, § 362; 2 Kent, Comm. 429; Halk. Max. 13.

DEBITOR NON PRAESUMITUR DOnare. A debtor is not presumed to make a gift. See 1 Kames, Eq. 212; Dig. 50. 16. 108; 1 P. Wms. 239.

DEBITORUM PACTIONIBUS, CREDItorum petitio nec tolli, nec minui potest. The right to sue of creditors cannot be taken away or lessened by the contracts of their debtors. Poth. Obl. 87. 108; Broom, Leg. Max. (3d London Ed.) 622.

DEBITRIX. A female debtor.

DEBITUM ET CONTRACTUS SUNT nullius loci. Debt and contract are of no particular place. 7 Coke, 61; 7 Man. & G. 1019, note; 1 Smith, Lead. Cas. (4th Am. Ed.) 528, note.

DEBITUM IN PRESENTI, SOLVENDUM in futuro. A present debt, to be discharged in the future. 2 Barb. (N. Y.) 457, 470; 16 Barb. (N. Y.) 171, 176; 19 Barb. (N. Y.) 442, 445.

DEBITUM SINE BREVI (Law Lat.) In old practice. Debt without writ. An action begun by original bill, instead of by writ.

DEBRUSER. (Law Fr.) To break in pieces.

To break down, as a hedge. *Ses haies debruseront.* Yearb. T. 1 Edw. II. 8.

Ceux queux ount debruse la prison; those who have broken the prison. Stat. Westm. 1, c. 15. Britt. c. 11.

DEBT. Any sum of money due under contract, express or implied. 20 Cal. 351.

Blackstone restricts the term to money due on express contract (3 Bl. Comm. 154), but it has been thought that he used the word "express" not so much in contradistinction to implied contracts, as to liabilities arising outside of contract. 2 Mo. App. 94.

The word includes not only debts of record or judgments and debts by specialty, but all that is due to a man under any form of promise. 3 Metc. (Mass.) 526.

In a strict sense, it is confined to sums fixed by agreement, and not dependent on after calculation (1 Yeates [Pa.] 70), but in common use, the absolute fixing of the amount is not necessary (2 Wash. C. C. [U. S.] 386).

"Debt" is a much narrower word than "demand." 2 Hill (N. Y.) 223.

Many qualifying terms are used with the word "debt," most of which are self-explanatory. A few of the more obscure may be given:

(1) Active debt is one due to a person. Used in the civil law.

(2) Doubtful debt is one of which the payment is uncertain. Clef des Lois Romaines.

(3) Hypothecary debt is one which is a lien upon an estate.

(4) Judgment debt is one which is evidenced by matter of record.

(5) Liquid debt is one which is immediately and unconditionally due.

(6) Passive debt is one which a person owes.

(7) Privileged debt is one which is to be paid before others, in case a debtor is insolvent.

(8) Debt of record is one proved to exist by the official records of a court of record, as a judgment or a recognizance.

——**In Practice.** A form of action which lies to recover a sum certain. 2 Greenl. Ev.

§ 279. It lies wherever the sum due is certain or ascertained in such a manner as to be readily reduced to a certainty, without regard to the manner in which the obligation was incurred or is evidenced. 3 Sneed (Tenn.) 145; 1 Dutch. (N. J.) 506; 26 Miss. 521; 3 McLean (U. S.) 150; 2 A. K. Marsh. (Ky.) 264; 1 Mason (U. S.) 243.

It is thus distinguished from "*assumpsit*," which lies as well where the sum due is uncertain as where it is certain, and from "covenant," which lies only upon contracts evidenced in a certain manner.

It is said to lie in the *debet* and *detinet*, when it is stated that the defendant owes and detains, or in the *detinet*, when it is stated merely that he detains. Debt in the *detinet* for goods differs from detinue, because it is not essential in this action, as in detinue, that the specific property in the goods should have been vested in the plaintiff at the time the action is brought. Dyer, 24b.

It is used for the recovery of a debt *eo nomine* and *in numero*, though damages, which are in most instances merely nominal, are usually awarded for the detention. 1 H. Bl. 550; Cowp. 588.

DEBT EX MUTUO. A species of debt or obligation mentioned by Glanville and Bracton, and which arose *ex mutuo*, out of a certain kind of loan. Glanv. lib. 10, c. 3; Bracton, fol. 99. See "Mutuum"; "Ex Mutuo."

DEBTEE. One to whom a debt is due; a creditor; as, debtee executor. 3 Bl. Comm.

DEBTOR. One who owes a debt; he who may be constrained to pay what he owes.

DEBTORS' ACT 1869. St. 32 & 33 Vict. c. 62, relating to insolvent debtors. See L. R. Ch. 152; L. R. 10 Ch. 76; 13 Ch. Div. 338; Id. 815.

DEBTOR'S SUMMONS. A summons under the seal of a court of bankruptcy in England, giving notice to the person to whom it is addressed (the debtor) that, unless he pays or compounds for a debt (not less than £50) due by him to a person therein named (the creditor) within a certain time, he will be liable to be adjudicated a bankrupt, unless he disproves the debt. Bankr. Act 1869, §§ 6, 7, form 4.

A trade debtor's summons is one for service on a trader, and differs from a non-trader debtor's summons in giving the debtor a shorter time for compliance with its terms. Id. §§ 4, 5.

DECANATUS, DECANIA, or **DECANA** (Lat.) A town or tithing, consisting originally of ten families of freeholders. Ten tithings compose a hundred. 1 Bl. Comm. 114.

Decanatus, a deanery, a company of ten. Spelman; Calv. Lex.

Decania, or *decana*, the territory under the charge of a dean.

DECANUS (Lat.) A dean; an officer having charge of ten persons. In Constantinople, an officer who has charge of the burial of the dead. Nov. Jus. 43. 59; Du Cange. The term is of extensive use, being found with closely related meanings in the old Roman, the civil, ecclesiastical, and old European law. It is used of civil and ecclesiastical, as well as military, affairs. There were a variety of *decani:*

Decanus monasticus, the dean of a monastery.

Decanus in majori ecclesia, dean of a cathedral church.

Decanus militaris, a military captain of ten soldiers.

Decanus episcopi, a dean presiding over ten parishes.

Decanus friborgi, dean of a fribourg, tithing, or association of ten inhabitants. A Saxon officer, whose duties were those of an inferior judicial officer. Du Cange; Spelman; Calv. Lex.

DECEASE. As a noun, death; departure from life.

As a verb, to die; to depart life, or from life. This has always been a common term in Scotch law. "Gif ane man deceasis." Skene de Verb. Sign.

DECEASED WIFE'S SISTER BILL. A proposed law seeking to legalize marriages between a man and a sister of his deceased wife. Many times brought before the English parliament and defeated by the bishops in the house of lords.

DECEDENT. A deceased person.

The signification of the word has become more extended than its strict etymological meaning. Strictly taken, it denotes a dying person, but is always used in the more extended sense given, denoting any deceased person, testate or intestate.

DECEIT. A fraudulent misrepresentation or contrivance, by which one man deceives another, who has no means of detecting the fraud, to the injury and damage of the latter.

It requires (1) a false representation; (2) inability of the person damaged to prevent the fraud; (3) resultant damage.

Deceit is a type of fraud (Bigelow, Frauds, § 1); fraud being the generic term, and deceit being active fraud by misrepresentation, or other positive contrivance.

DECEM TALES (Lat. ten such). In practice. A writ requiring the sheriff to appoint ten like men (*apponere decem tales*) to make up a full jury when a sufficient number do not appear.

DECEMVIRI LITIBUS JUDICANDIS. Ten judges (five being senators and five knights), appointed by Augustus to act as judges in certain cases. Calv. Lex.; Anthon, Rom. Ant.

DECENNARIUS (Lat.) One who held one-half a virgate of land. Du Cange. One of the ten freeholders in a *decennary*. Du Cange; Calv. Lex.

Decennier, one of the *decennarii*, or ten freeholders making up a tithing. Spelman; Du Cange, "Decenna"; 1 Bl. Comm. 114. See "Decanus."

DECENNARY (Lat. *decem*, ten). A district originally containing ten men with their families.

King Alfred, for the better preservation of the peace, divided England into counties, the counties into hundreds, and the hundreds into tithings or decennaries, the inhabitants whereof, living together, were sureties or pledges for each other's good behavior. One of the principal men of the latter number presided over the rest, and was called the chief pledge, borsholder, borrow's elder, or tything man.

DECEPTIS NON DECIPIENTIBUS, JURA subveniunt. The laws help persons who are deceived, not those deceiving. Tray. Lat. Max. 149.

DECERN. In Scotch law. To decree. "Decernit and ordainit." 1 How. St. Tr. 927. "Decerns." Shaw, 16.

DECESSUS (Lat. from *decedere*, to depart).

——**In the Civil Law.** Decease; death. Dig. 33. 2. 34. Rarely used.

——**In Old English Law.** Decease; death. *Post meum decessum*, after my decease. Fleta, lib. 3, c. 9, § 5; Id. c. 17, § 1.

Departure. 3 Salk. 123. See "Departure."

DECET TAMEN PRINCIPEM SERVARE leges, quibus ipse servatus est. It behooves, indeed, the prince to keep the laws by which he himself is preserved.

DECIES TANTUM (Lat.) An obsolete writ, which formerly lay against a juror who had taken money for giving his verdict. Called so because it was sued out to recover from him ten times as much as he took.

DECIMAE (Lat.) The tenth part of the annual profit of each living, payable formerly to the pope. There were several valuations made of these livings at different times. The *decimae* (tenths) were appropriated to the crown, and a new valuation established, by 26 Hen. VIII. c. 3. 1 Sharswood, Bl. Comm. 284.

DECIMAE DE DECIMATIS SOLVI NON debent. Tithes are not to be paid from that which is given for tithes.

DECIMAE DE JURE DIVINO ET CAnonica institutione pertinent ad personam. Tithes belong to the parson by divine right and canonical institution. Dal. 50.

DECIMAE DEBENTUR PAROCHO. Tithes are due to the parish priest.

DECIMAE NON DEBENT SOLVI, UBI non est annua renovatio, et ex annuatis renovantibus simul semel. Tithes ought not to be paid where there is an annual renovation, and from annual renovations once only. Cro. Jac. 42.

DECIMATION. The punishing every tenth soldier by lot, for mutiny or other failure of duty, was termed *"decimatio legionis"* by the Romans. Sometimes only the twentieth man was punished (*vicesimatio*), or the hundredth (*centesimatio*).

Also tithing or tenth part.

DECIME. A French coin, of the value of the tenth part of a franc, or nearly two cents.

DECIPI QUAM FALLERE EST TUTIUS. It is safer to be deceived than to deceive. Lofft, 396.

DECISION. In practice. A judgment given by a competent tribunal. The French lawyers call the opinions which they give on questions propounded to them, decisions. See Inst. 1. 2. 8; Dig. 1. 2. 2.

DECISIVE OATH. In the civil law. Where one of the parties to a suit, not being able to prove his charge, offered to refer the decision of the cause to the oath of his adversary, which the adversary was bound to accept, or tender the same proposal back again, otherwise the whole was taken as confessed by him. Code, 4. 1. 12.

DECLARANT. One who makes a declaration.

DECLARATION.

——**In Pleading.** A specification, in a methodical and logical form, of the circumstances which constitute the plaintiff's cause of action. 1 Chit. Pl. 248; Co. Litt. 17a, 303a; Bac. Abr. "Pleas" (B); Comyn, Dig. "Pleader" (C 7); Lawes, Pl. 35; Steph. Pl. 36; 6 Serg. & R. (Pa.) 28.

In real actions, it is most properly called the "count"; in a personal one, the "declaration." Steph. Pl. 36; Doctrina Plac. 83; Lawes, Pl. 33. See Fitzh. Nat. Brev. 16a, 60d. The latter, however, is now the general term, being that commonly used when referring to real and personal actions without distinction. 3 Bouv. Inst. note 2815.

In an action at law, the declaration answers to the bill in chancery, the libel (*narratio*) of the civilians, and the allegation of the ecclesiastical courts.

It may be general or special. For example, in debt on a bond, a declaration counting on the penal part only is general. One which sets out both the bond and the condition, and assigns the breach, is special. Gould. Pl. c. 4, § 50.

——**In Evidence.** An unsworn statement made out of court by a party in interest.

——**In Scotch Law.** The statement made before the magistrate by one arrested for crime.

DECLARATION OF INTENTION. The act of an alien who goes before a court of record, and in a formal manner declares that it is *bona fide* his intention to become a citizen of the United States, and to renounce forever all allegiance and fidelity to any foreign prince, potentate, state, or sovereignty whereof at the time he may be a citizen or subject. Act Cong. April 14, 1802, § 1.

DECLARATION OF PARIS. The name given to an agreement announcing four important rules of international law effected between the principal European powers and the Congress of Paris in 1856. These rules are: (1) Privateering is and remains abolished; (2) the neutral flag covers enemy's goods, except contraband of war; (3) neutral goods, except contraband of war, are not liable to confiscation under a hostile flag; (4) blockades, to be binding, must be effective. Abbott.

DECLARATION OF TRUST. The act by which an individual acknowledges that a property, the title of which he holds, does in fact belong to another, for whose use he holds the same.

The instrument in which such an acknowledgment is made.

DECLARATION OF WAR. The public proclamation of the government of a state, by which it declares itself to be at war with a foreign power, which is named, and which forbids all and every one to aid or assist the common enemy.

The power of declaring war is vested in congress by the constitution (article 1, § 8). There is no form or ceremony necessary except the passage of the act. A manifesto stating the causes of the war is usually published; but war exists as soon as the act takes effect. It was formerly usual to precede hostilities by a public declaration communicated to the enemy, and to send a herald to demand satisfaction. Potter, Grec. Ant. bk. 3, c. 7; Dig. 49. 15. 24. But that is not the practice of modern times.

A state of war, known as "imperfect" or "unsolemn" war, may exist without a declaration. Grotius de Jure Belli, bk. 1, c. 3, § 4. See 25 Wend. (N. Y.) 577.

DECLARATOR. In Scotch law. An action whereby a party prays something to be declared in his favor. Scotch Dict.

DECLARATOR OF TRUST. In Scotch law. An action resorted to against a trustee who holds property upon titles *ex facie* for his own benefit. Bell, Dict.

DECLARATORY. Something which explains or ascertains what before was uncertain or doubtful; as, a declaratory statute, which is one passed to put an end to a doubt as to what the law is, and which declares what it is, and what it has been. 1 Bl. Comm. 86.

DECLARATORY ACTION. In Scotch law. An action in which the right of the pursuer (or plaintiff) is craved to be declared, but nothing claimed to be done by the defender (defendant). Bell, Dict.; Ersk. Inst. 5. 1. 46. Otherwise called an "action of declarator."

DECLARATORY JUDGMENT (or DECREE). In practice. One which declares the rights of the parties, without ordering anything to be done.

DECLARATORY PART OF A LAW. That which clearly defines rights to be observed and wrongs to be eschewed. 1 Bl. Comm. 53.

DECLINATION. In Scotch law. A preliminary plea objecting to the jurisdiction on the ground that the judge is interested in the suit.

DECLINATORY PLEA. In English practice. The plea of sanctuary, or of benefit of clergy, before trial or conviction. 2 Hale, P. C. 236; 4 Bl. Comm. 333. Now abolished. 4 Steph. Comm. 400, note; Id. 436, note.

DECLINATURE. In Scotch practice. An objection to the jurisdiction of the judge. Bell, Dict.

DECOCTION. The operation of boiling certain ingredients in a fluid for the purpose of extracting the parts soluble at that temperature. The product of this operation.

In a case in which the indictment charged the prisoner with having administered to a woman a decoction of a certain shrub, called "savin," it appeared that the prisoner had administered an infusion, and not a decoction. The prisoner's counsel insisted that he was entitled to an acquittal on the ground that the medicine was misdescribed; but it was held that infusion and decoction are *ejusdem generis*, and that the variance was immaterial. 3 Campb. 74, 75.

DECOCTOR. In Roman law. A bankrupt; a person who squandered the money of the state. Calv. Lex.; Du Cange.

DECOLLATIO. Decollation; beheading.

DECONFES. In French law. A name formerly given to those persons who died without confession, whether they refused to confess, or whether they were criminals to whom the sacrament was refused. Droit de Canon, par M. l'Abbe Andre.

DECOY. A pond used for the breeding and maintenance of water fowl. 11 Mod. 74, 130; 3 Salk. 9; Holt, 14; 11 East, 571.

An article exposed for the purpose of affording an opportunity for the commission of a crime, and thereby detecting the perpetrator.

Particularly applied to letters sent through the mail to detect persons stealing or opening them in violation of the postal laws. Am. & Eng. Enc. Law (2d Ed.) tit. "Decoys."

DECREE.

——**In Practice.** The judgment of sentence of a court of equity, or of admiralty. It corresponds to the judgment of a court of law. It is either interlocutory or final. The former is given on some plea or issue arising in the cause which does not decide the main question; the latter settles the matter in dispute; and a final decree has the same effect as a judgment at law. 2 Madd. 462; 1 Chanc. Cas. 27; 2 Vern. 89; 4 Brown, Parl. Cas. 287. See 7 Viner, Abr. 394; 7 Comyn. Dig. 445; 1 Belt, Supp. to Ves. 223; Bouv. Inst. Index.

——**In Legislation.** In some countries, as in France, some acts of the legislature or of the sovereign, which have the force of law, are called "decrees"; as, the Berlin and Milan decrees.

——**In Scotch Law.** A final judgment or sentence of court, by which the question at issue between the parties is decided.

DECREE DATIVE. In Scotch law. The order of a court of probate appointing an administrator.

DECREE IN ABSENCE. In Scotch law. Judgment by default or *pro confesso.*

DECREE OF CONSTITUTION. In Scotch law. Any decree by which the extent of a debt or obligation is ascertained.

The term is, however, usually applied especially to those decrees which are required to found a title in the person of the creditor in the event of the death of either the debtor or the original creditor. Bell, Dict.

DECREE OF FORTHCOMING. In Scotch law. The decree made after an arrestment, ordering the debt to be paid or the effects to be delivered up to the arresting creditor. Bell, Dict.

DECREE OF LOCALITY. In Scotch law. The decree of a teind court allocating stipend upon different heritors. It is equivalent to the apportionment of a tithe rent charge.

DECREE OF MODIFICATION. In Scotch law. A decree of the teind court modifying or fixing a stipend.

DECREE OF REGISTRATION. In Scotch law. A proceeding by which the creditor has immediate execution. It is somewhat like a warrant of attorney to confess judgment. 1 Bell, Comm. 1. 1. 4.

DECREET. In Scotch law. The final judgment or sentence of court by which the question at issue between the parties is decided.

Decreet absolutor is one where the decision is in favor of the defendant.

Decreet condemnator is one where the decision is in favor of the plaintiff. Ersk. Inst. 4. 3. 5.

Decreet absolvitor is one dismissing a claim, or acquitting a defendant. 2 Kames, Eq. 367; 1 Forbes, Inst. pt. 4, bk. 1, c. 2, tit. 1, § 3.

Decreet arbitral is the award of arbitration; the form of promulgating such award. Bell, Dict. "Arbitration"; 2 Bell, H. L. Sc. 49.

DECREMENTUM MARIS (Lat.) In old English law. Decrease of the sea; the receding of the sea from the land. Callis, Sew. (53), 65. See "Reliction."

DECRETA. In the Roman law. Judicial sentences given by the emperor as supreme judge.

DECRETA CONCILIORUM NON LIGANT reges nostros. The decrees of councils bind not our kings. Moore, 906.

DECRETAL ORDER. In chancery practice. An order made by the court of chancery, upon a motion or petition, in the nature of a decree. 2 Daniell, Ch. Prac. 637.

DECRETALES BONIFACII OCTAVI. A supplemental collection of the canon law, published by Boniface VIII. in 1298. Called, also, *liber sextus decretalium,* sixth book of the decretals. 1 Kaufm. Mackeld. Civ. Law, 83, note. See "Decretals."

DECRETALES GREGORII NONI. The decretals of Gregory the Ninth. A collection of the laws of the church, published by order of Gregory IX. in 1227. It is composed of five books, subdivided into titles, and each title is divided into chapters. They are cited by using an X (or *extra*) thus: *Cap. & X de Regulis Juris,* etc. 1 Kaufm. Mackeld. Civ. Law, 83, note; Butler, Hor. Jur. 115.

DECRETALS. In ecclesiastical law. Canonical epistles, written by the pope alone, or by the pope and cardinals, at the instance or suit of one or more persons, for the ordering and determining some matter in controversy, and which have the authority of a law in themselves.

The decretals were published in three volumes. The first volume was collected by Raymundus Barcinius, chaplain to Gregory IX., about the year 1227, and published by him to be read in schools, and used in the ecclesiastical courts. The second volume is the work of Boniface VIII., compiled about the year 1298, with additions to and alterations of the ordinances of his predecessors. The third volume is called the "Clementines," because made by Clement V., and was published by him in the council of Vienna, about the year 1308. To these may be added the Extravagantes of John XXII. and other bishops of Rome, which, relatively to the others, are called *Novellae Consti-*

tutiones. Ridley's View, etc., 99, 100; 1 Fournel, Hist. des Avocats, 194, 195.

The false decretals were forged in the names of the early bishops of Rome, and first appeared about A. D. 845-850. The author of them is not known. They are mentioned in a letter written in the name of the council of Quierzy, by Charles the Bold, to the bishops and lords of France. See Van Espen Fleury, Droit de Canon, by Andre.

The decretals constitute the second division of the *Corpus Juris Canonici.*

DECRETO. In Spanish colonial law. An order emanating from some superior tribunal, promulgated in the name and by the authority of the sovereign, in relation to ecclesiastical matters. Schmidt, Civ. Law, 93, note.

DECRETUM.

——**In Civil Law.** A species of imperial constitution, being a judgment or sentence given by the emperor upon hearing of a cause, *quod imperator cognoscens decrevit.* Inst. 1. 2. 6.

——**In Canon Law.** An ecclesiastical law, in contradistinction to a secular law (*lex*). 1 Kaufm. Mackeld. Civ. Law, p. 81, § 93.

DECRETUM GRATIANI. A collection of ecclesiastical law made by Gratian, a Bolognese monk, in the year 1151. It is the oldest of the collections constituting the *Corpus Juris Canonici.* 1 Kaufm. Mackeld. Civ. Law, 81; 1 Bl. Comm. 82; Butler, Hor. Jur. 113.

DECRY. To cry down; to destroy the credit of. It is said that the king may at any time decry the coin of the realm. 1 Bl. Comm. 278.

DECURIO. In Roman law. One of the chief men or senators in the provincial towns. The *decuriones,* taken together, had the entire management of the internal affairs of their towns or cities, with powers resembling in some degree those of our modern city councils. 1 Spence, Eq. Jur. 54; Calv. Lex.

DEDBANA. An actual homicide or manslaughter.

DEDI (Lat. I have given.) A word used in deeds and other instruments of conveyance when such instruments were made in Latin.

The use of this word formerly carried with it a warranty in law, when in a deed; for example, if in a deed it was said, "*dedi* (I have given), etc., to A. B.," there was a warranty to him and his heirs. Brooke, Abr. "Guaranty," pl. 85. The warranty thus wrought was a special warranty, extending to the heirs of the feoffee during the life of the donor only. Co. Litt. 384b; 4 Coke, 81; 5 Coke, 17. *Dedi* is said to be the aptest word to denote a feoffment. 2 Sharswood, Bl. Comm. 310. The future, *dabo,* is found in some of the Saxon grants. 1 Spence, Eq. Jur. 44.

DEDI ET CONCESSI (Lat. I have given and granted). The aptest words to work a feoffment. They are the words ordinarily used, when instruments of conveyance were in Latin, in charters of feoffment, gift, or grant. These words were held the aptest, though others would answer. Co. Litt. 384b; 1 Steph. Comm. 114; 2 Bl. Comm. 53, 316.

DEDICATION. An appropriation of land to some public use, made by the owner, and accepted for such use by or on behalf of the public. Angell, Highways, c. 111, § 132.

There may be a dedication for pious and charitable purposes, as well as for public easements. 32 Barb. (N. Y.) 222.

Dedications are either—

(1) Statutory, being those in pursuance of a statute, or

(2) Common law, being that implied by acquiescence in the public user. It operates not by grant, but by estoppel. 9 Iowa, 451.

"In common-law dedication, no particular formality is necessary. It is not affected by the statute of frauds. It may be made, either with or without writing, by any act of the owner, such as throwing open his land to public travel, or platting it and selling lots bounded by streets designated in the plat, thereby indicating a clear intention to dedicate. Or an acquiescence in the use of his land for a highway, or his declared assent to such use, will be sufficient; the dedications being proved in most, if not all, of the cases by matter *in pais,* and not by deed. The vital principle of the dedication is the intention to dedicate; and whenever this is unequivocally manifested, the dedication, so far as the owner of the soil is concerned, has been made. Time, therefore, though often a very material ingredient in the evidence, is not an indispensable ingredient in the act of dedication. If accepted and used by the public in the manner intended, the dedication is complete, precluding the owner and all claiming in his right from asserting any ownership inconsistent with such use. Dedication, therefore, is a conclusion of fact to be drawn by the jury from the circumstances of each particular case; the whole question, as against the owner of the soil, being whether there is sufficient evidence of an intention on his part to dedicate the land to the public use as a highway." 14 Cal. 642.

DEDICATION DAY. The feast of dedication of churches, or rather the feast day of the saint and patron of a church, which was celebrated not only by the inhabitants of the place, but by those of all the neighboring villages, who usually came thither; and such assemblies were allowed as lawful. It was usual for the people to feast and to drink on those days. Cowell.

DEDIMUS ET CONCESSIMUS (Lat. we have given and granted). Words used by the king where there were more grantors than one, instead of *dedi et concessi.*

DEDIMUS POTESTATEM (Lat. we have given power). The name of a writ to commission private persons to do some act in the place of a judge; as, to administer an oath of office to a justice of the peace, to examine witnesses, and the like. Cowell; Comyn, Dig. "Chancery" (K 3), (P 2), "Fine" (E 7); Dane, Abr. Index; 2 Sharswood, Bl. Comm. 351.

DEDIMUS POTESTATEM DE ATTORNO faciendo (Lat.). The name of a writ which was formerly issued by authority of the crown in England to authorize an attorney to appear for a defendant.

By St. Westminster II. (13 Edw. I. c. 10), all persons impleaded may make an attorney to sue for them, in all pleas moved by or against them, in the superior courts there enumerated. 3 Man. & G. 184, note.

DEDITITII (Lat.) In Roman law. Criminals who have been marked in the face or on the body with fire or an iron so that the mark cannot be erased, and subsequently manumitted. Calv. Lex.

DEDUCTION FOR NEW. In maritime law. The allowance (usually one-third) on the cost of repairing a damage to the ship by the extraordinary operation of the perils of navigation, the renovated part being presumed to be better than before the damage. In some ports, by custom or by express provision in the policy, the allowance is not made on a new vessel during the first year, or on new sheating, or on an anchor or chain cables. 1 Phil. Ins. § 50; 2 Phil. Ins. §§ 1369, 1431, 1433; Benecke & S. Av. (Phil. Ed.) 167, note 238; 2 Serg. & R. (Pa.) 229; 1 Caines (N. Y.) 573; 18 La. 77; 2 Cranch, C. C. (U. S.) 218; 21 Pick. (Mass.) 456; 5 Cow. (N. Y.) 63.

DEED. A written instrument under seal, containing a contract or agreement which has been delivered by the party to be bound and accepted by the obligee or covenantee. Co. Litt. 171; 2 Bl. Comm. 295; Shep. Touch. 50.

A writing under seal, by which lands, tenements, or hereditaments are conveyed for an estate not less than a freehold. 2 Sharswood, Bl. Comm. 294.

Any instrument in writing under seal, whether it relates to the conveyance of real estate, or to any other matter,—as, for instance, a bond, single bill, agreement, or contract of any kind,—is as much a deed as is a conveyance of real estate, and, after delivery and acceptance, is obligatory. 2 Serg. & R. (Pa.) 504; 5 Dana (Ky.) 365; 2 Miss. 154. The term is, however, often used in the latter sense above given, and perhaps oftener than in its more general signification.

According to Sir William Blackstone (2 Comm. 313), deeds may be considered as conveyances at common law,—of which the original are feoffment, gift, grant, lease, exchange, partition; the derivatives are release, confirmation, surrender, assignment, defeasance,—or conveyances which derive their force by virtue of the statute of uses, namely, covenant to stand seised to uses; bargain and sale of lands; lease and release; deed to lead and declare uses; deed of revocation of uses.

DEED INDENTED. See "Indenture."

DEED OF COVENANT. Covenants are sometimes entered into by a separate deed, for title, or for the indemnity of a purchaser or mortgagee, or for the production of title deeds. A covenant with a penalty is sometimes taken for the payment of a debt, instead of a bond with a condition, but the legal remedy is the same in either case. Rapalje & L.

DEED POLL. A deed which is made by one party only.

A deed in which only the party making it executes it, or binds himself by it as a deed. 2 Washb. Real Prop. 588.

The distinction between "deed poll" and "indenture" has come to be of but little importance. The ordinary purpose of a deed poll is merely to transfer the rights of the grantor to the grantee. It was formerly called *charta de una parte,* and usually began with these words: *Sciant praesentes et futuri quod ego, A.*, etc.; and now begins, "Know all men by these presents that I, A. B., have given, granted, and enfeoffed, and by these presents do give, grant, and enfeoff," etc. Cruise, Dig. tit. 32, c. 1, § 23. See "Indenture."

DEED TO DECLARE USES. A deed made after a fine or common recovery, to show the object thereof.

DEED TO LEAD USES. A deed made before a fine or common recovery, to show the object thereof.

DEEMSTERS. Judges in the Isle of Man, who decide all controversies without process, writings, or any charges. These judges are chosen by the people, and are said by Spelman to be two in number. Spelman; Camden, Brit.; Cowell; Blount.

DEER FALD. A park or fold for deer.

DEER HAYES. Engines or great nets made of cord to catch deer. 19 Hen. VIII. c. 11.

DEFALCATION. The act of a defaulter. Embezzlement or misappropriation of public or trust funds.

The reduction of the claim of one of the contracting parties against the other, by deducting from it a smaller claim due from the former to the latter. See 1 Rawle (Pa.) 291; 3 Bin. (Pa.) 135.

DEFAMATION. The speaking or writing words of a person so as to hurt his good fame, *de bona fama aliquid detrahere.* Written defamation is termed "libel," and oral defamation "slander."

DEFAMES (Law Fr.) Infamous.

DEFAULT. The nonperformance of a duty, whether arising under a contract or otherwise. 2 Barn. & Ald. 516.

——**In Practice.** The nonappearance of a plaintiff or defendant at court within the time prescribed by law to prosecute his claim or make his defense.

DEFEASANCE. (Fr. *defaire,* to defeat). An instrument which defeats the force or operation of some other deed or estate. That which is in the same deed is called a condition, and that which is in another deed is a defeasance. Comyn, Dig. "Defeasance."

A collateral deed made at the same time with a feoffment or grant, containing certain conditions, upon the performance of which the estate created by such feoffment or grant may be defeated. 43 Me. 371.

An instrument collateral to a bond, and containing the condition thereof. 2 Bl. Comm. 342.

DEFEASIBLE. An estate is defeasible when subject to be defeated by the operation of a condition subsequent, or conditional limitation.

DEFECT. The want of something required by law. See 20 N. Y. 355; 40 Barb. (N. Y.) 574.

DEFECTUM. See "Propter Defectum."

DEFECTUS SANGUINIS. Failure of issue.

DEFENDANT. A party sued in a personal action. The term does not in strictness apply to the person opposing or denying the allegations of the demandant in a real action, who is properly called the "tenant." The distinction, however, is very commonly disregarded; and the term is further frequently applied to denote the person called upon to answer, either at law or in equity, and as well in criminal as civil suits.

DEFENDANT IN ERROR. The distinctive term appropriate to the party against whom a writ of error is sued out.

DEFENDER.

——**In French Law.** To deny; to defend; to conduct a suit for a defendant; to forbid; to prevent; to protect.

——**In Scotch and Canon Law.** A defendant.

DEFENDER OF THE FAITH. A peculiar title belonging to the sovereign of England, as that of "Catholic" to the king of Spain, and that of "Most Christian" to the king of France. These titles were originally given by the popes of Rome; and that of *Defensor Fidei* was first conferred by Pope Leo. X. on King Henry VIII., as a reward for writing against Martin Luther; and the bull for it bears date *quinto Idus Octob.,* 1521. Enc. Lond.

DEFENDERE SE PER CORPUS SUUM. To offer duel or combat as a legal trial and appeal. Abolished by 59 Geo. III., § 46. See "Battel."

DEFENDERE UNICA MANU. To wage law; a denial of an accusation upon oath. 3 Bl. Comm. 341; 3 Steph. Comm. 424.

DEFENDIT VIM ET INJURIAM. He defends the force and injury. Fleta, lib. 5, c. 39, § 1.

DEFENDOUR (Law Fr. a defender or defendant). The party accused in an appeal. Britt. c. 22.

DEFENERATION. The act of lending money on usury.

DEFENSA. A park or place fenced in for deer, and defended as a property, and peculiar for that use and service. Cowell.

DEFENSE.

——**In Torts.** A forcible resistance of an attack by force. See "Self-Defense."

——**In Pleading and Practice.** The denial of the truth or validity of the complaint. A general assertion that the plaintiff has no ground of action, which is afterwards extended and maintained in the plea. 3 Sharswood, Bl. Comm. 296; Co. Litt. 127.

In this sense it is similar to the *contestatio litis* of the civilians, and does not include justification. In a more general sense it denotes the means by which the defendant prevents the success of the plaintiff's action, or, in criminal practice, the indictment. The word is commonly used in this sense in modern practice.

Half defense was that which was made by the form "defends the force and injury, and says," *defendit vim et injuriam, et dicit.*

Full defense was that which was made by the form "defends the force and injury when and where it shall behoove him, and the damages and whatever else he ought to defend," *defendit vim et injuriam quando et ubi curia consideravit, et damna et quicquid quod ipse defendere debet, et dicit,* commonly shortened into "defends the force and injury when," etc. Gilb. C. P. 188; 8 Term R. 632; 3 Bos. & P. 9, note; Co. Litt. 127b; Willes, 41. It follows immediately upon the statement of appearance, "comes" (*venit*), thus: "comes and defends." By the general defense, the propriety of the writ, the competency of the plaintiff, and the jurisdiction of the court were allowed; by defending the force and injury, misnomer was waived; by defending the damages, all exceptions to the person of the plaintiff; and by defending either when, etc., the jurisdiction of the court was admitted. 3 Sharswood, Bl. Comm. 298.

The distinction between the forms of half and full defense was first lost sight of (8 Term. R. 633; Willes, 41; 3 Bos. & P. 9; 2 Saund. 209c), and no necessity for a technical defense exists, under the modern forms of practice.

DEFENSE AU FOND EN DROIT (called, also, *defence en droit*). A demurrer. 2 Low. (U. S.) 278. See, also, 1 Low. (U. S.) 216.

DEFENSE AU FOND EN FAIT. The general issue. 3 Low. (U. S.) 421.

DEFENSIVA. In old English law. A lord or earl of the marches, who was the warden and defender of his country. Cowell.

DEFENSIVE ALLEGATION. In ecclesiastical practice. The answer of the party defending to the allegations of the party moving the cause.

DEFENSIVE WAR. A war in defense of national right,—not necessarily defensive in its operations. 1 Kent, Comm. 50.

DEFENSO. See "Defensum."

DEFENSOR.

——**In Civil Law.** A defender; one who takes upon himself the defense of another's cause, assuming his liabilities.

An advocate in court. In this sense the word is very general in its signification, including *advocatus, patronus, procurator,* etc. A tutor or guardian. Calv. Lex.

——**In Old English Law.** A guardian or protector. Spelman. The defendant; a warrantor. Bracton.

——**In Canon Law.** The advocate of a church. The patron. See "Advocatus." An officer having charge of the temporal affairs of the church. Spelman.

DEFENSOR CIVITATIS (Lat. defender of the state). In Roman law. An officer whose business it was to transact certain business of the state.

Those officers were so called who, like the tribunes of the people at first, were chosen by the people in the large cities and towns, and whose duty it was to watch over the order of the city, protect the people and the *decuriones* from all harm, protect sailors and naval people, attend to the complaints of those who had suffered injuries, and discharge various other duties. As will be seen, they had considerable judicial power. Du Cange; Schmidt, Civ. Law, Introd. 16.

DEFENSUM (Law. Lat.) In old English law. An inclosure, or any fenced ground. 2 Mon. Ang. 114; 3 Mon. Ang. 306. *Inclusum et positum in defensum,* inclosed and put in defense or fence. Bracton, fol. 228. *Rationabilia defensa,* reasonable defenses. Fleta, lib. 4, c. 19, § 7.

A part of an open field, appropriated to a particular use, as for hay, which was hence said to be *in defenso.* Cowell.

A state of several occupancy or appropriation. Magna Charta, c. 16.

Defense, in the old sense of prohibition; a state of prohibition, or in which the use of a thing is prohibited by law. St. Westminster II. c. 47.

DEFICIENCY DECREES. One for the balance of the mortgage debt remaining after applying toward it the proceeds of the sale. 84 Ill. App. 36.

DEFICIENTE UNO SANGUINE NON potest esse haeres. One blood being wanted, he cannot be heir. 3 Coke, 41.

DEFINITIVE. That which terminates a suit; final. A definitive sentence or judgment is put in opposition to an interlocutory judgment.

DEFLORATION. The act by which a woman is deprived of her virginity.

When this is done unlawfully and against her will, it bears the name of "rape" (*q. v.*); when she consents, it is "fornication" (*q. v.*); or if the man be married, it is "adultery" on his part. 2 Greenl. Ev. § 48; 21 Pick. (Mass.) 509; 36 Me. 261; 11 Ga. 53; 2 Dall. (Pa.) 124.

DEFORCE.

——**In English Law.** To withhold wrongfully; to withhold the possession of lands from one who is lawfully entitled to them. 3 Bl. Comm. 172.

——**In Scotch Law.** To resist the execution of the law; to oppose by force a public officer in the execution of his duty. Bell, Dict.

DEFORCEMENT. The holding any lands or tenements to which another has a right.

In its most extensive sense, the term includes any withholding of any lands or tenements to which another person has a right (Co. Litt. 277); so that this includes as well an abatement, an intrusion, a disseisin, or a discontinuance, as any other species of wrong whatsoever, by which the owner of the freehold is kept out of possession. But, as contradistinguished from the former, it is only such a detainer of the freehold from him who has the right of property as falls within none of the injuries above mentioned. 3 Bl. Comm. 173; Archb. Civ. Pl. 13; Dane, Abr. Index.

——**In Scotch Law.** The opposition given, or resistance made, to messengers or other officers while they are employed in executing the law.

This crime is punished by confiscation of movables, the one half to the king and the other to the creditor at whose suit the diligence is used. Ersk. Prac. 4. 4. 32.

DEFORCIANT. One who wrongfully keeps the owner of lands and tenements out of the possession of them. 2 Bl. Comm. 350.

DEFORCIARE. To withhold lands or tenements from the rightful owner. This is a word of art which cannot be supplied by any other word. Co. Litt. 331b; 3 Thomas, Co. Litt. 3; Bracton, lib. 4, 238; Fleta, lib. 5, c. 11.

DEFOSSION. The punishment of being buried alive.

DEFRAUD. To withhold from another that which is justly due to him, or to deprive him of a right, by deception or artifice. 12 Barb. (N. Y.) 186.

DEFRAUDACION. In Spanish law. The crime committed by a person who fraudulently avoids the payment of some public tax.

DEFUER. (Law Fr.) To flee from; to run away; to elope. Kelham. *Defuiaunt;* running away. *Defuont;* run away. *Apres ceo que el avera defuy son baron;* after she shall have eloped from her husband. Britt. c. 42.

DEFUNCT. Deceased; a deceased person.

DEGASTER (Law Fr.) To waste. *Degast, degaste, degata,* wasted, destroyed. Kelham.

DEGRADATION. In ecclesiastical law. A censure by which a clergyman is deprived of the holy orders which he had as a priest or deacon.

DEGREE (Fr. *degre,* from Lat. *gradus,* a step in a stairway; a round of a ladder). A remove or step in the line of descent or consanguinity.

The state or civil condition of a person. The ancient English statute of additions, for example, requires that in process, for the better description of a defendant, his state, degree, or mystery shall be mentioned.

An honorable state or condition to which a student is advanced in testimony of proficiency in arts and sciences. They are of pontifical origin. See 1 Schmidt, Thesaurus, 144; Vicat, Doctores; Minshew, Dict. "Bacheler"; Merlin, Repert; Van Espen, pt. 1, tit. 10; Giannone, Istoria di Napoli, lib. xi. c. 2,—for a full account of this matter.

DEHORS (Fr. out of; without). Something out of the record, agreement, will, or other thing spoken of; something foreign to the matter in question.

DEI GRATIA (Lat. by the grace of God). An expression used in the titles of sovereigns, and considered as one of the prerogatives of royalty, *propria jura majestatis,* although anciently a part of the titles of inferior officers and magistrates, ecclesiastical and civil. Spelman.

DEI JUDICIUM (Lat. the judgment of God). A name given to the trial by ordeal.

DEJACION. In Spanish law. A general term applicable to the surrender of his property to his creditors by an insolvent; the renunciation of an inheritance; the release of a mortgage upon payment, and the abandonment of the property insured to the insurer.

DEJERATION. A taking of a solemn oath.

DEL BIEN ESTRE (Law Fr.; Law Lat. *de bene esse*). In old English practice. Of well being; of form. Britt. c. 39.

DEL CREDERE COMMISSION. An additional commission received by a factor in consideration of his engaging to insure to his principal not only the solvency of the debtor, but the punctual discharge of the debt. 104 Mass. 497; 47 Barb. (N. Y.) 9; 33 Mo. 412.

He was formerly held to be a principal debtor, but it is now well settled that his liability is only as a guarantor. Story, Ag. (9th Ed.) § 215; 5 Hill (N. Y.) 458.

DELATE. In Scotch law. To accuse. Bell, Dict.

DELATIO. In civil law. An accusation or information. Du Cange; Calv. Lex.

DELATOR. An accuser or informer. Du Cange.

DELATURA. In old English law. The reward of an informer. Whishaw.

DELECTUS PERSONAE (or **PERSONArum**). (Lat. the choice of the person.) A term applied to the doctrine that no new member can be introduced into a firm without the unanimous consent of the then partners. Shumaker, Partn. 9.

This doctrine excludes even executors and representatives of partners from succeeding to the state and condition of partners. 7 Pick. (Mass.) 237; 3 Kent, Comm. 55.

——**In Scotch Law.** The personal preference which is supposed to have been exercised by a landlord in selecting his tenant, by the members of a firm in making choice of partners, in the appointment of persons to office, and other cases. Nearly equivalent to personal trust, as a doctrine in law. Bell, Dict.

DELEGATA POTESTAS NON POTEST delegari. A delegated authority cannot be again delegated. Coke, 2d Inst. 597; 5 Bing. N. C. 310; 2 Bouv. Inst. note 1300; Story, Ag. § 13; 11 How. (U. S.) 233.

DELEGATE (Lat. *deligere,* to choose from). One authorized by another to act in his name; an agent or attorney.

A person elected, by the people of an organized territory of the United States, to congress, who has a seat in congress, and a right of debating, but not of voting. Ord. July 13, 1787 (3 Story, U. S. Laws, 2076).

A person elected to any deliberative assembly. It is, however, in this sense generally limited to occasional assemblies, such as conventions, and the like, and does not usually apply to permanent bodies, as houses of assembly, etc.

DELEGATION.

——In Civil Law. A kind of novation by which the original debtor, in order to be liberated from his creditor, gives him a third person, who becomes obliged in his stead to the creditor or to the person appointed by him. See "Novation."

Perfect delegation exists when the debtor who makes the delegation is discharged by the creditor.

Imperfect delegation exists when the creditor retains his rights against the original debtor. 2 Duv. note 169.

——At Common Law. The transfer of authority from one or more persons to one or more others.

All persons, *sui juris*, may delegate to another authority to act for them in a matter which is lawful and otherwise capable of being delegated. Comyn, Dig. "Attorney," c. 1; 9 Coke, 75b; Story, Ag. § 6.

——In Legislation. The whole number of the persons who represent a district, a state, and the like in a deliberative assembly; as, the delegation from Ohio, the delegation from the city of Philadelphia.

DELEGATUS DEBITOR EST ODIOSUS in lege. A delegated debtor is hateful in law. 3 Bulst. 148.

DELEGATUS NON POTEST DELEGARE. A delegate or deputy cannot appoint another. 2 Bouv. Inst. note 1936; Story, Ag. § 13; Broom, Leg. Max. (3d London Ed.) 756-758; 9 Coke, 77; 2 Scott, N. R. 509; 12 Mees. & W. 712; 6 Exch. 156; 8 C. B. 627.

DELETE. In Scotch law. To erase; to strike out. 1 How. St. Tr. 1381.

DELIBERANDUM EST DIU QUOD STATuendum est semel. That which is to be resolved once for all should be long deliberated upon. 12 Coke, 74.

DELIBERATE. To examine, to consult, in order to form an opinion. Thus, a jury deliberates as to their verdict.

DELIBERATION. The act of the understanding by which a party examines whether a thing proposed ought to be done or not to be done, or whether it ought to be done in one manner or another.

The deliberation relates to the end proposed, to the means of accomplishing that end, or to both. It is a presumption of law that all acts committed are done with due deliberation,—that the party intended to do what he has done. But he may show the contrary. In contracts, for example, he may show that he has been taken by surprise (*q. v.*); and when a criminal act is charged, he may prove that it was an accident, and not with deliberation,—that, in fact, there was no intention or will. In relation to crime, it implies a weighing of the motives for the act and its consequences, with a view to decision thereon. 28 Iowa 524.

"Deliberation" is not synonymous with "premeditation." "Deliberation is prolonged premeditation." 74 Mo. 247. See "Malice Aforethought."

It does not mean brooded over, reflected upon for a week, a day, or an hour, but it means an intent executed, not under the influence of violent passion, but in the furtherance of a formed design. 66 Mo. 13.

——In Legislation. The council which is held touching some business in an assembly having the power to act in relation to it.

DELICT. In civil law. The act by which one person, by fraud or malignity, causes some damage or tort to some other.

In its most enlarged sense, this term includes all kinds of crimes and misdemeanors, and even the injury which has been caused by another, either voluntary or accidentally, without evil intention. But more commonly by "delicts" are understood those small offenses which are punished by a small fine or a short imprisonment.

Private delicts are those which are directly injurious to a private individual.

Public delicts are those which affect the whole community in their hurtful consequences.

Quasi delicts are the acts of a person who, without malignity, but by an inexcusable imprudence, causes an injury to another. Poth. Obl. note 116; Ersk. Prac. 4. 4. 1.

DELICTUM (Lat.) A crime or offense; a tort or wrong, as in actions *ex delicto.* 1 Chit. Pl. A challenge of a juror *propter delictum* is for some crime or misdemeanor that affects his credit, and renders him infamous. 3 Bl. Comm. 363; 2 Kent, Comm. 241. Some offense committed, or wrong done. 1 Kent, Comm. 552; Cowp. 199. 200. A state of culpability. Occurring often, in the phrase *"in pari delicto melior est conditio defendentis."* So, where both parties to a broken contract have been guilty of unlawful acts, the law will not interfere, but will leave them *in pari delicto.* 2 Greenl. Ev. § 111.

DELIMIT. To mark or lay out the limits or boundary line of a territory or country.

DELINQUENS PER IRAM PROVOCAtus puniri debet mitius. A delinquent provoked by anger ought to be punished more mildly. 3 Inst. 55.

DELINQUENT. In civil law. He who has been guilty of some crime, offense, or failure of duty.

DELIRIUM FEBRILE. In medical jurisprudence. A form of mental aberration incident to febrile diseases, and sometimes to the last stages of chronic diseases.

DELIRIUM TREMENS (called, also, *mania-a-potu*). In medical jurisprudence. A form of mental disorder incident to habits of intemperate drinking, which generally appears as a sequel to a few days' abstinence from stimulating drink.

DELITO. In Spanish law. Crime; a crime, offense, or delict. White, New Recop. bk. 2, tit. 19, c. 1, § 4.

DELIVERANCE. In practice. A term used by the clerk in court to every prisoner who is arraigned and pleads not guilty, to whom he wishes a good deliverance. In modern practice this is seldom used.

DELIVERY.

——**Of Deed.** The transfer of a deed from the grantor to the grantee, or some person acting in his behalf, in such a manner as to deprive the grantor of the right to recall it at his option. Delivery may be (1) absolute, which is complete upon the actual transfer of the instrument from the possession of the grantor; or (2) conditional, which passes the deed from the possession of the grantor, but is not to be completed by possession in the grantee, or a third person as his agent, until the happening of a specified event.

——**Of Chattels.** The tradition or transfer of the possession of a chattel from one person to another. It may be actual or symbolical, as of goods in a storehouse by delivery of the key (39 Me. 496), or goods in the hands of a carrier by delivery of the bill of lading (5 Ohio, 88).

The word "delivery," as applied to sales, has been used in several senses, viz.:

(1) Delivery sufficient to pass title.

(2) Delivery sufficient to allow the seller to sue for goods sold and delivered.

(3) Delivery sufficient to destroy the vendor's lien.

(4) Delivery sufficient to determine the right of stoppage *in transitu*.

(5) Delivery sufficient under the statute of frauds.

(6) Delivery sufficient as against creditors or subsequent purchasers.

Unless the particular sense in which the word is used in each case be borne in mind, confusion will follow in reading the decisions. Benj. Sales, p. 649, note.

——**In Medical Jurisprudence.** The act of a woman giving birth to her offspring.

DELIVERY ORDER. An order addressed in England, by the owner of goods to a person holding them on his behalf, requesting him to deliver them to a person named in the order. Delivery orders are chiefly used in the case of goods held by dock companies, wharfingers, etc. Such an order is not a document of title, and therefore does not transfer the property, or divest the vendor's lien for the purchase money, until it is acted on by the holder's obtaining either (1) actual delivery, (2) an entry of his title in the wharfinger's books, or (3) the issue of a dock warrant in his name; which last operation would apparently presuppose the second. Until he does one of these things, the original owner may obtain delivery to himself, or transfer the property in the goods to some one else. 2 H. L. Cas. 309; 5 Ch. Div. 195; Benj. Sales, 684. See "Dock Warrant."

DELUSION. In medical jurisprudence. A diseased state of the mind, in which persons believe things to exist which exist only, or in the degree they are conceived of only, in their own imaginations, with a persuasion so fixed and firm that neither evidence nor argument can convince them to the contrary.

DEM. An abbreviation for "demise"; Jackson ex dem. Wood v. Wood, Jackson on the demise of Wood, etc. 6 Cow. (N. Y.) 586.

DEMAIN. See "Demesne."

DEMAND. A claim; a legal obligation.

Demand is a word of art of an extent greater in its signification than any other word except "claim." Co. Litt. 291; 2 Hill (N. Y.) 220; 9 Serg. & R. (Pa.) 124; 6 Watts & S. (Pa.) 226.

——**In Practice.** A requisition or request to do a particular thing specified under a claim of right on the part of the person requesting.

DEMAND IN RECONVENTION. A demand which the defendant institutes in consequence of that which the plaintiff has brought against him. Used in Louisiana. Prac. Code La. art. 374.

DEMANDA (Law Lat.)

——**In Old English Law.** A demand. Bracton, fols. 17, 35; Fleta, lib. 2, c. 39, § 1. *Si quis recuperaverit demandam suam,* if one shall recover his demand. St. Westminster II. c. 44. See 8 Coke, 153.

——**In Spanish Law.** The petition of a plaintiff, setting forth his demand. Las Partidas, pt. 3, tit. 10, lib. 3.

DEMANDANT. The plaintiff or party who brings a real action. Co. Litt. 127; Comyn, Dig.

DEMANDRESS. A female demandant.

DEMEASE. Death.

DEMEMBRATION. In Scotch law. Maliciously cutting off or otherwise separating one limb from another. 1 Hume, 323; Bell, Dict.

DEMENS (Lat.) One who has lost his mind through sickness or some other cause; one whose faculties are enfeebled. Dean, Med. Jur. 481. See "Dementia."

DEMENTENANT EN AVANT (Law Fr.) From this time forward. Kelham.

DEMENTIA. In medical jurisprudence. That form of insanity which is characterized by mental weakness and decrepitude, and by total inability to reason correctly or incorrectly.

DEMESNE. Lands of which the lord had the absolute property or ownership, as distinguished from feudal lands which he held of a superior. 2 Sharswood, Bl. Comm. 104; Cowell. Lands which the lord retained under his immediate control, for the purpose of supplying his table and the immediate needs of his household. Distinguished from that farmed out to tenants, called among the Saxons "bordlands." Blount; Co. Litt. 17a.

Own; original. *Son assault demesne,* his (the plaintiff's) original assault, or assault in the first place. 2 Greenl. Ev. § 633; 3 Bl. Comm. 120, 306.

DEMESNE AS OF FEE. A man is said to be seised in his demesne as of fee of a corporeal inheritance, because he has a property *dominicum* or demesne in the thing itself. 2 Bl. Comm. 106. But when he has no dominion in the thing itself, as in the case of an incorporeal hereditament, he is said to be seised as of fee, and not in his demesne as of fee. Litt. § 10; 17 Serg. & R. (Pa.) 196; Jones, Land tit. 166.

Formerly it was the practice in an action on the case—*e. g.* for a nuisance to real estate—to aver in the declaration the seisin of the plaintiff in demesne as of fee; and this is still necessary, in order to estop the record with the land, so that it may run with or attend the title. Archb. Civ. Pl. 104; Coke, Entr. 9, pl. 8; Lilly, Entr. 62; 1 Saund, 346; Willes, 508. But such an action may be maintained on the possession as well as on the seisin, although the effect of the record in this case upon the title would not be the same. Steph. Pl. 322; 1 Lutw. 120; 2 Mod. 71; 4 Term R. 718; 2 Wm. Saund. 113b; Cro. Car. 500, 575.

DEMESNE LANDS. A phrase meaning the same as "demesne."

DEMESNE LANDS OF THE CROWN. That share of lands reserved to the crown at the original distribution of landed property, or which came to it afterwards by forfeiture or otherwise. 1 Sharswood, Bl. Comm. 286; 2 Steph. Comm. 550.

DEMESNIAL. Pertaining to a demesne.

DEMI-MARK. A sum of money (6s., 8d., 3 Bl. Comm. App. v.) tendered and paid into court in certain cases in the trial of a writ of right by the grand assize. Co. Litt. 294b; Booth, Real Actions, 98.

It was paid by the tenant to obtain an inquiry by the grand assize into the time of the demandant's seisin. 1 Reeve, Hist. Eng. Law, 429; Stearns, Real Actions, 378, and note. It compelled the demandant to begin. 3 Chit. Pl. 1373. It is unknown in American practice. 13 Wend. (N. Y.) 546; Stearns, Real Actions, 378.

DEMINUTIO. In civil law. A taking away; loss or deprivation. See "Capitas Deminutio."

DEMI-OFFICIAL. Partly official or authorized.

DEMI-SANGUE, or **DEMY-SANGUE** (Law Fr.) Half blood.

DEMI-VILL. Half a tithing.

DEMIDIETAS. A word used in ancient records for a moiety, or one-half.

DEMIES. In some universities and colleges this term is synonymous with "scholars." Boyle, Char. 129.

DEMISE.

(1) A conveyance, either in fee for life or for years. A lease or conveyance for a term of years. According to Chief Justice Gibson, the term strictly denotes a posthumous grant, and no more. 5 Whart. (Pa.) 278. See 4 Bing. N. C. 678; 2 Bouv. Inst. note 1774 et seq.

(2) A term nearly synonymous with "death," appropriated in England especially to denote the decease of the king or queen.

DEMISE AND RE-DEMISE. A conveyance by mutual leases made from one to another on each side of the same land, or of something issuing from it. A lease for a given sum,—usually a mere nominal amount,—and a release for a larger rent. Toullier, Dr. Civ.; Whishaw; Jacob.

DEMISE OF THE KING. The natural dissolution of the king.

The term is said to denote in law merely a transfer of the property of the crown. 1 Bl. Comm. 249. By demise of the crown, we mean only that, in consequence of the disunion of the king's natural body from his body politic, the kingdom is transferred or demised to his successor, and so the royal dignity remains perpetual. Plowd. 117, 234.

A similar result, viz., the perpetual existence of the president of the United States, has been secured by the constitution and subsequent statutes. 1 Sharswood, Bl. Comm. 249.

DEMISI. I have demised or leased. *Demisi, concessi, et ad firmam tradidi,* have demised, granted, and to farm let. The usual operative words in ancient leases, as the corresponding English words are in the modern forms. 2 Bl. Comm. 317, 318.

DEMOLISH. To pull down or destroy, or begin to demolish, pull down or destroy. 50 L. J. M. C. 143. A substantial destruction is a demolition, even though a small part of the building be left uninjured. And a like meaning is to be given to "feloniously demolished, pulled down, or destroyed, wholly or in part." Car. & M. 602.

DEMONSTRATIO. Description.

Falsa demonstratio non nocet, a false description does not injure.

DEMONSTRATION. (Lat. *demonstrare,* to point out). Whatever is said or written to designate a thing or person.

Several descriptions may be employed to denote the same person or object; and the rule of law in such cases is that, if one of the descriptions be erroneous, it may be rejected, if, after it is expunged, enough will remain to identify the person or thing intended. For *falsa demonstratio non nocet.* The meaning of this rule is that, if there be an adequate description with convenient certainty of what was contemplated, a subsequent erroneous addition will not vitiate it. The complement of this maxim is, *non accipi debent verba in demonstrationem falsam quae competent in limitationem veram;* which means that if it stand doubtful upon the words whether they import a false reference or demonstration, or whether they be words of restraint that limit the generality of the former words, the law will never intend error or falsehood. If, therefore, there is some object wherein all the demonstrations are true, and some wherein part are true and part false, they shall be intended words of true limitation to ascertain that person or thing wherein all the circumstances are true. 4 Exch. 604, per Alderson, B.; 8 Bing. 244; Broom, Leg. Max. 490; Plowd. 191; 7 Cush. (Mass.) 460.

The rule that *falsa demonstratio* does not vitiate an otherwise good description applies to every kind of statement of fact. Some of the particulars in an averment in a declaration may be rejected if the declaration is sensible without them, and by their presence is made insensible or defective. Yelv. 182.

——**In Evidence.** That proof which excludes all possibility of error.

DEMONSTRATIVE LEGACY. A pecuniary legacy, coupled with a direction that it be paid out of a specific fund.

DEMPSTER, or **DEEMSTER.** In Scotch law. A doomsman; one who pronounced the sentence of court. 1 How. St. Tr. 937.

DEMURRAGE. The delay of a vessel by the freighter beyond the time allowed for loading, unloading, or sailing. 3 Kent. Comm. 203.

Payment for such delay.

Demurrage is an extended freight or reward to the vessel in compensation for earnings she is compelled to lose. Abb. Adm. (D. C.) 548.

The term is also applied to the payment for delay of railroad equipment.

DEMURRANT. One who demurs to a pleading or indictment.

DEMURRER (Lat. *demorari;* old Fr. *demorrer,* to stay; to abide).

——**In Pleading at Law.** An allegation that, admitting the facts of the preceding pleading to be true as stated by the party making it, he has yet shown no cause why the party demurring should be compelled by the court to proceed further. A declaration that the party demurring will go no further, because the other has shown nothing against him. 5 Mod. 232; Co. Litt. 71b. It imports that the objecting party will not proceed, but will wait the judgment of the court whether he is bound so to do. Co. Litt. 71b; Steph. Pl. 61.

A general demurrer is one which excepts to the sufficiency of a previous pleading in general terms; such a demurrer being sufficient if the objection is to matters of substance. Steph. Pl. 159.

A special demurrer is one which shows specifically the nature of the objection, and the ground of exception. Co. Litt. 72a.

——**In Equity Pleading.** An allegation of a defendant, which, admitting the matters of fact alleged by the bill to be true, shows that as they are therein set forth they are insufficient for the plaintiff to proceed upon or to oblige the defendant to answer; or, that, for some reason apparent on the face of the bill, or on account of the omission of some matter which ought to be contained therein, or for want of some circumstances which ought to be attendant thereon, the defendant ought not to be compelled to answer to the whole bill, or to some certain part thereof. Mitf. Eq. Pl. (Jeremy Ed.) 107.

Demurrers are general, where no particular cause is assigned except the usual formulary that there is no equity in the bill; or special, where the particular defects are pointed out. Story, Eq. Pl. § 455. General demurrers are used to point out defects of substance; special, to point out defects in form.

In many states, the grounds of demurrer and the requisites of a demurrer are regulated by statute. Thus, in Minnesota a complaint may be demurred to for (1) absence of jurisdiction; (2) lack of legal capacity in plaintiff to sue; (3) another action pending; (4) defect of parties; (5) misjoinder of causes of action; (6) failure to state facts sufficient to constitute a cause of action. The demurrer must distinctly specify the ground of objection as being one of those enumerated by Gen. St. Minn. 1878, c. 66, §§ 92, 93.

——**In Practice.** Demurrer to evidence is a declaration that the party making it will not proceed, because the evidence offered on the other side is not sufficient to maintain the issue. 28 Ala. (N. S.) 637. Upon joinder by the opposite party, the jury is generally discharged from giving any verdict (1 Archb. Prac. 186); and the demurrer, being entered on record, is afterwards argued and decided by the court in *banc;* and the judgment there given upon it may ultimately be brought before a court of error. See 2 H. Bl. 187; 4 Chit. Prac. 15; Gould, Pl. c. 9, pt. 2, § 47. It admits the truth of the evidence given, and the legal deductions therefrom. 14 Pa. St. 275. As to the right so to demur, and the practice, see 4 Iowa, 63.

Demurrer to interrogatories is the reason which a witness tenders for not answering a particular question in interrogatories. 2 Swanst. Ch. 194. It is not, strictly speaking, a demurrer, except in the popular sense of the word. Gresl. Eq. Ev. 61. The court are judicially to determine its validity. The witness must state his objection very carefully, for these demurrers are held to strict rules, and are readily overruled if they cover too much. 2 Atk. 524; 1 Younge & J. 132.

See, generally, as to demurrer, Bouv. Inst. Index.

DEMURRER BOOK. In English practice. A transcript of all the pleadings that have been filed or delivered between the parties made upon the formation of an issue at law. Steph. Pl. 95.

DEMY SANKE, or **DEMY SANGUE.** Half-blood. A corruption of *demi-sang.*

DEN AND STROND. Liberty for ships and vessels to run aground or come ashore,—strand themselves. Cowell.

DENARIATE. As much land as is worth one penny per annum. Rapalje & L.

DENARII. An ancient general term for any sort of *pecunia numerata,* or ready money. The French use the word *denier* in the same sense, *payer de ses propres deniers.*

DENARII DE CARITATE. Customary oblations made to a cathedral church at Pentecost.

DENARII S. PETRI. Commonly called "Peter's Pence." An annual payment on St. Peter's feast of a penny from every family to the pope, during the time that the Roman Catholic religion was established in England.

DENARIUS (Law Lat.; Fr. *denier*). A penny; an English penny. By the statute called *Compositio Mensurarum,* 51 Edw. I. (Hen. III.), it was declared that the penny sterling of England, *denarius Angliae qui nominatur sterlingus,* should weigh 32 grains of corn from the middle of the ear, and 20 pennies (penny weights) should make an ounce, and 12 ounces a pound. Spelman; Fleta, lib. 2, c. 12. See 2 Inst. 575.

——**In the Roman Law.** A silver coin of the value of ten asses, or ten pounds of brass. Its value in modern money is estimated at 7¾d. sterling, or about 14½ cents. Enc. Am. Brande.

DENARIUS DEI. A certain sum of money which is given by one of the contracting parties to the other as a sign of the completion of the contract.

It differs from *arrhae* in this, that the latter is a part of the consideration, while the *denarius Dei* is no part of it. 1 Duv. note 132; 3 Duv. note 49; Repert. de Jur. "Denier a Dieu."

It does not bind the parties, as he who received it may return it in a limited time, or the other may abandon it, and avoid the engagement.

DENARIUS TERTIUS COMITATUS (Law Lat.) In old English law. The third penny of the county; the third part of the fines and profits arising from the county court, which anciently were reserved to the *comes,* or earl, as his official stipend. Spelman, voc. "Comes"; LL. Edw. Conf. c. 1; Cowell.

DENIAL. In pleading. A traverse of the statement of the opposite party; a defense.

It may be general of all the allegations in a pleading, or a particular part thereof, or special of certain stated facts.

DENIER (Law Fr.) In old English law. Denial; refusal. *Denier* is when the rent (being demanded upon the land) is not paid. Finch, Law, bk. 3, c. 5.

DENIER A DIEU. In French law. A sum of money which the hirer of a thing gives to the other party as evidence, or for the consideration of the contract, which either party may annul within twenty-four hours; the one who gave the *denier a Dieu* by demanding, and the other by returning it. See "Denarius Dei."

DENIZATION. The act by which a foreigner becomes a subject, but without the rights either of a natural-born subject, or of one who has become naturalized. Bac. Abr. "Aliens" (B).

DENIZE. To make a denizen.

DENIZEN. In English law. An alien born who has obtained, *ex donatione legis,* letters patent to make him an English subject.

He is intermediate between a natural-born subject and an alien. He may take lands by purchase or devise, which an alien cannot; but he is incapable of taking by inheritance. 1 Bl. Comm. 374.

In South Carolina, and perhaps in other states, this civil condition is well known to the law, having been created by statute.

The right of making denizens is not exclusively vested in the king, for it is possessed by parliament, but is scarcely ever exercised but by royal power. It may be effected by conquest. 7 Coke, 6a; 2 Ventr. 6; Comyn, Dig. "Alien" (D 1); Chit. Com. Law, 120.

DENMAN'S (LORD) ACT. St. 6 & 7 Vict. 85. For the amendment of the law of evidence, which provides that no person offered as a witness shall thereafter be excluded by reason of incapacity, from crime or interest, from giving evidence. Wharton.

DENMAN'S (MR.) ACT. St. 28 & 29 Vict. 18. For amendment of procedure in criminal trials, allowing counsel to sum up the evidence in criminal as in civil trials, provided the prisoner be defended by counsel. Wharton.

DENOMBREMENT. n French feudal law. A minute or act drawn up, on the creation of a fief, containing a description of the fief, and all the rights and incidents belonging to it. Guyot, Inst. Feud. c. 3.

DENOMINATIO FIERI DEBET A DIGNIoribus. Denomination should be made from the more worthy.

DENOUNCEMENT. (In Mexican law.) A denouncement was a judicial proceeding, and though real property might be acquired by an alien in fraud of the law—that is without observing its requirements—he nevertheless retained his right and title to it, liable to be deprived of it by the proper proceeding of denouncement, which in its substantive characteristics was equivalent to the inquest of office found, at common law. 26 Cal. 477.

DENUMERATION. The act of present payment. Rapalje & L.

DENUNCIATION. In civil law. The act by which an individual informs a public officer, whose duty it is to prosecute offenders, that a crime has been committed. See 1 Brown, Civ. Law, 447; 2 Brown, Civ. Law, 389; Ayliffe, Par. 210; Poth. Proc. Cr. 2, § 2.

DENUNTIATIO. In old English law. A public notice or summons. Bracton, 202b.

DEODAND. Any personal chattel whatever which is the immediate cause of the death of a human creature, which is forfeited to the king, to be distributed in alms by his high almoner. 1 Bl. Comm. 301; 1 Hale, P. C. 422.

DEPART.

——**In Pleading.** To forsake or abandon the ground assumed in a former pleading, and assume a new one. See "Departure."

——**In Old English Law.** To divide or separate; to part. Cowell.

——**In Maritime Law.** To leave a port; to be out of a port. To depart imports more than to sail, or set sail. A warranty in a policy that a vessel shall depart on or before a particular day is a warranty not only that she shall sail, but that she shall be out of the port on or before that day. 3 Maule & S. 461; 3 Kent, Comm. 307. note. "To depart" does not mean merely to break ground, but fairly to set forward upon the voyage. 6 Taunt. 241.

DEPARTMENT. A portion of a country. In France, the country is divided into departments, which are somewhat similar to the counties in this country. The United States have been divided into military departments, including certain portions of the country. 1 Pet. (U. S.) 293. These departments are, for the purposes for which they are created, under the immediate government of some officer, who is, in turn, responsible to his superior.

A portion of the agents employed by the executive branch of the United States government, to whom a specified class of duties is assigned.

DEPARTURE.

——**In Maritime Law.** A deviation from the course prescribed in the policy of insurance. It may be justifiable. See "Deviation."

——**In Pleading.** The statement of matter in a replication, rejoinder, or subsequent pleading, as a cause of action or defense, which is not pursuant to the previous pleading of the same party, and which does not support and fortify it. 3 Bl. Comm. 301.

Where a party quits or departs from the case or defense he has just made, and has recourse to another. 13 N. Y. 89.

DEPARTURE IN DESPITE OF COURT. This took place where the tenant, having once made his appearance in court upon demand, failed to reappear when demanded. Co. Litt. 139a. As the whole term is, in contemplation of law, but a single day, an appearance on any day, and a subsequent failure to reappear at any subsequent part of the term, is such a departure. 8 Coke, 62a; 1 Rolle, Abr. 583; Metc. Yelv. 211; Roscoe, Real Actions, 283.

DEPASTURE. In old English law. To pasture. "If a man depastures unprofitable cattle in his ground." Bunb. 1, case 1.

DEPECULATION. A robbing of the prince or commonwealth; an embezzling of the public treasure.

DEPENDENCY. A territory distinct from the country in which the supreme sovereign power resides, but belonging rightfully to it, and subject to the laws and regulations which the sovereign may think proper to prescribe.

It differs from a "colony," because it is not settled by the citizens of the sovereign or mother state; and from "possession," because it is held by other title than that of mere conquest. For example, Malta was considered a dependency of Great Britain in the year 1813. 3 Wash. C. C. (U. S.) 286. See Act Cong. March 1, 1809, commonly called the "Nonimportation Law."

The state of being dependent for support. So used in Workmen's Compensation Acts.

DEPENDENT. One who depends; one who is sustained by another, or who relies on another for support or favor. 251 Ill. 256.

DEPENDENT CONTRACT. One which it is not the duty of the contractor to perform until some obligation contained in the same agreement has been performed by the other party. Hammond, Part. 17, 29, 30, 109.

DEPENDENT COVENANTS. Those in which the performance of one depends on the performance of the other.

DEPENDING. Sometimes used for "pending."

DEPESAS. In Spanish-American law. Spaces of ground in towns reserved for commons or public pasturage. 12 Pet. (U. S.) 443, note. White, New Recop. bk. 2, tit. 1, c. 6.

DEPONE. In Scotch practice. To depose; to make oath in writing.

DEPONENT. One who gives information, on oath or affirmation, respecting some facts known to him, before a magistrate; strictly, he who makes a deposition; but sometimes used for "affiant."

DEPONER. In old Scotch practice. A deponent. 3 How. St. Tr. 695.

DEPOPULATIO AGRORUM. In old English law. The crime of destroying, ravaging, or laying waste a country. 2 Hale, P. C. 333; 4 Bl. Comm. 373.

DEPOPULATION. In old English law. A species of waste, by which the population of the kingdom was diminished. Depopulation of houses was a public offense. 12 Coke, 30, 31.

DEPORTATIO (Lat.) In the civil law. A kind of banishment, where a condemned person was sent or carried away to some foreign country, usually to an island, *in insulam deportatur*, and thus taken out of the number of Roman citizens, *ex numero civium Romanorum tollitur*, being treated as though he were dead. Inst. 1. 12. 1. It was banishment for life, attended with the loss of civil rights, and the forfeiture of property. *Relegatio* was banishment for years, without the loss of civil rights. Dig. 48. 22; Calv. Lex. Bracton uses the term *deportatio* as synonymous with "exile," "abjuration of the realm," and "outlawry." Bracton, fol. 136b.

DEPORTATION. In Roman law. A perpetual banishment, depriving the banished of his rights as a citizen. It differed from "relegation" (*q. v.*) and "exile" (*q. v.*) 1 Brown, Civ. Law, 125, note; Inst. 1. 12. 1. 2; Dig. 48. 22. 14. 1.

In English law the word referred to sentences to servitude in penal colonies.

In American law the word usually refers to the compulsory removal from the country of undesirable aliens.

DEPOSE. To deprive an individual of a public employment or office against his will. Wolffius, Inst. § 1063. The term is usually applied to the deprivation of all authority of a sovereign.

To give a deposition.

DEPOSIT. A naked bailment of goods to be kept for the depositor without reward, and to be returned when he shall require it. Jones, Bailm. 36, 117; 9 Mass. 470.

A bailment of goods to be kept by the bailee without reward, and delivered according to the object or purpose of the original trust. Story, Bailm. § 41.

A contract by which one of the contracting parties gives a thing to another to keep, who is to do so gratuitously, and obliges himself to return it when he shall be requested.

To constitute a deposit, there must be (1) an actual delivery of the property; (2) the object must be to keep the property for the owner; (3) the custody must be gratuitous; (4) the deposit must be with another than the owner; and (5) there must be a voluntary undertaking by the bailee. Story, Bailm. §§ 55-60.

Deposits are divided in the civil law into necessary and voluntary.

(1) Necessary deposits are those made upon some sudden emergency, as of fire or shipwreck.

(2) Voluntary deposits are those made, in the absence of necessity, by contract of the parties. This distinction was unknown at common law.

Deposits are again divided in the civil law into simple deposits and sequestrations.

(3) Simple deposits are those made by one or more persons having a common interest.

(4) Deposits by sequestration are by persons having different or adverse interests in the property. Sequestrations are (a) conventional, by act of the parties, or (b) judicial, by order of a court in a judicial proceeding.

There are also certain contracts in the nature of deposits, and commonly regarded as such.

Irregular deposits, where money is deposited to be returned not in specie, but by an equal sum.

Quasi deposits, where one comes lawfully into the possession of goods of another by finding. Story, Bailm. §§ 41-85.

In modern usage, the term is most frequently used to denote the deposit of money in a banking institution. Deposits in bank are general if the money deposited becomes the property of the bank, and it undertakes to repay only an equal amount. Special, if the particular funds are to be returned.

DEPOSIT OF TITLE DEEDS. A pledge of land as security by giving the muniments of title to the pledgee. It is now seldom, if ever, used.

DEPOSITARY. One with whom anything is deposited (see "Deposit") or lodged in trust; as "depository" is the place where it is put. The obligation on the part of the depositary is that he keep the thing with reasonable care, and, upon request, restore it to the depositor, or otherwise deliver it, according to the original trust.

DEPOSITION. The testimony of a witness reduced to writing, in due form of law, by virtue of a commission or other authority of a competent tribunal, or according to the provisions of some statute law, to be used on the trial of some question of fact in a court of justice.

In some states it is applied to the testimony taken on a preliminary hearing, and reduced to writing by the committing magistrate.

In its generic sense, it embraces all written evidence verified by oath, and includes affidavits, but in legal language, a distinction is maintained between depositions and affidavits. 3 Blatchf. (U. S.) 456.

In its technical sense, it is confined to the written testimony of a witness given in a judicial proceeding. 53 Am. Dec. 270.

——**In Ecclesiastical Law.** The act of depriving a clergyman, by a competent tribunal, of his clerical orders, to punish him for some offense, and to prevent his acting in future in his clerical character. Ayliffe, Par. 206.

DEPOSITO. In Spanish law. A real contract by which one person confides to the custody of another an object on the condition that it shall be returned to him whenever he shall require it.

DEPOSITOR. He who makes a deposit.

DEPOSITUM (Lat. from *deponere*, to deposit). In the civil and common law. A naked bailment of goods, to be kept for the bailor without reward, and to be returned when he shall require it. Story, Bailm. §§ 4, 41; 2 Kent, Comm. 558, 559; Jones, Bailm. 36; Inst. 3. 15. 3; Bracton, fol. 100b; Dig. 16. 3; Code, 4. 34; Fleta, lib. 2, c. 56, § 7. Otherwise termed "deposit" (*q. v.*); the bailor being in this case termed the "depositor," and the bailee the "depositary." Bell, Dict.

DEPOT. In the French law. The *depositum* of the Roman, and the "deposit" of the English law. It is of two kinds, being either (1) *depot* simply so called, and which may be either voluntary or necessary, and (2) *sequestre*, which is a deposit made either under an agreement of the parties, and to abide the event of pending litigation regarding it, or by virtue of the direction of the court or a judge, pending litigation regarding it. Brown.

DEPRAVE. To defame; vilify; exhibit contempt for. In England, depraving the Lord's supper or the Book of Common Prayer is a criminal offense, punishable with fine and imprisonment. Steph. Crim. Dig. 99.

DEPREDATION. In French law. The pillage which is made of the goods of a decedent.

DEPRIVATION. In ecclesiastical law. A censure by which a clergyman is deprived of his parsonage, vicarage, or other ecclesiastical promotion or dignity. See Ayliffe, Par. 206; 1 Bl. Comm. 393.

DEPUTY. One authorized by an officer to exercise the office or right which the officer possesses, for and in place of the latter.

A deputy differs from an assignee in that an assignee has an interest in the office itself, and does all things in his own name, for whom his grantor shall not answer except in special cases, but a deputy has not any interest in the office, but is only the shadow of the officer in whose name he acts. And there is a distinction between doing an act by an agent or by a deputy. An agent can only bind his principal when he acts in the name of the principal. But a deputy may do the act, and sign his own name, and bind the principal, for a deputy has in law the whole power of his principal. Wharton.

DEPUTY STEWARD. A steward of a manor may depute or authorize another to hold a court; and the acts done in a court so holden will be as legal as if the court had been holden by the chief steward in person. So an under steward or deputy may authorize another as subdeputy, *pro hac vice*, to hold a court for him; such limited authority not being inconsistent with the rule *delegatus non potest delegare*. Wharton.

DERAIGN, DEREYN, or **DEREINE** (Law Lat. *derationare*, *dirationare*, or *disrationare;* Law Fr. *dereiner*, *derener*, *disreigner*, *disrener*, *contra* for *deraisner* or *deraisoner*). In old English law. To prove; to "*deraign* the warranty paramount." St. 31 Hen. VIII. c. 1; Cowell. See Glanv. lib. 2, c. 3; Id. c. 6, 20; 1 Reeve, Hist. Eng. Law, 123; Spelman, voc. "Dirationare."

In Texas, and perhaps other states, it is used to signify the assertion or proof of title from an ancestor or predecessor, *e. g.*, "to deraign title from the original patentee or pre-emptor."

To disprove or refute the assertion of an adverse party. Spelman makes this to be the proper meaning, relying in particular upon the etymology of *disrationare* (from *dis*, contrary, and *ratiocinari*, to reason).

To deny or refuse. "He cannot deraign battel." Dyer, 137. See Barr. Obs. St. 328.

To put out of place or order; to displace or disarrange; to turn one out of his order; to degrade. Some of the old books give the words this sense, deriving it either from the French *disarrayer*, to confound, or *derayer*, *desranger*, to derange or displace. Termes de la Ley; Cowell; Co. Litt. 136; Perkins,

c. 1, § 3 (G). This derivation, however, is not approved by Spelman.

DERECHO. In Spanish law. Law or right. White, New Recop. bk. 4, tit. 4. *Derecho comun,* common law. The civil law is so called. Id. bk. 2, tit. 13, c. 1, § 5. A right. *Derechos,* rights.

DERELICT. Abandoned; deserted; cast away.

Land left uncovered by the receding of water from its former bed. 2 Rolle, Abr. 170; 2 Bl. Comm. 262; 1 Crabb, Real Prop. 109.

When so left by degrees, the derelict land belongs to the owner of the soil adjoining; but when the sea retires suddenly, it belongs to the government. 2 Bl. Comm. 262; 1 Brown, Civ. Law, 239; 1 Sumn. (U. S.) 328, 490; 1 Gall (U. S.) 133; Bee, Adm. (U. S.) 62, 178, 260; Ware (U. S.) 332.

Personal property abandoned or thrown away by the owner in such manner as to indicate that he intends to make no further claim thereto. 2 Bl. Comm. 9; 2 Reeve, Hist. Eng. Law, 9; 1 C. B. 112; Broom, Leg. Max. Vessel 261.

DERELICTION (Lat. *derelictio*). The gaining of land from the water, in consequence of the sea shrinking back below the usual water mark; the opposite of *alluvion* (*q. v.*) 2 Rolle, Abr. 170; Dyer, 326b; 2 Bl. Comm. 262; 1 Steph. Comm. 419.

The abandonment of property. 2 Bl. Comm. 9.

DERIVATIVA POTESTAS NON POTEST esse major primitiva. The power which is derived cannot be greater than that from which it is derived. Wingate, Max. 36; Finch, Law, bk. 1, c. 3, p. 11.

DERIVATIVE. Coming from another; taken from something preceding; secondary; as, derivative title, which is that acquired from another person.

There is considerable difference between an original and a derivative title. When the acquisition is original, the right thus acquired to the thing becomes property, which must be unqualified and unlimited, and, since no one but the occupant has any right to the thing, he must have the whole right of disposing of it. But with regard to derivative acquisition it may be otherwise; for the person from whom the thing is acquired may not have an unlimited right to it, or he may convey or transfer it with certain reservations of right. Derivative title must always be by contract.

——**Derivative Conveyances.** Those which presuppose some precedent conveyance, and serve only to enlarge, confirm, alter, restrain, restore, or transfer the interest granted by such original conveyance. 3 Bl. Comm. 324.

DEROBARE. Law Lat. (from Fr. *desrobber, disrober*). In old European law. To steal; to pilfer. Spelman.

DEROGARE. (Lat. from *de*, from, and *rogare*, to pass a law). In the civil and old English law. To derogate or diminish; to take from or impair the authority, validity or effect of a law or contract; to repeal some clause of an old law by a new one.

DEROGATION. The partial abrogation of a law. To derogate from a law is to enact something which impairs its utility and force; to abrogate a law is to abolish it entirely. See "Abrogation."

DEROGATORY CLAUSE. In a will, this is a sentence or secret character inserted by the testator, of which he reserves the knowledge to himself, with a condition that no will he may make thereafter should be valid, unless this clause be inserted word for word. This is done as a precaution to guard against later wills being extorted by violence, or otherwise improperly obtained. By the law of England such a clause would be void, as tending to make the will irrevocable. Wharton.

DEROGATUR LEGI, CUM PARS DETRAhitur; abrogatur legi, cum prorsus tollitur. To derogate from a law is to take away part of it; to abrogate a law is to abolish it entirely. Dig. 50. 16. 102. See 1 Bouv. Inst. note 91.

DESAFUERO. In Spanish law. An irregular action committed with violence against law, custom, or reason.

DESCENDANTS. Those who have issued from an individual, including his children, grandchildren, and their children to the remotest degree. Amb. 327; 2 Brown, 30, 230; 3 Brown, 367, 1 Rop. Leg. 115; 2 Bouv Inst. note 1956.

The descendants from what is called the "direct descending line." The term is opposed to that of "ascendants."

"Descendants" is a good term of description in a will, and includes all who proceed from the body of the person named; as grandchildren and great-grandchildren. Amb. 397; 2 Vern. 108, note 2; 2 Hilliard, Real Prop. 242.

There is a difference between the number of ascendants and descendants which a man may have. Every one has the same order of ascendants, though they may not be exactly alike as to numbers, because some may be descended from a common ancestor. In the line of descendants they fork differently, according to the number of children, and continue longer or shorter, as generations continue or cease to exist. Many families become extinct, while others continue. The line of descendants is, therefore, diversified in each family.

DESCENDER. Descent. See "Formedon."

DESCENT. Hereditary succession.

Title by descent is the title by which one person, upon the death of another, acquires the real estate of the latter as his heir at law. 2 Bl. Comm. 201; Comyn, Dig. "Discent" (A).

It was one of the principles of the feudal system that, on the death of the tenant in fee, the land should descend, and not ascend. Hence the title by inheritance is in all cases called descent, although by statute law the title is sometimes made to ascend.

The English doctrine of primogeniture, by which by the common law the eldest son and his issue take the whole real estate, has been universally abolished in this country. So, with few exceptions, has been the distinction between male and female heirs.

Descent is either "lineal," as from father to son, or "collateral," as from brother to brother.

DESCENT CAST. The same as what the older writers called a "descent which tolls entry." Where a person who had acquired land by disseisin, abatement, or intrusion died seised of the land, the descent of it to his heir took away or "tolled" the real owner's right of entry, so that he could only recover the land by an action. Litt. § 385 et seq.; Co. Litt. 237b. The doctrine of descent cast was abolished by St. 3 & 4 Wm. IV. c. 27; Shelf. R. P. St. 228.

The term seems to have originally meant "the happening of any descent," because the law casts the land upon the heir. Litt. § 385; Watk. Desc. 33.

DESCRIPTIO PERSONAE. Description of the person. In wills, it frequently happens that the word "heir" is used as a *descriptio personae.* It is then a sufficient designation of the person. In criminal cases, a mere *descriptio personae* or addition, if false, can be taken advantage of only by plea in abatement. 1 Metc. (Mass.) 151.

The most common use of the term is in respect to designations as "agent," "executor," etc., attached to the name of one executing an instrument. If such designation is not sufficient to indicate that he is acting in an official or representative capacity, it is said to be *descriptio personae,* and he is bound personally. See 120 Mass. 92; 136 N. Y. 655; 5 Ill. 325; 19 Mo. 193.

DESCRIPTION. An account of the accidents and qualities of a thing. Ayliffe, Pand. 60.

A written account of the state and condition of personal property, titles, papers, and the like. It is a kind of inventory, but is more particular in ascertaining the exact condition of the property, and is without any appraisement of it.

——**In Pleading.** One of the rules which regulate the law of variance is that allegations of matter of essential description should be proved as laid. It is impossible to explain with precision the meaning of these words; and the only practical mode of understanding the extent of the rule is to examine some of the leading decisions on the subject, and then to apply the reasoning or ruling contained therein to other analogous cases. With respect to criminal law, it is clearly established that the name or nature of the property stolen or damaged is matter of essential description. Thus, for example, if the charge is one of firing a stack of hay, and it turns out to have been a stack of wheat, or if a man is accused of stealing a drake, and it is proved to have been a goose, or even a duck, the variance is fatal. 1 Tayl. Ev. § 233.

——**Of Persons.** Words identifying a person by reference to a fiduciary or official capacity, as "Executor," "Treasurer." Such a word, without more, is generally regarded as merely *descriptio personae,* and not as indicative of intention to act in the official or fiduciary capacity. See "Addition."

——**Of Land.** That part of a deed or other instrument that describes or identifies the property involved.

DESERT. (Lat. *deserere*). To leave or quit with an intention not to return; to forsake utterly; to abandon.

"In the common acceptance, both of the common and canon law, doth signify only a bare withdrawing, a temporary quitting of a thing, and neglect only; which leaveth the party at liberty of returning to it again." 26 Barb. (N. Y.) 501.

DESERTION. Abandonment; the abandonment of a duty or of a person as to whom the deserter is charged with a duty; as desertion by a seaman, or a soldier, or by a husband of his wife.

As a cause for divorce, is an unwarranted departure from the conjugal relation, intending not to return. The precise elements vary according to the statutes. In only one or two states is mere abstinence from sexual intercourse regarded as desertion.

The voluntary separation of one of the married parties from the other, or the voluntary refusal to renew a suspended cohabitation, without justification either in the consent or the wrongful conduct of the other. 122 Ill. App. 225.

DESERVIRE. (Law Lat.) To serve; as a feudal tenant did his lord. 2 Bl. Comm. 284.

DESIGN. In the law of evidence. Purpose or intention, combined with plan, or implying a plan in the mind. Burr Circ. Evid. 331; 95 Wis. 293.

——**As Term of Art.** The giving of a visible form to the conceptions of the mind, or, in other words, to the invention. 4 Wash. 52.

——**In Scotch Law.** To assign to; to make over.

DESIGNATIO PERSONAE. The description contained in a contract of the persons who are parties thereto.

DESIGNATIO UNIUS EST EXCLUSIO alterius, et expressum facit cessare tacitum. The appointment or designation of one is the exclusion of another; and that expressed makes that which is implied to cease. Co. Litt. 210.

DESIGNATION. The expression used by a testator to denote a person or thing, instead of the name itself.

A bequest of the farm which the testator bought of a person named, or of a picture which he owns, painted by a certain artist, would be a designation of the thing. A legacy " to the eldest son" of A. would be a designation of the person. See 1 Rop. Leg. c. 2.

DESLINDE. In Spanish law. The act of determining and indicating the boundaries of an estate, county, or province.

DESMEMORIADOS. In Spanish law. Persons without memory. White, New Recop. lib. 1, tit. 2, c. 1, § 4.

DESPACHEURS. The name given, in some countries, to persons appointed to settle cases of average. Ord. Hamb. tit. 21, art. 10.

DESPERATE. Of which there is no hope.

This term is used frequently in making an inventory of a decedent's effects, when a debt is considered so bad that there is no hope of recovering it. It is then called a desperate debt, and, if it be so returned, it will be *prima facie* considered as desperate. See Toller, Ex'rs., 248; 2 Williams, Ex'rs., 644; 1 Chit. Prac. 580; 11 Wend. (N. Y.) 361.

DESPITUS. A contemptible person. Fleta, lib. 4, c. 5, § 4.

DESPONSATION. The act of betrothing persons to each other.

DESPOSORIO. In Spanish law. Espousals; mutual promises of future marriage. White, New Recop. bk. 1, tit. 6, c. 1, § 1.

DESPOT. This word, in its original and most simple acceptation, signifies "master and supreme lord." It is synonymous with "monarch"; but taken in bad part, as it is usually employed, it signifies a "tyrant." In some states, "despot" is the title given to the sovereign, as king is given in others. Enc. Lond.

DESPOTISM. That abuse of government where the sovereign power is not divided, but united in the hands of a single man, whatever may be his official title. It is not, properly, a form of government. Rutherforth, Inst. bk. 1, c. 20, § 1.

DESRENABLE. Unreasonable. Britt. c. 121.

DESTINATION. The intended application of a thing.

For example, when a testator gives to a hospital a sum of money to be applied in erecting buildings, he is said to give a destination to the legacy. Mill stones taken out of a mill to be picked, and to be returned, have a destination, and are considered real estate, although detached from the freehold. Heirlooms, although personal chattels, are, by their destination, considered real estate; and money agreed or directed to be laid out in land is treated as real property. Newland, Cont. c. 3; 3 Wheat. (U. S.) 577; 2 Bell, Comm. 2; Ersk. Inst. 2. 2. 14; Fonbl. Eq. bk. 1, c. 6, § 9. See "Easement"; "Fixtures."

——**In Common Law.** The port at which a ship is to end her voyage is called her "port of destination."

The place for ultimate delivery of goods intrusted for carriage.

DESTRUCTION. A term used in old English law, generally in connection with "waste," and having, according to some, the same meaning. 1 Reeve, Hist. Eng. Law, 385; 3 Bl. Comm. 223. Britton, however, makes a distinction between waste of woods and destruction of houses. Britt. c. 66; St. Marlb. c. 17.

DESUBITO. To weary a person with continual barkings, and then to bite, provided against by old laws.

DESUETUDE. Disuse.

DETACHIARE. To seize or take into custody another's goods or person.

The word is given by Cowell, but seems a corruption of *attachiare.*

DETAINER. Detention; the act of keeping a person against his will, or of withholding the possession of goods or other personal or real property from the owner.

"Detainer" and "detention" are pretty much synonymous. If there be any distinction, it is perhaps that detention applies rather to the act considered as a fact; detainer to the act considered as something done by some person. Detainer is more frequently used with reference to real estate than in application to personal property.

——**In Practice.** A writ or instrument, issued or made by a competent officer, authorizing the keeper of a prison to keep in his custody a person therein named. A detainer may be lodged against one within the walls of a prison, on what account soever he is there. Comyn, Dig. "Process" (E) (3 B).

DETENTION. The act of retaining and preventing the removal of a person or property. See "Detainer."

DETERMINABLE. Liable to come to an end by the happening of a contingency: as, a determinable fee. See 2 Bouv. Inst. note 1695.

DETERMINABLE FEE (also called a "qualified" or "base" fee). One which has a qualification subjoined to it, and which must be determined whenever the qualification annexed to it is at an end. A limitation to a man and his heirs on the part of his father affords an example of this species of estate. Litt. § 254; Co. Litt. 27a, 220; 1 Preston, Est. 449; 2 Bl. Comm. 109; Cruise, Dig. tit. 1, § 82; 2 Bouv. Inst. note 1695.

DETERMINATE. That which is ascertained; what is particularly designated; as, if I sell you my horse Napoleon, the article sold is here determined. This is very different from a contract by which I would have sold you a horse, without a particular designation of any horse. 1 Bouv. Inst. notes 947, 950.

DETERMINATION. The decision of a court of justice.

The end, the conclusion, of a right of authority; as, the determination of a lease. Comyn, Dig. "Estates by Grant" (G 10, 11, 12).

The determination of an authority is the end of the authority given; the end of the return-day of a writ determines the authorty of the sheriff; the death of the principal determines the authority of a mere attorney.

DETERMINE. To come to an end. To bring to an end. 2 Bl. Comm. 121; 1 Washb. Real Prop. 380.

DETESTATIO (Lat.) In the civil law. A summoning made, or notice given, in the presence of witnesses, *denuntiatio facta cum testatione.* Dig. 50. 16. 40.

DETINET (Lat. *detinere,* to detain; *detinet,* he detains). In pleading. An action of debt is said to be in the *detinet* when it alleged merely that the defendant withholds or unjustly detains from the plaintiff the thing or amount demanded, as distinguished from actions in the *cepit* where a wrongful taking is alleged.

DETINUE (Lat. *ditinffere,*—*de,* and *tenere,*—to hold from; to withhold.) In practice. A form of action which lies for the recovery, in specie, of personal chattels from one who acquired possession of them lawfully, but retains it without right, together with damages for the detention. 3 Bl. Comm. 151.

It is generally laid down as necessary to the maintenance of this action that the original taking should have been lawful, thus distinguishing it from replevin, which lies in case the original taking is unlawful. Brooke, Abr. "Detinue," 21, 36, 63. It is said, however, by Chitty, that it lies in cases of tortious taking, except as a distress, and that it is thus distinguished from replevin, which lay originally only where a distress was made, as was claimed, wrongfully. 1 Chit. Pl. 112, 113. See 3 Sharswood, Bl. Comm. 152, and notes. In England this action has yielded to the more practical and less technical action trover, but was much used in the slaveholding states of the United States for the recovery of slaves. 4 Munf. (Va.) 72; 4 Ala. 221; 3 Bibb (Ky.) 510; 16 Overt. (Tenn.) 187; 10 Ired. (N. C.) 124.

DETINUE OF GOODS IN FRANK MARriage. An obsolete writ, by which, after a divorce, the wife might obtain the goods which were given with her in marriage.

DETINUIT (Lat. he detained). In pleading. An action of replevin is said to be in the *detinuit* when the plaintiff acquires possession of the property claimed by means of the writ. The right to retain is, of course, subject in such case to the judgment of the court upon his title to the property claimed. Buller, N. P. 521.

DETRACTARE (Law Lat.) In old English law. To draw, or drag; to draw along; to draw or drag a convict to the gallows or stake. *Detractentur et suspendentur,* they shall be drawn and hanged. Fleta, lib. 1, c. 37, § 4. *Detractari et comburi,* to be drawn and burned. Id. § 2.

DETUNICARI. To discover or lay open to the world. Matt. Westminster, 1240.

DEUNX (Lat. pl. *deunces*). In the Roman law. A division of the *as,* containing eleven *unciae* or duodecimal parts; the proportion of eleven-twelfths. 2 Bl. Comm. 462, note; Tayl. Civ. Law, 492.

DEUS SOLUS HAEREDEM FACERE POtest, non homo. God alone, and not man, can make an heir. Co. Litt. 7b; cited 5 Barn & C. 440, 454; Broom, Leg. Max. (3d London Ed.) 457.

DEUTEROGAMY. A second marriage.

DEVADIATUS, or DIVADIATUS. An offender without sureties or pledges. Cowell.

DEVASTATION. Wasteful use of the property of a deceased person; as, for extravagant funeral or other unnecessary expenses. 2 Bl. Comm. 508.

DEVASTAVERUNT (Lat. pl. of *devastavit*). They have wasted. A term applied in old English law to waste by executors and administrators, and to the process issued against them therefor. Cowell. See "Devastavit."

DEVASTAVIT. A mismanagement and waste by an executor, administrator, or other trustee, of the estate and effects trusted to him as such, by which a loss occurs.

Devastavit may be:

(1) By direct abuse, as when the executor, administrator, or trustee sells, embezzles, or converts to his own use the goods intrusted to him (Comyn, Dig. "Administration" [I 1]), releases a claim due to the estate (3 Bac. Abr. 700; Hob. 266; Cro. Eliz. 43; 7 Johns. [N. Y.] 404; 9 Mass. 352), or surrenders a lease below its value

(2 Johns. Cas. [N. Y.] 376; 3 P. Wms. 330).

(2) By maladministration, as by the payment of claims which were not due nor owing, or by paying others out of the order in which they ought to be paid, or by the payment of legacies before all the debts are satisfied. 4 Serg. & R. (Pa.) 394; 5 Rawle (Pa.) 266.

(3) By neglect, as by neglect to sell the goods at a fair price within a reasonable time, or, if they are perishable goods, before they are wasted; or a neglect to collect a doubtful debt which, by proper exertion, might have been collected. Bac. Abr. "Executors" (L).

DEVENERUNT (Lat. *devenire*, to come to). A writ directed to the king's escheators when any of the king's tenants *in capite* dies, and when his son and heir dies within age, and in the king's custody, commanding the escheat, or that by the oaths of twelve good and lawful men they shall inquire what lands or tenements by the death of the tenant have come to the king. Dyer, 360; Termes de la Ley; Keilw. 199a; Blount; Cowell.

DEVEST (Law Fr. *devester, descester;* Law Lat. *devestire*).

——**In Old English Law.** To take away; to deprive of, as a possession, title, or estate; the opposite of "invest." Termes de la Ley; Cowell. Sometimes written "divest," but "devest" has the support of the best authority. Co. Litt. 15a, 15b; Hale, Anal. § 32. See "Invest."

——**In Modern Law.** To take or draw away. "The whose estate was devested and drawn out of the feoffees." 4 Kent, Comm. 240. "The feoffment made by the feoffees devested all the estates." Id.

To strip or deprive. "The statute devested the feoffees of all the estate." Id. 239. See "Vest."

DEVIATION.

——**In Insurance.** Varying from the risks insured against, as described in the policy, without necessity or just cause, after the risk has begun. 1 Phil. Ins. § 977 et seq.

——**In Contracts.** A change made in the progress of a work from the original plan agreed on.

DEVISAVIT VEL NON. In practice. The name of an issue sent out of a court of chancery, or one which exercises chancery jurisdiction, to a court of law, to try the validity of a paper asserted and denied to be a will, to ascertain whether or not the testator did devise, or whether or not that paper was his will. 7 Brown, Parl. Cas. 437; 2 Atk. 424; 5 Pa. St. 21.

DEVISE. A gift of real property by a person's last will and testament.

The term "devise," properly and technically, applies only to real estate. The object of the devise must, therefore, be that kind of property. 1 Hill, Abr. c. 36, notes 62-74. But it is also sometimes improperly applied to a bequest or legacy. See 2 Bouv. Inst. note 2095 et seq.; 4 Kent, Comm. 489; 8 Viner, Abr. 41; Comyn, Dig. "Estates by Devise."

DEVISEE. A person to whom a devise has been made.

DEVISOR. A testator; one who devises real estate.

DEVOIR. Duty. It is used in the statute of 2 Rich. II. c. 3, in the sense of "duties" or "customs."

DEVOLUTION. In ecclesiastical law. The transfer, by forfeiture, of a right and power which a person has to another, on account of some act or negligence of the person who is vested with such right or power; for example, when a person has the right of presentation, and he does not present within the time prescribed, the right devolves on his next immediate superior. Ayliffe, Par. 331.

In the law of decedents' estates, it comprehends the processes whereby title is transmitted on the death of the owner of property.

DEVOLVE. "To devolve means to pass from a person dying to a person living." 1 Myline & K. 648.

DEVYER (Law Fr.) To die. *Deoya*, died. Y. B. I. 1 Edw. II. 11.

DEXTANS (Lat.) In Roman law. A division of the *as*, consisting of ten *unciae;* ten-twelfths, or five-sixths. 2 Bl. Comm. 462, note (m); Tayl. Civ. Law, 492.

DI COLONNA. In maritime law. A contract between the owner of a ship, the captain, and the mariners, that the voyage shall be for the benefit of all. The term is used in the Italian law. Targa, cc. 36, 37; Emerig. Mar. Loans, § 5.

DI. ET FI. (Law Lat.) In old writs. An abbreviation of *dilecto et fideli*, to his beloved and faithful. Reg. Orig. 17.

DIARIUM. Daily food, or as much as will suffice for the day. Du Cange.

DIATAXIS. In the civil law a constitution or ordinance. The novels of Justinian are all given this name.

DIATHEKE. In the civil law a will or testament.

DIATIM. In old records. Daily; every day; from day to day. Spelman.

DICA. In old English law. A tally for accounts, by number of cuts (*taillees*), marks or notches. Cowell. See "Tallia"; "Tally."

DICAST. An officer in ancient Greece answering nearly to our juryman.

DICTATOR. In Roman law. A magistrate at Rome invested with absolute power. His authority over the lives and fortunes of the citizens was without bounds. His office continued but for six months. Hist. de la Jur. Dig. 1. 2. 18. 1. 1. 1.

DICTUM. An opinion expressed by a court, but which, not being necessarily involved in the case, lacks the force of an adjudication. Usually given *obiter dictum.*

An opinion expressed by a court, upon a point in a case argued and deliberately passed on, though not essential to the disposition of a case, and hence lacks the force of an adjudication. 227 Ill. 337.

It frequently happens that, in assigning its opinion upon a question before it, the court discusses collateral questions, and expresses a decided opinion upon them. Such opinions, however, are frequently given without much reflection, or without previous argument at the bar; and as, moreover, they do not enter into the adjudication of the point before it, they have only that authority which may be accorded to the opinion, more or less deliberate, of the individual judge who announces it. It may be observed that in recent times, particularly in those jurisdictions where appeals are largely favored, the ancient practice of courts in this respect is much modified. Formerly, judges aimed to confine their opinion to the precise point involved, and were glad to make that point as narrow as it might justly be. Where appeals are frequent, however, a strong tendency may be seen to fortify the judgment given with every principle that can be invoked in its behalf,—those that are merely collateral, as well as those that are necessarily involved. In some courts of last resort, also, when there are many judges, it is not unfrequently the case that, while the court come to one and the same conclusion, the different judges may be led to that conclusion by different views of the law, so that it becomes difficult to determine what is to be regarded as the principle upon which the case was decided, and what shall be deemed mere *dicta.* According to the more rigid rule, an expression of opinion, however deliberate, upon a question, however fully argued, if not essential to the disposition that was made of the case, may be regarded as a *dictum;* but it is, on the other hand, said that it is difficult to see why, in a philosophical point of view, the opinion of the court is not as persuasive on all the points which were so involved in the cause that it was the duty of counsel to argue them, and which were deliberately passed over by the court, as if the decision had hung upon but one point. 1 Abb. N. Y. Dig. pref. iv. Consult 17 Serg. & R. (Pa.) 292; 1 Phillim. Ecc. Law, 406; 1 Eng. Ecc. 129; Ram, Judgm. c. 5, p. 36; Willes, 666; 1 H. Bl. 53-63; 2 Bos. & P. 375; 7 Pa. St. 287; 3 Barn. & Ald. 341; 2 Bing. 90. The doctrine of the courts of France on this subject is stated in 11 Toullier, Dr. Civ. 177, note 133. As to weight given to *dicta* in former decisions, see 6 Wheat. (U. S.) 399; 4 Heisk. (Tenn.) 419.

——**In French Law.** The report of a judgment made by one of the judges who has given it. Poth. Proc. Civ. pl. 1, c. 5, art. 2.

DICTUM DE KENILWORTH. The edict or declaration of Kenilworth. An edict or award between King Henry III. and all the barons and others who had been in arms against him; and so called because it was made at Kenilworth Castle, in Warwickshire, in the fifty-first year of his reign, containing a composition of five years' rent for the lands and estates of those who had forfeited them in that rebellion. Blount; 2 Reeve, Hist. Eng. Law, 62; Hale, Hist. Com. Law, 10, and note.

DIEI DICTIO (Lat.) In the Roman law. The notice given by a magistrate that he intended to impeach a certain citizen, whom he mentioned by name, of a certain crime, before the people, on a certain day. Halifax, Anal. bk. 3, c. 13, No. 40.

DIEM CLAUSIT EXTREMUM (Lat. he closed his last day,—died). A writ which lay on the death of a tenant *in capite,* to ascertain the lands of which he died seised, and reclaim them into the king's hands. It was directed to the king' escheators. Fitzh. Nat. Brev. 251 (K); 2 Reeve, Hist. Eng. Law, 327.

A writ of the same name, issuing out of the exchequer after the death of a debtor of the king, to levy the debt of the lands or goods of his heir, executor, or administrator. Termes de la Ley. This writ is still in force in England. 4 Steph. Comm. 47.

DIES (Lat.) A day; days; days for appearance in court; provisions or maintenance for a day. The king's rents were anciently reserved by so many days' provisions. Spelman; Cowell; Blount.

DIES A QUO (Lat.) In civil law. The day from which a transaction begins, the conclusion being the *dies ad quem.* Calv. Lex.; 1 Kaufm. Mackeld. Civ. Law, 168.

DIES AMORIS (Lat.) A day of favor. If obtained after a default by the defendant, it amounted to a waiver of the default. Co. Litt. 135a; 2 Reeve, Hist. Eng. Law, 60.

DIES CEDIT. The day begins; *dies venit,* the day has come. Two expressions in Roman law which signify the vesting or fixing of an interest, and the interest becoming a present one. Sandars, Just. Inst. (5th Ed.) 225, 232.

DIES COMMUNES IN BANCO (Lat.) Regular days for appearance in court; called also, "common return days." 2 Reeve, Hist. Eng. Law, 57.

DIES DATUS (Lat. a day given). A day or time given to a defendant in a suit, which is in fact a continuance of the cause. It is so called when given before a declaration. When it is allowed afterwards, it assumes the name of "imparlance." (*q. v.*)

Dies datus in banco, a day in bank. Co. Litt. 135. *Dies datus partibus*, a continuance; *dies datus prece partium*, a day given on prayer of the parties.

DIES DOMINICUS NON EST JURIDICUS. Sunday is not a day in law. Co. Litt. 135a; 2 Saund. 291; Broom, Leg. Max. (3d London Ed.) 21; Finch, Law, 7; Noy, Max. 2; Plowd. 265; 3 Dowl. & L. 328; 13 Mass. 327. See "Sunday."

DIES EXCRESCENS. In old English law. The added or increasing day in leap year. Bracton, fols. 359, 359b.

DIES FASTI (Lat.) In Roman law. Days on which courts might be held, and judicial and other business legally transacted. Calv. Lex.; Anthon, Rom. Ant.; 3 Bl. Comm. 424.

DIES FERIATI (Lat.) In the civil law. Holidays. Dig. 2. 12. 2. 9.

DIES GRATIAE (Lat.) In old English law. Days of grace. Co. Litt. 134b.

DIES IN BANCO (Law Lat.) In practice. A day (or days) in banc; a day in the bench or court of Common Bench. 3 Bl. Comm. 277. Bract. fol. 361, 362.

DIES INCEPTUS PRO COMPLETO HABETUR. A day begun is held as complete.

DIES INCERTUS PRO CONDITIONE HABETUR. A day uncertain is held as a condition. Bell, Dict. "Computation of Time."

DIES INTERCISI. In Roman law. Divided days; days on which the courts were open for a part of the day. Calv. Lex.; 1 Mackeld. Civ. Law, p. 24, § 35, note.

DIES LEGITIMUS. In the civil and old English law. A lawful or law day; a term day; a day of appearance. Halifax, Anal. bk. 3, c. 9, § 6; Bracton, fols. 334b, 359.

DIES MARCHIAE. In old English law. The day of meeting of English and Scotch, which was annually held on the marches or borders to adjust their differences and preserve peace. Cowell; Tomlin.

DIES NEFASTI (Lat.) In Roman law. Days on which it was unlawful to transact judicial affairs, and on which the courts were closed. Anthon, Rom. Ant.; Calv. Lex.; 1 Kaufm. Mackeld. Civ. Law, 24.

DIES NON (Lat.) An abbreviation of the phrase *dies nonjuridicus*, universally used to denote nonjudicial days. Days during which courts do not transact any business, as, Sunday, or the legal holidays. 3 Chit. Gen. Prac. 104; W. Jones, 156.

DIES NONJURIDICUS (Lat.) Nonjudicial days. See "Dies Non."

DIES PACIS (Lat. day of peace). The year was formerly divided into the days of the peace of the church, and the days of the peace of the king, including in the two divisions all the days of the year. Crabb, Hist. Eng. Law, 35.

DIES SOLARIS. In old English law. A solar day, as distinguished from what was called *"dies lunaris"* (a lunar day), both composing an artificial day. Bracton, fol. 264. See "Day."

DIES SOLIS. In the civil and old English law. Sunday, literally, the day of the sun. So called in Code, 3. 12. 7.

DIES UTILES (Lat. useful or available days). Days in which an heir might apply to the judge for an inheritance. Cooper, Inst.; Calv. Lex.; Du Cange.

DIET, or DYET. In Scotch practice. The sitting of a court. 3 How. St. Tr. 654.

An appearance day. Bell, Dict.

A day fixed for the trial of a criminal cause. 2 Alison, Prac. 343; 2 Brown, 240.

A criminal cause as prepared for trial. 1 Brown, 268; 2 Brown, 141. "Deserting the diet." Arkley, 481.

DIETA (Lat.) A day's journey; a day's work; a day's expenses. A reasonable day's journey is said to be twenty miles, by an old computation. Cowell; Spelman; Bracton, 235b; 3 Bl. Comm. 218.

DIETS OF COMPEARANCE. In Scotch law. The days allowed in which to appear after citation.

DIEU SON ACTE (Law Fr.) In old law. God, his act; God's act. An event beyond human foresight or control. Termes de la Ley.

DIFFACERE, or DISFACERE (Law Lat.; old Fr. *deffacer*). In old European law. To disfigure or deface; to mutilate; to destroy. Spelman; LL. Longobard, lib. 1, tit. 25. 1. 68.

Diffactio, a mutilating or maiming. Whishaw.

DIFFERENCE. A contention over a question of truth or fact, as distinguished from a non-agreement over a question.

DIFFICILE EST UT UNUS HOMO VICEM DUORUM SUSTINEAT. It is difficult that one man should sustain the place of two. 4 Coke, 118.

DIFFIDARE. To proclaim hostilities; to declare war; to defy; to outlaw. In feudal law to renounce fealty or allegiance; the opposite of affidare (*q. v.*)

DIFFORCIARE. In old English law. To deny, or keep from one. *Difforciare rectum*, to deny justice to any one, after having been required to do it. Matt. Par. A. D. 1164. Perhaps the same with *deforciare.*

DIGAMA, or DIGAMY. Second marriage; marriage to a second wife after the death of the first, as "bigamy," in law, is having two wives at once. Originally, a man who married a widow, or married again after the death of his wife, was said to be guilty of bigamy. Co. Litt. 40b, note.

DIGEST. A compilation arranged in an orderly manner.

The name is given to a great variety of topical compilations, abridgments, and analytical indices of reports, statutes, etc. When reference is made to "Digest," the Pandects of Justinian are intended, they being the authoritative compilation of the civil law. As to this Digest, and the mode of citing it, see "Pandects." Other digests are referred to by their distinctive names. For some account of digests of the civil and canon law, and those of Indian law, see "Civil Law," "Code," and "Canon Law."

The digests of English and American law are for the most part deemed not authorities, but simply manuals of reference, by which the reader may find his way to the original cases which are authorities. 1 Burrows, 364; 2 Wils. 1, 2. Some of them, however, which have been the careful work of scholarly lawyers, possess an independent value as original repositories of the law. Bacon's Abridgment, which has long been deservedly popular in this country, and Comyn's Digest, also often cited, are examples of these.

DIGNITARY. In eccleciastical law. An ecclesiastic who holds a dignity or benefice which gives him some pre-eminence over mere priests and canons, such as a bishop, archbishop, prebendary, etc. Swift; Burns.

DIGNITIES. In English law. Titles of honor.

They are considered as incorporeal hereditaments. The genius of our government forbids their admission into the republic.

DIJUDICATION. Judicial distinction.

DIKEREEVE. An officer appointed or confirmed by the English commissioners of sewers to take charge of the sluices and sea banks of fen or marsh land.

DILACION. In Spanish law. The time granted by law or by the judge to parties litigant for the purpose of answering a demand, or proving some disputed fact.

DILAPIDATION. A species of ecclesiastical waste which occurs whenever the incumbent suffers any edifices of his ecclesiastical living to go to ruin or decay. It is either voluntary, by pulling down, or permissive, by suffering the church, parsonage houses, and other buildings thereunto belonging, to decay. And the remedy for either lies either in the spiritual court, where the canon law prevails, or in the courts of common law. It is also held to be good cause of deprivation if the bishop, parson, or other ecclesiastical person dilapidates buildings or cuts down timber growing on the patrimony of the church, unless for necessary repairs; and that a writ of prohibition will also lie against him in the common-law courts. 3 Bl. Comm. 91.

DILATIO. (Lat. from *differre,* to put off). In old English law. Delay. *Sine dilatione*; without delay. Reg. Orig. 1.

DILATIONES IN LEGE SUNT ODIOSAE. Delays in law are odious. Branch, Princ.

DILATORY DEFENSE. In chancery practice. One the object of which is to dismiss, suspend, or obstruct the suit, without touching the merits, until the impediment or obstacle insisted on shall be removed. See "Defense."

DILATORY PLEA. One which goes to defeat the particular action brought, merely, and which does not answer as to the general right of the plaintiff.

DILIGENCE. In Scotch law. Process; execution.

——**Diligence Against the Heritage.** A writ of execution by which the creditor proceeds against the real estate of the debtor.

——**Diligence Incident.** A writ or process for citing witnesses and examining havers. It is equivalent to the English subpoena for witnesses, and rule or order for examination of parties and for interrogatories.

——**Diligence to Examine Havers.** A process to obtain testimony, equivalent to a bill of discovery in chancery, or a rule to compel oral examination and a subpoena *duces tecum* at common law.

——**Diligence Against the Person.** A writ of execution, by which the creditor proceeds against the person of the debtor; equivalent to the English *ca. sa.*

——**Second Diligence.** Second letters issued where the first have been disregarded. A similar result is produced in English practice by the attachment for contempt.

——**Summary Diligence.** Diligence issued in a summary manner, like an execution of a warrant of attorney, *cognovit actionem,* and the like, in English practice.

——**Diligence Against Witnesses.** Process to compel the attendance of witnesses; equivalent to the English subpoena. See Paterson, Comp.

DILIGIATUS (Law Lat. from *di,* away, and *ligius,* or *ligiatus,* under the protection of the law). In old English law. Cast out of the law's protection, *ejectus e patrocinio legis;* outlawed; an outlaw. Spelman; LL. Hen. I. c. 45.

DILLIGROUT. Pottage formerly made for the king's table on the coronation day. There was a tenure in serjeantry, by which lands were held of the king by the service of finding this pottage at that solemnity. 39 Hen. III.

DIMIDIETAS. The moiety or half of a thing.

DIMINUERE (Lat.) In old English law. To lessen or diminish; to take away, leave out, or omit. *De recordo diminuere;* to take from, or diminish a record. Bract., fol. 147.

DIMINUTIO. In the civil law. Diminution; a taking away; loss or deprivation. *Diminutio capitis,* loss of status or condition. See "Capitis Diminutio."

DIMINUTION OF THE RECORD. In practice. Incompleteness of the record of a case sent up from an inferior to a superior court.

DIMISI. In old conveyancing. I have demised. *Dimisi, concessi, et ad firmam tradidi,* have demised, granted, and to farm let. The usual words of operation in a lease. 2 Bl. Comm. 317, 318. Sometimes written *demisi.*

DIMISIT. In old conveyancing. He has demised. See "Dimisi."

DIMISSORIAE LITTERAE. In the civil law. Letters dimissory or dismissory, commonly called "apostles" (*quae vulgo apostoli dicuntur*). Dig. 50. 16. 106. See "Apostoli"; "Apostles."

DINARCHY. A government by two persons.

DINERO.

——**In Spanish Law.** Money. *Dinero contado,* money counted. White, New Recop. bk. 2, tit. 13, c. 1, § 1.

——**In Roman Law.** A civil division of the Roman empire, embracing several provinces. Calv. Lex.

DIOCESAN COURTS. Ecclesiastical courts taking cognizance of all matters arising within the diocese of each bishop. They consist of the consistorial court, and the courts of archdeacons, exercising general or limited jurisdictions, according to the terms of their patents, or to local customs, or to the authority of recent legislation. Phillim. Ecc. Law, 1202.

DIOCESE. The territorial extent of a bishop's jurisdiction; the circuit of every bishop's jurisdiction. Co. Litt. 94; 1 Bl. Comm. 111; 2 Burns, Ecc. Law, 158.

DIPLOMA. An instrument of writing, executed by a corporation or society, certifying that a certain person therein named is entitled to a certain distinction therein mentioned.

It is usually granted by learned institutions to their members, or to persons who have studied in them.

This word, which is also written "duploma," in the civil law signifies letters issued by a prince. They are so called, it is supposed, *a duplicatis tabellis,* to which Ovid is thought to allude (1 Arom. 12. 2. 27) when he says, *Tunc ego vos duplices rebus pro nomine sensi* (*Sueton. in Augustum,* c. 26). Seals also were called "diplomata." Vicat.

DIPLOMATICS. The art of judging of ancient charters, public documents, or diplomas, and discriminating the true from the false. Enc. Lond.

DIPSOMANIA. In medical jurisprudence. A disease produced by drunkenness, and, indeed, other causes, which overmasters the will of its victim, and irresistibly impels him to drink to intoxication. 1 Bish. Crim. Law, § 304. How far the law will hold a party responsible for acts committed while the mind is overwhelmed by the effects of liquor so taken is an open question.

DIPTYCHA. Diptychs; tablets of wood, metal, or other substance, used among the Romans for the purpose of writing, and folded like a book of two leaves. The diptychs of antiquity were especially employed for public registers. They were used in the Greek, and afterwards in the Roman, church, as registers of the names of those for whom supplication was to be made, and are ranked among the earliest monastic records. Hubback, Ev. Success. 567; Enc. Am. See Calv. Lex.; Brissonius.

DIRECT. Straightforward; immediate; not collateral. The direct line of descent is formed by a series of relationships between persons who descend successively one from the other.

Evidence is termed "direct" which applies immediately to the fact to be proved, without any intervening process, as distinguished from "circumstantial," which applies immediately to collateral facts supposed to have a connection, near or remote, with the fact in controversy.

The examination in chief of a witness is called the "direct examination."

Interrogatories propounded to a deponent by the party by whom the deposition is taken are called "direct interrogatories."

DIRECT ATTACK. An attempt to set aside or correct a judgment in some manner provided by law. 51 Ill. App. 476.

DIRECT CONTEMPT. Those contempts which are committed within the presence of the court while in session, or so near to the court as to interrupt its proceedings. 168 Ill. 106; 153 Ill. 647.

DIRECT LINE. In the law of descent. Direct lineal succession.

DIRECT TAX. See "Tax."

DIRECTION. The order and government of an institution; the persons who compose the board of directors are jointly called the "direction." Direction, in another sense, is nearly synonymous with instruction (*q. v.*).

——**In Practice.** That part of a bill in chancery which contains the address of the bill to the court. This must, of course, contain the appropriate and technical description of the court. See "Bill."

DIRECTORS. Persons appointed or elected according to law, authorized to manage and direct the affairs of a corporation or company. The whole of the directors collectively form the board of directors.

DIRECTORY. When a statute directs certain proceedings to be done in a certain way or at a certain time, and the form or the period does not appear essential to the judicial mind, the law will be regarded as directory, the time and manner not being of the essence of the thing to be done. 52 Ill. App. 360.

DIRECTORY TRUST. One where, by the terms of the trust, the trust fund is directed to be vested in a particular manner until the period arrives when the trust is to be terminated. 10 Yerg. (Tenn.) 272.

DIRIBITORES. In Roman law. Officers who distributed ballots to the people, to be used in voting. Tayl. Civ. Law, 192.

DIRIMANT IMPEDIMENTS. Those bars which annul a consummated marriage.

DISABILITY. The want of legal capacity.

"Disability implies want of power, not want of inclination. It refers to incapacity, and not to disinclination." 32 Barb. (N. Y.) 473.

Disabilities were anciently classified as general and special.

(1) A disability is called general when it disables a person from performing all acts of a given kind, as in the case of an outlaw.

(2) A disability is special when it disables him from doing a specific act, as where one renders himself incapable of performing a contract which he has entered into.

They are also classified as personal and absolute.

(3) A personal disability is confined to the person affected.

(4) An absolute disability descends to his heirs. The absolute disabilities such as attainder have been all abolished.

They are also classified as civil and canonical.

This classification existed only as to disability to enter the marriage contract. Civil were such as to render the marriage void, as prior marriage, consanguinity, etc., while a canonical disability, such as sterility, rendered the marriage voidable only. 2 Steph. Comm. 240.

DISABLING STATUTES. The acts of 1 Eliz. c. 19, 13 Eliz. c. 10, 14 Eliz. cc. 11, 14, 18 Eliz. c. 11, and 43 Eliz. c. 29, by which the power of ecclesiastical or eleemosynary corporations to lease their lands was restricted. 2 Bl. Comm. 319, 321; Co. Litt. 44a; 3 Steph. Comm. 140. Also called the "Restraining Statutes."

DISADVOCARE. To disavow.

DISAFFIRMANCE. The act by which a person who has entered into a voidable contract, as, for example, an infant, disagrees to such contract, and declares he will not abide by it.

Disaffirmance is express or implied,—the former, when the declaration is made in terms that the party will not abide by the contract; the latter, when he does an act which plainly manifests his determination not to abide by it; as where an infant made a deed for his land, and on coming of age he made a deed for the same land to another. 2 Dev. & B. (N. C.) 320; 10 Pet. (U. S.) 58; 13 Mass. 371, 375.

DISAFFOREST. To restore to their former condition lands which have been turned into forest. To remove from the operation of the forest laws. 2 Sharswood, Bl. Comm. 416.

DISAGREEMENT. The refusal by a grantee, lessee, etc., to accept an estate, lease, etc., made to him; the annulling of a thing that had essence before. No estate can be vested in a person against his will, consequently no one can become a grantee, etc., without his agreement. The law implies such an agreement until the contrary is shown, but his disagreement renders the grant, etc., inoperative. If an infant purchase an estate, he may, on coming to full age, disagree thereto; and, if he agree thereto, his heirs, after his death, may waive it. If a person of unsound mind purchase an estate, he cannot afterwards disagree thereto himself; but if he does not recover, or, after recovery, dies without agreement, his heir may disagree to it. If a *feme covert* purchase an estate, her husband may disagree thereto; and, if he neither agrees nor disagrees, the purchase is good during the coverture, but after his death, notwithstanding his agreement, the wife may disagree thereto, and so, after her death, may her heirs, if she does not herself agree thereto. Persons who purchase an estate under duress may disagree thereto when the duress ceases. See Co. Litt. 2b, 3a, 380b; 3 Prest. Abstr. 104; 2 Bl. Comm. 292; Viner, Abr.; Wharton.

DISALT. To disable a person.

DISAPPROPRIATION. This is where the appropriation of a benefice is severed, either by the patron presenting a clerk, or by the corporation which has the appropriation being dissolved. 1 Bl. Comm. 385.

DISAVOW. To deny the authority by which an agent pretends to have acted, as when he has exceeded the bounds of his authority.

It is the duty of the principal to fulfill the contracts which have been entered into by his authorized agent; and when an agent has exceeded his authority, he ought promptly to disavow such act, so that the other party may have his remedy against the agent. See "Agent"; "Principal."

DISBAR.

——**In English Law.** To expel a barrister from the bar.

——**In the United States.** To debar an attorney from the right to practice.

DISBENCH. To strike off the name of a person from the roll of the senior members of the Inns of Court in London.

DISBOCATIO. In old English law. A conversion of wood grounds into arable or pasture; an assarting. Cowell. See "Assart."

DISCARCARE, or **DISCARGARE** (Law Lat. from *dis, priv.,* and *carcare,* to load or charge). In old English law. To discharge; to unload; as a vessel. *Carcare et discarcare,* to charge and discharge; to load and unload. Cowell; Plac. Parl. 18 Edw. I.

In the Salian law it is written *discargare. Discarcatio,* a discharging or unloading of a vessel. Towns. Pl. 226.

DISCEPTATIO CAUSAE (Lat.) In Roman law and practice. The argument or disputation of a cause by the advocates on both sides. Halifax, Anal. bk. 3, c. 9, No. 39.

DISCEPTIO CAUSAE (Lat.) In Roman law. The arguments of a cause by the counsel on both sides. Calv. Lex.

DISCHARGE. To free from a charge or load; to remove; to satisfy or pay; to set free, dismiss, or absolve; to carry on or perform. The term has many applications, the principal being:

——**Of Cargo.** The unloading of a cargo from a ship. 5 Wall. (U. S.) 557.

——**Of Debt or Obligation.** Full and final release from and termination of the obligation in whatever manner; a receipt or other instrument acting as a discharge. 147 Mass. 585.

——**Of Prisoner.** The setting at liberty of one held in confinement under process of law. 68 Mich. 331.

——**Of Jury.** The dismissal of a jury when, for any cause, the rendition of a verdict becomes impossible.

DISCLAIMER. A disavowal; a renunciation; as, for example, the act by which a patentee renounces part of his title of invention.

——**Of Estates.** The act by which a party refuses to accept an estate which has been conveyed to him. Thus, a trustee is said to disclaim who releases to his fellow trustees his estate, and relieves himself of the trust. 1 Hilliard, Real Prop. 354.

——**Of Tenancy.** The act of a person in possession, who denies holding the estate of the person who claims to be the owner. 2 Nev. & M. 672. An affirmation, by pleading or otherwise, in a court of record, that the reversion is in a stranger. It works a forfeiture of the lease at common law (Co. Litt. 251; 1 Cruise, Dig. 109), but not, it is said, in the United States (1 Washb. Real Prop. 93). Equity, it is said, will not aid a tenant in denying his landlord's title. 1 Pet. (U. S.) 486.

——**In Pleading.** A renunciation by the defendant of all claim to the subject of the demand made by the plaintiff's bill. Cooper, Eq. Pl. 309; Mitf. Eq. Pl. (Jeremy Ed.) 318.

DISCLAMATION. In Scotch law. Disavowal of tenure; denial that one holds lands of another. Bell, Dict.; Skene de Verb. Sign.

DISCLOSE: DISCLOSURE. To disclose an offense, is not to state it or confess to it; but tc make the offense known for the first time. 28 L. J. M. C. 91.

To "disclose a defense upon the merits," means not merely to say there is a defense, but to show what the nature of it is; 27 L. J. C. p. 305; 25 L. J. Ex. 27; opening out and letting the judge see whether there really is a defense upon the merits. 93 Eng. C. L. 663.

The obligation to disclose arises in various ways. Where the parties to a contract stand in some pre-existing relationship to one another of a fiduciary character, full disclosure is required. Fry Specif. Perf. § 706.

The obligation may arise from an antecedent wrong done by the one party to the other. Fry Specif. Perf. § 707.

Sometimes the obligation to disclose arises from the character of the contract itself, where its nature demands a full disclosure of all material facts; such as contracts for marine insurance and partnership. In such cases silence may be fraud. Fry Specif. Perf. § 708.

In the case of a contract for the sale of a chattel having a latent defect, there exists an obligation to disclose the same. Fry Specif. Perf. § 708.

There are obligations to disclosure which arise from the contract itself; such as the duty of the vendor of land to honestly disclose his title.

Sometimes the obligation to disclose arises from the course of the negotiations, and where an incomplete or imperfect disclosure has been made, a full disclosure is necessary, as an imperfect statement may be a perfect untruth. Fry Specif. Perf. §§ 709-714.

DISCOMMON. To deprive commonable lands of their commonable quality, by inclosing and appropriating or improving them.

DISCONTINUANCE.

——**Of Estates.** An alienation made or suffered by the tenant in tail, or other tenant seised in *autre droit*, by which the issue in tail, or heir or successor, or those in reversion or remainder, are driven to their action, and cannot enter.

The term "discontinuance" is used to distinguish those cases where the party whose freehold is ousted can restore it only by action, from those in which he may restore it by entry. Co. Litt. 325a; 3 Bl. Comm. 171; Adams, Ej. 35-41; Comyn, Dig.; Bac. Abr.; Viner, Abr.; Cruise, Dig. Index; 2 Saund. Index.

——**In Pleading.** The chasm or interruption which occurs when no answer is given to some material matter in the preceding pleading, and the opposite party neglects to take advantage of such omission. See Comyn, Dig. "Pleader" (W); Bac. Abr. "Pleas" (P). It is distinguished from insufficient pleading by the fact that the pleading does not profess to answer all the preceding pleading in a case of discontinuance. 1 Wm. Saund. 28, note.

——**In Practice.** The chasm or interruption in proceedings occasioned by the failure of the plaintiff to continue the suit regularly from time to time, as he ought. 3 Bl. Comm. 296.

DISCONTINUOUS SERVITUDE, or **DIScontinuous easement.** An easement made up of repeated acts, instead of one continuous act, such as right of way, drawing water, etc.

DISCONVENABLE (Law Fr.) Improper; unfit. Kelham.

DISCOUNT.

——**In Contracts.** Interest reserved from the amount lent at the time of making a loan. An allowance sometimes made for prompt payment. As a verb, it is used to denote the act of giving money for a bill of exchange or promissory note, deducting the interest.

The taking legal interest in advance is not usurious; but it is only allowed for the benefit of trade, and where the bill or note discounted is meant for circulation, and is for a short term. 2 Cow. (N. Y.) 678, 712; 3 Wend. (N. Y.) 408.

There is a difference between "buying" a bill and "discounting" it. The former word is used when the seller does not indorse the bill, and is not accountable for its payment. See Poth. de l'Usure, note 128; 3 Pet. (U. S.) 40; Blydenburgh, Usury; Sewell, Banking.

——**In Practice.** A set-off or defalcation in an action. Viner, Abr.

DISCOVERT. Not covert; unmarried. The term is applied to a woman unmarried, or widow,—one not within the bonds of matrimony.

DISCOVERY (Fr. *decouvrir*, to uncover; to discover). The act of finding an unknown country.

The nations of Europe adopted the principle that the discovery of any part of America gave title to the government by whose subjects or by whose authority it was made, as against all European governments. This title was to be consummated by possession. 8 Wheat. (U. S.) 543; 16 Pet. (U. S.) 367; 2 Washb. Real Prop. 518.

An invention or improvement. Act Cong. July 4, 1836, § 6.

——**In Practice.** The disclosure of facts resting in the knowledge of the defendant, or the production of deeds, writings, or things in his possession or power, in order to maintain the right or title of the party asking it, in some suit or proceeding in another court.

It was originally an equitable form of procedure, and a "bill of discovery," strictly so called, was brought to assist parties to suits in other courts.

In modern practice, a statutory proceeding is generally substituted, by which an inspection of books and papers, or an examination of a party, may be had on motion.

DISCREDIT. To deprive one of credit or confidence.

The impeachment of a witness, as distinguished from a contradiction of his testimony. See "Impeachment."

DISCREPANCY. A difference between one thing and another; between one writing and another; a variance.

A material discrepancy exists when there is such a difference between a thing alleged and a thing offered in evidence as to show they are not substantially the same; as when the plaintiff in his declaration for a malicious arrest averred that "the plaintiff in that action did not prosecute his said suit, but therein made default," and the record was that he obtained a rule to discontinue.

An immaterial discrepancy is one which does not materially affect the cause; as where a declaration stated that a deed bore date in a certain year of our Lord, and the deed was simply dated "March 30, 1701." 2 Salk. 658; 19 Johns. (N. Y.) 49; 5 Taunt. 707; 2 Barn. & A. 301; 8 Miss. 428; 2 McLean (U. S.) 69; 1 Metc. (Mass.) 59; 21 Pick. (Mass.) 486.

DISCRETIO EST DISCERNERE PER legem quid sit justum. Discretion is to discern through law what is just. 5 Coke, 99, 100; 10 Coke, 140; Broom, Leg. Max. (3d London Ed.) p. 81; Coke, 4th Inst. 41; 1 W. Bl. 152; 1 Burrows, 570; 3 Bulst. 128; 6 Q. B. 700.

DISCRETIO EST SCIRE PER LEGEM quid sit justum. Discretion consists in knowing what is just in law. 4 Johns. Ch. (N. Y.) 352, 356.

DISCRETION.

——**In Practice.** The equitable decision of what is just and proper under the circumstances.

The power of a judge, in certain matters, to decide in accordance with his own judgment of the equities of the cases, unhampered by inflexible rules of law. The latitude allowed to judges as to the action to be taken on certain facts. See 34 Barb. (N. Y.) 291.

The discretion of a judge is said to be the law of tyrants. It is always unknown; it is different in different men; it is casual, and depends upon constitution, temper, and passion. In the best, it is oftentimes caprice; in the worst, it is every vice, folly, and passion to which human nature is liable. *Optima lex quae minimum relinquit arbitrio judicis; optimus judex qui minimum sibi.* Bac. Aph.; 1 Cas. (Pa.) 80, note; 1 Powell, Mortg. 247a; 2 Belt, Supp. to Ves. 391; Toullier, Dr. Civ. liv. 3, note 338; 1 Lilly, Abr. 447.

There is a species of discretion which is authorized by express law, and without which justice cannot be administered; for example, if an old offender, a man of much intelligence and cunning, whose talents render him dangerous to the community, induces a young man of weak intellect to commit a larceny in company with himself, they are both liable to be punished for the offense. The law, foreseeing such a case, has provided that the punishment should be proportioned so as to do justice, and it has left such apportionment to the discretion of the judge. It is evident that, without such discretion, justice could not be administered; for one of these parties assuredly deserves a much more severe punishment than the other.

And many matters relating to the trial, such as the order of giving evidence, granting of new trials, etc., are properly left mainly or entirely to the discretion of the judge.

As applied to executive officers, it means a power to decide on the propriety of certain actions, without any review by others.

——**In Criminal Law.** The ability to know and distinguish between good and evil, —between what is lawful and what is unlawful.

DISCRETIONARY TRUSTS. Those which cannot be duly administered without the application of a certain degree of prudence and judgment; as, when a fund is given to trustees to be distributed in certain charities to be selected by the trustees.

DISCUSSION. In civil law. A proceeding, on the part of a surety, by which the property of the principal debtor is made liable before resort can be had to the sureties. This is called the "benefit of discussion." This is the law in Louisiana. Civ. Code La. arts. 3014-3020. See Domat, 3. 4. 1-4; Burge, Sur. 329, 343, 348; 5 Toullier, Dr. Civ. 544; 7 Toullier, Dr. Civ. 93; 2 Bouv. Inst. note 1414.

DISEASE. For the purpose of furnishing an excuse for what would otherwise be a crime, "voluntary drunkenness is not regarded as a disease affecting the mind; but involuntary drunkenness, and diseases caused by voluntary drunkenness, fall, so far as they affect the mind, within that term." Steph. Cr. 22.

DISENTAILING DEED. An assurance by which a tenant in tail bars his estate tail, so as to convert it into an estate in fee, either absolute or base.

Disentailment is regulated by 3 & 4 Wm. IV. c. 74.

DISFIGURE. In an indictment for an assault to "disfigure" is to do some external injury which may detract from the personal appearance. Arch. Cr. 760.

DISFRANCHISEMENT. The act of depriving a member of a corporation of his right as such, by expulsion. 1 Bouv. Inst. note 192.

It differs from amotion (*q. v.*), which is applicable to the removal of an officer from office, leaving him his rights as a member. Willcock, Corp. note 708; Angell & A. Corp. 237. And see "Expulsion."

Also to deprive of the power of exercising the rights of citizenship, such as voting or holding office.

DISGAVEL. In English law. To deprive lands of that principal quality of gavelkind tenure by which they descend equally among all the sons of the tenant. 2 Wooddeson, Lect. 76; 2 Bl. Comm. 85; Robinson, Gavelkind, 97, note.

DISGRACE. Ignominy; shame; dishonor. No witness is required to disgrace himself. 13 How. St. Tr. 17, 334; 16 How. St. Tr. 161.

DISGRADING. In old English law. The depriving of an order or dignity. Termes de la Ley; Blount.

DISHERISON. Disinheritance; depriving one of an inheritance. Obsolete. See "Disinherison."

DISHERITOR. One who disinherits, or puts another out of his freehold. Obsolete.

DISHONOR. A term applied to the nonfulfillment of commercial engagements. To dishonor a bill of exchange or a promissory note is to refuse or neglect to pay it at maturity.

The holder is bound to give notice to the parties to such instrument of its dishonor; and his laches will discharge the indorsers. Chit. Bills, 256-278, 394, 395.

DISINCARCERATE. To set at liberty; to free from prison.

DISINHERISON. In civil law. The act of depriving a forced heir of the inheritance which the law gives him.

In Louisiana, forced heirs may be deprived of their legitime, or legal portion, and of the seisin granted them by law, for just cause. The disinherison must be made in proper form, by name and expressly, and for a just cause; otherwise it is null. See Civ. Code La. arts. 1609-1616.

DISINHERITANCE. The act by which a person deprives his heir of an inheritance, who, without such act, would inherit.

By the common law, any one may give his estate to a stranger, and thereby disinherit his heir apparent. Cooper, Just. Inst. 495; 7 East, 106.

DISINTERESTED WITNESS. One who has no interest in the cause or matter in issue, and who is lawfully competent to testify.

DISJUNCTIVE ALLEGATIONS. In pleading. Allegations which charge a party disjunctively, so as to leave it uncertain what is relied on as the accusation against him.

An indictment, information, or complaint which charges the defendant with one or other of two offenses, in the disjunctive, as that he murdered "or" caused to be murdered, forged "or" caused to be forged, wrote and published "or" caused to be written and published, is bad for uncertainty. 8 Mod. 330; 1 Salk. 342, 371; 2 Strange, 900; Cas. temp. Hardw. 370; 5 Barn. & C. 251; 2 Car. & K. 243; 1 Younge & J. 22.

DISJUNCTIVE TERM. One which is placed between two contraries, by the affirming of one of which the other is taken away. It is usually expressed by the word "or." See 3 Ves. 450; 7 Ves. 454; 2 Rop. Leg. 290; 1 P. Wms. 433; 2 P. Wms. 283; 2 Cox, Ch. 213; 2 Atk. 643; 3 Atk. 83, 85; 2 Ves. Sr. 67; 2 Strange, 1175; Cro. Eliz. 525; Poll. 645; 1 Bing. 500; 3 Term R. 470; Ayliffe, Pand. 56; 2 Miles (Pa.) 49.

In the civil law, when a legacy is given to Caius "or" Titius, the word "or" is considered "and," both Caius and Titius are entitled to the legacy in equal parts. 6 Toullier, Dr. Civ. note 704.

DISMISS. To remove; to send out of court. Formerly used in chancery of the removal of a cause out of court without any further hearing. The term is now used in courts of law also.

DISMORTGAGE. To redeem from mortgage.

DISORDERLY HOUSE. In criminal law. A house the inmates of which behave so badly as to become a nuisance to the neighborhood.

One kept in such a way as to disturb or scandalize the public generally, or the inhabitants of a particular neighborhood, or the passers by. 93 W. C. 608.

The term has a wide meaning, and includes bawdy houses, gambling houses, and the like.

A place kept for general resort for purposes injurious to the public morals or safety is a "disorderly house," in the legal sense, though there be no noise or disorder. 48 Ark. 60; 30 N. J. Law, 104; 120 Mass. 356; 83 N. Y. 587.

DISORDERLY PERSONS. A class of offenders, subjects of police regulation, described in the statutes which punish them. See 4 Bl. Comm. 169.

DISPARAGATION (Law Fr. disparagement). The matching an heir, etc., in marriage, under his or her degree or condition, or against the rules of decency. Kelham.

DISPARAGE (Law Lat. *disparagare*). To connect unequally; to match unsuitably. "The ward who is ward for knight's service land is accounted in law disparaged, if he be tendered a marriage of the burgher's parentage." Bac. Arg. Low's Case, Works, iv. 235. See "Disparagement."

DISPARAGEMENT. In old English law. An injury by union or comparison with some person or thing of inferior rank or excellence.

Marriage without disparagement was marriage to one of suitable rank and character. 2 Sharswood, Bl. Comm. 70; Co. Litt. 82b. The guardian in chivalry had the right of disposing of his infant ward in matrimony; and provided he tendered a marriage without disparagement or inequality, if the infant refused, he was obliged to pay a *valor maritagii* to the guardian.

Disparagare, to connect in an unequal marriage. Spelman. *Disparagatio*, disparagement. Used in Magna Charta (9 Hen. III.) c. 6. *Disparagation*, disparagement. Kelham. *Disparage*, to marry unequally. Used of a marriage proposed by a guardian between those of unequal rank, and injurious to the ward.

DISPARAGIUM. In old Scotch law. Inequality in blood, honor, dignity, or otherwise. Skene de Verb. Sign.

DISPARATA NON DEBENT JUNGI. Dissimilar things ought not to be joined. Jenk. Cent. Cas. 24.

DISPARK. To dissolve a park. Cro. Car. 59. To convert a park into ordinary ground.

DISPAUPER. In English law. To deprive a person of the privilege of suing *in forma pauperis*.

When a person has been admitted to sue *in forma pauperis*, and before the suit is ended it appears that the party has become the owner of a sufficient estate real or personal, or has been guilty of some wrong, he may be dispaupered.

DISPENSATIO EST VULNUS, QUOD vulnerat jus commune. A dispensation is a wound, because it wounds a common right. Dav. 69; Branch, Princ.

DISPENSATION. A relaxation of law for the benefit or advantage of an individual. In the United States, no power exists, except in the legislature, to dispense with law; and then it is not so much a dispensation as a change of the law.

DISPERSONARE. To scandalize or disparage. Blount.

DISPONE. In Scotch law. A technical word essential to the conveyance of heritable property, and for which no equivalent is accepted, however clear may be the meaning of the party. Paterson, Comp.

DISPOSING MIND. The mental capacity to know and understand what disposition he may wish to make of his property, and upon whom he will bestow his bounty. 117 Ill. 321.

Testamentary capacity (*q. v.*)

DISPOSITION. In Scotch law. A deed of alienation by which a right to property is conveyed. Bell, Dict.

DISPOSITIVE FACTS. Such as originate, transfer, or extinguish rights, known respectively as investitive, translative, and divestitive facts. These terms were coined by Bentham, and have not found their way into general use. Holland, Jur. 131.

DISPOSSESSION. Ouster; a wrong that carries with it the amotion of possession. An act whereby the wrongdoer gets the actual occupation of the land or hereditament. It includes abatement, intrusion, disseisin, discontinuance, deforcement. 3 Sharswood, Bl. Comm. 167.

DISPUNISHABLE. In old English law. Not answerable. Co. Litt. 27b, 53; 1 Steph. Com. 245; 2 Crabb's Real Prop. 47, § 1000.

Not punishable. "This murder is dispunishable." 1 Leon. 270.

DISPUTABLE PRESUMPTION. A presumption of law, which may be rebutted or disproved. Best, Pres. § 25; Burr. Circ. Ev. 47.

DISPUTATIO FORI (Lat.) Argument in court. Du Cange.

DISRATIONARE (Law Lat.; Law Fr. *desreigner*). In old English law. To prove; to deraign; to establish or make good a claim, charge, or accusation. Bracton, fol. 138. Spelman considers this as merely another form of *dirationare*, and makes its proper signification to be to disprove or refute, from *dis*, *priv*, and *ratiocinari*, to prove. It is, however, never employed in this sense by Bracton, who uses it frequently, but only in the sense first given. Bracton, fol. 138. See Id. fols. 101b, 119, 372b, 373b; Fleta, lib. 1, c. 31, § 6; Id. lib. 1, c. 21, § 2.

DISSASINA. In old Scotch law. Disseisin; dispossession. Skene de Verb. Sign.

DISSEISEE. One who is wrongfully put out of possession of his lands; one who is disseised.

DISSEISIN. A privation of seisin; a usurpation of the right of seisin and possession, and an exercise of such powers and privileges of ownership as to keep out or displace him to whom these rightfully belong. 2 Washb. Real Prop. 283.

The act of divesting the owner of his seisin and possession of the land, and substituting in its place the ownership and possession of the disseisor. The change in the meaning of the word, and the distinction between it and "deforcement," stated. 9 Cow. (N. Y.) 530, 552.

An actual and wrongful expulsion from a freehold. Dispossession may be by right or wrong. 6 Johns. (N. Y.) 197. And see 8 Barb. (N. Y.) 189, 194.

DISSEISINAM SATIS FACIT, QUI UTI non permittit possessorem, vel minus commode, licet omnino non expellat. He makes disseisin enough who does not permit the possessor to enjoy, or makes his enjoyment less commodious, although he does not expel altogether. Co. Litt. 331; Bracton, lib. 4, tr. 2.

DISSEISOR. One who puts another out of the possession of his lands wrongfully.

DISSEISORESS (Law Lat. *disseisitrix*). A woman that disseises another person. Litt. § 678; Co. Litt. 357b.

DISSENT. A disagreement to something which has been done. It is express or implied.

DISSIGNARE. In old law. To break open a seal. Whishaw.

DISSIMILIUM DISSIMILIS EST RATIO. Of dissimilars the rule is dissimilar. Co. Litt. 191.

DISSIMULATIONE TOLLITUR INJURIA. Wrong is wiped out by reconciliation. Ersk. Inst. bk. 4, tit. 4, § 108.

DISSOLUTION.

——**In Contracts.** The dissolution of a contract is the annulling thereof by the contracting parties.

——**Of Corporations.** The termination of the corporate existence in any manner, whether by expiration of the charter, decree of court, act of the legislature, etc.

——**In Practice.** The act of rendering a legal proceeding null, or changing its character; as, a foreign attachment in Pennsylvania is dissolved by entering bail to the action; injunctions are dissolved by the court.

DISSUADE. In criminal law. To induce a person not to do an act.

To dissuade a witness from giving evidence against a person indicted is an indictable offense at common law. Hawk. P. C. bk. 1, c. 21, § 15. The mere attempt to stifle evidence is also criminal, although the persuasion should not succeed, on the general principle that an incitement to commit a crime is in itself criminal. 1 Russ. Crimes, 44; 2 East, 5, 21; 6 East, 464; 2 Strange, 904; 2 Leach, C. C. 925.

DISTANCE. Where there are no special controlling words, distance is to be measured "as the crow flies," *i. e.*, by the shortest line that can be drawn from one place to another on a map without regard to the curvature or inequalities of the surface of the earth; and where the distance is to be ascertained between houses, the measurement is to be taken from the nearest point of the one house to the nearest point of the other, without regard to where the doors are situated. 28 L. J. Ch. 867; Johns. 446.

DISTINCTE ET APERTE. In old English practice. Distinctly and openly. Formal words in writs of error, referring to the return required to be made to them. Reg. Orig. 17.

DISTINGUENDA SUNT TEMPORA. The time is to be considered. 1 Coke, 16a; 14 N. Y. 380, 393.

DISTINGUENDA SUNT TEMPORA; ALiud est facere, aliud perficere. Times must be distinguished; it is one thing to do a thing, another to complete it. 3 Leon. 243; Branch, Princ.

DISTINGUENDA SUNT TEMPORA; DIStingue tempora, et concordabis leges. Times are to be distinguished; distinguish times, and you will attune laws. 1 Coke, 24.

DISTINGUISHING MARK. A mark placed upon the ballot by the voter by which his ballot can be identified. 250 Ill. 505.

Such a mark as will distinguish and separate the particular ballot from other ballots cast at the election—a mark put upon the ballot to indicate who cast it and to evade its secrecy. 235 Ill. 331.

DISTRACTED PERSON. A term used in the statutes of Illinois (Rev. Laws Ill. 1833, p. 332) and New Hampshire (Dig. N. H. Laws 1830, p. 339) to express a state of insanity.

DISTRACTIO. In civil law. The sale of a pledge by a debtor; the appropriation of the property of a ward by a guardian. Calv. Lex.

DISTRAHERE. To withdraw; to sell. *Distrahere controversias*, to diminish and settle quarrels; *distrahere matrimoniam*, to dissolve marriage; to divorce. Calv. Lex.

DISTRAIN. To take as a pledge property of another, and keep the same until he performs his obligation, or until the property is replevied by the sheriff. It was used to secure an appearance in court, payment of rent, performance of services, etc. 3 Bl. Comm. 231; Fitzh. Nat. Brev. 32 (B), (C), 223. See "Distress."

DISTRESS (Fr. *distraindre*, to draw away from). The taking of a personal chattel out of the possession of a wrongdoer into the custody of the party injured, to procure satisfaction for the wrong done. 3 Bl. Comm. 6. It is generally resorted to for the purpose of enforcing the payment of rent, taxes, or other duties, as well as to exact compensation for such damages as result from the trespasses of cattle.

This remedy is of great antiquity, and is said by Spelman to have prevailed among the Gothic nations of Europe from the breaking up of the Roman empire. The English statutes since the days of *Magna Charta* have, from time to time, extended and modified its features to meet the exigencies of the times.

It was at one time generally in vogue in the United States, but is now generally abolished, the remedy of attachment taking its place.

DISTRESS INFINITE. In English practice. A process commanding the sheriff to distrain a person from time to time, and continually afterwards, by taking his goods by way of pledge to enforce the performance of something due from the party distrained upon. In this case, no distress can be immoderate, because, whatever its value may be, it cannot be sold, but is to be immediately restored on satisfaction being made. 3 Bl. Comm. 231. It was the means anciently resorted to to compel an appearance. See "Attachment;" "Arrest."

DISTRIBUTEE. One entitled to take a share of the estate of a decedent under the statute of distribution.

DISTRIBUTION. In practice. The division by order of the court having authority, among those entitled thereto, of the residue of the personal estate of an intestate, after payment of the debts and charges. 13 Ill. App. 560.

The term sometimes denotes the division of a residue of both real and personal estate, and also the division of an estate according to the terms of a will.

DISTRIBUTIVE FINDING OF THE ISsue. The jury are bound to give their verdict for that party who, upon the evidence, appears to them to have succeeded in establishing his side of the issue. But there are cases in which an issue may be found distributively, *i. e.*, in part for plaintiff, and in part for defendant. Thus, in an action for goods sold and work done, if the defendant pleaded that he never was indebted, on which issue was joined, a verdict might be found for the plaintiff as to the goods, and for the defendant as to the work. Steph. Pl. (7th Ed.) 77d.

DISTRICT. A certain portion of the country, separated from the rest for some special purposes.

The United States are divided into judicial districts, in each of which is established a district court, these districts being subdivisions of the circuits (*q. v.*) They are also divided into election districts, collection districts, etc.

DISTRICT ATTORNEYS OF THE UNITed States. Officers appointed in each judicial district, whose duty it is to prosecute, in such district, all delinquents, for crimes and offenses cognizable under the authority of the United States, and all civil actions in which the United States shall be concerned, except in the supreme court, in the district in which the court shall be holden.

DISTRICT PARISHES. Ecclesiastical divisions of parishes in England, for all purposes of worship, and for the celebration of marriages, christenings, churchings, and burials, formed at the instance of the queen's commissioners for building new churches. See 3 Steph. Comm. 744.

DISTRICTIO. A distress; a distraint. Cowell.

DISTRINGAS. A writ directed to the sheriff, commanding him to distrain a person of his goods and chattels to enforce a compliance with what is required of him.

It is used to compel an appearance where the party cannot be found, and in equity may be availed of to compel the appearance of a corporation aggregate. 4 Bouv. Inst. note 4191; Comyn, Dig. "Process" (D 7); Chit. Prac.; Sellon, Prac.

A form of execution in the actions of detinue and assize of nuisance. Brooke, Abr. pl. 26; 1 Rawle (Pa.) 44.

DISTRINGAS JURATORES (Lat. that you distrain jurors). A writ commanding the sheriff to have the bodies of the jurors, or to distrain them by their lands and goods, that they may appear upon the day appointed. 3 Sharswood, Bl. Comm. 354. It issues at the same time with the *venire*, though in theory afterwards, founded on the supposed neglect of the juror to attend. 3 Steph. Comm. 590.

DISTRINGAS NUPER VICE COMITUM (Lat. that you distrain the late sheriff). A writ to distrain the goods of a sheriff who is out of office, to compel him to bring in the body of a defendant, or to sell goods attached under a *fi. fa.*, which he ought to have done while in office, but has failed to do. 1 Tidd, Prac. 313.

DISTRINGAS VICE COMITEM. A writ of *distringas*, directed to the coroner, may be issued against a sheriff if he neglects to execute a writ of *venditioni exponas*. Archb. Prac. 584.

DISTRINGERE (Lat.) In feudal and old English law. To distrain; to coerce or compel; literally, to bond fast, or strain hard. Spelman; Calv. Lex. *Nec villa nec homo distringatur facere pontes*, nor shall a vill nor a man be distrained to make bridges. Magna Charta (9 Hen. Ill.) c. 15; Id. (Johan.) c. 23. *Constringere* is used in this sense in old writs. Spelman.

DISTURBANCE. A wrong done to an incorporeal hereditament by hindering or disquieting the owner in the enjoyment of it. Finch, Law, 187; 3 Bl. Comm. 235; 1 Swift Dig. 522; Comyn, Dig. "Action upon the Case," "Pleader" (3 I 6); 1 Serg. & R. (Pa.) 298; 41 Me. 104. The remedy for a disturbance is an action on the case, or, in some instances in equity, by an injunction.

——**Disturbance of Common.** Any act done by which the right of another to his common is incommoded or hindered. The remedy is by distress (where beasts are put on his common), or by action on the case, provided the damages are large enough to admit of his laying an action with a *per quod*. Cro. Jac. 195; Co. Litt. 122; 3 Bl. Comm. 237; 1 Saund. 546; 4 Term R. 71.

——**Disturbance of Franchise.** Any acts done whereby the owner of a franchise has his property damnified, or the profits arising thence diminished. The remedy for such disturbance is a special action on the case. Cro. Eliz. 558; 2 Saund. 113b; 3 Sharswood, Bl. Comm. 236; 28 N. H. 438.

——**Disturbance of Patronage.** The hindrance or obstruction of the patron to present his clerk to a benefice. 3 Bl. Comm. 242. The principal remedy was a writ of right of advowson; and there were also writs of *darrein presentment* and of *quare impedit*. Coke, 2d Inst. 355; Fitzh. Nat. Brev. 31.

——**Disturbance of Tenure.** Breaking the connection which subsists between lord and tenant. 3 Bl. Comm. 242; 2 Steph. Comm. 513.

——**Disturbance of Ways.** This happens where a person who hath a right of way over another's ground by grant or prescription is obstructed by inclosures or other obstacles, or by ploughing across it, by which means he cannot enjoy his right of way, or at least in so commodious a manner as he might have done. 3 Sharswood, Bl. Comm. 242; 5 Gray (Mass.) 409; 7 Md. 352; 23 Pa. St. 348; 29 Pa. St. 22.

DISTURBER. If a bishop refuse or neglect to examine or admit a patron's clerk, without reason assigned or notice given, he is styled a "disturber" by the law, and shall not have any title to present by lapse; for no man shall take advantage of his own wrong. 2 Bl. Comm. 278.

DITES OUSTER (Law Fr. say over). The form of awarding a *respondeas ouster*, in the Year Books. Y. B. M. 6 Edw. III. 49.

DITTAY. In Scotch law. A technical term in civil law, signifying the matter of charge or ground of indictment against a person accused of crime. Taking up dittay is obtaining informations and presentments of crime in order to trial. Skene de Verb. Sign.; Bell, Dict.

DIVERSITE DES COURTS. A treatise on courts and their jurisdiction, written in French in the reign of Edward III., as is supposed, and by some attributed to Fitzherbert. It was first printed in 1525, and again in 1534. Crabb, Hist. Eng. Law, 330, 483; 3 Bl. Comm. 53; 3 Reeve, Hist. Eng. Law, 152; 3 Steph. Comm. 414.

DIVERSITY. A plea by a convict, in bar of execution; of "diversity of person," *i. e.*, that he is not the same person who was attainted. 4 Bl. Comm. 396.

DIVERSO INTUITU (Lat.) With a different view, purpose, or design; in a different view or point of view; by a different course or process. 1 W. Bl. 89; Cas. temp. Hardw. 132; 9 East, 311; 4 Kent, Comm. 211, note; 1 Pet. (U. S.) 500; 2 Gall. (U. S.) 318; Story, Bailm. § 57. See "Alio Intuitu."

DIVERSORIUM. In old English law. A lodging or inn. Towns. Pl. 38.

DIVES. In the practice of the English chancery division, "dives costs" are costs on the ordinary scale, as opposed to the costs formerly allowed to a successful pauper suing or defending *in forma pauperis*, and which consisted only of his costs out of pocket. Daniell, Ch. Pr. 43; Cons. Ord. xl. 5.

DIVEST. See "Devest."

DIVESTITIVE FACT. One which puts an end to a right or status. Thus, the right of a creditor is at an end when his debt is paid. Bentham divides divestitive facts into destitutive, abolishing rights, and exonerative, extinguishing duties. See "Dispositive Facts."

DIVIDE ET IMPERA, CUM RADIX ET vertex imperii in obedientium consensu ratae sunt. Divide and govern, since the foundation and crown of empire are established in the consent of the obedient. 4 Inst. 35.

DIVIDEND. A portion of the principal or profits divided among several owners of a thing.

The term is usually applied to the division of the profits arising out of bank or other stocks, or to the division among the creditors of the effects of an insolvent estate.

In another sense, according to some old authorities, it signifies one part of an indenture.

A corporate profit set aside, declared and ordered by the directors to be paid to the stockholders on demand or at a fixed time. 205 Ill. 313.

A cash dividend is a disbursement to the stockholder of accumulated earnings, and the corporation at once parts irrevocably with all interest therein. But a stock dividend involves no disbursement by the corporation. It parts with nothing, and the stockholder receives merely certificates of stock which evidence, with his former shares, his interest in the entire capital. Stock dividends represent an addition from accrued earnings to the capital of the company; but they do not represent income, but merely additions to the source of income. Hale, Private Corporations, 227.

DIVIDENDA. In old records. An indenture; one counterpart of an indenture.

DIVINARE (Lat.) To divine; to conjecture or guess; to foretell. *Divinatio*, a conjecturing or guessing.

DIVINATIO NON INTERPRETATIO est, quae omnino recedit a litera. It is a guess, not interpretation, which altogether departs from the letter. Bac. Max. reg. 3, p. 47.

DIVINE SERVICE. A species of feudal tenure, by which the tenant was required to say masses, to distribute such a sum in alms or the like. It differed from *frankalmoign* in that, for breach of a duty of divine service, the lord could destrain without complaint to the visitor; the particular service being always expressly defined and prescribed. 2 Bl. Comm. 102.

DIVISA, or DEVISA (Law Lat. from Fr. *diviser*, to divide). In old English law. A division or partition; a division or distribution of goods by will; a will or testament of goods or chattels. Spelman; Cowell; Glanv. lib. 12, c. 20; Id. lib. 7, c. 5. Hence the modern "devise," now confined to mean a will or disposition of real estate by will. See "Devise."

A division or boundary between neighboring or adjoining lands (Law Fr. *devise*, *q. v.*), such as a highway, a wall, ditch, or stream, a stake or stone. Bracton, fol. 180b. As to streams, see Fleta, lib. 4, c. 6, § 3.

DIVISIBILIS EST SEMPER DIVISIBILIS. A thing divisible may be forever divided.

DIVISIBLE. That which is susceptible of being divided.

A contract cannot, in general, be divided in such a manner that an action may be brought, or a right accrue, on a part of it. 2 Pa. St. 454. But some contracts are susceptible of division; as when a reversioner sells a part of the reversion to one man, and a part to another, each shall have an action for his share of the rent which may accrue on a contract to pay a particular rent to the reversioner. 3 Whart. (Pa.) 404. See "Apportionment." But when it is to do several things at several times, an action will lie upon every default. 15 Pick. (Mass.) 409. See 1 Me. 316; 6 Mass. 344.

DIVISIM. In old English law. Severally; separately. Bracton, fol. 47.

DIVISION. In English law. A particular and ascertained part of a county. In Lincolnshire, "division" means what "riding" does in Yorkshire.

DIVISION OF OPINION. Disagreement among those called upon to decide a matter.

When, in a company or society, the parties having a right to vote are so divided that there is not a plurality of the whole in favor of any particular proposition, or when the voters are equally divided, it is said there is division of opinion. The term is especially applied to a disagreement among the judges of a court, such that no decision can be rendered upon the matter referred to them.

When the judges of a court are divided into three classes, each holding a different opinion, that class which has the greatest number shall give the judgment. For example, on a *habeas corpus*, when a court is composed of four judges, and one is for remanding the prisoner, another is for discharging him on his own recognizance, and the two others are for discharging him absolutely, the judgment will be that he be discharged. Bac. Abr. When a division of opinion exists in the United States circuit court, the cause may be certified to the supreme court for decision. Act Cong. April 29, 1802, § 6.

DIVISUM IMPERIUM (Lat.) A divided empire or jurisdiction; a jurisdiction shared between two tribunals, or exercised by them alternately. This classic phrase is frequently applied in the books to the jurisdiction alternately exercised by the courts of common law and admiralty, between high and low water mark, where the sea ebbs and flows; the one having jurisdiction upon the water when it is full sea, and the other upon the land when it is an ebb. Finch, Law, bk. 2, c. 1, p. 78; 5 Coke, 107; 1 Bl. Comm. 110; Molloy de Jur. Mar. 231; 1 Kent, Comm. 366. It is applied, also, to the jurisdiction exercised by courts of common law and equity over the same subject. 4 Steph. Comm. 9.

DIVORCE. The dissolution or partial suspension, by law, of the marriage relation.

The dissolution is termed "divorce from the bond of matrimony," or, in the Latin form of the expression, *a vinculo matrimonii;* the suspension, divorce from bed and board, *a mensa et thoro.* The former divorce puts an end to the marriage; the latter leaves it in full force. Bish. Mar. & Div. § 292. The term "divorce" is sometimes also applied to a sentence of nullity, which establishes that a supposed or pretended marriage either never existed at all, or at least was voidable at the election of one or both of the parties.

The more correct modern usage, however, confines the signification of divorce to the dissolution of a valid marriage. What has been known as a divorce *a mensa et thoro* may more properly be termed a legal separation. So, also, a sentence or decree which renders a marriage void *ab initio,* and bastardizes the issue, should be distinguished from one which is entirely prospective in its operation; and for that purpose the former may be termed a "sentence of nullity."

DIVORTIUM DICITUR A DIVERTENDO, quia vir divertitur ab uxore. Divorce is called from *divertendo,* because a man is diverted from his wife. Co. Litt. 235.

DIXIEME (Fr.) Tenth; the tenth part. Ord. Mar. liv. 1, tit. 1, art. 9.

——**In Old French Law.** An income tax payable to the crown. Steph. Lect. 359.

DO (Lat. I give). The ancient and aptest word of feoffment and of gift. 2 Bl. Comm. 310, 316; Co. Litt. 9.

DO, DICO, ADDICO (Lat. I give, I say, I adjudge). Three words used in the Roman law to express the extent of the civil jurisdiction of the praetor. *Do* denoted that he gave or granted actions, exceptions, and judices; *dico,* that he pronounced judgment; *addico,* that he adjudged the controverted property, or the goods of the debtor, etc., to the plaintiff. Kaufm. Mackeld. Civ. Law, 187; Id. 24, § 35, note b; Calv. Lex.

DO, LEGO (Lat. I give, I bequeath; or, I give and bequeath). The formal words of making a bequest or legacy, in the Roman law. *Titio et Seio hominem Stichum do, lego;* I give and bequeath to Titius and Seius, my man Stichus. Inst. 2. 20. 8. 30. 31. The expression is literally retained in modern wills. According to Calvin, who quotes Spiegelius, either of these words separately imports as much as both together. Calv. Lex.; Tayl. Civ. Law, 240.

DO UT DES (Lat.) I give that you may give. Dig. 19. 4; Id. 19. 5. 5; 2 Bl. Comm. 444.

DO UT FACIAS (Lat. I give that you may do; I give [you] that you may do or make [for me]). A formula in the civil law, under which those contracts were classed, in which one party gave or agreed to give money, in consideration the other party did or performed certain work. Dig. 19. 5. 5; 2 Bl. Comm. 444. *Do tibi codicem, ut facias mihi scribi disgestum,* I give you a code, that you may have a digest written (or copied) for me. Bracton, fol. 19.

The particle *ut,* in this and the foregoing phrase, is considered as denoting or expressing a consideration; so much, that Blackstone has treated them as forms of consideration. 2 Bl. Comm. ubi supra. Strictly, however, *ut* denotes that the civilians called *modus* (qualification); *quia* being the particle employed to denote what they called *causa,* which is generally translated "consideration." Bracton, fol. 18b. See "Consideration;" "Causa." Britton calls these phrases or *formulae,* conditions, and repeats them after Bracton; but the passage in the original edition is much corrupted. Britt. c. 36.

DOCK. As a noun, the inclosed space occupied by prisoners in a criminal court; the space between two wharves.

As a verb, to curtail or diminish, as to dock an entail.

DOCK WARRANT. A document issued by a dock company or dock owner in England, stating that certain goods therein mentioned are deliverable to a person therein named, or to his assigns, by indorsement. Dock warrants in form resemble bills of lading (*q. v.*), but they differ from them in this, that, when goods are at sea, a purchaser who takes a bill of lading has done all that is possible to obtain possession of them, while a purchaser who takes a dock warrant can at any moment lodge it with the dock company, and so take actual or constructive possession of the goods. It therefore seems that the indorsement of a dock warrant does not, at common law, pass the ownership in the goods, or divest the vendor's lien if the goods have not been paid for, but merely operates as a constructive delivery of them as between the indorser and indorsee, until the dock company has "attorned" to the indorsee by agreeing to hold the goods for him. Benj. Sales, 573, 674; 3 C. P. Div. 373, 450. See "Delivery Order." Dock warrants, however, are included in the factors' acts among the "documents of title," the possession of which gives a factor power to confer a good title to the goods on persons dealing with him in good faith. Benj. Sales, 668. See "Factors' Acts."

DOCKAGE. The charge for use of a dock.

DOCKET. A formal record of judicial proceedings; a brief writing; a small piece of paper or parchment having the effect of a larger. Blount. An abstract. Cowell.

DOCKET, STRIKING A. In English bankruptcy practice. The filing of petition and bond to obtain the lord chancellor's fiat, allowing proceedings against an alleged bankrupt. Brown.

DOCTOR AND STUDENT. The title of a work written by St. Germain in the reign of Henry VIII., in which many principles of the common law are discussed in a popular manner. It is in the form of a dialogue between a doctor of divinity and a student in law, and has always been considered a book of merit and authority. 1 Kent, Comm. 504; Crabb, Hist. Eng. Law, 482.

DOCTORS COMMONS. An institution near St. Paul's cathedral, where the ecclesiastical and admiralty courts are held.

DOCUMENTS. The deeds, agreements, title papers, letters, receipts, and other written instruments used to prove a fact.

——**In Civil Law.** Evidence delivered in the forms established by law, of whatever nature such evidence may be. The term is, however, applied principally to the testimony of witnesses. Savigny, Hist. Rom. Law, § 165.

DODRANS (Lat.) In Roman law. A subdivision of the *as*, containing nine *unciae;* the proportion of nine-twelfths, or three-fourths. 2 Bl. Comm. 462, note; Tayl. Civ. Law, 492.

DOE, JOHN. Originally the name of the fictitious plaintiff in the action of ejectment. Now used as a fictitious name to designate any party whose name is unknown.

DOED BANA (Saxon). The actual perpetrator of a homicide.

DOER. In Scotch law. An agent or attorney. 1 Kames, Eq. 325.

DOG-DRAW. In forest law. Drawing after, that is, pursuing, a deer with a dog. One of the circumstances which constituted what was called the manifest deprehension of an offender against venison in a forest; that is, his being caught in the act of committing the offense, or taken with the mainour, as it was otherwise called. Manw. For. Law, pt. 2, c. 8. See "Mainour."

DOGMA. In civil law. This word is used in the first chapter, first section, of the second Novel, and signifies an ordinance of the senate. See, also, Dig. 27. 1. 6.

DOING BUSINESS. The expression "doing business" is equivalent to the expression "transacting business." 149 Ill. App. 511.

The expression as used in statutes regulating foreign corporations, has a settled and recognized meaning, referring only to the transaction of the ordinary business in which the corporation is engaged, and not including acts not constituting any part of its ordinary business. 244 Ill. 360.

DOITKIN, or **DOIT.** A foreign coin of small value, prohibited by St. 3 Hen. V. c. 1, from being introduced into England.

DOLE (Law Lat. *dola;* Saxon, *doel;* from *doelan,* to divide or distribute).

——**In Old English Law.** A part or portion. Spelman. Dole meadow was one in which several persons had a share. Cowell.

——**In Scotch Law.** Criminal intent; evil design. Bell, Dict. voc. "Crime."

DOLG (Saxon). A wound. Spelman.

DOLG BOTE. A recompense for a scar or wound. Cowell.

DOLI CAPAX. Capable of mischief; having knowledge of right and wrong. 4 Bl. Comm. 22, 23; 1 Hale, P. C. 26, 27.

DOLI INCAPAX (Lat.) Incapable of distinguishing good from evil. A child under fourteen is, *prima facie, incapax doli,* but may be shown to be *capax doli.* 3 Bl. Comm. 23.

DOLO. The Spanish form of *dolus.*

DOLOSUS VERSATUR IN GENERALIbus. A deceiver deals in generals. 2 Coke, 34; 2 Bulst. 226; Lofft, 782; 1 Rolle, Abr. 157; Wingate, Max. 636; Broom, Leg. Max. (3d London Ed.) 264.

DOLUM EX INDICIIS PERSPICUIS PRObari convenit. Fraud should be proved by clear tokens. Code, 2. 21. 6; 1 Story, Cont. (4th Ed.) p. 602.

DOLUS (Lat.) In civil law. A fraudulent address or trick used to deceive some one; a fraud. Dig. 4. 3. 1. Any subtle contrivance by words or acts with a design to circumvent. 2 Kent, Comm. 560; Code, 2. 21.

Dolus differs from *culpa* in this, that the latter proceeds from an error of the understanding, while to constitute the former there must be a will or intention to do wrong. Wolff. Inst. § 17.

It seems doubtful, however, whether the general use of the word *dolus* in the civil law is not rather that of very great negligence, than of fraud, as used in the common law.

Such acts or omissions as operate as a deception upon the other party, or violate the just confidence reposed by him, whether there be a deceitful intent (*malus animus*) or not. Poth. du Depot, notes 23, 27; Story, Bailm. § 20a; 2 Kent, Comm. 506, note.

DOLUS AUCTORIS NON NOCET SUCcessori. The fraud of a predecessor does not prejudice the successor.

DOLUS CIRCUITU NON PURGATOR. Fraud is not purged by circuity. Bac. Max. reg. 1; Noy, Max. 9, 12; Broom, Leg. Max. (3d London Ed.) 210.

DOLUS DANS LOCUM CONTRACTUI. Fraud or deceit giving occasion for the contract. This phrase is applied to a false representation, when it is such as to induce the contract. The phrase is commonly used in expressing the rule that a contract is not voidable for misrepresentations unless the representation was *dans locum contractui, i. e.*, unless it induced the misled party to enter into the contract. Therefore, if the person to whom the false representations were made did not rely on it, but made further inquiries, he could not afterwards make use of it to avoid the contract. 6 Clark & F. 444.

DOLUS EST MACHINATIO, CUM ALIUD dissimulat aliud agit. Deceit is an artifice since it pretends one thing and does another. Lane, 47.

DOLUS ET FRAUS NEMINI PATROCInentur; patrocinari debent. Deceit and fraud shall excuse or benefit no man; they themselves need to be excused. Y. B. 14 Hen. VIII. 8; Story, Eq. Jur. § 395; 3 Coke, 78; 2 Fonbl. Eq. bk. 2, c. § 3.

DOLUS MALUS (Lat. fraud; deceit with an evil intention). Distinguished from *dolus bonus,* justifiable or allowable deceit. Calv. Lex.; Broom, Leg. Max. 349; 1 Kaufm. Mackeld. Civ. Law, 165. Misconduct. *Magna negligentia culpa est; magna culpa dolus est,* great negligence is a fault; a great fault is fraud. 2 Kent, Comm. 560, note.

DOM. PROC. (*domus procerum*). The house of lords. Wharton.

DOMAIN. Dominion; territory governed; possession; estate; land about the mansion-house of a lord; the right to dispose at our pleasure of what belongs to us.

A distinction has been made between "property" and "domain." The former is said to be that quality which is conceived to be in the thing itself, considered as belonging to such or such person, exclusively of all others. By the latter is understood that right which the owner has of disposing of the thing. Hence, domain and property are said to be correlative terms; the one is the active right to dispose of the other a passive quality which follows the thing, and places it at the disposition of the owner. 3 Toullier, Dr. Civ., note 83. But this distinction is too subtle for practical use. Puffendorff, Law Nat. lib. 4, c. 4, § 2. See 1 Bl. Comm. 105, 106; 1 Bouv. Inst. note 456; Clef des Lois Rom.; Domat, Civ. Law; 1 Hilliard, Real Prop. 24; 2 Hill, Abr. 237.

DOMBOC, or **DOMBEC** (Saxon). The name of codes of laws among the Saxons. Of these, King Alfred's was the most famous. 1 Bl. Comm. 46; 4 Bl. Comm. 411.

The *Domboc* of King Alfred is not to be confounded with the Domesday Book of William the Conqueror.

DOME (Saxon). Doom; sentence; judgment; an oath; the homager's oath in the Black Book of Hereford. Blount.

DOME BOOK. A book or code said to have been compiled under the direction of Alfred, for the general use of the whole kingdom of England; containing, as is supposed, the principal maxims of the common law, the penalties for misdemeanors, and the forms of judicial proceedings. It is said to have been extant so late as the reign of Edward IV., but is now lost. 1 Bl. Comm. 64, 65.

This is stated by Blackstone on the authority of the early English historians, but Mr. Hallam considers the authority insufficient. 2 Hallam, Mid. Ages, 402.

DOMESDAY, or **DOMESDAY BOOK** (Saxon). An ancient record made in the time of William the Conqueror, and now remaining in the English exchequer, consisting of two volumes of unequal size, containing minute and accurate surveys of the lands in England. It has been printed, also. 2 Sharswood, Bl. Comm. 49, 50.

A variety of ingenious accounts are given of the origin of this term by the old writers. The commoner opinion seems to be that it was so called from the fullness and completeness of the survey making it a day of judgment for the value, extent, and qualities of every piece of land. See Spelman; Blount; Termes de la Ley.

It was practically a careful census taken and recorded in the exchequer of the kingdom of England.

DOMESMEN (Saxon). An inferior kind of judges; men appointed to doom (judge) in matters in controversy. Cowell. Suitors in a court of a manor in ancient demesne, who are judges there. Blount; Whishaw; Termes de la Ley.

DOMESTIC. Pertaining to domicile or family.

One who resides in the house with the master he serves. The term does not extend to workmen and laborers employed out of doors. 41 Tex. 558.

——**Animals.** An animal (whether a quadruped or not and not absolutely ferae naturae) which either by habit or training lives in association with man is a domestic animal.

Fowls and poultry are within the term, 3 B. & S. 386; 32 L. J. M. C. 95, as are pet birds, such as a canary or linnet. Parrots may become, but young unacclimated parrots are not. 50 L. J. M. C. 67; 120 D. B. 67.

A tame unconfined sea-gull which will go to its owner when called, feed out of the hand and submit to be photographed, being used by the owner for that purpose in the owner's business of a photographer, is not a "domestic animal" within the meaning of a statute providing that if any person shall cruelly ill-treat any domestic animal he shall be liable to a penalty [1896]. 1 Q. B. 166.

Performing lions, kept in a cage, are not domestic animals within the meaning of the same acts. 2 Q. B. 319; nor are wild rabbits caught in nets, and kept in confinement and fed during five or six days immediately following the capture. 2 Q. B. 57.

——**Products.** The word is appropriately used in an act of the state legislature to describe only a product exclusively belonging to, and within the sovereign jurisdiction of the state. 64 Pa. St. 103.

DOMESTIC ADMINISTRATION. See "Administration" (11).

DOMESTIC ATTACHMENT. A species of attachment against resident debtors who absent or conceal themselves, as foreign attachment (*q. v.*) is against nonresidents. 20 Pa. St. 144; 2 Kent, Comm. 403.

DOMESTIC BILL OF EXCHANGE. A bill of exchange drawn on a person residing in the same state with the drawer; or dated at a place in the state, and drawn on a person living within the state. 25 Miss. 143. It is the residence of the drawer and drawee which must determine whether a bill is domestic or foreign. Id.

DOMESTIC CORPORATIONS. Corporations transacting business in the state by which they are created.

DOMESTICS. Those who reside in the same house with the master they serve. The term does not extend to workmen or laborers employed out of doors. 5 Bin. (Pa.) 167; Merlin, Repert. The act of Congress of April 30, 1790 (section 25), uses the word "domestic" in this sense.

DOMESTICUS. In old European law. A *seneschal*, steward, or *major domo;* a judge's assistant; an assessor (*q. v.*) Spelman.

DOMICELLA. In old English law. A damsel. Fleta, lib. 1, c. 20, § 80.

DOMICELLUS (Law Lat. dim. of *dominus*). In old European law. A young lord; a title anciently given to the king's natural sons in France, and sometimes to the eldest sons of noblemen there. Spelman; Blount. Spelman says it answered to the Saxon "adeling," "aetheling."

DOMICILE. That place where a man has his true, fixed and permanent home and principal establishment, and to which, whenever he is absent, he has the intention of returning. Lieber, Enc. Am.; 10 Mass. 188; 11 La. 175; 5 Metc. (Mass.) 187; 4 Barb. (N. Y.) 505; 9 Ired. (N. C.) 99; 1 Tex. 673; 13 Me. 255; 27 Miss. 704; 1 Bosw. (N. Y.) 673; 74 Ill. 312.

The place in which one's habitation is fixed, without any present intention of removing therefrom. Story, Confl. Laws, § 43.

It is a more extensive term than "residence" or "habitation," not only residence, but intent to remain, being essential to domicile (4 Hun [N. Y.] 487; 4 Humph. [Tenn.] 346), though they have been considered convertible for certain purposes (17 Pick. [Mass.] 291).

Domicile may be either national or domestic. In deciding the question of national domicile, the point to be determined will be in which of two or more distinct nationalities a man has his domicile. In deciding the matter of domestic domicile, the question is in which subdivision of the nation does the person have his domicile. Thus, whether a person is domiciled in England or France would be a question of national domicile, whether in Norfolk or Suffolk county, a question of domestic domicile. The distinction is to be kept in mind, since the rules for determining the two domiciles, though frequently, are not necessarily, the same. See 2 Kent, Comm. 449; Story, Confl.

Laws, § 39 et seq.; Westl. Priv. Int. Law, 15; Wheat. Int. Law, 123 et seq.

The Romanists and civilians seem to attach about equal importance to the place of business and of residence as fixing the place of domicile. Story, Confl. Laws, § 42. This may go far towards reconciling the discrepancies of the common law and civil law as to what law is to govern in regard to contracts. But at common law the main question in deciding where a person has his domicile is to decide where he has his home, and where he exercises his political rights.

Legal residence, inhabitancy, and domicile are generally used as synonymous. 1 Bradf. Sur. (N. Y.) 70; 1 Har. (Del.) 383; 1 Spencer (N. J.) 328; 2 Rich. (S. C.) 489; 10 N. H. 452; 3 Wash. C. C. (U. S.) 555; 15 Mees. & W. 433; 23 Pick. (Mass.) 170; 5 Metc. (Mass.) 298; 4 Barb. (N. Y.) 505; 7 Gray (Mass.) 299. But much depends on the connection and purpose. 1 Wend. (N. Y.) 43; 5 Pick. (Mass.) 231; 17 Pick. (Mass.) 231; 15 Me. 58.

Commercial domicile is a domicile acquired by maintenance of a commercial establishment in a country, in relation to transactions connected with such establishments. 1 Kent, Comm. 82; 2 Kent, Comm. 11, 12.

DOMICILIATE. To fix or establish a domicile.

DOMIGERIUM. Power over another; also danger. Bracton, lib. 4, tit. 1, c. 10.

DOMINA. A title given to honorable women, who anciently, in their own right of inheritance, held a barony. Cowell.

DOMINANT. That to which a servitude or easement is due, or for the benefit of which it exists. Distinguished from "servient," that from which it is due. See "Easement."

DOMINANT TENEMENT. In civil and Scotch law. A term used in the constitution of servitudes, meaning the tenement or subject in favor of which the servitude is constituted. Bell, Dict.

DOMINATIO. In old English law. Lordship. Mem. in Scacc. H. 22 Edw. I.

DOMINICIDE. The act of killing one's lord or master.

DOMINICUM (Lat. domain; demain; demesne). A lordship; that of which one has the lordship or ownership; that which remains under the lord's immediate charge and control.

In this sense it is equivalent to the Saxon bordlands. Spelman; Blount. In regard to lands for which the lord received services and homage merely, the *dominicum* was in the tenant.

Property; domain; anything pertaining to a lord. Cowell.

——In Ecclesiastical Law. A church, or any other building consecrated to God. Du Cange.

DOMINICUM ANTIQUUM. In old English law. Ancient demesne. Bracton, fol. 369b.

DOMINIUM (Lat.) Perfect and complete property or ownership in a thing.

Plenum in re dominium,—plena in re potestas. This right is composed of three principal elements, viz., the right to use, the right to enjoy, and the right to dispose of the thing, to the exclusion of every other person. To use a thing, *jus utendi tantum,* consists in employing it for the purposes for which it is fit, without destroying it, and which employment can therefore be repeated; to enjoy a thing, *jus fruendi tantum,* consists in receiving the fruits which it yields, whether natural or civil, *quidquid ex re nascitur;* to dispose of a thing, *jus abutendi,* is to destroy it, or to transfer it to another. Thus, he who has the use of a horse may ride him, or put him in the plough to cultivate his own soil; but he has no right to hire the horse to another, and receive the civil fruits which he may produce in that way. On the other hand, he who has the enjoyment of a thing is entitled to receive all the profits or revenues which may be derived from it, either from natural or civil fruits. And, lastly, he who has the right of disposing of a thing, *jus abutendi,* may sell it, or give it away, etc., subject, however, to the rights of the usury or usufructuary, as the case may be.

These three elements, *usus, fructus, abusus* when united in the same person, constitute the *dominium;* but they may be, and frequently are, separated, so that the right of disposing of a thing may belong to *Primus,* and the rights of using and enjoying to *Secundus,* or the right of enjoying alone may belong to *Secundus,* and the right of using to *Tertius.* In that case, *Primus* is always the owner of the thing, but he is the naked owner, inasmuch as for a certain time he is actually deprived of all the principal advantages that can be derived from it. *Secundus,* if he has the use and enjoyment, *jus utendi et fruendi simul,* is called the "usufructuary," *usus-fructuarius;* if he has the enjoyment only, *jus fruendi tantum,* he is the *fructuarius.* And *Tertius,* who has the right of use, *jus utendi tantum,* is called the usuary,—*usuarius.* But this dismemberment of the elements of the *dominium* is essentially temporary. If no shorter period has been fixed for its duration, it terminates with the life of the usuary, fructuary, or usufructuary, for which reason the rights of use and usufruct are called "personal servitudes." Besides the separation of the elements of the *dominium* among different persons, there may also be a *jus in re,* or dismemberment, so far as real estates are concerned, in favor of other estates. Thus, a right of way over my land may exist in favor of your house. This right is so completely attached to the house that it can never be separated from it, except by its entire extinction. This class of *jura in re* is called "predial" or "real"' servitudes. To constitute this servitude, there must be two estates belonging to different owners. These estates are viewed in some measure as juridical persons, capable of acquiring rights and incurring obligations. The estate in favor of which the servitude exists is the creditor estate, and the estate by which the servitude is due, the debtor estate. 2 Mariade, 343 et seq.

DOMINIUM DIRECTUM (Lat.) legal ownership.

——**In the Civil Law.** Ownership, as distinguished from enjoyment.

——**In the Feudal Law.** The right of the lord.

DOMINIUM DIRECTUM ET UTILE (Lat.) Full ownership and possession united in one person.

DOMINIUM EMINENS. Eminent domain. Tayl. Civ. Law, 463.

DOMINIUM NON POTEST ESSE IN pendenti. Lordship cannot be in suspense, *i. e.*, property cannot remain in abeyance. Halk. Max. 39.

DOMINIUM PLENUM. Full ownership; the union of the *dominium directum* with the *dominium utile.* Tayl. Civ. Law, 478.

DOMINIUM UTILE (Lat.) The beneficial ownership; the use of the property.

DOMINO VOLENTE (Lat.) With the owner's consent.

DOMINUS (Lat.) The lord or master; the owner. Ainsworth. The owner or proprietor of a thing, as distinguished from him who uses it merely. Calv. Lex. A master or principal, as distinguished from an agent or attorney. Story, Ag. § 3; Ferriere.

——**In Civil Law.** A husband; a family. Vicat.

DOMINUS LITIS (Lat.) The master of a suit; the client, as distinguished from an attorney. And yet it is said, although he who has appointed an attorney is properly called *dominus litis*, the attorney himself, when the cause has been tried, becomes the *dominus litis*. Vicat.

DOMINUS NAVIS. In the civil law. The owner of a vessel. Dig. 39. 4. 11. 2.

DOMINUS NON MARITABIT PUPILLUM nisi semel. A lord cannot give a ward in marriage but once. Co. Litt. 9.

DOMINUS REX NULLUM HABERE POtest parem, multo minus superiorem. The king cannot have an equal, much less a superior. 1 Reeve, Hist. Eng. Law, 115.

DOMITAE (Lat.) Tame; subdued; not wild.

DOMO REPARANDA. A writ that lay for one against his neighbor, by the anticipated fall of whose house he feared a damage and injury to his own. Reg. Orig. 153; Termes de la Ley.

DOMUS (Lat.) In the civil and old English law. A house or dwelling; a habitation. Inst. 4. 4. 8; Towns. Pl. 183-185.

Held synonymous with "messuage." Cro. Jac. 634.

DOMUS CAPITULARIS. In old records. A chapter house; the chapter house. Dyer, 26b.

DOMUS CONVERSORUM (Law Lat. the house of the converts). An ancient house or institution (Spelman calls it *collegium*) established by Henry III. for the benefit of such Jews as were converted to the Christian faith. This continued to the reign of Edward III., who, having expelled the Jews from the kingdom, converted the building into a place for keeping the rolls and records of the chancery. Spelman; Cowell, voc. "Rolls." It is now called the "Rolls' Office in Chancery Lane," though in Latin the old name is sometimes retained. Id. voc. "Master of the Rolls."

DOMUS DEI. The house of God; applied to many hospitals and religious houses.

DOMUS PROCERUM. The house of lords; abbreviated into *Dom. Proc.* or *D. P.*

DOMUS SUA CUIQUE EST TUTISSImum refugium. Every man's house is his castle. 5 Coke, 91, 92; Dig. 2. 14. 18; Broom, Leg. Max. (3d London Ed.) 384; 1 Hale, P. C. 481; Fost. Hom. 320; 8 Q. B. 757; 16 Q. B. 546, 556; 19 How. St. Tr. 1030. See "Arrest."

DOMUS TUTISSIMUM CUIQUE REFUGium atque receptaculum. The habitation of each one is an inviolable asylum for him. Dig. 2. 4. 18.

DONA CLANDESTINA SUNT SEMPER suspiciosa. Clandestine gifts are always suspicious. 3 Coke, 81; Noy, Max. (9th Ed.) 152; 4 Barn. & C. 652; 1 Maule & S. 253; Broom, Leg. Max. (3d London Ed.) 264.

DONARI VIDETUR QUOD, NULLI JURE cogente conceditur. That is considered to be given which is granted when no law compels. Dig. 50. 17. 82.

DONATARIUS (Law Lat.) One to whom something is given; a donee.

DONATIO (Lat. a gift). A transfer of the title to property to one who receives it without paying for it. Vicat. The act by which the owner of a thing voluntarily transfers the title and possession of the same from himself to another person, without any consideration.

Its literal translation, gift, has acquired in real law a more limited meaning, being applied to the conveyance of estates tail. 2 Bl. Comm. 316; Litt. § 59; West, Symb. § 254; 4 Cruise, Dig. 51. There are several kinds of *donatio,*—as *donatio simplex et pura,* simple and pure gift, without compulsion or consideration; *donatio absoluta et larga,* an absolute gift; *donatio conditionalis,* a conditional gift; *donatio stricta et coarctura,* a restricted gift, as an estate tail.

——**Donatio Inter Vivos.** A gift between living persons. A contract which takes place by the mutual consent of the giver, who divests himself of the thing given in order to transmit the title of it to the donee gratuitously, and the donee, who accepts and acquires the legal title to it. This donation takes place when the giver is not in any immediate apprehension of death, which distinguishes it from a *donatio mortis causa.* 1 Bouv. Inst. note 712. See, also, Civ. Code La. art. 1453; Inst. 2. 7. 2; Cooper, Inst. notes 474, 475; U. S. Dig. tit. "Gift."

——**Donatio Mortis Causa.** A gift in prospect of death. A gift made by a person in sickness, who, apprehending his dissolution near, delivers, or causes to be delivered, to another, the possession of any personal goods, to keep as his own in case of the donor's decease. 2 Bl. Comm. 514. See Civ. Code La. art. 1455.

The civil law defines it to be a gift under apprehension of death; as when anything is given upon condition that if the donor dies, the donee shall possess it absolutely, or return it if the donor should survive, or should repent of having made the gift, or if the donee should die before the donor. 1 Miles (Pa.) 109-117.

A *donatio causa mortis* is sometimes considered as a species of legacy, and it is always accompanied with the implied trust or condition that, if the donor lives, the property shall revert to himself, being given only in contemplation of death. 2 Bl. Comm. 514. 1 White's Equity Cases, 602, 603. It is indispensable to its validity that it be accompanied and perfected by a present delivery of the subject of the gift, according to the manner in which it is capable of being delivered. 2 Kent's Com. 445-448, and notes.

It differs from a legacy, inasmuch as it does not require proof in the court of probate, 2 Strange, 77; 1 Bligh (N. S.) 531, and no assent is required from the executor to perfect the donee's title, 2 Ves. Jr. 120; 1 Sim. & S. 245. It differs from a gift *inter vivos* because it is ambulatory and revocable during the donor's life, because it may be made to the wife of the donor, and because it is liable for his debts.

Donations or gifts of this kind are derived entirely from the civil law, and were introduced into England as early as the time of Bracton, who closely follows the language of the Digests. Bract. fol. 60.

DONATIO NON PRAESUMITUR. A gift is not presumed. Jenk. Cent. Cas. 109.

DONATIO PERFICITUR POSSESSIONE accipientis. A gift is rendered complete by the possession of the receiver. See 1 Bouv. Inst. note 712; 2 Johns. (N. Y.) 52; 2 Leigh (Va.) 337; 2 Kent, Comm. 438.

DONATIO PROPTER NUPTIAS (Lat. gift on account of marriage). In Roman law. A gift made by the husband as a security for the marriage portion. The effect of the act of giving such a gift was different according to the relation of the parties at the time of making the gift. Vicat. Called, also, a "mutual gift."

The name was originally applied to a gift made before marriage, and was then called a *domatio ante nuptias;* but in process of time it was allowed to be made after marriage as well, and was then called a *donatio propter nuptias.*

DONATION. In ecclesiastical law. A mode of acquiring a benefice by deed of gift alone, without presentation, institution, or induction. 3 Steph. Comm. 81.

The act by which the owner of a thing voluntarily transfers the title and possession of the same from himself to another person, without any consideration. Ind. N. & S. R. R. Co. v. City of Attica, 56 Ind. 486. A donation, as defined by the civil law, is a contract whereby a person gratuitously dispossesses himself of something by transferring it to another to be his property, who accepts it. It is a contract or agreement, and must be accepted by the donee, otherwise it would be a mere offer. It must also be gratuitous, because otherwise, it would be a sale or exchange. 43 Texas, 343.

DONATIONUM ALIA PERFECTA, ALIA incepta, et non perfecta; ut si donatio, lecta fuit et concessa, ac traditio nondum fuerit subsecuta. Some gifts are perfect, others incipient and not perfect; as, if a gift were read and agreed to, but delivery had not then followed. Co. Litt. 56.

DONATIVE ADVOWSON. In ecclesiastical law. A species of advowson, where the benefice is conferred on the clerk by the patron's deed of donation, without presentation, institution, or induction. 2 Bl. Comm. 23; Termes de la Ley.

DONATOR (Lat. from *donare;* Law Fr. *donour*). In civil and old English law. A donor or giver; the party who makes a *donatio,* or gift. Bracton, fol. 11 et seq.; Fleta, lib. 3, c. 7, § 4.

Donatorius (properly, *donatarius*). A donee; a person to whom a gift is made; a purchaser. Bracton, fol. 13 et seq.; Fleta, ubi supra.

DONATOR NUNQUAM DESINIT POSSIdere antequam donatarius incipiat possidere. He that gives never ceases to possess until he that receives begins to possess. Dyer, 281; Bracton, 41b.

DONATORIUS. A donee; a person to whom a gift is made; a purchaser. Bracton, fol. 13 et seq.; Fleta, lib. 3, c. 7, § 4.

DONATORY. The person on whom the king bestows his right to any forfeiture that has fallen to the crown.

DONE. (Lat. *factum, actum*). Distinguished from "made." "A 'deed made' may no doubt mean an 'instrument made'; but a 'deed done' is not an 'instrument done,'—it is an 'act done'; and therefore these words, 'made and done' apply to acts as well as deeds." Lord Brougham, 4 Bell's Appeal Cases, 38.

DONEC. Lat. Until. Fleta, lib. 3, c. 12, § 6. A word of limitation in old conveyances. Co. Litt. 235a.

DONEE. He to whom a gift is made or a bequest given; one who is invested with a power of appointment. He is sometimes called an "appointee." 4 Kent, Comm. 316; 4 Cruise, Dig. 51.

DONIS, STATUTE DE. The statute of Westminster II. 2, namely, 13 Edw. I. c. 1, called the statute *de donis conditionalibus*. This statute revives, in some sort, the ancient feudal restraints which were originally laid on alienations. Its effect, by making a limitation in tail inalienable, was to defeat the former rule of construction by which a limitation to one and particular heirs was held to impose a condition which was fulfilled by the birth of such heirs, so that the fee conditional (fee tail) became a fee simple. Such estates were afterwards called "estates tail." See "Estates"; "Tail." 2 Bl. Comm. 110-113.

DONOR (from Law Fr. *donour;* Lat. *donator*).

——**In Old English Law.** He by whom lands were given to another; the party making a *donatio (q. v.)* See "Donator."

——**In Later Law.** He who gives lands or tenements to another in tail. Litt. § 57; Termes de la Ley.

——**In Modern Law.** He who makes a gift. See, also, "Power."

DONUM (Lat.) A gift.

The difference between *donum* and *numus* is said to be that *donum* is more general, while *numus* is specific. *Numus* is said to mean *donum* with a cause for the giving, though not a legal consideration, as on account of marriage, etc. *Donum* is said to be that which is given from no necessity of law or duty, but from free will, "from the absence of which, if they are not given, no blame arises, but, if they are given, praise is due." Vicat; Calv. Lex.

DOOM, or DOME. In Scotch practice. Judgment; sentence. The judgment of a court formerly pronounced by the mouth of an officer called a dempster (*q. v.*), and ending with the words, "And this I give (or pronounce) for doom." The term is still retained; sentences in criminal cases ending with the words, "Which is pronounced for doom." See 2 Brown, 128.

DORMANT. Sleeping; silent; not known; not acting.

——**Dormant Judgment.** One upon which itor delivers to the sheriff, with directions to levy only, and not to sell, until further orders, or until a junior execution is received.

——**Dormant Judgment.** One upon which no execution is issued until the time limited for issuing execution, as of course, has run out.

——**Dormant Partners.** A dormant partner is one whose name is not known, or does not appear as partner, but who nevertheless is a silent partner, and partakes of the profits, and thereby becomes a partner, either absolutely, to all intents and purposes, or at all events, in respect to third persons. According to Mr. Justice Story, dormant partners, in strictness of language, mean those who are merely passive in the firm, whether known or unknown, in contradistinction to those who are active and conduct the business of the firm as principals. Story, Partn. § 80.

DORMIUNT ALIQUANDO LEGES, NUNquam moriuntur. The laws sometimes sleep, but never die. Inst. 161.

DORSUM (Lat. the back). *In dorso recordi,* on the back of the record. 5 Coke, 44b.

DORTURE. A dormitory of a convent; a place to sleep in.

DOS (Lat.)

——**In Roman Law.** That which is received by or promised to the husband from the wife, or any one else by her influence, for sustaining the burdens of matrimony. There are three classes of *dos*. *Dos profectitia* is that which is given by the father or any male relative from his property or by his act. *Dos adventitia* is that which is given by any other person or from the property of the wife herself. *Dos receptitia* is where there is a stipulation connected with the gift relating to the death of the wife. Vicat; Calv. Lex.; Du Cange; 1 Washb. Real Prop. 147.

——**In English Law.** The portion bestowed upon a wife at her marriage by her husband. 1 Reeve, Hist. Eng. Law, 100; 1 Washb. Real Prop. 147; 1 Cruise, Dig. 152.

Dower generally. The portion which a widow has in the estate of her husband after his death. Park, Dower.

This use of the word in the English law, though, as Spelman shows, not strictly correct, has still the authority of Tacitus (de Mor. Germ. 18) for its use. And if the general meaning of marriage portion is given to it, it is strictly as applicable to a gift from the husband to the wife as to one from the wife to the husband. It occurs often in the phrase *dos de dote peti non debet,* dower should not be sought of dower. 1 Washb. Real Prop. 209.

DOS DE DOTE PETI NON DEBET. Dower ought not to be sought from dower. 4 Coke, 122; Co. Litt. 31; 4 Dane, Abr. 671; 1 Washb. Real Prop. 209.

DOS RATIONABILIS (Lat. a reasonable marriage portion). A reasonable part of her husband's estate, to which every widow is entitled, of lands of which her husband may have endowed her on the day of marriage. Co. Litt. 336. Dower, at common law. 2 Bl. Comm. 234.

DOS RATIONABILIS VEL LEGITIMA est cujuslibet mulieris de quocunque tenemento tertia pars omnium terrarum et tenementorum, quae vir suus tenuit in dominio suo ut de feodo, etc. Reasonable or legitimate dower belongs to every woman of a third part of all the lands and tenements of which her husband was seised in his demesne, as of fee, etc. Co. Litt. 336.

DOT. A French word adopted in Louisiana. The fortune, portion, or dowry which a woman brings to her husband by the marriage. 6 Mart. (La.; N. S.) 460.

DOTAGE. Dotage is that feebleness of the mental faculties which proceeds from old age. It is a diminution or decay of that intellectual power which was once possessed. It is the slow approach of death; of that irrevocable cessation, without hurt or disease, of all the functions which once belonged to the living animal. 1 Bland, Ch. (Md.) 389.

DOTAL PROPERTY. By the civil law in Louisiana, by this term is understood that property which the wife brings to the husband to assist him in bearing the expenses of the marriage establishment. Civ. Code La. art. 2315.

DOTALITIUM. In canon and feudal law. Dower. Spelman, voc. "Doarium;" Calv. Lex. 2 Bl. Comm. 129. Used as early as A. D. 841.

DOTATION. In French law. The act by which the founder of a hospital, or other charity, endows it with property to fulfill its destination.

DOTE. In Spanish law. The property and effects which a woman brings to her husband for the purpose of aiding him, with the rents and revenues thereof, to support the expenses of the marriage. Las Partidas, 4. 11. 1. "*Dos,*" says Cajas, "*est pecunia marito, nuptiarum causa, data vel promissa.*" The dower of the wife is inalienable, except in certain specified cases, for which see Escriche, Dic. Raz.

DOTE ASSIGNANDO. In English law. A writ which lay in favor of a widow, when it was found by office that the king's tenant was seised of tenements in fee or fee tail at the time of his death, and that he held of the king in chief.

DOTE UNDE NIHIL HABET. Dower *unde nihil habet (q. v.)*

DOTI LEX FAVET; PROEMIUM PUDORis est, ideo parcatur. The law favors dower; it is the reward of chastity, therefore let it be preserved. Co. Litt. 31; Branch, Princ.

DOTIS ADMINISTRATIO. Admeasurement of dower, where the widow holds more than her share, etc.

DOTISSA. A dowager.

DOUAY VERSION. A version of the Bible, of which the Old Testament was published by the English college at Douay, in France, in 1609, and the New Testament by the English college at Rheims in 1582. 245 Ill. 343.

DOUBLE AVAIL OF MARRIAGE. In Scotch law. Double the ordinary or single value of a marriage. Bell, Dict. See "Duplex Valor Maritagii."

DOUBLE BOND. In Scotch law. A bond with a penalty, as distinguished from a single bond. 2 Kames, Eq. 359.

DOUBLE COMPLAINT, or DOUBLE quarrel. A grievance made known by a clerk or other person, to the archbishop of the province, against the ordinary, for delaying or refusing to do justice in some cause ecclesiastical, as to give sentence, institute a clerk, etc. It is termed a "double complaint," because it is most commonly made against both the judge and him at whose suit justice is denied or delayed; the effect whereof is that the archbishop, taking notice of the delay, directs his letters, under his authentical seal, to all clerks of his province, commanding them to admonish the ordinary, within a certain number of days, to do the justice required, or otherwise to appear before him or his official, and there allege the cause of his delay; and to signify to the ordinary that if he neither perform the thing enjoined, nor appear nor show cause against it, he himself, in his court of audience, will forthwith proceed to do the justice that is due. Cowell.

DOUBLE (or TREBLE) COSTS. In England and some of the United States, ordinary costs, and fifty per cent. thereof in addition. 22 Mich. 5; 9 Wend. (N. Y.) 443. In other states, twice the ordinary costs. 16 Pa. St. 254; 34 N. J. Law, 145. Treble costs is either full costs, and seventy-five per cent. additional, or three times the ordinary costs, in different states.

DOUBLE (or TREBLE) DAMAGES. In some cases it is provided by statute that a party may recover double or treble damages. In these cases the jury find such damages as they think proper, and the court enhances them in the judgment. Brooke, Abr. "Damages," pl. 70; 2 Inst. 416; 1 Wils. 126; 1 Mass. 155. The damages are actually doubled or trebled, as the case may be; not assessed, like double or treble costs.

DOUBLE FINE. In old English law. A fine *sur done grant et render* was called a "double fine," because it comprehended the fine *sur cognizance de droit come ceo,* etc. and the fine *sur concessit.* 2 Bl. Comm. 353.

DOUBLE INSURANCE. Is where divers insurance are made upon the same interest in the same subject against the same risks in favor of the same assured, in proportions exceeding the value. 1 Phil. Ins. §§ 359, 366.

DOUBLE PLEA. The alleging, for one single purpose, two or more distinct grounds of defense, when one of them would be as effectual in law as both or all. See "Duplicity."

DOUBLE POSSIBILITY. A possibility based or dependent on another possibility. Used ordinarily in respect to the creation of contingent trusts and remainders. Thus, a bequest to testator's unborn "child" is valid, resting on a single possibility; while one to his unborn "son" is invalid, the possibility being double.

DOUBLE RENT. Required, by St. 11 Geo. II. c. 19, as a penalty of a tenant holding over after notice to quit. Wharton.

DOUBLE VOUCHER. A voucher which occurs when the person first vouched to warranty comes in and vouches over a third person. See a precedent, 2 Bl. Comm. Appendix V. p. xvii.

The necessity for double voucher arises when the tenant in tail is not the tenant in the writ, but is tenant by warranty; that is, where he is vouched, and comes in and confesses the warranty. Generally speaking, to accomplish this result a previous conveyance is necessary, by the tenant in tail, to a third person, in order to make such third person tenant to a writ of entry. Prest. Conv. 125, 126.

DOUBLE WASTE. When a tenant bound to repair suffers a house to be wasted, and then unlawfully fells timber to repair it, he is said to commit double waste. Co. Litt. 53. See "Waste."

DOUBT. The uncertainty which exists in relation to a fact, a proposition, or other thing; an equipoise of the mind arising from an equality of contrary reasons. Ayliffe, Pand. 121. See "Reasonable Doubt."

DOUBTFUL TITLE. A doubtful title is one which the court does not consider to be so clear that it will enforce its acceptance by a purchaser, nor so defective as to declare it a bad title, but only subject to so much doubt that a purchaser ought not to be compelled to accept it. 36 N. Y. Supp. 671.

DOUN, DON, or DONE (Law Fr.) A gift. The thirty-fourth chapter of Britton is entitled *"De Douns."*

DOWABLE. Entitled to dower.

DOWAGER. A widow endowed; one who has a jointure.

——**In England.** A title or addition given to the widows of princes, dukes, earls, and other noblemen, to distinguish them from the wives of the heir, who have a right to bear the title.

DOWAGER QUEEN. The widow of the king. As such she enjoys most of the privileges belonging to her as queen consort. It is not treason to conspire her death or violate her chastity, because the succession to the crown is not thereby endangered. No man, however, can marry her without a special license from the sovereign, on pain of forfeiting his lands or goods. 1 Bl. Comm. 233.

DOWER (Fr. *douer,* to endow). The provision which the law makes for a widow out of the lands or tenements of her husband, for her support and the nurture of her children. Co. Litt. 30a; 2 Bl. Comm. 130; 4 Kent, Comm. 35; Washb. Real Prop. 146.

The word "dower" has reference to real estate only. 36 Me. 216.

It has three stages: (1) Inchoate, from marriage to the death of the husband; (2) consummate, from the death of the husband to admeasurement; and (3) assigned from the time when it is set off to the widow. Stew. Husb. & Wife, §§ 262-264.

There were five species of dower in England:

(1) Dower by custom, where a widow became entitled to a specified portion of her husband's lands in consequence of some local or particular custom.

(2) Dower *ad ostium ecclesiae,* where a man of full age, on coming to the church door to be married, endowed his wife of a certain portion of his lands.

(3) Dower *ex assensu patris,* which differed from dower *ad ostium ecclesiae* only in being made out of the lands of the husband's father, and with his consent.

(4) Dower *de la plus belle,* where the widow, on suing the guardian in chivalry for dower, was required by him to endow herself of the fairest portion of any lands she might hold as guardian in socage, and thus release from dower the lands of her husband held in chivalry. This was abolished along with the military tenures, of which it was a consequence. 2 Bl. Comm. 132, note.

(5) Dower by common law, where the widow was entitled during her life to a third part of all the lands and tenements in fee simple or fee tail of which her hus-

band was seised at any time during the coverture, and of which any issue she might have had might by possibility have been heir.

Since the passage of the dower act in England (3 & 4 Wm. IV. c. 105), all these species of dower, except that by custom and by the common law, have ceased to exist. 2 Sharswood, Bl. Comm. 135, note. Dower in the United States, although regulated by statutes differing from each other in many respects, conforms substantially to that at the common law. 1 Washb. Real Prop. 149.

DOWER UNDE NIHIL HABET. A writ which lay for a widow to obtain an assignment of dower.

DOWLE STONES. Stones dividing lands, etc. Cowell.

DOWMENT. In old English law. Endowment; dower.

DOWRESS. A woman entitled to dower. See "Dower."

DOWRY. Formerly applied to mean that which a woman brings to her husband in marriage. This is now called a "portion." This word is sometimes confounded with "dower." See Co. Litt. 31; Civ. Code La. art. 2317; Dig. 23. 3. 76; Code, 5. 12. 20.

DOY (L. Fr.) Owe; ought.

Sauve la foy que jeo doy au roy; saving the faith which I owe to the king. Britt. c. 68.

DOYLE'S RULE. Doyle's rule for the measurement of logs is to deduct four inches from the diameter of the log, as an allowance for slab; square one-quarter of the remainder and multiply the result by the length of the log in feet. 199 Ill. App. 175.

DOZEIN (Law Fr. twelve). A person twelve years of age. St. 18 Edw. II.; Barr. Obs. St. 208.

DOZEN PEERS. Twelve peers assembled at the instance of the barons, in the reign of Henry III., to be privy counsellors, or rather conservators of the kingdom. Wharton.

DRACHMA. A term employed in old pleadings and records, to denote a groat. Towns. Pl. 180.

An Athenian silver coin, (Gr. *drachme*) of the value of about 7¾d. sterling.

DRACO REGIS. The standard, ensign, or military colors borne in war by the ancient kings of England, having the figure of a dragon painted thereon.

DRACONIAN LAWS. A code of laws prepared by Draco, the celebrated lawgiver of Athens. These laws were exceedingly severe, and the term is now sometimes applied to any laws of unusual harshness.

DRAFT. The common term for a bill of exchange.

DRAGOMAN. An interpreter employed in the east, and particularly at the Turkish court.

DRAIN. To conduct water from one place to another, for the purpose of drying the former.

The right of draining water through another man's land. This is an easement or servitude acquired by grant or prescription. See 3 Kent, Comm. 436; 7 Man. & G. 354; Washb. Easem. Index.

DRAINAGE DISTRICT. A local subdivision of the state created by law for the purpose of administering therein certain functions of local government. 240 Ill. 199.

DRAMATIC PERFORMANCE. The dramatic performances which are recognized as belonging to a theater, are those adapted to the stage, with the appropriate scenery for their representation. The stage with its machinery and appurtenances, forms an essential element in the definition of the term "theater." 22 Ala. 74.

DRAMSHOP. Places commonly known as tippling houses, where liquors are sold in small quantities for immediate use upon the premises, that use being the drinking of the liquor at the time and place of purchase, 203 Ill. 241.

DRAW. To drag, on a hurdle, to the place of execution. Anciently no hurdle was allowed, but the criminal was actually dragged along the road to the place of execution. A part of the ancient punishment of traitors was the being thus drawn. 4 Sharswood, Bl. Comm. 92, 377.

DRAWBACK. An allowance made by the government to merchants on the re-exportation of certain imported goods liable to duties, which in some cases consists of the whole, in others of a part, of the duties which had been paid upon the importation. For the various acts of congress which regulate drawbacks, see Brightly, Dig. U. S. Laws.

DRAWEE. A person to whom a bill of exchange is addressed, and who is requested to pay the amount of money therein mentioned. See "Bill of Exchange."

DRAWER. The party who makes a bill of exchange.

DRAWLATCHES. Thieves; robbers. Cowell.

DREIT DREIT. Double right; a union of the right of possession and the right of property. 2 Sharswood, Bl. Comm. 199.

DRENCHES, or DRENGES (Law Lat. *drengi*). A species of tenants mentioned in Domesday Book, whom Spelman supposes to have been military vassals or tenants by knight service. The same author quotes an old manuscript record of the family of Sharburn, in Norfolk, from which it would appear that the name was given to certain tenants *in capite*, who, at the coming of William the Conqueror, being put out of their estates, were afterwards, upon complaint being made to him, restored to them, on their making it appear that they were owners thereof, and had taken no part against him either by aid or counsel *in consilio et auxilio*. Spelman. According to Lord Coke, who spells the word *dreuchs*, they were free tenants of a manor. Co. Litt. 5b.

DRENGAGE. The tenure by which the drenches (*q. v.*) held their lands. Spelman.

DRIFT. In old English law. A driving. A term applied to cattle.

DRIFTS OF THE FOREST. A view or examination of what cattle are in a forest, chase, etc., that it may be known whether it be surcharged or not, and whose the beasts are, and whether they are commonable. These drifts are made at certain times in the year by the officers of the forest, when all cattle are driven into some pound or place inclosed, for the before-mentioned purposes, and also to discover whether any cattle of strangers be there, which ought not to common. Manw. For. Law. p. 2, c. 15.

DRIFTWAY. A road or way over which cattle are driven. 1 Taunt. 279; Selw. N. P. 1037; Woolr. Ways, 1. The term is in use in Rhode Island. 2 Hilliard, Real Prop. 33.

DRINCLEAN, or **DRINKLEAN** (Saxon). A contribution of tenants, in the time of the Saxons, towards a potation, or ale, provided to entertain the lord, or his steward. Cowell. See "Cervisarii."

DRIP. The right of drip is an easement by which the water which falls on one house is allowed to fall upon the land of another.

Unless the owner has acquired the right by grant or prescription, he has no right so to construct his house as to let the water drip over his neighbor's land. 1 Rolle, Abr. 107. See 3 Kent, Comm. 436; Dig. 43. 23. 4. 6; 11 Adol. & E. 40.

DROFDEN or **DROFDENE.** A grove or woody place where cattle are kept. Cowell; Blount.

DROFLAND, DRIFTLAND, or **DRYFland.** A yearly payment made by some to their landlords for driving their cattle through the manor to fairs and markets. Cowell.

DROIT (Fr.)

——**In French Law.** Law; the whole body of law, written and unwritten.

A right. No law exists without a duty. Toullier, Dr. Civ. note 96; Poth. Dr.

Droit d'accession. That property which is acquired by making a new species out of the material of another. *Modus acquirandi quo quis ex aliena materia suo nomine novam speciem faciens bona fide ejus speciei dominium consequitur.* It is a rule of the civil law that, if the thing can be reduced to the former matter, it belongs to the owner of the matter, *e. g.*, a statute made of gold, but, if it cannot so be reduced, it belongs to the person who made it, *e. g.*, a statute made of marble. This subject is treated of in the Code Nap. arts. 565, 577; Merlin, Repert. "Accession;" Malleville's Discussion, art. 565. See "Accession."

Droit d'Angarie. Angary, or Droit d'Angarie, is a contingent belligerent right, arising out of necessity of war, to dispose over, use and destroy, if need be, property belonging to neutral states. Encyc. Brit. XXXI, 129 (Neutrality).

Droit d'Aubaine. A rule by which all the property of a deceased foreigner, whether movable or immovable, was confiscated to the use of the state, to the exclusion of his heirs, whether claiming *ab intestato* or under a will of the deceased.

The word *aubaine* signifies *hospes loci, peregrinus advena*, a stranger. It is derived, according to some, from *alibi*, elsewhere, *natus*, born, from which the word *albinus* is said to be formed. Others, as Cujas, derive the word directly from *advena*, by which word *aubains* or strangers are designated in the capitularies of Charlemagne. See Du Cange; Trevoux. See "Aubaine."

Droit de bris. A right, formerly claimed by the lords of the coasts of certain parts of France, to shipwrecks, by which not only the property, but the persons of those who were cast away, were confiscated for the prince who was lord of the coast. Otherwise called *droit de bris sur le naufrages.* The right prevailed chiefly in Bretagne, and was solemnly abrogated by Henry III., as duke of Normandy, Aquitaine, and Guienne, in a charter granted A. D. 1226, preserved among the rolls at Bordeaux. Laws of Oleron, art. 26, note; Pet. Adm. Dec. Appendix. See "Bris."

Droit de garde. Right of ward; the guardianship of the estate and person of a noble vassal, to which the king, during his minority, was entitled. Steph. Lect. 250.

Droit de gite. The duty incumbent on a *roturier*, holding lands within the royal domain, of supplying board and lodging to the king and to his suite, while on a royal progress. Steph. Lect. 351.

Droit de greffe. The right of selling various offices connected with the custody of judicial records or notarial acts. Steph. Lect. 354. A privilege of the French kings.

Droit de maitrise. A charge payable to the crown by any one who, after having served his apprenticeship in any commercial guild or brotherhood, sought to become a master workman in it on his own account. Steph. Lect. 354.

Droit de prise. The duty (incumbent on a *roturier*) of supplying to the king on credit, during a certain period, such articles of domestic consumption as might be required for the royal household. Steph. Lect. 351.

Droit de quint. A relief payable by a noble vassal to the king as his *seigneur*, on every change in the ownership of his fief. Steph. Lect. 350.

——**In English Law.** Right. Co. Litt. 158. A person was said to have *droit droit, plurimum juris,* and *plurimum possessionis,* when he had the freehold, the fee, and the property in him. Crabb, Hist. Eng. Law, 406.

Droit close. The name of an ancient writ directed to the lord of ancient demesne, and which lies for those tenants in ancient demesne who hold their lands and tenements by charter in fee simple, in fee tail, for life, or in dower. Fitzh. Nat. Brev. 23.

DROIT DROIT (Law. Fr.; Law Lat. *jus duplicatum*). In old English law. A double right. The right of possession, united with the right of property. 2 Bl. Comm. 199; Co. Litt. 266a; 1 Reeve, Hist. Eng. Law, 476; 4 Kent, Comm. 373. See "Dreit Dreit."

DROIT ECRIT. In French law. The written law. The Roman civil law or *corpus juris civilis.* Steph. Lect. 130.

DROIT NE DONE PLUIS QUE SOIT DEmaunde. The law gives no more than is demanded. Coke, 2d Inst. 286.

DROIT NE POET PAS MORIER. Right cannot die. Jenk. Cent. Cas. 100.

DROITS CIVILS. This phrase in French law denotes private rights, the exercise of which is independent of the status (*qualite*) of citizen. Foreigners enjoy them; and the extent of that enjoyment is determined by the principle of reciprocity. Conversely, foreigners may be sued on contracts made by them in France. Brown.

DROITS OF ADMIRALTY. Rights claimed by the government over the property of an enemy. In England, it has been usual in maritime wars for the government to seize and condemn, as droits of admiralty, the property of an enemy found in her ports at the breaking out of hostilities. 1 C. Rob. Adm. 196; 13 Ves. 71; 1 Edw. Adm. 60; 3 Bos. & P. 191.

DROITURAL. What belongs of right; relating to right; as, real actions are either *droitural* or possessory,—*droitural* when the plaintiff seeks to recover the property. Finch, Law, 257.

DROP. In English practice. When the members of a court are equally divided on the argument showing cause against a rule *nisi,* no order is made, *i. e.,* the rule is neither discharged nor made absolute, and the rule is said to "drop." In practice, there being a right to appeal, it has been usual to make an order in one way, the junior judge withdrawing his judgment.

DROP LETTER. A letter addressed for delivery in the same city or district in which it is posted.

DROVE ROAD. A road for driving cattle. A right of way for carriages does not involve necessarily a right to drive cattle, or an easement of drove road.

DROVE STANCE. In Scotch law. A place adjoining a drove road, for resting and refreshing sheep and cattle on their journey. 7 Bell, App. Cas. 53, 57.

DROWN. To merge or sink; to extinguish by merging in something greater. "In some cases, a right of freehold shall *drown* in a chattel." Co. Litt. 266a, 321a. Perkins' Prof. bk. 9, §§ 584, 589.

Estates in land are properly drowned or confounded when a lesser estate concurs with a greater in the same person, and in the same right. J. Steph. Procurations, 54.

The reversionary interest coming to the possession drowns. Cruise, Dig. 4, 109.

DRU. A thicket of wood in a valley. Domesday Book.

DRUGGIST. One who deals in medicinal substances, vegetable, animal, or mineral, uncompounded.

In America, the term "druggist" is used synonymously with "apothecary," although, strictly speaking, a druggist is one who deals in medicinal substances, vegetable, animal, or mineral, without compounding or preparation, which composition and combination are really the business of the apothecary. The term has a much more limited and restricted meaning than "Apothecary." 28 La. Ann. 767. In England, an apothecary is a subphysician, or privileged practitioner. He is the ordinary medical man, or family medical attendant, in that country.

DRUNK. A man is drunk when he is overcome, stupefied, or frenzied by alcoholic liquors.

DRUNKARD. Synonymous with "habitual drunkard" (*q. v.*) 5 Gray (Mass.) 85.

He is a drunkard whose habit is to get drunk. "whose ebriety has become habitual." 5 Gray (Mass.) 86.

As for a drunkard, he is *voluntarius daemon;* he hath no privilege thereby; but what hurt or ill soever he doth, his drunkenness doth aggravate it. 9 Humph. (Tenn.) 665.

DRUNKENNESS. In medical jurisprudence. The condition of a man whose mind is affected by the immediate use of intoxicating drinks.

DRY CRAEFT. Witchcraft; magic.

DRY EXCHANGE. A term invented for disguising and covering usury, in which something was pretended to pass on both sides, when in truth nothing passed on one side; whence it was called "dry." St. 3 Hen. VII. c. 5; Wolff. Inst. § 657.

DRY MULTURES. In Scotch law. Corn paid to the owner of a mill, whether the payers grind or not. Wharton.

DRY RENT. Rent seck; a rent reserved without a clause of distress.

DUARCHY. A form of government where two reign jointly.

DUAS UXORES EODEM TEMPORE HAbere non potest. It is not lawful to have two wives at one time. Inst. 1. 10. 6; 1 Sharswood, Bl. Comm. 436.

DUBITANS, or DUBITANTE. Doubting. Dobbin, J., *dubitans.* 1 Show. 364.

DUBITATUR, or DUBITAVIT. It is doubted. A word frequently used in the reports to indicate that a point is considered doubtful. Vaughan, C. J., *dubitavit.* Freem. 150.

DUCAT. The name of a foreign coin.

The ducat, or sequin, was originally a gold coin of the middle ages, apparently a descendant from the bezant of the Greek-Roman empire. For many centuries it constituted the principal international currency, being intended, or supposed, to be made of pure gold, though subsequently settled at a basis a little below. It is now nearly obsolete in every part of the world. Its average value is about $2.26 of our money. It is said they appeared earliest in Venice, and that they bore the following motto: *Sit tibi, Christe, datus, quem tu regis, iste Ducatus,*—whence the name ducat.

The silver ducat was formerly a coin of Naples, weighing three hundred and forty-eight grains, eight hundred and forty-two thousandths fine; consequent value, in our money, about eighty-one cents; but it now exists only as a money of account.

DUCES TECUM (Law Lat. you bring with you). In practice. A term applied to certain writs, where a party summoned to appear in court is required to bring with him some piece of evidence, or other things that the court would view. Cowell; Termes de la Ley. See "Subpoena."

DUCES TECUM LICET LANGUIDUS. A writ directing the sheriff to bring a person whom he returned as so sick that he could not be brought without endangering his life. Blount; Cowell. The writ is now obsolete. See "Subpoena."

DUCHY COURT OF LANCASTER. A court of special jurisdiction in England, held before the chancellor of the duchy of Lancaster, or his deputy, concerning all matter of equity relating to lands holden of the king in right of the duchy of Lancaster. 3 Bl. Comm. 78; 3 Steph. Comm. 446. The proceedings in this court are the same as on the equity side in the courts of exchequer and chancery. Id.

DUCKING STOOL. See "Castigatory."

DUCROIRE. Guaranty; equivalent to *del credere (q. v.)*

DUE. Just and proper. A due presentment and demand of payment must be made. See 4 Rawle (Pa.) 307; 3 Leigh (Va.) 389; 3 Cranch (U. S.) 300.

What ought to be paid; what may be demanded; payable. 7 N. Y. 476.

It differs from "owing" in this, that sometimes what is owing is not due. A note payable thirty days after date is owing immediately after it is delivered to the payee, but it is not due until the thirty days have elapsed; but it has been held synonymous with "owing." 31 Mich. 219.

It may mean either "owing" or "payable," according to the context. 2 Ch. Div. 101.

DUE BILL. An acknowledgment of a debt in writing is so called. This instrument differs from a promissory note in many particulars. It is not payable to order, nor is it assignable by mere indorsement. See "Promissory Note."

DUE CARE. That degree of care that a reasonable and prudent person would exercise under all the circumstances of the case. 1 Ill. App. 421.

DUE COURSE OF LAW. Means such rules of action in relation to the rights and duties of the citizen, and such forms and modes of legal proceedings, of a general character, to ascertain and enforce duties, rights and remedies, as the legislature may deem fit, and which are not forbidden by the language or the spirit of other parts of the constitution. 38 Miss. 458.

DUE PROCESS OF LAW. Law in its regular course of administration through courts of justice. 3 Story, Const. 264, 661; 18 How. (U. S.) 272; 13 N. Y. 378.

It is the equivalent to "law of the land," as used in *Magna Charta.* Co. Inst. 50; 18 How. (U. S.) 272; 11 Mich. 129.

"Whatever difficulty may be experienced in giving to these terms a definition which will embrace every permissible exercise of power affecting private rights, and exclude such as is forbidden, there can be no doubt of their meaning as applied to judicial proceedings. They then mean a course of legal proceedings according to those rules and principles which have been established in our system of jurisprudence for the protection and enforcement of private rights." 96 U. S. 733.

"Such an exertion of the powers of government as the settled maxims of law permit and sanction, and under such safeguards for individual rights as those maxims prescribe for the class of cases to which the one in question belongs." Cooley, Const. Lim. § 356.

Due process of law is not any course of procedure that may at any time be established by the legislature (34 Ala. 216; 43 N. J. Law, 203), yet it is not a denial of due process of law for the legislature to make changes in the common law, or in modes of procedure (50 Miss. 468; 70 N. Y. 228; 160 U. S. 389).

Due process of law embraces only that which is fundamental, and to it is necessary an orderly legal proceeding, whereof the party affected shall have notice, and an opportunity to appear and be heard. 169 U. S. 366; 96 U. S. 97.

DUELLING. The fighting of two persons one against the other, at an appointed time and place, upon a precedent quarrel. It differs from an affray in this, that the latter occurs on a sudden quarrel, while the former is always the result of design.

DUELLUM. Trial by battle; judicial combat. Spelman.

DUFFER. To charge a pawnbroker with "duffing,"—*i. e.*, replenishing or doing up damaged pledges, and re-pledging them,—is actionable. 11 L. J. Ex. 341; 10 M. & W. 361; 2 Dowl. N. S. 270.

DUKE. The title given to those who are in the highest rank of nobility in England.

DULOCRACY. A government where servants and slaves have so much license and privilege that they domineer. Wharton.

DULY. In legal parlance, in a proper way, or regularly, or according to law. 5 Hun (N. Y.) 542, 543; 23 Barb. (N. Y.) 304; 3 Edw. Ch. 239; 59 Barb. (N. Y.) 531, 543; 15 Minn. 479, 484; 5 Hun (N. Y.) 543. Regularly; upon proper foundation as distinguished from mere form. 15 Mees. & W. 465. It does not relate to form merely, but includes form and substance both. 114 N. Y. 518, 527.

DUM (Lat. while). A word of limitation in old conveyances. Co. Litt. 235a; 10 Coke, 41b.

DUM BENE SE GESSERIT (Law Lat.) While he conducted himself well; during good behavior. 2 Bl. Comm. 252. The implied condition on which a feud or fee was originally given. Id. See "Quamdiu se Bene Gesserit."

DUM FERVET OPUS. While the work glows; in the heat of action. 1 Kent, Comm. 120.

DUM FUIT IN PRISONA (Law Lat.) In English law. A writ which lay for a man who had aliened lands under duress by imprisonment, to restore to him his proper estates. Coke, 2d Inst. 482.

DUM FUIT INFRA AETATEM (Lat.) The name of a writ which lies when an infant has made a feoffment in fee of his lands or for life, or a gift in tail.

It may be sued out by him after he comes of full age, and not before; but in the meantime he may enter, and his entry remits him to his ancestor's rights. Fitzh. Nat. Brev. 192; Co. Litt. 247, 337.

DUM NON FUIT COMPCS MENTIS (Lat.) The name of a writ which the heirs of a person who was *non compos mentis*, and who aliened his lands, might have sued out to restore him to his rights.

DUM RECENS FUIT MALEFICIUM. While the offense was fresh. A term employed in the old law of appeal of rape. Bracton, fol. 147.

DUM SOLA (Lat. while single or unmarried). A phrase applied to single women, to denote that something has been done, or may be done, while the woman is or was unmarried. Thus, when a judgment is rendered against a woman *dum sola*, and afterwards she marries, the *scire facias* to revive the judgment must be against both husband and wife.

DUMB BIDDING. In sales at auction, when the amount which the owner of the thing sold is willing to take for the article is written, and placed by the owner under a candlestick, or other thing, and it is agreed that no bidding shall avail unless equal to that, this is called dumb bidding. Bab. Auct. 44.

DUMMADO (Lat. provided that; so that). A word of limitation in old conveyancing. 10 Coke, 41b; Co. Litt. 235a. One of the apt words of reserving a rent. Co. Litt. 47a. *Dummodo solverit talem redditum*, provided he shall pay such a rent. Id. 235a.

DUNGEON. A cell under ground; a place in a prison built under ground, dark, or but indifferently lighted.

DUNIO. A double; a kind of base coin less than a farthing.

DUNNAGE. Pieces of wood or other material placed against the sides and bottom of the hold of a vessel, to preserve the cargo from the effect of leakage, according to its nature and quality. Abb. Shipp. 227.

DUO NON POSSUNT IN SOLIDO UNAM rem possidere. Two cannot possess one thing each in entirety. Co. Litt. 368; 1 Prest. Abstr. 318; 2 Prest. Abstr. 86, 326; 2 Dods. Adm. 157; 2 Carth. 76; Broom, Leg. Max. (3d London Ed.) 415.

DUO SUNT INSTRUMENTA AD OMNES res aut confirmandas aut impugnandas,—ratio et aucoritas. There are two instruments for confirming or impugning everything,—reason and authority. 8 Coke, 16.

DUODECEMVIRALE JUDICIUM. The trial by twelve men, or by jury. Applied to juries *de medietate linguae*. Molloy, de Jur. Mar. 448.

DUODECIMA MANUS (Lat. twelve hands). The oaths of twelve men, including himself, by whom the defendant was allowed to make his law. 3 Sharswood, Bl. Comm. 343.

DUODENA. In old records. A jury of twelve men. Cowell.

Generally, a dozen. *Duodena panis*, a dozen of bread. Towns. Pl. 170.

DUODENA MANU. Twelve witnesses to purge a criminal of an offense.

DUORUM IN SOLIDUM DOMINIUM VEL possessio esse non potest. Ownership or possession in entirety cannot be in two of the same thing. Dig. 13. 6. 5. 15; 1 Mackeld. Civ. Law, 245, § 236; Bracton, 28b.

DUPLEX QUERELA (Lat.) In ecclesiastical law. A complaint in the nature of an appeal from the ordinary to his next immediate superior for delaying or refusing to do justice in some ecclesiastical cause. 3 Bl. Comm. 247; Cowell; Jacob.

DUPLEX VALOR MARITAGII (Lat. double the value of a marriage). Guardians in chivalry had the privilege of proposing a marriage for their infant wards, provided it were done without disparagement; and if the wards married without the guardian's consent, they were liable to forfeit double the value of the marriage. Co. Litt. 82b; 2 Sharswood, Bl. Comm. 70.

DUPLICATE (Lat. *duplex*, double). The double of anything. A document which is essentially the same as some other instrument. 7 Man. & G. 93.

A duplicate writing has but one effect. Each duplicate is complete evidence of the intention of the parties. When a duplicate is destroyed, for example, in the case of a will, it is presumed both are intended to be destroyed; but this presumption possesses greater or less force, owing to circumstances. When only one of the duplicates is in the possession of the testator, the destruction of that is a strong presumption of an intent to revoke both; but if he possessed both, and destroys but one, it is weaker; when he alters one, and afterwards destroys it, retaining the other entire, it has been held that the intention was to revoke both. 1 P. Wms. 346; 13 Ves. 310. But that seems to be doubted. 3 Hagg. Ecc. 548.

A duplicate differs from a mere copy in having all the validity of an original.

——**In English Law.** The certificate of discharge given to an insolvent debtor who takes the benefit of the act for the relief of insolvent debtors.

DUPLICATE WILL. A term used in England, where a testator executes two copies of his will, one to keep himself, and the other to be deposited with another person. Upon application for probate of a duplicate will, both copies must be deposited in the registry of the court of probate.

DUPLICATIO (Lat. from *duplicarc*, to double, or follow as the second in order).

——**In the Civil Law.** The defendant's answer to the plaintiff's replication; corresponding to the rejoinder of the common law. Inst. 4. 14. 1; Heinec. Elem. Jur. Civ. lib. 4, tit. 14, § 1284. The fourth pleading in the series. 3 Bl. Comm. 310. Translated duplication. Halifax, Anal. bk. 3, c. 5, No. 7.

——**In Scotch Practice.** Duply (*q. v.*) Bracton and Fleta call this pleading *triplicatio*. Bracton, fols. 57b, 400b, 428b; Fleta, lib. 6, c. 36, § 10.

DUPLICATIONEM POSSIBILITATIS lex non patitur. The law does not allow a duplication of possibility. 1 Rolle, Abr. 321.

DUPLICATUM JUS. (Lat. a twofold or double right). Words which signify the same as *dreit dreit*, or *droit droit*, and which are applied to a writ of right, patent, and such other writs of right as are of the same nature, and do, as it were, flow from it as the writ of right. Booth, Real Actions, 87.

DUPLICITY (Lat. *duplex*, twofold; double). The union of more than one cause of action in one court in a writ, or more than one defense in one place, or more than a single breach in a replication. 1 Woodb. & M. (U. S.) 381.

DUPLY. In Scotch law. The defendant's answer to the plaintiff's replication. The same as *duplicatio*. Macl. Prac. 127.

To rejoin. "It is duplyed by the panel." 3 How. St. Tr. 471.

DURANTE (Lat. during). A word of limitation in old conveyances. Co. Litt. 234b. *Durante viduitate*, during widowhood; *durante virginitate*, during virginity; *durante vita*, during life.

DURANTE ABSENTIA. See "Administration."

DURANTE BENE PLACITO (Lat. during good pleasure). The ancient tenure of English judges was *durante bene placito*. 1 Sharswood, Bl. Comm. 267, 342.

DURANTE MINORE AETATE (Lat. during the minority). During his minority an infant can enter into no contracts, except those for his benefit. If he should be appointed an executor, administration of the estate will be granted, *durante minore aetate*, to another person. 2 Bouv. Inst. note 1555.

DURANTE VIDUITATE (Lat.) During widowhood.

DURESS. Personal restraint, or fear of personal injury or imprisonment. 2 Metc. (Ky.) 445.

Deprivation of one of his freedom of will and act by the unlawful acts of another.

Duress exists where one is induced by another's unlawful act to make a contract or perform some act under circumstances which prevent his exercising free will. 45 Mich. 569.

——**Duress of Imprisonment.** That which exists where a man actually loses his liberty. If a man be illegally deprived of his liberty until he sign and seal a bond, or the like, he may allege this duress, and avoid the bond. 2 Bay (S. C.) 211; 9 Johns. (N. Y.) 201; 10 Pet. (U. S.) 137. But if a man be illegally imprisoned, and, either to procure his discharge, or on any other fair account, seal a bond or a deed, this is not by duress of imprisonment, and he is not at liberty to avoid it. Coke, 2d Inst. 482; 3 Caines (N. Y.) 168; 6 Mass. 511; 1 Lev. 69; 1 Hen. & M. (Va.) 350; 17 Me. 338. Where the proceedings at law are a mere pretext, the instrument may be avoided. 1 Bl. Comm. 136.

——**Duress per Minas.** That which is either for fear or loss of life, or else for fear of mayhem or loss of limb, must be upon a sufficient reason. 1 Bl. Comm. 131. In this case, a man may avoid his own act. Lord Coke enumerates four instances in which a man may avoid his own act by reason of menaces,—for fear of loss of life; of member; of mayhem; of imprisonment. Coke, 2d Inst. 483; 2 Rolle, Abr. 124; Bac. Abr. "Duress," "Murder" (A); 2 Strange, 856; Fost, Crim. Law, 322; 2 Ld. Raym. 1578; Savigny, Dr. Rom. § 114.

——**Duress of Goods.** Restraint of goods under circumstances of peculiar hardship, which will avoid a contract. 2 Bay (S. C.) 211; 9 Johns. (N. Y.) 201; 10 Pet. (U. S.) 137. But see 2 Metc. (Ky.) 445; 2 Gall. (U. S.) 337.

DURESSOR. One who subjects another to duress; one who compels another to do a thing, as by menace. Bac. Max. 90, reg. 22.

DURING COVERTURE. Means while the marriage lasts. 4 Mo. 159.

There is frequently great difficulty in construing the words "during the coverture" when those words occur in an antenuptial marriage settlement and the wife, at the time of the marriage, is possessed of other property than that mentioned in the settlement. The question whether such other property is or is not comprised in the words is one the determination of which depends very much on the circumstances of each case and especially on the context. "The authorities seem to be such, upon the whole, as tend to show that the settlement should be taken to apply only to property which should come in futuro to the wife, and not to that which was hers before." 54 L. J. Q. B. 154. But in the same case it is observed: "Then—*i. e.*, where the covenant comprises property which the husband shall become entitled 'in her right'—the question would be, whether the words, 'at any time during her now intended coverture' would apply. Surely you cannot exclude from the duration of the coverture the first moment of its continuance. The moment that the marriage is complete by the performance of that which makes the parties husband and wife, that moment the coverture begins; and if at that moment he becomes entitled as her husband, in her right, we are totally unable to say that it is not during the intended coverture in a sense which the words will rightly, grammatically and reasonably bear." 54 L. J. Q. B. 148; 10 App. Cas. 1; 52 L. T. 662; 33 W. R. 373; 49 J. P. Distinguished 484; 33 Ch. D. 300 (*q. v.*)

DURING GOOD BEHAVIOR. While conducting oneself comformably to law. 240 Ill. 564.

DURSLEGI, or **DURSLEY.** In old English law. Blows without wounding or bloodshed; dry blows or beating. Spelman.

DUST MEASURE. A bushel, according to "dust measure," is composed of a half bushel heaped and a half bushel filled to the level, at the pit where the coal is made, coal dust being used because the measurement can be made more accurately with it than with lumps of coal. 4 Met. (Ky.) 124.

DUSTY FOOT. See "Court of Piepoudre."

DUTCH AUCTION. An auction at which the auctioneer fixes a price for the articles offered, which is gradually lowered until accepted. See 18 Hun (N. Y.) 475.

DUTIES. Things due and recoverable by law. The term, in its widest signification, is hardly less comprehensive than "taxes." It is applied, in its most restricted meaning, to customs; and in that sense is nearly the synonym of "imposts." 7 Wall. (U. S.) 445.

DUUMVIRI (from *duo*, two, and *viri*, men). A general appellation among the ancient Romans, given to any magistrates elected in pairs to fill any office, or perform any function. Brande.

Duumviri municipales were two annual magistrates in the towns and colonies, having judicial powers. Calv. Lex.

Duumviri navales were officers appointed to man, equip, and refit the navy. Id.

DUX (Lat.) From *ducere*, to lead.

——**In the Roman Law.** A leader or military commander; the commander of an army. Dig. 3. 2. 2. pr.

——**In Later Law.** A military governor of a province. See Code, 1. 27. 2. A military officer having charge of the borders or frontiers of the empire, called *dux limitis* (*duces limitum*). Code, 1. 49. 1. pr.; Id. 1. 46. 4; Id. 3. 26. 7. At this period, the word began to be used as a title of honor or dignity.

——**In Feudal and Old European Law.** Duke; a title of honor or order of nobility. 1 Bl. Comm. 397; Crabb, Hist. Eng. Law, 236. One who was invested by the prince with a dukedom or ducal fief (*ducatus*). Feud. lib. 2, tit. 10. The highest order of *capitanei regis* or crown vassals. Id. lib. 1, tit. 1, pr. The origin and history of this title are elaborately treated by Spelman, who observes that it was originally an official title, afterwards honorary, and finally feudal and hereditary. *Dux* is used in Bracton as descriptive of the first order of subjects in the kingdom. *Sub eis (regibus) duces, comites, barones*, etc., under them, dukes, earls, barons, etc. Bracton, fol. 5b.

DWELL. To have a domicile. 5 Pick. (Mass.) 379. As to one having no domicile, it signifies the place where he temporarily resides. L. R. 1 Exch. 133.

A corporation dwells in the place where its business is done. 15 Ill. 437.

DWELLING HOUSE. A building inhabited by man; a house usually occupied by the person there residing, and his family; the apartment, building, or cluster of buildings in which a man with his family resides. 1 Bish. Crim. Law, § 165.

The importance of an exact signification for this word is often felt in criminal cases; and yet it is very difficult to frame an exact definition which will apply to all cases. It is said to be quivalent to "mansion house." 3 Serg. & R. (Pa.) 199; 4 Strob. (S. C. 372; 13 Bost. Law Rep. 157; 7 Man. & G. 122. See 14 Mees. & W. 181; 4 C. B. 105; 4 Call (Va.) 109.

It must be a permanent structure (1 Hale, P. C. 557; 1 Russ. Crimes [Greaves Ed.] 798), it must be complete (20 Conn. 245), and it must be inhabited at the time (2 East, P. C. 496; 2 Leach, C. C. 1018, note; 33 Me. 30; 10 Cush. [Mass.] 479; 64 Mass. 478; 52 N. C. 167). It is sufficient if a part of the structure only be used for an abode. Russ. & R. 185; 2 Taunt. 339; 1 Moody, C. C. 248; 11 Metc. (Mass.) 295; 9 Tex. 42; 2 Bos. & P. 508; 27 Ala. (N. S.) 31.

Rooms in a tenement house are a dwelling. 80 N. Y. 327.

A jail has been held a dwelling house. 18 Johns. (N. Y.) 115; 4 Call (Va.) 109.

It includes buildings within the curtilage. 16 Mich. 142; 2 N. C. 118.

DYING DECLARATIONS. Declarations made by one at the point of death, or believing himself to be. They are admissible in evidence only when made by the victim of a homicide (56 N. Y. 103; 35 Ohio St. 78) as to facts relating to the homicide to which the dying person could have testified (30 Mich. 431; 124 Mo. 397), and under a full conviction of impending death (126 Ill. 81; 48 Mich. 474). They are admissible only in a prosecution for the killing of the declarant. 49 Iowa, 238.

DYING WITHOUT ISSUE. Not having issue living at the death of the decedent. 5 Paige, Ch. (N. Y.) 514. In England this is the signification, by St. 7 Wm. IV., and St. 1 Vict. c. 26, § 29. See 2 Washb. Real Prop. 362 et seq.

DYSNOMY. Bad legislation; the enactment of bad laws.

DYVOUR. In Scotch law. A bankrupt.

DYVOUR'S HABIT. In Scotch law. A habit which debtors who are set free on a *cessio bonorum* are obliged to wear, unless in the summons and process of *cessio* it be libelled, sustained, and proved that the bankruptcy proceeds from misfortune. And bankrupts are condemned to submit to the habit, even where no suspicion of fraud lies against them, if they have been dealers in an illicit trade. Ersk. Princ. 4. 3. 13.

E

E. Law Fr. A contraction of *et* (and). *Arisions e homicides.* Artic. sup. Chart. c. 17. *E volums ke;* and we will that. Conf. Cart. 25 Edw. I.

In Latin phrases. A preposition meaning "from" or "out of." It is used only before a consonant; "ex" being used with the same significance before a vowel.

E, at the commencement of words having the first syllable *En* or *Em,* properly denotes a derivation from the French, as I denotes a derivation from the Latin. Thus, *Enclose, Encumber, Endow, Enfranchise, Engross, Enjoin, Enlarge* and *Enroll* are closely formed from the L. Fr. *Enclorer, Encombrer, Endower, Enfranchir, Engrosser, Enjoyndre, Enlarger* and *Enrouler.* On the other hand, *Indict, Inform, Infringe, Inquire* follow the L. Lat. *Indictare Informare, Infringere* and *Inquirere.* The orthography, however, has not been uniform. Thus, there seems to have been a tendency, from an early period, to the use of I rather than E, even in words wholly and properly of French origin; as in *Imparl, Implead* and *Imprison,* which being derived from the pure L. Fr. *Emparler, Empleder* and *Emprisoner,* should properly have been spelled with an E. This may have arisen from the *sound* of the initial letter, the E being probably pronounced I, as it is at present. Hence we meet, in the old books, with *Ingross, Injoin, Inrol, Intitle, Inlarge, Imploy* and *Imbezzle,* which are no longer used. On the other hand we meet with such words as *Encur, Endebted, Endictment, Enfant, Enform, Entermarriage, Enterlining* and others, which are equally obsolete. On the whole, the gradual tendency in modern orthography has been to the use of I rather than E, as an initial letter. In a few cases, however, *both* forms are still employed. Thus, *Endorse* and *Indorse* continue to have their respective advocates, although the latter enjoys the support of standard authority.

E CONVERSO (Lat.) On the other hand; on the contrary.

EA (Saxon). The water or river; also the mouth of a river on the shore between high and low water mark.

EA EST ACCIPIENDA INTERPRETATIO, quae vitio caret. That interpretation is to be received which is free from fault. Bac. Max. reg. 3, p. 47.

EA INTENTIONE (Law Lat.) With that intent. Held not to make a condition, but a confidence and trust. Dyer, 138b.

EA QUAE COMMENDANDI CAUSA IN venditionibus dicuntur si palam appareant venditorem non obligant. Those things which, by way of commendation, are stated at sales, if they are openly apparent, do no bind the seller. Dig. 18. 43. m.

EA QUAE DARI IMPOSSIBILIA SUNT, vel quae in rerum natura non sunt, pro non adjectis habentur. Those things which cannot be given, or which are not in existence, are held as not expressed. Dig. 50. 17. 135.

EA QUAE IN CURIA NOSTRA RITE acta sunt debitae executioni demandari debent. Those things which are properly transacted in our court ought to be committed to a due execution. Co. Litt. 289.

EA QUAE RARO ACCIDUNT, NON TEmere in agendis negotiis computantur. Those things which rarely happen are not to be taken into account in the transaction of business, without sufficient reason. Dig. 50. 17. 64.

EACH. Every one of the two or more individuals composing the whole, considered separately from the rest. 102 Ill. 233.

EADEM CAUSA DIVERSIS RATIONIBUS coram judicibus ecclesiasticis et secularibus ventilatur. The same cause is argued upon different principles before ecclesiastical and secular judges. 2 Inst. 622.

EADEM EST RATIO, EADEM EST LEX. The same reason, the same law. 7 Pick. (Mass.) 493.

EADEM MENS PRAESUMITUR REGIS quae est juris quae esse debet, praesertim in dubiis. The mind of the sovereign is presumed to be coincident with that of the law, and with that which ought to be, especially in ambiguous matters. Hob. 154; Broom, Leg. Max. (3d London Ed.) 53.

EAGLE. A gold coin of the United States of the value of ten dollars.

EALDER, or **EALDING.** In old Saxon law. An elder or chief.

EALDERMAN (Saxon). A Saxon title of honor. It was a mark of honor very widely applicable, the ealdermen being of various ranks. It is the same as alderman (*q. v.*)

EALDOR BISCOP. A chief bishop or archbishop.

EALDORBURG (Saxon). The chief city.

EALEHUS. An ale house.

EALHORDA. The privilege of assizing and selling beer.

EAR WITNESS. One who attests to things he has heard himself.

EARL. In English law. A title of nobility next below a marquis, and above a viscount.

Earls were anciently called *comites*, because they were wont *comitari regem*, to wait upon the king for counsel and advice. They were also called "shiremen," because each earl had the civil government of a shire. After the Norman conquest they were called "counts,' whence the shires obtained the names of counties. They have now nothing to do with the government of counties, which has entirely developed on the sheriff, the earl's deputy, or *vice comes*.

EARL MARSHAL. An officer who formerly was of great repute in England. He held the court of chivalry alone as a court of honor, and, in connection with the lord high constable, as a court having criminal jurisdiction. 3 Bl. Comm. 68; 4 Bl. Comm. 467. The duties of the office now are restricted to the settlement of matters of form merely. It would appear, from similarity of duties, and from the derivation of the title, to be a relic of the ancient office of alderman of all England. See "Alderman."

EARLDOM. The dignity or jurisdiction of an earl. The dignity only remains now, as the jurisdiction has been given over to the sheriff. 1 Bl. Comm. 339.

EARLES PENNY. Earnest money.

EARMARK. A mark put upon a thing for the purpose of distinction. Money in a bag tied and labelled is said to have an earmark. 3 Maule & S. 575.

EARNEST. The payment of a part of the price of goods sold, or the delivery of part of such goods, for the purpose of binding the contract.

EARNINGS. That which is gained or merited by labor, service, or performance. 47 Wis. 113. It is a term of larger import than "wages," but in its general acceptation, does not mean net earnings unless qualified in some way. 182 Ill. 169; 102 Mass. 235. See "Gross Earnings."

EASEMENT. A right in the owner of one parcel of land, by reason of such ownership, to use the land of another for a special purpose not inconsistent with a general property in the owner. 2 Washb. Real Prop. 25.

A privilege, without profit, which the owner of one adjacent tenement hath of another, existing in respect of their several tenements, by which that owner against whose tenement the privilege exists is obliged to suffer or not to do something on or in regard to his own land for the advantage of him in whose land the privilege exists. Termes de la Ley; Bell, Dict. (Ed. 1838). "Easements," "Servitude"; 1 Serg. & R. (Pa.) 298; 3 Barn. & C. 339; 5 Barn. & C. 221; 3 Bing. 118; 2 McCord (S. C.) 451; 3 McCord (S. C.) 131, 194; 14 Mass. 49; 3 Pick. (Mass.) 408; 47 Md. 301.

In the civil law, the land against which the privilege exists is called the "servient tenement"; its proprietor, the "servient owner"; he in whose favor it exists, the "dominant owner"; his land, the "dominant tenement." And, as these rights are usually not personal, and do not change with the persons who may own the respective estates, it is very common to personify the estates as themselves owning or enjoying the easement. 4 Sandf. Ch. (N. Y.) 72; 3 Paige, Ch. (N. Y.) 254; 16 Pick. (Mass.) 522.

Easements have these essential qualities. There must be two tenements owned by several proprietors,—the dominant, to which the privilege is attached; the servient, upon which it is imposed. White & T. Lead. Cas. 108; 17 Mass. 443. Easements, strictly considered, exist only in favor of, and are imposed only on, corporeal property. 2 Washb. Real Prop. 25. They confer no right to any profits arising from the servient tenement. 4 Sandf. Ch. (N. Y.) 72; 4 Pick. (Mass.) 145; 5 Adol. & E. 758; 30 Eng. Law & Eq. 189; 3 Nev. & P. 257. They are incorporeal. By the common law, they may be temporary; by the civil law, the cause must be perpetual. They impose no duty on the servient owner, except not to change his tenement to the prejudice or destruction of the privilege. Gale, Easem. (3d Ed.) 1-18; Washb. Easem. Index.

Easements are either (1) positive or (2) negative, the former authorizing the commission of acts on the servient estate, and the latter merely forbidding the servient owner from doing some act to the detriment of the dominant owner, as to build to the obstruction of his light.

They are also (3) appurtenant, or (4) in gross, the former running with the land, and the latter attached to a person.

(5) *Quasi* easements. "There are rights mentioned in the books as *quasi* easements. (1) Where there has been an easement proper, with a dominant and servient tenement, and the ownership of such tenements has been unified. (2) Where the owner of land has constructed a way or drain over one portion of it for the benefit of another portion, and there has never been a separate ownership of a dominant and servient tenement. This class is again subdivided into those which are called 'continuous,' as a drain or sewer, which are used continuously without the intervention of man, and those which are called 'noncontinuous,' as a right of way, which can only be used by the intervention of man, repeated at intervals when user is desired." Goddard, Easem. 84; 68 N. Y. 66.

Easements are as various as the exigencies of domestic convenience, or the purposes to which buildings and land may be applied.

The following attach to land as incidents or appurtenances, viz.: The right of pasture on other land; of fishing in other waters; of taking game on other land; of way over other land; of taking wood, minerals, or other produce of the soil from other land; of receiving air, light, or heat from or over other land; of receiving or discharging water over, or having support to buildings from, other land (3 El., Bl. & El. 655); of going on other land to clear a mill stream, or repair its banks, or draw water from a spring there, or to do some other act not involving ownership; of carrying on an offensive trade (2 Bing. N. C. 134; 5 Metc. [Mass.] 8); of burying in a church, or a particular vault (Washb. Easem.; Civ. Code N. Y. pp. 149, 150; 8 H. L. Cas. 362; 3 Barn. & A. 735; 11 Q. B. 666).

An easement is distinguished from a license in that it carries an interest, and from a profit *a prendre* (*q. v.*) in that it is a privilege without profit.

EAST GREENWICH. The name of a royal manor in the county of Kent, England. Mentioned in royal grants or patents, as descriptive of the tenure of free socage. "To be holden of us, our heirs and successors, as of our manor of East Greenwich, in free and common socage."

EASTER OFFERINGS, or EASTER dues. In English law. Small sums of money paid to the parochial clergy by the parishioners at Easter as a compensation for personal tithes or the tithe for personal labor. 2 & 3 Edw. IV. c. 13; 2 & 3 Vict. c. 62, § 9.

EASTER TERM. In English practice one of the four terms of the superior courts in England, formerly called the movable term, but now fixed, beginning on the 15th of April, and ending on the 8th of May, in every year. St. 11 Geo. IV.; 1 Wm. IV. c. 70, 3 Chit. Gen. Prac. 91.

EASTERLING. A coin struck by Richard II., which is supposed to have given rise to the name of "sterling," as applied to English money. Wharton.

EAT INDE SINE DIE. Words used on an acquittal, or when a prisoner is to be discharged, "that he may go without day;" that is, that he be dismissed. Dane, Abr. Index.

EAVESDROPPERS. In criminal law. Such persons as wait under walls or windows or the eaves of a house, to listen to discourses and thereupon to frame mischievous tales. 4 Bl. Comm. 167.

EBBA. In old English law. Ebb (of the tide.) *Ebba et fluctus*, ebb and flow of tide; ebb and flood. Bracton, fols. 255, 338.

ECCHYMOSIS. In medical jurisprudence. Blackness. It is an extravasation of blood by rupture of capillary vessels, and hence it follows contusion; but it may exist, as in cases of scurvy and other morbid conditions, without the latter. Ryan, Med. Jur. 172.

ECCLESIA (Lat. an assembly). A Christian assembly; a church; a place of religious worship. Spelman.

ECCLESIA ECCLESIAE DECIMAS SOLvere non debet. It is not the duty of the church to pay tithes to the church. Cro. Eliz. 479.

ECCLESIA EST DOMUS MANSIONALIS Omnipotentis Dei. The church is the mansion house of the Omnipotent God. 2 Inst. 164.

ECCLESIA EST INFRA AETATEM ET in custodia domini regis, qui tenetur jura et haereditates ejusdem manu tene[illegible] et defendere. The church is under age, [illegible]d in the custody of the king, who is bo[illegible] to uphold and defend its rights and in[illegible]tances. 11 Coke, 49.

ECCLESIA FUNGITUR VICE MINORIS; meliorem conditionem suam facere potest, deteriorem nequaquam. The church enjoys the privilege of a minor; it can make its own condition better, but not worse. Co. Litt. 341.

ECCLESIA MAGIS FAVENDUM EST quam personae. The church is more to be favored than an individual. Godb. 172.

ECCLESIA NON MORITUR. The church does not die. 2 Inst. 3.

ECCLESIASTIC. A clergyman; one destined to the divine ministry; as, a bishop, a priest, a deacon. Domat, Civ. Law, liv. prel. tit. 2, § 2, note 14.

ECCLESIASTICAL. Pertaining to the church as distinguished from secular or civil.

ECCLESIASTICAL COMMISSIONERS. Commissioners established by statute, in England, principally for the purpose of preparing schemes for the improvement of the ecclesiastical system, especially as to the equalization of the revenues and duties of the various dioceses, and to provide for the cure of souls in parishes where assistance was required. Several of such schemes have been given effect to by orders in council. By later acts a fund has been vested in the commissioners to enable them to make provision for the cure of souls in populous districts, and provision is accordingly made for the creation of ecclesiastical districts and parishes, and the appointment of ministers therein. Phillim. Ecc. Law, 2090; 2 Steph. Comm. 748; St. 6 & 7 Wm. IV. c. 77; St. 13 & 14 Vict. c. 94; St. 29 & 30 Vict. c. 111, etc. See "Parish."

ECCLESIASTICAL CORPORATIONS. Such corporations as are composed of persons who take a lively interest in the advancement of religion, and who are associated and incorporated for that purpose. Angell & A. Corp. § 36.

Corporations whose members are spiritual persons are distinguished from lay corporations. 1 Bl. Comm. 470. They are generally called "religious corporations" in the United States. 2 Kent, Comm. 274; Angell & A. Corp. § 37.

ECCLESIASTICAL COURTS. In English ecclesiastical law. The generic name for certain courts in England, having cognizance mainly of spiritual matters. Also called "Courts Christian."

The jurisdiction which they formerly exercised in testamentary and matrimonial causes has been taken away. St. 20 & 21 Vict. c. 77, § 3, c. 85, § 2; 21 & 22 Vict. c. 95. See 3 Bl. Comm. 67.

They consist of the archdeacon's court, the consistory courts, the court of arches, the court of peculiars, the prerogative courts of the two archbishops, the faculty court, and, on appeal, the privy council.

ECCLESIASTICAL LAW. The law of the church. The existence in England of a separate order of ecclesiastical courts, and a separate system of law by them administered, may be traced back to the time of William the Conqueror, who separated the civil and the ecclesiastical jurisdictions, and forbade tribunals of either class from assuming cognizance of cases pertaining to the other. The elements of the English ecclesiastical law are the canon law, the civil law, the common law of England, and the statutes of the realm. The jurisdiction of the ecclesiastical tribunals extended to matters concerning the order of clergy and their discipline, and also to such affairs of the laity as "concern the health of the soul," and under this latter theory it grasped also cases of marriage and divorce, and testamentary causes. But in more recent times (1830-1858), these latter subjects have been taken from these courts, and they are now substantially confined to administering the judicial authority and discipline incident to a national ecclesiastical establishment. See, also, "Canon Law."

ECDICUS (Graeco-Lat.) The attorney, proctor, or advocate of a corporation. *Episcoporum ecdici*, bishops' proctors; church lawyers. 1 Reeve, Hist. Eng. Law, 65.

ECHANTILLON. In French law. One of the two parts or pieces of a wooden tally. That in possession of the debtor is properly called the "tally"; the other "*echantillon.*" Poth. Obl. pt. 4, c. 1, art. 2, § 8.

ECUMENICAL. General.

EDDERBRECHE. In Saxon law. The offense of hedge breaking.

EDESTIA. Buildings.

EDICT (Lat. *edictum*). A law ordained by the sovereign, by which he forbids or commands something. It extends either to the whole country, or only to some particular provinces.

Edicts are somewhat similar to public proclamations. Their difference consists in this, that the former have authority and form of law in themselves, whereas the latter are, at most, declarations of a law before enacted.

Among the Romans, this word sometimes signified a citation to appear before a judge. The edicts of the emperors, also called *constitutiones principium*, were new laws which they made of their own motion, either to decide cases which they had foreseen, or to abolish or change some ancient laws. They were different from "rescripts" or "decrees," which were answers given in deciding questions brought before them. These edicts contributed to the formation of the Gregorian, Hermogenian, Theodosian, and Justinian Codes. See Dig. 1. 4. 1. 1; Inst. 1. 2. 7; Code, 1. 1; Nov. 139.

EDICTS OF JUSTINIAN. Thirteen constitutions or laws of this prince, found in most editions of the *Corpus Juris Civilis*, after the Novels. Being confined to matters of police in the provinces of the empire, they are of little use.

EDICTUM (Lat.) In the Roman law. An edict; a mandate, or ordinance; an ordinance, or law, enacted by the emperor without the senate, belonging to the class of *constitutiones principis*. Inst. 1. 2. 6. An edict was a mere voluntary constitution of the emperor, differing from a rescript, in not being returned in the way of answer and from a decree, in not being given in judgment, and from both, in not being founded upon solicitation. Tayl. Civ. Law, 233.

A general order published by the praetor, on entering upon his office, containing the system of rules by which he would administer justice during the year of his office. Dig. 1. 2. 2. 10; Mackeld. Civ. Law, § 35; Tayl. Civ. Law, 214; Calv. Lex.

EDICTUM PERPETUUM (Lat.) The title of a compilation of all the edicts. The collection is in fifty books, and was made by Salvius Julianus, a jurist acting by command of Emperor Adrian.

Parts of this collection are cited in the Digest.

EDICTUM THEODORICI. This is the first collection of law that was made after the downfall of the Roman power in Italy. It was promulgated by Theodoric, king of the Ostrogoths, at Rome in A. D. 500. It consists of 154 chapters, in which we recognize parts taken from the Code and *Novellae* of Theodosius, from the *Codices Gregorianus* and Hermogenianus, and the *Sententiae* of Paulus. The edict was doubtless drawn up by Roman writers, but the original sources are more disfigured and altered than in any other compilation. This collection of law was intended to apply both to the Goths and the Romans, so far as its provisions went;

but, when it made no alteration in the Gothic law, that law was still to be in force. Savigny, Hist. Rom. Law; Wharton.

EDITUS, or AEDITUS (Law Lat.) In old English law. Put forth; published or promulgated; passed as a law. Reg. Jud. 2. 1. *Contra formam statuti—editi et provist;* against the form of the statute—made and provided. Rast. Entr. 598, 599.

Brought forth or born, as a child. Bracton, fol. 278.

EFFECTS. Property, or worldly substance. As thus used, it denotes property in a more extensive sense than goods. 2 Sharswood, Bl. Comm. 284; 223 Ill. 538. It includes all kinds of personalty (9 West. Rep. 403), unless limited by context (13 Ves. 39). Whether or not it includes realty depends on the context. In 89 N. C. 447, it was held to include realty. Contra, 15 Mees. & W. 450.

EFFECTUS SEQUITUR CAUSAM. The effect follows the cause. Wingate, Max. 226.

EFFICIENT CAUSE. The working cause, or that cause which produces effects or results. Ford v. Hine, etc., Co., 237 Ill. 469.

EFFIGY. The figure or representation of a person.

To make the effigy of a person with an intent to make him the object of ridicule is a libel (*q. v.*) Hawk. P. C. bk. 1, c. 73, § 2; 14 East, 227; 2 Chit. Crim. Law, 866.

In France an execution by effigy or in effigy is adopted in the case of a criminal who has fled from justice. By the public exposure or exhibition of a picture or representation of him on a scaffold on which his name and the decree condemning him are written, he is deemed to undergo the punishment to which he has been sentenced. Since the adoption of the Code Civil, the practice has been to affix the names, qualities, or addition, and the residence of the condemned person, together with an extract from the sentence of condemnation, to a post set upright in the ground instead of exhibiting a portrait of him on the scaffold.

EFFLUX. Running of time; expiration by lapse of time.

EFFLUXION OF TIME. When this phrase is used in leases, conveyances, and other like deeds, or in agreements expressed in simple writing, it indicates the conclusion or expiration of an agreed term of years specified in the deed or writing; such conclusion or expiration arising in the natural course of events, in contradistinction to the determination of the term by the acts of the parties, or by some unexpected or unusual incident or other sudden event. Brown.

EFFORCIALITER (Law Lat.) Forcibly.

EFFRACTION. A breach made by the use of force.

EFFRACTOR. One who breaks through; one who commits a burglary.

EFFRACTORES. In old English and civil law. Burglars or prison breakers.

EFFUSIO SANGUINIS (Law Lat.) In old English law. The shedding of blood; the mulct, fine, wite, or penalty imposed for the shedding of blood. Cowell; Tomlin. See "Bloodnit."

EFTERS. In Saxon law. Ways, walks, or hedges. Blount.

EGALITY. Owelty (*q. v.*) Co. Litt. 169a.

EGO, TALIS. I, such a one. Used in old forms to indicate where the name and description of a party should be inserted.

EGREDIENS ET EXEUNS (Law Lat.) In old pleading. Going forth and issuing out of land. Towns. Pl. 17.

EI INCUMBIT PROBATIO QUI DICIT, non qui negat. The burden of the proof lies upon him who affirms, not he who denies. Dig. 22. 3. 2; Tait; Ev. 1; 1 Phil. Ev. 194; 1 Greenl. Ev. § 74; 3 La. 83; 2 Daniell, Ch. Prac. 408; 4 Bouv. Inst. note 4411.

EI NIHIL TURPE, CUI NIHIL SATIS. Nothing is base to whom nothing is sufficient. 4 Inst. 53.

EIA, or EY. An island. So called, according to Spelman, from a supposed resemblance to an egg or eye.

EIGNE. A corruption of the French word *aine.* Eldest, or first-born.

It is frequently used in our old law books. *Bastard eigne* signifies an elder bastard when spoken of two children, one of whom was born before the marriage of his parents, and the other after. The latter is called *mulier puisne.* Litt. § 399.

EIK. In Scotch law. An addition; as, *eik* to a reversion, *eik* to a confirmation. Bell, Dict.

EINECIA. Eldership; the right or privilege of the first born.

EINETIUS, EINSNE, or EIGN. In English law. The oldest; the first born, Spelman.

EIRE, or EYRE. In English law. A journey.

Justices in eyre were itinerant judges, who were sent once in seven years with a general commission into divers counties, to hear and determine such causes as were called "pleas of the crown." See "Justices in Eyre."

EIRENARCHA. A name formerly given to a justice of the peace. Bac. Works, IV.

316. In the Digests, the word is written "*irenarcha.*"

EISDEM MODIS DISSOLVITUR OBLIGAtio quae nascitur ex contractu, vel quasi, quibus contrahitur. An obligation which arises from contract, or *quasi* contract, is dissolved in the same ways in which it is contracted. Fleta, lib. 2, c. 60, § 19.

EISNETIA, or **EINETIA** (Lat.) The share of the oldest son; the portion acquired by primogeniture. Termes de la Ley; Co. Litt. 166b; Cowell.

EITHER. Old forms: *either, eyther, aither, ayther.*

Each of two; the one and the other. 172 Ill. 68.

The word "either" is sometimes used in the sense of one or the other of several things, and not infrequently in the sense of one and the other, it being common to say on either hand, on either side, meaning, thereby, on each hand or side. 59 Ill. 89.

The term "either" does not include "both," nor does "both" the greater intend and therefore include the less "either." 4 Hawa. 429.

EJECTA. A woman ravished or deflowered, or cast forth from the virtuous. Blount.

EJECTIONE CUSTODIAE (Lat.) A writ which lay for a guardian to recover the land or person of his ward, or both, where he had been deprived of the possession of them. Fitzh. Nat. Brev. 139 (L); Co. Litt. 199.

EJECTIONE FIRMAE (Lat. ejectment from a farm). This writ lay where lands or tenements were let for a term of years, and afterwards the lessor, reversioner, remainderman, or a stranger ejected or ousted the lessee of his term. The plaintiff, if he prevailed, recovered the term with damages. This writ is the original foundation of the action of ejectment. 3 Sharswood, Bl. Comm. 199; Fitzh. Nat. Brev. 220 (F), (G); Gibson, Eject. 3; Stearns, Real Actions, 53, 400.

EJECTMENT (Lat. *e*, out of, *jacere*, to throw, cast; *ejicere*, to cast out, to eject). In practice. A form of action by which possessory titles to corporeal hereditaments may be tried and possession obtained.

A form of action which lies to regain the possession of real property, with damages for the unlawful detention.

In its origin, this action was an action of trespass which lay for a tenant for years, to recover damages against a person who had ousted him of his possession without right. To the judgment for damages, the courts soon added a judgment for possession, upon which the plaintiff became entitled to a writ of possession. As the disadvantages of real actions as a means of recovering lands for the benefit of the real owner from the possession of one who held them without title became a serious obstacle to their use, this form of action was taken advantage of by Rolle, C. J., to accomplish the same result.

In the original action, the plaintiff had been obliged to prove a lease from the person shown to have title, an entry under the lease, and an ouster by some third person. The modified action as sanctioned by Rolle was brought by a fictitious person as lessee against another fictitious person (the casual ejector) alleged to have committed the ouster. Service was made upon the tenant in possession, with a notice annexed from the casual ejector to appear and defend. If the tenant failed to do this, judgment was given by default, and the claimant put in possession. If he did appear, he was allowed to defend only by entering into the consent rule, by which he confessed the fictitious lease, entry, and ouster to have been made, leaving only the title in question. The tenant, by a subsequent statute, was obliged, under heavy penalties, to give notice to his lessor of the pendency of the action.

The action has been superseded in England by a form prescribed by the common law procedure act (1852, §§ 170-220), and has been materially modified in many of the states of the United States, though still retaining the name; but is retained in its original form in others, and in the United States courts for those states in which it existed when the circuit courts were organized. In some of the United States it has never been in use. See 3 Sharswood, Bl. Comm. 198-207; 1 Washb. Real Prop. (4th Ed.) 433.

EJECTUM. That which is thrown up by the sea. 1 Pet. Adm. (U. S.) 43.

EJECTUS. In old English law. A pimp or whoremonger.

EJERCITORIA. In Spanish law. The action which lies against the owner of a vessel for debts contracted by the master, or contracts entered into by him, for the purpose of repairing, rigging, and victualling the same.

EJIDOS (Spanish). Commons. 15 Cal. 554.

EJURARE. In feudal law. To abjure, renounce, or disclaim by oath.

EJUS EST INTERPRETARI CUJUS EST condere. It is his to interpret whose it is to enact. Tayl. Civ. Law. 96.

EJUS EST NOLLE, QUI POTEST velle. He who can will [exercise volition] has a right to refuse to will [to withhold consent]. Dig. 50. 7. 3.

EJUS EST NON NOLLE QUI POTEST velle. He may consent tacitly who may consent expressly. Dig. 50. 17. 3.

EJUS EST PERICULUM CUJUS EST DOminium aut commodum. He has the risk who has the right of property or advantage.

EJUS NULLA CULPA EST CUI PARERE necesse sit. No guilt attaches to him who is compelled to obey. Dig. 50. 17. 169.

EJUSDEM GENERIS (Lat.) Of the same kind.

In the construction of laws, wills, and other instruments, when certain things are enumerated, and then a phrase is used which might be construed to include other things, it is generally confined to things *ejusdem generis.* Thus, "clerical or other defects" includes only formal defects (40 Barb. [N. Y.] 574), and a statute providing for relief to women whose husbands fail to support them "from drunkenness, profligacy, or any other cause," means only causes of similar nature, and does not include physical incapacity. 20 Wis. 682.

ELABORARE (Law Lat.) In old European law. To gain, acquire, or purchase, as by labor and industry. *Elaboratus,* property acquired by labor. Spelman.

ELDER BRETHREN. See "Trinity Masters."

ELDER TITLE. That of two titles coming simultaneously into conflict which is of earlier date.

ELECTA UNA VIA, NON DATUR REcursus ad alteram. When there is concurrence of means, he who has chosen one cannot have recourse to another. 10 Toullier, Dr. Civ. note 170.

ELECTIO EST INTIMA [INTERNA], LIbera, et spontanea separatio unius rei ab alia, sine compulsione, consistens in animo et voluntate. Election is an internal, free, and spontaneous separation of one thing from another, without compulsion, consisting in intention and will. Dyer, 281.

ELECTIO SEMEL FACTA, ET PLACITum testatum, non patitur regressum. Election once made, and plea witnessed, suffers not a recall. Co. Litt. 146.

ELECTION. Choice; selection. The selection of one man from among more, to discharge certain duties in a state, corporation, or society.

The obligation imposed upon a party to choose between two inconsistent or alternative rights or claims, in cases where there is clear intention of the person from whom he derives one that he should not enjoy both.

——**Of Officers.** The choice of officers of a public or private body by the votes of the members, or a class thereof. It differs from "appointment," which implies the conferring of official station by one or more persons having power to represent the body in that regard. 25 Md. 215.

——**Of Rights.** The right or duty of one who, by contract or donation, is entitled to two or more rights in the alternative, to select that which he will accept as a substitute for the others. One form of this, sometimes known as "equitable election," arises when an instrument gives a right coupled with a burden, the donee of the right having an election whether to accept the same *cum onere,* but being compelled to accept thus, if at all.

——**Of Remedies.** The choice between two or more coexisting and inconsistent remedies for the same wrong. 2 Story, Eq. Jur. § 1078.

——**Between Criminal Charges.** The choice by a public prosecutor upon which of several offenses charged in a single indictment he will go to the jury.

ELECTION AUDITORS. In English law. Officers annually appointed, to whom was committed the duty of taking and publishing the account of all expenses incurred at parliamentary elections. See 17 & 18 Vict. c. 102, §§ 18, 26-28. But these sections have been repealed by 26 Vict. c. 29, which throws the duty of preparing the accounts on the declared agent of the candidate, and the duty of publishing an abstract of it on the returning officer. Wharton.

ELECTION JUDGES. In English law. Judges of the high court, selected in pursuance of 31 & 32 Vict. c. 125, § 11, and Judicature Act 1873, § 38, for the trial of election petitions.

ELECTION PETITIONS. Petitions for inquiry into the validity of elections of members of parliament, when it is alleged that the return of a member is invalid for bribery, or any other reason. These petitions are heard by a judge of one of the common-law divisions of the high court. Parl. El. Act 1868; Judicature Act 1873, § 38.

ELECTIONES FIANT RITE ET LIBERE sine interruptione aliqua. Elections should be made in due form, and freely, without any interruption. 2 Inst. 169.

ELECTIVE. Pertaining to elections, as the elective franchise.

Dependent on election, as an elective office.

ELECTOR. One who has the right to make choice of public officers; one who has a right to vote. See 10 Minn. 107; 53 Wis. 45.

ELECTORS OF PRESIDENT. Persons elected by the people, whose sole duty is to elect a president and vice president of the United States. Const. art. 2, § 1; Const. amend. art. 2.

ELEEMOSYNA REGIS (or ARATRI, or carucarum). A penny which King Ethelred ordered to be paid for every plow in England towards the support of the poor.

ELEEMOSYNAE. Possessions of the church. Blount.

ELEEMOSYNARIA. The place in a religious house where the common alms were deposited, and thence by the almoner distributed to the poor.

——**In Old English.** The *aumerie, aumbry,* or *ambry;* words still used in common speech in the north of England to denote a pantry or cupboard. Cowell.

The office of almoner. Cowell.

ELEEMOSYNARIUS (Lat.) An almoner. There was formerly a lord almoner to the kings of England, whose duties are described in Fleta, lib. 2, c. 23. A chief officer who received the eleemosynary rents and gifts, and in due method distributed them to pious and charitable uses. Cowell.

ELEEMOSYNARY CORPORATIONS. Such private corporations as are instituted for purposes of charity, their object being the perpetual distribution of the bounty of the founder of them to such persons as he directed. Of this kind are hospitals for the relief of the impotent, indigent, sick, and deaf or dumb. Angell & A. Corp. § 39; 1 Kyd. Corp. 26; 4 Conn. 272; 3 Bland, Ch. (Md.) 407; 1 Ld. Raym. 5; 2 Term R. 346. The distinction between ecclesiastical and eleemosynary corporations is well illustrated in the Darthmouth College Case, 4 Wheat. (U. S.) 681. See, also, Angell & A. Corp. § 39; 1 Sharswood, Bl. Comm. 471.

ELEGANTER (Lat.) In the civil law. Accurately; with discrimination. 3 Story (U. S.) 611, 636.

ELEGIT (Lat. *eligere,* to choose). A writ of execution directed to the sheriff, commanding him to make delivery of a moiety of the party's land and all his goods, beasts of the plough only excepted. The sheriff, on receipt of the writ, holds an inquest to ascertain the value of the lands and goods he has seized, and then they are delivered to the plaintiff, who retains them until the whole debt and damages have been paid and satisfied. During that term he is called "tenant by elegit." Co. Litt. 289. See Powell, Mortg. Index; Watson, Sheriffs, 206; 1 C. B. (N. S.) 568.

The name was given because the plaintiff has his choice to accept either this writ or a *fi. fa.*

By statute, in England, the sheriff is now to deliver the whole estate instead of the half. See 3 Sharswood, Bl. Comm. 418, note. The writ is still in use in the United States to some extent, and with somewhat different modifications in the various states adopting it. 4 Kent, Comm. 431, 436; 10 Grat. (Va.) 580; 1 Hilliard, Abr. 555, 556.

ELEMENTS. "Damage by the elements" has been held synonymous with "damage by act of God." "The elements are the means by which God acts." 35 Cal. 416.

Eligible, the term eligible relates to capacity of holding, as well as capacity of being elected to an office, 15 Ind. 331; 31 Neb. 707; legally qualified, 24 Ill. App. 612; or fit to be chosen, 30 L. J. Ch. 631; 8 H. L. Ca. 495.

ELIMINATION. Banishment; expulsion.

ELINGUATION. The punishment of cutting out the tongue.

ELISORS. In practice. Two persons appointed by the court to return a jury, when the sheriff and the coroner have been challenged as incompetent. In this case, the elisors return the writ of venire directed to them, with a panel of the jurors, names, and their return is final, no challenge being allowed to their array. 3 Bl. Comm. 355; 1 Cow. (N. Y.) 32; 3 Cow. (N. Y.) 296.

ELOGIUM (Lat.) In civil law. A will or testament.

ELOIGN, or **ELOIGNE.** To remove to a distance. See "Elongata."

ELONGATA. In practice. The return made by the sheriff to a writ of replevin, when the goods have been removed to places unknown to him. See, for the form of this return, Watson, Sheriffs, Append. c. 18, § 3, p. 454; 3 Bl. Comm. 148.

On this return, the plaintiff is entitled to a *capias in withernam.* See "Withernam"; Watson, Sheriffs, 300, 301. The word *eloigne* is sometimes used as synonymous with *elongata.*

ELONGATUS. A return to a writ *de homine replegiando,* that the man was out of the sheriff's jurisdiction.

ELONGAVIT. In England, where, in a proceeding by foreign attachment, the plaintiff has obtained judgment of appraisement, but by reason of some act of the garnishee the goods cannot be appraised (as where he has removed them from the city, or has sold them, etc.), the serjeant-at-mace returns that the garnishee has *eloigned* them, *i. e.,* removed them out of the jurisdiction, and on this return (called an "*elongavit*") judgment is given for the plaintiff that an inquiry be made of the goods *eloigned.* This inquiry is set down for trial, and the assessment is made by a jury after the manner of ordinary issues. Brant. For. Att. 124. The proceedings on the inquiry are also sometimes called the "*elongavit.*"

ELOPEMENT. The departure of a married woman from her husband, and dwelling with an adulterer. Cowell; Blount; Tomlin.

ELUVIONES. Spring tides.

EMANCIPATION. An act by which a person who was once in the power of another is rendered free.

This is of importance mainly in relation to the emancipation of minors from the parental control. See 3 Term R. 355; 6 Term R. 247; 8 Term R. 479; 3 East, 276; 10 East, 88; 11 Vt. 258, 477. See Cooper, Just. Inst. 441, 480; 2 Dall. (Pa.) 57, 58; Civ. Code La. bk. 1, tit. 8, c. 3; Ferriere, Dict. de Jur.; 15 Mass. 272; 8 Cow. (N. Y.) 184.

EMBARGO. A proclamation, or order of state, usually issued in time of war or threatened hostilities, prohibiting the departure of ships or goods from some or all the ports of such state, until further order. 2 Wheat. (U. S.) 148. It is in its nature and policy a temporary measure. 5 Johns. (N. Y.) 308. It is sometimes on the citizens of the power ordering it; sometimes on a foreign power as a means of coercing a settlement of difficulties that have not yet culminated in war, or of preparation for impending war. The former is called "civil," the latter "hostile," embargo.

EMBASSAGE, or **EMBASSY.** The message or commission given by a sovereign or state to a minister, called an "ambassador," empowered to treat or communicate with another sovereign or state; also the establishment of an ambassador.

EMBEZZLEMENT. The wrongful and fraudulent appropriation of property to his own use by one to whom it has been entrusted by or for the owner.

A breach of trust is the essence of the offense. To constitute embezzlement, the person appropriating the property must hold a relation of trust towards the owner, by virtue of which he had possession of such property. 31 Cal. 108; 68 Iowa, 593; 110 Mo. 209.

The appropriation must be with fraudulent intent, and by this embezzlement is distinguished from mere tortious conversion. 82 Ill. 425; 78 Ga. 340; 62 Mich. 276; 50 N. J. Law, 475.

The offense is a purely statutory one, and by many of the statutes is denominated "larceny," but it is commonly known as "embezzlement," and is distinct from larceny at common law, one of the essentials of which was a wrongful taking from the possession of the owner.

EMBLEMENTS. Crops. 65 Cal. 458. The growing crops of those vegetable productions of the soil which are not spontaneous, but require an outlay of cost and labor in one part of the year, the recompense for which is to arise in the shape of a crop in another part of the same year. The produce of grass, trees, and the like is not included. 76 Ind. 531.

EMBLERS DE GENTZ (Law Fr.) A stealing from the people. The phrase occurs in the old rolls of parliament: "Whereas divers murderers, *emblers de gentz*, and robberies are committed," etc. Rot. Parl. 21 Edw. III. note 62.

EMBRACEOR. In criminal law. He who, when a matter is on trial between party and party, comes to the bar with one of the parties, and, having received some reward so to do, speaks in the case, or privily labors the jury, or stands there to survey or overlook them, thereby to put them in fear and doubt of the matter. But persons learned in the law may speak in a case for their clients. Co. Litt. 369; Termes de la Ley.

EMBRACERY. In criminal law. An attempt to corrupt or influence a jury, or any way incline them to be more favorable to one side than to the other, by money, promises, threats, or persuasions, whether the juror on whom such attempt is made give any verdict or not, or whether the verdict be true or false. Hawk. P. C. 259; Bac. Abr. "Juries" (M 3); Co. Litt. 157b, 369a; Hob. 294; Dyer, 84a, pl. 19; Noy, 102; 1 Strange, 643; 11 Mod. 111, 118; Comyn, Dig. 601; 5 Cow. (N. Y.) 503.

EMBRING (or **EMBER**) **DAYS.** In ecclesiastical law. Those days which the ancient fathers called "*quatuor tempora jejunii*" are of great antiquity in the church. They are observed on Wednesday, Friday, and Saturday next after Quadragesima Sunday, or the first Sunday in Lent, after Whitsuntide, Holyrood Day, in September, and St. Lucy's Day, about the middle of December. Britt. c. 53. Our almanacs call the weeks in which they fall the "Ember Weeks," and they are now chiefly noticed on account of the ordination of priests and deacons; because the canon appoints the Sundays next after the Ember weeks for the solemn times of ordination, though the bishops, if they please, may ordain on any Sunday or holiday. Enc. Lond.

EMENDA (Lat.) Amends; that which is given in reparation or satisfaction for a trespass committed, or, among the Saxons, a compensation for a crime. Spelman.

EMENDALS. In English law. This ancient word is said to be used in the accounts of the inner temple, where so much in emendals at the foot of an account signifies so much in bank, in stock, for the supply of emergencies. Cunningham.

EMENDARE (Law Lat.) In Saxon law. To make amends or satisfaction for any crime or trespass committed; *emendam solvere*, to pay a fine; to be fined. Spelman. *Emendare se*, to redeem, or ransom one's life, by payment of a weregild.

To repair. Reg. Orig. 44b.

EMENDATIO (Lat.)

——**In Old English Law.** Amendment, or correction; the power of amending and correcting abuses, according to certain rules and measures. Cowell.

——**In Saxon Law.** A pecuniary satisfaction for an injury; the same as *emenda* (*q. v.*) Spelman.

EMENDATIO PANIS ET CEREVISIAE. The power of supervising and correcting the weights and measurers of bread and ale. Cowell.

EMERGENCY. Any event or occasional combination of circumstances which calls for immediate action or remedy; pressing necessity; exigency. 21 Ill. App. 274.

EMERGERE (Lat.) To arise; to come to light.

EMIGRANT. One who quits his country for any lawful reason, with a design to settle elsewhere, and who takes his family and property, if he has any, with him. Vattel, bk. 1, c. 19, § 224. See "Emigration."

EMIGRATION. The act of removing from one place to another.

It is sometimes used in the same sense as "expatriation," but there is some difference in the signification. Expatriation is the act of abandoning one's country; while emigration is, perhaps not strictly, applied to the act of removing from one part of the country to another. See 2 Kent, Comm. 36.

EMINENT DOMAIN. The power to take private property for public use, whether exercised by the sovereign directly, or by one to whom the sovereign power has been delegated for *quasi* public purposes.

The superior right of property subsisting in a sovereignty, by which private property may in certain cases be taken or its use controlled for the public benefit, without regard to the wishes of the owner.

The highest and most exact idea of property remaining in the government, or in the aggregate body of the people in their sovereign capacity, giving a right to resume the possession of the property in the manner directed by the constitution and the laws of the state whenever the public good requires it. 3 Paige, Ch. (N. Y.) 73.

The term was originated by Grotius (De Jure Belli, lib. 3, c. 20, VII).

EMISSION. In medical jurisprudence. The act by which any matter whatever is thrown from the body thus, it is usual to say, emission of urine, emission of semen, etc.

EMIT. To put out; to send forth.

The tenth section of the first article of the constitution contains various prohibitions, among which is the following: "No state shall emit bills of credit." To emit bills of credit is to issue paper intended to circulate through the community for its ordinary purposes, as money, which paper is redeemable at a future day. 4 Pet. (U. S.) 410, 432; 11 Pet. (U. S.) 257; Story, Const. § 1358.

EMMENAGOGUES. In medical jurisprudence. The name of a class of medicines which are believed to have the power of favoring the discharge of the menses. They are sometimes used for the criminal purpose of producing abortion (*q. v.*) 1 Beck, Med. Jur. 316; Dungl. Med. Dict.; Parr, Med. Dict.; 3 Paris & F. Med. Jur. 88.

EMOLUMENT. Any pecuniary advantage, profit, or gain arising from the possession of an office. It imports more than "salary" or "fees," and includes any perquisite, advantage, profit, or gain arising from the possession of an office. 105 Pa. St. 303.

EMOTIONAL INSANITY. The species of mental aberration produced by a violent excitement of the emotions or passions, though the reasoning faculties may remain unimpaired.

EMPALEMENT. In ancient law. A mode of inflicting punishment by thrusting a sharp pole up the fundament. Enc. Lond.

EMPANNEL. See "Impannel."

EMPARLANCE. See "Imparlance."

EMPARNOURS (Law Fr.) Undertakers of suits. Kelham.

EMPEROR. This word is synonymous with the Latin *imperator.* They are both derived from the verb *imperare.* Literally, it signifies "he who commands."

Under the Roman republic, the title "emperor" was the generic name given to the commanders-in-chief in the armies. But even then the application of the word was restrained to the successful commander, who was declared emperor by the acclamations of the army, and was afterwards honored with the title by a decree of the senate.

It is now used to designate some sovereign prince who bears this title. Ayliffe, Pand. tit. 23.

EMPHYTEOSIS (or EMPHYTEUSIS). In civil law. The name of a contract by which the owner of an uncultivated piece of land granted it to another, either in perpetuity, or for a long time, on condition that he should improve it by building, planting, or cultivating it, and should pay for it an annual rent, with a right to the grantee to alienate it, or transmit it by descent to his heirs, and under a condition that the grantor should never re-enter as long as the rent should be paid to him by the grantee or his assigns. Inst. 3. 25. 3; 18 Toullier, Dr. Civ. note 144.

EMPHYTEUTA. The grantee under a contract of *emphyteusis* or *emphyteosis.* Vicat; Calv. Lex.; 1 Hallam, Mid. Ages, c. 2, p. 1.

EMPHYTEUTICUS. In the civil law. Founded on, growing out of, or having the character of, an *emphyteusis;* held under an *emphyteusis.* 3 Bl. Comm. 232; Calv. Lex.

EMPLAZAMIENTO. In Spanish law. The citation given to a person by order of the judge, and ordering him to appear before his tribunal on a given day and hour.

EMPLEAD. See "Implead."

EMPLOYE. One who is employed. The term is general, but is rarely applied either to common laborers or to the higher officers of a corporation. 66 Wis. 481; 109 N. Y. 631.

EMPLOYERS' LIABILITY INSURANCE. There is a contract of indemnity called "employers' liability," etc., which has become familiar since the passing of employers' liability acts in England and America. It insures an employer against claim for compensation for damage on the part of an employee for injuries suffered (Encycl. Laws Eng.) These contracts are regulated by the same rules as fire and marine insurance.

EMPLOYMENT. A business or vocation. 16 Ala. 411; calling; office; service; commission trade; profession. 46 Ill. App. 373. The service of another. 72 Me. 455; the act of employing, in another sense, the state of being employed. 155 Ill. 103.

EMPRESTIDO. In Spanish law. A loan; something lent to the borrower at his request. Las Partidas, pt. 3, tit. 18, lib. 70.

EMPTIO, or **EMPTOR** (Lat. *emere,* to buy). *Emptio,* a buying; *emptor,* a buyer; *emptio et venditio,* buying and selling.
——**In Roman Law.** The name of a contract of sale. Du Cange; Vicat.

EMPTIO BONORUM. In the Roman law. The assignment of the estate and effects of an insolvent debtor, whether during his life or after his death, to a trustee for his creditors. Justinian deprived it of all its cumbrous formalities, but retained its effect, which is simply or very nearly that of an assignment upon bankruptcy in English law.

EMPTIO ET VENDITIO (Lat. buying and selling). In Roman law. The contract of sale. Sometimes it was compounded,—*emptio-venditio.*

EMPTOR (Lat.) Buyer.

EMPTOR EMIT QUAM MINIMO POtest, venditor vendit quam maximo potest. The buyer buys for as little as possible; the vendor sells for as much as possible. 2 Johns. Ch. (N. Y.) 252, 256, 486.

EN AUTRE DROIT (Fr.) In the right of another.

EN AVANT. (L. Fr.) In future; for the time to come; henceforward. Kelham.

EN BANKE (Law Fr.) In the bench. 1 And. 51.

EN DEMEURE (Fr.) In default. Used in Louisiana. 3 Mart. (La.; N. S.) 574.

EN ESCHANGE IL COVIENT QUE LES estates soient egales. In an exchange it is necessary that the estates be equal. Co. Litt. 50; 2 Hilliard, Real Prop. 298.

EN GROS (Fr.) In gross; by wholesale. Britt. c. 21.

EN JUICIO (Spanish). Judicially; in a court of law; in a suit at law. White, New Recop. bk. 2, tit. 8, c. 1.

EN MORT MEYNE (Law Fr.) In a dead hand; in mortmain. Britt. c. 43.

EN OWEL MAIN (Law Fr.) In equal hand. The word "owel" occurs also in the phrase "owelty of partition." See 1 Washb. Real Prop. 427.

EN VENTRE SA MERE (Fr.) In its mother's womb. For certain purposes, as of inheritance, etc., a child *en ventre sa mere* is to be considered as in being, in so far as its property rights are concerned, but not to the extent of permitting it to recover after its birth for prenatal injuries negligently inflicted.

EN VIE (Law Fr.) In life; alive. Britt. c. 50.

ENABLING POWERS. A term used in equity. When the donor of a power, who is the owner of the estate, confers upon persons not seised of the fee the right of creating interests to take effect out of it, which could not be done by the donee of the power unless by such authority, this is called an "enabling power." 2 Bouv. Inst. note 1628; 2 Bl. Comm. 319; Co. Litt. 44a; 3 Steph. Comm. 139.

ENABLING STATUTE. The act of 32 Henry VIII. c. 28, by which tenants in tail, husbands seised in right of their wives, were empowered to make leases for their lives or for twenty-one years, which they could not do before. 2 Bl. Comm. 319.

Applied generally to special acts conferring powers not previously possessed.

ENACT. To establish by law; to perform or effect; to decree. The usual formula in making laws is, "Be it enacted."

ENACTING CLAUSE. The section of a bill or statute which establishes the whole document as a law. 193 Ill. 193.

ENAJENACION. In Spanish law. The act by which one person transfers to another a property, either gratuitously, as in the case of a donation, or by an owner's title, as in the case of a sale or an exchange.

ENBREVER (Law Fr.) To write down in short; to abbreviate, or, in old language, imbreviate; to put into a schedule. Britt. c. 1.

ENCAUSTUM. See "Incaustum."

ENCEINTE (Fr.) Pregnant (*q. v.*)

ENCHESON, ENCHESSON, ENCHASON, enchison, or **acheson** (Law Fr.) Cause; reason; occasion. *Par quel encheson il se neya,* for what reason he drowned himself. Britt. c. 1. *Par encheson de matrimoyne,* in consideration of marriage. Id. c. 34. *Sans reasonable encheson,* without reasonable cause. St. Westminster I. c. 6.

ENCLOSURE. Imports land enclosed with something more than the imaginary boundary line, that there should be some visible or tangible obstruction, such as a fence, hedge, or ditch, or something equivalent, for the protection of the premises against encroachment by animals. 39 Vermont 331. See "Close."

ENCOMIENDA. A charge or mandate conferring certain important privileges on the four military orders of Spain, to wit, those of Santiago, Calatrava, Alcantara, and Montesa. In the legislation of the Indias, it signified the concession of a certain number of Indians for the purpose of instructing them in the Christian religion, and defending their persons and property.

ENCROACHMENT. An unlawful extension of one's right upon the lands of another.

An alteration by the owner of an easement of the dominant tenement, so as to impose an additional burden on the servient tenement. Gale, Easm. 615.

ENDENZIE, or **ENDENIZEN.** To make free; to enfranchise.

ENDORSE. See "Indorse."

ENDOW. Means giving a benefit to some existing thing; it supposes something to exist either at the time when the gift is made, or when the endowment is to take place; it has no reference at all to building or purchasing, 6 De G. M. & G. 83.

ENDOWMENT (Law Fr. and Eng.) The assignment or bestowment of dower to or upon a woman. 2 Bl. Comm. 135.

The providing for the officiating ministers of a church, by setting apart a certain portion of lands, etc., for their maintenance, etc. 2 Bl. Comm. 21; 1 Bl. Comm. 387; 3 Steph. Comm. 111. It has no reference to building or providing a site. 35 Eng. Law & Eq. 433.

The provision itself, so made (*dos ecclesiae*). Comyn, Dig. "Dismes" (B).

ENDOWMENT POLICY. In insurance; a policy of life insurance payable to the insured during his lifetime, if he arrive at a certain age.

In one aspect, it is a contract payable in the event of a continuance of life; in the other, in the event of death before the period specified. 86 N. Y. 17.

ENEMY. A nation which is at war with another; a citizen or a subject of such a nation; any of the subjects or citizens of a state in amity with the United States, who have commenced, or have made preparations for commencing, hostilities against the United States, and also the citizens or subjects of a state in amity with the United States, who are in the service of a state at war with them. See Salk. 635; Bac. Abr. "Treason" (G).

"An enemy is he with whom a nation is at war." Vattel, 387; 43 Pa. St. 493; 74 Mo. 418. "It does not embrace rebels in insurrection against their own government. An enemy is always the subject of a foreign power, who owes no allegiance to our government." 4 Sawy. (U. S.) 457.

A public enemy, where the whole body of the nation is at war with one another. 43 Pa. St. 493.

By the term "enemy" is also understood a person who is desirous of doing injury to another. The Latins had two terms to signify these two classes of persons: The first, or the public enemy, they called *hostis,* and the latter, or the private enemy, *inimicus.*

ENFEOFF. To make a gift of any corporeal hereditaments to another. See "Feoffment."

ENFRANCHISE. To make free; to incorporate a man in a society or body politic. Cunningham.

ENFRANCHISEMENT. Giving freedom to a person; admitting a person to the freedom of a city. A denizen of England, or a citizen of London, is said to be enfranchised. So, too, a villein is enfranchised when he obtains his freedom from his lord. Termes de la Ley; 11 Coke, 91; Jacob.

ENFRANCHISEMENT OF COPYHOLD. The change of the tenure by which lands are held from copyhold to freehold, as by a conveyance to the copyholder, or by a release of the seignorial rights. 1 Watk. Copyholds, 362; 1 Steph. Comm. 208; 2 Steph. Comm. 51.

ENGAGEMENT. In French law. A contract; the obligations arising from a *quasi* contract.

The terms "obligation" and "engagement" are said to be synonymous (17 Toullier, Dr. Civ. note 1), but the Code seems specially to apply the term "engagement" to those obligations which the law imposes on a man without the intervention of any contract, either on the part of the obligor or the obligee. Article 1370.

ENGLAND. In an Act of Parliament, includes Wales and Berwick-upon-Tweed (20 G. 2, c. 42, s. 3); but not Scotland or Ireland. 53 L. J. Ch. 1067.

ENGLESHIRE, or **ANGLESCHERIA.** A law was made by Canute, for the preservation of his Danes, that, when a man was killed, the hundred or town should be liable to be amerced, unless it could be proved that the person killed was an Englishman. This proof was called *engleshire*. It consisted, generally, of the testimony of two males on the part of the father of him who had been killed, and two females on the part of his mother. 1 Hale, P. C. 447; 4 Bl. Comm. 195. Spelman.

ENGLETERRE. England.

ENGLISH INFORMATION. In English law. A proceeding in the court of exchequer in matters of revenue. See 28 & 29 Vict. c. 104.

ENGLISH LANGUAGE. Combinations of letters do not of themselves constitute "language." They must be formed into words having a known meaning as part of the language and these words must be used in connection with other words in such relation that they convey intelligible meaning. 253 Ill. 199.

ENGROSS (Fr. *gros*). To copy the rude draught of an instrument in a fair, large hand; to write out, in a large, fair hand, on parchment. The term is applied to statutes, which, after being read and acted on a sufficient number of times, are ordered to be engrossed. Anciently, also, used of the process of making the indenture of a fine. 5 Coke, 39b.

——**In Criminal Law.** To buy up such large quantities of an article as to obtain a monopoly of it for the purpose of selling at an unreasonable price. The tendency of modern English law is very decidedly to restrict the application of the law against engrossing, and it is very doubtful if it applies at all except to obtaining a monopoly of provisions. 1 East, 143. Merely buying for the purpose of selling again is not necessarily engrossing. 14 East, 406; 15 East, 511. See 4 Sharswood, Bl. Comm. 159, note, for the law upon this subject.

ENGROSSER. One who engrosses or writes on parchment in a large, fair hand; one who purchases large quantities of any commodity in order to have the command of the market, and to sell them again at high prices.

ENGROSSING. The offense committed by an engrosser; writing on parchment in a large, fair hand. See "Engross."

ENITIA PARS (Law Lat.) The part of the eldest. Co. Litt. 166; Bac. Abr. "Coparceners" (C).

When partition is voluntarily made among coparceners in England, the eldest has the first choice, or primer election (*q. v.*), and the part which she takes is called *enitia pars*. This right is purely personal, and descends. It is also said that even her assignee shall enjoy it; but this has been doubted. The word *enitia* is said to be derived from the old French *eisne*, the eldest. Bac. Abr. "Coparceners" (C); Keilw. 1a, 49a; 2 And. 21; Cro. Eliz. 18.

ENJOIN. To command; to require; as, private individuals are not only permitted, but enjoined, by law, to arrest an offender when present at the time a felony is committed, or a dangerous wound given, on pain of fine and imprisonment if the wrongdoer escape through their negligence. 1 Hale, P. C. 587; 1 East, P. C. 298, 304; Hawk. P. C. bk. 2, c. 12, § 13; Ryan & M. 93.

To command or order a defendant in equity to do or not to do a particular thing by writ of injunction. See "Injunction."

ENLARGE. To extend; as, to enlarge a rule to plead is to extend the time during which a defendant may plead. To enlarge means, also, to set at liberty; as, the prisoner was enlarged on giving bail.

ENLARGER L'ESTATE. A species of release which inures by way of enlarging an estate, and consists of a conveyance of the ulterior interest to the particular tenant; as if there be tenant for life or years, remainder to another in fee, and he in the remainder releases all his right to the particular tenant and his heirs, this gives him the estate in fee. 1 Steph. Comm. 518.

ENLARGING. Extending, or making more comprehensive; as, an enlarging statute, which is one extending the common law.

ENLARGING STATUTE. See "Statute."

ENLISTMENT. The act of making a contract to serve the government in a subordinate capacity, either in the army or navy. It may signify either the complete fact of entering into the military service, or the first step taken by the recruit towards that end. 8 Allen (Mass.) 485. The contract so made is also called an "enlistment." See, as to the power of infants to enlist, 4 Bin. (Pa.) 487; 5 Bin. (Pa.) 423; 6 Bin. (Pa.) 255; 1 Serg. & R. (Pa.) 87; 11 Serg. & R. (Pa.) 93.

ENORMIA (Lat.) Wrongs. It occurs in the old Latin forms of pleading, where, after a specific allegation of the wrongs done by the defendant, the plaintiff alleges generally that the defendant did *alia enormia* (other wrongs), to the damage, etc. 2 Greenl. Ev. § 278; 1 Chit. Pl. 397. See "Alia Enormia."

ENPLEET. An old form of "implead."

ENQUETE. In canon law. An examination of witnesses in the presence of a judge authorized to sit for this purpose, taken in writing, to be used as evidence in the trial of a cause. The day of hearing must be specified in a notice to the opposite party. 9 Low. (U. S.) 392. It may be opened, in some cases, before the trial. 10 Low. (U. S.) 19.

ENROLL. To register; to enter on the rolls of chancery, or other courts; to make a record.

ENROLLMENT. In English law. The registering or entering on the rolls of chancery, king's bench, common pleas, or exchequer, or by the clerk of the peace in the records of the quarter sessions, of any lawful act, as, a recognizance, a deed of bargain and sale, and the like. Jacob.

ENS LEGIS (Law Lat.) A legal entity; an artificial person created by law as a corporation.

ENSCHEDULE. To insert in a list, account, or writing.

ENSEAL. To seal.

ENSERVER (Law Fr.) To make subject to a service or servitude. Britt. c. 54.

ENTAIL. A fee abridged or limited to the issue, or certain classes of issue, instead of descending to all the heirs. 1 Washb. Real Prop. 66; Cowell; 2 Sharswood, Bl. Comm. 112, note.

To restrict the inheritance of lands to a particular class of issue. 1 Washb. Real Prop. 66; 2 Sharswood, Bl. Comm. 113. See "Estates;" "Tail."

ENTAILED MONEY. That which is given to be used or invested in acquiring an "estate tail." 3 & 4 Wm. IV. c. 74, §§ 70-72.

ENTENCION. In old English law. The plaintiff's declaration.

ENTENDMENT. The old form of intendment (*q. v.*), derived directly from the French, and used by Cowell to denote the true meaning or signification of a word or sentence; that is, the understanding or construction of law.

ENTER. To go upon lands for the purpose of taking possession; to take possession. In a strict use of terms, "entry" and "taking possession" would seem to be distinct parts of the same act; but, practically, "entry" is now merged in "taking possession." 1 Washb. Real Prop. 10, 32; Stearns, Real Actions, 2.

To cause to be put down upon the record. An attorney is said to enter his appearance, or the party himself may enter an appearance. 74 Ind. 59.

To enter judgment is to formally enroll it or repose the evidence of it in the record or permanent memorial of the acts of the court.

ENTERCEUR (Law Fr.) A party challenging (claiming) goods; he who has placed them in the hands of a third person. Kelham.

ENTERPRISE. An undertaking of hazard; an arduous attempt; an undertaking; something projected and attempted; an attempt or project; particularly an undertaking of some importance or one requiring boldness, energy or perseverance; an arduous or hazardous attempt, as, a warlike enterprise. 271 Ill. 317.

ENTIRE CONTRACT. See "Contract."

ENTIRE TENANCY. A sole possession by one. Wharton.

ENTIRETY. This word denotes the whole, in contradistinction to moiety, which denotes the half part. A husband and wife, when jointly seised of land, are seised by entireties, and not *pur mie*, as joint tenants are. Jacob; 2 Kent, Comm. 132; 4 Kent, Comm. 362; 3 Pa. St. 350, 367.

ENTITLE. In its usual sense, to entitle is to give a right or title; therefore a person is said to be entitled to property when he has a right to it. L. R. 20 Eq. 534.

——**In Ecclesiastical Law.** To entitle is to give a title or ordination as a minister. Gibs. Code, 141, note.

——**In Practice.** To prefix to a document the title of the cause to which it relates.

ENTREBAT (Law Fr.) An intruder or interloper. Britt. c. 114.

ENTREGA. In Spanish law. Delivery.

ENTREPOT. A warehouse; a magazine where goods are deposited which are to be again removed.

ENTRY. The act of setting down the particulars of a sale, or other transaction, in a merchant's or tradesman's account books. Such entries are, in general, *prima facie* evidence of the sale and delivery, and of work done; but unless the entry be the original one, it is not evidence.

The submitting to the inspection of officers appointed by law, who have the collection of the customs, goods imported into the United States, together with a statement or description of such goods, and the original invoices of the same, for the purpose of estimating the duties to be paid thereon. Act March 2, 1799, § 36 (1 Story, U. S. Laws, 606), and Act March 1, 1823 (3 Story, U. S. Laws, 1881), regulate the manner of making entries of goods.

——**In Criminal Law.** The act of entering a dwelling house, or other building, in order to commit a crime. See "Burglary."

——**Of a Judgment.** A ministerial act which consists in spreading it upon the record or writing it at large, in English language (*q. v.*), 153 Ill. 199, in a docket or other official book. 191 Ill. App. 639; 195 Ill. App. 182.

——**Upon Real Estate.** The act of going upon the lands of another, or lands claimed as one's own, with intent to take possession. 1 Ala. 674.

ENTRY AD COMMUNEM LEGEM. In English law. A writ which lay in favor of the reversioner, when the tenant for term of life, tenant for term of another's life, tenant by the curtesy, or tenant in dower, had aliened and died. Tomlins.

ENTRY AD TERMINUM QUI PRAETERIIT. The writ of entry *ad terminum qui* *praeteriit* lies where a man leases land to another for a term of years, and the tenant holds over his term. And if lands be leased to a man for the term of another's life, and he for whose life the lands are leased dies, and the lessee holds over, then the lessor shall have this writ. Termes de la Ley.

ENTRY FOR MARRIAGE IN SPEECH. A writ of entry *causa matrimonii praeloquuti* lies where lands or tenements are given to a man upon condition that he shall take the donor to be his wife within a certain time, and he does not espouse her within the said term, or espouses another woman, or makes himself priest. Termes de la Ley.

ENTRY IN CASU CONSIMILI. A writ of entry *in casu consimili* lies where a tenant for life or by the curtesy aliens in fee. Termes de la Ley.

ENTRY IN THE CASE PROVIDED. A writ of entry *in casu proviso* lies if a tenant in dower alien in fee, or for life, or for another's life. Termes de la Ley.

ENTRY ON THE ROLL. In former times, the parties to an action, personally or by their counsel, used to appear in open court, and make their mutual statements *viva voce*, instead of, as at the present day, delivering their mutual pleadings, until they arrived at the issue or precise point in dispute between them. During the progress of this oral statement, a minute of the various proceedings was made on parchment by an officer of the court appointed for that purpose. The parchment then became the record; in other words, the official history of the suit. Long after the practice of oral pleading had fallen into disuse, it continued necessary to enter the proceedings in like manner upon the parchment roll, and this was called "entry on the roll," or making up the "issue roll." But by a rule of H. T. 4 Wm. IV., the practice of making up the issue roll was abolished, and it was only necessary to make up the issue in the form prescribed for the purpose by a rule of H. T. 1853, and to deliver the same to the court and to the opposite party. The issue which was delivered to the court was called the "*nisi prius* record;" and that was regarded as the official history of the suit, in like manner as the issue roll formerly was. Under the present practice, the issue roll or *nisi prius* record consists of the papers delivered to the court, to facilitate the trial of the action, these papers consisting of the pleadings simply, with the notice of trial. Brown.

ENTRY WITHOUT ASSENT OF THE chapter. A writ of entry *sine assensu capituli* lies where an abbot, prior, or such as has covent or common seal, aliens lands of the church without the assent of the chapter, and then dies. Termes de la Ley.

ENTRY, WRIT OF. In old practice. A real action brought to recover the possession of lands from one who wrongfully withholds possession thereof.

In general, the writ of entry is the universal remedy to recover possession when wrongfully withheld from the owner. 3 Bl. Comm. 183.

Such writs were said to be in the *quibus*, where the suit was brought against the party who committed the wrong; in the *per*, where the tenant against whom the action was brought was either heir or grantee of the original wrongdoer· in the *per* and *cui*, where there had been two descents, two alienations, or a descent and an alienation; in the *post*, where the wrong was removed beyond the degrees mentioned.

The above designations are derived from significant Latin words in the respective forms adapted to the cases given.

The writ was of many varieties, also, according to the character of the title of the claimant and the circumstances of the deprivation of possession. Booth enumerates and discusses twelve of these, of which some are *sur disseisin, sur intrusion, ad communem legem, ad terminum qui preterit, cui in vita, cui ante divortium*, etc. Either of these might, of course, be brought in any of the four degrees, as the circumstances of the case required. The use of writs of entry has been long since abolished in England; but they are still in use in a modified form in some of the United States, as the common means of recovering possession of realty against a wrongful occupant. 2 Pick. (Mass.) 473; 7 Pick. (Mass.) 36; 10 Pick. (Mass.) 359; 5 N. H. 450; 6 N. H. 555. See Stearns, Real Action; Booth, Real Actions; Reg. Brev. 229; Rast. Entr. 279b; Co. Litt. 238b.

Though the action was formerly a possessory one, it seems that title may be now tried therein. 141 Mass. 93.

ENUMERATIO INFIRMAT REGULAM in casibus non enumeratis. Enumeration disaffirms the rule in cases not enumerated. Bac. Aph. 17.

ENUMERATIO UNIUS EST EXCLUSIO alterius. Specification of one thing is an exclusion of the rest. 4 Johns. Ch. (N. Y.) 106, 113.

ENURE. To take or have effect; to serve to the use, benefit, or advantage of a person. The word is often written "inure." A release to the tenant for life enures to him in reversion; that is, it has the same effect for him as for the tenant for life. A discharge of the principal enures to the benefit of the surety.

ENVOY. In international law. A minister of the second rank, on whom his sovereign or government has conferred a degree of dignity and respectability which, without being on a level with an ambassador, immediately follows, and, among ministers, yields the pre-eminence to him alone.

Envoys are either ordinary or extraordinary. By custom, the latter is held in greater consideration. Vattel, liv. 4, c. 6, § 72.

EO INSTANTE (Lat.) At that instant.

EO INTUITU (Lat.) With that view or intent. Hale, Anal. § 2.

EO LOCI (Lat.) In civil law. In that place (*eo loco*); there. Dig. 5. 1. 19. 2.
In that state or condition. Calv. Lex.

EO NOMINE (Lat.) Under or by that name.

EODEM LIGAMINE QUO LIGATUM EST dissolvitur. A bond is released by the same formalities with which it is contracted. Co. Litt. 212b; Broom, Leg. Max. 891.

EODEM MODO QUO ORITUR, EODEM modo dissolvitur. It is discharged in the same way in which it arises. Bacon, Abr. "Release;" Cro. Eliz. 697; 2 Wm. Saund. 48. note 1; 11 Wend. (N. Y.) 28, 30; 24 Wend. (N. Y.) 294, 298.

EODEM MODO QUO QUID CONSTITUItur, eodem modo destruitur. In the same way in which anything is constituted, in that way is it destroyed. 6 Coke, 53.

EORLE (Saxon.) An earl. Blount; 1 Bl. Comm. 398.

EOTH (Saxon). Oath.

EPIMENIA. Expenses or gifts. Blount.

EPIQUEYA. In Spanish law. The benignant and prudent interpretation of the law according to the circumstances of the time, place, and person. This word is derived from the Greek, and is synonymous with the word "equity." See Murillo, notes 67, 68.

EPISCOPACY. In ecclesiastical law. A form of government by diocesan bishops; the office or condition of a bishop.

EPISCOPALIA (Law Lat.) In ecclesiastical law. Synodals, or payments due the bishop.

EPISCOPUS (Law Lat.) In civil law. A superintendent; an inspector. Those in each municipality who had the charge and oversight of the bread and other provisions which served the citizens for their daily food, were so called. Vicat; Du Cange.
A bishop. These bishops, or *episcopi*, were held to be the successors of the apostles, and have various titles at different times in history, and according to their different duties. It was applied generally to those who had authority, or were of peculiar sanctity. After the fall of the Roman empire, they came to have very considerable judicial powers. Du Cange; Vicat; Calv. Lex.

EPISCOPUS ALTERIUS MANDATO quam regis non tenetur obtemperare. A bishop need not obey any mandate save the king's. Co. Litt. 134.

EPISCOPUS PUERORUM. It was an old custom that, upon certain feasts, some lay person should plait his hair, and put on the garments of a bishop, and in them pretend to exercise episcopal jurisdiction, and do several ludicrous actions, for which reason he was called "bishop of the boys;" and this custom obtained in England long after several constitutions were made to abolish it. Blount. Such an officer is mentioned in the statutes of some of the cathedrals of the old foundation in England. Wharton.

EPISTOLA. A letter or epistle. Calv. Lex. An instrument in writing for the conveyance of lands, or the assurance of contracts. Spelman.

EPISTOLAE (Lat.) In civil law. Rescripts; opinions given by the emperors in cases submitted to them for decision.
Answers of the emperors to petitions.
The answers of counsellors (*juris consulta*), as Ulpian and others, to questions of law proposed to them, were also called *epistolae*.
Opinions written out. The term originally signified the same as *literae*. Vicat.

EPOCH, or EPOCHA. The time at which a computation is begun; the time whence dates are numbered. Enc. Lond.

EQUAL PROTECTION OF THE LAW. The guaranty of "equal protection of the laws," used in the fourteenth amendment to the Constitution of the United States, means that no person or class of persons shall be denied the same protection of the laws, which is enjoyed by other persons or other classes in the same place and in like circumstances. 272 Ill. 153.

EQUALITY. Likeness in possessing the same rights, and being liable to the same duties. See 1 Toullier, Dr. Civ. notes 170, 193.

EQUES. A knight. Used chiefly in heraldry; *miles*, being the technical legal term. 4 Inst. 5.

EQUILOCUS. An equal. It is mentioned in Simeon Dunelm, A. D. 882. Jacob.

EQUITABLE ASSETS. Such assets as are chargeable with the payment of debts or legacies in equity, and which do not fall under the description of "legal assets."
Those portions of the property which, by the ordinary rules of law, are exempt from debts, but which the testator has voluntarily charged as assets, or which, being non-existent at law, have been created in equity. Adams, Eq. 254 et seq.

EQUITABLE ASSIGNMENT. An assignment giving to the assignee a right enforceable only in equity. The term is now commonly applied to constructive assignments, though such are now generally enforceable at law. In this sense it is "such an appropriation of the subject-matter as to confer a complete and present right on the person intended to be provided for, even where the circumstances do not admit of its present exercise." 14 Wall. (U. S.) 69.

An order on a particular fund (120 U. S. 511; 78 Iowa, 426; 3 Me. 436), or an order by a creditor to pay the debt to a third person (7 Cal. 258; 18 Mass. 461; 18 Mont. 335), are examples of such assignments.

EQUITABLE CONSTRUCTION. A liberal construction, designed to reach the equities of the particular case.

EQUITABLE CONVERSION. See "Conversion."

EQUITABLE DEFENSE. A defense available only in equity, *e. g.*, duress in defense to a contract. In all states where codification prevails, the distinction between legal and equitable defenses is abolished.

EQUITABLE ELECTION. See "Election."

EQUITABLE ESTATE. A right or interest in land, which, not having the properties of a legal estate, but being merely a right of which courts of equity will take notice, requires the aid of such court to make it available.

These estates consist of uses, trusts, and powers (*q. v.*) See 2 Bouv. Inst. note 1884. They possess, in some respects, the qualities of legal estates at modern law. 1 Pet. (U. S.) 508; 13 Pick. (Mass.) 154; 5 Watts (Pa.) 113; 1 Johns. Ch. (N. Y.) 508; 2 Vern. 536; 1 Brown, 499; Williams, Real Prop. 134-136; 1 Spence, Eq. Jur. 501; 1 Washb. Real Prop. 130, 161.

EQUITABLE INTEREST. An interest which although lacking in the characteristics of a legal estate, the owner may enforce in a court of chancery. 82 Ill. 249.

EQUITABLE LIEN. One which a court of chancery recognizes, as distinct from strictly legal rights. 99 Ill. App. 243.

A lien such as exists in equity, and of which courts of equity alone take cognizance. 114 Ill. App. 564.

EQUITABLE MORTGAGE. A lien upon real estate of such a character that it is recognized in equity as a security for the payment of money, and is treated as a mortgage.

A transaction to which equity attaches the character of a mortgage, without regard to the intention of the parties. For example, a deposit of title deeds as security (Story, Eq. Jur. § 1020; 5 Wheat. [U. S.] 277), or the giving of an absolute deed as security (96 U. S. 332; 113 Mass. 149; 46 N. Y. 605).

A mortgage upon a purely equitable interest in lands.

EQUITABLE WASTE. Such acts to the detriment of the remainder or reversion as are within the legal rights of the tenant, but are not such as a prudent man would do in respect to his own property, though not necessarily done with evil motive. Equity will restrain such depredation, though no action at law would lie. 2 Story, Eq. Jur. § 915; 29 L. J. Ch. 598; 25 N. H. 361.

EQUITAS SEQUITUR LEGEM. Equity follows the law. 1 Story, Eq. Jur. 4; 5 Barb. (N. Y.) 277, 282.

EQUITATURA. In old English law. Needful equipments for riding or traveling.

EQUITY. A right which is established and enforced in accordance with the principles of equity jurisprudence under some general principle or acknowledged rule governing courts of equity. 208 Ill. 244.

A branch of remedial justice by and through which relief is afforded to suitors in the courts of equity.

In the broad sense in which this term is sometimes used, it signifies natural justice.

In a more limited application, it denotes equal justice between contending parties. This is its moral signification, in reference to the rights of parties having conflicting claims; but applied to courts and their jurisdiction and proceedings, it has a more restrained and limited signification.

One division of courts is into courts of law and courts of equity; and equity, in this relation and application, is a branch of remedial justice by and through which relief is afforded to suitors in the courts of equity.

The difference between the remedial justice of the courts of common law and that of the courts of equity is marked and material. That administered by the courts of law is limited by the principles of the common law (which are to a great extent positive and inflexible), and especially by the nature and character of the process and pleadings, and of the judgments which those courts can render; because the pleadings cannot fully present all the matters in controversy, nor can the judgments be adapted to the special exigencies which may exist in particular cases. It is not uncommon, also, for cases to fail in those courts, from the fact that too few or too many persons have been joined as parties, or because the pleadings have not been framed with sufficient technical precision.

The remedial process of the courts of equity, on the other hand, admits, and generally, requires, that all persons having an interest shall be made parties, and makes a large allowance for amendments by summoning and discharging parties after the commencement of the suit. The pleadings are usually framed so as to present to the consideration of the court the whole case, with its possible legal rights, and all its equities,—that is, all the grounds upon which the suitor is or is not entitled to relief upon the principles of equity. And its final remedial process may be so varied as to meet the requirements of these equities, in cases where the jurisdiction of the courts of equity exists, by "commanding what is right, and prohibiting what is wrong." In other words, its final process is varied so as to enable the courts to do that equitable justice between the parties which the case demands, either by commanding what is to be done, or prohibiting what is threatened to be done.

The principles upon which, and the modes and forms by and through which, justice is administered in the United States, are derived to a great extent from those which were in existence in England at the time of the settlement of this country, and it is therefore important to a correct understanding of the nature and character of our own jurisprudence, not only to trace it back to its introduction here on the early settlement of the colonies, but also to trace the English jurisprudence from its earliest inception as the administration of law founded on principles, down to that period. It is in this way that we are enabled to explain many things in our own practice which would otherwise be entirely obscure. This is particularly true of the principles which regulate the jurisdiction and practice of the courts of equity, and of the principles of equity as they are now applied and administered in the courts of law which at the present day have equitable jurisdiction conferred upon them by statutes passed for that purpose. And for the purpose of a competent understanding of the course of decisions in the courts of equity in England, it is necessary to refer to the origin of the equitable jurisdiction there, and to trace its history, inquiring upon what principles it was originally founded, and how it has been enlarged and sustained.

The study of equity jurisprudence, therefore, comprises an inquiry into the origin and history of the courts of equity; the distinctive principles upon which jurisdiction in equity is founded; the nature, character, and extent of the jurisdiction itself; its peculiar remedies; the rules and maxims which regulate its administration; its remedial process and proceedings, and modes of defense; and its rules of evidence and practice.

——**Origin and History.** The courts of equity may be said to have their origin as far back as the *aula* or *curia regis*, the great court in which the king administered justice in person, assisted by his counsellors. Of the officers of this court, the chancellor was one of great trust and confidence, next to the king himself, but his duties do not distinctly appear at the present day. On the dissolution of that court, he exercised separate duties.

On the introduction of seals, he had the keeping of the king's seal, which he affixed to charters and deeds; and he had some authority in relation to the king's grants,—perhaps annulling those which were alleged to have been procured by misrepresentation, or to have been issued unadvisedly.

As writs came into use, it was made his duty to frame and issue them from his court, which as early as the reign of Henry II. was known as the "chancery." And it is said that he exercised at this period a sort of equitable jurisdiction by which he mitigated the rigor of the common law,—to what extent it is impossible to determine. He is spoken of as one who "annuls unjust laws, and executes the rightful commands of the pious prince, and puts an end to what is injurious to the people or to morals," which would form a very ample jurisdiction; but it seems probable that this was according to the authority or direction of the king, given from time to time in relation to particular cases. He was a principal member of the king's council, after the Conquest, in which, among other things, all applications for the special exercise of the prerogative in regard to matters of judicial cognizance were discussed and decided upon. In connection with the council, he exercised a separate authority in cases in which the council directed the suitors to proceed in chancery. The court of chancery is said to have sprung from this council; but it may be said that it had its origin in the prerogative of the king, by which he undertook to administer justice, on petitions to himself, without regard to the jurisdiction of the ordinary courts, which he did through orders to his chancellor. The great council, or parliament, also sent matters relating to the king's grants, etc., to the chancery; and it seems that the chancellor, although an ecclesiastic, was the principal actor as regards the judicial business which the select or king's council, as well as the great council, had to advise upon or transact. In the reign of Edward I., the power and authority of the chancellor were extended by the statute of Westminster II.

In the time of Edward III., proceedings in chancery were commenced by petition or bill, the adverse party was summoned, the parties were examined, and chancery appears as a distinct court for giving relief in cases which required extraordinary remedies, the king having, "by a writ, referred all such matters as were of grace to be dispatched by the chancellor or by the keeper of the privy seal."

It may be considered as fully established, as a separate and permanent jurisdiction, from the 17th of Richard II.

In the time of Edward IV., the chancery had come to be regarded as one of the four principal courts of the kingdom. From this time, its jurisdiction and the progress of its jurisdiction become of more importance to us.

It is the tendency of any system of legal principles, when reduced to a practical application, to fail of effecting such justice between party and party as the special circumstances of a case may require, by reason of the minuteness and inflexibility of its rules, and the inability of the judges to adapt its remedies to the necessities of the controversy under consideration. This was the case with the Roman law, and, to remedy this, edicts were issued from time to time, which enabled the consuls and praetors to correct "the scrupulosity and mischievous subtlety of the law," and from these edicts a code of equitable jurisprudence was compiled.

So the principles and rules of the common law, as they were reduced to practice, became in their application the means of injustice in cases where special equitable circumstances existed, of which the judge could not take cognizance because of the precise nature of its titles and rights, the inflexible character of its principles, and the technicality of its pleadings and practice. And, in a manner somewhat analogous to the Roman mode of modification, in order to remedy such hardships, the prerogative of the king, or the authority of the great council, was exercised in ancient times to procure a more equitable measure of justice in the particular case, which was accomplished through the court of chancery.

This was followed by the "invention" of the writ of subpoena, by means of which the chancery assumed, upon a complaint made directly to that court, to require the attendance of the adverse party, to answer to such matters as should be objected against him. Notwithstanding the complaints of the commons, from time to time, that the course of proceeding in chancery "was not according to the course of the common law, but the practice of the holy church," the king sustained the authority of the chancellor, the right to issue the writ was recognized and regulated by statute, and other statutes were passed conferring jurisdiction where it had not been taken before. In this way, without any compilation of a code, a system of equitable jurisprudence was established in the court of chancery, enlarging from time to time; the decisions of the court furnishing an exposition of its principles, and of their application. It is said that the jurisdiction was greatly enlarged under the administration of Cardinal Wolsey, in the time of Henry VIII. A controversy took place between Chancellor Ellesmere and Lord Coke, C. J., of the king's bench, in the time of James I., respecting the right of the chancellor to interfere with the judgments of the courts of law. The king sustained the chancellor, and from that time the jurisdiction then claimed has been maintained.

It is from the study of these decisions, and the commentaries upon them, that we are enabled to determine, with a greater or less degree of certainty, the time when and the grounds upon which jurisdiction was granted or was taken in particular classes of cases, and the principles upon which it was administered. And it is occasionally of importance to attend to this; because we shall see that, chancery having once obtained jurisdiction, that jurisdiction continues until expressly taken away, notwithstanding the intervention of such changes as, if they had been made earlier, would have rendered the exercise of jurisdiction by that court incompatible with the principles upon which it is founded.

A brief sketch of some of the principal points in the origin and history of the court of chancery may serve to show that much of its jurisdiction exists independent of any statute, and is founded upon an assumption of a power to do equity, having its first inception in the prerogative of the king, and his commands to do justice in individual cases, extending itself, though the action of the chancellor, to the issue of a writ of summons to appear in his court without any special authority for that purpose, and, upon the return of the subpoena, to the reception of a complaint, to a requirement upon the party summoned to make answer to that complaint, and then to a hearing and decree, or judgment, upon the merits of the matters in controversy, according to the rules of equity and good conscience.

It appears as a noticeable fact that the jurisdiction of the chancery proceeded originally from, and was sustained by, successive kings of England against the repeated remonstrances of the commons, who were for adhering to the common law; though not perhaps, approving of all its rigors, as equity had been to some extent acknowledged as a rule of decision in the common-law courts.

This opposition of the commons may have been owing in part to the fact that the chancellor was in those days usually an ecclesiastic, and to the existing antipathy among the masses of the people to almost everything Roman.

The master of the rolls, who for a long period was a judicial officer of the court of chancery, second only to the chancellor, was originally a clerk or keeper of the rolls or records, but seems to have acquired his judicial authority from being at times directed by the king to take cognizance of and determine matters submitted to him.

——**Distinctive Principles.** It is quite apparent that some principles other than those of the common law must regulate the exercise of such a jurisdiction. That law could not mitigate its rigor upon its own principles. And as, down to the time of Edward III., and, with few exceptions, to the 21st of Henry VIII., the chancellors were ecclesiastics, much more familiar with the principles of the Roman law than with those of the common law, it was but a matter of course that there should be a larger adoption of the principles of that law, and the study of it is of some importance in this connection. Still, that law cannot be said to be of authority, even in equity proceedings. The commons were jealous of its introduction. "In the reign of Richard II., the barons protested that they would never suffer the kingdom to be governed by the Roman law, and the judges prohibited it from being any longer cited in the common-law tribunals."

This opposition of the barons and of the common-law judges furnished very sufficient reasons why the chancellors should not profess to adopt that law as the rule of decision. In addition to this, it was not fitted, in many respects, to the state of things existing in England; and so the chancellors were of necessity compelled to act upon equitable principles as expounded by themselves. In later times, the common-law judges in that country have resorted to the Roman law for principles of decision to a much greater extent than they have given credit to it.

Since the time of Henry VIII., the chancery bench has been occupied by some of the ablest lawyers which England has produced, and they have given to the proceedings and practice in equity definite rules and forms, which leave little to the personal discretion of the chancellor in determining what equity and good conscience require. The discretion of the chancellor is a judicial discretion, to be exercised according to the principles and practice of the court.

The avowed principle upon which the jurisdiction was at first exercised was the administration of justice according to honesty, equity, and conscience, which last, it is said, was unknown to the common law as a principle of decision.

In the 15th of Richard II., two petitions, addressed to the king and the lords of parliament, were sent to the chancery to be heard, with the direction, "Let there be done, by the authority of parliament, that which right and reason and good faith and good conscience demand in the case."

These may be said to be the general principles upon which equity is administered at the present day.

The distinctive principles of the courts of equity are shown, also, by the classes of cases in which they exercise jurisdiction and give relief; allowing it to be sought and administered through process and proceedings of less formality and technicality than are required in proceedings at law. This, however, has its limitations, some of its rules of pleading in defense being quite technical. And it is another peculiar feature that the relief is administered by a decree or process adapted to the exigencies of the particular case.

——**Jurisdiction.** It is difficult to reduce a jurisdiction so extensive, and of such diverse component parts, to a rigid and precise classification; but an approach to it may be made. The general nature of the jurisdiction has already been indicated. It exists—

First, for the purpose of compelling a discovery from the defendant, respecting the truth of the matters alleged against him, by an appeal to his conscience to speak the truth. The discovery is enforced by requiring an answer to the allegations in the plaintiff's complaint, in order that the plaintiff may use the matters disclosed in the answer as admissions of the defendant, and thus evidence for the plaintiff, either in connection with and in aid of other evidence offered by the plaintiff, or to supply the want of other evidence on his part; or it may be to avoid the expense to which the plaintiff must be put in procuring other evidence to sustain his case.

When the plaintiff's complaint, otherwise called a "bill," prays for relief in the same suit, the statements of the defendant in his answer are considered by the court in forming a judgment upon the whole case.

To a certain extent, the statements of the defendant in answer to the bill are evidence for himself also.

The discovery which may be required is not only of facts within the knowledge of the defendant, but may also be of deeds and other writings in his possession.

The right to discovery is not, however, an unlimited one; as, for instance, the defendant is not bound to make a discovery which would subject him to punishment, nor, ordinarily, to discover the title upon which he relies in his defense; nor is the plaintiff entitled to require the production of all papers which he may desire to look into. The limits of the right deserve careful consideration. The discovery, when had, may be the foundation of equitable relief in the same suit, in which case it may be connected with all the classes of cases in which relief is sought; or it may be for the purpose of being used in some other court, in which case the jurisdiction is designated as an "assistant jurisdiction."

Second, where the courts of law do not, or did not, recognize any right, and therefore could give no remedy, but where the courts of equity recognize equitable rights, and, of course, give equitable relief. This has been denominated the "exclusive jurisdiction." In this class are trusts, charities, forfeited and imperfect mortgages, penalties and forfeitures, imperfect consideration.

Uses and trusts have been supposed to have had their origin in the restrictions laid by parliament upon conveyances in mortmain,—that is, to the church for charitable, or rather for ecclesiastical, purposes.

It may well be that the doctrine of equitable titles and estates, unknown to the common law, but which could be enforced in chancery, had its origin in conveyances to individuals for the use of the church in order to avoid the operation of these restrictions; the conscience of the feoffee being bound to permit the church to have the use according to the design and intent of the feoffment. But conveyances in trust for the use of the church were not by any means the only cases in which it was desirable to convey the legal title to one for the use of another. In many instances, such a conveyance offered a convenient mode of making provision for those who, from any circumstances, were unable to manage property advantageously for themselves, or to whom it was not desirable to give the control of it; and the propriety in all such cases of some protection to the beneficiary is quite apparent. The court of chancery, by recognizing that he had an interest of an equitable character which could be protected and enforced against the holder of the legal title, exercised a jurisdiction to give relief in cases which the courts of common law could not reach consistently with their principles and modes of procedure.

Mortgages, which were originally estates conveyed upon condition, redeemable if the condition was performed at the day, but absolute on nonperformance, the right to redeem being thereby forfeited, owe their origin to the court of chancery, which, acting at first, perhaps, in some case where the nonperformance was by mistake or accident, soon recognized an equitable right of redemption after the day, as a general rule, in order to relieve against the forfeiture. This became known as an "equity of redemption,"—a designation in use at the present day, although there has long been a legal right of redemption in such cases.

Relief against penalties and forfeitures also was formerly obtained only through the aid of the court of chancery.

In most of the cases which fall under this head, courts of law now exercise a concurrent jurisdiction.

Third, where the courts of equity administer equitable relief for the infraction of legal rights, in cases in which the courts of law, recognizing the right, give a remedy according to their principles, modes, and forms, but the remedy is deemed by equity inadequate to the requirements of the case. This is sometimes called the "concurrent jurisdiction." This class embraces fraud, mistake, accident, administration, legacies, contribution, and cases where justice and conscience require the cancellation or reformation of instruments, or the rescission or the specific performance of contracts.

The courts of law relieve against fraud, mistake, and accident where a remedy can be had according to their modes and forms; but there are many cases in which the legal remedy is inadequate for the purposes of justice.

The modes of investigation, and the peculiar remedies of the courts of equity, are often of the greatest importance in this class of cases.

Transfers to defeat or delay creditors, and purchasers with notice of an outstanding title, come under the head of fraud.

It has been said that there is a less amount of evidence required to prove fraud, in equity, than there is at law, but the soundness of that position may well be doubted.

The court does not relieve in all cases of accident and mistake.

In many cases, the circumstances are such as to require the cancellation or reformation of written instruments, or the specific performance of contracts, instead of damages for the breach of them.

Fourth, where the court of equity administers a remedy because the relations of the parties are such that there are impediments to a legal remedy. Partnership furnishes a marked instance. Joint tenancy and marshalling of assets may be included.

From the nature of a partnership, there are impediments to suits at law between the several partners and the partnership in relation to matters involved in the partnership; and impediments of a somewhat similar character exist in other cases.

Fifth, where the forms of proceeding in the courts of law are not deemed adequate to the due investigation of the particulars and details of the case. This class includes account, partition, dower, ascertainment of boundaries.

Sixth, where, from a relation of trust and confidence, or from consanguinity, the parties do not stand on equal ground in their dealings with each other; as, the relations of parent and child, guardian and ward, attorney and client, principal and agent, executor and administrator, legatees and distributees, trustee and *cestui que trust*, etc.

Seventh, where the court grants relief from considerations of public policy, because of the mischief which would result if the court did not interfere. Marriage brokage agreements, contracts in restraint of trade, buying and selling public offices, agreements founded on corrupt considerations, usury, gaming, and contracts with expectant heirs, are of this class.

Cases of this and the preceding class are sometimes considered under the head of "constructive fraud."

Eighth, where a party, from incapacity to take care of his rights, is under the special care of the court of equity, as infants, idiots, and lunatics.

This is a branch of jurisdiction of very ancient date, and of a special character, said to be founded in the prerogative of the king.

In this country the court does not, in general, assume the guardianship, but exercises an extensive jurisdiction over guardians, and may hold a stranger interfering with the property of an infant accountable as if he were guardian.

Ninth, where the court recognizes an obligation on the part of a husband to make provision for the support of his wife, or to make a settlement upon her, out of the property which comes to her by inheritance, or otherwise.

This jurisdiction is not founded upon either trust or fraud, but is derived originally from the maxim that he who asks equity should do equity.

Tenth, where the equitable relief appropriate to the case consists in restraining the commission or continuance of some act of the defendant, administered by means of a writ of injunction.

Eleventh, the court aids in the procuration or preservation of evidence of the rights of a party, to be used, if necessary, in some subsequent proceeding, the court administering no final relief.

——**Peculiar Remedies, and the Manner of Administering Them.** Under this head are specific performance of contracts; re-execution, reformation, rescission, and cancellation of contracts or instruments; restraint by injunction; bills *quia timet;* bills of peace; protection of a party liable at law, but who has no interest, by bill of interpleader; election between two inconsistent legal rights; conversion; priorities; tacking; marshalling of securities; application of purchase money.

In recent periods, the principles of the court of chancery have in many instances been acted on and recognized by the courts of law (as, for instance, in relation to mortgages, contribution, etc.) so far as the rules of the courts of law admitted of their introduction.

In some states, the entire jurisdiction has, by statute, been conferred upon the courts of law, who exercise it as a separate and distinct branch of their authority, upon the principles and according to the modes and forms previously adopted in chancery.

In a few, the jurisdictions of the courts of law and of equity have been amalgamated, and an entire system has been substituted, administered more according to the principles and modes and forms of equity than the principles and forms of the common law.

——**Rules and Maxims.** In the administration of the jurisdiction, there are certain rules and maxims which are of special significance.

First, equity having once had jurisdiction of a subject matter because there is no remedy at law, or because the remedy is inadequate, does not lose the jurisdiction merely because the courts of law afterwards give the same or a similar relief.

Second, equity follows the law. This is true as a general maxim. Equity follows the law, except in relation to those matters which give a title to equitable relief because the rules of law would operate to sanction fraud or injustice in the particular case.

Third, when there is equal equity, the law must prevail. The ground upon which the suitor comes into the court of equity is that he is entitled to relief there. But if his adversary has an equally equitable case, the complainant has no title to relief.

Fourth, equality is equity. Applied to cases of contribution, apportionment of moneys due among those liable or benefited by the payment, abatement of claims on account of deficiency of the means of payment, etc.

Fifth, he who seeks equity must do equity. A party cannot claim the interposition of the court for relief unless he will do what it is equitable should be done by him as a condition precedent to that relief.

Sixth, equity considers that as done which ought to have been done. A maxim of much more limited application than might at first be supposed from the broad terms in which it is expressed. In favor of parties who would have had a benefit from something contracted to be done, and who have an equitable right to have the case considered as if it had been done, equity applies this maxim. Illustration: When there is an agreement for a sale of land, and the vendor dies, the land may be treated as money, and the proceeds of the sale, when completed, go to the distributees of personal estate, instead of to the heir. If the vendee dies before the completion of the purchase, the purchase money may be treated as land for the benefit of the heir.

——**Remedial Process and Defense.** A suit in equity is ordinarily instituted by a complaint or petition, called a "bill;" and the defendant is served with a writ of summons, requiring him to appear and answer, called a "subpoena."

The forms of proceedings in equity are such as to bring the rights of all persons interested before the court; and, as a general rule, all persons interested should be made parties to the bill, either as plaintiffs or defendants.

There may be amendments of the bill; or a supplemental bill, which is sometimes necessary when the case is beyond the stage for amendment.

In case the suit fails by the death of the party, there is a bill of revivor, and, after the cause is disposed of, there may be a bill of review.

The defense is made by demurrer, plea, or answer. If the defendant has no interest, he may disclaim. Discovery may be obtained from the plaintiff, and further matter may be introduced, by means of a cross bill, brought by the defendant against the plaintiff, in order that it may be considered at the same time.

If the plaintiff elects, he may file a replication to the defendant's answer.

The final process is directed by the decree, which, being a special judgment, can provide relief according to the nature of the case. This is sometimes by a perpetual injunction.

There may be a bill to execute or to impeach a decree.

——**Evidence and Practice.** The rules of evidence, except as to the effect of the answer and the taking of the testimony, are, in general, similar to the rules of evidence in cases at law; but to this there are exceptions.

The answer, if made on oath, is evidence for the defendant, so far as it is responsive to the calls of the bill for discovery, and as such it prevails, unless it is overcome by something more than what is equivalent to the testimony of one witness. If without oath, it is a mere pleading, and the allegations stand for proof.

If the answer is incomplete or improper, the plaintiff may except to it, and it must be so amended as to be made sufficient and proper.

The case may be heard on the bill and answer, if the plaintiff so elects, and sets the case down for a hearing in that mode.

If the plaintiff desires to controvert any of the statements in the answer, he files a replication by which he denies the truth of the allegations in the answer, and testimony is taken.

The testimony, according to the former practice in chancery, is taken upon interrogatories filed in the clerk's office, and propounded by the examiner, without the presence of the parties; but this practice has been very extensively modified.

If any of the testimony is improper, there is a motion to suppress it.

The case may be referred to a master to state the accounts between the parties, or to make such other report as the case may require; and there may be an examination of the parties in the master's office. Exceptions may be taken to his report.

The hearing of the case is before the equity judge, who may make interlocutory orders or decrees, and who pronounces the final decree or judgment. There may be a rehearing, if sufficient cause is shown.

At the present day, in England and in several of the United States, the proceedings are very much simplified.

EQUITY EVIDENCE. See "Evidence."

EQUITY OF A STATUTE. Where a class of cases is not within the words of a statute, but it is patent that it would have been included had it been within the mind of the legislature, it is included by construction, because it is said to be "within the equity of the statute."

EQUITY OF REDEMPTION. A right which the mortgagee of an estate has of redeeming it after it has been forfeited at law by the nonpayment, at the time appointed, of the money secured by the mortgage to be paid, by paying the amount of the debt, interest, and costs.

The phrase "equity of redemption" is indiscriminately, though often incorrectly, applied to the right of the mortgagor to regain his estate, both before and after breach of condition. In North Carolina, by statute, the former is called a "legal right of redemption," and the latter the "equity of redemption," thereby keeping a just distinction between these estates. 1 Rev. St. N. C. 266; 4 McCord (S. C.) 340. The interest is recognized at law for many purposes. As a subsisting estate, although the mortgagor, in order to enforce his right, is obliged to resort to an equitable proceeding, administered generally in courts of equity, but in some states by courts of law (11 Serg. & R. [Pa.] 223), or in some states he may pay the debt and have an action at law (18 Johns. [N. Y.] 7, 110; 1 Halst. [N. J.] 466; 2 Har. & McH. [Md.] 9).

EQUITY TO A SETTLEMENT. The right of a wife, in an action by her husband to reduce to his possession an equitable estate falling to her, to have the court inquire into the circumstances of the marriage, the marriage settlement, and the relation of the parties, and require part of the estate in controversy to be settled on her. Haynes, Eq. 114; White & T. Lead. Cas. 381.

EQUIVALENT. Of the same value. Some times a condition must be literally accomplished in *forma specifica;* but some may be fulfilled by an equivalent, *per aequipollens,* when such appears to be the intention of the parties. Rolle, Abr. 451; 1 Bouv. Inst. note 760.

——**In Patent Law.** As applied to machines, a device which performs the same result as another, in substantially the same way. 58 Fed. 281. As applied to the chemical action of fluids, it means "equally good." 7 Wall. (U. S.) 330.

EQUIVOCAL. Having a double sense.

In the construction of contracts, it is a general rule that, when an expression may be taken in two senses, that shall be preferred which gives it effect. See "Construction;" "Interpretation;" Dig. 22. 1. 4. 45. 1; Id. 80. 50. 17. 67.

EQUULEUS (Lat.) A kind of rack for extorting confessions. Enc. Lond.

ERASTIANS. The followers of Erastus. The sect obtained much influence in England, particularly among common lawyers in the time of Selden. They held that offenses against religion and morality should be punished by the civil power, and not by the censures of the church, or by excommunication. Wharton.

ERASURE. The obliteration of a writing, or part thereof. It will render it void or not under the same circumstances as an interlineation. See 5 Pet. (U. S.) 560; 11 Coke, 88; 4 Cruise, Dig. 368; 13 Viner, Abr. 41; Fitzg. 207; 5 Bing. 183; 3 Car. & P. 55; 2 Wend. (N. Y.) 555; 11 Conn. 531; 5 Mart. (La.) 190; 2 La. 291; 3 La. 56; 4 La. 270.

ERCISCUNDUS (Lat. *erciscere*). For dividing. *Familiae erciscundae actio,* an action for dividing away goods, or any matter of inheritance. Vicat; Calv. Lex.

EREGIMUS (Lat. we have erected). A word proper to be used in the creation of a new office by the sovereign. Bac. Abr. "Offices" (E).

ERGO (Lat.) Therefore.

ERGOLABI. In civil law. Undertakers of work; contractors. Code, 4, 59.

ERIACH. In the Brehon law. A pecuniary satisfaction or recompense, corresponding in some degree with the weregild of the Saxon law, which a party guilty of murder was condemned to pay to the wife or child or friends of the deceased. 4 Bl. Comm. 313. The same, probably, with *enach*, in old Scotch law. Skene de Verb. Sign. voc. "Enach."

EROSION. The gradual eating away of the soil by the operation of currents or tides. 100 N. Y. 433. It is distinguished from submergence (*q. v.*), and opposed to alluvion (*q. v.*)

EROTIC MANIA. In medical jurisprudence. A name given to a morbid activity of the sexual propensity. It is a disease or morbid affection of the mind, which fills it with a crowd of voluptuous images, and hurries its victim to acts of the grossest licentiousness, in the absence of any lesion of the intellectual powers. See "Mania."

Distinct from "nymphomania" (*q. v.*)

ERRANT Lat. *errare*, to wander). Wandering. Justices in eyre were formerly said to be *errant* (itinerant). Cowell.

ERRATICUM (Law Lat.) In old law. A waif or stray. Cowell.

ERRONICE (Lat.) Erroneously; through mistake. Yelv. 83.

ERROR. See "Mistake."

ERROR FUCATUS NUDA VERITATE in multis est probabilior, et saepe numero rationbus vincit veritatem error. Error artfully colored is in many things more probable than naked truth, and frequently error conquers truth by argumentation. 2 Coke, 73.

ERROR JURIS NOCET. Error of law is injurious. See 4 Bouv. Inst. note 3828; 1 Story, Eq. Jur. § 139, note.

ERROR NOMINIS NUNQUAM NOCET, si de identitate rei constat. Mistake in the name never injures, if there is no doubt as to the identity of the thing. 1 Duer, Ins. 171.

ERROR QUI NON RESISTITUR, APPROBatur. An error not resisted is approved. Doctor & Stud. c. 70.

ERROR SCRIBENTIS NOCERE NON debet. An error made by a clerk ought not to injure; a clerical error may be corrected. 1 Jenk. Cent. Cas. 324.

ERROR, WRIT OF. See "Writ of Error."

ERRORES AD SUA PRINCIPIA REFerre, est refellere. To refer errors to their origin is to refute them. 3 Inst. 15.

ERRORS EXCEPTED. A phrase appended to an account stated, in order to excuse slight mistakes or oversights. Often written "E. & O. E.," meaning errors and omissions excepted.

ERRORS OF LAW. When a person is truly acquainted with the existence or nonexistence of the facts, but is ignorant of the legal consequences, he is under an error of law. 1 Wend. (N. Y.) 360.

ERTHMIOTUM. In old English law. A meeting of the neighborhood to compromise differences among themselves, a court held on the boundary of two lands.

ERUBESCIT LEX FILIOS CASTIGARE parentes. The law blushes when children correct their parents. 8 Coke, 116.

ESBRANCATURA. Cutting off branches or boughs in forests, etc. Hov. Ann. 784.

ESCALDARE. To scald. It is said that to scald hogs was one of the ancient tenures in serjeanty.

ESCAMBIO. In old English law. A writ granting power to an English merchant to draw a bill of exchange on another who is in a foreign country. Reg. Orig. 194.

ESCAMBIUM. Exchange. (*q. v.*)

ESCAPE.

——**From Bodily Harm.** The ancient doctrine of the common law that the right of self-defense did not arise until every effort to escape, even to retreating until an impassable wall or something of that nature had been reached, has been supplanted in America by the doctrine that a man, if unlawfully assaulted in a place where he has a right to be, and put in danger, real or reasonably apparent, of losing his life or receiving great bodily harm, is not required to endeavor to escape from his assailant, but may stand his ground, and repel force with force, even to the taking of the life of his assailant, if necessary or in good reason apparently necessary, for the preservation of his own life or to protect himself from receiving great bodily harm. It is not necessary to the right of self-defense that a party having otherwise the right to exercise it, cannot "escape" the danger by fleeing from his assailant. 199 Ill. 173.

——**Of Prisoner.** The deliverance of a person, who is lawfully imprisoned, out of a prison, before such a person is entitled to such deliverance by law. 5 Mass. 310.

When one who is arrested gains his liberty before he is delivered in due course of law. 107 N. C. 858.

Departure of a prisoner from custody before he is discharged by due process of law.

Escape takes place without force; prison breach, with violence; rescue, through the intervention of third parties.

——**Actual Escapes.** Those which take place when the prisoner in fact gets out of prison, and unlawfully regains his liberty.

——**Constructive Escapes.** These take place when the prisoner obtains more liberty than the law allows, although he still remains in confinement. Bac. Abr. "Escape" (B); Plowd. 17; 5 Mass. 310; 2 Mason (U. S.) 486. This distinction obtains only as to arrest in civil actions.

——**Negligent Escape.** This takes place when the prisoner goes at large, unlawfully, either because the building or prison in which he is confined is too weak to hold him, or because the keeper, by carelessness, lets him go out of prison.

——**Voluntary Escape.** This takes place when the prisoner has given to him voluntarily any liberty not authorized by law. 5 Mass. 310; 2 N. Chip. (Vt.) 11; 25 N. H. 458.

ESCAPE WARRANT. A warrant issued in England against a person who, being charged in custody in the king's bench or Fleet prison, in execution or mesne process, escapes and goes at large. Jacob.

ESCAPIO QUIETUS. Delivered from that punishment which, by the laws of the forest, lay upon those whose beasts were found upon forbidden land. Jacob.

ESCAPIUM (Law Lat.) An escape. Reg. Orig. 312.

That which comes by chance or accident. Cowell.

ESCEPPA. A measure of corn. Cowell.

ESCHAETAE VULGO DICUNTUR QUAE decidentibus iis quae de rege tenent, cum non existit ratione sanguinis haeres, ad fiscum relabuntur. Those things are commonly called "escheats" which revert to the exchequer from a failure of issue in those who hold of the king, when there does not exist any heir by consanguinity. Co. Litt. 13.

ESCHEAT (Fr. *escheoir*, to happen).

——**Under the Feudal System.** An obstruction of the course of descent, and a consequent determination of the tenure by some unforeseen contingency, in which case the land naturally reverts back to the original grantor or lord of the fee. 2 Bl. Comm. 244.

Escheat grows out of the doctrine of tenure, which is the foundation of the feudal system, whereby a man was not an owner of land, but only of a demesne estate therein, based on allegiance to a superior lord.

Escheat is to be distinguished from "forfeiture." Forfeiture of land for crime was part of the Saxon system, and was not a consequence of any lordship paramount. It was not superseded by the introduction of the Norman tenures from which escheat resulted. "Escheat therefore operates in subordination to this more ancient and superior law of forfeiture." 2 Bl. Comm. 251.

The principal grounds of escheat were death intestate without heirs, alienage, illegitimacy, and attainder. 2 Bl. Comm. 246; 4 Kent, Comm. 424. Only the first two are generally in force in the United States, the third being generally abolished by statute, and the fourth by Const. U. S. art. 1, § 9, subd. 3. See 9 Mass. 363.

——**In Modern Law.** The reversion of land to the state by reason of failure of heirs or of the owner's incapacity to hold.

ESCHEAT, WRIT OF. A writ which anciently lay for a lord, to recover possession of lands that had escheated to him. Reg. Orig. 164b; Fitzh. Nat. Brev. 143; Termes de la Ley; 2 Bl. Comm. 245; 3 Bl. Comm. 194. Now abolished. 1 Steph. Comm. 401, note.

ESCHEATOR. The name of an officer whose duties are generally to ascertain what escheats have taken place, and to prosecute the claim of the sovereign for the purpose of recovering the escheated property. 10 Viner, Abr. 158; Co. Litt. 13b; Tomlins; Termes de la Ley. His office was to be retained but one year, and no one person could hold the office more than once in three years. Termes de la Ley.

ESCHECCUM. A jury or inquisition. Matt. Par.

ESCHIPARE. To build or equip. Du Cange.

ESCRIBANO. In Spanish law. The public officer who is lawfully authorized to reduce to writing and verify by his signature all judicial acts and proceedings, as well as all acts and contracts entered into between private individuals.

ESCRITURA. In Spanish law. A written instrument. Every deed that is made by the hand of a public *escribano*, or notary of a corporation or council (*concejo*), or sealed with the seal of the king or other authorized persons. White, New Recop. bk. 3, tit. 7, c. 5.

ESCROW. The delivery of a deed or other instrument (31 Ill. 538), actually executed and ready for delivery (42 Wis. 440) to a stranger to the instrument (13 Ohio St. 254), to be by him delivered to the person for whose benefit it is made, on the performance of a condition, or the happening of a contingency (90 Ala. 294), or to be redelivered to the depositor on failure thereof (24 Neb. 86).

ESCROWL. In old English law. An escrow; a scroll. "And deliver the deed to a stranger, as an escrowl." Perk. c. 1, § 9; Id. c. 2, §§ 137, 138.

ESCUAGE. In old English law. Service of the shield. Tenants who hold their land by escuage hold by knight's service. 1 Thomas, Co. Litt. 272; Litt. § 95, 86b.

ESKIPPAMENTUM. Tackle or furniture; outfit. Certain towns in England were bound to furnish certain ships at their own expense, and with double skippage or tackle. The modern word "outfit" would seem to render the passage quite as satisfactorily, though the conjecture of Cowell has the advantage of antiquity.

ESKIPPER, or ESKIPPARE. To ship. Kelham; Rast. Entr. 409.

ESKIPPESON. Shippage, or passage by sea. Spelled, also, "skippeson." Cowell.

ESLISORS. See "Elisors."

ESNE. In old law. A hireling of servile condition.

ESNECY. Eldership. In the English law, this word signifies the right which the eldest coparcener of lands has to choose one of the parts of the estate after it has been divided.

ESPERA. The period fixed by a competent judge within which a party is to do certain acts, as, *e. g.*, to effect certain payments, present documents, etc.; and more especially the privilege granted by law to debtors, allowing them certain time for the payment of their indebtedness.

ESPERONS. Spurs. 7 Coke, 13.

ESPLEES. The products which the land or ground yields; as, the hay of the meadows, the herbage of the pasture, corn or other produce of the arable, rents and services. Termes de la Ley. See 11 Serg. & R. (Pa.) 275; Dane, Abr. Index.

ESPOUSALS. A mutual promise between a man and a woman to marry each other at some other time. It differs from a marriage, because then the contract is completed. Wood, Inst. 57.

ESPURIO (Spanish). A spurious child; one begotten on a woman who has promiscuous intercourse with many men. White, New Recop. bk. 1, tit. 5, c. 2, § 1.

ESQUIRE. A title applied by courtesy to officers of almost every description, to members of the bar, and others. No one is entitled to it by law, and therefore it confers no distinction in law.

In England, it is a title next above that of a gentleman, and below that of a knight. Camden reckons up four kinds of esquires particularly regarded by the heralds: The eldest sons of knights, and their eldest sons in perpetual succession; the eldest sons of the younger sons of peers, and their eldest sons in like perpetual succession; esquires created by the king's letters patent, or other investiture, and their eldest sons; esquires by virtue of their office, as justices of the peace, and others who bear any office of trust under the crown.

ESSARTER (Law Fr.) To cut down woods; to clear land of trees and underwood; properly to thin woods by cutting trees, etc., at intervals. Spelman. Commonly written "assart" (*q. v.*)

ESSARTUM. Assarted or cleared woodland.

ESSENCE OF THE CONTRACT. A stipulation is said to be "of the essence of the contract" when a strict compliance with its terms is essential to due performance.

ESSENDI QUIETAM DE THEOLONIA (Lat. of being quit of toll). A writ which lay anciently for the citizens of burgesses of a town which was entitled to exemption from toll, in case toll was demanded of them. Fitzh. Nat. Brev. 226 (I).

ESSOIN, or ESSOIGN. In old English law. An excuse for not appearing in court at the return of the process; presentation of such excuse. Spelman; 1 Sellon, Prac. 4; Comyn, Dig. "Exoine" (B 1). Essoin is not now allowed at all in personal actions. 2 Term R. 16; 16 East, 7 (a); 3 Sharswood, Bl. Comm. 278, note.

ESSOIN DAY. Formerly, the first day in the term was essoin day; now practically abolished. Dowl. 448; 3 Sharswood, Bl. Comm. 278, note.

ESSOIN DE MALO VILLAE. When the defendant is in court the first day, but gone without pleading, and being afterwards surprised by sickness, etc., cannot attend, he may send two essoiners, who openly protest in court that he is detained by sickness in such a village, that he cannot come *pro lucrari* and *pro perdere;* and this will be admitted, for it lieth on the plaintiff to prove whether the essoin is true or not. Jacob.

ESSOIN ROLL. The roll containing the essoins and the day of adjournment. Roscoe, Real Actions, 162 et seq.

ESSOINIATOR, or ESSOINEOUR. An essioner. One who was sent to present an excuse for another. 1 Reeve, Hist. Eng. Law, 116, 118.

EST ALIQUID QUOD NON OPORTET, etiam si licet; quicquid vero non licet certe non oportet. There are some things which are not proper, though lawful; but certainly those things are not proper which are not lawful. Hob. 159.

EST ASCAVOIR (Lat.) It is to be understood or known; "it is to wit." Litt. §§ 9, 45, 46, 57, 59. A very common expression in Littleton, especially at the commencement of a section; and, according to Lord Coke, "it ever teacheth us some rule of law, or general or sure leading point." Co. Litt. 16. It seems to be derived from the *sciendum est (q. v.)* of the civil law.

EST AUTEM JUS PUBLICUM ET PRIvatum, quod ex naturalibus praeceptis aut gentium, aut civium est collectum; et quod in jure scripto jus appellatur, id in lege Angliae rectum esse dicitur. Public and private law is that which is collected from natural precepts, on the one hand of nations, on the other of citizens; and that which in the civil law is called *jus*, that in the law of England is said to be right. Co. Litt. 558.

EST AUTEM VIS LEGEM SIMULANS. Violence may also put on the mask of law.

EST BONI JUDICIS AMPLIARE JURISdictionem. It is the part of a good judge to extend the jurisdiction. Gilb. 14.

EST IPSORUM LEGISLATORUM TANquam viva vox; rebus et non verbis legem imponimus. The utterance of legislators themselves is like the living voice; we impose law upon things, not upon words. 10 Coke, 101.

EST QUIDDAM PERFECTIUS IN REbus licitis. There is something more perfect in things allowed. Hob. 159.

ESTABLISH. This word occurs frequently in the constitution of the United States, and it is there used in different meanings: (1) To settle firmly, to fix unalterably; as, to establish justice, which is the avowed object of the constitution. (2) To make or form; as, to establish a uniform rule of naturalization, and uniform laws on the subject of bankruptcies,—which evidently does not mean that these laws shall be unalterably established as justice. (3) To found, to create, to regulate; as, congress shall have power to establish post roads and post offices. (4) To found, recognize, confirm, or admit; as, congress shall make no law respecting an establishment of religion. (5) To create, to ratify, or confirm; as, "We, the people, etc., do ordain and establish this constitution." 1 Story, Const. § 454.

ESTABLISHMENT, or ESTABLISSEment. An ordinance or statute. Especially used of those ordinances or statutes passed in the reign of Edw. I. 2 Inst. 156; Britt. c. 21.

Establissement is also used to denote the settlement of dower by the husband upon his wife. Britt. c. 102.

ESTABLISHMENT OF DOWER. The assurance of dower made by the husband, or his friends, before or at the time of the marriage. Britt. cc. 102, 103.

ESTADAL. In Spanish law. In Spanish America this was a measure of land of sixteen square varas, or yards. 2 White, New Recop. 139.

ESTADIA. In Spanish law. The time for which the party who has chartered a vessel, or is bound to receive the cargo, has to pay demurrage on account of his delay in the execution of the contract. Called, also, *sobrestadia*.

ESTATE BY ELEGIT. See "Elegit."

ESTATE BY STATUTE MERCHANT. An estate whereby the creditor, under the custom of London, retained the possession of all his debtor's lands until his debts were paid. 1 Greenl. Cruise, Dig. 515. See "Statute Merchant."

ESTATE IN VADIO. An estate in pledge.

ESTATE TAIL, QUASI. When a tenant for life grants his estate to a man and his heirs, as these words, though apt and proper to create an estate tail, cannot do so, because the grantor, being only tenant for life, cannot grant *in perpetuum*, therefore they are said to create an estate tail *quasi*, or improper. Brown.

ESTATE UPON CONDITION. See "Condition."

ESTATES. The quantum and duration of proprietary rights in lands, tenements, and hereditaments; the theory of the common law being that the tenant or owner is entitled to an estate in the land rather than to the land iself. This doctrine of estates was not found in the Roman law, or the systems derived therefrom, and apparently owes its place in our law to the prevalence in England of the feudal system of tenures, by which the tenant was regarded as having interest short of absolute ownership, the landlord having a possibility of a reversion to him by the termination of the tenant's interest. Tiffany, Real Prop. § 17.

The various estates, classified with reference to their quantum or duration, may be tabulated as follows:

- I. Freehold estates.
  - A. Estates of inheritance.
    - (1) Fee simple.
    - (2) Fee tail.
  - B. Estates not of inheritance (life estates).
    - (1) Conventional life estates.
      - (a) Estates for life of the tenant.
      - (b) Estates *pur autre vie*.
    - (2) Legal life estates.
      - (a) Tenancy in tail after possibility of issue extinct.
      - (b) Dower.
      - (c) Curtesy.
      - (d) Estate during coverture.
- II. Estates less than freehold (leasehold estates, chattels real).
  - A. Estates for years.
  - B. Tenancy at will.
  - C. Tenancy from year to year.
  - D. Tenancy by sufferance.

Estates classified according as they give rights of present or future enjoyment are:

- I. Present estates.
- II. Future estates.
  - A. Reversions.
  - B. Remainders.
  - C. Contingent uses.
  - D. Springing uses.
  - E. Shifting uses.
  - F. Executory devises.

Classified according as they are owned by one or more persons, and according to the nature of the rights of several owners, they are:

I. Estates in severalty.

II. Joint estates.

A. Joint tenancy.

B. Tenancy in common.

C. Tenancy in coparcenary.

D. Tenancy in entirety.

——**Freehold.** An estate of freehold is one which is to endure for an uncertain period, which must, or at least may, last during the life of some person.

——**Estate of Inheritance.** An estate of inheritance is any estate which may descend to heirs. 1 Washb. Real Prop. 51. All freehold estates are estates of inheritance except estates for life. Crabb, Real Prop. § 945.

——**Estates in Fee Simple.** An estate in fee simple is that which a man has where lands are given to him and to his heirs absolutely, without any end or limit put to his estate. 2 Bl. Comm. 106; 1 Washb. Real Prop. 51.

The word "simple" does not add any significance, but is used to mark fully the distinction between an unqualified fee and any class of conditional estates.

——**Estate in Fee Tail.** An estate in fee tail or estate tail is an estate of inheritance which, if left to itself, will, after the death of the first owner, descend to his lawful issue as long as his posterity endures in a regular order of descent from one to another, and will terminate on the failure of such posterity. It derives its existence from the statute *de donis (q. v.)*

——**Estate for Life.** An estate for life is a freehold interest which cannot extend beyond the life or lives of some particular person or persons, but which may possibly endure for the period of such life or lives. The estate is generally for the tenant's own life, but made for the life of another person or persons, in which case it is called an estate *pur autre vie*.

——**Tenancy in Tail after Possibility of Issue Extinct.** Tenancy in tail after possibility of issue extinct is where, upon the death of the appointed wife of a donee in special tail, or of one of two donees in special tail without issue living, the donee or survivor of the two donees takes for his life, possibility of issue being extinct.

——**Dower.** An estate in dower is an estate which a widow has for her life in some portion of the lands and tenements of which her husband was seised at any time during coverture, and which her issue might have inherited if she had had any. 1 Washb. Real Prop. 149; 2 Bl. Comm. 129; 4 Kent, Comm. 41. See "Dower."

——**Curtesy.** An estate by curtesy is that estate to which a husband is entitled upon the death of his wife in the lands or tenements of which she was seised in fee in possession during their coverture, provided they have had lawful issue born alive, and possibly capable of inheriting her estate. 1 Washb. Real Prop. 128; Co. Litt. 30a; 2 Bl. Comm. 126. See "Curtesy."

——**Estate during Coverture.** An estate during coverture is that right or interest which a husband or wife has during coverture in the lands and tenements of his or her spouse.

——**Estate for Years.** An estate for years is an interest in lands by virtue of a contract for the possession of them for a definite and limited period of time. 2 Bl. Comm. 140. See "Tenancy."

——**Tenancy at Will.** An estate at will is an estate in lands which the tenant has, by entry made thereon under a demise, to hold during the joint wills of the parties to the same. 2 Bl. Comm. 145. See "Tenancy."

——**Tenancy from Year to Year.** A tenancy from year to year is an interest in lands for a term of one year certain, continuing for successive years, unless due notice be given to determine it at the end of the first or any subsequent year. See "Tenancy."

——**Tenancy by Sufferance.** An estate at sufferance is the interest of a tenant who has come rightfully into the possession of lands by permission of the owner, and continues to occupy the same after the period for which he is entitled to hold by such permission. 1 Washb. Real Prop. 392. See "Tenancy."

——**Estate in Possession.** An estate in possession is an estate where the tenant is in actual possession of the premises, or in receipt of the rents and other advances arising therefrom. 2 Bl. Comm. 163.

——**Estate in Expectancy.** An estate in expectancy is one giving a present or vested contingent right of future enjoyment. See "Expectancy."

——**Reversion.** An estate in reversion is the residue of an estate left in the grantor to commence in possession after the determination of some particular estate granted out by him. 2 Bl. Comm. 175. See "Reversion."

——**Remainders.** An estate in remainder is an estate limited to take effect in possession or in enjoyment, or in both, subject to a term of years or contingent interest to intervene, which intermediate interest is created by the same instrument out of the same subject of property. 2 Fearne, Cont. Rem. § 159. See "Remainder."

——**Springing, Shifting, and Contingent Uses.** See "Uses."

——**Executory Devises.** See "Devise."

——**Estate in Severalty.** An estate in severalty is one held by a person in his own right, without any other person being joined or connected with him in point of interest during his estate. 2 Bl. Comm. 179.

——**Joint Estate.** A joint estate is one in which two or more persons are joined in interest.

——**Joint Tenancy.** An estate of joint tenancy is that which subsists where several persons have any subject of property jointly between them in equal shares by purchase. 1 Bl. Comm. 180; Williams, Real Prop. 112. There must be unity of time, title, interest, and possession. See "Joint Tenants."

——**Tenancy in Common.** An estate in common one held in joint possession by two or more persons at the same time by several and distinct titles. This estate has the single unity of possession. 2 Bl. Comm. 191; 4 Kent, Comm. 366. See "Tenants in Common."

——**Estate in Coparcenary.** An estate which several persons hold as one heir, whether male or female. This estate has unity of time, title and possession, but the interest of the coparceners may be unequal. 2 Bl. Comm. 188; 4 Kent, Comm. 366.

——**Tenancy in Entirety.** The estate arising on a conveyance to a man and his wife jointly. They are seised, not of moieties, but of entireties. 16 Mass. 480; 14 N. Y. 430.

ESTATES OF THE REALM. The lords spiritual, the lords temporal, and the commons of Great Britain. 1 Bl. Comm. 153. Sometimes called the "three estates."

ESTER IN JUDGMENT. To appear before a tribunal either as plaintiff or defendant.

ESTOPPEL. The preclusion of a person from asserting a fact by previous conduct, inconsistent therewith, on his own part, or the part of those under whom he claims, or by a solemn establishment, which he cannot be allowed to call in question.

A preclusion, in law, which prevents a man from alleging or denying a fact, in consequence of his own previous act, allegation, or denial of a contrary tenor. Steph. Pl. 239.

"Estoppe cometh of the French word *estoupe*, from whence the English word 'stopped,' and it is called an 'estoppel' or 'conclusion' because a man's own act or acceptance stoppeth his mouth to allege or plead the truth." Co. Litt. 352a.

Estoppel is either by record, by deed, or by facts *in pais*.

(1) Estoppel by record is the preclusion of one to deny that which either appears by the roll of a legislature, or has been adjudicated by a court of competent jurisdiction. See "Former Adjudication."

(2) Estoppel by deed is the preclusion of one to deny that which he has asserted by an agreement or conveyance under seal. See 7 Conn. 214; 13 Pick. (Mass.) 670; 62 Ill. 344; 18 Johns. (N. Y.) 492.

(3) Estoppel by facts *in pais*, commonly called "estoppel *in pais*," is the preclusion of one to deny that which, by his conduct, he may have induced another to believe and act on to his prejudice. 129 Ill. 657; 60 Minn. 331; 22 N. J. Law, 619; 46 Ohio St. 255.

In the early common law, estoppel *in pais* was practically unrecognized (27 Conn. 282), the present doctrine being of equitable creation.

ESTOVERIA SUNT ARDENDI, ARANDI, construendi, et claudendi. Estovers are for burning, ploughing, building, and inclosing. 13 Coke, 68.

ESTOVERIIS HABENDIS. A writ which anciently lay for a wife, judicially separated from her husband, to recover her alimony or estovers.

ESTOVERS (*estouviers*, necessaries; from *estoffer*, to furnish). The right or privilege which a tenant has to furnish himself with so much wood from the demised premises as may be sufficient or necessary for his fuel, fences, and other agricultural operations. 2 Bl. Comm. 35; Woodf. Landl. & Ten. 232; 10 Wend. (N. Y.) 639.

ESTRAY. An animal of value, not wild, found wandering from its owner; cattle whose owner is unknown. 2 Kent, Comm. 359.

It is essential (1) that the animal should be by its nature tame or reclaimable (1 Bl. Comm. 298); (2) that it should be an animal upon which the law sets a value (Id.); (3) that it should not only be away from the owner, but running at large (36 N. J. Law, 235). The manner in which the animal escaped from the owner has been said to be immaterial. 70 Iowa, 509. But see 63 Ill. 88.

ESTREAT. A true copy or note of some original writing or record, and especially of fines and amercements imposed by a court, extracted from the record, and certified to a proper officer or officers, authorized and required to collect them. Fitzh. Nat. Brev. 57, 76. A forfeited recognizance taken out from among the other records for the purpose of being sent up to the exchequer, that the parties might be sued thereon, was said to be estreated. 4 Bl. Comm. 253.

ESTRECIATUS. Straightened, as applied to roads. Cowell.

ESTREPE. To strip; to commit waste.

ESTREPEMENT. A common-law writ for the prevention of waste.

The writ lay at common law to prevent a party in possession from committing waste on an estate the title to which was disputed, after judgment obtained in any real action, and before possession was delivered by the sheriff. But, as waste might be committed in some cases pending the suit, the statute of Gloucester gave another writ of estrepement *pendente placito*, commanding the sheriff firmly, to inhibit the tenant *"ne faciat vastum vel strepementum pendente placito dicto indiscusso."* By virtue of either of these writs, the sheriff may resist those who commit waste, or offer to do so; and he might use sufficient force for the purpose. 3 Bl. Comm. 225, 226.

This writ is sometimes directed to the sheriff and the party in possession of the lands, in order to make him amenable to the court as for a contempt in case of his disobedience to the injunction of the writ. At common law, the process proper to bring the tenant into court is a *venire facias*, and thereon an attachment. Upon the defendant's coming in, the plaintiff declares against him. The defendant usually pleads "that he has done no waste contrary to the prohibition of the writ." The issue on this plea is tried by a jury, and, in case they find against the defendant, they assess damages which the plaintiff recovers. But, as this verdict convicts the defendant of a contempt, the court proceed against him for that cause as in other cases. 2 Inst. 329; Rast. Entr. 317; Moore, 100; 1 Bos. & P. 121; 2 Lilly, Reg.; 5 Coke, 119; Reg. Brev. 76, 77.

In Pennsylvania, by legislative enactment, the remedy by estrepement is extended for the benefit of any owner of land leased for years or at will, at any time during the continuance or after the expiration of such demise, and due notice given to the tenant to leave the same, agreeably to law; or for any purchaser at sheriff or coroner's sale of lands, etc., after he has been declared the highest bidder by the sheriff or coroner; or for any mortgagee or judgment creditor, after the lands bound by such judgment or mortgage shall have been condemned by inquisition, or which may be subject to be sold by a writ of *venditioni exponas* or *levari facias*. See 10 Viner, Abr. 497; Woodf. Landl. & Ten. 447; Archb. Civ. Pl. 17; 7 Comyn. Dig. 659.

ET (Lat.) And.

ET ADJOURNATUR (or **ADJORNATUR**) (Law Lat. and it is adjourned). A phrase used in the old reports, where the argument of a cause was adjourned to another day, or where a second argument was had. Y. B. T. 3 Edw. III. 37; 1 Keb. 692, 754, 773; Keilw. 65; Hardr. 68; Cro. Eliz. 180; T. Raym. 55. See "Adjournatur."

ET AL. Abbreviation of *et alius*, or *alium*, and another. *Et als.*, abbreviation of *et alios*, and others.

Abbreviations used in entitling causes where there are two or more parties.

ET ALII E CONTRA (Lat. and others on the other side). A phrase constantly used in the Year Books, in describing a joinder in issue. Y. B. P. 1 Edw. II. *Prist; et alii e contra, et sic ad patriam*, ready; and others, *e contra*, and so to the country. Y. B. T. 3 Edw. III. 4.

ET DE CEO SE METTENT EN LE PAYS (Law Fr.) And of this they put themselves upon the country. Fet. Assaver, § 64.

ET DE HOC PONIT SE SUPER PATRIAM (Lat. and of this he puts himself upon the country). The Latin form of concluding a traverse. See 3 Bl. Comm. 313.

ET EI LEGITUR IN HAEC VERBA (Law Lat. and it is read to him in these words). Words formerly used in entering the prayer of oyer on record.

ET HABEAS IBI TUNC HOC BREVE (Law Lat. and have you then there this writ). A clause in old writs, expressive of the command to return to them. Reg. Jud. 1; Fleta, lib. 2, c. 64, § 19; Towns. Pl. 166. Literally translated in the modern forms.

ET HABUIT (Lat. and he had it). A common phrase in the Year Books, expressive of the allowance of an application or demand by a party. Parn. *demanda la view. Et habuit*, etc. Y. B. M. 6 Edw. III. 49.

ET HOC PARATUS EST VERIFICARE (Lat. and this he is prepared to verify). The Latin form of concluding a plea in confession and avoidance; that is, where the defendant has confessed all that the plaintiff has set forth, and has pleaded new matter in avoidance. 1 Salk. 2.

ET HOC PETIT QUOD INQUIRATUR per patriam (Lat. and this he prays may be inquired into by his country). The conclusion of a plea tendering an issue to the country. 1 Salk. 3.

ET INDE PETIT JUDICIUM (Lat. and thereupon [or thereof] he prays judgment). A clause at the end of pleadings, praying the judgment of the court in favor of the party pleading. It occurs as early as the time of Bracton, and is literally translated in the modern forms. Bracton, fol. 57b; Crabb, Hist. Eng. Law, 217.

ET INDE PRODUCIT SECTAM (Lat. and thereupon he brings suit). The Latin conclusion of a declaration, except against attorneys and other officers of the court. 3 Sharswood, Bl. Comm. 295.

ET MODO AD HUNC DIEM (Lat. and now at this day). The Latin form of the commencement of the record on appearance of the parties.

ET NON (Lat. and not). These words are sometimes employed in pleading to convey a pointed denial. They have the same effect as "without this," *absque hoc.*

ET SEQ. (Lat. *et sequentia*, and following). Ordinarily used with a reference to the first of several consecutive pages or chapters desired to be cited, as "page 246 et seq."

ET SIC (Law Lat. and so). The commencement of a formula, as, *et sic nil debet, et sic non est factum*, formerly used as a special conclusion to a plea in bar, in order to render it positive, and to avoid the fault of argumentativeness. Archb. Civ. Pl. 224; Mansel, Demurrer, 75.

ET SIC AD JUDICIUM. And so to judgment. Y. B. T. 1 Edw. II. 10.

ET SIC AD PATRIAM (Law Lat. and so to the country). A common phrase in the Year Books, in recording an issue to the country. *Il ne dona pas, prist, etc., et alii e contra; et sic ad patriam.* Y. B. M. 3 Edw. III. 29.

ET SIC FECIT (Lat.) And he did so. Y. B. P. 9 Hen. VI. 17.

ET SIC PENDET (Lat. and so it hangs). A term used in the old reports to signify that a point was left undetermined. T. Raym. 168. *Et sic pendet placitum,* and so the plea hangs. Y. B. T. 1 Edw. II. 8.

ET SIC ULTERIUS (Lat.) And so on; and so further; and so forth. Fleta, lib. 2, c. 50, § 27.

ET UX (Lat.) Abbreviation for *et uxor,* —"and wife."

ETCAETERA (Lat. and others; and other things). The abbreviation *etc.* was formerly much used in pleading to avoid the inconveniences attendant upon making full and half defense. See "Defense." It is not generally to be used in solemn instruments. See 6 Serg. & R. (Pa.) 427.

EUM QUI NOCENTEM INFAMAT, NON est aequum et bonum ob eam rem condemnari; delicta enim nocentium nota esse oportet et expedit. It is not just and proper that he who speaks ill of a bad man should be condemned on that account; for it is fitting and expedient that the crimes of bad men should be known. Dig. 47. 10. 17; 1 Bl. Comm. 125.

EUNDO, MORANDO ET REDEUNDO (Lat.) This Latin phrase signifies going, remaining, and returning. It is employed in cases where a person, either as a party, a witness, or one acting in some other capacity, as an elector, is privileged from arrest, in order to give him the freedom necessary to the performance of his respective obligations, to signify that he is protected from arrest *eundo, morando et redeundo.* See 3 Bouv. Inst. note 3380.

EUNOMY. Equal laws and a well-adjusted constitution of government.

EUNUCH. A male whose organs of generation have been so far removed or disorganized that he is rendered incapable of reproducing his species. Domat, Civ. Law, liv. prel. tit. 2, § 1, note 10.

EVASIO (Lat.) In old practice. Escape; an escape from prison or custody. Reg. Orig. 312; Fleta, lib. 1, c. 26, § 4.

EVASION (Lat. *evadere,* to avoid). A subtle device to set aside the truth or escape the punishment of the law; as, if a man should tempt another to strike him first, in order that he might have an opportunity of returning the blow with impunity. He is, nevertheless, punishable, because he becomes himself the aggressor in such a case. It is not a technical term. Hawk. P. C. c. 31, §§ 24, 25; Bac. Abr. "Fraud" (A).

EVENTUS EST QUI EX CAUSA SEQUItur; et dicitur eventus quia ex causis evenit. An event in that which follows from the cause, and is called an "event" because it eventuates from causes. 9 Coke, 81.

EVENTUS VARIOS RES NOVA SEMper habet. A new matter always produces various events. Co. Litt. 379.

EVERY. Every was formerly spelt "everich," that is, ever each, and the true meaning is "each one of all." 2 De G. F. & J. 172.

EVICTION. Depriving a person of the possession of his lands or tenements. Technically, the dispossession must be by judgment of law; if otherwise, it is an *ouster* (32 Iowa, 71), but in modern usage it is commonly applied to dispossession in any manner (44 N. Y. 382; 39 Cal. 360; 98 N. C. 239.)

Eviction may be total or partial.

(1) Total eviction takes place when the possessor is wholly deprived of his rights in the premises.

(2) Partial eviction takes place when the possessor is deprived of only a portion of them; as, if a third person comes in and ejects him from the possession of half his land, or establishes a right to some easement over it, by a title which is prior to that under which he holds.

It may be actual or constructive.

(3) Actual eviction is where one is, either by force or by process of law, actually put out of possession.

(4) Constructive eviction is such acts of wrongful interference as seriously impair the enjoyment of the premises. 132 Mass. 367; 20 N. Y. 281.

Thus, the erection by the landlord on the demised premises, of a permanent structure, which rendered two rooms in the demised house unfit for use, is a constructive eviction. 106 Mass. 201.

EVIDENCE. That which tends to prove or disprove any matter in question, or to influence the belief respecting it. Belief is produced by the consideration of something presented to the mind. The matter thus presented, in whatever shape it may come, and through whatever material organ it is derived is evidence. Prof. Parker, Lectures on Medical Jurisprudence, in Dartmouth College, N. H.

The word "evidence," in legal acceptation, includes all the means by which any alleged matter of fact, the truth of which is submitted to investigation, is established or disproved. 1 Greenl. Ev. c. 1, § 1.

That which is legally submitted to a jury, to enable them to decide upon the questions in dispute, or issues, as pointed out by the pleadings, and distinguished from all comment and argument, is termed "evidence." 1 Starkie, Ev. pt. 1, § 3.

"Any matter of fact the effect, tendency, or design of which is to produce in the mind a persuasion affirmative or disaffirmative of the existence of some other matter of fact." Best, Ev. § 11.

"Evidence" is to be distinguished from "proof." Evidence is not proof, but the medium of proof. Proof is the effect or result of evidence. 1 Greenl. Ev. § 1. "Proof is the perfection of evidence. Without evidence there can be no proof, though there may be evidence which does not amount to proof." Wills, Circ. Ev. 2.

It is also to be distinguished from "testimony," which excludes documentary evidence. Testimony embraces only the declaration of witnesses made under oath. "Testimony is but one of the several instruments of evidence, and cannot be considered the equivalent thereof, for evidence embraces not only testimony, but private writings and public documents." Thomp. Trials, § 2784; 3 Wyo. 388; 7 Ind. 94; 76 Hun (N. Y.) 427.

Evidence may be classified with reference to its instruments, its nature, its legal character, its effect, its object.

(1) The instruments of evidence, in the legal acceptation of the term, are:

(a) Judicial notice or recognition, being notice taken by the court, without the introduction of proof by the parties of matters, such as the territorial extent of their jurisdiction, local divisions of their own countries, seats of courts, etc. If the judge needs information on subjects, he will seek it from such sources as he deems authentic. See 1 Greenl. Ev. c. 2.

(b) Documentary evidence, including public records. The registers of official transactions made by officers appointed for the purpose; as, the public statutes, the judgments and proceedings of courts, etc. Judicial writings, such as inquisitions, depositions, etc. Public documents having a semi-official character, as, the statute books published under the authority of the government, documents printed by the authority of congress, etc. Private writings, as, deeds, contracts, wills.

(c) Parol evidence, being the testimony of witnesses.

(d) Real evidence, being that which is addressed to the senses of the court without the intervention of testimony, as by the production in court of an object.

(2) In its nature, evidence is direct or indirect.

(a) Direct evidence is that means of proof which tends to show the existence of a fact in question, without the intervention of the proof of any other fact.

It is that evidence which, if believed, establishes the truth of a fact in issue, and does not arise from any presumption. Evidence is direct and positive when the very facts in dispute are communicated by those who have the actual knowledge of them by means of their senses. 1 Phil. Ev. 116; 1 Starkie, Ev. 19; Burrill, Circ. Ev. 4; 1 Greenl. Ev. § 13.

(b) Indirect evidence is that which is applied to the principal fact indirectly by the proof of circumstances from which the principal fact is inferred. Indirect evidence is commonly known as "circumstantial evidence." See "Circumstantial Evidence."

Evidence has also been divided into real or demonstrative evidence, and moral evidence, the latter including all evidence which is not demonstrative. Brad. Ev. § 15; Gamb. Moral Ev. 121.

(3) With regard to its legal character, evidence is either primary or secondary.

(a) Primary, sometimes called "best," evidence is that which most certainly exhibits the true state of facts to which it relates. The rule is one of quality of evidence, not of quantity (17 Md. 67), and is not based on mere credibility, but on the degree of proximity of the proof to the principal fact to be proved. See "Best Evidence."

(b) Secondary evidence is any evidence suggesting in its nature that there is more direct evidence of the same fact. Hearsay evidence is a type of secondary evidence. See "Hearsay Evidence."

(4) As to its effect, evidence is either *prima facie* or conclusive.

(a) *Prima facie* evidence is that evidence which is sufficient proof respecting the matter in question until it is contradicted, but which may be contradicted or controlled.

Satisfactory evidence is that which produces the degree of certainty required in the case in hand. 1 Greenl. Ev. § 6; 70 Mo. 248.

(b) Conclusive evidence is that which establishes the fact, and is not subject to contradiction.

(5) As to its object, evidence is either substantive evidence, or evidence to credibility.

(a) Substantive evidence is that addressed directly to the point in controversy.

(b) Evidence to credibility is that which neither proves nor disproves the principal fact, but merely impeaches or sustains witnesses by whom the principal fact has been proved or disproved.

Among the kinds of substantive evidence are "cumulative evidence," which is further evidence of the same kind to the same point, and "corroborative evidence," which is further evidence of a different kind to the same point. Underh. Ev. § 2.

EVIDENCE, CIRCUMSTANTIAL. See "Circumstantial Evidence."

EVIDENCE, CONCLUSIVE. See "Conclusive Evidence."

EVIDENCE, DIRECT. See "Evidence."

EVIDENCE, EXTRINSIC. Extenral evidence, or that which is not contained in the body of a writing.

EVIDENCE OF DEBT. A written instrument given as an acknowledgment of an indebtedness, or as security therefor, and showing on its face the existence of the debt.

EVIDENCE OF TITLE. A deed or other document establishing the title to property, especially real estate; *quibus jus praediorum firmatur*. Spelman.

EVIDENTIARY. Having the quality of evidence; constituting evidence; evidencing. A term introduced by Bentham, and, from its convenience, adopted by other writers. Burrill, Circ. Ev. 3, and note.

EVIDENTIARY FACTS. The facts from which the existence of the principal facts is inferred, and which are mere evidence of such facts. 105 Ill. 48.

EVOCATION. In French law. The act by which a judge is deprived of the cognizance of a suit over which he had jurisdiction, for the purpose of conferring on other judges the power of deciding it. It is like the process by writ of *certiorari*.

EWAGE. A toll paid for water passage. Cowell. The same as *aquagium*.

EWBRICE. Adultery; spouse breach; marriage breach. Cowell; Tomlin.

EX (Lat.) From; of; out of; by or with; on; upon; according to; at or in.

EX ABUNDANTI CAUTELA (Lat.) Out of abundant caution. "The practice has arisen *abundanti cautela*." 8 East, 326; Lord Ellenborough, 4 Maule & S. 544.

EX ADVERSO (Lat.) On the other side. 2 Show. 461. Applied to counsel.

EX AEQUITATE (Lat.) According to equity; in equity. Fleta, lib. 3, c. 10, § 3.

EX AEQUO ET BONO (Lat.) In justice and good dealing. 1 Story, Eq. Jur. § 965.

EX ALTERA PARTE (Lat.) Of the other part. Y. B. H. 6 Edw. II. 191.

EX ANTECEDENTIBUS ET CONSEquentibus fit optima intepretatio. The best interpretation is made from antecedents and consequents. 2 Pars. Cont. 12, note (r); Broom, Leg. Max. (3d London Ed.) 513; 2 Inst. 317; 2 Sharswood, Bl. Comm. 379; 1 Bulst. 101; 15 East, 541.

EX ARBITRIO JUDICIS (Lat.) At, in, or upon the discretion of the judge. 4 Bl. Comm. 394. A term of the civil law. Inst. 4. 6. 31.

EX ASSENSU CURIAE (Law Lat.) With the consent of the court. "*Ex assensu totius curiae*, Crew, J., gave judgment." Latch. 139.

EX ASSENSU PATRIS (Lat.) By or with the father's consent. Litt. § 40; 2 Bl. Comm. 133. See Cro. Jac. 415, 587.

EX ASSENSU SUO (Law Lat. with his assent). Formal words in judgments for damages by default. Comb. 220.

EX BONIS (Lat. of the goods or property). A term of the civil law; distinguished from *in bonis*, as being descriptive of or applicable to property not in actual possession. Calv. Lex.

EX CAUSA (Law Lat.) By title.

EX CERTA SCIENTIA (Lat. of certain or sure knowledge). Formal words anciently used in letters patent, implying that the king had full knowledge and understanding of the matter. 1 Coke, 40b.

EX COLORE. Under color of.

EX COMITATE (Lat.) Out of comity or courtesy; by courtesy. 2 Kent, Comm. 457.

EX COMMODATO (Lat. from or out of loan). A term applied in the old law of England to a right of action arising out of a loan (*commodatum*). Glanv. lib. 10, c. 13; 1 Reeve, Hist. Eng. Law, 166.

EX COMPARATIONE SCRIPTORUM (Law Lat.) By a comparison of writings or handwritings; a term in the law of evidence. Best, Pres. 218.

EX CONCESSIS (Lat.) From things or premises granted.

EX CONSULTO (Lat.) With deliberation.

EX CONTINENTI (Lat.) Immediately; without any interval or delay; incontinently. A term of the civil law. Calv. Lex.

EX CONTRACTU. See "Action."

EX CURIA. Out of court.

EX DEBITO JUSTITIAE (Lat.) As a debt of justice; as a matter of legal right. 3 Bl. Comm. 48.

EX DEFECTU SANGUINIS (Law Lat.) From failure of blood; for want of issue. Hale, Anal. § 29.

EX DELICTO. See "Action."

EX DEMISSIONE (Law Lat.) From, or on the demise. Usually abbreviated *ex dem.*

EX DIRECTO (Law Lat.) Directly; immediately. Story, Bills, § 199.

EX DIUTURNITATE TEMPORIS, OMnia praesumuntur solemniter esse acta. From length of time, all things are presumed to have been done in due form. Co. Litt. 6; 1 Greenl. Ev. § 20; Best, Ev. § 43.

EX DOLO MALO (Lat.) Out of fraud or deceit. When a cause of action arises from fraud or deceit, it cannot be supported, *ex dolo malo non oritur actio.*

EX DOLO MALO NON ORITUR ACTIO. A right of action cannot arise out of fraud. Broom, Leg. Max. 349; Cowp. 343; 2 C. B. 501, 512, 515; 5 Scott, N. R. 558; 10 Mass. 276.

EX DONATIONIBUS AUTEM FEODA militaria vel magnum serjeantium non continentibus oritur nobis quoddam nomen generale, quod est socagium. From grants not containing military fees or grand serjeanty, a kind of general name is used by us, which is "socage." Co. Litt. 86.

EX EMPTO (Lat. out of purchase; founded on purchase). A term of the civil law, adopted by Bracton. Inst. 4. 6. 28; Bracton, fol. 102.

EX FACIE (Law. Lat.) On the face. 2 Steph. Comm. 158.

EX FACTO (Lat.) From, by, or in consequence of an act or thing done. Bracton, fol. 172. Applied generally to an act done in violation of law or right. A title is said to originate *ex facto* when it commences in an unlawful act. Id. Bracton uses it in the same sense with *de facto (q. v.)* Id.

EX FACTO JUS ORITUR. The law arises out of the fact. 2 Inst. 479; 2 Sharswood, Bl. Comm. 329; Broom, Leg. Max. (3d London Ed.) 99.

EX FICTIONE JURIS. Out of or by fiction of law. Bracton, fol. 53.

EX FREQUENTI DELICTO AUGETUR poena. Punishment increases with increasing crime. 2 Inst. 479.

EX GRATIA (Lat. of favor; of grace). Words used formerly at the beginning of royal grants, to indicate that they were not made in consequence of any claim of legal right.

EX GRAVI QUERELA (Law Lat. from or on the grievous complaint). In old English practice. The name of a writ (so called from its initial words) which lay for a person to whom any lands or tenements in fee were devised by will, within any city, town, or borough wherein lands were devisable by custom, and the heir of the devisor entered and detained them from him. Reg. Orig. 244b; Fitzh. Nat. Brev. 198 (L) et seq. 3 Reeve, Hist. Eng. Law, 49. Abolished by St. 3 & 4 Wm. IV. c. 27, § 36.

EX HYPOTHESI. Upon the hypothesis.

EX INDUSTRIA (Lat.) Intentionally; from fixed purpose.

EX INTEGRO. Anew; afresh. Bracton, fol. 293.

EX JUSTA CAUSA (Lat.) From a just or lawful cause; by a just or legal title.

EX LEGE. By law; by operation of law.

EX LEGIBUS (Lat. according to the laws). A phrase of the civil law, which means according to the intent or spirit of the law, as well as according to the words or letter Dig. 50. 16. 6. See Calv. Lex.

EX LICENTIA REGIS (Law Lat.) By the king's license. 1 Bl. Comm. 168, note.

EX LOCATO (Lat. from or out of lease or letting). A term of the civil law, applied to actions or rights of action arising out of the contract of *locatum.* Inst. 4. 6. 28. Adopted at an early period in the law of England. Bracton, fol. 102; 1 Reeve, Hist. Eng. Law, 168.

EX MALEFICIO (Lat.) On account of misconduct; by virtue of or out of an illegal act. Used in the civil law generally, and sometimes in the common law. Browne, St. Frauds, 110, note; Broom, Leg. Max. 351.

EX MALEFICIO NON ORITUR CONtractus. A contract cannot arise out of an act radically wrong and illegal. Broom, Leg. Max. (3d London Ed.) 660; 1 Term R. 734; 3 Term R. 422; 1 H. Bl. 324; 5 El. & Bl. 999, 1015.

EX MALIS MORIBUS BONAE LEGES natae sunt. Good laws arise from evil manners. 2 Inst. 161.

EX MERO MOTU (Lat.) Mere motion of a party's own free will. Generally applied to action by a court of its own motion. *Sua motu* and *sua sponte* are used as synonyms.

EX MORA (Lat.) From the delay; from the default.

EX MORE (Lat.) According to custom.

EX MULTITUDINE SIGNORUM, COLligitur identitas vera. From the great number of signs, true identity is ascertained. Brac. Max. reg. 25; Broom, Leg. Max. (3d London Ed.) 569.

EX MUTUO (Lat. from or out of loan). In the old law of England, a debt was said to arise *ex mutuo* when one lent another anything which consisted in number, weight, or measure. 1 Reeve, Hist. Eng. Law, 159; Bracton, fol. 99.

EX NECESSITATE (Lat.) Of necessity. 3 Rep. Ch. 123.

EX NECESSITATE LEGIS (Lat.) From the necessity of law.

EX NECESSITATE REI (Lat. from the necessity of the thing). Many acts may be done *ex necessitate rei* which would not be justifiable without it; and sometimes property is protected *ex necessitate rei* which, under other circumstances, would not be so.

EX NIHILO NIHIL FIT. From nothing nothing comes. 13 Wend. (N. Y.) 178, 221; 18 Wend. (N. Y.) 257, 301.

EX NUDO PACTO NON ORITUR ACTIO. No action arises on a contract without a consideration. Noy, Max. 24; 3 Burrows, 1670; 2 Sharswood, Bl. Comm. 445; Chit. Cont. (10th Am. Ed.) 25; 1 Story, Cont. § 525. See "Nudum Pactum."

EX OFFICIO (Lat. by virtue of his office). Many powers are granted and exercised by public officers which are not expressly delegated, or an office may be an incident to another, and filled by the incumbent thereof. Thus, the mayor may be *ex officio* a member of the city board of control. A judge, for example, may be *ex officio* a conservator of the peace and a justice of the peace.

EX OFFICIO INFORMATIONS. Proceedings filed in the English queen's bench division by the attorney general, at the direct and proper instance of the crown, in cases of such enormous misdemeanors as peculiarly tend to disturb or endanger the government, or to molest or affront the sovereign in discharging the royal functions. The information is tried by a jury of the county where the offense arose, and for that purpose, unless the case be of such importance as to be tried at bar, it is sent down by writ of *nisi prius* into that county and tried either by a common or special jury, like a civil action. 4 Steph. Comm. (7th Ed.) 374; Wharton.

EX OFFICIO OATH (Lat.) An oath taken by offending priests. Abolished by 13 Car. II. st. 1, c. 12.

EX PACTO ILLICITO NON ORITUR ACTIO. From an illicit contract no action arises. Broom, Leg. Max. (3d London Ed.) 666; 7 Clark & F. 729.

EX PARTE (Lat. of the one part.) Many things may be done *ex parte,* when the opposite party has had notice. An affidavit or deposition is said to be taken *ex parte* when only one of the parties attends to taking the same.

Many proceedings commenced by an *ex parte* application, as for writ of *habeas corpus,* are so entitled, as *Ex parte* Hartman, 9 Abb. Pr. (N. S.) 124.

EX PARTE MATERNA (Lat.) On the mother's side.

EX PARTE PATERNA (Lat.) On the father's side.

EX PARTE TALIS (Law Lat.) In old English practice. The name of a writ which lay for a bailiff or receiver, who, having auditors assigned to hear his account, could not obtain of them reasonable allowance, but was cast into prison by them. Cowell; Fitzh. Nat. Brev. 129 (F).

EX PAUCIS DICTIS INTENDERE PLURIMA POSSIS. You can imply many things from few expressions. Litt. § 384.

•**EX POST FACTO** (Lat. after the act). An estate granted may be made good or avoided by matter *ex post facto,* when an election is given to the party to accept or not to accept. 1 Coke, 146.

EX POST FACTO LAW. A statute which would render an act punishable in a manner in which it was not punishable when it was committed. 6 Cranch (U. S.) 138; 1 Kent, Comm. 408. A law made to punish acts committed before the existence of such law, and which had not been declared crimes by preceding laws. Dec. Rights Mass. pt. 1, § 24; Dec. Rights Md. art. 15.

"One which, in its operation, makes that criminal or penal which was not so at the time the action was performed, or which increases the punishment, or, in short, which, in relation to the offense or its consequences, alters the situation of the party to his disadvantage." 2 Wash. C. C. (U. S.) 366.

Laws under the following circumstances are to be considered *ex post facto* laws, within Const. art. 1, § 10: (1) Every law that makes an act done before the passing of the law, and which was innocent when done, criminal, and punishes such action. (2) Every law that aggravates a crime, or makes it greater than it was when committed. (3) Every law that changes the punishment, and inflicts a greater punishment than the law annexed to the crime when committed, though it would be otherwise of a law mitigating the punishment. 3 Story, Const. 212. (4) Every law that alters the legal rules of evidence, and receives less or different testimony than the law required at the time of the commission of the offense, in order to convict the offender, though it might be otherwise of a law merely modifying the remedy or mode of procedure. 3 Dall. (U. S.) 386; 16 Ga. 102. (5) A fifth class has been suggested to cover some exceptional cases, viz., laws that, in relation to the offense or its consequences, alter the situation of the party to his disadvantage. 7 Am. & Eng. Enc. Law, 528. As, for example, where, after a crime was committed, the law was so changed that a conviction of a lower degree was no longer a bar, on a new trial being granted, to a conviction of a higher degree. 107 U. S. 221.

A law mitigating the punishment of previously committed crimes is not *ex post facto,* within the meaning of the constitution. 12 Allen (Mass.) 421. Nor is a statute which regulates only mode of procedure. 110 U. S. 574; 137 U. S. 483.

There is a distinction between *ex post facto* laws and retrospective laws. Every *ex post facto* law must necessarily be retrospective, but every retrospective law is not an *ex post facto* law; the former only are prohibited.

It is fully settled that the term *ex post facto,* as used in the constitution, is to be taken in a limited sense as referring to criminal or penal statutes alone, and that the policy, the reason, and the humanity of the prohibition against passing *ex post facto* laws do not extend to civil cases, to cases that merely affect the private property of citizens. Some of the most necessary acts of legislation are, on the contrary, founded upon the principle that private rights must yield to public exigencies. 8 Wheat. (U. S.) 89; 17 How. (U. S.) 463; 6 Cranch (U. S.) 87; 8 Pet. (U. S.) 88; 11 Pet. (U. S.) 421. See 1 Cranch (U. S.) 109; 9 Cranch (U. S.) 374; 1 Gall. (U. S.) 105; 2 Pet. (U. S.) 380, 523, 627; 3 Story, Const. 212; Serg. Const. Law, 356; 2 Pick. (Mass.) 172; 11 Pick. (Mass.) 28; 9 Mass. 363; 2 Root (Conn.) 350; 5 T. B. Mon. (Ky.) 133; 1 J. J. Marsh. (Ky.) 563; 3 N. H. 475; 7 Johns. (N. Y.) 488; 6 Bin. (Pa.) 271; 2 Pet. (U. S.) 681. See "Retrospective Law."

EX PRAECOGITATA MALICIA (Law Lat.) Of malice aforethought. Reg. Orig. 102.

EX PROCEDENTIBUS ET CONSEquentibus optima fit interpretatio. The best interpretation is made from things preceding and following, *i. e.,* the context. 1 Rolle, Abr. 375.

EX PROPRIO MOTU (Lat.) Of his own accord.

EX PROPRIO VIGORE (Lat.) By its own force. 2 Kent, Comm. 457.

EX PROVISIONE HOMINIS (Law Lat.) By the provision of man; by the limitation of the party, as distinguished from the disposition of the law. 11 Coke, 80b.

EX PROVISIONE MARITI (Lat.) From the provision of the husband.

EX QUASI CONTRACTU (Lat.) From *quasi* contract. Fleta, lib. 2, c. 60.

EX RELATIONE (Lat. at the information of; by the relation). A bill in equity, for example, may in many cases be brought for an injunction to restrain a public nuisance *ex relatione* (by information of) the parties immediately interested in or affected by the nuisance. 18 Ves. 217; 2 Johns. Ch. (N. Y.) 382; 6 Johns. Ch. (N. Y.) 439; 13 How. (U. S.) 518; 12 Pet. (U. S.) 91.

EX RIGORE JURIS (Law Lat.) According to the rigor or strictness of law; in strictness of law. Fleta, lib. 3, c. 10, § 3.

EX SCRIPTIS OLIM VISIS (Law Lat. from writings formerly seen). A term used as descriptive of that kind of proof of handwriting where the witness has seen letters or documents professing to be the handwriting of a party, and has afterwards had correspondence or communication with such party, so as to induce a reasonable presumption that the letters or documents were actually his handwriting. 5 Adol. & E. 703, 730; Best, Pres. 219.

EX STATUTO (Law Lat.) According to the statute. Fleta, lib. 5, c. 11, § 1.

EX STIPULATU ACTIO (Lat.) In the civil law. An action of stipulation. An action given to recover marriage portions. Inst. 4. 6. 29.

EX TEMPORE (Lat.) From the time; without premeditation.

EX TESTAMENTO (Lat.) From, by, or under a will. Inst. 2. 9. 7; Code, 6. 30. 19.

EX TOTA MATERIA EMERGAT RESOlutio. The construction or explanation should arise out of the whole subject matter. Wingate, Max. 238.

EX TURPI CAUSA NON ORITUR ACTIO. No action arises out of an immoral consideration. Selw. N. P. 63; 2 Pet. (U. S.) 539.

EX UNA PARTE (Lat.) Of one part or side; on one side.

EX UNO DISCES OMNES. From one thing you can discern all.

EX UTRISQUE PARENTIBUS CONjuncti (Lat.) Related on the side of both parents; of the whole blood. Hale, Hist. Com. Law, c. 11.

EX VI TERMINI (Lat.) By force of the term.

EX VISCERIBUS (Lat. from the bowels). From the vital part; the very essence of the thing. 10 Coke, 24b; 2 Metc. (Mass.) 213). *Ex visceribus verborum,* from the mere words, and nothing else. 10 Johns. (N. Y.) 494; 1 Story, Eq. Jur. § 980.

EX VISITATIONE DEI (Lat. by or from the visitation of God). This phrase is frequently employed in inquisitions by the coroner, where it signifies that the death of the deceased was a natural one.

EX VISU SCRIPTIONIS (Lat. from sight of the writing; from having seen a person write). A term employed to describe one of the modes of proof of handwriting. Best, Pres. 218.

EX VOLUNTATE. Voluntarily.

EXACTION. A willful wrong done by an officer, or by one who, under color of his office, takes more fee or pay for his services than the law allows.

Between "extortion" and "exaction" there is this difference, that in the former case the officer extorts more than his due, when something is due to him; in the latter, he exacts what is not his due, when there is nothing due to him. Co. Litt. 368.

EXACTOR. In old English and civil law. A collector. *Exactor regis*, collector for the king. A collector of taxes or revenue. Vicat; Spelman. The term "exaction" early came to mean the wrong done by an officer, or one pretending to have authority, in demanding or taking any reward or fee for that matter, cause, or thing which the law allows not. Termes de la Ley.

EXACTOR REGIS. The king's exactor, who collected the taxes and other moneys due to the treasury. In the counties, this office was performed by the sheriff; in the seaports and cities by the publicans. Spelman.

EXALTARE (Law Lat.) In old English law. To raise or elevate. *Exaltare stagnum*, to raise a pool. Reg. Orig. 199; Fitzh. Nat. Brev. 184 (O). To raise the water in a pond by damming, so as to overflow another's land. Bracton, fol. 232; Fleta, lib. 4, c. 1, § 19.

EXAMEN (Law Lat.) A trial. *Examen computi*, the balance of an account. Towns. Pl. 223.

EXAMINATION. Interrogation; investigation. The interrogation of a person who is desirous of performing some act or claiming some privilege under the law, to ascertain if all the requirements of law have been complied with, conducted before an officer having authority for that purpose.

The interrogation of a party before a competent officer concerning some fact involved in a judicial proceeding.

——**In Practice.** The interrogation of a witness at the trial, or on the taking of his deposition.

——**In Criminal Law.** The investigation by an authorized magistrate of the grounds of accusation against a person arrested for crime, with a view of securing his appearance for trial before the proper court, should the evidence be sufficient to warrant it.

EXAMINED COPY. A phrase applied to designate a paper which is a copy of a record, public book, or register, and which has been compared with the original. 1 Campb. 469.

EXAMINERS. Persons appointed by law to examine into any matter of fact, to determine the advisability of action by public authorities pursuant to law. Thus, in many states there are examiners in law and medical examiners, to determine the qualifications of applicants for license to practice these professions; examiners of banks, charged with inspection to determine the solvency of banking institutions, etc.

EXAMINERS IN CHANCERY. Officers who examine, upon oath, witnesses produced on either side, upon such interrogatories as the parties to any suit exhibit for that purpose. Cowell.

The examiner is to administer an oath to the party, and then repeat the interrogatories, one at a time, writing down the answer himself. 2 Daniell, Ch. Prac. 1062. Anciently, the examiner was one of the judges of the court; hence an examination before the examiner is said to be an examination in court. 1 Daniell, Ch. Prac. 1053.

EXANNUAL ROLL. A roll containing the illeviable fines and desperate debts, which was read yearly to the sheriff, in the ancient way of delivering the sheriff's accounts, to see what might be gotten. Hale, Sheriffs, 67; Cowell.

EXCAMB. In Scotch law. To exchange. *Excambion*, exchange. The words are evidently derived from the Latin *excambium*. Bell, Dict. See "Exchange."

EXCAMBIATOR. An exchanger of lands; a broker. Obsolete.

EXCAMBIUM (Lat.) In English law. Exchange; a recompense. 1 Reeve, Hist. Eng. Law, 442.

EXCEPTANT. An exceptor; a party entering an exception to any proceeding.

EXCEPTIO.

——**In Roman Law.** An exception. In a general sense, a judicial allegation opposed by a defendant to the plaintiff's action. Calv. Lex., citing Hotoman.

A stop or stay to an action opposed by the defendant. Cowell; Halifax, Anal. bk. 3, c. 5.

Answering to the "defense" or "plea" of the common law.

In a stricter sense, an equitable "exception" to the general rule of law; the exclusion of an action that lay in strict law, on grounds of equity. Heinec. Elem. Jur. Civ. lib. 4, tit. 13, § 1277. A kind of limitation of an action, by which it was shown that the action, though otherwise just, did not lie in the particular case. Calv. Lex. A species of defense allowed in cases where, though the action as brought by the plaintiff was in itself just, yet it was unjust as against the particular party sued. Inst. 4. 13. pr.

A mode of defense to an action, consisting of facts which, though they do not *ipso jure* destroy the right of action, serve to protect the defendant on equitable grounds. 1 Mackeld. Civ. Law, p. 207, § 204; Id. p. 209, § 206, and note.

——**In Modern Civil Law.** Any objection of a defendant by which he alleges a new fact in order to defend himself against the action, as distinguished from a simple denial. 1 Mackeld. Civ. Law, p. 207, § 204.

Answering to the plea of confession and avoidance in the common law.

——**In the Early Common Law.** The first pleading in an action on the part of the defendant; an answer. Bracton, fol. 399b.

——**In the Canon Law.** The second pleading in an action. Corv. Jus. Canon. lib. iii. tit. 32.

——**In Old Practice.** An exception taken at the trial. Fleta, lib. 6, c. 55, § 8.

——**In Old Conveyancing.** An exception in a deed or other instrument. 9 Coke, 53.

EXCEPTIO DILATORIA (Lat.) In the civil law. A dilatory exception; called, also, "*temporalis*" (temporary); one which defeated the action for a time (*quae ad tempus nocet*), and created delay (*et temporis dilationem tribuit*); such as an agreement not to sue within a certain time, as five years. Inst. 4. 13. 10. See Dig. 44. 1. 3.

EXCEPTIO DOLI MALI (Lat.) In the civil law. An exception or plea of fraud. Inst. 4. 13. 1. 9; Dig. 44. 4; Bracton, fol. 100b.

EXCEPTIO EJUS REI CUJUS PETITUR dissolutio nulla est. A plea of that matter the dissolution of which is the object of the action is of no effect. Jenk. Cent. Cas. 37.

EXCEPTIO FALSI OMNIUM ULTIMA. A false plea is the basest of all things.

EXCEPTIO FIRMAT REGULAM IN CASIbus non exceptis. The exception affirms the rule in cases not excepted. Bac. Aph. 17.

EXCEPTIO FIRMAT REGULAM IN CONtrarium. The exception affirms the rule to be the other way. Bac. Aph. 17.

EXCEPTIO IN FACTUM (Lat.) In the civil law. An exception on the fact; an exception or plea founded on the peculiar circumstances of the case. Inst. 4. 13. 1; Calv. Lex.

EXCEPTIO JURISJURANDI (Lat.) In the civil law. An exception of oath; an exception or plea that the matter had been sworn to. Inst. 4. 13. 4. This kind of exception was allowed where a debtor, at the instance of his creditor (*creditore deferente*), had sworn that nothing was due the latter, and had notwithstanding been sued by him. Id.

EXCEPTIO METUS (Lat.) In the civil law. An exception or plea of fear or compulsion. Inst. 4. 13. 1. 9; Bracton, fol. 100b. Answering to the modern plea of duress.

EXCEPTIO NULLA EST VERSUS ACtionem quae exceptionem perimit. There can be no plea against an action which entirely destroys the plea. Jenk. Cent. Cas. 106.

EXCEPTIO PACTI CONVENTI (Lat.) In the civil law. An exception of compact; an exception or plea that the plaintiff had agreed not to sue. Inst. 4. 13. 3.

EXCEPTIO PECUNIAE NON NUMERAtae (Lat.) An exception or plea of money not paid; a defense which might be set up by a party who was sued on a promise to repay money which he had never received. Inst. 4. 13. 2.

EXCEPTIO PEREMPTORIA (Lat.)

——**In Civil Law.** A peremptory exception; called also "*perpetua*" (perpetual); one which forever destroyed the subject matter or ground of the action (*quae semper rem de qua agitur perimit*); such as the *exceptio doli mali*, the *exceptio metus*, etc. Inst. 4. 13. 9. See Dig. 44. 1. 3.

——**In Common Law.** A peremptory plea; a plea in bar. Bracton, fols. 240, 399b.

EXCEPTIO PROBAT REGULAM DE REbus non exceptis. An exception proves the rule concerning things not excepted. 11 Coke, 41.

EXCEPTIO QUAE FIRMAT LEGEM, EXponit legem. An exception which confirms the law expounds the law. 2 Bulst. 189.

EXCEPTIO QUOQUE REGULAM DECLArat. The exception also declares the rule. Bac. Aph. 17.

EXCEPTIO REI JUDICATAE (Lat.) In the civil law. An exception or plea of matter adjudged; a plea that the subject matter of the action had been determined in a previous action. Inst. 4. 13. 5; Dig. 44. 2.

This term is adopted by Bracton, and is constantly used in modern law to denote a defense founded upon a previous adjudication of the same matter. Bracton, fols. 100b, 177; 2 Kent, Comm. 120. A plea of a former recovery or judgment.

EXCEPTIO REI VENDITAE ET TRADItae. An exception or plea that the article claimed in an action was sold or delivered to the defendant. 1 Mackeld. Civ. Law, 315.

EXCEPTIO SEMPER ULTIMA PONENda est. An exception is always to be put last. 9 Coke, 53.

EXCEPTIO TEMPORIS (Lat.) In the civil law. An exception or plea analogous to that of the statute of limitations in our law; viz., that the time prescribed by law for bringing such actions has expired. Mackeld. Civ. Law, § 213. Answering to the modern plea of the statute of limitations.

EXCEPTION (Lat. *excipere; ex*, out of, *capere*, to take).

——**In Contracts.** A clause in a deed by which the lessor excepts something out of that which he granted before by the deed.

The exclusion of something from the effect or operation of the deed or contract which would otherwise be included.

An exception differs from a reservation, —the former being always of part of the thing granted, the latter of a thing not *in esse*, but newly created or reserved; the exception is of the whole of the part excepted; the reservation may be of a right or interest in the particular part affected by the reservation. See 5 R. I. 419; 41 Me. 177; 42 Me. 9; 42 Minn. 401; 142 N. Y. 561; 131 Ill. 490. An exception differs, also, from an explanation, which, by the use of a *videlicet*, proviso, etc., is allowed only to explain doubtful clauses precedent, or to separate and distribute generals into particulars. 3 Pick. (Mass.) 272. It differs also from a proviso, in that an exception is absolute, while a proviso is conditional. 53 Barb. (N. Y.) 522.

To make a valid exception, these things must concur: First, the exception must be by apt words, as, "saving and excepting," etc. See 30 Vt. 242; 5 R. I. 419; 41 Me. 177. Second, it must be of part of the thing previously described, and not of some other thing. Third, it must be of part of the thing only, and not of all, the greater part, or the effect of the thing granted. 11 Md. 339; 23 Vt. 395; 10 Mo. 426. An exception, therefore, in a lease which extends to the whole thing demised is void. Fourth, it must be of such thing as is severable from the demised premises, and not of an inseparable incident. 33 Pa. St. 251. Fifth, it must be of such a thing as he that excepts may have, and which properly belongs to him. Sixth, it must be of a particular thing out of a general, and not of a particular thing out of a particular thing. Seventh, it must be particularly described and set forth. A lease of a tract of land except one acre would be void, because that acre was not particularly described. Woodf. Landl. & Ten. 10; Co. Litt. 47a; 12 Me. 337; Wright (Ohio) 711; 3 Johns. (N. Y.) 375; 5 N. Y. 33; 8 Conn. 369; 6 Pick. (Mass.) 499; 6 N. H. 421; 4 Strobh. (S. C.) 208; 2 Tayl. (N. C.) 173. Exceptions against common right and general rules are construed as strictly as possible. 1 Bart. Conv. 68; 5 Jones (N. C.) 63.

——**In Equity Practice.** The allegation of a party, in writing, that some pleading or proceeding in a cause is insufficient.

——**In Civil Law.** A plea. Merlin, Repert.

Declinatory exceptions are such dilatory exceptions as merely decline the jurisdiction of the judge before whom the action is brought. Code Proc. La. 334.

Dilatory exceptions are such as do not tend to defeat the action, but only to retard its progress.

Peremptory exceptions are those which tend to the dismissal of the action.

——**In Practice.** The word "exceptions" has been given divers meanings in different jurisdictions. The most common is an objection formerly taken to a ruling made at the trial.

"Exception" is sometimes used for "bill of exceptions."

In Texas, an exception is a demurrer to a pleading; the term as so used being probably a relic of the civil law. See 85 Tex. 575.

EXCEPTION TO BAIL. An objection to the special bail put in by the defendant to an action at law made by the plaintiff, on grounds of the insufficiency of the bail. 1 Tidd, Prac. 255.

EXCEPTIS EXCIPIENDIS (Lat.) With all necessary exceptions.

EXCEPTOR. In old English law. A party who entered an exception or plea.

EXCERPTA, or EXCERPTS. Extracts.

EXCESS. In pleading. A replication to the plea *molliter manus imposuit*, that defendant used more force than was necessary.

EXCESSIVUM IN JURE REPROBATUR; excessus in re qualibet jure reprobatur communi. Excess in law is reprehended; excess in anything is reprehended at common law. Co. Litt. 44.

EXCHANGE.

——**In Commercial Law.** A negotiation by which one person transfers to another funds which he has in a certain place, either at a price agreed upon, or which is fixed by commercial usage.

This transfer is made by means of an instrument which represents such funds, and is well known by the name of a "bill of exchange." The price above the par value of the funds so transferred is called the "premium" of exchange, and if under that value the difference is called the "discount"; either being called the "rate" of exchange.

The rate of exchange, the difference in value of the same amount of money in different places, is sometimes known as "exchange."

——**Of Property.** An exchange of chattels is a transfer thereof for other chattels. This is commonly called "barter." Exchange of real estate is a mutual grant of equal interests in land, the one in consideration of the other. 2 Bl. Comm. 323; Litt. 62; Shep. Touch. 289; Watk. Conv. It is said that exchange in the United States does not differ from bargain and sale. 2 Bouv. Inst. note 2055.

——**At Common Law.** Five circumstances are necessary to an exchange: That the estates given be equal; that the word *excambium*, or exchange, be used, which cannot be supplied by any other words, or described by circumlocution; that there be an execution by entry or claim in the life of the parties; that, if it be of things which lie in grant, it be by deed; that, if the lands lie in several counties, or if the things lie in grant, though they be in one county, it be by deed indented. In practice this mode of conveyancing is nearly obsolete.

See Cruise, Dig. tit. 32; Comyn, Dig.; Co. Litt. 51; 1 Washb. Real Prop. 159; Hardin (Ky.) 593; 1 N. H. 65; 3 Har. & J. (Md.) 361; 3 Wils. 489; Watk. Conv. bk. 2, c. 5; 3 Wood, Conv. 243.

EXCHANGE, BILL OF. See "Bill of Exchange."

EXCHEQUER (Law Lat. *scaccarium;* Norman Fr. *eschequier*). In English law.

A department of the government which has the management of the collection of the king's revenue.

The name is said to be derived from the chequered cloth which covered the table on which some of the king's accounts were made up, and the amounts indicated by counters.

It consists of two divisions, one for the receipt of revenue, the other for administering justice. 4 Inst. 103-116; 3 Bl. Comm. 44, 45. See "Court of Exchequer"; "Court of Exchequer Chamber."

EXCHEQUER BILLS. Bills of credit issued by authority of parliament.

They constitute the medium of transaction of business between the bank of England and the government. The exchequer bills contain a guarantee from government which secures the holders against loss by fluctuation. Wharton.

EXCHEQUER, COURT OF. See "Court of Exchequer."

EXCISE. An inland imposition, laid sometimes upon the consumption of the commodity, sometimes on the manufacturer, sometimes upon the retail sale. 1 Bl. Comm. 318; Story, Const. § 950; 7 Wall. (U. S.) 445.

EXCLUSA, or **EXCLUSAGIUM.** In old English law. A sluice to carry off water; the payment to the lord for the benefit of such a sluice. Cowell; Reg. Orig. 96.

A place in a stream made narrow for the purpose of fishing. Spelman.

EXCLUSIVE (Lat. *ex*, out, *claudere*, to shut). Shutting out; debarring from participation. Shut out; not included.

An exclusive right or privilege, as a copyright or patent, is one which may be exercised and enjoyed only by the person authorized, while all others are forbidden to interfere.

A special grant of power is not exclusive merely because no one else happens to possess it, so long as there is nothing to prevent its granting to another. "An act does not grant an exclusive privilege or franchise unless it shuts out or excludes others from enjoying a similar privilege or franchise." 98 N. Y. 139.

EXCOMMENGEMENT (Lat.) Excommunication. Britt. c. 49.

EXCOMMUNICATION. In ecclesiastical law. An ecclesiastical sentence pronounced by a spiritual judge against a Christian man, by which he is excluded from the body of the church, and disabled to bring any action or sue any person in the common-law courts. Bac. Abr.; Co. Litt. 133, 134.

In early times it was the most frequent and most severe method of executing ecclesiastical censure, although proper to be used, said Justinian (Nov. 123), only upon grave occasions. The effect of it was to remove the excommunicated person not only from the sacred rites, but from the society of men. In a certain sense it interdicted the use of fire and water, like the punishment spoken of by Caesar (lib. 6, de Belli Gall.) as inflicted by the Druids. Innocent IV. called it the nerve of ecclesiastical discipline. On repentance, the excommunicated person was absolved and received again to communion. These are said to be the powers of binding and loosing,—the keys of the kingdom of heaven. This kind of punishment seems to have been adopted from the Roman usage of interdicting the use of fire and water. Fr. Duaren de Sacris Eccles. Ministeriis, lib. 1, c. 3. See Ridley, Civ. & Ecc. Law, 245, 246, 249.

EXCOMMUNICATO CAPIENDO (Lat. for taking an excommunicated person). In ecclesiastical law. A writ issuing out of chancery, founded on a bishop's certificate that the defendant had been excommunicated, returnable to the king's bench. 4 Bl. Comm. 415; Bac. Abr. "Excommunication" (E). See St. 3 Edw. I. c. 15; 9 Edw. II. c. 12; 2 & 3 Edw. VI. c. 13; 5 & 6 Edw. VI. c. 4; 5 Eliz. c. 23; 1 Hen. V. c. 5; Cro. Eliz. 224, 680; Cro. Car. 421; Cro. Jac. 567; 1 Vent. 146; 1 Salk. 293-295.

EXCOMMUNICATO INTERDICTUR OMnis actus legitimus, ita quod agere non potest, nec aliquem convenire, licet ipse ab aliis possit conveniri. Every legal act is forbidden an excommunicated person, so that he cannot act, nor sue any person, but he may be sued by others. Co. Litt. 133.

EXCULPATION, LETTERS OF. In Scotch law. A warrant granted at the suit of a prisoner for citing witnesses in his own defense.

EXCUSABLE HOMICIDE. Homicide committed under circumstances which constitute, not a justification, but merely an excuse.

It is of two sorts:

(1) *Per infortunium*, or by misadventure, where a person unfortunately kills another in doing a lawful act, without any intent to hurt, and without criminal negligence.

(2) *Se defendo*, or in self-defense, upon a sudden affray, where a person, after becoming engaged in a sudden affray, kills his antagonist to save himself from reasonably apparent danger of death or great bodily harm. 4 Bl. Comm. 182.

The latter sort was distinguished from justifiable homicide in self-defense by the fact that the perpetrator was deemed in some fault in being engaged in an affray. This distinction is now generally abolished.

Excusable homicide was anciently punished by forfeiture of goods (4 Bl. Comm. 182), but is not now punished. See "Justifiable Homicide."

EXCUSAT AUT EXTENUAT DELICTUM in capitalibus, quod non operatur idem in civilibus. That excuses or extenuates a wrong in capital causes which does not have effect in civil suits. Bac. Max. reg. 7; Broom, Leg. Max. (3d London Ed.) 291.

EXCUSATIO (Lat.) In civil law. Excuse; a cause for exemption from a duty, such as absence, insufficient age, etc. Vicat, and references there given.

EXCUSATOR (Lat.)

——**In English Law.** An excuser.

——**In Old German Law.** A defendant; he who utterly denies the plaintiff's claim. Du Cange.

EXCUSATOR QUIS QUOD CLAMEUM non opposuerit, ut si toto tempore litigii fuit ultra mare quacunque occasione. He is excused who does not bring his claim, if, during the whole period in which it ought to have been brought, he has been beyond sea for any reason. Co. Litt. 260.

EXCUSE. In a broad sense, a reason alleged for the doing or not doing a thing.

In a stricter sense, it does not include justification, but implies that, though the act complained of was improperly done, facts by way of mitigation relieve the doer from legal liability. In this sense, an excuse is facts mitigating the act, or depriving it of legal culpability. Compare, for example, "Excusable Homicide" and "Justifiable Homicide."

EXCUSS. To seize and detain by law.

EXCUSSIO (Lat.) In civil law. Exhausting the principal debtor before proceeding against the surety. Discussion is used in the same sense in Scotch law. Vicat, "Excusionis Beneficium."

EXECUTE. To complete; to make; to perform; to do; to follow out.

The term is frequently used in law; as, to execute a deed, which means to make a deed, including, especially, signing, sealing, and delivery. To execute a contract is to perform the contract. To execute a use is to merge or unite the equitable estate of the *cestui que use* in the legal estate, under the statute of uses. To execute a writ is to do the act commanded in the writ. To execute a criminal is to put him to death according to law, in pursuance of his sentence.

EXECUTED. Done; completed; effectuated; performed; fully disclosed; vested; giving present right of enjoyment. The term is used of a variety of subjects.

EXECUTED CONSIDERATION. See "Consideration."

EXECUTED CONTRACT. See "Contract."

EXECUTED ESTATE. An estate whereby a present interest passes to and resides in the tenant, not dependent upon any subsequent circumstances or contingency. They are more commonly called "estates in possession." 2 Sharswood, Bl. Comm. 162.

An estate where there is vested in the grantee a present and immediate right of present or future enjoyment. An estate which confers a present right of present enjoyment.

When the right of enjoyment in possession is to arise at a future period, only the estate is executed; that is, it is merely vested in point of interest. Where the right of immediate enjoyment is annexed to the estate, then, only, is the estate vested in possession. 1 Prest. Est. 62; Fearne, Cont. Rem. 392.

"Executed" is synonymous with "vested." 1 Washb. Real Prop. 11.

EXECUTED FINE. The fine *sur cognizance de droit, come ceo que il ad de son done;* or a fine upon acknowledgment of the right of the cognizee, as that which he has of the gift of the cognizor. Abolished by 3 & 4 Wm. IV. c. 74.

EXECUTED REMAINDER. One giving a present interest, though the enjoyment may be future. Fearne, Cont. Rem. 31; 2 Bl. Comm. 168. See "Remainder."

EXECUTED TRUST. A trust of which the scheme has in the outset been completely declared. Adams, Eq. 151. One in which the devise or trust is directly and wholly declared by the testator or settler, so as to attach on the lands immediately under the deed or will itself. 1 Greenl. Cruise, Dig. 385; 1 Jac. & W. 570.

EXECUTED USE. A use with which the possession and legal title have been united by statute. 1 Steph. Comm. 339; 2 Sharswood, Bl. Comm. 335, note; 7 Term R. 342; 12 Ves. 89; 4 Mod. 380; Comb. 312.

EXECUTED WRIT. A writ the command in which has been obeyed by the person to whom it was directed.

EXECUTIO (Lat.) The doing or following up of a thing; the doing a thing completely or thoroughly; management or administration.

——**In Old Practice.** Execution; the final process in an action.

EXECUTIO BONORUM (Lat.) In old English law. Management or administration of goods. *Ad ecclesiam et ad amicos pertinebit executio bonorum,* the execution of the goods shall belong to the church and to the friends of the deceased. Bracton, fol. 60b.

EXECUTIO EST EXECUTIO JURIS SEcundum judicium. An execution is the execution of the law according to the judgment. 3 Inst. 212.

EXECUTIO EST FINIS ET FRUCTUS legis. An execution is the end and the fruit of the law. Co. Litt. 289.

EXECUTIO JURIS NON HABET INJURIam. The execution of law does no injury. 2 Rolle, Abr. 301.

EXECUTION. The accomplishment of a thing; the completion of an act or instrument; the fulfillment of an undertaking. Thus, a contract is executed when the act to be done is performed; a deed is executed when it is signed, sealed, and delivered.

——**In Criminal Law.** Putting a convict to death, agreeably to law, in pursuance of his sentence. This is to be performed by the sheriff or his deputy. See 4 Sharswood, Bl. Comm. 403.

——**In Practice.** Putting the sentence of the law in force. 3 Bl. Comm. 412. The act of carrying into effect the final judgment or decree of a court.

The writ which directs and authorizes the officer to carry into effect such judgment.

Final execution is one which authorizes the money due on a judgment to be made out of the property of the defendant.

Execution *quousque* is such as tends to an end, but is not absolutely final; as, for example, a *capias ad satisfaciendum*, by virtue of which the body of the defendant is taken, to the intent that the plaintiff shall be satisfied his debt, etc., the imprisonment not being absolute, but until he shall satisfy the same. 6 Coke, 87. See "Facias."

EXECUTION PAREE. In French law. A right founded on an act passed before a notary, by which the creditor may immediately, without citation or summons, seize and cause to be sold the property of his debtor, out of the proceeds of which to receive his payment. It imports a confession of judgment, and is not unlike a warrant of attorney. Code Proc. La. art. 732; 6 Toullier, note 208; 7 Toullier, Dr. Civ. 99.

EXECUTIONER. The name given to him who puts criminals to death, according to their sentence; a hangman.

In the United States, executions are so rare that there are no executioners by profession. It is the duty of the sheriff or marshal to perform this office, or to procure a deputy to do it for him.

EXECUTIVE. That power in the government which causes the laws to be executed and obeyed.

The officer in whom the executive power is vested.

The constitution of the United States directs that "the executive power shall be vested in a president of the United States of America." Article 2, § 1. See Story, Const. bk. 3, c. 36.

EXECUTOR. One to whom another man commits by his last will the execution of that will and testament. 2 Bl. Comm. 503.

A person to whom a testator by his will commits the execution, or putting in force, of that instrument and its codicils. Fonbl. Rights & Wrongs, 307.

Lord Hardwicke, in 3 Atk. 301, says: "The proper term in the civil law, as to goods, is *haeres testamentarius;* and 'executor' is a barbarous term, unknown to that law." And again: "What we called 'executor and residuary legatee' is, in the civil law, 'universal heir.'" Id. 300.

The word "executor," taken in its broadest sense, has three acceptations: (1) *Executor a lege constitutus*, he is the ordinary of the diocese. (2) *Executor ab episcopo constitutus*, or *executor dativus*, and that is he who is called an administrator to an intestate. (3) *Executor a testator constitutus*, or *executor testamentarius*, and that is he who is usually meant when the term "executor" is used. 1 Wms. Ex'rs, 185.

——**General Executor.** One who is appointed to administer the whole estate, without any limit of time or place or of the subject matter.

——**Special Executor.** One who is appointed or constituted to administer either a part of the estate, or the whole for a limited time, or only in a particular place.

——**Instituted Executor.** One who is appointed by the testator without any condition, and who has the first right of acting when there are substituted executors.

——**Substituted Executor.** A person appointed executor if another person who has been appointed refuses to act.

An example will show the difference between an instituted and a substituted executor. Suppose a man makes his son his executor, but, if he will not act, he appoints his brother, and, if neither will act, his cousin. Here the son is the instituted executor in the first degree, the brother is said to be substituted in the second degree, the cousin in the third degree, and so on. See Swinb. Wills, pt. 4. § 19, pl. 1.

——**Rightful Executor.** One lawfully appointed by the testator, by his will. Deriving his authority from the will, he may do most acts before he obtains letters testamentary; but he must be possessed of them before he can declare in an action brought by him as such. 1 P. Wms. 768; Wms. Ex'rs, 173.

——**Executor de Son Tort.** One who, without lawful authority, undertakes to act as executor of a person deceased.

——**Executor to the Tenor.** A person who is not directly appointed by the will an executor, but who is charged with the duties which appertain to one; as, "I appoint A. B. to discharge all lawful demands against my will." 3 Phillim. Ecc. Law, 116; 1 Ecc. 374; Swinb. Wills, 247; Wentw. Ex'rs, pt. 4, § 4, p. 230.

EXECUTOR LUCRATUS (Lat.) An executor who has assets of his testator, who in his lifetime made himself liable by a wrongful interference with the property of another. 6 Jur. (N. S.) 543.

EXECUTORY. Executive; pertaining to the execution of official duty. Cent. Dict.

To be executed in the future; of such a nature as to take effect on a future contingency.

EXECUTORY CONSIDERATION. See "Consideration."

EXECUTORY CONTRACT. See "Contract."

EXECUTORY DEVISE. A limitation by will of a future estate in lands or chattels. 38 Pa. St. 294.

A devise of an estate to take effect upon some contingency subsequent to the testator's death.

As to chattels, it is more properly called an "executory bequest."

It differs from a remainder, in that it needs no particular estate to support it. See 6 Wall. (U. S.) 475.

EXECUTORY ESTATES. Interests which depend for their enjoyment upon some subsequent event or contingency. Such estate may be an executory devise, or an executory remainder, which is the same as a contingent remainder, because no present interest passes.

EXECUTORY FINES. These are the fines *sur cognizance de droit tantum; sur concessit;* and *sur done, grant et render.* Abolished by 3 & 4 Wm. IV. c. 74.

EXECUTORY INTERESTS. Include all future estates and interests in land or personalty, other than reversions and remainders. Rapalje & L.

EXECUTORY LIMITATION. Any limitation of a future estate, whether it be made by deed, or by way of executory devise (*q. v.*)

EXECUTORY PROCESS. (Lat. *via executoria*). In Louisiana. A process which can be resorted to in two cases, namely: (1) When the right of the creditor arises from an act importing confession of judgment, and which contains a privilege or mortgage in his favor. (2) When the creditor demands the execution of a judgment which has been rendered by a tribunal different from that within whose jurisdiction the execution is sought. Code Prac. art. 732.

EXECUTORY TRUSTS. A trust is called "executory" when some further act is requisite to be done by the author of the trust or his trustees to give it its full effect. See "Trust."

EXECUTORY USES. Springing uses which confer a legal title answering to an executory devise. See "Use."

EXECUTRESS. A female executor. Hardr. 165, 473. See "Executrix."

EXECUTRIX. A woman who has been appointed by will to execute such will or testament. See "Executor."

EXECUTRY. In Scotch law. The movable estate of a person dying, which goes to his nearest of kin. So called, as falling under the distribution of an executor. Bell, Dict.

EXEGENCE, or EXIGENCY. Probably a corruption of *exigents.* Demand; need; want. Thus, exigency of a writ, the command of the writ; exigency of a bond, that which the bond requires.

EXEMPLARY DAMAGES. See "Damages."

EXEMPLI GRATIA. For example. Abbreviated "*ex. gr.*," or "*e. g.*"

EXEMPLIFICATION. A perfect copy of a record or office book lawfully kept, so far as relates to the matter in question. 3 Bouv. Inst. note 3107. See, generally, 1 Starkie, Ev. 151; 1 Phil. Ev. 307; 7 Cranch (U. S.) 481; 9 Cranch (U. S.) 122; 3 Wheat. (U. S.) 234; 10 Wheat. (U. S.) 469; 2 Yeates (Pa.) 532; 1 Hayw. (N. C.) 359; 1 Johns. Cas. (N. Y.) 238.

A certified copy of a record or recorded instrument.

EXEMPLUM (Lat.) In civil law. A copy; a written authorized copy. Used also in the modern sense of "example:" *Ad exemplum constituti singulares non trahi,* exceptional things must not be taken for examples. Calv. Lex.; Vicat; Co. Litt. 24a.

EXEMPTION. Immunity; freedom from any charge, duty, burden, or liability. Generally used for exemption from process, which is a right given by law to a debtor to retain certain property free from execution, attachment, or other process.

The property exempt from execution.

EXEMPTS. Persons who are not bound by law, but excused from the performance of duties imposed upon others.

EXENNIUM, or EXHENIUM. A gift; a New Year's gift. Cowell.

EXEQUATUR (Lat.)

——**In French Law.** A Latin word which was, in the ancient practice, placed at the bottom of a judgment emanating from another tribunal, and was a permission and authority to the officer to execute it within the jurisdiction of the judge who put it below the judgment.

We have something of the same kind in our practice. When a warrant for the arrest of a criminal is issued by a justice of the peace of one county, and he flies into another, a justice of the latter county may indorse the warrant, and then the ministerial officer may execute it in such county. This is called "backing" a warrant.

——**In International Law.** A declaration made by the executive of a government near to which a consul has been nominated and appointed, after such nomination and appointment has been notified, addressed to the people, in which is recited the appointment of the foreign state, and that the executive, having approved of the consul as such, commands all the citizens to receive, countenance, and, as there may be occasion, favorably assist the consul in the exercise of his place, giving and allowing him all the privileges, immunities, and advantages thereto belonging. 3 Chit. Com. Law, 56; 3 Maule & S. 290; 5 Pardessus, note 1445.

EXERCITALIS (Lat.) A soldier; a vassal. Spelman.

EXERCITOR MARIS (Lat.) In civil law. One who fits out and equips a vessel, whether he be the absolute or qualified owner, or even a mere agent. Emerig. Mar. Loans, c. 1, § 1. We call him *exercitor* to whom all the returns come. Dig. 14. 1. 1. 15; Id. 14. 1. 7; 3 Kent, Comm. 161; Molloy de Jur. Mar. 243.

The managing owner, or ship's husband. These are the terms in use in English and American laws, to denote the same as *exercitor maris*. See "Managing Owner of Ship;" "Ship's Husband."

EXERCITOR NAVIS. The temporary owner or charterer of a ship.

EXERCITORIA ACTIO. See "Actio."

EXERCITORIAL POWER. The trust given to a ship master.

EXERCITUAL. A heriot paid only in arms, horses, or military accoutrements.

EXERCITUS.

——**In Old European Law.** An army; an armed force; a collection of thirty-five men and upwards. Laws Inae, apud Spelman.

A gathering of forty-two armed men. Laws Boior. tit. 3, c. 8.

A meeting of four men. Laws Longobard, lib. 1, tit. 17, c. 1. Spelman.

——**In Roman Law.** See Grotius de Jure Belli, lib. 2, c. 16, § 3.

EXETER (or **EXON**) **DOMESDAY.** The name given to a record preserved among the muniments and charters belonging to the dean and chapter of Exeter cathedral, which contains a description of the western parts of the kingdom, comprising the counties of Wilts, Dorset, Somerset, Devon, and Cornwall. The Exeter Domesday was published, with several other surveys, nearly contemporary, by order of the commissioners of the public records, under the direction of Sir Henry Ellis, in a volume supplementary to the Great Domesday, folio, London, 1816. Wharton.

EXFESTUCARE (Lat.) To abdicate; to resign by passing over a staff. Du Cange. To deprive oneself of the possession of lands, honors, or dignities, which was formerly accomplished by the delivery of a staff or rod. Said to be the origin of the custom of "surrender" as practised in England formerly in courts baron. Spelman. See, also, Vicat; Calv. Lex.

EXFREDIARE. In old English. To break the peace; to commit open violence. Cowell.

EXHAEREDATIO (Lat.) A disinheriting; the act by which a forced heir is deprived of his legitimate or legal portions; a disherison. Occurring in the phrase, in Latin pleadings, *ad exhaeredationem*, to the disherison, in case of abatement.

EXHAERES (Lat.) In civil law. One disinherited. Vicat; Du Cange.

EXHEREDATE. In Scotch law. To disinherit; to exclude from inheriting. 1 Kames, Eq. 247.

EXHIBERE (Lat.) To present a thing corporeally, so that it may be handled. Vicat. To appear personally to conduct the defense of an action at law.

EXHIBIT. As a verb, to produce a thing publicly, so that it may be taken possession of and seized. Dig. 10. 4. 2.

To file of record. Thus, it is the practice in England in personal actions, when an officer or prisoner of the king's bench is defendant, to proceed against such defendant in the court in which he is an officer, by exhibiting, that is, filing, a bill against him. Steph. Pl. 52, note (1); 2 Sellon, Prac. 74.

To administer; to cause a thing to be taken by a patient. Chit. Med. Jur. 9.

As a noun, a supplemental paper referred to in the principal instrument, identified in some particular manner, as by a capital letter, and generally attached to the principal instrument. 1 Strange, 674; 2 P. Wms. 410; Gresl. Eq. Ev. 98.

A paper referred to in and filed with the bill, answer, or petition in a suit in equity.

EXHIBITANT. A complainant in articles of the peace. 12 Adol. & E. 599.

EXHIBITIO BILLAE (Law Lat.) In old practice. A phrase formerly used in pleading, and generally equivalent to "the commencement of the suit;" the suit (where the proceedings were by bill) being anciently commenced by the exhibition of such a bill to the court.

EXHIBITION. In Scotch law. An action for compelling the production of writings. See "Discovery."

EXIGENCY OF A BOND. That upon which it is conditioned.

EXIGENDARY. In English law. An officer who makes out exigents.

EXIGENT, EXIGI FACIAS. In practice. A writ issued in the course of proceedings to outlawry, deriving its name and application from the mandatory words found therein, signifying, "that you cause to be exacted or required;" and it is that proceeding in an outlawry which, with the writ of proclamation, issued at the same time, immediately precedes the writ of *capias utlagatum*. 2 Va. Cas. 244.

EXIGENTER. An officer who made out exigents and proclamations. Cowell. The office is now abolished. Holthouse.

EXIGI FACIAS (Law Lat.) Another name of the writ of exigent; being the two emphatic words of that writ. Reg. Jud. 2.

EXIGIBLE. Demandable; that which may be exacted.

EXILE. Banishment; a person banished.

EXILIUM (Lat.) In old English law. Exile; setting free or wrongly ejecting bond-tenants. Waste is called *exilium* when bondmen (*servi*) are set free or driven wrongfully from their tenements. Co. Litt. 536. Destruction; waste. Du Cange. Any species of waste which drove away the inhabitants into exile, or had a tendency to do so. Bac. Abr. "Waste" (A); 1 Reeve, Hist. Eng. 386.

EXILIUM EST PATRIAE PRIVATIO, NATALIS SOLI MUTATIO, LEGUM NATIVARUM AMISSIO. Exile is a privation of country, a change of natal soil, a loss of native laws. 7 Coke, 20.

EXISTIMATIO (Lat.) The reputation of a Roman citizen; the decision of arbiters. Vicat; 1 Mackeld. Civ. Law, § 123.

EXIT (Lat.) It issues. Used in old records to indicate the granting of an application for a writ.

EXIT WOUND. The wound made in coming out by a weapon which has passed through the body, or any part of it. 2 Beck, Med. Jur. 119.

EXITUS (Lat.) An export duty; issue, child or offspring; rent or profits of land.

——**In Pleading.** The issue or the end, termination or conclusion, of the pleadings. So called because an issue brings the pleadings to a close. 3 Bl. Comm. 314.

EXLEGALITAS. In old English law. Outlawry. Laws Edw. Conf. c. 38; Spelman.

EXLEGARE. To outlaw.

EXLEGATUS, or **EXLEX.** An outlaw.

EXOINE. In French law. An act or instrument in writing which contains the reasons why a party in a civil suit, or a person accused, who has been summoned, agreeably to the requisitions of a decree, does not appear. Poth. Proc. Cr. § 3, art. 3.

EXONERATION.

(1) The taking off a burden or duty; the shifting of a burden from one person or one piece of property to another. Thus, it is a general rule in the distribution of an intestate's estate that the debts which he himself contracted, and for which he mortgaged his land as security, shall be paid out of the personal estate, in exoneration of the real.

(2) The right of one secondarily liable, who has paid the debt, to recourse in equity against the principal for reimbursement. Pom. Eq. Jur. p. 467, § 1416.

EXONERATUR (Lat.) In practice. A short note entered on a bail piece, that the bail is exonerated or discharged in consequence of having fulfilled the condition of his obligation, made by order of the court or of a judge upon a proper cause being shown. See "Recognizance."

EXPATRIATION. The voluntary act of abandoning one's country, and becoming the citizen or subject of another.

At common law, it is probable that a citizen of the United States had no right to expatriate himself. 2 Dall. (U. S.) 1; 7 Wheat. (U. S.) 283. But see 2 Paine (U. S.) 652. But Act Cong. July 27, 1868, declares that expatriation is a natural and inherent right. The effectiveness of this statute has been doubted. 56 Fed. 556.

Expatriation can only be accomplished by a removal from the country, and the acquirement of a domicile elsewhere. 56 Fed. 556; 8 Cranch (U. S.) 253; 7 Wheat. (U. S.) 283.

EXPECT (Lat. *expectare ex*, from, and *spectare*, to look). To look for; to wait for; to look forward to, as to something probable, intended, or contemplated; to be in readiness to operate. The word has sometimes been applied, in this sense, to instruments. Bacon's Arg. Case of Revocation of Uses; Works, iv. 248, 253. The words "expects to prove," in an affidavit, have been held insufficient. The party ought to say, "he firmly believes he can." 2 Littell's R. 230.

EXPECTANCY. The condition of being referred to a future time, or of dependence upon an expected event; contingency as to possession and enjoyment.

An estate giving a present or vested contingent right of future enjoyment; one in which the right of pernancy of the profits is postponed to some future period.

Of expectancies there are two sorts—one created by the act of the parties, called a "remainder;" the other by act of law, called a "reversion." 187 Ill. 58. See "Estates."

A mere hope unfounded in any limitation, provision, trust, or legal act whatever; such as the hope which an heir apparent has of succeeding to the ancestors' estate. Jeffers v. Lampson, 10 Ohio St. 106.

EXPECTANT. Contingent as to enjoyment. See "Estates."

EXPECTANT HEIR. An expectant heir, in the language of equity, is a person who has a reversionary right or hope or succession to property. Where he has but little or no property immediately available, and is exposed to the temptation of selling or mortgaging his right or expectation on unreasonable terms (*e. g.*, for much below its value, or at a usurious rate of interest), he is considered as entitled to the protection of the court against the enforcement of such "catching bargains," as they are called.

EXPECTATION OF LIFE. In the doctrine of life annuities, it is the share or number of years of life which a person of a given age may, upon an equality of chance, expect to enjoy. Wharton.

EXPEDIMENT. The whole of a person's goods and chattels, bag and baggage.

EXPEDIT REPUBLICAE NE SUA RE quis male utatur. It is for the interest of the state that a man should not use his own property improperly. Inst. 1. 8. 2; Broom, Leg. Max. (3d London Ed.) 328.

EXPEDIT REIPUBLICAE UT SIT FINIS litium. It is for the advantage of the state that there be an end of suits; it is for the public good that actions be brought to a close. Co. Litt. 303b.

EXPEDITATE. In forest law. To cut out the ball of a dog's fore feet, for the preservation of the royal game. Manw. For. Law, c. 16.

To cut the foot or root of a tree, so as to cause it to fall. Fleta, lib. 2, c. 41, § 32.

EXPEDITATION. A cutting off the claws or ball of the fore feet of mastiffs, to prevent their running after deer. Cart. de For. c. 17; Spelman; Cowell; 2 Bl. Comm. 393, 417.

EXPEDITIO. An expedition; an irregukind of army. Spelman.

EXPEDITIO BREVIS (Lat.) In old practice. The service of a writ. Towns. Pl. 43.

EXPENDITORS. Paymasters; those who expend or disburse certain taxes; especially the sworn officer who supervised the repairs of the banks of the canals in Romney Marsh. Cowell.

EXPENSAE LITIS (Lat.) Expenses of the suit; the costs, which are generally allowed to the successful party.

EXPERIENCE. Knowledge derived from proof furnished by one's own faculties or senses. 227 Ill. 444.

EXPERIENTIA PER VARIOS ACTUS legem facit. Magistra rerum experientia. Experience by various acts makes laws. Experience is the mistress of things. Co. Litt. 60; Branch. Princ.

EXPERTS (from Lat. *experti*, skilled by experience). Persons selected by the court or parties in a cause, on account of their knowledge or skill, to examine, estimate, and ascertain things, and make a report of their opinions. Merlin, Repert. Witnesses who are admitted to testify from a peculiar knowledge of some art or science, a knowledge of which is requisite or of value in settling the point at issue.

One who has made a subject a matter of study, practice, and observation, and has particular special knowledge on the subject. 41 N. H. 546.

Persons professionally acquainted with the science or practice in question. Strickl. Ev. 408. Persons conversant with the subject matter on questions of science, skill, trade, and others of like kind. Best, Ev. § 346.

A person skilled either by study (15 S. C. 408) or experience (12 Hun [N. Y.] 276) in respect to some matter on which a course of special study or experience is necessary to the formation of an opinion (Rog. Exp. Test. § 7), and who is accordingly admitted to testify to his opinion in relation thereto.

EXPILARE (Lat.) In the civil law. To spoil; to rob, or plunder. Applied to inheritances. Dig. 47. 19; Code, 9. 32.

EXPILATION. In civil law. The crime of abstracting the goods of a succession. This is said not to be a theft, because the property no longer belongs to the deceased, nor to the heir before he has taken possession. In the common law, the grant of letters testamentary, or letters of administration, relates back to the time of the death of the testator or intestate, so that the property of the estate is vested in the executor or administrator from that period.

EXPILATOR (Lat.) In the civil law. A robber; a spoiler or plunderer. *Expilatores sunt atrociores fures.* Dig. 47. 18. 1. 1.

EXPIRATION. Cessation; end; as, the expiration of a lease, of a contract or statute. It ordinarily implies termination by the running of an express limitation as to time, but has been used to signify termination in any manner. Plowd. 198a.

EXPIRY OF THE LEGAL. In Scotch law. The expiration of the term within which the subject of an adjudication may be redeemed on payment of the debt adjudged for. Bell, Dict.; 3 Jur. Styles (3d Ed.) 1107.

EXPLEES. The profits of an estate. See "Esplees."

EXPLETIA, or EXPLECIA (Lat. from *explere*, to complete or make perfect). Esplees or profit of land. Bracton, fols. 40, 44b.

EXPLICATIO (Lat.) In civil law. The fourth pleading. Equivalent to the surrejoinder of the common law. Calv. Lex.

EXPORTATION. The act of sending goods out of the country. It ordinarily implies a sending for commercial purposes. 5 Harr. (Del.) 501.

EXPOSE. A French word, sometimes applied to a written document containing the reasons or motives for doing a thing. The word occurs in diplomacy.

To place in an unprotected situation.

To exhibit. "Exposure for sale" implies an exhibition in a public place, not a private sale. 13 Wend. (N. Y.) 429.

EXPOSITIO (Lat.) Explanation; exposition; interpretation.

EXPOSITIO, QUAE EX VISCERIBUS causae nascitur, est aptissima et fortissima in lege. That exposition which springs from the vitals of a cause is the fittest and most powerful in law. 10 Coke, 24.

EXPOSITION DE PART. In French law. The abandonment of a child, unable to take care of itself, either in a public or private place.

If the child thus exposed should be killed in consequence of such exposure, as, if it should be devoured by animals, the person so exposing it would be guilty of murder. Rosc. Cr. Ev. 591.

EXPOSURE OF PERSON. See "Indecency."

EXPRESS. Stated or declared, as opposed to implied. That which is made known, and not left to implication.

EXPRESS ABROGATION. A direct repeal in terms by a subsequent law referring to that which is abrogated.

EXPRESS ASSUMPSIT. At common law an express assumpsit was an undertaking made orally, by writing not under seal or by matter of record, to perform an act or to pay a sum of money to another. 253 Ill. 172. See "Assumpsit."

EXPRESS COLOR. See "Color."

EXPRESS CONSIDERATION. See "Consideration."

EXPRESS CONTRACT. See "Contract."

EXPRESS MALICE. Actual malice or malice in fact, existing when one actually contemplates the injury or wrong which he inflicts. 1 Clark & Marshall, Crimes, p. 144. See "Malice."

EXPRESS NOTICE. Express notice embraces not only knowledge, but also that which is communicated by direct information, either written or oral, from those who are cognizant of the fact communicated. 78 Md. 235.

EXPRESS TRUST. See "Trust."

EXPRESS WARRANTY. See "Warranty."

EXPRESSA NOCENT; NON EXPRESSA non nocent. Things expressed may be prejudicial; things not expressed are not. Calv. Lex.; Dig. 50. 17. 19. 5.

EXPRESSA NON PROSUNT QUAE NON expressa proderunt. Things expressed may be prejudicial, which, not expressed, will profit. 4 Coke, 73.

EXPRESSIO EORUM QUAE TACITE INsunt nihil operatur. The expression of those things which are tacitly implied operates nothing. 2 Pars. Cont. 28; 4 Coke, 73; 5 Coke, 11; Hob. 170; 3 Atk. 138; 11 Mees. & W. 569; 7 Exch. 28.

EXPRESSIO UNIUS EST EXCLUSIO ALterius. The expression of one thing is the exclusion of another. Co. Litt. 210; Broom, Leg. Max. (3d London 7d.) 596; 2 pars. Cont. 28; 16 Mees. & W. 244; 2 Curt. (U. S.) 365; 6 Mass. 84; 11 Cush. (Mass.) 328.

That which is implied and is general is restricted by that which is expressed and is particular and specific. 163 Ill. 343.

EXPRESSUM FACIT CESSARE TACItum. That which is expressed puts an end to (renders ineffective) that which is implied. Smith, Cont. (2d Ed.) 390; 5 Bing. N. C. 185; 6 Barn. & C. 609; 2 Cromp. & M. 459; 2 El. & Bl. 856; 7 Mass. 106; 24 Me. 374; 6 N. H. 481; 1 Doug. (Mich.) 330; 4 Wash. C. C. (U. S.) 185.

EXPRESSUM SERVITIUM REGAT VEL declaret tacitum. Let service expressed rule, or declare what is silent.

EXPROMISSIO (Lat.) In civil law. The species of novation by which a creditor accepts a new debtor, who becomes bound instead of the old, the latter being released. 1 Bouv. Inst. note 802. See "Novation."

EXPROMISSOR. In civil law. The person who alone becomes bound for the debt of another, whether the latter were obligated or not. He differs from a surety, who is bound together with his principal. Dig. 12. 4. 4; Id. 16. 1. 13; Id. 24. 3. 64. 4; Id. 38. 1. 37. 8.

EXPROMITTERE (Lat.) In civil law. To undertake for another, with the view of becoming liable in his place. Calv. Lex.

EXPROPRIATION. Compulsorily depriving a person of a right of property belonging to him in return for a compensation. The term has been introduced from its use in foreign countries to denote a compulsory purchase of land, etc., for the purposes of a railway, canal, or the like. "*Expropriation pour cause d'utilite publique.*" Id.; 1 App. Cas. 384.

EXPULSION (Lat. *expellere*, to drive out). The act of depriving a member of a body politic or corporate, or of a society, of his right of membership therein, by the vote of such body or society, for some violation of his duties as such, or for some offense which renders him unworthy of longer remaining a member of the same.

It is sometimes loosely used in the sense of "eject."

The term is ordinarily applied only to voluntary associations and public bodies, "disfranchisement" (*q. v.*) being the appropriate term for expulsion of a member of a corporation.

EXPURGATION. The act of purging or cleansing.

EXPURGATOR. One who corrects by expurging.

EXQUAESTOR. In Roman law. One who had filled the office of *quaestor*. A title given to Tribonian. Inst. proem. § 3. Used only in the ablative case (*exquaestore*).

EXROGARE (Lat. *ex*, from, and *rogare*, to pass a law). In Roman law. To take something from an old law by a new law. Tayl. Civ. Law, 155. The same as *derogare*. See "Abrogation."

EXTENDI FACIAS (Lat. you cause to be extended). In English practice. The name of a writ of execution, derived from its two emphatic words; more commonly called an "extent." 2 Tidd, Prac. 1043; 4 Steph. Comm. 43.

EXTENSION. An enlargement, ordinarily, to time to do any act. This term is applied among merchants to signify an agreement made between a debtor and his creditors, by which the latter, in order to enable the former, embarrassed in his circumstances, to retrieve his standing, agree to wait for a definite length of time, after their several claims become due and payable, before they will demand payment.

Among the French, a similar agreement is known by the name of attermoiement. Merlin, Repert. mot "Attermoiement."

EXTENSORES (Law Lat.) In old English law. Extenders or appraisers; the name of certain officers appointed to appraise and divide or apportion lands. It was their duty to make a survey, schedule, or inventory of the lands, to lay them out under certain heads, and then to ascertain the value of each, as preparatory to the division or partition. Bracton, fols. 72b, 75; Britt. c. 71; Fleta, lib. 5, c. 9, § 5; Barr. Obs. St. 103, note.

EXTENT. A writ, issuing from the exchequer, by which the body, goods, and lands of the debtor may all be taken at once to satisfy the judgment.

It is so called because the sheriff is to cause the lands to be appraised at their full extended value before he delivers them to the plaintiff. Fitzh. Nat. Brev. 131. The writ originally lay to enforce judgments in case of recognizances or debts acknowledged on statutes merchant or staple (see St. 13 Edw. I. "de Mercatoribus;" 27 Edw. III. c. 9), and, by 33 Hen. VIII. c. 39, was extended to debts due the crown. The term is sometimes used in the various states of the United States to denote writs which give the creditor possession of the debtor's lands for a limited time till the debt be paid. 16 Mass. 186.

——**Extent in Aid.** An extent issued at the suit or instance of a crown debtor against a person indebted to himself. This writ was much abused, owing to some peculiar privileges possessed by crown debtors, and its use was regulated by St. 57 Geo. III. c. 117. See 3 Sharswood, Bl. Comm. 419.

——**Extent in Chief.** An extent issued to take a debtor's lands into the possession of the crown. See 2 & 3 Vict. c. 11; 5 & 6 Vict. c. 86, § 8.

EXTENTA MANERII (Law Lat.) The title of a statute passed 4 Edw. I. st. 1; being a sort of direction for making a survey or terrier of a manor, and all its appendages. 2 Reeve, Hist. Eng. Law, 140. Mr. Barrington observes that it is most certainly no act of parliament, in any sense of the word, but is merely a set of instructions to the king's extender, with regard to what he shall inquire into, and upon what heads and particulars he is to make his report. Barr. Obs. St. 103.

EXTENUATING CIRCUMSTANCES. Facts palliating or mitigating a crime. Sometimes applied to torts for which exemplary damages may be recovered.

EXTENUATION. That which renders a crime or tort less heinous than it would be without it. It is opposed to "aggravation."

EXTERRITORIALITY (Fr.) This term (*exterritorialite*) is used by French jurists to signify the immunity of certain persons, who, although in the state, are not amenable to its laws. Foreign sovereigns, ambassadors, ministers plenipotentiary, and ministers from a foreign power are of this class. Foelix, Droit Int. Prive, liv. 2 tit. 2, c. 2, § 4. See "Ambassador;" "Conflict of Laws;" "Minister;" "Privilege."

EXTERUS (Lat.) A foreigner or alien; one born abroad. The opposite of *civis*. Bac. Works, IV. 345.

EXTERUS NON HABET TERRAS. An alien holds no lands. Tray. Lat. Max. 203.

EXTINCT (Lat. *extinguere*, to destroy or put out). Extinguished. A rent is said to be extinguished when it is destroyed and put out. Co. Litt. 147b. See "Extinguishment."

EXTINCTO SUBJECTO, TOLLITUR ADJunctum. When the substance is gone, the adjuncts disappear. 16 Johns. (N. Y.) 438, 492.

EXTINGUISHMENT. The destruction of a right or contract; the act by which a contract is made void; the annihilation of a collateral thing or subject in the subject itself out of which it is derived. Prest. Merg. 9. For the distinction between an extinguishment and passing a right, see 2 Sharswood, Bl. Comm. 325, note.

An extinguishment may be by matter of fact and by matter of law. It is by matter of fact either express, as when one receives satisfaction and full payment of a debt, and the creditor releases the debtor (11 Johns.

[N. Y.] 513), or implied, as when a person hath a yearly rent out of lands, and becomes owner, either by descent or purchase, of the estate subject to the payment of the rent, and the latter is extinguished (3 Stew. [Ala.] 60); but the person must have as high an estate in the land as in the rent, or the rent will not be extinct (Co. Litt. 147b).

There are numerous cases where the claim is extinguished by operation of law. For example, where two persons are jointly but not severally liable for a simple contract debt, a judgment obtained against one is at common law an extinguishment of the claim on the other debtor. 1 Pet. C. C. (U. S.) 301; 2 Johns. (N. Y.) 213.

See, generally, Bouv. Inst. Index; Co. Litt. 147b; 1 Rolle, Abr. 933; 7 Viner, Abr. 367; 11 Viner, Abr. 461; 18 Viner, Abr. 493-515; 3 Nels. Abr. 818; Bac. Abr.; 5 Whart. (Pa.) 541; 2 Root (Conn.) 492; 3 Conn. 62; 6 Conn. 373; 1 Ohio, 187; 11 Johns. (N. Y.) 513; 1 Halst. (N. J.) 190; 4 N. H. 251; 31 Pa. St. 475.

EXTINGUISHMENT OF A DEBT. Destruction of a debt. This may be by the creditor's accepting a higher security. Plowd. 84; 1 Salk. 304; 1 Md. 492; 5 Md. 389; 24 Ala. (N. S.) 439. A judgment recovered extinguishes the original debt. 13 Mass. 148; 1 Pick. (Mass.) 118; Hill & D. (N. Y.) 392. A debt evidenced by a note may be extinguished by a surrender of the note. 10 Cush. (Mass.) 69; 29 Pa. St. 50; 3 Ind. 337. As to the effect of payment in extinguishing a debt, see "Payment." See, generally, 35 N. H. 421; 29 Vt. 488; 6 Fla. 25; 20 Ga. 403; 12 Barb. (N. Y.) 128.

EXTINGUISHMENT OF COMMON. Loss of the right to have common. This may happen from various causes,—by the owner of the common right becoming owner of the fee; by severance from the land; by release; by approvement. 2 Hilliard, Real Prop. 75; 2 Steph. Comm. 41; 1 Crabb, Real Prop. § 341 et seq.; Co. Litt. 280; Burton, Real Prop. 437; 1 Bac. Abr. 628; Cro. Eliz. 594.

EXTINGUISHMENT OF COPYHOLD. This takes place by a union of the copyhold and freehold estates in the same person; also by any act of the tenant showing an intention not to hold any longer of his lord. Hutt. 81; Cro. Eliz. 21; Williams, Real Prop. 287 et seq.; Watk. Copyholds, Index.

EXTINGUISHMENT OF RENT. A destruction of the rent by a union of the title to the lands and the rent in the same person. Termes de la Ley; Cowell; 3 Sharswood, Bl. Comm. 325, note.

EXTINGUISHMENT OF WAYS. Destruction of a right of way, effected usually by a purchase of the close over which it lies by the owner of the right of way. 2 Washb. Real Prop. Index.

EXTIRPATION. In English law. A species of destruction or waste, analogous to estrepement. See "Estrepement."

EXTIRPATIONE. A judicial writ, either before or after judgment, that lay against a person who, when a verdict was found against him for land, etc., maliciously overthrew any house, or extirpated any trees upon it. Reg. Jud. 13, 56.

EXTOCARE (Lat.) In old records. To grub woodland, and reduce it to arable or meadow; "to stock up," as it is rendered in Cowell. 5 Mon. Angl. 71.

EXTORSIVELY. A technical word used in indictments for extortion.

When a person is charged with extorsively taking, the very import of the word shows that he is not acquiring possession of his own. 4 Cox, C. C. 387. In North Carolina the crime may be charged without using this word. 1 Hayw. (N. C.) 406.

EXTORTIO EST CRIMEN QUANDO QUIS colore officii extorquet quod non est debitum, vel supra debitum, vel ante tempus quod est debitum. Extortion is a crime when, by color of office, any person extorts that which is not due, or more than is due, or before the time when it is due. 10 Coke, 102.

EXTORTION. The unlawful taking by any officer, by color of his office, of any money or thing of value that is not due to him, or more than is due, or before it is due. 4 Bl. Comm. 141; 1 Hawk. P. C. c. 68, § 1; 1 Russ. Crimes, 144*, 7 Pick. (Mass.) 279; 3 Ind. 93; 107 N. C. 921.

In a large sense, the term includes any injury under color of right; but it is generally and constantly used in the more limited technical sense above given; while "oppression" is used to signify injuries other than the extortion of things of value committed under color of office.

EXTRA (Lat. without; out of; beyond). Its opposite is *in* or *intra*. Calv. Lex.

EXTRA FEODUM (Lat.) Out of his fee; out of the seigniory, or not holden of him that claims it. Co. Litt. 1b; Reg. Orig. 97b.

EXTRA JUS (Lat.) Beyond the law; more than the law requires. *In jure, vel extra jus.* Bracton, fol. 169b.

EXTRA LEGEM. Out of the law; out of the protection of the law. Co. Litt. 130.

Outlaws (*utlagati*) are said to be *extra legem positi*, put out of the law. Fleta, lib. 1, c. 28, § 14.

EXTRA LEGEM POSITUS EST CIVILITER mortuus. One out of the pale of the law (an outlaw) is civilly dead. Co. Litt. 130.

EXTRA PRAESENTIAM MARITI (Lat.) Out of the presence of her husband.

EXTRA QUATUOR MARI (Lat. beyond four seas). Out of the realm. 1 Bl. Comm. 157.

EXTRA REGNUM (Lat.) Out of the realm. 7 Coke, 16a; 2 Kent, Comm. 42, note.

EXTRA TERRITORIUM. Outside territory (of a state or county). 2 Kent, Comm. 407.

EXTRA TERRITORIUM JUS DICENTI non paretur impune. One who exercises jurisdiction out of his territory cannot be obeyed with impunity. 10 Coke, 77; Dig. 2. 1. 20; Story, Confl. Laws, § 539.

EXTRA VIAM. Out of the way. When, in an action of trespass, the defendant pleads a right of way, the defendant may reply *extra viam*, that the trespass was committed beyond the way, or make a new assignment. 16 East, 343, 349.

EXTRA VIRES. Beyond powers. See "Ultra Vires."

EXTRACT. A part of a writing. In general, an extract is not evidence, because the whole of the writing may explain the part extracted, so as to give it a different sense; but sometimes extracts from public books are evidence, as extracts from the registers of births, marriages, and burials, kept according to law, when the whole of the matter has been extracted which relates to the cause or matter in issue.

EXTRACTA CURIAE. The issues or profits of holding a court, arising from the customary dues, fees, and amercements. Cowell.

EXTRADITION (Lat. *ex*, from, *traditio*, handing over). The surrender by one sovereign state to another, on its demand, of persons charged with the commission of crime within its jurisdiction, that they may be dealt with according to its laws.

——**International Extradition.** The surrender of persons charged with crime by one foreign state to another, on its demand, pursuant to treaty stipulations between them.

——**Interstate Extradition.** The surrender of persons by one federal state to another, on its demand, pursuant to their federal constitution and laws. Persons subject to extradition, see "Fugitive from Justice."

EXTRADOTAL PROPERTY. In Louisiana this term is used to designate that property which forms no part of the dowry of a woman, and which is also called "paraphernal property." Civ. Code La. art. 2315.

EXTRAHURA. In old English law. An estray. Spelman.

EXTRAJUDICIAL. That which does not belong to the judge or his jurisdiction, notwithstanding which he takes cognizance of it. Extrajudicial judgments and acts are absolutely void. See "Coram non Judice;" Merlin, Repert. "Exces de Pouvoir."

EXTRAJUDICIUM. Extrajudicial; out of the proper cause. Judgments rendered or acts done by a court which has no jurisdiction of the subject, or where it has no jurisdiction, are said to be "extrajudicial."

EXTRANEUS.

——**In Old English Law.** One foreign born; a foreigner. 7 Rep. 16.

——**In Roman Law.** An heir not born in the family of the testator; those of a foreign state. The same as *alienus*. Vicat; Du Cange.

EXTRANEUS EST SUBDITUS QUI EXtra terram, i. e., postestatem regis natus est. A foreigner is a subject who is born out of the territory, *i. e.*, government of the king. 7 Coke, 16.

EXTRAORDINARY CARE. The utmost possible diligence. It is that required of common carriers of passengers, and in a few other relations, and has been defined to be the doing of all that is possible to human sagacity and foresight under the circumstances. 85 Me. 34; 68 Mo. 340.

EXTRAORDINARY REMEDIES. The writs of *mandamus*, *habeas corpus*, *quo warranto*, and other special writs, not ancillary to an ordinary action, are sometimes so called.

EXTRAPAROCHIAL (Lat.) Out of a parish; not within the bounds or limits of any parish. 1 Bl. Comm. 113, 284.

EXTRATERRITORIALITY. That quality of laws which makes them operate beyond the territory of the power enacting them, upon certain persons or certain rights. See Wheaton, Int. Law (6th Ed.) 121 et seq.

EXTRAVAGANTES. In canon law. The name given to the constitutions of the popes posterior to the Clementines.

They are thus called, *quasi vagantes extra corpus juris*, to express that they were out of the canonical law, which at first contained only the decrees of Gratian. Afterwards the Decretals of Gregory IX., the Sexte of Boniface VIII., the Clementines, and at last the Extravagantes, were added to it. There are the Extravagantes of John XXII. and the common Extravagants. The first contain twenty epistles, decretals, or constitutions of that pope, divided under fifteen titles, without any subdivision into books. The others are epistles, decretals, or constitutions of the popes who occupied the holy see either before or after John XXII. They are divided into books, like the decretals.

EXTREME AND REPEATED CRUELTY. See Cruelty.

EXTREMIS (Lat.) When a person is sick beyond the hope of recovery, and near death, he is said to be *in extremis.*

A will made in this condition, if made without undue influence, by a person of sound mind, is valid. As to the effect of declarations of persons *in extremis,* see "Dying Declarations;" "Declaration."

EXTREMIS PROBATIS, PRAESUMUNtur media. Extremes being proved, intermediate things are presumed. Tray. Lat. Max. 207.

EXTUMAE (Law Lat.) In old records. Reliques. Cowell.

EXUERE PATRIAM (Lat). To throw off or renounce one's country or native allegiance; to expatriate one's self. Phillim. Dom. 18.

EXULARE (Lat.) In old English law. To exile or banish. *Nullus liber homo, exuletur, nisi,* etc., no freeman shall be exiled, unless, etc. Magna Charta, c. 29; 2 Inst. 47.

EY. A watery place; water. Co. Litt. 6.

EYE-WITNESS. One who saw the act or fact to which he testifies. When an eye-witness testifies, and is a man of intelligence and integrity, much reliance must be placed on his testimony, for he has the means of making known the truth.

EYOTT. A small island arising in a river. Fleta, lib. 3, c. 2, s. b; Bracton, lib. 2, c. 2. See "Island."

EYRE. See "Eire."

EYRER. To go about. See "Eire."

F

F. The sixth letter of the alphabet. A fighter or maker of frays, if he had no ears, was to be branded in the cheek with this letter. Cowell. Those who had been guilty of falsity were to be so marked. 2 Reeve, Hist. Eng. Law, 392.

F. O. B. Free on board. A mercantile term used in contracts of sale where the seller agrees to put the goods on board cars at a specified place, but freight is paid by the buyer.

FABRIC LANDS. In English law. Lands given for the repair, rebuilding, or maintenance of cathedrals or other churches.

It was the custom, says Cowell, for almost every one to give by will more or less to the fabric of the cathedral or parish church where he lived. These lands so given were called "fabric lands," because given *ad fabricam ecclesiae reparandam*, for repairing the fabric of the church. Called by the Saxons "timber lands." Cowell; Spelman.

FABRICA. In old English law. The making or coining of money. Mem. in Scacc. H. 12 Edw. I.

FABRICARE (Lat.) To make. Used of an unlawful making, as counterfeiting coin (1 Salk. 342), and also of a lawful coining.

FABULA. In old European law. A contract or formal agreement; but particularly used in the Lombardic and Visigothic laws to denote a marriage contract or a will. Spelman.

FAC SIMILE PROBATE. In England, where the construction of a will may be affected by the appearance of the original paper, the court will order the probate to pass in *fac simile*, as it may possibly help to show the meaning of the testator. 1 Williams, Ex'rs (7th Ed.) 331, 386, 566.

FACE. The face of an instrument is that which it shows without extrinsic explanation.

FACERE (Lat.) In civil law. To do; to make. A word of very comprehensive signification. Dig. 50. 16. 218. See Calv. Lex. "Brissonius." An important word formerly in the language of writs and contracts, and the general language of the law.

Facere defaltam, to make default. Bracton, fols. 238, 334b, 360b, 363.

Facere duellum, to make the duel; to engage in the combat, or make or do battle, as the phrase still is. Bracton, fol. 141b.

Facere finem, to make or pay a fine. Id. fol. 154.

Facere legem, to make one's law. Id. fols. 156b, 334b, 335b, 410.

Facere sacramentum, to make oath. Id. fols. 50b, 185b. See "Make."

FACIAS (Lat. *facere*, to make, to do). That you cause. Occurring in the phrases *scire facias*, that you cause to know, and *fieri facias*, that you cause to be made, etc. Used also in the phrases *do ut facias*, I give that you may do, and *facio ut facias*, I do that you may do, two of the four divisions of considerations made by Blackstone (2 Comm. 444).

FACIENDO (Law Lat. from *facere;* Law Fr. *fesaunt*). Doing, making, or paying; one of the apt words of reserving a rent, used in ancient deeds. Co. Litt. 47a. Applied usually to those services which consisted of acts done (*factiones*). *Faciendo inde talia servitia*, doing therefor such services. Bracton, fol. 35b; Fleta, lib. 3, c. 14, § 17.

FACIES (Lat.) The face, outward appearance or color of a thing; the inspection or view of a thing. *Prima facies*, the first face or appearance. *Prima facie*, on the first view or color,—at first blush, as the modern phrase is. Bracton, fols. 29, 280. See "Color."

FACILE. In Scotch law. Easily persuaded; easily imposed upon. Bell, Dict.

FACILITY. In Scotch law. Pliancy of disposition. Bell, Dict.

FACINUS QUOS INQUINAT AEQUAT. Guilt makes equal those whom it stains.

FACIO UT DES (Lat. I do that you may give). A species of contract which occurs when a man agrees to perform anything for a price either specifically mentioned, or left to the determination of the law to set a value on it; as when a servant hires himself to his master for certain wages, or an agreed sum of money. 2 Bl. Comm. 445.

FACIO UT FACIAS (Lat. I do that you may do). A species of contract in the civil law which occurs when I agree with a man to do his work for him if he will do mine for me; or if two persons agree to marry together, or to do any other positive acts on both sides; or it may be to forbear on one side in consideration of something done on the other. 2 Bl. Comm. 444.

FACT (Lat. *factum*). An action; a thing done; a circumstance.

"Fact" is much used in modern times in distinction from "law." Thus, in every case to be tried there are facts to be shown to exist to which the law is to be applied. If law is, as it is said to be, a rule of action, the fact is the action shown to have been done, and which should have been done in accordance with the rule. Fact, in this sense, means a thing done or existing.

Material facts are those which are essential to the right of action or defense.

Immaterial facts are those which are not essential to the right of action or defense.

Material facts must be shown to exist; immaterial facts need not. The existence of facts is generally determined by the jury; but there are many facts of which a court takes cognizance. See "Judge;" "Jury;" "Cognizance." As to pleading material facts, see Gould, Pl. c. 3, § 28. And see 3 Bouv. Inst. note 3150.

FACTA. In old English law. Deeds. *Facta armorum*, deeds or feats of arms; that is, jousts or tournaments. Cowell.

Facts. *Facta et casus*, facts and cases. Bracton, fol. 1b.

FACTA SUNT POTENTIORA VERBIS. Facts are more powerful than words.

FACTA TENENT MULTA QUAE FIERI prohibentur. Deeds contains many things which are prohibited to be done. 12 Coke, 124.

FACTIO TESTAMENTI (Lat.) In civil law. The power of making a will, including right and capacity. Also the power of receiving under a will. Vicat.

FACTO. In fact; by an act; by the act or fact. *Ipso facto*, by the act itself; by the mere effect of a fact, without anything superadded, or any proceeding upon it to give it effect. 3 Kent, Comm. 55, 58.

FACTOR. An agent employed to sell goods or merchandise consigned or delivered to him, by or for his principal, for a compensation, commonly called "factorage" or "commission." Paley, Ag. 13; 1 Livermore, Ag. 68; Story, Ag. § 33; Comyn, Dig. "Merchant" (B); Malynes, Lex. Merc. 81; Beawes, Lex. Merc. 44; 3 Chit. Com. Law, 193; 2 Kent, Comm. (3d Ed.) 622, note (d); 1 Bell, Comm. 385, §§ 408, 409; 2 Barn. & Ald. 143.

A domestic factor is one who resides in the same country with his principal.

A foreign factor is one who resides in a different country from his principal. 1 Term R. 112; 4 Maule & S. 576.

A "factor" differs from a "broker" in that he is intrusted with the possession and management of the goods to be sold, while a broker has only an agency to sell, or possession of documents. Story, Ag. § 33.

——**In Maritime Law.** A factor was anciently an agent who accompanied the ship, the cargo being consigned for sale, and he being empowered to purchase a return cargo out of the proceeds. Such an agent is usually called a "supercargo." Beawes, Lex. Merc. 44, 47.

FACTORAGE. The wages or allowances paid to a factor for his services. It is more usual to call this "commissions." 1 Bouv. Inst. note 1013; 2 Bouv. Inst. note 1288.

FACTORIZING PROCESS. A process for attaching effects of the debtor in the hands of a third party. It is substantially the same process known as the garnishee process, trustee process, process by foreign attachment. Drake, Attachm. § 451.

FACTORS' ACTS. A name given to certain English statutes, of which 40 & 41 Vict. c. 39, is the latest, validating pledges by factors to *bona fide* pledgees.

FACTORY. In Scotch law. A contract which partakes of a mandate and *locatio ad operandum*, and which is in the English and American law books discussed under the title of "Principal and Agent." 1 Bell, Comm. 259.

FACTUM. A man's own act and deed; a culpable or criminal act; an act not founded in law; a deed; a written instrument under seal. Called, also, *charta*. Spelman; 2 Bl. Comm. 295.

The difference between *factum* and *charta* originally would seem to have been that *factum* denoted the thing done, and *charta* the evidence thereof. Co. Litt. 9b. When a man denies by his plea that he made a deed on which he is sued, he pleads *non est factum*, he did not make it.

In wills, *factum* seems to retain an active signification, and to denote a making. See 11 How. (U. S.) 358.

A fact. *Factum probandum*, the fact to be proved. 1 Greenl. Ev. § 13.

A portion of land granted to a farmer; otherwise called a hide, *bovata*, etc. Spelman.

——**In French Law.** A memoir which contains, concisely set down, the fact on which a contest has happened, the means on which a party founds his pretensions, with the refutation of the means of the adverse party. See Vicat.

FACTUM A JUDICE QUOD AD EJUS OFficium non spectat, non ratum est. An act of a judge which does not pertain to his office is of no force. 10 Coke, 76; Dig. 50. 17. 170; Broom, Leg. Max. (3d London Ed.) 89.

FACTUM CUIQUE SUUM, NON ADVERsario, nocere debet. A man's actions should injure himself, not his adversary. Dig. 50. 17. 155.

FACTUM INFECTUM FIERI NEQUIT. What is done cannot be undone. 1 Kames, Eq. 96, 259.

FACTUM NEGANTIS NULLA PROBAtio. No proof is incumbent on him who denies a fact.

FACTUM NON DICITUR QUOD NON perseverat. That is not said to be done which does not last. 5 Coke, 96; Shep. Touch. (Prest. Ed.) 391.

FACTUM PROBANDUM. The fact to be proved.

FACTUM PROBANS. An evidentiary fact.

FACTUM UNIUS ALTERI NOCERE NON debet. The deed of one should not hurt another. Co. Litt. 152.

FACULTAS PROBATIONUM NON EST angustanda. The right of offering proof is not to be narrowed. 4 Inst. 279.

FACULTIES OF HUSBAND. His ability by earnings, or out of accumulated resources, to pay alimony which may be awarded to a wife suing for divorce. It should be alleged as a foundation for an allowance of alimony or support. Not in common use.

FACULTY.

——**In Canon Law.** A license; an authority. For example, the ordinary, having the disposal of all seats in the nave of a church, may grant this power, which, when it is delegated, is called a "faculty," to another.

Faculties are of two kinds: First, when the grant is to a man and his heirs in gross; second, when it is to a person and his heirs as appurtenant to a house which he holds in the parish. 1 Term R. 429, 432; 12 Coke, 106.

——**In Scotch Law.** Ability or power. The term "faculty" is more properly applied to a power founded on the consent of the party from whom it springs, and not founded on property. Kames, Eq. 504.

——**In American Colleges.** The faculty is the body of instructors.

FACULTY OF ADVOCATES. The college or society of advocates in Scotland.

FADERFIUM. A marriage gift coming from the father or brother of the bride.

FAEDER FEOH. The portion brought by a wife to her husband, and which reverted to a widow, in case the heir of her deceased husband refused his consent to her second marriage; *i. e.*, it reverted to her family in case she returned to them. Anc. Inst. Eng.

FAESTING MEN. Approved men who were strong armed. Subsequently the word seems to have been used in the sense of "rich," and hence it probably passed into its later and common meaning of pledges or bondsmen, which, by Saxon custom, were bound to answer for each other's good behavior. Cowell; Du Cange.

FAGGOT. A badge worn by persons who had recanted and abjured what was then adjudged to be heresy, as an emblem of what they had merited. Cowell.

FAGGOT VOTES. A faggot vote is where a man is formally possessed of a right to vote for members of parliament, without possessing the substance which the vote should represent; as if he is enabled to buy a property, and at the same moment mortgage it to its full value for the mere sake of the vote. Such a vote is called a "faggot vote." Wharton.

FAIDA. In Saxon law. Great and open hostility which arose on account of some murder committed. The term was applied only to that deadly enmity in deference to which, among the Germans and other northern nations, if murder was committed, punishment might be demanded from any one of kin to the murderer by any one of the kin of the murdered man. Du Cange; Spelman.

FAILING CIRCUMSTANCES. Means more than actual insolvency, for that is consistent with an honest belief of the insolvent debtor, of his wealth and prosperity; the words would seem to imply that the insolvent is about failing, and closing his affairs, from an inability to continue his business, and to meet his payments. 24 Conn. 310. Failing circumstances imply that the insolvent is about failing and closing his affairs, knowing his inability to continue in business and meet his payments. 35 Conn. 482.

FAILLITE (Fr.) Bankruptcy; failure; the condition of a merchant who ceases to pay his debts. 3 Masse, Dr. Comm. 171; Guyot, Rep. Univ.

FAILURE OF CONSIDERATION. Failure of a party to a contract, whether by fault or necessity, to perform that which he has obligated himself to do.

To constitute failure of consideration, there must be failure to perform that which was promised; subsequent depreciation of the thing promised (86 N. C. 498), though due to inherent defects (78 Ill. 578), not being a legal failure of consideration.

It is a phase of want of consideration, the contract being invalid for absence of consideration after the consideration has failed. But in another sense, want of consideration implies that there never was a consideration, while failure of consideration implies the existence of mutual promises at the making of the contract, and the subsequent breach of one party.

Failure of consideration differs from nonperformance or breach only as to the point of view; the same acts constituting a failure of consideration in respect to the effect to release the other party from his obligation, and a breach in respect to the effect to render the nonperforming party liable in damages.

FAILURE OF ISSUE. A want of issue to take an estate limited over by an executory devise.

Failure of issue is definite or indefinite. When the precise time for the failure of issue is fixed by the will, as in the case of a devise to Peter, but, if he dies without issue living at the time of his death, then to another, this is a failure of issue definite. An indefinite failure of issue is the very converse or opposite of this, and it signifies a general failure of issue, whenever it may happen, without fixing any time, or a certain or definite period, within which it must happen. 2 Bouv. Inst. note 1849. See "Dying Without Issue."

FAILURE OF RECORD. The neglect to produce the record after having pleaded it. When a defendant pleads a matter, and offers to prove it by the record, and then pleads *nul tiel record*, a day is given to the defendant to bring in the record. If he fails to do so, he is said to fail, and, there being a failure of record, the plaintiff is entitled to judgment. Termes de la Ley. See the form of entering it, 1 Wm. Saund. 92, note 3.

FAINT (or **FEIGNED**) **ACTION.** In old English practice. An action was so called where the party bringing it had no title to recover, although the words of the writ were true. A false action was properly where the words of the writ were false. Litt. § 689; Co. Litt. 361.

FAINT PLEADER. A false, fraudulent, or collusory manner of pleading, to the deception of a third person.

FAIR. A public mart or place of buying and selling. 1 Bl. Comm. 274. A greater species of market, recurring at more distant intervals.

A fair is usually attended by a greater concourse of people than a market, for the amusement of whom various exhibitions are gotten up. McCulloch; Wharton.

A solemn or greater sort of market, granted to any town by privilege, for the more speedy and commodious provision of such things as the subject needeth, or the utterance of such things as we abound in above our own uses and occasions. Cowell; Cunningham. A privileged market.

A fair is a franchise which is obtained by a grant from the crown. 2 Inst. 220; 3 Mod. 123; 3 Lev. 222; 1 Ld. Raym. 341; 2 Saund. 172; 1 Rolle, Abr. 106; Tomlins; Cunningham.

In the United States, fairs, in the ancient sense, are almost unknown. They are recognized in Alabama (Aik. Dig. 409, note), and in North Carolina, where they are regulated by statute (1 Rev. St. N. C. 282).

FAIR COMMENT. A fair comment (excusing what would otherwise be a libel) is a comment which is either true, or which, if false, expresses the real opinion of its author (as to the existence of matter of fact, or otherwise), such opinion having been formed with a reasonable degree of care and on reasonable grounds. Steph. Cr. 202.

FAIR-PLAY MEN. A local irregular tribunal which existed in Pennsylvania about the year 1769.

About the year 1769 there was a tract of country in Pennsylvania situate between Lycoming creek and Pine creek, in which the proprietaries prohibited the making of surveys, as it was doubtful whether it had or had not been ceded by the Indians. Although settlements were forbidden, yet adventurers settled themselves there. Being without the pale of ordinary authorities, the inhabitants annually elected a tribunal, in rotation, of three of their number, whom they denominated "fair-play men," who had authority to decide all disputes as to boundaries. Their decisions were final, and enforced by the whole community *en masse*. Their decisions are said to have been just and equitable. 2 Smith, Pa. Laws, 195; Sergeant, Land Laws Pa. 77.

FAIR PLEADER. The name of a writ given by the statute of Marlebridge, 52 Hen. III. c. 11. See "Beaupleader."

FAIT. Anything done; a deed lawfully executed. Comyn, Dig. *Femme de fait*, a wife *de facto*.

FAIT ENROLLE. A deed enrolled, as a bargain and sale of freeholds. 1 Keb. 568.

FAITOURS. Idle persons; idle livers; vagabonds. Termes de la Ley; Cowell; Blount; Cunningham.

FALCARE (Lat.) To cut or mow down. *Falcare prata*, to cut or mow down grass in meadows hayed (laid in for hay) was a customary service for the lord by his inferior tenants. Kennett.

Falcator, the tenant performing the service.

Falcatura, a day's mowing; *falcatura una*, once mowing the grass.

Falcatio, a mowing.

Falcata, that which was mowed. Kennett; Cowell; Jacob.

FALCIDIA. In Spanish law. The fourth portion of an inheritance, which legally belongs to the heir, and for the protection of which he has the right to reduce the legacies to three fourths parts of the succession, in order to protect his interest.

FALCIDIAN LAW. In Roman law. A statute or law restricting the right of disposing of property by will, enacted by the people during the reign of Augustus, on the proposition of Falcidius, who was a tribune in the year of Rome 714.

Its principal provision gave power to fathers of families to bequeath three-fourths of their property, but deprived them of the power to give away the other fourth, which was to descend to the heir. Inst. 2. 22. This fourth was termed the "Falcidian portion."

A similar principle has been adopted in Louisiana, where donations *inter vivos* or *mortis causa* cannot exceed two-thirds of the property of the disposer, if he leaves at his decease a legitimate child; one-half, if he leaves two children; and one-third, if he leaves three or a greater number. Civ. Code, art. 1480.

A similar principle prevailed in England in earlier times, and it was not until after the Restoration that the power of a father to dispose of all his property by will became fully established. 2 Bl. Comm. 11. As to the early history of testamentary law, see Maine, Anc. Law.

At the present day, by the common law, the power of the father to give all his property is unqualified. He may bequeath it to his children equally, to one in preference to another, or to a stranger in exclusion of all, except that his widow has a right of dower in his real property. In some of the states, the statutes authorizing bequests and devises to charitable corporations limit the amount which a testator may give, to a certain fraction of his estate.

FALCIDIAN PORTION. That portion of a testator's estate which, by the Falcidian law, was required to be left to the heir, amounting to at least one-fourth. Civ. Code La. art. 1608; 1 White, New Recop. 106.

FALDA (Spanish). The slope or skirt of a hill. 2 Wall. (U. S.) 673.

——**In Old English Law.** A sheep fold; the liberty of faldage, or setting up in a field a movable pen for sheep.

FALDAE CURSUS. A sheep walk. 2 Vent. 139.

FALDAGE. The privilege which anciently several lords reserved to themselves of setting up folds for sheep in any fields within their manors, the better to manure them, and this not only with their own, but their tenants' sheep. Called, variously, *secta faldare, fold-course, free-fold, faldagii.* Cunningham; Cowell; Spelman.

FALDATA. In old English law. A flock or fold of sheep. Cowell.

FALDFEY. A compensation paid by some customary tenants that they might have liberty to fold their own sheep on their own land. Cunningham; Cowell; Blount.

FALDISDORY. The bishop's seat or throne within the chancel.

FALDSOCA (Saxon). The liberty or privilege of foldage.

FALDSTOOL, or FOLDSTOOL. A place at the south side of the altar at which the sovereign kneels at his coronation.

FALDWORTH. A person of age that he may be reckoned of some decennary. Du Fresne.

FALERAE. In old English law. The tackle and furniture of a cart or wain. Blount.

FALESIA. In old English law. A hill, or down by the seaside. Co. Litt. 5b; Domesday Book.

FALK LAND. See "Folcland."

FALL. In Scotch law. To lose. To fall from a right is to lose or forfeit it. 1 Kames, Eq. 228.

FALL OF LAND. In English law. A quantity of land six ells square, superficial measure.

FALLO. In Spanish law. The final decree or judgment given in a lawsuit.

FALSA DEMONSTRATIO (Lat.) In the civil law. False designation; erroneous description of a person or thing in a written instrument. Inst. 2. 20. 30.

FALSA DEMONSTRATIO NON NOCET. A false description does not vitiate. 6 Term R. 676. See 2 Story (U. S.) 291; 1 Greenl. Ev. § 301; Broom, Leg. Max. (3d London Ed.) 562; 2 Pars. Cont. 62, note, 69, note, 72, note, 76, note; 4 C. B. 328; 11 C. B. 208; 14 C. B. 133.

FALSA DEMONSTRATIONE LEGATUM non perimi. A legacy is not destroyed by an incorrect description. 3 Bradf. Sur. (N. Y.) 144, 149.

FALSA MONETA. In civil law. False or counterfeit money. Code, 9. 24.

FALSA ORTHOGRAPHIA, SIVE FALSA grammatica, non vitiat concessionem. False spelling or false grammar does not vitiate a grant. 9 Coke, 48; Shep. Touch. 55.

FALSARE. To counterfeit. Bracton, fol. 276b.

FALSARIUS, or FOLSONARIUS. A counterfeiter. Towns. Pl. 260; Hov. Frauds, 424.

FALSE ACTION. See "Feigned Action."

FALSE CHARACTER. Personating the master or mistress of a servant, or any representative of such master or mistress, and giving a false character to the servant, is an offense punishable in England with a fine of £20. St. 32 Geo. III. c. 56.

FALSE FACT. In the law of evidence. The appearance or semblance of a fact; a fact existing only in statement, without any foundation in truth. Burr. Circ. Evid. 218, 219.

FALSE IMPRISONMENT. Any unlawful restraint of a man's liberty, whether in a place made use of for imprisonment generally, or in one used only on the particular occasion, or by words and an array of force, without bolts or bars, in any locality whatever. 2 Bish. Crim. Law, § 669; 8 N. H. 550; 9 N. H. 491; 7 Humph. (Tenn.) 43; 12 Ark. 43; 7 Q. B. 742; 5 Vt. 588; 3 Blackf. (Ind.) 46; 9 Johns. (N. Y.) 117; 1 A. K. Marsh. (Ky.) 345.

The characteristic of false imprisonment is the unlawfulness of the detention. If the person is detained under valid process, though it be erroneously or maliciously issued, it is not false imprisonment. 58 Wis. 276; 17 Kan. 436.

FALSE JUDGMENT (Law Lat. *falsum judicium; breve de falso judicio*). In English law. A writ which lies to the courts at Westminster to reverse the judgment of some inferior court not of record. 3 Bl. Comm. 34, 406; Fitzh. Nat. Brev. 18; Finch, Law, bk. 4, c. 47.

FALSE LATIN. In old practice. Ungrammatical Latin. Before the statute directing law proceedings to be in English, if a Latin word was significant, though not true or good Latin, yet an indictment, declaration, or fine should not be impeached or quashed on account of it, as where the word *proefato* was used for *proefatoe,* and the like. But if the word was not Latin, nor allowed by the law as *vocabulum artis* (a word or term of art), but was insensible there, if it were in a material point, as if *murdredum* was used for *murdrum,* in an indictment, or *burgariter* for *burglariter,* it made the whole vicious and insufficient. 5 Coke, 121b. See 4 Mod. 159; 5 Mod. 281; 11 Mod. 399.

FALSE NEWS. Spreading false news, whereby discord may grow between the sovereign of England and his people, or the great men of the realm, or which may produce other mischiefs, still seems to be a misdemeanor, under St. 3 Edw. I. c. 34. Steph. Dig. Crim. Law, § 95.

FALSE PERSONATION. See "Personation."

FALSE PRETENSES. In criminal law. False representations and statements, made with a fraudulent design to obtain "money, goods, wares, and merchandise," with intent to cheat. 2 Bouv. Inst. note 2308.

Such a fraudulent representation of a past or existing fact by one who knows it not to be true as is adapted to induce the person to whom it is made to part with something of value. 2 Bish. Crim. Law, § 415.

The offense is distinguished from "larceny" by the intent with which the injured person parts with his property. In larceny, the property is taken against the owner's will, while by false pretenses he is induced to voluntarily part with it. 77 N. Y. 114.

At common law it was not criminal to obtain property by false representation without false weights, measures, or tokens, but this is generally changed by statute. To constitute the offense of obtaining property by false pretenses:

(1) There must be an actual representation.

(2) The representation must be of a fact, not a prediction of future events, a promise, an expression of opinion, or mere dealer's talk.

(3) The pretense must be false at the time the property is obtained.

(4) It must be reasonably calculated to deceive, when considered with reference to the capacity of the person to whom it is made.

(5) It must be made (a) with knowledge that it is false; (b) with intent to defraud; (c) with intent to deprive the owner of his property.

(6) It must deceive the party to whom it is made; that is, it must be relied on.

(7) Negligence of the person defrauded is no defense.

(8) The property must be actually obtained.

(9) The person to whom the pretense was made must be defrauded.

(10) The thing obtained must be within the terms of the statutes. 2 Clark & Marshall, Crimes, 818.

FALSE RETURN. A return made by the sheriff, or other ministerial officer, to a writ, in which is stated a fact contrary to the truth, and injurious to one of the parties, or some one having an interest in it.

FALSE SWEARING. In English law. A misdemeanor consisting of making a willfully false oath, but not in a judicial proceeding, by which circumstance it is distinguished from perjury.

FALSE TOKEN. A false document or sign of the existence of a fact,—in general used for the purpose of fraud. See 2 Starkie, Ev. 563.

It must be something real and visible. 58 Ga. 409.

FALSEDAD. In Spanish law. Falsity; an alteration of the truth. Las Partidas, pt. 3, tit. 26, lib. 1.

Deception; fraud. Id. pt. 3, tit. 32, lib. 21.

FALSEHOOD. Any untrue assertion or proposition; a willful act or declaration contrary to the truth.

It does not always and necessarily imply a lie or willful untruth, but is generally used in the second sense here given. It is committed either by the willful act of the party, or by dissimulation, or by words. It is willful, for example, when the owner of a thing sells it twice, by different contracts, to different individuals, unknown to them; for in this the seller must willfully declare the thing is his own when he knows that it is not so. It is committed by dissimulation when a creditor, having an understanding with his former debtor, sells the land of the latter although he has been paid the debt which was due to him. Falsehood by word is committed when a witness swears to what he knows not to be true. See Rosc. Crim. Ev. 362.

FALSI CRIMEN. Fraudulent subornation or concealment, with design to darken or hide the truth, and make things appear otherwise than they are. It is committed (1) by words, as when a witness swears falsely; (2) by writing, as when a person antedates a contract; (3) by deed, as selling by false weights and measures. Wharton. See "Crimen Falsi."

FALSIFY.

——**In Chancery Practice.** To prove that an item in an account before the court as complete, which is inserted to the debit of the person falsifying, should have been omitted.

When a bill to open an account has been filed, the plaintiff is sometimes allowed to surcharge and falsify such account; and if anything has been inserted that is a wrong charge, he is at liberty to show it, and that is a falsification. 2 Ves. Jr. 565; 11 Wheat. (U. S.) 237. See "Surcharge."

——**In Criminal Law.** To alter or make false. The alteration or making false a record is punishable at common law by statute in the states, and, if of records of the United States courts, by act of congress of April 30, 1790. 1 Story, U. S. Laws, 86.

A fraudulent falsification of accounts is generally criminal. 140 Mass. 279; 18 Hun (N. Y.) 393.

——**In Practice.** To prove a thing to be false. Co. Litt. 104b.

FALSING. In Scotch law. Making or proving false. Bell, Dict.

FALSING OF DOOMS. In Scotch law. Protesting against a sentence, and taking an appeal to a higher tribunal. Bell, Dict.

An action to set aside a decree. Skene de Verb. Sign.

FALSO RETORNO BREVIUM (Law Lat.) In old English law. The name of a writ which might have been sued out against a sheriff for falsely returning writs. Cunningham.

FALSONARIUS. A forger; a counterfeiter. See "Falsarius." Hov. Frauds, 424.

FALSUM (Lat.) In civil law. A fraudulent imitation, perversion, or suppression of truth, such as an imitation of another's handwriting, or an instrument or writing belonging to him; a cutting out of a part of a writing.

FALSUS IN UNO, FALSUS IN OMNIbus. False in one thing, false in everything. 1 Sumn. (U. S.) 356; 7 Wheat. (U. S.) 338; 3 Wis. 645; 2 Jones (N. C.) 257.

FAMA, FIDES, ET OCULUS NON PATIuntur ludum. Fame, plighted faith, and eyesight do not endure deceit. 3 Bulst. 226.

FAMA, QUAE SUSPICIONEM INDUCIT, oriri debet apud bonos et graves, non quidem malevolos et maledicos, sed providas et fide dignas personas, non semel sed saepius, quia clamor minuit et defamatio manifestat. Report, which induces suspicion ought to arise from good and grave men; not, indeed, from malevolent and malicious men, but from cautious and credible persons; not only once, but frequently; for clamor diminishes, and defamation manifests. 2 Inst. 52.

FAMACIDE. A slanderer.

FAMILIA (Lat.)

——**In Roman Law.** A family.

This word had four different acceptations in the Roman law. In the first and most restricted sense it designated the *pater-familias*,—his wife, his children, and other descendants subject to his paternal power. In the second and more enlarged sense it comprehended all the *agnates*,—that is to say, all the different families who would all be subject to the paternal authority of a common chief if he were still living. Here it has the same meaning as *agnatio*. In a third acceptation it comprises the slaves and those who are *in mancipio* of the chief, although considered only as things, and without any tie of relationship. And, lastly, it signifies the whole fortune or patrimony of the chief. See "Pater-Familias;" 1 Ortolan, 28.

——**In Old English Law.** A household; all the servants belonging to one master. Du Cange; Cowell. A sufficient quantity of land to maintain one family. The same quantity of land is called sometimes *mansa* (a manse), *familia, carucata*. Du Cange; Cunningham; Cowell; Creasy, Church Hist.

FAMILIAE EMPTOR. In Roman law. An intermediate person who purchased the aggregate inheritance when sold *per aes et libram*, in the process of making a will under the Twelve Tables. This purchaser was merely a man of straw, transmitting the inheritance to the *haeres* proper. Brown.

FAMILIAE ERCISCUNDAE (Lat.) In civil law. An action which lay for any of the coheirs for the division of what fell to them by inheritance. Stair, Inst. lib. 1, tit. 7, § 15.

FAMILIARES REGIS. Persons of the king's household. The ancient title of the "six clerks" of chancery in England. Crabb, Com. Law, 184; 2 Reeve, Hist. Eng. Law, 249, 251. *Familier de la chauncery*. Kelham.

FAMILY. Persons collectively who live together in a house or under one head; a household. 90 Ill. 252; 26 Ill. App. 262.

Father, mother, and children, including the servants of the family. All the relations who descend from a common ancestor, or who spring from a common root. Code La. art. 3522, No. 16; 9 Ves. 323.

As used in homestead and exemption laws, it generally includes all persons resident under a roof whom the head of the family is under legal or moral duty to support. Thomp. Homest. & Ex. § 44.

In other connections it has been given a wider significance, having been held to include servants, but not boarders (53 Ill.

263), or even permanent boarders, but not visitors (13 Mass. 520).

In the construction of wills, the word "family," when applied to personal property, is synonymous with "kindred," or "relations," meaning next of kin, as applied to personalty (9 Ves. 323), and heirs at law, as applied to realty (17 Ves. 255). It may nevertheless be confined to particular relations by the context of the will, or may be enlarged by it, so that the expression may in some cases mean children, or next of kin, and in others may even include relations by marriage. 1 Rop. Leg. 115; 1 Hov. Supp. to Ves. 365, notes 6, 7; 2 Ves. Jr. 110; 4 Ves. 708; 5 Ves. 156; 17 Ves. 255; 3 East, 172; 5 Maule & S. 126. See "Legatee;" Dig. 50. 16. 195. 2.

FAMILY ARRANGEMENTS. An agreement made between a father and his son, or children, or between brothers, to dispose of property in a different manner to that which would otherwise take place.

In these cases, frequently, the mere relation of the parties will give effect to bargains otherwise without adequate consideration. 1 Chit. Prac. 67; 1 Turn. & R. 13.

FAMILY BIBLE. A Bible containing a record of the births, marriages, and deaths of the members of a family.

FAMILY MEETINGS, or FAMILY COUNCILS. In Louisiana. Meetings of at least five relations, or, in default of relations of minors or other persons on whose interest they are called upon to deliberate, then of the friends of such minors or other persons.

The appointment of the members of the family meeting is made by the judge. The relations or friends must be selected from among those domiciliated in the parish in which the meeting is held. The relations are selected according to their proximity, beginning with the nearest. The relation is preferred to the connection in the same degree; and among relations of the same degree the eldest is preferred. The under tutor must also be present. 6 Mart. (La.; N. S.) 455.

The family meeting is held before a justice of the peace, or notary public, appointed by the judge for the purpose. It is called for a fixed day and hour, by citations delivered at least three days before the day appointed for that purpose.

The members of the family meeting, before commencing their deliberations, take an oath before the officer before whom the meeting is held, to give their advice according to the best of their knowledge touching the interests of the person respecting whom they are called upon to deliberate. The officer before whom the family meeting is held must make a particular *proces verbal* of the deliberations, cause the members of the family meeting to sign it, if they know how to sign, and must sign it himself, and deliver a copy to the parties that they may have it homologated. Civ. Code La. arts. 305-311; Civ. Code, bk. 1, tit. 10, c. 2, § 4. See 31 La. Ann. 31; 14 La. Ann. 251; 10 La. 328.

FAMOSUS LIBELLUS (Lat.) Among the civilians, these words signified that species of *injuria* which corresponds nearly to libel or slander.

FANAL. Fr. In French Marine law. A large lantern, fixed upon the highest part of a vessel's stern. Ord. Mar. Appendix.

FANATICS. In old English law. Persons pretending to be inspired, and being a general name for Quakers, Anabaptists, and all other sectaries, and factious dissenters from the Church of England. St. 13 Car. II. c. 6; Jacob.

FANEGA. In Spanish law. A measure of land, which is not the same in every province. Dicc. de la Acad.; 2 White, Coll. 49. In Spanish America, the fanega consisted of six thousand four hundred square varas, or yards. 2 White, Coll. 138.

FARANDMAN. In Scotch law. A merchant stranger (*peregrinus mercator*). Skene de Verb. Sign. Spelman gives the word *faramannus*, from the law of the Burgundians (tit. 54, § 2), and derives it from Saxon *faran*, or *foeran*, to travel.

FARDEL. The fourth part of a yardland. Spelman. According to others, the eighth part. Noy, Compl. Lawy. 57; Cowell. See Cunningham.

FARDELLA. In old English law. A bundle or pack; a fardel. Fleta, lib. 1, c. 22, § 10.

FARDING DEAL. In old English law. The fourth part of an acre of land. Cowell. But Spelman considers it the same as fardel (*q. v.*)

FARE. A voyage or passage; the money paid for a voyage or passage. The latter is the modern signification. 1 Bouv. Inst. note 1036.

FARINAGIUM. A mill. L. Salic, tit. 32, § 3; Spelman.

FARLEU, or FARLEY. Money paid by tenants in lieu of a heriot. It was often applied to the best chattel, as distinguished from heriot, the best beast. Cowell.

FARLINGARII. Whoremongers and adulterers.

FARM.

Fearme, Ferm, Firm, (L. Lat. Firma; from Sax. fearme, feorme, food or provisions).

——**In English Law.** The rent of land under lease, anciently reserved and paid in provisions, (*in eduliis*), Spelman, voc. Firma. Cowell, voc. Ferme. 2 Bl. Comm. 318; when paid in money (*blanche firme*).

Spelman; 2 Bl. Comm. 42.

A term; a lease of lands; a leasehold interest. 2 Sharswood, Bl. Comm. 17; 1 Reeve, Hist. Eng. Law, 301, note; 6 Term R. 532; 2 Chit. Pl. 879, note (e). The land itself, let to farm or rent. 2 Bl. Comm. 368.

It is usually the chief messuage in a village or town whereto belongs great demesne of all sort. Cowell; Cunningham; Termes de la Ley.

A large tract or portion of land taken by a lease under a yearly rent payable by the tenant. Tomlins.

From this latter sense is derived its common modern signification of a large tract used for cultivation or other purposes, as raising stock, whether hired or owned by the occupant, including a messuage with outbuildings, gardens, orchard, yard, etc. Plowd. 195; Touch. 93.

——**In American or Modern Law.** A tract of land devoted, in part at least, to cultivation, without reference to its extent, or to the tenure by which it is held. 132 Ill. App. 277; 18 Pick. (Mass.) 553; 2 Bin. (Pa.) 238; 47 How. Pr. (N. Y.) 446.

FARM LET. Technical words in a lease creating a term for wears. Co. Litt. 45b; 2 Mod. 250; 1 Washb. Real Prop. Index, "Lease."

FARM OUT. To rent for a certain term. The collection of the revenue among the Romans was farmed out.

FARMER. The lessee of a farm. It is said that every lessee for life or years, although it be but of a small house and land, is called "farmer." This word implies no mystery, except it be that of husbandman. Cunningham; Cowell; 3 Sharswood, Bl. Comm. 318.

In common parlance, and as a term of description in a deed, "farmer" means one who cultivates a farm, whether he owns it or not. There may also be a farmer of the revenue, or of other personal property, as well as lands. Plowd. 195; Cunningham.

FARRAGO LIBELLI (Lat.) An ill-composed book containing a collection of miscellaneous subjects not properly associated nor scientifically arranged. Wharton.

FARRIER. One who takes upon himself the public employment of shoeing horses.

Like an innkeeper, a common carrier, and other persons who assume a public employment, a farrier is bound to serve the public as far as his employment goes, and an action lies against him for refusing, when a horse is brought to him at a reasonable time for such purpose, if he refuses (Oliph. Horses, 131), and he is liable for the unskillfulness of himself or servant in performing such work (1 Bl. Comm. 431), but not for the malicious act of the servant in purposely driving a nail into the foot of the horse with the intention of laming him (2 Salk. 440).

FARTHING. An English coin; the fourth part of a penny.

FARVAND. Standing by itself, this word signifies "passage by sea or water." In charter parties, it means voyage or passage by water. 18 C. B. 880.

FARYNDON INN. The ancient appelation of Serjeants' Inn. See "Inns of Court."

FAS (Lat.) Right; justice; the divine law. 3 Bl. Comm. 2; Calv. Lex.

FASIUS. A faggot of wood.

FAST BILL OF EXCEPTIONS. In Georgia, a bill of exceptions authorized in certain cases, in which the time for taking each step is much shorter than that prescribed in other cases, and a speedy review of the cases is made possible. See 66 Ga. 353.

FAST ESTATE. Real property; a term sometimes used in wills. 6 Johns. (N. Y.) 185; 9 N. Y. 502.

FASTERMANNES. Securities; bondsmen. Spelman.

FASTI. In Roman law. Lawful. *Dies fasti*, lawful days; days on which justice could lawfully be administered by the praetor. See "Dies Fasti."

FATETUR FACINUS QUI JUDICIUM fugit. He who flees judgment confesses his guilt. 3 Inst. 14; 5 Coke, 109b. But see Best, Pres. § 248.

FATHER. He by whom a child is begotten.

FATHOM. A measure of length, equal to six feet.

The word is probably derived from the Teutonic word "fad," which signifies the thread or yarn drawn out in spinning to the length of the arm, before it is run upon the spindle. Webster; Minsheu.

FATUA MULIER. A whore. Du Fresne.

FATUITAS. In old English law. Idiocy. Reg. Orig. 266.

FATUM (Lat.) Fate; a superhuman power; an event or cause of loss, beyond human foresight or means of prevention.

FATUOUS PERSON. One entirely destitute of reason; *is qui omnino desipit.* Ersk. Inst. bk. 1, tit. 7, § 48.

FATUUS. An idiot or fool. Braction, fol. 420b.

Foolish; absurd; indiscreet; or ill considered. *Fatuum judicium*, a foolish judgment or verdict. Bracton, fol. 289. Applied to the verdict of a jury which, though false, was not criminally so, or did not amount to perjury. Id.

FATUUS, APUD JURISCONSULTOS nostros, accipitur pro non compos mentis; et fatuus dicitur, qui omnino desipit. Fatuous, among our jurisconsults, is understood for a man not of right mind; and he is called *"fatuus"* who is altogether foolish. 4 Coke, 128.

FATUUS PRAESUMITUR QUI IN PROprio nomine errat. A man is presumed to be simple who makes a mistake in his own name. Code, 6. 24. 14; 5 Johns. Ch. (N. Y.) 148, 161.

FAUBOURG. A district or part of a town adjoining the principal city; as a faubourg of New Orleans. 18 La. 286.

FAUCES TERRAE (Lat. jaws of the land). Projecting headlands or promontories, including arms of the sea. Such arms of the sea are said to be inclosed within the *fauces terrae,* in contradistinction to the open sea. 1 Kent, Comm. 367. Where these *fauces* approach so near that a man standing on one shore can discern what another man is doing on the other shore, the water inclosed is *infra corpus comitatum,* within the body of the county. Andr. 231; 4 Inst. 140; 2 East, P. C. 804; 5 Wheat. (U. S.) 106; 5 Mason (U. S.) 290; 1 Story (U. S.) 259.

FAULT. An improper act or omission, which arises from ignorance, carelessness, or negligence. The act or omission must not have been meditated, and must have caused some injury to another. Lec. Elm. § 783. See "Dolus;" "Negligence;" 1 Miles (Pa.) 40.

Gross fault or neglect consists in not observing that care towards others which a man the least attentive usually takes of his own affairs. Such fault may, in some cases, afford a presumption of fraud, and in very gross cases it approaches so near as to be almost undistinguishable from it, especially when the facts seem hardly consistent with an honest intention. But there may be a gross fault without fraud. 2 Strange, 1099; Story, Bailm. §§ 18-22; Toullier, Dr. Civ. lib. 3, tit. 3, § 231.

Ordinary faults consist in the omission of that care which mankind generally pay to their own concerns; that is, the want of ordinary diligence.

A slight fault consists in the want of that care which very attentive persons take of their own affairs. This fault assimilates itself to, and in some cases is scarcely distinguishable from, mere accident or want of foresight.

This division has been adopted by common lawyers from the civil law. Although the civilians generally agree in this division, yet they are not without a difference of opinion. See Pothier, Observation generale sur le precedent Traite, et sur les suivants, printed at the end of his Traite des Obligations, where he cites Accurse, Alciat, Cujas, Duaren, D'Avezan, Vinnius, and Heineccius in support of this division. On the other side the reader is referred to Thomasius, tom. 2, Dissertationem, page 1006; Le Brun, cited by Jones, Bailm. 27; and Toullier, Dr. Civ. liv. 3, tit. 3, § 231.

——**In Maritime Law.** "Fault" is the technical term for negligence, particularly that contributing to a collision of vessels.

——**In the Law of Sale.** Defects, of any kind. 29 N. H. 343; 12 Ired. (N. C.) 49.

FAUTOR. In Spanish law. Accomplice; the person who aids or assists another in the commission of a crime.

FAUX. In French law. A falsification or fraudulent alteration or suppression of a thing by words, by writings, or by acts without either. Biret, Vocab.

Toullier says (tom. 9, note 188): *"Faux* may be understood in three ways: In its most extended sense, it is the alteration of truth, with or without intention; it is nearly synonymous with lying; in a less extended sense, it is the alteration of truth, accompanied with fraud, *mutatio veritatis cum dolo facta;* and lastly, in a narrow, or rather the legal, sense of the word, when it is a question to know if the *faux* be a crime, it is the fraudulent alteration of the truth in those cases ascertained and punished by the law." See "Crimen Falsi."

FAVOR. Bias; partiality; lenity; prejudice.

The grand jury are sworn to inquire into all offenses which have been committed, and into all violations of law, without fear, favor, or affection. See "Grand Jury." When a juror is influenced by bias or prejudice, so that there is not sufficient ground for a principal challenge, he may nevertheless be challenged for favor. See "Challenge;" Bac. Abr. "Juries" (E); Dig. 50. 17. 156. 4; 7 Pet. (U. S.) 160.

FAVORABILIA IN LEGE SUNT FISCUS, dos, vita, libertas. The treasury, dower, life, and liberty are things favored in law. Jenk. Cent. Cas. 94.

FAVORABILIORES REI POTIUS QUAM actores habentur. Defendants are rather to be favored than plaintiffs. Dig. 50. 17. 125. See 8 Wheat. (U. S.) 195, 196; Broom, Leg. Max. (3d London Ed.) 639.

FAVORABILIORES SUNT EXECUTIOnes aliis processibus quibuscunque. Executions are preferred to all other processes whatever. Co. Litt. 287.

FAVORES AMPLIANDI SUNT; ODIA restringenda. Favorable inclinations are to be enlarged; animosities restrained. Jenk. Cent. Cas. 186.

FEAL. Faithful. Britt. fol. 1.

FEAL AND DIVOT. A right in Scotland, similar to the right of turbary in England, for fuel, etc. Wharton.

FEALTY. That fidelity which every man who holds lands of another owes to him of whom he holds.

Under the feudal system, every owner of lands held them of some superior lord, from whom or from whose ancestors the tenant had received them. By this connection the lord became bound to protect the tenant in the enjoyment of the land granted to him; and, on the other hand, the tenant was bound to be faithful to his lord, and to defend him against all his enemies. This obligation was called *fidelitas,* or fealty. 1 Bl. Comm. 263; 2 Bl. Comm. 86; Co. Litt. 67b; 2 Bouv. Inst, note 1566.

This fealty was of two sorts,—that which is general, and is due from every subject to his prince; the other special, and required of such only as in respect of their fee are tied by this oath to their landlords. 1 Bl. Comm. 367; Cowell.

The oath or obligation of fealty was one of the essential requisites of the feudal relation. 2 Sharswood, Bl. Comm. 45, 86; Litt. §§ 117, 131; Wright, Ten. 35; Termes de la Ley; 1 Washb. Real Prop. 19. Fealty was due alike from freeholders and tenants for years as an incident to their estates, to be paid to the reversioner. Co. Litt. 67b. Tenants at will did not have fealty. 2 Flintoff, Real Prop. 222; Burton, Real Prop. 395, note; 1 Washb. Real Prop. 371.

It has now fallen into disuse, and is no longer exacted. 3 Kent, Comm. 510; Wright, Ten. 35, 55; Cowell.

FEAR. In criminal law. Dread; consciousness of approaching danger.

To constitute rape, the fear must be of death or great bodily harm. 39 Fla. 155; 45 Conn. 263; 139 Ind. 531.

Fear is an element of several crimes, and the nature and extent thereof varies with the crime. Thus, to constitute robbery, where the taking was by putting in fear, the fear may be of injury to the person (2 East, P. C. 712), of injury to property (2 East, P. C. 731), or of injury to character or reputation (12 Ga. 319). See "Putting in Fear."

FEASANCE. A doing; the doing of an act.

A making; the making of an indenture, release, or obligation. Litt. § 371; Dyer, (Fr. Ed.) 56b. The making of a statute. Keilw. 1b.

FEASANT. Doing or making.

FEASOR (Lat.) Doer; maker. *Feasors del estatute,* makers of the statute. Dyer, 3b.

FEASTS. Certain established periods in the Christian church. Formerly the days of the feasts of saints were used to indicate the dates of instruments and memorable events. 8 Toullier, Dr. Civ. note 81. These are yet used in England. There they have Easter term, Hilary term, etc.

FECIAL LAW. The law relating to declarations of war and treaties of peace among the Romans. So called from the *feciales (q. v.),* who were charged with its execution. 1 Kent, Comm. 6. See "Jus Feciale."

FECIALES. Amongst the ancient Romans, that order of priests who discharged the duties of ambassadors. Subsequently their duties appear to have related more particularly to the declaring war and peace. Calv. Lex.

FEDERAL. A term commonly used to express a league or compact between two or more states.

In the United States, the central government of the Union is federal. The constitution was adopted "to form a more perfect union" among the states, for the purpose of self-protection, and for the promotion of their mutual happiness.

FEE. A reward or wages given to one for the execution of his office, or for professional services, as those of a counsellor or physician. Cowell.

Fees differ from costs in this, that the former are, as above mentioned, a recompense to the officer for his services; and the latter, an indemnification to the party for money laid out and expended in his suit. 11 Serg. & R. (Pa.) 248; 9 Wheat. (U. S.) 262. See 4 Bin. (Pa.) 267.

That which is held of some superior on condition of rendering him services.

A fee is defined by Spelman (Feuds, c. 1) as the right which the tenant or vassal has to the use of lands, while the absolute property remained in a superior. But this early and strict meaning of the word speedily passed into its modern signification of an estate of inheritance. 2 Bl. Comm. 106; Cowell; Termes de la Ley; 1 Washb. Real Prop. 51; Co. Litt. 1b; 1 Prest. Est. 420; 3 Kent, Comm. 514. The term may be used of other property as well as lands. Old Nat. Brev. 41.

The term is generally used to denote as well the land itself so held as the estate in the land, which seems to be its stricter meaning. Wright, Ten. 19, 49; Cowell. The word "fee" is explained to signify that the land or other subject of property belongs to its owner, and is transmissible, in the case of an individual, to those whom the law appoints to succeed him, under the appellation of "heirs;" and, in the case of corporate bodies, to those who are to take on themselves the corporate function, and, from the manner in which the body is to be continued, are denominated "successors." 1 Co. Litt. 271b; Wright, Ten. 147, 150; 2 Bl. Comm. 104, 106; Bouv. Inst. Index. Sometimes used for "fee simple."

The compass or circuit of a manor or lordship. Cowell.

——**Fee Simple.** An estate belonging to a man and his heirs absolutely. An estate of inheritance. Co. Litt. 1b; 2 Bl. Comm. 106.

The word "simple" adds no meaning to the word "fee," standing by itself. But it excludes all qualification or restriction as to the persons who may inherit it as heirs, thus distinguishing it from a fee tail, as well as from an estate which, though inheritable, is subject to conditions or collateral determination. 1 Washb. Real Prop. 51; Wright, Ten. 146; 1 Prest. Est. 420; Litt. § 1.

It is the largest possible estate which a man can have, being an absolute estate in perpetuity. It is where lands are given to a man and to his heirs absolutely without any end or limitation put to the estate. Plowd. 557; Atk. Conv. 183; 2 Sharswood, Bl. Comm. 106.

——**Fee Tail.** One limited to particular classes of heirs. An inheritable estate which can descend to certain classes of heirs only. It is necessary that they should be heirs "of the body" of the ancestor. It corresponds with the *feudum talliatum* of the feudal law. The estate itself is said to have been derived from the Roman system of restricting estates. 1 Spence, Eq. Jur. 21; 1 Washb. Real Prop. 66; 2 Bl. Comm. 112, note. See, also, 2 Inst. 333; White & T. Lead. Cas. 607; 4 Kent, Comm. 14 et seq.

——**Determinable Fee.** One which is liable to be determined, but which may continue forever. 1 Plowd. 557; Shep. Touch. 97; 2 Bl. Comm. 109; Cro. Jac. 593; 10 Viner, Abr. 133; Fearne, Cont. Rem. 187; 3 Atk. 74; Ambl. 204; 9 Mod. 28. See "Determinable Fee."

——**Qualified Fee.** An interest given to a man and certain of his heirs at the time of its limitation. Litt. § 254; Co. Litt. 27a, 220; 1 Prest. Est. 449. See "Qualified Fee."

——**Conditional Fee.** This includes one that is either to commence or determine on some condition. 10 Coke, 95b; Prest. Est. 476; Fearne, Cont. Rem. 9. See "Condition."

FEE EXPECTANT. An estate where lands are given to a man and his wife, and the heirs of their bodies.

FEE FARM. Land held of another in fee; that is, in perpetuity by the tenant and his heirs at a yearly rent, without fealty, homage, or other services than such as are specially comprised in the feoffment. Cowell. Fealty, however, was incident to a holding in fee farm, according to some authors. Spelman; Termes de la Ley.

Land held at a perpetual rent. 2 Sharswood, Bl. Comm. 43.

FEE-FARM RENT. The rent reserved on granting a fee farm. It might be one-fourth the value of the land, according to Cowell; one-third, according to other authors. Spelman; Termes de la Ley.

FEGANGI (from Saxon *feh*, money or goods, and *gange*, to go). In old European law. A thief caught in the act of going off with the thing stolen. LL. Longobard, lib. 1, tit. 25, 1, 2; Spelman.

FEHMGERICHTE (or **VEHMGERICHT**). An irregular tribunal which existed and flourished in Westphalia during the thirteenth and fourteenth centuries.

From the close of the fourteenth century its importance rapidly diminished, and it was finally suppressed by Jerome Bonaparte in 1811.

FEIGNED ACTION. In practice. An action brought on a pretended right, when the plaintiff has no true cause of action, for some illegal purpose. In a feigned action, the words of the writ are true. It differs from "false action," in which case the words of the writ are false. Co. Litt. 361, § 689.

FEIGNED ISSUE. In practice. An issue brought by consent of the parties, or by the direction of a court of equity, or of such courts as possess equitable powers, to determine before a jury some disputed matter of fact which the court has not the power or is unwilling to decide. 3 Bl. Comm. 452; Bouv. Inst. Index.

FELAGUS (Lat.) One bound for another by oath; a sworn brother. Du Cange. A friend bound in the decennary for the good behavior of another. One who took the place of the deceased. Thus, if a person was murdered, the recompense due from the murderer went to the father or mother of the deceased; if he had none, to the lord; if he had none, to his *felagus*, or sworn brother. Cunningham; Cowell; Du Cange.

FELE. See "Feal."

FELIX QUI POTUIT RERUM COGNOSCERE CAUSAS. Happy is he who has been able to understand the causes of things. Co. Litt. 231.

FELLOW HEIR. A coheir; a partner of the same inheritance.

FELLOW SERVANTS. Certain servants of a common master, for injuries to one of whom by the negligence of another the master was not liable if he had exercised due care in the selection of the servants, and the providing of safe appliances.

The doctrine is an exception to the rule of *respondeat superior*, and rests upon the reason that coservants are better able to guard against each other's negligence than the master is to protect them. The earliest English case is found in 3 Mees. & W. 1. Earliest American cases are found in 1 McMull. (S. C.) 385, and 4 Metc. (Mass.) 49.

The question of who are fellow servants has given rise to a diversity of rules in different jurisdictions, making a general definition impossible.

FELO DE SE (Lat.) In criminal law. A felon of himself; a self-murderer. See "Suicide."

FELON. One convicted and sentenced for a felony (*q. v.*)

FELONIA (Lat.) Felony; the act or offense by which a vassal forfeited his fee. Spelman; Calv. Lex. *Per feloniam,* with a criminal intention. Co. Litt. 391.

Felonice was formerly used also in the sense of "feloniously." Cunningham.

FELONIA, EX VI TERMINI, SIGNIFICAT quodlibet capitale crimen felleo animo perpetratum. Felony, by force of the term, signifies some capital crime perpetrated with a malignant mind. Co. Litt. 391.

FELONIA IMPLICATUR IN QUOLIBET proditione. Felony is implied in every treason. 3 Inst. 15.

FELONIOUS HOMICIDE. The killing of a human creature, of my age or sex, without justification or excuse. It may include killing one's self, as well as any other person. 4 Sharswood, Bl. Comm. 188. See "Homicide."

FELONIOUSLY. In pleading. This is a technical word which must be introduced into every indictment for a felony, charging the offense to have been committed feloniously. No other word nor any circumlocution will supply its place. Comyn, Dig. "Indictment" (G 6); Bac. Abr. "Indictment" (G 1); 2 Hale, P. C. 172, 184; Hawk. P. C. bk. 2, c. 25, § 55; Cro. Car. 37; Williams, Just. "Indictment" (4); Cro. Eliz. 193; 5 Coke, 121; 1 Chit. Crim. Law, 242; 1 Bennett & H. Lead. Crim. Cas. 154.

FELONY.

——**At Common Law.** An offense which occasions a total forfeiture of either lands or goods, or both, to which capital or other punishment may be superadded, according to the degree of guilt. 4 Bl. Comm. 94, 95; 1 Russ. Crimes, 42; 1 Chit. Prac. 14; Co. Litt. 391; 1 Hawk. P. C. c. 37; 5 Wheat. (U. S.) 153, 159.

The common-law felonies were murder, manslaughter, rape, sodomy, robbery, larceny, arson, burglary, and perhaps mayhem. 1 Clark & Marshall, Crimes, 12; 2 Bish. New Crim. Law, § 1008.

——**In American Law.** The word has no clearly defined meaning, but includes offenses of a considerable gravity. 1 Park. Cr. R. (N. Y.) 39; 4 Ohio St. 542.

In the absence of a statute defining felonies, it is generally held that no statutory crime is a felony unless it is so declared by the statute creating it. 66 Fed. 290; 7 Mass. 245. In other jurisdictions it is enacted that all offenses punishable by death or by confinement in the penitentiary are felonies. See 99 N. Y. 210; 35 Wis. 308; 10 Mich. 169; 89 Va. 570; 48 Me. 218.

FEME, or **FEMME.** A woman.

FEME COVERT. A married woman.

FEME SOLE. An unmarried woman; includes widows and divorced women.

FEME SOLE TRADER. In English law. A married woman, who, by the custom of London, trades on her own account, independently of her husband; so called because, with respect to her trading, she is the same as a *feme sole.* Jacob; Cro. Car. 68.

The term is applied also to women deserted by their husbands, who do business as *femes sole.* 1 Pet. (U. S.) 105.

FEMICIDE. The killing of a woman. Wharton.

FEMININE. Of or belonging to females.

When the feminine is used, it is generally confined to females; as, if a man bequeathed all his mares to his son, his horses would not pass. See 3 Brev. (N. C.) 9.

FENATIO, or **FEONATIO.** In forest law. The fawning of deer; the fawning season. Spelman.

FENCE. A structure or erection between two contiguous estates, so as to divide them, or on the same estate, so as to divide one part from another.

——**In Scotch Law.** To hedge in or protect by certain forms. To fence a court, to open in due form. Pitc. Crim. Law, pt. 1, p. 75.

FENCE MONTH. A month in which it is forbidden to hunt in the forest. It begins fifteen days before midsummer, and ends fifteen days after. Manw. For. Laws, c. 23. There were also fence months for fish. Called, also, "defence month," because the deer are then defended from "scare or harm." Cowell; Spelman; Cunningham.

FENERATION. Usuary; the gain of interest; the practice of increasing money by lending.

FENGELD (Saxon). A tribute exacted for repelling enemies. Spelman.

FEOD. Said to be compounded of the two Saxon words *feoh* (stipend) and *odh* (property); by others, to be composed of *feoh* (stipend) and *hod* (condition). 2 Bl. Comm. 45; Spelman. See "Fee."

FEODAL. Belonging to a fee or feud; feudal. More commonly used by the old writers than "feudal."

FEODAL ACTIONS. Real actions. 3 Sharswood, Bl. Comm. 117.

FEODALITY. Fealty.

FEODARY. An officer in the court of wards, appointed by the master of that court, by virtue of St. 32 Hen. VIII. c. 46, to be present with the escheator at the finding offices, and to give in evidence for the king as to value and tenure. He was also to survey and receive rents of the ward lands, and assign dower to the king's widows. The office was abolished by St. 12 Car. II. c. 24; Kennett; Cowell.

FEODATORY, or FEUDATORY. The tenant who held his estate by feudal service. Termes de la Ley.

FEODI FIRMA (Law Lat.) Fee farm (*q. v.*)

FEODI FIRMARIUS. The lessee of a fee farm.

FEODUM. The form in use by the old English law writers instead of *feudum*, and having the same meaning. *Feudum* is used generally by the more modern writers and by the feudal law writers. Litt. § 1; Spelman. There were various classes of *feoda.*

Feodum militaris or *militare*, a knight's fee; *feodum improprium*, an improper or derivative feud; *feodum proprium*, a pure or proper fee; *feodum simplex*, a fee simple; *feodum talliatum*, a fee tail. 2 Bl. Comm. 58, 62; Litt. §§ 1, 13; Spelman.

FEODUM ANTIQUUM. An inherited feud, as distinguished from *feodum novum*, a feud acquired by the tenant.

FEODUM EST QUOD QUIS TENET EX quacunque causa; sive sit tenementum sive redditus. A fee is that which any one holds from whatever cause, whether tenement or rent. Co. Litt. 1.

FEODUM NOBILE. A fief for which the tenant did guard and owed homage. Spelman.

FEODUM NOVUM. See "Feodum Antiquum."

FEODUM SIMPLEX QUIA FEODUM idem est quod haereditas, et simplex idem est quod legitimum vel purum; et sic feodum simplex idem est quod haereditas legitima vel haereditas pura. A fee simple, so called because fee is the same as inheritance, and simple is the same as lawful or pure; and thus fee simple is the same as a lawful inheritance, or pure inheritance. Litt. § 1.

FEODUM TALLIATUM, i. e., HAEREDItas in quandam certitudinem limitata. Fee tail, *i. e.*, an inheritance limited in a definite descent. Litt. § 13.

FEOFFAMENTUM. A feoffment. 2 Bl. Comm. 310.

FEOFFARE. To bestow a fee. 1 Reeve, Hist. Eng. Law, 91.

FEOFFATOR. In old English law. A feoffer; one who gives or bestows a fee; one who makes a feoffment. Bracton, fols. 12b, 81.

FEOFFEE. He to whom a fee is conveyed. Litt. § 1; 2 Bl. Comm. 20.

FEOFFEE TO USES. A person to whom land was conveyed for the use of a third party. One holding the same position with reference to a use that a trustee does to a trust. 1 Greenl. Cruise, Dig. 333. He answers to the *haeres fiduciarius* of the Roman law.

FEOFFMENT. A gift of any corporeal hereditaments to another. It operates by transmutation of possession, and it is essential to its completion that the seisin be passed. Watk. Conv. 183.

The conveyance of a corporeal hereditament either by investiture or by livery of seisin. 1 Sullivan, Lect. 143; 1 Washb. Real Prop. 33.

The instrument or deed by which such hereditament is conveyed.

This was one of the earliest moods of conveyance used in the common law. It signified originally the grant of a fee or feud; but it came in time to signify the grant of a fee inheritance in fee, respect being had rather to the perpetuity of the estate granted than to the feudal tenure. 1 Reeve, Hist. Eng. Law, 90. The feoffment was likewise accompanied by livery of seisin. 1 Washb. Real Prop. 33. The conveyance by feoffment with livery of seisin has become infrequent, if not obsolete, in England, and in this country has not been used in practice. Cruise, Dig. tit. 32, c. 4, § 3; Shep. Touch. c. 9; 2 Bl. Comm. 20; Co. Litt. 9; 4 Kent, Comm. 467; Comyn, Dig.; 12 Viner, Abr. 167; Bac. Abr.; Dane, Abr. c. 104; 1 Washb. Real Prop. 33; 8 Cranch (U. S.) 229.

FEOFFOR. He who makes a feoffment. 2 Bl. Comm. 20; Litt. § 1.

FEOH (Saxon). A reward; wages; a fee. The word was in common use in these senses. Spelman, Feuds.

FEORME, or FEARME (Saxon; Law Lat. *firma*). Food, provisions. Spelman, voc. "Firma." An entertainment or feast. Id. *Herod gegeafwode mycle feorme*, Herod made a great feast. Sax. Evang. St. Marc. vi. 21.

Rent paid in provisions. Spelman, ubi supra; Cowell, voc. "Ferme;" 2 Bl. Comm. 318.

A manor. Spelman, ubi supra. Hence, the Law Latin *firma*, and English ferm, farm (*q. v.*)

FERAE BESTIAE. Wild beasts.

FERAE NATURAE (Lat. of a wild nature; untamed). A term used to designate animals not usually tamed, or not regarded as reclaimed, so as to become the subjects of property. 2 Bl. Comm. 390.

FERDFARE. A summons to serve in the army.

FERIA (Lat.) In old English law. A week day; a holiday; a day on which process may not be served; a fair; a ferry. Du Cange; Spelman; Cowell; 4 Reeve, Hist. Eng. Law, 17.

FERIAE (Lat.) In civil law. Holidays. Numerous festivals were called by this name in the early Roman empire. In the later Roman empire the single days occurring at intervals of a week apart, commencing with the seventh day of the ecclesiastical year, were so called. Du Cange.

FERIAL DAYS. Originally and properly days free from labor and pleading. In St. 27 Hen. VI. c. 5, working days. Cowell.

FERITA. A wound.

FERME (Saxon). A farm; a rent; a lease; a house or land, or both, taken by indenture or lease. Plowd. 195; Vicat; Cowell. See "Farm."

FERMER, or **FERMOR.** A lessee; a farmer; one who holds a term, whether of lands or an incorporeal right, such as customs or revenue.

FERMORY. A place in monasteries where the poor were fed. Spelman.

FERRI (Lat.) In the civil law. To be borne (on the person). Distinguished from *portari*, to be carried (on an animal). Dig. 50. 16. 235.

FERRIAGE. The toll or price paid for the transportation of persons and property across a ferry.

FERRY. A liberty to have a boat upon a river for the transportation of men, horses, and carriages, with their contents, for a reasonable toll. 42 Me. 9; 3 Zab. (N. J.) 206; Woolr. Ways, 217. The term is also used to designate the place where such liberty is exercised. 4 Mart. (La.; N. S.) 426; 30 Barb. (N. Y.) 311.

FERRYMAN. One employed in taking persons across a river or other stream, in boats or other contrivances, at a ferry. 3 Ala. 160; 8 Dana (Ky.) 158.

FESTINATIO JUSTITIAE EST NOVERca infortunii. The hurrying of justice is the stepmother of misfortune. Hob. 97.

FESTING MAN. A bondsman; a surety; a pledge; a frank pledge. It was one privilege of monasteries that they should be free from festing men, which Cowell explains to mean not to be bound for any man's forthcoming who should transgress the law. Cowell.

FESTING PENNY. Earnest given to servants when hired or retained. The same as "arles penny." Cowell.

FESTINUM REMEDIUM (Lat. a speedy remedy). A term applied to those cases where the remedy for the redress of an injury is given without any unnecessary delay. Bac. Arb. "Assise" (A). The action of dower is *festinum remedium*, and so is that of assise.

FETTERS. A sort of iron put on the leg of a malefactor or a person accused of crime.

FEU. In Scotch law. A holding or tenure where the vassal in place of military service makes his return in grain or money. Distinguished from "wardholding," which is the military tenure of the country. Bell, Dict.; Ersk. Inst. lib. 2, tit. 3, § 7.

FEU ANNUALS. In Scotch law. The *reddendo*, or annual return from the vassal to a superior in a feu holding. Wharton.

FEU ET LIEU (Fr.) In old French and Canadian law. Hearth and home. A term importing actual settlement upon land by a tenant.

FEU HOLDING. A holding by tenure of rendering grain or money in place of military service. Bell, Dict.

FEUAR. In Scotch law. The tenant of a feu; a feu vassal. Bell, Dict.

FEUD. Land held of a superior on condition of rendering him services. 2 Bl. Comm. 106.

A hereditary right to use lands, rendering services therefor to the lord, while the property in the land itself remains in the lord. Spelman, Feuds, c. 1.

The same as feod, fief, and fee. 1 Sullivan, Lect. 128; 1 Spence, Eq. Jur. 34; Dalr. Feud. Prop. 99; 1 Washb. Real Prop. 18.

In Scotland and the north of England, a combination of all the kin to revenge the death of any of the blood upon the slayer and all his race. Termes de la Ley; Whishaw.

FEUDA. Fees.

FEUDAL ACTIONS. Real actions. 3 Bl. Comm. 117.

FEUDAL LAW, or **FEODAL LAW.** A system of tenures of real property which prevailed in the countries of western Europe during the middle ages, arising from the peculiar political condition of those countries, and radically affecting the law of personal rights and of movable property.

Although the feudal system has never obtained in this country, and is long since extinct throughout the greater part of Europe, some understanding of the theory of the system is essential to an accurate knowledge of the English constitution, and of the doctrines of the common law in respect to real property. The feudal tenure was a right to lands on the condition of performing services and rendering allegiance to a superior lord. It had its origin in the military immigrations of the Northmen, who overran the falling Roman empire. Many writers have sought to trace the beginning of the system in earlier periods, and resemblances more or less distinct have been found in the tenures prevailing in the Roman republic and empire, in Turkey, in Hindostan, in ancient Tuscany, as well as in the system of Celtic clanship. 1 Hallam Mid. Ages; Stuart, Soc. in Europe;

Robertson, Hist. Charles V.; Pink. Diss.; Montesq. Esp. des Lois, liv. 30, c. 2; Meyer, des Inst. Judiciares, tom. 1, p. 4.

But the origin of the feudal system is so obvious in the circumstances under which it arose that perhaps there is no other connection between it and these earlier systems than that all are the outgrowth of political conditions somewhat similar. It has been said that the system is nothing more than the natural fruit of conquest; but the fact that the conquest was by immigrants, and that the conquerors made the acquired country their permanent abode, is an important element in the case, and in so far as other conquests have fallen short of this, the military tenures resulting have fallen short of the feudal system. The military chieftains of the northern nations allotted the lands of the countries they occupied among themselves and their followers, with a view at once to strengthen their own power and ascendency, and to provide for their followers.

Some lands were allotted to individuals as their own proper estates, and these were termed "allodial;" but, for the most part, those lands which were not retained by the chieftain he assigned to his comites, or knights, to be held by his permission, in return for which they assured him of their allegiance, and undertook for him military service.

It resulted that there was a general dismemberment of the political power into many petty nations and petty sovereignties. The violence and disorders of the times rendered it necessary both for the strong to seek followers, and for the weak to seek a protecting allegiance; and this operated on the one hand to lead the vassals to divide again among their immediate retainers the lands which they had received from the paramount lord, upon similar terms, and by this subinfeudation the number of fiefs was largely increased; and the same circumstances operated on the other hand to absorb the allodial estates by inducing allodial proprietors to surrender their lands to some neighboring chieftain, and receive them again from him under feudal tenure. Every one who held lands upon a feudal tenure was bound, when called upon by his benefactor or immediate lord, to defend him, and such lord was, in turn, subordinate to his superior, and bound to defend him, and so on upwards to the paramount lord or king, who in theory of the law was the ultimate owner of all the lands of the realm. The services which the vassals were bound to render to their lords were chiefly military; but many other benefits were required, such as the power of the lord or the good will of the tenant would sanction.

This system came to its height upon the continent in the empire of Charlemange and his successors. It was completely established in England in the time of William the Norman and William Rufus, his son; and the system thus established may be said to be the foundation of the English law of real property, and the position of the landed aristocracy, and of the civil constitution of the realm. And when we reflect that in the middle ages real property had a relative importance far beyond that of movable property, it is not surprising that the system should have left its traces for a long time upon the law of personal relations and personal property. The feudal tenures were originally temporary, at the will of the lord, or from year to year; afterwards they came more commonly to be held for the life of the vassal; and gradually they acquired an inheritable quality, the lord recognizing the heir of the vassal as the vassal's successor in his service.

The chief incidents of the tenure by military service were:

(1) Aids. A pecuniary tribute, required by the lord in an emergency, *e. g.*, a ransom for his person if taken prisoner, or money to make his son a knight, or to marry his daughter.

(2) Relief. The consideration which the lord demanded upon the death of a vassal for allowing the vassal's heir to succeed to the possession; and connected with this may be mentioned *primer seisin*, which was the compensation that the lord demanded for having entered upon the land, and protected the possession until the heir appeared to claim it.

(3) Fines upon alienation. A consideration exacted by the lord for giving his consent that the vassal should transfer the estate to another, who should stand in his place in respect to the services owed.

(4) Escheat. Where, on the death of the vassal, there was no heir, the land reverted to the lord; also, where the vassal was guilty of treason; for the guilt of the vassal was deemed to taint the blood, and the lord would no longer recognize him or his heirs.

(5) Wardship and marriage. Where the heir was a minor, the lord, as a condition of permitting the estate to descend to one who could not render military service, assumed the guardianship of the heir, and, as such, exercised custody both of his person and of the property, without accounting for the profits, until the heir, if a male, was twenty-one and could undertake the military services, or, if a female, until she was of a marriageable age, when, on her marriage, her husband might render the services. The lord claimed, in virtue of his guardianship, to make a suitable match for his ward, and if wards refused to comply they were mulcted in damages.

Feudal tenures were abolished in England by St. 12 Car. II. c. 24; but the principles of the system still remain at the foundation of the English and American law of real property. Although in many of the states of the United States all lands are held to be allodial, it is the theory of the law that the ultimate right of property is in the state; and in most of the states escheat is regulated by statute. "The principles of the feudal system are so interwoven with every part of our jurisprudence," says Tilghman, C. J., "that to attempt to eradicate them would be to destroy the whole." 3 Serg. & R. (Pa.) 447; 9 Serg. & R. (Pa.) 333. "Though our property is allodial," says Gibson, C. J., " yet feudal tenures may be said to exist among us in their consequences and the qualities which they originally imparted to estates; as, for instance, in precluding every limitation founded on an abeyance of the fee." 3 Watts (Pa.) 71; 1 Whart. (Pa.) 337; 7 Serg. & R. (Pa.) 188; 13 Pa. St. 35.

Many of these incidents are rapidly disappearing, however, by legislative changes of the law.

The principles of the feudal law will be found in Litt. Ten.; Wright, Ten.; 2 Bl. Comm. c. 5; Dalr. Feud. Prop.; Sullivan, Lect.; Book of Fiefs; Spelman, Feuds; Cruise, Dig.; Le Grand Coutumier; the Salic Laws; the Capitularies; Les Establissements de St. Louis; Assise de Jerusalem; Poth. des Fiefs; Merlin, Repert; Dalloz, Dict.; Guizot, Hist. de France, Essai 5.

The principal original collection of the feudal law of continental Europe is a digest of the twelfth century,—*feudorum consuetudines*,—which is the foundation of many of the subsequent compilations. The American student will perhaps find no more convenient source of information than 2 Sharswood, Bl. Comm. 43, and Greenl. Cruise, Dig. Introd.

FEUDAL TENURES. The tenures of land under the feudal system.

FEUDALISM. The feudal system.

FEUDALIZE. To reduce to a feudal tenure; to conform to feudalism. Webster.

FEUDARY. A feud; a feudal tenant.

FEUDATORY. See "Feodatory."

FEUDBOTE. A recompense for engaging in a feud, and the damages consequent, it having been the custom in ancient times for all the kindred to engage in their kinsman's quarrel. Jacob.

FEUDE, or **DEADLY FEUDE.** A German word, signifying implacable hatred, not to be satisfied but with the death of the enemy. Such was that among the people in Scotland and in the northern parts of England, which was a combination of all the kindred to revenge the death of any of the blood upon the slayer and all his race. Termes de la Ley.

FEUDIST. A writer on feuds, as Cujacius, Spelman, etc.

FEUDO. In Spanish law. Feud or fee. White, New Recop. bk. 2, tit. 2, c. 2.

FEUDUM. A feud, fief, or fee. A right of using and enjoying forever the lands of another, which the lord grants on condition that the tenant shall render fealty, military duty, and other services. Spelman. It is not properly the land, but a right in the land. This form of the word is used by the feudal writers. The earlier English writers generally prefer the form *feodum*, but the meaning is the same.

FEUDUM ANTIGUUM. A fee descended from the tenant's ancestors. 2 Bl. Comm. 212. One which had been possessed by the relations of the tenant for four generations. Spelman.

FEUDUM APERTUM. A fee which the lord might enter upon and resume either through failure of issue of the tenant, or any crime or legal cause on his part. Spelman; 2 Bl. Comm. 245.

FEUDUM FRANCUM. A free feud. One which was noble and free from talliage and other subsidies to which the *plebeia feuda* (vulgar feuds) were subject. Spelman.

FEUDUM HAUBERTICUM. A fee held on the military service of appearing fully armed at the *ban* and *arriere ban*. Spelman.

FEUDUM IMPROPRIUM. A derivative fee.

FEUDUM INDIVIDUUM. A fee which could descend to the eldest son alone. 2 Bl. Comm. 215.

FEUDUM LIGIUM. A liege fee. One where the tenant owed fealty to his lord against all other persons. Spelman; 1 Bl. Comm. 367.

FEUDUM MATERNUM. A fee descending from the mother's side. 2 Bl. Comm. 212.

FEUDUM NOBILE. A fee for which the tenant did guard and owed fealty and homage. Spelman.

FEUDUM NOVUM. One which began with the person of the feudatory, and did not come to him by descent.

FEUDUM NOVUM UT ANTIQUUM. A new fee held with the qualities and incidents of an ancient one. 2 Bl. Comm. 212.

FEUDUM PATERNUM. A fee which the paternal ancestors had held for four generations. Calv. Lex.; Spelman. One descendible to heirs on the paternal side only. 2 Bl. Comm. 223. One which might be held by males only. Du Cange.

FEUDUM PROPRIUM. A genuine original feud or fee, of a military nature, in the hands of a military person. 2 Sharswood, Bl. Comm. 57.

FEUDUM TALLIATUM. A restricted fee; one limited to descend to certain classes of heirs. 2 Bl. Comm. 112, note; 1 Washb.

Real Prop. 66; Spelman. See, generally, Le Grand Coutumier; Spelman, Feuds; Du Cange; Calv. Lex.; Dalr. Feud. Prop.; Poth. des Fiefs; Merlin, Repert. "Feodalite."

FI. FA. An abbreviation for *fieri facias* (*q. v.*)

FIANCER (Law Fr.) To pledge one's faith. Kelham.

FIANZA (Spanish). Surety; the contract by which one person engages to pay the debt or fulfill the obligations of another if the latter should fail to do so.

FIAR. In Scotch law. One whose property is charged with a life rent.

FIAR PRICES. The value of grain in the different counties of Scotland, fixed yearly by the respective sheriffs, in the month of February, with the assistance of juries. These regulate the prices of grain stipulated to be sold at the fiar prices, or when no price has been stipulated. Ersk. Inst. 1. 4. 6; Wharton.

FIAT. An order of a judge or of an officer whose authority, to be signified by his signature, is necessary to authenticate the particular acts. A short order or warrant of the judge, commanding that something shall be done. See 1 Tidd, Prac. 100, 108.

FIAT IN BANKRUPTCY. An order of the lord chancellor that a commission of bankruptcy shall issue. 1 Deac. Bankr. 106.

Fiats were abolished by 12 & 13 Vict. c. 116.

FIAT JUSTITIA. Let justice be done. Words formerly written by the king at the top of a petition for a warrant to bring a writ of error in parliament, signifying his assent. Jacob; Dyer, 375; Staund. Prerog. 22.

FIAT JUSTITIA RUAT COELUM. Let justice be done, though the heavens should fall. Branch, Princ. 161.

FIAT PROUT FIERI CONSUERIT; NIL temere novandum. Let it be done as formerly; let no innovation be made rashly. Jenk. Cent. Cas. 116; Branch, Princ.

FICTIO CEDIT VERITATI. FICTIO JUris non est, ubi veritas. Fiction yields to truth. Where truth is, fiction of law does not exist.

FICTIO EST CONTRA VERITATEM, sed pro veritate habetur. Fiction is against the truth, but it is to be esteemed truth.

FICTIO LEGIS INIQUE OPERATUR ALieni damnum vel injuriam. Fiction of law is wrongful if it works loss or injury to any one. 2 Coke, 35; 3 Coke, 36; Broom, Leg. Max. (3d London Ed.) 122.

FICTIO LEGIS NEMINEM LAEDIT. A fiction of law injures no one. 2 Rolle, Abr. 502; 3 Bl. Comm. 43; 17 Johns. (N. Y.) 348.

FICTION. The legal assumption that something which is or may be false is true.

It differs from a presumption in that a fiction is an assumption as true of something admittedly false; while a presumption is an attempt to arrive at the truth by inference.

FICTITIOUS ACTION. A suit brought on pretense of a controversy, when no such controversy in truth exists. Such actions have usually been brought on a pretended wager, for the purpose of obtaining the opinion of the court on a point of law. Courts of justice were constituted for the purpose of deciding really existing questions of right between parties; and they are not bound to answer impertinent questions which persons think proper to ask them in the form of an action on a wager. 12 East, 248. Such an attempt has been held to be a contempt of court; and Lord Hardwicke in such a case committed the parties and their attorneys. Lee temp. Hardw. 237. See, also, Comb. 425; 1 Coke, 83; 6 Cranch (U. S.) 147, 148. See, also, "Feigned Action."

FICTITIOUS PARTY. Where a suit is brought in the name of one who is not in being, or of one who is ignorant of the suit, and has not authorized it, it is said to be brought in the name of a fictitious plaintiff. To bring such a suit is deemed a contempt of court. 4 Bl. Comm. 133.

FICTITIOUS PAYEE. When a contract, such as negotiable paper, is drawn in favor of a fictitious person, and has been indorsed in such name, it is deemed payable to bearer as against all parties who are privy to the transaction, and a holder in good faith may recover on it against them. 2 H. Bl. 178, 288; 3 Term R. 174, 182, 481; 1 Camp. 130; 19 Ves. 311. And see 10 Barn. & C. 468; 2 Sandf. (N. Y.) 38; 2 Deur (N. Y.) 121.

FIDE JUBERE. In the civil law. To order a thing upon one's faith; to pledge one's self; to become surety for another. *Fide jubes? Fide jubeo:* Do you pledge yourself? I do pledge myself. Inst. 3. 16. 1. One of the forms of stipulation. Dig. 46. 1. 8. pr.; Inst. 3. 21. 7.

FIDE JUSSIO. An act by which any one binds himself as an additional security for another. This giving security does not destroy the liability of the principal, but adds to the security of the surety. Vicat.; Halifax, Anal. bk. 2, c. 16, note 10.

FIDE JUSSOR. In civil law. One who becomes security for the debt of another, promising to pay it in case the principal does not do so.

He differs from a co-obligor in this, that the latter is equally bound to a debtor with his principal, while the former is not liable till the principal has failed to fulfill his engagement. Dig. 12. 4. 4; Id. 16. 1. 13; Id. 24. 3. 64; Id. 38. 1. 37; Id. 50. 17. 110; Id.

6. 14. 20; Hall, Prac. 33; Dunl. Adm. Prac. 300; Clerke, Prax. tits. 63-65.

The obligation of the fide jussor was an accessory contract; for, if the principal obligation was not previously contracted, his engagement then took the name of "mandate." Lec. Elm. § 872; Code Nap. 2012.

FIDE PROMISSOR. See "Fide Jussor."

FIDEI COMMISSARIUS (Law Lat.) In civil law. One who has a beneficial interest in an estate which, for a time, is committed to the faith or trust of another. This term his nearly the same meaning as *cestui que trust* has in the common law. 1 Greenl. Cruise. Dig. 295; Story, Eq. Jur. § 966; Bouv. Inst. Index.

Fidei commissary and fide commissary, anglicized forms of this term, have been proposed to take the place of the phrase *cestui que trust*, but do not seem to have met with any favor.

According to Du Cange, the term was sometimes used to denote the executor of a will.

FIDEI COMMISSUM (Law Lat.) In civil law. A trust. A devise was made to some person (*haeres fiduciarius*), and a request annexed that he should give the property to some one who was incapable of taking directly under the will. Inst. 2. 23. 1; 1 Greenl. Cruise, Dig. 295; 15 How. (U. S.) 357. A gift which a man makes to another through the agency of a third person, who is requested to perform the will of the giver.

The rights of the beneficiary were merely rights in curtesy, to be obtained by entreaty or request. Under Augustus, however, a system was commenced, which was completed by Justinian, for enforcing such trusts. The trustee or executor was called *haeres fiduciarius*, and sometimes *fide jussor*. The beneficial heir was called *haeres fidei commissarius*.

The uses of the common law are said to have been borrowed from the Roman *fidei commissa*. 1 Greenl. Cruise, 295; Bac. Read. Uses, 19; 1 Madd. 446; Story, Eq. Jur. § 966. The *fidei commissa* are supposed to have been the origin of the common-law system of entails. 1 Spence, Eq. Jur. 21; 1 Washb. Real Prop. 60. This has been doubted by others. See 1 Bouv. Inst. note 1708.

FIDELIS. Faithful; trustworthy.

FIDELITAS. Fealty; fidelity.

FIDELITAS, DE NULLO TENEMENTO, quod tenetur ad terminum fit homagii; fit tamen inde fidelitatis sacramentum. Fealty. For no tenement which is held for a term is there the oath of homage, but there is the oath of fealty. Co. Litt. 67b.

FIDEM MENTIRI. When a tenant does not keep that fealty which he has sworn to the lord. Leg. Hen. I. c. 53.

FIDES EST OBLIGATIO CONSCIENTIAE alicujus ad intentionem alterius. A trust is an obligation of conscience of one to the will of another.

FIDES SERVANDA. Good faith must be observed. 1 Metc. (Mass.) 551; 3 Barb. (N. Y.) 323, 330; 23 Barb. (N. Y.) 521, 524.

FIDES SERVANDA EST; SIMPLICITAS juris genitum praevaleat. Good faith is to be preserved; the simplicity of the law of nations should prevail. Story, Bills, § 15.

FIDUCIA (Lat.) In civil law. A contract by which we sell a thing to some one—that is, transmit to him the property of the thing, with the solemn forms of emancipation—on condition that he will sell it back to us. This species of contract took place in the emancipation of children, in testaments, and in pledges. Poth. ad Pand.

FIDUCIARIUS TUTOR. In Roman law. The elder brother of an emancipated *pupillus*, whose father had died leaving him still under fourteen years of age.

FIDUCIARY. This term is borrowed from the civil law. The Roman laws called a fiduciary heir the person who was instituted heir, and who was charged to deliver the succession to a person designated by the testament. Merlin, Repert. But Poth. ad Pand. vol. 22, says that *fiduciarius haeres* properly signifies the person to whom a testator has sold his inheritance under the condition that he should sell it to another. Fiduciary may be defined "in trust," "in confidence."

A generic term embracing all persons acting in a fiduciary capacity.

FIDUCIARY CONTRACT. An agreement by which a person delivers a thing to another on the condition that he will restore it to him. The following formula was employed: *Ut inter bonos agere oportet, ne propter te fidemque tuam frauda.* Cicero de Offic. lib. 3, c. 13; Lec. Dr. Civ. §§ 237, 238. See 2 How. (U. S.) 202, 208; 6 Watts & S. (Pa.) 18; 7 Watts (Pa.) 415.

FIDUCIARY RELATION. That relation existing between parties where one holds the character of a trustee or a character analogous thereto, such as an agent, guardian, or the like, and the person stands in such a position that he has rights and powers which he is bound to exercise for the benefit of the other person. 227 Ill. 387.

FIEF. A fee, feod, or feud.

A fief was an organically complete brotherhood of associates whose proprietary and personal rights were inextricably blended together. It had much in common with an Indian village community and much in common with a Highland clan. Maine, Suc. L., 365.

FIEF D'HAUBERK. A fee held on the military tenure of appearing fully armed on the *ban* and *arriere-ban*. *Feudum hauber-*

ticum. Spelman; Calv. Lex.; Du Cange. A knight's fee. 2 Bl. Comm. 62.

FIEF TENANT. The holder of a fief or fee.

FIEL. In Spanish law. An officer who keeps possession of a thing deposited under authority of law. Las Partidas, pt. 3, tit. 9, lib. 1.

FIELD REEVE. An officer elected, in England, by the owners of a regulated pasture, to keep in order the fences, ditches, etc., on the land, to regulate the times during which animals are to be admitted to the pasture, and generally to maintain and manage the pasture, subject to the instructions of the owners. General Inclosure Act 1845, § 118.

FIELDAD. In Spanish law. Sequestration. This is allowed in six cases by the Spanish law where the title to property is in dispute. Las Partidas, pt. 3, tit. 3, liv. 1.

FIERDING COURTS. Ancient Gothic courts "in the lowest instance." So called because four were instituted within every superior district or hundred. Their jurisdiction was limited within forty shillings, or three marks. 3 Steph. Comm. 393; 3 Bl. Comm. 34; Stiernh. de Jur. Goth. lib. 1, c. 2.

FIERI FACIAS (Lat. that you cause to be made). In practice. A writ directing the sheriff to cause to be made of the goods and chattels of the judgment debtor the sum or debt recovered.

It receives its name from the Latin words in the writ, used when legal proceedings were conducted in Latin (*quod fieri facias de bonis et catallis,* that you cause to be made of the goods and chattels). It is the form of execution in common use where the judgment debtor has personal property.

FIERI FACIAS DE BONIS TESTATORIS. The writ issued on an ordinary judgment against an executor when sued for a debt due by his testator. If the sheriff returns to this writ *nulla bona,* and a *devastavit* (*q. v.*), the plaintiff may sue out a *fieri facias de bonis propriis,* under which the goods of the executor himself are seized. 1 Wm. Saund. 246; Smith, Action (11th Ed.) 368.

FIERI FECI (Law Lat.) In practice. The return which the sheriff or other proper officer makes to certain writs, signifying, "I have caused to be made."

When the officer has made this return, a rule may be obtained upon him after the return day, to pay the money into court, and, if he withholds payment, an action of debt may be had on the return, or *assumpsit* for money had and received may be sustained against him. 3 Johns. (N. Y.) 183.

FIERI NON DEBET, SED FACTUM VAlet. It ought not to be done, but done, it is valid. 5 Coke, 39; 1 Strange, 526; 19 Johns. (N. Y.) 84, 92; 12 Johns. (N. Y.) 11, 376.

FIFTEENTHS. A temporary aid, consisting of a fifteenth part of the personal property in every township, borough, and city in the kingdom. The valuation of the kingdom was fixed, and a record made in the exchequer of the amount (twenty-nine thousand pounds). This valuation was not increased as the property in the kingdom increased in value; whence the name came, in time, to be a great misnomer. 2 Inst. 77; 4 Inst. 34; 2 Sharswood, Bl. Comm. 309; Cowell.

FIGHTNITE, or **FIGHTWITE** (Saxon). A mulct or fine for making a quarrel to the disturbance of the peace. Called also by Cowell *forisfactura pugnae.* The amount was one hundred and twenty shillings. Cowell.

FILACER. An officer of the common pleas, whose duty it was to file the writs on which he made process. There were fourteen of them, and it was their duty to make out all original process. Cowell; Blount. The office is now abolished.

FILARE. In old English practice. To file. Towns. Pl. 67.

FILCH. The primary and ordinary meaning of the word "filch" is to steal, and carries with it also the idea of secrecy.

To steal privily; to pilfer; to steal, especially in a small, sly way; to take from another in an underhand way, as by violation of trust or good faith; to thieve; to rob; to purloin. 238 Ill. 124.

The term "filch" is ordinarily applied to things of little value. 141 Ill. App. 378.

FILE. A thread, string, or wire upon which writs and other exhibits in courts and offices are fastened or filed for the more safe keeping and ready turning to the same. Spelman; Cowell; Tomlins. Papers put together and tied in bundles. A paper is said also to be filed when it is delivered to the proper officer, and by him received to be kept on file. 13 Viner, Abr. 211; 1 Litt. 113; 1 Hawk. P. C. 7, 207.

FILEINJAID (Brit.) A name given to villeins in the laws of Hoel Dda. Barr. Obs. St. 302.

FILIATE. To declare whose child a bastard is. 2 W. Bl. 1017.

FILIATIO NON POTEST PROBARI. Filiation cannot be proved. Co. Litt. 126a. But see 7 & 8 Vict. c. 101.

FILIATION. In civil law. The descent of son or daughter, with regard to his or her father, mother, and their ancestors.

Nature always points out the mother by evident signs, and, whether married or not, she is always certain,—*mater semper certa est, etiamsi vulgo conceperit.* There is not the same certainty with regard to the father, and the relation may not know, or may feign ignorance as to the paternity. The law has therefore established a legal presumption to serve as a foundation for paternity and filiation.

When the mother is or has been married, her husband is presumed to be the father of the children born during the coverture, or within a competent time afterwards, whether they were conceived during the coverture or not,—*pater is est quem nuptiae demonstrant.*

——**In the Common Law.** The establishment of the paternity of a bastard.

FILICETUM. In old English law. A ferny or bracky ground; a place where fern grows. Co. Litt. 4b; Shep. Touch. 95.

FILIOLUS. In old records. A godson. Spelman.

FILIUS (Lat.) A son; a child.

As distinguished from heir, *filius* is a term of nature, *haeres* a term of law. 1 Powell, Dev. 311. In the civil law the term was used to denote a child generally. Calv. Lex.; Vicat. Its use in the phrase *nullius filius* would seem to indicate a use in the sense of legitimate son, a bastard being the legitimate son of nobody; though the word is usually rendered a son, whether legitimate or illegitimate. Vicat.

Filium eum definimus qui ex viro et uxore ejus nascitur, we define him to be a son who is born of a man and his wife. Dig. 1. 6. 6. *Praesumitur quis esse filius eo quod nascitur ex uxore*, one is presumed to be another's child because he is born of his wife. Bracton, fols. 6, 88. An alien may have a son, but no alien can have an heir. Id. See "Haeres."

A distinction was sometimes made, in the civil law, between *filii* and *liberi;* the latter word including grandchildren (*nepotes*), the former not. Inst. 1. 14. 5. But according to Paulus and Julianus, they were of equally extensive import. Dig. 50. 16. 84; Id. 50. 16. 201.

FILIUS EST NOMEN NATURAE, SED haeres nomen juris. Son is a name of nature, but heir a name of law. 1 Sid. 193; 1 Powell, Dev. 311.

FILIUS FAMILIAS (Lat.) A son who is under the control and power of his father. Story, Confl. Laws, § 61; Vicat.

FILIUS IN UTERO MATRIS EST PARS viscerum matris. A son in the mother's womb is part of the mother's vitals. 7 Coke, 8.

FILIUS MULIERATUS (Lat.) The first legitimate son born to a woman who has had a bastard son by her husband before her marriage. Called, also, *mulier*, and *mulier puisne.* 2 Bl. Comm. 248.

FILIUS NULLIUS (Lat. son of nobody). A bastard. Called, also, *filius populi*, son of the people. 1 Bl. Comm. 459; 6 Coke, 65a.

FILIUS POPULI (Lat.) A son of the people; a bastard.

FILUM (Lat.; Law Fr. *fil, file, q. v.*) In old practice. A thread, string, or wire used for passing through and connecting papers together; a file. Otherwise called *filacium* (Fr. *filacer, q. v.*) Spelman, voc. "Filacium."

A thread or line passing through a stream or road. See "Filum Aquae;" "Filum Viae." The English word "thread" has in ordinary speech this sense of running through; as in the expression "thread of a discourse or argument;" "to thread one's way," etc.

A line or mark, as the edge or border of a thing. *Filum forestae*, the edge of the forest. Manw. For. Laws, 371; 1 Crabb, Real Prop. 485. "To the very last *filum* of the plaintiff's lands." 5 Taunt. 133, arg. "Up to the extreme *filum* of the plaintiff's property." Id. 134, arg.

FILUM AQUAE (Lat. a thread of water). This may mean either the middle line or the outer line. *Altum filum* denotes high-water mark. Blount. *Filum* is, however, used almost universally in connection with *aquae* to denote the middle line of the stream. *Medium filum* is sometimes used with no additional meaning. See 4 Pick. (Mass.) 468; 24 Pick. (Mass.) 344; 3 Caines (N. Y.) 319; 6 Cow. (N. Y.) 579; 5 Wend. (N. Y.) 423; 26 Wend. (N. Y.) 404; 20 Johns. (N. Y.) 91; 4 Hill (N. Y.) 369; 4 Mason (U. S.) 397; 2 N. H. 369; 1 Halst. (N. J.) 1; 2 Conn. 481; 3 Rand. (Va.) 33; 8 Me. 253; 1 Ired. (N. C.) 535; Angell, Watercourses, § 11; 3 Dane, Abr. 4; Jacob; 2 Washb. Real Prop. 445. See "Ad Medium Filum Aquae."

FILUM FORESTAE (Lat.) The border of the forest. 2 Sharswood, Bl. Comm. 419; 4 Inst. 303; Manw. For. Law, "Purlieu."

FILUM VIAE (Lat.) The middle line of the way. 2 Smith, Lead. Cas. 98.

FIN. An end, or limit; a limitation, or period of limitation.

FIN DE NON RECEVOIR. In French law.

A legal bar to the maintenance of a claim. Ord. Mar. liv., tit. 12; Poth. Obl. p. 3, c. 8, art. 1.

An exception or plea founded on law, which, without entering into the merits of the action, shows that the plaintiff has no right to bring it, either because the time during which it ought to have been brought has elapsed, which is called "prescription," or that there has been a compromise, accord and satisfaction, or any other cause which has destroyed the right of action which once subsisted. Poth. Proc. Civ. pt. 1, c. 2, § 2, art. 2; Story, Confl. Laws, § 580.

FINAL. In practice. As applied to hearings, orders, decisions, etc., that which terminates the action, as distinguished from "interlocutory."

——**Final Decree.** A decree which finally disposes of the whole question, so that nothing further is left for the court to adjudicate upon. See 2 Daniell, Ch. Pr. (Perkins Ed.) 1199, note.

A decree which terminates all litigation on the same right. 1 Kent, Comm. 316.

A decree which disposes ultimately of the suit. Adams, Eq. 375. After such decree has been pronounced, the cause is at an end, and no further hearing can be had. Id. 388.

A decree which puts an end to the proceedings of the parties in that court. 44 Ala. 478; 95 N. C. 271.

A decree which so fixes the rights of the parties that it can be carried into effect without further inquiry thereon.

——**Final Judgment.** A judgment which puts an end to the action by declaring that the plaintiff has either entitled himself, or has not, to recover the remedy he sues for. 3 Bl. Comm. 398. A judgment which determines a particular cause, and terminates all litigation on the same right. 1 Kent, Comm. 316. A judgment which cannot be appealed from, but is perfectly conclusive as to the matter adjudicated upon. 24 Pick. (Mass.) 300; 2 Pet. (U. S.) 294; 6 How. (U. S.) 201, 209.

A determination of the rights of the parties to the particular suit, though not of all their rights with reference to the subject matter of the suit, is final. 1 Cal. 134.

To constitute a final judgment, the case must be finally disposed of as to all parties. 52 U. S. 22; 11 Or. 72; 1 Mo. App. 365.

——**Final Process.** Writs of execution; process issued for the execution of a final judgment. So called to distinguish them from "mesne process," which includes all process issuing before judgment rendered.

——**Final Sentence.** That pronounced on the conclusion of the case, as distinguished from the interlocutory sentences rendered during its progress

FINALIS CONCORDIA (Lat.) A decisive agreement; a fine; a final agreement.

A final agreement entered by the parties by permission of court in a suit actually brought for lands. Subsequently the bringing suit, entry of agreement, etc., became merely formal, but its entry upon record gave a firm title to the plaintiff. 1 Washb. Real Prop. 70; 1 Spence, Eq. Jur. 143; 2 Flintoff, Real Prop. 673; White & T. Lead. Cas. 689.

Finis est amicabilis compositio et finalis concordia ex consensu et concordia domini regis vel justiciarum, a fine is an amicable settlement and decisive agreement by consent and agreement of our lord the king or his justices. Glanv. lib. 8, c. 1.

Talis concordia finalis dicitur eo quod finem imposuit negotio, adeo ut neutra pars litigantium ab eo de cetero poterit recidere, such concord is called final because it puts an end to the business, so that neither of the litigants can afterwards recede from it. Glanv. lib. 9, c. 3; Cunningham.

FINANCES. The public revenue or resources of a government or state; the income or means of an individual or corporation. It is somewhat like the *fiscus* of the Romans. The word is generally used in the plural.

Money resources generally. The state of the finances of an individual or corporation, being his condition in a monetary point of view. The cash he has on hand, and that which he expects to receive, as compared with the engagements he has made to pay.

FINANCIER, or **FINANCIAN.** One who manages the finances or public revenue; persons skilled in matters appertaining to the judicious management of money affairs.

FINDER. One who lawfully comes to the possession of another's personal property, which was then lost.

FINDING. The result of the deliberations of a jury or a court. 1 Day (Conn.) 238; 2 Day (Conn.) 12.

The "findings of fact" of a judge, on which his decision is based.

FINE. In conveyancing. An amicable composition or agreement of a suit, either actual or fictitious, by leave of the court, by which the lands in question become, or are acknowledged to be, the right of one of the parties. Co. Litt. 120; 2 Bl. Comm. 349; Bac. Abr. "Fines and Recoveries."

A fine is so called because it puts an end not only to the suit thus commenced, but also to all other suits and controversies concerning the same matter. Such concords, says Doddridge (Eng. Lawy. 84, 85), have been in use in the civil law, and are called transactions, whereof they say thus: *Transactiones sunt de eis quae in controversia sunt, a lite futura aut pendente ad certam compositionem reducuntur, dando aliquid vel accipiendo.* Or, shorter, thus: *Transactio est de re dubia et lite ancipite ne dum ad finem ducta, non gratuita pactio.* It is commonly defined an assurance by matter of record, and is founded upon a supposed previously existing right, and upon a writ requiring the party to perform his covenant; although a fine may be levied upon any writ by which lands may be demanded, charged, or bound. It has also been defined an acknowledgment on record of a previous gift or feoffment, and *prima facie* carries a fee, although it may be limited to an estate for life or in fee tail. Prest. Conv. 200, 202, 268, 269; 2 Bl. Comm. 348, 349.

——**In Criminal Law.** Pecuniary punishment imposed by a lawful tribunal upon a person convicted of crime or misdemeanor. 1 Bish. Crim. Law, § 940; 4 Steph. Comm. 444. See "Amercement."

——**In Feudal Law.** Money exacted by the superior lord upon any change in the tenure, as upon alienation, endowment, etc. 2 Bl. Comm. 71, 135.

FINE AND RECOVERY ACT. St. 3. & 4 Wm. IV. c. 74. This act abolished fines and recoveries. 2 Sharswood, Bl. Comm. 364, note; 1 Steph. Comm. 514.

FINE ANNULLANDO LEVATO DE TENemento quod fuit de antiquo dominico. An abolished writ for disannulling a fine levied of lands in ancient demesne, to the prejudice of the lord. Reg. Orig. 15.

FINE FOR ALIENATION. A sum of money which a tenant by knight's service, or a tenant *in capite* by socage tenure, paid to his lord for permission to alienate his right in the estate he held to another, and by that means to substitute a new tenant for himself. 2 Bl. Comm. 71, 89. These fines are now abolished. In France, a similar demand from the tenant, made by the lord when the former alienated his estate, was called *lods et vente.* This imposition was abolished, with nearly every other feudal right, by the French Revolution.

FINE FOR ENDOWMENT. An old English law. grounded on the feudal exactions that a woman could not be endowed without a fine paid to the lord of the tenement. Abolished by Henry I., and afterwards by *Magna Charta* (chapter 7). 2 Bl. Comm. 135.

FINE FORCE. An absolute necessity or inevitable constraint. Old Nat. Brev. 78; Plowd. 94; 6 Coke, 11; Cowell.

FINE SUR COGNIZANCE DE DROIT come ceo que il ad de son done. A fine upon acknowledgment of the right of the cognizee as that which he hath of the gift of the cognizor. By this the deforciant acknowledges in court a former feoffment or gift in possession to have been made by him to the plaintiff. 2 Bl. Comm. 352; Cunningham; Shep. Touch. c. 2; Comyn, Dig. "Fine."

FINE SUR COGNIZANCE DE DROIT tantum. A fine upon acknowledgment of the right merely. Generally used to pass a reversionary interest which is in the cognizor. 2 Bl. Comm. 351; Jacob; Comyn, Dig.

FINE SUR CONCESSIT. A fine granted where the cognizor, in order to make an end of disputes, though he acknowledges no precedent right, yet grants to the cognizee an estate *de novo,* usually for life or years, by way of a supposed composition. 2 Bl. Comm. 353; Shep. Touch. c. 2.

FINE SUR DONE GRANT ET RENDER. A double fine, comprehending the fine *sur cognizance de droit come ceo,* and the fine *sur concessit.* It may be used to convey particular limitations of estates, and to persons who are strangers or not named in the writ of covenant; whereas the fine *sur cognizance de droit come ceo,* etc., conveys nothing but an absolute estate, either of inheritance, or at least freehold. Salk. 340. In this last species of fines, the cognizee, after the right is acknowledged to be in him, grants back again, or renders to the cognizor, or perhaps to a stranger, some other estate in the premises. 2 Bl. Comm. 353; Viner, Abr. "Fine;" Comyn, Dig. "Fine;" 1 Washb. Real Prop. 33.

FINEM FACERE (Lat.) To make or pay a fine. Bracton, 106; Skene de Verb. Sign.

FINES LE ROY. In old English law. A sum of money which any one is to pay the king for any contempt or offense; which fine any one that commits any trespass, or is convict that he falsely denies his own deed, or did anything in contempt of the law, shall pay to the king. Termes de la Ley; Cunningham.

FINIRE. In old English law. To fine, or pay a fine. Rog. Hov., cited in Cowell. To end or finish a matter.

FINIS EST AMICABILIS COMPOSITIO et finalis concordia ex consensu et concordia domini regis vel justicarium. A fine is an amicable settlement and decisive agreement by consent and agreement of our lord, the king, or his justices. Glanv. lib. 8, c. 1.

FINIS FINEM LITIBUS IMPONIT. A fine puts an end to litigation. 3 Inst. 78.

FINIS REI ATTENDENDUS EST. The end of a thing is to be attended to. 3 Inst. 51.

FINIS UNIUS DIEI EST PRINCIPIUM alterius. The end of one day is the beginning of another. 2 Bulst. 305.

FINITIO. In old records. An ending or finishing; death, as the end of life (*quia vita finitur morte*). Cowell; Holthouse.

FINIUM REGUNDORUM ACTIO. In civil law. An action for regulating boundaries. 1 Mackeld. Civ. Law, § 271.

FINORS. Refiners of gold and silver.

FIRDFARE (Saxon). See "Firdnite."

FIRDIRINGA (Saxon). A preparation to go into the army. Leg. Hen. 1.

FIRDNITE, or **FIRDWITE** (Saxon.) A mulct or penalty imposed on military tenants for their default in not appearing in arms, or coming to an expedition; a penalty imposed for murder committed in the army. Cowell.

FIRDSOCNE (Saxon.) Exemption from military service. Spelman.

FIRE. The common understanding of the word "fire" would never include heat, short of the degree of ignition, however produced. 30 Ill. App. 266.

Thus neither artificial nor solar heat, 6 Taunt. 436; 2 Marsh. 130; nor lightning, nor an explosion of gunpowder or of fire-damp, or of a steam-engine, nor the discharge of ordnance, nor a projectile from either a volcano or a gun, is "fire" within a fire policy, unless there be an actual setting on fire directly causing the injury insured against. 19 C. B. N. S. 133, 34 L. J. C. P. 301.

FIRE AND SWORD. Letters of fire and sword were the ancient means for dispossessing a tenant who retained possession contrary to the order of the judge and diligence of the law. They were directed to the sheriff, and ordered him to call the assistance of the county to dispossess the tenant. Bell, Dict.; Ersk. Inst. lib. 4, tit. 3, § 17.

FIRE INSURANCE. A contract of insurance by which the insurer agrees to indemnify the insured for injury by fire to goods named in the contract. See "Insurance."

FIRE ORDEAL. See "Ordeal."

FIRE POLICY. A policy of fire insurance. See "Fire Insurance."

FIREBARE. A beacon or high tower by the seaside, wherein are continual lights, either to direct sailors in the night, or to give warning of the approach of an enemy. Cowell.

FIREBOTE. An allowance of wood or estoves to maintain competent firing for the tenant. A sufficient allowance of wood to burn in a house. 1 Washb. Real Prop. 99. Tenant for life or years is entitled to it. 2 Bl. Comm. 35. Cutting more than is needed for present use is waste. 3 Dane, Abr. 238; 8 Pick. (Mass.) 312-315; Cro. Eliz. 593; 7 Bing. 640. The rules in England and in this country are different in relation to the kind of trees which the tenant may cut. 11 Metc. (Mass.) 504; 7 Pick. (Mass.) 152; 7 Johns. (N. Y.) 227; 6 Barb. (N. Y.) 9; 2 Zab. (N. J.) 521; 2 Ohio St. 180; 13 Pa. St. 438; 3 Leon. 16.

FIRKIN. A measure of capacity. equal to nine gallons. The word "firkin" is also used to designate a weight, used for butter and cheese, of fifty-six pounds avoirdupois.

FIRLOT. A Scotch measure of capacity, containing two gallons and a pint. Spelman.

FIRM. The persons composing a partnership, taken collectively.

The name or title under which the members of a partnership transact business.

The word is used as synonymous with "partnership." The words "house," "concern," and "company" are also used in the same sense. This name is, in point of law, conventional, and applicable only to the persons who, on each particular occasion when the name is used, are members of the firm. A firm is usually described, in legal proceedings, as certain persons trading or carrying on business under and using the name, style, and firm of, etc. Firm name, (*q. v.*) 9 Q. B. 361; 9 Mees. & W. 347; 1 Chit. Bailm. 49.

FIRM NAME. A firm name is such name as the copartners choose to adopt, and may disclose the names of all the partners or of none of them, or the name of but one of them may be used as the firm name. 189 Ill. 245.

FIRMA (Law Lat.) A farm or rent reserved on letting lands, anciently frequently reserved in provisions. Spelman; Cunningham.

A banquet; supper; provisions for the table. Du Cange.

A tribute or custom paid towards entertaining the king for one night. Domesday Book; Cowell.

A rent reserved to be paid in money, called then *alba firma*, white rents, money rents. Spelman.

A lease; a letting. *Ad firmam tradidi.* I have farm let. Spelman.

A messuage with the house, garden, or lands, etc., connected therewith. Co. Litt. 5a; Shep. Touch. 93. See "Farm."

FIRMA FEODI (Law Lat.) Fee farm. See "Feodi Firma."

FIRMAN. A passport granted by the great mogul to captains of foreign vessels to trade within the territories over which he has jurisdiction; a permit.

FIRMARATIO. The right of a tenant to his lands and tenements. Cowell.

FIRMARIUM. In old records. A place in monasteries, and elsewhere, where the poor were received and supplied with food. Spelman. Hence the word "infirmary."

FIRMARIUS (Law Lat.) A fermor; a lessee of a term. *Firmarii* comprehend all such as hold by lease for life or lives or for year, by deed or without deed. 2 Inst. 144, 145; 1 Washb. Real Prop. 107; 8 Pick. (Mass.) 312-315; 7 Adol. & E. 637.

FIRMATIO. In forest law. Doe season. Cowell.

FIRME. In old records. A farm.

FIRMIOR ET POTENTIOR EST OPERAtio legis quam dispositio hominis. The operation of law is firmer and more powerful than the will of man. Co. Litt. 102.

FIRMITAS. In old English law. An assurance of some privilege, by deed or charter.

FIRMURA. In old English law. Liberty to scour and repair a mill dam, and carry away the soil, etc. Blount.

FIRST CLASS. The term "first class" is a relative term, and depends upon the use of the thing to which it is applied, and the character of the persons who are to use it. 218 Ill. 90.

FIRST CLASS MISDEMEANANT. In English law, one convicted of misdemeanor who is designated by the judge to be treated with special favor. Such designation is in the discretion of the judge. 28 & 29 Vict. c. 126, § 67.

FIRST COUSIN. A person's first cousin is the child of his uncle or aunt; and only persons standing in that relationship to him will take under a gift to his "first cousins;" first cousins once removed will not be comprised, 8 L. J. Ch. 18; 25 L. J. Ch. 116; unless there be no first cousins properly so called. 1 Jarm. 153.

FIRST FRUITS. The first year's whole profits of the spiritual preferments. There were three valuations (*valor beneficium*) at different times, according to which these first fruits were estimated, made in 1253, 1288, and 1318. A final valuation was made by 26 Hen. VIII. c. 3.

They now form a perpetual fund, called "Queen Anne's Bounty," the income of which is used for the augmentation of poor livings. 1 Sharswood, Bl. Comm. 284, and notes; 2 Burn, Ecc. Law, 260.

FIRST IMPRESSION. First examination; first presentation to a court for examination or decision. A cause which presents a new question for the first time, and for which, consequently, there is no precedent, is said to be a case of the first impression.

FIRST PURCHASER. In the English law of descent, the first purchaser was he who first acquired an estate in a family which still owns it. A purchase of this kind signifies any mode of acquiring an estate, except by descent. 2 Bl. Comm. 220.

FISC. In civil law. The treasury of a prince; the public treasury. 1 Low. (U. S.) 361.

Hence, to confiscate a thing is to appropriate it to the fisc. Paillet, Dr. Pub. 21, note, says that *fiscus*, in the Roman law signified the treasure of the prince, and *aerarium* the treasurer of the state. But this distinction was not observed in France.

FISCAL. Belonging to the fisc, or public treasury.

FISCAL JUDGE (Law Lat. *judex fiscalis*). An officer named in the laws of the barbarous nations of Europe; the same with the *grafio, graf, greve,* or *greeve.* Spelman, voc. "Grafio." Called *fiscla,* because charged with the collection of public moneys, either directly, or by the imposition of fines. Id. In the Ripaurian law, he is said to be the same with the *comes* or count. L. Ripaur. tit. 35; Montesq. Esp. des Lois, liv. 30, c. 18.

FISCUS.

——**In Roman Law.** The treasury of the prince or emperor, as distinguished from "*aerarium,*" which was the treasury of the state. Spelman; Plin. Pand. 36; Tacit. vi. 2; Calv. Lex.

The treasury or property of the state, as distinguished from the private property of the sovereign. Dig. 49. 14; 1 Mackeld. Civ. Law, 149, § 144.

——**In English Law.** The king's treasury, as the repository of forfeited property. Bracton, fol. 150.

The treasury of a noble, or of any private person. Spelman.

The use of the word in the sense of a treasury is derived from its primary meaning, a wicker basket or hamper in which money was kept by the Romans. Burrill.

FISH. An animal which inhabits the water, breathes by means of gills, swims by the aid of fins, and is oviparous.

Fishes in rivers and in the sea are considered as animals *ferae naturae;* consequently, no one has any property in them until they have been captured, and, like other wild animals, if, having been taken, they escape and regain their liberty, the captor loses his property in them.

FISH ROYAL. A whale, porpoise, or sturgeon thrown ashore on the coast of England belonged to the king as a branch of his prerogative. Hence these fish are termed "royal fish." Hale, de Jur. Mar. pt. 1, c. 7; 1 Sharswood, Bl. Comm. 290; Plowd. 305; Bracton, lib. 3, c. 3.

FISHERY. A place prepared for catching fish with nets or hooks. This is commonly applied to the place of drawing a seine or net. 1 Whart. (Pa.) 131, 132.

A right or liberty of taking fish; a species of incorporeal hereditament, anciently termed "piscary," of which there are several kinds. 2 Bl. Comm. 34, 39; 3 Kent, Comm. 409-418; Angell, Watercourses, § 61 et seq.; Angell, Tide Waters, p. 124, c. 5.

A common of fishery is not an exclusive right, but one enjoyed in common with certain other persons. 3 Kent, Comm. 329.

A free fishery is said to be a franchise in the hands of a subject, existing by grant or prescription, distinct from an ownership in the soil. It is an exclusive right, and applies to a public navigable river, without any right in the soil. 3 Kent, Comm. 329.

A several fishery is one by which the party claiming it has the right of fishing, independently of all others, so that no person can have a coextensive right with him in the object claimed; but a partial and independent right in another, or a limited liberty, does not derogate from the right of the owner. 5 Burrows, 2814.

A distinction has been made between a common fishery (*commune piscarium*), which may mean for all mankind, as in the sea, and a common of fishery (*communium piscariae*), which is a right, in common with certain other persons, in a particular stream. 8 Taunt. 183. Mr. Angell seems to think that "common of fishery" and "free fishery" are convertible terms. Angell, Watercourses, c. 6, §§ 3, 4.

Mr. Woolrych says that sometimes a free fishery is confounded with a several, sometimes it is said to be synonymous with common, and again it is treated as distinct from either. Woolr. Waters, 97.

A several fishery, as its name imports, is an exclusive property. This, however, is not to be understood as depriving the territorial owner of his right to a several fishery when he grants to another person permission to fish; for he would continue to be the several proprietor, although he should suffer a stranger to hold a coextensive right with himself. Woolr. Waters, 96.

These distinctions in relation to several, free, and common of fishery are not strongly marked, and the lines are sometimes scarcely perceptible. "Instead of going into the black-letter books to learn what was a fishery, and a free fishery and a several fishery," says Huston, J., "I am disposed to regard our own acts, even though differing from old feudal law." 1 Whart. (Pa.) 132.

FISHGARTH. A dam or weir in a river for taking fish. Cowell.

FISK. In Scotch law. The revenue of the crown. Generally used of the personal estate of a rebel, which has been forfeited to the crown. Bell, Dict.

FISTUCA, or **FESTUCA** (Lat.) The rod which was transferred, in one of the ancient methods of feoffment, to denote a transfer of the property in land. Called, otherwise, *baculum, virga, fustis.* Spelman.

FISTULA. In the civil law. A pipe for conveying water. Dig. 8. 2. 18.

FIVE-MILE ACT. An act of parliament, passed in 1665, against nonconformists, whereby ministers of that body were prohibited from coming within five miles of any corporate town or place where they had preached or lectured. Brown.

FIXING BAIL. In practice. Rendering absolute the liability of special bail.

The bail are fixed upon the issue of a *ca. sa.* (*capias ad satisfaciendum*) against the defendant (2 Nott & McC. [S. C.] 569; 16 Johns. [N. Y.] 117; 3 Har. [N. J.] 9; 11 Tex. 15), and a return of *non est* thereto by the sheriff (4 Day [Conn.] 1; 2 Bailey [S. C.] 492; 3 Rich. [S. C.] 145; 1 Vt. 276; 7 Leigh [Va.] 371), made on the return day (2 Metc. [Mass.] 590; 1 Rich. [S. C.] 421), unless the defendant be surrendered within the time allowed *ex gratia* by the practice of the court (3 Conn. 316; 9 Serg. & R. [Pa.] 24; 2 Johns. [N. Y.] 101; 9 Johns. [N. Y.] 84; 1 Dev. [N. C.] 91; 11 Gill & J. [Md.] 92; 2 Hill [N. Y.] 216; 8 Cal. 552; 17 Ga. 88).

In New Hampshire (1 N. H. 472) and Massachusetts (2 Mass. 485) bail are not fixed till judgment on a *sci. fa.* is obtained against him, except by the death of the defendant after a return of *non est* to an execution against him.

The death of the defendant after a return of *non est* by the sheriff prevents a surrender and fixes the bail inevitably. 5 Bin. (Pa.) 332; 4 Johns. (N. Y.) 407; 3 McCord (S. C.) 49; 4 Pick. (Mass.) 120; 4 N. H. 29; 12 Wheat. (U. S.) 604. See 1 Overt. (Tenn.) 224; 1 Ohio, 35; 2 Ga. 331.

In Georgia and North Carolina, bail are not fixed till judgment is obtained against them. 3 Dev. (N. C.) 155; 2 Ga. 331.

FIXTURES. The word "fixtures" is used with three distinct meanings:

(1) Chattels affixed to the realty, without regard to the right to remove them.

(2) An article which was a chattel, but which, by being permanently annexed to the soil, becomes a part of the realty, and cannot be removed without the consent of the owner of the freehold. 40 N. Y. 287.

(3) Personal chattels affixed to real estate, which may be severed and removed by the party who has affixed them, or by his personal representative, against the will of the owner of the freehold. 8 Iowa, 544; Tayl. Landl. & Ten. § 544, note 1.

FLACO. A place covered with standing water.

FLAG. A symbol of nationality carried by soldiers, ships, etc., and used in many places where such a symbol is necessary or proper.

For the law upon the subject of nationality of a cargo as determined by the flag, see 5 East, 398; 9 East, 283; 3 Bos. & P. 201; 1 C. Rob. Adm. 1; 5 C. Rob. Adm. 16; 1 Dods. Adm. 81, 131; 9 Cranch (U. S.) 388; 2 Pars. Mar. Law, 114, 118, note 129.

FLAG, DUTY OF THE. Saluting the British flag, by striking the flag, and lowering the topsails of a vessel, exacted as a tribute to the sovereignty of England over the British seas.

FLAGELLAT. Whipped; scourged. An entry on old Scotch records. 1 Pitc. Crim. Tr. pt. 1, p. 7.

FLAGRANS. Burning; raging; in actual perpetration. *Flagrans bellum,* a war actually going on. *Flagrans crimen,* a crime in the act of perpetration, or just perpetrated.

FLAGRANS CRIMEN. In Roman law. A term denoting that a crime is being or has just been committed. For example, when a crime has just been committed, and the *corpus delictum* is publicly exposed, or if a mob take place, or if a house be feloniously burned, these are severally *flagrans crimen.*

The term used in France is *flagrant delit.* The Code of Criminal Instruction gives the following concise definition of it (article 41): *"Le delit qui se commet actuelle-*

ment ou qui vient de se commettre, est un flagrant delit."

FLAGRANT NECESSITY. A case of urgency rendering lawful an otherwise illegal act, as an assault to remove a man from impending danger.

FLAGRANTE BELLO. During an actual state of war.

FLAGRANTE DELICTO (Lat.) In the very act of committing the crime. 4 Bl. Comm. 307.

FLAT. The word "flat," as used with relation to stock transactions on the market, means "without interest." 205 Ill. 90.

Flats are as much separate dwellings as ordinary adjoining houses are. The difference is that flats are under one roof, and are divided one from another by a horizontal plane, but ordinary adjoining houses, by a perpendicular or vertical line. 117 Cal. 71.

When applied to lands, refers to the lands between the lines of high and low water. Gould, Waters, § 28.

FLAVIANUM JUS (Lat.) A treatise on civil law, which takes its name from its author, Cneius Flavius. It contains forms of actions. Vicat.

FLECTA. A feathered or fleet arrow. Cowell.

FLEDWITE. A discharge or freedom from amercements where one having been an outlawed fugitive cometh to the place of our lord of his own accord. Termes de la Ley.

The liberty to hold court and take up the amercements for beating and striking. Cowell.

The fine set on a fugitive as the price of obtaining the king's freedom. Spelman.

FLEE FROM JUSTICE. See "Fugitive from Justice."

FLEE TO THE WALL. A figurative expression used in the criminal law to express the duty of one assailed by violence to retreat as far as he safely may before making violent resistance. It probably originated from the language of Blackstone, who says: "The party assaulted must flee as far as he conveniently can, either by reason of some wall, ditch, or other impediment, or as far as the fierceness of the assault will permit him." 4 Bl. Comm. 185.

FLEET. A place of running water where the tide or float comes up.

A prison in London, so called from a river or ditch which was formerly there, on the side of which it stood.

FLEM. In Saxon and old English law. A fugitive bondman or villein. Spelman.

The privilege of having the goods and fines of fugitives. Id.

FLEMENE FRIT, FLEMENES FRINTHE, or **flymena frynthe.** The reception or relief of a fugitive or outlaw. Jacob.

FLEMESWHITE. The possession of the goods of fugitives. Fleta, lib. 1, c. 147.

FLET. House; home. Cowell.

FLETA. The title of an ancient law book, supposed to have been written by a judge while confined in the Fleet prison.

It is written in Latin, and is divided into six books. The author lived in the reigns of Edward II. and Edward III. See liber 2, c. 66, § *Item quod nullus;* liber 1, c. 20, § *Qui coeperunt;* 10 Coke, pref. Edward II. was crowned A. D. 1306. Edward III. was crowned 1326, and reigned till A. D. 1377. During this period the English law was greatly improved, and the lawyers and judges were very learned. Hale, Hist. Com. Law, 173. Blackstone (4 Comm. 427) says of this work "that it was for the most part law until the alteration of tenures took place." The same remark he applies to Britton and Hingham.

FLICHWITE. In Saxon law. A fine on account of brawls and quarrels. Spelman.

FLIGHT. In criminal law. The evading the course of justice by a man's voluntarily withdrawing himself. 4 Bl. Comm. 387. See "Fugitive from Justice."

FLOAT. A certificate authorizing the party possessing it to enter a certain amount of land. 20 How. (U. S.) 504. See 2 Washb. Real Prop.

FLOATABLE. A stream capable of floating logs, etc., is said to be floatable. 2 Mich. 519.

FLOATING DEBT. By the term "floating debt," as applied to a municipal corporation, is meant that mass of lawful and valid claims against the corporation, for the payment of which there is no money in the corporation treasury specially designed, nor any taxation or other means of providing money to pay, particularly provided. 34 Ill. App. 510; 71 N. Y. 371-374.

The term "floating indebtedness," as used in a resolution of a corporation, does not include the amount of a debt secured by mortgage on real estate, 34 Ill. App. 510.

FLOATING SECURITY. A floating security is "a security on the property of the company as a going concern, subject to the powers of the directors to dispose of the property of the company while carrying on its business in the ordinary course." 1 Ch. 434, 10 Ch. D. 530.

Debentures which allow a company to deal with its assets in the ordinary course of business until the company is wound up or stops business or a receiver is appointed at the instance of the debenture holders constitute a floating security. They constitute a charge and give a license to the company to carry on its business. 2 Ch. 118, 1 Ch. 641.

FLODEMARK. High-tide mark. Blount. The mark which the sea at flowing water and highest tide makes upon the shore. And. 189; Cunningham.

FLORENTINE PANDECTS. A copy of the Pandects discovered accidentally about the year 1137, at Amalphi, a town in Italy, near Salerno. From Amalphi, the copy found its way to Pisa, and, Pisa having submitted to the Florentines in 1406, the copy was removed in great triumph to Florence. By direction of the magistrates of the town, it was immediately bound in a superb manner, and deposited in a costly chest. Formerly, these Pandects were shown only by torch light, in the presence of two magistrates, and two Cistercian monks, with their heads uncovered. They have been successively collated by Politian, Bolognini, and Antonius Augustinus. An exact copy of them was published in 1553 by Franciscus Taurellus. For its accuracy and beauty, this edition ranks high among the ornaments of the press. Brenchman, who collated the manuscript about 1710, refers it to the sixth century. Butler, Hor. Jur. 90, 91.

FLORIN. A coin, originally made at Florence. Called, also, "gulder."

FLOTAGES. Things which float by accident on the sea or great rivers. Blount.

The commissions of water bailiffs. Cunningham.

FLOTSAM, or **FLOTSAN.** A name for the goods which float upon the sea when cast overboard for the safety of the ship, or when a ship is sunk. Distinguished from "jetsam" and "ligan." Bracton, lib. 2, c. 5; 5 Coke, 106; Comyn, Dig. "Wreck" (A); Bac. Abr. "Court of Admiralty" (B); 1 Bl. Comm. 292.

FLOUD MARKE. Flodemark (*q. v.*)

FLUMEN (Law Lat.) In civil law. The name of a servitude which consists in the right of turning the rain water, gathered in a spout, on another's land. Ersk. Inst. bk. 2, tit. 9, note 9; Vicat. See "Stillicidium."

FLUMINA ET PORTUS PUBLICA sunt; ideoque jus piscandi omnibus commune est. Rivers and ports are public; therefore the right of fishing there is common to all. Dav. Ir. K. B. 55; Branch, Princ.

FLUVIUS. (Lat.) In old English law. A river. *Fluvii regales*, royal streams. Public rivers for public passage (Fr. *haut stremes le roy*). So called, not in reference to the ownership of the river, but to the public use; all things of public safety and convenience being, in a special manner, under the king's care, supervision, and protection. Hale, de Jur. Mar. par. 1, c. 2.

Flood or flood tide. Fleta, lib. 6, c. 8, § 2.

FLUXUS. In old English law. Flow. *Per fluxum et refluxum maris*, by the flow and reflow of the sea. Dal. pl. 10.

FLYMA (Saxon). A fugitive or outlaw. Spelman.

FLYMAN FRYMTH. In old English law. The offense of harboring a fugitive, the penalty attached to which was one of the rights of the crown. Anc. Inst. Eng.

FOCAGE. House bote; fire bote. Cowell.

FOCALE (Law Lat.) In old English law. Firewood; the right of taking wood for the fire; fire bote. Cunningham.

FODERUM (Law Lat.) Food for horses or other cattle. Cowell.

——**In Feudal Law.** Fodder and supplies provided as a part of the king's prerogative for use in his wars or other expeditions. Cowell.

FODINA. A mine. Co. Litt. 6a.

FOEDUS (Lat.) A league; a compact.

FOEMINA VIRO CO-OPERTA. A *feme covert*.

FOEMINAE AB OMNIBUS OFFICIIS CIvilibus vel publicis remotae sunt. Women are excluded from all civil and public charges or offices. Dig. 50. 17. 2; 1 Exch. 645; 6 Mees. & W. 216.

FOEMINAE NON SUNT CAPACES DE publicis officiis. Women are not admissable to public offices (Jenk. Cent. Cas. 237); but a woman may be elected to the office of sexton (7 Mod. 263; Strange, 1114), or governor of a workhouse, and act by deputy (2 Ld. Raym. 1014), or an overseer (2 Term R. 395). See "Women."

FOENERATION. The act of putting out money at interest.

FOENUS NAUTICUS (Lat.) The name given to marine interest. The amount of such interest is not limited by law, because the lender runs so great a risk of losing his principal. Ersk. Inst. bk. 4, tit. 4, note 76. See "Marine Interest."

FOETICIDE. In medical jurisprudence. The act of criminal abortion. 1 Beck, Med. Jur. 288; Guy, Med. Jur. 133.

FOETURA (Law Lat.) In civil law. The produce of animals, and the fruit of other property, which are acquired to the owner of such animals and property by virtue of his right. Bowyer, Mod. Civ. Law, c. 14, p. 81.

FOETUS (Lat.) In medical jurisprudence. An unborn child; an infant *in ventre sa mere*.

FOGAGIUM. In old English law. Fogage or fog; a kind of rank grass of late growth, and not eaten in summer. Spelman; Cowell. Distinguished from "hay."

FOI. In French feudal law. Faith; fealty. Guyot, Inst. Feud. c. 2.

FOINESUN. In old English law. The fawning or fawning time of deer. Spelman.

FOIRFAULT. In old English law. To forfeit. 1 How. St. Tr. 927.

FOIRTHOCHT. In old Scotch law. Forethought; premeditated. 1 Pitc. Crim. Tr. pt. 1, p. 90.

FOITERERS. Vagrants.

FOLC LAND (Saxon). Land of the people. Spelman. Said by Blackstone to be land held by no assurance in writing, but to have been distributed amongst the common people at the pleasure of the lord, and resumable at his discretion. 2 Bl. Comm. 90; Cowell.

It was probably, however, land which belonged to the community, and which, being parcelled out for a term to people of all conditions, reverted again to the commons at the expiration of the term. 1 Spence, Eq. Jur. 8; Wharton.

FOLC MOTE, FOLK MOTE, or **FOLC GEmote** (Saxon, from folc, people, and mote, or gemote, meeting). In Saxon law. A meeting of the people; a general assembly of the people, to consider and order matters of the commonwealth. Somner; Spelman, voc. "Gemotum." Any popular or public meeting of all the folk or people of a place or district. Brande. See "Gemot."

The term was used to denote a court or judicial tribunal among the Saxons, which possessed substantially the powers afterwards exercised by the county courts and sheriff's tourn. These powers embraced the settlement of small claims, taking the oath of allegiance, preserving the laws, and making the necessary arrangements for the preservation of safety, peace, and the public weal. It appears that complaints were to be made before the folk gemote held in London annually, of any mismanagement by the mayor and aldermen of that city. It was called, also, a "burg gemote" when held in a burgh, and "shire gemote" when held for a county. See Manw. For. Laws; Spelman; De Brady; Cunningham.

A county court; an assembly of the people or freeholders of a county (*conventus comitatus*). Otherwise called the "shire mote." Spelman.

A city court; an assembly of the inhabitants of a city or borough (*conventus civitatis sea burgi*). Otherwise called the "burg mote." Spelman. The folc mote or city court of London is mentioned in ancient records. Id.; Crabb, Hist. Eng. Law, 141. The term seems to have been generally applied to all courts that were adapted to the convenience of the people within any district. Id. 26. See Cowell.

FOLC RIGHT. The common right of all the people. 1 Bl. Comm. 65, 67.

FOLD-COURSE. In English law. Land used as a sheep walk.

Land to which the sole right of folding the cattle of others is appurtenant. Sometimes it means merely such right of folding. The right of folding on another's land, which is called "common foldage." Co. Litt. 6a, note 1; W. Jones, 375; Cro. Car. 432; 2 Vent. 139.

FOLDAGE. A privilege possessed in some places by the lord of a manor, which consists in the right of having his tenant's sheep to feed on his fields, so as to manure the land.

The name of "foldage" is also given in parts of Norfolk to the customary fee paid to the lord for exemption at certain times from this duty. Elton, Commons, 45. 46.

FOLGARII. Menial servants; followers. Bracton.

FOLGERE. In old English law. A freeman, who has no house or dwelling of his own, but is the follower or retainer of another (*heorthfoest*), for whom he performs certain predial services. Anc. Inst. Eng.

FOLGOTH. Official dignity.

FOLIO. A leaf. The references to the writings of the older law authors are usually made by citing the folio, as it was the ancient custom to number the folio instead of the page, as is done in modern books.

A certain number of words specified by statute as a folio. Wharton. Originating, undoubtedly, in some estimate of the number of words which a folio ought to contain.

FONSADERA. In Spanish law. Any tribute or loan granted to the king for the purpose of enabling him to defray the expenses of a war.

FONTANA. A fountain or spring. Bracton, fol. 233.

FOOT. A measure of length, containing one-third of a yard, or twelve inches. Figuratively, it signifies the conclusion, the end; as, the foot of the fine, the foot of the account.

FOOT OF THE FINE. The fifth part of the conclusion of a fine. It includes the whole matter, reciting the names of the parties, day, year, and place, and before whom it was acknowledged or levied. 2 Bl. Comm. 351.

FOOTGELD. An amercement for not cutting out the ball or cutting off the claws of a dog's feet (expeditating him). To be quit of footgeld is to have the privilege of keeping dogs in the forest unlawed without punishment or control. Manw. For. Laws, pt. 1, p. 86; Cromp. Jur. 197; Termes de la Ley; Cunningham.

FOR. In French law. A tribunal. *Le for interieur*, the interior forum; the tribunal of conscience. Poth. Obl. pt. 1, c. 1, § 1, art. 3, § 4.

FOR A TURN. See "Gambling Contract."

FOR THAT, or **FOR THAT WHEREAS.** Words used in introduction in a declaration. "For that whereas" introduces recitals, "For that," positive allegations. Hammond, N. P. 9.

FOR THE USE OF. In an action at law by one for the use of another the expression "for the use of" is for the purpose of protecting the interest of the usee against the nominal plaintiff, and not for the benefit of the defendant, who is not interested in the declaration of use, and as far as defendant is concerned, the expression is surplusage. 183 Ill. 286; 188 Ill. App. 429.

FOR VALUE RECEIVED. Generally the expression "for value received" used in a note imports a consideration. 177 Ill. 291.

FORANEUS. One from without; a foreigner; a stranger. Calv. Lex.

FORATHE. One who can take oath for another who is accused of one of the lesser crimes. Manw. For. Laws, p. 3. Cowell.

FORBALCA. In old records. A forebalk; a balk (that is, an unplowed piece of land) lying forward or next the highway. Cowell.

FORBANER. To deprive forever; to shut out. 9 Rich. II. c. 2; 6 Hen. VI. c. 4; Cowell.

FORBARRER (Law Fr.) To bar out; to prevent or preclude; to estop. Cowell.

FORBATUDUS. In old English law. The aggressor slain in combat. Jacob.

FORBEARANCE. A delay in enforcing rights; the act by which a creditor waits for the payment of a debt due him by the debtor after it has become due. It is sufficient consideration to support *assumpsit*, or a guarantee. 27 L. J. Ex. 120; 2 H. & N. 517; 32 Ch. D. 289; 56 L. J. Q. B. 518; 57 L. T. 554; contra 1 Ex. 74; 16 L. J. Ex. 237.

A forbearance is a determination of the will, not to do some given external act. Or in not doing some given external act, and in not doing it in consequence of a determination of the will. Const. Jurisp. 1, 377.

FORCE. Restraining power; validity; binding effect.

A law may be said to be in force when it is not repealed, or, more loosely, when it can be carried into practical effect. An agreement is in force when the parties to it may be compelled to act, or are acting, under its terms and stipulations.

Strength applied; active power; power put in motion.

Actual force is where strength is actually applied, or the means of applying it are at hand.

The display of power to injure sufficient to put in bodily fear is force. 5 Blatchf. (U. S.) 18; 2 Whart. Crim. Law, 1698.

Implied force is that which is implied by law from the commission of an unlawful act. Every trespass *quare clausum fregit* is committed with implied force. 1 Salk. 641; Co. Litt. 57b, 161b, 162a; 1 Saund. 81, 140, note 4; 5 Term R. 361; 8 Term R. 78, 358; Bac. Abr. "Trespass;" 3 Wils. 18; Fitzh. Nat. Brev. 890; 6 East, 387; 5 Bos. & P. 365, 454.

Mere nonfeasance cannot be considered as force, generally. 2 Saund. 47; Co. Litt. 161; Bouv. Inst. Index.

FORCE AND ARMS. A phrase used in declarations of trespass and in indictments, but now necessary in declarations, to denote that the act complained of was done with violence. 2 Chit. Pl. 846, 850.

FORCED HEIRS. In Louisiana. Those persons whom the testator or donor cannot deprive of the portion of his estate reserved for them by law, except in cases where he has a just cause to disinherit them. Civ. Code La. art. 1482. As to the portion of the estate they are entitled to, see "Legitim." As to the causes for which forced heirs may be deprived of this right, see "Disinherison."

FORCED SALE. A sale under process of law, and against the consent of the owner. It does not embrace a sale under a power in a mortgage. 15 Fla. 336.

FORCHEAPUM. Pre-emption. Blount.

FORCIBLE ENTRY OR DETAINER. A forcible entry or detainer consists in violently taking or keeping possession of lands or tenements, by means of threats, force, or arms, and without authority of law. Comyn, Dig.; Gabbett, Crim. Law; 52 Barb. (N. Y.) 198; 4 Cush. (Mass.) 141.

Though generally referred to in the conjunctive, forcible entry and forcible detainer are distinct acts. 31 Cal. 122.

To authorize either a criminal prosecution or an action of forcible entry and detainer at common law, both entry and detainer must be forcible (93 Ind. 211); but a forcible entry will relate back to the entry, if that was unlawful, though peaceable; otherwise, if the entry was lawful (45 Cal. 597).

——**In Modern Usage.** The possessory action of forcible entry and detainer has been extended by statute to certain cases of constructive force, as where a tenant holds over after his term.

FORDA. In old records. A ford or shallow, made by damming or penning up the water. Cowell.

FORDAL (Saxon). A butt or headband; a piece.

FORDANNO. In old European law. He who first assaulted another. Spelman.

FORDIKA. In old records. Grass or herbage growing on the edge or bank of dykes or ditches. Cowell.

FORE (Saxon). Before (Fr.) Out. Kelham.

FORECLOSURE. To shut out; to bar. Used of the process of destroying an equity of redemption. 1 Washb. Real Prop. 589; Daniell, Ch. Pr. 1204; Coote, Mortg. 511; 9 Cow. (N. Y.) 382.

A proceeding in chancery by which the mortgagor's right of redemption of the mortgaged premises is barred or closed forever.

In the more comprehensive sense which modern usage requires, any proceeding by which mortgaged property is applied to the payment of the mortgage debt, and the equity of the mortgagor therein barred.

As so defined, foreclosure is divided into:

(1) Strict foreclosure, being foreclosure by a proceeding in chancery, by which the equity of redemption is barred within a certain time, and the title of the mortgagee becomes absolute.

(2) By entry, by the act of the mortgagee taking possession either by his own peaceable act, or under writ of entry.

(3) By sale, being by an action for the judicial sale of the mortgaged property, and the application of the proceeds to the payment of the mortgage debt. Sometimes called "foreclosure by action."

(4) By advertisement, being a sale under a power of sale in the mortgage, notice thereof being given by advertisement. Sometimes called "foreclosure under power of sale."

The two first-named varieties are practically unused in the United States, though they exist in a few states.

FOREFAULT. In Scotch law. To forfeit; to lose.

FOREGIFT. A premium for a lease.

FOREGOERS. Royal purveyors. 26 Edw. III. c. 5.

FOREHAND RENT. In English law. A species of rent which is a premium given by the tenant at the time of taking the lease, as on the renewal of leases by ecclesiastical corporations, which is considered in the nature of an improved rent. 1 Term R. 486; 3 Term R. 461; 3 Atk. 473; Crabb, Real Prop. § 155.

FOREIGN. That which belongs to another country; that which is strange. 1 Pet. (U. S.) 343.

Every nation is foreign to all the rest; and the several states of the American Union are foreign to each other with respect to their municipal laws. 2 Wash. C. C. (U. S.) 282; 4 Conn. 517; 6 Conn. 480; 2 Wend. (N. Y.) 411; 1 Dall. (Pa.) 458, 463; 6 Bin. (Pa.) 321; 12 Serg. & R. (Pa.) 203; 2 Hill (S. C.) 319; 1 D. Chip. (Vt.) 303; 7 T. B. Mon. (Ky.) 585; 5 Leigh (Va.) 471; 3 Pick. (Mass.) 293. And in respect to the distinction between foreign and inland bills of exchange. 112 U. S. 696; 41 Me. 302; 102 Mass. 141; 49 N. Y. 269.

But the reciprocal relations between the national government and the several states composing the United States are not considered as foreign, but domestic. 5 Pet. (U. S.) 398; 6 Pet. (U. S.) 317; 9 Pet. (U. S.) 607; 4 Cranch (U. S.) 384; 4 Gill & J. (Md.) 1, 63.

——**Foreign Administrator.** An administrator appointed in a state other than that in which the decedent resided. Lee, Admn.

——**Foreign Answer.** An answer not triable in the county where it is made. St. 15 Hen. VI. c. 5; Blount.

——**Foreign Apposer.** An officer in the exchequer who examines the sheriff's estreats, comparing them with the records, and apposeth (interrogates) the sheriff what he says to each particular sum therein. 4 Inst. 107; Blount; Cowell, "Foreigne." The word is written "opposer," "opposeth," by Lord Coke; and this signification corresponds very well to the meaning given by Blount, of examiner (interrogator) of the sheriff's accounts.

——**Foreign Assignment.** An assignment made in a foreign country, or in another state. 2 Kent, Comm. 405 et seq.

——**Foreign Attachment.** A process by virtue of which the property of an absent debtor is seized for the purpose of compelling an appearance, and, in default of that, to pay the claim of the plaintiff. See "Attachment."

——**Foreign Bill of Exchange.** A bill of exchange drawn in one state or country, and payable in another. N. Y. Neg. Inst. Law, § 213.

——**Foreign Coins.** Coins issued by the authority of a foreign government.

There were several acts of congress passed which rendered certain foreign gold and silver coins a legal tender in payment of debts upon certain prescribed conditions as to fineness and weight. In making a report in 1854 on this subject, the late director of the mint, Mr. Snowden, suggested that there was no propriety or necessity for legalizing the circulation of the coins of other countries, and that in no other nation, except in the case of some colonies, was this mixture of currencies admitted by law, either on the score of courtesy or convenience; and he recommended that if the laws which legalize foreign coins should be repealed, it would be proper to require an annual assay report upon the weight and fineness of such foreign coins as frequently reach our shores, with a view to settle and determine their marketable value. Ex. Doc. No. 68, 33d Cong., 1st Sess. This suggestion was subsequently repeated, and finally led to the passage of the act of February 21, 1857 (11 U. S. Stat. at Large, 163), the third section of which is as follows: "That all former acts authorizing the currency of foreign gold or silver coins, and declaring the same a legal tender in payment for debts, are repealed; but it shall be the duty of the director of the mint to cause assays to be made from time to time of such foreign coins as may be known to our commerce, to determine their average weight, fineness, and value, and to embrace in his annual report a statement of the results thereof."

——**Foreign Commerce.** Commerce or trade between the United States and foreign countries.

——**Foreign Corporation.** A corporation created by or under the laws of another state, government, or country. 2 Rev. St. N. Y. p. 375, § 15.

——**Foreign County.** Another county. It may be in the same kingdom, it will still be foreign. See Blount, "Foreign."

——**Foreign Creditor.** One who resides in a different state or country from the debtor.

——**Foreign Divorce.** A divorce granted in a state or country other than that in which one of the parties is domiciled.

A divorce granted in a state or country other than that in which its validity is called in question.

——**Foreign Domicile.** A domicile gained in a foreign country.

——**Foreign Enlistment Act.** St. 59 Geo. III. c. 69, for preventing British citizens from enlisting as sailors or soldiers in the service of a foreign power. Wharton; 4 Steph. Comm. 226.

——**Foreign Exchange.** Exchange between foreign states or countries.

——**Foreign Judgment.** The judgment of a foreign tribunal.

The various states of the United States are in this respect considered as foreign to each other. In Louisiana it has been decided that a judgment rendered by a Spanish tribunal under the former government of that state is not a foreign judgment. 4 Mart. (La.) 301, 310.

——**Foreign Jury.** A jury obtained from a county other than that in which issue was joined.

——**Foreign Laws.** The laws of a foreign country.

——**Foreign Matter.** Matter which must be tried in another county. Blount. Matter done or to be tried in another county. Cowell.

——**Foreign Plea.** See "Plea."

——**Foreign Port.** A port or place which is wholly without the United States. 19 Johns. (N. Y.) 375; 2 Gall. (U. S.) 4, 7; 1 Brock. (U. S.) 235. A port without the jurisdiction of the court. 1 Dods. Adm. 201; 4 C. Rob. Adm. 1; 1 W. Rob. Adm. 29; 6 Exch. 886; 1 Blatchf. & H. (U. S.) 66, 71. Practically, the definition has become, for most purposes of maritime law, a port at such distance as to make communication with the owners of the ship very inconvenient or almost impossible. See 1 Pars. Mar. Law, 512, note.

——**Foreign Service.** In feudal law. That whereby a mesne lord held of another, without the compass of his own fee, or that which the tenant performed either to his own lord or to the lord paramount out of the fee. Kitch. Cts. 299. Foreign service seems also to be used for knight's service, or escuage uncertain. Jacob.

——**Foreign Vessel.** A vessel owned by residents in, or sailing under the flag of, a foreign nation.

——**Foreign Voyage.** A voyage whose termination is within a foreign country. 3 Kent, Comm. 177, note. The length of the voyage has no effect in determining its character, but only the place of destination. 1 Story (U. S.) 1; 3 Sumn. (U. S.) 342; 2 Bost. Law Rep. 146; 2 Wall. C. C. (U. S.) 264; 1 Pars. Mar. Law, 31.

FOREIGNER. One who is not a citizen. Cowell.

——**In the Old English Law.** It seems to have been used of every one not an inhabitant of a city, at least with reference to that city. 1 H. Bl. 213. See, also, Cowell, "Foreigne."

——**In the United States.** Any one who was born in some other country than the United States, and who owes allegiance to some foreign state or country. 1 Pet. (U. S.) 343, 349. An alien. See "Alien;" "Citizen."

FOREIN. An old form of "foreign" (*q. v.*) Blount.

FOREJUDGE. To deprive a man of the thing in question by sentence of court.

Among foreign writers, says Blount, forejudge is to banish, to expel. In this latter sense, the word is also used in English law of an attorney who has been expelled from court for misconduct. Cowell; Cunningham.

FOREJUDGER. In English practice. A judgment by which a man is deprived or put out of a thing; a judgment of expulsion or banishment. See "Forejudge."

FOREMAN. The presiding member of a grand or petit jury.

FORENSIC. Belonging to courts of justice.

FORENSIC MEDICINE. Medical jurisprudence. "That science which teaches the application of every branch of medical knowledge to the purposes of the law; hence its limits are, on the one hand, the requirements of the law, and, on the other, the whole range of medicine. Anatomy, physiology, medicine, surgery, chemistry, physics, and botany lend their aid as necessity arises; and in some cases all these branches of science are required to enable a court of law to arrive at a proper conclusion on a contested question affecting life or property." Tayl. Med. Jur. 1.

FORENSIS. Forensic; belonging to court. *forensis homo*, a man engaged in causes. A pleader; an advocate. Vicat; Calv. Lex.

FORESAID. Used in Scotch law as "aforesaid" is in English, and sometimes, in a plural form, "foresaids." 2 How. St. Tr. 715. "Foresaidis" occurs in old Scotch records. "The Loirdis assesouris forsaidis." 1 Pitc. Crim. Tr. pt. 1, p. 107.

FORESCHOKE. Forsaken; Cowell.

FORESHORE. That part of the land adjacent to the sea which is alternately covered and left dry by the ordinary flow of the tides, *i. e.*, by the medium line between the greatest and least range of tide,—spring tides and neap tides. In the later English decisions it appears to denote the shore and bed of the sea, and of every channel, creek, bay, estuary, and of every navigable river of the United Kingdom, as far up the same as the tide flows. Gould, Water, § 27. In England it forms part of the adjoining county and is ordinarily and prima facie vested in the crown, subject to the rights of the queen's subjects of fishing and navigation, not only in the sea, but in all tidal navigable rivers, and of passing over the foreshore itself; but it may belong to a subject, either by itself, or as part of a manor. 10 Price, 350, 378; 46 L. J. Ch. 654. Chitty, Prerog. 207.

FOREST. A certain territory of wooded ground and fruitful pastures, privileged for wild beasts and fowls of forest, chase, and warren, to rest and abide in the safe protection of the prince for his princely delight and pleasure, having a peculiar court and officers. Manw. For. Laws, c. 1, No. 1; Termes de la Ley; 1 Bl. Comm. 289.

A royal hunting ground which lost its peculiar character with the extinction of its courts, or when a franchise passed into the hands of a subject. Spelman; Cowell; Manw. For. Laws, c. 1; 2 Bl. Comm. 83.

FOREST COURTS. In English law. Courts instituted for the government of the king's forests in different parts of the kingdom, and for the punishment of all injuries done to the king's deer or venison, to the vert or greensward, and to the covert in which the deer were lodged. They comprised the courts of attachments, of regard, of swein mote, and of justice seat; but since the revolution of 1688, these courts, it is said, have gone into absolute desuetude. 3 Steph. Comm. 439-441; 3 Bl. Comm. 71-74. But see 8 Q. B. 981.

FORESTAGIUM. A tribute payable to the king's foresters. Cowell.

FORESTALL. To intercept or obstruct a passenger on the king's highway. Cowell; Blount. To beset the way of a tenant so as to prevent his coming on the premises. 3 Bl. Comm. 170. To intercept a deer on his way to the forest before he can regain it. Cowell.

To commit the crime of forestalling the market.

FORESTALLER. One who commits the offense of forestalling. Used, also, to denote the crime itself, namely, the obstruction of the highway, or hindering a tenant from coming to his land. 3 Bl. Comp. 170.

FORESTALLING. Obstructing the way; intercepting a person on the highway.

FORESTALLING THE MARKET. Buying victuals on their way to the market before they reach it, with the intent to sell again at a higher price. Cowell; Blount; 4 Bl. Comm. 158. Every device or practice, by act, conspiracy, words, or news, to enhance the price of victuals or other provisions. 3 Inst. 196; Bac. Abr.; 1 Russ. Crimes, 169; 4 Bl. Comm. 158; Hawk. P. C. bk. 1, c. 80, § 1. See 13 Viner, Abr. 430; 1 East, 132; 14 East, 406; 15 East, 511; 3 Maule & S. 67; Dane, Abr. Index.

FORESTARIUS. A forester; an officer who takes care of the woods and forests. *De forestario apponendo*, a writ which lay to appoint a forester to prevent further commission of waste when a tenant in dower had committed waste. Bracton, 316; Du Cange.

FORESTER. A sworn officer of the forest, appointed by the king's letters patent to walk the forest, watching both the vert and the venison, attaching and presenting all trespassers against them within their own bailiwick or walk. These letters patent were generally granted during good behavior; but sometimes they held the office in fee. Blount; Cowell.

FORETHOUGHT FELONY. In Scotch law. Murder committed in consequence of a previous design. Ersk. bk. 4, tit. 4, c. 50; Bell, Dict.

FORFANG. A taking beforehand; a taking provisions from any one in fairs or markets before the king's purveyors are served with necessaries for his majesty. Blount; Cowell.

FORFEIT. To forfeit signifies the incurring of a forfeiture or penalty and is antagonistic to the idea of mere payment of compensation for damages for breach of contract. 172 Ill. App. 92.

To lose as the penalty of some misdeed or negligence. The word includes not merely the idea of losing, but also of having the property transferred to another without the consent of the owner and wrongdoer.

This is the essential meaning of the word, whether it be that an offender is to forfeit a sum of money, or an estate is to be forfeited to a former owner for a breach of condition, or to the king for some crime. Cowell says that forfeiture is general and confiscation a particular forfeiture to the king's exchequer. The modern distinction, however, seems to refer rather to a difference between forfeiture as relating to acts of the owner, and confiscation as relating to acts of the government. 1 Story (U. S.) 134; 13 Pet. (U. S.) 157; 11 Johns. (N. Y.) 293. Confiscation is more generally used of an appropriation of an enemy's property; forfeiture, of the taking possession of property to which the owner, who may be a citizen, has lost title through violation of law. See 1 Kent, Comm. 67; 1 Story (U. S.) 134.

FORFEITURE. A punishment annexed by law to some illegal act or negligence in the owner of lands, tenements, or hereditaments, whereby he loses all his interest therein, and they become vested in the party injured as a recompense for the wrong which he alone, or the public together with himself, hath sustained. 2 Bl. Comm. 267. A sum of money to be paid by way of penalty for a crime. 21 Ala. (N. S.) 672; 10 Grat. (Va.) 700. See "Confiscate."

Forfeiture by alienation. By the English law, estates less than a fee may be forfeited to the party entitled to the residuary interest by a breach of duty in the owner of the particular estate. 2 Bl. Comm. 274.

In this country, such forfeitures are almost unknown, and the more just principle prevails that the conveyance by the tenant operates only on the interest which he possessed, and does not affect the remainderman or reversioner. 4 Kent, Comm. 81, 82, 424; 3 Dall. (Pa.) 486; 5 Ohio, 30; 1 Pick. (Mass.) 318; 1 Rice (S. C.) 459; 2 Rawle (Pa.) 168; 1 Wash. (Va.) 381; 11 Conn. 553; 22 N. H. 500; 21 Me. 372. See, also, Stearns, Real Actions, 11; 4 Kent, Comm. 84; 2 Sharswood, Bl. Comm. 121, note; Williams, Real Prop. 25; 5 Dane, Abr. 6-8; 1 Washb. Real Prop. 92, 197.

Forfeiture for crimes. Under the constitution and laws of the United States (Const. art. 3, § 3; Act April 30, 1790, § 24 [1 Story, U. S. Laws, 88]), forfeiture for crimes is nearly abolished, and when it occurs, the state recovers only the title which the owner had. 4 Mason (U. S.) 174. See, also, Dalr. Feud. Prop. c. 4, pp. 145-154; Fost. Crim. Law, 95; 1 Washb. Real Prop. 92.

Forfeiture by nonperformance of conditions. An estate may be forfeited by a breach or nonperformance of a condition annexed to the estate, either expressed in the deed at its original creation, or implied by law, from a principle of natural reason. 2 Bl. Comm. 281; Litt. § 361; 1 Prest. Est. 478; White & T. Lead. Cas. 794, 795; 5 Pick. (Mass.) 528; 2 N. H. 120; 5 Serg. & R. (Pa.) 375; 32 Me. 394; 18 Conn. 535; 12 Serg. & R. (Pa.) 190. Such forfeiture may be waived by acts of the person entitled to take advantage of the breach. 1 Conn. 79; 1 Johns. Cas. (N. Y.) 126; Walk. Am. Law, 299; 1 Washb. Real Prop. 454.

Forfeiture by waste. Waste is a cause of forfeiture. 2 Bl. Comm. 283; 2 Inst. 299; 1 Washb. Real Prop. 118.

See, generally, 2 Bl. Comm. c. 18; 4 Bl. Comm. 382; Bouv. Inst. Index; 2 Kent, Comm. 318; 4 Kent, Comm. 422; 10 Viner, Abr. 371, 394; 13 Viner, Abr. 436; Bac. Abr. "Forfeiture;" Comyn, Dig.; Dane, Abr.; 1 Brown, Civ. Law, 252; Considerations on the Law of Forfeiture for High Treason (London Ed. 1746; 1 Washb. Real Prop. 91, 92, 118, 197.

FORFEITURE OF A BOND. A failure to perform the condition on which the obligee was to be excused from the penalty in the bond. Courts of equity and of law in modern practice will relieve from the forfeiture of a bond; and, upon proper cause shown, criminal courts will, in general, relieve from the forfeiture of a recognizance to appear. See 3 Yates (Pa.) 93; 2 Wash. C. C. (U. S.) 442; 2 Blackf. (Ind.) 104, 200; 1 Ill. 257.

FORFEITURE OF MARRIAGE. A penalty incurred by a ward in chivalry when he or she married contrary to the wishes of his or her guardian in chivalry. 2 Bl. Comm. 70.

FORFEITURES ABOLITION ACT. Another name for the English act of 1870, abolishing forfeitures on conviction of felony.

FORGAVEL. A small rent reserved in money; a quit rent.

FORGE. An establishment, or mechanical contrivance, by which iron is made, or manufactured from the ore. 1 Stock. Ch. (N. J.) 296.

To forge means, properly speaking, no more than *to make* or *form*, but in our law it is always taken in an evil sense. 2 East's P. C. 852, c. 19, § 1.

The French *fauxer* or *fauser*, however, which is a term employed by Britton, always radically imported a *false* making, and may have been the origin of the English word, instead of *forger*, to fashion.

To forge and *to counterfeit* are constantly used both in ancient and modern law, as synonymous terms. Britt. c. 4. The former, however, is usually applied to *writing* or written instruments, the latter to other subjects of imitation, especially money. See "Forgery."

——**In Criminal Law.** To make or fabricate a thing in imitation of another, with a view to deceive and defraud; to make falsely; to counterfeit.

FORGERY. The false making, with intent to defraud, or any writing which, if genuine, might apparently be of legal efficacy, or the foundation of a legal liability. 2 Bish. New Crim. Law, § 533.

Bishop (2 New Crim. Law, § 533) has collected seven definitions of forgery, and justly remarks that the books abound in definitions. Coke says the term is "taken metaphorically from the smith, who beateth upon his anvil, and forgeth what fashion and shape he will." 3 Inst. 169.

The elements are (1) a false making (46 N. H. 266; 28 Minn. 52), but this may consist of a material alteration (64 Wis. 432) (2) of an instrument apparently capable of defrauding (20 Iowa, 541, 118 Mass. 685) (3) with intent to defraud (51 Vt. 105, 15 Mass. 526).

FORHERDA. In old records. A herdland headland, or foreland. Cowell.

FORINSECUM MANERIUM. That part of a manor which lies without the town, and is not included within the liberties of it. Par. Ant. 351.

FORINSECUM SERVITIUM (Lat.) The payment of extraordinary aid. Kennett.

FORINSIC (Lat. *forinsecus*). Outward; on the outside; without; foreign; belonging to another manor. *Silio forinsecus,* the outward ridge or furrow. *Servitium forinsecum,* the payment of aid, scutage, and other extraordinary military services. *Forinsecum manerium,* the manor, or that part of it which lies outside the bars or town, and is not included within the liberties of it. Cowell; Blount; Cunningham; Jacob, "Foreign Service;" 1 Reeve, Hist. Eng. Law, 273.

FORIS. Abroad; out of doors; on the outside of a place; without; extrinsic.

FORIS DISPUTATIONES. In civil law. Arguments in court; disputations or arguments before a court. 1 Kent, Comm. 530; Vicat, "Disputatio."

FORISBANITUS, or **FORBANNITUS.** Banished; outlawed. Spelman.

FORISFACERE (Lat.) To forfeit; to lose on account of crime. It may be applied not only to estates, but to a variety of other things, in precisely the popular sense of the word "forfeit." Spelman; Du Cange.

To confiscate. Du Cange; Spelman.

To commit an offense; to do a wrong; to do something beyond or outside of (*foris*) what is right (*extra rationem*). Du Cange. To do a thing against or without law. Co. Litt. 59a.

To disclaim. Du Cange.

FORISFACTUM (Lat.) Forfeited. *Bona forisfacta,* forfeited goods. 1 Bl. Comm. 299. A crime. Du Cange; Spelman.

FORISFACTURA (Lat.) A crime or offense through which property is forfeited. Leg. Edw. Conf. c. 32.

A fine or punishment in money.

Forfeiture; the loss of property or life in consequence of crime. Spelman.

Forisfactura plena. A forfeiture of all a man's property; things which were forfeited. Du Cange; Spelman.

FORISFACTUS (Lat.) A criminal. One who has forfeited his life by commission of a capital offense. Spelman; Leg. Rep. c. 77; Du Cange. *Si quiespiam forisfactus poposcerit regis misericordiam,* etc., if any criminal shall have asked pardon of the king, etc. Leg. Edw. Conf. c. 18.

Forisfactus servus. A slave who has been a freeman, but has forfeited his freedom by crime. Leg. Athelstan, c. 3; Du Cange.

FORISFAMILIATED, or **FORISFAMILIatus.** In old English law. Portioned off. A son was *forisfamiliated* when he had a portion of his father's estate assigned to him during his father's life, in lieu of his share of the inheritance, when it was done at his request, and he assented to the assignment. The word etymologically denotes put out of the family, emancipated.

One who is no longer an heir of the parent. Du Cange; Spelman; Cowell. Similar in some degree to the modern practice of advancement.

FORISJUDICATIO (Lat.) In old English law. Forejudger; a forejudgment; a judgment of court whereby a man is put out of possession of a thing. Co. Litt. 100b; Cunningham.

FORISJUDICATUS (Lat.) Forejudged; sent from court; banished; deprived of a thing by judgment of court. Bracton, 250b; Co. Litt. 100b; Du Cange.

FORISJURARE (Lat.) To forswear; to abjure; to abandon.

Forisjurare parentilam. To remove one's self from parental authority. The person who did this lost his rights as heir. Du Cange; Leg. Hen. I. c. 88.

Provinciam forisjurare. To forswear the country. Spelman; Leg. Edw. Conf. c. 6.

FORJUDGE. See "Forejudge."

FORJURER (Law Fr.) In old English law. To forswear; to abjure. *Forjurer royalme,* to abjure the realm. Britt. cc. 1, 16.

FORLANDUM, *Forlanda.* Law Lat. In old records. Land extending beyond, or lybefore other land; or bordering or lying outward; a foreland; an extra allowance of land; an allowance in meeting and bounding, otherwise called *freebord.* 2 Mon. Angl. fol. 332. Blount; Cowell.

FORLER LAND. Land in the diocese of Hereford, which had a peculiar custom attached to it, but which has been long since disused, although the name is retained. Butl. Surv. 56.

FORM. In practice. The model of an instrument or legal proceeding, containing the substance and the principal terms, to be used in accordance with the laws.

The legal order or method of legal proceedings or construction of legal instruments.

FORMA DAT ESSE. Form gives being. Lord Henley, C., 2 Eden, 99.

FORMA LEGALIS FORMA ESSENTIALis. Legal form is essential form. 10 Coke, 100, 9 C. B. 493; 2 Hopk. 319.

FORMA NON OBSERVATA, INFERTUR adnullatio actus. When form is not observed, a nullity of the act is inferred. 12 Coke, 7.

FORMA PAUPERIS. See "In Forma Pauperis."

FORMALITIES. In England, robes worn by the magistrates of a city or corporation, etc., on solemn occasions. Enc. Lond.

FORMALITY. The conditions which must be observed in making contracts, and the words which the law gives to be used in order to render them valid. It also signifies the conditions which the law requires to make regular proceedings.

FORMATA. Canonical letters.

FORMATA BREVIA. Formed writs; writs of form. See "Brevia Formata."

FORMED ACTION. An action for which a form of words is provided, which must be exactly followed. 10 Mod. 140.

FORMEDON. An ancient writ provided by St. Westminster II. (13 Edw. I.) c. 1, for him who hath right to lands or tenements by virtue of a gift in tail. Stearns, Real Actions, 322.

It is a writ in the nature of a writ of right, and is the highest remedy which a tenant in tail can have. Co. Litt. 316.

This writ lay for those interested in an estate tail who were liable to be defeated of their right by a discontinuance of the estate tail, who were not entitled to a writ of right absolute, since none but those who claimed in fee simple were entitled to this. Fitzh. Nat. Brev. 255. It is called "formedon" because the plaintiff in it claimed *per forman doni.*

The writ was abolished in England by St. 3 & 4 Wm. IV. c. 27.

——**Formedon in the Descender.** A writ of formedon which lies where a gift is made in tail, and the tenant in tail aliens the lands, or is disseised of them and dies, for the heir in tail to recover them, against the actual tenant of the freehold. Fitzh. Nat. Brev. 211; Litt. § 595.

If the demandant claims the inheritance as an estate tail which ought to come to him by descent from some ancestor to whom it was first given, his remedy is by a writ of formedon in the descender. Stearns, Real Actions, 322.

It must have been brought within twenty years from the death of the ancestor who was disseised. 21 Jac. I. c. 16; 3 Brod. & B. 217; 6 East, 83; 4 Term R. 300; 2 Sharswood, Bl. Comm. 193, note.

——**Formedon in the Remainder.** A writ of formedon which lies where lands are given to one for life or in tail, with remainder to another in fee or in tail, and he who hath the particular estate dies without issue, and a stranger intrudes upon him in remainder, and keeps him out of possession. Fitzh. Nat. Brev. 211; Stearns, Real Actions, 323; Litt. § 597; 3 Bl. Comm. 293.

——**Formedon in the Reverter.** A writ of formedon which lies where there is a gift in tail, and afterwards, by death of the donee or his heirs without issue of his body, the reversion falls in upon the donor, his heirs or assigns.

In this case, the demandant must suggest the gift, his own right as derived from the donor, and the failure of heirs of the donee. 3 Sharswood, Bl. Comm. 293; Stearns, Real Actions, 323; Fitzh. Nat. Brev. 212; Litt. § 597.

FORMER ADJUDICATION. A previous determination of the matter in litigation by a competent court between the same parties. To constitute a former adjudication which will bar subsequent litigation, it is essential.

(1) That the judgment be final and upon the merits. 115 Ill. 29; 103 Mass. 280; 78 Mich. 234; 74 N. Y. 449; 82 N. Y. 55; 94 U. S. 351. Thus, a mere nonsuit (48 Me. 353) or dismissal because the action is premature (35 N. Y. 279) is not a bar to a subsequent action.

(2) The court must have had jurisdiction of the parties and the subject matter (93 U. S. 277; 132 Ill. 213), but it may be a foreign court (26 N. Y. 146).

(3) The same issues must have been involved (25 N. Y. 613), but the issues include every point which is either expressly in issue, or which must have been decided to support the judgment (24 Wis. 124. See 2 Smith's Lead. Cas. 63, and note); and the adjudication is conclusive not only as to what was actually litigated, but as to all that might have been litigated under the pleadings and issues made (70 Ill. 385; 102 N. Y. 452).

(4) As respects adjudications *in personam*, the adjudication must have been between the same parties or their privies (24 How. [U. S.] 241), and in the same capacity (58 N. Y. 463), but their position as plaintiff and defendant need not be the same if they be adversary parties (86 N. Y. 390; 61 Iowa, 290).

Privies of a party are bound to the same extent as the party himself. See "Privy." 69 Ill. 457; 68 Iowa 145.

Lessor and lessee (46 Mo. 444), bailor and bailee (12 N. Y. 343), assignor and assignee (17 Mass. 365), mortgagor and mortgagee (105 N. Y. 39), ancestor and heir (61 Ala. 472), are ordinarily privies, but husband

and wife (110 N. Y. 394), or guardian and ward (27 Pa. St. 226), are not.

A judgment *in rem* is conclusive as to the property in question and the title thereto without issues or parties. 23 Wall. (U. S.) 463.

FORMER RECOVERY. A recovery in a former action. See "Former Adjudication."

FORMIDO PERICULI (Lat.) Fear of danger. 1 Kent, Comm. 23; Huber de Jur. Civ. lib. 3, c. 7, § 4.

FORMS OF ACTION. The various classes of personal actions at common law, as *assumpsit*, trespass, case, detinue, trover, etc. (*q. v.*) The forms of action are now abolished in England by the judicature acts of 1873 and 1875, and in most of the United States.

FORMULA. In common-law practice, a set form of words used in judicial proceedings.

——In Civil Law. An action. Calv. Lex.

FORMULAE. In Roman law. When the *legis actiones* were proved to be inconvenient, a mode of procedure called "*per formulas*" (*i. e.*, by means of *formulae*) was gradually introduced, and eventually the *legis actiones* were abolished by the *Lex Aebutia*, B. C. 164, excepting in a very few exceptional matters. The *formulae* were four in number, namely: (1) The *Demonstratio*, wherein the plaintiff stated, *i. e.*, showed, the facts out of which his claim arose; (2) the *Intentio*, where he made his claim against the defendant; (3) the *Adjudicatio*, wherein the judex was directed to assign or adjudicate the property, or any portion or portions thereof, according to the rights of the parties; and (4) the *Condemnatio*, in which the judex was authorized and directed to condemn or to acquit according as the facts were or were not proved. These *formulae* were obtained from the magistrate (*in jure*), and were thereafter proceeded with before the judex (*in judicio*). Brown.

FORMULARIES. A collection of the forms of proceedings among the Franks and other early European nations. Co. Litt. Butler's note 77.

FORNAGIUM. The fee taken by a lord of his tenant, who was bound to bake in the lord's common oven (*in furno domini*), or for a commission to use his own.

FORNICATION. In criminal law. Unlawful carnal knowledge by an unmarried person of another, whether the latter be married or unmarried.

Fornication is distinguished from "adultery" by the fact that the guilty person is not married. Four cases of unlawful intercourse may arise: Where both parties are married; where the man only is married; where the woman only is married; where neither is married. In the first case, such intercourse must be adultery; in the second case the crime is fornication only on the part of the woman, but adultery on the part of the man; in the third case it is adultery in the woman, and fornication (by statute, in some states, adultery) in the man; in the last case it is fornication only in both parties.

In some states it is indictable by statute. 6 Vt. 311; 2 Tayl. (N. C.) 165; 2 Grat. (Va.) 555.

FORNO. In Spanish law. An oven. Las Partidas, pt. 3, tit. 32, lib. 18.

FORO. In Spanish law. The place where tribunals hear and determine causes,—*exercendarum litium locus.* This word, according to Varro, is derived from *ferendo*, and is so called because all lawsuits have reference to things that are vendible, which presupposes the administration of justice to take place in the markets

FOROS. In Spanish law. Emphyteutic rents. Schmidt, Civ. Law, 309.

FORPRISE. An exception; reservation; excepted; reserved. Anciently, a term of frequent use in leases and conveyances. Cowell; Blount.

In another sense, the word is taken for any exaction. Cunningham.

FORSPEAKER. An attorney or advocate; one who speaks for another. Blount.

FORSTAL. An intercepting or stopping in the highway. See "Forestall."

FORSTELLARIUS EST PAUPERUM DEpressor, et totius communitatis et patriae publicus inimicus. A forestaller is an oppressor of the poor, and a public enemy to the whole community and the country. 3 Inst. 196.

FORSWEAR. In criminal law. To swear to a falsehood.

This word has not the same meaning as "perjury." It does not, *ex vi termini*, signify a false swearing before an officer or court having authority to administer an oath, on an issue. A man may be forsworn by making a false oath before an incompetent tribunal, as well as before a lawful court. Hence, to say that a man is forsworn will or will not be slander, as the circumstances show that the oath was or was not taken before a lawful authority. Heard, Libel & S. §§ 16, 34; Cro. Car. 378; Lutw. 292; 1 Rolle, Abr. 39, pl. 7; Bac. Abr. "Slander" (B 3); Cro. Eliz. 609; 1 Johns. (N. Y.) 505; 2 Johns. (N. Y.) 10; 13 Johns. (N. Y.) 48, 80; 12 Mass. 496; 1 Hayw. (N. C.) 116.

FORTHCOMING. In Scotch law. The action by which an arrestment (attachment) of goods is made available to the creditor or holder.

The arrestee and common debtor are called up before the judge, to hear sentence given ordering the debt to be paid or the arrested goods to be given up to the creditor arresting. Bell, Dict.

FORTHCOMING BOND. A bond given for the security of the sheriff, conditioned to produce the property levied on when required. 2 Wash. (Va.) 189; 11 Grat. (Va.) 522.

FORTHWITH. As soon as, by reasonable exertion, confined to the object, it may be accomplished. This is the import of the term. Style, Pr. Reg. 452, 453.

The words "forthwith" and "immediately" have the same meaning. They are stronger than the expression "within a reasonable time," and imply prompt, vigorous action, without any delay, and whether there has been such action is a question of fact, having regard to the circumstances of the particular case. 4 Q. B. Div. 471; 4 Tyrwh. 837.

Where a judge has to do a thing "forthwith" after the happening of something else, the word will have a different meaning according as the act to be done is: (1) Ministerial and demandable ex debito justitiea; or (2) judicial. If the act comes within the first of these classes the word will mean, "forthwith upon the application of the party entitled to have the act done." 28 L. J. M. C. 196.

Where, however, the act to be done is judicial and discretionary, "forthwith" is synonymous with "immediately." 12 L. J. Q. B. 273; 23 L. J. Ex. 200; 29 L. J. Q. B. 191.

In a contract, and the ordinary transactions of life, "forthwith" does not usually mean "immediately," 34 L. J. C. P. 241; but means "with all reasonable celerity." 7 M. & G. 494.

In a rule of court it has been construed to mean twenty-four hours. 2 Edw. Ch. (N. Y.) 328. But no such construction has been given to the term when used in a statute. "Without delay" is a reasonable meaning in a statute. 39 How. Prac. (N. Y.) 392, affirming 11 Abb. Prac. (N. Y.) 473; 20 How. Prac. (N. Y.) 222.

FORTIA (Lat.) A word of art, signifying the furnishing a weapon of force to do the act, and by force whereof the act was committed, and he that furnished it was not present when the act was done. 2 Inst. 182.

The general meaning of the word is an unlawful force. Spelman; Du Cange.

FORTIA FRISCA. Fresh force (*q. v.*)

FORTILITY. A fortified place; a castle; a bulwark. Cowell.

FORTIOR (Lat.) Stronger. A term applied, in the law of evidence, to that species of presumption, arising from facts shown in evidence, which is strong enough to shift the burden of proof to the opposite party. Burrill, Circ. Ev. 64, 66.

FORTIOR EST CUSTODIA LEGIS QUAM hominis. The custody of the law is stronger than that of man. 2 Rolle, 325.

FORTIOR ET POTENTIOR EST DISPOSITIO legis quam hominis. The disposition of the law is stronger and more powerful than that of man. Co. Litt. 234; Broom, Leg. Max. (3d London Ed.) 622; 10 Q. B. 944; 18 Q. B. 87; 10 C. B. 561; 3 H. L. Cas. 507; 13 Mees. & W. 285, 306; 8 Johns. (N. Y.) 401.

FORTIORI. See "A Fortiori."

FORTIS. Strong. *Fortis et sana,* strong and sound; staunch and strong; as a vessel. Towns. Pl. 227.

FORTLETT. A place or port of some strength; a little fort. Old Nat. Brev. 45.

FORTUIT. Accidental.

FORTUITOUS COLLISION. An accidental collision.

FORTUITOUS EVENT. In civil law. That which happens by a cause which cannot be resisted. Code La. art. 2522, No. 7.

That which neither of the parties has occasioned or could prevent. Lois des Bat. pt. 2, c. 2. An unforeseen event which cannot be prevented. Dict. de Jur. "Cas Fortuit."

There is a difference between a fortuitous event, or inevitable accident, and irresistible force. By the former, commonly called the "act of God," is meant any accident produced by physical causes which are irresistible; such as a loss by lightning or storms, by the perils of the seas, by inundations and earthquakes, or by sudden death or illness. By the latter is meant such an interposition of human agency as is, from its nature and power, absolutely uncontrollable. Of this nature are losses occasioned by the inroads of a hostile army, or by public enemies. Story, Bailm. § 25; Lois des Bat. pt. 2, c. 2, § 1.

Fortuitous events are fortunate or unfortunate. The accident of finding a treasure is a fortuitous event of the first class. Lois des Bat. pt. 2, c. 2, § 2.

Involuntary obligations may arise in consequence of fortuitous events. For example, when, to save a vessel from shipwreck, it is necessary to throw goods overboard, the loss must be borne in common. There arises, in this case, between the owners of the vessel and of the goods remaining on board, an obligation to bear proportionably the loss which has been sustained. Lois des Bat. pt. 2, c. 2, § 2.

See, in general, Dig. 50. 17. 23; Id. 16. 3. 1; Id. 19. 2. 11; Id. 44. 7. 1; Id. 18. 6. 10; Id. 13. 6. 18; Id. 26. 7. 50.

FORTUNAM FACIUNT JUDICEM. They make fortune the judge. Co. Litt. 167. Spoken of the process of making partition among coparceners by drawing lots for the several purparts.

FORUM.

——**At Common Law.** A place; a place of jurisdiction; the place where a remedy is sought; jurisdiction; a court of justice.

Forum conscientiae. The conscience.

Forum contentiosum. A court. 3 Bl. Comm. 211.

Forum contractus. The courts of the place of making a contract. 2 Kent, Comm. 463.

Forum domesticum. A domestic court. 1 W. Bl. 82.

Forum domicilii. The court of the place of domicile. 2 Kent, Comm. 463.

Forum ecclesiasticum. An ecclesiastical court.

Forum rei gestae. The court of the place of transaction. 2 Kent, Comm. 463.

Forum rei sitae. The court of the place where the thing is situated.

Forum seculare. A secular court.

Forum ligeantiae rei. The court or jurisdiction of the county to which defendant owes allegiance.

Forum regium. The king's court. St. Westminster II. c. 43.

Forum rei, or *rei sitae* (Law Lat.) The *forum* or court of the thing (*res rei*); the court of the place where a thing claimed is; the tribunal where the property is. Story, Confl. Laws, § 325k. The place where a thing in controversy is situated, considered as a place of jurisdiction and remedy. 2 Kent, Comm. 463.

——**In Roman Law.** The paved open space in cities, particularly in Rome, where were held the solemn business assemblies of the people, the markets, the exchange (whence *cedere foro,* to retire from 'change, equivalent to "to become bankrupt"), and where the magistrates sat to transact the business of their office. It came afterwards to mean any place where causes were tried, *locus exercendarum litium.* Isidor. lib. 18, Orig. A court of justice.

The obligation and the right of a person to have his case decided by a particular court.

It is often synonymous with that signification of *judicium* which corresponds to our word "court" (*q. v.*) in the sense of jurisdiction; *e. g., foro interdicere* (l. 1, § 13, D. 1. 12; C. 9, § 4; D. 48. 19); *fori praescriptio* (l. 7, pr. D. 2, 8; l. 1, C. 3, 24); *forum rei accusator sequitur* (l. 5, pr. C. 3, 13). In this sense, the *forum* of a person means both the obligation and the right of that person to have his cause decided by a particular court. 5 Gluck, Pand. 237. What court should have cognizance of the cause depends, in general, upon the person of the defendant, or upon the person of some one connected with the defendant.

By modern writers upon the Roman law, jurisdiction dependent on the person of the defendant is distinguished as (1) that of common right, *forum commune,* and (2) that of special privilege, *forum privilegiatum.*

(1) *Forum commune.* The jurisdiction of common right was either general, *forum generale,* or special, *forum speciale.*

(a) *Forum generale.* General jurisdiction was of two kinds, the *forum originis,* which was that of the birthplace of the party, and the *forum domicilii,* that of his domicile. The *forum originis* was either *commune* or *proprium.* The former was that legal status which all free-born subjects of the empire, wherever residing, had at Rome when they were found there, and had not the *jus revocandi domum* (*i. e.,* the right of one absent from his domicile of transferring to the *forum domicilii* a suit instituted against him in the place of his temporary sojourn). L. 2, §§ 3, 4, 5, D. 5, 1; l. 28, § 4, D. 4, 6; 3 Gluck, Pand. 188. The *forum originis proprium,* or *forum originis speciale,* was the court of that place of which at the time of the party's birth his father was a citizen, though that might possibly be neither his own birthplace, nor the actual domicile of his father.

Forum domicilii. The place of the domicile exercised the greatest influence over the rights of the party. As to what constitutes domicile, see "Domicile." In general, one was subject to the laws and courts of his domicile alone, unless specially privileged. L. 29, D. 50, 1.

(b) *Forum speciale.* Particular jurisdiction. These were very numerous. The more important are: *Forum continentiae causarum.* Sometimes two or more actions or disputed questions are so connected that they cannot advantageously be tried separately, although in strictness they belong to different jurisdictions. In such cases the modern civil law permits them to be determined in a single court, although such court would be incompetent in regard to a portion of them taken singly. *Forum contractus,* the court having cognizance of the action on a contract.

Forum delicti, forum deprehensionis. The jurisdiction of the person of a criminal, and may be the court of the place where the offense was committed, or that of the place where the criminal was arrested.

Forum arresti. A jurisdiction unknown to the Roman law, but of frequent occurrence in the modern civil law. It is that over persons or things detained by a judicial order, and corresponds in some degree to the "attachment" of our practice.

Forum gestae administrationis. The jurisdiction over the accounts and administration of guardians, agents, and all persons appointed to manage the affairs of third parties. The court which appointed such administrator or wherein the cause was pending in which such appointment was made, or within whose territorial limits the business of the administration was transacted, had exclusive jurisdiction over all suits arising out of his acts, or brought for the purpose of compelling him to account, or brought by him to recover compensation for his outlays. L. 1, C. 3, 21; 6 Gluck, Pand. § 521.

(2) *Forum privilegiatum.* Privileged jurisdictions. In general, the privileged jurisdiction of a person held the same rank as the *forum domicilii*, and, like that, did not supplant the particular jurisdictions above named save in certain exceptional cases. The privilege was general in its nature, and applied to all cases not specially excepted, but it only arose when the person possessing it was sued by another; for he could not assert it when he was the plaintiff, the rule being, *actor sequitur forum rei*, the plaintiff must resort to the jurisdiction of the defendant. It was in general limited to personal actions; all real actions brought against the defendant in the character of possessor of the thing in dispute followed the *forum speciale*. The privilege embraced the wife of the privileged person and his children so long as they were under his *potestas*. And, lastly, when a *forum privilegiatum* purely personal conflicted with the *forum speciale*, the former must yield. 6 Gluck, Pand. 339-341.

Privileged persons were:

(a) *Personae miserabiles*, who were persons under the special protection of the law on account of some incapacity of age, sex, mind, or condition. These were entitled, whether as plaintiffs or defendants, to carry their causes directly before the emperor, and, passing over the inferior courts, to demand a hearing before his supreme tribunal, whenever they had valid grounds for doubting the impartiality or fearing the procrastination of the inferior courts, or for dreading the influence of a powerful adversary. 6 Gluck, Pand. § 522.

(b) *Clerici*, the clergy. The privilege of clerical persons to be impleaded only in the episcopal courts commenced under the Christian emperors.

(c) *Academici.* In the modern civil law, the officers and students of the universities are privileged to be sued before the university courts. This species of privilege was unknown to the Roman law. See 6 Gluck, Pand. § 524.

(d) *Milites.* Soldiers had special military courts as well in civil as criminal cases.

There are many classes of persons who are privileged in respect to jurisdiction under the modern civil law who were not so privileged by the Roman law. Such are officers of the court of the sovereign, including ministers of state and councillors, ambassadors, noblemen, etc. These do not require extended notice.

Jurisdiction ex persona alterius. A person might be entitled to be sued in a particular court on grounds depending upon the person of another. Such were (1) the wife, who, if the marriage had been legally contracted, acquired the *forum* of her husband (l. 65, D. 5, 1; l. ult. D. 50, 1; l. 19, D. 2, 1), and retained it until her second marriage (l. 22. § 1, D. 50, 1), or change of domicile. Section 93, Voet. Com. ad Pand. D. 5, 1. (2) Servants, who possessed the jurisdiction of their master as regarded the *forum domicilii*, and also the *forum privilegiatum*, so far at least as the privilege was that of the class to which such master belonged, and was not purely personal. Gluck, Pand. § 510b. (3) The *haeres*, who in many cases retained the jurisdiction of his testator. When sued in the character of heir in respect to causes of action upon which suit had been commenced before the testator's death, he must submit to the *forum* which had acquired cognizance of the suit. Ll. 30, 34, D. 5, 1.

FORWARDING MERCHANT. A person who receives and forwards goods, taking upon himself the expenses of transportation, for which he receives a compensation from the owners, but who has no concern in the vessels or wagons by which they are transported, and no interest in the freight.

Such a one is not deemed a common carrier, but a mere warehouseman or agent. 12 Johns. (N. Y.) 232; 7 Cow. (N. Y.) 497. He is required to use only ordinary diligence in sending the property by responsible persons. 2 Cow. (N. Y.) 593. See Story, Bailm.

FOSSA (Lat.) In English law. A ditch full of water, where formerly women who had committed a felony were drowned; the grave. Cowell.

FOSSAGIUM. The duty levied on the inhabitants for repairing the moat or ditch around a fortified town.

FOSSATORIUM OPERATIO (Lat.) The service or laboring done by the inhabitants and adjoining tenants, for repair and maintenance of the ditches round a city or town. A contribution in lieu of such work, called *fossagium*, was sometimes paid. Kennett; Cowell.

FOSSATUM (Law Lat. from *fossa, q. v.*) In old English law. A dyke; a bank of earth thrown up out of a ditch. Glanv. lib. 13, c. 34; Bracton, fol. 115; Fleta, lib. 1, c. 24, § 8; St. Westminster II. c. 46.

A ditch or trench. The same with *fossa*. Spelman; Rig. Orig. 92b, 198b, 199.

A moat or *fosse* around an encampment or fortified place. Spelman.

A canal or cut from a river. Cowell; Cart. 20 Hen. III.

A place fenced with a ditch. Cowell.

FOSSE WAY, or FOSSE. One of the four ancient Roman ways through England. Spelman, voc. "Ikenild Street."

FOSSELLUM. A small ditch. Cowell.

FOSTERLAND. Land given, assigned, or allotted to the finding of food or victuals for any person or persons; as in monasteries for the monks, etc. Cowell; Blount.

FOSTERLEAN. The remuneration fixed for the rearing of a foster child; also the jointure of a wife. Jacob.

FOUNDATION. The establishment of a charity; that upon which a charity is founded, and by which it is supported.

This word, in the English law, is taken in two senses,—*fundatio incipiens*, and *fundatio perficiens*. As to its political capacity, an act of incorporation is metaphorically called its foundation; but as to its dotation, the first gift of revenues is called the foundation. 10 Coke, 23a.

FOUNDER. One who endows an institution; one who makes a gift of revenues to a corporation. 10 Coke, 33; 1 Sharswood, Bl. Comm. 481.

In England, the king is said to be the founder of all civil corporations; and where there is an act of incorporation, he is called the "general founder," and he who endows is called the "perficient founder." 1 Sharswood, Bl. Comm. 481.

FOUNDEROSUS. Out of repair. Cro. Car. 366.

FOUNDLING. A new-born child abandoned by its parents, who are unknown. The settlement of such a child is in the place where found.

FOUR CORNERS. A metaphorical expression indicating the whole face or contents of an instrument, taken as an entirety.

FOUR SEAS. The seas surrounding England. These were divided into the western, including the Scotch and Irish; the northern, or North Sea; the eastern, being the German Ocean; the southern, being the British Channel. Selden, Mare Clausum, lib. 2, c. 1.

"Within the four seas" means within the jurisdiction of England. 4 Coke, 125; 2 Inst. 253. See "Beyond Sea."

FOURCHER (Fr. to fork). In English law. A method of delaying an action formerly practised by defendants.

When an action was brought against two, who, being jointly concerned, were not bound to answer till both appeared, and they agreed not to appear both in one day, the appearance of one excused the other's default, who had a day given him to appear with the other. The defaulter, on the day appointed, appeared; but the first then made default. In this manner they forked each other, and practised this for delay. See 2 Inst. 250; Booth, Real Actions, 16.

FOURCHING. The act of delaying legal proceedings. Termes de la Ley.

FOWL. The word comprehends all birds and poultry. 11 East, 577.

FOWLS OF WARREN. Such fowls are of two sorts, Terrestres and Aquatiles. Terrestres of two sorts, Silvestres, and Campestres; Campestres, as partridge, quaile, raile, etc.; Silvestres, as pheasant, woodcocke, etc.; Aquatiles, as mallard, herne, etc.; and are preserved under the game laws in warrens. Co. Litt. 233.

FOX'S ACT. St. 52 Geo. III. c. 60, which secured to juries, upon the trial of indictments or informations for libel, the right of pronouncing a general verdict of guilty or not guilty upon the whole matter in issue, and no longer bound them to find a verdict of guilty on proof of the publication of the paper charged to be a libel, and of the sense ascribed to it in the indictment.

FOY (Law Fr.) Faith; fidelity. Britt. 29; Oath. Britt. 70.

FRACTIO (Lat. from *frangere*, to break). A breaking; a breach. *Fractio fedei*, a breach of promise or of trust. 1 Rep. Ch. Append. 8.

FRACTION OF A DAY. A portion of a day; the dividing a day. Generally, the law does not allow the fraction of a day. 2 Sharswood, Bl. Comm. 141.

The day may be divided, however, to show which of two acts was actually done first. 3 Burrows, 1434; 4 Kent, Comm. 95, note; 11 H. L. Cas. 411.

FRACTIONEM DIEI NON RECIPET lex. The law does not regard a fraction of a day. Lofft, 572. But see "Day."

FRACTITIUM. Arable land. Mon Angl.

FRACTURA NAVIUM. Wreck of shipping at sea.

FRAIS DE JUSTICE. Costs incurred incidentally to the action. See 1 Tropl. Dr. Civ. 122, 135, note; 4 Low. (U. S.) 77.

FRANC. A French coin, of the value of about eighteen cents.

FRANC ALEU. In French law. An absolutely free inheritance; allodial lands. Generally, however, the word denotes an inheritance free from seignorial rights, though held subject to the sovereign. Dumoulin, "Cout. de Par." § 1; Guyot, Rep. Univ.; 3 Kent, Comm. 498, note; 8 Low. (U. S.) 95.

FRANCHILANUS. A freeman. Blount.

FRANCHISE. A special privilege conferred by government on individuals, and which does not belong to the citizens of the country generally by common right. Angell & A. Corp. § 4.

A particular privilege conferred by grant from government, and vested in individuals. 3 Kent, Comm. 458.

A branch of the king's prerogative subsisting in the hands of a subject. Finch, Law, lib. 2, c. 14; 2 Sharswood, Bl. Comm. 37.

In a popular sense, the word seems to be synonymous with "right" or "privilege"; as, the elective franchise. And it is commonly applied to those powers exercised by virtue of a grant of privilege.

"To be a corporation is a franchise. The various powers conferred on corporations are franchises. The execution of a policy of insurance by an insurance company, and the issuance of a bank note by an incorporated bank, are franchises." 15 Johns. (N. Y.) 387.

"The term [franchise] must be always considered in connection with the corporation or property to which it is supposed to appertain." 93 U. S. 223.

FRANCIGENA. A designation formerly given to aliens in England.

FRANCUS. Free; a freeman; a Frank. Spelman.

——**Francus Bancus.** Free bench (*q. v.*)

——**Francus Homo.** A free man.

——**Francus Plegius.** In old English law. A frank pledge, or free pledge. Spelman.

——**Francus Tenens.** In old English law. A frank or free tenant; a freeholder.

FRANK. In old English law. Free.

FRANK BANK. In old English law. Free bench. Litt. § 166; Co. Litt. 110b. See under "Francus."

FRANK CHASE. Free chase. The liberty or franchise of having a chase.

FRANK FEE. Lands not held in ancient demesne. Called "lands pleadable at common law." Reg. Orig. 12, 14; Fitzh. Nat. Brev. 161; Termes de la Ley.

That which a man holds to himself and his heirs, and not by such service as is required in ancient demesne, according to the custom of the manor. The opposite of copyhold. Cowell. A fine had in the king's court might convert demesne lands into frank fee. 2 Bl. Comm. 368.

FRANK FERME. Lands or tenements where the nature of the fee is changed by feoffment from knight's service to yearly service, and whence no homage but such as is contained in the feoffment may be demanded. Britt. c. 66, n. 3; Cowell; 2 Bl. Comm. 80.

FRANK FOLD. In old English law. Free fold; a privilege for the lord to have all the sheep of his tenants and the inhabitants within his seigniory, in his fold, in his demesnes, to manure his land. Keilw. 198; Y. B. H. 1 Edw. III. 4.

FRANK LAW (Law Fr. *fraunche ley;* Law Lat. *libera lex, lex terrae*). In old English law. The liberty of being sworn in courts, as a juror or witness; one of the ancient privileges of a freeman, or free and lawful man (*liber et legalis homo*). Otherwise called the law of the land (*lex terrae*), or simply law (*lex*). The nature of this privilege may be understood from Bracton's description of the consequences of losing it, among which the principal one was that the parties incurred perpetual infamy, so that they were never afterwards to be admitted to oath, because they were not deemed to be oathworthy (that is, not worthy of making oath), nor allowed to give testimony. *Perpetuam infamiam incurrant, et legem terrae amittant, et ita quod nunquam postea ad sacramentum admittantur, quia de coetero non erunt otheswortk, nec ad testimonium recipientur.* Bracton, fol. 292b. This was one of the punishments of jurors who had been convicted of perjury. Id.

This term has been very generally defined "the privilege of the law's protection," and "the benefit of the free and common law of the land." Holthouse; Wharton. But that it had a more particular and determinate meaning is clear both from the testimony of the ancient writers, and from the peculiar signification of the word "law," which, from a very early period, denoted an oath, or the taking or making of an oath; as in the common expressions "wager of law," and "making law." A lawful man (*legalis homo*) was one who was competent to be sworn as a juror or witness; and the word "lawful" is used in this sense in jury process to this day. 3 Bl. Comm. 340, 341, 352.

FRANK MARRIAGE. A species of estate tail where the donee had married one of kin (as daughter or cousin) to the donor, and held the estate subject to the implied condition that the estate was to descend to the issue of such marriage. On birth of issue, as in other cases of estate tail before the statute *De Donis*, the birth of issue was regarded as a condition performed, and the estate thereupon became alienable by the donee. 1 Cruise, Dig. 71; 1 Washb. Real Prop. 67.

The estate is said to be in frank marriage because given in consideration of marriage, and free from services for three generations of descendants. Blount; Cowell. See, also, 2 Sharswood, Bl. Comm. 115; 1 Steph. Comm. 232.

FRANK PLEDGE. A pledge or surety for freemen. Termes de la Ley.

The bond or pledge which the inhabitants of a tithing entered into for each one of their number that he should be forthcoming to answer every violation of law. Each boy, on reaching the age of fourteen, was obliged to find some such pledge, or be committed to prison. Blount; Cowell.

FRANK TENANT. A freeholder. Litt. § 91.

FRANK TENEMENT. In English law. A free tenement, freeholding, or freehold. 2 Bl. Comm. 61, 62, 104; 1 Steph. Comm. 217; Bracton, fol. 207. Used to denote both the tenure and the estate.

FRANKALMOIGNE. A species of ancient tenure, still extant in England, whereby a religious corporation, aggregate or sole, holds its lands of the donor, in consideration of the religious services it performs.

In the United States, religious corporations hold land by the same tenure with which all other corporations and individuals hold; and the only approach to a tenancy in frankalmoigne may be found in the exemption from taxation which is enjoyed by churches in common with charitable and scientific institutions.

FRANKING PRIVILEGE. The privilege of sending certain matter through the public mails without payment therefor.

It is enjoyed by various officers of the federal government, theoretically for the public good. See Brightly, Dig. U. S. Laws.

FRANKLEYN, FRANCLING, or **FRANKlin.** A freeman; a freeholder; a gentleman. Blount; Cowell.

FRASSETUM (Law Lat.) In old English law. A wood, or ground that is woody. Co. Litt. 4b; Shep. Touch. 95. Blount considers it a corruption of *fraxinetum*, a wood where ashes grow.

FRATER (Lat.) Brother.

——**Frater Consanguineus.** A brother born from the same father, though the mother may be different.

——**Frater Nutricius.** A bastard brother.

——**Frater Uterinus.** A brother who has the same mother, but not the same father. Blount; Vicat; 2 Bl. Comm. 232. See "Brother."

FRATER FRATRI UTERINO NON SUCcedet in haereditate paterna. A brother shall not succeed an uterine brother in the paternal inheritance. Fort. de Laud. Leg. Ang. by Amos, p. 15; 2 Sharswood, Bl. Comm. This maxim is now superseded in England by 3 & 4 Wm. IV. c. 106, § 9. Broom, Leg. Max. (3d London Ed.) 471; 2 Sharswood, Bl. Comm. 232.

FRATERNAL INSURANCE. A form of mutual life, and perhaps, also, health and accident, insurance. Its distinguishing characteristics seem to be (a) that it is written on members of a fraternal or beneficial society only, and (b) that the organization itself is the insurer. The premiums are usually paid by way of assessment or monthly dues, rather than by annual premium, and may or may not involve the creation of a reserve fund.

FRATERNIA. A fraternity or brotherhood.

FRATRIAGE. A younger brother's inheritance.

FRATRICIDE. The killing of a brother or sister.

One who has killed his brother or sister.

FRAUD. The unlawful obtaining of another's property by design, but without criminal intent, and with the assent of the owner obtained by artifice or misrepresentation. Any cunning deception or artifice used to circumvent, cheat, or deceive another. Story, Eq. Jur. § 186.

Fraud is sometimes used as a term synonymous with "covin," "collusion," and "deceit," but improperly so. Covin is a secret contrivance between two or more persons to defraud and prejudice another of his rights. Collusion is an agreement between two or more persons to defraud another under the forms of law, or to accomplish an illegal purpose. Deceit is a fraudulent contrivance by words or acts to deceive a third person, who, relying thereupon, without carelessness or neglect of his own, sustains damage thereby. Co. Litt. 357b; Bac. Abr.

Actual or positive fraud includes cases of the intentional and successful employment of any cunning, deception, or artifice, used to circumvent, cheat, or deceive another. 1 Story, Eq. Jur. § 186.

Legal or constructive fraud includes such contracts or acts as, though not originating in any actual evil design or contrivance to perpetrate a fraud, yet by their tendency to deceive or mislead others, or to violate private or public confidence, are prohibited by law. Thus, for instance, contracts against some general public policy or fixed artificial policy of the law; cases arising from some peculiar confidential or fiduciary relation between the parties, where advantage is taken of that relation by the person in whom the trust or confidence is reposed, or by third persons; agreements and other acts of parties which operate virtually to delay, defraud, and deceive creditors; purchases of property, with full notice of the legal or equitable title of other persons to the same property (the purchaser becoming, by construction, *particeps criminis* with the fraudulent grantor); and voluntary conveyances of real estate, as affecting the title of subsequent purchasers. 1 Story, Eq. Jur. c. 7.

——**In the Civil Law.** According to the civilians, positive fraud consists in doing one's self, or causing another to do, such things as induce the opposite party into error, or retain him there. The intention to deceive, which is the characteristic of fraud, is here present; the definition of "constructive fraud" being the same as at common law. Fraud was also divided into that which has induced the contract, *dolus dans causam contractui*, and incidental or accidental fraud. The former is that which has been the cause or determining motive of the contract, that without which the party defrauded would not have contracted, when the artifices practised by one of the parties have been such that it is evident that without them the other would not have contracted. Incidental or accidental fraud is that by which a person, otherwise determined to contract, is deceived on some accessories or incidents of the contract,—for example, as to the quality of the object of the contract, or its price,—so that he has made a bad bargain. Accidental fraud does not, according to the civilians, avoid the contract, but simply subjects the party to damages. It is otherwise where the fraud has been the determining cause of the contract, *qui causam dedit contractui*. In that case, the contract is void. Toullier, Dr. Civ. liv. 3, tit. 3, c. 2, note, § 5, note 86 et seq. See, also, 1 Mall. Anal. de la Disc. du Code Civ. pp. 15, 16; Bouv. Inst. Index.

——**In Equity.** It is sometimes inaccurately said that such and such transactions amount to fraud in equity, though not in law; according to the popular notion that the law allows or overlooks certain kinds of fraud which the more conscientious rules of equity condemn and punish. But, properly speaking, fraud in all its shapes is as odious in law as in equity. The difference is that, as the law courts are constituted, and as it has been found in centuries of experience that it is convenient they should be constituted, they cannot deal with fraud otherwise than to punish it by the infliction of damages. All those manifold varieties of fraud against which specific relief, of a preventive or remedial sort, is required for the purposes of substantial justice, are the subjects of equity and not of law jurisdiction.

The following classification of frauds as a head of equity jurisdiction is given by Lord Hardwicke (2 Ves. Jr. 155): (1) Fraud, or *dolus malus*, may be actual, arising from facts and circumstances of imposition. (2) It may be apparent from the intrinsic nature and subject of the bargain itself, such as no man in his senses and not under delusion would make, on the one hand, and no honest or fair man would accept, on the other. (3) It may be inferred from the circumstances and condition of the parties; for it is as much against conscience to take advantage of a man's weakness or necessity as of his ignorance. (4) It may be collected from the nature and circumstances of the transaction, as being an imposition on third persons.

——**In Criminal Law.** Without the express provision of any statute, all deceitful practices in defrauding or endeavoring to defraud another of his known right, by means of some artful device, contrary to the plain rules of common honesty, are condemned by the common law, and punishable according to the heinousness of the offense. Co. Litt. 3b; Dyer, 295; Hawk. P. C. c. 71.

FRAUDS, STATUTE OF. The name commonly given to St. 29 Car. II. c. 3, entitled, "An Act for the Prevention of Frauds and Perjuries"; and to statutes of the various states patterned thereon, and substantially to the same effect.

These statutes differ in detail, but generally provide that no action shall be brought on certain classes of contract unless some memorandum thereof be in writing, and signed by the party to be charged.

FRAUDULENT CONVEYANCE. A conveyance, the object, tendency, or effect of which is to defraud another, or the intent of which is to avoid some duty or debt due by or incumbent on the party making it. 2 Kent, Comm. 440; 4 Kent, Comm. 462.

There must be: (a) A creditor to be defrauded; but subsequent creditors are entitled to impeach a conveyance for fraud. 118 Mass. 527. (b) A conveyance by the debtor; but the form of the conveyance is immaterial. 89 Ind. 117. (c) Of property of value, out of which the creditor could have made a portion of his claim. 46 Mich. 243; 52 Vt. 45; 67 Me. 183. (d) With intent to hinder, delay, or defraud (88 N. Y. 669); but the fraud may arise from the nature and necessary result of the transaction, without regard to the actual intention of the parties (108 Ill. 502).

——**Statute of Fraudulent Conveyances.** Fraudulent conveyances received early attention; and the statutes of 13 Eliz. c. 5, and 27 Eliz. c. 4, made perpetual by 29 Eliz. c. 18, declared all conveyances made with intent to defraud creditors, etc., to be void. This statute, on which all subsequent legislation has been patterned, defined a fraudulent conveyance as "a conveyance, the object, tendency, or effect of which is to avoid some duty or debt due by or incumbent upon the party making the conveyance." By a liberal construction, it has become the settled English law that a voluntary conveyance shall be deemed fraudulent against a subsequent purchaser, even with notice. 9 East, 59; 2 Sharswood, Bl. Comm. 296; Roberts, Fraud. Conv. 2, 3.

Voluntary conveyances are not so construed in the United States, however, where the subsequent purchaser has notice, especially if there be a good consideration. 2 Gray (Mass.) 447.

These statutes have been generally adopted in the United States as the foundation of all the state statutes upon this subject. 1 Story, Eq. Jur. 353; 4 Kent, Comm. 462, 463.

FRAUDULENT PREFERENCES. See "Preferences."

FRAUNC, FRAUNCHE, or **FRAUNKE.** See "Frank."

FRAUNCHISE. A franchise.

FRAUS (Lat. fraud). More commonly called, in the civil law, "*dolus*" and "*dolus malus*" (*q v.*). A distinction, however, was sometimes made between "*fraus*" and "*dolus*"; the former being held to be of the most extensive import. Calv. Lex.

FRAUS EST CELARE FRAUDEM. It is a fraud to conceal a fraud. 1 Vern. 270.

FRAUS EST ODIOSA, ET NON PRAEsumenda. Fraud is odious, and not to be presumed. Cro. Car. 550.

FRAUS ET DOLUS NEMINI PATROCInari debent. Fraud and deceit should excuse no man. 3 Coke, 78.

FRAUS ET JUS NUNQUAM COHABITant. Fraud and justice never dwell together. Wingate, Max. 680.

FRAUS LATET IN GENERALIBUS. Fraud lies hid in general expressions.

FRAUS LEGIS. (Lat.) In civil law. Fraud of law; fraud upon law. See "In Fraudem Legis."

FRAUS MERETUR FRAUDEM. Fraud deserves fraud. Plowd. 110; Branch, Princ. This is very poor law.

FRAXINETUM. In old English law. A wood of ashes; a place where ashes grow. Co. Litt. 4b; Shep. Touch. 95.

FRAY. See "Affray."

FRECTUM. In Old English law. Freight. Blount.

FREDNITE. A liberty to hold courts and take up the fines for beating and wounding. Cowell; Cunningham.

To be free from fines.

FREDSTOLE, or FRIDSTOLE. Sanctuaries; seats of peace.

FREDUM. A fine paid for obtaining pardon when the peace had been broken. Spelman; Blount. A sum paid the magistrate for protection against the right of revenge. 1 Robertson, Hist. Charles V., Append. note xxiii.

FREE. Not bound to servitude; at liberty to act as one pleases. This word is put in opposition to slave. Const. U. S. art. 1, § 2. Used in distihction from being bound as an apprentice.

The Declaration of Independence asserts that all men are born free; and in this sense the term is usually supposed to mean all mankind, though this seems to be doubted in 19 How. (U. S.) 393.

Certain; as, free services. These were also more honorable.

Confined to the person possessing, instead of being held in common; as, free fishery.

FREE ALMS. Tenure by indefinite spiritual services; frankalmoigne (*q. v.*).

FREE BENCH. Copyhold lands which the wife has for dower after the decease of her husband. Kitch. Cts. 102; Bracton, lib. 4, tr. 6, c. 13, No. 2; Fitzh. Nat. Brev. 150; Plowd. 411.

Dower in copyhold lands. 2 Bl. Comm. 129. The quantity varies in different sections of England. Co. Litt. 110b. Incontinency was a cause of forfeiture, except on the performance of a ridiculous ceremony. Cowell; Blount.

FREE BORD. An allowance of land outside the fence, which may be claimed by the owner. An allowance, in some places, two and a half feet wide outside the boundary or inclosure. Blount; Cowell.

FREE CHAPEL. A chapel founded by the king, and exempted from the jurisdiction of the ordinary. It may be one founded or endowed by a private person under a grant from the king. Cowell; Termes de la Ley.

FREE COURSE. Having the wind from a favorable quarter. To prevent collision of vessels, it is the duty of the vessel having the wind free to give way to a vessel beating up to windward and tacking. 3 Hagg. Adm. 215. At sea, such vessel meeting another close hauled must give way, if necessary to prevent the danger of collision. 3 Car. & P. 528. See 9 Car. & P. 528; 2 W. Rob. Adm. 225; 2 Dods. Adm. 87.

FREE FISHERY. A franchise which gives an exclusive right of fishing in a public navigable river, without any ownership on the soil. 3 Kent, Comm. 329; 2 Sharswood, Bl. Comm. 39; 1 Salk. 637; Woolr. Waters, 97. Free fishery is the same as common of fishery. Co. Litt. Hargrave's notes, 122; 2 Sharswood, Bl. Comm. 39; 7 Pick. (Mass.) 79; Angell, Watercourses, c. 6, §§ 3, 4. See "Fishery."

FREE ON BOARD. Abbreviated f. o. b. in the law of sales. A sale free on board is one in which the seller agrees to deliver the goods on board cars or ship at a place named, at his own expense, free to be taken by the purchaser without any obstruction or impediment. 136 Wis. 495. See also F. O. B.

FREE SERVICES. Such as it was not unbecoming the character of a soldier or freeman to perform; as, to serve under his lord in the wars, to pay a sum of money, and the like. 2 Bl. Comm. 62; 1 Washb. Real Prop. 25.

FREE SHIPS. Neutral ships. "Free ships make free goods" is a phrase often used in treaties to denote that the goods on board neutral ships shall be free from confiscation, even though belonging to an enemy. Wheat. Int. Law, 507 et seq.; 1 Kent, Comm. 126. See 3 Phillim. Int. Law (3d Ed.) 238 et seq., for a full discussion of the subject.

FREE SOCAGE. Tenure in free socage is a tenure by certain and honorable services which yet are not military. 1 Spence, Eq. Jur. 52; Dalr. Feud. Prop. c. 2, § 1; 1 Washb. Real Prop. 25. Called, also, "free and common socage." See "Socage."

FREE SOCMEN. In old English law. Tenants in free socage. Glanv. lib. 3, c. 7; 2 Bl. Comm. 79.

FREE (or FRANK) TENURE. Freehold tenure. The opposite of the ancient villeinage or modern copyhold. 2 Bl. Comm. 89, 90.

FREE WARREN. A franchise for the preserving and custody of beasts and fowls of warren. 2 Sharswood, Bl. Comm. 39, 417;

Co. Litt. 233. This franchise gave the grantee sole right of killing, so far as his warren extended, on condition of excluding other persons. 2 Sharswood, Bl. Comm. 39.

FREE-BOROUGH MEN. Such great men as did not engage, like the frank-pledge men, for their decennier. Jacob.

FREEDMAN. In Roman law. A person who had been released from a state of servitude. See "Liberti."

FREEDOM. The power by which man can do what does not interfere with the rights of another; its basis is nature; its standard is justice; its protection is law; its moral boundary is the maxim, "Do not unto others that you do not wish they should do unto you." French Const. of 1793.

FREEHOLD. See "Estates."

FREEHOLD IN LAW. A freehold which has descended to a man, upon which he may enter at pleasure, but which he has not entered on. Termes de la Ley.

FREEHOLD LAND SOCIETIES. Societies in England designed for the purpose of enabling mechanics, artisans, and other working men to purchase, at the least possible price, a piece of freehold land of a sufficient yearly value to entitle the owner to the elective franchise for the county in which the land is situated. Wharton.

FREEHOLDER. The owner of a freehold estate. Such a man must have been anciently a freeman; and the gift to any man by his lord of an estate to him and his heirs made the tenant a freeman, if he had not been so before. See 1 Washb. Real Prop. 29, 45 et seq.

FREEMAN. One who is not a slave; one born free, or made so.

——**In Old English Law.** A freeholder, as distinguished from a villein.

An inhabitant of a city. St. 1 Hen. VI. c. 11; 3 Steph. Comm. 196, 197; Cunningham.

FREEMAN'S ROLL. A list of persons admitted as burgesses or freemen for the purposes of the rights reserved by the municipal corporation act (5 & 6 Wm. IV. c. 76). Distinguished from the burgess roll. 3 Steph. Comm. 197. The term was used, in early colonial history, of some of the American colonies.

FREIGHT. The amount due a carrier for the transportation of goods or live stock. Angell, Carr. § 391. Sometimes applied in a loose sense to the goods carried.

——**In Maritime Law.** The sum agreed on for the hire of a ship, entirely or in part, for the carriage of goods from one port to another. 13 East, 300. All rewards or compensation paid for the use of ships. 1 Pet. Adm. 206; 2 Boul. P. Dr. Com. tit. 8, § 1; 2 Bos. & P. 321; 4 Dall. (Pa.) 459; 2 Johns. (N. Y.) 346; 3 Johns. (N. Y.) 335; 3 Pardessus, note 705.

FREIGHTER. He to whom a ship or vessel has been hired, and who loads her under his contract; he who loads a general ship. 3 Kent, Comm. 173; 3 Pardessus, note 704.

FRENCHMAN. In early times, in English law, this term was applied to every stranger or "outlandish" man. Bracton, lib. 3, tr. 2, c. 15.

FRENDLESS MAN, or **FRENDLESMAN** (Saxon). The ancient name of an outlaw (*utlaughe*) in England. So called, according to Bracton, because he forfeited his friends (*quod forisfacit amicos*); all persons being forbidden to give him food or shelter, or to have any communication with him. Bracton, fol. 128b.

FRENDNITE, or **FRENDWITE.** A fine exacted from him who harbored an outlawed friend. Cowell; Cunningham. A quittance for forfang (exemption from the penalty of taking provisions before the king's purveyors had taken enough for the king's necessities). Cowell.

FRENETICUS. In old English law. A madman, or person in a frenzy. Fleta, lib. 1, c. 36.

FREOBORGH. A free surety or free pledge. Spelman. See "Frank Pledge."

FREQUENT. To visit often; to resort to often or habitually. 109 Ind. 176.

To "frequent" a place is to frequently go there, or to be in the habit of going there. Therefore a conviction cannot be sustained under the Vagrant Act for "frequenting" a street, etc., with intent to commit felony, where the evidence does not show that the person has been there more than once. 14 Q. B. D. 93; 49 J. P. 246. He must in fact be seen hanging about the street. 1 Times Rep. 109.

FREQUENTIA ACTUS MULTUM OPERatur. The frequency of an act effects much. 4 Coke, 78; Wingate, Max. 192.

FRESCA. In old records. Fresh water, or rain and land flood. Cowell.

FRESH DISSEISIN. Such disseisin as a man may seek to defeat of himself, and by his own power, without the help of the king or judges. There was no limit set to the time within which this might be done. It is set in one case at a disseisin committed within fifteen days. Bracton, lib. 4, c. 5. In another case it was held a fresh disseisin when committed within a year. Britt. cc. 43, 44; Cowell.

FRESH FINE. A fine levied within a year. St. Westminster II. (13 Edw. I.) c. 45; Cowell.

FRESH FORCE. Force done within forty days. Fitzh. Nat. Brev. 7; Old Nat. Brev.

4. The heir or reversioner in a case of disseisin by fresh force was allowed a remedy in chancery by bill before the mayor. Cowell.

FRESH PURSUIT. An immediate pursuit of an escaping criminal. The phrase does not imply instant pursuit, but pursuit without unreasonable delay. See 27 Cal. 574; 70 Miss. 253.

FRESH SUIT (Law Lat. *recens insecutio*). In English law. Immediate or speedy pursuit or prosecution. The pursuit of an offender or felon as a thief immediately or as soon as possible after the robbery, including the prosecution of such pursuit until the apprehension and conviction of the offender. The object of this was to enable the party to recover his goods, which otherwise would belong to the king. Britt. c. 15.

The early and speedy prosecution of a suit. St. Gloc. c. 9.

FRESH-WATER RIVER. A fresh-water river, like a tidal river, is composed of the alveus, or bed, and the water; but it has banks instead of shores. Gould Waters, § 45.

FRET (Fr.) In French marine law. Freight. Ord. Mar. liv. 3, tit. 3.

FRETER (Fr.) In French marine law. To freight a ship; to let it. Emerig. Ins. c. 11, § 3.

FRETEUR (Fr.) In French marine law. Freighter; the owner of a ship, who lets it to the merchant. Emerig. Ins. c. 11, § 3.

FRETTUM. In old English law. Freight money. Cowell.

FRETUM. A strait.

Fretum Britannicum, the strait between Dover and Calais. Otherwise called *Fretum Gallicum*. Cowell.

FRIARS. An order of religious persons of whom there were four principal branches, from whom the rest descend, viz.: (1) Franciscans, or Grey Friars; (2) Augustines; (3) Dominicans, or Black Friars; (4) Carmelites, or White Friars. Wharton.

FRIBUSCULUM. In civil law. A slight dissension between husband and wife, which produced a momentary separation, without any intention to dissolve the marriage, in which it differed from a divorce. Poth. Pand. lib. 50, § 106; Vicat. This amounted to a separation in our law. See "Separation."

FRIDBORG, or FRITHBORG. Frank pledge. Cowell. Security for the peace. Spelman.

FRIDHBURGUS (Saxon). A kind of frank pledge, whereby the principal men were bound for themselves and servants. Fleta, lib. 1, c. 47. Cowell says it is the same as frank pledge.

FRIDSTOLL. In Saxon law. A seat, chair or place of peace; an asylum, refuge, or sanctuary for offenders. Spelman; Cowell.

FRIEND OF THE COURT. See "Amicus Curiae."

FRIENDLY SOCIETIES. In England. Mutual benefit societies, supported by subscription of the members, the benefits being of various kinds,—the periodical division of assets, sick or funeral benefits, relief of widows and orphans, etc.

Regulated by "Friendly Society Act" of 1875.

FRIENDLY SUIT. A suit brought by a creditor in chancery against an executor or administrator, being really a suit by the executor or administrator, in the name of a creditor, against himself, in order to compel the creditors to take an equal distribution of the assets. 2 Williams, Ex'rs, 1915.

Also any suit instituted by agreement between the parties to obtain the opinion of the court upon some doubtful question in which they are interested, such as actions for construction of wills, partition suits, etc.

FRIGIDITY. Impotence.

FRILINGI. Persons of free descent, or freemen born; the middle class of persons among the Saxons. Spelman.

FRISCUS (Law Lat.; from Fr. *fresche*). In old English law. Recent or new. *Frisca fortia*, fresh force. Force recently committed, *vis nupera et recenter illata*. Spelman; Reg. Orig. 108a.

Fresh, as distinguished from salt. *Maricus friscus*, fresh marsh. Spelman. *Aqua frisca*, fresh water. Reg. Orig. 97.

Uncultivated, as ground. *Terra jacens frisca et ad warect*, land lying fresh and fallow. Towns. Pl. 69.

FRITHBORG. Frank pledge. Cowell.

FRITHBOTE. A satisfaction or fine for a breach of the peace.

FRITHBREACH. The breaking of the peace. Cowell.

FRITHGAR. The year of jubilee, or of meeting for peace and friendship. Jacob.

FRITHGILDA. Guildhall; a company or fraternity for the maintenance of peace and security; also a fine for breach of the peace. Jacob.

FRITHMAN. A member of a company or fraternity. Blount.

FRITHSOCUE. Surety of defense; jurisdiction of the peace; the franchise of preserving the peace. Cowell; Spelman.

FRITHSPLOT. A spot or plot of land, encircling some stone, tree, or well, considered sacred, and therefore affording sanctuary to criminals. Wharton.

FRIVOLOUS PLEA. Pleading interposed for delay, and its frivolous character indicates bad faith in the pleading. 51 Wis. 430.

FRODMORTEL, or FREOMORTEL. An immunity for committing manslaughter. Mon. Angl. tit. 1, p. 173.

FROM. As expressive of *place*, is always taken exclusively. Thus, "*from* a port" is exclusive of the port. The *terminus a quo* is the boundary line of the port, and when a vessel passes from that, she sails *from* the port, and is on the high seas. Story, J. 2 Mason's R. 130, 131.

Where the particular period sought is to begin or be computed "from" some recognized division of time, the date of beginning is to be excluded in making the computation unless a contrary intention appears. 46 Ill. 173; 41 Ill. 203. Used in a promissory note with reference to a named date, means a subsequent day. 165 Ill. 62.

The word simply expresses the general idea of separation. 103 Cal. 673.

FROM THE BODY OF THE COUNTY. It was not necessary that jurors should have been summoned from every township in the county, in order to comply with the statute requiring jurors to be summoned from the "body of the county." This language means, "from the county at large," "from the people of the county at large," competent to act as jurors. 39 Ia. 633; 10 Wyo. 476.

FRUCTUARIUS (Lat.) One entitled to the use of profits, fruits, and yearly increase of a thing; a lessee; a fermor. Bracton, 241; Vicat.

Sometimes, as applied to a slave, he of whom any one has the usufruct. Vicat.

FRUCTUS (Lat.) The right of using the increase or fruits; equivalent to usufruct.

That which results or springs from a thing; as, rents, interest, freight from a ship, etc.

All the natural return, increase, or additions which is added by nature or by the skill of man, including all the organic products of things. Vicat; 1 Mackeld. Civ. Law, § 154.

They were divided according to their nature into:

——**Fructus Civiles.** Civil fruits. All revenues and recompenses which, though not fruits, properly speaking, are recognized as such by the law. 1 Kauffm. Mackeld. Civ. Law, § 154; Calv. Lex.; Vicat.

——**Fructus Naturales.** Those products which are produced by the powers of nature alone; as, wool, metals, milk. 1 Kauffm. Mackeld. Civ. Law, § 154; Calv. Lex.

——**Fructus Industriales.** Those products which are obtained by the labor and cultivation of the occupant; as, corn. 1 Kauffm. Mackeld. Civ. Law, § 154, note. Emblements are such in the common law. 2 Steph. Comm. 258; Vicat.

According to their situation with respect to their source they were divided into:

——**Fructus Pendentes.** The fruits united with the thing which produces them. These form a part of the principal thing. 1 Kauffm. Mackeld. Civ. Law, § 154.

——**Fructus Separati.** Separate fruits; the fruits of a thing when they are separated from it. Dig. 7. 4. 13; 1 Mackeld. Civ. Law, p. 156, § 154.

FRUCTUS AUGENT HAEREDITATEM. Fruits enhance an inheritance.

FRUCTUS PENDENTES PARS FUNDI videntur. Hanging fruits make part of the land. Dig. 6. 1. 44; 2 Bouv. Inst. note 1578. See "Larceny."

FRUCTUS PERCEPTOS VILLAE NON esse constat. Gathered fruits do not make a part of the farm. Dig. 19. 1. 17. 1; 2 Bouv. Inst. note 1578.

FRUGES (Lat.) Anything produced from vines, underwood, chalk pits, stone quarries. Dig. 50. 16. 77.

Grains and leguminous vegetables. In a more restricted sense, any esculent growing in pods. Vicat; Calv. Lex.

FRUIT. The produce of a tree or plant which contains the seed, or is used for food.

The term in legal acceptation, is not confined to the produce of those trees which in popular language are called fruit trees; but applies also to the produce of oak, elm, and walnut trees. In the old books the lessee is stated to have an interest in the trees in respect of the shade for cattle, and the fruit thereof. 5 B. & C. 847.

FRUIT FALLEN. The produce of any possession detached therefrom, and capable of being enjoyed by itself. Thus, a next presentation, when a vacancy has occurred, is a fruit fallen from the advowson. Wharton.

FRUITS OF CRIME. In the law of evidence. Material objects acquired by means and in consequence of the commission of crime, and sometimes constituting the subject matter of the crime. Burrill, Circ. Ev. 445; 3 Benth. Jud. Ev. 31.

FRUMENTA QUAE SATA SUNT SOLO cedere intelliguntur. Grain which is sown is understood to form a part of the soil. Inst. 2. 1. 32.

FRUMENTUM. In the civil law. Grain; that which grows in an ear (*arista*). Dig. 50, 16, 77.

FRUMGYLD. The first payment made to the kindred of a slain person in recompense for his murder. Blount; Termes de la Ley; Leg. Edmundi, cap. ult.

FRUMSTOLL (Saxon). A chief seat, or mansion house. Cowell.

FRUSCA TERRA. In old records. Uncultivated and desert ground. 2 Mon. Angl. 327; Cowell.

FRUSSURA. A breaking; plowing. *Frussura domorum*, housebreaking. Cowell.

FRUSTRA AGIT QUI JUDICIUM PROSEqui nequit cum effectu. He in vain sues who cannot prosecute his judgment with effect. Fleta, lib. 6, c. 37, § 9.

FRUSTRA EXPECTATUR EVENTUS cujus effectus nullus sequitur. An event is vainly expected from which no effect follows.

FRUSTRA FERUNTUR LEGES NISI subditis et obedientibus. Laws are made to no purpose unless for those who are subject and obedient. 7 Coke, 13.

FRUSTRA FIT PER PLURA, QUOD fieri potest per pauciora. That is done vainly by many things, which might be accomplished by fewer. Jenk. Cent. Cas. 68; Wingate, Max. 177.

FRUSTRA LEGIS AUXILIUM QUAERIT qui in legem committit. Vainly does he who offends against the law seek the help of the law. 2 Hale, P. C. 386; Broom, Leg. Max. (3d London Ed.) 255.

FRUSTRA PETIS QUOD STATIM ALteri rederre cogeris. Vainly you ask that which you will immediately be compelled to restore to another. Jenk. Cent. Cas. 256; Broom, Leg. Max. (3d London Ed.) 310.

FRUSTRA PROBATUR QUOD PROBAtum non relevat. It is vain to prove that which, if proved, would not aid the matter in question. Broom, Leg. Max. (3d London Ed.) 255.

FRUSTRA [VANA] EST POTENTIA quae nunquam venit in actum. That power is to no purpose which never comes into act, or which is never exercised. 2 Coke, 51.

FRUSTRUM TERRAE (Law Lat.) In old English law. A piece or fragment of land; a piece of land left over after the measurement of a field (*residuum quiddam proeter campum mensuratum*). Spelman.

A large piece of land lying by itself, and unconnected with any field, town, or manor. Domesday Book. Spelman thinks it should be *frustum*. Co. Litt. 5b.

FRUTECTUM. In old records. A place overgrown with shrubs and bushes. Spelman; Blount.

FRUTOS. In Spanish law. Fruits; products; produce; grains; profits. White, New Recop. bk. 1, tit. 7, c. 5, § 2.

FRYTHE (Saxon). In old English law. A plain between woods. Co. Litt. 5b; Domesday Book.

An arm of the sea, or a strait between two lands (from Lat. *fretum*, a strait). Cowell.

FUAGE, or **FOCAGE.** Hearth money; a tax laid upon each fireplace or hearth. 1 Bl. Comm. 324; Spelman. An imposition of a shilling for every hearth, levied by Edward III. (the Black Prince) in the dukedom of Aquitaine.

FUER (Law Fr.; from Lat. *fugere*). In old English law. To fly or flee; to chase or drive. Kelham; Law Fr. Dict.

Flight. *Fuer en fait*, flight in fact, was when a man did apparently and corporally flee. *Fuer en ley*, flight in law, was when, being called in the county court, he failed to appear; for this was "flight," in interpretation of law. Staund. P. C. lib. 3, c. 22; Cowell.

FUERO. In Spanish law. Compilations or general codes of law.

The usages and customs which, in the course of time, had acquired the force of unwritten law.

Letters of privilege and exemption from payment of certain taxes, etc.

Charters granted to cities or towns on condition of their paying certain dues to the owner of the land of which they had enjoyment.

Acts of donation granted by some lord or proprietor in favor of individuals, churches, or monasteries.

Ordinances passed by magistrates in relation to the dues, fines, etc., payable by the members of a community.

Letters emanating from the king or some superior lord, containing the ordinances and laws for the government of cities and towns, etc.

This term has many and very various meanings, as is shown above, and is sometimes used in other significations besides those here given. See, also, Schmidt, Civ. Law, 64; Escriche, Dic. Raz.

——**Fuero de Castilla.** In Spanish law. The body of laws and customs which formerly governed the Castilians.

——**Fuero de Correos y caminos.** In Spanish law. A special tribunal taking cognizance of all matters relating to the post-office and roads.

——**Fuero de Guerra.** In Spanish law. A special tribunal taking cognizance of all matters in relation to persons serving in the army.

——**Fuero de Marina.** In Spanish law. A special tribunal taking cognizance of all matters relating to the navy, and to the persons employed therein. Spelled, also, *Jurisdiccion de Marina*.

——**Fuero Juzgo.** In Spanish law. The code of laws established by the Visigoths for the government of Spain, many of whose provisions are still in force. See the analysis of this work in Schmidt's Civ. Law, 30.

——**Fuero Municipal.** In Spanish law. The body of laws granted to a city or town for its government and the administration of justice.

——**Fuero Real.** In Spanish law. A code of laws promulgated by Alonzo el Sabio in 1255, and intended as an introduction to the larger and more comprehensive code called *Las Siete Partidas*, published eight years afterwards. For an analysis of this code, see Schmidt, Civ. Law, 67.

——**Fuero Viejo.** The title of a compilation of Spanish law, published about A. D. 992. Schmidt, Civ. Law, Introd. 65.

FUGA CATALLORUM. In old English law. A drove of cattle. Blount.

FUGACIA. In old English law. A chase. Spelman; Blount.

FUGAM FECIT (Lat. he fled). In old English law. A phrase in an inquisition, signifying that a person fled for treason or felony. The effect of this is to make the party forfeit his goods absolutely, and the profits of his lands, until he has been pardoned or acquitted.

FUGATOR. A driver. *Fugatores carrucarum,* drivers of wagons. Fleta, lib. 2, c. 78.

FUGITATE. In Scotch practice. To outlaw, by the sentence of a court; to outlaw for nonappearance in a criminal case. 2 Alis. Crim. Pr. 350.

FUGITATION. In Scotch law. Outlawry.

FUGITIVE FROM JUSTICE. One who, having committed a crime, flees from the jurisdiction within which it was committed, without waiting to abide the consequences of such crime.

All that is necessary is that the person shall be found in a state other than that in which he committed the crime; it being immaterial whether he left the latter state with intent to escape punishment. 106 Mass. 227; 116 U. S. 80.

FUGITIVE OFFENDER. In English law. One who, being accused of having committed a crime in one part of the British empire, has left there, and gone to another part thereof. See "Fugitive from Justice."

FUGITIVE SLAVE. One who, held in bondage, flees from his master's power.

FUGITIVUS. In the civil law. A fugitive; a runaway slave. Dig. 11. 4; Code, 6. 1. See the various definitions of this word in Dig. 21. 1. 17.

FULL. Complete; exhaustive; detailed.

FULL AGE. The age of twenty-one, by common law, of both males and females, and of twenty-five by the civil law. Litt. § 259; 1 Sharswood, Bl. Comm. 463; Vicat. Full age is completed on the day preceding the anniversary of birth. Salk. 44, 625; 1 Ld. Raym. 480; 2 Ld. Raym. 1096; 2 Kent, Comm. 263; 3 Har. (Del.) 557; 4 Dana (Ky.) 597. See "Age."

FULL BLOOD. A term of relation, denoting descent from the same couple. Brothers and sisters of full blood are those who are born of the same father and mother, or, as Justinian calls them, *"ex utroque parente conjuncti."* Nov. 118, cc. 2, 3; Mackeld. Civ. Law, § 145. The more usual term in modern law is "whole blood" (*q. v.*).

FULL COURT. In practice. A term applied to a court sitting in banc, and implying, strictly, the presence of all the judges. 3 Chit. Gen. Prac. 2. The term "full bench" is frequently used.

FULL DEFENSE. In pleading. The formula of defense in a plea, stated at length and without abbreviation, thus: "And the said C. D. by E. F. his attorney, comes and defends the force (or wrong) and injury when and where it shall behoove him, and the damages, and whatsoever else he ought to defend, and says," etc. Steph. Pl. (Am. ed. 1824) ch. i. sect. vii. rule v.

FULL LIFE. Life in fact and in law. See "In Full Life."

FULL PROOF. See "Plena Probatio."

FULLUM AQUAE. A stream of water, such as comes from a mill. Blount.

FULLY PAID UP SHARES. Shares upon which the whole amount that could be called up have been called up. [1897] A. C. 164.

FUMAGE. In old English law. The same as *fuage,* or smoke farthings. 1 Bl. Comm. 324. See "Fuage."

FUNCTION. The occupation of an office. By the performance of its duties, the officer is said to fill his function. Dig. 32. 65. 1.

FUNCTIONARY. One who is in office or in some public employment.

FUNCTUS OFFICIO (Lat.) A term applied to something which once has had life and power, but which has become of no virtue whatsoever.

For example, a warrant of attorney on which a judgment has been entered is *functus officio,* and a second judgment cannot be entered by virtue of its authority. When arbitrators cannot agree, and choose an umpire, they are said to be *functi officio.* Watson, Arb. 94. If a bill of exchange be sent to the drawee, and he passes it to the credit of the holder, it is *functus officio,* and cannot be further negotiated. 5 Pick. (Mass.) 85. When an agent has completed the business with which he was intrusted, his agency is *functus officio.* 2 Bouv. Inst. note 1382.

FUNDAMENTAL. This word is applied to those laws which are the foundation of society. Those laws by which the exercise of power is restrained and regulated are fundamental. The constitution of the United States is the fundamental law of the land. See Wolff. Inst. § 984.

FUNDAMUS. We found. One of the words by which a corporation may be created in England. 1 Bl. Comm. 473; 3 Steph. Comm. 173.

FUNDATIO (Lat.) A founding.

FUNDED DEBT. A public debt for the payment of which money has been specifically appropriated.

That part of the national debt for which certain funds are appropriated towards the payment of the interest. 14 N. Y. 367.

FUNDI PATRIMONIALES. Lands of inheritance.

FUNDING. The term "funding" has been sometimes applied in this country to the process of collecting together a variety of outstanding debts against corporations, the principal of which was payable at short periods, and borrowing money upon the bonds or stocks of the corporation to pay them off. 14 N. Y. 367.

FUNDING A DEBT. The pledging of a specific fund to keep down the interest, and ultimately discharge the principal. When the extinguishment of the debt is contemplated, it is called a "sinking fund."

FUNDING BONDS. Funding and refunding bonds are those issued to pay off prior indebtedness. If issued merely to pay floating indebtedness they are generally referred to as "funding" bonds, while if issued to take up other bonds they are usually called "refunding" bonds. 2 Fletcher Cyclopedia Corporations 1920.

FUNDITORES. Pioneers. Jacob.

FUNDS. In its most restricted sense, cash on hand. In a wider sense it includes commercial paper (3 B. Mon. [Ky.] 8); in a still more extended sense, property of every kind, when such property is contemplated as something to be used or applied in the payment of debts (69 Iowa, 278).

FUNDUS (Lat. land). A portion of territory belonging to a person; a farm; lands, including houses. 4 Coke, 87; Co. Litt. 5a; 3 Sharswood, Bl. Comm. 209.

FUNERAL EXPENSES. Money expended in procuring the interment of a corpse.

The nature and extent of the allowance for funeral expense varies with the solvency of the estate, and the discretion of the surrogate, so that it is impossible to define the scope of the terms. 3 Redf. Wills, 243.

"Funeral expenses have been held to include carriage hire to convey the family and friends to the place of interment (44 Miss. 124), suitable gravestones (30 Conn. 209), monuments (77 Pa. St. 49), burial plots (5 Redf. Sur. [N. Y.] 484), and vaults (14 Serg. & R. [Pa.] 64); also mourning apparel to enable the widow and children to attend decently at the funeral." 1 Ashm. (Pa.) 316; 2 Woerner, Admn. 761.

FUNGIBLE. A term applicable to things that are consumed by the use, as wine, oil, etc., the loan of which is subject to certain rules, and governed by the contract called *mutuum*. See Schmidt, Civ. Law, 145; Story, Bailm.; 1 Bouv. Inst. notes 987, 1098.

FUR (Lat. a thief). One who stole without using force, as distinguished from a robber. See "Furtum."

FUR MANIFESTUS (Lat.) In the civil law. A manifest thief; a thief who is taken in the very act of stealing, or in the place where the theft was committed. Inst. 4. 1. 3; Dig. 47. 2. 3.

FURANDI ANIMUS. See "Animus."

FURCA. A fork; a gallows or gibbet. Bracton, fol. 56.

FURCA ET FLAGELLUM (Lat. gallows and whip). The meanest of servile tenures, where the bondman was at the disposal of the lord for life and limb. Cowell.

FURCA ET FOSSA (Lat. gallows and pit). A jurisdiction of punishing felons,—the men by hanging, the women by drowning. Skene de Verb. Sign.; Spelman; Cowell.

FURIGELDUM. Mulct paid for theft. Jacob.

FURIOSI NULLA VOLUNTAS EST. A madman has no will. Dig. 50. 17. 5; Id. 1. 18. 13. 1; Broom, Leg. Max. (3d London Ed.) 282.

FURIOSITY. In Scotch law. Madness, as distinguished from fatuity or idiocy.

FURIOSUS (Lat.) An insane man; a madman; a lunatic.

In general, such a man can make no contract, because he has no capacity or will: *Furiosus nullum negotium gerere potest, quia non intelligit quod agit.* Inst. 3. 20. 8. Indeed, he is considered so incapable of exercising a will that the law treats him as if he were absent: *Furiosi nulla voluntas est. Furiosus absentis loco est.* Dig. 1. ult. 40. 124. 1. See "Insanity"; "Non Compos Mentis."

FURIOSUS ABSENTIS LOCO EST. A madman is considered as absent. Dig. 50. 17. 24. 1.

FURIOSUS NULLUM NEGOTIUM CONtrahere (gerere) potest (quia non intelligit quod agit). A lunatic cannot make a contract. Dig. 50. 17. 5; 1 Story, Cont. (4th Ed.) p. 76.

FURIOSUS SOLO FURORE PUNITUR. A madman is punished by his madness alone. Co. Litt. 247; Broom, Leg. Max. (3d London Ed.) 14; 4 Sharswood, Bl. Comm. 24, 25.

FURIOSUS STIPULARI NON POTEST nec aliquod negotium agere, qui non intelligit quid agit. An insane person who knows not what he does cannot make a bargain, nor transact any business. 4 Coke, 126.

FURLINGUS (Lat.) A furlong, or a furrow one-eighth part of a mile long. Co. Litt. 5b.

FURLONG. A measure of length, being forty poles, or one-eighth of a mile.

FURLOUGH. A permission given in the army and navy to an officer or private to absent himself for a limited time.

FURNAGE (from *furnus*, an oven). A sum of money paid to the lord by the tenants, who were bound by their tenure to bake at the lord's oven, for the privilege of baking elsewhere. The word is also used to signify the gain or profit taken and received for baking.

FURNITURE. Personal chattels in the use of a family. By the term "household furniture" in a will, all personal chattels will pass which may contribute to the use or convenience of the householder, or the ornament of the house; as, plate, linen, china (both useful and ornamental), and pictures. Ambl. 610; 1 Johns. Ch. (N. Y.) 329, 388; 1 Sim. & S. 189; 3 Russ. 301; 2 Williams, Ex'rs, 752; 1 Rop. Leg. 203, 204; 3 Ves. 312, 313.

"It [the word "furniture"] is very general both in meaning and application, and its meaning changes so as to take the color of, or to be in accord with the subject to which it is applied." The articles spoken of as furniture of different places, as of a house, a ship, or a store, "differ in kind according to the purposes which they are intended to subserve; yet, being put and employed in the several places as the equipment thereof for ornament, or to promote comfort or to facilitate the business therein done, and being kept or intended to be kept for those or some of those purposes, they pertain to such places, and constitute the furniture thereof." 63 Ala. 401.

FURNITURE OF A SHIP. This term includes everything with which a ship requires to be furnished or equipped to make her seaworthy. It comprehends all articles furnished by ship chandlers, which are almost innumerable. 1 Wall. Jr. (U. S.) 369.

FURNIVAL'S INN. Formerly an inn of chancery. See "Inns of Chancery."

FUROR CONTRAHI MATRIMONIUM non sinit, quia consensu opus est. Insanity prevents marriage from being contracted, because consent is needed. 1 Ves. & B. 140; 1 Bl. Comm. 439; 4 Johns. Ch. (N. Y.) 343, 345.

FURST AND FONDUNG (Saxon). Time to advise or take counsel. Laws Hen. I. c. 46; Whishaw.

FURTHER ADVANCE. A second or subsequent loan of money to a mortgagor by a mortgagee, either upon the same security as the original loan was advanced upon, or an additional security. Equity considers the arrears of interest on a mortgage security converted into principal, by agreement between the parties, as a further advance. Wharton.

FURTHER ASSURANCE. This phrase is frequently used in covenants when a covenantor has granted an estate, and it is supposed some further conveyance may be required. He then enters into a covenant for further assurance, that is, to make any other conveyance which may be lawfully required.

FURTHER DIRECTIONS. When a master ordinary in chancery made a report in pursuance of a decree or decretal order, the cause was again set down before the judge who made the decree or order, to be proceeded with. Where a master made a separate report, or one not in pursuance of a decree or decretal order, a petition for consequential directions had to be presented, since the cause could not be set down for further directions under such circumstances. See 2 Daniell, Ch. Pr. (5th Ed.) 1233, note; Rapalje & L.

FURTHER HEARING. In practice. Hearing at another time.

FURTHER MAINTENANCE OF ACtion, plea to. A plea of matter arising since the commencement of the suit.

FURTUM (Lat. theft). The fraudulent appropriation to one's self of the property of another, with an intention to commit theft, without the consent of the owner. Fleta, lib. 1, c. 36; Bracton, 150; 3 Inst. 107.

The thing which has been stolen. Bracton, 151.

FURTUM CONCEPTUM. (Lat.) The theft which was disclosed where, upon searching any one in the presence of witnesses in due form, the thing stolen is found. "Detected theft" is, perhaps, the nearest concise translation of the phrase, though not quite exact. Vicat.

FURTUM EST CONTRECTATIO REI alienae fraudulenta, cum animo furandi, invito illo domino cujus res illa fuerat. Theft is the fraudulent handling of another's property, with an intention of stealing, against the will of the proprietor, whose property it was. 3 Inst. 107.

FURTUM GRAVE (Lat. aggravated theft). Formerly, there were three classes of this theft: First, by landed men; second, by a trustee or one holding property under a trust; third, theft of the *majora animalia*, larger animals, including children. 1 Bouv. Civ. Law, 352, note; Bell, Dict.

FURTUM MANIFESTUM (Lat. open theft). Theft where a thief is caught with the property in his possession. Bracton, 150b.

FURTUM NON EST UBI INITIUM HAbet detentionis per dominum rei. It is not theft where the commencement of the detention arises through the owner of the thing. 3 Inst. 107.

FURTUM OBLATUM (Lat.) The theft committed when stolen property is offered any one and found upon him; the crime of receiving stolen property. Calv. Lex.; Vicat.

FUSTIGATIO. In old English law. A beating with sticks or clubs; one of the ancient kinds of punishment of malefactors. Bracton, fol. 104b, lib. 3, tr. 1, c. 6.

FUSTIS. In old English law. A staff, used in making livery of seisin. Bracton, fol. 40.

A baton, club, or cudgel. Spelman.

FUTURE DEBT. In Scotch law. A debt which is created, but which will not become due till a future day. 1 Bell, Comm. (5th Ed.) 315.

FUTURE ESTATE. An estate which is to commence in possession in the future (*in futuro*). It includes remainders, reversions, and estates limited to commence *in futuro* without a particular estate to support them, which last are not good at common law, except in the case of terms for years. See 2 Sharswood, Bl. Comm. 165. In New York law it has been defined as "an estate limited to commence in possession at a future day, either without the intervention of a precedent estate, or on the determination by lapse of time, or otherwise, of a precedent estate created at the same time," thus excluding reversions, which cannot be said to be created at the same time, because they are a remnant of the original estate remaining in the grantor. 11 Rev. St. N. Y. (3d Ed.) 9, § 10.

FUTURES. See "Gambling Contract."

FUTURI (Lat. those who are to be). Part of the commencement of old deeds. "*Sciant praesentes et futuri, quod ego, talis, dedi et concessi,*" etc., let all men now living and to come know that I, A. B., have, etc. Bracton, 34b.

FUZ, or FUST. A wood or forest.

FYHTWITE. One of the fines incurred for homicide.

FYLE, or FFYLE (Scotch). In old Scotch practice. To declare or find guilty; literally, to defile; to make or declare foul; as clenge was to acquit, literally to clean or cleanse. "Swa that he quha, of his conscience, can nocht clenge, he of neccessitie mon fyle." 1 Pitc. Crim. Tr. pt. 1, p. 314. "The assyise in ane voce ffylis the said R. W." 2 Pitc. Crim. Tr. 73.

FYLIT. In old Scotch practice. Fyled; found guilty. See "Fyle."

FYNDERINGA (Saxon). An offense or trespass for which the fine or compensation was reserved to the king's pleasure. Leg. Hen. I. c. 10. Its nature is not known. Spelman reads *fynderinga*, and interprets it "treasure trove"; but Cowell reads *fyrderinga*, and interprets it a joining of the king's fird or host, a neglect to do which was punished by a fine called "firdnite." See Cowell; Spelman. Du Cange agrees with Cowell.

FYRD. The military array or land force of the whole country. Contribution to the fyrd was one of the imposts forming the *trinoda necessitas*. Wharton.

FYRDWITE. The fine incurred by neglecting to join the fyrd; one of the rights of the crown. Anc. Inst. Eng.

G

G. In Law French. Frequently used at the beginning of words to express the English "W."; as "gage" for "wage," "gainage" for "wainage," and the like.

GABEL, GAFOL, or GAVEL. A tax, imposition, or duty. This word is said to have the same signification that *gabelle* formerly had in France. Cunningham. But this seems to be an error; for *gabelle* signified in that country, previous to its revolution, a duty upon salt. Merlin, Repert. Lord Coke says that *gabel* or *gavel, gablum, gabellum, gabelletum, galbelletum,* and *gavillettum,* signify a rent, duty, or service yielded or done to the king or any other lord. Co. Litt. 142a.

GABELLA. In old European law. A tax or duty on merchandise or personalty. Spelman; Cowell.

A tax on salt in France. Spelman; Brande.

GABLUM, GABULUM, or GABULA. The gable end of a building. Kennett, Par. Ant. p. 201; Cowell.

A tax. Du Cange.

GABULUS DENARIORUM. Rent paid in money. Seld. Tit. Hon. 321.

GAFOLGILD, or GAFFOLDGILD. The payment of rent or income.

Gafolgild, payment of such rent, etc. *Gafolland* was land liable to tribute or tax (Cowell); or land rented (Saxon Dict.). See Tayl. Hist. Gavelkind, pp. 26, 27, 1021; Anc. Inst. Eng.

GAGE, or GAGER (Law Lat. *vadium*). Personal property placed by a debtor in possession of his creditor as a security for the payment of his debt; a pledge or pawn (*q. v.*). Glanv. lib. 10, c. 6; Britt. c. 27.

To pledge; to wage. Webster.

Gager is used both as noun and verb; *e. g., gager del ley,* wager of law. Jacob. *Gager ley,* to wage law. Britt. c. 27. *Gager deliverance,* to put in sureties to deliver cattle distrained. Termes de la Ley; Kitch. Cts. fol. 145; Fitzh. Nat. Brev. fols. 67, 74.

A mortgage is a dead gage or pledge; for, whatsoever profit it yields, it redeems not itself, unless the whole amount secured is paid at the appointed time. Cowell.

GAGE, ESTATES IN. Estates held in security, of which mortgages are the most common example.

GAGER DE DELIVERANCE. When he who has distrained, being sued, has not delivered the cattle distrained, then he shall not only avow the distress, but *gager deliverance, i. e.,* put in surety or pledge that he will deliver them. Fitzh. Nat. Brev.

GAGER DEL LEY. Wager of law.

GAIN. Profits.

A mutual insurance company is an association for the purpose of "gain"; the reduction of a loss being a gain. 51 L. J. Ch. Div. 344.

GAINAGE. Wainage, or the draught oxen, horses, wain, plough, and furniture for carrying on the work of tillage. Also, the land tilled itself, or the profit arising from it. Old Nat. Brev. fol. 117.

Gainor, the sokeman that hath such land in occupation. Old Nat. Brev. fol. 12.

GAINERY. Tillage, or the profit of tillage. Blount.

GAJUM (from gagium). In old European law. A thick wood. Spelman.

GALE. In English law. The right to open and work a mine within the hundred of St. Briavels, or a stone quarry within the open lands of the forest of Dean, in Gloucestershire. The peculiar laws and customs of this district are regulated by St. 1 & 2 Vict. c. 43.

GALEA. A galley. Spelman.

GALENES. In old Scotch law. A kind of compensation for slaughter. Bell, Dict.

GALLI HALPENS, or GALLI HALFpence. A kind of coin which, with suskins and doitkins, was forbidden by St. 3 Hen. V. c. 1, 4 Bl. Comm. 99; 3 Reeve, Hist. Eng. Law, 261.

GALLOWS. An erection on which to hang criminals condemned to death.

GAMACTA (Law Lat.) In old European law. A stroke or blow. L. Boior, tit. 2, c. 4; Spelman.

GAMALIS (Law Lat.) In old European law. A child born in lawful wedlock; also one born to betrothed, but unmarried, parents. Spelman.

GAMBLING. See "Gaming."

GAMBLING CONTRACT. One in which the parties in effect stipulate that they shall gain or lose upon the happening of an uncertain event in which they have no interest except that arising from the possibility of such gain or loss. 153 Pa. St. 247.

Gambling contracts may be by bet or wager (*q. v.*), which is their simplest form; by lottery (*q. v.*); or they may be disguised in the form of a legitimate transaction, the ordinary form being by dealing in futures (*q. v.*) infra. The validity of such contracts depends on whether the intention of the parties at the inception is to deliver the goods bargained for, or to settle on the basis of difference in price (155 Ill. 617; 53 N. Y. 318; 59 Wis. 197). The course of speculative dealing has given rise to a number of technical terms, some of which are here defined.

"Bulls and Bears." See infra, this title, "Long"; "Short."

"Corner." An artificial scarcity created by holding property off the market for the extortion of abnormally high prices. Where the purchases of any party or parties exceed the amount of contract grain in regular warehouses on the last delivery day of the month for which such purchases have been made, the grain so bought is said to be cornered.

"Cover." The buying in of grain or stocks to fill short contracts is called "covering."

"Covering shorts." Buying in property to fill contracts (usually for future delivery) previously made.

"Delivery." When stock is brought to the buyer in exact accordance with the rules of the stock exchange it is called a "good delivery." When there are irregularities, the shares being of unacceptable issues, or the rules of the exchange being contravened in some particular, the delivery is pronounced "bad," and the buyer can appeal to the board. Also when warehouse receipts for grain are delivered in fulfillment of contracts.

"For a turn." Said of a speculative investment for a small profit or loss. A quick play. A "flyer." See infra, this title, "Scalping."

"Futures." Buyers of cash products protect themselves against possible loss by selling an agreed amount for future delivery in some general market. Such contracts are called "futures" because they do not terminate until some designated month in the future. These transactions pass from hand to hand, and may be turned over hundreds and thousands of times in an active market before maturity, and this is called "dealing in futures." Nearly all speculative operations are in futures.

"Hedge." The operation called "hedging" by speculators is practically the same as "straddling," though the terms are not synonymous. Traders hedge to avert a loss, and straddle for a profit. See infra, this title, "Straddle."

"Holding the market." Buying sufficient stock or commodities to keep the price from declining.

"In sight." Said of stocks of grain, cotton, coffee, or other merchandise available for immediate use. Grain stored in private warehouses, or held by producers, is not usually included in the supply "in sight."

"Insiders." Those who own a controlling interest or an important interest in the stocks of a concern, and who are therefore influential in directing its affairs.

"Investment buying." This phrase is generally used in contradistinction to buying for speculation, or for a quick turn in the market. It is understood to mean buying to hold for a considerable time.

"Long." One who has property bought in anticipation of a rise in price. Hence, for a trader to be "long" of stocks or grain presupposes him to be a "bull." Also used adjectively.

"Long interest." The aggregate amount of investment holdings in any speculative market.

"Long market." A market that is overbought, the volume of open contracts to buy property for future delivery being in dangerous excess of the probable demand.

"Margin." Money or collaterals deposited with a broker to protect contracts, usually for future delivery.

"Option." Property bought or sold at the call or demand of the buyer or seller, as may be specified; a conditional contract.

"Outsiders." The general trading public. The investors in stock or grain who base their judgment largely on the general situation.

"Pegged." Said of a market that refuses either to advance or to decline, because brokers have been supplied with selling or buying orders in excess of the demand.

"Privileges." "Puts" and "calls." A "put" is the privilege or option, which a person purchases, of "putting," *i. e.*, delivering property or contracts for property to the seller of such privilege, at a named price, within a stipulated time,—one or more days, weeks, or months. "Puts" are good (from the buyer's standpoint) when the market declines below the "put" price within the time covered by the privilege contract. The buyer can then buy the property at the cheaper figure, and "put" it to the person who sold him the risk, his profit being the difference between the "put" price and the quotation at which the property is bought with which to make the delivery. A "call" is the reverse of a "put," the purchaser of a "call" acquiring the right to "call" upon the seller of the privilege for property, or contracts for property, at a named price, within a stipulated time. "Calls" are good when the market advances above the call price, and the buyer of such privilege is enabled to sell at a profit the property "called" from the seller of the privilege. Trading in privileges is illegal in some states, notably in Illinois.

"Pyramiding." Enlarging one's operations by the use of profits which one has made.

"Scalper." One who trades in options continually, and, by reading the temper of the market at the moment, tries to get a profit out of the minor fluctuations.

"Scalping." Buying and selling on small fluctuations of the market. Taking a small profit or a small loss.

"Short," or "Short interest." The seller of a property which he does not possess and will not deliver until he has afterwards bought the same is called a "short." He is, by necessity, a "bear." The aggregate amount of such shortage by these sellers is called the "short interest."

"Short market." A market that is oversold; the volume of open contracts to deliver property being in dangerous excess of available supply.

"Short selling." The process of selling property for future delivery, in the expectation of being able to obtain the property cheaper before the maturity of contract, or of being able to close out the contract at a profit without the actual delivery of the property.

"Split." A transaction, one-half at one quotation and one-half at another. For instance, the quotation 53-⅝-¾ means that one-half of the quantity traded in was at 53⅝ and the other half at 53¾. This quotation is just half-way between 53⅝ and 53¾. Only an even number of thousand bushels can be traded in on a split, as, for instance, 2,000, 6,000, 10,000, etc.

"Spread." A "spread" is a double privilege entitling the holder to deliver to, or to demand from, the signer a certain amount of stock on the terms specified. Differences in prices, as between May and July wheat, or between the put and call price, or between the price of the same option in different cities.

"Squeezed." Said of "short sellers," who, by reason of having oversold the market, are forced to pay an artificially high price for property with which to fill contracts.

"Stop order." An operator may give his broker orders to close out his deals when the market goes against him, and when quotations reach a certain point, and in that case he is said to have given a "stop order." When a declining market is filled with "stop orders" to sell, the bears may make extraordinary efforts to force quotations down to a point which reaches the "stop orders," and which will thus throw on the market more securities or commodities. In the same way, on an advancing market, the bulls may endeavor to raise quotations to a point that will reach stop orders of short sellers, and force their brokers to become buyers.

"Straddle." A trader who is "long" of one option and "short" of another option has "straddled" the market. Example: A. buys corn for May delivery, and sells an equal amount for December delivery, in the expectation that the former will advance and the latter decline. It is also called a "straddle" when a trader buys property for future delivery in one market, and sells in another.

"Wash trades." Pretended trading. Trades made on an open market by parties between whom there is a tacit or private understanding that they shall be void. Done with a view to influence prices, and considered a reprehensible practice.

GAMBLING DEVICE, or **GAMING DEVICE.** Any appliance or contrivance used for the purpose of gambling.

The game played, the intangible result of the device, is to be distinguished from the device. Thus, the game of poker is not a "gambling device." 2 Orig. 238.

GAMBLING POLICY. A policy of life insurance issued to one as beneficiary who has no interest in the life of the insured.

GAME. Birds and beasts of a wild nature, obtained by fowling and hunting. Bac. Abr. See 11 Metc. (Mass.) 79.

All sorts of birds and beasts that are objects of the chase. Wharton.

——**Sports.** In our language, the word game has a very broad and comprehensive signification. It means sport of any kind, and means physical contests, whether of man or beast, when practiced for the purpose of deciding wagers or rewards, or for the purpose of diversion, as well as games of hazard or skill by means of instruments or devices. Such were the Olympic and Nemean games among the Greeks, the former of which are lately being revived, and Appollinarian and Capitoline games among the Romans. 23 Ill. 440.

GAME LAWS. Laws regulating the killing or taking of birds and beasts, as game.

The English game laws are founded on the idea of restricting the right of taking game to certain privileged classes, generally landholders. In 1831, the law was so modified as to enable any one to obtain a certificate or license to kill game, on payment of a fee. The laws relating to game in the United States are generally, if not universally, framed with reference to protecting the animals from indiscriminate and unreasonable havoc, leaving all persons free to take game, under certain restrictions as to the season of the year and the means of capture. The details of these regulations must be sought in the statutes of the several states. 60 N. Y. 10; 97 Ill. 320.

GAMING. A contract between two or more persons, by which they agree to play by certain rules at cards, dice, or other contrivance, and that one may be the loser, and another the winner.

To stake money on a chance. Whart. Crim. Law, § 1465.

Any sport or play carried on between two persons, depending on skill, chance, or the transpiring of an unknown future event, on the result of which some valuable thing is to be, without consideration, transferred from one to the other. Bish. St. Crimes, § 861.

The statutes against gaming are generally confined to games into which an element of chance enters. Thus, tenpins (8 Ired. [N. C.] 271), foot ball (1 Mod. 136), and wrestling (2 Car. & P. 376) have been held not to be gaming.

"Gaming" is synonymous with "gambling." Bish. St. Crimes, § 858.

It is to be distinguished from "bet" or "wager," which may be laid upon games, or things not games. 9 Ind. 14.

GAMING HOUSES. Houses kept for the purpose of permitting persons to gamble for money or other valuable thing. They are nuisances in the eye of the law, being detrimental to the public, as they promote cheating and other corrupt practices. 1 Russ. Crimes, 299; Rosc. Crim. Ev. 663; 3 Denio (N. Y.) 101.

A house, office, room, or other place kept for the purpose of betting between persons resorting thereto. Steph. Crim. Law, art. 182.

GANANCIAL. In Spanish law. Property held in community.

The property of which it is formed belongs in common to the two consorts, and, on the dissolution of the marriage, is divisible between them in equal shares. It is confined to their future acquisitions *durante el matrimonio*, and the *frutos* or rents and profits of the other property. 1 Burge, Confl. Laws, 418, 419; Aso & M. Inst. bk. 1, tit. 7, c. 5, § 1.

GANANCIAL PROPERTY. That which husband and wife, living together, acquire during matrimony, by a common title, lucrative or onerous; or those which husband and wife or either acquire by purchase, or by their labor and industry, as also the fruits of the separate property which each brings to the matrimony or acquires by lucrative title during the continuance of the partnership. 18 Tex. 634.

GANANCIAS (Spanish). In Spanish law. Gains or profits resulting from the employment of property held by husband and wife in common. White, New Recop. bk. 1, tit. 7, c. 5.

GANG WEEK. The time when the bounds of the parish are lustrated or gone over by the parish officers,—rogation week. Enc. Lond.; Rapalje & L.

GANGIATORI. Officers in ancient times, whose business it was to examine weights and measures. Skene de Verb. Sign.

GANTELOPE. A military punishment, in which the criminal running between the ranks receives a lash from each man. Enc. Lond. This was called "running the gauntlett," the word itself being pronounced "gauntlett."

GAOL. This word, now generally written "jail" is said to be derived from the Spanish *jaula*, a cage (derived from *caula*); in French, *geole*, gaol. 1 Man. & G. 222, note (a). A prison or building designated by law or used by the sheriff for the confinement or detention of those whose persons are judicially ordered to be kept in custody. See 6 Johns. (N. Y.) 22; 14 Viner, Abr. 9; Bac. Abr.; Dane, Abr. Index; 4 Comyn, Dig. 619. See "Jail."

GAOL DELIVERY. In English law. To insure the trial, within a certain time, of all prisoners, a patent, in the nature of a letter, is issued from the king to certain persons, appointing them his justices, and authorizing them to deliver his gaols. See "General Gaol Delivery."

GAOL LIBERTIES, or **GAOL LIMITS.** A space, marked out by limits, which is considered as a part of the prison, and within which prisoners are allowed to go at large on giving security to return. Owing to the rigor of the law which allowed *capias*, or attachment of the person, as the first process against a debtor, statutes were from time to time passed enlarging the gaol liberties, in order to mitigate the hardships of imprisonment. Thus, the whole city of Boston was held the "gaol liberties" of its county gaol. And so with a large part of New York City. Act March 13, 1830 (3 Rev. St. N. Y. 1829, App. 116). The prisoner, while within the limits, is considered as within the walls of the prison. 6 Johns. (N. Y.) 121.

GAOLER. The keeper of a gaol or prison; one who has the legal custody of the place where prisoners are kept. It is his duty to keep the prisoners in safe custody, and for this purpose he may use all necessary force. 1 Hale, P. C. 601. But any oppression of a prisoner under a pretended necessity will be punished; for the prisoner, whether he be a debtor or a criminal, is entitled to the protection of the laws from oppression.

GARANDIA, or **GARANTIA** (Law Lat.) A warranty. Spelman.

GARATHINX (Lomb.) In old Lombardic law. A gift; a free or absolute gift; a gift of the whole of a thing. Spelman.

GARAUNTOR. A warrantor or vouchee, who is obliged by his warranty (*garauntie*) to warrant (*garaunter*) the title of the warrantee (*garaunte*), that is, to defend him in his seisin, and if he do not defend, and the tenant be ousted, to give him land of equal value. Britt. c. 75.

GARBA (Law Lat.) In old English law. A bundle or sheaf. Applied to bundles of grain (Bracton, fol. 209), sheaves of arrows (Skene de Verb. Sign.), etc.

GARBALLO DECIMAE (Law Lat. from *garba*, a sheaf). In Scotch law. Tithes of corn; such as wheat, barley, oats, pease, etc. Also called parsonage tithes (*decimae rectoriae*). Ersk. Inst. bk. 11, tit. 10, § 13.

GARBLE. In old English statutes. To sort or cull out the good from the bad in spices, drugs, etc. Cowell; Blount.

GARBLER OF SPICES. An ancient officer in the city of London, who might enter into any shop, warehouse, etc., to view and search drugs and spices, and garble and make clean the same, or see that it be done. St. 6 Anne, c. 16.

GARD. A ward of a city.

GARDE. Custody; ward; care or keeping.

GARDEIN. A guardian. Britt. c. 35, 81. Used as an English word in Co. Litt. 38b.

GARDEN. A piece of ground appropriated to raising plants and flowers.

A garden is a parcel of a house, and passes with it. 2 Coke, 32; Plowd. 171; Co. Litt. 5b, 56a, 56b. But see F. Moore, 24; Bac. Abr. "Grants" (I).

GARDIANUS (Law Lat.) In old English law. A guardian, defender, or protector. In feudal law, *gardio.* Spelman.

A warden. *Gardianus ecclesiae*, a church-warden. *Gardianus Quinque Portuum*, warden of the Cinque Ports. Spelman.

GARDINUM (Law Lat.) In old English law. A garden. Reg. Orig. 1b, 2; Fleta, lib. 4, c. 19, § 8.

GARENE (Law Fr.) A warren; a privileged place for keeping animals. Britt. c. 19.

GARNISH.

——**In English Law.** Money paid by a prisoner to his fellow prisoners on his entrance into prison.

To warn. To garnish the heir is to warn the heir. Obsolete.

——**In Practice.** To attach by process of garnishment.

GARNISHEE. In practice. A person who has money or property in his possession belonging to a defendant, which money or property has been attached in his hands, and who has had notice of such attachment. He is so called because he has had warning or notice of the attachment.

Sometimes incorrectly used as a verb in place of "garnish."

GARNISHMENT.

——**In Old Practice.** A warning to any one for his appearance, in a cause in which he is not a party, for the information of the court and explaining a cause. For example, in the practice of Pennsylvania, when an attachment issues against a debtor, in order to secure to the plaintiff a claim due by a third person to such debtor, notice is given to such third person, which notice is a garnishment, and he is called the "garnishee."

——**In Modern Practice.** A writ or process by which money owing to a defendant is attached in the hands of the creditor, and the creditor is required to appear at a designated time, and disclose the nature and extent of the indebtedness.

In some states this process is called "trustee process," in Connecticut "factorizing process," and in New York the term "garnishment" is not used, it being classed as an attachment.

GARNISTURA. In old English law. Garniture; whatever is necessary for the fortification of a city or camp, or for the ornament of a thing. 8 Rymer, 328; Du Cange; Cowell; Blount.

GARSUMNE. In old English law. An amerciament or fine. Cowell. See "Gressume"; "Grossome"; "Gersume."

GARTER. See "Knights of the Garter."

GARTH. In English Law. A yard; a little close or homestead in the north of England. Cowell; Blount.

A dam or wear in a river, for the catching of fish. Id.

GARYTOUR. In old Scotch law. Warder. 1 Pitc. Crim. Tr. pt. 1, p. 8.

GASACHIO, *Gasachius.* (L. Lat.) In old European law. An adversary in a cause. L. Salic. tit. 52, § 2. Spelman.

GASTALDUS. A steward or bailiff. Spelman. Also applied to higher officers, as a governor of a city.

In the book of feuds it seems to have been used in the sense of "warden."

GASTINE (Law Fr.) Waste or uncultivated ground. Britt. c. 57.

GATE (Saxon, *geat*). At the end of names of places, signifies way or path. Cunningham.

In the words "beast gate" and "cattle gate," it means a right of pasture. These rights are local to Suffolk and Yorkshire, respectively. They are considered as corporeal hereditaments, for which ejectment will lie (2 Strange, 1084; 1 Term R. 137), and are entirely distinct from right of common. The right is sometimes connected with the duty of repairing the gates of the pasture, and perhaps the name comes from this.

GAUDIES. Double commons.

A term used in the English universities. Wharton.

GAUGEATOR (Law Lat.) In old English law. A gauger or gager. Cowell.

GAUGER. An officer appointed to examine all tuns, pipes, hogsheads, barrels, and tierces of wine, oil, and other liquids, and to give them a mark of allowance, as containing lawful measure.

GAUGETUM (Law Lat.) A gauge or gauging. Blount.

GAVEL. In old English law. Tribute; toll; custom; yearly revenue, of which there were formerly various kinds. Jacob; Tayl. Hist. Gavelkind, 26, 102. See "Gabel."

GAVELBRED. In English law. Rent reserved in bread, corn, or provisions; rent payable in kind. Cowell.

GAVELCESTER. A certain measure of rent ale. Cowell.

GAVELET. A customary process, whereby the lord of lands in gavelkind might seize the land in the nature of a distress, to be returned to the tenant in case he paid the rent. Crabb, Hist. Eng. Law, 203.

GAVELGELD (Saxon, *gavel*, rent, *geld*, payment). That which yields annual profit or toll; the tribute or toll itself. 3 Mon. Angl. 155; Cowell; Du Cange, "Gavelgida."

GAVELHERTE. A customary service of ploughing. Du Cange.

GAVELING MEN. Tenants who paid a reserved rent, besides some customary duties to be done by them. Cowell.

GAVELKIND. The tenure by which almost all lands in England were held prior to the Conquest, and which is still preserved in Kent.

All the sons of a tenant of gavelkind lands take equally, or their heirs male and female by representation. 104 Ill. App. 170. The wife of such tenant is dowable of one-half the lands. The husband of such tenant has curtesy, whether issue be born or not, but only of one-half while without issue. Such lands do not escheat, except for treason or want of heirs. The heir of such lands may sell at fifteen years old, but must himself give livery. The rule as to division among brothers in default of sons is the same as among the sons.

Lord Coke derives gavelkind from "gave all kinde"; for this custom gave to all the sons alike (1 Co. Litt. 140a); Lambard, from *gavel*, rent,—that is, land of the kind that pays rent or customary husbandry work, in distinction from lands held by knight service (Perambulations of Kent, 1656, p. 585).

GAVELLER. An officer of the English crown having the general management of the mines, pits, and quarries in the forest of Dean and hundred of St. Briavels, subject, in some respects, to the control of the commissioners of woods and forests. He grants gales to free miners in their proper order, accepts surrenders of gales, and keeps the registers required by the acts. There is a deputy gaveller, who appears to exercise most of the gaveller's functions. See "Gale." Rapalje & L.

GAVELMAN. A tenant who is liable to tribute. Somn. Gavelkind, p. 33; Blount. Gavelingmen were tenants who paid a reserved rent, besides customary service. Cowell.

GAVELMED. A customary service of mowing meadow land or cutting grass (*consuetudo falcandi*). Somn. Gavelkind, Append.; Blount.

GAVELREP. In old English law. Bedreap or bidreap; the duty of reaping at the bid or command of the lord. Somn. Gavelkind, 19, 21; Cowell.

GAVELWERK, or GAVELWEEK. A customary service, either *manuopera*, by the person of the tenant, or *carropera*, by his carts or carriages. Phill. Purv.; Blount; Somn. Gavelkind, 24; Du Cange.

GAYNAGE. (L. Fr.) Plough tackle, or implements of husbandy; wainage, Kelham.

GAZETTE. The official newspaper of the English government. It is published twice each week, and contains all the acts of state and proclamations, and also dissolutions of partnership and notices of proceedings in bankruptcy. Rapalje & L.

GEBOCCED (Saxon). From "boc," a writing conveyed.

GEBOCIAN (from Saxon boc). To convey boc land; the grantor being said to *gebocian* the grantee of the land. 1 Reeve, Hist. Eng. Law, 10. But the better opinion would seem to be that boc land was not transferable except by descent. See Du Cange.

GEBURSCIP, or GEBURSCRIPT. Neighborhood or adjoining district. Cowell.

GEBURUS. In old English law. A country neighbor; an inhabitant of the same geburscip or village. Cowell.

GELD (from Saxon *gildan*; Law Lat. *geldum*). A payment; tax; tribute. Laws Hen. I. c. 2; Charta Edredi Regis apud Ingulfum, c. 81; Mon. Angl. tit. 1, pp. 52, 211, 379; Id. tit. 2, pp. 161-163; Du Cange; Blount.

The compensation for a crime.

We find *geld* added to the word denoting the offense, or the thing injured or destroyed, and the compound taking the meaning of compensation for that offense, or the value of that thing. Capitulare 3, Anno 813, cc. 23, 25; Carl. Magn. So, *wergeld*, the compensation for killing a man, or his value; *orfgeld*, the value of cattle; *angeld*, the value of a single thing; *octogeld*, the value eight times over, etc. Du Cange, "Geldum."

GELDABILIS (Law Lat.) In old English law. Taxable; geldable.

GELDABLE (Law Fr.) Liable to pay *geld;* liable to be taxed. Kelham.

GEMMA (Lat.) In the civil law. A gem; a precious stone. Gems were distinguished by their transparency; such as emeralds, chrysolites, amethysts. Dig. 34. 2. 19. 17.

GEMOT, or GEMOTE. (Saxon, from *gemettand*, to meet or assemble; Law Lat. *gemotum*). An assembly; a mote or moot, meeting, or public assembly.

There were various kinds; as, the *witenagemot*, or meeting of the wise men; the *folcgemot*, or general assembly of the people; the *shiregemot*, or county court; the *burggemot*, or borough court; the *hundredgemot*, or hundred court; the *haligemot*, or court baron; the *halmote*, a convention of citizens in their public hall; the *holymote*, or holy court; *the sweingemote*, or forest court; the *wardmote*, or ward court. Cunningham.

GENEALOGY. The summary history or table of a house or family, showing how the persons there named are connected together.

GENEARCH. The head of a family. Rapalje & L.

GENEATH (Saxon.) In Saxon law. A villein, or agricultural tenant (*villanus villicus*); a hind or farmer (*firmarius rusticus*). Spelman.

GENER (Lat.) A son-in-law.

GENERAL. Principal; universal; common to all, or to the greatest number.

——**General Acceptance.** Of a bill of exchange. An absolute acceptance precisely in conformity to the tenor of the bill. 3 Bush (Ky.) 626.

——**General Agent.** One authorized to transact all his principal's business, or all his business of a particular class. 94 Ala. 346; 41 Ind. 438.

A "general agent" is so called in distinction from a "special agent," whose authority is for a particular purpose, and confined to a particular act (49 N. Y. 555), and "universal agent," who is authorized to do any and every act which the principal might do. Story, Ag. § 21.

——**General Appearance.** See "Appearance."

——**General Assembly.** A name given in some of the states to the senate and house of representatives, which compose the legislative body.

——**General Assignment.** An assignment of all the assignor's property; or one for the benefit of all his creditors.

——**General Average.** General average contribution is defined to be a contribution by all the parties in a sea adventure to make good the loss sustained by one of their number on account of sacrifices voluntarily made on part of the ship or cargo to save the residue and the lives of those on board from an impending peril, or for extraordinary expense necessarily incurred by one or more of the parties for the general benefit of all the interests embarked in the enterprise. Losses which give a claim to general average are usually divided into two great classes: (1). Those which arise from sacrifices of part of the ship or part of the cargo, purposely made in order to save the whole adventure from perishing. (2). Those which arise out of extraordinary expenses incurred for the joint benefit of ship and cargo. 9 Wallace (U. S.) 228. See also "Average."

——**General Charge.** The instructions given by the court of its own motion, usually on the general aspects of the case, as distinguished from those given on the request of a party.

——**General Covenant.** One which relates to lands generally, and places the covenantee in the position of a specialty creditor. Brown.

——**General Custom.** One which obtains through a whole country, as distinguished from those peculiar to localities.

——**General Damages.** See "Damages."

——**General Demurrer.** A demurrer not indicating the precise ground of objection. One going to substance. See "Demurrer."

——**General Deposit.** A general deposit is a deposit which is to be returned to the depositor in kind. 141 Ill. 267. See, also, "Deposit."

——**General Election.**

(1) An election of officers throughout a state. 17 Mo. 511.

(2) An election of officers for the full term, as distinguished from an election to fill a vacancy. 52 Cal. 154.

(3) An election at a time appointed by law, as distinguished from one called specially.

——**General Executor.** One having general charge of the estate of his testator, as distinguished from a special executor appointed for a particular purpose or a limited time.

——**General Gaol Delivery.** In English law. One of the four commissions issued to judges holding the assizes, which empowers them to try and deliverance make of every prisoner who shall be in the gaol when the judges arrive at the circuit town, whether an indictment has been preferred at any previous assize or not.

It was anciently the course to issue special writs of gaol delivery for each prisoner, which were called writs *de bono et malo;* but, these being found inconvenient and oppressive, a general commission for all the prisoners has long been established in their stead. 4 Steph. Comm. 333, 334; 2 Hawk. P. C. 14, 28.

Under this authority, the gaol must be cleared and delivered of all prisoners in it, whenever or before whomever indicted, or for whatever crime. Such deliverance takes place when the person is either acquitted, convicted, or sentenced to punishment. Bracton, 110.

——**General Guardian.** One who has full general charge of the subject of guardianship.

——**General Imparlance.** In pleading. One granted upon a prayer in which the defendant reserves to himself no exceptions. See "Imparlance."

——**General Issue.** In pleading. A plea which denies or traverses at once the whole indictment or declaration, without offering any special matter to evade it.

It is called the general issue because, by importing an absolute and general denial of what is alleged in the indictment or declaration, it amounts at once to an issue. 2 Bl. Comm. 305. In the early manner of pleading, the general issue was seldom used except where the party meant wholly to deny the charges alleged against him. When he intended to excuse or palliate the charge, a special plea was used to set forth the particular facts.

But now, since special pleading is generally abolished, the same result is secured by requiring the defendant to file notice of special matters of defense which he intends to set up on the trial, or obliging him to use a form of answer adapted to the plaintiff's declaration, the method varying in different systems of pleading.

In criminal cases, the general issue is, not guilty. In civil cases, the general issues are almost as various as the forms of action: In *assumpsit*, the general issue is *non assumpsit;* in debt, *nil debet;* in detinue, *non detinet;* in trespass, *non cul.* (not guilty); in replevin, *non cepit*, etc.

Where the forms of action are abolished, the term is, in strictness, incorrect, but it is commonly applied to the general denial.

——**General Jurisdiction.** Jurisdiction applying to all subjects within the object of its general organization, and to all parties who can be reached by its process. 37 Miss. 48.

A jurisdiction which is not, within the limits of the judicial power of the sovereignty creating it, limited as to nature of subject matter, amount in controversy, or character of parties.

It is the nature of the jurisdiction, not its territorial extent, which determines whether a court is of limited or general jurisdiction. 11 Wis. 50.

——**General Land Office.** A bureau in the United States government which has the charge of matters relating to the public lands.

It was established by the act of April 25, 1812 (2 Story, U. S. Laws, 1238). Another act was passed March 24, 1824 (3 Story, U. S. Laws, 1938), which authorized the employment of additional officers. And it was reorganized by an act entitled, "An act to reorganize the general land office," approved July 4, 1836. It was originally a bureau of the treasury department, but was transferred in 1859 to the department of the interior.

——**General Law.** A law framed in general terms and restricted to no locality, operating equally upon all of a group of objects which, having regard for the purposes of the legislation, are distinguished by characteristics sufficiently marked and important to make them a class by themselves. 266 Ill. 387.

——**General Legacy.** A pecuniary legacy, payable generally out of the assets of the testator. 2 Bl. Comm. 512.

——**General Lien.** A right to detain a chattel, etc., until payment be made, not only of any debt due in respect of the particular chattel, but of any balance that may be due on general account in the same line of business. 2 Steph. Comm. 132.

——**General Meeting.** A meeting of the largest class of persons concerned in a matter. Applied to meetings of stockholders, members, etc.

——**General Occupant.** The man who could first enter upon lands held *pur autre vie*, after the death of the tenant for life, living the *cestui que vie.* At common law he held the lands by right for the remainder of the term; but this is now altered by statute, in England, the term going to the executors if not devised. 29 Car. II. c. 3; 14 Geo. II. c. 20; 2 Sharswood, Bl. Comm. 258. This has been followed by some states (1 Code Md. 666, § 220, art. 93); in some states the term goes to heirs, if undevised (Gen. St. Mass. c. 91, § 1).

——**General Owner.** The person having the permanent or residuary title, as distinguished from a mere special or possessory right.

——**General Partnership.** One whose business includes all transactions of a particular class, as distinguished from special partnerships formed for a particular transaction. See 1 Cliff (U. S.) 32.

——**General Retainer.** A fee paid to retain the services of an attorney generally, and not in a particular case. "It binds the person retained not to take a fee from another against his retainer, but to do nothing except what he is asked to do, and for this he is to be distinctly paid." 6 R. I. 206.

——**General Sessions.** In England, a court of record, held by two or more justices of the peace, for the execution of the authority given them by the commission of the peace and certain statutes. General sessions held at certain times in the four quarters of the year pursuant to St. 2 Hen. V. are properly called "quarter sessions" (*q. v.*), but intermediate general sessions may also be held. Pritch. Quar. Sess.; Rapalje & L.

In the United States, a court of general criminal jurisdiction in some states.

——**General Ship.** One which is employed by the charterer or owner on a particular voyage, and is hired by a number of persons, unconnected with each other, to convey their respective goods to the place of destination. A ship advertised for general receipt of goods to be carried on a particular voyage. The advertisement should state the name of the ship and master, the general character of the ship, the time of sailing, and the proposed voyage. See 1 Pars. Mar. Law, 130; Abb. Shipp. (7th London Ed.) 123.

The shippers in a general ship generally contract with the master; but in law the owners and the master are separately bound to the performance of the contract, it being considered as made with the owners, as well as with the master. Abb. Shipp. (7th London Ed.) 319.

——**General Special Imparlance.** In pleading. One in which the defendant reserves to himself "all advantages and exceptions whatsoever." 2 Chit. Pl. 408. See "Imparlance."

——**General Statute, or General Law.** As opposed to "private," one relating to matters of public concern.

As opposed to "local," one operative throughout the jurisdiction of the legislative body.

As opposed to "special," one which affects equally all persons or things of the same class.

——**General Tail.** An estate tail where one parent only is specified, whence the issue must be derived, as to A. and the heirs of his body. Rapalje & L.

——**General Tenancy.** "Such tenancies only as are not fixed and made certain in point of duration by the agreement of the parties." 22 Ind. 122.

——**General Term.**

(1) A term held pursuant to law, as distinguished from one specially called.

(2) A term for the trial of cases, as distinguished from one for the hearing of motions.

(3) A sitting of the trial judges in banc, for appellate purposes.

——**General Traverse.** See "Traverse."

——**General Usage.** One which prevails generally throughout the country. See "General Custom," supra, this title.

——**General Verdict.** One finding generally for one of the parties, as distinguished from a special verdict finding the facts.

"A finding by the jury in the terms of the issue referred to them." 2 Tidd, Pr. 869.

——**General Warrant.** A process which used to issue from the state secretary's office, to take up (without naming any person in particular) the author, printer, and publisher of such obscene and seditious libels as were particularly specified in it. It was declared illegal and void for uncertainty by a vote of the house of commons. Com. Jour. 22d April, 1766; Wharton.

A writ of assistance. The issuing of these was one of the causes of the American Republic. They were a species of general warrant, being directed to "all and singular justices, sheriffs, constables, and all other officers and subjects," empowering them to enter and search any house for uncustomed goods, and to command all to assist them. These writs were perpetual, there being no return to them. They were not executed, owing to the eloquent argument of Otis before the supreme court of Massachusetts against their legality. See Tudor, Life of Otis, 66.

——**General Warranty.** A covenant whereby the grantor warrants and agrees to defend the title to the premises conveyed against all persons whatsoever, as distinguished from a "special warranty" against persons "by or from" the grantor.

GENERALE DICTUM GENERALITER est interpretandum. A general expression is to be construed generally. 8 Coke, 116; 1 Eden, 96.

GENERALE NIHIL CERTUM IMPLICAT. A general expression implies nothing certain. 2 Coke, 34; Wingate, Max. 164.

GENERALE TANTUM VALET IN GENERALIBUS, quantum singulare in singulis. What is general prevails, or is worth as much, among things general, as what is particular among things particular. 11 Coke, 59.

GENERALIA PRAECEDUNT; SPECIALIA sequuntur. Things general precede; things special follow. Reg. Brev.; Branch, Princ.

GENERALIA SPECIALIBUS NON DEROGANT. Things general do not derogate from things special. Jenk. Cent. Cas. 120.

GENERALIA SUNT PRAEPONDENDA singularibus. General things are to be put before particular things.

GENERALIA VERBA SUNT GENERALITER intelligenda. General words are understood in a general sense. 3 Inst. 76; Broom, Leg. Max. (3d London Ed.) 577.

GENERALIBUS SPECIALIA DEROGANT. Things special take from things general. Halk. Max. 51.

GENERALIS CLAUSULA NON PORRIGITUR ad ea quae antea specialiter sunt comprehensa. A general clause does not extend to those things which are previously provided for specially. 8 Coke, 154.

GENERALIS REGULA GENERALITER est intelligenda. A general rule is to be understood generally. 6 Coke, 65.

GENEROSA (Law Lat.) Gentlewoman. Cowell; 2 Inst. 668.

GENEROSI FILIUS. The son of a gentleman. Generally abbreviated "*gen fil.*"

GENEROSUS. Gentleman; a gentleman. Spelman.

GENICULUM. A degree of consanguinity. Spelman.

GENS (Lat.) In Roman law. A union of families, who bore the same name, who were of an ingenuous birth (*ingenui*), none of whose ancestors had been a slave, and who had suffered no *capitis diminutio.*

Gentiles sunt, qui inter se eodem nomine sunt; qui ab ingenuis oriundi sunt; quorum majorum nemo servitutem servivit; qui capite non sunt deminuti. This definition is given by Cicero (Topic 6), after Scaevola, the pontifex. But, notwithstanding this high authority, the question as to the organization of the *gens* is involved in great obscurity and doubt. The definition of Festus is still more vague and unsatisfactory. He says: "*Gentilis dicitur et ex eodem genere ortus, et is, qui simili nomine appellatur, ut ait Cincius; Gentiles mihi sunt, qui meo nomine appellantur."* *Gens* and *genus* are convertible terms; and Cicero defines the latter word: *"Genus autem est quod sui similes communione quadam, specie autem differentes, duas aut plures complectitur partes."* De Oratore 1, 42. The *genus* is that which comprehends two or more particulars, similar to one another by having something in common, but differing in species. From this it may fairly be concluded that the *gens* or race comprises several families, always of ingenuous birth, resembling each other by their origin, general name,—*nomen*,—and common sacrifices or sacred rites,—*sacra gentilitia (sui similes communione quadam)*,—but differing from each other by a particular name,—*cognomen* and *agnatio (specie autem differentes)*.

GENTES (Law Lat.) People. *Contra omnes gentes*, against all people. Bracton, fol. 37b. Words used in the clause of warranty in old deeds.

GENTILES. In Roman law. The members of a *gens* or common tribe.

GENTLEMAN. In English law. A person of superior birth.

According to Sir Edward Coke, he is one who bears coat armor, the grant of which adds gentility to a man's family. The eldest son had no exclusive claim to the degree; for, according to Littleton, "every son is as great a gentleman as the eldest." 2 Inst. 667. Sir Thomas Smith, quoted by Blackstone (1 Comm. 406), says: "As for gentlemen, they are made good cheap in this kingdom; for whosoever studies the laws of the realm, who studies in the universities, who professeth liberal sciences, and, to be short, who can live idly and without manual labor, and will bear the port, charge, and countenance of a gentleman, shall be called master, and be taken for a gentleman." In the United States, this word is unknown to the law; but in many places it is applied by courtesy to all men. See Poth. Proc. Cr. § 1, Append. § 3.

"It originally signified a man of gentle birth, but the use of the term has become changed, and it is often applied to denote persons of all ranks, from the upper down to the lowest verge of the middle class." 1 C. P. Div. 61. Thus, a coal agent out of employment (3 Hurl. & N. 798), or a medical student who had been in no business for several months (3 Hurl. & N. 382), is properly described as a "gent."

GENTLEWOMAN. An addition formerly appropriate in England to the state or degree of a woman. 2 Inst. 667.

GENUINE. Not spurious or counterfeit. Used in relation to a written instrument, it does not cover either the authority (149 N. Y. 182) or the capacity (37 N. Y. 487) of the maker.

GERECHTSBODE (Belg.) In old New York law. A court messenger or constable. O'Callaghan, New Neth. 322.

GEREFA. Reeve. (*q. v.*)

GERENS. Bearing. *Gerens datum*, bearing date. 1 Ld. Raym. 336; Hob. 19.

GERMAN. Whole or entire, as respects genealogy or descent; thus, "brother german" denotes one who is brother both by the father's and mother's side; "cousins german," those in the first and nearest degree, *i. e.*, children of brothers or sisters. Tech. Dict.; 4 Man. & G. 56.

GERMANUS (Lat.) Descended of the same stock, or from the same couple of ancestors; of the whole or full blood. Mackeld. Civ. Law, § 145.

GERONTOCOMI. In civil law. Officers appointed to manage hospitals for poor old persons. Clef des Lois Rom. "Administrateurs."

GERONTOCOMIUM. In the civil law. An institution or hospital for taking care of the old. Calv. Lex. Their managers are called "gerontocomi."

GERSUMARIUS. In old English. Fineable, or liable to be mulcted, fined, or amerced at the discretion of the lord. Cowell.

GERSUME (Saxon.) In old English law. Expense; reward; compensation; wealth; especially, the consideration or fine of a contract; *e. g., et pro hae concessione dedit nobis praedictus Jordanus* 100 *sol. sterling de gersume*. Old charter, cited Somn. Gavelkind, 177; Tabul. Reg. Ch. 377; 3 Mon. Angl. 126, 920. It is also used for a fine or compensation for an offense. 2 Mon. Angl. 973.

GEST, GUST or **GESTE.** In Saxon law. A guest.

GESTATION. See "Period of Gestation."

GESTIO (Lat.) In civil law. The doing or management of a thing. *Negotiorum gestio*, the doing voluntarily without authority business of another. *De neg. gest. Gester negotiorum*, one who so interferes with business of another without authority. *Gestio pro haerede*, behavior as heir; such conduct on the part of the heir as indicates acceptance of the inheritance, and makes him liable for ancestor's debts universally, *e. g.*, an entry upon, or assigning, or letting any of the heritable property, releasing any of the debtors of the estate, or meddling with the title deeds or heirship movables, etc. Ersk. Inst. 3. 8. 82 et seq.; Stair, Inst. 3. 6. 1.

GESTIO PRO HAEREDE. Behavior as heir. That conduct by which an heir renders himself liable for his ancestor's debts, as by taking possession of title deeds, receiving rents, etc. Bell, Dict.

GESTOR. In civil law. One who acts for another, or transacts another's business. Calv. Lex.

GESTUM (Lat.) In Roman law. A thing done; a transaction. Strictly, a thing done without words, and so distinguished from *actum*. A distinction was sometimes made between *"gestum"* and *"factum."*. Gaius, however, in the Digest (50. 16. 58) pronounces this to be subtile.

GEVILLOURIS. In old Scotch law. Gaolers. 1 Pitc. Crim. Tr. pt. 2, p. 234.

GEWINEDA. In Saxon law. The ancient convention of the people to decide a cause. Laws Aethel. c. 1.

GEWITNESSA (Saxon). In Saxon and old English law. The giving of evidence. Laws Aethel. c. 2.

GEWRITE. In Saxon law. Deeds or charters; writings. 1 Reeve, Hist. Eng. Law, 10.

GIFT. A voluntary conveyance; that is, a conveyance not founded on the consideration of money or blood.

The word denotes rather the motive of the conveyance, so that a feoffment or grant may be called a gift when gratuitous. A gift is of the same nature as a settlement,—neither denotes a form of assurance, but the nature of the transaction. Watk. Conv. (Preston Ed.) 199. The operative words of this conveyance are *do*, or *dedi*,—I give, or I have given. The maker of this instrument is called the donor, and he to whom it is made, the donee. 2 Bl. Comm. 316; Litt. 59; Shep. Touch. c. 11.

Gifts *inter vivos* are gifts made from one or more persons, without any prospect of immediate death, to one or more others. Gifts *causa mortis* are gifts made in prospect of death, and on the implied condition that they shall be of no effect if the donor shall recover. 49 N. Y. 17. See "Donatio."

GIFT ENTERPRISE. A scheme whereby gifts or premiums are distributed among the patrons of a business establishment, either the value of the premium, or the persons who shall receive the same, being determined by chance. See 165 Mass. 146; 73 Md. 529; 56 N. Y. 424; 48 Minn. 555.

GIFTA AQUAE. A stream of water. Blount.

GIFTOMAN. In Swedish law. He who has a right to dispose of a woman in marriage.

This right is vested in the father, if living; if dead, in the mother. They may nominate a person in their place; but for want of such nomination the brothers german, and for want of them the consanguine brothers, and in default of the latter the uterine brothers, have the right; but they are bound to consult the paternal or maternal grandfather. Swed. Code, "Marriage," c. 1.

GILD. See "Guild."

GILD HALL. See "Guildhall."

GILDA MERCATORIA (Law Lat.) A mercantile meeting.

If the king once grants to a set of men to have *gildam mercatoriam*, a mercantile meeting or assembly, this is alone sufficient to incorporate and establish them forever. 1 Sharswood, Bl. Comm. 473, 474. A company of merchants incorporated. St. Wm. Reg. Scot. c. 35; Leg. Burg. Scot. c. 99; Du Cange; Spelman; 8 Coke, 125a; 2 Ld. Raym. 1134.

GILDABLE. See "Geldable."

GILDO. In Saxon law. Member of a gild or decennary. Oftener spelled "congildo." Du Cange; Spelman, "Geldum."

GILL. A measure of capacity, equal to one-fourth of a pint.

GILOUR (Law Fr.) A cheat or deceiver. Applied in Britton to those who sold false or spurious things for good, as pewter for silver or latem for gold. Britt. c. 15.

GIRANTEM, or **GIRANTE.** In common law. An Italian word, which signifies the drawer. It is derived from *girare*, to draw, in the same manner as the English verb to murder is transformed into *murdrare* in our old indictments. Hall, Mar. Loans, 183, note.

GIRTH. A girth, or yard, is a measure of length. The word is of Saxon origin, taken from the circumference of the human body. Girth is contracted from *girdeth*, and signifies as much as girdle.

GIRTH AND SANCTUARY. In Scotch law. A refuge or place of safety given to those who had slain a man in heat of passion (*chaude melle*), and unpremeditatedly. Abolished at the Reformation. 1 Hume, Hist. Eng. 235; 1 Ross, Lect. 331.

GISEMENT. Agistment; cattle taken in to graze at a certain price; also the money received for grazing cattle. Rapalje & L.

GISER (Law Fr.) In old English law. To lie.

Giser et mason, to lie or lodge at a house. St. Westminster I. c. 1.

GISETAKER. An agister. See "Gisement."

GISIL, or **GISLE.** A pledge or hostage.

GIST (sometimes, also, spelled *git*).

——**In Pleading.** The essential ground or object of the action in point of law, without which there would be no cause of action. Gould, Pl. c. 4, § 12; 19 Vt. 102. In stating the substance or gist of the action, everything must be averred which is necessary to be proved at the trial. The moving cause of the plaintiff's bringing the action, and the matter for which he recovers the principal satisfaction, is frequently entirely collateral to the gist of the action. Thus, where a father sues the defendant for a trespass for the seduction of his daughter, the gist of the action is the trespass and the loss of his daughter's services; but the collateral cause is the injury done to his feelings, for which the principal damages are given. 1 Viner, Abr. 598; 2 Phil. Ev. 1, note; Bac. Abr. "Pleas" (B); Doct. Plac. 85. See "Damages."

——**Of an Action.** The cause for which an action will lie; the ground or foundation of a suit, and without which it would not be maintainable; the essential ground or object of a suit; without which it is not a cause of action. 199 Ill. 256.

GIVE. A term used in deeds of conveyance. At common law, it implied a covenant. 2 Hilliard, Real Prop. 366. So in Kentucky. 1 Pirtle, Dig. 211. In Maryland and Alabama it is doubtful. 7 Gill & J. (Md.) 311; 2 Ala. (N. S.) 555. In Ohio, in conveyance of freehold, it implies warranty for the grantor's life. 2 Hilliard, Real Prop. 366. In Maine it implies a covenant. 5 Me. 227; 23 Me. 219. In New York it does not, by statute. See 14 Wend. 38. It does not imply covenant in North Carolina. 1 Murph. 343. Nor in England, by St. 8 & 9 Vict. c. 106, § 4.

GIVER. He who makes a gift. By his gift the giver always impliedly agrees with the donee that he will not revoke the gift.

GIVING IN PAYMENT. In Louisiana. A term which signifies that a debtor, instead of paying a debt he owes in money, satisfies his creditor by giving in payment a movable or immovable. See "Dation en Paiement."

GIVING RINGS. A ceremony by gift of finger rings by a barrister on being made a serjeant-at-law.

GIVING TIME. An agreement by which a creditor gives his debtor a delay or time in paying his debt beyond that contained in the original agreement. When other persons are responsible to him, either as drawer, indorser, or surety, if such time be given without the consent of the latter, it discharges them for responsibility to him.

GLADIUS (Lat.) In old Latin authors, and in the Norman laws, this word was used to signify supreme jurisdiction,—*jus gladii.*

GLANS (Lat.) In the civil law. Acorns or nuts of the oak or other trees. Brissonius. In a larger sense, all fruits of trees. Dig. 43. 28.

GLANVILLE. The author of the oldest treatise on English law, written in Latin, about A. D. 1181, under the title of Tractatus de Legibus et Consuetudinibus Angliae (A Treatise of the Laws and Customs of England). The older writers are generally agreed that this was Ranulphus de Glanvilla, chief justitiary of England, to Henry II, who was equally eminent as a soldier and a judge, and died at the seige of Acre, in 1190. Hoveden in Hen. II, Staunf. Prær. c. 1, fol. 5. Catlin, C. J. Plowden, 368a. Cowell. 8 Co. pref. Crabb's Hist. Eng. Law, 70. The same opinion is adopted by Spelman and Sir Mathew Hale. Hist. Com. Law, c. 7. Lord Coke gives the arms and genealogy of Glanville, and speaks with the greatest confidence on the subject. 8 Co. ub. sup. Mr. Reeves, however, doubts the identity of these individuals, and thinks that the Glanville who wrote the treatise might have been a person of that name who was a justice itinerant. 1 Reeves' Hist. Eng. Law, 223.

As to the work itself, there is little doubt of its being the most ancient treatise on English law. Spelman remarks that Glanville was the first who attempted to make that law a lex scripta, or written law. But it possesses a higher interest even than this, from the fact of its being the oldest work of the kind in Europe. Dr. Robertson observes that it was the first undertaking in any country in Europe, to collect into one body the customs which then regulated the administration of justice, and thus to render the law fixed. 1 Robertson's Charles V. Appendix, Note xxv. Defontaines, the oldest law writer in France, composed his Conseil about half a century afterwards.

GLAVEA. A hand dart. Cowell.

GLEANING. The act of gathering such grain in a field where it grew as may have been left by the reapers after the sheaves were gathered.

There is a custom in England, it is said, by which the poor are allowed to enter and glean upon another's land after harvest, without being guilty of a trespass. 3 Bl. Comm. 212. But it has been decided that the community are not entitled to claim this privilege as a right. 1 H. Bl. 51. In the United States, it is believed, no such right exists. It seems to have existed in some parts of France. Merlin, Repert, "Glanage." As to whether gleaning would or would not amount to larceny, see Woodf. Landl. & Ten. 242; 2 Russ. Crimes, 99. The Jewish law may be found in the 19th chapter of Leviticus, verses 9 and 10. See Ruth ii. 2, 3; Isaiah xvii. 6.

GLEBA.

——**In the Civil Law.** A turf, sod, or clod of earth; the soil or ground; cultivated land in general.

——**In Old English Law.** Church land (*solum et dos ecclesiae*). Spelman. See "Glebe."

GLEBAE ASCRIPTITII. See "Adscriptiti."

GLEBARIAE. Turf or peat. Cowell.

GLEBE.

——**In Ecclesiastical Law.** The land which belongs to a church. It is the dowry of the church. *Gleba est terra qua consistit dos ecclesiae.* 9 Cranch (U. S.) 329.

——**In Civil Law.** The soil of an inheritance. There were serfs of the glebe, called *glebae addicti.* Code, 11. 47. 7. 21; Nov. 54, c. 1.

GLOMERELLS. Commissioners appointed to determine differences between scholars in a school or university and the townsmen of the place. Jacob.

GLOS (Lat.) In civil law. A husband's sister. Dig. 38. 10. 4. 6.

GLOSS (Lat. *glossa*). Interpretation; comment; explanation; remark intended to illustrate a subject,—especially the text of an author. See Webster.

——**In Civil Law.** *Glossae,* or *glossemata,* were words which needed explanation. Calv. Lex. The explanations of such words. Id. Especially used of the short comments or explanations of the text of the Roman law, made during the twelfth century by the teachers at the schools of Bologna, etc., who were hence called *glossators,* of which glosses Accursius made a compilation which possesses great authority, called *Glossa Ordinaria.* These glosses were at first written between the lines of the text (*glossae interlineares*), afterwards, on the margin, close by and partly under the text (*glossae marginales*). Cush. Introd. Rom. Law, 130-132.

GLOSSA VIPERINA EST QUAE CORRODIT VISCERA TEXTUS. That is a viperine gloss which eats out the vitals of the text. 10 Coke, 70; 2 Bulst. 79.

GLOSSATOR. A commentator or annotator of the Roman law. One of the authors of the Gloss.

GLOUCESTER, STATUTE OF. An English statute, passed 6 Edw. I., A. D. 1278. So called because it was passed at Gloucester. There were other statutes made at Gloucester which do not bear this name. See St. 2 Rich. II.

GLOVE SILVER. Extraordinary rewards formerly given to officers of courts, etc.; money formerly given by the sheriff of a county in which no offenders are left for execution to the clerk of assize and judges' officers. Jacob.

GLOVES. In was an ancient custom on a maiden assize, when there was no offender to be tried, for the sheriff to present the judge with a pair of white gloves. It is an immemorial custom to remove the glove from the right hand on taking oath. Wharton.

GLYN. A hollow between two mountains; a valley or glen. Co. Litt. 5b.

GO TO PROTEST. A term of the commercial law, indicating the dishonor of commercial paper by nonpayment or nonacceptance, whereby it becomes subject to protest (*q. v.*).

GO WITHOUT DAY. Words used to denote that a party is dismissed the court. He is said to go without day, because there is no day appointed for him to appear again.

GOAT, or GOTE (Law Lat. *gota;* German, *gote*). A canal or sluice for the passage of water. Charter of Roger, Duke de Basingham, *anno* 1220, in Tabularis S. Bertini; Du Cange.

A ditch, sluice, or gutter. Cowell; St. 23 Hen. VIII. c. 5. An engine for draining waters out of the land into the sea, erected and built with doors and percullesses of timber, stone, or brick,—invented first in Lower Germany. Callis, Sew. 66.

GOD AND MY COUNTRY. When a prisoner is arraigned, he is asked, "How will you be tried?" He answers, "By God and my country." This practice arose when the prisoner had the right to choose the mode of trial, namely, by ordeal or by jury, and then he elected by God or by his country, that is, by jury. It is probable that originally it was "By God or my country"; for the question asked supposes an option in the prisoner, and the answer is meant to assert his innocence by declining neither sort of trial. 1 Chit. Crim. Law, 416; Barr. Obs. St. 73, note.

GOD BOTE. In ecclesiastical law. An ecclesiastical or church fine imposed upon an offender for crimes and offenses committed against God.

GOD'S PENNY. In old English law. Money given to bind a bargain; earnest-money. So called because such money was anciently given to God,—that is, to the church and the poor. See "Denarius Dei."

GOGING STOLE. An old form of "cucking stool" (*q. v.*). Cowell.

GOING CONCERN. A business establishment which continues to transact its ordinary business, though it may be embarrassed, or even insolvent. 30 Fed. 865.

GOING THROUGH THE BAR. The act of the chief of an English common-law court in demanding of every member of the bar, in order of seniority, if he has anything to move. This was done at the sitting of the court each day in term, except special paper days, crown paper days in the queen's bench, and revenue paper days in the exchequer. On the last day of term this order is reversed, the first and second time round. In the exchequer the postman and tubman are first called on. Wharton.

GOING TO THE COUNTRY. When a party, under the common-law system of pleading, finished his pleading by the words, "and of this he puts himself upon the country," this was called "going to the country." It was the essential termination to a pleading which took issue upon a material fact in the preceding pleading. Rapalje & L.

GOING WITNESS. One who is going out of the jurisdiction of the court, although only into a state or country under the general sovereignty; as, for example, if he is going from one to another of the United States, or in Great Britain, from England to Scotland. 2 Dickens, 454.

GOLDA. A mine. Blount. A sink or passage for water. Cowell.

GOLDSMITH'S NOTES. In English law. Banker's notes. So called because the trades of banker and goldsmith were originally joined. Chit. Bills, 423.

GOOD. Reasonable; suitable; sufficient; valid; meeting all legal requirements. See 10 Gray (Mass.) 302; 36 Mo. App. 192.

——**As Applied to Commercial Paper.** Genuine; collectible. 4 Metc. (Mass.) 48; 1 N. J. Law, 99.

——**As Applied to Persons.** Of a debtor, solvent (21 Mo. App. 372); of a person in a representative or official capacity (1 Blackf. [Ind.] 396).

——**As Applied to Property Sold.** Reasonably sound and suitable. See 1 Idaho, 41.

GOOD ABEARING. See "Abearance."

GOOD AND LAWFUL MEN. Those qualified to serve on juries; that is, those of full age, citizens, not infamous or *non compos mentis;* and they must be resident in the county where the venue is laid. Bac. Abr. "Juries" (A); Cro. Eliz. 654; 3 Inst. 30; 2 Rolle, 82; Cam. & N. (N. C.) 38.

The expression "*good* and lawful *men*" continues to be used in modern law, and criers in American courts ordinarily address a jury as "You *good men*," etc.

GOOD BEHAVIOR. Conduct authorized by law. Surety of good behavior might at common law be demanded from any person justly suspected, upon sufficient grounds, of intending to commit a crime or misdemeanor. Surety for good behavior is somewhat similar to surety of the peace, but the recognizance is more easily forfeited, and it ought to be demanded with greater caution. 1 Bin. (Pa.) 98, note; 2 Yeates (Pa.) 437; 14 Viner, Abr. 21; Dane, Abr. Index. As to what is a breach of good behavior, see 2 Mart (La.; N. S.) 683; Hawk. P. C. bk. 1, c. 61, § 6; 1 Chit. Prac. 676.

GOOD CONSIDERATION. See "Consideration."

GOOD COUNTRY. In Scotch law. Good men of the country. A name given to a jury.

GOOD FAITH. Honesty; absence of fraud, collusion, or deceit. 91 Wis. 464. See "Bona Fide Purchaser."

GOOD MORAL CHARACTER. What constitutes good moral character may vary from one generation to another. It would seem that whatever is forbidden by the law of the land ought to be considered, for the time being, immoral. 22 Fed. Cas. 921.

GOOD TITLE. A perfect title, free and clear from any legal exception or charge thereon. 23 Barb. (N. Y.) 370.

GOOD WILL. The benefit which arises from the establishment of particular trades or occupations. The advantage or benefit which is acquired by an establishment, beyond the mere value of the capital, stocks, funds, or property employed therein, in consequence of the general public patronage and encouragement which it receives from constant or habitual customers, on account of its local position, or common celebrity, or reputation for skill or affluence or punctuality, or from other accidental circumstances or necessities, or even from ancient partialities or prejudices. Story, Partn. § 99. See 17 Ves. 336; 1 Hoff. Ch. (N. Y.) 68; 16 Am. Jur. 87.

It includes only that estimation and repute which is peculiar to the particular establishment. It is that species of connection in trade which induces customers to deal with a particular firm.

GOODS. The word goods, as a technical term of the law is *nomen generalissimum,* and has a very extensive meaning. 35 N. H. 483.

——**In Contracts.** The term "goods" is not so wide as "chattels," for it applies to inanimate objects, and does not include animals or chattels real, as a lease for years of house or land, which "chattels" does include. Co. Litt. 118; 1 Russ. 376.

Goods will not include fixtures. 2 Mass. 495; 4 J. B. Moore, 73. In a more limited sense, "goods" is used for articles of merchandise. 2 Sharswood, Bl. Comm. 389. It has been held in Massachusetts that promissory notes were within the term "goods" in the statute of frauds (3 Metc. [Mass.] 365; but see 24 N. H. 484; 4 Dud. [S. C.] 28); so stock or shares of an incorporated company (20 Pick. [Mass.] 9; 3 Har. & J. [Md.] 38; 15 Conn. 400); so, in some cases, bank notes and coin (2 Story [U. S.] 52; 5 Mason [U. S.] 537). See "Chattel."

——**In Penal Statutes.** In a strict sense, as the word is understood in penal statutes, it is limited to movables belonging to the property of some person, which have an intrinsic value, and does not include securities, which are not valuable in themselves, but merely represent value. 35 N. H. 483.

——**In Wills.** In wills, goods is *nomen generalissimum,* and, if there is nothing to limit it, will comprehend all the personal estate of the testator, as stocks, bonds, notes, money, plate, furniture, etc. 35 N. H. 483; 1 Atk. 180-182; 2 Atk. 62; 1 P. Wms. 267; 1 Brown, Ch. 128; 4 Russ. 370; Williams, Ex'rs, 1014; 1 Rop. Leg. 250. But in general it will be limited by the context of the will. See 2 Belt, Supp. Ves. 287; 1 Chit. Prac. 89, 90; 1 Ves. Jr. 63; 3 Ves. 212; Hammond, Parties, 182; 1 Yeates (Pa.) 101; 2 Dall. (Pa.) 142; Ayliffe, Pand. 296; Weskett, Ins. 260; Sugd. Vend. 493, 497; and the articles "Biens;" "Chattel"; "Furniture."

GOODS AND CHATTELS.

——**In Contracts.** A term which includes not only personal property in possession, but choses in action and chattels real, as a lease for years of house or land, or emblements. 12 Coke, 1; 1 Atk. 182; Co. Litt. 118; 1 Russ. 376.

——**In Criminal Law.** Choses in action, as bank notes, mortgage deeds, and money, do not fall within the technical definition of "goods and chattels." And if described in an indictment as "goods and chattels," these words may be rejected as surplusage. 4 Gray. (Mass.) 416; 3 Cox, C. C. 460; 1 Den. C. C. 450; 1 Dears. & B. C. C. 426; 2 Zab. (N. J.) 207; 1 Leach, C. C. 241 (4th Ed. 468). See 5 Mason (U. S.) 537.

——**In Wills.** If unrestrained, these words will pass all personal property. Williams, Ex'rs, 1014 et seq., Am. notes. See Add. Cont. 31, 201, 912, 914.

GOODS BARGAINED AND SOLD. A phrase used to designate the action of *assumpsit* brought on a contract of sale, where the purchaser has not accepted delivery of the goods.

GOODS SOLD AND DELIVERED. A phrase used to indicate the action of *assumpsit* brought when the sale and delivery of goods furnish the cause.

GOODS, WARES, AND MERCHANDISE. A phrase used in the statute of frauds, covering, generally, all classes of personal property. Fixtures do not come within it. 1 Cromp., M. & R. 275; 3 Tyrwh. 959; 1 Tyrwh. & G. 4. Growing crops of potatoes, corn, turnips, and other annual crops, are within it. 8 Dowl. & R. 314; 10 Barn. & C. 446; 4 Mees. & W. 347. *Per contra*, 2 Taunt. 38. See Add. Cont. 31, 32; 2 Dana (Ky.) 206; 2 Rawle (Pa.) 161; 5 Barn. & C. 829; 10 Adol. & E. 753. See, generally, 118 Mass. 285; 20 Mich. 357. Promissory notes and shares in an incorporated company, and, in some cases, money and bank notes, have been held within it. See 2 Pars. Cont. 330-332.

GOODTITLE. Sometimes used as the name of the fictitious tenant in ejectment, as "Doe" or "Jackson" is more usually employed.

GOVERNMENT (Lat. *gubernaculum*, a rudder. The Romans compared the state to a vessel, and applied the term *gubernator*, helmsman, to the leader or actual ruler of a state. From the Latin, this word has passed into most of the modern European languages). That institution or aggregate of institutions by which a state makes and carries out those rules of action which are necessary to enable men to live in a social state, or which are imposed upon the people forming a state.

We understand, in modern political science, by "state," in its widest sense, an independent society, acknowledging no superior, and by the term "government," that institution or aggregate of institutions, by which that society makes and carries out those rules of action which are necessary to enable men to live in a social state, or which are imposed upon the people forming that society by those who possess the power or authority of prescribing them. Government is the aggregate of authorities which rule a society. By "administration," again, we understand in modern times, and especially in more or less free countries, the aggregate of those persons in whose hands the reins of government are for the time being,—the chief ministers or heads of departments. But the terms "state," "government," and "administration" are not always used in their strictness. The government of a state being its most prominent feature, which is most readily perceived, "government" has frequently been used for "state"; and the publicists of the last century, almost always used the term "government," or "form of government," when they discussed the different political societies or states. On the other hand, "government" is often used, to this day, for "administration," in the sense in which it has been explained.

They are never actually created by agreement or compact. Even where portions of government are formed by agreement, as, for instance, when a certain family is called to rule over a country, the contracting parties must previously be conscious of having authority to do so. As society originates with the family, so does authority or government. Nowhere do men exist without authority among them, even though it were but in its mere incipiency. Men are forced into this state of things by the fundamental law that with them, and with them alone of all mammals, the period of dependence of the young upon its parents outlasts by many years the period of lactation, so that, during this period of post-lactational dependence, time and opportunity are given for the development of affection and the habit of obedience on the one hand, and of affection and authority on the other, as well as of mutual dependence. The family is a society, and expands into clusters of families, into tribes and larger societies, collecting into communities, always carrying the habit and necessity of authority and mutual support along with them. As men advance, the great and pervading law of mutual dependence shows itself more and more clearly, and acts more and more intensely. Man is eminently a social being, not only as to an instinctive love of aggregation, not only as to material necessity and security, but also as to mental and affectional development, and not only as to a given number of existing beings, or what we will call as to "extent," but also as to "descent" of generation after generation, or, as we may call it, "transmission." Society, and its government along with it, are continuous. Government exists and continues among men, and laws have authority for generations which neither made them, nor had any direct representation in making them, because the necessity of government—necessary according to the nature of social man and to his wants—is a continuous necessity. But the family is not only the institution from which once, at a distant period, society, authority, and government arose. The family increases in importance, distinctness, and intensity of action as man advances, and continues to develop authority, obedience, affection, and social adhesiveness, and thus acts with reference to the state as the feeder acts with reference to the canal. The state originates daily anew in the family.

Although man is an eminently social being, he is also individual, morally, intellectually, and physically; and, while his individuality will endure even beyond this life, he is necessitated, by his physical condition, to appropriate and to produce, and thus to imprint his individuality upon the material world around, to create property. But man is not only an appropriating and producing, he is also an exchanging, being. He always exchanges and always intercommunicates. This constant intertwining of man's individualism and socialism creates mutual claims of protection, rights, the necessity of rules, of laws,—in one word, as individuals and as natural members of society, men produce and require government. No society, no cluster of men, no individuals banded together even for a temporary purpose, can exist without some sort of government instantly springing up. Government is natural to man, and characteristic. No animals have a government; no authority exists among them; instinct and physical submission alone exist among them. Man alone has laws which ought to be obeyed, but may be disobeyed. Expansion, accumulation, development, progress, relapses, disintegration, violence, error, superstition, the necessity of intercommunication, wealth and poverty, peculiar disposition, temperament, configuration of the country, traditional types, pride and avarice, knowledge and ignorance, sagacity of individuals, taste, activity and sluggishness, noble or criminal bias, position, both geopraphical and chronological,—all that affects numbers of men affects their governments, and an endless variety of governments and political societies has been the consequence; but, whatever form of government may present itself to us, the fundamental idea, however rudely conceived, is always the protection of society and its members, security of property and person, the administration of justice therefor, and the united efforts of society to furnish the means to authority to carry out its objects,—contribution, which, viewed as imposed by authority, is taxation. Those bands of robbers which occasionally have risen in disintegrating societies, as in India, and who merely robbed and devastated, avowing that they did not mean to administer justice or protect the people, form no exception, although the extent of their soldiery, and the periodicity of their raids, caused them to be called governments. What little of government continued to exist was still the remnant of the communal government of the oppressed hamlets; while the robbers themselves could not exist without a government among themselves.

Aristotle classified governments according to the seat of supreme power, and he has been generally followed down to very recent times. Accordingly, we had monarchy, that government in which the supreme power is vested in one man, to which was added, at a later period, the idea of hereditariness. Aristocracy, the government, in which the supreme power is vested in the *aristoi*, which does not mean, in this case, the best, but the excelling ones, the prominent, *i. e.*, by property and influence. Privilege is its characteristic. Its corresponding degenerate government is the oligarchy (from *oligos*, little, few), that government in which supreme power is exercised by a few privileged ones, who generally have arrogated the power. Democracy, that government in which supreme power is vested in the people at large. Equality is one of its characteristics. Its degenerate correspondent is the ochlocracy (from *ochlos*, the rabble), for which at present the barbarous term "mobocracy" is frequently used.

But this classification was insufficient, even at the time of Aristotle, when, for instance, theocracies existed; nor is the seat of supreme power the only characteristic, nor, in all respects, by any means the chief characteristic. A royal government, for instance, may be less absolute than a republican government. In order to group together the governments and political societies which have existed, and are still existing, with philosophical discrimination, we must pay attention to the chief power holder (whether he be one or whether there are many), to the pervading spirit of the administration or wielding of the power, to the characteristics of the society, or the influencing interests of the same, to the limitation or entirety of public power, to the peculiar relations of the citizen to the state. Indeed, every principle, relation, or condition characteristically influencing or shaping society or government in particular may furnish us with a proper division. We propose, then, the following:

Grouping of Political Societies and Governments.

I. *According to the supreme power holder, or the placing of supreme power, whether really or nominally so.*

The power holder may be one, a few, many, or all; and we have, accordingly:

A. Principalities, that is, states the rulers of which are set apart from the ruled, or inherently differ from the ruled, as in the case of the theocracy.

(1) Monarchy.

(a) Patriarchy.

(b) Chieftain government (as our Indians).

(c) Sacerdotal monarchy (as the states of the church; former sovereign bishoprics).

(d) Kingdom, or principality proper.

(e) Theocracy (Jehovah was the chief magistrate of the Israelitic state).

(2) Dyarchy. It exists in Siam, and existed occasionally in the Roman empire; not in Sparta, because Sparta was a republic, although her two hereditary generals were called kings.

B. Republic.

(1) Aristocracy.

(a) Aristocracy proper.

(aa) Aristocracies which are democracies within the body of aristocrats (as the former Polish government).

(bb) Organic internal government (as Venice formerly).

(b) Oligarchy.

(c) Sacerdotal republic, or hierarchy.

(d) Plutocracy; if, indeed, we adopt this term from antiquity for a government in which it is the principle that the possessors of great wealth constitute the body of aristocrats.

(2) Democracy.

(a) Democracy proper.

(b) Ochlocracy (mob rule), "mob" meaning unorganized multitude.

II. *According to the unity of the public power, or its division and limitation.*

A. Unrestricted power, or absolutism.

(1) According to the form of government.

(a) Absolute monarchy, or despotism.

(b) Absolute aristocracy (Venice); absolute sacerdotal aristocracy, etc.

(c) Absolute democracy (the government of the Agora, or market democracy).

(2) According to the organization of the administration.

(a) Centralized absolutism. Centralism, called "bureaucracy" when carried on by writing; at least, bureaucracy has very rarely existed, if ever, without centralism.

(b) Provincial (satraps, pashas, proconsuls).

B. According to division of public power.

(1) Governments in which the three great functions of public power are separate, viz., the legislative, executive, judiciary. If a distinct term contradistinguished to centralism be wanted, we might call these "co-operative governments."

(2) Governments in which these branches are not strictly separate, as, for instance, in our government, but which are nevertheless not centralized governments; as Republican Rome, Athens, and several modern kingdoms.

C. Institutional government.

(1) Institutional government comprehending the whole, or constitutional government.

(a) Deputative government.

(b) Representative government.

(aa) Bicameral.

(bb) Unicameral.

(2) Local self-government. See V. We do not believe that any substantial self-government can exist without an institutional character and subordinate self-governments. It can exist only under an institutional government (see Lieber's Civil Liberty and Self-Government, under "Institution").

D. Whether the state is the substantive or the means, or whether the principle of socialism or individualism preponderates.

(1) Socialism, that state of society in which the socialist principle prevails, or in which government considers itself the substantive; the ancient states absorbing the individual or making citizenship the highest phase of humanity; absolutism of Louis XIV Indeed, all modern absolutism is socialistic.

(2) Individualism, that system in which the state remains acknowledged a means, and the individual the substantive; where primary claims, that is, rights, are felt to exist, for the obtaining and protection of which the government is established,—the government, or even society, which must not attempt to absorb the

individual. The individual is immortal, and will be of another world; the state is neither.

III. *According to the descent or transfer of supreme power.*

A. Hereditary governments.
Monarchies.
Aristocracies.
Hierarchies, etc.

B. Elective.
Monarchies.
Aristocracies.
Hierarchies.

C. Hereditary — elective — governments, the rulers of which are chosen from a certain family or tribe.

D. Governments in which the chief magistrate or monarch has the right to appoint the successor; as occasionally the Roman emperors, the Chinese, the Russian, in theory, Bonaparte when consul for life.

IV. *According to the origin of supreme power, real or theoretical.*

A. According to the primordial character of power.

(1) Based on *jus divinum.*

(a) Monarchies.

(b) Communism, which rests its claims on a *jus divinum,* or extrapolitical claim of society.

(c) Democracies, when proclaiming that the people, because the people, can do what they list, even against the law; as the Athenians once declared it, and Napoleon III., when he desired to be elected president a second time against the constitution.

(2) Based on the sovereignty of the people.

(a) Establishing an institutional government, as with us.

(b) Establishing absolutism (the Bonaparte sovereignty).

B. Delegated power.

(1) Chartered governments.

(a) Chartered city governments.

(b) Chartered companies, as the former great East India Company.

(c) Proprietary governments.

(2) Vice royalties; as Egypt, and, formerly, Algiers.

(3) Colonial government with constitution and high amount of self-government,—a government of great importance in modern history.

V. *Constitutions.* (*To avoid too many subdivisions, this subject has been treated here separately. See* II).

Constitutions, the fundamental laws on which governments rest, and which determine the relation in which the citizen stands to the government, as well as each portion of the government to the whole, and which, therefore, give feature to the political society, may be:

A. As to their origin.

(1) Accumulative; as the constitutions of England or Republican Rome.

(2) Enacted constitutions (generally, but not philosophically, called "written constitutions").

(a) Octroyed constitutions (as the French, by Louis XVIII).

(b) Enacted by the people, as our constitutions. ("We, the people, charter governments; formerly governments chartered the liberties of the people.")

(3) Pacts between two parties, contracts, as *Magna Charta,* and most charters in the Middle Ages. The medieval rule was that as much freedom was enjoyed as it was possible to conquer,—*expugnare* in the true sense.

B. As to extent or uniformity.

(1) Broadcast over the land. We may call them national constitutions, popular constitutions, constitutions for the whole state.

(2) Special charters. Chartered, accumulated and varying franchises, medieval character. (See article "Constitution" in the Encyclopaedia Americana.)

VI. *As to the extent and comprehension of the chief government.*

A. Military governments.

(1) Commercial government; one of the first in Asia, and that into which Asiatic society relapses, as the only remaining element, when barbarous conquerors destroy all bonds which can be torn by them.

(2) Tribal government.

(a) Stationary.

(b) Nomadic. We mention the nomadic government under the tribal government, because no other government has been nomadic, except the patriarchal government, which indeed is the incipiency of the tribal government.

(3) City government; that is, city states; as all free states of antiquity, and as the Hanseatic governments in modern times.

(4) Government of the Medieval Orders extending over portions of societies far apart; as the Templars, Teutonic Knights, Knights of St. John. Political societies without necessary territory, although they had always landed property.

(5) National states; that is, populous political societies spreading over an extensive and cohesive territory beyond the limits of a city.

B. Confederacies.

(1) As to admission of members, or extension.

(a) Closed, as the Amphictyonic council, Germany.

(b) Open, as ours.

(2) As to the federal character, or the character of the members, as states.

(a) Leagues.

(aa) Tribal confederacies; frequently observed in Asia; generally of a loose character.

(bb) City leagues, as the Hanseatic League, the Lombard League.

(cc) Congress of deputies, voting by states and according to instruction; as the Netherlands republic and our Articles of Confederation, Germanic Confederation.

(dd) Present "state system of Europe" (with constant congresses, if we may call this "system," a federative government in its incipiency).

(b) Confederacies proper, with national congress.

(aa) With *ecclesiae* or democratic congress (Achaean League).

(bb) With representative national congress, as ours.

C. Mere agglomerations of one ruler.

(1) As the early Asiatic monarchies, or Turkey.

(2) Several crowns in one head; as Austria, Sweden, Denmark.

VII. *As to the construction of society, the title of property and allegiance.*

A. As to the classes of society.

(1) Castes, hereditarily dividing the whole population, according to occupations and privileges. India, ancient Egypt.

(2) Special castes.

(a) Government with privileged classes or caste; nobility.

(b) Government with degraded or oppressed caste; slavery.

(c) Governments founded on equality of citizens (the uniform tendency of modern civilization).

B. As to property and production.

(1) Communism.

(2) Individualism.

C. As to allegiance.

(1) Plain, direct; as in unitary governments.

(2) Varied; as in national confederacies.

(3) Graduated or *encapsulated*; as in the feudal system, or as is the case with the serf.

D. Governments are occasionally called according to the prevailing interests or classes; as

Military states; for instance, Prussia under Frederick II.

Maritime state.

Commercial.

Agricultural.

Manufacturing.

Ecclesiastical, etc.

VIII. *According to simplicity or complexity, as in all other spheres, we have—*

A. Simple governments (formerly called "pure"; as "pure democracy").

B. Complex governments, formerly called "mixed."

GRACE. Favor or indulgence, as distinguished from right.

GRACE, DAYS OF. See "Days of Grace."

GRADATIM (Lat.) In old English law. By degrees or steps; step by step; from one degree to another. Bracton, fol. 64.

GRADUS (Lat. a step). A measure of space. Vicat. A degree of relationship (*distantia cognatorum*). Heinec. Elem. Jur. Civ. § 153; Bracton, fols. 134, 374; Fleta, lib. 6, c. 2, § 1; Id. lib. 4, c. 17, § 4.

A step or degree generally; *e. g.*, *gradus honorum*, degrees of honor. Vicat. A pulpit; a year; a generation. Du Cange.

A port; any place where a vessel can be brought to land. Du Cange.

GRADUS PARENTELAE. A pedigree; a table of relationship.

GRAFFER, or GRAFFARIUS. In old English law. A graffer, notary, or scrivener. St. 5 Hen. VIII. c. 1.

GRAFFIUM. A register; a leger book or cartulary of deeds and evidences.

GRAFIO. A baron, inferior to a count. 1 Mart. Anec. Collect. 13. A fiscal judge; an advocate. Du Cange; Spelman; Cowell. For various derivations, see Du Cange.

GRAFT. In equity. A term used to designate the right of a mortgagee in premises to which the mortgagor at the time of making the mortgage had an imperfect title, but who afterwards obtained a good title. In this case the new mortgage is considered a graft into the old stock, and as arising in consideration of the former title. 1 Ball & B. 40, 46, 57; 1 Powell, Mortg. 190. See 9 Mass. 34. The same principle has obtained by legislative enactment in Louisiana. If a person contracting an obligation towards another, says the Civil Code (article 2371), grants a mortgage on property of which he is not then the owner, this mortgage shall be valid if the debtor should ever acquire the ownership of the property, by whatever right.

GRAIN. The twenty-fourth part of a pennyweight.

For scientific purposes the grain only is used, and sets of weights are constructed in decimal progression, from ten thousand grains to one hundredth of a grain.

Wheat, rye, barley, or other corn sown in the ground. In Pennsylvania, a tenant for a certain term is entitled to the away-going crop. 2 Bin. (Pa.) 487; 5 Bin. (Pa.) 258, 289; 2 Serg. & R. (Pa.) 14. See "Away-Going Crop."

GRAINAGE. In English law. The name of an ancient duty collected in London, consisting of one-twentieth part of the salt imported into that city.

GRAMMATICA FALSA NON VITIAT chartam. False grammar does not vitiate a deed. 9 Coke, 48.

GRAMMATOPHYLACIUM (Graeco-Lat.) In the civil law. A place for keeping writings or records. Dig. 48. 19. 9. 6.

GRAMME. A French weight. The gramme is the weight of a cubic centimetre of distilled water at the temperature of zero. It is equal to 15.4441 grains troy, or 5.6481 drachms avoirdupois.

GRANATARIUS (Law Lat.) In old English law. An officer having charge of a granary. Fleta, lib. 2, c. 82, § 1; Id. c. 84.

GRAND ASSIZE. An extraordinary trial by jury, instituted by Henry II., by way of alternative offered to the choice of the tenant or defendant in a writ of right, instead of the barbarous custom of trial by battel. For this purpose, a writ *de magna assiza eliganda* was directed to the sheriff to return four knights, who were to choose twelve other knights to be joined with themselves; and these sixteen formed the grand assize, or great jury, to try the right between the parties. 3 Bl. Comm. 351.

GRAND BILL OF SALE. In English law. The name of an instrument used for the transfer of a ship while she is at sea. See "Bill of Sale"; 7 Mart. (La.) 318.

GRAND CAPE. In English law. A writ judicial which lieth when a man has brought a *praecipe quod reddat*, of a thing that toucheth plea of lands, and the tenant makes default on the day given him in the writ original, then this writ shall go for the king, to take the land into the king's hands, and, if he comes not at the day given him by the grand cape, he has lost his lands. Old Nat. Brev. fols. 161, 162; Reg. Jud. fol. 2b; Bracton, lib. 5, tr. 3, c. 1, Nos. 4, 5, 6. So called because its Latin form began with the word *cape*, "take thou," and because it had more words than the petit cape, or because petit cape summons to answer for default only. Petit cape issues after appearance to the original writ, grand cape before.

GRAND COUTUMIER. Two collections of laws bore this title. One, also called the "Coutumier of France," is a collection of the customs, usages, and forms of practice which had been used from time immemorial in France; the other, called the "Coutumier de Normandie" (which, indeed, with some alterations, made a part of the former), was composed about the fourteenth of Henry III., A. D. 1229, and is a collection of the Norman laws, not as they stood at the conquest of England by William the Conqueror, but some time afterwards, and contains many provisions probably borrowed from the old English or Saxon laws. Hale, Hist. Com. Law, c. 6.

GRAND DAYS. In English practice. Those days in the term which are solemnly kept in the inns of court and chancery, viz., Candlemas Day in Hilary term, Ascension Day in Easter term, St. John the Baptist's Day in Trinity term, and All Saints' Day in Michaelmas term, which are *dies nonjuridici*, or no days in court, and are set apart for festivity. Jacob.

GRAND DISTRESS. In English practice. A process which formerly issued where the defendant, after being attached, neglected to appear; its object being to compel an appearance by distraining his goods (3 Bl. Comm. 280). It is called "grand" from its extent and stringency. Blount.

GRAND JURY. In practice. A body of men, consisting of not less than twelve nor more than twenty-four, respectively returned by the sheriff of every county to every session of the peace, oyer and terminer, and general gaol delivery, to whom indictments are preferred. 4 Bl. Comm. 302; 1 Chit. Crim. Law, 310, 311.

There is reason to believe that this institution existed among the Saxons. Crabb, Hist. Eng. Law, 35. By the constitutions of Clarendon, enacted 10 Hen. II. (A. D. 1164), it is provided that, "if such men were suspected whom none wished or dared to accuse, the sheriff, being thereto required by the bishop, should swear twelve men of the neighborhood, or village, to declare the truth" respecting such supposed crime, the jurors being summoned as witnesses or accusers, rather than judges. It seems to be pretty certain that this statute either established grand juries, if this institution did not exist before, or recognized them if they already existed. 1 Spence, Eq. Jur. 63.

GRAND LARCENY.

——**At Common Law.** Simple larceny was divided into grand and petit. The former was committed by the stealing of property exceeding twelve pence in value; the latter, when the property was of the value of twelve pence or under. This distinction was not abolished till the reign of George IV. Grand larceny was a capital offense, but clergyable unless attended with certain aggravations. Petit larceny was punishable with whipping, "or some such corporal punishment less than death"; and, being a felony, it was subject to forfeiture, whether upon conviction or flight.

——**In the United States.** The distinction between grand and petit larceny is generally preserved; the amount necessary to be stolen to constitute grand larceny being ordinarily about twenty dollars. Grand larceny is a felony, and petit larceny a misdemeanor.

GRAND SERJEANTY. In English law. A species of tenure *in capite*, by certain personal and honorable services to the king, called "grand" in respect of the honor of so serving the king. Instances of such services are, the carrying of the king's banner, performing some service at his coronation, etc. The honorable parts of this tenure were retained, and its oppressive incidents swept away, by St. 12 Car. II. c. 24. Termes de la Ley; 2 Sharswood, Bl. Comm. 73; 1 Steph. Comm. 198.

GRANDCHILDREN. The children of one's children. Sometimes these may claim bequests given in a will to children, though, in general, they can make no such claim. 6 Coke, 16. See "Child"; "Construction."

GRANGE. A barn or granary; other outbuildings used in husbandry.

GRANGIARIUS, or **GRANGEARIUS.** A grange keeper.

GRANT.

——**At Common Law.** A transfer by deed of that which cannot pass by livery. Williams, Real Prop. 149.

A grant was proper to transfer an incorporeal hereditament or a reversion or vested remainder in land, but in England, before 1845, a grant was not effectual to transfer an estate in fee in land in possession. 7 W. Va. 235.

A grant is now sufficient to convey any estate. 12 Minn. 468.

——**In Modern Law.** A general term, including all sorts of conveyances. 4 Mason (U. S.) 69.

The term is properly applicable only to realty (1 Mont. 410), but it has been applied to personalty. 12 Minn. 468.

It is particularly applied to conveyances by the government, whether of lands or of incorporeal hereditaments, as franchises.

By the word "grant," in a treaty, is meant not only a formal grant, but any concession, warrant, order, or permission to survey, possess, or settle, whether written or parol, express, or presumed from possession. Such a grant may be made by law, as well as by a patent pursuant to a law. 12 Pet. (U. S.) 410. See 9 Adol. & E. 532; 5 Mass. 472; 9 Pick. (Mass.) 80.

"Office grant" applies to conveyances made by some officer of the law to effect certain purposes, where the owner is either unwilling or unable to execute the requisite deeds to pass the title.

"Private grant" is a grant by the deed of a private person.

"Public grant" is the mode and act of creating a title in an individual to lands which had previously belonged to the government.

The public lands of the United States, and of the various states, have been to a great extent conveyed by deeds or patents issued in virtue of general laws; but many specific grants have also been made, and are the usual method of transfer during the colonial period. See 2 Washb. Real Prop. 517-536; 4 Kent, Comm. 450, 494; 8 Wheat. (U. S.) 543; 6 Pet. (U. S.) 548; 16 Pet. (U. S.) 367; Brightly, Dig. U. S. Laws, "Lands"; "Patent."

Among the modes of conveyance included under office grant are levies and sales to satisfy execution creditors, sales by order or decree of a court of chancery, sales by order or license of court, sales for nonpayment of taxes, and the like. See Blackw. Tax Titles, passim; 2 Washb. Real Prop. 536-549.

With regard to private grants, see "Deed."

GRANT, BARGAIN, AND SELL. Words used in instruments of conveyance of real estate. See "Construction"; 8 Barb. (N. Y.) 463; 32 Me. 329; 1 T. B. Mon. (Ky.) 30; 1 Conn. 79; 5 Tenn. 124; 2 Bin. (Pa.) 95; 11 Serg. & R. (Pa.) 109; 1 Mo. 576; 1 Murph. (N. C.) 343.

GRANT OF PERSONAL PROPERTY. A method of transferring personal property, distinguished from a gift by being always founded on some consideration or equivalent. 2 Bl. Comm. 440, 441. Its proper legal designation is an "assignment," or "bargain and sale." 2 Steph. Comm. 102.

GRANT TO USES. This is common grant, with uses superadded, and has become the favorite mode of transferring realty. Wharton.

GRANTEE. He to whom a grant is made.

GRANTOR. He by whom a grant is made.

GRANTZ. In old English law. Noblemen.

GRASSHEARTH. In old English law. The name of an ancient customary service of tenants' doing one day's work for their landlord.

GRASSON. In feudal law. A fine paid on transfer of a copyhold.

GRATIFICATION. A reward given voluntarily for some service or benefit rendered, without being requested so to do, either expressly or by implication.

GRATIS (Lat.) Without reward or consideration.

GRATIS DICTUM (Lat.) A saying not required; a statement voluntarily made without necessity.

GRATUITOUS. Without valuable or legal consideration. A term applied to deeds of conveyance.

——**In Old English Law.** Voluntary; without force, fear, or favor. Bracton, fols. 11, 17.

GRATUITOUS CONTRACT. In civil law. One the object of which is for the benefit of the person with whom it is made, without any profit, received or promised, as a consideration for it; as, for example, a gift. 1 Bouv. Inst. note 709.

GRAVA. In old deeds, a little wood. In old English law, a grove; a small wood; a coppice or thicket. A thick wood of high trees. Co. Litt. 4b. Cowell; Blount; Spelman.

GRAVAMEN (Lat.) The grievance complained of; the substantial cause of the action. See Greenl. Ev. § 66.

GRAVATIO (Lat.) An accusation.

GRAVIS (Lat.) Grievous; great. *Ad grave damnum*, to the grievous damage. 11 Coke, 40.

GRAVIUS (Law Lat.) In old European law. A grave; a chief magistrate or officer. A term derived from the more ancient "*grafio*," and used in combination with various other words, as an official title in Germany; as *Margravius, Rheingravius, Landgravius*, etc. Spelman, voc. "Grafio."

GRAVIUS EST DIVINAM QUAM TEMPORALEM LAEDERE MAJESTATEM. It is more serious to hurt divine than temporal majesty. 11 Coke, 29.

GRAY'S INN. An inn of court. See "Inns of Court."

GREAT CATTLE. In English law. All manner of beasts, except sheep and yearlings. 2 Rolle, 173.

GREAT CHARTER. See "Magna Charta."

GREAT LAW. The name of an act of the legislature of Pennsylvania, passed at Chester immediately after the arrival of William Penn, December 7, 1682. Sergeant, Land Laws Pa. 24, 230.

GREAT SEAL. By act of union (article 24) it was provided that there should be one great seal for the United Kingdom, to be used in sealing writs, to summon parliament, foreign treaties, etc., in all public acts which concern the United Kingdom, and all acts which concern England, and that a seal should be kept in Scotland, to be used in all things relating to private rights or grants which had theretofore passed the Great Seal of Scotland. Wharton.

GREAT TITHES. In eccleciastical law. The more valuable tithes; as, corn, hay, and wood. 3 Burn, Ecc. Law, 680, 681; 3 Steph. Comm. 127.

GREE. Satisfaction for an offense committed, or injury done. Cowell.

GREEK. An important language in law, being the language of a large portion of the Corpus Juris Civilis.

The Novels of Justinian and his successors are, almost without exception, written in Greek; several of the constitutions in the Code are in the same language; and extracts from Greek writers, with numerous detached words and phrases, are scattered through the Pandects.

This Greek of the civil law, however, is, to a great extent, a corrupt and barbarous dialect, resembling in its uncouth combinations those varieties of the Latin and French, known as Law Latin and Law French, which were for so long a period the languages of the law and practice of England, and obviously framed on the same principles. Its peculiarities are (1) the conversion of Latin words into Greek, by simply writing them in Greek letters; (2) the mixture of Latin and Greek words together; and (3) the formation of new words by giving to Latin words Greek terminations.

GREEN CLOTH. An English board or court of justice, composed of the lord steward and inferior officers, and held in the royal household. So named from the cloth upon the board at which it is held.

GREEN GOODS. A slang term for counterfeit money. Usually used in connection with a swindle whereby, under a pretense of selling counterfeit money, some worthless substance is palmed off on the buyer. See 79 Hun (N. Y.) 310; 51 Hun (N. Y.) 624.

GREEN SILVER. A feudal custom in the manor of Writtel, in Essex, where every tenant whose front door opens to Greenbury shall pay a half-penny yearly to the lord, by the name of "green silver" or "rent." Cowell.

GREEN WAX. In English law. The name of the estreats of fines, issues and amercements in the exchequer, delivered to the sheriff under the seal of that court, which is made with green wax.

GREENBACKS. The term greenback is the popular and almost exclusive name applied to all United States treasury issues, and is not applied to any other species of paper currency. 23 Ind. 23.

GREEVE, GREF. (Law Fr.) Grievous; severe.

GREGORIAN EPOCH. The time from which the Gregorian calendar or computation dates, *i. e.*, from the year 1582.

GREMIO. In Spanish law. The union of merchants, artisans, laborers, or other persons who follow the same pursuits, and are governed by the same regulations. The word "guild," in English, has nearly the same signification.

GREMIUM (Lat.) Bosom. Ainsworth. *De gremio mittere,* to send from their bosom; used of one sent by an ecclesiastical corporation or body. *A latere mittere,* to send from his side, or one sent by an individual; as, a legate sent by the pope. Du Cange. In English law, an inheritance is said to be *in gremio legis,* in the bosom or under the protection of the law, when it is in abeyance. See "In Nubibus."

GRESSUME, GRESSAME, GRESSUM, or **grossome** (Scotch, *grassum*). In old English law. A fine due from a copyholder on the death of his lord. Plowd. fols. 271, 285; 1 Strange, 654. Cowell derives it from *gersum.*

GRETNA GREEN MARRIAGE. A marriage celebrated at Gretna, in Dumfries (bordering on the county of Cumberland), in Scotland. By the law of Scotland, a valid marriage may be contracted by consent alone, without any other formality. When the marriage act (26 Geo. II. c. 33) rendered the publication of banns, or a license, necessary in England, it became usual for persons who wished to marry clandestinely to go to Gretna Green, the nearest part of Scotland, and marry according to the Scotch law; so a sort of chapel was built at Gretna Green, in which the English marriage service was performed by the village blacksmith. 19 & 20 Vict. c. 96, § 1, now requires twenty-one days previous residence in Scotland, unless one of the parties has a usual place of residence therein. Wharton.

GREVA. (L. Lat.) In old records. The sea-shore, sand or beach. 2 Mon. Angl. 625. Cowell.

GREVE, *Gereve.* Sax. The contracted form of *gerefa* or *grefa,* used in the time of Edward the Confessor, to denote a chief magistrate or lord. Spelman.

GREVEMENT. (Law Fr.) Grievously; heavily, or severely.

GREVER. (Law Fr.) To hurt or harm. Britt. c. 22.

To prejudice or injure. Id. cc. 28, 39.

GRIEVED. Aggrieved. 3 East, 22.

GRIST. Grain carried to the mill to be ground separately for the owner; grain carried to the mill for grinding at one time. 119 Ill. App. 44.

GRITH (Saxon). Peace.

GRITHBRECH (Saxon, *grith,* peace, and *brych,* breaking). Breach of the king's peace, as opposed to *frithbrech,* a breach of the nation's peace with other nations. Leg. Hen. I. c. 36; Chart. Wilhelm, Conq. Eccl. St. Pauli in Hist. ejusd. fol. 90.

GRITHSTOLE (Saxon). In Saxon law. A seat, chair, or place of peace; a sanctuary; a stone within a church gate, to which an offender might flee. Skene writes the word "girtholl."

GROCER. In old English law. A merchant or trader who engrossed all vendible merchandise; an engrosser. St. 37 Edw. III. c. 5. See "Engrosser."

GROSS. Great or large; whole or entire; amount; the sum total; without deduction of any kind. 246 Ill. 209.

GROSS ADVENTURE. In maritime law. A maritime or bottomry loan. It is so called because the lender exposes his money to the perils of the sea, and contributes to the gross or general average. Poth.; Pardessus.

GROSS AVERAGE. In maritime law. That kind of average which falls on the ship, cargo, and freight, and is distinguished from "particular average." See "Average."

GROSS NEGLIGENCE. The omission of that care which even inattentive and thoughtless men never fail to take of their own property. Jones, Bailm.

The want of slight diligence. 103 Ill. 523.

Lata culpa, or, as the Roman lawyers most accurately called it, *dolo proxima,* is, in practice, considered as equivalent to *dolus,* or fraud itself. It must not be confounded, however, with fraud; for it may exist consistently with good faith and honesty of intention, according to common-law authorities.

GROSS WEIGHT. The total weight of goods or merchandise, with the chests, bags, and the like, from which are to be deducted tare and tret.

GROSSE BOIS. Great or large wood; timber. Cowell.

GROSSEMENT (Law Fr.) Largely; greatly. *Grossement enseint,* big with child. Plowd. 76.

GROSSOME. See "Gressume."

GROUND ANNUAL. In Scotch law. An annual rent of two kinds: First, the feu-duties payable to the lords of erection and their successors; second, the rents reserved for building lots in a city, where sub-feus are prohibited. This rent is in the nature of a perpetual annuity. Bell, Dict.; Ersk. Inst. 11. 3. 52.

GROUND LANDLORD. The person to whom ground rent is reserved.

GROUND RENT. Rent paid for the privilege of building on another man's land. Johnson; Webster. A rent reserved by the owner of unimproved land upon a lease of the land to be built upon, as contradistinguished from the rent paid to the lessee by his tenant of the premises where the buildings are erected, and from the ordinary rent paid by the tenant to his landlord upon a demise of lands and tenements.

A rent reserved to himself and his heirs, by the grantor of land in fee simple, out of the land conveyed. See 9 Watts (Pa.) 262; 8 Watts & S. (Pa.) 185; 2 Am. Law Reg. 577.

GROUND WRIT. By the English common-law procedure act of 1852 (chapter 121), "it shall not be necessary to issue any writ directed to the sheriff of the county in which the venue is laid, but writs of execution may issue at once into any county, and be directed to and executed by the sheriff of any county, whether a county palatine or not, without reference to the county in which the venue is laid, and without any suggestion of the issuing of a prior writ into such county." Before this enactment, a *ca. sa.* or *fi. fa.* could not be issued into a county different from that in which the venue in the action was laid, without first issuing a writ, called a "ground writ," into the latter county, and then another writ, which was called a "*testatum* writ," into the former. The above enactment abolished this useless process. Wharton.

GROUNDAGE. In maritime law. The consideration paid for standing a ship in a port. Jacob.

GROWTH HALF-PENNY. A rate paid in some places for the tithe of every fat beast, ox, or other unfruitful cattle. Rapalje & L.

GRUARII. The principal officers of a forest. Rapalje & L.

GUADIA, or WADIA. In old European law. A pledge. Spelman; Calv. Lex. A custom. Spelman.

GUARANTEE. He to whom a guaranty is made.

GUARANTOR. He who makes a guaranty.

GUARANTY. An undertaking to answer for another's liability, and collateral thereto. A collateral undertaking to pay the debt of another in case he does not pay it. Shaw, C. J., 24 Pick. (Mass.) 252. 194 Ill. App. 514.

It is distinguished from suretyship in being a secondary, while that is a primary, obligation; or, as sometimes defined, guaranty is an undertaking that the debtor shall pay; suretyship, that the debt shall be paid.

The undertaking is essentially in the alternative. A guarantor cannot be sued as a promisor, as the surety may; his contract must be specially set forth. A guarantor warrants the solvency of the promisor, which an indorser does not. 8 Pick. (Mass.) 423.

Guaranty, as distinguished from "suretyship," is an independent contract, while the surety is bound jointly with his principal. "A contract of suretyship is a direct liability for the act to be performed by the debtor, and a guaranty is a liability only for his ability to perform the act." 52 Pa. St. 440.

As distinguished from "indemnity," in that a principal obligation is essential to guaranty, while indemnity may be a primary contract.

Guaranties are either:

(1) General, running to any person dealing with the principal.

(2) Special, to a particular person.

(3) Limited, *i. e.*, covering only a particular transaction.

(4) Continuing, applicable to a class of future transactions.

(5) Absolute, conditioned only on the default of the principal.

(6) Conditional, dependent on some extraneous condition.

GUARANTY INSURANCE. A guaranty or insurance against loss in case a person named shall make a designated default, or be guilty of specified conduct. 9 Am. & Eng. Enc. Law, 65, quoted in 174 Ill. 310.

GUARDIAN. One who legally has the care and management of the person, or the estate, or both, of a child during its minority. Reeve, Dom. Rel. 311.

A person having the control of the property of a minor without that of his person is known in the civil law, as well as in some of the states of the United States, by the name of "curator." 1 Lec. Elm. 241; Rev. St. Mo. 1855, p. 823.

Guardians are also sometimes appointed of idiots, spendthrifts, etc.

The general classes of guardians are:

(1) Guardian by chancery. This guardianship, although unknown at the common law, is well established in practice now. It grew up in the time of William III., and had its foundation in the royal prerogative of the king as *parens patriae*. 2 Fonbl. Eq. (5th Ed.) 246.

This power the sovereign is presumed to have delegated to the chancellor. 10 Ves. 63; 2 P. Wms. 118; Reeve, Dom. Rel. 317.

By virtue of it, the chancellor appoints a guardian where there is none, and exercises a superintending control over all guardians, however appointed, removing them for misconduct, and appointing others in their stead. Co. Litt. 89; 2 Bulst. 679; 1 P. Wms. 703; 8 Mod. 214; 1 Ves. Jr. 160; 2 Kent, Comm. 227.

This power, in the United States, resides in courts of equity (1 Johns. Ch. [N. Y.] 99; 2 Johns. Ch. [N. Y.] 439), and in probate or surrogate courts (2 Kent, Comm. 226; 30 Miss. 458; 3 Bradf. Sur. [N. Y.] 133).

(2) Guardian by nature. The father, and, on his death, the mother. 2 Kent, Comm. 220; 2 Root (Conn.) 320; 7 Cow. (N. Y.) 36; 2 Wend. (N. Y.) 158; 4 Mass. 675.

(3) Guardian by nurture. This guardianship belonged to the father, then to the mother. The subject of it extended to the younger children, not the heirs apparent. In this country it does not exist, or, rather, it is merged in the higher and more durable guardianship by nature, because all the children are heirs, and, therefore, the subject of that guardianship. 2 Kent, Comm. 221; Reeve, Dom. Rel. 315; 6 Ga. 401. It extended to the person only (6 Conn. 494; 40 Eng. Law & Eq. 109), and terminated at the age of fourteen (1 Bl. Comm. 461).

(4) Guardian in socage. This guardianship arose when socage lands descended to an infant under fourteen years of age; at which period it ceased if another guardian was appointed, otherwise it continued. And. 313; 5 Johns. (N. Y.) 66.

The person entitled to it by common law was the next of kin, who could not by any possibility inherit the estate. 1 Bl. Comm. 461. Although formerly recognized in New York, it was never common in the United States (5 Johns. [N. Y.] 66; 7 Johns. [N. Y.] 157), because, by the statute of descents generally in force in this country, those who are next of kin may eventually inherit. Wherever it has been recognized, it has been in a form differing materially from its character at common law. 15 Wend. (N. Y.) 631.

(5) Guardians by statute. These are of two kinds: First, testamentary; second, those appointed by court in pursuance of some statute.

(6) Testamentary guardians. These are appointed by the deed or last will of the father, and they supersede the claims of all other guardians, and have control of the person and the real and personal estate of the child till he arrives at full age.

(7) Guardians appointed by court. The greater number of guardians among us, by far, are those appointed by court, in conformity with statutes which regulate their powers and duties. In the absence of special provisions, their rights and duties are governed by the general law on the subject of guardian and ward.

GUARDIAN AD LITEM. A guardian appointed for the purposes of a suit.

The appointment of such is incident to the power of every court to try a case (2 Cow. [N. Y.] 430), and the power is then confined to the particular case at bar (Co. Litt. 89, note 16). His duty is to manage the interest of the infant when sued, or to bring suit for him. In criminal cases, no guardian is appointed; the court acts as guardian. Reeve, Dom. Rel. 318.

GUARDIAN OF THE CINQUE PORTS. See "Warden of the Cinque Ports."

GUARDIAN OF THE PEACE. A warden or conservator of the peace. Rapalje & L.

GUARDIAN OF THE POOR. In English law. A person acting as overseer of a parish in matters relating to the management and relief of the poor.

GUARDIAN OF THE SPIRITUALITIES. In English ecclesiastical law. The person to whom the spiritual jurisdiction of a diocese is committed during the vacancy of the see. Cowell; Blount.

GUARDIAN OF THE TEMPORALITIES. The person to whose custody a vacant see or abbey was committed by the king, who, as steward of the goods and profits thereof, was to give an account to the escheator, and he into the exchequer. Tomlins.

GUARDIANSHIP. The power of protective authority given by law, and imposed on an individual who is free and in the enjoyment of his rights, over one whose weakness on account of his age or infirmity renders him unable to protect himself.

GUARDIANUS, or **GARDIANUS.** A guardian, warden, or keeper. Spelman; 3 Salk. 176.

GUARENTIGIO. In Spanish law. A term applicable to the contract or writing by which courts of justice are empowered to execute and carry into effect a contract in the same manner as if it were decreed by the court after the usual legal formalities. This clause, though formerly inserted in contracts of sale, etc., stipulating the payment of a sum of money, is at present usually omitted, as courts of justice ordinarily compel the parties to execute all contracts made by authentic acts, that is, acts passed before a notary, in the presence of two witnesses.

GUARNIMENTUM (Law Lat. from Fr. *garnement*). In old European law. A provision of necessary things. Spelman. A furnishing or garnishment.

GUASTALD. One who had the custody of the royal mansions. Rapalje & L.

GUBERNATOR (Lat.) A pilot of a ship.

GUERPI, or **GUERPY** (Law Fr.) Abandoned; left; deserted. Britt. c. 33.

GUERRA, GUARRA, or **GUERRE.** War, either public or private. Spelman.

GUERRILLA PARTY (Span. *guerra,* war; *guerrilla,* a little war). In military law. Self-constituted sets of armed men, in times of war, who form no integrant part of the organized army, do not stand on the regular payroll of the army, or are not paid at all, take up arms and lay them down at intervals, and carry on petty war, chiefly by raids, extortion, destruction, and massacre. Lieber, Guerr. Part. 18. See Halleck, Int. Law, 386; Woolsey, Int. Law, 299.

Partisan, free-corps, and guerrilla are terms resembling each other considerably in signification; and, indeed, partisan and guerrilla are frequently used in the same sense. See Halleck, Int. Law, 386.

GUEST. A traveler who stays at an inn from day to day, for pay, and without a special contract to board for any definite time.

If he is invited as a friend by the inn keeper, he is not a "guest" in the technical sense (Bac. Abr. "Inns," c. 5), and, if he stays under a contract for a definite time, he is not a guest, but a boarder (5 Barb. [N. Y.] 560; 26 Ala. [N. S.] 377; 26 Vt. 332).

The distinction between a guest and a boarder seems to be this: The guest comes without any bargain for time, remains without one, and may go when he pleases, paying only for the actual entertainment which he receives; and it is not enough to make a boarder, and not a guest, that he has stayed a long time in the inn in this way. 25 Ia. 555.

GUEST TAKER, or **GEST TAKER.** An agister.

GUET. In old French law. Watch. Ord. Mar. liv. 4, tit. 6.

GUIA. In Spanish law. A right of way for narrow carts. White, New Recop. lib. 2, c. 6, § 1.

GUIDAGE. In old law. That which was given for safe conduct through a strange territory, or another's territory. Cowell.

The office of guiding of travelers through dangerous and unknown ways. 2 Inst. 526.

GUIDON DE LA MER. The name of a treatise on maritime law, written in Rouen —then Normandy—in 1671, as is supposed. It was received on the continent of Europe almost as equal in authority to one of the ancient codes of maritime law. The author of this work is unknown. This tract or treatise is contained in the "Collection de Lois Maritimes," by J. M. Pardessus, vol. 2, p. 371 et seq.

GUILD, or **GILD.** A brotherhood or company governed by certain rules and orders made among themselves by king's license; a corporation, especially for purposes of commerce; so called because, on entering the guild, the members pay an assessment, or tax (gild) towards defraying its charges. Termes de la Ley; Du Cange. A guild held generally more or less property in common, —often a hall, called a "guild hall," for the purposes of the association. The name of "guild" was not, however, confined to mercantile companies, but was applied also to religious, municipal, and other corporations. A friborg, that is, among the Saxons, ten families' mutual pledges for each other to the king. Spelman.

GUILD HALL. (Law Lat. *gildhalla,* variously spelled *ghildhalla, guihalla, guihaula;* from Saxon *gild,* payment, company, and *halla,* hall). A place in which are exposed goods for sale. Charter of Count of Flanders; Hist. Guinensi, 202, 203; Du Cange. The hall of a guild or corporation; Du Cange; Spelman. The hall of the merchants of the Hanseatic League in London, otherwise called the "Stilyard." Id.

GUILT. In criminal law. That which renders criminal and liable to punishment.

That disposition to violate the law which has manifested itself by some act already done. The opposite of innocence. See Rutherforth, Inst. bk. 1, c. 18, § 10.

GUILTY. The state or condition of a person who has committed a crime, misdemeanor, or offense.

This word implies a malicious intent, and must be applied to something universally allowed to be a crime. Cowp. 275.

——**In Pleading.** A plea by which a defendant who is charged with a crime, misdemeanor, or tort admits or confesses it. In criminal proceedings, when the accused is arraigned, the clerk asks him, "How say you, A. B., are you guilty or not guilty?" His answer, which is given *ore tenus,* is called his "plea"; and when he admits the charge in the indictment, he answers or pleads "guilty."

GULE OF AUGUST. The first of August, the same as *St. Peter's Day ad Vincula.* Cowell.

GURGES. *Gurges,* a deep pit of water, a gors or gulf, consisteth of water and land; and therefore by the grant thereof by that name the soil doth pass. In Domesday it is called *guort, gort,* and *gors* plurally. Co. Litt. 5b.

GUST, GEST. (Sax.) In old English law. A guest; a person who lodged a second night with another was so called, among the ancient Saxons.

GUTI. Jutes; one of the three nations who migrated from Germany to Britain at an early period. According to Spelman, they established themselves chiefly in Kent and the Isle of Wight.

GWABR MERCHED. Maid's fee. A British word signifying a customary fine payable to lords of some manors on marriage of tenant's daughter, or otherwise on her incontinence. Cowell, "Marchet."

GWALSTOW (Saxon). A place of execution. Spelman.

GWAYF. Waif. Par. Ant. p. 196; Cowell.

GYLPUT. In old law. The name of a local court of the hundred of Pathbew, in Warwickshire.

GYLTWITE (Saxon). Compensation for fraud or trespass. Grant of King Edgar, A. D. 964; Cowell.

GYNARCHY. A government in which a woman holds, or is capable of holding, the position or chief executive.

GYVES. Fetters or shackles for the legs.

H

H is sometimes used in some Law Latin words in which it is more generally and properly omitted; thus, *Ostium* is sometimes written *Hostium; Coercio, Cohertio; Abundanti, Habundanti;* and the like. So, on the other hand, it is sometimes omitted where it should properly be used; thus, *Hutesium* occurs occasionally in the form *Utesium, Hypotheca* as *Ypotheca, Horreum* as *Orreum, Hordeum* as *Ordeum,* and the like.

HABE, or **HAVE** (Lat.) A form of the salutatory expression *Ave* (hail) in the titles of the constitutions of the Theodosian and Justinian Codes. Prateus; Calv. Lex.; Spelman.

HABEAS CORPORA (Lat. that you have the bodies). In English practice. A writ issued out of the common pleas, commanding the sheriff to compel the appearance of a jury in a cause between the parties. It answered the same purpose as a *distringas juratores* in the king's bench. It is abolished by the common-law procedure act.

HABEAS CORPUS (Lat. that you have the body). A writ directed to the person detaining another, and commanding him to produce the body of the prisoner at a certain time and place, with the day and cause of his caption and detention, to do, submit to, and receive whatsoever the court or judge awarding the writ shall consider in that behalf.

This is the most famous writ in the law; and, having for many centuries been employed to remove illegal restraint upon personal liberty, no matter by what power imposed, it is often called the great "writ of liberty." It takes its name from the characteristic words it contained when the process and records of the English courts were written in Latin:

Praecipimus tibi quod corpus A B in custodia vestra detentum, ut dicitur, una cum causa captionis et detentionis suae, quocunque nomine idem A B censeatur in eadem habeas coram nobis apud Westm. etc., ad subjiciendum et recipiendum ea, quae curia nostra de eo ad tunc et ibidem ordinari contigerit in hac parte, etc.

There were several other writs which contained the words *habeas corpus;* but they were distinguished from this and from one another by the specific terms declaring the object of the writ, which terms are still retained in the nomenclature of writs, as, *habeas corpus ad respondendum, ad testificandum, ad satisfaciendum, ad prosequendum,* and *ad faciendum et recipiendum, ad deliberandum et recipiendum.*

This writ was in like manner designated as *habeas corpus ad subjiciendum et recipiendum;* but, having acquired in public esteem a marked importance by reason of the nobler uses to which it has been devoted, it has so far appropriated the generic term to itself that it is now, by way of eminence, commonly called the "Writ of *Habeas Corpus.*"

The date of its origin cannot now be ascertained. Traces of its existence are found in Y. B. 48 Edw. III. 22; and it appears to have been familiar to, and well understood by, the judges in the reign of Henry VI. In its early history it appears to have been used as a means of relief from private restraint. The earliest precedents where it was used against the crown are in the reign of Henry VII. Afterwards the use of it became more frequent, and in the time of Charles I. it was held an admitted constitutional remedy. Hurd, Habeas Corpus, 145.

In process of time, abuses crept into the practice, which in some measure impaired the usefulness of the writ. The party imprisoning was at liberty to delay his obedience to the first writ, and might wait till a second and third were issued before he produced the party; and many other vexatious shifts were practised to detain state prisoners in custody. 3 Bl. Comm. 135.

Greater promptitude in its execution was required to render the writ efficacious. The subject was accordingly brought forward in parliament in 1668, and renewed from time to time until 1679, when the celebrated *habeas corpus* act of 31 Car. II. was passed. The passage of this act has been made the theme of the highest praise and congratulation by British authors, and is even said to have "extinguished all the resources of oppression." Hurd, Habeas Corpus, 93.

This act being limited to cases of commitments for "criminal or supposed criminal matters," every other species of restraint of personal liberty was left to the ordinary remedy at common law; but, doubts being entertained as to the extent of the jurisdiction of the judge to inquire into the truth of the return to the writ in such cases, an attempt was made, in 1757, in the house of lords, to render the jurisdiction more remedial. It was opposed by Lord Mansfield as unnecessary, and failed, for the time, of success. It was subsequently renewed, however; and the act of 56 Geo. III. c. 100, supplies, in England, all the needed legislation in cases not embraced by the act of 31 Car II. Hurd, Habeas Corpus.

The English colonists in America regarded the privilege of the writ as one of the "dearest birthrights of Britons," and sufficient indications exist that it was frequently resorted to. The denial of it in Massachusetts by Judge Dudley in 1689 to Rev. John Wise, imprisoned for resisting the collection of an oppressive and illegal tax, was made the subject of a civil action against the judge, and was, moreover, denounced, as one of the grievances of the people, in a pamphlet published in 1689 on the authority of "the gentlemen, merchants, and inhabitants of Boston and the country adjacent." In New York, in 1707, it served to effect the release of the Presbyterian ministers Makemie and Hampton from an illegal warrant of arrest issued by the governor, Cornbury, for preaching the gospel without license. In New Jersey, in 1710, the assembly denounced one of the judges for refusing the writ to Thomas Gordon, which, they said, was the "undoubted right and great privilege of the subject." In South Carolina, in 1692, the assembly adopted the act of 31 Car. II. This act was extended to Virginia by Queen Anne early in her reign, while in the assembly of Maryland in 1725 the benefit of its provisions was claimed, independent of royal favor, as the "birthright of the inhabitants." The refusal of parliament in 1774 to extend the law of *habeas corpus* to Canada was denounced by the continental congress in September of that year as oppressive, and was subsequently recounted in the Declaration of Independence as one of the manifestations on the part of the British government of tyranny over the colonies. Hurd, Habeas Corpus, 109-120.

It is provided in article 1, § 9, subd. 2, of the constitution of the United States that "the privilege of the writ of *habeas corpus* shall not be suspended, unless when, in cases of rebellion or invasion, the public safety may require it."

Similar provisions are found in the constitutions of most of the states. In Virginia and Vermont, however, it is forbidden to suspend the privilege of the writ in any case; but in the constitutions of Maryland, North Carolina, and South Carolina the writ is not mentioned.

Congress, by act of March 3, 1863, authorized the president to suspend the privilege of the writ throughout the whole or any part of the United States, whenever in his judgment the public safety might require it, during the Rebellion. A partial suspension took place.

Nor has the power of suspension ever been exercised by the legislature of any of the states, except that of Massachusetts, which, on the occasion of "Shay's Rebellion," suspended the privilege of the writ from November, 1786, to July, 1787.

HABEAS CORPUS ACT. The statute of 31 Chas. II. c. 2. 3 Bl. Comm. 135; 3 Steph. Comm. 699. This statute has been adopted in substance in the United States. 2 Kent, Comm. 27.

HABEAS CORPUS AD DELIBERANdum et recipiendum (Lat.) A writ which is issued to remove, for trial, a person confined in one county to the county or place where the offense of which he is accused was committed. Brac. Abr. "Habeas Corpus" (A); 1 Chit. Crim. Law, 132; Grady & S. Cr. Prac. 201. Thus, it has been granted to remove a person in custody for contempt to take his trial for perjury in another county. 1 Tyrwh. 185.

HABEAS CORPUS AD FACIENDUM ET recipiendum (Lat.) A writ usually issued in civil cases to remove an action from an inferior court, where the defendant is sued and imprisoned, to some superior court which has jurisdiction over the matter, in order that the cause may be determined there. This writ is commonly called *habeas corpus cum causa*, because it commands the judges of the inferior court to return the day and cause of the caption and detainer of the prisoner. Bac. Abr. "Habeas Corpus" (A); Bagl. Cham. Prac. 297; 3 Bl. Comm. 130; Tidd, Prac. 296.

This writ may also be issued at the instance of the bail of the defendant, to bring him up to be surrendered in their discharge, whether he is in custody in a civil suit or on a criminal accusation. Tidd, Prac. 298; 1 Chit. Crim. Law, 132.

HABEAS CORPUS AD PROSEQUENdum (Lat.) A writ which issues when it is necessary to remove a prisoner in order to prosecute in the proper jurisdiction wherein the fact was committed. 3 Bl. Comm. 130.

HABEAS CORPUS AD RESPONDENdum (Lat.) A writ which is usually employed in civil cases to remove a person out of the custody of one court into that of another, in order that he may be sued and answer the action in the latter. 2 Sellon, Prac. 259; 2 Mod. 198; 3 Bl. Comm. 129; Tidd, Prac. 300.

This writ lies also to bring up a person in confinement to answer a criminal charge. Thus, the court issued it to the warden of the fleet, to take the body of the prisoner confined there before a magistrate, to be examined respecting a charge of felony or misdemeanor. 5 Barn. & Ald. 730. But it was refused to bring up the body of a prisoner under sentence for a felony, for the purpose of having him tried for a previous felony.

HABEAS CORPUS AD SATISFACIENdum (Lat.) A writ which is issued to bring a prisoner from the prison of one court into that of another, in order to charge him in execution upon a judgment of the last court. 2 Sellon, Prac. 261; 3 Bl. Comm. 130; Tidd, Prac. 301.

HABEAS CORPUS AD SUBJICIENDUM. See "Habeas Corpus."

HABEAS CORPUS AD TESTIFICANdum (Lat.) A writ which lies to bring up a prisoner detained in any jail or prison, to give evidence before any court of competent jurisdiction. Tidd, Prac. 739; 3 Bl. Comm. 130; 2 Sellon, Prac. 261.

The allowance of this writ resting in the discretion of the court, it will be refused if the application appear to be in bad faith, or a mere contrivance. 3 Burrows, 1440.

It was refused to bring up a prisoner of war (2 Doug. 419), or a prisoner in custody for high treason (Peake, Add. Cas. 21).

It would of course be refused where it appeared from the application that the prisoner was under sentence for crime which rendered him incompetent as a witness.

The application for the writ is made upon affidavit, stating the nature of the suit and the materiality of the testimony, together with the general circumstances of restraint which render the writ necessary. Cowp. 672; Fost. Crim. Law, 396; 2 Cow. & H. notes to Phil. Ev. 658.

HABEAS CORPUS CUM CAUSA. See "Habeas Corpus ad Faciendum et Recipiendum."

HABEMUS OPTIMUM TESTEM, CONFItentem reum. We have the best witness, a confessing defendant. Fost. Crim. Law, 243. See 2 Hagg. 315; 1 Phil. Ev. 397.

HABENDUM (Lat. for having). In conveyancing. The clause usually following the granting part of the premises of a deed, which defines the extent of the ownership in the thing granted to be held and enjoyed by the grantee. 2 Washb. Real Prop. 642.

It commences with the words "to have and to hold." In Law French, these words are rendered "*aver et tener*," or "*a aver et tener*," and in Latin, "*habendum et tenendum*."

HABENDUM ET TENENDUM. In old conveyancing. To have and to hold. Formal words in deeds of land from a very early period. Bracton, fol. 17b.

HABENTES HOMINES (Lat.) Rich men. Du Cange.

HABERE (Lat.) In the civil law. To have. Sometimes distinguished from *tenere* (to hold), and *possidere* (to possess); *habere* referring to the right, *tenere* to the fact, and *possidere* to both.

Habere was likewise distinguished as referring to incorporeal things, *tenere* to corporeal, and *possidere* to both. Calv. Lex.

HABERE FACIAS POSSESSIONEM (Lat.) In practice. A writ of execution in the action of ejectment.

The sheriff is commanded by this writ that, without delay, he cause the plaintiff to have possession of the land in dispute which is therein described. A *fi. fa.* or *ca. sa.* for costs may be included in the writ. The duty of the sheriff in the execution and return of that part of the writ is the same as on a common *fi. fa.* or *ca. sa.* The sheriff is to execute this writ by delivering a full and actual possession of the premises to the plaintiff. For this purpose, he may break an outer or inner door of the house, and, should he be violently opposed, he may raise the *posse comitatus*. Watson, Sheriffs, 60, 215; 5 Coke, 91b; 1 Leon. 145; 3 Bouv. Inst. note 3375.

The name of this writ is abbreviated *hab. fa. poss.* See 10 Viner, Abr. 14; Tidd, Prac. (8th Eng. Ed.) 1081; 2 Archb. Prac. 58; 3 Bl. Comm. 412; Bing. Ex'ns, 115, 252; Bac. Abr.

HABERE FACIAS VISUM (Lat.) In practice. The name of a writ of execution, used in most real actions, by which the sheriff is directed that he cause the demandant to have seisin of the lands which he has recovered. 3 Bouv. Inst. note 3374.

This writ may be taken out at any time within a year and a day after judgment. It is to be executed nearly in the same manner as the writ of *habere facias possessionem*, and for this purpose the officer may break open the outer door of a house to deliver seisin to the demandant. 5 Coke, 91b; Comyn, Dig. "Execution" (E); Watson, Sheriffs, 238. The name of this writ is abbreviated *hab. fac. seis.* See Bing. Ex'ns, 115, 252; Bac. Abr.

HABERE FACIAS VISUM (Lat.) In practice. The name of a writ which lies when a view is to be taken of lands and tenements. Fitzh. Nat. Brev. Index, "View."

HABERE LICERE (Lat. to allow to have). In Roman law. A phrase denoting the duty of a seller to give possession.

HABERJECTS. A cloth of a mixed color, mentioned in Magna Charta, c. 26.

HABETO TIBI RES TUAS. Have or take your effects to yourself. One of the old Roman forms of divorcing a wife. Calv. Lex.

HABILIS (Lat.) Fit; suitable. 1 Sharswood, Bl. Comm. 436. Active; useful (of a servant). Du Cange. Proved; authentic (of Book of Saints). Du Cange. Fixed; stable (of authority of the king.) Du Cange.

HABIT. A disposition or condition of the body or mind acquired by custom or a frequent repetition of the same act. See 2 Mart. (La.; N. S.) 622; 18 Pa. St. 172; 5 Gray (Mass.) 851.

The habit of dealing has always an important bearing upon the construction of commercial contracts. A ratification will be inferred from the mere habit of dealing between the parties; as, if a broker has been accustomed to settle losses on policies in a particular manner, without any objection being made, or with the silent approbation of his principal, and he should afterwards settle other policies in the same manner, to which no objection should be made within a reasonable time, a just presumption would arise of an implied ratification; for, if the principal did not agree to such settlement, he should have declared his dissent. 2 Bouv. Inst. 1313, 1314.

HABIT AND REPUTE. Applied in Scotch law to a general understanding and belief of a certain thing having happened; *e. g.*, marriage may be constituted by habit and repute. Bell, Dict.

HABITATIO. A habitation or dwelling. Towns. Pl. 116.

——**In Civil Law.** The right of dwelling; the right of free residence in another's house. Inst. 2. 5; Dig. 7. 8.

HABITATION.

——**In Civil Law.** The right of a person to live in the house of another without prejudice to the property.

It differed from a usufruct in this, that the usufructuary might apply the house to any purpose,—as of a store or manufactory; whereas the party having the right of habitation could only use it for the residence of himself and family. 1 Brown, Civ. Law, 184; Domat. Civ. Law, lib. 1, tit. 11, § 2, note 7.

——**In Estates.** A dwelling house; a home stall. 2 Bl. Comm. 4; 4 Bl. Comm. 220. See 10 Grat. (Va.) 64.

HABITUAL CRIMINALS ACT. A name given to various statutes for the more severe punishment of repeated offenses. In England it was applied to St. 32 & 33 Vict. c. 99, giving power to apprehend, on suspicion, convicted persons holding a license under the penal servitude act. This statute is now repealed. 34 & 35 Vict. c. 112.

Also applied to statutes declaring professional criminals to be disorderly persons, and punishing them as such. Code Crim. Prac. N. Y. §§ 510-514, 899, subd. 9; Pen. Code N. Y. §§ 690-692.

HABITUAL DRUNKARD. A person given to ebriety or the excessive use of intoxicating drink, who has lost the power or the will, by frequent indulgence, to control his appetite for it. 5 Gray (Mass.) 85.

Occasional drunkenness is not enough (18 Pa. St. 172), yet daily intoxication is not required (112 Mass. 285).

HABLE. (Law Fr.) Able; competent. Dyer, 70b (Fr. ed.). In old English law. A port or harbor; a station for ships. Stat. 27 Hen. VI. c. 3.

HABUNDA. (Law Lat.) In old records. Abundance; plenty. Paroch. Ant. 548. Cowell.

HACCHE. (Sax. *hæca*, a hatch, or bolt). A hatch; a gate or door. Cowell.

HACHIA. (Law Lat.) In old records. A hack; a pick, or instrument for digging. Placita, 2 Edw. III. MS. Cowell.

HACIENDA. In Spanish law. A generic term, applicable to the mass of the property belonging to a state, and the administration of the same.

As a science, it is defined by Dr. Jose Canga Arguells, in his "Diccionario de Hacienda," to be that part of civil economy which teaches how to aggrandize a nation by the useful employment of its wealth.

A royal estate. Newman & B.

HADBOTE. In French law. A recompense or amends made for violence offered to a person in holy orders.

HADE. (Law Lat. *hada.*) In old records. A piece of land; a head of land, or headland. Cowell. See Butts, Caput terræ, Caputia, Headlands; Fitzherb, Husb. § 6.

HADERUNGA. Hatred; ill will; prejudice or partiality. Spelman; Cowell.

HADGONEL. A tax or mulct. Jacob.

HAEC EST CONVENTIO (Law Lat. this is an agreement). Words with which agreements anciently commenced. Y. B. H. 6 Edw. II. 191.

HAEC EST FINALIS CONCORDIA (Law Lat. this is the final agreement). The words with which the foot of a fine commenced. 2 Bl. Comm. 351.

HAEREDA. In Gothic law. A tribunal answering to the English court leet. 4 Bl. Comm. 274.

HAEREDE ABDUCTO. An ancient writ that lay for the lord, who, having by right the wardship of his tenant under age, could not obtain his person, the same being carried away by another person. Old Nat. Brev. 93.

HAEREDEM DEUS FACIT, NON HOMO. God, and not man, makes the heir. Bracton, 62b.

HAEREDEM EST NOMEN COLLECTIvum. Heir is a collective name.

HAEREDES (Lat. plural of *haeres*). In civil law. Heirs.

HAEREDES EXTRANEI (Lat.) In civil law. Extraneous or foreign heirs; that is, those who were not children or slaves of the testator. Those only could be extraneous heirs who had a capacity of accepting the inheritance both at the time of making the will and at the death of the testator. Halifax, Anal. bk. 11, c. 6, § 38 et seq.

HAEREDES NECESSARII (Lat.) In civil law. Necessary heirs. If slaves were made heirs, they had no choice, but on the death of the testator were necessarily free and his heirs. Calv. Lex.; Halifax, Anal. bk. 11, c. 6, § 38 et seq.; Heinec. Elem. Jur. Civ. § 587.

HAEREDES PROXIMI (Lat.) The children or descendants of the deceased. Dalr. Feud. Prop. 110.

HAEREDES REMOTIORES (Lat.) The kinsmen other than children or descendants. Dalr. Feud. Prop. 110.

HAEREDES SUI ET NECESSARII (Lat.) In civil law. Proper and necessary heirs; heirs by relationship and necessity. The descendants of an ancestor in direct line were so called, *sui* denoting the relationship, and *necessarii* the necessity of law which made them heirs without their election, and whether the ancestor died testate or intestate. Halifax, Anal. bk. 11, c. 6, § 38 et seq.; Mackeld, Civ. Law, §§ 681, 682; Heinec. Elem. Jur. Civ. § 588.

HAEREDIPETA (Law Lat.) In old English law. Next heir. Laws Hen. I.; Du Cange. One who seeks to be made heir (*qui cupit haereditatem*).

HAEREDIPETAE SUO PROPINQUO vel extraneo periculoso sane custodi nullus committatur. To the next heir, whether a relation or a stranger, certainly a dangerous guardian, let no one be committed. Co. Litt. 88b.

HAEREDITAS (Lat. from *haeres*).

——**In Civil Law.** "*Nihil aliud est haereditas, quam successio in universum jus, quod defunctus habuit.*" Inheritance is nothing else than succession to every right which the deceased possessed. Dig. 50. 17; Id. 50. 16; Id. 5. 2; Mackeld. Civ. Law, § 605; Bracton, 62b.

——**In Old English Law.** An estate transmissible by descent; an inheritance. Mart. Anec. Collect. tit. 3, p. 269; Co. Litt. 9; Glanv. lib. 7, c. 1.

HAEREDITAS, ALIA CORPORALIS, alia incorporalis; corporalis est, quae tangi potest et videri; incorporalis quae tangi non potest nec videri. An inheritance is either corporeal or incorporeal. Corporeal is that which can be touched and seen; incorporeal, that which can neither be touched nor seen. Co. Litt. 9.

HAEREDITAS DAMNOSA. See "Damnosa Haereditas."

HAEREDITAS EST SUCCESSIO IN UNIversum jus quod defunctus habuerat. Inheritance is the succession to every right which was possessed by the late possessor. Co. Litt. 237.

HAEREDITAS JACENS (Lat.)

——**In Civil Law.** A prostrate inheritance. The inheritance left to a voluntary heir was so called as long as he had not manifested, either expressly or by silence, his acceptance or refusal of the inheritance, which, by a fiction of law, was said to sustain the person (*sustinere personam*) of the deceased, and not of the heir. Mackeld. Civ. Law, § 685a. An estate with no heir or legatee to take. Code, 10. 10. 1; Bell, Dict.

——**In English Law.** An estate in abeyance; that is, after the ancestor's death, and before assumption of heir. Co. Litt. 342b. An inheritance without legal owner, and therefore open to the first occupant. 2 Sharswood, Bl. Comm. 259.

HAEREDITAS LUCTUOSA. In the civil law. A sad or mournful inheritance or succession; as that of a parent to the estate of a child, which was regarded as disturbing the natural order of mortality (*turbato ordine mortalitatis*). Code, 6. 25. 9; 4 Kent, Comm. 397.

HAEREDITAS NIHIL ALIUD EST, quam successio in universum jus, quod defunctus habuerit. The right of inheritance is nothing else than the faculty of succeeding to all the rights of the deceased. Dig. 50. 17. 62.

HAEREDITAS NUNQUAM ASCENDIT. The inheritance never ascends. Glanv. lib. 7, c. 1; Broom, Leg. Max. (2d London Ed.) 469; 2 Sharswood, Bl. Comm. 212, note; 3 Greenl. Cruise, Dig. 331; 1 Steph. Comm. 378. Abrogated by St. 3 & 4 Wm. IV. c. 106, § 6.

HAEREDUM APPELLATIONE VENIunt haeredes haeredum in infinitum. By the title of heirs, come the heirs of heirs to infinity. Co. Litt. 9.

HAERES. In Roman law. One who succeeds to the rights and occupies the place of a deceased person, being appointed by the will of the decedent. It is to be observed that the Roman *haeres* had not the slightest resemblance to the English "heir." He corresponded in character and duties almost exactly with the "executor" under the English law. The institution of the *haeres* was the essential characteristic of a testament. If this was not done, the instrument was called a *codicillus*. Mackeld. Civ. Law, §§ 632, 650.

HAERES ASTRARIUS (Law Lat.) In old English law. An heir in actual possession.

HAERES DE FACTO (Law Lat.) In old English law. Heir from fact; that is, from the deed or act of his ancestor, without or against right. Applied to an heir whose title originated in the wrongful act of his ancestor. An heir in fact, as distinguished from an heir *de jure*, or by law. Bracton, fol. 172.

HAERES EST ALTER IPSE, ET FILIUS est pars patris. An heir is another self, and a son is a part of the father.

HAERES EST AUT JURE PROPRIETAtis aut jure representationis. An heir is either by right of property or right of representation. 3 Coke, 40.

HAERES EST EADEM PERSONA CUM antecessore. The heir is the same person with the ancestor. Co. Litt. 22.

HAERES EST NOMEN COLLECTIVUM. "Heir" is a collective name or noun. 1 Vent. 215.

HAERES EST NOMEN JURIS; FILIUS est nomen naturae. "Heir" is a term of law; "son," one of nature.

HAERES EST PARS ANTECESSORIS. The heir is a part of the ancestor. Co. Litt. 22b; 3 Hill (N. Y.) 165, 167.

HAERES EX ASSE (Lat.) In civil law. An heir to the whole estate; a sole heir. Inst. 2. 23. 9.

HAERES EXTRANEUS (Lat.) In civil law. A strange or foreign heir; one who was not subject to the power of the testator, or person who made him heir. *Qui testatoris juri subjecti non sunt, extranei haeredes appellantur.* Inst. 2. 19. 3.

HAERES FACTUS (Lat.) In civil law. An heir made by will; a testamentary heir; the person created universal successor by will. Story, Confl. Laws, § 507; 3 Bl. Comm. 224. Otherwise called "*haeres ex testamento,*" and "*haeres institutus.*" Inst. 2. 9. 7; Id. 2. 14.

HAERES FIDEICOMMISSARIUS (Lat.) In the civil law. The person for whose benefit an estate was given to another, termed "*haeres fiduciarius*" (*q. v.*) by will. Inst. 2. 23. 6. 7. 9. Answering nearly to the *cestui que trust* of the English law.

HAERES FIDUCIARIUS. A fiduciary heir or heir in trust; a person constituted heir by will, in trust for the benefit of another, called the "*fideicommissarius.*" Inst. 2. 23. 1. 2. Corresponding nearly to the "trustee" of the English law. Crabb, Hist. Eng. Law, 397.

HAERES HAEREDIS MEI EST MEUS haeres. The heir of my heir is my heir. Wharton.

HAERES LEGITIMUS (Lat.) A lawful heir. Code, 6. 58.

HAERES LEGITIMUS EST QUEM NUPtiae demonstrant. He is the lawful heir whom the marriage demonstrates. Mirr. Just. 7; Fleta, lib. 6, c. 1; Dig. 2. 4. 5; Co. Litt. 7b; Broom, Leg. Max. (3d London Ed.) 457. As to the application of the principle when the marriage is subsequent to the birth of the child, see 2 Clark & F. 571; 6 Bing. (N. C.) 385; 5 Wheat. (U. S.) 226, 262, note.

HAERES MINOR UNO ET VIGINTI ANnis non respondebit, nisi in casu dotis. An heir minor, under twenty-one years of age, is not answerable, except in the matter of dower. F. Moore, 348.

HAERES NATUS (Lat.) In civil law. An heir born; one born heir, as distinguished from one made heir (*haeres factus, q. v.*); an heir at law, or by intestacy (*ab intestato*); the next of kin by blood, in cases of intestacy. Story, Confl. Laws, § 507; 3 Bl. Comm. 224.

HAERES NECESSARIUS (Lat.) In civil law. A necessary or compulsory heir. This name was given to the heir when, being a slave, he was named "heir" in the testament, because on the death of the testator, whether he would or not, he at once became free, and was compelled to assume the heirship. Inst. 2. 19. 1.

HAERES NON TENETUR IN ANGLIA ad debita antecessoris reddenda, nisi per antecessorem ad hoc fuerit obligatus, praeterquam debita regis tantum. In England, the heir is not bound to pay his ancestor's debts, unless he be bound to it by the ancestor, except debts due to the king. But now, by 3 & 4 Wm. IV. c. 104, he is liable. Co. Litt. 386.

HAERES RECTUS (Lat.) In old English law. A right heir. Fleta, lib. 6, c. 1, § 11.

HAERES SUUS (Lat.) In civil law. A man's own heir; a decedent's proper or natural heir. This name was given to the lineal descendants of the deceased. Inst. 3. 1. 4-5.

HAERETARE (Law Lat.) In old English law. To give a right of inheritance, or make the donation hereditary to the grantee and his heirs. Cowell.

HAERETICO COMBURENDO. See "De Haeretico Comburendo."

HAFNE COURTS (*hafne*, Danish, a haven, or port). Haven courts; courts anciently held in certain ports in England. Spelman.

HAGA. A house. Blount.
A military inclosure. Spelman.

HAGIA, or HAIA. A hedge or inclosure. Mon. Angl. tom. 2, p. 273.

HAIEBOTE. In old English law. A permission or liberty to take thorns, etc., to make or repair hedges. Blount.

HAILL. In Scotch law. Whole; the whole. "All and haill" are common words in conveyances. 1 Bell, App. Cas. 499.

HAILWORKFOLK. Holywork. Those who formerly held lands by the service of defending or repairing a church or monument. Rapalje & L. See "Halywercfolk."

HAIMHALDARE. In old Scotch law. To seek restitution of one's own goods and gear, and bring the same home again. Skene de Verb. Sign.

HAIMSUCKEN. In Scotch law. The crime of beating or assaulting a person in his own house. Bell, Dict.

HALF-BLOOD. A term denoting the degree of relationship which exists between those who have one parent only in common.
By the English common law, one related to an intestate of the half-blood only could

never inherit, upon the presumption that he is not of the blood of the original purchaser; but this rule has been greatly modified by 3 & 4 Wm. IV. c. 106.

In this country, the common-law principle on this subject may be considered as not in force, though in many states some distinction is still preserved between the whole and the half-blood. 4 Kent, Comm. 403, note; 2 Yerg. (Tenn.) 115; 1 McCord (S. C.) 456; 31 Pa. St. 289; Dane, Abr. Index; 2 Washb. Real Prop. 411. See "Descent."

HALF-BROTHER, or **HALF-SISTER.** Persons who have the same father, but different mothers; or the same mother, but different fathers.

HALF-DEFENSE. In common-law pleading. A name applied to the abbreviated form of words with which a plea is introduced.

HALF-ENDEAL. A moiety, or half of a thing. Rapalje & L.

HALF-KINEG. In Saxon law. Half-king (*semi-rex*). A title given to the aldermen of all England. Crabb, Hist. Eng. Law, 28; Spelman.

HALF-PROOF. In civil law. That which is insufficient as the foundation of a sentence or decree, although in itself entitled to some credit. Vicat, "Probatio."

HALF-SEAL. A seal used in the English chancery for the sealing of commissions to delegates appointed upon any appeal, either in ecclesiastical or marine causes.

HALF-TIMER. A child who, by the operation of the English factory and education acts, is employed for less than the full time in a factory or workshop, in order that he may attend some "recognized efficient school." See Factory and Workshop Act 1878, § 23; Elementary Education Act 1876, § 11. Wharton.

HALF-TONGUE. A jury, half of one tongue or nationality, and half of another. Vide "De Medietate Linguae," Jacob.

HALF-YEAR. In the computation of time, a half-year is not the same as six months, but "'Half a year' containeth one hundred and eighty-two dayes; for the oddie houres, in legall computation are rejected." Co. Litt. 135b; Rev. St. N. Y. pt. 1, c. 19, tit. 1, § 3. But in Woodf. (348), a half-year is stated to be 183 days.

"It is clear from a series of cases running back as far as the time of Henry VIII., that 'half a year's notice' means notice for half a year, and not for six months." 15 Q. B. D. 405.

HALI GEMOTE. Halle gemote.

HALIMASS. In English law. The feast of All Saints, on the 1st of November; one of the cross-quarters of the year was computed from Halimass to Candlemass. Wharton.

HALL. A public building used either for the meetings of corporations, courts, or employed to some public uses; as, the city hall, the town hall. Formerly this word denoted the chief mansion or habitation.

HALLAGE. In old English law. A fee or toll due for goods or merchandise vended in a hall. Jacob.

A toll due to the lord of a fair or market, for such commodities as were vended in the common hall of the place. Cowell; Blount.

HALLAZCO. In Spanish law. The finding and taking possession of something which previously had no owner, and which thus becomes the property of the first occupant. Las Partidas, 3. 5. 28; Id. 5. 48, 49; Id. 5. 20. 50.

HALLE GEMOTE. Hall assembly. A species of court baron.

HALLUCINATION. In medical jurisprudence. A species of mania by which an idea reproduced by the memory is associated and embodied by the imagination. This state of mind is sometimes called "delusion," or "waking dreams."

An attempt has been made to distinguish "hallucinations" from "illusions." The former are said to be dependent on the state of the intellectual organs, and the latter on that of those of sense. Ray, Med. Jur. § 99; 1 Beck, Med. Jur. 538, note. An instance is given of a temporary hallucination in the celebrated Ben Johnson, the poet. He told a friend of his that he had spent many a night in looking at his great toe, about which he had seen Turks and Tartars, Romans and Carthaginians, fight, in his imagination. 1 Colly. Lun. 34. If, instead of being temporary, this affection of his mind had been permanent, he would doubtless have been considered insane. See, on the subject of spectral illusions, Hibbert, Alderson, and Farrar's Essays; Scott on Demonology, etc.; 3 Bostock, Physiology, 91, 161; 1 Esquirol, Maladies Mentales, 159.

HALMOTE. See "Halle Gemote."

HALYMOTE, HOLIMOT, or **HALEGEmot** (from Saxon, *halg*, holy, and *gemot* or *mot*, a meeting). A holy or ecclesiastical court.

A court held in London before the lord mayor and sheriffs, for regulating the bakers.

It was anciently held on Sunday next before St. Thomas' day, and therefore called the *holymote*, or holy court. Cowell (Ed. 1727); Cunningham. See Spelman; 4 Inst. 321.

HALYWERCFOLK. Those who held by the service of guarding and repairing a church or sepulchre, and were excused from feudal services. Especially in the county of Durham, those who held by service of defending the corpse of St. Cuthbert. Jacob.

HAM. Properly a house; 4 Inst. 294; a vill; a piece of ground shaped like the ham of the leg; Spelman.

A piece of land; a home close, or little meadow; a narrow skirt, hem, or edge of meadow.

A collection of houses; a village or town. Hence the names of many places in England ending with *ham*, as Nottingham, Buckingham, etc. Spelman.

In Saxon and old English law. A house or dwelling; a home. *Æt ham;* at home. LL. Inea, c. 5. Spelman supposes the radical meaning to be an enclosure or circuit, something that goes around. Hence the *hem* of a garment.

HAMA. A piece of land. In old English law. A hook; an engine with which a house on fire is pulled down. Yelv. 60.

HAMALLARE. (Law Lat.) In old European law. To summon to court; to go to law with; to sue or implead. Spelman.

HAMALLUS. (Law Lat.) In old European law. One who was summoned to court. Spelman.

HAMBLING. In the forest law. The hoxing or hock sinewing of dogs; an old mode of laming or disabling dogs. Termes de la Ley.

HAMESUCKEN. In Scotch law. The crime of hamesucken consists in "the felonious seeking and invasion of a person in his dwelling house." 1 Hume, Hist. Eng. 312; Alis. Crim. Law, 199.

The mere breaking into a house, without personal violence, does not constitute the offense, nor does the violence without an entry with intent to commit an assault. It is the combination of both which completes the crime. It is necessary (1) that the invasion of the house should have proceeded from forethought malice; but it is sufficient if, from any illegal motive, the violence has been meditated, although it may not have proceeded from the desire of wreaking personal revenge, properly so called. (2) The place where the assault was committed must have been the proper dwelling house of the party injured, and not a place of business, visit, or occasional residence. (3) The offense may be committed equally in the day as in the night, and not only by effraction of the building by actual force, but by an entry obtained by fraud, with the intention of inflicting personal violence, followed by its perpetration. (4) But, unless the injury to the person be of a grievous and material character, it is not hamesucken, though the other requisites to the crime have occurred. When this is the case, it is immaterial whether the violence be done *lucri causa*, or from personal spite.

The punishment of hamesucken in aggravated cases of injury is death; in cases of inferior atrocity, an arbitrary punishment. Alis. Crim. Law, c. 6; Ersk. Inst. 4. 9. 23.

This term was formerly used in England instead of the now modern term "burglary." 4 Bl. Comm. 223.

But in Hale's Pleas of the Crown it is said: "The common genus of offenses that comes under the name of 'hamesucken' is that which is usually called 'house breaking'; which sometimes comes under the common appellation of 'burglary,' whether committed in the day or night to the intent to commit felony; so that house breaking of this kind is of two natures." 1 Hale, P. C. 547; 22 Pick. (Mass.) 4.

HAMFARE (Saxon, from *ham*, a house). In Saxon law. An assault made in a house; a breach of the peace in a private house. Spelman; Blount.

HAMLET. A small village; a part or member of a vill.

HAMMA. A close joining to a house; a croft; a little meadow. Cowell.

——**In Old English Law.** The right of security and privacy in a man's house. Du Cange. The breach of this privilege by a forcible entry of a house is breach of the peace. Anc. Inst. Eng.; Du Cange; Bracton, lib. 3, tr. 2, c. 2, § 3. The right to entertain jurisdiction of the offense. Will. Thorn. p. 2030; Spelman; Du Cange. Immunity from punishment for such offense. Id.; Fleta, lib. 1, c. 44, § 18. An insult offered in one's own house (*insultus factus in domo*). Brompton, p. 957; Du Cange. Variously spelled *hamsoca, hamsocua, hamsoken, haimsuken, hamesaken.*

HAMSOCA. (Law Lat.) In Saxon law. Hamsoken, or hamsocne. The privilege or liberty of a man's own house; a breach of such privilege by a violent entry. LL. Edmund. c. 6. See Hamma.

A fine for such entry; an immunity from such fine. Spelman.

HAMSOCNE *hamsokne, hamsockne, hamsoken, hamsockene, homesoken.* In Saxon law. The liberty, privilege, or immunity of a man's house. Spelman.

A breach of the immunity of a man's house by entering it against his will; the violent entry of a house. Spelman.

The offense of burglary. 4 Bl. Comm. 223.

A franchise or privilege granted to lords of manors, to hold pleas and take cognizance of the offence of entering a house against the will of the occupant, and of imposing and exacting fines therefor. Spelman; Blount.

A fine or amercement imposed for entering a house forcibly and without permission, and against the peace; an immunity or acquittance from such fine. See Hamma. Spelman.

HANAPER. A hamper or basket in which were kept the writs of the court of chancery relating to the business of a subject, and their returns. 5 & 6 Vict. c. 113; 10 Rich. II. c. 1. Equivalent to the Roman *fiscus*. Id. According to Spelman, the fees accruing on writs, etc., were there kept. Mon. Angl. tom. 1, p. 943; Du Cange.

HANAPER OFFICE. An office on the common-law side of the English court of chancery, in which the writs relating to the business of the subject, and the returns to them, were anciently kept. 3 Bl. Comm. 48.

So called, according to Blackstone, because the writs were kept in a basket or hamper, but Spelman says that the basket was for keeping the fees of the office, and not the writs.

This and the petty bag office (*q. v.*) were offices in which writs relating to the interests of the subject and the crown, respectively, were kept. For a discussion of the historic origin of the names, see 6 Johns. (N. Y.) 337, 363.

HAND. A measure of length, four inches long; used in ascertaining the height of horses.

HAND BOROW (from hand, and Saxon *borow*, a pledge.) Nine of a decennary or friborg were so called, being inferior to the tenth or head borow,—a decenna or friborga being ten freemen or frankpledges, who were mutually sureties for each other to the king for any damage. Du Cange, "Friborg," "Head Borow."

HAND GRITH (Saxon). Peace or protection given by the king with his own hand. Cowell.

HANDBILL. A written or printed notice displayed to inform those concerned of something to be done.

HANDHABEND. In Saxon law. One having a thing in his hand; that is, a thief found having the stolen goods in his possession,—*latro manifestus* of the civil law. See Laws Hen. I. c. 59; Laws Athelstane, § 6; Fleta, lib. 1, c. 38, § 1; Britt. p. 72; Du Cange.

Jurisdiction to try such thief. Id.

HANDSALE, or HANDSEL. Anciently, among all the northern nations, shaking of hands was held necessary to bind a bargain,—a custom still retained in verbal contracts. A sale thus made was called *handsale, venditio per mutuam manum complexionem*. In process of time, the same word was used to signify the price or earnest which was given immediately after the shaking of hands, or instead thereof. In some parts of the country it is usual to speak of hand money, as the part of the consideration paid or to be paid at the execution of a contract of sale. 2 Bl. Comm. 448; Heinec. Elem. Jur. Civ. lib. 2, § 335; Toullier, Dr. Civ. liv. 3, tit. 3, c. 2, note 33.

HANDWRITING. Anything written by a person. The manner in which a person writes, including the formation of the characters, the separation of the words, and other features distinguishing the written matter, as a mechanical result, from the writing of other persons.

HANGING IN CHAINS. In atrocious cases it was at one time usual, in England, for the court to direct a murderer, after execution, to be hanged upon a gibbet in chains near the place where the murder was committed, a practice quite contrary to the Mosaic law. Deut. xxi. 23. Abolished by 4 & 5 Wm. IV. c. 26. Wharton.

HANGMAN. An executioner. The name usually given to a man employed by the sheriff to put a man to death, according to law, in pursuance of a judgment of a competent court and lawful warrant.

HANGWITE (from Saxon *hangian*, to hang, and *wite*, fine). Fine, in Saxon law, for illegal hanging of a thief, or for allowing him to escape. Immunity from such fine. Du Cange.

HANIG. Customary labor.

HANSE. A commercial confederacy for the good ordering and protection of the commerce of its members; an imposition upon merchandise. Du Cange, "Hansa."

HANSE TOWNS. A number of towns in Europe which joined in a league for mutual protection of commerce as early as the twelfth century.

Amsterdam and Bremen were the first two that formed it, and they were joined by others in Germany, Holland, England, France, Italy, and Spain, till in 1200 they numbered seventy-two. They made war and peace to protect their commerce, and held countries in sovereignty, as a united commonwealth. They had a common treasury at Lubeck, and power to call an assembly as often as they chose. For purposes of jurisdiction, they were divided into four colleges or provinces. Great privileges were granted them by Louis VI. of France, and succeeding monarchs. One of their principal magazines was at London. Their power became so great as to excite the jealousy of surrounding nations, who forced the towns within their jurisdiction which belonged to the league to renounce it. Their number and power became thus gradually reduced, beginning from the middle of the fifteenth century; and at the present day only Bremen, Hamburg, Lubeck, and Frankfort-on-the-Main remain,—these being recognized by the act establishing the German Confederacy, in 1815, as free Hanseatic cities. Enc. Brit.

HANSE TOWNS, LAWS OF THE. The maritime ordinances of the Hanseatic towns, first published in German at Lubeck in 1597, and in May, 1614, revised and enlarged. The text of this digest, and a Latin translation, are published with a commentary by Kuricke; and a French translation has been given by Cleirac. See "Code."

HANSEATIC. Pertaining to the hanse towns.

HANSGRAVE. The chief of a company; the head man of a corporation.

HANTELOD. An arrest. Jacob.

HAP. To catch. Thus, "hap the rent," "hap the deed-poll," were formerly used. Tech. Dict.; Cowell.

HAPPEN. The word happen, in its strictest literal sense, signifies an unexpected event. It is also not uncommonly used as synonymous with "occur," "take place," "exist" and "happens to be." 51 N. J. Law, 192.

HARBOR (Saxon, *here berga*, station for an army). A place where ships may ride with safety; any navigable water protected by the surrounding country; a haven. It is public property. 1 Bouv. Inst. note 435.

Harbor is to be distinguished from "port," which has a reference to the delivery of cargo. See 7 Man. & G. 870; 9 Metc. (Mass.) 371-377; 2 Barn & Ald. 460. Thus, we have the "said harbor basin and docks of the port of Hull." 2 Barn. & Ald. 60. But they are generally used as synonymous. Webster.

——**In Torts.** To receive clandestinely or without lawful authority a person for the purpose of so concealing him that another having a right to the lawful custody of such person shall be deprived of the same; for example, the harboring of a wife or an apprentice in order to deprive the husband or the master of them; or, in a less technical sense, it is the reception of persons improperly. 10 N. H. 247; 5 Ill. 498.

The harboring of such persons will subject the harborer to an action for the injury; but, in order to put him completely in the wrong, a demand should be made for their restoration, for in cases where the harborer has not committed any other wrong than merely receiving the plaintiff's wife, child, or apprentice, he may be under no obligation to return them without a demand. 1 Chit. Prac. 564; Dane, Abr. Index; 2 N. C. Law Rep. 249; 5 How. (U. S.) 215, 227.

HARBOR AUTHORITY. In England, a harbor authority is a body of persons, corporate or unincorporate, being proprietors of, or intrusted with the duty of constructing, improving, managing, or lighting, any harbor St. 24 & 25 Vict. c. 47.

HARD LABOR. A phrase used in sentencing to confinement in institutions where labor is required of convicts. The word "hard" is surplusage. 29 Pa. St. 448.

HARDHEIDIS, or **HARDIES** (Scotch). In old Scotch law. Lions; coins formerly of the value of three half-pence. 1 Pitc. Crim. Tr. pt. 1, p. 64, note.

HARER, HARIER. (Law Fr.) To stir up; to provoke; to importune. Kelham.

HARNASCA (Law Lat.) In old European law. The defensive armor of a man; harness. Spelman.

HARO, or **HARROU** (Fr.) In Norman and early English law. An outcry, or hue and cry after felons and malefactors. Cowell.

HASP AND STAPLE. In old Scotch law. The form of entering an heir in a subject situated within a royal borough. It consisted of the heir's taking hold of the hasp and staple of the door (which was the symbol of possession), with other formalities. Bell, Dict.

HASPA.

——**In Old English Law.** The hasp of a door; by which the livery of seisin might anciently be made, where there was a house on the premises.

——**In Old Records.** The hasp or clasp of a book.

HASTA (Lat.)

——**In the Civil Law.** A spear; the badge of a sale by auction. *Hasta subjicere*, to put under the spear; to put up at auction. Calv. Lex.

——**In Feudal Law.** A spear; the symbol used in making investiture of a fief.

HAT MONEY. In maritime law. Primage; a small duty paid to the captain and mariners of a ship.

HAUR. In old English law. Hatred. LL. Gul. Conq. c. 16.

HAUSTUS (Lat. from *haurire*, to draw). In civil law. The right of drawing water, and the right of way to the place of drawing. Fleta, lib. 4, c. 27, § 9.

HAUT CHEMIN (Law Fr.) Highway. Y. B. M. 4 Hen. VI. 4.

HAUT ESTRET (Law Fr.) High street; highway. Y. B. P. 11 Hen. VI. 2.

HAVE (Lat.) A form of the salutory expression *Ave*, used in the titles of some of the constitutions of the Theodosian and Justinian Codes. See Code 7. 62. 9; Id. 9. 2. 11.

To possess corporally. "No one, at common law, was said to have or to be in possession of land, unless it were conveyed to him by the livery of seisin, which gave him the corporal investiture and bodily occupation thereof." Bl. Law Tr. 113.

HAVE AND HOLD. A common phrase in conveyancing, derived from the *habendum et tenendum* of the old common law. See "Habendum."

HAVEN. A place calculated for the reception of ships, and so situated, in regard to the surrounding land, that the vessel may ride at anchor in it in safety. Hale de Port. Mar. c. 2; 2 Chit. Com. Law, 2; 15 East, 304, 305. See "Port."

HAWKER. An itinerant or traveling trader, who carries small commodities about on his back or in a cart or wagon in order to sell them, and who actually sells them to purchasers, 132 Ill. 383, in contradistinction to a trader who has goods for sale, and sells them in a fixed place of business.

Superadded to this, though perhaps not essential, is generally understood one who not only carries goods for sale, but seeks for purchasers, either by outcry, which some lexicographers conceive as intimated by the derivation of the word, or by attracting notice and attention to them, as goods for sale, by an actual exhibition or exposure of them by placards or labels, or by a conventional signal, like the sound of a horn for the sale of fish. 12 Cush. (Mass.) 495.

HAY. In old English law. A hedge. Cowell.

A piece of ground enclosed with a hedge; an enclosure in forests and parks. Blount.

HAYBOTE (from *haye*, hedge, and *bote*, compensation). Hedgebote; one of the estovers allowed tenant for life or for years; namely, material to repair hedges or fences. 2 Sharswood, Bl. Comm. 35; 1 Washb. Real Prop. 99.

HAYWARD (from *haye*, Ledge, and *ward*, keeping). In old English law. An officer appointed in the lord's court to keep a common herd of cattle of a town. So called because he was to see that they did not break or injure the hedges of inclosed grounds. His duty was also to impound trespassing cattle, and to guard against pound breaches. Kitch. Cts. 46; Cowell.

HAZARDOUS CONTRACT. A contract in which the performance of that which is one of its objects depends on an uncertain event. Civ. Code La. art. 1769; 1 Bouv. Inst. note 707; 1 J. J. Marsh (Ky.) 596; 3 J. J. Marsh. (Ky.) 84. See "Maritime Loan."

HE, or HIS. The use of the masculine pronoun is not, as a rule of construction, conclusive that only males are embraced thereby. 71 Cal. 38.

HEAD COURTS. Certain tribunals in Scotland, abolished by 20 Geo. II. c. 50. Ersk. 1. 4. 5.

HEAD NOTE. The syllabus of a reported decision.

HEAD OF A FAMILY. Householder; one who provides for a family. 19 Wend. (N. Y.) 476. There must be the relation of father and child, or husband and wife. 3 Humph. (Tenn.) 216; 17 Ala. (N. S.) 486. *Per contra*, 20 Mo. 75. See "Family."

HEADBOROW, or HEADBOROUGH. In Saxon law. The head or principal man of a frank pledge decennary or tithing.

HEADLAND. In old English law. A narrow piece of unploughed land left at the end of a ploughed field for the turning of the plough. Called, also, "butt." Kennett, Par. Ant. 587; 2 Leon. 70, case 93; 1 Litt. 13.

HEAFODWEARD. A feudal service rendered by a thane, the nature of which is now unknown.

HEALGEMOTE. A court baron.

HEALSFANG (from German *hals*, neck, and *fangen*, to catch). A sort of pillory, by which the head of the culprit was caught between two boards, as feet are caught in a pair of stocks.

"The fine which every man would have to pay in commutation of this punishment, had it been in use," for it was very early disused, no mention of it occurring in the laws of the Saxon kings. Anc. Inst. Eng.; Spelman.

HEALTH LAWS. Laws designed to preserve the public health.

HEALTH OFFICER. An officer, usually municipal, charged with the enforcement of health laws.

HEAPED MEASURE. That kind of measure in which the commodities measured are *heaped* above the top of the vessel containing them.

HEARING. In legal contemplation, the word hearing, when used in connection with the trial of a lawsuit, includes not only the listening to the examination of the witnesses but the entire judicial examination of the issues, both of law and of fact, between the parties. 155 Ill. 232. Consequently the word embraces the listening to the arguments of counsel on both sides if oral arguments are made and the reading of the arguments if written or printed arguments are presented; and, also, the consideration of these arguments in respect to both points of law and of fact. 151 Ill. App. 505, 506.

——**In Chancery Practice.** The trial of a chancery suit.

The hearing is conducted as follows: When the cause is called on in court, the pleadings on each side are opened in a brief manner to the court by the junior counsel for the plaintiff; after which the plaintiff's leading counsel states the plaintiff's case and the points in issue, and submits to the court his arguments upon them. Then the depositions (if any) of the plaintiff's witnesses, and such parts of the defendant's answer as support the plaintiff's case, are read by the plaintiff's solicitor; after which the rest of the plaintiff's counsel address the court. Then the same course of proceedings is observed on the other side, excepting that no part of the defendant's answer can be read in his favor if it be replied to. The leading counsel for the plaintiff is then heard in reply; after which the court pronounces the decree. Newland, Prac. 153, 154; 14 Viner, Abr. 233; Comyn, Dig. "Chancery" (T. 1, 2, 3); Daniell, Ch. Prac.

——**In Criminal Law.** The examination of a prisoner charged with a crime or misdemeanor, and of the witnesses for the accused. See "Examination."

HEARSAY EVIDENCE. That kind of evidence which does not derive its value solely from the credit to be given to the witness himself, but rests also, in part, on the veracity and competency of some other person. 1 Phil. Ev. 185; 1 Greenl. Ev. § 99.

The term applies to written, as well as oral, matter. See "Evidence."

HEARTH MONEY. A tax, granted by 13 & 14 Car. II. c. 10, abolished 1 Wm. & Mary, st. 1, c. 10, of two shillings on every hearth or stove in England and Wales, except such as pay not to the church and poor. Jacob. Commonly called "chimney money." Id.

HEARTH SILVER. A sort of *modus* for tithes, viz., a prescription for cutting down and using for fuel the tithe of wood. 2 Burn, Ecc. Law, 304.

HEAT OF PASSION. In criminal law. *Furor brevis*, sudden passion caused by reasonable provocation. It is a characteristic of the crime of voluntary manslaughter, a killing without malice in heat of passion being manslaughter, not murder. 5 Mass. 295; 86 Va. 466.

It need not be so overpowering as for the time to shut out knowledge and destroy volition, but only sufficient to exclude deliberation and malice. 4 Dev. & B. (N. C.) 491; 10 Mich. 212.

HEBBERMAN. An unlawful fisher in the Thames below London bridge. So called because they generally fished at ebbing tide or water. 4 Hen. VII. c. 15; Jacob.

HEBBERTHEF. The privilege of having goods of thief and trial of him within such a liberty. Cart. S. Edmundi MS. 163; Cowell.

HEDAGIUM (Saxon, *heda, hitha*, port). A toll or custom paid at the hith, or wharf, for landing goods, etc., from which an exemption was granted by the king to some particular persons and societies. Cart. Abbatiae de Redinges; Cowell.

HEDGE. See "Gambling Contract."

HEDGE BOTE. Wood used for repairing hedges or fences. 2 Bl. Comm. 35; 16 Johns. (N. Y.) 15.

HEGIRA. The account of time used by the Turks and Arabians, who begin their computation of time from the day that Mahomet was compelled to escape from Mecca,—Friday, July 16, A. D. 622. Wharton.

HEIFER. A young cow which has not had a calf; a beast of this kind two years and a half old was held to be improperly described in the indictment as a cow. 2 East, P. C. 616; 1 Leach, C. C. 105.

HEINFAR. In Saxon law. The departure, flight, escape or loss of a servant. Spelman.

A fine paid for killing a man. Domesday. Spelman.

The right of taking cognizance of such an offence. Id.

HEIR.

——**At Common Law.** He who is born or begotten in lawful wedlock, and upon whom the law casts the estate in lands, tenements, or hereditaments immediately upon the death of his ancestor.

The term "heir" has a very different signification at common law from what it has in those states and countries which have adopted the civil law. In the latter, the term applies to all persons who are called to the succession, whether by the act of the party, or by operation of law. The person who is created universal successor by a will is called the "testamentary heir"; and the next of kin by blood is, in cases of intestacy, called the "heir at law," or "heir by intestacy." The executor of the common law is in many respects not unlike the testamentary heir of the civil law. Again, the administrator in many respects corresponds with the heir by intestacy. By the common law, executors—unless expressly authorized by the will—and administrators have no right except to the personal estate of the deceased; whereas the heir by the civil law is authorized to administer both the personal and real estate. 1 Brown, Civ. Law, 344; Story, Confl. Laws, § 508.

No person is heir of a living person. A person occupying a relation which may be that of heirship is, however, called "heir apparent" or "heir presumptive." 2 Bl. Comm. 208. A monster cannot be heir. Co. Litt. 7b. A bastard cannot be heir. 2 Kent, Comm. 208.

In the word "heirs" is comprehended heirs of heirs *in infinitum*. Co. Litt. 7b, 9a; Wood. Inst. 69.

According to many authorities, heir may be *nomen collectivum*, as well in a deed as in a will, and operate in both in the same manner as the word "heirs." 1 Rolle, Abr. 253; Ambl. 453; Godb. 155; T. Jones, 111; Cro. Eliz. 313; 1 Burrows, 38; 10 Viner, Abr. 233. But see 2 Prest. Est. 9, 10. In wills, in order to effectuate the intention of the testator, the word "heirs" is sometimes construed to mean the "next of kin" (1 Jac. & W. 388) and children (Ambl. 273). See, further, as to the force and import of this word, 2 Vent. 311; 1 P. Wms. 229; 2 P. Wms. 1, 369; 3 Brown, Parl. Cas. 60, 454; 2 W. Bl. 1010; 4 Ves. 26, 766, 794; 2 Atk. 89, 580; 5 East, 533; 5 Burrows, 2615; 11 Mod. 189.

——**In Civil Law.** He who succeeds to the rights and occupies the place of a deceased person. See "Haeres."

HEIR APPARENT. One who has an indefeasible right to the inheritance, provided he outlive the ancestor. 2 Bl. Comm. 208.

HEIR AT LAW. He who, after his ancestor's death intestate, has a right to all lands, tenements, and hereditaments which belonged to him or of which he was seised. The same as "heir general."

HEIR BENEFICIARY. One who accepts the succession under benefit of inventory (*q. v.*)

HEIR BY CUSTOM. In English law. One whose right of inheritance depends upon a particular and local custom, such as gavelkind, or borough English. Co. Litt. 140.

HEIR BY DEVISE. One to whom lands are devised by will; a devisee of lands. Answering to the *haeres factus* (*q. v.*) of the civil law.

HEIR, COLLATERAL. One who is not of the direct line of the deceased, but comes from a collateral line; as, a brother, sister, an uncle and aunt, a nephew, niece, or cousin, of the deceased.

HEIR, CONVENTIONAL. In civil law. One who takes a succession by virtue of a contract—for example, a marriage contract —which entitles the heir to the succession.

HEIR, GENERAL. Heir at common law.

HEIR INSTITUTE. One to whom the right of succession is ascertained by disposition or express deed of the deceased. 1 Forbes, Inst. pt. 3, p. 75.

HEIR, LEGAL. In civil law. A legal heir is one who is of the same blood as the deceased, and who takes the succession by force of law. This is different from a testamentary or conventional heir, who takes the succession in virtue of the disposition of man. See Civ. Code La. arts. 873, 875; Dict. de Jur. "Heritier Legitime." There are three classes of legal heirs, to-wit, the children and other lawful descendants, the fathers and mothers and other lawful ascendants, and the collateral kindred. Civ. Code La. art. 883.

HEIR MALE. In Scotch law. An heir institute, who, though not next in blood to the deceased, is his nearest male relation that can succeed to him. 1 Forbes, Inst. pt. 3, p. 76.

HEIR OF CONQUEST. In Scotch law. One who succeeds to the deceased in conquest, *i. e.*, lands or other heritable rights to which the deceased neither did nor could succeed as heir to his predecessor. Forbes, Inst. pt. 377.

One who succeeds to lands acquired by purchase. Bell, Dict.

HEIR OF LINE. In Scotch law. One who succeeds lineally by right of blood; one who succeeds to the deceased in his heritage; *i. e.*, lands and other heritable rights derived to him by succession as heir to his predecessor. 1 Forbes, Inst. pt. 3, p. 77.

An heir at law is so called because he succeeds according to certain lines of propinquity. Bell, Dict.

HEIR OF PROVISION. In Scotch law. One who succeeds as heir by virtue of a particular provision in a deed or instrument. Wharton.

HEIR OF TAILZIE. In Scotch law. He on whom an estate is settled that would not have fallen to him by legal succession. 1 Forbes, Inst. pt. 3, p. 75.

HEIR PRESUMPTIVE. One who, in the present circumstances, would be entitled to the inheritance, but whose rights may be defeated by the contingency of some nearer heir being born. 2 Bl. Comm. 208. In Louisiana, the presumptive heir is he who is the nearest relation of the deceased capable of inheriting. This quality is given to him before the decease of the person from whom he is to inherit, as well as after the opening of the succession, until he has accepted or renounced it. Civ. Code La. art. 876.

HEIR SPECIAL. In English law. The issue in tail, who claims *per formam doni*, by the form of the gift.

HEIR SUBSTITUTE, IN A BOND. In Scotch law. He to whom a bond is payable expressly in case of the creditor's decease, or after his death. 1 Forbes, Inst. pt. 3, p. 76.

HEIR, TESTAMENTARY. In civil law. One who is constituted heir by testament executed in the form prescribed by law. He is so called to distinguish him from the "legal heirs," who are called to the succession by the law; and from "conventional heirs," who are so constituted by a contract *inter vivos*. See "Haeres Factus"; "Devisee."

HEIRESS. A female heir to a person having an estate of inheritance. When there are more than one, they are called "coheiresses," or "coheirs."

HEIRLOOM. While the authorities generally credit the origin of the word to the

Saxon, some claim it was derived from "heier" or "heir," and "leoma," a limb or member; others are inclined to the opinion that it is a compound of the words "heir" and "loom," the latter being a frame to weave in; still others claim that it had its origin in the Saxon word "loma" or "geloma," which signifies utensils, or vessels generally.

The older authorities limited the application of the term to articles of household furniture or "dead chattels movable," but recent writers have given it a more general signification, until now it may be said that, in the common acceptance of the term, it includes all chattels which go to the heir, along with the inheritance, and necessary to its enjoyment, and which by custom, having belonged to a house, are seldom inventoried after the decease of the owner and do not go to the executor or administrator of the last proprietor.

Articles which are considered as annexed to the freehold and cannot be taken away without damaging or dismembering it; and utensils of the stronger or more ponderous kind which are not easily separated from the house are considered heirlooms.

Charters, deeds, and other evidences of the title of the land, together with the box or chest in which they are contained, the keys of a house, tables, presses, cupboards, bedsteads, and wainscots, fish in a pond, deer in a park and doves in a dovehouse have been held to have been heirlooms going with the inheritance. Co. Litt. 3a, 185b, 8a; 7 Coke, 17b; Cro. Eliz. 372; Brooke, Abr. "Charters," pl. 13; 2 Bl. Comm. 28, 427; 14 Viner, Abr. 291; 2 Kent's Com. 343; 1 Williams on Exec. 606, 607, 609; Bro. Abr. Descent, pl. 43; Termes de la Ley; Spelman.

HEIRS, BENEFICIARY. In civil law. Those who have accepted the succession under the benefit of an inventory regularly made. Civ. Code La. art. 879. If the heir apprehend that the succession will be burdened with debts beyond its value, he accepts with benefit of inventory, and in that case he is responsible only for the value of the succession.

HEIRS, FORCED. Those who cannot be disinherited. See "Forced heirs."

HEIRS, IRREGULAR. In Louisiana. Those who are neither testamentary nor legal, and who have been established by law to take the succession. See Civ. Code La. art. 874. When the deceased has left neither lawful descendants nor ascendants, nor collateral relations, the law calls to his inheritance either the surviving husband or wife, or his or her natural children, or the state. Id. art. 911. This is called an "irregular succession."

HEIRS OF THE BODY. Lineal descendants. 37 Ala. 178.

"The term 'heir of the body' is a well-established technical term, with which the words 'children' or 'issue' or 'lawful issue' are not synonymous." 115 Mass. 276.

Like all similar expressions, its technical sense is frequently subordinated to the evident intent.

Thus it has been construed as synonymous with "children." 147 Ind. 95; 8 Ga. 387.

HEIRS, UNCONDITIONAL. In Louisiana. Those who inherit without any reservation, or without making an inventory, whether their acceptance be express or tacit. Civ. Code La. art. 878.

HEIRSHIP MOVABLES. In Scotch law. The movables which go to the heir, and not to the executor, that the land may not go to the heir completely dismantled, such as the best of furniture, horses, cows, etc., but not fungibles. Hope, Minor Prac. p. 538; Ersk. Inst. 3. 8. 13-17 et seq; Bell, Dict.

HELL. The name given to a place under the exchequer chamber, where the king's debtors were confined. Rich. Dict.

HEMOLDBORH, or **HELMELBORCH.** A title to possession. The admission of this old Norse term into the laws of the Conqueror is difficult to be accounted for; it is not found in any Anglo Saxon law extant. Anc. Inst. Eng.

HENFARE. A fine for flight on account of murder. Domesday Book.

HENGHEN. In Saxon law. A prison, or house of correction. Anc. Inst. Eng.

HENGWYTE (Saxon). In old English law. An acquittance from a fine for hanging a thief. Fleta, lib. 1, c. 47, § 17.

HENRICUS VETUS. Henry the Old, or Elder. King Henry I. is so called in ancient English chronicles and charters, to distinguish him from the subsequent kings of that name. Spelman.

HERALD (from French, *herault*). An officer whose business it is to register genealogies, adjust ensigns armorial, regulate funerals and coronations, and, anciently, to carry messages between princes and proclaim war and peace.

HERALDS' COLLEGE. In 1450, the heralds in England were collected into a college by Richard II. The earl marshal of England was chief of the college, and under him were three kings-at-arms (styled Garter, Clarencieux, Norroy), six heralds-at-arms (styled of York, Lancaster, Chester, Windsor, Richmond, and Somerset), and four pursuivants-at-arms (styled Blue Mantle, Rouge Croix, Rouge Dragon, and Portcullis). This organization still continues. Enc. Brit.

HERBAGE. In English law. An easement which consists in the right to pasture cattle on another's ground.

HERBERY. An inn. *Herbergare,* to entertain at an inn. *Herbergatus,* entertained.

HERD WERCK, or **HEORDWERCH.** Customary uncertain services as herdsmen, shepherds, etc. A. D. 1166, Reg. Ecc. Christi Cant. MS.; Cowell.

HEREBANNUM. Calling out the army by proclamation; a fine paid by freemen for not attending the army; a tax for the support of the army. Du Cange.

HEREDAD. In Spanish law. A portion of land that is cultivated. Formerly it meant a farm, *hacienda de campo,* real estate.

HEREDAD YACENTE (Spanish, from Lat. "*haereditas jacens,*" *q. v.*). In Spanish law. An inheritance not yet entered upon or appropriated. White, New Recop. bk. 2, tit. 19, c. 2, § 8.

HEREDERO. In Spanish law. Heir; he who, by legal or testamentary disposition, succeeds to the property of a deceased person. "*Haeres censeatur cum defuncto una eademque persona.*" Las Partidas, 7. 9. 13.

HEREDITAMENTS. Things capable of being inherited. Co. Litt. 5b; 2 Bl. Comm. 17. By this term, such things are denoted as may be the subject matter of inheritance, but not the inheritance itself. It cannot, therefore, by its own intrinsic force, enlarge an estate *prima facie* a life estate into a fee. 2 Bos. & P. 251; 8 Term R. 503. See 4 Washb. Real Prop. Index.

Hereditaments are either (1) corporeal, such as are substantial and permanent, being comprehended under the general denomination "land"; (2) incorporeal, being heritable rights issuing out of things corporeal.

They include advowsons, tithes, dignities, pensions, franchises, offices, commons, ways, annuities, and rents. 2 Bl. Comm, 19 et seq.

Hereditaments are also divided into real, personal, and mixed. Challis, Real Prop. 39, 40.

HEREDITARY. That which is the subject of inheritance.

HEREGEAT. A heriot (*q. v.*). Spelman.

HEREGELD (Saxon). In old English law. A tribute or tax levied for the maintenance of an army. Spelman.

HERES. See "Haeres."

HERESCHIP (Scotch). In old Scotch law. Theft or robbery. 1 Pitc. Crim. Tr. pt. 2, pp. 26, 89.

HERESY. In English law. An offense against religion, consisting not in a total denial of Christianity, but of some of its essential doctrines, publicly and obstinately avowed. 4 Bl. Comm. 44, 45. An opinion on divine subjects devised by human reason, openly taught, and obstinately maintained. 1 Hale, P. C. 384. This offense is now subject only to ecclesiastical correction, and is no longer punishable by the secular law. 4 Steph. Comm. 233.

HERETOFORE. In the time before the present; down to this time; before this time. 167 Ill. 447; 117 N. Y. 150.

In times past; previous time; previously. 253 Ill. 539.

In times before the present; formerly. 167 Ill. 456.

HEREIN. Herein, as used in legal phraseology, is a locative adverb, and its meaning is to be determined by the context. It may refer to the section, the chapter, or the entire enactment in which it is used, and this rule is applicable to the construction of a document, as well as of a statute. 98 Cal. 608.

HERGE. In Saxon law. Persons who joined in a body of more than thirty-five to commit crimes.

HERIOT. In English law. A customary tribute of goods and chattels, payable to the lord of the fee on the decease of the owner of the land.

Heriot service is such as is due upon a special reservation in the grant or lease of lands, and therefore amounts to little more than a mere rent. Heriot custom arises upon no special reservation whatsoever, but depends merely upon immemorial usage and custom. See 2 Bl. Comm. 97, 422; Comyn, Dig. "Copyhold" (K. 18); Bac. Abr.; 2 Saund.; 1 Vern. 441.

HERISCHILD. A species of English military service.

HERISCHULDAE. A fine for disobedience to proclamation of warfare. Skene de Verb. Sign.

HERITABLE BOND. In Scotch law. A bond for a sum of money, to which is added, for further security of the creditor, a conveyance of land or heritage to be held by the creditor as pledge. 1 Ross, Lect. 76; 2 Ross, Lect. 324.

HERITABLE JURISDICTION. In Scotch law. Grants of criminal jurisdiction made to great families for the better execution of justice. Abolished by 20 Geo. II. c. 43. Bell, Dict.

HERITABLE RIGHTS. In Scotch law. Rights which go to the heir; generally, all rights in or connected with lands. Bell, Dict. "Heritable."

HERITAGE. In civil law. Every species of immovables which can be the subject of property, such as lands, houses, orchards, woods, marshes, ponds, etc., in whatever mode they may have been acquired, either by descent or purchase. 3 Toullier, Dr. Civ. 472. See Co. Litt. § 731.

HERITOR. In Scotch law. A land owner.

HERMANDAD. In Spanish law. A fraternity formed among different towns and villages to prevent the commission of crimes, and to prevent the abuses and vexations to which they were subjected by men in power.

To carry into effect the object of this association, each village and town elected two alcaldes,—one by the nobility, and the other by the community at large. These had under their order inferior officers, formed into companies, called *cuad villeros*. Their duty was to arrest delinquents and bring them before the alcaldes, when they were tried substantially in the ordinary form. This tribunal, established during the anarchy prevailing in feudal times, continued to maintain its organization in Spain for centuries; and various laws determining its jurisdiction and mode of proceeding were enacted by Ferdinand and Isabella and subsequent monarchs. Nov. Recop. tit. 35, bk. 12, § 7. The abuses introduced in the exercise of the functions of these tribunals caused their abolition, and the *santas hermandades* of Ciudad Rodrigo, Talavera, and Toledo, the last remnants of these anomalous jurisdictions, were abolished by the law of the 7th of May, 1835. Called, also, "Santa Hermandad."

HERMAPHRODITUS TAM MASCULO quam foeminae comparatur, secundum praevalentiam sexus incalescentis. An hermaphrodite is to be considered male or female according to the predominance of the exciting sex. Co. Litt. 8; Bracton, fol. 5.

HERMER. A great lord. Jacob.

HERRING SILVER. This was a composition in money for the custom of supplying herrings for the provision of a religious house. Rapalje & L.

HERUS. A master. *Servus facit ut herus det*, the servant does [the work] in order that the master may give [him the wages agreed on]. *Herus dat ut servus facit*, the master gives [or agrees to give, the wages] in consideration of, or with a view to, the servant's doing [the work]. 2 Bl. Comm. 445.

HESIA. An easement. Du Cange.

HEST CORN. In old records. Corn or grain given or devoted to religious persons or purposes. 2 Mon. Angl. 367b. Cowell.

HETERIA. In Roman law. A society or company.

HEUVELBORH. In Saxon law. A surety.

HEYBOTE, HAYBOTE. In English law. A liberty granted to a tenant, of cutting as much underwood and bushes on the premises, as was necessary for mending and maintaining the fences or hedges. Cowell. See Haybote.

HEYLODE. In feudal law. A duty of certain tenants to repair hedges (hays).

HIDAGE. In old English law. A tax levied, in emergencies, on every hide of land; the exemption from such tax. Bracton, lib. 2, c. 56. It was payable sometimes in money, sometimes in ships or military equipments; *e. g.*, in the year 994, when the Danes landed in England, every three hundred hides furnished a ship to king Ethelred, and every eight hides one pack and one saddle. Jacob.

HIDALGO, or HIJODALGO. In Spanish law. He who, by blood and lineage, belongs to a distinguished family, or is noble by descent. Las Partidas, 2. 12. 3. The origin of this word has given rise to much controversy; for which, see Escriche.

HIDALGUIA. In Spanish law. Nobility by descent or lineage. White, New Recop. bk. 1, tit. 5, c. 3, § 4. See "Hidalgo."

HIDE (from Saxon *hyden*, to cover; so, Lat. *tectum*, from *tegere*). In old English law. A building with a roof; a house.

As much land as might be ploughed with one plough. The amount was probably determined by usage of the locality. Some make it sixty, others eighty, others ninety-six, others one hundred or one hundred and twenty, acres. Co. Litt. 5; 1 Plowd. 167; Shep. Touch. 93; Du Cange.

As much land as was necessary to support a hide, or mansion house. Co. Litt. 69a; Spelman; Du Cange, "Hida"; 1 Introd. to Domesday Book, 145. At present, the quantity is one hundred acres. Anc. Inst. Eng.

HIDE AND GAIN. In English law. A term anciently applied to arable land. Co. Litt. 85b.

HIDE LANDS. In old English law. Lands appertaining to a hide, or mansion. See "Hide."

HIDEL. In old English law. A place of protection; a sanctuary. St. 1 Hen. VII. cc. 5, 6; Cowell.

HIDGILD. A sum of money paid by a villein or servant to save himself from a whipping. Fleta, lib. 1, c. 47, § 20.

HIGH BAILIFF. An officer attached to an English county court. His duties are to attend the court when sitting, to serve summonses, and to execute orders, warrants, writs, etc. St. 9 & 10 Vict. c. 95, § 33; Poll. Cir. Ct. Prac. 16. He also has similar duties under the bankruptcy jurisdiction of the county courts. Rapalje & L.

HIGH COMMISSION COURT. In English law. An ecclesiastical court of very extensive jurisdiction, for the vindication of the peace and dignity of the church, by reforming, ordering, and correcting the ecclesiastical state and persons, and all manner of errors, heresies, schisms, abuses, offenses, contempts, and enormities.

It was erected by St. 1 Eliz. c. 1, and abolished by 16 Car. II. c. 11.

HIGH CONSTABLE. An officer appointed in some cities with powers generally limited to matters of police, and not more extensive, in these respects, than those of constables. See "Constable."

HIGH CONSTABLE OF ENGLAND, Lord. His office has been disused (except only upon great and solemn occasions, as the coronation, or the like) since the attainder of Stafford, Duke of Buckingham, in the reign of Henry VII. Rapalje & L.

The origin and history of the office, duties of the incumbent and final disuse may be found in 1 Bl. Comm. 355, 356; Bacon's works iv. 309; Bract. fol. 337; Britt. fol. 2; Willcock's Off. Constable, 76, 78, 80; 1 Wooddes Lect. 152, 153 and Spelman. See also Constable.

HIGH COURT OF ADMIRALTY. See "Admiralty."

HIGH COURT OF DELEGATES. In English law. A tribunal which formerly exercised appellate jurisdiction over cases brought from the ecclesiastical and admiralty courts.

It was a court of great dignity, erected by St. 25 Hen. VIII. c. 19. It was abolished, and its jurisdiction transferred to the judicial committee of the privy council. See 2 & 3 Wm. IV. c. 92; 3 & 4 Wm. IV. c. 41; 6 & 7 Vict. c. 38; 3 Sharswood, Bl. Comm. 66.

HIGH COURT OF ERRORS AND APpeals. In American law. An appellate tribunal, and the court of last resort, in the state of Mississippi.

HIGH COURT OF JUSTICE. That branch of the English supreme court of judicature (*q. v.*) which exercises (1) the original jurisdiction formerly exercised by the court of chancery, the courts of queen's bench, common pleas, and exchequer, the courts of probate, divorce, and admiralty, the court of common pleas at Lancaster, the court of pleas at Durham, and the courts of the judges or commissioners of assize; and (2) the appellate jurisdiction of such of those courts as heard appeals from inferior courts. Judicature Act 1873, § 16; Rapalje & L.

HIGH COURT OF JUSTICIARY. See "Court of Justiciary."

HIGH COURT OF PARLIAMENT. In English law. The English parliament, as composed of the house of peers and house of commons.

The house of lords sitting in its judicial capacity.

This term is applied to parliament by most of the law writers. Thus, parliament is said by Blackstone to be the supreme court of the kingdom, not only for the making, but also for the execution, of the laws. 4 Bl. Comm. 259. Lord Coke and Lord Hale also apply the term "court" to the whole parliament. And see Finch, Law, 233; Fleta, lib. 2, c. 2. But, from the fact that in judicial proceedings, generally, the house of commons takes no part, but only in the trial of impeachments, and then only as prosecutor, and from the fact that the house of commons disclaimed possession of judicial powers at the deposition of Richard II., and the twelve judges made a similar decision in 1 Hen. VII., the propriety of this use of the term has been questioned. Bl. Comm. (Warren, Abr.) 215. The propriety of its application would seem to be derived from the claim of parliament to be considered as the successor of the *aula regis*, which was a judicial as well as a legislative body, and, if the succession is established, would be applicable, although the judicial power may have been granted to the various courts. See "Court."

The house of lords only acts in a judicial capacity in civil cases and in most criminal cases. See "House of Lords"; "Impeachment."

HIGH CRIMES AND MISDEMEANORS. A term used in Const. U. S. art. 2, § 4, and elsewhere, as a ground of impeachment. Its technical sense is parliamentary, and it includes many acts not constituting crimes. Cooley, Const. Lim. 159.

"High crimes and misdemeanors are such immoral and unlawful acts as are nearly allied and equal in guilt to felony, yet, owing to some technical circumstance, do not fall within the definition of 'felony.'" 1 Russ. Crimes, 61. And see 39 La. Ann. 186.

HIGH JUSTICE. In feudal law. The jurisdiction or right of trying crimes of every kind, even the highest. This was a privilege claimed and exercised by the great lords or barons of the middle ages. 1 Robertson, Hist. Charles V., Append. note 23.

HIGH JUSTICIER. In old French and Canadian law. A feudal lord who exercised the right called "high justice." Guyot, Inst. Feud. c. 26.

HIGH SEAS. The uninclosed waters of the ocean, and also those waters on the seacoast which are without the boundaries of low-water mark. 1 Gall. (U. S.) 624; 1 Mason (U. S.) 360; 5 Mason (U. S.) 290; 1 Bl. Comm. 110; 2 Hagg. Adm. 398; Dunl. Adm. Prac. 32, 33.

Waters within the ebb and flow of the sea (Gilp. 524), though in a harbor (Fed.

Cas. No. 14,509), but not in a landlocked haven (4 Mason [U. S.] 307; 5 Mason [U. S.] 290; 3 Blatchf. [U. S.] 435).

The open waters of the great lakes are "high seas" (150 U. S. 249), but the waters of an inland river flowing into the great lakes are not (7 Mich. 161).

HIGH STEWARD, COURT OF THE lord. In English law. A tribunal instituted for the trial of peers indicted for treason or felony, or for misprision of either, but not for any other offense. The office is very ancient, and was formerly hereditary, or held for life, or *dum bene se gesserit;* but it has been for many centuries granted *pro hac vice* only, and always to a lord of parliament. Wharton.

HIGH TREASON. In English law. The compassing of the king's death; the aiding and comforting of his enemies; the forging or counterfeiting of his coin; or the killing of the chancellor or either of the king's justices. 4 Bl. Comm. 73. See "Treason."

HIGH-WATER MARK. That part of the shore of the sea to which the waves ordinarily reach when the tide is at its highest. 6 Mass. 435; 1 Pick. (Mass.) 180; 1 Halst. (N. J.) 1; 1 Russ. Crimes, 107; 2 East, P. C. 803. See "Seashore"; "Tide."

——**Of Tidal Waters.** The ordinary high-water point. 60 Pa. St. 339. The point reached by the medium high tide between the spring and neap tides. 44 N. J. Eq. 398.

——**Of Nontidal Waters.** The highest point reached by the waters in the normal state, unaffected by freshets. 88 Me. 155. And see 56 Minn. 513.

HIGHER AND LOWER SCALE. In the practice of the English supreme court of judicature, there are two scales regulating the fees of the court and the fees which solicitors are entitled to charge. The lower scale applies (unless the court otherwise orders) to the following cases: All causes and matters assigned by the judicature acts to the queen's bench, or the probate, divorce, and admiralty divisions; all actions of debt, contract, or tort; and in almost all causes and matters assigned by the acts to the chancery division in which the amount in litigation is under £1,000. The higher scale applies in all other causes and matters, and also in actions falling under one of the above classes, but in which the principal relief sought to be obtained is an injunction. 5 Q. B. Div. 167, 431; 6 Q. B. Div. 190; Daniell, Ch. Prac. 1320.

HIGHNESS. A title of honor given to princes. The kings of England, before the time of James I., were not usually saluted with the title of "Majesty," but with that of "Highness." The children of crowned heads generally receive the style of "Highness." Wharton.

HIGHWAY. A passage, road, or street which every citizen has a right to use. 1 Bouv. Inst. note 442; 3 Kent, Comm. 432; 3 Yeates (Pa.) 421; Angell & D. Highways, § 2; 16 Mass. 33.

In a more abstract sense, a public easement or right of way.

The term "highway" is the generic name for all kinds of public ways, whether they be carriage ways, bridle ways, foot ways, bridges, turnpike roads, railroads, canals, ferries or navigable rivers. 6 Mod. 255; Angell & D. Highways, c. 1; 3 Kent, Comm. 432.

HIGHWAY ROBBERY. Robbery committed on a public highway was, under St. 23 Hen. VIII. c. 1, more severely punished than robbery committed elsewhere. This distinction was abolished by St. 3 & 4 Wm. & Mary, c. 9.

HIGHWAYMAN. A robber on the highway.

HIGLER. In English law. A person who carries from door to door, and sells by retail, small articles of provisions, and the like.

HIGUELA. In Spanish law. The written acknowledgment given by each of the heirs of a deceased person, showing the effects he has received from the succession.

HIKENILD STREET. A name sometimes given to Ikenild street (*q. v.*).

HILARY TERM. In English law. A term of court, beginning on the 11th and ending on the 31st day of January in each year.

HINDER AND DELAY. To hinder and delay is to do something which is an attempt to defraud, rather than a successful fraud; to put some obstacle in the path, or interpose some time, unjustifiably, before the creditor can realize what is owed out of his debtor's property. 10 Jones & S. (N. Y.) 63.

HINDU LAW. The system of native law prevailing among the Gentoos, and administered by the government of British India.

In all the arrangements for the administration of justice in India, made by the British government and the East India Company, the principle of reserving to the native inhabitants the continuance of their own laws and usages within certain limits has been uniformly recognized. The laws of the Hindus and Mohammedans have thus been brought into notice in England, and are occasionally referred to by writers on English and American law. The native works upon these subjects are very numerous. The chief English republications of the Hindu law are, Colebrooke's Digest of Hindu Law, London, 1801; Sir Wm. Jones' Institutes of Hindu Law, London, 1797. For a fuller account of the Hindu law, and of the original Digests and Commentaries, see Morley's Law of India, London, 1858, and

Macnaghten's Principles of Hindu and Mohammedan Law, London, 1860. The principal English republications of the Mohammedan law are Hamilton's Hedaya, London, 1791; Baillie's Digest, Calcutta, 1805; Precis de Jurisprudence Mussulmane Selon le Rite Malikite, Paris, 1848; and the treatises on succession and inheritance translated by Sir William Jones. An approved outline of both systems is Macnaghten's Principles of Hindu and Mohammedan Law; also contained in the "Principles and Precedents" of the same law previously published by the same author.

HINEFARE. The departure of a husbandry servant (*hine*) from his master.

HIPOTECA. In Spanish law. A mortgage of real property. Johnson, Civ. Law Spain, 156 [149]; White, New Recop. bk. 2, tit. 7.

HIRE. A bailment in which compensation is to be given for the use of a thing, or for labor and services about it. 2 Kent, Comm. 456; Story, Bailm. § 359. The divisions of this species of contract are denoted by Latin names.

Locatio operis faciendi is the hire of labor and work to be done, or care and attention to be bestowed, on the goods let by the hirer, for a compensation.

Locatio operis mercium vehendarum is the hire of the carriage of goods from one place to another, for a compensation. Jones, Bailm. 85, 86, 90, 103, 118; 2 Kent, Comm. 456; Civ. Code La. art. 1709-1711.

Locatio rei or *locatio conductio rei* is the bailment of a thing to be used by the hirer for a compensation to be paid by him.

This contract arises from the principles of natural law. It is voluntary, and founded in consent; it involves mutual and reciprocal obligations; and it is for mutual benefit. In some respects it bears a strong resemblance to the contract of sale; the principal difference between them being that in cases of sale the owner parts with the whole proprietary interest in the thing, and in cases of hire the owner parts with it only for a temporary use and purpose. In a sale, the thing itself is the object of the contract; in hiring, the use of the thing is its object. Vinnius. lib. 3, tit. 25, in pr.; Poth. de Contr. du Louage, notes 2-4; Jones, Bailm. 86; Story, Bailm. § 371; 2 Kent, Comm. 456.

HIRER. He who hires. See "Bailment."

HLAFORD (Saxon). A lord. *Hlafordsocna*, a lord's protection. *Hlafordswice*, the crime of betraying one's lord.

HLAFORDSWICE (Saxon, *hlaford*, lord, literally bread given, and *wice*). In old English law. Betraying one's lord; treason. Crabb, Hist. Eng. Law, 59, 301.

HLOTHBOTE (Saxon, *hloth*, company, and *bote*, compensation). In old English law. Fine for presence at an illegal assembly. Du Cange.

HLOTHE. An unlawful assembly of from eight to thirty-five persons. Cowell. See "Herge."

HOC (Lat.) This.

HOC PARATUS EST VERIFICARE. See "Et hoc, etc."

HOC SERVABITUR QUOD INITIO CONvenit. This shall be preserved which is useful in the beginning. Dig. 50. 17. 23; Bracton, 73b.

HOCCUS SALTIS. A hoke, hole, or lesser pit of salt. Cowell.

HOCK-TUESDAY MONEY. This was a duty given to the landlord that his tenants and bondmen might solemnize the day on which the English conquered the Danes, being the second Tuesday after Easter week. Cowell.

HODGE-PODGE ACT. A name given to a legislative act which embraces many subjects. Such acts, besides being evident proofs of the ignorance of the makers of them, or of their want of good faith, are calculated to create a confusion which is highly prejudicial to the interests of justice. Instances of this wretched legislation are everywhere to be found. See Barr. Obs. St. 449.

HOG HOWARDS. Township officers at one time elected in New York, whose duty was to catch hogs running at large, and put rings in their noses. 17 Wend. (N. Y.) 522.

HOGHENHYNE (from Saxon *hogh*, house, and *hine*, servant). A domestic servant. Among the Saxons, a stranger guest was, the first night of his stay, called *uncuth*, or unknown; the second, *gust*, guest; the third, *hoghenhyne;* and the entertainer was responsible for his acts as for those of his own servant. Bracton, 124b; Du Cange, "Agenhine"; Spelman, "Homehine."

HOGSHEAD. A liquid measure, containing half a pipe; the fourth part of a tun, or sixty-three gallons.

HOLD PLEAS. To hear or try causes. 3 Sharswood, Bl. Comm. 35, 298.

HOLDER. The holder of a bill of exchange is the person who is legally in the possession of it, either by indorsement or delivery, or both, and entitled to receive payment either from the drawee or acceptor, and is considered as an assignee. 4 Dall. (Pa.) 53.

HOLDING.

——**In English Law.** A piece of land held under a lease or similar tenancy for agricultural, pastoral, or similar purposes.

——**In Scotch Law.** The tenure or nature of the right given by the superior to the vassal. Bell, Dict.

HOLDING THE MARKET. See "Gambling Contract."

HOLIDAY. A day of cessation from labor; a day when public business is suspended; a nonjudicial day.

Primarily the term meant a "holy day," or religious festival. In modern usage it indicates a secular day on which, by statute, public business is suspended. It does not appropriately include Sunday. 51 N. J. Law, 255.

HOLOGRAFO. In Spanish law. Olographi; a term applicable to the paper, document, disposition, and more particularly to the last will of a person, which, in order to be valid, must be wholly written, signed, and dated by the testator. *"Holographum, apud testum, appellatur testamentum, quod totum manu testatoris scriptum est et subsignatum."*

HOLOGRAPH. What is written with one's own hand. See "Olograph."

HOLY ALLIANCE. A league entered into by Alexander I., the Czar of Russia, Francis I., emperor of Austria, and William III., King of Prussia.

The alliance was entered into at Paris, 26 Sept. 1815, twenty days before Napoleon landed at St. Helena. All creeds were to be united, Greek, Roman Catholic and Protestant, and all other powers were invited to join, except the Sultan, who was excluded because he was not Christian enough, and the pope, who was so conspicuously Christian that if admitted he would have to take the first place. Those included in it were subsequently joined by all the sovereigns of Europe, except the King of England.

The professed objects of the alliance were the union of Christian nations in a Christian brotherhood, and the application of Christian principles to the dealings of sovereign with sovereign and the relations of sovereign to subject.

These were no doubt to some extent the real objects, for motives are seldom wholly covert, even in the mind of a king.

But other objects there undoubtedly were in the background of consciousness which moved the contracting parties far more powerfully. These were, it cannot be doubted, the strengthening of defenses against the dreaded shape then just banished from the world they hoped to dominate, against him and his, a special clause barring the way to any European throne against any of the Bonaparte family in the erecting of barriers against the notions in regard to the rights of man and the sphere of government which since the first French revolution had been gradually making their way throughout Europe; the strengthening thus of their several dynasties against whatever might come against them.

The change that was then coming over the world had however gone too far. The alliance really fell before the new forces which it was created to control, enforced no doubt by the obvious fact that the conduct of princes was no more Christian than it was before, though to the casual eye, the causes of its dissolution were the French revolution of 1830, the European upheaval of 1848, and the re-establishment of the Napoleonic dynasty in 1850.

HOLY ORDERS. In ecclesiastical law. The orders or dignities of the church. Those within holy orders are archbishops, bishops, priests and deacons. The form of ordination must be according to the form in the book of Common Prayer. Besides these orders, the church of Rome had five others, viz., subdeacons, acolyths, exorcists, readers, and ostiaries. 2 Burn, Ecc. Law, 39, 40.

HOMAGE (anciently *hominium*, from *homo*). A mere acknowledgment of tenure made by a tenant by knight service upon investiture, in the following form:

The tenant in fee or fee tail that holds by homage shall kneel upon both his knees, ungirded, and the lord shall sit and hold both the hands of his tenant between his hands, and the tenant shall say, "I become your man (*homo*) from this day forward of life and member, of earthly honor, and to you shall be faithful and true, and shall bear to you faith for the lands that I claim to hold of you, saving that faith that I owe to our lord the king"; and then the lord so sitting shall kiss him. The kiss is indispensable, except sometimes in the case of a woman. Du Cange. After this the oath of fealty is taken; but this may be taken by the steward, homage only by the lord. Termes de la Ley. This species of homage was called *homagium planum* or *simplex* (1 Sharswood, Bl. Comm. 367), to distinguish it from *homagium ligium*, or liege homage, which included fealty and the services incident. Du Cange; Spelman.

Liege homage was that homage in which allegiance was sworn without any reservation, and was therefore due only to the sovereign; and, as it came in time to be exacted without any actual holding from him, it sunk into the oath of allegiance. Termes de la Ley.

The obligation of homage is mutual, binding the lord to protection of the vassal, as well as the vassal to fidelity. Fleta, lib. 3, c. 16.

HOMAGE ANCESTRAL. Homage was so called where time out of mind a man and his ancestors had held by homage; and in this case the lord who had received the homage was bound to acquit the tenant of all services to superior lords, and, if vouched, to warrant his title. If the tenant by homage ancestral aliened in fee, his alienee hold by homage, but not by homage ancestral. Termes de la Ley; 2 Sharswood, Bl. Comm. 300.

HOMAGE JURY. The jury of a lord's court, or court baron. So called because generally composed of those who owed homage to the lord, or the *pares curiae*. Kitch. Cts.; 2 Sharswood, Bl. Comm. 54, 366.

HOMAGER. One that is bound to do homage to another. Jacob.

HOMAGIUM. Homage. (*q. v.*)

HOMAGIUM LIGIUM. Liege homage; that kind of homage which was due to the sovereign alone as supreme lord, and which was done without any saving or exception of the rights of other lords. Spelman. So called from *ligando* (binding) because it could not be renounced like other kinds of homage.

HOMAGIUM, NON PER PROCURATORES nec per literas fieri potuit, sed in propria persona tam domini quam tenentis capi debet et fieri. Homage cannot be done by proxy, nor by letters, but must be paid and received in the proper person, as well of the lord as the tenant. Co. Litt. 68.

HOMAGIUM PLANUM. In feudal law. Plain homage; a species of homage which bound him who did it to nothing more than fidelity, without any obligation either of military service or attendance in the courts of his superior. 1 Robertson, Hist. Charles V., Append. note 8.

HOMAGIUM REDDERE. To renounce homage; to give it up or dissolve it. Bracton, fol. 81b.

HOMAGIUM SIMPLEX. In feudal law. Simple homage; that kind of homage which was merely an acknowledgment of tenure, with a saving of the rights of other lords. Harg. Co. Litt. note 18, lib. 2.

HOMBRE BUENO. In Spanish law. The ordinary judge of a district.

Hence, when the law declares that a contract, or some other act, is to be conformable to the will of the *hombre bueno*, it means that it is to be decided by the ordinary judge. Las Partidas, 7. 34. 31.

In matters of conciliation, it applies to the two persons, one chosen by each party, to assist the constitutional alcalde in forming his judgment of reconciliation. Article 1, c. 3, Decree of October 9, 1812.

Arbitrators chosen by litigants to determine their differences.

Persons competent to give testimony in a cause.

HOME. A place of abode from which one has no present intention of removing. 43 Me. 418; 124 Mass. 147.

HOME NE SERA PUNY PUR SUER DES briefes en court le roy, soit il a droit ou a tort. A man shall not be punished for suing out writs in the king's court, whether he be right or wrong. 2 Inst. 228.

HOME OFFICE. The department of state through which the English sovereign administers most of the internal affairs of the kingdom, especially the police, and communicates with the judicial functionaries.

HOME PORT. The port where the owner of a ship resides.

HOMESOKEN, or HOMSOKEN. See "Hamesucken."

HOMESTALL. The mansion house.

HOMESTEAD. The house and land constituting a family residence. 6 N. D. 482.

"'Stethe or sted,' says Lord Coke, 'betokeneth properly a bank of a river, and many times a place.' Co. Litt. 4, 6. The homestead, according to that definition, means the home place, the place where the house is, and such is its legal acceptation at the present day. It is the home, the house, and the adjoining land, where the head of the family dwells; the home farm." 36 N. H. 158.

The principal importance of the term is in respect to the exemption of the homestead from execution, and the nature and extent of such exemption is regulated in each state by the statutes allowing the same.

As a general rule, to constitute a homestead within the exemption laws the property must be actually occupied. (11 Allen [Mass.] 37; 51 Mich. 541; 23 Minn. 435) as a residence (27 Ill. 393) by the head of a family (10 Allen [Mass.] 425; 159 Ill. 148) who has a present possessory interest in the property (170 Ill. 115; 74 Iowa, 683), with the intention of making such property a homestead (6 Cal. 234; 53 Vt. 554).

HOMICIDE. Homicide is any killing of a human being. To constitute homicide, (1) the killing must be of a living human being; (2) the death must have been caused by the act or omission of the accused; (3) death must happen within a year and a day after the injury.

Homicide is either (1) justifiable; (2) excusable; or (3) felonious. Felonious homicide is either murder or manslaughter. 1 Clark & Marshall, Crimes, 466. See "Murder"; "Manslaughter."

HOMICIDIUM (Lat.) Homicide.

HOMINE CAPTO IN WITHERNAM. See "De Homine Capto in Withernam."

HOMINE ELIGENDO (Lat.) In English law. A writ directed to a corporation, requiring the members to make choice of a new man, to keep the one part of a seal appointed for statutes merchant. Tech. Dict.

HOMINE REPLEGIANDO. See "De Homine Replegiando."

HOMINES (Lat.) In feudal law. Men; feudatory tenants who claimed a privilege of having their causes, etc., tried only in their lord's court. Par. Ant. 15.

HOMINES LIGII. In feudal law. Liege men; feudal tenants or vassals, especially those who held immediately of the sovereign. 1 Bl. Comm. 367.

HOMINUM CAUSA JUS CONSTITUTUM est. Law is established for the benefit of man.

HOMIPLAGIUM. In old English law. The maiming of a man. Blount.

HOMMES DE FIEF (Fr.) In feudal law. Men of the fief; feudal tenants; the peers in the lords' courts. Montesq. Esp. des Lois, liv. 28, c. 27.

HOMMES FEODAUX (Fr.) In feudal law. Feudal tenants; the same with *hommes de fief* (*q. v.*). Montesq. Esp. des Lois, liv. 28, c. 36.

HOMO (Lat.) A human being, whether male or female. 2 Inst. 45.

——**In Feudal Law.** A vassal; one who, having received a feud, is bound to do homage and military service for his land. Variously called *vassalus, vassus, miles, cliens feudalis, tenens per servitium militare,* sometimes *baro,* and most frequently *leudes.* Spelman. *Homo* is sometimes also used for a tenant by socage, and sometimes for any dependent. A *homo* claimed the privilege of having his cause and person tried only in the court of his lord. Kennett, Par. Ant. p. 152.

HOMO CHARTULARIUS. One manumitted from slavery by charter.

HOMO COMMENDATUS. In feudal law. One who surrendered himself into the power of another for the sake of protection or support. L. Ripuar, tit. 72, § 5.

HOMO ECCLESIASTICUS. A church vassal; one who was bound to serve a church, especially to do service of an agricultural character. Spelman.

HOMO EXERCITALIS. A man of the army (*exercitus*); a soldier.

HOMO FEODALIS. A vassal or tenant; one who held a fee (*feodum*), or part of a fee. Spelman.

HOMO FISCALIS (or **FISCALINUS**). A servant or vassal belonging to the treasury or *fiscus.*

HOMO FRANCUS, HOMO INGENUUS, or homo liber. In old English law. A free man.

HOMO LIGIUS. A liege man; a subject; a king's vassal; the vassal of a subject. Spelman.

HOMO NOVUS. In feudal law. A new tenant or vassal; one who was invested with a new fee. Spelman.

HOMO PERTINENS. In feudal law. A feudal bondman or vassal; one who belonged to the soil (*qui glebae adscribitur*).

HOMO POTEST ESSE HABILIS ET INhabilis diversis temporibus. A man may be capable and incapable at divers times. 5 Coke, 98.

HOMO REGIUS. A king's vassal. L. Ripuar, tit. 11, § 3.

HOMO ROMANUS. A Roman. An appellation given to the old inhabitants of Gaul and other Roman provinces, and retained in the laws of the barbarous nations. L. Salis. tit. 34, § 3; Spelman.

HOMO TRIUM LITTERARUM. A man of three letters; *i. e.,* "f," "u," "r,"—a thief. Wharton.

HOMO VOCABULUM EST NATURAE; persona juris civilis. "Man" (*homo*) is a term of nature; "person" (*persona*) of the civil law. Calv. Lex.

HOMOLOGACION. In Spanish law. The tacit consent and approval, inferred by law from the omission of the parties, for the space of ten days, to complain of the sentences of arbitrators, appointment of syndics, or assignees, of insolvents, settlements of successions, etc. Also, the approval given by the judge of certain acts and agreements for the purpose of rendering them more binding and executory. Escriche, Dic. Raz.

HOMOLOGARE. In civil law. To confirm or approve; to consent or assent; to confess. Calv. Lex. Sometimes corruptly written "emologare."

HOMOLOGATE. In modern civil law. To approve; to confirm; as, a court homologates a proceeding. See "Homologation." Literally, to use the same words with another; to say the like. 9 Mart. (La.) 324. To assent to what another says or writes.

HOMOLOGATION.

——**In Civil Law.** Approbation; confirmation by a court of justice; a judgment which orders the execution of some act; as, the approbation of an award, and ordering execution on the same. Merlin, Repert.; Civ. Code La.; Dig. 4. 8; 7 Toullier, Dr. Civ. note 224. To homologate is to say the like, *similiter dicere.* 9 Mart. (La.) 324.

——**In Scotch Law.** An act by which a person approves a deed, so as to make it binding on him, though in itself defective. Ersk. Inst. 3. 3. 47 et seq.; 2 Bligh, 197; 1 Bell, Comm. 144.

HOMONYMIAE (Graeco-Lat.) A term applied in the civil law to cases where a law was repeated, or laid down in the same terms, or to the same effect, more than once.

Cases of iteration and repetition. Bac. Works, IV. 371. See 2 Kent, Comm. 489, note.

HONESTE VIVERE (Lat.) To live honorably, creditably, or virtuously. One of the three general precepts to which Justinian reduced the whole doctrine of the law (Inst. 1. 1. 3; Bracton, fols. 3, 3b), the others being *alterum non laedere,* not to injure others, and *suum cuique tribuere,* to render to every man his due.

This phrase is rendered by Blackstone, as well as Harris & Cooper, in their translations of the Institutes, "to live honestly," but this is not the proper meaning of *honeste.* Burrill.

HONOR.

——**In English Law.** The seigniory of a lord paramount. 2 Bl. Comm. 91.

——**In Common Law.** To accept a bill of exchange; to pay a bill accepted, or a promissory note, on the day it becomes due. 7 Taunt. 164; 1 Term R. 172.

HONOR COURTS. Tribunals held within honors. Cowell.

HONORABLE. A title of courtesy given in England to the younger children of earls, and the children of viscounts and barons, and, collectively, to the house of commons. In America, the word is used as a title of courtesy for judges, members of congress, and other high officials, but without any distinct rule for its application.

HONORARIUM. Something given in gratitude for services rendered.

It is so far of the nature of a gift that it cannot be sued for. 5 Serg. & R. (Pa.) 412; 1 Chit. Bailm. 38; 2 Atk. 332; 3 Bl. Comm. 28. Of this character were formerly in England, though never in the United States, the fees of counsellors at law and of physicians. See 3 Sharswood, Bl. Comm. 28.

HONORARY. Without fee, profit, or reward, either to or by the holder of the honorary position. 81 N. Y. 255.

HONORARY FEUDS. Titles of nobility, descendible to the eldest son, in exclusion of all the rest.

HONORARY SERVICES. Services by which lands in grand serjeantry were held; such as to hold king's banner, or to hold his head in the ship which carried him from Dover to Whitsand, etc. 2 Sharswood, Bl. Comm. 73, and note.

HONORARY TRUSTEES. Trustees to preserve contingent remainders. So called because they are bound, in honor only, to decide on the most proper and prudential course. Lewin, Trusts, 408.

HONTFONGENTHEF (Saxon). A thief taken with the stolen thing in his hand. See "Handhabend."

HORA AURORAE. In old English law. The morning bell. Cowell.

HORA NON EST MULTUM DE SUBstantia negotii, licet in appello de ea aliquando fiat mentio. The hour is not of much consequence as to the substance of business, although in appeal it is sometimes mentioned. 1 Bulst. 82.

HORAE JUDICIAE (Lat.) Hours judicial, or those in which judges sit in court. In Fortesque's time, these were from 8 to 11 a. m., and the courts of law were not open in the afternoon. Co. Litt. 135a; 2 Inst. 246; Fortesque, 51, p. 120, note.

HORCA. In Spanish law. A gallows; the punishment of hanging. White, New Recop. bk. 2, tit. 19, c. 4, § 1.

HORE. (Law Fr.) Now; hour; the present time. Kelham.

HORN. In old Scotch practice. A kind of trumpet used in denouncing contumacious persons, rebels, and outlaws, which was done with three blasts of the horn by the king's sergeant. This was called "putting to the horn," and the party so denounced was said to be "at the horn." Bell, Dict.; Skene de Verb. Sign.; 1 Pitc. Crim. Tr. pt. 2, pp. 77, 80.

HORN TENURE. Tenure by winding a horn on approach of enemy, called "tenure by cornage." If lands were held by this tenure of the king, it was grand serjeantry; if of a private person, knight service. Many anciently so held their lands towards the Picts' Wall. Co. Litt. § 156; Camden, Brit. 609.

HORN WITH HORN. A phrase used to describe the commoning together of horned beasts of different species.

HORNGELD. (Sax.) In old English law. A tax within a forest, paid for horned beasts. Cowell; Blount.

HORNING. In Scotch law. A process issuing on a decree of court of sessions, or of an inferior court, by which the debtor is charged to perform, in terms of his obligation, or on failure made liable to caption, that is, imprisonment. Bell, Dict. "Horning, Letters of"; "Diligence." The name comes from the ancient custom of proclaiming letters of horning not obeyed, and declaring the recusant a rebel, with three blasts of a horn, called "putting him to the horn." 1 Ross, Lect. 258, 308.

HORS (Law Fr.) Out; out of; without.

Hors son sen, out of his mind. Britt. c. 85.

HORS DE SON FEE (Fr. out of his fee). In old English law. A plea to an action brought by one who claimed to be lord for rent services as issuing out of his land, by which the defendant asserted that the land in question was out of the fee of the demandant. 9 Coke, 30; 2 Mod. 104.

HORS PRIS (Law Fr.) Except.

HORSE. Until a horse has attained the age of four years, he is called a "colt." 1 Russ. & R. 416. This word is sometimes used as a generic name for all animals of the horse kind. 3 Brev. (N. C.) 9. See Yelv. 67a.

HOSPES. (Lat.) In civil and old English law. A guest. 8 Co. 32, Calye's case.

A host or entertainer. Calv. Lex. More commonly *hospitator.*

HOSPITATOR (Lat.) A host or entertainer.

Hospitator communis, an innkeeper. 8 Coke, 32.

Hospitator magnus, the marshal of a camp.

HOSPITIA. Inns. *Hospitia communia,* common inns. Reg. Orig. 105. *Hospitia curiae,* inns of court. *Hospitia cancellariae,* inns of chancery. Crabb, Hist. Eng. Law, 428, 429; 4 Reeve, Hist. Eng. Law, 120.

HOSTAGE. A person delivered into the possession of a public enemy in the time of war, as a security for the performance of a contract entered into between the belligerents.

Hostages are frequently given as a security for the payment of a ransom bill, and if they should die, their death would not discharge the contract. 3 Burrows, 1734; 1 Kent, Comm. 106; Dane, Abr. Index.

HOSTELLAGIUM. In English law. A right reserved to the lords to be lodged and entertained in the houses of their tenants.

HOSTES. Enemies.

"Enemies are those who declare war against us, or against whom we declare war publicly; all others are pirates or robbers." Dig. 50. 16. 118. See "Enemy."

HOSTES SUNT QUI NOBIS VEL QUIbus nos bellum decernimus; caeteri traditores vel praedones sunt. Enemies are those upon whom we declare war, or who declare it against us; all others are traitors or pirates. 7 Coke, 24; Dig. 50. 16. 118; 1 Sharswood, Bl. Comm. 257.

HOSTICIDE. One who kills an enemy.

HOSTILE. Having the character of an enemy; standing in the relation of an enemy. See 1 Kent, Comm. c. 4.

HOSTILE EMBARGO. See "Embargo."

HOSTILE WITNESS. A witness who manifests so much hostility or prejudice under examination in chief that the party who has called him, or his representative, is allowed to cross-examine him, *i. e.,* to treat him as though he had been called by the opposite party. Rapalje & L.

HOSTILITY. A state of open enmity; open war. Wolff. Dr. Nat. § 1191.

Permanent hostility exists when the individual is a citizen or subject of the government at war.

Temporary hostility exists when the individual happens to be domiciliated or resident in the country of one of the belligerents. In this latter case, the individual may throw off the national character he has thus acquired by residence, when he puts himself in motion, *bona fide,* to quit the country *sine animo revertendi.* 3 C. Rob. Adm. 12; 3 Wheat. (U. S.) 14. See "Enemy"; "Domicile."

HOTCHPOT, HODGE-PODGE, or Hotchpotch. The blending and mixing property belonging to different persons, in order to divide it equally. 2 Bl. Comm. 190.

The bringing together all the personal estate of the deceased, with the advancements he has made to his children, in order that the same may be divided agreeably to the provisions of the statute for the distribution of intestates' estates.

In bringing an advancement into hotchpot, the donee is not required to account for the profits of the thing given. For example, he is not required to bring into hotchpot the produce of negroes, nor the interest of money. The property must be accounted for at its value when given. 1 Wash. (Va.) 224; 17 Mass. 358; 3 Pick. (Mass.) 450; 2 Desaus. (S. C.) 127; 3 Rand. (Va.) 117, 559. See "Advancement."

HOTEL. A public house for the entertainment of travelers and casual guests. 44 N. J. Law, 492.

The term is synonymous with "inn" or "tavern." 2 Daly (N. Y.) 17; 84 Ala. 452; 54 Barb. (N. Y.) 311.

HOT-WATER ORDEAL. See "Ordeal."

HOUR. (Lat. *hora*). The twenty-fourth part of a day, consisting of sixty minutes.

HOUR OF CAUSE. In Scotch practice. The hour when a court is met. 3 How. St. Tr. 603.

HOUSE. "In a general sense, a building or shed intended or used as a shelter or habitation for animals of any kind; but appropriately a building or edifice for the habitation of man; a dwelling place." Webster, quoted in 11 Abb. Pr. (N. Y.) 292.

Several buildings, so constructed that they may be used as an entirety, may constitute a "house." 9 Ch. Div. 425.

"House" has been variously held to mean "dwelling house" (11 Abb. Pr. [N. Y.] 292), or to include buildings used for other purposes (37 Tex. 412; 9 Ch. Div. 425), according to the context.

HOUSE BOTE. An allowance of necessary timber out of the landlord's woods for the repairing and support of a house or tenement. This belongs of common right to any lessee for years or for life. House bote is said to be of two kinds, *estoveriam uedificandi et ardendi.* Co. Litt. 41.

HOUSE OF COMMONS. One of the constituent houses of the English parliament.

It is composed of the representatives of the people, as distinguished from the house of lords, which is composed of the nobility. It consists of six hundred and seventy members, elected as follows: Four hundred and ninety-five from England and Wales, seventy-two from Scotland, and one hundred and three from Ireland. See "Parliament"; "High Court of Parliament."

HOUSE OF CORRECTION. A place for the imprisonment of those who have committed crimes of lesser magnitude.

HOUSE OF ILL FAME. A bawdy house (*q.v.*); a house resorted to for the purpose of prostitution and lewdness. 5 Ired. (N. C.) 603. See 3 Pick. (Mass.) 26; 21 N. H. 345; 33 Conn. 91.

HOUSE OF LORDS. One of the constituent houses of the English parliament.

This body is the supreme court of judicature in the kingdom. It has no original jurisdiction, but is the court of appeal in the last resort, with a few exceptions, and under some limitations as to the right, from the inferior courts upon appeal or writ of error for mistake of law. Appeals lie to this tribunal from Scotch and Irish courts, in some cases. See St. 4 Geo. IV. c. 85, as to Scotch, and St. 39 & 40 Geo. III. c. 67, art. 8, as to Irish, appeals.

This body, when sitting as a court of law, is presided over by the lord chancellor, whose attendance alone is in any respect compulsory, and is composed of as many of its members who have filled judicial stations as choose to attend. Three laymen also attend in rotation, but do not vote upon judicial matters. 11 Clark & F. 421. In the absence of the chancellor, deputy speakers, who were members of the profession, but not of the house, have been appointed. 3 Sharswood, Bl. Comm. 56.

It sits also to try impeachments. See "Impeachment"; "High Court of Parliament"; "Parliament."

HOUSE OF REFUGE. A prison for juvenile delinquents.

HOUSEBREAKING. In criminal law. The breaking and entering the dwelling house of another, by night or by day, with intent to commit some felony within the same, whether such felonious intent is executed or not. Housebreaking by night is burglary.

This crime is of a local character, and the evidence respecting the place must correspond with the allegation in the indictment.

HOUSEHOLD. Those who dwell under the same roof, and constitute a family. Webster. But it is not necessary that they should be under a roof, or that the father of the family be with it, if the mother and children keep together so as to constitute a family. 18 Johns. (N. Y.) 402.

Belonging to the house and family; domestic. Webster.

HOUSEHOLD FURNITURE. By this expression, in wills, all personal chattels will pass that may contribute to the use or convenience of the household, or the ornament of the house; as, plate, linen, china, both useful and ornamental, and pictures. But goods or plate in the hands of testator in the way of his trade will not pass, nor books, nor wines. 1 Jarm. Wills (Perkins Ed.) 591, 596, note; 1 Ves. Sr. 97; 2 Williams, Ex'rs (Am. Ed.) 1017; 1 Johns. Ch. (N. Y.) 329. See "Furniture."

HOUSEHOLD GOODS. In wills. This expression will pass everything of a permanent nature (that is, articles of household which are not consumed in their enjoyment) that were used or purchased, or otherwise acquired by the testator, for his house, but not goods in the way of his trade. Plate will pass by this term, but not articles of consumption found in the house, as malt, hops, or victuals, nor guns and pistols, if used in hunting or sport, and not for defense of house. A clock in the house, if not fixed to it, will pass. 1 Jarm. Wills (Perkins Ed.) 589; 1 Rop. Leg. 253. See "Goods."

HOUSEHOLD STUFF. Words sometimes used in a will. Plate will pass under the term (2 Freem. Ch. 64), but not apparel, books, cattle, victuals, and choses in action, which do not fall within the natural meaning of the word, unless there be an intention manifest that they should pass. 15 Ves. 319. Goods, as seven hundred beds in possession of testator for purposes of trade, do not pass under utensils of "household stuff." 2 P. Wms. 302. In general, "household stuff" will pass all articles which may be used for the convenience of the house. Swinb. Wills, pt. 7, § 10, p. 484.

HOUSEHOLDER. Master or chief of a family; one who keeps house with his family. Webster. It "means more than the mere occupant of a room or house. It implies the idea of a domestic establishment." 37 Ala. 145. But a man who has absconded from the state, and left his wife and children remaining together as a family, was for their benefit held to be a householder. 18 Johns. (N. Y.) 402. And a single man renting a house in which he lodged with a younger brother has been held a householder. 2 Tex. App. 432.

A keeper of a tavern or boarding house, or a master or mistress of a dwelling house. 1 Supp. Rev. St. Mass. 1836-1853, Index, p. 170. A person having and providing for a household. The character is not lost by a temporary cessation from housekeeping. 14 Barb. (N. Y.) 456; 19 Wend. (N. Y.) 475.

HOUSEKEEPER. One who occupies a house.

A person who occupies every room in the house, under a lease, except one, which is reserved for his landlord, who pays all the taxes, is not a housekeeper. 1 Chit. Bailm. 502. Nor is a person a housekeeper who takes a house which he afterwards underlets to another, whom the landlord refuses to accept as his tenant. In this case, the under tenant paid the taxes, and let to the tenant the first floor of the house, and the rent was paid for the whole house to the tenant, who paid it to the landlord. Id. note.

In order to make the party a housekeeper, he must be in actual possession of the house (1 Chit. Bailm. 288) and must occupy a whole house. See 1 Barn. & C. 178; 2 Term R. 406; 3 Petersd. Abr. 103, note; 2 Mart. (La.) 313.

The term is rarely, if ever, used in American law.

HOVEL. A place used by husbandmen to set their ploughs, carts, and other farming utensils out of the rain and sun. Law Lat. Dict. A shed; a cottage; a mean house.

HOYMAN. The master or captain of a hoy, or small coasting vessel.

Hoymen are liable as common carriers Story, Bailm. § 496.

HUDE-GELD. In old English law. A compensation for an assault (*transgressio illata*) upon a trespassing servant (*servus*). Supposed to be a mistake or misprint in Fleta for *hinegeld.* Fleta, lib. 1, c. 47, § 20. Also, the price of one's skin, or the money paid by a servant to save himself from a whipping. Du Cange.

HUE AND CRY. In old English law. A pursuit of one who had committed felony, by the highway.

The meaning of "hue" is said to be "shout," from the Saxon *huer;* but this word also means "to foot," and it may be reasonably questioned whether the term may not be "up foot and cry"; in other words, run and cry after the felon. We have a mention of hue and cry as early as Edward I.; and by the Statute of Winchester (13 Edw. I.), "immediately upon robberies and felonies committed, fresh suit shall be made from town to town, and county to county, by horsemen and footmen, to the seaside. The constable (the person being described, etc.) is to call upon the parishioners to assist him in the pursuit in his precinct, and to give notice to the next constable, who is to do the same as the first, etc. If the county will not answer the bodies of the offenders, the whole hundred shall be answerable for the robberies there committed, etc." A person engaged in the hue and cry apprehending a felon was, on the felon's conviction, entitled to forty pounds, on a certificate of the judge or justice before whom there was conviction, as well as to the felon's horse, furniture, arms, money, and other goods taken with him, subject to the rights of other persons therein. Wood, Inst. 370-373. See 2 Hale, P. C. 100.

HUEBRA. In Spanish law. An acre of land, or as much as can be ploughed in a day by two oxen. 2 White, New Coll. 49.

HUISSIER. An usher of the court; an officer who serves process.

In France, an officer of this name performs many of the duties of an English sheriff or constable. In Canada, there may be many huissiers in each county, whose acts are independent of each other; while there can be but one sheriff, who is presumed cognizant of the acts of his subordinates. The French huissier certifies his process; the Canadian merely serves what is put into his hands.

HUMBUG. Humbug is an imposition, imposture, deception; and as a verb, signifies to impose upon, to cozen, to swindle; all implying intention to misrepresent, by the assertion of what is not the actual condition or the suppression or concealment of what is. 65 Ill. App. 432, 433.

HUNDRED. In English law. A division of a county, which some make to have originally consisted of one hundred hides of land; others of ten tithings, or one hundred free families.

It differed in size in different parts of England. 1 Steph. Comm. 122. In many cases, when an offense is committed within a hundred, the inhabitants are liable to make good the damage if they do not produce the offender. See 12 East, 244.

This system was probably introduced by Alfred (though mentioned in the Poenitentiae of Egbert, where it seems to be the addition of a later age), being borrowed from the continent, where it was known to the Franks, under the name *centena*, in the sixth century. See Charlemagne, Cap. lib. 3, c. 10.

It had a court attached to it, called the "hundred court," or "hundred lagh," like a court baron, except in its larger territorial jurisdiction. It was governed by the hundredary (*hundredarius*). 9 Coke, 25. The jurisdiction of this court has devolved upon the county courts. Jacob; Du Cange. Hundred penny was a tax collected from the hundred by its lord or by the sheriff. Hundred setena signified the dwellers in the hundred. Charta Edg. Reg. Mon. Angl. tom. 1, p. 16.

HUNDRED COURT. An inferior court, whose jurisdiction extended to the whole territory embraced in a hundred. They were courts not of record; the freeholders were the judges; they were held before the steward of the manor as register; and they resembled courts baron in all respects except in their territorial jurisdiction. 3 Bl. Comm. 34, 35.

HUNDRED GEMOTE. An assembly among the Saxons of the freeholders of a hundred.

It met twelve times in the year, originally; though subsequently its meetings became less frequent.

It had an extensive jurisdiction, both civil and criminal, and was the predecessor of the county court and sheriff's tourn, and possessed very similar powers. Spelman, "Hundredum"; 1 Reeve, Hist. Eng. Law, 7.

HUNDRED LAGH (Saxon). Liability to attend the hundred court. Spelman. See Cowell; Blount.

HUNDRED PENNY. In old English law. A tax collected from the hundred, by the sheriff or lord of the hundred. Spelman, voc. "Hundredus."

HUNDRED SETENA. In Saxon law. The dwellers or inhabitants of a hundred. Cowell; Blount. Spelman suggests the reading of *sceatena* from Saxon *sceat*, a tax.

HUNDREDARIUS. In old English law. A hundredary or hundredor. A name given to the chief officer of a hundred, as well as to the freeholders who composed it. Spelman, voc. "Hundredus."

HUNDREDARY (Lat. *hundredarius*). The chief magistrate of a hundred. Du Cange.

HUNDREDORS. The inhabitants of a hundred, who, by several statutes, are held to be liable, in the cases therein specified, to make good the loss sustained by persons within the hundred by robbery or other violence, therein also specified. The principal of these statutes are 13 Edw. I. st. 2, c. 1, § 4; 28 Edw. III. c. 11; 27 Eliz. c. 13; 29 Car. II. c. 7; 8 Geo. II. c. 16; 22 Geo. II. c. 24.

Persons serving on juries, or fit to be impanelled thereon, dwelling within the hundred where the land in question lies. 35 Hen. VIII. c. 6. And some such were necessarily on every panel till 4 & 5 Anne, c. 16. 4 Steph. Comm. 370. Him that had the jurisdiction of the hundred; the bailiff of the hundred. Horne, Mirr. Just. lib. 1; Jacob.

HUNTING. The act of pursuing and taking wild animals; the chase.

The grant or reservation of "hunting, shooting, fishing and sporting" includes all things generally hunted, shot, fished, or sported after, in contradistinction to small birds and things of a similar character, e. g., rats and sparrows. 34 L. J. C. P. 261; 19 C. B. N. S. 264. Rabbits would be included in such a reservation. A covenant for quiet enjoyment in such a grant or reservation, does not imply any undertaking restricting the ordinary use of the land. 44 L. J. Ch. 334; 10 Ch. 355.

HURDLE. In English law. A species of sledge, used to draw traitors to execution.

HURTO. In Spanish law. Theft. White, New Recop. bk. 2, tit. 20.

HUSBAND. A man who has a wife.

HUSBAND OF A SHIP. See "Ship's Husband."

HUSBRECE. Housebreaking; burglary.

HUSCARLE. In old English law. A house servant or domestic; a man of the household. Spelman.

A king's vassal, thane, or baron; an earl's man or vassal. A term of frequent occurrence in Domesday Book.

HUSGABLUM. In old records. House rent; or a tax or tribute laid upon a house. 3 Mon. Angl. 254; Cowell; Blount.

HUSTINGS. In English law. The name of a court held before the lord mayor and aldermen of London. It is the principal and supreme court of the city. See 2 Inst. 327; St. Armand, Hist. Essay, Leg. Power Eng. 75. This name is also applied to some courts in Virginia.

The place of meeting to choose a member of parliament.

The term is used in Canadian as well as English law. The manner of conducting an election in Canada and England for a member of the legislative body is substantially as follows: Upon warrant from the proper officer, a writ issues from the clerk of the crown in chancery, directed to the sheriff, registrar, or other returning officer of the electoral division. He thereupon issues and posts in public places a proclamation appointing a day, place and hour for his holding an election, and also fixing a day when a poll will be opened, if one be demanded and granted. The first day is called "nomination day." On this day he proceeds to the hustings, which must be in the open air, and accessible to all the voters, proclaims the purpose of the election, and calls upon the electors present to name the person they require to represent them. The electors then make a show of hands, which may result in an election, or a poll may be demanded by a candidate or by any elector. On such demand, a poll is opened in each township, ward, or parish of the election district, at the places prescribed by statute.

HUTESIUM ET CLAMOR. Hue and cry (*q. v.*).

HYDRAULIC MINING. (Hydraulicing.) The process of mining gold and other precious minerals by forcing water, at great pressure though pipers or hose upon deposits of earth which contain the minerals. A considerable portion of the earth and debris is carried away through the sluices, at the bottom of which the heavier minerals remain. 81 Fed. 243; 9 Saw. 441; Raymond,

Gloss. Mining terms; Bancroft's Handbook Mining.

HYPOBOLUM (Lat.) In civil law. The name of the bequest or legacy given by the husband to his wife, at his death, above her dowry. Tech. Dict.

HYPOTHEC. In Scotch law. A right over a subject which is acquired by a creditor while the subject remains in the possession of the debtor.

HYPOTHECA. In civil law. That kind of pledge in which the possession of the thing pledged remains with the debtor; the obligation resting in mere contact. Dig. 1. 3. 7. 9. 2.

HYPOTHECARIA ACTIO. In civil law. An hypothecary action; an action for the enforcement of an *hypotheca*, or right of mortgage; or to obtain the surrender of the thing mortgaged. Inst. 4. 6. 7; Mackeld. Civ. Law, § 356. Adopted in the Civil Code of Louisiana, under the name of *"l'action hypothecarie"* (translated, "action of mortgage"). Article 3361.

HYPOTHECARII CREDITORES. In civil law. Hypothecary creditors; those who loaned money on the security of an *hypotheca* (*q. v.*). Calv. Lex.

HYPOTHECATE. To pledge a thing without delivering the possession of it to the pledgee. "The master, when abroad, and in the absence of the owner, may hypothecate the ship, freight, and cargo, to raise money requisite for the completion of the voyage." 3 Kent, Comm. 171.

HYPOTHECATION. A right which a creditor has over a thing belonging to another, and which consists in a power to cause it to be sold, in order to be paid his claim out of the proceeds.

There are two species of hypothecation, one called "pledge" (*pignus*), and the other properly denominated "hypothecation." Pledge is that species of hypothecation which is contracted by the delivery by the debtor to the creditor of the thing hypothecated. Hypothecation, properly so called, is that which is contracted without delivery of the thing hypothecated. 2 Bell, Comm. (5th Ed.) 25.

In the common law, cases of hypothecation, in the strict sense of the civil law,—that is, of a pledge of a chattel without possession by the pledgee,—are scarcely to be found; cases of bottomry bonds and claims for seamen's wages against ships are the nearest approach to it; but these are liens and privileges, rather than hypothecations. Story, Bailm. § 288. It seems that chattels not in existence, though they cannot be pledged, can be hypothecated, so that the lien will attach as soon as the chattel has been produced. 14 Pick. (Mass.) 497.

(1) Conventional hypothecations are those which arise by agreement of the parties. Dig. 20. 1. 5.

(2) General hypothecations are those by which the debtor hypothecates to his creditor all his estate which he has or may have.

(3) Legal hypothecations are those which arise without any contract therefor between the parties, express or implied.

(4) Special hypothecations are hypothecations of a particular estate.

(5) Tacit hypothecations are such as the law gives in certain cases, without the consent of the parties, to secure the creditor. They are a species of legal hypothecation.

Thus, the public treasury has a lien over the property of public debtors. Code, 8. 15. 1. The landlord has a lien on the goods in the house leased, for the payment of his rent. Dig. 20. 2. 2; Code, 8. 15. 7. The builder has a lien, for his bill, on the house he has built. Dig. 20. 1. The pupil has a lien on the property of the guardian for the balance of his account. Dig. 46. 6. 22; Code, 5. 37. 20. There is hypothecation of the goods of a testator for the security of the legacy. Code, 6. 43. 1.

See, generally, Poth. de l'Hyp.; Poth. Cont. (Cushing Ed.) 145, note 26; Merlin, Repert.; 2 Brown, Civ. Law, 195; Abb. Shipp.; Pars. Mar. Law.

HYPOTHECATION BOND. A bond given in the contract of bottomry or *respondentia*.

HYPOTHEQUE. In French law. Hypothecation; the right acquired by the creditor over the immovable property which has been assigned to him by his debtor as security for his debt, although he be not placed in possession of it.

HYPOTHETICAL. Based upon an assumption or hypothesis, as a hypothetical question is one which calls for the opinion of the witness upon facts assumed by the question.

HYSTEROPOTMOI. In Roman law. Those who, having been thought dead, unexpectedly returned. They were not permitted to enter their own houses by the door, but through a hole in the roof.

I

I, at the beginning of words having the first syllable *In,* commonly denotes a derivation from the Latin, as E, in a similar position, indicates a derivation from the French. But I and E were formerly, in many instances, used as initial letters indifferently, and in some words the practice continues to be retained. See E.

I. E. An abbreviation for *"id est,"* that is; that is to say.

I. O. U. In common law. A memorandum of debt in use among merchants. It is not a promissory note, as it contains no direct promise to pay. See 4 Car. & P. 324; 1 Man. & G. 46; 1 C. B. 543; 1 Esp. 426; Pars. Bills & Notes.

IBI SEMPER DEBET FIERI TRIATIO ubi juratores meliorem possunt habere notitiam. A trial should always be had where the jurors can be the best informed. 7 Coke, 1b.

IBIDEM (Lat.) In the same book or place; the same subject. Abbreviated *ib* or *ibid.*

ICTUS (Lat.) In old English law. A stroke or blow from a club or stone; a bruise, contusion, or swelling produced by a blow from a club or stone, as distinguished from *"plaga,"* a wound. Fleta, lib. 1, c. 41, § 3.

ICTUS ORBIS (Lat.) In medical jurisprudence. A maim, a bruise, or swelling; any hurt without cutting the skin.

When the skin is cut, the injury is called a "wound." Bracton, lib. 2, tr. 2, cc. 5, 24.

Ictus is often used by medical authors in the sense of *percussus.* It is applied to the pulsation of the arteries, to any external lesion of the body produced by violence; also to the wound inflicted by a scorpion or venomous reptile. *Orbis* is used in the sense of circle, circuit, rotundity. It is applied, also, to the eyeballs, *oculi dicuntur orbes.* Cast. Lex. Med.

ID CERTUM EST QUOD CERTUM REDDI potest. That is certain which may be rendered certain. 1 Bouv. Inst. note 929; 2 Bl. Comm. 143; 4 Kent, Comm. 462; 4 Pick. (Mass.) 179; Broom, Leg. Max. (3d London Ed.) 556.

ID CERTUM EST QUOD CERTUM REDDI potest, sed id magis certum est quod de semetipso est certum. That is certain which can be made certain, but that is more certain which is certain of itself. 9 Coke, 47a.

ID EST (Lat.) That is. Commonly abbreviated *"i. e."*

ID PERFECTUM EST QUOD EX OMNIbus suis partibus constat. That is perfect which is complete in all its parts. 9 Coke, 9.

ID POSSUMUS QUOD DE JURE POSSUmus. We are able to do that which we can do lawfully. Lane, 116.

ID QUOD EST MAGIS REMOTUM, NON trahit ad se quod est magis junctum, sed e contrario in omni casu. That which is more remote does not draw to itself that which is nearer, but the contrary in every case. Co. Litt. 164.

ID QUOD NOSTRUM EST, SINE FACTO nostro, ad alium transferri non potest. What belongs to us cannot be transferred to another without our act. Dig. 50. 17. 11. But this must be understood with this qualification, that the government may take property for public use, paying the owner its value. The title to property may also be acquired, without the consent of the owner, by a judgment of a competent tribunal.

ID SOLUM NOSTRUM QUOD DEBITIS deductis nostrum est. That only is ours which remains to us after deduction of debts. Tray. Lat. Max. 227.

IDEM (Lat. the same). According to Lord Coke, *idem* has two significations: *Idem syllabis seu verbis,* the same in syllables or words, and *idem re et sensu,* the same in substance and in sense. 10 Coke, 124a.

——**In Old Practice.** The said or aforesaid. Towns. Pl. 15, 16.

IDEM AGENS ET PATIENS ESSE NON potest. To be at once the person acting and the person acted upon is impossible. Jenk. Cent. Cas. 40.

IDEM EST FACERE, ET NOLLE PROhibere cum possis. It is the same thing to do a thing as not to prohibit it when in your power. 3 Co. Inst. 158.

IDEM EST NIHIL DICERE ET INSUFFIcienter dicere. It is the same thing to say nothing, and not to say sufficiently. 2 Inst. 178.

IDEM EST NON ESSE, ET NON APPArere. It is the same thing not to be as not to appear. Jenk. Cent. Cas. 207. Not to appear is the same thing as not to be. Broom, Leg. Max. 165.

IDEM EST NON PROBARI ET NON ESse; non deficit jus, sed probatio. What does not appear, and what is not, are the same; it is not the defect of the law, but the want of proof.

IDEM EST SCIRE AUT SCIRE DEBET aut potuisse. To be able to know is the same as to know. This maxim is applied to the duty of every one to know the law.

IDEM NON ESSE ET NON APPARERE. It is the same thing not to exist and not to appear. Jenk. Cent. Cas. 207.

IDEM SEMPER ANTECEDENTI PROXImo refertur. *Idem* always relates to the next antecedent. Co. Litt. 385.

IDEM SONANS. Sounding the same. A term applied to names which are spelled differently, but have substantially the same sound; the difference in spelling being held in such case not to constitute a variance. Thus, "Hutson" for "Hudson" (7 Miss. 142), "Keen" for "Keene" (Thach. C. C. [Mass.] 67), and "Deadema" for "Diadema" (2 Ired. [N. C.] 346).

IDENTIFICATION. The establishment of identity (*q. v.*).

IDENTITAS VERA COLLIGITUR EX multitudine signorum. True identity is collected from a number of signs. Bac. Reg. 29.

IDENTITATE NOMINIS. (Lat.) In English law. The name of a writ which lies for a person taken upon a *capias* or *exigent*, and committed to prison, for another man of the same name. This writ directs the sheriff to inquire whether he be the person against whom the action was brought, and if not, then to discharge him. Fitzh. Nat. Brev. 267. In practice, a party in this condition would be relieved by *habeas corpus*.

IDENTITY. Sameness; the state of being the same as something described; the fact that a person or thing is the same as it is represented or charged to be.

IDEO (Lat.) Therefore. Calv. Lex.

IDEO CONSIDERATUM EST (Law Lat.) Therefore it is considered. The initial words of the ancient entry of judgment in an action at law, and by which that part of the record is sometimes called in modern practice.

IDES (Lat.) In civil law. A day in the month from which the computation of days was made.

The divisions of months adopted among the Romans were as follows: The *calends* occurred on the first day of every month, and were distinguished by adding the name of the month; as, *calendis Januarii*, the first of January. The *nones* occurred on the fifth of each month, with the exception of March, July, October, and May, in which months they occurred on the seventh. The *ides* occurred always on the ninth day after the *nones*, thus dividing the month equally. In fact, the *ides* would seem to have been the primal division, occurring in the middle of the month, nearly. Other days than the three designated were indicated by the number of days which would elapse before the next succeeding point of division. Thus, the second of April is the *quarto nonas Aprilis;* the second of March, the *sexto nonas Martii;* the eighth of March, *octavius idus Martii;* the eighth of April, *sextus idus Aprilis;* the sixteenth of March, *decimus septimus calendis Aprilis.*

This system is still used in some chanceries in Europe, and we therefore give the following:

Table of the Calends, Nones, and Ides.

	Jan., Aug., Dec., 31 days.	March, May, July, Oct., 31 days.	April, June, Sept., Nov., 30 days.	February 28, bissextile, 29 days.
1	Calendis	Calendis	Calendis	Calendis
2	4 Nonas	6 Nonas	4 Nonas	4 Nonas
3	3 Nonas	5 Nonas	3 Nonas	3 Nonas
4	Prid. Non.	4 Nonas	Prid. Non.	Prid. Non.
5	Nonis	3 Nonas	Nonis	Nonis
6	8 Idus	Prid. Non.	8 Idus	8 Idus
7	7 Idus	Nonis	7 Idus	7 Idus
8	6 Idus	8 Idus	6 Idus	6 Idus
9	5 Idus	7 Idus	5 Idus	5 Idus
10	4 Idus	6 Idus	4 Idus	4 Idus
11	3 Idus	5 Idus	3 Idus	3 Idus
12	Prid. Idus	4 Idus	Prid. Idus	Prid. Idus
13	Idibus	3 Idus	Idibus	Idibus
14	19 Cal.	Prid. Idus	18 Cal.	16 Cal.
15	18 Cal.	Idibus	17 Cal.	15 Cal.
16	17 Cal.	17 Cal.	16 Cal.	14 Cal.
17	16 Cal.	16 Cal.	15 Cal.	13 Cal.
18	15 Cal.	15 Cal.	14 Cal.	12 Cal.
19	14 Cal.	14 Cal.	13 Cal.	11 Cal.
20	13 Cal.	13 Cal.	12 Cal.	10 Cal.
21	12 Cal.	12 Cal.	11 Cal.	9 Cal.
22	11 Cal.	11 Cal.	10 Cal.	8 Cal.
23	10 Cal.	10 Cal.	9 Cal.	7 Cal.
24	9 Cal.	9 Cal.	8 Cal.	6 Cal.
25	8 Cal.	8 Cal.	7 Cal.	5 Cal.
26	7 Cal.	7 Cal.	6 Cal.	4 Cal.
27	6 Cal.	6 Cal.	5 Cal.	3 Cal.
28	5 Cal.	5 Cal.	4 Cal.	Prid. Cal.
29	4 Cal.	4 Cal.	3 Cal.	
30	3 Cal.	3 Cal.	Prid. Cal.	
31	Prid. Cal.	Prid. Cal.		

IDIOCHIRA (Gr.) In civil law. An instrument privately executed, as distinguished from one publicly executed. Vicat.

IDIOCY. In medical jurisprudence. A form of insanity, resulting either from congenital defect, or some obstacle to the development of the faculties in infancy.

It is an imbecility or sterility of mind, and not a perversion of the understanding. Chit. Med. Jur. 327, note (s) 345; 1 Russ. Crimes, 6; Bac. Abr. "Idiot" (A); Brooke, Abr.; Co. Litt. 246, 247; 3 Mod. 44; 1 Vern. 16; 4 Coke, 126; 1 Bl. Comm. 302.

IDIOT. A person who has been without understanding from his nativity, and whom the law, therefore, presumes never likely to attain any. Shelf. Lun. 2.

IDIOTA INQUIRENDO, WRIT DE. This is the name of an old writ which directs the sheriff to inquire whether a man be an idiot or not. The inquisition is to be made by a jury of twelve men. Fitzh. Nat. Brev. 232.

IDONEARE (Law Lat.) To make or prove one's self innocent. Spelman.

IDONEUS (Lat.) Sufficient; fit; adequate. He is said to be *idoneus homo* who hath these three things, honesty, knowledge, and civility; and if an officer, etc., be not *idoneus*, he may be discharged. 8 Coke,

41. If a clerk presented to a living is not *persona idonea*, which includes ability in learning, honesty of conversation, etc., the bishop may refuse him. And to a *quare impedit* brought thereon, "*in literatura minus sufficiens* is a good plea, without setting forth the particular kind of learning." 5 Coke, 58; 6 Coke, 49b; 2 Inst. 631; 3 Lev. 311; 1 Show. 88; Wood. Inst. 32, 33.

So of things: *Idonea quantitas*. Calv. Lex. *Idonea paries*, a wall sufficient or able to bear the weight.

——**In Civil Law.** Rich; solvent; *e. g.*, *idoneus tutor, idoneus debitur.* Calv. Lex.

IDONIETAS (Law Lat.) In old English law. Ability or fitness (of a parson). Artic. Cleri, c. 13.

IGLISE. (Law. Fr.) A church. Kelham. Another form of *eglise*.

IGNIS JUDICIUM (Lat.) In old English law. The judicial trial by fire.

IGNITEGIUM (from *ignis*, fire, and *tegere*, to cover). In old English law. The curfew, or evening bell. Cowell. See "Curfew."

IGNOMINY. Public disgrace; infamy; reproach; dishonor. Ignominy is the opposite of esteem.

IGNORAMUS (Lat. we are ignorant or uninformed). In practice. The word which is written on a bill by a grand jury when they find that there is not sufficient evidence to authorize their finding it a true bill. Sometimes, instead of using this word, the grand jury indorse on the bill, "Not found." 4 Bl. Comm. 305.

IGNORANCE. The lack of knowledge.

Ignorance is distinguishable from "error" or "mistake." Ignorance is want of knowledge; error is the nonconformity or opposition of ideas to the truth. Considered as a motive of actions, ignorance differs but little from error. They are generally found together, and what is said of one is said of both. 1 Story, Eq. Jur. 108 et seq. See 4 Johns. Ch. (N. Y.) 567.

(1) Ignorance of fact is the want of knowledge as to the fact in question. It would be an error resulting from ignorance of fact, if a man believed a certain woman to be unmarried and free, when, in fact, she was a married woman, and were he to marry her under that belief, he would not be criminally responsible. 6 Allen (Mass.) 591. Ignorance of the laws of a foreign government, or of another state, is ignorance of fact. 9 Pick. (Mass.) 112. See, for the difference between ignorance of law and ignorance of fact, 9 Pick. (Mass.) 112.

(2) Ignorance of law consists in the want of knowledge of those laws which it is our duty to understand, and which every man is presumed to know. The law forbids any one to marry a woman whose husband is living. If any man, then, imagined he could marry such a woman, he would be ignorant of the law, and if he married her he would commit an error as to a matter of law. How far a party is bound to fulfill a promise to pay, upon a supposed liability, and in ignorance of the law, see 12 East, 38; 2 Jac. & W. 263; 5 Taunt. 143; 3 Barn. & C. 280; 1 Johns. Ch. (N. Y.) 512, 516; 6 Johns. Ch. (N. Y.) 166; 9 Cow. (N. Y.) 674; 4 Mass. 342; 7 Mass. 452, 488; 9 Pick. (Mass.) 112; 1 Bin. (Pa.) 27. Ignorance of law is a passive state, and is distinguished from actual mistake of law. 7 Ga. 70.

(3) Essential ignorance is ignorance in relation to some essential circumstance, so intimately connected with the matter in question, and which so influences the parties, that it induces them to act in the business. 2 Kent, Comm. 367.

(4) Nonessential or accidental ignorance is that which has not of itself any necessary connection with the business in question, and which is not the true consideration for entering into the contract; as, if a man should marry a woman whom he believed to be rich, and she proved to be poor, this fact would not be essential, and the marriage would therefore be good.

(5) Voluntary ignorance exists when a party might, by taking reasonable pains, have acquired the necessary knowledge. For example, every man might acquire a knowledge of the laws which have been promulgated. A neglect to become acquainted with them is therefore voluntary ignorance. Doctor & Stud. 1, 46; Plowd. 343.

(6) Involuntary ignorance is that which does not proceed from choice, and which could not have been avoided by any means at the party's command, as of a law not yet promulgated.

IGNORANCE OF LAW. See "Ignorance."

IGNORANTIA. Ignorance; want of knowledge. Distinguished from mistake, error or wrong conception. Mackeld. Civ. Law, § 165. Divided in the civil law into *ignorantia facti*, ignornace of fact, and *ignorantia juris*, ignorance of law. Dig. 22. 6. Lord Coke adopts this division, adding that the former is twofold,—*lectionis et linguae*, ignorance of reading, and ignorance of language. 2 Coke, 3b.

IGNORANTIA EORUM QUAE QUIS scire tenetur non excusat. Ignorance of those things which every one is bound to know excuses not. Hale, P. C. 42. See Tindal, C. J., 10 Clark & F. 210; Broom, Leg. Max. (3d London Ed.) 245; 4 Sharswood, Bl. Comm. 27.

IGNORANTIA EXCUSATUR, NON JURis sed facti. Ignorance of fact may excuse, but not ignorance of law. See "Ignorance."

IGNORANTIA FACTI EXCUSAT; IGNOrantia juris non excusat. Ignorance of facts excuses; ignorance of law does not excuse. 1 Coke, 177; 4 Bouv. Inst. note 3828; Broom,

Leg. Max. (3d London Ed.) 231; 1 Fonbl. Eq. (5th Ed.) 119, note. See "Ignorance."

IGNORANTIA JUDICIS EST CALAMITas innocentis. The ignorance of the judge is the misfortune of the innocent. 2 Inst. 591.

IGNORANTIA JURIS NON EXCUSAT. Ignorance of the law is no excuse. 8 Wend. (N. Y.) 267, 284; 18 Wend. (N. Y.) 586, 588; 6 Paige, Ch. (N. Y.) 189, 195; 1 Edw. Ch. (N. Y.) 467, 472.

The true meaning of that maxim is that parties cannot excuse themselves from liability from all civil or criminal consequences of their acts by alleging ignorance of the law, but there is no presumption that parties must be taken to know all the legal consequences of their acts, and especially where difficult questions of law, or of the practice of the court are involved. 13 App. Cas. 78.

IGNORANTIA JURIS QUOD QUISQUE scire tenetur, neminem excusat. Ignorance of law which every one is bound to know excuses no one. 2 Coke, 3b; 1 Plowd. 343; per Ld. Campbell, 9 Clark & F. 324; Broom, Leg. Max. (3d London Ed.) 232; 7 Car. & P. 456; 2 Kent, Comm. 491.

IGNORANTIA LEGIS NEMINEM EXCUsat. Ignorance of law excuses no one. See "Ignorance"; 4 Bouv. Inst. note 3828; 1 Story, Eq. Jur. § 111.

IGNORATIS TERMINIS, IGNORATUR et ars. Terms being unknown, the art also is unknown. Co. Litt. 2.

IGNORE. To be ignorant of. Webster. To pass over as if not in existence. A grand jury are said to ignore a bill when they do not find the evidence such as to induce them to make a presentment. Brande.

IGNOSCITUR EI QUI SANGUINEM SUum qualiter redemptum voluit. The law holds him excused who chose that his blood should be redeemed on any terms. Dig. 48. 21. 1; 1 Sharswood, Bl. Comm. 131.

IKENILD STREET. One of the four Roman roads in England.

ILL FAME. A technical expression, which not only means bad character as generally understood, but applies to every person, whatever may be his conduct and character in life, who visits bawdy houses, gaming houses, and other places which are of ill fame. 1 Rogers, City Hall Rec. (N. Y.) 67; 2 Hill (N. Y.) 558; 17 Pick. (Mass.) 80; Ayliffe, Par. 276; 1 Hagg. Ecc. 720, 767; 1 Hagg. Consist, 302; 2 Hagg. Consist. 24; 2 Greenl. Ev. § 44. See "House of Ill Fame."

ILLATA ET INVECTA. In Roman law. Things brought into the house by the tenant for his use, and which were liable to distress (jus hypothecae) by the landlord.

ILLEGAL. Contrary to law. Not synonymous with unlawful (*q. v.*).

ILLEGALITY. Signifies that which is contrary to the principles of law, and denotes a complete defect in the proceedings. 1 Abb. Pr. (N. S.; N. Y.) 432.

ILLEGITIMATE. That which is contrary to law. It is usually applied to children born out of lawful wedlock.

ILLEVIABLE. A debt or duty that cannot or ought not to be levied. *Nihil* set upon a debt is a mark for illeviable.

ILLICENCIATUS (Lat.) Without license.

ILLICIT. What is unlawful; what is forbidden by the law.

This word is frequently used in policies of insurance, where the assured warrants against illicit trade. By "illicit trade" is understood that "which is made unlawful by the laws of the country to which the object is bound." The assured, having entered into this warranty, is required to do no act which will expose the vessel to be legally condemned. 2 La. 337, 338. See "Insurance"; "Warranty."

ILLICITE. Unlawfully.

This word has a technical meaning, and is requisite in an indictment where the act charged is unlawful; as, in the case of a riot. 2 Hawk. P. C. 25, § 96.

ILLICITUM COLLEGIUM. An illegal corporation.

ILLITERATE. Unacquainted with letters.

ILLOCABLE. Incapable of being hired out.

ILLUD (Lat.) That.

ILLUD QUOD ALIAS LICITUM NON est, necessitas facit licitum, et necessitas inducit privilegium quod jure privatur. That which is not otherwise lawful necessity makes lawful, and necessity makes a privilege which supersedes the law. 10 Coke, 61.

ILLUD QUOD ALTERI UNITUR EXTINguitur, neque amplius per se vacare licet. That which is united to another is extinguished, nor can it be any more independent.

ILLUSION. A species of mania, in which the sensibility of the nervous system is altered, excited, weakened, or perverted.

The patient is deceived by the false appearance of things, and his reason is not sufficiently active and powerful to correct the error; and this last particular is what distinguishes the sane from the insane. Illusions are not unfrequent in a state of health, but reason corrects the errors, and dissipates them. A square tower, seen from a distance, may appear round, but, on approaching it, the error is corrected. A distant mountain may be taken for a cloud, but as we approach we discover the truth. To a person in the cabin of a vessel under sail, the shore appears to move; but reflection and a closer examination soon destroy this illusion. An insane individual is mistaken on the qualities, connections, and causes of the impressions he actually receives, and he forms wrong judgments as to his internal and external sensations; and his reason does not correct the error. 1 Beck, Med. Jur. 538; Esquirol, tom. 1, p. 202; Dict. des Sciences Medicales, "Hallucination." See "Hallucination."

ILLUSORY APPOINTMENT. Such an appointment or disposition of property under a power as is merely nominal, and not substantial.

ILLUSORY APPOINTMENT ACT. St. Wm. IV. c. 46, providing that no appointment shall be impeached in equity on the ground that it is unsubstantial, illusory, or nominal.

IMAGINE. In English law. In cases of treason, the law makes it a crime to imagine the death of the king. In order to complete the offense, there must, however, be an overt act,—the terms "compassing" and "imagining" being synonymous. It has been justly remarked that the words "to compass" and "imagine" are too vague for a statute whose penalty affects the life of a subject. Barr. Obs. St. 243. See "Fiction."

IMBASING. The act of reducing coin below the standard alloy. See 1 Hale, P. C. 102.

IMBECILITY. In medical jurisprudence, A form of insanity consisting in mental deficiency, either congenital, or resulting from an obstacle to the development of the faculties, supervening in infancy.

IMBEZZLE. Occasionally used for "embezzle."

IMBRACERY. See "Embracery."

IMMATERIAL. Not material; not essential or important.

IMMATERIAL AVERMENT. In pleading. A statement of unnecessary particulars in connection with, and as descriptive of, what is material. Gould, Pl. c. 3, § 186. Such averments must, however, be proved as laid, it is said (Doug. 665), though not if they may be struck out without striking out at the same time the cause of action, and when there is no variance. Gould, Pl. c. 3, § 188. See 1 Chit. Pl. 282.

IMMATERIAL ISSUE. In pleading. An issue taken upon some collateral matter, the decision of which will not settle the question in dispute between the parties in action. For example, if in an action of debt on bond, conditioned for the payment of ten dollars and fifty cents at a certain day, the defendant pleads the payment of ten dollars according to the form of the condition, and the plaintiff, instead of demurring, tenders issue upon the payment, it is manifest that, whether this issue be found for the plaintiff or the defendant, it will remain equally uncertain whether the plaintiff is entitled to maintain his action, or not; for in an action for the penalty of a bond, conditioned to pay a certain sum, the only material question is whether the exact sum were paid or not, and the question of payment of a part is a question quite beside the legal merits. Hob. 113; 5 Taunt. 386; Cro. Jac. 585; 2 Wm. Saund. 319b. A repleader will be ordered when an immaterial issue is reached, either before or after verdict. 2 Wm. Saund. 319b, note; 1 Rolle, Abr. 86; Cro. Jac. 585. See "Repleader."

IMMEDIATE. At once. "Though in strictness it excludes all mean times, it shall be construed such convenient time as is reasonably requisite for doing the thing." 2 Lev. 77.

It is stronger than the phrase "within a reasonable time," and implies prompt, vigorous action, without any delay. L. R. 4 Q. B. 469.

Acting with nothing interposed or between, or without the intervention of another object as a cause, means, medium or condition; producing its effect by direct agency. 60 Ill. App. 108.

IMMEDIATE DESCENT. Descents have long been distinguished as mediate and immediate, but these terms are susceptible of different interpretations, whence some confusion has been introduced into their legal discussion, since different judges have used them in different senses. In immediate descents there can be no impediment but what ariseth in the parties themselves, but in mediate descents, it is agreed, the disability of being an alien or attainted, in him that is the medius antecessor, will disable the other, though he have no such disability. Where the question is whether the inheritance by a brother from his brother, the father being an alien, is mediate or immediate, it is held after much discussion that the inheritance is immediate, so as not to be affected by the alienage of the father. It is held that in tracing the line of inheritance between brothers or their descendants it is not necessary to name the father as their common ancestor, and that alienism in any ancestor whom it was not necessary to name in tracing such inheritance or descent does not have the effect to impede it. 6 Pet. (U. S.) 112; 155 Ill. 604.

IMMEMORIAL. Time out of mind.

IMMEMORIAL POSSESSION. In Louisiana. Possession of which no man living has seen the beginning, and the existence of which he has learned from his elders. Civ. Code La. art. 762; 2 Mart. (La.) 214; 7 La. 46; 3 Toullier, Dr. Civ. p. 410; Poth. Cont. note 244; 3 Bouv. Inst. note 3069, note.

IMMEMORIAL USAGE. A usage which has existed from time immemorial.

IMMEUBLES. In French law. Immovables.

IMMIGRATION. The removing into one place from another. It differs from "emigration," which is the moving from one place into another.

IMMISCERE. (Lat.) In the civil law. To mix or mingle with; to meddle with; to join with; to take or enter upon an inheritance. Calv. Lex.

IMMISSIO. (Law Lat.) In old English law. A putting in; introduction. Fleta, lib. 3, c. 15, § 11.

IMMITTERE. (Lat.) In the civil law. To put or let into, as a beam into a wall. Calv. Lex. Dig. 50. 17. 242. 1.

In old English law. To put cattle on a common. Fleta, lib. 4, c. 20, § 7.

IMMOBILIA SITUM SEQUUNTUR. Immovables follow the law of their locality. 2 Kent, Comm. 67.

IMMOBILIS (Lat.) Immovable. *Immobilia*, or *res immobiles*, immovable things, such as lands and buildings. Mackeld. Civ. Law, p. 152, § 147; 2 Kent, Comm. 347.

IMMORAL. That which tends to subvert morality or decency. Contracts, etc., tending to sexual immorality furnish the most common examples, but a contract in derogation of religion was held "immoral" in England (L. R. 2 Exch. 230), as was a contract involving the removal of several thousand bodies from a burying ground (1 Cab. & El. 577).

IMMORAL CONSIDERATION. One contrary to good morals, and therefore invalid. For example, an agreement in consideration of future illicit cohabitation between the parties (3 Burrows, 1568; 1 Esp. 13; 1 Bos. & P. 340, 341), an agreement for the value of libellous and immoral pictures (4 Esp. 97), or for printing a libel (2 Starkie, 107), or for an immoral wager (Chit. Cont. 156), cannot, therefore, be enforced. For whatever arises from an immoral or illegal consideration is void, *quid turpi ex causa promissum est non valet.* Inst. 3. 20. 24.

IMMORALITY. That which is *contra bonos mores.*

In England, it is not punishable, in some cases, at the common law, on account of the ecclesiastical jurisdictions, *e. g.*, adultery. But except in cases belonging to the ecclesiastical courts, the court of king's bench is the *custos morum*, and may punish *delicto contra bonos mores.* 3 Burrows, 1438; 1 W. Bl. 94; 2 Strange, 788.

IMMOVABLES. In civil law. Property which, from its nature, destination, or the object to which it is applied, cannot move itself or be removed. Poth. des Choses, § 1.

IMMUNITY. Rights of exemption only—freedom from what otherwise would be a duty or burden. 3 Heisk. (Tenn.) 306

An exemption from serving in an office, or performing duties which the law generally requires other citizens to perform. See Dig. lib. 50, tit. 6; 1 Chit. Crim. Law, 821; 4 Har. & McH. (Md.) 341.

IMPAIRING THE OBLIGATION OF A contract. Any law, which enlarges, abridges, or in any manner changes the intention of the parties to the contract when it is discovered, necessarily impairs the contract itself, which is but the evidence of that intention. 11 Wheaton (U. S.) 256.

Any law impairs the obligation which renders the contract in itself less valuable or less enforcible, whether by changing its terms and stipulations, its legal qualities and conditions, or by regulating the remedy for its enforcement. 15 Rich. (S. C.) 105.

Whether the statute operates to impair debt or the remedy, the result is the same. 5 Lea (Tenn.) 112.

IMPANEL.

——In Old English Practice. To write the names of jurors on a panel, which is an oblong piece of parchment attached to the venire. This is done by the sheriff, or other officer lawfully authorized.

——In American Practice. The word is used of a jury drawn for trial of a particular cause by the clerk, as well as of the general list of jurors returned by the sheriff. Graham, Prac. 275. See 1 Arch. Prac. 365; 3 Sharswood, Bl. Comm. 354.

IMPANELLING. Has nothing to do with drawing, selecting, or swearing jurors, but means simply making the list of those who have been selected. 7 How. Pr. (N. Y.) 441.

IMPARCARE (Law Lat. from *in* and *parcus*, a pound or inclosed place). In old English law. To impound. Reg. Orig. 92b.

To shut up, or confine in prison. *Inducti sunt in carcerem et imparcati*, they were carried to prison and shut up. Bracton, fol. 124.

IMPARGAMENTUM. The right to impound cattle.

IMPARL. To have delay. Literally, to "speak with" (the plaintiff). The original object of an imparlance was to obtain time for an amicable adjustment. 3 Bl. Comm. 299. But the actual object has long been merely to obtain time to plead. 3 Chit. Prac. 700.

IMPARLANCE (from Fr. *parler*, to speak). In pleading and practice. Time given by the court to either party to answer the pleading of his opponent; as, either to plead, reply, rejoin, etc.

It is said to be nothing else but the continuance of the cause till a further day. Bac. Abr. "Pleas" (C). In this sense, imparlances are no longer allowed in English practice. 3 Chit. Prac. 700.

Time to plead. This is the common signification of the word. 2 Wm. Saund. 1, note 2; 2 Show. 310; Barnes, 346; Lawes, Civ. Pl. 93. In this sense, imparlances are not recognized in American law, the common practice being for the defendant to enter an appearance, when the cause stands continued, until a fixed time has elapsed within which he may file his plea. See "Continuance."

——**General Imparlance.** The entry of a general prayer and allowance of time to plead till the next term, without reserving to the defendant the benefit of any exception, so that after such an imparlance the defendant cannot object to the jurisdiction of the court, or plead any matter in abatement. This kind of imparlance is always from one term to another.

——**General Special Imparlance.** Contains a saving of all exceptions whatsoever, so that the defendant after this may plead not only in abatement, but he may also plead a plea which affects the jurisdiction of the court, as privilege. He cannot, however, plead a tender, and that he was always ready to pay, because by craving time he admits that he is not ready, and so falsifies his plea. Tidd, Prac. 418, 419.

——**Special Imparlance.** Reserves to the defendant all exception to the writ, bill, or count; and therefore after it the defendant may plead in abatement, though not to the jurisdiction of the court.

See Comyn, Dig. "Abatement" (I 19, 20, 21), "Pleader" (D); 1 Chit. Pl. 420; 1 Sellon, Prac. 265; Bac. Abr. "Pleas" (C).

IMPARSONEE. One in possession of a benefice.

IMPATRONIZATION. The act of a patron in putting one into possession of a benefice.

IMPEACH. To accuse; to question the sufficiency or genuineness of.

To proceed by impeachment (*q. v.*).

——**In the Law of Evidence.** To call in question the veracity of a witness, by means of evidence adduced for that purpose.

IMPEACHMENT.

——**In English Law.** The prosecution of a peer or commoner by the house of commons at the bar of the house of lords for treason, high crimes, or misdemeanors. 6 Enc. Laws Eng. 318.

——**In American Law.** A proceeding against a public civil officer, ordinarily prosecuted by the more numerous body of the legislature at the bar of the other, for the removal of such officer from office.

——**In Practice.** An attack on the testimony of a witness by showing his lack of veracity. It is to be distinguished from contradiction, which is an attack on testimony by showing that the facts at issue are other than as testified to.

IMPEACHMENT OF WASTE. A restraint from committing waste upon lands or tenements; or a demand of compensation for waste done by a tenant who has but a particular estate in the land granted, and therefore no right to commit waste.

All tenants for life or any less estate are liable to be impeached for waste, unless they hold without impeachment of waste; in the latter case they may commit waste without being questioned, or any demand for compensation for the waste done. 11 Coke, 82.

IMPECHIARE, or IMPESCARE (Law Lat.) To impeach or accuse. Cowell.

IMPEDIENS (Law Lat.) In old practice. One who hinders; an impedient. The defendant or deforciant in a fine was sometimes so called. Cowell; Blount.

IMPEDIMENTO. In Spanish law. A prohibition to contract marriage, established by law between certain persons.

The disabilities arising from this cause are twofold, viz.:

(1) *Impedimento dirimente,*—such disabilities as render the marriage null, although contracted with the usual legal solemnities.

Among these impediments, some are absolute, others relative. The former cannot be cured, and render the marriage radically null; others may be removed by previous dispensation.

(2) *Impedimento, impediente,* or *prohibitivo,*—such disabilities as impede the contracting of a marriage, but do not annul it when contracted.

For the effects of these impediments, see Escriche, Dict. Raz. "Impedimente Prohibitivo."

IMPEDIMENTS. Legal hindrances to making contracts. Some of these impediments are minority, want of reason, coverture, and the like. See "Contract"; "Incapacity."

——**In Civil Law.** Bars to marriage.

(1) Absolute impediments are those which prevent the person subject to them from marrying at all, without either the nullity of marriage or its being punishable.

(2) Dirimant impediments are those which render a marriage void; as, where one of the contracting parties is already married to another person.

(3) Prohibitive impediments are those which do not render the marriage null, but subject the parties to a punishment.

(4) Relative impediments are those which regard only certain persons with regard to each other; as, the marriage of a brother to a sister.

IMPEDITOR (Law Lat.) In old English law. A disturber in the action of *quare impedit.* St. Marlb. c. 12.

IMPENSAE (Lat.) In civil law. Expense; outlay. Divided into *necessariae*, for necessity, *utiles*, for use, and *voluptuariae*, for luxury. Dig. 79. 6. 14; Vocat.

IMPERATIVE. See "Mandatory."

IMPERATOR. Emperor. This was the title of the Roman emperor and of the English kings before the Conquest. 1 Bl. Comm. 242.

IMPERFECT OBLIGATIONS. Those which are not, in view of the law, of binding force.

IMPERFECT TRUST. A trust which has not been executed. See "Trust."

IMPERII MAJESTAS EST TUTELAE SAlus. The majesty of the empire is the safety of its protection. Co. Litt. 64.

IMPERITIA. Unskillfulness.

IMPERITIA CULPAE AENUMERATUR. Ignorance or want of skill is considered a fault, *i. e.*, a negligence, for which one who professes skill is responsible. Dig. 50. 17. 132; 1 Bouv. Inst. note 1004; 2 Kent, Comm. 588; 4 Ark. 523.

IMPERITIA EST MAXIMA MECHANEorum poena. Lack of skill is the greatest punishment of artisans. 11 Coke, 54a.

IMPERIUM. The right to command, which includes the right to employ the force of the state to enforce the laws. This is one of the principal attributes of the power of the executive. 1 Toullier, Dr. Civ. note 58.

IMPERSONALITAS NON CONCLUDIT nec ligat. Impersonality neither concludes nor binds. Co. Litt. 352.

IMPERTINENT (Lat. *in*, not, *pertinens*, pertaining or relating to).

——**In Equity Pleading.** A term applied to matters introduced into a bill, answer, or other proceeding in a suit which are not properly before the court for decision at that particular stage of the suit. 1 Sumn. (U. S.) 506; 3 Story (U. S.) 13; 1 Paige, Ch. (N. Y.) 555; 5 Blackf. (Ind.) 439. Impertinent matter is not necessarily scandalous; but all scandalous matter is impertinent.

——**In Pleading at Law.** A term applied to matters not necessary to constitute the cause of action or ground of defense. Cowp. 683; 5 East, 275; 2 Mass. 283. It constitutes surplusage (*q. v.*).

——**In Practice.** A term applied to evidence of facts which do not belong to the matter in question. That which is immaterial is, in general, impertinent, and that which is material is not, in general, impertinent. 1 McClel. & Y. 337. Impertinent matter in the interrogatories to witnesses or their answers, in equity, will be expunged after reference to a master at the cost of the offending party. 2 Younge & C. 445.

IMPESCARE. See "Impechiare."

IMPETITIO VASTI. Impeachment of waste (*q. v.*).

IMPETRARE (Lat.) In old English practice. To obtain by request, as a writ or privilege. Bracton, fols. 57, 172b. This application of the word seems to be derived from the civil law. Calv. Lex.

IMPETRATION. The obtaining anything by prayer or petition. In the ancient English statutes, it signifies a preobtaining of churches benefices in England from the church of Rome, which belonged to the gift of the king or other lay patrons.

IMPIER. Umpire.

IMPIERMENT (Law Fr.) Impairing or prejudicing. St. 23 Hen. VIII. c. 9. Blount; Kelham.

IMPIGNORATA (Law Lat.) Pledged; given in pledge (*pignori data*); mortgaged. A term applied in Bracton to land. Bracton, fol. 20.

IMPIUS ET CRUDELIS JUDICANDUS est qui libertati non favet. He is to be judged impious and cruel who does not favor liberty. Co. Litt. 124.

IMPLACITARE (Law Lat. from *in*, into, and *placitum*, a plea or suit). In old English law and practice. To subject to an action, or *placitum;* to implead or sue.

IMPLACITATUS (Law Lat.) Impleaded; sued.

IMPLEAD. In practice. To sue or prosecute by due course of law. 9 Watts (Pa.) 47.

IMPLEADED (Lat. *implacitatus*). Sued or prosecuted. Still used in practice.

The word is not synonymous with the expression "et al.," but when used in formal pleadings and in court records the word "impleaded" is properly used following the name of a defendant when there is more than one defendant and only one defendant appears, to designate that there are defendants other than the defendant who is then present in court.

In actions where there are more defendants than one and one answers, his name is sometimes stated thus in the title of his answer or plea: "Richard Roe, impleaded with John Doe," signifying that the two are sued together but one only interposed the plea. 250 Ill. 518, 519.

IMPLEMENTS (Lat. *impleo*, to fill). Such things as are used or employed for a trade, or furniture of a house. 11 Metc. (Mass.) 82.

Whatever may supply wants. Particularly applied to tools, utensils, vessels, instruments of labor; as, the implements of trade or of husbandry. Webster. Things of necessary use in any trade or mystery, without which the work cannot be performed. Also, the furniture of a house, as all household goods and implements, such as tables, presses, cupboards, etc. Termes de la Ley; Jacob; Tomlins; Williams.

The term does not apply to animals. 5 Ark. 41; 11 Metc. (Mass.) 79.

IMPLICATA (Lat.) Small adventures for which the freight contracted for is to be received, although the cargo may be lost. Targa, c. 34; Emerig. Mar. Loans, § 5.

IMPLICATION. An inference of something not directly declared, but arising from what is admitted or expressed. See terms defined under "Implied."

IMPLIED. Arising by intendment or inference, rather than by actual expression in words.

IMPLIED ABROGATION. See "Abrogation."

IMPLIED ASSUMPSIT. See "Assumpsit."

IMPLIED CONDITION. See "Condition."

IMPLIED CONSIDERATION. See "Consideration."

IMPLIED CONTRACT. See "Contract."

IMPLIED COVENANT. See "Covenant."

IMPLIED MALICE. Malice presumed or implied by law from the acts of a party and the circumstances of a case; malice inferred from any deliberate, cruel act committed by one person against another, however sudden. Whart. Hom. 38.

IMPLIED POWER. By an implied power is meant one that is directly and immediately appropriate to the execution of the specific power granted, and not one that has slight or remote relation to it. 130 Ill. 268.

IMPLIED TRUST. See "Trust."

IMPLIED USE. See "Resulting Use."

IMPLIED WARRANTY. See "Warranty."

IMPORTATION. In common law. The act of bringing goods and merchandise into a country from a foreign country. 5 Cranch (U. S.) 368; 9 Cranch (U. S.) 104, 120; 2 Man. & G. 155, note (a).

IMPORTS. Goods or other property imported or brought into a country from foreign territory. Story, Const. § 949. See (U. S.) Const. art. 1, § 10; 7 How. (U. S.) 477.

IMPORTUNITY. Urgent solicitation, with troublesome frequency and pertinacity. Generally applied to solicitation of a testator. Dane, Abr. c. 127, a. 14, s. 5, 6, 7; 2 Phillim. Ecc. 551, 552.

IMPOSITIO. (Lat.) In old English law. An imposition, tax, or tribute. The older expression was *maletot.* Stat. Confirm. Chartar. c. 7. 2 Inst. 530.

IMPOSITIONS. Imposts, taxes, or contributions.

IMPOSSIBILITY. That which, in the constitution and course of nature or the law, no man can do or perform.

Impossibility is of the following several sorts:

An act is physically impossible when it is contrary to the course of nature. Such an impossibility may be either absolute, *i. e.*, impossible in any case (*e. g.*, for A. to reach the moon), or relative (sometimes called "impossibility in fact"), *i. e.*, arising from the circumstances of the case (*e. g.*, for A. to make a payment to B., he being a deceased person). To the latter class belongs what is sometimes called "practical impossibility," which exists when the act can be done, but only at an excessive or unreasonable cost. An act is legally or juridically impossible when a rule of law makes it impossible to do it; *e. g.*, for A. to make a valid will before his majority. This class of acts must not be confounded with those which are possible, although forbidden by law, as to commit a theft. An act is logically impossible when it is contrary to the nature of the transaction, as where A. gives property to B. expressly for his own benefit, on condition that he transfers it to C. Rapalje & L.

IMPOSSIBILIUM NULLA OBLIGATIO est. There is no obligation to perform impossible things. Dig. 50. 18. 185; 1 Poth. Obl. pt. 1, c. 1, sec. 4, § 3; 2 Story, Eq. Jur. (6th Ed.) 763; Broom, Leg. Max. (3d London Ed.) 228.

IMPOSSIBLE CONTRACTS. Such contracts as cannot be performed, either because of the nature of the obligation undertaken, or because of some supervening event which renders the performance of the obligation either physically or legally impossible. 10 Am. & Eng. Enc. Law, 176.

IMPOSTS. Taxes, duties, or impositions. A duty on imported goods or merchandise. Federalist, No. 30; Elliott, Deb. 289; Story, Const. § 949; 12 Wheaton (U. S.) 437.

In a larger sense it is any tax or imposition. 7 Wallace (U. S.) 445.

IMPOTENCE. In medical jurisprudence. The incapacity for copulation or propagating the species. It has also been used as synonymous with "sterility."

The principal use of the term is as a ground of divorce, and as so used it signifies "the irremediable physical incapacity of one of the parties to a marriage for any reasonable sexual connection with the other." 1 Bish. Mar. & Div. § 766.

To avoid impotence, there must be capacity for "*copula vera,*" copulation in its natural and ordinary meaning, and not merely of incipient and imperfect coition. 33 Md. 405.

IMPOTENS (Lat.) Unable; impotent; without power or ability. *Impotens sui*, having no power of himself, unable to help himself. Bracton, fol. 15; Fleta, lib. 3, c. 7, § 1.

IMPOTENTIA (Lat.) Inability; impossibility.

IMPOTENTIA EXCUSAT LEGEM. Impossibility is an excuse in the law. Co. Litt. 29; Broom, Leg. Max. (3d London Ed.) 223.

IMPOTENTIAM. Impotence; impossibility.

IMPOTENTIAM, PROPERTY PROPTER. See "Property Propter Impotentiam."

IMPOUND. To place in a pound goods or cattle distrained or estray. 3 Bl. Comm. 12.

IMPRESCRIPTIBILITY. The state of being incapable of prescription.

A property which is held in trust is imprescriptible, that is, the trustee cannot acquire a title to it by prescription; nor can the borrower of a thing get a right to it by any lapse of time, unless he claims an adverse right to it during the time required by law.

IMPRESCRIPTIBLE RIGHTS. Rights to which no claim can be acquired by prescription.

IMPRESSMENT. A power possessed by the English crown of taking persons or property to aid in the defense of the country, with or without the consent of the persons concerned. It is usually exercised to obtain hands for the queen's ships in time of war, by taking seamen engaged in merchant vessels (1 Bl. Comm. 420; Maude & P. Shipp. 123), but in former times impressment of merchant ships was also practiced. The admiralty issues protections against impressment in certain cases, either under statutes passed in favor of certain callings (*e. g.*, persons employed in the Greenland fisheries), or voluntarily. Rapalje & L.

IMPRIMATUR (Lat.) A license or allowance to one to print.

At one time, before a book could be printed in England, it was requisite that a permission should be obtained. That permission was called an *imprimatur*. In some countries where the press is liable to censure, an *imprimatur* is required.

IMPRIMERY. In some of the ancient English statutes, this word is used to signify a printing office, the art of printing, a print or impression.

IMPRIMIS (Lat. in the first place). It is commonly used to denote the first clause in an instrument, especially in wills, *item* being used to denote the subsequent clauses. This is also its classical and literal meaning. Ainsworth. See Fleta, lib. 2, c. 54. *Imprimitus* and *imprimum* also occur. Du-Cange, Prec. Ch. 430; Cas. temp. Talb. 110; 6 Madd. 31; Magna Cart. 9 Hen. III.; 2 Anc. Inst. Eng. 506.

IMPRISONMENT. The restraint of a man's liberty. 2 Bish. Crim. Law, § 669.

The restraint of a person contrary to his will. 2 Inst. 589; 1 Baldw. (U. S.) 239, 600. Any forcible detention of a man's person, or control over his movements. 3 Harr. (Del.) 418.

Actual confinement is not essential, a forcible detention on the street being sufficient. 3 Bl. Comm. 127. Nor is actual manual violence. 100 Mass. 79.

Words are sufficient to constitute an imprisonment, if they impose a restraint upon the person, and the plaintiff is accordingly restrained; for he is not obliged to incur the risk of personal violence and insult by resisting, until actual violence is used. 9 N. H. 493.

IMPRISTI. Followers or adherents.

IMPROBATION. In Scotch law. An act by which falsehood and forgery are proved. Ersk. Inst. 4. 119; Stair, Inst. 4. 20; Bell, Dict.

IMPROPER FEUDS. Derivative feuds, such, for instance, as those that were originally bartered and sold to the feudatory for a price, or were held upon base or less honorable services, or upon a rent in lieu of military service, or were themselves alienable, without mutual license, or descended indifferently to males or females, or otherwise varied from the rules ordinarily pertaining to feudal tenure. Wharton.

IMPROPRIATE RECTOR. A lay rector.

IMPROPRIATE TITHES. Tithes in the hands of a lay owner.

IMPROPRIATION. In ecclesiastical law. The act of employing the revenues of a church living to one's own use. It is also a parsonage or ecclesiastical living in the hands of a layman, or which descends by inheritance. Tech. Dict.

IMPROVE. To impeach as false or forged; to cultivate. 4 Cow. (N. Y.) 190.

——**In Scotch Law.** To improve a lease means to grant a lease of unusual duration to encourage a tenant, when the soil is exhausted, etc. Bell, Dict.; Stair, Inst. p. 676, § 23.

IMPROVEMENT. An amelioration in the condition of real or personal property effected by the expenditure of labor or money for the purpose of rendering it useful for other purposes than those for which it was originally used, or more useful for the same purposes.

——**In Patent Law.** An addition of some useful thing to a machine, manufacture, or composition of matter.

The patent law of July 4, 1836, authorizes the granting of a patent for any new and useful improvement on any art, machine, manufacture, or composition of matter. Section 6. It is often very difficult to say what is a new and useful improvement, the cases often approaching very near to each other. In the present improved state of machinery it is almost impracticable not to employ the same elements of motion, and, in some particulars, the same manner of operation, to produce any new effect. 1 Gall. (U. S.) 478; 2 Gall. (U. S.) 51. See 4 Barn. & Ald. 540; 2 Kent, Comm. 370.

IMPRUIARE (Law Lat.) In old records. To improve land. *Impruiamentum*, the improvement so made of it. Chart. Abbat. MS. fol. 50a; Cowell.

IMPUBER (Lat.) In civil law. One who is more than seven years old, or out of infancy, and who has not attained the age of puberty; that is, if a boy, till he has attained his full age of fourteen years, and, if a girl, her full age of twelve years. Domat, Liv. Prel. tit. 2, § 2, note 8.

IMPUNITAS CONTINUUM AFFECTUM tribuit delinquenti. Impunity offers a continual bait to a delinquent. 4 Coke, 45.

IMPUNITAS SEMPER AD DETERIORA invitat. Impunity always invites to greater crimes. 5 Coke, 109.

IMPUTATIO (Lat.) In civil law. Legal liability.

IMPUTATION OF PAYMENT. In civil law. The application of a payment made by a debtor to his creditor.

The debtor may apply his payment as he pleases, with the exception that in case of a debt carrying interest it must be first applied to discharging the interest.

The creditor may apply the funds by informing the debtor at the time of payment.

The law imputes in the neglect of the parties to do so, and in favor of the debtor. It directs that imputation which would have been best for the debtor at the time of payment. Hence it applies the funds to obligations most burdensome to the debtor; *e. g.*, to a mortgage rather than to a book account, and to a debt which would render the debtor insolvent if unpaid, rather than to any less important one. If nothing else appears to control it, the rule of priority prevails.

In Louisiana the preceding civil law rules are in force. The statutory enactment (Civ. Code, art. 2159 et seq.) is a translation of the Code Napoleon (articles 1253-1256), slightly altered. See Poth. Obl. note 528, Translation by Evans, and the notes. Payment is imputed first to the discharge of interest. 1 Mart. (La.; N. S.) 571; 10 Rob. (La.) 51; 5 La. Ann. 738. But if the interest was not binding, being usurious, the payment must go to the principal.

IMPUTED NEGLIGENCE. Negligence of another than the injured person contributing to the injury, and imputed to him by law. As a general rule, contributory negligence will be imputed to another than the negligent person, so as to bar an action by such other for injuries received by him (1) if the negligent person was under the direction and control of the injured person (38 Me. 443), or (2) where the injured person is not *sui juris*, and the negligent person is responsible for him as parent or guardian. 75 Pa. St. 257.

IN (Law Fr. *eins*). A term used, from a very early period, to express the nature of a title, or the mode of acquiring an estate, or the ground upon which a seisin is founded. Thus, in Littleton, a tenant is said to be "in by lease of his lessor" (*eins per lease son lessor*), that is, his title or estate is derived from the lease. Litt. § 82. So, parceners are said to be "in by divers descents." Id. § 313. So, the issue of a husband is said to be "in by descent" (*eins per discent*). Id. § 403. So, two sisters are said to be "in by divers titles." Id. § 662. So, in modern law, parties are constantly said in the books to be "in by descent," "in by purchase." A dowress is said to be "in, of the seisin of her husband." 4 Kent, Comm. 69. A devisor is said to be "in, of his old estate." 1 Powell, Devises (by Jarman) 621, note. So, a lessor. Shaw, C. J., 1 Metc. (Mass.) 120. "If he has a freehold, he is in as freeholder. If he has a chattel interest, he is in as a termor. If he has no title, he is in as a trespasser." Lord Mansfield, 1 Burrows, 114.

IN ACTION. A thing is said to be in action when it is not in possession, and for its recovery, the possessor unwilling, an action is necessary. 2 Sharswood, Bl. Comm. 396. See "Chose."

IN ADVERSUM (Law Lat.) Against an adverse, unwilling, or resisting party. "A decree not by consent, but *in adversum*." 3 Story (U. S.) 318.

IN AEDIFICIIS LAPIS MALE POSITUS non est removendus. In buildings, a stone badly placed is not to be removed. 11 Coke, 69.

IN AEQUA (or AEQUALI) MANU (Law Lat.; Law Fr. *en owele mayn*). In equal hand; held equally or indifferently between two parties. Where an instrument was deposited by the parties to it in the hands of a third person, to keep on certain conditions, it was said to be held *in aequali manu*. Reg. Orig. 28.

IN AEQUALI JURE (Lat.) In equal right.

IN AEQUALI JURE MELIOR EST CONditio possidentis. When the parties have equal rights, the condition of the possessor is the better. Mitf. Eq. Pl. 215; Jeremy, Eq. Jur. 285; 1 Madd. Ch. Prac. 170; Dig. 50. 17. 128; Broom, Leg. Max. (3d London Ed.) 634; Plowd. 296.

IN ALIENO SOLO (Lat.) In another's land. 2 Steph. Comm. 20.

IN ALIO LOCO. See "Cepit in Alio Loco."

IN ALTA PRODITIONE NULLUS POtest esse accessorius sed principalis solummodo. In high treason, no one can be an accessary, but only principal. 3 Inst. 138.

IN ALTERNATIVIS ELECTIO EST DEbitoris. In alternatives, the debtor has the election.

IN AMBIGUA VOCE LEGIS EA POTIUS accipienda est significatio, quae vitio caret; praesertim cum etiam voluntas legis ex hoc colligi possit. When obscurities, ambiguities, or faults of expression render the meaning of an enactment doubtful, that interpretation shall be preferred which is most consonant to equity, especially where it is in conformity with the general design of the legislature. Dig. 1. 3. 19; Broom, Leg. Max. (3d London Ed.) 513; Bac. Max. reg. 3; 2 Inst. 173.

IN AMBIGUIS CASIBUS SEMPER praesumitur pro rege. In doubtful cases, the presumption is always in favor of the king.

IN AMBIGUIS ORATIONIBUS MAXIME sententia spectanda est ejus qui eas protulisset. When there are ambiguous expressions, the intention of him who uses them is especially to be regarded. This maxim of Roman law was confined to wills. Dig. 50. 17. 96; Broom, Leg. Max. (3d London Ed.) 506.

IN ANGLIA NON EST INTERREGNUM. In England there is no interregnum. Jenk. Cent. Cas. 205; Broom, Leg. Max. 50.

IN APERTA LUCE (Law Lat.) In open daylight; in the daytime. 9 Coke, 65b.

IN APICIBUS JURIS. Among the subtleties or extreme doctrines of the law. 1 Kames, Eq. 190. See "Apex Juris."

IN ARBITRIUM JUDICIS. In the discretion of the court.

IN ARCTA ET SALVA CUSTODIA (Law Lat.) In close and safe custody. 3 Bl. Comm. 415.

IN ARTICULO MORTIS. In the article of death; at the point of death. 1 Johns. (N. Y.) 159.

IN ATROCIORIBUS DELICTIS PUNITUR affectus licet non sequatur effectus. In more atrocious crimes, the intent is punished, though the effect does not follow. 2 Rolle, 89.

IN AUTER SOILE. (Law Fr.) In or on another's land. Dyer, 36b (Fr. ed.)

IN AUTRE DROIT (Law Fr.) In another's right; as representing another. An executor, administrator, or trustee sues *in autre droit.*

IN BANCO (Law Lat.) In bank; in the bench. See "Banc."

IN BLANK. Without restriction. Applied to indorsements on promissory notes where no indorsee is named.

IN BONIS (Lat.) Among the goods or property; in actual possession. Inst. 4. 2. 2; Tayl. Civ. Law, 479.

IN CAMERA. In private; in chambers.

IN CAPITA (Lat.) To or by the heads or polls. Thus, where persons succeed to estates *in capita,* they take each an equal share. So, where a challenge to a jury is *in capita,* it is to the polls, or to the jurors individually, as opposed to a challenge to the array. 3 Sharswood, Bl. Comm. 361. *Per capita* is also used.

IN CAPITE (Lat.) In chief. A tenant *in capite* was one who held directly of the crown (2 Sharswood, Bl. Comm. 60), whether by knight's service or socage. But tenure *in capite* was of two kinds,—general and special; the first from the king (*caput regni*), the second from a lord (*caput feudi*). A holding of an honor in king's lands, but not immediately of him, was yet a holding *in capite.* Kitch. Cts. 127; Dyer, 44; Fitzh. Nat. Brev. 5. Abolished by 12 Car. II. c. 24.

IN CASU EXTREMAE NECESSITATIS omnia sunt communia. In cases of extreme necessity, everything is in common. Hale, P. C. 54; Broom, Leg. Max. 1.

IN CASU PROVISO (Law Lat.) In a (or the) case provided. *In tali casu editum et provisum,* in such case made and provided. Towns. Pl. 164, 165.

IN CAUSA. In the cause, as distinguished from *in initialibus* (*q. v.*). A term in Scotch practice. 1 Brown, Ch. 252.

IN CHIEF. Principal; primary; directly obtained. A term applied to the evidence obtained from a witness upon his examination in court by the party producing him, in relation to the matter in issue at the trial. The examination so conducted for this purpose.

Evidence or examination in chief is to be distinguished from evidence given on cross-examination, and from evidence given upon the *voir dire.*

Evidence in chief should be confined to such matters as the pleadings and the opening warrant, and a departure from this rule will be sometimes highly inconvenient, if not fatal. Suppose, for example, that two assaults have been committed, one in January and the other in February, and the plaintiff prove his cause of action to have been the assault in January; he cannot abandon that, and afterwards prove another committed in February, unless the pleadings and openings extend to both. 1 Campb. 473. See, also, 6 Car. & P. 73; 1 Moody & R. 282.

This matter, however, is one of practice; and a great variety of rules exist in the different states of the United States, the leading object, however, being in all cases the same,—to prevent the plaintiff from introducing in evidence a different case from the one which he had prepared the defendant to expect from the pleadings.

IN CIVILIBUS MINISTERIUM EXCUSAT, in criminalibus non item. In civil matters, agency or service excuses, but not so in criminal matters. Lofft, 228; Tray. Lat. Max. 243.

IN CLARIS NON EST LOCUS CONJECTURIS. In things obvious there is no room for conjecture.

IN COMMENDAM (Lat.) The state or condition of a church living which is void or vacant, and which is commended to the care of some one. In Louisiana there is a species of partnership called "partnership *in commendam.*" See "Commendam."

IN COMMODATO HAEC PACTIO, NE dolus praestetur, rata non est. If in a contract for a loan there is inserted a clause that fraud should not be accounted of, such clause is void. Dig. 13. 7. 17.

IN COMMUNI (Law Lat.) In common. Fleta, lib. 3, c. 4, § 2.

IN CONJUNCTIVIS, OPORTET UTRAMque partem esse veram. In conjunctives, each part must be true. Wingate, Max. 13.

IN CONSIDERATIONE INDE (Law Lat.) In consideration thereof. 3 Salk. 64, pl. 5.

IN CONSIDERATIONE LEGIS (Law Lat.) In consideration or contemplation of law; in abeyance. Dyer, 102b.

IN CONSIDERATIONE PRAEMISSORUM (Law Lat.) In consideration of the premises. 1 Strange, 535.

IN CONSIMILI CASU CONSIMILE DEbet esse remedium. In similar cases, the remedy should be similar. Hardr. 65.

IN CONSUETUDINIBUS NON DIUTURnitas temporis sed soliditas rationis est consideranda. In customs, not the length of time, but the strength of the reason, should be considered. Co. Litt. 141.

IN CONTINENTI (Lat.) Immediately; without any interval or intermission. Calv. Lex. Sometimes written as one word, *incontinenti.*

IN CONTRACTIBUS, BENIGNA; IN TEStamentis, benignior; in restitutionibus, benignissima interpretatio facienda est. In contracts, the interpretation or construction should be liberal; in wills, more liberal; in restitutions, most liberal. Co. Litt. 112a.

IN CONTRACTIBUS, REI VERITAS POtius quam scriptura perspici debet. In contracts, the truth of the matter ought to be regarded, rather than the writing. Code, 4. 22. 1.

IN CONTRACTIBUS TACITE INSUNT quae sunt moris et consuetudinis. In contracts, those things which are of custom and usage are tacitly implied. Broom, Leg. Max. (3d London Ed.) 759; 3 Bing. N. C. 814, 818; Story, Bills, § 143; 3 Kent, Comm. 260.

IN CONTRAHENDA VENDITIONE, AMbiguum pactum contra venditorem interpretandum est. In negotiating a sale, an ambiguous agreement is to be interpreted against the seller. Dig. 50. 17. 172; Id. 18. 1. 21.

IN CONVENTIONIBUS CONTRAHENTIum voluntatem potius quam verba spectari placuit. In agreements, the rule is to regard the intention of the contracting parties, rather than their words. Dig. 50. 16. 219; 2 Kent, Comm. 555; Broom, Leg. Max. (3d London Ed.) 491; 17 Johns. (N. Y.) 150.

IN CORPORE (Lat.) In body or substance; in a material thing or object. *Sive consistant in corpore, sive in jure,* whether they consist in or belong to a material object, or a mere right. Bracton, fol. 37b.

IN CRASTINO (Law Lat.) On the morrow. *In crastino Animarum,* on the morrow of All Souls. 1 Bl. Comm. 342.

IN CRIMINALIBUS, PROBATIONES DEbent esse luce clariores. In criminal cases, the proofs ought to be clearer than the light. 3 Inst. 210.

IN CRIMINALIBUS SUFFICIT GENERAlis malitia intentionis cum facto paris gradus. In criminal cases, a general malice of intention is sufficient, with an act of equal or corresponding degree. Bac. Max. reg. 15; Broom, Leg. Max. (3d London Ed.) 291.

IN CRIMINALIBUS VOLUNTAS REPUtabitur pro facto. In criminal acts, the will will be taken for the deed. 3 Inst. 106.

IN CUJUS REI TESTIMONIUM. In testimony whereof.

IN CUSTODIA LEGIS. In the custody of the law. A term applied to property which has been lawfully seized by or committed to the care of an officer of a court for some purpose incident to an action. 10 Pet. (U. S.) 400. The property must be legally held by the officer. Thus, where the clerk of court received money paid in to keep a tender good, without an order to that effect, it was held that the money was not *in custodia legis*. 49 Minn. 133.

IN DELICTO. In fault; culpable; guilty. See "In Pari Delicto."

IN DIEM. (Lat.) For a day; for the space of a day. Calv. Lex. Spiegelius.

On, or at a day. *In diem debitum;* a debt due at a certain day. Calv. Lex. Brissonius.

IN DISJUNCTIVIS SUFFICIT ALTERAM partem esse veram. In disjunctives, it is sufficient if either part be true. Wingate, Max. 13; Co. Litt. 225a; 10 Coke, 50; Dig. 50. 17. 110.

IN DOMINICO (Law Lat.) In demesne. *In dominico suo, ut de feodo,* in his demesne as of fee. Bracton, fols. 253b, 261b; Fleta, lib. 2, c. 54, § 18; 1 Reeve, Hist. Eng. Law, 428; Co. Litt. 17a; 2 Bl. Comm. 105, 106.

IN DORSO. On the back. 2 Bl. Comm. 468; 2 Steph. Comm. 164. *In dorso recordi,* on the back of the record. 5 Coke, 45. Hence the English "indorse," "indorsement," etc.

IN DUBIIS (Lat.) In doubtful cases; in matters or cases of doubt.

IN DUBIIS BENIGNIORA PRAEFEREN da sunt. In doubtful matters, the more favorable are to be preferred. Dig. 50. 17. 56; 2 Kent, Comm. 557.

IN DUBIIS MAGIS DIGNUM EST ACCIPiendum. In doubtful cases, the more worthy is to be taken. Branch, Princ.

IN DUBIIS NON PRAESUMITUR PRO testamento. In doubtful cases, there is no presumption in favor of the will. Cro. Car. 51.

IN DUBIO (Lat.) In doubt; in a state of uncertainty; in a doubtful case.

IN DUBIO HAEC LEGIS CONSTRUCTIO quam verba ostendunt. In a doubtful case, that is the construction of the law which the words indicate.

IN DUBIO PARS MELIOR EST SEQUENda. In doubt, the gentler course is to be followed.

IN DUBIO SEQUENDUM QUOD TUTIUS est. In doubt, the safer course is to be adopted.

IN DUPLO. In double. *Damna in duplo,* double damages. Fleta, lib. 4, c. 10, § 1.

IN EADEM CAUSA (Lat.) In the same state or condition. Calv. Lex.

IN EMULATIONEM VICINI (Lat.) In envy or hatred of a neighbor. Where an act is done, or action brought, solely to hurt or distress another, it is said to be *in emulationem vicini.* 1 Kames, Eq. 56.

IN EO QUOD PLUS SIT SEMPER INEST et minus. The less is always included in the greater. Dig. 50. 17. 110.

IN EQUITY. According to equitable doctrines.

IN ESSE (Lat.) In being; in existence. An event which may happen is *in posse;* when it has happened, it is *in esse.* The term is often used of liens or estates. A child in its mother's womb is, for some purposes, regarded as *in esse.*

IN EXCAMBIO (Law Lat.) In exchange. Formal words in old deeds of exchange.

IN EXITU (Lat.) In issue. *De materia in exitu,* of the matter in issue. 12 Mod. 372.

IN EXPOSITIONE INSTRUMENTORUM, mala grammatica, quod fieri potest, vitanda est. In the construction of instruments, bad grammar is to be avoided as much as possible. 6 Coke, 39; 2 Pars. Cont. 26.

IN EXTENSO. At length; in full.

IN EXTREMIS (Lat.) At the very end; in the last moments.

IN FACIE CURIAE (Law Lat.) In the face of the court. Dyer, 28.

IN FACIE ECCLESIAE (Lat.) In the face or presence of the church. A marriage is said to be made *in facie ecclesiae* when made in a consecrated church or chapel, or by a clerk in orders elsewhere; and one of these two things is necessary to a marriage in England in order to the wife's having dower, unless there be a dispensation or license. Bright, Husb. & Wife, pp. 370, 371, 391. But see 6 & 7 Wm. IV. c. 85; 1 Vict. c. 22; 3 & 4 Vict. c. 72. It was anciently the practice to marry at the church door, and there make a verbal assignment of dower. These verbal assignments, to prevent fraud, were necessarily held valid only when made *in facie et ad ostium ecclesiae.* See 2 Sharswood, Bl. Comm. 103; Taylor.

IN FACIENDO (Lat.) In doing. Story, Eq. Jur. § 1308.

IN FACT. Actual; not based on legal fiction or intendment of law.

IN FACTO In fact; in deed. *In facto dicit,* in fact says. 1 Salk. 22, pl. 1.

Depending on fact. Calv. Lex.

IN FACTO QUOD SE HABET AD BOnum et malum magis de bono quam de malo lex intendit. In a deed which may be considered good or bad, the law looks more to the good than to the bad. Co. Litt. 78.

IN (or EN) FAIT (Law Fr.) In fact; in deed. Lord Coke distinguishes "matters of record" from "matters *in fait.*" Co. Litt. 380b.

IN FAVORABILIBUS MAGIS ATTENDItur quod prodest quam quod nocet. In things favored, what does good is more regarded than what does harm. Bac. Max. reg. 12.

IN FAVOREM LIBERATIS (Lat.) In favor of liberty.

IN FAVOREM VITAE (Lat.) In favor of life.

IN FAVOREM VITAE, LIBERTATIS, ET innocentiae omnia praesumuntur. In favor of life, liberty, and innocence, all things are to be presumed. Lofft, 125.

IN FEODO (Law Lat.) In fee. Bracton, fol. 207; Fleta, lib. 2, c. 64, § 15. *Seisitus in feodo,* seised in fee. Fleta, lib. 3, c. 7, § 1.

IN FICTIONE JURIS SEMPER AEQUItas existit. A legal fiction is always consistent with equity. 11 Coke, 51; Broom, Leg. Max. (3d London Ed.) 120, 123; 17 Johns. (N. Y.) 348; 3 Bl. Comm. 43, 283.

IN FIERI (Lat.) In being done; in process of completion. A thing is said to rest *in fieri* when it is not yet complete; *e. g.,* the records of a court were anciently held to be *in fieri,* or incomplete, till they were recorded on parchment, but now till the giving of judgment, after which they can be amended only during the same term. 2 Barn. & Adol. 791; 3 Sharswood, Bl. Comm. 407. It is also used of contracts.

IN FINE. At the end.

IN FORMA PAUPERIS (Lat.) In the character or form of a poor man.

When a person is so poor that he cannot bear the charges of suing at law or in equity, upon making oath that he is not worth five pounds, and bringing a certificate from a counsellor at law that he believes him to have a just cause, he is permitted to sue *in forma pauperis,* in the manner of a pauper; that is, he is allowed to have original writs and subpoenas gratis, and counsel assigned him without fee. 3 Bl. Comm. 400. And in most if not all the states, provision is made by statute for suing *in forma pauperis,* the manner of obtaining such privilege varying with the statutes. See 3 Johns. Ch. (N. Y.) 65; 1 Paige, Ch. (N. Y.) 588; 3 Paige, Ch. (N. Y.) 273; 5 Paige, Ch. (N. Y.) 58; 2 Molloy, 475.

IN FORMA PRAEDICTA (Law Lat.) In form aforesaid. Perk. c. 3, § 242.

IN FORO (Lat.) In a (or the) forum, court, or tribunal.

IN FORO CONSCIENTIAE (Lat.) Before the tribunal of conscience; conscientiously. The term is applied to moral obligations, as distinct from the obligations which the law enforces. In the sale of property, for example, the concealment of facts by the vendee which may enhance the price is wrong *in foro conscientiae,* but there is no legal obligation on the part of the vendee to disclose them, and the contract will be good if not vitiated by fraud. Poth. Vente. pt. 2, c. 2, note 233; 2 Wheat. (U. S.) 185, note (c).

IN FORO CONTENTIOSO. In the forum of contention or litigation.

IN FORO ECCLESIATICO (Law Lat.) In an ecclesiastical forum; in the ecclesiastical court. Fleta, lib. 2, c. 57, § 13.

IN FORO SAECULARI (Law Lat.) In a secular forum or court. Fleta, lib. 2, c. 57, § 14; 1 Bl. Comm. 20.

IN FRAUDEM CREDITORUM (Lat.) In fraud of creditors; with intent to defraud creditors. Inst. 1. 6. pr. 3.

IN FRAUDEM LEGIS (Lat.) In fraud of the law; contrary to law. Taylor. Using process of law for a fraudulent purpose; and if a person gets an affidavit of service of declaration in ejectment, and thereupon gets judgment, and turns the tenant out, when he has no manner of title in a house, he is liable as a felon, for he used the process of law *in fraudem legis.* 1 Ld. Raym. 276; Sid. 254.

An act done *in fraudem legis* cannot give right of action in the courts of the country whose laws are evaded. 1 Johns. (N. Y.) 433.

IN FULL LIFE. Neither physically nor civilly dead. The term "life" alone has also been taken in the same sense, as including natural and civil life; *e. g.,* a lease made to a person "during life" is determined by a civil death, but if "during natural life," it would be otherwise. 2 Coke, 48. It is a translation of the French phrase *en plein vie.* Law Fr. Dict.

IN FUTURO (Lat.) In future; at a future time; the opposite of *in praesenti.* 2 Bl. Comm. 166, 175.

IN GENERALI PASSAGIO (Law Lat.) In the general passage; *passagium* being a journey, or, more properly, a voyage, and especially when used alone or with the adjectives *magnum, generale,* etc.,—the journey to Jerusalem of a crusader, especially of a king. 36 Hen. III.; 3 Prynne, Collect. 767; Du Cange.

In generali passagio was an excuse for nonappearance in a suit, which put off the hearing *sine die;* but *in simplici peregrinatione* or *passagio*—*i. e.,* being absent on a private pilgrimage to the Holy Land—put off the hearing for a shorter time. Bracton, 338.

IN GENERALIBUS VERSATUR ERROR. Error dwells in general expressions. 3 Sumn. (U. S.) 290.

IN GENERE (Lat.) In kind; of the same kind. Things which, when bailed, may be restored *in genere,* as distinguished from those which must be returned *in specie,* or specifically, are called *fungibles.* Kaufm. Mackeld. Civ. Law, § 148, note.

Heinec. Elem. Jur. Civ. § 619, defines *genus* as what the philosophers call "species," viz., a kind. See Dig. 12. 1. 2. 1.

IN GENERE QUICUNQUE ALIQUID DIcit, sive actor sive reus, necesse est ut probat. In general, whoever says anything, whether plaintiff or defendant, must prove it. Best, Ev. 294, § 252.

IN GREMIO LEGIS (Lat. in the bosom of the law). This is a figurative expression, by which is meant that the subject is under the protection of the law; as, where land is in abeyance.

IN GROSS. At large; not appurtenant or appendant, but annexed to a man's person, *e. g.,* common granted to a man and his heirs by deed is common in gross; or common in gross may be claimed by prescriptive right. 2 Bl. Comm. 34.

IN HAC PARTE (Law Lat.) In this behalf. Reg. Orig. 25.

IN HAEC VERBA. In these words; in the same words. Dig. 34. 4. 30.

IN HAEREDES NON SOLENT TRANSIre actiones quae poenales ex maleficio sunt. Penal actions arising from anything of a criminal nature do not pass to heirs. 2 Inst. 442.

IN HIS ENIM QUAE SUNT FAVORAbilia animae, quamvis sunt damnosa rebus, flat aliquando extentio statuti. In things that are favorable to the spirit, though injurious to property, an extension of the statute should be sometimes made. 10 Coke, 101.

IN HIS QUAE DE JURE COMMUNI OMnibus conceduntur, consuetudo alicujus patriae vel loci non est alleganda. In those things which, by common right, are conceded to all, the custom of a particular country or place is not to be alleged. 11 Coke, 85.

IN HOC. In this.

IN IISDEM TERMINIS (Lat.) In the same terms. 9 East, 487.

IN INDIVIDUO (Law Lat.) In the distinct, identical, or individual form; *in specie.* Story, Bailm. § 97.

In special; particular.

IN INFINITUM. Infinitely or indefinitely.

IN INITIALIBUS (Lat.) In Scotch law. In the preliminaries. Before a witness is examined as to the cause in which he is to testify, he must deny bearing malice or ill will, being instructed what to say, or having been bribed, and these matters are called *initialia testimonii,* and the examination on them is said to be *in initialibus.* It is similar to our *voir dire.* Bell, Dict. "Initialia Testimonii"; Ersk. Inst. p. 451; Halk. Tech. Terms.

IN INITIO (Lat.) In or at the beginning. *In initio litis,* at the beginning, or in the first stage of the suit. Bracton, fol. 400.

IN INTEGRUM (Lat.) The original condition. See "Restitutio in Integram." Vicat, "Integer."

IN INVITUM (Lat.) Unwillingly. Taylor. Against an unwilling party, or one who has not given his consent, by operation of law. Wharton.

IN IPSIS FAUCIBUS (Lat.) In the very throat or entrance. *In ipsis faucibus* of a port, actually entering a port. 1 C. Rob. Adm. 233. 234.

IN ITINERE (Lat.) On a journey; on the way. Justices *in itinere* were justices in eyre, who went on circuit through the kingdom for the purpose of hearing causes. 3 Sharswood, Bl. Comm. 351; Spelman. *In itinere* is used in the law of lien, and is there equivalent to *in transitu;* that is, not yet delivered to vendee.

IN JUDICIIS MINORI AETATI SUCCURritur. In judicial proceedings, infancy is aided or favored. Jenk. Cent. Cas. 46.

IN JUDICIO (Lat.) In or by a judicial proceeding; in court. *In judicio non creditur nisi juratis,* in judicial proceedings no one is believed unless on oath. Cro. Car. 64. See Bracton, fols. 98b, 106, 287b, et passim.

——**In Civil Law.** The proceedings before a praetor, from the bringing the action till issue joined, were said to be *in jure;* but after issue joined, when the cause came before the *judex,* the proceedings were said to be *in judicio.* See "Judex."

IN JUDICIO NON CREDITUR NISI JURAtis. In law, none is credited unless he is sworn. All the facts must, when established by witnesses, be under oath or affirmation. Cro. Car. 64.

IN JURE (Lat.) In law.

——**In Civil Law.** A phrase which denotes the proceedings in a cause before the praetor, up to the time when it is laid before a *judex;* that is, till issue joined (*litis contestatio*); also the proceedings in causes tried throughout by the praetor (*cognitiones extraordinariae*). Vicat, "Jus."

——**In English Law.** In law; rightfully; in right. *In jure, non remota causa, sed proxima, spectatur.* Broom, Leg. Max. 104. Incorporeal hereditaments, as right of jurisdiction, are said to exist only *in jure,* in right, or contemplation of law, and to admit of only a symbolical delivery. See Halk. Tech. Terms.

IN JURE ALTERIUS (Lat.) In another's right. Hale, Anal. § 26.

IN JURE NON REMOTA CAUSA, SED proxima, spectatur. In law, the proximate and not the remote cause is to be looked to. Bac. Max. reg. 1; Broom, Leg. Max. (3d London Ed.) 202. See 2 Pars. Cont. 455.

IN JURE PROPRIO (Lat.) In one's own right. Hale, Anal. § 26.

IN JUS VOCARE (Lat.) To call, cite, or summon to court. Inst. 4. 16. 3; Calv. Lex. *In jus vocando*, summoning to court. Dig. 2. 4; 3 Bl. Comm. 279.

IN KIND. Of the same sort. Return of property is "in kind," as distinguished from *in specie*, where an article of the same kind, but not the identical one obtained, is returned.

IN LAW. Implied by law; depending on legal fiction or intendment.

IN LECTO MORTALI (Lat.) On the death bed. Fleta, lib. 5, c. 28, § 12.

IN LIMINE (Lat.) In or at the beginning. This phrase is frequently used; as, the courts are anxious to check crimes *in limine*.

IN LITEM (Lat. *ad litem*). For a suit; to the suit. Greenl. Ev. § 348.

IN LOCO (Lat.) In place; in lieu; in stead; in the place or stead. Towns. Pl. 38.

IN LOCO PARENTIS (Lat.) In the place of a parent; as, the master stands towards his apprentice *in loco parentis*.

IN MAJORE SUMMA CONTINETUR MInor. In the greater sum is contained the less. 5 Coke, 115.

IN MAJOREM CAUTELAM (Lat.) For greater security. 1 Strange, 105, arg.

IN MALEFICIIS VOLUNTAS SPECTAtur non exitus. In offenses, the intention is regarded, not the event. Dig. 48. 8. 14; Bac. Max. reg. 7; Broom, Leg. Max. (3d London Ed.) 292.

IN MALEFICIO RATIHABITO MANDAto comparetur. In a tort, ratification is equivalent to a command. Dig. 50. 17. 152. 2.

IN MAXIMA POTENTIA MINIMA LICENtia. In the greatest power there is the least liberty. Hob. 159.

IN MEDIO (Law Lat.) Intermediate. A term applied, in Scotch practice, to a fund held between parties litigant.

IN MERCIBUS ILLICITIS NON SIT COMmercium. No commerce should be in illicit goods. 3 Kent, Comm. 262, note.

IN MERCY. To be in mercy is to be at the discretion of the king, lord, or judge in punishing any offense not directly censured by the law. Thus, to be in the grievous mercy of the king is to be in hazard of a great penalty. 11 Hen. VI. c. 6. So, where the plaintiff failed in his suit, he and his pledges were in the mercy of the lord, *pro falso clamore suo*. This is retained nominally on the record. 3 Sharswood, Bl. Comm. 376. So the defendant is in mercy if he fail in his defense. Id. 398.

IN MISERICORDIA (Lat. in mercy). The entry on the record where a party was in mercy was, *Ideo in misericordia*, etc. The phrase was used because the punishment in such cases ought to be moderate. See Magna Cart. c. 14; Bracton, lib. 4, tr. 5, c. 6. Sometimes *misericordia* means the being quit of all amercements.

IN MITIORI SENSU (Lat. in a milder acceptation). A phrase denoting a rule of construction formerly adopted in slander suits, the object of which was to construe phrases, if possible, so that they would not support an action.

IN MODUM ASSISAE (Law Lat.) In the manner or form of an assize. Bracton, fol. 183b. *In modum juratae*, in manner of a jury. Id. fol. 181b.

IN MORA (Lat.) In delay.

IN MORTUA MANU (Lat. in a dead hand). Property owned by religious societies was said to be held *in mortua manu*, or in mortmain, since religious men were *civiliter mortui*. 1 Sharswood, Bl. Comm. 479; Taylor.

IN NOMINE DEI, AMEN (Lat.) In the name of God, Amen. A solemn form of introduction, anciently used in wills and many other instruments, public and private. The Proemia to the Institutes and Digests of Justinian commence, *In nomine Domini nostri Jesu Christi*, "In the name of our Lord Jesus Christ." The confirmation of the Code and several of the Novels are introduced with the same form. Some old wills began, *In nomine Patris, et Filii, et Spiritus Sancti, Amen*. Blount, voc. "Will." Mercantile instruments, such as protests, policies, procurations, etc., frequently began, *In Dei nomine, Amen*.

IN NOVO CASU, NOVUM REMEDIUM apponendum est. A new remedy is to be applied to a new case. 2 Inst. 3.

IN NUBIBUS (Lat.) In the clouds; in abeyance; in custody of law. *In nubibus, in mare, in terra vel in custodia legis*, in the air, earth, or sea, or in the custody of the law. Taylor. In case of abeyance, the inheritance is figuratively said to rest *in nubibus*, or *in gremio legis; e. g.*, in case of a grant of life estate to A., and afterwards to heirs of Richard, Richard in this case, being alive, has no heirs until his death, and, consequently, the inheritance is considered as resting *in nubibus*, or in the clouds, till the death of A., when the contingent remainder either vests or is lost, and the inheritance goes over. See 2 Sharswood, Bl. Comm. 107, note; 1 Coke, 137.

IN NULLIUS BONIS (Lat.) Among the goods or property of no person; belonging to no person, as treasure trove and wreck were anciently considered. Bracton, fol. 120.

IN NULLO EST ERRATUM (Lat.) In pleading. A plea to errors assigned on proceedings in error, by which the defendant in error affirms there is no error in the record. As to the effect of such plea, see 1 Vent. 252; 1 Strange, 684; 9 Mass. 532; 1 Burrows, 410; T. Raym. 231. It is a general rule that the plea *in nullo est erratum* confesses the fact assigned for errors (Yelv. 57; Dane, Abr. Index), but not a matter assigned contrary to the record (7 Wend. [N. Y.] 55; Bac. Abr. "Error" [G]).

IN OBSCURA VOLUNTATE MANUMITTENTIS favendum est libertati. Where the expression of the will of one who seeks to manumit a slave is ambiguous, liberty is to be favored. Dig. 50. 17. 179.

IN OBSCURIS INSPICI SOLERE QUOD verisimilius est, aut quod plerumque fieri solet. Where there is obscurity, we usually regard what is probable or what is generally done. Dig. 50. 17. 114.

IN OBSCURIS QUOD MINIMUM EST SEquimur. In obscure cases, we follow that which is least so. Dig. 50. 17. 9.

IN OCTAVIS, or OCTABIS. (Law Lat.) On the octave. One of the ancient return days in the English courts. 3 Bl. Comm. 277, 278.

IN ODIUM SPOLIATORIS (Lat.) In hatred of a despoiler. All things are presumed against a despoiler or wrongdoer, *in odium spoliatoris omnia praesumuntur.*

IN OMNI ACTIONE UBI DUAE CONCURrunt districtiones, videlicet in rem et in personam, illa districtio tenenda est quae magis timetur et magis ligat. In every action where two distresses concur, as those *in rem* and *in personam,* that is to be chosen which is most dreaded, and which binds most firmly. Bracton, 372; Fleta, lib. 6, c. 14, § 28.

IN OMNI RE NASCITUR RES QUAE IPsam rem exterminat. In everything, the thing is born which destroys the thing itself. 2 Inst. 15.

IN OMNIBUS CONTRACTIBUS, SIVE nominatis, sive innominatis, permutatio continetur. In every contract, whether nominate or innominate, there is implied an exchange, *i. e.,* a consideration.

IN OMNIBUS OBLIGATIONIBUS, IN quibus dies non ponitur, praesenti die debetur. In all obligations, when no time is fixed for the payment, the thing is due immediately. Dig. 50. 17. 14.

IN OMNIBUS POENALIBUS JUDICIIS, et aetati et imprudentiae succurritur. In all trials for penal offenses, allowance is made for youth and lack of discretion. Dig. 50. 17. 108; Broom, Leg. Max. (3d London Ed.) 282.

IN OMNIBUS QUIDEM MAXIME TAMEN in jure, aequitas spectanda sit. In all affairs indeed, but principally in those which concern the administration of justice, equity should be regarded. Dig. 50. 17. 90.

IN PACE DEI ET REGIS (Law Lat.) In the peace of God and the king. Fleta, lib. 1, c. 31, § 6. Formal words in old appeals of murder.

IN PAIS. Out of court, or without judicial process. Matter *in pais* is distinguished from matter of record. 2 Bl. Comm. 294. Conveyances were either by matter *in pais* or deed which was an assurance transacted between two or more private persons out of court, or by matter of record which was an assurance transacted in a court of record. 1 Steph. Comm. 466. Notice *in pais* is notice given without the intervention of the court. Story, Bailm. § 348.

Without writing, by act or conduct, as distinguished from "by deed." Thus, estoppels are said to be by record, by deed, or by matter *in pais.* See "Estoppel."

IN PAPER. In English practice. A term used of a record until its final enrollment on the parchment record. 3 Sharswood, Bl. Comm. 406; 10 Mod. 88; 2 Lilly, Abr. 322; 4 Geo. II.

IN PARI CAUSA (Lat.) In an equal cause. It is a rule that when two persons have equal rights in relation to a particular thing, the party in possession is considered as having the better right, *in pari causa possessor potior est.* Dig. 50. 17. 128; 1 Bouv. Inst. note 952.

IN PARI CAUSA POSSESSOR POTIOR haberi debet. When two parties have equal rights, the advantage is always in favor of the possessor. Dig. 50. 17. 128.

IN PARI DELICTO. Equally in fault. A term applied to parties who have participated equally in a transaction which is illegal, fraudulent, or contrary to public policy, neither of whom can for that reason obtain relief in equity from any injury suffered from the other in respect to such transaction. Thus, one making a conveyance of his property to defraud creditors cannot set aside the conveyance if his accomplice subsequently refuse to reconvey. 64 Fed. 195; 36 Mich. 229. But to put parties *in pari delicto* there must be equality of turpitude. See 124 N. Y. 160.

Though both parties assent to the illegal transaction, if there is great disparity of intelligence or condition, they are not *in pari delicto.* 59 Ill. 470; 82 Ky. 564; 9 Md. 348; 69 Mo. 115.

IN PARI DELICTO MELIOR EST CONDItio possidentis. When the parties are equally in the wrong, the condition of the possessor is better. 11 Wheat. (U. S.) 258; 3 Cranch (U. S.) 244; Cowp. 341; Broom, Leg. Max. 325; 4 Bouv. Inst. note 3724.

IN PARI DELICTO POTIOR EST CONDItio defendentis (et possidentis). Where both parties are equally in fault, the condition of the defendant is preferable. 11 Mass. 376; Broom, Leg. Max. (3d London Ed.) 265; 1 Story, Cont. (4th Ed.) 591, 592.

IN PATRIMONIO (Lat.) As a subject of property. Fleta, lib. 3, c. 1, § 2.

IN PECTORE JUDICIS (Lat.) In the breast of the judge. Latch, 180. A phrase applied to a judgment.

IN PEJOREM PARTEM (Law Lat.) In the worst part; on the worst side. Latch, 159, 160.

IN PENDENTI (Lat.) In suspension or abeyance. Bracton, fols. 12, 19b. Written in Fleta as one word, *inpendenti* and *impendenti.* Fleta, lib. 3, c. 9, § 7.

IN PERPETUAM REI MEMORIAM (Lat.) For the perpetual memory or remembrance of a thing. Gilb. For. Rom. 118.

IN PERSONAM (Lat.) A remedy where the proceedings are against the person, in contradistinction to those which are against specific things, or *in rem.* 1 Bouv. Inst. note 2646.

IN PERSONAM ACTIO EST, QUA CUM eo agimus qui obligatus est nobis ad faciendum aliquid vel dandum. The action *in personam* is that by which we sue him who is under obligation to us to do something or give something. Dig. 44. 7. 25; Bracton, 101b.

IN PIOS USUS (Law Lat.) For pious uses; for religious purposes. 2 Bl. Comm. 505.

IN PLENA VITA (Law Lat.) In full life. Y. B. P. 18 Hen. VI. 2.

IN PLENO COMITATU (Law Lat.) In full county court. 2 Bl. Comm. 36.

IN POENALIBUS CAUSIS BENIGNIUS interpretandum est. In penal cases, the more favorable interpretation is to be made. Dig. 50. 17. 155. 2; Plowd. 86b; 2 Hale, P. C. 365.

IN POSSE (Lat.) In possibility; not in actual existence; used in contradistinction to *in esse.*

IN POTESTATE PARENTIS (Lat.) In the power of a parent. Inst. 1. 8; pr.; Id. 1. 9; 2 Bl. Comm. 498.

IN PRAEMISSORUM FIDEM (Law Lat.) In confirmation or attestation of the premises. A notarial phrase.

IN PRAEPARATORIIS AD JUDICIUM favetur actori. In things preparatory before trial, the plaintiff is favored. 2 Inst. 57.

IN PRAESENTI (Lat.) At the present time; used in opposition to *in futuro.* A marriage contracted in words *de praesenti* is good; as, "I take Paul to be my husband" is a good marriage; but words *de futuro* would not be sufficient, unless the ceremony was followed by consummation. 1 Bouv. Inst. note 258.

IN PRAESENTIA MAJORIS POTESTAtis, minor potestas cessat. In the presence of the superior power, the minor power ceases. Jenk. Cent. Cas. 214; Cas. temp. Hardw. 28; 13 How. (U. S.) 142; 13 Q. B. 740.

IN PRENDER (Law Fr. in taking). A term applied to such incorporeal hereditaments as a party entitled to them was to take for himself; such as common. 2 Steph. Comm. 23; 3 Bl. Comm. 15.

IN PRETIO EMPTIONIS ET VENDITIOnis naturaliter licet contrahentibus se circumvenire. In the price of buying and selling, it is naturally allowed to the contracting parties to overreach each other. 1 Story, Cont. (4th Ed.) 606.

IN PRIMIS. (Law Lat.) In the first place. Mag. Cart. Johan. c. 1.

IN PRINCIPIO (Lat. at the beginning). This is frequently used in citations; as, Bac. Abr. "Legacies in pr."

IN PROPRIA CAUSA NEMO JUDEX. No one can be judge in his own cause. 12 Coke, 13.

IN PROPRIA PERSONA (Lat.) In his person; himself; as, the defendant appeared *in propria persona;* the plaintiff argued the cause *in propria persona.*

IN QUINDENA (Law Lat.) In fifteen days. One of the return days in the old practice of the English courts. 2 Reeves' Hist. Eng. Law, 57-61.

IN QUO QUIS DELINQUIT, IN EO DE jure est puniendus. In whatever thing one offends, in that he is rightfully to be punished. Co. Litt. 233b.

IN RE (Lat.) In the matter; as *in re* A. B., in the matter of A. B.

IN RE COMMUNI NEMINEM DOMINOrum jure facere quicquam, invito altero, posse. One co-proprietor can exercise no authority over the common property against the will of the other. Dig. 10. 3. 28.

IN RE COMMUNI POTIOR EST CONDItio prohibentis. In a partnership, the condition of one who forbids is the more favorable.

IN RE DUBIA BENIGNIOREM INTERpretationem sequi, non minus justius est, quam tutius. In a doubtful case, to follow the milder interpretation is not less the more just than it is the safer course. Dig. 50. 17. 192. 2; Id. 28. 4. 3.

IN RE DUBIA MAGIS INFICIATO QUAM affirmatio intelligenda. In a doubtful matter, the negative is to be understood, rather than the affirmative. Godb. 37.

IN RE LUPANARI, TESTES LUPANAres admittentur. In a matter concerning a brothel, prostitutes are admitted as witnesses. 6 Barb. (N. Y.) 320, 324.

IN RE PARI, POTIOREM CAUSAM ESSE prohibentis constat. Where a thing is owned in common, it is agreed that the cause of him prohibiting its use is the stronger. Dig. 10. 3. 28; 3 Kent, Comm. 45; Poth. Con. de Soc. note 90; 16 Johns. (N. Y.) 438, 491.

IN RE PROPRIA INIQUUM ADMODUM est aliculi licentiam tribuere sestentiae. It is extremely unjust that any one should be judge in his own cause.

IN REBUS (Lat.) In things, cases, or matters.

IN REBUS MANIFESTIS ERRAT QUI auctoritates legum allegat, quia perspicua vera non sunt probanda. He errs who alleges the authorities of law in things manifest, because obvious truths need not be proved. 5 Coke, 67.

IN REM (Lat.) A technical term used to designate proceedings or actions instituted against the thing, in contradistinction to personal actions, which are said to be *in personam.*

Proceedings *in rem* include not only those instituted to obtain decrees or judgments against property as forfeited in the admiralty or the English exchequer, or as prize, but also suits against property to enforce a lien or privilege in the admiralty courts, and suits to obtain the sentence, judgment, or decree of other courts upon the personal status or relations of the party, such as marriage, divorce, bastardy, settlement, or the like. 1 Greenl. Ev. §§ 525, 541.

Courts of admiralty enforce the performance of a contract, when its performance is secured by a maritime lien or privilege, by seizing into their custody the very subject of hypothecation. In these suits, generally, the parties are not personally bound, and the proceedings are confined to the thing *in specie.* Brown, Civ. & Adm. Law, 98. And see 2 Gall. C. C. (U. S.) 200; 3 Term R. 269, 270.

There are cases, however, where the remedy is either *in personam* or *in rem.* Seamen, for example, may proceed against the ship or freight for their wages, and this is the most expeditious mode; or they may proceed against the master or owners. 4 Burrows, 1944; 2 Brown, Civ. & Adm. Law, 396. See, generally, 1 Phil. Ev. 254; 1 Starkie, Ev. 228; Dane, Abr.; Serg. Const. Law, 202, 203, 212; Pars. Mar. Law.

"Various definitions have been given of a judgment *in rem,* but all are criticised as either incomplete or comprehending too much. It is generally said to be a judgment declaratory of the status of some subject matter, whether this be a person or a thing. Thus, the probate of a will fixes the status of the document as a will. The personal rights and interests which follow are mere incidental results of the status or character of the paper, and do not appear on the face of the judgment. So, a decree establishing or dissolving a marriage is a judgment *in rem,* because it fixes the status of the person. A judgment of forfeiture, by the proper tribunal, against specific articles or goods, for a violation of the revenue laws, is a judgment *in rem.* But it is objected that the customary definition does not fit such a case, because there is no fixing of the status of anything, the whole effect being a seizure, whatever the thing may be. In the foregoing instances, and many others, the judgment is conclusive against all the world, without reference to actual presence or participation in the proceedings. If the expression 'strictly *in rem*' may be applied to any class of cases, it should be confined to such as these. A very able writer says: 'The distinguishing characteristic of judgments *in rem* is that, wherever their obligation is recognized and enforced as against any person, it is equally recognized and enforced as against all persons. It seems to us that the true definition of a judgment *in rem* is "an adjudication" against some person or thing, or "upon the status of some subject matter," which, wherever and whenever binding upon any person, is equally binding upon all persons.'" 10 Mo. App. 78.

IN REM ACTIO EST PER QUAM REM nostram quae ab alio possidetur petimus, et semper adversus eum est qui rem possidet. The action *in rem* is that by which we seek our property which is possessed by another, and is always against him who possesses the property. Dig. 44. 7. 25; Bracton, 102.

IN RENDER. A thing in a manor is said to lie *in render* when it must be rendered or given by the tenant, *e. g.,* rent; to lie *in prender,* when it may be taken by the lord or his officer when it chance. West, Symb. pt. 2, "Fines," § 126.

IN REPUBLICA MAXIME CONSERVANda sunt jura belli. In the state, the laws of war are to be greatly preserved. 2 Inst. 58.

IN RERUM NATURA (Lat.) In the nature or order of things; in existence. Not *in rerum natura* is a dilatory plea, importing that the plaintiff is a fictitious person.

——**In Civil Law.** A broader term than *in rebus humanis; e. g.,* before quickening, an infant is *in rerum natura,* but not *in rebus humanis;* after quickening, he is *in rebus* *humanis,* as well as *in rerum natura.* Calv. Lex.

IN RESTITUTIONEM, NON IN POENAM, haeres succedit. The heir suceeds to the restitution, not the penalty. 2 Inst. 198.

IN RESTITUTIONIBUS BENIGNISSIMA interpretatio facienda est. The most favorable construction is to be made in restitutions. Co. Litt. 112.

IN ROBERIA. (Law Lat.) In or by robbery. Bract. fol. 146b.

IN SATISFACTIONIBUS NON PERMITtitur amplius fieri quam semel factum est. In payments, more must not be received than has been received once for all. 9 Coke, 53.

IN SCRINIO JUDICIS (Law Lat.) In the writing case of the judge; among the judge's papers. "That is a thing that rests *in scrinio judicis,* and does not appear in the body of the decree." Hardr. 51.

IN SEPARALI (Law Lat.) In several; in severalty. Fleta, lib. 2, c. 54, § 20.

IN SIGHT. See "Gambling Contract."

IN SIMILI MATERIA. Dealing with the subject matter of the same kind.

IN SIMPLICI PEREGRINATIONE (Lat.) In simple pilgrimage. Bracton, fol. 338. A phrase in the old law of essoins. See "In Generali Passagio."

IN SIVE JUXTA. In or near. 14 Q. B. D. 253.

IN SOLIDUM, or **IN SOLIDO** (Lat.) In civil law. For the whole; as a whole. An obligation or contract is said to be *in solido* or *in solidum* when each is liable for the whole, but so that a payment by one is payment for all; *i. e.,* it is a joint and several contract.

Possession is said to be *in solidum* when it is exclusive. *"Duo in solidum precario habere non magis possunt, quam duo in solidum vi possidere aut clam; nam neque justae neque injustae possessiones duae concurrere possunt."* Savigny, lib. 3, § 11.

IN SOLO (Lat.) In the soil or ground. *In solo alieno,* in another's ground. *In solo proprio,* in one's own ground. 2 Steph. Comm. 20.

IN SPECIE (Lat.) In the same form; *e. g.,* a ship is said to no longer exist *in specie* when she no longer exists as a ship, but as a mere congeries of planks. 8 Barn. & C. 561; Arnould, Ins. 1012. To decree a thing *in specie* is to decree the performance of that thing specifically.

IN STATU QUO (Lat.) In the same situation as; in the same condition as.

IN STIPULATIONIBUS CUM QUAERItur quid actum sit verba contra stipulatorem interpretanda sunt. In contracts, when the question is what was agreed upon, the terms are to be interpreted against the party offering them. Dig. 45. 1. 38. 18. Chancellor Kent remarks that the true principle appears to be "to give the contract the sense in which the person making the promise believes the other party to have accepted it, if he in fact did so understand and accept it." 2 Kent, Comm. (7th Ed.) 721; 2 Day (Conn.) 281; 1 Duer, Ins. 159, 160; Broom, Leg. Max. (3d London Ed.) 534; Dig. 45. 1. 38. § 18.

IN STIPULATIONIBUS ID TEMPUS spectatur quo contrahimus. In agreements, reference is had to the time at which they were made. Dig. 50. 17. 144. 1.

IN STIRPES. According to roots or stocks; by representation. See "Per Stirpes."

IN STRICTO JURE. (Lat.) In strict law; in strict right.

IN SUBSIDIUM. In aid.

IN SUO QUISQUE NEGOTIO HEBETIOR est quam in alieno. Every one is more dull in his own business than in that of another. Co. Litt. 377.

IN SUPERFICIE. (Lat.) In the surface.

IN TANTUM (Law Lat.) In so much; so much; so far; so greatly. Reg. Orig. 97, 106.

IN TERMINIS TERMINANTIBUS (Law Lat.) In terms of determination; exactly in point. 11 Coke, 40b. In express or determinate terms. 1 Leon. 93.

IN TERROREM (Lat.) By way of threat, terror, or warning. For example, when a legacy is given to a person upon condition not to dispute the validity or the dispositions in wills and testaments, the conditions are not, in general, obligatory, but only *in terrorem.* If, therefore, there exist *probabilis causa litigandi,* the nonobservance of the conditions will not be a forfeiture. 2 Vern. 90; 1 Hill, Abr. 253; 3 P. Wms. 344; 1 Atk. 404.

IN TERROREM POPULI (Lat. to the terror of the people). A technical phrase necessary in indictments for riots. 4 Car. & P. 373.

Lord Holt has given a distinction between those indictments in which the words *in terrorem populi* are essential, and those wherein they may be omitted. He says that, in indictments for that species of riots which consist in going about armed, etc., without committing any act, the words are necessary, because the offense consists in terrifying the public; but in those riots in which an unlawful act is committed, the words are useless. 11 Mod. 116; 10 Mass. 518.

IN TESTAMENTIS PLENIUS TESTAtoris intentionem scrutamur. In testaments, we should seek diligently the will of the testator. "But," says Dodderidge, C. J., "this is to be observed with these two limitations: (1) His intent ought to be agreeable to the rules of the law; (2) his intent ought to be collected out of the words of the will." 3 Bulst. 103; Broom, Leg. Max. (3d London Ed.) 494.

IN TESTAMENTIS PLENIUS VOLUNtates testantium interpretantur. In testaments, the will of the testator should be liberally construed. That is to say, a will shall receive a more liberal construction than its strict meaning, if alone considered, would permit. Dig. 50. 17. 12; Cujac. ad loc., cited 3 Poth. Pand. 46; Broom, Leg. Max. (3d London Ed.) 507.

IN TESTAMENTIS RATIO TACITA NON debet considerari, sed verba solum spectari debent; adeo per divinationem mentis a verbis recedere durum est. In wills, an unexpressed meaning ought not to be considered, but the words alone ought to be looked to, so hard is it to recede from the words by guessing at the intention.

IN TESTIMONIUM (Lat.) In witness whereof.

IN THE COURSE OF EMPLOYMENT. While engaged generally in the service of the master. 97 Minn. 312, 313; 162 Mass. 66.

IN TOTIDEM VERBIS (Lat.) In just so many words; as, the legislature has declared this to be a crime *in totidem verbis.*

IN TOTO (Lat.) In the whole; wholly; completely; as, the award is void *in toto.* In the whole, the part is contained, *in toto et pars continetur.* Dig. 50. 17. 123.

IN TOTO ET PARS CONTINETUR. A part is included in the whole. Dig. 50. 17. 113.

IN TRADITIONIBUS SCRIPTORUM chartarum non quod dictum est, sed quod gestum factum est, inspicitur. In the delivery of writings (deeds), not what is said, but what is done, is to be considered. 9 Coke, 137.

IN TRAJECTU (Lat.) In the passage over; on the voyage over. See Sir William Scott, 3 Rob. Adm. 141.

IN TRANSITU (Lat.) During the transit or removal from one place to another. See "Stoppage in Transitu."

IN VADIO (Lat.) In pledge; in gage.

IN VENTRE SA MERE (Law Fr.) In his mother's womb.

IN VERAM QUANTITATEAM FIDEJUSser teneatur, nisi pro certa quantitate accessit. Let the surety be holden for the true quantity, unless he agreed for a certain quantity. 17 Mass. 597.

IN VERBIS NON VERBA SED RES ET ratio quaerenda est. In words, not the words, but the thing and meaning is to be inquired after. Jenk. Cent. Cas. 132.

IN VINCULIS (Lat.) In chains; in actual custody. Gilb. For. Rom. 97.

Applied also, figuratively, to the condition of a person who is compelled to submit to terms which oppression and his necessities impose on him. 1 Story, Eq. Jur. § 302.

IN VOCIBUS VIDENDUM NON A QUO sed ad quid sumatur. In discourses, it is to be seen not from what, but to what, it is advanced. Ellesmere, Postn. 62.

IN WITNESS WHEREOF. These words, which, when conveyancing was in the Latin language, were *in cujus rei testimonium,* are the initial words of the concluding clause in deeds: "In witness whereof the said parties have hereunto set their hands," etc.

INADEQUATE PRICE. A term applied to indicate the want of a sufficient consideration for a thing sold, or such a price as, under ordinary circumstances, would be considered insufficient.

INADMISSIBLE. What cannot be received in evidence.

INAEDIFICATIO (Lat.) In civil law. Building on another's land with own materials, or on own land with another's materials. Heinec. Elem. Jur. Civ. § 363. The word is especially used of a private person's building so as to encroach upon the public land. Calv. Lex. The right of possession of the materials yields to the right to what is on the soil. Id.

INALIENABLE. A word denoting the condition of those things the property in which cannot be lawfully transferred from one person to another. Public highways and rivers are inalienable. There are also many rights which are inalienable, as the rights of liberty or of speech.

INAUGURATION. A word applied by the Romans to the ceremony of dedicating a temple, or raising a man to the priesthood, after the *augurs* had been consulted.

It was afterwards applied to the installation of emperors, kings, and prelates, in imitation of the ceremonies of the Romans when they entered the temple of the *augurs.* It is applied in the United States to the installation of the chief magistrate of the republic, and of the governors of the several states.

INBOARD. In marine policy. Not projecting over the rail of the vessel. 46 Jones & S. (N. Y.) 175, 181, 85 N. Y. 473.

INBORH (Saxon.) In old English law. A security, pledge, or *hypotheca,* consisting of the chattels of a person unable to obtain a personal "borg," or surety.

INCAPACITY. The want of a quality legally to do, give, transmit, or receive something. See "Capacity."

INCAUSTUM, or ENCAUSTUM (Lat.) Ink; a fluid anciently used for writing, of which, as appears from the following passage of Bracton, there were two kinds,—the black (*incaustum nigrum*), and the red (*incaustum rubrum*), the former being also termed *atramentum* (from *ater*, black), which is the Latin word generally used for "ink." *Item diversitas incausti et atramenti, ut si una pars scribatur incausto nigro, et altera pars incausto rubro, non atramento.* Bracton, fol. 398b.

INCAUTE FACTUM PRO NON FACTO habetur. A thing done unwarily or unadvisedly will be taken as not done. Dig. 28. 4. 1.

INCENDIARY (Lat. *incendium*, a kindling). One who maliciously and willfully sets another person's building on fire; one guilty of the crime of arson.

INCENDIUM AERE ALIENO NON exuit debitorum. A fire does not release a debtor from his debt. Code, 4. 2. 11.

INCEPTION. The commencement; the beginning. In making a will, for example, the writing is its inception. 3 Coke, 31b; Plowd. 343.

INCERTA PRO NULLIS HABENTUR. Things uncertain are held for nothing. Dav. 33.

INCERTA QUANTITAS VITIAT ACTUM. An uncertain quantity vitiates the act. 1 Rolle, 465.

INCERTI TEMPORIS. (Lat.) Of uncertain time or date. A title given to some English statutes enacted between Magna Charta and the reign of Edward III.; their period not being ascertained. 2 Reeves' Hist. Eng. Law, 85, 312.

INCEST. The carnal copulation of a man and a woman related to each other in any of the degrees within which marriage is prohibited by law. Bish. Mar. & Div. 214-221.

INCH (Lat. *uncia*). A measure of length, containing one-twelfth part of a foot.

INCH OF CANDLE. A mode of sale at one time in use among merchants. A notice is first given upon the exchange, or other public place, as to the time of sale. The goods to be sold are divided into lots, printed papers of which, and the conditions of sale, are published. When the sale takes place, a small piece of candle, about an inch long, is kept burning, and the last bidder, when the candle goes out, is entitled to the lot or parcel for which he bids. Wharton.

INCHARTARE. To grant by a writing.

INCIDENT. This term is used both substantively and adjectively of a thing which, either usually or naturally and inseparably, depends upon, appertains to, or follows another that is more worthy. For example, rent is usually incident to a reversion (1 Hilliard, Real Prop. 243), while the right of alienation is necessarily incident to a fee-simple at common law, and cannot be separated by a grant (1 Washb. Real Prop. 54). So a court baron is inseparably incident to a manor, in England. Kitch. Cts. 36; Co. Litt. 151. All nominate contracts and all estates known to common law have certain incidents which they draw with them, and which it is not necessary to reserve in words. See Jacob.

INCIDERE (Lat. from *in*, into or upon, and *cadere*, to fall). In the civil and old English law. To fall into. Calv. Lex.; Brissonius.

To fall out; to happen; to come to pass. Calv. Lex.

To fall upon or under; to become subject or liable to. *Incidere in legem*, to incur the penalty of a law. Brissonius. *Quibus modis quis incidat in assisam*, in what ways a person may become liable to an assize. Bracton, fols. 170b, 171. *Incidere in misericordiam*, to fall into mercy; to become liable to amercement. Fleta, lib. 2, c. 44, § 2.

INCIPITUR (Lat.) In practice. This word which means "it is begun," signifies the commencement of the entry on the roll on signing judgment, etc.

INCIVILE EST, NISI TOTA LEGE PROSpecta, una aliqua particula ejus proposita, judicare, vel respondere. It is improper, unless the whole law has been examined, to give judgment or advice upon a view of a single clause of it. Dig. 1. 3. 24. See Hob. 171a.

INCIVILE EST NISI TOTA SENTENTIA inspecta, de aliqua parte judicare. It is improper to pass an opinion on any part of a sentence without examining the whole. Hob. 171.

INCLAMARE (Law Lat. from *in*, to or upon, and *clamare*, to cry). In old European law. To cry out for a person, as a crier does in court; to summon to court. *Inclamatus*, proclaimed; called or summoned by proclamation (*in jus exactus*). Edict. Theod. c. 145; Spelman.

INCLOSURE. In English law. Inclosure is the act of freeing land from rights of common, commonable rights, and generally all rights which obstruct cultivation and the productive employment of labor on the soil.

Also, an artificial fence around one's estate. 39 Vt. 34, 326; 36 Wis. 42. See "Close."

INCLUSIO UNIUS EST EXCLUSIO ALterius. The inclusion of one is the exclusion of another. 11 Coke, 58.

INCLUSIVE. Comprehended in computation. In computing time, as ten days from a particular time, one day is generally to be included, and one excluded. See "Exclusive."

INCOLA (Lat. from *incolere*, to inhabit, to dwell in). In the civil law. An inhabitant; a dweller or resident. Properly, one who has transferred his domicile to any country. One who comes from abroad, and takes up his abode in a place, with the view of residing there. The peculiar sense of the word seems to be derived from the component particle "in," having the sense of "into," or "entry." Domicile made a person an *incola*, as birth made him *civis* (a citizen). Code, 10. 40. 7; Phillim. Dom. 25, 26.

——**In Old English Law.** A subject. St. Marlb. pr.; Fleta, lib. 2, c. 47, § 13.

INCOLA DOMICILIUM FACIT. Residence creates domicile. 1 Johns. Cas. (N. Y.) 363, 366. See "Domicile."

INCOME. The gain which proceeds from labor, business, or property of any kind. 44 Pa. St. 347. It is as large a word as can be used to denote a person's receipts (21 Ch. Div. 85), and means "gross income," not "profits" (18 Wend. [N. Y.] 605), though the contrary has been held (5 Metc. [Mass.] 596).

INCOME BONDS. As the term is ordinarily used, income bonds are bonds which carry interest only so far as the interest is earned from the net income of the corporation, within an interest period. They bear a close resemblance to capital stock. Such interest is ordinarily not cumulative. 2 Fletcher Cyclopedia Corporations 1922.

INCOMMODUM NON SOLVIT ARGUMENTUM. An inconvenience does not solve an argument.

INCOMMUNICACION. In Spanish law. The condition of a prisoner who is not permitted to see or to speak with any person visiting him during his confinement. A person accused cannot be subjected to this treatment unless it be expressly ordered by the judge, for some grave offense, and it cannot be continued for a longer period than is absolutely necessary. Art. 7, Reglamento de 26 Setiembre, 1835. This precaution is resorted to for the purpose of preventing the accused from knowing beforehand the testimony of the witnesses, or from attempting to corrupt them, and concert such measures as will efface the traces of his guilt. As soon, therefore, as the danger of his doing so has ceased, the interdiction ceases likewise. Escriche, Dic. Raz.

INCOMPATIBILITY. Incapability of existing or being exercised together.

Thus, the relations of landlord and of tenant cannot exist in one man at the same time in reference to the same land. Two offices may be incompatible, either from their nature or by statutory provisions. Const. U. S. art. 6, § 3, note 5; Id. art. 1, § 6, note 2; 4 Serg. & R. (Pa.) 277; 17 Serg. & R. (Pa.) 219. See "Office."

INCOMPETENCY.

——**Of Officers.** Lack of ability or fitness to discharge the required duty.

Judges and jurors are said to be incompetent from having an interest in the subject matter. A judge is also incompetent to give judgment in a matter not within his jurisdiction. See "Jurisdiction."

——**Of Witness.** Want of legal capacity to testify.

——**Of Evidence.** Not proper to be received. Incompetency relates to the evidence itself, not to the fact to be proved thereby.

——**In French Law.** Inability or insufficiency of a judge to try a cause brought before him, proceeding from lack of jurisdiction.

INCONCLUSIVE. Not finally decisive. Inconclusive presumptions are capable of being overcome by opposing proof. 3 Bouv. Inst. 3063.

INCONSULTO. (Lat.) In the civil law. Unadvisedly; unintentionally. Dig. 28. 4. 1.

INCONTINENCE. Impudicity; indulgence in unlawful carnal connection.

INCORPORALIA BELLO NON ADQUIRUNTUR. Things incorporeal are not acquired by war. 6 Maule & S. 104.

INCORPORATE.

(1) To form into a corporation; to procure or to grant a corporate franchise.

(2) To include in any writing the contents of any other writing, whether by actual insertion, or by mere reference to the document to be incorporated.

INCORPORATION. The act of creating a corporation.

——**In Civil Law.** The union of one domain to another.

INCORPOREAL. Having no body or corpus; not material or tangible; not an object of sense, but existing solely in contemplation of law.

INCORPOREAL CHATTELS. A class of incorporeal rights growing out of or incident to things personal; such as patent rights and copyrights. 2 Steph. Comm. 72.

INCORPOREAL HEREDITAMENTS. Anything, the subject of property, which is inheritable, and not tangible or visible. 2 Woodeson, Lect. 4. A right issuing out of a thing corporate, whether real or personal, or concerning or annexed to or exercisable within the same. 2 Sharswood, Bl. Comm. 20; 1 Washb. Real Prop. 10. See "Hereditaments."

INCORPOREAL PROPERTY. In civil law. That which consists in legal right merely.

The same as choses in action at common law.

INCORRIGIBLE ROGUE. A species of rogue or offender, described in St. 5 Geo. IV. c. 83, and St. 1 & 2 Vict. c. 38. 4 Steph. Comm. 309.

INCREASE, COSTS OF. In English law. It was formerly a practice with the jury to award to the successful party in an action the nominal sum of 40s. only for his costs; and the court assessed by their own officer the actual amount of the successful party's costs; and the amount so assessed, over and above the nominal sum awarded by the jury, was thence called "costs of increase." Lush, Com. Law Prac. 775. The practice has now wholly ceased. Rapalje & L.

INCREMENTUM. In old English law. Increase; addition; accretion. Cowell.

INCROACHMENT. See "Encroachment."

INCULPATE. To impute blame or guilt; to accuse.

INCULPATORY. In the law of evidence. Going or tending to establish guilt; intended to establish guilt; criminative. Burrill, Circ. Ev. 251, 252.

INCUMBENT. From the verb incumbo, that is, to be diligently resident; and when it is written encumbent, it is falsely written. Co. Litt. 119b. See Termes de la Ley.

One who is in possession of an office and is legally authorized to discharge the duties of that office; as, the present incumbent. 11 Ohio 50.

In Ecclesiastical Law. A clerk resident on his benefice with cure. He is so called because he does, or ought to, bend the whole of his studies to his duties.

INCUMBRANCE. Any right to, or interest in, land which may subsist in third persons, to the diminution of the value of the estate of the tenant, but consistently with the passing of the fee. 5 Conn. 527; 2 Greenl. Ev. § 242.

INCUMBRANCER. One who holds an incumbrance upon another's estate.

INCUR. To become subject to; to bring on. 4 Denio (N. Y.) 103. "Men contract debts; they incur liabilities." 15 How. Pr. (N. Y.) 48.

INCURRERE, or **INCURRAMENTUM.** To become liable to or subject to. Cowell.

INDE. Thereof; therefrom; therefore or therewith.

INDE DATAE LEGES NE FORTIOR OMnia posset. Laws were made lest the stronger should have unlimited power. Dav. 36.

INDEBITATUS. (Law Lat.) Indebted. *Nunquam indebitatus*, never indebted. The title of the plea substituted in England for *nil debet.*

INDEBITATUS ASSUMPSIT (Lat.) In pleading. That species of action of *assumpsit* in which the plaintiff alleges, in his declaration, first a debt, and then a promise in consideration of the debt to pay the amount to the plaintiff.

It is so called from the words in which the promise is laid in the Latin form, translated in the modern form, "being indebted he promised." The promise so laid is generally an implied one only. See 1 Chit. Pl. 334; Steph. Pl. 318; 4 Robinson, Prac. 490 et seq.; Yelv. 21; 4 Coke, 92b. This form of action is brought to recover in damages the amount of the debt or demand. Upon the trial the jury will, according to evidence, give verdict for whole or part of that sum. 3 Sharswood, Bl. Comm. 155; Selw. N. P. 68, 69 et seq.

Indebitatus assumpsit is in this distinguished from "debt" and "covenant," which proceed directly for the debt, damages being given only for the detention of the debt. Debt lies on contracts by specialty as well as by parol, while *indebitatus assumpsit* lies only on parol contracts, whether express or implied. Browne, Actions at Law, 317.

For the history of this form of action, see 3 Reeve, Hist. Com. Law; 2 Comyn, Cont. 549-556; 1 H. Bl. 550, 551; 3 Bl. Comm. 154; Yelv. 70. See "Assumpsit."

INDEBITI SOLUTIO (Lat.) In civil law. The payment to one of what is not due to him. If the payment was made by mistake, the civilians recovered it back by an action called *condictio indebiti.* With us, such money may be recovered by an action of *assumpsit.*

INDEBITUM (Lat.) In civil law. Not due or owing. Dig. 12. 6; Calv. Lex.

INDEBTEDNESS. A word of large meaning. It is used to denote almost every kind of pecuniary obligation originating in contract. 12 R. I. 179.

The state of being in debt, without regard to the ability or inability of the party to pay the same. See 1 Story, Eq. Jur. 343; 2 Hill, Abr. 421.

But in order to create an indebtedness, there must be an actual liability at the time, either to pay then or at a future time. If, for example, a person were to enter and become surety for another, who enters into a rule of reference, he does not thereby become a debtor to the opposite party until the rendition of the judgment on the award. 1 Mass. 134. See Debt.

INDECENCY. An act tending to obscenity. "The term [indecent] is said to signify more than 'indelicate,' and less than 'immodest,'—to mean something unfit for the eye or ear." 12 Fed. 671.

INDECENT EXPOSURE. Willful or negligent exposure of the person, or the private parts thereof, in a public place. 2 Clark & Marshall, Crimes, 1130; 2 Gray (Mass.) 72; 32 Mo. 560; 56 Ind. 328.

To constitute an offense at common law, the offense must be in such a place that a number of persons may be offended thereby. 11 Cox, C. C. 659; 18 Vt. 574.

INDECIMABLE. Not tithable.

INDEFEASIBLE. That which cannot be defeated or undone. This epithet is usually applied to an estate or right which cannot be defeated.

INDEFENSUS (Lat.) One sued or impleaded who refuses or has nothing to answer.

INDEFINITE FAILURE OF ISSUE. See "Failure of Issue."

INDEFINITE NUMBER. A number which may be increased or diminished at pleasure.

When a corporation is composed of an indefinite number of persons, any number of them consisting of a majority of those present may do any act, unless it be otherwise regulated by the charter or by-laws.

INDEFINITE PAYMENT. That which a debtor who owes several debts to a creditor makes without making an appropriation. In that case the creditor has a right to make such appropriation.

INDEFINITUM AEQUIPOLLET UNIVERsali. The undefined is equivalent to the whole. 1 Vent. 368.

INDEFINITUM SUPPLET LOCUM UNIversalis. The undefined supplies the place of the whole. 4 Coke, 77.

INDEMNIFY. To save harmless; to secure against loss or damage; to make good; to put one in the situation he was in before sustaining a loss.

INDEMNIS (Lat.) Without loss, damage, or harm.

INDEMNITEE. The person who is protected by a contract of indemnity.

INDEMNITOR. The person who, by a contract of indemnity, agrees to protect another.

INDEMNITY. That which is given to a person to prevent his suffering damage. 2 McCord (S. C.) 279.

Security to save harmless. A contract whereby one party agrees to secure another against an anticipated loss or damage, and the liability under which is coterminous with the liability it is intended to cover. 53 L. J. Q. B. 321; 12 Q. B. D. 152.

For distinction between "indemnity" and "guaranty," see "Guaranty."

INDEMPNIS (Law Lat.) The old form of writing *indemnis*. Towns. Pl. 19. So, *indempnificatus* for *indemnificatus*.

INDENIZATION. The act of making a denizen.

INDENT (Lat. *in*, and *dens*, tooth). To cut in the shape of teeth.

Deeds of indenture were anciently written on the same parchment or paper as many times as there were parties to the instrument, the word *chirographum* being written between, and then the several copies cut apart in a zigzag or notched line (whence the name), part of the word *chirographum* being on either side of it, and each party kept a copy. The practice now is to cut the top or side of the deed in a waving or notched line. 2 Sharswood, Bl. Comm. 295.

To bind by indentures; to apprentice; as to indent a young man to a shoemaker. Webster.

——**In American Law.** An indented certificate issued by the government of the United States at the close of the Revolution, for the principal or interest of the public debt. Ramsay; Hamilton; Webster; Eliot, Funding System, 35; 5 McLean (U. S.) 178; Act April 30, 1790, Sess. 2, c. 9, § 14; Act March 3, 1825, Sess. 2, c. 65, § 17. The word is no longer in use in this sense.

INDENTURE. A formal written instrument made between two or more persons in different interests, as opposed to a deed poll, which is one made by a single person, or by several having similar interests.

Its name comes from a practice of indenting or scolloping such an instrument on the top or side in a waving line. This is not necessary in England at the present day, by St. 8 & 9, Vict. c. 106, § 5, but was in Lord Coke's time, when no words of indenture would supply its place. 5 Coke, 20. In this country it is a mere formal act, not necessary to the deed's being an indenture. See Bac. Abr. "Leases" (E 2); Comyn, Dig. "Fait" (C, and note d); Litt. § 370; Co. Litt. 143b, 229a; Cruise, Dig. tit. 32, c. 1, § 24; 2 Sharswood, Bl. Comm. 294; 2 Washb. Real Prop. 587 et seq.; 1 Steph. Comm. 447. The ancient practice was to deliver as many copies of an instrument as there were parties to it. And as early as King John it became customary to write the copies on the same parchment, with the word *chirographum*, or some other word, written between them, and then to cut them apart through such word, leaving part of each letter on either side the line, which was at first straight, afterwards indented or notched. 1 Reeve, Hist. Eng. Law, 89; Du Cange; 2 Washb. Real Prop. 587 et seq. See "Indent."

INDENTURE OF APPRENTICESHIP. A contract in two parts, by which a person is bound to serve another in his trade, art, or occupation, on condition of being instructed in it. See "Apprentice."

INDEPENDENT CONTRACT. One in which the mutual acts or promises have no relation to each other, either as equivalents or considerations. Civ. Code La. art. 1762; 1 Bouv. Inst. note 699.

INDEPENDENT COVENANTS. Covenants in an instrument which are independent of each other, or where the performance of one does not depend on the performance of the other. 1 Seld. 247.

INDEPENDENTER SE HABET ASSECU-ratio a viaggio navis. The voyage insured is an independent or distinct thing from the voyage of the ship. 3 Kent, Comm. 318, note.

INDETERMINATE. That which is uncertain, or not particularly designated; as, if I sell you one hundred bushels of wheat, without stating what wheat. 1 Bouv. Inst. note 950.

INDEX ANIMI SERMO. Speech is the index of the mind.

INDIAN TRIBE. A separate and distinct community or body of the aboriginal Indian race of men found in the United States. See 5 Pet. (U. S.) 1, 16, 17; 20 Johns. (N. Y.) 193; 3 Kent, Comm. 308-318; Story, Const. § 1096; 4 How. (U. S.) 567; 1 McLean (U. S.) 254; 6 Hill (S. C.) 546; 3 Ala. (N. S.) 48.

INDICARE (Law Lat. from *index*, a shower or pointer). In the civil law. To show or discover.

To fix or tell the price of a thing. Calv. Lex.

To inform against; to accuse. Dig. 50. 16. 197.

INDICATIF. An abolished writ by which a prosecution was in some cases removed from a court christian to the queen's bench. Enc. Lond.

INDICATION. In the law of evidence. A sign or token; a fact pointing to some inference or conclusion. Burrill, Circ. Ev. 251, 252, 263, 275.

INDICAVIT (Lat. from *indicare*, to show). In English practice. A writ of prohibition that lies for a patron of a church, whose clerk is sued in the spiritual court by the clerk of another patron, for tithes amounting to a fourth part of the value of the living. 3 Bl. Comm. 91; 3 Steph. Comm. 711. So termed from the emphatic word of the Latin form. Reg. Orig. 35b, 36.

INDICIA (Lat.) Signs; marks. Conjectures which result from circumstances not absolutely certain and necessary, but merely probable, and which may turn out not to be true, though they have the appearance of truth.

The term is much used in the civil law in a sense nearly or entirely synonymous with "circumstantial evidence." It denotes facts which give rise to inferences, rather than the inferences themselves. However numerous *indicia* may be, they only show that a thing may be, not that it has been. An *indicium* can have effect only when a connection is essentially necessary with the principal. Effects are known by their causes, but only when the effects can arise only from the causes to which they are attributed. When several causes may have produced one and the same effect, it is therefore unreasonable to attribute it to any particular one of such causes.

The term is much used in common law of signs or marks of identity. For example, in replevin it is said that property must have *indicia*, or ear marks, by which to distinguish it from other property of the same kind. So it is much used in the phrase "*indicia* of crime," in a sense similar to that of the civil law.

INDICIUM (Lat.) Singular of *indicia* (*q. v.*). In civil law. A sign or mark; a species of proof, answering very nearly to the "circumstantial evidence" of the common law. Best, Pres. p. 13, § 11, note; Wills, Circ. Ev. 34.

INDICTED. Having had an indictment found against him.

INDICTEE. A person indicted.

INDICTIO (Lat.) In old public law. A declaration; a proclamation. *Indictio belli*, a declaration or indiction of war. Molloy de Jur. Mar. 17.

INDICTION. The space of fifteen years. It was used in dating at Rome and in England. It began at the dismission of the Nicene council, A. D. 312. The first year was reckoned the first of the first indiction, and so on till fifteen years afterwards. The sixteenth year was the first year of the second indiction; the thirty-first year was the first year of the third indiction, etc.

INDICTMENT. In criminal practice. A written accusation against one or more persons of a crime or misdemeanor, presented to, and preferred upon oath or affirmation by, a grand jury legally convoked. 4 Bl. Comm. 299; Co. Litt. 126; 2 Hale, P. C. 152; Bac. Abr.; Comyn, Dig.; 1 Chit. Crim. Law, 168.

An accusation at the suit of the crown, found to be true by the oaths of a grand jury.

A written accusation of one or more persons of a crime or misdemeanor, preferred to and presented on oath by a grand jury, and by assent of twelve at least. 12 Conn. 452.

The word is said to be derived from the old French word *inditer*, which signifies to indicate, to show, or point out. Its object is to indicate the offense charged against the accused. Rey des Inst. l'Angl. tom. 2, p. 347.

A distinction has been taken between "indictment" and "presentment," the former being a bill of indictment presented to the grand jury by the prosecuting officer, and by it found to be "a true bill"; while the latter is a return made by the grand jury of its own motion, upon which a bill of indictment was subsequently framed. 4 Bl. Comm. 301; 7 Grat. (Va.) 631. This distinction is no longer of much practical importance; an indictment in modern practice being both a finding and a presentment. See 9 Gray (Mass.) 290.

INDICTOR. He who causes another to be indicted. The latter is sometimes called the "indictee."

INDIFFERENT. To have no bias or partiality. 7 Conn. 229. A juror, an arbitrator, and a witness ought to be indifferent; and when they are not so they may be challenged. See 9 Conn. 42.

INDIGENA (Lat. from *inde*, in, and *geno*, *gigno*, to beget). A native; born or bred in the same country or town. Ainsworth. A subject born, or naturalized by act of parliament. Opposed to *alienigena*. Rymer, tom. 15, p. 37; Co. Litt. 8a.

INDIRECT EVIDENCE. Evidence which does not prove the fact in question, but one from which it may be presumed. See "Evidence."

INDISTANTER. Instanter.

INDITEE (Law Fr.) In old English law. An indictee. 9 Coke, pref.

INDIVIDUUM (Lat.) In civil law. That cannot be divided. Calv. Lex.

INDIVISIBLE. Which cannot be separated; entire.

INDIVISUM (Lat.) That which two or more persons hold in common without partition; undivided.

INDORSAT. In old Scotch law. Indorsed. 2 Pitc. Crim. Tr. 41.

INDORSE. To write on the back. Bills of exchange and promissory notes are indorsed by a party's writing his name on the back. Writs in Massachusetts are indorsed in some cases by a person's writing his name on the back, in which case he becomes liable to pay the costs of the suit.

INDORSEE. The person to whom a negotiable instrument is transferred by indorsement.

INDORSEMENT.

——**In Commercial Law.** That which is written on the back of an instrument in writing, and which has relation to it.

Writing one's name on the back of a promissory note or other negotiable instrument. 20 Vt. 499.

An indorsement is generally made primarily for the purpose of transferring the rights of the holder of the instrument to some other person. It has, however, various results, such as rendering the indorser liable in certain events; and hence an indorsement is sometimes made merely for the purpose of additional security. This is called an "accommodation indorsement" when done without consideration other than an exchange of indorsements. See "Accommodation."

(1) A blank indorsement is one in which the name of the indorser only is written upon the instrument. It is commonly made by writing the name of the indorser on the back (13 Serg. & R. [Pa.] 315), but a writing across the face may answer the same purpose (18 Pick. [Mass.] 63; 16 East, 12).

(2) An indorsement in full is one in which mention is made of the name of the indorsee. Chit. Bills, 170.

(3) A conditional indorsement is one made subject to some condition without the performance of which the instrument will not be or remain valid. 4 Taunt. 30.

(4) A qualified indorsement is one which restrains, or limits, or qualifies, or enlarges the liability of the indorser, in any manner different from what the law generally imports as his true liability, deducible from the nature of the instrument. Chit. Bills (8th Ed.) 261; 7 Taunt. 160. The words commonly used are *sans recours*, without recourse. 3 Mass. 225; 12 Mass. 14.

(5) A restrictive indorsement is one which restrains the negotiability of the instrument to a particular person, or for a particular purpose. 1 Rob. (La.) 222.

——**In Criminal Law.** An entry made upon the back of a writ or warrant.

When a warrant for the arrest of a person charged with a crime has been issued by a justice of the peace of one county, which is to be executed in another county, it is necessary, in some states, that it should be indorsed by a justice of the county where it is to be executed. This indorsement is called "backing."

INDORSER. The person who makes an indorsement.

INDUCEMENT.

——**In Contracts.** The benefit which the obligor is to receive from a contract is the inducement for making it.

——**In Criminal Law.** The motive. Confessions are sometimes made by criminals under the influence of promises or threats. When these promises or threats are made by persons in authority, the confessions cannot be received in evidence. See "Confession."

——**In Pleading.** The statement of matter which is introductory to the principal subject of the declaration or plea, and which is necessary to explain or elucidate it. See "Colloquium."

INDUCIAE (Lat.)

——**In Civil Law.** A truce; cessation from hostilities for a time agreed upon. Also, such agreement itself. Calv. Lex. So in international law. Grotius de Jure Belli, lib. 3, c. 2, § 11; Huber, Jur. Civ. p. 743, § 22.

——**In Old Practice.** A delay or indulgence allowed by law. Calv. Lex.; Du Cange; Bracton, fol. 352b; Fleta, lib. 4, c. 5, § 8. See Bell, Dict.; Burton, Law Scot. 561. So used in old maritime law; *e. g.*, an *induciae* of twenty days after safe arrival of vessel was allowed in case of a bottomry bond, to raise principal and interest. Locc. de Jure Mar. lib. 2, c. 6, § 11.

INDUCIAE LEGALES (Lat.) In Scotch law. The days between the citation of the defendant and the day of appearance; the days between the teste day and day of return of the writ.

INDUCING. The words "inducing" and "persuading" as used in an information for pandering, are practically synonymous and charge only one offense. 198 Ill. App. 361.

INDUCTION. In ecclesiastical law. The giving a clerk, instituted to a benefice, the actual possession of its temporalities, in the nature of livery of seisin. Ayliffe, Par. 299.

INDULGENCE. A favor granted.

It is a general rule that where a creditor gives indulgence, by entering into a binding contract with a principal debtor, by which the surety is or may be damnified, such surety is discharged, because the creditor has put it out of his power to enforce immediate payment, when the surety would have a right to require him to do so. 6 Dow, Parl. Cas. 238; 3 Mer. 272; Bac. Abr. "Oblig." (D).

INDULTO. In Spanish law. The condonation or remission of the punishment imposed on a criminal for his offense. L. 1, tit. 32, pt. 7. This power is exclusively vested in the king.

INDUMENT. Endowment. (*q. v.*)

INDUSTRIAL PURSUITS. The expression industrial pursuit is broader than "trading" or "manufacturing." It includes both, and something more. It has been held that a statute authorizing corporations for "industrial pursuits" authorizes a corporation for carrying on the express business, and a corporation for carrying on a mercantile business for the sale of goods, mining supplies, etc. Fletcher Cyclopedia Corporations 131.

INDUSTRIAM. See "Per Industriam."

INEBRIATE. An habitual drunkard. A person rendered unfit, by habitual intoxication, to transact business.

INELIGIBILITY. The incapacity to be lawfully elected to an office.

INESSE POTEST DONATIONI, MODUS, conditio sive causa; ut modus est; si conditio; quia causa. In a gift there may be manner, condition, and cause; as (*ut*), introduces a manner; if (*si*), a condition; because (*quia*), a cause. Dyer, 138.

INEST DE JURE. It is implied by law.

INEVITABLE ACCIDENT. A term used in the civil law, nearly synonymous with fortuitous event. 10 Miss. 572.

Any accident which cannot be foreseen and prevented. Though used as synonymous with "act of God," it would seem to have a wider meaning, including not only accidents resulting from natural forces, but those originating from human agencies. 4 Doug. 287, 290, per Lord Mansfield; 21 Wend. (N. Y.) 198, per Cowen, J.; 3 Blackf. (Ind.) 222; 2 Ga. 349; 10 Miss. 572; 1 Pars. Cont. 635; Whart. Neg. 553.

——**In the Law of Maritime Collisions.** Inevitable accident, "an occurrence which the party charged with the collision could not possibly prevent by the exercise of ordinary care, caution, and maritime skill." 2 Wall. (U. S.) 550.

INFALISTATUS (Law Lat. from *in*, and Fr. *falaize*, the seashore). In old English law. Exposed upon the sands or seashore. A species of punishment mentioned in Hengham. Summa Parva, c. 3; Cowell.

INFAMARE. (Lat.) In the civil law. To defame; to attack or injure one's character by word or writing. Brissonius; 3 Bl. Com. 125.

INFAMIS (Lat.) In Roman law. One who, in consequence of the application of a general rule, and not by virtue of an arbitrary decision of the censors, lost his political rights, but preserved his civil rights. Savigny, Dr. Rom. § 79.

INFAMOUS CRIME. A crime which works infamy in one who has committed it.

——**In the United States.** It has been held that only those crimes are infamous that were so at common law (1 Dak. 289), but the general rule is that any offense is infamous that may be punished by death, or by imprisonment in the penitentiary, with or without hard labor. 128 U. S. 393; 8 Gray (Mass.) 349; 75 Mich. 611.

A crime which subjects the party to a disqualification to hold office, in case he is convicted of such crime. 171 Ill. 73.

The test is the possible punishment, and not that awarded in a particular case. 114 U. S. 417.

——**At Common Law.** Treason and all felonies, and certain misdemeanors affecting the public interest most closely, were infamous crimes, the nature of the crime being the test. 1 Greenl. Ev. § 373; 114 U. S. 417.

INFAMOUS PERSONS. Such as may be challenged as jurors *propter delictum*, and therefore shall never be admitted to give evidence to inform that jury with whom they were too scandalous to associate. 59 Pa. St. 116.

INFAMOUS PUNISHMENT. Disqualification from holding office, if inflicted as a punishment for crime, is an infamous punishment. 171 Ill. 73.

INFAMY. That state which is produced by the conviction of an infamous crime, and the loss of honor, which renders the infamous person incompetent as a witness or juror. 3 Watts & S. (Pa.) 342.

INFANGTHEFE (from *in*, within, *fang*, taken, and *thef*, or *theof*, a thief). In old English law. A thief taken in, or within; *i. e.*, within the manor or liberty of any man having jurisdiction to try him. Spelman; Fleta, lib. 6, c. 37, § 2. A thief taken on any one's lands, being one of his own men or tenants, found in possession of the thing stolen. Bracton, fol. 154b; 2 Reeve, Hist. Eng. Law, 40.

The privilege or liberty, anciently granted to lords of certain manors, to try such offenders. Id.; Cowell; LL. Gul. Conq. lib. 3, note.

INFANS NON MULTUM A FURIOSO distat. An infant does not differ much from a lunatic. Bracton, lib. 3, c. 2, § 8; Dig. 50. 17. 5. 40; 1 Story, Eq. Jur. §§ 223, 224, 242.

INFANT. At common law, one of either sex under the age of twenty-one years. Co. Litt. 171. By statute, the age at which females reach their majority has been lowered in some states. See "Age."

INFANTIA (Lat. from *infans*). In the civil law. The age from birth till the completion of seven years. 4 Bl. Comm. 22; Calv. Lex.; Heinec. Elem. Jur. Civ. lib. 1, tit. 21, § 247.

INFANTICIDE. The murder of a newborn infant. It is thus distinguishable from "abortion" and "foeticide," which are limited to the destruction of the life of the *foetus in utero.*

INFANZON. In Spanish law. A person of noble birth, who exercises within his domains and inheritance no other rights and privileges than those conceded to him.

INFEFT. In Scotch law. To give seisin or possession of lands; to invest or enfeoff. 1 Kames, Eq. 215.

INFEFTMENT.

——**In Old Scotch Law.** Investiture or infeudation, including both charter and seisin. 1 Forbes, Inst. pt. 2, p. 110.

——**In Later Law.** *Sasine*, or the instrument of possession. Bell. Dict.

INFENSARE CURIAM (Law Lat.) An expression applied to a court when it suggested to an advocate something which he had omitted through mistake or ignorance. Spelman.

INFEOFFMENT. The act or instrument of feoffment. In Scotland it is synonymous with *sasine*, meaning the instrument of possession. Formerly it was synonymous with "investiture." Bell, Dict. See "Enfeoffment."

INFERENCE. A conclusion drawn by reason from premises established by proof.

INFERIOR. One who, in relation to another, has less power and is below him; one who is bound to obey another. He who makes the law is the superior; he who is bound to obey it, the inferior. 1 Bouv. Inst. note 8.

INFERIOR COURTS. By this term are understood all courts except the supreme courts. An inferior court is a court of limited jurisdiction, and it must appear on the face of its proceedings that it has jurisdiction, or its proceedings will be void. 3 Bouv. Inst. note 2529.

INFICIARI, or INFITIARI (Lat.) In the civil law. To deny; to deny one's liability; to refuse to pay a debt or restore a pledge; to deny the allegation of a plaintiff; to deny the charge of an accuser. Calv. Lex.

INFICIATIO (Lat.) In civil law. Denial; denial of fact alleged by plaintiff,—especially, a denial of debt or deposit. Vocat; Calv. Lex.

INFIDEL. One who does not believe in the existence of a God who will reward or punish in this world, or that which is to come. Willes, 550. One who professes no religion that can bind his conscience to speak the truth. 1 Greenl. Ev. § 368.

This term has been very indefinitely applied. Under the name of "infidel," Lord Coke comprises Jews and heathens (2 Inst. 506; 3 Inst. 165), and Hawkins includes among infidels such as do not believe either in the Old or New Testament (Hawk. P. C. bk. 2, c. 46, § 148).

INFIDELITAS (Lat.) In feudal law. Infidelity; faithlessness to one's feudal oath. Spelman.

INFIDUCIARE (Law Lat.) In old European law. To pledge property. Spelman.

INFIHT (Saxon). An assault upon an inhabitant of same dwelling. Anc. Inst. Eng.

INFINITUM IN JURE REPROBATUR. That which is infinite or endless is reprehensible in law. 9 Coke, 45.

INFIRMATIVE. Weakening. Webster. Tending to weaken or render infirm; disprobabilizing. 3 Benth. Jud. Ev. 13, 14. Exculpatory is used by some authors as synonymous. See Wills, Circ. Ev. 120 et seq.; Best, Pres. § 217 et seq.

INFIRMATIVE CONSIDERATION. In the law of evidence. A consideration, supposition, or hypothesis of which the criminative facts of a case admit, and which tends to weaken the inference or presumption of guilt deducible from them. Burrill, Circ. Ev. 153-155.

INFIRMATIVE FACT. In the law of evidence. A fact set up, proved, or even supposed, in opposition to the criminative facts of a case, the tendency of which is to weaken the force of the inference of guilt deducible from them. 3 Benth. Jud. Ev. 14; Best, Pres. § 217 et seq.; Burrill, Circ. Ev. 154.

Otherwise called an "exculpatory fact."

INFIRMATIVE HYPOTHESIS. In the law of evidence. An hypothesis upon which the criminative circumstances may be explained consistently with the innocence of the accused.

INFORMAL. Deficient in matters of form.

INFORMALITY. Want of legal form.

INFORMATION. The communication of material facts for the first time. 4 M. & W. 24.

——**In French Law.** The act or instrument which contains the depositions of witnesses against the accused. Poth. Proc. Civ. § 2, art. 5.

——**In Practice.** A criminal information is an accusation or a complaint exhibited against a person for some criminal offense. It differs principally from an indictment in this, that an indictment is found upon the oath of twelve men and an information is only the allegation of the officer who exhibits it. 4 Bl. Comm. 308. It is a prosecution originating with an officer, but may originate with a private citizen, but its object is, not compensation to the informer, but solely the public advantage. 67 Mo. 379.

Informations "are of two sorts; first, those which are partly at the suit of the king and partly at that of a subject; and secondly, such as are only in the name of the king." And the last "are of two kinds; first those which are truly and properly his own suits, and filed ex officio by his own officer, the Attorney-General; and secondly, those in which, though the King is the nominal prosecutor, yet it is at the relation of some private person or common informer. 12 Conn. 452.

Criminal informations are analogous to declarations for the redress of a personal injury, except that the latter are at the suit of a subject for the satisfaction of a private wrong, and the former are in the name of the King, for the punishment of offences affecting the interests of the public. 20 N. H. 296.

The process has not been formally put in motion by congress for misdemeanors, but is common in civil prosecutions for penalties and forfeitures. 3 Story, Const. 659. The information is usually made upon knowledge given by some other person than the officer, called the "relator."

The term is also applied to the pleading by which proceedings by the government, particularly those of a *quasi* criminal character. are begun.

INFORMATION IN THE NATURE OF A quo warranto. A proceeding against the usurper of a franchise or office. See "Quo Warranto."

INFORMATION OF INTRUSION. A proceeding instituted by the state prosecuting officer against intruders upon the public domain. See Gen. St. Mass. c. 141; 3 Pick. (Mass.) 224; 6 Leigh (Va.) 588.

INFORMATUS NON SUM (Lat.) In practice. I am not informed. A formal answer made in court or put upon record by an attorney when he has nothing to say in defense of his client. Styles, Reg. 372.

INFORMER. A person who informs or prefers an accusation against another, whom he suspects of the violation of some penal statute.

INFORTIATUM (Lat.) In civil law. The second part of the Digest or Pandects of Justinian. See "Digest."

This part, which commences with the third title of the twenty-fourth book, and ends with the thirty-eighth book, was thus called because it was the middle part, which, it was said, was supported and fortified by the two others. Some have supposed that this name was given to it because it treats of successions, substitutions, and other important matters, and, being more used than the others, produced greater fees to the lawyers.

INFRA (Lat.) Below; under; beneath; underneath. The opposite of *supra*, above. Thus, we say, *primo gradu est*,—supra, *pater, mater*, infra, *filius, filia;* in the first degree of kindred in the ascending line, above is the father and the mother, below, in the descending line, son and daughter. Inst. 3, 6. 1.

In another sense, this word signifies "within"; as, *infra corpus civitatis*, within the body of the county; *infra praesidia*, within the guards; *infra clausum*, within the close. So of time, "during"; *infra furorem*, during the madness. This use is not classical. The sole instance of the word in this sense in the Code, *infra anni spatium* (Code, bk. 5, tit. 9, § 2), is corrected to *intra anni spatium*, in the edition of the Corpus Jur. Civ. of 1833, at Leipsic. The use of *infra* for *intra* seems to have sprung up among the barbarians after the fall of the Roman empire. In Italian, the preposition *fra*, which is a corruption of *infra*, is used in the sense of *intra*. Bonetti, Ital. Dict.

INFRA AETATEM (Lat.) Within or under age.

INFRA ANNOS NUBILES (Law Lat.) Under marriageable years; not yet of marriageable age. 6 Coke, 22.

INFRA ANNUM LUCTUS (Lat.) Within the year of grief or mourning. 1 Sharswood, Bl. Comm. 457; Code, 5. 9. 2. But *intra* *anni spatium* is the phrase used in the passage in the Code referred to. See Corp. Jur. Civ. 1843, Leipsic. *Intra tempus luctus* occurs in Novella 22, c. 40. This year was at first ten months, afterwards twelve. 1 Beck, Med. Jur. 612.

INFRA BRACHIA (Lat.) Within her arms. Used of a husband *de jure* as well as *de facto*. 2 Inst. 317. Also, *inter brachia*. Bracton, fol. 148b. It was in this sense that a woman could only have an appeal for murder of her husband *inter brachia sua*. Woman's Lawy., pp. 332, 335.

INFRA CIVITATEM. Within the state.

INFRA CORPUS COMITATUS (Lat.) Within the body of the county.

The common-law courts have jurisdiction *infra corpus comitatus*. The admiralty, on the contrary, has no such jurisdiction, unless, indeed, the tide water may extend within such county. 5 How. (U. S.) 441, 451. See "Admiralty"; "Fauces Terrae."

INFRA DIGNITATEM CURIAE (Lat.) Below the dignity of the court. Example: In equity a demurrer will lie to a bill on the ground of the triviality of the matter in dispute, as being below the dignity of the court. See 4 Johns. Ch. (N. Y.) 183; 4 Paige, Ch. (N. Y.) 364; 4 Bouv. Inst. note 4237.

INFRA FUROREM (Law Lat.) During madness; while in a state of insanity. Bracton, fol. 19b; Fleta, lib. 3, c. 9, § 17.

INFRA HOSPITIUM (Lat.) Within the inn. When once a traveler's baggage comes *infra hospitium*, that is, in the care and under the charge of the innkeeper, it is at his risk. See 1 Coke, 32; 14 Johns. (N. Y.) 175; 21 Wend. (N. Y.) 282; 25 Wend. (N. Y.) 642; 8 N. H. 408; 1 Smith, Lead. Cas. 47; 9 Pick. (Mass.) 280; 7 Cush. (Mass.) 417; 1 Adol. & E. 522; 3 Nev. & M. 576; 2 Kent, Comm. 593 (9th Ed.) Story, Bailm. § 478; 1 Pars. Cont. 631, notes. See "Guest"; "Innkeeper."

INFRA JURISDICTIONEM (Law Lat.) Within the jurisdiction. 2 Strange, 827; Latch, 214.

INFRA LIGEANTIAM REGIS (Law Lat.) Within the king's ligeance. Comb. 212.

INFRA METAS (Law Lat.) Within the bounds or limits. *Infra metas forestae*, within the bounds of the forest. Fleta, lib. 2, c. 41, § 12. *Infra metas hospitii*, within the limits of the household; within the verge. Id. lib. 2, c. 2, § 2.

INFRA PRAESIDIA (Lat. within the walls). A term used in relation to prizes, to signify that they had been brought completely in the power of the captors; that is, within the towns, camps, ports, or fleet of the captors. Formerly the rule was, and perhaps still in some countries is, that the act of bringing a prize *infra praesidia* changed the property; but the rule now established is that there must be a sentence of condemnation to effect this purpose. 1 C. Rob. Adm. 134; 1 Kent, Comm. 104; Chit. Law Nat. 98; Abb. Shipp. 14; Hugo, Dr. Rom. § 90.

INFRA QUATUOR MARIA (Lat.) Within the four seas. Litt. § 157.

According to classical style, the phrase ought to be *"intra,"* etc. Harg. Co. Litt. lib. 2, note 115.

INFRA REGNUM (Law Lat.) Within the realm. Reg. Orig. 25.

INFRA TEMPUS SEMESTRE (Law Lat.) Within six months (*infra sex menses*). St. Westminster II. c. 5, 2 Inst. 361; 2 Reeve, Hist. Eng. Law, 195; 3 Bl. Comm. 249.

INFRA TRIDUUM (Law Lat.) Within three days. Formal words in old appeals. Fleta, lib. 1, c. 31, § 6; Id. c. 35, § 3.

INFRACTION (Lat. *infrango*, to break in upon). The breach of a law or agreement; the violation of a compact. In the French law this is the generic expression to designate all actions which are punishable by the Code of France.

INFRINGEMENT. In patent law. A word used to denote the act of trespassing upon the incorporeal right secured by a patent. Any person who, without legal permission, shall make, use, or sell to another to be used, the thing which is the subject matter of any existing patent, is guilty of an infringement.

To constitute an infringement, there need not be a precise duplication, but only an adoption of the "operative principle" (1 Fish. Pat. Cas. [U. S.] 319); a mere change in the mechanical incidents, while retaining the principle, being an infringement. By the "principle" of a machine is not meant the original elementary principles of motion, but the *modus operandi*,—the peculiar device or manner of producing the effect. 1 Gall. (U. S.) 478.

The term is also applied to the unlawful or unauthorized use of copyrighted matter or of a trade-mark or trade name.

INFUGARE. To cause to flee.

INFUSION. In medical jurisprudence. A pharmaceutical operation, which consists in pouring a hot or cold fluid upon a substance whose medical properties it is desired to extract. The product of this operation.

Although "infusion" differs from "decoction," they are said to be *ejusdem generis*; and in the case of an indictment which charged the prisoner with giving a decoction, and the evidence was that he had given an infusion, the difference was held to be immaterial. 3 Campb. 74.

INGENIUM (Lat. of middle ages). A net or hook (Du Cange); hence, probably, the meaning given by Spelman of artifice, fraud (*ingin*). A machine (Spelman), especially for warlike purposes; also, for navigation of a ship (Du Cange).

INGENUI (Lat.) In civil law. Those freemen who were born free. Vicat.

They were a class of freemen, distinguished from those who, born slaves, had afterwards legally obtained their freedom. The latter were called, at various periods, sometimes *liberti*, sometimes *libertini*. An unjust or illegal servitude did not prevent a man from being *ingenuus*.

INGENUITAS (Law Lat.) Manumission; liberty.

INGENUITAS REGNI (Law Lat.) In old English law. The freemen, yeomanry, or commonalty of the kingdom. Cowell. Applied sometimes also to the barons. Id.

INGRESS, EGRESS, AND REGRESS. These words are frequently used in leases to express the right of the lessee to enter, go upon, and return from the lands in question.

INGRESSU (Lat.) An ancient writ of entry, by which the plaintiff or complainant sought an entry into his lands. Tech. Dict.

INGRESSUS (Lat.) In old English law. Ingress; entry. The relief paid by an heir to the lord was sometimes so called. Cowell.

INGROSSATOR (Law Lat.) An engrosser. *Ingrossator magni rotuli*, engrosser of the great roll; afterwards called "clerk of the pipe." Spelman; Cowell.

INGROSSING. In practice. The act of copying, from a rough draft, a writing, in order that it may be executed; as, ingrossing a deed.

INHABITANT (Lat. *in*, in, *habeo*, to dwell). One who has a habitation at a given place. It embraces locality of existence; refers to the place of a person's actual residence and excludes the idea of occasional or temporary residence. 3 Ill. 396, 403. See "Habitation."

The term is one whose meaning varies with the context. 10 Am. & Eng. Enc. Law, 771.

Used in the tax laws as convertible with "resident." In making residence a test of taxability, the statute looks only to an actual inhabitancy for some permanent period and purpose, at a prescribed time. 48 Barb. (N. Y.) 51.

INHABITED HOUSE DUTY. A tax assessed in England on inhabited dwelling-houses, according to their annual value (St. 14 & 15 Vict. c. 36; 32 & 33 Vict. c. 14, § 11), which is payable by the occupier, the landlord being deemed the occupier where the house is let to several persons (St. 48 Geo. III. c. 55, Schedule B). Houses occupied solely for business purposes are exempt from duty, although a caretaker may dwell therein, and houses partially occupied for business purposes are to that extent exempt. Rapalje & L.

INHERENT POWER. An authority possessed without its being derived from another; a right, ability, or faculty of doing a thing, without receiving that right, ability, or faculty from another.

INHERETRIX. The old term for "heiress." Co. Litt. 13a.

INHERIT. To take by inheritance; to take as heir on the death of the ancestor. "To inherit to" a person is a common expression in the books. 3 Coke, 41; 2 Bl. Comm. 254, 255.

INHERITABLE BLOOD. Blood of an ancestor which, while it makes the person in whose veins it flows a relative, will also give him the legal rights of inheritance incident to that relationship. See 2 Sharswood, Bl. Comm. 254, 255. Descendants can derive no title through a person whose blood is not inheritable. Such, in England, are persons attainted and aliens. But attainder is not known in this country. Id. See 4 Kent, Comm. 413, 424; 1 Hilliard Real Prop. 148; 2 Hilliard, Real Prop. 190.

INHERITANCE. A perpetuity in lands to a man and his heirs; the right to succeed to the estate of a person who dies intestate. Dig. 50. 16. 24. The term is applied to lands.

The property which is inherited is called an inheritance.

The term "inheritance" includes not only lands and tenements which have been acquired by descent, but every fee simple or fee tail which a person has acquired by purchase may be said to be an inheritance, because the purchaser's heirs may inherit it. Co. Litt. § 9. See "Estate."

——**In Civil Law.** The succession to all the rights of the deceased. It is of two kinds: That which arises by testament when the testator gives his succession to a particular person; and that which arises by operation of law, which is called "succession *ab intestat*." Heinec. Lec. Elem. §§ 484, 485.

INHERITANCE ACT. The English statute of 3 & 4 Wm. IV. c. 106, regulating the law of inheritance. 2 Chit. St. 575; 2 Sharswood, Bl. Comm. 37; 1 Steph. Comm. 500.

INHIBITION.

——**In Civil Law.** A prohibition which the law makes or a judge ordains to an individual. Halifax, Anal. p. 126.

——**In English Law.** The name of a writ which forbids a judge from further proceeding in a cause depending before him. It is in the nature of a prohibition. Termes de la Ley; Fitzh. Nat. Brev. 39.

——**In Scotch Law.** A personal prohibition which passes by letters under the signet, prohibiting the party inhibited to contract any debt or do any act by which any part of the heritable property may be aliened or carried off, in prejudice of the creditor inhibiting. Ersk. Prac. bk. 2, tit. 2, § 2. See "Diligence."

INHIBITION AGAINST A WIFE. In Scotch law. A writ in the sovereign's name, passing the signet, which prohibits all and sundry from having transactions with a wife, or giving her credit. Bell, Dict.; Ersk. Inst. 1. 6. 26.

INHOC, or **INHOKE** (Saxon; Law Lat. *inhokium*). In old records. A nook or corner of a common or fallow field, inclosed and cultivated. Kennett Par. Ant. 297, 298; Cowell.

INHONESTUS (Lat.) In old English law. Unseemly; not in due order. Fleta, lib. 1, c. 31, § 8.

INIQUISSIMA PAX EST ANTEPONENda justissimo bello. The most unjust peace is to be preferred to the justest war. 18 Wend. (N. Y.) 257, 305.

INIQUITY In Scotch Practice. A technical expression applied to the decision of an inferior judge who has decided contrary to law. He is said to have committed iniquity. Bell, Dict.

INIQUUM EST ALIOS PERMITTERE, alios inhibere mercaturam. It is inequitable to permit some to trade, and to prohibit others. 3 Inst. 181.

INIQUUM EST ALIQUEM REI SUI ESSE judicem. It is unjust for any one to be judge in his own cause. 12 Coke, 13.

INIQUUM EST INGENUIS HOMINIBUS non esse liberam rerum suarum alienationem. It is against equity for freemen not to have the free disposal of their own property. Co. Litt. 223. See 1 Bouv. Inst. notes 455, 460.

INITIAL (from Lat. *initium*, beginning). Beginning; placed at the beginning. Webster. Thus, the initials of a man's name are the first letters of his name.

There is no presumption of sex from use of initials. 180 Ill. App. 578.

The middle initial is no part of a name, and it will be presumed, after many years, in absence of evidence to contrary, that a person who attested a will, signing his first name with an initial for middle name, was the same person who testified, signing by initials of first and middle names, where the first initial is the first letter of the given name in the attestation, although the middle initial, when testifying, was different. 253 Ill. 58.

INITIALIA TESTIMONII (Lat.) In Scotch law. A preliminary examination of a witness to ascertain what disposition he bears towards the parties,—whether he has been prompted what to say, whether he has received a bribe, and the like. It resembles in some respects an examination on *voir dire* in English practice.

INITIATE. Commenced.

A husband was, in feudal law, said to be tenant by the curtesy *initiate* when a child who might inherit was born to his wife, because he then first had an inchoate right as tenant by the curtesy, and did homage to the lord as one of the *pares curiae*, peers of the court; whence "curtesy." This right became consummated on the death of the wife before the husband. See 2 Sharswood, Bl. Comm. 127; 1 Steph. Comm. 247.

INITIATIVE. In French law. The name given to the important prerogative conferred by the Charte Constitutionnelle (article 16) on the late king to propose through his ministers projects of laws. 1 Toullier, Dr. Civ. note 39. See "Veto."

INITIUM. (Lat.) A, or the beginning; the origin, cause or foundation of a thing, act or contract.

INJUNCTION. A prohibitory writ, issued by the authority of, and generally under the seal of, a court of equity, to restrain one or more of the defendants or parties, or *quasi* parties, to a suit or proceeding in equity, from doing, or from permitting his servants or others who are under his control to do, an act which is deemed to be unjust or inequitable so far as regards the rights of some other party or parties to such suit or proceedings in equity. Eden, Inj. c. 1; Jeremy, Eq. Jur. bk. 3, c. 2, § 1; Story, Eq. Jur. § 861; Willard, Eq. Jur. 341; 4 Bouv. Inst. 120; 2 Green, Ch. (N. J.) 136; 1 Madd. 126.

(1) Preliminary injunctions are used to restrain the party enjoined from doing or continuing to do the wrong complained of, either temporarily or during the continuance of the suit or proceeding in equity in which such injunction is granted, and before the rights of the parties have been definitely settled by the decision and decree of the court in such suit or proceeding.

(2) Final or perpetual injunctions are awarded, or directed to be issued, or the preliminary injunction already issued is made final or perpetual, by the final decree of the court, or when the rights of the parties so far as relates to the subject of the injunction are finally adjudicated and disposed of by the decision and the order or decree of the court. 2 Freem. Ch. 106; 4 Johns. Ch. (N. Y.) 69; 3 Yerg. (Tenn.) 366; 1 Bibb (Ky.) 184; 4 Bouv. Inst. 123.

In England, injunctions were divided into "common injunctions" and "special injunctions," Eden. Inj. (3d Am. Ed.) 178, note; Willard, Eq. Jur. 342; Saxt. (N. J.) 504. The common injunction was obtained of course when the defendant in the suit in equity was in default for not entering his appearance, or for not putting in his answer to the complainant's bill within the time prescribed by the practice of the court. Eden, Inj. (3d Am. Ed.) 59-61, 68-72, 93, note; Story, Eq. Jur. § 892; 18 Ves. 523; Jeremy, Eq. Jur. bk. 3, c. 2, § 1, p. 339; Gilb. For. Rom. 194; Newby, Chanc. Prac. c. 4, § 7. Special injunctions were founded upon the oath of the complainant, or other evidence of the truth of the charges contained in his bill of complaint. They were obtained upon a special application to the court, or to the officer of the court who was authorized to allow the issuing of such injunctions, and usually upon notice of such application given to the party whose proceedings were sought to be enjoined. Story, Eq. Jur. § 892; 4 Eden, Inj. 78, 290; Jeremy, Eq. Jur. 339, 341, 342; 3 Mer. 475; 18 Ves. 522, 523. In the United States courts, and in the equity courts of most of the states of the Union, the English practice of granting the common injunction has been discontinued or superseded, either by statute or by the rules of the courts. And the preliminary injunctions are therefore all special injunctions in the courts of this country, where such English practice has been superseded.

INJURIA ABSQUE (or SINE) DAMNO. Wrong without damage; an actionable wrong not resulting in any legal damage.

The doctrine of *injuria absque damno* applies only in those cases where, though there was a wrongful act, it did not amount to an invasion of a substantial right, the tendency of modern law being to presume nominal damages from every infraction of a legal right, though no actual damage result. Whether nominal damages will be presumed, or the rule of *injuria absque damno* applied, depends on the disposition of the court to invoke the maxim "*de minimis*," etc. See 75 Cal. 182; 30 Vt. 443. And this will be done generally, only where the right infringed was in itself trivial, as where an officer, on attaching hay, used for a few moments, without leave, a fork belonging to the attachment debtor, and then returned it uninjured. 22 Vt. 231. See Sedgw. Dam. § 96; Suth. Dam. § 3; "Nominal Damages."

INJURIA FIT EI CUI CONVICIUM DICtum est, vel de eo factum carmen famosum. An injury is done to him of whom a reproachful thing is said, or concerning whom an infamous song is made. 9 Coke, 60.

INJURIA NON EXCUSAT INJURIAM. A wrong does not excuse a wrong. Broom. Leg. Max. (3d London Ed.) 247, 343, 349; 11 Exch. 822; 15 Q. B. 276; 6 El. & Bl. 76; Branch, Princ.

INJURIA NON PRAESUMITUR. A wrong is not presumed. Co. Litt. 232.

INJURIA PROPRIA NON CADET IN beneficium facientis. No one shall profit by his own wrong.

INJURIA SERVI DOMINUM PERTINGIT. The master is liable for injury done by his servant. Lofft, 229.

INJURIOUS WORDS. In Louisiana. Slander, or libellous words. Civ. Code La. art. 3501.

INJURY (Lat. *in*, negative, *jus*, a right). A wrong or tort.

Relative injuries are injuries to those rights which a person possesses in relation to the person who is immediately affected by the wrongful act done.

Absolute injuries are injuries to those rights which a person possesses as being a member of society.

Private injuries are infringements of the private or civil rights belonging to individuals, considered as individuals.

Public injuries are breaches and violations of rights and duties which affect the whole community as a community.

Injuries to personal property are the unlawful taking and detention thereof from the owner; and other injuries are some damage affecting the same while in the claimant's possession, or that of a third person, or injuries to his reversionary interests.

Injuries to real property are ousters, trespasses, nuisances, waste, subtraction of rent, disturbance of right of way, and the like.

It is obvious that the divisions overlap each other, and that the same act may be, for example, a relative, a private, and a public injury at once. For many injuries of this character, the offender may be obliged to suffer punishment for the public wrong, and to recompense the sufferer for the particular loss which he has sustained. The distinction is more commonly marked by the use of the terms civil injuries to denote private injuries, and of crimes, misdemeanors, etc., to denote the public injury done, though not always; as, for example, in case of a public nuisance which may be also a private nuisance.

——**In Civil Law.** A delict committed in contempt or outrage of any one, whereby his body, his dignity, or his reputation is maliciously injured. Voet. Com. ad Pand. 47, tit. 10, note 1.

A real injury is inflicted by any act by which a person's honor or dignity is affected; as, striking one with a cane, or even aiming a blow without striking; spitting in one's face; assuming a coat of arms, or any other mark or distinction, proper to another, etc. The composing and publishing defamatory libels may be reckoned of this kind. Ersk. Prac. 4. 4. 45.

A verbal injury, when directed against a private person, consists in the uttering contumelious words, which tend to injure his character by making him littl or ridiculous. Where the offensive words are uttered in the heat of a dispute, and spoken to the person's face, the law does not presume any malicious intention in the utterer, whose resentment generally subsides with his passion; and yet, even in that case, the truth of the injurious words seldom absolves entirely from punishment. Where the injurious expressions have a tendency to blacken one's moral character, or fix some particular guilt upon him, and are deliberately repeated in different companies, or handed about in whispers to confidants, the crime then becomes slander, agreeably to the distinction of the Roman law. Dig. 15. § 12, "De Injur."

INJUSTUM EST, NISI TOTA LEGE INspectae, de una aliqua ejus particula proposita judicare vel respondere. It is unjust to give judgment or advice concerning any particular clause of a law without having examined the whole law. 8 Coke, 117b.

INLAGARE, or **INLEGIARE.** To restore to protection of law. Opposed to *utlagare.* Bracton, lib. 3, tr. 2, c. 14, § 1; Du Cange.

INLAGATION. Restoration to the protection of law.

INLAGHE. A person subject to the law; under the protection of the law.

INLAND. Within the same country.

INLAND BILL OF EXCHANGE. One drawn upon a person living in the same state or country with the drawer.

INLAND NAVIGATION. Includes navigation upon rivers (6 Biss. [U. S.] 364), but not on the Great Lakes (24 How. [U. S.] 1).

INLANDTAL, or **INLANTAL** (Saxon). The same with inland (*q. v.*). Cowell.

INLAUGHE. See "Inlaghe."

INLAW. To place under the protection of the law. Swearing obedience to the king in a leet, which doth inlaw the subject." Bac. Works, IV. 328.

INLIGARE (Law Lat.) In old European law. To confederate; to join in a league (*in ligam coire*). Spelman.

INMATE. One who dwells in a part of another's house, the latter dwelling, at the same time, in the said house. Kitch. Cts. 45b; Comyn, Dig. "Justices of the Peace" (B 85); 1 Barn. & C. 578; 8 Barn. & C. 71; 9 Barn. & C. 335; 2 Dowl. & R. 743; 2 Man. & R. 227; 4 Man. & R. 151; 2 Russ. Crimes, 937; 1 Deac. Crim. Law, 185; 2 East, P. C. 499, 505; 1 Leach, Crim. Law, 90, 237, 427; Alc. Reg. Cas. 21; 1 Man. & G. 83. See "Lodger."

INN. A house where a traveller is furnished with everything he has occasion for while on his way. Bac. Abr. "Inns" (B); 12 Mod. 255; 3 Barn. & Ald. 283; 4 Camp. 77; 2 Chit. Bailm. 484; 9 B. Mon. (Ky.) 72; 3 Chit. Comm. Law, 365, note 6. A public house of entertainment for all who choose to visit it. 5 Sandf. (N. Y.) 247.

INNAMIUM. A pledge.

INNATURALITAS. (Law Lat.) In old records. Unnatural usage. Cowell.

INNAVIGABLE. A term applied in foreign insurance law to a vessel not navigable, through irremediable misfortune by a peril of the sea. The ship is relatively innavigable when it will require almost as much time and expense to repair her as to build a new one. Targa, c. 54, p. 238, c. 60, p. 256; Emerig. tom. 1, pp. 577, 591; 3 Kent, Comm. 323, note.

INNER BARRISTER. One admitted to plead within the bar.

INNINGS. Lands gained from the sea by draining. Cunningham.

INNKEEPER. The keeper of a common inn for the lodging and entertainment of travelers and passengers, their horses and attendants, for a reasonable compensation. Bac. Abr. "Inns," etc.; Story, Bailm. § 475. But one who entertains strangers occasionally, although he may receive compensation for it, is not an innkeeper. 2 Dev. & B. (N. C.) 424; 7 Ga. 296.

INNOCENCE. The absence of guilt (*q. v.*).

INNOCENT CONVEYANCES. In English law. A technical term used to signify those conveyances made by a tenant of his leasehold which do not occasion a forfeiture. These are conveyances by lease and release, bargain and sale, and a covenant to stand seised by a tenant for life. 1 Chit. Prac. 243, 244.

INNOMINATE (Lat.) In civil law. Not named or classed; belonging to no specific class; ranking under a general head. A term applied to those contracts for which no certain or precise remedy was appointed, but a general action on the case only. Dig. 2. 1. 4. 7. 2; Id. 19. 4. 5.

INNOMINATE CONTRACTS. In civil law. Contracts which have no particular names, as permutation and transaction. Inst. 2. 10. 13. There are many innominate contracts; but the Roman lawyers reduced them to four classes, namely, *do ut des, do ut facias, facio ut des,* and *facio ut facias.* Dig. 2. 14. 7. 2.

INNONIA (Law Lat.) In old English law. A close or inclosure (*clausum, inclausura*). Spelman.

INNOTESCIMUS (Lat.) In English law. An epithet used for letters patent, which are always of a charter of feoffment, or some other instrument not of record, concluding with the words, *innotescimus per praesentes,* etc. Tech. Dict.

INNOVATION. In Scotch law. The exchange of one obligation for another, so that the second shall come in the place of the first. Bell, Dict. The same as "novation,"

INNS OF CHANCERY. So called because anciently inhabited by such clerks as chiefly studied the framing of writs, which regularly belonged to the cursitors, who were officers of the court of chancery. There are nine of them,—Clement's, Clifford's and Lyon's Inn; Furnival's, Thavies', and Symond's Inn, New Inn; and Barnard's and Staples' Inn. These were formerly preparatory colleges for students, and many entered them before they were admitted into the inns of court. They consist chiefly of solicitors, and possess corporate property, hall, chambers, etc., but perform no public functions like the inns of court. Wharton.

INNS OF COURT. The name given to the colleges of the English professors and students of the common law.

The four principal inns of court are the Inner Temple and Middle Temple (formerly belonging to the Knights Templar), Lincoln's Inn, and Gray's Inn (anciently belonging to the earls of Lincoln and Gray). The other inns are the two Sergeants' Inns. See "Inns of Chancery."

INNUENDO (Lat. *innuere*, to nod at, to hint at; meaning). The word was used when pleadings were in Latin, and has been translated by "meaning."

——**In Pleading.** A clause in a declaration, indictment, or other pleading containing an averment which is explanatory of some preceding word or statement.

It derives its name from the leading word by which it was always introduced when pleadings were in Latin. It is mostly used in actions of slander, and is then said to be a subordinate averment, connecting particular parts of the publication with what has gone before, in order to elucidate the defendant's meaning more fully. 1 Starkie, Sland. & L. 431.

Its object is to explain the defendant's meaning by reference to previous matter. See "Colloquium." It may be used to point to the plaintiff as the person intended in the defendant's statement. It may show that a general imputation of crime is intended to apply to the plaintiff (Heard, Lib. & Sland. § 226; 1 H. L. Cas. 637; 2 Hill [N. Y.] 282), but it cannot be allowed to give a new sense to words where there is no such charge (8 Q. B. 825; 7 C. B. 280).

It may point to the injurious and actionable meaning, where the words complained of are susceptible of two meanings (8 Q. B. 841; Moore & S. 727), and generally explain the preceding matter (1 Dowl. [N. S.] 602; 7 C. B. 251; 15 C. B. 360; 1 Mees. & W. 245; 5 Bing. 17; 10 Bing. 250; 12 Adol. & E. 317), but cannot enlarge and point the effect of language beyond its natural and common meaning in its usual acceptation (Heard, Lib. & Sland. § 219; Metc. Yelv. 22; 2 Salk. 513; 1 Ld. Raym. 256; 2 Cowp. 688; 4 Per. & D. 161; 6 Barn. & C. 154; 4 Nev. & M. 841; 4 Dowl. 703; 9 Adol. & E. 282; 12 Adol. & E. 719; 15 Pick. [Mass.] 335), unless connected with the proper introductory averments (1 Cromp. & J. 143; 1 Adol. & E. 554; 9 Adol. & E. 282, 286, note; 1 C. B. 728; 6 C. B. 239; 1 Saund. 242; 2 Pick. [Mass.] 320; 13 Pick. [Mass.] 198; 15 Pick. [Mass.] 321; 16 Pick. [Mass.] 1; 11 Metc. [Mass.] 473; 8 N. H. 246; 12 Vt. 51; 1 Bin. [Pa.] 537; 5 Bin. [Pa.] 218; 11 Serg. & R. [Pa.] 343; 5 Johns. [N. Y.] 211).

INOFFICIOSUM (Lat.) In civil law. Inofficious; contrary to natural duty or affection. Used of a will of a parent which disinherited a child without just cause, or of that of a child which disinherited a parent, and which could be contested by *querela inofficiosi testamenti*. Dig. 2, 5, 3, 13; Paulus, lib. 4, tit. 5, § 1.

INOFFICIOUS TESTAMENT. A will not in accordance with the natural affections and ties of relationship of the testator.

INOFICIOCIDAD. In Spanish law. Everything done contrary to a duty or obligation assumed, as well as in opposition to the piety and affection dictated by nature, *inofficiosum dicitur id omne quod contra pietatis officium factum est.* The term applies especially to testaments, donations, dower, etc., which may be either revoked or reduced when they affect injuriously the rights of creditors or heirs.

INOPS CONSILII (Lat.) Destitute or without counsel. In the construction of wills, a greater latitude is given, because the testator is supposed to have been *inops consilii.*

INPENY AND OUTPENY. In old English law. A customary payment of a penny on entering into and going out of a tenancy (*pro exitu de tenura, et pro ingressu*). Spelman; Cowell.

INQUEST OF OFFICE. An inquiry made by the king's officer, his sheriff, coroner, or escheator, either *virtute officii,* or by writ sent to him for that purpose, or by commissioners specially appointed, concerning any matter that entitles the king to the possession of lands or tenements, goods or chattels. It is done by a jury of no determinate number,—either twelve, or more, or less. 3 Sharswood, Bl. Comm. 258; Finch, Law, 323-325. An inquest of office was bound to find for the king upon the direction of the court. The reason given is that an inquest concluded no man of his right, but only gave the king an opportunity to enter, so that he could have his right tried. 3 Sharswood, Bl. Comm. 260; 4 Steph. Comm. 61; F. Moore, 730; Vaughan, 135; 3 Hen. VII. 10; 2 Hen. IV. 5; 3 Leon. 196. An inquest of office was also called, simply, "office." As to "office" in the United States, see 1 Caines (N. Y.) 426; 7 Cranch (U. S.) 603; 2 Kent, Comm. 16, 23.

INQUILINUS. In civil law. The hirer of a house in the city; a city tenant, as *colonus* was a country tenant. Bracton, fol. 42b.

INQUIRY, WRIT OF. A writ sued out by a plaintiff in a case where the defendant has let the proceedings go by default, and an interlocutory judgment has been given for damages generally, where the damages do not admit of calculation. It issues to the sheriff of the county in which the venue is laid, and commands him to inquire, by a jury of twelve men, concerning the amount of damages. The sheriff thereupon tries the cause in his sheriff's court, and some amount must always be returned to the court. But the return of the inquest merely informs the court, which may, if it choose, in all cases assess damages, and thereupon give final judgment. 2 Archb. Prac. (Waterman Ed.) 952; 3 Sharswood, Bl. Comm. 398; 3 Chit. St. 495, 497.

INQUISITIO (Lat.) In old English law. An inquisition or inquest. *Inquisitio post mortem*, an inquisition after death. An inquest of office held, during the continuance of the military tenures, upon the death of every one of the king's tenants, to inquire of what lands he died seised, who was his heir, and of what age, in order to entitle the king to his marriage, wardship, relief, primer seisin, or other advantages, as the circumstances of the case might turn out. 3 Bl. Comm. 258. *Inquisitio patriae*, the inquisition of the country; the ordinary jury, as distinguished from the grand assize. Bracton, fol. 15b.

INQUISITION. In practice. An examination of certain facts by a jury impanelled by the sheriff for the purpose. The instrument of writing on which their decision is made is also called an inquisition. The sheriff or coroner, and the jury who make the inquisition, are called the "inquest." The term "inquest" is now generally used instead of "inquisition."

INQUISITOR. A designation of sheriffs, coroners *super visum corporis*, and the like, who have power to inquire into certain matters.

——**In Ecclesiastical Law.** The name of an officer who is authorized to inquire into heresies, and the like, and to punish them; a judge.

INROLMENT, or **ENROLLMENT** (Law Lat. *irrotulatio*). The act of putting upon a roll.

Formerly, the record of a suit was kept on skins of parchment, which, best to preserve them, were kept upon a roll, or in the form of a roll. What was written upon them was called the "inrolment." After, when such records came to be kept in books, the making up of the record retained the old name of "inrolment." Thus, in equity, the inrolment of a decree is the recording of it, and will prevent the rehearing of the cause, except on appeal to the house of lords, or by bill of review. The decree may be inrolled immediately after it has been passed and entered, unless a *caveat* has been entered. 2 Freem. 179; 4 Johns. Ch. (N. Y.) 199; 14 Johns. (N. Y.) 501. And before signing and inrolment, a decree cannot be pleaded in bar of a suit, though it can be insisted on by way of answer. 3 Atk. 809; 2 Ves. Jr. 577; 4 Johns. Ch. (N. Y.) 199. See Saund. Ord. Chanc.

Transcribing upon the records of a court deeds, etc., according to the statutes on the subject. See 1 Chit. St. 425, 426; 2 Chit. St. 69, 76-78; 3 Chit. St. 1497. Placing on file or record generally, as annuities, attorneys, etc.

INSANITY. Unsoundness or derangement of mind.

Insanity is the general term, and includes all mental unsoundness, whether complete or partial, and whether congenital or induced.

It may be divided into (1) idiocy or imbecility, being the state of one who has been from birth without reason, and (2) lunacy, the state of one who once possessed reason, but has lost it in whole or in part.

"Lunacy" may be either (1) impulsive, consisting in an unnatural and sometimes irresistible impulse to certain acts, apart from or against all reason, and (2) delusive, consisting in persistent and incorrigible hallucinations as to matters of fact.

Further subdivisions have been sometimes made, as into the various manias,—homicidal, suicidal, etc.

Moral or emotional insanity is a perverted condition of the emotional or moral nature, inducing criminal acts, and not accompanied by intellectual delusion. It is the negative aspect of "irresistible impulse."

"Insanity" is frequently used in the sense of "lunacy," and as excluding "idiocy," and "imbecility."

The forms of insanity have been tabulated by a distinguished alienist as follows:

I. Defective development of faculties.
- (1) Idiocy.
  - (a) Resulting from congenital defect.
  - (b) Resulting from an obstacle to the development of the faculties, supervening in infancy.
- (2) Imbecility.
  - (a) Resulting from congenital defect.
  - (b) Resulting from an obstacle to the development of the faculties, supervening in infancy.

II. Lesion of the faculties subsequent to their development.
- (1) Mania.
  - (a) Intellectual.
    - (aa) General.
    - (bb) Partial.
  - (b) Affective.
    - (aa) General.
    - (bb) Partial.
- (2) Dementia.

(a) Consecutive to mania, or injuries of the brain.
(b) Senile, peculiar to old age.

1 Ray, Med. Jur. "Insanity" (3d Ed.) p. 71.

INSANUS EST QUI, ABJECTA RAtione, omnia cum impetu et furore facit. He is insane who, reason being thrown away, does everything with violence and rage. 4 Coke, 128.

INSCRIBERE. In the Roman law. To subscribe an accusation. The subscriber was bound to substantiate his charge, or suffer the penalty appropriate to such charge. Calv. Lex.

INSCRIPTIO (Lat.) In civil law. A written accusation; an undertaking to suffer the punishment of the accused in case of a failure to prove him guilty. Calv. Lex.

INSCRIPTION.

——**In Civil Law.** An engagement which a person who makes a solemn accusation of a crime against another enters into that he will suffer the same punishment, if he has accused the other falsely, which would have been inflicted upon him had he been guilty. Code, 9. 1. 10; Id. 9. 2. 16. 17.

——**In Evidence.** Something written or engraved.

Inscriptions upon tombstones and other proper places, as rings, and the like, are held to be evidence of pedigree. Buller, N. P. 233; Cowp. 591; 10 East, 120; 13 Ves. 145. See "Declaration"; "Hearsay Evidence."

INSCRIPTIONES (Lat.) The name given by the old English law to any written instrument by which anything is granted. Blount.

INSENSIBLE. In pleading. That which is unintelligible is said to be insensible. Steph. Pl. 378.

INSIDERS. See "Gambling Contract."

INSIDIATORES VIARUM (Lat.) Persons who lie in wait in order to commit some felony or other misdemeanor.

INSIMUL (Lat.) Together; jointly. Towns Pl. 44.

INSIMUL COMPUTASSENT (Lat.) They had accounted together. See "Account."

INSIMUL TENUIT. In old English practice. The name of a species of the writ of *formedon* in the descender, which lay for a cotenant against a stranger.

INSINUACION. In Spanish law. The presentation of a public document to a competent judge, in order to obtain his approbation and sanction of the same, and thereby giving it judicial authenticity.

"*Insinuatio est ejus quod traditur, sive agitur, coram quocumque judice in scripturam redactio.*"

This formality is requisite to the validity of certain donations *inter vivos.* Escriche, Dic. Raz.

INSINUARE. In civil law. To put into; to deposit a writing in court, answering nearly to the modern expression "to file." To transcribe an act in the public registers; to record. *Si non mandatum actis insinuatum est,* if the power or authority be not deposited among the records of the court. Inst. 4. 11. 3.

To declare or acknowledge before a judicial officer; to give an act an official form. Calv. Lex.

To make known; to give information. Id.

INSINUATIO (Law Lat.) In old English law. Information or suggestion. *Ex insinuatione,* on the information. Reg. Jud. 25, 50.

INSINUATION. In civil law. The transcription of an act on the public registers, like our recording of deeds. It was not necessary in any other alienation but that appropriated to the purpose of donation. Inst. 2. 7. 2; Poth. Tr. des Donations, Entre Vifs, sec. 2, art. 3, § 3; Encyclopedie; 8 Toullier, Dr. Civ. note 198.

INSINUATION OF A WILL. In civil law. The first production of it; or, leaving it in the hands of the register in order to its probate. 21 Hen. VIII. c. 5; Jacob.

INSOLIDE (Law Lat.) Solidly; without any separation of possession or ownership.

A term used by Bracton to express that impossible or impracticable kind of possession where two persons hold a thing at the same time exclusively. Bract. fol. 45.

INSOLVENCY. The state of a person who is unable, from any cause, to pay his debts. Two tests of insolvency prevail, their application generally being governed by the purpose for which the fact of insolvency is ascertained, though there is some confusion in the cases in this respect.

Generally, for the purpose of enabling the debtor or his creditors to take advantage of insolvent acts, one is insolvent who is unable to meet his obligations as they accrue in due course of trade, and is unable to proceed in business without making some arrangement with his creditors, without regard to the ultimate sufficiency of his assets in liquidation. 112 Pa. St. 294; 98 Iowa, 321; 86 Me. 246; 3 Gray (Mass.) 600; 116 Mo. 226.

Within the rule relating to conveyances by insolvent persons, it is generally held that one is insolvent whose obligation could not be collected by legal means out of his property. 43 N. Y. 75; 31 Mo. 73. If one has means from which payment could be enforced, he is not insolvent, even though he is in embarrassed circumstances, and unable to make present payment (136 N. Y. 104; 52 Mo. App. 282), or has even been compelled to suspend business (63 Hun

[N. Y.] 632). Property so situated that it cannot be reached by creditors is not to be considered in determining the issue of solvency (*q. v.*).

Distinction between "insolvency" and "bankruptcy," see "Bankruptcy."

INSOLVENT. One who is in a state of insolvency (*q. v.*)

INSPECTATOR. An adverse party.

INSPECTION (Lat. *inspicere*, to look into). The examination of certain articles made by law subject to such examination, so that they may be declared fit for commerce. The decision of the inspectors is not final. The object of the law is to protect the community from fraud, and to preserve the character of the merchandise abroad. 8 Cow. (N. Y.) 45. See 1 Johns. (N. Y.) 205; 13 Johns. (N. Y.) 331; 2 Caines (N. Y.) 312; 3 Caines (N. Y.) 207.

——**In Practice.** Examination.

——**Books and Records.** The inspection of all public records is free to all persons who have an interest in them, upon payment of the usual fees. 7 Mod. 129; 1 Strange, 304, 2 Strange, 260, 954, 1005. But it seems a mere stranger, who has no such interest, has no right at common law. 8 Term R. 390.

A stockholder has, as a general rule, the right to inspect the books and records of his corporation.

INSPECTION, TRIAL BY. A mode of trial formerly in use in England, by which the judges of a court decided a point in dispute, upon the testimony of their own senses, without the intervention of a jury. This took place in cases where the fact upon which issue was taken must, from its nature, be evident to the court from ocular demonstration, or other irrefragable proof, and was adopted for the greater expedition of a cause. 3 Bl. Comm. 331. In this way questions whether a party were an infant or not, whether an injury was mayhem or not, etc., were determined; but this has been long out of use. 3 Steph. Comm. 582.

INSPECTOR. The name given to certain officers whose duties are to examine and inspect things over which they have jurisdiction; as, inspector of bark, one who is by law authorized to examine bark for exportation, and to approve or disapprove of its quality. Inspectors of customs are officers appointed by the general government. As to their duties, see 1 Story, U. S. Laws, 590, 605, 609, 610, 612, 619, 621, 623, 650; 2 Story, U. S. Laws, 1490, 1516; 3 Story, U. S. Laws, 1650, 1790.

INSPECTORSHIP, DEED OF. In English law. An agreement between an insolvent and his creditors, by which a certain person is appointed to supervise the winding up of the estate.

INSPEXIMUS (Lat. we have seen). A word sometimes used in letters patent, reciting a grant, *inspeximus* such former grant, and so reciting it *verbatim*. It then grants such further privileges as are thought convenient. 5 Coke, 54.

INSTALLATION, or INSTALMENT. The act by which an officer is put in public possession of the place he is to fill. The president of the United States, or a governor, is installed into office, by being sworn agreeably to the requisition of the constitution and laws.

INSTANCE. Literally; standing on; hence, urging, solicitation. Webster.

——**In Civil and French Law.** In general, all sorts of actions and judicial demands. Dig. 44. 7. 58.

——**In Ecclesiastical Law.** Causes of instance are those proceeded in at solicitation of some party, as opposed to causes of office, which run in the name of the judge. Halifax, Anal. p. 122.

——**In Scotch Law.** That which may be insisted on at one diet or course of probation. Wharton.

INSTANCE COURT. In English law. That branch of the admiralty court which has the jurisdiction of all matters except those relating to prizes.

An "instance court" takes cognizance of contracts made and injuries committed on the high seas; a "prize court" has jurisdiction of prizes, etc. 18 Johns. (N. Y.) 257.

The term is sometimes used in American law for purposes of explanation, but has no proper application to admiralty courts in the United States, where the powers of both instance and prize courts are conferred without any distinction. 3 Dall. (U. S.) 6; 1 Gall. (U. S.) 563; 3 Kent, Comm. 355, 378. See "Admiralty."

INSTANCIA. In Spanish law. The institution and prosecution of a suit from its inception until definitive judgment. The first instance, *primera instancia*, is the prosecution of a suit before the judge competent to take cognizance of it at its inception; the second instance, *secunda instancia*, is the exercise of the same action before the court of appellate jurisdiction; and the third instance, *tercera instancia*, is the prosecution of the same suit, either by an application of revision before the appellate tribunal, that has already decided the cause, or before some higher tribunal, having jurisdiction of the same.

All civil suits must be tried and decided, in the first instance, within three years; and all criminal, within two years.

As a general rule, three instances are admitted in all civil and criminal cases. Const. 1812, art. 285.

INSTANS EST FINIS UNIUS TEMPORIS et principium alterius. An instant is the end of one time, and the beginning of another. Co. Litt. 185.

INSTANTER (Lat.) Immediately; presently; instantly; forthwith; without any delay or the allowance of any time. This term, it is said, means that the act to which it applies shall be done within twenty-four hours; but a doubt has been suggested by whom is the account of the hours to be kept, and whether the term "instanter," as applied to the subject matter, may not be more properly taken to mean "before the rising of the court," when the act is to be done in court, or "before the shutting of the office the same night," when the act is to be done there. 1 Taunt. 343; 6 East, 587, note (e); Tidd. Prac. (3d Ed.) 508, note; 3 Chit. Prac. 112. See 3 Burrows, 1809; Co. Litt. 157; Styles, Reg. 452; 20 Ill. App. 110.

——**Pleading.** An order that the defendants plead instanter technically means within the judicial day then begun. 1 Bouvier Law Dic. 645; 20 Ill. App. 110. It is probably true that the term, as ordinarily used, is understood to mean instantly, immediately, or at once, so that upon such a rule, a default may follow the entry of the rule, and this, in effect, makes the rule unnecessary, for the default might as well be entered without it. 53 Ill. App. 160, 161.

INSTAR (Lat.) Like; resembling; equivalent; as, *instar dentium*, like teeth; *instar omnium*, equivalent to all.

INSTAURUM (Law Lat.) In old English deeds. A stock or store of cattle, and other things; the whole stock upon a farm, including cattle, wagons, ploughs, and all other implements of husbandry. 1 Mon. Angl. 548; Fleta, lib. 2, c. 68, § 1; Id. c. 72, § 7. *Terra instaurata*, land already stocked, or furnished with all things necessary to carry on the use or occupation of a farm.

INSTIGATION. The act by which one incites another to do something; as, to injure a third person, or to commit some crime or misdemeanor, to commence a suit, or to prosecute a criminal. See "Accomplice."

INSTIRPARE. To establish.

INSTITOR (Lat.) In civil law. A clerk in a store; an agent.

He was so called because he watched over the business with which he was charged; and it is immaterial whether he was employed in making a sale in the store, or whether charged with any other business. *Institor appellatus est ex eo, quod negotio gerendo instet; nec multum facit tabernae sit praepositus, an cuilibet alii negotiationi.* Dig. 14. 3. 1. 3. Mr. Bell says that the charge given to a clerk to manage a store or shop is called "institorial power." 1 Bell, Comm. (5th Ed.) 479; Ersk. Inst. 3. 3. 46; 1 Stair, Inst. (by Brodie) bk. 1, tit. 11, §§ 12, 18, 19; Story, Ag. § 8.

INSTITORIA ACTIO (Lat.) In the civil law. The name of an action given to those who had contracted with an *institor* (*q. v.*) to compel the principal to performance. Inst. 4. 7. 2; Dig. 14. 3. 1; Story, Ag. § 426.

INSTITUTE.

——**In Scotch Law.** The person first called in the "tailzie"; the rest, or the heirs of tailzie, are called "substitutes." Ersk. Prac. 3. 8. 8. See "Substitutes."

——**In Civil Law.** One who is appointed heir by testament, and is required to give the estate devised to another person, who is called the "substitute."

To name or to make an heir by testament. Dig. 28. 5. 65. To make an accusation; to commence an action.

INSTITUTES. Elements of jurisprudence; text books containing the principles of law made the foundation of legal studies.

The word was first used by the civilians to designate those books prepared for the student, and supposed to embrace the fundamental legal principles arranged in an orderly manner. Two books of Institutes were known to the civil lawyers of antiquity,—Gaius and Justinian..

(1) Coke's Institutes. Four volumes of commentaries upon various parts of the English law.

Sir Edward Coke hath written four volumes of "Institutes," as he is pleased to call them, though they have little of the institutional method to warrant such a title. The first volume is a very extensive commentary upon a little excellent treatise of tenures, compiled by Judge Littleton in the reign of Edw. IV. This comment is a rich mine of valuable common-law learning, collected and heaped together from the ancient reports and Year Books, but greatly defective in method. The second volume is a comment on many old acts of parliament, without any systematical order; the third, a more methodical treatise on the pleas of the crown; and the fourth, an account of the several species of courts. These Institutes are usually cited thus: The first volume as Co. Litt., or 1 Inst.; the second, third, and fourth as 2, 3, or 4 Inst., without any author's name. 1 Bl. Comm. 72.

(2) Gaius' Institutes. A tractate upon the Roman law, ascribed to Caius or Gaius.

Of the personal history of this jurist nothing is known. Even the spelling of his name is matter of controversy, and he is known by no other title than Gaius, or Caius. He is believed to have lived in the reign of Marcus Aurelius. The history of Gaius' Institutes is remarkable. In 1816, Niebuhr was sent to Rome by the king of Prussia. On his way thither, he spent two days in the cathedral library of Verona, and at this time discovered these Institutes, which had been lost to the jurists of the middle ages. In 1817, the Royal Academy of Berlin charged Goeschen, Bekker, and Hollweg with the duty of transcribing the discovered manuscript. In 1819, Goeschen gave the first completed edition, as far as the manuscript could be deciphered, to his fellow jurists. It created an unusual sensation, and became a fruitful source of comment. It formed a new era in the study of Roman law. It gave the modern jurist the signal advantage of studying the source of the Institutes of Justinian. It is believed by the best modern scholars that Gaius' was the first original tractate of the kind, not being compiled from former publications. The language of Gaius is clear, terse, and technical,—evidently written by a master of law, and a master of the Latin tongue. The Institutes were unquestionably practical. There is no attempt at criticism or philosophical discussion. The disciple of Sabinus is content to teach law as he finds it. Its arrangement is solid and logical, and Justinian follows it with an almost servile imitation.

The best editions of Gaius are Goeschen's second edition, Berlin, 1824, in which the text was again collated by Bluhme, and the third edition of Goeschen, Berlin, 1842, edited by Lachman from a critical revision by Goeschen, which had been interrupted by his death. In France, Gaius attracted equal attention, and we have three editions and translations: Boulet, Paris, 1824; Domenget, 1843; and Pellat, 1844.

In 1859, Francesco Lisi, a learned Italian scholar, published, at Bologna, a new edition of the first book of Gaius, with an Italian translation, *en regard*. The edition is accompanied and enriched by many valuable notes, printed in both Latin and Italian. Perhaps this must be considered, so far as printed, the most complete edition of the old civilian that modern scholars have yet produced.

The reader who may wish to pursue his Gaiian studies should consult the list of some thirty-odd treatises and commentaries mentioned in Mackeldey's Lehrbuch des Rom. Rechts, p. 47, note (b), (13th Ed.) Wein, 1851; Huschke, Essay Zur Kritik und Interp. von Gaius Inst., Breslau, 1830; Haubold's Inst. Jur. Rom. Prev. Line pp. 151, 152, 505, 506, Lipsiae, 1826; Boecking's Gaius, Preface, pp. 11-18, Leps. 1845; Lisi's Gaius, Preface, pp. x. xi., Bologna, 1859.

(3) Justinian's Institutes. An abridgment of the Code and Digest, composed by order of that emperor, and under his guidance, with an intention to give a summary knowledge of the law to those persons not versed in it, and particularly to students. Inst. Proem. § 3.

The lawyers employed to compile it were Tribonian, Theophilus, and Dorotheus. The work was first published on the 21st of November in the year 533, and received the sanction of statute law by order of the emperor. It is divided into four books; each book is divided into titles, and each title into separate paragraphs or sections, preceded by an introductory part. The first part is called *principium*, because it is the commencement of the title; those which follow are numbered, and called "paragraphs." The work treats of the rights of persons, of things, and of actions. The first book treats of persons; the second, third, and the first five titles of the fourth book, of things; and the remainder of the fourth book, of actions. The method of citing the Institutes should be understood, and is now commonly by giving the number of the book, title, and section, thus: Inst. I. 2. 5,—thereby indicating book I. title 2, section 5. Where it is intended to indicate the first paragraph, or *principium*, thus: Inst. B. I. 2. pr. Frequently the citation is simply I. or J. I. 2. 5. A second mode of citation is thus: § 5, Inst. or I. I. 2,—meaning book I. title 2, paragraph 5. A third method of citation, and one in universal use with the older jurists, was by giving the name of the title and the first words of the paragraph referred to, thus: § senatusconsultum est I de jure nat. gen. et civil,—which means, as before, Inst. B. I. tit. 2, § 5. See 1 Colquhoun, § 61.

The first printed edition of the Institutes is that of Schoyffer, fol. 1468. The last critical German edition is that of Schrader, Berlin, 1832. This work of Schrader is the most learned and most elaborate commentary on the text of Justinian in any language, and was intended to form a part of the Berlin Corpus Juris, but nothing further has been published. It is impossible in this brief article to name all the commentaries on these Institutes, which in all ages have commanded the study and admiration of jurists. More than one hundred and fifty years ago, one Homberg printed a tract De Multitudine nimia Commentatorum in Instutiones Juris. But we must refer the reader to the best recent French and English editions. Ortolan's Institutes de l'Empereur Justinien avec le texte, la traduction en regard, et les explications sous chaque paragraphe, Paris, 1857, 3 vols. 8vo, sixth edition. This is, by common consent of scholars, regarded as the best historical edition of the Institutes ever published. Du Caurroy's Institutes de Justinean traduites et expliquees par A. M. Du Caurroy, Paris, 1851, 8th ed. 2 vols. 8vo. The Institutes of Justinian, with English Introduction, Translation, and Notes, by Thomas Collet Sandars, M. A., London, 1853, 8vo; 2d Ed., 1860. This work has been prepared expressly for beginners, and is founded mainly upon Ortolan, with a liberal use of La Grange. Du Caurroy, Warnkoenig, and Puchta, as well as Harris and Cooper. A careful study of this edition will result in the student's abandoning its pages, and betaking himself to Schrader and Ortolan. The English edition of Harris, and the American one of Cooper, have ceased to attract attention.

(4) Theophilus' Institutes. A paraphrase of Justinian, made, it is believed, soon after A. D. 533.

It is generally supposed that in A. D. 534, 535, and 536, Theophilus read his commentary in Greek to his pupils in the law school of Constantinople. He is conjectured to have died some time in A. D. 536. This paraphrase maintained itself as a manual of law until the eighth or tenth century.

This text was used in the time of Hexabiblos of Harmenipulus, the last of the Greek jurists. It is also conjectured that Theophilus was not the editor of his own paraphrase, but that it was drawn up by some of his pupils after his explanations and lectures, inasmuch as it contains certain barbarous phrases, and the texts of the manuscripts vary greatly from each other.

It has, however, always been somewhat in use, and jurists consider that its study aids the text of the Institutes; and Cujas and Hugo have both praised it. The first edition was that of Zuichem, fol. Basle, 1531; the best edition is that of Reitz, 2 vols. 4to, 1751, Haag. There is a German translation by Wusterman, 1823, 2 vols. 8vo; and a French translation by Mons. Ilregier, Paris, 1847, 8vo, whose edition is prefaced by a learned and valuable introduction and dissertation. Consult Mortreuil, Hist. du Droit Byzan., Paris, 1843; Smith, Dict. Biog. London, 1849, 3 vols. 8vo; 1 Kent, Comm. 533; Profession d'Avocat, tom. ii. note 536, p. 95; Introd. a l'Etude du Droit Romain, p. 124; Dict. de Jurisp.; Merlin, Repert.; Enc. d'Alembert.

INSTITUTIO HAEREDIS (Lat.) In Roman law. The appointment of the *haeres* in the will. See "Haeres."

INSTITUTION (Lat. *instituere*, to form, to establish).

——**In Civil Law.** The appointment of an heir; the act by which a testator nominates one or more persons to succeed him in all his rights, active and passive. Halifax, Anal. 39; Poth. Tr. des Donations Testamentaires, c. 2, sec. 1, § 1; Civ. Code La. art. 1598; Dig. 28. 5. 1; Id. 1. 28. 6. 1. 2. 4.

——**In Ecclesiastical Law.** To become a parson or vicar, four things are necessary, viz., holy orders, presentation, institution, induction. Institution is a kind of investiture of the spiritual part of the benefice; for by institution the care of the souls of the parish is committed to the charge of the clerk, previous to which the oath against simony and of allegiance and supremacy are to be taken. By institution the benefice is full, so that there can be no fresh presentation (except the patron be the king), and the clerk may enter on parsonage house and glebe, and take the tithes; but he cannot grant or let them, or bring an action for them, till induction. See 1 Sharswood, Bl. Comm. 389-391; 1 Burns, Ecc. Law, 169-172.

——**In Political Law.** A law, rite, or ceremony enjoined by authority as a permanent rule of conduct or of government; as, the Institutions of Lycurgus. Webster. An organized society, established either by law or the authority of individuals, for promoting any object, public or social. Webster.

——**In Practice.** The commencement of an action; as, A. B. has instituted a suit against C. D. to recover damages for trespass.

INSTITUTIONES (Lat. from *instituere*, to instruct, or educate). Works containing the elements of any science; institutions, or institutes. One of Justinian's principal law collections, and a similar work of the Roman jurist Gaius, are so entitled. See "Institutes."

INSTRUCTIONS.

——**In the Law of Agency.** Orders given by a principal to his agent in relation to the business of his agency.

The agent is bound to obey the instructions he has received, and when he neglects so to do he is responsible for the consequences, unless he is justified by matter of necessity. 4 Bin. (Pa.) 361; 1 Livermore, Ag. 368. See "Agent."

——**In English Practice.** The statements of a cause of action, given by a client to his attorney, and which, where such is the practice, are sent to his pleader to put into legal form of a declaration. Warren, Law Stud. 284.

Instructions to counsel are their indemnity for any aspersions they may make on the opposite party; but attorneys who have a just regard to their own reputation will be cautious, even under instructions, not to make any unnecessary attack upon a party or witness. For such unjustifiable conduct the counsel will be held responsible. Eunom. Dial. 2, § 43, p. 132. For a form of instructions, see 3 Chit. Prac. 117, 120, note.

——**In American Practice.** The charge or directions as to the law, given by the court to the jury.

——**In French Law.** The means used and formality employed to prepare a case for trial. It is generally applied to criminal cases, and is then called "criminal instruction." It is then defined as the acts and proceedings which tend to prove positively a crime or delict, in order to inflict on the guilty person the punishment which he deserves.

INSTRUMENT. The writing which contains some agreement, and is so called because it has been prepared as a memorial of what has taken place or been agreed upon.

Something reduced to writing as a means of evidence. Abbott. A will has been held to be an "instrument." 14 Eq. Cas. 402.

The agreement and the instrument in which it is contained are very different things,—the latter being only evidence of the existence of the former.

INSTRUMENT OF APPEAL. The document by which an appeal is brought in an English matrimonial cause from the president of the probate, divorce, and admiralty division to the full court. It is analogous to a petition. Browne, Div. 322.

INSTRUMENT OF EVIDENCE. Instruments of evidence are the *media* through which the evidence of facts, either disputed or required to be proved, is conveyed to the mind of a judicial tribunal; and they comprise persons, as well as writings. Best, Ev. § 123.

INSTRUMENTA (Lat.) That kind of evidence which consists of writings not under seal; as, court rolls, accounts, and the like. 3 Co. Litt. (Thomas Ed.) 487.

INSUFFICIENCY. In chancery practice. After filing of defendant's answer, the plaintiff has six weeks in which to file exceptions to it for insufficiency, which is the fault of not replying specifically to specific charges in the bill. Smith, Ch. Prac. 344; Mitf. Eq. Pl. 376, note; Saunders, Ord. Chanc. Index.

INSULA (Lat. island). A house not connected with other houses, but separated by a surrounding space of ground. Calv. Lex.

INSUPER (Lat.) Moreover; over and above.

An old exchequer term, applied to a charge made upon a person in his account. Blount.

INSURABLE INTEREST. Such an interest in a subject of insurance as will entitle the person possessing it to obtain insurance.

In the law of fire insurance, an insurable interest may be defined as such an interest as would entail a pecuniary loss were the property destroyed. 62 N. Y. 47.

In the law of life insurance, an insurable interest in the life of another is such a relation that the death of such person would entail pecuniary loss. Any relationship resulting in dependence, or giving a right to service or support, gives an insurable interest to the person benefited. 12 Mass. 115; 57 Vt. 496; 66 Mo. 63. A creditor has an insurable interest in the life of his debtor. 23 Conn. 244.

INSURANCE. A contract whereby, for an agreed premium, one party undertakes to indemnify the other against loss on a specified subject by specified perils. The party agreeing to make the indemnity is usually called the "insurer" or "underwriter;" the other, the "insured' or "assured;" the agreed consideration, the "premium"; the written contract, a "policy"; the events insured against, "risks" or "perils"; and the subject, right, or interest to be protected, the "insurable interest." 1 Phil. Ins. §§ 1-5. Called, also, "assurance."

Insurance is classified according to the nature of the risk insured against, or the nature of the property insured, the principal sorts being (1) fire insurance, being against injury to property by fire; (2) life insurance, being against injury by the death of one in whose interest the assured has a pecuniary interest; (3) marine insurance, being against injury to vessels or their cargo by any peril of navigation; and (4) accident insurance, being against loss from accidental personal injury.

Many other varieties, however, have become common in recent years, as against injury to crops by hail; against loss by defalcation; against defects of title to land, etc.

INSURANCE AGENT. An agent for effecting insurance may be such by appointment, or the recognition of his acts done as such. 2 Phil. Ins. § 1848; 4 Cow. (N. Y.) 645. He may be agent for either of the parties to the policy, or for distinct purposes for both. 16 T. B. Mon. (Ky.) 252; 20 Barb. (N. Y.) 68.

INSURED. The person who procures an insurance.

INSURER. The underwriter in a policy of insurance; the party agreeing to make indemnity to the other. Sometimes applied improperly to denote the party insured.

INSURGENT. One who is concerned in an insurrection. He differs from a rebel in this, that "rebel" is always understood in a bad sense, or one who unjustly opposes the constituted authorities; insurgent may be one who justly opposes the tyranny of constituted authorities. The colonists who opposed the tyranny of the English government were insurgents, not rebels.

INSURRECTION. A rebellion of citizens or subjects of a country against its government.

An insurrection may constitute treason (2 Dall. [U. S.] 348), and, if extensive, may amount to civil war. 67 U. S. 635.

INTAKERS. In English law. The name given to receivers of goods stolen in Scotland, who take them to England. 9 Hen. V. c. 27.

INTEGER (Lat.) Whole; untouched. *Res integra* means a question which is new and undecided. 2 Kent, Comm. 177.

INTEMPERANCE. Habitual immoderate use of intoxicants does not necessarily imply drunkenness. 76 Ill. 213.

INTEND (from Lat. *intendere*, from *in*, to or towards, and *tendere*, to stretch or strain). To fix the mind upon a thing; to mean; to determine; to act with a full knowledge of consequences, and with a determination or willingness to produce such consequences. 1 Greenl. Ev. § 18; 3 Maule & S. 11, 15; Burrill, Circ. Ev. 38, 47.

INTENDANT. One who has the charge, management, or direction of some office, department, or public business.

INTENDED TO BE RECORDED. This phrase is frequently used in conveyancing, in deeds which recite other deeds which have not been recorded. In Pennsylvania, it has been construed to be a covenant, on the part of the grantor, to procure the deed to be recorded in a reasonable time. 2 Rawle (Pa.) 14.

INTENDENTE. In Spanish law. The immediate agent of the minister of finance, or the chief and principal director of the different branches of the revenue, appointed in the various departments in each of the provinces of the Spanish monarchy. See Escriche, Dic. Raz.

INTENDMENT OF LAW. The true meaning, the correct understanding, or intention, of the law; a presumption or inference made by the courts. Co. Litt. 78.

INTENT. Intention (*q. v.*).

That the terms are synonymous, see 2 Jones (N. C.) 414.

INTENTIO (Lat.)

——**In Civil Law.** The formal complaint or claim of a plaintiff before the praetor. "*Reus exceptionem velut intentionem implete*"; *id est, reus in exceptione actor est*, the defendant makes up his plea as if it were a declaration; *i. e.*, the defendant is plaintiff in the plea.

——**In Old English Law.** A count or declaration in a real action (*narratio*). Bracton, lib. 4, tr. 2, c. 2; Fleta, lib. 4, c. 7; Du Cange.

INTENTIO CAECA MALA. A hidden intention is bad. 2 Bulst. 179.

INTENTIO INSERVIRE DEBET LEGIbus, non leges intentioni. Intentions ought to be subservient to the laws, not the laws to intentions. Co. Litt. 314.

INTENTIO MEA IMPONIT NOMEN OPeri meo. My intent gives a name to my act. Hob. 123.

INTENTION. A design, resolve, or determination of the mind.

The exercise of an intelligent will, the mind being fully aware of the nature and consequences of the act which is about to be done, and with such knowledge, and with full liberty of action, willing and electing to do it. 2 Lea (Tenn.) 619.

It implies contractual obligation to carry out the intention, and is to be distinguished from "promise." 24 N. J. Law, 430.

It is not synonymous with "motive" (131 Mo. 397), nor with "attempt" (3 Dev. [N. C.] 330).

INTER. In Latin phrases. A preposition, meaning among; between.

INTER ALIA (Lat.) Among other things; as, "the said premises, which, *inter alia*, Titius granted to Caius."

INTER ALIAS CAUSAS ACQUISItiones magna, celebris, et famosa est causa donationis. Among other methods of acquiring property, a great, much-used, and celebrated method is that of gift. Bracton, 11.

INTER ALIOS (Lat.) Between other parties, who are strangers to the proceeding in question.

INTER ALIOS RES GESTAS ALIIS NON posse praejudicium facere saepe constitutum est. It has been often settled that things which took place between other parties cannot prejudice. Code, 7. 60. 1. 2.

INTER APICES JURIS. See "Apex Juris."

INTER CAETEROS (Lat.) Among others; in a general clause; not by name (*nominatim*). A term applied, in the civil law, to clauses of disinheritance in a will. Inst. 2. 13. 1; Id. 2. 13. 3.

INTER CANEM ET LUPUM (Lat. between the dog and the wolf). The twilight; because then the dog seeks his rest, and the wolf his prey. 3 Inst. 63.

INTER CONJUGES. Between husband and wife.

INTER PARTES (Lat. between the parties). A phrase signifying an agreement professing in the outset, and before any stipulations are introduced, to be made between such and such persons; as, for example, "This indenture, made the ——— day of ———, 1848, between A. B., of the one part, and C. D., of the other." It is true that every contract is in one sense *inter partes*, because to be valid there must be two parties at least, but the technical sense of this expression is as above mentioned. Add. Cont. 9.

INTER REGALIA. Among the regalia (*q. v.*).

INTER SE, INTER SESE (Lat.) Among themselves. Story, Partn. § 405.

INTER VIVOS (Lat.) Between living persons; as, a gift *inter vivos*, which is a gift made by one living person to another. See "Gifts." It is a rule that a fee cannot pass by grant or transfer *inter vivos*, without appropriate words of inheritance. 2 Prest. Est. 64. See "Donatio Mortis Causa."

INTERCALARE (Lat.) In civil law. To introduce or insert among or between others; to introduce a day or month into the calendar; to intercalate. Dig. 50. 16. 98. pr.

INTERCHANGEABLY (Law Lat. *alternatim*). In the way, mode, or form of exchange or interchange. A term constantly used in the concluding clause of indentures, —in witness whereof, the said parties have hereunto interchangeably set their hands and seals,—and properly importing not only an execution by all the parties, but an actual interchange of signatures and seals, such as take place in the case of instruments executed in duplicate, or in part and counterpart, where the signature and seal of each party are affixed to the part given to the other. It is used, however, every day in deeds signed by the grantor only, but will not be held to import a signature by the grantee. 7 Pa. St. 329.

INTERCOMMON. To enjoy a right of common mutually with the inhabitants of a contiguous town, vill, or manor. 2 Sharswood, Bl. Comm. 33; Termes de la Ley.

INTERCOMMONING. A mutual privilege between the tenants of adjoining manors, of pasturing their cattle on the commons of each other.

INTERCOURSE (Lat. *intercursus*, from *inter*, between, and *currere*, to run). Communication; literally, a running or passing between persons or places; commerce. 7 How. (U. S.) 283-573.

INTERDICT.

——**In Civil Law.** The formula according to which the praetor ordered or forbade anything to be done in a cause concerning true or *quasi* possession until it should be decided definitely who had a right to it. But in modern civil law it is an extraordinary action, by which a summary decision is had in questions of possession or *quasi* possession. Heinec. Elem. Jur. Civ. § 1287. Interdicts are either prohibitory, restorative, or exhibitory; the first being a prohibition, the second a decree for restoring possession lost by force (*interdict unde vi.*, 50 Ill. 465), the third a decree for the exhibiting of accounts, etc. Id. 1290. Interdicts were decided by the praetor without the intervention of a *judex*, differing in this from actions (*actiones*).

The etymology of the word, according to Justinian, is *quod inter duos dicitur;* according to Isidorus, *quod interim dicitur.* Vocat; Sand. Just. 589; Mackeld. Civ. Law, §§ 195, 230, 235. Like an injunction, the interdict was merely personal in its effects; and it had also another similarity to it, by being temporary or perpetual. Dig. 43. 1. 1. 3. 4. See Story, Eq. Jur. § 865; Halifax, Anal. c. 6. See "Injunction."

——**In Ecclesiastical Law.** An ecclesiastical censure, by which divine services are prohibited either to particular persons or particular places. These tyrannical edicts, issued by ecclesiastical powers, have been abolished in England since the reformation, and were never known in the United States. See 2 Burns, Ecc. Law, 340, 341. Baptism was allowed during an interdict; but the holy eucharist was denied, except in the article of death, and burial in consecrated ground was denied, unless without divine offices.

INTERDICTION. In civil law. A judicial decree, by which a person is deprived of the exercise of his civil rights.

The condition of the party who labors under this incapacity.

INTERDICTUM SALVIANUM (Lat.) In civil law. The Salvian interdict. A process which lay for the owner of a farm to obtain possession of the goods of his tenant who had pledged them to him for the rent of the land. Inst. 4. 15. 3.

INTERDUM EVENIT UT EXCEPTIO quae prima facie justa videtur, tamen inique noceat. It sometimes happens that a plea which seems *prima facie* just, nevertheless is injurious and unequal. Inst. 4. 14; Id. 4. 14. 1. 2.

INTERESSE (Lat.) The interest of money, as distinguished from the principal.

An interest in land.

INTERESSE TERMINI (Lat.) An interest in the term. The demise of a term in land does not vest any estate in the lessee, but gives him a mere right of entry on the land, which right is called his interest in the term, or *interesse termini.* See Co. Litt. 46; 2 Bl. Comm. 144; 10 Viner, Abr. 348; Dane, Abr. Index; Watk. Conv. 15; 1 Washb. Real Prop. Index.

INTEREST. (Lat.) It concerns; it is of advantage.

——**In Contracts.** The right of property which a man has in a thing. See "Insurable Interest."

——**On Debts.** The compensation which is paid by the borrower of money to the lender for its use, and, generally, by a debtor to his creditor in recompense for his detention of the debt.

INTEREST, MARITIME. See "Marine Interest."

INTEREST OR NO INTEREST. A provision in a policy of insurance, which imports that the policy is to be good though the insured have no insurable interest in the subject matter. This constitutes a "wager policy," which is bad in England, by St. 19 Geo. II. c. 37, and, generally, from the policy of the law. 2 Pars. Mar. Law, 89, note.

INTEREST REIPUBLICAE NE MALEFICIA remaneant impunita. It concerns the commonwealth that crimes do not remain unpunished. Jenk. Cent. Cas. 30, 31.

INTEREST REIPUBLICAE NE SUA quis male utatur. It concerns the republic that no one misuse his property. 6 Coke, 36.

INTEREST REIPUBLICAE QUOD HOMINES conserventur. It concerns the commonwealth that we be preserved. 12 Coke, 62.

INTEREST REIPUBLICAE RES JUDICATAS non rescindi. It concerns the commonwealth that things adjudged be not rescinded. See "Res Judicata."

INTEREST REIPUBLICAE SUPREMA hominum testamenta rata haberi. It concerns the commonwealth that men's last wills be sustained. Co. Litt. 236.

INTEREST REIPUBLICAE UT CARCERES sint in tuto. It concerns the commonwealth that prisons be secure. 2 Inst. 589.

INTEREST REIPUBLICAE UT PAX IN regno conservetur, et quaecunque paci adversentur provide declinentur. It benefits the state to preserve peace in the kingdom, and to prudently decline whatever is adverse to it. 2 Inst. 158.

INTEREST REIPUBLICAE UT QUALIbet re sua bene utatur. It concerns the commonwealth that every one use his property properly. 6 Coke, 37.

INTEREST REIPUBLICAE UT SIT FInis litium. It concerns the commonwealth that there be a limit to litigation. Co. Litt. 303.

INTEREST SUIT. In English probate law. A suit to determine which of several persons is by interest entitled to administer an estate.

INTERFERENCE. The state of things which exists when a person applies for a patent which, if granted, would cover any of the patentable ground occupied by any existing patent, or by any patent for which an application is then pending. An investigation is ordered by the commissioner of patents, for the purpose of determining which of the parties was the first to make the invention, or that portion of it from which the interference results. When the controversy is between two applications, a patent will be finally granted to him who is shown to be the first inventor, and will be denied to the other applicant so far as the point thus controverted is concerned. But if the interference is between an application on the one hand and an actual patent on the other, as there is no power in the patent office to cancel the existing patent, all that can be done is to grant or withhold from the applicant the patent he asks. If the patent is granted to him, there will be two patents for the same thing. The two parties will stand upon a footing of equality, and must settle their rights by a resort to the courts, in the manner provided by the act of congress. In interference-cases, each party is allowed to take the testimony of witnesses in accordance with rules established by the patent office. See Act July 4, 1836, §§ 8, 16.

INTERIM (Lat.) In the meantime; meanwhile. An assignee *ad interim* is one appointed between the time of bankruptcy and appointment of the regular assignee. 2 Bell, Comm. 355.

INTERIM COMMITTATUR. In the meantime let him be committed.

INTERIM CURATOR. An officer appointed to have the temporary management of the property of a convict, since the abolition of escheats. 4 Steph. Comm. 462.

INTERIM FACTOR. In Scotch law. A judicial officer elected or appointed under the bankruptcy law to take charge of and preserve the estate until a fit person shall be elected trustee. 2 Bell, Comm. 357.

INTERIM OFFICER. One appointed to fill a temporary vacancy.

INTERLAQUEARE. In old practice. To link together, or interchangeably. Writs were called *"interlaqueata"* where several were issued against several parties residing in different counties, each party being summoned by a separate writ to warrant the tenant, together with the other warrantors. Fleta, lib. 5, c. 4, § 2. They were, in other words, *simul cum* writs.

INTERLINEATION. Writing between two lines.

INTERLOCUTOR. In Scotch practice. An order or decree of court; an order made in open court. 2 Swint. 362; Arkley, 32.

INTERLOCUTOR OF RELEVANCY. In Scotch practice. A decree as to the relevancy of a libel or indictment in a criminal case. 2 Alis. Crim. Pr. 373.

INTERLOCUTORY. Something which is done between the commencement and the end of a suit or action which decides some point or matter, which, however, is not a final decision of the matter in issue; as, interlocutory judgments, or decrees, or orders.

——**Interlocutory Costs.** Costs accruing upon proceedings in the intermediate stages of a cause, as distinguished from final costs; such as the costs of motions. 3 Chit. Gen. Prac. 597.

——**Interlocutory Decree.** A provisional or preliminary decree, which is not final, and does not determine the suit, but directs some further proceedings preparatory to the final decree. A decree pronounced for the purpose of ascertaining matter of law or fact preparatory to a final decree. 1 Barb. Ch. Prac. 326, 327.

——**Interlocutory Judgment.** A preliminary or intermediate judgment. A judgment given in the course of an action upon some plea, proceeding, or default which is only intermediate, and does not determine or complete the suit, as upon a demurrer or plea in abatement, or where the right of the plaintiff is established, but the quantum of damages is not ascertained. 1 Tidd, Prac. 568. See "Final."

——**Interlocutory Order.** An order made during the progress of a cause upon some incidental matter which arises out of the proceedings.

——**Interlocutory Sentence.** In civil law. A sentence on some indirect question arising from the principal cause. Halifax, Civ. Law, bk. 3, c. 9, No. 40.

INTERLOPERS. Persons who interrupt the trade of a company of merchants, by pursuing the same business with them in the same place, without lawful authority.

INTERN. To restrict a person to a limited territory; to forbid departure from the realm.

INTERNATIONAL LAW. The system of rules which Christian states acknowledge to be obligatory upon them in their relations to each other and to each other's subjects. It is the *jus inter gentes,* as distinguished from the *jus gentium.*

The rules of conduct regulating the intercourse of states. Halleck, Int. Law, 41; Davis, Int. Law, § 2. It consists of those rules of conduct which reason deduces as consonant to justice from the nature of the society existing among independent nations, with such definitions and modifications as may be established by mutual consent. Wheaton, Int. Law, § 14.

International law has been divided into (1) public, and (2) private, under which division public international law is the law of nations as above defined, while private international law consists of the rules by which courts determine within what national jurisdiction an action or proceeding falls, or by what national law it should be decided. Glenn, Int. Law, § 2.

Various divisions of international law have been proposed, but none are of any great importance. One has been into natural and voluntary law, in which latter conventional or treaty law and customary are embraced. Another, somewhat similar, separates international rules into those which are deducible from general natural *jus,* those which are derived from the idea of estate, and those which grow out of simple compact. Whatever division be made, it is to be observed that nations are voluntary, first, in deciding the question what intercourse they will hold with each other; second, that they are voluntary in defining their rights and obligations, moral claims and duties, although these have an objective existence beyond the control of the will of nations; and third, that, when international law has arisen by the free assent of those who enter into certain arrangements, obedience to its provisions is as truly in accordance with natural law, which requires the observance of contracts, as if natural law had been intuitively discerned or revealed from heaven, and no consent had been necessary at the outset.

INTERNUNCIO. A minister of a second order, charged with the affairs of the court of Rome, where that court has no nuncio under that title.

INTERNUNCIUS (Lat. from *inter,* between, and *nuncius,* a messenger). A messenger between two parties; a go-between. Applied to a broker, as the agent of both parties. 4. Rob. Adm. 204.

INTERPOLATION. In civil law. The act by which, in consequence of an agreement, the party bound declares that he will not be bound beyond a certain time. Wolff. Inst. § 752.

In the case of a lease from year to year, or to continue as long as both parties please, a notice given by one of them to the other of a determination to put an end to the contract would bear the name of "interpolation."

INTERPLEADER.

——At Common Law. A proceeding in the action of detinue, by which the defendant states the fact that the thing sued for is in his hands, and that it is claimed by a third person, and that whether such person or the plaintiff is entitled to it is unknown to the defendant, and thereupon the defendant prays that a process of garnishment may be issued to compel such third person so claiming to become defendant in his stead. 3 Reeve, Hist. Eng. Law, c. 23; Mitf. Eq. Pl. (Jeremy Ed.) 141; Story, Eq. Jur. §§ 800, 801, 802.

——In Equity. A bill whereby one from whom two or more persons claim the same duty or thing can compel them to interplead, and have their several claims adjudged, lest he be twice compelled to render the same debt, duty, or property. 77 Ill. 139.

——In Modern Law. Several statutory remedies have been substituted in various states. In some, a complaint in the nature of a bill of interpleader (see 17 Mo. 499), and in others a formal collateral proceeding to try title to property (130 Ill. 87).

INTERPRETARE ET CONCORDARE LEges legibus est optimus interpretandi modus. To interpret and reconcile laws so that they harmonize is the best mode of construction. 8 Coke, 169.

INTERPRETATIO CHARTARUM BENIGne facienda est, ut res magis valeat quam pereat. The interpretation of deeds is to be liberal, that the thing may rather have effect than fail. Broom, Leg. Max. 543.

INTERPRETATIO FIENDA EST UT RES magis valeat quam pereat. Such a construction is to be made that the subject may have an effect, rather than none. Jenk. Cent. Cas. 198.

INTERPRETATIO TALIS AMBIGUIS semper fienda est, ut evitetur inconveniens et absurdum. In ambiguous things, such a construction should be made that what is inconvenient and absurd may be avoided. 4 Inst. 328.

INTERPRETATION. The act of finding out the true sense of any form of words—that is, the sense which their author intended to convey—and of enabling others to derive from them the same idea which the author intended to convey. 14 How. Pr. R. (N. Y.) 272.

The discovery and representation of the true meaning of any signs used to convey ideas. Lieber, Leg. & Pol. Herm.

"Construction" is sometimes used as a synonym (Jones, Const. p. 3), though it has been said that "construction" is the broader term, and includes also the legal effect (2 Pars. Cont. 491, note a).

The "true meaning" of any signs is that meaning which those who used them were desirous of expressing. A person adopting or sanctioning them "uses" them as well as their immediate author. Both parties to an agreement equally make use of the signs declaratory of that agreement, though one only is the originator, and the other may be entirely passive. The most common signs used to convey ideas are words. When there is a contradiction in signs intended to agree, resort must be had to construction,—that is, the drawing of conclusions from the given signs, respecting ideas which they do not express.

(1) Close interpretation (*interpretatio restricta*) is adopted if just reasons, connected with the formation and character of the text, induce us to take the words in their narrowest meaning. This species of interpretation has generally been called "literal," but the term is inadmissible. Lieber, Leg. & Pol. Herm. 66.

(2) Extensive interpretation (*interpretatio extensiva,* called, also, "liberal interpretation") adopts a more comprehensive signification of the word.

(3) Extravagant interpretation (*interpretatio excedens*) is that which substitutes a meaning evidently beyond the true one. It is therefore not genuine interpretation.

(4) Free or unrestricted interpretation (*interpretatio soluta*) proceeds simply on the general principles of interpretation in good faith, not bound by any specific or superior principle.

(5) Limited or restricted interpretation (*interpretatio limitata*) is when we are influenced by other principles than the strictly hermeneutic ones. Ernesti, Inst. Interp.

(6) Predestined interpretation (*interpretatio predestinata*) takes place if the interpreter, laboring under a strong bias of mind, makes the text subservient to his preconceived views or desires. This includes artful interpretation (*interpretatio vafer*), by which the interpreter seeks to give a meaning to the text other than the one he knows to have been intended.

The civilians divide interpretation into:

(1) Authentic (*interpretatio authentica*), which proceeds from the author himself.

(2) Usual (*interpretatio usualis*), when the interpretation is on the ground of usage.

(3) Doctrinal (*interpretatio doctrinalis*), when made agreeably to rules of science. Doctrinal interpretation is subdivided into extensive, restrictive, and declaratory,—extensive, whenever the reason of a proposition has a broader sense than its terms, and it is consequently applied to a case which had not been explained; restrictive, when the expressions have a greater latitude than the reasons; and declaratory, when the reasons and terms agree, but it is necessary to settle the meaning of some term or terms to make the sense complete.

INTERPRETATION CLAUSE. A clause in a statute defining words used therein, or prescribing rules for its interpretation.

INTERPRETER. One employed to make a translation.

An interpreter should be sworn before he translates the testimony of a witness. 4 Mass. 81; 5 Mass. 219; 2 Caines (N. Y.) 155.

A person employed between an attorney and client to act as interpreter is considered merely as the organ between them, and is not bound to testify as to what he has acquired in those confidential communications. 1 Pet. C. C. (U. S.) 356; 4 Munf. (Va.) 273; 3 Wend. (N. Y.) 337.

INTERREGNUM (Lat.) The period, in case of an established government, which elapses between the death of a sovereign and the election of another, is called "interregnum." The vacancy which occurs when there is no government.

INTERROGATOIRE. In French law. An act or instrument which contains the interrogatories made by the judge to the person accused, on the facts which are the object of the accusation, and the answers of the accused. Poth. Proc. Crim. sec. 4, art. 2, § 1.

INTERROGATORIES. Material and pertinent questions, in writing, to necessary points, not confessed, exhibited for the examination of witnesses or persons who are to give testimony in the cause.

Interrogatories are exhibited in various proceedings, as in a bill of equity by way of discovery, on a statutory discovery, on the taking of a deposition.

Interrogatories to a witness are either original and direct on the part of him who produces the witnesses, or cross and counter, on behalf of the adverse party, to examine witnesses produced on the other side. Either party, plaintiff or defendant, may exhibit original or cross interrogatories.

INTERRUPTIO (Lat. from *interrumpere,* to break through or apart). Interruption. A term used both in the civil and common law of prescription. Calv. Lex.

INTERRUPTIO MULTIPLEX NON TOLlit praescriptionem semel obtentam. Repeated interruptions do not defeat a prescription once obtained. 2 Inst. 654.

INTERRUPTION. The effect of some act or circumstance which stops the course of a prescription or act of limitations. 3 Bligh (N. S.) 444; 4 Mees. & W. 497.

Civil interruption is that which takes place by some judicial act.

Natural interruption is an interruption in fact. 4 Mason (U. S.) 404; 2 Younge & J. 285. See "Easement"; "Limitations"; "Prescription."

——**In Scotch Law.** The true proprietor's claiming his right during the course of prescription. Bell, Dict.

INTERSTATE COMMERCE. Commerce between persons or places in different states. The exchange of property in one state for property in another, its essential characteristic being that it involves the moving of property from one state to another. 223 Ill. 590. See "Commerce." A shipment from one state to another under a contract for continuous carriage is interstate commerce, even as to so much of the journey as is within the limits of a single state (102 U. S. 541), or though the journey is temporarily interrupted before leaving the state (116 U. S. 517); but a shipment between points in the same state is not interstate commerce, though the goods are carried out of the state en route (145 U. S. 192).

INTERSTATE COMMERCE ACT. Act Cong. Feb. 4, 1888, regulating interstate commerce, designed to secure reasonable and uniform charges for carriage of freight and passengers, and prevent rebates, preferences, and pooling.

INTERSTATE COMMERCE COMMISSION. A commission created by the interstate commerce act to enforce its provisions.

INTERVALLUM. (Lat.) In old English law. An interval of time or place.

INTERVENER. A party who seeks to interpose in a suit. See "Intervention."

INTERVENTION (Lat. *intervenio,* to come between or among).

——**In Civil Law.** The act by which a third party becomes a party in a suit pending between other persons.

The intervention is made either to be joined to the plaintiff, and to claim the same thing he does, or some other thing connected with it; or to join the defendant, and with him to oppose the claim of the plaintiff, which it is his interest to defeat. Poth. Proc. Civ. c. 2, sec. 6, § 3.

——**In Modern Practice.** The term is sometimes used in the same sense as in the civil law.

——**In English Ecclesiastical Law.** The proceeding of a third person, who, not being originally a party to the suit or proceeding, but claiming an interest in the subject matter in dispute, in order the better to protect such interest, interposes his claim. 2 Chit. Prac. 492; 3 Chit. Com. Law, 633; 2 Hagg. Const. 137; 3 Phillim. Ecc. Law, 586; 1 Add. Ecc. Law, 5; 4 Hagg. Ecc. Law, 67; Dunl. Adm. Prac. 74. The intervener may come in at any stage of the cause, and even after judgment, if an appeal can be allowed on such judgment. 2 Hagg. Const. 137; 1 Eng. Ecc. Law, 480; 2 Eng. Ecc. Law, 13.

INTESTABILIS. An incompetent or disqualified witness.

INTESTABLE. One who cannot lawfully make a testament.

An infant, an insane person, or one civilly dead cannot make a will, for want of capacity or understanding. A married woman cannot make such a will without some special authority, because she is under the power of her husband. They are all intestable.

INTESTACY. The state or condition of dying without a will.

INTESTATE. One who, having lawful power to make a will, has made none, or one which is defective in form. In that case, he is said to die intestate, and his estate descends to his heir at law.

This term comes from the Latin *intestatus.* Formerly, it was used in France indiscriminately with *de-confess;* that is, without confession. It was regarded as a crime, on account of the omission of the deceased person to give something to the church, and was punished by privation of burial in consecrated ground. This omission, according to Flournel, Hist. de Avocats, vol. 1, p. 116, could be repaired by making an ampliative testament in the name of the deceased. Vely, tom. 6, p. 145; Henrion de Pansey, Authorite Judiciaire, 129, and note. See "Descent"; "Distribution"; "Will."

INTESTATE SUCCESSION. The succession or devolution of interest of the property of one dying intestate. In Louisiana, the term "succession" is applied to the estate as a whole.

INTESTATO. In the civil law. Intestate; without a will. Calv. Lex.

INTESTATUS. In the civil and old English law. An intestate; one who dies without a will. Dig. 50. 17. 7.

INTESTATUS DECEDIT, QUI AUT OMNINO TESTAMENTUM NON FECIT AUT NON JURI FECIT, AUT ID QUOD FECERAT RUPTUM IRRITUMVE FACTUM EST, AUT NEMO EX EO HAERES EXSTITIT. He dies intestate who either has made no will at all, or has not made it legally, or whose will which he had made has been annulled or become ineffectual, or from whom there is no living heir. Inst. 3. 1, pr.; Dig. 38. 16. 1; Id. 50. 16. 64.

INTIMATION.

——**In Civil Law.** The name of any judicial act by which a notice of a legal proceeding is given to some one; but it is more usually understood to mean the notice or summons which an appellant causes to be given to the opposite party, that the sentence will be reviewed by the superior judge.

——**In Scotch Law.** An instrument of writing, made under the hand of a notary, and notified to a party, to inform him of a right which a third person had acquired; for example, when a creditor assigns a claim against his debtor, the assignee or cedent must give an intimation of this to the debtor, who, till then, is justified in making payment to the original creditor. Kames, Eq. bk. 1, p. 1, § 1.

INTITLE. An old form of entitle. 6 Mod. 304.

INTOL AND UTTOL. In old records. Toll or custom paid for things imported and exported, or bought in and sold out. Cowell.

INTOXICATED. Drunk from the use of intoxicating liquors. See 47 Vt. 294.

INTOXICATING LIQUORS. Such liquors as will, if used as a beverage, produce drunkenness. 25 Kan. 767.

It includes all liquors, whether spirituous, vinous, or malt (70 Mass. 20), of which the human stomach can contain enough to produce intoxication. 21 N. Y. 173.

INTRA. In Latin phrases. A preposition, meaning in; near; within. *Infra* or *inter* has taken the place of *intra* in many of the more modern Latin phrases.

INTRA ANNI SPATIUM. Within the space of a year. Code, 5. 9. 2. *Intra annale tempus.* Id. 6. 30. 19.

INTRA FIDEM. Within belief; credible. Calv. Lex.

INTRA LUCTUS TEMPUS (Lat.) Within the time of mourning. Code, 9. 1.

INTRA MAENIA (Lat. within the walls of a house). A term applied to domestic or menial servants. 1 Bl. Comm. 425.

INTRA PARIETES (Lat.) Between walls; among friends; out of court; without litigation. Calv. Lex.

INTRA PRAESIDIA (Lat.) Within the defenses. Dig. 49. 15. 5. 1. See "Infra Praesidia."

INTRA QUATUOR MARIA (Lat.) Within the four seas. Shep. Touch. 378.

INTRA VIRES. Within the power. The opposite of *ultra vires* (*q. v.*).

An act which might be done by the managing board of a corporation or by a majority of the stockholders in meeting assembled. The act in intra vires although done by the managing board of directors, and in opposition to the will of a majority of the stockholders. 113 Ill. App. 609.

INTRINSIC VALUE. "Its true, inherent, and essential value, not depending upon accident, place, or person, but the same everywhere, and to every one." 5 Ired. (N. C.) 698.

INTROMISSION. In Scotch law. The assuming possession of property belonging to another, either on legal grounds, or without any authority. In the latter case it is called "vicious" intromission. Bell, Dict.

INTRONISATION. In French ecclesiastical law. The installation of a bishop in his episcopal see. Clef des Lois Rom.

INTRUDER. One who, on the death of the ancestor, enters on the land, unlawfully, before the heir can enter.

INTRUSION. The entry of a stranger after the determination of a particular estate of freehold, before the entry of him in reversion or remainder. Intrusion or usurpation, and trespass are not synonymous terms. 96 Ill. 255.

The entry and interposition of the stranger differs from an abatement in this, that an abatement is always to the prejudice of an heir or immediate devisee; an intrusion is always to the prejudice of him in remainder or reversion. 3 Sharswood, Bl. Comm. 169; Fitzh. Nat. Brev. 203; Archb. Civ. Pl. 12; Dane, Abr. Index; 3 Steph. Comm. 443.

The name of a writ brought by the owner of a fee simple, etc., against an intruder. New Nat. Brev. 453. Abolished by 3 & 4 Wm. IV. c. 57.

——**At Common Law.** Intrusion at the common law is one of the modes of ouster of the freehold, and is defined to be "an entry by a stranger after a particular estate of freehold is determined before him in reversion or remainder; as when a tenant for life dieth seized of certain lands and tenements, and a stranger cometh thereon, after such death of the tenant, and before any entry of him in reversion or remainder. 3 Ch. Bl. 169.

——**Trespass Distinguished.** Trespass is an entry on another's ground without lawful authority, and doing some damage however inconsiderable to his real property. This broad distinction does not exist under our statute dispensing with livery of seizin; but the only distinction apparent to my mind between an intrusion and a trespass is, that the former implies an unlawful possession of lands, while the latter may amount to a mere entry upon land without retaining possession, but doing some damage. Hulick v. Scovil, 9 Ill. 170, 171.

INTUITUS (Lat. from *intueri*, to look upon or view). A view; regard; contemplation. *Diverso intuitu (q. v.)*, with a different view.

View or sight. *Intuitu Dei*, in the sight of God. Magna Charta, pr.

INURE. To take effect; to result.

INUTILIS LABOR, ET SINE FRUCTU, non est effectus legis. Useless labor and without fruit is not the effect of law. Co. Litt. 127; Wingate, Max. 38.

INVADIARE (Law Lat.) In feudal and old European law. To pledge; to engage or pledge lands; to mortgage.

INVADIATIO (Law Lat.) A pledge or mortgage.

INVADIATUS (Law Lat.) One who is under pledge; one who has had sureties or pledges given for him. Spelman.

A person acquitted.

INVALID. Not valid; of no binding force.

INVASION. The entry of a country by a public enemy, making war.

INVECTA ET ILLATA (Lat.) In civil law. Things carried and brought in; things brought into a building hired (*aedes*), or into a hired estate in the city (*praedium urbanum*), which are held by a tacit mortgage for the rent. Vocat; Domat, Civ. Law.

INVEIGLE. To inveigle, in a legal sense, is to induce a party to come within the jurisdiction of the court, by some scheme, subterfuge, fraud, trick, device, or misrepresentation, that he may be served with process. 106 Mich. 525; 13 N. Y. Supp. 570.

INVENIENS LIBELLUM FAMOSUM ET non corrumpens punitur. He who finds a libel, and does not destroy it, is punished. F. Moore, 813.

INVENTIO.

——In Civil Law. Finding; one of the modes of acquiring title to property by occupancy. Heinec, lib. 2, tit. 1, § 350. Sometimes rendered in English "invention."

——In Old English Law. A thing found; as goods, or treasure trove. Cowell. The plural, *inventiones*, is also used.

INVENTION. In patent law. The act or operation of finding out something new; the contrivance of that which did not before exist. The word is also used to denote the thing itself which has been so contrived, and which is the subject matter of a patent.

The test of novelty to determine whether a given contrivance is an "invention" is whether an ordinary mechanic would, without other suggestion than his knowledge of the art, make such a contrivance. If so, it is not an invention. 3 Fish. Pat. Cas. (U. S.) 98; 27 Fed. 219.

An invention differs from a "discovery," inasmuch as this latter term is used to signify the finding out of something which existed before. Thus, we speak of the discovery of the properties of steam, or of electricity; but the first contrivance of any machinery by which those discoveries were applied to practical use was an invention; the former always existed, though not before known; the latter did not previously exist.

INVENTIONES. A word used in some ancient English charters to signify treasure trove.

INVENTOR. One who finds out something new, or who contrives or produces a thing which did not before exist; one who makes an invention. The word is generally used to denote the author of such contrivances as are by law patentable. See "Invention."

INVENTORY. A list, schedule, catalogue, or enumeration in writing, containing, article by article, the goods and chattels, rights and credits, and, in some cases, the lands and tenements, of a person or persons, without attempt to describe the same in detail. 217 Ill. 169. But enumerating them with reasonable particularity according to the well understood usage of business men. 20 Q. B. D. 114; 58 L. T. 34. A conservatory act, which is made to ascertain the situation of an intestate's estate, the estate of an insolvent, and the like, for the purpose of securing it to those entitled to it.

INVENTUS (Lat.) Found. *Thesaurus inventus*, treasure trove. *Non est inventus*, he is not found.

INVERITARE. To verify or prove.

INVEST (Lat. *investire*, to clothe). to put in possession of a fief upon taking the oath of fealty or fidelity to the prince or superior lord.

INVESTITIVE FACT. One by means of which a right comes into existence. Holland, Jur. 132.

They are divided by Bentham into collative, conferring rights, and impositive, imposing duties.

INVESTITURE. The act of giving possession of lands by actual seisin.

When livery of seisin was made to a person by the common law, he was invested with the whole fee. This the foreign feudists, and sometimes our own law writers, call "investiture"; but, generally speaking, it is termed by the common-law writers the "seisin of the fee." 2 Bl. Comm. 209, 313; Ferne, Cont. Rem. 223, note (z).

By the canon law, investiture was made *per baculum et annulum*, by the ring and crosier, which were regarded as symbols of the Episcopal jurisdiction. Ecclesiastical and secular fiefs were governed by the same rule in this respect,—that previously to investiture neither a bishop, abbot, or lay lord could take possession of a fief conferred upon them by the prince.

Pope Gregory VI. first disputed the right of sovereigns to give investiture of ecclesiastical fiefs, A. D. 1045; but Pope Gregory VII. carried on the dispute with much more vigor, A. D. 1073. He excommunicated the emperor Henry IV. The popes Victor III., Urban II., and Paul II. continued the contest. This dispute, it is said, cost Christendom sixty-three battles, and the lives of many millions of men.

INVESTMENT BUYING. See "Gambling Contract."

INVIOLABILITY. That which is not to be violated. The persons of ambassadors are inviolable. See "Ambassador."

INVITO (Lat.) Being unwilling.

INVITO BENEFICIUM NON DATUR. No one is obliged to accept a benefit against his consent. Dig. 50. 17. 69; Broom, Leg.

Max. (3d London Ed.) 625. But if he does not dissent, he will be considered as assenting. See "Assent."

INVITO DEBITORE (Lat.) Against the will of the debtor.

INVITO DOMINO (Lat.) In criminal law. Without the consent of the owner.

In order to constitute larceny, the property stolen must be taken *invito domino;* this is the very essence of the crime. Cases of considerable difficulty arise when the owner has, for the purpose of detecting thieves, by himself or his agents, delivered the property taken, as to whether they are larcenies or not. The distinction seems to be this, that when the owner procures the property to be taken, it is not larceny; and when he merely leaves it in the power of the defendant to execute his original purpose of taking it, in the latter case it will be considered as taken *invito domino.* 2 Bailey (S. C.) 569; 2 Russ. Crimes, 66, 105; 2 Leach, C. C. 913; 2 East, P. C. 666; Bac. Abr. "Felony" (C); Alis. Crim. Prac. 273; 2 Bos. & P. 508; 1 Car. & M. 217. See "Larceny."

INVOICE. In commercial law. An account of goods or merchandise sent by merchants to their correspondents at home or abroad, in which the marks of each package, with other particulars, are set forth. Marsh. Ins. 408; Dane, Abr. Index. 47 Miss. 76. An invoice ought to contain a detailed statement, which should indicate the nature, quantity, quality, and price of the things sold, deposited, etc. 1 Pardessus, Dr. Com. note 248. See "Bill of Lading"; 2 Wash. C. C. (U. S.) 113, 155.

An invoice of goods sometimes means the goods themselves, and invoice price or cost sometimes means the prime price or cost of goods, although there is no invoice in fact. 6 Jones & Spencer (N. Y.) 342.

INVOICE BOOK. A book in which invoices are copied.

INVOLUNTARY. An involuntary act is that which is performed with constraint (*q. v.*), or with repugnance, or without the will to do it. An action is involuntary, then, which is performed under duress. Wolff. Inst. § 5.

The term is frequently used in connection with various proceedings to denote an adverse proceeding. Thus, involuntary bankruptcy proceedings are those instituted by a creditor, and not by the bankrupt.

A nonsuit allowed on the motion of the defendant and against the plaintiff's will is an involuntary nonsuit. 223 Ill. 174; 180 Ill. 191.

INVOLUNTARY MANSLAUGHTER. Homicide committed unintentionally, but without excuse, and not under such circumstances as to raise the implication of malice. 1 Clark & Marshall, Crimes, 562.

INVOLUNTARY PAYMENT. A payment of money upon an illegal or unjust demand, where a party is advised of all the facts, can only be considered involuntary when it is made to secure the release of person or property from detention, or where the payee is armed with apparent authority to seize upon one or the other and to prevent this the payment is made. 57 Ill. App. 240; 94 Ill. App. 526.

What shall constitute the compulsion or coercion which the law will recognize as sufficient to render the payments involuntary, may often be a question of difficulty. It may be said in general that there must be some actual or threatened exercise of power, possessed or supposed to be possessed by the party exacting or receiving the payment, over the person or property of another, from which the latter has no other means of immediate relief. 100 Pa. St. 346; 18 Cal. 272, 407; 46 Cal. 598; 94 Ill. App. 526; 2 Dillon on Municipal Corporations (4th Ed.), § 943.

INWADIARE. (Law Lat.) In old European law. To pledge. LL. Longob. lib. 1, tit. 14, l. 10.

IOTA. The ninth and smallest letter of the Greek alphabet; hence any minute or insignificant thing.

IPSAE LEGES CUPIUNT UT JURE REgantur. The laws themselves desire that they should be governed by right. Co. Litt. 174b, quoted from Cato.

IPSE (Lat.) I (before verbs of first person); thou (before verbs of second person); he himself, she herself, he alone, etc.; the very one; *e. g., ipsum corpus,* the very thing itself. Halk. Tech. Terms. *Ipsae [etenim] leges cupiunt ut jures regantur,* for the very laws themselves wish that they should be ruled by right,—a line, quoted from Cato, which occurs in the decision of Chief Justice Wray and the whole court in the Case of Bankrupts, 2 Coke, 25b.

IPSE DIXIT. He himself said it. Applied as a substantive to the unsupported assertion of one person.

IPSISSIMIS VERBIS (Lat.) In the identical words; opposed to "substantially." 7 How. (U. S.) 719; 5 Ohio St. 346.

IPSO FACTO (Lat.) By the fact itself; by the mere fact.

IPSO JURE (Lat.) By the operation of law; by mere law.

IRA FUROR BREVIS EST. Anger is a short insanity. 4 Wend. (N. Y.) 336, 355.

IRA MOTUS (Lat.) Moved or excited by anger or passion. A term sometimes formerly used in the plea of *son assault demesne.* 1 Tidd, Prac. 645.

IRE AD LARGUM (Lat.) To go at large.

IRENARCHA. In Roman law. An officer whose duties are described in Dig. 5. 4. 18. 7. See Id. 48. 3. 6; Code, 10. 75. Literally, a peace officer or magistrate.

IRREGULAR. Not according to rule. See "Irregularity."

IRREGULAR DEPOSIT. See "Deposit."

IRREGULAR PROCESS. Such as a court has general jurisdiction to issue, but which is unauthorized in the particular case by reason of the existence or nonexistence of some fact or circumstance rendering it improper in such a case. 103 N. Y. 84, 90.

IRREGULARITY. In practice. The doing or not doing that, in the conduct of a suit at law, which, conformably with the practice of the court, ought or ought not to be done. 115 Ill. 590.

It is the technical term for every defect in proceedings or the mode of conducting an action or defense. It is a comprehensive term, including all formal objections to matters of practice.

An irregularity is a formal but a nullity is a substantial defect. One applies chiefly to the manner, the other to the matter or merits of the proceeding; the former is voidable, the latter absolutely void. As a general rule whenever there is any doubt upon the matter it will always be safer to treat the defect as an irregularity rather than as a nullity. 130 Ill. App. 588; Macnamara on Nullities and Irregularities in Law, 20.

IRRELEVANT. Matter in a pleading which has no substantial relation to the controversy in suit. 3 Sandf. Ch. (N. Y.) 743; 6 How. Pr. (N. Y.) 312.

Equivalent to "impertinent." Includes "Scandalous" matter in a pleading. 5 How. Pr. (N. Y.) 53.

IRRELEVANT EVIDENCE. That which does not support the issue, and which, of course, must be excluded.

IRREPARABLE INJURY. An injury is "irreparable," within the rule that injunction will issue to prevent only such injuries, not only where the injury, from its nature, cannot be compensated by damages, or the damages cannot be ascertained by any certain measure 4 N. J. Eq. 449, or when the wrongdoer is insolvent and for that reason incapable of responding in damages. 210 Ill. 464; 218 Ill. 87; 51 Iowa, 385; 42 Neb. 238.

That species of injury, whether great or small, that ought not to be submitted to on the one hand or inflicted on the other; and because it is so large on the one hand or so small on the other, is of such constant and frequent recurrence, that no fair or reasonable redress can be had therefor in a court of law. 76 Ill. 326; 149 Ill. 570; 181 Ill. 611; 246 Ill. 534; 52 Ill. App. 615.

IRREPLEVIABLE. That cannot be replevied or delivered on sureties. Spelled, also, "irreplevisable." Co. Litt. 145; 13 Edw. I. c. 2.

IRRESISTIBLE FORCE. A term applied to such an interposition of human agency as is, from its nature and power, absolutely uncontrollable; as, the inroads of a hostile army. Story, Bailm. § 25; Lois des Batim. pt. 2, c. 2, § 1. It differs from "inevitable accident" (*q. v.*).

IRREVOCABLE. Which cannot be revoked or recalled. A power of attorney in which the attorney has an interest granted for consideration is irrevocable. See "Will."

IRRIGATION. The act of wetting or moistening the ground by artificial means; the application of water to land by artificial means for the raising of crops and other products of the soil. Long, Irrigation, § 1; 111 Cal. 476.

IRRITANCY. In Scotch law. The happening of a condition or event by which a charter, contract, or other deed, to which a clause irritant is annexed, becomes void. Ersk. Inst. bk. 2, tit. 5, note 25. Irritancy is a kind of forfeiture. It is legal or conventional. Burton, Real Prop. 298.

IRRITANT. In Scotch law. Avoiding or making void; as an irritant clause. See "Irritancy."

IRRITANT CLAUSE. In Scotch law. A provision by which certain prohibited acts specified in a deed are, if committed, declared to be null and void.

IRROGARE. In civil law. To impose or set upon, as a fine. Calv. Lex. To inflict, as a punishment. To make or ordain, as a law.

IRROTULATIO (Law Lat.) An inrolling; a record. 2 Rymer, Foed. 673; Du Cange; Law Fr. & Lat. Dict.; Bracton, fol. 293; Fleta, lib. 2, c. 65, § 11.

ISH. In Scotch law. The period of the termination of a tack or lease. 1 Bligh, 522.

ISLAND. A body of land surrounded by water. The title to islands in navigable waters is in the state (53 Am. Rep. 215); but an island in private waters belongs to the owners of the nearest mainland, unless otherwise appropriated (9 Cush. [Mass.] 548).

ISSINT (Norman Fr. thus, so). In pleading. A term formerly used to introduce a statement that special matter already pleaded amounts to a denial.

In actions founded on deeds, the defendant may, instead of pleading *non est factum* in the common form, allege any special matter which admits the execution of the writing in question, but which, nevertheless, shows that it is not in law his deed, and may conclude with, "and so it is not his deed," as, that the writing was delivered to A. B. as an escrow, to be delivered over on certain conditions, which have not been complied with, "and so it is not his act"; or that, at the time of making the writing the defendant was a *feme covert*, "and so it is not her act." Bac. Abr. "Pleas" (H 3), (I 2); Gould, Pl. c. 6, pt. 1, § 64.

An example of this form of plea, which is sometimes called the "special general issue," occurs in 4 Rawle (Pa.) 83, 84.

ISSUABLE. In practice. Leading or tending to an issue. An issuable plea is one upon which the plaintiff can take issue and proceed to trial.

ISSUABLE PLEA. A plea in chief to the merits, upon which the plaintiff may take issue and go to trial.

ISSUABLE TERMS. Hilary and Trinity terms are so called from the making up of the issues, during those terms, for the assizes, that they may be tried by the judges, who generally go on circuit to try such issues after these two terms. But for town causes all four terms are issuable. 3 Sharswood, Bl. Comm. 350; 1 Tidd, Prac. 121.

ISSUE.

——**In Real Property Law.** Lineal descendants; all persons who have descended from a common ancestor. 3 Ves. 257; 17 Ves. 481; 19 Ves. 547; 1 Rop. Leg. 90.

In a will it may be held to have a more restricted meaning, to carry out the testator's intention. 7 Ves. 522; 19 Ves. 73; 1 Rop. Leg. 90; 173 Ill. 229; 255 Ill. 357, 358. See "Heirs of the Body."

——**In Pleading.** A single, certain, and material point, deduced by the pleadings of the parties, which is affirmed on the one side, and denied on the other.

The entry of the pleadings. 1 Chit. Pl. 630.

Several connected matters of fact may go to make up the point in issue.

A collateral issue is one framed upon some matter not directly in the line of the pleadings; as, for example, upon the identity of one who pleads diversity in bar of execution. 4 Bl. Comm. 396.

A common issue is that which is formed upon the plea of *non est factum* to an action of covenant broken.

An actual issue is one formed in an action brought in the regular manner, for the purpose of trying a question of right between the parties.

A feigned issue is one formed in a fictitious action, under direction of the court, for the purpose of trying before a jury some question of fact.

Such issues are generally ordered by a court of equity, for which no jury is summoned, to ascertain the truth of some disputed fact. They are also frequently used in courts of law, by the consent of the parties, to determine some disputed rights without the formality of pleading; and by this practice much time and expense are saved in the decision of a cause. 3 Bl. Comm. 452. Suppose, for example, it is desirable to settle a question of the validity of a will in a court of equity. For this purpose an action is brought, in which the plaintiff, by a fiction, declares that he laid a wager for a sum of money with the defendant, for example, that a certain paper is the last will and testament of A., then avers it is his will, and therefore demands the money; the defendant admits the wager, but avers that it is not the will of A.; and thereupon that issue is joined, which is directed out of chancery to be tried; and thus the verdict of the jurors at law determines the fact in the court of equity.

The name is a misnomer, inasmuch as the issue itself is upon a real, material point in question between the parties, and the circumstances only are fictitious. It is a contempt of the court in which the action is brought to bring such an action, except under the direction of some court. 4 Term R. 402.

(1) A formal issue is one which is framed according to the rules required by law, in an artificial and proper manner.

(2) An informal issue is one which arises when a material averment is traversed in an improper or inartificial manner. Bac. Abr. "Pleas" (G 2, N 5); 2 Wm. Saund. 319a, note 6.

(3) An issue in fact is one in which the truth of some fact is affirmed and denied.

In general, it consists of a direct affirmative allegation on one side, and a direct negative on the other. Co. Litt. 126 a; Bac. Abr. "Pleas" (G 1); 2 W. Bl. 1312; 8 Term R. 278; 5 Pet. (U. S.) 149. But an affirmative allegation which completely excludes the truth of the preceding may be sufficient. 1 Wils. 6; 2 Strange, 1177. Thus, the general issue in a writ of right, called the "mise," is formed by two affirmatives, the demandant claiming a greater right than the tenant, and the tenant a greater than the demandant. 3 Bl. Comm. 195, 305. And in an action of dower, the count merely demands that the third part of [ ] acres of land, etc., as the dower of the demandant of the endowment of A. B., heretofore the husband, etc., and the general issue is that A. B. was not seised of such estate, etc., and that he could not endow the demandant thereof, etc.; which mode of denial, being argumentative, would not, in general, be allowed. 2 Saund. 329.

(4) A general issue is one which denies in direct terms the whole declaration; as, for example, where the defendant pleads *nil debet*, that he owes the plaintiff nothing, or *nul disseisin*, no disseisin committed. 3 Greenl. Ev. § 9; 3 Bl. Comm. 305. See "General Issue."

(5) A special issue is one formed by the defendant's selecting any one substantial point, and resting the weight of his cause upon that. It is contrasted with the general issue. Comyn, Dig. "Pleader" (R 1, 2).

(6) A material issue is one properly formed on some material point which will, when decided, decide the question between the parties.

(7) An immaterial issue is one formed on some immaterial matter, which, though found by the verdict, will not determine the merits of the cause, and will leave the court at a loss how to give judgment. 2 Wm. Saund. 319, note 6. See "Immaterial Issue."

(8) An issue in fact is an issue taken upon or consisting of matter of fact, the fact only, and not the law being disputed, and which is to be tried by a jury. 3 Bl. Comm. 314, 315; Co. Litt. 126a; 3 Steph. Comm. 572.

(9) An issue in law is an issue upon matter of law, or consisting of matter of law, being produced by a demurrer on the one side, and a joinder in demurrer on the other. 3 Bl. Comm. 314; 3 Steph. Comm. 572, 580.

ISSUE ROLL. In English law. The name of a record which contains an entry of the term of which the demurrer book, issue, or paper book is entitled, and the warrants of attorney supposed to have been given by the parties at the commencement of the cause, and then proceeds with the transcript of the declaration and subsequent proceedings, continuances, and award of the mode of the decision as contained in the demurrer, issue or paper book. Steph. Pl. 98, 99. After final judgment, the issue roll is no longer called by that name, but assumes that of judgment roll. 2 Archb. Prac. 206.

ISSUES. In English law. The goods and profits of the lands of a defendant against whom a writ of distringas or distress infinite has been issued, taken by virtue of such writ, are called "issues." 3 Bl. Comm. 280; 1 Chit. Crim. Law. 351.

IT IS CONSIDERED. The language of courts in pronouncing judgment. 100 Ill. 490.

ITA EST (Lat. so it is). Among the civilians, when a notary dies, leaving his register, an officer who is authorized to make official copies of his notarial acts writes, instead of the deceased notary's name, which is required when he is living, *ita est.*

ITA LEX SCRIPTA EST. The law is so written. 26 Barb. (N. Y.) 374, 380.

The law must be obeyed, notwithstanding the apparent rigor of its application. 3 Bl. Comm. 430. We must be content with the law as it stands, without inquiring into its reasons. 1 Bl. Comm. 32.

ITA QUOD (Lat.) The name or condition in a submission, which is usually introduced by these words, "so as the award be made of and upon the premises," which, from the first words, is called the *ita quod.*

When the submission is with an *ita quod,* the arbitrator must make an award of all matters submitted to him of which he had notice, or the award will be entirely void. 7 East, 81; Cro. Jac. 200; 2 Vern. 109; Rolle, Abr. "Arbitrament" (L 9).

ITA SEMPER FIAT RELATIO UT VALEAT DISPOSITIO. Let the relation be so made that the disposition may stand. 6 Coke, 76.

ITA TE DEUS ADJUVET (Lat. so help you God). The old form of administering an oath in England, generally in connection with other words, thus: *Ita te Deus adjuvet, et sacrosancta Dei Evangelia,* so help you God, and God's holy Evangelists. *Ita te Deus adjuvet et omnes sancti,* So help you God and all the saints. Willes, 338.

ITA UTERE TUO UT ALIENUM NON LAEDAS. Use your own property and your own rights in such a way that you will not hurt your neighbor, or prevent him from enjoying his. Frequently written, "*Sic utere tuo,*" etc. (*q. v.*)

ITEM (Lat.) Also; likewise; in like manner; again; a second time. These are the various meanings of this Latin adverb.

It is used to introduce a new paragraph, or chapter, or division; also to denote a particular in an account. It is used when any article or clause is added to a former, as if there were here a new beginning. Du Cange. Hence the rule that a clause in a will introduced by item shall not influence or be influenced by what precedes or follows, if it be sensible, taken independently (1 Salk. 239), or there is no plain intent that it should be taken in connection, in which cases it may be construed conjunctively, in the sense of "and," or "also," in such a manner as to connect sentences. If, therefore, a testator bequeath a legacy to Peter, payable out of a particular fund, or charged upon a particular estate, *item,* a legacy to James, James' legacy as well as Peter's will be a charge upon the same property. 1 Atk. 436; 3 Atk. 256; 1 Brown, Ch. 482; 1 Rolle, Abr. 844; 1 Mod. 100; Cro. Car. 368; Vaughan, 262; Rop. Leg. 349; 1 Salk. 234.

The word is commonly used and well understood as a separate entry in an account or a schedule, or a separate particular in an enumeration of a total which is separate and distinct from the other particulars or entries. 277 Ill. 131.

ITER. (Lat.)

——**In Civil Law.** A way; a right of way belonging as a servitude to an estate in the country (*praedium rusticum*). The right of way was of three kinds: (1) *Iter,* a right to walk, or ride on horseback or in a litter; (2) *actus,* a right to drive a beast or vehicle; (3) *via,* a full right of way, comprising right to walk or ride, or drive beast or carriage. Heinec. Elem. Jur. Civ. § 408. Or, as some think, they were distinguished by the width of the objects which could be rightfully carried over the way; *e. g.*, *via*, eight feet; *actus*, four feet, etc. Mackeld. Civ. Law, § 290; Bracton, 232; 4 Bell, H. L. Sc. 390.

Iter est jus eundi, ambulandi hominis; non etiam jumentum agendi vel vehiculum. Iter is the right of going or walking, and does not include the right of driving a beast of burden or a carriage. Co. Litt. 56a; Inst. 2. 3. pr.; 1 Mackeld. Civ. Law, p. 343, § 314.

——**In Old English Law.** A journey, especially a circuit made by a justice in eyre, or itinerant justice, to try causes according to his own mission. Du Cange; Bracton, lib. 3, cc. 11, 12, 13; Britt. c. 2; Cowell. See "Justices in Eyre."

ITERATIO. Again; a second time.

ITERUM (Lat.) In the civil law. A second time. Dig. 2. 13. 7. 1.

ITINERA (Lat. pl. of *iter*). Eyres, or circuits. 1 Reeve, Hist. Eng. Law, 52.

ITINERANT. Wandering; travelling; who makes circuits. See "Justices in Eyre."

ITINERANTES (Law Lat.) Itinerant; travelling; in eyre. A term applied to justices instituted by Hen. II.

ITINERATIO (Law Lat.) In old English law. An eyre, or circuit; the same with *iter.* Spelman. *Si infra diem illum incipiat itineratio*, if the eyre begins within that day. Bracton, fol. 110.

J

J. P. These letters are commonly used and understood to indicate the office of justice of the peace. 12 Ill. 200; 5 Ill. 481.

JA (Law Fr.) Yet; never; nevertheless. Kelham; Britt. c. 49, 93.

JACENS (Lat.) Lying; fallen; prostrate; in abeyance. Bracton, fol. 84.

JACENS HAEREDITAS. An inheritance which is in abeyance.

JACTITATION. Throwing out; a false boasting.

JACTITATION OF MARRIAGE. In English ecclesiastical law. The boasting by an individual that he or she has married another, from which it may happen that they will acquire the reputation of being married to each other.

The ecclesiastical courts may in such cases entertain a libel by the party injured, and, on proof of the facts, enjoin the wrongdoer to perpetual silence, and, as a punishment, make him pay the costs. 3 Bl. Comm. 93; 2 Hagg. Consist. 285, 423; 2 Chit. Prac. 459.

JACTITATION OF TITHES. The boasting by a man that he is entitled to certain tithes, to which he has legally no title.

JACTIVUS. One who is in default, or loses by default. Spelman.

JACTURA (Lat. *jaceo*, to throw). A jettison.

JACTUS (Lat.) A throwing goods overboard to lighten or save the vessel, in which case the goods so sacrificed are a proper subject for general average. Dig. 14. 2, *de lege Rhodia de jactu;* 1 Pardessus, 104 et seq.; Kuricke, Inst. Mar. Hanseat. tit. 8; 1 Pars. Mar. Law, 288, note.

JACTUS LAPILLI. In the civil law. The throwing down of a stone (of a structure being erected on land). One of the means whereby the true owner might assert his title, and interrupt the running of an adverse possession.

JAIL. A term generally substituted in modern usage for "gaol" (*q. v.*).

JAIL DELIVERY. See "Gaol Delivery."

JAIL LIBERTIES. See "Gaol Liberties."

JALO. (Law Lat.) In old English law. A gallon. Fleta, lib. 2, c. 11.

JAMUNLINGI, or **JAMUNDILINGI.** Freemen who delivered themselves and property to the protection of a more powerful person, in order to avoid military service and other burdens. Spelman. Also a species of serfs among the Germans. Du Cange. The same as *commendati.*

JANITOR (Lat.) In old English law. A doorkeeper. Fleta, lib. 2, c. 24.

JAVELOUR. In Scotch law. Jailer or gaoler. 1 Pitc. Crim. Tr. pt. 1, p. 33.

JECT. (Law Fr.) In old practice. Cast; thrown; overthrown or defeated in law. Litt. §§ 448, 680, 682, 684. A term derived from the old practice in trial by battel, and literally signifying thrown to the ground; unhorsed.

JEDBURGH JUSTICE. Lynch law. Rapalje & L.

JEO DONE. (Law Fr.) I give; I do.

JEOFAILE (Law Fr.) I have failed; I am in error.

Certain statutes are called statutes of amendments and jeofailes, because, where a pleader perceives any slip in the form of his proceedings, and acknowledges the error (jeofaile), he is at liberty, by those statutes, to amend it. The amendment, however, is seldom made; but the benefit is attained by the court's overlooking the exception. 3 Bl. Comm. 407; Steph. Pleading, C. I. 93, note (i); 1 Saund. 228, note 1; Doct. Plac. 297; Dane, Abr. These statutes do not apply to indictments.

JEOPARDY. Peril; danger. See Baldw. (U. S.) 93.

The usual technical use of the term is in connection with the rule of criminal law, that no person shall be twice put in jeopardy for the same offense. Const. U. S. art. 5, Amend.

A person is "in jeopardy," within this rule, when a trial jury is impanelled and sworn to try his case (83 Ind. 331; 18 N. Y. 128; 105 Pa. St. 1) upon issue joined (111 Ind. 47) by plea to a valid indictment (105 Mass. 53; 5 Md. 82) in a court of competent jurisdiction (7 Mich. 162; 48 N. J. Law, 371), and the jury has been charged with his deliverance (23 Pa. St. 12; 2 Kelly [Ga.] 60). Where the practice of charging the jury with the deliverance of the prisoner at the outset does not obtain, jeopardy attaches when the jury is sworn.

There are some holdings that jeopardy does not attach till after verdict. 5 Litt. (Ky.) 137; 1 Walk. (Miss.) 134.

JERGUER. In English law. An officer of the custom house, who oversees the waiters. Tech. Dict.

JET (Fr.) In French law. Jettison. Ord. Mar. liv. 3, tit. 8; Emerig. Tr. des Assur. c. 12, § 40.

JETSAM. Goods cast out from a ship by way of jettison, and which sink, being thus distinguished from *flotsam*, jettisoned goods which float, and *ligan*, jettisoned goods, bound to some buoyant substance. 1 Bl. Comm. 292.

JETTISON. The throwing overboard of part of the cargo, or any article on board a ship, or the cutting and casting away of masts, spars, rigging, sails, or other furniture, for the purpose of lightening or relieving the ship in case of necessity or emergency. Gourlie, Gen. Av. 74.

In its largest sense, it signifies any throwing overboard; but, in its ordinary sense, it means throwing overboard for the preservation of the ship and cargo, and most jurists treat of it in this sense under the head of general average. 3 B. & Ald. 400, Termes de la Ley, Jetsam.

JEUX DE BOURSE. In French law. A kind of gambling or speculation, which consists of sales and purchases which bind neither of the parties to deliver the things which are the object of the sale, and which are settled by paying the difference in the value of the things sold between the day of the sale and that appointed for delivery of such things. 1 Pardessus, Dr. Com. note 162.

JOB. The whole of a thing which is to be done. In this sense it is employed in the Civil Code of Louisiana (article 2727): "To build by plot, or to work by the job," says that article, "is to undertake a building for a certain stipulated price." See Duranton, Cont. liv. 3, tit. 8, notes 248, 263; Poth. Cont. notes 392, 394. See "Deviation."

JOBBER. In commercial law. One who buys and sells articles for others.

One who buys from importers, and sells to retailers. 4 Sandf. Ch. (N. Y.) 587.

One who sells to any one who comes to him at a fraction above the market price, and buys of any one at a fraction below the market price. L. R. 7 P. C. 104.

JOCALIA (Lat.) Jewels. This term was formerly more properly applied to those ornaments which women, although married, call their own. When these *jocalia* are not suitable to her degree, they are assets for the payment of debts. 1 Rolle, Abr. 911.

JOCLET. In old English law. A little farm or manor. Cowell; Blount.

JOCUS (Lat.) In old English law. A game of hazard. Reg. Orig. 290.

JOCUS PARTITUS. In old English practice. A divided game, risk, or hazard. An arrangement which the parties to a suit were anciently sometimes allowed to make by mutual agreement upon a certain hazard (*sub periculo*); as that one should lose if the case turned out in a certain way, and, if it did not, that the other should gain (*quod unus amittat si ita sit, et si non sit, quod alius lucretur*). Bracton, fols. 211b, 379b, 432, 434, 200b.

This arrangement, however, was altogether a voluntary and extrajudicial one.

JOHN DOE. A name given in legal proceedings to a party whose true name is unknown. It was the name which was usually given to the fictitious lessee of the plaintiff in the mixed action of ejectment. He was sometimes called "Goodtitle," or "Jackson." So the Romans had their fictitious personages in law proceedings, as *Titius, Seius.*

JOINDER. A joining or uniting together; persons or things together; as of several persons as plaintiffs or defendants in one suit, or of several causes of action, or counts, in one declaration. 1 Chit. Pl. 8, 41, 64, 84, 199.

JOINDER IN DEMURRER. The formal answer made to a demurrer at common law.

JOINDER IN ERROR. A joinder in error is equivalent to a demurrer to the assignments of error, and raises a question of law whether there are such errors in the record as the assignments of error allege. Cass v. Duncan, 260 Ill. 228; Tobias v. Tobias, 193 Ill. App. 98.

JOINDER OF ACTIONS. Joinder of two or more causes of action in the same complaint or declaration.

JOINDER OF CAUSES OF ACTION. See "Joinder of Actions."

JOINDER OF ISSUE. The acceptance by one party of an issue of fact tendered by the other.

JOINDER OF OFFENSES. The uniting of several distinct offenses in one indictment or information.

JOINDER OF PARTIES. The uniting of two or more persons as coparties, either plaintiff or defendant.

JOINT ACTION. An action brought by two or more as plaintiffs, or against two or more as defendants.

JOINT ADVENTURE. An enterprise undertaken by several persons jointly to carry out a single business enterprise for profit. 206 Mich. 153.

JOINT AND SEVERAL BOND. A bond of two or more obligors, who bind themselves jointly and severally to the obligees, who can sue all the obligors jointly, or any one of them separately, for the whole amount, but cannot bring a joint action against part, that is, treat it as joint as to some, and several as to others. Upon the payment of the whole by one of such obligors, a right to contribution arises in his favor against the other obligors.

JOINT BOND. The bond of two or more obligors, the action to enforce which must be joint against them all.

JOINT CONTRACT. One in which the contractors are jointly bound to perform the promise or obligation therein contained, or entitled to receive the benefit of such promise or obligation.

JOINT CREDITORS. Persons jointly holding the same debt or demand.

JOINT DEBTORS. Persons united in a joint liability or indebtedness.

JOINT EXECUTORS. Those who are joined in the execution of a will.

JOINT FIAT. A fiat in bankruptcy, issued against two or more trading partners. Wharton.

JOINT FINE. In old English law. "If a whole vill is to be fined, a joint fine may be laid, and it will be good for the necessity of it; but, in other cases, fines for offenses are to be severally imposed on each particular offender, and not jointly upon all of them." Jacob.

JOINT HEIR. A coheir.

JOINT INDICTMENT. One indictment brought against two or more offenders, charging the defendants jointly. It may be where there is a joint criminal act, without any regard to any particular personal default or defect of either of the defendants. Thus, there may be a joint indictment against the joint keepers of a gaming house. 1 Vent. 302; 2 Hawk. P. C. 240.

JOINT LIVES. This expression, which is met with more frequently in English books, applies when a right is granted to two or more persons, to be enjoyed while both or all of them shall live. Abbott.

JOINT-STOCK BANKS. In English law. A species of *quasi* corporations, or companies regulated by deeds of settlement.

In some respects they stand in the same situation as other unincorporated bodies; but they differ from the latter in this, that they are invested by certain statutes with powers and privileges usually incident to corporations. These enactments provide for the continuance of the partnership notwithstanding a change of partners. The death, bankruptcy, or the sale by a partner of his share does not affect the identity of the partnership. It continues the same body, under the same name, by virtue of the act of parliament, notwithstanding these changes. 7 Geo. IV. c. 46, § 9.

JOINT-STOCK COMPANY. A partnership having a capital stock divided into transferable shares. Shumaker, Partnership, 447.

JOINT-STOCK CORPORATION. A term used sometimes instead of "stock corporation" to indicate those corporations (including substantially all corporations for pecuniary profit) which have a capital stock divided into shares.

JOINT TENANTS. Two or more persons who acquire together lands or tenements to be held jointly between them in equal shares, the interests of all uniting and forming one ownership.

Joint tenants differ from tenants in common, in that the title of the former must have been acquired at the same time, by the same conveyance or act, while the latter hold by several titles; and also in that the shares of the former are equal, while those of the latter need not be so.

JOINT TRESPASSERS. Two or more who unite in committing a trespass.

JOINT TRUSTEES. Two or more persons charged jointly with the execution of a trust.

JOINT WILL. A joint will contained in a single instrument is the will of each of the makers, and at the death of one may be probated as his will and be again probated at the death of the other as the will of the latter. Wills may be joint or mutual or both joint and mutual. A joint will is one where the same instrument is made the will of two or more persons and is jointly signed by them. It is not necessarily either mutual or reciprocal. Mutual wills may be defined as the separate wills of two persons which are reciprocal in their provisions. A will that is both joint and mutual is one executed jointly by two or more persons, the provisions of which are reciprocal, and which shows on its face that the devises are made one in consideration of the other. These several classes of wills have some characteristics that distinguish them one from the other. A joint will which is not reciprocal is simply the individual personal will of each of the persons signing the same and is subject to the same rules that would apply if the will were several. Mutual wills,—that is, where two persons execute wills reciprocal in their provisions but separate instruments,—may or may not be revocable at the pleasure of either party, according to the circumstances and understanding upon which they were executed. To deprive either party of the right to revoke such mutual will it is necessary to prove, by clear and satisfactory evidence, that such wills were executed in pursuance of a contract or a compact between the parties, and that each is the consideration for the other; and even in cases where mutual wills have been executed in pursuance of a compact or agreement between the parties, the law appears to be well settled that either party may, during the lifetime of both, withdraw from the compact and revoke the will as to him. A joint and mutual will is revocable during the joint lives of either party, so far as relates to his own disposition, upon giving notice to the other.

but it becomes irrevocable after the death of one of them if the survivor takes advantage of the provision made by the other. 30 Am. & Eng. Ency. of Law (2d ed.), 621, 1 Redfield on Wills, 182, 183; Walpole v. Orford, 3 Ves. Jr. 402; Schouler on Wills, § 455 et seq.

When mutual or joint wills first came up for consideration, the courts of England, both common law and spiritual, pronounced against them, and the same unfavorable position was taken by some of the earlier American cases, but the later and better opinions in both countries now sustain such wills where they have been executed with the necessary formalities and have not been revoked by some later instrument. Schouler on Wills, 456. In a leading case in England on this subject (1 Dick. 419) it was held that a joint and mutual will might be revoked by both jointly or that it might be revoked separately, provided the party intending it had given notice to the other of such revocation, but that neither of them could, during their joint lives, revoke it secretly, nor could it be done by the survivor after the death of the other; that such wills constituted a mutual contract between the parties which could not be rescinded by the survivor after the death of one, on the theory that the first that dies carries his part of the contract into execution. In such a case the courts will not permit the other party to afterwards break the contract. The doctrine of this case has been approved in a number of well considered cases in this country. 86 Wis. 364; 155 N. Y. 55; 72 Mich. 76; 198 Mo. 289; 243 Ill. 84, 85.

JOINTRESS, or JOINTURESS. A womas who has an estate settled on her by her husband, to hold during her life, if she survive him. Co. Litt. 46.

JOINTURE. A joint estate limited to both husband and wife. A competent livelihood of freehold for the wife, of lands and tenements, to take effect, in profit or possession, presently after the death of the husband, for the life of the wife at least.

Jointures are regulated by the statute of 27 Hen. VIII. c. 10, commonly called the "Statute of Uses."

To make a good jointure, the following circumstances must concur, namely: It must take effect, in possession or profit, immediately from the death of the husband. It must be for the wife's life, or for some greater estate. It must be limited to the wife herself, and not to any other person in trust for her. It must be made in satisfaction for the wife's whole dower, and not of part of it only. The estate limited to the wife must be expressed or averred to be in satisfaction of her whole dower. It must be made before marriage. A jointure attended with all these circumstances is binding on the widow, and is a complete bar to the claim of dower, or, rather, it prevents its ever arising. But there are other modes of limiting an estate to a wife, which, Lord Coke says, are good jointures within the statute, provided the wife accepts of them after the death of the husband. She may, however, reject them, and claim her dower. Cruise, Dig. tit. 7; 2 Bl. Comm. 137. In its more enlarged sense, a jointure signifies a joint estate limited to both husband and wife. 2 Bl. Comm. 137. See 14 Viner, Abr. 540; Bac. Abr.; 2 Bouv. Inst., note 1761 et seq.; Washb. Real Prop.

JORNALE (Law Lat.) In old European law. As much ground as might be ploughed in one day. Spelman.

JOUR. A French word, signifying day. It is used in our old law books; as, *tout jours*, forever. It is also frequently employed in the composition of words; as, journal, a day book; journeyman, a man who works by the day; journeys account.

JOUR EN BANC. In old practice. A day *in banc*. Distinguished from *"jour en pays,"* a day in the country, otherwise called *"jour en nisi prius."* Y. B. H. 11 Hen. VI. 1.

JOURNAL.

——**In Maritime Law.** The book kept on board of a ship or other vessel, which contains an account of the ship's course, with a short history of every occurrence during the voyage. Another name for log book. Chit. Law Lat. 199.

——**In Commercial Law.** A book used among merchants, in which the contents of the waste book or day book are separated every month, and entered on the debtor and creditor side, for more convenient posting in the ledger.

——**In Legislation.** An account of the proceedings of a legislative body.

JOURNEY. The term originally signified a day's travel (see "Jour"), but now means travel, without regard to duration.

JOURNEYS ACCOUNT. In English practice. A new writ which the plaintiff was permitted to sue out within a reasonable time after the abatement, without his fault, of the first writ. This time was computed with reference to the number of days which the plaintiff must spend in journeying to reach the court; hence the name of "journeys account,"—that is, journeys *accomptes* or counted. This writ was *quasi* a continuance of the first writ, and so related back to it as to oust the defendant or tenant of his voucher, plea of nontenure, joint tenancy fully administered, or any other plea arising upon matter happening after date of the first writ. Co. Litt. fol. 9b.

JUBERE (Lat.) In civil law. To order, direct, or command. Calv. Lex. The word *jubeo*, I order, in a will, was called a "word of direction," as distinguished from "precatory words." Code, 6. 43. 2.

To assure or promise. Calv. Lex.

To decree or pass a law. Adam, Rom. Ant.

JUBILACION. In Spanish law. The right of a public officer to retire from office, retaining his title and his salary, either in whole or in part, after he has attained the age of fifty years, and been in public service at least twenty years, whenever his infirmities prevent him from discharging the duties of his office.

JUDAEUS. A Jew.

JUDAISMUS (Lat.) The religion and rites of the Jews. Du Cange. A quarter set apart for residence of Jews. Du Cange. A usurious rate of interest. 1 Mon. Angl. 839; 2 Mon. Angl. 10, 665. *Sex marcus sterlingorum ad acquietandam terram praedictum de Judaismo, inquo fuit impignorata.* Du Cange. An income anciently accruing to the king from the Jews. Blount.

JUDEX (Lat.)

——**In Roman Law.** One who, either in own right, or by appointment of the magistrate for the special case, judged causes.

Thus, the praetor was formerly called *judex.* But, generally, praetors and magistrates who judge of their own right are distinguished from *judices,* who are private persons, appointed by the praetor, on application of the plaintiff, to try the cause, as soon as issue is joined, and furnished by him with instructions as to the legal principles involved. They were variously called *judices delegati,* or *pedanei,* or *speciales.* They resemble in many respects jurors. Thus, both are private persons, brought in at a certain stage of the proceedings, viz., issue joined, to try the cause, under instructions from the judge as to the law of the case. But civilians are not clear whether the *judices* had to decide the fact alone, or the law and fact. The *judex* resembles in many respects the *arbitrator,* or arbiter, the chief differences being, first, that the latter is appointed in cases of trust and confidence, the former in cases where the relations of the parties are governed by strict law (*in practionibus strictis*); second, the latter has the whole control of case, and decides according to equity and good conscience, the former by strict formulae; third, that the latter may be a magistrate, the former must be a private person; fourth, that the award of the arbiter derives its force from the agreement of submission, while the decree of the *judex* has its sanction in the command of the praetor to try the cause. Calv. Lex.; 1 Spence, Eq. Jur. 210, note; Kaufm. Mackeld. Civ. Law, § 193, note.

There was generally one *judex,* sometimes three,—in which case the decision of two, in the absence of the third, had no effect. Calv. Lex. Down to the time of handing over the cause to the *judex,* that is, till issue joined, the proceedings were before the praetor, and were said to be *in jure;* after that, before the *judex,* and were said to be *in judicio.* In all this we see the germ of the Anglo-Saxon system of judicature. 1 Spence, Eq. Jur. 67.

——**In Civil Law.** A judge who conducts the trial from beginning to end; *magistratus.* The practice of calling in *judices* was disused before Justinian's time; therefore, in the Code, Institutes, and Novels, *judex* means judge in its modern sense. Heinec. Elem. Jur. Civ. § 1327.

——**In Old English Law.** A juror. Spelman. A judge, in modern sense, especially—as opposed to *justiciarius, i. e.,* a common-law judge,—to denote an ecclesiastical judge. Bracton, fols. 401, 402.

JUDEX A QUO. The judge from whom an appeal is taken. See "A Quo."

JUDEX AD QUEM. A judge to whom an appeal is taken. See "A Quo."

JUDEX AEQUITATEM SEMPER SPECtare debet. A judge ought always to regard equity. Jenk. Cent. Cas. 45.

JUDEX ANTE OCULOS AEQUITATEM semper habere debet. A judge ought always to have equity before his eyes. Jenk. Cent. Cas. 58.

JUDEX BONUS NIHIL EX ARBITRIO suo faciat, nec propositione domesticae voluntatis, sed juxta leges et jura pronunciet. A good judge should do nothing from his own arbitrary will, or from the dictates of his private wishes; but he should pronounce according to law and justice. 7 Coke, 27a.

JUDEX DAMNATUR CUM NOCENS ABsolvitur. The judge is condemned when the guilty are acquitted.

JUDEX DATUS. In Roman law. A judge given, that is, assigned or appointed, by the praetor to try a cause.

JUDEX DEBET JUDICARE SECUNDUM allegata et probata. The judge ought to decide according to the allegations and the proofs.

JUDEX DELEGATUS (Lat.) In civil law. A delegated judge; a special judge.

JUDEX EST LEX LOQUENS. The judge is the speaking law. 7 Coke, 4a.

JUDEX FISCALIS. In old European law. A fiscal judge; a judge having cognizance of matters pertaining to the *fiscus,* or public treasury.

JUDEX HABERE DEBET DUOS SALES,—salem sapientiae, ne sit insipidus, et salem conscientiae, ne sit diabolus. A judge should have two salts,—the salt of wisdom, lest he be insipid; and the salt of conscience, lest he be devilish. 3 Inst. 147.

JUDEX NON POTEST ESSE TESTIS IN propria causa. A judge cannot be a witness in his own cause. 4 Inst. 279.

JUDEX NON POTEST INJURIAM SIBI datam punire. A judge cannot punish a wrong done to himself. 12 Coke, 114.

JUDEX NON REDDIT PLUS QUAM quod petens ipse requirit. The judge does not give more than the plaintiff demands. 2 Inst. 286, case 84.

JUDEX ORDINARIUS (Lat.) In civil law. A judge who had jurisdiction by his own right, not by another's appointment. Calv. Lex.; Vicat. Blackstone says that *judices ordinarii* decided only questions of fact, while questions of law were referred to the *centumviri;* but this would seem to be rather the definition of *judices selecti;* and not all questions of law were referred to the *centumviri,* but particular actions, *e. g., querela inofficiosi testamenti.* See 2 Sharswood, Bl. Comm. 315; Vicat, "Centumviri."

JUDEX PEDANEUS. In Roman law. A name given to the judge appointed by the praetor to try a cause from the law seat which he occupied at the foot of the tribunal or praetor's bench.

JUDGE. A public officer lawfully appointed to decide litigated questions according to law.

An officer so named in his commission, and who presides in some court.

In its most extensive sense, the term includes all officers appointed to decide litigated questions while acting in that capacity, including justices of the peace, and even jurors, it is said, who are judges of the facts. 4 Dall. (Pa.) 229; 3 Yeates (Pa.) 300. In ordinary legal use, however, the term is limited to the sense of the second of the definitions here given (15 Ill. 388), unless it may be that the case of a justice or commissioner acting judicially is to be considered an extension of this meaning. See 3 Cush. (Mass.) 584.

JUDGE ADVOCATE. An officer of a court martial who is to discharge some duties at the trial of offenders. His duties are to prosecute in the name of the United States; but he shall so far consider himself as counsel for the prisoner, after the prisoner shall have made his plea, as to object to leading questions to any of the witnesses, or any question to the prisoner the answer to which might tend to criminate himself. He is, further, to swear the members of the court before they proceed upon any trial. Rules & Articles of War, art. 69; 2 Story, U. S. Laws, 1001; Holt, Dig. passim.

JUDGE ORDINARY. By St. 20 & 21 Vict. c. 85, § 9, the judge of the court of probate was made judge of the court for divorce and matrimonial causes created by that act, under the name of the "judge ordinary."

JUDGE'S CERTIFICATE. In English practice. The written statement of the judge who tried the cause, that one of the parties is entitled to costs in the action. It is very important in some cases that these certificates should be obtained at the trial. See Tidd, Prac. 879; 3 Chit. Prac. 458, 486; 3 Camp. 316; 5 Barn. & Ald. 796. A statement of the opinion of the court, signed by the judges, upon a question of law submitted to them by the chancellor for their decision. See 3 Sharswood, Bl. Comm. 453. See "Case Stated."

JUDGE'S NOTES. Short statements, noted by a judge on the trial of a cause, of what transpires in the course of such trial.

JUDGMENT. In practice. The conclusion of law upon facts found, or admitted by the parties, or upon their default in the course of the suit. Tidd, Prac. 930.

The decision or sentence of the law, given by a court of justice or other competent tribunal, as the result of proceedings instituted therein for the redress of an injury.

A final decision entered in a book of judgments under the signature of the judge (3 Green [N. J.] 383), or, as is the practice in many jurisdictions, under the signature of the clerk.

A final or definitive sentence or decision, by which a cause is determined, though not capable of being enrolled, so as to constitute what is technically called a "record," is a judgment. 10 Wend. (N. Y.) 44.

Judgments are either *in rem,* or *in personam.* See "In Rem"; "In Personam."

They are either final, or interlocutory. See "Final Judgment"; "Interlocutory Judgment."

Accordingly, as they are rendered for various causes, and at various stages of the proceedings without trial, or on a partial trial of the issues, judgments are:

(1) Judgment by default. A judgment rendered in consequence of the nonappearance of the defendant.

(2) Judgment by *nil dicit.* One rendered against a defendant for want of a plea.

(3) Judgment by confession. A judgment entered for the plaintiff in case the defendant, instead of entering a plea, confesses the action, or, at any time before trial, confesses the action and withdraws his plea.

(4) Judgment of retraxit. One given against the plaintiff, where, after appearance, he withdraws his suit. It differs from nonsuit in being a voluntary renunciation of the claim, and will bar a subsequent action. 3 Bl. Comm. 396.

(5) Judgment of nonsuit. A judgment rendered against a plaintiff when he, on trial by jury, fails to be present. See "Nonsuit."

(6) Judgment of *nolle prosequi.* A judgment entered against the plaintiff where, after appearance, he refuses to further prosecute his suit.

(7) Judgment by *non sum informatus.* One which is rendered when defendant's attorney, instead of entering a plea, says that he is not informed of any answer to be given to the action.

(8) Judgment of *non prosequitur*. One given against a plaintiff for neglect to take any of the steps which it is incumbent upon him to take in due time.

Among the different judgments rendered in particular actions, or on particular pleas, are:

(9) Judgment *quod recuperet*. A judgment in favor of the plaintiff that he do recover, which is rendered when plaintiff has prevailed upon an issue in fact or an issue in law other than one arising on a dilatory pleading.

(10) Judgment *quod partitio fiat*. The interlocutory judgment in a writ of partition, that partition be made.

(11) Judgment *partitio facto, firma et stablis in perpetuum*. The final judgment in partition.

(12) Judgment *quod computet*. A judgment in an action of account render that the defendant account.

(13) Judgment *pro retorno habendo*. A judgment in an action for the possession of goods, that plaintiff have a return thereof.

(14) Judgment of *nil capiat per breve*, or *per billam*. A judgment in favor of a defendant upon an issue raised upon a declaration or peremptory plea.

(15) Judgment of *cassetur breve* (that the writ be quashed). A judgment rendered in favor of a party pleading in abatement to a writ.

(16) Judgment of error. A judgment rendered by an appellate court on a record sent up from an inferior court.

(17) Judgment of *respondeat ouster*. One rendered against a defendant that he do answer over after he has failed to establish a dilatory plea.

(18) Judgment *quod partes replacitant*. A judgment for repleader.

(19) Judgment *nul tiel record*. One rendered upon a plea denying the existence of a record.

(20) Judgment *capiatur*. One formerly rendered against a defendant in a civil action for a wrong *vi et armis*, rendering him liable to arrest and imprisonment until a fine was paid to the king for the breach of the peace.

(21) Judgment *non obstante veredicto*. A judgment rendered without regard to a verdict rendered in the action. See "Non Obstante Veredicto."

JUDGMENT CREDITOR. One who is entitled to enforce a judgment by execution (*q. v.*). The owner of an unsatisfied judgment.

JUDGMENT DEBTOR. One against whom a judgment stands unsatisfied.

JUDGMENT DEBTOR SUMMONS. Under the English bankruptcy act of 1861 (sections 76-85), these summonses might be issued against both traders and nontraders, and, in default of payment of, or security or agreed composition for, the debt, the debtors might be adjudicated bankrupt. This act was repealed by 32 & 33 Vict. c. 83, § 20. 32 & 33 Vict. c. 71, however (bankruptcy act 1869), provides (section 7) for the granting of a "debtor's summons," at the instance of creditors, and, in the event of failure to pay or compound, a petition for adjudication may be presented, unless in the events provided for by that section. Rapalje & L.

JUDGMENT DEBTS. Debts, whether on simple contract or by specialty, for the recovery of which judgment has been entered up, either upon a *cognovit*, or upon a warrant of attorney, or as the result of a successful action.

JUDGMENT NISI. A judgment entered on the return of the *nisi prius* record with the postea indorsed, which will become absolute according to the terms of the "postea" unless the court out of which the *nisi prius* record proceeded shall, within the first four days of the following term, otherwise order.

Under the compulsory arbitration law of Pennsylvania, on filing the award of the arbitrators, judgment *nisi* is to be entered, which judgment is to be valid as if it had been rendered on a verdict of a jury, unless an appeal is entered within the time required by law.

JUDGMENT NOTE. A promissory note given in the usual form, and containing, in addition, a power of attorney to appear and confess judgment for the sum therein named.

JUDGMENT PAPER. In English practice. An *incipitur* of the pleadings, written on plain paper, upon which the master will sign judgment. 1 Archb. Prac. 229, 306, 343.

JUDGMENT RECORD.

——**In English Practice.** A parchment roll, on which are transcribed the whole proceedings in the cause, deposited and filed of record in the treasury of the court, after signing of judgment. 3 Steph. Comm. 632.

——**In American Practice.** A record signed, filed, and docketed by the clerk, all of which is necessary to suing out execution. Graham, Prac. 341.

JUDGMENT ROLL. In English law. A record made of the issue roll (*q. v.*), which, after final judgment has been given in the cause, assumes this name. Steph. Pl. 133; 3 Chit. St. 514.

JUDICANDUM EST LEGIBUS NON EXEMPLIS. We are to judge by the laws, not by examples. 4 Coke, 33b; 4 Sharswood, Bl. Comm. 405; 19 Johns. (N. Y.) 513.

JUDICATIO (Lat.) In civil law. Judging; the pronouncing of sentence, after hearing a cause. Halifax, Anal. bk. 3, c. 8, No. 7.

JUDICATORES TERRARUM. Persons in the county palatine of Chester, who, on a writ of error, were to consider of the judgment given there, and reform it; otherwise they forfeited £100 to the crown by custom. Jenk. Cent. Cas. 71.

JUDICATURE. The state of those employed in the administration of justice; and in this sense it is nearly synonymous with "judiciary." This term is also used to signify a tribunal; and sometimes it is employed to show the extent of jurisdiction; as, the judicature is upon writs of error, etc. Comyn, Dig. "Parliament" (L 1). And see Comyn, Dig. "Courts" (A).

JUDICATURE ACTS. A series of acts of parliament reforming and consolidating the English courts, and simplifying the procedure therein. St. 36 & 37 Vict. c. 66, and St. 38 & 39 Vict. c. 77, and amendments. Also applied to similar acts adopted by the various states.

JUDICES NON TENENTUR EXPRIMERE causam sententiae suae. Judges are not bound to explain the reason of their sentence. Jenk. Cent. Cas. 75.

JUDICES ORDINARII (Lat.) In civil law. Ordinary *judices;* the common *judices* appointed to try causes, and who, according to Blackstone, determined only questions of fact. 3 Bl. Comm. 315.

JUDICES PEDANEOS (Lat.) In Roman law. Judges chosen by the parties.

Among the Romans, the praetors and other great magistrates did not themselves decide the actions which arose between private individuals. These were submitted to judges chosen by the parties, and these judges were called *judices pedaneos.* In choosing them, the plaintiff had the right to nominate, and the defendant to accept or reject those nominated. Heinec. Ant. Rom. lib. 4, tit. b. note 40; 7 Toullier, Dr. Civ. note 353.

JUDICES SELECTI (Lat.) In civil law. Select or selected *judices* or judges; those who were used in criminal causes, and between whom and modern jurors many points of resemblance have been noticed. 3 Bl. Comm. 366.

JUDICI OFFICIUM SUUM EXCEDENTI per paretur. To a judge who exceeds his office or jurisdiction no obedience is due. Jenk. Cent. Cas. 139.

JUDICI SATIS POENA EST QUOD deum habet ultorem. It is punishment enough for a judge that he is responsible to God. 1 Leon. 295.

JUDICIA (Lat.) In Roman law. Judicial proceedings; trials. *Judicia publica,* criminal trials. Dig. 48. 1.

JUDICIA IN CURIA REGIS NON ADNIhilentur, sed stent in robore suo quousque per errorem aut attinctum adnullentur. Judgments in the king's courts are not to be annihilated, but to remain in force until annulled by error or attaint. 2 Inst. 539.

JUDICIA IN DELIBERATIONIBUS CREbro maturescunt, in accelerate processu nunquam. Judgments frequently become matured by deliberation, never by hurried process. 3 Isst. 210.

JUDICIA POSTERIORA SUNT IN LEGE fortiora. The latter decisions are stronger in law. 8 Coke, 97.

JUDICIA SUNT TANQUAM JURIS DICta, et pro veritate accipiuntur. Judgments are, as it were, the *dicta* or sayings of the law, and are received as truth. 2 Inst. 537.

JUDICIAL. Belonging to the office of a judge; as judicial authority.

Relating to or connected with the administration of justice; as a judicial officer.

Having the character of judgment or formal legal procedure; as a judicial act.

Proceeding from a court of justice; as a judicial writ, a judicial determination.

Constituting the basis of a judgment; as a judicial opinion.

Whatever emanates from a judge as such, or proceeds from a court of justice, is judicial. A power which, when exercised by officers not connected with the judiciary, would be regarded as purely administrative, becomes at once judicial when exercised by a court of justice.

Where any power is conferred upon a court of justice, to be exercised by it as a court, in the manner and with the formalities used in its ordinary proceedings, the action of such court is to be regarded as judicial, irrespective of the original nature of the power. 22 N. Y. 67, 82, 84; 11 Abb. Pr. (N. Y.) 301, 315.

JUDICIAL ACTION. An act performed by a court, touching the rights of parties, or property, brought before it by voluntary appearance, or by the prior action of ministerial officers, in short, by ministerial acts. 17 Ind. 173.

JUDICIAL ACTS. Acts requiring the exercise of some judicial discretion, as distinguished from ministerial acts, which require none. Rapalje & L.

JUDICIAL ADMISSIONS. Admissions of the party which appear of record as the admissions of the party.

JUDICIAL COMMITTEE OF THE PRIVY council. In English law. A tribunal, composed of members of the privy council, which exercises the entire appellate jurisdiction of the sovereign in council, and also advises him upon any matters which he may refer to it.

Its jurisdiction extends to cases in civil, ecclesiastical, and maritime law, in equity, and to many of the colonial cases, including cases arising under the Hindoo and Mohammedan law. It consists of eminent lawyers, chiefly of judicial station. When questions arise which belong to any peculiar jurisdiction, as the ecclesiastical or civil, the attendance and aid of judges in that branch are required; and in case of questions under the Hindoo or other peculiar systems of law, assistance is, in like manner, derived from those skilled in such proceedings.

Allegations and proofs are made before this committee, which thereupon reports to the sovereign in council, by whom judgment is finally rendered. Bl. Comm. (Warren, Abr.) 220.

JUDICIAL CONFESSIONS. In criminal law. Those voluntarily made before a magistrate, or in a court, in the due course of legal proceedings. A preliminary examination, taken in writing, by a magistrate lawfully authorized, pursuant to a statute, or the plea of guilty made in open court to an indictment, are sufficient to found a conviction upon them.

JUDICIAL CONVENTIONS. Agreements entered into in consequence of an order of court; as, for example, entering into a bond on taking out a writ of sequestration. 6 Mart. (La.; N. S.) 494.

JUDICIAL DECISIONS. The opinions or determinations of the judges in causes before them. Hale, Hist. Crim. Law, 68; Willes, 666; 3 Barn. & Ald. 122; 1 H. Bl. 63; 5 Maule & S. 185. See "Dictum."

JUDICIAL DEPARTMENT. That department of government which interprets, construes and applies the laws. 270 Ill. 510.

JUDICIAL DISCRETION. See "Discretion."

JUDICIAL DOCUMENTS. Proceedings relating to litigation. They are divided into (1) judgments, decrees, and verdicts; (2) depositions, examinations, and inquisitions taken in the course of a legal process; (3) writs, warrants, pleadings, etc., which are incident to any judicial proceedings.

JUDICIAL MORTGAGE. In Louisiana. The lien resulting from judgments, whether these be rendered on contested cases, or by default, whether they be final or provisional, in favor of the person obtaining them. Civ. Code La. art. 3289.

JUDICIAL NOTICE. The cognizance taken by a court of matters of fact, without the production of evidence thereof. The matters of fact of which judicial notice will be taken are, in general, those of general notoriety, immemorial usage, or uniform national occurrence.

JUDICIAL POWER. The authority vested in the judges or courts, as distinguished from that vested in other departments of government. That power by which judicial tribunals construe the constitution, and laws of the United States, or of the states, and determine the rights of parties, and application of the laws. 14 Abb. Pr. (N. S.; N. Y.) 165; 65 Barb. (N. Y.) 444; 270 Ill. 510, 511; 256 Ill. 621; 192 Ill. 612.

JUDICIAL PROCEEDINGS. A proceeding which takes place in or under the authority of a court of justice, or which relates in any way to the administration of justice, or which legally ascertains any right or liability. 197 Ill. 228.

JUDICIAL SALE. A sale, by authority of some competent tribunal, by an officer authorized by law for the purpose. In a strict sense, an execution sale is not a judicial sale (18 Vt. 394), but it is generally so regarded (66 Ind. 505).

JUDICIAL WRITS. In English practice. The *capias* and all other writs subsequent to the original writ not issuing out of chancery, but from the court to which the original was returnable.

Being grounded on what had passed in that court in consequence of the sheriff's return, they are called "judicial" writs, in contradistinction to the writs issued out of chancery, which were called "original" writs. 3 Bl. Comm. 282.

JUDICIARY. That which is done while administering justice; the judges taken collectively; as, the liberties of the people are secured by a wise and independent judiciary. See "Court"; 3 Story, Const. bk. 3, c. 38.

JUDICIARY ACT. The name ordinarily given to Act Cong. Sept. 24, 1789, establishing the system of federal courts.

JUDICIIS POSTERIORIBUS FIDES EST adhibenda. Faith or credit is to be given to the later decisions. 13 Coke, 14.

JUDICIS EST IN PRONUNTIANDO SEqui regulam, exceptione non probata. The judge in his decision ought to follow the rule, when the exception is not proved.

JUDICIS EST JUDICARE SECUNDUM allegata et probata. A judge ought to decide according to the allegations and proofs. Dyer, 12a; Halk. Max. 73.

JUDICIS EST JUS DICERE NON DARE. It is the duty of a judge to declare the law, not to enact it. Lofft, 42.

JUDICIS OFFICIUM EST OPUS DIEI IN die suo perficere. It is the duty of a judge to finish the work of each day within that day. Dyer, 12.

JUDICIS OFFICIUM EST UT RES ITA tempora rerum quaerere, quaesito tempore tutus eris. It is the duty of a judge to inquire the times of things, as well as into things; by inquiring into the time you will be safe. Co. Litt. 171.

JUDICIUM. A court; judicial power; a judicial proceeding; sometimes applied in this sense to an action generally, and sometimes to a determination therein, as a verdict or judgment.

JUDICIUM A NON SUO JUDICE DATUM nullius est momenti. A judgment given by an improper judge is of no moment. 10 Coke, 76b; 2 Q. B. 1014; 13 Q. B. 143; 14 Mees. & W. 124; 11 Clark & F. 610.

JUDICIUM CAPITALE. In old English law. Judgment of death; capital judgment. Fleta, lib. 1, c. 39, § 2. Called, also, "*judicium vitae amissionis*," judgment of loss of life. Id. lib. 2, c. 1, § 5.

JUDICIUM DEI (Lat. the judgment or decision of God). In old English law. A term applied to trials by ordeal; for, in all trials of this sort, God was thought to interfere in favor of the innocent, and so decide the cause. These trials are now all abolished.

JUDICIUM EST QUASI JURIS DICTUM. Judgment is, as it were, a saying of the law. Co. Litt. 168.

JUDICIUM NON DEBET ESSE ILLUSOrium; suum effectum habere debet. A judgment ought not to be illusory; it ought to have its proper effect. 2 Inst. 341.

JUDICIUM PARIUM. In old English law. Judgment of the peers; judgment of one's peers; trial by jury. Magna Charta, c. 29.

JUDICIUM REDDITUR IN INVITUM. Judgment is given against one, whether he will or not. Co. Litt. 248b.

JUDICIUM REDDITUR IN INVITUM, IN praesumptione legis. In presumption of law, a judgment is given against inclination. Co. Litt. 248b, 314b.

JUDICIUM SEMPER PRO VERITATE accipitur. A judgment is always taken for truth. 2 Inst. 380; 17 Mass. 237.

JUGERUM (Lat.) An acre. Co. Litt. 5b. As much as a yoke (*jugum*) of oxen could plough in one day.

JUGES D'INSTRUCTION. In French law. Officers subject to the *procureur imperial* or *general*, who receive in cases of criminal offenses the complaints of the parties injured, and who summon and examine witnesses upon oath, and, after communication with the *procureur imperial*, draw up the forms of accusation. They have also the right, subject to the approval of the same superior officer, to admit the accused to bail. They are appointed for three years, but are re-eligible for a further period of office. They are usually chosen from among the regular judges. Brown.

JUGULATOR. In old records. A cutthroat or murderer. Cowell.

JUGUM (Lat.) In the civil law. A yoke; a measure of land; as much land as a yoke of oxen could plough in a day. Nov. 17, c. 8. Called, also, *jugerum*, *jugalium* and *zygocephalum*. Id. See Brissonius.

JUGUM TERRAE (Law Lat.) In old English law. A yoke of land; half a plough land. Domesday Book; Co. Litt. 5a; Cowell.

JUICIO. In Spanish law. A trial or suit. White, New Recop. bk. 3, tit. 4, c. 1.

JUICIO DE APEO. In Spanish law. The decree of a competent tribunal directing the determining and marking the boundaries of lands or estates.

JUICIO DE CONCURSO DE ACREEDOres. In Spanish law. The decree obtained by a debtor against his creditors, or by the creditors against their debtor, for the payment of the amounts due, according to the respective rank of each creditor, when the property of the debtor is insufficient to pay the whole of his liabilities.

JUMENT. In old Scotch law. An ox used for tillage. 1 Pitc. Crim. Tr. pt. 2, p. 89.

JUMENTA. In civil law. Beasts of burden; animals used for carrying burdens. This word did not include "oxen." Dig. 32. 65. 5.

JUMP BAIL. A colloquial expression, meaning to abscond in violation of the obligation of a bail bond.

JUNCTA JUVANT. Things joined have effect. 11 East, 220.

JUNCTURA. (Lat.) In old English law. A joining together; the uniting, putting together, or including of several covenants in one stipulation or contract. Bract. fol. 100b. A jointure; a joint estate. 4 Co. 2a.

JUNIOR. Younger; subsequent to in point of time. Thus, junior creditor, one whose claim accrued after that of another; junior judgment, one entered after another against the same person; junior writ, one issued after another against the same person.

The term is no part of the name of a person. It is a term used to designate and describe the person, as the name of his residence is sometimes used for the same purpose. 131 Mass. 184.

As applied to a manufactured article, it indicates the later or more recent product, or a smaller type or model of a machine that has been on the market. 249 Fed. 52.

JURA (Lat. pl. of *jus*, *q. v.*) Rights; laws. 1 Bl. Comm. 123. Freedoms or abilities. Bac. Works, iii. 265.

JURA ECCLESIASTICA LIMITATA sunt infra limites separatos. Ecclesiastical laws are limited within separate bounds. 3 Bulst. 53.

JURA EODEM MODO DESTITUUNTUR quo constituuntur. Laws are abrogated or repealed by the same means by which they are made. Broom, Leg. Max. (3d London Ed.) 785.

JURA FISCALIA (Lat.) In English law. Fiscal rights; rights of the exchequer. 3 Bl. Comm. 45.

JURA IN RE (Lat.) In civil law. Rights in a thing, as opposed to rights to a thing (*jura ad rem*). Rights in a thing which are not gone upon loss of possession, and which give a right to an action *in rem* against whoever has the possession. These rights are of four kinds: *Dominium, hereditas, servitus, pignus.* Heinec. Elem. Jur. Civ. § 333. See "Jus in Re."

JURA MIXTI DOMINII. In old English law. Rights of mixed dominion. The king's right or power of jurisdiction was so termed. Hale, Anal. § 6.

JURA NATURAE SUNT IMMUTABILIA. The laws of nature are unchangeable. Branch, Princ.; Oliver, Forms, 56.

JURA PERSONARUM (Lat.) In civil law. Rights which belong to men in their different characters or relations, as father, apprentice, citizen, etc. 1 Sharswood, Bl. Comm. 122, note.

JURA PRAEDIORUM. In civil law. The rights of estates. Dig. 50. 16. 86.

JURA PUBLICA ANTEFERENDA PRIvatis. Public rights are to be preferred to private. Co. Litt. 130.

JURA PUBLICA EX PRIVATO PROMIScue decidi non debent. Public rights ought not to be decided promiscuously with private. Co. Litt. 181b.

JURA REGALIA (or **REGIA**) (Lat.) Royal rights. 1 Sharswood, Bl. Comm. 117, 119, 240; 3 Sharswood, Bl. Comm. 45. See 21 & 22 Vict. c. 45.

JURA REGIS SPECIALIA NON CONCEduntur per generalia verba. The special rights of the king are not granted by general words. Jenk. Cent. Cas. 103.

JURA RERUM. Rights of things; the rights of things; rights which a man may acquire over external objects or things unconnected with his person. 1 Bl. Comm. 122; 2 Bl. Comm. 1.

JURA SANGUINIS NULLO JURE CIVILI dirimi possunt. The right of blood and kindred cannot be destroyed by any civil law. Dig. 50. 17. 9; Bac. Max. reg. 11; Broom, Leg. Max. (3d London Ed.) 474.

JURA SUMMI IMPERII. Rights of supreme dominion; rights of sovereignty. 1 Bl. Comm. 49; 1 Kent, Comm. 211.

JURAMENTAE CORPORALES (Lat.) Corporal oaths. These oaths are so called because the party making oath must touch the Bible, or other thing, by which he swears.

JURAMENTUM (Lat.) In civil law. An oath.

JURAMENTUM CALUMNIAE (Lat. oath of calumny). In civil and canon law. An oath required of plaintiff and defendant, whether the parties themselves insist on it or not, that they are not influenced in seeking their right by malice, but believe their cause to be just. It was also required of the attorneys and procurators of the parties. Called also, *jusjurandum* or *sacramentum calumniae.* Calv. Lex.; Vicat; Clerke, Prax. tit. 42.

JURAMENTUM EST INDIVISIBLE; ET non est admittendum in parte verum et in parte falsam. An oath is indivisible; it is not to be held partly true and partly false. 4 Inst. 274.

JURAMENTUM JUDICIALE (Lat.) In civil law. An oath which the judge, of his own accord, defers to either of the parties.

It is of two kinds: First, that which the judge defers for the decision of the cause, and which is understood by the general name *juramentum judiciale,* and is sometimes called suppletory oath, *juramentum suppletorium;* second, that which the judge defers in order to fix and determine the amount of the condemnation which he ought to pronounce, and which is called *juramentum in litem.* Poth. Obl. p. 4, c. 3, § 3, art. 3.

JURAMENTUM NECESSARIUM. In Roman law. A necessary (compulsory) oath. A statement under oath which might be required of a party on his adversary agreeing to be bound thereby.

JURAMENTUM VOLUNTARIUM. In Roman law. A voluntary oath, which a party might make on the offer of his adversary to be bound thereby. He was not, however, compelled to accept the offer, as in case of the *juramentum necessarium.*

JURARE. To swear; to take an oath.

JURARE EST DEUM IN TESTEM VOcare, et est actus divini cultus. To swear is to call God to witness, and is an act of religion. 3 Inst. 165. See 3 Bouv. Inst. 3180, note; 1 Benth. Jud. Ev. 376, 371, note.

JURAT. In practice. That part of an affidavit where the officer certifies that the same was "sworn" before him, and when and where.

JURATA (Lat.) In old English law. A jury of twelve men sworn. Especially, a jury of the common law, as distinguished from the *assiza,* or jury established or reestablished by St. Hen. II.

The *jurata,* or common-law jury, was a jury called in to try the cause, upon the prayer of the parties themselves, in cases where a jury was not given by St. Hen. II., and, as the jury was not given under the statute of Henry II., the writ of attaint provided in that statute would not be against a *jurata* for false verdict. It was common for the parties to a cause to request that the cause might be decided by the *assiza,* sitting as a *jurata,* in order to save trouble of summoning a new jury, in which case "*cadit assiza et vertitur in juratam,*" and the cause is said to be decided *non in modum assizae,* but *in modum juratae.* 1 Reeve, Hist. Eng. Law, 335, 336; Glanv. lib. 13, c. 20; Bracton, lib. 3, c. 30. But this distinction has been long obsolete.

Juratae were divided into: First, *jurata dilatoria,* which inquires out offenses against the law, and presents the offenders' names, together with their offenses, to the judge, and which is of two kinds,—major and minor, according to the extent of its jurisdiction; second, *jurata judicaria,* which gives verdict as to the matter of fact in issue, and is of two kinds,—*civilis,* in civil causes, and *criminalis,* in criminal causes. Du Cange.

A clause in *nisi prius* record called the "jury clause," so named from the word *jurata,* with which its Latin form begins.

A jurat.

JURATION. The act of swearing; the administration of an oath.

JURATO CREDITUR IN JUDICIO. He who makes oath is to be believed in judgment. 3 Inst. 79.

JURATOR. A juror; a compurgator (*q. v.*).

JURATORES DEBENT ESSE VICINI, sufficientes et minus suspecti. Jurors ought to be neighbors, of sufficient estate, and free from suspicion. Jenk. Cent. Cas. 141.

JURATORES SUNT JUDICES FACTI. Jurors are the judges of the facts. Jenk. Cent. Cas. 68.

JURATORY CAUTION. A security sometimes taken in Scotch proceedings, when no better can be had, viz., an inventory of effects given up upon oath, and assigned in security of the sums which may be found due. Bell, Dict.

JURATS (Law Lat. *jurati*). Sworn men; officers of certain municipal corporations in England, in the nature of aldermen or assistants. Cowell; Blount. So called from their official oaths. See Dugdale, Imbanking, 18 et seq.

JURE (Lat.) By right; in right; by the law; according to the law.

JURE BELLI. By the right or law of war. 1 Kent, Comm. 126; 1 C. Rob. Adm. 289.

JURE CIVILI. By the civil law. Inst. 1. 3. 4; 1 Bl. Comm. 423.

JURE ECCLESIAE. In right of the church. 1 Bl. Comm. 401.

JURE EMPHYTEUTICO. By the right or law of *emphyteosis.* 3 Bl. Comm. 232. See "Emphyteosis."

JURE GENTIUM. By the law of nations. Inst. 1. 3. 4; 1 Bl. Comm. 423.

JURE NATURAE AEQUUM EST, NEMInem cum alterius detrimento, et injuria fiere locupletiorem. According to the laws of nature, it is just that no one should be enriched with detriment and injury to another, *i. e.,* at another's expense. Dig. 50. 17. 200.

JURE PROPINQUITATIS (Lat.) By right of relationship. Co. Litt. 10b.

JURE REPRESENTATIONIS (Lat.) By right of representation. See "Per Stirpes." 2 Sharswood, Bl. Comm. 219, note 14, 224.

JURE UXORIS (Lat.) By right of a wife.

JURI NON EST CONSONUM QUOD ALIquis accessorius in curia regis convincatur antequam aliquis de facto fuerit attinctus. It is not consonant to justice that any accessory should be convicted in the king's court before any one has been attainted of the fact. 2 Inst. 183.

JURIDICAL (Lat. *juridicus, q. v.*) Relating to the administration of justice. A juridical day is one on which courts sit for the administration of justice.

Belonging to the office of a judge. See "Judicial."

JURIDICUS (Lat. from *jus,* law, and *dicere,* to say, or pronounce). Belonging to law; relating to the administration of justice in or by a court. *Dies juridicus,* a day on which courts can lawfully sit; a juridical day; a law or court day.

JURIS EFFECTUS IN EXECUTIONE consistit. The effect of a law consists in the execution. Co. Litt. 289b.

JURIS ET DE JURE (Lat. of right and by law). A presumption is said to be *juris et de jure* when it is conclusive, *i. e.,* when no evidence will be admitted to rebut it, in contradistinction to a presumption, which is simply *juris, i e.,* rebuttable by evidence. 1 Greenl. Ev. § 15, note; Wills, Circ. Ev. 29; Best, Pres. p. 20, § 17; Best. Ev. p. 43, § 48.

JURIS ET SEISINAE CONJUNCTIO (Lat.) The union of seisin, or possession, and the right of possession, forming a complete title. 2 Sharswood, Bl. Comm. 199, 311.

JURIS POSITIVI. Positive, as destinguished from natural, law.

JURIS PUBLICI (Lat.) Of common right; of common or public use; such things as, at least in their own use, are common to all the king's subjects; as common highways, common bridges, common rivers, and common ports. Hale, Anal. § 23. The phrase *publici juris* is also used. Hale de Jur. Mar. par. 1, c. 3.

JURIS UTRUM (Law Lat.) In English law. A writ which lay for the incumbent of a benefice, to recover the lands or tenements belonging to the church, which were aliened by his predecessor. Termes de la Ley; 48 Fitzh. Nat. Brev. 49. Sometimes called "the parson's writ of right," being the highest writ he could have. 3 Bl. Comm. 252.

JURISCONSULTUS (Lat. skilled in the law). In civil law. A person who has such knowledge of the laws and customs which prevail in a state as to be able to advise, act, and to secure a person in his dealings.

The early jurisconsults gave their opinions gratuitously, and were also employed in drawing up written documents. From Augustus to Adrian, only those allowed by the emperor could be jurisconsults. Before and after those emperors, any could be jurisconsults who chose. If their opinion was unanimous, it had the force of law; if not, the praetor could follow which opinion he chose. Vicat.

There were two sects of jurisconsults at Rome,—the Proculeians and Labinians. The former were founded by Labeo, and were in favor of innovation; the latter by Capito, and held to the received doctrine. Cush. Rom. Law, §§ 5, 6.

JURISDICTIO EST POTESTAS DE PUBlico introducta, cum necessitate juris dicendi. Jurisdiction is a power introduced for the public good, on account of the necessity of dispensing justice. 10 Coke, 73a.

JURISDICTION (Lat. *jus*, law, *dicere*, to say). The authority by which judicial officers take cognizance of and decide causes; power to hear and determine a cause. 3 Ohio, 494; 6 Pet. (U. S.) 591. And it has been considered that it is essential to jurisdiction that the court should not only have power to hear and determine the case generally, but that, in the course of the hearing, and in the particular judgment rendered, it keep within its power. 93 U. S. 282.

Jurisdiction is either (1) general over all matters within the judicial power of the sovereignty creating it, or (2) limited to certain specified subject matters or persons. See "General Jurisdiction."

It is either (3) original, being that of the tribunal in which an action is commenced in the first instance, or (4) appellate, being that of the tribunal to which the action is removed by proceedings for review.

It is either (5) exclusive in some particular court, (6) concurrent in being possessed at the same time by two or more separate tribunals, or (7) assistant, being that possessed by a tribunal in aid of proceedings in another separate tribunal.

It is either (8) criminal, that which exists for the punishment of crimes, or (9) civil, over subject matters not of a criminal nature.

JURISDICTION CLAUSE. In equity practice. That part of a bill which is intended to give jurisdiction of the suit to the court, by a general averment that the acts complained of are contrary to equity, and tend to the injury of the plaintiff, and that he has no remedy, or not a complete remedy, without the assistance of a court of equity, is called the "jurisdiction clause." Mitf. Eq. Pl. (Jeremy Ed.) 43.

This clause is unnecessary; for if the court appear from the bill to have jurisdiction, the bill will be sustained without this clause; and if the court have not jurisdiction, the bill will be dismissed, though the clause may be inserted. Story, Eq. Pl. § 34.

JURISDICTIONAL. Pertaining to; essential to or conferring jurisdiction.

JURISPERITUS (Lat. from *jus*, law [*juris*, of law], and *peritus*, skilled). Skilled or learned in the law.

JURISPRUDENCE. The science of the law; the practical science of giving a wise interpretation to the laws, and making a just application of them to all cases as they arise.

By science, in the first definition, is understood that connection of truths which is founded on principles either evident in themselves, or capable of demonstration,—a collection of truths of the same kind, arranged in methodical order. In the latter sense, it is the habit of judging the same questions in the same manner, and by this course of judgments forming precedents. 1 Ayliffe, Pand. 3; Toullier, Dr. Civ. tit. prel. § 1, note 1, 12, 99; Merlin, Repert.; 19 Am. Jur. 3.

JURISPRUDENTIA (Lat. from *jus*, law [*juris*, of law] and *prudentia*, wisdom, knowledge). In the civil and common law. Jurisprudence, or legal science.

JURISPRUDENTIA EST DIVINARUM atque humanarum rerum notitia; justi atque injusti scientia. Jurisprudence is the knowledge of things divine and human; the science of the just and the unjust. Dig. 1. 1. 10. 2; Inst. 1. 1. 1; Bracton, 3; 8 Johns. (N. Y.) 290, 295.

JURISPRUDENTIA LEGIS COMMUNIS Angliae est scientia socialis et copiosa. The jurisprudence of the common law of England is a science sociable and copious. 7 Coke, 28a.

JURIST. One versed in the science of the law; one skilled in the civil law; one skilled in the law of nations.

JURISTIC ACT. One of legal efficacy.

JURO. In Spanish law. A certain pension granted by the king on the public revenues, and more especially on the salt works, by favor, either in consideration of meritorious services, or in return for money loaned the government, or obtained by it through forced loans. It is a portion of the yearly revenue of the state, assigned as a rightful indemnity, either in perpetuity or as an annuity.

JUROR (Lat. *juro*, to swear). A man who is sworn or affirmed to serve on a jury.

JURY (Lat. *jurata*, sworn). In practice. A body of men who are sworn to declare the facts of a case as they are delivered from the evidence placed before them.

It is applied loosely to a number of bodies, as coroners' juries, etc.

As applied to petit juries, its most common use, the full number of twelve men is essential to a common-law jury. 18 N. Y. 128.

The origin of this venerable institution of the common law is lost in the obscurity of the middle ages. Antiquarians trace it back to an early period of English history; but, if known to the Saxons, it must have existed in a very crude form, and may have been derived to them from the mode of administering justice by the peers of litigant parties, under the feudal institutions of France, Germany, and the other northern nations of Europe. The ancient ordeals of red-hot iron and boiling water, practiced by the Anglo-Saxons to test the innocence of a party accused of crime, gradually gave way to the wager of battle, in the days of the Normans; while this latter mode of trial disappeared in civil cases in the thirteenth century, when Henry II. introduced into the assizes a trial by jury. It is referred to in *Magna Charta* as an institution existing in England at that time, and its subsequent history is well known. See "Grand Assize"; 3 Bl. Comm. 349; 1 Reeve, Hist. Eng. Law, 23, 84; Glanv. c. 9; Bracton, 155.

A jury de medietate linguae is one composed half of aliens and half of denizens.

Such juries might formerly be claimed, both in civil and criminal cases, where the party claiming the privilege was an alien born, by virtue of 28 Edw. III. c. 13. And see 8 Hen. VI. c. 29; 3 Geo. III. c. 25, by which latter statute the right is thought to be taken away in civil cases. See 3 Sharswood, Bl. Comm. 360; 4 Sharswood, Bl. Comm. 352. A provision of a similar nature, providing for a jury one-half of the nationality of the party claiming the privilege, where he is a foreigner, exists in some of the states of the United States.

A grand jury is one organized for certain preliminary purposes. See "Grand Jury."

A petit jury is a jury who try the question in issue, and pass finally upon the truth of the facts in dispute. The term "jury" is ordinarily applied to this body distinctively.

A common jury is one drawn in the usual manner.

A special or struck jury is one selected by the assistance of the parties.

This is granted in some cases upon motion and cause shown, under various local provisions. See 33 Eng. Law & Eq. 406. The method at common law was for the officer to return the names of forty-eight principal freeholders to the prothonotary or proper officer. The attorneys of the respective parties, being present, strike off each twelve names, and from the remaining twenty-four the jury is selected. A similar course is pursued in those states where such juries are allowed. See 3 Sharswood, Bl. Comm. 357.

JURY BOX. A place set apart for the jury to sit in during the trial of a cause.

JURY LIST. A paper containing the names of jurors impanelled to try a cause, or it contains the names of all the jurors summoned to attend court.

JURY OF MATRONS. See "Jury Women."

JURY PROCESS. In practice. The writs for summoning a jury, viz., in England, *venire juratores facias*, and *distringas juratores*, or *habeas corpora juratorum*. These writs are now abolished, and jurors are summoned by precept. 1 Chit. Archb. Prac. (by Prent.) 344; Com. Law Proc. Act 1852, §§ 104, 105; 3 Chit. St. 519.

JURY WHEEL. A revolving box, from which names are drawn by chance to form the jury list (*q. v.*).

JURY WOMEN. A jury of women was given in two cases, viz., on writ *de ventre inspiciendo*, in which case the jury was made up of men and women, but the search is made by the latter (1 Madd. 11; 2 P. Wms. 591); and where pregnancy was pleaded by condemned criminal in delay of execution, in which case a jury of twelve discreet women was formed, and on their returning a verdict of *enseinte*, the execution was delayed till birth, and sometimes the punishment commuted to perpetual exile. But if the criminal be *privement enseinte*, and not "quick," there is no respite. 2 Hale, P. C. 412. As to time of quickening, see 1 Beck, Med. Jur. 229.

JURYMAN. A juror; one who is impanelled on a jury. Webster.

JUS. Right in general or in the abstract; justice or equity.

Law in general; law as distinguished from equity.

A rule of law; a statute or regulation.

Power or authority.

An action; a court or judicial tribunal.

JUS ABUTENDI (Lat. the right to abuse). By this phrase is understood the right to abuse property, or having full dominion over property. 3 Toullier, Dr. Civ. note 86. Used in contradistinction to the *jus utendi* (*q. v.*).

JUS ACCRESCENDI (Lat.) The right of survivorship.

At common law, when one of several joint tenants died, the entire tenancy or estate went to the survivors, and so on to the last survivor, who took an estate of inheritance. This right, except in estates held in trust, has been abolished by statute in most of the United States.

JUS ACCRESCENDI INTER MERCATOres locum non habet, pro beneficio commercii. The right of survivorship does not exist among merchants for the benefit of commerce. Co. Litt. 182; 1 Bouv. Inst. note 682.

JUS ACCRESCENDI PRAEFERTUR oneribus. The right of survivorship is preferred to incumbrances. Co. Litt. 185.

JUS ACCRESCENDI PRAEFERTUR ULtimae voluntati. The right of survivorship is preferred to a last will. Co. Litt. 185b.

JUS AD REM (Lat.) A right which belongs to a person only mediately and relatively, and has for its foundation an obligation incurred by a particular person.

The *jus in re*, by the effect of its very nature, is independent and absolute, and is exercised *per se ipsum*, by applying it to its object; but the *jus ad rem* is the faculty of demanding and obtaining the performance of some obligation by which another is bound to me *ad aliquid dandum, vel faciendum, vel praestandum.* Thus, if I have the ownership of a horse, the usufruct of a flock of sheep, the right of habitation of a house, a right of way over your land, etc., my right in the horse, in the flock of sheep, in the house, or the land, belongs to me directly, and without any intermediary; it belongs to me absolutely, and independently of any particular relation with another person; I am in direct and immediate relation with the thing itself which forms the object of my right, without reference to any other relation. This constitutes a *jus in re.* If, on the other hand, the horse is lent to me by you, or if I have a claim against you for a thousand dollars, my right to the horse or to the sum of money exists only relatively, and can only be exercised through you; my relation to the object of the right is mediate, and is the result of the immediate relation of debtor and creditor existing between you and me. This is a *jus ad rem.* Every *jus in re*, or real right, may be vindicated by the *actio in rem* against him who is in possession of the thing, or against any one who contests the right. It has been said that the words *jus in re* of the civil law convey the same idea as "thing in possession" at common law. This is an error, arising from a confusion of ideas as to the distinctive characters of the two classes of rights. Nearly all the common-law writers seem to take it for granted that by the *jus in re* is understood the title or property in a thing in the possession of the owner; and that by the *jus ad rem* is meant the title or property in a thing not in the possession of the owner. But it is obvious that possession is not one of the elements constituting the *jus in re*, although possession is generally, but not always, one of the incidents of this right, yet the loss of possession does not exercise the slightest influence on the character of the right itself, unless it should continue for a sufficient length of time to destroy the right altogether by prescription. In many instances the *jus in re* is not accompanied by possession at all; the usuary is not entitled to the possession of the thing subject to his use; still, he has a *jus in re.* So with regard to the right of way, etc. See "Dominium."

A mortgage is considered by most writers as a *jus in re;* but it is clear that it is a *jus ad rem.* It is granted for the sole purpose of securing the payment of a debt, or the fulfillment of some other personal obligation. In other words, it is an accessory to a principal obligation and corresponding right. It can have no separate and independent existence. The immovable on which I have a mortgage is not the object of the right, as in the case of the horse of which I am the owner, or the house of which I have the right of habitation, etc. The true object of my right is the sum of money due to me, the payment of which I may enforce by obtaining a decree for the sale of the property mortgaged. 2 Marcade, 350 et seq.

JUS AESNECIAE. The right of primogeniture.

JUS ALBINATUS. The *droit d'aubaine* (*q. v.*). See "Albinatus Jus."

JUS ANGLORUM. The laws and customs of the West Saxons, in the time of the Heptarchy, by which the people were for a long time governed, and which were preferred before all others. Wharton.

JUS AQUAEDUCTUS (Lat.) In civil law. The name of a servitude which gives to the owner of land the right to bring down water through or from the land of another, either from its source, or from any other place.

JUS BANCI. In old English law. The right of bench; the right or privilege of having an elevated and separate seat of judgment, anciently allowed only to the king's judges, who hence were said to administer "high" justice, *summam administrant justitiam.* Blount.

JUS BELLI. The law of war; the law of nations as applied to a state of war, defining in particular the rights and duties of the belligerent powers themselves, and of neutral nations.

The right of war; that which may be done without injustice with regard to an enemy. Grotius de Jure Belli, lib. 1, c. 1, § 3.

JUS BELLUM DICENDI. The right to declare war.

JUS CANONICUM. The canon law.

JUS CIVILE (Lat.) In Roman law. The private law, in contradistinction to the public law, or *jus gentium.* 1 Savigny, Dr. Rom. c. 1, § 1.

JUS CIVILE EST QUOD SIBI POPULUS constituit. The civil law is what a people establishes for itself. 1 Johns. (N. Y.) 424, 426.

JUS CIVITATIS (Lat.) In Roman law. The collection of laws which are to be observed among all the members of a nation. It is opposed to *jus gentium,* which is the law which regulates the affairs of nations among themselves. 2 Lepage, c. 5, p. 1.

JUS CLOACAE. (Lat.) In civil law. The name of a servitude which requires the party who is subject to it to permit his neighbor to conduct the waters which fall on his grounds over those of the servient estate.

JUS COMMUNE.

——In Civil Law. Common right; the common and natural rule of right, as opposed to *jus singulare* (*q. v.*). Mackeld. Civ. Law, § 196.

——In English Law. The common law, answering to the Saxon "folcright." 1 Bl. Comm. 67.

JUS CONSTITUI OPORTET IN HIS quae ut plurimum accidunt non quae ex inopinato. Laws ought to be made with a view to those cases which happen most frequently, and not to those which are of rare or accidental occurrence. Dig. 1. 3. 3; Broom, Leg. Max. 43.

JUS CORONAE. In English law. The right of the crown, or, rather, to the crown; the right of succession to the throne. 1 Bl. Comm. 191; 2 Steph. Comm. 434.

JUS CUDENDAE MONETAE. In old English law. The right of coining money. 2 How. St. Tr. 118.

JUS CURIALITATIS. In English law. The right of curtesy. Spelman.

JUS DARE (Lat.) To give or to make the law. *Jus dare* belongs to the legislature; *jus dicere,* to the judge.

JUS DELIBERANDI (Lat.) The right of deliberating given to the heir, in those countries where the heir may have "benefit of inventory" (*q. v.*), in which to consider whether he will accept or renounce the succession.

In Louisiana, he is allowed ten days before he is required to make his election. Civ. Code La. art. 1028.

JUS DESCENDIT, ET NON TERRA. A right descends, not the land. Co. Litt. 345.

JUS DICERE (Lat.) To declare the law. It is the province of the court *jus dicere,* to declare what the law is.

JUS DICERE, NON JUS DARE. To declare the law, not to make it. 7 Term R. 696; Arg. 10 Johns. (N. Y.) 566; 7 Exch. 543; 2 Edw. Ch. (N. Y.) 29; 4 C. B. 560, 561; Broom, Leg. Max. (3d London Ed.) 140.

JUS DISPONENDI (Lat.) The right to dispose of a thing.

JUS DIVIDENDI. The right of disposing of realty by will. Du Cange.

JUS DUPLICATUM (Lat. double right). When a man has the possession as well as the property of anything, he is said to have a double right, *jus duplicatum.* Bracton, lib. 4, tr. 4, c. 4; 2 Bl. Comm. 199.

JUS EST ARS BONI ET AEQUI. Law is the science of what is good and just. Dig. 1. 1. 1. 1.

JUS EST NORMA RECTI; ET QUICquid est contra normam recti est injuria. The law is the rule of right; and whatever is contrary to the rule of right is an injury. 3 Bulst. 313.

JUS ET FRAUS NUNQUAM COHABItant. Right and fraud never live together.

JUS EX INJURIA NON ORITUR. A right cannot arise from a wrong. 4 Bin. 639.

JUS FALCANDI. (Lat.) In old English law. The right of mowing or cutting. Fleta, lib. 4, c. 27, § 1.

JUS FECIALE (Lat.) In Roman law. That species of international law which had its foundation in the religious belief of different nations, such as the international law which now exists among the Christian people of Europe. Savigny, Dr. Rom. c. 2, § 11.

JUS FIDUCIARUM (Lat.) In civil law. A right to something held in trust; for this there was a remedy in conscience. 2 Bl. Comm. 328.

JUS FLAVIANUM. In old Roman law. A body of laws drawn up by Cneius Flavius, a clerk of Appius Claudius, from the materials to which he had access. It was a popularization of the laws. Mackeld. Civ. Law, § 39.

JUS FLUMINUM. In civil law. The right to the use of rivers. Locc. de Jur. Mar. lib. 1, c. 6.

JUS FODIENDI (Lat.) In the civil and old English law. A right of digging on another's land. Inst. 2. 3. 2; Bracton, fol. 222; Fleta, lib. 4, c. 19, § 6.

JUS GENTIUM (Lat.) The law of nations. Although the Romans used these words in the sense we attach to "law of nations," yet among them the sense was much more extended. Falck, Enc. Jur. 102, note 42.

Modern writers have made a distinction between the laws of nations which have for their object the conflict between the laws of different nations, which is called *jus gentium privatum,* or private international law, and those laws of nations which regulate those matters which nations, as such, have with each other, which is denominated *jus gentium publicum*, or public international law. Foelix, Droit Int. Prive, note 14. See "International Law."

JUS GLADII (Lat. the right of the sword). Supreme jurisdiction; the right to absolve from or condemn a man to death.

JUS HABENDI (Lat.) The right to have a thing.

JUS HABENDI ET RETINENDI. A right to have and to retain the profits, tithes, and offerings, etc., of a rectory or parsonage. Rapalje & L.

JUS HAEREDITATIS. The right of inheritance. Rapalje & L.

JUS HAURIENDI. (Lat.) In civil and old English law. The right of drawing water. Fleta, lib. 4, c. 27, § 1.

JUS HONORARIUM. The body of Roman law, which was made up of edicts of the supreme magistrates, particularly the praetors.

JUS IMMUNITATIS. In civil law. The law of immunity or exemption from the burden of public office. Dig. 50. 6.

JUS IN PERSONAM. A right against a person; a right which gives its possessor a power to oblige another person to give or procure, to do or not to do, something. Rapalje & L.

JUS IN RE (Lat.) A right which belongs to a person, immediately and absolutely, in a thing, and which is the same against the whole world,—*idem erga omnes*. See "Jus ad Rem."

JUS IN RE INHAERIT OSSIBUS USUfructuarii. A right in the thing cleaves to the person of the usufructuary.

JUS IN RE PROPRIA. The right of enjoyment which is incident to full ownership or property, and is often used to denote the full ownership or property itself. It is distinguished from *jus in re aliena*, which is a mere easement or right in or over the property of another.

JUS INCOGNITUM (Lat.) An unknown law. This term is applied by the civilians to obsolete laws, which, as Bacon truly observes, are unjust; for the law, to be just, must give warning before it strikes. Bac. Aph. 8, § 1; Bowyer, Mod. Civ. Law, 33. But until it has become obsolete, no custom can prevail against it. See "Obsolete."

JUS INDIVIDUUM (Law Lat.) An individual or indivisible right; a right incapable of division. 36 Eng. Law & Eq. 25.

JUS JURANDI FORMA VERBIS DIFfert, re convenit; hunc enim sensum habere debet, ut Deus invocetur. The form of taking an oath differs in language, agrees in meaning; for it ought to have this sense,—that the Deity is invoked. Grotius de Jure Belli, lib. 2, c. 13, § 10.

JUS LATII. In Roman law. The right of Latium or of the Latins. The principal privilege of the Latins seems to have been the use of their own laws, and their not being subject to the edicts of the praetor, and that they had occasional access to the freedom of Rome, and a participation in her sacred rites. Butler, Hor. Jur. 41.

JUS LEGITIMUM (Lat.) In civil law. A legal right which might have been enforced by due course of law. 2 Bl. Comm. 328.

JUS MARITI (Lat.) In Scotch law. The right of the husband to administer, during the marriage, his wife's goods and the rents of her heritage.

In the common law, by *jus mariti* is understood the rights of the husband, as *jus mariti* cannot attach upon a bequest to the wife, although given during coverture, until the executor has assented to the legacy. 1 Bailey, Eq. (S. C.) 214.

JUS MERUM (Lat.) A simple or bare right; a right to property in land, without possession, or the right of possession.

JUS NATURAE. The law of nature. See "Jus Naturale."

JUS NATURALE. Natural law; the rule and dictate of right reason, showing the moral deformity or moral necessity there is in any act according to its suitableness to a reasonable nature. Grotius de Jure Belli, lib. 1, c. 1, c. 3.

The term is used interchangeably with *jus gentium*. Tayl. Civ. Law, 128.

JUS NATURALE EST QUOD APUD HOmines eandem habet potentiam. Natural right is that which has the same force among all men. 7 Coke, 12.

JUS NAVIGANDI. The right of navigating or navigation; the right of commerce by ships or by sea. Locc. de Jur. Mar. lib. 1, c. 3.

JUS NEC INFLECTI GRATIA, NEC frangi potentia, nec adulterari pecunia potest; quod si non modo oppressum, sed desertum aut negligentia asservatum fuerit, nihil est quod quisquam se habere certum, aut a patre accepturum, aut liberis esse relicturum, arbitretur. Favor ought not to be able to bend justice, power to break it, nor money to corrupt it; for not only if it be overborne, but if it be abandoned or negligently observed, no one can think that he holds anything securely, or that he will inherit anything from his father, or be able to leave anything to his children. Cicero.

JUS NECIS. In Roman law. The right of death, or of putting to death; a right which a father anciently had over his children. 3 Gibb. Rom. Emp. 169.

JUS NON HABENTI, TUTE NON PARETUR. It is safe not to obey him who has no right. Hob. 1. 46.

JUS NON PATITUR UT IDEM BIS SOLVATUR. Law does not suffer that the same thing be twice paid.

JUS NON SCRIPTUM. The unwritten law. 1 Bl. Comm. 64.

JUS PAPIRIANUM. The civil law of Papirius. The title of the earliest collection of Roman *leges curiatae*, said to have been made in the time of Tarquin, the last of the kings, by a *pontifex maximus* of the name of Sextus or Publius Papirius. Dig. 1. 2. 2. 2. Very few fragments of this collection now remain, and the authenticity of these has been doubted. 1 Kent, Comm. 517; Mackeld. Civ. Law, p. 14, § 21.

JUS PASCENDI. (Lat.) In civil and old English law. The right of pasturing cattle. Bract. fol. 53b, 222.

JUS PATRONATUS (Lat.) In ecclesiastical law. A commission from the bishop, directed usually to his chancellor and others of competent learning, who are required to summon a jury, composed of six clergymen and six laymen, to inquire into and examine who is the rightful patron. 3 Bl. Comm. 246.

JUS PERSONARUM (Lat.) The right of persons. See "Jure Personarum."

JUS POSSESSIONIS (Lat.) A (or the) right of possession, or seisin. Bracton, fol. 3; Fleta, lib. 4, c. 1, § 2; Co. Litt. 266a; 3 Bl. Comm. 177, 191.

JUS POSTLIMINII.

—**In Civil Law.** The right of postliminy; the right or claim of a person who had been restored to the possession of a thing, or to a former condition, to be considered as though he had never been deprived of it. Dig. 49. 15. 5; 3 Bl. Comm. 107, 210.

—**In International Law.** The right by which property taken by an enemy, and recaptured or rescued from him by the fellow subjects or allies of the original owner, is restored to the latter upon certain terms. 1 Kent, Comm. 108.

JUS PRAESENS. In civil law. A present or vested right; a right already completely acquired. Mackeld. Civ. Law, p. 174, § 183.

JUS PRAETORIUM. In civil law. The discretion of the praetor, as distinct from the *leges*, or standing laws. 3 Bl. Comm. 49. That kind of law which the praetors introduced for the purpose of aiding, supplying, or correcting the civil law for the public benefit. Dig. 1. 1. 7. Called, also, *jus honorarium* (*q. v.*).

JUS PRECARIUM (Lat.) In civil law. A right to a thing held for another, for which there was no remedy. 2 Bl. Comm. 328.

JUS PRIVATUM. The king's private property in the soil covered by navigable water. 202 Ill. 433.

JUS PROJICIENDI (Lat.) In civil law. The name of a servitude by which the owner of a building has a right of projecting a part of his building towards the adjoining house, without resting on the latter. It is extended merely over the ground. Dig. 50. 16. 242; Id. 8. 2. 25; Id. 8. 5. 8. 5.

JUS PROPRIETATIS. The right of property, as distinguished from the *jus possessionis*, or right of possession. Bracton, fol. 3. Called by Bracton "*jus merum*," the mere right. Id.; 2 Bl. Comm. 197; 3 Bl. Comm. 19, 176.

JUS PROTEGENDI (Lat.) In civil law. The name of a servitude. It is a right by which a part of the roof or tiling of one house is made to extend over the adjoining house. Dig. 50. 16. 242. 1; Id. 8. 2. 25; Id. 8. 5. 8. 5.

JUS PUBLICUM. The right to have the water kept free from obstructions for the purpose of navigation. 202 Ill. 433.

—**In the Roman Law.** Public law; that which regards the condition of the Roman state (*quod ad statum rei Romanae spectat*). Inst. 1. 1. 4; Dig. 1. 1. 1. 2. This definition is borrowed by Bracton, who accommodates it to the English jurisprudence. *Est jus publicum quod ad statum reipublicae pertinet.* Bracton, fol. 3b.

JUS PUBLICUM ET PRIVATUM QUOD ex naturalibus praeceptis aut gentium aut civilibus est collectum; et quod in jure scripto jus appellatur, id in lege Angliae rectum esse dicitur. Public and private law is that which is collected from natural principles, either of nations or in states; and that which in the civil law is called *jus*, in the law of England is said to be "right." Co. Litt. 185.

JUS PUBLICUM PRIVATORUM PACTIS mutari non potest. A public right cannot be changed by agreement of private parties.

JUS QUAESITUM (Lat.) A right to ask or recover; for example, in an obligation there is a binding of the obligor, and a *jus quaesitum* in the obligee. 1 Bell, Comm. (5th Ed.) 323.

JUS QUIRITIUM. The old law of Rome, that was applicable originally to patricians only, and, under the Twelve Tables, to the entire Roman people, was so called, in contradistinction to the *jus praetorium* (*q. v.*), or equity. Brown.

JUS QUO UNIVERSITATES UTUNTUR est idem quod habent privati. The law which governs corporations is the same which governs individuals. 16 Mass. 44.

JUS RELICTAE (Lat.) In Scotch law. The right of a wife, after her husband's death, to a third of movables if there be children, and to one-half if there be none.

JUS RERUM (Lat.) The right of things. Its principal object is to ascertain how far a person can have a permanent dominion over things, and how that dominion is acquired. See Bl. Comm.

JUS RESPICIT AEQUITATEM. Law regards equity. Co. Litt. 24b; Broom, Leg. Max. (3d London Ed.) 143; 17 Q. B. 292.

JUS SCRIPTUM.

——**In Roman Law.** Written law. Inst. 1. 2. 3. All law that was actually committed to writing, whether it had originated by enactment or by custom, in contradistinction to such parts of the law of custom as were not committed to writing. Mackeld. Civ. Law, p. 125, § 113.

——**In English Law.** Written law, or statute law, otherwise called *lex scripta*, as distinguished from the common law, *lex non scripta*. 1 Bl. Comm. 62.

Jus scriptum is used in Fleta to denote the civil law, as distinguished from the common law of England. Liber 6, c. 1, § 1.

JUS SINGULARE. In civil law. A peculiar or individual rule, differing from the *jus commune*, or common rule of right, and established for some special reason. Mackeld. Civ. Law, p. 181, § 188.

JUS STAPULAE. In old European law. The law of staple; the right of staple; a right or privilege of certain towns of stopping imported merchandise, and compelling it to be offered for sale in their own markets. Locc. de Jur. Mar. lib. 1, c. 10.

JUS STRICTUM (Lat.) A Latin phrase, which signifies law interpreted without any modification, and in its utmost rigor.

JUS SUPERVENIENS AUCTORI ACcressit successori. A right growing to a possessor accrues to a successor. Halk. Max. 76.

JUS TERTII. The right or interest of a third party.

JUS TESTAMENTORUM PERTINET ordinario. Y. B. 4 Hen. VII., 13b. The right of testaments belongs to the ordinary.

JUS TRIPERTITUM. In the Roman law. The law of wills. Sir Henry Maine says that it is so called because of its three-fold derivation from the imperial constitutions, the civil law, and the praetorian edicts. Anc. Law, 207.

JUS TRIPLEX EST,—PROPRIETATIS, possessionis, et possibilitatis. Right is threefold,—of property, of possession, and of possibility.

JUS TRIUM LIBERORUM. In Roman law. A right or privilege allowed to the parent of three or more children. 2 Kent, Comm. 85; 2 Bl. Comm. 247. These privileges were an exemption from the trouble of guardianship, priority in bearing offices, and a treble proportion of corn. Adams, Rom. Ant. (Am. Ed.) 227.

JUS UTENDI (Lat.) The right to use property without destroying its substance. It is employed in contradistinction to the *jus abutendi*. 3 Toullier, Dr. Civ. note 86.

JUS VENANDI ET PISCANDI. The right of hunting and fishing.

JUS VENDIT QUOD USUS APPROBAVit. The law dispenses what use has approved. Ellesmere, Postn. 35.

JUSJURANDI FORMA VERBIS DIFfert, re convenit; hunc enim sensum habere debet, ut Deus invocetur. The form of taking an oath differs in language, agrees in meaning; for it ought to have this sense, that the Deity is invoked. Grotius de Jure Belli, bk. 2, c. 13, § 10.

JUSJURANDUM (Lat.) In civil law. An oath.

Juramentum is the usual law Latin word.

JUSJURANDUM INTER ALIOS FACtum nec nocere nec prodesse debet. An oath made in another cause ought neither to hurt nor profit. 4 Inst. 279.

JUST COMPENSATION. As used in the constitution, means a full and fair equivalent for the loss sustained by the taking for public use. It may be more, or it may be less, than the mere money value of the property actually taken. The exercise of the power being necessary for the public good, and all property being held subject to its exercise when and as the public good requires it, it would be unjust to the public that it should be required to pay the owner more than a fair indemnity for the loss he sustains by the appropriation of his property for the general good. On the other hand, it would be equally unjust to the owner if he should receive less than a fair indemnity for such loss. To arrive at this fair indemnity, the interests of the public and of the owner, and all the circumstances of the particular appropriation, should be taken into consideration. Lewis, Em. Dom. § 462.

Compensation for the actual loss in dollars and cents. 157 Ill. 56.

JUSTA CAUSA (Lat.) In the civil law. A just cause; a lawful ground; a legal transaction of some kind. 1 Mackeld. Civ. Law, 287, § 274. See Grotius de Jure Belli, lib. 2, c. 23, § 13.

JUSTICE. The constant and perpetual disposition to render every man his due. Inst. bk. 1. tit. 1: 2 Inst. 56. The conformity of our actions and our will to the law. Toullier, Dr. Civ. tit. prel. note 5.

In the most extensive sense of the word, it differs little from "virtue"; for it includes within itself the whole circle of virtues. Yet the common distinction between them is that which considered positively and in itself is called "virtue," when considered relatively and with respect to others has the name of "justice." But justice, being in itself a part of virtue, is confined to things simply good or evil, and consists in a man's taking such a proportion of them as he ought.

Toullier exposes the want of utility and exactness in this division of distributive and commutative justice, adopted in the compendium or abridgments of the ancient doctors, and prefers the division of internal and external justice,—the first being a conformity of our will, and the latter a conformity of our actions, to the law, their union making perfect justice. Exterior justice is the object of jurisprudence; interior justice is the object of morality. Dr. Civ. tit. prel. notes 6, 7.

According to the Frederician Code (part 1, bk. 1, tit. 2, § 27), justice consists simply in letting every one enjoy the rights which he has acquired in virtue of the laws. And, as this definition includes all the other rules of right, there is properly but one single general rule of right, namely, give every one his own.

Commutative justice is that virtue whose object it is to render to every one what belongs to him, as nearly as may be, or that which governs contracts. To render commutative justice, the judge must make an equality between the parties, that no one may be a gainer by another's loss.

Distributive justice is that virtue whose object it is to distribute rewards and punishments to each one according to his merits, observing a just proportion by comparing one person or fact with another, so that neither equal persons have unequal rights, nor unequal persons things equal. Toullier's learned note, Droit Civ. tit. prel. n. 7. note.

——**In Norman French.** Amenable to justice. Kelham.

——**In Feudal Law.** Feudal jurisdiction, divided into high (*alta justitia*), and low (*simplex, inferior justitia*), the former being a jurisdiction over matters of life and limb; the latter over smaller causes. Leg. Edw. Conf. c. 26; Du Cange. Sometimes high, low, and middle justice or jurisdiction were distinguished.

An assessment. Du Cange. Also, a judicial fine. Du Cange.

——**In Practice.** A title given in England and America to judges of common-law courts, being a translation of *justitia*, which was anciently applied to common-law judges, while *judex* was applied to ecclesiastical judges and others; *e. g.*, *judex fiscalis*. Leg. Hen. I. §§ 24, 63; Anc. Inst. Eng. Index; Co. Litt. 71b.

The judges of king's bench and common pleas, and the judges of almost all the supreme courts in the United States, are properly styled "justices."

The term "justice" is also applied to the lowest judicial officers; *e. g.*, a trial justice; a justice of the peace.

JUSTICE AYRES. In Scotch law. The circuits through the kingdom made for the distribution of justice. Ersk. Inst. 1. 3. 25.

JUSTICES COURTS. In American law. Inferior tribunals, with limited jurisdiction, both civil and criminal. There are courts so called in the states of Massachusetts and New Hampshire, and probably other states.

JUSTICES IN EYRE. Certain judges established, if not first appointed, A. D. 1176, 22 Hen. II.

England was divided into certain circuits, and three justices in eyre—or "justices itinerant," as they were sometimes called—were appointed to each district, and made the circuit of the kingdom once in seven years, for the purpose of trying causes. They were afterwards directed, by *Magna Charta*, c. 12, to be sent into every county once a year. The itinerant justices were sometimes mere justices of assize or dower, or of general gaol delivery, and the like. 3 Bl. Comm. 58; Crabb, Hist. Eng. Law, 103, 104.

JUSTICES OF ASSIZE. These justices, or, as they are sometimes called, "justices of *nisi prius*," are judges of the superior English courts, who go on circuit into the various counties of England and Wales for the purpose of disposing of such causes as are ready for trial at the assizes. Rapalje & L.

JUSTICES OF GAOL DELIVERY. Those justices who are sent with a commission to hear and determine all causes appertaining to persons, who, for any offense, have been cast into gaol. Part of their authority was to punish those who let to mainprise those prisoners who were not bailable by law, and they seem formerly to have been sent into the country upon this exclusive occasion, but afterwards had the same authority given them as the justices of assize. Brown.

JUSTICES OF LABORERS. In old English law. Justices appointed to try the cases of laboring men who would not work for the wages prescribed by the statute of laborers. 23 Edw. III.

JUSTICES OF NISI PRIUS. In English law. This title is now usually coupled with that of "justices of assize"; the judges of the superior courts acting on their circuits in both these capacities. 3 Bl. Comm. 58, 59. Formerly there was a distinction made, justices of assize having power to render judgments, but justices of *nisi prius* having power only to receive verdicts.

JUSTICES OF OYER AND TERMINER. Certain persons appointed by the king's commission, among whom were usually two judges of the courts at Westminster, and who went twice in every year to every county of the kingdom (except London and Middlesex), and, at what was usually called the "assizes," heard and determined all treasons, felonies, and misdemeanors.

JUSTICES OF THE BENCH. The justices of the court of common bench or common pleas.

JUSTICES OF THE FOREST. In old English law. Officers who had jurisdiction over all offenses committed within the forest against vert or venison. The court wherein these justices sat and determined such causes was called the "justice seat of the forest." They were also sometimes called the "justices in eyre of the forest."

JUSTICES OF THE HUNDRED. Hundredors; lords of the hundreds; they who had the jurisdiction of hundreds, and held the hundred courts.

JUSTICES OF THE JEWS. Justices appointed by Richard I. to carry into effect the laws and orders which he had made for regulating the money contracts of the Jews.

JUSTICES OF THE PAVILION (*justiciarii pavilionis*). Certain judges of court of piepoudre, of a most transcendent jurisdiction, authorized by the bishop of Winchester, at a fair held at St. Giles Hills near that city, by virtue of letters patent granted by Edw. IV. Prynne on 4 Inst. fol. 191.

JUSTICES OF THE PEACE. Public officers invested with judicial powers for the purpose of preventing breaches of the peace, and bringing to punishment those who have violated the law. 58 N. Y. 530. They have also a limited jurisdiction in civil matters.

JUSTICES OF TRAIL BASTON. A sort of justice in eyre, with large and summary powers, appointed by Edw. I. during his absence in war. Old. Nat. Brev. fol. 52; 12 Coke, 25. For derivation, see Cowell.

JUSTICIAR, or **JUSTICIER.** In old English law. A judge or justice. Baker, fol. 118; Cron. Angl. One of several persons learned in the law, who sat in the *aula regis*, and formed a kind of court of appeal in cases of difficulty.

The chief justiciar (*capitalis justicarius totius Angliae*) was a special magistrate, who presided over the whole *aula regis*, who was the principal minister of state, the second man in the kingdom, and, by virtue of his office, guardian of the realm in the king's absence. 3 Sharswood, Bl. Comm. 37; Spelman, 330, 331, 332; 2 Hawk. P. C. 6. The last who bore this title was Philip Basset, in the time of Hen. III.

JUSTICIARE, or **JUSTITIARE** (Law Lat. from *justicia* or *justitia*, justice). In old English law. To justice; to do justice or right; to compel a person to appear in court. Bracton, fol. 308b; 1 Reeves, Hist. Eng. Law, 125, 173, 174. Hence the writ of *justicies* (*q. v.*) *Justiciari*, to be justiced; to have justice. St. Marlb. c. 1.

JUSTICIARII ITINERANTES (Lat.) In English law. Justices who formerly went from county to county to administer justice. They were usually called justices in eyre, to distinguish them from justices residing at Westminster, who were called *justicii residentes*. Co. Litt. 293.

JUSTICIARII RESIDENTES (Lat.) In English law. Justices or judges who usually resided in Westminster. They were so called to distinguish them from justices in eyre. Co. Litt. 293.

JUSTICIARIUS, or **JUSTITIARIUS** (Law Lat.) In old English law. A justice. Magna Charta, 9 Hen. III. cc. 12, 13.

JUSTICIARY. Another name for a judge. In Latin, he was called *justicairius*, and in French *justicier*. Not used. Brac. Abr. "Courts" (A).

JUSTICIARY COURT. The chief criminal court of Scotland.

JUSTICIATUS (Law Lat. from *justiciare*, *q. v.*) In old English law. Judicature, prerogative, or jurisdiction. Blount.

JUSTICIES (from *justiciare*). In English law. A special writ, in the nature of a commission, empowering a sheriff to hold plea in his county court of a cause which he could not take jurisdiction of without this writ; *e. g.*, trespass *vi et armis* for any sum, and all personal actions above forty shillings. 1 Burn, Just. 449. So called from the Latin word *justicies*, used in the writ, which runs, "*praecipimus tibi quod justicies A. B.*," etc.; we command you to do A. B. right, etc. Bracton, lib. 4, tr. 6, c. 13; Kitch. Cts. 74; Fitzh. Nat. Brev. 117; 3 Sharswood, Bl. Comm. 3, 6.

JUSTIFIABLE HOMICIDE. Justifiable homicide is the necessary killing of another in the performance of the legal duty, or the exercise of a legal right, the slayer not being at all in fault. Homicide is justifiable (1) in the execution of a capital sentence pronounced by a competent court; (2) to prevent the commission of a felony; (3) to suppress a riot; (4) to effect the arrest of a felon, or prevent his escape after arrest; (5) where one who is feloniously assaulted, and who is himself without fault, kills his assailant to save himself from death or great bodily harm then appearing reasonably imminent. 1 Clark & Marshall, Crimes, 582.

JUSTIFICATION.

——**In Torts.** Facts making the act charged legally justifiable.

——**In Pleading.** The allegation of matter of fact by the defendant, establishing his legal right to do the act complained of by the plaintiff.

Justification admits the doing of the act charged as a wrong, but alleges a right to do it on the part of the defendant, thus denying that it is a wrong. Excuse merely shows reasons why the defendant should not make good the injury which the plaintiff has suffered from some wrong done. See "Avowry."

——**In Practice.** The proceeding by which sureties establish their ability to perform the undertaking of the bond or recognizance.

JUSTIFICATORS. A kind of compurgators, or those who, by oath, justified the innocence or oaths of others, as in the case of wagers of law.

JUSTIFYING BAIL. In practice. The production of bail in court, who there justify themselves against the exception of the plaintiff. See "Bail."

JUSTITIA (Lat.) Justice; a jurisdiction, or the office of a judge.

JUSTITIA DEBET ESSE LIBERA, QUIA nihil iniquius venali justitia; plena, quia justitia non debt claudicare; et celeris, quia dilatio est quaedam negatio. Justice ought to be unbought, because nothing is more hateful than venal justice; full, for justice ought not to halt; and quick, for delay is a kind of denial. 2 Inst. 56.

JUSTITIA EST CONSTANS ET PERPEtua voluntas ius suum cuique tribuendi. Justice is a steady and unceasing disposition to render to every man his due. Inst. 1. 1. pr.; Dig. 1. 1. 10.

JUSTITIA EST DUPLEX, VIZ., SEVERE puniens et vere praeveniens. Justice is double; punishing severely, and truly preventing.

JUSTITIA EST VIRTUS EXCELLENS, et Altissimo complacens. Justice is an excellent virtue and pleasing to the Most High. 4 Inst. 58.

JUSTITIA FIRMATUR SOLIUM. By justice the throne is established. 3 Inst. 140.

JUSTITIA NEMINI NEGANDA EST. Justice is to be denied to none. Jenk. Cent. Cas. 178.

JUSTITIA NON EST NEGANDA, NON differenda. Justice is not to be denied nor delayed. Jenk. Cent. Cas. 76.

JUSTITIA NON NOVIT PATREM NEC matrem; solum veritatem spectat justitia. Justice knows neither father nor mother; justice looks to truth alone. 1 Bulst. 199.

JUSTITIA PIEPOUDROUS. Speedy justice. Bracton, 333b.

JUSTITIUM. In civil law. A suspension or intermission of the administration of justice in courts; vacation time. Calv. Lex.

JUSTIZA. In old Spanish law. A supreme judge; a judicial magistrate peculiar to the kingdom of Aragon.

JUSTUM NON EST ALIQUEM ANTENAtum mortuum facere bastardum, qui pro tota vita sua pro legitimo habetur. It is not just to make a bastard after his death one elder born, who all his life has been accounted legitimate. 8 Coke, 101.

JUVENES. (Lat.) (Youths or young men.) In old English law. Inferior clerks of chancery, so called. Crabb's Hist. Eng. Law, 184.

JUXTA (Lat.) According to. 1 Ld. Raym. 415. The same as *secundum*, in the civil law. 12 Mod. 218.

Juxta formam statuti, according to the form of the statute. Reg. Orig. 16. The established phrase by which reference to a statute was expressed in old writs and records.

Juxta tenorem sequentem, according to the tenor following. 2 Salk. 417. A phrase used in the old books, when the very words themselves referred to were set forth. Id.; 1 Ld. Raym. 415.

Juxta conventionem, according to the covenant. Fleta, lib. 4, c. 16, § 6.

Juxta ratam, at or after the rate. Dyer, 82.

JUZGADO. In Spanish law. The collective number of judges that concur in a decree, and more particularly the tribunal having a single judge.

K

K. B. An abbreviation for "king's bench" (*q. v.*).

KAIA (Law Lat.) A key, kay, or quay. Spelman.

KAIAGIUM (Law Lat.) Kayage or wharfage. Spelman.

KAIN. In Scotch law. A payment of fowls, etc., reserved in a lease. It is derived from *canum*, a word used in ancient grants to signify fowls or animals deliverable by the vassal to his superior as part of the *reddendum*. Ersk. Inst. 11. 10. 32; 2 Ross, Lect. 236, 405.

KALENDAE. Rural chapters, or conventions of the rural deans and parochial clergy, which were formerly held on the calends of every month; hence the name. Par. Ant. 604.

KALENDAR. The original form of "calendar."

KALENDARIUM (Lat.) In civil law. A calendar; a book of accounts, memorandum book, or debt books; a book in which accounts were kept of moneys loaned out on interest. Dig. 32. 64. So called because the Romans used to let out their money, and receive the interest on the calends of each month. Calv. Lex.

KALENDS. See "Calends."

KARAXARE. (*Charaxare*, Law Lat.) In old records. To mark; to put down in characters or letters; to write. Spelman.

KARL (Saxon). In Saxon and old English law. A man; a serving man. *Buskarl*, a seaman. *Huskarl*, a house servant. Spelman.

KARRATA (Law Lat.) In old records. A cartload. Cowell; Blount.

KAST (Swed.) In Swedish law. Jettison; a literal translation of the Latin *jactus* (*q. v.*). Locc. de Jur. Mar. lib. 2, c. 7, § 1.

KAST GELD (Swed.) Contribution for a jettison; average. Locc. de Jur. Mar. lib. 2, c. 8, § 1.

KE (Law Fr. that). A corruption of *que*. *E volums ke meismes celes chartres*, and we will that these same charters. Conf. Cart. 25 Edw. I.

KEELAGE. The right of demanding money for the bottom of ships resting in a port or harbor. The money so paid is also called "keelage."

KEELHALE, KEELHAUL, or **KEEL-rake.** To drag a person under the keel of a ship by means of ropes from the yard- arms, a punishment formerly practiced in the navy. Enc. Lond.

KEELS. This word is applied, in England, to vessels employed in the carriage of coals. Jacob.

KEEP. A strong tower or hold in the middle of any castle or fortification, wherein the besieged make their last efforts of defense, was formerly, in England, called a "keep"; and the inner pile within the castle of Dover, erected by King Henry II. about the year 1153, was termed the "King's Keep"; so at Windsor, etc. It seems to be something of the same nature with what is called abroad a "citadel." Jacob.

KEEP AND BEAR ARMS. The words "bear arms" as used in the constitutional provision have reference to their military use, and the wearing of them in war or in peace, 3 Heisk. 194, and were not employed to mean wearing them about the person as part of the dress. 2 Hump. 158.

The "arms" are such as are needful to, and ordinarily used by the militia; weapons ordinarily used in battle, and such as are necessary and suitable to enable a free people to resist oppression, prevent usurpation, repel invasion, etc.; and include guns of every kind, swords, bayonets, pistols, etc.; with the right to load and shoot them and use them as such things are ordinarily used in battle. 53 Ga. 474; 1 Ga. 251; 31 Ark. 458; 11 La. Ann. 633; 35 Tex. 476.

KEEP OPEN. As applied to a place of business, implies "a readiness to carry on the usual business therein." 16 Mich. 477.

KEEP THE PEACE. To refrain from any breach of the peace (*q. v.*).

KEEPER. One who has the care, custody or superintendence of anything. 67 Ill. 590.

KEEPER OF THE FOREST (called, also, the "chief warden of the forest"). An officer who had the principal government over all officers within the forest, and warned them to appear at the court of justice seat on a summons from the lord chief justice in eyre. Manw. For. Law, pt. 1, p. 156; Jacob.

KEEPER OF THE GREAT SEAL. A judicial officer who is, by virtue of his office, a lord and a member of the privy council. Through his hands pass all charters, commissions, and grants of the crown, to be sealed with the great seal, which is under his keeping. The office was consolidated with that of lord chancellor by 5 Eliz. c. 18, and the lord chancellor is appointed by delivery of the great seal, and taking oath. 4 Inst. 87; 1 Hale, P. C. 171, 174; 3 Sharswood, Bl. Comm. 47.

KEEPER OF THE PRIVY SEAL. The officer through whose hands go all charters, pardons, etc., signed by the king before going to the great seal, and some which do not go there at all. He is of the privy council *virtute officii*. He was first called clerk of the privy seal, then guardian, then lord privy seal, which is his present designation. 12 Rich. II. c. 12; Rot. Parl. 11 Hen. IV.; St. 34 Hen. VIII. c. 4; 4 Inst. 55; 2 Sharswood, Bl. Comm. 347.

KEEPER OF THE TOUCH. The master of the assay in the English mint. 12 Hen. VI. c. 14.

KEEPING HOUSE. In English bankruptcy law. The act of a trader in withdrawing to a secret part of the house, refraining from going to business, or confining himself to the house for the purpose of avoiding his creditors. It is an act of bankruptcy. Robs. Bankr. 107 et seq.

KEEPING TERM. It was necessary for students in the Inns of Court to keep twelve terms, comprising three years, for admission to the English bar. Each term was three or four weeks, including one grand week. "Keeping the term" was to dine in the hall once in each grand week, and once in each of two half weeks. The terms so kept need not have been consecutive. Robinson, "Bench and Bar."

KENILWORTH EDICT. An edict or award between Henry III. and those who had been in arms against him; so called because made at Kenilworth Castle, in Warwickshire, A. D. 1266. It contained a composition of those who had forfeited their estates in that rebellion, which composition was five years' rent of the estates forfeited. Hale, Com. Law, 10, note (d).

KENNING TO A TERCE. In Scotch law. The ascertainment by a sheriff of the just proportion of the husband's lands which belongs to the widow in virtue of her terce or third. An assignment of dower by sheriff. Ersk. Inst. 11. 9. 50; Bell, Dict.

KENTLAGE. In maritime law. A permanent ballast, consisting usually of pigs of iron, cast in a particular form, or other weighty material, which, on account of its superior cleanliness, and the small space occupied by it, is frequently preferred to ordinary ballast. Abb. Shipp. 5.

KENTREF. The division of a county; a hundred in Wales. See "Cantred."

KEPT MISTRESS. The expression as used in modern times, amounts to the same thing as "concubine." 124 Ill. 616.

KERNES. Idlers; vagabonds.

KEYAGE. A toll paid for loading and unloading merchandise at a key or wharf.

KEYS.

——**Of Court.** In old Scotch law. Certain officers of courts. See "Claves Curiae."

——**Of the Isle of Man.** The twenty-four chief commoners, who form the local legislature. 1 Steph. Comm. 99.

——**In Old English Law.** A guardian or warden.

KEYUS. A guardian, warden, or keeper. Mon. Angl. tom. 2, p. 71.

KIDDER. An engrosser of corn to enhance its price.

KIDNAPPING. The forcible abduction or stealing away of a man, woman, or child from their own country, and sending them into another. 4 Bl. Comm. 219. Statutory definitions are somewhat different.

Actual force is not necessary; fraud or intimidation may suffice. 88 N. Y. 182. But the taking must be against the will of the person, and consent is a defense unless the person was incapable of consenting (8 N. H. 550; 25 N. Y. 272), or the consent was obtained by fraud (20 Ill. 315).

KILDERKIN. A measure of capacity, equal to eighteen gallons.

KILKETH. An ancient servile payment made by tenants in husbandry. Cowell.

KILL.

(1) A Dutch word, meaning the channel or bed of a stream. Sometimes applied to the stream itself. 1 Const. (N. Y.) 107.

(2) An Irish word, meaning church or cemetery. Enc. Lond.

KILLYTHSTALLION. A custom by which lords of manors were bound to provide a stallion for the use of their tenants' mares. Spelman.

KIN. Relation or relationship by blood or consanguinity. "The nearness of kin is computed according to the civil law." 2 Kent, Comm. 413.

KINDERGARTEN. A garden of children was devised by Froebel, a German philosopher and educator, to apply to a system which he elaborated for the instruction of children of very tender years. "Children's garden" ought to be taken in its allegorical sense. The child is a plant, the school is a garden and Froebel calls teachers "gardeners of children." 107 Cal. 190. Compayré, History of Pedagogy, § 537, Payne's translation.

KINDRED. Relations by blood.

Nature has divided the kindred of every one into three principal classes: (1) His children, and their descendants. (2) His father, mother, and other ascendants. (3) His collateral relations; which include, in the first place, his brothers and sisters, and their descendants; and, secondly, his uncles, cousins, and other relations of either sex, who have not descended from a brother or sister of the deceased. All kindred, then, are descendants, ascendants, or collaterals. A husband or wife of the deceased, therefore, is not his or her kindred. 14 Ves. 372. See Wood. Inst. 50; Ayliffe, Par. 325; Dane, Abr.; 2 Bl. Comm. 516, note; Poth. des Success. c. 1, art. 3.

It has been held to include an adopted child (4 S. W. 683), but not an illegitimate child (38 Me. 153).

KING. The chief magistrate of a kingdom, vested usually with the executive power.

The following table of the reigns of English and British kings and queens, commencing with the Conquest, is added, to assist the student in many points of chronology:

	Accession.
William I	1066
William II	1087
Henry I.	1100
Stephen	1135
Henry II.	1154
Richard I.	1189
John	1199
Henry III.	1216
Edward I.	1272
Edward II.	1307
Edward III.	1327
Richard II.	1377
Henry IV.	1399
Henry V.	1413
Henry VI.	1422
Edward IV.	1461
Edward V.	1483
Richard III.	1483
Henry. VII.	1485
Henry VIII.	1509
Edward VI.	1547
Mary	1553
Elizabeth	1558
James I.	1603
Charles I.	1625
Charles II.	1660
James II.	1685
William III.	1689
Anne	1702
George I.	1714
George II.	1727
George III.	1760
George IV.	1820
William IV.	1830
Victoria	1837
Edward VII.	1901
George V.	1910

KING GELD. A royal aid; an escuage (*q. v.*).

KING JAMES VERSION. A version of the Bible published in London in 1611. 245 Ill. 343.

KINGDOM. A country where an officer called a "king" exercises the powers of government, whether the same be absolute or limited. Wolff. Inst. § 994. In some kingdoms the executive officer may be a woman, who is called a "queen."

KING'S BENCH. See "Court of King's Bench."

KING'S CHAMBERS. Those portions of the seas, adjacent to the coasts of Great Britain, which are inclosed within headlands, so as to be cut off from the open sea by imaginary straight lines drawn from one promontory to another. Rapalje & L.

KING'S (or QUEEN'S) COUNSEL. Barristers or serjeants who have been called within the bar, and selected to be the king's counsel. They answer in some measure to the *advocati fisci*, or advocates of the revenue, among the Romans. They must not be employed against the crown without special leave, which is, however, always granted, at a cost of about nine pounds. 3 Sharswood, Bl. Comm. 27, note.

KING'S (or QUEEN'S) EVIDENCE. In English law. An accomplice in a felony, who, on an implied promise of pardon if he fully and fairly discloses the truth, is admitted as evidence for crown against his accomplices. See "State's Evidence."

KING'S (or QUEEN'S) SILVER. A fine or payment due to the king for leave to agree in order to levying a fine (*finalis concordia*). 2 Sharswood, Bl. Comm. 350; Dyer, 320, pl. 19; 1 Leon, 249, 250; 2 Leon, 56, 179, 233, 234; 5 Coke, 39.

KING'S WIDOW. In feudal law. A widow of the king's tenant. She was not allowed to remain without the king's consent, lest she thereby induct the king's enemy into the tenure.

KINSBOTE (from *kin*, and *bote*, a composition). In Saxon law. A composition for killing a kinsman. Anc. Inst. Eng. Index, "Bote."

KINTLIDGE. A term used by merchants and seafaring men to signify a ship's ballast. Merc. Dict.

KIRBY'S QUEST. An ancient record remaining with the remembrancer of the English exchequer. So called from being the inquest of John de Kirby, treasurer to Edward I.

KISSING THE BOOK. A ceremony used in taking the corporal oath; the object being, as the canonists say, to denote the assent of the witness to the oath in the form it is imposed. The witness kisses either the whole Bible, or some portion of it; or a cross, in some countries. See the ceremony explained in Oughton's Ordo, tit. lxxx.; Consitt. Courts pt. 3, sec. 1, § 3; Junkin, Oath, 173, 180; 2 Poth. Obl. (Evans Ed.) 234.

KLEPTOMANIA. A mania to steal.

KNAVE. A false, dishonest, or deceitful person. This signification of the word has arisen by a long perversion of its original meaning, which was merely "servant" or "attendant."

KNAVESHIP. In old English law. The portion of grain given to the servant in charge of a mill by tenants who were thirled to the mill.

KNIGHT. In English law. The next personal dignity after the nobility. Of knights there are several orders and degrees. The first in rank are Knights of the Garter, instituted by Edward III. in 1344; next follows, a knight banneret; then come knights of the Bath, instituted by Henry IV., and revived by George I.; and they were so called from a custom of bathing the night before their creation. The last order are knights bachelors, who, though the lowest, are yet the most ancient, order of knighthood; for we find that King Alfred conferred this order upon his son Athelstan. 1 Bl. Comm. 403. These are sometimes called "knights of the chamber," being such as are made in time of peace, and so called because knighted in the king's chamber, and not in the field. 2 Inst. 666. Of the more recently established orders are the knights of St. Michael and St. George, established in 1818, and the knights of St. Patrick, an Irish order instituted in 1763. These last have no rank in England. Knights were called *equites*, because they always served on horseback; *aurati*, from the gilt spurs they wore; and *milites*, because they formed the royal army, in virtue of their feudal tenures.

KNIGHTENCOURT. A court which used to be held twice a year by the bishop of Hereford.

KNIGHTENGUILD, or KNIGHTENGYLD. An ancient guild or society formed by King Edgar.

KNIGHTHOOD. The character, dignity, or status of a knight.

KNIGHTS BACHELORS. See "Knight."

KNIGHTS BANNERET. See "Knight."

KNIGHT'S FEE. The word is a compound word, and may comprehend many things. And therefore by the grant of this may pass land, meadow and pasture as parcel of it. Anciently so much of an inheritance in land as was sufficient to maintain a knight; and every man possessed of such an estate was obliged to be knighted, and attend the king in his wars, or pay a pecuniary sum in lieu thereof, called "escuage." In the time of Henry II. the estate was estimated at twenty pounds a year; but Lord Coke, in his time, states it to be an estate of six hundred and eighty acres. Co. Litt. 69, 69a.

According to Selden, however, it did not consist of land of a fixed extent or value, but it was as much as the king was pleased to grant, upon the condition of having the service of one knight. Tit. of Hon. part 2, §§ 17, 26.

KNIGHTS HOSPITALLERS. An order of knights that had their name from a hospital erected at Jerusalem for the use of pilgrims coming to the Holy Land, and dedicated to St. John Baptist. They were afterwards called "Knights of St. John of Jerusalem," and their first business was to provide for and protect such pilgrims as came to that hospital. Afterwards, being driven out of the Holy Land, they settled at Rhodes, and then at Malta, and were then called "Knights of Malta." Many of them came to England in the year 1100, where, in process of time, they became of so much wealth and dignity that their superior was the first lay baron, and had a seat among the lords in parliament.

KNIGHTS OF ST. MICHAEL AND ST. George. See "Knight."

KNIGHTS OF ST. PATRICK. See "Knight."

KNIGHTS OF THE BATH. See "Knight."

KNIGHTS OF THE CHAMBER. See "Knight."

KNIGHTS OF THE GARTER. See "Knight."

KNIGHTS OF THE POST. Hireling witnesses.

KNIGHTS OF THE SHIRE. In English law. Members of parliament representing counties or shires, in contradistinction to citizens or burgesses, who represent boroughs or corporations. So called because, as the terms of the writ for election still require, it was formerly necessary that he should be a knight. 2 Steph. Comm. 362, 392.

KNIGHT'S SERVICE. Upon the Norman conquest, all the lands in England were divided into knight's fees, in number above sixty thousand; and for every knight's fee a knight was bound to attend the king in his wars forty days in a year, in which space of time, before war was reduced to a science, a campaign was generally finished. If a man only held half a knight's fee, he was only bound to attend twenty days; and so in proportion. But this personal service, in process of time, grew into pecuniary commutations, or aids, until at last, with the military part of the feudal system, it was abolished at the restoration, by St. 12 Car. II. c. 24, 1 Bl. Comm. 410; 2 Bl. Comm. 62.

KNIGHTS TEMPLARS. An order of knights so called from having their first residence in some apartments adjoining the temple at Jerusalem; and their employment was to guard the roads for the security of pilgrims in the Holy Land. They came into England in the reign of Stephen, where they increased so much in wealth and power that they were considered dangerous to the state, and the order was suppressed in 1312.

KNOCK DOWN. To accept a bid at an auction. So called from the fact that the auctioneer's acceptance of the bid is commonly signified by a stroke of his hammer. "Knocked down" is synonymous with "struck off." 7 Hill (N. Y.) 439.

KNOW ALL MEN. In conveyancing. A form of public address, of great antiquity, and with which many written instruments, such as bonds, letters of attorney, etc., still commence.

KNOWINGLY. In pleading. The word "knowingly," or "well knowing," will supply the place of a positive averment, in an indictment or declaration, that the defendant knew the facts subsequently stated. If notice or knowledge be unnecessarily stated, the allegation may be rejected as surplusage. See Comyn, Dig. "Indictment" (G 6); 2 Cush. (Mass.) 577; 2 Strange, 904; 2 East, 452; 1 Chit. Pl. 367.

It implies actual personal knowledge. 4 Lans. (N. Y.) 22.

In an indictment it signifies that defendant, at the time of committing the offense charged, well knew what he was doing. 14 Fed. 127.

KNOWLEDGE. Positive assurance of a fact.

It is not synonymous with "information," 21 Pac. 39, or "notice," 1 So. 777, and differs from "belief" in degree. The act or state of knowing; clear perception of fact; that which is or may be known. Acquainted with things ascertained or ascertainable; specific information, 28 Ind. App. 367; a firm belief, 9 Gray (Mass.) 271. It implies actual notice as distinguished from constructive notice. 176 Iowa 316.

Believe; to exercise trust or confidence; to be persuaded upon evidence, arguments and deductions, or by other circumstances other than personal knowledge. 28 Ind. App. 367.

KNOWN MEN. A title formerly given to the Lollards. Cowell.

KNUCKLES. See "Brass Knuckles."

KURDI. A certain kind of shells used among many of the native tribes on the headwaters of the Niger, as currency or a circulating medium, about 2500 kurdi representing the value of a dollar. 27 Ill. 507.

KYTH. Kin or kindred.

L

L. S. An abbreviation for *locus sigilli* (*q. v.*).

When appearing in the margin of an instrument, in the place where a seal is usually found, indicate a seal. 36 Ill. 164; 155 Ill. 431. See Seal.

LA (Law Fr.) There. Dyer (Fr. Ed.) 62. *La ou*, there where; whereas. Kelham; Law Fr. Dict. *Que la*, until that. Kelham.

LA. (Fr.) The definite article feminine.

LA CONSCIENCE EST LA PLUS CHANgeante des regles. Conscience is the most changeable of rules.

LA LEY FAVOUR LA VIE D'UN HOME. The law favors a man's life. Y. B. Hen. VI. 51.

LA LEY FAVOUR L'INHERITANCE d'un home. The law favors a man's inheritance. Y. B. Hen. VI. 51.

LA LEY VOIT PLUS TOST SUFFER UN mischiefe que un inconvenience. The law would rather suffer a mischief than an inconvenience. Litt. § 231.

LABEL. A narrow slip of paper or parchment affixed to a deed or writing, hanging at or out of the same. This name is also given to an appending seal. See 2 Fed. 217. It is also a mark, or design, or statement placed on goods to indicate their origin or contents.

LABOR. Continued operation; work; manual work.

The act of doing what requires a painful exertion of strength; pains; toil; work to be done; work done; performance; exercise; motion with some degree of violence; childbirth; travail. 2 Ohio St. 400. Biddle's Lexicon.

LABOR A JURY. To tamper with a jury; to persuade jurymen not to appear. It seems to come from the meaning of "labor," to prosecute with energy, to urge; as, to labor a point. Dyer, 48; Hob. 294; Co. Litt. 157b; 14 & 20 Hen. VII. 30, 11. The first lawyer that came from England to practice in Boston was sent back for laboring a jury. Washb. Jud. Hist.

LABORARIIS. An ancient writ against persons who refused to serve and do labor, and who had no means of living; or against such as, having served in the winter, refused to serve in the summer. Reg. Orig. 189.

LABORER. One who performs manual labor, 10 Am. & Eng. R. R. Cas. 642, not requiring special knowledge or skill. 17 Ill. App. 200.

A contractor is not (6 Am. & Eng. R. R. Cas. 619), nor is an architect who merely provides plans (90 Pa. St. 47); but one who directs the work is (35 Pa. St. 42).

Clerks, bookkeepers, traveling salesmen, etc., are not. 44 Ill. App. 338, 341. See Servant.

LABORERS, STATUTES OF. St. 23 Edw. III., St. 12 Rich. II., 5 Eliz. c. 4, and St. 26 & 27 Vict. c. 125, making regulations as to laborers, servants, apprentices, etc.

LACHES (Fr. *lacher*, to slacken; to let slip). Negligent delay in enforcing a right.

"Inexcusable negligence and inattention to one's interests." 16 N. J. Eq. 242.

"Laches presupposes not only lapse of time, but also the existence of circumstances which render negligence imputable, and unless reasonable diligence is shown in the prosecution of a claim to equitable relief, the court, acting on the maxim *vigilantibus non dormientibus subveniunt leges*, will decline to interfere." Lindl. Partn. 902.

LACTA (Law Lat.) In old English law. Defect in the weight of money; lack of weight. This word and the verb *lactare* are used in an assize or statute of the sixth year of King John. Spelman.

LACUS (Lat.)

——**In the Civil Law.** A lake; a receptacle of water which is never dry. Dig. 43. 14. 1. 3.

——**In Old English Law.** Allay or alloy of silver with base metal. Fleta, lib. 1, c. 22, § 6. This word is not found either in Spelman or Cowell.

LADA (from Saxon *ladian*, to purge).

——**In Saxon Law.** A purgation, or mode of trial by which one purged himself of an accusation; as by oath or ordeal. Spelman.

A watercourse; a trench or canal for draining marshy grounds. In old English, a *lade* or *load*. Spelman; Cowell.

——**In Old English Law** (from Saxon *lathian*, to assemble). A court of justice; a lade or lath. Cowell.

LADE, or LODE. The mouth of a river.

LADEN IN BULK. Freighted with a cargo which is neither in casks, boxes, bales, nor cases, but lies loose in the hold, being defended from wet or moisture by a number of mats and a quantity of dunnage. Cargoes of corn, salt, etc., are usually so shipped. Wharton.

LADY. The title pertaining to a peer's wife, and (by courtesy) to the wife of a baronet or knight, and the daughter of an earl. Webster.

LADY COURT. The court of a lady of the manor.

LADY DAY. The feast of the Annunciation, March twenty-fifth.

LADY'S FRIEND. The name of a functionary in the British house of commons. When the husband sues for a divorce, or asks the passage of an act to divorce him from his wife, he is required to make a provision for her before the passage of the act. It is the duty of the lady's friend to see that such a provision is made. Macq. Husb. & Wife, 213.

LAESA MAJESTAS (Lat.) Lese majesty, or injured majesty; high treason. It is a phrase taken from the civil law, and anciently meant any offense against the king's person or dignity, defined by 25 Edw. III. c. 6. Glanv. lib. 5, c. 2; 4 Sharswood, Bl. Comm. 75; Bracton, 118. See "Crimen."

LAESIO ULTRA DIMIDIUM VEL ENORmis. In Roman law. The injury sustained by one of the parties to an onerous contract when he had been overreached by the other to the extent of more than one-half of the value of the subject matter; *e. g.*, when a vendor had not received half the value of property sold, or the purchaser had paid more than double value. Colq. Civ. Law, § 2094.

LAESIONE FIDEL, SUITS PRO. Suits or actions for breach of faith in civil contracts which the clergy, in the reign of Stephen, introduced into the spiritual courts, by means of which they took cognizance of many matters of contract belonging to the temporal courts under a pretext that faith solemnly plighted was of a religious nature, the breach of which belonged to the spiritual tribunals. 1 Reeve, Hist. Eng. Law, 74.

LAESIWERP. In old English law. A thing surrendered into the hands or power of another; a thing given or delivered. Spelman.

LAGA. The law.

LAGAN (Saxon *liggan, cubare*). Goods found at such a distance from shore that it was uncertain what coast they would be carried to, and therefore belonging to the finder. Bracton, 120. See "Ligan."

LAGE DAY. In old English law. A law day; a day of open court.

LAGE MAN. A juror. Cowell.

LAGU. In old English law. Law; also used to express the territory or district in which a particular law was in force, as *Dena lagu*, the district under Danish law, etc.

LAHLSLIT (Saxon). A breach of law. Cowell. A mulct for an offense, viz., twelve "ores." 1 Anc. Inst. Eng. 169.

LAHMAN (Saxon). A lawyer. Domesday Book, I. 189.

LAICUS. A layman.

LAIRESITE. The name of a fine imposed upon those who committed adultery or fornication. Tech. Dict.

LAITY. Those persons who do not make a part of the clergy. In the United States the division of the people into clergy and laity is not authorized by law, but is merely conventional.

LAKE. Fresh-water lakes are bodies of standing water distinguishable from rivers chiefly by the fact that they have no current. The fact that there is a current from a higher to a lower level does not make that a river which would otherwise be a lake, nor does a lake lose its distinctive character because there is a current in it for a certain distance tending towards a river which forms its outlet. Gould Waters, § 79.

LAMBETH DEGREE. A degree given by archbishop of Canterbury. 1 Sharswood, Bl. Comm. 381, note. Although he can confer all degrees given by the two universities, the graduates have many privileges not shared by the recipients of his degrees.

LAME DUCK. A lame duck is one who is unable to meet his contracts in the exchange,—an insolvent. Biddle, Br. 71.

The expression "lame duck" would be actionable if applied to a person on the stock exchange, because there it has acquired a particular meaning. 27 L. J. Ex. 412; 3 H. & N. 376; 31 L. T. O. S. 217.

LAMMAS LANDS. Lands over which there is a right of pasturage by persons other than the owner from about Lammas, or reaping time, until sowing time. Wharton.

LANCETI. In feudal law. Vassals who were obliged to work for their lord one day in the week, from Michaelmas to autumn, either with fork, spade, or flail, at the lord's option. Spelman.

LAND, or LANDS. A term comprehending any ground, soil, or earth whatsoever; as, meadows, pastures, woods, waters, marshes, furzes, and heath. 170 Ill. 256.

An estate of frank tenement at the least. Shep. Touch. 92.

In the technical sense, freeholds are not included within the word "lands." 3 Madd. 535. The term *terra* in Latin was used to denote land, from *terendo, quia vomere teritur* (because it is broken by the plough), and, accordingly, in fines and recoveries, land, *i. e., terra,* has been held to mean arable land. Salk. 256; Cowp. 346; Co. Litt. 4a; 11 Coke, 55a. But see Cro. Eliz. 476; 4 Bing. 90; Burton, Real Prop. 196. See, also, 2 P. Wms. 458, note; 5 Ves. 476; 20 Viner, Abr. 203.

"'Land' comprehendeth in its legal significance any ground, soil, or earth whatsoever. It includes, also, all castles, houses, or other buildings, for they consist of two things,—land, which is the foundation, and structures thereon. Land hath also, in its legal signification, an indefinite extent upwards, as well as downwards." 1 Inst. 4a; 2 P. Wms. 458, note; 5 Ves. 476; 20 Viner, Ired. L. (N. C.) 280; 49 Am. Dec. 379.

"Lands" is not as broad a term as "tenements" or "hereditaments," but has been sometimes used as including these. 1 Washb. Real Prop. 9. It does not include incorporeal hereditaments issuing out of lands. 5 Denio (N. Y.) 324.

LAND CEAP, or **LAND CHEAP** (land, and Saxon *ceapan*, to buy). A fine payable in money or cattle, upon the alienation of land, within certain manors and liberties. Cowell.

LAND CLAUSES CONSOLIDATION acts. Certain English statutes (8 Vict. C. 8, amended by 23 & 24 Vict. c. 106, and 32 & 33 Vict. c. 18), to provide legislative clauses in a convenient form for incorporation by reference in future special acts of parliament for taking lands, with or without the consent of their owners, for the promotion of railways, and other public undertakings. Mozley & W.

LAND COURT. The name of a court in the city of St. Louis, state of Missouri, having sole jurisdiction in St. Louis county in suits respecting lands, and in actions of ejectment, dower, partition.

LAND GABEL (or **GABLE**). A tax or rent issuing out of land. Blount. A ground rent. Cowell.

LAND-REEVE. A person whose business it is to overlook certain parts of a farm or estate; to attend not only to the woods and hedge timber, but also to the state of the fences, gates, buildings, private roads, driftways, and watercourses; and likewise to the stocking of commons, and encroachments of every kind, as well as to prevent or detect waste and spoil in general, whether by the tenants or others, and to report the same to the manager or land steward. Enc. Lond.

LAND TAX. A tax on beneficial proprietor of land. So far as a tenant is beneficial proprietor, and no farther, does it rest on him. It has superseded all other methods of taxation in Great Britain. Sugd. Vend. 268. It was first imposed in 1693, a new valuation of the lands in the kingdom having been made in 1692, which has not since been changed. In 1798 it was made perpetual, at a rate of four shillings in a pound of valued rent. See Enc. Brit. "Taxation"; Wharton.

LAND TENANT (commonly called *terre tenant*). He who actually possesses the land.

LAND WAITER. In English law. An officer of the custom house, whose duty is, upon landing any merchandise, to examine, taste, weigh, or measure it, and to take an account thereof. In some ports they also execute the office of a coast waiter. They are likewise occasionally styled "searchers," and are to attend and join with the patent searchers in the execution of all cockets for the shipping of goods to be exported to foreign parts; and, in cases where drawbacks on bounties are to be paid to the merchant on the exportation of any goods, they, as well as the patent searchers, are to certify the shipping thereof on the debentures. Enc. Lond.

LANDATOR. A witness to character.

LANDBOC (Saxon, from *land*, and *boc*, a writing). In Saxon law. A charter or deed by which lands or tenements were given or held. Spelman; Cowell; 1 Reeve, Hist. Eng. Law, 10; 1 Spence, Ch. 22.

LANDEFRICUS. A landlord.

LANDEGANDMAN (Saxon.) In old English law. A kind of customary tenant or inferior tenant of a manor. Spelman.

LANDIMER (Scotch; Lat. *agrimensor*). In old Scotch law. A measurer of land. Skene de Verb. Sign. voc. "Particata."

LANDIRECTA. In Saxon law. Services and duties laid upon all that held land, including the three obligations called "*trinoda necessitas*" (*q. v.*); *quasi* land rights. Cowell.

LANDLORD.

——**In Old Law.** The lord or proprietor of land, who, under the feudal system, retained the dominion or ultimate property of the feud, or fee of the land; while his grantee, who had only the possession and use of the land, was styled the "feudatory," or "vassal," which was only another name for the tenant or holder of it.

——**In Modern Law.** The lessor of lands or tenements.

Not the lord of the soil, but the person between whom and the tenant the relation of landlord and tenant exists. 2 Hurlst. & N. 450.

LANDMARK. A monument set up in order to ascertain the boundaries between two contiguous estates. For removing a landmark an action lies. 1 Thomas, Co. Litt. 787. See "Monument."

LANDS, TENEMENTS, AND HEREDITAments. The technical and most comprehensive description of real property, as "goods and chattels" is of personalty. Williams, Real Prop. 5.

LANDSLAGH. In Swedish law. A body of common law, compiled about the thirteenth century, out of the particular customs of every province; being analogous to the common law of England. 1 Bl. Comm. 66.

LANDWARD. (Scotch). Rural.

LANGUAGE. The medium for the communication of perceptions and ideas.

Spoken language is that wherein articulate sounds are used.

Written language is that wherein written characters are used, and especially the system of characters called "letters and figures."

LANGUIDUS (Lat.) In practice. The name of a return made by the sheriff when a defendant, whom he has taken by virtue of process, is so dangerously sick that to remove him would endanger his life or health.

LANGUOR. (Law Lat.) In old English practice. Sickness; a confirmed and lingering sickness, as distinguished from a transient indisposition. Bract. fol. 340, 344b, 352b, 357b. Skene defines it to be "a vehement sickness of body or of mind." Reg. Maj. lib. 1, c. 8. If it continued over a year, it was called *morbus sonticus*. Bract. fol. 344b.

LANIS DE CRESCENTIA WALLIAE traducendis absque custuma, etc. An ancient writ that lay to the customer of a port to permit one to pass wool without paying custom, he having paid it before in Wales. Reg. Orig. 279.

LANZAS. In Spanish law. A certain contribution in money paid by the grandees and other high officers in lieu of the soldiers they ought to furnish government in time of war.

LAPIS MARMORIUS. A marble stone about twelve feet long and three feet broad, placed at the upper end of Westminster Hall, where was likewise a marble chair erected on the middle thereof, in which the English sovereigns anciently sat at their coronation dinner, and at other times the lord chancellor. Rapalje & L.

LAPSE. To glide; to pass slowly, silently, or by degrees, to slip; to deviate from the proper path. Webster. See "Lapsed Devise"; "Lapsed Legacy."

——**In Ecclesiastical Law.** The transfer, by forfeiture, of a right to present or collate to a vacant benefice from a person vested with such right to another, in consequence of some act of negligence by the former. Ayliffe, Par. 331.

Upon six months' neglect of the patron, the right lapses to the bishop; upon six months' neglect of bishop, to archbishop; upon his six months' neglect, to king. The day on which the vacancy occurs is not counted, and the six months are calculated as a half-year. 2 Burn, Ecc. Law 355.

LAPSE PATENT. A patent issued to petitioner for land; a patent for which land to another party has lapsed through neglect of patentee. The lapse patent relates to date of original patent, and makes void all mesne conveyances. 1 Wash. (Va.) 39, 40.

LAPSED DEVISE. A devise which has lapsed, or does not take effect because of the death of devisee before testator.

LAPSED LEGACY. A legacy which, on account of the death of the legatee before the period arrives for the payment of the legacy, lapses or deviates from the course prescribed by the testator, and falls into the residuum. 1 Williams, Ex'rs, 1036.

A distinction exists between a lapsed devise and a lapsed legacy. A legacy which lapses does not fall into the residue unless so provided by the will, but descends to the heir at law; on the contrary, personal property passes by the residuary clause where it is not otherwise disposed of. 2 Bouv. Inst. 2154-2156. See "Lapsed Devise."

LARCENY. In criminal law. The wrongful and fraudulent taking and carrying away by one person of the mere personal goods of another from any place, with a felonious intent to convert them to his, the taker's, use, and make them his property without the consent of the owner. 2 East, P. C. 553; 4 Wash. C. C. (U. S.) 700.

In a recent English case, Mr. Baron Parke said that this definition, which was the most complete of any, was defective, in not stating what is the meaning of the word "felonious," which, he said, "may be explained to mean that there is no color of right or excuse for the act; and the 'intent' must be to deprive the owner, not temporarily, but permanently, of his property." 2 Car. & K. 942; 1 Den. C. C. 370; Templ. & M. C. C. 40. It is safer to be guided by the cases than by the definitions given by text writers.

Larceny is of two kinds, namely, simple larceny, and compound larceny.

(1) Simple larceny at common law is the taking and carrying away of the mere personal goods of another of any value, from any place, with a felonious intent to steal the same. This definition includes the following elements:

(a) The subject of the offense must be the mere personal goods of another, though, at common law, other things are made the subject of larceny by statute.

Therefore—

(i) It must be personal, as distinguished from real property.

(ii) It must be something which the law recognizes as property, and the subject of ownership.

(iii) It must be of some value; but the least value to the owner is sufficient.

(iv) It must be the property of another; but a special property in another is sufficient, even as against the general owner;

and mere possession is enough as against others than the owner.

(b) The goods must be taken, and the taking must be under such circumstances as to amount technically to a trespass.

(c) There must be some asportation or carrying away of the goods.

(d) Both the taking and the carrying away must be with a felonious intent,—an intent to steal,—existing at the time.

Grand and petit larceny. By statute in some jurisdictions, larceny has been divided, according to the value of the property or other circumstances, into grand larceny and petit larceny.

(2) Compound larcenies are larcenies committed under certain aggravating circumstances. Thus:

(a) At common law, robbery, which is larceny from the person or in the presence of another by violence, or by putting him in fear, is a compound larceny.

(b) By statute in most jurisdictions, it is a compound larceny, punished more severely than simple larceny, to steal (1) from the person of another, or (2) from a dwelling house, or certain other places specified in the statute. 2 Clark & Marshall, Crimes, 649.

LARCENY BY BAILEE. A statutory offense existing in one or two states, consisting of the fraudulent conversion of property by a bailee thereof. The offense is covered by the ordinary statutes against embezzlement.

LARGE (Law Fr.) Broad; the opposite of *estreyte*, strait or strict. *Pures et larges.* Britt. c. 34.

LARGURE. (*Largeur.* Law Fr. from *large.*) Breadth. According to the breadth and length. Britt. c. 63, c. 103.

LARGUS. (Lat.) Large; broad; comprehensive. Bract, fol. 37b.

LARON, or LARUN. In old English law. A thief; thieves. *Petits larons*, petty thieves. Britt. c. 29.

LAS PARTIDAS. The name of a code of Spanish law. It is sometimes called *las siete partidas*, or the seven parts, from the number of its principal divisions. It is a compilation from the civil law, the customary law of Spain, and the canon law. It was compiled by four Spanish jurisconsults, under the eye of Alphonso X., A. D. 1250, and published in Castille in 1263, but first promulgated as law by Alphonso XI., A. D. 1348. The maritime law contained in it is given in volume 6, Pardessus, Col. Mar. Law. He follows the edition of 1807, at Paris. It has been translated into English. Such of its provisions as are applicable are in force in Florida, Louisiana, and Texas. 1 Bl. Comm. 66; 1 White, New Recop. 354.

LASCIVIOUS CARRIAGE. In Connecticut. A term including those wanton acts between persons of different sexes, who are not married to each other, that flow from the exercise of lustful passions, and which are not otherwise punished as crimes against chastity and public decency. 2 Swift. Dig. 343; 2 Swift, Syst. 331.

Lascivious carriage may consist not only in mutual acts of wanton and indecent familiarity between persons of different sexes, but in wanton and indecent actions against the will and without the consent of one of them; as, if a man should forcibly attempt to pull up the clothes of a woman. 5 Day (Conn.) 81.

LASHITE, or LASHLITE. A kind of forfeiture during the government of the Danes in England. Enc. Lond.

LAST (Law Lat. *lastus, lestus*). In English law. A burden; a weight or measure of various commodities, as of pitch, hides, fish, corn, wool, leather, etc. Cowell.

LAST ANTECEDENT. The last antecedent is the last word which can be made an antecedent, without impairing the meaning of a sentence. 190 Mich. 313.

LAST COURT. A court held by the twenty-four jurats in the marshes of Kent, and summoned by the bailiffs, whereby orders were made to lay and levy taxes, impose penalties, etc., for the preservation of the said marshes. Enc. Lond.

LAST HEIR. He to whom the lands come if they escheat for want of lawful heirs, viz., sometimes the lord of whom the lands are held, sometimes the king. Bracton, lib. 5, c. 17.

LAST RESORT. A court from which there is no appeal is called the "court of last resort."

LAST SICKNESS. That of which a person dies. The last sickness includes the whole of the sickness of which the person dies, no matter of how long duration. 8 Me. 167.

The expenses of this sickness are generally entitled to a preference in payment of debts of an insolvent estate. Civ. Code La. art. 3166.

To prevent impositions, the statute of frauds requires that nuncupative wills shall be made during the testator's last sickness. Roberts, Frauds, 556; 20 Johns. (N. Y.) 502.

LAST WILL (Lat. *ultima voluntas*). A disposition of real estate, to take effect after death.

It is strictly distinguishable from "testament," which is applied to personal estate (1 Williams, Ex'rs, 6, note [b] Am. Notes); but the words are generally used together, "last will and testament," in a will, whether real or personal estate is to be disposed of.

Those words do not, of themselves, revoke a former will, 9 Moo. P. C. 131; 5 D. G. M. & G. 704; 23 L. J. Ch. 838; but may be confirmatory proof of an intention to revoke. 16 Bea. 173; 22 L. J. ch. 185; 1 W. R. 3. See "Will."

LASTAGE, or LESTAGE. A custom exacted in some fairs and markets to carry things bought whither one will. But it is more accurately taken for the ballast or lading of a ship. Also custom paid for wares sold by the last, as herrings, pitch, etc.

LATA CULPA DOLO AEQUIPARATUR. Gross negligence is equal to fraud.

LATE. Recently; last. 7 Cal. 226. Defunct. 17 Ala. 190.

LATELY. This word has been held to have "a very large retrospect, as we say 'lately deceased' of one dead ten or twenty years." 2 Show. 294.

LATENS (Lat. from *latere,* to lie hid). Latent; hidden; not apparent.

LATENT AMBIGUITY. One which does not appear from the words of an instrument, but only from the application of the words to the subject matter. See 117 U. S. 221.

A latent ambiguity may arise from the fact that there are two or more persons or objects to which a perfect description will apply. Thus, where lands were conveyed to one by name, and it appeared that there were two of that name, it was held a latent ambiguity. 131 Mass. 179. Or it may arise from a misdescription not apparent on the face of the instrument, whereby two persons or objects or none at all are described. 117 U. S. 221.

A mere mistake in a description, whereby it is made to apply to something other than was intended, is not an ambiguity. 11 Johns. (N. Y.) 201.

LATENT DEED. One kept for twenty years or more in a man's scrutoire or strong box, accompanied by no distinctive possession. 7 N. J. Law, 177.

LATENT DEFECT. One not discoverable by external examination. 13 N. Y. 9.

The term is used both in personal injury law, and in the law of sales.

——**In Personal Injury Law.** An employee (108 Ind. 286) and *a fortiori* a third person is not bound to take notice of latent defects, while the owner of the defective appliance is bound to use due care and diligence to discover the same, if it can be done by any appropriate test (Wood, Mast. & S. § 368); while a carrier is held to every test dictated by the utmost possible care (119 Mass. 412).

——**In the Law of Sales.** A seller is bound to disclose latent defects known to him, but does not impliedly warrant against latent defects except under peculiar circumstances, as where the goods are of his own manufacture. 21 N. Y. 552.

LATERAL SUPPORT. The support of land by the adjoining land; so called in contradistinction from "subjacent support," that of the soil beneath. The right to such lateral support exists as a natural incident of real property (25 N. J. Law, 356; 122 Mass. 199); and an adjoining landowner who, by excavation on his own land, removes such lateral support, is liable in damages (135 Mass. 150; 57 Minn. 493).

LATERARE (Law Lat. from *latus,* a side). In old English law. To lie sideways; literally, to side; the opposite of *capitare,* to head or abut. Cowell. See "Capitare."

LATHE, or LATH (Law Lat. *laestrum* or *leda*). A division of certain counties in England, intermediate between a county or shire and a hundred, sometimes containing three or four hundreds, as in Kent and Sussex. Cowell. But in Sussex the word used for this division is "rape." 1 Bl. Comm. 116. There was formerly a lathe reeve or bailiff in each lathe. Id. This division into lathes continues to the present day. See 12 East, 244. In Ireland, the lathe was intermediate between the tything and the hundred. Spencer, Ireland. See Termes de la Ley.

LATHE REEVE, LATHREVE, or LEIDgreve (Saxon.) An officer under the Saxon government, who had authority over a lathe. Cowell; 1 Bl. Comm. 116.

LATIDEMEO. In Spanish law. The tax paid by the possessor of land held by quit rent or *emphyteusis* to the owner of the estate, when the tenant alienates his right in the property.

LATIFUNDIUM (Lat.) In civil law. Great or large possessions; a great or large field; a common. Ainsworth. A great estate made up of smaller ones (*fundus*), which began to be common in the latter times of the empire. Schmidt, Civ. Law, Introd. p. 17.

LATIFUNDUS (Lat. *late possidens*). A possessor of a large estate made up of smaller ones. Du Cange.

LATIN. An important language in the law; being the language not only of the civil and canon law, but of the early European codes, of much of the ancient common law of England and Scotland, and of a large proportion of the public, civil and maritime law of later times. The Code and Institutes exhibit the language in the periods of its decline and decay, and the Latin of most of the subsequent law belongs to that peculiar and technical dialect known as *low Latin,* or *law Latin.* The value of the Latin has always consisted in its peculiar expressiveness as a language of law terms, in its superior conciseness which has made it the appropriate language of law maxims, and in its almost unlimited capacity of condensation by means of abbreviations and contractions, many of which are retained in popular use at the present day.

LATINI JUNIANI (Lat.) In Roman law. A class of freedmen (*libertini*) intermediate between the two other classes of freedmen called, respectively, "*Cives Romani*" and "*Dediticii.*" Slaves under thirty years of age at the date of their manumission, or manumitted otherwise than by *vindicta*, *census*, or *testamentum*, or not the quiritary property of their manumissors at the time of manumission, were called "*Latini.*" By reason of one or other of these three defects, they remained slaves by strict law even after their manumission, but were protected in their liberties first by equity, and eventually by the *Lex Junia Norbana*, A. D. 19, from which law they took the name of "*Juniani*" in addition to that of "*Latini.*" Brown.

LATITAT (Lat. he lies hid.) In English law. The name of a writ calling a defendant to answer to a personal action in the king's bench. It derives its name from a supposition that the defendant lurks and lies hid, and cannot be found in the county of Middlesex (in which the said court is holden) to be taken there, but is gone into some other county, and therefore requiring the sheriff to apprehend him in such other county. Fitzh. Nat. Brev. 78.

LATITATIO. In the civil law and old English practice. A lying hid; lurking, or concealment of the person. Dig. 42. 4. 7. 5; Bracton, fol. 126.

LATRO. In the civil and old English law. A robber. Dig. 50. 16. 118; Fleta, lib. 1, c. 38, § 1. A thief.

LATROCINATION. The act of robbing; a depredation.

LATROCINIUM. Larceny or theft. Reg. Orig. 268b.

A thing stolen. Fleta, lib. 1, c. 38, § 7.

The liberty of infangthef, or privilege of judging and executing thieves.

LATROCINY. Larceny.

LAUDARE.

——**In Civil Law.** To name; to cite or quote; to show one's title or authority. Calv. Lex.

——**In Feudal Law.** To determine or pass upon judicially. Feud. lib. 1, tit. 22. *Laudamentum*, the finding or award of a jury. 2 Bl. Comm. 285.

LAUDATIO. In Roman law. Testimony adduced in favor of the character of an accused person. Halifax, Anal. bk. 3, c. 13.

LAUDATOR. A witness to the good character of an accused person.

LAUDEMIUM, or LAUDATIOREM (Lat. *a laudando domino*). A fiftieth part of the purchase money, or (if no sale) of the value of the estate paid to the landlord (*dominus*) by a new *emphyteuta* on his succession to the estate, not as heir, but as singular successor. Voet. Com. ad Pand. lib. 6, tit. 3, §§ 26-35; Mackeld. Civ. Law, 297.

——**In Old English Law.** The tenant paid a *laudemium* or acknowledgment money to new landlord on the death of the old. See Blount, "Acknowledgment Money."

LAUDUM. An arbitrament or award. Rapalje & L.

——**In Old Scotch Law.** Sentence or judgment; dome or doom. 1 Pitc. Crim. Tr. pt. 2, p. 8.

LAUGEMANNI (Law Lat.) Lords of manors, according to Coke's definition, who writes the word *launemanni*. Domesday Book; Co. Litt. 5a.

LAUGHE. Frank pledge. 2 Reeve, Hist. Eng. Law, 17.

LAUGHLESMAN (Saxon). In old English law. An outlaw. Bracton, fol. 125.

LAUNCEGAY. A kind of offensive weapon, now disused, and prohibited by 7 Rich. II. c. 13.

LAUNCH. The movement by which a ship or boat descends from the shore into the water when she is first built, or afterwards.

A large, long, low, flat-bottomed boat. Mar. Dict. The long-boat of a ship; a small vessel employed to carry the cargo of a large one to and from the shore.

LAUS DEO (Lat.) Praise be to God. An old heading to bills of exchange. West, Symb. pt. 1, lib. 2, § 660.

LAVOR NUEVA (Spanish). In Spanish law. A new work. Las Partidas, pt. 3, tit. 32, lib. 1.

LAW. That which is established; a rule or method of action.

A distinction is to be observed in the outset between the abstract and the concrete meaning of the word. In the broadest sense which it bears when used in the abstract law, it is the science which treats of the theory of government.

In a stricter sense, but still in the abstract, it is the aggregate of those rules and principles enforced and sanctioned by the governing power in a community, and according to which it regulates, limits, and protects the conduct of members of the community. In the abstract sense, it includes the decisions of courts. 164 Wis. 228.

Used in the concrete, law is a rule of action prescribed by a superior. 1 Bl. Comm. 38.

In a stricter concrete sense, it is a rule of civil conduct prescribed by the supreme power in a state. 1 Steph. Comm. 25.

In the strictest sense, it is a statute; a rule prescribed by the legislative power. 10 Pet. (U. S.) 18.

Used without an article prefixed, the abstract sense is generally intended; with an article, the sense is usually concrete.

Law is used to denote the system of the common law, as distinguished from equity. See "Equity."

It is also used in contradistinction to "fact." See "In Law."

Arbitrary law. A law or provision of law so far removed from considerations of abstract justice that it is necessarily founded on the mere will of the law-making power, so that it is rather a rule established than a principle declared. The principle that an infant shall not be bound by his contract is not arbitrary; but the rule that the limit of infancy shall be twenty-one years, not twenty nor twenty-two, is arbitrary.

The term is also sometimes used to signify an unreasonable law,—one that is in violation of justice.

Irrevocable laws. All laws which have not in their nature or in their language some limit or termination provided are, in theory, perpetual; but the perpetuity is liable to be defeated by subsequent abrogation. It has sometimes been attempted to secure an absolute perpetuity by an express provision forbidding any abrogation. But it may well be questioned whether one generation has power to bind their posterity by an irrevocable law. See this subject discussed by Benth. Works, vol. 2, pp. 402-407; and see Dwarr. St. 479.

Municipal law is a system of law proper to any single state, nation, or community. See "Municipal Law."

Penal law is one which inflicts a penalty for its violation.

Positive law is the system naturally established by a community, in distinction from "natural law."

A private law is one which relates to private matters which do not concern the public at large.

A prospective law or statute is one which applies only to cases arising after its enactment, and does not affect that which is already past.

A public law is one which affects the public, either generally or in some classes.

A retrospective law or statute is one that turns backward to alter that which is past, or to affect men in relation to their conduct before its enactment. These are also called "retroactive law." In general, whenever a retroactive statute would take away vested rights, or impair the obligation of contracts, it is in so far void. 3 Dall. (Pa.) 391. But laws which only vary the remedies, or merely cure a defect in proceedings otherwise fair, are valid. 10 Serg. & R. (Pa.) 102, 103; 15 Serg. & R. (Pa.) 72; 2 Pet. (U. S.) 380, 627; 8 Pet. (U. S.) 88; 11 Pet. (U. S.) 420. See "Ex Post Facto."

For matters peculiar to the following classes of laws, see their several titles: "Adjective Law"; "Brehon Law"; "Bretts and Scotts, Laws of the"; "Canon Law"; "Civil Law"; "Code"; "Colonial Laws"; "Commercial Law"; "Consuetudinary Law"; "Corn Laws"; "Criminal Law"; "Crown Law"; "Ecclesiastical Law"; "Ex Post Facto Law"; "Fecial Law"; "Feudal Law"; "Foreign Law"; "Game Laws"; "Hindu Law"; "Insolvency"; "Laws of Oleron"; "Military Laws"; "Retrospective Law"; "Rhodian Laws."

LAW ALWAYS CONSTRUETH THINGS to the best. Wingate, Max. p. 720, max. 193.

LAW BORGH. In old Scotch law. A pledge or surety for appearance.

LAW BURROWS. In Scotch law. Security for the peaceful behavior of a party; security to keep the peace. This process was much resorted to by the government of Charles II. for political purposes.

LAW CHARGES. In Louisiana. Costs.

LAW COURT OF APPEALS. In American law. An appellate tribunal, in the state of South Carolina, for hearing appeals from the courts of law.

LAW DAY. The day fixed in a mortgage or defeasible deed for the payment of the debt secured. 24 Ala. (N. S.) 149; 10 Conn. 280.

The phrase formerly marked the time when all legal rights were lost by the mortgagor's default. There is now no such time, until foreclosure; and the term serves only to engender confusion. 21 N. Y. 343, 345, 365, 367.

——**In Old English Law.** Law day or lage day denoted a day of open court; especially the more solemn courts of a county or hundred. The court leet, or view of frankpledge.

LAW FRENCH. From the time of William the Norman down to that of Edward III., all public proceedings and documents in England, including the records of the courts, the arguments of counsel, and the decisions of the judges, were in the language of the Norman French. After Latin and English were substituted in the records and proceedings, however, the cases and decisions continued until the close of the seventeenth century to be reported in French; the first reports published in England being those of Style, in 1658. The statutes of the reign of Henry III., and some of the subsequent reigns, are partly or wholly in this language; but English was substituted in the reign of Henry VII. Of the law treatises in French, the Mirrour and Britton, and the works of Littleton, may be mentioned.

LAW LATIN. Edward III. substituted the Latin language for the Norman French in the records, and the English in other proceedings. The Latin was used by virtue of its being the language of scholars of all European nations; but, in order to adapt it to the purposes of the profession, the English terms of legal art in most frequent use were Latinized by the simple addition of a Latin termination, and the diverse vocabulary thus collected was arranged in English idioms. But this barbarous dialect commended itself by a semblance of scholarly sound, and more by the precision which attaches to technical terms that are never used in popular language. During the time of Cromwell, English was used; but with the restoration Latin was reinstated, and held its place till 4 Geo. II. c. 26, when it was enacted that, since the common people ought to know what was done for and against them, proceedings should be in English. It was found, however, that certain technical terms had become so fixed that, by a subsequent act, such words were allowed to continue in use. 6 Geo. II. c. 14. Hence a large class of Latin words are still in use of which *nisi prius, habeas corpus, lis pendens,* are examples. Consult 3 Bl. Comm. 318-323, and as to particular words and phrases, Termes de la Ley; Taylor; Law French & Law Latin Dict.; Kelham; Du Cange.

LAW LIST. An annual English publication of a *quasi* official character, comprising various statistics of interest in connection with the legal profession. It includes (among other information) the following matters: A list of judges, queen's counsel, and serjeants at law; the judges of the county courts; benchers of the inns of court; barristers, in alphabetical order; the names of counsel practicing in the several circuits of England and Wales; London attorneys; county attorneys; officers of the courts of chancery and common law; the magistrates and law officers of the city of London; the metropolitan magistrates and police; recorders; county court officers and circuits; lord lieutenants and sheriffs; colonial judges and officers; public notaries. Mozley & W.

LAW LORDS. Peers in the British parliament who have held high judicial office, or have been distinguished in the legal profession. Mozley & W.

LAW MARTIAL. The military law or articles of war.

LAW MERCHANT.

——**In England.** The general body of commercial usages in matters relative to commerce. Blackstone calls it the "custom of merchants," and ranks it under the head of the particular customs of England, which go to make up the great body of the common law. 1 Bl. Comm. 75. Since, however, its character is not local, nor its obligation confined to a particular district, it cannot with propriety be considered as a "custom" in the technical sense. 1 Steph. Comm. 54. It is a system of law which does not rest exclusively on the positive institutions and local customs of any particular country, but consists of certain principles of equity and usages of trade which general convenience and a common sense of justice have established, to regulate the dealings of merchants and mariners in all the commercial countries of the civilized world. 3 Kent, Comm. 2.

——**In the United States.** The law merchant of England, consisting of the body of usages, the decisions of the English courts construing the same, and statutes confirming and modifying the same prior to the Declaration of Independence, are a part of the common law of the United States. 19 Ill. 598; 1 Morris (Iowa) 128.

LAW OF ARMS. That law which gives precepts and rules concerning war, how to make and observe leagues and truce, to punish offenders in the camp, and such like. Cowell; Blount. Now more commonly called the "law of war."

LAW OF CITATIONS. In Roman law. An act of Valentinian, passed A. D. 426, providing that the writings of only five jurists, viz., Papinian, Paul, Gaius, Ulpian, and Modestinus, should be quoted as authorities. The majority was binding on the judge. If they were equally divided, the opinion of Papinian was to prevail, and in such a case, if Papinian was silent upon the matter, then the judge was free to follow his own view of the matter. Brown.

LAW OF MARQUE. Law authorizing reprisal against the goods of another, where justice cannot be had in ordinary course. See "Letter of Marque and Reprisal."

LAW OF NATIONS. See "International Law."

LAW OF NATURE. That law which God, the sovereign of the universe, has prescribed to all men, not by any formal promulgation, but by the internal dictate of reason alone. It is discovered by a just consideration of the agreeableness or disagreeableness of human actions to the nature of man, and it comprehends all the duties which we owe either to the Supreme Being, to ourselves, or to our neighbors; as, reverence to God, self-defense, temperance, honor to our parents, benevolence to all, a strict adherence to our engagements, gratitude, and the like. Ersk. Prac. Scotch Law, 1. 1. 1. See Ayliffe, Pand. tit. 2, p. 2; Cicero, de Leg. lib. 1.

The primitive laws of nature may be reduced to six, namely, comparative sagacity, or reason; self-love; the attraction of the sexes to each other; the tenderness of parents towards their children; the religious sentiment; sociability. See "Jus Naturale."

LAW OF THE FLAG. The flag is used, in the prosecution of commerce upon the high seas, as a symbol of nationality. The nationality of a ship is determined by the flag which it carries. A ship, navigating under the flag and pass of a foreign country, is to be considered as bearing the national character of the country under whose flag she sails. Under what is called, in international law, "the law of the flag," a shipowner who sends his vessel into a foreign port gives notice by his flag to all who enter into contracts with the ship-master, that he intends the law of that flag to regulate those contracts, and that they must either submit to its operation or not contract with him or his agent at all. 185 Ill. 144.

LAW OF THE LAND. The law of the land has been defined to be the general law; a law which hears before it condemns; which proceeds upon inquiry, and renders judgment only after trial. The meaning is that every citizen shall hold his life, liberty, property, and immunities, under the protection of the general rules which govern society. Everything, which may pass under the form of an enactment is not, therefore, to be considered the law of the land. 207 Ill. 368.

Lord Coke says that the words "by the law of the land," mean by the course and process of law by indictment or presentment of good and lawful men, where such deeds be done in due manner or by original writ of the common law. 20 Barb. (N. Y.) 199.

Due process of law (*q. v.*). 2 Yerg. (Tenn.) 50; 6 Pa. St. 86; 4 Hill (N. Y.) 140.

LAW OF THE ROAD. The rules of law regulating the conduct of persons on highways to avoid collision with or other injury to other persons thereon. It cannot be stated in rules, but is a general duty to observe in speed, vigilance, etc., what due and ordinary care may require under the circumstances of the particular case. An illustration is that meeting vehicles should each turn to the right of the center of the road (28 Mich. 32; 195 Pa. St. 190), though nonobservance may be justified by circumstances (9 App. Div. [N. Y.] 68), and the rule does not apply as between vehicles and pedestrians (147 Mo. 679)..

LAW OF THE STAPLE. See "Law Merchant."

LAW SPIRITUAL. The ecclesiastical law, or law Christian. Co. Litt. 344.

LAW WORTHY. Being entitled to, or having the benefit and protection of, the law.

LAWFUL. Legal; that which is not contrary to law; that which is sanctioned or permitted by law; that which is in accordance with law. 101 Ill. 215. The terms "lawful," "unlawful," and "illegal" are used with reference to that which is in its substance sanctioned or prohibited by the law. The term "legal" is occasionally used with reference to matters of form alone. Thus, an oral agreement to convey land, though void by law, is not properly to be said to be unlawful, because there is no violation of law in making or in performing such an agreement; but it is said to be not legal, or not in lawful form, because the law will not enforce it, for want of that written evidence required in such cases.

LAWFUL AGE. Majority; usually the age of twenty-one years.

LAWFUL MAN. A freeman, unattainted, and capable of bearing oath; a *legalis homo*.

LAWFUL MONEY. Money which is a legal tender in payment of debts; *e. g.*, gold and silver coined at the mint. 2 Salk. 446; 5 Mod. 7; 3 Ind. 358; 2 How. (U. S.) 244; 3 How. (U. S.) 717; 16 Ark. 83. See 1 Hempst. (U. S.) 236.

LAWING OF DOGS. Mutilating the forefeet of mastiffs, to prevent them from running after deer. 3 Bl. Comm. 71.

LAWLESS COURT. An ancient local English court, said to have been held in Essex once a year, at cock crowing, without a light or pen and ink, and conducted in a whisper.

LAWLESS MAN. An outlaw.

LAWS OF OLERON. A maritime code said to have been drawn up by Richard I. at the Isle of Oleron, whence its name. See Fed. Cas. vol. 30, Appendix, for a copy.

LAWSUIT. An action at law, or litigation.

LAWYER. One skilled in the law.

A popular term for a person engaged in the practice of law. See "Attorney."

LAY.

——**In English Law.** That which relates to persons or things not ecclesiastical. In the United States, the people are not by law divided, as in England, into ecclesiastical and lay. The law makes no distinction between them.

——**In Pleading.** To state or to allege. The place from whence a jury are to be summoned is called the "venue," and the allegation in the declaration of the place where the jury is to be summoned is, in technical language, said to "lay the venue." 3 Steph. Comm. 574; 3 Bouv. Inst. note 2826. To state at the conclusion of a declaration the amount of damages which the plaintiff claims is to "lay damages."

LAY CORPORATION. A corporation composed of lay persons, or for lay purposes. Angell & A. Corp. 28-30; 1 Bl. Comm. 470.

According to the line of demarcation drawn by Blackstone, all corporations other than ecclesiastic are called "lay corporations." They are created for a variety of temporal or secular purposes, and are according to their object either eleemosynary or civil. 1 Fletcher Cyclopedia Corporations 85.

LAY DAMAGES. See "Lay."

LAY DAYS. In maritime law. The time allowed to the master of a vessel for loading and unloading the same. In the absence of any custom to the contrary, Sundays are to be computed in the calculation of lay days at the port of discharge. 10 Mees. & W. 331. See 3 Esp. 121. See "Demurrage."

LAY FEE. A fee held by ordinary feudal tenure, as distinguished from the ecclesiastical tenure of frankalmoign, by which an ecclesiastical corporation held of donor. The tenure of frankalmoign is reserved by St. 12 Car. II., which abolished military tenures. 1 Bl. Comm. 101.

LAY IMPROPRIATOR. Lay rector, to whom the greater tithes are reserved, the lesser going to the vicar. 1 Burn, Ecc. Law, 75, 76.

LAY OUT. This has always been regarded as an appropriate expression for the location and establishment of a highway. 133 Mass. 329.

LAY PEOPLE. Jurymen. Finch, Law, 381.

LAYING THE VENUE. See "Lay."

LAYMAN. In ecclesiastical law. One who is not an ecclesiastic nor a clergyman.

LAZARET, or LAZARETTO. A place, selected by public authority, where vessels coming from infected or unhealthy countries are required to perform quarantine.

LE CONGRES. A species of proof on charges of impotency in France, *coitus coram testibus*. Abolished A. D. 1677. Rapalje & L.

LE CONTRAT FAIT LA LOI. The contract makes the law.

LE GUIDON (or **LE GUIDON DE LA mer**). The title of a celebrated French treatise on the law of insurance, being the earliest work extant on that subject. It was prepared for the use of the merchants of Rouen at least as early as the sixteenth century, but its author's name has not been preserved. It was published by Cleirac in 1671, in his collection entitled *Les Us et Coutumes de la Mer*. 3 Kent, Comm. 346; 1 Buer, Ins. Introd. Disc. Lect. ii.

LE LEY DE DIEU ET LE LEY DE TERre sont tout un, et l'un et l'autre preferre et favour le common et publique bien del terre. The law of God and the law of the land are all one, and both preserve and favor the common and public good of the land. Keilw. 191.

LE LEY EST LE PLUS HAUT ENHERItance que le roy ad, car par le ley, il mesme et touts ses sujets sont rules, et si le ley ne fuit, nul roy ne nul enheritance serra. The law is the highest inheritance that the king possesses; for by the law both he and all his subjects are ruled; and, if there were no law, there would be neither king nor inheritance.

LE ROI LE VEUT. The king assents. This is the formula used in England, and formerly in France, when the king approved of a bill passed by the legislature. 1 Toullier, Dr. Civ. note 52.

LE ROI S'AVISERA. The king will consider of it. This phrase is used by the English monarch when he gives his dissent to an act passed by the lords and commons. The same formula was used by the late king of the French for the same purpose. 1 Toullier, Dr. Civ. note 52. See "Veto."

LE ROI VEUT EN DELIBERER. The king will deliberate on it. This is the formula which the late French king used when he intended to veto an act of the legislative assembly. 1 Toullier, Dr. Civ. note 42.

LE ROY (or **LA REINE**) **REMERCIE SES loyal sujets, accepte leur benevolence, et aussi le veut** (Law Fr.) The king (or queen) thanks his (or her) loyal subjects, accepts their benevolence, and wills it to be so. The form of the royal assent to a bill of declaring the use of a fine; *i. e.*, specifying to whose use the fine shall inure before the supply. 1 Bl. Comm. 184.

LEADING A USE. A term applied to deeds declaring the use of a fine; that is, specifying to whose use the fine shall inure before the fine is levied. 2 Bl. Comm. 363. See "Deed."

LEADING CASE. A case decided by a court of last resort, which decides some particular point in question, and to which reference is constantly or frequently made, for the purpose of determining the law in similar questions.

Many elements go to the constitution of a case as a leading case, among which are the priority of the case, the character of the court, the amount of consideration given to the question, the freedom from collateral matters or questions. The term is applied to cases as leading either in a particular state, or at common law. A very convenient means of digesting the law upon any subject is found to be the selection of a leading case upon the subject, and an arrangement of authorities illustrating the questions decided. See Bennett & H. Lead. Cr. Cas.; Smith, Lead. Cas.; Hare & W. Sel. Dec.; White & T. Lead. Cas.; and a variety of others.

LEADING COUNSEL. That one of two or more counsel employed on the same side in a cause who has the principal management of the cause. So called as distinguished from the other, who is called the "junior counsel."

LEADING QUESTION. In practice. A question which puts into the witness' mouth the words to be echoed back, or plainly suggests the answer which the interrogating party desires or expects. 164 Ill. App. 612; 7 Serg. & R. (Pa.) 171; 4 Wend. (N. Y.) 247. In that case the examiner is said to lead him to the answer. It is not always easy to determine what is or is not a leading question.

These questions cannot, in general, be put to a witness in his examination in chief. 3 Bin. (Pa.) 130; 6 Bin. (Pa) 483; 1 Phil. Ev. 221; 1 Starkie, Ev. 123. But, in an examination in chief, questions may be put to lead the mind of the witness to the subject of inquiry; and they are allowed when it appears the witness wishes to conceal the truth, or to favor the opposite party, or where, from the nature of the case, the mind of the witness cannot be directed to the subject of inquiry without a particular specification of such subject. 1 Campb. 43; 1 Starkie, 100.

In cross-examinations, the examiner has generally the right to put leading questions. 1 Starkie, Ev. 132; 3 Chit. Prac. 892; Rosc. Civ. Ev. 94; 3 Bouv. Inst. notes 3203, 3204.

LEAGUE. A measure of length, which consists of three geographical miles. The jurisdiction of the United States extends into the sea a marine league. See Acts Congress June 5, 1794 (1 Story, U. S. Laws, 352), and April 20, 1818 (3 Story, U. S. Laws, 1694); 1 Wait, State Papers, 195.

——**In Criminal Law.** A conspiracy to do an unlawful act. The term is but little used.

——**In International Law.** An agreement between states. Leagues between states are of several kinds: First, leagues offensive and defensive, by which two or more nations agree not only to defend each other, but to carry on war against their common enemies. Second, defensive, but not offensive, obliging each to defend the other against any foreign invasion. Third, leagues of simple amity, by which one contracts not to invade, injure, or offend the other. This usually includes the liberty of mutual commerce and trade, and the safeguard of merchants and traders in each other's domain. Bac. Abr. "Prerogative" (D 4). See "Confederacy;" "Conspiracy;" "Truce;" "War."

LEAKAGE. The waste which has taken place in liquids, by their escaping out of the casks or vessels in which they were kept.

By Act March 2, 1799, § 59 (1 Story, U. S. Laws, 625), it is provided that there be an allowance of two per cent. for leakage on the quantity which shall appear by the gauge to be contained in any cask of liquors subject to duty by the gallon, and ten per cent. on all beer, ale, and porter in bottles, and five per cent. on all other liquors in bottles, to be deducted from the invoice quantity, in lieu of breakage; or it shall be lawful to compute the duties on the actual quantity, to be ascertained by tale, at the option of the importer, to be made at the time of entry.

LEAL. Loyal; that which belongs to the law.

LEALTE (Law Fr.) Legality; the condition of a *legalis homo*, or lawful man. LL. Gul. Conq. lib. 16.

LEAP YEAR. See "Bissextile."

LEARNED IN THE LAW. A qualification usually prescribed by statute for judges and district attorneys. Admission to the bar is the only and conclusive test of legal learning within such a requirement. 12 S. D. 16.

LEASE. A contract by which a person owning or controlling lands or tenements permits another to occupy the same for a period less than that to which the right of the lessor extends. The person so permitting the occupation of premises is called the "lessor"; the person contracting for possession is called the "lessee." Regarded with respect not to the making of the lease, but of the relation created thereby, the parties are known respectively as "landlord" and "tenant."

LEASE AND RELEASE. A species of conveyance much used in England, consisting theoretically of two instruments, but which are practically united in the same instrument.

It was invented by Sergeant Moore, soon after the enactment of the statute of uses. It is thus contrived: A lease, or rather bargain and sale upon some pecuniary consideration for one year, is made by the tenant of the freehold to the lessee or bargainee. This, without any enrollment, makes the bargainor stand seised to the use of the bargainee, and vests in the bargainee the use of the term for one year, and then the statute immediately annexes the possession. Being thus in possession, he is capable of receiving a release of the freehold and reversion, which must be made to the tenant in possession, and accordingly the next day a release is granted to him.

The lease and release, when used as a conveyance of the fee, have the joint operation of a single conveyance. 2 Bl. Comm. 339; 4 Kent, Comm. 482; Co. Litt. 207; Cruise, Dig. tit. 32, c. 11.

LEASEHOLD. The estate held by virtue of a lease.

For the various kinds of leasehold estates, see "Tenancy."

LEASING MAKING. In Scotch law. Verbal sedition, viz., slanderous and untrue speeches to the disdain, reproach, and contempt of his majesty, his council and proceedings, etc. Bell, Dict.; Ersk. Inst. 4. 4. 29.

LEAUTE (Law Fr.) Legality; sufficiency in law. Britt. c. 109.

LEAVE. To give or dispose of by will. "The word 'leave,' as applied to the subject matter, *prima facie* means a disposition by will." 10 East, 438.

LEAVE AND LICENSE. A defense to an action in trespass setting up the consent of the plaintiff to the trespass complained of.

LEAVE OF COURT. Permission granted by the court to do something which, without such permission, would not be allowable.

LECHERWITE, LAIRWITE, or LEGERwite. A fine for adultery or fornication, anciently paid to the lords of certain manors. 4 Inst. 206.

LECTOR DE LETRA ANTIQUA. In Spanish law. The person duly authorized by the government to read and decipher ancient documents and titles, in order to entitle them to legal effect in courts of justice.

The importance of the functions of this officer caused the queen of Spain to issue an ordinance on the 2d of July, 1838, ordering that no person should be permitted to exercise it unless he justified, first, that he was a man of good character; second, that he was twenty-five years of age, and submitted to a strict examination, justifying that he was acquainted with the Latin language, and especially with the idioms of it used in writings and documents of the middle ages, also with the Romance or ancient Castilian, the Limousin, used in the ancient provinces of Arragon, paleology, Spanish history and chronology; and, third, that he could decipher the ancient manuscripts preserved in the archives of Spain, the ancient modes of writing, and the changes introduced in it by time. This examination to be conducted under the superintendence of the *Chefe Politico*, and the *proces verbal* forwarded to the queen, together with the observations of the board of examiners. Escriche, Dic. Raz.

LEDE. (Law Fr.) Grievous. Kelham. Afflicted; impaired or damaged in appearance.

LEDENGE. (Law Fr.) Damaged. Kelham.

LEDER. (L. Fr.) To hurt. *Ledera;* shall shall hurt. *Ledez;* hurt. Kelham.

LEDGER BOOK. In ecclesiastical law. The name of a book kept in the prerogative courts in England. It is considered as a roll of the court, but, it seems, it cannot be read in evidence. Bac. Abr.

LEDGREVIUS (Law Lat.) In old English law. A lathe reeve, or chief officer of lathe. Spelman.

LEES. (Law Fr. from *lesser*, to let.) A lease.

A leash by which dogs were led. Yearb. M. 18 Hen. VI. 6.

LEET. In English law. The name of a court of criminal jurisdiction, formerly of much importance, but latterly fallen into disuse. See "Court Leet."

LEGA (Law Lat.) In old English law. The alloy of money. Cowell; Blount.

A termination of the names of places in old records, supposed by Spelman to signify "place."

LEGABILIS. In old English law. That which may be bequeathed. Cowell.

LEGACY. A gift by last will. The term is more commonly applied to money or personal property, although sometimes used with reference to a charge upon real estate. 2 Williams, Ex'rs, 947; 5 Term R. 716; 1 Burrows, 268; 7 Ves. 391, 522.

——**Absolute Legacy.** One given without condition, to vest immediately. 1 Vern. 254; 2 Vern. 181; 5 Ves. 461; 19 Ves. 86; Comyn, Dig. "Chancery" (I 4).

——**Additional Legacy.** One given to a legatee to whom a legacy has already been given. It may be either by an increase in a codicil of a prior legacy given in the will, or by another legacy added to that already given by the will. 6 Mod. 31; 2 Ves. Jr. 449; 3 Mer. 154.

——**Alternative Legacy.** One by which the testator gives one of two or more things, without designating which.

——**Conditional Legacy.** A bequest whose existence depends upon the happening or not happening of some uncertain event, by which it is either to take place or be defeated. 1 Rop. Leg. (3d Ed.) 645.

——**Demonstrative Legacy.** A bequest of a certain sum of money with reference to a particular fund for payment. Williams, Ex'rs, 995.

——**General Legacy.** One so given as not to amount to a bequest of a particular thing or money of the testator, distinguished from all others of the same kind. 1 Rop. Leg. (3d Ed.) 170.

——**Indefinite Legacy.** A bequest of things which are not enumerated or ascertained as to numbers or quantities; as, a bequest by a testator of all his goods, all his stocks in the funds. Lowndes, Leg. 84; Swinb. Wills, 485; Ambl. 641; 1 P. Wms. 697.

——**Lapsed Legacy.** One which, in consequence of the death of the legatee before the testator, or before the period for vesting, has never vested.

——**Legacy for Life.** One in which the legatee is to enjoy the use of the legacy for life.

——**Model Legacy.** A bequest accompanied with directions as to the mode in which it should be applied for the legatee's benefit; for example, a legacy to Titius to put him an apprentice. 2 Vern. 431; Lowndes, Leg. 151.

——**Pecuniary Legacy.** One of money. Pecuniary legacies are most usually general legacies, but there may be a specific pecuniary legacy; for example, of the money in a certain bag. 1 Rop. Leg. 150, note.

——**Residuary Legacy.** A bequest of all the testator's personal estate not otherwise effectually disposed of by his will. Lowndes, Leg. 10; Bac. Abr. "Legacies" (I).

——**Specific Legacy.** A bequest of a specified part of the testator's personal estate, distinguished from all others of the same kind. 3 Beav. Rolls, 349.

LEGAL Opposed (1) to that which is unlawful; (2) to that which is equitable; (3) to that which is actual. See "In Law."

As a prefix, it ordinarily implies sufficient in point of law; thus, legal consideration, legal debts, legal defenses, etc.

LEGAL ASSETS. Such property of a testator in the hands of his executor as is liable to debts in temporal courts, and to legacies in the spiritual by course of law. Equitable assets are such as are liable only by help of a court of equity. 2 Williams, Ex'rs, 1408-1431 (Am. Notes). No such distinction exists in Pennsylvania. 1 Ashm. (Pa.) 347. See Story, Eq. Jur. § 551; 2 Jarm. Wills, 543.

LEGAL DEFINITIONS. Legal definitions are, for the most part, inductive generalizations derived from our juridical experience; and, in order to be complete and adequate, they must sum up the results of all that experience, as they are to be found in the special cases that belong to the class to be defined. 1 Grant's Cases (Pa.) 328.

LEGAL ESTATE. One the right to which may be enforced in a court of law.

It is distinguished from an equitable estate, the right to which can be established only in a court of equity. 2 Bouv. Inst. note 1688.

The party who has the legal title has alone the right to seek a remedy for a wrong to his estate, in a court of law, though he may have no beneficial interest in it. The equitable owner is he who has not the legal estate, but is entitled to the beneficial interest.

The person who holds the legal estate for the benefit of another is called a "trustee." He who has the beneficiary interest and does not hold the legal title is called the "beneficiary," or, more technically, the *cestui que trust*.

When the *cestui que trust* has a claim, he must enforce his right in a court of equity, for he cannot sue any one at law in his own name (1 East, 497; 8 Term R. 332; 1 Saund. 158, note 1; 2 Bing. 20), still less can he in such court sue his own trustee. (1 East, 497).

LEGAL INTEREST. That rate of interest which is allowed by law in the absence of an express contract.

LEGAL MALICE. Constructive or implied malice. See "Malice."

LEGAL MEMORY. See "Memory."

LEGAL REPRESENTATIVE. Sometimes used for "personal representative" (*q. v.*).

LEGAL REVERSION. In Scotch law. The period within which a proprietor is at liberty to redeem land adjudged from him for debt. Bell, Dict.

LEGAL TENDER. Lawful money which may be tendered in payment of debt. Under the laws of the United States, gold coin is full legal tender, silver coin is legal tender in payments of not to exceed five dollars, the minor coins in payments not to exceed twenty-five cents. Treasury notes, etc., are full legal tender except in payment of duties on imports and interest on the public debt. U. S. Rev. St., § 3584 et seq.

LEGALIS HOMO (Lat.) A person who possesses all his civil rights; a lawful man; one who stands *rectus in curia*, not outlawed nor infamous. In this sense are the words *probi et legales homines*.

LEGALIS MONETA ANGLIAE. Lawful money of England. 1 Inst. 207.

LEGALITY, or LEGALNESS. Lawfulness.

LEGALIZATION. The act of making lawful.

By legalization is also understood the act by which a judge or competent officer authenticates a record, or other matter, in order that the same may be lawfully read in evidence. See 102 Mass. 127.

LEGALLY. See "Legal."

LEGANTINE CONSTITUTIONS. The name of a code of ecclesiastical laws, enacted in national synods, held under legates from Popes Gregory IX. and Clement IV., in the reign of Hen. III., about the years 1220 and 1268. I Bl. Comm. 83. Burns says, 1237 and 1268. 2 Burn, Ecc. Law, 30d.

LEGARE (Lat.) In the civil and old English law. To bequeath; to leave or give by will; to give in anticipation of death. In Scotch phrase, to legate. Bracton, fol. 18b. Applied to real, as well as personal, property.

LEGATARIUS. (Lat.) In the civil law. One to whom a thing is bequeathed; a legatee, or legatary. Bract. fol. 40. In old European law. A legate, messenger, or envoy. Spelman.

LEGATARIUS PARTIARIUS. A legatee to whom the testator has in his will instructed his heir to give a definite share of his universal succession.

This kind of legacy was called a legacy of partition (legatum partitionis), because the legatee divided the inheritance with the heir. Inst. 2, 23, 5.

LEGATARY. One to whom anything is bequeathed; a legatee. This word is sometimes, though seldom, used to designate a legate or nuncio.

LEGATEE. The person to whom a legacy is given. See "Legacy."

LEGATES. Legates are extraordinary ambassadors sent by the pope to Catholic countries to represent him, and to exercise his jurisdiction. They are distinguished from the ambassadors of the pope who are sent to other powers.

Legates a latere hold the first rank among those who are honored by a legation. They are always chosen from the college of cardinals, and are called *a latere,* in imitation of the magistrates of ancient Rome, who were taken from the court, or side of the emperor.

Legati missi are simple envoys.

Legati nati are those who are entitled to be legates by birth. See "A Latere."

LEGATION. An embassy; a mission. All persons attached to a foreign legation, lawfully acknowledged by the government of this country, whether they are ambassadors, envoys, ministers, or attaches, are protected by the act of April 30, 1790 (1 Story, U. S. Laws, 83), from violence, arrest, or molestation. 1 Dall. (Pa.) 117; 1 Wash. C. C. (U. S.) 232; 2 Wash. C. C. (U. S.) 435; 4 Wash. C. C. (U. S.) 531; 11 Wheat. (U. S.) 467; 1 Miles (Pa.) 366; 1 Nott & McC. (S. C.) 217; 1 Baldw. (U. S.) 240; Wheat. Int. Law, 167. See "Ambassador"; "Arrest"; "Privilege."

LEGATORY. The third part of a freeman's personal estate, which by the custom of London, in case he had a wife and children, the freeman might always have disposed of by will. Bac. Abr. "Customs of London" (D 4).

LEGATOS VIOLARE CONTRA JUS GENtium est. It is contrary to the law of nations to do violence to ambassadors. Branch, Princ.

LEGATUM.

——**In Civil Law.** A legacy; a gift left by will. Dig. 3136. A gift left by a deceased person to be executed by the heir. Inst. 2. 20. 1.

——**In Common Law.** A legacy.

——**In Old Ecclesiastical Law.** A soul scot or a gift to the church. Cowell.

LEGATUM MORTE TESTATORIS TANtum confirmatur, sicut donatio inter vivos traditione sola. A legacy is confirmed by the death of the testator, in the same manner as a gift from a living person is by delivery alone. Dyer, 143.

LEGATUS, REGIS VICE FUNGITUR A quo destinatur, et honorandus est sicut ille cujus vicem gerit. An ambassador fills the place of the king by whom he is sent, and is to be honored as he is whose place he fills. 12 Coke, 17.

LEGEM AMITTERE. To lose one's law; to become infamous or outlaw.

LEGEM ENIM CONTRACTUS DAT. The contract makes the law. 22 Wend. (N. Y.) 215, 233.

LEGEM FACERE (Law Lat.) In old English law. To make law, or oath. *Legem vadiare,* to wage law. *Legem habere,* to have law; to be capable of giving evidence upon oath. *Legem amittere,* to lose the law, or privilege of being admitted to oath. *Legem terrae amittentes perpetuam infamiae notam inde merito incurrunt,* they who lose the *lex terrae* (law of the land) justly incur therefor the perpetual brand of infamy. 3 Inst. 221. In Branch's Maxims, the peculiar meaning of *lex terrae,* in this passage, has been misapprehended.

LEGEM FERRE (Lat.) In the Roman law. To propose a law to the people for their adoption. Heinec. Ant. Rom. lib. 1, tit. 2; Tayl. Civ. Law, 9.

LEGEM HABERE. To have one's law; to be a legal person.

LEGEM JUBERE (or **SCISCERE).** In the Roman law. To give consent and authority to a proposed law; to make or pass it. Tayl. Civ. Law, 9.

LEGEM TERRAE AMITTENTES PERpetuam infamiae notam inde merito incurrunt. Those who do not preserve (or who lose) the law of the land, thence justly incur the ineffaceable brand of infamy. 3 Inst. 221.

LEGEM VADIARE. To wage one's law.

LEGES (Lat.)

——**In Civil Law.** Laws proposed by a magistrate of the senate, and adopted by the whole people in *comitia centuriata.* See "Populiscitum"; "Lex."

——**In English Law.** Laws.

Leges scriptae, written or statute laws. Hale's Hist. Com. Law, 1, 2.

Leges non scriptae, unwritten or customary laws; the common law, including general customs, or the common law, properly so called; and also particular customs of certain parts of the kingdom, and those particular laws that are, by custom, observed only in certain courts and jurisdictions. 1 Bl. Comm. 67. "These parts of law are therefore styled *leges non scriptae,* because their original institution and authority are not set down in writing, as acts of parliament are, but they receive their binding power and the force of laws by long and immemorial usage." 1 Steph. Comm. 40, 66. It is not to be understood, however, that they are merely oral, for they have come down to us in reports and treatises.

LEGES ANGLIAE SUNT TRIPARTITAE: jus commune, consuetudines, ac decreta comitiorum. The laws of England are threefold: Common law, customs, and decrees of parliament.

LEGES FIGENDI ET REFIGENDI CONsuetudo est periculosissima. The custom of making and unmaking laws is a most dangerous one. 4 Coke, pref.

LEGES HUMANAE NASCUNTUR, VIvunt, et moriuntur. Human laws are born, live, and die. 7 Coke, 25; 2 Atk. 674; 11 C. B. 767; 1 Bl. Comm. 89.

LEGES NATURAE PERFECTISSIMAE sunt et immutabiles; humani vero juris conditio semper in infinitum decurrit, et nihil est in eo quod perpetuo stare possit. Leges humanae nascuntur, vivunt, moriuntur. The laws of nature are most perfect and immutable; but the condition of human law is an unending succession, and there is nothing in it which can continue perpetually. Human laws are born, live, and die. 7 Coke, 25.

LEGES NON VERBIS SED REBUS SUNT impositae. Laws are imposed on things, not words. 10 Coke, 101.

LEGES POSTERIORES PRIORES CONtrarias abrogant. Subsequent laws repeal prior conflicting ones. 2 Rolle, 410; 11 Coke, 626, 630.

LEGES SUUM LIGENT LATOREM. Laws should bind the proposers of them. Fleta, bk. 1, c. 17, § 11.

LEGES TABELLARIAE (Lat.) Roman laws regulating the mode of voting by ballot (*tabella*). 1 Kent, Comm. 232, note.

LEGES VIGILANTIBUS, NON DORMIENtibus subveniunt. The laws aid the vigilant, not the negligent. Fanning; Dunham; 5 Johns. Ch. (N. Y.) 122, 145; Toole; Cook; 16 How. Pr. (N. Y.) 142, 144.

LEGIBUS SOLUTUS (Lat.) Released from the laws; not bound by the laws. An expression applied in the Roman civil law to the emperor. Calv. Lex.; 3 Gibb. Rom. Emp. 157.

LEGIBUS SUMPTIS DESINENTIBUS, lege naturae utendum est. When laws imposed by the state fail, we must act by the law of nature. 2 Rolle, 298.

LEGIS CONSTRUCTIO NON FACIT INjuriam. The construction of law does no wrong. Co. Litt. 183.

LEGIS INTERPRETATIO LEGIS VIM OBtinet. The construction of law obtains the force of law. Branch, Princ.

LEGIS MINISTER NON TENETUR, IN executione officii sui, fugere aut retrocedere. The minister of the law is not bound, in the execution of his office, either to fly or retreat. 6 Coke, 68.

LEGISLATIVE POWER. The authority, under the constitution, to make laws, and to alter or repeal them.

LEGISLATOR. One who makes laws; a member of the legislature (*q. v.*).

LEGISLATORUM EST VIVA VOX, REbus et non verbis, legem imponere. The voice of legislators is a living voice, to impose laws on things, and not on words. 10 Coke, 101.

LEGISLATURE. That body of men in the state which has the power of making laws.

LEGISPERITUS (Law Lat.) A person skilled or learned in the law; a lawyer or advocate. Feud. lib. 2, tit. 1.

LEGIT UT CLERICUS. He reads as a clerk. The answer made by the ordinary to the question *legit vel non*, importing that the prisoner could read, and was entitled to benefit of clergy. Dyer, 205.

LEGIT VEL NON? Does he read or not? The question asked of the ordinary on the trial, whether a prisoner claiming benefit of clergy could read. 1 Salk. 61.

LEGITIM (called, otherwise, "Bairn's Part of Gear"). In Scotch law. The legal share of father's free movable property, due on his death to his children. If widow and children are left, it is one-third; if children alone, one-half. Ersk. Inst. 3. 9. 20; 4 Bell, H. L. Sc. 286.

LEGITIMACY. The state of being born in wedlock; that is, in a lawful manner.

LEGITIMATE. That which is according to law; as, legitimate children are lawful children, born in wedlock, in contradistinction to bastards; legitimate authority, or lawful power, in opposition to usurpation.

LEGITIMATION. The act of giving the character of legitimate children to those who were not so born. This was formerly effected (1) By subsequent marriage of the parents, Hunter, Introd. Rom. Law, 29, introduced by Constantine (A. D. 335), abrogated by Zeno (A. D. 476), and revived and amplified by Justinian (A. D. 529). (2) By offering the natural child to the curia (per oblationem curiae); making a son a decurio, or a member of the class that furnished the magistrates in provincial towns, or giving a daughter in marriage to a decurio. (3) By rescript of the emperor; introduced by Justinian.

Legitimation of bastards, either by subsequent marriage or by an act of the government (*Rescriptum principiis*), is nothing but a legal equalization of certain children illegitimately begotten with legitimate children. 96 Cal. 560; Bar on International Law, p. 434.

LEGITIMATION PER SUBSEQUENS matrimonium. The legitimation of a bastard by the subsequent marriage of his parents. Bell, Dict.

LEGITIME. In civil law. That portion of a parent's estate of which he cannot disinherit his children without a legal cause.

The Civil Code of Louisiana declares that donations *inter vivos* or *mortis causa* cannot exceed two-thirds of the property of the disposer, if he leaves at his decease a legitimate child; one-half if he leaves two children; and one-third if he leaves three, or a greater number. Under the name of "children" are included descendants of whatever degree they may be. It must be understood that they are only counted for the child they represent. Civ. Code La. art. 1480.

LEGITIME IMPERANTI PARERE NEcesse est. One who commands lawfully must be obeyed. Jenk. Cent. Cas. 120.

LEGITIMUS. Lawful; legitimate. *Legitimus haeres et filius est quem nuptiae demonstrant*, a lawful son and heir is he whom the marriage points out to be lawful. Bracton, fol. 63.

LEGO (Lat.) In Roman law. I bequeath. A common term in wills. Dig. 30. 36. 81 et seq.

LEGULEIUS (Lat.) A person skilled in law (*in legibus versatus*); one versed in the forms of law. Calv. Lex.; Cicero de Orat. i. 55.

LEIDGREVE. In Saxon law. An officer who had jurisdiction over a lathe. Cowell.

LEIPA (Law Lat.) In old English law. A fugitive or runaway. LL. Hen. I. c. 43. Spelman. Possibly the root of "elope."

LENDER. He from whom a thing is borrowed; the bailor of an article loaned.

LEOD (Saxon). People; a people; a nation. Spelman, voc. "Leodes."

LEODES (Law Lat.; from Saxon *Leod*). In old European law. A vassal, or liege man (*vassallus; homo ligeus*). Spelman.

Service (*servitium*). Id.; Marculf. lib. 1, form. 40.

A were or weregild (*wera, wergildum*). Spelman.

LEOHT GESCEOT. A tax for lighting the church.

LEONINA SOCIETAS (Lat.) An attempted partnership, in which one party was to bear all the losses, and have no share in the profits. This was a void partnership in Roman law; and, apparently, it would also be void as a partnership in English law, as being inherently inconsistent with the notion of partnership. Dig. 17. 2. 29. 2; Brown.

LEPRA. (Lat.) In old English law. Leprosy. *Leprosus;* a leper. Fleta, lib. 6, c. 40, § 3.

LEPROSO AMOVENDO. A writ which anciently lay to remove a leper who attended at church or public meetings, to the danger and annoyance of the inhabitants.

LES FICTIONS NAISSENT DE LA LOI, et non la loi des fictions. Fictions arise from the law, and not law from fictions.

LES LOIS NE SE CHARGENT DE PUNIR que les actions exteriures. Laws do not undertake to punish other than outward actions. Montesq. Esp. de Lois, bk. 12, c. 11; Broom, Leg. Max. (3d London Ed.) 279.

LESE MAJESTY, *Laese Majesty.* (Law Fr. *leze majest.*) The old English and Scotch translation of *læsa majestas*, or high treason. 2 Reeves' Hist. Eng. Law, 6. See "Leze Majesty."

LESION. In civil law. A term used to signify the injury suffered, in consequence of inequality of situation, by one who does not receive a full equivalent for what he gives in a commutative contract.

The remedy given for this injury is founded on its being the effect of implied error or imposition; for in every commutative contract equivalents are supposed to be given and received. Code La. art. 1854. Persons of full age, however, are not allowed, in point of law, to object to their agreements as being injurious, unless the injury be excessive. Poth. Obl. p. 1, c. 1, sec. 1, art. 3, § 4. But minors are admitted to restitution, not only against any excessive inequality, but against any inequality whatever. Id. § 5; Code La. art. 1858. See "Fraud"; "Guardian"; "Sale."

LESPEGEND (Saxon). A lessor thane or baron. Const. Canuti Regis de Foresta, art. 2. Spelman prefers to write it "lesthegen."

LESSEE. He to whom a lease is made; he who holds an estate by virtue of a lease. See "Lease."

LESSOR. He who grants a lease. See "Lease."

LESTAGE, or **LASTAGE** (Saxon *last*, burden). A custom for carrying things in fairs and markets. Fleta, lib. 1, c. 47; Termes de la Ley.

LESWES. *Lesues.* Pastures. Domesday. Co. Litt. 4b. A term often inserted in old deeds and conveyances. Cowell.

LET. Hindrance; obstacle; obstruction. To lease; to grant the use and possession of a thing for compensation. It is the correlative of "hire." See "Hire."

LETRADO (Spanish). In Spanish law. An advocate. White's New Recop. bk. 1, tit. 1, c. 1, § 3, note.

LETTER. He who, being the owner of a thing, lets it out to another for hire or compensation. Story, Bailm. § 369. See "Hire."

LETTER CARRIER. A person employed to carry letters from the post office to the persons to whom they are addressed. Provisions were made by the act of March 3, 1851 (11 U. S. St. at Large, 591), for the appointment of letter carriers in cities and towns, and by chapter 21, § 2, of the same act, for letter carriers in Oregon and California.

LETTER MISSIVE. In English law. A request addressed to a peer, peeress, or lord of parliament, against whom a bill has been filed, desiring the defendant to appear and answer the bill. It is issued by the lord chancellor, on petition, after the filing of the bill; and a neglect to attend to this places the defendant, in relation to such suit, on the same ground as other defendants who are not peers, and a subpoena may then issue. Newland, Prac. 9; 2 Madd. Ch. Prac. 196; Cooper, Eq. Pl. 16.

LETTER OF ADVICE. A letter containing information of any circumstances unknown to the person to whom it is written; generally informing him of some commercial transaction by the writer of the letter.

It is usual and perfectly proper for the drawer of a bill of exchange to write a letter of advice to the drawee, as well to prevent fraud or alteration of the bill, as to let the drawee know what provision has been made for the payment of the bill. Chit. Bills, 185.

LETTER OF ADVOCATION. In Scotch law. The decree or warrant of the supreme court or court of sessions, discharging the inferior tribunal from all further proceedings in the matter, and advocating the action to itself. This proceeding is similar to a *certiorari* issuing out of a superior court for the removal of a cause from an inferior.

LETTER OF ATTORNEY. A written instrument, by which one or more persons, called the "constituents," authorize one or more other persons, called the "attorneys," to do some lawful act for or instead, and in the place of, the former. 1 Moody, C. C. 52, 70. It may be parol or under seal. See "Power of Attorney."

LETTER OF CREDENCE. In international law. A written instrument addressed by the sovereign or chief magistrate of a state to the sovereign or state to whom a public minister is sent, certifying his appointment as such, and the general object of his mission, and requesting that full faith and credit may be given to what he shall do and say on the part of his court.

When it is given to an ambassador, envoy, or minister accredited to a sovereign, it is addressed to the sovereign or state to whom the minister is delegated. In the case of a *charge d'affaires*, it is addressed by the secretary or minister of state charged with the department of foreign affairs to the minister of foreign affairs of the other government. Wheat. Int. Law, pt. 3, c. 1, § 7; Wicq. de l'Ambassadeur. lib. 1, § 15.

LETTER OF CREDIT. A letter whereby one person requests another to advance money or give credit to a third, and agrees to reimburse or indemnify the person making the advance, or giving the credit.

At first it was practically confined to merchants, and was designed to enable a merchant to obtain goods or money to buy the same.

In modern times it is much used as a convenience by travelers in foreign parts to avoid carrying large sums of money; a sum being deposited with a bank, which issues a letter of credit to its correspondents in foreign parts.

Letters of credit are special if addressed to some particular person; general if addressed to any one giving credit to the bearer.

LETTER OF LICENSE. An instrument or writing made by creditors to their insolvent debtor, by which they bind themselves to allow him a longer time than he had a right to, for the payment of his debts, and that they will not arrest or molest him in his person or property till after the expiration of such additional time.

LETTER OF MARQUE AND REPRISAL. A commission granted by the government to a private individual, to take the property of a foreign state, or of the citizens or subjects of such state, as a reparation for an injury committed by such state, its citizens or subjects. A vessel loaded with merchandise, on a voyage to a friendly port, but armed for its own defense in case of attack by an enemy, is also called a "letter of marque." 1 Boul. P. Dr. Com. tit. 3, § 2, p. 300.

By the constitution (article 1, § 8, cl. 11), congress have power to grant letters of marque and reprisal. See Chit. Law Nat. 73; 1 Bl. Comm. 251; Viner, Abr. "Prerogative" (B 4); Comyn, Dig. "Prerogative" (B 4); Molloy, bk. 1, c. 2, § 10; 2 Wooddeson, Lect. 440; 2 C. Rob. Adm. 224; 5 C. Rob. Adm. 9, 260. And see "Reprisal."

LETTER OF RECALL. A written document addressed by the executive of one government to the executive of another, informing the latter that a minister sent by the former to him has been recalled.

LETTER OF RECOMMENDATION. An instrument given by one person to another, addressed to a third, in which the bearer is represented as worthy of credit. 1 Bell, Comm. (5th Ed.) 371; 3 Term R. 51; 7 Cranch (U. S.) 69; Fell, Guar. c. 8; 6 Johns. (N. Y.) 181; 13 Johns. (N. Y.) 224; 1 Day (Conn.) 22. See "Recommendation."

LETTER OF RECREDENTIALS.. A document delivered to a minister by the secretary of state of the government to which he was accredited. It is addressed to the executive of the minister's country. This is in reply to the "letter of recall."

LETTERS. Epistles; despatches; written messages, usually on paper, folded up and sealed, and sent by one person to another. 1 Caines (N. Y.) 582.

LETTERS AD COLLIGENDUM BONA DEFUNCTI. In practice. In default of the representatives and creditors to administer the estate of an intestate, the officer entitled to grant letters of administration may grant, to such person as he approves, "letters to collect the goods of the deceased," which neither make him executor nor administrator; his only business being to collect the goods, and keep them in his safe custody. 2 Bl. Comm. 505.

LETTERS CLOSE. Close letters are grants of the king, and, being of private concern, they are thus distinguished from "letters patent."

LETTERS OF ADMINISTRATION. An instrument in writing, granted by the judge or officer having jurisdiction and power of granting such letters, thereby giving the administrator (naming him) "full power to administer the goods, chattels, rights, and credits, which were of the said deceased, in the county or district in which the said judge or officer has jurisdiction; as also to ask, collect, levy, recover, and receive the credits whatsoever of the said deceased, which at the time of his death were owing, or did in any way belong, to him, and to pay the debts in which the said deceased stood obliged, so far forth as the said goods and chattels, rights and credits, will extend, according to the rate and order of law." See "Letters Testamentary."

LETTERS OF FIRE AND SWORD. See "Fire and Sword."

LETTERS OF HORNING. See "Horning."

LETTERS OF REQUEST. In English ecclesiastical law. An instrument by which a judge of an inferior court waives or remits his own jurisdiction in favor of a court of appeal immediately superior to it.

Letters of request, in general, lie only where an appeal would lie, and lie only to the next immediate court of appeal, waiving merely the primary jurisdiction to the proper appellate court, except letters of request from the most inferior ecclesiastical court, which may be direct to the court of arches, although one or two courts of appeal may by this be ousted of their jurisdiction as courts of appeal. 2 Add. Ecc. 406. The effect of letters of request is to give jurisdiction to the appellate court in the first instance. See a form of letters of request in 2 Chit. Prac. 498, note (h).

LETTERS OF SAFE-CONDUCT. No subject of a nation at war with England can, by the law of nations, come into the realm, nor can travel himself upon the high seas, or send his goods and merchandise from one place to another, without danger of being seized, unless he has "letters of safe-conduct," which, by divers old statutes, must be granted under the great seal, and enrolled in chancery, or else are of no effect; the sovereign being the best judge of such emergencies as may deserve exemption from the general law of arms. But passports or licenses from the ambassadors abroad are now more usually obtained, and are allowed to be of equal validity. Wharton.

LETTERS OF SLAINS (or SLANES). Letters subscribed by the relatives of a person who had been slain, declaring that they had received an assythment, and concurring in an application to the crown for a pardon to the offender. These or other evidences of their concurrence were necessary to found the application. Bell, Dict.

LETTERS PATENT. The name of an instrument granted by the government to convey a right to the patentee; as, a patent for a tract of land; or to secure to him a right which he already possesses, as, a patent for a new invention or discovery. Letters patent are matter of record. They are so called because they are not sealed up, but are granted open. See "Patent."

LETTERS ROGATORY. An instrument sent in the name and by the authority of a judge or court to another, requesting the latter to cause to be examined, upon interrogatories filed in a cause depending before the former, a witness who is within the jurisdiction of the judge or court to whom such letters are addressed.

LETTERS TESTAMENTARY. The formal instrument in writing granted to an executor by the judge or officer having jurisdiction of the probate of wills, stating his appointment as executor, and authorizing him to proceed.

LETTING OUT. In American law. The act of awarding a contract.

This term is much used in the United States, and most frequently in relation to contracts to construct railroads, canals, or other mechanical works. When such an undertaking has reached the point of actual construction, a notice is generally given that proposals will be received until a certain period, and thereupon a letting out, or award of portions of the work to be performed according to the proposals, is made. See 35 Ala. (N. S.) 55.

LETTRE (Law Fr.) In old English law. A letter; conveyance or grant, so called from its form. *A toutz ceux que ceste lettre verrount ou orrount,* A. *de* B. *salut: Saches moy aver done a* P. *etc.* To all those who shall see or hear this letter, A. of B. greeting: Know that I have given to P., etc. Britt. c. 41.

LEUCA, LEUGA, or **LEGA** (Law Lat.)

——**In Old French Law.** A league, consisting of fifteen hundred paces. Spelman.

——**In Old English Law.** A league or mile of a thousand paces. Domesday Book; Spelman; Fleta, lib. 2, c. 2, § 2.

A privileged space around a monastery of a league or mile in circuit. Spelman.

LEUDIS, *Leodis.* (Law Lat.) In old European law. A vassal; a liege man or feudal dependant; a retainer; a feudal tenant; a crown vassal or baron; a layman; a common or illiterate person. Spelman.

LEVANDAE NAVIS CAUSA (Lat.) In civil law. For the sake of lightening the ship. Goods thrown overboard with this purpose are subjects of a general average.

LEVANT ET COUCHANT (Law Fr.) Rising up and lying down. A term applied to trespassing cattle which have remained long enough upon land to have laid down to rest and risen up to feed, which, in general, is held to be a night and a day. 3 Bl. Comm. 9.

LEVANTES ET CUBANTES. Same as *levant et couchant.*

Applied by Bracton to villeins, who lived on their lord's estate. Bracton, fol. 6b.

LEVARI FACIAS (Lat. that you cause to be levied).

——**In Practice.** A writ of execution directing the sheriff to cause to be made of the lands and chattels of the judgment debtor the sum recovered by the judgment.

Under this writ, the sheriff was to sell the goods and collect the rents, issues, and profits of the land in question. It has been generally superseded by the remedy by *elegit,* which was given by St. Westminster II. (13 Edw. I.) c. 18. In case, however, the judgment debtor is a clerk, upon the sheriff's return that he has no lay fee, a writ in the nature of a *levari facias* goes to the bishop of the diocese, who thereupon sends a sequestration of the profits of the clerk's benefice, directed to the church wardens, to collect and pay them to the plaintiff till the full sum be raised. Yet the same course is pursued upon a *fi. fa.* 2 Burns, Ecc. Law, 329. See 2 Tidd, Prac. 1042; Comyn, Dig. "Execution" (C 4); Finch, Law, 471; 3 Bl. Comm. 471.

——**In American Law.** A writ used to sell lands mortgaged, after a judgment has been obtained by the mortgagee, or his assignee, against the mortgagor, under a peculiar proceeding authorized by statute. 3 Bouv. Inst. note 3396.

LEVARI FACIAS DAMNA DE DISSEISItoribus. A writ formerly directed to the sheriff for the levying of damages, which a disseisor had been condemned to pay to the disseisee. Cowell.

LEVARI FACIAS QUANDO VICECOMES returnavit quod non habuit emptores. An old writ commanding the sheriff to sell the goods of a debtor which he had already taken, and had returned that he could not sell them; and as much more of the debtor's goods as would satisfy the whole debt. Cowell.

LEVARI FACIAS RESIDUUM DEBITI. An old writ directed to the sheriff for levying the remnant of a partly-satisfied debt upon the lands and tenements or chattels of the debtor. Cowell.

LEVATO VELO (Lat.) An expression used in the Roman law (Code, 11. 4. 5), and applied to the trial of wreck and salvage. Commentators disagree about the origin of the expression, but all agree that its general meaning is that these causes shall be heard summarily. The most probable solution is that it refers to the place where causes were heard. A sail was spread before the door, and officers employed to keep strangers from the tribunal. When these causes were heard, this sail was raised, and suitors came directly to the court, and their causes were heard immediately. As applied to maritime courts, its meaning is that causes should be heard without delay. These causes require despatch, and a delay amounts practically to a denial of justice. Emerig. Tr. des Assur. c. 26, § 3.

LEVIABLE. That which may be levied.

LEVIR. A husband's brother. Vicat.

LEVITICAL DEGREES. Those degrees of kindred, set forth in the eighteenth chapter of Leviticus, within which persons are prohibited to marry.

LEVY. To raise. Webster. To levy a nuisance, *i. e.,* to raise or do a nuisance (9 Coke, 55); to levy a fine, *i. e.,* to raise or acknowledge a fine (2 Bl. Comm. 357; 1 Steph. Comm. 236); to levy a tax, *i. e.,* to raise or collect a tax; to levy war, *i. e.,* to raise or begin war, to take arms for attack (4 Bl. Comm. 81); to levy an execution, *i. e.,* to raise or levy so much money on execution (Reg. Orig. 298).

——**In Practice.** The raising of the money for which an execution has been issued. The seizing of property under an execution.

LEVYING WAR. In criminal law. The assembling of a body of men for the purpose of effecting by force a treasonable object; and all who perform any part, however minute, or however remote from the scene of action, and who are leagued in the general conspiracy, are considered as engaged in levying war, within the meaning of the constitution. 4 Cranch (U. S.) 473, 474; Const. art. 3, § 3. See "Treason"; Fed. Cas. No. 14,692. This is a technical term, borrowed from the English law, and its meaning is the same as it is when used in St. 25 Edw. III. 4 Cranch (U. S.) 471; Hall, Law J. 351; 1 East, P. C. 62-77; Alis. Crim. Law, 606; 9 Car. & P. 129.

LEWDNESS. Licentiousness; an offense against the public economy, when of an open and notorious character; as, by frequenting houses of ill fame, which is an indictable offense, or by some grossly scandalous and public indecency, for which the punishment at common law is fine and imprisonment. The various acts which constituted lewdness at common law are now generally covered by a variety of statutory offenses, as "indecent exposure," "lascivious cohabitation," etc.

LEX (Lat.) The law; a law for the government of mankind in society. Among the ancient Romans this word was frequently used as synonymous with right, *jus*. When put absolutely, it means the law of the Twelve Tables.

LEX AELIA SENTIA. The Aelian Sentian law, respecting wills, proposed by the consuls Aelius and Sentius, and passed A. U. 756, restraining a master from manumitting his slaves in certain cases. Calv. Lex.; Halifax, Anal. bk. 1, c. 3.

LEX AEQUITATE GAUDET; APPETIT perfectum; est norma recti. The law delights in equity; it covets perfection; it is a rule of right. Jenk. Cent. Cas. 36.

LEX AGRARIA. In Roman law. The agrarian law. A law proposed by Tiberius Gracchus, A. U. 620, that no one should possess more than five hundred acres of land, and that three commissioners should be appointed to divide among the poorer people what any one had above that extent. Liv. Epit. 58.

LEX ALAMANNORUM (or **ALEMANNOrum**). The law of the Alemanni; first reduced to writing from the customs of the country by Theodoric, king of the Franks, A. D. 512. Amended and re-enacted by Clotaire II. Spelman; Butler, Hor. Jur. 84.

LEX ALIQUANDO SEQUITUR AEQUItatem. The law sometimes follows equity. 3 Wils. 119.

LEX AMISSA. One who is an infamous, perjured, or outlawed person. Bracton, lib. 4, c. 19.

LEX ANGLIAE. The law of England; the common law; or, the curtesy of England.

LEX ANGLIAE EST LEX MISERICORdiae. The law of England is a law of mercy. 2 Inst. 315.

LEX ANGLIAE NON PATITUR ABSURdum. The law of England does not suffer an absurdity. 9 Coke, 22.

LEX ANGLIAE NUNQUAM MATRIS SED semper patris conditionem imitari partum judicat. The law of England rules that the offspring shall always follow the condition of the father never that of the mother. Co. Litt. 123.

LEX ANGLIAE NUNQUAM SINE PARliamento mutari potest. The law of England cannot be changed but by parliament. 2 Inst. 218, 619.

LEX APPARENS. In old English and Norman law. Apparent or manifest law. A term used to denote the trial by battel or duel, and the trial by ordeal, "*lex*" having the sense of process of law (*process litis*). Spelman. Called "apparent" because the plaintiff was obliged to make his right clear by the testimony of witnesses before he could obtain an order from the court to summon the defendant.

LEX AQUILIA. In the Roman law. The Aquilian law; a celebrated law passed on the proposition of the tribune C. Aquilius Gallus, A. U. 672, regulating the compensation to be made for that kind of damage called "injurious," in the cases of killing or wounding the slave or beast of another. Inst. 4. 3; Dig. 9. 2; Code, 3. 35; Calv. Lex.

LEX ATILIA. In the Roman law. The Atilian law; a law passed on the proposition of the tribune L. Atilius Regulus, A. U. 443, authorizing the praetor, with a majority of the tribunes, to appoint guardians. Changed by Justinian. Inst. 1. 20. 3. 4.

LEX ATINIA. In the Roman law. The Atinian law; a law declaring that the property in things stolen should not be acquired by prescription (*usucapione*). Inst. 2. 6. 2; Adam, Rom. Ant. 207.

LEX BAIUVARIORUM (BAIORIORUM, or Boiorum). The law of the Bavarians, a barbarous nation of Europe, first collected (together with the law of the Franks and Alemanni) by Theodoric I., and finally completed and promulgated by Dagobert. Spelman.

LEX BARBARA. The barbarian law. A term applied to the laws of those nations that were not in subjection to the Roman empire, such as the Burgundian and Salian law, the law of the Lombards, etc. Spelman.

LEX BENEFICIALIS REI CONSIMILI remedium praestat. A beneficial law affords a remedy in a similar case. 2 Inst. 689.

LEX BREHONIA (Law Lat.) The Brehon law. See "Brehon Law."

LEX BRETOYSE (or **BRETOISE**). The law of the ancient Britons, or Marches of Wales.

LEX BURGUNDIONUM. The law of the Bergundians, a barbarous nation of Europe, first compiled and published by Gundebald, one of the last of their kings, about A. D. 500. Spelman; Butler, Hor. Jur. 84.

LEX CITIUS TOLERARE VULT PRIVAtum damnum quam publicum malum. The law would rather tolerate a private loss than a public evil. Co. Litt. 152b.

LEX COMITATUS (Law Lat.) In old English law. The law of the county, or the law administered in the county court before the earl (*comes*) or his deputy. Spelman.

LEX COMMISSORIA. In Roman law. A law by which a debtor and creditor might agree, where a thing had been pledged to the latter to secure the debt, that, if the debtor did not pay at the day, the pledge should become the absolute property of the creditor. This was abolished by a law of Constantine. Kent, Comm. 583.

A law according to which a seller might stipulate that, if the price of the thing sold were not paid within a certain time, the sale should be void. Dig. 18. 3.

LEX COMMUNIS. The common law. See "Jus Commune."

LEX CONTRA ID QUOD PRAESUMIT, probationem non recipit. The law admits no proof against that which it presumes. Lofft, 573.

LEX CORNELIA DE FALSO (or **FALSis**). In Roman law. The Cornelian law respecting forgery or counterfeiting. Passed by the dictator Sylla. Dig. 48. 10; Calv. Lex.

LEX CORNELIA DE INJURIIS. In Roman law. The Cornelian law respecting injuries; a law passed by the dictator L. Cornelius Sylla, providing remedies for certain injuries, as for battery, forcible entry of another's house, etc. Calv. Lex. Being the most important of the Cornelian laws, it is sometimes known generally as "Lex Cornelia."

LEX CORNELIA DE SICARIIS ET VENEficis. In Roman law. The Cornelian law respecting assassins and poisoners. Passed by the dictator Sylla. Dig. 48. 8; Calv. Lex.

LEX DANORUM. The law of the Danes; Dane-law or Dane-lage. Spelman.

LEX DE FUTURO; JUDEX DE PRAETErito. The law provides for the future; the judge for the past.

LEX DEFICERE NON POTEST IN JUStitia exhibenda. The law ought not to fail in dispensing justice. Co. Litt. 197.

LEX DERAISNIA. The proof of a thing which one denies to be done by him, where another affirms it; defeating the assertion of his adversary, and showing it to be against reason or probability. This was used among the old Romans, as well as the Normans. Cowell.

LEX DILATIONES SEMPER EXHORret. The law always abhors delay. 2 Inst. 240.

LEX DOMICILII (Lat.) The law of the domicile. 2 Kent, Comm. 112, 433.

LEX EST AB AETERNO. The law is from everlasting. Branch, Princ.

LEX EST DICTAMEN RATIONIS. Law is the dictate of reason. Jenk. Cent. Cas. 117.

LEX EST NORMA RECTI. Law is a rule of right.

LEX EST RATIO SUMMA, QUAE JUBET quae sunt utilia et necessaria, et contraria prohibet. Law is the perfection of reason, which commands what is useful and necessary, and forbids the contrary. Co. Litt. 319b.

LEX EST SANCTIO SANCTA, JUBENS honesta, et prohibens contraria. Law is a sacred sanction, commanding what is right, and prohibiting the contrary. 2 Inst. 587.

LEX EST TUTISSIMA CASSIS; SUB clypeo legis nemo decipitur. Law is the safest helmet; under the shield of the law no one is deceived. 2 Inst. 56.

LEX ET CONSUETUDO PARLIAMENTI. The law and custom of parliament. The houses of parliament constitute a court not only of legislation, but also of justice, and have their own rules, by which the court itself and the suitors therein are governed. May, Parl. Prac. (6th Ed.) 38-61. See 1 Bl. Comm. 163.

LEX ET CONSUETUDO REGNI. The law and custom of the realm; one of the names of the common law.

LEX FALCIDIA. See "Falcidian Law."

LEX FAVET DOTI. The law favors dower. 3 & 4 Wm. IV. c. 105.

LEX FINGIT UBI SUBSISTIT AEQUITas. Law feigns where equity subsists. 11 Coke, 90; Branch, Princ.

LEX FORI (Lat. the law of the forum). The law of the country, to the tribunal in which an action is brought. 5 Clark & F. 1.

LEX FRANCORUM. The law of the Franks; promulgated by Theodoric I., son of Clovis I., at the same time with the law of the Alemanni and Bavarians. Spelman. This was a different collection from the Salic law.

LEX FRISIONUM. The law of the Frisians, promulgated about the middle of the eighth century. Spelman.

LEX FURIA (or **FUSIA**) **CANINIA.** In Roman law. The Furian Caninian law; a law passed in the consulship of P. Furius Camillus and C. Caninius Gallus, A. U. 752, prohibiting masters from manumitting by will more than a certain number or proportion of their slaves. This law was abrogated by Justinian. Inst. 1. 7; Code, 7. 3; Heinec. Elem. Jur. Civ. lib. 1, tit. 7.

LEX GOTHICA. The Gothic law, or law of the Goths. First promulgated in writing, A. D. 466. Spelman.

LEX HOSTILIA. The Hostilian law, passed in the consulship of A. Hostilius, authorizing actions of theft to be brought in the name of captives or persons absent on the business of the state. Inst. 4. 10. pr.; Calv. Lex.

LEX IMPERATORIA. The Imperial or Roman law. Quoted under this name by Fleta, lib. 1, c. 38, § 15; Id. lib. 3, c. 10, § 3.

LEX INTENDIT VICINUM VICINI FACta scire. The law presumes that one neighbor knows the actions of another. Co. Litt. 78b.

LEX JUDICAT DE REBUS NECESSARIO faciendis quasi re ipsa factis. The law judges of things which must necessarily be done as if actually done. Branch, Princ.

LEX JUDICIALIS. An ordeal. Leg. H. 1.

LEX JULIA MAJESTATIS. In Roman law. The Julian law of majesty; a law promulgated by Julius Caesar, and again published with additions by Augustus, comprehending all the laws before enacted to punish transgressors against the state. Halifax, Anal. bk. 3, c. 12; Calv. Lex.

LEX LOCI (Lat.) The law of the place. This may be either *lex loci contractus aut actus*, the law of the place of making the contract or of the thing done; *lex loci rei sitae*, the law of the place where the thing is situated; *lex loci domicilii*, the law of the place of domicile.

In general, however, *lex loci* is only used for *lex loci contractus aut actus*.

LEX LOCI DELICTUS. The law of the place where an offense was committed.

LEX LOCI SOLUTIONIS. The law of the place where payment or performance of a contract is, by its terms, to be made.

LEX LONGOBARDORUM (Lat.) The name of an ancient code in force among the Lombards. It contains many evident traces of feudal policy. It survived the destruction of the ancient government of Lombardy by Charlemagne, and is said to be still partially in force in some districts of Italy.

LEX MANIFESTA. Manifest or open law; the trial by duel or ordeal. The same as *lex apparens* (*q. v.*).

LEX MERCATORIA (Lat.) That system of laws which is adopted by all commercial nations, and which, therefore, constitutes a part of the law of the land. See "Law Merchant."

LEX NECESSITATIS EST LEX TEMPOris, i. e., instantis. The law of necessity is the law of time, that is, time present. Hob. 159.

LEX NEMINEM COGIT AD VANA SEU inutilia peragenda. The law forces no one to do vain or useless things. Wingate, Max. 600; 3 Bl. Comm. 144; 2 Bing. (N. C.) 121; 13 East, 420; 7 Pa. St. 206, 214; 3 Johns. (N. Y.) 598.

LEX NEMINEM COGIT OSTENDERE quod nescire praesumitur. The law forces no one to make known what he is presumed not to know. Lofft, 569.

LEX NEMINI FACIT INJURIAM. The law does wrong to no one. Branch, Princ.

LEX NEMINI OPERATUR INIQUUM, NEmini facit injuriam. The law never works an injury, or does him a wrong. Jenk. Cent. Cas. 22.

LEX NIL FACIT FRUSTRA, NIL JUBET frustra. The law does nothing and commands nothing in vain. 3 Bulst. 279; Jenk. Cent. Cas. 17.

LEX NON A REGE EST VIOLANDA. The law is not to be violated by the king. Jenk. Cent. Cas. 7.

LEX NON COGIT AD IMPOSSIBILIA. The law requires nothing impossible. Co. Litt. 231b; Hob. 96; 1 Bouv. Inst. note 851.

LEX NON CURAT DE MINIMIS. The law does not regard small matters. Hob. 88.

LEX NON DEFICIT IN JUSTITIA EXIbenda. The law does not fail in showing justice. Jenk. Cent. Cas. 31.

LEX NON EXACTE DEFINIT, SED ARbitrio boni viri permittit. The law does not define exactly, but trusts in the judgment of a good man. 9 Mass. 475.

LEX NON FAVET VOTIS DELICATOrum. The law favors not the wishes of the dainty. 9 Coke, 58a.

LEX NON INTENDIT ALIQUID IMPOSsibile. The law intends not anything impossible. 12 Coke, 89a.

LEX NON PATITUR FRACTIONES ET divisiones statuum. The law suffers no fractions and divisions of estates. 1 Coke, 87; Branch, Princ.

LEX NON PRAECIPIT INUTILIA, QUIA inutilis labor stultus. The law commands not useless things, because useless labor is foolish. Co. Litt. 197; 5 Coke, 89a.

LEX NON REQUIRIT VERIFICARE quod apparet curiae. The law does not require that to be proved which is apparent to the court. 9 Coke, 54.

LEX NON SCRIPTA. (Lat.) Law not written; unwritten law; a law originating in custom, and having its force from long and immemorial usage. The term is applied to the common law of England, not in the literal sense of an unwritten or *oral* law, but in that of a law not derived from express legislative enactment. 1 Bl. Comm. 63, 64, 67.

LEX ORDINANDI. The same as *lex fori* (*q. v.*).

LEX PAPIA POPPAEA. In Roman law. The Papian Poppaean law; a law proposed by the consuls Papius and Poppaeus at the desire of Augustus, A. U. 762, enlarging the *lex Praetoria* (*q. v.*). Inst. 3. 8. 2; Halifax, Anal. bk. 2, c. 10.

LEX PLUS LAUDATUR QUANDO RAtione probatur. The law is the more praised when it is consonant to reason. 3 Term R. 146; 7 Term R. 252; 7 Adol. & E. 657; Broom, Leg. Max. (3d London Ed.) 151.

LEX POSTERIOR DEROGAT PRIORI. A prior statute shall give place to a later. Mackeld. Civ. Law, 5; Broom, Leg. Max. (3d London Ed.) 27.

LEX PRAETORIA. In Roman law. The Praetorian law; a law by which every freedman who made a will was commanded to leave a moiety to his patron. Inst. 3. 8. 1.

L. C. B. Gilbert has applied the term to the rules that govern in a court of equity. Gilb. Ch. pt. 2.

LEX PROSPICIT, NON RESPICIT. The law looks forward, not backward. Jenk. Cent. Cas. 284. See "Retrospective Law."

LEX PUNIT MENDACIUM. The law punishes falsehood. Jenk. Cent. Cas. 15.

LEX REGIA. A law by which it was claimed that the legislative power was transferred by the Roman people to the emperor. Inst. 1. 2. 6. Whether such a law was passed has been doubted. 1 Kent, Comm. 544; Tayl. Civ. Law, 236, note.

LEX REI SITAE (Lat.) The law of the place of situation of the thing.

LEX REJICIT SUPERFLUA, PUGNANtia, incongrua. The law rejects superfluous, contradictory, and incongruous things. Jenk. Cent. Cas. 133, 140, 176.

LEX REPROBAT MORAM. The law disapproves of delay.

LEX RESPICIT AEQUITATEM. Law regards equity. See 14 Q. B. 504, 511, 512.

LEX RHODIA. The Rhodian law, particularly the fragment of it on the subject of jettison (*de jactu*), preserved in the Pandects. Dig. 14. 2. 1; 3 Kent, Comm. 232, 233.

LEX SACRAMENTALIS. Purgation by oath. Leg. H. 1.

LEX SALICA. The Salic law; the law of the Salian Franks, a people of Germany who settled in Gaul in the fifth century. It is the oldest of the barbarian codes, being said to have been framed about A. D. 422. The most celebrated provision of this code, one excluding females from inheritance, is often referred to alone as the Salic law.

According to Spelman, many provisions of the laws of Henry I. were taken from this source.

LEX SCRIPTA. The statutory law. 20 Ill. App. 288.

LEX SCRIPTA SI CESSET, ID CUSTODIri oportet quod moribus et consuetudine inductum est; et, si qua in re hoc defecerit, tunc id quod proximum et consequens ei est; et, si id non appareat, tunc jus quo urbs Romana utitur servari oportet. If the written law be silent, that which is drawn from manners and custom ought to be observed; and, if that is in any manner defective, then that which is next and analogous to it; and, if that does not appear, then the law which Rome uses should be followed. 7 Coke, 19. This maxim of Lord Coke is so far followed at the present day that, in cases where there is no precedent of the English courts, the civil law is always heard with respect, and often, though not necessarily, followed. Wharton.

LEX SEMPER DABIT REMEDIUM. The law will always give a remedy. 3 Bouv. Inst. note 2411; Bac. Abr. "Actions in General" (B); Branch, Princ.; Broom, Leg. Max. (3d London Ed.) 181; 12 Adol. & E. 266; 7 Q. B. 451.

LEX SEMPER INTENDIT QUOD CONvenit rationi. The law always intends what is agreeable to reason. Co. Litt. 78.

LEX SITUS. Modern law Latin for "the law of the place where property is situated." The general rule is that lands and other immovables are governed by the *lex situs*, *i. e.*, by the law of the country in which they are situated. Westl. Priv. Int. Law, 62.

LEX SPECTAT NATURAE ORDINEM. The law regards the order of nature. Co. Litt. 197; Broom, Leg. Max. (3d London Ed.) 231.

LEX SUCCURRIT IGNORANTI. The laws succor the ignorant. Jenk. Cent. Cas. 15.

LEX SUCCURRIT MINORIBUS. The law assists minors. Jenk. Cent. Cas. 57.

LEX TALIONIS (Lat.) The law of retaliation, an example of which is given in the law of Moses,—an eye for an eye, a tooth for a tooth, etc.

Amicable retaliation includes those acts of retaliation which correspond to the acts of the other nation under similar circumstances.

Jurists and writers on international law are divided as to the right of one nation punishing with death, by way of retaliation, the citizens or subjects of another nation. In the United States, no example of such barbarity has ever been witnessed; but prisoners have been kept in close confinement in retaliation for the same conduct towards American prisoners. See Rutherford, Inst. bk. 2, c. 9; Mart. Law Nat. bk. 8, c. 1, § 3, note; 1 Kent, Comm. 93; Wheaton, Int. Law, pt. 4, c. 1, § 1.

Vindictive retaliation includes those acts which amount to a war.

LEX TERRAE (Lat.) The law of the land. See "Due Process of Law."

LEX UNO ORE OMNES ALLOQUITUR. The law speaks to all with one mouth. 2 Inst. 184.

LEX VIGILANTIBUS, NON DORMIENTIbus subvenit. Law assists the wakeful, not the sleeping. 1 Story, Cont. (4th Ed.) 502.

LEX WALLENSICA. The Welsh law; the law of Wales. Blount.

LEX WISIGOTHORUM. The law of the Visigoths, or Western Goths, who settled in Spain; first reduced to writing A. D. 466. They were made by Euric, amended by Chindaswindus and Recaswindus. A revision of these laws was made by Egigas. Spelman.

LEY (Old Fr.; a corruption of *loi*). Law. For example, Termes de la Ley,—Terms of the Law. In another, and an old technical, sense, *ley* signifies an oath, or the oath with compurgators; as, *il tend sa ley aiu pleyntiffe*. Britt. c. 27.

LEY CIVILE. In old English law. The civil or Roman law. Y. B. H. 8 Edw. III. 42. Otherwise termed *ley escripte*, the written law. Y. B. 10 Edw. III. 24.

LEY GAGER. Wager of law; an offer to make an oath denying the cause of action of the plaintiff, confirmed by compurgators (*q. v.*), which oath used to be allowed in certain cases. When it was accomplished, it was called the "doing of the law," *fesans de ley*. Termes de la Ley, "Ley"; 2 Barn. & C. 538; 3 Bos. & P. 297; 3 & 4 Wm. IV. c. 42, § 16.

LEYES DE ESTILLO. In Spanish law. Laws of the age; a book of explanations of the *Fuero Real*, to the number of two hundred and fifty-two, formed under the authority of Alonzo X. and his son Sancho, and of Fernando el Emplazado, and published at the end of the thirteenth century or beginning of the fourteenth, and some of them are inserted in the New Recopilacion. See 1 White, New Recop. p. 354.

LEZE MAJESTY. An offense against sovereign power; treason; rebellion. See "Lese Majesty."

LI. LO. An abbreviation of *licentia loquendi*, formerly used in practice to signify an imparlance. Towns. Pl. 159.

LIABILITY. Responsibility; the state of one who is bound in law and justice to do something which may be enforced by action. This liability may arise from contracts either express or implied, or in consequence of torts committed.

LIBEL.

——**In Practice.** A written statement by a plaintiff, in ecclesiastical and admiralty courts, of his cause of action, and of the relief he seeks to obtain in a suit. Law, Ecc. Law, 17; Ayliffe, Par. 346; Shelf. Mar. & Div. 506; Dunl. Adm. Prac. 111. It performs substantially the same office in the ecclesiastical courts, and those courts which follow the practice of the ecclesiastical courts, as the bill in chancery and the declaration in common-law practice.

——**In Torts.** That which is written or printed, and published, calculated to injure the character of another by bringing him into ridicule, hatred, or contempt. Parke, J., 15 Mees. & W. 344.

Everything, written or printed, which reflects on the character of another, and is published without lawful justification or excuse, is a libel, whatever the intention may have been. 15 Mees. & W. 437.

A malicious defamation, expressed either in printing or writing, or by signs or pictures, and tending either to blacken the memory of one who is dead, or the reputation of one who is alive, and expose him to public hatred, contempt, or ridicule. 1 Hawk. P. C. bk. 1, c. 73, § 1; 4 Mass. 168; 2 Pick. (Mass.) 115; 9 Johns. (N. Y.) 214; 1 Denio (N. Y.) 347; 24 Wend. (N. Y.) 434; 9 Barn & C. 172; 4 Man. & R. 127; 2 Kent, Comm. 13.

It has been defined, perhaps, with more precision, to be a censorious or ridiculous writing, picture, or sign made with a malicious or mischievous intent towards government, magistrates, or individuals. 3 Johns. Cas. (N. Y.) 354; 9 Johns. (N. Y.) 215; 5 Bin. (Pa.) 340.

Any publication not oral, which exposes a person to hatred, contempt, ridicule, or obloquy, or tends to injure him in his business or calling, impairing his standing in society, or cause him to be shunned or avoided by his neighbors. Odgers, Libel & S. 22.

LIBEL OF ACCUSATION. In Scotch law. The instrument which contains the charge against a person accused of a crime. Libels are of two kinds, namely, indictments and criminal letters.

Every libel assumes the form of what is termed, in logic, a "syllogism." It is first stated that some particular kind of act is criminal; as, that "theft is a crime of a heinous nature, and severely punishable." This proposition is termed the "major." It is next stated that the person accused is guilty of the crime so named, "actor, or art and part." This, with the narrative of the manner in which, and the time when, the offense was committed, is called the "minor" proposition of the libel. The "conclusion" is that, all or part of the facts being proved, or admitted by confession, the panel "ought to be punished with the pains of the law, to deter others from committing the like crime in all time coming." Burton, Pub. Laws, 300, 301.

LIBELLANT. The party who files a libel in an ecclesiastical or admiralty case, corresponding to the plaintiff in actions in the common-law courts.

LIBELLEE. A party against whom a libel has been filed in proceedings in an ecclesiastical court or in admiralty, corresponding to the defendant in a common-law suit.

LIBELLUS (Lat.)

——**In Civil Law.** A little book. *Libellus supplex,* a petition, especially to emperor, all petitions to whom must be in writing. L. 15, Dig. *in jus voc. Libellum rescribere,* to mark on such petition the answer to it. L. 2, § 2, Dig. *de jur. fisc. Libellum agere,* to assist or counsel the emperor in regard to such petitions, L. 12, Dig. *de distr. pign.;* and one whose duty it is to do so is called *magister libellorum.* There were also *promagistri.* L. 1, Dig. *de offic. praef. pract. Libellus accusatorius,* an information and accusation of a crime. L. 17, § 1, and L. 29, § 8, Dig. *ad leg. Jul de adult. Libellus divortii,* a writing of divorcement. L. 7, Dig. *de divort. et repud. Libellus rerum,* an inventory. Calv. Lex. *Libellus* or *oratio consultoria,* a message by which emperors laid matters before senate. Calv. Lex.; Suet. Caes. 56.

A writing in which is contained the names of the plaintiff (*actor*) and defendant (*reus*), the thing sought, the right relied upon, and name of the tribunal before which the action is brought. Calv. Lex.

Libellus appellatorius, an appeal. Calv. Lex.; L. 1, § ult., Dig. ff. *de appellat.*

——**In English Law** (sometimes called *libellus conventionalis*). A bill. Bracton, fol. 112.

LIBELLUS CONVENTIONIS. In the civil law. The statement of a plaintiff's claim in a petition presented to the magistrate, who directed an officer to deliver it to the defendant.

LIBELLUS FAMOSUS (Lat.) A libel; a defamatory writing. L. 15, Dig. *de poen.;* Vocat. sub "*famosus.*" It may be without writing; as, by signs, pictures, etc. 5 Rep. *de famosis libellis.*

LIBELOUS. Constituting a libel.

LIBER (Lat.)

——**In Civil Law.** A book, whatever the material of which it is made; a principal subdivision of a literary work; thus, the Pandects, or Digest of the Civil Law, is divided into fifty books. L. 52, Dig. *de legat.*

——**In Civil and Old English Law.** Free; *e. g.,* a free (*liber*) bull. Jacob. Exempt from service or jurisdiction of another, *e. g.,* a free (*liber*) man. L. 3, Dig. *de statu hominum.*

LIBER ASSISARUM (Lat.) The book of assigns or pleas of the crown; being the fifth part of the Year Books.

LIBER BANCUS (Law Lat.) In old English law. Free bench. Bracton, fol. 97b.

LIBER ET LEGALIS HOMO (Lat.) A free and lawful man; one worthy of being a juryman. *Liberi homines,* freemen; owners of land. Wright on Tenures, 66, and note. He must neither be infamous nor a bondman. 3 Bl. Comm. 340, 362; Bracton, fol. 14b; Fleta, lib. 6, c. 25, § 4; Id. lib. 4, c. 5, § 4.

One must only be a freeman and not bound, but also one that hath such freedom of mind that he stands indifferent as he stands unsworn. 144 Ill. 163. See Liber Homo.

LIBER FEUDORUM (Lat.) A code of the feudal law, which was compiled by direction of the emperor Frederick Barbarossa, and published in Milan, in 1170. It was divided into five books, of which the first, second, and some fragments of the others still exist, and are printed at the end of all the modern editions of the *Corpus Juris Civilis.* Giannone, bk. 13, c. 3; Cruise, Dig. prel. diss. c. 1, § 31.

LIBER HOMO (Lat.) A free man; a freeman lawfully competent to act as juror. Ld. Raym. 417; Keb. 563. One must not only be a freeman and not bound, but also one that hath such freedom of mind that he stands indifferent as he stands unsworn. 144 Ill. 163. See, also, Liber Et Legalis Homo.

In London, a man can be a *liber homo* either (1) by service, as having served his apprenticeship; or (2) by birthright, being a son of a *liber homo;* or (3) by redemption, *i. e.,* allowance of mayor and aldermen. There was no intermediate state between *villein* and *liber homo.* Fleta, lib. 4, c. 11, § 22. But a *liber homo* could be vassal of another. Bracton, fol. 25.

——**In Old European Law.** An allodial proprietor, as opposed to a feudatory. Calv. Lex. "Alode."

LIBER JUDICIARUM (Lat.) The book of judgment, or doom book. The Saxon Domboc. Conjectured to be a book of statutes of ancient Saxon kings. See Jacob, "Domboc"; 1 Bl. Comm. 64.

LIBER NIGER (Lat.) Black book. A name given to several ancient records. See "Black Book of the Exchequer."

LIBER NIGER SCACCARII (Law Lat.) The Black Book of the Exchequer, attributed to Gervase of Tillbury. 1 Reeve, Hist. Eng. Law, 220, note.

LIBER RUBER SCACCARII (Law Lat.) The Red Book of the Exchequer. 1 Reeve, Hist. Eng. Law, 220, note. See "Red Book of the Exchequer."

LIBERA BATELLA (Law Lat.) In old records. A free boat; the right of having a boat to fish in a certain water; a species of free fishery. Plac. Itin, apud Cestriam, 14 Hen. VII.

LIBERA ELEEMOSYNA (Law Lat.) In old English law. Free alms; frankalmoign. Bracton, fol. 27b.

LIBERA FALDA (Law Lat.) In old English law. Frank fold; free fold; free foldage. 1 Leon. 11.

LIBERA LEX (Law Lat.) In old English law. Frank law; free law; otherwise called *lex terrae* (*q. v.*). Called *libera*, according to Lord Coke, to distinguish men who enjoy it, and whose best and freest birthright it is, from them that by their offenses have lost it. Co. Litt. 94b. *Amittere liberam legem*, to lose one's frank law. 3 Bl. Comm. 340; 4 Bl. Comm. 136; Crabb, Hist. Eng. Law, 318, 319; Co. Litt. 294b; Fleta, lib. 4, c. 8, § 2.

LIBERA PISCARIA (Law Lat.) In old English law. A free fishery (*q. v.*). Co. Litt. 122a.

LIBERA WARRENA (Law Lat.) In old English law. Free warren (*q. v.*)

LIBERAM LEGEM AMITTERE. To lose one's free law (called the villainous judgment) to become discredited or disabled as juror and witness, to forfeit goods and chattels and lands for life, to have those lands wasted, houses razed, trees rooted up, and one's body committed to prison. It was anciently pronounced against conspirators, but is now disused, the punishment substituted being fine and imprisonment. Hawk. P. C. 61, c. 72, § 9; 3 Inst. 221.

LIBERARE.

——**In the Civil Law.** To free or set free; to liberate; to give one his liberty. Calv. Lex.

——**In Old English Law.** To deliver, transfer, or hand over. Applied to writs, panels of jurors, etc. Bracton, fols. 116, 176b.

LIBERATA PECUNIA NON LIBERAT offerentem. Money being restored does not set free the party offering. Co. Litt. 207.

LIBERATE (Lat.) In English practice. A writ which issues on lands, tenements, and chattels, being returned under an extent on a statute staple, commanding the sheriff to deliver them to the plaintiff, by the extent and appraisement mentioned in the writ of extent, and in the sheriff's return thereto. See Comyn, Dig. "Statute Staple" (D 6).

LIBERATIO.

——**In Old English Law.** Livery; money paid for the delivery or use of a thing.

——**In Old Scotch Law.** Livery; a fee given to a servant or officer. Skene de Verb. Sign.

Money, meat, drink, clothes, etc., yearly given and delivered by the lord to his domestic servants. Blount.

LIBERATION. In civil law. The extinguishment of a contract, by which he who was bound becomes free or liberated. Wolff. Dr. Nat. § 749. Synonymous with "payment." Dig. 50. 16. 47.

LIBERI.

——**In Saxon Law.** Freemen; the possessors of allodial lands. 1 Reeve, Hist. Eng. law, 5.

——**In the Civil Law.** Children. The term included "grandchildren."

LIBERI CHASEA (or **CHACIA**) (Law Lat.) In old English law. A free chase. Reg. Jud. 37; Fleta, lib. 2, c. 41, § 51.

LIBERTAS. Liberty; freedom; a privilege; a franchise.

LIBERTAS ECCLESIASTICA. Church liberty, or ecclesiastical immunity.

LIBERTAS EST NATURALIS FACULtas ejus quod cuique facere libet, nisi quod de jure aut vi prohibetur. Liberty is the natural power of doing whatever one pleases, except that which is restrained by law or force. Co. Litt. 116.

LIBERTAS INAESTIMABILIS RES EST. Liberty is an inestimable good. Dig. 50. 17. 106; Fleta, lib. 2, c. 51, § 13.

LIBERTAS NON RECIPIT AESTIMAtionem. Freedom does not admit a valuation. Bracton, 14.

LIBERTAS OMNIBUS REBUS FAVORAbilior est. Liberty is more favored than all things. Dig. 50. 17. 122.

LIBERTAS REGALES AD CORONAM spectantes ex concessione regum a corona exierunt. Royal franchises relating to the crown have emanated from the crown by grant of kings. 2 Inst. 496.

LIBERTATIBUS ALLOCANDIS. A writ lying for a citizen or burgess, impleaded contrary to his liberty, to have his privilege allowed. Reg. Orig. 262.

LIBERTATIBUS EXIGENDIS IN ITINEre. An ancient writ, whereby the king commanded the justices in eyre to admit of an attorney for the defense of another's liberty. Reg. Orig. 19.

LIBERTI, or **LIBERTINI.** In Roman law. The condition of those who, having been slaves, had been made free. 1 Brown, Civ. Law, 99.

There is some distinction between these words. By *libertus* was understood the freedman when considered in relation to his patron, who had bestowed liberty upon him;

and he was called *libertinus* when considered in relation to the state he occupied in society subsequent to his manumission, Lec. Dr. Civ. § 93.

LIBERTICIDE. A destroyer of liberty.

LIBERTIES. Privileged districts exempt from the sheriff's jurisdiction.

LIBERTINUM INGRATUM LEGES CIViles in pristinam servitutem redigunt; sed leges Angliae semel manumissum semper liberum judicant. The civil laws reduce an ungrateful freedman to his original slavery; but the laws of England regard a man once manumitted as ever after free. Co. Litt. 137.

LIBERTY (Lat. *liber*, free; *libertas*, freedom, liberty). Freedom from restraint; the faculty of willing, and the power of doing what has been willed, without influence from without.

As used in the constitution means not only freedom of the citizen from servitude and restraint, but embraces the right of every man to be free in the use of his powers and faculties, and to adopt and pursue such calling as he may choose, subject only to the restraints necessary to secure the common welfare. 231 Ill. 346; 193 Ill. 345; 185 Ill. 139; 161 Ill. 296; 217 Ill. 248; 155 Mass. 117; 109 N. Y. 389; 16 Wall. 36; 113 Pa. St. 431; 33 W. Va. 179.

A privilege held by grant or prescription, by which some men enjoy greater privileges than ordinary subjects.

A territory with some extraordinary privilege.

A part of a town or city; as, the Northern Liberties of Philadelphia. See "Faubourg."

Civil liberty is the greatest amount of absolute liberty which can, in the nature of things, be equally possessed by every citizen in a state.

The term is frequently used to denote the amount of absolute liberty which is actually enjoyed by the various citizens under the government and laws of the state as administered. 1 Bl. Comm. 125.

The fullest political liberty furnishes the best possible guaranty for civil liberty.

Lieber defines civil liberty as guaranteed protection against interference with the interests and rights held dear and important by large classes of civilized men, or by all the members of a state, together with an effectual share in the making and administration of the laws, as the best apparatus to secure that protection, including Blackstone's divisions of civil and political under this head.

Natural liberty is the right which nature gives to all mankind of disposing of their persons and property after the manner they judge most consonant to their happiness, on condition of their acting within the limits of the law of nature, and so as not to interfere with an equal exercise of the same rights by other men. Burlam. Nat. Law, c. 3, § 15; 1 Bl. Comm. 125. It is called by Lieber "social" liberty, and is defined as the protection of unrestrained action in as high a degree as the same claim of protection of each individual admits of.

Personal liberty consists in the power of locomotion, of changing situation, or removing one's person to whatever place one's inclination may direct, without imprisonment or restraint, unless by due course of law. 1 Bl. Comm. 134.

Political liberty is an effectual share in the making and administration of the laws. Lieber, Civ. Lib.

Liberty, in its widest sense, means the faculty of willing, and the power of doing what has been willed, without influence from without. It means self-determination, unrestrainedness of action. Thus defined, one being only can be absolutely free, namely, God. So soon as we apply the word "liberty" to spheres of human action, the term receives a relative meaning, because the power of man is limited; he is subject to constant influences from without. If the idea of unrestrainedness of action is applied to the social state of man, it receives a limitation still greater, since the equal claims of unrestrained action of all necessarily involves the idea of protection against interference by others. We thus come to the definition, that liberty of social man consists in the protection of unrestrained action in as high a degree as the same claim of protection of each individual admits of, or in the most efficient protection of his rights, claims, interests, as man or citizen, or of his humanity, manifested as a social being. See "Right." The word "liberty," applied to men in their political state, may be viewed with reference to the state as a whole, and in this case means the independence of the state, of other states; or it may have reference to the relation of the citizen to the government, in which case it is called "political" or "civil" liberty; or it may have reference to the status of a man as a political being, contradistinguished from him who is not considered master over his body, will, or labor,—the slave. This is called "personal" liberty, which, as a matter of course, includes freedom from prison.

LIBERTY OF THE PRESS. The right to print and publish the truth, from good motives and for justifiable ends. 3 Johns. Cas. (N. Y.) 394. The right to print without previous license or restraint, subject to the consequences of law. 1 Cow. (N. Y.) 628; 13 W. Va. 182.

LIBERTY OF THE RULES. A privilege to go out of the Fleet and Marshalsea prisons within certain limits, and there reside. Abolished by 5 & 6 Vict. c. 22.

LIBERTY TO HOLD PLEAS. The liberty of having a court of one's own. Thus, certain lords had the privilege of holding pleas within their own manors.

LIBERUM CORPUS AESTIMATIONEM non recipit. The body of a freeman does not admit of valuation. Dig. 9. 3. 7.

LIBERUM EST CUIQUE APUD SE EXplorare an expediat sibi consilium. Every one is free to ascertain for himself whether a recommendation is advantageous to his interests. 6 Johns. (N. Y.) 181, 184.

LIBERUM MARITAGIUM (Lat.) In old English law. Frank marriage (*q. v.*). 2 Bl. Comm. 115; Litt. § 17; Bracton, fol. 21.

LIBERUM SERVITIUM. Free service; service of a warlike sort by a feudatory tenant; sometimes called *servitium liberum armorum.* Somn. Gavelkind, p. 56; Jacob; 4 Coke, 9.

Service not unbecoming character of freemen and soldiers to perform; as, to serve under the lord in his wars, to pay a sum of money, and the like. 2 Bl. Comm. 60. The tenure of free service does not make a villein a free man, unless homage or manumission precede, any more than a tenure by villein services makes a freeman a villein. Bracton, fol. 24.

LIBERUM SOCAGIUM. In old English law. Free socage. Bracton, fol. 207; 2 Bl. Comm. 61, 62.

LIBERUM TENEMENTUM.

——**In Real Law.** Freehold; frank tenement. 2 Bouv. Inst. note 1690; 1 Washb. Real Prop. 46.

——**In Pleading.** A plea in justification by the defendant in an action of trespass, by which he claims that he is the owner of the close described in the declaration, or that it is the freehold of some third person, by whose command he entered. 2 Salk. 453; 7 Term R. 355; 1 Wm. Saund. 299b, note.

It has the effect of compelling the plaintiff to a new assignment, setting out the abuttals where he has the *locus in quo* only generally in his declaration (11 East, 51, 72; 16 East, 343; 1 Barn. & C. 489); or to set forth tenancy in case he claims as tenant of the defendant, or the person ordering the trespass (1 Saund. 299b). It admits possession by the plaintiff, and the fact of the commission of a trespass as charged. 2 McCord (S. C.) 226.

LIBLAC. In Saxon law. Witchcraft, particularly that kind which consisted in the compounding and administering of drugs and philters.

LIBLACUM. In Saxon law. Bewitching any person; also a barbarous sacrifice.

LIBRA ARSA (Law Lat.) In old English law. A pound burned; that is, melted, or assayed by melting, to test its purity. *Librae arsae et pensatae,* pounds burned and weighed. A frequent expression in Domesday Book, to denote the purer coin in which rents were paid. Spelman; Cowell.

LIBRA NUMERATA (Law Lat.) In old English law. A pound counted; that is, paid or reckoned by tale (*ad numerum*), instead of being weighed. Spelman.

LIBRA PENSA (or **PENSATA**) (Law Lat.) In old English law. A pound weighed, or tried by weight. Spelman. See "Libra Arsa."

LIBRARIUS (Lat.) In the Roman law. A writer or amanuensis; a copyist. Dig. 50. 17. 92. See Calv. Lex.

LIBRATA (Law Lat. from *libra,* a pound). In old English law. A quantity of land yielding a pound rent per annum; a pound land. Bracton, fol. 16; Reg. Orig. 1b, 94; Fleta, lib. 5, c. 5, 41; Cowell, voc. "Fardingdeal."

LIBRIPENS (Lat.) In the Roman law. A weigher, or balance holder; the person who held a brazen balance in the ceremony of emancipation *per aes et libram.* Inst. 2. 10. 1; Adam, Rom. Ant. 52.

LIBRORUM APPELLATIONE CONTInentur omnia volumnia, sive in charta, sive in membrana sint, sive in quavis alia materia. Under the name of books are contained all volumes, whether upon paper, or parchment, or any other material. Dig. 32. 52. pr. et per tot.

LICENCIADO. In Spanish law. Lawyer or advocate. By a decree of the Spanish government of 6th November, 1843, it was declared that all persons who have obtained diplomas of "Licentiates in Jurisprudence" from any of the literary universities of Spain are entitled to practice in all the courts of Spain without first obtaining permission by the tribunals of justice.

Their title is furnished them by the minister of the interior, to whom the universities forward a list of those whom they think qualified.

This law does not apply to those already licensed, who may, however, obtain the benefit of it, upon surrendering their license and complying with certain other formalities prescribed by the law.

LICENSE (Lat. *licere,* to permit).

——**By Government.** An authorization by the government to an individual to do certain acts, or carry on a certain business. Thus, marriage licenses, saloon keepers' licenses, pilots' licenses, etc.

——**In Contracts.** A permission; a right given by some competent authority to do an act which, without such authority, would be illegal.

An authority to do a particular act or series of acts on another's land without possessing any estate therein. 11 Mass. 533; 4 Sands. Ch. (N. Y.) 72; 1 Washb. Real Prop. 148.

The written evidence of the grant of such right.

An executed license exists where the licensed act has been done.

An executory license exists where the licensed act has not been performed.

An express license is one which is granted in direct terms.

An implied license is one which is presumed to have been given from the acts of the party authorized to give it.

It is distinguished from an easement, which implies an interest in the land to be affected, and a lease, or right to take the profits of land. It may be, however, and often is, coupled with a grant of some interest in the land itself, or right to take the profits. 1 Washb. Real Prop. 148.

A license may be by specialty (2 Pars. Cont. 22); by parol (13 Mees. & W. 838; 4 Maule & S. 562; 7 Barb. [N. Y.] 4; 1 Washb. Real Prop. 148); or by implication from circumstances, as opening a door in response to a knock (Hob. 62; 2 Greenl. Ev. § 427).

——**In International Law.** Permission granted by a belligerent state to its own subjects, or to the subjects of the enemy, to carry on a trade interdicted by war. Wheaton. Int. Law, 475.

——**In Patent Law.** A right granted by a patentee to another to use or vend the patented article.

——**In Pleading.** A plea of justification to an action of trespass, that the defendant was authorized by the owner of the freehold to commit the trespass complained of.

A license must be specially pleaded to an action of trespass (2 Term R. 166), but may be given in evidence in an action on the case (2 Mod. 6; 8 East, 308).

LICENSEE. A person to whom a license has been granted.

——**Invitation.** In a strict and legal sense there is a distinction between a mere licensee and one who comes upon the premises of another by invitation, express or implied. While in a general sense one upon the premises of another by invitation is a licensee, in a legal sense an invitation gives the visitor a different status from that of a licensee, and entitles him to a somewhat higher degree of care from the owner. 141 Ill. App. 437; 200 Ill. 122; 235 Ill. 526.

——**Naked Licensee.** A person on premises by permission of law but without invitation from the owner is a mere naked licensee. 179 Ill. App. 604; 143 Ill. 189.

LICENSOR. The grantor of a license.

LICENTIA. Lat. [from *licere*, to be lawful.] License; liberty; permission.

LICENTIA CONCORDANDI (Lat. leave to agree). One of the formal steps in the levying a fine. When an action is brought for the purpose of levying a fine, the defendant, knowing himself to be in the wrong, is supposed to make overtures of accommodation to the plaintiff, who accepts them, but, having given pledges to prosecute his suit, applies to the court, upon the return of the writ of covenant, for leave to make the matter up. This, which is readily granted, is called the *licentia concordandi.* 5 Coke, 39; Cruise, Dig. tit. 35, c. 2, 22.

LICENTIA LOQUENDI. Imparlance.

LICENTIA SURGENDI. In old English law. Liberty of rising; a liberty or space of time given by the court to a tenant, who is essoined, *de malo lecti,* in a real action, to arise out of his bed. Also, the writ thereupon. If the demandant can show that the tenant was seen abroad before leave of court, and before being viewed by the knights appointed by the court for that purpose, such tenant shall be taken to be deceitfully essoined, and to have made default. Bracton, lib. 5; Fleta, lib. 6, c. 10.

LICENTIA TRANSFRETANDI. A writ or warrant directed to keeper of port of Dover, or other seaport, commanding him to let the person who has this license of the king pass over sea. Reg. Orig. 93.

LICENTIATE. One who has license to practice any art or faculty.

LICENTIOUSNESS. The doing what one pleases, without regard to the rights of others. It differs from liberty in this, that the latter is restrained by natural or positive law, and consists in doing whatever we please not inconsistent with the rights of others, whereas the former does not respect those rights. Wolff. Inst. § 84.

In a narrower sense, lewdness or lasciviousness.

LICERE, or LICERI (Lat.) In Roman law. To offer a price for a thing; to bid for it.

LICET (Lat.) It is lawful; not forbidden by law.

Id omne licitum est, quod non est legibus prohibitum, quamobrem, quod, lege permittente, fit, poenam non meretur. Licere dicimus quod legibus, moribus, institutisque conceditur. Cic. Philip. 13; L. 42, D. ff. *de ritu nupt. Est aliquid quod non oporteat; tametsi licet; quicquod vero non licet certe non oportet.* L. *verbum oportere,* ff. *de verb. et rer. sign.*

Although. Calv. Lex. An averment that "although such a thing is done or not done" is not implicative of the doing or not doing, but a direct averment of it. Plowd. 127.

LICET DISPOSITIO DE INTERESSE FUturo sit inutilis tamen potest fieri declaratio praecedens quae sortiatur effectum interveniente novo actu. Although the grant of a future interest be inoperative, yet a declaration precedent may be made which may take effect, provided a new act intervene. Bac. Max. reg. 14; Broom, Leg. Max. London Ed.) 600.

LICET SAEPIUS REQUISITUS (Lat. although often requested). In pleading. A formal allegation in a declaration that the defendant has been often requested to perform the acts of nonperformance of which is complained of.

It is usually alleged in the declaration that the defendant, *licet saepius requisitus*, etc., he did not perform the contract the violation of which is the foundation of the action. This allegation is generally sufficient when a request is not parcel of the contract. Indeed, in such cases it is unnecessary even to lay a general request; for the bringing of the suit is itself a sufficient request. 1 Saund. 33, note 2; 2 Saund. 118, note 3; Plowd. 128; 1 Wils. 33; 2 H. Bl. 131; 1 Johns. Cas. (N. Y.) 99, 319; 7 Johns. (N. Y.) 462; 18 Johns. (N. Y.) 485; 3 Maule & S. 150. See "Demand."

LICITA BENE MISCENTUR, FORMULA nisi juris obstet. Lawful acts may well be fused into one, unless some form of law forbid; *e. g.*, two having a right to convey, each a moiety, may unite and convey the whole. Bac. Max. 94; Crabb, Real Prop. 179.

LICITACION. In Spanish law. The sale made at public auction by coproprietors, or coheirs, of their joint property which is not susceptible of being advantageously divided in kind.

LICITARE (Lat.) In Roman law. To offer a price at a sale; to bid; to bid often; to make several bids, one above another. Calv. Lex.

LICITATION. In civil law. An offering for sale to the highest bidder, or to him who will give most for a thing. An act by which coheirs or other coproprietors of a thing in common and undivided between them put it to bid between them, to be adjusted and to belong to the highest and last bidder, upon condition that he pay to each of his coproprietors a part in the price equal to the undivided part which each of the said coproprietors had in the estate licited, before the adjudication. Poth. Cont. Sale, notes 516, 638.

LICITATOR. In Roman law. A bidder at a sale.

LIDFORD LAW. See "Lynch Law."

LIEGE (from *liga*, a bond, or *litis*, a man wholly at command of his lord). In feudal law. Bound by a feudal tenure; bound in allegiance to the lord paramount, who owned no superior.

The term was applied to the lord, or liege lord, to whom allegiance was due, since he was bound to protection and a just government, and also to the feudatory, liegeman, or subject bound to allegiance, for he was bound to tribute and due subjection. 34 & 35 Hen. VIII. So lieges are the king's subjects. St. 8 Hen. VI. c. 10; 14 Hen. VIII. c. 2. So in Scotland. Bell, Dict. But in ancient times private persons, as lords of manors, had their lieges. Jacob; 1 Bl. Comm. 367.

Liege, or *ligius*, was used in old records for full, pure, or perfect; *e. g.*, *ligia potestas*, full and free power of disposal. Par. Ant. 280. Probably in this sense derived from *legitima*. So in Scotland. See "Liege Poustie."

LIEGE HOMAGE. Homage based on allegiance, as opposed to that which implied merely an acknowledgment of tenure. The former was due to the sovereign alone, while the latter was rendered to any superior lord of whom lands were held. 1 Bl. Comm. 367.

LIEGE LORD. A sovereign; a superior lord.

LIEGE POUSTIE (*legitima potestas*). In Scotch law. That state of health which gives a person full power to dispose of, *mortis causa*, or otherwise, his heritable property. Bell, Dict.

LIEGEMAN. He that oweth allegience. Cowell.

LIEGER, or LEGER. A resident ambassador.

LIEGES, or LIEGE PEOPLE. Subjects.

LIEN. A French word which originally signified a string, tie, or band, and in the metaphorical sense in which the law now uses it, it signifies the hold or claim which one person has upon the property of another as security for the satisfaction of a debt, duty or demand, by which he may, if in possession of the property, detain it until the same is satisfied. 2 South. (N. J.) 441. Actual possession by the lien claimant being essential. 62 Barb. (N. Y.) 323; 26 Wend. (N. Y.) 467.

The term may be defined as a charge imposed on specific property, real or personal, by which it is made security for the performance of an act. 4 Cliff. (U. S.) 225.

In every case in which property, either real or personal, is charged with the payment of a debt or duty, every such charge may be denominated a lien on the property. It differs from an estate in or title to the property, as it may be discharged at any time by payment of the sum for which the lien attaches. It differs from a mortgage in the fact that a mortgage is made and the property delivered, or otherwise, for the express purpose of security; while the lien attaches as incidental to the main purpose of the bailment, or, as in case of a judgment, by mere act of the law, without any act of the party. In this general sense, the word is commonly used by English and American law writers to include those preferred or privileged claims given by statute or by admiralty law, and which seem to have been adopted from the civil law, as well as the security existing at common law, to which the term more exactly applies.

Liens are divided, in respect to their origin and nature, into common law, civil law, equitable, maritime, and statutory.

(1) Common-law liens. As distinguished from the other classes, they consist in a mere right to retain possession until the debt or charge is paid.

In the case of a factor, an apparent exception exists, as he is allowed a lien on the proceeds of goods sold, as well as on the goods themselves. But this seems to result from the relation of the parties, and the purposes of the bailment; to effectuate which, and at the same time give a security to the factor, the law considers the possession, or right to possession, of the proceeds, the same thing as the possession of the goods themselves.

A particular lien is a right to retain the property of another on account of labor employed or money expended on that specific property. Whit. Liens, 9.

A general lien is a right to retain the property of another on account of a general balance due from the owner. 3 Bos. & P. 494.

(2) Civil-law liens. The civil law embraces, under the head of mortgages and privilege, the peculiar securities which, in the common and maritime law, and equity, are termed "liens."

In regard to privilege, Domat says: "We do not reckon in the number of privileges the preference which the creditor has on the movables that have been given him in a pawn, and which are in his custody. The privilege of a creditor is the distinguishing right which the nature of his credit gives him, and which makes him to be preferred before other creditors, even those who are prior in time, and who have mortgages." Domat. Civ. Law, pt. 1, lib. iii. tit. i. § v.

These privileges are of two kinds: One gives a preference on all the goods, without any particular assignment on any one thing; the other gives to the creditors their security on certain things, and not on the other goods.

(3) Equitable liens. Such as exist in equity, and of which courts of equity alone take cognizance.

A lien is neither a *jus in re* nor a *jus ad rem.* It is not property in the thing, nor does it constitute a right of action for the thing. It more properly constitutes a charge upon the thing. In regard to these liens, it may be generally stated that they arise from constructive trusts. They are, therefore, wholly independent of the possession of the thing to which they are attached as an incumbrance, and they can be enforced only in courts of equity. Story, Eq. Jur. § 1217.

An equitable lien on a sale of realty is very different from a lien at law, for it operates after the possession has been changed, and is available by way of charge instead of detainer. Adams, Eq. Jur. 127.

(4) Maritime liens. Maritime liens do not include or require possession. The word lien is used in maritime law, not in the strict legal sense in which we understand it in courts of common law, in which case there could be no lien where there was no possession, actual or constructive; but to express, as if by analogy, the nature of claims which neither presuppose nor originate in possession. 22 Eng. Law & Eq. 62. See 15 Bost. Law Rep. 555; 16 Bost. Law Rep. 1, 264; 17 Bost. Law Rep. 93, 421. A distinction is made in the United States between qualified maritime liens, which depend upon possession, and absolute maritime liens, which do not require nor depend upon possession. 7 How. (U. S.) 729.

(5) Statutory liens. Under this head it is convenient to consider some of those liens which subsist at common law, but have been extensively modified by statutory regulations, as well as those which subsist entirely by force of statutory regulations.

The principal liens of this class are judgment liens, and liens of materialmen and builders.

Liens, whether common-law, equitable, or statutory, are either conventional, *i. e.*, by express agreement of the parties, or by operation of law, by legal implication from the acts of parties.

LIEN OF A COVENANT. The commencement of a covenant stating the names of the covenantors and covenantees, and the character of the covenant, whether joint or several.

LIENOR. One who holds or owns a lien.

LIEU, LEU, LIU, or **LYU** (Law Fr.; from Lat. *locus*). A place. Britt. c. 27.

LIEU CONUS (Law Fr.) In old pleading. A known place; a place well known and generally taken notice of by those who dwell about it, as a castle, a manor, etc. Whishaw; 1 Ld. Raym. 259. "A liberty is in the nature of a *lieu conus.*" North, C. J., 2 Mod. 48; Wishaw, 1 Ld. Raym. 259.

LIEUTENANT. This word has now a narrower meaning than it formerly had. Its true meaning is a deputy, a substitute, from the French *lieu* (place or post) and *tenant* (holder). Among civil officers we have lieutenant governors, who in certain cases perform the duties of governors, lieutenants of police, etc. Among military men, "lieutenant general" was formerly the title of a commanding general, but now it signifies the degree above major general. Lieutenant colonel is the officer between the colonel and the major. Lieutenant, simply, signifies the officer next below a captain.

LIFE ANNUITY. An annual income to be paid during the continuation of a particular life. See "Annuity."

LIFE ASSURANCE. An insurance of a life upon the payment of a premium. This may be for the whole life, or for a limited time. On the death of the person whose life has been insured during the time for which it is insured, the insurer is bound to pay to the beneficiary the money agreed upon. 1 Bouv. Inst. note 1231. See "Loss."

LIFE ESTATE. An estate whose duration is limited to the life of the party holding it, or of some other person; a freehold estate, not of inheritance. 4 Kent, Comm. 23, 25.

LIFE INSURANCE. A contract of insurance wherein the insurer agrees to pay a specified sum in the event of the death of a particular person, if it occurs at a time and under circumstances within the terms of the contract.

LIFE INTEREST. An interest, limited by the term of the life, either of the person in whom the right is vested, or of another.

LIFE, LIBERTY AND PROPERTY. This phrase embraces every personal, political and civil right or liberty which any person within the state may possess, including the right to labor, to make and terminate contracts and to acquire property, right of self-defense, freedom of speech, religious and political freedom, exemption from arbitrary arrests, the right to buy and sell as others may. By no authority can any person be deprived of any of these rights or restricted in their exercise except by due process of law, by a statute general in its operation and affecting in the same way all persons similarly situated. 249 Ill. 514.

LIFE PEERAGE. Letters patent, conferring the dignity of baron for life only, do not enable the grantee to sit and vote in the house of lords, not even with the usual writ of summons to the house. Wharton.

LIFE POLICY. A policy of life insurance.

LIFE RENT. In Scotch law. A right to use and enjoy a thing during life, the substance of it being preserved.

A life rent cannot, therefore, be constituted upon things which perish in the use; and though it may upon subjects which gradually wear out by time, as household furniture, etc., yet it is generally applied to heritable subjects. Life rents are divided into conventional and legal.

The conventional are either simple or by reservation. A simple life rent, or by a separate constitution, is that which is granted by the proprietor in favor of another. A life rent by reservation is that which a proprietor reserves to himself in the same writing by which he conveys the fee to another. Life rents by law are the terce and the curtesy (*q. v.*).

LIFE RENTER. In Scotch law. A tenant for life without waste. Bell, Dict.

LIGA (Law Lat.) On old European law. A league or confederation (*foedus, confoederatio*). Spelman.

LIGAN, or LAGAN. Goods cast into the sea tied to a buoy, so that they may be found again by the owners, are so denominated. When goods are cast into the sea in storms or shipwrecks, and remain there, without coming to land, they are distinguished by the barbarous names of jetsam, flotsam, and ligan. 5 Coke, 108; Harg. St. Tr. 48; 1 Bl. Comm. 292.

LIGARE (Lat.) To tie, or bind. Bracton, fol. 369b.

To enter into a league or treaty (*inire foedus*). Spelman.

LIGEA (Law Lat.) In old English law. A liege woman; a female subject. Reg. Orig. 312b.

LIGEANCE. The true and faithful obedience of a subject to his sovereign, of a citizen to his government. It signifies, also, the territory of a sovereign. See "Allegiance."

LIGEANTIA EST QUASI LEGIS ESSENtia; est vinculum fidei. Allegiance is, as it were, the essence of the law; it is the bond of faith. Co. Litt. 129.

LIGEANTIA NATURALIS, NULLIS claustris coercetur, nullis metis refraenatur, nullis finibus premitur. Natural allegiance is restrained by no barriers, curbed by no bounds, compressed by no limits. 7 Coke, 10.

LIGHTERMAN. The owner or manager of a lighter; a lighterman is considered as a common carrier. See "Lighters."

LIGHTERS. Small vessels employed in loading and unloading larger vessels.

The owners of lighters are liable like other common carriers for hire. It is a term of the contract on the part of the carrier or lighterman, implied by law, that his vessel is tight and fit for the purpose or employments for which he offers and holds it forth to the public. It is the immediate foundation and substratum of the contract that it is so; the law presumes a promise to that effect on the part of the carrier, without actual proof; and every principle of sound policy and public convenience requires it should be so. 5 East. 428; Abb. Shipp. 225; 1 Marsh. Ins. 254; Park, Ins. 23; Weskett, Ins. 328; Pars. Mar. Law.

LIGHTS. Those openings in a wall which are made rather for the admission of light than to look out of. 6 J. B. Moore, 47; 9 Bing. 305. See "Ancient Lights."

Lamps carried on board vessels, under statutory regulations or otherwise, for the purpose of preventing collisions at night.

Lamps or lights placed in lighthouses, or other conspicuous positions, as aids to navigation at night.

LIGIUS. A tie or bond allegiance.

LIGNA ET LAPIDES SUB "ARMORUM" appellatione non continentur. Sticks and stones are not contained under the name of arms. Bracton, 144b.

LIGULA. In old English law. A copy, exemplification, or transcript of a court roll or deed. Cowell.

LIMB. Ordinarily, only a member useful in fight, and the loss of which would amount to mayhem at common law. 1 Bl. Comm. 130.

Sometimes metaphorically used for general physical safety.

LIMENARCHA (Graeco-Lat.) In the Roman law. An officer who had charge of a harbor or port. Dig. 50. 4. 18. 10; Code 7. 16. 38.

LIMITATION OF ASSIZE. In old practice. A certain time prescribed by statute, within which a man was required to allege himself or his ancestor to have been seised of lands sued for by a writ of assize. Cowell.

LIMITATION, WORDS OF. See "Words of Limitation."

LIMITATIONS.

——**Of Actions.** The statutory restriction of the time within which action may be brought.

——**Of Criminal Prosecutions.** The statutory restriction of the time within which indictment may be found for an offense.

——**Of Estates.** A circumscription of the quantity of time comprised in any estate. 1 Prest. Est. 25.

The definition or circumscription, in any conveyance, of the interest which the grantee is intended to take. The term is used by different writers in different senses. Thus, it is used by Lord Coke to denote the express definition of an estate by the words of its creation, so that it cannot endure for any longer time than till the contingency happens upon which the estate is to fail. Co. Litt. 23b. In the work of Mr. Sanders on Uses, the term is used, however, in a broader and more general sense, as given in the second definition above. 1 Sanders, Uses (4th Ed.) 121 et seq. And, indeed, the same writers do not always confine themselves to one use of the term, though the better usage is undoubtedly given by Mr. Stephen in his note below cited. And see Fearne, Cont. Rem. (Butler's note [n]; 9th Ed.) 10; 1 Steph. Comm. (5th Ed.) 304, note. For the distinctions between limitations and remainders, see "Conditional Limitation"; "Contingent Remainder."

Consult, generally, Angell, Ballantine, and Price, on Limitations; Flintoff and Washburn on Real Property; Barbour and Bishop on Criminal Law.

LIMITED. Restricted; bounded; prescribed; confined within positive bounds; restricted in duration, extent, or scope.

LIMITED ADMINISTRATION. Special administration. See "Administration."

LIMITED DIVORCE. A divorce *a mensa et thoro*. See "Divorce."

LIMITED FEE. A general term, opposed to fee simple, and covering all qualified or conditional estates of inheritance in lands. It includes base fees, conditional fees, and fees tail. 2 Bl. Comm. 109.

LIMITED JURISDICTION. See "Jurisdiction."

LIMITED OWNER. One whose title in lands is less than a fee simple.

LIMITED PARTNERSHIP. One wherein the liability of one or more of the members is, by compliance with certain statutory provisions, limited to the amount of their contribution to the capital stock. The term "special partnership" is sometimes used; but "limited partnership" seems better, for "particular partnerships," or partnerships for a single transaction, are sometimes called "special partnerships."

LINARIUM (Law Lat. from *linum*, flax). In old records. A place where flax is sown; a flax plat. Pat. 22 Hen. IV. par. 1, m. 33; Blount.

LINE.

——**In Descents.** The series of persons who have descended from a common ancestor, placed one under the other, in the order of their birth. It connects successively all the relations by blood to each other. See "Consanguinity"; "Degree."

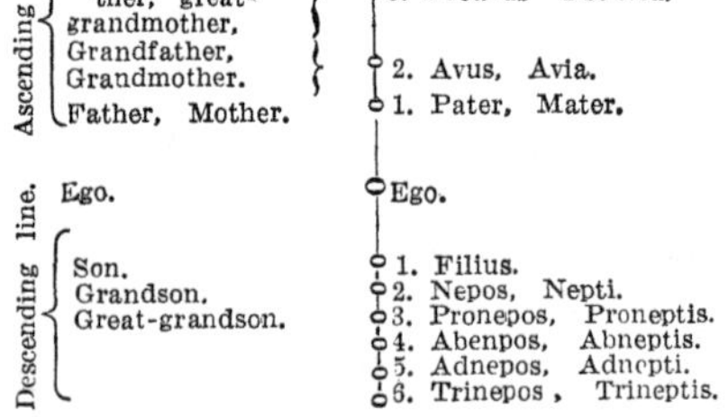

The line is either direct or collateral. The direct line is composed of all the persons who are descended from each other. If, in the direct line, any one person is assumed as the *propositus*, in order to count from him upwards and downwards, the line will be divided into two parts, the ascending and descending lines. The ascending line is that which, counting from the *propositus*, ascends to his ancestors, to his father, grandfather, great-grandfather, etc. The descending line is that which, counting from the same person, descends to his children, grandchildren, great-grandchildren, etc. The preceding table is an example.

The collateral line, considered by itself, and in relation to the common ancestor, is a direct line. It becomes collateral when placed alongside of another line below the common ancestor, in whom both lines unite. For example:

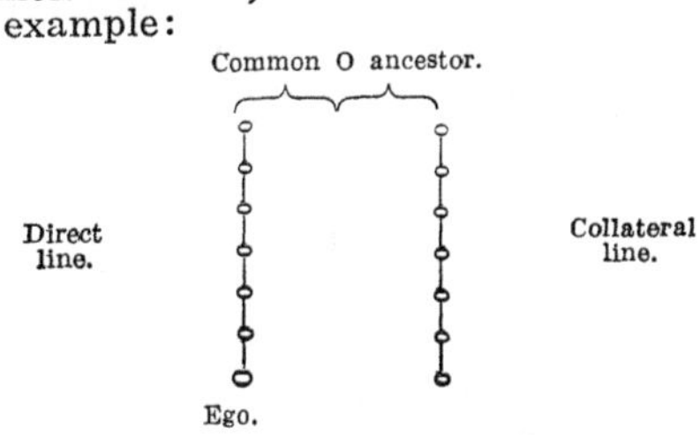

These two lines are independent of each other; they have no connection except by their union in the person of the common ancestor. This reunion is what forms the relation among the persons composing the two lines.

A line is also paternal or maternal. In the examination of a person's ascending line, the line ascends first to his father, next to his paternal grandfather, his paternal great-grandfather, etc., so on from father to father. This is called the paternal line. Another line will be found to ascend from the same person to his mother, his maternal grandmother, and so from mother to mother. This is the maternal line. These lines, however, do not take in all the ascendants; there are many others who must be imagined.

See 2 Bl. Comm. 200 bk. 2, c. 14; Poth. des Success. c. 1, art. 3, § 2; "Ascendants."

——**Boundary Lines.** The division between two estates. Limit; border; boundary.

——**Measures.** A line is a lineal measure, containing the one-twelfth part of an inch.

LINEA (Lat.) In civil and old English law. A line; a series of persons descending from a common stock (*series personarum a communi stipite descendentium*). Heinec. Elem. Jur. Civ. lib. 1, tit. 10, § 153. It was *ascendens* as well as *descendens*. Hale, Anal. § 18; Fleta, lib. 6, c. 1, § 11.

LINEA RECTA (Lat.) The perpendicular line; the direct line; the line of ascent, through father, grandfather, etc., and of descent, through son, grandson, etc. Co. Litt. 10, 158; Bracton, fol. 67; Fleta, lib. 6, c. 1, § 11. This is represented in a diagram by a vertical line.

Persons springing from another immediately, or mediately through a third person, are said to be in the direct line (*linea recta*), and are called "ascendants" and "descendants." Mackeld. Civ. Law, § 129.

LINEA RECTA EST INDEX SUI ET OBliqui; lex est linea recti. A right line is an index of itself and of an oblique; law is a line of right. Co. Litt. 158.

LINEA RECTA SEMPER PRAEFERTUR transversali. The right line is always preferred to the collateral. Co. Litt. 10; Fleta, lib. 6, c. 1; 1 Steph. Comm. (4th Ed.) 406.

LINEA TRANSVERSALIS (Lat.) A line crossing the perpendicular lines. Where two persons are descended from a third, they are called "collaterals," and are said to be related in the collateral line (*linea transversa* or *obliqua*).

LINEAL. In a direct line.

LINEAL CONSANGUINITY. That kind of consanguinity which subsists between persons of whom one is descended in a direct line from the other; as between a particular person and his father, grandfather, great-grandfather, and so upward, in the direct ascending line; or between the same person and his son, grandson, great-grandson, and so downwards, in the direct descending line. 2 Bl. Comm. 203; 198 Ill. 317.

LINEAL DESCENT. Descent in a right line, as where an estate descends from ancestor to heir in one line of succession, as opposed to collateral descent, which is descent in a transverse or zigzag line, namely, up through the common ancestor, and then down from him.

LINEAL WARRANTY. A warranty by ancestor from whom the title did or might have come to heir. 2 Bl. Comm. 301; Rawle, Cov. 30; 2 Hilliard, Real Prop. 360. Thus, a warrant by an elder son during lifetime of father was lineal to a younger son, but a warranty by younger son was collateral to elder; for, though the younger might take the paternal estate through the elder, the elder could not take it through the younger. Litt. § 703. Abolished. 3 & 4 Wm. IV. c. 74, § 14.

LINES AND CORNERS. In deeds and surveys. Boundary lines and their angles with each other. 17 Miss. 459; 21 Ala. 66; 9 Fost. & H. (N. H.) 471; 10 Grat. (Va.) 445; 16 Ga. 141.

LINGUA. (Lat.) A tongue; speech. Applied, in old English law, to the verdict of a jury.

LIQUERE (Lat.) In the civil law. To be clear, evident, or satisfactory. When a *judex* was in doubt how to decide a case, he represented to the praetor, under oath, *sibi non liquere*, that it was not clear to him, and was thereupon discharged. Calv. Lex.

LIQUET. It is clear or apparent; it appears. *Satis liquet*, it sufficiently appears. 1 Strange, 412.

LIQUEUR. A liquor compounded of alcohol, water, sugar, and different aromatic substances. 28 Fed. Cas. 141.

LIQUIDATE. To pay; to settle. Webster; 8 Wheat. (U. S.) 322.

To ascertain or make certain in amount. 20 Ga. 53.

LIQUIDATED ACCOUNT. A liquidated account is one the amount of which is agreed upon by the parties or is fixed by operation of law. 61 Conn. 568; 15 Ga. 321; 43 Conn. 469.

LIQUIDATED DAMAGES. Liquidated damages are ascertained damages. 48 Ill. 408.

LIQUIDATED DEBT. A debt is liquidated when its amount and the fact that it is due are certain. 69 Ill. 523.

LIQUIDATING PARTNER. The member of a dissolved partnership who winds up its business. Shumaker, Partn. 128.

LIQUIDATION. A fixed and determinate valuation of things which before were uncertain.

LIQUIDATOR. A person appointed to carry out the winding up of a company.

LIRRA. (Law Fr.) It shall be lawful. *Lirroit;* it should be lawful. Kelham.

LIS (Lat.) A controversy or dispute. See "Lis Mota."

A suit at law; an action; a controversy carried on in form of law. In the civil law, this was a more general term than *actio. Litis nomen omnem actionem significat,* the term *lis* signifies every kind of action. Dig. 50. 16. 36; Co. Litt. 292.

LIS ALIBI PENDENS. A suit pending elsewhere. The fact that proceedings are pending between a plaintiff and defendant in one court in respect to a given matter is frequently a ground for preventing the plaintiff from taking proceedings in another court against the same defendant for the same object, and arising out of the same cause of action. Rapalje & L.

LIS MOTA (Lat.) A controversy begun *i. e.,* on the point at issue, and prior to commencement of judicial proceedings. Such controversy is taken to arise on the advent of the state of facts on which the claim rests; and after such controversy has arisen (*post litem motam*), no declarations of deceased members of family as to matters of pedigree are admissible. 6 Car. & P. 560; 4 Campb. 417; 2 Russ. & M. 161; Greenl. Ev. §§ 131, 132; 4 Maule & S. 497; 1 Pet. (U. S.) 337; 26 Barb. (N. Y.) 177.

LIS PENDENS (Lat.) A pending suit.

The control which a court has, during the pendency of an action, over property involved therein. Bennett, Lis Pendens, § 2.

The property involved is the *res.* Its character remains fixed during the litigation, and this litigated or contested quality is called *res litigiosa. Lis pendens, notice of lis pendens,* and *rule lis pendens,* when used without reference to a statute defining their meaning, are synonymous terms. Bennett, Lis Pendens, §§ 2, 59.

One who purchases property pending an action concerning it (*pendente lite, q. v.*) takes subject to the event of the action, the maxim of the law being *pendente lite nihil innovetur.*

All real property is subject to *lis pendens* (45 N. H. 517), and all personalty (37 Pa. St. 353; 23 Wis. 1), except negotiable paper (103 U. S. 806; 48 N. Y. 613).

To constitute *lis pendens* there must be an action actually commenced (27 Mo. 560) in a court of competent jurisdiction, involving the title to particular property (13 R. I. 102), to which the claimant of the property is a party (24 Iowa 155), and the property must be sufficiently described in the pleadings so that it can be identified by reasonable inquiry (4 Johns. Ch. [N. Y.] 39).

LIST. A table of cases arranged for trial or argument; as, the trial list, the argument list. 3 Bouv. Inst. note 3031. See "Calendar."

LISTERS. This word is used in some of the states to designate the persons appointed to make lists of taxables. See Rev. St. Vt. 538.

LITE PENDENTE (Lat.) Pending the suit. Fleta, lib. 2, c. 54, § 23.

LITEM SUAM FACERE (Lat.) To make a suit his own. Where a *judex,* from partiality or enmity, evidently favored either of the parties, he was said *litem suam facere.* Calv. Lex.

LITERA (Lat.) A letter; the letter of a law, as distinguished from its spirit. See "Letter."

LITERA PISANA. The Pisan letter. A term applied to the old character in which the copy of the Pandects formerly kept at Pisa, in Italy, was written. Spelman.

LITERAE. Letters. A term applied in old English law to various instruments in writing, public and private.

LITERAE DIMISSORIAE. Dimissory letters. See "Dimissoriae Litterae."

LITERAE HUMANIORES. A term including Greek, Latin, general philology, logic, moral philosophy, metaphysics; the name of the principal course of study in the University of Oxford. Wharton.

LITERAE MORTUAE. Dead letters; fulfilling words of a statute. Lord Bacon observes that "there are in every statute certain words which are as veins, where the life and blood of the statute cometh, and where all doubts do arise, and the rest are *literae mortuae,* fulfilling words." Bac. St. Uses, (Works, iv. 189).

LITERAE PATENTES. Letters patent; literally, open letters.

LITERAE PATENTES REGIS NON erunt vacuae Letters patent of the king shall not be void. 1 Bulst. 6.

LITERAE PROCURATORIAE (Lat.) In civil law. Letters procuratory; a written authority, or power of attorney (*litera attornati*), given to a procurator. Vicat; Bracton, fols. 40-43.

LITERAE RECOGNITIONIS. In maritime law. A bill of lading. Jacobsen, Sea Laws, 172.

LITERAE SCRIPTAE MANENT. Written words last.

LITERAE SIGILLATAE. In old English law. Sealed letters. The return of a sheriff was so called. Fleta, lib. 2, c. 64, § 19.

LITERAL CONTRACT. In civil law. A contract the whole of the evidence of which is reduced to writing. This contract is perfected by the writing, and binds the party who subscribed it, although he has received no consideration. Lec. Elm. § 887.

LITERAL PROOF. In civil law. Written evidence.

LITERARY PROPERTY. The interest of an author, or those who claim under him, in his work before or after publication, and with or without copyright. Drone, Copyright, 97.

Literary property is the common-law ownership of the original work. Copyright is the statutory right to make all the copies of it that shall be made for a term of years. Abbott.

The scope of such property is, in the absence of copyright laws, that an author has the sole right of first printing and publishing his writings. 4 Burrows, 2408. The author's property right is lost as soon as he prints and publishes the manuscript (8 Pet. [U. S.] 591); though a private use or circulation of a manuscript, as for the purpose of instructing students, will not forfeit the author's literary property.

By statute, a penalty is denounced against the publication of a manuscript without the author's consent. Rev. St. U. S. § 4966.

LITERATURA (Lat. from *litera*, a letter). In old English law. Education; learning; knowledge of letters. *Ad literaturam ponere*, to put to learning; to put to school. Par. Ant. 401; Cowell. *Minus sufficiens in literatura*, deficient in education.

LITERIS OBLIGATIO. In Roman law. The contract of *nomen*, which was constituted by writing (*scriptura*). It was of two kinds, viz.: (1) *A re in personam*, when a transaction was transferred from the daybook (*adversaria*) into the ledger (*codex*) in the form of a debt under the name or heading of the purchaser or debtor (*nomen*); and (2) a *persona in personam*, where a debt already standing under one *nomen* or heading was transferred in the usual course of *novatio* from that *nomen* to another and substituted *nomen*. By reason of this transferring, these obligations were called *nomina transcriptitia*. No money was, in fact, paid to constitute the contract. If ever money was paid, then the *nomen* was *arcarium, i. e.*, a real contract, *re contractus*, and not a *nomen proprium*. Brown.

LITIGANT. One engaged in a suit; one fond of litigation.

LITIGARE (Lat.) To litigate; to carry on a suit (*litem agere*), either as plaintiff or defendant; to claim or dispute by action; to test or try the validity of a claim by action.

LITIGATE. To contend in form of law.

LITIGATION. A contest, authorized by law, in a court of justice, for the purpose of enforcing a right.

LITIGIOSA RES. See "Lis Pendens."

LITIGIOSITY. In Scotch law. The pendency of a suit. It is an implied prohibition of alienation, to the disappointment of an action, or of diligence, the direct object of which is to obtain possession, or to acquire the property of a particular subject. The effect of it is analogous to that of inhibition. 2 Bell, Comm. (5th Ed.) 152. See "Lis Pendens."

LITIGIOUS. That which is the subject of a suit or action; that which is contested in a court of justice. In another sense, litigious signifies a disposition to sue; a fondness for litigation.

LITIGIOUS RIGHTS. In French law. Those which are or may be contested either in whole or in part, whether an action has been commenced, or when there is reason to apprehend one. Poth. Vente, note 584; 9 Mart. (La.) 183; Tropl. de la Vente, note 984 a 1003; Eva. Civ. Code, art. 2623; Eva Civ. Code, art. 3522, note 22. See "Contentious Jurisdiction."

LITIS AESTIMATIO. The measure of damages.

LITIS CONTESTATIO.

——**In the Civil and Canon Law.** Contestation of suit; the process of contesting a suit by the opposing statements of the respective parties; the process of coming to an issue; the attainment of an issue; the issue itself.

——**In the Practice of the Ecclesiastical Courts.** The general answer made by the defendant, in which he denies the matter charged against him in the libel. Halifax, Civ. Law, bk. 3, c. 11, No. 9.

LITIS DOMINIUM. In civil law. Ownership, control, or direction of a suit. A fiction of law by which the employment of an attorney or proctor (*procurator*) in a suit was authorized or justified, he being supposed to become, by the appointment of his principal (*dominus*) or client, the *dominus litis*. Heinec. Elem. Jur. Civ. lib. 4, tit. 10, §§ 1246, 1247.

LITIS NOMEN ACTIONEM SIGNIFICAT, sive in rem, sive in personam sit. The word *lis, i. e.,* a lawsuit, signifies every action, whether *in rem* or *in personam.* Co. Litt. 292.

LITISPENDENCE. An obsolete term for the time during which a lawsuit is going on.

LITISPENDENCIA. In Spanish law. The condition of a suit pending in a court of justice.

In order to render this condition valid, it is necessary that the judge be competent to take cognizance of the cause; that the defendant has been duly cited to appear, and fully informed, in due time and form, of the nature of the demand, or that, if he has not, it has been through his own fault or fraud.

The *litispendencia* produces two effects: The legal impossibility of alienating the property in dispute during the pendency of the suit; the accumulation of all the proceedings in the cause, in the tribunal where the suit is pending, whether the same be had before the same judge or other judges or notaries. This cumulation may be required in any stage of the cause, and forms a valid exception to the further proceeding, until the cumulation is effected. Escriche, Dic. Raz.

LITRE. A French measure of capacity. It is of the size of a decimetre, or one-tenth part of a cubic metre. It is equal to 61.028 cubic inches. See "Measure."

LITTORAL (*litus*). Belonging to shore; as, of sea and great lakes. Webster. Corresponding to riparian proprietors on a stream or small pond are littoral proprietors on a sea or lake. Although used coextensively with "riparian," 7 Cush. (Mass.) 94, its employment is preferred to "riparian," in respect to the shores of the sea, and also, according to important authorities, as including "riparian." Gould Waters, § 148; 2 Ex. D. 63; 17 How. 432, 433; 7 Allen 158, 167; Smith v. Power, 14 Texas 146.

LITTORAL PROPRIETOR. One whose lands border upon tide waters, as distinguished from lands bounding on a watercourse. See "Riparian Proprietors." There appears to be no word or phrase of sufficiently broad meaning to include both riparian and littoral, although each is sometimes used to denote the other. Gould Waters, § 148. See "Littoral."

LITURA. In civil law. An obliteration or blot in a will or other instrument. Dig. 28. 4. 1. 1.

LITUS EST QUOUSQUE MAXIMUS fluctus a mari pervenit. The shore is where the highest wave from the sea has reached. Dig. 50. 16. 96; Angell, Tide Waters, 67.

LITUS MARIS (Lat.)

——**In Civil Law.** Shore; beach. *Qua fluctus eluderet.* Cic. Top. c. 7. *Qua fluctus adludit.* Quinct. lib. 5, c. ult. *Quousque maximus fluctus a mari pervenit.* Celsus. Said to have been first so defined by Cicero, in an award as arbitrator. L. 92, D, *de verb. signif. Qua maximus fluctus exaestuat.* L. 112, D., *eod. tit. Quatenas hibernus fluctus maximus excurrit.* Inst. lib. 2, *de rer. divis. et qual.* § 3. That is to say, as far as the largest winter wave runs up. Vocab.

——**At Common Law.** The shore between common high-water mark and low-water mark. Hale de Jur. Mar. cc. 4, 5, 6; 3 Kent, Comm. 427; 2 Hilliard, Real Prop. 90.

Shore is also used of a river. 5 Wheat. (U. S.) 385; 20 Wend. (N. Y.) 149. See 13 How. (U. S.) 381; 28 Me. 180; 14 Pa. St. 171.

LIVERY. In English law. The delivery of possession of lands to those tenants who hold of the king *in capita* or by knight's service.

The name of a writ which lay for the heir of age to obtain possession of the seisin of his lands at the king's hands. Fitzh. Nat. Brev. 155; 2 Bl. Comm. 68.

The distinguishing dress worn by the servants of a gentleman or nobleman, or by the members of a particular guild. "Livery or clothing." Sayer, 274. By St. 1 Rich. II. c. 7, and St. 16 Rich. II. c. 4, none but the servants of a lord, and continually dwelling in his house, or those above rank of yeomen, should wear the lord's livery.

Privilege of a particular company or guild. Wharton.

LIVERY OF SEISIN. In estates. A delivery of possession of lands, tenements, and hereditaments unto one entitled to the same. This was a ceremony used in the common law for the conveyance of real estate; and livery was in deed, which was performed by the feoffor and the feoffee going upon the land, and the latter receiving it from the former; or in law, where the same was not made on the land, but in sight of it. 2 Bl. Comm. 315, 316.

In most of the states, livery of seisin is unnecessary, it having been dispensed with either by express law or by usage. The recording of the deed has the same effect. Washb. Real Prop. 14, 35. In Maryland, however, it seems that a deed cannot operate as a feoffment without livery of seisin. 5 Har. & J. (Md.) 158. See 4 Kent, Comm. 381; 1 Mo. 553; 1 Pet. (U. S.) 508; 1 Bay (S. C.) 107; 5 Har. & J. (Md.) 158; 11 Me. 318; Dane, Abr. See "Seisin."

LIVERY STABLE. A place where horses and vehicles are kept to be let to the public. See 30 La. Ann. 1095.

Though some other related business may be carried on, as the boarding of horses for hire, the keeper of the stable is, as to such, an agister, etc., as the case may be, not a livery stable keeper.

LIVORARE. (Law Lat.) In old European law. To beat; to bruise by beating. Marculf. lib. 1, form. 29.

LIVRE TOURNOIS. In common law. A coin used in France before the revolution. It is to be computed, in the *ad valorem* duty on goods, etc., at eighteen and a half cents. Act March 2, 1798, § 61 (1 Story, U. S. Laws, 629). See "Foreign Coins."

LLOYDS. A mutual fire and marine insurance association, the members underwriting each other's policies.

LOADMANAGE. The pay to loadsmen; that is, persons who sail or row before ships, in barks or small vessels, with instruments for towing the ship and directing her course, in order that she may escape the dangers in her way. Poth. des Avaries, note 137; Guidon de la Mer, c. 14; Bac. Abr. "Merchant and Merchandise" (F). It is not in use in the United States.

LOAN. A bailment without reward; a bailment of an article for use or consumption without reward; the thing so bailed.

A loan, in general, implies that a thing is lent without reward; but in some cases a loan may be for a reward; as, the loan of money. 7 Pet. (U. S.) 109.

It would be an inquiry too purely speculative whether this use of the term "loan" originated in the times when taking interest was considered usury, and improper, the bailment of money which was to be returned in kind. The supposition would furnish a reasonable explanation of the exception to the general rule that loan includes properly only those bailments where no reward is given or received by the bailee.

In order to make a contract usurious, there must be a loan (Cowp. 112, 770; 1 Ves. Jr. 527; 2 Bl. 859; 3 Wils. 390), and the borrower must be bound to return the money at all events (2 Schoales & L. 470). The purchase of a bond or note is not a loan (3 Schoales & L. 469; 9 Pet. [U. S.] 103); but if such a purchase be merely colorable, it will be considered as a loan (2 Johns. Cas. [N. Y.] 60, 66; 12 Serg. & R. [Pa.] 46; 15 Johns. [N. Y.] 44).

LOAN FOR CONSUMPTION. A contract by which the owner of a personal chattel, called the "lender," delivers it to the bailee, called the "borrower," to be returned in kind. For example, if a person borrows a bushel of wheat, and at the end of a month returns to the lender a bushel of equal value. This class of loans is commonly considered under the head of "bailments," but it lacks the one essential element of bailment —that of a return of the property. It is more strictly a barter or an exchange; the property passes to the borrower. 4 N. Y. 76; 8 N. Y. 433; 1 Ohio St. 98; 3 Mason (U. S.) 478; 1 Blackf. (Ind.) 353; Story, Bailm. § 439. Those cases sometimes called *mutuum* (the corresponding civil-law term), such as where corn is delivered to a miller to be ground into wheat, are either cases of hiring of labor and service, as where the miller grinds and returns the identical wheat ground into flour, retaining a portion for his services, or constitute a mere exchange, as where he mixes the wheat with his own, undertaking to furnish an equivalent in corn. It amounts to a contract of sale; payment being stipulated for in a specified article instead of money.

LOAN FOR USE. A bailment of an article to be used by the borrower without paying for the use. 2 Kent, Comm. (4th Ed.) 573.

Loan for use (called *commodatum* in the civil law) differs from a loan for consumption (called *mutuum* in the civil law) in this, that the *commodatum* must be specifically returned; the *mutuum* is to be returned in kind. In the case of a *commodatum*, the property in the thing remains in the lender; in a *mutuum*, the property passes to the borrower.

LOAN SOCIETIES. In English law. A kind of club formed for the purpose of advancing money on loan to the industrial classes. They are of comparatively recent origin in England, and are authorized and regulated by 3 & 4 Vict. c. 110, and 21 Vict. c. 19.

LOBBYING. Personal solicitation of a member of a legislative body during a session thereof, by one not a member, with reference to any matter pending in the legislature, so called from the fact that such solicitation is supposed to take place in the "lobby" of the legislative hall.

The term is generally used in a bad sense, as including only secret or wrongful solicitation, and not the submission of petitions, or the presentation of arguments, at a proper time and place.

As a general rule, all contracts for personal solicitation of legislators, or the use of personal influence with them, are void, though no bribery or other corrupt practice is contemplated. 36 N. Y. 241; 101 U. S. 108. But the professional services of a lawyer may be employed for legitimate purposes connected with pending legislation, such as the presentation of evidence or argument openly, and at proper times and places. 80 Va. 475; 21 Wall. (U. S.) 441.

L'OBLIGATION SANS CAUSE, OU SUR une fausse cause, ou sur cause illicite, ne peut avoir aucun effet. An obligation without consideration, or upon a false consideration (which fails), or upon unlawful consideration, cannot have any effect. Code, 3. 3. 4; Chit. Cont. (10th Am. Ed.) 25, note.

LOCAL (Law Lat. *localis*, from *locus*, place). Relating to place; expressive of place; belonging or confined to a particular place. Distinguished from *general*, *personal* and *transitory*.

LOCAL ACTION. In practice. An action the cause of which could have arisen in some particular county only.

All local actions must be brought in the county where the cause of action arose.

In general, all actions are local which seek the recovery of real property (2 W. Bl. 1070; 4 Term R. 504; 7 Term R. 589), whether founded upon contract or not; or damages for injury to such property, as waste, under the statute of Cloucester, trespass *quare clausum fregit*, trespass or case for injuries affecting things real, as for nuisances to houses or lands, disturbance of rights of way or of common, obstruction or diversion of ancient watercourses (1 Chit. Pl. 271; Gould, Pl. c. 3, §§ 105, 106, 107); but not if there were a contract between the parties on which to ground an action (15 Mass. 284; 1 Day [Conn.] 263).

Many actions arising out of injuries to local rights are local; as, *quare impedit*. 1 Chit. Pl. 241. The action of replevin is also local. 1 Wm. Saund. 247, note 1; Gould, Pl. c. 3, § 111; Comyn, Dig. "Action." See "Transitory Action."

LOCAL ALLEGIANCE. The allegiance due to a government from an alien while within its limits. 1 Bl. Comm. 370; 2 Kent, Comm. 63, 64.

LOCAL CHATTEL. A fixture.

LOCAL COURT. A court whose jurisdiction is limited to a particular locality. Sometimes applied to the courts of the home jurisdiction, as opposed to foreign courts.

LOCAL CUSTOM. One whose observance is confined to a particular locality.

LOCAL GOVERNMENT. Government confined to a certain locality. The autonomous government of a minor subdivision of a state or country, as opposed to the general government.

LOCAL IMPROVEMENTS. Improvements made in a particular locality, by which the real estate in that locality is specially benefited. Cooley, Tax'n, 109, 177, 419.

The question whether an improvement is local depends not on whether it is of use to the general public, but on the special benefit which will result to the real property adjoining or near the locality in which it is made. 22 Minn. 507. See "Special Assessments."

LOCAL OPTION. A privilege granted to a locality of determining by popular vote whether a general law shall be effective in that locality. Usually applied to the determination by popular vote whether or not the sale of intoxicating liquor shall be allowed in a particular locality.

LOCAL PREJUDICE. A prejudice against a litigant, or in favor of his adversary, prevailing in a particular locality, and tending to prevent a fair trial there. Such prejudice is ground for change of venue.

LOCAL STATUTES. Statutes whose operation is intended to be restricted within certain limits, much less than the limits of the legislative jurisdiction. A statute is not local because it excludes from its operation one or two counties in the state. See 86 N. Y. 7; Dwarr. St. p. 384. It may be either public or private. 1 Bl. Comm. 85, 86, note. "Local statutes" is used by Lord Mansfield as opposed to "personal statutes," which relate to personal transitory contracts; whereas local statutes refer to things in a certain jurisdiction alone; *e. g.*, the statute of frauds relates only to things in England. 1 W. Bl. 246.

LOCAL TAXES. Taxes (more often called "assessment") limited to certain civil divisions of the state or city.

LOCAL VENUE. The venue of a local action (*q. v.*).

LOCALITY. In Scotch law. This name is given to a life rent created in marriage contracts in favor of the wife, instead of leaving her to her legal life rent of terce. 1 Bell, Comm. 55. See "Jointure."

LOCARE. To let for hire; to deliver or bail a thing for a certain reward or compensation. Bracton, fol. 62.

LOCARIUM. In old European law. The price of letting; money paid for the hire of a thing; rent. Spelman.

LOCATARIUS. In civil law. A depositary.

LOCATE. To fix or definitely determine.

LOCATIO (Lat.) In civil law. Letting for hire. Calv. Lex.; Vocat. The term is also used by text writers upon the law of bailment at common law. 1 Pars. Cont. 602. In Scotch law it is translated "location." Bell, Dict.

LOCATIO-CONDUCTIO. In civil law. A compound word used to denote the contract of bailment for hire, expressing the action of both parties, viz., a letting by the one, and a hiring by the other. 2 Kent, Comm. 586, note; Story, Bailm. § 368.

LOCATIO CUSTODIAE. A letting to keep; a bailment or deposit of goods for hire. Story, Bailm. § 442.

LOCATIO MERCIUM VEHENDARUM (Lat.) In civil law. The carriage of goods for hire.

In respect to contracts of this sort entered into by private persons not exercising the business of common carriers, there does not seem to be any material distinction varying the rights, obligations, and duties of the parties from those of other bailees for hire. Every such private person is bound to ordinary diligence and a reasonable exercise of skill; and of course he is not responsible for any losses not occasioned by ordinary negligence, unless he has expressly, by the terms of his contract, taken upon himself such risk. 2 Ld. Raym. 909, 917, 918; 4 Taunt. 787; 6 Taunt. 577; 2 Marsh. 293; Jones, Bailm. 103, 106, 121; 2 Bos. & P. 417; 1 Bouv. Inst. note 1020. See "Common Carriers."

LOCATIO OPERIS (Lat.) In civil law. The hiring of labor and services.

It is a contract by which one of the parties gives a certain work to be performed by the other, who binds himself to do it for the price agreed between them, which he who gives the work to be done promises to pay to the other for doing it. Poth. du Contr. de Louage, note 392. This is divided into two branches: First, *locatio operis faciendi;* and, secondly, *locatio mercium vehendarum* (*q. v.*).

LOCATIO OPERIS FACIENDI (Lat.) In civil law. Hire of services to be performed.

There are two kinds: First, the *locatio operis faciendi,* strictly so called, or the hire of labor and services; such as the hire of tailors to make clothes, and of jewelers to set gems, and of watchmakers to repair watches. Jones, Bailm. 90, 96, 97. Secondly, *locatio custodiae,* or the receiving of goods on deposit for a reward, which is properly the hire of care and attention about the goods. Story, Bailm. §§ 422, 442; 1 Bouv. Inst. note 994.

In contracts for work, it is of the essence of the contract, first, that there should be work to be done; secondly, for a price or reward; and, thirdly, a lawful contract between parties capable and intending to contract. Poth. du Contr. de Louage, notes 395-403.

LOCATIO REI (Lat.) In civil law. The hiring of a thing. It is a contract by which one of the parties obligates himself to give to the other the use and enjoyment of a certain thing for a period of time agreed upon between them, and in consideration of a price which the latter binds himself to pay in return. Poth. du Contr. de Louage, note 1.

LOCATION. In the apportionment of public lands, the selection and designation of lands which the person making the location claims under the law.

——**In Scotch Law.** A contract by which the temporary use of a subject, or the work or service of a person, is given for an ascertained hire. 1 Bell, Comm. bk. 2, pt. 3, c. 2, sec. 4, art. 2, § 1, p. 255. See "Bailment"; "Hire."

LOCATIVE CALLS. Calls describing certain means by which the land to be located can be identified.

Reference to physical objects in entries and deeds by which the land to be located is exactly described. 2 Bibb (Ky.) 145; 3 Bibb (Ky.) 414.

Special, as distinguished from general, calls or descriptions. 3 Bibb (Ky.) 414; 2 Wheat. (U. S.) 211; 10 Wheat. (U. S.) 463; 7 Pet. (U. S.) 171; 18 Wend. (N. Y.) 157; 16 Johns. (N. Y.) 257; 17 Johns. (N. Y.) 29; 10 Grat. (Va.) 445; Jones Law (N. C.) 469; 16 Ga. 141; 5 Ind. 302; 15 Mo. 80; 2 Bibb (Ky.) 118.

LOCATOR. In civil law. He who leases or lets a thing to hire to another. His duties are, first, to deliver to the hirer the thing hired, that he may use it; second, to guarantee to the hirer the free enjoyment of it; third, to keep the thing hired in good order in such manner that the hirer may enjoy it; fourth, to warrant that the thing hired has not such defects as to destroy its use. Poth. du Contr. de Louage, note 53.

LOCKMAN. An officer in the Isle of Man to execute the orders of the governor, something like our undersheriff. Wharton.

LOCKOUT. The closing of a factory or workshop by an employer, usually in order to bring the workmen to satisfactory terms by a suspension of wages. 202 Ill. 398.

LOCK UP HOUSE. A place used temporarily as a prison.

LOCO PARENTIS. See "In Loco Parentis."

LOCOCESSION (Lat.) In the civil law. The act of giving place.

LOCUM TENENS (Lat.) Holding the place. Applied to a deputy.

LOCUPLES (Lat.) In civil law. Able to respond in an action; good for the amount which the plaintiff might recover. Dig. 50. 16. 234. 1.

LOCUS (Lat.) A place; the place where a thing is done.

LOCUS CONTRACTUS. See "Lex Loci."

LOCUS CONTRACTUS REGIT ACTUM. The place of the contract governs the act. 2 Kent, Comm. 458.

LOCUS CRIMINIS. The locality of a crime; the place where a crime was committed.

LOCUS DELICTI. The place where the tort, offense, or injury has been committed.

LOCUS IN QUO (Lat. the place in which). In pleading. The place where anything is alleged to have been done. 1 Salk. 94.

LOCUS PARTITUS. In old English law. A place divided; a division made between two towns or counties to make out in which the land or place in question lies. Fleta, lib. 4, c. 15, § 1; Cowell.

LOCUS PRO SOLUTIONE REDITUS aut pecuniae secundum conditionem dimissionis aut obligationis est stricte observandus. The place for the payment of rent or money is to be strictly observed according to the condition of the lease or obligation. 4 Coke, 73.

LOCUS PUBLICUS. In civil law. A public place. Dig. 43. 8. 1; Id. 43. 8. 2. 3.

LOCUS REGIT ACTUM. In private international law. The rule that, when a legal transaction complies with the formalities required by the law of the country where it is done, it is also valid in the country where it is to be given effect, although by the law of that country other formalities are required. 8 Savigny, System, § 381; Westl. Priv. Int. Law, 159.

LOCUS REI SITAE. See "Lex Rei Sitae."

LOCUS SIGILLI. The place of the seal. The letters L. S. (an abbreviation of *locus sigilli*), surrounded by a scroll, is in some states held a good seal (5 Wis. 549), but in others a common-law seal is required. See "Seals."

LOCUS STANDI. A place of standing; standing in court. A right of appearance in a court of justice, or before a legislative body, on a given question.

LODEMAN. In old English law. A kind of pilot who navigated a vessel within a harbor. Jacob.

LODEMANAGE. Pilotage fees paid to a lodeman.

LODGER. One who inhabits a portion of a house of which another has the general possession and custody. It is by this retention of general possession and control by another that a "lodger" is distinguished from a "tenant." 40 L. J. C. P. 188; L. R. 6 C. P. 360. A lodger has no interest in the real estate. 117 Cal. 71.

It is difficult, in the present state of the law, to state exactly the distinctions between a "lodger," a "guest," and a "boarder." A person may be a guest at an inn without being a lodger. 1 Salk. 388; 9 Pick. (Mass.) 280; 25 Wend. (N. Y.) 653; 5 Sandf. (N. Y.) 242; 16 Ala. (N. S.) 666; 8 Blackf. (Ind.) 535; 14 Barb. (N. Y.) 193; 6 C. B. 132. And boarder includes one who regularly takes his meals with, and forms in some degree a part of, the householder's family. 25 Eng. Law & Eq. 76.

LODGING HOUSE. A lodging house is distinguished from a hotel in that the keeper specially deals with his customers by contracting personally with the customer for the nature of the accommodation to be provided, the duration of the stay, and exercises the right to reject all applicants at his pleasure. 168 Wis. 119. See "Hotel."

LODS ET RENTES. A fine payable to the seigneur upon every sale of lands within his seigniory. 1 Low. (U. S.) 59.

Any transfer of lands for a consideration gives rise to the claim (1 Low. [U. S.] 79): as, the creation of a *rente viagire* (life rent) (1 Low. [U. S.] 84); a transfer under *bail emphyteotique* (1 Low. [U. S.] 295); a promise to sell, accompanied by transfer of possession (9 Low. [U. S.] 272). It does not arise on a transfer by a father to his son subject to a payment by the son of a life rent to the father, and of the father's debts (8 Low. [U. S.] 5, 34, 324); nor where property is required for public uses (1 Low. [U. S.] 91).

LOG BOOK. A ship's journal. It contains a minute account of the ship's course, with a short history of every occurrence during the voyage. 1 Marsh. Ins. 408.

LOG ROLLING. A name given to a legislative practice of obtaining the passage of several measures by a combination of minorities. The original method was to embody the different measures in a single bill, and pass the same by a united vote of the minorities favoring each. This practice is now rendered impossible by constitutional provision in most of the states, that no bill shall embrace more than one subject. The term is now applied to the practice of agreement by minorities favoring several bills to vote for all. 106 Ill. 206.

LOGIA or **LOGIUM.** A small house.

LOGOGRAPHUS. In Roman law. A public clerk or accountant.

LOIAL. (Law Fr.) Lawful. Kelham.

LOLLARDS A body of primitive Wesleyans, who assumed importance about the time of John Wycliffe (1360), and were very successful in disseminating evangelical truth; but, being implicated (apparently against their will) in the insurrection of the villeins in 1381, the statute *De Haeretico Comburendo* (2 Hen. IV. c. 15) was passed against them, for their suppression. Brown.

LOMBARDS. A name given to the merchants of Italy, numbers of whom, during the twelfth and thirteenth centuries, were established as merchants and bankers in the principal cities of Europe.

LONG. See "Gambling Contract."

LONG INTEREST. See "Gambling Contract."

LONG MARKET. See "Gambling Contract."

LONG PARLIAMENT. The name usually given to the parliament which met in November, 1640, under Charles I., and was dissolved by Cromwell on the 10th of April, 1653. The name "Long Parliament" is, however, also given to the parliament which met in 1661, after the restoration of the monarchy, and was dissolved on the 30th of December, 1678. This latter parliament is sometimes called, by way of distinction, the "long parliament of Charles II." Mozley & W.

LONG QUINTO, THE. An expression used to denote part second of the Year Book which gives reports of cases in 5 Edw. IV.

LONG VACATION. The recess of the English courts from August 10th to October 24th.

LONGA PATIENTIA TRAHITUR AD consensum. Long sufferance is construed as consent. Fleta, lib. 4, c. 26, § 4.

LONGA POSSESSIO EST PACIS JUS. Long possession is the law of peace. Co. Litt. 6.

LONGA POSSESSIO JUS PARIT. Long possession begets right. Fleta, lib. 3, c. 15, § 6.

LONGA POSSESSIO PARIT JUS POSSIdendi, et tollit actionem vero domino. Long possession produces the right of possession, and takes away from the true owner his action. Co. Litt. 110.

LONGUM TEMPUS, ET LONGUS USUS qui excedit memoria hominum, sufficit pro jure. Long time, and long use beyond the memory of man, suffices for right. Co. Litt. 115.

LOOSE WOMAN. A loose woman, a woman of loose character, is an unchaste woman in the ordinary signification of those terms. By an unchaste woman is meant a sexually impure woman, ordinarily. 68 Vt. 320.

LOPWOOD. A right in the inhabitants of a parish, within a manor in England, to lop for fuel, at certain periods of the year, the branches of trees growing upon the waste lands of the manor.

LOQUELA (Lat.) In practice. An imparlance, *loquela sine die,* a respite in law to an indefinite time. Formerly by *loquela* was meant the allegations of fact mutually made on either side, now denominated the "pleadings." Steph. Pl. 29.

LOQUENDUM UT VULGUS; SENTIENdum ut docti. We should speak as the com mon people; we should think as the learned. 7 Coke, 11.

LORD.

——**In Feudal Law.** The superior of whom land is held by feudal tenure.

——**In English Law.** A title belonging to the degree of baron, but sometimes applied to all persons of nobility. 1 Bl. Comm. 396.

LORD ADVOCATE. The chief public prosecutor of Scotland. 2 Alis. Crim. Pr. 84.

LORD CHIEF BARON. The chief judge of the English court of exchequer, prior to the judicature acts.

LORD CHIEF JUSTICE. See "Justice."

LORD HIGH CHANCELLOR. See "Chancellor, The Lord High."

LORD HIGH STEWARD. In England, when a person is impeached, or when a peer is tried on indictment for treason or felony before the house of lords, one of the lords is appointed lord high steward, and acts as speaker *pro tempore.* Sweet.

LORD HIGH TREASURER. An officer formerly existing in England, who had the charge of the royal revenues and customs duties, and of leasing the crown lands. His functions are now vested in the lord's commissioners of the treasury. Mozley & W.

LORD IN GROSS. In feudal law. He who is lord, not by reason of any manor, but as the king in respect of his crown, etc. "Very lord" is he who is immediate lord to his tenant; and "very tenant," he who holds immediately of that lord. So that, where there is lord paramount, lord mesne, and tenant, the lord paramount is not very lord to the tenant. Wharton.

LORD JUSTICE CLERK. The second judicial officer in Scotland.

LORD KEEPER. Originally another name for the lord chancellor. After Henry II.'s reign they were sometimes divided, but now there cannot be a lord chancellor and lord keeper at the same time, for by St. 5 Eliz. c. 18, they are declared to be the same office. Com. Dig. "Chancery" (B 1).

LORD MAYOR'S COURT. In English law. One of the chief courts of special and local jurisdiction in London. It is a court of the queen, held before the lord mayor and aldermen. Its practice and procedure are amended, and its powers enlarged, by 20 & 21 Vict. c. 157. In this court, the recorder, or, in his absence, the common serjeant, presides as judge; and from its judgments error may be brought in the exchequer chamber. 3 Steph. Comm. 449, note (l).

LORD OF A MANOR. The grantee or owner of a manor.

LORD ORDINARY. In Scotch law. A judge of sessions officiating for the time being as the judge of first instance.

LORDS APPELLANTS. Five peers who for a time superseded Richard II. in his government, and whom, after a brief control of the government, he in turn superseded in 1397, and put the survivors of them to death. Richard II.'s eighteen commissioners (twelve peers and six commoners) took their place, as an embryo privy council acting with full powers, during the parliamentary recess. Brown.

LORD'S DAY. Sunday. Co. Litt. 135.

LORDS MARCHERS. Those noblemen who lived on the marches of Wales or Scotland, who in times past had their laws and power of life and death, like petty kings.

Abolished by 27 Hen. VIII. c. 26, and 6 Edw. VI. c. 10. Wharton.

LORDS OF ERECTION. On the reformation in Scotland, the king, as proprietor of benefices formerly held by abbots and priors, gave them out in temporal lordships to favorites, who were termed "lords of erection." Wharton.

LORDS OF PARLIAMENT. Those who have seats in the house of lords. During bankruptcy, peers are disqualified from sitting or voting in the house of lords. 34 & 35 Vict. c. 50. Wharton.

LORDS ORDAINERS. Lords appointed in 1312, in the reign of Edward II., for the control of the sovereign and the court party, and for the general reform and better government of the country. Brown.

LORDS SPIRITUAL. The archbishops and bishops who have seats in the house of lords.

LORDS TEMPORAL. Those lay peers who have seats in the house of lords.

LORDSHIP. Dominion, manor, seigniory, domain; also a title of honor used to a nobleman not being a duke. It is also the customary titulary appellation of the judges and some other persons in authority and office. Wharton.

LOSS. In insurance. The destruction of or damage to the insured subject by the perils insured against, according to the express provisions and construction of the contract.

These accidents, or misfortunes, or perils, as they are usually denominated, are all distinctly enumerated in the policy. And no loss, however great or unforeseen, can be a loss within the policy unless it be the direct and immediate consequence of one or more of these perils. Marsh. Ins. 1, c. 12.

Loss under a life policy is simply the death of the subject by a cause the risk of which is not expressly excepted in the policy, and where the loss is not fraudulent, as where one assured, who assures the life of another for his own benefit, procures the death.

Loss in insurance against fire must, under the usual form of policy, be by the partial or total destruction or damage of the thing insured by fire.

In maritime insurance, in which loss by fire is one of the risks usually included, the loss insured against may be absolutely or constructively total, or a partial or general average loss, or a particular average.

A partial loss is any loss or damage short of, or not amounting to, a total loss; for if it be not the latter, it must be the former. See 4 Mass. 374; 6 Mass. 102, 122, 317; 12 Mass. 170, 288; 8 Johns. (N. Y.) 237; 10 Johns. (N. Y.) 487; 5 Bin. (Pa.) 595; 2 Serg. & R. (Pa.) 553.

A total loss is such destruction of, or damage to, the thing insured that it is of little or no value to the owner.

Partial losses are sometimes denominated average losses, because they are often in the nature of those losses which are the subject of average contributions; and they are distinguished into general and particular averages. See "Average."

Total losses, in maritime insurance, are absolutely such when the entire thing perishes or becomes of no value. Constructively, a loss may become total where the value remaining is of such a small amount that the whole may be surrendered. See "Abandonment."

Consult Phil. Ins.; Arnold, Ind.; Pars. Mar. Law. See "Total Loss."

LOST, OR NOT LOST. A phrase in policies of insurance, signifying the contract to be retrospective and applicable to any loss within the specified risk, provided the same is not already known to either of the parties, and that neither has any knowledge or information not equally obvious or known to the other. The clause has been adopted only in maritime insurance; though a fire or life policy is not unfrequently retrospective, or under a different phraseology, by a provision that the risk is to commence at some time prior to its date. 1 Phil. Ins. § 925.

LOST PAPERS. Papers which have been destroyed (107 Mass. 546), or so mislaid that they cannot be found after diligent search (1 Vt. 470; 9 Gray [Mass.] 351).

LOT. That which fortuitously determines what we are to acquire.

When it can be certainly known what are our rights, we ought never to resort to a decision by lot; but when it is impossible to tell what actually belongs to us, as if an estate is divided into three parts, and one part given to each of three persons, the proper way to ascertain each one's part is to draw lots. Wolff. Dr. Nat. § 669.

LOT AND SCOT. In English law. Certain duties which must be paid by those who claim to exercise the elective franchise within certain cities and boroughs, before they are entitled to vote. It is said that the practice became uniform to refer to the poor rate as a register of "scot and lot" voters; so that the term, when employed to define a right of election, meant only the payment by a parishioner of the sum to which he was assessed on the poor rate. Brown.

LOT OF GROUND. A small piece of land in a town or city, usually employed for building a yard, a garden, or such other urban use. 2 Ohio St. 124; 25 Ark. 101. Lots are "in-lots," or those within the boundary of the city or town, and "out-lots," or those which are out of such boundary, and which are used by some of the inhabitants of such town or city.

LOTHERWITE, or LEYERWIT. In old English law. A liberty or privilege to take amends for lying with a bondwoman without license.

LOTTERY. A scheme for the distribution of prizes by lot to persons buying chances. 49 Ala. 396. A scheme whereby one, on paying money or other valuable thing to another, becomes entitled to receive from him such a return in value or nothing as some formula of chance may determine. Bish. St. Crimes, § 952.

A lottery has been distinguished from a mere bet or wager in that the latter is executory on both sides, and determined by an independent event; while in case of the former, a price is paid for a chance of a prize, and it is determined by the manager of the game, according to a prearranged scheme, whether he who pays the money is to have a prize. 137 Mass. 250.

A gift enterprise (*q. v.*) is a lottery (37 Tenn. 507), as is any enterprise by which prizes are paid by lot to persons paying to become members of an association (8 N. Y. 228; 33 N. H. 329; 59 Ill. 160).

L'OU LE LEY DONE CHOSE, LA CEO done remedie a vener a ceo. Where the law gives a right, it gives a remedy to recover. 2 Rolle, 17.

LOUAGE (Fr.) This is the contract of hiring and letting in French law, and may be either of things or of labor. The varieties of each are the following:

(1) Letting of things; *bail a loyer* being the letting of houses; *bail a ferme* being the letting of lands.

(2) Letting of labor; *loyer* being the letting of personal service; *bail a cheptel* being the letting of animals. Brown.

LOUDRES (Law Fr.) London.

LOVE DAY. The day on which any dispute between neighbors was amicably settled, or a day on which one neighbor helped another without hire. Wharton.

LOW JUSTICE. In old European law. Jurisdiction of petty offenses, as distinguished from "high justice" (*q. v.*).

LOW-WATER MARK. That part of the shore of the sea to which the waters recede when the tide is lowest. 125 Ill. 26. Where the water usually stands when free from disturbing causes. 94 Wis. 642.

The ordinary low-water mark, independent of spring or neap tides on the ocean, or of drought or freshet in respect to rivers. 60 Pa. St. 343. See "High-Water Mark."

LOWBOTE. Recompense for the death of one killed in an affray.

LOYAL. Legal, or according to law; as, loyal matrimony, a lawful marriage.

"Uncore n'est loyal a homme de faire un tort," it is never lawful for a man to do a wrong. Dyer, fol. 36, § 38. *"Et per curiam n'est loyal,"* and it was held by the court that it was not lawful. T. Jones, 24. Also spelled *loayl.* Dyer, fol. 36, § 38; Law Fr. & Lat. Dict. The Norman spelling is *"loyse."* Kelham.

Faithful to a prince or superior; true to plighted faith or duty. Webster.

LOYALTY. Adherence to law; faithfulness to the existing government.

LUBRICUM LINGUAE NON FACILE trahendum est in poenam. The slipperiness of the tongue, *i. e.*, its liability to err, ought not lightly to be subjected to punishment. Cro. Car. 117.

LUCID INTERVALS. In medical jurisprudence. Periods in which a lunatic is so far free from his disease that the ordinary legal consequences of insanity do not apply to acts done therein.

LUCRATIVA CAUSA (Lat.) In Roman law. A consideration which is voluntary; that is to say, a gratuitous gift, or such like. It was opposed to *onerosa causa,* which denoted a valuable consideration. It was a principle of the Roman law that two lucrative causes could not concur in the same person as regarded the same thing; that is to say, that, when the same thing was bequeathed to a person by two different testators, he could not have the thing (or its value) twice over. Brown.

LUCRATIVA USUCAPIO (Lat.) This species of *usucapio* was permitted in Roman law only in the case of persons taking possession of property upon a decease of its late owner, and in exclusion or deforcement of the heir, whence it was called *"usucapio pro haerede."* The adjective *"lucrativa"* denoted that property was acquired by this *usucapio* without any consideration or payment for it by way of purchase; and, as the possessor who so acquired the property was a *mala fide* possessor, his acquisition, or *usucapio,* was called also *"improba," i. e.,* dishonest; but this dishonesty was tolerated (until abolished by Hadrian) as an incentive to force the *haeres* to take possession, in order that the debts might be paid and the sacrifices performed; and, as a further incentive to the *haeres,* this *usucapio* was complete in one year. Brown.

LUCRATIVE SUCCESSION. In Scotch law. The passive title of *praeceptio haereditatis,* by which, if an heir apparent receive gratuitously a part, however small, of the heritage which would come to him as heir, he is liable for all grantor's precontracted debts. Ersk. Inst. 3. 8. 87-89; Stair, Inst. 3. 7.

LUCRI CAUSA (Lat. for the sake of gain). In criminal law. A term descriptive of the intent of deriving personal gain with which property is taken in cases of larceny, robbery, and other crimes against property. It is generally held not to be essential (34 Minn. 221; 52 Ala. 411; 17

Tex. 521), though the contrary has been held (1 McAll. [U. S.] 196).

LUCRUM CESSANS. In Scotch law. A cessation of gain. Opposed to *damnum emergens*, an actual loss.

LUCRUM FACERE EX PUPILLI TUTELA tutor non debet. A guardian ought not to make money out of the guardianship of his ward. 1 Johns. Ch. (N. Y.) 527, 535.

LUCTUOSA HAEREDITAS. A mournful inheritance. See "Haereditas Luctuosa."

LUGGAGE. This term is synonymous with "baggage;" the latter being in more common use in this country, while the former seems to be almost exclusively used in England. It may consist of any article intended for the use of a passenger while traveling, or for his personal equipment. 85 Cal. 330. See "Baggage."

LUM. L. Fr. A man. LL. Gul. Conq. l. 41.

LUMEN. In the civil law. Light; an easement of light. The plural form was *lumina.*

LUNACY. Lunacy is that condition or habit in which the mind is directed by the will, but is wholly or partially misguided, or erroneously governed by it; or it is the impairment of any one or more faculties of the mind, accompanied with, or inducing a defect in the comparing faculty. 1 Bland Ch. (Md.) 386. See "Insanity."

LUNATIC. One who is insane. See "Insanity."

LUNATICUS, QUI GAUDET IN LUCIDIS intervallis. He is a lunatic who enjoys lucid intervals. 1 Story, Cont. (4th Ed.) 70.

LUNDRESS. In old English law. A silver penny, so called because it was to be coined only at London, and not at the country mints. Lowndes' Essay on Coins, 17. Cowell.

LUPANATRIX. In Roman law. A bawd.

LUPINUM CAPUT GERERE (Lat.) To be outlawed, and have one's head exposed, like a wolf's, with a reward to him who should take it. Cowell.

LUPULICETUM (Law Lat.) In old English law. A hop ground, or place where hops grow. Co. Litt. 4 b.

LUXURY. Excess and extravagance, which was formerly an offense against the public economy, but is not now punishable. 1 Jac. I. c. 25.

LYEF GELD. In Saxon law. Leave money; a small sum paid by customary tenant for leave to plough, etc. Cowell; Somn. Gavelkind, p. 27.

LYING IN FRANCHISE. Things derelict, such as waifs, wrecks, estrays, and the like, which may be seized without suit or action. 3 Steph. Comm. 258.

LYING IN GRANT. Capable of being passed by grant without livery or seisin.

Incorporeal rights and things which cannot be transferred by livery of possession, but which exist only in idea, in contemplation of law, are said to lie in grant, and pass by the mere delivery of the need.

LYING IN LIVERY. Incapable of being passed by grant without livery.

LYING IN WAIT. Hiding in ambush or concealment. 122 Ia. 125.

For the purpose of murdering another. 8 W. Va. 769.

To constitute lying in wait, three things must concur, to wit, waiting, watching, and secrecy; and these facts must be established beyond a reasonable doubt, to authorize the conclusion that there was such lying in wait. 9 Humph. (Tenn.) 651.

LYNCH LAW. A common phrase used to express the vengeance of a mob inflicting an injury and committing an outrage upon a person suspected of some offense. In England this is called "Lidford Law." See also "Jedburgh Justice."

LYNDHURST'S (LORD) ACT. This statute (5 & 6 Wm. IV. c. 54) renders marriages within the prohibited degrees absolutely null and void. Theretofore such marriages were voidable merely.

LYON KING OF ARMS. In Scotch law. The chief herald.

LYTAE. In the old Roman law. A name given to students of the civil law in the fourth year of their course, from their being supposed capable of solving any difficulty in law. Tayl. Civ. Law, 39.

M

M. Persons convicted of manslaughter, in England, were formerly marked with this letter on the brawn of the thumb.

This letter is sometimes put on the face of treasury notes of the United States, and signifies that the treasury note bears interest at the rate of one mill per centum, and not one per centum interest. 13 Pet. (U. S.) 176.

MACE BEARER. In English law. An officer attending the court of session.

MACE PROOF. Secure against arrest.

MACEDONIAN DECREE. In Roman law. A decree of the Roman senate, which derived its name from that of a certain usurer, who was the cause of its being made, in consequence of his exactions.

It was intended to protect sons who lived under the paternal jurisdiction from the unconscionable contracts which they sometimes made on the expectations after their fathers' deaths; another, and perhaps the principal, object, was to cast odium on the rapacious creditors. It declared such contracts void. Dig. 14. 6. 1; Domat, Civ. Law, liv. 1, tit. 6, § 4; Fonbl. Eq. bk. 1, c. 2, § 12, note. See "Catching Bargain;" "Post Obit."

MACEGRIEF, or MACEGREF. In old English law. One who bought stolen meats, knowing it to be stolen. Spelman.

MACER. A mace bearer; an officer attending the court of session in Scotland.

MACHINATION. The act by which some plot or conspiracy is contrived or set on foot; an artful design.

MACHINE. In patent law.

In its broadest signification, this term is applied to any contrivance which is used to regulate or modify the relations between force, motion, and weight. "The term 'machine' includes every mechanical device or combination of mechanical powers and devices to perform some function and produce a certain effect or result." 15 How. (U. S.) 267.

What are sometimes called the "simple machines" are six in number: The lever, the pulley, the wheel and axle, the wedge, the screw, and the inclined plane. These are sometimes known as the mechanical powers, though neither these nor any other machinery can ever constitute or create power. They can only economize, control, direct, and render it useful.

Machines, as generally seen and understood, are compounded of these simple machines in some of their shapes and modifications. Such a combination as, when in operation, will produce some specific final result, is regarded as an entire machine. It is so treated in the patent law; for, although a new machine, or a new improvement of a machine, is an invention, and although only one invention can be included in a single patent, still, several different contrivances, each of which is in one sense a machine, may all be separately claimed in a single patent, provided they all contribute to improve or to constitute one machine, and are intended to produce a single ultimate result; and a new combination of machines is patentable, whether the machines themselves be new or old. 3 Wash. C. C. (U. S.) 69; 1 Story (U. S.) 273, 568; 2 Story (U. S.) 609; 1 Mason (U. S.) 474; 1 Sumn. (U. S.) 482; 3 Wheat. (U. S.) 454.

MACHINERY. This term is said to be more comprehensive than "machine," including the appurtenances necessary to its working. 111 Mass. 540.

MACTATOR. A murderer.

MADE KNOWN. Words used as a return to a *scire facias* when it has been served on the defendant.

MAEC BURGH (Saxon). Family.

MAEGBOTE, or MAEGBOT. In Saxon law. A recompense or satisfaction for the slaying or murder of a kinsman. Spelman.

MAEREMIUM (Law Lat. from Law Fr. *marisme*, timber). In old English law. Timber; wood for the construction of houses or ships. Blount; Bract. fol. 122.

MAGIS (Lat.) More.

MAGIS DE BONO QUAM DE MALO LEX intendit. The law favors a good rather than a bad construction. Co. Litt. 78b. Where the words used in an agreement are susceptible of two meanings, the one agreeable to, the other against, the law, the former is adopted. Thus, a bond conditioned "to assign all offices" will be construed to apply to such offices only as are assignable. Chit. Cont. 78.

MAGIS DIGNUM TRAHIT AD SE MINUS dignum. The more worthy draws to itself the less worthy. Y. B. 20 Hen. VI. 2, arg.

MAGISTER (Lat.) A master; a ruler; one whose learning and position make him superior to others. Thus, one who has attained to a high degree or eminence in science and literature is called a "master;" as, master of arts.

MAGISTER AD FACULTATES (Lat.) In English ecclesiastical law. The title of an officer who grants dispensations; as, to marry, to eat flesh on days prohibited, and the like. Bac. Abr. "Ecclesiastical Courts" (A 5).

MAGISTER CANCELLARIAE. In old English law. Master in chancery.

MAGISTER EQUITUM. In Roman law. Master of the horse.

MAGISTER LIBELLORUM. In Roman law. Master of requests.

MAGISTER NAVIS (Lat.) In civil law. Master of a ship; he to whom the whole care of a ship is given up, whether appointed by the owner, or charterer, or master. Calv. Lex.; Story, Ag. § 36.

MAGISTER RERUM USUS. Use is the master of things. Co. Litt. 229b. Usage is a principal guide in practice.

MAGISTER RERUM USUS; MAGISTRA rerum experientia. Use is the master of things; experience is the mistress of things. Co. Litt. 69, 229; Wingate, Max. 752.

MAGISTER SOCIETATIS (Lat.) In civil law. Managing partner. Vicat; Calv. Lex. Especially used of an officer employed in the business of collecting revenues, who had power to call together the tything men (*decumands*), as it were a senate, and lay matters before them, and keep account of all receipts, etc. He had, generally, an agent in the province, who was also sometimes called *magister societatis*. Id.; Story, Partn. § 95.

MAGISTERIAL. Pertaining to a magistrate.

MAGISTRACY. In its most enlarged signification, this term includes all officers, legislative, executive, and judicial. For example, in most of the state constitutions will be found this provision: "The powers of the government are divided into three distinct departments, and each of these is confided to a separate magistracy, to wit, those which are legislative, to one; those which are executive, to another; and those which are judiciary, to another." In a more confined sense, it signifies the body of officers whose duty it is to put the laws in force; as, judges, justices of the peace, and the like. In a still narrower sense, it is employed to designate the body of justices of the peace. It is also used for the office of a magistrate.

MAGISTRALIA BREVIA (Lat.) Writs adapted to special cases, and so called because drawn by the masters in chancery. 1 Spence, Eq. Jur. 239. For the difference between these and judicial writs, see Bracton, 413b.

MAGISTRATE. A public civil officer, invested with some part of the legislative, executive or judicial power given by the constitution. 32 Ark. 127.

The president of the United States is the chief magistrate of this nation; the governors are the chief magistrates of their respective states.

In a narrower sense, an inferior judicial officer, as a justice of the peace. 32 Ark. 127. The term generally applies to judicial officers having power to issue warrants for the arrest of persons charged with crime, but the use of the term has been held not to necessarily imply such a power. 32 Ark. 124.

MAGISTRATE'S COURT. The court of a magistrate (*q. v.*)

——**In South Carolina.** A court having exclusive jurisdiction in matters of contract of and under twenty dollars.

MAGISTRATUS. In civil law. A magistrate. Calv. Lex.

MAGNA ASSISA. The grand assize.

MAGNA ASSISA ELIGENDA. See "De Magna, etc."

MAGNA AVENA. Great beasts (oxen, etc.)

MAGNA CENTUM. The great hundred, or six score. Wharton.

MAGNA CHARTA. The great charter of English liberties, so called, but which was really a compact between the king and his barons, and almost exclusively for the benefit of the latter, though confirming the ancient liberties of Englishmen in some few particulars, was wrung from King John by his barons assembled in arms, on the 15th of June, 1215, and was given by the king's hand, as a confirmation of his own act, on the little island in the Thames, within the county of Buckinghamshire, which is still called "*Magna Charta* Island."

The preliminary interview was held in the meadow of Running Mede, or Runny Mede (from Saxon *rune*, council), that is, council meadow, which had been used constantly for national assemblies, and which was situated on the southwest side of the Thames, between Staines and Windsor. Though such formalities were observed, the provisions of the charter were disregarded by John and succeeding kings, each of whom, when wishing to do a popular thing, confirmed this charter. There were thirty-two confirmations between 1215 and 1416, the most celebrated of which were those by Hen. III. (1225) and Edw. I., which last confirmation was sealed with the great seal of England at Ghent, on the 5th of November, 1297. The *Magna Charta* printed in all the books as of 9 Hen. III. is really a transcript of the roll of parliament of 25 Edw. I. There were many originals of *Magna Charta* made, two of which are preserved in the British Museum.

Magna Charta consists of thirty-seven chapters, the subject matter of which is various. Chapter 1 provides that the Anglican church shall be free, and possess its rights unimpaired, probably referring chiefly to immunity from papal jurisdiction. Chapter 2 fixes relief which shall be paid by king's tenant of full age. Chapter 3 relates to heirs and their being in ward. Chapter 4. Guardians of wards within age are by this chapter restrained from waste of ward's estate, *"vasto hominum et rerum,"* waste of men and of things, which shows that serfs were regarded as slaves even by this much-boasted charter; and as serfs and freemen were at this time the divisions of society, and as freemen included, almost without exception, the nobility alone, we can see somewhat how much this charter deserves its name. Chapter 5 relates to the land and other property of heirs, and the delivering them up when the heirs are of age. Chapter 6 relates to the marriage of heirs. Chapter 7 provides that widow shall have quarantine of forty days in her husband's chief house, and shall have her dower set out to her at once, without paying anything for it, and in meanwhile to have reasonable estovers; the dower to be one-third of lands of husband, unless wife was endowed of less at the church door; widow not to be compelled to marry, but to find surety that she will not marry without consent of the lord of whom she holds. Marriage settlements have now in England taken the place, in great measure, of dower. Chapter 8. The goods and chattels of crown debtor to be exhausted before his rents and lands are distrained; the surety not to be called upon if the principal can pay. If sureties pay the debt, they to have the rents and lands of debtor till the debt is satisfied. Chapter 9 secures to London and other cities and boroughs and town barons of the five ports, and all other ports, to have their ancient liberties. Chapter 10 prohibits excessive distress for more services or rent than was due. Chapter 11 provides that court of common pleas should not follow the court of the king, but should be held in a certain place. They have been, accordingly, located at Westminster. Chapter 12 declares the manner of taking assizes of *novel disseisin* and *mort d'ancestor*. These were actions to recover lost seisin (*q. v.*), now abolished. Chapter 13 relates to assizes *darein presentment* brought by ecclesiastics to try right to present to ecclesiastical benefice. Abolished. Chapter 14 provides that amercement of a freeman for a fault shall be proportionate to his crime, and not excessive, and that the villein of any other than the king shall be amerced in same manner, his farm, utensils, etc., being preserved to him (*salvo wanagio suo*); for otherwise he could not cultivate lord's land. Chapter 15 and chapter 16 relate to making of bridges, and keeping in repair of sewers and sea walls. This is now regulated by local parochial law. Chapter 17 forbids sheriffs and coroners to hold pleas of the crown. Pleas of the crown are criminal cases which it is desirable should not be tried by an inferior and perhaps ignorant magistrate. Chapter 18 provides that, if any one holding a lay fee from crown die, the king's bailiff, on showing letters patent of summons for debt from the king, may attach all his goods and chattels, so that nothing be moved away till the debt to crown be paid off clearly, the residue to go to executors to perform the testament of the dead; and if there be no debt owing to crown, all the chattels of the deceased to go to executors, reserving, however, to the wife and children their reasonable parts. Debts to the government have precedence in United States, as well as in England. A man can now in England will away his whole personal property from wife and children, but not in some of the United States. See Gen. St. Mass. 1560. Chapter 19 relates to purveyance of king's house. Chapter 20 relates to the castle guard. Chapter 21 relates to taking horses, carts, and wood for use of royal castles. The three last chapters are now obsolete. Chapter 22 provides that the lands of felons shall go to the king for a year and a day; afterwards to the lord of the fee. So in France. The day is added to prevent dispute as to whether the year is exclusive or inclusive of its last day. Chapter 23 provides that the weirs shall be pulled down in the Thames and Medway, and throughout England, except on the seacoast. These weirs destroyed fish, and interrupted the floating of wood and the like down stream. Chapter 24 relates to the writ of *praecipe in capite* for lords against their tenants offering wrong, etc. Now abolished. Chapter 25 provides a uniform measure. See 5 & 6 Wm. IV. c. 63. Chapter 26 relates to inquisitions of life and member, which are to be granted freely. Now abolished. Chapter 27 relates to knight service and other ancient tenures, now abolished. Chapter 28 relates to accusations, which must be under oath. Chapter 29 provides that "no freeman shall be taken, or imprisoned, or disseised from his freehold, or liberties, or immunities, nor outlawed, nor exiled nor in any manner destroyed, nor will we come upon him or send against him, except by legal judgment of his peers or the law of the land. We will sell or deny justice to none, nor put off right or justice." This clause is very much celebrated, as confirming the right to trial by jury. By common law, the twelve jurors must be unanimous. Lord Campbell, in England, introduced a bill changing this, and, in certain cases, allowing the majority to decide. In some jurisdictions in the United States statutes have been enacted doing away in certain cases with the requirement for a unanimous verdict. Chapter 30 relates to merchant strangers, who are to be civilly treated, and, unless previously prohibited, are to have free passage through, and exit from, and dwelling in, England, without any manner of extortions, except in time of war. If they are of a country at war with England, and found in England at the beginning of the war, they are to be kept safely until it is found out how English merchants are treated in their country, and then are to be treated accordingly. Chapter 31 relates to escheats. Chapter 32 relates to the power of alienation in a freeman, which is limited. Chapter 33 relates to patrons of abbeys, etc. Chapter 34 provides that no appeal shall be brought by a woman except for death of her husband. This was because the defendant could not defend himself against a woman in single combat. The crime of murder or homicide is now inquired into by indictment. Chapter 35 relates to rights of holding county courts, etc. Obsolete. Chapter 36 provides that a gift of lands in mortmain shall be void, and lands so given go to lord of fee. Chapter 37 relates to escuage and subsidy. Chapter 38 confirms every article of the charter.

Magna Charta is said by some to have been so called because larger than the *Charta de Foresta*, which was given about the same time. Spelman. But see Cowell. *Magna Charta* is mentioned casually by Bracton, Fleta, and Britton. Glanville is supposed to have written before *Magna Charta*. The Mirror of Justices (chapter 315 et seq.) has a chapter on its defects. See 2 Inst.; Barr. Obs. St.; 4 Bl. Comm. 423. See a copy of *Magna Charta* in 1 Laws S. C. edited by Judge Cooper (page 78). In the Penny Magazine for the year 1833 (page 229), there is a copy of the original seal of King John affixed to this instrument; a specimen of a *fac simile* of the writings of *Magna Charta*, beginning at the passage, *Nullus liber homo capietur vel imprisonetur*, etc. A copy of both may be found in the Magasin Pittoresque for the year 1834 (pages 52, 53). See 8 Enc. Brit. 722; 6 Enc. Brit. 332; Wharton.

MAGNA CHARTA AND CHARTA DE foresta are called les deux grand charters. *Magna Charta* and the Charter of the Forest are called the two great charters. 2 Inst. 570.

MAGNA CULPA DOLUS EST. Great neglect is equivalent to fraud. Dig. 50. 16. 226; 2 Spears (S. C.) 256; 1 Bouv. Inst. note 646.

MAGNA NEGLIGENTIA CULPA EST; magna culpa dolus est. Gross negligence is a fault; gross fault is a fraud. Dig. 50. 16. 226. *Culpa* is an intermediate degree of negligence between *negligentia*, or lack of energetic care, and *dolus*, or fraud, seeming to approach nearly to our "negligence" in meaning.

MAGNA SERJEANTIA. In old English law. Grand serjeanty. Fleta, lib. 2, c. 4, § 1.

MAGNUM CAPE. Grand cape (*q. v.*)

MAGNUM CENTUM. (L. Lat.) In old records. The great hundred; six-score, or one hundred and twenty. Cart. 20. Cowell.

MAGNUM CONCILIUM. In old English law. The great council; the general council of the realm; afterwards called "parliament." 1 Bl. Comm. 148; 1 Reeve, Hist. Eng. Law, 62; Spelman.

The king's great council of barons and prelates. Spelman; Crabb, Hist. Eng. Law, 228.

MAGNUS ROTULUS STATUTORUM. The great statute roll. The first of the English statute rolls, beginning with *Magna Charta*, and ending with Edward III. Hale, Hist. Com. Law, 16, 17.

MAGRE, *Maugre*. L. Fr. Against the will; in spite of; notwithstanding. Kelham.

MAHEMIUM EST HOMICIDIUM INCHOatum. Mayhem is incipient homicide. 3 Inst. 118.

MAHLBRIEF. Germ. In maritime law. A contract for the building of a vessel, specifying the denomination and size of the vessel, the time when she is to be completed, and the time and manner of payment. Jacobsen's Sea Laws, 2-8. There is no corresponding term for this contract in English.

MAIDEN ASSIZE. In English practice. An assize at which no capital conviction takes place. In such a case, the sheriff of the county presents the judges with white gloves. Wharton's Lex.

MAIDEN RENTS. In old English law. A fine paid to lords of some manors, on the marriage of tenants, originally given in consideration of the lord's relinquishing his customary right of lying the first night with the bride of a tenant. Cowell.

MAIHEM. See "Mayhem;" "Maim."

MAIHEMATUS. Maimed.

MAIHEMIUM, or **MAIHEM.** Mayhem (*q. v.*)

MAIHEMIUM EST INTER CRIMINA MAjora minimum, et inter minora maximum. Mayhem is the least of great crimes, and the greatest of small. Co. Litt. 127.

MAIHEMIUM EST MEMBRI MUTILAtio, et dici poterit, ubi aliquis in aliqua parte sui corporis effectus sit inutilis ad pugnandum. Mayhem is the mutilation of a member, and can be said to take place when a man is injured in any part of his body so as to be useless in fight. Co. Litt. 126.

MAIL (Fr. *malle*, a trunk). Originally used in reference to the bag or valise which postillions had behind them, and in which they carried letters. In modern usage it is a general term to express the carriage of letters by public authority. 6 Daly (N. Y.) 558. It is used also in reference to the whole or any part of the matter so carried. 41 Fed. 130.

MAILE. In old English law. A small piece of money; a rent or tribute.

MAILS AND DUTIES. In Scotch law. Rents of an estate. Stair, Inst. 2. 12: 32; 2 Ross, Lect. 235, 381, 431-439.

MAIM. In criminal law. To deprive a person of such part of his body as to render him less able in fighting or defending himself than he would have otherwise been. See "Mayhem."

MAINAD. Perjury. Cowell.

MAINE PORT. A small tribute, commonly of loaves of bread, which in some places the parishioners paid to the rector in lieu of small tithes. Cowell.

MAINOUR. In criminal law. The thing stolen found in the hands of the thief who has stolen it.

Hence, when a man is found with property which he has stolen, he is said to be taken with the *mainour*, that is, it is found in his hands.

Formerly there was a distinction made between a larceny, when the thing stolen was found in the hands of the criminal, and when the proof depended upon other circumstances not quite so irrefragable. The former properly was termed *pris ove maynovere*, or *ove mainer*, or *mainour*, as it is generally written. Barr. Obs. St. 315, 316, note.

MAINOVRE, or MAINOEUVRE. A trespass committed by hand. See 7 Rich. II. c. 4.

MAINPERNABLE. Capable of being bailed; one for whom bail may be taken; bailable.

MAINPERNORS. In English law. Those persons to whom a man is delivered out of custody or prison, on their becoming bound for his appearance.

Mainpernors differ from bail. A man's bail may imprison or surrender him up before the stipulated day of appearance; mainpernors can do neither, but are merely sureties for his appearance at the day. Bail are only sureties that the party be answerable for all the special matter for which they stipulate; mainpernors are bound to produce him to answer all charges whatsoever. 6 Mod. 231; 7 Mod. 77, 85, 98; 3 Bl. Comm. 128. See Dane, Abr.

MAINPRISE. In English law. The taking a man into friendly custody, who might otherwise be committed to prison, upon security given for his appearance at a time and place assigned. Wood. Inst. bk. 4, c. 4.

MAINSWORN. Forsworn, by making false oath with hand (*main*) on book. Used in the North of England. Brownl. & G. 4; Hob. 125.

MAINTAINED. In pleading. A technical word indispensable in an indictment for maintenance. 1 Wils. 325.

MAINTAINORS. In criminal law. Those who maintain or support a cause depending between others, not being retained as counsel or attorney. For this they may be fined and imprisoned. 2 Swift, Dig. 328; 4 Bl. Comm. 124; Bac. Abr. "Barrator."

MAINTENANCE. Aid, support, assistance; the support which one person, who is bound by law to do so, gives to another for his living; for example, a father is bound to find maintenance for his children; and a child is required by law to maintain his father or mother, when they cannot support themselves, and he has ability to maintain them. 1 Bouv. Inst. notes 284-286.

——**In Criminal Law.** A malicious, or, at least, officious, interference in a suit in which the offender has no interest, to assist one of the parties to it against the other, with money or advice to prosecute or defend the action without any authority of law. 1 Russ. Crimes, 176. See 3 Cow. (N. Y.) 623.

The intermeddling of a stranger in a suit for the purpose of stirring up strife and continuing the litigation. 2 Pars. Cont. 266. See 4 Term. R. 340; 6 Bing. 299; 4 Q. B. 883.

There must be assistance actually rendered (1 Hempst. [Ark.] 300), though the suit need not be pending (13 Ired. [N. C.] 201), and under the modern doctrine, the assistance must be either in giving or hiring legal advice, or the bearing part of the expenses.

But there are many acts in the nature of maintenance which become justifiable from the circumstances under which they are done. They may be justified, first, because the party has an interest in the thing in variance, as when he has a bare contingency in the lands in question, which possibly may never come *in esse* (Bac. Abr. "Maintenance." And see 11 Mees. & W. 675; 9 Metc. [Mass.] 489; 13 Metc. [Mass.] 262; 1 Me. 292; 6 Me. 361; 11 Me. 111); second, because the party is of kindred or affinity, as father, son, or heir apparent, or husband or wife (3 Cow. [N. Y.] 623); third, because the relation of landlord and tenant or master and servant subsists between the party to the suit and the person who assists him; fourth, because the money is given out of charity (1 Bailey [S. C.] 401); fifth, because the person assisting the party to the suit is an attorney or counsellor; the assistance to be rendered must, however, be strictly professional, for a lawyer is not more justified in giving his client money than another man (1 Russ. Crimes, 179; Bac. Abr. "Maintenance;" Broke, Abr. "Maintenance"). See "Champerty."

MAINZIE (Scotch). Mayhem.

MAIRE.

——**In Old English Law.** A mayor; an officer classed with justices and sheriffs.

——**In Old Scotch Law.** An officer to whom process was directed. Otherwise called *"mair of fie"* (fee), and classed with the *serjand.* Skene de Verb. Sign.

MAISON DE DIEU (Fr. house of God). A hospital; an almshouse; a monastery. St. 39 Eliz. c. 5.

MAISTER. An old form of *master.*

MAJESTAS. In Roman law. The magesty or prerogative of the sovereign or state.

MAJESTY. A term used of kings and emperors as a title of honor. It sometimes means power; as when we say, the majesty of the people. See Wolff. Inst. § 998.

MAJOR. One who has attained his full age, and has acquired all his civil rights; one who is no longer a minor; an adult.

——**In Military Law.** The officer next in rank above a captain.

MAJOR ANNUS. The greater year; the bissextile year, consisting of 366 days. Bracton, fol. 359b.

MAJOR-GENERAL. In military law. An officer next in rank above a brigadier general. He commands a division consisting of several brigades, or even an army.

MAJOR HAEREDITAS VENIT UNICUIque nostrum a jure et legibus quam a parentibus. A greater inheritance comes to every one of us from right and the laws than from parents. 2 Inst. 56.

MAJOR NUMERUS IN SE CONTINET minorem. The greater number contains in itself the less. Bracton, 16.

MAJORA REGALIA. See "Regalia."

MAJORE POENA AFFECTUS QUAM legibus statuta est, non est infamis. One affected with a greater punishment than is provided by law is not infamous. 4 Inst. 66.

MAJORES.

——**In Roman Law and Genealogical Tables.** The male ascendants beyond the sixth degree.

——**In Old English Law.** Greater persons; persons of higher condition or estate.

MAJORI CONTINET IN SE MINUS. The greater includes the less. 19 Viner, Abr. 379.

MAJORI SUMMAE MINOR INEST. The lesser is included in the greater sum. 2 Kent, Comm. 618; Story, Ag. § 172.

MAJORITY. The state or condition of a person who has arrived at full age. He is then said to be a "major," in opposition to "minor," which is his condition during infancy.

The greater number; more than all the opponents; more than half of the whole number or group. 146 Iowa, 215.

MAJUS DIGNUM TRAHIT AD SE minus dignum. The more worthy or the greater draws to it the less worthy or the lesser. 5 Viner, Abr. 584, 586; Co. Litt. 43, 355b; 2 Inst. 307; Finch, Law, 22.

MAJUS EST DELICTUM SEIPSUM OCcidere quam alium. It is a greater crime to kill one's self than another.

MAJUS JUS. In old practice. Greater right, or more right. A plea in the old real actions. 1 Reeve, Hist. Eng. Law, 476. *Majus jus merum,* more mere right. Bracton, fol. 31.

MAKE. To perform or execute; as, to make his law is to perform that which a man had bound himself to do; that is, to clear himself of an action commenced against him, by his oath and the oath of his neighbors. Old Nat. Brev. 161. To make a contract is to execute the same. To make default is to fail to appear in proper trial. To make oath is to swear according to the form prescribed by law. To make money on an execution is to collect the same. It is also used intransitively of persons and things, to have effect, to tend; *e. g.,* "That case makes for me." Hardr. 133; Webster. See "Facias."

MAKER. A term applied to one who makes a promissory note, and promises to pay it when due.

He who makes a bill of exchange is called the "drawer;" and frequently in common parlance and in books of reports we find the word "drawer" inaccurately applied to the maker of a promissory note. See "Promissory Note."

MAKING HIS LAW. A phrase used to denote the act of a person who wages his law. Bac. Abr. "Wager of Law."

MALA (Lat.) Bad.

MALA FIDES (Lat.) Bad faith. It is opposed to *bona fides,* good faith.

MALA GRAMMATICA NON VITIAT chartam; sed in expositione instrumentorum mala grammatica quoad fieri possit evitanda est. Bad grammar does not vitiate a deed; but in the construction of instruments, bad grammar, as far as it can be done, is to be avoided. 6 Coke, 39; 9 Coke, 48; Viner, Abr. "Grammar" (A); Lofft, 441; Broom, Leg. Max. (3d London Ed.) 612.

MALA IN SE. That which is wrong in itself, without regard to statutory prohibition, because of its palpable and proximate injury to the public peace, order, or morals.

A distinction was formerly made, in respect of contracts, between *mala prohibita* and *mala in se;* but that distinction has been exploded, and it is now established that when the provisions of an act of the legislature have for their object the protection of the public, it makes no difference, with respect to contracts, whether the thing be prohibited absolutely or under a penalty. 5 Barn. & Ald. 335, 340; 10 Barn. & C. 98; 3 Starkie, 61; 13 Pick. (Mass.) 518; 2 Bing. N. C. 636, 646. The distinction is, however, important in criminal law in some cases with reference to the question of intent. 1 Bish. Crim. Law, § 2157.

Thus, one who kills another by accident in committing a misdemeanor *mala in se* is guilty of manslaughter, but otherwise if the misdemeanor was *mala prohibita*. 1 Clark & Marshall, Crimes, 20.

Crimes *mala in se* include all common-law offenses, for the common law punishes no act not in itself wrong. See 114 Mass. 323.

MALA PRAXIS. Malpractice (*q. v.*)

MALA PROHIBITA. That which is wrong only because it is prohibited by statute. 1 Bl. Comm. 57. See "Mala in Se."

MALANDRINUS. In old English law. A thief.

MALBERGE. A hill where the people assembled at a court, like the English assizes, which by the Scotch and Irish were called "parley hills." Du Cange.

MALE. Of the masculine sex; of the sex that begets young; the sex opposed to the female.

MALE CREDITUS. In old English law. Unfavorably thought of; in bad repute or credit. Bracton, fols. 116, 154.

MALE FAME. (L. Fr.) Bad character. Stat. Westm. 1, c. 12.

MALEDICTA EXPOSITIO QUAE CORrumpit textum. It is a cursed construction which corrupts the text. 2 Coke, 24; 4 Coke, 35; 11 Coke, 34; Wingate, Max. 26.

MALEDICTION (Lat.) In ecclesiastical law. A curse which was anciently annexed to donations of lands made to churches and religious houses against those who should violate their rights.

MALEFACTOR (Lat.) He who has been guilty of some crime; in another sense, one who has been convicted of having committed a crime.

MALEFICIA NON DEBENT REMANere impunita, et impunitas continuum affectum tribuit delinquenti. Evil deeds ought not to remain unpunished, and impunity affords continual incitement to the delinquent. 4 Coke, 45.

MALEFICIA PROPOSITIS DISTINguuntur. Evil deeds are distinguished from evil purposes. Jenk. Cent. Cas. 290.

MALEFICIUM (Lat.) In civil law. Waste damage; torts; injury. Dig. 5. 18. 1.

MALESON, or MALISON. A curse. Bailey.

MALFEASANCE. The unjust performance of some act which the party had no right, or which he had contracted not, to do. 33 Com. 115. It differs from misfeasance and nonfeasance (*q. v.*) See 1 Chit. Prac. 9; 1 Chit. Pl. 134.

MALFETRIA. In Spanish law. Offense. White, New Recop. bk. 2, tit. 19, c. 1, § 1.

MALICE.

——**In Crimes.** In its broadest legal sense, the term is substantially synonymous with "criminal intent," and means the state of mind of a person, irrespective of his motive, whenever he consciously violates the law. In this sense, every person who is *sui juris*, and who, without justification or excuse, willfully does an act which is prohibited and made punishable by law as a crime, does the act maliciously. 1 Clark & Marshall, Crimes, 139.

Malice, in its legal sense, characterizes all acts done intentionally with an evil disposition, a wrong and unlawful motive and purpose; the willful doing an injurious act without lawful excuse. 9 Metc. (Mass.) 93, or just cause, 194 Mich. 197; 4 B. & C. 255; 107 Mich. 215.

Malice implies not only willfulness, but an absence of lawful excuse. 12 Fla. 117.

In relation to particular crimes, the term is sometimes used in a narrower sense. Thus, as applied to the offense of malicious mischief, it implies a sense of resentment or ill will towards the owner of the property injured. 3 Cush. (Mass.) 558.

Malice is either express or implied. Express malice is actual malice, and exists where a person actually contemplates the injury or wrong which he inflicts. Implied malice, otherwise called "constructive malice," or "malice in law," is that which is imputed by the law from the nature of the act done, irrespective of the actual intent of the party. See 10 N. Y. 120.

——**In Torts.** Generally, malice implies no more than an absence of legal excuse (4 Wend. [N. Y.] 13); a mind not sufficiently cautious before it inflicts injury upon another (11 Serg. & R. [Pa.] 39); but in some connections, as, for example, to authorize the allowance of punitive damages, there must be either actual ill will, or a wanton disregard of consequences (37 Mich. 34; 77 Ill. 280).

Malice, to render one liable in punitive damages, contemplates not merely an injurious act, but an act conceived in a spirit of mischief, or of willful indifference to civil obligations. See 91 U. S. 489.

Specific ill will is not essential (27 Mo. 28); but a general wanton desire to annoy is sufficient to constitute malice (2 Hilt. [N. Y.] 40).

MALICE AFORETHOUGHT. Wicked purpose. These words in the description of murder do not imply deliberation, or the lapse of considerable time between the malicious intent to take and the actual execution of that intent, but rather denote purpose and design, in contradistinction to accident and mischance. 5 Cush. (Mass.) 306. And see 8 Car. & P. 616; 2 Mason (U. S.) 60; 1 Dev. & B. (N. C.) 121, 163; 6 Blackf. (Ind.) 299; 3 Ala. (N. S.) 497. They do not imply evil design against a particular person, but evil design in general, the dictate of a wicked, depraved, and malignant heart. 49 N. H. 399.

The term implies more than "malice" (1 Clark & Marshall, Crimes, 492). It includes not only a willful doing of wrong without lawful excuse, but an evil purpose, general or particular therein. 2 Moody, 40. See 9 Yerg. (Tenn.) 342.

MALICE PREPENSE. Malice aforethought (*q. v.*)

MALICIOUS. Done with malice (*q. v.*)

MALICIOUS ARREST. A wanton arrest made without probable cause by a regular process and proceeding. See "Malicious Prosecution."

MALICIOUS MISCHIEF. The wanton or reckless destruction of property.

The word "malicious" is not sufficiently defined as the willfully doing of any act prohibited by law, and for which the defendant has no lawful excuse. In order to a conviction of the offense of malicious mischief, the jury must be satisfied that the injury was done either out of a spirit of wanton cruelty, or of wicked revenge. Jacob. "Mischief," "Malicious;" Alis. Sc. Cr. Law, 448; 3 Cush. (Mass.) 558; 2 Metc. (Mass.) 21; 3 Dev. & B. (N. C.) 130; 5 Ired. (N. C.) 364; 8 Leigh (Va.) 719; 3 Me. 177. Authorities are divided as to whether wantonness or general malice is sufficient. That it is not, see 79 N. C. 656; 44 Ala. 380; 49 Miss. 331. Contra, 28 Ga. 380; 44 N. H. 392.

MALICIOUS PROSECUTION. A judicial proceeding instituted without probable cause (97 U. S. 642; 59 Ind. 500), and with malicious intent (7 Ill. App. 181; 30 N. Y. 625).

While malice may be inferred by the jury from absence of probable cause, the presence of malice in fact is essential. 44 Cal. 144.

At common law, the malicious prosecution of a civil action was actionable (Co. Litt. 161), but in most of the states only the malicious institution of a criminal proceeding is the subject of an action. (4 N. J. Law, 330).

MALIGNARE. To malign or slander; also to maim.

MALITIA (Lat.) Malice. 4 Bl. Comm. 199.

MALITIA EST ACIDA; EST MALI ANIMI affectus. Malice is sour; it is the quality of a bad mind. 2 Bulst. 49.

MALITIA PRAECOGITATA. Malice aforethought. 4 Bl. Comm. 198.

MALITIA SUPPLET AETATEM. Malice supplies age. Dyer, 104; 1 Bl. Comm. 464; 4 Bl. Comm. 22, 23, 312; Broom, Leg. Max. (3d London Ed.) 284. See "Malice."

MALITIIS HOMINUM EST OBVIANDUM. The wicked or malicious designs of men must be thwarted. 4 Coke, 15b.

MALLUM. In old European law. A court of the higher kind (*placitum majus*), in which the more important business of the county was dispatched by the count or earl (*comes*). Spelman. A public national assembly. 1 Robertson, Hist. Chas. V. Append. note xl.

MALO ANIMO. With evil intent.

MALO SENSU. In an evil sense.

MALPRACTICE. Bad or unskillful practice in a physician or other professional person, whereby the health of the patient is injured.

Physicians and surgeons impliedly contract that they are reasonably and ordinarily qualified to practice the medical profession, and for a failure to possess and exercise such qualifications they are liable. 17 Ind. 115; 21 Minn. 464; 75 N. Y. 12.

Willful malpractice takes place when the physician purposely administers medicines or performs an operation which he knows and expects will result in damage or death to the individual under his care; as in the case of criminal abortion. Elwell, Malprac. 243 et seq.; 2 Barb. (N. Y.) 216.

Negligent malpractice comprehends those cases where there is no criminal or dishonest object, but gross negligence of that attention which the situation of the patient requires; as, if a physician should administer medicines, while in a state of intoxication, from which injury would arise to his patient.

Ignorant malpractice is the administration of medicines calculated to do injury, which do harm, and which a well-educated and scientific medical man would know were not proper in the case. Elwell, Malprac. 198 et seq.; 7 Barn. & C. 493, 497; 6 Bing. 440; 6 Mass. 134; 5 Car. & P. 333; 1 Moody & R. 405; 5 Cox, C. C. 587.

MALTREATMENT. Synonymous with bad treatment. 2 Allen (Mass.) 143.

MALT TAX, or MALT SCOT. In English law. An excise duty on malt.

MALUM HOMINUM EST OBVIANDUM. The malicious plans of men must be avoided. 4 Coke, 15.

MALUM IN SE. An act wrong in itself. The plural form is *mala in se (q. v.)*

MALUM NON HABET EFFICIENTEM, sed deficientem causam. Evil has not an efficient, but a deficient, cause. 3 Inst. Proeme.

MALUM NON PRAESUMITUR. Evil is not presumed. 4 Coke, 72; Branch, Princ.

MALUM PROHIBITUM. A thing wrong only because prohibited by law. The plural form is *mala prohibita (q. v.)*

MALUM QUO COMMUNIUS EO PEJUS. The more common the evil, the worse. Branch, Princ.

MALUM VENIENDI (Fr. *mal de venue.*) Misfortune or sickness, or accident happening to a party on his way to court. Bract. fol. 339.

MALUS USUS EST ABOLENDUS. An evil custom is to be abolished. Co. Litt. 141; Broom, Leg. Max. (3d London Ed.) 827; Litt. § 212; 5 Q. B. 701; 12 Q. B. 845; 2 Myline & K. 449.

MALVEILLES. Ill will. In some ancient records, this word signifies malicious practices, or crimes and misdemeanors.

MALVEIS PROCURORS. Such as used to pack juries, by the nomination of either party in a cause, or other practice. Art. Sup. Chart. c. x. Cowell.

MALVERSATION. In French law. This word is applied to all punishable faults committed in the exercise of an office, such as corruptions, exactions, extortions, and larceny. Merlin, Repert.

MAN. A human being; a person of the male sex; a male of the human species above the age of puberty, as distinguished from a woman or a boy. 106 Wis. 346.

In its most extended sense, the term includes not only the adult male sex of the human species, but women and children. Examples: "Of offenses against man, some are more immediately against the king, others more immediately against the subject." Hawk. P. C. bk. 1, c. 2, § 1. "Offenses against the life of man come under the general name of 'homicide,' which in our law signifies the killing of a man by a man." Id. bk. 1, c. 8, § 2.

In a statute prohibiting fornication it will be held to include all male persons who have arrived at the age of puberty. 106 Wis. 346.

It was considered in the civil or Roman law that, although "man" and "person" are synonymous in grammar, they had a different acceptation in law. All persons were men, but not all men—for example, slaves—were not persons, but things. See Barr. Obs. St. 216, note.

MAN OF STRAW. See "Straw Men."

MANAGER. A person appointed or elected to manage the affairs of another. A term applied to those officers of a corporation who are authorized to manage its affairs. 1 Bouv. Inst. note 190; 17 Mass. 29.

In England and Canada, the chief executive officer of a branch bank is called a "manager." His duties are those of our presidents and cashiers combined. His signature is necessary to every contract binding on the bank, except entries in the passbooks of customers. He indorses bills, signs bills of exchange and drafts, and conducts the correspondence of the bank. He is under the control of the board of directors of the bank, and there is usually a local or branch board of directors, at which he acts as presiding officer. Sewell, Bank.

One of the persons appointed on the part of the house of representatives to prosecute impeachments before the senate.

MANAGING AGENT. The managing agent of a corporation is one exercising general powers and having general supervision over its affairs. 16 Wis. 220.

MANAGING OWNER OF SHIP. The managing owner of a ship is one of several co-owners, to whom the others, or those of them who join in the adventure, have delegated the management of the ship. He has authority to do all things usual and necessary in the management of the ship and the delivery of the cargo, to enable her to prosecute her voyage and earn freight, with the right to appoint an agent for the purpose. 6 Q. B. Div. 93; L. R. 1 C. P. 649.

MANAGIUM. A mansion house or dwelling place. Cowell.

MANBOTE. A compensation paid the relations of a murdered man by the murderer or his friends.

MANCEPS. In Roman law. A purchaser; one who took the articles sold in his hand (*qui manu cepit*); a formality observed in certain sales; a farmer of the public taxes. Calv. Lex.; Adams, Rom. Ant. 55.

MANCHE PRESENT. A bribe; a present from the donor's own hand.

MANCIPARE. In the Roman law. To sell, alienate, or make over to another; to sell with certain formalities.

To sell a person; one of the forms observed in the process of emancipation.

MANCIPATIO (Lat. from *mancipare, q. v.*) In the Roman law. A kind of sale in the presence of five witnesses, accompanied with delivery of possession or seisin; the purchaser taking the thing sold in his hand. It took place among Roman citizens only, and was confined to certain property called *res mancipi* or *mancipia*. Calv. Lex.; Adams, Rom. Art. 55, 58.

The imaginary sale of a son in the ceremony of emancipation; so called because the natural father gave over (*mancipabat, i. e., manu tradebat*) his son to the purchaser, adding these words, *Mancupo tibi hunc filium qui meus est.* Adams, Rom. Ant. 52; Cooper, Just. Inst. notes, *442, 443.

MANCIPI RES (Lat.) In old Roman law. A name given to one of the leading divisions of private property, the precise meaning of which is not settled. Ulpian defines or describes it as embracing estates in Italy (*praedia in Italico solo*) which were acquired by mancipation, usucapion, or adjudication, those rights of country estates called servitudes, slaves, and working animals. Calv. Lex. Gibbon explains it to mean things originally taken in war (*manu capti*), and which were sold in the particular form called *mancipatio*, in order to assure the purchaser that they had been the property of an enemy, and not of a fellow citizen. 3 Gibb. Rom. Emp. (Am. Ed. 1844) 176.

MANCIPIUM. The power acquired over a freeman by the *mancipatio*.

To form a clear conception of the true import of the word in the Roman jurisprudence, it is necessary to advert to the four distinct powers which were exercised by the *pater-familias*, viz.: The *manus*, or martial power; the *mancipium*, resulting from the *mancipatio*, or *alienatio per aes et libram*, of a freeman; the *dominica potestas*, the power of the master over his slaves, and the *patria potestas*, the paternal power. When the *pater-familias* sold his son, *venum dare, mancipare*, the paternal power was succeeded by the *mancipium*, or the power acquired by the purchaser over the person whom he held *in mancipio*, and whose condition was assimilated to that of a slave. What is most remarkable is that, on the emancipation from the *mancipium*, he fell back into the paternal power, which was not entirely exhausted until he had been sold three times by the *pater-familias. Si pater filium ter venum duit, filius a patre liber esto.* Gaius speaks of the *mancipatio* as *imaginaria quaedam venditio*, because in his time it was only resorted to for the purpose of adoption or emancipation. See "Adoption;" "Pater-Familias;" 1 Ortolan, 112 et seq.

MANCOMUNAL. In Spanish law. An obligation is said to be *mancomunal* when one person assumes the contract or debt of another, and makes himself liable to pay or fulfill it. Schmidt, Civ. Law, 120.

MANDAMIENTO. In Spanish law. Commission; authority or power of attorney; a contract of good faith, by which one person commits to the gratuitous charge of another his affairs, and the latter accepts the charge. White, New Recop. bk. 2, tit. 12, c. 1.

MANDAMUS. In practice. This is a high prerogative writ, usually issuing out of the highest court of general jurisdiction in a state, in the name of the sovereignty, directed to any natural person, corporation, or inferior court of judicature within its jurisdiction, requiring them to do some particular thing therein specified, and which appertains to their office or duty. 3 Bl. Comm. 110; 4 Bac. Abr. 495; Opinion of Marshall, C. J., 1 Cranch (U. S.) 137, 168.

It is a proper remedy to compel the performance of a specific act where the act is ministerial in its character (12 Pet. [U. S.] 524; 34 Pa. St. 293; 26 Ga. 665; 7 Iowa, 186, 390); but where the act is of a discretionary (6 How. [U. S.] 92; 11 How. [U. S.] 272; 17 How. [U. S.] 284; 12 Cush. [Mass.] 403; 20 Tex. 60; 10 Cal. 376; 5 Har. [Del.] 108; 12 Md. 329; 4 Mich. 187; 5 Ohio St. 528) or judicial nature (14 La. Ann. 60; 7 Cal. 130; 18 B. Mon. [Ky.] 423; 7 El. & Bl. 366), it will lie only to compel action generally (11 Cal. 42; 30 Ala. [N. S.] 49; 28 Mo. 259); and where the necessity of acting is a matter of discretion, it will not lie even to compel action (6 How. [U. S.] 92; 5 Iowa, 380).

The writ of *mandamus* is either alternative or peremptory. The former usually issued at the commencement of the suit, commanding in the alternative that defendant do the specified act, or show cause why he should not, and the latter, issued after hearing, commanding the performance of the decree without alternative.

MANDANS. In civil law. The employing party in a contract of mandate. One who gives a thing in charge to another; one who requires, requests, or employs another to do some act for him. Inst. 3. 27. 1. et seq.

MANDANT. The bailor in a contract of mandate.

MANDATA LICITA STRICTAM RECIPIunt interpretationem, sed illicita latam et extensam. Lawful commands receive a strict interpretation, but unlawful, a wide or broad construction. Bac. Max. reg. 16.

MANDATAIRE. In French law. A mandatary.

MANDATARIUS TERMINOS SIBI POSItos transgredi non potest. A mandatary cannot exceed the bounds of his authority. Jenk. Cent. Cas. 53.

MANDATARY, or MANDATARIUS. One who undertakes to perform a mandate. Jones, Bailm. 53.

MANDATE.

——**In Practice.** A judicial command or precept issued by a court or magistrate, directing the proper officer to enforce a judgment, sentence, or decree. Commonly applied to the precept issued by an appellate court after decision of the cause, commanding the lower court to proceed therein.

——**In Contracts.** A bailment of property in regard to which the bailee engages to do some act without reward. Story, Bailm. § 137; 148 Ill. 186.

The contract of mandate in the civil law is not limited to personal property, nor does it require a delivery of personal property when it relates to that. Poth. de Mand. note 1; Civ. Code La. arts. 2954-2964. It is, however, restricted to things of a personal nature at common law, and of these there must be a delivery, actual or constructive. Story, Bailm. § 142; 3 Strob. (S. C.) 343.

Mandates and deposits closely resemble each other; the distinction being that in mandates the care and service are the principal, and the custody the accessory; while in deposits the custody is the principal thing and the care and service are merely accessory. Story, Bailm. § 140.

——**In Civil Law.** The instructions which the emperor addressed to a public functionary, and which were to serve as rules for his conduct. These mandates resembled those of the proconsuls, the *mandata jurisdictio*, and were ordinarily binding on the legates or lieutenants of the emperor of the imperial provinces, and there they had the authority of the principal edicts. Savigny, Dr. Rom. c. 3, § 24, note 4.

——**International Law.** The authority under which former German colonies were taken over and administered under the treaty of Versailles.

MANDATO. In Spanish law. The contract of mandate. Escriche, Dic. Raz., Schmidt, Civ. Law, 197.

MANDATOR. The person who consigns property to another under a contract of mandate. Story, Bailm. § 138.

MANDATORY. Containing a command; peremptory. As applied to statutes, a provision is mandatory if proceedings in disregard of it are absolutely void. 1 Duer (N. Y.) 79.

MANDATORY INJUNCTION. One which commands the doing of some affirmative act by the person to whom it is directed. See 14 Abb. Pr. (N. Y.) 106; 25 Fed. 654; High, Inj. § 478.

MANDATUM. In the civil law. Mandate (*q. v.*)

MANDATUM NISI GRATUITUM NULlum est. Unless a mandate is gratuitous, it is not a mandate. Dig. 17. 1. 1. 4; Inst. 3. 27; 1 Bouv. Inst. note 1070.

MANDAVI BALLIVO. In English practice. The return made by a sheriff when he has committed the execution of a writ to a bailiff of a liberty, who has the right to execute the writ.

MANENS (pl. *manentes;* Law Lat. from *manere*, to remain or stay). In Saxon and old English law. A kind of tenant inhabiting a manse (*mansi incola*); an agricultural tenant (*qui hydan colit*). Spelman. The ceorls are mentioned in the later Anglo-Saxon charters, under the name of *manentes.* 1 Spence, Ch. 50.

MANERA. In Spanish law. Manner or mode. Las Partidas, pt. 4, tit. 4, lib. 2.

MANERIUM DICITUR A MANENDO, SEcundum excellentiam, sedes magna, fixa, et stabilis. A manor is so called from *manendo*, according to its excellence, a seat, great, fixed, and firm. Co. Litt. 58.

MANHOOD. In feudal law. A term denoting the ceremony of doing homage by the vassal to his lord. The formula used was *devenio vester homo*, I become your man. 2 Bl. Comm. 54. See "Homage."

MANIA. In medical jurisprudence. This is the most common of all the forms of recent insanity, and consists of one or both of the following conditions, viz., intellectual aberration, and morbid or affective obliquity.

In other words, the maniac either misapprehends the true relations between persons and things, in consequence of which he adopts notions manifestly absurd, and believes in occurrences that never did and never could take place, or his sentiments, affections, and emotions are so perverted that whatever excites their activity is viewed through a distorting medium; or, which is the most common fact, both these conditions may exist together, in which case their relative share in the disease may differ in such a degree that one or the other may scarcely be perceived at all. According as the intellectual or moral element prevails, the disease is called "intellectual" or "moral" mania. Whether the former is ever entirely wanting has been stoutly questioned, less from any dearth of facts than from some fancied metaphysical incongruity. The logical consequence of the doubt is that, in the absence of intellectual disturbance, there is really no insanity,—the moral disorders proceeding rather from unbridled passions than any pathological condition. Against all such reasoning it will be sufficient here to oppose the very common fact that in every collection of the insane may be found many who exhibit no intellectual aberration, but in whom moral disorders of the most flagrant kind present a marked contrast to the previous character and habits of life.

Both forms of mania may be either general or partial. In the latter, the patient has adopted some notion having a very limited influence upon his mental movements, while outside of that no appearance of impairment or irregularity can be discerned. Pure "monomania," as this form of insanity has been often called,—that is, a mania confined to a certain point, the understanding being perfectly sound in every other respect, —is, no doubt, a veritable fact, but one of very rare occurrence. The peculiar notions of the insane, constituting insane belief, are of two kinds,—"delusions" and "hallucinations." By the former is meant a firm belief in something impossible, either in the nature of things or in the circumstances of the case, or, if possible, highly improbable, and associated in the mind of the patient with consequences that have to it only a fanciful relation. By "hallucination" is meant an impression supposed by the patient, contrary to all proof or possibility, to have been received through one of the senses. For instance, the belief that one is Jesus Christ or the pope of Rome is a delusion; the belief that one hears voices speaking from the walls of the room, or sees armies contending in the clouds, is a hallucination. The latter implies some morbid activity of the perceptive powers; the former is a mistake of the intellect exclusively.

MANIA A POTU. See "Delirium Tremens."

MANIFEST.

——**In Commercial Law.** A written instrument containing a true account of the cargo of a ship or a commercial vessel.

As to the requirements of the United States laws in respect to manifests, see 1 Story, U. S. Laws, 593, 594.

The want of a manifest, where one is required, and also the making a false manifest, are grave offenses.

——**In Evidence.** That which is clear and requires no proof; that which is notorious.

MANIFESTA PROBATIONE NON INDIgent. Manifest things require no proof. 7 Coke, 40b.

MANIFESTO. A solemn declaration, by the constituted authorities of a nation, which contains the reasons for its public acts towards another.

On the declaration of war, a manifesto is usually issued, in which the nation declaring the war states the reasons for so doing. Vattel, lib. 3, c. 4, § 64; Wolff. Dr. Nat. § 1187.

MANKIND. Persons of the male sex; the human species. St. 25 Hen. VIII., c. 6, makes it felony to commit sodomy with mankind or beast. Females as well as males are included under the term "mankind." Fortescue, 91; Bac. Abr. "Sodomy."

MANNER. Manner has a broader meaning than "method." The word is derived from the Latin, *manus*, the hand, and in a wider sense embraces both method and mode. 20 Ill. App. 326.

MANNER AND FORM. In pleading. After traversing any allegation in pleading, it is usual to say, "in manner and form as he has in his declaration in that behalf alleged," which is as much as to include in the traverse not only the mere fact opposed to it, but that in the manner and form in which it is stated by the other party. These words, however, only put in issue the substantial statement of the manner of the fact traversed, and do not extend to the time, place, or other circumstances attending it, if they were not originally material and necessary to be proved as laid. 3 Bouv. Inst. 297. See "Modo et Forma."

MANNIRE. To cite any person to appear in court and stand in judgment there. It is different from *bannire;* for, though both of them are citations, this is by the adverse party, and that is by the judge. Du Cange.

MANNOPUS. (Lat.) An ancient word, which signifies goods taken in the hands of an apprehended thief.

MANOR. This word is derived from the French *manoir*, and signifies a house, residence, or habitation. At present its meaning is more enlarged, and includes not only a dwelling house, but also lands. See Co. Litt. 58, 108; 2 Rolle, Abr. 121; Merlin, Repert, "Manoir." See Sergeant, Land Laws Pa. 195.

——**In English Law.** A tract of land originally granted by the king to a person of rank, part of which (*terrae tenementales*) were given by the grantee or lord of the manor to his followers; the rest he retained, under the name of his demesnes (*terrae dominicales*). That which remained uncultivated was called the "lord's waste," and served for public roads, and commons of pasture for the lord and his tenants. The whole fee was called a "lordship," or "barony," and the court appendant to the manor the "court baron." The tenants, in respect to their relation to this court and to each other, were called *pares curiae;* in relation to the tenure of their lands, copyholder (*q. v.*), as holding by a copy of the record in the lord's court.

The franchise of a manor, *i. e.*, the right to jurisdiction and rents and services of copyholders. Cowell. No new manors were created in England after the prohibition of subinfeudation by St. Quia Emptores, in 1290. 1 Washb. Real Prop. 30.

——**In American Law.** A manor was formerly a tract held of a properietor by a fee-farm rent in money or in kind, and descending to oldest son of proprietor, who in New York was called a "patroon."

"Manor" is derived originally either from Latin *manendo*, remaining, or from British *maer*, stones, being the place marked out or inclosed by stones. Webster.

MANQUELLER (Saxon). A murderer.

MANRENT, or **MANRED.** In Scotch law. The service of a man or vassal. A bond of manrent was an instrument by which a person, in order to secure the protection of some powerful lord, bound himself, "in manrent and service, to be leil and trew man and servant," specifying the service.

MANSE. Habitation; farm and land. Spelman. Parsonage or vicarage house. Paed. Ant. 431; Jacob. So in Scotland. Bell, Dict.

MANSER. A bastard. Cowell.

MANSIO L. Lat. [from *manere,* to stay.] In old European law. An inn; a place of entertainment and accommodation for travelers. Spelman.

In old English law. A dwelling; a mansion; which might be constructed of several houses. Bract. fol. 434.

MANSION HOUSE. Any house of dwelling, in the law of burglary, etc. 3 Inst. 64.

The term "mansion house," in its common sense, not only includes the dwelling house, but also all the buildings within the curtilage, as the dairy house, the cow house, the stable, etc.; though not under the same roof nor contiguous. Burn, Inst. "Burglary;" 1 Thomas, Co. Litt. 215, 216; 1 Hale, P. C. 558; 4 Bl. Comm. 225. See 3 Serg. & R. (Pa.) 199; 4 Strob. (S. C.) 372; 13 Bost. Law Rep. 157; 4 Call. (Va.) 109; 14 Mees. & W. 181; 4 C. B. 105.

MANSLAUGHTER. Manslaughter is homicide committed without excuse or justification, and without malice aforethought, expressed or implied. 1 Hawk. P. C. c. 30, §§ 2, 3; Steph. Dig. Crim. Law, art. 223.

Voluntary manslaughter is an intentional homicide in sudden passion or heat of blood caused by reasonable provocation, and not with malice aforethought. 1 Hale, P. C. 466.

To constitute voluntary manslaughter, (1) the killing must be intentional; (2) it must be without malice; (3) the provocation must be so great as to reasonably excite passion in an ordinary man, and cause him to act rashly and without reflection, and so immediate as not to afford reasonable cooling time.

Involuntary manslaughter is homicide committed unintentionally, but without excuse, and not under such circumstances as to raise the implication of malice. 23 Iowa, 154; 62 Mich. 29. It may arise (1) from the doing of a criminal act not amounting to a felony, nor naturally tending to cause death or great bodily harm; (2) from the doing of a lawful act with gross negligence; (3) from the omission to perform a legal duty under circumstances showing gross negligence.

By statutes in the various states, the degrees of manslaughter and the elements of each degree have been variously altered.

MANSUETUS. Tame. See "Animals."

MANSUM CAPITALE. The manor house.

MANTHEOFF (Saxon). A horse thief.

MANU BREVI (Lat.) In civil law. With a short hand. A term used in the civil law, signifying shortly; directly; by the shortest course; without circuity. Calv. Lex.

MANU FORTI. With strong hand. Used in writs of trespass.

MANU LONGA. In civil law. With a long hand; indirectly or circuitously. Calv. Lex.

MANUAL LABOR. The term manual labor, in its ordinary and usual meaning and acceptation, means labor performed by and with the hand or hands, and implies the ability for such sustained exercise and use of the hand or hands at labor as will enable a person thereby to earn or assist in earning a livelihood. 206 Ill. 211.

MANUCAPERE. L. Lat. [from *manus,* hand, and *capere,* to take.] In old law and practice. To become surety; to offer one's self as a surety to redeem another from imprisonment, and to have him in court at an appointed day. Spelman.

MANUCAPTIO. A writ which lay to admit to bail one taken on suspicion of felony, and who could not be admitted to bail by the sheriff.

MANUCAPTORS. Mainpernors (*q. v.*)

MANUFACTURE. Primarily, something made by hand as distinguished from a natural growth, but as machinery has largely supplanted this primitive method the word is now ordinarily used to denote an article upon the material of which labor has been expended to make the finished product. 255 Ill. 272.

To manufacture is to make or fabricate, as anything for use, especially in considerable quantities or numbers, or by the aid of many hands or machinery; to make wares or merchandise by hand or machinery or by other agency. 188 Ill. 495.

MANUFACTURING CORPORATIONS. Such as are engaged in "the production of some article, thing, or object, by skill or labor, out of raw material, or from matter which has already been subjected to natural forces." 99 N. Y. 184.

It has been held to include a company for the manufacture and supply of illuminating gas (89 N. Y. 409); but otherwise as to a company supplying natural gas (108 Pa. 111). It includes a company preparing ice by artificial refrigeration, but not one cutting and storing natural ice. 99 N. Y. 181. It includes a company engaged in refining oil (101 Mass. 385); a milling company (17 Ill. 54); but not a mining company (106 Mass. 131), nor a dry-dock company engaged in repairing vessels (92 N. Y. 487). A company engaged in publishing a newspaper is not a manufacturing company (51 N. J. Law, 75; 60 Minn. 82; 18 Nat. Bankr. Reg. 319); but a book and job printing company is (47 N. J. Law, 36; 51 N. J. Law, 75; 6 Nat. Bankr. Reg. 238).

A company dealing in the articles of its manufacture is not engaged exclusively in manufacturing. 66 Minn. 234.

MANUMISSION. The act of releasing from the power of another; the act of giving liberty to a slave.

——**In the Roman Law.** It was a generic expression, equally applicable to the enfranchisement from the *manus*, the *mancipium*, the *dominica potestas*, and the *patria potestas*.

MANUNG, or **MONUNG.** In old English law. The district within the jurisdiction of a reeve, apparently so called from his power to exercise therein one of his chief functions, viz., to exact (*amanian*) all fines.

MANURABLE. In old English law. Capable of being had or held in hand; capable of manual occupation; capable of being cultivated; capable of being touched; tangible; corporeal. Hale, Anal. § 24.

MANUS (Lat. hand). Anciently signified the person taking an oath as a compurgator. The use of this word probably came from the party laying his hand on the New Testament. *Manus* signifies, among the civilians, power, and is frequently used as synonymous with *potestas*. Lec. Elm. § 94.

MANUS MEDIAE. Men of low degree.

MANUS MORTUA. A dead hand; mortmain. Spelman.

MANUSCRIPT. An unpublished writing, or one that has been published without the consent of the person entitled to control it.

MANUTENENTIA. In old English law. Maintenance.

MANWORTH. In old English law. The price or value of a man's life or head. Cowell.

MARASTRE. (L. Fr.) A mother-in-law. Kelham. A step-mother. Britt. c. 119.

MARAUDER. One who, while employed in the army as a soldier, commits a larceny or robbery in the neighborhood of the camp, or while wandering away from the army. Merlin, Repert. See Halleck, Int. Law; Lieber, Guerrilla Parties; 37 Mo. 328.

MARC-BANCO. The name of a coin. The marc-banco of Hamburg, as money of account, at the custom house, is deemed and taken to be of the value of thirty-five cents. Act March 3, 1843.

MARCH. In Scotch law. A boundary line. Bell, Dict.; Ersk. Inst. 2. 6. 4.

MARCHERS. In old English law. Nobles who lived on the Marches, and had their own laws, and power over life and death, as if they were petty princes. Camden; Jacob. Abolished by St. 27 Hen. VIII. c. 26, 1 Edw. VI. c. 10, and 1 & 2 Philip & M. c. 15. They were also called "Lords Marchers."

MARCHES. In old English law. Boundaries or frontiers of a state.

MARCHETA.

——**In Old Scotch Law.** A custom for the lord of a fee to lie the first night with the bride of his tenant. Abolished by Malcolm III. Spelman; 2 Bl. Comm. 83.

A fine paid by the tenant for the remission of such right, originally a mark or half a mark of silver. Spelman.

——**In Old English Law.** A fine paid for leave to marry, or to bestow a daughter in marriage. Cowell.

The etymology of the term is variously traced from Scotch *march*, a horse, Latin *marca*, a mark, and British *merch*, a maid. The first of these is approved by Skene.

MARCHIONESS. A dignity in a woman corresponding to that of marquis in a man, and obtained either by creation or by marriage with a marquis. Wharton.

MARESCALLUS (from German, *march*, horse, and *schalch*, master). A groom of the stables, who also took care of the diseases of the horses. Du Cange.

An officer of the imperial stable, *magister equorum*. Du Cange.

A military officer, whose duty it was to keep watch on the enemy, to choose place of encampment, to arrange or marshal the army in order of battle, and, as master of the horse to commence the battle. This office was second to that of *comes stabuli*, or constable. Du Cange.

An officer of the court of exchequer. 51 Hen. III. 5.

An officer of a manor, who oversaw the hospitalities (*mansionarius*). Du Cange; Fleta, lib. 2, c. 74.

Marescallus aulae. An officer of the royal household, who had charge of the person of the monarch and peace of the palace. Du Cange.

MARETUM (Lat.) Marshy ground overflowed by the sea or great rivers. Co. Litt. 5.

MARGIN. See "Gambling Contract."

MARGINAL PURCHASE. By a marginal purchase of an article is usually meant a purchase where the full price is not given at the time of the execution of the order, without regard to the percentage of the unpaid balance thereon and without regard to whether the purchase is made as an investment with the expectation of later making full payment and acquiring possession of the article or as a speculation with the intention of selling upon a rise in the market and without any intention of making full payment therefor or acquiring possession of the article purchased. 171 Mich. 38.

MARINARIUS (Law Lat.) An ancient word which signified a mariner or seaman. In England, *marinarius capitaneus* was the admiral or warden of the ports.

MARINE. Belonging to the sea; relating to the sea; naval. A soldier employed, or liable to be employed, on vessels of war, under the command of an officer of marines, who acts under the direction of the commander of the ship. See "Marine Corps." It is also used as a general term to denote the whole naval power of a state or country.

MARINE CONTRACT. One which relates to business done or transacted upon the sea and in seaports, and over which the courts of admiralty have jurisdiction concurrent with the courts of common law. See "Maritime Contract;" Pars. Mar. Law; 2 Gall. (U. S.) 398.

MARINE CORPS. A body of officers and soldiers under an organization separate and distinct from that of the army, and intended for service, in detached portions, on board of ships of war.

MARINE INSURANCE. A contract of indemnity by which one party, for a stipulated premium, undertakes to indemnify the other, to the extent of the amount insured, against all perils of the sea, or certain enumerated perils, to which his ship, cargo, and freight, or some of them, may be exposed during a certain voyage, or a fixed period of time.

MARINE INTEREST. A compensation paid for the use of money loaned on bottomry or respondentia. Provided the money be loaned and put at risk, there is no fixed limit to the rate which may be lawfully charged by the lender; but courts of admiralty, in enforcing the contract, will mitigate the rate when it is extortionate and unconscionable.

MARINE LEAGUE. A measure equal to the twentieth part of a degree of latitude. Bouch. Inst. note 1845. It is generally conceded that a nation has exclusive territorial jurisdiction upon the high seas for a marine league from its own shores. 1 Kent, Comm. 29.

MARINER. One whose occupation it is to navigate vessels upon the sea. Surgeons, engineers, clerks, stewards, cooks, porters, and chamber maids, on passenger steamers, when necessary for the service of the ship or crew, are also deemed mariners, and permitted as such to sue in the admiralty for their wages. 1 Conkl. Adm. 107. See "Seaman."

MARIS ET FOEMINAE CONJUNCTIO est de jure naturae. The union of male and female is founded on the law of nature. 7 Coke, 13.

MARITAGIO AMISSO PER DEFALTAM. An obsolete writ for the tenant in frank marriage to recover lands, etc., of which he was deforced.

MARITAGIUM (Lat.) A portion given with a daughter in marriage.

During the existence of the feudal law, it was the right which the lord of the fee had, under certain tenures, to dispose of the daughters of his vassal in marriage. Beames, Glanv. 138, note; Bracton, 21a; Spelman; 2 Bl. Comm. 69; Co. Litt. 21b, 76a.

MARITAGIUM EST AUT LIBERUM aut servitio obligatum; liberum maritagium dicitur ubi donator vult quod terra sic data quieta sit et libera ab omni seculari servitio. A marriage portion is either free or bound to service; it is called "frank marriage" when the giver wills that land thus given be exempt from all secular service. Co. Litt. 21.

MARITAGIUM HABERE. To have the free disposal of an heiress in marriage.

MARITAL. That which belongs to marriage; as, marital rights, marital duties.

MARITAL PORTION. In Louisiana. The name given to that part of the deceased husband's estate to which the widow is entitled. Civ. Code La. 334, art. 55; 3 Mart. (La.; N. S.) 1.

MARITAL RIGHTS. The rights of a husband. Chiefly applied to the right of sexual intercourse.

MARITIMA ANGLIAE. In old English law. The emolument or revenue coming to the king from the sea, which the sheriffs anciently collected, but which was afterwards granted to the admiral. Spelman.

MARITIMA INCREMENTA. In old English law. Marine increases; lands gained from the sea. Hale de Jur. Mar. pt. 1, c. 4.

MARITIME. Pertaining to the sea. Ordinarily, the term is synonymous with "marine."

MARITIME CAUSE. A cause arising from a maritime contract, whether made at sea or on land.

The term includes such causes as relate to the business, commerce, or navigation of the sea; as charter parties, bills of lading, and other contracts of affreightment; bottomry and respondentia contracts; and contracts for maritime services in repairing, supplying, and navigating ships and vessels; contracts and *quasi* contracts respecting averages, contributions, and jettisons, when the party prosecuting has a maritime lien; and also those arising from torts and injuries committed on the high seas, or on other navigable waters within the admiralty jurisdiction.

MARITIME CONTRACT. One which relates to the business of navigation upon the sea, or to business appertaining to commerce or navigation to be transacted or done upon the sea, or in seaports, and over which courts of admiralty have jurisdiction concurrent with the courts of common law.

Such contracts, according to the civilians, include, among others, charter parties, bills of lading, marine hypothecations, contracts for services in building, repairing, supplying, and navigating ships, contracts respecting averages, jettisons, etc.

In an early opinion by Story, J., these views were generally adopted (2 Gall. [U. S.] 398), but it has been since held that the contract for building a vessel is not a maritime contract. (20 How. [U. S.] 393; 22 How. [U. S.] 129).

MARITIME COURT. A court of admiralty jurisdiction.

MARITIME INTEREST. Marine interest (*q. v.*)

MARITIME LAW. That system of law which particularly relates to the affairs and business of the sea, to ships, their crews and navigation, and to the marine conveyance of persons and property. See 21 Wall. (U. S.) 558.

MARITIME LIEN. See "Lien."

MARITIME LOAN. A contract or agreement by which one, who is the lender, lends to another, who is the borrower, a certain sum of money, upon condition that, if the thing upon which the loan has been made should be lost by any peril of the sea, or *vis major*, the lender shall not be repaid unless what remains shall be equal to the sum borrowed; and if the thing arrive in safety, or in case it shall not have been injured but by its own defects, or the fault of the master or mariners, the borrower shall be bound to return the sum borrowed, together with a certain sum agreed upon as the price of the hazard incurred. Emerig. Mar. Loans, c. 1, § 2. See "Bottomry;" "Gross Adventure;" "Marine Interest;" "Respondentia."

MARITIME PROFIT. A term used by French writers to signify any profit derived from a maritime loan.

MARITIME STATE. In English law. The officers and enlisted men of the English navy.

MARITIME TORT. One committed on the high seas, or otherwise within admiralty jurisdiction.

MARK. A sign, traced on paper or parchment, which stands in the place of a signature; usually made by persons who cannot write. It is most often the sign of the cross, made in a little space left between the Christian name and surname. 2 Bl. Comm. 305; 2 Curt. 324; Moody & M. 516; 12 Pet. (U. S.) 150; 7 Bing. 457; 2 Ves. Sr. 455; 1 Ves. & B. 362; 1 Ves. Jr. 11. A mark is now held to be a good signature, though the party was able to write. 8 Adol. & E. 94; 3 Nev. & P. 228; 3 Curt. 752; 5 Johns. (N. Y.) 144; 2 Bradf. Sur. (N. Y.) 385; 24 Pa. St. 502; 29 Pa. St. 221; 19 Mo. 609; 21 Mo. 17; 18 Ga. 396; 16 B. Mon. (Ky.) 102; 1 Jarm. Wills (Perkins Ed.) 69, 112, note; 1 Williams, Ex'rs, 63. See St. Pa. 1848.

MARKET (Lat. *merx*, merchandise; anciently, *mercat*). A public place and appointed time for buying and selling. A public place appointed by public authority, where all sorts of things necessary for the subsistence or for the convenience of life are sold. 14 N. Y. 356. All fairs are markets, but not *vice versa*. Bracton, lib. 2, c. 24; Co. Litt. 22; 2 Inst. 401; 4 Inst. 272. Markets are generally regulated by local laws.

The franchise by which a town holds a market, which can only be by royal grant or immemorial usage. 21 Barb. (N. Y.) 296, 2 Bl. Comm. 37.

By the term "market" is also understood the demand there is for any particular article; as, the cotton market in Europe is dull. See 15 Viner, Abr. 42; Comyn, Dig.

MARKET GELD. The toll of a market.

MARKET OVERT. An open or public market; that is, a place appointed by law or custom for the sale of goods and chattels at stated times in public. "An open, public, and legally constituted market." Jervis, C. J., 9 J. Scott, 601.

The market place is the only market overt out of London; but in London every shop is a market overt. 5 Coke, 83; F. Moore, 300. In London, every day except Sunday is market day. In the country, particular days are fixed for market days. 2 Bl. Comm. 449.

The term is of importance in English law, because of the protection afforded purchasers in good faith in market overt. 5 Coke, 83.

MARKET PRICE. See "Market Value."

MARKET TOWNS. Those towns which are entitled to hold markets. 1 Steph. Comm. (7th Ed.) 130.

MARKET VALUE. The price established by public sales, or sales in the way of ordinary business, 99 Mass. 345; what the property will sell for as between one who wants to purchase and one who wants to sell. 151 Wis. 224.

MARKET ZELD, or **MARKET GELD.** The toll of a market.

MARKETABLE TITLE. A title not subject to such reasonable doubt as would create a just apprehension of invalidity in the mind of a reasonable, prudent and intelligent person; one that a person of reasonable prudence and intelligence, guided by competent legal advice, would be willing to take and pay fair value for. 154 Ill. 607; 27 Ill. App. 280.

A title which is not only good, but as to which there is no reasonable doubt as to matter of either law or fact. Such a title as dealers in real estate, banks, etc., would be willing to invest in. 46 Hun (N. Y.) 638.

MARKSMAN. In practice and conveyancing. One who makes his mark; a person who cannot write, and only makes his mark in executing instruments. Archb. N. P. 13; 2 Chit. 92.

MARLBRIDGE, STATUTE OF, An important English statute (52 Hen. III. [1267]) relating to the tenures of real property, and to procedure. It derived its name from the town in Wiltshire in which parliament sat when it was enacted, now known as Marlborough. Compare 2 Reeve, Hist. Eng. Law, 62; Crabb, Com. Law, 156; Barr. Obs. St. 66.

MARQUE AND REPRISAL. See "Letter of Marque and Reprisal."

MARQUIS. A nobleman next in rank to a duke.

MARRIAGE. The word marriage is used to signify either the act of entering into the marital condition, or the condition itself. In the latter and more frequent legal sense, it is a civil status, existing in one man and one woman, legally united for life for those civil and social purposes, which are based in the distinction of sex. Its source is the law of nature whence it has flowed into the municipal laws of every civilized country, and into the general law of nations. And since it can exist only in pairs, and since no persons are compelled, but all who are capable are permitted to assume it, marriage may be said to proceed from a civil contract between one man and one woman of the needful physical and civil capacity. 30 Georgia 176.

As applied to the act of becoming married, marriage is the acts, whether of private contract or official or religious ceremonial, by which a man and a woman lawfully enter into the married state.

As distinguished from the agreement to marry, and the act of becoming married, is the civil status of one man and one woman united in law for the discharge to each other and the community of the duties legally incumbent on husband and wife. See Bish. Mar. & Div. § 3.

Marriage is generally referred to as a contract, but, under modern doctrine, its contractual nature is confined to the formation of the relation, such formation being wholly a matter of contract. But, when formed, marriage is not a contract, but a status. 30 Ga. 176; 3 Heisk. (Tenn.) 307; 53 Mo. 578; 9 Ind. 37.

MARRIAGE ARTICLES. Articles of agreement between parties contemplating marriage, in accordance with which the marriage settlement is afterwards to be drawn up. They are to be binding in case of marriage. They must be in writing, by statute of frauds. Burton, Real Prop. 484; Crabb, Real Prop. § 1809; 4 Cruise, Dig. 274, 323. See 2 Washb. Real Prop. Append.

MARRIAGE BROKERAGE. The act by which a person interferes, for a consideration to be received by him, between a man and a woman, for the purpose of promoting a marriage between them. 83 Ill. App. 509. The money paid for such service is also known by this name.

It is a doctrine of the courts of equity that all marriage brokage contracts are utterly void, as against public policy, and are therefore, incapable of confirmation. 1 Fonbl. Eq. bk. 1, c. 4, § 10, note (s); 2 Story, Eq. Jur. § 263; Newland, Cont. 469. But where a party is established in business as a marriage broker, one dealing with him is not *in pari delicto*, and can recover back money deposited on a contract. 124 N. Y. 156.

MARRIAGE LICENSE. A license required in some states to be obtained from a public officer by persons intending to marry.

MARRIAGE PORTION. That property which is given to a woman on her marriage. See "Dowry."

MARRIAGE, PROMISE OF. A promise of marriage is a contract entered into between a man and woman that they will marry each other.

MARRIAGE SETTLEMENT. An agreement made by the parties in contemplation of marriage, by which the title to certain property is changed, and the property to some extent becomes inalienable. 1 Rice, Eq. (S. C.) 315. See 2 Hill Ch. (S. C.) 3; 8 Leigh (Va.) 29; 1 Dev. & B. Eq. (N. C.) 389; 2 Dev. & B. Eq. (S. C.) 103; 1 Baldw. (U. S.) 344; 15 Mass. 106; 1 Yeates (Pa.) 221; 7 Pet. (U. S.) 348; 4 Bouv. Inst. note 3947. See 2 Washb. Real Prop. Append.

MARSH. Marsh is equivalent to meadow. It does not appear to have been used in the earlier records or in grants. 155 N. Y. 303.

MARSHAL. An officer of the United States, whose duty it is to execute the process of the courts of the United States. His duties within the district for which he is appointed are very similar to those of a sheriff. See U. S. St. at Large, Index; Sergeant, Const. Law, c. 25; 2 Dall. (U. S.) 402; Burr's Trial, 365; 1 Mason (U. S.) 100; 2 Gall (U. S.) 101; 4 Cranch (U. S.) 96; 7 Cranch (U. S.) 276; 9 Cranch (U. S.) 86, 212; 6 Wheat. (U. S.) 194; 9 Wheat. (U. S.) 645.

MARSHALLING. Arranging; putting in proper order; *e. g.*, "the law will marshal words, *ut res magis valeat.*" Hill, B., Hardr. 92. So to marshal assets. See "Assets." So to marshal coat armor. This now belongs to heralds. Wharton.

MARSHALLING ASSETS. Such an arment of creditors into classes with respect all parties having equities therein to receive their due proportions, notwithstanding the intervening interests of particular persons to prior satisfaction out of a part of the funds. 1 Story, Eq. 558. The doctrine does not apply unless there are two funds in existence to which claim is made by several having diverse rights. L. R. 3 Eq. 668. But it is immaterial what is the nature of the property which constitutes the fund.

MARSHALLING SECURITIES. An arrangement of creditors into classes with respect to their satisfaction out of the assets of the common debtor in such manner as to compel the creditor having a right of resort to two or more different funds to satisfy his claim first from the fund to which no other creditor has a right to resort. 1 Story, Eq. 633.

MARSHALSEA. In English law. A prison belonging to the king's bench. It has now been consolidated with others, under the name of the queen's prison.

MARSHALSEA, COURT OF. A court originally held before the steward and marshal of the royal household.

It was instituted to administer justice between the servants of the king's household, that they might not be drawn into other courts, and their services lost. It was anciently ambulatory; but Charles I. erected a court of record, by the name of *curia palatii*, to be held before the steward of the household, etc., to hold pleas of all personal actions which should arise within twelve miles of the royal palace at Whitehall, not including the city of London. This court was held weekly, to determine causes involving less than twenty pounds, together with the ancient court of Marshalsea, in the borough of Southwark. A writ of error lay thence to the king's bench. Both courts were abolished by St. 12 & 13 Vict. c. 101, § 13. See Jacob; Wishaw.

MARTE SUO DECURRERE (Lat. to run by its own force). A term applied in the civil law to a suit when it ran its course to the end, without any impediment. Calv. Lex.; Brissonius.

MARTIAL LAW. That military rule and authority which exists in time of war, and is conferred by the laws of war, in relation to persons and things under and within the scope of active military operations, in carrying on the war, and which extinguishes or suspends civil rights and the remedies founded upon them, for the time being, so far as it may appear to be necessary in order to the full accomplishment of the purposes of the war. Prof. Joel Parker, in N. A. Rev., Oct., 1861.

It depends on the just but arbitrary power and pleasure of the king, who may not make laws without the consent of parliament, yet in time of war, by reason of the necessity of it, to guard against dangers that often arise, he uses absolute power; so that his word is law. 21 Ind. 377.

The phrases, "martial law" and "military law," are sometimes carelessly used as meaning the same thing, but there is a broad distinction between them.

Acting under constitutional authority, congress has passed divers acts prescribing the rules and articles of war, which constitute the military law, but apply only to persons in the military or naval service of the government.

Martial law, when once established, applies alike to citizens and soldiers. In a proper sense it is not law, but merely the will of the military commander, who is responsible to his government or superior officer. Hale's Hist. C. L. 54.

War being simply an appeal to force, necessarily suspends and displaces the ordinary laws, and martial law prevails as an inavoidable necessity to restrain disloyal acts and preserve the authority of the government. This is true not only in the actual field of military operations, but also in remote districts where the inhabitants may be so far in sympathy with the public enemy as to obstruct the administration of the laws by the civil tribunals and render resort to military power necessary.

But where the civil courts, in the midst of loyal communities, are exercising their ordinary jurisdiction, the appeal to the military arm or to martial law is needless. 44 Ill. 159.

MASCULINE. Belonging to, or descriptive of the male sex.

The masculine frequently includes the feminine; as "man" includes "woman." The masculine sex always includes the feminine. Dig. 32. 62.

MASSA. In the civil law. A mass; raw material.

MASSACHUSETTS TRUST. A trust created for the operation and conduct of a business enterprise; also known as common law companies, and business trusts.

MAST. To fatten with mast (acorns, etc.) 1 Leon. 186.

MAST SELLING. In old English law. The practice of selling the goods of dead seamen at the mast. Held void. 7 Mod. 141.

MASTER. One who has control over an apprentice.

A master stands in relation to his apprentices *in loco parentis*, and is bound to fulfill that relation, which the law generally enforces. He is also entitled to be obeyed by his apprentices as if they were his children. Bouv. Inst. Index. See "Apprenticeship."

One who is employed in teaching children; known, generally, as a "schoolmaster."

One who has in his employment one or more persons hired by contract to serve him, either as domestic or common laborers.

MASTER AT COMMON LAW. In English law. An officer of the superior courts of common law (each court having five), whose principal duties, when attending court, consists in taking affidavits sworn in court, in administering oaths to attorneys on their admission, and in certifying to the court, in cases of doubt or difficulty, what the practice of the court is. Their principal duties out of court consist in taxing attorneys' costs, in computing principal and interest on bills of exchange, promissory notes, and other documents, under rules to compute, in examining witnesses who are going abroad for the purpose of obtaining their testimony, in hearing and determining rules referred to them by the court in the place of the court itself, and in reporting to the court their conclusions with reference to the rules so referred to them. Holthouse.

MASTER IN CHANCERY (anciently **master of the chancery**) (Law Lat. *magister cancellariae*). In equity practice. An important officer of courts of equity, who acts as assistant to the chancellor or judge, and whose principal duty consists in inquiring into various matters referred to him for the purpose, and reporting thereon to the court. Wharton; Holthouse. 180 Ill. App. 538; 169 Ill. 495. In England, there are twelve of these masters, of whom the master of the rolls is the chief.

These officers were originally the chief clerks of the chancery (*clerici de prima forma*), 180 Ill. App. 538; 169 Ill. 495; who acted as the assessors or council of the lord chancellor (*collaterales et socii cancellarii*). 2 Reeve, Hist. Eng. Law, 251. According to Mr. Spence, they obtained the title of "masters" in the reign of Edward III. 1 Spence, Ch. 360. But they appear to have had the title of *praeceptores* at a much earlier period. 2 Reeve, Hist. Eng. Law, ubi supra; Crabb, Hist. Eng. Law, 184.

MASTER OF A SHIP. In maritime law. The commander or first officer of a merchant ship; a captain.

MASTER OF THE CROWN OFFICE. In English law. The queen's coroner and attorney in the criminal department of the court of queen's bench, who prosecutes at the relation of some private person, or common informer, the crown being the nominal prosecutor. Wharton.

MASTER OF THE ROLLS. (Law Lat. *magister rotulorum*). In English law. An assistant judge of the court of chancery, who holds a separate court ranking next to that of the lord chancellor, and has the keeping of the rolls and grants which pass the great seal, and the records of the chancery. He was originally appointed only for the superintendence of the writs and records appertaining to the common-law department of the court, and is still properly the chief of the masters in chancery. 3 Steph. Comm. 417; Wharton.

MASURA. (L. Lat.) In old English law. A house and ground; a piece of ground belonging to a house; a house in a city. Spelman.

An old decayed house or wall; the ruins of a building. Cowell.

MATE. In maritime law. The officer next in rank to the master on board a merchant ship or vessel.

In such vessels there is always one mate, and sometimes a second, third, and fourth mate, according to the vessel's size, and the trade in which she may be engaged. When the word "mate" is used without qualification, it always denotes the first mate; and the others are designated as above. On large ships the mate is frequently styled "first officer," and the second and third mates, "second" and "third" officers. Parlish, Sea Off. Man. 83-140.

MATER-FAMILIAS. In civil law. The mother of a family; the mistress of a family.

A chaste woman, married or single. Calv. Lex.

MATERIA (Lat.)

——**In the Civil Law.** Materials; as distinguished from species, or the form given by labor and skill. Dig. 41. 1. 7. 7-12; Fleta, lib. 3, c. 2, § 14.

Materials (wood) for building, as distinguished from "*lignum*." Dig. 32. 55. pr.

——**In English Law.** Matter; substance; subject matter. 3 Bl. Comm. 322.

MATERIAL.

(1) That which enters into the erection or repair of any structure. It does not include tools or facilities used. 71 Pa. St. 293.

(2) That which is essential or important.

MATERIAL FACT. Material facts are those which relate to the merits of the cause of action or defense—facts which are within the issues to be tried and which may be made available on the trial as completing the cause of action or defense. 54 Ill. App. 353.

MATERIALITY. The property of substantial importance or influence, especially as distinguished from formal requirement. Capability of properly influencing the result of the trial.

MATERIALMEN. Persons who furnish materials to be used in the erection of buildings, ships, etc.

By the general American law, materialmen have a lien on a foreign ship (9 Wheat. [U. S.] 409), but not on a domestic ship (20 How. [U. S.] 393). By statute, materialmen have a lien on a building. See "Mechanic's Lien."

MATERNA MATERNIS (Lat. from the mother to the mother's). In French law. A term denoting the descent of property of a deceased person derived from his mother to the relations on the mother's side.

MATERNAL. That which belongs to, or comes from, the mother; as, maternal authority, maternal relation, maternal estate, maternal line. See "Line."

MATERNAL ANCESTOR. The words maternal ancestor are manifestly limited to progenitors, or ancestors in the direct ascending line, according to their common meaning and the only sense in which the word "ancestor" is used throughout the statute of descents, the rules of which statute are declared to be those of the statute of distributions also. 108 Mass. 42.

MATERNAL PROPERTY. That which comes from the mother of the party, and other ascendants of the maternal stock. Domat, Liv. Prel. tit. 3, § 2, note 12.

MATERNITY. The state or condition of a mother.

It is either legitimate or natural. The former is the condition of the mother who has given birth to legitimate children; while the latter is the condition of her who has given birth to illegitimate children. Maternity is always certain; while the paternity is only presumed.

MATHEMATICAL EVIDENCE. That evidence which is established by a demonstration. It is used in contradistinction to "moral evidence."

MATIMA. A godmother.

MATRICIDE. The murder of a mother; or one who has slain his mother.

MATRICULA. In civil law. A register in which are inscribed the names of persons who become members of an association or society. Dig. 50. 3. 1. In the ancient church there were *matricula clericorum*, which was a catalogue of the officiating clergy, and *matricula pauperum*, a list of the poor to be relieved; hence, to be entered in the university is to be matriculated.

MATRIMONIA DEBENT ESSE LIBERA. Marriages ought to be free. Halk. Max. 86; 2 Kent, Comm. 102.

MATRIMONIAL CAUSES. In the English ecclesiastical courts there are five kinds of causes which are classed under this head, viz.: Causes for a malicious jactitation; suits for nullity of marriage, on account of fraud, incest, or other bar to the marriage (2 Hagg. Consist. 423); suits for restitution of conjugal rights; suits for divorces on account of cruelty or adultery, or causes which have arisen since the marriage; suits for alimony.

MATRIMONIUM. In civil law. A legal marriage. A marriage celebrated in conformity with the rules of the civil law was called *justum matrimonium;* the husband *vir*, the wife *uxor*. It was exclusively confined to Roman citizens, and to those to whom the *connubium* had been conceded. It alone produced the paternal power over the children, and the marital power—*manus*—over the wife. The *farreum*, the *coemptio*, or the *usus* was indispensable for the formation of this marriage. See "Pater-Familias."

MATRIMONIUM SUBSEQUENS TOLLIT peccatum praecedens. A subsequent marriage cures preceding criminality.

MATRIMONY. The nuptial state.

MATRIX. In civil law. The protocol or first draft of a legal instrument, from which all copies must be taken. See 16 S. W. 53.

MATRON. A woman who is a mother. See "Jury Women."

MATTER EN LEY NE SERRA MISE EN bouche del jurors. Matter of laws shall not be put into the mouth of jurors. Jenk. Cent. Cas. 180.

MATTER IN CONTROVERSY. The subject of litigation; the amount demanded and for which the suit is brought and upon which issue is joined, and in relation to which jurors are called and witnesses examined. 1 Wallace (U. S.) 339; 1 Serg. & R. (Pa.) 269.

MATTER IN DEED. Such matter as may be proved or established by a deed or specialty. Matter of fact, in contradistinction to matter of law. Co. Litt. 320; Steph. Pl. 197.

MATTER IN DISPUTE. See Matter in Controversy.

MATTER IN ISSUE. That matter upon which the plaintiff bases his action and which the defendant denies or controverts by his pleadings. 132 Ill. 339; 165 Mich. 380. See Issue; Matter in Controversy.

MATTER IN PAIS (literally, matter in the country). Matter of fact, as distinguished from matter of law or matter of record. See "In Pais."

MATTER OF AGGRAVATION. Matter of aggravation, correctly understood, does not consist in acts of the same kind and description as those constituting the gist of the action, but in something done by the defendant, on the occasion of committing the trespass, which is, to some extent, of a different legal character from the principal act complained of. As where the plaintiff declares in trespass for breaking and entering his dwelling-house, and alleges, in addition, that the defendant also destroyed his goods in the house, assaulted and beat his domestics, or debauched his daughter, or servant. 19 Vt. 107. See Gist.

MATTER OF AVOIDANCE. Matter of avoidance in pleading is new matter which admits the declaration to be true, but shows nevertheless, either that the defendant was never liable to the recovery claimed against him or that he has been discharged from his original liability, by something supervenient. 31 Conn. 177. See Confession and Avoidance; Pleas; Special Plea in Bar.

MATTER OF COURSE. See "Of Course."

MATTER OF FACT. In pleading. Matter the existence or truth of which is determined by the senses, or by reasoning based upon their evidence. The decision of such matters is referred to the jury. Hob. 127; 1 Greenl. Ev. § 49.

MATTER OF FORM. See "Form."

MATTER OF LAW. Matter of truth or falsity of which is determined by the established rules of law or reasoning based on them. 70 N. C. 167.

MATTER OF RECORD. Those facts which may be proved by the production of a record. It differs from matter in deed, which consists of facts which may be proved by specialty. See "Record."

MATTER OF SUBSTANCE. See "Substance."

MATTERS OF SUBSISTENCE FOR man. Comprehends all articles or things, whether animal or vegetable, living or dead, which are used for food, and whether they are consumed in the form in which they are bought from the producer, or are only consumed after undergoing a process of preparation, which is greater or less, according to the character of the article. 19 Grat. (Va.) 813.

MATURIORA SUNT VOTA MULIERUM quam virorum. The wishes of women are of quicker growth than those of men; *i. e.*, women arrive at maturity earlier than men. 6 Coke, 71a; Bracton, 86b.

MATURITY. The time when a bill or note becomes due.

MAUNDER. (L. Fr.) In old English law. To command; to return (a writ). Stat. Westm. 1, c. 45.

MAXIM. An established principle or proposition; a principle of law universally admitted, as being just and consonant with reason. The wisdom of many, but the wit of one.

Maxims in law are somewhat like axioms in geometry. 1 Bl. Comm. 68. They are principles and authorities, and part of the general customs or common law of the land, and are of the same strength as acts of parliament, when the judges have determined what is a maxim; which belongs to the judges and not the jury. Termes de la Ley; Doctor & Stud. Dial. 1, c. 8. Maxims of the law are holden for law, and all other cases that may be applied to them shall be taken for granted. Co. Litt. 11, 67. See Plowd. 27b.

The application of the maxim to the case before the court is generally the only difficulty. The true method of making the application is to ascertain how the maxim arose, and to consider whether the case to which it is applied is of the same character, or whether it is an exception to an apparently general rule.

*The most important of the maxims of law will be found alphabetically arranged through this book.

MAXIME ITA DICTA QUIA MAXIMA est ejus dignitas et certissima auctoritas, atque quod maxime omnibus probetur. A maxim is so called because its dignity is chiefest, and its authority the most certain, and because universally approved by all. Co. Litt. 11.

MAXIME PACI SUNT CONTRARIA, VIS et injuria. The greatest enemies to peace are force and wrong. Co. Litt. 161.

MAXIMUS ERRORIS POPULUS MAGISter. The people is the greatest master of error.

MAY. See also "Shall."

——**Construction in General.** That "may" always means "must" is a misconception, 44 Ch. D. 270. It is ordinarily permissive, 52 N. Y. 96; 107 Mass. 196. It gives a power as to the exercise of which there is discretion. 44 Ch. D. 270. An enabling and discretionary power. 174 Mass. 245; is permitted to; has liberty to.

In the absence of any controlling consideration the word is not considered as mandatory, 122 Iowa 669, but when the power is given in the interest of public justice; or whenever the object of the power is to effectuate the public interests, or a private, or legal right; where the public or third persons have a claim, de jure, that the power shall be exercised, 77 Ill. 273; 56 N. J. L. 300; 68 N. Y. 119; 21 Wis. 371; 49 L. J. Q. B. 577; 2 Q. B. 274; or to carry out the intention of a contract, the word will be construed as compulsory. 84 Ill. 471; 44 Conn. 534.

Where a power is deposited with a public officer for the purpose of being used for the benefit of persons who are specifically pointed out, or with regard to whom the legislature has supplied the conditions upon which they are entitled to call for the exercise of the power, the courts will require it to be exercised. 49 L. J. Q. B. 577, 585.

When the point in controversy is not covered by authority, those who contend that an obligation for exercise of the power exists must show something which creates such obligation. 49 L. J. Q. B. 577.

The word "may" may be interchangeably used with "shall" or "will." State v. Starr, 24 N. M. 180, 173 Pac. 674.

While colloquially the words "may" and "will" are used interchangeably and are commonly so understood, in grammatical construction they perform entirely different distinct offices, and therefore convey essentially different meanings, the one importing a mere possibility or vague or indefinite speculation as to the existence of some fact or thing, the other the unqualified or unconditional existence of some fact or thing; or, in other words, the one meaning an existence in possibility, and the other an existence in actuality. Scally v. W. T. Garratt & Co., 11 Cal. App. 138.

——**Construction of Statutes.** The word "may" in a statute is sometimes mandatory, but not necessarily so, 86 Iowa 352. It is to be construed as "must" where the evident purpose of the statute, the object of the provision and the context so require. 136 Iowa 445; 51 L. J. M. C. 27, 132; 8 Q. D. B. 306; 9 Q. D. B. 238, and in all cases where the statute imposes a positive and absolute duty, devoid of any discretion; 1 Peters 46, 64; 3 Hill (N. Y.) 612, 615; or where public justice, 2 Salk. 609; 204 Ill. 462, public interests, or rights of persons depend on the exercise of the power, or the performance of the duty to which it refers. 130 Ill. 490; 270 Ill. 145; 2 Pet. (U. S.) 64; 12 Ala. 693; 1 Vern. 153; 1 Kent's Com. 467, note. In such statutes "may" or "shall" may be read interchangeably, as will best express the legislative intention. 77 Ill. 273; 181 Ill. App. 290; 219 Ill. 174.

May should not be construed as mandatory when inconsistent with the manifest intention of the legislature, or repugnant to the text of the statute, and only when necessary to give effect to the clear policy and intention of the enacting body. 123 Iowa 660. Where persons or the public have an interest in having the act done by a public body, "may" in such a statute means "must." 52 N. Y. 27.

The word "will" as used in an act providing that "any citizen of the state may, within ten days, by written notice to the secretary of state and to the party or parties who file such petition, protest against the same, at which time he will hear testimony and arguments for and against the sufficiency of such petition," means "shall" and is mandatory, and, being addressed to a public official, excludes the idea of discretion. Russell v. Harrison, 33 Okla. 225.

MAYHEM. In criminal law. The act of unlawfully and violently depriving another of the use of such of his members as may render him less able, in fighting, either to defend himself or annoy his adversary. 8 Car. & P. 167; 4 Bl. Comm. 205. The cutting or disabling, or weakening, a man's hand or finger, or striking out his eye or fore tooth, or depriving him of those parts the loss of which abates his courage, are held to be mayhems. But cutting off the ear or nose, or the like, are not held to be mayhems at common law. 4 Bl. Comm. 205. The offense has been extended by statute to these and other injuries. See 87 N. C. 509; 70 Iowa, 505.

MAYHEMAVIT. Maimed. This is a term of art which cannot be supplied in pleadings by any other word, as *mutilavit, truncavit*, etc. 3 Thomas, Co. Litt. 548; 7 Mass. 247.

MAYNOVER (from Fr. *mayn*, hand). Anything produced by manual labor.

MAYOR. (Lat. *major; meyr, miret*, or *maer*, one that keeps guard; old English, *maier, potestas*, power or authority, 25 Wend. [N. Y.] 50.) The chief governor or executive magistrate of a city. The old word was "portgreve." The word "mayor" first occurs in 1189, when Richard I. substituted a mayor for the two bailiffs of London. The word is common in Bracton. Bracton, 57. In London, York, and Dublin, he is called "lord mayor." Wharton.

MAYORALTY. The office or dignity of a mayor.

MAYORAZGO. In Spanish law. A species of entail known to Spanish law. 1 White, New Recop. 119.

The right to the enjoyment of certain aggregate property, left with the condition therein imposed, that they are to pass in their integrity perpetually, successively to the eldest son. Schmidt's Civ. Law, 62.

MAYOR'S COURT. The name of a court usually established in cities, composed of a mayor, recorder, and aldermen, generally having jurisdiction of offenses committed within the city, and of other matters specially given them by the statute.

MEAL RENT. A rent formerly paid in meal.

MEAN. See "Mesne."

MEANDER. To wind, as a river or stream. Webster.

The winding or bend of a stream.

To survey a stream according to its meanders or windings. Rev. St. Wis. c. 34, § 1; 2 Wis. 317.

MEANDER LINE. A line designed to point out the sinuosities of the bank or shore, and a means of ascertaining the quantity of land in the fraction which is to be paid for by the purchaser. 241 Ill. 319.

MEASE, or **MESE** (Norman French). A house. Litt. §§ 74, 251.

MEASON DUE. A corruption of *Maison de Dieu.*

MEASURE. A means or standard for computing amount; a certain quantity of something, taken for a unit, and which expresses a relation with other quantities of the same thing.

MEASURE OF DAMAGES. In practice. The rules by which the damage sustained is to be estimated or measured; the quantum of damage allowed by law.

MECHANIC'S LIEN. A statutory lien in favor of persons who have performed labor or furnished material for the erection or repair of any building, upon the building and the land on which it is situated.

MEDFEE. In old English law. A bribe or reward; a compensation given in exchange where the things exchanged were not of equal value. Cowell.

MEDIA ANNATA. In Spanish law. Half-yearly profits of land. 5 Tex. 34, 79.

MEDIA NOX. Midnight.

MEDIAE ET INFIRMAE MANUS HOMInes. Men of a middle and base condition. Blount.

MEDIATE DESCENT. See Immediate Descent.

MEDIATE POWERS. Those incident to primary powers, given by a principal to his agent. For example, the general authority given to collect, receive, and pay debts due by or to the principal is a primary power. In order to accomplish this, it is frequently required to settle accounts, adjust disputed claims, resist those which are unjust, and answer and defend suits. These subordinate powers are sometimes called "mediate powers." Story, Ag. § 58. See 1 Campb. 43, note; 4 Campb. 163; 6 Serg. & R. (Pa.) 149.

MEDIATE TESTIMONY. Secondary evidence (*q. v.*).

MEDIATION. The act of some mutual friend of two contending parties, who brings them to agree, compromise, or settle their disputes. Vattel, Dr. des Gens, liv. 2, c. 18, § 328.

MEDIATOR. One who interposes between two contending parties, with their consent, for the purpose of assisting them in settling their differences. Sometimes this term is applied to an officer who is appointed by a sovereign nation to promote the settlement of disputes between two other nations. See "Minister."

MEDIATORS OF QUESTIONS. In English law. Six persons authorized by statute (27 Edw. III. st. 2, c. 24), who, upon any question arising among merchants relating to unmerchantable wool, or undue packing, etc., might, before the mayor and officers of the staple, upon their oath certify and settle the same; to whose determination therein the parties concerned were to submit. Cowell.

MEDICAL EVIDENCE. Testimony given by physicians or surgeons in their professional capacity as experts, or derived from the statements of writers of medical or surgical works.

This kind of evidence was first recognized by Charles V. of Germany, and incorporated in the "Caroline Code," framed at Ratisbon in 1532, wherein it was ordained that the opinion of medical men—at first surgeons only—should be received in cases of death by violent or unnatural means, when suspicion existed of a criminal agency. The publication of this code encouraged the members of the medical profession to renewed activity, tending greatly to advance their sciences and the cause of justice generally. Many books soon appeared on the subject of medical jurisprudence, and the importance of medical evidence was more fully understood. Elwell, Malprac. 285.

MEDICINE. The art of understanding diseases and curing or relieving them when possible. It is that branch of physic which relates to the healing of diseases. It is not restricted to any particular methods or remedies. 71 Ill. App. 239.

The term "medicine" is not limited to substances supposed to possess curative or remedial properties, but has also the meaning of the healing art,—the science of preserving health and treating disease for the purpose of cure,—whether such treatment involves the use of medical substances or not. 278 Ill. 257.

MEDICINE CHEST. A box containing an assortment of medicines.

Statutory provisions in the United States require all vessels above a certain size to keep a medicine chest. 1 Story, U. S. Laws, 106; 2 Story, U. S. Laws, 971.

MEDIETAS LINGUAE. In old practice. Moiety of tongue; half-tongue. Applied to a jury, impaneled in a cause, consisting the one-half of natives, and the other half of foreigners.

MEDIO ACQUIETANDO. A judicial writ to distrain a lord for the acquitting of a mesne lord from a rent, which he had acknowledged in court not to belong to him. Reg. Jur. 129.

MEDITATIO FUGAE. In Scotch law. Contemplation of flight; intention to abscond. 2 Kames, Eq. 14, 15.

MEDIUM TEMPUS. In old English law. Meantime; mesne profits. Cowell.

MEDIUS. (Lat.) In old English law; mean, intermediate; between two; a mesne; an intermediate lord; a tenant having a mesne between himself and the chief lord. Stat. Westm. 2, c. 6.

In old continental law. A man of middle condition. L. Alam. tit. 67.

MEDLETUM. In old English law. A mixing together; a medley or *melee;* an affray or sudden encounter; an offense suddenly committed in an affray. The English word "medley" is preserved in the term "chance medley." An intermeddling, without violence, in any matter of business. Spelman.

MEDLEY. An affray; a sudden or casual fighting; a hand to hand battle; a *melee.* See "Chance Medley;" "Chaud Medley.

MEDSCEAT. In old English law. A bribe; hush money.

MEETING. The word meeting implies a concurrence, or coming face to face of at least two persons. 46 L. J. Q. B. 104; W. N. (77) 223; 2 Q. B. D. 26; 25 W. R. 66; 36 L. T. 188. There is speaking generally, no meeting of shareholders or other bodies if only one attends; though no doubt in a particular statute the word might be used in a special sense, so that the attendance of one might satisfy. 46 L. J. Q. B. 104.

MEGBOTE. A recompense for the murder of a relative.

MEIGNE. A family.

MEINDRE AGE. Lesser age; minority.

MEJORADO. In Spanish law. Preferred; advanced. White, New Recop. lib. 3, tit. 10, c. 1, § 4.

MELANCHOLIA. In medical jurisprudence. A name given by the ancients to a species of partial intellectual mania, now more generally known by the name of "monomania." It bore this name because it was supposed to be always attended by dejection of mind and gloomy ideas. See "Mania."

MELDFEOH (Saxon). A fee paid to an informer.

MELIOR (Lat.) Better.

MELIOR EST CAUSA POSSIDENTIS. The cause of the possessor is preferable. Dig. 50. 17. 126. 2.

MELIOR EST CONDITIO DEFENDENTis. The cause of the defendant is the better. Broom, Leg. Max. (3d London Ed.) 639, 642; Dig. 50. 17. 126. 2; Hob. 199; 1 Mass. 66.

MELIOR EST CONDITIO POSSIDENTIS et rei quam actoris. Better is the condition of the possessor and that of the defendant than that of the plaintiff. 4 Inst. 180; Vaughan, 58, 60; Hob. 103.

MELIOR EST CONDITIO POSSIDENTIS, ubi neuter jus habet. Better is the condition of the possessor where neither of the two has a right. Jenk. Cent. Cas. 118.

MELIOR EST JUSTITIA VERE PRAEVEniens quam severe puniens. That justice which justly prevents a crime is better than that which severely punishes it.

MELIORATIONS. In Scotch law. Improvements of an estate, other than mere repairs; betterments. 1 Bell, Comm. 73.

MELIOREM CONDITIONEM ECCLESIAE suae facere potest praelatus, deteriorem nequaquam. A bishop can make the condition of his own church better, but by no means worse. Co. Litt. 101.

MELIOREM CONDITIONEM SUUM FACere potest minor, deteriorem nequaquam. A minor can improve or make his condition better, but never worse. Co Litt. 337b.

MELIUS EST IN TEMPORE OCCURRE-re, quam post causam vulneratum remedium quaerere. It is better to restrain or meet a thing in time, than to seek a remedy after a wrong has been inflicted. 2 Inst. 299.

MELIUS EST JUS DEFICIENS QUAM jus incertum. Law that is deficient is better than law that is uncertain. Lofft, 395.

MELIUS EST OMNIA MALA PATI quam consentire. It is better to suffer every wrong or ill than to consent to it. 3 Inst. 23.

MELIUS EST PETERE FONTES QUAM sectari rivulos. It is better to go to the fountain head than to follow little streamlets.

MELIUS EST RECURRERE QUAM MAlo currere. It is better to recede than to proceed wrongly. 4 Inst. 176.

MELIUS INQUIRENDUM VEL INQUIrendo. In old English practice. A writ which, in certain cases, issued after an imperfect inquisition returned on a *capias utligatum* in outlawry. This *melius inquirendum* commanded the sheriff to summon another inquest in order that the value, etc., of lands, etc., might be better or more correctly ascertained.

MELLER. (L. Fr.) To mix or blend; to meddle with; to interfere or interpose. Kelham.

MEMBER. A limb of the body useful in self-defense. *Membrum est pars corporis habens destinatum operationem in corpore.* Co. Litt. 126a.

An individual who belongs to a firm, partnership, company, or corporation.

One who belongs to a legislative body, or other branch of the government; as, a member of the house of representatives; a member of the court.

MEMBER OF CONGRESS. A member of the senate or house of representatives of the United States.

MEMBERS. In English law. Places where a custom house has been kept of old time, with officers or deputies in attendance; and they are lawful places of exportation or importation. 1 Chit. Com. Law, 726.

MEMBRANA (Lat.) In civil and old English law. Parchment; a skin of parchment. Vocat.; Du Cange. The English rolls were composed of several skins, sometimes as many as forty-seven. Hale, Hist. Com. Law, 17.

MEMORANDUM (Lat. from *memorare*, to remember). A note to assist the memory. 32 Conn. 509. An informal instrument recording some fact or agreement; so called from its beginning, when it was made in Latin. It is sometimes commenced with this word, though written in English; as, "Memorandum, that it is agreed;" or it is headed with the words, "Be it remembered that," etc.

——**In English Practice.** The commencement of a record in king's bench, now written in English, "Be it remembered," and which gives name to the whole clause.

It is only used in proceedings by bill, and not in proceedings by original, and was introduced to call attention to what was considered the bye-business of the court. 2 Tidd. Prac. 775. Memorandum is applied, also, to other forms and documents in English practice; *e. g.*, "memorandum in error," a document alleging error in fact, and accompanied by an affidavit of such matter of fact. 15 & 16 Vict. c. 76, § 158. Also, a "memorandum of appearance," etc., in the general sense of an informal instrument, recording some fact or agreement.

A writing required by the statute of frauds. Vide "Note or Memorandum."

——**In Insurance.** A clause in a policy limiting the liability of the insurer.

MEMORANDUM CHECK. It is not unusual among merchants, when one makes a temporary loan to another, to give the lender a check on a bank, with the express or implied agreement that it shall be redeemed by the maker himself, and that it shall not be presented at the bank for payment; such understanding being denoted by the word "memorandum" upon it. If passed to a third person, it will be valid in his hands like any other check. 4 Duer (N. Y.) 122; 11 Paige, Ch. (N. Y.) 612.

MEMORANDUM CLAUSE. In a policy of marine insurance, the memorandum clause is a clause inserted to prevent the underwriters from being liable for injury to goods of a peculiarly perishable nature, and for minor damages. It begins as follows: "N. B. Corn, fish, salt, fruit, flour, and seed are warranted free from average, unless general, or the ship be stranded;" meaning that the underwriters are not to be liable for damage to these articles caused by sea water or the like.

MEMORANDUM OF ALTERATION. Formerly, in England, where a patent was granted for two inventions, one of which was not new or not useful, the whole patent was bad, and the same rule applied when a material part of a patent for a single invention had either of those defects. To remedy this, St. 5 & 6 Wm. IV. c. 83, empowers a patentee (with the fiat of the attorney general) to enter a disclaimer (*q. v.*) or a memorandum of an alteration in the title or specification of the patent, not being of such a nature as to extend the exclusive right granted by the patent, and thereupon the memorandum is deemed to be part of the letters patent or the specification. Johns. Pat. 151; St. 15 & 16 Vict. c. 83, § 39.

MEMORANDUM OF ASSOCIATION. A document by the registration of which a company is formed under the English companies act of 1862.

MEMORIAL. A petition or representation made by one or more individuals to a legislative or other body. When such instrument is addressed to a court, it is called a "petition."

MEMORITER (Lat.) From memory.

MEMORY. Understanding; a capacity to make contracts, a will, or to commit a crime, so far as intention is necessary.

Memory is sometimes employed to express the capacity of the understanding, and sometimes its power. When we speak of a retentive memory, we use it in the former sense; when of a ready memory, in the latter. Shelf. Lun. Introd. 29, 30.

The reputation, good or bad, which a man leaves at his death.

This memory, when good, is highly prized by the relations of the deceased, and it is therefore libellous to throw a shade over the memory of the dead, when the writing has a tendency to create a breach of the peace, by inciting the friends and relations of the deceased to avenge the insult offered to the family. 4 Term R. 126; 5 Coke, 125; Hawk. P. C. bk. 1, c. 73, § 1.

MEMORY, TIME OF. According to the English common law, which has been altered by 2 & 3 Wm. IV. c. 71, the time of memory commenced from the reign of Richard I., A. D. 1189. 2 Bl. Comm. 31.

But proof of a regular usage for twenty years, not explained or contradicted, is evidence upon which many public and private rights are held, and sufficient for a jury in finding the existence of an immemorial custom or prescription. 2 Saund. 175a, 175d; Peake, Ev. 336; 2 Price, 450; 4 Price, 198.

MEN OF STRAW. "See Straw Men."

MENACE. A threat; a declaration of an intention to cause evil to happen to another.

When menaces to do an injury to another have been made, the party making them may, in general, be held to bail to keep the peace; and when followed by any inconvenience or loss, the injured party has a civil action against the wrongdoer. Comyn. Dig. "Battery" (D); Viner, Abr.; Bac. Abr. "Assault;" Co. Litt. 161a, 162b, 253b; 2 Lutw. 1428.

MENDACIUM (Lat.) In old English law. Falsehood; a falsehood or lie; a false statement made with intent to deceive. Fleta, lib. 5, c. 22, § 6.

MENIAL. This term is applied to servants who live under their master's roof. See St. 2 Hen. IV. c. 21.

MENS (Lat.) Mind.

MENS LEGISLATORIS. The intent of the legislators.

MENS REA (Lat.) A guilty mind.

MENS TESTATORIS IN TESTAMENTIS spectanda est. In wills, the intention of the testator is to be regarded. Jenk. Cent. Cas. 277.

MENSA (Lat.) An obsolete term, comprehending all goods and necessaries for livelihoods.

MENSA ET THORO. See "Divorce."

MENSOR. In the civil law. A surveyor.

MENSULARIUS. In the civil law. A money changer.

MENSURA. A measure.

MENSURA DOMINI REGIS. "The measure of our lord the king." The standard of weights and measures, established under King Richard I., 1197. 1 Bl. Comm. 275.

MENTAL INCAPACITY. Lack of sufficient mind and memory on the part of a grantor or testator to comprehend the nature and character of the transaction in which he was engaged. 230 Ill. 586; 93 Ill. 516.

MENTAL RESERVATION. A silent exception to the general words of a promise or agreement not expressed, on account of a general understanding on the subject. But the word has been applied to an exception existing in the mind of the one party only, and has been degraded to signify a dishonest excuse for evading or infringing a promise. Wharton.

MENTAL SUFFERING. A mental emotion arising from a physical injury; any mental anguish connected with bodily injury. Braun v. Craven, 175 Ill. 408; Tomasi v. Donk Bros. Coal Co., 257 Ill. 75.

MENTIRI (Lat.) To lie; to assert a falsehood. Calv. Lex.; 3 Bulst. 260.

MENTIRI EST CONTRA MENTEM IRE. To lie is to go against the mind. 3 Bulst. 260.

MENTITION. The act of lying; a falsehood.

MERA NOCTIS. Midnight.

MERCANDISA, *Merchandisa, Mercandisia.* L. Lat. In old English law. Merchandise; all goods and wares exposed to sale in fairs or markets. Brac. fol. 57.

MERCANTILE. Having to do with or engaged in trade, or the buying and selling of commodities; pertaining to the business of merchants; concerned with trade or the buying and selling of commodities; pertaining to trade; commercial; 255 Ill. 273, 563; 167 Ill. App. 147.

MERCANTILE LAW. That branch of law which defines and enforces the rights, duties, and liabilities arising out of mercantile transactions and relations. See "Law Merchant."

MERCANTILE PAPER. Commercial paper (*q. v.*)

MERCANTILE PARTNERSHIP. One formed for trading purposes.

MERCAT. A market. An old form of the latter word common in Scotch law, formed from the Latin *mercatum.*

MERCATIVE. Belonging to trade.

MERCATUM (Lat.) A market. Du Cange. A contract of sale. Id. Supplies for an army (*commeatus*). Id. See Bracton, 56; Fleta, lib. 4, c. 28, §§ 13, 14.

MERCEN-LAGE. The law of the Mercians. One of the three principal systems of laws which prevailed in England about the beginning of the eleventh century. It was observed in many of the midland counties, and those bordering on the principality of Wales. 1 Bl. Comm. 65.

MERCENARIUS. A mercenary.

MERCES (Lat.) In civil law. Reward of labor in money or other things. As distinguished from *pensis*, it means the rent of farms (*praedia rustici*). Calv. Lex.

MERCHANDISE (Lat. *merx*). A term including all those things which merchants sell, either wholesale or retail; as, dry-goods, hardware, groceries, drugs, etc. It is usually applied to personal chattels only, and to those which are not required for food or immediate support but such as remain after having been used, or which are used only by a slow consumption. See Pardessus, note 8; Dig. 13. 3. 1; Id. 19. 4. 1; Id. 50. 16. 66; 8 Pet. (U. S.) 277; 6 Wend. (N. Y.) 335.

Mere evidences of value, as bank bills, are not merchandise. "The fact that a thing is sometimes bought and sold does not make it merchandise." Story, J., 2 Story, C. C. (U. S.) 10, 53, 54. See 2 Mass. 467; 20 Pick. (Mass.) 9; 3 Metc. (Mass.) 367; 2 Pars. Cont. 331, note (w).

Nor are baggage (6. Fed. 413) tools or facilities (26 Ind. 294), or animals kept for use; though otherwise if they were imported for purpose of sale only (22 Vt. 655).

MERCHANDISE MARKS ACT 1862. St. 25 & 26 Vict. c. 88. Its principal provision is that making it a misdemeanor to forge or falsely apply any trade-mark or indication of quality, or to sell any goods falsely marked.

MERCHANT (Lat. *mercator; merx*). A man who traffics or carries on trade with foreign countries, or who exports and imports goods, and sells them by wholesale. Webster; Lex. Merc. 23. These are known by the name of "shipping merchants." See Comyn, Dig.; Dyer, 279b; Bac. Abr.

"Merchants," in the statute of limitations, means not merely those trading beyond sea, as formerly held (1 Chanc. Cas. 152; 1 Watts & S. [Pa.] 469); but whether it includes common retail tradesmen, *quaere* (1 Mod. 238; 4 Scott, N. R. 819; 2 Pars. Cont. 369, 370. See, also, 5 Cranch [U. S.] 15; 6 Pet. [U. S.] 151; 12 Pet. [U. S.] 300; 5 Mason [U. S.] 505).

According to an old authority, there are four species of merchants, namely, merchant adventurers, merchants dormant, merchant travelers, and merchant residents. 2 Brownl. 99. See, generally, 9 Salk. 445; Bac. Abr.; Comyn, Dig.; 1 Bl. Comm. 75, 260; 1 Pardessus, Dr. Com. note 78; 2 Show. 326; Bracton, 334.

One whose business it is to buy and sell merchandise. This applies to all persons who habitually trade in merchandise. 1 Watts & S. (Pa.) 469; 2 Salk. 445.

The term does not include those who buy goods for the purpose of manufacture and subsequent sale. 33 Mo. 424. A commercial traveler is not a merchant (58 Miss. 478), nor is a farmer who raises produce for the market (3 T. B. Mon. [Ky.] 330), nor a speculator in stocks (8 Ben. [U. S.] 563).

MERCHANTABLE TITLE. A merchantable title must be good beyond a reasonable doubt, and this must appear from the abstract itself. That the title may, in fact, be good, or that it may be made good is insufficient. The abstract on its face must show that there is no reasonable doubt about it. The opinion of the court that it is probably good, is not sufficient. It must be such a title as will not detract from the salability of the land, or depreciate its value on the market, or expose the vendee to possible litigation or to the danger of being defeated in an action concerning it. If there is even a color of outstanding title which may prove substantial a purchaser will not be required to take it and thus encounter the hazard of litigation with an adverse claimant over whom the court has no jurisdiction. Where the vendor in a contract for the sale of land has agreed to furnish an abstract of title showing good merchantable title in him, all the vendee need do to defeat a bill by the vendor for specific performance is to show that that title which the vendor was prepared to convey was doubtful in character. 241 Ill. 514.

On the other hand, an objection cannot be founded on unsubstantial trifles; and a bare possibility that the title may be affected by the existing causes which may subsequently be developed when the highest evidence of which the case admits, amounting to a moral certainty, is given that no such cause exists, is not to be regarded as a sufficient ground for a refusal to perform the contract. 156 Ill. App. 137, 138.

MERCHANTS' SHIPPING ACTS. English statutes for the amelioration of the condition of seamen on merchant vessels, and the general improvement of shipping, and vesting a control of merchant shipping in the board of trade to that end.

MERCHET. Marcheta (*q. v.*)

MERCIAMENT. An amerciament.

MERCIMONIATUS ANGLIAE. In old records. The impost of England upon merchandise. Cowell.

MERCIS APPELLATIO AD RES MOBILes tantum pertinet. The term "merchandise" belongs to movable things only. Dig. 50. 16. 66.

MERCIS APPELLATIONE HOMINES non continere. Under the name of "merchandise," men are not included. Dig. 50. 16. 207.

MERCY (Law Fr. *merci;* Lat. *misericordia*).

——**In Practice.** The arbitrament of the king or judge in punishing offenses not directly censured by law. 2 Hen. VI. c. 2; Jacob. So, to be in mercy signifies to be liable to punishment at the discretion of the judge.

——**In Criminal Law.** The total or partial remission of a punishment to which a convict is subject. When the whole punishment is remitted, it is called a "pardon;" when only a part of the punishment is remitted, it is frequently a "conditional pardon;" or, before sentence, it is called "clemency" or "mercy." See Rutherforth, Inst. 224; 1 Kent, Comm. 265; 3 Story, Const. § 1488.

As to the construction of "mercy" in the exception to the Sunday laws in favor of deeds of necessity and mercy, see 2 Pars. Cont. 262, notes.

MERE (Fr.) Mother. This word is frequently used; as, *en ventre sa mere*, which signifies a child unborn, or in the womb.

MERE MOTION. See "Ex Mero Motu."

MERE RIGHT. An abstract right of property without possession or right thereto. 2 Bl. Comm. 197.

MERE STONE. A boundary stone.

MEREMIUM. (Law Lat. [from L. Fr. *meresme, mereme.*]) In old English and Scotch law, Timber.

MERETRICIOUS. Illicit, as applied to sexual relations.

MERGER. The absorption of a thing of lesser importance by a greater, whereby the lesser ceases to exist, but the greater is not increased.

There appears to be a distinction recognized by most of the authorities between a "merger," strictly speaking, and a "consolidation," but the terms are not always used with strict accuracy. 256 Ill. 522.

——**In Estates.** When a greater estate and less coincide and meet in one and the same person, without any intermediate estate, the less is immediately merged, that is, sunk or drowned, in the latter. For example, if there be a tenant for years, and the reversion in fee simple descends to or is purchased by him, the term of years is merged in the inheritance, and no longer exists; but they must be to one and the same person, at one and the same time, in one and the same right. 2 Bl. Comm. 177; Latch, 153; Poph. 166; 6 Madd. 119; 1 Johns. Ch. (N. Y.) 417; 3 Johns, Ch. (N. Y.) 53; 3 Mass. 172.

——**In Contracts.** Merger, in the law of contracts, is the absorption or extinguishment of a security of a lower legal degree in another of a higher legal degree. 120 Ill. App. 554.

——**Of Rights.** Rights or demands merged in a judgment for their enforcement (65 Ind. 243; 25 Pa. St. 200; 41 Mo. 205), or in a security of a higher nature (10 Iowa, 443; 14 Mo. 450). Rights are also said to be merged when the same person who is bound to pay is also entitled to receive. 117 Ill. 338. This is more properly called a "confusion of rights," or "extinguishment."

——**In Torts.** Where a person, in committing a felony, also commits a tort against a private person, the wrong was, under the old law, sunk in the felony, and, by modern law, is suspended until after the felon's conviction. 1 Chit. Prac. 10. The rule is generally changed by statute.

——**In Crimes.** At common law, if an act included several offenses of different degree (*i. e.*, misdemeanors and felony), the misdemeanors merged in the felony (5 Mass. 106; 1 Mich. 217; 26 N. J. Law, 213); but if the offenses were of the same grade, there was no merger, and the prosecution might elect on which to prosecute (48 Me. 238; 4 Wend. [N. Y.] 265; 93 Fed. 452).

The doctrine of merger of offenses is now repudiated in England (11 Q. B. 929), and in some of the United States (57 Conn. 461; 51 Minn. 382).

MERIDIES. Noon.

MERITS. The strict legal rights of the parties, as distinguished from matters of practice and matters resting in the discretion of the court. 4 How. Pr. (N. Y.) 329; Id. 432; 2 Daly (N. Y.) 203.

A cause of action or defense on the merits is one resting on matters of substance, not on form or technicality. See 12 Wis. 588. A judgment on the merits is one decisive of some strictly legal right of the party. 12 Minn. 357; 26 S. C. 119.

MERITS, AFFIDAVIT OF. See "Affidavit of Merits."

MERO MOTU. See "Ex Mero Motu."

MERTON, STATUTE OF. An ancient English ordinance or statute (20 Hen. III. [1253]), which took its name from the place in the county of Surrey where parliament sat when it was enacted. 2 Inst. 79; Barr. Obs. St. 41, 46; Hale, Hist. Com. Law, 9, 10, 18.

MERUM (Lat.) In old English law. Mere; naked or abstract. *Merum jus*, mere right. Bracton, fol. 31. *Majus jus merum*, more mere right. Id. See "Mere Right."

MERX EST QUIDQUID VENDI POtest. Merchandise is whatever can be sold. 3 Metc. (Mass.) 365. See "Merchandise."

MES. tof. mo. co. gar. ter. pra. pas. bos. brue. mora.

Junca. maris. alne. rus. re. sectare priora.

A rhyming couplet artificially constructed by the old practitioners in real actions, for the more easy remembrance of the rule requiring the various parcels of land which might be demanded in a writ of right to be named in a certain order. It consists of the first syllables of the following words: *Messuagium, toftum, molendinum, columbare, gardinum, terra, pratum, pastura, boscus, bruera, mora, Juncaria, mariscus, alnetum, ruscaria, reditus* (in English, messuage, toft, mill, dovehouse, garden, land, meadow, pasture, wood, heath, moor, rush ground, marsh, alder ground, broom ground, rent); the words *sectare priora* (follow the first syllables) denoting how it was to be read. Fitzh. Nat. Brev. 2 (C). In the register, the complementary syllables are written over each of the abbreviations. Reg. Orig. 2.

MESAGUIM. A messuage.

MESCROYANT. Used in our ancient books. An unbeliever.

MESE. An ancient word used to signify "house;" probably from the French *maison*. It is said that by this word the buildings, curtilage, orchards, and gardens will pass. Co. Litt. 56.

MESNALITY. The estate of a mesne tenant.

MESNE. Intermediate; the middle between two extremes; that part between the commencement and the end, as it relates to time.

In England, the word "mesne" also applies to a dignity; those persons who hold lordships or manors of some superior, who is called "lord paramount," and grant the same to inferior persons, are called "mesne lords."

MESNE LORD. A middle or intermediate lord. 2 Bl. Comm. 59; 1 Steph. Comm. 168, 174. See "Mesne."

MESNE PROCESS. In practice. All writs necessary to a suit between its beginning and end, that is, between primary process or summons and final process, or execution, whether for the plaintiff, against the defendant, or for either against any party whose presence is necessary to the suit.

MESNE PROFITS. The value of land during the period of a wrongful possession thereof; that is to say, from the time of wrongful entry to dispossession. 3 Bl. Comm. 205.

The net rental value or value of the use and occupation of premises during the period of a wrongful occupation. 101 N. Y. 13.

MESNE, WRIT OF. The name of an ancient writ, which lies when the lord paramount distrains on the tenant paravail. The latter shall have a writ of mesne against the lord who is mesne. Fitzh. Nat. Brev. 316.

MESPRISION. (Law Fr.) Mistake; a mistaking.

MESQUE (Law Fr.) Except; unless. Fet. Assaver, § 23.

MESS BRIEF. In Danish law. A certificate of admeasurement granted by competent authority at home port of vessel. Jacobsen, Sea Laws, 50.

MESSENGER. An employe or officer whose duty is to bear messages or communications.

——**In English Law.** An officer who takes possession of an insolvent or bankrupt estate.

MESSENGER ASSOCIATION. An association engaged in the business of furnishing messengers for hire to any who may desire them. Such associations are held to be common carriers. 31 Abb. N. C. 147; 6 Misc. Rep. (N. Y.) 534.

MESSIS SEMENTEM SEQUITUR. The harvest follows the sowing. Ersk. Inst. 174. 26; Bell, Dict.

MESSUAGE. A term used in conveyancing, and nearly synonymous with "dwelling house." A grant of a messuage with the appurtenances will not only pass a house, but all the buildings attached or belonging to it, as also its curtilage, garden, and orchard, together with the close on which the house is built. Co. Litt. 5b; 2 Saund. 400; Hammond, N. P. 189; 4 Cruise, Dig. 321; 2 Term. R. 502; 4 Blackf. (Ind.) 331. But see the cases cited in 9 Barn. & C. 681. This term, it is said, includes a church. 11 Coke, 26; 2 Esp. 528; 1 Salk. 256; 8 Barn. & C. 25. And see 3 Wils. 141; 2 W. Bl. 726; 4 Mees. & W. 567; 2 Bing. (N. C.) 617; 1 Saund. 6.

META (Lat.) The goal of a Roman racecourse; a mark or object about which the chariots turned, and where the course ended.

——**In Old English Law.** A boundary line; a border or terminus. Properly, a visible object, standing upon the line, as a stone or tree, and showing where it ended; a butt. See "Butts and Bounds." *Bundae et metae, et rationabiles divisae quae ponuntur in terminis et finibus agrorum, ad distinguendum praedia et dominia vicinorum,* bounds and metes and reasonable divisions which are set on the borders and limits of lands, in order to distinguish the estates and properties of neighbors. Bracton, fols. 166b, 167; Fleta, lib. 2, c. 41, § 30. *Pro metis et terminis ponendis.* Mag. Rot. 3 Hen. III. rot. 14b.

METALLUM (Lat.) In the Roman law. Metal; a mine.

Labor in mines, as a punishment for crime. Dig. 40. 5. 24. 5; Calv. Lex.

METATUS (Law Lat.) In old European law. A dwelling; a seat; a station; quarters; the place where one lives or stays. Spelman.

METAYER SYSTEM. A system of agricultural holdings, under which the land is divided, in small farms, among single families, the landlord generally supplying the stock which the agricultural system of the country is considered to require, and receiving, in lieu of rent and profit, a fixed proportion of the produce. This proportion, which is generally paid in kind, is usually one-half. 1 Mill. Pol. Econ. 296, 363; 2 Smith, Wealth of Nations, 3, c. 2; Wharton.

METECORN. A measure of corn given by a lord to customary tenants as a reward for labor.

METEGAVEL. A rent paid in victuals.

METES AND BOUNDS. The boundary lines of land, with their terminal points and angles. Courses and distances control, unless there is matter of more certain description, *e. g.,* natural monuments. 42 Me. 209.

The boundary line may be pointed out and ascertained by reference to permanent objects either natural or artificial, and so situated that they may conveniently be used for the purpose of indicating its extent. Such objects, when so used in a description, are called monuments; streams, trees, walls, fences, streets and highways, or railroad tracks, or other objects may be referred to as monuments. 46 Ill. App. 128; 25 Ill. 152.

A joint tenant cannot convey by metes and bounds. 1 Hilliard, Real Prop. 582. See "Boundary."

METHEL (Saxon). Speech.

METHOD. See "Process."

METROPOLIS (Graeco-Lat. and Eng.) A mother city; one from which a colony was sent out. Calv. Lex.

The capital of a province. Id.

METROPOLITAN. In English law. One of the titles of an archbishop. Derived from the circumstance that archbishops were consecrated at first in the metropolis of a province. 4 Inst. 94.

METUS (Lat.) A reasonable fear of an intolerable evil, as of loss of life or limb, such as may fall upon a brave man (*virum constantem*). 1 Bl. Comm. 131; Calv. Lex. And this kind of fear alone will invalidate a contract as entered into through duress. Calv. Lex.

In a more general sense, fear.

MEU (Law Fr.) Moved; commenced, as a suit. Kelham; Britt. c. 126.

MEUBLES. In French law. Movables (*q. v.*) *Meubles meublans*, household utensils and ornaments.

MEUM EST PROMITTERE, NON DIMittere. It is mine to promise, not to discharge. 2 Rolle, 39.

MICHAELMAS TERM. In English law. One of the four terms of the courts. It begins on the 2d day of November, and ends on the 25th of November. It was formerly a movable term. St. 11 Geo. IV. and 1 Wm. IV. c. 70.

MICHEL GEMOT, or **MICEL GEMOTE** (Saxon, great meeting or assembly). One of the names of the general council immemorially held in England. 1 Bl. Comm. 147.

One of the great councils of a king and noblemen in Saxon times.

These great councils were severally called *wittena gemotes*, afterwards *micel synods*, and *micel gemotes*. Cowell (Ed. 1727); Cunningham. See "Michel Synoth."

MICHEL SYNOTH (Saxon, great council). One of the names of the general council immemorially held in England. 1 Bl. Comm. 147.

The Saxon kings usually called a "synod," or mixed council, consisting both of ecclesiastics and the nobility, three times a year, which was not properly called a "parliament" till Henry III.'s time. Cowell (Ed. 1727); Cunningham.

MICHERY. Theft; dishonesty.

MIDDLE OF THE RIVER. The phrases "middle of the river' and "middle of the main channel" are equivalent expressions and both mean the main line of the channel, or, as is frequently expressed, the middle thread of the current. 270 Ill. 422. See "Middle Thread."

MIDDLE THREAD (Law Lat. *medium filum;* Law Fr. *fil de myleu*). An imaginary line drawn through the middle of a stream in the direction of its length. Story, J., 3 Sumn. 170, 178.

MIDDLEMAN. One who has been employed as an agent by a principal, and who has employed a subagent under him by authority of the principal, either express or implied. He is not, in general, liable for the wrongful acts of the subagent, the principal being alone responsible. 3 Campb. 4; 6 Term R. 411; 14 East, 605.

A person who is employed both by the seller and purchaser of goods, or by the purchaser alone, to receive them into his possession, for the purpose of doing something in or about them.

MIDWIFE. In medical jurisprudence. A woman who practices midwifery; a woman who pursues the business of an *accoucheuse.*

MIESES (Spanish). Crops.

MILE. A length of a thousand paces, or seventeen hundred and sixty yards, or five thousand two hundred and eighty feet. It contains eight furlongs, every furlong being forty poles, and each pole sixteen feet six inches. 2 Starkie, 89.

MILEAGE. A compensation of so much per mile allowed to officers traveling on the public business, or to any person authoritatively summoned in respect to a matter of public importance, as to a witness.

MILES.

——**In Civil Law.** A soldier. *Vel a "militia," aut a "multitudine," aut a numero, "mille hominum."* Vocat.

——**In Old English Law.** A knight, because military service was part of the feudal tenure. Also, a tenant by military service, not a knight. 1 Bl. Comm. 404; Seld. Tit. Hon. 334.

MILITARY CAUSES. In English law. Causes of action or injuries cognizable in the court military, or court of chivalry. 3 Bl. Comm. 103.

MILITARY COURTS. In English law. Include the ancient court of chivalry and modern court-martial (*q. v.*) 3 Bl. Comm. 68, 103.

MILITARY FEUDS. The genuine or original feuds which were in the hands of military men, who performed military duty for their tenures.

MILITARY LANDS. In American law. Lands granted to soldiers for military services.

MILITARY LAW. A system of regulation by acts of congress prescribing the rules and articles of war, and providing for the government of the army and discipline of the troops. 1 Kent, Comm. 377, note; 44 Ill. 153.

That branch of the laws which respects military discipline and the government of persons employed in the military service. De Hart, Courts-Martial, 16.

Military law is to be distinguished from martial law. Martial law extends to all persons; military law to all military persons only, and not to those in a civil capacity. 44 Ill. 142. Martial law supersedes and suspends the civil law, but military law is superadded and subordinate to the civil law. See 2 Kent, Comm. 10; 34 Me. 126. See Martial Law.

The body of the military law of the United States is contained in the act of April 30, 1806, and the amendatory acts.

MILITARY OFFENSES. Those offenses which are cognizable by the courts military, as insubordination, sleeping on guard, desertion, etc.

MILITARY SERVICE. A statute releasing an attachment issued against any property of any "soldiers in the actual military service of the United States" does not include a person in the naval service. One may be in the naval service, or connected with the navy without being a soldier, as when he belongs to merchantmen or the merchant's service. A soldier in the military service, on the contrary, means one belonging to the soldiery, militia or army of a nation or state. 18 Iowa 513.

MILITARY STATE. The soldiery of the kingdom of Great Britain.

MILITARY STATION. Is synonymous with the term "military post," and means a place where troops are assembled, where military stores, animate and inanimate, are kept or distributed, where military duty is performed or military protection afforded,—where something in short, more or less closely connected with arms or war is kept or is to be done. 4 Otto (U. S.) 222.

MILITARY TENURES. The various tenures by knight service, grand serjeanty, cornage, etc., are frequently called "military tenures," from the nature of the services which they involve. 1 Steph. Comm. 204.

MILITARY TESTAMENT. In English law. A nuncupative will,—that is, one made by word of mouth,—by which a soldier may dispose of his goods, pay, and other personal chattels, without the forms and solemnities which the law requires in other cases. St. 1 Vict. c. 26, § 11.

MILITES. Knights, and, in Scotch law, freeholders.

MILITIA. A body of persons enlisted and trained to military duty, but not kept in service, being subject only to service on call, as in case of invasion, insurrection, or riot. 94 Ill. 120.

MILL. A complicated engine or machine for grinding and reducing to fine particles grain, fruit, or other substance, or for performing other operations by means of wheels and a circular motion.

The house or building that contains the machinery for grinding, etc. Webster.

MILLBANK PRISON. Formerly called the "Penitentiary at Millbank." A prison at Westminster, for convicts under sentence of transportation, until the sentence or order shall be executed, or the convict be entitled to freedom, or be removed to some other place of confinement. This prison is placed under the inspectors of prisons, appointed by the secretary of state, who are a body corporate, "The inspectors of the Millbank Prison." The inspectors make regulations for the government thereof, subject to the approbation of the secretary of state, and yearly reports to him, to be laid before parliament. The secretary also appoints a governor, chaplain, medical officer, matron, etc. Wharton.

MILLEATE, or MILL LEAT. A trench to convey water to or from a mill. St. 7 Jac. I. c. 19.

MILLED MONEY. This term means merely coined money, and it is not necessary that it should be marked or rolled on the edges. Leach, C. C. 708.

MILREIS. The name of a coin. The milreis of Portugal is taken as money of account, at the custom house, to be of the value of one hundred and twelve cents. The milreis of Azores is deemed of the value of eighty-three and one-third cents. The milreis of Madeira is deemed of the value of one hundred cents. Act March 3, 1843 (5 U. S. St. at Large, 625).

MINA (Law Lat.) In old English law. A measure of corn or grain. Cowell; Spelman.

MINARE (Law Lat.) In old records. To mine or dig mines. Cowell. *Minator*, a miner. Id.

To drive. Spelman. *Minator carucae*, a plough driver. Cowell.

MINATUR INNOCENTIBUS QUI PARcit nocentibus. He threatens the innocent who spares the guilty. 4 Coke, 45.

MIND AND MEMORY. A testator must have a sound and disposing mind and memory. In other words, he "ought to be capable of making his will with an understanding of the nature of the business in which he is engaged, a recollection of the property he means to dispose of, of the persons who are the object of his bounty, and the manner in which it is to be distributed between them." Washington, J., 3 Wash. C. C. (U. S.) 585, 586; 4 Wash. C. C. (U. S.) 262; 1 Green, Ch. (N. J.) 82, 85; 2 Green, Ch. (N. J.) 563, 604; 26 Wend. (N. Y.) 255, 306, 311, 312; 8 Conn. 265; 9 Conn. 105.

MINERALS (Law Lat. *minera*, a vein of metal). The term mineral is not confined to metallic substances. 233 Ill. 62.

All fossil bodies or matters dug out of mines or quarries, whence anything may be dug; such as beds of stone which may be quarried. 14 Mees. & W. 859, in construing 55 Geo. III. c. 18; Broom, Leg. Max. 175, 176.

Any natural production, formed by the action of chemical affinities, and organized when becoming solid by the powers of crystallization. Webster. But see 5 Watts (Pa.) 34; 1 Crabb, Real Prop. 95.

Including every kind of stone, flint, marble, slate, brick earth, chalk, gravel and sand when found under the surface and not lying loosely upon it.

The following substances have been held to be minerals: Brick clay, 22 Q. D. B. 555; 58 L J. Q. B. 573; whether got under ground or by open workings, 51 L. J. Ch. 570; 55 L. J. Ch. 745; 5 App. Ca. 820; 43 L. T. 513; china clay, 417 L. J. Ch. 761; coal and ironstone, 35 L. J. Ch. 337; 37 Ch. D. 386; 15 App. Ca. 19; coprolites, 46 L. J. Ch. 654; 5 Ch. D. 750; freestone and limestone got by open workings, 1 Shaw, App. 225; 9 Ir. C. L. Rep. 223; granite, 1 Times Rep. 549; oil and gas, 233 Ill. 62; 240 Ill. 367; stone got by quarrying, 4 Eq. Cas. 19; 14 M. & W. 859; 20 L. J. Ex. 313; 6 Ex. 644; 17 L. T. O. S. 185; petroleum, 237 Ill. 337; stratum of clay, 1 Ch. 427.

The following have been held not to be minerals: Boat, ancient and embedded, but unpetrified, 55 L. J. Ch.; 33 Ch. D.; brine formed by the percolation of rain-water through rock salt, 26 S. J. 359; clay and sand, 48 L. J. P. C. 36; 4 App. Ca. 294; 40 L. T. 764; clay subsoil, 13 App. Ca. 657; 37 W. R. 627; 31 L. J. C. P. 201; freestone quarry, 1 Shaw App. 225; limestone, 9 Ir. C. L. Rep. 223.

MINERATOR. In old records. A miner.

MINIMA POENA CORPORALIS EST MAjor qualibet pecuniaria. The smallest bodily punishment is greater than any pecuniary one. 2 Inst. 220.

MINIME MUTANDA SUNT QUAE CERtam habuerunt interpretationem. Things which have had a certain interpretation are to be altered as little as possible. Co. Litt. 365.

MINIMENT. An old form of muniments (*q. v.*) Blount.

The least possible quantity, amount or degree that can be assigned in a given case or under fixed conditions. 283 Ill. 554.

MINIMUM EST NIHILO PROXIMUM. The least is next to nothing. Bac. Arg. Low's Case of Tenures.

MINING PARTNERSHIP. An association between the tenants in common of a mine, who work it together, and divide the profits in proportion to their several interests. 1 Mont. 224; 23 Cal. 198.

It has been said not to be a true partnership, but rather a cross between a tenancy in common and a partnership proper (Bates, Partn. § 14. And see 35 Cal. 365), for the reason that it has no *delectus personarum*. 102 U. S. 641; 52 Cal. 540.

MINISTER.

——**In Governmental Law.** An officer who is placed near the sovereign, and is invested with the administration of some one of the principal branches of the government.

Ministers are responsible to the king or other supreme magistrate who has appointed them. 4 Conn. 134.

——**In Ecclesiastical Law.** One ordained by some church to preach the Gospel.

Ministers are authorized in the United States, generally, to solemnize marriage, and are liable to fines and penalties for marrying minors contrary to the local regulations. As to the right of ministers or parsons, see 3 Am. Jur. 268; Shep. Touch. (Anthon Ed.) 564; 2 Mass. 500; 10 Mass. 97; 14 Mass. 333; 11 Me. 487.

——**In International Law.** An officer appointed by the government of one nation, with the consent of two other nations who have a matter in dispute, with a view by his interference and good office to have such matter settled.

A name given to public functionaries who represent their country with foreign governments, including ambassadors, envoys, and residents.

A custom of recent origin has introduced a new kind of ministers, without any particular determination of character. These are simply called "ministers," to indicate that they are invested with the general character of a sovereign's mandatories, without any particular assignment of rank or character.

The minister represents his government in a vague and indeterminate manner, which cannot be equal to the first degree, and he possesses all the rights essential to a public minister.

There are also "ministers plenipotentiary," who, as they possess full powers, are of much greater distinction than simple ministers. These, also, are without any particular attribution of rank and character, but by custom are now placed immediately below the ambassador, or on a level with the envoy extraordinary. Vattel, liv. 4, c. 6, § 74; 1 Kent, Comm. (10th Ed.) 48; Merlin, Repert.

Formerly no distinction was made in the different classes of public ministers, but the modern usage of Europe introduced some distinctions in this respect, which, on account of a want of precision, became a source of controversy. To obviate these, the congress of Vienna, and that of Aix-la-Chapelle, put an end to these disputes by classing ministers as follows: (1) Ambassadors and papal legates or nuncios; (2) envoys, ministers, or others accredited to sovereigns (*aupres des souverains*); (3) ministers resident, accredited to sovereigns; (4) *Charges d'Affaires*, accredited to the minister of foreign affairs. Recez du Congres de Vienne, du 19 Mars, 1815; Protocol du Congres d'Aix-la-Chapelle, du 21 Novembre, 1818; Wheaton, Int. Law, pt. 3, c. 1, § 6. See "Ambassador."

MINISTERIAL. That which is done under the authority of a superior; opposed to judicial; as, the sheriff is a ministerial officer bound to obey the judicial commands of the court.

When an officer acts in both a judicial and ministerial capacity, he may be compelled to perform ministerial acts in a particular way; but when he acts in a judicial capacity, he can only be required to proceed; the manner of doing so is left entirely to his judgment. 10 Me. 377; Bac. Abr. "Justices of the Peace" (E); 1 Conn. 295; 3 Conn. 107; 9 Conn. 275; 12 Conn. 464. See "Mandamus."

MINISTERIAL OFFICE. Ministerial offices are those which give the officer no power to judge of the matter to be done, and which require him to obey some superior, many of which are merely employments requiring neither a commission nor a warrant of appointment, as temporary clerks or messengers. 7 Court of Claims R. 293.

MINISTERIAL POWERS. A phrase used in English conveyancing to denote powers given for the good, not of the donee himself exclusively, or of the donee himself necessarily at all, but for the good of several persons, including or not including the donee also. They are so called because the donee of them is as a minister or servant in his exercise of them.

MINISTERIAL TRUSTS. Those which demand no further exercise of reason or understanding than every intelligent agent must necessarily employ; as, to convey an estate. They are a species of special trusts, distinguished from discretionary trusts, which necessarily require much exercise of the understanding. 2 Bouv. Inst. note 1896. Called, also, "instrumental trusts."

MINISTRANT. The party cross-examining a witness was so called, under the old system of the ecclesiastical courts.

MINISTRI REGIS (Lat.) In old English law. Ministers of the king, applied to the judges of the realm, and to all those who hold ministerial offices in the government. 2 Inst. 208.

MINOR (Lat. less; younger). A minor; one not a major, *i. e.*, not twenty-one. 2 Inst. 291; Co. Litt. 88, 128, 172b; 6 Coke, 67; 3 Bulst. 143; Bracton, 340b; Fleta, lib. 2, c. 60; § 26.

Of less consideration; lower. Calv. Lex. "Major" and "minor" belong rather to civil law. The common-law terms are "adult" and "infant."

MINOR AETAS (Lat.) Minority or infancy. Cro. Car. 516. Literally, lesser age.

MINOR ANTE TEMPUS AGERE NON potest in casu proprietatis, nec etiam convenire. A minor before majority cannot act in a case of property, nor even agree. 2 Inst. 291.

MINOR FACT. In the law of evidence. A relative, collateral or subordinate fact; a circumstance. Wills, Circ. Ev. 27; Burrill, Circ. Ev. p. 121, note 582.

MINOR JURARE NON POTEST. A minor cannot make oath. Co. Litt. 172b. An infant cannot be sworn on a jury. Litt. 289.

MINOR MINOREM CUSTODIRE NON debet; alios enim praesumitur male regere qui seipsum regere nescit. A minor ought not to be guardian of a minor, for he is presumed to govern others ill who does not know how to govern himself. Co. Litt. 88.

MINOR NON TENETUR RESPONDERE durante minori aetati; nisi in causa dotis, propter favorem. A minor is not bound to answer during his minority, except as a matter of favor in a cause of dower. 3 Bulst. 143.

MINOR, QUI INFRA AETATEM 12 ANnorum fuerit, utlagari non potest, nec extra legem poni, quia ante talem aetatem, non est sub lege aliqua, nec in decenna. A minor who is under twelve years of age cannot be outlawed, nor placed without the laws, because, before such age, he is not under any laws, nor in a decennary. Co. Litt. 128.

MINOR 17 ANNIS, NON ADMITTITUR fore executorem. A minor under seventeen years of age is not admitted to be an executor. 6 Coke, 67.

MINORITY. The state or condition of a minor; a status; infancy, depending for its existence upon the laws of the state in which the person is domiciled. 57 Ill. App. 496.

The lesser number of votes of a deliberative assembly; opposed to "majority (*q. v.*)

MINT. The place designated by law where money is coined by authority of the government.

MINTAGE. The charge at the mint for coining.

MINUS SOLVIT, QUI TARDIUS SOLVit; nam et tempore minus solvitur. He does not pay who pays too late; for, from the delay, he is judged not to pay. Dig. 50. 16. 12. 1.

MINUTE.

——**In Measures.** In divisions of the circle or angular measures, a minute is equal to sixty seconds, or one-sixtieth part of a degree.

In the computation of time, a minute is equal to sixty seconds, or the sixtieth part of an hour. See "Measure."

——**In Practice.** A memorandum of what takes place in court, made by authority of the court. From these minutes the record is afterwards made up.

Toullier says they are so called because the writing in which they were originally was small; that the word is derived from the Latin *minuta* (*scriptura*), in opposition to copies which were delivered to the parties, and which were always written in a larger hand. 8 Toullier, Dr. Civ. note 413.

Minutes are not considered as any part of the record. 1 Ohio, 268. See 23 Pick. (Mass.) 184, though in some states, notably New York, they are by statute made part of the judgment-roll. Code Crim. Proc. N. Y. § 485.

MINUTE BOOK. A book kept by the clerk or prothonotary of a court, in which minutes of its proceedings are entered.

MINUTE TITHES. Small tithes, usually belonging to the vicar; *e. g.*, eggs, honey, wax, etc. 3 Burn, Ecc. Law, 680; 6 & 7 Wm. IV. c. 71, §§ 17, 18, 27.

MINUTES.

——**In Scotch Practice.** A pleading put into writing before the lord ordinary, as the ground of his judgment. Bell, Dict.

——**In Business Law.** Memoranda or notes of a transaction or proceeding. Thus, the record of the proceedings at a meeting of directors or shareholders of a company is called the "minutes."

MINUTIO. In the civil law. Diminution.

MIRROR DES JUSTICES. The Mirror of Justices, a treatise written during the reign of Edward II. Andrew Horne is its reputed author. It was first published in 1642, and in 1768 it was translated into English by William Hughes. Some diversity of opinion seems to exist as to its merits. Pref. to 9 and 10 Coke. As to the history of this celebrated book, see St. Armand's Essays on the Legislative Power of England, 58, 59.

MISA.

——**In Old English Law.** The mise or issue in a writ of right. Spelman.

——**In Old Records.** A compact or agreement; a form of compromise. Cowell.

MISADVENTURE. An accident by which an injury occurs to another.

When applied to homicide, misadventure is the act of a man who, in the performance of a lawful act, without any intention to do harm, and after using proper precaution to prevent danger, unfortunately kills another person. The act upon which the death ensues must be neither *malum in se* nor *malum prohibitum*. The usual examples under this head are: (1) When the death ensues from innocent recreations; (2) from moderate and lawful correction *in foro domestico;* (3) from acts lawful and indifferent in themselves, done with proper and ordinary caution. 4 Bl. Comm. 182; 1 East, P. C. 221. See "Homicide;" "Manslaughter."

MISALLEGE. To cite falsely as a proof or argument.

MISAPPROPRIATION. Wrongful conversion of property by one to whom it has been intrusted. Steph. Dig. Crim. Law, 275.

Somewhat similar to embezzlement in certain cases, as the misapplication of funds intrusted to a person for a particular purpose, by devoting them to some unauthorized purpose. 108 Cal. 426.

MISBEHAVIOR. Improper or unlawful conduct. See 2 Mart. (La.; N. S.) 683.

Generally applied to a breach of duty or propriety by an officer, witness, juror, etc., not amounting to a crime.

MISCARRIAGE.

——**In Medical Jurisprudence.** The expulsion of the ovum or embryo from the uterus within the first six weeks after conception. Between that time, and before the expiration of the sixth month, when the child may possibly live, it is termed "abortion." When the delivery takes place soon after the sixth month, it is denominated "premature labor." But the criminal act of destroying the foetus at any time before birth is termed, in law, "procuring miscarriage." Chit. Med. Jur. 410; 2 Dungl. Hum. Phys. 364. See "Abortion."

——**In Practice.** A term used in the statute of frauds to denote that species of wrongful act for the consequences of which the wrongdoer would be responsible at law in a civil action. 2 Barn. & Ald. 613; 2 Day (Conn.) 457; 63 N. C. 198; Browne, St. Frauds, § 155.

MISCASTING. An error in auditing and numbering. It does not include any pretended miscasting or misvaluing. 4 Bouv. Inst. note 4128.

MISCEGENATION. Marriage between persons of different races.

MISCOGNIZANT. Ignorant, or not knowing. St. 32 Hen. VIII. c. 9. Little used.

MISCONTINUANCE. In practice. A continuance of a suit by undue process. Its effect is the same as a discontinuance. 2 Hawk. P. C. 299; Kitch. Cts. 231; Jenk. Cent. Cas. 57.

MISCREANT. In old English law. An apostate; an unbeliever; one who totally renounced Christianity. 4 Bl. Comm. 44.

MISCREAUNTES. (L. Fr.) In old English law. Apostates; unbelievers; infidels. Classed by Britton with the worst criminals; as murderers, robbers, prison-breakers, sorcerers, poisoners, etc. Britt. c. 29. Hence the term *miscreant.* 4 Bl. Comm. 44.

MISDEMEAN. In old English law. To use improperly; to abuse. "If he misdemean an authority." Finch, Law, bk. 1, c. 3, No. 63.

MISDEMEANMENT. A person guilty of a misdemeanor.

MISDEMEANOR. Every offense inferior to felony. See "Felony."

MISE (Lat. *mittere,* through the French *mettre,* to place).

——**In Pleading.** The issue in a writ of right. The tenant in a writ of right is said to "join the mise on the mere right" when he pleads that his title is better than the demandant's. 2 Wm. Saund. 45h, 45i. It was equivalent to the general issue; and everything except collateral warranty might be given in evidence under it by the tenant. Booth, Real Actions, 98, 114; 3 Wils. 420; 7 Wheat. (U. S.) 31; 3 Pet. (U. S.) 133; 7 Cow. (N. Y.) 52; 10 Grat. (Va.) 350. The payee in aid, on coming into court, joined in the mise together with the tenant. 2 Wm. Saund. 45d, note. It was the more common practice, however, for the demandant to traverse the tenant's plea when the cause could be tried by a common jury instead of the grand assize.

——**In Practice.** Expenses. It is so commonly used in the entries of judgments, in personal actions; as, when the plaintiff recovers, the judgment is *quod recuperet damna sua,* that he recovers his damages, and *pro mises et custagiis,* for costs and charges, so much, etc.

MISERA EST SERVITUS, UBI JUS EST vagum aut incertum. It is a miserable slavery where the law is vague or uncertain. 4 Inst. 246; 9 Johns. (N. Y.) 427; 11 Pet. (U. S.) 286.

MISERABILE DEPOSITUM (Lat.) In civil law. The name of an involuntary deposit, made under pressing necessity; as, for instance, shipwreck, fire, or other inevitable calamity. Poth. Proc. Civ. pt. 5, c. 1, § 1; Code La. art. 2935.

MISERERE. The name and first word of one of the penitential psalms (Ps. li., 1), being that which was commonly used to be given by the ordinary to such condemned malefactors as were allowed the benefit of clergy; whence it is also called the "psalm of mercy." Wharton.

MISERICORDIA (Lat.) An arbitrary or discretionary amercement.

To be in mercy is to be liable to such punishment as the judge may, in his discretion, inflict. According to Spelman, *misericord* is so called because the party is in mercy, and to distinguish this fine from redemptions, or heavy fines. Spelman. See Co. Litt. 126b; Madd. c. 14.

MISERICORDIA COMMUNIS. In old English law. A fine on the whole community.

MISFEASANCE. The performance of an act which might lawfully be done, in an improper manner, by which another person receives an injury.

It differs from malfeasance or nonfeasance. See, generally, 2 Viner, Abr. 35; 2 Kent, Comm. 443; Doct. Plac. 62; Story, Bailm. § 9.

It seems to be settled that there is a distinction between misfeasance and nonfeasance in the case of mandates. In cases of nonfeasance, the mandatary is not generally liable, because, his undertaking being gratuitous, there is no consideration to support it, but in cases of misfeasance the common law gives a remedy for the injury done, and to the extent of that injury. 5 Term R. 143; 4 Johns. (N. Y.) 81; 2 Johns. Cas. (N. Y.) 92; 1 Esp. 74; 2 Ld. Raym. 909; Story, Bailm. § 165; Bouv. Inst. Index.

MISFORTUNE. An adverse event not immediately dependent on the action or will of him who suffers from it, and of such a character that no prudent man would take it into his calculation in reference to the interest of himself or of others.

Homicide by misfortune. See "Excusable Homicide."

MISJOINDER. An improper joinder, whether of actions, causes of action, offenses, parties, etc. See "Joinder."

MISKENNING (Fr. *mis,* wrong, and Saxon *cennan,* summon). A wrongful citation; a variance in a plea. 1 Mon. Angl. 237; Chart. Hen. II.; Jacob; Du Cange.

MISNOMER. The use of a wrong name in designating any person in any instrument or proceeding. In contracts and deeds, a misnomer is generally immaterial if the person intended can be ascertained. 11 Coke, 20; 1 Ld. Raym. 304.

In a pleading, a misnomer of a party is ground of abatement, while misnomer of a third person is or is not a fatal variance, accordingly as it is or is not material. See "Idem Sonans."

MISPLEADING. Pleading incorrectly, or omitting anything in pleading which is essential to the support or defense of an action, is so called. 198 Ill. 466.

Pleading "Not guilty" to an action of debt is an example of the first; setting out a defective title is an example of the second. See 3 Salk. 365.

It comprehends misdeclaring, whether the error is in separate counts, or in the misjoining of counts. 22 Wend. (N. Y.) 369, 375.

MISPRISION. In criminal law. A term used to signify every considerable misdemeanor which has not a certain name given to it by law. 3 Inst. 36.

The concealment of a crime.

Misprision of felony is the like concealment of felony, without giving any degree of maintenance to the felon (Act Cong. April 30, 1790, § 6; 1 Story, U. S. Laws, 84); for if any aid be given him, the party becomes an accessory after the fact.

Misprision of treason is the concealment of treason by being merely passive. Act Cong. April 30, 1790 (1 Story, U. S. Laws, 83; 1 East, P. C. 139). If any assistance be given to the traitor, it makes the party a principal, as there are no accessories in treason.

Negative misprision consists in the concealment of something which ought to be revealed.

Positive misprision consists in the commission of something which ought not to be done. 4 Bl. Comm. c. 9.

MISRECITAL. The incorrect recital of a matter of fact, either in an agreement or a plea. Under the latter term is here understood the declaration and all the subsequent pleadings. See "Recital."

MISREPRESENTATION. The assertion of that which is not true.

The nature of misrepresentations to entitle a party injured thereby varies with the nature of the relief sought, but in general the misrepresentation for which relief will be granted must be a willfully false statement respecting a matter ot fact (not of law or opinion), which was reasonably calculated to mislead the party to his prejudice in respect to the business in hand, and which did actually have that effect.

MISSILIA (Lat. from *mittere*, to send or throw). In the Roman law. Gifts or liberalities, which the praetors and consuls were in the habit of throwing among the people. Inst. 2. 1. 45.

MISSING SHIP. A ship which has been at sea and unheard from for so long a time as to give rise to the presumption that she has perished with all on board.

There is no precise time fixed as to when the presumption is to arise; and this must depend upon the circumstances of each case. 2 Strange, 1199; Park, Ins. 63; Marsh. Ins. 488; 2 Johns. (N. Y.) 150; 1 Caines (N. Y.) 525; Holt, 242.

MISSIO (Lat. from *mittere*, to send or put). In the civil law. A sending or putting. *Missio in bona*, a putting the creditor in possession of the debtor's property. 1 Mackeld. Civ. Law, 378, § 344; 4 Reeve, Hist. Eng. Law, 20; 2 Kames, Eq. 208.

Missio judicum in consilium, a sending out of the *judices* (or jury) to make up their sentence. Halifax, Anal. bk. 3, c. 13, No. 31.

MISSIVES. In Scotch practice. Writings passed between parties as evidence of a transaction. Bell, Dict.

MISSTAICUS (Lat.) In old records. A messenger.

MISTAKE. An erroneous conception, conviction, or belief in respect to matter of either fact or law, arising from ignorance, surprise, imposition, or misplaced confidence. See Story, Eq. Jur. § 110. 159 Iowa 529.

That result of ignorance of law or fact which has misled a person to commit that which, if he had not been in error, he would not have done. Jeremy, Eq. Jur. bk. 2, pt. 2, p. 358. An erroneous mental condition, conception, or conviction induced by a misapprehension of the truth, without which the act complained of would not have taken place. 159 Iowa 529.

Distinction between "mistake" and "ignorance," see "Ignorance."

MISTAKE OF FACT. Mistake of fact has been defined to be a mistake, not caused by the neglect of a legal duty on the part of the person making the mistake, and consisting in an unconscious ignorance or forgetfulness of a fact, past or present, material to the contract, or belief in the present existence of a thing material to the contract which does not exist, or in the past existence of a thing which has not existed. 151 Ill. 224.

MISTAKE OF LAW. An erroneous conclusion as to the legal effect of known facts. 151 Ill. 223.

MISTERY. An old form of mystery (*q. v.*)

MISTRESS. The style of the wife of an esquire or gentleman.

MISTRIAL. A trial which is erroneous on account of some defect in the persons trying, as if the jury come from the wrong county, or because there was no issue formed, as if no plea be entered, or some other defect of jurisdiction. 3 Croke, 284; 2 Maule & S. 270.

MISUSER. An unlawful use of a right.

In cases of public offices and franchises, a misuser is sufficient to cause the right to be forfeited. 2 Bl. Comm. 153; 5 Pick. (Mass.) 163.

MITIGATION. Reduction; diminution; lessening of the amount of a penalty or punishment.

Circumstances which do not amount to a justification or excuse of the act committed may yet be properly considered in mitigation of the punishment; as, for example, the fact that one who stole a loaf of bread was starving.

In actions for the recovery of damages, matters may often be given in evidence in mitigation of damages which are no answer to the action itself. See "Damages;" "Character."

MITIOR SENSUS. See "In Mitiori Sensu."

MITIUS IMPERANTI MELIUS PARETUR. The more mildly one commands, the better is he obeyed. 3 Inst. 24.

MITTENDO MANUSCRIPTUM PEDIS finis. An abolished judicial writ addressed to the treasurer and chamberlain of the exchequer to search for and transmit the foot of a fine acknowledged before justices in eyre into the common pleas. Reg. Orig. 14.

MITTER (Law Fr.) To put, to send, or to pass; as, *mitter l'estate,* to pass the estate; *mitter le droit,* to pass a right. 2 Bl. Comm. 324; Bac. Abr. "Release" (C); Co. Litt. 193, 273b. *Mitter a large,* to put or set at large.

MITTER AVANT (Law Fr.) In old practice. To put before; to present before a court; to produce in court. *Mist avant un fait,* produced a deed. Y. B. M. 5 Edw. III. 119.

MITTIMUS.

——**In Old English Law.** A writ inclosing a record sent to be tried in a county palatine. It derives its name from the Latin word *mittimus,* "we send." It is the jury process of these counties, and commands the proper officer of the county palatine to command the sheriff to summon the jury for the trial of the cause, and to return the record, etc. 1 Mart. (La.) 278; 2 Mart. (La.) 88.

——**In Criminal Practice.** A precept in writing, under the hand and seal of a justice of the peace, or other competent officer, directed to the jailer or keeper of a prison, commanding him to receive and safely keep a person charged with an offense therein named, until he shall be delivered by due course of law. Co. Litt. 590.

MIXED ACTION. In practice. An action partaking of the nature both of a real and of a personal action, by which real property is demanded, and also damages for a wrong sustained. An ejectment is of this nature. 4 Bouv. Inst. note 3650. See "Action."

MIXED CONTRACT. In civil law. A contract in which one of the parties confers a benefit on the other, and requires of the latter something of less value than what he has given; as, a legacy charged with some thing of less value than the legacy itself. Poth. Obl. note 12.

MIXED GOVERNMENT. A government established with some of the powers of a monarchical, aristocratical, and democratical government.

MIXED JURY. A bilingual jury; a jury of the half-tongue.

Also a jury composed partly of negroes and partly of white men.

MIXED LARCENY. Compound larceny. See "Larceny."

MIXED LAWS. A name sometimes given to those which concern both persons and property.

MIXED PRESUMPTIONS. Presumptions partaking of the nature both of presumptions of law and presumptions of fact; *i. e.,* presumptions of fact recognized by law.

MIXED PROPERTY. That kind of property which is not altogether real nor personal, but a compound of both. Heirlooms, tombstones, monuments in a church, and title deeds to an estate, are of this nature. 1 Bl. Comm. 428; 3 Barn. & Adol. 174; 4 Bing. 106. See "Mixed Subjects of Property."

MIXED SUBJECTS OF PROPERTY. Such as fall within the definition of things real, but which are attended, nevertheless, with some of the legal qualities of things personal, as emblements, fixtures, and shares in public undertakings, connected with land. Besides these, there are others which, though things personal in point of definition, are, in respect of some of their legal qualities, of the nature of things real; such are animals, *ferae naturae,* charters and deeds, court rolls, and other evidences of the land, together with the chests in which they are contained, ancient family pictures, ornaments, tombstones, coats of armor, with pennons and other ensigns, and especially heirlooms. Wharton.

MIXED TITHES. In ecclesiastical law. "Those which arise not immediately from the ground, but from those things which are nourished by the ground;" *e. g.,* colts, chickens, calves, milk, eggs, etc. 3 Burn, Ecc. Law. 380; 2 Bl. Comm. 24.

MIXED WAR. A mixed war is one which is made on one side by public authority, and on the other by mere private persons. 1 Hill (N. Y.) 377, 415.

MIXTION. The putting of different goods or chattels together in such a manner that they can no longer be separated; as, putting the wines of two different persons into the same barrel, the grain of several persons into the same bag, and the like.

The intermixture may be occasioned by the willful act of the party, or owner of one of the articles, by the willful act of a stranger, by the negligence of the owner or a stranger, or by accident. See "Confusion."

MIXTUM IMPERIUM (Lat.) In old English law. Mixed authority; a kind of civil power. A term applied by Lord Hale to the "power" of certain subordinate civil magistrates, as distinct from "jurisdiction." Hale, Anal. § 11.

MOB. An unorganized assemblage of many persons bent on unlawful violence; a riot involving a multitude. Abbott.

MOBBING AND RIOTING. In Scotch law. A general term, including all those convocations of the lieges for violent and unlawful purposes which are attended with injury to the persons or property of the lieges, or terror and alarm to the neighborhood in which it takes place. The two phrases are usually placed together; but, nevertheless, they have distinct meanings, and are sometimes used separately in legal language,—the word "mobbing" being peculiarly applicable to the unlawful assemblage and violence of a number of persons, and that of "rioting" to the outrageous behavior of a single individual. Alis. Crim. Law, c. 23, p. 509.

MOBILIA. See "Movables."

MOBILIA NON HABET SITUM. Movables have no *situs*. 4 Johns Ch. (N. Y.) 472.

MOBILIA PERSONAM SEQUUNTUR; immobilia situm. Movable things follow the person; immovable, their locality. Story, Confl. Laws (3d Ed.) 638, 639.

MOBILIA SEQUUNTUR PERSONAM. Movables follow the person. Story, Confl. Laws (3d Ed.) 638, 639; Broom, Leg. Max. (3d London Ed.) 462.

MODALIS. (L. Lat. from *modus*). In old English law. Having the character of a *modus*; qualified; enlarged or restricted.

MODERAMEN INCULPATAE TUTELAE (Lat.) In Roman law. The regulation of justifiable defense. A term used to express that degree of force in defense of the person or property which a person might safely use, although it should occasion the death of the aggressor. Calv. Lex.; Bell, Dict.

MODERATA MISERICORDIA. A writ founded on *Magna Charta*, which lies for him who is amerced in a court, not of record, for any transgression beyond the quality or quantity of the offense. It is addressed to the lord of the court, or his bailiff, commanding him to take a moderate amerciament of the parties. New Nat. Brev. 167; Fitzh. Nat. Brev. 76.

MODERATE CASTIGAVIT. In pleading. The name of a plea in trespass by which the defendant justifies an assault and battery, because he moderately corrected the plaintiff, whom he had a right to correct. 2 Chit. Pl. 576; 2 Bos. & P. 224; 15 Mass. 347; 2 Phil. Ev. 147; Bac. Abr. "Assault" (C).

This plea ought to disclose, in general terms, the cause which rendered the correction expedient. 3 Salk. 47.

MODERATOR. A person appointed to preside at a popular meeting. Sometimes he is called a "chairman." The presiding officer of town meetings in New England is so called.

MODICA CIRCUMSTANTIA FACTI JUS mutat. A small circumstance attending an act may change the law.

MODIUS (Lat.) In old English law. A bushel. Cowell; Spelman.

A larger measure, of uncertain quantity. Id.

A measure of land. Id.

MODO ET FORMA (Lat. in manner and form). In pleading. Technical words used to put in issue such concomitants of the principal matters as time, place, etc., where these circumstances were material. Their use when these circumstances were immaterial was purely formal. The words were translated literally, when pleadings began to be made in English, by "in manner and form." See Lawes, Pl. 120; Gould, Pl. c. 6, § 22; Steph. Pl. 213; Dane, Abr. Index; Viner, Abr. "Modo et forma."

MODUS.

——**In Civil Law.** Manner; means; way. Ainsworth. A rhythmic song. Du Cange.

——**In Old Conveyancing.** Manner; *e. g.*, the manner in which an estate should be held, etc. A qualification, whether in restriction or enlargement of the terms of the instrument; especially with relation to the kind of grant called "*donatio*,"—the making those *quasi* heirs who were not in fact heirs, according to the ordinary form of such conveyances. And this *modus* or qualification of the ordinary form became so common as to give rise to the maxim, *modus et conventio vincunt legem*. Co. Litt. 19a; Bracton, 17b; 1 Reeve, Hist. Eng. Law, 293. A consideration. Bracton, 17, 18.

——**In Ecclesiastical Law.** A peculiar manner of tithing, growing out of custom. See "Modus Decimandi."

MODUS DE NON DECIMANDO. In ecclesiastical law. A custom or prescription not to pay tithes, which is not good, except in case of abbey lands. 2 Bl. Comm. 31, note.

MODUS DE NON DECIMANDO NON VAlet. A *modus* (prescription) not to pay tithes is void. Lofft, 427; Cro. Eliz. 511; 2 Bl. Comm. 31.

MODUS DECIMANDI. In ecclesiastical law. A peculiar manner of tithing, arising from immemorial usage, and differing from the payment of one-tenth of the annual increase.

To be a good *modus*, the custom must be, first, certain and invariable; second, beneficial to the parson; third, a custom to pay something different from the thing compounded for; fourth, of the same species; fifth, the thing substituted must be in its nature as durable as the tithes themselves; sixth, it must not be too large,—that would be a *rank modus*. 2 Bl. Comm. 30. See 2 & 3 Wm. IV. c. 100; 13 Mees. & W. 822.

MODUS ET CONVENTIO VINCUNT LEgem. The form of agreement and the convention of the parties overrule the law. 2 Coke, 73.

MODUS HABILIS. A good or valid manner.

MODUS LEGEM DAT DONATIONI. The manner gives law to a gift. Co. Litt. 19a; Broom, Leg. Max. (3d London Ed.) 615.

MODUS LEVANDI FINES. The manner of levying fines; the title of a short statute in French, passed in the eighteenth year of Edward I. 2 Inst. 510; 2 Bl. Comm. 349.

MODUS TENENDI. The manner of holding; *i. e.*, the different species of tenures by which estates are held.

MODUS TRANSFERRENDI. The manner of transferring.

MODUS VACANDI. The manner of vacating. How and why an estate has been relinquished or surrendered by a vassal to his lord might well be referred to by this phrase. See Tray. Lat. Max. s. v.

MODUS VIVENDI. In international law. An agreement between nations not rising to the dignity of a treaty, regulating their conduct in respect to a particular matter. Ordinarily applied to agreements to preserve the *status quo* pending the negotiation of a final treaty.

MOERDA. The secret killing of another; murder. 4 Bl. Comm. 194.

MOHATRA. In French law. The name of a fraudulent contract made to cover a usurious loan of money.

It takes place when an individual buys merchandise from another on a credit at a high price, to sell it immediately to the first seller, or to a third person who acts as his agent, at a much less price for cash. 16 Toullier, Dr. Civ. note 44; 1 Bouv. Inst. note 1118.

MOIETY. The half of anything; as, if a testator bequeath one moiety of his estate to A., and the other to B., each shall take an equal part. Joint tenants are said to hold by moieties. Litt. 125; 3 C. B. 274, 283.

MOLESTATION. In Scotch law. The name of an action competent to the proprietor of a landed estate against those who disturb his possession. It is chiefly used in questions of commonty, or of controverted marches. Ersk. Inst. 4. 1. 48.

MOLITURA. Toll paid for grinding at a mill; multure. Not used.

MOLITURA LIBERA. Free grinding; a liberty to have a mill without paying tolls to the lord. Jacob.

MOLLITER MANUS IMPOSUIT (Lat.) He laid his hands on gently.

——**In Pleading.** Technical words in a plea in justification of a trespass to the person, that defendant used no more force than was reasonably necessary (20 Johns. [N. Y.] 427; 4 Denio [N. Y.] 448; 2 Strob. [S. C.] 232; 17 Ohio, 454), in defense of property (3 Cush. [Mass.] 154; 3 Ohio. St. 159; 9 Barb. [N. Y.] 652; 23 Pa. St. 424. See 19 N. H. 562; 25 Ala. [N. S.] 41; 4 Cush. [Mass.] 597), or the prevention of crime (2 Chit. Pl. 574).

MOLMUTIAN LAWS. The laws of Dunvallo Molmutius, a legendary or mythical king of the Britons, who is supposed to have begun his reign about 400 B. C. These laws were famous in the land until the Conquest. Tomlins; Mozley & W.

MOMENTUM. In the civil law. An instant; an indivisible portion of time. Calv. Lex.

A portion of time that might be measured, a division or subdivision of an hour, answering in some degree to the modern "minute," but of longer duration. According to Accursius, ten moments (*momenta*) made a point (*punctum*), and four points an hour. Calv. Lex. Hence, no doubt, the rule stated in Bracton, that an hour consists of forty moments (*hora fit ex quadraginta momentis*), which has been so far misunderstood as to be pronounced a misprint. Bracton, fols. 264, 359b; Fleta, lib. 5, c. 5, § 31.

MONARCHY. That government which is ruled, really or theoretically, by one man, who is wholly set apart from all other members of the state.

MONASTERIUM (Graeco-Lat. and Law Lat.) In civil and old English law. A monastery; a church. Nov. 5; Spelman. Hence, according to Spelman, the Saxon *mynster* and *munster*, and probably, also, the Law French *monstre*.

MONETA (Lat.) In civil and old English law. Money. Said to be derived from *monere*, to warn, because by the impression upon it we are warned whose it is, that is, by whom coined, and what is its value. *Falsa moneta*, counterfeit money. Code, 9, 24. *Monetam conterfactam*. Mem. in Scacc. M. 22 Edw. I. *De moneta et chambio domini regis*, of the money and exchange of the lord the king. Bracton, fol. 117.

MONETA EST JUSTUM MEDIUM ET mensura rerum commutabilium, nam per medium monetae fit omnium rerum conveniens, et justa aestimatio. Money is the just medium and measure of all commutable things, for by the medium of money a convenient and just estimation of all things is made. See 1 Bouv. Inst. note 922.

MONETANDI JUS COMPREHENDITUR in regalibus quae nunquam a regio sceptro abdicantur. The right of coining is comprehended amongst those rights of royalty which are never relinquished by the kingly sceptre. Dav. 18.

MONEY. A representative of value, established by law, and made a legal tender in the payment of debts. 65 N. C. 415.

In a strict sense, gold and silver coin. Const. U. S. art. 1, §§ 8, 10. See 44 Tex. 622.

In a broader sense, the common medium of exchange in a civilized nation. 45 Tex. 309; 5 Humph. (Tenn.) 15.

The term is used to designate the whole volume of the medium of exchange, recognized by law or the custom of merchants. 34 Fed. 681. It is generally held to include banknotes. 3 Mass. 403; 71 Ala. 544; 47 Wis. 557. But see, contra, 3 Conn. 534.

As used in wills, it has been construed as synonymous with personalty, to effect the intent of the testator. Jarm. Wills, c. 24.

MONEY CLAIMS. In English practice. Under the judicature act of 1875, claims for the price of goods sold, for money lent, for arrears of rent, etc., and other claims where money is directly payable on a contract express or implied, as opposed to the cases where money is claimed by way of damages for some independent wrong, whether by breach of contract or otherwise. These "money claims" correspond very nearly to the "money counts" hitherto in use. Mozley & W.

MONEY COUNTS. In pleading. The common counts in an action of *assumpsit.*

They are so called because they are founded on express or implied promises to pay money in consideration of a precedent debt They are of four descriptions, the *indebitatis assumpsit,* the *quantum meruit,* the *quantum valebant,* and the account stated.

MONEY DEMAND. A demand which is certain beforehand, or ascertainable by calculation.

MONEY HAD AND RECEIVED. In pleading. The technical designation of a form of declaration in *assumpsit,* wherein the plaintiff declares that the defendant had and received certain money, etc.

An action of *assumpsit* will lie, without regard to privity of contract, to recover money to which the plaintiff is entitled, and which in justice and equity, when no rule of policy or strict law prevents it, the defendant ought to refund to the plaintiff, and which he cannot with good conscience retain, on a count for money had and received. 6 Serg. & R. (Pa.) 369; 10 Serg. & R. (Pa.) 219; 1 Dall. (Pa.) 148; 2 Dall. (Pa.) 154; 3 J. J. Marsh. (Ky.) 175; 1 Har. (N. J.) 447; 1 Har. & G. (Md.) 258; 7 Mass. 288; 6 Wend. (N. Y.) 290; 13 Wend. (N. Y.) 488; Add. Cont. 230.

MONEY JUDGMENT. One which requires the payment of money, as distinguished from one directing some act to be done.

MONEY LENT. In pleading. The technical name of a declaration in an action of *assumpsit* for that the defendant promised to pay the plaintiff for money lent.

To recover, the plaintiff must prove that the defendant received his money, but it is not indispensable that it should be originally lent. If, for example, money has been advanced upon a special contract, which has been abandoned and rescinded, and which cannot be enforced, the law raises an implied promise from the person who holds the money to pay it back as money lent. 7 Bing. 266; 3 Mees. & W. 434; 9 Mees. & W. 729. See 1 N. Chip. (Vt.) 214; 3 J. J. Marsh. (Ky.) 37.

MONEY MADE. The return on execution that the amount has been collected thereon.

MONEY OF ADIEU. In French law. Earnest money. So called because given at parting, in completion of the bargain. Poth. Sale, 507. *Arrhes* is the usual French word for earnest money; "money of adieu" is a provincialism found in the province of Orleans.

MONEY PAID. In pleading. The technical name of a declaration in *assumpsit,* in which the plaintiff declares for money paid for the use of the defendant.

MONEYED CORPORATION. In New York law corporations formed under or subject to the banking or insurance law, and they include every corporation having banking powers, or having the power to make loans upon pledges or deposits, or authorized by law to make contracts of insurance. 1 Rev. St. N. Y. 731; 3 N. Y. 479. Fletcher Cyclopedia Corporations 133.

MONIER, or MONEYER (Law Lat. *monetarius*). In old English law. A minister of the mint, who made and coined the king's money. There were several of these *moniers* or workmen; "some to shear the money, some to forge it, others to beat it broad, some to round it, and some to stamp or coin it." Cowell, voc. "Moniers;" "Mint."

A banker; one who dealt in money. Cowell.

MONITION. In practice. A process in the nature of a summons, which is used in the civil law, and in those courts which derive their practice from the civil law.

A general monition is a citation or summons to all persons interested, or, as is commonly said, to the whole world, to appear and show cause why the libel filed in the case should not be sustained, and the prayer of relief granted. This is adopted in prize cases, admiralty suits for forfeitures, and other suits *in rem,* when no particular individuals are summoned to answer. In such cases, the taking possession of the property libelled, and this general citation of monition, served according to law, are considered constructive notice to the world of the pendency of the suit; and the judgment rendered thereupon is conclusive upon the title of the property which may be affected. In form, the monition is substantially a warrant of the court, in an admiralty cause, directed to the marshal or his deputy, commanding him, in the name of the president of the United States, to give public notice, by advertisements in such newspapers as the court may select, and by notifications to be posted in public places, that a libel has been filed in a certain admiralty cause pending, and of the time and place appointed for the trial. A brief statement of the allegations in the libel is usually contained in the monition. The monition is served in the manner directed in the warrant.

A mixed monition is one which contains directions for a general monition to all persons interested, and a special summons to particular persons named in the warrant. This is served by newspaper advertisements, by notifications posted in public places, and by delivery of a copy attested by the officer to each person specially named, or by leaving it at his usual place of residence.

A special monition is a similar warrant, directed to the marshal or his deputy, requiring him to give special notice to certain persons, named in the warrant, of the pendency of the suit, the grounds of it, and the time and place of trial. It is served by delivery of a copy of the warrant, attested by the officer, to each one of the adverse parties, or by leaving the same at his usual place of residence; but the service should be personal, if possible. Clerke, Prax. tit. 21; Dunl. Adm. Prac. 135. See Conkl. Adm.; Pars. Mar. Law.

MONITORY LETTER. In ecclesiastical law. The process of an official, a bishop, or other prelate having jurisdiction, issued to compel, by ecclesiastical censures, those who know of a crime, or other matter which requires to be explained, to come and reveal it. Merlin, Repert.

MONOCRACY. A government by one person only.

MONOCRAT. A monarch who governs alone; an absolute governor.

MONOGAMY. The state of having only one husband or one wife at a time.

A marriage contracted between one man and one woman, in exclusion of all the rest of mankind. The term is used in opposition to "bigamy" and "polygamy." Wolff. Dr. Nat. § 857.

MONOGRAM. A character or cipher composed of one or more letters interwoven, being an abbreviation of a name.

A signature made by monogram would perhaps be binding provided it could be proved to have been made and intended as a signature. 1 Denio (N. Y.) 471.

There seems to be no reason why such a signature should not be as binding as one which is altogether illegible.

MONOMACHY. Single combat.

MONOMANIA. In medical jurisprudence. Insanity only upon a particular subject, and with a single delusion of the mind.

The most simple form of this disorder is that in which the patient has imbibed some single notion, contrary to common sense, and to his own experience, and which seems, and no doubt really is, dependent on errors of sensation. It is supposed the mind in other respects retains its intellectual powers. In order to avoid any civil act done or criminal responsibility incurred, it must manifestly appear that the act in question was the effect of monomania. Cyc. Prac. Med. "Soundness and Unsoundness of Mind;" Ray, Ins. § 203; 13 Ves. 89; 3 Brown, Ch. 444; 1 Add. Ecc. 283; 2 Add. Ecc. 402; Hagg. 18; 2 Add. 79, 94, 209; 5 Car. & P. 168; Burrows, Ins. 484, 485. See "Delusion;" "Mania."

MONOMANIACS. Persons who are insane upon some one or more subjects, and apparently sane upon all others. 2 Redf. Sur. (N. Y.) 34, 37.

MONOPOLIA DICITUR, CUM UNUS SOlus aliquod genus mercaturae universum emit, pretium ad suum libitum statuens. It is said to be a monopoly when one person alone buys up the whole of one kind of commodity, fixing a price at his own pleasure. 11 Coke, 86.

MONOPOLIUM (Graeco-Lat.) The sole power, right, or privilege of sale; monopoly; a monopoly. Calv. Lex.; Code, 4, 59; Grotius de Jure Belli, lib. 2, c. 12, § 16.

MONOPOLY (from Lat. *monopolium, q. v.*) An exclusive right granted to a few, of something which was before of common right. 11 Peters (U. S.) 607.

The exclusive privilege of selling any commodity. Defined in English law to be "a license or privilege allowed by the king for the sole buying and selling, making, working, or using of anything whatsoever, whereby the subject in general is restrained from that liberty of manufacturing or trading which he had before." 4 Bl. Comm. 159; 4 Steph. Comm. 291.

Any exclusive right or privilege.

The term also indicates the possession of total (or in some cases a dominating control of a commodity, etc.

MONSTER. An animal which has a conformation contrary to the order of nature. 2 Dungl. Hum. Phys. 422.

A monster, although born of a woman in lawful wedlock, cannot inherit. Those who have, however, the essential parts of the human form, and have merely some defect of conformation, are capable of inheriting, if otherwise qualified. 2 Bl. Comm. 246;

1 Beck, Med. Jur. 366; Co. Litt. 7, 8; Dig. 1. 5. 14; 1 Swift, System, 331; Fred. Code. pt. 1, bk. 1, tit. 4, § 4.

No living human birth, however much it may differ from human shape, can be lawfully destroyed. Traill, Med. Jur. 47. See Briand, Med. Leg. pt. 1, c. 6, art. 2, § 3; 1 Fodere, Med. Leg. §§ 402-405.

MONSTRANS DE DROIT (Fr. showing of right). A common-law process by which restitution of personal or real property is obtained from the crown by a subject. Chit. Prerog. Cr. 345; 3 Bl. Comm. 256. By this process, when the facts of the title of the crown are already on record, the facts on which the plaintiff relies, not inconsistent with such record, are shown, and judgment of the court prayed thereon. The judgment, if against the crown, is that of *ouster le main*, which vests possession in the subject without execution. Bac. Abr. "Prerogative" (E); 1 And. 181; 5 Leigh (Va.) 512; 12 Grat. (Va.) 564.

MONSTRANS DE FAIT (Fr. showing of a deed). A profert. Bac. Abr. "Pleas" (I 12, note 1).

MONSTRAVERUNT, WRIT OF. In English law. A writ which lies for the tenants of ancient demesne who hold by free charter, and not for those tenants who hold by copy of court roll, or by the rod, according to the custom of the manor. Fitzh. Nat. Brev. 31.

MONTES PIETATIS, or **MONTS DE PIete.** Institutions established by public authority for lending money upon pledge of goods.

In these establishments a fund is provided, with suitable warehouses, and all necessary accommodations. They are managed by directors. When the money for which the goods pledged is not returned in proper time, the goods are sold to reimburse the institutions. They are found principally on the continent of Europe. With us, private persons, called "pawnbrokers," perform this office,—sometimes with doubtful fidelity. See Bell, Inst. 5. 2. 2.

MONTH. A space of time variously computed, as it is applied to astronomical, civil or solar, or lunar months.

The astronomical month contains one-twelfth part of the time employed by the sun in going through the zodiac. In law, when a month simply is mentioned, it is never understood to mean an astronomical month.

The civil, solar or calendar month is that which agrees with the Gregorian calendar; and these months are known by the names of January, February, March, etc. They are composed of unequal portions of time. There are seven of thirty-one days each, four of thirty, and one which is sometimes composed of twenty-eight days, and in leap years of twenty-nine.

The lunar month consists of twenty-eight days.

By the law of England, a month means ordinarily, in common contracts, as in leases, a lunar month. A contract, therefore, made for a lease of land for twelve months would mean a lease for forty-eight weeks only. 2 Bl. Comm. 141; 6 Coke, 62; 6Term R. 224; 1 Maule & S. 111; 1 Bing. 307. A distinction has been made between "twelve months" and "a twelve-months." The latter has been held to mean a year. 6 Coke, 61.

But in mercantile contracts in England, and for any purpose in the United States, a month simply signifies a calendar month, Chit. Bills, 406; 3 Brod. & B. 187; 1 Maule & S. 111; Story, Bills, § 143; Story, Partn. § 213; 2 Mass. 170; 4 Mass. 460; 6 Watts & S. (Pa.) 179; 1 Johns. Cas. (N. Y.) 99; 4 Wend. (N. Y.) 512; 15 Johns. (N. Y.) 358; 2 Cow. (N. Y.) 518, 605; 2 Dall. (Pa.) 302; 4 Dall. (Pa.) 143; 4 Mass. 461; 4 Bibb (Ky.) 105, which ends on the corresponding day in the month succeeding its beginning, less one day. 279 Ill. 401.

In England, in the ecclesiastical law, months are computed by the calendar. 3 Burrows, 1455; 1 Maule & S. 111.

MONUMENT. A thing intended to transmit to posterity the memory of some one. A tomb where a dead body has been deposited.

In this sense it differs from a "cenotaph," which is an empty tomb. Dig. 11. 7. 2. 6; Id. 11. 7. 2. 42.

A permanent landmark, whether natural or artificial, established for the purpose of indicating a boundary.

MONUMENTA QUAE NOS RECORDA vocamus sunt veritatis et vetustatis vestigia. Monuments, which we call "records," are the vestiges of truth and antiquity. Co. Litt. 118.

MOORING. In maritime law. The securing of a vessel by a hawser or chain, or otherwise, to the shore, or to the bottom by a cable and anchor. The being "moored in safety," under a policy of insurance, is being moored in port, or at the usual place for landing and taking in cargo, free from any immediate impending peril insured against. 1 Phil. Ins. 968; 3 Johns. (N. Y.) 88; 11 Johns. (N. Y.) 358; 2 Strange, 1243; 5 Mart. (La.) 637; 6 Mass. 313; Code de Comm. 152.

MOOT (from Saxon *gemot*, meeting together). In English law. A term used in the inns of court, signifying the exercise of arguing imaginary cases, which young barristers and students used to perform at certain times, the better to be enabled by this practice to defend their clients' cases. Orig. Jur. 212.

To plead a mock cause. Also spelled "meet," from Saxon *motain*, to meet; the sense of debate being from meeting, encountering. A moot question is one which has not been decided.

MOOT COURT. A court where moot questions are argued. Webster.

In law schools this is one of the methods of instruction. An undecided point of law is argued by students appointed as counsel on either side of the cause, one or more of the professors sitting as judge in presence of the school. The argument is conducted as in cases reserved for hearing before the full bench.

MOOT HILL. Hill of meeting (*gemot*), on which the Britons used to hold their courts, the judge sitting on the eminence, the parties, etc., on an elevated platform below. Enc. Lond.

MOOT MAN. One of those who used to argue the reader's cases in the inns of court.

MORA (Lat.) In the civil law. Delay; default; neglect; culpable delay or default. Calv. Lex.

MORA REPROBATUR IN LEGE. Delay is disapproved of in law. Jenk. Cent. Cas. 51.

MORAL CERTAINTY. This expression has been introduced into our jurisprudence from the publicists and metaphysicians, and signifies only a very high degree of probability. 118 Mass. 23.

That degree of certainty which will justify a jury in grounding on it their verdict. It is only probability; but it is called "certainty," because every sane man assents to it necessarily, from a habit produced by the necessity of acting. Nothing else but a strong presumption grounded on probable reasons, and which very seldom fails and deceives us. Puffendorff, Law Nat. bk. 1, c. 2, § 11. A reasonable and moral certainty; a certainty that convinces and directs the understanding, and satisfies the reason and judgment, of those who are bound to act conscientiously upon it. A certainty beyond a reasonable doubt. Shaw, C. J., Com. v. Webster, Bemis., Report of the trial, 469, 470. Such a certainty "as convinces beyond all reasonable doubt." Parke, B., Best, Pres. 257, note; 6 Rich. Eq. (S. C.) 217.

MORAL DURESS. Moral duress consists in imposition, oppression, undue, influence, or the taking of undue advantage of the business or financial stress or extreme necessities or weakness of another; the theory under which relief is granted being that the party profiting thereby has received money, property or other advantage, which in equity and good conscience he ought not to be permitted to retain. 164 Ill. App. 258; 114 Ill. App. 255.

MORAL FRAUD. Fraud involving actual turpitude, as distinguished from mere constructive fraud.

MORAL OBLIGATION. A duty which one owes, and which he ought to perform, but which he is not legally bound to fulfill.

These obligations are of two kinds: (1) Those founded on a natural right; as, the obligation to be charitable, which can never be enforced by law. (2) Those which are supported by a good or valuable antecedent consideration; as, where a man owes a debt barred by the act of limitations, this cannot be recovered by law, though it subsists in morality and conscience; but if the debtor promise to pay it, the moral obligation is a sufficient consideration for the promise, and the creditor may maintain an action of *assumpsit* to recover the money. 1 Bouv. Inst. note 623. See "Consideration."

MORARI (Lat.) In old English law. To delay; to pause or rest. *Moratur in lege*, (he) rests or pauses in law; (he) demurs.

MORBOSUS (Lat. from *morbus*). In the civil law. Diseased. See Dig. 21. 1. 1-16.

MORBUS SONTICUS (Lat.) In the civil law. A sickness which rendered a man incapable of attending to any business (*qui cuique rei nocet*). Dig. 50. 16. 113; 1 Mackeld. Civ. Law, 137, § 127, note. A sickness of the severer kind, having the power of causing great pain. A. Gellius, Noct. Att. lib. 20, c. 1. A sickness which excused a nonappearance in court. Calv. Lex.; Adams, Rom. Ant. 245, 272. Bracton uses this term in treating of the law of essoins, but gives it the meaning of an incurable disease. Bracton, fol. 344b.

MORE COLONICO (Lat.) In old pleading. In husbandlike manner. Towns. Pl. 108.

MORE OR LESS. Words, in a conveyance of lands or contract to convey lands, importing that the quantity is uncertain and not warranted, and that no right of either party under the contract shall be affected by a deficiency or excess in the quantity. 17 Ves. 394; Powell, Powers, 397. So in contracts of sale generally. 2 Barn. & Adol. 106.

MORGANATIC MARRIAGE. A lawful and inseparable conjunction of a single man of noble and illustrious birth with a single woman of an inferior or plebeian station, upon this condition, that neither the wife nor children should partake of the title, arms, or dignity of the husband, nor succeed to his inheritance, but should have a certain allowance assigned to them by the morganatic contract.

This relation was frequently contracted during the middle ages. The marriage ceremony was regularly performed, the union was for life and indissoluble and the children were considered legitimate, though they could not inherit. Fred. Code, bk. 2, art. 3; Poth. du Mar. 1, c 2, § 2; Shelf. Mar. & Div. 10; Pruss. Code, art. 835.

MORGANGIVA, or **MORGENGEBA** (Law Lat.; Lomb. *morgingap;* Saxon, *morgan gyfe;* from *morgin*, morning, and *gab*, a gift). In old European law. A gift made to a wife on the morning of the nuptial day; a species of dower, which Spelman compares to the English dower *ad ostium ecclesiae*. This word occurs in the laws of the Burgundians, Alemanni, Ripuarians, and Lombards, and also in the laws of Canute. LL. Canuti, c. 71. Spelman.

MORGEN (Anglo-Dutch). In old New York law. A measure of land, equal to about two acres. O'Callaghan's New Netherlands, vol. 2, Append. 593.

MORS (Lat.) Death.

MORS DICITUR ULTIMUM SUPPLICIum. Death is denominated the extreme penalty. 3 Inst. 212.

MORS OMNIA SOLVIT. Death dissolves all things.

MORT CIVILE. In French law. Civil death, as upon conviction for felony. It was nominally abolished by a law of the 31st of May, 1854, but something very similar to it, in effect, at least, still remains. Thus, the property of the condemned, possessed by him at the date of his conviction, goes and belongs to his successors (*heritiers*), as in case of an intestacy, and his future acquired property goes to the state by right of its prerogative (*par droit de desherence*), but the state may, as a matter of grace, make it over in whole or in part to the widow and children. Brown.

MORT D'ANCESTOR. An ancient and now almost obsolete remedy in the English law. An assize of *mort d'ancestor* was a writ which was sued out where, after the decease of a man's ancestor, a stranger abated, and entered into the estate. Co. Litt. 159. The remedy in such case is now to bring ejectment.

MORTALITY. The word "mortality" may, under certain circumstances, include every description of death, every termination of life to which mortals are subject. It applies generally, however, to that description of death which is not occasioned by violent means. 5 B. & Ald. 110, 112; 3 B. & C. 793.

MORTALITY (or **MORTUARY**) **TABLES.** Tables showing the duration of human life, as based on observations and records of vital statistics. The records of deaths kept at certain places for long periods form the basis of the tables more commonly known as "Carlisle Tables," or "Northampton Tables" (*q. v.*)

MORTGAGE. The conveyance of an estate or property by way of pledge for the security of debt, and to become void on payment of it. 4 Kent, Comm. 136.

An estate created by a conveyance absolute in its form, but intended to secure the performance of some act, such as the payment of money, and the like, by the grantor or some other person, and to become void if the act is performed agreeably to the terms prescribed at the time of making such conveyance. 1 Washb. Real Prop. 475.

By the law of several states, a mortgage is no longer a conveyance by which an estate passes, but a mere pledge creating only a lien. Holmes, Mortg. § 1.

Two general theories prevail as to the nature of the estate created by mortgage. The common-law theory that a mortgage passes title to the mortgagee subject to defeat by the performance of the condition subsequent has been adopted in Alabama (69 Ala. 442), Arkansas (65 Ark. 174), Connecticut (19 Conn. 218), Illinois (1 Scam. 140), Maine (2 Me. 132), Maryland (6 Gill & J. 72), Massachusetts (5 Mass. 120), New Hampshire (5 N. H.) 420), North Carolina (66 N. C. 477), Ohio (10 Ohio, 71), Pennsylvania (77 Pa. St. 250), Rhode Island (6 R. I. 542), Tennessee (10 Humph. 214), and Virginia (4 Rand. 245).

The common-law theory, in a somewhat modified form, prevails in Delaware (1 Houst. 320), Mississippi (24 Miss. 368), Missouri (10 Mo. 229), New Jersey (40 N. J. Law, 417), and Vermont (44 Vt. 294).

The equitable doctrine that a mortgage conveys only a lien is adopted in California (2 Cal. 491; 64 Cal. 514), Colorado (Laws 1887, § 263, p. 174), Florida (17 Fla. 698), Georgia (76 Ga. 384), Idaho (Rev. St. 1887, § 3350), Indiana (27 Ind. 472), Iowa (30 Iowa, 268), Kansas (35 Kan. 120), Kentucky (14 Bush, 788), Michigan (65 Mich. 598), Minnesota (12 Minn. 330), Montana (6 Mont. 596), Nebraska (14 Neb. 246), Nevada (1 Nev. 179), New York (54 N. Y. 599), North Dakota (Rev. Code, § 1733), Oregon (11 Or. 534), South Carolina (27 S. C. 309), South Dakota (Rev. Code 1877, § 1733), Utah (Comp. Laws 1876, p. 478), Washington (3 Wash. T. 318), Wisconsin (7 Wis. 566), 1 Pingrey, Mortg. 16.

Both real and personal property may be mortgaged, and in substantially the same manner, except that, a mortgage being in its nature a transfer of title, the laws respecting the necessity of possession of personal property and the nature of instruments of transfer, being different, require the transfer to be made differently in the two cases. See "Chattel Mortgage."

A mortgage may in form be either a conveyance with provision for a defeasance, or a conveyance absolute in form, with a collateral agreement for a defeasance. 15 Johns. (N. Y.) 555; 2 Me. 152; 12 Mass. 456.

An equitable mortgage is one in which the mortgagor does not actually convey the property, but does some act by which he manifests his determination to bind the same as a security. See "Equitable Mortgage."

A legal mortgage is a conveyance of property intended by the parties at the time of making it to be a security for the performance of some prescribed act. 1 Washb. Real Prop. 479.

MORTGAGE OF GOODS. A conveyance of goods in gage, or mortgage, by which the whole legal title passes conditionally to the mortgagee; and if the goods are not redeemed at the time stipulated, the title becomes absolute in law, although equity will interfere to compel a redemption. Story, Bailm. § 287. It is distinguished from a pledge by the circumstance that possession by the pledgee is not, or may not be, essential to create or to support the title. Id. See 2 Kent, Comm. 522-532; 4 Kent, Comm. 138.

MORTGAGEE. He to whom a mortgage is made. See "Mortgage."

MORTGAGOR. He who makes a mortgage. See "Mortgage."

MORTH (Saxon). Murder, answering exactly to the French "*assassinat*" or "*meurtre de guet-apens.*"

MORTHLAGA. A murderer. Cowell.

MORTHLAGE. Murder. Cowell.

MORTIFICATION. In Scotch law: A term nearly synonymous with "mortmain."

MORTIS CAUSA (Lat.) By reason of death; in contemplation of death. Thus used in the phrase, *donatio mortis causa* (*q. v.*)

MORTIS MOMENTUM EST ULTIMUM vitae momentum. The last moment of life is the moment of death. 4 Bradf. Sur. (N. Y.) 245, 250.

MORTMAIN. Mortmain, so called by resemblance to a man in his last moments, who holds whatever he takes in his hand *mortuo manu*, that is, so fast that he never quits it until he is dead. Plowden 193.

A term applied to denote the possession of lands or tenements by any corporation, sole or aggregate, ecclesiastical or temporal. These purchases having been chiefly made by religious houses, in consequence of which lands became perpetually inherent in one dead hand, this has occasioned the general appellation of "mortmain" to be applied to such alienations. 2 Bl. Comm. 268; Co. Litt. 2b; Ersk. Inst. 2. 4. 10; Barr. Obs. St. 27, 97. See Story, Eq. Jur. § 1137; Shelf. Mortm.

MORTMAIN ACTS. These acts had for their object to prevent lands getting into the possession or control of religious corporations, or, as the name indicates, *in mortua manu.* After numerous prior acts dating from the reign of Edward I., it was enacted by St. 9 Geo. II. c. 36 (called the "Mortmain Act" *par excellence*), that no lands should be given to charities unless certain requisites should be observed. Brown.

MORTUARY. In ecclesiastical law. A burial place. A kind of ecclesiastical heriot, being a customary gift of the second-best living animal belonging to the deceased, claimed by and due to the minister in many parishes, on the death of his parishioners, whether buried in the church yard or not. These mortuaries, like lay heriots, were originally voluntary bequests to the church in lieu of tithes or ecclesiastical dues neglected in lifetime. See "Soulscot." They were reduced to a certain amount by 21 Hen. VIII. c. 6. They were sometimes payable to the lord. Par. Ant. 470. The mortuary seems to have been carried to church with the corpse, and was therefore sometimes called corpse present. 2 Burn, Ecc. Law, 563. Anciently, a parishioner could not make a valid will without an assignment of a sufficient mortuary or gift to the church. 2 Bl. Comm. 427.

MORTUUM VADIUM. A mortgage.

MORTUUS (Lat.) Dead. Ainsworth. So in sheriff's return *mortuus est*, he is dead. O. Bridg. 469; Brooke, Abr. "Retórne de Briefe," pl. 125; 19 Viner, Abr. "Return," lib. 2, pl. 12.

MORTUUS EXITUS NON EST EXITAS. To be dead-born is not to be born. Co. Litt. 29. See 2 Paige, Ch. (N. Y.) 35; Domat, liv, prel. tit. 2 § 1, note 4, 6; 2 Bouv. Inst. notes 1721, 1935.

MOS RETINENDUS EST FIDELISSIMAE vetustatis. A custom of the truest antiquity is to be retained. 4 Coke, 78.

MOSTRENCOS. In Spanish law. Strayed goods; estrays. White, New Recop. bk. 2, tit. 2, c. 6.

MOT BELL (Saxon). Meeting bell; a bell used by the Saxons to summon the people to the *folc mote.* Spelman. See "Folc Mote."

MOTE (Saxon). A meeting; an assembly. Used in composition, as burgmote, folkmote, etc.

MOTEER. The customary payment at the court (*mote*) of a feudal lord.

MOTION. In practice. An application to a court by one of the parties in a cause, or his counsel, in order to obtain some rule or order of court which he thinks becomes necessary in the progress of the cause, or to get relieved in a summary manner from some matter which would work injustice. Properly, an oral application for a rule or order (41 Cal. 650), but the term is now generally applied to applications, whether written or oral.

MOTION FOR NEW TRIAL. A motion designed to bring in review before the trial court the occurrences of the trial, and to present for consideration alleged errors during the course of the trial. 217 Ill. 82, 177 Ill. 333.

MOTIVE. (from Lat. *movere*, to move or stir). In the law of evidence. That which moves or influences the mind or will; an emotion, passion, or desire which incites or impels to action.

——**In Criminal Evidence.** An unlawful desire or emotion, awakened by the perception or contemplation of some external object, or end to be attained by action. This ultimate object is, in fact, the cause or spring of the motive itself, and has sometimes been called the "exterior" or "external" motive, as distinguished from the desire or passion it creates, which is termed the "interior" or "internal" motive. See 3 Benth. Jud. Ev. 183. It is, in other words, the inducement, or that which leads or tempts the mind to indulge the criminal desire. Burrill, Circ. Ev. 283, 284.

MOTWORTHY (Old Eng.) A common councilman. Cowell, voc. "Concionator."

MOURNING. The apparel worn at funerals, and for a time afterwards, in order to manifest grief for the death of some one, and to honor his memory.

The expenses paid for such apparel.

It has been held, in England, that a demand for mourning furnished to the widow and family of the testator is not a funeral expense. 2 Car. & P. 207. See 14 Ves. 346; 1 Ves. & B. 364. See 2 Bell. Comm. 156.

MOVABLES. Such subjects of property as attend a man's person wherever he goes, in contradistinction to things immovable.

Things movable by their nature are such as may be carried from one place to another, whether they move themselves, as cattle, or cannot be removed without an extraneous power, as inanimate things. So in the civil law *mobilia;* but this term did not properly include living movables, which were termed *moventia.* Calv. Lex. But these words, *mobilia* and *moventia,* are also used synonymously, and in the general sense of "movables." Id. Movables are further distinguished into such as are in possession, or which are in the power of the owner, as a horse in actual use, a piece of furniture in a man's own house, or such as are in possession of another, and can only be recovered by action, which are therefore said to be in action, as a debt. See "Personal Property;" Fonbl. Eq. Index; Powell, Mortg. Index; 2 Bl. Comm. 384; Civ. Code La. arts. 464-472; 1 Bouv. Inst. note 462; 2 Steph. Comm. 67; Shep. Touch. 447; 1 P. Wms. 267.

In a will, "movables" is used in its largest sense, but will not pass growing crop, nor building materials on ground. 2 Williams, Ex'rs, 1014; 3 A. K. Marsh. (Ky.) 123; 1 Yeates (Pa.) 101; 2 Dall. (Pa.) 142.

——**In Scotch Law.** Every right which a man can hold which is not heritable. Opposed to "heritage." Bell, Dict.

MOVANT. One who moves; one who makes a motion before a court; the applicant for a rule or order.

MOVING FOR AN ARGUMENT. Making a motion on a day which is not motion day, in virtue of having argued a special case; used in the exchequer after it became obsolete in the queen's bench. Wharton.

MR. The word "Mr." indicates only a man. 15 Ill. App. 103.

MRS. The designation "Mrs." is not a name but usually distinguishes the person referred to as a married woman. 240 Ill. 110.

MUEBLES. In Spanish law. Movables; all sorts of personal property. White, New Recop. bk. 1, tit. 3, c. 1, § 2.

MUIRBURN. In Scotch law. The offense of setting fire to a muir or moor. 1 Brown, Ch. 78, 116.

MULATTO. A person born of one white and one black parent. 7 Mass. 88; 2 Bailey (S. C.) 558.

MULCT. A fine imposed on the conviction of an offense.

An imposition laid on ships or goods by a company of trade for the maintenance of consuls and the like. It is obsolete in the latter sense, and but seldom used in the former.

MULCTA DAMNUM FAMAE NON IRROgat. A fine does not impose a loss of reputation. Code, 1. 54; Calv. Lex.

MULIER. Of ancient time, "mulier" was taken for a wife, as it is commonly used for a woman, and sometimes for a widow; but it has been held that a virgin is included under the name "mulier." Co. Litt. 170, 243; 2 Bl. Comm. 248.

The term is used always in contradistinction to a bastard, *mulier* being always legitimate (Co. Litt. 243), and seems to be a word corrupted from *melior*, or the French *meilleur*, signifying lawful issue born in wedlock. But by Glanville, lawful issue are said to be *mulier*, not from *melior*, but because begotten *e muliere* and not *ex concubina*, for he calls such issue *filios mulieratos*, opposing them to bastards. Glanv. lib. 7, c. 1. If the said lands "should, according to the queen's lawes, descend to the right heire, then in right it ought to descend to him, as next heire being *mulierlie* borne, and the other not so borne." Holinshead, Chron. Ireland, an. 1558.

MULIER PUISNE (Law Fr.) When a man has a bastard son, and afterwards marries the mother, and by her has also a legitimate son, the elder son is *bastard eigne*, and the younger son is *mulier puisne*.

MULTA CONCEDUNTUR PER OBLIQUUM quae non conceduntur de directo. Many things are conceded indirectly which are not allowed directly. 6 Coke, 47.

MULTA FIDEM PROMISSA LEVANT. Many promises lessen confidence. 11 Cush. (Mass.) 350.

MULTA IGNORAMUS QUAE NOBIS non laterent si veterum lectio nobis fuit familiaris. We are ignorant of many things which would not be hidden from us if the reading of old authors were familiar to us. 10 Coke, 73.

MULTA IN JURE COMMUNI CONTRA rationem disputandi pro communi utilitate introducta sunt. Many things have been introduced into the common law, with a view to the public good, which are inconsistent with sound reason. Co. Litt. 70; Broom, Leg. Max. (3d London Ed.) 150; 2 Coke, 75. See 3 Term R. 146; 7 Term R. 252.

MULTA MULTO EXERCITATIONE FAcilius quam regulis percipes. You will perceive many things much more easily by practice than by rules. 4 Inst. 50.

MULTA NON VETAT LEX, QUAE TAmen tacite damnavit. The law fails to forbid many things which yet it has silently condemned.

MULTA TRANSEUNT CUM UNIVERSItate quae non per se transeunt. Many things pass as a whole which would not pass separately. Co. Litt. 12a.

MULTI MULTA; NEMO OMNIA NOVIT. Many men know many things; no one knows everything. 4 Inst. 348.

MULTI UTILIUS EST PAUCA IDONEA effundere, quam multis inutilibus homines gravari. It is much more useful to pour forth a few useful things than to oppress men with many useless things. 4 Coke, 20.

MULTIFARIOUSNESS. In equity pleading. The demand in one bill of several matters of a distinct and independent nature against several defendants. Cooper, Eq. Pl. 182; 18 Ves. 80; 2 Mason (U. S.) 201; 4 Cow. (N. Y.) 682; 2 Gray (Mass.) 467.

The uniting in one bill against a single defendant several matters perfectly distinct and unconnected. This latter is more properly called "misjoinder" (*q. v.*)

The subject admits of no general rules, but the courts seem to consider the circumstances of each case with reference to avoiding on one hand a multiplicity of suits, and on the other inconvenience and hardship to the defendants from being obliged to answer matters with which they have, in great part, no connection, and the complication and confusion of evidence. 1 Mylne & C. 618; 5 Sim. 288; 3 Story, C. C. (U. S.) 25; 2 Gray (Mass.) 471; Story, Eq. Pl. §§ 274, 530. It is to be taken advantage of by demurrer (2 Anstr. 469), or by plea and answer previous to a hearing (Story, Eq. Pl. 530, note), or by the court of its own acccod at any time (1 Myline & K. 546; 3 How. [U. S.] 412; 5 How. [U. S.] 127). See, generally, Story, Eq. Pl. §§ 274-290, 530-540; 4 Bouv. Inst. note 4243.

MULTIPLE POINDING. In Scotch law. Double distress; a name given to an action which may be brought by a person in possession of goods claimed by different persons pretending a right thereto, calling the claimants and all others to settle their claims, so that the party who sues may be liable only "in once and single payment." Bell, Dict.; 2 Bell, Comm. 299; Stair, Inst. 3. 1. 39.

MULTIPLEX ET INDISTINCTUM PARIT confusionem; et questiones quo simpliciores, eo lucidiores. Multiplicity and indistinctness produce confusion; the more simple questions are, the more lucid they are. Hob. 335.

MULTIPLICATA TRANSGRESSIONE crescat poenae inflicto. The infliction of punishment should be in proportion to the increase of crime. 2 Inst. 479.

MULTIPLICITY (from Lat. *multiplex*, from *multus*, many, and *plicare*, to fold). A state of being many. Webster. That quality of a pleading which involves a variety of matters or particulars; undue variety. 2 Saund. 410.

A multiplying or increasing. Story, Eq. Pl. § 287.

MULTIPLICITY OF SUITS. A multiplicity of suits does not mean a multitude of suits. It does not apply to a situation where each of several parties jointly and severally liable may be independently sued, but where one party may be sued several times in relation to the same subject matter, in its entirety or in respect to some element or elements thereof. 133 Wis. 561.

MULTITUDE. The meaning of this word is not very certain. By some it is said that, to make a multitude, there must be ten persons, at least, while others contend that the law has not fixed any number. Co. Litt. 257.

MULTITUDINEM DECEM FACIUNT. Ten make a multitude. Co. Litt. 247.

MULTITUDO ERRANTIUM NON PARIT errori patrocinium. The multitude of those who err is no protection for error. 11 Coke, 75.

MULTITUDO IMPERITORUM PERDIT curiam. A multitude of ignorant practitioners destroys a court. 2 Inst. 219.

MULTURE (Law Lat. *multura, molitura,* from *molere,* to grind). In old English law. A grinding of grain at a mill; the grain ground.

The toll or fee due for grinding grain. 2 Mon. Angl. 825; Cowell. Called *multer* in an old award. 28 Hen. IV. cited by Blount.

——**In Scotch Law.** A duty paid for grinding in any mill. 1 Forbes, Inst. pt. 2, p. 140. A quantity of grain payable to the proprietor of a mill for grinding grain. Bell, Dict.

MUND. Peace.

MUNDBRYE. A breach of the peace.

MUNERA. The name given to grants made in the early feudal ages, which were merely tenancies at will, or during the pleasure of the grantor. Dalr. Feud. Prop. 198, 199; Wright, Ten. 19.

MUNICEPS (Lat. from *munus,* office, and *capere,* to take). In Roman law. Eligible to office.

A freeman born in a municipality or town other than Rome, who had come to Rome, and, though a Roman citizen, yet was looked down upon as a provincial, and not allowed to hold the higher offices (*dignitates.*)

The inhabitants of a municipality entitled to hold municipal offices. Vocat; Calv. Lex.

MUNICIPAL. Strictly, this word applies only to what belongs to a city.

Among the Romans, cities were called *municipia.* These cities voluntarily joined the Roman republic in relation to their sovereignty only, retaining their laws, their liberties, and their magistrates, who were thence called "municipal magistrates." With us this word has a more extensive meaning; for example, we call "municipal law" not the law of a city only, but the law of the state. 1 Bl. Comm. "Municipal" is used in contradistinction to "international." Thus, we say, an offense against the law of nations is an international offense, but one committed against a particular state or separate community is a municipal offense.

MUNICIPAL AID. A contribution of money, lands, municipal bonds, etc., by a municipality to some private enterprise deemed to be of general benefit, to procure or encourage the construction thereof.

MUNICIPAL CORPORATION. A public corporation, created by government for political purposes, and having subordinate and local powers of legislation; *e. g.,* a county, town, city, etc. 2 Kent, Comm. 275; Angell & A. Corp. 9, 29; 1 Baldw. (U. S.) 222.

An incorporation of persons, inhabitants of a particular place, or connected with a particular district, enabling them to conduct its local civil government. Glover, Mun. Corp. 1.

The incorporation, by authority of the government, of the inhabitants of a particular place, and authorizing them, in their corporate capacity, to exercise certain specified powers with respect to their local government. Dill. Mun. Corp. § 2.

In modern usage, the term is somewhat narrower, and is generally confined to bodies politic, specially organized or chartered, and excluding the ordinary political divisions of the state. In this sense, it includes cities and villages, but excludes counties, townships, or school districts. 44 Wis. 489; 34 Iowa, 84; 52 Mo. 309. But see 36 Minn. 430.

——**In English Law.** A body of persons in a town having the powers of acting as one person, of holding and transmitting property, and of regulating the government of the town. Such corporations existed in the chief towns of England (as of other countries) from very early times, deriving their authority from "incorporating" charters granted by the crown. Wharton.

MUNICIPAL CORPORATIONS ACT. In English law. A general statute (5 & 6 Wm. IV. c. 76), passed in 1835, prescribing general regulations for the incorporation and government of boroughs.

MUNICIPAL COURTS. Courts whose jurisdiction extends only to the limits of a municipality. They are sometimes so called in the statutes creating them, but sometimes have other designations.

MUNICIPAL LAW. In contradistinction to international law is the system of law proper to any single nation or state. It is the rule or law by which a particular district, community, or nation is governed. 1 Bl. Comm. 44.

Municipal law contrasts with international law, in that it is a system of law proper to a single nation, state, or community. In any one state, the municipal law of another state is foreign law. A conflict of laws arises where a case arising in one state involves foreign persons or interests, and the foreign and the domestic law do not agree as to the proper rule to be applied.

The various provinces of municipal law are characterized according to the subjects with which they respectively treat; as, "criminal or penal law," "civil law," "military law," and the like. "Constitutional law," "commercial law," "parliamentary law," and the like, are departments of the general province of civil law, as distinguished from criminal and military law.

MUNICIPAL ORDINANCE. An ordinance of a municipal corporation.

MUNICIPAL SECURITIES. Municipal securities are evidences of municipal indebtedness issued by the municipality.

They are of two general classes:

(1) Municipal bonds, being written and usually sealed obligations executed by the proper officers of the municipality, binding it to pay a specified sum at a particular time. Such bonds are ordinarily negotiable.

(2) Municipal warrants, being instruments generally in the form of a bill of exchange drawn by a municipal officer, upon the treasurer directing him to pay a specified amount to a person named, or to bearer.

MUNICIPALITY. The body of officers, taken collectively, belonging to a city, who are appointed to manage its affairs, and defend its interests.

MUNICIPIUM (Lat. from *munus*, office or honor, and *capere*, to take).

——**In Roman Law.** A foreign town to which the freedom of the city of Rome was granted, and whose inhabitants had the privilege of enjoying offices and honors there; a free town. Butler, Hor. Jur. 29; Adams, Rom. Ant. 47, 77.

A free or privileged town; one that had the right of being governed by its own laws and customs. Id. 77. Hence the Latin *municipalis*, and English "municipal" (*q. v.*)

——**In Old English Law.** A castle. Spelman.

MUNIMENTS. The instruments of writing and written evidences which the owner of lands, possessions, or inheritances has, by which he is enabled to defend the title of his estate. Termes de la Ley; 3 Inst. 170.

MUNUS. A gift; an office; a benefice, or feud; a gladiatorial show or spectacle. Calv. Lex.; Du Cange.

MUR, or **MURE** (Law Fr. from *murus*). A wall. *Par mure ou par haye*, by a wall or by a hedge. Britt. c. 61. *Mur abatu*, a wall beaten or thrown down. Id.

MURAGE. A toll formerly levied in England for repairing or building public walls. St. Westminster I. c. 30.

MURAL MONUMENTS. Monuments made in walls.

Owing to the difficulty or impossibility of removing them, secondary evidence may be given of inscriptions on walls, fixed tables, gravestones, and the like. 2 Starkie, 274.

MURDER. In criminal law. The willful killing of any subject whatever, with malice aforethought, whether the person slain shall be an Englishman or a foreigner. Hawk. P. C. bk. 1, c. 13, § 3. Russell says, the killing of any person under the king's peace, with malice prepense or aforethought, either express or implied by law. 1 Russ. Crimes, 421; 5 Cush. (Mass.) 304. When a person of sound mind and discretion unlawfully killeth any reasonable creature in being, and under the king's peace, with malice aforethought, either express or implied. 3 Inst. 47.

This latter definition, which has been adopted by Blackstone (4 Comm. 195), Chitty (2 Crim. Law, 724), and others, has been severely criticized. What, it has been asked, are "sound memory and understanding?" What has soundness of memory to do with the act? Be it ever so imperfect, how does it affect the guilt? If discretion is necessary, can the crime ever be committed? For is it not the highest indiscretion in a man to take the life of another, and thereby expose his own? If the person killed be an idiot or a new-born infant, is he a reasonable creature? Who is in the king's peace? What is malice aforethought? Can there be any malice afterthought? Livingston, Pen. Law, 186. It is, however, apparent that some of the criticisms are merely verbal, and others are answered by the construction given in the various cases to the requirements of the definition. See, especially, 5 Cush. (Mass.) 304.

According to Coke's definition, there must be: First, sound mind and memory in the agent. By this is understood there must be a will and legal discretion. Second, an actual killing; but it is not necessary that it should be caused by direct violence; it is sufficient if the acts done apparently endanger life and eventually prove fatal. Hawk. P. C. bk. 1, c. 31, § 4; 1 Hale, P. C. 431; 1 Ashm. (Pa.) 289; 9 Car. & P. 356; 2 Palmer, 545. Third, the party killed must have been a reasonable being, alive and in the king's peace. To constitute a birth, so as to make the killing of a child murder, the whole body must be detached from that of the mother; but if it has come wholly forth, but is still connected by the umbilical cord, such killing will be murder. 2 Bouv. Inst. note 1722. Foeticide would not be such a killing; he must have been *in rerum natura*. Fourth, malice, either express or implied. It is this circumstance which distingushes murder from every description of homicide. See "Malice."

In some of the states, by legislative enactments, murder has been divided into degrees, according to the degree of premeditation.

MURDRARE (Law Lat.) In old criminal law. To murder. 3 Bl. Comm. 321. *Murdravit*, murdered. A necessary word in old indictments for murder. 4 Bl. Comm. 307; 5 Coke, 122b; Lord Kenyon, 2 East, 30.

To hide, conceal, or stifle. *Nullam veritatem celabo, nec celari permittam, vel murdrari*, I will conceal no truth, nor will I permit it to be concealed or stifled. Fleta, lib. 1, c. 18, § 4. Words of the oath of an inquisitor or juror. And see Id. §§ 8, 10.

MURDRE (Law Fr.) Murder. LL. Gul. Conq. lib. 26.

A fine so called. Id. See "Murdrum."

MURDRITOR (Law Lat. from *murdrare*, *q. v.*) In old English law. A murderer. *Murdritores*, murderers. Bracton, fol. 115b.

MURDRUM. In old English law. During the times of the Danes, and afterwards till the reign of Edward III., murdrum was the killing of a man in a secret manner, and in that it differed from simple homicide.

When a man was thus killed, and he was unknown, by the laws of Canute he was presumed to be a Dane, and the vill was compelled to pay forty marks for his death. After the Conquest, a similar law was made in favor of Frenchmen, which was abolished by 3 Edw. III.

The fine formerly imposed in England upon a person who had committed homicide *per infortunium* or *se defendendo*. Prin. Pen. Law 219, note (r).

MURORUM OPERATIO. The service of work and labor done by inhabitants and adjoining tenants in building or repairing the walls of a city or castle; their personal service was commuted into *murage* (*q. v.*) Cowell.

MURTHRUM. In old Scotch law. Murther or murder. Skene de Verb. Sign.

MUSEUM. By tracing the Greek word from which "museum" is derived to its root it is found to signify amusement, or to amuse; and thus, the term museum would appear to embrace not only collections of curiosities for the entertainment of the sight, but also such as would interest, amuse and instruct the mind. But see Webster. 5 Stev. & Port. (Ala.) 109.

MUSTER ROLL. In maritime law. A list or account of a ship's company, required to be kept by the master or other person having care of the ship, containing the names, ages, national character, and quality of every person employed in the ship. Abb. Shipp. 191, 192; Jacobsen, Sea Laws, 161.

MUSTIZO. A name given to the issue of an Indian and a negro. Dudley (S. C.) 174.

MUTA CANUM (Law Lat.) In old English law. A pack of hounds. Spelman. See 2 How. St. Tr. 1164.

MUTATIO NOMINIS (Lat.) In the civil law. Change of name. Code, 9. 25.

MUTATION. In French law. This term is synonymous with "change," and is particularly applied to designate the change which takes place in the property of a thing in its transmission from one person to another. Permutation therefore happens when the owner of the thing sells, exchanges, or gives it. It is nearly synonymous with transfer. Merlin, Repert.

MUTATION OF LIBEL. In practice. An amendment allowed to a libel, by which there is an alteration of the substance of the libel, as by propounding a new cause of action, or asking one thing istead of another. Dunl. Adm. Prac. 213; Law, Ecc. Law, 165-167; 1 Paine (U. S.) 435; 1 Gall. (U. S.) 123; 1 Wheat. (U. S.) 261.

MUTATIS MUTANDIS (Lat.) The necessary changes. This is a phrase of frequent practical occurrence, meaning that matters or things are generally the same, but to be altered when necessary, as to names, offices, and the like.

MUTE (Lat. *mutus*). See "Standing Mute."

MUTILATION. In criminal law. The depriving a man of the use of any of those limbs which may be useful to him in fight, the loss of which amounts to mayhem. 1 Bl. Comm. 130.

MUTINY. In criminal law. The unlawful resistance to a superior officer, or the raising of commotions and disturbances on board of a ship against the authority of its commander, or in the army in opposition to the authority of the officers; a sedition; a revolt.

MUTINY ACT. In English law. A statute, annually passed, to punish mutiny and desertion, and for the better payment of the army and their quarters. It was first passed April 12, 1689. See 22 Vict. cc. 4, 5. The passage of this bill is the only provision for the payment of the army, and, like our appropriation bills, it must be passed, or the wheels of government will be stopped. There is a similar act with regard to the navy. 1 Bl. Comm. 416, 417, note.

MUTUAL. Reciprocal; reciprocally giving and receiving. Applied to contracts and relations by which reciprocal duties are imposed.

MUTUAL ACCOUNT. See "Account."

MUTUAL AND OPEN ACCOUNT CURrent. A mutual and open account current is one consisting of credits as well as debits between the parties. 73 W. 545.

MUTUAL CONTRACT. To constitute a mutual contract both parties must be bound. Without this reciprocal obligation no contract can be constituted. If for any reason a contract cannot be enforced against one party, that party is incapable of enforcing it against the other. 157 Ill. 342.

MUTUAL CREDITS. Credits given by two persons mutually, *i. e.*, each giving credit to the other. It is a more extensive phrase than "mutual debts." Thus, the sum credited by one may be due at once; that by the other payable *in futuro;* yet the credits are mutual, though the transaction would not come within the meaning of mutual debts. 1 Atk. 230; 7 Term R. 378. And it is not necessary that there should be intent to trust each other. Thus, where an acceptance of A. came into the hands of B. who bought goods of A., not knowing the acceptance to be in B.'s hands, it was held a mutual credit. 3 Term R. 507, note; 4 Term R. 211; 3 Ves. 65; 8 Taunt. 156, 499; 1 Holt, 408; 2

Smith, Lead. Cas. 179; 26 Barb. (N. Y.) 310; 4 Gray (Mass.) 284.

MUTUAL INSURANCE. A form of life insurance in which the insurer is an association in which all the policy holders are members, and the losses are met by assessments levied upon the members either periodically, or as the exigency arises. See 50 Miss. 662.

MUTUAL MISTAKE. The phrase "mutual mistake," as used in equity, means a mistake common to all the parties to a written contract or instrument, and it usually relates to a mistake concerning the contents or the legal effect of the contract or instrument. 150. Mass. 30. See "Mistake."

MUTUAL PROMISES. Promises simultaneously made by two parties to each other, each promise being the consideration of the other. Hob. 88; 14 Mees. & W. 855; Add. Cont. 22. If one of the promises be voidable, it will yet be good consideration; but not if void. Story, Cont. § 81; 2 Steph. Comm. 114.

MUTUALITY. Reciprocity; acting in return. Add. Cont. 622; 26 Md. 37. See "Consideration."

MUTUANT. The person who lends chattels in the contract of *mutuum* (*q. v.*)

MUTUARI. To borrow; *mutuatus*, a borrowing. 2 Archb. Prac. 25.

MUTUARY. A person who borrows personal chattels to be consumed by him, and returned to the lender in kind; the person who receives the benefit arising from the contract of *mutuum*. Story, Bailm. § 47.

MUTUS (Lat.) In civil and old English law. Dumb; mute; a dumb person. Dig. 50. 17. 124; Inst. 3. 20. 7; Fleta, lib. 2, c. 56, § 19. *Mutus et surdus*, dumb and deaf. Cro. Jac. 105.

MUTUUM. A loan of personal chattels to be consumed by the borrower, and to be returned to the lender in kind and quantity; as, a loan of corn, wine, or money, which are to be used or consumed, and are to be replaced by other corn, wine, or money. Story, Bailm. § 228. See "Loan for Consumption"; "Loan and Use."

MY (Law Fr.) Half; middle. *En my leu*, in the middle place; in the middle. Britt. c. 119. *Per my et per tout*, by the half or moiety, and by all. 2 Bl. Comm. 182.

MYALGIA. A nervous disease affecting the muscles. 244 Ill. 342.

MYELITIS. Inflammation of the spinal cord. 193 Ill. 279; 41 Ill. App. 273.

MYNUTE (Law Fr.) Midnight. Britt. c. 80.

MYS (Law Fr. from *mitter*, to put). Put; sent; put in or inserted. *Mys a lour penaunce*, put to their penance. Britt. c. 4. *Mys en ferges*, put in irons. Id. c. 11. *P'oles mys en escritz*, words put in writings. Id. c. 39. *Que date soit mys del jour*, that a date be put in of the day. Id. *Mys en la gaole*. Id. c. 100. *Mys en certaine*, put in certain. Dyer, 55b.

MYSTERY (said to be derived from the French *mestier*, now written *metier*, a trade). A trade, art, or occupation. 2 Inst. 668.

Masters frequently bind themselves in the indentures with their apprentices to teach them their art, trade, and mystery. See Hawk. P. C. c. 23, § 11.

MYSTIC TESTAMENT. A will under seal. 5 Mart. (La.) 182; 5 La. 396; 10 La. 328; 15 La. 88.

So called from the fact that it is sealed up or enclosed by the testator before attestation. Civ. Code La. arts. 1567, 1584.

N

N. An abbreviation of *Novellæ*, the Novels of Justinian; used in citing them. Tayl. Civ. Law, 24.

N. E. I. An abbreviation for *non est inventus* (*q. v.*)

N. L. An abbreviation of *non liquet* (*q. v.*)

NACION. (L. Fr.) Birth; origin.

NAIF (Law Fr.; Law Lat. *nativus*, a born slave). A villein; a born slave (*nee serfe*). Britt. c. 31; LL. Gul. Conq. lib. 33.

NAKED. As used in legal phrases, the term means either without consideration or legal formality, or without support or corroboration.

NAKED CONFESSION. A confession of crime unsupported by extrinsic evidence showing the commission of the crime.

NAKED POWER. A right, power or authority disconnected from any interest or estate of the donee in the subject-matter to which it relates. 1 Caines Cas. (N. Y.) 15; 47 Miss. 534.

NAKED TRUST. A passive trust.

NAM, or NAAM.

——**In Old English Law.** The taking of a pledge; a distress. A component part of the word "withernam" (*q. v.*)

——**In Latin Phrases.** For. Used as introductory to the quotation of a maxim, and sometimes erroneously treated as part of the maxim itself.

NAMARE (Law Lat.) To take; to distrain. Spelman. The derivatives *namptus* and *namptum* were also used.

NAMATO (Law Lat.) In old English and Scotch law. A distraining or taking of a distress; an impounding. Spelman.

The English namation is given by Cowell and Blount.

NAME. One or more words habitually used to distinguish a particular individual.

A letter of the alphabet does not constitute a name. 232 Ill. 228.

The name of a person consists, among Anglo-Saxon peoples, of one family name, surname, or patronymic, by which all members of the immediate family are known, and one Christian, baptismal, or surname bestowed upon one by his parents, to distinguish him from others of the same family. 5 Robt. 599.

Only one Christian name is recognized in law, and for all legal purposes the use of a middle name is surplusage. 31 Minn. 385; 78 Iowa, 519; 39 Barb. (N. Y.) 479.

For all practical and legal purposes, the name by which a person is known and called in the community in which he lives and is best known, is his name. 149 Iowa 672, 31 L. R. A. (N. S.) 1112.

The word "junior" or "jr" forms no part of a person's name, but is merely descriptive. 182 Ill. 424; 192 Ill. 184.

NAME AND ARMS CLAUSE. The popular name in English law for the clause, sometimes inserted in a will or settlement by which property is given to a person, for the purpose of imposing on him the condition that he shall assume the surname and arms of the testator or settlor, with a direction that if he neglects to assume or discontinues the use of them, the estate shall devolve on the next person in remainder, and a provision for preserving contingent remainders. 3 Dav. Prec. Conv. 277.

NAMELY. In a strict grammatical sense a difference exists between "namely" and "including." The former imports interpretation, *i. e.*, indicates what is included in the previous term; but "including" imports addition, *i. e.*, indicates something not included. 1 Jarm. 753; 2 Jarm. 229; 14 Bea. 626; as to its antecedents, Dy. 77b, pl. 38; Hob. 173.

NAMIUM. An old word which signifies the taking or distraining another person's movable goods. 2 Inst. 140; 3 Bl. Comm. 149. A distress. Dalr. Feud. Prop. 113.

NAMIUM VETITUM. An unjust taking of the cattle of another, and driving them to an unlawful place, pretending damage done by them. 3 Bl. Comm. 149.

NARR (an abbreviation of the word *narratio*). A declaration in a cause.

NARRATOR. A pleader who draws *narrs*. *Serviens narrator*, a serjeant-at-law. Fleta, lib. 2, c. 37. Obsolete.

NARROW SEAS. In English law. Those seas which adjoin the coast of England. Bac. Abr. "Prerogative" (B 3).

NASCITURUS (Lat. from *nasci*, to be *born*). In the civil law. An unborn child; a child to be born, or about to be born. 1 Kaufm. Mackeld. Civ. Law, 128, § 118; Tayl. Civ. Law, 248.

NASTRE (Law Fr.) Born. *Fols nastres*, born fools; idiots from birth. Britt. c. 34.

NATALE. The state or condition of a man acquired by birth.

NATI ET NASCITURI (Lat.) Born and to be born. An expression including all heirs, near and remote. Fleta, lib. 3, c. 8. See Comb. 154.

NATIO (Lat.) In old records. A native place. Cowell.

NATION. An independent body politic; a society of men united together for the purpose of promoting their mutual safety and advantage by the joint efforts of their combined strength.

But every combination of men who govern themselves independently of all others will not be considered a nation. A body of pirates, for example, who govern themselves, are not a nation. To constitute a nation, another ingredient is required. The body thus formed must respect other nations in general, and each of their members in particular. Such a society has her affairs and her interests; she deliberates and takes resolutions in common,—thus becoming a moral person, who possesses an understanding and will peculiar to herself, and is susceptible of obligations and rights. Vattel, Prelim. §§ 1, 2; 5 Pet. (U. S.) 52. See 1 Idaho (N. S.) 612.

NATIONAL BANKS. National banks are, and are not, foreign corporations. They are incorporated and exist under acts of congress and are agencies of the federal government, domesticated in the state. 192 Mich. 640.

NATIONAL CORPORATIONS (sometimes called "federal corporations"). Those incorporated under acts of congress.

NATIONAL DOMAIN. See "Public Domain."

NATIONAL DOMICILE. Domicile considered with respect to the nation within which one is domiciled, rather than with respect to the particular locality.

NATIONALITY. Character, status, or condition with reference to the rights and duties of a person as a member of some one state or nation, rather than another.

The term is in frequent use with regard to ships. See, generally, "Citizen;" "Denizen;" "Domicile;" "Naturalization."

NATIVA (Law Lat.) In old English law. A neife, or female villein. So called, because for the most part bond by nativity. Co. Litt. 122b.

NATIVE, or **NATIVE CITIZEN.** A natural-born subject. 1 Bl. Comm. 366. A person born within the jurisdiction of the United States, whether after Declaration of Independence or before, if he did not withdraw before the adoption of the constitution; or the child of a citizen born abroad, if his parents have ever resided here; or the child of an alien born abroad, if he be in the country at the time his father is naturalized. 8 Paige, Ch. (N. Y.) 433; Act Cong. Feb. 10, 1855; 2 Kent, Comm. (9th Ed.) 38 et seq.

NATIVI (Law Lat.) Vassals or feudal tenants. So called, even before feuds became hereditary. Wright, Ten. 14.

Villeins. Fleta, lib. 2, c. 51. See "Nativus."

NATIVITAS. In old English law. Villenage; that state in which men were born slaves. 2 Mon. Angl. 643. Called by Britton *naifte.* Britt. c. 31.

NATIVO HABENDO. A writ which lay for a lord whose villein had run away, commanding the sheriff to apprehend the villein, and restore him to the lord.

NATIVUS. A born villein.

NATURA APPETIT PERFECTUM, ITA et lex. Nature aspires to perfection, and so does the law. Hob. 144.

NATURA FIDE JUSSIONIS SIT STRICTissimi juris et non durat, vel extendatur de re ad rem, de persona ad personam, de tempore ad tempus. The nature of the contract of suretyship is *strictissimi juris,* and cannot endure nor be extended from thing to thing, from person to person, or from time to time, Burge, Sur. 40.

NATURA NON FACIT SALTUM, ITA nec lex. Nature makes no leap, nor does the law. Co. Litt. 238.

NATURA NON FACIT VACUUM; NEC lex supervacuum. Nature makes no vacuum; the law nothing purposeless. Co. Litt. 79.

NATURAE VIS MAXIMA; NATURA BIS maxima. The force of nature is greatest; nature is doubly great. 2 Inst. 564.

NATURAL AFFECTION. The affection which a husband, a father, a brother, or other near relative naturally feels towards those who are so nearly allied to him sometimes supplies the place of a valuable consideration in contracts, and natural affection is a good consideration in a deed. See "Bargain and Sale;" "Covenant to Stand Seised to Uses."

NATURAL ALLEGIANCE.

——**In English Law.** That kind of allegiance which is due from all men born within the king's dominions, immediately upon their birth, which is intrinsic and perpetual, and cannot be divested by any act of their own. 1 Bl. Comm. 369; 2 Kent, Comm. 42.

——**In American Law.** The allegiance due from citizens of the United States to their native country, and also from naturalized citizens, and which cannot be renounced without the permission of government, to be declared by law. 2 Kent, Comm. 43-49.

NATURAL-BORN SUBJECTS. In English law. Such persons as are born within the dominions of the crown of England, or rather within the allegiance of the king.

NATURAL CHILDREN. Bastards; children born out of lawful wedlock.

——**In Civil Law.** Children by procreation, as distinguished from children by adoption.

——**In Louisiana.** Illegitimate children who have been adopted by the father. Civ. Code La. art. 220.

NATURAL DAY. That space of time included between the rising and the setting of the sun. See "Day."

NATURAL EQUITY. That which is founded in natural justice, in honesty and right, and which arises *ex aequo et bono.*

It corresponds precisely with the definition of justice or natural law, which is a constant and perpetual will to give to every man what is his. This kind of equity embraces so wide a range that human tribunals have never attempted to enforce it. Every code of laws has left many matters of natural justice or equity wholly unprovided for, from the difficulty of framing general rules to meet them, from the almost impossibility of enforcing them, and from the doubtful nature of the policy of attempting to give a legal sanction to duties of imperfect obligation, such as charity, gratitude, or kindness. 4 Bouv. Inst. note 3720.

NATURAL FOOL. An idiot; one born without the reasoning powers, or a capacity to acquire them.

NATURAL FRUITS. The natural production of trees, bushes, and other plants, for the use of men and animals, and for the reproduction of such trees, bushes, or plants.

This expression is used in contradistinction to artificial or figurative fruits. For example, apples, peaches, and pears are natural fruits; interest is the fruit of money, and this is artificial.

NATURAL INFANCY. A period of nonresponsible life, which ends with the seventh year.

NATURAL LAW. The law of nature; the divine will, or the dictate of right reason, showing the moral deformity or moral necessity there is in any act, according to its suitableness or unsuitableness to a reasonable nature. A proposition naturally recognized, pointing out actions which are the source of common good. Cumberland, De Lege Nat. V. 1. Sometimes used of the law of human reason, in contradistinction to the revealed law, and sometimes of both, in contradistinction to positive law.

They are independent of any artificial connections, and differ from mere presumptions of law in this essential respect, that the latter depend on and are a branch of the particular system of jurisprudence to which they belong; but mere natural presumptions are derived wholly by means of the common experience of mankind, without the aid or control of any particular rule of law, but simply from the course of nature and the habits of society. These presumptions fall within the exclusive province of the jury, who are to pass upon the facts. 3 Bouv. Inst. note 3064; Greenl. Ev. § 44.

NATURAL LIBERTY. The power of acting as one thinks fit, without any restraint or control, unless by the law of nature. 1 Bl. Comm. 125.

NATURAL LIFE. The period between birth and natural death, as distinguished from civil death (*q. v.*)

NATURAL OBLIGATION. One which in honor and conscience binds the person who has contracted it, but which cannot be enforced in a court of justice. Poth. notes 173, 191. See "Obligation."

NATURAL PERSONS. Such as are formed by the Deity, as distinguished from artificial persons, or corporations, formed by human laws for purposes of society and government.

NATURAL PRESUMPTIONS. In evidence. Presumptions of fact; those which depend upon their own form and efficacy in generating belief or conviction in the mind, as derived from those connections which are pointed out by experience. See also "Natural Law."

NATURAL YEAR. In old English law. That period of time in which the sun was supposed to revolve in its orbit, consisting of three hundred and sixty-five days and one-fourth of a day, or six hours. Bracton, fol. 359b.

NATURALE EST QUIDLIBET DISSOLVI eo modo quo ligatur. It is natural for a thing to be unbound in the same way in which it was bound. Jenk. Cent. Cas. 66; 4 Denio (N. Y.) 414, 417; Broom, Leg. Max. (3d London Ed.) 785.

NATURALEZA. In Spanish law. The state of a natural-born subject. White, New Recop. bk. 1, tit. 5, c. 2. Called *naturalidad.*

NATURALIZATION. The process of conferring citizenship on an alien.

NATURALIZED CITIZEN. One who, being born an alien, has lawfully become a citizen of the United States under the constitution and laws.

He has all the rights of a natural-born citizen, except that of being eligible as president or vice president of the United States. In foreign countries he has a right to be treated as such, and will be so considered even in the country of his birth, at least for most purposes. 1 Bos. & P. 430. See "Citizen."

NAUCLERUS (Lat.) Master or owner of a vessel. Vicat; Calv. Lex.

NAUFRAGE. In French maritime law. When, by the violent agitation of the waves, the impetuosity of the winds, the storm, or the lightning, a vessel is swallowed up, or so shattered that there remain only the pieces, the accident is called *naufrage.*

It differs from *echouement,* which is when the vessel remains whole, but is grounded; or from *bris,* which is when it strikes against a rock or a coast; or from *sombrer,* which is the sinking of a vessel in the sea when it is swallowed up, and which may be caused by any accident whatever. Pardessus, note 643. See "Wreck."

NAUFRAGIUM (Lat.) Shipwreck.

NAUGHT. In old practice. Bad; defective. "The bar is naught." 1 Leon. 77. "The avowry is naught." 5 Mod. 73. "The plea is undoubtedly naught." 10 Mod. 329. See 11 Mod. 179. Sometimes written "naughty." Brownl. & G. 97.

NAULAGE. The freight of passengers in a ship. Johnson; Webster.

NAULUM (Lat.) Freight or passage money. 1 Pars. Mar. Law, 124, note; Dig. 1. 6. 1, *qui potiores in pignore.*

NAUTA (Lat.) One who charters (*exercet*) a ship. L. 1, § 1, ff. *nautae, caupo;* Calv. Lex. Any one who is on board a vessel for the purpose of navigating her. 3 Sumn. (U. S.) 213; Vicat; 2 Enmerig. 448; Poth. ad Pand. lib. 4, tit. 9, note 2; Id. lib. 47, tit. 5, notes 1-3, 8, 10. A carrier by water. 2 Ld. Raym. 917.

NAUTICAL ASSESSORS. Persons experienced in navigation, who are called upon by an admiralty judge to sit with him in cases involving questions of correct navigation, and advise him thereon. 2 Curt. C. C. (U. S.) 369.

NAVAGIUM. A duty on certain tenants to carry their lord's goods in a ship. 1 Mon. Angl. 922.

NAVAL. Appertaining to the navy (*q. v.*)

NAVAL COURTS. Courts held abroad in certain cases to inquire into complaints by the master or seamen of a British ship, or as to the wreck or abandonment of a British ship. A naval court consists of three, four, or five members, being officers in her majesty's navy, consular officers, masters of British merchant ships, or British merchants. It has power to supersede the master of the ship with reference to which the inquiry is held, to discharge any of the seamen, to decide questions as to wages, send home offenders for trial (Merch. Ship. Act 1854, § 260), or try certain offenses in a summary manner (Merch. Ship. Act 1855, § 28).

NAVAL COURTS-MARTIAL. Tribunals for the trial of offenses arising in the management of public war vessels.

NAVAL LAW. A system of regulations for the government of the navy. 1 Kent, Comm. 377, note. Consult Act April 3, 1800; Act Dec. 21, 1861; Act July 16, 1862; Homans, Nav. Laws; De Hart, Courts-Martial.

NAVAL OFFICER. An officer of the customs of the United States.

His office relates to the estimating duties, countersigning permits, clearances, etc., certifying the collectors' returns, and similar duties.

NAVARCHUS, or **NAVICULARIUS** (Lat.) In civil law. The master of an armed ship. *Navicularius* also denotes the master of a ship (*patronus*) generally; also, a carrier by water (*exercitor navis*). Calv. Lex.

NAVIGABLE. Capable of being navigated. In English law, only waters in which the tide flows are navigable in the technical sense. 5 Taunt. 705; Davies, 149.

In American law, any water is navigable which is used as a means of useful commerce. 112 Ill. 611; 42 Minn. 532; 110 N. Y. 380.

The navigation need not be by boats. Waters used for floating rafts or logs are public highways for that purpose. 31 Mich. 336; 58 N. H. 304; 72 N. Y. 211.

The capacity for navigation need not be perennial. 42 Wis. 203; 17 Ore. 165. Nor need it be continuous through the entire length of the stream. 31 Me. 9.

The Niagara river has been held navigable, notwithstanding the obstruction of the falls. 37 Hun. (N. Y.) 537.

"Those only are navigable waters where the public pass and repass upon them with vessels or boats in the prosecution of useful occupations. There must be some commerce or navigation which is essentially valuable. A hunter or fisherman, by drawing his boat through the waters of a brook or shallow creek, does not create navigation, or constitute their waters channels of commerce. 20 Conn. 217.

NAVIGATION. The science or art of conducting a ship from one place to another This includes the supply of necessary implements and skillful mariners. The instruments are useless without the skillful mariners, and conversely, navigation includes two things,—the supply of the instruments or organs of the ship, and the living instruments, or seamen. If either of these is wanting by the negligence of the owner, or of those for whom he is responsible, there is improper navigation. 53 L. J. P. D. & A. 66; 9 P. D. 145.

NAVIGATION ACT. St. 12 Car. II, c. 78. It was repealed by 6 Geo. IV. cc. 109, 110, 114. See 16 & 17 Vict. c. 107; 17 & 18 Vict. c. 120.

NAVIRE (Fr.) In French law. A ship. Emerig. Tr. des. Assur. c. 6, § 1.

NAVIS (Lat.) A ship; a vessel. Dig. 21. 2. 44; Id. 47. 9.

NAVIS BONA (Lat.) A good ship; one that was staunch and strong, well caulked, and stiffened to bear the sea, obedient to her helm, swift, and not unduly affected by the wind. Calv. Lex., citing Seneca, lib. 5, p. 77.

NAVY. The whole shipping, taken collec tively, belonging to the government of an independent nation, and appropriated for the purposes of naval warfare. It does not include ships belonging to private individuals, nor (in the United States, at least) revenue vessels or transports in the service of the war department. See Brightly, Dig. U. S. Laws.

NAZERANNA. A sum paid to government as an acknowledgment for a grant of lands, or any public office. Enc. Lond.

NE ADMITTAS (Lat.) The name of a writ, so called from the first words of the Latin form, by which the bishop is "forbidden to admit" to a benefice the other party's clerk during the pendency of a *quare impedit*. It ought to be issued within six months after avoidance of the benefice, before title to present has devolved upon the bishop by lapse, or it will be useless. Fitzh. Nat. Brev. 37; Reg. Orig. 31; 3 Bl. Comm. 248; 1 Burn, Ecc. Law, 31.

NE BAILA PAS. He did not deliver. In pleading. A plea in detinue, by which the defendant denies the delivery to him of the thing sued for.

NE DISTURBA PAS. In pleading. The general issue in *quare impedit*. Hob. 162. See Rast. Entr. 517; Winch, Entr. 703.

NE DONA PAS, NON DEDIT. In pleading. The general issue in formedon. It is in the following formula: "And the said C. D., by J. K., his attorney, comes and defends the right, when, etc., and says that the said E. F. did not give the said manor, with the appurtenances, or any part thereof, to the said G. B. and the heirs of his body issuing, in manner and form as the said A. B. hath in his count above alleged. And of this the said C. D. puts himself upon the country." 10 Wentw. Pl. 182.

NE EXEAT.

——**In Old English Law.** A high prerogative writ, generally called *ne exeat regno*, issued out of chancery to forbid a subject from leaving the realm. Originally it was issued for political reasons only. 1 Bl. Comm. 162, 319.

——**In Modern Law.** The name of a writ issued by a court of chancery, directed to the sheriff, reciting that the defendant in the case is indebted to the complainant, and that he designs going quickly into parts without the state, to the damage of the complainant, and then commanding him to cause the defendant to give bail in a certain sum that he will not leave the state without leave of the court, and for want of such bail that he, the sheriff, do commit the defendant to prison.

The writ has been abolished in most of the United States.

NE GIST PAS EN BOUCHE (Law Fr.) It does not lie in the mouth. A common phrase in the old books. Y. B. M. 3 Edw. II. 50.

NE LUMINIBUS OFFICIATUR (Lat.) In civil law. The name of a servitude which restrains the owner of a house from making such erections as obstruct the light of the adjoining house. Dig. 8. 4. 15. 17.

NE RECIPIATUR (Lat. that it be not received). A caveat or words of caution given to a law officer, by a party in a cause, not to receive the next proceedings of his opponent. 1 Sellon, Prac. 8.

NE RECTOR PROSTERNET ARBORES (Law Lat.) St. 35 Edw. I. § 2, prohibiting rectors, *i. e.*, parsons, from cutting down the trees in church yards. In 1 Keb. 557, it was extended to prohibit them from opening new mines, and working the minerals therein. Brown.

NE RELESSA PAS (Law Fr.) The name of a replication to a plea of release, by which the plaintiff insists he "did not release." 2 Bulst. 55.

NE UNJUSTE VEXES (Lat.) In old English law. The name of a writ which issued to relieve a tenant upon whom his lord had distrained for more services than he was bound to perform.

It was a prohibition to the lord, not unjustly to distrain or vex his tenant. Fitzh. Nat. Brev.

NE UNQUES ACCOUPLE (Law Fr.) In pleading. A plea by which the party denies that he ever was lawfully married to the person to whom it refers. See the form, 2 Wils. 118; 10 Wentw. Pl. 158; 2 H. Bl. 145; 3 Chit. Pl. 599.

NE UNQUES EXECUTOR. In pleading. A plea by which the party who uses it denies that the plaintiff is an executor, as he claims to be; or that the defendant is executor, as the plaintiff in his declaration charges him to be. 1 Chit. Pl. 484; 1 Saund. 274, note 3; Comyn, Dig. "Pleader" (2 D 2); 2 Chit. Pl. 498.

NE UNQUES SEISIE QUE DOWER. In pleading. A plea by which a defendant denies the right of a widow who sues for and demands her dower in lands, etc., late of her husband, because the husband was not, on the day of her marriage with him, or at any time afterwards, seised of such estate, so that she could be endowed of the same. See 2 Saund. 329; 10 Wentw. Pl. 159; 3 Chit. Pl. 598, and the authorities there cited.

NE UNQUES SON RECEIVER. In pleading. The name of a plea in an action of account render, by which the defendant affirms that he never was receiver of the plaintiff. 12 Viner, Abr. 183.

NE VARIETUR (Lat. that it be not changed). A form sometimes written by notaries public upon bills or notes, for the purpose of identifying them. This does not destroy their negotiability. 8 Wheat. (U. S.) 338.

NEAT, or **NET.** The exact weight of an article, without the bag, box, keg, or other thing in which it may be enveloped.

NEAT CATTLE. Oxen or heifers. The term is not as broad as "beeves." 36 Tex. 324.

NEAT LAND. Land let out to the yeomanry. Cowell.

NEATNESS. In pleading. The statement in apt and appropriate words of all the necessary facts, and no more. Lawes, Pl. 62.

NEC CURIA DEFICERET IN JUSTITIA exhibenda. Nor should the court be deficient in showing justice. 4 Inst. 63.

NEC TEMPUS NEC LOCUS OCCURRIT regi. Neither time nor place bars the king. Jenk. Cent. Cas. 190.

NEC VENIAM EFFUSO SANGUINE, CAsus habet. Where blood is spilled, the case is unpardonable. 3 Inst. 57.

NEC VENIAM, LAESO NUMINE, CASUS habet. Where the Divinity is insulted, the case is unpardonable. Jenk. Cent. Cas. 167.

NECATION. The act of killing.

NECESSARIES. Such things are as proper and necessary for the sustenance of man.

As used to describe those things for which an infant may lawfully contract, necessaries are such articles, suitable to the infant's station in life, as are needful to supply the personal requirements of the infant, whether of body or mind. 12 Metc. (Mass.) 561. It includes board and lodging (23 Vt. 378), medical attendance (42 Conn. 203), or education suitable to the infant's station in life (16 Vt. 683). It does not include services essential to the improvement or protection of his property rights (12 Metc. [Mass.] 559; 32 N. H. 345), but does include services essential to secure or protect his personal rights (68 Hun [N. Y.] 589; 12 Kan. 463).

As used to describe those things for which a wife may pledge her husband's credit, it has a slightly narrower significance, excluding instruction (40 Conn. 75), and including only those things which are presently needful for the present support of the wife (63 Mo. App. 191), or to maintain her personal rights (50 Ill. App. 27); but the nature of the support for which she is entitled to contract depends on the husband's means and station in life (114 Mass. 429).

As used to describe those things for which a master may hypothecate the ship, it includes such articles fit and proper for the ship as the owner would, in the exercise of reasonable prudence, have ordered, if present. Maude & P. Shipp, 71.

NECESSARIUM EST QUOD NON POtest aliter se habere. That is necessary which cannot be otherwise.

NECESSARIUS (Lat.) Necessary; unavoidable; indispensable; not admitting of choice or the action of the will; needful. See "Necessity."

NECESSARY. Necessary is often employed as a term somewhat analogous to "expedient," or "appropriate," or "reasonably convenient." 115 Ia. 734.

NECESSARY DEPOSITS. See "Deposit."

NECESSARY DOMICILE. That kind of domicile which exists by operation of law, as distinguished from voluntary domicile or domicile of choice. Phillim. Dom. 27-97.

NECESSARY INTROMISSION. In Scotch law. That kind of intromission or interference where a husband or wife continues in possession of the other's goods, after their decease, for preservation. Wharton.

NECESSARY REPAIRS. Include not only those absolutely indispensable to the safety of the ship, but such as are reasonably fit and proper under the circumstances. 3 Sumn. (U. S.) 237.

NECESSITAS. In the civil law. Necessity; *vis major.*

NECESSITAS CULPABILIS. Culpable or blameworthy necessity; that kind of necessity which excuses a man who kills another *se defendendo.* So called by Lord Bacon to distinguish it from the necessity of killing a thief or malefactor. Bac. Com. Law, c. 5; 4 Bl. Comm. 187.

NECESSITAS EST LEX TEMPORIS ET loci. Necessity is the law of a particular time and place. 8 Coke, 69; Hale, P. C. 54.

NECESSITAS EXCUSAT AUT EXTENUat delictum in capitalibus, quod non operatur idem in civilibus. Necessity excuses or extenuates delinquency in capital cases, but not in civil. See "Necessity."

NECESSITAS FACIT LICITUM QUOD alias non est licitum. Necessity makes that lawful which otherwise is unlawful. 10 Coke, 61.

NECESSITAS INDUCIT PRIVILEGIUM quoad jura privata. With regard to private rights, necessity privileges. Bac. Max. reg. 5.

NECESSITAS NON HABET LEGEM. Necessity has no law. Plowd. 18. See "Necessity." 15 Viner, Abr. 534; 22 Viner, Abr. 540.

NECESSITAS PUBLICA MAJOR EST quam privata. Public necessity is greater than private. Bac. Max. reg. 5; Noy, Max. (9th Ed.) 34; Broom, Leg. Max. (3d London Ed.) 18.

NECESSITAS, QUOD COGIT, DEFENDIT. Necessity defends what it compels. Hale, P. C. 54.

NECESSITAS SUB LEGE NON CONTInetur, quia quod alias non est licitum necessitas facit licitum. Necessity is not restrained by law; since what otherwise is not lawful, necessity makes lawful. 2 Inst. 326, Fleta, lib. 5, c. 23, § 14.

NECESSITAS VINCIT LEGEM. Necessity overcomes the law. Hob. 144.

NECESSITAS VINCIT LEGEM; LEGUM vincula irridet. Necessity overcomes law; it derides the fetters of law. Hob. 144.

NECESSITY (Lat. *necessitas*). Irresistible power; compulsive force, physical or moral. Webster.

The influence or operation of superior power or irresistible force; the influence of a cause which cannot be avoided nor controlled.

A constraint upon the will, whereby a man is urged to do that which his judgment disapproves, and which, it is to be presumed, his will (if left to itself) would reject. It is highly just and equitable, therefore, that a man should be excused for those acts which are done through unavoidable force and compulsion. 4 Bl. Comm. 27.

NECK VERSE. A cant term for the verse which the ordinary gave a malefactor who prayed his clergy to read, and by reading which he escaped hanging. The first verse of the 51st Psalm, being that ordinarily given, was called the "neck verse."

NEFAS (Lat.) That which is against right or the divine law (*fas*). A wicked or impious thing or act. Calv. Lex.

NEFASTUS (Lat.) In Roman law. A term applied to a day on which it was unlawful to administer justice. Adams, Rom. Ant. 129.

NEGATIO CONCLUSIONIS EST ERROR in lege. The denial of a conclusion is error in law. Wingate, Max. 268.

NEGATIO DESTRUIT NEGATIONEM, et ambae faciunt affirmationem. A negative destroys a negative, and both make an affirmative. Co. Litt. 146.

NEGATIO DUPLEX EST AFFIRMATIO. A double negative is an affirmative.

NEGATIVE AVERMENT. In pleading. An averment in some of the pleadings in a case in which a negative is asserted.

NEGATIVE CONDITION. One where the thing which is the subject of it must not happen. 1 Bouv. Inst. note 751.

NEGATIVE COVENANT. One in negative form, whereby the covenantor binds himself not to do a particular thing.

NEGATIVE EASEMENT. One which consists in a prohibition upon the owner of the servient estate of some act which would be detrimental to the dominant estate.

NEGATIVE PREGNANT. In pleading. Such a form of negative expression as may imply or carry within it an affirmative. Thus, where a defendant pleaded a license from the plaintiff's daughter, and the plaintiff rejoined that he did not enter by her license, the rejoinder was objected to successfully as a negative pregnant. Cro. Jac. 87. The fault here lies in the ambiguity of the rejoinder, since it does not appear whether the plaintiff denies that the license was given, or that the defendant entered by the license. Steph. Pl. 381.

This ambiguity constitutes the fault (Hob. 295), which, however, does not appear to be of much account in modern pleading (1 Lev. 88; Comyn, Dig. "Pleader" [R 6]; Gould, Pl. c. 6, § 36).

NEGATIVE STATUTE. One which is enacted in negative terms, and which so controls the common law that it has no force in opposition to the statute. Bac. Abr. "Statutes" (G); Brooke, Abr. "Parliament," pl. 72.

NEGLIGENCE. The breach of a legal noncontractual duty to use care, with no precise intention of producing a particular injury thereby. See Shear. & R. Neg. § 3; Beven, Emp. Liab.

An inadvertent imperfection by a responsible human agent in the discharge of a legal duty, which produces, in an orderly and natural sequence, a damage to another. Whart. Neg. § 3.

Any lack of carefulness in one's conduct, whether in doing, or in abstaining from doing, wherefrom by reason of its not filling the full measure of the law's requirement in the particular circumstances there comes to another a legal injury. Bish. Non-Cont. Law, § 436.

Negligence has been defined as the doing or omission of something which a reasonable prudent person would not have done or omitted under the circumstances (95 U. S. 439); but this is rather a statement of what constitutes proper care, and moreover omits the element of a duty imposed by law which is broken by the negligent act or omission (Pollock, Torts, 352).

NEGLIGENT ESCAPE. The omission on the part of a gaoler to take such care of a prisoner as he is bound to take, when in consequence thereof the prisoner departs from his confinement without the knowledge or consent of the gaoler, and eludes pursuit.

For a negligent escape, the sheriff or keeper of the prison is liable to punishment, in a criminal case; and in a civil case, he is liable to an action for damages at the suit of the plaintiff. In both cases the prisoner may be retaken. 3 Bl. Comm. 415. See "Escape."

NEGLIGENTIA (Lat. from *negligere*, to neglect). In the civil law. Negligence, want or omission of care or attention; inattention. This term hardly seems to correspond with what is called in English simple "negligence," since it took a high degree of it to constitute *culpa*, or fault. *Magna negligentia culpa est.* Dig. 50. 16, 226. See "Culpa."

NEGLIGENTIA SEMPER HABET INFORtuniam comitem. Negligence always has misfortune for a companion. Co. Litt. 246; Shep. Touch. 476.

NEGOTIABILITY. In mercantile law. Transferable quality. That quality of bills of exchange and promissory notes, which renders them transferable from one person to another, and from possessing which, they are emphatically termed "negotiable paper." 3 Kent, Comm. 74, 77, 89, et seq. See Story, Bills, § 60.

NEGOTIABLE INSTRUMENT. Any written instrument which may be transferred by indorsement and delivery, or by delivery alone, so as to give the indorsee the legal title, and enable him to sue in his own name. 15 Mo. 337.

In a narrower sense, those instruments the indorsee of which, under the law merchant, takes free of certain equities and defenses between the original parties.

NEGOTIABLE WORDS. See "Words of Negotiability."

NEGOTIATION. The deliberation which takes place between the parties touching a proposed agreement.

That which transpires in the negotiation makes no part of the agreement, unless introduced into it. It is a general rule that no evidence can be given to add, diminish, contradict, or alter a written instrument. 1 Dall. (Pa.) 426; 4 Dall. (Pa.) 340; 3 Serg. & R. (Pa.) 609.

——**In Mercantile Law.** The act by which a bill of exchange or promissory note is put into circulation by being passed by one of the original parties to another person.

Until an accommodation bill or note has been negotiated, there is no contract which can be enforced on the note; the contract, either express or implied, that the party accommodated will indemnify the other, is, till then, conditional. 2 Man. & G. 911.

NEGOTIORUM GESTIO (Lat.) In the civil law. Literally, a doing of business or businesses; a species of spontaneous agency, or an interference by one in the affairs of another, in his absence, from benevolence or friendship, and without authority. 2 Kent, Comm. 616, note; Inst. 3. 28. 1; Dig. 3. 5.

The intervention of a person acting without authority in transacting the affairs of another.

NEGOTIORUM GESTOR (Lat.) In civil law. One who spontaneously, and without authority, undertakes to act for another, during his absence, in his affairs.

In cases of this sort, as he acts wholly without authority, there can, strictly speaking, be no contract; but the civil law raises a *quasi* mandate by implication for the benefit of the owner in many such cases. Mackeld. Civ. Law, § 460; 2 Kent, Comm. 616, note; Story, Bailm, §§ 82,189.

NEGRO. Generally a person belonging to the African race, and having such a proportion of African blood as will identify him with that race. 5 Jones, Law (N. C.) 11; 80 Va. 544.

It has been held to mean a black man and not to include a mulatto. 18 Ala. 20.

NEIF. In old English law. A woman who was born a villein, or a bond woman.

NEIGHBORHOOD. The immediately adjacent locality. See 27 Mo. App. 584; 63 N. H. 246; as applied to place, signifies nearness, as opposed to remoteness, 63 N. H. 246. Vicinity does not denote so close a connection as neighborhood. A neighborhood is a more immediate vicinity. 27 Mo. App. 584, 190 Ill. 625.

NEMBA (Teut.) In Swedish and Gothic law. A jury. 3 Bl. Comm. 349, 359; Barr. Obs. St. 18, note (z).

NEMINE CONTRADICENTE (usually abbreviated *nem. con.*) Words used to signify the unanimous consent of the house to which they are applied. In England, they are used in the house of commons; in the house of lords, the words used to convey the same idea are *nemine dissentiente.*

NEMI. See "Nerny."

NEMINEM OPORTET ESSE SAPIENTIOrem legibus. No man need be wiser than the laws. Co. Litt. 97.

NEMO ADMITTENDUS EST INHABILItare seipsum. No one is allowed to incapacitate himself. Jenk. Cent. Cas. 40. But see "To Stultify;" 5 Whart. (Pa.) 371; 2 Kent, Comm. 451, note.

NEMO AGIT IN SEIPSUM. No man acts against himself (Jenk. Cent. Cas. 40); therefore no man can be a judge in his own cause (Broom, Leg. Max. [3d London Ed.]

201, note; 4 Bing. 151; 2 Exch. 595; 18 C. B. 253; 2 Barn. & Ald. 822).

NEMO ALIENAE REI, SINE SATISDAtione, defensor idoneus intelligitur. No man is considered a competent defender of another's property, without security. 1 Curt. C. C. (U. S.) 202.

NEMO ALIENO NOMINE LEGE AGERE potest. No man can sue at law in the name of another. Dig. 50. 17. 123.

NEMO ALIQUAM PARTEM RECTE INtelligere potest, antequam totum iterum atque iterum perlegit. No one can properly understand any part of a thing till he has read through the whole again and again. 3 Coke, 59.

NEMO ALLEGANS SUAM TURPITUDInem, audiendus est. No one alleging his own turpitude is to be heard as a witness. 4 Inst. 279; 3 Story (U. S.) 514, 516.

NEMO BIS PUNITUR PRO EODEM DElicto. No one can be punished twice for the same crime or misdemeanor. 2 Hawk. P. C. 377; 4 Bl. Comm. 315.

NEMO COGITATIONIS POENAM PATItur. No one suffers punishment on account of his thoughts. Tray. Lat. Max. 362.

NEMO COGITUR REM SUAM VENdere, etiam justo pretio. No one is bound to sell his property, even for a just price. But see "Eminent Domain."

NEMO CONTRA FACTUM SUUM VEnire potest. No man can contradict his own deed. 2 Inst. 66.

NEMO DAMNUM FACIT, NISI QUI ID facit quod facere jus non habet. No one is considered as doing damage unless he who is doing what he has no right to do. Dig. 50. 17. 151.

NEMO DARE POTEST QUOD NON HAbet. No man can give that which he has not. Fleta, lib. 3, c. 15, § 8.

NEMO DAT QUI NON HABET. No one can give who does not possess. Jenk. Cent. Cas. 250.

NEMO DE DOMO SUA EXTRAHI DEbet. A citizen cannot be taken by force from his house to be conducted before a judge or to prison. Dig. 50. 17. 103. This maxim in favor of Roman liberty is much the same as that every man's house is his castle. Broom, Leg. Max. (3d London Ed.) 384.

NEMO DEBET ALIENA JACTURA LOcupletari. No one ought to gain by another's loss. 2 Kent, Comm. 336.

NEMO DEBET BIS PUNIRI PRO UNO delicto. No one ought to be punished twice for the same offense. 4 Coke, 43; 11 Coke, 59b.

NEMO DEBET BIS VEXARI PRO [UNA et] eadem causa. No one should be twice harassed for the same cause. 2 Johns. (N. Y.) 24, 27, 182; 13 Johns. (N. Y.) 153; 8 Wend. (N. Y.) 10, 38; 2 Hall (N. Y.) 454; 3 Hill (N. Y.) 420; 6 Hill (N. Y.) 133; 2 Barb. (N. Y.) 285; 6 Barb. (N. Y.) 32; 5 Pet. (U. S.) 61; 1 Archb. Prac. (Chit. Ed.) 476; 2 Mass. 355; 17 Mass. 425.

NEMO DEBET BIS VEXARI, SI CONstat curiae quod sit pro una et eadem causa. No man ought to be twice punished, if it appear to the court that it is for one and the same cause. 5 Coke, 61; Broom, Leg. Max. (3d London Ed.) 294.

NEMO DEBET ESSE JUDEX IN PROpria causa. No one should be judge in his own cause. 12 Coke, 114; Broom, Leg. Max. (3d London Ed.) 111.

NEMO DEBET IMMISCERE SE REI alienae ad se nihil pertinenti. No one should interfere in what no way concerns him. Jenk. Cent. Cas. 18.

NEMO DEBET IN COMMUNIONE INVItus teneri. No one should be retained in a partnership against his will. 2 Sandf. Ch. (N. Y.) 568, 593; 1 Johns. (N. Y.) 106, 114.

NEMO DEBET LOCUPLETARI EX ALterius incommodo. No one ought to be made rich out of another's loss. Jenk. Cent. Cas. 4; 10 Barb. (N. Y.) 626, 633.

NEMO DEBET REM SUAM SINE FACTO aut defectu suo amittere. No one should lose his property without his act or negligence. Co. Litt. 263.

NEMO DUOBUS UTATUR OFFICIIS. No one should fill two offices. 4 Inst. 100.

NEMO EJUSDEM TENEMENTI SIMUL potest esse haeres et dominus. No one can be at the same time heir and lord of the same fief. 1 Reeve, Hist. Eng. Law, 106.

NEMO ENIM ALIQUAM PARTEM RECte intelligere possit antequam totum iterum atque iterum perlegerit. No one is able rightly to understand one part before he has again and again read through the whole. Broom, Leg. Max. 593.

NEMO EST HAERES VIVENTIS. No one is an heir to the living. Co. Litt. 22b; 2 Bl. Comm. 70, 107, 208; Viner, Abr. "Abeyance"; 2 Bouv. Inst. 1694; 1832; 2 Johns. (N. Y.) 36.

NEMO EST SUPRA LEGES. No one is above the law. Lofft, 142.

NEMO EX ALTERIUS FACTO PRAEgravari debet. No man ought to be burdened in consequence of another's act. 2 Kent, Comm. 646; Poth. Obl. (Evans' Ed.) 133.

NEMO EX CONSILIO OBLIGATUR. No man is bound for the advice he gives. Story, Bailm. § 155.

NEMO EX DOLO SUO PROPRIO RELEvetur, aut auxilium capiat. Let no one be relieved or gain an advantage by his own fraud. A civil-law maxim.

NEMO EX PROPRIO DOLO CONSEQUItur actionem. No one acquires a right of action from his own wrong. Broom, Leg. Max (3d London Ed.) 270.

NEMO EX SUO DELICTO MELIOREM suam conditionem facere potest. No one can improve his condition by his own wrong. Dig. 50. 17. 134. 1.

NEMO IN PROPRIA CAUSA TESTIS ESse debet. No one can be a witness in his own cause. But to this rule there are many exceptions. 1 Bl. Comm. 443; 3 Bl. Comm. 370.

NEMO INAUDITUS CONDEMNARI DEbet, si non sit contumax. No man ought to be condemned unheard, unless he be contumacious. Jenk. Cent. Cas. 18.

NEMO JUS SIBI DICERE POTEST. No one can declare the law for himself. No one is entitled to take the law into his own hands. Tray. Lat. Max. 366.

NEMO MILITANS DEO IMPLICETUR secularibus negotiis. No man warring for God should be troubled by secular business. Co. Litt. 70.

NEMO NASCITUR ARTIFEX. No one is born an artificer. Co. Litt. 97.

NEMO PATRIAM IN QUA NATUS EST exuere, nec ligeantiae debitum ejurare possit. No man can renounce the country in which he was born, nor adjure the obligation of his allegiance. Co. Litt. 129a; 3 Pet. (U. S.) 155; Broom, Leg. Max. (3d London Ed.) 72. See "Allegiance;" "Expatriation;" "Naturalization."

NEMO PLUS COMMODI HEREDI SUO relinquit quam ipse habuit. No one leaves a greater benefit to his heir than he had himself. Dig. 50. 17. 120.

NEMO PLUS JURIS AD ALIENUM transferre potest, quam ipse habet. One cannot transfer to another a larger right than he himself has. Co. Litt. 309b; Wingate, Max. 56; 2 Kent, Comm. 324; 1 Story, Cont. (4th Ed.) 417, note; 5 Coke, 113; 10 Pet. (U. S.) 161, 175.

NEMO POTEST CONTRA RECORDUM verificare per patriam. No one can verify by the country against a record. The issue upon a record cannot be tried by a jury. 2 Inst. 380.

NEMO POTEST ESSE DOMINUS ET haeres. No one can be both owner and heir. Hale, Hist. Com. Law, c. 7.

NEMO POTEST ESSE SIMUL ACTOR et judex. No one can be at the same time judge and suitor. Broom, Leg. Max. (3d London Ed.) 112; 13 Q. B. 327; 17 Q. B. 1; 15 C. B. 796; 1 C. B. (N. S.) 323.

NEMO POTEST ESSE TENENS ET DOminus. No man can be at the same time tenant and landlord (of the same tenement). Gilb. Ten. 102.

NEMO POTEST FACERE PER ALIUM quod per se non potest. No one can do that by another which he cannot do by himself. Jenk. Cent. Cas. 237.

NEMO POTEST FACERE PER OBLIquum quod non potest facere per directum. No one can do that indirectly which cannot be done directly. 1 Eden, 512.

NEMO POTEST MUTARE CONSILIUM suum in alterius injuriam. No one can change his purpose to the injury of another. Dig. 50. 17. 75; Broom, Leg. Max. (3d London Ed.) 33; 7 Johns. (N. Y.) 477.

NEMO POTEST PLUS JURIS AD ALIUM transferre quam ipse habet. No one can transfer a greater right to another than he himself has. Co. Litt. 309; Wingate, Max. 56.

NEMO POTEST SIBI DEBERE. No one can owe to himself. See "Confusion of Rights."

NEMO PRAESENS NISI INTELLIGAT. One is not present unless he understands. See "Presence."

NEMO PRAESUMITUR ALIENAM POSteritatem suae praetulisse. No one is presumed to have preferred another's posterity to his own. Wingate, Max. 285.

NEMO PRAESUMITUR DONARE. No one is presumed to give.

NEMO PRAESUMITUR ESSE IMMEMOR suae aeternae salutis, et maxime in articulo mortis. No man is presumed to be forgetful of his eternal welfare, and particularly at the point of death. 6 Coke, 76.

NEMO PRAESUMITUR LUDERE IN EXtremis. No one is presumed to trifle at the point of death.

NEMO PRAESUMITUR MALUS. No one is presumed to be bad.

NEMO PROHIBETUR PLURES NEGOtiationes sive artes exercere. No one is restrained from exercising several kinds of business or arts. 11 Coke, 54.

NEMO PROHIBETUR PLURIBUS DEfensionibus uti. No one is restrained from using several defenses. Co. Litt. 304; Wingate, Max. 479.

NEMO PRUDENS PUNIT UT PRAETERita revocentur, sed ut futura praeveniantur.

No wise one punishes that things done may be revoked, but that future wrongs may be prevented. 3 Bulst. 17.

NEMO PUNITUR PRO ALIENO DELICto. No one is to be punished for the crime or wrong of another. Wingate, Max. 336.

NEMO PUNITUR SINE INJURIA, FACto, seu defalto. No one is punished unless for some wrong, act, or default. 2 Inst. 287.

NEMO, QUI CONDEMNARE POTEST, absolvere non potest. No one who may condemn is unable to acquit. Dig. 50. 17. 37.

NEMO SIBI ESSE JUDEX VEL SUIS JUS dicere debet. No man ought to be his own judge, or to administer justice in cases where his relations are concerned. 12 Coke, 113; Code, 3. 5. 1; Broom, Leg. Max. (3d London Ed.) 111.

NEMO SINE ACTIONE EXPERITUR, ET hoc non sine breve sive libello conventionali. No one goes to law without an action, and no one can bring an action without a writ or bill. Bracton, 112.

NEMO TENETUR AD IMPOSSIBILE. No one is bound to an impossibility. Jenk. Cent. Cas. 7.

NEMO TENETUR ARMARE ADVERSArium contra se. No one is bound to arm his adversary. Wingate, Max. 665.

NEMO TENETUR DIVINARE. No one is bound to foretell. 4 Coke, 28; 10 Coke, 55a.

NEMO TENETUR EDERE INSTRUMENta contra se. No man is bound to produce writings against himself. Bell, Dict.

NEMO TENETUR INFORMARE QUI nescit sed quisquis scire quod informat. No one who is ignorant of a thing is bound to give information of it, but every one is bound to know that which he gives information of. Branch, Princ.; Lane, Exch. 110.

NEMO TENETUR JURARE IN SUAM turpitudinem. No one is bound to testify to his own baseness.

NEMO TENETUR PRODERE SEIPSUM. No one is bound to betray himself. In other words, no one can be compelled to criminate himself. Broom, Leg. Max. 968.

NEMO TENETUR SEIPSUM ACCUSARE. No one is bound to accuse himself. Wingate, Max. 486; Broom, Leg. Max. (3d London Ed.) 871, 1 Bl. Comm. 443; 14 Mees. & W. 286.

NEMO TENETUR SEIPSUM INFORTUniis et periculis exponere. No one is bound to expose himself to misfortune and dangers. Co. Litt. 253.

NEMO UNQUAM JUDICET IN SE. No one can ever be a judge in his own cause.

NEMO UNQUAM VIR MAGNUS FUIT sine aliquo divino afflatu. No one was ever a great man without some divine inspiration. Cicero.

NEMO VIDETUR FRAUDARE EOS QUI sciunt, et consentiunt. No one is considered as deceiving those who know and consent. Dig. 20. 17. 145.

NEMY, or **NEMI** (Law Fr.) Not. *Nemy come heire,* not as heir. Litt. § 3.

NEPHEW. The son of a brother or sister, Ambl. 514; 1 Jac. 207, whether such brother or sister be of the whole or only of the half-blood. 22 L. J. Ch. 625; 10 Hare, 63.

The Latin *nepos,* from which "nephew" is derived, was used in the civil law for nephew, but more properly for grandson; and we accordingly find *neveu,* the original form of nephew, in the sense of grandson. Britton, c. 119.

NEPUOY (Old Scotch). In Scotch law. A grandson. Skene de Verb. Sign. voc. "Eneya."

NET. Clear of anything extraneous, with all deductions (such as charges, expenses, discounts, commissions, taxes, etc.) made; after deductions made; clear of all charges; free from expenses. 198 Ill. 311.

NETHER HOUSE OF PARLIAMENT. The house of commons was so called in the time of Henry VIII.

NEUTRALITY. The state of a nation which takes no part between two or more other nations at war with each other. The strict definition rather imports the duty which a neutral owes to a belligerent, than the relative situation in which that belligerent chooses to place her. But as it rests with every belligerent to determine, according to its views of expediency, in what way it will deal with neutrals who have acted in violation of their duty; neturality, therefore, in a more enlarged sense, may signify that permitted relation between any two states, after the right to its continuance has been forfeited by one of them. 1 M. & S. 459.

Neutrality consists in the observance of a strict and honest impartiality, so as not to afford advantage in the war to either party, and particularly in so far restraining its trade to the accustomed course which is held in time of peace as not to render assistance to one of the belligerents in escaping the effects of the other's hostilities. Even a loan of money to one of the belligerent parties is considered a violation of neutrality. 9 J. B. Moore, 586. A fraudulent neutrality is considered as no neutrality.

NEVER INDEBTED (Law Lat. *nunquam indebitatus*). In English practice. A form of plea in actions of debt on simple contract, substituted by the late pleading rules in place of the plea of *nil debet* (*q. v.*) Reg. Hillary Term, 4 Wm. IV.; Steph. Pl. 156. The substance of it is that the defendant "never was indebted in manner and form as in the declaration alleged." Id. It is made the proper form of plea in cases where the defendant means to deny, in point of fact, the existence of any express contract to the effect alleged in the declaration, or to deny the matters of fact from which such contract would, by law, be implied. Wharton.

NEW ASSIGNMENT. A restatement of the cause of action by the plaintiff, with more particularity and certainty, but consistently with the general statement in the declaration. Steph. Pl. 241; 20 Johns. (N. Y. 43.

Its purpose is to avoid the effect of an evasive plea which apparently answers the declaration, though it does not really apply to the matter which the plaintiff had in view. 1 Wm. Saund. 299b, note 6. Thus, if a defendant has committed two assaults on the plaintiff, one of which is justifiable, and the other not, as the declaration may not distinguish one from the other, the defendant may justify, and the plaintiff, not being able either to traverse, demur, or confess and avoid, must make a new assignment.

NEW FOR OLD. A term used in the law of insurance in cases of adjustment of a loss when it has been but partial. In making such adjustment, the rule is to apply the old materials towards the payment of the new, by deducting the value of them from the gross amount of the expenses for repairs, and to allow the deduction of one-third new for old upon the balance. See 1 Cow. (N. Y.) 265; 4 Cow. (N. Y.) 245; 4 Ohio, 284; 7 Pick. (Mass.) 259; 14 Pick. (Mass.) 141.

NEW INN. An inn of chancery. See "Inns of Chancery."

NEW MATTER. In pleading. Matter extrinsic to the matter in the pleading to which the party introducing the same answers or replies. 7 Hun (N. Y.) 482.

Facts different from those alleged in the complaint, and not embraced within the judicial inquiry into their truth. 16 S. C. 586.

Thus, payment (16 N. Y. 297; 25 Ohio St. 276), fraud in obtaining the instrument sued on (20 Minn. 411), or limitations (57 Iowa, 307) constitute new matter.

NEW PROMISE. A contract made after the original promise has, for some cause, been rendered invalid, by which the promiser agrees to fulfill such original promise.

NEW STYLE. The modern system of computing time was introduced into Great Britain A. D. 1752, the 3d of September of that year being reckoned as the 14th.

NEW TRIAL. In practice. A rehearing of the legal rights of the parties, upon disputed facts, before another jury, granted by the trial court, or a reviewing on application of the party dissatisfied with the result of the previous trial, upon a proper case being presented for the purpose. 4 Chit. Prac. 30; 2 Graham & W. New Tr. 32.

NEW TRIAL PAPER. In English practice. A paper containing a list of causes in which rules *nisi* have been obtained for a new trial, or for entering a verdict in place of a nonsuit, or for entering judgment *non obstante veredicto*, or for otherwise varying or setting aside proceedings which have taken place at *nisi prius*. These are called on for argument in the order in which they stand in the paper, on days appointed by the judges for the purpose. Brown.

NEW WORK. In the civil law. An edifice or other work newly commenced on any ground whatever. Civ. Code La. art. 852.

NEWLY-DISCOVERED EVIDENCE. Proof of some new material fact in a case, ascertained since the decision.

To constitute such newly-discovered evidence as is ground for a new trial, the evidence must be new and material, not merely impeaching (125 Ill. 122; 24 Pick. [Mass.] 246; 67 Barb. [N. Y.] 411; 36 Minn. 323), nor cumulative (20 Conn. 306; 43 Barb. [N. Y.] 203). It must have been discovered since the former trial (39 Me. 263; 37 How. Pr. [N. Y.] 524), and reasonable diligence must have been used, without success, to discover it in time for the trial (113 Ill. 82; 34 Minn. 351; 35 Hun [N. Y.] 95).

NEWSPAPER. A printed publication, issued in numbers at stated intervals, conveying intelligence of passing events. The term "newspaper" is commonly applied to such publications only as are issued in a single sheet, and at short intervals, as daily or weekly. 4 Op. Attys. Gen. U. S. 10; 7 Exch. 97.

As used in statutes regulating the publication of legal notices, etc., a newspaper must contain matter of general interest; a journal confined to the interests of a single trade or profession not being within the term. 25 Minn. 147. But see 75 Ill. 51. But where, though the main body of the paper is devoted to some special interest, there is in each issue one or more columns of general news and reading matter and advertisements confined to no one calling or trade, the publication is a newpaper. 126 Ill. 219 (law journal); 38 Minn. 349 (religious weekly); 43 N. Y. Supp. 720 (daily mercantile journal).

NEXI. In Roman law. Persons bound (*nexi*); that is, insolvents, who might be held in bondage by their creditors until their debts were discharged. Vicat; Heinec. Ant. Rom. lib. 3. tit. 330; Calv. Lex.; Mackeld. Civ. Law, § 486a.

NEXT. Next is only an abbreviation of the word "nearest." 1 Coll. C. C. 9; 13 L. J. Ch. 147; 36 L. J. Ch. 793; L. R. 4 Eq. 359. It means nearest or nighest; not in the sense of propinquity alone, as, for example, three persons on three chairs, one in the midst, those on each side of the middle one are equally near, each "next" to the center one. But it signifies also order, or succession, or relation as well as propinquity. 27 L. J. Ch. 654.

NEXT FRIEND. One who, without being regularly appointed guardian, acts for the benefit of an infant, married woman, or other person not *sui juris*. Same as *prochein ami* (*q. v.*)

NEXT OF KIN. The next of kin of a deceased person are his nearest blood relatives. It has been held that the next of kin included all blood relatives who took under the statute of distribution (28 How. Pr. [N. Y.] 417); but the more modern holding is that it includes only the nearest in blood, excluding some who may be within the statute (150 Mass. 225). It includes relatives of the half blood.

The term does not include a surviving husband or wife, they not being related by blood. 113 Mass. 431; 44 Ill. 446; 69 N. Y. 36.

NEXUM (Lat.) In Roman law. The transfer of the ownership of a thing, or the transfer of a thing to a creditor as a security.

In one sense, *nexum* includes *mancipium;* in another sense, *mancipium* and *nexum* are opposed, in the same way as sale and mortgage or pledge are opposed. The formal part of both transactions consisted in a transfer *per aes et libram.* The person who became *nexus* by the effect of a *nexum* placed himself in a servile condition, not becoming a slave, his *ingenuitas* being only in suspense, and was said to be *nexum inire.* The phrases *nexi datio, nexi liberatio,* respectively express the contracting and the release from the obligation.

NICHIL. An old form of *nihil* (*q. v.*)

NIECE. The daughter of a brother or sister. Ambl. 514; 1 Jac. 207.

NIEFE. In old English law. A woman born in vassalage.

NIENT (Law Fr.) Nothing; not; null.

NIENT COMPRISE (Law Fr. not included). An exception taken to a petition because the thing desired is not contained in that deed or proceeding whereon the petition is founded. Tomlins.

NIENT CULPABLE (Law Fr. not guilty). The name of a plea used to deny any charge of a criminal nature, or of a tort.

NIENT DEDIRE (Law Fr. to say nothing). Words used to signify that judgment be rendered against a party because he does not deny the cause of action; *i. e.*, by default.

When a fair and impartial trial cannot be had in the county where the venue is laid, the practice in the English courts is, on an affidavit of the circumstances, to change it in transitory actions; or, in local actions, they will give leave to enter a suggestion on the roll, with a *nient dedire,* in order to have the trial in another county. 1 Tidd, Prac. (8th Ed.) 655.

NIENT LE FAIT (Law Fr.) In pleading. The same as *non est factum,* a plea by which the defendant asserts that the deed declared upon is not his deed.

NIENT SEISI. In old pleading. Not seised. The general plea in the writ of annuity. Crabb, Hist. Eng. Law, 424.

NIGER LIBER. The black book of register in the exchequer; chartularies of abbeys, cathedrals, etc.

NIGHT. That space of time during which the sun is below the horizon of the earth, except that short space which precedes its rising and follows its setting, during which, by its light, the countenance of a man may be discerned. At common law, the night, for the purpose of burglary, does not begin until after and ceases when there is daylight enough to discern a man's countenance. 1 Hale, P. C. 550; 4 Bl. Comm. 224; 10 N. H. 105; 42 Vt. 629. See "Daytime."

NIGHT MAGISTRATE. A constable of the night; the head of a watch house.

NIGHT WALKERS. Persons who sleep by day and walk by night (5 Edw. III. c. 14); that is, persons of suspicious appearance and demeanor, who walk by night.

Watchmen may undoubtedly arrest them; and it is said that private persons may also do so. 2 Hawk. P. C. 120. Women walking up and down the streets to pick up men. 3 Taunt. 14, 15. See Hammond, N. P. 135; 15 Viner, Abr. 555; Dane, Abr. Index.

NIGRUM NUNQUAM EXCEDERE DEBET RUBRUM. The black should never go beyond the red; *i. e.*, the text of a statute should never be read in a sense more comprehensive than the rubric, or title. Tray. Lat. Max. 373.

NIHIL, NICHIL, or **NIL** (Lat.) Nothing.

——**In Practice.** A return made by a sheriff to a writ of *scire facias*, that the bail or defendants have nothing (*nihil habent*) by which he can make known to them. 2 Tidd, Prac. 1124.

A return formerly made to process of attachment and *distringas* to compel the appearance of a defendant. 3 Bl. Comm. 282.

A return or answer formerly made by a sheriff, on being opposed (that is, interrogated) in the exchequer concerning illeviable debts, that they were worth nothing. Cowell.

——**In American Law.** A return to an attachment in garnishee process. 4 Pa. St. 232.

NIHIL ALIUD POTEST REX QUAM quod de jure potest. The king can do nothing but what he can do justly. 11 Coke, 74.

NIHIL CAPIAT PER BREVE (Lat. that he take nothing by his writ). In practice. The form of judgment against the plaintiff in an action, either in bar or in abatement. When the plaintiff has commenced his proceedings by bill, the judgment is *nihil capiat per billam.* Co. Litt. 363.

NIHIL CONSENSUI TAM CONTRARIUM est quam vis atque metus. Nothing is so contrary to consent as force and fear. Dig. 50. 17. 116.

NIHIL DAT QUI NON HABET. He gives nothing who has nothing.

NIHIL DE RE ACCRESCIT EI QUI NIHIL in re quando jus accresceret habet. Nothing accrues to him who, when the right accrues, has nothing in the subject matter. Co. Litt. 188.

NIHIL DICIT (Lat. he says nothing). The name of the judgment rendered against a defendant who fails to put in a plea or answer to the plaintiff's declaration by the day assigned. In such a case, judgment is given against the defendant of course, as he says nothing why it should not. See 15 Viner, Abr. 556; Dane, Abr. Index.

NIHIL EST ENIM LIBERALE QUOD non idem justum. For there is nothing generous which is not at the same time just. 2 Kent, Comm. 441, note (a).

NIHIL EST MAGIS RATIONI CONSENtaneum quam eodem modo quodque dissolvere quo conflatum est. Nothing is more consonant to reason than that everything should be dissolved in the same way in which it was made. Shep. Touch. 323.

NIHIL FACIT ERROR NOMINIS CUM DE corpore constat. An error in the name is nothing when there is certainty as to the thing. 11 Coke, 21; 2 Kent, Comm. 292.

NIHIL HABET (Lat. he has nothing). The name of a return made by a sheriff, marshal, or other proper officer, to a *scire facias* or other writ, when he has not been able to serve it on the defendant. 5 Whart. (Pa.) 367.

Two returns of *nihil* are, in general, equivalent to a service. Yelv. 112; 1 Cow. (N. Y.) 70; 1 Law Rep. (N. C.) 491; 4 Blackf. (Ind.) 188; 2 Bin. (Pa.) 40.

NIHIL HABET FORUM EX SCENA. The court has nothing to do with what is not before it.

NIHIL IN LEGE INTOLERABILIUS EST, eandem rem diverso jure censeri. Nothing in law is more intolerable than that the same case should be subject (in different courts) to different views of the law. 4 Coke, 93.

NIHIL INFRA REGNUM SUBDITOS MAgis conservat in tranquilitate et concordia quam debita legum administratio. Nothing preserves in tranquillity and concord those who are subjected to the same government better than a due administration of the laws. 2 Inst. 158.

NIHIL INIQUIUS QUAM AEQUITATEM nimis intendere. Nothing is more unjust than to extend equity too far. Halk. Max. 103.

NIHIL MAGIS JUSTUM EST QUAM quod necessarium est. Nothing is more just than what is necessary. Dav. 12.

NIHIL NEQUAM EST PRAESUMENDUM. Nothing wicked is to be presumed. 2 P. Wms. 583.

NIHIL PERFECTUM EST DUM ALIQUID restat agendum. Nothing is perfect while something remains to be done. 9 Coke, 9.

NIHIL PETI POTEST ANTE ID TEMpus, quo per rerum naturam persolvi possit. Nothing can be demanded before that time when, in the nature of things, it can be paid. Dig. 50. 17. 186.

NIHIL POSSUMUS CONTRA VERITAtem. We can do nothing against truth. Doctor & Stud. dial. 2, c. 6.

NIHIL PRAESCRIBITUR NISI QUOD possidetur. There is no prescription for that which is not possessed. 5 Barn. & Ald. 277.

NIHIL QUOD EST CONTRA RATIONEM est licitum. Nothing against reason is lawful. Co. Litt. 97.

NIHIL QUOD EST INCONVENIENS EST licitum. Nothing inconvenient is lawful. 4 H. L. Cas. 145, 195.

NIHIL SIMUL INVENTUM EST ET PERfectum. Nothing is invented and perfected at the same moment. Co. Litt. 230; 2 Bl. Comm. 298, note.

NIHIL TAM CONVENIENS EST NATUrali aequitati quam unumquodque dissolvi eo ligamine quo ligatum est. Nothing is so consonant to natural equity as that each thing should be dissolved by the same means by which it was bound. 2 Inst. 360; Broom, Leg. Max. (3d London Ed.) 785. See Shep. Touch. 323.

NIHIL TAM CONVENIENS EST NATUrali aequitati, quam voluntatem domini vo-

lentis rem suam in alium transferre, ratam haberi. Nothing is more conformable to natural equity than to confirm the will of an owner who desires to transfer his property to another. Inst. 2. 1. 40; 1 Coke, 100.

NIHIL TAM NATURALE EST, QUAM EO genere quidque dissolvere, quo colligatum est. Nothing is so natural as that an obligation should be dissolved by the same principles which were observed in contracting it. Dig. 50. 17. 35. See 1 Coke, 100; 2 Inst. 359.

NIHIL TAM PROPRIUM IMPERIO QUAM legibus vivere. Nothing is so becoming to authority as to live according to the law. Fleta, lib. 1. c. 17, § 11; 2 Inst. 63.

NIL AGIT EXEMPLUM LITEM QUOD lite resolvit. An example does no good which settles one question by another. 15 Wend. (N. Y.) 44, 49.

NIL DEBET (Lat. he owes nothing). In pleading. The general issue in debt on simple contract. It is in the following form: "And the said C. D., by E. F., his attorney, comes and defends the wrong and injury, when, etc., and says that he does not owe the said sum of money above demanded, or any part thereof, in manner and form as the said A. B. hath above complained. And of this the said C. D. puts himself upon the country." When, in debt on specialty, the deed is the only inducement to the action, the general issue is *nil debet*. Steph. Pl. 174, note; 8 Johns. (N. Y.) 83; Dane, Abr. Index.

NIL FACIT ERROR NOMINIS SI DE corpore constat. An error in the name is immaterial if the body is certain. Broom, Leg. Max. (3d London Ed.) 566; 11 C. B. 406.

NIL HABUIT IN TENEMENTIS (Lat.) In pleading. A plea by which the defendant, who is sued by his landlord in debt for rent upon a lease, but by deed indented, denies his landlord's title to the premises, alleging "that he has no interest in the tenements." 2 Lilly, Abr. 214; 12 Viner, Abr. 184; 15 Viner, Abr. 556.

NIL SINE PRUDENTI FECIT RATIONE vetustas. Antiquity did nothing without a good reason. Co. Litt. 65.

NIL TEMERE NOVADUM. Nothing should be rashly changed. N. Jenk. Cent. Cas. 163.

NIMIA CERTITUDO CERTITUDINEM IPsam destruit. Too great certainty destroys certainty itself. Lofft, 244.

NIMIA SUBTILITAS IN JURE REPRObatur. To much subtlety in law is discountenanced. Wingate, Max. 26.

NIMIA SUBTILITAS IN JURE REPRObatur, et talis certitudo certitudinem confundit. Too great subtlety is disapproved of in law; for such nice pretense of certainty confounds true and legal certainty. Broom, Leg. Max. (3d London Ed.) 175; 4 Coke, 5.

NIMIUM ALTERCANDO, VERITAS amittitur. By too much altercation, truth is lost. Hob. 344.

NIMMER. A thief; a pilferer.

NISI (Lat. unless). A word frequently affixed to the words "order," "rule," etc., to indicate that such order or rule is conditional, being operative unless the party shall show cause to the contrary.

NISI PRIUS (Lat. unless before). In practice. For the purpose of holding trials by jury. Important words in the writ (*venire*) directing the sheriff to summon jurors for the trial of causes depending in the superior courts of law in England, which have come to be adopted, both in England and the United States, to denote those courts or terms of court held for the trial of civil causes with the presence and aid of a jury. The origin of the use of the term is to be traced to a period anterior to the institution of the commission of *nisi prius* in its more modern form. By *Magna Charta* it was provided that the common pleas should be held in one place, and should not follow the person of the king; and by another clause, that assizes of novel disseisin and of *mort d'ancestor*, which were the two commonest forms of actions to recover land, should be held in the various counties before the justices in eyre. A practice obtained very early, therefore, in the trial of trifling causes, to continue the cause in the superior court from term to term, provided the justices in eyre did not sooner (*nisi justiciarii diu*) come into the county where the cause of action arose, in which case they had jurisdiction when they so came. Bracton, lib. 3, c. 1, § 11. By the statute of *nisi prius* (13 Edw. I. c. 30, enforced by 14 Edw. III. c. 16), justices of assize were empowered to try common issues in trespass and other suits, and return them, when tried, to the superior court, where judgment was given. The clause was then left out of the continuance and inserted in the *venire*, thus: "*Praecipimus tibi quod venire facias coram justiciaris nostris apud Westm. in Octabis Scti Michaelis, nisi talis et talis, tali die et loco, ad partes illas venerint, duodecim,*" etc. We command you that you cause to come before our justices at Westminster, on the octave of Saint Michael, unless such and such a one, on such a day and place, shall come to those parts, twelve, etc. Under the provisions of 42 Edw. III. c. 11, the clause is omitted from the *venire*, and the jury is respited in the court above, while the sheriff summons them to appear before the justices, upon a *habeas corpora juratorum*, or, in the king's bench, a *distringas*. See Sellon, Prac. Introd. lxv;

1 Spence, Eq. Jur. 116; 3 Bl. Comm. 352-354; 1 Reeve, Hist. Eng. Law, 245, 382.

See, also "Assize;" "Courts of Assize and Nisi Prius;" "Jury."

NISI PRIUS ROLL. In practice. The transcript of a case made from the record of the superior court in which the action is commenced, for use in the *nisi prius* court.

It includes a history of all the proceedings in the case, including the declaration, plea, replication, rejoinder, issue, etc. It must be presented in proper manner to the *nisi prius* court. When a verdict has been obtained and entered on this record, it becomes the *postea,* and is returned to the superior court.

NISI PRIUS WRIT. The old name of the writ of *venire,* which originally, in pursuance of the statute of Westminster II., contained the *nisi prius* clause. Reg. Jud. 28, 75; Cowell. The clause, however, as it appears in the forms, was not in the original *nisi prius* form, but in the alternative, the jury being directed to be summoned to come before the justices at Westminster, etc., or before the justices of assize if they should sooner come to the place of trial, on the day designated. The emphatic Latin words were not *nisi prius,* but *vel si prius.* See Reg. Jud. ubi supra.

NO AWARD. The name of a plea to an action or award. 2 Ala. 520; 1 N. Chip. (Vt.) 131; 3 Johns. (N. Y.) 367.

NO BILL. Words frequently indorsed on a bill of indictment by the grand jury when they have not sufficient cause for finding a true bill. They are equivalent to "Not found," or "Ignoramus" (*q. v.*) 2 Nott & McC. (S. C.) 558.

NO PAR VALUE. Stock issued without any expressed par value. Fletcher Cyclopedia Corporations, § 3456.

NOBILE OFFICIUM. In Scotch law. An equitable power of the court of sessions, by which it is able, to a certain extent, to give relief when none is possible at law. Stair, Inst. bk. 4, tit. 3, § 1; Ersk. Inst. 1. 3. 22; Bell, Dict.

NOBILES MAGIS PLECTUNTUR PECUNIA; plebes vero in corporo. The higher classes are more punished in money; but the lower in person. 3 Inst. 220.

NOBILES SUNT QUI ARMA GENTILITIA antecessorum suorum proferre possunt. The gentry are those who are able to produce armorial bearings derived by descent from their own ancestors. 2 Inst. 595.

NOBILIORES ET BENIGNIORES PRESUMPTIONES in dubiis sunt praeferendae. When doubts arise, the most generous and benign presumptions are to be preferred. Reg. Jur.

NOBILITAS EST DUPLEX,—SUPERIOR et inferior. There are two sorts of nobility,—the higher and the lower. 2 Inst. 583.

NOBILITY. A division of the civil state, comprising persons exalted to some title or dignity. It is the opposite of "commonalty," and in England includes dukes, marquises, earls, viscounts, and barons. 1 Bl. Comm. 396.

NOCENT (from Lat. "*nocere*"). Guilty. "The *nocent* person." 1 Vern. 429.

NOCTANTER. By night. An abolished writ which issued out of chancery, and returned to the queen's bench, for the prostration of inclosures, etc.

NOCTES and NOCTEM DE FIRMA. Entertainment of meat and drink for so many nights. Domesday Book.

NOCUMENTUM (Lat. harm, nuisance). In old English law. A thing done whereby another man is annoyed in his free lands or tenements. Also, the assize or writ lying for the same. Fitzh. Nat. Brev. 183; Old Nat. Brev. 108, 109. Manw. For. Laws, c. 17, divides *nocumentum* into *generale, commune, speciale.* Reg. Orig. 197, 199; Coke, Will Case. *Nocumentum* was also divided into *damnosum,* for which no action lay, it being done by an irresponsible agent, and *injuriosum et damnosum,* for which there were several remedies. Bracton, 221; Fleta, lib. 4, c. 26, § 2.

NOLENS VOLENS (Lat.) Whether willing or unwilling.

NOLISSEMENT (Fr. from *nolis*). In French marine law. Affreightment. Ord. Mar. liv. 3, tit. 1.

NOLLE (Lat.) To be unwilling; to will not do a thing; to refuse to do a thing. Used, in the civil law, to denote a voluntary act under full knowledge. Calv. Lex. A distinction was made between *nolle* and *non velle.* Id. *Ejus est nolle, quie potest velle* (*q. v.*).

NOLLE PROSEQUI. In practice. An entry made on the record, by which the prosecutor or plaintiff declares that he will proceed no further. It was formerly used in both civil and criminal proceedings, but in the former is now superseded by the practice of discontinuance.

NOLO CONTENDERE. I will not contend. A plea to an indictment on which the defendant might be sentenced, but which did not estop him in a civil proceeding for the same cause.

NOMEN (Lat.)

——**In Civil Law.** A name of a person or thing. In a stricter sense, the name which declared the *gens* or family, as, Porcius, Cornelius; the *cognomen* being the name which marked the individual, as Cato, Marcus; *agnomen*, a name added to the *cognomen* for the purpose of description. The name of the person himself; *e. g.*, *nomen curiis addere*. The name denoting the condition of a person or class; *e. g.*, *nomen liberorum*, condition of children. Cause or reason (*pro causa aut ratione*); *e. g.*, *nomine culpae*, by reason of fault. A mark or sign of anything, corporeal or incorporeal. *Nomen supremum*, *i. e.*, God. Debt, or obligation of debt; a debtor. See Vicat; Calv. Lex.

——**In Old English Law.** A name; the Christian name, *e. g.*, John, as distinguished from the family name. It is also called *praenomen*. Fleta, lib. 4, c. 10, §§ 7, 9; Law Fr. & Lat. Dict.

——**In Scotch Law.** *Nomen debiti*, right to payment of a debt.

NOMEN COLLECTIVUM (Lat.) A word in the singular number, which is to be understood in the plural in certain cases.

Misdemeanor, for example, is a word of this kind, and when in the singular may be taken as *nomen collectivum*, and including several offenses. 2 Barn. & Adol. 75. "Heir," in the singular, sometimes includes all the heirs. "Felony" is not such a term.

NOMEN EST QUASI REI NOTAMEN. A name is, as it were, the note of a thing. 11 Coke, 20.

NOMEN GENERALE (Lat.) A general name; the name of a *genus*. Fleta, lib. 4, c. 19, § 1.

NOMEN GENERALISSIMUM (Lat.) A most universal or comprehensive term; *e. g.*, land. 2 Bl. Comm. 19; 3 Bl. Comm. 172; Taylor. So, "goods." 2 Williams, Ex'rs, 1014.

NOMEN JURIS. A name of the law; a legal name or designation; a technical legal term. 2 Swinton, 429.

NOMEN NON SUFFICIT SI RES NON sit de jure aut de facto. A name does not suffice if the thing do not exist by law or by fact. 4 Coke, 107.

NOMINA SI NESCIS PERIT COGNITIO rerum. If you know not the names of things, the knowledge of things themselves perishes. Co. Litt. 86.

NOMINA SUNT MUTABILIA, RES AUtem immobiles. Names are mutable, but things immutable. 6 Coke, 66.

NOMINA SUNT NOTAE RERUM. Names are the notes of things. 11 Coke, 20.

NOMINA SUNT SYMBOLA RERUM. Names are the symbols of things.

NOMINA VILLARUM (Lat.) Names of the villages. The name of a return made by the sheriffs of England into the exchequer, in the reign of Edward II. of the names of all the villages and their possessors in every county. Cowell; Blount.

NOMINAL. Existing in name only; formal, and not substantial.

NOMINAL DAMAGES. In practice. A trifling sum awarded where a breach of duty or an infraction of the plaintiff's right is shown, but no serious loss is proved to have been sustained. See "Injuria Absque Damno." Practically no damages at all. Such as exist only in name, and not in amount. They are such as are to be awarded in a case where there has been a breach of contract and no actual damages whatever have been or can be shown. 59 Conn. 272; 21 Am. St. Rep. 110; 188 Ill. 241, 242.

NOMINAL PARTNER. One who is apparently or ostensibly a member of a firm, but who is not really so.

The term "ostensible partner" has been used in the sense of nominal partner (67 Tex. 383), but it is better to confine the term "ostensible partner" to one who is really a partner, and known as such, and apply "nominal partner" to one who is not really a partner, but only apparently so.

NOMINAL PLAINTIFF. One who is named as the plaintiff in an action, but who has no interest in it, having assigned the cause or right of action to another, for whose use it is brought.

NOMINARE (Lat. from *nomen*, name). To name; to nominate; to appoint. Calv. Lex.

NOMINATE. To appoint. Applied in this sense to the designation by a person of one to act as fiduciary or personal representative. Thus it is the customary term in designating the executor by a testator.

To make a candidate for election. See "Candidate."

NOMINATE CONTRACT. A contract distinguished by a particular name, the use of which name determines the rights of all the parties to the contract; as, purchase and sale, hiring, partnership, loan for use, deposit, and the like. The law thus supersedes the necessity for special stipulations, and creates an obligation in the one party to perform, and a right in the other to demand, whatever is necessary to the explication of that contract. In Roman law there were twelve nominate contracts, with a particular action for each. Bell, Dict. "Nominate and Innominate;" Mackeld. Civ. Law, §§ 395, 408; Dig. 2, 14. 7. 1.

NOMINATING AND REDUCING. A mode of obtaining a panel of special jurors in England, from which to select the jury to try a particular action. The proceeding takes place before the under sheriff or secondary, and in the presence of the parties' solicitors. Numbers denoting the persons on the sheriff's list are put into a box and drawn until forty-eight unchallenged persons have been nominated. Each party strikes off twelve, and the remaining twenty-four are returned as the "panel" (*q. v.*) This practice is now only employed by order of the court or judge. Smith, Actions, 130; Juries Act 1870, § 17; Rapalje & L.

NOMINATIVUS PENDENS (Lat.) A nominative case grammatically unconnected with the rest of the sentence in which it stands. The opening words in the ordinary form of a deed *inter partes*, "This indenture," etc., down to "whereas," though an intelligible and convenient part of the deed, are of this kind. Wharton.

NOMINE POENAE (Lat. in the nature of a penalty).

——**In Civil Law.** A condition annexed to heirship by the will of the deceased person. Domat, Civ. Law; Halifax, Anal.

——**At Common Law.** A penalty fixed by covenant in a lease for nonperformance of its conditions. 2 Lilly, Abr. 221.

It is usually a gross sum of money, though it may be anything else, appointed to be paid by the tenant to the reversioner, if the duties are in arrear, in addition to the duties themselves. Hammond, N. P. 411, 412.

NOMINEE. One who has been nominated. See "Nominate."

NOMOCANON.

(1) A collection of canons and imperial laws relative or conformable thereto. The first nomocanon was made by Johannes Scholasticus in 554. Photius, patriarch of Constantinople, in 883, compiled another nomocanon, or collation of the civil laws with the canons; this is the most celebrated. Balsamon wrote a commentary upon it in 1180.

(2) A collection of the ancient canons of the apostles, councils, and fathers, without any regard to imperial constitutions. Such is the nomocanon by M. Cotelier. Enc. Lond.

NOMOGRAPHER. One who writes on the subject of laws.

NOMOGRAPHY. A treatise or description of laws.

NOMOTHETA. A lawgiver; such as Solon and Lycurgus among the Greeks, and Caesar, Pompey, and Sylla among the Romans. Calv. Lex.

NON (Lat.) Not; no.

NON ACCEPTAVIT (Lat. he did not accept). In pleading. The name of a plea to an action of *assumpsit* brought against the drawee of a bill of exchange upon a supposed acceptance by him. See 4 Man. & G. 561.

NON ACCIPI DEBENT VERBA IN DEMonstrationem falsam, quae competunt in limitationem veram. Words ought not to be accepted to import a false description, which may have effect by way of true limitation. Bac. Max. reg. 13; 2 Pars. Cont. 62-65; Broom, Leg. Max. (3d London Ed.) 573; 3 Barn. & Adol. 459; 4 Exch. 604; 3 Taunt. 147.

NON ALIO MODO PUNIATUR ALIQUIS, quam secundum quod se habet condemnatio. A person may not be punished differently than according to what the sentence enjoins. 3 Inst. 217.

NON ALITER A SIGNIFICATIONE VERborum recedi oportet quam cum manifestum est, aliud sensisse testatorem. We must never depart from the signification of words, unless it is evident that they are not conformable to the will of the testator. Dig. 32. 69. pr.; Broom, Leg. Max. (3d London Ed.) 500; 2 De Gex., M. & G. 313.

NON ASSUMPSIT (Lat. he did not undertake). In pleading. The general issue in an action of *assumpsit*.

Its form is: "And the said C. D., by E. F., his attorney, comes and defends the wrong and injury, when, etc., and says that he did not undertake or promise, in manner and form as the said A. B. hath above complained. And of this he puts himself upon the country."

NON ASSUMPSIT INFRA SEX ANNOS. (Lat. he has not undertaken within six years). In pleading. The plea by which, when pleadings were in Latin, the defendant alleged that the obligation was not undertaken and the right of action had not accrued within six years, the period of limitation of the right to bring suit.

NON AUDITUR PERIRE VOLENS. One who wishes to perish ought not to be heard. Best, Ex. § 385.

NON BIS IN IDEM. In civil law. A phrase which signifies that no one shall be twice tried for the same offense; that is, that when a party accused has been once tried by a tribunal in the last resort, and either convicted or acquitted, he shall not again be tried. Code, 9. 2. 9. 11; Merlin, Repert. See "Jeopardy."

NON CEPIT MODO ET FORMA (Lat. he did not take in manner and form). In pleading. The plea which raises the general issue in an action of replevin.

Its form is: "And the said C. D., by E. F., his attorney, comes and defends the wrong and injury, when, etc., and says that he did not take the said cattle (or, goods and chattels, according to the subject of the action) in the said declaration mentioned, or any of them, in manner and form as the said A. B. hath above complained. And of this the said C. D. puts himself upon the country."

It denies the taking the things, and having them in the place specified in the declaration, both of which are material in this action. Steph. Pl. 183, 184; 1 Chit. Pl. 490.

NON COMPOS MENTIS (Lat. not of sound mind, memory, or understanding). A generic term, including all the species of madness, whether it arise from idiocy, sickness, lunacy, or drunkenness. Co. Litt. 247; 4 Coke, 124; 1 Phil. 100; 4 Comyn, Dig. 613; 5 Comyn, Dig. 186; Shelf. Lun. 1. See "Idiocy;" "Insanity."

NON CONCEDANTUR CITATIONES PRIusquam exprimatur super qua re fieri decet citatio. Summonses or citations should not be granted before it is expressed upon what ground a citation ought to be issued. 12 Coke, 47.

NON CONCESSIT (Lat. he did not grant). In English law. The name of a plea by which the defendant denies that the crown granted to the plaintiff by letters patent the rights which he claims as a concession from the king; as, for example, when a plaintiff sues another for the infringement of his patent right, the defendant may deny that the crown has granted him such a right.

It does not deny the grant of a patent, but of the patent as described in the plaintiff's declaration. 3 Burrows, 1544; 6 Coke, 15b.

NON CONSENTIT QUI ERRAT. He who errs does not consent. 1 Bouv. Inst. note 581; Bracton, 44.

NON CONSTAT (Lat. it does not appear). Words frequently used, particularly in argument, to express dissatisfaction with the conclusions of the other party; as, it was moved in arrest of judgment that the declaration was not good, because *non constat* whether A. B. was seventeen years of age when the action was commenced. Swinb. pt. 4, § 22, p. 331.

NON CULPABILIS (Lat.) In pleading. Not guilty. It is usually abbreviated *non cul.* 16 Viner, Abr. 1; 2 Gabbett, Crim. Law, 317.

NON DAMNIFICATUS (Lat. not injured). In pleading. A plea to an action of debt on a bond of indemnity, by which the defendant asserts that the plaintiff has received no damage. 1 Bos. & P. 640, note (a); 1 Taunt. 428; 1 Saund. 116, note 1; 2 Saund. 81; 7 Wentw. Pl. 615, 616; 1 H. Bl. 253; 2 Lilly, Abr. 224; 14 Johns. (N. Y.) 177; 5 Johns. (N. Y.) 42; 20 Johns. (N. Y.) 153, 3 Cow. (N. Y.) 313; 10 Wheat. (U. S.) 396, 405; 3 Halst. (N. J.) 1.

NON DAT QUI NON HABET. He gives nothing who has nothing. Broom, Leg. Max. (3d London Ed.) 417.

NON DEBEO MELIORIS CONDITIONIS esse, quam auctor meus a quo jus in me transit. I ought not to be in better condition than he to whose rights I succeed. Dig. 50. 17. 175. 1.

NON DEBET ADDUCI EXCEPTIO EJUS rei cujus petitur dissolutio. A plea of the same matter the dissolution of which is sought ought not to be made. Bac. Max. reg. 2; Broom, Leg. Max. (3d London Ed.) 157; 3 P. Wms. 317; 1 Ld. Raym. 57; 2 Ld. Raym. 1433.

NON DEBET ALII NOCERE, QUOD INter alios actum est. A person ought not to be prejudiced by what has been done between others. Dig. 12. 2. 10.

NON DEBET ALTERI PER ALTERUM iniqua conditio inferri. A burdensome condition ought not to be brought upon one man by the act of another. Dig. 50. 17. 74.

NON DEBET, CUI PLUS LICET, QUOD minus est, non licere. He who is permitted to do the greater may with greater reason do the less. Dig. 50. 17. 21; Broom, Leg. Max. (3d London Ed.) 165.

NON DEBET DICI TENDERE IN PRAEjudicium ecclesiasticae libertatis quod pro rege et republica necessarium videtur. That which seems necessary for the king and the state ought not to be said to tend to the prejudice of spiritual liberty. 2 Inst. 625.

NON DEBET ACTORI LICERE, QUOD reo non permittitur. That which is not permitted to the defendant ought not to be to the plaintiff. Dig. 50. 17. 41.

NON DECET HOMINES DEDERE CAUSA non cognita. It is unbecoming to surrender men when no cause is shown. 4 Johns. Ch. (N. Y.) 106, 114; 3 Wheeler, Cr. R. (N. Y.) 473, 482.

NON DECIPITUR QUI SCIT SE DECIPI. He is not deceived who knows himself to be deceived. 5 Coke, 60.

NON DEDIT. In pleading. The general issue in formedon. See "Ne Dona Pas, Non Debit."

NON DEFINITUR IN JURE QUID SIT conatus. What an attempt is, is not defined in law. 6 Coke, 42.

NON DEMISIT (Lat. he did not demise). In pleading. A plea proper to be pleaded to an action of debt for rent, when the plaintiff declares on a parol lease. Gilb. Debt, 436, 438; Buller, N. P. 177; 1 Chit. Pl. 477.

It cannot be pleaded when the demise is stated to have been by indenture. 12 Viner, Abr. 178; Comyn, Dig. "Pleader" (2 W. 48).

NON DETINET (Lat. he does not detain). In pleading. The general issue in an action of detinue. Its form is as follows: "And the said C. D., by E. F., his attorney, comes and defends the wrong and injury, when, etc., and says that he does not detain the said goods and chattels (or "deeds and writings," according to the subject of the action) in the said declaration specified, or any part thereof, in manner and form as the said A. B. hath above complained. And of this the said C. D. puts himself upon the country."

NON DIFFERUNT QUAE CONCORDANT re, tametsi non in verbis iisdam. Those things which agree in substance, though not in the same words, do not differ. Jenk. Cent. Cas. 70.

NON DUBITATUR, ETSI SPECIALITER venditor evictionem non promiserit, re evicta, ex empto competere actionem. It is certain that, although the vendor has not given a special guaranty, an action *ex empto* lies against him, if the purchaser is evicted. Code, 8. 45. 6. But see Doctor & Stud. bk. 2, c. 47; Broom, Leg. Max. (3d London Ed.) 690.

NON EFFICIT AFFECTUS NISI SEQUAtur effectus. The intention amounts to nothing unless some effect follows. 1 Rolle, 226.

NON ERIT ALIA LEX ROMAE, ALIA Athenis; alia nunc, alia posthac; sed et omnes gentes, et omni tempore, una lex, et sempiterna, et immortalis continebit. There will not be one law at Rome, another at Athens; one law now, another hereafter; but one eternal and immortal law shall bind together all nations throughout all time. Cicero, Frag. de Repub. lib. 3; 3 Kent, Comm. 1.

NON EST ARCTIUS VINCULUM INTER homines quam jusjurandum. There is no stronger link among men than an oath. Jenk. Cent. Cas. 126.

NON EST CERTANDUM DE REGULIS juris. There is no disputing about rules of law.

NON EST CONSONUM RATIONI, QUOD cognitio accessorii in curia christianitatis impediatur, ubi cognitio causae principalis ad forum ecclesiasticum noscitur pertinere. It is unreasonable that the cognizance of an accessory matter should be impeded in an ecclesiastical court, when the cognizance of the principal cause is admitted to appertain to an ecclesiastical court. 12 Coke, 65.

NON EST DISPUTANDUM CONTRA principia negantem. There is no disputing against a man denying principles. Co. Litt. 343.

NON EST FACTUM (Lat. is not his deed). In pleading. A plea to an action of debt on a bond or other specialty.

Its form is: "And the said C. D., by E. F., his attorney, comes and defends the wrong and injury, when, etc., and says that the said supposed writing obligatory (or "indenture," or "articles of agreement," according to the subject of the action) is not his deed. And of this he puts himself upon the country." 6 Rand. (Va.) 86; 1 Litt. (Ky.) 158.

NON EST INVENTUS (Lat. I have not found him). In practice. The sheriff's return to a writ requiring him to arrest the person of the defendant, which signifies that he is not to be found within his jurisdiction. The return is usually abbreviated N. E. I. Chit. Prac.

NON EST JUSTUM ALIQUEM ANTENAtum post mortem facere bastardum, qui toto tempore vitae suae pro legitimo habebatur. It is not just to make an elder born a bastard after his death, who during his lifetime was accounted legitimate. 12 Coke, 44.

NON EST NOVUM UT PRIORES LEGIS ad forum ecclesiasticum noscitur pertinere. thing that prior statutes shall give place to later ones. Dig. 1. 3. 26; Id. 1. 1. 4; Broom, Leg. Max. (3d London Ed.) 27.

NON EST RECEDENDUM A COMMUNI observanti. There should be no departure from a common observance. 2 Coke, 74.

NON EST REGULA QUIN FALLAT. There is no rule but what may fail. Off. Exec. 212.

NON EST SINGULIS CONCEDENDUM, quod per magistratum publice possit fieri, ne occasio sit majoris tumultus faciendi. That is not to be conceded to private persons which can be publicly done by the magistrate, lest it be the occasion of greater tumults. Dig. 50. 17. 176.

NON EX OPINIONIBUS SINGULORUM, sed ex communi usu, nomina exaudiri debent. Names of things ought to be understood according to common usage, not according to the opinions of individuals. Dig. 33. 10. 7. 2.

NON FACIES MALUM, UT INDE VEniat bonum. You are not to do evil that good may come of it. 11 Coke, 74a.

NON FECIT (Lat. he did not make it). The name of a plea, for example, in an action of *assumpsit* on a promissory note. 3 Man. & G. 446.

NON FECIT VASTUM CONTRA PROHIbitionem (Lat. he did not commit waste against the prohibition). In pleading. The name of a plea to an action founded on a writ of estrepement, that the defendant did not commit waste contrary to the prohibition. 3 Bl. Comm. 226, 227.

NON IMPEDIT CLAUSULA DEROGATOria, quo minus ab eadem potestate res dissolvantur a quibus constituuntur. A derogatory clause does not prevent things or acts from being dissolved by the same power by which they were originally made. Bac. Max. reg. 19.

NON IMPEDIVIT (Lat. he did not impede). In pleading. The plea of the general issue in *quare impedit.* 3 Bl. Comm. 305; 3 Wooddeson, Lect. 36. In law French, *ne disturba pas.*

NON IMPLACITANDO ALIQUEM DE libero tenemento sine brevi. A writ to prohibit bailiffs, etc., from distraining or impleading any man touching his freehold without the king's writ. Reg. Orig. 171.

NON IN LEGENDO SED IN INTELLIgendo leges consistunt. The laws consist not in being read, but in being understood. 8 Coke, 167.

NON INFREGIT CONVENTIONEM (Lat. he has not broken the covenant). In pleading. A plea in an action of covenant. This plea is not a general issue; it merely denies that the defendant has broken the covenants on which he is sued. It being in the negative, it cannot be used where the breach is also in the negative. Bac. Abr. "Covenant" (L); 3 Lev. 19; 2 Taunt. 278; 1 Aik. (Vt.) 150; 4 Dall. (Pa.) 436; 7 Cow. (N. Y.) 71.

NON INTERFUI. I was not present. A reporter's note. T. Jones, 10.

NON INTROMITTANT CLAUSE. In English law. A clause of a charter of a municipal borough, whereby the borough is exempted from the jurisdiction of the justices of the peace for the county.

NON INTROMITTENDO, QUANDO BREve praecipe in capite subdole impetratur. A writ addressed to the justices of the bench, or in eyre, commanding them not to give one who, under color of entitling the king to land, etc., as holding of him *in capite,* had deceitfully obtained the writ called "*praecipe in capite,*" any benefit thereof, but to put him to his writ of right. Reg. Orig. 4.

NON JURIDICUS. Not judicial. See "Dies Non."

NON JUS EX REGULA, SED REGULA ex jure. The law does not arise from the rule, or maxim, but the rule from the law. Tray. Lat. Max. 384.

NON JUS, SED SEISINA FACIT STIPItem. Not right, but seisin, makes a stock from which the inheritance must descend. Fleta, lib. 6. cc. 14, 2, § 2; Noy, Max. (9th Ed.) 72, note (b); Broom, Leg. Max. (3d London Ed.) 466; 2 Bl. Comm. 209; 1 Steph. Comm. 365, 368, 394; 4 Kent, Comm. 383, 389; 4 Scott, N. R. 468.

NON LICET QUOD DISPENDIO LICET. That which is permitted only at a loss is not permitted to be done. Co. Litt. 127.

NON LIQUET (Lat. it is not clear). In civil law. Words by which the judges (*judices*) in a Roman trial were accustomed to free themselves from the necessity of deciding a cause when the rights of the parties were doubtful. On the tablets which were given to the judges wherewith to indicate their judgment, was written "*N. L.*" Vicat.

NON MERCHANDIZANDA VICTUALIA. An ancient writ addressed to justices of assize, to inquire whether the magistrates of a town sold victuals in gross or by retail during the time of their being in office, which was contrary to an obsolete statute; and to punish them if they did. Reg. Orig. 184.

NON MOLESTANDO. A writ that lay for a person who was molested contrary to the king's protection granted to him. Reg. Orig. 184.

NON NASCI, ET NATUM MORI, PARIA sunt. Not to be born, and to be dead born, are the same.

NON OBLIGAT LEX NISI PROMULgata. A law is not obligatory unless it be promulgated.

NON OBSERVATA FORMA, INFERTUR adnullatio actus. When the form is not observed, it is inferred that the act is annulled. 12 Coke, 7.

NON OBSTANTE. In English law. These words, which literally signify "notwithstanding," are used to express the act of the English king by which he dispenses with the law, that is, authorizes its violation.

He cannot by his license or dispensation make an offense dispunishable which is *malum in se;* but in certain matters which are *mala prohibita* he may, to certain persons and on special occasions, grant a *non obstante.* Vaughan, 330-359; Lev. 217; Sid. 6, 7; 12 Coke, 18; Bac. Abr. "Prerogative" (D 7). See "Judgment."

NON OBSTANTE VEREDICTO. Notwithstanding the verdict. See "Judgment."

NON OFFICIT CONATUS NISI SEQUAtur effectus. An attempt does not harm unless a consequence follow. 11 Coke, 98.

NON OMITTAS (Lat. more fully, *non omittas propter libertatem,* do not omit on account of the liberty or franchise). In practice. A writ which lies when the sheriff returns on writ to him directed, that he hath sent to the bailiff of such a franchise, which hath return of writs, and he hath not served the writ; then the plaintiff shall have this writ directed to the sheriff, that he "omit not on account of any franchise," but himself enter into the franchise, and execute the king's writ. Termes de la Ley.

This clause is now usually inserted in all processes addressed to sheriffs. Wharton; 2 Wm. IV. c. 39; 3 Chit. St. 494; 3 Chit. Prac. 190, 310.

NON OMNE DAMNUM INDUCIT INJURiam. Not every loss produces an injury, *i. e.*, gives a right of action. See 3 Bl. Comm. 219; 1 Smith, Lead. Cas. 131; Broom, Leg. Max. 93; 2 Bouv. Inst. note 2211.

NON OMNE QUOD LICET HONESTUM est. It is not everything which is permitted that is honorable. Dig. 50. 17. 144.

NON OMNIUM QUAE A MAJORIBUS nostris constituta sunt ratio reddi potest. A reason cannot always be given for the institutions of our ancestors. 4 Coke, 78; Broom, Leg. Max. (3d London Ed.) 149; Branch, Princ.

NON PERTINET AD JUDICEM SECUlarem cognoscere de iis quae sunt mere spiritualia annexa. It belongs not to the secular judge to take cognizance of things which are merely spiritual. 2 Inst. 488.

NON PONENDIS IN ASSISIS ET JURAtis. A writ formerly granted for freeing and discharging persons from serving on assizes and juries. Fitzh. Nat. Brev. 165.

NON POSSESSORI INCUMBIT NECESsitas probandi possessiones ad se pertinere. It is not incumbent on the possessor of property to prove his right to his possessions. Code, 4. 9. 2; Broom, Leg. Max. (3d London Ed.) 639.

NON POTEST ADDUCI EXCEPTIO ejusdem rei cujus petitur dissolutio. A plea of the same matter, the dissolution of which is sought by the action, cannot be brought forward. Bac. Max. reg. 2. When an action is brought to annul a proceeding, the defendant cannot plead such proceeding in bar. Broom, Leg. Max. (3d London Ed.) 154; Wingate, Max. 647; 3 P. Wms. 317.

NON POTEST PROBARI QUOD PROBAtum non relevat. That cannot be proved which, proved, is irrelevant. See 1 Exch. 91, 92, 102.

NON POTEST QUIS SINE BREVI agere. No one can sue without a writ. Fleta, lib. 2, c. 13, § 4.

NON POTEST REX GRATIAM FACERE cum injuria et damno aliorum. The king cannot confer a favor which occasions injury and loss to others. 3 Inst. 236; Broom, Leg. Max. (3d London Ed.) 60; Vaughan, 338; 2 El. & Bl. 874.

NON POTEST REX SUBDITUM RENItentem onerare impositionibus. The king cannot load a subject with imposition against his consent. 2 Inst. 61.

NON POTEST VIDERI DESISSE HAbere, qui nunquam habuit. He cannot be considered as having ceased to have a thing, who never had it. Dig. 50. 17. 208.

NON PRAESTAT IMPEDIMENTUM quod de jure non sortitur effectum. A thing which has no effect in law is not an impediment. Jenk. Cent. Cas. 162; Wingate, Max. 727.

NON PROS. An abbreviation of *non prosequitur*, he does not pursue. Where the plaintiff, at any stage of the proceedings, fails to prosecute his action, or any part of it, in due time, the defendant enters *non prosequitur*, and signs final judgment, and obtains costs against the plaintiff, who is said to be *non pros'd*. 2 Archb. Prac. (Chit. Ed.) 1409; 3 Bl. Comm. 296; 1 Tidd. Prac. 458; Graham, Prac. 763; 3 Chit. Prac. 10; 1 Penn. Prac. 84; Caines Prac. 102. The name *non pros.* is applied to the judgment so rendered against the plaintiff. 1 Sellon, Prac., and authorities above cited.

NON QUOD DICTUM EST, SED QUOD factum est, inspicitur. Not what is said, but what is done, is to be regarded. Co. Litt. 36; 6 Bing. 310; 1 Metc. (Mass.) 353; 11 Cush. (Mass.) 536.

NON REFERT AN QUIS ASSENSUM suum praefert verbis, an rebus ipsis et factis. It is immaterial whether a man gives his assent by words or by acts and deeds. 10 Coke, 52.

NON REFERT QUID EX AEQUIPOLlentibus fiat. It matters not what becomes of equipollent expressions. 5 Coke, 122.

NON REFERT QUID NOTUM SIT JUDIci, si notum non sit in forma judicii. It matters not what is known to the judge, if it is not known to him judicially. 3 Bulst. 115.

NON REFERT VERBIS AN FACTIS FIT revocatio. It matters not whether a revocation be by words or by acts. Cro. Car. 49; Branch, Princ.

NON REMOTA CAUSA SED PROXIMA spectatur. See "Causa Proxima, etc".

NON RESPONDEBIT MINOR, NISI IN causa dotis, et hoc pro favore doti. A minor shall not answer unless in a case of dower, and this in favor of dower. 4 Coke, 71.

NON REUS NISI MENS SIT REA. Not guilty unless the intent be guilty. 1 Story, Cont. (4th Ed.) 87.

NON SANAE MENTIS (Lat.) Of unsound mind. Fleta, lib. 6, c. 40, § 1.

NON SANE MEMORY. Unsound memory; unsound mind. A term essentially law French. See "Memory."

NON SEQUITUR (Lat.) It does not follow.

NON SOLENT QUAE ABUNDANT VITIare scripturas. Surplusage does not usually vitiate writings. Dig. 50. 17. 94; Broom, Leg. Max. (3d London Ed.) 559, note.

NON SOLUM QUID LICET, SED QUID est conveniens considerandum, quia nihil quod inconveniens est licitum. Not only what is permitted, but what is convenient, is to be considered, because what is inconvenient is illegal. Co. Litt. 66a.

NON SOLVENDO PECUNIAM AD quam clericus mulctatur pro non residentia. A writ prohibiting an ordinary to take a pecuniary mulct imposed on a clerk of the sovereign for nonresidence. Reg. Writs. 59.

NON SUBMISSIT (Lat.) The name of a plea to an action of debt, or a bond to perform an award, by which the defendant pleads that he did not submit. Bac. Abr. "Arbitration, etc." (G).

NON SUI JURIS (Lat.) The opposite of *sui juris* (*q. v.*)

NON SUM INFORMATUS. See "Judgment."

NON SUNT LONGA UBI NIHIL EST quod demere possis. There is no prolixity where there is nothing that can be omitted. Vaughan, 138.

NON TEMERE CREDERE, EST NERvus sapientae. Not to believe rashly is the nerve of wisdom. 5 Coke, 114.

NON TENENT INSIMUL. (Lat. they do not hold together). In pleading. A plea to an action in partition, by which the defendant denies that he holds the property which is the subject of the suit, together with the complainant or plaintiff.

NON TENUIT (Lat. he did not hold). In pleading. The name of a plea in bar in replevin, when the plaintiff has avowed for rent arrear, by which the plaintiff avows that he did not hold in manner and form as the avowry alleges.

NON VALEBIT FELONIS GENERATIO, nec ad haereditatem paternam vel maternam; si autem ante feloniam generationem fecerit, talis generatio succedit in haereditate patris vel matris a quo non fuerit felonia perpetrata. The offspring of a felon cannot succeed either to a maternal or paternal inheritance; but, if he had offspring before the felony, such offspring may succeed as to the inheritance of the father or mother by whom the felony was not committed. 3 Coke, 41.

NON VALENTIA AGERE (Law Lat.) Inability to sue. 5 Bell, App. Cas. 172.

NON VALET CONFIRMATIO, NISI ille, qui confirmat, sit in possessione rei vel juris unde fieri debet confirmatio; et eodem modo, nisi ille cui confirmatio fit sit in possessione. Confirmation is not valid unless he who confirms is either in possession of the thing itself, or of the right of which confirmation is to be made, and, in like manner, unless he to whom confirmation is made is in possession. Co. Litt. 295.

NON VALET EXCEPTIO EJUSDEM REI cujus petitur dissolutio. A plea of that of which the dissolution is sought is not valid. 2 Eden, 134.

NON VALET IMPEDIMENTUM QUOD de jure non sortitur effectum. An impediment is of no avail which by law has no effect. 4 Coke, 31a.

NON VERBIS SED IPSIS REBUS, LEges imponimus. Not upon words, but upon things themselves, do we impose law. Code, 6. 43. 2.

NON VIDENTUR QUI ERRANT CONsentire. He who errs is not considered as consenting. Dig. 50. 17. 116; Broom, Leg. Max. (3d London Ed.) 240; 2 Kent, Comm. 477; 14 Ga. 207.

NON VIDENTUR REM AMITTERE QUIbus propria non fuit. They are not considered as losing a thing whose own it was not. Dig. 50. 17. 85.

NON VIDETUR CONSENSUM RETINuisse si quis ex praescripto minantis aliquid immutavit. He does not appear to have retained his consent, who has changed anything at the command of a party threatening. Bac. Max. reg. 22; Broom, Leg. Max. (3d London Ed.) 254.

NON VIDETUR PERFECTE CUJUSQUE id esse, quod ex casu auferri potest. That does not truly belong to any one which can be taken from him upon occasion. Dig. 50. 17. 159. 1.

NON VIDETUR QUISQUAM ID CApere, quod ei necesse est alii restituere. One is not considered as acquiring property in a thing which he is bound to restore. Dig. 50. 17. 51.

NON VIDETUR VIM FACERE, QUI jure suo utitur, et ordinaria actione experitur. He is not judged to use force who exercises his own right, and proceeds by ordinary action. Dig. 50. 17. 155. 1.

NONACCESS. The nonexistence of sexual intercourse between a husband and wife is generally expressed by the words "nonaccess of the husband to the wife;" which expressions, in a case of bastardy, are understood to mean the same thing. 2 Starkie, Ev. 218, note. See "Access."

NONAGE. By this term is understood that period of life from the birth till the arrival of twenty-one years. In another sense, it means under the proper age to be of ability to do a particular thing; as, when nonage is applied to one under the age of fourteen, who is unable to marry. See "Age."

NONAGIUM, or NONAGE. A ninth part of movables which was paid to the clergy on the death of persons in their parish, and claimed on pretense of being distributed to pious uses. Blount.

NONAPPARENT EASEMENT. A discontinuous easement. See "Apparent Easement."

NONCLAIM. An omission or neglect by one entitled to make a demand within the time limited by law; as, when a continual claim ought to be made, a neglect to make such claim within a year and a day.

NONCONFORMISTS. In English law. A name given to certain dissenters from the rites and ceremonies of the church of England.

NONCONTINUOUS EASEMENT. A nonapparent or discontinuous easement. See "Apparent Easement."

NONES. In the Roman calendar. The fifth, and, in March, May, July, and October the seventh, day of the month. So called because, counting inclusively, they were nine days from the Ides. Adams, Rom. Ant. 355, 357. See "Ides."

NONFEASANCE. The neglect or failure of a person to do some act which he ought to do. The term is not generally used to denote a breach of contract, but rather the failure to perform a duty towards the public whereby some individual sustains special damage, as where a sheriff fails to execute a writ. 3 Bl. Comm. 165; Broom, Com. Law, 655.

When a legislative act requires a person to do a thing, its nonfeasance will subject the party to punishment; as, if a statute require the supervisors of the highways to repair such highways, the neglect to repair them may be punished. See 1 Russ. Crimes, 48. See also, "Mandate."

NONISSUABLE PLEAS. Those upon which a decision would not determine the action upon the merits, as a plea in abatement. 1 Chit. Archb. Prac. (12th Ed.) 249.

NONJOINDER. Omission of a necessary or proper party. See "Joinder."

NONJURORS. In English law. Persons who refuse to take the oaths, required by law, to support the government. See 1 Dall. (Pa.) 170.

NONPLEVIN. In old English law. A neglect to replevin land taken into the hands of the king upon default, within fifteen days, by which seisin was lost, as by default. Heugh. de Magna Charta, c. 8. By 9 Edw. III. c. 2, no man shall lose his land by nonplevin.

NONRESIDENCE. In ecclesiastical law. The absence of spiritual persons from their benefices.

NONRESIDENT. A nonresident is one who does not reside in or is not a resident of a particular place. One may be a nonresident of the United States or of a state, or of a county, or of any particular place. 169 Ill. 42, 43; 69 Ill. App. 423.

NONRESIDENTIA PRO CLERICO REGIS. A writ, addressed to a bishop, charging him not to molest a clerk employed in the royal service, by reason of his nonresidence; in which case he is to be discharged. Reg. Orig. 58.

NONSENSE. That which in a written agreement or will is unintelligible.

NONSUIT. A judgment given against the plaintiff when he is unable to prove his case, or, when he neglects or refuses to proceed to trial, judgment of nonsuit dismisses the action, but does not determine the issues.

Voluntary nonsuit is an abandonment of his cause by the plaintiff either before the trial is commenced, or during the presentation of his case.

Involuntary nonsuit is judgment of nonsuit ordered by the court where plaintiff fails to appear, or where he has given no evidence on which a verdict in his favor could be rendered.

NONSUMMONS, WAGER OF LAW OF. The mode in which a tenant or defendant in a real action pleaded, when the summons which followed the original was not served within the proper time. 31 Eliz. c. 3, § 2; 2 Saund. 45.

NONTENURE. In pleading. A plea in a real action, by which the defendant asserted that he did not hold the land, or at least some part of it, as mentioned in the plaintiff's declaration (1 Mod. 250); in which case the writ abates as to the part with reference to which the plea is sustained (8 Cranch [U. S.] 242). It may be pleaded with or without a disclaimer. It was a dilatory plea, though not strictly in abatement (2 Saund. 44, note 4; Dyer, 210; Booth, Real Actions, 179; 3 Mass. 312; 11 Mass. 216), but might be pleaded as to part along with a plea in bar as to the rest (1 Lutw. 716; Rast. Entr. 231a, 231b), and was subsequently considered as a plea in bar (14 Mass. 239; 1 Me. 54; 2 N. H. 10; Bac. Abr. "Pleas" [I 9]).

NONTERM. The vacation between two terms of a court.

NONTERMINUS. The vacation between term and term, formerly called the time or days of the king's peace.

NONUSER. Neglect to make use of a franchise, privilege, or right. See 23 Pick. (Mass.) 141.

NOOK OF LAND (Law Lat. *noka,* or *nocata terrae*). In old records. A measure or description of land, of uncertain quantity. Blount observes that he had seen an old deed of Sir Walter de Pedwardyn, wherein twelve acres and a half were granted for a noke of land, but he thought the quantity was not certain.

NOON. The middle of the day, the time when the sun is in the meridian, and is to be determined by mean sun time, and not by arbitrary standard time, in the absence of any evidence that standard time was intended. 110 Iowa 75.

NORTH. Unless qualified or controlled by other words, "north" means due north. 96 Cal. 508.

NORTHAMPTON TABLES. Longevity and annuity tables compiled from bills of mortality kept in All Saints Parish, England, in 1735-1780.

NOSAUNCE, *Noysaunce.* L. Fr. (from *noier*, or *nuire*, to hurt). A nuisance; an act done by one to the injury of another's freehold; an act by which a person is prevented from enjoying his tenement as conveniently or freely as he ought to do. Britt. c. 61.

NOSCITUR A SOCIIS. It is known from its associates. The meaning of a word may be ascertained by reference to the meaning of words associated with it. Broom, Leg. Max. (3d London Ed.) 523; 9 East, 267; 13 East, 531; 6 Taunt. 294; 1 Vent. 225; 1 Barn. & C. 644; Arg. 10 Barn. & C. 496, 519; 18 C. B. 102, 893; 5 Man. & G. 639, 667; 3 C. B. 437; 5 C. B. 380; 4 Exch. 511, 519; 5 Exch. 294; 11 Exch. 113; 3 Term R. 87; 8 Term R. 118; 1 N. Y. 47, 69; 11 Barb. (N. Y.) 43, 63; 20 Barb. (N. Y.) 644.

NOSCITUR EX SOCIO, QUI NON COGnoscitur ex se. He who cannot be known from himself may be known from his associate. F. Moore, 817; 1 Vent. 225; 3 Term R. 87; 9 East, 267; 13 East, 531; 6 Taunt. 294; 1 Barn. & C. 644.

NOSOCOMI. In civil law. Persons who have the management and care of hospitals for paupers. Clef Lois Rom. mot "Administrateurs."

NOT FOUND. Words indorsed on a bill of indictment by a grand jury, when they have not sufficient evidence to find a true bill. See "Ignoramus."

NOT GUILTY.

——**In Pleading.** The general issue in several sorts of actions of tort.

——**In Criminal Law.** The general traverse of the accusation by the accused.

NOT POSSESSED. In pleading. A plea sometimes used in actions of trover, when the defendant was not possessed of the goods at the commencement of the action. 3 Man. & G. 101, 103.

NOT PROVEN. In Scotch criminal law. It is a peculiarity of the Scotch jury system in criminal trials that it admits a verdict of "Not proven," corresponding to the *Non liquet* of the Roman law. The legal effect of this is equivalent to "Not guilty;" for a prisoner in whose case it is pronounced cannot be tried again. According to the homely but expressive maxim of the law, no man can be made to thole an assize twice. But, although the verdict of "Not proven" is so far tantamount to an acquittal that the party cannot be tried a second time, it falls very far short of it with regard to the effect upon his reputation and character. He goes away from the bar of the court with an indelible stigma upon his fame. There stands recorded against him the opinion of a jury that the evidence respecting his guilt was so strong that they did not dare to pronounce a verdict of acquittal. So that many of the evil consequences of a conviction follow, although the jury refuses to convict. When Sir Nicholas Throckmorton was tried and acquitted by an English jury in 1554, he said: "It is better to be tried than to live suspected." But in Scotland a man may be not only tried, but acquitted, and yet live suspected, owing to the sinister influence of a verdict of "Not proven." Forsyth, Hist. Trial by Jury, 334-339.

NOTA (Lat.)

——**In Civil Law.** A mark or brand put upon a person by the law. 1 Mackeld. Civ. Law, 134, 135.

——**In Old English Conveyancing.** A note or memorandum of a charter or deed, drawn up preparatory to the execution of the charter itself. *Si autem dicant testes quod praesentes fuerint confectioni notae in quam utraque pars consentit, donator et donatorius, hoc sufficit ad probationem, licet praesentes non essent ubi charta scripta fuit et assignata* [*signata*]. But if the witnesses say that they were present at the making of the note, to which each party agreed, donor and donee, this is sufficient for proof, though they were not present when the charter was written and sealed. Bracton, fol. 398; Fleta, lib. 6, c. 34, § 2.

A promissory note. 11 Mod. 340.

NOTAE (Lat.) In civil and old European law. Shorthand characters or marks of contraction, in which one person wrote what was said by another, or in which the emperors' secretaries took down what they dictated. Spelman; Calv. Lex. See "Notarius."

NOTARE INFAMIA (Lat.) In the civil law. To mark or brand with infamy, or disgrace. Dig. 3. 2. For a description of the persons who were so branded (*de his qui notantur infamia*), see Id.

NOTARIAL. Belonging to a notary; made or done by a notary.

NOTARIUS.

——**In Civil Law.** One who took notes or draughts in shorehand of what was said by another, or of proceedings in the senate or in a court. One who draughted written instruments, wills, conveyances, etc. Vicat; Calv. Lex.

——**In English Law.** A notary. Law Fr. & Lat. Dict.; Cowell.

NOTARY, or NOTARY PUBLIC. An officer appointed by the executive or other appointing power, under the laws of different states, having power generally to attest writings for the purpose of establishing their authenticity, to administer oaths, etc.

NOTATION. In English probate practice, notation is the act of making a memorandum of some special circumstance on a probate or letters of administration. Thus, where a grant is made for the whole personal estate of the deceased within the United Kingdom, which can only be done in the case of a person dying domiciled in England, the fact of his having been so domiciled is noted on the grant. Coote, Prob. Prac. 36.

NOTE OF A FINE. The fourth step of the proceedings in acknowledging a fine, which is only an abstract of the writ of covenant and the concord, naming the parties, the parcel of land, and the agreement, and enrolled of record in the proper office. 2 Bl. Comm. 351, Append. note iv. § 3; 1 Steph. Comm. 518.

NOTE OF ALLOWANCE. This was a note delivered by a master to a party to a cause, who alleged that there was error in law in the record and proceedings, allowing him to bring error. See Com. Law Prac. Act 1852, § 149.

NOTE OF HAND. A popular name for a promissory note.

NOTE OF PROTEST. A note or minute of the protest, made by the notary, at time of protest on the bill, to be completed or filled out at his leisure. Byles, Bills (5th Ed.) 9.

NOTE OR MEMORANDUM. No form of language used in a writing is necessary in order to comply with the Statute of Frauds, requiring some "note or memorandum" as evidence of a contract not in writing, provided that from the writing the intention may be gathered, and any writing from a solemn deed down to hasty notes or memoranda in books, papers, or letters will satisfy the statute, provided that the writing contains on its face or by reference to other writings, the names of the parties, a description of the property, sufficient for its identification, together with the terms, conditions and consideration. 209 Ill. 478.

NOTHUS (Lat.) A natural child, or a person of spurious birth.

NOTICE. Information, whether actual or presumptive, and whether direct or indirect, respecting a matter of fact.

Notice is either (1) actual, consisting of information actually received, or (2) constructive, consisting of facts which, by implication of law, constitute notice without regard to whether they actually impart information.

Actual notice is either (a) express, consisting of direct positive knowledge of the fact in question, or (b) implied, consisting of information sufficient to put one on inquiry as to the fact in question.

"Notice" is a broader term than "knowledge," which includes only express actual notice. 81 Ala. 140; 79 Me. 195.

NOTICE OF APPEARANCE. A notice by defendant to plaintiff that he appears in the action, or by an attorney that he appears for defendant. See "Appearance."

NOTICE OF DISHONOR. A notice given to a drawer or indorser of a bill, or an indorser of a negotiable note, by a subsequent party, that it has been dishonored either by nonacceptance in the case of a bill, or by nonpayment in the case of an accepted bill or a note.

NOTICE OF JUDGMENT. A written notice of the entry of judgment required in some states to be given to the judgment debtor to start the running of time to appeal.

NOTICE OF LIS PENDENS. See "Lis Pendens."

NOTICE OF MOTION. A notice in writing to the adverse party to an action that a specified motion will be made at a time stated.

NOTICE OF PROTEST. A notice given to the drawer or indorser of a bill, or to an indorser of a note, by a prior party, that the bill has been protested for refusal of payment or acceptance. See "Notice of Dishonor."

NOTICE OF TRIAL. A notice by one party to his adversary that he will bring the cause on for trial at the next term of court.

NOTICE TO ADMIT. In the practice of the English high court, either party to an action may call on the other party by notice to admit the existence and execution of any document, in order to save the expense of proving it at the trial; and the party refusing to admit must bear the costs of proving it unless the judge certifies that the refusal to admit was reasonable. No costs of proving a document will in general be allowed, unless such a notice is given. Rules of Court, xxxii. 2.

NOTICE TO PLEAD. Written notice to defendant, requiring him to plead within a certain time. It must always be given before plaintiff can sign judgment for want of a plea. 1 Chit. Archb. Prac. (Prent. Ed.) 221. Notice to plead, indorsed on the declaration, or delivered separately, is sufficient without demanding plea or rule to plead, in England, by statute. See 3 Chit. St. 515.

NOTICE TO PRODUCE PAPERS. In practice. When it is intended to give secondary evidence of a written instrument or paper which is in the possession of the opposite party, it is in general, requisite to give him notice to produce the same on the trial of the cause, before such secondary evidence can be admitted.

NOTICE TO QUIT. A request by a landlord to his tenant to quit the leased premises, and give possession thereof to the landlord at a time therein mentioned. 3 Wend. (N. Y.) 357; 7 Halst. (N. J.) 99.

NOTING. A term denoting the act of a notary in minuting on a bill of exchange, after it has been presented for acceptance or payment, the initials of his name, the date of the day, month, and year when such presentment was made, and the reason, if any has been assigned, for nonacceptance or nonpayment, together with his charge. The noting is not indispensable, it being only a part of the protest; it will not supply the protest. 4 Term R. 175.

NOTIO (Lat. from *noscere,* to know). In the civil law. The power of hearing and trying a matter of fact; the power or authority of a *judex;* the power of hearing causes and of pronouncing sentence, without any degree of jurisdiction. Halifax, Anal. bk. 3, c. 8, Nos. 3, 6; Calv. Lex.

In a more general sense, *notio* included both *cognitio* (cognizance) and *jurisdictio* (jurisdiction). Dig. 50. 16. 99, pr.; Calv. Lex.

NOTITIA (Lat. from *notus,* known, or *noscere,* to know). In the civil law. Knowledge; information; intelligence.

——**In Old Practice.** Notice. *Inde notitiam habuit,* had notice thereof. .1 Ld. Raym. 70, 70. *Notitia non debet claudicare,* notice ought not to be lame or imperfect. 6 Coke, 29b.

NOTITIA DICITUR A NOSCENDO; ET notitia non debet claudicare. Notice is called from a knowledge being had; and notice ought not to halt, *i. e.,* be imperfect. 6 Coke, 29.

NOTORIAL. The Scotch form of "notarial" (*q. v.*). Bell, Dict.

NOTORIOUS. Primarily "notorious" means "generally known and talked of by the public." 151 Mass. 426.

NOTOUR. In Scotch law. Open; notorious. A notour bankrupt is a debtor who, being under diligence by horning and caption of his creditor, retires to sanctuary, or absconds, or defends by force, and is afterwards found insolvent by court of sessions. Bell, Dict.; Burton, Law of Scotland, 601.

NOVA CONSTITUTIO FUTURIS FORmam imponere debet, non praeteritis. A new enactment ought to impose form upon what is to come, not upon what is past. 2 Inst. 292; Broom, Leg. Max. (3d London Ed.) 33, 36; T. Jones, 108; 2 Show. 16; 6 Mees. & W. 285; 7 Mees. & W. 536; 2 Mass. 122, 2 Gall. (U. S.) 139; 2 N. Y. 245; 7 Johns. (N. Y.) 503 et seq.,—where this rule is fully considered and the authorities reviewed.

NOVA CUSTOMA. An imposition or duty. See "Antiqua Custuma."

NOVA STATUTA. New statutes. A term including all statutes passed in the reign of Edw. III. and subsequently.

NOVAE NARRATIONES. "New counts or tallys." A book of such pleadings as were then in use, published in the reign of Edw. III. 3 Bl. Comm. 297; 3 Reeve, Hist. Eng. Law, 151.

NOVALE (Lat.) Land newly ploughed, or that had not been tilled before within the memory of man. Cowell; Spelman.

NOVALIS (Lat. from *novus,* new). In the civil law. Land that rested a year after the first ploughing. Dig. 50. 16. 30. 2.

NOVATIO (Lat. from *novare,* to make new, from *novus,* new). In the civil law. Literally, a making new. A change of a former debt or obligation into another of the same or a different kind, either by a change of the persons, called *delegatio,* or by a change in the obligation, the persons continuing the same. Inst. 3. 30. 3; Dig. 46. 2; Code, 8. 42; Halifax, Anal. bk. 2, c. 20, No. 8; Heinec. Elem. Jur. Civ. lib. 3, tit. 30, § 1011 et seq. This term, translated or converted into "novation," is extensively used in modern civil law, and in the jurisprudence of Holland, Spain, France, Scotland, and the state of Louisiana. Burge, Sur. 166. Called in Fleta, *innovatio.* Fleta, lib. 2, c. 60, § 12. See "Novation."

NOVATIO NON PRAESUMITUR. A novation is not presumed. Halk. Max. 104.

NOVATION. The substitution of a new obligation for an old, which is thereby extinguished. 57 Wis. 534. The term is of civil law origin, and is rarely used in the common law.

Novation is of three sorts:

(1) Where the debtor and creditor remain the same, but a new debt takes the place of the old one. Here, either the subject matter of the debt may be changed, or the conditions of time, place, etc., of payment.

(2) Where the debt remains the same, but a new debtor is substituted for the old. This novation may be made without the in-

tervention or privity of the old debtor (in this case the new agreement is called *expromissio*, and the new debtor *expromissor*), or by the debtor's transmission of his debt to another, who accepts the obligation, and is himself accepted by the creditor. This transaction is called *delegatio*. Domat lays down the essential distinction between a delegation and any other novation, thus: That the former demands the consent of all three parties, but the latter that only of the two parties to the new debt.

(3) Where the debt remains the same, but a new creditor is substituted for the old. This also is called *delegatio*, for the reason adduced above, to wit, that all three parties must assent to the new bargain. It differs from the *cessio nominis* of the civil law by completely cancelling the old debt, while the *cessio nominis* leaves the creditor a claim for any balance due after assignment. See Civ. Code Cal. §§ 1530, 1532.

To constitute a novation there must be (1) a valid pre-existing obligation; (2) consent of capable parties; (3) express intention to innovate.

The release of the old obligation is a sufficient consideration. 37 Ohio St. 279.

NOVEL ASSIGNMENT. See "New Assignment."

NOVEL DISSEISIN. See "Assize of Novel Disseisin."

NOVELLAE LEONIS. The ordinances of Emperor Leo, which were made from the year 887 till the year 893, are so called. These Novels changed many rules of the Justinian law. This collection contains one hundred and thirteen Novels, written originally in Greek, and afterwards, in 1560, translated into Latin by Agilaeus.

NOVELS, or NOVELLAE CONSTITUTIONES. In civil law. The name given to the constitutions or laws of Justinian and his immediate successors, which were promulgated soon after the Code of Justinian.

It appears to have been the intention of Justinian, after the completion of the second and revised edition of the Code, to supply what had not been foreseen in the preceding laws, together with any necessary amendments or alterations, not by revising the Code, but by supplementary laws. Such laws he promulgated from time to time; but no official compilation of them is known to have been made until after his death, when his laws, one hundred and fifty-nine in number, with those of the reigns of Justin II. and Tiberias, nine in number, were collected, together with some local edicts, under this name. They belong to various times between 535 and 565 A. D.

NOVERINT UNIVERSI PER PRAESENTES (Law Lat.) Know all men by these presents. Words with which deeds, obligations, letters of attorney, and other instruments were formerly commenced. Litt. § 445; West, Symb. pars 1, lib. 2, §§ 102, 518, 522-525.

NOVI OPERIS NUNCIATIO (Lat.) In the civil law. A protest against or prohibition of a new work. Where a person began to build up or to pull down something (which was technically called *novum opus*, a new work), another person, who feared that his right would be impaired thereby, might extrajudicially hinder the completion of the work, by protesting before the workmen on the spot, or before some one present representing the owner, against the prosecution of the work, and forbidding the same. Dig. 39. 1; Id. 43. 24; Code, 8. 11. See "Opus Novum."

NOVIGILD. In Saxon law. A pecuniary satisfaction for an injury, amounting to nine times the value of the thing for which it was paid. Spelman.

NOVISIMA RECOPILACION. Span. (Latest compilation). The title of a collection of Spanish law compiled by order of Don Carlos IV. in 1805. 1 White's Recop. 355.

NOVITAS NON TAM UTILITATE PRODEST quam novitate perturbat. Novelty benefits not so much by its utility as it disturbs by its novelty. Jenk. Cent. Cas. 167.

NOVITER PERVENTA, or NOVITER ad notitiam perventa. In ecclesiastical procedure. Facts "newly come" to the knowledge of a party to a cause. Leave to plead facts *noviter perventa* is generally given, in a proper case, even after the pleadings are closed. Phillim. Ecc. Law, 1257; Rog. Ecc. Law, 723.

NOVODAMUS (Law Lat.) In old Scotch law. We give anew. The name given to a charter or clause in a charter, granting a renewal of a right. Bell, Dict.

NOVUM JUDICIUM NON DAT NOVUM jus, sed declarat antiquum. A new judgment does not make a new law, but declares the old. 10 Coke, 42.

NOVUM OPUS (Lat.) In the civil law. A new work. See "Novi Operis Nunciatio;" "Opus Novum."

NOVUS HOMO (Lat. a new man). This term is applied to a man who has been pardoned of a crime, by which he is restored to society and is rehabilitated.

NOXA (Lat.) In civil law. Damages resulting from an offense committed by an irresponsible agent; the offense itself; the punishment for the offense; the slave or animal who did the offense, and who is delivered up to the person aggrieved (*datur noxae*) unless the owner choose to pay the damage. The right of action is against whoever becomes the possessor of the slave or animal (*noxa caput sequitur*). Vicat; Calv. Lex.

NOXA SEQUITUR CAPUT. The injury (*i. e.*, liability to make good an injury caused by a slave) follows the head or person, *i. e.*, attaches to his master. Heinec. Elem. Jur. Civ. lib. 4, tit. 8, § 1231.

NOXALIS ACTIO. See "Actio Noxalis."

NOXIA (Lat.) In the civil law. An offense committed or damage done by a slave. Inst. 4. 8. 1.

NUBILIS (Lat.) In civil law. One who is of a proper age to be married. Dig. 32. 51.

NUDA (Lat.) Bare or mere. *Nuda patientia*, mere sufferance. *Nuda possessio*, mere possession.

NUDA PACTIO OBLIGATIONEM NON parit. A naked promise does not create an obligation. Dig. 2. 14. 7. 4; Code, 4. 65. 27; Broom, Leg. Max. (3d London Ed.) 670; Brisson. "Nudus."

NUDA RATIO ET NUDA PACTIO NON ligant aliquem debitorem. Naked reason and naked promise do not bind any debtor. Fleta, lib. 2, c. 60, § 25.

NUDE. Naked. Figuratively, this word is applied to various subjects.

A nude contract, *nudum pactum*, is one without a consideration. Nude matter is a bare allegation of a thing done, without any evidence of it.

NUDUM PACTUM. A contract made without consideration. See "Consideration."

It is a mere agreement, without the requisites necessary to confer upon it a legal obligation to perform. In the Roman Law, an agreement not made by specialty so as to support an action of covenant, or falling within one of certain classes so as to support an action of debt. Early English law gave it the same meaning. Pollock, Princ. Cont. 695. 3 McLean (U. S.) 330; 2 Denio (N. Y.) 403; 6 Ired. (N. C.) 480; 1 Strobh. (S. C.) 329; 1 Ga. 294; 1 Doug. (Mich.) 188. The term, and the rule which decides upon the nullity of its effects, are borrowed from the civil law; yet the common law has not in any degree been influenced by the notions of the civil law in defining what constitutes a *nudum pactum*. Dig. 19. 5. 5. See, on this subject, a learned note in Fonbl. Eq. 335, and 2 Kent, Comm. 364. Toullier defines *nudum pactum* to be an agreement not executed by one of the parties. Toullier, Dr. Civ. tom. 6, note 13, page 10.

It is of no consequence whether the agreement be oral or written (7 Term R. 350; 7 Brown, Parl. Cas. 550; 4 Johns. [N. Y.] 235; 5 Mass. 301, 392; 2 Day [Conn.] 22); but a contract under seal cannot be held a *nudum pactum* for lack of consideration, since the seal imports consideration (2 Barn. & Ald. 551). See "Consideration;" 2 Bl. Comm. 445; 16 Viner, Abr. 16.

NUDUM PACTUM EST UBI NULLA subest causa propter conventionem; sed ubi subest causa, fit obligatio, et parit actionem. *Nudum pactum* is where there is no consideration for the undertaking or agreement; but when there is a consideration, an obligation is created, and an action arises. Dig. 2. 14. 7. 4; 2 Bl. Comm. 445; Broom, Leg. Max. (3d London Ed.) 669; Plowd. 309; 1 Powell, Cont. 330 et seq.; 3 Burrows, 1670 et seq.; Viner, Abr. "Nudum Pactum" (A); 1 Fonbl. Eq. (5th Ed.) 335a.

NUDUM PACTUM EX QUO NON ORItur actio. *Nudum pactum* is that upon which no action arises. Code, 2. 3. 10; Id. 5. 14. 1; Broom, Leg. Max. (3d London Ed.) 676.

NUE. (L. Fr.) Nude; naked; bare.

NUEVA RECOPILACION. Span. The title of a code of Spanish law, promulgated in the year 1567. Schmidt's Civ. Law, Introd. 79-81.

NUISANCE. A nuisance is anything that unlawfully worketh hurt, inconvenience, or damage. 3 Bl. Comm. 216.

Any offensive erection, which, from its nature, may be an annoyance, and from its situation actually becomes so, is a nuisance. Tayl. Landl. & Ten. § 201.

——**Public Nuisance.** Such an inconvenience or troublesome offense as annoys the whole community in general, and not merely some particular person. 4 Bl. Comm. 166. Such an annoyance as infringes on rights common to the public. 7 Mich. 432. Some considerable portion of the community must be affected, for while that is a public nuisance which injures generally such citizens as may be so circumstanced as to come within its influence (43 N. J. Eq. 478; 8 Cow. [N. Y.] 146), it must be in a public place, where members of the community are liable to come within its influence (7 Blackf. [Ind.] 534; 34 Tex. 230; 36 N. J. Law, 283). The test is not the number of persons annoyed, but the possibility of invasion of the public rights. 5 Rand. (Va.) 691.

——**Private Nuisance.** Anything done or maintained whereby special annoyance or injury is done to another.

A public nuisance may be private, as well, and such have been termed "mixed nuisances." Wood, Nuisance, § 17.

The exact amount of annoyance or inconvenience necessary to constitute a private nuisance has never been settled. In general terms, the injury should cause an inconvenience "materially interfering with the ordinary comfort, physically, of human existence; not merely according to elegant or dainty modes and habits of living, but according to plain, sober, and simple notions." 4 Eng. Law & Eq. 15.

The filling of the air with smoke or noxious vapor, to the detriment of health (11 Mo. 517; 12 L. T. [N. S.] 776), or with noisome odors (20 N. J. Eq. 201; 23 N. J. Eq. 251), the production of great noise and clangor in a quiet neighborhood (14 Mo. App. 590), the maintenance of excessive heat, rendering adjoining premises uninhabitable (46 Ala. 381), the keeping of explosives or inflammable substances (35 N. J. Law, 17), are well-recognized forms of private nuisance.

NUISANCE, ASSISE OF. See "Assize of Nuisance."

NUL. No; none. A law French negative particle, commencing many phrases.

NUL AGARD (Law Fr. no award). In pleading. A plea to an action on an arbitration bond, when the defendant avers that there was no legal award made. 3 Burrows, 1730; 2 Strange, 923.

NUL CHARTER, NUL VENTE, NE NUL done vault perpetualment, si le donor n'est seise al temps de contracts de deux droits, sc. del droit de possession et del droit de propertie. No grant, no sale, no gift is valid forever, unless the donor, at the time of the contract, is seised of two rights, namely, the right of possession, and the right of property. Co. Litt. 266.

NUL DISSEISIN. In pleading. No disseisin. A plea in a real action, by which the defendant denies that there was any disseisin. It is a species of the general issue.

NUL NE DOIT S'ENRICHIR AUX DEpens des autres. No one ought to enrich himself at the expense of others.

NUL PRENDRA ADVANTAGE DE SON tort demesne. No one shall take advantage of his own wrong. Broom, Leg. Max. (3d London Ed.) 265.

NUL SANS DAMAGE AVERA ERROR ou attaint. No one shall have error or attaint unless he has sustained damage. Jenk. Cent. Cas. 323.

NUL TIEL CORPORATION. No such corporation exists. The form of a plea denying the existence of an alleged corporation.

NUL TIEL RECORD (Fr. no such record). In pleading. A plea which is proper when it is proposed to rely upon facts which disprove the existence of the record on which the plaintiff founds his action.

Any matters may be introduced under it which tend to destroy the validity of the record as a record, provided they do not contradict the recitals of the record itself. 10 Ohio, 100. It is frequently used to enable the defendant to deny the jurisdiction of the court from which the alleged record emanates. 2 McLean, C. C. (U. S.) 129; 22 Wend. (N. Y.) 293.

It is said to be the proper plea to an action on a foreign judgment, especially if of a sister state, in the United States (2 Leigh [Va.] 72; 6 Leigh [Va.] 570; 17 Vt. 302; 6 Pick. [Mass.] 232; 11 Miss. 210; 1 Pa. St. 499; 2 South. [S. C.] 778; 2 Breese [Ill.] 2), though it is held that *nil debet* is sufficient (33 Me. 268; 3 J. J. Marsh. [Ky.] 600), especially if the judgment be that of a justice of the peace (3 Har. [N. J.] 408). See "Conflict of Laws."

NUL TORT (Law Fr. no wrong). In pleading. A plea to a real action, by which the defendant denies that he committed any wrong. It is a species of general issue.

NUL WASTE. In pleading. The general issue in an action of waste. 3 Inst. 700a, 708a. The plea of *nul waste* admits nothing, but puts the whole declaration in issue; and in support of this plea the defendant may give in evidence anything which proves that the act charged is no waste, as that it happened by tempest, lightning, and the like. Co. Litt. 283a; 3 Wm. Saund. 238, note 5.

NULL. Properly, that which does not exist; that which is not in the nature of things. In a figurative sense, it signifies that which has no more effect than if it did not exist. 8 Toullier, Dr. Civ. note 320.

NULLA BONA (Law Lat. no goods). The return made to a writ of *fieri facias* by the sheriff, when he has not found any goods of the defendant on which he could levy. 3 Bouv. Inst. note 3393.

NULLA CURIA QUAE RECORDUM non habet potest imponere finem, neque aliquem mandare carceri, quia ista spectant tantummodo ad curias de recordo. No court which has not a record can impose a fine, or commit any person to prison, because those powers belong only to courts of record. 8 Coke, 60.

NULLA EMPTIO SINE PRETIO ESSE potest. There can be no sale without a price. 4 Pick. (Mass.) 189.

NULLA IMPOSSIBILIA AUT INHONESta sunt praesumenda; vera autem et honesta et possibilia. No impossible or dishonorable things are to be presumed, but things true, honorable, and possible. Co. Litt. 78.

NULLA PACTIONE EFFICI POTEST ne dolus praestetur. By no agreement can it be effected that there shall be no accountability for fraud. Dig. 2. 14. 27. 3; Broom, Leg. Max. (3d London Ed.) 622, 118, note; 5 Maule & S. 466.

NULLA VIRTUS, NULLA SCIENTIA, locum suum et dignitatem conservare potest sine modestia. Without modesty, no virtue, no knowledge, can preserve its place and dignity. Co. Litt. 394.

NULLE REGLE SANS FAUTE. There is no rule without a fault.

NULLE TERRE SANS SEIGNEUR. No land without a lord. Guyot, Inst. Feud. c. 28.

NULLI ENIM RES SUA SERVIT JURE servitutis. No one can have a servitude over his own property. Dig. 8. 2. 26; 17 Mass. 443; 2 Bouv. Inst. note 1600.

NULLITY. An act or proceeding which has absolutely no legal effect whatever. See Chit. Cont. 228.

NULLIUS FILIUS (Lat.) The son of no one; a bastard.

NULLIUS HOMINIS AUCTORITAS apud nos valere debet, ut meliora non sequeremur si quis attulerit. The authority of no man ought to avail with us, that we should not follow better opinions, should any one present them. Co. Litt. 383b.

NULLIUS JURIS. In old English law. Of no legal force. Fleta, lib. 2, c. 60, § 24.

NULLUM ARBITRIUM (Lat.) In pleading. The name of a plea to an action on an arbitration bond for not fulfilling the award, by which the defendant asserts that there is no award.

NULLUM CRIMEN MAJUS EST INOBEdientia. No crime is greater than disobedience. Jenk. Cent. Cas. 77.

NULLUM EXEMPLUM EST IDEM OMnibus. No example is the same for all purposes. Co. Litt. 212a.

NULLUM FECERUNT ARBITRIUM (Lat.) In pleading. The name of a plea to an action of debt upon an obligation for the performance of an award, by which the defendant denies that he submitted to arbitration, etc. Bac. Abr. "Arbiter, etc." (G).

NULLUM INIQUUM EST PRAESUMENdum in jure. Nothing unjust is to be presumed in law. 4 Coke, 72.

NULLUM MATRIMONIUM, IBI NULLA dos. No marriage, no dower. 4 Barb. (N. Y.) 192, 194.

NULLUM SIMILE EST IDEM. Nothing which is like another is the same, *i. e.*, no likeness is exact identity. 2 Story, C. C. (U. S.) 512; Story, Partn. 90; Co. Litt. 3a; 2 Bl. Comm. 162.

NULLUM SIMILE EST IDEM NISI QUAtuor pedibus currit. No like is identical, unless it run on all fours. Co. Litt. 3.

NULLUM SIMILE QUATUOR PEDIBUS currit. No simile runs upon four feet, or, as ordinarily expressed, "on all fours." Co. Litt. 3a; Eunom. Dial. 2, p. 155; 1 Story, C. C. 143.

NULLUM TEMPUS ACT. St. 3 Geo. III. c. 16. See 32 Geo. III. c. 58, and 7 Wm. III. c. 3. It was so called because the right of the crown to sue, etc., was limited by it to sixty years, in contradiction to the Maxim, *Nullum tempus occurrit regi.* 3 Chit. St. 63.

NULLUM TEMPUS AUT LOCUS OCcurrit regi. No time or place affects the king. 2 Inst. 273; Jenk. Cent. Cas. 83; Broom, Leg. Max. 65.

NULLUM TEMPUS OCCURRIT REGI. Lapse of time does not bar the right of the crown. 2 Inst. 273; 1 Bl. Comm. 247; Broom, Leg. Max. (3d London Ed.) 62; Hob. 347; 2 Steph. Comm. 504; 1 Mass. 355; 2 Brock. C. C. (U. S.) 393; 18 Johns. (N. Y.) 227; 10 Barb. (N. Y.) 139.

One of the ancient maxims of the common law, being a natural offshoot of the maxim, "rex non potest peccare." 97 Ill. 88.

NULLUM TEMPUS OCCURRIT REIpublicae. Lapse of time does not bar the commonwealth. 11 Grat. (Va.) 572; Hilliard, Real Prop. 173; 8 Tex. 410; 16 Tex. 305; 5 McLean, C. C. (U. S.) 133; 19 Mo. 667.

NULLUS ALIUS QUAM REX POSSIT episcopo demandare inquisitionem faciendam. No other than the king can command the bishop to make an inquisition. Co. Litt. 134.

NULLUS COMMODUM CAPERE POtest de injuria sua propria. No one shall take advantage of his own wrong. Co. Litt. 148b; Broom, Leg. Max. (3d London Ed.) 265; 4 Bing. N. C. 395; 4 Barn. & Ald. 409; 10 Mees. & W. 309; 11 Mees. & W. 680.

NULLUS DEBET AGERE DE DOLO, ubi alia actio subest. Where another form of action is given, no one ought to sue in the action *de dolo.* 7 Coke, 92.

NULLUS DICITUR ACCESSORIUS post feloniam sed ille qui novit principalem feloniam fecisse, et illum receptavit et comfortavit. No one is called an accessory after the fact but he who knew the principal to have committed a felony, and received and comforted him. 3 Inst. 138.

NULLUS DICITUR FELO PRINCIPALIS nisi actor, aut qui praessens est, abettans aut auxilians actorem ad feloniam faciendam. No one shall be called a principal felon except the party actually committing the felony, or the party present aiding and abetting in its commission. 3 Inst. 138.

NULLUS IDONEUS TESTIS IN RE SUA intelligitur. No one is understood to be a competent witness in his own cause. Dig. 22. 5. 10; 1 Sumn. (U. S.) 328, 344.

NULLUS JUS ALIENUM FORISFAcere potest. No man can forfeit another's right. Fleta, lib. 1, c. 28, § 11.

NULLUS RECEDAT E CURIA CANCELlaria sine remedio. No one ought to depart out of the court of chancery without a remedy. Y. B. 4 Hen. VII. 4.

NULLUS VIDETUR DOLO FACERE qui suo jure utitur. No man is to be esteemed a wrongdoer who avails himself of his legal right. Dig. 50. 17. 55; Broom, Leg. Max. (3d London Ed.) 124, 118, note q; 14 Wend. (N. Y.) 339, 492.

NUMBER. A collection of units.

NUMERATA PECUNIA (Lat.) In civil law. Money counted or paid; money given in payment by count. L. 3, 10, C. *de non numerat. pecun.;* Vicat.

NUMMATA TERRAE (Law Lat.) In old records. A quantity of land, thought to contain an acre. Cowell.

NUNC PRO TUNC (Lat. now for then). A phrase used to express that a thing is done at one time as if or with the same effect as if performed at another.

NUNCIATIO. In civil law. A formal proclamation or protest. It may be by acts (*realis*) or by words. Mackeld. Civ. Law, § 237. Thus, *nunciatio novi operis* was an injunction which one man could place on the erection of a new building, etc., near him, until the case was tried by the praetor. Id.; Calv. Lex. An information against a criminal. Calv. Lex.

NUNCIO. The name given to the pope's ambassador. Nuncios are ordinary or extraordinary; the former are sent upon usual missions, the latter upon special occasions.

NUNCIUS. In international law. A messenger; a minister; the pope's legate, commonly called a "nuncio."

NUNCUPATE. To declare publicly and solemnly.

NUNCUPATIVE WILL. An oral will, declared by a testator, *in extremis*, before witnesses, and afterwards reduced to writing. 4 Kent, Comm. 576; 2 Bl. Comm. 500; 1 Jarm. Wills (Perkins Ed.) 130-136. See 1 Wm. IV. c. 20; 1 Vict. c. 26, §§ 9, 11; 11 Eng. Law & Eq. 596,—by which the privilege of making a nuncupative will is only allowed to soldiers and seamen in actual service. So in almost all the states. See, in general, 27 Ala. (N. S.) 296, 596; 26 N. H. 372; 9 N. Y. 196; 10 Grat. (Va.) 548; 27 Miss. 119, 725; 2 R. I. 133; 4 Bradf. Sur. (N. Y.) 154; 22 Ga. 293, 603; 12 La. Ann. 114, 603; 1 Sneed (Tenn.) 616; 1 Williams, Ex'rs, 59; Swinb. Wills; Ayliffe, Pand. 359; Roberts, Wills; 2 Bouv. Inst. note 436; 1 Brown, Civ. Law, 288.

NUNDINAE (Law Lat.) In civil and old English law. Fair or fairs. Dion Halic. lib. 2, p. 98; Vicat; Law Fr. & Lat. Dict.

NUNQUAM (Lat.) Never. *Nunquam fuit ballivus ejus, vel mercator, vel denariorum suorum receptor, vel administrator*, never was his bailiff or merchant, or receiver of his moneys, or his administrator (manager). Fleta, lib. 2, c. 70, § 9.

NUNQUAM CRESCIT EX POST FACTO praeteriti delicti aestimatio. The quality of a past offense is never aggravated by that which happens subsequent. Dig. 50. 17. 138. 1; Bac. Max. reg. 8; Broom, Leg. Max. (3d London Ed.) 41.

NUNQUAM DECURRITUR AD EXTRAordinarium sed ubi deficit ordinarium. We are never to recur to what is extraordinary till what is ordinary fails. 4 Inst. 84.

NUNQUAM FICTIO SINE LEGE. There is no fiction without law.

NUNQUAM INDEBITATUS (Lat. never indebted). In pleading. A plea to an action of *indebitatus assumpsit*, by which the defendant asserts that he is not indebted to the plaintiff. 6 Car. & P. 545; 1 Mees. & W. 542; 1 Q. B. 77.

NUNQUAM NIMIS DICITUR QUOD nunquam satis dicitur. What is never sufficiently said is never said too much. Co. Litt. 375.

NUNQUAM PRAESCRIBITUR IN FALso. There is never prescription in case of falsehood (*crimen falsi*). Bell, Dict.

NUNQUAM RES HUMANAE PROSpere succedunt ubi negliguntur divinae. Human things never prosper when divine things are neglected. Co. Litt. 95; Wingate, Max. 2.

NUNTIUS, or NUNCIUS. In old English practice. One who made excuse for absence of one summoned; an apparitor, beadle, or sergeant. Cowell. A messenger or legate, *e. g.*, pope's nuncio. Jacob. *Essoniator* was sometimes wrongly used for *nuntius* in the first sense. Bracton, fol. 345, § 2.

NUPER OBIIT (Lat. he or she lately died). In practice. The name of a writ which in the English law lies for a sister co-heiress dispossessed by her coparcener of lands and tenements whereof their father, brother, or any common ancestor died seised of an estate in fee simple. Termes de la Ley; Fitzh. Nat. Brev. 197.

NUPTIAE (Lat. from *nubere*, to cover or veil). In the civil law. Marriage; nuptials; the union of man and woman; companionship for all life (*conjunctio maris et feminae, et consortium omnis vitae*). Dig. 23. 2. 1. See Code, 5. 4. Justinian uses *nuptiae* and *matrimonium* as synonymous. Inst. 1. 9. 1. Properly, the nuptial ceremony. Calv. Lex.; Tayl. Civ. Law, 269, 274. See "Consensus Non, etc."

NUPTIAE SECUNDAE (Lat.) In the canon law. A second marriage; any marriage after the first. The canon law put a mark of disapprobation upon *nuptiae secundae*, for so they termed every marriage after the first. No benediction could be pronounced, nor could any priest be present at the celebration of them. Corvin. Jus.

Canon. 108, 109, 110; Launc. Inst. Jur. Can. lib. 2, tit. 16; 4 Reeve, Hist. Eng. Law, 63.

NUPTIAL. Of or pertaining to the marital relation.

NUPTIAS NON CONCUBITUS, SED consensus facit. Not cohabitation, but consent, makes the marriage. Dig. 50. 17. 30; 1 Bouv. Inst. note 239; Co. Litt. 33.

NURTURE. The rearing and care of children.

NUSANCE. The old form of "nuisance." Hale, Anal. § xlii.

NUTAUNTRE, NUTANDER, or NUICtander (Law Fr.) By night. *Ou nutauntre ou de jour*, by night or by day. Britt. c. 47; Y. B. P. 10 Edw. III. 37.

NUYT, or NUTE (Law Fr.) Night. Britt. c. 80.

NYMPHOMANIA. Erotic insanity manifested in a female. It is said to be distinguished from erotomania, in that it proceeds from some sexual disorder as an exciting cause. Wharton.

O

O. C. In the civil law. An abbreviation for "*ope consilio*" (*q. v.*)

O. K. The abbreviation "O. K." has a well-defined meaning and signifies "all right," "correct," its effect being determined from the circumstances of the situation. 204 Ill. App. 398.

O. NI. It was the course of the English exchequer, as soon as the sheriff entered into and made up his account for issues, amerciaments, etc., to mark upon each head "*O. Ni.*" which denoted *oneratur, nisi habeat sufficientem exonerationem,* and presently he became the king's debtor, and a *debet* was set upon his head; whereupon the parties *paravaile* became debtors to the sheriff, and were discharged against the king, etc. 4 Inst. 116. But sheriffs now account to the commissioners for auditing the public accounts. Wharton.

OATH. An outward pledge given by the person taking it that his attestation or promise is made under an immediate sense of his responsibility to God. Tyler, Oaths, 15.

The term has been variously defined: As, "a solemn invocation of the vengeance of the Deity upon the witness if he do not declare the whole truth, so far as he knows it." 1 Starkie, Ev. 22. Or, "a religious asseveration by which a person renounces the mercy and imprecates the vengeance of Heaven if he do not speak the truth." 2 Leach, C. C. 482. Or, as "a religious act by which the party invokes God not only to witness the truth and sincerity of his promise, but also to avenge his imposture or violated faith, or, in other words, to punish his perjury if he shall be guilty of it." 10 Toullier, Dr. Civ. notes 343-348; Puffendorff, bk. 4, c. 2, § 4. The essential idea of an oath would seem to be, however, that of a recognition of God's authority by the party taking it, and an undertaking to accomplish the transaction to which it refers as required by His laws.

In its broadest sense, the term is used to include all forms of attestation by which a party signifies that he is bound in conscience to perform the act faithfully and truly. In a more restricted sense, it excludes all those forms of attestation or promise which are not accompanied by an imprecation.

——**Assertory Oaths.** Those required by law other than in judicial proceedings, and upon induction to office, such, for example, as custom-house oaths.

——**Promissory Oaths.** Oaths taken by authority of law, by which the party declares that he will fulfill certain duties therein mentioned; as, the oath which an alien takes, on becoming naturalized, that he will support the constitution of the United States; the oath which a judge takes that he will perform the duties of his office. The breach of this does not involve the party in the legal crime or punishment of perjury. 3 Zab. (N. J.) 49.

——**Extrajudicial Oaths.** Those taken without authority of law. Though binding *in foro conscientiae,* they do not, when false, render the party liable to punishment for perjury.

——**Judicial Oaths.** Those administered in judicial proceedings.

OATH AGAINST BRIBERY. One which could have been administered to a voter at an election for members of parliament. Abolished by 17 & 18 Vict. c. 102. Wharton.

OATH DECISORY. In civil law. An oath which one of the parties defers or refers back to the other for the decision of the cause.

OATH EX OFFICIO. The oath by which a clergyman charged with a criminal offense was formerly allowed to swear himself to be innocent; also the oath by which the compurgators swore that they believed in his innocence. 3 Bl. Comm. 101, 447; Mozley & W.

OATH IN LITEM. An oath which, in the civil law, was deferred to the complainant as to the value of the thing in dispute, on failure of other proof, particularly when there was a fraud on the part of the defendant, and he suppressed proof in his possession. See Greenl. Ev. § 348; Tait, Ev. 280; 1 Vern. 207; 1 Eq. Cas. Abr. 229; 1 Me. 27; 1 Yeates (Pa.) 34; 12 Viner, Abr. 24.

OATH OF CALUMNY. In civil law. An oath which a plaintiff was obliged to take that he was not actuated by a spirit of chicanery in commencing his action, but that he had *bona fide* a good cause of action. Poth. ad Pand. lib. 5, tits. 16, 17, § 124. This oath is somewhat similar to our affidavit of a cause of action. See Dunl. Adm. Prac. 289, 290.

OATH PURGATORY. An oath by which one destroys the presumptions which were against him, for he is then said to purge himself when he removes the suspicions which were against him; as, when a man is in contempt for not attending court as a witness, he may purge himself of the contempt by swearing to a fact which is an ample excuse. See "Purgation."

OATH RITE. The form used at the taking of an oath.

OATH SUPPLETORY. In civil and ecclesiastical law. An oath required by the judge from either party in a cause, upon half proof already made, which, being joined to half proof, supplies the evidence required to enable the judge to pass upon the subject. See Strange, 80; 3 Bl. Comm. 270.

OATHWORTHY. Worthy of making an oath; credible.

OB. On account of; for. A few Latin phrases and maxims commence with this word, but *in* is more commonly used.

OB CAUSAM ALIQUAM A RE MARItima ortam. For some cause arising out of a maritime matter. 1 Pet. Adm. (U. S.) 92. Said to be Selden's translation of the French definition of admiralty jurisdiction, "*pour le fait de la mer.*" Id.

OB CONTINENTIAM DELICTI. On account of contiguity to the offense; a ground for extending the operation of a decree of maritime condemnation. Thus, a cargo of a vessel condemned for carrying dispatches for the enemy may be condemned *ob continentiam delicti.* 6 Rob. Adm. 440.

OB CONTINGENTIAM. In Scotch law. On account of connection; by reason of similarity. A ground for the consolidation of actions. 7 Bell, App. Cas. 163.

OB FAVOREM MERCATORUM. In favor of merchants. Fleta, lib. 2, c. 63, § 12.

OB INFAMIAM NON SOLET JUXTA LEgem terrae aliquis per legem apparentem se purgare, nisi prius convictus fuerit vel confessus in curia. On account of evil report it is not usual, according to the law of the land, for any person to purge himself, unless he have been previously convicted, or confessed in court. Glanv. lib. 14, c. 2.

OB TURPEM CAUSAM. For a base or immoral cause or consideration.

OBAERATUS. In Roman law. A debtor who was obliged to serve his creditor till his debt was discharged.

OBEDIENTIA. (Lat.) Obedience; submission.

In old records. A kind of rent. Cowell.

In the canon law. An office, or the administration of an office. Id.

OBEDIENTIA EST LEGIS ESSENTIA. Obedience is the essence of the law. 11 Coke, 100.

OBIIT SINE PROLE. (Lat.) (He) died without issue. Y. B. M. 1 Edw. II. 1.

OBIT. That particular solemnity or office for the dead which the Roman Catholic church appoints to be read or performed over the body of a deceased member of that communion before interment; also, the office which, upon the anniversary of his death, was frequently used as a commemoration or observance of the day. 2 Cro. 51; Dyer, 313.

OBITER (Lat. from *obire*, to pass). By the way; in passing. "This point was not the principal question in the case of Clere and Brooke, but the law concerning it is delivered *obiter* only, and in the course of argument, by Justice Manwoode." 2 Bl. Comm. 238.

OBITER DICTUM. See "Dictum."

OBJECT. Anything which comes within the cognizance or scrutiny of the senses; especially anything tangible or visible. Anything, whether concrete or abstract, real or imaginary, that may be perceived or apprehended by the mind; that of which the understanding has knowledge. 83 N. J. L. 641, 85 Atl. 194, Ann. Cas. 1914 B 847.

OBJECT OF ACTION. The thing sought to be attained by the action; the remedy demanded, or relief prayed for. It differs from the subject of the action, which is the subject matter out of which the cause of action arose. 18 Kan. 406.

OBJECTION. The act by which a party questions the propriety of evidence offered or proceedings proposed to be had in the course of the trial.

OBJECTS OF A POWER. A name given to the members of a class among whom one is empowered to appoint the power.

OBLATI ACTIO (Lat.) In the civil law. An action given to a party against another who had offered to him a stolen thing, which was found in his possession. Inst. 3. 1. 4.

OBLATIO (Lat.) In civil law. A tender of money in payment of debt made by debtor to creditor. L. 9, C. *de solut.* Whatever is offered to the church by the pious. Calv. Lex.; Vicat.

OBLIGACION (Law Fr.) Obligation. *Obligacion est un lien de droit*, obligation is a bond of law. Britt. c. 28. See "Obligation."

OBLIGATIO. In Roman law. A legal bond which obliges us to the performance of something in accordance with the law of the land. Ortolan, Inst. 2, § 1179.

It corresponded nearly to our word "contract." Justinian says, "*Obligatio est juris vinculum, quo necessitate adstringimur alicujus solvendae rei, secundum nostrae civitatis jura.*" Pr. Just. 3. 13.

The Romans considered that obligations derived their validity solely from positive law. At first the only ones recognized were those established in special cases in accordance with the forms prescribed by the strict *jus civilis.* In the course of time, however, the praetorian jurisdiction, in mitigation of the primitive rigor of the law, introduced new modes of contracting obligations, and provided the means of enforcing them; hence the twofold division made by Justinian of *obligationes civiles*, and *obligationes praetoriae*. Inst. 1. 3. 13. But there was a third class, the *obligationes naturales*, which derived their validity from the law of nature and nations, or the natural reason of mankind. These had not the binding force of the other classes, not being capable of enforcement by action, and are, therefore, not noticed by Justinian in his classification; but they had, nevertheless, a certain efficacy even in the civil law. For instance, though a debt founded upon a natural obligation could not be recovered by an action, yet if it was voluntarily paid by the debtor, he could not recover it back, as he might do in the case of money paid by mistake, etc., where no natural obligation existed. L. 38, pr. D. 12. 6. And see Ortolan, Inst. 2, § 1180.

The second classification of obligations made by Justinian has regard to the way in which they arise. They were, in this aspect, either *ex contractu* or *quasi ex contractu*, or *ex maleficio* or *quasi ex maleficio*. Inst. 2. 3. 13.

OBLIGATION (Lat. *obligo; ligo*, to bind). A legal bond, whereby constraint is laid upon a person or group of persons to act or forbear on behalf of another person or group. Savigny, Obl. §§ 2-4; Anson, Cont. § 2.

Secondarily applied to an instrument whereby one binds himself, under penalty, to an act or forbearance (2 Serg. & R. [Pa.] 502; 6 Vt. 40), and sometimes in modern usage to all written contracts (22 Ohio St. 111).

——**Absolute Obligation.** One which gives no alternative to the obligor, but requires fulfillment according to the engagement.

——**Accessory Obligation.** One which is dependent on the principal obligation. For example, if I sell you a house and lot of ground, the principal obligation on my part is to make you a title for it; the accessory obligation is to deliver you all the title papers which I have relating to it, to take care of the estate till it is delivered to you, and the like.

——**Alternative Obligation.** Where a person engages to do or to give several things in such a manner that the payment of one will acquit him of all.

——**Civil Obligation.** One which has a binding operation in law, and which gives to the obligee the right of enforcing it in a court of justice. In other words, it is an engagement binding on the obligor. 4 Wheat. (U. S.) 197; 12 Wheat. (U. S.) 318, 337.

Civil obligations are divided into express and implied, pure and conditional, primitive and secondary, principal and accessory, absolute and alternative, determinate and indeterminate, divisible and indivisible, single and penal, and joint and several. They are also purely personal, purely real, or mixed.

——**Conditional Obligation.** One, the execution of which is suspended by a condition which has not been accomplished, and subject to which it has been contracted.

——**Determinate Obligation.** One which has for its object a certain thing; as, an obligation to deliver a certain horse, named "Bucephalus." In this case, the obligation can only be discharged by delivering the identical horse.

——**Divisible Obligation.** One which, being a unit, may nevertheless be lawfully divided with or without the consent of the parties.

——**Express or Conventional Obligations.** Those by which the obligor binds himself in express terms to perform his obligation.

——**Imperfect Obligations.** Those which are not binding on us as between man and man, and for the nonperformance of which we are accountable to God only, such as charity or gratitude. In this sense, an obligation is a mere duty. Poth. Obl. art. prel. note 1.

——**Implied Obligation.** One which arises by operation of law; as, for example, if I send you daily a loaf of bread, without any express authority, and you make use of it in your family, the law raises an obligation on your part to pay me the value of the bread.

——**Indeterminate Obligation.** One where the obligor binds himself to deliver one of a certain species; as, to deliver a horse, where the delivery of any horse will discharge the obligation.

——**Indivisible Obligation.** One which is not susceptible of division; as, for example, if I promise to pay you one hundred dollars, you cannot assign one-half of this to another, so as to give him a right of action against me for his share. See "Divisible."

——**Joint Obligation.** One by which several obligors promise to the obligee to perform the obligation. When the obligation is only joint, and the obligors do not promise separately to fulfill their engagement, they must be all sued, if living, to compel the performance; or, if any be dead, the survivors must all be sued. See "Parties."

——**Natural or Moral Obligation.** One which cannot be enforced by action, but which is binding on the party who makes it in conscience and according to natural justice.

As, for instance, when the action is barred by the act of limitation, a natural obligation still subsists, although the civil obligation is extinguished. 5 Bin. (Pa.) 573. Although natural obligations cannot be enforced by action, they have the following effect: First, no suit will lie to recover back what has been paid or given in compliance with a natural obligation (1 Term R. 285, 1 Dall. [Pa.] 184); second, a natural obligation is a sufficient consideration for a new contract (2 Bin. [Pa.] 591; 5 Bin. [Pa.] 33; Yelv. 41a, note 1; Cowp. 290; 2 Bl. Comm. 445; 3 Bos. & P. 249, note; 2 East, 506; 3 Taunt. 311; 5 Taunt. 36; 3 Pick. [Mass.] 207; Chit. Cont. 10). See "Consideration."

——**Penal Obligation.** One to which is attached a penal clause, which is to be enforced if the principal obligation be not performed. See "Damages."

——**Perfect Obligation.** One which gives a right to another to require us to give him something, or not to do something. These obligations are either natural or moral, or they are civil.

——**Personal Obligation.** One by which the obligor binds himself to perform an act, without directly binding his property for its performance.

It also denotes an obligation in which the obligor binds himself only, not including his heirs or representatives.

——**Primitive Obligation.** This obligation, which, in one sense, may also be called a "principal obligation," is one which is contracted with a design that it should itself be the first fulfilled.

——**Principal Obligation.** One which is the most important object of the engagement of the contracting parties.

——**Pure** (or **Simple**) **Obligation.** One which is not suspended by any condition, either because it has been contracted without condition, or, having been contracted with one, it has been fulfilled.

——**Real Obligation.** One by which real estate, and not the person, is liable to the obligee for the performance.

A familiar example will explain this: When an estate owes an easement as a right of way, it is the thing, and not the owner, who owes the easement. Another instance occurs when a person buys an estate which has been mortgaged, subject to the mortgage. He is not liable for the debt, though his estate is. In these cases the owner has an interest only because he is seised of the servient estate or the mortgaged premises, and he may discharge himself by abandoning or parting with the property. The obligation is both personal and real when the obligor has bound himself and pledged his estate for the fulfillment of his obligations.

——**Secondary Obligation.** One which is contracted and is to be performed in case the primitive cannot be. For example, if I sell you my house, I bind myself to give a title; but if I find I cannot, as the title is in another, then my secondary obligation is to pay you damages for my nonperformance of my obligation.

——**Several Obligation.** One by which one individual, or, if there be more, several individuals, bind themselves separately to perform the engagement. In this case, each obligor may be sued separately; and if one or more be dead, their respective executors may be sued. See "Parties."

——**Single Obligation.** One without any penalty; as, where I simply promise to pay you one hundred dollars. This is called a "single bill," when it is under seal.

OBLIGATION OF CONTRACT. The duty imposed by law on the parties to a contract to perform the same. 4 Wheat. (U. S.) 197.

The remedy by which the contract can be enforced is deemed a part of its obligation, within the constitutional prohibition of its impairment, to the extent that its adequacy must be maintained (47 N. Y. 157; 97 U. S. 293), but the mere form of the remedy (157 U. S. 219), or the rules of evidence (108 Mo. 303), are not.

OBLIGATORY WRITING. See "Writing Obligatory."

OBLIGEE. The person in favor of whom an obligation is contracted.

OBLIGOR. The person who has engaged to perform some obligation. Code La. art. 3522, No. 12. One who makes a bond.

OBLIQUUS (Lat.)

——**In the Old Law of Descents.** Oblique; cross; transverse; collateral. The opposite of *rectus*, right, or upright. Fleta, lib. 5, c. 7, § 2.

——**In the Law of Evidence.** Indirect; circumstantial. Vinn. Juris. Cont. lib. 4, c. 25.

OBLITERATION. The destruction of words in an instrument by erasure, blotting, or striking out. They need not be completely effaced. The term is most commonly applied to wills which may be revoked by obliteration. 29 Car. II. c. 3, § 6.

OBLOQUY. Censure; odium, reproach. See 70 Cal. 275.

OBRA (Spanish; from Lat. *opera*). In Spanish law. Work. *Obras*, works or trades; those which men carry on in houses or covered places. White, New Recop. bk. 1, tit. 5, c. 3, § 6.

OBREPTIO (Lat. from *obrepere*, to creep upon). The obtaining a thing by fraud or surprise. Calv. Lex. Called, in Scotch law, *"obreption."*

OBREPTION. Acquisition of escheats, etc., from sovereign, by making false representations. Bell, Dict. "Subreption;" Calv. Lex.

OBROGARE (Lat. from *ob*, and *rogare*, to pass a law). In the civil law. To pass a law contrary to a former law, or to some clause of it; to change a former law in some part of it. Calv. Lex.; Tayl. Civ. Law, 155.

OBROGATION. The annulling a law, in whole or in part, by passing a law contrary to it; the alteration of a law. Vicat; Calv. Lex.

OBSCENITY. In criminal law. Such indecency as is calculated to promote the violation of the law and the general corruption of morals. It may consist in written or spoken words, conduct, pictures, or effigies. It need not be couched in obscene or vulgar terms if the idea conveyed tends to produce indecency. 16 Blachf. (U. S.) 362.

OBSERVE. In civil law. To perform that which has been prescribed by some law or usage. Dig. 1. 3. 32.

OBSES (Lat.) In the law of war. A hostage. Grotius de Jure Belli, lib. 3, c. 20, § 52. *Obsides,* hostages. Id. Magna Carta Johan. c. 49.

OBSESSUM (Lat. from *obsidere,* to besiege or block up). In the law of war. Besieged. *Oppidum obsessum,* a town besieged. Grotius de Jure Belli, lib. 3, c. 1, § 5; 1 Kent, Comm. 144.

OBSIGNARE (Lat.) In the civil law. To seal up, as money that had been tendered and refused. Heinec. Elem. Jur. Civ. lib. 3, tit. 30, § 1007.

OBSOLETE. Fallen into disuse. A term applied to laws which, by change in conditions or subject matter, or by long neglect, have lost their efficacy without being repealed.

A positive statute, unrepealed, can never be repealed by nonuser alone. 4 Yeates (Pa.) 181, 215; 1 P. A. Browne (Pa. App.) 28; 13 Serg. & R. (Pa.) 447. The disuse of a law is at most only presumptive evidence that society has consented to such a repeal. However this presumption may operate on an unwritten law, it cannot, in general, act upon one which remains as a legislative act on the statute book, because no presumption can set aside a certainty. A written law may indeed become obsolete when the object to which it was intended to apply, or the occasion for which it was enacted, no longer exists. 1 P. A. Browne (Pa. App.) 28. "It must be a very strong case," says Chief Justice Tilghman, "to justify the court in deciding that an act standing on the statute book, unrepealed, is obsolete and invalid. I will not say that such case may not exist where there has been a nonuser for a great number of years, where, from a change of times and manners, an ancient sleeping statute would do great mischief if suddenly brought into action, where a long practice inconsistent with it has prevailed, and especially where, from other and later statutes, it might be inferred that in the apprehension of the legislature the old one was not in force." 13 Serg. & R. (Pa.) 452; Rutherford, Inst. bk. 2, c. 6, § 19; Merlin, Repert. "Desuetude."

OBSTA PRINCIPIIS. Withstand or resist beginnings.

OBSTANTE. Withstanding; hindering. See "Non Obstante."

OBSTRICTION. Obligation; bond.

OBTAIN. To get hold of; to obtain possession of; to acquire; to maintain a hold upon; to keep; to possess. 39 Ill. App. 562.

OBTEMPERANDUM EST CONSUETUdini rationabili tanquam legi. A reasonable custom is to be obeyed like law. 4 Coke, 38.

OBTORTO COLLO (Lat.) In Roman law. Taking by the neck or collar; as a plaintiff was allowed to drag a reluctant defendant to court. Adams, Rom. Ant. 242; Gilb. For. Rom. 20.

OBTULIT SE (Lat. offered himself). In old practice. The emphatic words of entry on the record where one party offered himself in court against the other, and the latter did not appear. 1 Reeve, Hist. Eng. Law, 417.

OBVENTIO (Lat. *obvenire,* to fall in).

—**In Civil Law.** Rent or profit accruing from a thing, or from industry. It is generally used in the plural.

—**In Old English Law.** The revenue of spiritual living, so called. Cowell. Also, in the plural, offerings. 2 Inst. 661.

OCASION, or **OCCASION** (Spanish). In Spanish law. Accident. Las Partidas, pt. 3, tit. 32, lib. 21; White, New Recop. bk. 2, tit. 9, c. 2.

OCCASIO (Law Lat.) In old English law. Molestation; trouble; hindrance; vexation by suit. Spelman; Carta de Foresta, c. 12; Barr. Obs. St. 38, 39, note (k).

OCCASIONARE (Law Lat.) In old practice. To trouble or molest; to vex or haress with litigation. Spelman; Fleta, lib. 2, c. 66, § 20; Cart. Conf. 49 Hen. III.

OCCASIONES (Law Lat.) In old English law. Assarts. Spelman.

OCCISION (Law Fr. from Lat. *occisio,* from *occidere,* to kill). A killing or slaying. *Murdre est occision de home.* Britt. c. 6.

OCCULTATIO (Lat.) In old English law. A hiding. *Occultatio thesauri inventi fraudulosa,* the fraudulent concealment of treasure trove. Bracton, fol. 119b; 3 Inst. 133.

OCCUPANCY. The taking possession of those things corporeal which are without an owner, with an intention of appropriating them to one's own use.

Pothier defines it to be the title by which one acquires property in a thing which belongs to nobody, by taking possession of it with design of acquiring it. Tr. du Dr. de Propriete, note 20. The Civil Code of Louisiana (article 3375), nearly following Pothier, defines occupancy to be "a mode of acquiring property by which a thing which belongs to nobody becomes the property of the person who took possession of it with an intention of acquiring a right of ownership in it."

Sometimes used in the sense of actual possession of things corporeal.

"Occupancy and possession, when applied to land, are synonymous." 21 Ill. 178.

A distinction is sometimes made in the use of "occupation" to indicate mere possession and "occupancy" for the acquirement of title by the taking of possession (Abbott), but it is not generally observed.

OCCUPANT, or OCCUPIER. One who has the actual use or possession of a thing. Occupancy implies the exclusion of every one else from enjoyment. 25 Barb. (N. Y.) 54.

Tenant in possession. 11 Abb. Pr. (N. Y.) 97, 101.

OCCUPANTIS FIUNT DERELICTA. Things abandoned become the property of the first occupant. 1 Pet. Adm. (U. S.) 53.

OCCUPARE (Lat.) In the civil law. To seize or take possession of; to enter upon a vacant possession; to take possession before another. Calv. Lex.

OCCUPATIO Lat. from *occupare*, to occupy). In the civil law. A taking possession of a thing which before belonged to nobody (*quod ante nullius est*); as of wild beasts and other wild animals, property and persons captured in war, gems and other things found upon the seashore, etc. Inst. 2. 1. 12. 17. 18. See Fleta, lib. 3, c. 2.

OCCUPATION. That which occupies or engages the time or attention; the principal business of one's life; vocation; employment; calling; trade. 134 Ill. 234. See "Occupancy."

OCCUPAVIT (Lat.) In old practice. The name of a writ which lies to recover the possession of lands when they have been taken from the possession of the owner by occupation.

OCCUR. In its general and most popular sense the word "occur" means to "happen." When used in a contract limiting the time within which an action may be brought to a certain time after the happening of a particular event, should be given the sense of "accrue." 61 How. § 146; 91 Ill. 92.

OCCURRERE. (Lat.) To meet; to run against; to stop, or bar.

OCCYS. (L. Fr. from Lat. *occisus*). Slain; killed. Britt. c. 5.

OCHIERN (Scotch; Law Lat. *ogetharius*). In old Scotch law. A name of dignity and of a freeholder. Skene de Verb. Sign.

OCHLOCRACY. A government where the authority is in the hands of the multitude; the abuse of a democracy. Vaumene, Dict. du Language Politique.

OCTABIS (Law Lat. from *octo*, eight). In old practice. The octave. Fleta, lib. 2, c. 35. See "Octave."

OCTAVE (Law Lat. *utas*). In old English practice. The eighth day inclusive after a feast. 3 Bl. Comm. 277.

OCTO TALES (Lat. eight such). If, when a trial at bar is called on, the number of jurors in attendance is too small, the trial must be adjourned, and a *decem* or *octo tales* awarded, according to the number deficient; as, at common law, namely, a writ to the sheriff to summon eight more such men as were originally summoned. 3 Bl. Comm. 364.

OCTROI (Fr.) In old French law. Originally, a duty, which, by the permission of the seigneur, any city was accustomed to collect on liquors and some other goods, brought within its precincts, for the consumption of the inhabitants. Afterwards appropriated to the use of the king. Steph. Lect. p. 361.

ODHALL RIGHT. The same as "allodial."

ODIO ET ATIA. See "De Odio et Atia."

ODIOSA ET INHONESTA NON SUNT in lege praesumanda. Odious and dishonest acts are not presumed in law. Co. Litt. 78; 6 Wend. (N. Y.) 228, 231; 18 N. Y. 295, 300.

ODIOSA NON PRAESUMUNTUR. Odious things are not presumed. Burr. Sett. Cas. 190.

OECONOMICUS. An executor.

OECONOMUS (Lat.) In the civil law. A manager or administrator. Calv. Lex.

OEPS, or OES (Law Fr.) Use. *A nostre oeps*, to our use. Britt. c. 21; St. Westminster I. c. 48. *A son oeps demesne.* Dyer, 5. See "Opus."

OF COUNSEL. A term applied to the counsel employed by a party in a cause, or whose name appears upon the papers. Derived probably from the Latin *a consiliis* (*q. v.*) and expressed by the Law Latin *de consilio* (Law French *de counsel*). Dyer, 34b, 38. The modern phrase "of counsel for" a party was formerly expressed "of counsel with." "The counsellor should give his counsel to him with whom he is of counsel." 5 Coke, 20.

OF COURSE. A term applied to those acts in the course of a judicial proceeding which may be done without leave of court, or which will be granted by the court on application without inquiry.

OF NEW. A Scotch expression, closely translated from the Latin "*de novo*" (*q. v.*).

OFFA EXECRATA (Law Lat.) In old English law. The morsel of execration; the corsned (*q. v.*). 1 Reeve, Hist. Eng. Law, 21.

OFFENSE. In criminal law. The doing that which a penal law forbids to be done, or omitting to do what it commands. In this sense, it is nearly synonymous with "crime." In a more confined sense, it may be considered as having the same meaning with "misdemeanor;" but it differs from it in this, that it is not indictable, but punishable summarily by the forfeiture of a penalty. 1 Chit. Prac. 14.

OFFER. The word offer is frequently used by courts and text writers as synonymous with "tender," and it may properly be so used with reference to articles capable of manual delivery and actually produced. But with respect to heavy articles of merchandise, situated at a distance from the place to which they must be transported if restored to the vendor, the phrase "offer to return" is more commonly or aptly applied to express a willingness, or to make a proposal, to rescind the contract and return the goods. 156 Ill. App. 476.

OFFICE. A right to exercise a function or employment, and take the fees and emoluments belonging to it. 3 Serg. & R. (Pa.) 149; 23 Ind. 449; 36 Miss. 273.

The term is ordinarily used with respect to the power conferred on individuals to exercise public functions, and in this connection "public office" is a more discriminating term. An "office" in this sense implies a delegation of a part of the sovereign power to an individual. See 3 Me. 481.

The office exists and survives as an entity apart from the incumbent (28 Cal. 382; 29 Ohio St. 347), but it has been said that the essence of the office is the power and jurisdiction of the officer (62 Pa. St. 343).

Offices are either civil or military. Civil offices are either executive, judicial, or legislative.

OFFICE COPY. A copy of a writing or record made and certified or authenticated by the officer legally intrusted with its custody or control. Such a copy is admissible in evidence to prove the original. 1 Greenl. Ev. § 507.

OFFICE FOUND.

——**In English Law.** When an inquisition is made to the king's use of anything, by virtue of office of him who inquires, and the inquisition is found, it is said to be "office found."

——**In American Law.** An action by the state or national government, or its proper officer, for the enforcement of escheat.

OFFICE GRANT. A conveyance made by a public officer in certain cases, where the owner is either unwilling or unable to execute the requisite deeds to pass title. See 3 Washb. Real Prop. *537.

OFFICER. The incumbent of an office. The term is ordinarily applied to the incumbent of a public office, though it may be otherwise applied, as to the officer of a corporation.

A public officer is one occupying a public office, to whom a portion of the sovereign power is delegated, and whose duties are continuous in their nature, and prescribed by law.

The distinction between an officer and a government employee is that the duties of the former are fixed by law, and not by contract. 22 Conn. 379; 36 Miss. 273; 42 N. Y. Super. Ct. 481.

——**Executive Officers.** Those whose duties are mainly to cause the laws to be executed. For example, the president of the United States of America, and the several governors of the different states, are executive officers. Their duties are pointed out in the national constitution, and in the constitutions of the several states.

——**Legislative Officers.** Those whose duties relate mainly to the enactment of laws, such as members of congress and of the several state legislatures.

These officers are confined in their duties, by the constitution, generally to make laws; though sometimes, in cases of impeachment, one of the houses of the legislature exercises judicial functions somewhat similar to those of a grand jury, by presenting to the other articles of impeachment, and the other house acts as a court in trying such impeachments. The legislatures have, besides, the power to inquire into the conduct of their members, judge of their elections, and the like.

——**Judicial Officers.** Those whose duties are to decide controversies between individuals, and accusations made in the name of the public against persons charged with a violation of the law.

——**Ministerial Officers.** Those whose duty it is to execute the mandates, lawfully issued, of their superiors.

——**Military Officers.** Those who have command in the army.

——**Naval Officers.** Those who are in command in the navy.

OFFICER DE FACTO. One whose acts, though not those of lawful officer, the law upon principles of policy and justice will hold valid so far as they involve the interests of the public and third persons, where the duties of the office were exercised, (1) without a known appointment or election, but under such circumstances of reputation or acquiescence as were calculated to induce people, without inquiry, to submit to or invoke his action, supposing him to be the officer he assumed to be; (2) under color of a known and valid appointment or election, but where the officer had failed to conform to some precedent requirement or condition, as to take an oath, give a bond, or the like; (3) under color of a known election or appointment void because the officer was not eligible, or because there was a want of power in the electing or appointing body, or, by reason of some defect or irregularity in its exercise, such ineligibility, want of power or defect, being unknown to the public; (4) under color of an election or appointment by or pursuant to a public unconstitutional law before the same is adjudged to be such. 38 Conn. 449.

The most generally accepted of the short definitions of the term is that of Lord Ellenborough: "An officer *de facto* is one who has the reputation of being the officer he assumes to be, and yet is not a good officer in point of law." 6 East, 356.

OFFICER DE JURE. One having the legal right to an office; generally applied to such officers when not in possession of the office.

OFFICIA JUDICIALIA NON CONCEDANtur antequam vacent. Judicial offices ought not to be granted before they are vacant. 11 Coke, 4.

OFFICIA MAGISTRATUS NON DEBENT esse venalia. The offices of magistrates ought not to be sold. Co. Litt. 234.

OFFICIAL. An officer (*q. v.*)

——**In Old Civil Law.** The person who was the minister of, or attendant upon, a magistrate.

——**In Canon Law.** The person to whom the bishop generally commits the charge of his spiritual jurisdiction bears this name. Wood, Inst. 30, 505; Merlin, Repert.

OFFICIAL ACT. By an official act is not simply meant a lawful act of the officer—it means any act done by the officer in his official capacity, under color and by virtue of his office. 154 Ill. 601, 52 Ill. App. 345; 137 Mass. 191.

OFFICIAL BOND. The bond of a public officer; though more loosely it is often applied to any bond legally required of one exercising a given function, *e. g.*, an executor's or trustee's bond.

OFFICIAL USE. An active use. Wharton.

OFFICIARIIS NON FACIENDIS VEL amovendis. A writ addressed to the magistrates of a corporation, requiring them not to make such a man an officer, or to put one out of the office he has until inquiry is made of his manners, etc. Reg. Orig. 126.

OFFICINA JUSTITIAE. The workshop or office of justice.

——**In English Law.** The chancery is so called, because all writs issue from it, under the great seal, returnable into the courts of common law. See "Court of Chancery."

OFFICIOUS WILL. A testament by which a testator leaves his property to his family. Sandars, Just. Inst. 207. See "Inofficious Testament."

OFFICIT CONATUS SI EFFECTUS sequitur. The attempt becomes of consequence if the effect follows.

OFFICIUM NEMINI DEBET ESSE DAMnosum. An office ought to be injurious to no one. Bell, Dict.

OIL, *Oile, Oyl, Oyel.* (L. Fr.) Yes; yea. Schard. The assent of the commons in 28 Edw. III. Kelham.

Oil is a mineral and part of the realty. Owing to its fugitive nature, a grant of oil under the ground is a grant, not of the oil in place in the earth, but of such oil as the grantee may find there and save. 240 Ill. 367; 233 Ill. 12. See "Minerals."

OIR (Spanish; from Lat. *audire,* to hear). In Spanish law. To hear; to take cognizance. White, New Recop. bk. 3, tit. 1, c. 7.

OLD STYLE. See "New Style."

OLD TENURES. The title of a small tract, which, as its title denotes, contains an account of the various tenures by which land was holden in the reign of Edward III. This tract was published in 1719, with notes and additions with the eleventh edition of the First Institutes, and reprinted in 8vo, in 1764, by Serjeant Hawkins, in a Selection of Coke's Law Tracts.

OLERON, LAWS OF. A maritime code promulgated by Eleanor, duchess of Guienne, mother of Richard I., at the Isle of Oleron,—whence their name. They were modified and enacted in England under Richard I., and again promulgated under Henry III. and Edward III., and are constantly quoted in proceedings before the admiralty courts, as are also the Rhodian Laws. Co. Litt. 2. See Code, § 25.

OLIGARCHY (Gr. the government of a few). A name given to designate the power which a few citizens of a state have usurped, which ought by the constitution to reside in the people. Among the Romans, the government degenerated several times into an oligarchy; for example, under the decemvirs, when they became the only magistrates in the commonwealth.

OLOGRAPH. A term which signifies that an instrument is wholly written by the party from whom it emanates. See Civ. Code La. art. 1581; Civ. Code, 970; 5 Toullier, Dr. Civ. note 357; 1 Stuart, K. B. 327; 2 Bouv. Inst. note 2139.

OLOGRAPHIC WILL. One that is entirely written, dated and signed by the hand of the testator himself. Belcher, 100 Cal. 207.

OM, or **OMME** (Law Fr.) Man; a man or person. Corrupted forms of "home" (*q. v.*) Kelham.

OME BUENO (Spanish). In Spanish law. A good man; a substantial person. Las Partidas, pt. 5, tit. 13, lib. 38.

OMISSIO (Lat. from *omittere*). Omission; a leaving out.

OMISSIO EORUM QUAE TACITE INsunt nihil operatur. The omission of those things which are silently expressed is of no consequence. 2 Bulst. 131.

OMISSION. Neglect to perform an act required by law.

OMISSIS OMNIBUS ALIIS NEGOTIIS (Lat.) Laying aside all other businesses. 9 East, 347.

OMIT. To fail to use or to do; neglect; disregard; to fail, forbear, neglect to mention or to speak of; say nothing of; to leave out; forbear, fail to assert or include, as to omit an item from a list. 146 Ia. 360, 373; 140 Am. St. Rep. 282.

OMNE ACTUM AB INTENTIONE AGENtis est judicandum. Every act is to be estimated by the intention of the doer. Branch, Princ.

OMNE CRIMEN EBRIETAS ET INCENdit et detegit. Drunkenness inflames and reveals every crime. Co. Litt. 247.

OMNE JUS AUT CONSENSUS FECIT, aut necessitas constituit, aut firmavit consuetudo. All law has either been derived from the consent of the people, established by necessity, or confirmed by custom. Dig. 1. 3. 40; Broom, Leg. Max. (3d London Ed.) 616, note.

OMNE MAGIS DIGNUM TRAHIT AD SE minus dignum sit antiquius. Every worthier thing draws to it the less worthy, though the latter be more ancient. Co. Litt. 355.

OMNE MAGNUM EXEMPLUM HABET aliquid ex iniquo, quod publica utilitate compensatur. Every great example has some portion of evil, which is compensated by its public utility. Hob. 279.

OMNE MAJUS CONTINET IN SE MInus. The greater contains in itself the less. 5 Coke, 115a; Wingate, Max. 206; Story, Ag. § 172; Broom, Leg. Max. (3d London Ed.) 173.

OMNE MAJUS DIGNUM CONTINET IN se minus dignum. The more worthy contains in itself the less worthy. Co. Litt. 143.

OMNE MAJUS MINUS IN SE COMPLECtitur. Every greater embraces in itself the minor. Jenk. Cent. Cas. 208.

OMNE PRINCIPALE TRAHIT AD SE accessorium. Every principal thing draws to itself the accessory. 17 Mass. 425; 1 Johns. (N. Y.) 580.

OMNE QUOD INAEDIFICATUR SOLO cedit. Everything belongs to the soil which is built upon it. Dig. 41. 1. 7. 10; Id. 47. 3. 1; Inst. 2. 1. 29; Broom, Leg. Max. (3d London Ed.) 355; Fleta, lib. 3, c. 2, § 12.

OMNE SACRAMENTUM DEBET ESSE de certa scientia. Every oath ought to be founded on certain knowledge. 4 Inst. 279.

OMNE TESTAMENTUM MORTE CONsummatum est. Every will is consummated by death. 3 Coke, 29b; 4 Coke, 61b; 2 Bl. Comm. 500; Shep. Touch. 401.

OMNES ACTIONES IN MUNDO INFRA certa tempora habent limitationem. All actions in the world are limited within certain periods. Bracton, 52.

OMNES HOMINES AUT LIBERI SUNT aut servi. All men are freemen or slaves. Inst. 1. 3. pr.; Fleta, lib. 1, c. 1, § 2.

OMNES LICENTIAM HABERE HIS quae pro se indulta sunt, renunciare. All shall have liberty to renounce those things which have been established in their favor. Code, 2. 3. 29; Id. 1. 3. 51; Broom, Leg. Max. (3d London Ed.) 625.

OMNES PRUDENTES, ILLA ADMITtere solent quae probantur iis qui in arte sua bene versati sunt. All prudent men are accustomed to admit those things which are approved by those who are well versed in the art. 7 Coke, 19.

OMNES SORORES SUNT QUASI UNUS haeres de una haereditate. All sisters are, as it were, one heir to one inheritance. Co. Litt. 67.

OMNIA DELICTA IN APERTO LEVIORA sunt. All crimes committed openly are considered lighter. 8 Coke, 127.

OMNIA PERFORMAVIT (Lat. he has done all). In pleading. A good plea in bar where all the covenants are in the affirmative. 1 Me. 189.

OMNIA PRAESUMUNTUR CONTRA spoliatorem. All things are presumed against a wrongdoer. Broom, Leg. Max. (3d London Ed.) 843.

OMNIA PRAESUMUNTUR LEGITIME facta donec probetur in contrarium. All things are presumed to be done legitimately until the contrary is proved. Co. Litt. 232.

OMNIA PRAESUMUNTUR RITE ESSE acta. All things are presumed to be done in due form. Co. Litt. 6.

OMNIA PRAESUMUNTUR RITE ET SOlemniter esse acta. All things are presumed to have been rightly and regularly done. Co. Litt. 232b; Broom, Leg. Max. (3d London Ed.) 847; 12 C. B. 788; 3 Exch. 191; 6 Exch. 716. *Omnia rite esse acta praesumuntur.* 11 Cush. (Mass.) 441; 2 Ohio St. 246, 247; 4 Ohio St. 148; 6 Ohio St. 293.

OMNIA PRAESUMUNTUR RITE ET SOlemniter esse acta donec probetur in contrarium. All things are presumed to have been done regularly and with due formality until the contrary is proved. Broom, Leg. Max. (3d London Ed.) 157, 849; 3 Bing. 381; 2 Campb. 44; 1 Cromp. & M. 461; 17 C. B.

183; 5 Barn. & Adol. 550; 12 Mees. & W. 251; 12 Wheat. (U. S.) 69, 70.

OMNIA PRAESUMUNTUR SOLEMNIter esse acta. All things are presumed to have been done rightly. Co. Litt. 6.

OMNIA QUAE JURE CONTRAHUNTUR, contrario jure pereunt. Obligations contracted under a law are destroyed by a law to the contrary. Dig. 50. 17. 100.

OMNIA QUAE SUNT UXORIS SUNT ipsius viri. All things which are the wife's belong to the husband. Co. Litt. 112; 2 Kent, Comm. 130, 143.

OMNIBUS AD QUOS PRAESENTES literae pervenerint, salutem. To all to whom the present letters shall come, greeting. A form of address with which charters and deeds were anciently commenced.

OMNIS ACTIO EST LOQUELA. Every action is a complaint. Co. Litt. 292.

OMNIS CONCLUSIO BONI ET VERI JUdicii sequitur ex bonis et veris praemissis et dictis juratorum. Every conclusion of a good and true judgment arises from good and true premises, and the verdicts of jurors. Co. Litt. 226.

OMNIS CONSENSUS TOLLIT ERROrem. Every consent removes error. 2 Inst. 123.

OMNIS DEFINITIO IN JURE CIVILI periculosa est, parum est enim ut non subverti possit. Every definition in the civil law is dangerous, for there is very little that cannot be overthrown. There is no rule in the civil law which is not liable to some exception; and the least difference in the facts of the case renders its application useless. Dig. 50. 17. 202; 2 Wooddeson, Lect. 196.

OMNIS DEFINITIO IN JURE PERICUlosa est; parum est enim ut non subverti posset. Every definition in law is perilous, for it is within an ace of being subverted. Dig. 50. 17. 202; 2 Wooddeson, Lect. 196.

OMNIS EXCEPTIO EST IPSA QUOQUE regula. An exception is in itself also a rule.

OMNIS INDEMNATUS PRO INNOXIS legibus habetur. Every uncondemned person is held by the law as innocent. Lofft, 121.

OMNIS INNOVATIO PLUS NOVITATE perturbat quam utilitate prodest. Every innovation disturbs more by its novelty than it benefits by its utility. 2 Bulst. 338; 1 Salk. 20.

OMNIS INTERPRETATIO SI FIERI POtest ita fienda est in instrumentis, ut omnes contrarietates amoveantur. The interpretation of instruments is to be made, if they will admit of it, so that all contradictions may be removed. Jenk. Cent. Cas. 96.

OMNIS INTERPRETATIO VEL DEClarat, vel extendit, vel restringit. Every inpretation either declares, extends, or restrains.

OMNIS NOVA CONSTITUTIO FUTURIS formam imponere debet, non praeteritis. Every new statute ought to prescribe a form to future, not to past, acts. Bracton, fol. 228; 2 Inst. 95.

OMNIS PERSONA EST HOMO, SED non vicissim. Every person is a man, but not every man a person. Calv. Lex.

OMNIS PRIVATIO PRAESUPPONIT habitum. Every privation presupposes former enjoyment. Co. Litt. 339.

OMNIS QUERELA ET OMNIS ACTIO injuriarum limitata est infra certa tempora. Every plaint and every action for injuries is limited within certain times. Co. Litt. 114.

OMNIS RATIHABITIO RETRO TRAHItur et mandato aequiparatur. Every subsequent ratification has a retrospective effect, and is equivalent to a prior command. Co. Litt. 207a; Story, Ag. (4th Ed.) 102; Broom, Leg. Max. (3d London Ed.) 715; 2 Bouv. Inst. 25; 4 Bouv. Inst. 26; 8 Wheat. (U. S.) 363; 7 Exch. 726; 10 Exch. 845; 9 C. B. 532, 607; 14 C. B. 53.

OMNIS REGULA SUAS PATITUR EXceptiones. Every rule of law is liable to its own exceptions.

OMNIUM (Lat.) In mercantile law. A term used to express the aggregate value of the different stocks in which a loan is usually funded. 2 Esp. 361; 7 Term R. 630.

OMNIUM CONTRIBUTIONE SARCIAtur quod pro omnibus datum est. What is given for all shall be compensated for by the contribution of all. 4 Bing. 121; 2 Marsh. 309.

OMNIUM RERUM QUARUM USUS est, potest esse abusus, virtute sola excepta. There may be an abuse of everything of which there is a use, virtue only excepted. Dav. 79.

ON. Where an act is to be done on a particular day, the party has the whole of that day in which to perform it. 14 Ill. 333.

When used as indicating relative situation or position, "on" means at, near, or adjacent to, without implying contact or support. 143 Ia. 297, 300. See "From."

ON ACCOUNT OF WHOM IT MAY CONcern, or For whom it may concern. A clause in policies of insurance, under which all are insured who have an insurable interest at the time of effecting the insurance, and who were then contemplated by the party effecting the insurance. 2 Pars. Mar. Law, 30.

ON CALL. On demand. 22 Grat. (Va.) 609.

ON DEMAND. When requested. A promissory note payable "on demand" is payable immediately without demand, *i. e.*, is always due.

ONCE IN JEOPARDY. See "Jeopardy."

ONE HUNDRED THOUSAND POUNDS clause. A precautionary stipulation inserted in a deed making a good tenant to the *praecipe* in a common recovery. See 1 Prest. Conv. 110.

ONERANDO PRO RATA PORTIONIS. A writ that lay for a joint tenant or tenant in common who was distrained for more rent than his proportion of the land comes to. Reg. Orig. 182.

ONERARI NON (Lat. ought not to be burdened). In pleading. The name of a plea by which the defendant says that he ought not to be charged. It is used in an action of debt. 1 Saund. 290, note (a).

ONERATUR NISI. See "O. Ni."

ONERIS FERENDI (Lat. of bearing a burden). In civil law. The name of a servitude by which the wall or pillar of one house is bound to sustain the weight of the buildings of the neighbor.

The owner of the servient building is bound to repair and keep it sufficiently strong for the weight it has to bear. Dig. 8. 2. 23; 2 Bouv. Inst. note 1627.

ONEROUS. A contract, lease, share, or other right is said to be "onerous" when the obligations attaching to it counterbalance or exceed the advantage to be derived from it, either absolutely or with reference to the particular possessor. Rapalje & L.

ONEROUS CAUSE. In civil law. A valuable consideration.

ONEROUS CONTRACT. In civil law. One made for a consideration given or promised, however small. Civ. Code La. art. 1767.

ONEROUS DEED. In Scotch law. A deed given for valuable consideration. Bell, Dict. See "Consideration."

ONEROUS GIFT. The gift of a thing subject to certain charges imposed by the giver on the donee. Poth. Obl.

ONOMASTIC. A term applied to a signature which is in a different handwriting from the body of the instrument. 2 Benth. Jud. Ev. 460, 461.

ONUS PROBANDI (Lat.) In evidence. The burden of proof.

OPE CONSILIO (Lat.) By aid and counsel. A civil law term applied to accessories, similar in import to the "aiding and abetting" of the common law. Often written "*ope et consilio.*"

OPEN A CREDIT. To accept or pay the draft of a correspondent who has not furnished funds. Pardessus, note 296.

OPEN ACCOUNT. A running or unsettled account.

OPEN CORPORATION. One in which all members have a vote to choose officers, as distinguished from a "close corporation," wherein the officers fill vacancies. 3 Bland, Ch. (Md.) 416, note.

The latter term in common use means that all stock is closely held, usually by a few persons, so that no one else can, by purchase of shares, obtain a voice in the policy of the corporation.

OPEN COURT. A court formally opened and engaged in the transaction of all judicial functions.

A court to which all persons have free access as spectators while they conduct themselves in an orderly manner.

The term is used in the first sense as distinguishing a court from a judge sitting in chambers or informally for the transaction of such matters as may be thus transacted. See "Chambers;" "Court."

In the second sense, all courts in the United States are open; but in England, formerly, while the parties and probably their witnesses were admitted freely in the courts, all other persons were required to pay in order to obtain admittance. St. 13 Edw. I. cc. 42, 44; Barr. Obs. St. 126, 127. See Princ. Pen. Law, 165.

OPEN DOORS. In Scotch law. "Letters of open doors" are process which empower the messenger or officer of the law to break open doors of houses or rooms in which the debtor has placed his goods. Bell, Dict.

OPEN LAW. The trial by duel or ordeal. See "Lex Manifesta."

OPEN POLICY. An open policy is one in which the amount of the interest of the insured is not fixed by the policy, and is to be ascertained in case of loss. See "Policy."

OPEN THEFT. In Saxon law. The same with the Latin *furtum manifestum* (*q. v.*)

OPENING.

——**In American Practice.** The beginning; the commencement; the first address of the counsel. The opening is made immediately upon the impaneling of the jury. It embraces the reading of such of the pleadings as may be necessary, and a brief outline of the case as the party expects to prove it, where there is a trial, or of the argument, where it is addressed to the court.

——**In English Practice.** The address made immediately after the evidence is closed. Such address usually states, first, the full extent of the plaintiff's claims, and the circumstances under which they are made, to show that they are just and reasonable; second, at least an outline of the evidence by which those claims are to be established; third, the legal grounds and authorities in favor of the claim or of the proposed evidence; fourth, an anticipation of the expected defense, and statement of the grounds on which it is futile, either in law or justice, and the reasons why it ought to fail. But the court will sometimes restrict counsel from an anticipation of the defense. 3 Chit. Prac. 881; 3 Bouv. Inst. note 3044 et seq.

OPENING A COMMISSION. An entering upon the duties under a commission, or commencing to act under a commission, is so termed. Thus, the judges of assize and *nisi prius* derive their authority to act under or by virtue of commissions directed to them for that purpose; and, when they commence acting under the powers so committed to them, they are said to open the commissions; and the day on which they so commence their proceedings is thence termed the "commission day of the assizes." Brown.

OPENING A JUDGMENT. Taking off the bar of finality so as to permit the reconsideration of the judgment and of the cause on which it was founded. It does not abrogate the judgment, as does "vacation of judgment."

OPENING A POLICY OF INSURANCE. The question has been made whether, and in what cases, if any, the valuation in a valued policy shall be opened. The valuation, being a part of the agreement of the parties, is not to be set aside as between them in any case. The question is, how shall it be treated where only a part of the subject insured and valued is put at a risk, and also in the settlement of a particular average? and the answer is the same in both cases, viz., when the proportion or rate per centum put at risk or loss is ascertained, the agreed valuation of the whole is to be applied to the part put at risk; or the proportion lost, *pro rata.* 2 Phil. Ins. 1203.

OPENING A RULE. The act of restoring or recalling a rule which has been made absolute to its conditional state, as a rule *nisi*, so as to readmit of cause being shown against the rule. Thus, when a rule to show cause has been made absolute under a mistaken impression that no counsel had been instructed to show cause against it, it is usual for the party at whose instance the rule was obtained to consent to have the rule opened, by which all the proceedings subsequent to the day when cause ought to have been shown against it are in effect nullified, and the rule is then argued in the ordinary way. Brown.

OPENING BIDDINGS. Ordering a resale. When estates are sold under decree of equity to the highest bidder, the court will, on notice of an offer of a sufficient advance on the price obtained, open the biddings, *i. e.*, order a resale; but this will not generally be done after the confirmation of the certificate of the highest bidder. So, by analogy, a resale has been ordered of an estate sold under bankruptcy. Sugd. Vend. 90; 22 Barb. (N. Y.) 167; 8 Md. 322; 9 Md. 228; 13 Grat. (Va.) 639; 4 Wis. 242; 31 Miss. 514.

OPENING THE PLEADINGS. Making an opening statement to the jury of the issues at the beginning of a trial.

OPERARIUS (Law Lat. from *opus*, work). In old English law. A workman or laborer. Fleta, lib. 2, c. 73, § 4.

OPERATION OF LAW. A term applied to indicate the manner in which a party acquires rights without any act of his own, as, the right to an estate of one who dies intestate is cast upon the heir at law, by operation of law. When a lessee for life enfeoffs him in reversion, or when the lessee and lessor join in a feoffment, or when a lessee for life or years accepts a new lease or demise from the lessor, there is a surrender of the first lease by operation of law. 5 Barn. & C. 269; 9 Barn. & C. 298; 2 Barn. & Adol. 119; 5 Taunt. 518. See "Descent;" "Purchase."

OPERATIVE. A workman; one employed to perform labor for another. See 2 Cush. (Mass.) 371.

OPERATIVE PART. In a written instrument, that which carries out the main object of the instrument, as distinguished from the recitals, formal conclusion, etc. Sometimes everything that follows the recitals is called the operative part.

OPERATIVE WORDS. Those by which the purpose of an instrument is effected. Generally applied to those words in a deed by which an estate is passed, viz., "grant," "quitclaim," "demise," "bargain and sell," etc.

OPERIS NOVI NUNTIATIO. In the civil law. A protest or warning against (of) a new work. Dig. 39. 1.

OPINIO EST DUPLEX, SCILICET, opinio vulgaris, orta inter graves et discretos, et quae vultum veritatis habet, et opinio tantum orta inter leves et vulgares homines, absque specie veritatis. Opinion is of two kinds, namely, common opinion, which springs up among grave and discreet men, and which has the appearance of truth, and opinion which springs up only among light and foolish men, without the semblance of truth. 4 Coke, 107.

OPINIO QUAE FAVET TESTAMENTO est tenenda. That opinion is to be followed which favors the will.

OPINION.

——**In Evidence.** An inference or conclusion stated by a witness, as distinguished from a statement of matters of fact.

——**In Practice.** The statement of reasons delivered by a judge or court for giving the judgment which is pronounced upon a case. The judgment itself is sometimes called an opinion, and sometimes the opinion is spoken of as the judgment of the court.

A declaration, usually in writing, made by a counsel to his client of what the law is, according to his judgment, on a statement of facts submitted to him.

An opinion is in both the above cases a decision of what principles of law are to be applied in the particular case, with the difference that judicial opinions pronounced by the court are law and of authority, while the opinions of counsel, however eminent, are merely advice to his client or argument to the court.

OPORTET (Lat.) It behooves; it is needful or necessary. *Oportebit* (the future form) had, in the civil law, the sense of *oportet.* Dig. 50. 16. 8. And as to the meaning of *oportere,* see Dig. 50. 16.

OPORTET QUOD CERTA RES DEDUcatur in donationem. It is necessary that a certain thing be brought into the gift, or made the subject of the conveyance. Bracton, fol. 15b.

OPORTET QUOD CERTA RES DEDUcatur in judicium. A thing, to be brought to judgment, must be certain or definite. Jenk. Cent. Cas. 84; Bracton, fol. 15b.

OPORTET QUOD CERTA SIT RES quae venditur. A thing, to be sold, must be certain or definite.

OPORTET QUOD CERTAE PERSONAE, terrae, et certi status, comprehendantur in declaratione usuum. It is necessary that certain persons, lands, and estates be comprehended in a declaration of uses. 9 Coke, 9.

OPP'. A contraction of *obtulit* or *optulit,* in the old books. A. *opp' see versus* B. *quarto die,* A. offered himself against B. on the fourth day. Fleta, lib. 2, c. 65, § 11; Id. c. 67, § 2.

OPPIDUM (Lat.) A town. Dig. 50. 16. 239. 7.

OPPIGNERARE (Lat.) In the civil law. To pledge. Calv. Lex.

OPPOSER (Law Lat. *oppositor*). In old English law. An officer in the court of exchequer. See "Foreign Apposer." Sometimes treated as a corrupted form of *apposer* (*q. v.*), but there are good reasons for considering it as the genuine word.

OPPOSITA JUXTA SE POSITA MAGIS elucescunt. Opposites placed next each other appear in a clearer light. 4 Bac. Works, 256, 258, 353.

OPPOSITION. In bankruptcy practice. The act of a creditor who declares his dissent to a debtor's being discharged under the bankrupt laws.

OPPRESSION. The act of an officer in inflicting upon any person, with improper motive, any bodily harm, imprisonment, or other injury, not constituting extortion. Steph. Dig. art. 119; 4 Q. B. 475.

OPTIMA ENIM EST LEGIS INTERPRES consuetudo. Usage is the best interpreter of law. 2 Inst. 18; Broom, Leg. Max. (3d London Ed.) 823.

OPTIMA EST LEX, QUAE MINIMUM relinquit arbitrio judicis. That is the best system of law which confides as little as possible to the discretion of the judge. Bac. Aph. 46.

OPTIMA STATUTI INTERPRETATRIX est (omnibus particulis ejusdem inspectis) ipsum statutum. The best interpretress of a statute is (all the separate parts being considered) the statute itself. 8 Coke, 117; Wingate, Max. 239, max. 68.

OPTIMAM ESSE LEGEM, QUAE MINImum relinquit arbitrio judicis; id quod certitudo ejus praestat. That law is the best which leaves the least discretion to the judge; and this is an advantage which results from its certainty. Bac. Aph. 8.

OPTIMUS INTERPRES RERUM USUS. Usage is the best interpreter of things. 2 Inst. 282.

OPTIMUS INTERPRETANDI MODUS est sic legis interpretare ut leges legibus accordant. The best mode of interpreting laws is to make them accord. 8 Coke, 169.

OPTIMUS JUDEX, QUI MINIMUM SIBI. He is the best judge who relies as little as possible on his own discretion. Bac. Aph. 46.

OPTIMUS LEGUM INTERPRES CONsuetudo. Custom is the best interpreter of laws. 4 Inst. 75; 2 Pars. Cont. 53.

OPTION. A right of choice or election. Sometimes applies specifically to contracts whereby one purchases the right for a certain time, at his election, to demand and receive or to deliver property at a stated price. See "Gambling Contract."

OPTIONAL WRIT. An original writ in the alternative, commanding either to do a thing, or show cause why it has not been done. 3 Bl. Comm. 274; Finch, Law, 257.

OPTOMETRY. The employment of subjective and objective mechanical means to determine the accommodative and refractive states of the eye and the scope of its functions in general; the employment of any means, other than the use of drugs, for the measurement of the powers or range of human vision and the adaptation of lenses or frames for the aid thereof; measurement of the powers of vision in general, as acuteness of perception of form and color or the extent of the field. 280 Ill. 21.

OPTULIT. An old form of *obtulit*, used in Bracton. Bracton, fols. 354, 354b.

OPUS (Lat. and Law Lat.) In civil and old English law. Work; labor; benefit; advantage. This word seems to have been framed from the Law French *oeps* (*q. v.*) A thing made or done by labor.

OPUS LOCATUM (Lat.) In civil law. A work, *i. e.*, the result of work, let to another to be used. A work, *i. e.*, something to be completed by work, hired to be done by another. Vicat, "Opus," "Locare;" L. 51, § 1, D. "Locat.;" L. 1, § 1, D. ad leg. Rhod.

OPUS MAGNIFICIUM (or **MANIFICIUM**) (from Lat. *opus*, work; *manus*, hand). In old English law. Manual labor. Fleta, lib. 2, c. 48, § 3.

OPUS NOVUM. In civil law. A new work. A new (*i. e.*, late or recent) construction on land, or alteration in works already there. Dig. 39. 1. 1. 11.

OR. Ordinarily a disjunctive particle. 249 Ill. 117; 99 Ill. 560. To further the intent of the parties, however, it has often been construed as conjunctive. 98 U. S. 143; 30 Ohio St. 407; 36 Wis. 466; 3 Gill (Md.) 492; 1 Yeates (Pa.) 316; 14 Daly (N. Y.) 361; 55 Ill. 239; 181 Ill. App. 715.

It is sometimes used also to introduce a synonymous or further expression in explanation of what precedes. 91 U. S. 362; 8 Mass. 59.

The usual province of the word is to disjoin the parts of a sentence, and while it suggests an alternative it also denotes opposition. 54 N. J. Law, 133.

Used in its ordinary and disjunctive sense, it corresponds with either, "meaning one or the other of two, but not both." 143 Ill. 100.

The word "or" is often construed "and," and vice versa, to further the intent of the parties in legacies, devises, deeds, bonds and writings. 213 Ill. 130; 249 Ill. 117.

In such cases it may usually be determined from the context that the wrong word was mistakenly used. 51 L. J. Q. B. 557; 9 Q. D. B. 643.

Instances in which "or" should be read "and." 2 Ves. 243; 6 D. & R. 257; 30 L. J. M. C. 245; 10 C. B. N. S. 317; 21 L. J. Ch. 434; 2 Sim. N. S. 212; 6 Ir. Eq. Rep. 118.

Instances in which "and" should not be read "or." 3 Rep. 80a; 12 East, 228; 26 L. J. Ch. 473; 6 H. L. Ca. 61; 28 Bea. 440; L. R. 11 Eq. 514; 40 L. J. Ch. 355; L. R. 2 Eq. 400; 33 L. J. Ch. 279; 33 Bea. 353; 22 L. J. Ex. 144; 8 Ex. 578; L. R. 1 Eq. 675.

"Or" sometimes means "nor." 51 L. J. M. C. 22; 8 Q. D. B. 445.

ORACULUM (Lat.) In civil law. The name of a kind of decision given by the Roman emperors.

ORAL. Spoken, in contradistinction to written; as, oral evidence, which is evidence delivered verbally by a witness.

ORANDO PRO REGE ET REGNO. An ancient writ which issued, while there was no standing collect for a sitting parliament, to pray for the peace and good government of the realm.

ORATIO SIGNIFICATIVA. (Lat.) In old English law. The meaning of an instrument, as distinguished from the mere letters (*literoe*) in which it was written. Fleta, lib. 2, c. 56, § 20.

ORATOR.

——**In Chancery Practice.** The party who files a bill.

——**In Roman Law.** An advocate. Code 1. 3. 33. 1.

ORATRIX. The feminine form of "orator."

ORCINUS LIBERTUS (Lat.) In Roman law. A freedman who obtained his liberty by the direct operation of the will or testament of his deceased master was so called, being the freedman of the deceased (*orcinus*), not of the *haeres*. Brown.

ORDAIN. To ordain is to make an ordinance, to enact a law.

The preamble to the constitution of the United States declares that the people "do ordain and establish this constitution for the United States of America." The third article of the same constitution declares that "the judicial power shall be vested in one supreme court, and in such inferior courts as the congress may from time to time ordain and establish." See 1 Wheat. (U. S.) 304, 324; 4 Wheat. (U. S.) 316, 402.

ORDAINED. When the word is applied to a clergymen, it means, that he has been invested with ministerial functions, or sacerdotal power. 4 Conn. 139.

ORDEAL. An ancient superstitious mode of trial.

When in a criminal case the accused was arraigned, he might select the mode of trial either by God and his country,—that is, by jury,—or by God only,—that is, by ordeal.

The trial by ordeal was either by fire or by water. Those who were tried by the former passed barefooted and blindfolded over nine hot, glowing ploughshares, or were to carry burning irons in their hands, and accordingly as they escaped or not they were acquitted or condemned. The water ordeal was performed either in hot or cold water.

In cold water, the parties suspected were adjudged innocent if their bodies were not borne up by the water contrary to the course of nature; and if, after putting their bare arms or legs into scalding water, they came out unhurt, they were taken to be innocent of the crime. It was supposed that God would, by the mere contrivance of man, exercise his power in favor of the innocent. 4 Bl. Comm. 342; 2 Am. Jur. 280. For a detailed account of the trial by ordeal, see Herbert, Ant. Inns of Court, 146.

ORDEFFE. A liberty whereby one claims ore found on his own land.

ORDENAMIENTO (Spanish). In Spanish law. An order emanating from the sovereign, and differing from a *cedula* only in form, and in the mode of its promulgation. Schmidt, Civ. Law, Introd. 93, note.

ORDENAMIENTO DE ALCALA (Spanish). A collection of Spanish law, promulgated by the Cortes in the year 1348. Schmidt, Civ. Law, Introd. 75.

ORDER. Command; direction.

An informal bill of exchange or letter of request requiring the party to whom it is addressed to deliver property of the person making the order to some one therein described.

A designation of the person to whom a bill of exchange or negotiable promissory note is to be paid.

This order, in the case of negotiable paper, is usually by indorsement, and may be either express, as, "Pay to C. D.," or implied merely, as by writing A. B. (the payee's name). See "Indorsement."

——**In French Law.** The act by which the rank of preferences of claims, among creditors who have liens over the price which arises out of the sale of an immovable subject, is ascertained. Dalloz.

——**In Governmental Law.** By this expression is understood the several bodies which compose the state. In ancient Rome, for example, there were three distinct orders, namely, that of the senators, that of the patricians, and that of the plebeians. In the United States there are no orders of men; all men are equal in the eye of the law. See "Rank."

ORDER NISI. A conditional order, which is to be confirmed unless something be done, which has been required, by a time specified. Eden, Inj. 122. See "Nisi."

ORDER OF FILIATION. The judgment rendered in a bastardy proceeding, whereby a certain man is adjudged the father of a bastard child.

ORDER OF HARUGARI. An order composed of German-speaking persons, whose general object is to preserve and spread the German language wherever the order exists, to facilitate and promote the intellectual and material welfare of its members and improve and elevate social conditions among German families.

ORDERS OF THE DAY. Any member of the English house of commons who wishes to propose any question, or to "move the house," as it is termed, must, in order to give the house due notice of his intention, state the form or nature of his motion on a previous day, and have it entered in a book termed the "order book;" and the motions so entered, the house arranges, shall be considered on particular days, and such motions or matters, when the day arrives for their being considered, are then termed the "orders of the day." Brown; May, Parl. Prac.

ORDINANCE.

——**In Modern Usage.** A law passed by the legislative body of a municipal corporation for the government of such municipality. 117 Ind. 221.

——**In Old Law.** The term was applied to laws of other than municipal bodies.

The following account of the difference between a statute and an ordinance is extracted from Bac. Abr. "Statute" (A): "Where the proceeding consisted only of a petition from parliament and an answer from the king, these were entered on the parliament roll; and if the matter was of a public nature, the whole was then styled an 'ordinance.' If, however, the petition and answer were not only of a public, but a novel, nature, they were then formed into an act by the king, with the aid of his council and judges, and entered on the statute roll." See Co. Litt. 159b, Butler's note; 3 Reeve, Hist. Eng. Law, 146.

According to Lord Coke, the difference between a statute and an ordinance is that the latter has not had the assent of the king, lords, and commons, but is made merely by two of these powers. 4 Inst. 25. See Barr. Obs. St. 41, note (x).

It is distinguished from a "resolution" by the same body by the fact that an ordinance prescribes a permanent rule of government, while a resolution is of a temporary character. 11 Ohio St. 96; 114 Ind. 336; 174 Ill. 445; 184 Ill. 51; 262 Ill. 396. Thus matters upon which a city council wishes to legislate must be put in the form of an ordinance, but all acts that are done in its ministerial capacity may be in the form of resolutions. Resolutions are special and temporary, applicable only to a single matter of passing moment; ordinances are permanent regulations, applicable to all states of facts thereafter arising within the scope of their provisions. 186 Ill. 571.

Certain enactments in the nature of constitutions have also been referred to as ordinances, as, for example, the "ordinance for the government of the Northwest Territory," passed by congress in 1787.

ORDINANCE OF THE FOREST. In English law. A statute made touching matters and causes of the forest. 33 & 34 Edw. I.

ORDINANDI LEX. The law of procedure, as distinguished from the substantial part of the law.

ORDINARIUS ITA DICITUR QUIA HAbet ordinariam jurisdictionem, in jure proprio, et non propter deputationem. The ordinary is so called because he has an ordinary jurisdiction in his own right, and not a deputed one. Co. Litt. 96.

ORDINARY. In ecclesiastical law. An officer who has original jurisdiction in his own right, and not by deputation.

In England, the ordinary is an officer who has immediate jurisdiction in ecclesiastical causes. Co. Litt. 344.

In the United States, the ordinary possesses, in those states where such officer exists, powers vested in him by the constitution and acts of the legislature. In South Carolina, the ordinary is a judicial officer. 1 Const. (S. C.) 267; 2 Const. (S. C.) 384.

ORDINARY CARE. Such a degree of care, skill and diligence as men of ordinary prudence, under similar circumstances, usually employ (31 Pa. St. 512; 3 Mass. 132; 2 Wis. 316; 23 Conn. 443; 28 Vt. 150; 9 N. Y. 416), and is to be determined with reference to all the attendant circumstances of the transaction (35 N. Y. 27; 47 Super. Ct. 292, 296).

ORDINARY CONVEYANCES. Those deeds of transfer which are entered into between two or more persons, without an assurance in a superior court of justice.

ORDINARY COURSE OF BUSINESS. The rules or questions prevailing in business generally, or in a particular business. See 14 Q. B. Div. 386.

ORDINARY DILIGENCE. The degree which men of ordinary prudence generally exercise.

ORDINARY NEGLIGENCE. Absence of ordinary care (*q. v.*)

ORDINARY OF ASSIZE AND SESSIONS. In old English law. A deputy of the bishop of the diocese, anciently appointed to give malefactors their neck verses, and judge whether they read or not; also to perform divine services for them, and assist in preparing them for death. Wharton.

ORDINARY OF NEWGATE. The clergyman who is attendant upon condemned malefactors in that prison to prepare them for death. He records the behavior of such persons. Formerly it was the custom of the ordinary to publish a small pamphlet upon the execution of any remarkable criminal. Wharton.

ORDINARY SKILL. Such skill as a person conversant with the matter undertaken might be reasonably supposed to have. 11 Mees. & W. 113; 20 Mart. (La.) 68, 75; 1 H. Bl. 158, 161; 6 Ga. 213, 219; 8 B. Mon. (Ky.) 515; 3 Barb. (N. Y.) 380; 13 Johns. (N. Y.) 211; 4 Burrows, 2060; 3 Campb. 17, 19; 7 Car. & P. 289; 6 Bing. 460; 2 Bing. (N. C.) 625; 16 Serg. & R. (Pa.) 368; 15 Mass. 316; 15 Pick. (Mass.) 440; 2 Cush. (Mass.) 316; 8 Car. & P. 479; 3 Campb. 451; 4 Barn. & C. 345.

ORDINATION. The act of conferring the orders of the church upon an individual.

ORDINATIONE CONTRA SERVIENTES. A writ that lay against a servant for leaving his master contrary to the ordinance of St. 23 & 24 Edw. III. Reg. Orig. 189.

ORDINATUM EST (Lat.) It is ordered. The initial words are of the record entry of an order.

ORDINE PLACITANDI SERVATO, SERVatur et jus. The order of pleading being preserved, the law is preserved. Co. Litt. 303.

ORDINES MAJORES ET MINORES. In ecclesiastical law. The holy orders of priest, deacon, and subdeacon, any of which qualified for presentation and admission to an ecclesiastical dignity or cure were called "*ordines majores;*" and the inferior orders of chanters, psalmists, ostiary, reader, exorcist, and acolyte were called "*ordines minores.*" Persons ordained to the *ordines minores* had their *prima tonsura,* different from the *tonsura clericalis.* Cowell.

ORDINIS BENEFICIUM. See "Beneficium Ordinis."

ORDINUM FUGITIVI. In old English law. Those of the religious who deserted their houses, and, throwing off the habits, renounced their particular order in contempt of their oath and other obligations. Par. Ant. 388.

ORDO ALBUS. The friars. *Ordo Griseus,* the gray friars; *ordo Niger,* the black friars.

ORDO ATTACHIAMENTORUM. The order of attachments.

ORDO JUDICIORUM. In the canon law. The order of judgments; the rule by which the due course of hearing each cause was prescribed. 4 Reeve, Hist. Eng. Law, 17.

ORE. The word "ore" has a definite signification, and designates a compound of metal and other substance; metal unrefined, yet in its fossil state. 147 N. Y. 501; 1 Ch. 432.

ORE TENUS (Lat.) Verbally; orally.

Formerly the pleadings of the parties were *ore tenus;* and the practice is said to have been retained till the reign of Edward III. 3 Reeve, Hist. Eng. Law, 95; Steph. Pl. 29. And see Bracton, 372b.

In chancery practice, a defendant may demur at the bar *ore tenus* (3 P. Wms. 370) if he has not sustained the demurrer on the record (1 Swanst. 288; Mitf. Pl. 176; 6 Ves. 779; 8 Ves. 405; 17 Ves. 215, 216).

ORFGILD (Saxon *orf*, cattle, *gild*, payment. Also called "cheapgild"). A payment for cattle, or the restoring them. Cowell.

A restitution made by the hundred or county of any wrong done by one that was in pledge. Lambard, Arch. 125, 126.

A penalty for taking away cattle. Blount.

ORGANIC LAW. The written or unwritten constitution; the underlying rules and principles on which the government is established.

ORGILD (Saxon). Without recompense; as where no satisfaction was to be made for the death of a man killed, so that he was judged lawfully slain. Spelman.

ORIGINAL. That which is first in order; an authentic instrument of something, and which is to serve as a model or example to be copied or imitated. It also means first, or not deriving any authority from any other source; as, original jurisdiction, original writ, original bill, and the like.

ORIGINAL AND DERIVATIVE ESTATES. An original is the first of several estates, bearing to each other the relation of a particular estate and a reversion. An original estate is contrasted with a derivative estate; and a derivative estate is a particular interest carved out of another estate of larger extent. Prest. Est. 125.

ORIGINAL BILL. In chancery practice. A bill relating to a matter not before brought before the court by the same parties, standing in the same interests. Mitf. Eq. Pl. 33; Willis, Pl. 13 et seq.

Proceedings in a court of chancery are either commenced by way of information, when the matter concerns the state or those under its protection, or by original petition or bill, when the matter does not concern the state or those under its protection. The original bill states simply the cause of complaint, and asks for relief. It is composed of nine parts (Story, Eq. Pl. 7, 8), and is the foundation of all subsequent proceedings before the court (1 Daniell, Chanc. Prac. 351). See "Bill."

ORIGINAL BILL IN THE NATURE OF SUPPLEMENTAL BILL. A bill embracing in some degree the qualities of both an original and a supplemental bill. It is founded on an event occurring after the filing of the original bill, of such a nature that the suit cannot be continued as to all the parties, as by a supplemental bill.

ORIGINAL CHARTER. In Scotch law. One by which the first grant of land is made. On the other hand, a charter by progress is one renewing the grant in favor of the heir or singular successor of the first or succeeding vassals. Bell, Dict.

ORIGINAL CONVEYANCES (called, also, primary conveyances). Those conveyances by means whereof the benefit or estate is created or first arises, viz., feoffment, gift, grant, lease, exchange, partition. 2 Bl. Comm. 309, 310*; 1 Steph. Comm. 466.

ORIGINAL JURISDICTION. See "Jurisdiction."

ORIGINAL PACKAGE. The term "original package" as employed by law, admits of no precise definition applicable to all. Generally, it is said to be a parcel, bundle, bale, box, or case made up of or "packed" with some commodity with a view to its safety and convenient handling and transportation. It does not necessarily mean that goods shall be inclosed in a tight or sealed receptacle. It relates wholly to goods as prepared for transportation, and has no necessary reference whatever to the package originally prepared or put up by the manufacturer. Indeed the idea of the "original package" may well be made to cover certain forms of property which do not ordinarily admit of being packed or incased in any other manner than in the car or vessel in which they are transported; such, for instance, as steel beams, threshing machines, and other bulky articles. 170 Fed. 449, 99 C. C. A. 667; 119 Ia. 384, 93 N. W. 372, 373; 179 U. S. 343, 45 Law. ed. 224.

Within the meaning of interstate commerce regulations, the original unbroken package imported into a state from another state or a foreign country before it becomes by sale or otherwise part of the general mass of property in the state. 135 U. S. 100.

ORIGINAL PROCESS. That process which issues for defendant's appearance. See "Process."

ORIGINAL WRIT. In English practice. A mandatory letter issued in the king's name, sealed with his great seal, and directed to the sheriff of the county wherein the injury was committed or supposed to have been done, requiring him to command the wrongdoer, or party accused, either to do justice to the complainant, or else to appear in court and answer the accusation against him. This writ is deemed necessary to give the courts of law jurisdiction.

In modern practice, however, it is often dispensed with, by recourse, as usual, to fiction, and a proceeding by bill is substituted. In this country, our courts derive their jurisdiction from the constitution, and require no original writ to confer it. Improperly speaking, the first writ which is issued in a case is sometimes called an original writ; but it is not so in the English sense of the word. See 3 Bl. Comm. 273; Walk. Am. Law, 514.

ORIGINALIA (Lat.) In English law. The transcripts and other documents sent to the office of the treasurer remembrancer in exchequer are called by this name to distinguish them from *recorda,* which contain the judgments of the barons.

ORIGINE PROPRIA NEMINEM POSSE voluntate sua eximi manifestum est. It is manifest that no one by his own will can renounce his origin (put off or discharge his natural allegiance). Code, 10. 34. 4. See 1 Bl. Comm. c. 10; 20 Johns. (N. Y.) 313; 3 Pet. (U. S.) 122, 246; Broom, Leg. Max. (3d London Ed.) 74.

ORIGO REI INSPICI DEBET. The origin of a thing ought to be inquired into. 1 Coke, 99.

ORNERY. The word "ornery" is not recognized by lexicographers. It is generally understood to be of uncertain meaning, but used to express the opposite of good qualities. 78 Iowa 79.

ORNEST. In old English law. The trial by battle, which does not seem to have been usual in England before the time of the Conqueror, though originating in the kingdoms of the north, where it was practiced under the name of "holmgang," from the custom of fighting duels on a small island or holm. Wharton.

ORPHAN. A minor or infant who has lost both of his or her parents. Sometimes the term is applied to such a person who has lost only one of his or her parents. 3 Mer. 48; 2 Sim. & S. 93; Aso & M. Inst. bk. 1, tit. 2, c. 1. See 14 Hazz. Pa. Reg. 188, 189, for a correspondence between the Hon. Joseph Hopkinson and ex-President J. Q. Adams as to the meaning of the word "orphan." See, also, Hob. 247.

ORPHANAGE. In English law. The share reserved to an orphan by the custom of London.

By the custom of London, when a freeman of that city dies, his estate is divided into three parts, as follows: One-third part to the widow; another to the children advanced by him in his lifetime, which is called the "orphanage;" and the other third part may be by him disposed of by will. Now, however, a freeman may dispose of his estate as he pleases; but in cases of intestacy, the statute of distribution expressly excepts and reserves the custom of London. Lovelace, Wills, 102, 104; Bac. Abr. "Custom of London" (C).

ORPHANAGE PART. That portion of an intestate's effects which his children were entitled to by the custom of London. This custom appears to have been a remnant of what was once a general law all over England, namely, that a father should not by his will bequeath the entirety of his personal estate away from his family, but should leave them a third part at least, called the "children's part," corresponding to the "bairns' part" or *legitim* of Scotch law, and also (although not in amount) to the *legitima quarta* of Roman law. Inst. 2. 18. This custom of London was abolished by St. 19 & 20 Vict. c. 94. Brown.

ORPHANOTROPHI. In civil law. Persons who have the charge of administering the affairs of houses destined for the use of orphans. Clef des Lois Rom. "Administrateurs."

ORPHANS' COURT. In American law. Courts of more or less extended probate jurisdiction.

ORRAY (Law Fr. from *oyer,* to hear). Shall hear. *Orrount* (plur.) Britt. c. 41.

ORWIGE, SINE WITA. In old English law. Without war or feud, such security being provided by the laws, for homicides under certain circumstances, against the foehth, or deadly feud, on the part of the family of the slain. Anc. Inst. Eng.

OSTENDIT VOBIS (Law Lat.) In old pleadings. Shows to you. Formal words with which a demandant began his count. Fleta, lib. 5, c. 38, § 2.

OSTENSIBLE PARTNER. One whose name appears in a firm as a partner, and who is really such. See "Nominal Partner."

OSTENSURUS (Law Lat.) To show. A formal word in old writs. Reg. Orig. 36; Fet. Assaver, § 21.

OSTENTUM (Lat.) In the civil law. A monstrous or prodigious birth. Dig. 50. 16. 38.

OSTEOPATHY. Osteopathy is a system of treatment of physical ailments based on the theory that diseases are generally due to deranged mechanism of the joints, nerves, blood vessels and other tissues, and can be remedied by manipulations of those parts. 155 Wis. 55.

OSTER (Law Fr.) To take away; to take out or off. *Oste del file,* taken off the file. Y. B. H. 20 Hen. VI. 1.

OSTER LA TOUAILLE (Old Fr.) In the laws of Oleron. To deny a seaman his mess. Article 13. Literally, to deny the table cloth or victuals for three meals. See 1 Pet. Adm. (U. S.) Append. xxvii.; 2 Pet. Adm. (U. S.) Append. lxxxv.

OSTIA REGNI (Lat.) Gates of the kingdom. The ports of the kingdom of England are so called by Sir Matthew Hale. Hale de Jur. Mar. pt. 2, c. 3.

OSTIUM ECCLESIAE (Law Lat.) In old English law. The door or porch of the church, where dower was anciently conferred. See "Ad Ostium Ecclesiae."

OSWALD'S LAW. The law by which was effected the ejection of married priests, and the introduction of monks into churches, by Oswald, bishop of Worcester, about A. D. 964. Wharton.

OSWALD'S LAW HUNDRED. An ancient hundred in Worcestershire, so called from Bishop Oswald, who obtained it from King Edgar, to be given to St. Mary's Church in Worcester. It was exempt from the sheriff's jurisdiction, and comprehends three hundred hides of land. Camd. Brit.

OTHERWISE. A different manner; in another way differently; in other respects in a different manner; in different respects; in a different manner or way; differently; in other respects. 187 Ill. 268.

OTHESWORTHE (Saxon, *eoth*, oath). Worthy to make oath. Bracton, 185, 192.

OULTRE LE MERE (Law Fr.) Beyond the sea. Y. B. P. 1 Edw. III. 27.

OURLOP. The lierwite or fine paid to the lord by the inferior tenant when his daughter was debauched. Cowell.

OUST (from L. Fr. *ouster, q. v.*) In old English law. To take away.

To put out; to turn out or eject. 3 Bl. Com. 201, 202.

In modern law. To deprive, as ousting a corporation of its franchises. 12 Mod. 18, 19.

OUSTER (Law Fr. *outre, oultre;* Lat. *ultra*, beyond). Out; beyond; besides; farther; also; over and more. *Le ouster*, the uppermost. Over,—*respondeat ouster*, let him answer over. Britt. c. 29. *Ouster le mer*, over the sea. Jacob. *Ouster eit*, he went away. 6 Coke, 41b; 9 Coke, 120.

To put out; to oust. *Il oust*, he put out or ousted. *Oustes*, ousted. 6 Coke, 41b.

"Judgment of ouster," in some states, is used to denote the judgment in *quo warranto*, by which one is held not entitled to an office; in others to the judgment in summary proceedings for possession of property.

——**In Torts.** The actual turning out or keeping excluded the party entitled to possession of any real property corporeal.

OUSTER LE MAIN (Law Fr. to take out of the hand). In old English law. A livery of lands out of the hands of the lord after the tenant came of age. If the lord refused to deliver such lands, the tenant was entitled to a writ to recover the same from the lord. This recovery out of the hands of the lord was called *ouster le main*.

OUSTER LE MER. Beyond the sea; a cause of excuse if a person, being summoned, did not appear in court. Cowell.

OUT OF THE STATE. Beyond sea (*q. v.*)

OUT OF TIME. In marine insurance. Missing. Generally speaking, a ship may be said to be missing or out of time when she has not been heard of after the longest ordinary time in which the voyage is safely performed. 1 Arnould, Ins. 540; 2 Duer, Ins. 469, note.

OUTER BAR. In the English courts, barristers at law have been divided into two classes, viz., queen's counsel, who are admitted within the bar of the courts, in seats specially reserved for themselves, and junior counsel, who sit without the bar; and the latter are thence frequently termed barristers of the "outer bar," or "utter bar," in contradistinction to the former class.

OUTER HOUSE. The name given to the great hall of the parliament house in Edinburgh, in which the lords ordinary of the court of session sit as single judges to hear causes. The term is used colloquially as expressive of the business done there, in contradistinction to the "Inner House," the name given to the chambers in which the first and second divisions of the court of sessions hold their sittings. Bell, Dict.

OUTFANGTHEF. A liberty or privilege in the ancient common law, whereby a lord was enabled to call any man dwelling in his manor, and taken for felony in another place out of his fee, to judgment in his own court. Du Cange.

OUTFIT.

——**In Maritime Law.** That part of a ship's apparel which ordinarily perishes or is consumed in the course of her voyage. Lowndes, Av. 11.

——**In the Diplomatic Service.** An allowance made by the government of the United States to a minister plenipotentiary, or *charge des affaires*, on going from the United States to any foreign country.

OUTHOUSES. Buildings adjoining or belonging to dwelling houses.

Buildings subservient to, yet distinct from, the principal mansion house, located either within or without the curtilage. 1 Bish. Crim. Law, § 175; 4 Conn. 46; 4 Gill & J. (Md.) 402; 2 Craw. & D. 479.

Any house standing out and apart from houses where people reside, or where business is transacted. 15 Tex. 260.

A building appurtenant to some main building. A school house is not an outhouse. 10 Conn. 143.

OUTLAND. The Saxon thanes divided their hereditary lands into inland, such as lay nearest their dwelling, which they kept to their own use, and outland, which lay beyond the demesnes, and was granted out to tenants, at the will of the lord, like copyhold estates. This outland they subdivided into two parts. One part they disposed among those who attended their persons, called "theodans," or lesser thanes; the other part they allotted to their husbandmen, or churls. Jacob.

OUTLAW. In English law. One who is put out of the protection or aid of the law. 22 Viner, Abr. 316; 1 Phil. Ev. Index; Bac. Abr. "Outlawry;" 2 Sellon, Prac. 277; Doct. Plac. 331; 3 Bl. Comm. 283, 284.

OUTLAWED. Applied to debts, barred by limitations. See 37 Me. 389.

OUTLAWRY. In English law. The act of being put out of the protection of the law, by process regularly sued out against a person who is in contempt in refusing to become amenable to the court having jurisdiction. The proceedings themselves are also called the "outlawry."

Outlawry may take place in criminal or in civil cases. 3 Bl. Comm. 283; Co. Litt. 128; 4 Bouv. Inst. note 4196.

In the United States, outlawry in civil cases is unknown, and if there are any cases of outlawry in criminal cases, they are very rare. Dane, Abr. c. 193a, 34. See Bac. Abr. "Abatement" (B), "Outlawry;" Gilb. Hist. 196, 197; 2 Va. Cas. 244; 2 Dall. (Pa.) 92.

OUTPARTERS. A name given in old English statutes to certain depredators from Redesdale, on the northern border of England, who made incursions into Scotland, and brought back to their accomplices at home (called intakers) any booty they had taken. Spelman voc. "Intakers;" St. 9 Hen. V. c. 8.

OUTRAGE. A grave injury; a serious wrong. A generic word which is applied to everything which is injurious in a great degree to the honor or rights of another. 44 Iowa 314.

OUTRIDERS. In English practice. Bailiffs employed by the sheriffs and their deputies to ride to the farthest places of their counties or hundreds, to summon such as they thought good to attend their county or hundred court.

OUTROPER. Old English. A person to whom the business of selling by auction was confined by statute. 2 H. Bl. 557.

OUTSETTER. Scotch. Publisher. 3 How. St. Tr. 603.

OUTSIDERS. See "Gambling Contract."

OUTSUCKEN MULTURES. In Scotch law. Out-town multures; multures, duties, or tolls paid by persons voluntarily grinding corn at any mill to which they are not thirled, or bound by tenure. 1 Forbes, Inst. pt. 2, p. 140; Bell, Dict. voc. "Multures."

OVELTY. In old English law. Equality of service in subordinate tenures.

OVER. In conveyancing, the word "over" is used to denote a contingent limitation intended to take effect on the failure of a prior estate. Thus, in what is commonly called the "name and arms clause" in a will or settlement, there is generally a proviso that, if the devisee fails to comply with the condition, the estate is to go to some one else. This is a limitation or gift over. Watson, Comp. Eq. 1110.

OVERCYTED, or OVERCYHSED. Proved guilty or convicted. Blount.

OVERDRAW. To obtain by bills or checks upon an individual, bank, or other depository, a greater amount of funds than the party who draws is entitled to.

OVERHERNISSA. In Saxon law. Contumacy or contempt of court. Leg. Aethel. c. 25.

OVERPLUS. What is left beyond a certain amount; the residue; the remainder of a thing. The same as "surplus."

OVERREACHING CLAUSE. In a resettlement, a clause which saves the powers of sale and leasing annexed to the estate for life created by the original settlement, when it is desired to give the tenant for life the same estate and powers under the resettlement. The clause is so called because it provides that the resettlement shall be overreached by the exercise of the old powers. If the resettlement were executed without a provision to this effect, the estate of the tenant for life and the annexed powers would be subject to any charges for portions, etc., created under the original settlement. 3 Dav. Conv. 489; Rapalje & L.

OVERRULE. To annul; to make void.

This word is frequently used to signify that a case has been decided directly opposite to a former case. When this takes place, the first-decided case is said to be overruled as a precedent, and cannot any longer be considered as of binding authority.

It also signifies that a majority of the judges have decided against the opinion of the minority, in which case the latter are said to be overruled.

OVERSAMESSA. In old English law. A forfeiture for contempt or neglect in not pursuing a malefactor. 3 Inst. 116.

OVERSEERS OF HIGHWAYS. Officials of the local division of government, as towns, who supervise and direct the maintenance or construction of highways.

OVERSEERS OF THE POOR. Persons appointed or elected to take care of the poor with moneys furnished to them by the public authority.

The duties of these officers are regulated by local statutes. In general, the overseers are bound to perform those duties, and the neglect of them will subject them to an indictment. See 1 Bl. Comm. 360; 16 Viner, Abr. 150; 1 Mass. 459; 3 Mass. 436; 1 Pennington (N. J.) 6, 136; Comyn, Dig. "Justices of the Peace" (B 63-65).

OVERSMAN. In Scotch law. A person commonly named in a submission, to whom power is given to determine in case the arbiters cannot agree in the sentence. Sometimes the nomination of the oversman is left to the arbiters. In either case, the oversman has no power to decide unless the arbiters differ in opinion. Ersk. Inst. 4. 3. 16. The office of an oversman very much resembles that of an umpire.

OVERT, OVERTE, or **OUVERTE** (Law Fr. and Eng.) Open. Pound overt, an open or uncovered pound. 3 Bl. Comm. 12. Market overt, open market. 2 Id. 449. *Lettres ouvertes,* open letters; letters patent (*q. v.*)

OVERT ACT (Law Lat. *apertum factum*). In criminal law. An open, manifest act, from which criminality may be implied. 193 Ill. App. 128. Brande. An open act, which must be manifestly proved. 3 Inst. 12.

OVERVERT. In old English law. High wood. See "Vert."

OVES (Lat. [pl. of *ovis*], sheep). In the civil law. Under a bequest of sheep (*ovibus*), lambs and rams were not included. Dig. 32. 65. 7; Id. 32. 81. 4. But under the name of a flock of sheep (*ovium grege*), both were included. Id. 32. 81. 5.

OVESQUE (Law Fr.) With. Litt. § 240; Britt. c. 38.

For. *Il voile av' argue ovesque le lease,* he would have argued for the lease. Dyer, 126b.

OWEL, or **OWELE** (Law Fr. from Lat. *aequalis*). Equal. *En owele mayn,* in equal hand. Britt. c. 39. *Owelment,* equally. Id. c. 119.

OWELTY. The difference which is paid or secured by one coparcener to another for the purpose of equalizing a partition. Litt. § 251; Co. Litt. 169a; 1 Watts (Pa.) 265; 1 Whart. (Pa.) 292; Cruise, Dig. tit. 19, § 32; 1 Vern. 133; Plowd. 134; 16 Viner, Abr. 223, pl. 3; Brooke, Abr. "Partition," § 5; 99 Tex. 51, 97 S. W. 334, Ann. Cas. 1914 A650; 117 Ill. 351; 160 Ill. 602.

OWING. Something unpaid. A debt, for example, is owing while it is unpaid, and whether it be due or not.

In a business sense, in correspondence or contracts, a legal obligation is implied. In ordinary transactions between debtor and creditor it does not necessarily imply an enforceable obligation. 155 Mich. 567.

OWLER. In English law. One guilty of the offense of owling.

OWLING. In English law. The offense of transporting wool or sheep out of the kingdom.

The name is said to owe its origin to the fact that this offense was carried on in the night, when the owl was abroad.

OWNER. He who has dominion of a thing, real or personal, corporeal or incorporeal, which he has a right to enjoy and do with as he pleases, even to spoil or destroy it, as far as the law permits, unless he be prevented by some agreement or covenant which restrains his right. 31 Cal. 649.

The term has no exact technical meaning. Hare, Am. Const. Law, 355.

As applied to lands, it has been said to include all who had an interest therein, though it fall short of ownership of the fee. (38 Mich. 171; 2 Ohio St. 114), and it has been applied both to the holder of the legal title (6 Hun [N. Y.] 553) and of an equitable estate (21 Minn. 107).

In like manner, as applied to personalty, it has been held to include one having a temporary right of possession. 44 Conn. 298. Such persons are ordinarily designated as "special owner," in contradistinction from "general owner," in whom is the full title. See 10 Cush. (Mass.) 399; 50 Mich. 249.

OWNERSHIP. The right by which a thing belongs to some one in particular to the exclusion of all others. Civ. Code La. art. 480. See "Owner."

OXFILD. A restitution anciently made by a hundred or county for any wrong done by one that was within the same. Lambard, Arch. 125.

OXGANG (from Saxon, *gang,* going, and ox; Law Lat. *bovata*). In old English law. So much land as an ox could till. According to some, fifteen acres. Co. Litt. 69a; Cromp. Jur. 220. According to Balfour, the Scotch oxengang, or oxgate, contained twelve acres; but this does not correspond with ancient charters. See Bell, Dict. "Ploughgate." Skene says thirteen acres. Cowell.

OYER. The reading to a party of a written instrument stated in the pleadings of the opposite party. In modern practice a copy of the writing is ordered furnished on application. See "Profert in Curia."

OYER AND TERMINER. See "Assize;" "Court of Oyer and Terminer."

OYER DE RECORD. A petition made in court that the judges, for better proofs, compel the production of a record for inspection.

OYER ET TERMINER (Law Fr.) To hear and determine. *A oyer et terminer toutes quereles,* to hear and determine all complaints. Britt. fol. 1. *De oyr et determiner.* Art. Sup. Chart.

OYEZ (Fr. hear ye). The introduction to any proclamation or advertisement by public crier. It is wrongly and usually pronounced "oh yes." 4 Bl. Comm. 340, note.

P

P. H. V. *Pro hac vice*, for this occasion.

P. P. S. An abbreviation used in insurance for the words "policy proof of interest." It amounts to an agreement that in the event of loss, the insured shall be recognized, without further proof, to have had the interest named in the policy in the subject-matter insured. 279 Fed. 893.

PAAGE. A toll for passage through another's land.

PACARE. In old records. To pay.

PACATIO. Payment. Mat. Par. A. D. 1248.

PACE. A measure of length, containing two feet and a half. The geometrical pace is five feet long. The common pace is the length of a step; the geometrical is the length of two steps, or the whole space passed over by the same foot from one step to another.

PACEATUR (Lat.) Let him be freed or discharged.

PACI SUNT MAXIME CONTRARIA, VIS et injuria. Force and wrong are especially contrary to peace. Co. Litt. 161.

PACIFICATION (Lat. *pax*, peace, *facere*, to make). The act of making peace between two countries which have been at war; the restoration of public tranquillity.

PACK. To deceive by false appearances; to counterfeit; to delude; as, packing a jury. See "Jury;" Bac. Abr. "Juries" (M); 12 Conn. 262.

PACKED PARCELS. The name for a consignment of goods, consisting of one large parcel made up of several small ones, each bearing a different address, collected from different persons by the immediate consignor (a carrier), who unites them into one for his own profit, at the expense of the railway by which they are sent, since the railway company would have been paid more for the carriage of the parcels singly than together.

PACT. In civil law. An agreement made by two or more persons on the same subject, in order to form some engagement, or to dissolve or modify one already made. *Conventio est duorum in idem placitum consensus de re solvenda, id est facienda vel praestanda.* Dig. 2. 14; Clef des Lois Rom.; Ayliffe, Pand. 558; Merlin, Repert, "Pacte."

PACTA CONVENTA, QUAE NEQUE contra leges, neque dolo malo inita sunt, omni modo observanda sunt. Contracts which are not illegal, and do not originate in fraud, must in all respects be observed. Code, 2. 3. 29; Broom, Leg. Max. (3d London Ed.) 624.

PACTA DANT LEGEM CONTRACTUI. Agreements give the law to the contract. Halk. Max. 118.

PACTA PRIVATA JURI PUBLICO DErogare non possunt. Private contracts cannot derogate from the public law. 7 Coke, 23.

PACTA QUAE CONTRA LEGES CONSTItutionesque vel contra bonos mores fiunt, nullam vim habere, indubitati juris est. It is indubitable law that contracts against the laws or good morals have no force. Code, 2. 3. 6; Broom, Leg. Max. (3d London Ed.) 620.

PACTA QUAE TURPEM CAUSAM CONtinent non sunt observanda. Contracts founded upon an immoral consideration are not to be observed. Dig. 2. 14. 27. 4; 2 Pet. (U. S.) 539; Broom, Leg. Max. (3d London Ed.) 658.

PACTIO (Lat. from *pangere*, to strike). In civil law. A bargaining or agreeing of which *pactum* (the agreement itself) was the result. Calv. Lex. It is used, however, as the synonym of *pactum*.

PACTIONS. In international law. Contracts between nations which are to be performed by a single act, and of which execution is at an end at once. 1 Bouv. Inst. note 100.

PACTIS PRIVATORUM JURI PUBLICO non derogatur. Private contracts do not derogate from public law. Broom, Leg. Max. (3d London Ed.) 621; per Dr. Lushington, Arg. 4 Clark & F. 241; Arg. 3 Clark & F. 621.

PACTITIOUS. Settled or governed by agreement.

PACTO ALIQUOD LICITUM EST, QUID sine pacto non admittitur. By a contract, something is permitted, which, without it, could not be admitted. Co. Litt. 166.

PACTUM (Lat.) In the civil law. A pact; an agreement or convention without specific name, and without consideration, which, however, might, in its nature produce a civil obligation. Heinec. Elem. Jur. Civ. lib. 3, tit. 14, § 775.

A pact was distinguished from a contract (*contractus*), which had a specific name or present consideration, and carried with it a civil obligation, both being a species of *conventio* (convention) which was the general term. *Do ut des*, I give that you may give, was a contract. *Dabo ut des*, I will give that you may give, was a pact.

PACTUM CONSTITUTAE PECUNIAE (Lat.) In civil law. An agreement by which a person appointed to his creditor a certain day, or a certain time, at which he promised to pay; or it may be defined simply an agreement by which a person promises a creditor to pay him.

When a person by this pact promises his own creditor to pay him, there arises a new obligation, which does not destroy the former by which he was already bound, but which is accessory to it; and by this multiplicity of obligations the right of the creditor is strengthened. Poth. Obl. pt. 2, c. 6, § 9.

There is a striking conformity between the *pactum constitutae pecuniae*, as above defined, and our *indebitatus assumpsit*. The *pactum constitutae pecuniae* was a promise to pay a subsisting debt, whether natural or civil, made in such a manner as not to extinguish the preceding debt, and introduced by the praetor to obviate some formal difficulties. The action of *indebitatus assumpsit* was brought upon a promise for the payment of a debt. It was not subject to the wager of law and other technical difficulties of the regular action of debt, but by such promise the right to the action of debt was not extinguished nor varied. 4 Coke, 91, 95. See 1 H. Bl. 550-555, 850; Doug. 6, 7; 3 Wood, Inst. 168, 169, note (c); 1 Viner, Abr. 270; Brooke, Abr. "Action sur le Case" (pl. 7, 69, 72); Fitzh. Nat. Brev. 94 (a), note (a), 145 (g); 4 Bos. & P. 295; 1 Chit. Pl. 89; Toullier, Dr. Civ. lib. 3, tit. 3, c. 4, notes 388, 396.

PACTUM DE NON PETANDO (Lat.) In civil law. An agreement made between a creditor and his debtor that the former will not demand from the latter the debt due. By this agreement, the debtor is freed from his obligation. This is not unlike the "covenant not to sue," of the common law. Wolff. Dr. Nat. § 755.

PACTUM DE QUOTA LITIS (Lat.) In civil law. An agreement by which a creditor of a sum difficult to recover promises a portion—for example, one-third—to the person who will undertake to recover it. In general, attorneys will abstain from making such a contract, yet it is not unlawful at common law.

PADDER. A robber; a foot highwayman.

PAGA (Spanish). In Spanish law. Payment. Las Partidas, pt. 5, tit. 14, lib. 1, *pagamento*, satisfaction.

PAGODA. In commercial law. A denomination of money in Bengal. In the computation of *ad valorem* duties it is valued at one dollar and ninety-four cents. Act March 2, 1799, § 61 (1 Story, U. S. Laws, 626).

PAGUS. A county. Jacob.

PAIN, *Peyne.* [Lat. *poena.*] A penalty. "To incur a *pain*"; "to pay a *pain*." 1 Leon. 203. "Under pain," "pains and penalties," are expressions still used.

PAINE FORTE ET DURE. See "Peine Forte et Dure."

PAINS AND PENALTIES, BILLS OF. See "Bill of Pains and Penalties."

PAIRING OFF. A legislative practice, said to have originated in the time of Cromwell, whereby legislators of opposite opinions agree not to vote on a given measure. Usually resorted to in order to relieve a member from the necessity of remaining constantly present to await a vote.

PAIS, or **PAYS.** A French word, signifying "country." In law, matter *in pais* is matter of fact, in opposition to matter of record; a trial *per pais* is a trial by the country,— that is, by a jury. See "In Pais."

PAIS, CONVEYANCES IN. In old English law. Ordinary conveyances between two or more persons in the country, *i. e.*, upon the land to be transferred.

PALACE COURT. In English law. A court which had jurisdiction of all personal actions arising between any parties within twelve miles of Whitehall, not including the city of London.

It was erected in the time of Charles I., and was held by the steward of the household, the knight marshal and steward of the court, or his deputy. It had its sessions once a week, in the borough of Southwark. It was abolished by 12 & 13 Vict. c. 101, § 13.

PALAGIUM. A duty to lords of manors for exporting and importing vessels of wine at any of their ports. Jacob.

PALATINE. Possessing royal privileges, See "County Palatine."

PALATINE COURTS. Formerly the court of common pleas at Lancaster, the chancery court of Lancaster, and the court of pleas at Durham, the second of which alone now exists.

PALATIUM (Lat.) A palace. The emperor's house in Rome was so called from the *Mons Palatinus* on which it was built. Adams, Rom. Ant. 613.

——**In Old English Law.** A paling; a fence. Fleta, lib. 4, c. 18, § 1.

PALEFRETUM (Law Lat.) In old English law. A palfrey. Fleta, lib. 2, c. 73, § 19.

PALINGMAN. In old English law. A merchant denizen; one born within the English pale. Blount.

PALLIO COOPERIRE. In old English law. An ancient custom, where children were born out of wedlock, and their parents afterwards intermarried. The children, together with the father and mother, stood under a cloth extended while the marriage was solemnized. It was in the nature of adoption. The children were legitimate by the civil, but not by the common, law. Jacob.

PALMER'S ACT. A name given to the English statute 19 & 20 Vict. c. 16, enabling a person accused of a crime committed out of the jurisdiction of the central criminal court to be tried in that court.

PANDECTS. In civil law. The name of an abridgment or compilation of the civil law, made by Tribonian and others, by order of the emperor Justinian, and to which he gave the force of law A. D. 533.

It is also known by the name of the Digest, because in his compilation of writings of the jurists were reduced to order and condensed *quasi digestiae.* The emperor, in 530, published an ordinance entitled *De Conceptione Digestorum,* which was addressed to Tribonian, and by which he was required to select some of the most distinguished lawyers to assist him in composing a collection of the best decisions of the ancient lawyers, and compile them in fifty books, without confusion or contradiction. The instructions of the emperor were to select what was useful, to omit what was antiquated or superfluous, to avoid contradictions, and, by the necessary changes, to produce a complete body of law. This work was a companion to the Code of Justinian, and was to be governed in its arrangement of topics by the method of the Code. Justinian allowed the commissioners, who were sixteen in number, ten years to compile it; but the work was completed in three years, and promulgated in 533. A list of the writers from whose works the collection was made, and an account of the method pursued by the commissioners, will be found in Smith Dict. Gr. & R. Ant. The Digest, although compiled in Constantinople, was originally written in Latin, and afterwards translated into Greek.

The Digest is divided in two different ways: The first into fifty books, each book into several titles, and each title into several extracts or *leges,* and at the head of each series of extracts is the name of the lawyer from whose work they were taken.

The first book contains twenty-two titles. The subject of the first is *De Justicia et Jure,* of the division of persons and things, of magistrates, etc. The second, divided into fifteen titles, treats of the power of magistrates and their jurisdiction, the manner of commencing suits, of agreements and compromises. The third, composed of six titles, treats of those who can and those who cannot sue, of advocates and attorneys and syndics, and of calumny. The fourth, divided into nine titles, treats of causes of restitution, of submissions and arbitrations, of minors, carriers by water, innkeepers, and those who have the care of the property of others. In the fifth there are six titles, which treat of jurisdiction and inofficious testaments. The subject of the sixth, in which there are three titles, is actions. The seventh, in nine titles, embraces whatever concerns usufructs, personal servitudes, habitations, the uses of real estate and its appurtenances, and of the sureties required of the usufructuary. The eighth book, in six titles, regulates urban and rural servitudes. The ninth book, in four titles, explains certain personal actions. The tenth in four titles, treats of mixed actions. The object of the eleventh book, containing eight titles, is to regulate interrogatories, the cases of which the judge was to take cognizance, fugitive slaves, of gamblers, of surveyors who made false reports, and of funerals and funeral expenses. The twelfth book, in seven titles, regulates personal actions in which the plaintiff claims the title of a thing. The thirteenth, in seven titles, and the fourteenth, in six titles, regulate certain actions. The fifteenth, in four titles, treats of actions to which a father or master is liable in consequence of the acts of his children or slaves, and those to which he is entitled, of the *peculium* of children and slaves, and of the actions on this right. The sixteenth, in three titles, contains the law relating to the *senatus consultum Velleianum,* of compensation or set-off, and of the action of deposit. The seventeenth, in two titles, expounds the law of mandates and partnership. The eighteenth book, in seven titles, explains the contract of sale. The nineteenth, in five titles, treats of the actions which arise on a contract of sale. The law relating to pawns, hypothecation, the preference among creditors, and subrogation, occupy the twentieth book, which contains six titles. The twenty-first book explains, under three titles, the edict of the *ediles* relating to the sale of slaves and animals, then what relates to evictions and warranties. The twenty-second book, in six titles, treats of interest, profits, and accessories of things, proofs, presumptions, and of ignorance of law and fact. The twenty-third, in five titles, contains the law of marriage, and its accompanying agreements. The twenty-fourth, in three titles, and the twenty-fifth, in seven titles, regulate donations between husband and wife, divorces, and their consequence. The twenty-sixth and twenty-seventh, each in two titles, contain the law relating to tutorship and curatorship. The twenty-eighth, in eight titles, and the twenty-ninth, in seven, contain the law on last will and testaments. The thirtieth, thirty-first, and thirty-second, each divided into two titles, contain the law of trusts and specific legacies. The thirty-third, thirty-fourth, and thirty-fifth—the first divided into ten titles, the second into nine titles, and the last into three titles—treat of various kinds of legacies. The thirty-sixth, containing four titles, explains the *senatus consultum Trebellianum,* and the time when trusts become due. The thirty-seventh book, contains fifteen titles, has two objects,—to regulate successions, and to declare the respect which children owe their parents, and freedmen their patrons. The thirty-eighth book, in seventeen titles, treats of a variety of subjects,—of successions, and of the degree of kindred in successions; of possession; and of heirs. The thirty-ninth explains the means which the law and the praetor take to prevent a threatened injury, and donations *inter vivos* and *mortis causa.* The fortieth, in sixteen titles, treats of the state and condition of persons, and of what relates to freedmen and liberty. The different means of acquiring and losing title to property are explained in the forty-first book, in ten titles. The forty-second, in eight titles, treats of the *res judicata,* and of the seizure and sale of the property of a debtor. Interdicts, or possessory actions, are the object of the forty-third book, in three titles. The forty-fourth contains an enumeration of defenses which arise in consequence of the *res judicata,* from the lapse of time, prescription, and the like. This occupies six titles; the seventh treats of obligations and actions. The forty-fifth speaks of stipulations, by freedmen or by slaves. It contains only three titles. The forty-sixth, in eight titles, treats of securities, novations and delegations, payments, releases, and acceptilations. In the forty-seventh book are explained the punishments inflicted for private crimes, *de privatis delictis,* among which are included larcenies, slander, libels, offenses against religion and public manners, removing boundaries, and similar offenses. The forty-eighth book treats of public crimes, among which are enumerated those of *laesae-majestatis,* adultery, murder, poisoning, parricide, extortion, and the like, with rules for procedure in such cases. The forty-ninth, in eighteen titles, treats of appeals, of the rights of the public treasury, of those who are in captivity, and of their repurchase. The fiftieth and last book, in seventeen titles, explains the rights of municipalities, and then treats of a variety of public officers.

These fifty books are allotted in seven parts: The first contains the first four books; the second, from the fifth to the eleventh book, inclusive; the third, from the twelfth to the nineteenth, inclusive; the fourth, from the twentieth to the twenty-seventh, inclusive; the fifth, from the twenty-eighth to the thirty-sixth, inclusive; the sixth commences with the thirty-seventh, and ends with the forty-seventh book; and the seventh, or last, is composed of the last six books.

The division into *digestum vetus* (book first to and including title second of book twenty-fourth), *digestum infortiatum* (title third of book twenty-fourth, to and including book thirty-eighth), and *digestum novum* (from book thirty-ninth to the end), has reference to the order in which these three parts appeared.

The Pandects are more usually cited by English and American jurists by numbers, thus: Dig. 23. 3. 5. 6, meaning book 23, title 3, law or fragment 5, section 6; sometimes, also, otherwise, as, D. 23. 3. fr. 5, § 6; or fr. 5, § 6. D. 23. 3. The old mode of citing was by titles and initial words, thus: D. *de jure dotium,* L. *profectitia,* § *si pater;* or the same references in reverse order. From this afterwards originated the following: L. *profectitia,* 5. § *se pater,* 6. D. *de jure dotium,* and, lastly, L. 5. § 6. D. *de jure dotium,*—which is the form commonly used by the continental jurists of Europe. 1 Hackeld. Civ. Law, pp. 54, 55, § 65. And see Tayl. Civ. Law, 24, 25. The abbreviation *ff.* was commonly used instead of Dig. or Pandects.

The Pandects—as well, indeed, as all Justinian's laws, except some fragments of the Code and Novels—were lost to all Europe for a considerable period. During the pillage of Amalfi, in the war between the two soi-disant popes Innocent II. and Anaclet II., a soldier discovered an old manuscript, which attracted his attention by its envelope of many colors. It was carried to the Emperor Clothaire, and proved to the Pandects of Justinian. The work was arranged in its present order by Warner, a German, whose Latin name is Irnerius, who was appointed by that emperor Professor of Roman Law at Bologna. 1 Fournel, Hist. des Ovocats, 44, 46, 51. The style of the work is very grave and pure, and contrasts in this respect with that of the Code, which is very far from classical. On the other hand, the learning of the Digest stands rather in the discussing of subtle questions of law, and enumerations of the variety of opinions of ancient lawyers thereupon, than in practical matters of daily use, of which the Code so simply and directly treats. See Ridley, View, pt. 1, cc. 1, 2.

PANDOXARE (Law Lat.) In old records. to brew. Cowell.

Pandoxatrix, an ale wife; a woman that both brewed and sold ale and beer. Id.

PANEL (diminutive from either *pane,* apart, or *page, pagella*).

——**In Practice.** A schedule or roll, containing the names of jurors summoned by virtue of a writ of *venire facias,* and annexed to the writ. It is returned into the court whence the *venire* issued. Co. Litt. 158b; 3 Bl. Comm. 353.

——**In Scotch Law.** The prisoner at the bar, or person who takes his trial before the court of justiciary for some crime. So called from the time of his appearance. Bell, Dict. Spelled, also, *pannel.* See "Impanel."

PANIER. A waiter at table at English bar dinners.

PANIS (Lat.) In old English law. Bread; loaf; a loaf. Fleta, lib. 2, c. 9.

PANNAGE. In old English law. Food that swine fed on in the woods, as mast of beech, acorns, &c. which some called *pawns*. Cowell.

A duty for feeding in woods. Fleta, lib. 2, c. 41, § 31.

PANNAGIUM EST PASTUS PORCORUM, in nemoribus et in silvis, ut puta, de glandibus, etc. A pannagium is a pasture of hogs, in woods and forests, upon acorns, and so forth. 1 Bulst. 7.

PANNELLATION. The act of impaneling a jury.

PAPER BLOCKADE. A blockade proclaimed, but not maintained by a naval force sufficient to render it effective. See "Blockade."

PAPER BOOK. In appellate practice. A book or paper, usually printed, containing a transcript or an abstract, as may be required, of all the evidence and proceedings submitted to the appellate court.

PAPER DAYS. In English law. Days on which special arguments are to take place. Tuesdays and Fridays in term time are paper days appointed by the court. Lee, Dict.; Archb. Prac. 101.

PAPER MONEY. The engagements to pay money which are issued by governments and banks, and which pass as money. Pardesus, Dr. Com. note 9. Bank notes are generally considered as cash, and will answer all the purposes of currency; but paper money is not a legal tender if objected to. See "Legal Tender."

PAPER OFFICE. In English law. An ancient office in the palace of Whitehall, where all the public writings, matters of state and council, proclamations, letters, intelligences, negotiations of the queen's ministers abroad, and generally all the papers and dispatches that pass through the office of the secretaries of state, are deposited. Also an office or room in the court of queen's bench, where the records belonging to that court are deposited; sometimes called "paper mill." Wharton.

PAPER TITLE. A claim of title unfounded in fact, but founded on a conveyance or chain of conveyances showing an apparently good title.

PAR. In common law. Equal. It is used to denote a state of equality or equal value. An equality of actual with nominal value. 9 Baxt. (Tenn.) 410, 99 Miss. 859; 35 L. R. A. (N. S.) 791; 156 N. Y. 363, 50 N. E. 973. Bills of exchange, stocks, and the like, are at par when they sell for their nominal value; above par, or below par, when they sell for more or less.

PAR DELICTUM (Lat.) Equal guilt. "This is not a case of *par delictum*. It is oppression on one side, and submission on the other. It never can be predicated as *par delictum* when one holds the rod and the other bows to it." 6 Maule & S. 165. See "In Pari Delicto."

PAR IN PAREM IMPERIUM NON HAbet. An equal has no power over an equal. Jenk. Cent. Cas. 174. Example, one of two judges of the same court cannot commit the other for contempt.

PAR OF EXCHANGE. The par of the currencies of any two countries means the equivalence of a certain amount of the currency of the one in the currency of the other, supposing the currency of both to be of the precise weight and purity fixed by their respective mints. 26 Wend. (N. Y.) 224. The exchange between the two countries is said to be at par when bills are negotiated on this footing, *i. e.*, when a bill for £100 drawn on London sells in Paris for 2,520 frs., and *vice versa*. Bowen, Pol. Econ. 321. See 11 East, 267.

PAR ONERI. Equal to the damage.

PAR VALUE. In its customary and commercial sense, with reference to exchange between different states or countries, par value has been defined to be "the equivalency of a certain amount of the currency of one country in the currency of the other." 26 Wend. (N. Y.) 224.

By the par value of stock is generally understood the value expressed on the face of the certificate.

PARACIUM. The tenure between parceners, viz., that which the youngest owes to the eldest without homage or service. Domesday Book.

PARAGE. Equality of blood, name, or dignity, but more especially of land in the partition of an inheritance between coheirs. Co. Litt. 166b. Hence "disparage," and "disparagement." Blount.

——**In Feudal Law.** Where heirs took of the same stock and by same title, but from right of primogeniture, or some other cause, the shares were unequal, the younger was said to hold of the elder, *jure et titulo paragii*, by right and title of parage, being equal in everything but the quantity, and owning no homage or fealty. Calv. Lex.

PARAGIUM (Lat. *par*, equal, and (*aqium*). 1 Thomas, Co. Litt. 681. Equality.

——**In Ecclesiastical Law.** The portion which a woman gets on her marriage. Ayliffe, Par. 336.

PARAGRAPH. A part or section of a statute, pleading, affidavit, etc., which contains one article, the sense of which is complete. Wharton.

PARAMOUNT (*par*, by, *mounter*, to ascend). Above; upwards. Kelham. *Para-*

mount especifie, above specified. Plowd. 209a.

That which is superior; usually applied to the highest lord of the fee of lands, tenements, or hereditaments. Fitzh. Nat. Brev. 135. Where A. lets lands to B. and he underlets them to C., in this case A. is the paramount and B. is the mesne landlord. 2 Bl. Comm. 91; 1 Thomas, Co. Litt. 484, note 79, 485, note 81. The estate which is entitled to the benefit of an easement is known as the "paramount estate."

PARANOIA. A form of insanity, the principal characteristic of which is that the sufferer possesses insane delusions. 227 Ill. 192.

PARAPHERNA (Lat.) In civil law. Goods brought by wife to husband over and above her dower (*dos*). Vocat; Fleta, lib. 5, c. 23, § 6; Mackeld. Civ. Law, § 529.

PARAPHERNAL. Belonging or pertaining to the parapherna.

PARAPHERNALIA. Apparel and ornaments of a wife, suitable to her rank and degree. 2 Bl. Comm. 435.

PARAPHERNAUX, BIENS (Fr.) In French law. All the wife's property which is not subject to the *regime dotal* is called by this name, and of these articles the wife has the entire administration; but she may allow the husband to enjoy them, and in that case he is not liable to account. Brown.

PARASYNEXIS. In the civil law, a conventicle or unlawful meeting.

PARATITLA (Lat.) In civil law. An abbreviated explanation of some titles or books of the Code or Digest.

PARATUM HABEO (Lat. I have ready). In practice. A return made by the sheriff to a *capias ad respondendum,* which signified that he had the defendant ready to bring into court. This was a fiction, where the defendant was at large. Afterwards he was required, by statute, to take bail from the defendant, and he returned *cepi corpus* and bail bond. But still he might be ruled to bring in the body. 7 Pa. St. 535.

PARATUS EST VERIFICARE. In old pleading. This he is ready to verify.

PARAVAIL. Tenant paravail is the lowest tenant of the fee, or he who is the immediate tenant to one who holds of another. He is called tenant paravail because it is presumed he has the avails or profits of the land. Fitzh. Nat. Brev. 135; 2 Inst. 296.

PARCEL. A part of the estate. 1 Comyn, Dig. "Abatement" (H 51), "Grant" (E 10). To parcel is to divide an estate. Bac. Abr. "Conditions" (O).

A small bundle. It is the diminutive of package. 1 Hughes (U. S.) 529.

The word "parcel" is not a sufficient description of the property alleged in an indictment to have been stolen. The prisoner was indicted for stealing "one parcel, of the value of one shilling, of the goods," etc. The parcel in question was taken from the hold of a vessel, out of a box broken open by the prisoner. Held an insufficient description. 7 Cox, C. C. 13.

PARCEL MAKERS. Two officers in the exechequer who formerly made the parcels or items of the escheators' accounts, wherein they charged them with everything they had levied for the sovereign's use during the term of their office, and delivered the same to the auditors to make up their accounts therewith.

PARCELLA TERRAE. A parcel of land.

PARCELS, BILL OF. An account of the items composing a parcel or package of goods, transmitted with them to the purchaser.

PARCENARY. The state or condition of holding title to lands jointly by parceners, before the common inheritance has been divided. See "Coparcenary, Estates in."

PARCENERS. The daughters of a man or woman seised of lands and tenements in fee simple or fee tail, on whom, after the death of such ancestor, such lands and tenements descend, and they enter. See "Coparceners."

PARCHMENT (Fr.; Law Lat. *pergamenum*). Sheep skins dressed for writing; so called because invented at Pergamus, in Asia Minor, by King Eumenes, when the exportation of paper, which was made in Egypt only, was forbidden by Ptolemy.

PARCO FRACTO (Lat.) In English law. The name of a writ against one who violently breaks a pound and takes from thence beasts which, for some trespass done, or some other just cause, were lawfully impounded.

PARCUS (Lat.) A park.

PARDON. An act of grace, proceeding from the power intrusted with the execution of the laws, which exempts the individual on whom it is bestowed from the punishment the law inflicts for a crime he has committed. 7 Pet. (U. S.) 160.

Every pardon granted to the guilty is in derogation of the law. If the pardon be equitable, the law is bad; for where legislation and the administration of the law are perfect, pardons must be a violation of the law. But, as human actions are necessarily imperfect, the pardoning power must be vested somewhere, in order to prevent injustice when it is ascertained that an error has been committed.

(1) An absolute pardon is one which frees the criminal without any condition whatever.

(2) A conditional pardon is one to which a condition is annexed, performance of which is necessary to the validity of the pardon. 1 Bailey (S. C.) 283; 10 Ark. 284; 1 McCord (S. C.) 176; 1 Park. Cr. Cas. (N. Y.) 47.

(3) A general pardon, more properly called "amnesty" (*q. v.*), is one which extends to all offenders of the same kind. It may be express, as when a general declaration is made that all offenders of a certain class shall be pardoned, or implied, as in case of the repeal of a penal statute. 2 Overt. (Tenn.) 423.

"The distinction between pardon, amnesty, and reprieve seems to be that pardon permanently discharges the individual designated from some or all special penal consequences of his crime, but does not affect the legal character of the offense committed; while amnesty obliterates the effect, and declares that government will not consider the thing done punishable, and hence operates in favor of all persons involved in it, whether mentioned or not; and reprieve only temporarily suspends execution of punishment, leaving the legal character of the act unchanged, and the individual subject to its consequences in time to come." Abbott.

PARENS. A parent. This was the original and proper sense of the word.

In the civil law, any relative in the direct ascending line, either male or female.

PARENS EST NOMEN GENERALE AD omne genus cognationis. Parent is a general name for every kind of relationship. Co. Litt. 80; Litt. § 108; Magna Carta Johan. c. 50.

PARENS PATRIAE (Lat.) Father of his country. In England, the king, in America, the state, 94 Kan. 115; the people, 3 Bl. Comm. 427; 2 Steph. Comm. 528; 4 Kent, Comm. 508, note; 17 How. (U. S.) 393; Shelf. Ins. 12; 94 Kan. 115, Ann. Cas. 1916E 1024.

PARENTAGE. Kindred in the direct ascending line. See 2 Bouv. Inst. note 1955.

PARENTS. The lawful father and mother of the party spoken of. 1 Murph. (N. C.) 336; 11 Serg. & R. (Pa.) 93.

The term "parent" differs from that of "ancestor;" the latter embracing not only the father and mother, but every person in an ascending line. It differs also from "predecessor." Wood Inst. 68; 7 Ves. 522; 1 Murph. (N. C.) 336; 6 Bin. (Pa.) 255. See "Father."

By the civil law, grandfathers and grandmothers, and other ascendants, were, in certain cases, considered parents. Dict. de Jur. "Parente." See 1 Ashm. (Pa.) 55; 2 Kent, Comm. 159; 5 East, 223; Bouv. Inst. Index.

PARENTUM EST LIBEROS ALERE etiam nothos. It is the duty of parents to support their children, even when illegitimate. Lofft, 222.

PARES (Lat.) A man's equals; his peers. 3 Bl. Comm. 349.

PARES CURIAE (Lat.) In feudal law. Those vassals who were bound to attend the lord's court. Ersk. Inst. bk. 2, tit. 3, § 17; 1 Washb. Real Prop.

PARES REGNI. The peers of the realm.

PARESIS. A progressive disease, manifesting itself at first by a slight loss of memory, dropping of words or carelessness as to dress or person, these conditions becoming more marked as the disease progresses and affecting in an increasing degree the memory, judgment and mental functions, until, at an advanced stage of the disease, the mental powers of the victim are wholly destroyed. 250 Ill. 176.

PARI DELICTO (Lat.) In criminal law. In a similar offense or crime; equal in guilt.

A person who is *in pari delicto* with another differs from a *particeps criminis* in this, that the former term always includes the latter, but the latter does not always include the former. 8 East, 381, 382; 124 N. Y. 156. See "In Pari Delicto."

PARI MATERIA (Lat.) Of the same matter; on the same subject; as, laws *pari materia* must be construed with reference to each other. Bac. Abr. "Statute" (I 3).

PARI PASSU (Lat.) By the same gradation. Used especially of creditors who, in marshalling assets, are entitled to receive out of the same fund, without any precedence over each other.

PARI RATIONE (Lat.) For the like reason; by like mode of reasoning.

PARIA COPULANTUR PARIBUS. Similar things unite with similar.

PARIBUS SENTENTIIS REUS ABSOLvitur. When opinions are equal, a defendant is acquitted. 4 Inst. 64.

PARIENTES. In Spanish law. Relations. White, New Recop. bk. 1, tit. 7, c. 5, § 2.

PARIES. In the civil law. A wall. Dig. 50. 16. 157.

PARIES COMMUNIS. In the civil law. A common wall; a party wall. Dig. 29. 2. 39.

PARISH. A district of country, of different extents.

——**In Ecclesiastical Law.** The territory committed to the charge of a parson, or vicar, or other minister. Ayliffe, Par. 404; 2 Bl. Comm. 112.

——**In Louisiana.** Divisions corresponding to counties. The state is divided into parishes.

——**In New England.** Divisions of a town, originally territorial, but which now constitute *quasi* corporations, consisting of those connected with a certain church. See 2 Mass. 501; 7 Mass. 447; 16 Mass. 457, 488, 492 et seq.; 1 Picfl. (Mass.) 91.

PARISH APPRENTICE. The children of poor persons in England who are bound by the overseers of the parish, with the consent of two justices. 2 Steph. Comm. 230.

PARISH CONSTABLE. A petty constable exercising his functions within a given parish. Mozley & W.

PARISH COURT. In Louisiana. A court established in each parish, having general probate jurisdiction, and a limited civil jurisdiction.

PARISH OFFICERS. Church wardens, overseers, and constables.

PARIUM EADEM EST RATIO, IDEM jus. Of things equal, the reason is the same, and the same is the law.

PARIUM JUDICIUM (Lat. the decision of equals). The right of trial by one's peers, *i. e.*, by jury in the case of a commoner, by the house of peers in the case of a peer.

PARK (Law Lat. *parcus*).

——**In Old Law.** An inclosure. 2 Bl. Comm. 38. A pound. Reg. Orig. 166; Cowell. *Pairk* is still retained in Ireland for "pound."

——**In English Law.** An inclosed chase extending only over a man's own grounds. 13 Car. II. c. 10; Manw. For. Laws; Cromp. Jur. fol. 148; 2 Bl. Comm. 38.

——**In American Law.** A piece of ground in a city or village set apart for ornament, or to afford the benefit of air, exercise, or amusement. 36 N. Y. 120.

PARK BOTE. To be quit of inclosing a park, or any part thereof.

PARLE HILL (also called Parling Hill). A hill where courts were held in old times. Cowell.

PARLER. (L. Fr.) To speak. Kelham.

PARLIAMENT (said to be derived from *parler la ment*, to speak the mind, or *parum lamentum*). In English law. The legislative branch of the government of Great Britain, consisting of the house of lords and the house of commons.

PARLIAMENTARY AGENTS. Persons (usually solicitors) who transact the technical business connected with passing private bills through parliament. They are required to sign a declaration and give security for compliance with the rules of parliament.

PARLIAMENTARY TAXES. Such taxes as are imposed directly by act of parliament, *i. e.*, by the legislature itself, as distinguished from those which are imposed by private individuals or bodies under the authority of an act of parliament. Thus, a sewers rate, not being imposed directly by act of parliament, but by certain persons termed "commissioners of sewers," is not a parliamentary tax; whereas the income tax, which is directly imposed, and the amount also fixed, by act of parliament, is a parliamentary tax.

PARLIAMENTUM DIABOLICUM. A parliament held at Coventry, 3 Hen. VI., wherein Edward, Earl of March (afterwards King Edward IV.), and many of the chief nobility were attainted, was so called; but the acts then made were annulled by the succeeding parliament. Jacob.

PARLIAMENTUM INDOCTUM (Law Lat.) Unlearned or lack learning parliament. A name given to a parliament held at Coventry in the sixth year of Henry IV., under an ordinance requiring that no lawyer should be chosen knight, citizen or burgess; "by reason whereof," says Sir Edward Coke, "this parliament was fruitless, and never a good law made thereat." 4 Inst. 48; 1 Bl. Comm. 177.

PARLIAMENTUM INSANUM. A parliament assembled at Oxford, 41 Hen. III., so styled from the madness of their proceedings, and because the lords came with armed men to it, and contentions grew very high between the king, lords, and commons, whereby many extraordinary things were done. Jacob.

PARLIAMENTUM RELIGIOSORUM. In most convents there has been a common room into which the brethren withdrew for conversation; conferences there being termed *parliamentum*. Likewise, the societies of the two temples, or inns of court, call that assembly of the benchers or governors wherein they confer upon the common affairs of their several houses a "parliament." Jacob.

PAROCHIA EST LOCUS IN QUO DEGIT populus alicujus ecclesiae. A parish is a place in which the population of a certain church resides. 5 Coke, 67.

PAROL (more properly *parole*, a French word, meaning literally "word" or "speech"). Oral; by word of mouth.

——**In Contracts.** Verbal or merely written, as distinguished from sealed. 1 Chit. Cont. 1; 3 Johns. Cas. (N. Y.) 60.

——**In Evidence.** Parol evidence is that delivered verbally by witnesses in court.

PAROLE.

——**In International Law.** The agreement of persons who have been taken by an enemy that they will not again take up arms against those who captured them, either for a limited time or during the continuance of the war. Vattel, liv. 3, c. 8, § 151.

——**In Criminal Law.** A form of conditional pardon, by which the convict is released before the expiration of his term, to remain subject, during the remainder thereof, to supervision by the public authorities, and to return to imprisonment on violation of the conditions of the parole.

PAROLS FONT PLEA. Words make the plea. 5 Mod. 458; Y. B. 19 Hen. VI. 48.

PARRICIDE (from Lat. *pater*, father, and *caedere*, to slay). In civil law. One who murders his father; one who murders his mother, his brother, his sister, or his children. Merlin, Repert.; Dig. 48. 9. 1. 3, 4.

The common law does not define the crime and makes no difference in punishment between it and other murders. 1 Hale, P. C. 380.

In colloquial use, the term is applied according to its derivative, rather than its civil-law meaning, to the slayer of a father only.

PARRICIDIUM. In the civil law. Parricide; the murder of a parent. Dig. 48. 9. 9.

PARS (Lat.) A party (to a suit). *Pars actrix*, a party plaintiff. Reg. Orig. 9a; Fleta, lib. 2, c. 63, § 11; Clerke, Prax. Cur. Adm. tit. 4. Singularly translated in Dyer (179a), part actress. *Pars agens*. 3 How. St. Tr. 863.

Pars rea, a party defendant. St. Marlb. c. 13.

PARS ENITIA (Lat.) In old English law. The share of the eldest daughter where lands were parted between daughters by lot, she having her first choice after the division of the inheritance. Co. Litt. 166b; Glanv. lib. 7, c. 3; Fleta, lib. 5, c. 10, § "In Divisionem."

PARS GRAVATA. In old practice. A party aggrieved; the party aggrieved. Hardr. 50; 3 Leon. 237.

PARS PRO TOTO. Part for the whole; the name of a part used to represent the whole; as the roof for the house, ten spears for ten armed men, etc.

PARS RATIONABILIS (Lat. reasonable part). That part of a man's goods which the law gave to his wife and children. 2 Bl. Comm. 492; Magna Charta; 9 Hen. III. c. 18; 2 Steph. Comm. 228, 254.

PARSON. In ecclesiastical law. One that hath full possession of all the rights of a parochial church. So called because the church, which is an invisible body, is represented by his person. In England he is himself a body corporate, in order to protect and defend the church (which he personates) by a perpetual succession. Co. Litt. 300.

PARSON IMPARSONA (Lat.) A *persona*, or parson, may be termed "*impersonata*," or "impersonee," only in regard to the possession he hath of the rectory by the act of another. Co. Litt. 300. One that is inducted and in possession of a benefice, *e. g.*, a dean and chapter. Dyer, 40, 221. He that is in possession of a church, be it presentative or appropriate, and with whom the church is full,—*persona* in this case meaning the patron who gives the title, and *persona impersonata* the parson to whom the benefice is given in the patron's right. Reg. Jud. 24.

PARSONAGE. A parsonage is a house in which a minister of the gospel resides. 189 Mich. 408.

PART. A share; one of the portions equal or unequal into which anything is divided, or regarded as divided; a piece; a fragment, division, a member, a constituent, 9 Ill. App. 407; a purpart. This word is also used in contradistinction to counterpart, and is synonymous with section. 9 Ill. App. 407. Covenants were formerly made in a script and rescript, or part and counterpart.

PART AND PERTINENT. In Scotch law. A term in a conveyance including lands or servitudes held for forty years as part of, or pertinent to, lands conveyed, natural fruits before they are separated, woods and parks, etc., but not steelbow stock, unless the lands have been sold on a rental. Bell, Dict.; Ersk. Inst. 2. 5. 3. et seq.

PART OWNERS. Those who own a thing together or in common.

——**In Maritime Law.** A term applied to two or more person who own a vessel together, and not as partners.

In general, when a majority of the part owners are desirous of employing such a ship upon a particular voyage or adventure, they have a right to do so upon giving security in the admiralty by stipulation to the minority, if required, to bring her back and restore the ship, or, in case of her loss, to pay them the value of their respective shares. 4 Bouv. Inst. note 3780; Abb. Shipp. 70; 3 Kent, Comm. (4th Ed.) 151; Story, Partn. § 489; 11 Pet. (U. S.) 175. When the majority do not choose to employ the ship, the minority have the same right, upon giving similar security. 11 Pet. (U. S.) 175; 1 Hagg. Adm. 306; Jacobsen, Sea Laws, 442.

PARTE NON COMPARENTE (Lat.) The party not having appeared. The condition of a cause called "default."

PARTE QUACUMQUE INTEGRANTE sublata, tollitur totum. An integral part being taken away, the whole is taken away. 8 Coke, 41.

PARTEM ALIQUAM RECTE INTELLIGERE nemo potest, antequam totum, iterum atque iterum, perlegerit. No one can rightly understand any part until he has read the whole again and again. 3 Coke, 52.

PARTES FINIS NIL HABUERUNT (Lat. the parties to the fine had nothing, *i. e.*, nothing which they could convey). In old English pleading. The plea to a fine levied by a stranger, and which only bound parties and privates. 2 Bl. Comm. 356*; Hob. 334; 1 P. Wms. 520; 1 Wooddeson, Lect. 315.

PARTIAL LOSS. A loss of a part of a thing, or of its value, as contrasted with a total loss.

——**In Maritime Law.** Where this happens by damage to an article, it is also called a particular average (*q. v.*)

PARTICEPS (Lat. plur. *participes;* from *pars*, a part, and *capere*, to take). Literally, a part-taker; a partaker or sharer; one jointly interested with another; an associate or accomplice.

In old English law. A part-owner; a parcener.

PARTICEPS CRIMINIS. A sharer or partaker in crime. Applied, also, to persons participating in an illegal or immoral transaction or contract not criminal. One may be *particeps criminis*, and not *in pari delicto*. 124 N. Y. 156.

PARTICEPS PLURES SUNT QUASI unum corpus in eo quod unum jus habent, et oportet quod corpus sit integrum, et quod in nulla parte sit defectus. Many parceners are as one body, inasmuch as they have one right, and it is necessary that the body be perfect, and that there be a defect in no part. Co. Litt. 4.

PARTICULA (Law Lat.) In old English law. Parcel. Perk. c. 10, §§ 674, 676, 679.

PARTICULAR AVERAGE. Every kind of expense or damage, short of total loss, which regards a particular concern, and which is to be wholly borne by the proprietor of that concern or interest alone. 2 Phil. Ins. § 354; 1 Pars. Mar. Law, 284. See "Average."

PARTICULAR AVERMENT. See "Averment."

PARTICULAR CUSTOM. A custom which only affects the inhabitants of some particular district.

To be good, a particular custom must have been used so long that the memory of man runneth not to the contrary; must have been continued; must have been peaceable; must be reasonable; must be certain; must be consistent with itself; must be consistent with other customs. 1 Bl. Comm. 74, 79.

PARTICULAR ESTATE. An estate which is carved out of a larger, and which precedes a remainder; as, an estate for years to A., remainder to be for life; or an estate for life to A., remainder to B. in tail. This precedent estate is called the "particular estate." 2 Bl. Comm. 165; 4 Kent, Comm. 226; 16 Viner, Abr. 216; 4 Comyn, Dig. 32; 5 Comyn, Dig. 346. See "Remainder."

PARTICULAR LIEN. A right which a person has to retain property in respect of money or labor expended on such particular property. See "Lien."

PARTICULAR MALICE. Malice against a particular person. See "Malice."

PARTICULAR STATEMENT. In Pennsylvania pleading and practice. A statement particularly specifying the date of a promise, book account, note, bond (penal or single), bill, or all of them, on which an action is founded and the amount believed by the plaintiff to be due from the defendant. 6 Serg. & R. (Pa.) 21. It is founded on the provisions of a statute passed March 21, 1806. See 4 Smith, Pa. Laws, 328. It is an unmethodical declaration, not restricted to any particular form. 2 Serg. & R. (Pa.) 537; 3 Serg. & R. (Pa.) 405; 8 Serg. & R. (Pa.) 316, 567; 2 Browne (Pa.) 40.

PARTICULAR TENANT. The holder of a particular estate (*q. v.*).

PARTICULARS. See "Bill of Particulars."

PARTICULARS OF CRIMINAL charges. A prosecutor, when a charge is general is frequently ordered to give the defendant a statement of the acts charged, which is called, in England, the "particulars" of the charges.

In the United States, a bill of particulars is often ordered for the same purpose.

PARTICULARS OF SALE. When property such as land, houses, shares, reversions, etc., is to be sold by auction, it is usually described in a document called the "particulars" copies of which are distributed among intending bidders. They should fairly and accurately describe the property. Dart, Vend. 113; 1 Dav. Conv. 511.

PARTIES (Lat. *pars*, a part. Those who take part in the performance of an act, as, making a contract, carrying on an action. A party in law may be said to be those united in interest in the performance of an act. It may then be composed of one or more persons. "Parties" includes every party to an act. It is also used to denote all the individual separate persons engaged in the act—in which sense, however, a corporation may be a party.

——**To Contracts.** Those persons who engage themselves to do or not to do the matters and things contained in an agreement.

——**In Actions.** The persons seeking relief, and those against whom relief is sought, in any action. Parties are either "of record," being those in whose name the suit is brought, or who are named as defendants, and "not of record," those not so named, but who have a beneficial interest in the subject matter. 6 Abb. Pr. (N. S.; N. Y.) 147.

PARTITION. The division which is made between several persons of lands, tenements, or hereditaments, or of goods and chattels, which belong to them as coheirs or coproprietors. The term is more technically applied to the division of real estate made between coparceners, tenants in common, or joint tenants.

Compulsory partition is that which takes place by a judicial proceeding for that purpose, without regard to the wishes of one or more of the owners.

Voluntary partition is that made by the owners by mutual consent.

PARTNER. One who is a member of a partnership (*q. v.*)

——**Ostensible Partners.** Those held out and known as partners, and who in reality are such.

——**Secret Partners.** Those whose relation to the partnership is concealed.

——**Active Partners.** Those who take an active part in the conduct of the business. They may be either ostensible or secret partners.

——**Silent Partners.** Those who take no active part in the management of the business. They may be either ostensible or secret partners.

——**Dormant Partners.** Such as are both secret and silent partners. The term is sometimes applied, however, as meaning merely a secret partner, and sometimes as meaning a silent partner. Pars. Partn. § 31.

——**Nominal Partners.** Such as are apparently partners, but really are not.

——**General Partners.** Those members of a limited partnership whose liability is not limited by special agreement.

——**Special Partners.** Those members of a limited partnership whose liability is limited. See "Partnership." Shumaker, Partnership, 124.

PARTNERSHIP. The relation subsisting between two or more persons who have contracted together to share as common owners the profits of a business carried on by all or any of them on behalf of all of them. Shumaker, Partnership, 2.

Elements:

The essential elements of a partnership are (1) a contract between the partners; a true partnership being always formed by contract, not by operation of law. 138 Ill. 74; 43 Mo. 391; 63 Pa. St. 273. The so-called partnership by estoppel or holding out is only an apparent exception; it not being a true partnership *inter se*, but only a liability of individuals to third persons as if they were partners. (2) A sharing of profits; but the profits must be shared between the partners as common owners thereof, not because of a portion thereof being due to a party as a debt. 8 H. L. Cas. 268; 5 Colo. 564; 30 Me. 384; 38 Cal. 205; 28 Ohio St. 319. But community of ownership in the stock or capital by means of which profits are earned is not essential. 15 Conn. 67.

Test:

Profit sharing, therefore, is not a test, nor is mutual agency, for mutual agency results from partnership, not partnership from agency. The true test is the intention of the parties to share in the profits as common owners. An agreement to share both profits and losses is *prima facie* but not conclusive evidence of intention to form a partnership (97 Ill. 303), as is an agreement to share profits with nothing said about losses (145 U. S. 611), or with a stipulation against the liability of one of the parties for losses (18 Fed. 888); but not an agreement to share gross returns (15 Ill. 31; 20 N. Y. 93), or to share losses or expenses only (92 Ill. 103; 132 Mass. 423). The common ownership of property does not create a partnership unless it be employed in business for common profit. 27 Iowa, 131.

Classification:

Partnerships classified with reference to the nature of the association are either (1) ordinary partnerships, (2) limited partnerships, being those wherein the liability of one or more partners is, by compliance with certain statutory provisions, limited to the amount of their contribution to the capital stock, or (3) joint-stock companies, being partnerships with a capital stock divided into transferable shares.

Partnerships classified with reference to their extent are either (1) universal partnerships, being those in which the parties bring into the firm all their property, of whatever nature, and employ all their services for the common benefit, (2) general partnerships, being those formed to transact some general class of business, or (3) special or particular partnerships, being those formed for a particular transaction.

Partnerships classified with reference to their business are either (1) trading or commercial partnerships, being those whose business consists in buying or preparing for sale and selling commodities for profit, or (2) nontrading partnerships.

PARTNERSHIP IN COMMENDAM. In Louisiana law. Partnership *in commendam* is formed by a contract by which one person or partnership agrees to furnish another person or partnership a certain amount, either in property or money, to be employed by the person or partnership to whom it is furnished, in his or their own name or firm, on condition of receiving a share in the profits, in the proportion determined by the contract, and of being liable to losses and expenses to the amount furnished, and no more. Civ. Code La. art. 2839.

PARTURITION. The act of giving birth to a child. See "Birth."

PARTUS (Lat.) The child just before it is born, or immediately after its birth; off-spring.

PARTUS EX LEGITIMO THORO NON certius noscit matrem quam genitorem suam. The offspring of a legitimate bed knows not his mother more certainly than his father. Fortescue, c. 42.

PARTUS SEQUITUR VENTREM. The off-spring follows the condition of the mother. Inst. 2. 1. 19. This is the law in the case of slaves and animals (1 Bouv. Inst. notes 167, 502), but with regard to freemen, children follow the condition of the father.

PARTY. See "Parties."

PARTY JURY. A jury *de medietate linguae* (*q. v.*)

PARTY STRUCTURE. A structure separating buildings, stories, or rooms which belong to different owners, or which are approached by distinct staircases or separate entrances from without, whether the same be a partition, arch, floor, or other structure. St. 18 & 19 Vict. c. 122, § 3. Mozley & W.

PARTY WALL. A wall erected on the line between two adjoining estates, belonging to different persons, for the use of both estates. 2 Bouv. Inst. note 1615.

It is ordinarily owned in common by the adjoining owners, but may be divided longitudinally or divided latitudinally, the sections being subject to mutual easements, or it may belong to one owner, and be subject to an easement in favor of the other. 50 N. Y. 646; 75 Ill. 118.

PARUM CAVET NATURA. Nature takes little heed. 2 Johns. Cas. (N. Y.) 127, 166.

PARUM CAVISSE VIDETUR. In Roman law. He seems to have taken too little care. A form used by judges in pronouncing sentence.

PARUM DIFFERUNT QUAE RE CONcordant. Things differ but little which agree in substance. 2 Bulst. 86.

PARUM EST LATAM ESSE SENTENtiam, nisi mandetur executioni. It is not enough that sentence should be given, unless it be committed to execution. Co. Litt. 289.

PARUM PROFICIT SCIRE QUID FIERI debet, si non cognoscas quomodo sit facturum. It avails little to know what ought to be done, if you do not know how it is to be done. 2 Inst. 503.

PARVA SERJANTIA (Law Lat.) In old English law. Petty serjeanty. Fleta, lib. 1, c. 11. Called also, *parva serjanteria*. Magna Carta, 9 Hen. III. c. 27.

PARVUM CAPE. See "Petit Cape."

PAS (Fr.) Precedence.

PASCHA (Law Lat.; Law Fr. *pasche*). In old English law and practice. Easter *De termino Paschae*, of the term of Easter. Bracton, fol. 246b. *A die Paschae in quindecim dies*, from the day of Easter in fifteen days; after fifteen days of Easter. Reg. Jud. 36; 3 Bl. Comm. Append. No. iii. § 3.

PASCUA SILVA (Lat.) In the civil law. A feeding wood; a wood devoted to the feeding of cattle (*quae pastui pecudum destinata est*). Dig. 50. 16. 30. 5.

PASS.

——**In Practice.** To proceed; to be entered. A verdict or judgment is said "to pass for" a party where it is delivered in his favor. This term is directly taken from the old French *passer*.

——**In Conveyancing.** To go from one person to another; to be transferred. "The names of things by which they pass in assurances." Hale, Anal. § xxiv. " By what names things pass." Id. § xxxv.

To convey or transfer. "To pass an estate." "Effectual words to pass the interest." Id. § xxxv. "The passing of estates." Id.

PASSAGE MONEY. The sum claimable for the conveyance of a person, with or without luggage, on the water.

The difference between freight and passage money is this, that the former is claimable for the carriage of goods, and the latter for the carriage of the person. The same rules which govern the claim for freight affect that for passage money. 3 Chit. Com. Law, 424; 1 Pet. Adm. (N. Y.) 126; 3 Johns. (N. Y.) 335. See "Common Carriers of Passengers."

PASSAGIO. An ancient writ addressed to the keepers of the ports to permit a man who had the king's leave to pass over sea. Reg. Orig. 193.

PASSAGIUM (Law Lat.; Law Fr. *passage*, from *passer*, to pass. In old English law. Passage; a passing over sea; a voyage. Reg. Orig. 193b. A term frequently used in the law of essoins, in the days of the Crusades. Bracton, fol. 339; Fleta, lib. 6, c. 8.

PASSATOR. He who has the interest or command of the passage of a river; or a lord to whom a duty is paid for passage. Wharton.

PASSENGER. One who has taken a place in a public conveyance for the purpose of being transported from one place to another. One who is so conveyed from one place to another.

Though the relation of passenger and carrier is in a sense a matter of contract, on account of the duty of the carrier to receive all persons without discriminations, the implications of contract are broader than in other cases. Thus, one is a passenger on a train which he took by mistake. 64 Tex. 536; 40 Ind. 37.

One who is carried gratuitously is a passenger, as is one who has not yet paid his fare (57 N. Y. Super. Ct. 348; 46 Mo. App. 555), but not one who designs evading payment of fare (157 Mass. 377), even by using a pass issued to another (107 Ind. 442).

An employe of the carrier not engaged in the management of the particular train is a passenger (69 Ga. 715; but see 95 N. Y. 267), as is an employe of another carrier under contract, as an express messenger (56 Ark. 594), or a postal clerk (95 N. Y. 562; 57 Fed. 165).

The relation of passenger and carrier begins the moment one goes on the carrier's premises to take passage on one of its trains (58 Ga. 461; 36 Fed. 72; 40 Barb. [N. Y.] 546), and is not ended until the passenger leaves the conveyance and the carrier's premises (55 Kan. 582; 146 Mass. 241; 9 Tex. Civ. App. 599).

PASSIVE DEBTS. In the civil law. All the sums of which one is a debtor, as distinguished from "active debt,"—those which are owed to one; the terms being used in the same sense as "bills payable" and "bills receivable." The term "passive debt" is also used to indicate one upon which no interest is payable, as distinguished from "active debt,"—one which draws interest.

PASSIVE TRUST. See "Trust."

PASSIVE USE A permissive use (*q. v.*)

PASSPORT (Fr. *passer*, to pass, *port*, harbor or gate).

——**In Maritime Law.** A paper containing a permission from the neutral state to the captain or master of a ship or vessel to proceed on the voyage proposed. It usually contains his name and residence, the name, property, description, tonnage, and destination of the ship, the nature and quantity of the cargo, the place from whence it comes, and its destination, with such other matters as the practice of the place requires.

It is also called a "sea brief," or "sea letter." But Marshall distinguishes sea letter from passport, which latter, he says, is intended to protect the ship, while the former relates to the cargo, destination, etc. See Jacobsen, Sea Laws, 66, note. This document is indispensably necessary in time of war for the safety of every neutral vessel. Marsh. Ins. bk. 1, c. 9, § 6, 317, 406b.

A Mediterranean pass or protection against the Barbary powers. Jacobsen, Sea Laws, 66, note; Act Cong. 1796.

——**In International Law.** A document granted in time of war to protect persons or property from the general operation of hostilities. Wheaton, Int. Law, 475; 1 Kent, Comm. 161; 6 Wheat. (U. S.) 3.

An official letter of identification, given to travelers in most countries of continental Europe. These are intended to protect them on their journey from all molestation while they are obedient to the laws. Passports are also granted by the secretary of state to persons traveling abroad, certifying that they are citizens of the United States. 9 Pet. (U. S.) 692. See 1 Kent, Comm. 162, 182; Merlin, Repert.

PASTO (Spanish; from Lat. *pastus*, *q. v.*) In Spanish law. Feeding; pasture; a right of pasture. White, New Recop. bk. 2, tit. 1, c. 6, § 4.

PASTURES. Lands upon which beasts feed themselves. By a grant of pastures, the land itself passes. 1 Thomas, Co. Litt. 202.

PASTUS. The procuration or provision which feudal tenants were bound to make for their lords at certain times, or as often as they made a progress to their lands. It was often converted into money. Wharton.

PATEAT UNIVERSIS PER PRAESENtes. Know all men by these presents.

PATENT. A grant of some privilege, property, or authority, made by the government or sovereign of a country to one or more individuals. Phil. Pat. 1.

As the term was originally used in England, it signified certain written instruments emanating from the king, and sealed with the great seal. These instruments conferred grants of lands, honors, or franchises; they were called "letters patent," from being delivered open, and by way of contradistinction from instruments like the French *lettres de cachet*, which went out sealed.

In the United States the word "patent" is sometimes understood to mean the title deed by which a government, either state or federal, conveys its lands. But in its more usual acceptation it is understood as referring to those instruments by which the United States secures to inventors for a limited time the exclusive use of their own inventions.

PATENT AMBIGUITY. One arising from the words of an instrument, and hence obvious on its face before attempting to apply the words to the subject matter. See "Latent Ambiguity."

PATENT OF PRECEDENCE. Letters patent granted, in England, to such barristers as the crown thinks fit to honor with that mark of distinction, whereby they are entitled to such rank and preaudience as are assigned in their respective patents, which is sometimes next after the attorney general, but more usually next after her majesty's counsel then being. These rank promiscuously with the king's (or queen's) counsel, but are not the sworn servants of the crown. 3 Bl. Comm. 28; 3 Steph. Comm. 274.

PATENT RIGHT. A right of exclusive sale or manufacture secured by a patent.

PATENT ROLLS. In English law. Rolls containing the records of letters patent granted by the crown since the year 1516. The earlier of these records are deposited in the Tower, the others are in the Rolls' Chapel. Hubback, Ev. Success. 616, 617, where a particular description is given.

PATENT WRIT. In old practice. An open writ; one not closed or sealed up. See "Close Writs."

PATER (Lat.) A father; the father. In the civil law, this word sometimes included *avus* (grandfather). Dig. 50. 16. 201.

PATER-FAMILIAS (Lat.) In civil law. One who was *sui juris*, and not subject to the paternal power.

In order to give a correct idea of what was understood in the Roman law by this term, it is proper to refer briefly to the artificial organization of the Roman family,—the greatest moral phenomenon in the history of the human race. The comprehensive term *familia* embraced both persons and property. Money, lands, houses, slaves, children, all constituted part of this artificial family, this juridical entity, this legal patrimony, the title to which was exclusively vested in the chief or *pater-familias*, who alone was *capax dominii*, and who belonged to himself, *sui juris*.

The word *pater-familias* is by no means equivalent to the modern expression father of a family, but means "proprietor," in the strongest sense of that term. It is he, *qui in domo dominium habet*, in whom were centered all property, all power, all authority. He was, in a word, the lord and master whose authority was unlimited. No one but he who was *sui juris*, who was *pater-familias*, was capable of exercising any right of property, or wielding any superiority or power over anything, for nothing could belong to him who was himself *alieni juris*. Hence the children of the *filii-familias*, as well as those of slaves, belonged to the *pater-familias*. In the same manner, everything that was acquired by the sons or slaves formed a part of the *familia*, and, consequently, belonged to its chief. This absolute property and power of the *pater-familias* only ceased with his life, unless he voluntarily parted with them by a sale; for the alienation by sale is invariably the symbol resorted to for the purpose of dissolving the stern dominion of the *pater-familias* over those belonging to the *familia*. Thus, both emancipation and adoption are the results of imaginary sales,—*per imaginarias venditiones*. As the daughter remained in the family of her father, grandfather, or great-grandfather, as the case might be, notwithstanding her marriage, it followed as a necessary consequence that the child never belonged to the same family as its mother. There is no civil relationship between them; they are natural relations,—*cognati*,—but they are not legally related to each other,—*agnati*, and therefore the child never inherits from its mother, nor the mother from her child. There was, however, a means by which the wife might enter into the family and subject herself to the power of her husband, *in manu mariti*, and thereby establish a legal relationship between herself and her husband. This marital power of the husband over the wife was generally acquired either *coemptione*, by the purchase of the wife by the husband from the *pater-familias*, or *usu*, by the prescription based on the possession of one year,—the same by which the title to movable property was acquired according to the principles governing the *usucapio* (*usu capere*, to obtain by use). Another mode of obtaining the same end was the *confarreatio*, a sacred ceremony performed by the breaking and eating of a small cake, *farreum*, by the married couple. It was supposed that by an observance of this ceremony the marital power was produced by the intervention of the gods. This solemn mode of celebrating marriages was peculiar to the patrician families. By means of these fictions and ceremonies, the wife became, in the eye of the law, the daughter of her husband, and the sister of the children to whom she gave birth, who would otherwise have been strangers to her. Well might Gaius say, *Fere nulli alii sunt homines qui talem in liberos habeant potestatem, qualem nos habemus.*

This extraordinary organization of the Roman family, and the unlimited powers and authority vested in the *pater-familias*, continued until the reign of Justinian, who, by his 118th Novel, enacted on the 9th of August, 544, abolished the distinction between the *agnatio* and *cognatio*, and established the order of inheritance, which, with some modifications, continues to exist at the present day in all countries whose jurisprudence is based on the civil law. See "Patria Potestas."

PATER IS EST QUEM NUPTIAE DEmonstrant. The father is he whom the marriage points out. 1 Bl. Comm. 446; 7 Mart. (N. S.; La.) 548, 553; Dig. 2. 4. 5; 1 Bouv. Inst. notes 273, 304, 322; Broom, Leg. Max. (3d London Ed.) 458.

PATER PATRIAE. Father of the country. See "Parens Patriae."

PATERNA PATERNIS (Lat. the father's to the father's). In French law. An expression used to signify that, in a succession, the property coming from the father of the deceased descends to his paternal relations.

PATERNAL. That which belongs to the father or comes from him; as, paternal power, paternal relation, paternal estate, paternal line. See "Line."

PATERNAL POWER. The authority lawfully exercised by parents over their children. See "Father."

PATERNAL PROPERTY. That which descends or comes from the father and other ascendants or collaterals of the paternal stock. Domat, tit. 3, § 2, note 11.

PATERNITY. The state or condition of a father.

PATIBULATED. Hanged.

PATIBULUM. In old English law. A gallows or gibbet. Fleta, lib. 2, c. 3, § 9.

PATIENS. In the civil law, the passive party to a transaction. The correlative term is *agens*. See "Agent and Patient."

PATRIA (Lat.) The country; the men of the neighborhood competent to serve on a jury; a jury. This word is nearly synonymous with *pais (q. v.)*

PATRIA LABORIBUS ET EXPENSIS non debet fatigari. A jury ought not to be harassed by labors and expenses. Jenk. Cent. Cas. 6.

PATRIA POTESTAS (Lat.) In civil law. The paternal power; the authority which the law vests in the father over the persons and property of his legitimate children.

One of the effects of marriage is the paternal authority over the children born in wedlock. In the early period of the Roman history, the paternal authority was unlimited. The father had the absolute control over his children, and might even, as the domestic magistrate of his family, condemn them to death. They could acquire nothing except for the benefit of the *paterfamilias (q. v.)*, and they were even liable to be sold and reduced to slavery by the author of their existence. But in the progress of civilization, this stern rule was gradually relaxed. The voice of nature and humanity was listened to on behalf of the oppressed children of a cruel and heartless father. A passage in the 37th book (title 12, § 5) of the Pandects informs us that, in the year 870 of Rome, the emperor Trajan compelled a father to release his son from the paternal authority, on account of cruel treatment. The same emperor sentenced a father to transportation because he had killed his son in a hunting party, although the son had been guilty of adultery with his stepmother; for, says Marcianus, who reports the case, *patria potestas in pietate debet, non in atrocitate, consistere.* Ulpianus says that a father is not permitted to kill his son without a judgment from the prefect or the president of the province. In the year 981 of Rome, the emperor Alexander Severus addressed a constitution to a father, which is found in book 8, tit. 47, § 3, of the Justinian Code, in which he says: "Your paternal authority authorizes you to chastise your son, and, if he persists in his misconduct you may bring him before the president of the province, who will sentence him to such punishment as you may desire." In the same book and title of the Code we find a constitution of the emperor Constantine, dated in the year of Rome 1065, which inflicts the punishment denounced against parricide on the father who shall be convicted of having killed his son. The power of selling the child, which at first was unlimited, was also much restricted, and finally altogether abolished, by subsequent legislation, especially during the empire. Paulus, who wrote about the middle of the tenth century of Rome, informs us that the father could only sell his child in case of extreme poverty,—*contemplatione extremae necessitatis aut alimentarum gratia.* In 1039 of Rome, Diocletian and Maximian declare in a rescript that it is beyond doubt (*manifestissimi juris*) that a father can neither sell nor pledge nor donate his children. Constantine, in 1059, permitted the sale by the father of his child at its birth, and when forced to do so by abject poverty,—*propter nimiam paupertatem egestatemque victus;* and the same law is re-enacted in the Code of Justinian. Code, 4. 43. 2. 3.

The father, being bound to indemnify the party who had been injured by the offenses of his child, could release himself from this responsibility by an abandonment of the offender, in the same manner as the master could abandon his slave for a similar purpose,—*noxali causa mancipare.* This power of abandonment continued to exist, with regard to male children, up to the time of Gaius, in the year 925 of Rome. But by the Institutes of Justinian it is forbidden. Inst. 4. 8. 7.

With regard to the rights of the father to the property the child might acquire, it was originally as extensive and absolute as if it had been acquired by a slave. The child could possess nothing nor acquire anything that did not belong to the father. It is true, the child might possess a *peculium*, but of this he had only a precarious enjoyment, subject to the will and pleasure of the father. Under the first emperors, a distinction was made in favor of the son as to such property as had been acquired by him in the army, which was called *castrense peculium*, to which the son acquired a title in himself. Constantine extended this rule by applying it to such property as the child had acquired by services in offices held in the state, or by following a liberal profession. This was denominated *quasi castrense peculium.* He also created the *peculium adventitium*, which was composed of all property inherited by the son from his mother, whether by will or *ab intestat;* but the father had the usufruct of this *peculium.* Arcadius and Honorius extended it to everything the son acquired by succession or donations from his grandfather or mother or other ascendants in the maternal life. Theodosius and Valentinian embraced in it whatever was given by one of the spouses to the other, and Justinian included in it everything acquired by the son, except such as was produced by property belonging to the father himself. It is thus seen that, by the legislation of Justinian and his predecessors, the paternal power with regard to property was almost entirely destroyed.

The *pater-familias* had not only under his paternal power his own children, but also the children of his sons and grandsons,—in fact, all his descendants in the male line; and this authority continued in full force and vigor, no matter what might be the age of those subject to it. The highest offices in the government did not release the incumbent from the paternal authority. The victorious general or consul to whom the honors of a triumph were decreed by the senate was subject to the paternal power in the same manner and to the same extent as the humblest citizen. It is to be observed, however, that the domestic subjection did not interfere with the capacity of exercising the highest public functions in the state. The children of the daughter were not subject to the paternal authority of her father,—they entered into the family of her husband. Women could never exercise the paternal power. And even when a woman was herself *sui juris*, she could not exercise the paternal power. It is for this reason, Ulpian observes, that the family of which a woman, *sui juris*, was the head, *mater-familias*, commenced and ended with her,—*mulier autem familiae suae et caput et finis est*. 1 Ortolan, 191 et seq.

The modern civil law has hardly preserved any features of the old Roman jurisprudence concerning the paternal power. Article 233 of the Louisiana Code provides, it is true, that a child, whatever be its age, owes honor and respect to its father and mother; and the next article adds that the child remains under the authority of the father and mother until his majority or emancipation, and that, in case of a difference of opinion between the parents, the authority of the father shall prevail. In the succeeding article, obedience is enjoined on the child to the orders of the parents as long as he remains subject to the paternal authority. But article 236 renders the foregoing rules in a great measure nugatory, by declaring that "a child under the age of puberty cannot quit the paternal house without the permission of his father and mother, who have a right to correct him, provided it be done in a reasonable manner." So that the power of correction ceases with the age of fourteen for boys and twelve for girls. Nay, at these ages the children may leave the paternal roof in opposition to the will of their parents. It is seen that, by the modern law, the paternal authority is vested in both parents, but practically it is generally exercised by the father alone, for, wherever there is a difference of opinion, his will prevails. The great object to be attained by the exercise of the paternal power is the education of the children to prepare them for the battle of life, to make them useful citizens and respectable members of society. During the marriage, the parents are entitled to the enjoyment of the property of their minor children, subject to the obligation of supporting and educating them, and of paying the taxes, making the necessary repairs, etc. Donations made to minors are accepted by their parents or other ascendants. The father has under his control all actions which it may be necessary to bring for his minor children during the marriage. When the marriage is dissolved by the death of one of the spouses, the paternal power ceases, and the tutorship is opened; but the surviving parent is the natural tutor, and can at his death appoint a testamentary tutor to his minor children. See "Pater-Familias."

PATRIA POTESTAS IN PIETATE DEBet, non in atrocitate consistere. Paternal power should consist in affection, not in atrocity.

PATRICIDE. One guilty of killing his father. See "Parricide."

PATRICIUS. In Roman law. A nonhereditary title to nobility conferred by the emperor.

PATRIMONIAL. A thing which comes from the father, and, by extension, from the mother or other ancestor.

PATRIMONIUM. In civil law. That which is capable of being inherited.

Things capable of being possessed by a single person exclusively of all others are, in the Roman or civil law, said to be *in patrimonio;* when incapable of being so possessed, they are *extra patrimonium.*

Most things may be inherited; but there are some which are said to be *extra patrimonium,* or which are not in commerce. These are such as are common, as the light of heaven, the air, the sea, and the like; things public, as rivers, harbors, roads, creeks, ports, arms of the sea, the seashore, highways, bridges, and the like; things which belong to cities and municipal corporations, as public squares, streets, market houses, and the like. See 1 Bouv. Inst. notes 421-446.

PATRIMONY. Any kind of property; such estate as has descended in the same family; estates which have descended or been devised in a direct line from the father, and, by extension, from the mother or other ancestor.

The father's duty to take care of his children. Swinb. Wills, pt. 3, § 18, note 31, p. 235.

PATRIMUS (Lat. from *pater*, father. In the civil law. One who had a father living. Calv. Lex.; Spelman.

PATRINUS (Law Lat. from *pater*, father). In old ecclesiastical law. A godfather. Spelman.

PATROCINIUM (Lat.) In the Roman law. Patronage; protection; defense. The business or duty of a patron or advocate. See "Patronus."

PATRON.

——**In Ecclesiastical Law.** He who has the disposition and gift of an ecclesiastical benefice.

——**In Roman Law.** The former master of a freedman. Dig. 2. 4. 8. 1.

PATRONAGE. The right of appointing to office; as, the patronage of the president of the United States, if abused, may endanger the liberties of the people.

——**In Ecclesiastical Law.** The right of presentation to a church or ecclesiastical benefice. 2 Bl. Comm. 21.

PATRONATUS (Lat. from *patronus*, *q. v.*)

——**In the Roman Law.** The condition, relation, right, or duty of a patron.

——**In Ecclesiastical Law.** Patronage (*q. v.*)

PATRONUM FACIUNT DOS, AEDIFICAtio, fundus. Endowment, building, and land make a patron. Dod. Adv. 7.

PATRONUS (Lat.) In Roman law. A modification of the Latin word *pater*, father. A denomination applied by Romulus to the first senators of Rome, and which they always afterwards bore. Romulus at first appointed a hundred of them. Seven years afterwards, in consequence of the association of Tatius to the Romans, a hundred more were appointed, chosen from the Sabines. Tarquinius Priscus increased the number to three hundred. Those appointed by Romulus and Tatius were called *patres majorum gentium*, and the others were called *patres minorum gentium*. These and their descendants constituted the nobility of Rome. The rest of the people were called the "plebeians," every one of whom was obliged to choose one of these fathers as his patron. The relation thus constituted involved important consequences. The plebeian, who was called *cliens* (a client), was obliged to furnish the means of maintenance to his chosen patron, to furnish a portion for his patron's daughters, to ransom him and his sons, if captured by an enemy, and pay all sums recovered against him by judgment of the courts. The patron, on the other hand, was obliged to watch over the interests of his client, whether present or absent, to protect his person and property, and especially to defend him in all actions brought against him for any cause. Neither could accuse or bear testimony against the other, or give contrary votes, etc. The contract was of a sacred nature; the violation of it was a sort of treason, and punishable as such. According to Cicero (De Repub. ii. 9), this relation formed an integral part of the governmental system, *Et habuit plebem in clientelas principum descriptum*, which he affirms was eminently useful. Blackstone traces the system of vassalage to this ancient relation of patron and client. It was, in fact, of the same nature as the feudal institutions of the middle ages, designed to maintain order in a rising state by a combination of the opposing interests of the aristocracy and of the common people, upon the principle of reciprocal bonds for mutual interests. Dumazeau, Barreau Romain, § iii. Ultimately, by force of radical changes in the institution, the word *patronus* came to signify nothing more than an advocate. Id. iv.

PATROON. In old New York law. The lord of a manor.

PATRUELIS (Lat.) In civil law. A cousin german by the father's side; the son or daughter of a father's brother. Dig. 38. 10. 1.

PATRUUS (Lat.) In civil law. An uncle by the father's side; a father's brother. Dig. 38. 10. 10. *Patruus magnus* is a grandfather's brother,—grand uncle. *Patruus major* is a great-grandfather's brother. *Patruus maximus* is a great-grandfather's father's brother.

PAUPER. One so poor that he must be supported at the public expense.

A person who, being unable to support himself or herself and his or her children, applies to the public authorities for relief, becomes by so doing a pauper. 159 Ill. 500. 12 Metc. (Mass.) 35; Garland v. Dover, 19 Me. 44; Clinton v. York, 26 Me. 167; Green v. Brookfield, 3 Greenl. 136; East Haddam v. Lyme, 14 Cow. 394; Northfield v. Roxbury, 15 Vt. 622.

PAUPERIES (Lat.) In civil law. Poverty. In a technical sense, *damnum absque injuria, i. e.*, a damage done without wrong on the part of the doer; *e. g.*, damage done by an irrational being, as an animal. L. 1, § 3, D. *si quod paup. fec.*; Vicat; Calv. Lex.

PAVIAGE. A contribution or tax for paving streets or highways.

PAWN. A pledge. A pledge includes, in Louisiana, a pawn and an antichresis; but sometimes pawn is used as the general word, including pledge and antichresis. Civ. Code La. art. 3101; Hennen, Dig. "Pledge."

PAWNBROKER. One whose business it is to lend money, usually in small sums, upon pawn or pledge.

PAWNEE. He who receives a pawn or pledge.

PAWNOR. One who, being liable to an engagement, gives to the person to whom he is liable a thing to be held as a security for the payment of his debt or the fulfillment of his liability.

PAX (Lat.) In old English law. Peace; the peace. A state of order and quiet, in the preservation of which the whole community was concerned; otherwise called the "king's peace" (*pax regis*), he being the principal conservator of the peace of the kingdom. 1 Bl. Comm. 268, 349, 350. *Quod pax nostra teneatur*, that our peace be maintained. Magna Carta, 9 Hen. III. c. 35. The term occurs also in feudal law. Feud. Lib. 2, tits. 27, 53.

Freedom from molestation by another. Fleta, lib. 2, c. 51, §§ 2, 3.

The privilege of a member of a legislative assembly. See 1 Bl. Comm. 165.

PAX ECCLESIAE (Law Lat.) In old English law. The peace of the church. See "Peace of God and the Church."

A particular privilege attached to a church; sanctuary (*q. v.*) Crabb, Hist. Eng. Law, 41; Cowell.

PAX REGIS (Lat.) The peace of the king. That peace or security for life and goods which the king promises to all persons under his protection. Bracton, lib. 3, c. 11; 6 Rich. II. st. 1, c. 13.

In ancient times there were certain limits which were known by this name. The *pax regis*, or verge of the court, as it was afterwards called, extended from the palace gate to the distance of three miles, three furlongs, three acres, nine feet, nine palms, and nine barleycorns (Crabb, Com. Law, 41); or from the four sides of the king's residence, four miles, three furlongs, nine acres in breadth, nine feet, nine barleycorns, etc. (LL. Edw. Conf. c. 12 et LL. Hen. I.)

PAYABLE. A sum of money is said to be payable when a person is under an obligation to pay it. "Payable" may therefore signify an obligation to pay at a future time, but, when used without qualification, "payable" means that the debt is payable at once, as opposed to "owing." 2 Ch. Div. 103.

PAYEE. The person in whose favor a note or bill of exchange is made payable.

PAYMENT. The fulfillment of a promise, or the performance of an agreement.

The discharge in money of a sum due.

In its most general sense, the rendition by the person under an obligation (68 Cal. 41) to the person to whom the same is due, or one lawfully authorized to represent him (6 How. Pr. [N. Y.] 161), of the exact act or thing required by such obligation (23 La. Ann. 84; 3 Duer [N. Y.] 441; 1 Cush. [Mass.] 76), with the assent of both parties that the same is rendered and received in satisfaction of such obligation, and not for another purpose (50 Mich. 112; 6 Heisk. [Tenn.] 131).

In a more restricted sense, payment is the rendition of a sum of money due. As so used, payment in cash is implied, and the giving of a note or check is not payment. 26 Conn. 487; 70 Iowa, 406; 42 N. Y. 538.

PAYMENT INTO COURT. Deposit of a sum of money with a proper officer of court for the benefit of the adverse party, and by way of a continuing tender thereof to him in answer to his claim.

PAYS. Country. Trial *per pays*, trial by jury (the country). See "Pais."

PEACE (Law Fr. *peas, pees;* Lat. *pax*). Quiet, orderly behavior; the quiet, orderly behavior of the citizens or subjects of a community towards one another, and towards the government, which is said to be broken by acts of a certain kind. See "Breach of Peace." Defined in the old books, "a quiet and harmless behavior toward the king and his people." Lambard, Eiren, lib. 1, c. 2; Cowell.

PEACE OF GOD AND THE CHURCH. The freedom from suits at law between the terms. Spelman; Jacob.

PECCATA CONTRA NATURAM SUNT gravissima. Offenses against nature are the heaviest. 3 Inst. 20.

PECCATUM PECCATO ADDIT QUI CULpae quam facit patrocinium defensionis adjungit. He adds one offense to another who, when he commits a crime, joins to it the protection of a defense. 5 Coke, 49.

PECK. A measure of capacity, equal to two gallons. See "Measure."

PECORA (Lat.; pl. of *pecus*). In the Roman law. Cattle; beasts. The term included all quadrupeds that fed in flocks. Dig. 32. 65. 4.

PECULATION.

——**In Civil Law.** The unlawful appropriation, by a depositary of public funds, of the property of the government intrusted to his care, to his own use or that of others. Domat, Supp. au. Dr. Pub. lib. 3, tit. 5.

——**In American Law.** An offense defined by statute in New York, essentially the same as in the civil law.

PECULATUS. In the civil law. The offense of stealing or embezzling the public money. Hence the common English word "peculation;" but "embezzlement" is the proper legal term. 4 Bl. Comm. 121, 122.

PECULIAR. In ecclesiastical law. A parish or church in England which has jurisdiction of ecclesiastical matters within itself, and independent of the ordinary.

They may be either:

(1) Royal, which include the sovereign's free chapels.

(2) Of the archbishops, excluding the jurisdiction of the bishops and archdeacons.

(3) Of the bishops, excluding the jurisdiction of the bishop of the diocese in which they are situated.

(4) Of the bishops in their own diocese, excluding archdiaconal jurisdiction.

(5) Of deans, deans and chapters, prebendaries, and the like, excluding the bishop's jurisdiction in consequence of ancient compositions.

The court of peculiars has jurisdiction of causes arising in such of these peculiars as are subject to the metropolitan of Canterbury. In other peculiars the jurisdiction is exercised by commissaries. 1 Phillim. Ecc. Law, 202, note 245; Skin. 589; 3 Bl. Comm. 65.

PECULIUM (Lat.) In civil law. The most ancient kind of *peculium* was the *peculium profectitium* of the Roman law, which signified that portion of the property acquired by a son or slave which the father or master allowed him, to be managed as he saw fit. In modern civil law there are other kinds of *peculium*, viz., *peculium castrense*, which includes all movables given to a son by relatives and friends on his going on a campaign, all the presents of comrades, and his military pay and the things bought with it; *peculium quasi castrense*, which includes all acquired by a son by performing the duties of a public or spiritual office or of an advocate, and also gifts from the reigning prince; *peculium adventitium*, which includes the property of son's mother and relatives on that side of the house, and all which comes to him on a second marriage of his parents, and, in general, all his acquisitions which do not come from his father's property, and do not come under *castrense* or *quasi castrense peculium.*

The *peculium profectitium* remains the property of the father. The *peculium castrense* and *quasi castrense* are entirely the property of the son. The *peculium adventitium* belongs to the son, but he cannot alien it nor dispose of it by will; nor can the father, unless under peculiar circumstances, alien it without consent of son. Mackeld. Civ. Law, §§ 557-559; Vicat; Inst. 2. 9. 1; Dig. 15. 1. 5. 3; Poth. ad Pand. lib. 50, tit. 17, c. 2, art. 3.

PECULIUM CASTRENSE. That property which a minor son who was in the army might hold by reason thereof, or which he acquired in war.

PECUNIA (Lat.) In civil law. Property, real or personal, corporeal or incorporeal. Things in general, *omnes res.* So the law of the Twelve Tables said, *uti quisque paterfamilias legasset super pecunia tutelave rei suae, ita jus esto,* in whatever manner a father of a family may have disposed of his property, or of the tutorship of his things, let this dispostion be law. 1 Lec. Elm. 288. But Paulus (liber 5, D. de Verb. Signif.) gives it a narrower sense than *res,* which he says means what is not included within patrimony; *pecunia* what is. Vicat. In a still narrower sense, it means those things only which have measure, weight, and number and most usually strictly money. Id. The general sense of property occurs, also, in the old English law. Leg. Edw. Confess. c. 10.

Flocks were the first riches of the ancients; and it is from *pecus* that the words *pecunia, peculium,* and *peculatus* are derived. In old English law, *pecunia* often retains the force of *pecus.* So often in Domesday Book,—*pastura ibidem pecuniae villae, i. e.,* pasture for cattle of the village. So *vivae pecuniae,* live stock. Leg. Edw. Confess. c. 10; Emendat. Willielmi Primi ad Leges Edw. Confess.; Cowell.

PECUNIA CONSTITUTA. In Roman law. Money owing (even upon a moral obligation) upon a day being fixed (*constituta*) for its payment became recoverable upon the implied promise to pay on that day, in an action called "*de pecunia constituta,*" the implied promise not amounting (of course) to a *stipulatio.*

PECUNIA DICITUR A PECUS, OMNES enim veterum divitiae in animalibus consistebant. Money (*pecunia*) is so called from cattle (*pecus*), because all the wealth of our ancestors consisted in cattle. Co. Litt. 207.

PECUNIA NONNUMERATA (Lat.) Money not paid or numbered. The *exception nonnumeratae pecuniae* (plea of money not paid) is allowed to the principal or surety by the creditor. Calv. Lex.

PECUNIA NUMERATA (Lat.) Money given in payment of a debt. Properly used of the creditor, who is properly said to number, *i. e.,* count out, the money to the debtor which he must pay, and improperly of the debtor, who is said to number or count out the money to the creditor, *i. e.,* to pay it. Vicat; Calv. Lex.

PECUNIA SEPULCHRALIS. Money anciently paid to the priest at the opening of a grave for the good of the deceased's soul.

PECUNIA TRAJECTITIA (Lat.) A loan of money which, either itself or in the shape of goods bought with it, is to be carried over the sea, the lender to take the risk from the commencement of voyage till arrival at port of destination, and on that account to have higher interest; which interest is not essential to the contract, but, if reserved, is called *foenus nauticum.* Mackeld. Civ. Law, § 398b. The term *foenus nauticum* is sometimes applied to the transaction as well as the interest, making it coextensive with *pecunia trajectitia*.

PECUNIARY. That which relates to money.

PECUNIARY CAUSES. Causes in ecclesiastical courts where satisfaction is sought for withholding ecclesiastical dues, or the doing or neglecting some act connected with the church. 3 Bl. Comm. 88. For what causes are ecclesiastical, see 2 Burn, Ecc. Law, 39.

PECUNIARY LEGACY. A bequest of money.

PECUNIARY LOSS. A loss of money, or of that by which money or something of money value may be acquired. 32 Barb. (N. Y.) 33.

PECUS (Lat.; pl. *pecudes*). In the Roman law. Cattle; a beast. Under a bequest of *pecudes* were included oxen and other beasts of burden. Dig. 32. 81. 2.

PEDAGIUM, or **PEDAGE** (Lat. from *pes*, foot). Money paid for passing by foot or horse through any forest or country. Pupilla Oculi, p. 9, c. 7; Cassan de Coutum. Burgund. p. 118; Rot. Vasc. 22 Edw. III. m. 34.

PEDANEUS (Lat. from *pes*, foot). In the Roman law. On, or at the foot; occupying a low position. A term applied to the *judices* appointed by the praetor to determine causes; either from their not occupying a tribunal or elevated seat, or because they were occupied with small or less important causes. See "Judex Pedaneus."

PEDAULUS (Lat. from *pes*, foot). In civil law. A judge who sat at the foot of the tribunal, *i. e.*, on the lowest seats, ready to try matters of little moment at command of praetor. Calv. Lex.; Vicat.

PEDDLER. A word is commonly used to describe one who travels about retailing small wares. It carries the idea of pettiness as respects the character of the business transacted. The original root of the word is "ped," meaning "basket" in old English and descriptive of the receptacle in which a peddler carries his goods about for sale. 65 Conn. 292. See "Pedlars."

PEDE PULVEROSUS. In old English and Scotch law. Dusty foot. A term applied to itinerant merchants, chapmen, or peddlers who attended fairs. "Ane merchand or cremar quha hes ne certaine dwelling place quhair the dust may be dicht fra his feet or schone." Skene de Verb. Sign.

PEDEM PONERE. (L. Lat.) In civil and old English law. To put or place the foot. A figurative expression used to denote the taking possession of lands; which was done by standing upon or walking over them, or symbolically by merely placing the foot upon the ground. Britt. cc. 35, 36, 42, 43.

PEDIGREE. A succession of degrees from the origin. It is the state of the family as far as regards the relationship of the different members, their births, marriages, and deaths. This term is applied to persons or families who trace their origin or descent.

PEDIS ABSCISSIO (Lat.) In old criminal law. The cutting off a foot; a punishment anciently inflicted instead of death. Fleta, lib. 1, c. 38.

PEDIS POSITIO (Lat. a planting or placing of the foot). A term used to denote an actual corporal possession. *Possessio est quasi pedis positio*, possession is, as it were, a planting of the foot. 3 Coke, 42; 8 Johns. (N. Y.) per Kent, C. J.; 5 Pa. St. 303; 2 Nev. & M. 343. See "Pedis Possessio."

PEDIS POSSESSIO (Lat.) A foothold; an actual possession. To constitute adverse possession, there must be *pedis possessio*, or a substantial inclosure. 2 Bouv. Inst. note 2193; 2 Nott. & McC. (S. C.) 343.

PEDLARS. Persons who travel about the country with merchandise for the purpose of selling it.

One is a pedlar who carries his goods about the country for sale by public conveyance. 4 Barn. & A. 510.

One who solicits orders by sample for one who ships the same from an established place of business is not a pedlar. 34 Kan. 434.

Persons, except those peddling newspapers, Bibles, or religious tracts, who sell, or offer to sell, at retail, goods, wares, or other commodities, traveling from place to place, in the street, or through different parts of the country. Act Cong. July 1, 1862. See "Peddler."

PEERS (Lat. *pares*). The vassals of a lord; the freeholders of a neighborhood, before whom livery of seisin was to be made, and before whom, as the jury of the county, trials were had. 2 Bl. Comm. 316. Trial by a man's peers or equals is one of the rights reserved by *Magna Charta*. 4 Bl. Comm. 349. These vassals were called *pares curiae* (*q. v.*) 1 Washb. Real Prop. 23. One's equals in rank and condition.

The nobility of England, who, though of different ranks, viz., dukes, marquises, earls, viscounts, and barons, yet are equal in their privilege of sitting and voting in the house of lords; hence they are called "peers of the realm." They are created by writ summoning them to attend the house of lords by the title intended to be given, or by letters patent directly conferring the dignity. The former is the more ancient way, but the grant by patent is more certain. See Sullivan, Lect. 19a; 1 Wooddeson, Lect. 37.

Peers are tried by their peers in cases of treason, felony, and misprision of the same. In cases of treason, felony, and breach of the peace, they have no privilege from arrest. 1 Bl. Comm. 401*, note 11.

Bishops who sit in parliament are peers; but the word "spiritual" is generally added: *e. g.*, "lords temporal and spiritual." 1 Bl. Comm. 401*, note 12.

PEERS OF FEES. Vassals or tenants of the same lord, who were obliged to serve and attend him in his courts, being equal in function. These were termed "peers of fees," because holding fees of the lord, or because their business in court was to sit and judge, under their lords, of disputes arising upon fees; but, if there were too many in one lordship, the lord usually chose twelve, who had the title of peers, by way of distinction; whence, it is said, we derive our common juries and other peers. Cowell.

PEGGED. See "Gambling Contract."

PEINE FORTE ET DURE (Law Fr.) In English law. A punishment formerly inflicted in England on a person who, being arraigned of felony, refused to plead and put himself on his trial, and stubbornly stood mute; the purpose of standing mute being, of course, to avoid the confiscation of estate which would follow on conviction. He was to be laid down, naked, on his back, on the ground, his feet, head, and loins covered, his arms and legs drawn apart by cords, and as much weight of iron or stone as he could bear placed on his chest. He was to have the next day three morsels of barley bread, without drink; the next, three draughts, as much each time as he could drink, of the nearest stagnant water to the prison, without bread; and such was to be his diet on alternate days till he died. It was vulgarly called "pressing to death." 2 Reeve, Hist. Eng. Law, 134; 4 Bl. Comm. 324; Cowell; Britt. c. 4, fol. 11*. This punishment was introduced between 31 Edw. III. and 8 Hen. IV. 4 Bl. Comm. 324; Y. B. 8 Hen. IV. 1. Standing mute was now,, by statute, in England, equivalent to a confession or a verdict of guilty 12 Geo. III. c. 20. Subsequently it was provided that where the accused stood mute, the court might record a plea of "Not guilty," and such plea would have the same effect as if it had been made by the accused. 7 and 8 Geo. IV, c. 28, s. 2. See "Standing Mute."

The only instance in which this punishment has ever been inflicted in this country is that of Giles Cory, of Salem, who refused to plead when arraigned for witchcraft. Washb. Jud. Hist. 142; 1 Chand. Am. Crim. Tr. 122.

PELLEX (Lat.) In the Roman law. A concubine. Dig. 50. 16. 144.

PELLS, CLERK OF THE. An officer in the English exchequer, who entered every seller's bill on the parchment rolls, the roll of receipts, and the roll of disbursements.

PENAL (from Lat. *poenalis*, from *poena*, punishment or penalty). Enacting punishment. Webster. Imposing a punishment or penalty. See "Penal Statutes."

Connected with a penalty, either as the object or consequence of an action.

PENAL ACTION. An action for recovery of statute penalty; "penalty" in this case being used in its narrowest sense of a pecuniary punishment for a noncriminal act. 3 Steph. Comm. 535. See Hawk. P. C. "Informatio." It is distinguished from a popular or *qui tam* action, in which the action is brought by the informer, to whom part of the penalty goes. A penal action or information is brought by an officer, and the penalty goes to the king. 1 Chit. Gen. Prac. 25, note; 2 Archb. Prac. 188.

PENAL BILL. The old name for a bond with condition, by which a person is bound to pay a certain sum of money or do a certain act, or, in default thereof, pay a certain sum of money by way of penalty. Jacob, "Bill."

PENAL LAWS. Laws imposing a penalty; the term being used, like "penalty," in several senses.

PENAL STATUTES. Those which inflict a penalty for the violation of some of their provisions.

PENAL SUM. A sum payable as a penalty. Usually applied to the sum fixed by a bond to be paid on breach of its condition.

PENALTY. The punishment inflicted by law for an illegal act. The term is used loosely to embrace all the consequences visited by law on those who violate police regulations. 26 Mich. 482.

In a narrower sense it is confined to pecuniary penalties. "The terms fine, forfeiture and penalty are often used loosely and even confusedly. But when a discrimination is made, the word 'penalty' is found to be generic in its character, including both fine and forfeiture." 4 Iowa, 300.

In its narrowest sense, it includes only pecuniary punishment imposed by statute for such unlawful acts as do not constitute crimes or which are for this purpose regarded in other than their criminal aspect.

——**In Contracts.** A clause in an agreement, by which the obligor agrees to pay a certain sum of money if he shall fail to fulfill the contract contained in another clause of the same agreement.

A penal obligation differs from an alternative obligation, for this is but one in its essence; while a penalty always includes two distinct engagements, and when the first is fulfilled the second is void.

When a breach has taken place, the obligor has his option to require the fulfillment of the first obligation, or the payment of the penalty, in those cases which cannot be relieved in equity, when the penalty is considered as liquidated damages.

PENANCE. In ecclesiastical law. An ecclesiastical punishment inflicted by an ecclesiastical court for some spiritual offense. Ayliffe, Par. 420.

PENDENCY. The state of being pending or undecided.

PENDENS (Lat. from *pendere*, to hang). Hanging; pending. See "Lis Pendens."

PENDENTE LITE (Lat.) Pending the continuance of an action while litigation continues. See "Lis Pendens."

PENDENTE LITE NIHIL INNOVETUR. During a litigation, nothing should be changed. Co. Litt. 344. See 20 How. (U. S.) 106; Cross, Liens, 140; 1 Story, Eq. Jur. § 406; 2 Johns. Ch. (N. Y.) 441; 6 Barb. (N. Y.) 33.

PENDENTES (Lat.) In civil law. The fruits of the earth not yet separated from the ground; the fruits hanging by the roots. Ersk. Inst. bk. 2, lib. 2, § 4.

PENDING. As applied to judicial proceedings, remaining undecided (4 N. H. 386), and an action has been held to be pending till the judgment is satisfied (41 N. Y. 159).

PENETRATION. In criminal law. In rape and some other sexual crimes, actual carnal knowledge is requisite, but the slightest penetration is sufficient (102 N. Y. 234), it being enough if any part of the virile member be within the labia of the pudendum (1 Car. & K. 393). Rupture of the hymeneal membrane is not requisite, though, in the absence of such rupture, proof of penetration should be clear. 8 Car. & P. 641.

PENITENTIARY. A prison in which persons convicted of serious offenses (felonies), or sentenced for long terms of imprisonment, are confined.

PENNYWEIGHT. A troy weight which weighs twenty-four grains, or one-twentieth part of an ounce.

PENSA (Law Lat. from Lat. *pendere, to* weigh).

——**In Old English Law.** A weight. *Ad pensam*, by weight. The ancient way of paying into the exchequer as much money for a pound of sterling as weighed twelve ounces troy. Lowndes' Essay upon Coin, 4; Cowell. This was distinguished from payment *de numero*, by count.

——**In Old Records.** A wey (weigh) of salt or cheese, containing two hundred and fifty-six pounds. Cowell.

PENSIO (Lat. from *pendere*).

——**In the Civil Law.** A payment, properly, for the use of a thing. Calv. Lex.

A rent; a payment for the use and occupation of another's house. Calv. Lex.

PENSION. A stated and certain allowance granted by the government to an individual, or those who represent him, for valuable services performed by him for the country. It is sometimes loosely used in the sense of "annuity."

——**In Spanish Law.** Rent; a rent, White, New Recop. bk. 2, c. 2, § 3.

PENSIONER. One who is supported by an allowance at the will of another. It is more usually applied to him who receives an annuity or pension from the government.

PEONAGE. The holding of any person to service or labor against his will. Prohibited by U. S. Rev. St. § 1990.

PEONIA. In Spanish law. A portion of land which was formerly given to a simple soldier on the conquest of a country. It is now a quantity of land of different size in different provinces. In the Spanish possessions in America, it measured fifty feet front and one hundred feet deep. 2 White, Coll. 49; 12 Pet. (U. S.) 444, notes.

PEOPLE. A state; as, the people of the state of New York. A nation in its collective and political capacity. 4 Term R. 783. See 6 Pet. (U. S.) 467.

The word "people" occurs in a policy of marine insurance. The insurer insures against "detainments of all kings, princes, and people." He is not by this understood to insure against any promiscuous or lawless rabble which may be guilty of attacking or detaining a ship. 2 Marsh. Ins. 508. See "Body Politic;" "Nation."

PEPPERCORN. A dried pepper berry. In England, the payment of a peppercorn is sometimes stipulated where a nominal consideration is intended.

PER. In Latin phrases. A preposition meaning by or through.

PER AES ET LIBRAM (Lat. *aes*, brass, *libram*, scale). In civil law. A sale was said to be made *per aes et libram* when one called *libripens* held a scale (*libra*), which the one buying struck with a brazen coin (*aes*), and said, "I say, by the right of a Roman, this thing is mine," and gave the coin to the vendor, in presence of at least three witnesses. This kind of sale was used in the emancipation of a son or slave and in making a will. Calv. Lex. "Mancipatio;" Vicat, "Mancipatio."

PER ALLUVIONEM (Lat.) In civil law. By alluvion, or the gradual and imperceptible increase arising from deposit by water. Vocab. Jur. Utr. "Alluvio;" Angell & A. Watercourses, 53-57.

PER ALLUVIONEM ID VIDETUR ADJICI, quad ita paulatim adjicitur, ut intelligere non possumus quantum quoquo momento temporis adjiciatur. That is said to be added by alluvion which is so added little by little that we cannot tell how much is added at any one moment of time. Dig. 41. 1. 7. 1; Hale de Jur. Mar. par. 1, c. 4; Fleta, lib. 3, c. 2, § 6.

PER AND CUI. When a writ of entry is brought against a second alienee or descendant from the disseisor, it is said to be in the *per* and *cui*, because the form of the writ is that the tenant had not entry but by and under a prior alienee, to whom the intruder himself demised it. 2 Bl. Comm. 181.

PER AND POST. To come in in the *per* is to claim by or through the person last entitled to an estate; as the heirs or assigns of the grantee. To come in in the *post* is to claim by a paramount and prior title; as the lord by escheat.

PER ANNULUM ET BACULUM (Lat.) In ecclesiastical law. The symbolical investiture of an ecclesiastical dignity was *per annulum et baculum, i. e.*, by staff and crosier. 1 Bl. Comm. 378, 379; 1 Burn, Ecc. Law, 209.

PER ANNUM (Lat.) By the year; for the space of a year. Fleta, lib. 2, c. 71, §§ 3-12. A common expression still in use.

PER AUTRE VIE (Law Fr.) For or during another's life.

PER AVERSIONEM (Lat.) In civil law. By turning away. Applied to a sale not by measure or weight, but for a single price for the whole in gross; *e. g.*, a sale of all the wine of a vineyard for a certain price. Vocab. Jur. Utr. "Aversio." Some derive the meaning of the phrase from a turning away of the risk of a deficiency in the quantity from the seller to the buyer; others, from turning away the head, *i. e.*, failure to make a particular examination; others think *aversio* is for *adversio*. Calv. Lex.; 2 Kent, Comm. 640; 4 Kent, Comm. 517.

PER BOUCHE (L. Fr.) By the mouth; orally. 3 How. St. Trials, 1024.

PER CAPITA (Lat. by the head or polls). When descendants take as individuals, and not by right of representation (*per stirpes*), they are said to take *per capita*. For example, if a legacy be given to the issue of A. B. and A. B., at the time of his death, shall have two children and two grandchildren, his estate shall be divided into four parts, and the children and grandchildren shall each have one of them. 3 Ves. 257; 13 Ves. 344; 2 Bl. Comm. 218; 6 Cush. (Mass.) 158, 162; 2 Jarm. Wills (Perkins' Notes) 47; 3 Beav. Rolls, 451; 4 Beav. Rolls, 239; 2 Steph. Comm. 253; 3 Steph. Comm. 197; 2 Wooddeson, Lect. 114. See "Capitation."

PER CONSEQUENS. By consequence; consequently. Y. B. M. 9 Edw. III. 8.

PER CONSIDERATIONEM CURIAE. In old practice. By the consideration (judgment) of the court. Y. B. M. 1 Edw. II. 2.

PER CURIAM (Lat. by the court). A phrase which occurs in all the reports. It is sometimes translated. See 3 Barb. (N. Y.) 353.

PER EUNDEM. By the same. This phrase is commonly used to express "by, or from the mouth of, the same judge." So "*per eundem in eadem*" means "by the same judge in the same case."

PER EXTENSUM. In old practice. At length.

PER FORMAM DONI (Lat by the form of the gift.) According to the line of descent prescribed in the conveyance of the ancestor or donor of estate tail. 2 Bl. Comm. 113*; 3 Har. & J. (Md.) 323; 1 Washb. Real Prop. 74, 81.

PER FRAUDEM (Lat.) A replication to a plea where something has been pleaded which would be a discharge if it had been honestly pleaded that such a thing has been obtained by fraud; for example, where, on debt on a statute, the defendant pleads a prior action depending, if such action has been commenced by fraud, the plaintiff may reply *per fraudem*. 2 Chit. Pl. *675.

PER INCURIAM. Through inadvertence. 35 Eng. Law & Eq. 302.

PER INFORTUNIUM (Lat. by misadventure). In criminal law. Homicide *per infortunium*, or by misadventure, is said to take place when a man in doing a lawful act, without any intent to hurt, unfortunately kills another. Hawk. P. C. bk. 1, c. 11; Fost. Crim. Law, 258, 259; 3 Inst. 56.

PER LEGEM ANGLIAE. By the law of England; by the curtesy. Fleta, lib. 2, c. 54, § 18.

PER LEGEM TERRAE (Lat.) By the law of the land; by indictment or presentment of good and lawful men. 7 Ill. 519.

PER METAS ET BUNDAS (Law Lat.) old English law. By metes and bounds.

PER MINAS (Lat. by threats). When a man is compelled to enter into a contract by threats or menaces, either for fear of loss of life or mayhem, he may avoid it afterwards. 1 Bl. Comm. 131; Bac. Abr. "Duress," "Murder" (A). See "Duress."

PER MISADVENTURE (Lat. and Eng.) In old English law. By mischance. 4 Bl. Comm. 182. The same with *per infortunium (q. v.)*

PER MY ET PER TOUT (Law Fr. by the moiety, or half, and by the whole). The mode in which joint tenants hold the joint estate, the effect of which, technically considered, is that for purposes of tenure and survivorship each is the holder of the whole, but for purposes of alienation each has only his own share, which is presumed in law to be equal. 1 Washb. Real Prop. 406; 2 Bl. Comm. 182.

——**In partnerships.** Each partner has a joint interest in the whole but not a separate interest in any particular part of the partnership property; and being so possessed, and because the title of partners is undivided, it follows that all have a moiety or the same species of interest in the stock in trade, whether each individual partner contributes exactly in the same proportion or not. But their several degrees of interest must be regulated according to the stipulated proportions and the different conditions of the partnership. 213 Ill. 480; 80 Ill. 300.

PER PROCURATION. By proxy; by letter of attorney. Used in connection with the signature of an agent or attorney in fact. It is notice that the agent has but a limited authority to sign. Byles, Bills, 33. Commonly abbreviated "*per proc.*"

The term is little used in the United States, though it has been adopted by the negotiable instrument laws. Neg. Inst. Law, § 40.

PER QUAE SERVITIA. A real action by which the grantee of a seigniory could compel the tenants of the grantor to attorn to himself. Shep. Touch. 254. It was abolished by St. 3 & 4 Wm. IV. c. 27, § 35.

PER QUOD. By which. Used in common-law pleading to introduce a conclusion. Sometimes used as the name of the clause averring special damages.

PER QUOD CONSORTIUM AMISIT (Lat. by which he lost her company). If a man's wife is so injured that thereby he loses her company and assistance for any time, he has a separate remedy by an action of trespass (in the nature of an action on the case) *per quod consortium amisit*, in which he shall recover satisfaction in damages. 3 Bl. Comm. 140; Cro. Jac. 501, 538; 1 Chit. Gen. Prac. 59.

PER QUOD SERVITIUM AMISIT (Lat. by which he lost her or his service). Where a servant has been so beaten or injured that his or her services are lost to the master, the master has an action of trespass *vi et armis, per quod servitium amisit*, in which he must allege and prove the special damage he has sustained. 3 Bl. Comm. 142. This action is commonly brought by the father for the seduction of his daughter, in which case very slight evidence of the relation of master and servant is necessary; but still some loss of service, or some expense, must be shown. 5 East, 45; 6 East, 391; 11 East, 23; T. Raym. 459; 3 Wils. 18; 2 Term R. 4; 5 Bos. & P. 466; Peake, 253; 1 Starkie, 287; 2 Starkie, 493; 3 Esp. 119; 5 Price, 641; 11 Ga. 603; 15 Barb. (N. Y.) 279; 18 Barb. (N. Y.) 212; 8 N. Y. 191; 11 N. Y. 343; 14 N. Y. 413; 20 Pa. St. 354; 5 Md. 211; 1 Wis. 209; 3 Sneed (Tenn.) 29.

PER RATIONES PERVENITUR AD LEgitimam rationem. By reasoning we come to legal reason. Litt. § 386.

PER RERUM NATURAM, FACTUM NEgantis nulla probatio est. It is in the nature of things that he who denies a fact is not bound to give proof.

PER SALTUM (Lat.) By a leap or bound; by a sudden movement; passing over certain proceedings. "The parties have proceeded *per saltum.*" Lord Ellenborough, 8 East, 511.

PER SE. By itself; of itself. Fraud *per se*. 3 Pick. (Mass.) 257.

PER SERVITIUM. (L. Lat.) By the service.

PER STIRPES (Lat. *stirps*, trunk or root of a tree or race). By or according to stocks or roots; by right of representation. Gen. St. Mass. 1860; c. 9, § 12; 6 Cush. (Mass.) 158, 162; 2 Bl. Comm. 217, 218; 2 Steph. Comm. 253; 2 Wooddeson, Lect. 114, 115; 2 Kent, Comm. 425.

PER TOTAM CURIAM. By the whole court.

PER TOUT ET NON PER MY (Law Fr.) By the whole, and not by the moiety. 2 Bl. Comm. 182. See "Per My et per Tout."

PER UNIVERSITATEM (Lat. by the whole). Used of the acquisition of any property as a whole, in opposition to an acquisition by parts; *e. g.*, the acquisition of an inheritance, or of the separate property of the son (*peculium*), etc. Calv. Lex. "Universitas."

PER VADIUM ET SALVOS PLEGIOS. In old practice. By gage and safe pledge. Words in the old writ of attachment or pone commanding the sheriff to summon the defendant by gage (taking of his goods) and safe pledges (requiring sureties) for appearance. 3 Bl. Comm. 280.

PER VARIOS ACTUS, LEGEM EXPERIentia facit. By various acts experience frames the law. 4 Inst. 50.

PER VERBA DE FUTURO. By words of the future (tense). 1 Bl. Comm. 439; 2 Kent, Comm. 87.

PER VERBA DE PRAESENTI. By words of the present (tense). 1 Bl. Comm. 439.

PER VISUM ECCLESIAE. In old English law. By view of the church; under the supervision of the church. The disposition of intestates' goods *per visum ecclesiae* was one of the articles confirmed to the prelates by King John's *Magna Charta.* 3 Bl. Comm. 96.

PER VIVAM VOCEM (Law Lat.) In old English law. By the living voice; the same with *viva voce.* Bracton, fol. 95.

PERAMBULATION. The act of walking over and about the boundaries of a district manor, parish, or piece of land with or without witnesses, either for the purpose of determining them, or of preserving evidence of them, and to see that no encroachments have been made, or that landmarks have not been removed. Thus, in many parishes in England, it is the custom for the parishioners to perambulate the boundaries of the parish in rogation week in every year. Such a custom entitles them to enter any man's land and abate nuisances in their way. Phillim. Ecc. Law, 1867; Hunt, Boundaries, 103; Britt. 124b; 57 N. Hamp. 392.

PERAMBULATIONE FACIENDA, WRIT de. In English law. The name of a writ which is sued by consent of both parties when they are in doubt as to the bounds of their respective estates. It is directed to the sheriff to make perambulation, and to set the bounds and limits between them in certainty. Fitzh. Nat. Brev. 309.

"The writ *de perambulatione facienda* is not known to have been adopted in practice in the United States," says Professor Greenleaf (Greenl. Ev. § 146, note), "but in several of the states, remedies somewhat similar in principle have been provided by statutes."

PERCENNARIUS (Law Lat.) In old English law. A parcener; one of several commoners. Fleta, lib. 4, c. 24, § 11.

PERCEPTION (from *per* and *capere*). The taking possession of. For example, a lessee or tenant before perception of the crops, *i. e.,* before harvesting them, has a right to offset any loss which may happen to them against the rent; but after the perception they are entirely at his risk. Mackeld Civ. Law, § 378. Used of money, it means the counting out and payment of a debt. Also used for food due to soldiers. Vicat.

PERCEPTURA (Law Lat.) In old records. A weir; a place in a river made up with banks, dams, etc., for the better convenience of preserving and taking fish. Par. Ant. 120; Cowell.

PERCH. The length of sixteen feet and a half; a pole or rod of that length. Forty perches in length and four in breadth make an acre of land.

PERCOLATING WATERS. Flowing, seeping, or moving subterraneous waters.

PERDONATIO UTLAGARIAE (Lat.) In English law. A pardon for a man who, for contempt in not yielding obedience to the process of the king's courts, is outlawed, and afterwards, of his own accord, surrenders.

PERDUELLIO (Lat.) In civil law. At first, an honorable enmity to the republic; afterwards, a traitorous enmity of a citizen; consisting in being of a hostile disposition towards the republic, *e. g.,* treason aiming at the supreme power, violating the privileges of a Roman citizen by beating him, etc., attempting anything against the person of the emperor, and, in general, any open hostility to the republic. Sometimes used for the enemy or traitor himself. *Perduellio* was distinguished from *crimen imminutae majestatis,* as being an attempt against the whole republic, punishable in *comitia centuriata,* by crucifixion and by infamy after death. Calv. Lex.; Vicat.

PERDURABLE (old Fr. *perdurable,* eternal, from Lat. *per,* intensive, and *durabilis,* lasting). As applied to an estate, *perdurable* signifies lasting long or forever. Thus, a disseisor or tenant in fee upon condition has as high and great an estate as the rightful owner or tenant in fee simple absolute, but not so *perdurable.* The term is chiefly used with reference to the extinguishment of rights by unity of seisin, which does not take place unless both the right and the land out of which it issues are held for equally high and *perdurable* estates. Co. Litt. 313a, 313b; Gale, Easem. 582.

PEREGRINI (Lat.) In civil law. Under the denomination of *peregrini* were comprehended all who did not enjoy any capacity of the law, namely, slaves, alien enemies, and such foreigners as belonged to nations with which the Romans had not established relations. Savigny, Dr. Rom. § 66.

PEREMPTORIUS (Lat. from *perimere,* to destroy). In civil law. That which takes away or destroys forever; hence, *exceptio peremptoria,* a plea which is a perpetual bar. See "Peremptory." Bracton, lib. 4, c. 20; Fleta, lib. 6, c. 36, § 3; Calv. Lex.

PEREMPTORY. Absolute; positive. A final determination to act without hope of renewing or altering. Joined to a substantive, this word is frequently used in law; as, peremptory action (Fitzh. Nat. Brev. 35, 38, 104, 108); peremptory nonsuit (Id. 5, 11); peremptory exception (Bracton, lib. 4, c. 20); peremptory undertaking (3 Chit. Prac. 112, 793); peremptory challenge of jurors (Inst. 4. 13. 9; Code, 7. 50. 2; Id. 8. 36. 8; Dig. 5. 1. 70. 73).

PEREMPTORY CHALLENGE. A challenge without cause given, allowed to prisoner's counsel in criminal cases, up to a certain number of jurors. 11 Chit. Stat. 59, 689; 2 Harg. St. Tr. 808; 4 Harg. St. Tr. 1; Fost. Crim. Law, 42; 4 Bl. Comm. 353*. See "Challenge."

PEREMPTORY DEFENSE. A defense which insists that the plaintiff never had the right to institute the suit, or that, if he had, the original right is extinguished or determined. 4 Bouv. Inst. note 4206.

PEREMPTORY EXCEPTION. Any defense which denies entirely the ground of action. 1 White, New Recop. 283. So of a demurrer. 1 Tex. 364.

PEREMPTORY INSTRUCTION. A binding instruction by the court to the jury. Usually the direction of a verdict.

PEREMPTORY MANDAMUS. A *mandamus* requiring a thing to be done absolutely. It is usually granted after failure to show satisfactory cause on an alternative *mandamus.* No other return will be permitted but absolute obedience. 3 Bl. Comm. 110*; Tapping, Mand. 400 et seq. See "Mandamus."

PEREMPTORY NONSUIT. An involuntary nonsuit. See "Nonsuit."

PEREMPTORY PAPER. A list of the causes which were enlarged at the request of the parties, or which stood over from press of business in court to a day which was specified in the paper, and which day was peremptory.

PEREMPTORY PLEA. A plea which goes to destroy the right of action itself; a plea in bar or to the action. 3 Steph. Comm. 576; 3 Wooddeson, Lect. 57; 2 Saund. Pl. & Ev. 645; 3 Bouv. Inst. note 2891.

PEREMPTORY RULE. An absolute rule, as distinguished from a rule *nisi.*

PEREMPTORY WRIT. An original writ, called from the words of the writ a *"si te fecerit securum,"* and which directed the sheriff to cause the defendant to appear in court without any option given him, provided the plaintiff gave the sheriff security effectually to prosecute his claim. The writ was rarely used, and where nothing was specifically demanded, but only a satisfaction in general; as in the case of writs of trespass on the case, wherein no debt or other specific thing was sued for, but only damages to be assessed by a jury. Brown.

PERFECT. Complete.

This term is applied to rights and obligations in order to distinguish those which may be enforced by law, which are called "perfect," from those which cannot be so enforced, which are said to be "imperfect." 37 Ga. 128.

PERFECT ABSTRACT. An abstract is said to be perfect where it shows a complete title, 2 Hare. 111, that is, when it shows that a vendor is either himself competent to convey, or can otherwise procure to be vested in him, the legal and equitable estates free from encumbrance. 8 Ves. 436; Dart. Vend. & P. 303; 2 Exch. 783. See "Mercantile Title"; "Perfect Title."

PERFECT OBLIGATION. One which is enforceable by law.

PERFECT TITLE. A title which is good both at law and in equity. 21 Conn. 449. See "Merchantable Title."

PERFECT TRUST. An executed trust (*q. v.*).

PERFECTING BAIL. Justification of bail. See "Justifying Bail."

PERFECTUM EST CUI NIHIL DEEST secundum suae perfectionis vel naturae modum. That is perfect which wants nothing according to the measure of its perfection or nature. Hob. 151.

PERFIDY. The act of one who has engaged his faith to do a thing, and does not do it, but does the contrary. Wolff. § 390.

PERFORMANCE. Such a fulfillment of an obligation as puts an end thereto by leaving nothing more to be done.

PERICULOSUM EST RES NOVAS ET INusitatas inducere. It is dangerous to introduce new and unaccustomed things. Co. Litt. 379.

PERICULOSUM EXISTIMO QUOD BOnorum vivorum non comprobatur exemplo. I think that dangerous which is not warranted by the example of good men. 9 Coke, 97.

PERICULOSUS (Lat.) Dangerous.

PERICULUM (Lat.) In the civil law. Peril; danger; hazard; risk.

PERICULUM REI VENDITIAE, NONdum traditae, est emptoris. The purchaser runs the risk of the loss of a thing sold, though not delivered. 1 Bouv. Inst. note 939; 2 Kent, Comm. 498, 499; 4 Barn. & C. 481, 941.

PERIL. Danger; the accident by which a thing is lost. Lec. Elm. § 911.

——**In Insurance.** The risk, contingency, or cause of loss insured against in a policy of insurance.

PERILS OF THE RIVER. A term used in respect to river navigation in the United States, and having the same significance as "perils of the sea." 8 Ala. 176.

PERILS OF THE SEA. One of the perils insured against in marine insurance, and from which bills of lading usually exempt the carrier. It signifies "all marine casualties resulting from the violent action of the elements, as distinguished from their natural silent influence on the fabric of the vessel; casualties which may, and not consequences which must, occur." L. R. 9 Q. B. 596.

Loss by foundering (3 Wheat. [U. S.] 168), or stranding (57 Me. 170), injury to the vessel by ice (15 Wall. [U. S.] 202), or to cargo from water shipped in a storm (16 Me. 207), or loss of property overboard (16 Mo. 98), or loss of property are perils of the sea. But damages by rats. (1 Wils. 281) or worms (2 Mass. 429), or the breakage of packages, are not.

PERINDE VALERE (Law Lat. to be equally valid). In English ecclesiastical law. The name of a writ of dispensation granted to a clerk who, being defective in his capacity to a benefice or other ecclesiastical function, was, *de facto*, admitted to it. So called from the emphatic words of the Latin form, the faculty being declared to be equally effectual to the party dispensed with as if he had been actually capable of the thing for which he was dispensed with, at the time of his admission. St. 25 Hen. VIII. c. 21; Cowell.

PERIOD. A space of time; any portion of complete time.

"The word 'period' has its etymological meaning, but it also has a distinctive signification, according to the subject with which it may be used in connection. It may mean any portion of complete time, from a thousand years or less to the period of a day; and when used to designate an act to be done or to be begun, though its completion may take an uncertain time, as for instance the act of exportation, it must mean the day on which the exportation commences, or it would be an unmeaning and useless word in its connection in the statute." Wayne, J., 20 How. (U. S.) 579.

PERIPHRASIS. Circumlocution; the use of other words to express the sense of one.

Some words are so technical in their meaning that, in charging offenses in indictments, they must be used, or the indictment will not be sustained. For example, an indictment for treason must contain the word "traitorously;" an indictment for burglary, "burglariously;" and "feloniously" must be introduced into every indictment for felony. 1 Chit. Crim. Law, 242, 3 Inst. 15; Carth. 319; 2 Hale, P. C. 172, 184; 4 Bl. Comm. 307; Hawk. P. C. bk. 2, c. 25, § 55; 1 East, P. C. 115; Bac. Abr. "Indictment" (G 1); Comyn, Dig. "Indictment" (G 6); Cro. Car. c. 37.

PERISHABLE GOODS. Goods which are lessened in value and become worse by being kept.

PERISHABLE PROPERTY. Perishable property in its most enlarged sense, would mean all personal, as distinguished from real property; whilst in its most restricted sense, it would only mean such personal property as had in itself the elements of destruction or decomposition, as for instance, fruits, or such productions from the labor and skill of man as are ephemeral in their existence, or evanescent and changeable in their value. 23 Ala. 768.

PERJURI SUNT QUI SERVITIS VERBIS juramenti decipiunt aures eorum qui accipiunt. They are perjured who, preserving the words of an oath, deceived the ears of those who receive it. 3 Inst. 166.

PERJURY. Perjury at common law is the willful and corrupt taking of a false oath in a judicial proceeding in regard to a matter material to the issues. 1 Hawk. P. C. c. 69, § 1; 4 Bl. Comm. 153. It is extended by statute in most jurisdictions to false swearing in certain proceedings not judicial. To constitute the offense, (1) the testimony must be false, or believed to be false, or the witness must not know whether it be true or false (42 Vt. 152; 17 N. H. 373); (2) the taking of the false oath must be both willful and corrupt; (3) the matter sworn to must be material to the issue or question in controversy (12 Mass. 273; 54 Vt. 146); (4) some form of oath or its equivalent must have been duly administered by an authorized officer (86 N. Y. 154; 107 U. S. 671; 76 N. Y. 220); (5) the oath itself, as well as the facts sworn to, must have been material (45 Mich. 543; 17 Ohio, 365); (6) to constitute perjury in a judicial proceeding, the court or tribunal must have jurisdiction (49 Me. 412; 8 Pick. [Mass.] 453; 96 Ky. 407).

PERMANENT ALIMONY. Permanent alimony is a provision for the support and maintenance of a wife out of her husband's estate during her lifetime, ordered by a court on decreeing a divorce. 188 Mich. 195.

PERMANENT IMPROVEMENT. Permanent improvements are not necessarily everlasting in character, but are such as rest upon, or are attached to, the soil, are reasonably enduring and not intended for removal at the end of a limited term. 153 Iowa, 397.

PERMANENT TRESPASS. A trespass consisting of trespasses of one and the same kind, committed on several days, which are in their nature capable of renewal or continuation, and are actually renewed or continued from day to day, so that the particular injury done on each particular day cannot be distinguished from what was done on another day. In declaring for such trespasses, they may be laid with a *continuando*. 3 Bl. Comm. 212; Bac. Abr. "Trespass" (B 2, I 2); 1 Saund. 24, note 1. See "Continuando;" "Trespass."

PERMISSION. Leave or license to do any act. It ordinarily implies consent actually given (105 Ill. 558), but has been held to mean "allow," by not prohibiting (9 Allen [Mass.] 266).

PERMISSIVE. Allowed; that which may be done; as, permissive waste, which is the permitting real estate to go to waste. 2 Bouv. Inst. note 2400. See "Waste."

PERMISSIVE USE. A passive use which was resorted to before the statute of uses, in order to avoid a harsh law; as that of mortmain or a feudal forfeiture. It was a mere invention in order to evade the law by secrecy; as a conveyance to A. to the use of B. A. simply held the possession, and B. enjoyed the profits of the estate.

PERMISSIVE WASTE. Waste suffered by omission of care, not by actual depredation; the mere neglect or omission to do what will prevent injury, as, to suffer a house to go to decay for want of repairs; and voluntary waste consists in the commission of destructive acts, as, pulling down a house, or plowing up a flower garden. 57 Ill. App. 663. See Waste.

PERMIT. A license or warrant to do something not forbidden by law; as, to land goods imported into the United States, after the duties have been paid or secured to be paid. Act Cong. March 2, 1799, § 49, cl. 2. See form of such a permit. Gordon, Dig. Append. II. 46.

PERMUTATIO (Lat. from *permutare*, to exchange). In the civil law. Exchange; barter. Dig. 19. 4; Code, 4. 64.

PERMUTATION. In civil law. Exchange; barter.

This contract is formed by the consent of the parties; but delivery is indispensable, for without it, it is a mere agreement. Dig. 31. 77. 4; Code, 4. 64. 3.

Permutation differs from sale in this, that in the former a delivery of the articles sold must be made, while in the latter it is unnecessary. It agrees with the contract of sale, however, in the following particulars: That he to whom the delivery is made acquires the right or faculty of prescribing (Dig. 41. 3. 4. 17); that the contracting parties are bound to guaranty to each other the title of the things delivered (Code, 4. 64. 1); and that they are bound to take back the things delivered when they have latent defects which they have concealed (Dig. 21. 1. 63).

PERMUTIONE. A writ commanding an ordinary to admit a clerk on exchange of benefices.

PERNANCY (from Fr. *prendre*, to take). A taking or receiving.

PERNOR (from Law Fr. *parnour*, or *pernour*, *q. v.*) A taker. *Pernor* of profits is the taker or receiver of the profits of an estate. Cowell.

PERNOR OF PROFITS. He who receives the profits of lands, etc. A *cestui que use*, who is legally entitled and actually does receive the profits, is the *pernor* of profits.

PERNOUR (Law Fr.) A taker. *Le pernour ou le detenour*, the taker or the detainer. Britt. c. 27.

PERPETUA LEX EST, NULLAM LEGEM humanam ac positivam perpetuam esse; et clausula quae abrogationem excludit ab initio non valet. It is a perpetual law that no human or positive law can be perpetual; and a clause in a law which precludes the power of abrogation is void *ab initio*. Bac. Max. reg. 19; Broom, Leg. Max. (3d London Ed.) 27.

PERPETUAL. That which is to last without limitation as to time; as, a perpetual statute, which is one without limit as to time, although not expressed to be so.

PERPETUAL CURACY. The office of a curate, in a parish where there is no spiritual rector or vicar, but where the curate is appointed to officiate for the time by the impropriator. 2 Burn, Ecc. Law, 55.

The church of which the curate is perpetual. 2 Ves. Sr. 425, 429. See 2 Steph. Comm. 76; 2 Burn, Ecc. Law, 55; 9 Adol. & E. 556. As to whether such curate may be removed, see 2 Burn, Ecc. Law, 55.

PERPETUAL INJUNCTION. Opposed to an injunction *ad interim;* an injunction which finally disposes of the suit, and is indefinite in point of time.

PERPETUAL LEASE. A lease without limitation as to term; a grant in fee, subject to a reserved rent.

PERPETUAL STATUTE. One not subject to repeal or expiration at any future time.

PERPETUATING TESTIMONY. The act by which testimony is reduced to writing as prescribed by law, so that the same shall be read in evidence in some suit or legal proceedings to be thereafter instituted.

The origin of this practice may be traced to the canon law (chapter 5, X *ut lite non contestata*, etc.) Bockmer, note 4; 8 Toullier, Dr. Civ. note 22. Statutes exist in most of the states for this purpose. Equity also furnishes means, to a limited extent, for the same purpose.

PERPETUITY. Any limitation tending to take the subject of it out of commerce for a longer period than a life or lives in being, and twenty-one years beyond, and, in case of a posthumous child, a few months more, allowing for the term of gestation. Rand. Perp. 48. Such a limitation of property as renders it unalienable beyond the period allowed by law. Gilb. Uses (Sugd. Ed.) 260, note.

An interest subject to a condition precedent, which condition is not to be fulfilled within twenty-one years after some life in being at the creation of the interest. Gray, Perp. § 216.

Mr. Justice Powell, in 12 Mod. 278, distinguished perpetuities into two sorts,—absolute and qualified; meaning thereby, as it is apprehended, a distinction between a plain, direct, and palpable perpetuity, and the case where an estate is limited on a contingency, which might happen within a reasonable compass of time, but where the estate nevertheless, from the nature of the limitation, might be kept out of commerce longer than was thought agreeable to the policy of the common law. But this distinction would not now lead to a better understanding or explanation of the subject; for whether an estate be so limited that it cannot take effect until a period too much protracted, or whether on a contingency which may happen within a moderate compass of time, it equally falls within the line of perpetuity, and the limitation is therefore void; for it is not sufficient that an estate may vest within the time allowed, but the rule requires that it must. Rand. Perp. 49. See Cruise, Dig. tit. 32, c. 23; 1 Belt, Supp. Ves. 406; 2 Ves. Jr. 357; 3 Saund. 388; Comyn Dig. "Chancery" (4 G 1); 3 Chanc. Cas. 1; 2 Bouv. Inst. note 1890.

PERPETUITY OF THE KING. That fiction of the English law which, for certain political purposes, ascribes to the king in his political capacity the attribute of immortality; for, though the reigning monarch may die, yet by this fiction the king never dies, *i. e.*, the office is supposed to be reoccupied for all political purposes immediately on his death.

PERQUIRERE (Law Lat. from *per*, through, and *quaerere*, to obtain). In feudal law. To gain or acquire; to acquire by one's own act; to purchase. *Breve perquirere*, to purchase a writ. Cowell.

PERQUISITES. In its most extensive sense, perquisites signifies anything gotten by industry or purchased with money, different from that which descends from a father or ancestor. Bracton, lib. 2, c. 30, note 3; Id. lib. 4, c. 22. In a more limited sense, it means something gained by a place or office beyond the regular salary or fee. 201 Mich. 468.

PERQUISITIO. Purchase. 2 Bl. Comm. 241. Acquisition by one's own act or agreement, and not by descent. Id. See "Purchase."

PERQUISITOR. A purchaser; one who first acquired an estate to his family; one who acquired an estate by sale, by gift, or by any other method, except only that of descent. 2 Bl. Comm. 220.

PERQUISITUM. Purchase. Bracton, fol. 65. Co. Litt. 3b, 18b. An estate acquired by purchase, that is, by one's own act, and not by descent; *praedium quod quis non a patre vel majoribus possidet, sed quo sua industria vel pecuniis comparato gaudet.* Spelman.

PERSECUTIO (Lat. from *persequi, q. v.*) In the civil law. A following after; a pursuing at law; a suit or prosecution.

Properly, that kind of judicial proceeding before the praetor which was called "extraordinary." Calv. Lex.

In a general sense, any judicial proceeding, including not only actions (*actiones*) properly so called, but other proceedings also. Calv. Lex.

PERSEQUI (Lat.) In the civil law. To follow after; to pursue or claim in form of law. An action is called a *jus persequendi.* See "Actio."

PERSEWAR (Old Scotch). In old Scotch law. Pursuer; plaintiff or prosecutor. See "Pursuer."

PERSON. A man considered according to the rank he holds in society, with all the rights to which the place he holds entitles him, and the duties which it imposes. 1 Bouv. Inst. note 137.

A corporation, which is an artificial person. 1 Bl. Comm. 123; 4 Bing. 669; Woodeson, Lect. 116; 1 Mod. 164; 22 N. Y. 352; 10 Ill. 48; 32 Conn. 216; 118 U. S. 394. And it has been held to include a partnership association. 108 Pa. St. 147. It includes both sexes. 136 Mass. 580.

PERSONA (Lat.) In civil law. Character, in virtue of which certain rights belong to a man, and certain duties are imposed upon him. Thus, one man may unite many characters (*personae*); as, for example, the characters of father and son, of master and servant. Mackeld. Civ. Law, § 117.

In its original signification, a mask; afterwards, a man in reference to his condition or character (*status*). Vicat. It is used metaphorically of things, among which are counted slaves. It is often opposed to *res;* as, *actio in personam* and *actio in rem.*

Power and right belonging to a person in a certain character (*pro jure et potestate personae competente*). Vicat. Its use is not confined to the living, but is extended to the dead and to angels. Id. A statue in a fountain whence water gushes.

PERSONA CONJUNCTA AEQUIPARATUR interesse proprio. The interest of a personal connection is sometimes regarded in law as that of the individual himself. Bac. Max. reg. 18; Broom, Leg. Max. (3d London Ed.) 474.

PERSONA EST HOMO, CUM STATU quodam consideratus. A person is a man considered with reference to a certain *status.* Heinec. Elem. Jur. Civ. lib. 1, tit. 2, § 75.

PERSONA NON GRATA. A person not acceptable. Applied to diplomatic representatives who are not acceptable at the court to which they are accredited.

PERSONA REGIS MERGITUR PERSONA ducis. The person of duke merges in that of king. Jenk. Cent. Cas. 160.

PERSONA STANDI IN JUDICIO. Capacity of standing in court or in judgment; capacity to be a party to an action; capacity or ability to sue.

A phrase probably derived from Bracton (folios 155b, 196). See 15 Johns. (N. Y.) 83.

PERSONABLE (Law Lat. *personabilis*, from *persona*, capacity). In old English law. Able to maintain a plea in court; having capacity to sue. Cowell. Derived probably from the phrase *persona standi in judicio* (*q. v.*)

Of capacity to take a thing granted or given. Plowd. 27a, arg. But in the case here cited, it is used as two words, "person able." "There is a maxim that when a remainder is appointed to one, he to whom it is appointed ought at that time to be 'a person able,' and to have capacity to take the remainder, or else it shall be void." Id.

PERSONAE VICE FUNGITUR MUNICIPium et decuria. Towns and boroughs act as if persons. 23 Wend. (N. Y.) 103, 144.

PERSONAL. Belonging to the person.

This adjective is frequently employed in connection with substantives, as personal services (see 59 N. H. 551), personal goods (see 5 Mason [U. S.] 356), etc. Personal rights are those which belong to the person; personal duties are those which are to be performed in person.

PERSONAL ACTION.

——**In the Civil Law.** An action in which one person (the *actor*) sues another (the *reus*) in respect of some obligation which he is under to the *actor* either *ex contractu* or *ex delicto*. It will be seen that this includes all actions against a person, without reference to the nature of the property involved. In a limited sense of the word "action" in the civil law, it includes only personal actions, all others being called "petitions." See "Real Action."

——**At Common Law.** An action brought for the recovery of personal property, for the enforcement of some contract or to recover damages for its breach, or for the recovery of damages for the commission of an injury to the person or property. Such arise either upon contracts, as account, *assumpsit*, covenant, debt, and detinue (*q. v.*), or for wrongs, injuries, or torts, as trespass, trespass on the case, replevin, trover (*q. v.*) Other divisions of personal actions are made in the various states; and in Vermont and Connecticut an action is in use called the "action of book debt." 71 Me. 287. See "Action."

PERSONAL ASSETS. Chattels, money, and other personal property belonging to a bankrupt, insolvent, or decedent estate, which go to the assignee or executor.

PERSONAL CHATTELS. Strictly and properly speaking, things movable, which may be annexed to or attendant on the person of the owner and carried about with him from one part of the world to another. 2 Bl. Comm. 388*. See Chattel; Personal Effects.

PERSONAL CONTRACT. A contract as to personal property. A covenant (or contract) personal relates only to matters personal as distinguished from real, and is binding on the covenantor (contractor) during his life, and on his personal representatives after his decease, in respect of assets. Angell & A. Watercourses, 305; Co. Litt. 22.

PERSONAL COVENANT. A covenant which binds only the covenantor and his personal representatives in respect to assets, and can be taken advantage of only by the covenantee.

A covenant which must be performed by the covenantor in person. Fitzh. Nat. Brev. 340.

All covenants are either personal or real, but some confusion exists in regard to the division between them. Thus, a covenant may be personal as regards the covenantor, and real as regards the covenantee; and different definitions have been given, according to whether the rights and liabilities of the covenantor or the covenantee have been in consideration. It is apprehended, however, that the prevalent modern usage is to hold a covenant real, if it is real,—that is, runs with the land, so as to apply to an assignee, either as regards the covenantor or the covenantee. See Platt, Cov. 61; 4 Bl. Comm. 304, note, 305, note; 3 N. J. 260; 7 Gray (Mass.) 83.

All covenants which relate to personalty merely are of this class. 30 Miss. 145.

PERSONAL EFFECTS. Without qualifying words, "personal effects" generally include such tangible property as is worn or carried about the person, but for the most part, as used in wills, the phrase derives its meaning from descriptions of articles and classifications immediately preceding. 66 Ark. 381. See Personal Chattels.

PERSONAL ESTATE. Personal property.

PERSONAL KNOWLEDGE. Knowledge derived at first hand from actual sight or hearing of the matter in question, and not from hearsay.

PERSONAL LAW. As opposed to territorial law, personal law is the law applicable to persons not subject to the law of the territory in which they reside. It is only by permission of the territorial law that personal law can exist at the present day; *e. g.*, it applies to British subjects resident in the Levant and in other Mohammedan and barbarous countries. Under the Roman Empire, it had a very wide application. Brown.

PERSONAL LIBERTY. The right or power of locomotion, of changing situation, or moving one's person to whatsoever place one's own inclination may direct, without imprisonment or restraint, unless by due courst of law. 1 Bl. Comm. 134. Its modern definition is wider, embracing the right of the individual to do as he pleases, unrestricted save by the right of the public to subordinate his freedom of action to the welfare of the public.

PERSONAL PROPERTY. Chattels (*q. v.*)

PERSONAL REPLEVIN. A proceeding which succeeded to the court *de homine replegiando*, and was in turn succeeded by the writ of *habeas corpus*.

PERSONAL REPRESENTATIVES. The executors or administrators of the person deceased. 6 Mod. 155; 5 Ves. 402; 1 Madd. 108.

In wills, these words are sometimes construed to mean "next of kin." 2 Jarm. Wills, 28; 1 Beav. Rolls, 46; 1 Russ. & M. 587.

PERSONAL RIGHTS. The right of personal security, comprising those of life, limb, body, health, reputation, and the right of personal liberty. Wharton.

PERSONAL SECURITY. A person's legal and uninterrupted enjoyment of his life, his limbs, his body, his health, and his reputation. 1 Bl. Comm. 129.

PERSONAL SERVICE. Service of process on one by actual delivery thereof to him, as distinguished from substituted service at his residence or constructive service by publication.

PERSONAL SERVITUDE. Servitudes in gross; *i. e.*, belonging to a person, and not appurtenant to an estate.

PERSONAL STATUTE. A law whose principal, direct, and immediate object is to regulate the condition of persons.

The term is not properly in use in the common law, although Lord Mansfield, in 2 W. Bl. 234, applied it to those legislative acts which respect personal transitory contracts, but is occasionally used in the sense given to it in civil law, and which is adopted as its definition. It is a law, ordinance, regulation, or custom, the disposition of which affects the person, and clothes him with a capacity or incapacity which he does not change with his abode. See 2 Kent, Comm. (10th Ed.) 613.

PERSONAL THINGS. In the old books, include personal rights and duties.

PERSONALIA PERSONAM SEQUUNtur. Personal things follow the person. 10 Cush. (Mass.) 516.

PERSONALIS ACTIO. See "Actio."

PERSONALITER. In old English law. Personally.

PERSONALITY. In foreign and modern civil law. That quality of a law which concerns the condition, state, and capacity of persons. By the personality of laws, foreign jurists generally mean all laws which concern the condition, state, and capacity of persons. Story, Confl. Laws, § 16.

PERSONALTY. Personal property.

PERSONATION. The offense of falsely representing one's self as another person, and thereby obtaining some material advantage.

The offense of personating a voter is complete as soon as a person has, to the proper officer, falsely represented himself as the person entitled to vote, even though he stop short of voting. 33 L. J. M. C. 81; 4 B. & S. 15.

PERSONE (Law Fr.) A parson. *En mesme la manere est de persone de un esglise*, in the same manner is it with the parson of a church. Britt. c. 48.

PERSONERO (Spanish). In Spanish law. An attorney. So called, because he represents the person of another, either in or out of court. Las Partidas, pt. 3, tit. 5, lib. 1.

PERSONNE (Fr.) A person. This term is declared by the Civil Code of Louisiana to be applicable to men and women, or to either. Article 3522, No. 25.

PERSPICUA VERA NON SUNT PRObanda. Plain truths need not be proved. Co. Litt. 16.

PERTAIN. To belong or pertain, whether by right of nature, appointment or custom; to relate, as "things pertaining to life." 174 Ill. 182.

PERTICA, PERTICATA, or PARTICATA (Law Lat. from *pertica*). In old Scotch law. A perch. Skene de Verb. Sign.

PERTINENT (from Lat. *pertineo*, belonging to). Belonging to or related to the subject or matter in hand; fit or appropriate in any way; adapted to the end proposed; opposite; material; relevant. 174 Mich. 351. That which tends to prove or disprove the allegations of the parties. Willes. 319. Matters which have no such tendency are called "impertinent." 8 Toullier, Dr. Civ. note 22.

PERTINENTIAE (Law Lat. from *pertinere*, to belong). In old English law. Appurtenances, or, as anciently written, "appertinances;" in Scotch law, pertinents; things belonging or incident to another (principal) thing. Reg. Orig. 1; Fleta, lib. 3, c. 14, § 11. Appurtenances had sometimes their own appurtenances, called *pertinentiae pertinentiarum*. Thus, to the right of feeding and pasture, themselves appurtenant to a tenement, were appurtenant the right of way, and free ingress and egress; *habent hujusmodi pertinentiae suas pertinentias, sicut ad jus pascendi et ad pasturam pertinent via et liber ingressus et egressus.* Bracton, fol. 232. See Fleta, lib. 4, c. 18, § 3.

PERTINENTS. In Scotch law. Appurtenances. "Parts and pertinents," "parts pendicles and pertinents," are formal words in old deeds and charters. 1 Forbes, Inst. pt. 2, pp. 112, 118.

PERTURBATION. This is a technical word which signifies disturbance or infringement of a right. It is usually applied to the disturbance of pews or seats in a church. In the ecclesiastical courts, actions for these disturbances are technically called "suits for perturbation of seat." 1 Phillim. Ecc. Law, 323. See "Pew."

PERTURBATRIX. A woman who breaks the peace.

PERVISE, or PARVISE. The palace yard at Westminster.

A place where counsel used to advise with their clients.

An afternoon exercise or moot for the instruction of students. Cowell; Blount.

PESAGE. In England, a toll charged for weighing avoirdupois goods other than wool. 2 Chit. Com. Law, 16.

PESQUISIDOR. In Spanish law. Coroner. White, New Recop. bk. 1, tit. 1, § 3.

PESSIMI EXEMPLI. Of the worst example.

PESSONA (Law Lat.) In old English law. Mast, including acorns, nuts, and other similar produce of trees. Bracton, fol. 222b.

PETENS (Lat.; Fr. *petere,* to demand). In old English law. A demandant; the plaintiff in a real action. Bracton, fols. 102, 106b; Fleta, lib. 6, c. 6, § 1.

PETER FUNK SALE. A fraudulent auction sale. 27 Abb. N. C. (N. Y.) 378.

PETIT (sometimes corrupted into "petty"). A French word signifying little, small. It is frequently used; as, petit larceny, petit jury, petit treason.

PETIT CAPE. When the tenant is summoned on a plea of land, and comes on the summons, and his appearance is recorded, if at the day given him he prays the view, and, having it given him, makes default, then shall this writ issue from the king. Old Nat. Brev. 162; Reg. Jud. fol. 2; Fleta, lib. 2, c. 44. See "Grand Cape."

PETIT JUDICIUM. (Lat.) In old practice. Prays judgment. 6 Mod. 236. 10 Id. 210, 211.

PETIT (or PETTY) JURY. The ordinary jury of twelve, as opposed to the grand jury, which was of a larger number, and whose duty it was to find bills for the petit jury to try. 3 Bl. Comm. 351*.

A body of twelve men, who are sworn to try the facts of a case as they are presented in the evidence placed before them. Any less than this number of twelve would not be a common law jury and not such a jury as the Constitution guarantees to accused parties, when a less number is not allowed in express terms; and the necessity of a full panel could not be waived—at least in the case of felony—even by consent. The infirmity in the case of a trial by a jury of less than twelve, by consent, would be that the tribunal would be one unknown to the law, created by mere voluntary act of the parties; and it would in effect be an attempt to submit to a species of arbitration the question whether the accused has been guilty of an offense against the State. Cooley's Const. Lim. 319; 128 Ill. 593.

PETIT (or PETTY) LARCENY. In old English law, based on St. Westminster I. c. 15, larceny where the value of the property stolen was twelve pence or less. The distinction between grand and petit larceny has been abolished in England. 24 & 25 Vict. c. 96, § 4.

In the United States there are statutes in some states making a distinction between grand and petty larceny based on the value of the property stolen.

PETIT SERJEANTY. A tenure by which lands are held of the crown by the service of rendering yearly some small implement of war, as a lance, an arrow, etc. 2 Bl. Comm. 82. Though St. 12 Car. II. took away the incidents of livery and primer seisin, this tenure still remains a dignified branch of socage tenure, from which it only differs in name on account of its reference to war. Such is the tenure of the grants to the dukes of Marlborough and Wellington.

PETIT (or PETTY) TREASON. In English law. The killing of a master by his servant, a husband by his wife, a superior by a religious man. 4 Bl. Comm. 73. In the United States this is like any other murder. See "Treason."

PETITE ASSIZE. Used in contradistinction from the "grand assize," which was a jury to decide on questions of property. *Petite assize,* a jury to decide on questions of possession. Britt. c. 42; Glanv. lib. 2, c. 6, 7; Horne, Mir. lib. 2, c. "De Novel Disseisin."

PETITIO (Lat. from *petere,* to ask or demand).

——**In the Civil Law.** The plaintiff's or *actor's* statement of his cause of action, in an action *in rem.* Dig. 44. 7. 28; Calv. Lex.

——**In Old English Law.** Petition or demand; the count in a real action; the form of words in which a title to land was stated by the demandant, and which commenced with the word *peto* (*q. v.*) 1 Reeve, Hist. Eng. Law, 176. Obviously borrowed from the civil law.

PETITION. An instrument of writing or printing, containing a prayer from the person presenting it, called the "petitioner," to the body or person to whom it is presented, for the redress of some wrong, or the grant of some favor which the latter has the right to give. 48 Miss. 36.

——**In Practice.** An application to a court in writing; in contradistinction to a "motion," which may be *viva voce*. Shaw, C. J., 4 Metc. (Mass.) 376. A motion stated in writing.

——**In Equity Practice.** An application in writing for an order of the court, stating the circumstances upon which it is founded; a proceeding resorted to whenever the nature of the application to the court requires a fuller statement than can be conveniently made in a notice of motion. 1 Barb. Ch. (N. Y.) 578. See 3 Daniell, Chanc. Prac. (Perkins' Ed.) 1801.

PETITION DE DROIT (Law Fr.) In English practice. A petition of right; a form of proceeding to obtain restitution from the crown of either real or personal property, being of use where the crown is in possession of any hereditaments or chattels, and the petitioner suggests such a right as controverts the title of the crown, grounded on facts disclosed in the petition itself. 3 Bl. Comm. 256; 8 Adol. & E. (N. S.) 208.

PETITION OF RIGHT. In English law. A proceeding in chancery by which a subject may recover property in the possession of the king.

This is in the nature of an action against a subject, in which the petitioner sets out his right to that which is demanded by him, and prays the king to do him right and justice; and, upon a due and lawful trial of the right, to make him restitution. It is called a "petition of right," because the king is bound of right to answer it, and let the matter therein contained be determined in a legal way, in like manner as causes between subject and subject. The petition is presented to the king, who subscribes it with these words, *soit droit fait al partie*, and thereupon it is delivered to the chancellor to be executed according to law. 4 Inst. 419, 422b; Mitf. Eq. Pl. 30, 31; Cooper, Eq. Pl. 22, 23.

PETITION OF RIGHTS. A parliamentary declaration of the liberties of the people, assented to by King Charles I. in 1629. It is to be distinguished from the bill of rights (1689), which has passed into a permanent constitutional statute.

PETITIONING CREDITOR. The creditor at whose instance an adjudication of bankruptcy is made against a bankrupt.

PETITOR (Lat. from *petere*, to demand). In Roman law. A plaintiff or *actor*, particularly in an action *in rem;* a demandant. Calv. Lex. *Actor est qui agit in personam, petitor, qui agit in rem,* an *actor* is one who prosecutes against a person, a demandant one who prosecutes against a thing. Cujac. Observ. lib. 7, c. 26.

PETITORY. That which demands or petitions; that which has the quality of a prayer or petition; a right to demand.

A petitory suit or action is understood to be one in which the mere title to property is to be enforced by means of a demand, petition, or other legal proceeding, as distinguished from a suit where only the right of possession and not the mere right of property is in controversy. 1 Kent, Comm. 371; 7 How. (U. S.) 846; 10 How. (U. S.) 257. Admiralty suits touching property in ships are either petitory, in which the mere title to the property is litigated, or possessory, to restore the possession to the party entitled thereto.

The American courts of admiralty exercised unquestioned jurisdiction in petitory as well as possessory actions; but in England the courts of law, some time after the restoration in 1660, claimed exclusive cognizance of mere questions of title, until the statute of 3 & 4 Vict. c. 65. By that statute, the court of admiralty was authorized to decide all questions as to the title to or ownership of any ship or vessel, or the proceeds thereof remaining in the registry in any cause of possession, salvage, damage, wages, or bottomry, instituted in such court after the passing of that act. Ware, Dist. Ct. 232; 18 How. (U. S.) 267; 2 Curt. C. C. (U. S.) 426.

——**In Scotch Law.** Actions in which damages are sought.

This class embraces such actions as *assumpsit*, debt, covenant, and detinue, at common law. See Patterson, Comp. 1058, note.

PETITORY SUIT (or ACTION).

——**In Admiralty Law.** A suit in which the mere title to property is litigated and sought to be enforced, as distinguished from a possessory action (*q. v.*) 5 Mason (U. S.) 465; 1 Kent, Comm. 371. See "Petitory."

——**In Scotch Law.** An action wherein the pursuer (plaintiff) claims something as due or belonging to him by the defender (defendant). 1 Forbes, Inst. pt. 4, p. 163; Bell, Dict.

PETO (Lat.)

——**Roman Law.** I request. A common word by which a *fideicommissum*, or trust, was created in a will. Inst. 2. 24. 3.

——**In Old English Law.** I demand. The word with which a demandant's count commenced.

PETRA (Lat.) In old English law. Stone. Fleta, lib. 1, c. 20, § 114.

A stone. A weight of twelve pounds and a half. Fleta, lib. 2, c. 12, § 1.

PETTIFOGGER. One who pretends to be a lawyer, but possesses neither knowledge of the law nor conscience.

An unprincipled practitioner of law, whose business is confined to petty cases. See 40 Mich. 256. See, also, "Shyster."

PETTIFOGGING. Practicing the arts of a pettifogger, like the raising of unprofessional or dishonorable quibbles, practicing petty deceptions on the court, attempting to bring scandalous or impertinent issues into the trial, etc.

PETTY. Small; inferior. A word framed from the Fr. *petit*, and sometimes used indiscriminately with it.

PETTY AVERAGE (called, also, "customary average"). Several petty charges which are borne partly by the ship and partly by the cargo, such as the expense of tonnage, beaconage, etc. Abb. Shipp. (7th Ed.) 404; 2 Pars. Mar. Law, 312; 1 Bell, Comm. 567; 2 Magens, 277. See "Average."

PETTY BAG OFFICE. In English law. An office in the court of chancery, appropriated for suits against attorneys and officers of the court, and for process and proceedings by extent on statutes, recognizances *ad quod damnum*, and the like. Termes de la Ley. See "Hanaper Office."

PETTY CONSTABLE. The ordinary constable, as distinguished from the high constable of the hundred. 1 Bl. Comm. 355; Bac. Law Tr. 181, "Office of Constable;" Willcock, Const. c. 1, § 1. See "Constable."

PEW. A seat in a church, separated from all others, with a convenient place to stand therein. It is derived from *puye*, and signifies primarily an inclosed seat in a church. L. R. 5 C. P. 224.

It is an incorporeal interest in the real property. And although a man has the exclusive right to it, yet it seems he cannot maintain trespass against a person entering it (1 Term R. 430); but case is the proper remedy (3 Barn. & Ald. 361; 8 Barn. & C. 294).

In Connecticut and Maine, pews are considered real estate. In Massachusetts and New Hampshire, they are personal property. Gen. St. Mass. c. 30, § 38; 1 Smith, St. 145. The precise nature of such property does not appear to be well settled in New York. 15 Wend. (N. Y.) 218; 16 Wend. (N. Y.) 28; 5 Cow. (N. Y.) 494. See 10 Mass. 323; 17 Mass. 438; 7 Pick. (Mass.) 138; 4 N. H. 180; 4 Ohio, 515; 4 Har. & McH. (Md.) 279; Best, Pres. 111; Crabb, Real Prop. §§ 481-497; Washb. Easem.

PEWTER. An alloy of lead and tin. 28 L. Cas. 326.

PHAROS. (Lat.) In maritime law. A light-house. Mar. lib. 2, c. 1, sec. 7.

PHYSICAL FACT. A fact the existence of which may be perceived by the senses, such as the sound of a pistol shot, a man running, impressions of feet on the ground. Burrill, Circ. Ev. 130.

PHYSICIAN. A person who has received the degree of doctor of medicine from an incorporated institution.

One lawfully engaged in the practice of medicine.

The term is not limited to any of the schools of practitioners recognized by law. 62 Wis. 289.

PIA FRAUS. A pious fraud. A term applied to evasions of the statute of mortmain, and other frauds in the interest of religious institutions.

PICCAGE (Law Lat. *piccagium*, from Fr. *piquer*, to perforate, or pick). In old English law. Money paid at fairs for leave to break the ground, to set up booths or stalls. Cowell; Spelman.

PICKERY. In Scotch law. Stealing of trifles, punishable arbitrarily. Bell, Dict.; Tait, Inst. "Theft."

PICKET. A relay of guards in front of a factory or place of business of an employer for the purpose of watching who enters or leaves it, or the establishment and maintenance of an organized espionage upon the works and upon those going to and from them, 178 Mich. 305; it has also been defined as "a body of men belonging to a trade union sent to watch and annoy nonunion workers in a shop or against which a strike is in progress," but the word originally had no such meaning. 118 Mich. 497.

PICKPOCKET. A thief; one who in a crowd or in other places steals from the pockets or person of another, without putting him in fear. This is generally punished as simple larceny, but by some states larceny from the person, committed privily, is made a distinct crime. Pen. Code Ga. § 175; Pen. Code Tex. art. 879.

PIEDPOUDRE. See "Court of Piepoudre."

PIERAGE. Toll for using a marine pier. Webster; Smart.

PIGNORATIO (Lat. from *pignorare*, to pledge). In civil law. The obligation of a pledge. L. 9 D. "De Pignor." Sealing up (*obsignatio*). A shutting up of an animal caught in one's field, and keeping it till the expenses and damage have been paid by its master. New Dec. 1. 34. 13.

PIGNORATITIA ACTIO. See "Actio Pignoraticia."

PIGNORATIVE CONTRACT. In civil law. A contract by which the owner of an estate engages it to another for a sum of money, and grants to him and his successors the right to enjoy it until he shall be reimbursed, voluntarily, that sum of money. Poth. Obl.

PIGNORIS CAPTIO (Lat.) In Roman law. The name given to one of the *legis actiones* of the Roman law. It consisted chiefly in the taking of a pledge, and was, in fact, a mode of execution. It was confined to special cases determined by positive law or by custom, such as taxes, duties, rents, etc., and is comparable in some respects to distresses at common law. The proceeding took place in the presence of a praetor.

PIGNUS (Lat.) In civil law. Pledge, or pawn; the contract of pledge; the right in the thing pledged.

"It is derived" says Gaius, "from *pugnum*, the fist, because what is delivered in pledge is delivered in hand." Dig. 50. 16. 238. 2. This is one of several instances of the failure of the Roman jurists when they attempted etymological explanations of words. The elements of *pignus* (*pig*) are contained in the word *pan*(*g*)-*o* and its cognate forms. See Smith.

Though pledge is distinguished from mortgage (*hypotheca*), as being something delivered in hand, while mortgage is good without possession, yet a pledge (*pignus*) may also be good without possession. Domat, Civ. Law, bk. iii. tit. 1, § 5; Calv. Lex. *Pignus* is properly applied to movables, *hypotheca* to immovables; but the distinction is not always preserved. Id.

PILFERAGE. Pilferage has but one meaning, and it is one form of stealing. 207 Ill. App. 492.

PILLAGE. A robbery by force or violence; and not a simple larceny merely. 26 Wend. 573. The taking by violence of private property by a victorious army from the citizens or subjects of the enemy. This in modern times is seldom allowed, and then only when authorized by the commanding or chief officer at the place where the pillage is committed. The property thus violently taken belongs, in general, to the common soldiers. Dalloz. "Propriete," art. 3, § 5; Wolff. § 1201. See "Booty;" "Prize."

PILLORY. An instrument of punishment, consisting of a wooden machine, in which the neck of the culprit is inserted, he being ordinarily exposed in a public place while so secured.

PILOT. An officer serving on board of a ship during the course of a voyage, and having the charge of the helm and of the ship's route. An officer authorized by law, who is taken on board at a particular place for the purpose of conducting a ship through a river, road, or channel, or from or into port. 10 Abb. Pr. (N. Y.) 30.

Pilots of the second description are established by legislative enactments at the principal seaports in this country, and have rights, and are bound to perform duties, agreeably to the provisions of the several laws establishing them; the principal being the obligation of every vessel entering the port to take on a licensed pilot of the port, usually the first who offers his services (118 U. S. 90; 12 Fed. 81; 10 Fed. 135), or pay pilotage to the pilot so offering.

PILOTAGE. The compensation given to a pilot for conducting a vessel in or out of port. Poth. des Avaries, note 147.

Pilotage is a lien on the ship, when the contract has been made by the master or *quasi* master of the ship, or some other person lawfully authorized to make it (1 Mason [U. S.] 598; 32 Fed. 486), and the admiralty court has jurisdiction when services have been performed at sea (Id.; 10 Wheat. [U. S.] 428; 6 Pet. [U. S.] 682; 10 Pet. [U. S.] 108). And see 1 Pet. Adm. Dec. (U. S.) 227.

PIMP. A procurer; a panderer; a man who has intercourse with a loose woman, and usually she is taking care of him,—supporting him. The word has no technical meaning. 75 Mich. 131.

PIMP TENURE. A very singular and odious kind of tenure mentioned by the old writers, "*Wilhelmus Hoppeshort tenet dimidiam virgatam terrae per servitium custodiendi sex damisellas, scil. meretrices ad usum domini regis.*" 12 Edw. I.

PIN MONEY. Money allowed by a man to his wife to spend for her own personal comforts. 9 Beav. 55; 2 Clark & F. 654.

It has been conjectured that the term "pin money" has been applied to signify the provision for a married woman, because anciently there was a tax laid for providing the English queen with pins. Barr. Obs. St. 181.

PINT. A liquid measure, containing half a quart, or the eighth part of a gallon.

PIOUS USES. See "Charitable Uses."

PIPE. In English law. The name of a roll in the exchequer, otherwise called the "Great Roll" or "pipe roll." Spelman. A measure, containing two hogsheads. One hundred and twenty-six gallons is also called a pipe.

PIPE LINES. A line or series of pipes designed for the transportation of water, gas, etc.

PIPOWDER, or PIEPOUDRE (Ft. *pied-poudre*). In English law. The name of a court held for fairs and markets. See "Court of Piepoudre." *Pipowder* courts were formerly appointed to be held at fairs in the town and borough of Westchester, New York. Bolton, Hist. Westchester, i. 194.

PIRACY.

——**In Criminal Law.** A robbery or forcible depredation on the high seas, without lawful authority, done *animo furandi*, in the spirit and intention of universal hostility. 3 Wheat. (U. S.) 610; 5 Wheat. (U. S.) 153, 163; 3 Wash. C. C. (U. S.) 209. This is the definition of this offense by the law of nations. 1 Kent, Comm. 183.

"A pirate is one who roves the seas in an armed vessel, without any commission from any sovereign, and for the purpose of seizing by force and appropriating to himself every vessel which he may meet." Trial of Savannah Privateers, p. 371.

The commission upon the high seas of such acts of robbery and depredation as would, if committed on land, have amounted to a felony. 4 Bl. Comm. 72.

——**In Torts.** By piracy is understood the plagiarisms of a book, engraving, or other work for which a copyright has been taken out.

When a piracy has been made of such a work, an injunction will be granted. 4 Ves. 681; 5 Ves. 709; 12 Ves. 270. See "Copyright."

PIRATA EST HOSTIS HUMANI GENERIS. A pirate is an enemy of the human race. 3 Inst. 113.

PIRATE. A sea robber, who, to enrich himself, by subtlety or open force, setteth upon merchants and others trading by sea, despoiling them of their loading, and sometimes bereaving them of life and sinking their ships. Ridley, View, pt. 2, c. 1, § 3. One guilty of the crime of piracy. Merlin, Repert. See, for the etymology of this word, Bac. Abr. "Piracy."

PIRATICALLY. In pleading. This is a technical word, essential to charge the crime of piracy in an indictment, which cannot be supplied by another word or any circumlocution. Hawk. P. C. bk. 1, c. 37, § 15; 3 Inst. 112; 1 Chit. Crim. Law, *244.

PISCARY. The right of fishing in the waters of another. Bac. Abr.; 5 Comyn, Dig. 366. See "Fishery."

PISTAREEN. A small Spanish coin. It is not made current by the laws of the United States. 10 Pet. (U. S.) 618.

PIT. A hole dug in the earth, which was filled with water, and in which women thieves were drowned, instead of being hung. The punishment of the pit was formerly common in Scotland.

PIT AND GALLOWS (Law Lat. *fossa et furca*). In Scotch law. A privilege of inflicting capital punishment for theft, given by King Malcolm, by which a woman could be drowned in a pit (*fossa*) or a man hanged on the gallows (*furca*). Bell, Dict.; Stair, Inst. 277, § 62.

PIX (Lat.) A mode of testing coin. The ascertaining whether coin is of the proper standard is, in England, called "pixing" it; and there are occasions on which resort is had for this purpose to an ancient mode of inquisition called the "trial of the pix," before a jury of members of the Goldsmith's Company. 2 Steph. Comm. 540, note.

PIXIS (Law Lat.) In old pleading. A box. Cro. Jac. 664. "Trover was brought *de una pixide, Anglice*, a box full of bands," etc. Id. A box for deeds and muniments. Latch, 195.

PLACE. See "Venue."

PLACE OF ABODE. By place of abode is usually meant the place of residence. A man's residence, where he lives with his family and sleeps at night, is always his place of abode in the full sense of that expression. 21 L. J. Q. B. 153; 17 Q. B. 772.

PLACE OF BUSINESS. The place where a man usually transacts his affairs or business.

A place of business is a place actually occupied, either continually or at regular intervals, by a person, or those in his employment, for the transaction of business; the mere occasional transaction of business at a place, not at stated periods, not being sufficient. 8 Port. (Ala.) 155.

A place in the house of another, where one is employed two or three days a week in settling up his old business, is not a place of business. 1 Pet. (U. S.) 578.

The term implies a particular place appropriated exclusively to a local business. 38 Tex. 599.

When a man keeps a store, shop, counting room, or office, independently and distinctly from all other persons, that is deemed his place of business; and when he usually transacts his business at the counting house, office, and the like, occupied and used by another, that will also be considered his place of business, if he has no independent place of his own. But when he has no particular right to use a place for such private purpose, as in an insurance office, an exchange room, a banking room, a post office, and the like, where persons generally resort, these will not be considered as the party's place of business, although he may occasionally or transiently transact business there. 1 Pet. (U. S.) 582; 2 Pet. (U. S.) 121; 10 Johns. (N. Y.) 501; 11 Johns. (N. Y.) 231; 16 Pick. (Mass.) 392.

PLACE OF CONTRACT. See "Lex Loci."

PLACEA. (Law Lat.) In old records. A place.

PLACITA. The convening order of the court. 63 Ill. 497.

PLACITA COMMUNIA (Lat.) Common pleas. All civil actions between subject and subject. 3 Bl. Comm. 38, 40*; Cowell, "Plea." See "Placitum."

PLACITA CORONAE (Lat.) Pleas of the crown. All trials for crimes and misdemeanors, wherein the king is plaintiff, on behalf of the people. 3 Bl. Comm. 40*; Cowell, "Plea."

PLACITA DE TRANSGRESSIONE CONtra pacem regis, in regno Angliae vi et armis facta, secundum legem et consuetudinem Angliae sine brevi regis placitari non debent. Pleas of trespass against the peace of the king in the kingdom of England, made with force and arms, ought not, by the law and custom of England, to be pleaded without the king's writ. 2 Inst. 311.

PLACITA JURIS (Lat.) Arbitrary rules of law. Bac. Law Tr. 73; Bac. Max. reg. 12.

PLACITA NEGATIVA DUO EXITUM non faciunt. Two negative pleas do not form an issue. Lofft, 415.

PLACITABILE (Law Lat.) In old English law. Pleadable. Spelman.

PLACITAMENTUM (Law Lat.) In old records. The pleading of a cause. Spelman.

PLACITARE (Law Lat. from *placitum, q. v.*) In old English law. To plead; to state to a court in form of law. *Placitantur placita,* pleas are pleaded. Bracton, fol. 106. *Placitavit* (he) pleaded. Y. B. M. 1 Edw. II.

To litigate; to make the subject of a plea or action; to implead or prosecute. Breve Gul. Conq. apud Hale, Hist. Com. Law, 120.

PLACITATOR (Law Lat. from *placitare, q. v.*) In old records. A pleader. Cowell; Spelman.

PLACITUM (Lat. from *placere*).

——**In Civil Law.** Any agreement or bargain; a law; a constitution or rescript of the emperor; the decision of a judge or award of arbitrators. Vicat; Calv. Lex.; Dupin, Notions Sur le Droit.

——**In Old English Law** (Ger. *plats;* Lat. *plateae, i. e.,* fields or streets). An assembly of all degrees of men, where the king presided, and they consulted about the great affairs of the kingdom. First held, as the name would show, in the fields or street. Cowell.

So on the continent. Hinc. de Ordine Palatii, c. 29; Bertinian, Annals of France, A. D. 767; Const. Car. Mag. c. ix.; Hinc. Epist. 197, 227; Laws of the Longobards, passim.

A lord's court. Cowell.

An ordinary court. *Placita* is the style of the English courts at the beginning of the record at *nisi prius.* In this sense, *placita* are divided into pleas of the crown and common pleas (*q. v.*) Cowell.

A trial or suit in court. Cowell. Jacobs.

A fine. Black Book of Exchequer, lib. 2, tit. 13; 1 Hen. I. cc. 12, 13.

A plea. This word is *nomen generalissimum,* and refers to all the pleas in the case. 1 Saund. 388, note 6; Skin. 554; Carth. 334; Yelv. 65. By *placitum* is also understood the subdivisions in abridgements and other works, where the point decided in a case is set down separately, and generally numbered. In citing, it is abbreviated as follows: Viner, Abr. "Abatement," pl. 3.

Placitum nominatum is the day appointed for a criminal to appear and plead.

Placitum fractum is a day past or lost to the defendant. 1 Hen. I. c. 59.

PLAGIARISM. The act of appropriating the ideas and language of another, and passing them for one's own. When this amounts to piracy, the party who has been guilty of it will be enjoined when the original author has a copyright. See "Copyright;" "Piracy;" "Quotation;" Pardessus, Dr. Com. note.

PLAGIARIUS (Lat.) In civil law. He who fraudulently concealed a freeman or slave who belonged to another.

The offense itself was called *plagium.* It differed from larceny or theft in this, that larceny always implies that the guilty party intended to make a profit, whereas the *plagiarius* did not intend to make any profit. Dig. 48. 15. 6; Code, 9. 20. 9. 15.

PLAGIUM (Lat.) Man stealing; kidnapping. This offense is the *crimen plagii* of the Romans. Alis. Crim. Law, 280, 281.

PLAIDEUR (Old Fr.) A pleader; an advocate.

PLAIN STATEMENT. One that may be readily understood, not merely by lawyers, but by all who are sufficiently acquainted with the language in which it is written. 5 Sandf. Ch. (N. Y.) 557, 564.

PLAINT. In English law. The exhibiting of any action, real or personal, in writing. The party making his plaint is called the plaintiff.

PLAINTIFF. He who complains. He who, in a personal action, seeks a remedy for an injury to his rights. 3 Bl. Comm. 25.

——**In Code Practice.** The person by whom a civil action is brought.

PLAINTIFF IN ERROR. A party who sues out a writ of error; and this, whether in the court below he was plaintiff or defendant.

PLANT. The fixtures and tools necessary to carry on any trade or mechanical business. 77 Ga. 748.

PLANTATIONS.

——**In English Law.** Colonies; dependencies. 1 Bl. Comm. 107. If this use of the term was ever current in America, it is now obsolete. See 7 Conn. 201.

In England, this word, as it is used in St. 12 Car. II. c. 18, is never applied to any of the British dominions in Europe, but only to the colonies in the West Indies and America. 1 Marsh. Ins. bk. 1, c. 3, § 2, p. 64. The title of the state of Rhode Island, at the time of the Articles of Confederation, was "Rhode Island and Providence Plantations."

——**In American Law.** A large estate, cultivated chiefly by negroes, who live in a distinct community on the estate, under the control of the proprietor. 79 Ga. 721. Apparently the term is applied in Maine to a minor civil subdivision. Webster.

PLAT. A map of a piece of land, on which are marked the courses and distances of the different lines, and the quantity of land it contains.

Such a plat may be given in evidence in ascertaining the position of the land and what is included, and may serve to settle the figure of a survey and correct mistakes. 5 T. B. Mon. (Ky.) 160. See 17 Mass. 211; 5 Me. 219; 7 Me. 61; 4 Wheat. (U. S.) 444; 14 Mass. 149.

PLATEA. (Latin.) A wide place; a court yard; a barn-yard. In old English law. A clear or open space of ground; a plat or plot of ground.

PLAY. (L. Fr.) In old English law. A plea, or action.

PLAZA. (Spanish derivation.) A plat of ground in a city or village dedicated to the use of the general public for a market place, a common or a park. 79 Ill. App. 441.

PLEA.

——**In Equity.** A special answer showing or relying upon one or more things as a cause why the suit should be either dismissed, or delayed, or barred. Mitf. Eq. Pl. (Jeremy Ed.) 219; Cooper, Eq. Pl. 223; Story, Eq. Pl. § 649.

The modes of making defense to a bill in equity are said to be by "demurrer," which demands of the court whether, from the matter apparent from the bill, the defendant shall answer at all; by "plea," which, resting on the foundation of new matter offered, demands whether the defendant shall answer further; by "answer," which responds generally to the charges of the bill; by "disclaimer," which denies any interest in the matters in question. Mitf. Eq. Pl. (Jeremy Ed.) 13; 2 Story (U. S.) 59; Story, Eq. Pl. § 437. Pleas are said to be "pure" which rely upon foreign matter to discharge or stay the suit, and "anomalous" or "negative" which consist mainly of denials of the substantial matters set forth in the bill. Story, Eq. Pl. §§ 651, 667; 2 Daniell, Ch. Pr. 97, 110; Beames, Eq. Pl. 123; Adams, Eq. 236.

(1) Pleas to the jurisdiction assert that the court before which the cause is brought is not the proper court to take cognizance of the matter.

(2) Pleas to the person may be to the person of the plaintiff or defendant. Those of the former class are mainly outlawry, excommunication, popish recusant convict, which are never pleaded in America, and very rarely now in England; attainder, which is now seldom pleaded (2 Atk. 399); alienage, which is not a disability unless the matter respect lands, when the alien may not hold them, or he be an alien enemy not under license (2 Ves. & B. 323); infancy, coverture, and idiocy, which are pleadable as at law (see "Abatement"); bankruptcy and insolvency, in which case all the facts necessary to establish the plaintiff as a legally declared bankrupt must be set forth (3 Mer. 667), though not necessarily as of the defendant's own knowledge (Younge, 331; 4 Beav. Rolls, 554; 1 Younge & C. 39); want of character in which he sues, as that he is not an administrator (2 Dick. 510; 1 Cox, 198), is not heir (2 Ves. & B. 159; 2 Brown, Ch. 143; 3 Brown, Ch. 489), is not a creditor (2 Sim. & S. 274), is not a partner (6 Madd. 61), as he pretends to be, that the plaintiff named is a fictitious person, or was dead at the commencement of the suit (Story, Eq. Pl. § 727). Those to the person of the defendant may show that the defendant is not the person he is alleged to be, or does not sustain the character given by the bill (6 Madd. 61; Rep. temp. Finch, 334), or that he is bankrupt, to require the assignees to be joined (Story, Eq. Pl. § 732). These pleas to the person are pleas in abatement, or, at least, in the nature of pleas in abatement.

(3) Pleas to the bill or the frame of the bill object to the suit as framed, or contend that it is unnecessary. These may be the pendency of another suit, which is analogous to the same plea at law, and is governed in most respects by the same principles (Story, Eq. Pl. § 736; 2 Mylne & C. 602; 1 Phil. Ch. 82; 1 Ves. Jr. 544; 4 Ves. Jr. 357; 1 Sim. & S. 491; Mitf. Eq. Pl. [Jeremy Ed.] 248; see "Lis Pendens"). and the other suit must be in equity, and not at law (Beames, Eq. Pl. 146-148); want of proper parties, which goes to both discovery and relief, where both are prayed for (Story, Eq. Pl. § 745; see 3 Younge & C. 447), but not to a bill of discovery merely (2 Paige [N. Y.] 280; 3 Paige [N. Y.] 222; 3 Cranch [U. S.] 220); a multiplicity of suits (1 P. Wms. 428; 2 Mason [U. S.] 190); multifariousness, which should be taken by way of demurrer, when the joining or confession of the distinct matters appears from the face of the bill, as it usually does (Story, Eq. Pl. § 271).

(4) Pleas in bar rely upon a bar created by statute, as, the statute of limitations (1 Sim. & S. 4; 2 Sim. 45; 3 Sumn. [U. S.] 152), which is a good plea in equity as well as at law, and with similar exceptions (Coop. Eq. Pl. 253; see "Statute of Limitations"), the statute of frauds, where its provisions apply (1 Johns. Ch. [N. Y., 425; 2 Johns. Ch. [N. Y.] 275; 4 Ves. 24, 720; 2 Brown, Ch. 559), or some other

public or private statute (2 Story, Eq. Jur. § 768); matter of record or as of record in some court, as, a common recovery (1 P. Wms. 754; 2 Freem. Ch. 180; 1 Vern. 13); a judgment at law (1 Keen, 456; 2 Mylne & C. 602; Story, Eq. Pl. § 781, note), the sentence or judgment of a foreign court or a court not of record (12 Clark & F. 368; 14 Sim. 265; 3 Hare, 100; 1 Younge & C. 464), especially where its jurisdiction is of a peculiar or exclusive nature (12 Ves. 307; Ambl. 756; 2 How. [U. S.] 619), with limitations in case of fraud (1 Ves. Jr. 284; Story, Eq. Pl. § 788), or a decree of the same or another court of equity (Cas. temp. Talb. 217; 7 Johns. Ch. [N. Y.] 1; 2 Sim. & S. 464; 2 Younge & C. 43); matters purely *in pais*, in which case the pleas may go to discovery, relief, or either, both, or part of either, of which the principal (though not the only) pleas are, account, stated or settled (2 Atk. 1; 13 Price, 767; 7 Paige [N. Y.] 573; 1 Mylne & K. 231), accord and satisfaction (1 Hale, 564), award (2 Ves. & B. 764), purchase for valuable consideration (2 Sumn. [U. S.] 507; 2 Younge & C. 457), release (3 P. Wms. 315), lapse of time, analogous to the statute of limitations (1 Ves. Jr. 264; 10 Ves. 466; 1 Younge & C. 432, 453; 2 Jac. & W. 1; 1 Hare, 594; 1 Russ. & M. 453; 2 Younge & C. 58; 1 Johns. Ch. [N. Y.] 46; 10 Wheat. [U. S.] 152; 1 Schoales & L. 721; 6 Madd. 61; 3 Paige [N. Y.] 273; 5 Paige [N. Y.] 26; 7 Paige [N. Y.] 62), title in the defendant (Story, Eq. Pl. § 812).

——**At Law.** The defendant's answer by matter of fact to the plaintiff's declaration, as distinguished from a demurrer, which is an answer by matter of law.

It includes as well the denial of the truth of the allegations on which the plaintiff relies, as the statement of facts on which the defendant relies. In an ancient use, it denoted action, and is still used sometimes in that sense; as, "summoned to answer in a plea of trespass." Steph. Pl. 38, 39, note; Warren, Law Stud. 272, note (w); Oliver, Prec. 97. In a popular, and not legal, sense, the word is used to denote a forensic argument. It was strictly applicable in a kindred sense when the pleadings were conducted orally by the counsel. Steph. Pl. Append. note 1.

Pleas are either dilatory, which tend to defeat the particular action to which they apply on account of its being brought before the wrong court, by or against the wrong person or in an improper form, or peremptory, which impugn the right of action altogether, or which answer the plaintiff's allegations of right conclusively. Pleas are also said to be to the jurisdiction of the court, in suspension of the action, in abatement of the writ, in bar of the action. The first three classes are dilatory, the last peremptory. Steph. Pl. 63; 1 Chit. Pl. 425; Lawes, Pl. 36.

Pleas are of various kinds,—in abatement (see "Abatement"); in avoidance, called, also, "confession and avoidance," which admits, in words or in effect, the truth of the matters contained in the declaration, and alleges some new matter to avoid the effect of it, and show that the plaintiff is, notwithstanding, not entitled to his action (1 Chit. Pl. 540; Lawes, Pl. 122), see "Confession and Avoidance"; in bar, which deny that the plaintiff has any cause of action (1 Chit. Pl. 407; Co. Litt. 303b). The term is often used in a restricted sense to denote what are with propriety called "special pleas in bar." These pleas are of two kinds,—the general issue, and special pleas in bar. See "Special Plea in Bar."

The parts of a plea are: First, the title of the court. Second, the title of the term. Third, the names of the parties in the margin. These, however, do not constitute any substantial part of the plea. The surnames only are usually inserted, and that of the defendant precedes the plaintiff's; as, "Roe ads. Doe." Fourth, the commencement, which includes the statement of the name of the defendant, the appearance, the defense (see "Defense"), the *actio non* (see "Actio Non"). Fifth, the body, which may contain the inducement, the protestation (see "Protestation"), ground of defense, *quae est eadem*, the traverse. Sixth, the conclusion.

(1) Dilatory pleas go to destroy the particular action, but do not affect the right of action in the plaintiff, and hence delay the decision of the cause upon its merits. Gould, Pl. c. ii. § 33. This class includes pleas to the jurisdiction, to the disability of the parties, and all pleas in abatement. All dilatory pleas must be pleaded with the greatest certainty, must contain a distinct, clear, and positive averment of all material facts, and must, in general, enable the plaintiff to correct the deficiency or error pleaded to. 1 Chit. Pl. 365. See "Abatement;" "Jurisdiction."

(2) Pleas in discharge admit the demand of the plaintiff, and show that it has been discharged by some matter of fact. Such are pleas of judgment, release, and the like.

(3) Pleas in excuse admit the demand or complaint stated in the declaration, but excuse the noncompliance with the plaintiff's claim, or the commission of the act of which he complains, on account of the defendant's having done all in his power to satisfy the former, or not having been the culpable author of the latter. A plea of tender is an example of the former, and a plea of *son assault demesne* an instance of the latter.

(4) Foreign pleas go to the jurisdiction, and their effect is to remove the action from the county in which the venue is originally laid. Carth. 402. Previous to the statute of Anne, an affidavit was required. 5 Mod. 335; Carth. 402; 1 Saund. Pl. 98, note 1; Viner, Abr. "Foreign Pleas;" 1 Chit. Pl. 382; Bac. Abr. "Abatement" (R).

(5) Pleas of justification, which assert that the defendant has purposely done the act of which the plaintiff complains, and in the exercise of his legal rights. 8 Term R. 78; 3 Wils. 71. No person is bound to justify who is not *prima facie* a wrongdoer. 1 Leon. 301; 2 Leon. 83; Cowp. 478; 4 Pick. (Mass.) 126; 13 Johns. (N. Y.) 443, 579; 1 Chit. Pl. 436.

(6) Pleas *puis darrein continuance*, which introduce new matter of defense, which has arisen or come to the plaintiff's knowledge since the last continuance. In most of the states, the actual continuance of a cause from one term to another, or from one particular day in term to another day in the same term, is practically done away with, and the prescribed times for pleading are fixed without any reference to terms of court. Still, this right of a defendant to change his plea so as to avail himself of facts rising during the course of the litigation remains unimpaired; and though there be no continuance, the plea is still called a plea *puis darrein continuance*, meaning, now, a plea upon facts arising since the last stage of the suit.

——**In Criminal Law.** The formal answer of the defendant to the indictment.

Pleas are either general or special; the general pleas being "guilty," "not guilty," and "*nollo contendere*," and all other pleas being special. Special pleas are either in bar, being, if found true, a bar to further prosecution, or in abatement, those which go merely to abate or suspend the proceeding. See "Pleading."

PLEA IN ABATEMENT. See "Plea."

PLEA IN BAR. See "Plea."

PLEA OF LIBERUM TENEMENTUM. A plea that at the time of the alleged trespass the plaintiffs were in the lawful possession of the premises as tenants of the defendant. 115 Ill. 180.

PLEA OF SET-OFF. A plea of set-off is in the nature of a cross-action, and the same principles apply as in the case of an original suit on the claim pleaded as a set-off. 88 Ill. App. 30. See Set-off.

PLEA SIDE. The plea side of a court is that branch or department of the court which entertains or takes cognizance of civil actions and suits, as distinguished from its criminal or crown department. Thus, the court of queen's bench is said to have a plea side and a crown or criminal side; the one branch or department of it being devoted to the cognizance of civil actions, the other to criminal proceedings and matters peculiarly concerning the crown. So the court of exchequer is said to have a plea side and a crown side; the one being appropriated to civil actions, the other to matters of revenue. Brown.

PLEAD ISSUABLY. To plead in such manner as to make an issue of law and fact.

PLEAD OVER. To interpose a general plea after a special plea or demurrer has been disposed of.

PLEADER (Law Fr. *pleador, pledor;* old Fr. *pleideoir;* Law Lat. *placitans advocatus*). A person professionally employed to manage another's cause for him, particularly to plead orally, or argue for him in court. The use of professional pleaders or advocates may be traced, among some of the continental nations, to a period extremely remote. Steph. Pl. Append. note (8). In the assizes of Jerusalem, the term "pleader" (*pledeoir*), is used as nearly synonymous with "counsel" (*conseill*).

PLEADING.

——**In Chancery Practice.** Consists in making the formal written allegations or statements of the respective parties on the record to maintain the suit, or to defeat it, of which, when contested in matters of fact, they propose to offer proofs, and in matters of law to offer arguments to the court. Story, Eq. Pl. § 4, note. The substantial object of pleading is the same, but the forms and rules of pleading are very different, at law and in equity.

——**In Civil Practice.** The stating in a logical and legal form the facts which constitute the plaintiff's cause of action or the defendant's ground of defense. It is the formal mode of alleging that on the record which constitutes the support or the defense of the party in evidence. 3 Term R. 159; Doug. 278; Comyn, Dig. "Pleader" (A); Bac. Abr. "Pleas and Pleading;" Comp. 682. Pleading is used to denote the act of making the pleadings.

——**In Criminal Practice.** The rules of pleading are the same as in civil practice. There is, however, less liberty of amendment of the indictment. The order of the defendant's pleading is as follows: First, to the jurisdiction; second, in abatement; third, special pleas in bar, as former jeopardy or pardon; fourth, the general issue.

See, generally, Lawes, Chitty, Stephen, and Gould on Pleading; 3 Bl. Comm. 301 et seq., and notes; Co. Litt. 303; Comyn, Dig. "Pleader;" Bac. Abr. "Plea and Pleading."

PLEADING, SPECIAL. By special pleading is meant the allegation of special or new matter, as distinguished from a direct denial of matter previously alleged on the opposite side. Gould, Pl. c. 1, § 18. See "Special Pleading."

PLEADINGS.

——**In Chancery Practice.** The written allegations of the respective parties in the suit. The pleadings in equity are less formal than those at common law.

The parts of the pleadings are (1) the bill, which contains the plaintiff's statement of his case. or information, where the suit is brought by a public officer in behalf of the sovereign; (2) the demurrer, by which the defendant demands judgment of the court, whether he shall be compelled to answer the bill or not; (3) the plea, whereby he shows some cause why the suit should be dismissed or barred; (4) the answer, which, controverting the case stated by the bill, confesses and avoids it, or traverses and denies the material allegations in the bill, or, admitting the case made by the bill, submits to the judgment of the court upon it, or relies upon a new case, or upon new matter stated in the answer, or upon both; (5) disclaimer, which seeks at once a termination of the suit by the defendants, disclaiming all right and interest in the matter sought by the bill. Story, Eq. Pl. § 546; Mitf. Eq. Pl. (Jeremy Ed.) 13, 106; Cooper, Eq. Pl. 108; 2 Story (U. S.) 59.

——**In Common-Law Civil Practice.** The statements of the parties, in legal and proper manner, of the causes of action and grounds of defense. The result of pleading. They were formerly made by the parties or their counsel, orally, in open court, under the control of the judge. They were then called the "parole." 3 Bl. Comm. 293; 2 Reeve, Hist. Eng. Law, 267.

The regular parts are (1) the declaration or count; (2) the plea, which is either to the jurisdiction of the court, or suspending the action, as in the case of a parol demurrer, or in abatement, or in bar of the action, or in replevin, an avowry or cognizance; (3) the replication, and, in case of an evasive plea, a new assignment, or, in replevin, the plea in bar to the avowry or cognizance; (4) the rejoinder, or, in replevin the replication to the plea in bar; (5) the sur-rejoinder, being in replevin the rejoinder; (6) the rebutter; (7) the sur-rebutter (Viner, Abr. "Pleas and Pleading" [C]; Bac. Abr. "Pleas and Pleadings" [A]); (8) pleas *puis darrein continuance*, when the matter of defense arises pending the suit.

The irregular or collateral parts of pleading are stated to be (1) demurrers to any part of the pleadings above mentioned; (2) demurrers to evidence given at trials; (3) bills of exceptions; (4) pleas in *scire facias;* (5) and please in error. Viner, Abr. "Pleas and Pleadings" (C); Bouv. Inst. Index.

——**In Civil Practice under the Codes.** The pleadings are (1) the complaint, (2) the answer, (3) the reply, and (4) the demurrer, which lies to either complaint, answer or reply.

——**In Criminal Practice.** The pleadings are (1) the indictment; (2) the plea, either special or general.

PLEAS OF THE CROWN. In English law. A phrase now employed to signify criminal causes in which the king is a party. Formerly it signified royal causes for offenses of a greater magnitude than mere misdemeanors.

These were left to be tried in the courts of the barons; whereas the greater offenses, or royal causes, were to be tried in the king's courts, under the appellation of "pleas of the crown." 1 Robertson, Hist. Charles V. 48.

PLEAS ROLL. In English practice. A record which contains the declaration, plea, replication, rejoinder, and other pleadings, and the issue. Eunom. Dial. 2, § 29, p. 111.

PLEBEIAN. One who is classed among the common people, as distinguished from the nobles.

PLEBEYOS. In Spanish law. Commons; those who exercise any trade, or who cultivate the soil. White, New Recop. bk. 1, tit. 5, c. 3, § 6, and note.

PLEBISCITE. A submission to the popular vote of a law or governmental policy.

PLEBISCITUM (Lat.) In Roman law. A law established by the people (*plebs*), on the proposal of a popular magistrate, as a tribune. Vicat; Calv. Lex.; Mackeld. Civ. Law, §§ 27, 37.

PLEBITY. The plebeians.

PLEBS (Lat.) In the Roman law. The commonalty, or citizens, exclusive of the patricians and senators. *Plebis appellatione, sine patriciis et senatoribus, caeteri cives significantur.* Inst. 1. 2. 4; Dig. 50. 16. 238, pr.

PLEDABLE (Law Fr.) That may be brought or conducted, as an action, or "plea," as it was formerly called. Britt. c. 32.

PLEDGE, or PAWN. A bailment of personal property as security for some debt or engagement. 41 N. Y. 241.

A deposit of personal property as security, with an implied power of sale in case of default. Jones, Pl. § 1.

A pledge or pawn (Lat. *pignus*), according to Story, is a bailment of personal property as security for some debt or engagement. Story, Bailm. § 286, which see for the less comprehensive definitions of Sir Wm. Jones, Lord Holt, Pothier, etc. Domat broadly defines it as an appropriation of the thing given for the security of an engagement. But the term is commonly used as Sir Wm. Jones defines it, to wit, as a bailment of goods by a debtor to his creditor, to be kept till the debt is discharged. Jones, Bailm. 117; 2 Ld. Raym. 909; Poth. de Naut. art. prelim. 1; Civ. Code, art. 2071; Domat, bk. 3, tit. 1, § 1, note 1; Civ. Code La. art. 3100; 6 Ired. (N. C.) 309. The pledgee secures his debt by the bailment, and the pledgor obtains credit or other advantage. See 1 Pars. Cont. 591 et seq.

Pledge and pawn. At common law, the terms were synonymous, but in modern usage "pawn" generally indicates the pledging of goods with a pawnbroker (*q. v.*)

Pledge and mortgage. A pledge is distinguished from a chattel mortgage in that it depends for its validity on possession of the subject matter.

Pledge and hypothecation. Hypothecation (*q. v.*) is a special form of pledge wherein the possession remains in the debtor.

——In Louisiana. There are two kinds of pledges,—the pawn and the antichresis. The former relates to movable securities, and the latter to immovables. If a creditor have not a right to enter on the land and reap the fruits, the security is not an antichresis. 3 La. 157. A pledge of negotiable paper is not valid against third parties without transfer from debtor to creditor. 2 La. 387. See, in general, 13 Pet. (U. S.) 351; 5 Mart. (La.; N. S.) 618; 18 La. 543; 1 La. Ann. 340; 2 La. Ann. 872.

PLEDGEE. One to whom a thing is pledged.

PLEDGERY. Suretyship.

PLEDGES. In pleading. Those persons who became sureties for the plaintiff's prosecution of the suit. Their names were anciently appended at the foot of the declaration. In time it became purely a formal matter, because the plaintiff was no longer liable to be amerced for a false claim, and the fictitious persons John Doe and Richard Roe became the universal pledges, or they might be omitted altogether (1 Tidd, Prac. 455; Archb. Civ. Pl. 171), or inserted at any time before judgment (4 Johns. [N. Y.] 90), and are now omitted.

PLEDGES TO RESTORE. In England, before the plaintiff in foreign attachment can issue execution against the property in the hands of the garnishee, he must find "pledges to restore," consisting of two householders, who enter into a recognizance for the restoration of the property, as a security for the protection of the defendant; for, as the plaintiff's debt is not proved in any stage of the proceedings, the court guards the rights of the absent defendant by taking security on his behalf, so that, if he should afterwards disprove the plaintiff's claim, he may obtain restitution of the property attached. Brand, For. Attachm. 93.

PLEDGOR. The party who makes a pledge.

PLEE (Law Fr.) In old English law. An action or suit; a "plea" in the ancient sense of the word. *Parsonels plees pledables par attachments*, personal actions which may be prosecuted by attachments. Britt. c. 32. *En plees realx, et auxi en plees personals*, in real actions, and also in personal actions. Litt. § 464.

A plea, in the modern sense. *Plee en barre*, a plea in bar. Litt. § 492.

PLEGIABILIS (Law Lat.) In old English law. That may be pledged; the subject of pledge or security. Fleta, lib. 1, c. 20, § 98.

PLEGII DE PROSEQUENDO. Pledges to prosecute with effect an action of replevin.

PLEGII DE RETORNO HABENDO. Pledges to return the subject of distress, should the right be determined against the party bringing the action of replevin. 3 Steph. Comm. (7th Ed.) 422, note.

PLEGIIS ACQUIETANDIS, WRIT DE. The name of an ancient writ in the English law, which lies where a man becomes pledge or surety for another to pay a certain sum of money at a certain day. After the day, if the debtor does not pay the debt, and the surety be compelled to pay, he shall have this writ to compel the debtor to pay the same. Fitzh. Nat. Brev. 321.

PLENA AETAS. Of full age.

PLENA ET CELERIS JUSTITIA FIAT partibus. Let full and speedy justice be done to the parties. 4 Inst. 67.

PLENA FORISFACTURA. A forfeiture of all that one possesses.

PLENA PROBATIO. In civil law. A term used to signify full proof, in contradistinction to *semi-plena probatio*, which is only a presumption. Code, 4. 19. 5. et seq.; 1 Greenl. Ev. § 119.

PLENARTY. In ecclesiastical law. Signifies that a benefice is full. See "Avoidance."

PLENARY. Full; complete.

In the courts of admiralty, and in the English ecclesiastical courts, causes or suits in respect of the different course of proceedings in each are termed "plenary" or "summary." Plenary, or full and formal, suits are those in which the proceedings must be full and formal; the term "summary" is applied to those causes where the proceedings are more succinct and less formal. 2 Chit. Prac. 481.

PLENE ADMINISTRAVIT (Lat. he has fully administered). In pleading. A plea in bar entered by an executor or administrator, by which he affirms that he had not in his possession at the time of the commencement of the suit, nor has had at any time since, any goods of the deceased to be administered. When the plaintiff replies that the defendant had goods, etc., in his possession at that time, and the parties join issue, the burden of the proof will be on the plaintiff. See 15 Johns. (N. Y.) 323; 6 Term R. 10; 1 Barn. & Ald. 254; 11 Viner, Abr. 349; 12 Viner, Abr. 185; 2 Phil. Ev. 295; 6 Comyn, Dig. 311.

PLENE ADMINISTRAVIT PRAETER (Lat. he has fully administered except). In pleading. A plea by which a defendant executor or administrator admits that there is a balance remaining in his hands unadministered.

PLENE COMPUTAVIT (Lat. he has fully accounted). In pleading. A plea in an action of account render, by which the defendant avers that he has fully accounted. Bac. Abr. "Accompt" (E). This plea does not admit the liability of the defendant to account. 15 Serg. & R. (Pa.) 153.

PLENIPOTENTIARY. Possessing full powers; as, a minister plenipotentiary is one authorized fully to settle the matters connected with his mission, subject, however, to the ratification of the government by which he is authorized.

PLENUM DOMINIUM (Lat.) The unlimited right which the owner has to use his property as he deems proper, without accountability to any one.

PLEYNTYFE (L. Fr. from *pleyndre*, to complain). In old English law. Plaintiff; a complaining party.

PLEYTO. In Spanish law. The pleadings in a cause. White, New Recop. bk. 3, tit. 7.

PLIGHT. An old English word, used sometimes for the estate with the habit and quality of the land. Co. Litt. 221. It extends to a rent charge, and to a possibility of dower. Id.; 1 Rolle, Abr. 447; Litt. § 289.

PL'IT'M. A contraction of *placitum*. *Pl'ito*, of *placito*. 1 Inst. Cl. 11.

PLOUGH BOTE. An allowance made to a rural tenant of wood sufficient for ploughs, harrows, carts, and other instruments of husbandry.

PLOUGH LAND. In old English law. An uncertain quantity of land. According to some opinions, it contains one hundred and twenty acres. Co. Litt. 69a.

PLOUGH SILVER. Money paid by tenants in composition of a duty to plough.

PLUMBATURA (Lat. from *plumbum*, lead). In the civil law. Soldering. Dig. 6. 1. 23. 5.

PLUMBUM (Lat.) In the civil law. Lead. Dig. 50. 16. 242. 2.

PLUNDER. The capture of personal property on land by a public enemy, with a view of making it his own. The property so captured is called "plunder."

The taking by open force, as by pirates.

It has been used in the sense of aggravated and open larceny. 8 Fed. 232.

PLUNDERAGE. In maritime law. The embezzlement of goods on board of a ship is known by the name of "plunderage."

The rule of the maritime law in such cases is that the whole crew shall be responsible for the property thus embezzled, because there must be some negligence in finding out the depredator. Abb. Shipp. 457; 3 Johns. (N. Y.) 17; 1 Pet. Adm. (U. S.) 200, 239, 243; 4 Bos. & P. 347.

PLURAL. Words implying the plural may be construed to include the singular: the greater includes the less. 1 Iowa, 282; 60 Mich. 462; 54 Mich. 245.

PLURALIS NUMERUS EST DUOBUS contentus. The plural number is contained in two. 1 Rolle, 476.

PLURALITER. In the plural; plurally.

PLURALITY. The greatest number of votes given for any one person.

Plurality has the meaning, as used in governmental law, given above. Thus, if there are three candidates, for whom four hundred, three hundred and fifty, and two hundred and fifty votes are respectively given, the one receiving four hundred has a plurality, while five hundred and one would be a majority of the votes cast.

PLURES COHAEREDES SUNT QUASI unum corpus, propter unitatem juris quod habent. Several coheirs are as one body, by reason of the unity of right which they possess. Co. Litt. 163.

PLURES PARTICIPES SUNT QUASI unum corpus, in eo quod unum jus habent. Several part owners are as one body, by reason of the unity of their rights. Co. Litt. 164.

PLURIES (Lat. many times). A writ issued subsequently to a first and second (*alias*) of the same kind, which have proved ineffectual. The name is given to it from the word *pluries* in the Latin form of the writ: "We command you, as we have often (*pluries*) commanded you before," which distinguishes it from those which have gone before. *Pluries* is variously translated, in the modern forms of writs, by "formerly," "more than once," "often." The next writ to the *pluries* is called the second *pluries*," and so on. 3 Bl. Comm. 283, Append. 15; Nat. Brev. 33.

PLURIS PETITIO (Lat.) In Scotch practice. An excessive demand.

PLUS EXEMPLA QUAM PECCATA NOcent. Examples hurt more than offenses.

PLUS PECCAT AUCTOR QUAM ACtor. The instigator of a crime is worse than he who perpetrates it. 5 Coke, 99.

PLUS PETITIO. In Roman law. A phrase denoting the offense of claiming more than was just in one's pleadings. This "more" might be claimed in four different respects, viz.: (1) *Re*, *i. e.*, in amount (*e. g.*, £50 for £5); (2) *loco*, *i. e.*, in place (*e. g.*, delivery at some place more difficult to effect than the place specified); (3) *tempore*, *i. e.*, in time (*e. g.*, claiming payment on the 1st of August of what is not due till the 1st of September); and (4) *causa, i. e.*, in quality (*e. g.*, claiming a dozen of champagne, when the contract was only for a dozen of wine generally). Prior to Justinian's time, this offense was in general fatal to the action; but, under the legislation of the emperors Zeno and Justinian, the offense (if *re, loco*, or *causa*) exposed the party to the payment of three times the damage, if any, sustained by the other side, and (if *tempore*) obliged him to postpone his action for double the time, and to pay the costs of his first action before commencing a second. Brown.

PLUS VALET CONSUETUDO QUAM concessio. Custom is more powerful than grant.

PLUS VALET UNUS OCULATUS TEStis, quam auriti decem. One eye witness is better than ten ear ones. 4 Inst. 279.

PLUS VIDENT OCULI QUAM OCULUS. Eyes see more than one eye. 4 Inst. 160.

PO. LO. SUO. An old abbrevation for the words "*ponit loco suo*," put in his place, used in warrants of attorney. Towns. Pl. 431.

POACHING. Unlawful taking of game from the land of another. Unlawfully entering land, in nighttime, armed, with intent to destroy game. 1 Russ. Crimes, 469; 2 Steph. Comm. 82; 2 Chit. St. 221-245.

POBLADOR. In Spanish law. A colonizer; he who peoples; the founder of a colony.

POCKET JUDGMENT. A statute merchant which was enforceable at any time after nonpayment on the day assigned, without further proceedings. Wharton.

POCKET SHERIFF. In English law. A sheriff appointed by sole authority of the crown, not being one of the three nominated by the judges in the exchequer. 1 Bl. Comm. 342*.

POENA AD PAUCOS, METUS AD OMnes perveniat. If punishment be inflicted on a few, a dread comes to all.

POENA CORPORALIS. Corporal punishment.

POENA EX DELICTO DEFUNCTI, HAEres teneri non debet. The heir ought not to be bound in a penalty inflicted for the crime of the ancestor. 2 Inst. 198.

POENA NON POTEST, CULPA PERENnis erit. Punishment cannot be, crime will be, perpetual. 21 Viner, Abr. 271.

POENA PILLORALIS. In old English law. Punishment of the pillory. Fleta, lib. 1, c. 38, § 11.

POENAE POTIUS MOLLIENDAE QUAM exasperandae sunt. Punishments should rather be softened than aggravated. 3 Inst. 220.

POENAE SINT RESTRINGENDAE. Punishments should be restrained. Jenk. Cent. Cas. 29.

POENAE SUOS TENERE DEBET ACTOres et non alios. Punishment ought to be inflicted upon the guilty, and not upon others. Bracton, 380b; Fleta, lib. 1, c. 38, § 12; Id. lib. 4, c. 17, § 17.

POENALIS (Lat. from *poena*). In the civil law. Penal; imposing a penalty; claiming or enforcing a penalty. *Actiones poenales*, actions for penalties; penal actions. Inst. 4. 6. 12.

POENITENTIA (Lat. from *poenitere*, to repent). In the civil law. Repentance; a change of mind or purpose; the rescinding of a contract.

POER, *Poeir, Poair.* L. Fr. Power; authority.

POET, *Poit, Puit, Pout.* L. Fr. May; can.

POINDING. In Scotch law. That diligence (*q. v.*) affecting movable subjects by which their property is carried directly to the creditor. Poinding is real or personal. Ersk. Inst. 3. 6. 11.

——**Personal.** Poinding of the goods belonging to the debtor, and of those goods only.

It may have for its warrant either letters of horning, containing a clause for poinding, and then it is executed by messengers; or precepts of poinding, granted by sheriffs, commissaries, etc., which are executed by their proper officers. No cattle pertaining to the plough, nor instrument of tillage, can be poinded in the time of laboring or tilling the ground, unless where the debtor has no other goods they may be poinded. Ersk. Inst. 3. 6. 11. This process is somewhat similar to distress.

——**Real.** Poinding of the ground. Though it be properly a diligence, this is generally considered by lawyers as a species of real action, and is so called to distinguish it from personal poinding, which is founded merely on an obligation to pay.

Every *debitum fundi*, whether legal or conventional, is a foundation for this action. It is therefore competent to all creditors in debts which make a real burden on lands. As it proceeds on a real right, it may be directed against all goods that can be found on the lands burdened; but goods brought upon the ground by strangers are not subject to this diligence. Even the goods of a tenant cannot be poinded for more than his term's rent. Ersk. Inst. 4. 1. 3.

POINT. A single distinct proposition or principle of law.

POINT RESERVED. A point or question of law which the court, not being fully satisfied how to decide, in the hurried trial of a cause, rules in favor of the party offering it, but subject to revision on a motion for a new trial. If, after argument, it be found to have been ruled correctly, the verdict is supported; if otherwise, it is set aside.

POISON. In medical jurisprudence. A substance having an inherent deleterious property which renders it, when taken into the system, capable of destroying life. Whart. & S. Med. Jur. § 493; Tayl. Poisons (2d Am. Ed.) 18.

POLE. A measure of length, equal to five yards and a half.

POLICE. That species of superintendence by magistrates which has principally for its object the maintenance of public tranquillity among the citizens. The officers who are appointed for this purpose are also called the police.

"Police is in general a system of precaution either for the prevention of crime or of calamities." Bentham.

The due regulation and domestic order of the kingdom, whereby the individuals of the state, like members of a well-governed family, are bound to conform their general behavior to the rules of propriety. 4 Bl. Comm. 162.

The word "police" has three significations. The first relates to the measures which are adopted to keep order, the laws and ordinances on cleanliness, health, the markets, etc. The second has for its object to procure to the authorities the means of detecting even the smallest attempts to commit crime, in order that the guilty may be arrested before their plans are carried into execution, and delivered over to the justice of the country. The third comprehends the laws, ordinances, and other measures which require the citizens to exercise their rights in a particular form.

Police has also been divided into "administrative police," which has for its object to maintain constantly public order in every part of the general administration; and "judiciary police," which is intended principally to prevent crimes by punishing the criminals. Its object is to punish crimes which the administrative police has not been able to prevent.

POLICE JURY. In Louisiana. A name given to certain officers who collectively exercise jurisdiction in certain cases of police; as, levying taxes, regulating roads, etc.

POLICE JUSTICE. A magistrate having criminal jurisdiction of minor offenses similar to that of a justice of the peace, but charged exclusively with the duties incident to the common-law office of the conservator of the peace. The prefix "police" serves merely to distinguish them from justices having also civil jurisdiction. 58 N. Y. 530. Usually a city officer.

POLICE POWER. The general power of government in the administration of its police (*q. v.*), to preserve and promote the welfare of the public, even at the expense of infringing the private rights of individuals. Cooley, Const. Lim. 704.

It is an exception to the right of the citizen to conduct himself and use his property in such manner as he may see fit.

"It involves a provision and means of enforcing the legal maxim which underlies all law,—*sic utere tuo ut alienum non laedas*. The power of the government to impose this restraint is called 'police power'." Tiedeman, Lim. Police Power, § 1.

"The police power of a state extends to the protection of the lives, limbs, health, comfort, and quiet of all persons, and to the protection of all property within the state, and hence to the making of all regulations promotive of domestic order, morals, health, and safety." 95 U. S. 465.

POLICY. In insurance. The instrument whereby insurance is made by an underwriter in favor of an assured, expressed, implied, or intended, against some risk, peril, or contingency in reference to some subject. It is usually either marine, or against fire, or on a life.

(1) An interest policy is one where the insured has a real, substantial, assignable interest in the thing insured.

(2) An open policy is one on which the value is to be proved by the assured. 1 Phil. Ins. §§ 4, 6, 7, 27, 439, 948, 1178. By an "open policy" is also sometimes meant, in the United States, one in which an aggregate amount is expressed in the body of the policy, and the specific amounts and subjects are to be indorsed from time to time. 12 La. Ann. 259; 19 N. Y. 305; 6 Gray (Mass.) 214.

(3) A valued policy is one where a value has been set on the ship or goods insured, and this value inserted in the policy in the nature of liquidated damages. In such a policy, the value of the subject is expressly agreed, or is, as between the parties, the amount insured.

(4) A wager policy is a pretended insurance, founded on an ideal risk, where the insured has no interest in the thing insured, and can therefore sustain no loss by the happening of any of the misfortunes insured against. These policies are strongly reprobated. 3 Kent, Comm. 225.

POLICY OF THE LAW. Public policy (*q. v.*)

POLITIAE LEGIBUS NON LEGES POLITIIS ADAPTANDAE. Politics are to be adapted to the laws, and not the laws to politics. Hob. 154.

POLITICAL. Pertaining to policy, or the administration of the government. 90 Ill. 563. Political rights are those which may be exercised in the formation or administration of the government; "rights" being synonymous with "power." 90 Ill. 563. They are distinguished from civil rights, which are the rights which a man enjoys as regards other individuals, and not in relation to the government. A political corporation is one which has principally for its object the administration of the government, or to which the powers of government, or a part of such powers, have been delegated. 1 Bouv. Inst. notes 182, 197, 198.

POLITICAL ARITHMETIC. An expression sometimes used to signify the art of making calculations on matters relating to a nation; the revenues, the value of land and effects; the produce of lands and manufactures; the population, and the general statistics of a country. Wharton.

POLITICAL OFFENSES. A class of offenses excluded from many extradition treaties, and including, generally, crimes against the government as such, and crimes incident to political uprisings. Treason, sedition, *lese majestae*, etc., are examples. Spear, Extradition, 48.

The nature of political offenses is open to treaty definition, and in some treaties it has been defined to exclude the assassination of the ruler.

POLITICAL OFFICES. Such as are not immediately connected with the administration of justice, or with the execution of the orders of a superior, as the president or the head of a department. 13 Wall. (U. S.) 568, 575.

POLITICAL OR CIVIL LIBERTY. Natural liberty, so far restrained by human laws as is necessary and expedient for the general advantage of the public. 1 Bl. Comm. 125.

POLITICAL QUESTIONS. Questions involving executive policy, and within the power of the executive to determine, such as the recognition of a particular government in a foreign state. Such questions will not be decided by the courts. See 7 How. (U. S.) 39.

POLITICAL RIGHTS. Rights which may be exercised in the formation or administration of the government, the word "rights," as so used, being synonymous with "power." 90 Ill. 563.

A political right is a right exercisable in the establishment or administration of government, while a civil right is a right accorded to every member of a distinct community or nation with reference to property, family or marriage, and the like. Political rights consist in the power to participate, directly or indirectly, in the establishment or management of government. 203 Ill. 104; 151 Ill. 41; 122 N. E. 344. See Civil Rights; Political.

POLITICS. The science and art of government; the science dealing with the organization, regulation and administration of a state in both its internal and external affairs. 264 Ill. 313.

POLL. A head. Hence poll tax is the name of a tax imposed upon the people at so much a head.

To poll a jury is to require that each juror shall himself declare what is his verdict. This may be done, at the instance of either party, at any time before the verdict is recorded, according to the practice in some states. See 3 Cow. (N. Y.) 23; 18 Johns. (N. Y.) 188; 1 Ill. 109; 7 Ill. 342; 9 Ill. 336. In some states it lies in the discretion of the judge. 1 McCord (S. C.) 24, 525; 22 Ga. 431.

——**In Conveyancing.** A deed poll, or single deed, is one made by a single party, whose edges are polled, or shaved even, in distinction from an "indenture," whose sides are indented, and which is executed by more than one party. 2 Bl. Comm. 296. See "Deed Poll."

POLLICITATION. In civil law. A promise not yet accepted by the person to whom it is made. It differs from a contract, inasmuch as the latter includes a concurrence of intention in two parties, one of whom promises something to the other, who accepts, on his part, of such promise. Grotius de Jure Belli, lib. 2, c. 2; Poth. Obl. pt. 1, c. 1, sec. 1, art. 1, § 2.

POLLS. The place where electors cast in their votes.

POLYANDRY. The state of a woman who has several husbands. Polyandry is legalized only in Thibet.

POLYGAMIA EST PLURIUM SIMUL VIrorum uxorumve connubium. Polygamy is the marriage with many husbands or wives at one time. 3 Inst. 88.

POLYGAMY. The act or state of a person who, knowing that he has two or more wives, or that she has two or more husbands, marries another.

It differs fom "bigamy" (*q. v.*) Comyn, Dig. "Justices" (S 5); Dict. de Jur.; 3 Inst. 88.

But "bigamy" is now commonly used even where "polygamy" would be strictly correct. 1 Russ. Crimes, 186, note. On the other hand, "polygamy" is used where "bigamy" would be strictly correct. Gen. St. Mass. 1860, p. 817.

POLYGARCHY. A term used to express a government which is shared by several persons; as, when two brothers succeed to the throne, and reign jointly.

POND. A body of stagnant water; a pool, either natural or artificial. 13 Pick. (Mass.) 265. A pond differs from a lake only in size.

PONDERANTUR TESTES NON NUMErantur. Witnesses are weighed, not counted.

1 Starkie, Ev. 554; Best, Ev. 426, § 389; 14 Wend. (N. Y.) 105, 109.

PONDUS (Lat.) In old English law. Poundage; literally, weight. A duty anciently paid to the king.

PONDUS REGIS (Lat.) In old English law. The king's weight; the standard weight appointed by the king. Cowell; 1 Bl. Comm. 276.

PONE (Lat. *ponere*, to put). In English practice. An original writ issuing out of chancery, for the purpose of removing a plaint from an inferior court into the superior courts at Westminster. The word signifies "put,"—put by gages, etc. The writ is called from the words it contained when in Latin, *pone per vadium et salvos plegios*, etc., put by gage and safe pledges, etc. See Fitzh. Nat. Brev. 69, 70a; Wilkinson, Repl. Index.

PONE PER VADIUM. In English practice. An obsolete writ to the sheriff to summon the defendant to appear and answer the plaintiff's suit, on his putting in sureties to prosecute. It was so called from the words of the writ, "*pone per vadium et salvos plegios*," "put by gage and safe pledges, A. B., the defendant." It issued out of the common pleas, being grounded on the non-appearance of the defendant at the return of the original writ, and commanded the sheriff to take certain of his goods, which he should forfeit if he did not appear or make him find sureties. 3 Bl. Comm. 210.

PONENDIS IN ASSISIS. An obsolete writ to impanel a jury.

PONENDUM IN BALLIUM. A writ commanding that a prisoner be bailed in cases bailable. Reg. Orig. 133.

PONENDUM SIGILLUM AD EXCEPTIonem. A writ by which justices were required to put their seals to exceptions exhibited by a defendant against a plaintiff's evidence, verdict, or other proceedings, before them, according to St. Westminster II. (13 Edw. I. st. 1, c. 31).

PONERE (Lat.) To put. The word is used in the old law in various connections, in all of which it can be translated by the English verb "put." See Glanv. lib. 2, c. 3.

PONIT SE (Lat. puts himself). In English criminal practice. When the defendant pleads "not guilty," his plea is recorded by the officer of the court, either by writing the words "*po. se*," an abbreviation of the words *ponit se super patriam*, puts himself upon his country, or, as at the central criminal court, *non cul.* 2 Den. C. C. 392. See "Arraignment."

PONTAGE. A contribution towards the maintenance, rebuilding, or repairs of a bridge. The toll taken for this purpose also bears this name. Obsolete.

PONTIBUS REPARANDIS. An old writ directed to the sheriff, requiring him to charge one or more to repair a bridge. Reg. Orig. 153.

POOL. A pond (*q. v.*)

A combination of independent persons or corporations for the division of earnings. See "Pooling Contract."

A pool or trust is a combination having the intention and power, or tendency, to monopolize business, or to control production, or to interfere with trade, or to fix and regulate prices, and the like. The primary object of a pool or trust is to secure a monopoly. The law does not call for proof of monopoly in order to declare such combinations unlawful. 114 Ill. App. 112.

POOLING CONTRACT. Strictly, an agreement between common carriers to divide their earnings on an agreed basis, irrespective of the proportions which such earnings bore to each other, the same being put into a common fund or "pool" (15 Fed. 667; 23 Fed. 306); but the term is loosely applied to other combinations of carriers. See 126 Ind. 348.

POOR DEBTOR. One who, being imprisoned in a civil action, has no property to pay the debt whereon the same was issued, and who is accordingly entitled to his release on making oath to such fact, and on other conditions variously affixed by statute.

POOR DEBTOR'S OATH. An oath of poverty, on taking which one imprisoned on execution is entitled to release.

POPE. The bishop of Rome and the head of the Roman Catholic church. He is a temporal prince. He is elected by certain officers called "cardinals," and remains in power during life. In the 9th Collation of the Authentics, it is declared the bishop of Rome hath the first place of sitting in all assemblies, and the bishop of Constantinople the second. Ridley, Civ. & Ecc. Law, pt. 1, c. 3, § 10.

POPULAR ACTION. An action given by statute to any one who will sue for the penalty. A *qui tam* action. Dig. 47. 23. 1.

POPULISCITUM (Lat.) An act of the commons; same as *plebiscitum.* Ainsworth.

A law passed by the whole people assembled in *comitia centuriata,* and at the proposal of one of the senate, instead of a tribune, as was the case with a *plebiscitum.* Tayl. Civ. Law, 178; Mackeld. Civ. Law, §§ 26, 37.

POPULUS (Lat.) In the Roman law. The people; the whole body of the citizens, including, with the *plebs* or commonalty, the patricians and senators; *appellatione populi universi cives significantur, connumeratis etiam patriciis et senatoribus.* Inst. 1. 2. 4.

PORCION. In Spanish law. A part or portion; a lot or parcel; an allotment of land. See 16 S. W. 49.

PORT. A place to which the officers of the customs are appropriated, and which includes the privileges and guidance of all members and creeks which are allotted to them. 1 Chit. Com. Law, 726; Postlethwaite.

A proper place for the lading or unlading of vessels, recognized and supervised for maritime purposes by the public authorities.

A port differs from a haven, and includes something more. First, it is a place at which vessels may arrive and discharge or take in their cargoes. Second, it comprehends a ville, city, or borough, called in Latin *caput corpus*, for the reception of mariners and merchants, for securing the goods and bringing them to market, and for victualling the ships. Third, it is impressed with its legal character by the civil authority. Hale de Port. Mar. c. 2; 1 Harg. Tr. 46, 73; Bac. Abr. "Prerogative" (D 5); Comyn, Dig. "Navigation" (E); 4 Inst. 148; Callis, Sewers, 56; 2 Chit. Com. Law, 2; Dig. 50. 16. 59; Id. 43. 12. 1. 13; Id. 47. 10. 15. 7; Id. 39. 4. 15.

PORT TOLL. The toll paid for bringing goods into a port.

PORTARE. (L. Lat.) In old English practice. To bear; to bring.

PORTATICA (Law Lat.) In English law. The generic name for port duties charged to ships. Harg. Tr. 74.

PORTER. The name of an ancient English officer who bore or carried a rod before the justices. The door keeper of the English parliament also bears this name.

One who is employed as a common carrier to carry goods from one place to another in the same town is also called a porter. Such person is, in general, answerable as a common carrier. Story, Bailm. § 496.

PORTGREVE (from Saxon *gerefa*, reeve or bailiff, and port). A chief magistrate in certain maritime towns. The chief magistrate of London was anciently so called, as appears from a charter of King William I. Instead of this portgreve of London, the succeeding kings appointed two bailiffs, and afterwards a mayor. Camden, Hist. 325.

PORTMEN. The burgesses of Ipswich and of the Cinque Ports were so called.

PORTMOTE. In old English law. A court held in ports or haven towns, and sometimes in inland towns also. Cowell; Blount.

PORTORIA (Lat.) In civil law. Duties paid in ports on merchandise. Code, 4. 61. 3. Taxes levied in old times at city gates; tolls for passing over bridges. Vicat; Spelman.

PORTSALES. Auctions were anciently so called, because they took place in ports.

PORTSOKA, or **PORTSOKEN.** The suburbs of a city, or any place within its jurisdiction. Somner; Cowell.

POSITIVE. Express; absolute; not doubtful. This word is frequently used in composition.

POSITIVE CONDITION. One in which the thing which is the subject of it must happen; as, if I marry. It is opposed to a negative condition, which is where the thing which is the subject of it must not happen; as, if I do not marry.

POSITIVE EVIDENCE. That which, if believed, establishes the truth or falsehood of a fact in issue, and does not arise from any presumption. It is distinguished from circumstantial evidence (*q. v.*) 3 Bouv. Inst. note 3057.

POSITIVE FRAUD. The intentional and successful employment of any cunning, deception, or artifice to circumvent, cheat, or deceive another. 1 Story, Eq. Jur. 186; Dig. 4. 3. 1. 2; Id. 2. 14. 7. 9. It is cited in opposition to constructive fraud.

POSITIVE LAW. Law actually ordained or established, under human sanctions, as distinguished from the law of nature or natural law, which comprises those considerations of justice, right, and universal expediency that are announced by the voice of reason or of revelation. Municipal law is chiefly, if not essentially, positive; while the law of nations has been deemed by many of the earlier writers as merely an application of the law of nature. That part of the law of nations which rests on positive law may be considered in a threefold point of view: First, the universal voluntary law, or those rules which become law by the uniform practice of nations in general, and by the manifest utility of the rules themselves; second, the customary law, or that which, from motives of convenience, has, by tacit but implied agreement, prevailed not necessarily among all nations nor with so permanent a utility as to become a portion of the universal voluntary law, but enough to have acquired a prescriptive obligation among certain states so situated as to be mutually benefited by it (1 Taunt. 241); third, the conventional law, or that which is agreed between particular states by express treaty, a law binding on the parties among whom such treaties are in force. 1 Chit. Com. Law, 28.

POSITIVI JURIS (Law Lat.) Of positive law. "That was a rule *positivi juris;* I do not mean to say an unjust one." Lord Ellenborough, 12 East, 639.

POSITO UNO OPPOSITORUM NEGAtur alterum. One of two opposite positions being affirmed, the other is denied. 3 Rolle, 422.

POSSE. This word is used substantively to signify a possibility. For example, such a thing is *in posse*, that is, such a thing may possibly be. When the thing is in being, the phrase to express it is, *in esse*.

POSSE COMITATUS (Lat.) The power of the county.

Citizens summoned by the sheriff to assist him in the execution of process.

POSSESSED. This word is applied to the right and enjoyment of a termor, or a person having a term, who is said to be possessed, and not seised. Bac. Tr. 335; Poph. 76; Dyer, 369.

POSSESSIO (Lat.)

——**In Civil Law.** The detention of a thing; divided into, first, natural, or the naked detention of a thing, without intention to acquire ownership; second, civil, or the detention of a thing to which one has a right, or with intention of acquiring ownership. Heinec. Elem. Jur. Civ. § 1288; Mackeld. Civ. Law, §§ 210, 213.

——**In Old English Law.** Possession; seisin. Law Fr. & Lat. Dict.; 2 Bl. Comm. 227; Bracton, lib. 2, c. 17; Cowell, "Possession." But *seisina* cannot be of an estate less than freehold; *possessio* can. New England Sheriff, 141; 1 Metc. (Mass.) 450; 6 Metc. (Mass.) 439.

POSSESSIO BONA FIDE (Lat.) Possession in good faith.

POSSESSIO BONORUM (Lat.) In the civil law. The possession of goods. More commonly termed *bonorum possessio*.

POSSESSIO CIVILIS. In Roman law. A legal possession, *i. e.*, a possessing accompanied with the intention to be or to thereby become owner, and, as so understood, it was distinguished from "*possessio naturalis*," otherwise called "*nuda detentio*," which was a possessing without any such intention. *Possessio civilis* was the basis of *usucapio* or of *longi temporis possessio*, and was usually, but not necessarily, adverse possession. Brown.

POSSESSIO EST QUASI PEDIS POSITIO. Possession is, as it were, the position of the foot. 3 Coke, 42.

POSSESSIO FRATRIS (Lat. the brother's possession). A technical phrase applied in the English law relating to descents, to denote the possession by one in such privity with a person as to be considered the person's own possession.

POSSESSIO FRATRIS DE FEODO SIMPLICI FACIT SOROREM ESSE HAEREDEM. Possession of the brother in fee simple makes the sister to be heir. 3 Coke, 42; 2 Bl. Comm. 227; Broom, Leg. Max. (3d London Ed.) 473.

POSSESSIO NATURALIS. See "Possessio Civilis."

POSSESSIO PACIFICA POUR ANNS 60 FACIT JUS. Peaceable possession for sixty years gives a right. Jenk. Cent. Cas. 26.

POSSESSION. The detention or enjoyment of a thing which a man holds or exercises by himself, or by another who keeps or exercises it in his name.

The owning or having a thing in one's power. 64 N. Y. 80. "Possession of land is the holding of and exercise of exclusive dominion over it." 25 Iowa, 177.

By the possession of a thing, we always conceive the condition in which not only one's own dealing with the thing is physically possible, but every other person's dealing with it is capable of being excluded. Thus, the seaman possesses his ship, but not the water in which it moves, although he makes each subserve his purpose.

(1) Actual possession exists where the thing is in the immediate occupancy of the party. 3 Dev. (N. C.) 34.

(2) Constructive possession is that which exists in contemplation of law, without actual personal occupation. 11 Vt. 129; 64 N. Y. 80. And see 1 McLean (U. S.) 214, 265; 2 Bl. Comm. 116.

(3) Adverse possession is possession inconsistent with the right of the true owner. See "Adverse Possession."

(4) Naked possession, called also "bare possession," is actual possession without shadow or pretense of right. 3 Colo. 360.

——**In Louisiana.**

(1) Civil possession exists when a person ceases to reside in a house or on the land which he occupied, or to detain the movable which he possessed, but without intending to abandon the possession. It is the detention of a thing by virtue of a just title, and under the conviction of possessing as owner. Civ. Code La. arts. 3392, 3394.

(2) Natural possession is that by which a man detains a thing corporeal; as, by occupying a house, cultivating ground, or retaining a movable in his possession. Natural possession is also defined to be the corporeal detention of a thing which we possess as belonging to us, without any title to that possession, or with a title which is void. Civ. Code La. arts. 3391, 3393.

POSSESSION MONEY. An allowance to one put in possession of goods taken under writ of *fieri facias*. Holthouse.

POSSESSION VAUT TITRE (Fr.) In English law, as in most systems of jurisprudence, the fact of possession raises a *prima facie* title or a presumption of the right of property in the thing possessed. In other words, the possession is as good as the title (about). Brown.

POSSESSION, WRIT OF. Process to put into execution a judgment in ejectment for delivery of the premises. 2 Rev. St. N. Y. p. 310, § 37.

POSSESSOR. He who holds, detains, or enjoys a thing, either by himself or his agent, which he claims as his own.

In general, the possessor of personal chattels is presumed to be the owner; and in case of real estate he has a right to receive the profits until a title adverse to his possession has been established, leaving him subject to an action for the mesne profits.

POSSESSOR BONA FIDE. See "Bona Fide Possessor, etc."

POSSESSORY. Relating to possession; founded on possession; contemplating or claiming possession.

POSSESSORY ACTION.

——**In Old English Law.** A real action, in which the plaintiff, called the "demandant," sought to recover the possession of land, tenements, and hereditaments. On account of the great nicety required in its management, and the introduction of more expeditious methods of trying titles by other actions, it has been laid aside. Finch, Laws, 257; 2 Bouv. Inst. note 2640.

——**In Louisiana.** An action by which one claims to be maintained in the possession of an immovable property, or of a right upon or growing out of it, when he has been disturbed; or to be reinstated to that possession, when he has been divested or evicted. 2 La. 227, 254.

——**In Scotch Law.** An action by which the possession of heritable or movable property may be recovered and tried. An action of molestation is one of them. Paterson, Comp. § 1058, note.

POSSESSORY JUDGMENT. In Scotch practice. A judgment which entitles a person who has uninterruptedly been in possession for seven years to continue his possession until the question of right be decided in due course of law. Bell, Dict.

POSSIBILITAS (Lat.) In old English law. Possibility; a possibility. *Possibilitas post dissolutionem executionis nunquam reviviscatur,* a possibility will never be revived after the dissolution of its execution. 1 Rolle, 321. After a possibility has become executed, it will not be revived by a dissolution of the estate, as by a divorce. *Post executionem status, lex non patitur possibilitatem,* after the execution of an estate, the law does not suffer a possibility. 3 Bulst. 108.

POSSIBILITY. An uncertain thing which may happen. Lilly, Reg. An expectancy which is not founded on any limitation, provision, or trust, such as the expectancy of an heir apparent, who may be disinherited by will, or may not survive the ancestor.

(1) A bare possibility is one that is not coupled with an interest, as that a son may inherit the lands of his father, who is living.

(2) A possibility coupled with an interest is where the person who is to take an estate upon the happening of a contingency is ascertained and fixed.

(3) A near or common possibility is such as death or death without issue.

(4) A remote possibility is such as a remainder to the heirs of a person not in being. 4 Kent, Comm. 206, 262.

POSSIBILITY ON A POSSIBILITY. See "Double Possibility."

POSSIDERE. (Lat.) To possess.

POSSIDERE PRO HEREDE. To possess in the belief that one is heir. Inst. 4, 15, 3.

POSSIDERE PRO POSSESSORE. To possess a part or the whole of an inheritance, without any right, and with the knowledge that it does not belong to one. Inst. 4, 15, 3.

POSSUMUS. We can; we can or may do.

POST (Lat.) After.

——**In Real-Estate Law.** When two or more alienations or descents have taken place between an original intruder and the tenant or defendant in a writ of entry, the writ is said to be in the post, because it states that the tenant had not entry unless after the ouster of the original intruder. 3 Bl. Comm. 182.

——**In Military Law.** A station where military duty is performed, or stores are kept, or something connected with military affairs is done. 94 U. S. 219.

——**In Latin Phrases.** A preposition meaning "after."

POST-ACT. An after-act; an act done afterwards.

POST CONQUESTUM. After the Conquest. Words first used in the king's title by King Edward I., 1328, to distinguish the Edwards after the Conquest from those before it, and constantly used in the time of Edward III. Tomlins.

POST DATE. To date an instrument a time after that on which it is made. See "Date."

POST DIEM (Lat.) After the day; as a plea of payment *post diem,*—after the day when the money became due. Comyn, Dig. "Pleader" (2 W 29).

POST DISSEISIN. In English law. The name of a writ which lies for him who, having recovered lands and tenements by force of a novel disseisin, is again disseised by a former disseisor. Jacob.

POST ENTRY. In maritime law. An entry made by a merchant upon the importation of goods, after the goods have been weighed, measured, or gauged, to make up the deficiency of the original or prime entry. The custom of making such entries has arisen from the fact that a merchant in making the entry at the time of importation is not or may not be able to calculate exactly the duties which he is liable to pay. He therefore makes an approximately correct entry, which he subsequently corrects by the post entry. See Chit. Com. Law, 746.

POST EXECUTIONEM STATUS LEX non patitur possibilitatem. After the execution of the estate, the law suffers not a possibility. 3 Bulst. 108.

POST FACTO (Lat.) After the fact. See "Ex Post Facto."

POST-FACTUM. An after-act; an act done afterwards; a post-act.

POST FINE. In old conveyancing. A fine or sum of money, otherwise called the "king's silver," formerly due on granting the *licentia concordandi*, or leave to agree, in levying a fine of lands. It amounted to three-twentieths of the supposed annual value of the land, or ten shillings for every five marks of land. 2 Bl. Comm. 350.

POST LITEM MOTAM (Lat.) After the commencement of the suit.

Declarations or acts of the parties made *post litem motam* are presumed to be made with reference to the suit then pending, and, for this reason, are not evidence in favor of the persons making them; while those made before an action has been commenced, in some cases, as when a pedigree is to be proved, may be considered as evidence. 4 Campb. 401.

POST MORTEM (Lat.) After death; as, an examination *post mortem* is an examination made of a dead body to ascertain the cause of death; an inquisition *post mortem* is one made by the coroner.

POST-NATUS (Lat.) Literally, afterborn. It is used by the old law writers to designate the second son.

POST NOTES. A species of banknotes payable at a distant period, and not on demand. 2 Watts & S. (Pa.) 463. A kind of banknotes intended to be transmitted a distance by post. See 24 Me. 36.

POST NUPTIAL. Something which takes place after marriage; as, a post-nuptial settlement, which is a conveyance made generally by the husband for the benefit of the wife.

POST OBIT (Lat.) An agreement by which the obligor borrows a certain sum of money, and promises to pay a larger sum, exceeding the lawful rate of interest, upon the death of a person from whom he has some expectation, if the obligor be then living. 7 Mass. 119; 6 Madd. 111; 5 Ves. 57; 19 Ves. 628; 62 Barb. (N. Y.) 95.

Equity will, in general, relieve a party from these unequal contracts, as they are fraudulent on the ancestor. See 1 Story, Eq. Jur. § 342; 2 P. Wms. 182, 2 Sim. 183, 192; 5 Sim. 524. But relief will be granted only on equitable terms; for he who seeks equity must do equity. 1 Fonbl. Eq. bk. 1, c. 2, § 13, note (p); 1 Story, Eq. Jur. § 344. See "Catching Bargain;" "Macedonian Decree."

POST PROLEM SUSCITATAM. After issue born. Co. Litt. 19b.

POST-TERMINAL SITTINGS. Sittings after term. See "Sittings After Term."

POST TERMINUM. After term, or post term. The return of a writ not only after the day assigned for its return, but after the term also, for which a fee was due. The fee itself. Cowell.

POSTEA (Lat. afterwards). In practice. The indorsement, on the *nisi prius* record purporting to be the return of the judge before whom a cause is tried, of what has been done in respect of such record.

It states the day of trial, before what judge, by name, the cause is tried, and also who is or was an associate of such judge. It also states the appearance of the parties by their respective attorneys, or their defaults, and the summoning and choice of the jury, whether those who were originally summoned, or those who were tales, or taken from the standers-by. It then states the finding of the jury upon oath, and the assessment of the damages, with the occasion thereof, together with the costs.

POSTERIORA DEROGANT PRIORIBUS. Posterior things derogate from things prior. 1 Bouv. Inst. note 90.

POSTERIORES (Lat.) This term was used by the Romans to denote the descendants in a direct line beyond the sixth degree. It is still used in making genealogical tables.

POSTERIORITY. Being or coming after. It is a word of comparison, the correlative of which is "priority;" as, when a man holds lands from two landlords, he holds from his ancient landlord by priority, and from the other by posteriority. 2 Inst. 392.

These terms, "priority" and "posteriority," are also used in cases of liens. The first are prior liens, and are to be paid in the first place; and the last are posterior liens, and are not entitled to payment until the former have been satisfied.

POSTERITY. All the descendants of a person in a direct line.

POSTHUMOUS CHILD. One born after the death of its father, or, when the Caesarian operation is performed, after that of the mother.

POSTLIMINIUM (Lat. from *post*, after, and *limen*, a threshold).

——**In the Civil Law.** The return or restoration of a person to a former estate or right; sometimes, in English, "postliminy."

A fiction applied in the case of a person who had been taken prisoner by an enemy, and afterwards returned from captivity, by which he was supposed never to have been abroad, and was on this ground restored to his former rights. *Postliminium fingit eum qui captus est in civitate semper fuisse*, postliminy supposes that he who was taken prisoner had always been in the state. Inst. 1. 12. 5. See Dig. 49. 15.

Postliminium included things as well as persons. Paulus, in the Digests, defines it to be *jus amissae rei recipiendae ab extraneo, et in statum pristinum restituendae, inter nos ac liberos populos regesque moribus, legibus constitutum. Nam quod bello amisimus, aut etiam citra bellum, hoc si rursus recipiamus dicimur postliminio recipere*, the right of receiving a lost thing from a foreigner, and of restoring it to its former state, established between us and free nations and kings, by customs and by laws. For whatever we have lost in war, or even not in war, if we receive it again, we are said to receive it *postliminio*. Dig. 49. 15. 19, pr.

Postliminium is thus analyzed and explained in the Institutes: It is called *postliminium* from *limen* (threshold), and *post* (after). Wherefore we properly say of one who was taken by an enemy, and afterwards came into our borders or limits, that he has returned *postliminio*. For as the threshold of a house makes, as it were, the limit or boundary of it, so the ancients chose to call the boundary or border of the empire its threshold. Hence *limen* (a threshold) came to be used in the sense of a limit (*finis*), and boundary (*terminus*). And hence the word *postliminium* was framed, and used to signify that a person had returned to the same threshold which he had lost; *ab eo postliminium dictum est, quia ad idem limen revertebatur quod amiserat*. So that now a prisoner who is recovered from an enemy, and returns home, is supposed to have returned in postliminy, that is, in the way explained. Inst. 1. 12. 5.

——**In the Law of Nations.** A right which arises from a return *in limen*, that is, to the borders of one's country. Grotius de Jur. Belli, lib. 3, c. 9, § 2. A term derived from the Roman law, and extensively used in public law. See its etymology explained by Grotius de Jure Belli lib. 3, c. 9, § 1. See his whole chapter, "De Postliminio." The term is used in maritime law. See Locc. de Jur. Mar. lib. 2, c. 4.

POSTLIMINIUM FINGIT EUM QUI CAPtus est in civitate semper fuisse. Postliminy feigns that he who has been captured has never left the state. Inst. 1. 12. 5; Dig. 49. 15.

POSTMAN. A senior barrister in court of exchequer, who has precedence in motions. Sc called from the place where he sits. 2 Bl. Comm. 28; Wharton. A letter carrier. Webster.

POSTMARK. A stamp or mark put on letters in the post office.

Postmarks are evidence of a letter's having passed through the post office. 2 Campb. 620; 2 Bos. & P. 316; 15 East, 416; 1 Maule & S. 201; 15 Conn. 206.

POSTNATI (Lat. those born after). Applied to American and British subjects born after the separation of England and the United States; also to the subjects of Scotland born after the union of England and Scotland. Those born after an event, as opposed to *antenati*, those born before. 2 Kent, Comm. 56-59; 2 Pick. (Mass.) 394; 5 Day (Conn.) 169*. See "Antenati."

POSTNUPTIAL SETTLEMENT. A settlement made after marriage upon a wife or children; otherwise called a "voluntary" settlement. 2 Kent, Comm. 173.

POSTPONEMENT. The putting over of a cause for trial to another term. Considerable confusion exists in the use of the words, "continuance," "adjournment," and "postponement." In exact phraseology, "continuance" means the revival of a cause after it has abated, "adjournment" the putting over of a cause from day to day within the term, and "postponement" the putting over of a cause from term to term.

POSTREMO GENITURE. Borough English (*q. v.*)

POSTULATIO (Lat.) In Roman law. The name of the first act in a criminal proceeding.

A person who wished to accuse another of a crime appeared before the praetor and requested his authority for that purpose, designating the person intended. This act was called *postulatio*. The postulant (*calumnium jurabat*) made oath that he was not influenced by a spirit of calumny, but acted in good faith, with a view to the public interest. The praetor received this declaration, at first made verbally, but afterwards in writing, and called a "libel." The *postulatio* was posted up in the forum, to give public notice of the names of the accuser and the accused. A second accuser sometimes appeared, and went through the same formalities.

Other persons were allowed to appear and join the postulant or principal accuser. These were said *postulare subscriptionem*, and were denominated *subscriptores*. Cicero, Caecil. Divinatio, 15. But commonly such persons acted concurrently with the postulant, and inscribed their names at the time he first appeared. Only one accuser, however, was allowed to act; and if the first inscribed did not desist in favor of the second, the right was determined, after discussion, by judges appointed for the purpose. Cicero, Verres, i. 6. The preliminary proceeding was called *divinatio*, and is well explained in the oration of Cicero entitled *Divinatio*. See Aulus Gellius, Att. Noct. lib. ii. c. 4.

The accuser having been determined in this manner, he appeared before the praetor, and formally charged the accused by name, specifying the crime. This was called *nominis et criminis delatio.* The magistrate reduced it to writing, which was called *inscriptio,* and the accuser and his adjuncts, if any, signed it, *subscribebant.* This proceeding corresponds to the indictment of the common law.

If the accused appeared, the accuser formally charged him with the crime. If the accused confessed it, or stood mute, he was adjudged to pay the penalty. If he denied it, the *inscriptio* contained his answer, and he was then *in reatu* (indicted, as we should say), and was called *reus,* and a day was fixed, ordinarily after an interval of at least ten days, according to the nature of the case, for the appearance of the parties. In the case of Verres, Cicero obtained one hundred and ten days to prepare his proofs, although he accomplished it in fifty days, and renounced, as he might do, the advantage of the remainder of the time allowed him.

At the day appointed for the trial, the accuser and his adjuncts or colleagues, the accused, and the judges, were summoned by the herald of the praetor. If the accuser did not appear, the case was erased from the roll. If the accused made default, he was condemned. If both parties appeared, a jury was drawn by the praetor or *judex quaestionis.* The jury was called *jurati homines,* and the drawing of them *sortitio,* and they were taken from a general list made out for the year. Either party had a right to object to a certain extent to the persons drawn, and then there was a second drawing, called *subsortitio,* to complete the number.

In some tribunals, *quaestiones* (the jury) were *editi* (produced) in equal number by the accuser and the accused, and sometimes by the accuser alone, and were objected to or challenged in different ways, according to the nature of the case. The number of the jury also varied according to the tribunal (*quaestio*). They were sworn before the trial began; hence they were called *jurati.*

The accusers, and often the *subscriptores,* were heard, and afterwards the accused, either by himself or by his advocates, of whom he commonly had several. The witnesses, who swore by Jupiter, gave their testimony after the discussions or during the progress of the pleadings of the accuser. In some cases it was necessary to plead the cause on the third day following the first hearing, which was called *comperendinatio.*

After the pleadings were concluded, the praetor or the *judex quaestionis* distributed tablets to the jury, upon which each wrote, secretly, either the letter A. (*absolvo*), or the letter C. (*condemno*), or N. L. (*non liquet*). These tablets were deposited in an urn. The president assorted and counted the tablets. If the majority were for acquitting the accused, the magistrate declared it by the words *fecisse non videtur,* and by the words *fecisse videtur* if the majority were for a conviction. If the tablets marked N. L. were so many as to prevent an absolute majority for a conviction or acquittal, the cause was put off for more ample information, *ampliatio,* which the praetor declared by the word *amplies.* Such, in brief, was the course of proceedings before the *quaestiones perpetuae.*

The forms observed in the *comitia centuriata* and *comitia tributa* were nearly the same, except the composition of the tribunal and the mode of declaring the vote.

POSTULATIO ACTIONIS (Lat.) In civil law. Demand of an action (*actio*) from the praetor, which some explain to be a demand of a *formula,* or form of the suit; others, a demand of leave to bring the cause before the judge. Tayl. Civ. Law, 80; Calv. Lex. "Actio."

POSTUMUS. A child of a testator, born after his death, who if born in his lifetime, would have been entitled to succeed him if he died intestate; a child of a testator conceived before the date of the will, but born afterwards, and before the testator's death. See "Posthumous Child."

POSTUMUS ALIENUS. A posthumous stranger; a posthumous child that would not have been under the testator's power if born in his lifetime. Inst. 2, 20, 28.

POT-DE-VIN. In French law. A sum of money frequently paid, at the moment of entering into a contract, beyond the price agreed upon. It differs from *arrha* in this, that it is no part of the price of the thing sold, and that the person who has received it cannot, by returning double the amount, or the other party by losing what he has paid, rescind the contract. 18 Toullier, Dr. Civ. note 52.

POTENTATE. One who has a great power over an extended country; a sovereign.

By the naturalization laws of the United States, an alien is required, before he can be naturalized, to renounce all allegiance and fidelity to any foreign prince, potentate, state, or sovereign whatever.

POTENTIA (Lat.) Possibility; power.

POTENTIA DEBET SEQUI JUSTITIAM, non antecedere. Power ought to follow, not to precede, justice. 3 Bulst. 199.

POTENTIA EST DUPLEX, REMOTA ET propinqua; et potentia remotissima et vana est quae nunquam venit in actum. Possibility is of two kinds, remote and near; that which never comes into action is a power the most remote and vain. 11 Coke, 51.

POTENTIA INUTILIS FRUSTRA EST. Useless power is vain.

POTENTIA NON EST NISI AD BONUM. Power is not conferred but for the public good.

POTENTIA PROPINQUA. Common possibility. See "Possibility."

POTEST QUIS RENUNCIARE PRO SE, et suis, jus quod pro se introductum est. A man may relinquish, for himself and those claiming under him, a right which was introduced for his own benefit. See 1 Bouv. Inst. note 83.

POTESTAS (Lat.) In civil law. Power; authority; domination; empire. *Imperium*, or the jurisdiction of magistrates. The power of the father over his children, *patria potestas*. The authority of masters over their slaves, which makes it nearly synonymous with *dominium*. See Inst. 1. 9. 12; Dig. 2. 1. 13. 1; Id. 14. 1; Id. 14. 4. 1. 4.

POTESTAS STRICTE INTERPRETATur. Power should be strictly interpreted. Jenk. Cent. Cas. 17.

POTESTAS SUPREMA SEIPSUM DISsolvare potest, ligare non potest. Supreme power can dissolve, but cannot bind itself. Bac. Max. reg. 19.

POTIOR EST CONDITIO DEFENDENTis. Better is the condition of the defendant than that of the plaintiff. Broom, Leg. Max. (3d London Ed.) 664; 15 Pet. (U. S.) 471.

POTIOR EST CONDITIO POSSIDENTIS. Better is the condition of the possessor. Broom, Leg. Max. (3d London Ed.) 201, note.

POTWALLOPER. A term formerly applied to voters in certain boroughs of England, where all who boil (wallop) a pot were entitled to vote. Webster.

POULTRY COUNTER (or **COMPTER**). The name of a prison formerly existing in London. 2 Mod. 306; 6 Mod. 247. See "Counter."

POUND. *Ex vi termini* is an enclosed piece of land, secured by a firm structure of stone, or of posts and timber, placed in the ground. 2 Cush. (Mass.) 309.

A place, inclosed by public authority, for the temporary detention of stray animals. 4 Pick. (Mass.) 258; 5 Pick. (Mass.) 514; 9 Pick. (Mass.) 14.

——**In Weights.** There are two kinds of weights, namely, the troy and the avoirdupois. The pound avoirdupois is the greater, being seven thousand grains, the troy pound, five thousand seven hundred and sixty. The troy pound contains twelve ounces; that of avoirdupois sixteen ounces.

——**In Money.** The sum of twenty shillings. Previous to the establishment of the federal currency, the different states made use of the pound in computing money. It was of different value in the several states.

Pound sterling is a denomination of money of Great Britain. It is of the value a sovereign. In calculating the rates of duties, the pound sterling was, by statute, considered and taken as of the value of four dollars and eighty cents. Act March 3, 1883.

Under the same act the pound sterling of Ireland was to be computed, in calculating said duties, at four dollars and ten cents.

POUND BREACH. The offense of breaking a pound in order to take out the cattle impounded. 3 Bl. Comm. 146. The writ *de parco fracto*, or pound breach, lies for recovering damages for this offense; also case. Id. It is also indictable.

POUNDAGE. In practice. The amount allowed to the sheriff, or other officer, for commissions on the money made by virtue of an execution. This allowance varies in different states, and to different officers.

POUR COMPTE DE QUI IL APPARtient (Fr.) For account of whom it may concern. Emerig. Tr. des Assur. c. 11, sec. 4, § 3. A phrase in insurance law.

POUR SEISIR TERRES (Law Fr. for seizing the lands). In old practice. A writ by which the king seized the land which the wife of a tenant *in capite*, deceased, had for her dower, if she married without his leave. Cowell.

POURPARLER. In French law. The conversations and negotiations which have taken place between the parties in order to make an agreement. These form no part of the agreement. Pardessus, Dr. Com. 142.

POURPARTY (Law Fr.; Law Lat. *propars, propartis, propartia*). In old English law. Division; a divided share. Literally, "for," or as "divided" (*pour parti*); a close translation of the Latin phrase *pro diviso*. To make *pourparty* is to divide and sever the lands that fall to parceners, which, before partition, they held jointly and *pro indiviso*. Cowell.

POURPRESTURE. See Purpresture."

POURSUIVANT. A follower; a pursuer. In the ancient English law, it signified an officer who attended upon the king in his wars, at the council table, exchequer, in his court, etc., to be sent as a messenger. A poursuivant was, therefore, a messenger of the king.

POURVEYANCE (Law Fr. and Eng.; from Fr. *pourvoire*, to provide). In old English law. The providing corn (grain), fuel, victual, and other necessaries for the king's house. Cowell. See "Purveyance."

POURVEYOR (from Fr. *pourvoire*, to provide). In old English law. An officer of the king or queen, or other great personage, that provided corn (grain) and other victual for their house. Cowell. See "Purveyor."

POUSTIE, or POISTEE (Scotch). In Scotch law. Power. 1 Pitc. Crim. Tr. pt. 1, p. 162. See "Liege Poustie." A word formed from the Latin *potestas*.

POVERTY AFFIDAVIT. A term used in a few states for an affidavit *in forma pauperis*. See "In Forma Pauperis."

POWER. The right, ability, or faculty of doing something.

An authority by which one person enables another to do some act for him. 2 Lilly, Abr. 339.

In a more technical sense, an authority vested in one person to dispose of an estate which is vested in another.

(1) Inherent powers are those which are enjoyed by the possessors of natural right, without having been received from another. Such are the powers of a people to establish a form of government, of a father to control his children. Some of these are regulated and restricted in their exercise by law, but are not technically considered in the law as powers.

(2) Derivative powers are those which are received from another. This division includes all the powers technically so called. They are of the following classes:

a) Naked, being a right of authority disconnected from any interest of the donee in the subject matter. 3 Hill (N. Y.) 365.

(b) Coupled with an interest, being a right or authority to do some act, together with an interest in the subject on which the power is to be exercised. Marshall, C. J., 8 Wheat. (U. S.) 203.

A power of this class survives the person creating it, and, in case of an excess in execution, renders the act valid so far as the authority extends, leaving it void as to the remainder only. It includes powers of sale conferred on a mortgagee.

——**Powers under the Statute of Uses.** An authority enabling a person, through the medium of the statute of uses, to dispose of an interest in real property, vested either in himself or another person. 52 N. Hamp. 271.

Methods of causing a use, with its accompanying estate, to spring up at the will of a given person. Williams, Real Prop. 245; 2 Washb. Real Prop. 300.

The right to designate the person who is to take a use. Co. Litt. 271b, Butler's note, 231, § 3, pl. 4.

A right to limit a use. 4 Kent, Comm. 334.

An authority to do some act in relation to lands, or the creation of estates therein, or of charges thereon, which the owner granting or reserving such power might himself lawfully perform. Rev. St. N. Y.

Powers are divided generally into powers of appointment, being those which are to create new estates and powers of revocation, which are to divest or abridge an existing estate. But as every appointment must divest an existing estate, the distinction is of doubtful exactness.

They are distinguished as:

(1) Appendant, being those which the donee is authorized to exercise out of the estate limited to him, and which depend for their validity upon the estate which is in him. 2 Washb. Real Prop. 304. A life estate limited to a man, with a power to grant leases in possession, is an example. Hardr. 416; 1 Caines, Cas. (N. Y.) 15; Sugd. (Pow. Ed. 1856) 107; Burton, Real Prop. § 179.

(2) Collateral, being those in which the donee has no estate in the land. 2 Washb. Real Prop. 305.

(3) General, being those by which the donee is at liberty to appoint whom he pleases.

(4) Special, being those in which the donee is restricted to an appointment to or among particular objects only. 2 Washb. Real Prop. 307.

(5) In gross, being those which give a donee, who has an estate in the land, authority to create such estates only as will not attach on the interest limited to him, or take effect out of his own interest. 2 Cow. (N. Y.) 236; White & T. Lead. Cas. 293; Watk. Conv. 260.

(6) Beneficial, when by its terms no person other than the donee has any interest in its execution. See "Beneficial Power."

(7) In trust, when any person or class of persons is designated to receive the benefit.

——**Designation of Parties.** The person bestowing a power is called the "donor;" the person on whom it is bestowed is called the "donee;" the person who receives the estate by appointment of the donee is called the "appointee." When referred to in connection with the appointee, the donee is sometimes called the "appointor."

By statute in New York, the term "grantor of a power" is used to denote the person by whom a power is created, and "grantee of a power" to denote the person in whom it is vested. 4 Rev. St. N. Y. § 135, p. 2451.

POWER OF ATTORNEY. An instrument authorizing a person to act as the attorney in fact of the person granting it.

A general power authorizes the agent to act generally in behalf of the principal.

A special power is one limited to particular acts.

POYNDING. See "Poinding."

POYNINGS' LAWS. A set of statutes enacted in the tenth year of Henry VII. (so called from Sir Edward Poynings, being then lord deputy), regulating the method of passing statutes in Ireland. By another of these laws it was provided that all acts of parliament before made in England should be in force within the realm of Ireland. 1 Bl. Comm. 102, 103.

P'P'M. A contraction of *perpetuum.* 1 Inst. Cler. 11.

PRACTICA. (L. Lat.) Practice; the practice of a court. Clerke's Prax. Cur. Adm. tit. 42.

PRACTICAL CONSTRUCTION.

——**Of a Statute.** One determined by long-established procedure under it, to which deference will be paid by the courts in interpreting the statute, if possible, without doing violence to its terms. 16 Ohio, 559; 49 Mo. 404; 93 Ill. 191.

——**Of a Contract.** That given to the contract by the parties, and under which they acted in performing it. Such an interpretation will be effectuated by the court, if possible. 76 U. S. 50; 80 U. S. 608; 41 Minn. 308; 41 Neb. 56; 67 Vt. 1.

PRACTICAL LOCATION. Mutual acquiescence in a known boundary line for a long period of time. 47 Barb. (N. Y.) 287.

PRACTICE. The form, manner, and order of conducting and carrying on suits or prosecutions in the courts through their various stages, according to the principles of law and the rules laid down by the respective courts.

PRACTICE COURT. In English law. A court attached to the court of king's bench, which hears and determines common matters of business and ordinary motions for writs of *mandamus*, prohibition, etc.

It was formerly called the "bail court." It is held by one of the puisne justices of the king's bench.

PRACTICES. A succession of acts of a similar kind, or in a like employment. Webster.

PRACTICKS. In Scotch law. The decisions of the court of session, as evidence of the practice or custom of the country. Bell, Dict.

PRAEBENDA (Law Lat.) In old English law. A prebend. Bracton, fol. 442b; Fleta, lib. 2, c. 54, § 10; Id. c. 69, § 3.

An allowance of fodder for horses and cattle. Fleta, lib. 2, c. 76, § 8.

PRAECEPTORES (Lat.) Heretofore masters in chancery were so called, as having the direction of making out remedial writs. Fleta, 76; 2 Reeve, Hist. Eng. Law, 251. A species of benefice, so called from being possessed by the principal templars (*praeceptores templi*), whom the chief master by his authority created. 2 Mon. Angl. 543.

PRAECEPTORIES. A kind of feudal benefices; so called because they were possessed by the more eminent templars, whom the chief master by his authority created and called *Praeceptores Templi.* 2 Mon. Angl. 543.

PRAECIPE, or **PRECIPE** (Lat.) A slip of paper upon which the particulars of a writ are written. It is lodged in the office out of which the required writ is to issue. Wharton.

PRAECIPE IN CAPITE. A writ of chancery which lay (in case of his deforcement) for a tenant holding of the crown *in capite,* viz., in chief. Magna Charta, c. 24.

PRAECIPE QUOD REDDAT (Lat.) Command him to return. An original writ, of which *praecipe* is the first word, commanding the person to whom it is directed to do a thing, or to show cause why he has not done it. 3 Bl. Comm. 274; Old Nat. Brev. 13. It is as well applied to a writ of right as to other writs of entry and possession.

PRAECIPE QUOD TENEAT CONVENtionem. The writ which commenced the action of covenant in fines. Abolished by 3 & 4 Wm. IV. c. 74.

PRAECIPITIUM. The punishment of casting headlong from some high place.

PRAECIPUT CONVENTIONNEL. In the French law, under the *regime en communaute,* when that is of the conventional kind, if the surviving husband or wife is entitled to take any portion of the common property by a paramount title, and before partition thereof, this right is called by the somewhat barbarous title of the conventional *praeciput,* from *prae,* before, and *capere,* to take. Brown.

PRAECO (Lat.)

——**In Roman Law.** A herald or crier. Adams, Rom. Ant. 189, 190.

——**In Later Practice.** The crier of a court. Bac. Works, iv. 316.

PRAECOGNITA. Things to be previously known in order to the understanding of something which follows.

PRAEDA BELLICA (Lat.) Booty; property seized in war.

PRAEDIA (Lat.) In civil law. Lands.

Praedia urbana, those lands which have buildings upon them and are in the city.

Praedia rustica, those lands which are without buildings or in the country. Vocat.

It indicates a more extensive domain than *fundus.* Calv. Lex.

PRAEDIA STIPENDIARIA. In the civil law, provincial lands belonging to the people.

PRAEDIA TRIBUTARIA. In the civil law, provincial lands belonging to the emperor.

PRAEDIAL. That which arises immediately from the ground; as, grain of all sorts, hay, wood, fruits, herbs, and the like; as praedial tithes. 2 Bl. Comm. 23.

PRAEDIAL (or PREDIAL) SERVITUDE. A right which is granted for the advantage of one piece of land over another, and which may be exercised by every possessor of the land entitled against every possessor of the servient land. It always presupposes two pieces of land (*praedia*) belonging to different proprietors; one burdened with the servitude, called "*praedium serviens*," and one for the advantage of which the servitude is conferred, called "*praedium* dominans." Mackeld. Civ. Law, § 306; Inst. 2. 3; Dig. 8. 1-6.

PRAEDIAL TITHES. Arising out of or from land. Natural products not principally produced by care and nurture, as corn, grass, hops, wood. 2 Bl. Comm. 24.

PRAEDICTUS, PRAEDICTA, or PRAEdictum (Lat.) In old pleading. Aforesaid. Abbreviated in old entries *praed.*, *praedict.*, *p'dc'us*, etc. Hob. 117; 10 Coke, 65.

Of the three words, *idem*, *praedictus*, and *praefatus* (all corresponding to the English aforesaid), *idem* was most usually applied to plaintiffs or demandants; *praedictus*, to defendants or tenants, places, towns, or lands; and *praefatus*, to persons named, not being actors or parties. Towns. Pl. 15.

PRAEDIUM DOMINANS (Lat. the ruling estate). In civil law. The name given to an estate to which a servitude is due. It is called the ruling estate.

PRAEDIUM RUSTICUM (Lat. a country estate). In civil law. By this is understood all heritages which are not destined for the use of man's habitation; such, for example, as lands, meadows, orchards, gardens, woods, even though they should be within the boundaries of a city.

PRAEDIUM SERVIENS (Lat.) In civil law. The name of an estate which suffers or yields a service to another estate.

PRAEDIUM URBANUM (Lat.) In civil law. By this term is understood buildings and edifices intended for the habitation and use of man, whether they be built in cities or whether they be constructed in the country.

PRAEDO (Lat.) In Roman law. A robber. See Dig. 50. 17. 126.

PRAEFATUS. In old pleadings. Aforesaid. Sometimes abbreviated to *praefat.* and *p. fat.* See "Praedictus."

PRAEFECTUS (Lat.)

——**In the Roman Law.** A chief officer; a governor or commander. The tilte of various officers and magistrates. Dig. 1. 11; Id. 1. 12; Id. 1. 15; Code, 1. 28; Calv. Lex.

——**In Old English Law.** The chief officer of a hundred, and other divisions. Spelman, voc. "Praepositus."

PRAEFECTUS VIGILIUM (Lat.) In Roman law. The chief officer of the night watch. His jurisdiction extended to certain offenses affecting the public peace, and even to larcenies; but he could inflict only slight punishments.

PRAEFINE. The fee paid on suing out the writ of covenant, on levying fines, before the fine was passed. 2 Bl. Comm. 350.

PRAEJUDICIALIS (Lat. from *prae*, before, and *judicare*, to judge). In the civil law. That which is to be predetermined, or decided before something else. See "Actio Praejudicialis."

PRAEJUDICIUM (Law Lat.) In old English law. Prejudice; detriment; disparagement. Bracton, fol. 19. *Sine praejudicio melioris sententiae*, without prejudice to the better opinion. Id. fol. 48. A common phrase used by Bracton, when expressing his own opinion on any point.

PRAEJURAMENTUM (Law Lat.) In old English law. A preparatory oath.

PRAEMIUM (Lat.) Reward; compensation. *Praemium assecurationis*, compensation for insurance; premium of insurance. Locc. de Jur. Mar. lib. 2, c. 5, § 6. Now used in the law of insurance, in the form "premium," as a common English word.

PRAEMIUM PUDICITIAE (Lat.) The price of chastity; or compensation for loss of chastity. A term applied to bonds and other engagements given for the benefit of a seduced female. Sometimes called *premium pudoris*. 2 Wils. 339, 340.

PRAEMUNIRE (Lat.) In order to prevent the pope from assuming the supremacy in granting ecclesiastical livings, a number of statutes were made in England, during the reigns of Edward I. and his successors, punishing certain acts of submission to the papal authority therein mentioned. In the writ for the execution of these statutes, the words *praemunire facias*, being used to command a citation of the party, gave not only to the writ, but to the offense itself of maintaining the papal power, the name of *praemunire*. Co. Litt. 129; Jacob.

PRAENOMEN (Lat.) Forename, or first name. The first of the three names by which the Romans were commonly distinguished. It marked the individual, and was commonly written with one letter; as A. for Aulus; C. for Caius, etc. Adams, Rom. Ant. 35. See Fleta, lib. 4, c. 10, § 9; Butler, Hor. Jur. 28.

PRAEPOSITUS. An officer next in authority to the alderman of a hundred called *praepositus regius*; or a steward or bailiff of an estate, answering to the *wicnere*.

Also the person from whom descents are traced under the old canons.

One who was set over others; a presiding officer.

PRAEPOSITUS ECCLESIAE. A church reeve, or warden. Spelman.

PRAEPOSITUS VILLAE. A constable of a town, or petty constable.

PRAEPROPERA CONSILIA, RARO sunt prospera. Hasty counsels are seldom prosperous. 4 Inst. 57.

PRAEROGATIVA REGIS. (L. Lat.) In old English law. The king's prerogative. Crabb's Hist. 204.

PRAESCRIPTIO (Lat.) In the civil law. That mode of acquisition whereby one becomes proprietor of a thing on the ground that he has for a long time possessed it as his own; prescription. Dig. 41. 3; 1 Mackeld. Civ. Law, p. 290, § 276. It was anciently distinguished from "*usucapio*," (*q. v.*), but was blended with it by Justinian. Heinec. Elem. Jur. Civ. lib. 2, tit. 6, § 438.

PRAESCRIPTIO EST TITULUS EX USU et tempore substantiam capiens ab auctoritate legis. Prescription is a title by authority of law, deriving its force from use and time. Co. Litt. 113.

PRAESCRIPTIO ET EXECUTIO NON pertinent ad valorem contractus, sed ad tempus et modum actionis instituendae. Prescription and the execution of a contract do not affect the validity of the contract, but the time and manner of bringing an action. 3 Mass. 84; 3 Johns. Ch. (N. Y.) 190, 219.

PRAESCRIPTIONES. In Roman law. Forms of words (of a qualifying character) inserted in the *formulae* in which the claims in actions were expressed, and, as they occupied an early place in the *formulae*, they were called by this name, *i. e.*, qualifications preceding the claim. For example, in an action to recover the arrears of an annuity, the claim was preceded by the words "so far as the annuity is due and unpaid," or words to the like effect (*cujus rei dies fuit*). Brown.

PRAESENTARE NIHIL ALIUD EST quam praesto dare seu offerre. To present is no more than to give or offer on the spot. Co. Litt. 120.

PRAESENTIA CORPORIS TOLLIT ERrorem nominis, et veritas nominis tollit errorem demonstrationis. The presence of the body cures the error in the name; the truth of the name cures an error in the description. Bac. Max. reg. 25; Broom, Leg. Max. (3d London Ed.) 568; 6 Coke, 66; 3 Barn. & Adol. 640; 6 Term R. 675; 11 C. B. 996; 1 H. L. Cas. 792; 3 De Gex, M. & G. 140.

PRAESES (Lat.) In the Roman law. A president, or governor. Dig. 1. 18. 1. Called a *nomen generale*, including proconsuls, legates, and all who governed provinces. Id.

PRAESIDIUM (Lat.) In the civil law. A guard; a fortress; a defense, aid, or shelter.

In records of the middle ages, all household stuff or effects, including particularly gold and silver. Spelman. Every kind of property, real as well as personal (*omnis vis bonorum, tam immobilium quam mobilium*). Id.

PRAESTARE (Lat.)

——**In Old English Law.** To pay, or render; to make or execute; to perform. *Praestitit sacramentum*, made oath, or took an oath. T. Raym. 34; 2 Ld. Raym. 1376; Mem. in Scacc. P. 16 Edw. I.

To make good. *Praestare tenetur quodcunque damnum obveniens in mari*, the insurer is bound to make good any loss happening on the sea. 3 Kent, Comm. 291.

——**In Old European Law.** To lease, or let to farm. Chart. Alaman. 75; Spelman.

PRAESTAT CAUTELA QUAM MEDELA. Prevention is better than cure. Co. Litt. 304.

PRAESUMATUR PRO JUSTITIA SENtentiae. The justice of a sentence should be presumed. Best, Ev. Introd. 42; Mascardus de Prob. Conc. 1237, note 2.

PRAESUMITUR PRO LEGITIMATIONE. Legitimacy is to be presumed. 5 Coke, 98b; 1 Bl. Comm. 457.

PRAESUMITUR PRO NEGANTE. It is presumed for the negative. The rule of the house of lords when the numbers are equal on a motion. Wharton.

PRAESUMPTIO, EX EO QUOD PLERumque fit. Presumptions arise from what generally happens. 22 Wend. (N. Y.) 425, 475.

PRAESUMPTIO FORTIOR (Lat.) A strong (literally, stronger) presumption (of fact). One which determines the tribunal in its belief of an alleged fact, without, however, excluding the belief of the possibility of its being otherwise; the effect of which is to shift the burden of proof to the opposite party, and if this proof be not made, the presumption is held for truth. Hub. Prael. J. C. lib. 22, tit. 3, note 16; Burrill, Circ. Ev. 66.

PRAESUMPTIO HOMINIS (Lat.) The presumption of the man or individual; that is, natural presumption unfettered by strict rule. Heinec. ad Pand. par. 4, § 124.

PRAESUMPTIO JURIS (Lat.) In Roman law. A deduction from the existence of one fact as to the existence of another which admits of proof to the contrary. A rebuttable presumption. An intendment of law which holds good until it is weakened by proof or a stronger presumption. Best, Pres. 29.

PRAESUMPTIO JURIS ET DE JURE (Lat.) In Roman law. A deduction drawn, by reason of some rule of law, from the existence of one fact as to the existence of another, so conclusively that no proof can be admitted to the contrary. A conclusive presumption.

PRAESUMPTIO VIOLENTA, PLENA probatio. Violent presumption is full proof.

PRAESUMPTIO VIOLENTA VALET IN lege. Strong presumption avails in law. Jenk. Cent. Cas. 58.

PRAESUMPTIONES SUNT CONJECTURAE ex signo verisimili ad probandum assumptae. Presumptions are conjectures from probable proof, assumed for purposes of evidence. J. Voct. Com. ad Pand. lib. 22, tit. 3, note 14.

PRAETEXTU LICITI NON DEBET ADmitti illicitum. Under pretext of legality, what is illegal ought not to be admitted. 10 Coke, 88.

PRAETOR. In Roman law. A municipal officer of Rome, so called because (*praeiret populo*) he went before or took precedence of the people.

The consuls were at first called *praetors.* Liv. Hist. iii. 55. He was a sort of minister of justice, invested with certain legislative powers, especially in regard to the forms or formalities of legal proceedings. Ordinarily, he did not decide causes as a judge, but prepared the grounds of decision for the judge, and sent to him the questions to be decided between the parties. The judge was always chosen by the parties, either directly, or by rejecting, under certain rules and limitations, the persons proposed to them by the *praetor.* Hence the saying of Cicero (*pro Cluentis,* 43) that no one could be judged except by a judge of his own choice. There were several kinds of officers called *praetors.* See Vicat.

Before entering on his functions, he published an edict announcing the system adopted by him for the application and interpretation of the laws during his magistracy. His authority extended over all jurisdictions, and was summarily expressed by the words *do, dico, addico, i. e., do,* I give the action; *dico,* I declare the law, I promulgate the edict; *addico,* I invest the judge with the right of judging. There were certain cases which he was bound to decide himself, assisted by a council chosen by himself,—perhaps the *decemvirs;* but the greater part of causes brought before him he sent either to a judge, an arbitrator, or to recuperators (*recuperatores*), or to the *centumvirs,* as before stated. Under the empire, the powers of the *praetor* passed by degrees to the prefect of the *praetorium,* or the prefect of the city, so that this magistrate, who at first ranked with the consuls, at last dwindled into a director or manager of the public spectacles or games.

Till lately, there were officers in certain cities of Germany denominated *praetors.* See 1 Kent, Comm. 528.

PRAETOR FIDEI COMMISSARIUS (Lat.) In the civil law. A special *praetor* created to pronounce judgment in cases of trusts or *fidei commissa.* Inst. 2. 23. 1; 2 Story, Eq. Jur. § 966. Called, by Lord Bacon, a "particular chancellor for uses." Bac. Law Tr. 315; 4 Kent, Comm. 290.

PRAEVARICATOR (Lat.) In the civil law. One who betrays his trust, or is unfaithful to his trust. An advocate who aids the opposite party by betraying his client's cause. Dig. 47. 15. 1. Used in Spanish law. Las Partidas, pt. 3, tit. 6, lib. 15.

PRAEVENTO TERMINO. In old Scotch practice. A form of action known in the forms of the court of session, by which a delay to discuss a suspension or advocation was got the better of. Bell, Dict.

PRAGMATIC SANCTION.

——**In French Law.** An expression used to designate those ordinances which concern the most important object of the civil or ecclesiastical administration. Merlin, Repert.; 1 Fournel, Hist. de Avocats, 24, 38, 39.

——**In Civil Law.** The answer given by the emperors on questions of law, when consulted by a corporation or the citizens of a province or of a municipality, was called a "pragmatic sanction." Lec. Elm. § 53. This differed from a "rescript."

PRAGMATICA (Spanish). In Spanish colonial law. An order emanating from the sovereign, and differing from a *cedula* only in form and in the mode of promulgation. Schmidt, Civ. Law, Introd. 93, note.

PRAXIS JUDICUM EST INTERPRES LEgum. The practice of the judges is the interpreter of the laws. Hob. 96; Branch. Princ.

PRAY IN AID. In old English practice. To call upon for assistance. In real actions, the tenant might pray in aid or call for assistance of another, to help him to plead, because of the feebleness or imbecility of his own estate. 3 Bl. Comm. 300. See "Aid Prayer."

PRAYER. In equity practice. The request in a bill that the court will grant the aid which the petitioner desires. That part of the bill which asks for relief. The word denotes, strictly, the request, but is very commonly applied to that part of the bill which contains the request.

PREAMBLE. An introduction prefixed to a statute, reciting the intention of the legislature in framing it, or the evils which led to its enactment.

A preamble is said to be the key of a statute, to open the minds of the makers as to the mischiefs which are to be remedied, and the objects which are to be accomplished, by the provisions of the statute. 4 Inst. 330; 6 Pet. (U. S.) 301. In modern legislative practice, preambles are much less used than formerly, and in some of the United States are rarely, if ever, now inserted in statutes. In the interpretation of a statute, though resort may be had to the preamble, it cannot limit or control the express provisions of the statute. Dwarr. St. 504-508. Nor can it by implication enlarge what is expressly fixed. 1 Story, Const. bk. 3, c. 6; 3 McCord (S. C.) 298; 15 Johns. (N. Y.) 89; Busb. (N. C.) 131; 2 Ware (U. S.) 38.

PREAPPOINTED EVIDENCE. Evidence whose nature and quantity are prescribed beforehand by law, as for the attestation of wills.

PREAUDIENCE. The right of being heard before another. A privilege belonging to the English bar, the members of which are entitled to be heard in their order, according to rank, beginning with the queen's attorney general, and ending with barristers at large. 3 Bl. Comm. 28, note; 3 Steph. Comm. 387, note.

PREBEND. In ecclesiastical law. The stipend granted to an ecclesiastic, in consideration of officiating in the church. It is in this distinguished from a "canonicate," which is a mere title, and may exist without stipend. The prebend may be a simple stipend, or a stipend with a dignity attached to it, in which case it has some jurisdiction belonging to it. 2 Burn, Ecc. Law, 88; Strange, 1082; 1 Term R. 401; 2 Term R. 630; 1 Wils. 206; Dyer, 273a; 7 Barn. & C. 113; 8 Bing. 490; 5 Taunt. 2.

PREBENDARY (Lat. *praebendarius*, from *praebenda*). In English ecclesiastical law. One that has a prebend (*q. v.*) Cowell. The stipendiary of a cathedral or collegiate church. Webster.

PRECARIOUS RIGHT. The right which the owner of a thing transfers to another, to enjoy the same until it shall please the owner to revoke it.

If there is a time fixed during which the right may be used, it is then vested for that time, and cannot be revoked until after its expiration. Wolff. Inst. § 333.

PRECARIUM (Lat.) The name of a contract among civilians, by which the owner of a thing, at the request of another person, gives him a thing to use as long as the owner shall please. Poth. note 87. See Yelv. 172; Cro. Jac. 236; 9 Cow. (N. Y.) 687; Rolle, 128; Bac. Abr. "Bailment" (C); Ersk. Inst. 3. 1. 9; Wolff. Inst. § 333.

A tenancy at will is a right of this kind.

PRECARIAE, or PRECES (Law Lat.) In old English law. Days' works, which the tenants of some manors were bound, by reason of their tenure, to do for the lord in harvest. Vulgarly called "bind days," which Spelman supposes to be a corruption of "biden days," which in Saxon, answered to *dies precariae* (literally, pray days, or prayed days), the Saxon *biden* signifying to pray. Spelman; Cowell.

PRECATORY TRUST. A trust created by certain words which are more like words of entreaty and permission than of command or certainty. Words of entreaty when coupled with discretionary words, 15 L. J. Ch. 182; 20 L. J. Ch. 280; 17 Bea. 156; 18 Bea. 215; L. R. 4 Eq. 151, 4 Ch. D. 238, 40 L. J. Ch. 447, 6 Ch. 597, or with an absolute gift do not create such trust. *E. g.*, "They are hereby enjoined to take care of my nephew J. J. as may seem best in the future," 55 L. J. Ch. 418; "feeling confident that she will act justly," 51 L. J. P. C. 72, 7 App. Ca. 321; "agreeably to my wishes," 46 L. J. Ch. 880, 5 Ch. D. 225, 36 L. T. 498. Examples of such words, which the courts have held sufficient to constitute a trust, are "having full confidence, I hereby request," 59 Wis. 172; "recommend and request," 127 U. S. 300; "request," 82 N. Y. 405; "hope and trust," 109 U. S. 725; "advise him to settle," 5 L. J. Ch. 98; "well assured," 1 Atk. 389, 1 Amb. 520; "have full assurance and confident hope," 17 Bea. 299; "authorise and empower", 4 Ves. 708, 5 Ib. 495, 8 Ib. 561, 18 Ib. 192, 11 L. J. Ch. 219, 5 Bea. 241; "beg," Ir. Rep. 7 Eq. 456; "in the full belief," W. N. (75) 140; "most heartily beseech," 1 Sim. 553; "confide," 11 L. J. Ch. 219, 5 Bea. 241, 2 J. & H. 766; "have the fullest confidence," 32 Bea. 143, 60 L. T. 140; 17 Ves. 255, 19 Ib. 299, 21 L. J. Ch. 625; 2 Sim. N. S. 267. Where the words expressing "confidence" are preceded by an absolute gift. 52 L. J. Ch. 758, 24 Ch. D. 199, 6 Ch. 597; 8 Ch. D. 540, 51 L. J. P. C. 72, 7 App. Ca. 321.

"In consideration the legatee has promised to give," 1 Amb. 519; "under the firm conviction," 26 L. J. Ch. 92, 2 Jur. N. S. 1127; "of course the legatee will give," 6 Mad. 194, 2 My. & K. 198; "desire," 1 Atk. 469, Amb. 4, 2 Vern. 708, 3 Ves. 7, 9 Ves. 319; "do not doubt," 18 Ves. 476, 2 V. & B. 378; "entreat," 2 Mad. 458, 1 Sim. 553, 555; "hope," 1 Bro. C. C. 142, L. R. 4 Eq. 151; "well know," 7 L. J. Ch. 268, 9 Sim. 323, 1 Bro. C. C. 489, 3 Mac. & G. 546, 46 L. J. Ch. 880, 36 L. T. 498; "order and direct," 2 Sch. & Lef. 189; "recommend," Jac. 317, 19 Ves. 656, 1 S. & S. 387, 8 Ves. 280, 3 Ves. 150, 1 Sim. 553, 2 Hogan 166, 14 Sim. 590, 18 Bea. 215, 15 Sim. 33.

That "recommend" may amount to a command and create a binding trust is certain. It is equally certain that the word is susceptible of a different interpretation. It must depend upon the language of the particular instrument in which this word is found, in which of the two senses it is to be taken, 17 L. J. Ch. 438, 2 D. G. & S. 356; "request," 2 Bro. C. C. 38, 3 Ir. Ch. Rep. 26, Johns. 276; "trusting," 38 L. J. Ch. 635, L. R. 8 Eq. 673; "trusting and confiding," 5 L. J. Ch. 361, 6 Ib. 366, 2 My. & C. 684, 12 Sim. 114; "will," Pr. Ch. 200, 1 Vern. 411; "will and declare," 11 Ir. Ch. Rep. 218; "will and desire," 3 V. & B. 198; "wish and desire," 29 L. J. Ch. 619, 28 Bea. 266; "wish and request," 5 Sim. 138, 2 My. & K. 138.

But any of the foregoing or similar phrases might easily be controlled the other way by a context, 52 L. J. Ch. 761, 24 Ch. D. 199; and at the present time, the courts are not disposed to enlarge the number of such phrases, so as to create a trust. 2 Pom. Eq. Jur. § 1016.

PRECATORY WORDS. Words which create a precatory trust (*q. v.*)

PRECEDENCE, PATENT OF. In English law. A grant from the crown to such barristers as it thinks proper to honor with that mark of distinction, whereby they are entitled to such rank and preaudience as are assigned in their respective patents. 3 Steph. Comm. 274.

PRECEDENT CONDITION. A precedent condition is one which must be performed before the estate can vest. 260 Ill. 102. See "Condition."

PRECEDENTS. Authorities to be followed in courts of justice. A term particularly applied to judicial decisions upon points of law arising in any given case. 1 Kent, Comm. 475, 476. These are recognized in equity as well as at law. 1 Story, Eq. Jur. § 18. The old books are full of expressions in support of precedents. Jenk. Cent. Cas. viii. See "Stare Decisis."

Written forms of proceedings which have been approved by the courts, or by long professional usage, and are to be (usually strictly) followed. Steph. Pl. 392. Lord Bacon observes that there are political as well as legal precedents. Bac. Works, iv. 354.

PRECEPT (Lat. *precipio*, to command). A writ directed to the sheriff, or other officer, commanding him to do something.

PRECEPT OF CLARE CONSTAT. In Scotch feudal law. An acknowledgment by the lord of the right of an heir of the tenant to succeed to his right.

PRECES (Lat.) In the Roman law. Prayers. One of the names of an application to the emperor. Tayl. Civ. Law, 230.

PRECINCT.

——**In English Law.** The district for which a high or petty constable is appointed. Wilcox, Const. xii.

——**In American Law.** A district, usually of a subordinate character, marked out for governmental purpose. See 113 U. S. 516; 124 Mass. 172.

PRECIPE. See "Praecipe."

PRECIPUT. In French law. An object which is ascertained by law or the agreement of the parties, and which is first to be taken out of property held in common, by one having a right, before a partition takes place.

The *preciput* is an advantage or a principal part to which some one is entitled *praecipium jus*, which is the origin of the word *preciput*. Dalloz; Poth. Obl. By *preciput* is also understood the right to sue out the *preciput*.

PRECLUDI NON (Lat.) In pleading. A technical allegation contained in a replication which denies or confesses and avoids the plea.

It is usually in the following form: "And the said A. B., as to the plea of the said C. D., by him secondly above pleaded, says that he, the said A. B., by reason of anything by the said C. D. in that plea alleged, ought not to be barred from having and maintaining his aforesaid action thereof against the said C. D., because he says that," etc. 2 Wils. 42; 1 Chit. Pl. 573.

PRECOGNITION. In Scotch law. The examination of witnesses who were present at the commission of a criminal act, upon the special circumstances attending it, in order to know whether there is ground for a trial, and to serve for direction to the prosecutor. But the persons examined may insist on having their declaration cancelled before they give testimony at the trial. Ersk. Inst. 4. 4. note 49.

PRECOGNOSCE (Scotch; from Lat. *praecognoscere*). In Scotch practice. To examine beforehand. Arkley, 232.

PRECONTRACT. An engagement entered into by a person which renders him unable to enter into another; as, a promise or covenant of marriage to be had afterwards. When made *per verba de presenti*, it is in fact a marriage, and in that case the party making it cannot marry another person.

PREDECESSOR. One who has preceded another.

This term is applied in particular to corporators who are now no longer such, and whose rights have been vested in their successor. The word "ancestor" is more usually applicable to common persons. The predecessor in a corporation stands in the same relation to the successor that the ancestor does to the heir.

One who has filled an office or station before the present incumbent.

PREDIAL SERVITUDE. See "Praedial Servitude."

PRE-EMPTION. In international law. The right of pre-emption is the right of a nation to detain the merchandise of strangers passing through her territories or seas, in order to afford to her subjects the preference of purchase. 1 Chit. Com. Law, 103; 2 Bl. Comm. 287.

This right is sometimes regulated by treaty. In that which was made between the United States and Great Britain, bearing date the 19th day of November, 1794, ratified in 1795, it was agreed (article 18), after mentioning that the usual munitions of war, and also naval materials, should be confiscated as contraband, that "whereas the difficulty of agreeing on precise cases in which alone provisions and other articles not generally contraband may be regarded as such renders it expedient to provide against the inconveniences and misunderstandings which might thence arise, it is further agreed that whenever any such articles so being contraband according to the existing laws of nations shall for that reason be seized, the same shall not be confiscated, but the owners thereof shall be speedily and completely indemnified; and the captors, or, in their default, the government under whose authority they act, shall pay to the masters or owners of such vessel the full value of all articles, with a reasonable mercantile profit thereon, together with the freight, and also the damages incident to such detention." See Manning, Comm. bk. 3, c. 8.

PRE-EMPTION RIGHT. The right given to settlers upon the public lands of the United States to purchase them at a limited price, in preference to others.

PREFECT. In French law. A chief officer invested with the superintendence of the administration of the laws in each department. Merlin, Repert.

PREFERENCE. Priority of payment, or right thereto. Preferences may be either involuntary, being the right which a creditor obtains by law to be first paid out of the assets of the debtor, as by obtaining a judgment which is a lien on his lands, or voluntary, being the paying or securing to one or more of his creditors by a debtor (usually insolvent) the whole or a part of their claims, to the exclusion of the rest.

PREFERENCE SHARES. A name sometimes given in England to preferred stock.

PREFERENTIAL ASSIGNMENT. An assignment for the benefit of creditors, giving preferences (*q. v.*)

PREFERRED CREDITOR. One to whom the debtor has given a preference (*q. v.*), or to whom he has directed that a preference be given.

PREFERRED STOCK. Corporate stock entitled to priority in payment of dividends, or to a higher rate of dividends.

PREGNANCY, PLEA OF. A plea by a woman under sentence of death, on which, if she be found quick with child, execution is stayed. 4 Bl. Comm. 394.

PREGNANT. See "Affirmative Pregnant;" "Negative Pregnant."

PREJUDICE. (Lat. *prae*, before, *judicare*, to judge). A forejudgment. A leaning towards one side of a cause formed before the person entertaining the same is called upon to hear and determine the cause. See "Bias."

PRELATE. The name of an ecclesiastical officer. There are two orders of prelates—the first is composed of bishops, and the second, of abbots, generals of orders, deans, etc.

PRELEVEMENT. In French law. The portion which a partner is entitled to take out of the assets of a firm before any division shall be made of the remainder of the assets between the partners.

The partner who is entitled to a *prelevement* is not a creditor of the partnership,—on the contrary, he is a part owner; for, if the assets should be deficient, a creditor has a preference over the partner. On the other hand, should the assets yield any profit, the partner is entitled to his portion of it, whereas the creditor is entitled to no part of it, but he has a right to charge interest when he is in other respects entitled to it.

PRELIMINARY. Something which precedes; as, preliminaries of peace, which are the first sketch of a treaty, and contain the principal articles on which both parties are desirous of concluding, and which are to serve as the basis of the treaty.

PRELIMINARY ACT. In English admiralty practice. A document narrating the particulars of a collision, required to be filed by each solicitor in actions for damages in such collision. Wharton.

PRELIMINARY INJUNCTION. Sometimes called an *ad interim* injunction. One issued at the commencement of a suit, to restrain the commission of some act pending the suit.

PREMEDITATION. A design formed to commit a crime or to do some other thing before it is done.

Premeditation differs essentially from "will," which constitutes the crime; because it supposes, besides an actual will, a deliberation and a continued persistence, which indicate more perversity.

It is also to be distinguished from "deliberation." "Premeditation" implies merely previous contrivance or formed design, and does not necessarily exclude acts on a sudden impulse. "Deliberation" implies reflection upon the act before committing it. Fixed and determined purpose, as distinguished from sudden impulse. 58 Pa. St. 9.

PREMISES (Lat. *prae*, before, *mittere*, to put, to send). That which is put before; the introduction; statements previously made. See 1 East, 456.

——**In Conveyancing.** That part of a deed which precedes the *habendum*, in which are set forth the names of the parties, with their titles and additions, and in which are recited such deeds, agreements, or matters of fact as are necessary to explain the reasons upon which the contract then entered into is founded; and it is here, also, the consideration on which it is made is set down, and the certainty of the thing granted. 2 Bl. Comm. 298; 8 Mass. 174; 6 Conn. 289.

——**In Equity Pleading.** The stating part of a bill. It contains a narrative of the facts and circumstances of the plaintiff's case, and the wrongs of which he complains, and the names of the persons by whom done, and against whom he seeks redress. Cooper, Eq. Pl. 9; Bart. Suit in Eq. 27; Mitf. Eq. Pl. (Jeremy Ed.) 43; Story, Eq. Pl. § 27.

Every material fact to which the plaintiff intends to offer evidence must be stated in the premises; otherwise, he will not be permitted to offer or require evidence of such fact. 1 Brown, Ch. 94; 3 Swanst. 472; 3 P. Wms. 276; 2 Atk. 96; 1 Vern. 483; 11 Ves. 240; 2 Hare, 264; 6 Johns. (N. Y.) 565; 9 Ga. 148.

——**In Estates.** Lands and tenements. 1 East, 453; 3 Maule & S. 169.

PREMIUM (from Lat. *praemium*, reward). The sum paid or agreed to be paid by an assured to the insurers, as the consideration for the insurance; being a certain rate per cent. on the amount insured. 1 Phil. Ins. 205; 3 Kent, Comm. 253.

The price of a risk.

PREMIUM PUDICITIAE (Lat. the price of chastity). The consideration of a contract by which a man promises to pay to a woman with whom he has illicit intercourse a certain sum of money. In the civil law, sometimes applied to the compensation recovered for loss of chastity.

PREMUNIRE. See "Praemunire."

PRENDA. In Spanish law. Pledge. White, New Recop. bk. 2, tit. 7.

PRENDER, or **PRENDRE** (Law Fr. to take). This word is used to signify the right of taking a thing before it is offered; hence the phrase of law, "it lies in render, but not in prender." Gale & W. Easem.; Washb. Easem.

PRENDER DE BARON (Law Fr.) In old English law. A taking of husband; marriage. An exception or plea which might be used to disable a woman from pursuing an appeal of murder against the killer of her former husband. Staundf. P. C. lib. 3, c. 59.

PRENOMEN (Lat.) The first or Christian name of a person. Benjamin is the *prenomen* of Benjamin Franklin. See Cas. temp. Hardw. 286; 1 Tayl. (N. C.) 148.

PREPENSE. Aforethought. See 2 Chit. Crim. Law, *784.

PREPONDERATE. To "preponderate" is to "outweigh." There may be evidence which, standing by itself, establishes a certain state of facts, but the evidence does not preponderate in favor of any given state of facts unless it is sufficient to outweigh all the testimony introduced in opposition thereto. 138 Ill. 13.

PREROGATIVE.

——**In Civil Law.** The privilege, preeminence, or advantage which one person has over another; thus, a person vested with an office is entitled to all the rights, privileges, prerogatives, etc., which belong to it.

——**In English Law.** The royal prerogative is an arbitrary power vested in the executive to do good, and not evil. Rutherforth, Inst. 279; Co. Litt. 90; Chit. Prerog.; Bac. Abr.

PREROGATIVE COURT.

——**In English Law.** An ecclesiastical court held in each of the two provinces of York and Canterbury, before a judge appointed by the archbishop of the province.

Formerly in this court testaments were proved, and administrations granted where a decedent left chattels to the value of five pounds (*bona notabilia*) in two distinct dioceses or jurisdictions within the province, and all causes relating to the wills, administrations, or legacies of such persons were originally cognizable. This jurisdiction was transferred to the court of probate by 20 & 21 Vict. c. 77, § 4, and 21 & 22 Vict. c. 95.

An appeal lay formerly from this court to the king in chancery, by St. 25 Hen. VIII, c. 19, but lies now to the privy council, by St. 2 & 3 Wm. IV, c. 92; 2 Steph. Comm. 237, 238; 3 Bl. Comm. 65, 66.

——**In American Law.** A court having a jurisdiction of probate matters in the state of New Jersey.

PREROGATIVE LAW. That part of the common law of England which is more particularly applicable to the king. Com. Dig. tit. "Ley" (A).

PREROGATIVE WRIT. A writ issued upon some extraordinary occasion, and for which it is necessary to apply by motion to the court. 3 Bl. Comm. 132. The writs of *procedendo*, *mandamus*, prohibition, *quo warranto*, *habeas corpus*, and *certiorari* belong to this class. 3 Steph. Comm. 681.

Prerogative writs have also been distinguished from writs ministerially directed, viz., those issued to the sheriff; the prerogative writs being generally directed to no sheriff or officer of the court, but to the public or private parties, whose acts are the subject of complaint. 2 Burrows, 855.

PRES (Law Fr.) Near, *Cy pres*, so near; as near. See "Cy Pres."

PRESBYTER (Lat.) In civil and ecclesiastical law. An elder; a presbyter; a priest. Code, 1. 3. 6. 20; Nov. 6.

PRESCRIBABLE. To which a right may be acquired by prescription.

PRESCRIPTION. A mode of acquiring title to incorporeal hereditaments by immemorial or long-continued enjoyment.

The distinction between a prescription and a custom is that a custom is a local usage, and not annexed to a person. A prescription is a personal usage, confined to the claimant and his ancestors or grantors. The theory of prescription was that the right claimed must have been enjoyed beyond the period of the memory of man, which for a long time, in England, went back to the time of Richard I. To avoid the necessity of proof of such long duration, a custom arose of allowing a presumption of a grant on proof of usage for a long term of years. In modern practice, the period of legal limitation for adverse possession of lands is generally adopted. 100 N. Y. 455.

To acquire title by prescription, the user must be adverse (117 Ill. 532), exclusive (7 Metc. [Mass.] 33), peaceable (31 N. J. Eq. 706), notorious (7 Allen [Mass.] 368), and continuous (2 Cush. [Mass.] 191).

PRESCRIPTION ACT. St. 2 & 3 Wm. IV, c. 71, passed to limit the period of prescription in certain cases.

PRESCRIPTION, TIME OF. See "Time Immemorial."

PRESENCE. The being in a particular place.

In many contracts and judicial proceedings it is necessary that the parties should be present in order to render them valid; for example, a party to a deed, when it is executed by himself, must personally acknowledge it, when such acknowledgment is required by law, to give it its full force and effect, and his presence is indispensable, unless, indeed, another person represent him as his attorney, having authority from him for that purpose.

Presence at a particular transaction is in a measure relative. Thus, a crime is committed in the presence of a police officer if he can detect the act, and could have seen the persons had it been light (53 Mich. 493); and a married woman executes a deed in the presence of her husband, if he was under the same roof, though not in the same room (112 Mass. 287).

Actual presence is being bodily in the precise spot indicated.

Constructive presence is being so near to or in such relation with the parties actually in a designated place as to be considered in law as being in the place. Thus, a man was held constructively present at a stage robbery, where he built a fire on a mountain forty miles distant as a notice to the robber of the leaving of the stage. 13 Nev. 386.

PRESENT. A gift, or, more properly, the thing given.

PRESENT ESTATE. An estate in possession; one presently vested.

PRESENT USE. One which has an immediate existence, and is at once operated upon by the statute of uses.

PRESENTATION. In ecclesiastical law. The act of a patron offering his clerk to the bishop of the diocese to be instituted in a church or benefice.

PRESENTEE. In ecclesiastical law. A clerk who has been presented by his patron to a bishop in order to be instituted in a church.

PRESENTLY. Immediately; in the present tense.

PRESENTMENT.

——**In Criminal Practice.** The written notice taken by a grand jury of any offense, from their own knowledge or observation, without any bill of indictment laid before them at the suit of the government. 4 Bl. Comm. 301; 109 Cal. 448; 183 Mich. 207.

Upon such presentment, when proper, the officer employed to prosecute afterwards frames a bill of indictment, which is then sent to the grand jury, and they find it to be a true bill. In an extended sense, presentments include not only what are properly so called, but also inquisitions of office and indictments found by a grand jury. 2 Hawk. P. C. c. 25, § 1.

The difference between a presentment and an inquisition is this: that the former is found by a grand jury authorized to inquire of offenses generally, whereas the latter is an accusation found by a jury specially returned to inquire concerning a particular offense. 2 Hawk. P. C. c. 25, § 6. See, generally, Comyn, Dig. "Indictment" (B); Bac. Abr. "Indictment" (A); 1 Chit. Crim. Law, 163; 7 East, 387; 1 Meigs (Tenn.) 112; 11 Humph. (Tenn.) 12.

The chief distinction between an indictment and a presentment at common law was that the former was made at the suggestion of the crown, while the latter was made upon the knowledge of one or more of the jurors, and instead of being indorsed "a true bill" by the foreman alone, was signed by all of the jurors.

The writing which contains the accusation so presented by a grand jury. 1 Brock. (U. S.) 156.

——**In Contracts.** The production of a bill of exchange or promissory note to the party on whom the former is drawn, for his acceptance, or to the person bound to pay either, for payment.

PRESENTS. This word signifies the writing then actually made and spoken of; as, these presents; know all men by these presents; to all to whom these presents shall come.

PRESS. In old practice. A piece or skin of parchment, several of which used to be sewed together in making up a roll or record of proceedings. See 1 Bl. Comm. 183; Towns. Pl. 486.

PRESSING TO DEATH. See "Peine Forte et Dure."

PREST (and afterwards **PRIST**) (Law Fr.; from Lat. *paratus*).

——**In Old Pleading and Practice.** Ready. *Prest averrer*, ready to prove. Y. B. P. 11 Hen. VI 8; Y. B. M. 12 Hen. VI. 13. *Prest de prover*. Britt. c. 22. A formal word at the conclusion of pleas and replications, expressive of a tender and acceptance of issue. *Prest*, etc., was a mere common form. See Y. B. 8 Edw. III. 20; Y. B. T. 8 Edw. III. 11.

Prest a passer, ready to pass, that is, to give a verdict. Y. B. M. 3 Edw. II. 56. See "Passer."

—**In Old English Law.** A duty in money to be paid by the sheriff upon his account in the exchequer, or for money left or remaining in his hands. Cowell.

PRESTATION (Lat. *praestatio*, from *praestare, q. v.*) In old English law. A payment or performance; the rendering of a service; a toll, custom or duty.

PRESUMPTIVE EVIDENCE. See "Circumstantial Evidence."

PRESUMPTIVE HEIR. One who, if the ancestor should die immediately, would, under existing condition of things, be his heir, but whose right of inheritance may be defeated by the contingency of some nearer heir being born; as, a brother, who is the presumptive heir, may be defeated by the birth of a child to the ancestor. 2 Bl. Comm 208

PRESUMPTIVE TITLE. That which arises from mere occupation, with no pretense of right to hold possession. It is the very lowest order of title.

PRET (Fr.) Loan.

PRET A USAGE (Fr. loan for use). A phrase used in the French law instead of *commodatum*.

PRETENSED, or PRETENCED (Law Lat. *praetensum*). In old English law. Pretended; claimed. Where a party out of possession of lands or tenements claimed or sued for the possession, he was said to have a pretensed right and title (*jus praetensum*). Cowell; Dyer, 74b.

PRETENSED TITLE STATUTE. The English statute 32 Hen. VIII. c. 9, § 2. It enacts that no one shall sell or purchase any pretended right or title to land, unless the vendor has received the profits thereof for one whole year before such grant, or has been in actual possession of the land, or of the reversion or remainder, on pain that both purchaser and vendor shall each forfeit the value of such land to the king and the prosecutor. See 4 Broom & H. Comm. 150.

PRETENSES. In equity pleading. Allegations sometimes made in a bill for the purpose of negativing an anticipated defense. Hunt, Eq. pt. 1, c. 1.

PRETENSION. In French law. The claim made to a thing which a party believes himself entitled to demand, but which is not admitted or adjudged to be his.

The words "rights," "actions," and "pretensions" are usually joined; not that they are synonymous, for "right" is something positive and certain, "action" is what is demanded, while "pretension" is sometimes not even accompanied by a demand.

PRETER LEGAL. Not agreeable to law.

PRETERITION (Lat. *praeter* and *eo*, to go by). In civil law. The omission by a testator of some one of his heirs who is entitled to a *legitime* (*q. v.*) in the succession.

Among the Romans, the preterition of children when made by the mother was presumed to have been made with design. The preterition of sons by any other testator was considered as a wrong, and avoided the will, except the will of a soldier in service, which was not subject to so much form.

PRETERMISSION. In the law of wills. The intentional passing over without making provision for a child or legal heir or next of kin. Same as "preterition," which is the strictly proper term.

PRETEXT (Lat. *praetextum*, woven before). The reasons assigned to justify an act, which have only the appearance of truth, and which are without foundation, or which, if true, are not the true reasons for such act. Vattel, liv. 3, c. 3, § 32.

An ostensible reason or motive assigned or assumed as a color or cover for the real motive or reason. 27 Neb. 601.

PRETIUM, or PRECIUM (Lat. price; value). In the civil law. The price of a thing sold, which properly consisted in counted money; *pretium in numerata pecunia consistere debet*. Inst. 3. 24. 2. *Pretium constitui oportet, nam nulla emptio sine pretio esse potest*, the price ought to be fixed for there can be no purchase without a price. Id.; Dig. 18. 1. 2; 2 Kent, Comm. 477.

PRETIUM AFFECTIONIS (Lat.) An imaginary value put upon a thing by the fancy of the owner in his affection for it, or for the person from whom he obtained it. Bell, Dict.

PRETIUM SUCCEDIT IN LOCUM REI. The price stands in the place of the thing sold. 1 Bouv. Inst. note 939; 2 Bulst. 312.

PRETORIUM. In Scotch law. A court house, or hall of justice. 3 How. St. Tr. 425.

PREVARICATION. In civil law. The acting with unfaithfulness and want of probity. The term is applied principally to the act of concealing a crime. Dig. 47. 15. 6.

PREVENTION (Lat. *preveniato*, to come before). In civil law. The right of a judge to take cognizance of an action over which he has concurrent jurisdiction with another judge.

In Pennsylvania it has been ruled that a justice of the peace cannot take cognizance of a cause which has been previously decided by another justice. 2 Dall. (Pa.) 77, 114.

PREVENTION OF CRIMES ACT. The statute 34 & 35 Vict. c. 112, passed for the purpose of securing a better supervision over habitual criminals. This act provides that a person who is for a second time convicted of crime may, on his second conviction, be subjected to police supervision for a period of seven years after the expiration of the punishment awarded him. Penalties are imposed on lodging house keepers, etc., for harboring thieves or reputed thieves. There are also provisions relating to receivers of stolen property, and dealers in old metals who purchase the same in small quantities. This act repeals the habitual criminals act of 1869 (32 & 33 Vict. c. 99). Brown.

PRICE. See "Value."

PRICKING FOR SHERIFFS. In England, when the yearly list of persons nominated for the office of sheriff is submitted to the queen, she took a pin, and to insure impartiality, as it is said, she let the point of it fall upon one of the three names nominated for each county, etc., and the person upon whose name it chanced to fall was sheriff for the ensuing year. This is called "pricking for sheriffs." Atk. Sheriffs, 18.

PRIMA FACIE. At first view; from the appearance, without contradiction or explanation.

PRIMA FACIE CASE. A case established by *prima facie* evidence (*q. v.*)

PRIMA FACIE EVIDENCE. Such as is, in judgment of law, sufficient to establish the fact, and, if not rebutted remains sufficient for the purpose.

PRIMA PARS AEQUITATIS AEQUALItas. The radical element of justice is equality.

PRIMA TONSURA (Lat.) A grant of a right to have the first crop of grass. 1 Chit. Prac. 181.

PRIMAE IMPRESSIONIS (Law Lat.) Of the first impression; without precedent. A term applied to a new case, or one which has not occurred before, or to a question which is raised for the first time. Eyre, J., 5 Mod. 23; 1 Vern. 94; Platt, J., 19 Johns. (N. Y.) 310. "The question here, as there, is *primae impressionis*; the case here, as there, is the first of its kind." Story, J., 3 Mason (U. S.) 116, 125. The expression is applied to actions, returns, motions, and other proceedings. Freem. 431; Holt, C. J., 5 Mod. 21; Mansfield, C. J., 4 Taunt. 3; 1 Taunt. 492, arg. The Gunpowder Plot was called by Lord Coke, in his argument as attorney general in the case, an offense *primae impressionis*. 2 How. St. Tr. 167.

PRIMAE (or **PRIMARIAE**) **PRECES** (Lat.) In the civil law. An imperial prerogative, by which the emperor exercised the right of naming to the first prebend that became vacant after his accession, in every church of the empire. Goldast. Constit. Imper. tom. 3, p. 406; 1 Bl. Comm. 381.

PRIMAGE. In mercantile law. A duty payable to the master and mariners of a ship or vessel,—to the master for the use of his cables and ropes to discharge the goods of the merchant; to the mariners for lading and unlading in any port or haven. Abb. Shipp. 270.

This payment appears to be of very ancient date, and to be variously regulated in different voyages and trades. It is sometimes called the "master's hat money." 3 Chit. Com. Law, 431.

PRIMARY. That which is first or principal; as, primary evidence, that evidence which is to be admitted in the first instance, as distinguished from secondary evidence, which is allowed only when primary evidence cannot be had.

PRIMARY CONVEYANCES. See "Conveyance."

PRIMARY EVIDENCE. The best evidence of which the case in its nature is susceptible. 3 Bouv. Inst. note 3053. See "Evidence."

PRIMARY OBLIGATION. An obligation which is the principal object of the contract; for example, the primary obligation of the seller is to deliver the thing sold, and to transfer the title to it. It is distinguished from the accessory or secondary obligation to pay damages for not doing so. 1 Bouv. Inst. note 702.

PRIMARY POWERS. The principal authority given by a principal to his agent. It differs from "mediate powers." Story, Ag. § 58.

PRIMATE. In ecclesiastical law. An archbishop who has jurisdiction over one or several other metropolitans.

PRIME SERJEANT. The queen's first serjeant at law.

PRIMER ELECTION. A term used to signify first choice.

In England, when coparcenary lands are divided, unless it is otherwise agreed, the eldest sister has the first choice of the purparts. This part is called the *enitia pars.* Sometimes the oldest sister makes the partition, and in that case, to prevent partiality, she takes the last choice. Hob. 107; Litt. §§ 243-245; Bac. Abr. "Coparceners" (U).

PRIMER FINE. In old English practice. A fine or payment which was due to the king on suing out the writ of *praecipe,* at the commencement of the proceedings to levy a fine of lands. 2 Bl. Comm. 350.

PRIMER SEISIN. In English law. The right which the king had, when any of his tenants died seised of a knight's fee, to receive of the heir, provided he were of full age, one whole year's profits of the lands, if they were in immediate possession, and half a year's profits, if the lands were in reversion, expectant on an estate for life. 2 Bl. Comm. 66.

PRIMITIAE (Lat.) In English law. First fruits; the first year's whole profits of a spiritual preferment. 1 Bl. Comm. 284; Crabb, Hist. Eng. Law, 252.

PRIMO EXCUTIENDA EST VERBI VIS, ne sermonis vitio obstruitur oratio, sive lex sine argumentis. The force of a word is to be first examined, lest by the fault of diction the sentence be destroyed, or the law be without arguments. Co. Litt. 68.

PRIMOGENITURE. The state of being first born; the eldest.

Formerly primogeniture gave a title in cases of descent to the oldest son in preference to the other children. This unjust distinction has been generally abolished in the United States.

PRIMOGENITUS (Lat. from *primo,* first, and *genitus,* born or begotten). In old English law. A first born or eldest son. Bracton, fol. 33; 1 Ves. Sr. 290. And see 3 Maule & S. 25; 8 Taunt. 468; 3 Vern. 660.

PRIMUM DECRETUM (Lat.) In the courts of admiralty, this name is given to a provisional decree. Bac. Abr. "Court of Admiralty" (E).

PRINCE. In a general sense, a sovereign; the ruler of a nation or state. The son of a king or emperor, or the issue of a royal family; as, princes of the blood. The chief of any body of men.

By a clause inserted in policies of insurance, the insurer is liable for all losses occasioned by "arrest or detainment of all kings, princes, and people, of what nation, condition, or quality soever." 1 Bouv. Inst. note 1218.

PRINCEPS (Lat.) In the civil law. The prince; the emperor. *Quod principi placuit, legis habet vigorem,* the emperor's pleasure has the force of law. Inst. 1. 2. 6.

PRINCEPS ET RESPUBLICA EX JUSTA causa possunt rem meam auferre. The king and the commonwealth, for a just cause, can take away my property. 12 Coke, 13.

PRINCEPS LEGIBUS SOLUTUS EST. The emperor is free from laws. Dig. 1. 3. 31; Halifax, Anal. pref. vi., vii., note.

PRINCEPS MAVULT DOMESTICOS MILites quam stipendiarios bellicis opponere casibus. A prince, in the chances of war, had better employ domestic than stipendiary troops. Co. Litt. 69.

PRINCIPAL. Leading; chief; more important.

This word has several meanings. It is used in opposition to "accessary," to show the degree of crime committed by two persons.

In estates, "principal" is used as opposed to "incident" or "accessory," to denote the more important subject to which others are appurtenant or ancillary, as in the rule: "The incident shall pass by the grant of the principal, but not the principal by the grant of the incident,—*accessorium non ducit, sed sequitur suum principale.*" Co. Litt. 152a.

It is used in opposition to "agent," and in this sense it signifies that the principal is the prime mover.

It is used in opposition to "interest;" as, the principal being secured, the interest will follow.

It is used also in opposition to "surety," to denote the person for whom the surety is bound. Thus, we say, the principal is answerable before the surety.

Principal is used also to denote the more important; as, the principal person.

In the English law, the chief person in some of the inns of chancery is called "principal of the house." Principal is also used to designate the best of many things; as, the principal bed, the principal table, and the like.

——**In Contracts.** One who, being competent *sui juris* to do any act for his own benefit or on his own account, confides it to another person to do for him. 1 Domat, bk. 1, tit. 15, Introd.; Story, Ag. § 3.

——**In Criminal Law.** Principals in crime are either in the first or second degree.

A principal in the first degree is the one who actually commits the crime, either by his own hand, or by an inanimate agency (4 Bl. Comm. 34; 2 Sumn. [U. S.] 482), or by an innocent human agent (1 N. Y. 173; 1 Mass. 136).

A principal in the second degree is one who, being present at the commission of a crime by another, aids and abets him therein. There must be a guilty principal in the first degree. The principal in the second must be present, but constructive presence, as by keeping watch at a distance, is sufficient (83 N. Y. 408; 13 Nev. 386), and the principal in the second degree must in some manner assist or abet the principal offender; mere presence and acquiescence not being enough (81 Ill. 333; 45 Cal. 293). See "Aiding and Abetting;" "Presence."

The distinction between principals and accessaries is not recognized in treason or in misdemeanors. 4 Bl. Comm. 35, 36.

PRINCIPAL CHALLENGE. A principal challenge was grounded on such manifest presumption of partiality that if the fact alleged was proved to be true, the disqualification of the juror followed as a legal conclusion, incapable of being rebutted. 144 Ill. 164. See Challenge.

PRINCIPAL CONTRACT. One entered into by both parties on their own accounts, or in the several qualities they assume.

PRINCIPAL FACT. The main fact in issue. The fact ultimately to be proved.

PRINCIPAL LEGATEE. In the statute as to right to letters of administration with will annexed means general, rather than chief or most important. 2 How. Pr. (N. S.; N. Y.) 194.

PRINCIPAL OBLIGATION. That obligation which arises from the principal object of the engagement which has been contracted between the parties. It differs from an accessory obligation. For example, in the sale of a horse, the principal obligation of the seller is to deliver the horse; the obligation to take care of him till delivered is an accessory engagement. Poth. Obl. note 182. By principal obligation is also understood the engagement of one who becomes bound for himself, and not for the benefit of another. Poth. Obl. note 186.

PRINCIPALIS. (Lat. from *princeps*, first or chief). In civil and old English law. Principal; a principal debtor. *Principalis debitor*. Fleta, lib. 2, c. 63, § 5. Called *capitalis debitor* (chief debtor). Id.

PRINCIPALIS DEBET SEMPER EXCUTI antequam perveniatur ad fidei jussores. The principal should always be exhausted before coming upon the sureties. 2 Inst. 19.

PRINCIPIA DATA SEQUUNTUR CONcomitantia. Given principles are followed by their concomitants.

PRINCIPIA PROBANT, NON PROBANtur. Principles prove, they are not proved. 3 Coke, 40. See "Principles."

PRINCIPIIS OBSTA. Oppose beginnings. Branch, Princ.

PRINCIPIORUM NON EST RATIO. There is no reasoning of principles. 2 Bulst. 239. See "Principles."

PRINCIPIUM (Lat. from *princeps*, first). In civil and old English law. A beginning. *In principio donationis*, at the commencement of the gift. Bracton, fol. 17b.

A principle; a maxim. Analyzed by Lord Coke, in his peculiar manner, to be *quasi primum caput* (the first head), from which many cases have their origin or beginning. Co. Litt. 303a.

PRINCIPIUM EST POTISSIMA PARS cujusque rei. The beginning is the most powerful part of a thing. 10 Coke, 49.

PRINCIPLES. By this term is understood truths or propositions so clear that they cannot be proved nor contradicted unless by propositions which are still clearer.

They are of two kinds: One when the principle is universal, and these are known as "axioms" or "maxims;" as, "no one can transmit rights which he has not;" "the accessory follows the principal," etc. The other class are simply called "first principles." These principles have known marks, by which they may always be recognized. These are, first, that they are so clear that they cannot be proved by anterior and more manifest truths; second, that they are almost universally received; third, that they are so strongly impressed on our minds that we conform ourselves to them whatever may be our avowed opinions.

First principles have their source in the sentiment of our own existence, and that which is in the nature of things. A principle of law is a rule or axiom which is founded in the nature of the subject, and it exists before it is expressed in the form of a rule. Domat, Lois Civ. liv. prel. tit. 1, § 2; Toullier, Dr. Civ. tit. prel. note 17. "The right to defend one's self continues as long as an unjust attack" was a principle before it was ever decided by a court; so that a court does not establish, but recognizes, principles of law.

That which constitutes the essence of a body, or its constituent parts. 8 Term R. 107. See "Patent."

PRIOR PETENS (Lat.) The first applicant. *Priori petenti*, to the first applicant.

PRIOR TEMPORE, POTIOR JURE. He who is first in time is preferred in right. Co. Litt. 14a; 2 P. Wms. 491; 1 Term R. 733; 9 Wheat. (U. S.) Append. 24.

PRIORITY. Precedence. Thus, claims are said to be allowed priority where they are satisfied from a fund before other claims against the same are allowed to participate.

PRISAGE. An ancient hereditary revenue of the crown, consisting in the right to take a certain quantity from cargoes of wine imported into England. In Edward I.'s reign it was converted into a pecuniary duty called "butlerage." 2 Steph. Comm. 561.

PRISE (Fr.)

——**In French Law.** Prize; captured property. Ord. Mar. liv. 3, tit. 9. See "Prize."

Capture, by a naval force. Emerig. Tr. des Assur. c. 12, sec. 18, § 1.

——**In Old English Law.** Things taken of the king's subjects by purveyors; provisions taken for the king's use. Cowell; Artic. sup. Chart. c. 2; 2 Reeve, Hist. Eng. Law, 233; Fleta, lib. 2, c. 50, § 21.

PRISEL EN AUTER LIEU (Law Fr.) A taking in another place; a plea in abatement in the action of replevin. 2 Ld. Raym. 1016, 1017.

PRISO (Law Lat.; Law Fr. *prison,* from *prise,* taken). In old English law. A prisoner; a captive in war. Spelman.

A prisoner, or imprisoned malefactor. *Prisones vero, sic imprisonati,* but prisoners so imprisoned. Bracton, fol. 123. See Fleta, lib. 1, c. 26, § 5.

PRISON. A public building for confining persons, either to insure their production in court, as accused persons and witnesses, or to punish, as criminals.

The root is French, as is shown by the Norman *prisons,* prisoners (Kelham), and French *prisons,* prisons (Britt. c. 11, "De Prisons"). Originally it was distinguished from "gaol," which was a place for confinement, not for punishment. See Jacob, "Gaol." But at present there is no such distinction.

It is a general term to include jails, penitentiaries, etc.

PRISON BONDS. See "Gaol Liberties."

PRISON BREACH. The act of one who is lawfully detained on a criminal charge, or under sentence for a crime, in breaking out of the place in which he is detained, against the will of the person by whom he is detained.

It is something more than an escape,—adding thereto a breaking out of custody. The breaking must be actual, but need not be intentional. Thus, if loose bricks on top of a prison wall are thrown by a convict in climbing over the same, it is a breach. Rus. & R. 458. The opening of a window or unlocking of a door in the course of an escape constitutes a breach. 53 N. J. Law, 488.

PRISONER. One held in confinement against his will.

PRISONER OF WAR. One who has been captured while fighting under the banner of some state. He is a prisoner, although never confined in a prison. Not only such persons as a belligerent can lawfully kill, but all who may be separated from the mass of noncombatants by their importance to the enemy's state, or by their usefulness to him in his war, may be made prisoners of war. Glenn, Int. Law, 187.

Any person captured and held by the military power while carrying on war, and held as an enemy prisoner, whether rightly or wrongfully so held. 1 Bish. Crim. Law, § 65, note.

PRIST (Law Fr. ready). A formal word used in the days of oral pleading, to express a tender of or joinder in issue.

PRIUS VITIIS LABORAVIMUS, NUNC legibus. We labored first with vices, now with laws. 4 Inst. 76.

PRIVATE. Affecting or belonging to individuals, as distinct from the public generally; not clothed with office.

PRIVATE ACT. An act operating only upon particular persons and private concerns, and rather an exception than a rule. Opposed to "public act." 1 Bl. Comm. 86; 1 Term R. 125; Plowd. 28; Dyer, 75, 119; 4 Coke, 76. Private acts ought not to be noticed by courts unless pleaded.

PRIVATE BANKERS. Such as engage in the business of banking, without having any special grant of authority from the state. 80 N. Y. 225.

PRIVATE BILL OFFICE. An office of the English parliament where the business of obtaining private acts of parliament is conducted.

PRIVATE CARRIER. A carrier who is not a common carrier, because he does not hold himself out as ready to carry all persons who may employ him.

PRIVATE CORPORATION. A corporation founded by a private individual, or the stock of which is owned by private persons, such as a hospital or college, a bank, an insurance, turnpike, or railroad company. 2 Kent, Comm. 275.

PRIVATE EASEMENT. One the enjoyment of which is restricted to certain individuals.

PRIVATE HOUSE. A dwelling place, not open for the accommodation of all applicants who come lawfully and pay regularly. A boarding house for the accommodation of such only as are accepted by the proprietor is a private house. 3 Brewst. (Pa.) 344.

PRIVATE INTERNATIONAL LAW. Is a convenient expression for such rules as, in the jurisprudence of most civilized nations, are applied, *ex comitate,* to the solution of questions depending upon foreign status, foreign laws, or foreign contracts. But no law, binding *proprio vigore* upon any independent state, can be established by generalization from the jurisprudence of other nations. 10 App. Cas. 513. See "Conflict of Laws;" "International Law."

PRIVATE NUISANCE. See "Nuisance."

PRIVATE PERSON. One not an officer.

PRIVATE PROPERTY. Within the constitutional requirement of compensation for "private property taken for public use," it includes, of course, all property owned by individuals, and also certain property held by public bodies, such as municipal corporations, which is held not for the performance of the public duties devolving upon it, but for purposes not deemed strictly public and political.

PRIVATE RIGHTS. Those rights which relate to the person, or to personal or real property of particular individuals. 1 Chit. Gen. Prac. 3.

PRIVATE STATUTE. A statute which operates only upon particular persons and private concerns. 1 Bl. Comm. 86. See "General Statute."

PRIVATE WAY. An easement of one person, or of any number of persons less than the public at large, to pass over the servient land of another in the manner, at the times, on the location, and for the purpose allotted or agreed for the particular way. Bish. Non-Cont. Law, § 866.

Private ways are either (1) appurtenant, *i. e.*, pertaining to some particular land, or (2) in gross, *i. e.*, personal to some particular individual or individuals. 3 Bl. Comm. 241.

PRIVATE WRONGS. A private wrong, otherwise termed a "tort" or "civil injury," is an infringement or privation of the civil rights which belong to individuals, considered merely as individuals. 4 Bl. Comm. 5. See "Public Wrongs."

PRIVATEER. A vessel owned by one or more private individuals, armed and equipped at his or their expense, for the purpose of carrying on a maritime war, by the authority of one of the belligerent parties. The commissions issued to such vessels are generally called "letters of marque."

The treaty of Paris (*q. v.*) provides for the discontinuance of the use of privateers except as against such powers (of which the United States is one) as did not accede to such treaty, and the general policy of the United States is against their use. See 1 Kent, Comm. 97.

PRIVATIO PRAESUPPONIT HABITUR. A deprivation presupposes a possession. 2 Rolle, 419.

PRIVATIS PRACTIONIBUS NON DUBIum est non laedi jus caeterorum. There is no doubt that the rights of others cannot be prejudiced by private agreements. Dig. 2. 15. 3. pr.; Broom, Leg. Max. (3d London Ed.) 623.

PRIVATORUM CONVENTIO JURI PUBlico non derogat. Private agreements cannot derogate from public law. Dig. 50. 17. 45. 1.

PRIVATUM COMMODUM PUBLICO CEdit. Private yields to public good. Jenk. Cent. Cas. 273.

PRIVATUM INCOMMODUM PUBLICO bono pensatur. Private inconvenience is made up for by public good.

PRIVEMENT ENCEINTE (Law Fr.) A term used to signify that a woman is pregnant, but not quick with child. Wood, Inst. 662.

PRIVIES. By privies are meant heirs, executors, administrators, terre-tenants, or those having an interest in remainder or reversion, or one who is made a party by the law. 7 Ency. of Pl. & Pr. 857; 232 Ill. 168; 173 Ill. 117.

In judgments or decrees which do not determine status, but relate to rights or interests of parties in and to certain property, "privies" are those who succeed to the ownership of the property or some right or interest therein, under one of the parties to the litigation, directly or by mesne conveyance, by gift, by kinship, or by operation of law. Privity in such cases has reference to persons in their relation to property. 153 Wis. 69. See "Privy."

PRIVIGNUS (Lat.) In civil law. Son of a husband or wife by a former marriage; a stepson. Calv. Lex.; Vicat.

PRIVILEGE. An exemption or immunity peculiar to a particular person or body. Commonly applied to the various special rights and immunities of legislators, and to the privilege of witnesses from testifying to certain facts as self-incriminating ones. See "Privileged Communications."

——**In Civil Law.** A right which the nature of a debt gives to a creditor, and which entitles him to be preferred before other creditors. Code La. art. 3153; Dalloz, "Privilege;" Domat, Lois Civ. liv. 2, tit. 1, § 4, note 1.

——**In Maritime Law.** An allowance to the master of a ship of the general nature with primage, being compensation, or rather a gratuity, customary in certain trades, and which the law assumes to be a fair and equitable allowance, because the contract on both sides is made under the knowledge of such usage by the parties.

PRIVILEGE, WRIT OF. A process to enforce or maintain a privilege. Cowell.

PRIVILEGED COMMUNICATIONS.

——**In the Law of Slander.** A communication made *bona fide* upon any subject matter in which the party communicating has an interest, or in reference to which he has a duty, if made to a person having a corresponding interest or duty, although it contain criminatory matter which, without this privilege, would be slanderous and actionable.

——**In Evidence.** Communication which the law refuses, on grounds of public policy, to allow to be disclosed in evidence. The policy prohibiting such disclosure may be (1) political, as that restraining the disclosure of secrets of state, (2) judicial, as that which prohibits the disclosure of proceedings in the jury room, (3) professional, as that which forbids the disclosure of statements by client to attorney, or (4) social, as that which restricts the disclosure of communications between husband and wife. Best, Ev. § 578.

PRIVILEGED COPYHOLDS. Those copyholds which are held according to the customs of the manor, and not according to the will of the lord. They include ancient demesne and customary freehold. 2 Woddeson, Lect. 33-49; Lee, Real Prop. 63; 1 Crabb, Real Prop. 709, 919; 2 Bl. Comm. 100.

PRIVILEGED DEED. In Scotch law. An instrument, for example, a testament, in the execution of which certain statutory formalities usually required are dispensed with, either from necessity or expediency. Ersk. Inst. 3. 2. 22; Bell, Dict.

PRIVILEGED VILLENAGE. In old English law. A species of villenage in which the tenants held by certain and determinate services; otherwise called "villein socage." Bracton, fol. 209. Now called "privilege copyhold," including the tenure in ancient demesne. 2 Bl. Comm. 99, 100.

PRIVILEGES. See "Gambling Contract."

PRIVILEGES AND IMMUNITIES. The "privileges and immunities" which are protected by the constitutional inhibition concern the personal and private rights of the citizen, such as his right to acquire and possess property, to pursue ordinary callings and secure happiness and safety, etc., and do not include within their meaning the right to hold office. The State may decline to confer official power on residents of other states without depriving such nonresidents of any privilege or immunity protected by the constitution of the general government, or of liberty or property within the meaning of those words as used in our state Constitution. 217 Ill. 248; 175 Ill. 611.

PRIVILEGIA QUAE RE VERA SUNT IN praejudicium reipublicae, magis tamen habent speciosa frontispicia, et boni publici praetextum, quam bonae et legales concessiones; sed praetextu liciti non debet admitti illictum. Privileges which are truly in prejudice of public good have, however, a more specious front and pretext of public good than good and legal grants; but, under pretext of legality, that which is illegal ought not to be admitted. 11 Coke, 88.

PRIVILEGIUM (*priva lex, i. e., de uno homine*). In civil law. A private law inflicting a punishment or conferring a reward. Calv. Lex.; Cicero, de Lege, 3, 19, pro Domo, 17; Vicat. Every peculiar right by which one creditor or class of creditors is preferred to another in personal actions. Vicat. Every privilege granted by law in derogation of common right. Mackeld. Civ. Law, §§ 188, 189. A claim or lien on a thing, which, once attaching, continued till waiver or satisfaction, and which existed apart from possession. So at the present day in maritime law, *e. g.*, the lien of seamen on ship for wages. 2 Pars. Mar. Law, 561-563.

PRIVILEGIUM CLERICALE (Lat.) Benefit of clergy.

PRIVILEGIUM EST BENEFICIUM PERsonale et extinguitur cum persona. A privilege is a personal benefit, and dies with the person. 3 Bulst. 8.

PRIVILEGIUM EST QUASI PRIVATA lex. A privilege is, as it were, a private law. 2 Bulst. 189.

PRIVILEGIUM NON VALET CONTRA rempublicam. A privilege avails not against the commonwealth. Bac. Max. 25; Broom, Leg. Max. (3d London Ed.) 17; Noy, Max. (9th Ed.) 34.

PRIVITY (Law. Fr. *privitie*). Connection; interest; mutuality of interest; such as subsists between the immediate parties to a contract, as between lessor and lessee; otherwise called "personal privity," or "privity of contract." 3 Coke, 23a; Litt. §§ 460, 461. But this does not seem to be privity in its proper sense, for privies are they who are not parties. See "Privy."

A derivative kind of interest, founded upon or growing out of the contract of another, as that which subsists between an heir and his ancestor, between an executor and testator, and between a lessor or lessee and his assignee. 3 Coke, 23a.

The mutual or successive relationship to the same rights of property. 1 Greenl. Ev. § 189; 6 How. (U. S.) 60; 246 Ill. 573; 127 Ill. 571; 161 Mich. 503. See "Privy."

PRIVY. One who is a partaker or has any part or interest in any action, matter, or thing. Co. Litt. 271a.

One who has an interest in an estate created by another, or in a contract or conveyance to which he is not a party.

A mutual or successive relationship of persons. 263 Ill. 203; 246 Ill. 573.

Privy may be:

(1) Of contract, being the relation which exists between the immediate parties to a contract.

(2) In estate, as between lessor and lessee.

(3) In blood, as between an heir and his ancestor.

(4) In representation, as between a testator and his executors.

(5) In tenure, as between a lord and his feudal tenants.

(6) In person, as between husband and wife or trustee and beneficiary.

(7) In possession, as between joint tenants or tenants in common.

(8) In law, as where the law casts land upon another without privity of blood or estate, as by escheat.

A more general division has been made into privies in estate, privies in blood, and privies in law. 1 Greenl. Ev. § 189.

PRIVY COUNCIL. The chief council of the sovereign, called, by pre-eminence, "The Council," composed of those whom the king appoints. 1 Bl. Comm. 229-232.

By St. Charles II., in 1679, the number was limited to thirty,—fifteen the chief officers of the state *ex virtute officii*, the other fifteen at the king's pleasure; but the number is now indefinite. A committee of the privy council is a court of ultimate appeal in admiralty causes and causes of lunacy and idiocy (3 P. Wms. 108), and from all dominions of the crown except Great Britain and Ireland (1 Wooddeson, Lect. 157b; 2 Steph. Comm. 479; 3 Steph. Comm. 425, 432).

PRIVY SEAL. In English law. A seal which the king uses to such grants or things as pass the great seal. 2 Inst. 554.

PRIVY SIGNET. The seal which is first used in making grants, etc., of the crown. It is always in custody of the secretary of state. 2 Bl. Comm. 347; 1 Wooddeson, Lect. 250; 1 Steph. Comm. 571.

PRIVY VERDICT. In practice. A verdict given privily to the judge out of court, but which was of no force unless afterwards affirmed by a public verdict given openly in court. 3 Bl. Comm. 377. Now disused.

PRIZE.

——**In Maritime Law.** The apprehension and detention at sea of a ship or other vessel, by authority of a belligerent power, either with the design of appropriating it, with the goods and effects it contains, or with that of becoming master of the whole or a part of its cargo. 1 C. Rob. Adm. 228.

The vessel or goods thus taken.

Goods taken on land from a public enemy are called "booty;" and the distinction between a prize and booty consists in this, that the former is taken at sea, and the latter on land.

——**In Contracts.** A reward which is offered to one of several persons who shall accomplish a certain condition, 81 N. Y. 539; as if an editor should offer a silver cup to the individual who shall write the best essay in favor of peace. In this case there is a contract subsisting between the editor and each person who may write such essay that he will pay the prize to the writer of the best essay. Wolff. Dr. Nat. § 675.

A thing which is won by putting into a lottery.

PRIZE COURT. In English law. That branch of admiralty which adjudicates upon cases of maritime captures made in time of war. A special commission issues in England, in time of war, to the judge of the admiralty court, to enable him to hold such court. See "Admiralty."

Some question has been raised whether the prize court is or is not a separate court from the admiralty court. Inasmuch as the commission is always issued to the judge of that court, and the forms of proceeding are substantially those of admiralty, while the law applicable is derived from the same sources, the fact that the commission of prize is only issued occasionally would hardly seem to render the distinction a valid one.

In the United States, the admiralty courts discharge the duties both of a prize and an instance court.

PRIZEFIGHT. A personal combat between men, without weapons, in public and by agreement, for a prize or reward. 67 Miss. 352.

PRO. In Latin phrases. A preposition meaning "for."

PRO BONO ET MALO. For good and for evil.

PRO CONFESSO (Lat. as confessed). In equity practice. A decree taken where the defendant has either never appeared in the suit, or, after having appeared, has neglected to answer. 1 Daniell, Ch. Prac. 479; Adams, Eq. 327, 374; 1 Smith, Ch. Prac. 254.

PRO CORPORA COMITATUS. Latin words meaning "for the body of the county." Watt v. People, 126 Ill. 33.

PRO DEFECTU EMPTORUM. For want (failure) of purchasers.

PRO DEFECTU EXITUS. For, or in case of, default of issue. 2 Salk. 620.

PRO DEFECTU HAEREDIS. For want of an heir.

PRO DEFECTU JUSTITIAE. For defect or want of justice. Fleta, lib. 2, c. 62, § 2.

PRO DEFENDENTE (Law Lat.) For the defendant. Vaughan, 65. Commonly abbreviated, *pro. def.* Hardr. passim. "Morton, *pro querent*. Blackstone, *pro def.*" 1 W. Bl. 532.

PRO DERELICTO (Lat.) As derelict or abandoned. A species of usucaption in the civil law. The title of Dig. 41. 7. *Quod pro derelicto habitum est,* what is held as derelict. Id. 41. 7. 4.

PRO DIGNITATE REGALI. In consideration of the royal dignity. 1 Bl. Comm. 223.

PRO DIVISO. As divided, *i. e.*, in severalty.

PRO DONATO. As a gift; as in case of gift; by title of gift. A species of usucaption in the civil law. Dig. 41. 6. See Id. 5. 3. 13. 1.

PRO DOTE. As a dowry; by title of dowry. A species of usucaption. Dig. 41. 9. See Id. 5. 3. 13. 1.

PRO EMPTORE. As a purchaser; by the title of a purchaser. A species of usucaption. Dig. 41. 4. See Id. 5. 3. 13. 1.

PRO EO QUOD (Lat.) In pleading. For this that. This is a phrase of affirmation, and is sufficiently direct and positive for introducing a material averment. 1 Saund. 117, note 4; 2 Chit. Pl. 369-393; Gould, Pl. c. 3, § 34.

PRO FACTI. As a fact.

PRO FALSO CLAMORE SUO. A nominal amercement of a plaintiff for "his false claim," which used to be inserted in a judgment for the defendant. Obsolete.

PRO FORMA. As a matter of form. 3 East, 232; 2 Kent, Comm. 245.

PRO HAC VICE. For this turn; for this one particular occasion.

PRO ILLA VICE. For that turn. 3 Wils. 233, arg.

PRO INDEFENSO. As undefended; as making no defense. A phrase in old practice. Fleta, lib. 1, c. 41, § 7.

PRO INDIVISO (Lat.) For an undivided part. The possession or occupation of lands or tenements belonging to two or more persons, and where, consequently, neither knows his several portion till divided. Bracton, lib. 5.

PRO INTERESSE SUO (Lat.) According to his interest.

PRO LAESIONE FIDEI. For breach of faith. 3 Bl. Comm. 52.

PRO LEGATO. As a legacy; by the title of a legacy. A species of usucaption. Dig. 41. 8.

PRO LUCRARI (Law Lat.) For to gain. Fleta, lib. 6, c. 7, § 12.

PRO MAJORI CAUTELA. For greater caution.

PRO NON SCRIPTO (Lat.) As not written; as though it had not been written; as never written. Ambl. 139. *Pro non scriptis*, as void. 7 Wils. & S. 523.

PRO OPERE ET LABORE (Law Lat.) For work and labor.

PRO PARTIBUS LIBERANDIS. An ancient writ for partition of lands between coheirs. Reg. Orig. 316.

PRO POSSE SUO. To the extent of his power or ability. Bracton, fol. 109.

PRO POSSESSORE. As a possessor; by title of a possessor. Dig. 41. 5. See Id. 5. 3. 13.

PRO POSSESSORE HABETUR QUI dolo injuriave desiit possidere. He is esteemed a possessor whose possession has been disturbed by fraud or injury. Off. Exec. 166.

PRO QUERENTE (Lat.) For the plaintiff; usually abbreviated *pro quer.*, or *p. q.*

PRO RATA (Lat.) According to the rate, proportion, or allowance. A creditor of an insolvent estate is to be paid *pro rata* with creditors of the same class.

PRO RE NATA (Lat.) For the occasion as it may arise.

PRO SALUTE ANIMAE. For the good of his soul. All prosecutions in the ecclesiastical courts are *pro salute animae;* hence it will not be a temporal damage founding an action for slander that the words spoken put any one in danger of such a suit. 3 Steph. Comm. (7th Ed.) 309n, 437; 4 Steph. Comm. 207.

PRO SE. For himself; in his own behalf; in person.

PRO SOCIO. For a partner; the name of an action in behalf of a partner. A title of the civil law. Dig. 17. 2; Code, 4. 37.

PRO SOLIDO. For the whole; as one; jointly; without division. Dig. 50. 17. 141. 1.

PRO TANTO (Lat.) For so much. See 17 Serg. & R. (Pa.) 400.

PRO TEMPORE. For the time being; temporarily; provisionally.

PROBABILITY. Likelihood; consonance to reason; for sample, there is a strong probability that a man of good moral character, and who has heretofore been remarkable for truth, will, when examined as a witness under oath, tell the truth; and, on the contrary, that a man who has been guilty of perjury will not under the same circumstances, tell the truth. The former will therefore be entitled to credit, while the latter will not.

It is not as strong an expression as "proof." "Demonstration produces certain knowledge; proof produces belief and probability opinion." 19 S. C. 39.

PROBABLE. Having the appearance of truth; appearing to be founded in reason. That which is probable is that which has more evidence for than against it; which inclines the mind to believe a fact although it leaves some room for doubt. Probability is that quality or state which presents an appearance of truth. 269 Ill. 319.

PROBABLE CAUSE. Such a state of facts as to make it a reasonable presumption that their supposed existence was the cause of action.

The principal technical use of the phrase is to define the degree of certainty which will justify one in instituting a criminal prosecution, and relieve from liability for malicious prosecution should the charge prove unfounded.

As so used, "probable cause" is such a state of facts known to and influencing the prosecutor as would lead a man of ordinary caution and prudence, acting conscientiously, impartially, reasonably, and without prejudice, to believe, or entertain an honest and strong suspicion, that the person accused is guilty. Hilliard, Torts, c. 12, § 18; 81 Ala. 220; 62 N. Y. 19.

Belief in the guilt of the person accused must exist (67 Wis. 350), but is not in itself sufficient (56 Mich. 367), if ordinary care, diligence, and impartiality were not exercised (60 Miss. 916).

PROBABLE EVIDENCE. Presumptive evidence is so called, from its foundation in probability. Butler, Anal. Introd.

PROBABLE REASONING (Lat. *argumentum verisimile*). In the law of evidence. Reasoning founded on the probability of the fact or proposition sought to be proved or shown; reasoning in which the mind exercises a discretion in deducing a conclusion from premises. Burr. Circ. Ev. 22, 23.

PROBANDI NECESSITAS INCUMBIT illi qui agit. The necessity of proving lies with him who sues. Inst. 2. 20. 4.

PROBATE COURTS. See "Court of Probate."

PROBATE OF A WILL. The proof before an officer or court authorized by law that an instrument offered to be proved or recorded is the last will and testament of the deceased person whose testamentary act it is alleged to be.

In some jurisdictions, the term is loosely used to denote the proof of claim against estates, etc.

PROBATIO (Lat.) Proof; more particularly direct, as distinguished from indirect, or circumstantial, evidence.

PROBATIO MORTUA. Dead proof; that is, proof by inanimate objects, such as deeds or other written evidence.

PROBATIO PLENA. In the civil law. Full proof; proof by two witnesses, or a public instrument. Halifax, Civ. Law, bk. 3, c. 9, No. 25; 3 Bl. Comm. 370.

PROBATIO SEMI-PLENA. In the civil law. Half-full proof; half-proof. Proof by one witness, or a private instrument. Halifax, Civ. Law, bk. 3, c. 9, No. 25; 3 Bl. Comm. 370.

PROBATIO VIVA. Living proof; that is, proof by the mouth of living witnesses.

PROBATION. The evidence which proves a thing. It is either by record, writing, the party's own oath, or the testimony of witnesses. Proof. It also signifies the time of a novitiate; a trial. Nov. 5.

PROBATIONES DEBENT ESSE EVIdentes, id est, perspicuae et faciles intelligi. Proofs ought to be made evident, that is, clear and easy to be understood. Co. Litt. 283.

PROBATIS EXTREMIS, PRAESUMITUR media. The extremes being proved, the intermediate proceedings are presumed. 1 Greenl. Ev. § 20.

PROBATIVE. In the law of the evidence. Having the effect of proof.

PROBATIVE FACT. In the law of evidence. A fact which actually has the effect of proving a fact sought; an evidentiary fact. 1 Benth. Jud. Ev. 18.

PROBATOR. In old English law. Strictly, an accomplice in felony who, to save himself, confessed the fact, and charged or accused any other as principal or accessary, against whom he was bound to make good his charge. It also signified an approver, or one who undertakes to prove a crime charged upon another. Jacob.

PROBATORY TERM. In the British courts of admiralty, after the issue is formed between the parties, a time for taking the testimony is assigned. This is called a "probatory term."

This term is common to both parties, and either party may examine his witnesses. When good cause is shown, the term will be enlarged. 2 Brown, Civ. Law, 418; Dunl., Adm. Prac. 217.

PROBI ET LEGALES HOMINES (Lat.) Good and lawful men; persons competent, in point of law, to serve on juries. Cro. Eliz. 654, 751; Cro. Jac. 635; Mart. & Y. (Tenn.) 147; Hardin (Ky.) 63; Bac. Abr. "Juries" (A).

PROBITY. Justice; honesty. A man of probity is one who loves justice and honesty, and who dislikes the contrary. Wolff. Dr. Nat. § 772.

PROCEDENDO (Lat.) In practice. A writ which issues where an action is removed from an inferior to a superior jurisdiction by *habeas corpus, certiorari,* or writ of privilege, and it does not appear to such superior court that the suggestion upon which the cause has been removed is sufficiently proved; in which case, the superior court by this writ remits the cause to the court from whence it came, commanding the inferior court to proceed to the final hearing and determination of the same. See 1 Chit. 575; 2 W. Bl. 1060; 1 Strange, 527; 6 Term R. 365; 4 Barn. & Ald. 535; 16 East, 387.

It also issues where an inferior court unwarrantably delays in giving judgment. 3 Bl. Comm. 109; 4 Minor, Inst. 276, 301.

PROCEDENDO ON AID PRAYER. If one pray in aid of the crown in real action, and aid be granted, it shall be awarded that he sue to the sovereign in chancery, and the justices in the common pleas shall stay until this writ of *procedendo de loquela* come to them. So, also, on a personal action. New Nat. Brev. 154.

PROCEDURE. The rule of pleading and practice by which rights are enforced. It is generally considered as not including the law of evidence.

PROCEEDING. In its general acceptation, this word means the form in which actions are to be brought and defended, the manner of intervening in suits, of conducting them, the mode of deciding them, of opposing judgments, and of executing.

In a narrower sense, any act, in the course of an action, done to achieve a given end.

A prescribed mode of action to carry into effect a right. 1 Duer (N. Y.) 620.

Ordinary proceedings intend the regular and usual mode of carrying on a suit by due course at common law.

Summary proceedings are those where the matter in dispute is decided without the intervention of a jury. These must be authorized by the legislature, except, perhaps, in cases of contempt, for such proceedings are unknown to the common law.

In Louisiana there is a third kind of proceeding, known by the name of "executory proceeding," which is resorted to in the following cases: When the creditor's right arises from an act importing a confession of judgment, and which contains a privilege or mortgage in his favor; or when the creditor demands the execution of a judgment which has been rendered by a tribunal different from that within whose jurisdiction the execution is sought. Code La. art. 732.

In New York, and some other states, the code of practice divides remedies into actions and special proceedings. An action is a regular judicial proceeding, in which one party prosecutes another party for the enforcement or protection of a right, the redress or prevention of a wrong, or the punishment of a public offense. Every other remedy is a special proceeding. Code N. Y. § 2.

PROCEEDS. Money or articles of value arising or obtained from the sale of property. Goods purchased with money arising from the sale of other goods, or obtained on their credit, are proceeds of such goods. 2 Pars. Mar. Law, 201, 202. The sum, amount, or value of goods sold, or converted into money. Wharton.

It is a term of equivocal import, depending on the context. 89 Pa. St. 46.

PROCERES (Lat.) The name by which the chief magistrates in cities were formerly known. St. Armand, Hist. Eq. 88.

PROCES VERBAL. In French law. A true relation in writing, in due form of law, of what has been done and said verbally in the presence of a public officer, and what he himself does upon the occasion. It is a species of inquisition of office.

The *proces verbal* should be dated, contain the name, qualities, and residence of the public functionary who makes it, the cause of complaint, the existence of the crime, that which serves to substantiate the charge, point out its nature, the time, the place, the circumstances, state the proofs and presumptions, describe the place,—in a word, everything calculated to ascertain the truth. It must be signed by the officer. Dalloz.

PROCESS.

——**In Practice.** The means of compelling a defendant to appear in court, after suing out the original writ, in civil, and, after indictment, in criminal, cases. In a broader sense all writs and mandates issued in the course of the proceeding. 15 Fla. 410.

The method taken by law to compel a compliance with the original writ or commands of the court.

In a strict sense, "process" is confined to the mandate of a court under its seal, whereby a party or an officer of the court is commanded to do certain acts. Thus, the summons used in many states, signed by plaintiff's attorney only, is not process. 12 Minn. 80; 17 Ore. 564.

In civil causes, in all real actions and for injuries not committed against the peace, the first step was a summons, which was served in personal actions by two persons called summoners, in real actions by erecting a white stick or wand on the defendant's grounds. If this summons was disregarded, the next step was an attachment of the goods of the defendant, and in case of trespasses the attachment issued at once without a summons. If the attachment failed, a distringas issued, which was continued till he appeared. Here process ended in injuries not committed with force. In case of such injuries, an arrest of the person was provided for. See "Arrest." In modern practice some of these steps are omitted; but the practice of the different states is too various to admit tracing here the differences which have resulted from retaining different steps of the process.

In the English law, process in civil causes is called "original" process, when it is founded upon the original writ; and also to distinguish it from mesne or intermediate process, which issues pending the suit, upon some collateral interlocutory matter, as, to summon juries, witnesses, and the like. "Mesne" process is also sometimes put in contradistinction to "final" process, or process of execution; and then it signifies all process which intervenes between the beginning and end of a suit. 3 Bl. Comm. 279. And this is the modern usage. 31 N. J. Law, 231.

——**In Patent Law.** The art or method by which any particular result is produced.

A process, *eo nomine,* is not made the subject of a patent in our act of congress. It is included under the general term "useful art." Where a result or effect is produced by chemical action, by the operation or application of some element or power of nature, or of one substance to another, such modes, methods, or operations are called "processes." A new process is usually the result of discovery; a machine, of invention. The arts of tanning, dyeing, making waterproof cloth, vulcanizing india rubber, smelting ores, and numerous others, are usually carried on by "processes," as distinguished from "machines." But the term "process" is often employed more vaguely in a secondary sense, in which it cannot be the subject of a patent. Thus, we say that a board is undergoing the process of being planed, grain of being ground, iron of being hammered or rolled. Here the term is used subjectively or passively, as applied to the material operated on, and not to the method or mode of producing that operation, which is by mechanical means, or the use of a machine, as distinguished from a process. In this use of the term it represents the function of a machine, or the effect produced by it on the material subjected to the action of the machine, and does not constitute a patentable subject matter, because there cannot be a valid patent for the function or abstract effect of a machine, but only for the machine which produces it. 15 How. (U. S.) 267, 268. See 2 Barn. & Ald. 349.

PROCESS OF GARNISHMENT. See "Garnishment."

PROCESS OF LAW. See "Due Process of Law."

PROCESS ROLL. In practice. A roll used for the entry of process to save the statute of limitations. 1 Tidd, Prac. 161, 162.

PROCESSIONING. A term used to denote the manner of ascertaining the boundaries of land. It consists in a survey of the lands in the presence of all persons interested who shall have been previously given notice. Comp. St. Tenn. 548. The term is also used in North Carolina (3 Murph. 504; 3 Dev. 268), and Georgia (69 Ga. 53).

It is similar to the English "perambulation" (*q. v.*)

PROCESSUM CONTINUANDO. In English practice. A writ for the continuance of process after the death of the chief justice or other justices in the commission of oyer and terminer. Reg. Orig. 128.

PROCESSUS LEGIS EST GRAVIS VEXAtio, executio legis coronat opus. The process of the law is a grievous vexation; the execution of the law crowns the work. Co. Litt. 289.

PROCHEIN (Law Fr.) Next. A term somewhat used in modern law, and more frequently in the old law; as, *prochein ami prochein cousin.* Co. Litt. 10.

PROCHEIN AMI (Law Fr.; spelled, also, *prochein amy* and *prochain amy*). Next friend. He who, without being appointed guardian, sues in the name of an infant for the recovery of the rights of the latter, or does such other acts as are authorized by law; as, in Pennsylvania, to bind the infant apprentice. 3 Serg. & R. (Pa.) 172; 1 Ashm. (Pa.) 27. For some of the rules with respect to the liability or protection of a *prochein ami,* see 3 Madd. 468; 4 Madd. 461; 2 Strange, 709; 1 Dick. 346; 1 Atk. 570; Mosely, 47, 85; 1 Ves. Jr. 409; 7 Ves. 425; 10 Ves. 184; Edwards, Parties, 182-204.

PROCHEIN AVOIDANCE. Next vacancy. Used in respect to appointments to ecclesiastical vacancies.

PROCINCTUS (Lat. from *procingi* [properly, *praecingi*], to be girt about). In the Roman law. A girding or preparing for battle. *Testamentum in procinctu,* or *testamentum procinctum,* a will made by a soldier, while girding himself, or preparing to engage in battle. A. Gell. Noct. Att. lib. xv. c. 27, note 4; Adams, Rom. Ant. 62; Calv. Lex. This mode of making a will had become obsolete in the time of Justinian. Inst. 2. 10. 1.

PROCLAMARE (Lat.)

——**In the Civil Law.** To cry out, or proclaim; to give warning. Inst. 4. 3. 5.

To assert a claim. Calv. Lex.

——**In Old European Law.** To appeal (to a higher court). Flod. lib. 3, c. 23; Capit. lib. 6, c. 299; Spelman.

PROCLAMATION. The act of causing some state matters to be published or made generally known. A written or printed document in which are contained such matters, issued by proper authority; as, the president's proclamation, the governor's proclamation, the mayor's proclamation. The word "proclamation" is also used to express the public nomination made of any one to a high office; as, such a prince was proclaimed emperor.

The giving of publicity is essential to the idea of a proclamation, no paper being such until it is in some manner published. 101 U. S. 770.

——**In Practice.** The declaration made by the crier, by authority of the court, that something is about to be done.

It usually commences with the French word *oyez* (hear ye), in order to attract attention. It is particularly used on the meeting or opening of the court, and at its adjournment. It is also frequently employed to discharge persons who have been accused of crimes or misdemeanors.

PROCLAMATION OF EXIGENTS. In old English practice. On awarding an exigent, in order to outlawry, a writ of proclamation issued to the sheriff of the county where the party dwelt, to make three proclamations for the defendant to yield himself or be outlawed.

PROCLAMATION OF REBELLION. In old English practice. When a party neglected to appear upon a subpoena, or an attachment in the chancery, a writ bearing this name issued, and, if he did not surrender himself by the day assigned, he was reputed and declared a rebel.

PROCLAMATION OF RECUSANTS. A proceeding whereby such persons were formerly convicted, on nonappearance at the assizes. Jacob.

PROCREATION. The generation of children. It is an act authorized by the law of nature. One of the principal ends of marriage is the procreation of children. Inst. tit. 2. pr.

PROCTOR. One appointed to represent in judgment the party who empowers him, by writing under his hand, called a "proxy." The term is used chiefly in the courts of civil, ecclesiastical, and admiralty law. The proctor is somewhat similar to the attorney. Ayliffe, Par. 421.

PROCURACY. The writing or instrument which authorizes a procurator to act. Cowell; Termes de la Ley.

PROCURARE (Lat. from *pro*, for, and *curare*, to take care of). To take care of another's affairs for him, or in his behalf; to see to the affairs of another; to govern; to manage; to take care of, or superintend. Dig. 17. 1. 34.

PROCURATIO (Lat. from *procurare*, to manage). Management of another's affairs by his direction, and in his behalf; procuration; administration; agency. See "Procuration."

A taking care of another. Spelman.

PROCURATION. In civil law. The act by which one person gives power to another to act in his place, as he could do himself. A letter of attorney.

An express procuration is one made by the express consent of the parties. An implied or tacit procuration takes place when an individual sees another managing his affairs and does not interfere to prevent it. Dig. 17. 1. 6. 2; Id. 50. 17. 60; Code, 7. 32. 2.

Procurations are also divided into those which contain absolute power, or a general authority, and those which give only a limited power. Dig. 3. 3. 58; Id. 17. 1. 60. 4. Procurations are ended in three ways: First, by the revocation of the authority; second, by the death of one of the parties; third, by the renunciation of the mandatory, when it is made in proper time and place, and it can be done without injury to the person who gave it. Inst. 3. 27; Dig. 17. 1; Code. 4. 35. See "Authority;" "Letter of Attorney;" "Mandate."

PROCURATION FEE (or **MONEY**). In English law. Brokerage or commission allowed to scriveners and solicitors, for obtaining loans of money. 4 Bl. Comm. 157.

PROCURATIONS. In ecclesiastical law. Certain sums of money which parish priests pay yearly to the bishops or archdeacons *ratione visitationis*. Dig. 3. 39. 25; Ayliffe, Par. 429; 17 Viner, Abr. 544.

PROCURATOR. In civil law. A proctor; a person who acts for another by virtue of a procuration. *Procurator est, qui aliena negotia mandata Domini administrat.* Dig. 3. 3. 1. See "Attorney;" "Authority."

PROCURATOR, FISCAL. In Scotch law. A public prosecutor. Bell, Dict.

PROCURATOR IN REM SUAM. In Scotch law. A term which imports that one is acting as attorney as to his own property. When an assignment of a thing is made, as a debt, and a procuration or power of attorney is given to the assignee to receive the same, he is in such case procurator *in rem suam*. 3 Stair, Inst. 1. 2. 3, etc.; 3 Ersk. Inst. 3. 5. 2; 1 Bell, Dict. bk. 5, c. 2, sec. 1, § 2.

PROCURATOR LITIS (Lat.) In civil law. One who, by command of another, institutes and carries on for him a suit. Vicat. Procurator is properly used of the attorney of *actor* (the plaintiff), *defensor* of the attorney of *reus* (the defendant). It is distinguished from *advocatus*, who was one who undertook the defense of persons, not things, and who was generally the patron of the person whose defense he prepared, the person himself speaking it. It is also distinguished from *cognitor*, who conducted the cause in the presence of his principal, and generally in cases of citizenship; whereas the procurator conducted the cause in the absence of his principal. Calv. Lex.

PROCURATOR NEGOTIORUM (Lat.) In the civil law. The manager of another's business or affairs; an agent; an attorney in fact. Calv. Lex.

PROCURATOR PROVINCIAE (Lat.) In the Roman law. A provincial officer who managed the affairs of the revenue, and had a judicial power in matters that concerned the revenue. Adams, Rom. Ant. 178.

PROCURATORIUM (Lat.) The proxy or instrument by which a proctor is constituted and appointed.

PROCURATORY OF RESIGNATION. In Scotch law. A form of proceeding by which a vassal authorizes the feu to be returned to his superior. Bell, Dict. It is analogous to the surrender of copyholds in England. Wharton.

PROCUREUR. In French law. An attorney; one who has received a commission from another to act on his behalf. There were in France two classes of *procureurs*: *Procureurs ad negotia*, appointed by an individual to act for him in the administration of his affairs; persons invested with a power of attorney; corresponding to "attorneys in fact." *Procureurs ad lites* were person appointed and authorized to act for a party in a court of justice. These corresponded to attorneys at law (now called, in England, "solicitors of the supreme court"). The order of *procureurs* was abolished in 1791, and that of *avoues* established in their place. Mozley & W.

PROCUREUR GENERAL. In French law. An officer of the French court, who either personally or by his deputy prosecutes every one who is accused of a crime, according to the forms of French law. His functions appear to be confined to preparing the case for trial at the assizes, assisting in that trial, demanding the sentence in case of a conviction, and being present at the delivery of the sentence. He has a general superintendence over the officers of police and of the *juges d'instruction*, and he requires from the *procureur du roi* a general report once in every three months. Brown.

PRODES HOMINES. The barons of the realm.

PRODIGUS. In civil law. A person who, though of full age, is incapable of managing his affairs, and of the obligations which attend them, in consequence of his bad conduct, and for whom a curator is therefore appointed.

PRODITION. Treason; treachery.

PRODITOR. A traitor.

PRODITORIE (Lat.) Treasonably. This is a technical word formerly used in indictments for treason, when they were written in Latin.

PRODUCENT. In ecclesiastical law. He who produces a witness to be examined.

PRODUCTIO SECTAE (Law Lat.) In old English law. Production of suit; the production, by a plaintiff, of his *secta* or suit, that is, a number of persons prepared to confirm what he had stated in his count (or *intentio*). This was done at the time of counting, or immediately after, and was expressed by the phrase at the end of the count or declaration: "*Et inde producit sectam,*" and thereupon, or thereof, he produces suit. Translated in the modern forms: "And therefore he brings suit." *Et inde statim producat sectam sufficientem, duos ad minus, vel tres, vel plures, si possit,* and thereupon he should immediately produce a sufficient suit, two at least, or three or more, if he can. Bracton, fol. 410. See Id. 159, 314b; Steph. Pl. 429, and note.

PRODUCTION OF SUIT (*productio sectae*). The concluding clause of all declarations is, "and thereupon he brings his suit." In old pleading this referred to the production by the plaintiff of his *secta* or suit, *i. e.,* persons prepared to confirm what he had stated in the declaration.

The phrase has remained; but the practice from which it arose is obsolete. 3 Bl. Comm. 295; Steph. Pl. 428.

PROFANE. That which has not been consecrated. By a profane place is understood one which is neither sacred, nor sanctified, nor religious. Dig. 11, 7. 2. 4.

PROFANELY. In a profane manner. In an indictment, under the act of assembly of Pennsylvania, against profanity, it is requisite that the words should be laid to have been spoken profanely. 11 Serg. & R. (Pa.) 394.

PROFANENESS, or **PROFANITY.** In criminal law. Imprecations in the name of the Deity.

It is a form of blasphemy. 8 Conn. 375.

PROFECTITUS (Lat.) In civil law. That which descends to us from our ascendants. Dig. 23. 3. 5.

PROFER (Law. Lat. *proferus, profrus,* from Law Fr. *proferer,* to produce). In old English law. An offer or proffer; an offer or endeavor to proceed in an action, by any man concerned to do so. Cowell. A judicial offer to do some act.

A return made by a sheriff of his accounts into the exchequer; a payment made on such return. Cowell.

PROFERT IN CURIA (Lat. he produces in court. Sometimes written *profert in curiam,* with the same meaning). In pleading. A declaration on the record that a party produces the deed under which he makes title in court. In ancient practice, the deed itself was actually produced; in modern times, the allegation only is made in the declaration, and the deed is then constructively in possession of the court. 3 Salk. 119; 6 Man. & G. 277; 11 Md. 322.

Profert is, in general, necessary when either party pleads a deed and claims rights under it, whether plaintiff (2 Dutch. [N. J.] 293) or defendant (17 Ark. 279). to enable the court to inspect and construe the instrument pleaded, and to entitle the adverse party to oyer thereof (10 Coke, 92b; 1 Chit. Pl. 414; 1 Archb. Prac. 164), and is not necessary when the party pleads it without making title under it (Gould, Pl. c. 7, p. 2, § 47). But a party who is actually or presumptively unable to produce a deed may plead it without profert, as in suit by a stranger (Comyn, Dig. "Pleader" [O 8]; Cro. Jac. 217; Cro. Car. 441; Carth. 316), or one claiming title by operation of law (Co. Litt. 225; Bac. Abr. "Pleas" [I 12]; 5 Coke, 75), or where the deed is in the possession of the adverse party, or is lost. In all these cases, the special facts must be shown, to excuse the want of profert. See Gould, Pl. c. 8, p. 2; Lawes, Pl. 96; 1 Saund. 9a, note. Profert and oyer are abolished in England by the common-law procedure act (15 & 16 Vict. c. 76), and a provision exists (14 & 15 Vict. c. 99) for allowing inspection of all documents in the possession or under the control of the party against whom the inspection is asked. See 25 Eng. Law & Eq. 304. In many of the states of the United States profert has been abolished, and in some instances the instrument must be set forth in the pleading of the party relying upon it. The operation of profert and oyer, where allowed, is to make the deed a part of the pleadings of the party producing it. 11 Md. 322; 3 Cranch (U. S.) 234. See 7 Cranch (U. S.) 176.

PROFESSION. A public declaration respecting something. Code, 10. 41. 6. A state, art, or mystery; as, the legal profession. Dig. 1. 18. 6. 4; Domat, Dr. Pub. lib. 1, tit. 9, § 1, note 7. See 41 Mich. 155.

——**In Ecclesiastical Law.** The act of entering into a religious order. See 17 Viner, Abr. 545.

PROFICUUM. (L. Lat.) In old English law. Profit.

PROFIT A PRENDRE. A right to take products or emblements from the lands of another.

"Under the term 'profit' is comprehended the produce of the soil, whether it arise above or below the surface, as herbage, wood, turf, coal, minerals, stones; also fish in a pond or stream." 9 S. E. 562.

Profits a prendre are distinguished from easements, in that they are rights of profit, while an easement is a right without profit. See "Easement."

PROFITS. An excess of the value of returns over the value of expenditures. The net amount made after deducting any proper expenses incident to the transaction. 2 Sneed (Tenn.) 452; 15 Minn. 519.

The expenses to be deducted are ordinarily the current expenses incident to the business; not such items as the depreciation of buildings in which the business is carried on. 94 U. S. 500.

This is a word of very extended signification. In commerce, it means the advance in the price of goods sold beyond the cost of purchase. In distinction from the wages of labor, it is well understood to imply the net return to the capital or stock employed, after deducting all the expenses, including not only the wages of those employed by the capitalist, but the wages of the capitalist himself for superintending the employment of his capital or stock. Smith, Wealth of Nations, bk. i. c. 6, and McCulloch's notes; Mill, Pol. Econ. c. 15. After indemnifying the capitalist for his outlay, there commonly remains a surplus, which is his profit, the net income from his capital. 1 Mill, Pol. Econ. c. 15. The word "profit" is generally used by writers on political economy to denote the difference between the value of advances and the value of returns made by their employment.

The profit of the farmer and the manufacturer is the gain made by the sale of produce or manufactures, after deducting the value of the labor, materials, rents, and all expenses, together with the interest of the capital employed,—whether land, buildings, machinery, instruments, or money. The rents and profits of an estate, the income or the net income of it, are all equivalent expressions. The income or the net income of an estate means only the profit it will yield after deducting the charges of management. 5 Me. 202, 203; 35 Me. 420, 421.

Under the term "profit" is comprehended the produce of the soil, whether it arise above or below the surface; as, herbage, wood, turf, coals, minerals, stones; also fish in a pond or running water. Profits are divided into *profits a prendre*, or those taken and enjoyed by the mere act of the proprietor himself, and *profits a vendre*, namely, such as are received at the hands of and rendered by another. Hammond, N. P. 172.

Profits are divided by writers on political economy into gross and net,—gross profits being the whole difference between the value of advances and the value of returns made by their employment, and net profits being so much of that difference as is attributable solely to the capital employed. What remains as the clear gains in any business venture after deducting the capital invested, the expense incurred and the loss sustained. 83 Mich. 63.

The remainder of the difference, or in other words, the gross profits minus the net profits, has no particular name; but it represents the profits attributable to industry, skill, and enterprise. See Malthus, Def. Pol. Econ.; McCulloch, Pol. Econ. (4th

Ed.) 563. But the word "profit" is generally used in a less extensive signification, and presupposes an excess of the value of returns over the value of advances.

PROGRESSION (Lat. *progressio;* from *pro* and *gredior*, to go forward). That state of a business which is neither the commencement nor the end. Some act done after the matter has commenced, and before it is completed. Plowd. 343.

PROHAEREDES. (L. Lat.) In old European law. Persons acting for heirs, or in place of heirs.

Remote heirs. Spelman.

PROHIBETUR NE QUIS FACIAT IN SUO quod nocere possit alieno. It is prohibited to do on one's own property that which may injure another's. 9 Coke, 59.

PROHIBITIO DE VASTO, DIRECTA PARti. A judicial writ which used to be addressed to a tenant, prohibiting him from waste pending suit. Reg. Jud. 21; Moore, 917.

PROHIBITION (Lat. *prohibition;* from *pro* and *habeo*, to hold back). In practice. The name of a writ issued by a superior court, directed to the judge and parties of a suit in an inferior court, commanding them to cease from the prosecution of the same, upon a suggestion that the cause originally, or some collateral matter arising therein, does not belong to that jurisdiction, but to the cognizance of some other court. 3 Bl. Comm. 112; Comyn, Dig.; Bac. Abr.; Saund. Index; Viner, Abr.; 2 Sellon, Prac. 308; Ayliffe, Par. 434; 2 H. Bl. 533.

The writ is based on absence of jurisdiction, and will issue only where the lower court has either no jurisdiction of the action (47 Cal. 584; 4 Minn. 366; 60 N. Y. 31), or where, having jurisdiction of a cause, it proceeds to some act beyond its power (20 N. Y. 531). But where the lower court has jurisdiction of all matters involved, mere error in its decision is no ground for prohibition. 100 Mo. 59; 13 Ind. 235.

"The writ of prohibition, as its name imports, is one which commands the person to whom it is directed not to do something which, by the suggestion of the relator, the court is informed he is about to do. If the thing be already done, it is manifest that the writ of prohibition cannot undo it, for that would require an affirmative act, and the only effect of a writ of prohibition is to prevent any further proceedings in the prohibited direction." 4 Wall. (U. S.) 159.

PROHIBITIVE IMPEDIMENTS. Those impediments to a marriage which are only followed by a punishment, but do not render the marriage null. Bowyer, Mod. Civ. Law, 44.

PROJECT (Fr.) In international law. The draft of a proposed treaty or convention.

PROJECTIO (Lat. from *projicere*, to cast up). In old English law. A throwing up of earth by the sea. Used by Sir Matthew Hale a synonym of *alluvio.*

PROLEM ANTE MATRIMONIUM NAtam, ita ut post legitimam, lex civilis succedere facit in haereditate parentum; sed prolem, quam matrimonium non parit, succedere non sinit lex Anglorum. The civil law permits the offspring born before marriage [provided such offspring be afterwards legitimized] to be the heirs of their parents; but the law of the English does not suffer the offspring not produced by the marriage to succeed. Fortescue, c. 39.

PROLES (Lat.) Progeny; such issue as proceeds from a lawful marriage, and, in its enlarged sense, it signifies any children.

PROLES SEQUITUR SORTEM PATERnam. The offspring follows the condition of the father. 1 Sandf. Ch. (N. Y.) 583, 660.

PROLETARIUS. In civil law. One who had no property to be taxed, and paid a tax only on account of his children (*proles*); a person of mean or common extraction. The word has become Frenchified, *proletaire* signifying one of the common people.

PROLICIDE (Lat. *proles*, offspring, *cedere*, to kill). In medical jurisprudence. A word used to designate the destruction of the human offspring. Jurists divide the subject into "foeticide," or the destruction of the foetus *in utero*, and "infanticide," or the destruction of the new-born infant. Ryan, Med. Jur. 137.

PROLIXITY. The unnecessary and superfluous statement of facts in pleading or in evidence. This will be rejected as impertinent. 7 Price, 278, note.

PROLOCUTOR (Lat. *pro* and *loquor*, to speak before). In ecclesiastical law. The president or chairman of a convocation.

PROLONGATION. Time added to the duration of something.

When the time is lengthened during which a party is to perform a contract, the sureties of such a party are, in general, discharged, unless the sureties consent to such prolongation.

In the civil law, the prolongation of time to the principal did not discharge the surety. Dig. 2. 14. 27; Id. 12. 1. 40.

PROLYTAE (Lat.) In Roman law. The term used to denominate students of law during the fifth and last year of their studies. They were left during this year very much to their own direction, and took the name *prolytae omnino soluti.* They studied chiefly the Code and the imperial constitutions. See Dig. Pref. Prim. Const. 2; Calv. Lex.

PROMISE. An engagement by which the promisor contracts towards another for the performance of some act. 1 Denio (N. Y.) 226.

"We are in the habit of considering as the essential feature of contract a promise by one party to another, or by two parties to one another, to do or forbear from doing certain acts. We are further in the habit of using the word 'promise' to signify a binding promise, as opposed to the offer of a promise, or, to use the cumbrous terminology of Austin, a pollicitation. * * * There are then three stages necessary to the making of that sort of agreement which results in contract: There must be an offer, there must be an acceptance of the offer resulting in a promise, and the law must attach a binding force to the promise, so as to invest it with the character of an obligation." Anson, Cont. 4.

PROMISE OF MARRIAGE. A contract between a man and a woman to marry each other at some future time. The implied agreement is, if no time be expressed, to marry within a reasonable time. 42 Mich. 346; 97 Pa. St. 465.

The agreement need not be in any set form (53 N. Y. 267), nor in express terms, but may be inferred from conduct (71 Hun [N. Y.] 137; 85 Ill. 222; 23 Barb. [N. Y.] 639).

To render the contract valid, the parties must be competent to contract generally (8 Mich. 318; 26 Barb. [N. Y.] 615), and, moreover, must be able to enter into the marriage relation; a promise by one already married (60 N. Y. Super. Ct. 222), or one who is impotent (41 N. J. Law, 13), being void; but precontract to marry another does not invalidate the promise (18 Mo. 389).

PROMISEE. A person to whom a promise has been made.

PROMISOR. One who makes a promise.

PROMISSORY NOTE. A written promise to pay a certain sum of money at a future time, unconditionally. Bailey, Bills, 1; 3 Kent, Comm. 74; 7 Watts & S. (Pa.) 264; 2 Humph. (Tenn.) 143; 10 Wend. (N. Y.) 675; 1 Ala. 263; 7 Mo. 42; 2 Cow. (N. Y.) 536; 6 N. H. 364; 7 Vern. 22.

A written engagement to pay absolutely to a person named, or to order or bearer, at a specified time or on demand, a certain sum of money. 10 Ill. 252; 15 Mass. 387; 127 N. Y. 92.

No particular form of expression is required. 37 Ill. 137; 7 Vt. 22.

A date is not essential. 32 Ind. 375; 30 Vt. 11; 76 Ala. 339.

The promise must be unconditional. 30 Minn. 441; 6 Wis. 209.

The promise to pay may be implied from a phrase such as "good for," etc. (33 Ill. 424; 6 N. H. 364), or "due to," etc. (88 Hun [N. Y.] 535; 27 Ill. 337; 17 Ga. 574).

To be a promissory note, the instrument must be for the payment of money only. 40 Ark. 344; 20 N. Y. 272; 17 Wis. 139.

The payee must be clearly designated (13 Ga. 55; 6 Mo. App. 583; 1 Ill. 18); but this may be done by description, without naming him (16 Ill. 169).

The consideration need not be expressed. 127 N. Y. 92; 26 Or. 315; 8 Cal. 288.

The place of payment need not be stated. 31 Tex. 614.

The time of payment must be designated, unless the note is payable "on demand" (86 U. S. 560). But see 8 Miss. 176; 1 Pin. (Wis.) 643.

The amount payable must be certain (60 Mich. 432), but the addition of "current exchange" (9 Mich. 241; 54 Minn. 184; 10 Wis. 34), or "attorneys' fees" (82 Ind. 370), does not prevent the instrument being a note.

The decisions are in conflict as to whether negotiability is an essential of a promissory note. That it is not, see 1 Ga. 226; 46 Me. 387; 10 Gill & J. 299; 6 Cush. (Mass.) 172; 34 Vt. 402. Contra, 1 Ill. 18; 8 N. J. Law, 262; 66 N. Y. 14.

PROMOTERS.

——**In English Law.** Those who, in popular or penal actions, prosecute in their own names and the king's, having part of the fines and penalties.

——**In Modern Corporation Law.** Those persons who manage the incorporation of a company, issuing prospectuses, procuring the stock subscriptions, organizing, etc. Any one who actively assists in doing this, whether as a business or in a single instance, is a promoter. 1 Fletcher Cyclopedia Corporations 264.

PROMOVENT. A plaintiff in a suit of *duplex querela* (*q. v.*) 2 Prob. Div. 192.

PROMULGATION. The order given to cause a law to be executed, and to make it public. It differs from "publication." 1 Bl. Comm. 45; St. 6 Hen. VI. c. 4.

PROMUTUUM (Lat.) In civil law. A *quasi* contract, by which he who receives a certain sum of money, or a certain quantity of fungible things, which have been paid to him through mistake, contracts towards the payer the obligation of returning him as much. Poth. de l'Usure, pt. 3, § 1, a. 1.

This contract is called *promutuum*, because it has much resemblance to that of *mutuum*. This resemblance consists in this: First, that in both a sum of money or some fungible things are required; second, that in both there must be a transfer of the property in the thing; third, that in both there must be returned the same amount or quantity of the thing received. But, though there is this general resemblance between the two, the *mutuum* differs essentially from the *promutuum*. The former is the actual contract of the parties, made expressly, but the latter is a *quasi* contract, which is the effect of an error or mistake. 1 Bouv. Inst. notes 1125, 1126.

PRONUNCIATIO (Lat. From *pronunciare,* to pronounce.) In old English law. Delivery of judgment on a verdict. Bract. fol. 289.

PROOF. The conviction or persuasion of the mind of a judicial tribunal by the exhibition of evidence of the reality of a fact alleged. See "Evidence."

PROPER FEUDS. The original and genuine feuds held by pure military service.

PROPERTY. The right and interest which a man has in lands and chattels, to the exclusion of others. 6 Bin. (Pa.) 98; 4 Pet. (U. S.) 511; 17 Johns. (N. Y.) 283; 59 N. Y. 192; 31 Cal. 637; 11 East, 290, 518; 14 East, 370.

The right to possess, use, enjoy, and dispose of a thing in any manner not forbidden by law (56 N. Y. 268; 31 Cal. 637); the power of disposition being essential (13 N. Y. 396; 70 Mich. 537).

The term is frequently applied to that which is the subject of property and in this sense it includes everything corporeal or incorporeal which is the subject of ownership. 26 Conn. 449; 84 N. Y. 565. It includes choses in action. 23 Minn. 239.

Within legal and constitutional provisions for the protection of "property," it has been held to include the right to labor (33 Hun [N. Y.] 374), to practice a profession (90 Pa. St. 477), the right to take an appeal (57 Cal. 464). See "Real Property;" "Chattel Property."

PROPERTY PER INDUSTRIAM. A qualified property in animals acquired by reclaiming or confining them.

PROPERTY PROPTER IMPOTENTIAM. A qualified property which one has in animals *ferae naturae,* which are on his premises, and unable, by immaturity, to leave them. It is lost when such animals become able to leave.

PROPERTY PROPTER PRIVILEGIUM. A qualified property in wild animals by reason of a privilege of hunting them, to the exclusion of others. 2 Bl. Comm. 394.

PROPINQUIOR EXCLUDIT PROPINquum; propinquus remotum; et remotus remotiorem. He who is nearer excludes him who is near; he who is near, him who is remote; he who is remote, him who is more remote. Co. Litt. 10.

PROPINQUITY (Lat.) Kindred; parentage. See "Affinity;" "Consanguinity."

PROPINQUUS (Lat.) In old English law. Near; near of kin.

PROPIOS, or PROPRIOS. In Spanish law. Certain portions of ground laid off and reserved when a town was founded in Spanish America, as the unalienable property of the town, for the purpose of erecting public buildings, markets, etc., or to be used in any other way, under the direction of the municipality, for the advancement of the revenues or the prosperity of the place. 12 Pet. (U. S.) 442, note.

PROPONE.

——**In Scotch Law.** To state. To propone a defense is to state or move it. 1 Kames, Eq. pref.

——**In Ecclesiastical and Probate Law.** To bring forward for adjudication; to exhibit as basis of a claim; to proffer for judicial action.

PROPONENT. In ecclesiastical law. One who propounds a thing; as, "the party proponent doth allege and propound." 6 Ecc. 356, note.

He who propounds a will for probate.

PROPORCITAS, *Proportatio.* L. Lat. In old records. The purport, tenor or substance of a thing; a report or relation of a matter. Called *proport.* Spelman.

In old Scotch law. A verdict; called the *proport* or *report* of the jury or assise. Spelman.

PROPORTUM. In old records. Purport; intention or meaning. Cowell.

PROPOSAL. An offer; a formal offer to perform some undertaking, stating the time and manner of performance, and price demanded, or one or more of these particulars, either directly or by implied or direct reference to some announcement requesting such an offer. See 35 Ala (N. S.) 33. A proposal of this character is not to be considered as subject to different rules from any other offer. Pierce, Am. Ry. Law, 364.

PROPOSITION. An offer to do something. Until it has been accepted, a proposition may be withdrawn by the party who makes it, and, to be binding, the acceptance must be in the same terms, without any variation. See "Acceptance;" 1 La. 190; 4 La. 80.

PROPOSITUM INDEFINITUM AEQUIpollet universali. An indefinite proposition is equal to a general one.

PROPOSITUS (Lat.) The person proposed. In making genealogical tables, the person whose relations it is desired to find out is called the *propositus.*

PROPOUND. In the law of wills. To offer for probate.

PROPRES. In French law. The term *propres* or *biens propres* is used to denote that property which has come to an individual from his relations, either in a direct line, ascending or descending, or from a collateral line, whether the same have come by operation of law or by devise. *Propres* is used in opposition to *acquets*. Poth. des Propres; 2 Burge, Confl. Laws, 61.

PROPRIA PERSONA (Lat. in his own person). It is a rule in pleading that pleas to the jurisdiction of the court must be pleaded *in propria persona*, because, if pleaded by attorney, they admit the jurisdiction, as an attorney is an officer of the court, and he is presumed to plead after having obtained leave, which admits the jurisdiction. Lawes, Pl. 91.

An appearance may be *in propria persona*, and need not be by attorney.

PROPRIEDAD. In Spanish law. Property. White, New Recop. bk. 1, tit. 7, c. 5, § 2.

PROPRIETARY. Belonging or pertaining to a proprietor. See 117 U. S. 487.

PROPRIETARY MEDICINES. Proprietary medicines are described as those "prepared, put up and marked and ready for use by the public so soon as they leave the hands of the manufacturer. They are in packages or bottles, are labeled with the name, and are accompanied with wrappers containing directions for their use and the conditions for which they are claimed to be specifics. 176 Ill. App. 628.

PROPRIETARY RIGHTS. Those rights which an owner of property has by virtue of his ownership. When proprietary rights are opposed to acquired rights, such as easements, franchises, etc., they are more often called "natural rights."

PROPRIETAS (Lat.) In the civil and old English law. Property; that which is one's own; ownership.

——**Proprietas Nuda.** Naked or mere property or ownership; the mere title, separate from the usufruct.

——**Proprietas Plena.** Full property, including not only the title, but the usufruct, or exclusive right to the use. Calv. Lex.

PROPRIETAS TOTIUS NAVIS CARINAE causam sequitur. The property of the whole ship follows the ownership of the keel. Dig. 6. 1. 61. Provided it had not been constructed with the materials of another. Id.; 2 Kent, Comm. 362.

PROPRIETAS VERBORUM EST SALUS proprietatum. The propriety of words is the safety of property.

PROPRIETATE PROBANDA. The name of a writ. See "De proprietate Probanda."

PROPRIETATES VERBORUM OBSERvandae sunt. The proprieties (*i. e.*, proper meanings) of words are to be observed. Jenk. Cent. Cas. 136.

PROPRIETOR. An owner; the holder of the legal title; the person who has the legal right or exclusive title to anything, whether in possession or not. Latham v. Roach, 72 Ill. 181.

PROPRIO VIGORE (Lat.) By its own force or vigor. An expression frequently used in construction. A phrase is said to have a certain meaning *proprio vigore*.

PROPTER AFFECTUM (Lat.) For or on account of some affection or prejudice. A juryman may be challenged *propter affectum;* as, because he is related to the party, has eaten at his expense, and the like. See "Challenge."

PROPTER DEFECTUM (Lat.) On account of or for some defect. This phrase is frequently used in relation to challenges. See "Challenge."

PROPTER DEFECTUM SANGUINIS. On account of failure of blood.

PROPTER DELICTUM (Lat.) For or on account of crime. A juror may be challenged *propter delictum* when he has been convicted of an infamous crime. See "Challenge."

PROPTER HONORIS RESPECTUM. On account of respect of honor or rank. See "Challenge."

PROROGATED JURISDICTION. In Scotch law. That jurisdiction which, by the consent of the parties, is conferred upon a judge who, without such consent, would be incompetent. Ersk. Inst. 1. 2. 15.

At common law, when a party is entitled to some privilege or exemption from jurisdiction, he may waive it, and then the jurisdiction is complete; but the consent cannot give jurisdiction.

PROROGATION (Lat.) Putting off to another time. It is generally applied to the English parliament, and means the continuance of it from one day to another. It differs from "adjournment," which is a continuance of it from one day to another in the same session. 1 Bl. Comm. 186.

——**In Civil Law.** The giving time to do a thing beyond the term prefixed. Dig. 2. 14. 27. 1. See "Prolongation."

PROSCRIBED (Lat. *proscribo*, to write before). In civil law. Among the Romans, a man was said to be proscribed when a reward was offered for his head; but the term was more usually applied to those who were sentenced to some punishment which carried with it the consequences of civil death. Code, 9. 49.

PROSECUTION. The conducting or carrying forward of a judicial proceeding.

The means adopted to bring a supposed offender against the criminal law to punishment by due course of law.

PROSECUTOR. In practice. He who prosecutes another for a crime in the name of the government.

The public prosecutor is an officer appointed by the government to prosecute all offenses,—he is the attorney general or his deputy.

A private prosecutor is one who prefers an accusation against a party whom he suspects to be guilty.

PROSEQUI (Lat.) To follow up or pursue. See "Nolle Prosequi."

PROSPECTIVE (Lat. *prospicio*, to look forward). That which is applicable to the future. It is used in opposition to retrospective. To be just, a law ought always to be prospective. 1 Bouv. Inst. note 116.

PROSPECTIVE DAMAGES. Such as will naturally result from the injury complained of, but have not accrued at the time of the trial; such, for example, as the loss of wages from a personal injury which will result where plaintiff has not, at the time of the trial, recovered his earning capacity.

PROSTERNERE. (Lat.) In old English law. To throw down; to break or pull down; to abate.

PROSTITUTE. A female given to indiscriminate lewdness for gain.

PROSTITUTION. The common lewdness of a woman for gain. The act of permitting a common and indiscriminate sexual intercourse for hire. 12 Metc. (Mass.) 97; 8 Barb. (N. Y.) 610; 102 Ind. 161; 154 Ill. 647. In Iowa, the term seems to be used in a wider sense than elsewhere prevails. 56 Iowa, 432; 78 Iowa, 492.

In a figurative sense, it signifies the bad use which a corrupt judge makes of the law, by making it subservient to his interest; as, the prostitution of the law, the prostitution of justice.

PROTECTIO TRAHIT SUBJECTIONEM, subjectio protectionem. Protection draws to it subjection; subjection, protection. Co. Litt. 65.

PROTECTION.

——**In Mercantile Law.** The name of a document generally given by notaries public to sailors and other persons going abroad, in which is certified that the bearer therein named is a citizen of the United States.

——**In Governmental Law.** That benefit or safety which the government affords to the citizens.

——**In English Law.** A privilege granted by the king to a party to an action, by which he is protected from a judgment which would otherwise be rendered against him. Of these protections there are several kinds. Fitzh. Nat. Brev. 65.

PROTECTION OF INVENTIONS ACT. St. 33 & 34 Vict. c. 27. By this act it is provided that the exhibition of new inventions shall not prejudice patent rights, and that the exhibition of designs shall not prejudice the right to registration of such designs.

PROTECTION ORDER. In English probate practice. An order for the protection of the property of a deserted wife.

PROTECTIONIBUS, STATUTE DE. The English statute 33 Edw. I. st. 1, allowing a challenge to be entered against a protection, etc.

PROTECTOR OF SETTLEMENT. One who may be appointed by the settler of an estate tail, without whose consent the tenant in tail cannot bar the entail except as against his own issue.

PROTECTORATE. Government by a protector. The period of his rule. Specially so used with reference to the period of English history during which Oliver and Richard Cromwell held the title of "Lord Protector."

——**In International Law.** A relation assumed by a strong nation toward a weak one, whereby the former protects the latter from hostile invasion or dictation, and interferes more or less in its domestic concerns. Cent. Dict. Such, for example, is the supervision assumed jointly by the United States, Germany, and Great Britain over Samoa. See Davis, Int. Law, 247.

PROTEST.

——**In Mercantile Law.** A notarial act, made for want of payment of a promissory note, or for want of acceptance or payment of a bill of exchange by a notary public, in which it is declared that all parties to such instruments will be held responsible to the holder for all damages, exchanges, re-exchange, etc.

——**In Legislation.** A declaration made by one or more members of a legislative body that they do not agree with some act or resolution of the body. It is usual to add the reasons which the protestants have for such a dissent.

——**In Maritime Law.** A writing, attested by a justice of the peace, a notary public, or a consul, made and verified by the master of a vessel, stating the severity of a voyage by which a ship has suffered, and showing that it was not owing to the neglect or misconduct of the master. See Marsh. Ins. 715, 716; 1 Wash. C. C. (U. S.) 145, 238, 408, note; 1 Pet. C. C. (U. S.) 119; 1 Dall. (Pa.) 6, 10, 317; 2 Dall. (Pa.) 195; 3 Watts & S. (Pa.) 144.

PROTESTANDO. See "Protestation."

PROTESTATION.

——**In Pleading.** The indirect affirmation or denial, by means of the word "protesting" (in the Latin form of pleadings, *protestando*), of the truth of some matter which cannot with propriety or safety be positively affirmed, denied, or entirely passed over. See 3 Bl. Comm. 311.

The exclusion of a conclusion. Co. Litt. 124.

Its object was to secure to the party making it the benefit of a positive affirmation or denial in case of success in the action, so far as to prevent the conclusion that the fact was admitted to be true as stated by the opposite party, and at the same time to avoid the objection of duplicity to which a direct affirmation or denial would expose the pleading. 19 Johns. (N. Y.) 96; 2 Saund. 103; Comyn, Dig. "Pleader" (N); Plowd. 276; Lawes, Pl. 171. Matter which is the ground of the suit upon which issue could be taken could not be protested. Plowd. 276; 3 Wils. 109; 2 Johns. (N. Y.) 227. But see 2 Wm. Saund. 103, note. Protestations are no longer allowed (3 Bl. Comm. 312), and were generally an unnecessary form (3 Lev. 125).

The common form of making protestations is as follows: "Because protesting that," etc., excluding such matters of the adversary's pleading as are intended to be excluded in the *protestando*, if it be matter of fact; or, if it be against the legal sufficiency of his pleading, "because protesting that the plea by him above pleaded in bar" (or by way of reply, or rejoinder, etc., as the case may be) "is wholly insufficient in law." See, generally, 1 Chit. Pl. 534; Archb. Civ. Pl. 245; Comyn, Dig. "Pleader" (N); Steph. Pl. 235.

——**In Practice.** An asserveration made by taking God to witness. A protestation is a form of asseveration which approaches very nearly to an oath. Wolff. Inst. § 375.

PROTESTED FOR NONPAYMENT. These words, in mercantile law, have come to have a technical meaning. In them is included not only the idea that the bill is past due, but that payment of it has been demanded; and not being paid, it is therefore dishonored. They mean that the process necessary to dishonor the bill, to-wit, demand, refusal of payment and the drawing up of a formal protest, has been gone through with. All this is included in and meant by the term "protested." 2 Douglas' (Mich.) R. 425; 8 Cal. 637; 28 N. Y. 554; 12 Barb. 250.

PROTHONOTARY. The title given to an officer who officiates as principal clerk of some courts. Viner, Abr. The office exists in Pennsylvania.

In the ecclesiastical law, the name of "prothonotary" is given to an officer of the court of Rome. He is so called because he is the first notary,—the Greek word *protos*, signifying *primus*, or first. These notaries have pre-eminence over the other notaries, and are put in the rank of prelates. There are seven of them. Dalloz.

PROTOCOL. A record or register. Among the Romans, *protocollum* was a writing at the head of the first page of the paper used by the notaries or tabellions. Nov. 44.

In France, the minutes of notarial acts were formerly transcribed on registers, which were called "protocols." Toullier, Dr. Civ. liv. 3, tit. 3, c. 6, § 1, note 413.

By the German law it signifies the minutes of any transaction. Enc. Am. "Protocol." In the latter sense, the word has of late been received into international law. Id.

PROTOCOLLUM (Graeco-Lat.) In the civil law. A brief note or memorandum of a transaction made by a notary, for the purpose of being afterwards extended or written out in full (*quod breviter et succincte notatur a tabellione, ut extendi deinde atque absolvi possit*). Calv. Lex. A hasty note of a transaction, as it were *prima collectio rerum*, the first getting together of matters. Id.

Protocollum, among the Romans, seems to have originally signified a formal caption or heading of instruments drawn by *tabelliones* (notaries); or, more particularly, a writing at the head of the paper used by these officers, containing the name of the *comes sacrarum largitionum* (chief officer of the imperial treasury), and the time when the instrument was made. Nov. 44. It seems to have served the purpose of an official stamp. In the forty-fourth Novel, the *tabelliones* are forbidden to write their instruments upon any other paper than such as contained this *protocollum* at the head.

PROTOCOLO. In Spanish law. The original draft or writing of an instrument which remains in the possession of the *escribano*, or notary. White, New Recop. lib. 3, tit. 7, c. 5, § 2.

PROTUTOR (Lat.) In civil law. He who, not being the tutor of a pupil or minor, has administered his property or affairs as if he had been, whether he thought himself legally invested with the authority of a tutor or not.

He who marries a woman who is tutrix becomes, by the marriage, a protutor. The protutor is equally responsible as the tutor.

PROUT PATET PER RECORDUM (Lat.) As appears by the record. This phrase is frequently used in pleading; as, for example, in debt on a judgment or other matter of record, unless when it is stated as an inducement, it is requisite, after showing the matter of record, to refer to it by the *prout patet per recordum*. 1 Chit. Pl. *356; 10 Me. 127.

PROVE. To make proof of; to establish by evidence.

PROVER. In old English law. One who undertakes to prove a crime against another. 28 Edw. I.; 5 Hen. IV. One who, being indicted and arraigned for treason or felony, confesses before plea pleaded, and accuses his accomplices to obtain pardon; state's evidence. 4 Bl. Comm. 329, 330*. To prove. Law Fr. & Lat. Dict.; Britt. c. 22.

PROVINCE. Sometimes this signifies the district into which a country has been divided; as, the province of Canterbury, in England; the province of Languedoc, in France. Sometimes it means a dependency or colony, as the province of New Brunswick. It is sometimes used figuratively to signify power or authority; as, it is the province of the court to judge of the law, that of the jury to decide on the facts.

PROVINCIAL CONSTITUTIONS. The decrees of provincial synods held under divers archbishops of Canterbury, from Stephen Langton, in the reign of Henry III., to Henry Chichele, in the reign of Henry V., and adopted also by the province of York in the reign of Henry VI.

PROVING OF THE TENOR. In Scotch practice. An action for proving the tenor of a lost deed. Bell, Dict.

PROVISION.

——**In Common Law.** The property which a drawer of a bill of exchange places in the hands of a drawee; as, for example, by remittances, or when the drawee is indebted to the drawer when the bill becomes due, provision is said to have been made. Acceptance always presumes a provision. See Code de Comm. arts. 115-117.

——**In French Law.** An allowance granted by a judge to a party for his support,—which is to be paid before there is a definitive judgment. In a civil case, for example, it is an allowance made to a wife who is separated from her husband. Dalloz.

PROVISIONAL ASSIGNEES. Those who, under the old bankruptcy practice of England, were appointed to take charge of bankrupt estates until the creditors' assignees were appointed.

PROVISIONAL ORDER. In English law. Under various acts of parliament, certain public bodies and departments of the government are authorized to inquire into matters which, in the ordinary course, could only be dealt with by a private act of parliament, and to make orders for their regulation. These orders have no effect unless they are confirmed by an act of parliament, and are hence called "provisional orders." Several orders may be confirmed by one act. The object of this mode of proceeding is to save the trouble and expense of promoting a number of private bills.

PROVISIONAL REMEDY. A remedy adopted to meet a particular exigency. The term is ordinarily applied to process issued at the commencement or during the pendency of a suit to preserve some status until the rights of the parties are adjudicated. Preliminary injunction, attachment, arrest on mesne process, garnishment, etc., are provisional remedies.

PROVISIONAL SEIZURE.

——**In Louisiana.** A term which signifies nearly the same as attachment of property.

It is regulated by the Code of Practice as follows, namely: The plaintiff may, in certain cases, hereafter provided, obtain the provisional seizure of the property which he holds in pledge, or on which he has a privilege, in order to secure a payment of his claim. Code La. art. 284.

Provisional seizure may be ordered in the following cases: First, in executory proceedings, when the plaintiff sues on a title importing confession of judgment; second, when a lessor prays for the seizure of furniture or property used in the house, or attached to the real estate which he has leased; third, when a seaman, or other person, employed on board of a ship or water craft, navigating within the state, or person having furnished materials for or made repairs to such ship or water craft, prays that the same may be seized, and prevented from departing, until he has been paid the amount of his claim; fourth, when the proceedings are *in rem*, that is to say, against the thing itself which stands pledged for the debt, when the property is abandoned or in cases where the owner of the thing is unknown or absent. Code La. art. 285. See 6 Mart. (La.; N. S.) 168; 7 Mart. (La.; N. S.) 153; 8 Mart. (La.; N. S.) 320; 1 Mart. (La.) 168; 12 Mart. (La.) 32.

PROVISIONS OF EMPOWERIZATION. Provisions granting power. 146 Ill. App. 420.

PROVISIONS OF OXFORD. Certain provisions made in the parliament of Oxford, 1258, for the purpose of securing the execution of the provisions of *Magna Charta* against the invasions thereof by Henry III. The government of the country was in effect committed by these provisions to a standing committee of twenty-four, whose chief merit consisted in their representative character, and their real desire to effect an improvement in the king's government. Brown.

PROVISO. A proviso is a limitation or exception to a grant made or authority conferred, the effect of which is to declare that the one shall not operate or the other be exercised unless in case provided. 187 Mich. 516, 525.

The name of a clause inserted in an act of the legislature, a deed, a written agreement, or other instrument, which generally contains a condition that a certain thing shall or shall not be done, in order that an agreement contained in another clause shall take effect.

"This word hath divers operations. Sometimes it worketh a qualification or limitation, sometimes a condition, and sometimes a covenant." Co. Litt. 146b, 203b.

It always implies a condition, unless subsequent words change it to a covenant; but when a proviso contains the mutual words of the parties to a deed, it amounts to a covenant. 2 Coke, 72; Cro. Eliz. 242; Moore, 707.

A proviso differs from an exception. 1 Barn. & Ald. 99. An exception exempts, absolutely, from the operation of an engagement or an enactment; a proviso defeats their operation conditionally. An exception takes out of an engagement or enactment something which would otherwise be part of the subject matter of it; a proviso avoids them by way of defeasance or excuse. 8 Am. Jur. 242; Plowd. 361; Carth. 99; 1 Saund. 234a, note; Lilly, Reg., and the cases there cited. See, generally, Am. Jur. No. 16, art. 1; Bac. Abr. "Conditions" (A); Comyn, Dig. "Condition" (A 1), (A 2); Dwarr. St. 660.

PROVISO EST PROVIDERE PRAESENtia et futura, non praeterita. A proviso is to provide for the present and the future, not the past. 2 Coke, 72; Vaughan, 279; Broom, Leg. Max. (3d London Ed.) 275.

PROVISOR. He that hath the care of providing things necessary, but more especially one who sued to the court of Rome for a provision. Jacob; 25 Edw. III. One nominated by the pope to a benefice before it became void, in prejudice of right of true patron. 4 Bl. Comm. 111*.

PROVOCATION (Lat. *provoco*, to call out). The act of inciting another to do something. Such conduct as tends to arouse passions which may lead to the commission of an act.

Provocation is no defense for crime, but may mitigate the damages for an assault (3 E. D. Smith [N. Y.] 518), and if adequate to arouse in the mind of a reasonable man such passion as to cause him to act rashly and without reflection, it will reduce homicide from murder to manslaughter. See "Cool Blood."

PROVOST. A title given to the chief of some corporations or societies. In France, this title was formerly given to some presiding judges. The word is derived from the Latin *praepositus*.

PROVOST MARSHAL. A military officer appointed to arrest and secure deserters and other offenders, to prevent pillaging, indict offenders, and see to the passage and execution of sentence, and also to perform other certain duties pertaining to the police and discipline of the service. The provost marshal of the navy has charge of prisoners, etc. Webster.

PROXENETAE (Lat.) In the civil law. Among the Romans, these were persons whose functions somewhat resembled those of the brokers of modern commercial nations. Dig. 50. 14. 3; Domat, lib. 1, tit. 17, § 1, art. 1.

PROXIMATE CAUSE. That which, in a natural and continuous sequence, unbroken by a new cause, produced an event, and without which that event would not have occurred. Shear. & R. Neg. § 261.

PROXIMATE DAMAGES. Proximate damages are such as are the ordinary and natural results of the omission or commission of acts of negligence, and such as are usual and might have been reasonably expected. 123 Ill. App. 24-25; 175 Ill. 406. See "Remote Damages."

PROXIMITY (Lat.) Kindred between two persons. Dig. 38. 16. 8.

PROXIMUS EST CUI NEMO ANTECEdit; supremus est quem nemo sequitur. He is next whom no one precedes; he is last whom no one follows. Dig. 50. 16. 92.

PROXY. A person appointed in the place of another, to represent him.

The instrument by which a person is appointed so to act. It is said to be a contraction of "procuracy."

——**In Ecclesiastical Law.** A judicial proctor, or one who is appointed to manage another man's law concerns, is called a "proxy." Ayliffe, Par.

An annual payment made by the parochial clergy to the bishop, etc., on visitations. Tomlins. See Rutherforth, Inst. 253; Hall, Prac. 14.

PRUDENTER AGIT QUI PRAECEPTO legis obtemperat. He acts prudently who obeys the commands of the law. 5 Coke, 49.

PRYK. A kind of service of tenure. Blount says it signifies an old-fashioned spur, with one point only, which the tenant holding land by this tenure was to find for the king. Wharton.

PSYCHOLOGICAL FACT. In the law of evidence. A fact which can only be perceived mentally; such as the motive by which a person is actuated. Burrill, Circ. Ev. 130, 131.

PUBERTY. In civil law. The age in boys of fourteen and in girls of twelve years. Ayliffe, Pand. 63; Hall, Prac. 14; Toullier, Dr. Civ. tom. 5, p. 100; Inst. 1. 22; Dig. 1. 7. 40. 1; Code, 5. 60. 3; 1 Bl. Comm. 436.

PUBLIC. The whole body politic, or all the citizens of the state. It is inapplicable to a municipal corporation or other political subdivision; the people are the public. 21 Mich. 335. It does not necessarily mean all of the inhabitants of a state, a county or a community. 184 Ill. App. 156; 169 Ill. 84.

This term is sometimes joined to other terms, to designate those things which have a relation to the public; as, a public officer, a public road, a public passage, a public house.

A distinction has been made between the terms "public" and "general;" they are sometimes used as synonymous. The former term is applied strictly to that which concerns all the citizens and every member of the state; while the latter includes a lesser, though still a large, portion of the community. Greenl. Ev. § 128.

PUBLIC ADMINISTRATOR. One appointed to administer the estates of intestates where there is no person interested in them competent and willing to take the administration. He is generally a standing officer, or an officer of court acting *ex officio*, as the sheriff in Arkansas (23 Ark. 304), or the clerk of the superior court in Georgia (20 Ga. 775); but the term is also applied to an administrator appointed for the occasion in default of any application for administration.

PUBLIC AUCTION. This phrase is frequently used, but it is difficult to conceive of a private auction, so the word "public" seems to add nothing. See "Auction."

PUBLIC BRIDGE. One forming part of a public highway; one erected for common use or public convenience, as distinguished from one erected for the use and convenience of a private person.

Common use on special occasion will constitute a public bridge. 4 Campb. 189.

PUBLIC BUILDINGS. Buildings ordinarily used in or indispensable to the conduct of the public business. 41 Pa. St. 270.

PUBLIC CARRIER. A common carrier (*q. v.*)

PUBLIC CHARITY. Any charity whose objects are undefined; one for the benefit of an indefinite number of unselected persons. See "Charitable Uses."

PUBLIC COMPANY. A term used in the English law for an open corporation. "What a 'public company' is has not been defined, but one test is whether the members have a right to transfer their shares." Buckl. 3; 12 Ch. Div. 655.

PUBLIC CORPORATIONS. Public corporations are political corporations, such as are founded wholly for public purposes, and the whole interest in which is in the public. All corporations, whether public or private, are, in contemplation of law, founded upon the principle that they will promote the interest or convenience of the public. 71 Ill. 322.

PUBLIC DEBT. That which is due or owing by the government.

PUBLIC DOMAIN. In its most general sense, all landed property owned by the public. In peculiar context it has been limited to unappropriated public lands. 68 Tex. 547.

PUBLIC EASEMENT. An easement, such as a public right of way, the enjoyment of which belongs to the public generally, and not to the owner of a particular dominant estate.

PUBLIC ENEMY. This word, used in the singular number, designates a nation at war with the United States, and includes every member of such nation. Vattel, bk. 3, c. 5, § 70.

To make a public enemy, the government of the foreign country must be at war with the United States; for a mob, howsoever numerous it may be, or robbers, whoever they may be, are never considered as a public enemy. 2 Marsh. Ins. 508; 3 Esp. 131, 132.

A common carrier is exempt from responsibility whenever a loss has been occasioned to the goods in his charge by the act of a public enemy; but the burden of proof lies on him to show that the loss was so occasioned. 3 Munf. (Va.) 239; 4 Bin. (Pa.) 127; 2 Bailey (S. C.) 157.

Bills of lading exempting the carrier from liability for losses arising from the act of God or the "public enemy," refer, by the expression quoted, to the enemy of the country, and not to that of the carrier, and do not include mobs and riots. 242 Ill. 188. See "Common Carriers."

PUBLIC LAND. In its most general sense, all lands owned by the government. In the more limited sense in which it is ordinarily used, it signifies such lands as are subject to sale or other disposition by the government under general laws. 92 U. S. 761; 98 U. S. 118.

PUBLIC LAW. In one sense, international law. In another sense, a general law.

PUBLIC MINISTERS. A general term of the international law, which includes all diplomatic representatives, but excludes consuls.

PUBLIC NOTICE. Notice given to the public generally, as by advertisement or posting, and not to some particular individual.

PUBLIC NUISANCE. See "Nuisance."

PUBLIC OFFENSE. Includes all criminal offenses, including violations of municipal ordinances. 34 Minn. 1.

PUBLIC PASSAGE. A right to pass over a body of water. This term is synonymous with "public highway," with this difference: by the latter is understood a right to pass over the land of another; by the former is meant the right of going over the water which is on another's land. Carth. 193; Hammond, N. P. 195.

PUBLIC PEACE. "Public tranquillity; that quiet, order, and freedom from disturbance which is guarantied by the laws." The determination of what acts disturb the public peace rests in the sound discretion of the legislature. 6 Daly (N. Y.) 276, 280.

PUBLIC POLICY. The criterion by which the courts condemn contracts as opposed to the public will, or as tending to subvert the public welfare.

Thus, public policy invalidates contracts tending to immorality, as for the rental of a brothel (27 Mo. App. 649), or in consideration of future illicit cohabitation (58 Ala. 303; 57 Hun [N. Y.] 292); contracts facilitating divorce (89 Ill. 349; 25 Minn. 72); contracts in unreasonable restraint of trade (49 N. J. Eq. 217); combinations to restrict competition (90 Cal. 110; 68 N. Y. 558); contracts to unfairly influence an appointment or election to public office (8 Kan. 601; 23 Mo. App. 555); to unlawfully influence legislation (88 Mass. 152); to limit the jurisdiction of courts, as by agreeing not to sue in a particular court (94 U. S. 535); to compound a criminal offense (83 Ill. 418); to restrict competition at a public sale, as by agreeing not to bid thereat (47 Ga. 479). And the agreement need only tend to illegality. Thus, an agreement for witness' fees contingent on the success of the party for whom the witness is to testify (10 Ala. 206), or for a fee to a private prosecutor contingent on a conviction (62 Ky. 207), or by an attorney to defend against offenses to be committed in the future (41 Kan. 364), are void as against public policy.

PUBLIC RECORD. A record maintained by public authorities, or open to the inspection of the public.

PUBLIC RIVER. A navigable river. See "Navigable."

PUBLIC ROAD. A road dedicated to, and kept up by the public, as contradistinguished from private ways or neighborhood roads, which are not so kept up. 20 Ala. 88.

PUBLIC SALE. A sale conducted on notice to the public, at which the public is invited to attend and purchase.

PUBLIC SCHOOLS. Schools maintained at the public expense by taxation.

PUBLIC SEAL. The official seal of a public officer. See "Seals."

PUBLIC STOCKS. Public obligations or securities.

PUBLIC TRIAL. A trial which, under reasonable limitations, the public are freely admitted to attend. The attendance may be limited to the reasonable seating capacity of the courtroom (92 Mo. 542), and persons whose attendance as a class would probably tend to disorder may be excluded (Fed. Cas. No. 14680), but the exclusion of all persons except officers of the court is a violation of the right to a public trial (103 Cal. 242), as is an order to an officer to admit only "respectable persons," where it appears that proper persons were excluded (89 Mich. 276).

"The requirement of a public trial is for the benefit of the accused, that the public may see he is fairly dealt with, and not unjustly condemned, and that the presence of interested spectators may keep his triers keenly alive to a sense of their responsibility and to the importance of their functions; and the requirement is fairly observed if, without partiality or favoritism, a reasonable proportion of the public is suffered to attend, notwithstanding that those persons whose presence could be of no service to the accused, and who would only be drawn thither by a prurient curiosity, are excluded altogether." Cooley, Const. Lim. *312.

PUBLIC USE. The nature of the "public use" for which private property may be taken is "flexible" (43 N. J. Law, 384), "dependent somewhat on the situation and wants of the community for the time being" (1 N. J. Eq. 694), and not reducible to any set of rules or principles of certain and uniform application (7 W. Va. 195). It has been limited to use by the public themselves (21 W. Va. 534), and, on the other hand, extended to any use for the public utility or advantage (16 Gray [Mass.] 417). The use may be by a private person for the public benefit (17 N. H. 57), and it is immaterial that such person may derive private profit therefrom (39 N. Y. 171).

The establishment of public highways is an undisputed public use (103 Mass. 120), as is the establishment of a railway line (23 Wall. [U. S.] 108; 9 N. Y. 100), and its various facilities, as depots (111 Mass. 125), but spur tracks for private advantage have been held not to be (40 Ohio St. 504; 48 Fed. 615). Canals (39 N. Y. 171), public wharves (110 N. Y. 569), drains necessary to preserve the public health (72 N. Y. 1), irrigation (4 Colo. 100), public cemeteries (66 N. Y. 569), public grain elevators (68 N. Y. 208), have been held to be public purposes.

PUBLIC VERDICT. A verdict delivered by the jury in open court, as distinguished from a privy verdict sealed and delivered by the jury when court is not in session.

PUBLIC WAR. See "War."

PUBLIC WAYS. Highways (*q. v.*)

PUBLIC WORSHIP. "May mean the worship of God, conducted and observed under public authority; or it may mean worship in an open or public place, without privacy or concealment; or it may mean the performance of religious exercises, under a provision for an equal right in the whole public to participate in its benefits; or it may be used in contradistinction to worship in the family or the closet. In this country, what is called 'public worship' is commonly conducted by voluntary societies, constituted according to their own notions of ecclesiastical authority and ritual propriety, opening their places of worship, and admitting to their religious services such persons, and upon such terms, and subject to such regulations, as they may choose to designate and establish. A church absolutely belonging to the public, and in which all persons without restriction have equal rights, such as the public enjoy in highways or public landings, is certainly a very rare institution, if such a thing can be found." 14 Gray (Mass.) 586, 602.

PUBLIC WRONGS. A public wrong, otherwise termed a "crime," is a breach and violation of the public rights and duties due to the whole community, considered as a community in its social aggregate capacity. 4 Bl. Comm. 5; Thatcher's Cr. Cas. 550.

Thus, an entry on the land of another without committing a breach of the peace is a mere trespass (8 Grat. [Va.] 708; 5 Denio [N. Y.] 277), but an entry upon the land of another in such manner as to cause a breach of the public peace is a public wrong, criminally punishable (8 Grat. [Va.] 708). See 1 Clark & Marshall, Crimes, 4.

PUBLICAN. In civil law. A farmer of the public revenue; one who held a lease of some property from the public treasury. Dig. 39. 4. 1. 1; Id. 39. 4. 12. 3; Id. 39. 4. 13.

PUBLICANUS (Lat.) In the Roman law. A farmer of the customs; a publican (*qui publico fructur*). Dig. 39. 4. 1; Id. 50. 16. 16; Calv. Lex.

PUBLICATION. The act by which a thing is made public.

Printing without circulation is not publication (5 Fed. 729), and circulation in manuscript is publication (3 Fed. 486). See, also, "Literary Property."

It differs from "promulgation" (*q. v.*) And see, also, Toullier, Dr. Civ. tit. "Preliminaire," note 59, for the difference in the meaning of these two words.

Publication has different meanings. When applied to a law, it signifies the rendering public the existence of the law; when it relates to the opening of the depositions taken in a case in chancery, it means that liberty is given to the officer in whose custody the depositions of witnesses in a cause are lodged, either by consent of parties, or by the rules or orders of the court, to show the depositions openly, and to give out copies of them. Prac. Reg. 297; Blake, Ch. Prac. 143. When spoken of a will, it signifies that the testator has done some act from which it can be concluded that he intended the instrument to operate as his will. Cruise, Dig. tit. 38, c. 5, § 47; 3 Atk. 161; 4 Me. 220; 3 Rawle (Pa.) 15; Comyn, Dig. "Estates by Devise" (E 2), "Chancery" (Q).

——**In the Law of Libel and Slander.** The communication of the defamatory words to some third person.

The sending of a letter to the person defamed is not publication. 68 Iowa, 726. Nor is the speaking of slanderous words where no third person could hear them. 13 Gray (Mass.) 304.

PUBLICI JURIS (Lat.) Of public right. As applied to a thing or right means that it is open to or exercisable by all persons.

When a thing is common property, so that any one can make use of it who likes, it is said to be "*publici juris;*" as in the case of light, air, and public water.

PUBLICIANA (Lat.) In civil law. The name of an action introduced by the *praetor* Publicius, the object of which was to recover a thing which had been lost. Inst. 4. 6. 4; Dig. 6. 2. 1. 16. 17. Its effects were similar to those of our action of trover.

PUBLICUM JUS (Lat.) In the civil law. Public law; that law which regards the state of the commonwealth (*quod ad statum rei Romanae spectat*). Inst. 1. 1. 4.

PUBLISHER. One who, by himself or his agent, makes a thing publicly known, one engaged in the circulation of books, pamphlets, and other papers.

PUDICITY. Chastity; the abstaining from all unlawful carnal commerce or connection. A married woman or a widow may defend her pudicity as a maid may her virginity. See "Chastity;" "Rape."

PUDZELD. In old English law. To be free from the payment of money for taking of wood in any forest. Co. Litt. 233a. The same as "woodgeld."

PUEBLO. In Spanish law. People; all the inhabitants of any country or place, without distinction. A town, township, or municipality. Las Partidas, pt. 1, tit. 2, l. 5; White, New Recop. bk. 2, tit. 1, c. 6, § 4; Schmidt, Civ. Law, 44, 185; 10 Otto (U. S.) 251.

PUER (Lat.) A boy; a child. In its enlarged sense, this word signifies a child of either sex, though in its restrained meaning it is applied to a boy only.

A case once arose which turned upon this question, whether a daughter could take lands under the description of *puer;* and it was decided by two judges against one that she was entitled. Dyer, 337b. In another case, it was ruled the other way. Hob. 33.

PUERI SUNT DE SANGUINE PARENTUM, sed pater et mater non sunt de sanguine puerorum. Children are of the blood of their parents, but the father and mother are not of the blood of their children. 3 Coke, 40.

PUERILITY. In civil law. A condition which commenced at the age of seven years, the end of the age of infancy, and lasted till the age of puberty,—that is, in females till the accomplishment of twelve years, and in males till the age of fourteen years fully accomplished. Ayliffe, Pand. 63.

The ancient Roman lawyers divided puerility into *proximus infantiae*, as it approached infancy, and into *proximus pubertati*, as it became nearer to puberty. 6 Toullier, Dr. Civ. note 100.

PUERITIA (Lat.) In civil law. Age from seven to fourteen. 4 Bl. Comm. 22; Wharton. The age from birth to fourteen years in the male, or twelve in the female. Calv. Lex. The age from birth to seventeen. Vicat.

PUFFER. A person employed by the owner of property which is sold at auction to bid it up, who does so accordingly, for the purpose of raising the price upon *bona fide* bidders.

This is a fraud, which, at the choice of the purchaser, invalidates the sale. 3 Madd. 112; 5 Madd. 37, 440; 12 Ves. 483; 1 Fonbl. Eq. 227, note; 2 Kent, Comm. 423; Cowp. 395; 3 Ves. 628; 3 Term R. 963; 6 Term R. 642; 2 Brown, Ch. 326; 1 P. A. Browne (Pa.) 346; 11 Serg. & R. (Pa.) 89; 2 Hayw. (N. C.) 328; 4 Har. & McH. (Md.) 282; 2 Dev. (N. C.) 126; 2 Const. (S. C.) 821. See "Auction;" "Bidder."

PUFFING. Exaggerated statements of value such as a vendor is allowed to make use of. 85 Ill. 275.

PUIS, PUYS, PUES, PUS, or **PUZ** (Law Fr.) After; since; afterwards. Kelham.

PUIS DARREIN CONTINUANCE (Law. Fr. since last continuance). In pleading. A plea which is put in after issue joined, for the purpose of introducing new matter, or matter which has come to the knowledge of the party pleading it subsequently to such joinder.

There is a distinction between a plea setting up matter of defense, which has arisen since the commencement of the action but before plea pleaded, and pleas alleging matters of defense originating after pleas pleaded. A plea of the former kind is not, properly speaking, a plea of puis darrein continuance. Such a plea differs from a plea in bar in this only, that it cannot destroy the original cause of action, and cannot be pleaded in bar generally, but must be pleaded to the further maintenance of the suit. 8 Ill. 103. See "Plea."

PUISNE (Law Fr.) Younger; junior; associate.

PULSARE (Lat.) In the civil law. To beat, without giving pain.

To accuse or charge; to proceed against at law. Calv. Lex.

PULSATOR. In the civil law. A name sometimes applied to the *actor.*

PUNCTUM (Lat.) A point; an indivisible point of time. See "Punctum Temporis."

A quarter of an hour, according to the old computation. Ten moments (*momenta*) made a point (*punctum*), and four points an hour. See "Momentum."

PUNCTUM TEMPORIS (Lat.) A point of time; an indivisible period of time; the shortest space of time; an instant. Calv. Lex.

A point or period from which a computation of time is made. 2 Alis. Crim. Prac. 188.

PUNDBRECH. In old English law. Pound breach (*q. v.*).

PUNIR L. Fr. (from Lat. *punire*). To punish. *Puni, puny;* punished. Britt. c. 68.

PUNISHMENT. In criminal law. Some pain or penalty warranted by law, inflicted on a person for the commission of a crime or misdemeanor, or for the omission of the performance of an act required by law, by the judgment and command of some lawful court.

Punishments are either corporal or not corporal.

The former are: Death, which is usually denominated "capital punishment;" imprisonment, which is either with or without labor (see "Penitentiary"); whipping, in some states; and banishment.

The punishments which are not corporal are: Fines, forfeitures; suspension or deprivation of some political or civil right; deprivation of office, and being rendered incapable to hold office; compulsion to remove nuisances.

PUNITIVE DAMAGES. Exemplary damages.

PUPIL.

—**In Civil Law.** One who is in his or her minority. See Dig. 1. 7.; Id. 26. 7. 1. 2; Id. 50. 16. 239; Code, 6. 30. 18. One who is in ward or guardianship.

—**At Common Law.** One who is under tuition in any school, or under a private instructor.

PUPILLARIS SUBSTITUTIO (Lat.) In civil law. The nomination of another besides his son pupil to succeed, if the son should not be able or inclined to accept the inheritance, or should die before he came of age to make a testament.

If the child survive the age of puberty, though he made no testament, the substitute had no right of succession. See Bell, Dict. "Substitution;" Dig. 28. 6.

PUPILLARITY. In civil law. That age of a person's life which included infancy and puerility.

PUPILLUS PATI POSSE NON INTELLIGITUR. A pupil is not considered able to do an act which would be prejudicial to him. Dig. 50. 17. 110. 2; 2 Kent, Comm. 245.

PUR. A corruption of the French word *par*, by or for. It is frequently used in old French law phrases, as, *pur autre vie.* It is also used in the composition of words, as, purparty, purlieu, purview.

PUR AUTRE VIE (Old Fr. for another's life). An estate is said to be *pur autre vie* when a lease is made of lands or tenements to a man to hold for the life of another person. 2 Bl. Comm. 259; 10 Viner, Abr. 296; 2 Belt, Supp. Ves. 41.

PUR TANT QUE (Law Fr.) Forasmuch as; because; to the intent that. Kelham.

PURCHASE. In the broadest sense, the transmission of property from one person to another by their voluntary agreement on a valuable consideration. 4 Kent, Comm. 509.

In a stricter sense, a term including every mode of acquisition of estate known to the law, except that by which an heir on the death of his ancestor becomes substituted in his place as owner by operation of law. 2 Washb. Real Prop. 401.

There are six ways of acquiring a title by purchase, namely: By deed; by devise; by execution; by prescription; by possession or occupancy; by escheat. In its more limited sense, "purchase" is applied only to such acquisitions of lands as are obtained by way of bargain and sale for money or some other valuable consideration. Cruise, Dig. tit. 30, §§ 1-4; 1 Dall. (Pa.) 20. In common parlance, purchase signifies the buying of real estate and of goods and chattels.

PURCHASE MONEY. The consideration in money which is agreed to be paid by a purchaser.

PURCHASE MONEY MORTGAGE. A mortgage given on the purchase of land by the purchaser to the vendor to secure the payment of the purchase money, or the unpaid balance thereof.

PURCHASE, WORDS OF. Those by which, taken absolutely, without reference to or connection with any other words, an estate first attaches, or is considered as commencing in point of title, in the person described by them, such as the words "son," "daughter." Words which create a title in certain persons, as distinguished from those which merely limit or define the quantum of estate. See "Shelley's Case, Rule in."

PURCHASER. A buyer; a vendee. The term is applied indifferently to persons acquiring, by purchase, either realty or personalty, but in the interest of exact nomenclature it should be applied only with respect to the sale of realty; "buyer" being the appropriate term for one who obtains personalty by sale.

PURCHASER OF A NOTE OR BILL. The person who buys a promissory note or bill of exchange from the holder without his indorsement. Bayley, Bills, 370.

PURE DEBT. In Scotch law. A debt actually due, in contradistinction to one which is to become due at a future day certain, which is called a "future debt," and one due provisionally, in a certain event, which is called a "contingent debt." 1 Bell, Comm. (5th Ed.) 315.

PURE OBLIGATION. One which is not suspended by any condition, whether it has been contracted without any condition, or, when thus contracted, the condition has been performed. Poth. Obl. note 176.

PURE PLEA. In equity pleading. One which relies wholly on some matter dehors the bill; as, for example, a plea of a release on a settled account.

Pleas not pure are so called in contradistinction to pure pleas. They are sometimes also denominated "negative pleas." 4 Bouv. Inst. note 4275.

PURE VILLENAGE. A base tenure, where a man holds upon terms of doing whatsoever is commanded of him, nor knows in the evening what is to be done in the morning, and is always bound to an uncertain service. 1 Steph. Comm. (7th Ed.) 188.

PURGATION (Lat. *purgo;* from *purum* and *ago*, to make clean). The clearing one's self of an offense charged, by denying the guilt on oath or affirmation.

Canonical purgation was the act of justifying one's self, when accused of some offense, in the presence of a number of persons worthy of credit, generally twelve, who would swear they believed the accused. See "Compurgator."

Vulgar purgation consisted in superstitious trials by hot and cold water, by fire, by hot irons, by battle, by corsned, etc.

In modern times, a man may purge himself of an offense in some cases where the facts are within his own knowledge; for example, when a man is charged with a contempt of court, he may purge himself of such contempt by swearing that in doing the act charged he did not intend to commit a contempt.

PURGED OF PARTIAL COUNSEL. In Scotland, every witness, before making oath or affirmation, is "purged of partial counsel," *i. e.*, cleared by examination on oath of having instigated the plea, of having been present with the party for whom he testifies at consultations of lawyers, where it might be shown what was necessary to be proved, or of having acted as his agent in any of the proceedings. So, in a criminal case, he who is agent of prosecutor, or who tampers with the panel, cannot be heard to testify, because of "partial counsel." Stair, Inst. p. 768, § 9; Bell, Dict. "Partial Counsel."

PURGING A TORT. This is like the ratification of a wrongful act by a person who has power of himself to lawfully do the act; but, unlike ratification, the purging of the tort may take place even after commencement of the action. 1 Brod. & B. 282.

PURGING CONTEMPT. See "Purgation."

PURLIEU. In English law. A space of land near a forest, known by certain boundaries, which was formerly part of a forest, but which has been separated from it.

The history of purlieus is this: Henry II., on taking possession of the throne, manifested so great a taste for forests that he enlarged the old ones wherever he could, and by this means enclosed many estates which had no outlet to the public roads; and things increased in this way until the reign of King John, when the public reclamations were so great that much of this land was disforested,—that is, no longer had the privileges of the forests; and the land thus separated bore the name of "purlieu."

PURLIEU MEN. Those who have ground within the purlieu to the yearly value of 40s. a year freehold are licensed to hunt in their own purlieus. Manw. For. Law, c. 20, § 8.

PURPARTY. That part of an estate which, having been held in common by parceners, is by partition allotted to any of them. To make purparty is to divide and sever the lands which fall to parceners. Old Nat. Brev. 11.

PURPORT. In pleading. The substance of a writing as it appears on the face of it to the eye that reads it. It differs from tenor (*q. v.*) 2 Russ. Crimes, 365; 1 East, 179; and therefore, where the instrument is stated according to its tenor, the purport of it must necessarily appear. 9 Yerg. (Tenn.) 394.

To "purport" means "to intend to show; to intend; to mean; to signify." 39 Ill. App. 594.

PURPOSE. Something intended to be done. 22 Q. B. D. 296.

PURPRESTURE. An inclosure by a private individual of a part of a common or public domain.

According to Lord Coke, purpresture is a close or inclosure, that is, when one encroaches or makes several to himself that which ought to be in common to many; as, if an individual were to build between high and low water mark on the side of a public river. In England this is a nuisance, and in cases of this kind an injunction will be granted, on *ex parte* affidavits, to restrain such a purpresture and nuisance. 2 Bouv. Inst. note 2382; 4 Bouv. Inst. note 3798; 2 Inst. 28. And see Skene de Verb. Sign.; Glanv. lib. 9, c. 11. p. 239, note; Spelman; Hale de Port Mar.; Harg. Tr. 84; 2 Anstr. 606; Callis, Sew. 174.

PURPRISUM (Law Lat.; from Law Fr. *pourpris*, an inclosure). In old records. A close or inclosure. Cowell.

The whole compass of a manor. Cowell.

PURQ' (Law Fr. wherefore). A word used in old practice, at the end of pleas, arguments, and judgments. Very common in the Year Books. *Purq', pur defaut de r'ns, no' d'dons judgt, et prions nos dam'*, wherefore, for want of an answer, we demand judgment and pray our damages. The clause is sometimes abbreviated, *purq', etc.*

PURSER. The person appointed by the master of a ship or vessel, whose duty it is to take care of the ship's books, in which everything on board is inserted, as well the names of mariners as the articles of merchandise shipped. Roccius, Ins. note.

PURSUE (from Lat. *persequi*). To follow a matter judicially, as a complaining party. In Scotch law, to prosecute criminally. 3 How. St. Tr. 425.

PURSUER. The name by which the complainant or plaintiff is known in the ecclesiastical courts. 3 Ecc. 350.

PURUS (Lat.) In old English law. Pure; clear; simple; free of any qualification or condition. *Donationum quaedam libera et pura, et quaedam sub conditione vel sub modo*, of gifts, one kind is free and pure, and another under a condition or qualification. Bracton, fol. 11b.

Absolute. *Purus idiota*, a clear or absolute idiot. 1 Bl. Comm. 303.

PURVEYANCE (Law Fr. and Eng.; from *pourvoire*, to provide. In old English law. A providing of necessaries for the king's house. Cowell. A buying at the king's price. Hale, Anal. § viii. See "Pourveyance."

PURVEYOR. One employed in procuring provisions. See Code, 1. 34.

PURVIEW. That part of an act of the legislature which begins with the words, "Be it enacted," etc., and ends before the repealing clause. Cooke (Tenn.) 330; 3 Bibb (Ky.) 181. According to Cowell, this word also signifies a conditional gift or grant. It is said to be derived from the French *pourvu*, provided. It always implies a condition.

PUT.

——**In Pleading.** To select; to demand; as, "the said C. D. puts himself upon the country;" that is, he selects the trial by jury as the mode of settling the matter in dispute, and does not rely upon an issue in law. Gould, Pl. c. 6, pt. 1, § 19.

——**In Mercantile Usage.** A term of the stock markets, signifying an option to sell to another certain goods within a specified time, at a specified price. See "Gambling Contract."

PUT IN SUIT. Applied to a chose in action, to sue on.

PUT IN URE. In old statutes. To put in practice or effect; to carry into effect. Sometimes written to "put in use."

PUT OUT. To open. To put out lights; to open or cut windows. 11 East, 372.

PUT UPON (Law Lat. *ponere super*). In practice. To rest upon; to submit to; as a defendant "puts himself upon the country."

PUTATIVE. Reputed to be that which is not. The word is frequently used; as, putative father, putative marriage, putative wife, and the like. And Toullier (Dr. Civ. tom. 7, note 29) uses the words putative owner, *proprietaire putatif*. Lord Kames uses the same expression (Eq. 391).

PUTATIVE FATHER. The reputed father. This term is most usually applied to the father of a bastard child.

PUTATIVE MARRIAGE. In the civil law. A marriage which is forbidden, but which has been contracted in good faith and ignorance of the impediment on the part of at least one of the contracting parties.

PUTEUS. (Lat.) In old English law. A well. Fleta, lib. 4, c. 27, § 8.

PUTS AND CALLS. See "Gambling Contract."

PUTTING IN FEAR. The causing of such reasonable apprehension of death or serious injury as will excuse the person so threatened from running the risk of incurring the same by resistance to unlawful aggression. In the crime of robbery, such putting in fear is accounted constructive violence. The fear inspired to compel a man to surrender his property may be of injury to his person (2 East, P. C. 712), or to his property (Id. 729). Fear of injury to character or reputation is not sufficient (7 Humph. [Tenn.] 45, 12 Ga. 293), with the single exception of a threat to accuse of an unnatural crime (1 Car. & P. 479).

PUTURE. A custom claimed by keepers in forests, and sometimes by bailiffs of hundreds, to take man's meat, horse's meat, and dog's meat of the tenants and inhabitants within the perambulation of the forest, hundred, etc. The land subject to this custom was called *"terra putura."* Others, who call it *"pulture,"* explain it as a demand in general, and derive it from the monks, who, before they were admitted, *pulsabant*, knocked at the gates for several days together. 4 Inst. 307; Cowell.

PYKERIE (Scotch). In old Scotch law. Petty theft. 2 Pitc. Crim. Tr. 43.

PYRAMIDING. See "Gambling Contract."

Q

Q. A letter used in the Roman law, in various abbreviations. An abbreviation used in writing out decrees of the senate. Tayl. Civ. Law, 576. Calv. Lex.

Q. C. An abbreviation of "queen's counsel" (*q. v.*)

Q. C. F. An abbreviation of *quare clausum fregit*. See "Trespass."

Q. V. *Quod vide*, which see. Used after the mention of a title, chapter, etc., to refer the reader thereto.

QAR (Law Fr.) For Fet. Assaver, § 45,

Q'D. A contraction of *quod*, in old pleading. 1 Inst. Cler. 12.

QUA. As; in the character or capacity of. "The judge *qua* judge cannot know." Vaughan, 147.

QUACK. One who, without sufficient knowledge, study, or previous preparation, undertakes to practice medicine or surgery, under the pretense that he possesses secrets in those arts.

The origin of the word "quack" is not clearly ascertained. Johnson derives it from the words "to quack," or gabble like a goose. Butler uses this verb as descriptive of the encomiums empirics heap upon their nostrums. Thus, in Hudibras, "To quack of universal cures."

The Egyptian hieroglyphic for a doctor was a duck, and it has been a question whether this may not form a clue to the derivation of the word "quack." The English quack—or "quacksalber," as it was originally written—is from the German *quacksalber*, or rather the Dutch *kwaksalver*, which Bilderdyk states should be more properly *kwabsalver*, from *kwab*, a wen, and *zalver*, to salve or anoint. 5 Notes & Queries.

QUACUNQUE VIA DATA (Lat.) Whichever way you take it; in whichever view of the case. 2 Burrows, 980; 2 Gall. (U. S.) 26.

QUADRAGESIMA (Lat.) The fortieth. The first Sunday in Lent is so called because it is about the fortieth day before Easter. Cowell.

QUADRAGESMS. The third volume of the Year Books of the reign of Edward III. So called, because beginning with the fortieth year of the reign. Crabb, Hist. Eng. Law, 327; Hale, Hist. Com. Law, c. 8.

QUADRANS (Lat.)

——**In Civil Law.** The fourth part of the whole. Hence the heir *ex quadrante;* that is to say, of the fourth part of the whole.

——**In Old English Law.** A farthing; a fourth part or quarter of a penny.

Before the reign of Edward I. the smallest coin was a sterling or silver penny marked with a cross or traverse strokes, by the guidance of which a penny, upon occasion, might be cut in halves for a half penny, or into quarters for farthings or fourth parts, till, to avoid the fraud of unequally cutting, King Edward I., A. D. 1279, coined half pence and farthings in round distinct pieces. Cowell; Spelman, voc. "Denarius," citing Stow, p. 306, where some curious old verses are given.

QUADRANT. In angular measures, a quadrant is equal to ninety degrees. See "Measure."

QUADRANTALIS (Law Lat.; from *quadrans, q. v.*) In old English law. Of the value or price of a quarter or farthing. *Panis quadrantalis*, the farthing loaf. Fleta, lib. 2, c. 9. Britton, in the parallel passage, has the word *ferlinges*. Britt. c. 30. But the word is not taken notice of either by Spelman or Cowell.

QUADRANTATA TERRAE (Law Lat.) The fourth part of an acre, according to Cowell. But Spelman makes it to be the fourth part of a yard land. Spelman voc. "Fardella."

QUADRARIUM (Law Lat.) In old records. A quarry or stone pit. Par. Ant. 208; Cowell.

QUADRIENNIUM (Lat. from *quatuor*, four, and *annus*, year). The four years' course of studying the civil law, before arriving at the code or imperial constitutions. Inst. proem; Tayl. Civ. Law, 39.

QUADRIENNIUM UTILE (Lat.) In Scotch law. The four years of a minor between his age of twenty-one and twenty-five years are so called. During this period he is permitted to impeach contracts made against his interest previous to his arriving at the age of twenty-one years. Ersk. Inst. 1. 7. 19. 35; 1 Bell, Comm. (5th Ed.) 135.

QUADRIPARTITE (Lat.) Having four parts, or divided into four parts; as, this indenture *quadripartite*, made between A. B., of the one part, C. D., of the second part, E. F., of the third part, and G. H., of the fourth part.

QUADROON. A person who is descended from a white person and another person who has an equal mixture of the European and African blood. 2 Bailey (S. C.) 558. See "Mulatto."

QUADRUPLICATION. In pleading. Formerly this word was used instead of "surrebutter." 1 Brown, Civ. Law, 469, note.

QUAE AB HOSTIBUS CAPIUNTUR, STAtim capientium fiunt. Things taken from public enemies immediately become the property of the captors. Inst. 2. 1. 17; Grotius de Jure Belli, lib. 3, c. 6, § 12.

QUAE AB INITIO INUTILIS FUIT INstitutio, ex post facto convalescere non potest. An institution void in the beginning cannot acquire validity from after-matter. Dig. 50. 17. 210.

QUAE AB INITIO NON VALENT, EX post facto convalescere non possunt. Things invalid from the beginning cannot be made valid by subsequent act. Tray. Lat. Max. 482.

QUAE ACCESSIORIUM LOCUM OBTInent, extinguuntur cum principales res peremptae fuerint. When the principal is destroyed, those things which are accessory to it are also destroyed. Poth. Obl. pt. 3, c. 6, art. 4; Dig. 33. 8. 2; Broom, Leg. Max. (3d London Ed.) 439.

QUAE AD UNUM FINEM LOQUUTA sunt, non debent ad alium detorqueri. Words spoken to one end ought not to be perverted to another. 4 Coke, 14.

QUAE COHAERENT PERSONAE A PERsona separari nequeunt. Things which belong to the person ought not to be separated from the person. Jenk. Cent. Cas. 28.

QUAE COMMUNI LEGI DEROGANT stricte interpretantur. Laws which derogate from the common law ought to be strictly construed. Jenk. Cent. Cas. 221.

QUAE CONTRA RATIONEM JURIS INtroducta sunt, non debent trahi in consequentiam. Things introduced contrary to the reason of the law ought not to be drawn into precedents. 12 Coke, 75.

QUAE DUBITATIONIS CAUSA TOLLENdae inseruntur communem legem non laedunt. Whatever is inserted for the purpose of removing doubt does not hurt or affect the common law. Co. Litt. 205.

QUAE DUBITATIONIS TOLLENDAE causa contractibus inseruntur, jus commune non laedunt. Particular clauses inserted in agreements to avoid doubts and ambiguity do not prejudice the common law. Dig. 50. 17. 81.

QUAE EST EADEM (Lat. which is the same). In pleading. A clause containing a statement that the trespass, or other fact mentioned in the plea, is the same as that laid in the declaration, where from the circumstances there is an apparent difference between the two. 1 Chit. Pl. 473; Gould, Pl. c. 3, §§ 79, 80; 29 Vt. 455.

The form is as follows: "Which are the same assaulting, beating, and ill-treating, the said John, in the said declaration mentioned, and whereof the said John hath above thereof complained against the said James." See 1 Saund. 14, 208, note 2; 2 Saund. 5a, note 3; Archb. Civ. Pl. 217; Comyn, Dig. "Pleader" (E 31); Cro. Jac. 372; 1 Chit. Pl. 473.

QUAE IN CURIA ACTA SUNT RITE AGI praesumuntur. Whatever is done in court is presumed to be rightly done. 3 Bulst. 43.

QUAE IN PARTES DIVIDI NEQUEUNT solida, a singulis praestantur. Things (i. e., services and rents) which cannot be divided into parts are rendered entire by each severally. 6 Coke, 1.

QUAE IN TESTAMENTO ITA SUNT scripta ut intelligi non possunt, perinde sunt ac si scripta non essent. Things which are so written in a will that they cannot be understood are as if they had not been written. Dig. 50. 17. 73. 3.

QUAE INCONTINENTER VEL CERTO fiunt in esse videntur. Whatever things are done at once and certainly appear part of the same transaction. Co. Litt. 236.

QUAE INTER ALIOS ACTA SUNT NEMini nocere debent, sed prodesse possunt. Transactions between strangers may benefit, but cannot injure, persons who are parties to them. 6 Coke, 1.

QUAE LEGI COMMUNI DEROGANT NON sunt trahenda in exemplum. Things derogatory to the common law are not to be drawn into precedent. Branch, Princ.

QUAE LEGI COMMUNI DEROGANT stricte interpretantur. Those things which derogate from the common law are to be construed strictly. Jenk. Cent. Cas. 29.

QUAE MALA SUNT INCHOATA IN principio vix bono peragantur exitu. Things bad in the commencement seldom end well. 4 Coke, 2.

QUAE NIHIL FRUSTRA. (Law Lat.) Which (does or requires) nothing in vain; which requires nothing to be done, that is to no purpose. 2 Kent, Comm. 53.

QUAE NON FIERI DEBENT, FACTA VAlent. Things which ought not to be done are held valid when they have been done. Tray. Lat. Max. 484.

QUAE NON VALEANT SINGULA, JUNCta juvant. Things which may not avail singly, when united have an effect. 3 Bulst. 132.

QUAE PLURA (Law Lat. what more). In old English practice. A writ which lay where an inquisition had been made by an escheator in any county of such lands or tenements as any man died seised of, and all that was in his possession was imagined not to be found by the office; the writ commanding the escheator to inquire what more (*quae plura*) lands and tenements the party held on the day when he died, etc. Fitzh. Nat. Brev. 255a; Reg. Orig. 293; Cowell.

QUAE PRAETER CONSUETUDINEM ET morem majorum fiunt, neque placent, neque recta videntur. What is done contrary to the custom and usage of our ancestors, neither pleases nor appears right. 4 Coke, 78.

QUAE PROPTER NECESSITATEM RE-cepta sunt, non debent in argumentum trahi. Things which are tolerated on account of necessity ought not to be drawn into precedent. Dig. 50. 17. 162.

QUAE RERUM NATURA PROHIBEN-tur, nulla lege confirmata sunt. What is prohibited in the nature of things can be confirmed by no law. Finch, Law, 74.

QUAE SINGULA NON PROSUNT, JUNC-ta juvant. Things which, taken singly, are of no avail, afford help when taken together. Tray. Lat. Max. 486.

QUAE SUNT MINORIS CULPAE SUNT majoris infamiae. Things which are of the smaller guilt are of the greater infamy. Co. Litt. 6.

QUAECUNQUE INTRA RATIONEM LE-gis inveniuntur, intra legem ipsam esse judicantur. Whatever appears within the reason of the law is considered within the law itself. 2 Inst. 689.

QUAELIBET CONCESSIO DOMINI RE-gis capi debet stricte contra dominum regem, quando potest intelligi duabus viis. Every grant of our lord the king ought to be taken strictly against our lord the king, when it can be understood in two ways. 3 Leon. 243.

QUAELIBET CONCESSIO FORTISSIME contra donatorem interpretanda est. Every grant is to be taken most strongly against the grantor. Co. Litt. 183a.

QUAELIBET JURISDICTIO CANCEL-los suos habet. Every jurisdiction has its bounds. Jenk. Cent. Cas. 139.

QUAELIBET PARDONATIO DEBET CA-pi secundum intentionem regis, et non ad deceptionem regis. Every pardon ought to be taken according to the intention of the king, and not to the deception of the king. 3 Bulst. 14.

QUAELIBET POENA CORPORALIS, quamvis minima, major est qualibet poena pecuniaria. Every corporal punishment, although the very least, is greater than any pecuniary punishment. 3 Inst. 220.

QUAERAS DE DUBIIS, LEGEM BENE discere si vis. Inquire into doubtful points if you wish to understand the law well. Litt. § 443.

QUAERE (Lat.) In practice. A word frequently used to denote that an inquiry ought to be made of a doubtful thing. 2 Lilly, Abr. 406.

QUAERE DE DUBIIS, QUIA PER RATIO-nes pervenitur ad legitimam rationem. Inquire into doubtful points, because by reasoning we arrive at legal reason. Litt. § 377.

QUAERENS. In old practice. A plaintiff; the plaintiff.

QUAERENS NON INVENIT PLEGIUM (Lat.) In practice. The plaintiff has not found pledge. The return made by the sheriff to a writ directed to him with this clause, namely, *Si A facerit B securem de clamore suo prosequando*, when the plaintiff has neglected to find sufficient security. Fitzh. Nat. Brev. 38.

QUAERERE DAT SAPERE QUAE SUNT legitima vere. To investigate is the way to know what things are really lawful. Litt. § 443.

QUAESTIO (Lat.) In Roman law. A sort of commission (*ad quaerendum*) to inquire into some criminal matter given to a magistrate or citizen, who was called *quaesitor* or *quaestor*, who made report thereon to the senate or the people, as the one or the other appointed him. In progress of time he was empowered (with the assistance of a counsel) to adjudge the case, and the tribunal thus constituted was called *quaestio*.

This special tribunal continued in use until the end of the Roman republic, although it was resorted to, during the last times of the republic, only in extraordinary cases.

The manner in which they were constituted was this: If the matter to be inquired of was within the jurisdiction of the *comitia*, the senate, on the demand of the consul, or of a tribune, or of one of its members, declared by a decree that there was cause to prosecute a citizen. Then the consul *ex auctoritate senatus* asked the people in *comitia* (*rogabat rogatio*) to enact this decree into a law. The *comitia* adopted it, either simply or with amendment, or they rejected it.

The increase of population and of crimes rendered this method, which was tardy at best, onerous, and even impracticable. In the year 149 B. C., under the consulship of Censorinus and Manilius, the tribune Calpurnius Piso procured the passage of a law establishing a *questio perpetua*, to take cognizance of the crime of extortion committed by Roman magistrates against strangers *de pecuniis repetundis*. Cicero, Brut. 27; Cicero de Off. ii. 21; Cicero in Verr. iv. 25.

Many such tribunals were afterwards established, such as *quaestiones de majestate, de ambitu, de peculatu, de vi, de sodalitiis*, etc. Each was composed of a certain number of judges taken from the senators, and presided over by a *praetor*, although he might delegate his authority to a public officer, who was called *judex quaestionis*. These tribunals continued a year only; for the meaning of the word *perpetuus* is (*non interruptus*), not interrupted during the term of its appointed duration.

The establishment of these *quaestiones* deprived the *comitia* of their criminal jurisdiction, except the crime of treason. They were, in fact, the depositories of the judicial power during the sixth and seventh centuries of the Roman republic, the last of which was remarkable for civil dissensions, and replete with great public transactions. Without some knowledge of the constitution of the *quaestio perpetua*, it is impossible to understand the forensic speeches of Cicero, or even the political history of that age. But when Julius Caesar, as dictator, sat for the trial of Ligarius, the ancient constitution of the republic was, in fact, destroyed, and the criminal tribunals, which had existed in more or less vigor and purity until then, existed no longer but in name. Under Augustus, the concentration of the triple power of the consuls, proconsuls, and tribunes in his person transferred to him, as of course, all judicial powers and authorities.

QUAESTIONES PERPETUAE. In the Roman law. Commissions (or courts) of inquisition into crimes alleged to have been committed. They were called "*perpetuae*," to distinguish them from "occasional" inquisitions, and because they were permanent courts for the trial of offenders. Brown.

QUAESTOR (Lat.) The name of a magistrate of ancient Rome.

QUAESTORES CLASSICI (Lat.) In Roman law. Officers intrusted with the care of the public money.

Their duties consisted in making the necessary payments from the *aerarium*, and receiving the public revenues. Of both they had to keep correct accounts in their *tabulae publicae*. Demands which any one might have on the *aerarium*, and outstanding debts, were likewise registered by them. Fines to be paid to the public treasury were registered and exacted by them. They were likewise to provide proper accommodations for foreign ambassadors and such persons as were connected with the republic by ties of public hospitality. Lastly, they were charged with the care of the burials and monuments of distinguished men, the expenses for which had been decreed by the senate to be paid by the treasury. Their number at first was confined to two, but this was afterwards increased as the empire became extended. There were *quaestores* of cities and of provinces, and *quaestores* of the army; the latter were in fact paymasters.

QUAESTORES PARRICIDII (Lat.) In Roman law. Public accusers, two in number, who conducted the accusation of persons guilty of murder or any other capital offense, and carried the sentence into execution. They ceased to be appointed at an early period. Smith.

QUAESTUS. That estate which a man has by acquisition or purchase, in contradistinction to "*haereditas*," which is what he has by descent. Glanv. 1, 7, c. 1.

QUALE JUS (Lat.) In old English law. A judicial writ, which lay where a man of religion had judgment to recover land before execution was made of the judgment. It went forth to the escheator between judgment and execution, to inquire what right the religious person had to recover, or whether the judgment were obtained by the collusion of the parties, to the intent that the lord might not be defrauded. Reg. Jud. 8.

QUALIFICATION. Having the requisite qualities for a thing; as, to be president of the United States, the candidate must possess certain qualifications.

The natural endowment or acquirement which fits a person for a place, office, or employment. See 4 Wall. (U. S.) 319.

QUALIFIED ELECTOR. One entitled to vote.

QUALIFIED FEE. One which has a qualification subjoined to it, and which must be determined whenever the qualification annexed to it is at an end. A limitation to a man and "his heirs on the part of his father" affords an example of this species of estate. Litt. § 254; 2 Bouv. Inst. note 1695.

QUALIFIED INDORSEMENT. A transfer of a bill of exchange or promissory note to an indorsee, without any liability to the indorser. The words usually employed for this purpose are *sans recours*, without recourse. 1 Bouv. Inst. note 1138.

QUALIFIED PROPERTY. Property not in its nature permanent, but which may sometimes subsist and at other times not subsist. A defeasible and precarious ownership, which lasts as long as the thing is in actual use and occupation; *e. g.*, first, property in animals *ferae naturae*, or in light, or air, where the qualified property arises from the nature of the thing; second, property in a thing held by any one as a bailee, where the qualified property arises not from the nature of the thing, but from the peculiar circumstances under which it is held. 2 Bl. Comm. 391, 395*; 2 Kent, Comm. 347; 2 Wooddeson, Lect. 385.

Any ownership not absolute.

QUALITAS QUAE INESSE DEBET, FAcile praesumitur. A quality which ought to form a part is easily presumed.

QUALITER (Lat.) In what manner. A word used in old writs. Fleta, lib. 2, c. 64, § 19.

QUALITY.

——**Of Persons.** The state or condition of a person.

Two contrary qualities cannot be in the same person at the same time. Dig. 41, 10. 4. Every one is presumed to know the quality of the person with whom he is contracting. In the United States the people happily are all upon an equality in their civil rights.

——**In Pleading.** That which distinguishes one thing from another of the same kind.

QUALITY OF ESTATE. The period when, and the manner in which, the right of enjoying an estate is exercised. It is of two kinds: (1) The period when the right of enjoying an estate is conferred upon the owner, whether at present or in future; and (2) the manner in which the owner's right of enjoyment of his estate is to be exercised, whether solely, jointly, in common, or in coparcenary. Wharton.

QUAM LONGUM DEBET ESSE "RATIOnabile tempus," non definitur in lege, sed pendet ex discretione justiciariorum. What is "reasonable time" the law does not define; it is left to the discretion of the judges. Co. Litt. 56. See 11 Coke, 44.

QUAM RATIONABILIS DEBET ESSE finis, non definitur, sed omnibus circumstantiis inspectis pendet ex justiciariorum discretione. What a reasonable fine ought to be is not defined, but is left to the discretion of the judges, all the circumstances being considered. 11 Coke, 44.

QUAMDIU (Lat.) As long as; so long as. A word of limitation in old conveyances. Co. Litt. 235a; 10 Coke, 41b; Shep. Touch. 125.

QUAMDIU SE BENE GESSERIT (Lat. as long as he shall behave himself well). A clause inserted in commissions, when such instruments were written in Latin, to signify the tenure by which the officer held his office.

QUAMVIS ALIQUID PER SE NON SIT malum, tamen si sit mali exempli, non est faciendum. Although in itself a thing may not be bad, yet if it holds out a bad example it is not to be done. 2 Inst. 564.

QUAMVIS LEX GENERALITER LOQUItur, restringenda tamen est, ut cessante ratione et ipsa cessat. Although the law speaks generally, it is to be restrained, since when the reason on which it is founded fails, it fails. 4 Inst. 330.

QUANDO ABEST PROVISIO PARTIS, adest provisio legis. When a provision of the party is lacking, the provision of the law is at hand. 13 C. B. 960.

QUANDO ACCIDERINT (Lat. when they fall in). In practice. When a defendant, executor or administrator, pleads *plene administravit,* the plaintiff may pray to have judgment of assets *quando acciderint.* Buller, N. P. 169; Bac. Abr. "Executor" (M).

By taking a judgment in this form, the plaintiff admits that the defendant has fully administered to that time. 1 Pet. C. C. (U. S.) 442, note. See 11 Viner, Abr. 379; Comyn, Dig. "Pleader" (2 D. 9).

QUANDO ALIQUID CONCEDITUR, CONceditur id sine quo illud fieri non possit. When anything is granted, that also is granted without which it cannot be of effect. 9 Barb. (N. Y.) 516, 518; 10 Barb. (N. Y.) 354, 359.

QUANDO ALIQUID MANDATUR, MANdatur et omne per quod pervenitur ad illud. When anything is commanded, everything by which it can be accomplished is also commanded. 5 Coke, 116. See 7 C. B. 886; 14 C. B. 107; 6 Exch. 886, 889; 10 Exch. 449; 2 El. & Bl. 301; Story, Ag. (4th Ed.) 110, 179, 242, 299; Broom, Leg. Max. (3d London Ed.) 431.

QUANDO ALIQUID PER SE NON SIT malum, tamen si sit mali exempli, non est faciendum. When anything by itself is not evil, and yet may be an example for evil, it is not to be done. 2 Inst. 564.

QUANDO ALIQUID PROHIBETUR EX directo, prohibetur et per obliquum. When anything is prohibited directly, it is also prohibited indirectly. Co. Litt. 223.

QUANDO ALIQUID PROHIBETUR, PROhibetur omne per quod devenitur ad illud. When anything is prohibited, everything by which it is reached is prohibited. 2 Inst. 48; Broom, Leg. Max. (3d London Ed.) 432; Wingate, Max. 618. See 7 Clark & F. 509, 546; 4 Barn. & C. 187, 193; 2 Term R. 251, 252; 8 Term R. 301, 415; 15 Mees. & W. 7; 11 Wend. (N. Y.) 329.

QUANDO ALIQUIS ALIQUID CONCEDit, concedere videtur et id sine quo res uti non potest. When a person grants a thing, he is supposed to grant that also without which the thing cannot be used. 3 Kent, Comm. 421.

QUANDO CHARTA CONTINET GENERalem clausulam, posteaque descendit ad verba specialia quae clausulae generali sunt consentanea, interpretanda est charta secundum verba specialia. When a deed contains a general clause, and afterwards descends to special words, consistent with the general clause, the deed is to be construed according to the special words. 8 Coke, 154.

QUANDO DE UNA ET EADEM RE, DUO onerabiles existunt, unus, pro insufficientia alterius, de integro, onerabitur. When two persons are liable concerning one and the same thing, if one makes default, the other must bear the whole. 2 Inst. 277.

QUANDO DISPOSITIO REFERRI POtest ad duas res, ita quod secundum rela-

tionem unam vitiatur et secundum alteram utilis sit, tum facienda est relatio ad illam ut valeat dispositio. When a disposition may be made to refer to two things, so that, according to one reference, it would be vitiated, and by the other it would be made effectual, such a reference must be made that the disposition shall have effect. 6 Coke, 76b.

QUANDO DIVERSI DESIDERANTUR actus ad aliquem statum perficiendum, plus respicit lex actum originalem. When different acts are required to the formation of an estate, the law chiefly regards the original act. 10 Coke, 49.

QUANDO DUO JURA CONCURRUNT IN una persona, aequum est ac si essent in diversis. When two rights concur in one person, it is the same as if they were in two separate persons. 4 Coke, 118.

QUANDO JUS DOMINI REGIS ET SUBditi concurrunt jus regis praeferri debet. When the right of the sovereign and of the subject concur, the right of the sovereign ought to be preferred. 1 Coke, 129; Co. Litt. 30b; Broom, Leg. Max. (3d London Ed.) 66.

QUANDO LEX ALIQUID ALICUI CONCEdit, concedere videtur id sine quo res ipsa esse non potest. When the law gives anything, it gives the means of obtaining it. 5 Coke, 47; 3 Kent, Comm. 421.

QUANDO LEX ALIQUID ALICUI CONcedit, omnia incidentia tacite conceduntur. When the law gives anything, it gives tacitly what is incident to it. 2 Inst. 326; Hob. 234.

QUANDO LEX ALIQUID ALIQUO CONcedit, conceditur et id sine qua res ipsa esse non potest. When the law grants a thing to any one, it grants that also without which the thing itself cannot exist. 15 Barb. (N. Y.) 153, 160.

QUANDO LEX EST SPECIALIS, RATIO autem generalis, generaliter lex est intelligenda. When the law is special, but its reason is general, the law is to be understood generally. 2 Inst. 83; 10 Coke, 101.

QUANDO LICET ID QUOD MAJUS, VIDEtur licere id quod minus. When the greater is allowed, the less seems to be allowed also. Shep. Touch. 429.

QUANDO MULIER NOBILIS NUPSERIT ignobili, desinit esse nobilis nisi nobilitas nativa fuerit. When a noble woman marries a man not noble, she ceases to be noble, unless her nobility was born with her. 4 Coke, 118.

QUANDO PLUS FIT QUAM FIERI DEbet, videtur etiam illud fieri quod faciendum est. When more is done than ought to be done, that too shall be considered as performed which should have been performed; as, if a man, having a power to make a lease for ten years, make one for twenty years, it shall be void only for the surplus. Broom, Leg. Max. (3d London Ed.) 166; 5 Coke, 115; 8 Coke, 85a.

QUANDO QUOD AGO NON VALET UT ago, valeat quantum valere potest. When that which I do does not have effect as I do it, let it have as much effect as it can. 16 Johns. (N. Y.) 172, 178; 3 Barb. Ch. (N. Y.) 242, 261.

QUANDO RES NON VALET UT AGO, valeat quantum valere potest. When a thing is of no force as I do it, it shall have as much as it can have. Cowp. 600; Broom, Leg. Max. (3d London Ed.) 483; 2 Smith, Lead. Cas. 294; 6 East, 105; 1 Vent. 216; 1 H. Bl. 614, 620.

QUANDO VERBA ET MENS CONgruunt, non est interpretationi locus. When the words and the mind agree, there is no place for interpretation.

QUANDO VERBA STATUTI SUNT SPEcialia, ratio autem generalis, generaliter statutum est intelligendum. When the words of a statute are special, but the reason or object of it general, the statute is to be construed generally. 10 Coke, 101b.

QUANTI MINORIS (Lat.) The name of a particular action in Louisiana. An action *quanti minoris* is one brought for the reduction of the price of a thing sold, in consequence of defects in the thing which is the object of the sale.

Such action must be commenced within twelve months from the date of the sale, or from the time within which the defect became known to the purchaser. 3 Mart. (La.; N. S.) 287; 11 Mart. (La.) 11.

QUANTITY. In pleading. That which is susceptible of measure.

It is a general rule that, when the declaration alleges an injury to goods and chattels, or any contract relating to them, their quantity should be stated. Gould, Pl. c. 4, § 35. And in actions for the recovery of real estate, the quantity of the land should be specified. Bracton, 431a; 11 Coke, 25b, 55a; Doct. Plac. 85, 86; 1 East, 441; 8 East, 357; 13 East, 102; Steph. Pl. 314, 315.

QUANTUM DAMNIFICATUS (Lat.) In equity practice. An issue directed by a court of equity to be tried in a court of law, to ascertain by a trial before a jury the amount of damages suffered by the nonperformance of some collateral undertaking which a penalty has been given to secure. When such damages have thus been ascertained, the court will grant relief upon their payment. 4 Bouv. Inst. note 3913.

QUANTUM MERUIT (Lat.) In pleading. As much as he has deserved.

When a person employs another to do work for him, without any agreement as to his compensation, the law implies a promise from the employer to the workman that he will pay him for his services as much as he may deserve or merit. In such case, the plaintiff may suggest in his declaration that the defendant promised to pay him as much as he reasonably deserved, and then aver that his trouble was worth such a sum of money, which the defendant has omitted to pay. This is called an *assumpsit* on a *quantum meruit.* 2 Bl. Comm. 162, 163; 1 Viner, Abr. 346; 2 Phil. Ev. 82.

QUANTUM TENENS DOMINO EX HOmagio, tantum dominus tenenti ex dominio debet praeter solam reverentiam; mutua debet esse dominii et homagii fidelitatis connexio. As much as the tenant by his homage owes to his lord, so much is the lord, by his lordship, indebted to the tenant, except reverence alone; the tie of dominion and of homage ought to be mutual. Co. Litt. 64.

QUANTUM VALEBAT (Lat. as much as it was worth). In pleading. When goods are sold without specifying any price, the law implies a promise from the buyer to the seller that he will pay him for them as much as they were worth.

The plaintiff may, in such case, suggest in his declaration that the defendant promised to pay him as much as the said goods were worth, and then aver that they were worth so much, which the defendant has refused to pay. See the authorities cited under the article "Quantum Meruit."

QUARANTINE

——**In Maritime Law.** The space of forty days, or less, during which the crew of a ship or vessel coming from a port or place infected or supposed to be infected with disease are required to remain on board after their arrival, before they can be permitted to land.

The term is applied in modern usage to any isolation by law of infected persons or places.

——**In Real Property.** The space of forty days, during which a widow has a right to remain in her late husband's principal mansion immediately after his death. The right of the widow is also called her "quarantine."

QUARE (Lat.) In pleading. Wherefore.

This word is sometimes used in the writ in certain actions, but is inadmissible in a material averment in the pleadings, for it is merely interrogatory; and therefore, when a declaration began with complaining of the defendant, "wherefore with force, etc., he broke and entered" the plaintiff's close, it was considered ill. Bac. Abr. "Pleas" (B 5, 4); Gould, Pl. c. 3, § 34.

QUARE CLAUSUM FREGIT. See "Trespass."

QUARE EJECIT INFRA TERMINUM. See "Ejectment."

QUARE IMPEDIT (Lat. why he hinders). In English law. A real possessory action which can be brought only in the court of common pleas, and lies to recover a presentation when the patron's right is disturbed, or to try a disputed title to an advowson. See "Disturbance;" Mireh. Advowson, 265; 2 Saund. 336a.

QUARE INCUMBRAVIT (Lat. why he incumbered). A writ or action which lay against a bishop after judgment in an action *quare impedit,* where he had incumbered the church with a clerk pending the action. 3 Bl. Comm. 248.

QUARE INTRUSIT (Lat. why he intruded). A writ that formerly lay where the lord proffered a suitable marriage to his ward, who rejected it, and entered into the land, and married another, the value of his marriage not being satisfied to the lord. Abolished by 12 Car. II. c. 24.

QUARE NON ADMISIT (Lat. wherefore he did not admit). A writ to recover damages against a bishop who does not admit a plaintiff's clerk. It is, however, rarely or never necessary; for it is said that a bishop, refusing to execute the writ *ad admittendum clericum,* or making an insufficient return to it, may be fined. Watson, Cler. Law, 302.

QUARE NON PERMITTIT. An ancient writ, which lay for one who had a right to present to a church for a turn against the proprietary. Fleta, lib. 5, c. 6.

QUARE OBSTRUXIT. (Lat. why he obstructs.) The name of a writ formerly used in favor of one who, having a right to pass through his neighbor's grounds, was prevented enjoying such right, because the owner of the grounds had obstructed the way.

QUARREL. A dispute; a difference. In law, particularly in releases, which are taken most strongly against the releasor, when a man releases all quarrel he is said to release all actions, real and personal. 8 Coke, 153.

QUARRY. A place whence stones are dug for the purpose of being employed in building, making roads, and the like.

When a farm is let with an open quarry, the tenant may, when not restrained by his contract, take out the stone; but he has no right to open new quarries. See "Waste."

QUARTER DAYS. The four days of the year on which rent payable quarterly becomes due.

QUARTER SALES. In New York a certain fraction of the purchase money is often conditioned to be paid back on alienation of the estate; and this fine on alienation is expressed as a "tenth sales," a "quarter sales," etc. 7 Cow. (N. Y.) 285; 7 Hill (N. Y.) 253; 7 N. Y. 490.

QUARTER SEAL. In Scotch law. The seal kept by the director of the chancery in Scotland is so called. It is in the shape and impression of the fourth part of the great seal. Bell, Dict.

QUARTER SESSIONS. A court bearing this name, mostly invested with the trial of criminals. It takes its name from sitting quarterly, or once in three months.

The English courts of quarter sessions were erected during the reign of Edward III. See St. 36 Edw. III.; Crabb, Hist. Eng. Law, 278.

QUARTER YEAR. In the computation of time, a quarter year consists of ninety-one days. Co. Litt. 135b; 2 Rolle, Abr. 521, lib. 40; Rev. St. N. Y. pt. 1, c. 19, tit. 1, § 3.

QUARTERING. A barbarous punishment formerly inflicted on criminals by tearing them to pieces by means of four horses, one attached to each limb.

QUARTERING OF SOLDIERS. Furnishing soldiers with board or lodging or both. Const. U. S. Amend. art. 3, provides that "no soldier shall, in time of peace, be quartered in any house without the consent of the owner, nor in time of war but in a manner to be prescribed by law."

QUARTEROON. One who has had one of his grandparents of the black or African race.

QUARTO DIE POST (Lat. fourth day after). Appearance day, which is the fourth day inclusive from the return of the writ; and if the person summoned appears on that day, it is sufficient. On this day, also, the court begins to sit for despatch of business. These three days were originally given as an indulgence. 3 Bl. Comm. 278; Tidd, New Prac. 134. But this practice is now altered. 15 & 16 Vict. c. 76.

QUASH. In practice. To overthrow or annul.

Distinguished from "dismiss." The term "quash," as applied to writs, is predicated of some defect in the writ itself, or in the form of the writ, which defect does not reach the merits of the case; the usual practice being to grant a new writ on the original petition. Dismissal is applied to the removal or disposal of the cause itself, and not to the mere annulment of the writ. 24 Miss. 457.

QUASHAL. The act of quashing.

QUASI (Lat. as if; almost). A term used to mark a resemblance, and which supposes a little difference between two objects. Dig. 11. 7. 1. 8. 1; 60 Ill. 402. Civilians use the expressions *quasi contractus, quasi delictum, quasi possessio, quasi traditio,* etc.

QUASI AFFINITY. In civil law. The affinity which exists between two persons, one of whom has been betrothed to the kindred of the other, but who have never been married. For example, my brother is betrothed to Maria, and afterwards, before marriage, he dies. There then exists between Maria and me a *quasi* affinity.

The history of England furnishes an example of this kind. Catherine of Arragon was betrothed to the brother of Henry VIII. Afterwards, Henry married her, and under the pretense of this *quasi* affinity he repudiated her, because the marriage was incestuous.

QUASI CONTRACT. A liability similar to that created by contract, but not really arising by the consent of the parties.

Quasi contracts are said to be founded in general.

(1) On a record, as the liability on a judgment.

(2) On a statutory, official, or customary duty, as the obligation of a husband for necessaries furnished his wife, even against his orders; or the liability of a vessel for half pilotage on refusing the first pilot offering himself. 2 Wall. (U. S.) 450.

(3) On the doctrine that no one shall be permitted to enrich himself unjustly at the expense of another; as the liability of an infant to pay for necessaries (141 Mass. 530), or the liability to repay money paid by mistake (Keener, Quasi Cont. 16).

The distinction between "*quasi* contract" and "implied contract" appears to be one of degree, rather than of principle. It has been said that implied contract extends to those cases where there was an intent to contract, or at least no intent not to contract; but in many cases commonly assigned to implied contracts, the only evidence of intent to contract is in the imputed knowledge that the law would impose a given liability, and this element is absent from but few *quasi* contracts. On the other hand, the test of definite intention not to contract would exclude many liabilities properly classified as *quasi* contractual, *e. g.*, that for money paid by mistake.

It may be said, generally, that *quasi* contracts embrace those cases where there was a positive intention not to contract, and cases where there was no intent to contract, and the party was more remote from any inferred intent than in cases of implied contract, but the exact line of demarcation cannot, in the present state of legal nomenclature, be drawn.

QUASI CONTRACTUS (Lat.) In civil law. The act of a person, permitted by law, by which he obligates himself towards another, or by which another binds himself to him, without any agreement between them.

By article 2272 of the Civil Code of Louisiana, which is translated from article 1371 of the *Code Civil, quasi* contracts are defined to be "the lawful and purely voluntary acts of a man, from which there results any obligation whatever to a third person, and sometimes a reciprocal obligation between the parties." In contracts, it is the consent of the contracting parties which produces the obligation; in *quasi* contracts no consent is required, and the obligation arises from the law or natural equity, on the facts of the case. These acts are called "*quasi* contracts" because, without being contracts, they bind the parties as contracts do.

Bracton makes use of the term "*quasi ex contractu*," and includes contracts that impliedly arise from the relations of agency, wardship, the division of common property, the distribution of an inheritance, an action growing out of a testament, a suit to require a sum paid not due, and such like. 253 Ill. 173.

There is no term in the common law which answers to that of "*quasi* contract." Many *quasi* contracts may doubtless be classed among "implied contracts." There is, however, a difference to be noticed. For example, in case money should be paid by mistake to a minor, it may be recovered from him by the civil law, because his consent is not necessary to a *quasi* contract; but by the common law, if it can be recovered, it must be upon an agreement to which the law presumes he has consented, and it is doubtful, upon principle, whether such recovery could be had.

Quasi contracts may be multiplied almost to infinity. They are, however, divided into five classes,—such as relate to the voluntary and spontaneous management of the affairs of another, without authority (*negotiorum gestio*); the administration of tutorship; the management of common property (*communio bonorum*); the acquisition of an inheritance; and the payment of a sum of money or other thing by mistake, when nothing was due (*indebiti solutio*).

Each of these *quasi* contracts has an affinity with some contract. Thus, the management of the affairs of another without authority, and tutorship, are compared to a mandate; the community of property, to a partnership; the acquisition of an inheritance, to a stipulation; and the payment of a thing which is not due, to a loan.

QUASI CORPORATIONS. A term applied to those bodies which, though not vested with the general powers of corporations, are yet recognized by statutes or immemorial usage as persons or corporations aggregate, with power to sue and be sued in their aggregate capacity. 2 Kent, Comm. 274; 9 Mass. 247; 1 Me. 361.

A body having capacity to make contracts in respect to county affairs, and having perpetual succession, is a *quasi* corporation (2 Wall. [U. S.] 501), *e. g.*, the overseers of the poor (18 Johns. [N. Y.] 407).

QUASI DELICT. In civil law. An act whereby a person, without malice, but by fault, negligence, or imprudence not legally excusable, causes injury to another.

A *quasi* delict may be public or private. The neglect of the affairs of a community, when it is our duty to attend to them, may be a crime; the neglect of a private matter, under similar circumstances, may be the ground of a civil action. Bowyer, Mod. Civ. Law, c. 43, p. 265.

QUASI DEPOSIT. A kind of involuntary bailment, which takes place where a person acquires possession of property lawfully, by finding. Story, Bailm. § 85.

QUASI EASEMENT. An "easement," in the proper sense of the word, can only exist in respect of two adjoining pieces of land occupied by different persons, and can only impose a negative duty on the owner of the servient tenement. Hence an obligation on the owner of land to repair the fence between his and his neighbor's land is not a true easement, but is sometimes called a "*quasi* easement." Gale, Easem. 516.

QUASI ENTAIL. A *quasi* entail exists when an estate *pur autre vie* is limited to a person and the heirs of his body.

QUASI EX CONTRACTU. See "Quasi Contractus."

QUASI FEE. An estate gained by wrong; for wrong is unlimited and uncontained within rules. Wharton.

QUASI OFFENSES, or QUASI CRIMES. Wrongs against the general or local public which have not been declared crimes (68 Ill. 375); *e. g.*, bastardy proceedings, which are commonly said to be *quasi* criminal.

Offenses for which some person other than the actual perpetrator is responsible, the perpetrator being presumed to act by command of the responsible party.

Injuries which have been unintentionally caused.

QUASI PARTNERS. Partners of lands, goods, or chattels, who are not actual partners, are sometimes so called. Poth. de Societe, Append. note 184. See "Part Owners."

QUASI PERSONALTY. Things which are movable in point of law, though fixed to things real, either actually, as emblements (*fructus industriales*), fixtures, etc., or fictitiously, as chattels real, leases for years, etc.

QUASI POSSESSION. Such use as is to a right what possession is to a thing. When the enjoyment is exercised by means of possession of the thing, which is the subject of the right, the idea of *quasi* possession does not arise, and the term is confined to those rights which merely give a limited power of using the thing, as in case of easements. The term is little used, "enjoyment" being more frequently employed.

QUASI POSTHUMOUS CHILD. In civil law. One who, born during the life of his grandfather or other male ascendant, was not his heir at the time he made his testament, but who, by the death of his father, became his heir in his lifetime. Inst. 2. 13. 2; Dig. 28. 3. 13.

QUASI PURCHASE. This term is used in the civil law to denote that a thing is to be considered as purchased from the presumed consent of the owner of a thing; as, if a man should consume a cheese, which is in his possession and belonging to another, with an intent to pay the price of it to the owner, the consent of the latter will be presumed, as the cheese would have been spoiled by keeping it longer. Wolff. Dr. Nat. § 691.

QUASI REALTY. Things which are fixed in contemplation of law to realty, but movable in themselves, as heirlooms (or limbs of the inheritance), title deeds, court rolls, etc. Wharton.

QUASI TENANT AT SUFFERANCE. An under tenant, who is in possession at the determination of an original lease, and is permitted by the reversioner to hold over.

QUASI TORT. Though not a recognized term of English law, it may be conveniently used in those cases where a man who has not committed a tort is liable as if he had. Thus, a master is liable for wrongful acts done by his servant in the course of his employment. Broom, Com. Law, 690; Underh. Torts, 29. Austin rejects "*quasi* torts," or "*quasi* delict," altogether. Austin, Jur. 959.

QUASI-TRADITIO (Lat.) In civil law. A term used to designate that a person is in the use of the property of another, which the latter suffers and does not oppose. Lec. Elm. § 396. It also signifies the act by which the right of property is ceded in a thing to a person who is in possession of it; as, if I loan a boat to Paul, and deliver it to him, and afterwards I sell him the boat, it is not requisite that he should deliver the boat to me to be again delivered to him. There is a *quasi* tradition or delivery.

QUASI TRUSTEE. A person who reaps a a benefit from a breach of trust, and so becomes answerable as a trustee. Lewin, Trusts (4th Ed.) 592, 638.

QUASI USUFRUCT. In the civil law. A name given to a usufructuary interest in consumable things. See "Usufruct."

QUATER COUSIN. "The very name of *cater*, or (as it is more properly written) *quater* cousins, is grown into a proverb, to express, by way of irony, the last and most trivial degree of intimacy and regard." Bl. Law Tr. 6.

QUATUOR PEDIBUS CURRIT (Law Lat.) Runs upon four feet; runs upon all fours. A term used to denote an exact correspondence. See "All Fours." *Nullum simile quatuor pedibus currit*, no simile holds in everything. Co. Litt. 3a. "It does not follow that they (a trust and an equity of redemption) run *quatuor pedibus*." 1 W. Bl. 145.

QUATUORVIRI (Lat. four men). In Roman law. Magistrates who had the care and inspection of roads. Dig. 1. 2. 3. 30.

QUAY. A wharf at which to load or land goods. Sometimes spelled "key."

In its enlarged sense, the word "quay" means the whole space between the first row of houses of a city and the sea or river. 5 La. 152, 215. So much of the quay as is requisite for the public use of loading and unloading vessels is public property, and cannot be appropriated to private use, but the rest may be private property.

QUE EST MESME (Law Fr.) Which is the same. See "Quae est Eadem."

QUE ESTATE (Lat. *quem statum*, or which estate). A plea by which a man prescribes in himself and those whose estate he holds. 2 Bl. Comm. 270; 18 Viner, Abr. 133-140; Co. Litt. 121a; Hardr. 459; 2 Bouv. Inst. note 499.

QUEAN. A worthless woman; a strumpet. The meaning of this word, which is now seldom used, is said not to be well ascertained. 2 Rolle, Abr. 296; Bac. Abr. "Slander" (U 3).

QUEEN. A female sovereign.

QUEEN ANNE'S BOUNTY. By St. 2 Anne, c. 11, all the revenue of first fruit and tenths was vested in trustees forever, to form a perpetual fund for the augmentation of poor livings. 1 Bl. Comm. 286; 2 Burn, Ecc. Law, 260-268.

QUEEN CONSORT. The wife of a reigning king. 1 Bl. Comm. 218. She is looked upon by the law as a *feme sole*, as to her power of contracting, suing, etc. Id.

QUEEN DOWAGER. The widow of the king. She has most of the privileges belonging to a queen consort. 1 Bl. Comm. 229.

QUEEN GOLD. A royal revenue belonging to every queen consort during her marriage with the king, and due from every person who has made a voluntary fine or offer to the king of ten marks or upwards, in consideration of any grant or privilege conferred by the crown. It is due of record on the recording of the fine. It was last exacted in the reign of Charles I. It is now quite obsolete. 1 Bl. Comm. 220-222; Fortesc. de Laud. 398; Jacob.

QUEEN REGNANT. She who holds the crown in her own right. She has the same duties and prerogatives, etc., as a king. St. 1 Mar. I. st. 3, c. 1; 1 Bl. Comm. 218; 1 Wooddeson, Lect. 94.

QUEEN'S (or KING'S) ADVOCATE. An English advocate who holds, in the courts in which the rules of the canon and civil law prevail, a similar position to that which the attorney general holds in the ordinary courts, *i. e.*, he acts as counsel for the crown is ecclesiastical, admiralty, and probate cases, and advises the crown on questions of international law. In order of precedence, it seems that he ranks after the attorney general. 3 Steph. Comm. 275, note; Man. S. ad L. 19 Append. IV.

QUEEN'S BENCH. The English court of king's bench is so called during the reign of a queen. 3 Steph. Comm. 403.

QUEEN'S (or KING'S) COUNSEL. In English law. Barristers called within the bar, and selected to be the queen's (or king's) counsel, learned in the law; answering in some measure to the advocates of the revenue (*advocati fisci*) among the Romans. They cannot be employed in any cause against the crown, without special license. 3 Bl. Comm. 27; 3 Steph. Comm. 386.

QUEEN'S (or KING'S) EVIDENCE. Testimony of an accomplice in a felony, admitted as evidence for the crown against his accomplices. 4 Steph. Comm. 398. See "State's Evidence."

QUEEN'S PRISON. In English law. A prison appropriated to the debtors and criminals confined under process, or by authority of the superior courts at Westminster, the Marshalsea court and Palace court, and the high court of admiralty, and also to persons imprisoned under the bankrupt law. It was established by St. 5 & 6 Vict. c. 22, consolidating into one the queen's bench, the Fleet, and the Marshalsea prisons. 3 Steph. Comm. 254.

QUEM REDDITUM REDDIT. A real action, by which the grantee of a rent could compel the tenants to attorn to him.

QUEMADMODUM AD QUAESTIONEM facti non respondent judices, ita ad quaestionem juris non respondent juratores. In the same manner that judges do not answer to questions of fact, so jurors do not answer to questions of law. Co. Litt. 295.

QUERELA (Lat.) An action preferred in any court of justice. The plaintiff was called *querens*, or complainant, and his brief, complaint, or declaration was called *querela*. Jacob. See "Audita Querela."

QUERELA CORAM REGE A CONCILIO discutienda et terminanda. A writ by which one is called to justify a complaint of a trespass made to the king himself, before the king and his council. Reg. Orig. 124.

QUERELA INOFFICIOSI TESTAMENTI (Lat. complaint of an undutiful or unkind will). In civil law. A species of action allowed to a child who had been unjustly disinherited, to set aside the will, founded on the presumption of law, in such cases, that the parent was not in his right mind. Calv. Lex.; 2 Kent, Comm. 327; Bell, Dict.

QUERENS (Lat. from *queri*, to complain). In old English practice. A plaintiff; the plaintiff or complaining party. Bracton, fols. 98b, 214, 240, et passim; 8 Coke, 153b. The complaining party in a personal action; as *petens* (demandant) was, in a real action. *Actor, sive sit petens sive querens.* Bracton, fol. 106b. But *querens* was used in assizes. Fleta, lib. 4, c. 7.

QUESTA (Law Lat.) In old records. A quest; an inquest, inquisition, or inquiry, upon the oaths of an impanelled jury. Cowell.

QUESTION.

——**In Old Criminal Law.** A means sometimes employed in some countries, by torture, to compel supposed great criminals to disclose their accomplices or to acknowledge their crimes.

This torture is called "question" because, as the unfortunate person accused is made to suffer pain, he is asked questions as to his supposed crime or accomplices. This is unknown in the United States. See Poth. Proc. Crim. sec. 5, art. 2, § 3.

——**In Evidence.** An interrogation put to a witness, requesting him to declare the truth of certain facts as far as he knows them.

Questions are either general or leading. By a general question is meant such a one as requires the witness to state all he knows, without any suggestion being made to him; as, "Who gave the blow?" A leading question is one which leads the mind of the witness to the answer, or suggests it to him; as, "Did A. B. give the blow?"

The Romans called a question by which the fact or supposed fact which the interrogator expected or wished to find asserted in and by the answer was made known to the proposed respondent a "suggestive" interrogation; as, "Is not your name A. B.?" See "Leading Question."

——**In Practice.** A point on which the parties are not agreed, and which is submitted to the decision of a judge and jury.

When the doubt or difference arises as to what the law is on a certain state of facts, this is said to be a "legal question;" and when the party demurs, this is to be decided by the court. When it arises as to the truth or falsehood of facts, this is a "question of fact," and is to be decided by the jury.

QUESTUS EST NOBIS. A writ of nuisance which lay against one who acquired, by descent or alienation, the thing which caused the nuisance. It was given by 15 Edw. I. Formerly only the person causing it was liable. Cowell.

QUI ABJURAT REGNUM AMITTIT REGnum, sed non regem; patriam, sed non patrem patriae. He who abjures the realm leaves the realm, but not the king; the country, but not the father of the country. 7 Coke, 9.

QUI ACCUSAT INTEGRAE FAMAE SIT et non criminosus. Let him who accuses be of clear fame, and not criminal. 3 Inst. 26.

QUI ACQUIRIT SIBI ACQUIRIT HAEREdibus. He who acquires for himself acquires for his heirs. Tray. Lat. Max. 496.

QUI ADIMIT MEDIUM DIRIMIT FINEM. He who takes away the means destroys the end. Co. Litt. 161.

QUI ALIQUID STATUERIT PARTE INaudita altera, aequum licet dixerit, haud aequum facerit. He who decides anything, a party being unheard, though he should decide right, does wrong. 6 Coke, 52; 4 Bl. Comm. 483.

QUI ALTERIUS JURE UTITUR, EODEM jure uti debet. He who uses the right of another ought to use the same right. Poth. Tr. de Change, pt. 1, c. 4, § 114; Broom, Leg. Max. (3d London Ed.) 421.

QUI APPROBAT NON REPROBAT. He who approbates does not reprobate, *i. e.*, he cannot both accept and reject the same thing.

QUI BENE DISTINGUIT BENE DOCET. He who distinguishes well, learns well. 2 Inst. 470.

QUI BENE INTERROGAT BENE DOCET. He who questions well, learns well. 3 Bulst. 227.

QUI CADIT A SYLLABA CADIT A TOTA causa. He who fails in a syllable fails in his whole cause. Bracton, fol. 211; St. Wales, 12 Edw. I.; 3 Bl. Comm. 407.

QUI CONCEDIT ALIQUID, CONCEDERE videtur et id sine quo concessio est irrita, sine quo res ipsa esse non potuit. He who grants anything is considered as granting that without which his grant would be idle, without which the thing itself could not exist. 11 Coke, 52; Jenk. Cent. Cas. 32.

QUI CONFIRMAT NIHIL DAT. He who confirms does not give. 2 Bouv. Inst. note 2069.

QUI CONTEMNIT PRAECEPTUM CONtemnit praecipientem. He who contemns the precept contemns the party giving it. 12 Coke, 96.

QUI CUM ALIO CONTRAHIT, VEL EST, vel debet esse non ignarus conditionis ejus. He who contracts knows, or ought to know, the quality of the person with whom he contracts, otherwise he is not excusable. Dig. 50. 17. 19; 2 Hagg. Consist.; Story, Confl. Laws, § 76.

QUI DAT FINEM DAT MEDIA AD FINEM necessaria. He who gives an end gives the means to that end. 3 Mass. 129.

QUI DESTRUIT MEDIUM DESTRUIT FInem. He who destroys the means destroys the end. 11 Coke, 51; Shep. Touch. 342; Co. Litt. 161a.

QUI DOIT INHERITER AL PERE DOIT inheriter al fiz. He who ought to inherit from the father ought to inherit from the son. 2 Bl. Comm. 250, 273; Broom, Leg. Max. (3d London Ed.) 459.

QUI EVERTIT CAUSAM EVERTIT CAUsatum futurum. He who overthrows the cause overthrows its future effects. 10 Coke, 51.

QUI EX DAMNATO COITU NASCUNTUR inter liberos non computentur. They who are born of an illicit union should not be counted among children. Co. Litt. 8. See 1 Bouv. Inst. note 289; Bracton, 5; Broom, Leg. Max. (3d London Ed.) 460.

QUI FACIT ID QUOD PLUS EST FACIT id quod minus est, sed non convertitur. He who does that which is more does that which is less, but not *vice versa*. Bracton, 207b.

QUI FACIT PER ALIUM FACIT PER SE. He who acts by or through another acts himself; *i. e.*, the acts of an agent are the acts of the principal. 1 Bl. Comm. 429; Story, Ag. § 440; 2 Bouv. Inst. notes 1273, 1335, 1336; 7 Man. & G. 32, 33; 16 Mees. & W. 26; 8 Scott, N. R. 590; 6 Clark & F. 600; 10 Mass. 155.

QUI HABET JURISDICTIONEM ABSOLvendi habet jurisdictionem ligandi. He who has jurisdiction to loosen has jurisdiction to bind. 12 Coke, 59.

QUI HAERET IN LITERA HAERET IN cortice. He who adheres to the letter adheres to the bark. Co. Litt. 289; 5 Coke, 4b; 11 Coke, 34b; 12 East, 372.

QUI IGNORAT QUANTUM SOLVERE DEbeat non potest improbus videre. He who does not know what he ought to pay does not want probity in not paying. Dig. 50. 17. 99.

QUI IN JUS DOMINIUMVE ALTERIUS succedit jure ejus uti debet. He who succeeds to the right or property of another ought to use his right, *i. e.*, holds it subject to the same rights and liabilities as attached to it in the hands of the assignor. Dig. 50. 17. 177; Broom, Leg. Max. (3d London Ed.) 420, 425.

QUI IN UTERO EST PRO JAM NATO habetur quoties de ejus commodo quaeritur. He who is in the womb is considered as born whenever his benefit is concerned.

QUI JURE SUO UTITUR NEMINI FACIT injuriam. He who uses his legal rights harms no one.

QUI JUSSU JUDICIS ALIQUOD FECERIT non videtur dolo malo fecisse, quia parere necesse est. He who does anything by command of a judge will not be supposed to have acted from an improper motive, because it was necessary to obey. 10 Coke, 76; Dig. 50. 17. 167. 1.

QUI MALE AGIT ODIT LUCEM. He who acts badly hates the light. 7 Coke, 66.

QUI MANDAT IPSE FECISSE VIDETUR. He who commands a thing to be done is held to have done it himself. Story, Bailm. § 147.

QUI MELIUS PROBAT MELIUS HABET. He who proves most recovers most. 9 Viner, Abr. 235.

QUI MOLITUR INSIDIAS IN PATRIAM id facit quod insanus nauta perforans navem in qua vehitur. He who betrays his country is like the insane sailor who bores a hole in the ship which carries him. 3 Inst. 36.

QUI NASCITUR SINE LEGITIMO MATRImonio matrem sequitur. He who is born out of lawful matrimony follows the condition of the mother.

QUI NON CADUNT IN CONSTANTEM virum vani timores sunt aestimandi. Those are to be esteemed vain fears which do not affect a man of a firm mind. 7 Coke, 27.

QUI NON HABET, ILLE NON DAT. Who has not, he gives not. Shep. Touch. 248; 4 Wend. (N. Y.) 619.

QUI NON HABET IN AERE LUAT IN corpore, ne quis peccetur impune. He who cannot pay with his purse must suffer in his person, lest he who offends should go unpunished. 2 Inst. 173; 4 Bl. Comm. 20.

QUI NON HABET POTESTATEM ALIEnandi habet necessitatem retinendi. He who has not the power of alienating is obliged to retain. Hob. 336.

QUI NON IMPROBAT APPROBAT. He who does not disapprove approves. 3 Inst. 27.

QUI NON LIBERE VERITATEM PROnunciat proditor est veritatis. He who does not freely speak the truth is a betrayer of the truth.

QUI NON NEGAT FATETUR He who does not deny admits. A well-known rule of pleading. Tray. Lat. Max. 503.

QUI NON OBSTAT QUOD OBSTARE POtest facere videtur. He who does not prevent what he can seems to commit the thing. 2 Inst. 146.

QUI NON PROHIBET CUM PROHIBERE possit jubet. He who does not forbid when he can forbid commands. 1 Bl. Comm. 430.

QUI NON PROHIBET QUOD PROHIbere potest assentire videtur. He who does not forbid what he can forbid seems to assent. 2 Inst. 308; 8 Exch. 304.

QUI NON PROPULSAT INJURIAM quando potest, infert. He who does not repel a wrong when he can, occasions it. Jenk. Cent. Cas. 271.

QUI OBSTRUIT ADITUM DESTRUIT commodum. He who obstructs an entrance destroys a conveniency. Co. Litt. 161.

QUI OMNE DICIT, NIHIL EXCLUDIT. He who says all excludes nothing. 4 Inst. 81.

QUI PARCIT NOCENTIBUS INNOCENTIbus punit. He who spares the guilty punishes the innocent. Jenk. Cent. Cas. 126.

QUI PECCAT EBRIUS LUAT SOBRIUS. He who offends drunk must be punished when sober. Cary, 133.

QUI PER ALIUM FACIT PER SEIPSUM facere videtur. He who does anything through another is considered as doing it himself. Co. Litt. 258.

QUI PER FRAUDEM AGIT, FRUSTRA agit. He who acts fraudulently acts in vain. 2 Rolle, 17.

QUI POTEST ET DEBET VETARE, JUbet. He who can and ought to forbid, and does not, commands.

QUI PRIMUM PECCAT ILLE FACIT rixam. He who first offends causes the strife.

QUI PRIOR EST TEMPORE POTIOR est jure. He who is first or before in time is stronger in right. Co. Litt. 14a; 1 Story, Eq. Jur. § 64d; Story, Bailm. § 312; 1 Bouv. Inst. note 952; 4 Bouv. Inst. 3728; 1 Smith, Lead. Cas. (4th Hare & W. Ed.) 440; 3 East, 93; 24 Miss. 208.

QUI PRO ME ALIQUID FACIT, MIHI FEcisse videtur. He who does any benefit (to another) for me is considered as doing it to me. 2 Inst. 501.

QUI PROVIDET SIBI PROVIDET HAEREdibus. He who provides for himself provides for his heirs.

QUI RATIONEM IN OMNIBUS QUAErunt rationem subvertunt. He who seeks a reason for everything subverts reason. 2 Coke, 75; Broom, Leg. Max. (3d London Ed.) 149.

QUI SCIENS SOLVIT INDEBITUM DOnandi consilio id videtur fecisse. One who knowingly pays what is not due is supposed to have done it with the intention of making a gift. 17 Mass. 388.

QUI SEMEL ACTIONEM RENUNCIAverit, amplius repetere non potest. He who renounces his action once cannot any more bring it. 8 Coke, 59. See "Retraxit."

QUI SEMEL MALUS SEMPER PRAEsumitur esse malus in eodem genere. He who is once bad is presumed to be always so in the same degree. Cro. Car. 317; Best, Ev. 345.

QUI SENTIT COMMODUM SENTIRE DEbet et onus. He who derives a benefit from a thing ought to bear the disadvantages attending it. 2 Bouv. Inst. note 1433; 2 Woodb. & M. (U. S.) 217; 1 Story, Const. 78; Broom, Leg. Max. (3d London Ed.) 630.

QUI SENTIT ONUS SENTIRE DEBET et commodum. He who bears the burden of a thing ought also to experience the advantage arising from it. 1 Coke, 99a; Broom, Leg. Max. (3d London Ed.) 638; 1 Serg. & R. (Pa.) 180; Coote, Mortg. (3d Ed.) 517d; Francis, Max. 5.

QUI TACET CONSENTIRE VIDETUR. He who is silent appears to consent. Jenk. Cent. Cas. 32.

QUI TACET CONSENTIRE VIDETUR ubi tractatur de ejus commodo. He who is silent is considered as assenting, when his advantage is debated. 9 Mod. 38.

QUI TACET NON UTIQUE FATETUR, sed tamen verum est eum non negare. He who is silent does not indeed confess, but yet it is true that he does not deny. Dig. 50. 17. 142.

QUI TAM (Lat. who as well). An action under a statute which imposes a penalty for the doing or not doing an act, and gives that penalty in part to whosoever will sue for the same, and the other part to the commonwealth, or some charitable, literary, or other institution, and makes it recoverable by action. The plaintiff describes himself as suing as well for the commonwealth, for example, as for himself. Esp. Pen. Actions. 5, 6; 1 Viner, Abr. 197; 1 Salk. 29, note; Bac. Abr.

QUI TARDIUS SOLVIT MINUS SOLVIT. He who pays tardily pays less than he ought. Jenk. Cent. Cas. 38.

QUI TIMENT CAVENT ET VITANT. They who fear take care and avoid. Off. Ex. 162; Branch, Princ.

QUI TOTUM DICIT NIHIL EXCIPIT. He who says all excepts nothing.

QUI VULT DECIPI, DECIPIATUR. Let him who wishes to be deceived be deceived. De Gex, M. & G. 687, 710; Shep. Touch. 56.

QUIA (Lat.) In pleading. Because. This word is considered a term of affirmation. It is sufficiently direct and positive for introducing a material averment. 1 Saund. 117, note 4; Comyn, Dig. "Pleader" (C 77).

QUIA DATUM EST. NOBIS INTELLIGI. Because it is given to us to understand. Formal words in old writs. Rat. Parl. 4 Hen. IV.

QUIA DOMINUS REMISIT CURIAM (Law Lat.) In old practice. Because the lord hath remised or remitted his court. A clause inserted at the conclusion of a writ of right, where it was brought, in the first instance, in the king's court; the lord in whose court baron it regularly ought to be first brought having waived or remitted his right. 3 Bl. Comm. 195; Id. Append. No. i. § 4.

QUIA EMPTORES (Lat. because the purchasers). The title of St. Westminster III. (18 Edw. I. c. 1), which provided that from thenceforth it should be lawful for every freeman or freeholder to sell his lands or tenements or part thereof at his pleasure, so that, however, the feoffee should hold such lands or tenements of the chief lord of the same fee, by the same services and customs by which his feoffor before held them. So called from its initial words: *Quia emptores terrarum et tenementorum de feodis magnatum*, etc. 2 Bl. Comm. 91; Barr. Obs. St. 167. See the New York case, 2 Seld. 467.

QUIA ERRONICE EMANAVIT. Because it issued erroneously, or through mistake. A term in old English practice. Yelv. 83

QUIA TIMET (Lat. because he fears). A term applied to preventive or anticipatory remedies. According to Lord Coke, "there be six writs of law that may be maintained *quia timet*, before any molestation, distress, or impleading; as, first, a man may have his writ or mesne before he be distrained; second, a *warrantia chartae*, before he be impleaded; third, a *monstraverunt*, before any distress or vexation; fourth, an *audita querela*, before any execution sued; fifth, a *curia claudenda*, before any default of inclosure; sixth, a *ne injuste vexes*, before any distress or molestation. And these are called *brevia anticipantia*, writs of prevention." Co. Litt. 100. And see 7 Brown, Parl. Cas. 125.

These writs are generally obsolete. In chancery, when it is contemplated to prevent an expected injury, a bill *quia timet* is filed. See "Bill Quia Timet."

QUICK DISPATCH. A term used in charter parties to express the promptness with which the cargo will be delivered to the vessel for loading. It signifies delivery as rapidly as the vessel can receive it. 2 Fed. 607.

It is a stronger term than "customary quick dispatch," and supersedes the custom of the port. 2 Low. (U. S.) 361.

QUICK WITH CHILD. The state of a woman pregnant with a quick child, *i. e.*, a foetus which has quickened. 9 Metc. (Mass.) 263. A woman's condition from the time of conception and the commencement of gestation. 49 N. Y. 89. In an English case, "quick with child" was distinguished from "with quick child," the former phrase being said to signify merely "having conceived" (8 Car. & P. 262), but this distinction is not recognized (22 N. J. Law, 57).

QUICQUID ACQUIRITUR SERVO, ACquiritur domino. Whatever is acquired by the servant is acquired for the master. 15 Viner, Abr. 327.

QUICQUID DEMONSTRATAE REI ADDItur satis demonstratae frustra est. Whatever is added to the description of a thing already sufficiently described is of no effect. Dig. 33. 4. 1. 8; Broom, Leg. Max. (3d London Ed.) 562.

QUICQUID EST CONTRA NORMAM RECti est injuria. Whatever is against the rule of right is a wrong. 3 Bulst. 313.

QUICQUID IN EXCESSU ACTUM EST, lege prohibitur. Whatever is done in excess is prohibited by law. 2 Inst. 107.

QUICQUID JUDICIS AUCTORITATI SUBjicitur novitati non subjicitur. Whatever is subject to the authority of a judge is not subject to innovation. 4 Inst. 66.

QUICQUID PLANTATUR SOLO, SOLO cedit. Whatever is affixed to the soil belongs to it. Wentw. Off. Ex'r, 145; Ambl. 113; 3 East, 51. See "Fixtures."

QUICQUID RECIPITUR, RECIPITUR SEcundum modum recipientis. Whatever is received is received according to the intention of the recipient. Broom, Leg. Max. (3d London Ed.) 727; Halk. Max. 149; Law Mag. 1855, p. 21; 2 Bing. (N. C.) 461; 2 Barn. & C. 72; 14 Sim. 522; 2 Clark & F. 681; 2 Cromp. & J. 678; 14 East, 239, 243c.

QUICQUID SOLVITUR, SOLVITUR SEcundum modum solventis. Whatever is paid is to be applied according to the intention of the payor. 2 Vern. 606. See "Appropriation."

QUICQUID SOLVITUR, SOLVITUR SEcundum modum solventis; quicquid recipitur, recipitur secundum modum recipientis. Whatever money is paid is paid according to the direction of the payor; whatever money is received is received according to that of the recipient. 2 Vern. 606; Broom, Leg. Max. 810.

QUICUNQUE HABET JURISDICTIONEM ordinariam est illius loci ordinarius. Whoever has an ordinary jurisdiction is ordinary of that place. Co. Litt. 344.

QUICUNQUE JUSSU JUDICIS ALIQUID fecerit non videtur dolo malo fecisse, quia parere necesse est. Whoever does anything by the command of a judge is not reckoned to have done it with an evil intent, because it is necessary to obey. 10 Coke, 71.

QUID JURIS CLAMAT (Law Lat. what right he claims). In old English practice. A writ which lay for the grantee of a reversion or remainder, where the particular tenant would not attorn, for the purpose of compelling him. Termes de la Ley; Cowell.

QUID PRO QUO (Lat.) What for what; something for something. An equivalent, or consideration; that which is given in exchange for another thing; that which is done in consideration of another thing. Cowell; 2 P. Wms. 219.

QUID SIT JUS, ET IN QUO CONSISTIT injuria, legis est definire. What constitutes right, and what injury, it is the business of the law to declare. Co. Litt. 158b.

QUIDAM (Lat. some one; somebody). In French law. A term used to express an unknown person, or one who cannot be named.

A *quidam* is usually described by the features of his face, the color of his hair, his height, his clothing, and the like, in any process which may be issued against him. Merlin, Repert.

QUIDQUID ENIM SINE DOLO ET CULPA venditoris accidit in eo venditor securus est. For concerning anything which occurs without deceit and wrong on the part of the vendor, the vendor is secure. 4 Pick. (Mass.) 198.

QUIET ENJOYMENT. The name of a covenant in a lease, by which the lessor agrees that the lessee shall peaceably enjoy the premises leased. This covenant goes to the possession, and not to the title. 3 Johns. (N. Y.) 471; 5 Johns. (N. Y.) 120; 2 Dev. (N. C.) 388; 3 Dev. (N. C.) 200. A covenant for quiet enjoyment does not extend as far as a covenant of warranty. 1 Aik. (Vt.) 233.

The covenant for quiet enjoyment is broken only by an entry, or unlawful expulsion from, or some actual disturbance in, the possession. 3 Johns. (N. Y.) 471; 8 Johns. (N. Y.) 483; 7 Wend. (N. Y. 281; 2 Hill (N. Y.) 105; 9 Metc. (Mass.) 63; 4 Whart. (Pa.) 86; 4 Cow. (N. Y.) 340. But the tortious entry of the covenantor, without title, is a breach of the covenant for quiet enjoyment. 7 Johns. (N. Y.) 376.

QUIETA NON MOVERE. Not to unsettle things which are established. 28 Barb. (N. Y.) 9, 22.

QUIETARE (Law Lat.) To quit, acquit, discharge, or save harmless. A formal word in old deeds of donation and other conveyances. Cowell.

QUIETE CLAMARE, or **QUIETUM CLAmare.** To quitclaim or renounce all pretensions of right and title. Cowell; Fleta.

QUIETUS (Lat. freed or acquitted).

——**In English Law.** A discharge; an acquittance.

An instrument by the clerk of the pipe and auditors in the exchequer, as proof of their acquittance or discharge as accountants. Cowell.

Discharge of a judge or attorney general. 3 Mod. 99.

——**In American Law.** The discharge of an executor by the probate court. 4 Mason (U. S.) 131.

QUIETUS REDDITUS. In old English law. Quit rent (*q. v.*) Spelman.

QUILIBET POTEST RENUNCIARE JURI pro se inducto. Any one may renounce a law introduced for his own benefit. To this rule there are some exceptions. See 1 Bouv. Inst. note 83; 3 Curt. C. C. (U. S.) 393; 1 Exch. 657.

QUINQUE PORTUS. The Cinque Ports (*q. v.*).

QUINQUEPARTITE. In five parts.

QUINSIEME, or **QUINZIME** (Law Fr. and Eng.) In old English law. A fifteenth; a tax so called. Cowell. See "Fifteenths."

QUINTO EXACTUS (Lat.) In old English law. The fifth call or last requisition of a defendant sued to outlawry.

QUIRE OF DOVER. In English law. A record in the exchequer, showing the tenures for guarding and repairing Dover Castle, and determining the services of the Cinque Ports. 3 How. St. Tr. 868.

QUIRITARIAN OWNERSHIP. In Roman law. Ownership in the strict forms of law; legal title, as distinguished from the equitable title known as "Bonitarian ownership."

QUISQUIS EST QUI VELIT JURIS CONsultus haberi, continuet studium, velit a quocunque doceri. Whoever wishes to be held a jurisconsult, let him continually study, and desire to be taught by everybody.

QUISQUIS PRAESUMITUR BONUS; ET semper in dubiis pro reo respondendum. Every one is presumed good; and in doubtful cases the resolution should be ever for the accused.

QUIT RENT. A rent paid by the tenant of the freehold, by which he goes quit and free,—that is, discharged from any other rent. 2 Bl. Comm. 42.

In England, quit rents were rents reserved to the king or a proprietor, on an absolute grant of waste land, for which a price in gross was at first paid, and a mere nominal rent reserved as a feudal acknowledgment of tenure. Inasmuch as no rent of this description can exist in the United States, when a quit rent is spoken of, some other interest must be intended. 5 Call (Va.) 364. A perpetual rent reserved on a conveyance in fee simple is sometimes known by the name of "quit rent" in Massachusetts. See "Ground Rent;" "Rent."

QUITCLAIM. In conveyancing. A form of deed of the nature of a release, containing words of grant as well as release. 2 Washb. Real Prop. 606.

The term is in constant and general use in American law to denote a deed substantially the same as a release in English law. It presupposes a previous or precedent conveyance, or a subsisting estate and possession. Thornton, Conv. 44. It is a conveyance at common law, but differs from a release in that it is regarded as an original conveyance in American law, at least in some states. 6 Pick, (Mass.) 499; 14 Pick. (Mass.) 374; 3 Conn. 398; 9 Ohio, 96; 5 Ill. 117; Rev. St. Me. c. 73, § 14; Code Miss. 1857, p. 309, art. 17. The operative words are "remise, release, and forever quitclaim." Thornton, Conv. 44. Covenants of warranty against incumbrances by the grantor are usually added.

QUITE CLAMAUNCE (Law Fr.) Quitclaim. Britt. c. 85.

QUITTANCE. A discharge or release; abbreviated from "acquittance."

QUO ANIMO (Lat. with what intention). The intent; the mind with which a thing has been done; 17 Ill. 501; as, the *quo animo* with which the words were spoken may be shown by the proof of conversations of the defendant relating to the original defamation. 19 Wend. (N. Y.) 296.

QUO JURE, WRIT OF. In English law. The name of a writ commanding the defendant to show by what right he demands common of pasture in the land of the complainant who claims to have a fee in the same. Fitzh. Nat. Brev. 299.

QUO LIGATUR, EO DISSOLVITUR. By the same mode by which a thing is bound, by that is it released. 2 Rolle, 21.

QUO MINUS (Lat.) The name of a writ. In England, when the king's debtor is sued in the court of the exchequer, he may have a writ *quo minus* by which he avers the wrong done by him by defendant, *quo minus sufficiens existit* (by which he is less able) to pay the king's debt. This was originally necessary to give jurisdiction to the court of exchequer.

QUO MODO QUID CONSTITUITUR EOdem modo dissolvitur. In the same manner by which anything is constituted, by that it is dissolved. Jenk. Cent. Cas. 74.

QUO WARRANTO (Lat. by what authority).

——**In Old Practice.** The name of a writ (and also of the whole pleading) by which the government commences an action to recover an office or franchise from the person or corporation in possession of it.

The writ commands the sheriff to summon the defendant to appear before the court to which it is returnable, to show (*quo warranto*) by what authority he claims the office or franchise. It was a writ of right, a civil remedy to try the mere right to the franchise or office, where the person in possession never had a right to it, or has forfeited it by neglect or abuse. 33 Miss. 523; 3 Bl. Comm. 262, 263.

The action of *quo warranto* was prescribed by the statute of Gloucester (6 Edw. I), and is a limitation upon the royal prerogative. Before this statute, the king, by virtue of his prerogative,, sent commissions over the kingdom to inquire into the right to all franchises, *quo jure quove nomine illi retinent*, etc.; and, as they were grants from the crown, if those in possession of them could not show a charter, the franchises were seized into the king's hands without any judicial proceeding. Like all other original civil writs, the writ of *quo warranto* issued out of chancery, and was returnable alternatively before the king's bench or justices in eyre. 2 Inst. 277-283, 494-499; 2 Term R. 549. See 4 Term R. 381; 2 Strange, 819, 1196.

——**In Modern Practice.** The writ of *quo warranto* has given place to an information in the nature of *quo warranto*. 3 Bl. Comm. 263; 1 Serg. & R. (Pa.) 382; 58 N. H. 113. Such informations ordinarily issue in the name of the attorney general, either *ex officio*, or on the relation of some private person.

The remedy by *quo warranto* is the proper one to try title to public (1 Ark. 279; 33 Miss. 509) or corporate office (20 Fla. 784; 61 Pa. 339), or to revoke a charter or franchise (8 Vt. 489; 45 Wis. 579).

The judgment on an information in the nature of *quo warranto* is not punitive, but extends only to ouster from the office or franchise usurped. 3 Bl. Comm. 263; 4 Wis. 567.

QUOAD HOC (Lat. as to this; with respect to this). A term frequently used to signify, as to the thing named, the law is so and so.

QUOCUMQUE MODO VELIT, QUOCUMque modo possit. In any way he wishes, in any way he can. 14 Johns. (N. Y.) 484, 492.

QUOD A QUOQUE POENAE NOMINE exactum est id codem restituere nemo cogitur. That which has been exacted as a penalty no one is obliged to restore. Dig. 50. 17. 46.

QUOD AB INITIO NON VALET, IN TRACtu temporis non convalescet. What is not good in the beginning cannot be rendered good by time. Merlin, Repert. verb. Regle de Droit. This, though true in general, is not universally so. 4 Coke, 26; Broom, Leg. Max. (3d London Ed.) 166, 172, note.

QUOD AD JUS NATURALE ATTINET, omnes homines aequales sunt. All men are equal as far as the natural law is concerned. Dig. 50. 17. 32.

QUOD AEDIFICATUR IN AREA LEGATA cedit legato. Whatever is built upon land given by will passes with the gift of the land. Amos & F. Fixt. (2d Ed.) 246; Broom, Leg. Max. (3d London Ed.) 377.

QUOD ALIAS BONUM ET JUSTUM EST, si per vim vel fraudem petatur, malum et injustum efficitur. What is otherwise good and just, if sought by force or fraud, becomes bad and unjust. 3 Coke, 78.

QUOD ALIAS NON FUIT LICITUM NEcessitas licitum facit. Necessity makes that lawful which otherwise were unlawful. Fleta, lib. 5, c. 23, § 14.

QUOD APPROBO NON REPROBO. What I accept I do not reject. Broom, Leg. Max. (3d London Ed.) 636.

QUOD ATTINET AD JUS CIVILE, SERVI pro nullis habentur, non tamen et jure naturali, quia, quod ad jus naturale attinet, omnes homines aequali sunt. So far as the civil law is concerned, slaves are not reckoned as persons, but not so by natural law, for, so far as regards natural law, all men are equal. Dig. 50. 17. 32.

QUOD BILLA CASSETUR. That the bill be quashed. The common-law form of a judgment sustaining a plea in abatement, where the proceeding is by bill, *i. e.*, by a *capias* instead of by original writ.

QUOD CLERICI BENEFICIATI DE CANcellaria. A writ to exempt a clerk of the chancery from the contribution towards the proctors of the clergy in parliament, etc. Reg. Orig. 261.

QUOD CLERICI NON ELIGANTUR IN officio ballivi, etc. A writ which lay for a clerk who, by reason of some land he had, was made, or was about to be made, bailiff, beadle, reeve, or some such officer, to obtain exemption from serving the office. Reg. Orig. 187.

QUOD COMPUTET (Lat. that he account). The name of an interlocutory judgment in an action of account render. Also the name of a decree in the case of creditors' bills against executors or administrators. Such a decree directs the master to take the accounts between the deceased and all his creditors, to cause the creditors, upon due and public notice, to come before him to prove their debts, at a certain place and within a limited period, and also directs the master to take an account of all personal estate of the deceased in the hands of the executor or administrator. Story, Eq. Jur. § 548. See "Judgment."

QUOD CONSTAT CLARE, NON DEBET verificari. What is clearly apparent need not be proved. 10 Mod. 150.

QUOD CONSTAT CURIAE OPERE TEStium non indiget. What appears to the court needs not the help of witnesses. 2 Inst. 662.

QUOD CONTRA JURIS RATIONEM REceptum est, non est producendum ad consequentias. What has been admitted against the reason of the law ought not to be drawn into precedents. Dig. 50. 17. 141; 12 Coke, 75.

QUOD CONTRA LEGEM FIT, PRO INfecto habetur. What is done contrary to the law is considered as not done. 4 Coke, 31. No one can derive any advantage from such an act.

QUOD CUM (Lat.) In pleading. For that whereas. A form of introducing matter of inducement in those actions in which introductory matter is allowed to explain the nature of the claim; as, *assumpsit* and case. Hardr. 1; 2 Show, 180.

This form is not allowable to introduce the matter which constitutes the gravamen of the charge, as such matter must be stated by positive averment, while *quod cum* introduces the matter which depends upon it by way of recital merely. Hence, in those actions, as trespass *vi et armis*, in which the complaint is stated without matter of inducement, *quod cum* cannot be properly used. 2 Bulst. 214. But its improper use is cured by verdict. 1 Browne (Pa.) 68; Comyn, Dig. "Pleader" (C 86).

QUOD CURIA CONCESSIT. L. Lat. Which the court granted. A phrase in the old reports. Yearb. M. 4 Hen. VI. 19. Id. M. 9 Hen. VI. 40. 6 Mod. 28.

QUOD DATUM EST ECCLESIAE, DAtum est Deo. What is given to the church is given to God. 2 Inst. 590.

QUOD DEMONSTRANDI CAUSA ADDItur rei satis demonstratae, frustra fit. What is added to a thing sufficiently palpable, for the purpose of demonstration, is vain. 10 Coke, 113.

QUOD DUBITAS, NE FECERIS. When you doubt about a thing, do not do it. 1 Hale, P. C. 310.

QUOD EI DEFORCEAT (Lat.) In English law. The name of a writ given by St. Westminster II. (13 Edw. I. c. 4), to the owners of a particular estate, as for life, in dower, by the curtesy, or in fee tail, who are barred of the right of possession by a recovery had against them through their default or nonappearance in a possessory action, by which the right was restored to him who had been thus unwarily deforced by his own default. 3 Bl. Comm. 193.

QUOD ENIM SEMEL AUT BIS EXISTIT praetereunt legislatores. That which never happens but once or twice, legislators pass by. Dig. 1. 3. 17.

QUOD EST EX NECESSITATE NUNquam introducitur, nisi quando necessarium. What is introduced of necessity is never introduced except when necessary. 2 Rolle, 512.

QUOD EST INCONVENIENS, AUT CONtra rationem non permissum est in lege. What is inconvenient or contrary to reason is not allowed in law. Co. Litt. 178.

QUOD EST NECESSARIUM EST LICItum. What is necessary is lawful. Jenk. Cent. Cas. 76.

QUOD FACTUM EST, CUM IN OBSCURO sit, ex affectione cujusque capit interpretationem. When there is doubt about an act or expression, it receives interpretation from the (known) feelings or affections of the actor or writer. Dig. 50. 17. 168. 1.

QUOD FIERI DEBET FACILE PRAEsumitur. That is easily presumed which ought to be done. Halk. Max. 153.

QUOD FIERI NON DEBET, FACTUM VAlet. What ought not to be done, when done, is valid. 5 Coke, 38; 12 Mod. 438; 6 Mees. & W. 58; 9 Mees. & W. 636.

QUOD FUIT CONCESSUM. Which was granted.

QUOD IN JURE SCRIPTO "JUS" APPELlatur, id in lege Angliae "rectum" esse dicitur. What in the civil law is called *"jus,"* in the law of England is said to be *"rectum"* (right). Co. Litt. 260; Fleta, lib. 6, c. 1, § 1.

QUOD IN MINORI VALET, VALEBIT IN majori; et quod in majori non valet, nec valebit in minori. What avails in the less will avail in the greater; and what will not avail in the greater will not avail in the less. Co. Litt. 260.

QUOD IN UNO SIMILIUM VALET, VAlebit in altere. What avails in one of two similar things will avail in the other. Co. Litt. 191.

QUOD INCONSULTO FECIMUS, CONsultius devocemus. What is done without consideration or reflection, upon better consideration we should revoke or undo. Jenk. Cent. Cas. 116.

QUOD INITIO VITIOSUM EST, NON POtest tractu temporis convalescere. Time cannot render valid an act void in its origin. Dig. 50. 17. 29.

QUOD IPSIS, QUI CONTRAXERUNT, OBstat; et successoribus eorum obstabit. That which bars those who have contracted will bar their successors also. Dig. 50. 17. 103.

QUOD JUSSU (Lat.) In civil law. The name of an action given to one who had contracted with a son or slave, by order of the father or master, to compel such father or master to stand to the agreement. Halifax, Civ. Law, bk. 3, c. 2, No. 3; Inst. 4. 7. 1; Dig. 15. 4.

QUOD JUSSU ALTERIUS SOLVITUR pro eo est quasi ipsi solutum esset. That which is paid by the order of another is, so far as such person is concerned, as if it had been paid to himself. Dig. 50. 17. 180.

QUO LIGATUR, EO DISSOLVITUR. As a thing is bound, so it is unbound. 2 Rolle, 21.

QUOD MEUM EST, SINE FACTO SIVE defectu nostro, amitti seu in alium transferri non potest. That which is ours cannot be lost or transferred to another without our own act or default. 8 Coke, 92; Broom, Leg. Max. (3d London Ed.) 415; 1 Prest. Abstr. 147, 318.

QUOD MEUM EST SINE ME AUFERRI non potest. What is mine cannot be taken away without my consent. Jenk. Cent. Cas. 251. But see "Eminent Domain."

QUOD MINUS EST IN OBLIGATIONEM videtur deductum. That which is the less is held to be imported into the contract; *e. g.*, A. offers to hire B.'s house at six hundred dollars at the same time B. offers to let it for five hundred dollars; the contract is for five hundred dollars. 1 Story, Cont. (4th Ed.) 481.

QUOD NATURALIS RATIO INTER OMnes homines constituit, vocatur jus gentium. That which natural reason has established among all men is called the law of nations. Dig. 1. 1. 9; Inst. 1. 2. 1; 1 Bl. Comm. 43.

QUOD NECESSARIE INTELLIGITUR ID non deest. What is necessarily understood is not wanting. 1 Bulst. 71.

QUOD NECESSITAS COGIT, DEFENDIT. What necessity forces, it justifies. Hale, P. C. 54.

QUOD NON APPARET NON EST, ET non apparet judicialiter ante judicium. What appears not does not exist, and nothing appears judicially before judgment. 2 Inst. 479; Jenk. Cent. Cas. 207.

QUOD NON CAPIT CHRISTUS, CAPIT fiscus. What the church does not take, the treasury takes. Y. B. 19 Hen. VI. 1.

QUOD NON FUIT NEGATUM (Law Lat. which was not denied). A phrase found in the old reports. Latch, 213. Otherwise stated *quod nemo negavit*, which no one denied.

QUOD NON HABET PRINCIPIUM NON habet finem. What has no beginning has no end. Co. Litt. 345; Broom, Leg. Max. (3d London Ed.) 170, 171.

QUOD NON LEGITUR, NON CREDITUR. What is not read is not believed. 4 Coke, 304.

QUOD NON VALET IN PRINCIPALIA, IN accessoria seu consequentia non valebit; et quod non valet in magis propinquo, non valebit in magis remoto. What is not good as to things principal will not be good as to accessories or consequences; and what is not of force as regards things near will not be of force as to things remote. 8 Coke, 78.

QUOD NOTA (Lat.) Which note; which mark. A reporter's note in the old books, directing attention to a point or rule. Dyer, 23.

QUOD NULLIUS ESSE POTEST ID UT alicujus fieret nulla obligatio valet efficere. No agreement can avail to make that the property of any one which cannot be acquired as property. Dig. 50. 17. 182.

QUOD NULLIUS EST, EST DOMINI REgis. That which belongs to nobody belongs to our lord the king. Fleta, lib. 3; Broom, Leg. Max. (3d London Ed.) 317; Bac. Abr. "Prerogative" (B); 2 Bl. Comm. 260.

QUOD NULLIUS EST ID RATIONE NAturali occupanti conceditur. What belongs to no one, by natural reason belongs to the first occupant. Inst. 2. 1. 12; 1 Bouv. Inst. note 491; Broom, Leg. Max. (3d London Ed.) 316.

QUOD NULLUM EST NULLUM PRODUcit effectum. That which is null produces no effect. Tray. Lat. Max. 519.

QUOD OMNES TANGIT, AB OMNIBUS debet supportari. That which concerns all ought to be supported by all. 3 How. St. Tr. 818, 1087.

QUOD PARTES REPLACITENT. (Lat. that the parties do replead). The form of the judgment on award of a repleader. 2 Salk. 579.

QUOD PARTITIO FIAT. See "Judgment."

QUOD PENDET, NON EST PRO EO, quasi sit. What is in suspense is considered as not existing during such suspense. Dig. 50. 17. 169. 1.

QUOD PER ME NON POSSUM, NEC PER alium. What I cannot do in person, I cannot do through the agency of another. 4 Coke, 24b; 11 Coke, 87a.

QUOD PER RECORDUM PROBATUM non debet esse negatum. What is proved by the record ought not to be denied.

QUOD PERMITTAT (Lat.) In English law. That he permit. The name of a writ which lies, for the heir of him who is disseised of his common of pasture, against the heir of the disseisor, he being dead. Termes de la Ley.

QUOD PERMITTAT PROSTERNERE (Lat. that he give leave to demolish). In English law. The name of a writ which commands the defendant to permit the plaintiff to abate the nuisance of which complaint is made, or otherwise to appear in court and to show cause why he will not. On proof of the facts, the plaintiff is entitled to have judgment to abate the nuisance and to recover damages. This proceeding, on account of its tediousness and expense, has given way to a special action on the case.

QUOD POPULUS POSTREMUM JUSSIT, id jus ratum esto. What the people have last enacted, let that be the established law. 1 Bl. Comm. 89.

QUOD PRIMUM EST INTENTIONE ULtimum est in operatione. That which is first in intention is last in operation. Bac. Max.

QUOD PRINCIPI PLACUIT LEGIS HAbet vigorem. That which has pleased the prince has the force of law. The emperor's pleasure has the force of law. Dig. 1. 4. 1; Inst. 1. 2. 6. A celebrated maxim of imperial law.

QUOD PRINCIPI PLACUIT, LEGIS HAbet vigorem; utpote cum lege regia, quae de imperio ejus lata est, populus ei et in eum omne suum imperium et potestatem conferat. The will of the emperor has the force of law; for, by the royal law which has been made concerning his authority, the people has conferred upon him all its own sovereignty and power. Dig. 1. 4. 1; Inst. 1. 2. 1; Fleta, lib. 1, c. 17; § 7, Bracton, 107; Seld. Diss. ad Flet. c. 3, §§ 2-5.

QUOD PRIUS EST VERIUS EST; ET quod prius est tempore potius est jure. What is first is truest; and what comes first in time is best in law. Co. Litt. 347.

QUOD PRO MINORE LICITUM EST ET pro majore licitum est. What is lawful in the less is lawful in the greater. 8 Coke, 43.

QUOD PROSTRAVIT (Lat.) The name of a judgment upon an indictment for a nuisance, that the defendant abate such nuisance.

QUOD PURE DEBETUR PRAESENTI die debetur. That which is due unconditionally is due now. Tray. Leg. Max. 519.

QUOD QUIS EX CULPA SUA DAMNUM sentit, non intelligitur damnum sentire. He who suffers a damage by his own fault is not held to suffer damage. Dig. 50. 17. 203.

QUOD QUIS SCIENS INDEBITUM DEDIT hac mente, ut postea repeteret, repetere non potest. What one has paid knowing it not to be due, with the intention of recovering it back, he cannot recover back. Dig. 2. 6. 50.

QUOD QUISQUIS NOVIT IN HOC SE EXerceat. Let every one employ himself in what he knows. 11 Coke, 10.

QUOD RECUPERET (Lat. that he recover). The form of a judgment that the plaintiff do recover. See "Judgment."

QUOD REMEDIO DESTITUITUR IPSA re valet si culpa absit. What is without a remedy is by that very fact valid if there be no fault. Bac. Max. reg. 9; 3 Bl. Comm. 20.

QUOD SEMEL AUT BIS EXISTIT PRAEtereunt legislatores. Legislators pass over what happens (only) once or twice. Dig. 1. 3. 6; Broom, Leg. Max. (3d London Ed.) 45.

QUOD SEMEL MEUM EST AMPLIUS meum esse non potest. What is once mine cannot be mine more completely. Co. Litt. 49b; Shep. Touch. 212; Broom, Leg. Max. (3d London Ed.) 415, note.

QUOD SEMEL PLACUIT IN ELECTIONE, amplius displicere non potest. That which, in making his election, a man has once been pleased to choose, he cannot afterwards quarrel with. Co. Litt. 146.

QUOD SI CONTINGAT (Law Lat. that if it happen). Words by which a condition might formerly be created in a deed. Litt. § 330.

QUOD SOLO INAEDIFICATUR SOLO CEdit. Whatever is built on the soil is an accessory of the soil. Inst. 2. 1. 29; 16 Mass. 449; 2 Bouv. Inst. note 1571.

QUOD SUB CERTA FORMA CONCESsum vel reservatum est, non trahitur ad valorem vel compensationem. That which is granted or reserved under a certain form is not to be drawn into valuation or compensation. Bac. Max. reg. 4.

QUOD SUBINTELLIGITUR NON DEEST. What is understood is not wanting. 2 Ld. Raym. 832.

QUOD TACITE INTELLIGITUR DEESSE non videtur. What is tacitly understood does not appear to be wanting. 4 Coke, 22.

QUOD VANUM ET INUTILE EST, LEX non requirit. The law does not require what is vain and useless. Co. Litt. 319.

QUOD VERO CONTRA RATIONEM JUris receptum est, non est producendum ad

consequentias. But that which has been admitted contrary to the reason of the law ought not to be drawn into precedents. Dig. 1. 3. 14; Broom, Leg. Max. (3d London Ed.) 150.

QUOD VOLUIT NON DIXIT. He did not say what he intended to. 1 Kent, Comm. 468, note; 4 Maule & S. 522, arg.; 1 Johns. Ch. (N. Y.) 235.

QUODCUNQUE ALIQUIS OB TUTELAM corporis suit fecerit jure id fecisse videtur. Whatever one does in defense of his person, that he is considered to have done legally. 2 Inst. 590.

QUODQUE DISSOLVITUR EODEM MOdo quo ligatur. In the same manner that a thing is bound, it is unbound. 2 Rolle, 39; Broom, Leg. Max. (3d London Ed.) 788; 2 Man. & G. 729.

QUOMODO QUID CONSTITUITUR EOdem modo dissolvitur. In whatever mode a thing is constituted, in the same manner is it dissolved. Jenk. Cent. Cas. 74.

QUONIAM ATTACHIAMENTA (Law Lat.) Since the attachments. One of the oldest books in the Scotch law; so called from the two first words of the volume. Bell, Dict. Still sometimes cited in argument, in the Scotch courts. 7 Wilson & S. 9.

QUORUM. Used substantively, quorum signifies the number of persons belonging to a legislative assembly, a corporation, society, or other body, required to transact business. There is a difference between an act done by a definite number of persons, and one performed by an indefinite number. In the first case, a majority is required to constitute a quorum, unless the law expressly directs that another number may make one. 88 Pa. St. 42; 9 Wend. (N. Y.) 394; 7 Cow. (N. Y.) 402. In the latter case, any number who may be present may act, the majority of those present having, as in other cases, the right to act. 1 Barn. & C. 492.

In the absence of special provision, a majority is a quorum (12 Metc. [Mass.] 99; 13 Ind. 581), but sometimes the law requires a greater number than a bare majority to form a quorum. In such case, no quorum is present until such a number convene.

In the absence of a rule of procedure to the contrary, the presence of a quorum in a legislative body can only be ascertained from the votes recorded on the particular matter submitted (117 N. C. 158); but a rule authorizing the presiding officer to count members present and not voting to make up a quorum is within the power of a legislative body (144 U. S. 1).

QUORUM PRAETEXTA, NEC AUGET nec minuit sententiam, sed tantum confirmat prae missa. "*Quorum praetexta*" neither increases nor diminishes the meaning, but only confirms that which went before. Plowd. 52.

QUORUM UNUS. One of the quorum. In England it was formerly the practice to appoint certain justices of the peace, one of whom must be present for the transaction of certain business, such justices being named in the commission of all the justices (*quorum aliquem vestrum A. B., C. D., etc., unum esse volumus*). Such justices were called "justices of the quorum." The present practice is to name all the justices, so that the designation is of no practical importance.

QUOT. In Scotch law. The twentieth part of the movables, computed without computation of debts, was so called.

Formerly the bishop was entitled, in all confirmations, to the quot of the testament. Ersk. Inst. 3. 9. 11.

QUOTA. A proportionate share of anything required to be paid, supplied, or furnished.

QUOTATION. The listed price bid, offered, or paid for properties or commodities currently dealt in.

QUOTIENS DUBIA INTERPRETATIO LIbertatis est, secundum libertatem respondendum erit. Whenever there is a doubt between liberty and slavery, the decision must be in favor of liberty. Dig. 50. 17. 20.

QUOTIENS IDEM SERMO DUAS SENtentias exprimit, ea potissimum excipiatur, quae rei gerendae aptior est. Whenever the same words express two meanings, that is to be taken which is the better fitted for carrying out the proposed end. Dig. 50. 17. 67.

QUOTIES IN STIPULATIONIBUS AMbigua oratio est, commodissimum est id accipi quo res de quo agitur, in tuto sit. Whenever in stipulations the expression is ambiguous, it is most proper to give it that interpretation by which the subject matter may be in safety. Dig. 41. 1. 80; Id. 50. 16. 219.

QUOTIES IN VERBIS NULLA EST AMbiguitas ibi nulla expositio contra verba fienda est. When there is no ambiguity in the words, then no exposition contrary to the words is to be made. Co. Litt. 147; Broom, Leg. Max. (3d London Ed.) 850.

QUOTUPLEX (Lat.) Of how many kinds; of how many fold. A term of frequent occurrence in Sheppard's Touchstone. Shep. Touch. 37, 50, 117, 160 et passim.

QUOUSQUE. A Latin adverb, which signifies how long, how far, until.

In old conveyances, it is used as a word of limitation. 10 Coke, 41.

In practice, it is the name of an execution which is to have force until the defendant shall do a certain thing. Of this kind is the *capias ad satisfaciendum,* by virtue of which the body of the defendant is taken into execution, and he is imprisoned until he shall satisfy the execution. 3 Bouv. Inst. note 3371.

QUOVIS MODO (Lat.) In whatever manner. 10 East, 476.

QUUM (Lat.) When.

QUUM DE LUCRO DUORUM QUAERAtur, melior est conditio possidentis. When the gain of one of two is in question, the condition of the possessor is the better. Dig. 50. 17. 126. 2.

QUUM IN TESTAMENTO AMBIGUE AUT etiam perperam scriptum est, benigne interpretari et secundum id quod credibile et cogitatum, credendum est. When in a will an ambiguous or even an erroneous expression occurs, it should be construed liberally, and in accordance with what is thought the probable meaning of the testator. Dig. 34. 5. 24; Broom, Leg. Max. (3d London Ed.) 437. See Brissonius, "Perperam."

QUUM (CUM) PRINCIPALIS CAUSA non consistit ne ea quidem quae sequuntur locum habent. When the principal does not hold its ground, neither do the accessories find place. Dig. 50. 17. 129. 1; Broom, Leg. Max. (3d London Ed.) 438; 1 Poth. Obl. 413.

QUUM QUOD AGO NON VALET UT ago, valeat quantum valere potest. When what I do is of no force as to the purpose for which I do it, let it be of force to as great a degree as it can. 1 Vent. 216.

QUYKE. In old records. Quick; living; a quick or live beast. Cowell.

QY (Law Fr.) Who; which. Kelham.

R

RACHAT (Fr.) Ransom; relief. Ord. Mar. liv. 3, tit. 3, art. 19; Emerig. Tr. des Assur. c. 12, § 21; Guyot, Inst. Feud. c. 5.

RACHATER (Law Fr.) To redeem; to repurchase, or buy back. Kelham.

RACHETUM (Fr. *racheter,* to redeem). In Scotch law. Ransom; corresponding to Saxon *weregild,* a pecuniary composition for an offense. Skene de Verb. Sign.; Jacob.

RACHIMBURGII, or **RACHINBURGII** (Law Lat.) In old European law. Rachenburgers or Rakenburghs; judges among the Salians, Ripuarians, and some other nations of Germany who sat with the count (*comes*) in his court called *mallum,* and were generally associated with him in all matters. L. Salic. tits. 52, 59; L. Ripuar. tit. 32, § 3; Capit. Carol. lib. 5, c. 14; Spelman. The word was found by Spelman in an old MS. copy of the laws of Canute. Montesquieu writes it *rathimburges.* Esprit des Lois, liv. 30, c. 18.

RACK. An engine with which to torture a supposed criminal, in order to extort a confession of his supposed crime, and the names of his supposed accomplices. It is unknown in the United States, but, known by the nickname of the "Duke of Exeter's Daughter," was in use in England. Barr. Obs. St. 366; 12 Serg. & R. (Pa.) 227.

RACK RENT. In English law. The full extended value of land left by lease, payable by a tenant for life or years. Wood, Inst. 192.

RADECHENISTRES. A word used in Domesday Book, which Spelman interprets to mean "freemen." Domesday Book, fol. 18, tit. "Glowc. Berchelay;" Spelman.

RADOUR. In French law. A term including the repairs made to a ship, and a fresh supply of furniture and victuals, munitions, and other provisions required for the voyage. Pardessus, note 602.

RAENCON (Law Fr.) A ransom, or fine. *Ou par ranceoun ou par amercement.* Artic. sup. Chart.

RAFFLE. A form of lottery by which the price of an article is divided into shares, and the article awarded by chance to one of the shareholders. Cent. Dict.

RAGEMAN, or **RAGMAN.** A statute, so called, of justices assigned by Edw. I. and his council, to go a circuit through all England, and to hear and determine all complaints of injuries done within five years next before Michaelmas, in the fourth year of his reign. Spelman.

RAGMAN'S ROLL, or **RAGIMUND'S roll.** A roll, called from one Ragimund, or Ragimont, a legate in Scotland, who, summoning all the beneficed clergymen in that kingdom, caused them on oath to give in the true value of their benefices, according to which, they were afterwards taxed by the court of Rome. Wharton.

RAILROAD, or **RAILWAY.** The terms "railroad" and "railway" are synonymous. 30 Minn. 524. Their significance varies with the context, being used sometimes to include all appurtenances (173 Ill. 521, 46 N. J. Law, 289; 58 Pa. St. 252), and sometimes as including only the immovable structure, graded and railed for the use of trains (93 U. S. 442). Ordinarily, when used without qualifying words, the term "railroad" means those railroads specially laid out and graded having parallel rails of iron or steel for the wheels of carriages drawn by steam or other motive power, to run upon, 156 Ill. 294, but in some connections it has been held to include street or horse railroads. 24 Ill. 52.

RAISE. To create; to bring into existence. The term is used in various senses, thus, to "raise" a use is to create it; to "raise" an issue is to file such a plea as to make an issue. Facts are said to "raise" a presumption when they give rise thereto.

RAISING PORTIONS. A term used in old English law for the charging of a devise to one child of testator, with the payment of certain sums to others.

RAN (Saxon). Open theft or robbery. Cowell.

RANGE. In the United States government surveys of lands, the "townships" (*q. v.*) are ranged in tiers east or west of a given meridian, such ranges therefore being a row of towns in a north and south direction. The "towns" are tiers lying at right angles to the ranges.

RANGER. A sworn officer of the forest to inquire of trespasses, and to drive the beasts of the forest out of the deforested ground into the forest. Jacob.

RANK. The order or place in which certain officers are placed in the army and navy, in relation to others. The term is sometimes applied to debts or securities to indicate their precedence in respect to order of payment.

——**In English Law.** Excessive; too large in amount; as a *rank modus.* 2 Bl. Comm. 30.

RANKING. In Scotch law. Determining the order in which the debts of a bankrupt ought to be paid.

RANSOM. A price of redemption of a captive or prisoner of war, or of captured property.

——**In Old English Law.** A price paid for the pardon of some great offense. It differs from amercement in that it excuses from corporal punishment. Cowell.

RANSOM BILL. A contract for payment of ransom of a captured vessel, with stipulations of safe-conduct, if she pursue a certain course and arrive in a certain time. If found out of time or course, the safe-conduct is void. Wheaton, Int. Law, 107*. The payment cannot be enforced in England, during war, by an action on the contract, but can in this country. 1 Kent, Comm. 104, 105; 4 Wash. C. C. (U. S.) 141; 2 Gall. (U. S.) 325.

RAPE.

——**In Criminal Law.** Unlawful carnal knowledge of a woman by force and without her consent.

(1) Carnal knowledge is essential (67 Wis. 552), but by statute in most states, the slightest penetration is enough (see 45 Conn. 256; 102 N. Y. 234), though, at common law, emission was essential (1 East, P. C. 439). (2) The carnal knowledge must be unlawful; thus, forcible carnal knowledge by a man of his wife against her will is not rape. 1 Hale, P. C. 629. (3) The carnal knowledge must be by force, but constructive force, as by threats or intimidation, is sufficient (39 Fla. 155; 45 Conn. 263; 139 Ind. 531); and where the woman is insane or insensible, it has been said that the force necessary to accomplish the act is sufficient (53 Ark. 425; 50 Iowa, 189); but the weight of authority is that fraud (2 Swan [Tenn.] 394; 6 Ala. 765), as by personating the woman's husband (11 Cox, C. C. 191; 7 Conn. 54), will not take the place of force (but see 94 Ind. 96). (4) The carnal knowledge must be without the woman's consent. The phrase "against her will" is sometimes substituted, but it means no more than "without her consent." 22 Wis. 445; 25 Mich. 356. Unless asleep or insensible (12 Cox, C. C. 311), or intimidated by threats (9 Car. & P. 748), the woman must resist "to the uttermost" (19 Wend. [N. Y.] 192; 13 Mich. 427), to the point of inability longer to resist (59 N. Y. 374); and acquiescence, however tardy or reluctant, prevents the offense from being rape (82 Va. 653; 124 Ill. 576).

——**In Old English Law.** A division of a county similar to a hundred, but oftentimes containing in it more hundreds than one.

RAPE OF THE FOREST (Law Lat. *raptus forestae*). In old English law. Trespass committed in a forest by violence. Cowell; Spelman; LL. Hen. I. c. 11.

RAPE REEVE. In English law. The chief officer of a rape (*q. v.*) 1 Bl. Comm. 116.

RAPINA (Lat. from *rapere*, to drag, or carry away forcibly).

——**In the Civil Law.** The violent taking from the person of another of money or goods for the sake of gain; robbery from the person. Halifax, Anal. bk. 2, c. 23, Nos. 1, 2; Heinec. Elem. Jur. Civ. lib. 4, tit. 2, § 1071.

——**In Old English Law.** Open and violent larceny from the person; robbery. St. 14 Car. II. c. 22; Cowell; 4 Bl. Comm. 242.

RAPTOR. In old English law, a ravisher.

RAPTU HAEREDIS. A writ for taking away an heir holding in socage, of which there were two sorts: One when the heir was married; the other when he was not. Reg. Orig. 163.

RAPUIT (Lat. from *rapere*, to ravish). In old English law. Ravished. A technical word in old indictments. 2 East, 30; Wharton, Am. Crim. Law, § 401.

RASE (Law Lat. *raseria;* from Lat. *rasus*, shaved or scraped). In old English law. Strike; struck measure; that in which the commodity measured was made even with the top of the measure, by scraping or striking off all that was above it. An old ordinance for bakers, brewers, etc., provided that toll should be taken "by the rase, and not by the heap or cantel." Cowell quotes the provision, but strangely overlooks the meaning it so clearly expresses, and makes rase (*raseria*) to be "a measure of corn, now disused."

RASURA (Law Lat.; from Lat. *radere*, to scrape). In old English law. A rasure. Fleta, lib. 4, c. 10, §§ 3, 4.

RASURE (Law Fr. *rassure, rasoure*; from Lat. *rasura*, from *radere*, to scrape). A scraping off; the removal of one or more words from an instrument, by scraping the writing off or out. One of the modes by which a deed or other instrument may be avoided, or rendered of no effect. 2 Bl. Comm. 308; Shep. Touch. 55, 63, 71; Fleta, lib. 6, c. 29, § 4. "Rasure" is properly distinguished from "obliteration," which is effected by marking out the writing with pen and ink, or blotting it out by other means; but the terms are sometimes used as synonymous. See 18 Johns. (N. Y.) 499.

RASUS, or RASUM (Law Lat. from *radere*). In old English law. Rased; erased. Fleta, lib. 2, c. 54, § 12. A rase; a measure of onions, containing twenty flones, and each flonis twenty-five heads. Fleta, lib. 2, c. 12, § 12.

Struck; scraped off. *Mensura rasa*, struck measure. Fleta, lib. 2, c. 82, § 1.

RATAM REM HABERE (Lat.) In the civil law. To hold a thing ratified; to ratify or confirm it (*comprobare, agnoscere*). Dig. 46. 8. 12. 1, et per tot.

RATE OF EXCHANGE. In commercial law. The actual price at which a bill, drawn in one country upon another country, can be bought or obtained in the former country at any given time. Story, Bills, § 31.

RATE TITHES. Tithes charged *pro rata* on personal property kept within the parish for less than a year.

RATIFICATION. An agreement to adopt an act performed by another for us.

Express ratifications are those made in express and direct terms of assent. Implied ratifications are such as the law presumes from the acts of the principal; as, if Peter buy goods for James, and the latter, knowing the fact, receive them and apply them to his own use.

It is applied in the sense of "confirmation" to various transactions, but it has been said that it applies properly only to agency. 73 Me. 487.

RATIHABITIO(Lat. from *ratus*, approved, and *habere*, to hold). In civil and old English law. A holding as approved; approval or ratification.

RATIHABITIO MANDATO AEQUIPARAtur. Ratification is equal to a command. Dig. 46. 3. 12. 4; Broom, Leg. Max. (3d London Ed.) 771; Story, Ag. (4th Ed.) 302.

RATIHABITION. Confirmation; approbation of a contract; ratification.

RATING.

——**In Commerce.** The estimate put on the credit and financial resources of a person. There are various institutions or persons who furnish ratings. They are called "mercantile agencies."

——**In Shipping.** The order or class of a vessel according to her magnitude or force.

RATIO (Lat.) A reason; a cause; a reckoning of an account.

RATIO DECIDENDI. The ground of decision.

RATIO EST FORMALIS CAUSA CONsuetudinis. Reason is the source and mold of custom.

RATIO EST LEGIS ANIMA; MUTATA legis ratione mutatur et lex. Reason is the soul of the law; the reason of the law being changed, the law is also changed. 7 Coke, 7.

RATIO EST RADIUS DIVINI LUMINIS. Reason is a ray of divine light. Co. Litt. 232.

RATIO ET AUCTORITAS DUO CLARISsima mundi lumina. Reason and authority are the two brightest lights in the world. 4 Inst. 320.

RATIO IN JURE AEQUITAS INTEGRA. Reason in law is perfect equity.

RATIO LEGIS. The reason or occasion of a law; the occasion of making a law. Bl. Law Tr. 3.

Grotius distinguishes between "ratio" and "*mens*," the meaning or intent of a law.

RATIO LEGIS EST ANIMA LEGIS. The reason of the law is the soul of the law. Jenk. Cent. Cas. 45.

RATIO NON CLAUDITUR LOCO. Reason is not confined to any place.

RATIO POTEST ALLEGARI DEFICIENte lege, sed vera et legalis et non apparens. Reason may be alleged when the law is defective, but it must be true and legal reason, and not merely apparent. Co. Litt. 191.

RATIONABILE ESTOVERIUM. Alimony.

RATIONALIBUS DIVISIS, WRIT DE. The name of a writ which lies properly when two men have lands in several towns or hamlets, so that the one is seised of the land in one town or hamlet, and the other of the other town or hamlet by himself, and they do not know the bounds of the town or hamlet, nor of their respective lands. This writ lies by one against the other, and the object of it is to fix the boundaries. Fitzh. Nat. Brev.

RATIONE (Lat.) By reason; on account.

Ratione impotentiae, on account of inability. A ground of qualified property in some animals *ferae naturae*, as in the young ones, while they are unable to fly or run. 2 Bl. Comm. 394; Hale, Anal. § xxvi.

Ratione loci, by reason of place. A ground of ownership in rabbits and hares. Hale, Anal. § xxvi.

Ratione privilegii, by reason of privilege. A ground of ownership in birds or beasts of warren. Hale, Anal. § xxvi.

Ratione soli, on account of the soil; with reference to the soil. Said to be the ground of ownership in bees. 2 Bl. Comm. 393.

Ratione tenurae, by reason of tenure; as a consequence of tenure. 3 Bl. Comm. 230; 1 Maule & S. 435. A phrase in old pleading. Not the same as "by reason of being owner and proprietor." Le Blanc, J., 1 Maule & S. 441. *Ratione tenurae* implies *ex vi termini*, something originally annexed to the holding. Id.

RATIONE MATERIAE (Lat.) By reason of the subject matter.

RATIONE PERSONAE (Lat.) By reason of the person concerned; from the character of the person.

RATIONE TENURAE (Law Lat.) By reason of tenure; as a consequence of tenure. 3 Bl. Comm. 230.

RATIONES. In old law. The pleadings in a suit. *Rationes exercere*, or *ad rationes stare*, to plead.

RATTENING. The act of trade unionists in causing the tools, clothes, or other property of a workman to be taken away or hidden, in order to compel him to join the union or cease working. It is an offense punishable by fine or imprisonment. 38 & 39 Vict. c. 86, § 7.

RAUNSOM, or **RAUNSOME** (Law Fr.) In old English law. Ransom; a fine; a severe kind of fine. *Sur peyne de raunsome*, on pain of ransom. Britt. c. 11. *Per raunsome simple ou graund, solonc le fait*, by an ordinary or a great ransom, according to the fact. Id. *Puny par prison et greve raunsom.* Id. c. 48.

RAVISHED. In pleading. A technical word necessary in an indictment for rape.

No other word or circumlocution will answer. The defendant should be charged with having "feloniously ravished" the prosecutrix, or woman mentioned in the indictment. Bac. Abr. "Indictment" (G 1); Comyn, Dig. "Indictment" (G 6); Hawk. P. C. 2, c. 25, § 56; Cro. Car. 37; 1 Hale, P. C. 628; 2 Hale, P. C. 184; Co. Litt. 184, note (p); 2 Inst. 180; 1 East, P. C. 447. The words "feloniously did ravish and carnally know" imply that the act was done forcibly and against the will of the woman. 12 Serg. & R. (Pa.) 70. See 3 Chit. Crim. Law, 812.

RAVISHMENT. In criminal law. An unlawful taking of a woman, or of an heir in ward; rape.

RAVISHMENT DE GARD (Law Fr.) An abolished writ, which lay for a guardian by knight's service or in socage, against a person who took from him the body of his ward. Fitzh. Nat. Brev. 140; 12 Car. II. c. 3.

RAVISHMENT OF WARD. In English law. The marriage of an infant ward without the consent of the guardian. It is punishable by St. Westminster II. c. 35.

RE (Lat.) In the matter of.

RE, verbis, scripto, consensu, traditione, junctura, vestes, sumere pacta solent.

From the thing [itself], from words, from writing, from consent, from delivery, from union, agreements usually take their vestments. A couplet formerly in use, framed to express (in aid of the memory) the six different modes in which obligation might be contracted, which were fancifully termed its "vestments," or garments, that is, the forms in which it was clothed. It is twice quoted by Bracton, who explains the six forms in detail. Bracton, fol. 16b; Id. fols. 99-101. It is thus expressed in the prose of Britton: *Obligation doit estre vestue de v. maneres de garnementz; de chose, de parole, de escript, de unite, de volounte, debail, de joynture.* Britt. c. 28. It seems to be a mere extension of the fourfold division of the Institutes; *Aut* re, *aut* verbis, *aut* literis, *aut* consensu. Inst. 3. 14. 2. And see Dig. 44. 7. 52.

RE. FA. LO. An abbreviation of *recordari facias loquelam* (*q. v.*)

REAL.

——**At Common Law.** A term which is applied to land in its most enlarged signification. "Real security," therefore, means the security of mortgages or other incumbrances affecting lands. 2 Atk. 806; 2 Ves. Sr. 547.

——**In Civil Law.** That which relates to a thing, whether it be movable or immovable, lands or goods; thus, a "real injury" is one which is done to a thing, as a trespass to property, whether it be real or personal, in the common-law sense. A real statute is one which relates to a thing, in contradistinction to such as relate to a person.

REAL ACTION.

——**In the Civil Law.** One by which a person seeks to recover his property which is in the possession of another. Dig. 50. 16. 16. It is to be brought against the person who has possession.

——**At Common Law.** One brought for the specific recovery of lands, tenements, or hereditaments. Steph. Pl. 3.

They are droitural when they are based upon the right of property, and possessory when based upon the right of possession. They are either writs of right; writs of entry, which lie in the *per*, the *per et cui*, or the *post*, upon disseisin, intrusion, or alienation; writs ancestral possessory, as *mort d'ancestor, aiel, besaiel, cosinage*, or *nuper obiit.* Comyn, Dig. "Actions" (D 2).

These actions were always local, and were to be brought in the county where the land lay. Bracton, 189, 414. They are now pretty generally laid aside in practice, upon account of the great nicety required in their management, and the inconvenient length of their process,—a much more expeditious method of trying titles being since introduced by other actions, personal and mixed. See Stearns, Real Actions; Booth, Real Actions; Bac. Abr. "Actions;" Comyn, Dig. "Actions;" 3 Bl. Comm. 118.

REAL ASSETS. Lands or real estate in the hands of an heir, chargeable with the payment of the debts of the ancestor. 2 Bl. Comm. 244, 302; 2 Williams, Ex'rs, 436. See "Assets."

REAL BURDEN. In Scotch law. Where a right to lands is expressly granted under the burden of a specific sum, which is declared a burden on the lands themselves, or where the right is declared null if the sum be not paid, and where the amount of the sum, and the name of the creditor in it, can be discovered from the records, the burden is said to be real. Bell, Dict.

REAL CHATTELS. See "Chattel."

REAL CHYMIN (Law Fr.) In old English law. The royal way; the king's highway (*regia via*). Y. B. P. 6 Edw. III. 48.

REAL COMPOSITION. An agreement made, in England, between the owner of land and the incumbent of a parish, with the consent of the ordinary and the patron of the living, that the land shall for the future be discharged from payment of tithes, by reason of some land or other real recompense given in lieu and satisfaction thereof. But since St. 13 Eliz. c. 10, no real composition can be made for any longer term than three lives, or twenty-one years, and such compositions are now rarely heard of. 2 Bl. Comm. 28. See St. 2 & 3 Wm. IV. c. 100, § 2, making valid all compositions confirmed in a certain manner.

REAL CONTRACT.

——**At Common Law.** A contract respecting real property. 3 Rawle (Pa.) 225.

——**In Civil Law.** Those contracts which require the interposition of a thing (*rei*) as the subject of them; for instance, the loan for goods to be "specifically returned."

Contracts are divided into those which are formed by the mere consent of the parties and therefore are called "consensual," such as sale, hiring, and mandate, and those in which it is necessary that there should be something more than mere consent, such as the loan of money, deposit, or pledge, which, from their nature, require the delivery of the thing, whence they are called "real." Poth. Obl. p. 1, c. 1, § 1, art. 2.

REAL COVENANT. A covenant connected with a conveyance of realty, whereby an obligation to pass something real is created, or which is so connected with the realty that he who has the latter is entitled to the benefit of, or is bound to perform, the former. Fitzh. Nat. Brev. 145; Shep. Touch. 161; Platt, Cov. 60, 62.

A covenant which is so connected with the realty as to apply to the owner thereof, either in reference to benefit or obligation, whether he be a party to the instrument creating the covenant or not.

A covenant by which the obligor undertakes to pass something real. Co. Litt. 384b; Stearns, Real Actions, 134. See 4 Kent, Comm. 472.

A covenant by which the covenantor binds his heirs. 2 Bl. Comm. 304.

Very considerable confusion exists among the authorities in the use of the term "real covenants." The definition of Blackstone, which determines the character of covenants from the insertion or noninsertion of the word "heir" by the covenantor, is pretty generally rejected. See Platt, Cov. 61; 2 Bl. Comm. 304, note, 305, note. Of the other definitions, that which makes a real covenant an obligation to pass realty is the most ancient. Upon such a covenant the remedy was by voucher or *warrantia chartae*, and not by the action of covenant.

Together with the disuse of real actions, these covenants gave place to the more modern covenants which furnish the basis of a personal action for damages, and the term "real covenants" lost its ancient signification, and acquired its modern one, as given in the latter part of the first and in the second definition. The covenant to stand seised approaches perhaps more nearly than any covenant still in use to the ancient real covenant.

Covenants are real only when they have entered into the consideration for which land, or some interest therein to which the covenant is annexed, passed between the covenantor and covenantee. 2 Washb. Real Prop. 662, 663.

In England, all covenants for title are held to be real covenants; in the United States, those only which are future in their operation come under this description. 10 Ga. 311.

The object of these covenants is, usually, either to preserve the inheritance, as to keep in repair (3 Lev. 92; 9 Barn. & C. 505; 8 Cow. [N. Y.] 206; 17 Wend. [N. Y.] 148; 1 Dall. [U. S.] 210; 6 Yerg. [Tenn.] 512; 6 Vt. 276; 25 Pa. St. 257; 38 Eng. Law & Eq. 462; to keep buildings insured, and reinstate them if burned (Platt, Cov. 185; 5 Barn. & Adol. 1; 6 Gill & J. [Md.] 372); to continue the relation of landlord and tenant, as to pay rent (5 East, 575; 1 Doug. 183; 1 Wash. C. C. [U. S.] 375; do suit to the lessor's mill (5 Coke, 18; 1 Barn. & C. 410; grind the tenant's corn (2 Yeates [Pa.] 74; 9 Vt. 91); for the renewal of leases (12 East, 469); or to protect the tenant in his enjoyment of the premises, as to warrant and defend (Shep. Touch. 161; 2 Mass. 433; 5 Cow. [N. Y.] 137; 1 Paige, Ch. [N. Y.] 455); to make further assurance (Cro. Car. 503); for quiet enjoyment (Cro. Eliz. 373; 3 Barn. & Ald. 392; 1 C. B. 402; 1 Dev. & B. [N. C.] 94; 23 Me. 383); never to claim or assert title (7 Me. 97; 3 Metc. [Mass.] 121); to remove incumbrances (17 Mass. 586); to release suit and service (Co. Litt. 384b); to produce title deeds in defense of the grantee's title (4 Greenl. Cruise, Dig. 393; 10 Law Mag. 353-357; 1 Sim. & S. 449); to supply water to the premises (4 Barn. & Ald. 266); to draw water off from a mill pond (19 Pick. [Mass.] 449); not to establish another mill on the same stream (17 Wend. [N. Y.] 136); not to erect buildings on adjacent land (4 Paige, Ch. [N. Y.] 510); to use the land in a specified manner (13 Sim. 228); generally to create or preserve easements for the benefit of the land granted (4 E. D. Smith [N. Y.] 122; 1 Brandf. [N. Y.] 40; 2 Greenl. Ev. § 240; 2 Washb. Real Prop. 648). See "Covenant."

REAL ESTATE. Landed property, including all estates and interests in lands which are held for life or for some greater estate, and whether such lands be of freehold or copyhold tenure. Wharton.

REAL-ESTATE BROKER. One who engages in the purchase and sale of real estate as a business and occupation, and so holds himself out to the public in that character and capacity.

REAL EVIDENCE. All evidence of which things (or persons regarded as things) is the source; evidence arising from physical indications or appearances. Thus, the production of a dead body is real evidence of the *corpus delicti.*

REAL INJURY. In the civil law. An injury arising from an unlawful act, as distinguished from a verbal injury, which was done by words. Halifax, Civ. Law, bk. 2, c. 15, notes 3, 4.

REAL LAW.

——**At Common Law.** A popular term used to denote such parts of the system of common law as concern or relate to real property.

——**In Civil Law.** A law which relates to specific property, whether movable or immovable.

If real law in any given case relate to immovable property, it is limited in its operation to the territory within which that is situate, real estate being, both by the common and continental laws, subject exclusively to the laws of the government within whose territory it is situate. Story, Confl. Laws, 426, 428. See "Lex Rei Sitae."

REAL PARTY. Practice statutes frequently require that actions be brought in the name of the "real party in interest." As so used, the term means the person having the real beneficial interest in the obligation sued on. Thus, the assignee of a demand is the real party in interest (68 N. Y. 30), as is the person for whose benefit a contract is made by another (138 N. Y. 468; 112 N. Y. 1).

REAL PROPERTY. Something which may be held by tenure, or will pass to the heir of the possessor at his death, instead of his executor, including lands, tenements, and hereditaments, whether the latter be corporeal or incorporeal. 1 Atk. Conv.

In respect to property, "real" and "personal" correspond very nearly with "immovables" and "movables" of the civil law. By the latter, "*biens*" is a general term for property; and these are classified into movable and immovable, and the latter are subdivided into corporeal and incorporeal. Guyot, Rep. Univ. "Biens."

By "immovables" the civil law intended property which could not be removed at all, or not without destroying the same, together with such movables as are fixed to the freehold, or have been so fixed and are intended to be again united with it, although at the time severed therefrom. Tayl. Civ. Law, 475.

The same distinction and rules of law as to the nature and divisions of property are adopted in Scotland, where, as by the Roman law, another epithet is applied to immovables. They are called "heritables," and go to the heir, as distinguished from "movables," which go to executors or administrators. So, rights connected with or affecting heritable property, such as tithes, servitudes, and the like, are themselves heritable, and in this it coincides with the common law. Ersk. Inst. 192.

In another respect, the Scotch coincides with the common law, in declaring growing crops of annual planting and culture not to be heritable, but to go to executors, etc., although so far a part of the real estate that they would pass by a conveyance of the land. Ersk. Inst. 193; Williams, Ex'rs, 600.

Though the term "real," as applied to property, in distinction from "personal," is now so familiar, it is one of a somewhat recent introduction. While the feudal law prevailed, the terms in use in its stead were "lands," "tenements," or "hereditaments;" and these acquired the epithet of "real" from the nature of the remedy applied by law for the recovery of them, as distinguished from that provided in case of injuries, contracts broken, and the like. In the one case, the claimant or demandant recovered the real thing sued for,—the land itself,—while, ordinarily, in the other he could only recover recompense in the form of pecuniary damages.

The term, it is said as a means of designation, did not come into general use until after the feudal system had lost its hold, nor till even as late as the commencement of the seventeenth century. One of the earliest cases in which the courts applied the distinctive terms of "real" and "personal" to estates, without any words of explanation, is said to have been that of Wind c. Jekyl (A. D. 1719) 1 P. Wms. 575; Williams, Real Prop. 6, 7. See "Land;" "Tenement;" "Hereditaments;" "Fixtures."

REAL REPRESENTATIVE. He who represents or stands in the place of another with respect to his real property is so termed, in contradistinction to him who stands in the place of another with regard to his personal property, and who is termed the "personal representative." Thus, the heir is the real representative of his deceased ancestor, and the executor or administrator is the personal representative.

REAL RIGHT. In Scotch law. That which entitles him who is vested with it to possess the subject as his own, and, if in the possession of another, to demand from him its actual possession.

It is distinguished from a personal right, which is that of action against a debtor, but without any right in the subject which the debtor is obliged to transfer to him. Real rights affect the subject itself; personal rights are founded in obligation. Ersk. Inst. 479.

By analogy, the right which a claimant in an action of replevin seeks to enforce at common law would be a real one, while the compensation which a plaintiff seeks in an action of *assumpsit* or of trover, being a pecuniary one, would be personal.

REAL SECURITY. Security consisting of a lien on realty.

REAL SERVITUDE. Praedial servitude (*q. v.*).

REAL STATUTES. In the civil law. Statutes which have property for their principal object, and do not speak of persons, except in relation to property. Story, Confl. Laws, § 13.

REAL THINGS, or THINGS REAL. In common law. Such things as are permanent, fixed, and immovable, which cannot be carried out of their place; as lands and tenements. 2 Bl. Comm. 15. Things substantial and immovable, and the rights and profits annexed to or issuing out of them. 1 Steph. Comm. 156. This expression is in strictness clearly pleonastic, the sense of thing (*res*) being already implied in the word "real," as will at once appear by giving it a Latin form, *res reales.*

REAL WARRANDICE. In Scotch law, an enfeoffment of one tenement given in security of another.

REAL WRONG. In old English law. An injury to the freehold.

REALITY. In foreign law. That quality of laws which concerns property or things (*quae ad rem spectant*). Story, Confl. Laws, § 16. See "Personalty."

REALM. A kingdom; a country. 1 Taunt. 270; 4 Campb. 289; Rose, 387.

REALTY. A term sometimes used as a collective noun for real property or estate,—more generally to imply that that of which it is spoken is of the nature or character of real property or estate.

The quality of being real, or relating to lands and tenements; things real. 1 Steph. Comm. 156.

REASONABLE ACT. This term signifies such an act as the law requires. When an act is unnecessary, a party will not be required to perform it as a reasonable act. 9 Price, 43; Yelv. 44; Platt, Cov. 342, 157; 42 Mo. 88.

REASONABLE AID. The ordinary or customary aids were so termed. See "Aids."

REASONABLE AND PROBABLE CAUSE. A term sometimes used to express the cause which will justify the institution of a criminal prosecution. It does not appear to differ in meaning from "probable cause," which is the more usual expression. 97 U. S. 642. See "Probable Cause."

REASONABLE CARE. Such care and diligence as an ordinarily prudent man would exercise under the same circumstances. It is synonymous with "ordinary care." 34 Wis. 318; 79 Ga. 44.

The term is altogether a relative one, dependent on the circumstances, and the nature of the duty owed. See 25 Md. 521.

REASONABLE CERTAINTY. To establish a fact to a reasonable certainty requires that degree of proof of certainty which the jurors would be willing to act upon in their own grave and important concerns; that is, the degree of proof should be such that the fact is established beyond a reasonable doubt. "A reasonable doubt" and "reasonable certainty" and "moral certainty" mean one and the same thing. 72 Ill. App. 579.

REASONABLE DOUBT. "The term 'reasonable doubt' is almost incapable of any definition which will add much to what the words themselves imply." Mitchell, J., in 38 Minn. 439.

The most commonly quoted definition is that of Chief Justice Shaw: "An abiding conviction to a moral certainty" (5 Cush. [Mass.] 320); but it has been held that "moral certainty is not equivalent to an absence of reasonable doubt" (47 Ala. 78). It has been defined by negation as not a vague or whimsical doubt (34 Iowa, 520), not a mere conjecture (36 Ala. 211), etc. A practical definition upheld in some jurisdictions is that it is such a doubt as would cause a man to hesitate before acting in his own most important business concerns (10 Minn. 407); but this has been disapproved (1 Dak. 452), and, in general, no affirmative equivalent has ever been given which has not been disapproved in another jurisdiction.

REASONABLE PART. In old English law. That share of a man's goods which the law gave to his wife and children after his decease. Fitzh. Nat. Brev. 122.

REASONABLE TIME. The term is entirely relative and dependent on circumstances. "*Quam longum debet esse rationabile tempus non definitur in lege, sed pendet ex discretione justiciariorum.*" Co. Litt. 50.

So much time as is necessary under the circumstances for a reasonably prudent and diligent man to do, conveniently, what the contract or duty requires should be done, having a regard for the rights and possibility of loss, if any, to the other party to be affected. 126 Ark. 38, 189 S. W. 361, Ann. Cas. 1917 E 521.

REASONABLY. The adverb reasonably, whatever it may originally have meant, as now used, qualifies the condition of things as well as the conduct of persons. One of its definitions is, "in a moderate degree not fully, moderately, tolerably." 3 Ill. App. 610.

REASSURANCE. When an insurer is desirous of lessening his liability, he may procure some other insurer to insure him from loss, for the insurance he has made. This is called "reassurance."

REATTACHMENT. A second attachment of him who was formerly attached, and dismissed the court without day, by the not coming of the justices, or some such casualty. Reg. Orig. 35.

REBATE. In mercantile law. Discount; the abatement of interest in consequence of prompt payment; the repayment of a part on compliance with some condition.

REBEL. A citizen or subject who unjustly and unlawfully takes up arms against the constituted authorities of the nation, to deprive them of the supreme power, either by resisting their lawful and constitutional orders in some particular matter, or to impose on them conditions. Vattel, liv. 3, § 328. In another sense, it signifies a refusal to obey a superior, or the commands of a court.

REBELLION. In criminal law. The taking up arms traitorously against the government; the forcible opposition and resistance to the laws and process lawfully issued.

If the rebellion amount to treason, it is punished by the laws of the United States with death. If it be a mere resistance of process, it is generally punished by fine and imprisonment. See Dalloz; Pen. Code, 209.

REBELLION, COMMISSION OF. In old English practice. A writ issuing out of chancery to compel the defendant to appear.

REBELLIOUS ASSEMBLY. A gathering of twelve persons or more, intending, going about, or practicing unlawfully and of their own authority to change any laws of the realm; or to destroy the inclosure of any park or ground inclosed, banks of fish ponds, oneys in any warren, dove houses, the same shall remain void, or that they shall have way in any of the said grounds; or to destroy the deer in any park, fish in ponds, conveys in any warren, dove houses, etc.; or to burn sacks of corn; or to abate rents or prices of victuals, etc. See Cowell.

REBOUTER. To repel or bar. The action of the heir by the warranty of his ancestor is called "rebut" or "repel."

REBUS SIC STANTIBUS (Lat.) At this point of affairs; in the condition of things.

REBUT. To contradict; to do away. Thus, every homicide is presumed to be murder unless the contrary appears from evidence which proves the death; and this presumption it lies on the defendant to rebut, by showing that it was justifiable or excusable. Alis. Sc. Crim. Law, 48.

REBUTTABLE PRESUMPTION. In the law of evidence. A presumption which may be rebutted by evidence. Otherwise called a "disputable" presumption. A species of legal presumption which holds good until disproved. Best, Pres. § 25; 1 Greenl. Ev. § 33.

REBUTTER. In pleading. The defendant's third pleading, being his answer to the surrejoinder.

REBUTTING EVIDENCE. That evidence which is given by a party in the cause to explain, repel, counteract, or disprove facts given in evidence on the other side. The term "rebutting evidence" is more particularly applied to that evidence given by the plaintiff to explain or repel the evidence given by the defendant.

RECALL A JUDGMENT. To reverse a judgment on a matter of fact. The judgment is then said to be recalled or revoked; and when it is reversed for an error of law, it is said simply to be reversed, *quod judicium reversetur.*

RECAPTION. The act of a person who has been deprived of the custody of another, to which he is legally entitled, by which he peaceably regains the custody of such person; or of the owner of personal or real property, who has been deprived of his possession, by which he peaceably retakes possession.

The rule of law is that one who has been wrongfully deprived of a person to whose custody he has a right (3 Bl. Comm. 4; 15 Barb. [N. Y.] 590; 13 Pick. [Mass.] 36; 19 Ga. 27), or of property, real or personal, to the possession of which he is entitled (11 N. H. 540; 13 Wend. [N. Y.] 256; 25 Vt. 620; 18 Minn. 355; 5 Watts [Pa.] 543), may, without legal process, retake the same wherever he may find it, if he can do so without a breach of the peace (11 Pick. [Mass.] 387; 73 N. Y. 529), though it is held in England (10 C. B. [N. S.] 713), and in some states (6 Rand. [Va.] 457; 59 Ill. 234), that so much force as is necessary may be used.

RECAPTURE. The recovery from the enemy, by a friendly force, of a prize by him captured.

RECEDITUR A PLACITIS JURIS, POTIus quam injuriae et delicta maneant impunita. Positive rules of law will be receded from rather than crimes and wrongs should remain unpunished. Bac. Max. reg. 12; Broom, Leg. Max. (3d London Ed.) 9. This applies only to such maxims as are called *placita juris.* These will be dispensed with rather than crimes should go unpunished, *quia salus populi suprema lex,* because the public safety is the supreme law.

RECEIPTOR. In Massachusetts. A name given to the person who, on a trustee process being issued and goods attached, becomes surety to the sheriff to have them forthcoming on demand, or in time to respond the judgment, when the execution shall be issued; upon which the goods are bailed to him. Story, Bailm. § 124. See "Attachment."

RECEIVER. One who receives money to the use of another to render an account. Story, Eq. Jur. § 446.

A person standing indifferent between the parties, who is appointed by the court to take the charge and management of property pending litigation, or for the benefit of the persons who may ultimately be entitled to it. 16 Wend. (N. Y.) 421; 80 Ill. 468.

Receivers are appointed in various proceedings and for various special purposes, but the general design of a receiver is to hold and protect the subject of litigation, whether it be specific property, or the assets of an insolvent.

RECEIVER GENERAL OF THE DUCHY of Lancaster. An officer of the duchy court, who collects all the revenues, fines, forfeitures, and assessments within the duchy.

RECEIVER GENERAL OF THE PUBLIC revenue. In English law. An officer appointed in every county to receive the taxes granted by parliament, and remit the money to the treasury.

RECEIVER OF THE FINES. An English officer who receives the money from persons who compound with the crown on original writs sued out of chancery. Wharton.

RECEIVERS AND TRIERS OF PETItions. The mode of receiving and trying petitions to parliament was formerly judicial rather than legislative, and the triers were committees of prelates, peers, and judges, and, latterly, of the members generally. Brown.

RECEIVERS' CERTIFICATES. Certificates of indebtedness issued by a receiver, as surety for money borrowed, to carry on the receivership. They are usually made a first lien on the property. See 117 U. S. 434.

RECEIVERS OF WRECK. Persons appointed by the English board of trade. The duties of a receiver of wreck are to take steps for the preservation of any vessel stranded or in distress within his district; to receive and take possession of all articles washed on shore from the vessel; to use force for the suppression of plunder and disorder; to institute an examination on oath with respect to the vessel; and, if necessary, to sell the vessel, cargo, or wreck. Merch. Ship. Act 1854, § 439 et seq.

RECEIVING STOLEN GOODS. The offense of receiving stolen goods, knowing them to have been stolen.

(1) The property must have been received, but constructive receipt is sufficient (95 N. C. 626; 6 Cox, C. C. 353), and at common law it must have been received from the thief (13 Ired. [N. C.] 338); but under the statutes, the rule seems otherwise (38 Fla. 3; 52 Neb. 727). (2) The property must have been, at the time, stolen property in fact and law. 9 Cush. 284. (3) The receiver must know at the time that it was stolen (78 N. C. 491; 60 Ill. 119), but knowledge of circumstances from which any man of ordinary observation could have known that it was stolen is enough (33 Ala. 434; 96 Iowa, 299). (4) The property must be received with fraudulent intent, but the intent need not be *lucri causa*, an intent to aid the thief being sufficient. 101 Ill. 16; 26 Tex. App. 205. An intent to hold for a reward is a fraudulent intent. 37 Ohio St. 63.

RECENS SECTA (or **INSECUTIO**) (Law Lat.) In old English law. Fresh suit; fresh pursuit; pursuit of a thief immediately after the discovery of the robbery. 1 Bl. Comm. 297.

RECEPTUS (Lat.) In civil law. The name sometimes given to an arbitrator, because he had been received or chosen to settle the differences between the parties. Dig. 4. 8; Code, 2. 56.

RECESSION. A regrant; the act of a returning the title of a country to a government which formerly held it, by one which has it at the time; as, the recession of Louisiana, which took place by the treaty between France and Spain, of October 1, 1800. See 2 White, Coll. 516.

RECESSUS (Lat. from *recedere*, to go back). In old English law. A going from; a going off or out of land. *Cum libero accessu et recessu*, with free access and recess [ingress and egress]. Bracton, fol. 231b.

RECESSUS MARIS (Lat.) In old English law. A going back; reliction or retreat of the sea. Hale de Jur. Mar. par. 1, c. 6.

RECETOUR, or **RECETTOUR** (Law Fr.) In old English law. A receiver or harborer of a felon; an accessary after the fact. Britt. c. 24. One who received and concealed a returned outlaw. Id. c. 12.

RECETTEMENT (Law Fr.) In old English law. Receiptment; the receiving and harboring a felon. *Del consentment ou del recettement de ceux felons a escient*, of consenting to or harboring such felons knowingly. Britt. c. 1.

RECHASER (Law Fr.) To drive back. Y. B. M. 11 Hen. VI. 4.

RECHATE (Law Fr.) Ransom. *Faire rechat' du char et du saunk*, to make ransom of flesh and of blood. Y. B. M. 7 Edw. II. 214.

RECHATER (Law Fr.) To ransom; to buy back. Kelham.

RECIDIVE. In French law. The state of an individual who commits a crime or misdemeanor, after having once been condemned for a crime or misdemeanor; a relapse.

Many statutes provide that, for a second offense, punishment shall be increased. In those cases the indictment should set forth the crime or misdemeanor as a second offense.

The second offense must have been committed after the conviction for the first. A defendant could not be convicted of a second offense, as such, until after he had suffered a punishment for the first. Dalloz.

RECIPROCAL CONTRACT. In civil law. One by which the parties enter into mutual engagements.

They are divided into perfect and imperfect. When they are perfectly reciprocal, the obligation of each of the parties is equally a principal part of the contract, such as sale, partnership, etc. Contracts imperfectly reciprocal are those in which the obligation of one of the parties only is a principal obligation of the contract; as, mandate, deposit, loan for use, and the like. In all reciprocal contracts, the consent of the parties must be expressed. Poth. Obl. note 9; Civ. Code La. arts. 1758, 1759.

RECIPROCITY. Mutuality; state, quality, or character of that which is reciprocal.

RECITAL. The repetition of some former writing, or the statement of something which has been done. It is useful to explain matters of fact which are necessary to make the transaction intelligible. 2 Bl. Comm. 298.

——**In Contracts.** The preliminary statement of facts explanatory of the purpose for which the contract is made, or the reasons which led to its execution.

——**In Pleading.** A statement of matter introductory to an averment.

RECLAIM. To demand again; to insist upon a right, as, when a defendant for a consideration received from the plaintiff has covenanted to do an act, and fails to do it, the plaintiff may bring covenant for the breach, or *assumpsit* to reclaim the consideration. 1 Caines (N. Y.) 47.

RECLAIMING BILL. In Scotch law. A petition for review of an interlocutor, pronounced in a sheriff's or other inferior court. It recites verbatim the interlocutor, and, after a written argument, ends with a prayer for the recall or alteration of the interlocutor, in whole or in part. Bell, Dict. "Reclaiming Petition;" Shaw, Dig. 394.

RECOGNITION. Adoption; ratification (*q. v.*) An acknowledgment that something which has been done by one man in the name of another was done by authority of the latter.

A recognition by the principal of the agency of another in the particular instance, or in similar instances, is evidence of the authority of the agent, so that the recognition may be either express or implied. As an instance of an implied recognition may be mentioned the case of one who subscribes policies in the name of another, and, upon a loss happening, the latter pays the amount. 1 Campb. 43, note (a); 4 Campb. 88; 1 Esp. 61.

RECOGNITIONE ADNULLANDA PER vim et duritiam facta. A writ to the justices of the common bench for sending a record touching a recognizance, which the recognizor suggests was acknowledged by force and duress; that if it so appear the recognizance may be annulled. Reg. Orig. 183.

RECOGNITORS. In English law. The name by which the jurors impaneled on an assize are known. 17 Serg. & R. (Pa.) 174.

RECOGNIZANCE. An obligation of record, entered into before a court or officer duly authorized for that purpose, with a condition to do some act required by law, which is therein specified. 2 Bl. Comm. 341; 53 Ill. 436; 68 Ill. App. 203.

The liability of bail above in civil cases, and of the bail in all cases in criminal matters, must be evidenced by a recognizance, as the sheriff has no power to discharge upon a bail bond being given to him in these cases. See 4 Bl. Comm. 297.

RECOGNIZE. To try; to examine in order to determine the truth of a matter. 3 Bl. Comm. Append. No. III. § 4; Bracton, 179.

To enter into a recognizance.

RECOGNIZEE. He for whose use a recognizance has been taken.

RECOGNIZOR. He who enters into a recognizance.

RECOLEMENT. In French law. The reading and re-examination by a witness of a deposition, and his persistence in the same, or his making such alteration as his better recollection may enable him to do after having read his deposition. Without such re-examination, the deposition is void. Poth. Proc. Crim. § 4, art. 4.

RECOMMENDATION. A commendatory account given by a person of another to a third person.

——**In Feudal Law.** A transfer of allodial lands by the owner to the king, and the return of the same to be held on feudal tenure

RECOMMENDATORY. Advisory. "Precatory" is the more usual term.

RECOMPENSATION. In Scotch law. An allegation by the plaintiff of compensation on his part, made in answer to a compensation or set-off pleaded by the defendant in answer to the plaintiff's demand.

RECOMPENSE. A reward for services; remuneration for goods or other property.

In maritime law, there is a distinction between "recompense" and "restitution." When goods have been lost by jettison, if at any subsequent period of the voyage the remainder of the cargo be lost, the owner of the goods lost by jettison cannot claim restitution from the owners of the other goods; but in the case of expenses incurred with a view to the general benefit, it is clear that they ought to be made good to the party, whether he be an agent employed by the master in a foreign port, or the shipowner himself.

RECOMPENSE OF RECOVERY IN value. A phrase applied to the matter recovered in a common recovery, after the vouchee has disappeared, and judgment is given for the demandant. 2 Bouv. Inst. note 2093.

RECONDUCTION. In civil law. A renewing of a former lease; relocation. Dig. 19. 2. 13. 11; Code Nap. arts. 1737-1740.

RECONTINUANCE. This word seems to be used to signify that a person has recovered an incorporeal hereditament of which he had been wrongfully deprived. Thus, "A. is disseised of a mannor, whereunto an advowson is appendant, an estranger [*i. e.*, neither A. nor the disseisor] usurpes to the advowson; if the disseisee [A.] enter into the mannor, the advowson is recontinued again, which was severed by the usurpation. * * * And so note a diversitie between a recontinuance and a remitter; for a remitter cannot be properly, unless there be two titles; but a recontinuance may be where there is but one." Co. Litt. 363b.

RECONVENIRE (Lat.) In the canon and civil law. To make a cross demand upon the *actor* or plaintiff. 4 Reeve, Hist. Eng. Law, 14, and note (r).

RECONVENTIO (Lat. from *reconvenire*, *q. v.*) In the civil and canon law. A cross demand by the *reus* (defendant) upon the *actor* (plaintiff); a proceeding in the nature of a cross bill in equity. Halifax, Anal. bk. 3, c. 1, note 40; Calv. Lex.; Fleta, lib. 4, c. 22, § 9; Gilb. For. Rom. 45, 46; Story, Eq. Pl. § 402. Considered to be the origin of a cross bill. Id.

RECONVENTION.

——**In the Civil Law.** A species of cross bill. Story, Eq. Pl. § 402.

——**In Louisiana and Texas.** A plea in the nature of set-off, by which any matter connected with or incident to the subject of the main action may be asserted. See 11 La. 309; 5 Tex. 502.

RECONVERSION. That imaginary process by which a prior constructive conversion is annulled, and the converted property restored, in contemplation of law, to its original state. Rapalje & L.

RECOPILACION DE INDIAS (Spanish). A collection of Spanish colonial law, promulgated A. D. 1680. See Schmidt, Civ. Law, introd. 94.

RECORD. Record, in its broadest sense, is a written memorial, public or private, of what has been said or done. It is ordinarily applied to public records only, in which sense it is a written memorial made by a public officer, judicial, legislative, or executive, authorized by law to perform that function, and intended to serve as evidence of something written, said, or done. 6 Call (Va.) 78; 1 Dana (Ky.) 595; 49 Maine 345; 101 Ill. App. 490.

Any record required by law to be kept by an officer, or which he keeps as necessary or convenient to the discharge of his official duty, is a public record. 15 Wall. (U. S.) 123; 123 Ind. 197; 1 Pa. St. 224.

A judicial record is the written memorial of proceedings had in court, kept by the proper officers of the court.

The common-law record was an enrollment of the pleadings, a statement in formal language of each proceeding had in the progress of the cause, and the judgment. Steph. Pl. 61.

The more common modern practice is to file the pleadings, etc., with the clerk's entries of proceedings on the trial without enrollment.

——**In Appellate Practice.** The term "record" is used in two senses, as comprising, generally, all the matters certified and transmitted by the lower court to show the proceedings therein, and in a more limited sense as signifying only the record proper, and not the abstract or bill of exceptions. In this limited sense, it includes the pleadings (22 Ill. 326), the process, and the return thereof (22 Me. 442), the verdict (60 Ill. App. 580) or findings (34 Minn. 330), and judgment (60 Ill. App. 580), but not the clerk's minutes (94 N. Y. 508), the opinion of the court below (140 Ill. 637), interlocutory motions or orders (82 Ind. 524; 109 Ill. 245), the evidence (23 Mich. 526; 91 U. S. 127), though documentary (87 Ind. 221), nor the instructions (72 U. S. 663; 119 Ind. 35).

RECORD, CONVEYANCES BY. Extraordinary assurances; as private acts of parliament, and royal grants.

RECORD, COURTS OF. Those whose judicial acts and proceedings are enrolled in parchment, for a perpetual memorial and testimony, which rolls are called the "records of the court," and are of such high and supereminent authority that their truth is not to be called in question. Every court of record has authority to fine and imprison for contempt of its authority. 3 Broom & H. Comm. 21, 30. See "Court."

RECORD, DEBTS OF. Those which appear to be due by the evidence of a court of record; such as a judgment, recognizance, etc. 2 Broom & H. Comm. 655.

RECORD OF NISI PRIUS. In English law. A transcript from the issue roll. It contains a copy of the pleadings and issue. Steph. Pl. 105.

RECORD, TRIAL BY. See "Trial."

RECORDA SUNT VESTIGIA VETUSTAtis et veritatis. Records are vestiges of antiquity and truth. 2 Rolle, 296.

RECORDARI. A writ in vogue in North Carolina to bring up the proceedings of a justice of the peace into a court of record. It is an adoption of the English writ, *Recordari facias loquelam* (*q. v.*). It is used to review matters apparent of record, or when the remedy by appeal is lost without the fault of the party, its general nature and scope being similar tc that of *certiorari.* See 65 N. C. 211; 82 N. C. 236; 89 N. C. 198.

RECORDARI FACIAS LOQUELAM (Lat.) In English practice. A writ commanding the sheriff that he cause the plaint to be recorded which is in his county, without writ, between the parties there named, of the cattle, goods, and chattels of the complainant taken and unjustly distrained as it is said, and that he have the said record before the court on a day therein named, and that he prefix the same day to the parties, that then they may be there ready to proceed in the same plaint. 2 Sellon, Prac. 166.

RECORDATUR (Lat.) An order or allowance that the verdict returned on the *nisi prius* roll be recorded. Bac. Abr. "Arbitration," etc. (D).

RECORDER. A judicial officer of some cities, possessing generally the powers and authority of a judge. 3 Yeates (Pa.) 300; 4 Dall. (Pa.) 299. But see 1 Const. (S. C.) 45.

The recorder in New York city was the chief judge of the criminal courts. There were recorders in various other cities in New York state, and also in the counties thereof, having various powers. See Rev. St. N. Y.

Anciently, "recorder" signified to recite or testify on recollection, as occasion might require, what had previously passed in court; and this was the duty of the judges, thence called "recordeurs." Steph. Pl. note 11.

An officer appointed to make record or enrollment of deeds and other legal instruments authorized by law to be recorded.

RECOUPE, or RECOUP (from Law Fr. *recouper*, to cut again, or to cut out and keep back). To diminish a claim for damages by cutting out or keeping back a part. Cowell interprets it, "to defalk or discount." Where a man had ten pounds issuing out of certain lands, and he disseised the tenant of the land, in an assize brought by the disseisee, the disseisor might *recoupe* the rent in the damages, in order to avoid circuity of action. 5 Coke, 30a. An executor *de son tort* is not allowed to retain or *recoupe* any part of the deceased's goods to satisfy his own debt. Id.; 3 Campb. 282.

This old word has been revived to a considerable extent in modern law. "Where a man brings an action for breach of a contract between him and the defendant, and the latter can show that some stipulation in the same contract was made by the plaintiff, which he has violated, the defendant may if he choose, instead of suing in his turn, *recoupe* his damages, arising from the breach committed by the plaintiff, whether they be liquidated or not. The law will cut off so much of the plaintiff's claim as the cross damages may come to." Cowen, J., 22 Wend. (N. Y.) 156. See "Recoupment."

RECOUPMENT (Fr. *recouper*, to cut again). In practice. That right of the defendant, in the same action, to claim damages from the plaintiff, either because he has not complied with some cross obligation of the contract upon which he sues, or because he has violated some duty which the law imposed upon him in the making or performance of that contract. 4 Wend. (N. Y.) 483; 8 Wend. (N. Y.) 109; 10 Barb. (N. Y.) 55; 13 N. Y. 151; 3 Ind. 72, 265; 4 Ind. 533; 7 Ind. 200; 9 Ind. 470; 7 Ala. (N. S.) 753; 13 Ala. (N. S.) 587; 16 Ala. (N. S.) 221; 27 Ala. (N. S.) 574; 12 Ark. 699; 16 Ark. 97; 17 Ark. 270; 6 B. Mon. (Ky.) 528; 13 B. Mon. (Ky.) 239; 15 B. Mon. (Ky.) 454; 3 Mich. 281; 4 Mich. 619; 39 Me. 382; 16 Ill. 495; 11 Mo. 415; 18 Mo. 368; 25 Mo. 430.

"Recoupment is distinguished from set-off in these three essential particulars: (1) In being confined to matters arising out of and connected with the transaction or contract on which suit is brought; (2) in having no regard to whether such matters are liquidated or unliquidated; (3) in not being the subject of statutory regulation, but controlled by the common law." 3 Mich. 281. Recoupment belongs to cases where the same contract lays mutual duties and obligations on two parties, and on an action by one for a breach of duty, the other presents a claim of breach of duty under the same contract. In set-off, the position of the defendant is that, though he may owe the plaintiff what he claims, a part or the whole of such debt is paid in reason and justice by a distinct unconnected debt which plaintiff owes him. 2 Pars. Cont. 740.

This is not a new title in the law, although it seems recently to have assumed a new signification. Originally it implied a mere deduction from the claim of the plaintiff, on account of payment in whole or in part, or a former recovery, or some analogous fact. 3 Coke, 65; 4 Coke, 94; 5 Coke, 2, 31; 11 Coke, 51, 52. See note to 6 Nev. & M. 467; Viner, Abr. "Discount," pl. 3, 4, 9, 10; 28 Vt. 413. This meaning has been retained in many modern cases, but under the name of "deduction" or "reduction of damages." 11 East, 232; 1 Maule & S. 318, 323; 5 Maule & S. 6, 10; 4 Burrows, 2133. See "Set-Off."

RECOURSE. See "Without Recourse."

RECOUSSE (Fr.) In French law. Recapture. Emerig. Tr. des Assur. c. 12, § 23.

RECOVEREE. In old conveyancing. The party who suffered a common recovery.

RECOVERER. The demandant in a common recovery, after judgment has been given in his favor, assumes the name of "recoverer."

RECOVERY. The restoration of a former right, by the solemn judgment of a court of justice. 3 Murph. (N. C.) 169.

A common recovery is a judgment obtained in a fictitious suit, brought against the tenant of the freehold, in consequence of a default made by the person who is last vouched to warranty in suit suit. Bac. Tr. 148.

A true recovery, usually known by the name of "recovery" simply, is the procuring a former right by the judgment of a court of competent jurisdiction; as, for example, when judgment is given in favor of the plaintiff when he seeks to recover a thing or a right.

Common recoveries are considered as mere forms of conveyance or common assurances. Although a common recovery is a fictitious suit, yet the same mode of proceeding must be pursued, and all the forms strictly adhered to, which are necessary to be observed in an adversary suit. The first thing, therefore, necessary to be done in suffering a common recovery is that the person who is to be the demandant, and to whom the lands are to be adjudged, shall sue out a writ or *praecipe* against the tenant of the freehold; when such tenant is usually called the "tenant to the *praecipe*." In obedience to this writ, the tenant appears in court, either in person or by his attorney; but, instead of defending the title to the land himself, he calls on some other person, who, upon the original purchase, is supposed to have warranted the title, and prays that the person may be called in to defend the title which he warranted, or otherwise to give the tenant lands of equal value to those he shall lose by the defect of his warranty. This is called the "voucher *vocatio*," or "calling to warranty." The person thus called to warrant, who is usually called the "vouchee," appears in court, is impleaded, and enters into the warranty, by which means he takes upon himself the defense of the land. The defendant then desires leave of the court to imparl, or confer with the vouchee in private, which is granted of course. Soon after the demandant returns into court, but the vouchee disappears or makes default, in consequence of which it is presumed by the court that he has no title to the lands demanded in the writ, and therefore cannot defend them; whereupon judgment is given for the demandant, now called the "recoverer," to recover the lands in question against the tenant, and for the tenant to recover against the vouchee lands of equal value in recompense for those so warranted by him, and now lost by his default. This is called the "recompense of recovery in value;" but as it is customary for the crier of the court to act, who is hence called the "common vouchee," the tenant can only have a nominal and not a real recompense for the land thus recovered against him by the demandant. A writ of *habere facias* is then sued out, directed to the sheriff of the county in which the lands thus recovered are situated, and on the execution and return of the writ the recovery is completed. The recovery here described is with single voucher; but a recovery may be, and is frequently, suffered with double, treble, or further voucher, as the exigency of the case may require, in which case there are several judgments against the several vouchees.

Common recoveries were invented by the ecclesiastics in order to evade the statute of mortmain, by which they were prohibited from purchasing, or receiving under the pretense of a free gift, any land or tenements whatever. They have been used in some states for the purpose of breaking the entail of estates. See, generally, Cruise, Dig. tit. 36; 2 Wm. Saund. 42, note 7; 4 Kent, Comm. 487; Pigot, Comm. Rec. passim.

All the learning in relation to common recoveries is nearly obsolete, as they are out of use. Rey, a French writer, in his work Des Institutions Judiciares de l'Angleterres (tom. ii. p. 221), points out what appears to him the absurdity of a common recovery. As to common recoveries, see 3 Serg. & R. (Pa.) 435; 9 Serg. & R. (Pa.) 330; 1 Yeates (Pa.) 244; 4 Yeates (Pa.) 413; 1 Whart. (Pa.) 139, 151; 2 Rawle (Pa.) 168; 6 Pa. St. 45; 2 Halst. (N. J.) 47; 5 Mass. 438; 6 Mass. 328; 8 Mass. 34; 3 Har. & J. (Md.) 292.

RECREANT. A coward; a poltroon. 3 Bl. Comm. 340.

RECRIMINATION. In the law of divorce. The defense that the plaintiff has been guilty of such a matrimonial offense as is a ground for divorce. At common law only an offense of the same nature as that for which plaintiff sued was available in recrimination (1 Hagg. Consist. 144; 4 Ecc. 360); but in the United States, the courts refuse, in the absence of statute, to measure the comparative turpitude of the several statutory grounds of divorce, and any one may be pleaded in recrimination (21 N. J. Eq. 331; 72 Wis. 136).

Recrimination is based on the maxim that suitors in equity must come with clean hands, and, if established, is a complete defense.

RECTE (Lat.) In the civil law. Rightly. Dig. 50. 16. 73. As to the interpretation of this word, see Id.

RECTITUDO. Right or justice; legal dues; tribute or payment. Cowell.

RECTO (Lat.) Right. *Breve de recto*, writ of right.

RECTO DE ADVOCATIONE ECCLESIAE. A writ which lay at common law where a man had right of advowson of a church, and, the parson dying, a stranger had presented. Fitzh. Nat. Brev. 30.

RECTO DE CUSTODIA TERRAE ET haeredis. A writ of right of ward of the land and heir. Abolished.

RECTO DE DOTE. A writ of right of dower, which lay for a widow who had received part of her dower, and demanded the residue, against the heir of the husband or his guardian. Abolished. See 23 & 24 Vict. c. 126, § 26.

RECTO DE DOTE UNDE NIHIL HABET. A writ of right of dower whereof the widow had nothing, which lay where her deceased husband, having divers lands or tenements, had assured no dower to his wife, and she thereby was driven to sue for her thirds against the heir or his guardian. Abolished.

RECTO DE RATIONABILI PARTE. A writ of right of the reasonable part, which lay between privies in blood; as brothers in gavelkind, sisters, and other coparceners, for land in fee simple. Fitzh. Nat. Brev. 9.

RECTO QUANDO (or QUIA) DOMINUS remisit curiam. A writ of right, when or because the lord had remitted his court, which lay where lands or tenements in the seigniory of any lord were in demand by a writ of right. Fitzh. Nat. Brev. 16.

RECTO SUR DISCLAIMER. An abolished writ on disclaimer.

RECTOR. In ecclesiastical law. One who rules or governs. A name given to certain officers of the church.

RECTOR PROVINCIAE (Lat.) In the Roman law. The governor of a province. Code, 1. 40.

RECTORY. In English law. Corporeal real property, consisting of a church, glebe lands, and tithes. 1 Chit. Prac. 163.

RECTUM (Lat.) Right; also a trial or accusation. Bracton; Cowell.

RECTUM ESSE. To be right in court.

RECTUM ROGARE. To ask for right; to petition the judge to do right.

RECTUM, STARE AD. To stand trial or abide by the sentence of the court.

RECTUS IN CURIA (Lat. right in court). The condition of one who stands at the bar, against whom no one objects any offense, or prefers any charge.

When a person outlawed has reversed his outlawry, so that he can have the benefit of the law, he is said to be *rectus in curia*. Jacob.

RECUPERATIO, i. e., AD REM, PER INjuriam extortam sive detentam, per sententiam judicis restitutio. Recovery, *i. e.*, restitution by sentence of a judge of a thing wrongfully extorted or detained. Co. Litt. 154a.

RECUPERATIO EST ALICUJUS REI IN causam, alterius adductae per judicem acquisitio. Recovery is the acquisition by sentence of a judge of anything brought into the cause of another. Co. Litt. 154a.

RECUPERATORES (Lat.) In Roman law. A species of judges originally established, it is supposed, to decide controversies between Roman citizens and strangers concerning the right to the possession of property requiring speedy remedy, but gradually extended to questions which might be brought before ordinary judges.

After the enlargement of their powers, the difference between them and judges, it is supposed, was simply this: If the *praetor* named three judges, he called them *recuperatores;* if one, he called him *judex.* But opinions on this subject are various. Colman, *De Romano judicio recuperatorio.* Cicero's oration (Pro Coecin. 1, 3) was addressed to recuperators.

RECURRENDUM EST AD EXTRAORDInarium quando non valet ordinarium. We must have recourse to what is extraordinary when what is ordinary fails.

RECUSANT. In English law. A person who refuses to make the declarations against Catholicism, and promotes, encourages or professes the Catholic religion.

RECUSATIO TESTIS. In the civil law. Rejection of a witness on the ground of incompetency.

RECUSATION. In civil law. A plea or exception by which the defendant requires that the judge having jurisdiction of the cause should abstain from deciding, upon the ground of interest, or for a legal objection to his prejudice.

A recusation is not a plea to the jurisdiction of the court, but simply to the person of the judge. It may, however, extend to all the judges, as when the party has a suit against the whole court. Poth. Proc. Civ. ch. 2, § 5. It is a personal challenge of the judge for cause. See 2 La. 390; 6 La. 134.

The challenge of jurors. Code Prac. La. arts. 499, 500. An act, of what nature soever it may be, by which a strange heir, by deeds or words, declares he will not be heir. Dig. 29. 2. 95. See, generally, 1 Hopk. Ch. (N. Y.) 1; 5 Mart. (La.) 292.

RED BOOK OF THE EXCHEQUER. An ancient record, wherein are registered the holders of lands *per baroniam* in the time of Henry III., the number of hides of land in certain counties before the Conquest, and the ceremonies on the coronation of Eleanor, wife of Henry III., compiled by Alexander de Swenford, archdeacon of Salop, and treasurer of St. Paul's, who died in 1246, 31 Hen. III; Jacob; Cowell.

REDDENDO SINGULA SINGULIS (Lat.) Referring particular things to particular persons. For example, when two descriptions of property are given together in one mass, both the next of kin and the heir cannot take, unless in cases where a construction can be made *reddendo singula singulis*, that the next of kin shall take the personal estate, and the heir-at-law the real estate. 14 Ves. 490. See 11 East, 513, note; Bac. Abr. "Conditions" (L).

REDDENDUM (Lat.) That clause in a deed by which the grantor reserves something new to himself out of that which he granted before. It usually follows the *tenendum*, and is generally in these words, "yielding and paying." In every good *reddendum* or reservation these things must concur, namely: It must be in apt words; it must be of some other thing issuing or coming out of the thing granted, and not a part of the thing itself, nor of something issuing out of another thing; it must be of a thing on which the grantor may resort to distrain; it must be made to one of the grantors, and not to a stranger to the deed. See 2 Bl. Comm. 299; Co. Litt. 47; Shep. Touch. 80; Cruise, Dig. tit. 32, c. 24, § 1; Dane, Abr. Index.

REDDENS CAUSAM SCIENTIAE. Giving the reason of his knowledge.

——**In Scotch Practice.** A formal phrase used in depositions, preceding the statement of the reason of the witness' knowledge. 2 How. St. Tr. 715.

REDDERE, NIL ALIUD EST QUAM ACceptum restituere; seu, reddere est quasi retro dare, et redditur dicitur a redeundo, quia retro it. To render is nothing more than to restore that which has been received; or, to render is, as it were, to give back, and it is called "rendering" from "returning," because it goes back again. Co. Litt. 142.

REDDIDIT SE (Lat.) In English practice. An indorsement made on the bail piece when a certificate has been made by the proper officer that the defendant is in custody. Comyn, Dig. "Bail" (Q 4).

REDDITARIUM (Law Lat. from *redditus*). In old records. A rental, or rent roll. Cowell.

REDDITION. A judicial confession or acknowledgment that the thing in demand belongs to the demandant, and not to the person surrendering. Cowell.

REDDITUS SICCUS. See "Reditus Siccus."

REDDOUR (Law Fr.) A rendering. Kelham.

REDEEM. See "Redemption."

REDEEMABLE RIGHTS. Rights which return to the conveyor or disposer of land, etc., upon payment of the sum for which such rights are granted.

REDELIVERY. A yielding and delivering back of a thing.

REDEMISE. A regranting of land demised or leased.

REDEMPTIO (Law Lat.) In old English law. A ransom, or fine. St. Marlb. c. 1. Spelman calls it the heaviest kind of fine (*mulcta gravissima*), and makes it to be the same with the Saxon "were" or "weregild."

REDEMPTION (Lat. *re, red*, back, *emptio*, a purchase). A purchase back by the seller from the buyer. It is applied to denote the performance of the conditions upon performance of which a conditional sale is to become ineffective as a transfer of title, or, more strictly, a right to demand a reconveyance becomes vested in the seller. In the case of mortgages, this right is a legal right until a breach of conditions, when it becomes an equitable right, and is called the "equity of redemption."

The term is applied to the statutory right of one whose property is sold at various forced sales other than mortgage foreclosure (*e. g.*, for taxes) to buy the same back within a fixed time, ordinarily for the price paid by the purchaser, with interest and costs.

REDEMPTION, EQUITY OF. See "Equity of Redemption."

REDEMPTIONES (Lat.) Heavy fines. Distinguished from *misericordia* (*q. v.*).

REDEUNDO (Lat.) Returning; in returning; while returning. 3 East, 89; 2 Strange, 985.

REDHIBERE (Lat.) In the civil law. To have again; to have back; to cause a seller to have again what he had before. Dig. 21. 1. 21. pr.

The returning of a thing purchased to the seller.

REDHIBITION. In civil law. The returning of a thing purchased to the seller, on the ground of some defect or fraud. Calv. Lex. The avoidance of a sale on account of some vice or defect in the thing sold, which renders its use impossible, or so inconvenient and imperfect that it must be supposed that the buyer would not have purchased it had he known of the vice. Civ. Code La. art. 2496.

This is essentially a civil-law right. The effect of the rule expressed by the maxim *caveat emptor* is to prevent any such right at common law, except in cases of express warranty. 2 Kent, Comm. 374; Sugd. Vend. 222.

REDHIBITORY ACTION. In civil law. An action instituted to avoid a sale on account of some vice or defect in the thing sold which renders its use impossible, or so inconvenient and imperfect that it must be supposed the buyer would not have purchased it had he known of the vice. Civ. Code La. art. 2496.

REDHIBITORY DEFECT (or VICE). In the civil law. A defect in an article sold, for which the seller may be compelled to take it back; a defect against which the seller is bound to warrant. Poth. Contr. Sale, No. 203.

REDISSEISIN. In old English law. A second disseisin of a person of the same tenements, and by the same disseisor, by whom he was before disseised. 3 Bl. Comm. 188; Fleta, lib. 4, c. 29. Called in the statute of Marlbridge (chapter 8) a repeated disseisin.

The name of a writ which lay in such case (*breve de redisseisina*). Reg. Orig. 206b.

REDITUS ALBI (Lat.) A rent payable in money; sometimes called "white rent," or "blanchefarm." See "Alba Firma."

REDITUS ASSISUS. A set or standing rent.

REDITUS CAPITALES. Chief rent paid by freeholders to go quit of all other services.

REDITUS NIGRI. A rent payable in grain, work, and the like. It was also called "black mail." This name was given to it to distinguish it from *reditus albi*, which was payable in money.

REDITUS QUIETI. Quit rents (*q. v.*)

REDITUS SICCUS. Rent seck. See "Rent."

REDMEN. Customary tenants required to ride on the business or errands of their lord.

REDOBATORES (Law Lat.) Those that buy stolen cloth, and turn it into some other color or fashion, that it may not be recognized; redubbers. Barr. Obs. St. (2d Ed.) 87, note; 3 Inst. 134; Britt. c. 29.

REDRAFT. In commercial law. A bill of exchange drawn at the place where another bill was made payable, and where it was protested, upon the place where the first bill was drawn, or, when there is no regular commercial intercourse rendering that practicable, then in the next best or most direct practicable course. 1 Bell, Comm. (5th Ed.) 406. See "Re-Exchange."

REDRESS. The act of receiving satisfaction for an injury sustained. For the mode of obtaining redress, see "Remedies;" 1 Chit. Prac. Anal. Table.

REDUBBOURS (Law Fr.; Law Lat. *redobatores, q. v.*) In old English law. Persons who knowingly bought stolen clothes, and changed them into another form; *achatauntz ascient dras embles, et les attirent en auter forme.* Britt. c. 29; Cowell.

REDUCTION. In Scotch law. An action brought for the purpose of rescinding, annulling, or cancelling some deed, bond, contract, or other instrument in writing. 1 Forbes, Inst. pt. 4. pp. 158, 159. See Bell, Dict.

REDUCTION EX CAPITE LECTI. By the law of Scotland, the heir in heritage was entitled to reduce all voluntary deeds granted to his prejudice by his predecessor within sixty days preceding the predecessor's death; provided the maker of the deed, at its date, was laboring under the disease of which he died, and did not subsequently go to kirk or market unsupported. Bell, Dict. Abolished 34 & 35 Vict. c. 81.

REDUCTION IMPROBATION. In Scotch law. One form of the action of reduction, in which falsehood and forgery are alleged against the deed or document sought to be set aside. Bell, Dict.

REDUCTION INTO POSSESSION. The act of exercising the right conferred by a chose in action, so as to convert it into a chose in possession; thus, a debt is reduced into possession by payment.

REDUNDANCY. In pleading. The averment of matter foreign to the issue, or the needless repetition of immaterial averments. 5 Sandf. (N. Y.) 660.

RE-ENTRY. The resuming or retaking of that possession of lands and tenements which one has lately foregone. See "Entry."

REEVE. An ancient English officer of justice, inferior in rank to an alderman. He was a ministerial officer appointed to execute process, keep the king's peace, and put the laws in execution. He witnessed all contracts and bargains, brought offenders to justice, and delivered them to punishment, took bail for such as were to appear at the county court, and presided at the court or folcmote. He was also called "gerefa."

There were several kinds of reeves; as, the shire gerefa, shire reeve, or sheriff; the heh gerefa, or high sheriff, tithing reeve, burgh or borough reeve.

RE-EXCHANGE. The expense incurred by a bill's being dishonored in a foreign country, where it is made payable and returned to that country in which it was made or indorsed, and there taken up. 11 East, 265; 2 Campb. 65.

It is the sum for which a sight bill must be drawn at the time and place of dishonor at the then rate of exchange on the place where the drawer or indorser sought to be charged resides, in order to realize, at the place of dishonor, the amount of the dishonored bill, and the expenses consequent on its dishonor. 2 Daniell, Neg. Inst. § 1445. See "Redraft."

REFALO. A word composed of the three initial syllables, *re. fa. lo.*, for *recordari facias loquelam.* 2 Sellon, Prac. 160; 8 Dowl. 514.

REFECTION (Lat. *re*, again, *facio*, to make). In civil law. Reparation; re-establishment of a building. Dig. 19. 1. 6. 1.

REFEREE. The person to whom a reference (*q. v.*) is made.

REFEREE IN CASE OF NEED. A person whose name may be inserted in a bill of exchange by the drawer or an indorser, to whom the holder may resort in case the bill is dishonored by nonacceptance or nonpayment. The usual form is "in case of need, apply to ———." Chit. Bills, 165; N. Y. Neg. Inst. Law, § 215.

REFERENCE. A sending or direction to a person or place.

——**In Contracts.** A statement in a writing, wherein it points to another for the matters therein contained.

——**In Mercantile Law.** A direction or request by a party who asks a credit to the person from whom he desires it to some other person named, in order to ascertain the character or mercantile standing of the former.

——**In Practice.** The sending of a pending cause, or some question therein, by the court in which it is pending, to a private person to hear and determine the cause, or some question therein, or to take evidence and report the same, with or without his opinion thereon, to the court.

Distinguished from arbitration. The submission of a controversy to a private person by the parties is sometimes called "reference," but the term "reference" properly applies only to reference by a court in the exercise of its powers as such, whether it be with or without the consent of the parties. The cases in which reference may be made, and the powers and duties of referees, are governed by varying statutes. Generally speaking, any cause may be referred with the consent of the parties, and any cause in which there is no constitutional right to a jury trial may be referred, in the discretion of the court. Whether the referee merely report evidence or determine the cause, his report must be confirmed by the court appointing him, and the court has extensive power of revision on motion to confirm.

REFERENCE IN CASE OF NEED. See "Referee in Case of Need."

REFERENCE TO RECORD. Under the English practice, when an action is commenced, an entry of it is made in the cause book according to the year, the initial letter of the surname of the first plaintiff, and the place of the action, in numerical order among those commenced in the same year, *e. g.*, "1876, A. 26;" and all subsequent documents in the action (such as pleadings and affidavits) bear this mark, which is called the "reference to the record."

REFERENDARIUS (Lat.) An officer by whom the order of causes was laid before the Roman emperor, the desires of petitioners made known, and answers returned to them. Vicat; Calv. Lex.

REFERENDARY. In Saxon law. A master of requests; an officer to whom petitions to the king were referred. Spelman.

REFERENDO SINGULA SINGULIS (Lat.) Referring individual or separate words to separate subjects; making a distributive reference of words in an instrument; construing distributively. 11 East, 322; 2 Powell, Dev. 112.

REFERENDUM (Lat.) In international law. A note addressed by an ambassador to his government, submitting to its consideration propositions made to him touching an object over which he has no sufficient power, and is without instructions. When such a proposition is made to an ambassador, he accepts it *ad referendum;* that is, under the condition that it shall be acted upon by his government, to which it is referred.

——**In Political Economy.** A system of legislation, whereby proposed laws are submitted to the popular vote.

REFORM. To reorganize; to rearrange. Thus, the jury "shall be reformed by putting to and taking out of the persons so impanelled." St. 3 Hen. VIII. c. 12; Bac. Abr. "Juries" (A).

To reform an instrument in equity is to make a decree that a deed or other agreement shall be made or construed as it was originally intended by the parties, when an error or mistake as to a fact has been committed. A contract has been reformed although the party applying to the court was in the legal profession, and he himself drew the contract, it appearing clear that it was framed so as to admit of a construction inconsistent with the true agreement of the parties. 1 Sim. & S. 210; 3 Russ. 424. But a contract will not be reformed in consequence of an error of law. 1 Russ. & M. 418; 1 Chit. Prac. 124.

REFORMATORY. All places and institutions in which efforts are made either to cultivate the intellect, instruct the conscience, or improve the conduct; places in which persons voluntarily assemble, receive instruction, and submit to discipline, or are detained therein for either of these purposes by force. 49 Conn. 35. Ordinarily applied to penal or *quasi* penal institutions; but it was said in the case above cited to be a term of too uncertain signification to support a bequest for the purpose of building a reformatory.

REFRESH THE MEMORY. To revive the recollection of a subject by referring to something connected with it. Commonly applied to the right of a witness to refer, even on the stand, to memoranda made by him at the time of a transaction, but which are not of themselves evidence, to refresh his recollection. See 5 Wend. (N. Y.) 301; 6 Pick. (Mass.) 222; 2 Conn. 213.

REFRESHER. In English practice. A fee paid to counsel on the trial of an action, in addition to the retainer paid him with his brief. In the practice of the queen's bench division, a refresher is usually paid to counsel for every day a trial lasts after the first day.

REFULLUM (Law Lat.) In old English law. A flowing back. Fleta, lib. 4, c. 27, § 4.

REFUND. To pay back by the party who has received it, to the party who has paid it, money which ought not to have been paid.

On a deficiency of assets, executors and administrators *cum testamento annexo* are entitled to have refunded to them legacies which they may have paid, or so much as may be necessary to pay the debts of the testator; and in order to insure this they are generally authorized to require a refunding bond. See Bac. Abr. "Legacies" (H).

REFUSAL. The act of declining to receive or to do something. In some cases, a neglect to perform a duty will be construed as a refusal; but, ordinarily, demand is essential to refusal. 6 Gray (Mass.) 224.

Refusal is sometimes used in the sense of "option;" thus, to "give a refusal" of property means to give an option of buying it.

REFUTANTIA (Law Lat.) In old records. An acquittance or acknowledgment of renouncing all future claim. Cowell.

REG. GEN. An abbreviation of *regula generalis*. 6 East, 1.

REGAL FISH. Whales and sturgeons. 2 Steph. Comm. 19, note 448.

REGALE (Law Lat.) In old French law. A payment made to the seigneur of a fief, on the election of every bishop or other ecclesiastical feudatory, corresponding with the relief paid by a lay feudatory. Steph. Lect. 235.

REGALIA. This seems to be an abbreviation of "*jura regalia*," royal rights, or those rights which a king has by virtue of his prerogative. Hence owners of counties palatine were formerly said to have "*jura regalia*" in their counties as fully as the king in his palace. 1 Bl. Comm. 117.

Some writers divide the royal prerogative into *majora* and *minora regalia*, the former including the regal dignity and power, the latter the revenue or fiscal prerogatives of the crown. 1 Bl. Comm. 117.

REGALIA FACERE. To do homage or fealty to the sovereign by a bishop when he is invested with the regalia.

REGALITY. A territorial jurisdiction in Scotland conferred by the crown. The lands were said to be given *in liberam regalitatem*, and the persons receiving the right were termed "lords of regality." Bell, Dict.

REGARD (Law Fr.) Reference; relation. Kelham. Respect. Id. Reward; fee; a perquisite or allowance. Id.

REGARD, COURT OF. See "Court of Regard."

REGARD OF THE FOREST. In old English law. The oversight or inspection of it, or the office and province of the regarder, who is to go through the whole forest, and every bailiwick in it, before the holding of the sessions of the forest, or justice seat, to see and inquire after trespassers, and for the survey of dogs. Manw. For. Law.

REGARDANT (Fr. seeing or vigilant). A villein *regardant* was one who had the charge to do all base services within the manor, and to see the same freed of annoyances. Co. Litt. 120; 2 Bl. Comm. 93*.

REGARDATOR (Law Lat.) In old forest law. A regarder (*q. v.*) *Regardatores nos-*

tri eant per forestas ad faciendum regardum, our regarders shall go through the forests to make regard. Cart. de Foresta, 9 Hen. III. c. 5.

REGARDER (Law Lat. *regardator;* from Law Fr. *regardeur*, an inspector). In forest law. An officer of the forest, appointed to supervise all other officers. Cromp. Jur. 153; Manw. For. Laws; Cowell.

REGE INCONSULTO (Lat.) In English law. A writ issued from the sovereign to the judges, not to proceed in a cause which may prejudice the crown, until advised. Jenk. Cent. Cas. 97.

REGENCY. The authority of the person in monarchical countries invested with the right of governing the state, in the name of the monarch, during his minority, absence, sickness, or other inability.

REGENT. A ruler; a governor. The term is usually applied to one who governs a regency, or rules in the place of another.

In the canon law, it signifies a master or professor of a college. Dict. Canonique.

It sometimes means simply a ruler, director, or superintendent; as in New York, where the board who have the superintendence of all the colleges, academies, and schools are called the "Regents of the University of the State of New York."

REGIA DIGNITAS EST INDIVISIBILIS, et quaelibet alia derivativa dignitas est similiter indivisibilis. The kingly power is indivisible, and every other derivative power is similarly indivisible. 4 Inst. 243.

REGIA VIA (Lat.; Law Fr. *real chymin*). In old English law. The royal way; the king's highway. Co. Litt. 56a.

REGIAM MAJESTATEM (Lat.) An ancient book purporting to contain the law of Scotland, and said to have been compiled by King David, who reigned 1124-1153. It is not part of the law of Scotland, though it was ordered to be revised with other ancient laws of Scotland by parliaments of 1405 and 1407. Stair, Inst. p. 12, § 16; Id. p. 508, § 27. So Craig, Inst. 1. 8. 11; Scott, Border Antiq. prose works, 7, 30; but Ersk. Inst. bk. 1, tit. 1, § 32, and Ross, Lect. 11, p. 60 et seq. maintain its authenticity. It is cited in some modern Scotch cases. 2 Swin. 409; 3 Bell, H. L. Sc. It is, according to Dr. Robertson, a servile copy of Glanville. Robertson, Hist. Charles V., vol. 1, note 25, p. 262; Ersk. Inst. 1. 1. 3.

REGICIDE (Lat. *rex*, king, *cedere*, to kill, slay). The killing of a king, and, by extension, of a queen. Theorie des Lois Criminelles, vol. 1, p. 300.

REGIDOR. In Spanish law. One of a body, never exceeding twelve, who formed a part of the *ayuntamiento*, or municipal council, in every capital of a jurisdiction in the colonies of the Indies. The office of *regidor* was held for life; that is to say, during the pleasure of the supreme authority. In most places the office was purchased. In some cities, however, they were elected by persons of the district, called *capitulares*. 12 Pet. (U. S.) 442, note.

REGIME DOTAL. In French law. The *dot*, being the property which the wife brings to the husband as her contribution to the support of the burdens of the marriage, and which may either extend as well to future as to present property, or be expressly confined to the present property of the wife, is subject to certain regulations which are summarized in the phrase *"regime dotal."* The husband has the entire administration during the marriage; but, as a rule, where the *dot* consists of immovables, neither the husband nor the wife, nor both of them together, can either sell or mortgage it. The *dot* is returnable upon the dissolution of the marriage, whether by death or otherwise. Brown.

REGIMIENTO. In Spanish law. The body of *regidores*, who never exceeded twelve, forming a part of the municipal council, or *ayuntamiento*, in every capital of a jurisdiction. 12 Pet. (U. S.) 442, note.

REGISTER, or REGISTRAR. An officer authorized by law to keep a record called a "register" or "registry;" as, the register for the probate of wills.

REGISTER OF WRITS. A book preserved in the English court of chancery, in which were entered, from time to time, all forms of writs once issued. St. Westminster II. c. 25.

It is spoken of as one of the most ancient books of the common law. Co. Litt. 159; 4 Inst. 150; 8 Coke, pref.; 3 Bl. Comm. 183*. It was first printed and published in the reign of Hen. VIII. This book is still in authority, as containing, in general, an accurate transcript of the forms of all writs as then framed, and as they ought still to be framed in modern practice. But many of the writs now in use are not contained in it; and a variation from the register is not conclusive against the propriety of a form, if other sufficient authority can be adduced to prove its correctness. Steph. Pl. 7, 8.

REGISTERED BONDS. A "registered" bond is one which is payable to a particular individual whose name is entered on the books of the corporation debtor as the registered owner. 2 Fletcher Cyclopedia Corporations 1920.

REGISTER'S COURT. In American law. A court in the state of Pennsylvania, which has jurisdiction in matters of probate.

REGISTRARIUS (Lat.) An ancient name given to a notary. In England this name is confined to designate the officer of some court the records or archives of which are in his custody.

REGISTRUM BREVIUM (Lat.) The name of an ancient book which was a collection of writs. See "Register of Writs."

REGISTRY. A book, authorized by law, in which writings are registered or recorded.

REGLAMENTO (Spanish). In Spanish colonial law. A written instruction given by a competent authority, without the observance of any peculiar form. Schmidt, Civ. Law, introd. 93, note.

REGNAL YEARS. A table of the English regnal years will be found in this work under title "King."

REGNANT. One having authority as a king; one in the exercise of royal authority.

REGNI POPULI. A name given to the people of Surrey and Sussex, and on the sea coasts of Hampshire. Blount.

REGNUM ECCLESIASTICUM. The ecclesiastical kingdom. 2 Hale, P. C. 324.

REGNUM NON EST DIVISIBLE. The kingdom is not divisible. Co. Litt. 165.

REGRANT. In the English law of real property, when, after a person has made a grant, the property granted comes back to him (*e. g.*, by escheat or forfeiture), and he grants it again, he is said to have regranted it. The phrase is chiefly used in the law of copyholds. Thus, before the fines and recoveries act, one mode of barring an entail in copyhold was a preconcerted forfeiture by the tenant, followed by a regrant to him in fee by the lord.

REGRATING. In criminal law. Every practice or device, by act, conspiracy, words, or news, to enhance the price of victuals or other merchandise, is so denominated. 3 Inst. 196; 1 Russ. Crimes, 169.

In the Roman law, persons who monopolized grain, and other produce of the earth, were called *dardanarii*, and were variously punished. Dig. 47. 11. 6.

REGRESS. Returning; going back; opposed to "ingress."

REGULA (Lat.) In practice. A rule. *Regula generalis*, a general rule; a standing rule or order of a court. Frequently abbreviated *Reg. Gen.*

REGULA CATONIANA (Lat.) In the Roman law. The rule of Cato; a rule respecting the validity of dispositions by will. See Dig. 34. 7.

REGULA EST, JURIS QUIDEM IGNOrantiam cuique nocere, facti vero ignorantiam non nocere. The rule is, that ignorance of law does not excuse, but that ignorance of a fact may excuse a party from the legal consequences of his conduct. Dig. 22. 6. 9; Broom, Leg. Max. (3d London Ed.) 232. See Irving, Civ. Law (4th Ed.) 74.

REGULA PRO LEGE, SI DEFICIT LEX. In default of the law, the maxim rules.

REGULAR CLERGY. Monks who lived according to the rules of their respective houses or societies, in contradistinction to the parochial clergy, who did their duties "*in seculo*," and hence were called secular clergy. 1 Bl. Comm. 387, note.

REGULAR DEPOSIT. One where the thing deposited must be returned. It is distinguished from an "irregular deposit." See "Deposit."

REGULAR PROCESS. Regular process is that which has been lawfully issued by a court or magistrate having competent jurisdiction.

REGULARITER (Law Lat.) In old English law. Regularly; strictly; according to rule; as a general rule. Bracton, fol. 87b. 223.

REGULARITER, NON VALET PACTUM de re mea non alienanda. Regularly, a contract not to alienate my property is not binding. Co. Litt. 223.

REGULARS. In ecclesiastical law. Those who profess and follow a certain rule of life (*regula*), belong to a religious order, and observe the three approved vows of poverty, chastity, and obedience. Wharton.

REGULATE. To direct, govern, or restrict. A governmental power to regulate does not include a power to prohibit. 39 N. J. Law, 44; 70 Mich. 396.

REGULUS (Lat.) In Saxon law. A title sometimes given to the earl or *comes*, in old charters. Spelman.

REHABERE FACIAS SEISINAM (Lat. do you cause to regain seisin). When a sheriff in the *habere facias seisinam* had delivered seisin of more than he ought, this judicial writ lay to make him restore seisin of the excess. Reg. Jud. 13. 51. 54.

REHABILITATION. The act by which a man is restored to his former ability, of which he had been deprived by a conviction, sentence, or judgment of a competent tribunal.

REHEARING.

——**In Appellate Practice.** A second consideration, on further argument, given to a cause after decision.

——**In Chancery Practice.** A retrial of the issues; a new trial. See "New Trial."

REI (Lat.; plur. of *reus*, *q. v.*) In the civil law. In a special sense, persons from whom a thing is demanded (*ii unde petitur*). Heinec. Elem. Jur. Civ. lib. 3, tit. 17, § 841. Defendants. In a general sense, parties to an action; litigating parties (*ii quorum de re disceptatur*), including both the *actor* and the *reus* proper. Id. Parties to a contract. Id.

REI INTERVENTUS (Lat.) When a party is imperfectly bound in an obligation, he may, in general, annul such imperfect obligation; but when he has permitted the opposite party to act as if his obligation or agreement were complete, such things have intervened as to deprive him of the right to rescind such obligation. These circumstances are the *rei interventus*. 1 Bell, Comm. (5th Ed.) 328, 329; Burton, Man. Scot. 128.

REI TURPIS NULLUM MANDATUM est. A mandate of an illegal thing is void Dig. 17. 1. 6. 3.

REIF (Scotch; from Saxon *reaf*). In old Scotch law. Robbery. Skene ad Leg. Alexandri R. c. 2, par. 2; Cowell.

REINSURANCE. Insurance effected by an underwriter upon a subject against certain risks with another underwriter, on the same subject, against all or a part of the same risks, not exceeding the same amount. In the original insurance, he is the insurer; in the second, the assured.

REIPUBLICAE INTEREST VOLUNTATes defunctorum effectum sortiri. It concerns the state that the wills of the dead should have their effect.

REISA. L. Lat. (from Sax. *raese*, a rush). In old European law. A sudden military expedition; a sally. Spelman.

REISSUABLE NOTES. Bank notes which, after having been once paid, may again be put into circulation.

They cannot properly be called "valuable securities" while in the hands of the maker, but, in an indictment, may properly be called "goods and chattels." Ryan & M. 218. See 5 Mason (U. S.) 537; 2 Russ. Crimes, 147. And such notes would fall within the description of "promissory" notes. 2 Leach, C. C. 1090, 1093; Russ. & R. 232.

REJOINDER. In common-law pleading. The defendant's answer to the plaintiff's replication. The second pleading of defendant in the common-law series.

REJOINING GRATIS. Rejoining within four days from the delivery of the replication, without a notice to rejoin or demand of rejoinder. Wharton, "Rejoinder;" 1 Archb. Prac. 280, 317; 10 Mees. & W. 12. But judgment cannot be signed without demanding rejoinder. 3 Dowl. 537.

RELATIO EST FICTIO JURIS ET INtenta ad unum. Relation is a fiction of law, and intended for one thing. 3 Coke, 28.

RELATIO SEMPER FIAT UT VALEAT dispositio. Reference should always be had in such a manner that a disposition in a will may avail. 6 Coke, 76.

RELATION (Lat. *re*, back, *fero*, to bear).

——**In Civil Law.** The report which the judges made of the proceedings in certain suits to the prince were so called. These relations took place when the judge had no law to direct him, or when the laws were susceptible of difficulties. It was then referred to the prince, who was the author of the law, to give the interpretation. They were made in writing, and contained the pleadings of the parties and all the proceedings. together with the judge's opinion, and prayed the emperor to order what should be done. This ordinance of the prince thus required was called a "*rescript*." Their use was abolished by Justinian (Nov. 125).

——**In Contracts and Conveyances.** A fiction of law whereby an act done at one time operates as if done at another time. 79 Ill. 467. An act so operating is said to do so by relation.

All the several parts and ceremonies necessary to complete a conveyance shall be taken together as one act, and operate from the substantial part by relation. Thus a deed given by a sheriff, upon a previous sale on execution, relates back to, and, in judgment of law, is executed at the time of the sale. 79 Ill. 467. An entry in a United States land office on which a patent issues relates to the entry, and takes date with it. 21 How. 228.

A deed not acknowledged until long after its execution has been held to take effect from its date, the acknowledgment operating as of that time by relation. 75 Mo. 613.

RELATIVE. One connected with another by blood or affinity; a relation; a kinsman or kinswoman. In an adjective sense, having relation or connection with some other person or thing; as, relative rights, relative powers.

RELATIVE FACT. In the law of evidence. A fact having relation to another fact; a minor fact; a circumstance. Burr. Circ. Ev. 121, note (d).

RELATIVE POWERS. Those which relate to land. So called to distinguish them from those which are collateral to it.

These powers are appendant; as, where a tenant for life has a power of making leases in possession. They are in gross when a person has an estate in the land, with a power of appointment, the execution of which falls out of the compass of his estate, but, notwithstanding, is annexed in privity to it, and takes effect in the appointee out of an interest appointed in the appointer. 2 Bouv. Inst. note 1930.

RELATIVE RIGHTS. Those to which a person is entitled in consequence of his relation with others; such as the rights of a husband in relation to his wife; of a father as to his children; of a master as to his servant; of a guardian as to his ward.

In general, the superior may maintain an action for an injury committed against his relative rights. 2 Bouv. Inst. notes 2277-2296; 3 Bouv. Inst. note 3491; 4 Bouv. Inst. notes 3615-3618. See "Action."

RELATIVORUM COGNITO UNO, COGnoscitur et alterum. Of things relating to each other, one being known, the other is known. Cro. Jac. 539.

RELATOR. A rehearser or teller; one who, by leave of court, brings an information in the nature of a *quo warranto*, or other writ issuing in the name of the state, on the relation of a private person.

RELATRIX (Law Lat. and Eng.) In practice. A female relator, or petitioner. 14 Pet. (U. S.) 500, 517.

RELAXARE (Law Lat.) In old conveyancing. To release. *Relaxavi, relaxasse*, have released. Litt. § 445. In 10 Coke, 52b, reference was made to a case in 4 Edw. VI., where it was said that *laxare* is properly to set prisoners in fetters at liberty, and *relaxare* is to do it quickly; and *metaphorice relaxare* is to set at liberty fettered estates and interests, and to make them free and absolute.

RELAXATIO (Law Lat. from *relaxare*, *q. v.*) In old conveyancing. A release; an instrument by which a person relinquishes to another his right in anything. Y. B. P. 18 Hen. VI. 9; Spelman. A deed of release. See "Release."

RELAXATION. In old Scotch practice. Letters passing the signet (*q. v.*) by which a debtor was relaxed (released) from the horn; that is, from personal diligence. Bell, Dict. See "Horning."

RELEASE. The giving up or abandoning a claim or right to the person against whom the claim exists, or the right is to be exercised or enforced.

Releases may either give up, discharge, or abandon a right of action, or convey a man's interest or right to another who has possession of it, or some estate in the same. Shep. Touch. 320; Litt. 444; Nelson, Abr.; Bac. Abr.; Viner, Abr.; Rolle, Abr. In the former class, a mere right is surrendered; in the other, not only a right is given up, but an interest in the estate is conveyed and becomes vested in the release.

An express release is one directly made in terms by deed or other suitable means.

An implied release is one which arises from acts of the creditor or owner, without any express agreement. See Poth. Obl. notes 608, 609.

A release by operation of law is one which, though not expressly made, the law presumes in consequence of some act of the releasor; for instance, when one of several joint obligors is expressly released, the others are also released by operation of law. 3 Salk. 298; Hob. 10, 66; 4 Mod. 380; 7 Johns. (N. Y.) 207.

——In Estates. The conveyance of a man's interest or right which he hath unto a thing, to another that hath the possession thereof, or some estate therein. Shep. Touch. 320. The relinquishment of some right or benefit to a person who has already some interest in the tenement, and such interest as qualifies him for receiving or availing himself of the right or benefit so relinquished. Burton, Real Prop. 15*. A discharge or conveyance of a man's right in lands or tenements to one that held some former estate in possession. 2 Bl. Comm. 324.

The words generally used in such conveyance are "remised, released, and forever quitclaimed." Litt. § 445.

Releases of land are, in respect of their operation, divided into five sorts:

(1) Releases that inure by way of passing the estate, or *mitter l'estate; e. g.*, a release by joint tenant to co-joint tenant, which conveyance will pass a fee without words of limitation.

(2) Releases that inure by way of passing the right, or *mitter le droit; e. g.*, by disseisee to disseisor.

(3) Releases that inure by enlargement of the estate. Here there must be an actual privity of estate at the time between releasor and releasee, who must have an estate actually vested in him capable of enlargement.

(4) Releases that inure by way of extinguishment; *e. g.*, a lord releasing his seignorial rights to his tenant.

(5) Releases that inure by way of feoffment and entry; *e. g.* if there are two disseisors, a release to one will give him a sole estate, as if the disseisee had regained seisin by entry, and enfeoffed him. 2 Bl. Comm. 325*. See 4 Cruise, Dig. 71; Gilb. Ten. 82; Co. Litt. 264; 3 Brock. (U. S.) 185; 2 Sumn. (U. S.) 487; 4 Pick. (Mass.) 143; 10 Pick. (Mass.) 195; 7 Mass. 381; 5 Har. & J. (Md.) 158; 2 N. H. 402; 5 Paige, Ch. (N. Y.) 299; 10 Johns. (N. Y.) 456.

The technicalities of English law as to releases are not generally applicable in the United States. The corresponding conveyance is a quitclaim deed. 2 Bouv. Inst. 416; 21 Ala. (N. S.) 125.

——In Admiralty. An instrument under seal of the court, commanding the marshal to release a ship or other property arrested in a proceeding *in rem* on the giving of bail by the owner.

RELEASE BY WAY OF ENLARGING AN estate. See "Release."

RELEASE BY WAY OF ENTRY AND feoffment. See "Release."

RELEASE BY WAY OF EXTINGUISHment. See "Release."

RELEASE BY WAY OF PASSING A right. See "Release."

RELEASE BY WAY OF PASSING AN Estate. See "Release."

RELEASE TO USES. The conveyance by a deed of release to one party to the use of another is so termed. Thus, when a conveyance of lands was effected, by those instruments of assurance termed a "lease" and "release," from A. to B. and his heirs, to the use of C. and his heirs, in such case C. at once took the whole fee simple in such lands; B., by the operation of the statute of uses, being made a mere conduit pipe for conveying the estate to C., and B. was called the "releasee to uses."

RELEASEE. A person to whom a release is made.

RELEASOR. He who makes a release.

RELEGATIO (Lat.) A kind of banishment known to the civil law, which did not take away the rights of citizenship, which *deportatio* did.

Some say that *relegatio* was temporary, *deportatio* perpetual; that *relegatio* did not take away the property of the exile, and that *deportatio* did; but these distinctions do not seem always to exist. There was one sort of *relegatio* for slaves, viz., *in agros;* another for freedom, viz., *in provincias. Relegatio* only exiled from certain limits; *deportatio* confined to a particular place (*locus poenae*). Calv. Lex.

RELEGATION (from Lat. *relegatio, q. v.*) In old English law. Banishment for a time only. Co. Litt. 133.

RELEVAMEN (Law Lat. from *relevare,* to lift up). In old English law. Relief; one of the incidents of the feudal tenure. Lib. Rames, § 310; Spelman. In Domesday Book it is called *relevamentum;* in the laws of Edward the Confessor, *relevatio;* in *Magna Charta,* and generally in old English and Scotch law *relevium.* Domesday Book, tit. "Berocscire, Walingford;" LL. Edw. Conf. c. 35.

RELEVANCY. Applicability to the issue joined. That quality of evidence which renders it properly applicable in determining the truth or falsity of the matters in issue between the parties to a suit. See 1 Greenl. Ev. § 49.

RELEVANT. In the law of evidence. Having relation; applicable. Relevant evidence is evidence applicable to the issue.

RELEVER. (L. Fr.) To relieve; to pay a relief. Britt. c. 69.

RELEVIUM. L. Lat. [from L. Fr. *relever,* to raise or lift again.] In old English and Scotch law. Relief; one of the incidents of the feudal tenure. Bract. fol. 84. Spelman.

RELICT. A widow; as A. B., relict of C. B.; A. B., widow of C. B.

RELICTA VERIFICATIONE (Lat. his pleading being abandoned). In pleading. A confession of judgment made after plea pleaded, viz., a *cognovit actionem,* accompanied by a withdrawal of the plea.

RELICTION (Lat. *relinquo,* to leave behind). An increase of the land by the retreat or recession of the sea or a river. Sometimes called "dereliction."

If the reliction be gradual, the land belongs to the riparian owner, but if it be sudden, and considerable, it belongs to the state (13 N. Y. 296; 1 Gill & J. [Md.] 249), unless the land has been previously lost by submergence (100 N. Y. 424).

RELIEF.

——**In Feudal Law.** A sum payable by the new tenant, the duty being incident to every feudal tenure, by way of fine or composition with the lord for taking up the estate which was lapsed or fallen in by the death of the last tenant. At one time, the amount was arbitrary; but afterwards the relief of a knight's fee became fixed at one hundred shillings. 2 Bl. Comm. 65.

——**In Practice.** A general name for the remedy sought or allowed in any action, legal or equitable.

RELIEVE. In feudal law. To hold or depend; thus, a tenant was said to relieve of the crown. Now obsolete.

RELIGION (Lat. *re,* back, *ligo,* to bind). Real piety in practice, consisting in the performance of all known duties to God and our fellow men.

Any system of faith and worship; as the religion of the Turks, of Hindoos, of Christians; true and false religion. 200 Ill. 572.

RELIGIOUS CORPORATION. Any corporation the charter powers of which are to be used in aid of the propagation and practice of a religious belief, but the fact that a corporation is under the control of members of a particular church does not make it a religious corporation. Nor does the fact that a board of trustees of a corporation college is to be elected by an association of churches, constitute it a sectarian or religious corporation. Corporations organized under acts authorizing the incorporation of religious societies or congregations are not to be classified as ecclesiastical corporations, but are civil corporations and subject to the same principles of law, and the same control by the civil courts, as any other civil corporation. 1 Fletcher Cyclopedia Corporations 141.

RELIGIOUS LIBERTY. As secured by the provisions of the constitution of the United States, and of the several states, means freedom from any establishment of a religion, from compulsory support of religious instruction, from compulsory attendance on religious worship, and from restraints on the free exercise of religion according to the dictates of conscience, or upon the expression of religious belief. See Cooley, Const. Lim. 575.

The full and free right to entertain any religious belief, to practice any religious principle, and to teach any religious doctrine which does not violate the laws of morality and propriety, or infringe personal rights. 13 Wall. (U. S.) 728. But freedom from restraint on the exercise of religion does not permit one to break the law, violate peace and good order, or interfere with another's liberty of action, 63 Mich. 396, because his unlawful acts were in the exercise of his religion, or according to the dictates of his conscience. 98 U. S. 166.

RELIGIOUS MEN (Law Lat. *religiosi*). Such as entered into some monastery or convent. In old English deeds, the vendee was often restrained from aliening to "Jews or religious men," lest the lands should fall into mortmain. Religious men were civilly dead. Blount.

RELIGIOUS TEST. A belief in certain dogmas of religion which are prerequisite to the holding of a civil office, or the exercise of any civil right. "No religious test shall ever be required as a qualification to any office or public trust under the United States." Const. art. 6, § 3.

RELIGIOUS USE. See "Charitable Uses."

RELINQUISHMENT. A forsaking, abandoning, or giving over a right; for example, a plaintiff may relinquish a bad count in a declaration, and proceed on a good; a man may relinquish a part of his claim in order to give a court jurisdiction. The word has no exact technical significance.

RELIQUA. The remainder or debt which a person finds himself debtor in upon the balancing or liquidation of an account. Hence *reliquary*, the debtor of a *reliqua;* as also a person who only pays piecemeal. Enc. Lond.

RELIQUI (Lat.) In the civil law. The rest. Held to signify "all" (*universos, omnes*). Dig. 50. 16. 95. 160.

RELOCATIO (Lat.) In civil law. A renewal of a lease on its determination on like terms as before. It may be either express or tacit. The latter is when the tenant holds over with the knowledge and without objection of the landlord. Mackeld. Civ. Law, § 379.

RELOCATION. In Scotch law. A reletting or renewal of a lease; a tacit relocation is permitting a tenant to hold over without any new agreement.

REM domino vel non domino vendente duobus.

In jure est potior venditione prior.

Where one, whether owner or not owner, sells a thing to two persons, the party who is first sold to has the better right. A Latin couplet quoted in Fleta (lib. 3, c. 15, § 8).

REMAINDER. The remnant of an estate in lands or tenements expectant on a particular estate created together with the same at one time. Co. Litt. 143a.

To constitute a valid remainder at common law, the estate in remainder must be created (1) on purchase (2 Washb. Real Prop. 586); (2) at the same time with a particular estate (2 Bl. Comm. 167); (3) less than a fee (Id. 164); and (4) must vest in the grantee during the continuance of the particular estate, or *eo instanti* that it determines, so that the freehold shall not remain in abeyance (Id. 168); but (5) the remainder must rest on the natural termination of the particular estate, and not be in defeasance of it (Fearne, Cont. Rem. 13).

——**In the United States.** The term "remainder" is applied to various estates in expectancy, limited on precedent estates which do not fulfill all the requirements of the common law.

Remainders are either vested or contingent.

(1) A vested remainder is one by which a present interest passes to the party, though to be enjoyed in the future, and by which the estate is invariably fixed to remain to a determinate person after the particular estate is spent. A determinate remainderman *in esse* at the time of its creation is essential to a vested remainder.

A future estate is vested where there is a person in being who would have an immediate right to the lands on the ceasing of the immediate or precedent estate. 1 Rev. St. N. Y. c. 1, tit. 2, § 13. This definition has been justly criticised so far as it is intended to be declaratory of the common law, in that it omits the essential that the person who shall take the remainder shall be ascertained before the termination of the particular estate.

(2) A contingent remainder is one where the estate in remainder is limited to take effect either to a dubious and uncertain person, or upon a dubious and uncertain event, so that the particular estate may chance to be determined, and the remainder never take effect. 2 Bl. Comm. 169.

A remainder which, as regards the possession or enjoyment, depends on a contingency other than the survival of the remainderman. Smith, Ex. Int. § 171.

It is not the uncertainty of enjoyment in future, but the uncertainty of the right to that enjoyment, which marks the difference between a vested and a contingent interest. 4 Kent, Comm. 206; 2 Cruise, Dig. 270.

REMAINDERMAN. One who is entitled to the remainder of the estate after a particular estate carved out of it has expired.

REMALLARE. (L. Lat.) In old European law. To summon to court a second time; to resummon. Spelman.

REMAND. To send back.

——**Of Prisoner.** The ordering of a prisoner's return to custody pending proceedings, or on a determination that he is not entitled to release.

——**Of a Cause.** The sending it back to the same court out of which it came, for the purpose of having some action on it there. March, 100.

REMANENT PRO DEFECTU EMPTORUM (Lat. *remanent*, they remain, *pro defectu*, through lack, *emptorum*, or buyers). In practice. The return made by the sheriff to a writ of execution when he has not been able to sell the property seized, that the same remains unsold for want of buyers; in that case, the plaintiff is entitled to a *venditioni exponas*. Comyn, Dig. "Execution" (C 8).

REMANENTIA (Law Lat. from *remanere*, *q. v.*) In old English law. A remainder. Spelman.

A perpetuity, or perpetual estate (*pro perpetuo*). Glanv. lib. 7, c. 1; Bracton, fol. 244; Reg. Maj. lib. 2, c. 23.

REMANERE (Lat.)

——**In Old English Practice.** To remain; to stop or stay; to "demur," in the old sense of the word. *Primo queratur a tenente si aliquid velit vel sciat dicere quare assisa debeat remanere*, it first should be inquired of the tenant if he will or know to say anything why the assize should stay,—that is, why it should not proceed. Bracton, fol. 184b. *Non propter minorem aetatem petentium remanebit assisa*, the assize shall not stay on account of the nonage of the demandants. Id. fol. 276. Hence the term *remanet*, in modern practice.

REMANET (Lat.) In practice. The causes which are entered for trial, and which cannot be tried during the term, are *remanets*. Lee, "Trial;" 1 Sellon, Prac. 434; 1 Phil. Ev. 4.

REMEDIAL LAW. That part of the body of the law which contains the remedies by which rights are enforced and wrongs redressed, and the rules by which the substantive law (*q. v.*) is applied.

REMEDIAL STATUTE. A statute having for its object either to redress some existing grievance, or to introduce some regulation or proceeding conducive to the public good. 58 Ill. 247; 30 Ill. App. 109; or remove some defect in the law, and thus giving a more perfect remedy for private wrongs. Used usually in contradistinction to "penal statute," but sometimes to "declaratory statute."

A penal law may be also remedial, and a statute may be remedial in one part and penal in another. 103 Ill. 390.

REMEDY. The means employed to enforce a right or redress an injury. "The being put in possession of that right whereof the party injured is deprived." 6 Wheat. (U. S.) 407.

The procedure whereby redress is secured, as distinguished from the right to be enforced. 103 U. S. 717.

It includes every original application to a court of justice for a judgment or an order. Thus, the application for admission to practice as an attorney or counsellor is a remedy. 22 N. Y. 67, 87.

——**In Old English Law.** A remainder. Co. Litt. 49a; 2 Coke, 51a.

(1) Equitable remedies are those obtainable only in a court of equity.

(2) Legal remedies in the technical sense of the term, are those which may be awarded in a court of law; in a broader sense, any remedy allowed by the law of the land.

(3) Cumulative or concurrent remedies are such as are provided in addition to other existing remedies, and whose existence does not preclude a resort to the old remedy. A resort to one of the two remedies, however, precludes a subsequent resort to the other. See "Election."

(4) Specific or exclusive remedies are such as repeal all pre-existing remedies for the same wrong.

REMEDY OVER. The remedy of him who is primarily liable against him who is secondarily liable for the same debt.

REMEMBRANCERS. In English law. Officers of the exchequer, whose duty it is to remind the lord treasurer and the justices of that court of such things as are to be called and attended to for the benefit of the crown. Cowell; St. 3 & 4 Wm. IV. c. 99.

REMENAUNT (Law Fr.) Remaining; to come after; remainder. A *remenaunt*, for ever after. Kelham.

REMISE, RELEASE, AND QUITCLAIM. The ordinary effective words in a release. These words are, in this country, sufficient to pass the estate in a primary conveyance. 7 Conn. 250; 24 N. H. 460; 21 Ala. (N. S.) 125; 7 N. Y. 422. "Remise" is a French word synonymous with "release." See "Quitclaim."

REMISSION (Lat. *re*, back, *mitto*, to send).

——**In Civil Law.** A release of a debt. It is conventional when it is expressly granted to the debtor by a creditor having a capacity to alienate; or tacit, when the creditor voluntarily surrenders to his debtor the original title, under private signature, constituting the obligation. Civ. Code La. art. 2195.

Forgiveness or pardon of an offense.

It has the effect of putting back the offender into the same situation he was before the commission of the offense. Remission is generally granted in cases where the offense was involuntary, or committed in self-defense. Poth Prcc. Civ. sec. 7, art. 2, § 2.

——**At Common Law.** The act by which a forfeiture or penalty is forgiven. 10 Wheat. (U. S.) 246.

REMISSIUS IMPERANTI MELIUS PARETUR. A man commanding not too strictly is better obeyed. 3 Inst. 233.

REMIT. To annul a fine or forfeiture. This is generaly done by the courts where they have a discretion by law; as, for example, when a juror is fined for nonattendance in court, after being duly summoned, and, on appearing, he produces evidence to the court that he was sick and unable to attend, the fine will be remitted by the court.

——**In Commercial Law.** To send money, bills, or something which will answer the purpose of money.

REMITTANCE. In commercial law. Money sent by one merchant to another, either in specie, bill of exchange, draft, or otherwise.

REMITTEE. A person to whom a remittance is made. Story, Bailm. § 75.

REMITTER. To be placed back in possession.

When one having a right to lands is out of possession, and afterwards the freehold is cast upon him by some defective title, and he enters by virtue of that title, the law remits him to his ancient and more certain right, and, by an equitable fiction, supposes him to have gained possession under it. 3 Bl. Comm. 190; Comyn, Dig. "Remitter."

REMITTERE (Lat. from *re*, again, and *mittere*, to send). In old English practice. To send back; to give up or relinquish; to remise or release. *Postea jus suum remisit, et quietum clamavit*, afterwards remised and quitclaimed his right. Bracton, fol. 313b.

To remand on *habeas corpus*. 3 How. St. Tr. 161.

REMITTIT DAMNA (Lat. he releases damages). An entry on the record, by which the plaintiff declares that he remits the damages or a part of the damages which have been awarded him by the jury, is so called.

In some cases, a misjoinder of actions may be cured by the entry of a *remittit damna*. 1 Chit. Pl. *207.

REMITTITUR DAMNUM (or DAMNA). In practice. The act of the plaintiff upon the record, whereby he abates or remits the excess of damages found by the jury beyond the sum laid in the declaration. See 1 Saund. 285, note 6; 4 Conn. 109; Bouv. Inst. Index.

REMITTITUR OF RECORD. After a record has been removed to the supreme court, and a judgment has been rendered, it is to be remitted or sent back to the court below, for the purpose of retrying the cause, when the judgment has been reversed, or of issuing an execution when it has been affirmed. The act of so returning the record, and the writ issued for that purpose, bear the name of "remittitur."

REMITTOR. A person who makes a remittance to another.

REMONSTRANCE. A petition to a court or deliberative or legislative body, in which those who have signed it request that something which it is in contemplation to perform shall not be done.

REMOTE CAUSE. See "Proximate Cause."

REMOTE DAMAGES. Damages are too remote to be actionable when not the legal and natural consequence of the act complained of. Sweet.

Remote damages are such as are the unusual and unexpected result, not reasonably to be anticipated from an accidental or unusual combination of circumstances, —a result beyond and over which the negligent party has no control. 175 Ill. 406; 131 Ill. App. 295; 123 Ill. App. 25. See "Damages;" "Proximate Damages."

REMOTE EVIDENCE. Evidence so disconnected from the fact to be proved as to be irrelevant thereto. See "Evidence."

REMOTO IMPEDIMENTO, EMERGIT ACTIO. The impediment being removed, the action arises. 5 Coke, 76; Wingate, Max. 20.

REMOVAL OF CAUSE. The removal of a cause from the court in which it was commenced to another court, in which it thereafter proceeds. The term seems literally to include change of venue and removal to a reviewing court, but to these it is rarely applied, being ordinarily used to denote the removal of a cause from a state to a federal court, where a federal question is involved, or the parties are citizens of different states, or one of them is an alien (see Act Cong. March 3, 1887), or to proceedings under state statutes for the transfer of a cause to another of concurrent jurisdiction.

REMOVER. In practice. A transfer of a suit or cause out of one court into another, which is effected by writ of error, *certiorari*, and the like. 11 Coke, 41.

REMUNERATION. Reward; recompense; salary. Dig. 17. 1. 7.

RENANT, or RENIANT. In old English law. Denying. 32 Hen. VIII. c. 2.

RENCOUNTER. A sudden meeting; as opposed to a duel, which is deliberate.

RENDER. In the civil law. To yield; to return; to give again. It is the reverse of "prender." See "Rendition of Judgment."

RENDITION OF A JUDGMENT. The judicial act of the court in pronouncing the sentence of the law upon the facts in controversy as ascertained by the pleadings and verdict. 195 Ill. App. 181.

The announcement of the decision of the court, as by a verbal decision entered in the minutes, the filing of findings, etc.

It differs from "entry of judgment," which is the formal entry of the judgment upon the records. 80 Cal. 166. But see 9 Minn. 318.

RENEGADE. One who has changed his profession of faith or opinion; one who has deserted his church or party.

RENEWAL. A change of something old for something new; as, the renewal of a note; the renewal of a lease. See "Novation;" 1 Bouv. Inst. note 800.

RENOUNCE. To give up a right; for example, an executor may renounce the right of administering the estate of the testator; a widow, the right to administer to her intestate husband's estate.

RENOUNCING PROBATE. Giving up the right to be executor of a will, wherein he has been appointed to that office, by refusing to take out probate of such will. Toller, Ex'rs, 42; 1 Williams, Ex'rs, 230, 231; 20 & 21 Vict. c. 77, § 79; 21 & 22 Vict. c. 94, § 16.

RENOVARE (Lat.) In old English law. To renew. *Annuatim renovare,* to renew annually. A phrase applied to profits which are taken and the product renewed again. Amb. 131.

RENT. A return or compensation for the possession of some corporeal inheritance, and is a certain profit, either in money, provisions, or labor, issuing out of lands and tenements, in return for their use.

Some of its common-law properties are that it must be a profit to the proprietor, certain in its character, or capable of being reduced to a certainty, issuing yearly, that is, periodically, out of the thing granted, and not be part of the land or thing itself. Co. Litt. 47; 2 Bl. Comm. 41.

At common law there were three species of rent,—rent service, having some corporeal service attached to the tenure of the land, to which the right of distress was necessarily incident; rent charge, which was a reservation of rent, with a clause authorizing its collection by distress; and rent seck, where there was no such clause, but the rent could only be collected by an ordinary action at law. These distinctions, however, for all practical purposes, have become obsolete, in consequence of various statutes both in England and in this country, allowing every kind of rent to be distrained for without distinction. See Tayl. Landl. & Ten. § 370.

RENT CHARGE. See "Rent."

RENT ROLL. A list of rents payable to a particular person or public body.

RENT SECK. See "Rent."

RENT SERVICE. See "Rent."

RENTS, ISSUES, AND PROFITS. The profits arising from property generally (Gen. St. Mass. 1860, p. 537; Rev. St. N. Y. st. 1849), for better protection of property of married women.

This phrase in the Vermont statute has been held not to cover "yearly profits." 26 Vt. 741.

RENTS OF ASSIZE. The certain and determined rents of the freeholders and ancient copyholders of manors are called "rents of assize," apparently because they were assized or made certain, and so distinguished from a *redditus mobilis,* which was a variable or fluctuating rent. 3 Cruise, Dig. 314; Brown.

RENTS RESOLUTE. Rents anciently payable to the crown from the lands of abbeys and religious houses; and after their dissolution, notwithstanding that the lands were demised to others, yet the rents were still reserved and made payable again to the crown. Cowell.

RENTAL. A roll or list of the rents of an estate, containing the description of the lands let, the names of the tenants, and other particulars connected with such estate. This is the same as "rent roll," from which it is said to be corrupted.

Derived from or pertaining to rent, as rental value.

RENTAL BOLLS. In Scotch law. When the tithes (tiends) have been liquidated and settled for so many bolls of corn yearly. Bell, Dict.

RENTAL RIGHTS. In English law. A species of lease usually granted at a low rent and for life. Tenants under such leases were called "rentalers" or "kindly tenants."

RENTE. In French law. A word nearly synonymous with our word "annuity."

RENTE FONCIERE. In French law. A rent which issues out of land; and it is of its essence that it be perpetual, for if it be made but for a limited time, it is a lease.

It may, however, be extinguished. Civ. Code La. arts. 2750, 2759. See "Ground Rent."

RENTE VIAGERE. In French law. An annuity for life. Civ. Code La. art. 2764.

REO ABSENTE (Lat.) Defendant being absent.

REP SILVER. In old records. Money paid by servile tenants for exemption from the customary duty of reaping for the lord. Cowell.

REPAIRS. That work which is done to an estate to keep it in good order. It does not include additions and adaptions of the premises to new uses. 24 N. J. Eq. 358.

REPARATION. The redress of an injury; amends for a tort inflicted. See "Remedy."

REPARATIONE FACIENDA, WRIT DE (Lat.) The name of an ancient writ, which lies by one or more joint tenants against the other joint tenants, or by a person owning a house or building against the owner of the adjoining building, to compel the reparation of such joint property. Fitzh. Nat. Brev. 295.

REPATRIATION. The regaining of a nationality once lost; the converse of "expatriation."

REPEAL. The abrogation or destruction of a law by a legislative act.

A repeal is "express," as, when it is literally declared by a subsequent law, or "implied," when the new law contains provisions contrary to or irreconcilable with those of the former law, or which, though reconcilable, are manifestly designed to furnish an exclusive rule.

A law may be repealed by implication, by an affirmative as well as by a negative statute, if the substance, is inconsistent with the old statute. 1 Ohio, 10; 2 Bibb (Ky.) 96; Harper (S. C.) 101; 4 Wash. C. C. (U. S.) 691.

Repeal is express where the repealing act explicity refers to an existing law, and declares its repeal.

Where statutes are repugnant, there is, of course, an implied repeal. An implied repeal also results from an act covering the whole subject matter, and obviously designed as a substitute (84 Ill. 590; 123 N. Y. 485), or by a revision or codification of the law (78 Wis. 457; 30 Vt. 344).

REPELLITUR A SACRAMENTO INFAMIS. An infamous person is repelled or prevented from taking an oath. Co. Litt. 158; Bracton, 185.

REPELLITUR EXCEPTIONE CEDENDARUM ACTIONUM. He is defeated by the plea that the actions have been assigned. 1 Johns. Ch. (N. Y.) 409, 414.

REPERTORY. In French law. A word used to denote the inventory or minutes which notaries are required to make of all contracts which take place before them. Dalloz.

REPETITION.

——**In Civil Law.** The act by which a person demands and seeks to recover what he has paid by mistake or delivered on a condition which has not been performed. Dig. 12. 4. 5.

The name of an action which lies to recover the payment which has been made by mistake, when nothing was due.

Repetition is never admitted in relation to natural obligations which have been voluntarily acquitted, if the debtor had capacity to give his consent. 6 Toullier, Dr. Civ. 386.

In order to entitle the payer to recover back money paid by mistake, it must have been paid by him to a person to whom he did not owe it, for otherwise he cannot recover it back,—the creditor having, in such case, the just right to retain the money. *Repetitio nulla est ab eo qui suum recepit.*

How far money paid under a mistake of law is liable to repetition has been discussed by civilians; and opinions on this subject are divided. 2 Poth. Obl. (Evans Ed.) 369, 408-437; 1 Story, Eq. Pl. § 111, note 2.

——**In Scotch Law.** The act of reading over a witness' deposition, in order that he may adhere to it or correct it, at his choice. The same as *recolement* (*q. v.*) in the French law. 2 Benth. Ev. bk. 3, c. 12, p. 239. See "Legacy."

REPETITUM NAMIUM. A repeated, second or reciprocal distress; withernam. 3 Bl. Comm. 148.

REPETUNDAE, or PECUNIAE REPETUNDAE. In Roman law. The terms used to designate such sums of money as the *socii* of the Roman state, or individuals, claimed to recover from *magistratus*, *judices*, or *publici curatores*, which they had improperly taken or received in the *provinciae*, or in the *urbs Roma*, either in the discharge of their *jurisdictio*, or in their capacity of *judices*, or in respect of any other public function. Sometimes the word "*repetundae*" was used to express the illegal act for which compensation was sought. Wharton.

REPETUNDARUM CRIMEN (Lat.) In the Roman law. The crime of bribery or extortion in a magistrate, or person in any public office. Calv. Lex.; Halifax, Anal. bk. 3, c. 12, No. 73; Dig. 48. 11; Code, 9. 27.

REPLEADER. In pleading. Making a new series of pleadings.

Judgment of repleader differs from a judgment *non obstante veredicto* in this, that it is allowed by the courts to do justice between the parties where the defect is in the form or manner of stating the right, and the issue joined is on an immaterial point, so that it cannot tell for whom to give judgment (7 Mass. 312; 3 Pick. [Mass.] 124; 19 Pick. [Mass.] 419); while judgment *non obstante* is given only where it is clearly apparent to the court that the party who has succeeded has, upon his own showing, no merits, and cannot have by any manner of statement (1 Chit. Pl. 568). See 19 Ark. 194.

REPLEGIARE (Lat.) To replevy; to redeem a thing detained or taken by another, by putting in legal sureties. See "De Homine Replegiando."

REPLEGIARE DE AVERIIS (Lat.) A writ brought by one whose cattle are impounded or distrained, upon security given to the sheriff to pursue or answer the action at law. 7 Hen. VIII. c. 4; Fitzh. Nat. Brev. 68; New Book of Entries, "Replevin;" Dyer, 173; Reg. Orig. 81.

REPLEGIARE FACIAS (Lat.) A writ of replevin, which issued out of chancery, commanding the sheriff to deliver the distress to the owner, and afterwards to do justice in regard to the matter in his own county court. It was abolished by statute of Marlbridge, which provided a shorter process. 3 Bl. Comm. 147*.

REPLEVIABLE, or REPLEVISABLE. Property is said to be repleviable or replevisable when proceedings in replevin may be resorted to for the purpose of trying the right to such property. Brown.

REPLEVIN.

——**At Common Law.** A form of action which lay to regain the possession of personal chattels taken from the plaintiff unlawfully.

It differs from "detinue" in this, that it requires an unlawful taking as the foundation of the action; and from all other personal actions in that it is brought to recover the possession of the specific property claimed to have been unlawfully taken.

——**In the United States.** By statutes in nearly all the states, the actions of replevin and detinue have been merged, the action being usually called "replevin," but sometimes "claim and delivery," so that such action lies for either the unlawful taking or the unlawful detention of property, *i. e.*, either in the *cepit* or the *detinet.*

REPLEVISH. In old English law. To let one to mainprise upon surety. Cowell.

REPLEVY. To redeliver goods which have been distrained to the original possessor of them, on his giving pledges in an action of replevin. It signifies, also, the bailing or liberating a man from prison, on his finding bail to answer. See "Replevin."

REPLIANT. One who makes a replication.

REPLICATIO (Lat.) In the civil law and old English pleading. The plaintiff's answer to the defendant's exception or plea; corresponding with and giving name to the replication in modern pleading. Inst. 4. 14. pr.

REPLICATION (Lat. *replicare,* to fold back).

——**In Pleading.** The plaintiff's answer to the defendant's plea or answer.

——**In Equity.** The plaintiff's avoidance or denial of the answer or defense. Story, Eq. Pl. § 877.

A general replication is a general denial of the truth of the defendant's plea or answer, and of the sufficiency of the matte ralleged in it to bar the plaintiff's suit, and an assertion of the truth and sufficiency of the bill. Cooper, Eq. Pl. 329, 330.

A special replication was one which introduced new matter to avoid the defendant's answer. It might be followed by rejoinder, surrejoinder, and rebutter. Special replications have been superseded by the practice of amending bills. 1 How. (U. S.) Introd. 55; 17 Pet. (U. S.) Append. 68. A replication must be made use of where the plaintiff intends to introduce evidence, and a subpoena to the defendant to rejoin must be added, unless he will appear gratis. Story, Eq. Pl. § 879.

A replication may be filed *nunc pro tunc* after witnesses have been examined under leave of court. Story, Eq. Pl. § 881; Mitf. Eq. Pl. (by Jeremy) 323.

——**At Law.** The plaintiff's reply to the defendant's plea. It contains a statement of matter, consistent with the declaration, which avoids the effect of the defendant's plea, or constitutes a joinder in issue thereon.

REPLY. In its general sense, a reply is what the plaintiff, petitioner, or other person who has instituted a proceeding says in answer to the defendant's case.

——**In Code Pleading.** The second pleading of the plaintiff, corresponding to the common-law replication.

——**In Trial Practice.** The argument of plaintiff in answer to that of defendant.

REPONE (from Lat. *reponere,* to put back). In Scotch practice. To replace; to restore to a former state or right. 2 Alis. Crim. Prac. 351.

REPORT. An official or formal statement of facts or proceedings.

A printed or written account of the judicial determination of a case. In this sense, the term is used ordinarily in the plural to denote the published volumes of reports of decisions.

REPORTARE (Law Lat.) In old English practice. To report.

REPOSITION OF THE FOREST. In old English law. An act whereby certain forest grounds, being made *purlieu* upon view, were by a second view laid to the forest again,—put back into the forest. Manw. For. Law; Cowell.

REPRESENT. To state or assert.

To act as substitute or agent for another.

REPRESENTATION.

——**In Practice.** A doctrine by which a particular party, though not before the court in person, is so far represented by others that his interest receives such actual and efficient protection that the decree may be held to be binding upon him. 209 Ill. 141.

——**In Insurance.** The stating of facts by one applying for a policy of insurance, whether in writing or orally, expressly or by plain implication, preliminary and in reference to making the insurance, obviously tending to influence the insurer as to entering into the contract. 1 Phil. Ins. § 524; 12 Md. 348; 11 Cush. (Mass.) 324; 2 N. H. 551; 6 Gray (Mass.) 221.

A representation is to be distinguished from a "warranty," which is a statement of facts by the insured, which is a part of the contract. 21 Conn. 19; 49 Me. 200.

There is no certain rule to determine whether particular statements are representations or warranties. Statements expressly declared to be warranties (78 Hun. [N. Y.] 222), or incorporated in the policy, actually (39 N. J. Law, 89) or by reference (45 N. Y. 80), are warranties, but otherwise the question is one of intent; the use of the word "warrant" not being conclusive (59 N. Y. 557), and a statement will be declared a representation unless the contrary intent is clear (98 Mass. 381).

The importance of the distinction lies in the fact that breach of any warranty avoids the policy, while breach of a representation is fatal only when such representation is material to the risk. 98 Mass. 381.

——**In Scotch Law.** The name of a plea or statement presented to the lord ordinary of the court of session when his judgment is brought under review.

REPRESENTATION OF PERSONS. A fiction of the law, the effect of which is to put the representative in the place, degree, or right of the person represented.

The heir represents his ancestor (Bac. Abr. "Heir and Ancestor" [A]; the devisee, his testator; the executor, his testator; the administrator, his intestate; the successor in corporations, his predecessor; and, generally speaking, they are entitled to the rights of the persons whom they represent, and bound to fulfill the duties and obligations which were binding upon them in those characters.

Representation was unknown to the Romans, and was invented by the commentators and doctors of the civil law. Toullier, Dr. Civ. liv. 3, tit. 1, c. 3, note 180. See Ayliffe, Pand. 397; Dalloz, "Succession," art. 4, § 2.

REPRESENTATIVE. One who represents or is in the place of another. One having lawful authority to act in behalf of the property and bind the owner in regard thereto. 104 Ill. 554.

In legislation, it signifies one who has been elected a member of that branch of the legislature called the "house of representatives."

The executor or administrator of a deceased person is called the "personal representative," to distinguish him from the "real representative," or heir at law. 39 Barb. (N. Y.) 520.

REPRESENTATIVE ACTION OR SUIT. A representative action or suit is one brought by a member of a class of persons on behalf of himself and the other members of the class.

REPRESENTATIVE DEMOCRACY. A form of government where the powers of the sovereignty are delegated to a body of men, elected from time to time, who exercise them for the benefit of the whole nation. 1 Bouv. Inst. note 31.

REPRESENTATIVE PEERS. Those who, at the commencement of every new parliament, are elected to represent Scotland and Ireland in the British house of lords. Brown.

REPRIEVE (from Fr. *reprendre*, to take back). In criminal practice. The withdrawing of a sentence for an interval of time, which operates in delay of execution. 4 Bl. Comm. 394. It is a deferring of sentence to a definite day, as opposed to an indefinite "suspension." 1 Park. Cr. R. 266. See "Pardon."

REPRISALS. The forcibly taking a thing by one nation which belonged to another, in return or satisfaction for an injury committed by the latter on the former. Vattel, bk. 2, c. 18, § 342; 1 Bl. Comm. c. 7.

(1) General reprisals take place by virtue of commissions delivered to officers and citizens of the aggrieved state, directing them to take the persons and property belonging to the offending state wherever found.

(2) Negative reprisals take place when a nation refuses to fulfill a perfect obligation which it has contracted, or to permit another state to enjoy a right which it justly claims.

(3) Positive reprisals consist in seizing the persons and effects belonging to the other nation, in order to obtain satisfaction.

(4) Special reprisals are such as are granted in times of peace to particular individuals who have suffered an injury from the citizens or subjects of the other nation.

Reprisals are used between nation and nation to do themselves justice, when they cannot otherwise obtain it. Congress has the power to grant letters of marque and reprisal. Const. U. S. art. 1, § 8. cl. 11.

Reprisals are made in two ways,—either by embargo, in which case the act is that of the state, or by letters of marque and reprisal, in which case the act is that of the citizen, authorized by the government. See 2 Brown, Civ. Law, 334.

REPRISES. The deductions and payments out of lands, annuities, and the like are called "reprises," because they are taken back. When we speak of the clear yearly value of an estate, we say it is worth so much a year *ultra reprises,* besides all reprises.

In Pennsylvania, lands are not to be sold when the rents can pay the incumbrances in seven years, beyond all reprises.

REPROBATA PECUNIA LIBERAT SOLventum. Money refused liberates the debtor. 9 Coke, 79. But this must be understood with a qualification. See "Tender."

REPROBATION. In ecclesiastical law. The propounding exceptions either against facts, persons, or things; as, to allege that certain deeds or instruments have not been duly and lawfully executed; or that certain persons are such that they are incompetent as witnesses; or that certain things ought not, for legal reasons, to be admitted.

REPROBATOR, ACTION OF. In Scotch law. An action or proceeding intended to convict a witness of perjury, to which the witness must be made a party. Bell, Dict.

REPROBUS. (Lat.) In old English law. Bad or spurious; reprobate. A term applied to money which might be rejected or refused.

REPUBLIC. A commonwealth; that form of government in which the administration of affairs is open to all the citizens. In another sense, it signifies the state, independently of its form of government. 1 Toullier, Dr. Civ. n. 28, and n. 202, note.

REPUBLICATION. An act done by a testator, from which it can be concluded that he intended that an instrument which had been revoked by him should operate as his will; or it is the re-execution of a will by the testator, with a view of giving it full force and effect.

The republication is express when there has been an actual re-execution of it (1 Ves. Jr. 440; 2 Rand. [Va.] 192; 9 Johns. [N. Y.] 312); it is implied when, for example, the testator by a codicil executed according to the statute of frauds, reciting that he had made his will, added, "I hereby ratify and confirm my said will, except in the alterations after mentioned" (3 Brown, Parl. Cas. 85). The will might be at a distance, or not in the power of the testator, and it may be thus republished. 1 Ves. Sr. 437; 3 Bing. 614; 1 Ves. Jr. 486; 4 Brown, Ch. 2.

REPUDIATION.

——**In Civil Law.** A term used to signify the putting away of a wife or a woman betrothed.

Properly, "divorced" is used to point out the separation of married persons; "repudiation," to denote the separation either of married people, or those who are only affianced. *Divortium est repudium et separatio maritorum; repudium est renunciatio sponsalium, vel etiam est divortium.* Dig. 50. 16. 101.

A determination to have nothing to do with any particular thing; as, a repudiation of a legacy is the abandonment of such legacy, and a renunciation of all right to it.

——**In Ecclesiastical Law.** The refusal to accept a benefice which has been conferred upon the party repudiating.

REPUDIUM (Lat.) In Roman law. A breaking off of the contract of espousals, or of a marriage intended to be solemnized. Sometimes translated "divorce," but this was not the proper sense. Dig. 50. 16. 191.

REPUGNANCY (Lat. *re,* back, against, *pugnare,* to fight).

——**In Contracts.** A disagreement or inconsistency between two or more clauses of the same instrument. In deeds, and other instruments *inter vivos,* the earlier clause prevails, if the inconsistency be not so great as to avoid the instrument for uncertainty. Hardw. 94; Owen, 84; 2 Taunt. 109; 15 Sim. 118; 2 C. B. 830; 13 Mees. & W. 534.

In wills, the latter clause prevails, under the same exceptions. Co. Litt. 112b; Plowd. 541; 2 Taunt. 109; 6 Ves. 100; 2 Mylne & K. 149; 1 Jarm. Wills, 411. See 23 Am. Jur. 277; 1 Pars. Cont. 26.

Repugnancy in a condition renders it void. 2 Salk. 463; 2 Mod. 285; 11 Mod. 191; 1 Hawks (N. C.) 20; 7 J. J. Marsh. (Ky.) 192. And see, generally, 3 Pick. (Mass.) 272; 4 Pick. (Mass.) 54; 6 Cow. (N. Y.) 677.

——**In Pleading.** An inconsistency or disagreement between the statements of material facts in a declaration or other pleading; as, where certain timber was said to be for the completion of a house already built. 1 Salk. 213.

Repugnancy of immaterial facts, or of redundant and unnecessary matter, if it does not contradict material allegations, will not, in general, vitiate the pleadings. Co. Litt. 303b; 10 East, 142; 1 Chit. Pl. 233. See Lawes, Pl. 64; Steph. Pl. 378; Comyn, Dig. "Abatement" (H 6); 1 Viner, Abr. 36; 19 Viner, Abr. 45; Bac. Abr. "Amendments, etc," (E 2), "Pleas" (I 4).

REPUGNANT (Lat. *repugnans,* from *repugnare,* to fight against). Contrary to; in conflict with. A condition repugnant to the nature of the estate to which it is annexed is void. 1 Steph. Comm. 281.

REPUTABLE. Reputable means "worthy of repute or distinction," "held in esteem," "honorable," "praiseworthy." 123 Ill. 245.

The term "reputable person" has reference to a person's real character as distinguished from his reputation. 165 Ia. 189, 144 N. W. 1021.

REPUTATIO EST VULGARIS OPINIO ubi non est veritas. Reputation is a common opinion where there is no certain knowledge. 4 Coke, 107.

REPUTATION. The opinion generally entertained in a community regarding any matter. Thus, certain matters of pedigree may be proved by common repute.

Most commonly used in the sense of personal reputation, the opinion entertained regarding a man in a community.

"Reputation" is to be distinguished from "character" (*q. v.*) Character is what a person is; reputation is what he is supposed to be. Character is injured by temptations and wrongdoings; reputation, by slanders and libels. Abbott. See 26 N. Y. 203.

REPUTED. Accepted by general, vulgar, or public opinion. Thus, land may be reputed part of a manor, though not really so, and a certain district may be reputed a parish or a manor, or be a parish or a manor in reputation, although it is in reality no parish or manor at all. Brown.

REPUTED MANOR. In feudal law. A name sometimes applied to a manor which has, by becoming separated from the services by which it was formerly held, ceased to be a manor in fact.

REQUEST (Lat. *requiro*, to ask for).

——**In Contracts.** A notice of a desire on the part of the person making it that the other party shall do something in relation to a contract. Generally, when a debt is payable immediately, no request need be made. 10 Mass. 230; 3 Day (Conn.) 327; 1 Johns. Cas. (N. Y.) 319.

——**In Pleading.** The statement in the plaintiff's declaration that a demand or request has been made by the plaintiff of the defendant to do some act which he was bound to perform, and for which the action is brought.

A general request is that stated in the form, "although often requested so to do" (*licet saepe, requisitus*), generally added in the common breach to the money counts. Its omission will not vitiate the declaration. 2 H. Bl. 131; 1 Wils. 33; 1 Bos. & P. 59; 1 Johns. Cas. (N. Y.) 100.

A special request is one provided for by the contract expressly or impliedly. Such a request must be averred (5 Term R. 409; 1 East, 204; 3 Bulst. 297; 3 Campb. 549; 2 Barn. & C. 685) and proved (1 Saund. 32, note 2). It must state time and place of making, and by whom it was made, that the court may judge of its sufficiency. 1 Strange, 89; Comyn, Dig. "Pleader" (C 69, 70); 1 Saund. 33, note; 2 Vent. 75. See "Demand."

In wills, see "Precatory Words."

REQUEST, LETTERS OF. See "Letters of Request."

REQUEST NOTES. In English law. Certain notes or requests from persons amenable to the excise laws, to obtain a permit for removing any excisable goods or articles from one place to another.

REQUISITION. The act of demanding a thing to be done by virtue of some right.

The demand made by the governor of one state on the governor of another for a fugitive from justice.

The term "requisition" is sometimes used to denote the surrender of fugitives from one state to another; "extradition" being confined to surrender of fugitives by a foreign country.

When, as is more common, "extradition" is used to embrace both interstate and international extradition, "requisition" is applied to the formal request of the governor for the surrender, and not to the other proceedings.

REQUISITIONS ON TITLE. In English conveyances. Objections to the title shown by an abstract pointed out by the purchaser's solicitor to the vendor's solicitor.

REREFIEFS. In Scotch law. Inferior fiefs; portions of a fief or feud granted out to inferior tenants. 2 Bl. Comm. 57.

RERUM ORDO CONFUNDITUR, SI UNIcuique jurisdictio non servatur. The order of things is confounded if every one preserves not his jurisdiction. 4 Inst. Proem.

RERUM PROGRESSU OSTENDUNT multa, quae in initio praecaveri seu praevideri non possunt. In the course of events, many mischiefs arise which at the beginning could not be guarded against or foreseen. 6 Coke, 40.

RERUM SUARUM QUILIBET EST MODerator et arbiter. Every one is the manager and disposer of his own matters. Co. Litt. 223.

RES (Lat. things). It has a general signification, including both corporeal and incorporeal things. 3 Inst. 182.

The terms *res*, *bona*, *biens*, used by jurists who have written in the Latin and French languages, are intended to include movable or personal, as well as immovable or real, property. 1 Burge, Confl. Laws, 19. See "Biens;" "Bona;" "Things."

By *res*, according to the modern civilians, is meant everything that may form an object of rights, as in opposition to *persona*, which is regarded as a subject of rights. *Res*, therefore, in its general meaning, comprises actions of all kinds; while in its restricted sense it comprehends every object of rights except actions. 1 Mackeld. Civ. Law, 151, § 146. This has reference to the fundamental division of the institutes that all law relates either to persons, to things, or to actions.

The term is used in many special senses, among these being a business matter or question (Dig. 48. 19. 38. 5); equity (Dig. 48. 8. 1. 3); an inheritance (Calv. Lex.); a suit; the subject matter of a suit (Story, Confl. Laws, § 592a); substance; property; ownership (Calv. Lex.); a contract (Dig. 50 16, 6); truth (Dig. 48. 10. 1. 4); empire (Tayl. Civ. Law, 62).

These have been variously divided and classified in law, *e. g.*, in the following ways: (1) Corporeal and incorporeal things; (2) movables and immovables; (3) *res mancipi* and *res nec mancipi;* (4) things real and things personal; (5) things in possession and choses (*i. e.*, things) in action; (6) fungible things and things not fungible (*fungibiles vel non fungibiles*); and (7) *res singulae* (*i. e.*, individual objects) and *universitates rerum* (*i. e.*, aggregates of things). Also persons are for some purposes and in certain respects regarded as things.

RES ACCENDENT LUMINA REBUS. One thing throws light upon others. 4 Johns. Ch. (N. Y.) 149.

RES ACCESSORIA (Lat.) In the civil law. An accessory thing; that which belongs to a principal thing, or is in connection with it. 1 Mackeld. Civ. Law, 155, § 152. Otherwise termed *accessio.* Id. § 153.

RES ACCESSORIA SEQUITUR REM principalem. An accessory follows its principal. Broom, Leg. Max. (3d London Ed.) 433. For a definition of *res accessoria*, see Mackeld. Civ. Law, 155.

RES ADJUDICATA. See "Res Judicata."

RES CADUCA. In the civil law. A fallen or escheated thing; an escheat. Halifax, Civ. Law, bk. 2, c. 9, No. 60.

RES COMMUNES (Lat.) In civil law. Those things which, though a separate share of them can be enjoyed and used by every one, cannot be exclusively and wholly appropriated; as, light, air, running water. Mackeld. Civ. Law, § 156; Ersk. Inst. 1. 1. 5. 6.

RES CONTROVERSA. In the civil law. A matter controverted; a matter in controversy; a point in question; a question for determination. Calv. Lex.

RES CORONAE. In old English law. Things of the crown; such as ancient manors, homages of the king, liberties, etc. Fleta, lib. 3, c. 6, § 3.

RES CORPORALES. In the civil law. Corporeal things; things which can be touched, or are perceptible to the senses. Dig. 1. 8. 1. 1; Inst. 2. 2; Bracton, fols. 7b, 10b, 13b.

RES DENOMINATUR A PRINCIPALIOri parte. A thing is named from its principal part. 5 Coke, 47.

RES EST MISERA UBI JUS EST VAGUM et incertum. It is a miserable state of things where the law is vague and uncertain. 2 Salk. 512.

RES FUNGIBILES (Lat.) In the civil law. Fungible things.

RES FURTIVAE (Law Lat.) In Scotch law. Goods which have been stolen. Bell, Dict.

RES, GENERALEM HABET SIGNIFICAtionem, quia tam corporea, quam incorporea, cujuscunque sunt generis, naturae sive speciei, comprehendit. The word "things" has a general signification, because it comprehends as well corporeal as incorporeal objects, of whatever nature, sort, or species. 3 Inst. 482; 1 Bouv. Inst. note 415.

RES GESTAE. The facts surrounding or accompanying a transaction which is the subject of legal proceedings.

The phrase is generally used in the law of evidence; the rule being that evidence of words or acts may be admissible (notwithstanding the rule against derivative evidence) on the ground that they are part of the *res gestae*, provided that the act they accompanied is in itself admissible in evidence, and that they reflect light upon or qualify that act. Thus, the declaration of a railroad engineer as to the cause of an accident, made immediately thereafter, was held admissible in an action against the railroad company. 55 Pa. St. 396. And in criminal cases, remarks of defendant (25 Grat. [Va.] 921), or by the injured person (10 Mo. App. 111; 34 Iowa, 131), are admissible if connected with the transaction, and connected with both in point of time and causal connection; but remarks of persons not in some manner connected with the transaction are inadmissible (99 Mass. 438).

No inflexible rule can be laid down as to the necessary proximity in point of time between the declaration and the act under investigation. See 9 Tex. App. 440; Id. 619; 71 Ga. 128. Perhaps the most extreme holding is that declarations of a deceased some hours before the homicide, that she was to meet defendant on business that evening, were held admissible as part of the *res gestae* in connection with evidence that she went out that evening to meet some one. 62 Minn. 474.

RES IMMOBILES. In the civil law. Immovable things; including land and that which is connected therewith, either by nature or art, such as trees and buildings. Mackeld. Civ. Law, § 160.

RES INCORPORALES. In the civil law. Incorporeal things; things which cannot be touched; such as those things which consist in right. Inst. 2. 2; Bracton, fols. 7b, 10b. Such things as the mind alone can perceive.

RES INTEGRA (Lat. an entire thing; an entirely new or untouched matter). A term applied to those points of law which have not been decided, which are untouched by dictum or decision. 3 Mer. 269; 1 Burge, Confl. Laws, 241.

RES INTER ALIOS ACTA (Lat.) A technical phrase which signifies acts of others or transactions between others.

Neither the declarations nor any other acts of those who are mere strangers, or, as it is usually expressed, any *res inter alios acta*, are admissible in evidence against anyone. When the party against whom such acts are offered in evidence was privy to the act, the objection ceases; it is no longer *res inter alios*. 1 Starkie, Ev. 52; 3 Starkie, Ev. 1300; 4 Man. & G. 282. See 1 Metc. (Mass.) 55.

RES INTER ALIOS ACTA ALTERI NOcere non debet. Things done between strangers ought not to injure those who are not parties to them. Co. Litt. 132; 3 Curt. C. C. (U. S.) 403; 11 Q. B. 1028.

RES INTER ALIOS JUDICATAE NULlum aliis praejudicium faciant. Matters adjudged in a cause do not prejudice those who were not parties to it. Dig. 44. 2. 1.

RES IPSA LOQUITUR. The thing speaks for itself. A phrase used in actions for injury by negligence, where no proof of negligence is required beyond the accident itself, which is such as necessarily to involve negligence.

RES JUDICATA. A legal or equitable issue which has been decided by a court of competent jurisdiction.

To constitute a matter *res judicata*, so that, in a subsequent action, it cannot be drawn in question, (1) the court deciding the issue must have had jurisdiction (10 Pet. [U. S.] 474); (2) there must be identity of the subject matter of the action (7 Johns. [N. Y.] 20); (3) identity of the cause of action (8 Conn. 268; 3 Pick. [Mass.] 429), though the form of action may be different if it be of the same general class, or if the remedies be concurrent (12 Gray [Mass.] 428; 28 Minn. 450; 82 Ky. 505); (4) identity of parties (4 Mass. 441; 5 Me. 410; 23 Barb. [N. Y.] 464), but privies of the parties are bound (see "Privy;" 52 N. H. 162; 98 N. Y. 351); (5) identity of capacity in which they sue or are sued (4 C. B. 884; 21 Ala. 813); (6) and there must have been a final determination of the issues (143 Mass. 413; 104 Ill. 369); (7) on the merits (91 U. S. 526; 42 Mich. 459); (8) upon the particular issue (7 Gray [Mass.] 502), but the adjudication is final upon every matter which might have been litigated under the issues made (102 N. Y. 452).

——**In Proceedings in Rem.** Identity of parties is not essential, the adjudication attaching to the *res*. See 1 Metc. (Mass.) 204.

RES JUDICATA FACIT EX ALBO NIgrum, ex nigro album, ex curvo rectum, ex recto curvum. A thing adjudged makes white, black; black, white; the crooked, straight; the straight, crooked. 1 Bouv. Inst. note 840.

RES JUDICATA PRO VERITATE ACCIpitur. A thing adjudged must be taken for truth. Co. Litt. 103; Dig. 50. 17. 207; 2 Kent, Comm. 120; 13 Mees. & W. 679. See "Res Judicata."

RES MANCIPI (Lat.) In Roman law. Those things which might be sold and alienated, or of which the property might be transferred from one person to another.

The division of things into *res mancipi* and *res nec mancipi* was one of ancient origin, and it continued to a late period in the empire. *Res mancipi* (Ulph. Frag. *xix.*) are *praedia in italico solo*, both rustic and urban; also, *jura rusticorum praediorum* or *servitutes*, as *via*, *iter*, *aquaeductus;* also slaves, and four-footed animals, as oxen, horses, etc., *quae collo dorsove domantur*. Smith. To this list may be added children of Roman parents, who were, according to the old law, *res mancipi.* The distinction between *res mancipi* and *nec mancipi* was abolished by Justinian in his Code. Id.; Cooper, Inst. 442.

RES MOBILES. In the civil law. Movable things; things which may be transported from one place to another, without injury to their substance and form. Things corresponding with the chattels personal of the common law. 2 Kent, Comm. 347.

RES NOVA (Lat.) Something new; something not before decided.

RES NULLIUS (Lat.) A thing which has no owner. A thing which has been abandoned by its owner is as much *res nullius* as if it had never belonged to any one.

The first possessor of such a thing becomes the owner; *res nullius fit primi occupantis*. Bowyer, Comm. 97.

RES PER PECUNIAM AESTIMATUR, et non pecunia per res. The value of a thing is estimated by its worth in money, and the value of money is not estimated by reference to the thing. 9 Coke, 76; 1 Bouv. Inst. note 922.

RES PERIIT DOMINO (Lat. the thing is lost to the owner). A phrase used to express that, when a thing is lost or destroyed, it is lost to the person who was the owner of it at the time. For example, an article is sold; if the seller have perfected the title of the buyer so that it is his, and it be destroyed, it is the buyer's loss; but if, on the contrary, something remains to be done before the title becomes vested in the buyer, then the loss falls on the seller.

RES PERIT DOMINO SUO. The destruction of the thing is the loss of its owner. 2 Bouv. Inst. notes 1456, 1466; Story, Bailm. 426; 2 Kent, Comm. 591.

RES PRIVITAE (Lat.) In the civil law. Things the property of one or more individuals. Mackeld. Civ. Law, § 157.

RES PROPRIA EST QUAE COMMUNIS non est. A thing is private which is not common. 8 Paige, Ch. (N. Y.) 261, 270.

RES PUBLICAE (Lat.) In the civil law. Things the property of the state. Mackeld. Civ. Law, § 157; Ersk. Inst. 2. 1. 5. 6.

RES QUAE INTRA PRAESIDIA PERductae nondum sunt, quanquam ab hostibus occupatae, ideo postliminii non egent, quia dominum nondum mutarunt ex gentium jure. Things which have not yet been introduced within the enemy's lines, although held by the enemy, do not need the fiction of postliminy on this account, because their ownership by the law of nations has not yet changed. Grotius de Jure Belli, lib. 3, c. 9, § 16; Id. lib. 3, c. 6, § 3.

RES RELIGIOSAE (Lat.) In civil law. Things pertaining to religion; places where the dead were buried. Thevenot Dessaules, Dict. du Dig. "Chose."

RES SACRA NON RECIPIT AESTIMAtionem. A sacred thing does not admit of valuation. Dig. 1. 8. 9. 5.

RES SACRAE (Lat.) In civil law. Those things which had been publicly consecrated.

RES SANCTAE (Lat.) In civil law. Those things which were especially protected against injury of man.

RES SUA NEMINI SERVIT. No one can have a servitude over his own property. 4 Macq. H. L. Cas. 151.

RES TRANSIT CUM SUO ONERE. The thing passes with its burden. Fleta, lib. 3, c. 10, § 3.

RES UNIVERSATIS (Lat.) Those things which belong to cities or municipal corporations. They belong so far to the public that they cannot be appropriated to private use, such as public squares, market houses, streets, and the like. 1 Bouv. Inst. note 446.

RESCEIT, or RECEIT. The admission or receiving of a third person to plead his right in a cause formerly commenced between two other persons; as, when an action is brought against a tenant for life or years, or any other particular tenant, and he makes default, in such case the reversioner may move that he may be received to defend his right, and to plead with the demandant. Jacob; Cowell.

The admittance of a plea when the controversy is between the same two persons. Co. Litt. 192; 3 Nelson, Abr. 146.

RESCEU, or RESCUE (Law Fr.) Received. Novae Narr. 5b; Kitch. Cts. Resceux (plur.); Britt. c. 2.

RESCISSIO (Lat. from *rescindere*, to annul or avoid). In the civil law. An annulling, avoiding, or making void; abrogation; rescission. Code, 4. 44; Poth. Contr. No. 331.

RESCISSION OF CONTRACTS. The abrogation or annulling of contracts. It differs from the waiving of some of the terms of the contract. 59 Conn. 561.

The term is generally, but not uniformly, applied to abrogation by the parties, either by consent, or by one party; "cancellation" being the usual term for abrogation by decree of court. It requires concurrent action by both parties; a meeting of minds. 59 Conn. 561. See Waiver.

RESCISSORY ACTIONS. In Scotch law. Actions which are brought to set aside deeds. Patterson, Comp. 1058, note.

Proper improbation is an action brought for declaring writing false or forged.

Reduction improbation is an action whereby a person who may be hurt or affected by a writing insists on producing or exhibiting it in court, in order to have it set aside, or its effects ascertained under the certification that the writing, if not produced, shall be declared false and forged.

In an action of simple reduction, the certification is only temporary, declaring the writings called for null until they be produced, so that they recover their full force after their production. Ersk. bk. 4, tit. 1, § 5; Id. bk. 4, tit. 1, § 8.

RESCOUS. An old term, synonymous with "rescue" (*q. v.*).

RESCRIPT.

——**In Canon Law.** A term including any form of apostolical letter emanating from the pope. The answer of the pope in writing. Dict. Dr. Canonique.

——**In Civil Law.** The answer of the prince, at the request of the parties, respecting some matter in dispute between them, or to magistrates, in relation to some doubtful matter submitted to him.

The rescript was differently denominated according to the character of those who sought it. They were called "annotations" or "subnotations," when the answer was given at the request of private citizens; "letters" or "epistles," when he answered the consultation of magistrates; "pragmatic sanctions," when he answered a corporation, the citizens of a province, or a municipality. See "Code."

——**At Common Law.** A counterpart.

In Massachusetts it is used to denote the statement of the decision of the supreme judicial court as an appellate tribunal, and the accompanying brief statement of the reasons for the decision sent to the court from which the case was brought.

RESCRIPTION. In French law. A rescription is a letter by which the maker requests some one to pay a certain sum of money, or to account for him to a third law. To rescue. *Rescussit,* he rescued. Reg. 225.

According to this definition, bills of exchange are a species of rescription. The difference appears to be this, that a bill of exchange is given when there has been a contract of exchange between the drawer and the payee; whereas the rescription is sometimes given in payment of a debt, and at other times it is lent to the payee.

RESCUE.

——**In Criminal Law.** The forcibly and knowingly freeing another from arrest or imprisonment. 4 Bl. Comm. 131.

A deliverance of a prisoner from lawful custody by a third person. 2 Bish. Crim. Law, § 911.

Taking and setting at liberty, against law, a distress taken for rent, services, or damage feasant. Bac. Abr. "Rescous." See "Resceu."

——**In Maritime Law.** The retaking by a party captured of a prize made by the enemy. There is still another kind of rescue which partakes of the nature of a recapture,—it occurs when the weaker party, before he is overpowered, obtains relief from the arrival of fresh succors, and is thus preserved from the force of the enemy. 1 C. Rob. Adm. 224, 271; Halleck, Int. Law, cxxxv.

"Rescue" differs from "recapture." The rescuers do not, by the rescue, become owners of the property, as if it had been a new prize, but the property is restored to the original owners by the right of *postliminium.*

RESCUSSOR. The party making a rescue is sometimes so called; but more properly he is a "rescuer."

RESCUSSUS (Law Lat.; from Law Fr. *rescous*). In old English law. Rescue; forcible liberation or release. Spelman.

RESCUTERE (Law Lat.) In old English law. To rescue. *Rescussit,* he rescued. Reg. Orig. 117; 3 P. Wms. 484. *Rescusserunt,* they rescued. Reg. Orig. 118.

RESCYT (Law Fr.) Resceit; receipt; the receiving or harboring a felon, after the commission of crime. Britt. c. 23.

RESEANTISA (Law Lat.; from Law Fr. *reseance*). In old English and Scotch law. Residence. Fleta, lib. 6, c. 3, § 2; Spelman.

RESEAUNT, or **RESEANT** (Law Fr.) Abiding; dwelling; residing. Britt. c. 98.

RESEISER (Law Lat. *reseisire*). In old English law. A taking back of seisin. A taking again of lands into the hands of the king, whereof a general livery or *ouster le main* was formerly issued, contrary to the form and order of law. Staundf. Pr. Reg. 26; Cowell.

RESERVANDO. Reserving. In old conveyancing. An apt word of reserving a rent. Co. Litt. 47a.

RESERVATIO NON DEBET ESSE DE proficuis ipsis quia ea conceduntur, sed de redditu novo extra proficua. A reservation ought not to be of the annual increase itself, because it is granted, but of new rent apart from the annual increase. Co. Litt. 142.

RESERVATION. That part of a deed or instrument which reserves a thing not *in esse* at the time of the grant, but newly created. 2 Hilliard, Abr. 359.

The creation of a right or interest which had no prior existence as such in a thing or part of a thing granted, by means of a clause inserted by the grantor in the instrument of conveyance.

A "reservation" is distinguished from an "exception" in that it is of a new right or interest; thus, a right of way reserved at the time of conveying an estate, which may have been enjoyed by the grantor as owner of the estate, becomes a new right. 42 Me. 9.

A reservation may be of a life estate (28 Vt. 10; 33 N. H. 18; 3 Jones [N. C.] 37, 38; 23 Mo. 373; 3 Md. Ch. 230); of a right of flowage (41 Me. 298); right to use water (41 Me. 177; 9 N. Y. 423; 16 Barb. [N. Y.] 212); right of way (25 Conn. 331; 6 Cush. [Mass.] 254; 10 Cush. [Mass.] 313; 10 B. Mon. [Ky.] 463); and many other rights and interests (33 N. H. 507; 9 B. Mon. [Ky.] 163; 5 Pa. St. 317). See 6 Cush. (Mass.) 162; 4 Pa. St. 173; 9 Johns. (N. Y.) 73.

RESET. The receiving or harboring an outlawed person. Cowell.

RESET OF THEFT. In Scotch law. The receiving and keeping stolen goods, knowing them to be stolen, with a design of feloniously retaining them from the real owner. Alis. Crim. Law, 328.

RESETTER. In Scotch law. A receiver of stolen goods, knowing them to have been stolen.

RESIANCE. In old English law. A man's residence or permanent abode. Such a man is called a "resiant." Kitch. Cts. 33.

RESIANT, RESIENT, or **RESYAUNT** (from Law Fr. *reseant,* resident). In old English law. Continually dwelling or abiding in a place; resident; a resident. Kitch. Cts. 33; Cowell; 2 Inst. 99. "*Resiants* and inhabitants within a manor." 3 Leon. 8, case 21.

RESIANTIA, or **RESEANTIA** (Law Lat.) In old English law. Resiance; residence. Spelman. See "Resiance."

RESIDENCE (Lat. *resedeo*). Personal presence in a fixed and permanent abode. 20 Johns. (N. Y.) 208; 1 Metc. (Mass.) 251; 105 Mass. 93; 23 Wis. 607.

A residence is different from a domicile, although it is a matter of great importance in determining the place of domicile. 13 Mass. 501; 5 Pick. (Mass.) 370; 1 Metc. (Mass.) 251; 2 Gray (Mass.) 490; 19 Wend. (N. Y.) 11; 11 La. 175; 5 Me. 143. See "Domicile." "Residence" and "habitancy" are usually synonymous. 2 Gray (Mass.) 490; 2 Kent, Comm. (10th Ed.) 574, note. "Residence" indicates permanency of occupation, as distinct from lodging, or boarding, or temporary occupation, but does not include so much as "domicile," which requires an intention continued with residence. 19 Me. 293; 2 Kent, Comm. (10th Ed.) 576.

RESIDENT. One who has his residence (*q. v.*) in a place.

RESIDENT FREEHOLDER. One who resides within a certain city, county, or state, and owns a freehold estate in lands therein. 29 Wis. 419; 68 Ind. 214.

RESIDENT MINISTER. In international law. The second or intermediate class between ambassadors and envoys, created by the conference of the five powers at Aix-la-Chapelle, in 1818. They are accredited to the sovereign. 2 Phillim. Int. Law, 220*. They are said to represent the affairs, and not the person, of the sovereign, and so to be of less dignity. Vattel, bk. 4, c. 6, § 73. The fourth class is *charges-d'affaires*, accredited to the minister of foreign affairs. 2 Phillim. Int. Law, 220; Wheaton, Int. Law, pt. 3, c. 1, § 6.

RESIDERE (Lat.) In old English law. To sit down; to sit still; to rest; to remain or continue. See "Resident."

RESIDUARY CLAUSE. The clause in a will by which that part of the property is disposed of which remains after satisfying previous bequests and devises. 4 Kent, Comm. 541*; 2 Williams, Ex'rs, 1014, note 2.

RESIDUARY DEVISEE. The person to whom the residue of a testator's real estate is devised after satisfying previous devises.

RESIDUARY ESTATE. What remains of testator's estate after deducting the debts and the bequests and devises.

RESIDUARY LEGATEE. He to whom the residuum of the estate is devised or bequeathed by will. Rop. Leg. Index; Powell, Mortg. Index. See "Legacy."

RESIDUE. That which remains of something after taking away a part of it; as, the residue of an estate, that which remains after payment of debts, charges, and particular legacies and devises. 68 Pa. St. 332.

A will bequeathing the general residue of personal property passes to the residuary legatee everything not otherwise effectually disposed of; and it makes no difference whether a legacy falls into the estate by lapse, or as void at law, the next of kin is equally excluded. 15 Ves. 416; 2 Mer. 392. See 7 Ves. 391; 1 Brown, Ch. 589; 4 Brown, Ch. 55; Rop. Leg. Index; Jarm. Wills.

RESIGNATION (Lat. *resignatio; re*, back, *signo*, to sign). The act of an officer by which he declines his office, and renounces the further right to use it. It differs from "abdication" (*q. v.*)

As offices are held at the will of both parties, if the resignation of an officer be not accepted, he remains in office. 4 Dev. (N. C.) 1.

RESIGNATION BOND. In ecclesiastical law. A bond given by an incumbent to resign on a certain contingency. It may be conditioned to resign for good and sufficient reason, and therefore lawful; *e. g.*, to resign if he take a second benefice, or on request, if patron present his son or kinsman when of age to take the living, etc. Cro. Jac. 249, 274. But equity will generally relieve the incumbent. 1 Rolle, Abr. 443.

RESIGNATION EST JURIS PROPRII spontanea refutatio. Resignation is the spontaneous relinquishment of one's own right. Godb. 284.

RESIGNEE. One in favor of whom a resignation is made. 1 Bell, Comm. 125, note.

RESILIRE (Lat.) In old English law. To draw back from a contract before it is made binding. Literally, to leap back or start back. *Adhunc possunt partes resilire*, the parties may yet draw back. Bracton, fol. 38; Fleta, lib. 2, c. 58, § 3. The Scotch law, with its accustomed closeness, renders this word *resile*.

RESIST. (Lat.) The opposition of force to force. The word retains the exact classical meaning. 37 Wis. 201.

RESOLUCION. In Spanish colonial law. An opinion formed by some superior authority on matters referred to its decision, and forwarded to inferior authorities for their instruction and government. Schmidt, Civ. Law, 93, note 1.

RESOLUTION (Lat. *re*, back, again, *solvo*, to loose, to free). A solemn judgment or decision of a court. This word is frequently used in this sense in Coke and some of the more ancient reporters. An agreement to a law or other thing adopted by a legislature or popular assembly.

——**Governing Bodies.**

Acts that are done by a city council in its ministerial capacity may be in the form of resolutions. Resolutions are special and temporary, applicable only to a single matter of passing moment. 186 Ill. 571; 174 Ill. 445; 184 Ill. 51; 262 Ill. 396. Distinction between "resolution" and "ordinance." See "Ordinance."

——**Distinguished from By-law.**

While a by-law may be in the form of a resolution, a resolution is not necessarily a by-law. The distinction between the two has been said to lie in the fact that a resolution applies to a single act of the corporation whereas a by-law is a permanent and continuing rule which is to be applied on all future occasions. 1 Fletcher Cyclopedia Corporations 977.

——**In Civil Law.** The act by which a contract which existed and was good is rendered null.

"Resolution" differs essentially from "rescission." The former presupposes the contract to have been valid, and it is owing to a cause posterior to the agreement that the resolution takes place; while rescission, on the contrary, supposes that some vice or defect annulled the contract from the beginning. Resolution may be by consent of the parties, or by the decision of a competent tribunal; rescission must always be by the judgment of a court. 7 Tropl. de la Vente, note 689; 7 Toullier, Dr. Civ. 551; Dalloz.

RESOLUTIVE. In Scotch conveyancing. Having the quality or effect of resolving or extinguishing a right. Bell, Dict.

RESOLUTO JURE CONCEDENTIS RE-solvitur jus concessum. The right of the grantor being extinguished, the right granted is extinguished. Mackeld. Civ. Law, 179; Broom, Leg. Max. (3d London Ed.) 417.

RESOLUTORY CONDITION. One which has for its object, when accomplished, the revocation of the principal obligation; for example, I will sell you my crop of cotton if my ship America does not arrive in the United States within six months. My ship arrives in one month; my contract with you is revoked. 1 Bouv. Inst. note 764.

RESON (Law Fr.) Reason; truth; right; title; justice; act; argument; charge; expression; method; case; article; point. Kelham.

RESORT (from Fr. *resorter, q. v.*) To go back. "It resorted to the line of the mother." Hale, Hist. Com. Law, c. 11.

The act of visiting; assembly; meeting; concourse; frequent assembling. 90 Ill. 220.

RESORTER (Law Fr.) In old English law. To go back. *A force resortera le tenement au seigniour del fee*, the tenement must necessarily go back to the lord of the fee. Britt. c. 119.

RESPECTARE, or RESPECTUARE (Law Lat.) In old English law. To respite. Fortescue de L. L. Angliae, c. 53, note; Reg. Orig. 319. *Respectuabitur*, shall be put off. Fleta, lib. 6, c. 23, § 21.

RESPECTU COMPUTI VICECOMITIS habendo. A writ for respiting a sheriff's account, addressed to the treasurer and barons of the exchequer. Reg. Orig. 139.

RESPICIENDUM EST JUDICANTI, NE quid aut durius aut remissius construatur quam causa deposcit; nec enim aut severitatis aut clementiae gloria affectanda est. It it a matter of import to one adjudicating that nothing should be either more leniently or more severely construed than the cause itself demands; for the glory neither of severity nor clemency should be affected. 3 Inst. 220.

RESPIRATION (Lat. *re*, back, *spiro*, to breathe). Breathing, which consists of the drawing into, inhaling, or, more technically, "inspiring," atmospheric air into the lungs, and then forcing out, expelling, or technically, "expiring," from the lungs the air therein. Chit. Med. Jur. 92, 416, note (n).

RESPITE.

——**In Civil Law.** An act by which a debtor who is unable to satisfy his debts at the moment transacts (*i. e.*, compromises) with his creditors and obtains from them time or delay for the payment of the sums which he owes to them. Code La. art. 3051.

A forced respite takes place when a part of the creditors refuse to accept the debtor's proposal, and when the latter is obliged to compel them, by judicial authority, to consent to what the others have determined in the cases directed by law.

A voluntary respite takes place when all the creditors consent to the proposal of the debtor to pay in a limited time the whole or a part of his debt.

A delay, forbearance, or continuation of time.

——**In Criminal Law.** A temporary suspension of the execution of a sentence. It differs from a "pardon," which is an absolute suspension, and from a "reprieve," in that it is ordinarily for an indefinite time.

RESPITE OF HOMAGE. To dispense with the performance of homage by tenants who held their lands in consideration of performing homage to their lords. Cowell.

RESPONDE BOOK. In Scotch law. A book of record of the chancellary, in which are entered all nonentry and relief duties payable by heirs who take precepts from chancery. Stair, Inst. p. 296, § 28; Ersk. Inst. 11. 5. 50.

RESPONDEAT OUSTER (that he answer over). In practice. A form of judgment anciently used when an issue in law upon a dilatory plea was decided against the party pleading it. See "Abatement."

RESPONDEAT RAPTOR, QUI IGNOrare non potuit quod pupillum alienum abduxit. Let the ravisher answer, for he could not be ignorant that he has taken away another's ward. Hob. 99.

RESPONDEAT SUPERIOR. Let the principal answer. 4 Inst. 114; 2 Bouv. Inst. note 1337; 4 Bouv. Inst. Note 3586; 3 Lev. 352; 1 Salk. 408; 1 Bing. N. C. 418; 4 Maule & S. 259; 10 Exch. 656; 2 El. & Bl. 216; 7 El. & Bl. 426; 1 Bos. & P. 404; 1 C. B. 578; 6 Mees. & W. 302; 10 Exch. 656.

He who expects to derive advantage from an act which is done by another person for him must answer for any injury which such person may inflict upon a third party. 243 Ill. 488.

RESPONDENT. One who answers a judicial proceeding. Applied to the party against whom a writ as of *quo warranto* is brought.

——**In Chancery Practice.** The party who makes an answer to a bill or other proceeding in chancery. The correlative is "petitioner" or "complainant."

——**In Appellate Practice.** The party who answers an appeal. Sometimes called "appellee." The correlative is "appellant."

——**In Civil Law.** One who answers or is security for another; a fidejussor. Dig. 2. 8. 6.

RESPONDENTIA. In maritime law. A loan of money, on maritime interest, on goods laden on board of a ship, upon the condition that, if the goods be wholly lost in the course of the voyage, by any of the perils enumerated in the contract, the lender shall lose his money; if not, that the borrower shall pay him the sum borrowed, with the interest agreed upon.

The contract is called "respondentia" because the money is lent mainly, or most frequently, on the personal responsibility of the borrower. It differs principally from bottomry (*q. v.*) in the following circumstances: Bottomry is a loan on the ship; respondentia is a loan upon the goods. The money is to be repaid to the lender, with maritime interest, upon the arrival of the ship in the one case, and of the goods in the other. In most other respects, the contracts are nearly the same, and are governed by the same principles. In the former, the ship and tackle, being hypothecated, are liable, as well as the borrower; in the latter, the lender has, in general, it is said, only the personal security of the borrower. Marsh. Ins. bk. 2, c. 1, p. 734. The general term, including both respondentia and bottomry, is "hypothecation" (*q. v.*)

RESPONDERA SON SOVERAIGNE. His superior or master shall answer. Articuli sup. Charta, c. 18.

RESPONDERE NON DEBET (Lat. ought not to reply). In pleading. The prayer of a plea where the defendant insists that he ought not to answer, as, when he claims a privilege; for example, as being a member of congress or a foreign ambassador. 1 Chit. Pl. *433.

RESPONSA PRUDENTUM (Lat.) In Roman law. Opinions given by Roman lawyers.

Before the time of Augustus, every lawyer was authorized, *de jure*, to answer questions put to him; and all such answers, *responsa prudentum*, had equal authority, which had not the force of law, but the opinion of a lawyer. Augustus was the first prince who gave to certain distinguished jurisconsults the particular privilege of answering in his name, and from that period their answers required greater authority. Adrian determined in a more precise manner the degree of authority which these answers should have, by enacting that the opinions of such authorized jurisconsults, when unanimously given, should have the force of law (*legis vicem*), and should be followed by the judges, and that when they were divided, the judge was allowed to adopt that which to him appeared the most equitable. The opinions of other lawyers held the same place they had before—they were considered merely as the opinions of learned men. Mackeld. Man. Introd. § 43; Mackeld. Hist. Dr. Rom. §§ 40, 49; Hugo, Hist. Dr. Rom. § 313; Inst. 1. 2. 8; Inst. Expl. note 39.

RESPONSALIS (Law Lat.)

——**In Old English Law.** One who answered or gave answer for another (*qui responsum defert*). The term seems to be used by Glanville in the sense of "attorney." Glanv. lib. 12, c. 1; Steph. Pl. Append. note (5). But Bracton makes a clear distinction between the two offices, and is followed by Fleta. Bracton, fol. 212b. But see Id. fol. 361b; Fleta, lib. 4, c. 6. Lord Coke defines *responsalis* to be "he that was appointed by the tenant or defendant, in case of extremity and necessity, to allege the cause of the party's absence, and to certify the court upon what trial he will put himself, viz., the combat or the country." Co. Litt. 128a.

——**In the Canon Law.** A proctor; one who excuses an absent party. Cowell.

RESPONSALIS AD LUCRANDUM VEL petendum. He who appears and answers for another in court at a day assigned; a proctor, attorney, or deputy. 1 Reeve, Hist. Eng. Law, 169.

RESPONSIBILITY. The obligation to answer for an act done, either civilly or criminally, and to repair any injury it may have caused.

RESPONSIBLE. Able to pay the sum which may be required of him; able to discharge an obligation. Webster; 26 N. H. 527.

RESPONSIO (Lat.) An answer.

RESPONSIO UNIUS NON OMNINO AUDITUR. The answer of one witness shall not be heard at all. 1 Greenl. Ev. § 260. This is a maxim of the civil law, where everything must be proved by two witnesses.

RESTITUTIO IN INTEGRAM (Lat.) In civil law. A restoring parties to the condition they were in before entering into a contract or agreement on account of fraud, infancy, force, honest mistake, etc. Calv. Lex. The going into a cause anew from the beginning. Calv. Lex.

RESTITUTION. The return of property to the owner or person entitled to it.

——**In Maritime Law.** The placing back or restoring articles which have been lost by jettison. This is done when the remainder of the cargo has been saved, at the general charge of the owners of the cargo; but when the remainder of the goods is afterwards lost, there is not any restitution. Stev. Av. pt. 1, c. 1, § 1, art. 1, note 8.

RESTITUTION OF CONJUGAL RIGHTS. In ecclesiastical law. A compulsory renewal of cohabitation between a husband and wife who have been living separately.

A suit may be brought in the divorce and matrimonial court for this purpose whenever either the husband or wife is guilty of the injury of subtraction, or lives separate from the other without sufficient reason, by which the party injured may compel the other to return to cohabitation. 3 Bl. Comm. 94; 3 Steph. Comm. 11; 1 Add. Ecc. 505; 3 Hagg. Ecc. 619.

RESTITUTION OF MINORS. In Scotch law. A minor, on attaining majority, may obtain relief against a deed previously executed by him, which may be held void or voidable, according to circumstances. This is called "restitution of minors." Bell, Dict.

RESTITUTION, WRIT OF.

——**In Common-Law Practice.** A writ which lies, after the reversal of a judgment, to restore a party to all that he has lost by occasion of the judgment. 2 Tidd, Prac. 1186.

——**In Criminal Practice.** A writ which lay on conviction of an offense involving the asportation of property to compel the criminal to restore the same.

RESTITUTIONE TEMPORALIUM. A writ addressed to the sheriff, to restore the temporalities of a bishopric to the bishop elected and confirmed. Fitzh. Nat. Brev. 169.

RESTORE. To return what has been unjustly taken; to place the owner of a thing in the state in which he formerly was.

RESTRAINING ORDER. An order restraining the doing of any act; more commonly called an "injunction."

——**In English Law.** An order under St. 5 Vict. c. 5, § 4, by which the Bank of England, or any other public company, may be restrained from permitting a transfer of shares until the rights of certain parties thereto have been adjudged.

RESTRAINT OF ALIENATION. Restriction of the power of aliening realty. See "Perpetuity."

RESTRAINT OF TRADE. Restriction of freedom of traffic. Restraint of trade of individuals may be general, or may be partial, in being limited as to time or territory. Contracts in general restraint of trade are void (8 Mass. 223); while those in partial restraint are valid (42 N. J. Eq. 185; 11 Ohio St. 349; 68 N. Y. 300), unless the time be so long, or the territory so extensive, that it amounts to a general restraint (36 Cal. 342). Contracts or combinations which operate in restraint of public trade are ordinarily void, though the restraint be put partial. 68 N. Y. 558.

RESTRICTIVE INDORSEMENT. An indorsement which confines the negotiability of a promissory note or bill of exchange by using express words to that effect, as, by indorsing it payable to A. B. only. 1 Wash. C. C. (U. S.) 512; 2 Murph. (N. C.) 138; 1 Bouv. Inst. note 1138.

RESTS. Periodical balancings of an account (particularly in mortgage and trust accounts), made for the purpose of converting interest into principal, and charging the party liable thereon with compound interest. Mozley & W.

RESULTING TRUST. A trust raised by implication or construction of law, and presumed to exist from the supposed intention of the parties and the nature of the transaction.

All trusts created by implication or construction of law are often included under the general term "implied trust;" but these are commonly distinguished into implied or resulting and constructive trusts; resulting or presumptive trusts being those which are implied or presumed from the supposed intention of the parties and the nature of the transaction; constructive trusts, such as are raised independently of any such intention, and which are forced on the conscience of the trustee by equitable construction and the operation of law. Story, Eq. Jur. § 1095; Hill, Trustees, 91; 1 Spence, Eq. Jur. 510; 2 Spence, Eq. Jur. 198; 3 Swanst. 585; 1 Ohio, 321; 6 Conn. 285; 2 Edw. Ch. (N. Y.) 373; 6 Humph. (Tenn.) 93. See "Trust."

RESULTING USE. A use raised by equity for the benefit of a feoffor who has made a voluntary conveyance to uses without any declaration of the use. 2 Washb. Real Prop. 100.

The doctrine, at first limited to the case of an apparently voluntary conveyance with no express declaration, became so extended that a conveyance of the legal estate ceased to imply an intention that the feoffee should enjoy the beneficial interest therein; and if no intent to the contrary was expressed, and no consideration proved or implied, the use always resulted to the feoffor. 2 Washb. Real Prop. 100. And if part only of the use was expressed, the balance resulted to the feoffor. 2 Atk. 150; 2 Rolle, Abr. 781; 1 Spence, Eq. Jur. 451; Co. Litt. 23a. And, under the statute, where a use has been limited by deed, and expires, or cannot vest, it results back to the one who declared it. 4 Wend. (N. Y.) 494; 15 Me. 414; 5 Watts & S. (Pa.) 323; 3 Johns. (N. Y.) 388. And see Cro. Jac. 200; White & T. Lead. Cas. 258; 2 Washb. Real Prop. 132 et seq. See "Use."

RESUME WORK. In mining law, is to actually begin work anew with a bona fide intention of prosecuting it as required by the statute (U. S. Rev. Stat. § 2324). 104 Cal. 229.

RESUMMONS (Law Lat. *resummonitio*). In practice. A second summons. The calling a person a second time to answer an action, where the first summons is defeated upon any occasion, as the death of a party, or the like. Cowell.

RESUMPTION (Law Lat. *resumptio*). In old English law. The taking again into the king's hands such lands or tenements as before, upon false suggestion or other error, he had delivered to the heir or granted by letters patent to any man. St. 31 Hen. VI. c. 7; Cowell.

RESURRENDER. Where copyhold land has been mortgaged by surrender, and the mortgagee has been admitted, then, on the mortgage debt being paid off, the mortgagor is entitled to have the land reconveyed to him, by the mortgagee surrendering it to the lord to his use. This is called a "resurrender." 2 Dav. Conv. 1332n.

RETAIL. To sell by small parcels, and not in the gross. 5 Mart. (La.; N. S.) 279; 7 Metc. (Mass.) 308.

RETAIN. In practice. To engage the services of an attorney or counsellor to manage a cause. See "Retainer."

RETAINER. The act of withholding what one has in one's own hands, by virtue of some right. See "Administrator;" "Executor;" "Lien."

——**In Practice.** The act of a client by which he engages an attorney or counsellor to manage a cause, either by prosecuting it, when he is plaintiff, or defending it, when he is defendant. 200 Ill. 353.

The word is also used to denote the fee which the client pays his attorney when he retains him to act for him, and thereby prevents him from acting for his adversary. 200 Ill. 353; 38 Kan. 668.

In English practice, a much more formal retainer is usually required than in America. Thus it is said by Chitty (3 Prac. 116, note [m]), that, although it is not indispensable that the retainer should be in writing, unless required by the other side, it is very expedient. It is therefore recommended, particularly when the client is a stranger, to require from him a written retainer, signed by himself, and, in order to avoid the insinuation that it was obtained by contrivance, it should be witnessed by one or more respectable persons. When there are several plaintiffs, it should be signed by all, and not by one for himself and the others, especially if they are trustees or assignees of a bankrupt or insolvent. The retainer should also state whether it be given for a general or a qualified authority. See 9 Wheat. (U. S.) 738, 830; 6 Johns. (N. Y.) 34, 296; 11 Johns. (N. Y.) 464; 1 N. H. 23; 28 N. H. 302; 7 Har. & J. (Md.) 275; 27 Miss. 567.

RETAINING FEE. A fee given to counsel on being consulted, in order to insure his future services. See "Retainer."

RETAKING. The taking one's goods, wife, child, etc., from another, who, without right, has taken possession thereof. See "Recaption."

RETALIATION. In international law. A term including both reprisal and retorsion (*q. v.*)

RETALLIA (Law Lat.; from Law Fr. *retailler*, to cut again). In old English law. Retail; the cutting up again, or division of a commodity into smaller parts. *Nec in grosso, nec ad retalliam*, neither in gross (by wholesale), nor at retail. Reg. Orig. 184.

RETARE (Law Lat.) In old English law. To suspect; to accuse. *Retatus de murdro*, accused of murder. Assis. de Clarendon, temp. Hen. II. § 1; Spelman. *De furto retatus*, charged with theft. Cowell.

RETENTION. In Scotch law. The right which the possessor of a movable has of holding the same until he shall be satisfied for his claim either against such movable or the owner of it; a lien.

General retention is the right to withhold or detain the property of another, in respect of any debt which happens to be due by the proprietor to the person who has the custody, or for a general balance of accounts arising on a particular train of employment. 2 Bell, Comm. (5th Ed.) 90, 91.

Special retention is the right of withholding or retaining property or goods which are in one's possession under a contract, till indemnified for the labor or money expended on them.

RETONSOR (Law Lat. from *retandere*, *q. v.*) In old English law. A clipper of money. Fleta, lib. 1, c. 20, § 122.

RETORNA BREVIUM. In old English law. The return of writs by sheriffs and bailiffs, which is only a certificate delivered to the court on the day of return, of that which he hath done touching the execution of their writ directed to him. This must be indorsed on back of writ by officer. 2 Lilly, Abr. 476. Each term has return days, fixed, as early as 51 Hen. III., at intervals of about a week, on which all original writs are returnable. The first return day is regularly the first day in the term; but there are three days' grace. 2 Bl. Comm. 277.

RETORNO HABENDO. In practice. A writ issued to compel a party to return property to the party to whom it has been adjudged to belong, in an action of replevin.

Thus, where the property taken was cattle, it recites that the defendant was summoned to appear to answer the plaintiff in a plea whereof he took the cattle of the said plaintiff, specifying them, and that the said plaintiff afterwards made default; wherefore it was then considered that the said plaintiff and his pledges of prosecuting should be in mercy, and that the said defendant should go without day, and that he should have return of the cattle aforesaid. It then commands the sheriff that he should cause to be returned the cattle aforesaid to the said defendant without delay, etc. 2 Sellon, Prac. 168.

RETORSION. The name of the act employed by a government to impose the same hard treatment on the citizens or subjects of a state that the latter has used towards the citizens or subjects of the former, for the purpose of obtaining the removal of obnoxious measures. Vattel, liv. 2, c. 18, § 341; De Martens, Precis, liv. 8, c. 2, § 254; Kluber, Dr. des Gens, sec. 2, c. 1, § 234; Manning, Comm. 105.

RETOUR. In Scotch law. To return a writ or brieve to the office in chancery from which it issued. Hubback, Ev. Success. 597. See "Retour of Service."

RETOUR OF SERVICE. In Scotch law. An authenticated copy of the verdict of a jury (called a "service") taken under a brieve of succession, by which the legal character of a party as heir is judicially established. Hubback, Ev. Success. 597; 1 Forbes, Inst. pt. 3, p 80. See Bell, Dict.

RETRACTATION, or RETRACTION. In probate practice. A withdrawal of a renunciation.

RETRACTO O TANTEO. In Spanish law. The right of revoking a contract of sale; the right of redemption of a thing sold. White, New Recop. bk. 2, tit. 13, c. 2, § 4.

RETRACTUS AQUAE (Law Lat.) In old English law. Retreat of the water; ebb, or low water; the retreat of tide. Plac. Cor. Rege, Pasch.; 30 Edw. I. apud Cantuar. Rot. 58; Cowell.

RETRACTUS FEUDALIS (Law Lat.) In old Scotch law. The power which a superior possessed of paying off a debt due to an adjudging creditor, and taking a conveyance to the adjudication. Bell, Dict.

RETRAHERE (Lat. from *re*, back, and *trahere*, to draw). In old English practice. To draw back; to withdraw. *Si simpliciter se retrahat a brevi, non tamen se retrahit ab actione,—nisi expresse dicat quod se retrahat ab utroque*, if he merely withdraw himself from the writ, he does not thereby withdraw himself from the action, unless he expressly says that he withdraws himself from both. Bracton, fol. 182b. See Fleta, lib. 4, c. 7, § 1.

RETRAIT (Fr. from *retraire*, to draw back). In old French and Canadian law. The taking back of a fief by the seignior, in case of alienation by the vassal. Dunkin's Address, 93.

A right of pre-emption by the seignior, in case of sale of the land by the grantee. Id. 40.

RETRAXIT (Lat. he has withdrawn.) In practice. The act by which a plaintiff withdraws his suit. It is so called from the fact that this was the principal word used when the law entries were in Latin.

A "*retraxit*" differs from a "nonsuit;" the former being the act of the plaintiff himself, for it cannot even be entered by attorney (8 Coke, 58; 3 Salk. 245; 8 Pa. St. 157, 163), and it must be after declaration filed (3 Leon. 47; 8 Pa. St. 163); while the latter occurs in consequence of the neglect merely of the plaintiff. A *retraxit* also differs from a *nolle prosequi*. The effect of a *retraxit* is a bar to all actions of a like or a similar nature (Bac. Abr. "Nonsuit" [A]); a *nolle prosequi* is not a bar even in a criminal prosecution (2 Mass. 172). See 2 Sellon, Prac. 338; Bac. Abr. "Nonsuit;" Comyn, Dig. "Pleader" (X 2).

RETREAT TO THE WALL. A figurative phrase used to express the duty of one assailed to retreat as far as he can with safety before resisting the assault with force, such a retreat being essential to the right to kill in self-defense. 4 Bl. Comm. 185.

RETRO (Lat.) Back; backward; behind. *Retrofeodum*, a rere fief, or arriere fief. Spelman.

RETROACTIVE. The same as "retrospective" (*q. v.*)

RETROCESSION. In civil law. When the assignee of heritable rights conveys his rights back to the cedent, it is called a "retrocession." Ersk. Inst. 3. 5. 1; Dict. de Jur.

RETROSPECTIVE. Looking backward. A retroactive law is one which applies to cases existing at its passage, so as to impose new duties or attach new disabilities with reference to past transaction, or to impair vested rights.

RETTE (Law Fr.) In old English law. An accusation or charge. *Quant clerk est prise par rette de felony*, when a clerk is taken on a charge of felony. St. Westminster I. c. 2.

RETTER (Law Fr.) In old English law. To accuse; to charge; to lay to the charge; to account; in old English, to arret, or arrect. *Ceo purra il retter a sa negligence*, he must charge this to his own negligence. Britt. c. 59. *Ceo poies retter a vostre folly demesne*, you may lay this to your own folly. Y. B. H. 10 Edw. III. 8. *Il serra rette la folly*, it shall be accounted the folly. Litt. § 261.

RETTUM (Law Lat.; from Law Fr. *rette*, *q. v.*) In old English law. An accusation; a charge. *Si clericus aliquis pro crimine aliquo vel retto—arrestatus fuerit*, if any clerk shall have been arrested for any crime or charge. St. Marlb. c. 28 (27).

RETURN.

——**Of Writs or Process.** The redelivery of a writ or process by the officer charged with its execution to the court from which it issued, with an account of the manner in which he has executed it. The account indorsed on or affixed to process or writs by the officer, stating the manner of its execution.

——**To Writs.** The answer made by one to whom an alternative writ (as of *habeas corpus* or *quo warranto*) is directed.

——**On Appeal or Error.** The papers or record transmitted from the lower to the appellate court.

RETURN DAY. A day appointed by law when all writs are to be returned which have issued since the preceding return day. The sheriff is, in general, not required to return his writ until the return day. After that period he may be ruled to make a return.

RETURN OF PREMIUM. In insurance. A repayment of a part or the whole of the premium paid. Policies of insurance, especially those on marine risks, not unfrequently contain stipulations for a return of the whole or a part of the premium in certain contingencies (2 Phil. Ins. xxii. § 11); but in the absence of any such stipulation, in a case free of fraud on the part of the assured, if the risk does not commence to run, he is entitled to a return of it, if paid, or an exoneration from his liability to pay it, subject to deduction settled by stipulation or usage; and so, *pro rata*, if only a part of the insured subject is put at risk (2 Phil. Ins. c. xxii. § 1); and so an abatement of the excess of marine interest over the legal rate is made in hypothecation of ship or cargo in like case (Id. § 7; Boul. P. Dr. Com. tit. 9, § 13, tom. 3, p. 63 (Ed. of 1822); Poth. Cont. a la Grosse, note 39.

RETURNUM AVERIORUM. A judicial writ, similar to the *retorno habendo*. Cowell.

RETURNUM IRREPLEGIABILE. A judicial writ addressed to the sheriff for the final restitution or return of cattle to the owner when unjustly taken or distrained, and so found by verdict. It is granted after a nonsuit in a second deliverance. Reg. Jud. 27.

REUS (Lat.) In civil law. A party to a suit, whether plaintiff or defendant. *Reus est qui cum altero litem contestatem habet, sive id egit, sive cum eo actum est.*

A party to a contract. *Reus credendi* is he to whom something is due, by whatever title it may be; *reus debendi* is he who owes, for whatever cause. Poth. ad Pand. lib. 50.

REUS EXCIPIENDO FIT ACTOR. The defendant, by a plea, becomes plaintiff. Bannier, Tr. des Preuves, §§ 152, 320; Best, Ev. 294, § 252.

REUS LAESAE MAJESTATIS PUNITUR, ut pereat unus ne pereant omnes. A traitor is punished that one may die lest all perish. 4 Coke, 124.

REUS PROMITTENDI. See "Reus Stipulandi."

REUS STIPULANDI. In the civil law. The party to a stipulation is so called if he is the creditor or obligee, and the debtor or obligor to such a stipulation is called the "*reus promittendi*." Where there are several creditors or several debtors jointly entitled to or jointly liable under a stipulation, they were respectively called "*correi*;" *i. e.*, joint *rei*. Brown.

REVE, or GREVE (Lat. *gerefa*, or *refa*, from *raefan*, to seize). In English law. A chief officer or superintendent (*praepositus*, *praefectus*). Properly, according to Spelman, a collector or exactor of public moneys or fines.

Shire reve, the reve or chief officer of the shire (*pagi praepositus*). Hence, sheriff.

Tun greve, the reve or chief officer of a town (*villae praepositus*). Afterwards simply called "reve," and bailiff. Spelman. See "Reeve."

REVE LAND. In Domesday Book we find land put down as "thane lands," which were afterwards converted into reve lands, *i. e.*, such lands as, having reverted to the king upon death of his thane, who had it for life, were not since granted out to any by the king, but vested in charge upon account of the reve or bailiff of the manor. Spelman, Feuds, c. 24. Coke was mistaken in thinking it was land held in socage.

REVE MOTE. In Saxon law. The court of the reve, reeve, or shire reeve. 1 Reeve, Hist. Eng. Law, 6.

REVENDICATION. In civil law. An action by which a man demands a thing of which he claims to be owner. It applies to immovables as well as movables; to corporeal or incorporeal things. Merlin, Repert.

Revendication, in another sense, corresponds very nearly to the "stoppage *in transitu*" of the common law. It is used in that sense in Code de Commerce, art. 577. Revendication, says that article, can take place only when the goods sold are on the way to their place of destination, whether by land or water, and before they have been received into the warehouse of the insolvent (*failli*) or that of his factor or agent authorized to sell them on account of the insolvent. See Dig. 14. 4. 15; Id. 18. 1. 19. 53; Id. 19. 1. 11.

REVENUE. (L. Fr. and Eng.) That which returns, or is returned; a rent. Income; annual profit received from lands or other property. Cowell.

REVERSAL.

——**In International Law.** A declaration by which a sovereign promises that he will observe a certain order, or certain conditions, which have been once established, notwithstanding any changes that may happen to cause a deviation therefrom; as, for example, when the French court consented for the first time, in 1745, to grant to Elizabeth, the czarina of Russia, the title of empress, it exacted as a reversal a declaration purporting that the assumption of the title of an imperial government by Russia should not derogate from the rank which France had held towards her.

Letters by which a sovereign declares that, by a particular act of his, he does not mean to prejudice a third power. Of this we have an example in history. Formerly the emperor of Germany, whose coronation, according to the Golden Bull, ought to have been solemnized at Aix-la-Chapelle, gave to that city, when he was crowned elsewhere, reversals, by which he declared that such coronation took place without prejudice to its rights, and without drawing any consequences therefrom for the future.

——**In Practice.** The decision of a superior court by which the judgment, sentence, or decree of the inferior court is annulled.

REVERSER. In Scotch law. The propritor of an estate who grants a wadset (or mortgage) of his lands, and who has a right, on repayment of the money advanced to him, to be replaced in his right. Bell, Dict.

REVERSIO (Law Lat. from *reverti*, to return). In old English law. The returning of land to the donor. Fleta, lib. 3, cc. 10, 12.

REVERSION. The residue of an estate left in the grantor, to commence in possession after the determination of some particular estate granted out by him. The return of land to the grantor and his heirs after the grant is over. Co. Litt. 142b.

The reversion arises by operation of law, and not by deed or will, and it is a vested interest or estate, and in this it differs from a "remainder," which can never be limited unless by either deed or devise. 2 Bl. Comm. 175; Cruise, Dig. tit. 17; Plowd. 151; 4 Kent, Comm. 349; 19 Viner, Abr. 217. A reversion is said to be an incorporeal hereditament. 4 Kent, Comm. 354; 1 Washb. Real Prop. 37, 47, 63; 2 Bouv. Inst. note 1850. See "Remainder."

REVERSIONARY INTEREST. The interest which one has in the reversion of lands or other property. The residue which remains to one who has carved out of his estate a lesser estate. See "Reversion." An interest in the land when possession shall fail. Cowell.

REVERSIONARY LEASE. One to take effect *in futuro*. A second lease, to commence after the expiration of a former lease. Wharton.

REVERSIONER. A person who is entitled to an estate in reversion.

REVERSOR. In Scotch law. A debtor who makes a wadset, and to whom the right of reversion is granted. Ersk. Inst. 2. 8. 1. A reversioner. Jacob.

REVERTER. Reversion. A possibility of reverter is that species of reversionary interest which exists when the grant is so limited that it may possibly terminate. See 1 Washb. Real Prop. 63.

REVEST. To vest again. A seisin is said to revest, where it is acquired a second time by the party out of whom it has been divested. 1 Roper, Husb. & Wife, 353.

It is opposed to "divest." The words "revest" and "divest" are also applicable to the mere right or title, as opposed to the possession. Brown.

REVESTIRE (Law Lat.) In old European law. To return or resign an investiture, seisin, or possession that has been received; to reinvest; to re-enfeoff. Spelman.

REVIEW. A second examination of a matter; ordinarily applied to a re-examination of a judicial or official determination. It is a general term, embracing re-examination obtained by every variety of procedure, as by motion for new trial, appeal, writ of error, bill of review, etc.

REVIEW, BILL OF. In equity practice. A bill in the nature of a writ of error, filed to procure an examination and alteration or reversal of a decree made upon a former bill, which decree has been signed and enrolled. Story, Eq. Pl. § 403.

REVISING BARRISTERS. In English law. Barristers appointed to revise the list of voters for county and borough members of parliament, and who hold courts for that purpose throughout the country, being appointed in July or August. 6 Vict. c. 18; 3 Chit. St.

REVIVAL.

——**Of Contracts.** An agreement to renew the legal obligation of a just debt after it has been barred by the act of limitation or lapse of time is called its "revival."

——**Of Judgment.** At common law, the act by which a judgment which has lain dormant or without any action upon it for a year and a day is again restored to its original force.

When a judgment is more than a day and a year old, no execution can issue upon it at common law; but till it has been paid, or the presumption arises from lapse of time that it has been satisfied, it may be revived and have all its original force, which was merely suspended. This may be done by a *scire facias*, or an action of debt on the judgment. See "Scire Facias."

Where the common-law rule is not in force, the bringing of suit on a judgment to prevent the bar of the statute of limitations is termed "revival."

——**Of Action.** The continuation of an action which has abated by the death or disability of a party, or a transfer of the cause of action. At common law, this was effected by a bill in equity (see "Bill of Revivor"), but in most of the states, a proceeding on application to the court in which the action was pending has been substituted.

REVIVOR. In equity practice. A bill used to renew an original bill which, for some reason, has become inoperative.

The purpose of a revivor is to renew a dormant judgment and to give it its original force as a lien on the judgment debtor's property. 209 Ill. 249. See "Bill of Revivor."

REVOCATION OF AGENCY. An agency is dissolved or determined in several ways:

I. By the act of the principal, either
  (a) Express, as
    (1) By direct and formal writing, publicly advertised;
    (2) By informal writing to the agent privately;
    (3) By parol. 6 Pick. (Mass.) 198.
  (b) Implied from circumstances, as by appointing another person to do the same act, where the authority of both would be incompatible. 78 Ky. 413.

The exceptions to the power of the principal to revoke his agent's authority at mere pleasure are

(1) When the principal has expressly stipulated that the authority shall be irrevocable, and the agent has also an interest in its execution. 86 Ill. 142.

(2) Where an authority or power is coupled with an interest, or is given for a valuable consideration, or is a part of a security, unless there is an express stipulation that it shall be revocable. 40 Ill. 109.

(3) Where an agent's act in pursuance of his authority has become obligatory, for *nemo potest mutare consilium suum in alterius injuriam.* 121 N. Y. 582.

II. By the agent's giving notice to his principal that he renounces the agency; but the principal must sustain no damage thereby; otherwise the agent would be responsible therefor. 37 Mich. 481.

III. By operation of law, as
  (a) By the expiration of the period during which the agency was to exist or to have effect. 62 Ga. 216.
  (b) By a change of condition or of state, producing an incapacity of either the principal or the agent, as
    (1) Marriage of a *feme sole* principal. 22 Tex. 365.
    (2) Mental disability established by inquisition, or where the party is placed under guardianship. 2 Hall (N. Y.) 495.
    (3) Bankruptcy, except as to such rights as do not pass to the trustee under the adjudication. 6 Biss. (U. S.) 405.
    (4) Death, unless the authority is coupled with an interest in the thing vested in the agent. 18 Beav. 179.
    (5) Extinction of the subject of the agency.
    (6) Cessation of the principal's powers.
    (7) Complete execution of the trust confided to the agent, who then is *functus officio.* 100 N. Y. 413; Wharton.
    (8) A state of war also terminates all agencies requiring intercourse between belligerent nations. 100 Mass. 561.

REVOCATION OF PROBATE. The vacation or recall of an order admitting a will to probate.

REVOCATIONE PARLIAMENTI. An ancient writ for recalling a parliament. 4 Inst. 44.

REVOCATUR (Lat. recalled). A term used to denote that a judgment is annulled for an error in fact. The judgment is then said to be recalled, *revocatur;* not "reversed," which is the word used when a judgment is annulled for an error in law. Tidd, Prac. 1126.

REVOLT. The endeavor of the crew of a vessel, or any one or more of them, to overthrow the legitimate authority of her com-

who held cottages and lands by the services of plowing, and other labors of agriculture, for the lord. Par. Ant. 136; Cowell.

RUSTICUM JUDICIUM (Law Lat.) In maritime law. A rough or rude judgment or decision. 3 Kent, Comm. 231; Story, Bailm. § 608a.

RUTA ET CAESA (Lat.) In the civil law. Things dug, as sand and lime, and things cut, as wood, coal, etc. Dig. 19. 1. 17. 6. Words used in conveyancing.

RUTARII, or RUTTARII (Law Lat.) In old records. Stipendiary forces; mercenary soldiers. Cowell. This word occurs in the articles of King John's *Magna Charta*, (chapter 4), but is omitted in the charter itself.

RYBAUD (Law Fr.) In old English law. A ruffian; a vagabond. Brownl. pt. 2. 340.

S

S. A common abbreviation of *scilicet* in the old books.

S. C. An abbreviation for "same case," indicating, when inserted between two citations of cases, that the case is reported in both places.

S. F. S. In the civil law, an abbreviation of *sine fraude sua,* without fraud on his part.

S. P. An abbreviation of *sine prole,* without issue.

An abbreviation of "same point," or "same principle," indicating, when inserted between two citations of cases, that the second one involves the same doctrine as the first.

SS. An abbreviation used in that part of a record, pleading, or affidavit, called the statement of the venue, or county in which it is made, as "City and County of New York, ss." Commonly translated or read, "to wit," and supposed to be a contraction of *scilicet.*

It has been otherwise explained to be a mark used to denote a separate section or paragraph. 1 Chit. Pl. (6th Am. Ed.) 305, note (t).

SA ET LA (Law Fr.) Here and there. Kelham.

SABBATH. Commonly used for "Sunday." Though such use is incorrect, it is sanctioned by usage. See 64 N. C. 591.

SABBATH BREAKING. Violation of penal laws regulating the observance of the Sabbath.

SABBATUM. The Sabbath; also peace. Domesday Book.

SABINIANS. A sect of lawyers whose first chief was Atteius Capito, and the second Caelius Sabinus, from whom they derived their name. Clef des Lois Rom.

SABLE. The heraldic term for black. It is called "Saturn" by those who blazon by planets, and "diamond" by those who use the names of jewels. Engravers commonly represent it by numerous perpendicular and horizontal lines, crossing each other. Wharton.

SABULONARIUM (Law Lat. from *sabulo*). In old records. A gravel pit, or the free use of it. Cowell.

SAC, or SAK (Law Lat. *saca, sacha;* from Saxon, *sac,* a cause, sake). In old English and Scotch law. The cognizance which a lord had in his court of causes and suits arising among his vassals or tenants. The privilege which a lord had, within his manor, of holding pleas of trespasses and other controversies arising there, and of imposing levying, and collecting of his tenants, fines, and amercements in regard of the same. Spelman; Bracton, fol. 154b. A privilege touching plea, or correction of trespasses of men within a manor. Minshew, cited in Cowell; Rastal, Expos.

A forfeiture. Id.

SACABURTH, or SACABERE (from *sac, cause,* and *burth,* pledge. He that is robbed and puts in surety to prosecute the felon with fresh suit. Britton, c. 15, 29; Bracton, lib. 3, c. 32; Cowell.

SACCABOR, SACABURTH, or SACABERE. In old English law. He that is robbed and puts in surety to prosecute the felon with fresh suit.

SACCULARII (Lat. from *saccus,* a bag or purse). In the civil law. Persons who cheated in wares or money, by means of sacks or bags which they carried with them (*vetitas in sacculo artes exercentes*). Dig. 47. 11. 7 and glossary in margin. Blackstone, referring to this passage, translates the word "cutpurses." 4 Bl. Comm. 242. But this is hardly warranted by the text.

SACCUS (Law Lat.) In old English law. A sack; a quantity of wool weighing thirty or twenty-eight stone. Fleta, lib. 2, c. 79, § 10. According to Cowell, twenty-six stone. Two ways made a sack, and twelve sacks a last. Fleta, lib. 2, c. 12, § 2.

A sack or pack; a pack saddle. Fleta, lib. 2, c. 21.

In a MS. compotus or household book of Bolton Priory, in the possession of the Duke of Devonshire, the *ductor sacorum* is mentioned among the *liberi servientes* (free servants) of the priory, and is translated "sackman."

SACCUS CUM BROCHIA. In old English law. A service or tenure of finding a sack and a broach (pitcher) to the sovereign for the use of the army. Bracton, lib. 2, c. 16.

SACQUIER. In maritime law. The name of an ancient officer, whose business was to load and unload vessels laden with salt, corn, or fish, to prevent the ship's crew defrauding the merchant by false tale, or cheating him of his merchandise otherwise. Laws of Oleron, art. 11, published in an English translation in an appendix to 1 Pet. Adm. xxv. See "Arrameur;" "Stevedore."

SACRA (Lat.) In the Roman law. The right to participate in the sacred rites of the city. Butler, Hor. Jur. 27.

SACRAMENTALES (Law Lat. *sacramentum*, oath). *Compurgatores* (*q. v.*); jurors. Law Fr. & Lat. Dict.

SACRAMENTI ACTIO. In the Roman law. General *legis actio*, to which resort might be had failing a right to use any of the four shorter forms of action.

SACRAMENTUM (Law Lat.)

——**In Civil Law.** A gage in money laid down in court by both parties that went to law, returned to him who had the verdict on his side, but forfeited by the party who was cast, to the exchequer, to be laid out *in sacris rebus*, and therefore so called. Varro, lib. 4, de Ling. Lat. c. 36.

An oath, as a very sacred thing. Ainsworth; Vicat.

The oath taken by soldiers to be true to their general and country. Id.

——**In Old Common Law.** An oath. Carpentier; Cowell; Jacob.

SACRAMENTUM DECISIONIS (Lat.) The voluntary or decisive oath of the civil law, where one of the parties to a suit, not being able to prove his case, offers to refer the decision of the cause to the oath of his adversary, who is bound to accept or make the same offer on his part, or the whole is considered as confessed by him. 3 Bl. Comm. 342.

SACRAMENTUM FIDELITATIS. In old English law. The oath of fealty. Reg. Orig. 303.

SACRAMENTUM HABET IN SE TRES comites, veritatem, justitiam et judicium; veritas habenda est in jurato; justitia et justicium in judice. An oath has in it three component parts,—truth, justice, and judgment; truth in the party swearing; justice and judgment in the judge administering the oath. 3 Inst. 160.

SACRAMENTUM SI FATUUM FUERIT, licet falsum, tamen non committit perjurium. A foolish oath, though false, makes not perjury. 2 Inst. 167.

SACRILEGE (from Lat. *sacrilegium*, from *sacra*, sacred things, or *sacrum*, sacred, and *legere*, to steal).

——**In English Criminal Law.** Larceny from a church. 4 Steph. Comm. 164. The crime of breaking a church or chapel, and stealing therein. 1 Russ. Crimes, 843. See "Sacrilegium." This does not seem to be recognized as a distinct crime, in American jurisprudence.

——**In Old English Law.** Profanation of holy things; the alienation to laymen or to profane or common purposes of what was given to religious persons, and to pious uses. Cowell.

SACRILEGIUM (Lat. from *sacrum*, sacred, and *legere*, to steal). In the civil law. The stealing of sacred things, or things dedicated to sacred uses; the taking of things out of a holy place. Calv. Lex.; Brissonius.

The violation of an imperial rescript or constitution. *Sacrilegii instar est rescripto principis obviari*, it amounts to sacrilege to oppose or hinder the execution of the prince's rescript. Code, 1. 23. 5; 1 Bl. Comm. 74. The text of the Code here referred to, reads, *Sacrilegii instar est—divinis obviare beneficiis.*

SACRILEGUS (Lat.) In the civil and common law. A sacrilegious person; one guilty of sacrilege; he who takes away anything that is given for the divine and true service of God.

SACRILEGUS OMNIUM PRAEDORUM cupiditatem et scelerem superat. A sacrilegious person transcends the cupidity and wickedness of all other robbers. 4 Coke, 106.

SACRISTAN. A sexton, anciently called *sagerson*, or *sagiston;* the keeper of things belonging to divine worship.

SADBERGE. A denomination of part of the county palatine of Durham. Camd. Brit.

SAEMEND. An umpire, or arbitrator. Anc. Inst. Eng.

SAEPE CONSTITUTUM EST, RES INter alios judicatas aliis non praejudicare. It has often been settled that matters adjudged between others ought not to prejudice those who were not parties. Dig. 42. 1. 63.

SAEPE VIATOREM NOVA NON VETUS orbita fallit. Often it is the new track, not the old one, which deceives the traveller. 4 Inst. 34.

SAEPENUMERO UBI PROPRIETAS verborum attenditur, sensus veritatis amittitur. Frequently, where the propriety of words is attended to, the meaning of truth is lost. 7 Coke, 27.

SAEVITIA (Lat.) Cruelty of one spouse to the other. To constitute *saevitia* there must be such a degree of cruelty as to endanger the party's suffering bodily hurt. 1 Hagg. Consist. 35; 2 Mass. 150; 3 Mass. 321; 4 Mass. 587.

SAEVITIAM. (Lat.) Cruelty. 16 Ill. 90.

SAFE-CONDUCT. A passport or permission from a neutral state to persons who are thus authorized to go and return in safety, and, sometimes, to carry away certain things in safety.

According to common usage, the term "passport" is employed on ordinary occasions for the permission given to persons when there is no reason why they should not go where they please; and "safe-conduct" is the name given to the instrument which authorizes certain persons, as enemies, to go into places where they could not go without danger unless thus authorized by the government.

The name of an instrument given to the captain or master of a ship to proceed on a particular voyage. It usually contains his name and residence, the name, description, and destination of the ship, with such other matters as the practice of the place requires. This document is indispensably necessary for the safety of every neutral ship.

Act Cong. April 30, 1790, § 27, punishes the violation of any safe-conduct or passport granted under the authority of the United States, on conviction, with imprisonment, not exceeding three years, and a fine at the discretion of the court. See "Passport;" 18 Viner, Abr. 272.

SAFEGUARD. A protection of the king to one who is a stranger, who fears violence from some of his subjects for seeking his right by course of law. Reg. Orig. 26.

SAFE-PLEDGE. A surety given that a man shall appear upon a certain day. Bracton, lib. 4, c. 1.

SAGES DE LA LEY (Law Fr.) Sages of the law; persons learned in the law. A term applied to the chancellor and justices of the king's bench.

SAGIBARO (Law Lat. from *sac*, or *sag*, a cause, and *baro*, a man). In old European law. A judge or justice; literally, a man of causes (*vir causarum*), or having charge or supervision of causes (*causis et litibus praepositus*). Spelman. One who administered justice and decided causes in the *mallum*, or public assembly. Id.; L. Salic. tit. 56, §§ 2-4; LL. Inae, c. 6.

SAID. Before mentioned. A word of reference to what has been already spoken of or specified. 172 Ill. 465.

In contracts and pleadings it is usual and proper, when it is desired to speak of a person or thing before mentioned, to designate them by the term "said" or "aforesaid," or by some similar term; otherwise the latter description will be ill for want of certainty. 2 Lev. 207; Comyn, Dig. "Pleader" (C 18); Gould, Pl. c. 3, § 63.

If there is a question as to which of the antecedent things or propositions specified is referred to, it is generally, 172 Ill. 465, but not necessarily, held to be the last. 10 Ind. 372.

SAIGA (Law Lat.) In old European law. A German coin of the value of a penny, or of three pence. L. Alaman. tit. 6, æ 2; L. Boior. tit. 8, c. 2, § 3; Spelman.

SAIL. In insurance law. To move, on the prosecution of a voyage; to make a movement for the purpose of proceeding to sea. Cowen, J., 3 Hill (N. Y.) 126; Lord Denman, C. J., 1 Cromp., M. & R. 809, 818. The least locomotion, with readiness of equipment and clearance satisfies a warranty to sail. 3 Barn. & Adol. 514.

SAILING INSTRUCTIONS. In maritime law. Written or printed directions, delivered by the commanding officer of a convoy to the several masters of the ships under his care, by which they are enabled to understand and answer his signals, to know the place of rendezvous appointed for the fleet in case of dispersion by storm, by an enemy, or by any other accident.

Without sailing instructions, no vessel can have the full protection and benefit of convoy. Marsh. Ins. 368.

SAILORS. Seamen; mariners. See "Seaman."

SAINT MARTIN LE GRAND, COURT of. A writ of error formerly lay from the sheriff's courts in the city of London to the court of hustings, before the mayor, recorder, and sheriffs, and thence to justices appointed by the royal commission, who used to sit in the church of St. Martin le Grand, and from the judgment of those justices a writ of error lay immediately to the house of lords. Fitzh. Nat. Brev.

SAINT SIMONISM. An elaborate form of noncommunistic socialism. It is a scheme which does not contemplate an equal, but an unequal, division of the produce. It does not propose that all should be occupied alike, but differently, according to their vocation or capacity; the function of each being assigned, like grades in a regiment, by the choice of the directing authority, and the remuneration being by salary, proportioned to the importance, in the eyes of that authority, of the function itself, and the merits of the person who fulfills it. 1 Mill, Pol. Econ. 258.

SAIO (Law Lat.) In Gothic law. The ministerial officer of a court or magistrate, who brought parties into court (*qui reos protraxit in judicium*), and executed the orders of his superior. Spelman thinks the word may be derived from the Saxon *sagol*, or *saiol*, a staff, giving it the sense of the modern "tipstaff."

SAIREMENT (Law Fr.) An oath. Kelham.

SAISIE ARRET. In French law. An attachment of property in the possession of a third person.

SAISIE EXECUTION. In French law. A writ of execution by which the creditor places under the custody of the law the movables of his debtor, which are liable to seizure, in order that out of them he may obtain payment of the debt due by him. Code Prac. La. art. 641; Dalloz. It is a writ very similar to the *fieri facias* of the common law.

SAISIE FORAINE. In French law. A permission given by the proper judicial officer to authorize a creditor to seize the property of his debtor in the district which he inhabits. Dalloz. It has the effect of an attachment of property, which is applied to the payment of the debt due.

SAISIE GAGERIE. In French law. A conservatory act of execution, by which the owner or principal lessor of a house or farm causes the furniture of the house or farm leased, and on which he has a lien, to be seized, in order to obtain the rent due to him. It is similar to the "distress" of the common law. Dalloz.

SAISIE IMMOBILIERE. In French law. A writ by which the creditor puts in the custody of the law the immovables of his debtor; that out of the proceeds of their sale he may be paid his demand.

SAISINA (Law Lat.) An old form of *seisina (q. v.)*

SAKE. In old English law. A lord's right of amercing his tenants in his court. Kielw. 145.

Acquittance of suit at county courts and hundred courts. Fleta, lib. 1, c. 47, § 7.

SALADINE TENTH. A tax imposed in England and France, in 1888, by Pope Innocent III., to raise a fund for the crusade undertaken by Richard I., of England, and Philip Augustus, of France, against Saladin, sultan of Egypt, then going to besiege Jerusalem. By this tax, every person who did not enter himself a crusader was obliged to pay a tenth of his yearly revenue, and of the value of all his movables, except his wearing apparel, books, and arms. The Carthusians, Bernardines, and some other religious persons, were exempt.

SALARIUM (Lat. from *sal*, salt).

——**In the Civil Law.** An allowance of provisions. Calv. Lex.

A stipend, wages, or compensation for service. Id.; Dig. 7. 1. 7. 2; Id. 44. 7. 61. 1.

An annual allowance or compensation. Id.

——**In Old European Law.** The rents or profits of a *sala*, hall or house. Cowell.

SALARY (from "salarium," *sal*, salt, the medium of payment to the Roman soldiers). The periodical allowance or compensation to a person for his official or professional services or for his regular work. 193 Mich. 476; 105 Cal. 212; 10 Ind. 85.

A reward or recompense for services performed.

It is applied to the reward paid to a public officer for the performance of his official duties.

Salary is also applied to the reward paid for the performance of other services; but if it be not fixed for each year, it is called "honorarium." Poth. ad Pand. According to M. Duvergier, the distinction between "honorarium" and "salary" is this: By the former is understood the reward given to the most elevated professions for services performed; and by the latter, the price of hiring of domestic servants and workmen. 19 Toullier, Dr. Civ. n. 268, p. 292, note.

There is this difference between "salary" and "price,"—the former is the reward paid for services or for the hire of things; the latter is the consideration paid for a thing sold. Lec. Elm. §§ 907, 908.

"Salary" and "wages" have been held to be synonymous (24 Fla. 29), but in other cases, distinctions have been suggested,—one, that salary is per annum compensation (42 Alb. Law J. 332), and another, that the difference lies in the more or less honorable character of the services for which they are paid. 99 Pa. St. 542.

SALE. An agreement by which one of two contracting parties, called the "seller," gives a thing and passes the title to it, in exchange for a certain price in current money, to the other party, who is called the "buyer" or "purchaser," who, on his part, agrees to pay such price. Pardessus, Dr. Com. note 6; Noy, Max. c. 42; Shep. Touch. 244; 2 Kent, Comm. 363; Poth. Vente, note 1. A transfer of the absolute or general property in a thing for a price in money. Benj. Sales, § 1.

This contract differs from a barter or exchange in this, that in the latter the price or consideration, instead of being paid in money, is paid in goods or merchandise susceptible of a valuation. 3 Salk. 157; 12 N. H. 390; 10 Vt. 457. It differs from "accord and satisfaction," because in that contract the thing is given for the purpose of quieting a claim, and not for a price. An onerous gift, when the burden it imposes is the payment of a sum of money, is, when accepted, in the nature of a sale. When partition is made between two or more joint owners of a chattel, it would seem the contract is in the nature of a barter. See 11 Pick. (Mass.) 311.

(1) An absolute sale is one made and completed without any condition whatever.

(2) A conditional sale is one which depends for its validity upon the fulfillment of some condition. See 4 Wash. C. C. (U. S.) 588; 10 Pick. (Mass.) 522; 18 Johns. (N. Y.) 141; 8 Vt. 154; 2 Rawle (Pa.) 326; Coxe (N. J.) 292; 2 A. K. Marsh. (Ky.) 430.

(3) A forced sale is one made without the consent of the owner of the property, by some officer appointed by law, as by a marshal or a sheriff, in obedience to the mandate of a competent tribunal. This sale has the effect to transfer all the rights the owner had in the property, but it does not, like a voluntary sale of personal property, guaranty a title to the thing sold; it merely transfers the rights of the person as whose property it has been seized. This kind of a sale is sometimes called a "judicial sale."

(4) A private sale is one made voluntarily, and not by auction.

(5) A public sale is one made at auction to the highest bidder. Auction sales sometimes are voluntary, as, when the owner chooses to sell his goods in this way, and

then as between the seller and the buyer the usual rules relating to sales apply; or they are involuntary or forced, when the same rules do not apply.

(6) A voluntary sale is one made freely without constraint by the owner of the thing sold. This is the common case of sales, and to this class the general rules of the law of sale apply.

SALE AND RETURN. When goods are sent from a manufacturer or wholesale dealer to a retail trader, in the hope that he may purchase them, with the understanding that what he may choose to take he shall have as on a contract of sale, and what he does not take he will retain as a consignee for the owner, the goods are said to have been sent on "sale and return."

The goods taken by the receiver as on sale will be considered as sold, and the title to them is vested in the receiver of them. The goods he does not buy are considered as a deposit in the hands of the receiver of them, and the title is in the person who sent them. 1 Bell, Comm. (5th Ed.) 268.

SALE NOTE. A memorandum given by a broker to a seller or buyer of goods, stating the fact that certain goods have been sold by him on account of a person called the "seller" to another person called the "buyer." Sale notes are also called "bought and sold notes." See "Bought Note."

SALFORD HUNDRED COURT OF RECord. An inferior and local court of record having jurisdiction in personal actions, where the debt or damage sought to be recovered does not exceed £50, if the cause of action arise within the Hundred of Salford. St. 31 & 32 Vict. c. 130; 2 Exch. 346. See "Hundred."

SALIQUE (or SALIC) LAW. The name of a code of laws, so called from the Salians, a people of Germany who settled in Gaul under their king Pharamond.

The most remarkable law of this code, which is sometimes itself called the Salic law, is that which regards succession. *De terra vero salica nulla portio haereditatis transit in mulierem, sed hoc virilis sextus acquirit; hoc est, filii in ipsa haereditate succedunt,* no part of the salique land passes to females, but the males alone are capable of taking; that is, the sons succeed to the inheritance. This has ever excluded females from the throne of France.

SALOON. The term does not necessarily imply a place for the sale of intoxicants. 36 Tex. 364. But see 105 Mass. 40.

SALT SILVER. One penny paid at the feast day of St. Martin, by the tenants of some manors, as a commutation for the service of carrying their lord's salt from market to his larder. Par. Ant. 496.

SALUS (Lat.) Health; prosperity; safety.

SALUS POPULI EST SUPREMA LEX. The safety of the people is the supreme object of the law. Bac. Max. reg. 12; Broom, Leg. Max. 1; 13 Coke, 139, 196 Ill. 503.

SALUS UBI MULTI CONSILIARII. In many counsellors there is safety. 4 Inst. 1.

SALUTE (Lat. *salus*). A gold coin stamped by Henry V. in France, after his conquests there, whereon the arms of England and France were stamped quarterly. Stow. Chron. 589; Cowell.

SALUTEM (Lat.) Health; greeting; prosperity; salvation. An expression of salutation used by the Romans in the commencement of their letters or epistles, generally abbreviated. *S.* *"C. Plinius Cornelio Tacito suo, S."* Plin. Ep. i. 6 et passim. In legal instruments, it was written at length, *Titius Seio salutem.* Dig. 17. 1. 60. *Ille illi salutem.* Id. 59.

A formal word in the commencement of Roman deeds and charters, which, during the later periods of the empire, were written in an epistolary form. See "Epistola." After Christianity had become established, *salutem* seems to have been used in its religious sense of "salvation."

A formal word in the commencement of old English deeds, probably derived from the Roman practice above noticed. *Omnibus Christi fidelibus ad quos praesentes literae indentatae pervenerint, A. de B. salutem in Domino sempiternam; Sciatis me dedisse, etc.,* to all Christian people to whom these presents [present letters] indented shall come, A. of B. sends greeting [or salvation], in our Lord everlasting. Litt. § 372.

A formal word invariably used in the address of old English writs, which commenced in the epistolary form. *Rex vice comiti, etc., salutem,* the king to the sheriff, etc., greeting. Reg. Orig. & Jud. per tot. Translated "greeting," and retained in modern English and American writs. See "Breve." Called by Finch the "salutation" of the writ. Finch, Law, bk. 4, c. 1.

SALVA GARDIA (Law Lat.) Safeguard. Reg. Orig. 26. See "Safeguard."

SALVAGE. In maritime law. A compensation given by the maritime law for service rendered in saving property or rescuing it from impending peril on the sea or wrecked on the coast of the sea, or, in the United States, on a public navigable river or lake, where interstate or foreign commerce is carried on. 1 Sumn. (U. S.) 210, 416; 12 How. (U. S.) 466; 1 Blatchf. (U. S.) 420; 5 McLean (U. S.) 359.

Occasionally used to designate the property saved. 2 Phil. Ins. § 1488; 2 Pars. Mar. Law, 595.

There are three things essential to the right to salvage:

(1) The peril. In order to found a title to salvage, the peril from which the prop-

erty was saved must be real, not speculative merely (1 Cranch [U. S.] 1); but it need not be such that escape from it by any other means than by the aid of the salvors was impossible. It is sufficient that the peril was something extraordinary,—something differing in kind and degree from the ordinary perils of navigation. 1 Curt. [U. S.] 353; 2 Curt. [U. S.] 350. All services rendered at sea to a vessel in distress are salvage services. 1 W. Rob. Adm. 174; 3 W. Rob. Adm. 71. But the peril must be present and pending, not future, contingent, and conjectural. 1 Sumn. (U. S.) 216; 3 Hagg. Adm. 344. It may arise from the sea, rocks, fire, pirates, or enemies (1 Cranch [U. S.] 1), or from the sickness or death of the crew of master (1 Curt. [U. S.] 376; 2 Wall. Jr. [U. S.] 59; 1 Swab. 84).

(2) The saving. In order to give a title to salvage, the property must be effectually saved; it must be brought to some port of safety, and it must be there in a state capable of being restored to the owner, before the service can be deemed completed. 1 Sumn. (U. S.) 417; 1 W. Rob. Adm. 329, 406. It must be saved by the instrumentality of the asserted salvors, or their services must contribute in some certain degree to save it (4 Wash. C. C. [U. S.] 651; Olc. Adm. [U. S.] 462); though, if the services were rendered on the request of the master or owner, the salvor is entitled to salvage, though the services were slight, and the property was saved mainly by a providential act (5 McLean [U. S.] 359; 1 Newb. Adm. [U. S.] 130; 2 W. Rob. Adm. 91; Bee, Adm. [U. S.] 90; 9 Lond. Jur. 119).

(3) The place. In England it has been held that the services must be rendered on the high seas, or, at least, *extra corpus comitatus*, in order to give the admiralty court jurisdiction to decree salvage; but in this country it is held that the district courts of the United States have jurisdiction to decree salvage for services rendered on tide waters and on the lakes or rivers where interstate or foreign commerce is carried on, although *infra corpus comitatus*. 12 How. (U. S.) 466; 1 Blatchf. (U. S.) 420; 5 McLean (U. S.) 359.

SALVAGE CHARGES. In insurance. All those costs, expenses, and charges necessarily incurred in and about the saving and preservation of the property imperilled, and which, if the property be insured, are eventually borne by the underwriters. Stev. Av. c. 2, § 1.

SALVAGE LOSS. That kind of loss which it is presumed would, but for certain services rendered and exertions made, have become a total loss. It also means, among underwriters and average adjusters, a mode of settling a loss, under a policy, in cases where the goods have been necessarily sold at a port short of the port of destination, in consequence of the perils insured against. In such cases, though the property be not abandoned to the underwriter, the principle of abandonment is assumed in the adjustment of the loss. The underwriter pays a total loss. The net proceeds of the sale of the goods, after deducting all expenses, are retained by the assured, and he credits the underwriter with the amount. 2 Phil. Ins. § 1480; Stev. Av. c. 2, § 1.

SALVAGE SERVICE. In maritime law. Any service rendered in saving property on the sea, or wrecked on the coast of the sea. Story, J., 1 Sumn. (U. S.) 210.

SALVIAN INTERDICT. See "Interdictum Salvianum."

SALVO (Lat.) Saving; excepting; without prejudice to. *Salvo me et haeredibus meis*, except me and my heirs. *Salvo jure cujuslibet*, without prejudice to the rights of any one.

SALVOR. In maritime law. A person who saves property or rescues it from impending peril on the sea or when wrecked on the coast of the sea, or, in the United States, on a public navigable river or lake where interstate commerce is carried on, and who is under no pre-existing contract or obligation of duty by his relation to the property to render such services. 1 Hagg. Adm. 236; 1 Curt. (U. S.) 378.

SALVUS PLEGIUS (Law Lat.) A safe pledge; called, also, "*certus plegius*," a sure pledge. Bracton, fol. 160b.

SAME. The ordinary meaning of the word "same" is "identical;" "identical in substance or numerically;" "of one nature, degree or amount." 248 Ill. 166.

"The same" generally refers to the next preceding antecedent. Co. Litt. 20b, 385b; 26 Bea. 160; but the word "same" may grammatically refer to more than one antecedent. 45 L. J. Ch. 216; 1 Ch. D. 605.

SAMPLE. A small quantity of any commodity or merchandise, exhibited as a specimen of a larger quantity, called the "bulk." A fair representation of the whole; a part shown as a specimen. 33 Gratt. (Va.) 904.

When a sale is made by sample, and it afterwards turns out that the bulk does not correspond with it, the purchaser is not, in general, bound to take the property on a compensation being made to him for the difference. 1 Campb. 113. See 2 East, 314; 4 Campb. 22; 9 Wend. (N. Y.) 20; 12 Wend. (N. Y.) 413, 566; 5 Johns. (N. Y.) 395; 6 N. Y. 73, 95; 13 Mass. 139; 2 Nott & McC. (S. C.) 538; 3 Rawle (Pa.) 37; 14 Mees & W. 651.

SANAE MENTIS (Lat.) In old English law. Of sound mind. Fleta, lib. 3, c. 7, § 1.

SANCTIO (Lat.) In the civil law. That part of a law by which a penalty was ordained against those who should violate it. Inst. 2. 1. 10.

SANCTION. That part of a law which inflicts a penalty for its violation, or bestows a reward for its observance. Sanctions are of two kinds,—those which redress civil injuries, called "civil sanctions," and those which punish crimes, called "penal sanctions." 1 Hoffm. Leg. Outl. 279; Rutherforth, Inst. bk. 2, c. 6, § 6; Toullier, Dr. Civ. tit. prel. 86; 1 Bl. Comm. 56.

SANCTUARY. A place of refuge, where the process of the law cannot be executed.

Sanctuaries may be divided into religious and civil. The former were very common in Europe,—religious houses affording protection from arrest to all persons, whether accused of crime or pursued for debt. 4 Bl. Comm. 332. This kind was never known in the United States.

Civil sanctuary, or that protection which is afforded to a man by his own house, was always respected in this country. The house protects the owner from the service of all civil process in the first instance, but not if he is once lawfully arrested and takes refuge in his own house. See "House;" "Arrest."

No place affords protection from arrest in criminal cases. A man may therefore, be arrested in his own house in such cases, and the doors may be broken for the purpose of making the arrest. See "Arrest."

SANCTUS, or **SANCTUM** (Lat. from *sancire*). In the civil law. That which is guarded and fenced round against injury (*quod ab injuria hominum defensum atque munitum est*). Dig. 1. 8, pr. Derived by Marcian, in the Digests, from *sagmina*, which were certain herbs carried by the legates of the Roman people to secure them from harm. Id. § 1.

SAND GAVEL. A payment due to the lord of the manor of Rodley, in the county of Gloucester, for liberty granted to the tenants to dig sand for their common use. Cowell.

SANE (Law Fr. and Eng.; from Lat. *sanus*). Sound. *De non sane memorie* of unsound memory, *non compos mentis*. Litt. § 405.

SANG, or **SANC.** Blood. These words are nearly obsolete.

SANGUINE, or **MURREY.** An heraldic term for "blood color," called, in the arms of princes, "dragon's tail," and, in those of lords, "sardonyx." It is a tincture of very infrequent occurrence, and not recognized by some writers. In engraving, it is denoted by numerous lines in saltire. Wharton.

SANGUINEM EMERE (Lat.) In feudal law. A redemption by villeins, of their blood or tenure, in order to become freemen.

SANGUINIS CONJUNCTIO BENEVOLentia devincit homines et caritate. A tie of blood overcomes men through benevolence and family affection. 5 Johns. Ch. (N. Y.) 1, 13.

SANIS. A kind of punishment among the Greeks, inflicted by binding the malefactor fast to a piece of wood. Enc. Lond.

SANITARY. Pertaining to, or designed to secure, sanity or health; relating to the preservation of health. 133 Ill. 579.

SANITARY AUTHORITIES. In the English law bodies having jurisdiction over their respective districts in regard to sewerage, drainage, scavenging, the supply of water, the prevention of nuisances and offensive trades, etc., all of which come under the head of "sanitary matters" in the special sense of the words. Sanitary authorities also have jurisdiction in matters coming under the head of "local government" (*q. v.*) Public Health Act 1875, passim.

SANITY. The state of a person who has a sound understanding; the reverse of insanity (*q. v.*)

SANS CEO QUE. The same as *absque hoc* (*q. v.*)

SANS IMPEACHMENT DE WAST (Law Fr.) Without impeachment of waste. Litt. § 152. See "Absque Impetitione Vasti."

SANS JOUR (L. Fr.) Without day.

SANS NOMBRE (Fr. without number). In English law. A term used in relation to the right of putting animals on a common. The term common *sans nombre* does not mean that the beasts are to be innumerable, but only indefinite, not certain (Willes, 227); but they are limited to the commoner's own commonable cattle, *levant et couchant*, upon his lands, or as many cattle as the land of the commoner can keep and maintain in winter. 2 Brownl. 101; Ventr. 54; 5 Term R. 48; 1 Wm. Saund. 28, note 4.

SANS RECOURS (Fr. without recourse). Words which are sometimes added to an indorsement by the indorsee to avoid incurring any liability. Chit. Bills, 179; 7 Taunt. 160; 3 Cranch (U. S.) 193; 7 Cranch (U. S.) 159; 12 Mass. 172; 14 Serg. & R. (Pa.) 325. See "Without Recourse."

CANUS (Lat.) Sound. 151 Ill. 165.

SAPIENS INCIPIT A FINE; ET QUOD primum est in intentione, ultimum est in executione. A wise man begins with the last; and what is first in intention is last in execution. 10 Coke, 25.

SAPIENS OMNIA AGIT CUM CONSILIO. A wise man does everything advisedly. 4 Inst. 4.

SAPIENTIA LEGIS NUMMARIO PRETIO NON EST AESTIMANDA. The wisdom of the law cannot be valued by money. Jenk. Cent. Cas. 168.

SAPIENTIS JUDICIS EST COGITARE tantum sibi esse permissum, quantum commissum et creditum. It is the duty of a wise judge to think so much only permitted to him as is committed and intrusted to him. 4 Inst. 163.

SARCULATURA (Law Lat.) In old records. Weeding corn; a tenant's service of weeding for the lord. Cowell.

SART. In old English law. A piece of woodland, turned into arable. Cowell. See "Assart."

SARUM (Law Lat.) In old records. The city of Salisbury in England. Spelman.

SASINE. In Scotch law. The symbolical delivery of land, answering to the livery of seisin of the old English law. 4 Kent, Comm. 459.

SASSONS. The corruption of Saxons. A name of contempt formerly given to the English, while they affected to be called "Angles." They are still so called by the Welsh. Apparently this corresponds to the Scotch and Irish rendering of "Saxon" by the word "Sassenach."

SATISDARE. In the civil law, to guaranty the obligation of a principal.

SATISDATIO (Lat. *satis*, and *dare*). In civil law. Security given by a party to an action to pay what might be adjudged against him. It is a satisfactory security, in opposition to a naked security or promise. Vicat; 3 Bl. Comm. 291.

SATISFACTION (Lat. *satis*, enough, *facio*, to do, to make). In practice. An entry made on the record, by which a party in whose favor a judgment was rendered declares that he has been satisfied and paid.

SATISFACTION PIECE. In English practice. An instrument of writing in which it is declared that satisfaction is acknowledged between the plaintiff and defendant. It is signed by the attorney, and on its production and the warrant of attorney to the clerk of the judgments, satisfaction is entered on payment of certain fees.

SATISFACTORY EVIDENCE. That which is sufficient to induce a belief that the thing is true; in other words, it is credible evidence. 3 Bouv. Inst. note 3049.

SATISFIED OUTSTANDING TERM. Where a long term had been created in trustees to raise money for a purpose, and the money had been paid, but the trustees had not released to the freeholder, and the lease had not provided for its own extinguishment on the purpose becoming satisfied, the estate so remaining in the trustees was called a "satisfied outstanding term." It came to be a mode of protecting the rightful owner of the freehold, but the estate was abolished by 8 & 9 Vict. c. 112, § 2, and it never existed in the United States. 1 Washb. Real Prop. *311.

SATIUS EST PETERE FONTES QUAM sectari rivulos. It is better to seek the fountain than to follow rivulets. 10 Coke, 118. It is better to drink at the fountain than to sip in the streams.

SATURDAY'S STOP. A space of time from evensong on Saturday till sun rising on Monday, in which it was not lawful to take salmon in Scotland and the northern parts of England. Cowell.

SAUNKEFIN (Law Fr.) End of blood; failure of the direct line in successions. Spelman; Cowell.

SAUVAGINE (Law Fr.) Wild animals. *De pessons et de autre sauvagine.* Britt. c. 33, fol. 85.

The wild disposition of an animal (*fera natura*). *Mes si ele eschape et repreigne la sauvagine en son natural estate,* but if it escape, and resume its wildness, in its natural estate. Id.

SAUVEMENT (Law Fr.) Safely. *Sauvement gardes,* safely kept. Britt. c. 87.

SAVANT. (L. Fr.) Saving; knowing. Kelham.

SAVER-DE-FAULT. To excuse. Termes de la Ley.

SAVING THE STATUTE OF LIMITATIONS. A creditor is said to "save the statute of limitations" when he saves or preserves his debt from being barred by the operation of the statute. Holthouse. Thus, in the case of a simple contract debt, if a creditor commence an action for its recovery within six years from the time when the cause of action accrued, he will be in time to save the statute.

SAVINGS BANKS. In American law. Institutions for the safe custody and increase of the savings of the industrious poor, and persons of small means. They are banks to receive deposits of money, however small, which is to accumulate at interest, and to be paid out to the depositors as required.

Any institution in the nature of a bank formed for the purpose of receiving deposits of money for the benefit of the persons depositing; to accumulate the produce of so much thereof as shall not be required by the depositors, their executors or administrators, at compound interest, and to return the whole, or any part of such deposit, and the produce thereof, to the depositors, or their personal representatives, deducting out of such produce so much as shall be required for the necessary expenses attending the management of such institution, but deriving no power whatsoever from any such deposit or the produce thereof. 2 Bradwell (Ill.) 274.

SAVOUR. To partake of the nature of; to bear affinity to.

SAVOY. One of the old privileged places, or sanctuaries. 4 Steph. Comm. (7th Ed.) 227, note.

SAXON LAGE. The law of the West Saxons.

SC., or SCIL. An abbreviation for "*scilicet*," that is to say.

SCABINI. In old European law. The judges or assessors of the judges in the court held by the count. Assistants or associates of the count; officers under the count. The permanent selected judges of the Franks. Judges among the Germans, Franks, and Lombards, who were held in peculiar esteem. Spelman.

SCACCARIUM. A chequered cloth, resembling a chess board, which covered the table in the exchequer, and on which, when certain of the king's accounts were made up, the sums were marked and scored with counters. Hence the court of exchequer, or *curia scaccarii*, derived its name. 3 Bl. Comm. 44.

SCALAM. The old way of paying money into the exchequer. Cowell.

SCALE. In early American law. To adjust, graduate or value according to a scale. "The court scaled the debt." Marshall, arg. Wash. (Va.) 5, 6. A term used after the establishment of American independence, to signify a process of adjusting the difference in value between paper money and specie, rendered necessary by the great depreciation of the former. The act of assembly of Virginia of February 10, 1781, establishing a scale of depreciation, and declaring that outstanding current money contracts should be regulated by such scale, as at the date of such contracts, is called "An act for scaling paper money contracts." 2 Wash. (Va.) [41] 52; Id. [98, 99] 127; Id. [103, 104] 132, 134.

SCALPER, or SCALPING. See "Gambling Contract."

SCAMNUM (or SCANNUM) CADUCUM (Law Lat.) In old records. The cucking stool, or ducking stool. Cowell.

SCANDAL. A scandalous verbal report or rumor respecting some person.

SCANDALOUS MATTER. In equity pleading. Unnecessary matter criminatory of the defendant or any other person, alleged in the bill answer, or other pleading, or in the interrogatories to or answers by witnesses. Adams, Eq. 306. Matter which is relevant can never be scandalous (Story, Eq. Pl. § 270, 15 Ves. 477); and the degree of relevancy is of no account in determining the question (Cooper, Eq. Pl. 19; 2 Ves. Jr. 24; 6 Ves. 514; 11 Ves. 256; 15 Ves. 477). Where scandal is alleged, whether in the bill (2 Ves. Jr. 631), answer (Mitf. Eq. Pl. [Jeremy Ed.] 313), or interrogatories to or answers of witnesses (2 Younge & C. 445), it will be referred to a master at any time (2 Ves. Jr. 631), and, by leave of court, even upon the application of a stranger to the suit (6 Ves. 514; 5 Beav. Rolls, 82), and matter found to be scandalous by him will be expunged (Story, Eq. Pl. §§ 266, 862; 4 Hen. & M. [Va.] 414), at the cost of counsel introducing it, in some cases (Story, Eq. Pl. § 266). The presence of scandalous matter in the bill is no excuse for its being in the answer. 19 Me. 214.

SCANDALUM MAGNATUM (Law Lat. slander of great men). In old English law. Words spoken in derogation of a peer, a judge, or other great officer of the realm. 1 Vent. 60. This was distinct from mere slander in the earlier law, and was considered a more heinous offense. Buller, N. P. 4. See 3 Bl. Comm. 124; 64 Ill. 296. The doctrine never prevailed in the United States (151 Mass. 50), and is said to be obsolete in England (Odgers, Lib. & Sland. 136).

SCAPELLARE (Law Lat.) In old European law. To chop; to chip or haggle. Spelman.

SCAPHA (Lat.) In the Roman law. A boat; a lighter. Dig. 14. 2. 4, pr. A ship's boat. Id. 6. 1. 3. 1; Id. 21. 2. 44; Loce. de. Jur. Mar. lib. 1, c. 2, § 6.

SCARA (Law Lat.) In old European law. A troop (*turma*); a division of an army. A phalanx (*cuneus*). Spelman.

SCAVAGE, SCHEVAGE, SCHEWAGE, or shewage. A kind of toll or custom, exacted by mayors, sheriffs, etc., of merchant strangers, for wares showed or offered for sale within their liberties. Prohibited by 19 Hen. VII. c. 7. Cowell.

SCAVAIDUS. The officer who collected the scavage money. Cowell.

SCAVER, *Scavoir*. L. Fr. to know; knows. Kelham.

SCEATTA, or SCAETTA (Saxon). A Saxon coin of less denomination than a shilling. Spelman.

SCHAN PENNY, SCHARN PENNY, or schorn penny. A small duty or compensation. Cowell.

SCHEDULE. In practice. When an indictment is returned from an inferior court in obedience to a writ of *certiorari*, the statement of the previous proceedings sent with it is termed the "schedule." 1 Saund. 309a, note 2.

Schedules are also frequently annexed to answers in a court of equity, and to depositions and other documents, in order to show more in detail the matter they contain than could otherwise be conveniently shown.

The term is frequently used instead of "Inventory."

SCHEME. In English law, a scheme is a document containing provisions for regulating the management or distribution of property, or for making an arrangement between persons having conflicting rights. Thus, in the practice of the chancery division, where the execution of a charitable trust in the manner directed by the founder is difficult or impracticable, or requires supervision, a scheme for the management of the charity will be settled by the court. Tud. Char. Trusts, 257; Hunt, Eq. 248; Daniel, Ch. Prac. 1765.

SCHETES. Usury. Cowell.

SCHIREMAN. A sheriff; the ancient name for an earl.

SCHIRRENS GELD. A tax paid to sheriffs for keeping the shire or county court. Cowell.

SCHISM BILL. The name of an act passed in the reign of Queen Anne, which restrained Protestant dissenters from educating their own children, and forbade all tutors and schoolmasters to be present at any conventicle or dissenting place of worship. The queen died on the day when this act was to have taken effect (August 1, 1714), and it was repealed in the fifth year of Geo. I. Wharton.

SCIENCE. Science signifies knowledge, the knowledge of many. It springs from the recognition of the existence of general truths or laws, to which the relation of things and their operation upon each other conform. These laws or truths ascertained by the investigation of men devoted to particular departments of inquiry, methodically digested and arranged so as to be attainable, constitute science. 3 Bosworth (N. Y.) 13. It is not synonymous with "art". Eg., Rifle shooting, though it may be an art, is not a science. Fletcher Encyclopedia Corporations 241.

SCIENDUM (Lat.) In English law. The name given to a clause inserted in the record, by which it is made "known that the justice here in court, in this same term, delivered a writ thereupon to the deputy sheriff of the county aforesaid, to be executed in due form of law." Lee, Dict. "Record."

SCIENDUM EST (Lat. it is to be known, or understood). A phrase frequently used in the civil law, in the commencement of paragraphs or other divisions of a subject, as preliminary to some explanation, or as calling attention to some particular rule. *Sciendum itaque est, omnia fidei commissa primis temporibus infirma fuisse,* it is to be known, then, that all trusts were, in their origin, weak. Inst. 2. 23. 1.

SCIENTER (Lat. knowingly). The allegation of knowledge on the part of a defendant or person accused, which is necessary to charge upon him the consequences of the crime or tort.

A man may do many acts which are justifiable or not, as he is ignorant or not ignorant of certain facts. He may pass a counterfeit coin, when he is ignorant of its being counterfeit, and is guilty of no offense; but if he knew the coin to be counterfeit, which is called the *scienter,* he is guilty of passing counterfeit money.

SCIENTIA SCIOLORUM EST MIXTA IGnorantia. The knowledge of smatterers is mixed ignorance. 8 Coke, 159.

SCIENTIA UTRIUSQUE PAR PARES contrahentes facit. Equal knowledge on both sides makes the contracting parties equal. 3 Burrows, 1910.

SCIENTII ET VOLUNTI NON FIT INJUria. A wrong is not done to one who knows and wills it.

SCI. FA. An abbreviation of *scire facias.* (*q. v.*)

SCILICET (Lat. *scire,* to know, *licet,* it is permitted; you may know; translated by "to wit," in its old sense of "to know"). That is to say; to wit; namely. It is often abbreviated *"sc."* or *"scil."*

It is a clause to usher in the sentence of another, to particularize that which was too general before, distribute what was too gross, or to explain what was doubtful and obscure. It neither increases nor diminishes the premises or *habendum,* for it gives nothing of itself. It may make a restriction when the preceding words may be restrained. Hob. 171; 1 P. Wms. 18; Co. Litt. 180b, note 1.

When the *scilicet* is repugnant to the precedent matter, it is void; for example, when a declaration in trover states that the plaintiff on the third day of May was possessed of certain goods which, on the fourth day of May, came to the defendant's hands, who afterwards, to wit, on the first day of May, converted them, the *scilicet* was rejected as surplusage. Cro. Jac. 428. And see 6 Bin. (Pa.) 15; 3 Saund. 291, note 1.

Stating material and traversable matter under a *scilicet* will not avoid the consequences of a variance (1 McClel. & Y. 277; 4 Taunt. 321; 6 Term R. 462; 2 Bos. & P. 170, note 2; 1 Cow. [N. Y.] 676; 4 Johns. [N. Y.] 450; 2 Pick. [Mass.] 223); nor will the mere omission of a *scilicet* render immaterial matter material (2 Saund. 206a; 3 Term R. 68; 1 Chit. Pl. 276, even in a criminal proceeding (2 Campb. 307, note). See 3 Term R. 68; 3 Maule & S. 173.

SCINTILLA (Lat.) A spark; a remaining particle; the least particle. "A *scintilla* of equity." Henley, Lord Keeper, 1 W. Bl. 180. "There is not a *scintilla* of intention, upon the face of the will, to show the contrary." Lord Ellenborough, 11 East, 322. "Not a *scintilla* of benefit." Id.; 1 Maule & S. 509. See 6 Maule & S. 180.

SCINTILLA JURIS (Lat. a spark of law or right). A legal fiction resorted to for the purpose of enabling feoffees to uses to support contingent uses when they come into existence, thereby to enable the statute of uses (27 Hen. VIII.) to execute them. For example, a shifting use; a grant to A. and his heirs to the use of B. and his heirs, until C. perform an act, and then to the use of C. and his heirs. Here the statute executes the use in B., which, being coextensive with A.'s seisin, leaves no actual seisin in A. When, however, C. performs the act, B.'s use ceases, and C.'s springs up, and he enjoys the fee simple; upon which the question arises, out of what seisin C.'s use is served. It is said to be served out of A.'s original seisin; for upon the cessor of B.'s use it is contended that the original seisin reverted to A., for the purpose of serving C.'s use, and is a possibility of seisin, or *scintilla juris*. See 4 Kent, Comm. 238 et seq., and the authorities there cited, for the learning upon this subject; Burton, Real Prop. 48, 49; Wilson, Springing Uses, 59, 60; Washb. Real Prop.

SCINTILLA OF EVIDENCE. Any material evidence which, taken as true, would tend to establish the issue in the mind of a juror. It has been stated that to warrant the submission of a case to the jury "a mere scintilla of evidence is sufficient." The propriety of this test has been emphatically denied. Wigni. Ev. § 2494.

SCIRE DEBES CUM QUO CONTRAHIS. You ought to know with whom you deal. 11 Mees. & W. 405, 632; 13 Mees. & W. 171.

SCIRE FACIAS (Lat. that you make known). The name of a writ (and of the whole proceeding) founded on some public record.

Its principal use was to revive a judgment on which execution had not issued for a year and a day (see "Revival"), or to enforce some obligation of record, as a recognizance on appeal (24 Pa. St. 69).

Scire facias is also used by government as a mode to ascertain and enforce the forfeiture of a corporate charter, where there is a legal existing body capable of acting, but who have abused their power. It cannot, like *quo warranto* (which is applicable to all cases of forfeiture), be applied where there is a body corporate *de facto* only, who take upon themselves to act, but cannot legally exercise their powers. In *scire facias* to forfeit a corporate charter, the government must be a party to the suit; for the judgment is that the parties be ousted, and the franchises be seized into the hands of the government. 2 Kent, Comm. 313; 10 Barn. & C. 240; Yelv. 190; 5 Mass. 230; 16 Serg. & R. (Pa.) 140; 4 Gill & J. (Md.) 1; 9 Gill & J. (Md.) 365; 4 Gill (Md.) 404.

Scire facias is also used to suggest further breaches on a bond with a condition, where a judgment has been obtained for some, but not all, of the breaches, and to recover further installments where a judgment has been obtained for the penalty before all the installments are due. 1 Wm. Saund. 58, note 1; 4 Md. 375.

As to the effects of the judgment, and the principle of forfeiture, see "Quo Warranto."

The pleadings in *scire facias* are peculiar. The writ recites the judgment or other record, and also the suggestions which the plaintiff must make to the court to entitle him to the proceeding by *scire facias*. The writ, therefore, presents the plaintiff's whole case, and constitutes the declaration, to which the defendant must plead. 1 Blackf. (Ind.) 297. And when the proceeding is used to forfeit a corporate charter, all the causes of forfeiture must be assigned in distinct breaches in the writ. And the defendant must either disclaim the charter, or deny its existence, or deny the facts alleged as breaches, or demur to them. The suggestions in the writ disclosing the foundation of the plaintiff's case must also be traversed if they are to be avoided. The *scire facias* is founded partly upon them and partly upon the record. 2 Inst. 470, 679. They are substantive facts, and can be traversed by distinct pleas embracing them alone, just as any other fundamental allegation can be traversed alone. All the pleadings after the writ or declaration are in the ordinary forms. There are no pleadings in *scire facias* to forfeit a corporate charter to be found in the books, as the proceeding has been seldom used. There is a case in 1 P. Wms. 207, but no pleadings. There is a case also in 9 Gill (Md.) 379, with a synopsis of the pleadings. Perhaps the only other case is in Vermont, and it is without pleadings. A defendant cannot plead more than one plea to a *scire facias* to forfeit a corporate charter. St. 4 & 5 Anne, c. 16, and St. 9 Anne, c. 20, allowing double pleas, do not extend to the crown. 1 Chit. Pl. 479; 1 P. Wms. 220.

There are various special forms of the writ designated in accordance with the purpose for or the record on which it is brought. The principal are:

Scire facias sur mortgage, being a writ of *scire facias* issued upon the default of a mortgagor, requiring him to show cause why the mortgage should not be foreclosed.

Scire facias ad disprobandum debitum, being a writ in use in Pennsylvania, which lies by a defendant in foreign attachment against the plaintiff, in order to enable him, within a year and a day next ensuing the time of payment to the plaintiff in the attachment, to disprove or avoid the debt recovered against him. Act relating to the commencement of actions (section 61), passed June 13, 1836.

Scire facias ad audiendum errores, being a writ which is sued out after the plaintiff in error has assigned his errors. Fitzh. Nat. Brev. 20; Bac. Abr. "Error" (F).

Scire facias ad rehabendam terram, being a writ which lay for an execution debtor to recover back his land taken on execution after he has satisfied the debt. Fost. Scire Facias, 58.

SCIRE FECI (Lat. I have made known). In practice. The return of the sheriff, or other proper officer, to the writ of *scire facias*, when it has been served.

SCIRE FIERI INQUIRY. In English law. The name of a writ formerly used to recover the amount of a judgment from an executor.

The history of the origin of the writ is as follows: When, on an execution *de bonis testatoris* against an executor, the sheriff returned *nulla bona* and also a *devastavit*, a *fieri facias, de bonis propriis*, might formerly have been issued against the executor, without a previous inquisition finding a *devastavit* and a *scire facias*. But the most usual practice upon the sheriff's return of *nulla bona* to a *fieri facias de bonis testatoris* was to sue out a special writ of *fieri facias de bonis testatoris*, with a clause in it, *et si tibi constare, poterit*, that the executor had wasted the goods, then to levy *de bonis propriis*. This was the practice in the king's bench till the time of Charles I.

In the common pleas, a practice had prevailed in early times upon a suggestion in the special writ of *fieri facias* of a *devastavit* by the executor, to direct the sheriff to inquire by a jury whether the executor had wasted the goods, and if the jury found he had, then a *scire facias* was issued out against him, and, unless he made a good defense thereto, an execution *de bonis propriis* was awarded against him.

The practice of the two courts being different, several cases were brought into the king's bench on error, and at last it became the practice of both courts, for the sake of expedition, to incorporate the *fieri facias* inquiry and *scire facias* into one writ, thence called a "*scire fieri* inquiry,"—a name compounded of the first words of the two writs of *scire facias* and *fieri facias*, and that of inquiry, of which it consists.

This writ recites the *fieri facias de bonis testatoris* sued out on the judgment against the executor, the return of *nulla bona* by the sheriff, and then, suggesting that the executor had sold and converted the goods of the testator to the value of the debt and damages recovered, commands the sheriff to levy the said debt and damages of the goods of the testator in the hands of the executor, if they could be levied thereof; but if it should appear to him by the inquisition of a jury that the executor had wasted the goods of the testator, then the sheriff is to warn the executor to appear, etc. If the judgment had been either by or against the testator or intestate, or both, the writ of *fieri facias* recites that fact, and also that the court had adjudged, upon a *scire facias* to revive the judgment, that the executor or administrator should have execution for the debt, etc. Clift, Entr. 659; Lilly, Entr. 664.

Although this practice is sometimes adopted, yet the most usual proceeding is by action of debt on the judgment, suggesting a *devastavit*, because in the proceeding by *scire fieri* inquiry the plaintiff is not entitled to costs unless the executor appears and pleads to the *scire facias*. 1 Saund. 219, note 8. See 2 Archb. Prac. 934.

SCIRE LEGES, NON HOC EST VERBA earum tenere, sed vim et potestatem. To know the laws is not to observe their mere words, but their force and power. Dig. 1. 3. 17.

SCIRE PROPRIE EST, REM RATIONE et per causam cognoscere. To know properly is to know a thing by its cause and in its reason. Co. Litt. 183.

SCITE. The setting or standing of any place; the seat or situation of a capital messuage, or the ground on which it stood. Jacob.

SCOLD. A woman who, by her habit of scolding, becomes a nuisance to the neighborhood, is called a "common scold." See "Common Scold."

SCOLDING. Scolding is mere clamor, railing, personal reproof. 137 Wis. 506, 517.

SCOT (Law Lat. *scottum, scottus, scotta;* from Saxon *sceat*, a part or portion). In old English law. A tax, or tribute; one's share of a contribution. Or rather, a contribution of several.

Camden, following Matthew of Westminster, defines this word to mean, "that which is gathered together into one heap, from several things" (*illud quod ex diversis rebus in unum acervum aggregatur*). Cowell. Spelman observes that it properly signifies what the authors of the middle ages called *conjectus* (a throwing together), because it was thrown together by several into one (from Saxon *sceote*, to throw or cast, whence *sceotan*, to shoot). It is found associated with the word "lot," in the laws of William the Conqueror, and other early records; scot and lot (or, in the Saxon form, *an hlot & an scote*), signifying a customary contribution laid upon all subjects, according to their ability. Cowell; Spelman, voc. "Scot," "Lot."

SCOT AND LOT. In English law. The name of a customary contribution laid upon all the subjects according to their ability.

SCOTALE. An extortion by officers of the forests who kept ale houses, and compelled people to drink there under fear of their displeasure. Charta de Foresta, c. 7; Manw. For. Laws, pt. 1, 216.

SCOTCH PEERS. Peers of the kingdom of Scotland. Of these sixteen are elected by the rest, and represent the whole body. They are elected for one parliament only. See 6 Anne, c. 23, amended by 10 & 11 Vict. c. 52, 14 & 15 Vict. c. 87, and 15 & 16 Vict. c. 35.

SCOTS. Assessments by commissioners of sewers.

SCOTTARE. To pay scot, tax, or customary dues. Cowell.

SCRAWL. A mark which is to supply the place of a seal. 2 Pars. Cont. 100. See "Scroll."

SCRIBA (Lat. from *scribere,* to write). A scribe; a secretary. *Scriba regis,* a king's secretary; a chancellor. Spelman.

SCRIBERE EST AGERE. To write is to act. 2 Rolle, 89; 4 Bl. Comm. 80.

SCRIP. A certificate or schedule. Evidence of the right to obtain shares in a public company; sometimes called "scrip certificate," to distinguish it from the real title to shares. Wharton; 15 Ark. 12. The possession of such scrip is *prima facie* evidence of ownership of the shares therein designated. Add. Cont. 203*. It is not goods, wares, or merchandise, within the statute of frauds. 16 Mees. & W. 66.

SCRIPT. The original or principal instrument, where there are part and counterpart.

SCRIPTAE OBLIGATIONES SCRIPTIS tolluntur, et nudi consensus obligatio, contrario consensu dissolvitur. Written obligations are dissolved by writing, and obligations of naked agreement by naked agreement to the contrary.

SCRIPTORIUM (Law Lat. from *scribere,* to write). In old records. A place in monasteries, where writing was done. Spelman.

SCRIPTUM (Lat. from *scribere,* to write). In old conveyancing. A writing; a thing written. Fleta, lib. 2, c. 60, § 25. This word, alone, does not import or signify a deed, that is, an instrument under seal. 2 Strange, 814.

Scriptum indentatum, a writing indented; an indenture or deed. Reynolds, J., 2 Strange, 815.

Scriptum obligatorium, a writing obligatory. The technical name of a bond in old pleadings. T. Raym. 393. Any writing under seal. Id.

SCRIPTUM INDENTATUM (Law Lat.) A writing indented; an indenture or deed.

SCRIPTURA (Lat. from *scribere,* to write). In old English law. The act or fact of writing. Fleta, lib. 2, c. 60, § 25.

SCRIVENER. A person whose business it is to write deeds and other instruments for others; a conveyancer.

Money scriveners are those who are engaged in procuring money to be lent on mortgages and other securities, and lending such money accordingly. They act, also, as agents for the purchase and sale of real estates.

To be considered a money scrivener, a person must be concerned in carrying on the trade or profession as a means of making a livelihood. He must, in the course of his occupation, receive other men's moneys into his trust and custody, to lay out for them as occasion offers. 3 Campb. 538; 2 Esp. Cas. 555.

SCROLL. A printed or written mark intended to supply the place of a seal. See "Seal."

SCRUET ROLL (called, also, *scruet finium,* or simply *scruet*). In old English law. A record of the bail accepted in cases of *habeas corpus.* The award was set down in the remembrance roll, together with the cause of commitment, the writ and return were put on file, the bail was recorded in the *scruet.* 3 How. St. Tr. 134, 135, arg. For remembrance roll, see Reg. Michael. 1654, § 15.

SCRUTATOR (Lat. from *scrutari,* to search). In old English law. A bailiff whom the king of England appointed in places that were his in franchise or interest, whose duty was to look after the king's water rights; as flotsam, jetsam, wreck, etc. 1 Harg. Tr. p. 23; Pat. 27 Hen. VI. parte 2, m. 20; Pat. 8 Ed. IV. parte 1, m. 22.

SCUTAGE (from Lat. *scutum,* a shield). Knight service. Litt. § 99. The tax which those who, holding by knight service, did not accompany the king, had to pay on its being assessed by parliament. Escuage certain was a species of socage where the compensation for service was fixed. Litt. §§ 97, 98; Reg. Orig. 88; Wright, Ten. 121-134.

SCUTAGIO HABENDO. See "De Scutagio Habendo."

SCYRA (Law Lat.) In old English law. Shire; county; the inhabitants of a county. Writ cited, Hale, Hist. Com. Law, 119.

A fine imposed upon such as neglected to attend the *scyre gemote* courts, which all tenants were bound to do.

SCYRE GEMOTE. The name of a court among the Saxons. It was the court of the shire, in Latin called *curia comitatus,* and the principal court among the Saxons. It was holden twice a year for determining all causes, both ecclesiastical and secular.

SE DEFENDENDO (Lat.) Defending himself.

Homicide *se defendendo* may be justifiable. See "Self-Defense."

SEA. The ocean; the great mass of water which surrounds the land, and which extends from pole to pole, covering nearly three-quarters of the globe. Waters within the ebb and flow of the tide are to be considered the sea. Gilp. Dist. Ct. 526.

A large body of salt water communicating with the ocean is also called a sea; as, the Mediterranean sea, etc.

Very large inland bodies of salt water are also called seas; as, the Caspian sea, etc.

The open sea is public and common property, and any nation or person has ordinarily an equal right to navigate it or to fish therein (1 Kent, Comm. 27; Angell, Tide Waters, 44-49; 1 Bouv. Inst. 170, 174), and to land upon the seashore (1 Bouv. Inst. 173, 174); but it is generally conceded that every nation has jurisdiction to the distance of a cannon shot, or marine league, over the waters adjacent to its shore (2 Cranch [U. S.] 187, 234; Bynkershoek, Qu. Pub. Jur. 61; Vattel, 207).

SEA BATTERIES. Assaults by masters in the merchant service upon seamen at sea.

SEA LAWS. Maritime laws, as those of Oleron, Wisbuy, and the Hanse Towns.

SEA LETTER, or SEA BRIEF. In maritime law. A document which should be found on board of every neutral ship. It specifies the nature and quantity of the cargo, the place from whence it comes, and its destination. Chit. Law Nat. 197; 1 Johns. (N. Y.) 192.

SEA REEVE. An officer in maritime towns and places, who takes care of the maritime rights of the lord of the manor, watches the shore, and collects the wreck.

SEAL. Anciently, wax with an impression. *Sigillum est cera impressa quia cera sine impressione non est sigillum.* 3 Inst. 169; 21 Pick. (Mass.) 417; 2 Caines (N. Y.) 362.

In more modern law, wax, wafer, or any tenacious substance upon which an impression may be made. 5 Cush. (Mass.) 359; 5 Johns. (N. Y.) 239.

In many of the states, a scroll made with a pen or printed (4 Ill. 12), such as the letters "L. S.") (5 Wis. 549), or the word "Seal" (28 Grat. [Va.] 627), is held sufficient, and in some states this holding is independent of statute (4 Ark. 195; 5 Cal. 315). See "L. S."

SEAL OF THE UNITED STATES. The seal used by the United States in congress assembled shall be the seal of the United States, viz.:

Arms: Paleways of thirteen pieces, argent and gules; a chief azure; the escutcheon on the breast of the American eagle displayed proper, holding in his dexter talon an olive branch, and in his sinister a bundle of thirteen arrows, all proper, and in his beak a scroll, inscribed with this motto, "*E Pluribus unum.*"

For the Crest: Over the head of the eagle which appears above the escutcheon, a glory, or breaking through a cloud proper, and surrounding thirteen stars, forming a constellation argent on an azure field.

Reverse: A pyramid unfinished. In the zenith, an eye in a triangle, surrounded with a glory proper. Over the eye, these words, "*Annuit coeptis.*" On the base of the pyramid, the numerical letters MDCCLXXVI, and underneath, the following motto, "*Novus ordo seclorum.*" Resolution of Congress, June 20, 1782; Gordon, Dig. art. 207.

SEAL OFFICE. In English practice. The office at which certain judicial writs are sealed with the prerogative seal, and without which they are of no authority. The officer whose duty it is to seal such writs is called "sealer of writs."

SEAL PAPER. A document issued by the lord chancellor, previously to the commencement of the sittings, detailing the business to be done for each day in his court, and in the courts of the lords justices and vice chancellors. The master of the rolls in like manner issued a seal paper in respect of the business to be heard before him. Smith, Ch. Prac. 9.

SEALS. In Louisiana. A method of taking the effects of a deceased person into public custody.

On the death of a person, according to the laws of Louisiana, if the heir wishes to obtain the benefit of inventory and the delays for deliberating, he is bound, as soon as he knows of the death of the deceased to whose succession he is called, and before committing any act of heirship, to cause the seals to be affixed on the effects of the succession by any judge or justice of the peace. Civ. Code La. art. 1027.

In ten days after this affixing of the seals, the heir is bound to present a petition to the judge of the place in which the succession is opened, praying for the removal of the seals, and that a true and faithful inventory of the effects of the succession be made. Civ. Code La. art. 1028.

In case of vacant estates, and estates of which the heirs are absent and not represented, the seals, after the decease, must be affixed by a judge or justice of the peace within the limits of his jurisdiction, and may be fixed by him either *ex officio* or at the request of the parties. Civ. Code La. art. 1070. The seals are affixed at the request of the parties when a widow, a testamentary executor, or any other person who pretends to have an interest in a succession or community of property, requires it. Id. art. 1071. They are affixed *ex officio* when the presumptive heirs of the deceased do not all reside in the place where he died, or if any of them happen to be absent. Id. art. 1072.

The object of placing the seals on the effects of a succession is for the purpose of preserving them, and for the interest of third persons. Code Civ. La. art. 1068.

The seals must be placed on the bureaus, coffers, armoires, and other things which contain the effects and papers of the deceased, and on the doors of the apartments which contain these things, so that they cannot be opened without tearing off, breaking, or altering the seals. Code Civ. La. art. 1069.

The judge or justice of the peace who affixes the seals is bound to appoint a guardian, at the expense of the succession, to take care of the seals and of the effects, of which an account is taken at the end of the *proces verbal* of the affixing of the seals. The guardian must be domiciliated in the place where the inventory is taken. Code Civ. La. art. 1079. And the judge, when he retires, must take with him the keys of all things and apartments upon which the seals have been affixed. Id.

The raising of the seals is done by the judge of the place, or justice of the peace appointed by him to that effect, in the presence of the witnesses of the vicinage, in the same manner as for the affixing of the seals. Code Civ. La. art. 1084.

SEALED AND DELIVERED. In conveyancing. The common formula of attestation of deeds and other instruments, written immediately over the witnesses' names. This has been retained without change from the old practice, when sealing alone, without signing, constituted a sufficient execution or authentication. 2 Bl. Comm. 306. See 15 Ohio, 107.

In England, it has been held that the words "sealed and delivered," in an attestation, does not import signing. 5 Maule & S. 581; 3 Maule & S. 512; 4 Taunt. 213. But the contrary has recently been held in the supreme court of the United States. 8 How. (U. S.) 10, citing 6 Man. & G. 386.

SEALED INSTRUMENT. A writing, the maker of which has affixed his seal, or that which is the legal equivalent of a seal, in addition to his signature. Formerly the seal alone was sufficient if it identified the maker.

SEALING A VERDICT. In practice. The putting a verdict in writing, and placing it in an envelope, which is sealed. To relieve jurors after they have agreed, it is not unusual for the counsel to agree that the jury shall seal their verdict and then separate. When the court is again in session, the jury come in and give their verdict in all respects as if it had not been sealed; and a juror may dissent from it if since the sealing he has honestly changed his mind. 8 Ohio, 405; 1 Gilm. 333; 3 Bouv. Inst. note 3257.

SEAMAN. A sailor; a mariner; one whose business is navigation. 2 Boul. P. Dr. Com. 232; Code de Commerce, art. 262; Laws of Oleron, art. 7; Laws of Wisbuy, art. 19.

In a statute, it has been held to include persons engaged in fresh-water navigation. 2 Pet. Adm. (U. S.) 268.

The term "seamen," in its most enlarged sense, includes the captain as well as other persons of the crew; in a more confined signification, it extends only to the common sailors. 3 Pardessus, note 667. But the mate (1 Pet. Adm. [U. S.] 246), the cook and steward (2 Pet. Adm. [U. S.] 268), and engineers, clerks, carpenters, firemen, deck hands, porters, and chamber maids, on passenger steamers, when necessary for the service of the ship (1 Conkl. Adm. 107; 2 Pars. Mar. Law, 582; 1 Sumn. [U. S.] 170), are considered, as to their rights to sue in the admiralty, as common seamen; and persons employed on board of steamboats and lighters engaged in trade or commerce on tide water are within the admiralty jurisdiction; while those employed in ferryboats are not (Gilp. Dist. Ct. 203, 532). Persons who do not contribute their aid in navigating the vessel or to its preservation in the course of their occupation, as musicians, are not to be considered as seamen, with a right to sue in the admiralty for their wages. Gilp. Dist. Ct. 516. See "Lien."

SEAMANSHIP. The skill of a good seaman; an acquaintance with the art of navigating and managing a ship or other vessel.

SEARCH.

——**In Criminal Law.** An examination of a man's house, premises, or person, for the purpose of discovering stolen or contraband goods, or proof of his guilt in relation to some crime or misdemeanor of which he is accused.

The constitution of the United States (Amend. art. 4) protects the people from unreasonable searches and seizures. 3 Story, Const. § 1895; Rawle, Const. c. 10, p. 127; 10 Johns. (N. Y.) 263; 11 Johns. (N. Y.) 500; 1 U. S. St. at Large, 651; 3 Cranch (U. S.) 447.

——**In Practice.** An examination made in the proper lien office for mortgages, liens, judgments, or other incumbrances against real estate. The certificate given by the officer as to the result of such examination is also called a "search."

Conveyancers and others who cause searches to be made ought to be very careful that they should be correct with regard to the time during which the person against whom the search has been made owned the premises, to the property searched against, which ought to be properly described, and to the form of the certificate of search.

SEARCH, RIGHT OF. In international law. The right existing in a belligerent to examine and inspect the papers of a neutral vessel at sea. On the continent of Europe this is called the "right of visit." Dalloz, "Prises Maritimes," notes 104-111.

The right does not extend to examine the cargo, nor does it extend to a ship of war, it being strictly confined to the searching of merchant vessels. The exercise of the right is to prevent the commerce of contraband goods. Although frequently resisted by powerful neutral nations, yet this right appears now to be fixed beyond contravention. The penalty for violently resisting this right is the confiscation of the property so withheld from visitation. Unless in extreme cases of gross abuse of his right by a belligerent, the neutral has no right to resist a search. 1 Kent, Comm. 154; 2 Brown, Civ. & Adm. Law, 319.

The right of search—or rather of visitation—in time of peace, especially in its connection with the efforts of the British government for the suppression of the slave trade, has been the subject of much discussion (Wheaton, Right of Search; Life of General Cass [by Smith] cc. 25, 26; Webster, Works, vol. 6, 329, 335, 338), and the documents relating to this subject communicated to congress from time to time, and most of the works on international law, may be profitably examined by those who desire to trace the history and understand the merits of the questions involved in the proposed exercise of this right. See, also, Edinburgh Review, vol. 11, p. 9; Foreign Quarterly Review, vol. 35, p. 211; 3 Phillim. Int. Law, Index, tit. "Visit and Search."

SEARCH WARRANT. In practice. A warrant requiring the officer to whom it is addressed to search a house, or other place, therein specified, for stolen, contraband or illicit property therein, and, if the same shall be found upon such search, to bring the goods so found, together with the body of the person occupying the same, who is named, before the justice or other officer granting the warrant, or some other justice of the peace, or other lawfully authorized officer.

SEARCHER. In English law. An officer of the customs, whose duty it is to examine and search all ships outward bound, to ascertain whether they have any prohibited or unaccustomed goods on board.

SEASHORE. That space of land on the border of the sea which is alternately covered and left dry by the rising and falling of the tide; or, in other words, that space of land between high and low water mark. Harg. Tr. 12; 6 Mass. 435, 439; 1 Pick. (Mass.) 180, 182; 5 Day (Conn.) 22; 12 Me. 237; 2 Zab. (N. J.) 441; 27 Eng. Law & Eq. 242; 4 De Gex, M. & G. 206. See "Tide;" "Tide Water."

SEATED LANDS. In the early land legislation of some of the United States, "seated" is used, in connection with "improved," to denote lands of which actual possession was taken. 5 Pet. (U. S.) 468.

SEAWANT. In old American law. The Dutch name for *wampum*, or Indian money, which consisted of perforated beads, manufactured from the inside of shells, and strung together. O'Callaghan's N. Netherlands, i. 60, 61. Id. ii. 543.

SEAWEED. A species of grass which grows in the sea. When cast upon land, it belongs to the owner of the land adjoining the seashore, upon the grounds that it increases gradually, that it is useful as manure and a protection to the ground, and that it is some compensation for the encroachment of the sea upon the land. 2 Johns. (N. Y.) 313, 323. See 5 Vt. 223.

The French differs from our law in this respect, as seaweeds there, when cast on the beach, belong to the first occupant. Dalloz, "Propriete," art. 3, § 2, note 128.

SEAWORTHINESS. In maritime law. The sufficiency of the vessel in materials, construction, equipment, officers, men, and outfit, for the trade or service in which it is employed. 5 M. & W. 414, 9 L. J. Ex. 48.

Any sort of disrepair left in the ship, by which she or the cargo may suffer, is a breach of the warranty of seaworthiness. A deficiency of force in the crew, or of skill in the master, mate, etc., is a want of seaworthiness. 1 Campb. 1; 14 East, 481; 4 Duer (N. Y.) 234.

If the assurance attaches before the voyage commences, it is enough that the state of the ship be commensurate to the then risk; and, if the voyage be such as to require a different complement of men, or state of equipment in different parts of it, as if it were a voyage down a canal or river and thence across to the open sea, it would be enough if the vessel were, at the commencement of each stage of the navigation, properly manned and equipped for it. 5 M. & W. 414; 8 Ib. 895; 9 L. J. Ex. 48. And if there was once a sufficient crew, their temporary absence will not be considered a breach of the warranty. 2 Barn. & Ald. 73; 1 Johns. Cas. (N. Y.) 184; 1 Pet. (U. S.) 183. A vessel may be rendered not seaworthy by being overloaded. 2 Barn. & Ald. 320.

It can never be settled by positive rules of law how far this obligation of seaworthiness extends in any particular case, for the reason that improvements and changes in the means and modes of navigation frequently require new implements, or new forms of old ones; and these, though not necessary at first, become so when there is an established usage that all ships of a certain quality, or those to be sent on certain voyages, or used for certain purposes, shall have them. 2 Pars. Mar. Law, 134. Seaworthiness is, therefore, in general, a question of fact for the jury. Id.

137; 1 Pet. (U. S.) 170, 184; 1 Bouv. Inst. 441.

SEBASTOMANIA. In medical jurisprudence. Religious insanity; demonomania.

SECK. A want of remedy by distress. Litt. § 218. See "Rent." Want of present fruit or profit, as in the case of the reversion without rent or other service, except fealty. Co. Litt. 151b, note 5.

SECOND DELIVERANCE. In practice. The name of a writ given by the statute of Westminster II. (13 Edw. I. c. 2), founded on the record of a former action of replevin, 2 Inst. 341. It commands the sheriff, if the plaintiff make him secure of prosecuting his claim and returning the chattels which were adjudged to the defendant by reason of the plaintiff's default, to make deliverance. On being nonsuited, the plaintiff in replevin might, at common law, have brought another replevin, and so *ad infinitum*, to the intolerable vexation of the defendant. The statute of Westminster restrains the plaintiff, when nonsuited, from so doing, but allows him this writ, issuing out of the original record, in order to have the same distress delivered again to him, on his giving the like security as before. 3 Bl. Comm. 150; Fitzh. Nat. Brev. 68.

SECOND DISTRESS. By 17 Car. II. c. 7, § 4, in all cases where the value of the cattle distrained shall not be found to be of the full value of the arrears distrained for, the party to whom such arrears are due, his executors or administrators, may distrain again for the said arrears; but a second distress cannot, it seems, be at all justified, where there is enough which might have been taken upon the first, if the distrainer had then thought proper; for a man who has an entire duty, as rent, for example, shall not split the entire sum, and distrain for one part of it at one time, and for the other part of it at another time, and so *toties quoties* for several times, for that would be great oppression. Wharton.

SECOND-HAND EVIDENCE. Hearsay, because the facts were perceived or discovered by some other than the witness testifying or by an agency extraneous to that producing the evidence offered.

SECOND SURCHARGE, WRIT OF. The name of a writ issued in England against a commoner who has a second time surcharged the common. 3 Bl. Comm. 239.

SECONDS. Assistants at a duel. They are equally guilty with the principals under many of the statutes against duelling. See "Duelling."

SECONDARY. In English law. An officer who is second or next to the chief officer; as, secondaries to the prothonotaries of the courts of king's bench or common pleas· secondary of the remembrancer in the exchequer, etc. Jacob.

——**In Medical Practice.** Secondary is the term for a disease which is not the primary cause of death. 39 L. J. Ex. 214; L. R. 5 Ex. 302; 34 L. J. C. P. 28; 17 C. B. N. S. 122.

SECONDARY (or DERIVATIVE) CONVEYANCES. Those which presuppose some other conveyance precedent, and only serve to enlarge, confirm, alter, restrain, restore, or transfer the interest granted by such original conveyance. 2 Bl. Comm. 324*.

SECONDARY EASEMENT. A kind of appendancy or appurtenancy of one easement to or upon another easement, passing with the principal easement, as being necessary or convenient to the enjoyment of the same. 116 Ill. 20.

SECONDARY EVIDENCE. That species of proof which is admissible on the loss of primary evidence, and which becomes by that event the best evidence. 3 Bouv. Inst. note 3055. See "Evidence."

SECONDARY USE. A use limited to take effect in derogation of a preceding estate, otherwise called a "shifting use," as a conveyance to the use of A. and his heirs, with a proviso that, when B. returns from India, then to the use of C. and his heirs. 1 Steph. Comm. 546.

SECRET COMMITTEE. A secret committee of the house of commons is a committee specially appointed to investigate a certain matter, and to which secrecy being deemed necessary in furtherance of its objects, its proceedings are conducted with closed doors, to the exclusion of all persons not members of the committee. All other committees are open to members of the house, although they may not be serving upon them. Brown.

SECRET PARTNERSHIP. See "Partner."

SECRET TRUSTS. Where a testator gives property to a person, on a verbal promise by the legatee or devisee that he will hold it in trust for another person, this is called a "secret trust." The English rule is, that if the secret trust would have been valid as an express trust, it will be enforced against the legatee or devisee, while if it would have been invalid as an express trust, *e. g.*, by contravening the provisions of the mortmain act, the gift fails altogether, so that neither the devisee or legatee, nor the object of the trust, takes any benefit by it. Lewin, Trusts, 51; Watson, Comp. Eq. 54.

SECRETARY OF DECREES AND INJUNCTIONS. An officer of the English court of chancery. The office was abolished by St. 15 & 16 Vict. c. 87, § 23.

SECRETARY OF LEGATION. An officer employed to attend a foreign mission, and to perform certain duties as clerk.

His salary is fixed by the act of congress of May 1, 1810 (section 1), at such a sum as the president of the United States may allow, not exceeding two thousand dollars.

The salary of a secretary of embassy, or the secretary of a minister plenipotentiary, is the same as that of a secretary of legation.

Private secretaries of a minister must not be confounded with secretaries of embassy or of legation. Such private secretaries are entitled to protection only as belonging to the suite of the ambassador.

The functions of a secretary of legation consist in his employment by his minister for objects of ceremony; in making verbal reports to the secretary of state or other foreign ministers; in taking care of the archives of the mission; in ciphering and deciphering despatches; in sometimes making rough draughts of the notes or letters which the minister writes to his colleagues or to the local authorities; in drawing up *proces verbaux;* in presenting passports to the minister for his signature, and delivering them to the persons for whom they are intended; and, finally, in assisting the minister, under whom he is placed, in everything concerning the affairs of the mission. In the absence of the minister, he is admitted to conferences, and to present notes signed by the minister.

SECRETARY OF STATE. The word "secretary" is synonymous with the word "clerk" or "scribe," and it means a person employed to write orders, records and the like, so that the title "Secretary of State," in and of itself implies an officer who is charged with the duties of keeping the official records of the State,—not only as regards the acts and doings of the chief executive, but of the legislative branch as well. 254 Ill. 34.

SECTA (Lat. *sequor,* to follow). The persons, two or more in number, whom the plaintiff produced in court, in the ancient form of proceedings, immediately upon making his declaration, to confirm the allegations therein, before they were called in question by the defendant's plea. Bracton, 214a. The word appears to have been used as denoting that these persons followed the plaintiff into court; that is, came in a matter in which the plaintiff was the leader, or one principally concerned. The actual production of "suit" was discontinued very early (3 Bl. Comm. 295), but the formula "*et inde producit sectam*" (for which, in more modern pleadings, "and thereupon he brings suit" is substituted) continued till the abolition of the Latin form of pleadings (Steph. Pl. 429, 430). The count in dower and writs of right did not so conclude, however. 1 Chit. Pl. 399. A suit or action. Hob. 20; Bracton, 399b. A suit of clothes. Cowell; Spelman.

SECTA AD CURIAM. A writ that lay against him who refused to perform his suit either to the county court or the court baron. Cowell.

SECTA AD FURNUM. Suit due a public bake house.

SECTA AD JUSTICIAM FACIENDAM. In old English law. A service which a man is bound to perform by his fee.

SECTA AD MOLENDRINUM. A service arising from the usage, time out of mind, of carrying corn to a particular mill to be ground. 3 Bl. Comm. 235. A writ adapted to the injury lay at the old law. Fitzh. Nat. Brev. 123.

SECTA AD TORRALE. Suit due a man's kiln or malt house. 3 Bl. Comm. 235.

SECTA CURIAE. Suit at court. The service due from tenants to the lord of attending his courts baron, both to answer complaints alleged against themselves, and for the trial of their fellow tenants. 2 Bl. Comm. 54.

SECTA EST PUGNA CIVILIS; SICUT actores armantur actionibus, et quasi accinguntur gladiis, ita rei (e contra) muniuntur exceptionibus, et defenduntur quasi clypeis. A suit is a civil battle, for as the plaintiffs are armed with actions, and, as it were, girt with swords, so, on the other hand, the defendants are fortified with pleas, and defended, as it were, by helmets. Hob. 20; Bracton, 339b.

SECTA FACIENDA PER ILLAM QUAE habet eniciam partem. A writ to compel the heir, who has the elder's part of the coheirs, to perform suit and services for all the coparceners. Reg. Orig. 177.

SECTA QUAE SCRIPTO NITITUR A scripto variari non debet. A suit which relies upon a writing ought not to vary from the writing. Jenk. Cent. Cas. 65.

SECTA REGALIS. A suit so called by which all persons were bound twice in the year to attend in the sheriff's tourn, in order that they might be informed of things relating to the public peace. It was so called because the sheriff's tourn was the king's leet, and it was held in order that the people might be bound by oath to bear true allegiance to the king. Cowell.

SECTA UNICA TANTUM FACIENDA pro pluribus haereditatibus. A writ for an heir who was distrained by the lord to do more suits than one, that he should be allowed to do one suit only in respect of the land of divers heirs descended to him. Cowell.

SECTATORES. Suitors of court who, among the Saxons, gave their judgment or verdict in civil suits upon the matter of fact and law. 1 Reeve, Hist. Eng. Law, 22.

SECTION. A division of land one mile square, containing six hundred and forty acres, established by the United States government survey of the public domain. See "Range;" "Section of Land;" "Township."

SECTION OF LAND. A parcel of government land containing six hundred and forty acres. The lands of the United States are surveyed into parcels of six hundred and forty acres; each such parcel is called a "section."

These sections are divided into half-sections, each of which contains three hundred and twenty acres, and into quarter-sections of one hundred and sixty acres each. See 2 Washb. Real Prop.

SECTORES (Lat.) In Roman law. Bidders at an auction. Bab. Auct. 2.

SECUNDUM. According to.

——**Secundum Aequum et Bonum.** According to what is just and right.

——**Secundum Allegata et Probata.** According to that which is alleged and proved.

——**Secundum Consuetudinem Manerii.** According to the custom of the manor.

——**Secundum Formam Statuti.** According to the form of the charter (deed).

——**Secundum Formam Doni.** According to the form of the gift or grant. See "Formedon."

——**Secundum Formam Statuti.** According to the form of the statute.

——**Secundum Legem Communem.** According to the common law.

——**Secundum Naturam est, Commoda Cujusque rei eum Sequi, quem Sequuntur Incommoda.** It is natural that he who bears the charge of a thing should receive the profits. Dig. 50. 17. 10.

——**Secundum Normam Legis.** According to the rule of law; by the rule of law.

——**Secundum Regulam.** Accordinf to the rule; by rule.

——**Secundum Subjectam Materiam.** According to the subject matter. 1 Bl. Comm. 229. All agreements must be construed *secundum subjectam materiam,* if the matter will bear it. 2 Mod. 80, arg. Delivery must be *secundum subjectam materiam.* 2 Kent, Comm. 439.

SECURITAS.

——**In old English Law.** Security; surety.

——**In the Civil Law.** An acquittance or release. Spelman; Calv. Lex.

SECURITATEM INVENIENDI. An ancient writ, lying for the sovereign, against any of his subjects, to stay them from going out of the kingdom to foreign parts; the ground whereof is that every man is bound to serve and defend the commonwealth as the crown shall think fit. Fitzh. Nat. Brev. 115.

SECURITATIS PACIS. In old English law. Security of the peace. A writ that lay for one who was threatened with death or bodily harm by another, against him who so threatened. Reg. Orig. 88.

SECURITY. That which renders a matter sure; an instrument which renders more certain the performance of a contract. Anything that makes money more assured in its payment, or more readily recoverable, as distinguished from a mere evidence of debt.

A person who becomes the surety for another, or who engages himself for the performance of another's contract. See 3 Blackf. (Ind.) 431.

SECURITY FOR COSTS. Security given by a party to an action to pay any costs which may be adjudged against him therein.

Such security is required by statute in various cases, as on appeal, on the bringing of suit by a nonresident, etc.

SECURITY FOR GOOD BEHAVIOR. Giving surety of the peace (*q. v.*)

SECURIUS EXPEDIUNTUR NEGOTIA commissa pluribus, et plus vident oculi quam oculus. Business intrusted to several speeds best, and several eyes see more than one eye. 4 Coke, 46.

SECUS (Lat.) Otherwise.

SED NON ALLOCATUR (Lat. but it is not allowed). A phrase used in the old reports to signify that the court disagreed with the arguments of counsel. "It was argued," etc., "*sed non allocatur.*"

SED PER CURIAM (Lat. but by the court). An expression sometimes found in the reports, after the opinion of a single judge, to introduce that of the court which differs from that of the single judge.

SED VIDE (Lat.) But see.

SEDERUNT, ACTS OF. In Scotch law. Certain ancient ordinances of the court of session, conferring upon the courts power to establish general rules of practice. Bell, Dict.

SEDITION. In criminal law. The raising commotions or disturbances in the state. 195 Mich. 293. It is a revolt against legitimate authority. Ersk. Inst. 4. 4. 14; Dig. 49. 16. 3. § 19, not amounting to insurrection. Excitement of discontent against the government, or of resistance to lawful authority; conduct tending to treason, but without an overt act. 195 Mich. 293.

The distinction between "sedition" and "treason" consists in this, that though the ultimate object of sedition is a violation of the public peace, or at least such a course of measures as evidently engenders it, yet it does not aim at direct and open violence against the laws, or the subversion of the constitution. Alis. Crim. Law, 580.

The obnoxious act of July 14, 1798 (1 Story, U. S. Laws, 543), was called the "sedition law," because its professed object was to prevent disturbances.

In the Scotch law, sedition is either verbal or real. Verbal is inferred from the uttering of words tending to create discord between the king and his people; real sedition is generally committed by convocating together any considerable number of people, without lawful authority, under the pretense of redressing some public grievance, to the disturbing of the public peace. Ersk. Inst. 4. 4. 14.

SEDUCTION.

——**As a Tort.** At common law, the act of a man in inducing a woman to have unlawful sexual intercourse with him. The use of seductive arts was not essential. The woman herself had no action for damages except in case of a breach of a marriage promise, the only civil remedy being that of her parent, based on loss of services. 89 Ill. 543; 49 Mich. 540.

By statute in many states, the woman has the right to sue in her own name, but such statutes generally provide that the seduction must be under promise of marriage, or by seductive arts and devices.

——**As a Crime.** The crime is statutory, and consists generally in inducing an unmarried female of previous chaste character to submit to sexual intercourse by promise of marriage, or, in some states, by other seductive means.

"The exact amount or what kind of seductive art is necessary to establish the offense cannot be defined. Every case must stand on its own peculiar circumstances, together with the condition in life, advantages, age, and intelligence of the parties." 32 Iowa, 262. The intercourse must be accomplished by artifice and deception, and not by a yielding of the woman from mere lust. 79 Ala. 14.

Where a promise of marriage is required, it need not be valid, if it is believed by the woman to be so. 26 N. Y. 203. The woman must be induced by the promise to submit. 108 Ind. 406.

"No one can contend with any degree of plausibility that a virtuous female can be seduced without any of those arts, wiles, and blandishments so necessary to win the hearts of the weaker sex. To say that such a one was seduced by simply a blunt offer of wedlock *in futuro*, in exchange for sexual favors *in presenti* is an announcement that smacks too much of a bargain and barter, and not enough of betrayal. This is hire or salary, not seduction." 97 Mo. 668.

SEIGNIOR, or **SEIGNEUR.** Among the feudists, this name signified lord of the fee. Fitzh. Nat. Brev. 23. The most extended signification of this word includes not only a lord or per of parliament, but is applied to the owner or proprietor of a thing; hence the owner of a hawk, and the master of a fishing vessel, is called a "seigneur." 37 Edw. III. c. 19; Barr. Obs. St. 258.

SEIGNIOR IN GROSS. A lord without a manor, simply enjoying superiority and service

SEIGNIORAGE. A royalty or prerogative of the sovereign, whereby an allowance of gold and silver, brought in the mass to be exchanged for coin, is claimed.

——**In the United States.** The mint charge for coining bullion.

SEIGNIORESS. A female superior.

SEIGNIORY. In English law. The rights of a lord, as such, in lands. Swinb. Wills, 174.

SEISED IN DEMESNE AS OF FEE. The precise technical phrase to express a fee simple in possession in a corporeal hereditament, the words "in demesne" signifying that he is seised as owner of the land itself, and not merely of the seigniory or services; and the words "as of fee" importing that he is seised of an estate of inheritance in fee simple. 2 Bl. Comm. 105; Steph. Comm. 22.

SEISI. In old English law. Seised; possessed.

SEISIN. The completion of the feudal investiture, by which the tenant was admitted into the feud, and performed the rites of homage and fealty. Stearns, Real Actions, 2.

Possession with an intent on the part of him who holds it to claim a freehold interest. 8 N. H. 58; 1 Washb. Real Prop. 35; 115 Ill. 183.

Immediately upon the investiture or livery of seisin, the tenant became tenant of the freehold; and the term "seisin" originally contained the idea of possession derived from a superior lord of whom the tenant held. There could be but one seisin, and the person holding it was regarded for the time as the rightful owner. Litt. § 701; 1 Spence, Eq. Jur. 136. In the early history of the country, livery of seisin seems to have been occasionally practiced. See 1 Washb. Real Prop. 34, note; Colony Laws (Mass.) 85, 86; Smith, Landl. & Ten. (Morris Ed.) 6, note.

Seisin and ownership, as to corporeal hereditaments, in the common law sense of the term, mean practically the same thing. 115 Ill. 182.

In Connecticut, Massachusetts, Pennsylvania, and Ohio, seisin means merely "ownership," and the distinction between seisin in deed and in law is not known in practice. Walk. Am. Law, 324, 330; 4 Day (Conn.) 305; 4 Mass. 489; 14 Pick. (Mass.) 224; 6 Metc. (Mass.) 439. A patent by the commonwealth, in Kentucky, gives a right of entry, but not actual seisin. 3 Bibb (Ky.) 57.

Seisin in fact is possession with intent on the part of him who holds it to claim a freehold interest.

Seisin in law is a right of immediate possession according to the nature of the estate. Cowell; Comyn, Dig. "Seisin" (A 1, 2). See "Livery of Seisin."

SEISIN, LIVERY OF. See "Livery of Seisin."

SEISIN OX. In Scotch law. A perquisite formerly due to the sheriff when he gave possession to an heir holding crown lands. It was long since converted into a payment in money, proportioned to the value of the estate. Bell, Dict.

SEISINA (Law Lat.) Seisin.

SEISINA FACIT STIPITEM. Seisin makes the stock. 2 Bl. Comm. 209; Broom, Leg. Max. (3d London Ed.) 466; 1 Steph. Comm. 367; 4 Kent, Comm. 388, 389; 13 Ga. 238.

SEISINA HABENDA. A writ for delivery of seisin to the lord, of lands and tenements, after the sovereign, in right of his prerogative, had had the year, day, and waste on a felony committed, etc. Reg. Orig. 165.

SEIZIN. See "Seisin."

SEIZING OF HERIOTS. Taking the best beast, etc., where an heriot is due, on the death of the tenant. 2 Bl. Comm. 422.

SEIZURE. In practice. A forcible taking possession. 52 L. J. Q. B. 343; 10 Q. B. D. 432. The act of taking possession of the property of a person condemned by the judgment of a competent tribunal to pay a certain sum of money, by a sheriff, constable, or other officer lawfully authorized thereto, by virtue of an execution, for the purpose of having such property sold according to law to satisfy the judgment. The taking possession of goods for a violation of a public law; as, the taking possession of a ship for attempting an illicit trade. 2 Cranch (U. S.) 187; 4 Wheat. (U. S. 100); 1 Gall. (U. S.) 75; 2 Wash. C. C. (U. S.) 127, 567; 6 Cow. (N. Y.) 404.

SELECT. Choice; to choose; to take one thing rather than another. 61 Ill. 119. To pick out or take from among a number. There can be no selection, where there is nothing left. One may take the whole, but he cannot select the whole. 21 Ill. 104.

SELECTI JUDICES (Lat.) In Roman law. Judges who were selected very much like our juries. They were returned by the *praetor*, drawn by lot, subject to be challenged and sworn. 3 Bl. Comm. 366.

SELECTMEN. The name of certain town officers in several states of the United States, who are invested by the statutes of the states with extensive powers for the conduct of the town business.

SELF-DEFENSE. The protection by force of one's person or property from unlawful injury. The force used must be no more than is reasonably necessary to repel the threatened injury, and must be proportioned to the nature of the injury apprehended. Thus, an assault with the hand cannot be repelled by the use of a deadly weapon. 77 Ind. 274; 34 Ohio St. 98.

As a general rule, an assault threatening death or serious bodily injury, the infliction of which would amount to a felony, may be resisted to the taking of life (29 Ohio St. 186; 8 Mich. 150), but not an assault which is but a misdemeanor (2 N. Y. 193).

Unlawful injury to property may be resisted by force short of the taking of life (148 Mass. 529; 56 Vt. 703), but the taking of life in defense of property is only justifiable when it is necessary in order to prevent a felony attempted by violence or surprise, as burglary, robbery, or arson (4 Bl. Comm. 180; 25 Grat. [Va.] 887; 31 Conn. 479), but not secret felonies, such as larceny (71 Ala. 330).

SELF-DESTRUCTION. See "Suicide."

SELF-EXECUTING—CONSTITUTIONAL provisions. Constitutional provisions are self-executing when it appears they shall take immediate effect, and ancillary legislation is not necessary to the enjoyment of the right thus given, or the enforcement of the duty thus imposed; a provision complete in itself. 265 Mo. 26; 175 S. W. 940; Ann. Cas. 1916 D 6; 54 Colo. 117; 129 Pac. 198.

——**Order.** A self-executing order is one requiring no ministerial act to become effective. 164 Iowa 417.

SELF-REGARDING EVIDENCE. Evidence which either serves or disserves the party is so called. This species of evidence is either self-serving (which is not in general receivable), or self-disserving, which is invariably receivable, as being an admission against the party offering it, and that either in court or out of court. Brown.

SELION OF LAND. A ridge of ground rising between two furrows, containing no certain quantity, but sometimes more and sometimes less. Termes de la Ley.

SELLER. One who disposes of a thing in consideration of money; a vendor.

This term is more usually applied in the sale of chattels; that of "vendor" in the sale of estates. See "Sale."

SELLER THE MONTH. The term as used on the board of trade means that the seller has until the last day of the month in which to make a delivery of any grain contracted to be sold. 79 Ill. 353.

SEMAYNE'S CASE. This case decided, in 2 Jac. I., that "every man's house [meaning his dwelling-house only] is his castle," and that the defendant may not break open outer doors in general, but only inner doors, but that (after request made) he may break open even outer doors to find goods of another wrongfully in the house. Brown.

SEMBLE (Fr. it seems). A term frequently used before the statement of a point of law which has not been directly settled, but about which the court have expressed an opinion, and intimated what a decision would be.

SEMEL CIVIS SEMPER CIVIS. Once a citizen always a citizen. Tray. Lat. Max. 555.

SEMEL MALUS SEMPER PRAESUMItur esse malus in eodem genere. Whoever is once bad is presumed to be so always in the same degree. Cro. Car. 317.

SEMESTRIA. In the civil law, the collected decisions of the emperors in their councils.

SEMESTRIS, or **SEMESTRE** (Lat. from *sex*, six, and *mensis*, month). Of, or for six months. Dig. 27. 1. 41; St. Westminster II. c. 5; 2 Inst. 361.

SEMI-MATRIMONIUM (Lat.) In Roman law. Half-marriage. Concubinage was so called. Tayl. Civ. Law, 273.

SEMI-NAUFRAGIUM (Lat.) A term used by Italian lawyers, which literally signifies "half-shipwreck," and by which they understand the jetsam, or casting merchandise into the sea to prevent shipwreck. Locre, Esp. du Code de Com. art. 409. The state of a vessel which has been so much injured by tempest or accident that to repair the damages, after being brought into port, and prepare her for sea, would cost more than her worth. 4 Bost. Law Rep. 120.

SEMI-PROOF. In civil law. Presumption of fact. This degree of proof is thus defined: *"Non est ignorandum, probationem semiplenam eam esse, per quam rei gestae fides aliqua fit judici; non tamen tanta ut jure debeat in pronuncianda sententia eam sequi."* Mascardus, de Prob. vol. 1, quaest. 11, note 1, 4.

SEMPER (Lat.) Always.

SEMPER IN DUBIIS BENIGNIORA praeferunda sunt. In dubious cases, the more liberal constructions are always to be preferred. Dig. 50. 17. 56.

SEMPER IN DUBIIS ID AGENDUM EST, ut quam tutissimo loco res sit bona fide contracta, nisi quum aperte contra leges scriptum est. Always, in doubtful cases, that is to be done by which a *bona fide* contract may be in the greatest safety, except when its provisions are clearly contrary to law. Dig. 34. 5. 21.

SEMPER IN OBSCURIS QUOD MINImum est sequimur (sequere). In obscure cases we always follow that which is least. Dig. 50. 17. 9; Broom, Leg. Max. (3d London Ed.) 613, note; 3 C. B. 962.

SEMPER IN STIPULATIONIBUS ET IN caeteris contractibus id sequimur quod actum est. In stipulations and other contracts we always follow that which was done (*i. e.*, agreed). Dig. 50. 17. 34.

SEMPER ITA FIAT RELATIO UT VAleat dispositio. Let the reference always be so made that the disposition may avail. 6 Coke, 76.

SEMPER NECESSITAS PROBANDI INcumbit ei qui agit. The claimant is always bound to prove; the burden of proof lies on him.

SEMPER PARATUS (Lat. always ready). In pleading. The name of a plea by which the defendant alleges that he has always been ready to perform what is demanded of him. 3 Bl. Comm. 303. The same as *tout temps prist.*

SEMPER PRAESUMITUR PRO LEGITImatione puerorum, et filiatio non potest probari. The presumption is always in favor of legitimacy, for filiation cannot be proved. Co. Litt. 126. See 1 Bouv. Inst. note 303; 5 Coke, 98b.

SEMPER PRAESUMITUR PRO MATRImonio. The presumption is always in favor of the validity of a marriage.

SEMPER PRAESUMITUR PRO NEGANte. The presumption is always in favor of the one who denies. See 10 Clark & F. 534; 3 El. & Bl. 723.

SEMPER PRAESUMITUR PRO SENTENtia. Presumption is always in favor of the sentence. 3 Bulst. 42.

SEMPER QUI NON PROHIBET PRO SE intervenire, mandare creditur. He who does not prohibit the intervention of another in his behalf is supposed to authorize it. 2 Kent, Comm. 616; Dig. 14. 6. 16; Id. 43. 3. 12. 4.

SEMPER SEXUS MASCULINUS ETIAM foemininum continet. The male sex always includes the female. Dig. 32. 62.

SEMPER SPECIALIA GENERALIBUS insunt. Special clauses are always comprised in general ones. Dig. 50. 17. 147.

SEN. This is said to be an ancient word which signified "justice." Co. Litt. 61a.

SENATE. The name of the less numerous of the two bodies constituting the legislative branch of the government of the United States, and of the several states.

SENATOR. A member of a senate.

SENATORES SUNT PARTES CORPORIS regis. Senators are part of the body of the king. Staundf. 72 (E); 4 Inst. 53, in marg.

SENATORS OF THE COLLEGE OF JUStice. The judges of the court of session in Scotland are so called. Act 1540, c. 93.

SENATUS CONSULTA. Ordinances (public acts) of the Roman senate.

SENATUS CONSULTUM MARCIANUM (Lat.) In the civil law. The Marcian decree of the senate. A decree enacted in the consulate of Qnintus Marcius and Spurius Postumus, in relation to the celebration of the Bacchanalian mysteries. This decree has been preserved entire to the present day, and is given in full by Dr. Taylor, with a commentary abounding in curious learning. Tayl. Civ. Law, 546-584. It was obtained from a copper plate dug up about the year 1640, in the territories of J. Bapt. Cigala, in the kingdom of Naples, and now in the imperial library at Vienna. Id. 547.

SENATUS CONSULTUM ORFICIANUM (Lat.) In the civil law. The Orfician decree of the senate. A decree enacted in the consulate of Orficius and Rufus, in the reign of the Emperor Marcus Antonius, by which children, both sons and daughters, were admitted to the inheritance of their intestate mothers. Inst. 3. 4. pr.

SENATUS CONSULTUM PEGASIANUM (Lat.) In the civil law. The Pegasian decree of the senate. A decree enacted in the consulship of Pegasus and Pusio, in the reign of Vespasian, by which an heir, who was requested to restore an inheritance, was allowed to retain one-fourth of it for himself. Inst. 2. 23. 5. This was declared by Justinian to be superseded by the *Senatus Consultum Trebellianum* (*q. v.*) Id. 2. 23. 7; Heinec. Elem. Jur. Civ. lib. 2, tit. 23, § 668.

SENATUS CONSULTUM TREBELLIANum (Lat.) In the civil law. The Trebellian decree of the senate. A decree enacted in the consulate of Trebellius Maximus and Annaeus Seneca, in the reign of Nero, by which it was provided that, if an inheritance was restored under a trust, all actions which, by the civil law, might be brought by or against the heir should be given to and against him to whom the inheritance was restored. Inst. 2. 23. 4; Dig. 36. 1. See the words of the decree, Id. § 2.

SENATUS CONSULTUM ULTIMAE NEcessitatis (Lat.) A decree of the senate of the last necessity. The name given to the decree which usually preceded the nomination of a dictator. 1 Bl. Comm. 136.

SENATUS CONSULTUM VELLEIANUM (Lat.) In the civil law. The Velleian decree of the senate. A decree enacted in the consulship of Velleius, by which married women were prohibited from making contracts. Dig. 16, 1; Story, Confl. Laws, § 425.

SENATUS DECRETA. In the civil law. Decisions of the senate; private acts concerning particular persons merely.

SENDA. In Spanish law. A path; the right of a path; the right of foot or horse path. White, New Recop. bk. 2, tit. 6, § 1.

SENESCHALLO ET MARESHALLO quod non teneat placita de libero tenemento. A writ addressed to the steward and marshal of England, inhibiting them to take cognizance of an action in their court that concerns freehold. Reg. Orig. 185. Abolished.

SENESCHALLUS (Lat.) A steward. Co. Litt. 61a.

SENILE DEMENTIA. A gradual impairment of the mental faculties by reason of physical decay and resulting in second childhood.

SENILITY. Old age; a state of mental impairment resulting from old age. See 2 Johns. Ch. (N. Y.) 232.

SENIOR. The elder. This addition is sometimes made to a man's name, when two persons bear the same, in order to distinguish them. In practice, when nothing is mentioned, the senior is intended. 3 Miss. 59.

Used in reference to securities conveyances, etc., it signifies first in point of time.

SENORIO. In Spanish Law. Dominion or property.

SENSU HONESTO. To interpret words *sensu honesto* is to take them so as not to impute impropriety to the person concerned.

SENSUS VERBORUM EST ANIMA LEgis. The meaning of words is the spirit of the law. 5 Coke, 2.

SENSUS VERBORUM EST DUPLEX, MItis et asper, et verba semper accipienda sunt in mitiore sensu. The meaning of words is twofold, mild and harsh; and words are to be received in their milder sense. 4 Coke, 13.

SENSUS VERBORUM EX CAUSA DIcendi accipiendus est, et sermones semper accipiendi sunt secundum subjectam materiam. The sense of words is to be taken from the occasion of speaking them, and discourses are always to be interpreted according to the subject matter. 4 Coke, 14.

SENTENCE. A judgment or judicial declaration made by a judge in a cause. The term "judgment" is more usually applied to civil, and "sentence" to criminal, proceedings. A sentence (in criminal proceedings) is the order of court made in the presence of the defendant, and entered of record, pronouncing the judgment, and ordering the same to be carried into execution in the manner prescribed by law. Clark, Crim. Law Tex. 580.

Sentences are final, when they put an end to the case; or interlocutory, when they settle only some incidental matter which has arisen in the course of its progress. See Aso & M. Inst. bk. 3, tit. 8, c. 1.

SENTENTIA (Lat.) In civil law. Sense; import; as distinguished from mere words. Calv. Lex.

The deliberate expression of one's will. Tayl. Civ. Law, 532.

The sentence of a judge or court. Inst. 4. 11. 4.

SENTENTIA A NON JUDICE LATA NEmini debet nocere. A sentence pronounced by one who is not a judge should not harm any one. Fleta, lib. 6, c. 6, § 7.

SENTENTIA CONTRA MATRIMONIUM nunquam transit in rem judicatam. A sentence against marriage never passes into a judgment (conclusive upon the parties). 7 Coke, 43.

SENTENTIA FACIT JUS, ET LEGIS INterpretatio legis vim obtinet. The sentence makes the law, and the interpretation has the force of law.

SENTENTIA FACIT JUS, ET RES JUDIcata pro veritate accipitur. Judgment creates the right, and what is adjudicated is taken for truth. Ellesmere, Postn. 55.

SENTENTIA INTERLOCUTORIA REVOcari potest, definitiva non potest. An interlocutory sentence or order may be revoked, but not a final. Bac. Max. reg. 20.

SENTENTIA NON FERTUR DE REBUS non liquidis. Sentence is not given upon a thing which is not clear.

SEPARALE. (L. Lat.) In old English law. Several; a several or separate share or portion. A separate property.

SEPARALITER (Lat. separately). A word sometimes used in indictments to show that the defendants are charged separately with offenses which, without the addition of this word, would seem, from the form of the indictment, to be charged jointly; as, for example, when two persons are indicted together for perjury, and the indictment states that A. and B. came before a commissioner, etc., this is alleging that they were both guilty of the same crime, when by law their crimes are distinct, and the indictment is vicious; but if the word *separaliter* is used, then the affirmation is that each was guilty of a separate offense. 2 Hale, P. C. 174.

SEPARATE ACKNOWLEDGMENT. A married woman's acknowledgment of a deed, taken apart and privately from her husband.

SEPARATE DEMISE IN EJECTMENT. A demise in a declaration in ejectment used to be termed a "separate demise" when made by the lessor separately or individually, as distinguished from a demise made jointly by two or more persons, which was termed a "joint demise." No such demise, either separate or joint, is now necessary in this action. Brown.

SEPARATE ESTATE. That which belongs to one only of several persons; as, the separate estate of a partner, which does not belong to the partnership. 2 Bouv. Inst. note 1519.

The separate estate of a married woman is that which belongs to her, and over which her husband has no right in equity. It may consist of lands or chattels. 4 Barb. (N. Y.) 407; 1 Const. (S. C.) 452; 4 Bouv. Inst. note 3996.

SEPARATE EXAMINATION. See "Separate Acknowledgment."

SEPARATE MAINTENANCE. The maintenance of a woman by her husband on an agreement to live separately. An allowance made by a husband to his wife for her separate support and maintenance. Bouvier. See 2 Rop. Husb. & Wife, 267 et seq.; 2 Steph. Comm. 309.

SEPARATIM. In old conveyancing. Severally. A word which made a several covenant. 5 Coke, 23a.

SEPARATION. A cessation of cohabitation of husband and wife by mutual agreement.

SEPARATION A MENSA ET THORO. A partial dissolution of the marriage relation.

By the ecclesiastical or canon law of England, which had exclusive jurisdiction over marriage and divorce, marriage was regarded as a sacrament, and indissoluble. This doctrine originated with the Church of Rome, and became established in England while that country was Catholic; and though, after the Reformation, it ceased to be the doctrine of the Church of England, yet the law remained unchanged until the recent statute of 20 & 21 Vict. (1857) c. 85. Bish. Mar. & Div. §§ 274, 278. Hence, as has been seen in the article on divorce, a valid marriage could not be dissolved in England except by what has been termed the "omnipotent power of parliament."

This gave rise, in the ecclesiastical courts, to the practice of granting divorces "from bed and board," as they used to be called, or "judicial separation," as they are called in 20 & 21 Vict. c. 85, § 7. Bish. Mar. & Div. §§ 277, 278. From England this practice was introduced into this country; and though in some of the states it has entirely given way to the divorce *a vinculo matrimonii*, in others it is still in use, being generally granted for causes which are not sufficient to authorize the latter. See "Divorce."

SEPARATION ORDER. In England, where a husband is convicted of an aggravated assault upon his wife, the court or magistrate may order that the wife shall be no longer bound to cohabit with him. Such an order has the same effect as a judicial decree of separation on the ground of cruelty. It may also provide for the payment of a weekly sum by the husband to the wife and for the custody of the children. Sweet.

SEPARATISTS. Seceders from the Church of England. They, like Quakers, solemnly affirm, instead of taking the usual oath, before they give evidence. See 3 & 4 Wm. IV. c. 82.

SEPTUM. An inclosure; any place paled in. Cowell.

SEPULCHRE. The place where a corpse is buried. The violation of sepulchres is a misdemeanor at common law.

SEPULTURA. An offering to the priest for the burial of a dead body.

SEQUAMUR VESTIGIA PATRUM NOSTRORUM. Let us follow the footsteps of our fathers. Jenk. Cent. Cas.

SEQUATUR SUB SUO PERICULO. A writ that lay where a summons *ad warrantizandum* was awarded, and the sheriff returned that he had nothing whereby he might be summoned, then issued an *alias* and a *pluries*, and if he came not in on the *pluries*, this writ issued. Old Nat. Brev. 163.

SEQUELA (Law Lat.) In old English law. Suit; process or prosecution. *Sequela causae*, the process of a cause. Cowell.

SEQUELA CURIAE. Suit of court. Cowell. See "Suit."

SEQUELA VILLANORUM. The family retinue and appurtenances to the goods and chattels of villeins, which were at the absolute disposal of the lord. Par. Ant. 216.

SEQUELS. Small allowances of meal or manufactured victuals made to the servants at a mill where corn was ground, by tenure, in Scotland. See "Thirlage."

SEQUESTER.

——**In Civil and Ecclesiastical Law.** To renounce. Example: When a widow comes into court and disclaims having anything to do or to intermeddle with her deceased husband's estate, she is said to "sequester." Jacob.

——**In Chancery Practice.** To take possession under a writ of sequestration. See "Sequestration."

SEQUESTRARI FACIAS. A writ issued for the purpose of enforcing a judgment against a beneficed clergyman when a *fi. fa.* has been issued and returned *nulla bona*. It commands the bishop of the diocese to enter into the benefice, and sequester the rents, tithes, and profits until the debt is satisfied. The bishop executes the writ by issuing a sequestration. Chit. Gen. Prac. 1284; Daniell, Ch. Prac. 927; Smith, Actions (11th Ed.) 397. See "Levari Facias;" "Writ."

SEQUESTRATIO. In the civil law. The separating or setting aside of a thing in controversy, from the possession of both parties that contend for it. It is twofold,—"voluntary," done by consent of all parties; and "necessary," when a judge orders it. Brown.

SEQUESTRATION.

——**In Chancery Practice.** A remedy by writ for the taking of property, and the rents and profits thereof, either to enforce a decree, 19 Ency. of Pl. & Pr. 540, or to preserve the subject matter of the suit. See 3 Bl. Comm. 444. The writ issued sometimes to the sheriff, but usually to four or more commissioners.

While the remedy is now practically superseded by executions against real estate, receivership proceedings and kindred remedies, it has not been abolished or prohibited and may be resorted to whenever it is deemed necessary. 19 Ency. of Pl. & Pr. 540. See 6 Fed. 766; 11 Paige (N. Y.) 603.

——**In Contracts.** A species of deposits which two or more persons, engaged in litigation about anything, make of the thing in contest with an indifferent person, who binds himself to restore it, when the issue is decided, to the party to whom it is adjudged to belong. Code La. art. 2942; Story, Bailm. § 45. See 19 Viner, Abr. 325; 1 Vern. 58, 420; 2 Ves. Jr. 23.

——**In Louisiana.** A mandate of the court, ordering the sheriff, in certain cases, to take into his possession, and to keep, a thing of which another person has the possession, until after the decision of a suit, in order that it be delivered to him who shall be adjudged entitled to have the property or possession of that thing. This is what is properly called a "judicial sequestration." See 1 Mart. (La.) 79; 1 La. 439; Civ. Code La. arts. 2941, 2948.

In this acceptation, the word "sequestration" does not mean a "judicial deposit," because sequestration may exist together with the right of administration, while mere deposit does not admit it.

SEQUESTRATOR. One to whom a sequestration is made.

A depositary of this kind cannot exonerate himself from the care of the thing sequestered in his hands, unless for some cause rendering it indispensable that he should resign his trust. Civ. Code La. art. 2947. See "Stakeholder."

Officers appointed by a court of chancery, and named in a writ of sequestration. As to their powers and duties, see 2 Madd. Ch. Prac. 205; Blake, Ch. Prac. 103.

SEQUESTRO HABENDO. In English ecclesiastical law. A judicial writ for the discharging a sequestration of the profits of a church benefice, granted by the bishop at the sovereign's command, thereby to compel the parson to appear at the suit of another. Upon his appearance, the parson may have this writ for the release of the sequestration. Reg. Jur. 36.

SEQUI DEBET POTENTIA JUSTITIAM, non praecedere. Power should follow justice, not precede it. 2 Inst. 454.

SERF. In feudal law. A term applied to a class of persons who were bound to perform very onerous duties towards others. Poth. des Personnes, pt. 1, tit. 1, a. 6, § 4.

There is this essential difference between a "serf" and a "slave:" The serf was bound simply to labor on the soil where he was born, without any right to go elsewhere without the consent of his lord, but he was free to act as he pleased in his daily action; the slave, on the contrary, is the property of his master, who may require him to act as he pleases in every respect, and who may sell him as a chattel. Lepage, c. 3, art. 2, § 2.

SERGEANT-AT-ARMS. An officer appointed by a legislative body, whose duties are to enforce the orders given by such bodies, generally under the warrant of its presiding officer.

SERIATIM (Lat.) In a series; severally; as, the judges delivered their opinions *seriatim.*

SERIOUS ILLNESS. An illness attended by danger, giving rise to apprehension; any permanent or material impairment of health. The term does not include the ordinary diseases of the country, but refers to those severe attacks which often leave a permanent injury and tend to shorten life. 24 Okla. 218, 20 Ann. Cas. 288; 85 Ill. 542; 65 Mich. 306, 32 N. W. 610.

SERJEANTIA IDEM EST QUOD SERVITium. Serjeanty is the same as service. Co. Litt. 105.

SERJEANT OF THE MACE. In English law. An officer who attends the lord mayor of London, and the chief magistrates of other corporate towns. Holthouse.

SERJEANTS-AT-LAW. A very ancient and the most honorable order of advocates at the common law.

They were called, formerly, "countors," or "serjeant-countors," or "countors of the bench" (in the old law Latin phrase, *banci narratores*), and are mentioned by Matthew Paris in the life of John II., written in 1255. They are limited to fifteen in number, in addition to the judges of the courts of Westminster, who are always admitted before being advanced to the bench.

The most valuable privilege formerly enjoyed by the serjeants was the monopoly of the practice in the court of common pleas. A bill was introduced into parliament for the purpose of destroying this monopoly, in 1755, which did not pass. In 1834, a warrant under the sign manual was directed to the judges of the common pleas, commanding them to open the court to the bar at large. The order was received and complied with. In 1839, the matter was brought before the court and decided to be illegal. 10 Bing. 571; 6 Bing. N. C. 187, 232, 235. St. 9 & 10 Vict. c. 54, has since extended the privilege to all barristers. 3 Bl. Comm. 27, note.

SERJEANTS' INN. The inn to which the serjeants at law belonged, near Chancery Lane; formerly called "Faryndon Inn."

SERJEANTY. In English law. A species of service which cannot be due or performed from a tenant to any lord but the king, and is either grand or petit serjeanty.

SERMO INDEX ANIMI. Speech is an index of the mind. 5 Coke, 118.

SERMO RELATA AD PERSONAM, INtelligi debet de conditione personae. A speech relating to the person is to be understood as relating to his condition. 4 Coke, 16.

SERMONES SEMPER ACCIPIENDI sunt secundum subjectam materiam, et conditionem personarum. Language is always to be understood according to its subject matter, and the condition of the person. 4 Coke, 14.

SERVAGE. In feudal law. Where a tenant, besides payment of a certain rent, found one or more workmen for his lord's service. Tomlins.

SERVANDA EST CONSUETUDO LOCI ubi causa agitur. The custom of the place where the action is brought is to be observed. 3 Johns. Ch. (N. Y.) 190, 219.

SERVANT. One who serves; one who serves another (termed his master), under a contract of hire; one who serves or undertakes to serve another for a stipulated consideration or wage. 2 Kent's Com. 258-261; one employed to perform an inferior and menial service, 17 Ill. App. 200; a hireling who makes a part of a man's family, employed for *money*, to assist in the economy of the family, or in matters connected with it. 3 S. & R. (Pa.) 353.

Bequests to servants construed. Williams Exs. 1152; 27 Bea. 226; 26 Bea. 1472; L. J. Ch. 162; 9 Hare 551; 2 Vern. 546; 16 Ves. 486; 11 L. J. Ch. 223. Servants who take priority in bankruptcy. Mont. & McA. 95, 194; 6 Jur. 898; 42 L. J. Bank. 49; 21 W. R. 523.

SERVANT IN HUSBANDRY. A person, whether male or female, whose *chief* employment is in works of husbandry. 3 E. & E. 549; L. J. M. C. 84; 23 L. J. M. C. 138.

SERVI. Bondsmen, or servile tenants. They were of four sorts: (1) Such as sold themselves for a livelihood; (2) debtors sold because they were unable to pay their debts; (3) captives in war, retained and employed as perfect slaves; (4) *nativi*, servants born as such, solely belonging to the lord. There were also said to be *servi testamentales* those which were afterwards called "covenant servants." Cowell.

SERVI REDEMPTIONE. Criminal slaves in the time of Henry I. 1 Kemble, Sax. 197 (1849).

SERVICE.

——**In Feudal Law.** That duty which the tenant owed to his lord by reason of his fee or estate.

The services, in respect of their quality, were either free or base, and in respect of their quantity, and the time of exacting them, were either certain or uncertain. 2 Bl. Comm. 62.

——**In Civil Law.** A servitude.

——**In Practice.** The execution of a writ or process. Thus, to serve a writ of *capias* signifies to arrest a defendant under the process (Kirby [Conn.] 48; 2 Aik. [Vt.] 338; 11 Mass. 181); to serve a summons is to deliver a copy of it at the house of the party, or to deliver it to him personally, or to read it to him. Notices and other papers are served by delivering the same at the house of the party, or to him in person.

Service of process is either (1) actual, or (2) constructive; constructive service being such as is by law conclusively presumed to give notice, e. g., by publication or posting.

Actual service is either (a) personal, by actual delivery of the process to the person to be served, or (b) substituted, being by such a disposition as the law deems to be the equivalent of personal service, *e. g.*, by leaving at his dwelling house.

When the service of a writ is prevented by the act of the party on whom it is to be served, it will, in general, be sufficient if the officer do everything in his power to serve it. 1 Man. & G. 238.

SERVICE OF AN HEIR. By the former law of Scotland, before an heir could regularly acquire a right to the ancestor's estate, he had to be served heir. See Bell, Dict.

SERVICE, SECULAR. Worldly service, as contrasted with spiritual or ecclesiastical. Cowell.

SERVICES FONCIERS. These are in French law the easements of English law.

SERVIDUMBRE. In Spanish law. A servitude. The right and use which one man has in the buildings and estates of another, to use them for the benefit of his own. Las Partidas, 3. 31. 1.

SERVIENS-AD-CLAVAM. A serjeant- at-mace.

SERVIENS AD LEGEM. Sergeant-at-law.

SERVIENS DOMINI REGIS (Law Lat.) In old English law. King's serjeant; a public officer, who acted sometimes as the sheriff's deputy, and had also judicial powers. Bracton, fols. 145b, 150b, 330, 358.

SERVIENT. In civil law. A term applied to an estate or tenement by or in respect of which a servitude is due to another estate or tenement. See "Easement."

SERVILE EST EXPILATIONIS CRIMEN; sola innocentia libera. The crime of theft is slavish; innocence alone is free. 2 Inst. 573.

SERVITIA PERSONALIA SEQUUNTUR personam. Personal services follow the person. 2 Inst. 374; Fleta, lib. 3, c. 11, § 1.

SERVITIIS ACQUIETANDIS. A judicial writ for a man distrained for services to one, when he owes and performs them to another, for the acquittal of such services. Reg. Jur. 27.

SERVITIUM. In feudal and old English law. The duty of obedience and performance which a tenant was bound to render to his lord by reason of his fee. Spelman. See Co. Litt. 65a.

SERVITIUM FEODALE ET PRAEDIALE. A personal service, but due only by reason of lands which were held in fee. Bracton, lib. 2, c. 16.

SERVITIUM FORINSECUM. A service due, not to the chief lord, but to the king.

SERVITIUM, IN LEGE ANGLIAE, REGULariter accipitur pro servitio quod per tenentes dominis suis debetur ratione feodi sui. Service, by the law of England, means the service which is due from the tenants to the lords by reason of their fee. Co. Litt. 65.

SERVITIUM INTRINSECUM. The ordinary service due the chief lord from his tenants.

SERVITIUM LIBERUM. A service to be done by feudatory tenants, who were called "*liberi homines*," and distinguished from vassals, as was their service, for they were not bound to any of the base services of plowing the lord's land, etc., but were to find a man and horse, or go with the lord into the army, or to attend the court, etc.

It was called, also, "*servitium liberum armorum.*"

SERVITIUM MILITARE. Knight service; military service. 2 Bl. Comm. 62.

SERVITIUM REGALE. Royal service, or the rights and prerogatives that, within a royal manor, belong to the lord of the same, which are generally reckoned to be the following, viz.: Power of judicature, in matters of property, and of life and death, in felonies and murder, a right to waifs and strays; assessments; minting of money; and assize of bread, beer, and weights and measures. Cowell.

SERVITIUM SCUTI. Service of the shield; that is, knight service.

SERVITIUM SOKAE. Service of the plow; that is, socage.

SERVITORS OF BILLS. Such servants or messengers of the marshal belonging to the king's bench as were heretofore sent abroad with bills or writs to summon men to that court, being now called "tipstaves." Blount; 2 Hen. IV. c. 23.

SERVITUDE.

——**In Civil Law.** The subjection of one person to another person, or of a person to a thing, or of a thing to a person, or of a thing to a thing.

A right which subjects a land or tenement to some service for the use of another land or tenement which belongs to another master. Domat, Civ. Law (Cushing Ed.) § 1018.

(1) A mixed servitude is the subjection of persons to things, or things to persons.

(2) A natural servitude is one which arises in consequence of the natural condition or situation of the soil.

(3) A personal servitude is the subjection of one person to another. If it consists in the right of property which a person exercises over another, it is slavery. When the subjection of one person to another is not slavery, it consists simply in the right of requiring of another what he is bound to do or not to do. This right arises from all kinds of contracts or *quasi* contracts. Lois des Bat. p. 1, c. 1, art. 1.

(4) A real or predial servitude is a charge laid on an estate for the use and utility of another estate belonging to another proprietor. Code La. art. 643. When used without any adjunct, the word "servitude" means a real or predial servitude. Lois des Bat. p. 1, c. 1. Real servitudes are divided into rural and urban.

(a) Rural servitudes are those which are due by an estate to another estate, such as the right of passage over the serving estate, or that which owes the servitude, or to draw water from it, or to water cattle there, or to take coal, lime, and wood from it, and the like.

(b) Urban servitudes are those which are established over a building for the convenience of another, such as the right of resting the joists in the wall of the serving building, of opening windows which overlook the serving estate, and the like. Dalloz.

This term is used as a translation of the Latin term *servitus* in the French and Scotch law (Dalloz; Paterson, Comp.), and by many common-law writers (3 Kent, Comm. 434; Washb. Easem.), and in the Civil Code of Louisiana. "Service" is used by Wood, Taylor, Harris, Cowper, and Cushing in his translation of Domat. Much of the common-law doctrine of easements is closely analogous to, and probably in part derived from, the civil-law doctrine of servitudes.

——**In Modern Law.** Real servitudes are known as "easements," the term "servitude" being used only in the sense of the burden imposed by an easement.

SERVITUS (Lat.) In Roman law. Servitude; slavery; a state of bondage; a disposition of the law of nations by which, against common right, one man has been subjected to the dominion of another. Inst. 1. 2. 3; Bracton, 4b; Co. Litt. 116.

A service or servitude; a burden imposed by law, or the agreement of parties, upon one estate for the advantage of another, or for the benefit of another person than the owner.

Servitus actus, a right of way on horseback or in a carriage. Inst. 2. 3. pr.

Servitus altius non tollendi, a servitude preventing the owner of a house from building higher than his neighbor. Inst. 2. 3. 4; Paterson, Comp.

Servitus aquae ducendae, a right of leading water to one's own land over that of another. Inst. 2. 3. pr.

Servitus aquae educendae, a right of conducting water from one's own land unto a neighbor's. Dig. 8. 3. 29.

Servitus aquae hauriendae, a right of drawing water from another's spring or well. Inst. 2. 3. 2.

Servitus cloacae mittendae, a right of having a sewer through a neighbor's estate. Dig. 8. 1. 7.

Servitus fumi immitendi, a right of conducting smoke or vapor through a neighbor's chimney or over his ground. Dig. 8. 5. 8.

Servitus itineris, a right of way on horseback or in a carriage. This includes a *servitus actus*. Inst. 2. 3.

Servitus luminum, a right to have an open place for receiving light into a chamber or other room. Domat, 1. 1. 4; Dig. 8. 2. 4.

Servitus oneris ferendi, a servitude of supporting a neighbor's building.

Servitus pascendi, a right of pasturing one's cattle on another's land. Inst. 2. 3. 2.

Servitus pecoris ad aquam adpulsam, a right of driving one's cattle on a neighbor's land to water.

Servitus praedii rustici, a rural servitude.

Servitus praedii urbani, an urban servitude.

Servitus praediorum, a servitude on one estate for the benefit of another. See "Praedia."

Servitus projiciendi, a right of building a projection into the open space belonging to a neighbor. Dig 8. 2. 2.

Servitus prospectus, a right of prospect. Dig. 8. 2. 15. This may be either to give one a free prospect over his neighbor's land or to prevent a neighbor from having a prospect over one's own land. Domat, 1. 1. 6.

Servitus stillicidii, a right of having the water drip from the eaves of one's house upon a neighbor's house or ground.

Servitus tigni immitendi, a right of inserting beams in a neighbor's wall. Inst. 2. 3. 1. 4; Dig. 8. 2. 2.

Servitus viae, a right of way on foot or horseback, or with a loaded beast or wagon, over a neighbor's estate. Inst. 2. 3.

See, generally, Inst. 2. 3; Dig. 8. 2; Dict. de Jur.; Domat, Civ. Law; Bell, Dict.; Washb. Easem.

SERVITUS EST CONSTITUTIO JURE gentium qua quis domino alieno contra naturam subjicitur. Slavery is an institution by the law of nations, by which a man is subjected to the dominion of another, contrary to nature. Inst. 1. 3. 2; Co. Litt. 116.

SERVITUS NE LUMINIBUS OFFICIAtur. A servitude not to hinder lights; the right of having one's lights or windows unobstructed or darkened by a neighbor's building, etc. Inst. 2. 3. 4.

SERVITUS NE PROSPECTUS OFFENDatur. A servitude not to obstruct one's prospect. Dig. 8. 2. 15.

SERVITUS TIGNI IMMITTENDI. The servitude of letting in a beam; the right of inserting beams in a neighbor's wall. Inst. 2. 3. 1. 4; Dig. 8. 2. 2.

SERVITUS VIAE. The servitude or right of way; the right of walking, riding, and driving over another's land. Inst. 2. 3. pr.

SERVUS. A slave.

SESS, or ASSESS. Rate or tax.

SESSIO. A sitting; a session. *Sessio parliamenti*, the sitting of parliament. Cowell.

SESSION. The time during which a legislative body, a court, or other assembly sits for the transaction of business; as, a session of congress, which commences on the day appointed by the constitution, and ends when congress finally adjourns before the commencement of the next session; the session of a court, which commences at the day appointed by law, and ends when the court finally rises. A term.

SESSION COURT. See "Court of Session."

SESSION, GREAT, OF WALES. A court which was abolished by St. 1 Wm. IV. c. 70. The proceedings now issue out of the courts at Westminster, and two of the judges of the superior courts hold the circuits in Wales and Cheshire, as in other English counties.

SESSIONS. A sitting of justices in court upon their commission, or by virtue of their appointment, and most commonly for the trial of criminal cases. The title of several courts in England and the United States, chiefly those of criminal jurisdiction.

SESSIONS OF THE PEACE. In English law. Sittings of justices of the peace for the execution of the powers which are confided to them as such.

(1) Petty sessions (or petit sessions) are sittings held by one or more justices for the trial of minor offenses, admitting to bail prisoners accused of felony, and the like purposes.

When sitting for purposes of preliminary inquiry, the public cannot claim admittance; but it is otherwise when sitting for purposes of adjudication.

(2) Special sessions are sittings of two or more justices on a particular occasion for the exercise of some given branch of their authority, upon reasonable notice given to the other magistrates of the hundred or other division of the county, city, etc., for which they are convened. See St. 7 & 8 Vict. c. 33.

The counties are distributed into divisions, and authority given by various statutes to the justices acting for the several divisions to transact different descriptions of business, such as licensing alehouses, or appointing overseers of the poor, surveyors of the highways, etc., at special sessions. 3 Steph. Comm. 43, 44.

(3) General sessions of the peace are courts of record, holden before the justices, whereof one is of the *quorum*, for execution of the general authority given to the justices by the commission of the peace and certain acts of parliament.

The only description of general sessions now usually held is the court of general quarter sessions of the peace; but in the county of Middlesex, besides the four quarter sessions, four general sessions are held in the intervals, and original intermediate sessions occasionally take place. They may be called by any two justices in the jurisdiction, one being of the *quorum*, or by the *custos rotulorum* and one justice, but not by one justice or the *custos rotulorum* alone.

(4) General quarter sessions of the peace. See "Court of General Quarter Sessions of the Peace."

SESSIONAL ORDERS. Certain resolutions which are agreed to by both houses at the commencement of every session of the English parliament, and have relation to the business and convenience thereof; but they are not intended to continue in force beyond the session in which they are adopted. They are principally of use as directing the order of business. Brown.

SET. This word appears to be nearly synonymous with "lease." A lease of mines is frequently termed a "mining set." Brown.

SET ASIDE. To annul; to make void; as, to set aside an award.

When proceedings are irregular, they may be set aside on motion of the party whom they injuriously affect.

SET LINE. A line with baited hooks fastened to it set or anchored for taking fish;

a line to which a number of baited hooks are attached and which supported by a buoy, is extended on the surface of the water. 3 Johns Univ. Cyc., 390; 69 Vt. 413; 4 Encyc. Dic., 4216.

SET OF EXCHANGE. The different parts of a bill of exchange, taken together. Each part is a perfect instrument by itself; but the parts are numbered successively, and upon payment of any one, the others become useless. See Chit. Bills (1836 Ed.) 175; Pars. Notes & Bills.

SET-OFF. In practice. A demand, growing out of a distinct transaction, which a defendant makes against the plaintiff in the suit for the purpose of liquidating the whole or a part of his claim. See 7 Fla. 329.

A set-off was unknown to the common law, according to which mutual debts were distinct, and inextinguishable except by actual payment or release. 1 Rawle (Pa.) 293; Babington, Set-Off, 1.

St. 2 Geo. II. c. 22, which has been generally adopted in the United States, with some modifications, in cases of mutual debts, however, allowed the defendant to set his debt against the other, either by pleading it in bar, or giving it in evidence, when proper notice had been given of such intention, under the general issue. The statute, being made for the benefit of the defendant, is not compulsory (8 Watts [Pa.] 39); the defendant may waive his right, and bring a cross action against the plaintiff (2 Campb. 594; 5 Taunt. 148; 9 Watts [Pa.] 179).

It seems, however, that in some cases of intestate estates and of insolvent estates, perhaps owing to the peculiar wording of the law, the statute has been held to operate on the rights of the parties before action brought or an act done by either of them. 2 Rawle (Pa.) 293; 3 Bin. (Pa.) 135; Bac. Abr. "Bankrupt" (K). See 7 Gray (Mass.) 191, 425.

Set-off takes place only in actions on contracts for the payment of money, as, *assumpsit*, debt, and covenant. A set-off is not allowed in actions arising *ex delicto;* as upon the case, trespass, replevin, or detinue. Buller, N. P. 181; 4 E. D. Smith (N. Y.) 162.

The matters which may be set off may be mutual liquidated debts or damages; but unliquidated damages cannot be set off. 3 Bosw. (N. Y.) 560; 34 Pa. St. 239; 34 Ala. (N. S.) 659; 20 Tex. 31; 2 Head (Tenn.) 467; 2 Metc. (Ky.) 143; 3 Iowa 163; 8 Iowa 325; 1 Blackf. (Ind.) 394; 8 Conn. 325; 6 Halst. (N. J.) 397; 5 Wash. C. C. (U. S.) 232. The statutes refer only to mutual unconnected debts; for at common law, when the nature of the employment, transaction, or dealings necessarily constitutes an account consisting of receipts and payments, debts and credits, the balance only is considered to be the debt, and therefore in an action it is not necessary in such cases either to plead or give notice of set-off. 4 Burrows, 2221.

Distinguished from counterclaim and recoupment. Counterclaim is a term of statutory origin, and includes both set-off and recoupment, and something more. It embraces all sorts of claims which a defendant may have against a plaintiff in the nature of a cross action or demand, or for which a cross or separate action would lie. 13 How. Pr. (N. Y.) 84.

In recoupment, the defendant's claim must arise from the same transaction as the plaintiff's, and in this it is distinguished from set-off, which must arise in a distinct claim. See "Recoupment."

SETTER. In Scotch law. The grantor of a tack or lease. 1 Forbes, Inst. pt. 2, p. 153.

SETTLEMENT. A residence under such circumstances as to entitle a person to support or assistance in case of becoming a pauper.

It is obtained in various ways, to wit: By birth; by the legal settlement of the father, in the case of minor children; by marriage; by continued residence; by the payment of requisite taxes; by the lawful exercise of a public office; by hiring and service for a specified time; by serving an apprenticeship; and perhaps some others, which depend upon the local statutes of the different states. See 1 Bl. Comm. 363; 1 Doug. 9; 6 Serg. & R. (Pa.) 103, 565; 10 Serg. & R. (Pa.) 179.

——**In Contracts.** A determination by agreement. 113 Iowa 211. An agreement by which two or more persons who have dealings together so far arrange their accounts as to ascertain the balance due from one to the other; payment in full.

The conveyance of an estate for the benefit of some person or persons.

See "Marriage Settlement."

SETTLEMENT, ACT OF. See "Act of Settlement."

SETTLEMENT, DEED OF. A deed made for the purpose of settling property, *i. e.*, arranging the mode and extent of the enjoyment thereof. The party who settles property is called the "settlor;" and usually his wife and children or his creditors or his near relations are the beneficiaries taking interests under the settlement.

SETTLEMENT, EQUITY OF. See "Equity to a Settlement."

SETTLING DAY. The day on which transactions for the "account" are made up on the English stock exchange. In consols, they are monthly; in other investments, twice in the month.

SEVER. In practice. To separate; to insist upon a plea distinct from that of other codefendants.

SEVERAL. Separate; distinct. A several agreement or covenant is one entered into by two or more persons separately, each binding himself for the whole; a several action is one in which two or more persons are separately charged; a several inheritance is one conveyed so as to descend or come to two persons separately by moieties. "Several" is usually opposed to "joint."

SEVERAL ACTIONS. Separate actions, the opposite of "joint actions," in which the plaintiffs combine their causes. See "Joinder of Actions."

SEVERAL COUNTS. See "Count;" "Indictment."

SEVERAL COVENANT. A covenant by two or more, separately; a covenant made so as to bind the parties to it severally or individually.

SEVERAL DEMISES. Prior to the common-law procedure acts of 1852-1860, it was necessary, in England, that the plaintiff in ejectment should make a demise, and that he should have the legal estate in him for that purpose. Wherefore, in case of any doubt whether the legal estate was in A., or in B., or in C., it was usual, in framing the declaration, to insert a demise by each, and the declaration was then said to contain several demises; but now no demise at all is necessary to an action of ejectment. See "Ejectment."

SEVERAL FISHERY. A right to fish in private water, either exclusively, or in conjunction with the owner of the soil. 1 Kent, Comm. 410, and note.

SEVERAL INHERITANCE. An inheritance conveyed so as to descend to two persons severally, by moieties, etc.

SEVERAL TAIL. An entail severally to two; as, if land is given to two men and their wives, and to the heirs of their bodies begotten. Here the donees have a joint estate for their two lives, and yet they have a several inheritance, because the issue of the one shall have his moiety, and the issue of the other the other moiety. Cowell.

SEVERAL TENANCY. A tenancy which is separate, and not held jointly with another person.

SEVERALLY. To separate is to disunite, to divide, to disconnect, to sever. 9 Ill. App. 370.

SEVERALTY, ESTATE IN. An estate which is held by the tenant in his own right only, without any other being joined or connected with him in point of interest during the continuance of his estate. 2 Bl. Comm. 179; Cruise, Dig. 479, 480.

SEVERANCE. The separation of a part of a thing from another; for example, the separation of machinery from a mill is a severance, and in that case the machinery, which, while annexed to the mill, was real estate, becomes by the severance personalty, unless such severance be merely temporary. 8 Wend. (N. Y.) 587.

——**In Pleading.** When an action is brought in the name of several plaintiffs, in which the plaintiffs must of necessity join, and one or more of the persons so named do not appear, or make default after appearance, the other may have judgment of severance, or, as is technically called, judgment *ad sequendum solum.*

But in personal actions, with the exception of those by executors, and of detinue for charters, there can be no summons and severance. Co. Litt. 139.

After severance, the party severed can never be mentioned in the suit, nor derive any advantage from it.

When there are several defendants, each of them may use such plea as he may think proper for his own defense; and they may join in the same plea, or sever, at their discretion (Co. Litt. 303a), except, perhaps, in the case of dilatory pleas (Hob. 245, 250). But when the defendants have once united in the plea, they cannot afterwards sever at the rejoinder, or other later stage of the pleading. See, generally, Brooke, Abr. "Summ. and Sev."; 2 Rolle, 488; Archb. Civ. Pl. 59.

——**Of Estates.** The destruction of any one of the unities of a joint tenancy. It is so called because the estate is no longer a joint tenancy, but is severed.

A severance may be effected in various ways, namely: By partition, which is either voluntary or compulsory; by alienation of one of the joint tenants, which turns the estate into a tenancy in common; by the purchase or descent of all the shares of the joint tenants, so that the whole estate becomes vested in one only. Comyn, Dig. "Estates by Grant" (K 5); 1 Bin. (Pa.) 175.

SEWAGE. That which passes through a sewer. A secondary meaning is derived from the usual character of the contents of a sewer and as used in that sense the word signifies the refuse and foul matter solid or liquid, which it so carried off. 67 Conn. 494.

SEWER (Law Lat. *sewera, severa*). A fresh-water trench compassed in on both sides with a bank. Callis, Sewers (80) 99. Callis calls it "a small current or little river;" "a diminutive of a river;" "a common public stream." Id. 100. A passage to carry water into the sea or a river. Cowell. A ditch or trench carried through marshy places, to carry off the water. Spelman.

In its modern and more usual sense, a sewer means an underground or covered channel used for the drainage of two or more separate buildings, as opposed to a "drain," which is a channel used for carrying off the drainage of one building or set of buildings in one curtilage. See "Drain" (2).

SEXTANS (Lat.) In the Roman law. A subdivision of the *as*, containing two *unciae;* the proportion of two-twelfths, or one-sixth. Tayl. Civ. Law, 492; 2 Bl. Comm. 462, note.

SEXTERY LANDS. Lands given to a church or religious house for maintenance of a sexton or sacristan. Cowell.

SEXTUS DECRETALIUM. The sixth decretal.

SEYSINA. (L. Lat.) In old English law. Seisin; possession of lands; or of a freehold estate in lands. Bract. fol. 38b, 39.

SHACK, COMMON OF. The right of persons occupying lands lying together in the same common field to turn out their cattle after harvest to feed promiscuously in such field.

SHALL.

——**British Cases.** Great care is to be employed in using or construing this word. Its various meanings range under two general classes according as it is used, as implying futurity; or as implying a mandate, or giving permission or direction.

——**Futurity.** If something is agreed to be done if or when something else "shall" happen, this contemplates futurity. Past occurrences will not satisfy the condition precedent. 3 Drew. 617; 25 L. J. Ch. 850; 27 L. T. O. S. 289; 29 L. J. Ch. 911; 7 W. R. 135; 5 Jur. N. S. 56.

"Shall be born," in the absence of a context, are words of futurity; and, in a will, mean persons born after its date. 50 L. J. P. C. 45; 6 App. Ca. 471.

The phrase, in a divesting clause, if donee of property "shall become bankrupt" seems "to mean, simply being bankrupt," 29 L. J. Ch. 843; and it is immaterial whether the bankruptcy has happened before, or shall have happened after, the making of the instrument. 1 D. G. & S. 282; 16 L. J. Ch. 245. So, too, in an independent testamentary gift to issue of a deceased member of a class, the words "shall die" or "shall happen to die" do not necessarily point to a future death, so as inevitably to exclude the issue of a member of the class who may have died before the date of the will. 30 L. J. Ch. 789; 1 Dr. & Sm. 497; 1 Mer. 320; 2 Jarm. 771. So "a surrender to such uses as the testator 'shall' by will appoint, applied to a will antecedently executed, it being considered that the surrender referred to that will which should be in existence at testator's death." 1 Jarm. 58; 1 T. R. 435n. See May.

——**Whether Mandatory or Directory.** In its ordinary signification, "shall" is mandatory and not permissive. It is to be so construed unless by the context it appears that a different meaning was intended or when it is necessary to effectuate the chief purpose of the statute. 122 N. E. 268 (Mass.); 217 Mass. 430; 106 N. E. 618.

——**"Shall" and "May."** "Shall" and "May" are often held to be convertible terms in ascertaining legislative intention. 108 Ill. App. 614, 615; 77 Ill. 271; 184 Ill. 597.

As where, in a statute, no right or benefit to anyone depends upon its imperative use it may be held to be directory. 249 Ill. 294.

The word has not often been construed as "may," and as importing only power or authority. 153 Mass. 200.

——**Mandatory.** Whenever a statute declares that a thing "shall" be done, the natural and proper meaning is that a peremptory mandate is enjoined. But where the thing has reference to the time or formality of completing any public act, not being a step in a litigation, or accusation; or, of creating an executed contract whereof the benefit has been, or but for the act of the beneficiary might be, received, the enactment will generally be regarded as merely directory, unless there be words making the thing done void if not done in accordance with the prescribed requirements.

The word "shall" has been held mandatory as regards time for appeals from justice's courts, 4 C. B. N. S. 264; 27 L. J. C. P. 224; 29 L. J. M. C. 108; 31 L. J. M. C. 92; except when the appeal is hindered by the offices of the court being closed, L. R. 2 Q. B. 410; 9 B. & S. 27, note; or by respondent not being found, 27 L. J. M. C. 273; E. B. & E. 469. As regards time for appeal from county court, 27 L. J. Q. B. 319; 51 L. J. Q. B. 110. As regards application for special case, 19 Q. B. D. 168; 56 L. J. M. C. 122; 57 L. T. 368; 21 Q. B. D. 188; 36 W. R. 800. As regards requirements for creating mortgage of a ship, 29 L. J. Ch. 827. As regards contracts being under seal, 27 L. J. C. P. 314; 51 L. J. Q. B. 292; 16 Q. B. D. 446. As regards provisions for arbitration, 57 L. J. Q. B. 181; 36 W. R. 468; 2 L. J. Ex. 150. As regards sealing and signing by directors of contracts by railway and dock companies, 18 L. J. Ex. 345; 5 Ex. 442; 21 L. J. Ex. 117. As regards building contracts, 18 L. J. Ex. 282.

——**Directory.** In the following cases the word "shall" was sustained as being directory merely as regards the time fixed for the appointment of overseers. 2 Stra. 1123; 10 L. J. M. C. 166; 9 Dowl. 1001; and as regards the time for the election of guardians for the Borough of Norwich, 1 B. & Ad. 310; for appointment of surveyors of highways, 4 East 142; for holding quarter sessions, 5 L. J. O. S. M. C. 95; 7 B. & C. 6.

As regards the transmission of a conviction by justices to the next quarter sessions. 13 Q. B. 216; 18 L. J. M. C. 78.

As regards the time and manner of making out the lists of persons entitled to vote, or the time when the lists of voters are to be signed and delivered to the sheriff or returning officer. 25 L. J. C. P. 141; 17 C. B. 334; 30 L. J. C. P. 33; 9 C. B. N. S.

1; 55 L. J. Q. B. 12; 16 Q. B. D. 244; 54 L. T. 183; 50 J. P. 631.

As regards stamping the official mark on the back of a ballot paper. 55 L. J. Q. B. 273; 16 Q. B. D. 739; 54 L. T. 651; 34 W. R. 609; 50 J. P. 519.

As regards consent of father to the marriage of a minor. 8 B. & C. 29; 6 L. J. O. S. M. C. 67; 2 M. & R. 230.

As regards the questions to be asked a recruit. 16 Q. B. 48; 20 L. J. Q. B. 73.

As regards the particulars to be stated in a doctor's certificate for the detention of a lunatic. 16 L. J. M. C. 18; 9 Q. B. 651.

As regards the formalities prior to a sale by a bankruptcy assignee. 2 L. J. Ex. 179; 1 Cr. & M. 450; 3 Tyr. 339.

As regards the provisions in a private act as to the mode of keeping the register of proprietors in an incorporated company. 1 M. & G. 448; 2 Ib. 606.

As regards the countersigning, by secretary, of a bill or note of a joint-stock company. 9 C. B. 574; 19 L. J. C. P. 305; 1 H. & N. 165; 25 L. J. Ex. 348.

SHAM PLEA. One which is palpably false in fact, though it be good in form.

SHARE. A portion of anything. Sometimes shares are equal; at other times they are unequal.

In companies and corporations, the whole of the capital stock is usually divided into equal portions, called "shares." See "Capital Stock." The proportion which descends to one of several children from his ancestor is called a "share." The term "share and share alike" signifies in equal proportions.

SHARE AND SHARE ALIKE. In equal shares or proportions.

SHARE WARRANT. A share warrant to bearer is a warrant or certificate under the seal of the company, stating that the bearer of the warrant is entitled to a certain number or amount of fully paid up shares or stock.

SHARPING CORN. A customary gift of corn, which, at every Christmas, the farmers in some parts of England give to their smith for sharpening their plow irons, harrow tines, etc. Blount.

SHAVE. Sometimes used to denote the act of obtaining the property of another by oppression and extortion; but it also denotes the buying of existing notes and other securities for money, at a discount. 2 Denio (N. Y.) 293, 300.

SHEADING. A riding, tithing, or division in the Isle of Man, where the whole island is divided into six sheadings, in each of which there is a coroner or chief constable appointed by a delivery of a rod at the Tinewald Court or annual convention. King, Isle of Man, 7.

SHEEP SILVER. A service turned into money, which was paid because anciently the tenants used to wash the lord's sheep.

SHELLEY'S CASE, RULE IN. "When the ancestor, by any gift or conveyance, taketh an estate of freehold, and in the same gift or conveyance an estate is limited, either mediately or immediately, to his heirs in fee or in tail, 'the heirs' are words of limitation of the estate, and not words of purchase." 1 Coke, 104.

This rule has been the subject of much comment. It is given by Mr. Preston (1 Prest. Est. pp. 263-419) as follows: "When a person takes an estate of freehold, legally or equitably, under a deed, will, or other writing, and in the same instrument there is a limitation by way of remainder, either with or without the interposition of another estate, of the same legal or equitable quality, to his heirs, or heirs of his body, as a class of persons to take in succession from generation to generation, the limitation to the heirs entitles the ancestor to the whole estate." See 15 B. Mon. (Ky.) 282; Harg. Tr. 489, 551; 2 Kent, Comm. 214.

If the limitation be to "heirs of the body," he takes an estate tail; if to "heirs" generally, a fee simple. 1 Day (Conn.) 299; 2 Yeates (Pa.) 410.

It does not apply where the ancestor's estate is equitable, and that of the heirs legal. 1 Curt. C. C. (U. S.) 419.

SHEPWAY, COURT OF. A court held before the lord warden of the Cinque Ports. A writ of error lay from the mayor and jurats of each port to the lord warden in this court, and thence to the queen's bench. The civil jurisdiction of the Cinque Ports was abolished by 18 & 19 Vict. c. 48.

SHEREFFE. The body of the lordship of Caerdiff in South Wales. Pow. Hist. Wal. 123.

SHERIFF (Sax. *scyre*, shire, *reve*, keeper). A county officer representing the executive or administrative power of the state within his county.

The office is said by Camden to have been created by Alfred when he divided England into counties; but Lord Coke is of opinion that it is of still greater antiquity, and that it existed in the time of the Romans, being the deputy of the earl (*comes*), to whom the custody of the shire was originally committed, and hence known as *vice comes*. Camden, 156; Co. Litt. 168a; Dalton, Sheriff, 5.

The office was anciently of great dignity, and conferred considerable judicial power. 1 Bl. Comm. 117; 3 Bl. Comm. 80.

In the United States, he is the chief peace officer of the county, is the custodian of the county jail, and executes the civil and criminal process and mandates of the courts within his county.

SHERIFF CLERK. The clerk of the sheriff's court in Scotland.

SHERIFF DEPUTE. In Scotch law. The principal sheriff of a county, who is also a judge.

SHERIFF GELD. A rent formerly paid by a sheriff, and it is prayed that the sheriff in his account may be discharged thereof. Rot. Parl. 50 Edw. III.

SHERIFF TOOTH. In English law. A tenure by the service of providing entertainment for the sheriff at his county courts; a common tax, formerly levied for the sheriff's diet. Wharton.

SHERIFF'S COURT. In Scotch law. A court having an extensive civil and criminal jurisdiction.

Its judgments and sentences are subject to review by the court of session and court of justiciary. Alis. Prac. 25; Paterson, Comp. 941, note.

SHERIFF'S COURT IN LONDON. A tribunal having cognizance of personal actions under the London (city) small debts act of 1852 (21 & 22 Vict. c. 157, § 3). See 11 & 12 Vict. c. 121; 15 & 16 Vict. c. 127; 18 & 19 Vict. c. 122, § 99; 20 & 21 Vict. c. 157.

The sheriff's court in London is one of the chief of the courts of limited and local jurisdiction in London. 3 Steph. Comm. 449, note (1); 3 Bl. Comm. 80, note (j).

SHERIFF'S JURY. In practice. A jury composed of no determinate number, but which may be more or less than twelve, summoned by the sheriff for the purposes of an inquisition or inquest of office. 3 Bl. Comm. 258.

SHERIFF'S OFFICERS. Bailiffs, who are either bailiffs of hundreds or bound bailiffs.

SHERIFF'S TOURN. A court of record in England, held twice each year, within a month after Easter and Michaelmas, before the sheriff, in different parts of the county.

It is, indeed, only the turn or circuit of the sheriff to keep a court leet in each respective hundred. It is the great court leet of the county, as the county court is the court baron; for out of this, for the ease of the sheriff, was taken the court leet or view of frank pledge (*q. v.*) 4 Steph. Comm. 339; 4 Bl. Comm. 273.

SHERIFFALTY. The office of sheriff.

SHERIFFWICK. The jurisdiction of a sheriff. Doctor & Stud. dial 2, c. 42, p. 232. Called, in modern law, "bailiwick." The office of a sheriff. Finch, Law, bk. 4, c. 25.

SHERRERIE. A word used by the authorities of the Roman Church, to specify contemptuously the technical parts of the law, as administered by nonclerical lawyers. Bac. Abr.

SHEWER. In the practice of the English high court, when a view by a jury is ordered, persons are named by the court to show the property to be viewed, and are hence called "shewers." There is usually a shewer on behalf of each party. Archb. Prac. 339 et seq.

SHEWING. In English law. To be quit of attachment in a court, in plaints shewed and not avowed. Obsolete.

SHIFTING CLAUSE. A shifting clause in a settlement is a clause by which some other mode of devolution is substituted for that primarily prescribed. Examples of shifting clauses are: The ordinary name and arms clause, and the clause of less frequent occurrence, by which a settled estate is destined as the foundation of a second family, in the event of the elder branch becoming otherwise enriched. 3 Dav. Conv. 273. These shifting clauses take effect under the statute of uses.

SHIFTING USE. Such a use as takes effect in derogation of some other estate, and is limited expressly by the deed, or is allowed to be created by some person named in the deed. Gilb. Uses (Sugden Ed.) 152, note; 2 Washb. Real Prop. 284.

For example, a feoffment in fee is made to the use of W. and his heirs till A. pays £40 to W., and then to the use of A. and his heirs. A very common application is in the case of marriage settlements. Williams, Real Prop. 243. The doctrine of shifting uses furnished a means of evading the principle of law that a fee could not be limited after a fee. See 2 Washb. Real Prop. 284 et seq.; Williams, Real Prop. 242; 1 Spence, Eq. Jur. 452; 1 Vern. 402; 1 Edw. Ch. 34; Plowd. 25; Poll. 65. See "Use."

SHIP. A vessel employed in navigation; for example, the terms the ship's papers, the ship's husband, shipwreck, and the like, are employed whether the vessel referred to be a brig, a schooner, a sloop, or a three-masted vessel.

A vessel with three masts, employed in navigation. 4 Wash. C. C. (U. S.) 530; Weskett, Ins. 514. The boats and rigging (2 Marsh. Ins. 727), together with the anchors, masts, cables, and such-like objects, are considered as part of the ship (Pardessus, note 599; Dig. 22. 2. 44).

SHIP BREAKING. In Scotch law. The offense of breaking into a ship. Arkley, 461.

SHIP BROKER. One who transacts business relating to vessels and their employment between the owners of vessels and merchants who send cargoes.

SHIP DAMAGE. In the charter parties with the English East India Company these words occur. Their meaning is, damage from negligence, insufficiency, or bad stowage in the ship. Doug. 272; Abb. Shipp. 204.

SHIP MASTER. The captain or master of a ship. He controls and manages the ship and cargo, and represents the owners for certain purposes.

SHIP MONEY. A tax levied on ports, towns, cities, boroughs, and counties to provide money for equipping the navy. It existed in England, and was finally abolished in the reign of Charles I. after he had attempted to restore it. This attempt, and Hampden's resistance, was one cause which led to the king's death.

SHIP'S HUSBAND. In maritime law. An agent appointed by the owner of a ship, and invested with authority to make the requisite repairs, and attend to the management, equipment, and other concerns of the ship. He is the general agent of the owners in relation to the ship, and may be appointed in writing or orally. He is usually, but not necessarily, a part owner. 1 Pars. Mar. Law, 97. He must see to the proper outfit of the vessel in the repairs adequate to the voyage, and in the tackle and furniture necessary for a seaworthy ship; must have a proper master, mate, and crew for the ship, so that in this respect it shall be seaworthy; must see to the due furnishing of provisions and stores according to the necessities of the voyage; must see to the regularity of the clearances from the custom house, and the regularity of the registry; must settle the contracts, and provide for the payment of the furnishings which are requisite to the performance of those duties; must enter into proper charter parties, or engage the vessel for general freight under the usual conditions, and settle for freight and adjust averages with the merchant; and must preserve the proper certificates, surveys, and documents, in case of future disputes with insurers and freighters, and to keep regular books of the ship. Bell, Comm. § 428; 4 Barn. & Adol. 375; 13 East, 538; 1 Younge & C. 326; 8 Wend. (N. Y.) 144; 16 Conn. 12. These are his general powers; but of course they may be limited or enlarged by the owners; and it may be observed that, without special authority, he cannot borrow money generally for the use of the ship, though, as above observed, he may settle the accounts for furnishings, or grant bills for them, which form debts against the concern, whether or not he has funds in his hands with which he might have paid them. 1 Bell, Comm. § 499. Although he may, in general, levy the freight which is by the bill of lading payable on the delivery of the goods, it would seem that he would not have power to take bills for the freight, and give up the possession of the lien over the cargo, unless it has been so settled by the charter party.

He cannot insure or bind the owners for premiums. 17 Me. 147; 2 Maule & S. 485; 13 East, 274; 7 B. Mon. (Ky.) 595; 11 Pick. (Mass.) 85; 5 Burrows, 2627; Paley, Ag. (Lloyd Ed.) 23, note 8; Abb. Shipp. pt. 1, c. 3, § 2; Marsh. Ins. bk. 1, c. 8, § 2; Livermore, Ag. 72, 73.

As the power of the master to enter into contracts of affreightment is superseded in the port of the owners, so it is by the presence of the ship's husband, or the knowledge of the contracting parties that a ship's husband has been appointed. 2 Bell, Comm. 199. The ship's husband, as such, has no lien on the vessel or proceeds. 2 Curt. C. C. (U. S.) 427.

SHIP'S PAPERS. The papers or documents required for the manifestation of the ownership and national character of a vessel and her cargo, and to show her compliance with the revenue and navigation laws of the country to which she belongs.

The want of these papers or any of them renders the character of a vessel suspicious (2 Boul. P. Dr. Com. 14); and the use of false or simulated papers frequently subjects the vessel to confiscation (15 East, 46, 70, 364; Molloy, bk. 2, c. 2, § 9), or avoids an insurance unless the insurer has stipulated that she may carry such papers (Id.)

A ship's papers are of two sorts: First, those required by the law of the particular country to which the ship belongs; as, the certificate of registry or of enrollment, the license, the crew list, the shipping articles, clearance, etc.; and, second, such as are required by the law of nations to be on board of neutral ships as evidence of their title to that character; as the sea brief or letter, or passport, the proofs of property in the ship, as bills of sale, etc., the charter party, the bills of lading, the invoices, the crew list or muster roll, the log book, and the bill of health. McCulloch, Comm. Dict. "Ship's Papers." See Glenn, Int. Law, Append. p. 365, for a list of ship's papers required by the laws of various nations.

SHIPPER. The consignor of goods to a ship or common carrier for transportation.

SHIPPING. A generic term for all marine craft, and for the things and matters which are incident to it.

SHIPPING ARTICLES. An agreement, in writing or print, between the master and seamen or mariners on board his vessel (except such as shall be apprenticed or servant to himself or owners), declaring the voyage or voyages, term or terms of time, for which such seamen or mariners shall be shipped. It is also required that at the foot of every such contract there shall be a memorandum, in writing, of the day and the hour on which each seaman or mariner who shall so ship and subscribe shall render himself on board to begin the voyage agreed upon.

SHIPWRECK. The loss of a vessel at sea, either by being swallowed up by the waves, by running against another vessel or thing at sea, or on the coast.

SHIRE. In English law. A district or division of country. Co. Litt. 50a.

SHIRE CLERK. He that keeps the county court.

SHIRE GEMOT (spelled also, *scire gemote, scir gemot, scyre gemote, shire mote;* from the Saxon *scir* or *scyre,* county, *shire,* and *gemote,* a court, an assembly).

The Saxon county court.

It was held twice a year before the bishop and alderman of the shire, and was the principal court. Spelman. "Gemotum;" Cunningham, "Shire;" Crabb, Hist. Eng. Law, 28.

SHIRE MAN, or **SCYRE MAN.** Before the Conquest, the judge of the county, by whom trials for land, etc., were determined.

SHOP. A building in which goods and merchandise are sold at retail; where a retail trade is carried on; a blacksmith's shop is rather a warehouse than a shop. 7 J. P. 132. See "Stores".

SHOPA. In old records, a shop. Cowell.

SHORE (Lat. *litus, littus*). Land on the margin of the sea, or a lake, or river. That space of land which is alternately covered and left dry by the rising and falling of the tide; the space between high and low water marks. Hale de Jur. Mar. par. 1. c. 6; Angell, Tide Waters, 67, c. 3; 8 Mich. 27. See "Seashore." The shore of a fresh water river is where the land and water ordinarily meet. 6 Cow. (N. Y.) 547. But this is more properly called the "bank" (*ripa*). A river in which the tide does not ebb and flow has no "shores," in the legal sense of the term. Walworth, C., 4 Hill (N. Y.) 375. And a lake without tides cannot properly be said to have a shore. Angell, Tide Waters, ubi supra. And see 3 Grat. (Va.) 655; 13 How. (U. S.) 391.

SHORE LINE. The term "shore line," in natural fresh water rivers, is usually used as meaning low water mark. 224 Ill. 57.

SHORT CAUSE. In English chancery practice, and in some of the United States, a cause the trial of which will take but a short time, and which may accordingly be put on a special calendar for speedy trial. See 8 Misc. Rep. (N. Y.) 94; 247 Ill. 112.

SHORT INTEREST. See "Gambling Contract."

SHORT MARKET. See "Gambling Contract."

SHORT NOTICE. In English practice. Four days' notice of trial. Wharton, "Notice of Trial at Common Law;" 3 Chit. St. 148; 1 Cromp. & M. 499. Where short notice has been given, two days is sufficient notice of continuance. Wharton.

SHORT SELLING. See "Gambling Contract."

SHORT SUMMONS. Process returnable in a shorter time than the ordinary summons or writ. It exists in New York and in other states.

SHOULD. A mandatory word. 163 Ill. 315.

SHOWING CAUSE. The presentation, on a hearing appointed for that purpose, of reasons and facts to control the action of the court in respect to a certain specified order or determination.

SHRIEVALTY. The office of sheriff; the period of that office.

SHYSTER. A lawyer who conducts business in a knavish or dishonest way.

SI. In Latin phrases. If.

SI A JURE DISCEDAS VAGUS ERIS, ET erunt omnia omnibus incerta. If you depart from the law, you will wander without a guide, and everything will be in a state of uncertainty to every one. Co. Litt. 227.

SI ALICUJUS REI SOCIETAS SIT, ET finis negotio impositus est, finitur societas. If there is a partnership in any matter, and the business is ended, the partnership ceases. 16 Johns. (N. Y.) 438, 489.

SI ALIQUID EX SOLEMNIBUS DEFICIat, cum aequitas poscit subveniendum est. If anything be wanting from required forms, when equity requires, it will be aided. 1 Kent, Comm. 157.

SI ASSUETIS MEDERI POSSIS NOVA non sunt tentanda. If you can be relieved by accustomed remedies, new ones should not be tried. 10 Coke, 142.

SI CONSTET DE PERSONA. If it be certain who is the person meant.

SI CONTINGAT (Lat. if it happen). Words of condition in old conveyances. 10 Coke, 42a.

SI INGRATUM DIXERIS, OMNIA DIXeris. If you affirm that one is ungrateful, in that you include every charge. A Roman maxim. Tray. Lat. Max.

SI ITA EST. If it be so. Emphatic words in the old writ of *mandamus* to a judge, commanding him, if the fact alleged be truly stated (*si ita est*), to affix his seal to a bill of exceptions. 5 Pet. (U. S.) 192.

SI JUDICAS, COGNOSCE. If you judge, understand.

SI MELIORES SUNT QUOS DUCIT amor, plures sunt quos corrigit timor. If those are better who are led by love, those are the greater number corrected by fear. Co. Litt. 392.

SI NON APPAREAT QUID ACTUM EST erit consequens, ut id sequamur quod in regione in qua actum est, frequentatur. If it does not appear what was agreed upon, the consequence will be that we must follow that which is the usage of the place where the agreement was made. Dig. 50. 17. 34.

SI NON OMNES (Lat. if all cannot). In English practice. A writ of association of justices whereby, if all in commission cannot meet at the day assigned, it is allowed that two or more may proceed with the business. Cowell; Fitzh. Nat. Brev. 111 (C), 186a; Reg. Orig. 202, 206.

SI NULLA SIT CONJECTURA QUAE DUcat alio, verba intelligenda sunt ex proprietate, non grammatica sed populari ex usu. If there be no inference which leads to a different result, words are to be understood according to their proper meaning, not in a grammatical, but in a popular and ordinary, sense. 2 Kent, Comm. 555.

SI PLURES CONDITIONES ASCRIPtae fuerunt donationi conjunctim, omnibus est parendum; et ad veritatem copulative requiritur quod utraque pars sit vera, si divisim, cuilibet vel alteri eorum satis est obtemperare; et in disjunctivis, sufficit alteram partem esse veram. If some conditions are conjunctively written in a gift, the whole of them must be complied with; and with respect to their truth, it is necessary that every part be true, taken jointly; if the conditions are separate, it is sufficient to comply with either one or other of them; and being disjunctive, that one or the other be true. Co. Litt. 225.

SI PLURES SINT FIDEJUSSORES, quodque erunt numero, singuli in solidum tenentur. If there are more sureties than one, how many soever they shall be, they shall each be held for the whole. Inst. 3. 21. 4; Id. 4. 116; 1 W. Bl. 388.

SI PRIUS (Law Lat.) In old practice. If before. Formal words in the old writs for summoning juries. Fleta, lib. 2, c. 65, § 12.

SI QUID UNIVERSITATI DEBETUR SINgulis non debetur, nec quod debet universitas singuli debent. If anything is due to a corporation, it is not due to the individual members of it, nor do the members individually owe what the corporation owes. Dig. 3. 4. 7; 1 Bl. Comm. 484.

SI QUIDEM IN NOMINE, COGNOMINE, praenomine, agnomine legatarii erraverit; cum de persona constat, nihilominus valet legatum. If the testator has erred in the name, cognomen, praenomen, or title of the legatee, whenever the person is rendered certain, the legacy is nevertheless valid. Inst. 2. 20. 29; Broom, Leg. Max. (3d London Ed.) 574; 2 Domat, bk. 2, tit. 1, s. 6, §§ 10, 19.

SI QUIS (Lat.) In the civil law. If any one. Formal words in the praetorian edicts. The word *"quis,"* though masculine in form, was held to include women. Dig. 50. 16. 1.

SI QUIS CUSTOS FRAUDEM PUPILLO fecerit, a tutela removendus est. If a guardian behave fraudulently to his ward, he shall be removed from the guardianship. Jenk. Cent. Cas. 39.

SI QUIS PRAEGNANTEM UXOREM REliquit, non videtur sine liberis decessisse. If a man dies, leaving his wife pregnant, he shall not be considered as having died childless.

SI QUIS UNUM PERCUSSERIT, CUM alium percutere vellet, in felonia tenetur. If a man kill one, meaning to kill another, he is held guilty of felony. 3 Inst. 51.

SI RECOGNOSCAT (Lat. if he acknowledge). In old practice. A writ which lay for a creditor against his debtor for money numbered (*pecunia numerata*) or counted; that is, a specific sum of money, which the debtor had acknowledged in the county court, to owe him, as received *in pecuniis numeratis.* Cowell.

SI SUGGESTIO NON SIT VERA, LITErae patentes vacuae sunt. If the suggestion of a patent is false, the patent itself is void. 10 Coke, 113.

SI TE FECERIT SECURUM (Lat. if he make you secure). Words which occur in the form of writs, which originally required, or still require, that the plaintiff should give security to the sheriff that he will prosecute his claim, before the sheriff can be required to execute such writ.

SIB (Saxon). A relative or kinsman. Used in the Scotch tongue, but not now in English. A trace of it is found in the word "gossip" which originally was "God's sib," meaning God's kin.

SIC (Lat.) Thus; so; in such manner.

SIC ENIM DEBERE QUEM MELIOREM agrum suum facere, ne vicini deteriorem faciat. Every one ought so to improve his land as not to injure his neighbor's. 3 Kent, Comm. 441.

SIC INTERPRETANDUM EST UT VERba accipiantur cum effectu. Such an interpretation is to be made that the words may have an effect. 3 Inst. 80.

SIC SUBSCRIBITUR (Lat.) In Scotch practice. So it is subscribed. Formal words at the end of depositions, immediately preceding the signature. 1 How. St. Tr. 1379.

SIC UTERE TUO UT ALIENUM NON laedas. So use your own as not to injure another's property. 1 Bl. Comm. 306; Broom, Leg. Max. (3d London Ed.) 206, note, 246, 327, 332, 336, 340, 348, 353; 2 Bouv. Inst. note 2379; 5 Exch. 797; 12 Q. B. 739; 4 Adol. & E. 384; 15 Johns. (N. Y.) 218; 17 Johns. (N. Y.) 99; 17 Mass. 334; 4 McCord (S. C.) 472; 9 Coke, 59; 22 Ill. 510. Applied to the use of water powers. 90 Wis. 370, 28 L. R. A. 443.

SICH. A little current of water, which is dry in summer; a water furrow or gutter. Cowell.

SICIUS. A sort of money current among the ancient English, of the value of 2d.

SICKNESS. The state of being sick or suffering from disease; a diseased condition of the system; illness; ill health; a disease; a malady; a particular kind of disorder; a diseased, distracted, or enfeebled state. Inability to work from mere old age is not. 51 J. P. 227; pregnancy is not; 26 L. J. C. M. 169; but a woman may be "ill" from pregnancy. Color blindness and incurable blindness have been held to be sickness. 7 E. & B. 794; 90 Neb. 114; Ann. Cas. 1913 A 765; 3 El. & Bl. 587; 28 Eng. L. & Eq. 176.

SICUT (Lat.) As.

SICUT ALIAS. As at another time, or heretofore. This was a second writ sent out when the first was not executed.

SICUT ALIAS PRAECIPIMUS. As we have formerly commanded you. 70 Ill. App. 179; 172 Ill. 196.

SICUT ME DEUS ADJUVET (Lat.) So help me God. Fleta, lib. 1, c. 18, § 4.

SICUT NATURA NIL FACIT PER SALtum, ita nec lex. As nature does nothing by a bound or leap, so neither does the law. Co. Litt. 238.

SIDE. See "Plea Side."

SIDE-BAR RULES. In English practice. Rules which were formerly moved for by attorneys on the side bar of the court, but now may be had of the clerk of the rules, upon a *praecipe*. These rules are, that the sheriff return his writ, that he bring in the body, for special imparlance, to be present at the taxing of costs, and the like.

SIDELINGS (L. Lat.) In old records. Unploughed pieces of land on the sides of fields. Meres or balks on the side of arable lands. Cowell.

SIDESMEN (*testes, synodales*). In ecclesiastical law. A kind of impanelled jury, consisting of two, three, or more persons, in every parish, who were, upon oath, to present all heretics and irregular persons. In process of time they became standing officers in many places, especially cities. They were called "synodsmen,"—by corruption, "sidesmen;" also "questmen." But their office has become absorbed in that of church warden. 1 Burn, Ecc. Law, 399.

SIENS. Scions or descendants.

SIERVO (Spanish). In Spanish law. A slave. Las Partidas, pt. 4, tit. 21, lib. 1.

SIETE PARTIDAS (Spanish). Seven parts. See "Las Partidas."

SIGHT. Presentment. Bills of exchange are frequently drawn payable at sight, or a certain number of days or months after sight.

SIGILLUM (Lat.) A seal.

SIGILLUM EST CERA IMPRESSA, QUIA cera sine impressione non est sigillum. A seal is a piece of wax impressed, because wax without an impression is not a seal. 3 Inst. 169. But see "Seal."

SIGLA (Lat.) In Roman law. Marks or signs of abbreviation used in writing. Code, 1. 17. 11. 13.

SIGN. To make a mark. The signature is the sign thus made. 140 Iowa 80.

Signing does not necessarily mean a written signature, as distinguished from a signature by mark, by print, by stamp, or by the hand of another. 157 Mass. 439. See "Signature."

A token of anything; a note or token given without words.

SIGN MANUAL. In English law. The signature of the king to grants or letters patent, inscribed at the top. 2 Bl. Comm. 347*.

Any one's name written by himself. Webster; Wharton. The sign manual is not good unless countersigned, etc. 9 Mod. 54.

SIGNA (Lat.) In civil law. Those species of *indicia* which come more immediately under the cognizance of the senses; such as stains of blood on the person of one accused of murder, indications of terror at being charged with the offense, and the like.

Signa, although not to be rejected as instruments of evidence, cannot always be relied upon as conclusive evidence, for they are frequently explained away. In the instance mentioned, the blood may have been that of a beast; and expressions of terror have been frequently manifested by innocent persons who did not possess much firmness. See Best, Pres. Ev. 13, note (f); Denisart.

SIGNARE (Lat.) In the civil law. To seal; to affix a seal; to confirm by a seal.

In old English law. To seal a measure. Fleta, lib. 2, c. 82, § 1.

SIGNATORIUS ANNULUS (Lat.) In the civil law. A signet ring; a seal ring. Dig. 50. 16. 74.

SIGNATURE.

——**In Ecclesiastical Law.** The name of a sort of rescript, without seal, containing the supplication, the signature of the pope or his delegate, and the grant of a pardon. Dict. Dr. Canonique.

——**In Practice.** By signature is understood the act of putting down a man's name at the end of an instrument, to adopt its statements, or attest its validity. The name thus written is also called a "signature." It must be the actual writing of the name, or the doing of some act intended by the person to be equivalent to the actual signature of the name. Fry Specif. Perf. § 517; 3 Mer. 2.

It is not necessary that a party should write his name himself, to constitute a signature; nor is it necessary that it be written as distinguished from signing by mark, by print, by stamp, or by the hand of another, 157 Mass. 439; or another may, with the signer's consent, guide his hand. 4 Wash. C. C. (U. S.) 262, 269.

A mark is sufficient even though the party is able to write. 8 Adol. & E. 94; 3 Nev. & P. 228; 3 Curt. C. C. (U. S.) 752; 2 Johns. (N. Y.) 144; and a printed name, if ratified and adopted, will suffice. Fry. Spec. Perf. § 518; 2 B. & P. 239; 27 W. R. 706; 48 L. J. Ch. 567; 2 M. & S. 286. See Sign.

SIGNET. A seal commonly used for the sign manual of the sovereign. Wharton. The signet is also used for the purpose of civil justice in Scotland. Bell, Dict.

SIGNIFICATION (Lat. *signum*, a sign, *facere*, to make). In French law. The notice given of a decree, sentence, or other judicial act.

SIGNIFICAVIT (Lat.) In ecclesiastical law. When this word is used alone, it means the bishop's certificate to the court of chancery in order to obtain the writ of excommunication; but where the words *writ of significavit* are used, the meaning is the same as *writ de excommunicato capiendo*. 2 Burn, Ecc. Law, 248; Shelf. Mar. & Div. 502.

SIGNING JUDGMENT.

——**In English Practice.** The plaintiff or defendant, when the cause has reached such a stage that he is entitled to a judgment, obtains the signature or allowance of the proper officer; and this is called "signing judgment," and is instead of the delivery of judgment in open court. Steph. Pl. 111. It is the leave of the master of the office to enter up judgment, and may be had in vacation. 3 Barn. & C. 317; Tidd, Prac. 616.

——**In American Practice.** It is an actual signing of the judgment on the record, by the judge or other officer duly authorized. Graham, Prac. 341.

SIGNUM (Lat.)

——**In the Roman and Civil Law.** A sign; a mark; a seal. The seal of an instrument. Calv. Lex.

——**In the Saxon Law.** The sign of a cross prefixed as a sign of assent and approbation to a charter or deed.

SILENT LEGES INTER ARMA. Laws are silent amidst arms. 4 Inst. 70.

SILK GOWN. The professional robe worn by those barristers who have been appointed queen's counsel (*q. v.*) It is the distinctive badge of queen's or king's counsel.

SILVA CAEDUA (Lat.) By these words, in England, is understood every sort of wood, except gross wood of the age of twenty years. Bac. Abr. "Tythes" (C).

SIMILITER (Lat. likewise). In pleading The plaintiff's reply that, as the defendant has put himself upon the country, he, the plaintiff, does the like. It occurs only when the plea has the conclusion to the country, and its effect is to join the plaintiff in the issue thus tendered by the defendant. Co. Litt. 126a. The word *similiter* was the effective word when the proceedings were in Latin. 1 Chit. Pl. 519; Archb. Civ. Pl. 250. See Steph. Pl. 255; 2 Saund. 319b; Cowp. 407; 1 Strange, 551; 11 Serg. & R. (Pa.) 32.

SIMILITUDO LEGALIS EST, CASUUM diversorum inter se collatorum similis ratio; quod in uno similium valet, valebit in altero. Dissimilium, dissimilis est ratio. Legal similarity is a similar reason which governs various cases when compared with each other, for what avails in one similar case will avail in the other. Of things dissimilar, the reason is dissimilar. Co. Litt. 191.

SIMONIA EST VOLUNTAS SIVE DESIderium emendi vel vendendi spiritualia vel spiritualibus adhaerentia. Contractus ex turpi causa et contra bonos mores. Simony is the will or desire of buying or selling spiritualities, or things pertaining thereto. It is a contract founded on a bad cause, and against morality. Hob. 167.

SIMONY. In ecclesiastical law. The selling and buying of holy orders or an ecclesiastical benefice. Bac. Abr. By "simony" is also understood an unlawful agreement to receive a temporal reward for something holy or spiritual. Code, 1. 3. 31; Ayliffe, Par. 496.

SIMPLE AVERAGE. Particular average (*q. v.*)

SIMPLE CONTRACT. A contract the evidence of which is merely oral or in writing, not under seal nor of record. 1 Chit. Cont. 1; 1 Chit. Pl. 88. And see 11 Mass. 30; 11 East, 312; 4 Barn. & Ald. 588; 3 Starkie, Ev. 995; 2 Bl. Comm. 472.

SIMPLE DEPOSIT. A deposit made, according to the civil law, by one or more persons having a common interest.

SIMPLE LARCENY. The felonious taking and carrying away the personal goods of another, unattended by acts of violence. It is distinguished from "compound larceny," which is stealing from the person or with violence. See "Larceny."

SIMPLE OBLIGATION. An unconditional obligation; one which is to be performed without depending upon any event provided by the parties to it.

SIMPLE TRUST. A simple or passive trust corresponds with the ancient use, and is where property is simply vested in one person for the use of another, and the nature of the trust, not being qualified by the settler, is left to the construction of law. It differs from a "special trust," in that the trustee performs no duty. 7 Watts & S. (Pa.) 25; 2 Bouv. Inst. note 1896. See "Trust."

SIMPLE WARRANDICE. In Scotch law. An obligation to warrant or secure from all subsequent or future deeds of the grantor. Whishaw. A simple warranty against the grantor's own acts.

SIMPLEX (Lat.) Simple or single; as, *charta simplex* is a deed poll or single deed. Jacob.

SIMPLEX BENEFICIUM. In ecclesiastical law. A minor dignity in a cathedral or collegiate church, or any other ecclesiastical benefice, as distinguished from a cure of souls. It may therefore be held with any parochial cure, without coming under the prohibitions against pluralities.

SIMPLEX COMMENDATIO NON OBLIGAT. A simple recommendation does not bind. Dig. 4. 3. 37; 2 Kent, Comm. 485; Broom, Leg. Max. (3d London Ed.) 700; 4 Taunt. 488; 16 Q. B. 282, 283; Cro. Jac. 4; 5 Johns. (N. Y.) 354; 4 Barb. (N. Y.) 95.

SIMPLEX DICTUM. In old English practice. Simple averment; mere assertion without proof. Bracton, fol. 320.

SIMPLEX ET PURA DONATIO DICI POTERIT, UBI NULLA EST ADJECTA CONDITIO NEC MODUS. A gift is said to be pure and simple when no condition or qualification is annexed. Bracton, 1.

SIMPLEX JUSTITIARIUS (Law Lat.) In old records. Simple justice. A name sometimes given to a *puisne* justice. Cowell.

SIMPLEX LOQUELA. In old English practice. Simple speech; the mere declaration or plaint of a plaintiff. Called in Fleta, *simplex vox*. Lib. 2, c. 63, § 9.

SIMPLEX OBLIGATIO. A single obligation; a bond without a condition. 2 Bl. Comm. 340.

SIMPLEX PEREGRINATIO (Law Lat.) In old English law. Simple pilgrimage. Fleta, lib. 4, c. 2, § 2.

SIMPLICITAS EST LEGIBUS AMICA, ET NIMIA SUBTILITAS IN JURE REPROBATUR. Simplicity is favorable to the law, and too much subtlety is blameworthy in law. 4 Coke, 8.

SIMPLICITER (Lat.) Simply; without ceremony; in a summary manner.

SIMUL CUM (Lat. together with). In pleading. Words used in indictments and declarations of trespass against several persons, when some of them are known and others are unknown.

In cases of riots, it is usual to charge that A. B., together with others unknown, did the act complained of. 2 Chit. Crim. Law, 488; 2 Salk. 593.

When a party sued with another pleads separately, the plea is generally entitled in the name of the person pleading, adding, "sued with ———," naming the other party. When this occurred, it was, in the old phraseology, called pleading with a *simul cum*.

SIMUL ET SEMEL (Lat.) Together and at one time. Fleta, lib. 2, c. 47, § 5; 1 Saund. 323a, note (6).

SIMULATED FACT. In the law of evidence. A fabricated fact; an appearance given to things by human device, with a view to deceive and mislead. Burrill, Circ. Ev. 131.

SIMULATIO LATENS. A species of feigned disease, in which disease is actually present, but where the symptoms are falsely aggravated, and greater sickness is pretended than really exists. Beck, Med. Jur. 3.

SIMULATION (Lat. *simul*, together). In French law. The concert or agreement of two or more persons to give to one thing the appearance of another, for the purpose of fraud. Merlin, Repert.

With us, such act might be punished by indictment for a conspiracy, by avoiding the pretended contract, or by action to recover back the money or property which may have been thus fraudulently obtained.

SINE (Lat.) Without.

SINE ANIMO REVERTENDI. Without the intention of returning.

SINE ASSENSU CAPITULI (Lat. without the consent of the chapter). In old English practice. A writ which lay where a dean, bishop, prebendary, abbot, prior, or master of a hospital aliened the lands holden in the right of his house, abbey, or priory, without the consent of the chapter; in which case his successor might have this writ. Fitzh. Nat. Brev. 195.

SINE CONSIDERATIONE CURIAE (Lat.) Without the judgment of the court.

SINE DECRETO (Lat.) Without authority of a judge. 2 Kames, Eq. 115.

SINE DIE (Lat.) Without day. A judgment for a defendant in many cases is *quod eat sine die*, that he may go without day. While the cause is pending and undetermined, it may be continued from term to term by *dies datus*. See "Continuance;" Co. Litt. 362b, 363a. When the court or other body rise at the end of a session or term, they adjourn *sine die.*

SINE HOC QUOD (Law Lat. without this, that). A technical phrase in old pleading, of the same import with the phrase "*absque hoc*" (*q. v.*)

SINE JUDICIO (Law Lat.) Without judgment; without a judicial sentence. Fleta, lib. 4, c. 14, § 1.

SINE LIBERIS (Lat.) Without children. For the construction of this phrase in the civil law, see Dig. 50. 16. 148; Id. 50. 17. 187.

SINE NUMERO (Law Lat. without stint or limit). A term applied to common. Fleta, lib. 4, c. 19, § 8.

SINE POSSESSIONE USUCAPIO PROcedere non potest. There can be no prescription without possession.

SINE PROLE. Without issue. Used in genealogical tables.

SINECURE. In ecclesiastical law. A term used to signify that an ecclesiastical officer is without a charge or cure.

In common parlance, it means the receipt of a salary for an office when there are no duties to be performed.

SINGLE BILL. One without any condition, and which does not depend upon any future event to give it validity. 5 Ill. 483.

SINGLE BOND. A bond without a condition.

SINGLE COMBAT, TRIAL BY. See "Battel."

SINGLE ORIGINAL. An original instrument which is not executed in duplicate.

SINGULAR SUCCESSOR. A purchaser is so termed in the Scotch law, in contradistinction to the heir of the landed proprietor, who succeeds to the whole heritage by regular title of succession, whereas the purchaser acquires rights solely by the single title of the former proprietor.

SINGULI IN SOLIDUM TENENTUR. Each is bound for the whole. 6 Johns. Ch. (N. Y.) 242, 252.

SINKING FUND. A fund arising from particular taxes, imposts, or duties, which is appropriated towards the payment of the interest due on a public loan, and for the gradual payment of the principal. 9 Neb. 453.

SIST. In Scotch practice. A stay or suspension of proceedings, an order for a stay of proceedings. Bell, Dict.

SISTER. A female person considered in the relation to another person having the same parents. 193 Ill. App. 617.

SITHCUNDMAM. The high constable of a hundred.

SITTINGS AFTER TERM. Sittings *in banc* after term were held by authority of St. 1 & 2 Vict. c. 32. The courts were at liberty to transact business at their sittings as in term time, but the custom was to dispose only of cases standing for argument or judgment. Wharton.

SITTINGS IN BANK (or BANC). The sittings which the respective superior courts of common law hold during every term for the purpose of hearing and determining the various matters of law argued before them.

They are so called in contradistinction to the sittings at *nisi prius*, which are held for the purpose of trying issues of fact. The former are usually held, in England, before four of the judges, while at the latter one judge only presides. Holthouse; 3 Steph. Comm. 423.

In America, the practice is essentially the same, all the judges, or a majority of them, usually, sitting *in banc*, and but one holding the court for jury trials, and the term has the same application here as in England.

SITTINGS IN CAMERA. See "Chambers."

SITUS (Lat.) Situation; location. 5 Pet. (U. S.) 524.

Real estate has always a fixed *situs*, while personal estate has no such fixed *situs;* the law *rei sitae* regulates real, but not the personal, estate. Story, Confl. Laws, § 379.

The rules as to the *situs* of personal property have been stated as follows:

(1) Movable and tangible chattels are of the county where they may be at the time.

(2) Shares in corporations or joint-stock companies are of the county where the chief office of the company is situated.

(3) Judgments and other debts of record are of the county where the record is kept.

(4) Bonds and negotiable securities are of the county where they happen to be at the time.

(5) Promissory notes, bills of exchange, and all simple contracts are of the county where the debtor resides.

(6) Demands against a commonwealth are of the county wherein is situated the seat of government. 2 Minor, Inst. 853.

SIVE TOTA RES EVINCATUR, SIVE pars habet regressum emptor in venditorem. The purchaser who has been evicted in whole or in part has an action against the vendor. Dig. 21. 2. 1; Broom, Leg. Max. (3d London Ed.) 690.

SIX ACTS, THE. The acts passed in 1819, for the pacification of England, are so called. They, in effect, prohibited the training of persons to arms; authorized general searches and seizure of arms; prohibited meetings of more than fifty persons for the discussion of public grievances; repressed with heavy penalties and confiscations seditious and blasphemous libels; and checked pamphleteering by extending the newspaper stamp duty to political pamphlets. Brown.

SIX CLERKS IN CHANCERY. Officers who received and filed all proceedings, signed office copies, attended court to read the pleadings, etc. Abolished by 5 Vict. c. 5. 3 Bl. Comm. 443*; Spence, Eq. Jur.; Fleta, lib. 2, c. 13, § 15.

SIXHINDI. Servants of the same nature as rodknights. Anc. Inst. Eng.

SKELETON BILL. In commercial law. A blank paper, properly stamped, in those countries where stamps are required, with the name of a person signed at the bottom.

In such case, the person signing the paper will be held as the drawer or acceptor, as it may be, of any bill which shall afterwards be written above his name, to the sum of which the stamp is applicable. 1 Bell, Comm. (5th Ed.) 390.

SKIAGRAPH. A skiagraph is not a picture of the object or substance itself, but of the shadow merely, which is cast by such object or substance. 149 Ill. App. 445.

SLAINS. See "Letters of Slains."

SLANDER. In torts. Words maliciously spoken or written of another, imputing to him some crime, or tending to exclude him from society, and cause him to be avoided (see 87 N. C. 300), or which tend to his prejudice in his profession, trade, or business (36 Wis. 515). See "Slut."

SLANDER OF TITLE. In torts. A statement tending to cut down the extent of title. See 60 Cal. 160. An action for slander of title is not properly an action for words spoken, or for libel written and published, but an action on the case for special damage sustained by reason of the speaking or publication of the slander of the plaintiff's title. An action is permitted against one who falsely and maliciously disparages the title of another to property, whether real or personal, and thereby causes him some special pecuniary loss or damage. 90 Cal. 537. This action is ranged under that division of actions in the digests and other writers on the text law, and is so held by the courts at the present day. An action for slander of title is a sort of metaphorical expression. Slander of title may be of such a nature as to fall within the scope of ordinary slander. Slander of title ordinarily means a statement tending to cut down the extent of title, which is injurious only if it is false. It is essential, to give a cause of action, that the statement should be false. It is essential, also, that it should be malicious, —not malicious in the worst sense, but with intent to injure the plaintiff. If the statement be true, if there really be the infirmity in the title that is suggested, no action will lie, however malicious the defendant's intention might be. Heard, Lib. & Sland. §§ 10, 59 et seq.

SLANDERER. A calumniator who maliciously and without reason imputes a crime or fault to another, of which he is innocent.

For this offense, when the slander is merely verbal, the remedy is an action on the case for damages; when it is reduced to writing or printing, it is a libel.

SLAVE. One over whose life, liberty, and property another has unlimited control. The *jus vitae et necis* is included in pure or absolute slavery. Such a power has no foundation in natural law, and hence the Justinian Code declared it *contra naturam esse.* Inst. 1. 4. 2.

Every limitation placed by law upon this absolute control modifies and to that extent changes the condition of the slave. In every slaveholding state of the United States, the life and limbs of a slave were protected from violence inflicted by the master or third persons.

Among the Romans, the slave was classed among things (*res*). He was *homo sed non persona.* Heinec. Elem. Jur. Civ. lib. 1, § 75. He was considered *pro nullo et mortuo, quia nec statu familiae nec civitatis nec libertatis gaudet.* Id. § 77. See, also, 4 Dev. (N. C.) 340; 9 Ga. 582. In the United States, as a person, he was capable of committing crimes, of receiving his freedom, of being the subject of homicide, and of modifying by his volition, very materially, the rules applicable to other species of property. His existence as a person being recognized by the law, that existence was protected by the law. 1 Hawks (N. C.) 217; 2 Hawks (N. C.) 454; 1 Ala. 8; 1 Miss. 83; 11 Miss. 518; 2 Va. Cas. 394; 5 Rand. (Va.) 678; 1 Yerg. (Tenn.) 156; 11 Humph. (Tenn.) 172.

In the slaveholding states, the relations of husband and wife and parent and child were recognized by statutes in relation to public sales, and by the courts in all cases where such relations were material to elucidate the motives of their acts.

A slave has no political rights, the government being the judgment who shall be its citizens. His civil rights, though necessarily more restricted than the freeman's, are based upon the same foundation,—the law of the land. He has none but such as are by that law and the law of nature given to him. The civil-law rule "*partus sequitur ventrem*" was adopted in all the slaveholding states, the status of the mother at the time of birth deciding the status of the issue. 1 Hen. & M. (Va.) 134; 2 Rand. (Va.) 246; 4 Rand. (Va.) 600; 1 Hayw. (N. C.) 234; 1 Cooke (Tenn.) 381; 2 Bibb (Ky.) 298; 2 Dana (Ky.) 432; 5 Dana (Ky.) 207; 2 Mo. 71; 3 Mo. 540; 8 Pet. (U. S.) 220; 14 Serg. & R. (Pa.) 446; 15 Serg. & R. (Pa.) 18; 2 Brev. (N. C.) 307; 3 Har. & McH. (Md.) 139; 20 Johns. (N. Y.) 1;

12 Wheat. (U. S.) 568; 2 How. (U. S.) 265, 496. In South Carolina, Georgia, Mississippi, Virginia, Louisiana, and perhaps Maryland, this rule was adopted by statute.

The slave cannot acquire property; his acquisitions belong to his master. 5 Cow. (N. Y.) 397; 1 Bailey (S. C.) 633; 2 Hill, Ch. (S. C.) 397; 2 Rich. (S. C.) 424; 6 Humph. (Tenn.) 299; 2 Ala. 320; 5 B. Mon. (Ky.) 186. The *peculium* of the Roman slave was *ex gratia*, and not of right. Inst. 2. 9. 3; Heinec. Elem. Jur. Civ. lib. ii. tit. xviii. In like manner, negro slaves in the United States were, as a matter of fact, sometimes permitted by their masters, *ex gratia*, to obtain and retain property. The same was true of ancient villeins in England. The slave could not be a witness, except for and against slaves or free negroes. This was, perhaps, the rule of the common law. None but a freeman was *otheswortk.* The privilege of being sworn was one of the characteristics of a *"liber et legalis homo."* To lose this privilege, *amittere liberam legem*, was a severe punishment. 3 Bl. Comm. 340; Fortesc. c. xxvi.; Co. Litt. 6b. With this the civil law agreed. Huberus, Praelec. lib. xxv. tit. v. § 2. In the United States, the rule of exclusion mentioned was enforced in all cases where the evidence was offered for or against free white persons. 6 Leigh (Va.) 74. In most of the states this exclusion was by express statutes, while in others it existed by custom and the decision of the courts. 10 Ga. 519. In the slaveholding states, and in Ohio, Indiana, Illinois, and Iowa, by statute, the rule was extended to include free persons of color or emancipated slaves. 14 Ohio, 199; 3 Har. & J. (Md.) 97. The slave could be a suitor in court only for his freedom. For all other wrongs, he appeared through his master, for whose benefit the recovery was had. 9 Gill & J. (Md.) 19; 1 Litt. (Ky.) 326; 1 Mo. 608; 4 Yerg. (Tenn.) 303; 3 Brev. (N. C.) 11; 4 Gill (Md.) 249; 9 La. 156; 4 T. B. Mon. (Ky.) 169. The suit for freedom is favored. 1 Hen. & M. (Va.) 143; 8 Pet. (U. S.) 44; 2 A. K. Marsh. (Ky.) 467; 2 Call (Va.) 350; 4 Rand. (Va.) 134. Lapse of time worked no forfeiture by reason of his dependent condition (3 Dana [Ky.] 382; 8 B. Mon. [Ky.] 631; 1 Hen. & M. [Va.] 141), and such was the civil law (Code, 7. 22. 2. 3). The master was bound to maintain, support, and defend his slave, however helpless or impotent. If he failed to do so, public officers were provided to supply his deficiency at his expense. In Tennessee, the master in such a case was responsible for all that he stole.

Cruel treatment was a penal offense of a high grade. Emancipation of the slave was the consequence of conviction in Louisiana; and the sale of the slave to another master was a part of the penalty in Alabama and Texas. In some of the ancient German states, and also by the "Code noir," another and more effectual penalty was a total disqualification of the master forever to hold slaves.

Among the ancient Lombards, if a master debauched his slave's wife, the slave and his wife were thereby emancipated. Among the Romans, double damages were given for the corruption of a slave. The enfranchisement of a slave is called "manumission." The word is expressive of the idea. Thus, Litt. § 204, *"manumittere quod idem est, quod extra manum, vel potestem alterius ponere."* Manumission being merely the withdrawal of the dominion of the master, the right to manumit exists everywhere, unless forbidden by law. No one but the owner can manumit (4 J. J. Marsh. [Ky.] 103; 10 Pet. [U. S.] 583), and the effect is simply to make a freeman, not a citizen. The state must decide who shall be citizens. See "Servus."

SLAVE TRADE. The traffic in slaves, or the buying and selling of slaves for profit. It is either foreign or domestic. The former is when the trade includes transportation from a foreign state; the latter, when confined within a single state or states connected in a federal union.

SLAVERY. The status or condition of a slave. The keeping of slaves as a practice or legal institution.

SLEEPING PARTNER. See "Partner."

SLEEPING RENT. An expression used in English coal-mine leases to indicate a fixed rent, as distinguished from a rent based on the output. It is said to be so called because payable though the mine was "sleeping" (unworked).

SLIP. In insurance law. An informal memorandum of the particulars of a contract of insurance to be afterwards included, usually called in the United States a "binding slip."

SLIPPA. A stirrup. There is a tenure of land in Cambridgeshire by holding the sovereign's stirrup.

SLOUGH. A swale or slough is a natural depression or natural water course into which surface water may be cast by open or covered drains wholly upon one's own land, without incurring liability to owner of lower land. 157 Iowa 6.

SLOUGH SILVER. A rent paid to the castle of Wigmore in lieu of certain days' work in harvest, heretofore reserved to the lord from his tenants. Cowell.

SLUT. An untidy woman, a slattern, and also a female dog, the same as "bitch." Such terms when applied to a woman, do not amount to a charge of crime or of want of chastity, and are not, therefore, in their common meaning, slanderous words. 27 Ill. App. 398.

SMALL. Small is a comparative term, denoting things of little size as compared with other things of the same class. 201 Ill. 97.

SMALL DEBTS COURTS. The several county courts established by 9 & 10 Vict. c. 95, for the purpose of bringing justice home to every man's door.

SMALL TITHES. All personal and mixed tithes, and also hops, flax, saffrons, potatoes, and sometimes, by custom, wood. Otherwise called "privy tithes." 2 Steph. Comm. (7th Ed.) 726.

SMART MONEY. Vindictive or exemplary damages given beyond the actual damage, by way of punishment and example, in cases of gross misconduct of defendant. 15 Conn. 225; 14 Johns. (N. Y.) 352; 6 Hill (N. Y.) 466. That it cannot be given by jury, see 2 Greenl. Ev. (4th Ed.) § 253, note. See "Damages."

SMOKE-FARTHINGS. In old English law. An annual rent paid to cathedral churches; another name for the pentecostals or customary oblations offered by the dispersed inhabitants within a diocese, when they made their processions to the mother cathedral church. Cowell.

SMOKE SILVER. A modus of sixpence in lieu of tithe wood. Twisdale, Hist. Vindicat. 77.

SMUGGLING. The fraudulent taking into a country, or out of it, merchandise which is lawfully prohibited. More specifically, a secret introduction of goods into a state with intent to avoid payment of duty thereon. Bac. Abr.

SO HELP ME GOD. A formal invocation of the Deity to witness, by which an oath is concluded.

SOBRE JUEZES. In Spanish law. Superior judges. Las Partidas, pt. 3, tit. 4, lib. 1.

SOBRINI, or **SOBRINAE** (Lat.) In the civil law. The children of cousins german in general. Cooper, Just. Inst. notes,* 573; Dig. 38. 10, 3, pr.

SOC, SOK, or **SOKA.** In Saxon law. Jurisdiction; a power or privilege to administer justice and execute the laws; also a shire, circuit, or territory. Cowell.

SOCA. A seigniory or lordship, enfranchised by the king, with liberty of holding a court of his *socmen* or *socagers, i. e.*, his tenants.

SOCAGE. This word, according to the earlier common-law writers, originally signified a service rendered by a tenant to his lord, by the *soke* or ploughshare; but Mr. Somner's etymology, referred to by Blackstone, seems more apposite, who derives it from the Saxon word soc, which signifies liberty or privilege, denoting thereby a free or privilege tenure. A species of English tenure, whereby the tenant held his lands of the lord by any certain service in lieu of all other services, so that the service was not a knight's service. Its principal feature was its certainty; as, to hold by fealty and a certain rent, or by fealty homage and a certain rent, or by homage and fealty without rent, or by fealty and certain corporal service, as ploughing the lord's land for a specified number of days. 2 Bl. Comm. 80.

The term "socage" was afterwards extended to all services which were not of a military character, provided they were fixed; as, by the annual payment of a rose, a pair of gilt spurs, a certain number of capons, or of so many bushels of corn. Of some tenements, the service was to be hangman, or executioner of persons condemned in the lord's court; for in olden times such officers were not volunteers, nor to be hired for lucre, and could only be bound thereto by tenure. There were three different species of these socage tenures,—one in frank tenure, another in ancient tenure, and the third in base tenure. The second and third kinds are now called, respectively, "tenure in ancient demesne," and "copyhold tenure." The first is called "free and common socage," to distinguish it from the other two; but, as the term "socage" has long ceased to be applied to the two latter, "socage" and "free and common socage" now mean the same thing. Bracton; Co. Litt. 17, 86.

By St. 12 Car. II. c. 24, the ancient tenures by knight's service were abolished, and all lands, with the exception of copyholds and of ecclesiastical lands, which continued to be held in free alms (frankalmoigne), were turned into free and common socage, and the great bulk of real property in England is now held under this ancient tenure. Many grants of land in the United States, made, previous to the Revolution, by the British crown, created the same tenure among us, until they were formally abolished by the legislatures of the different states. In 1787, the state of New York converted all feudal tenure within its boundaries into a tenure by free and common socage; but in 1830 it abolished this latter tenure, with all its incidents, and declared that from thenceforth all lands in the state should be held upon a uniform allodial tenure, and vested an absolute property in the owners according to their respective estates. Similar provisions have been adopted by other states; and the ownership of land throughout the United States is now essentially free and unrestricted. See "Tenure."

SOCAGER. A tenant by socage.

SOCAGIUM IDEM EST QUOD SERVItum socae; et soca, idem est quod caruca. Socage is the same as service of the soc;

and "soc" is the same thing as a plow. Co. Litt. 86.

SOCER (Lat.) The father of one's wife; a father-in-law.

SOCIDA (Lat.) In civil law. The name of a contract by which one man delivers to another, either for a small recompense, or for a part of the profits, certain animals, on condition that, if any of them perish, they shall be replaced by the bailer, or he shall pay their value.

A contract of hiring, with the condition that the bailee takes upon him the risk of the loss of the thing hired. Wolff. § 638.

SOCIEDAD. In Spanish law. Partnership. Schmidt, Civ. Law, 153, 154.

SOCIETAS (Lat.) In civil law. A contract in good faith made to share in common the profit and loss of a certain business or thing, or of all the possessions of the parties. Calv. Lex.; Inst. 3. 26; Dig. 17. 21. See "Partnership."

Also, companionship or partnership in good or evil. Cicero, pro S. Rosc. 34; Fleta, lib. 1, c. 38, § 18.

SOCIETAS LEONINA (Lat.) In Roman law. That kind of society or partnership by which the entire profits should belong to some of the partners, in exclusion of the rest.

It was so called in allusion to the fable of the lion and other animals, who, having entered into partnership for the purpose of hunting, the lion appropriated all the prey to himself. Dig. 17. 2. 29. 2; Poth. Traite de Societe, note 12. See 2 McCord (S. C.) 421; 6 Pick. (Mass.) 372.

SOCIETAS NAVALIS (Lat.) In European law. Naval partnership or company; the sailing of a number of vessels in company, for mutual protection. Otherwise called *admiralitas*. Locc. de Jur. Mar. lib. 2, c. 2; Id. lib. 3, c. 7.

SOCIETE (Fr.) In French law. Partnership. See "Commendam."

SOCIETE ANONYME. In French law. An association where the liability of all the partners is limited. It had in England until lately no other name than that of "chartered company," meaning thereby a joint-stock company whose shareholders, by a charter from the crown, or a special enactment of the legislature, stood exempted from any liability for the debts of the concern, beyond the amount of their subscriptions. 2 Mill, Pol. Econ. 485.

SOCIETE EN COMMENDITE. In Louisiana. A partnership formed by a contract by which one person or partnership agrees to furnish another person or partnership a certain amount, either in property or money, to be employed by the person or partnership to whom it is furnished, in his or their own name or firm, on condition of receiving a share in the profits, in the proportion determined by the contract, and of being liable to losses and expenses to the amount furnished, and no more. Civ. Code La. art. 2810; Code de Comm. 26, 33. 4 Pardessus, Dr. Com. note 1027; Dalloz, "Societe Commerciale," note 166. See "Commendam."

SOCIETY. In its abstract sense (used with no article prefixed), the public at large; the people; the body politic. In a concrete sense, a voluntary unincorporated association of persons for a common purpose.

SOCII MEI SOCIUS, MEUS SOCIUS non est. The partner of my partner is not my partner. Dig. 50. 17. 47. 1.

SOCIUS. In the civil law, a partner.

SOCMAN. A tenant by socage.

SOCMANRY. Free tenure by socage.

SOCNA. A privilege, liberty, or franchise. Cowell.

SODOMITE. One who has been guilty of sodomy. Formerly, such offender was punished with great severity, and was deprived of the power of making a will.

SODOMY. A carnal copulation by human beings with each other against nature, or with a beast. 2 Bish. Crim. Law, § 1029.

A distinction not generally recognized has been made between bestiality and sodomy, the former being defined as carnal connection between a human being and a brute, and the latter as carnal connection between two human beings against the order of nature. 10 Ind. 355.

It has generally been held that at common law the crime of sodomy was committed by penetration per anum, and not per os. A penetration of the mouth is not sodomy. Bishop's New Criminal Law, Vol. 2, § 1194; 2 Russell on Crimes, p. 638; McClain's Crim. Law, § 1153; 86 Neb. 237, 21 Am. & Eng. Ann. Cas. 336; 133 Ky. 720, 118 S. W. 943.

SOIT BAILE AUX COMMONS (Law Fr. let it be delivered to the commons). The form of indorsement on a bill when sent to the house of commons. Dyer, 93a.

SOIT BAILE AUX SEIGNEURS (Law Fr. let it be delivered to the lords). The form of indorsement on a bill in parliament when sent to the house of lords. Hob. 111a.

SOIT DROIT FAIT AL PARTIE. In English law. Let right be done to the party. A phrase written on a petition of right, and subscribed by the king. See "Petition of Rights."

SOIT FAIT COMME IL EST DESIRE (Law Fr. let it be as it is desired). The royal assent to private acts of parliament,

SOJOURNING (Fr. *sejourner*). Literally, dwelling for a day. "The term 'sojourning' means something more than 'traveling,' and applies to a temporary, as contradistinguished from a permanent residence." 1 Wheat. (U. S.) 5.

SOKE REEVE. The lord's rent gatherer in the soca. Cowell.

SOKEMANRIES. Lands and tenements which were not held by knight service, nor by grand serjeantry, nor by petit, but by simple services; being, as it were, lands enfranchised by the king or his predecessors from their ancient demesne. Their tenants were "sokemans." Wharton.

SOKEMANS. In English law. Those who held their land in socage. 2 Bl. Comm. 100.

SOLA AC PER SE SENECTUS DONATIONEM testamentum aut transactionem non vitiat. Old age does not alone and of itself vitiate a will or a gift. 5 Johns. Ch. (N. Y.) 148, 158.

SOLAR DAY. That period of time which begins at sunrise and ends at sunset; the same as "artificial day." Co. Litt. 135a; 3 Chit. St. 1376, note.

SOLAR MONTH. A calendar month; the mean quantity of which is thirty days, ten hours, twenty minutes, and five seconds, being one twelfth of the time composing the whole year. 1 Jones L. (N. C.) 87; Co. Litt. 135b; 1 W. Bl. 450; 1 Maule & S. 111; 1 Bing. 307; 3 Chit. St. 1375, note.

SOLARES. In Spanish law. Lots of ground. This term is frequently found in grants from the Spanish government of lands in America. 2 White, Coll. 474.

SOLARIUM (Lat.) In the civil law. A rent paid for the ground, where a person built on the public land. A ground rent. Spelman; Calv. Lex.

SOLATIUM. Compensation; damages allowed for injury to the feelings.

SOLD NOTE. The name of an instrument in writing, given by a broker to a buyer of merchandise, in which it is stated that the goods therein mentioned have been sold to him; or one given to the buyer by a broker employed to sell goods, in his own name, as agent of both seller and buyer, whereby they are respectively bound. 167 Ill. 372. 1 Bell, Comm. (5th Ed.) 435; Story, Ag. § 28. Some confusion may be found in the books as to the name of these notes. They are sometimes called "bought notes."

SOLD SHORT. See "Gambling Contract."

SOLE. Alone, single; used in contradistinction to "joint" or "married." A sole tenant, therefore, is one who holds lands in his own right, without being joined with any other. A *feme sole* is a single woman; a sole corporation is one composed of only one natural person.

SOLE CORPORATION. A corporation consisting of one person and his legal successors, thus having the attribute of perpetuity, as a bishop of the Roman Catholic Church or of the Church of England.

SOLE TENANT. He that holds lands by his own right only, without any other person being joined with him. Cowell.

SOLEMN. Formal; in regular form.

SOLEMN FORM. In English law. Probate may be granted either in solemn form or in common form.

Probate in solemn form is only employed when there is or is likely to be a dispute as to the validity of the will, and in such a case the person who wishes its validity to be established commences an action against the person who disputes it. The action proceeds as to pleadings, trial, etc., in the same way as an ordinary action. If the plaintiff makes out his case, the court pronounces for the validity of the will, and the executor may then take probate of it as if it had not been disputed. Coote, Prob. Prac. 250, 308. As a general rule, probate in solemn form is conclusive on all who are parties to the proceedings, or cognizant of them. Browne, Prob. Prac. 101.

Probate in common form is that "form which is slight and summary for ordinary and undisputed cases."

SOLEMN WAR. A war made in form by public declaration. See "War."

SOLEMNES LEGUM FORMULAE (Lat.) In the civil law. Solemn forms of laws; forms of forensic proceedings and of transacting legal acts. One of the sources of the unwritten law of Rome. Butler, Hor. Jur. 47.

SOLEMNITAS ATTACHIAMENTORUM (Law Lat.) In old English practice. Solemnity or formality of attachments. The issuing of attachments in a certain formal and regular order. Bracton, fols. 439, 440; 1 Reeve, Hist. Eng. Law, 480; Fleta, lib. 2, c. 65, § 5.

SOLEMNITATES JURIS SUNT OBSERVANDAE. The solemnities of law are to be observed. Jenk. Cent. Cas. 13.

SOLEMNITY. The formality established by law to render a contract, agreement, or other act valid.

A marriage, for example, would not be valid if made in jest and without solemnity. See "Marriage;" Dig. 4. 1. 7; Id. 45. 1. 30.

SOLICITATION OF CHASTITY. The asking a person to commit adultery or fornication.

This, of itself, is not an indictable offense. Salk. 382; 2 Chit. Prac. 478. The contrary doctrine, however, has been held in

Connecticut. 7 Conn. 267. In England, the bare solicitation of chastity is punished in the ecclesiastical courts. 2 Chit. Prac. 478. See 2 Strange, 1100; 10 Mod. 384; Sayer, 33; 1 Hawk. P. C. c. 74; 2 Ld. Raym. 809.

The civil law punished arbitrarily the person who solicited the chastity of another. Dig. 47. 11. 1. See 3 Phillim. Ecc. Law, 508.

SOLICITOR. A person whose business is to be employed in the care and management of suits depending in courts of chancery.

A solicitor, like an attorney, will be required to act with perfect good faith towards his clients. He must conform to the authority given him. It is said that, to institute a suit, he must have a special authority, although a general authority will be sufficient to defend one. The want of a written authority may subject him to the expenses incurred in a suit. 3 Mer. 12; Hovenden, Frauds, c. 2, pp. 28-61. See 1 Phil. Ev. 102; 2 Chit. Prac. 2. See "Attorney."

SOLICITOR-GENERAL. In English law. A law officer of the crown, appointed by patent during the royal pleasure, and who assists the attorney general in managing the law business of the crown. Selden, 1. 6. 7. He is first in right of preaudience. 3 Bl. Comm. 28, n. (a), n. 9; Enc. Brit.

SOLICITOR OF THE TREASURY. The title of one of the officers of the United States, created by Act May 29, 1830 (4 U. S. St. at Large, 414), which prescribed his duties and his rights.

His powers and duties as originally fixed were: First those which were by law vested and required from the agent of the treasury of the United States. Second, those which theretofore belonged to the commissioner or acting commissioner of the revenue, relating to the superintendence of the collection of outstanding direct and internal duties. Third, to take charge of all lands which shall be conveyed to the United States, or set off to them in payment of debts, or which are vested in them by mortgage or other security; and to release such lands which had, at the passage of the act, become vested in the United States, on payment of the debt for which they were received. Fourth, generally to superintend the collection of debts due to the United States, and receive statements from different officers in relation to suits or actions commenced for the recovery of the same. Fifth, to instruct the district attorneys, marshals, and clerks of the circuit and district courts of the United States, in all matters and proceedings appertaining to suits in which the United States are a party or interested, and to cause them to report to him any information he may require in relation to the same. Sixth, to report to the proper officer from whom the evidence of debt was received the fact of its having been paid to him, and also all credits which have, by due course of law, been allowed on the same. Seventh, to make rules for the government of collectors, district attorneys, and marshals, as may be requisite. Eighth, to obtain from the district attorneys full accounts of all suits in their hands, and submit abstracts of the same to congress.

His rights were: First to call upon the attorney general of the United States for advice and direction as to the manner of conducting the suits, proceedings, and prosecutions aforesaid. Second, to receive a salary of three thousand five hundred dollars per annum. Third, to employ, with the approbation of the secretary of the treasury, a clerk, with a salary of one thousand five hundred dollars, and a messenger, with a salary of five hundred dollars. Fourth, to receive and send all letters, relating to the business of his office, free of postage.

SOLICITOR TO THE SUITORS' FUND. An officer of the English court of chancery, who is appointed in certain cases guardian *ad litem.*

SOLIDO. See "In Solidum."

SOLIDUM (Lat.) In the civil law. A whole; an entire or undivided thing. See "In Solidum."

SOLINUM (Law Lat.) In old English law. Two plough lands, and somewhat less than a half. Co. Litt. 5a. Spelman defines it a plough land.

SOLO CEDIT QUOD SOLO IMPLANTATUR. What is planted in the soil belongs to the soil. Inst. 2. 1. 32; 2 Bouv. Inst. note 1572.

SOLO CEDIT QUOD SOLO INAEDIFICATUR. Whatever is built on the soil belongs to the soil. Inst. 2. 1. 29. See 1 Mackeld. Civ. Law, § 268; 2 Bouv. Inst. note 1571.

SOLUM PROVINCIALE. In Roman law. The *solum italicum* (an extension of the old *Ager Romanus*) admitted full ownership, and of the application to it of *usucapio;* whereas the *solum provinciale* (an extension of the old *Ager Publicus*) admitted of a possessory title only, and of *longi temporis possessio* only. Justinian abolished all distinctions between the two, sinking the *italicum* to the level of the *provinciale.* Brown.

SOLUM REX HOC NON FACERE POTEST, quod non potest injuste agere. This alone the king cannot do,—he cannot act unjustly. 11 Coke, 72.

SOLUS DEUS HAEREDEM FACIT. God alone makes the heir. Co. Litt. 5.

SOLUTIO (Lat. release). In civil law. Payment. By this term is understood every species of discharge or liberation, which is called "satisfaction," and with which the creditor is satisfied. Dig. 46. 3. 54; Code 8. 43. 17; Inst. 3. 30. This term has rather a reference to the substance of the obligation than to the numeration or counting of the money. Dig. 50. 16. 176.

SOLUTIO INDEBITI (Lat.) In civil law. The case where one has paid a debt, or done an act or remitted a claim, because he thought that he was bound in law to do so, when he was not. In such cases of mistake there is an implied obligation (*quasi ex contractu*) to pay back the money, etc. Mackeld. Civ. Law, § 468.

SOLUTIO PRETII EMPTIONIS LOCO habetur. The payment of the price stands in the place of a sale. Jenk. Cent. Cas. 56.

SOLUTIONE FEODI MILITIS PARLIAmenti, or **Feodi burgensis parliamenti.** Old writs whereby knights of the shire and burgesses might have recovered their wages or allowance if it had been refused. 35 Hen. VIII. c. 11.

SOLUTUS (Lat. from *solvere*, to loose). ——**In the Civil Law.** Loosed; freed from confinement; set at liberty. Dig. 50. 16. 48. ——**In Scotch Practice.** Purged. A term used in old depositions. See "Purged of Partial Counsel."

SOLVABILITE (Fr.) In French law. Ability to pay; solvency. Emerig. Tr. des Assur. c. 8, § 15.

SOLVENCY. The state of a person who is able to pay all his debts; the opposite of "insolvency" (*q. v.*)

Imports adequate means of a person to pay his debts, which embraces within its meaning the opportunity by reasonable diligence to convert and apply to such purpose. In other words, a person is deemed insolvent who at the time in question is unable to pay his debts in the ordinary course of business.

It means that the debtor is in such a condition that the demand may be collected out of his property by due course of law. Ability to raise money on credit for the payment of debts does not constitute solvency. 13 Wend. (N. Y.) 375, 377; 4 Hill (N. Y.) 650.

SOLVENDO (Lat. paying). An apt word of reserving a rent in old conveyances. Co. Litt. 47a.

SOLVENDO ESSE. To be in a state of solvency, *i. e.*, able to pay.

SOLVENDO ESSE NEMO INTELLIGItur nisi qui solidum potest solvere. No one is considered to be solvent unless he can pay all that he owes. Dig. 50. 16. 114.

SOLVENDUS (Lat.) In old English law. To be paid. Fleta, lib. 2, c. 64, § 3.

SOLVENT. One who has sufficient to pay his debts and all obligations. Dig. 50. 16. 114. The opposite of insolvent (*q. v.*)

SOLVERE (Lat. to unbind; to untie). To release; to pay. *Solvere dicimus eum qui fecit quod facere promisit.* 1 Bouv. Inst. note 807.

SOLVIT. (Lat. from *solvere, q. v.*) He paid. 10 East, 206.

SOLVIT AD DIEM (Lat. he paid at the day). In pleading. The name of a plea to an action on a bond, or other obligation to pay money, by which the defendant pleads that he paid the money on the day it was due. See 1 Strange, 652; Rep. temp. Hardw. 133; Comyn, Dig. "Pleader" (2 W 29).

This plea ought to conclude with an averment, and not to the country. 1 Sid. 215; 12 Johns. (N. Y.) 253. See 2 Phil. Ev. 92; Coxe (N. J.) 467.

SOLVIT POST DIEM (Lat. he paid after the day). In pleading. The name of a special plea in bar to an action of debt on a bond, by which the defendant asserts that he paid the money after the day it became due. 1 Chit. Pl. 480, 555; 2 Phil. Ev. 93.

SOLVITUR ADHUC SOCIETAS ETIAM morte socii. A partnership is moreover dissolved by the death of a partner. Inst. 3. 26. 5; Dig. 17. 2.

SOLVITUR EO LIGAMINE QUO LIGAtur. In the same manner that a thing is bound it is unloosed. 4 Johns. Ch. (N. Y.) 582.

SOMERSETT'S CASE. A celebrated decision of the English king's bench, in 1771-72, affirming the extinction of villeinage, and the nonexistence of any other form of slavery in England.

SON ASSAULT DEMESNE (Law Fr. his own first assault). In pleading. A form of a plea to justify an assault and battery, by which the defendant asserts that the plaintiff committed an assault upon him, and the defendant merely defended himself.

When the plea is supported by evidence, it is a sufficient justification, unless the retaliation by the defendant were excessive, and bore no proportion to the necessity, or to the provocation received. 1 East, P. C. 406; 1 Chit. Prac. 595.

SONS. The words "sons," "daughters," "child," and "children" are not technical legal terms, to which a fixed and determined meaning must be given regardless of the sense in which they are employed, but they are flexible and subject to construction, to give effect to the intention of the testator. 230 Ill. 270.

SONTAGE. A tax of forty shillings anciently laid upon every knight's fee. Cowell.

SONTICUS (Lat.) In the civil law. That which hurts or hinders; that which tends to delay or put off.

SOREHON, or SORN. An arbitrary exaction, formerly existing in Scotland and Ireland. Whenever a chieftain had a mind to revel, he came down among the tenants with his followers, by way of contempt called "*gilliwitfitts*," and lived on free quarters. See Bell, Dict.

SORNER. In Scotch law. A person who takes meat and drink from others by force or menaces, without paying for it. Bell, Dict.

SORS (Lat.)

——**In Civil Law.** A lot; chance; fortune. Calv. Lex.; Ainsworth. Sort; kind. The little scroll on which the thing to be drawn by lot was written. Carpentier. A principal or capital sum; *e. g.*, the capital of a partnership. Calv. Lex.

——**In Old English Law.** A principal lent on interest, as distinguished from the interest itself. Pryn, Collect. tom. 2, p. 161; Cowell.

SORTITIO (Lat. from *sortiri*, to cast or draw lots). In the civil law. A casting or drawing of lots; a determination or choice by lot. *Sortitio judicum*, a drawing of judges (*judices*) on criminal trials, resembling the modern practice of drawing a jury. Halifax, Anal. bk. 3, c. 13, No. 20; 3 Bl. Comm. 366.

SOUL SCOT. A mortuary, or customary gift due ministers, in many parishes of England, on the death of parishioners. It was originally voluntary, and intended as amends for ecclesiastical dues neglected to be paid in the lifetime. 2 Bl. Comm. 425*.

SOUND MIND. That state of a man's mind which is adequate to reason, and comes to a judgment upon ordinary subjects like other rational men.

SOUNDING IN DAMAGES. When an action is brought, not for the recovery of lands, goods, or sums of money (as is the case in real or mixed actions, or the personal action of debt or detinue), but for damages only, as in covenant, trespass, etc., the action is said to be sounding in damages. Steph. Pl. 126, 127.

SOUS SEING PRIVE. In Louisiana. An act or contract evidenced by writing under the private signature of the parties to it. The term is used in opposition to the "authentic act," which is an agreement entered into in the presence of a notary or other public officer.

The form of the instrument does not give it its character so much as the fact that it appears or does not appear to have been executed before the officer. 5 Mart. (La.; N. S.) 196; 7 Mart. (La.; N. S.) 548.

The effect of a *sous seing prive* is not the same as that of the "authentic act." The former cannot be given in evidence until proved, and, unless accompanied by possession, it does not, in general, affect third persons. 6 Mart. (La.; N. S.) 429, 432. The latter, or authentic acts, are full evidence against the parties and those who claim under them. 8 Mart. (La.; N. S.) 132.

SOUTH SEA FUND. The produce of the taxes appropriated to pay the interest of such part of the English national debt as was advanced by the South Sea Company and its annuitants. The holders of South Sea annuities have been paid off, or have received other stock in lieu thereof. 2 Steph. Comm. (7th Ed.) 578.

SOVEREIGNTY. The union and exercise of all human power possessed in a state. It is a combination of all power; it is the power to do everything in a state without accountability,—to make laws, to execute and to apply them, to impose and collect taxes and levy contributions, to make war or peace, to form treaties of alliance or of commerce with foreign nations, and the like. Story, Const. § 207.

Abstractly, sovereignty resides in the body of the nation, and belongs to the people; but these powers are generally exercised by delegation.

When analyzed, sovereignty is naturally divided into three great powers, namely, the legislative, the executive, and the judiciary. The first is the power to make new laws, and to correct and repeal the old; the second is the power to execute the laws, both at home and abroad; and the last is the power to apply the laws to particular facts, to judge the disputes which arise among the citizens, and to punish crimes.

Strictly speaking, in our republican forms of government the absolute sovereignty of the nation is in the people of the nation; and the residuary sovereignty of each state, not granted to any of its public functionaries, is in the people of the state. 2 Dall. (U. S.) 471. And see, generally, 2 Dall. (U. S.) 433, 455; 3 Dall. (U. S.) 93; 1 Story, Const. § 208; 1 Toullier. Dr. Civ. note 20; Merlin, Repert.

SOWMING and ROWMING. In Scotch law. Terms used to express the form by which the number of cattle brought upon a common by those having a servitude of pasturage may be justly proportioned to the rights of the different persons possessed of the servitude. Bell, Dict.

SOWNE. In old English law. To be leviable. An old exchequer term applied to sheriff's returns. "Estreats that sowne not" were such as could not be collected. 4 Inst. 107; Cowell; Spelman.

SPADONES (Lat.) In civil law. Those who, on account of their temperament or some accident they have suffered, are unable to procreate. Inst. 1. 11. 9; Dig. 1. 7. 2. 1. And see "Impotence."

SPARSIM (Lat.) Here and there; in a scattered manner; sparsedly; dispersedly.

It is sometimes used in law; for example, the plaintiff may recover the place wasted, not only where the injury has been total, but where trees growing *sparsim* in a close are cut. Bac. Abr. "Waste" (M); Brownl. 240; Co. Litt. 54a; 4 Bouv. Inst. note 3690.

SPATAE PLACITUM. A court for the speedy execution of justice upon military delinquents. Cowell.

SPEAKING DEMURRER. In pleading. One which alleges new matter in addition to that contained in the bill as a cause for demurrer. 4 Brown, Ch. 254; 2 Ves. Jr. 83; 4 Paige, Ch. (N. Y.) 374.

SPECIAL. That which relates to a particular species or kind, or is confined to a particular person, object or class, opposed to general; as, special verdict and general verdict; special imparlance and general imparlance; special jury, or one selected for a particular case, and general jury; special issue and general issue, etc.

SPECIAL ACCEPTANCE. A qualified acceptance of a bill of exchange, as by stipulating for payment at a certain time or place.

SPECIAL ACT. A private statute (*q. v.*)

SPECIAL ADMINISTRATION. See "Administration."

SPECIAL AGENT. An agent whose authority is confined to a particular or an individual instance. It is a general rule that he who is invested with a special authority must act within the bounds of his authority, and he cannot bind his principal beyond what he is authorized to do. 2 Bouv. Inst. note 1299; 2 Johns. (N. Y.) 48; 5 Johns. (N. Y.) 48; 15 Johns. (N. Y.) 44; 8 Wend. (N. Y.) 494; 1 Wash. C. C. (U. S.) 174. See "Agent."

SPECIAL ALLOWANCES. In taxing the costs of an action as between party and party, the taxing officer is, in certain cases, empowered to make special allowances; *i. e.*, to allow the party costs which the ordinary scale does not warrant.

SPECIAL APPEARANCE. See "Appearance."

SPECIAL ASSESSMENT. A species of taxation to pay for local improvements for public purposes upon real property, which recognizes the general public interest, but rests upon the theory that such property, by reason of locality, is specially benefited by the improvement. 246 Ill. 52; 190 Ill. 476; 155 Ill. 271; 133 Ill. 469.

SPECIAL ASSUMPSIT. In practice. An action of *assumpsit* brought on a special contract, which the plaintiff declares upon, setting out its particular language or its legal effect.

It is distinguished from a general *assumpsit*, where the plaintiff, instead of setting out the particular language or effect of the original contract, declares as for a debt arising out of the execution of the contract, where that constitutes the debt. 3 Bouv. Inst. note 3426.

SPECIAL BAIL. See "Bail."

SPECIAL BASTARD. One born of parents before marriage, the parents afterwards intermarrying. See "Bastard."

SPECIAL BENEFITS. Any benefits not conjectural or speculative, which result to the market value of property as a result of an improvement are special benefits. 267 Ill. 124.

SPECIAL CASE. The name given in English practice to an agreed statement of facts, on which a cause is submitted to the court without trial. Also the statement of facts on which a point reserved for further consideration or for reference to another court is heard.

SPECIAL CLAIM. In English law. A claim not enumerated in the orders of 22d April, 1850, which required the leave of the court of chancery to file it. Such claims are abolished.

SPECIAL COMMISSION. In English law. An extraordinary commission of oyer and terminer and gaol delivery, issued by the crown to the judges when it is necessary that offenses should be immediately tried and punished. Wharton.

SPECIAL CONSTABLE. A person appointed and sworn as a constable in an emergency to augment the constabulary, or to serve during disability or disqualification of the constable.

SPECIAL CONTRACT. A specialty.

SPECIAL COUNT. A statement of the facts of the particular case, as opposed to the common counts (*q. v.*)

SPECIAL CUSTOM. A local custom. See "Custom."

SPECIAL DAMAGES. The damages recoverable for the actual injury incurred through the peculiar circumstance of the individual case, above and beyond those presumed by law from the general nature of the wrong. See "Damages."

SPECIAL DEMURRER. In pleading. One which excepts to the sufficiency of the pleadings on the opposite side, and shows specifically the nature of the objection and the particular ground of the exception. 3 Bouv. Inst. note 3022. See "Demurrer."

SPECIAL DEPOSIT. A deposit made of a particular thing with the depositary. It is distinguished from an irregular deposit.

——**In Banking Law.** A deposit which is to be returned in specie.

SPECIAL ELECTION. An election specially called for an emergency, as opposed to general election (*q. v.*)

SPECIAL ERRORS. Special pleas in error are those which assign for error matters in confession and avoidance, as a release of errors, the act of limitations, and the like, to which the plaintiff in error may reply or demur.

SPECIAL EXAMINER. An examiner in chancery appointed to take evidence in a particular suit.

SPECIAL EXECUTION. A special execution is process upon which a sale of property is had which has already been levied upon by writ of attachment and is in the custody of the law. 198 Ill. 494.

SPECIAL EXECUTOR. See "Executor."

SPECIAL FINDING. A finding by the jury of a particular ultimate fact material to the issue.

SPECIAL GUARANTY. See "Guaranty."

SPECIAL GUARDIAN. A guardian of limited or temporary power in respect of his ward, or of his ward's estate. A guardian of a particular fund, appointed because of the general guardian's adverse interest, or one who exercises general powers during a limited time, as where the general guardian is disqualified or incapacitated, are examples. In the broadest sense, guardians *ad litem* are special, but the term is not usually applied to them, and under the laws of some states, notably New York, they are distinct.

SPECIAL IMPARLANCE. In pleading. An imparlance which contains the clause, "saving to himself all advantages and exceptions, as well to the writ as to the declaration aforesaid." 2 Chit. Pl. 407, 408. See "Imparlance."

SPECIAL INDORSEMENT. An indorsement of a note or bill, naming the indorsee.

SPECIAL INDORSEMENT OF WRIT. In English practice. The writ of summons in an action may, under Order iii. 6, be indorsed with the particulars of the amount sought to be recovered in the action, after giving credit for any payment or set-off; and this special indorsement (as it is called) of the writ is applicable in all actions where the plaintiff seeks merely to recover a debt or liquidated demand in money payable by the defendant, with or without interest, arising upon a contract, express or implied, as, for instance, on a bill of exchange, promissory note, check, or other simple contract debt, or on a bond or contract under seal for payment of a liquidated amount of money, or on a statute where the sum sought to be recovered is a fixed sum of money, or in the nature of a debt, or on a guaranty, whether under seal or not. Brown.

SPECIAL ISSUE. In pleading. A plea to the action which denies some particular material allegation, which is in effect a denial of the entire right of action. It differs from the general issue, which traverses or denies the whole declaration or indictment. Gould, Pl. c. 2, § 38. See "General Issue."

SPECIAL JURISDICTION. Limited jurisdiction.

SPECIAL JURY. One selected in a particular way by the parties. See "Jury."

SPECIAL LAW. See "Statute."

SPECIAL LEGACY. A "specific legacy" (*q. v.*)

SPECIAL LIEN. A particular lien. See "Lien."

SPECIAL LIMITATION. A qualification serving to make out the bounds of an estate, so as to determine it ipso facto in a given event without action, entry or claim, before it would, or might, otherwise expire by force of, or according to, the general limitation. A special limitation may be created by the words "until," "so long," "if," "whilst" and "during." 59 Pa. St. 340.

SPECIAL MALICE. Express malice. See "Malice."

SPECIAL MATTER. Matter of special defense admitted under the general issue by a relaxation of the common-law rules of pleading. 3 Bl. Comm. 306. See "Special Plea."

SPECIAL MEETING. A meeting called for and limited to the transaction of a specified business. Applied to corporate meetings, including meetings of municipal councils or assembles.

SPECIAL MOTION. A special motion is a motion addressed to the discretion of the court, and which must be heard and determined, as distinguished from one which may be granted of course. 173 Mich. 109.

SPECIAL NON EST FACTUM. The name of a plea by which the defendant says that the deed which he has executed is not his own, or binding upon him, because of some circumstance which shows that it was not intended to be his deed, or because it was not binding upon him for some lawful reason; as, when the defendant delivered the deed to a third person as an escrow to be delivered upon a condition, and it has been delivered without the performance of the condition, he may plead *non est factum*, state the fact of the conditional delivery, the nonperformance of the condition, and add, "and so it is not his deed;" or if the defendant be a *feme covert*, she may plead *non est factum*, that she was a *feme covert* at the time the deed was made, "and so it is not her deed." Bac. Abr. "Please," etc. (H 3, I 2); Gould, Pl. c. 6, pt. 1, § 64. See "Issint."

SPECIAL OCCUPANT. When an estate is granted to a man and his heirs during the life of *cestui que vie*, and the grantee die without alienation, and while the life for which he held continues, the heir will succeed, and is called a "special occupant." 2 Bl. Comm. 259. In the United States, the statute provisions of the different states vary considerably upon this subject. In New York and New Jersey, special occupancy is abolished. Virginia, and probably Maryland, follow the English statutes. In Massachusetts and other states, where the real and personal estates of intestates are distributed in the same way and manner, the question does not seem to be material. 4 Kent, Comm. 27.

SPECIAL OFFICER. One who has been appointed a constable for a particular occasion, as in the case of an actual tumult or a riot, or for the purpose of serving a particular process.

SPECIAL OWNER. One having a special property. See "Property."

SPECIAL PAPER. A list kept in the English courts of common law, and now in the queen's bench, common pleas, and exchequer divisions of the high court, in which list demurrers, special cases, etc., to be argued are set down. It is distinguished from the new trial paper, peremptory paper, crown paper, revenue paper, etc., according to the practice of the particular division.

SPECIAL PARTNER. See "Partner."

SPECIAL PARTNERSHIP. See "Partnership."

SPECIAL PLEA. A plea which alleged matter to distinguish away or palliate the charge in the declaration. They were various, limitations and estoppel being examples of matters so to be pleaded.

SPECIAL PLEA IN BAR. One which advances new matter. It differs from the general in this, that the latter denies some material allegation, but never advances new matter. Gould, Pl. c. 2, § 38.

SPECIAL PLEADER. In English practice. A lawyer whose professional occupation is to give verbal or written opinions upon statements submitted to him, either in writing or verbally, and to draw pleadings, civil or criminal, and such practical proceedings as may be out of the general course. 2 Chit. Prac. 42.

SPECIAL PLEADING. The science of pleading.

The allegation of special or new matter to avoid the effect of the previous allegations of the opposite party, as distinguished from a direct denial of matter previously alleged on the opposite side. Gould, Pl. c. 1, § 18; 3 Wheat. (U. S.) 246; Comyn, Dig. "Pleader" (E 15).

SPECIAL PROCEEDINGS. A phrase used in the codes of procedure to denote all proceedings other than actions; generally, any proceeding in a court which was not under the common law and equity practice either an action at law or a suit in chancery is a special proceeding. 117 Cal. 387; Ency. of Pl. & Pr. 112.

SPECIAL PROPERTY. That property in a thing which gives a qualified or limited right. See "Property."

SPECIAL REQUEST. A request actually made, at a particular time and place. This term is used in contradistinction to a "general request," which need not state the time when nor place where made. 3 Bouv. Inst. note 2843.

SPECIAL RESTRAINT OF TRADE. See "Restraint of Trade."

SPECIAL RULE. A rule or order of court made in a particular case, for a particular purpose. It is distinguished from a "general rule," which applies to a class of cases. It differs also from a "common rule," or "rule of course."

SPECIAL SERVICE. In Scotch law. That form of service by which the heir is served to the ancestor who was feudally vested in the lands. Bell, Dict.

SPECIAL SESSIONS. In English law. A meeting of two or more justices of the peace, held for a special purpose (such as the licensing of alehouses), either as required by statute, or when specially convoked, which can only be convened after notice to all the other magistrates of the division, to give them an opportunity of attending. See "Statute."

SPECIAL STATUTE. A private statute. See "Statute."

SPECIAL TAIL. Where an estate tail is limited to the children of two given parents, as to "A. and the heirs of his body by B., his wife." 1 Steph. Comm. 244.

SPECIAL TERM. A term of court called for a special occasion, as distinguished from the regular terms held at times appointed by law.

SPECIAL TRAVERSE. See "Traverse."

SPECIAL TRUST. A special trust is one where a trustee is interposed for the execution of some purpose particularly pointed out, and is not, as in the case of a simple trust, a mere passive depositary of the estate, but is required to exert himself actively in the execution of the settlor's intention; as, where a conveyance is made to trustees upon trust to reconvey, or to sell for the payment of debts. 2 Bouv. Inst. note 1896. 115 Ill. 668. See "Trust."

SPECIAL VERDICT. In practice. A special verdict is one by which the facts of the case are put on the record, and the law is submitted to the judges, as where the jury instead of finding for either party, find and state all the facts at issue, and conclude conditionally, that if upon the whole matter thus found, the court should be of the opinion that the plaintiff has a good cause of action, they then find for the plaintiff, and assess his damages; if otherwise, then for the defendant. 129 Ill. 142. See "Verdict."

SPECIALIA GENERALIBUS DEROGANT. Special words derogate from general words. A special provision as to a particular subject matter is to be preferred to general language, which might have governed in the absence of such special provision. L. R. 1 C. P. 546.

SPECIALTY. A writing sealed and delivered, containing some agreement. 2 Serg. & R. (Pa.) 503; Willes, 189; 1 P. Wms. 130; 10 Ga. 167. A writing sealed and delivered, which is given as a security for the payment of a debt, in which such debt is particularly specified. Bac. Abr. "Obligation" (A).

Although in the body of the writing it is not said that the parties have set their hands and seals, yet if the instrument be really sealed, it is a specialty, and, if it be not sealed, it is not a specialty, although the parties in the body of the writing make mention of a seal. 2 Serg. & R. (Pa.) 504; 2 Coke, 5a. See "Bond;" "Debt;" "Obligation."

SPECIALTY DEBT. A debt due or acknowledged to be due by deed or instrument under seal. 2 Bl. Comm. 465.

SPECIE. Metallic money issued by public authority.

This term is used in contradistinction to "paper money," which in some countries is emitted by the government, and is a mere engagement which represents specie. Bank paper in the United States is also called "paper money." See "In Specie."

SPECIES (Lat.) In the civil law. Form; figure; fashion or shape; a form or shape given to materials. 1 Mackeld. Civ. Law, 277, § 265.

A particular thing; as distinguished from "genus."

——**Zoology.** A species embraces individuals of the same kind, and all of the individuals having the same characteristics. It embraces all individuals that are precisely alike in every character, and not capable of change by any accidental circumstances, and capable of uniform, invariable and permanent continuance by natural propagation. Or, it is founded on identity of form and structure, both external and internal—the principal characteristics of species in animals being the power to produce beings like themselves, and who are themselves naturally productive. 69 Ill. 471.

SPECIES FACTI (Lat.) The particular kind of act. Ainsworth.

SPECIFIC. Having a certain form or designation; observing a certain form; particular; precise. Burrill.

SPECIFIC DEVISES. Devises of lands particularly specified in the terms of the devise, as opposed to general and residuary devises of land, in which the local or other particular descriptions are not expressed. For example, "I devise my Hendon Hall estate" is a specific devise; but "I devise all my lands," or, "all other my lands," is a general devise or a residuary devise. But all devises are, in effect, specific; even residuary devises being so. L. R. 3 Ch. 420; L. R. 10 Ch. 136; Brown.

SPECIFIC LEGACY. A bequest of a particular thing, so described that it may be identified. The description may be such as to distinguish a particular article among several of the class owned by testator, or it may embrace all the property of a class owned by him. Thus, a legacy of "one set of blacksmith's tools" is general (8 N. Y. 520); but a legacy of "the diamond ring presented to me by A.," or of "all the personal property on the farm or in the house at the time of my death" (30 Hun [N. Y.] 531), is specific.

SPECIFIC PERFORMANCE. The actual accomplishment of a contract by the party bound to fulfill it.

An equitable remedy to compel the precise or substantial performance of a contract.

The right to the remedy was in its origin dependent on the inadequacy of the legal remedy by suit for damages, but this rule has been very much relaxed. 2 N. Y. 60; 7 Ill. 327.

SPECIFICATIO (Lat.) In civil law. The process by which, from material either of one kind or different kinds, either belonging to the person using them or to another, a new form or thing is created; as, if from gold or gold and silver a cup be made, or from grapes' wine. Calv. Lex. Whether the property in the new article was in the owner of the materials, or in him who effected the change, was a matter of contest between the two great sects of Roman lawyers. Stair, Inst. p. 204, § 41; Mackeld. Civ. Law, § 241.

SPECIFICATION. A particular and detailed account of a thing.

For example, in order to obtain a patent for an invention, it is necessary to file a specification or an instrument of writing, which must lay open and disclose to the public every part of the process by which the invention can be made useful. If the specification does not contain the whole truth relative to the discovery, or contains more than is requisite to produce the desired effect, and the concealment or addition was made for the purpose of deception, the patent would be void; for if the specification were insufficient on account of its want of clearness, exactitude, or good faith, it would be a fraud on society that the patentee should obtain a monopoly without giving up his invention. 2 Kent, Comm. 300; 1 Bell, Comm. pt. 2, c. 3, § 1, p. 112; Perpigna, Pat. 67; Renouard des Brevets d'Inv. 252. See "Patent."

——**In Military Law.** The clear and particular description of the charges preferred against a person accused of a military offense. Tytler, Mil. Law, 109.

SPECIFY. To mention specifically or explicitly, to state in full or explicit terms or explicitly and in detail, name expressly, distinctly and particularly. 145 Iowa 424, 431.

SPECIMEN. A sample; a part of something by which the other may be known.

Act Cong. July 4, 1836, § 6, requires the inventor or discoverer of an invention or discovery to accompany his petition and specification for a patent with specimens of ingredients, and of the composition of matter, sufficient in quantity for the purpose of experiment, where the invention or discovery is of the composition of matter.

SPECULATION. The hope or desire of making a profit by the purchase and resale of a thing. Pardessus, Dr. Com. note 12. The profit so made; as, he made a good speculation.

SPECULATIVE DAMAGES. See "Damages."

SPECULUM (Lat.) Mirror or looking glass. The title of several of the most ancient law books or compilations. One of the ancient Icelandic books is styled *Speculum Regale*. In the preface to this work, four others, bearing the same title of *Speculum*, are referred to. There is also a collection of the ancient laws of Pomerania and Prussia, under the same title. Barr. Obs. St. 1, 2, note (b).

SPEEDY EXECUTION. An execution which, by the direction of the judge at *nisi prius*, issues forthwith, or on some early day fixed upon by the judge for that purpose after the trial of the action. Brown.

SPEEDY TRIAL. A trial brought on as speedily as the prosecution can reasonably be expected or required to be ready for it. 4 Nev. 113; 74 Iowa 369.

SPENDTHRIFT. A person who, by excessive drinking, gaming, idleness, or debauchery of any kind, shall so spend, waste, or lessen his estate as to expose himself or his family to want or suffering, or expose the town to charge or expense for the support of himself or family. Rev. St. Vt. c. 65, § 9.

SPENDTHRIFT TRUST. A trust created for the purpose of providing for the maintenance of a person, and at the same time putting the property from which such maintenance is derived beyond the reach of the improvidence of the beneficiary. It is generally held that such trusts are ineffective, on the ground that the beneficial interest of the *cestui que trust*, whatever it may be, is liable for his debts (5 [Wall.] U. S. 441; 15 Ohio St. 419); but in some states, such trust provisions have been upheld (20 Mo. App. 1; 86 Tenn. 81).

SPERATE (Lat. *spero*, to hope.) That of which there is hope.

In the accounts of an executor and the inventory of the personal assets, he should distinguish between those which are sperate and those which are desperate. He will be *prima facie* responsible for the former, and discharged for the latter. 1 Chit. Prac. 520; 2 Williams, Ex'rs, 644; Toller, Ex'rs, 248. See "Desperate."

SPES EST VIGILANTIS SOMNIUM. Hope is the dream of the vigilant. 4 Inst. 203.

SPES IMPUNITATIS CONTINUUM AFfectum tribuit delinquendi. The hope of impunity holds out a continual temptation to crime. 3 Inst. 236.

SPES RECUPERANDI (Lat. the hope of recovery). A term applied to cases of capture of an enemy's property as a booty or prize, while it remains in a situation in which it is liable to be recaptured. As between the belligerent parties, the title to the property taken as a prize passes the moment there is no longer any hope of recovery. 2 Burrows, 683.

SPINSTER. An addition given, in legal writings, to a woman who never was married. Lovelace, Wills, 269.

SPIRITUAL CORPORATIONS. Corporations, the members of which are entirely spiritual persons, and incorporated as such, for the furtherance of religion, and perpetuating the rights of the church. They are of two sorts,—sole, as bishops, certain deans, parsons, and vicars, or aggregate, as dean and chapter, prior and convent, etc.

SPIRITUAL COURTS. Ecclesiastical courts (*q. v.*)

SPIRITUAL LORDS. The archbishops and bishops of the house of lords. 2 Steph. Comm. (7th Ed.) 328.

SPIRITUALISM. A belief in the power of departed spirits to communicate with the living by means of mediums. 160 Ill. App. 642.

SPIRITUALITY OF BENEFICES. The tithes of land, etc.

SPIRITUOUS LIQUORS. These are intoxicating liquids produced by distillation, and forming an article of commerce. 1 Exch. 281. The term does not include fermented liquors. 5 Blackf. (Ind.) 118.

SPITAL, or SPITTLE. A charitable foundation; a hospital for diseased people. Cowell.

SPITE FENCE. A fence erected maliciously and with no other purpose than to shut out the light and air from a neighbor's window. Such a fence is a nuisance, for no man has a right to build and maintain an entirely useless structure for the sole purpose of injuring his neighbor. 151 N. C. 434, 440, 19 Ann. Cas. 473, 475. 68 Ill. 479.

SPLIT. See "Gambling Contract."

SPLITTING A CAUSE OF ACTION. The bringing an action for only a part of the cause of action. This is not permitted either at law or in equity. 4 Bouv. Inst. note 4167.

SPOLIATION.
——**In English Ecclesiastical Law.** The name of a suit sued out in the spiritual court to recover for the fruits of the church, or for the church itself. Fitzh. Nat. Brev. 85.

A waste of church property by an ecclesiastical person. 3 Bl. Comm. 90.

——**In Torts.** Destruction of a thing by the act of a stranger; as, the erasure or alteration of a writing by the act of a stranger is called "spoliation;" as contradistinguished from "alteration." 5 Sneed (Tenn.) 344. This has not the effect to destroy its character or legal effect. 1 Greenl. Ev. § 566.

——**In Admiralty Law.** By spoliation is also understood the total destruction of a thing; as, the spoliation of papers by the captured party is generally regarded as a proof of guilt; but in America it is open to explanation except in certain cases, where there is a vehement presumption of bad faith. 2 Wheat. (U. S.) 227, 241; 1 Dods. Adm. 480, 486. See "Alteration."

SPOLIATOR (Lat. from *spoliare,* to despoil). In old English law. A despoiler; a disseisor. Fleta, lib. 4, c. 2, §§ 19, 20, 22.

A destroyer (of a deed). See "In Odium Spoliatoris."

——**Of Evidence.** One who wilfully withholds evidence in his possession or under his control, such as books, maps, contracts, etc., is a spoliator of evidence; his conduct being attributed to his supposed knowledge that the truth would have operated against him. 138 Ill. 539.

SPOLIATUS DEBET ANTE OMNIA RESTITUTI. He who has been despoiled ought to be restored before anything else. 2 Inst. 714; 4 Bl. Comm. 353.

SPOLIUM. In the civil and common law. A thing violently or unlawfully taken from another. 1 Mackeld. Civ. Law, 261, note.

SPONDEO (Lat.) In the civil law. I undertake; I engage. Inst. 3. 16. 1.

SPONDES? SPONDEO (Lat.) Do you undertake? I do undertake. The most common form of verbal stipulation in the Roman law. Inst. 3. 16. 1.

SPONDET PERITIAM ARTIS. He promises to use the skill of his art. Poth. de Contr. du Louage, note 425; Jones, Bailm. 22, 53, 62, 97, 120; Domat, liv. 1, tit. 4, § 8, note 1; 1 Story, Bailm. § 431; 1 Bell, Comm. (5th Ed.) 459; 1 Bouv. Inst. note 1004.

SPONSALIA, or STIPULATIO SPONSALITIA (Lat.) A promise lawfully made between persons capable of marrying each other, that at some future time they will marry. See "Espousals;" Ersk. Inst. 1. 6. 3.

SPONSIA JUDICIALIS. The feigned issue of the Romans. See "Feigned Issue."

SPONSIO (Lat.) In the civil law. An engagement or undertaking; particularly such as was made in the form of an answer to a formal interrogatory by the other party. Calv. Lex.; Dig. 50. 16. 7.

An engagement to pay a certain sum of money to the successful party in a cause. Calv. Lex.

SPONSIO LUDICRA (Lat.)
——**In Scotch Law.** A trifling or ludicrous engagement, such as a court will not sustain an action for. 1 Kames, Eq. Introd. 34.

——**In the Civil Law.** An informal undertaking, or one made without the usual formula of interrogation. Calv. Lex.

SPONSIONS. In international law. Agreements or engagements made by certain public officers, as generals or admirals, in time of war, either without authority or by exceeding the limits of authority under which they purport to be made.

Before these conventions can have any binding authority on the state, they must be confirmed by express or tacit ratification. The former is given in positive terms and in the usual forms; the latter is justly implied from the fact of acting under the agreement as if bound by it, and from any other circumstance from which an assent may be fairly presumed. Wheaton, Int. Law, pt. 3, c. 2, § 3; Grotius de Jure Belli, lib. 2, c. 15, § 16; Id. lib. 3, c. 22, §§ 1-3; Vattel. Law Nat. bk. 2, c. 14, §§ 209-212; Wolff. Inst. § 1156.

SPONSOR. In civil law. He who intervenes for another voluntarily and without being requested. The engagement which he enters into is only accessory to the principal. See Dig. 17. 1. 18; Nov. 4. 1; Code de Comm. arts. 158, 159; Code Nap. 1236; Wolff. Inst. § 1556.

SPONTE OBLATA. A free gift or present to the crown.

SPONTE VIRUM FUGIENS MULIER ET adultera facta, doti sua careat, nisi sponte retracta. A woman leaving her husband of her own accord, and committing adultery, loses her dower, unless her husband takes her back of his own accord. Co. Litt. 37.

SPORTING HOUSES. Houses of ill fame. 202 Ill. 66.

SPORTULA, or **SPORTELLA.** A dole or largess, either of meat or money, given by princes or great men to the poor. It was properly the pannier or basket in which the meat was brought, or with which the poor went to beg it, thence the word was transferred to the meat itself, and thence to money sometimes given in lieu of it. Enc. Lond.

SPOUSALS. In old English law. Mutual promises to marry.

SPOUSE BREACH. In old English law. Adultery. Cowell.

SPREAD. See "Gambling Contract."

SPRINGING USE. A use limited to arise on a future event, where no preceding use is limited, and which does not take effect in derogation of any other interest than that which results to the grantor, or remains in him in the meantime. Gilb. Uses (Sugden Ed.) 153, note; 2 Crabb, Real Prop. 498.

A future use, either vested or contingent, limited to arise without any preceding limitation. Cornish, Uses, 91.

It differs from a remainder in not requiring any other particular estate to sustain it than the use resulting to the one who creates it, intermediate between its creation and the subsequent taking effect of the springing use. Dyer, 274; Poll. 65; 1 Edw. Ch. (N. Y.) 34; 4 Dru. & W. 27; 1 Mod. 238; 1 Me. 271. It differs from an executory devise in that a devise is created by will, a use by deed. Fearne, Cont. Rem. 385 (Butler's note); Wilson, Uses. It differs from a shifting use, though often confounded therewith. See, generally, 2 Washb. Real Prop. 281. See "Use."

SPULZIE (*spoliatio*). In Scotch law. The taking away movables without the consent of the owner or order of law. Stair, Inst. 96, § 16; Bell, Dict.

SPURIUS (Lat.) In the civil law. A bastard; the offspring of promiscuous cohabitation, otherwise called *vulgo quaesitus*, or *conceptus*. Inst. 1. 10. 12.

One born of an unlawful intercourse (*ex nuptiis injustis*, or *ex damnato coitu*). Inst. 1. 10. 12; Bracton, fol. 63.

SPY. One who penetrates secretly or in disguise or by false pretenses within military lines for the purpose of obtaining information to be used to the disadvantage of the forces so spied upon.

SQUATTER. One who settles on the lands of others without any legal authority. This term is applied particularly to persons who settle on the public land. 3 Mart. (La.; N. S.) 293; 5 Biss. (U. S.) 530.

SQUEEZED. See "Gambling Contract."

STAB. To make a wound with a pointed instrument. A stab differs from a cut or a wound. 3 La. Ann. 514; Russ. & R. 356; Russ. Crimes, 597; Bac. Abr. "Maihem" (B).

STABILIA. A writ called by that name, founded on a custom in Normandy, that where a man in power claimed land in the possession of an inferior, he petitioned the prince that it might be put into his hands till the right was decided, whereupon he had this writ. Wharton.

STABIT PRAESUMPTIO DONEC PRObetur in contrarium. A presumption will stand good until the contrary is proved. Hob. 297; 3 Bl. Comm. 371; Broom, Leg. Max. (3d London Ed.) 852; 16 Mass. 87.

STABLE STAND. In forest law. One of the four evidences or presumptions whereby a man was convicted of an intent to steal the king's deer in the forest. This was when a man was found at his standing in the forest with a cross-bow or long-bow bent, ready to shoot at any deer, or else standing close by a tree with greyhounds in a leash, ready to slip. Cowell.

STABULARII (Lat. pl. of *stabularius*). In the civil law. Stable keepers; hostlers; *qui stabulum exercent*. Dig. 4. 9. 1. 5; Story, Bailm. § 464.

STAGE RIGHT. Words which it has been attempted to introduce as a substitute for "the right of representation and performance," but it can hardly be said to be an accepted term of English or American law.

STAGNUM (Lat.) A pool. It is said to consist of land and water, and therefore by the name of *stagnum* the water and the land may be passed. Co. Litt. 5.

STAKE. A sum of money or other valuable thing, the ownership of which is in dispute, or to which one or more have contributed, or own, who agree that it shall become the sole property of some person or persons upon the happening, in the future of an event at present uncertain. The person chosen as custodian of the property is called the stateholder (*q. v.*) 81 N. Y. 539.

STAKEHOLDER. A third person chosen by two or more persons to keep in deposit property the right or possession of which is contested between them, and to be delivered to the one who shall establish his right to it. Thus, each of them is considered as depositing the whole thing. This distinguishes this contract from that which takes place when two or more tenants in common deposit a thing with a bailee. Domat, Lois Civ. liv. 1, tit. 7, § 4; 1 Vern. 44, note 1.

A person having in his hands money or other property claimed by several others is considered in equity as a stakeholder. 1 Vern. 144.

The stakeholder cannot be regarded as a party to an illegal contract, or in pari delicto. He is a mere depositary, with a naked authority to deliver it over on the proposed contingency. If the authority is actually revoked before the money or thing is paid over or delivered, it remains a naked deposit to the use of the depositor. 32 Ill. App. 116; 2 Ill. 32.

STALE DEMAND. A claim which has been for a long time undemanded; as, for example, where there has been a delay of twelve years unexplained. 3 Mason (U. S.) 161.

STALLAGE (Saxon, *stal*). The liberty or right of pitching or erecting stalls in fairs or markets, or the money paid for the same. Blount; Wharton; 6 Q. B. 31.

STALLARIUS (Lat.) In Saxon law. The *praefectus stabuli*, now master of the horse (Saxon, *stalstabulum*). Blount. Sometimes one who has a stall in a fair or market. Fleta, lib. 4, c. 28, p. 13.

STAMP. An impression made by order of the government, on paper, which must be used in reducing certain contracts to writing, for the purpose of raising a revenue. See Starkie, Ev.; 1 Phil. Ev. 444.

A paper bearing an impression or device authorized by law, and adapted for attachment to some subject of duty or excise.

The term in American law is used often in distinction from "stamped paper," which latter meaning, as well as that of the device or impression itself, is included in the broader signification of the word.

Stamps or stamped paper are prepared under the direction of officers of the government, and sold at a price equal to the duty or excise to be collected. The stamps are affixed and cancelled; and where stamped paper is used, one use obviously prevents a second use. The internal revenue acts of the United States of 1862 and subsequent years require stamps to be affixed to a great variety of subjects, under severe penalties in the way of fines, and also under penalty of invalidating written instruments, and rendering them incapable of being produced in evidence.

STAND. To abide by a thing; to submit to a decision; to comply with an agreement; to have validity; as, the judgment must stand.

STANDARD.

——**In War.** An ensign or flag used in war.

——**In Measures.** A weight or measure of certain dimensions, to which all other weights and measures must correspond; as, a standard bushel. Also, the quality of certain metals, to which all others of the same kind ought to be made to conform; as, standard gold, standard silver.

STANDING ASIDE. A practice prevailing in England and a few of the United States in the selection of jurors in a criminal case, whereby the prosecuting attorney may peremptorily put aside a juror without challenge until the panel is exhausted, at which time the jurors so put aside are called, and cause must be shown against them.

STANDING MUTE. Refusal of one charged with crime to plead to the charge, or, after plea of not guilty, to put himself upon the country.

STANDING SEISED TO USES. See "Covenant to Stand Seized to Uses."

STANNARY COURTS (*stannary*, from Lat. *stannum*, Cornish, *stean*, tin,—a tin mine). In English law. Courts of record, in Devonshire and Cornwall, England, for the administration of justice among the tinners therein. They are of the same limited and exclusive nature as those of the counties palatine.

STAPLE. In international law. The right of staple, as exercised by a people upon foreign merchants, is defined to be that they may not allow them to set their merchandises and wares to sale, but in a certain place.

This practice is not in use in the United States. 1 Chit. Com. Law, 103; 4 Inst. 238; Malone, Lex. Merc. 237; Bac. Abr. "Execution" (B 1). See "Statute Staple."

STAR CHAMBER. See "Court of Star Chamber."

STARE DECISIS. To abide by or adhere to decided cases. It is a general rule that, when a point has been settled by a decision, it becomes a precedent which should be followed in subsequent cases before the same court. The rule is based wholly on policy, in the interest of uniformity and certainty of the law, but is frequently departed from. See "Rule of Property."

STARE DECISIS, ET NON QUIETA MOvere. To adhere to precedents, and not to unsettle things which are established. 9 Johns. (N. Y.) 395, 428; 11 Wend. (N. Y.) 504, 507; 23 Wend. (N. Y.) 336, 340; 25 Wend. (N. Y.) 119, 142; 4 Hill (N. Y.) 271, 323; 4 Hill (N. Y.) 592, 595; 22 Barb. (N. Y.) 97, 106.

STARE IN JUDICIO (Lat.) To appear before a tribunal, either as plaintiff or defendant.

STAT PRO RATIONE VOLUNTAS. The will stands in place of a reason. 1 Barb. (N. Y.) 408, 411; 16 Barb. (N. Y.) 514, 525.

STAT PRO RATIONE VOLUNTAS POpuli. The will of the people stands in place of a reason. 25 Barb. (N. Y.) 344, 376.

STATE (Lat. *stare*, to place, establish).

——**In Governmental Law.** A self-sufficient body of persons united together in one community for the defense of their rights, and to do right and justice to foreigners. In this sense, the state means the whole people united into one body politic; and the "state," and the "people of the state," are equivalent expressions. 1 Pet. Cond. Rep. (U. S.) 37-39; 2 Dall. (Pa.) 425; 3 Dall. (Pa.) 93; 2 Wilson, Lect. 120; Dane, Abr. Append. § 50, p. 63; 1 Story, Const. § 361. A body governmental and politic, comprising all the human beings within a certain defined territory, organized for the purpose of governing, and which does supremely govern, within the limits of that territory. The positive or actual organization of the legislative or judicial powers; thus, the actual government of the state is designated by the name of the state; hence the expression, the state has passed such a law or prohibited such an act. The section of territory occupied by a state; as, the state of Pennsylvania.

One of the commonwealths which form the United States of America.

——**In Practice.** To make known specifically; to explain particularly; as, to state an account, or to show the different items in an account; to state the cause of action in a declaration.

STATE OF FACTS AND PROPOSAL. In English lunacy practice, when a person has been found a lunatic, the next step is to submit to the master a scheme called a "state of facts and proposal," showing what is the position in life, property, and income of the lunatic, who are his next of kin and heir at law, who are proposed as his committees, and what annual sum is proposed to be allowed for his maintenance, etc. From the state of facts and the evidence adduced in support of it, the master frames his report. Elmer, Lun. 22; Pope, Lun. 79. A similar practice formerly prevailed in chancery.

STATE TRIALS. Trials of political offenders. Also the name of a series of reports of such trials held in England.

STATE'S EVIDENCE. A term used in the United States corresponding to the king's (or queen's) evidence of England.

STATED ACCOUNT. An acknowledgment of or agreement to an existing condition of liability of the parties, from which the law implies that all items therein are true and a promise to pay the balance thus acknowledged to be due. 246 Ill. 241; 121 Cal. 590; 71 Cal. 60.

STATED TERM. A regular term of court, held at the time fixed by law or rule.

STATEMENT. See "Particular Statement."

STATEMENT OF AFFAIRS. In English bankruptcy practice, a bankrupt or debtor who has presented a petition for liquidation or composition must produce at the first meeting of creditors a statement of his affairs, giving a list of his creditors, secured and unsecured, with the value of the securities, a list of bills discounted, and a statement of his property. Bankruptcy Act 1869, § 19.

STATEMENT OF CLAIM. A written or printed statement by the plaintiff in an action in the English high court, showing the facts on which he relies to support his claim against the defendant, and the relief which he claims. It is delivered to the defendant or his solicitor. The delivery of the statement of claim is usually the next step after appearance, and is the commencement of the pleadings. A somewhat similar procedure has been adopted in some courts in the United States.

STATEMENT OF DEFENSE. In the practice of the English high court, where the defendant in an action does not demur to the whole of the plaintiff's claim, he delivers a pleading called a "statement of defense." The statement of defense deals with the allegations contained in the statement of claim (or the indorsement on the writ, if there is no statement of claim), admitting or denying them, and, if necessary, stating fresh facts in explanation or avoidance of those alleged by the plaintiff.

STATEMENT OF PARTICULARS. In English practice, when the plaintiff claims a debt or liquidated demand, but has not indorsed the writ specially (*i. e.*, indorsed on it the particulars of his claim under Order iii. r. 6), and the defendant fails to appear, the plaintiff may file a statement of the particulars of his claim, and after eight days enter judgment for the amount, as if the writ had been specially indorsed. Rules of Court xiii. 5.

STATIM (Lat.) Immediately.

STATING PART OF A BILL. See "Bill."

STATION. In civil law. A place where ships may ride in safety. Dig. 49. 12. 1. 13; Id. 50. 15. 59.

STATIONERS' HALL. St. 5 & 6 Vict. c. 45, authorizes, in every case of copyright, the registration of the title of the proprietor at Stationers' Hall, and provides that, without previous registration, no action shall be commenced, though an omission to register is not otherwise to affect the copyright itself. It was founded A. D. 1553. 2 Hall, Hist. Lit. pt. 2, c. 8. p. 366; 3 Steph. Comm. (7th Ed.) 37.

STATU LIBERI (Lat.) In Louisiana. Slaves for a time, who have acquired the right of being free at a time to come, or on a condition which is not fulfilled, or in a certain event which has not happened, but who in the meantime remain in a state of slavery. Civ. Code La. art. 37. See 3 La. 176; 6 La. 571; 4 Mart. (La.) 102; 7 Mart. (La.) 351; 8 Mart. (La.) 219. This is substantially the definition of the civil law. Hist. de la Jur. lib. 40; Dig. 40. 7. 1; Code, 7. 2. 13.

STATUS (Lat.) The condition of persons. It also means "estate," because it signifies the condition or circumstances in which the owner stands with regard to his property. 2 Bouv. Inst. note 1689.

STATUS DE MANERIO. The assembly of the tenants in the court of the lord of a manor, in order to do their customary suit.

STATUS QUO (Lat.) The existing state of things at any given date. *Status quo ante bellum,* the state of things before the war.

STATUTA PRO PUBLICO COMMODO late interpretantur. Statutes made for the public good ought to be liberally construed. Jenk. Cent. Cas. 21.

STATUTA SUO CLAUDUNTUR TERRItorio, nec ultra territorium disponunt. Statutes are confined to their own territory, and have no extraterritorial effect. 4 Allen (Mass.) 324.

STATUTABLE, or **STATUTORY.** That which is introduced or governed by statute law, as opposed to the common law or equity. Thus, a court is said to have statutory jurisdiction when jurisdiction is given to it in certain matters by statute.

STATUTE. A law established by the act of the legislative power; an act of the legislature; the written will of the legislature, solemnly expressed according to the forms necessary to constitute it the law of the state.

This word is used to designate the written law, in contradistinction to the unwritten law. See "Common Law."

Among the civilians, the term "statute" is generally applied to laws and regulations of every sort. Every provision of law which ordains, permits, or prohibits anything is designated a "statute," without considering from what source it arises. Sometimes the word is used in contradistinction from the imperial Roman law, which, by way of eminence, civilians call the "common law."

——**In Old Common Law.** A bond or obligation of record. See "Statute Merchant;" "Statute Staple."

Classification:

(1) An affirmative statute is one which is enacted in affirmative terms. Such a statute does not necessarily take away the common law. 2 Inst. 200; Dwarr. St. 474. If, for example, a statute without negative words declares that, when certain requisites shall have been complied with, deeds shall have a certain effect as evidence, this does not prevent their being used in evidence, though the requisites have not been complied with, in the same manner as they might have been before the statute was passed. 2 Caines (N. Y.) 169. Nor does such an affirmative statute repeal a precedent statute if the two can both be given effect. Dwarr. St. 474.

(2) A declaratory statute is one which is passed in order to put an end to a doubt as to what is the common law or the meaning of another statute, and which declares what it is and ever has been.

(3) A negative statute is one expressed in negative terms, and so controls the common law that it has no force in opposition to the statute. Bac. Abr. "Statute" (G).

(4) Penal statutes are those which command or prohibit a thing under a certain penalty. Espinasse, Pen. Act. 5; Bac. Abr. See, generally, Bac. Abr.; Comyn, Dig. "Parliament;" Viner, Abr.; Dane, Abr. Index; Chit. Prac.; 1 Kent, Comm. 447-459; Barr. Obs. St.; Boscawen, Pen. St.; Espinasse, Pen. Act.; Dwarr. St.; Sedgw. Const. Law. A statute affixing a penalty to an act, though it does not in words prohibit it, thereby makes it illegal. 14 Johns. (N. Y.) 273; 1 Bin. (Pa.) 110; 37 Eng. Law & Eq. 475; 14 N. H. 294; 4 Iowa 490; 7 Ind. 77.

(5) Mandatory statutes are such as imperatively require compliance.

(6) Directory statutes are such as may be violated without invalidating the acts done in violation of it.

(7) Permissive statutes are those which allow something without requiring it.

(8) A perpetual statute is one for the continuance of which there is no limited time, although it be not expressly declared to be so.

If a statute which did not itself contain any limitation is to be governed by another which is temporary only, the former will also be temporary and dependent upon the existence of the latter. Bac. Abr. "Statute" (D).

(9) A temporary statute is one which is limited in its duration at the time of its enactment.

It continues in force until the time of its limitation has expired, unless sooner repealed. A statute which by reason of its nature, has only a single and temporary operation—*e. g.*, an appropriation bill—is also called a "temporary statute."

The most ancient English statute extant is *Magna Charta*. Formerly the statutes enacted after the beginning of the reign of Edw. III. were called *Nova Statuta*, or new statutes, to distinguish them from the ancient statutes. The modern English statutes are divided into public general acts, local and personal acts declared public, private acts printed, and private acts not printed. In parliamentary practice are adopted other distinctions, resting upon different grounds.

(10) A remedial statute is one made to supply such defects and abridge such superfluities in the common law as may have been discovered. 1 Bl. Comm. 86.

These remedial statutes are themselves divided into

(a) "Enlarging" statutes, by which the common law is made more comprehensive and extended than it was before, and into

(b) "Restraining" statutes, by which it is narrowed down to that which is just and proper. The term "remedial statute" is also applied to those acts which give the party injured a remedy, and in some respects such statutes are penal. Espinasse, Pen. Act. 1.

(11) Public statutes are those which affect the public at large, whether their operation be throughout the state, or in a particular locality. 93 N. C. 600.

(12) Private statutes are such as affect in a peculiar manner certain persons or classes. 43 N. Y. 10.

By the civilians, statutes are considered as real, personal, or mixed.

(1) Mixed statutes are those which concern at once both persons and property; but in this sense almost all statutes are mixed, there being scarcely any law relative to persons which does not at the same time relate to things.

(2) Personal statutes are those which have principally for their object the person, and treat of property only incidentally. Such are those which regard birth, legitimacy, freedom, the right of instituting suits, majority as to age, incapacity to contract, to make a will, to plead in person, and the like. A personal statute is universal in its operation, and in force everywhere.

(3) Real statutes are those which have principally for their object property, and which do not speak of persons except in relation to property. Story, Confl. Laws, § 13. Such are those which concern the disposition which one may make of his property either alive or by testament. A real statute, unlike a personal one, is confined in its operation to the country of its origin.

STATUTE FAIR. In English law. A fair at which laborers of both sexes stood and offered themselves for hire; sometimes called, also, "Mop."

STATUTE MERCHANT. A security enentered before the mayor of London, or some chief warden of a city, in pursuance of 13 Edw. I. st. 3, c. 1, whereby the lands of the debtor are conveyed to the creditor till out of the rents and profits of them his debt may be satisfied. Cruise, Dig. tit. 14, § 7; 2 Bl. Comm. 160.

STATUTE OF ALLEGIANCE DE FACTO. Act 11 Hen. VII. c. 1, requiring subjects to give their allegiance to the actual king for the time being, and protecting them in so doing.

STATUTE OF DISTRIBUTION. A statute regulating the distribution of the estate of an intestate.

STATUTE OF ELIZABETH. St. 13 Eliz. c. 5, relating to fraudulent conveyances.

STATUTE OF FRAUDS. See "Frauds, Statute of."

STATUTE OF USES. See "Use."

STATUTE OF WILLS. The statute 32 Hen. VIII. c. 1, by which the right of testamentary disposal of property in lands is created. 2 Bl. Comm. 375.

STATUTE ROLL. A roll upon which an English statute, after receiving the royal assent, was formerly entered.

STATUTE STAPLE. The statute of the staple (27 Edw. III. st. 2) confined the sale of all commodities to be exported to certain towns in England, called "estaple" or "staple," where foreigners might resort. It authorized a security for money, commonly called "statute staple," to be taken by traders for the benefit of commerce. The mayor of the place is entitled to take a recognizance of a debt in proper form, which has the effect to convey the lands of the debtor to the creditor till out of the rents and profits of them he may be satisfied. 2 Bl. Comm. 160; Cruise, Dig. tit. 14, § 10; 2 Rolle, Abr. 446; Bac. Abr. "Execution" (B 1); 4 Inst. 238.

STATUTI (Lat.) In Roman law. Those advocates whose names were inscribed in the registers of matriculation, and formed a part of the college of advocates. The number of advocates of this class was limited. They were distinguished from the supernumeraries from the time of Constantine to Justinian. See Calv. Lex.

STATUTORY EXPOSITION. When the language of a statute is ambiguous, and any subsequent enactment involves a particular interpretation of the former act, it is said to contain a statutory exposition of the former act.

STATUTORY RELEASE. A conveyance which superseded the old compound assurance by lease and release. It was created by St. 4 & 5 Vict. c. 21, which abolished the lease for a year.

STATUTUM (Lat. *statuere,* to establish).

——**In the Civil Law.** Established; determined. A term applied to judicial action. Dig. 50. 16. 46. pr.

——**In Old English Law.** A statute; an act of parliament. Fleta, lib. 2, c. 47, § 10.

STATUTUM AFFIRMATIVUM NON DErogat communi legi. An affirmative statute does not take from the common law. Jenk. Cent. Cas. 24.

STATUTUM DE MERCATORIBUS. The statute of Acton Burnell (*q. v.*)

STATUTUM EX GRATIA REGIS DICItur, quando rex dignatur cedere de jure suo regio, pro commodo et quiete populi sui. A statute is said to be by the grace of the king when the king deigns to yield some portion of his royal rights for the good and quiet of his people. 2 Inst. 378.

STATUTUM GENERALITER EST INtelligendum quando verba statuti sunt specialia, ratio autem generalis. When the words of a statute are special, but the reason of it general, it is to be understood generally. 10 Coke, 101.

STATUTUM HIBERNIAE DE COHAEredibus. St. 14 Hen. III. The third public act in the statute book. It has been pronounced not to be a statute. In the form of it, it appears to be an instruction given by the king to his justices in Ireland, directing them how to proceed in a certain point where they entertained doubt. It seems the justices itinerant in that country had a doubt, when land descended to sisters, whether the younger sisters ought to hold of the eldest, and do homage to her for their several portions, or of the chief lord, and do homage to him; and certain knights had been sent over to know what the practice was in England in such a case. 1 Reeve, Hist. Eng. Law, 259.

STATUTUM SESSIONEM. In old English law. The statute session; a meeting in every hundred of constables and householders, by custom, for the ordering of servants, and debating of differences between masters and servants, rating of wages, etc. 5 Eliz. c. 4.

STATUTUM SPECIALE STATUTO SPEciali non derogat. One special statute does not take away from another special statute. Jenk. Cent. Cas. 199.

STATUTUM WALLIAE (Lat.) The statute of Wales. The title of a statute passed in the twelfth year of Edw. I., being a sort of constitution for the principality of Wales, which was thereby, in a great measure, put on the footing of England with respect to its laws and the administration of justice. 2 Reeve, Hist. Eng. Law, 93-99.

STAY. The arresting of a judicial proceeding or process.

STAY LAWS. Laws suspending remedies against debtors. They are adopted during periods of financial distress or depression. There were numerous instances in acts passed by the legislatures of the American states which had been in rebellion against the Union during the few years which ensued after the war of the rebellion had closed. Adoption of similar measures of relief was practiced by a number of governments during the World War.

STAY OF EXECUTION. An arrest of the issuance of execution process on a judgment. It may be by direction of the judgment creditor for some cause which he conceives to be to his advantage, or it may be by composition or agreement, or it may be by way of a remedy in favor of the judgment debtor, by which, on the giving of approved security usually, the issue of process is postponed for a time fixed by statute. The statutory stay by giving security is the most commonly observed, and is the one to which the term usually refers.

STAY OF PROCEEDING. A suspension of proceedings in a cause, either by an order of the court in the cause, or by some proceeding such as (in some states) an appeal which operates *ipso facto* as a suspension.

STEALING. This term imports, *ex vi termini,* nearly the same as larceny (2 G. Greene [Iowa] 311) but in common parlance it does not always import a felony; as, for example, you stole an acre of my land.

In slander cases, it seems that the term "stealing" takes its complexion from the subject matter to which it is applied, and will be considered as intended of a felonious stealing, if a felony, could have been committed of such subject matter. Starkie, Sland. & L. 80; 12 Johns. (N. Y.) 239; 3 Bin. (Pa.) 546.

STEALTH. Theft is so called by Finch. "Stealth is the wrongful taking of goods without pretense of title." Finch, Law, bk. 3, c. 17.

STEELBOW GOODS. Instruments of husbandry, cattle, corn, etc., delivered by a landlord to his tenant on condition that the like number of goods of like quality should be returned on expiration of the lease. Bell, Dict.; Stair, Inst. 285, § 81.

STELLONATUS. In civil law. A name given generally to all species of frauds committed in making contracts.

This word is said to be derived from the Latin *stellio*, a kind of lizard remarkable for its cunning and the change of its color, because those guilty of frauds used every art and cunning to conceal them. But more particularly it was the crime of a person who fraudulently assigned, sold, or engaged the thing which he had before assigned, sold, or engaged to another, unknown to the person with whom he was dealing. Dig. 47. 20. 3; Code, 9. 34. 1; Merlin, Repert.; Civ. Code La. art. 2069; 1 Brown, Civ. Law, 426.

STEP-RATE SYSTEM. A system of fraternal insurance by which the member pays each year or group of years according to the actual cost of the society of the protection furnished him, and thus increases each year or group of years as age increases, as distinguished from the level rate by which the member pays more than the actual cost in the earlier years and less than the actual cost in the later years. 188 Ill. App. 273, 274.

STERBRECHE, or **STREBRICH.** The breaking, obstructing, or straitening of a way. Termes de la Ley.

STERE. A French measure of solidity, used in measuring wood. It is a cubic meter. See "Measure."

STERILITY. Barrenness; incapacity to produce a child. It is curable and incurable. See "Impotence."

Incapacity of the male to impregnate, or of the female to conceive, when copulation is natural and complete. Keysor, Med. Leg. Manual, 219.

STERLING. Current money of Great Britain, but anciently a small coin worth about one penny, and so called, as some suppose, because it was stamped with the figure of a small star, or, as others suppose, because it was first stamped in England in the reign of King John by merchants from Germany, called "Esterlings." "Pounds sterling" originally signified so many pounds in weight of these coins. Thus, we find in Matthew Paris, A. D. 1242, the expression, *Accepit a rege pro stipendio tredecim libras esterlingorum.* The secondary or derived sense is a certain value in current money, whether in coins or other currency. Lowndes, 14; Watts.

STET BILLA. If the plaintiff in a plaint in the mayor's court of London has attached property belonging to the defendant, and obtained execution against the garnishee, the defendant, if he wishes to contest the plaintiff's claim, and obtain restoration of his property, must issue a *scire facias ad disprobandum debitum.* If the only question to be tried is the plaintiff's debt, the plaintiff, in appearing to the *scire facias*, prays *stet billa* "that his bill original," *i. e.*, his original plaint, "may stand, and that the defendant may plead thereto." The action then proceeds in the usual way as if the proceedings in attachment (which are founded on a fictitious default of the defendant in appearing to the plaint) had not taken place. Brand. For. Attachm. 115, and forms. See "Attachment."

STET PROCESSUS (Lat.) In practice. An order made, upon proper cause shown, that the process remain stationary. As, where a defendant, having become insolvent, would, by moving judgment in the case of nonsuit, compel a plaintiff to proceed, the court will, on an affidavit of the fact of insolvency, award a *stet processus.* See 7 Taunt. 180; 1 Chit. Bailm. 738; 10 Wentw. Pl. 43.

STEVEDORE. A person employed in loading and unloading vessels. He has no maritime lien on the ship for wages. Dunl. Adm. Prac. 98.

STEWARD OF ALL ENGLAND. In old English law. An officer who was invested with various powers, and, among others, it was his duty to preside on the trial of peers.

STEWS. In English law. Places formerly permitted in England to women of professed lewdness, and who for hire would prostitute their bodies to all comers.

These places were so called because the dissolute persons who visited them prepared themselves by bathing,—the word stews being derived from the old French estuves, stove, or hot bath. 3 Inst. 205.

STIFLING A PROSECUTION. Agreeing, in consideration of receiving a pecuniary or other advantage, to abstain from prosecuting a person for an offense not giving rise to a civil remedy, *e. g.*, perjury. As a general rule, such an agreement invalidates any transaction of which it forms part. 6 Q. B. 308; 1 Campb. 45; L. R. 1 H. L. 200.

STILLICIDIUM (Lat.) In civil law. The rainwater that falls from the roof or eaves of a house by scattered drops. When it is gathered into a spout, it is called *flumen.*

Without the constitution of one or other of these servitudes, no proprietor can build so as to throw the rain that falls from his house directly on his neighbor's grounds; for it is a restriction upon all property, *nemo potest immittere in alienum;* and he who, in building, breaks through that restraint, truly builds on another man's property; because to whomsoever the area belongs, to him also belongs whatever is above it, *cujus est solum, ejus est usque ad coelum.* 3 Burge, Confl. Laws, 405. See "Servitus;" Inst. 3. 2. 1; Dig. 8. 2. 2.

STINT. The proportionable part of a man's cattle which he may keep upon the common. The general rule is that the commoner shall not turn more cattle upon the common than are sufficient to manure and stock the land to which his right of common is annexed. There may be such a thing as common without stint or number; but this is seldom granted, and a grantee cannot grant it over. 3 Bl. Comm. 239; 1 Ld. Raym. 407.

STIPENDIARY ESTATES. Estates granted in return for services, generally of a military kind. 1 Steph. Comm. 174.

STIPENDIARY MAGISTRATES. In English law. Paid magistrates.

STIPULATED DAMAGE. Liquidated damage. See "Damages."

STIPULATIO (Lat.) In Roman law. A contract made in the following manner, viz.: The person to whom the promise was to be made proposed a question to him from whom it was to proceed, fully expressing the nature and extent of the engagement, and, the question so proposed being answered in the affirmative, the obligation was complete.

It was essentially necessary that both parties should speak (so that a dumb man could not enter into a stipulation), that the person making the promise should answer conformably to the specific question proposed, without any material interval of time, and with the intention of contracting an obligation. No consideration was required.

STIPULATIO AQUILIANA (Lat.) In Roman law, a particular application of the *stipulatio*, which was used to collect together into one verbal contract all the liabilities of every kind and quality of the debtor, with a view to their being released or discharged by an *acceptilatio*, that mode of discharge being applicable only to the verbal contract. Brown.

STIPULATION. A material article in an agreement.

The term appears to have derived its meaning from the use of *stipulatio* above given; though it is applied more correctly and more conformably to its original meaning to denote the insisting upon and requiring any particular engagement. 2 Poth. Obl. (Evans Ed.) 19. It is commonly applied to agreements between counsel in respect to matters of proceeding.

——**In Admiralty Practice.** A recognizance of certain persons (called in the old law *fide jussors*) in the nature of bail for the appearance of a defendant. 3 Bl. Comm. 108.

These stipulations are of three sorts, namely: *Judicatum solvi*, by which the party is absolutely bound to pay such sum as may be adjudged by the court; *de judicio sisti*, by which he is bound to appear from time to time during the pendency of the suit, and to abide the sentence; *de ratio*, or *de rato*, by which he engages to ratify the acts of his proctor. This stipulation is not usual in the admiralty courts of the United States.

The securities are taken in the following manner, namely: *Cautio fide jussoria*, by sureties; *pignoratitia*, by deposit; *juratoria*, by oath,—this security is given when the party is too poor to find sureties, at the discretion of the court; *nude promissoria*, by bare promise,—this security is unknown in the admiralty courts of the United States. Hall, Adm. Prac. 12; Dunl. Adm. Prac. 150, 151. See 17 Am. Jur. 51.

STIPULATOR. In the civil law, the party who asked the question in the contract of stipulation; the other party, or he who answered, being called the "promissor." But, in a more general sense, the term was applied to both the parties. Calv. Lex.

STIRPES (Lat.) Descents. The root, stem, or stock of a tree. Figuratively, it signifies in law that person from whom a family is descended, and also the kindred or family. See "Per Stirpes." 2 Bl. Comm. 209.

STOCK. The capital of a merchant or tradesman, including his money, merchandise, and credits. See "Capital." The goods and wares he has for sale and traffic.

——**Of Corporations.** The amount of money or property subscribed and paid in, or agreed to be paid in, by the shareholders. It is ordinarily divided into equal shares of a determined value, and apportioned among the stockholders in proportion to the amount which they have paid in, or for which they are liable.

Distinction has been made between the capital stock, which is an asset of the corporation, and the shares of stock, which are the property of the several shareholders. 34 Eng. & Am. Corp. Cas. 223.

STOCK BROKER. See "Brokers."

STOCK CERTIFICATES. A written acknowledgment by the corporation of the interest of a shareholder in the corporate property and franchises. It expresses the contract between the shareholder and the corporation and his co-shareholders. It is in the nature of an instrument evidencing a chose in action, but, properly speaking, it is not a chose in action. 5 Fletcher Cyclopedia Corporations 5604.

STOCK DIVIDENDS. Dividends consisting of the issue of certificates of stock.

There is a clear distinction between a stock dividend and an extraordinary cash dividend, the latter being a disbursement to the stockholder of accumulated earnings, where the corporation at once parts irrevocably with all interest therein, while the former involves no disbursement by the corporation, which parts with nothing to the stockholder, the latter receiving, not an actual dividend, but certificates of stock which evidence in a new proportion his interest in the entire capital, including such as by investment of accumulated profits has been added to the original capital. 205 Ill. 314.

STOCK EXCHANGE. A building or room in which stock brokers meet to transact their business of purchasing or selling stocks.

An association of stock brokers for the purpose of transacting their business.

In large cities, the stock business is transacted through the medium of the members of the board of brokers. This is an association of stock brokers governed by rules and regulations made by themselves, to which all the members are obliged to subject themselves. Admission is procured by ballot, and a member defaulting in his obligations forfeits his seat. A regular register of all the transactions is kept by an officer of the association, and questions arising between the members are generally decided by an arbitration committee. The official record of sales is the best evidence of the price of any stock on any particular day. The stocks dealt in at the sessions of the board are those which are placed on the list by a regular vote of the association; and when it is proposed to add a stock to the list, a committee is appointed to examine into the matter, and the board is generally guided by the report of such committee. Sewell, Bankr.

STOCK JOBBING. A fictitious transaction in stocks by way of speculation. Also the title of an act relating to such transaction. See "Gambling Contract."

STOCK SUBSCRIPTION. A contract of subscription to the stock of a corporation by which the subscriber agrees to take a certain number of shares of the capital stock of a corporation, paying for the same, or expressly or impliedly promising to pay for the same. The effect of such a contract, the company being in existence at the time of the subscription, and having accepted the same, and the subscription being unconditional, is to make the subscriber a stockholder in the corporation, and to bind him to pay for his stock in accordance with the terms of his contract. 2 Fletcher Cyclopedia Corporations 1120.

STOCKS. In criminal law. A machine, commonly made of wood, with holes in it, in which to confine persons accused of or guilty of crime.

It was used either to confine unruly offenders by way of security, or convicted criminals for punishment. This barbarous punishment has been generally abandoned in the United States.

STOCKHOLDER. The holder of shares of stock in a corporation or joint-stock com pany.

STOP ORDER.

——**In English Chancery Practice.** An order to prevent a fund in court from being paid out or otherwise deal with without notice to a claimant.

——**In Commercial Usage.** An order to buy or sell on margins and close out at a set price. See under "Gambling Contract."

STOPPAGE IN TRANSITU. A resumption by the seller of the possession of goods not paid for, while on their way to the vendee, and before he has acquired actual possession of them. 15 Me. 314.

For most purposes, the possession of the carrier is considered to be that of the buyer; but by virtue of this right, which is an extension of the right of lien, the vendor may reclaim the possession before they reach the vendee, in case of the insolvency of the latter. 12 Pick. (Mass.) 313; 4 Gray (Mass.) 336; 2 Caines (N. Y.) 98; 8 Mees. & W. 341.

To give a right of stoppage *in transitu*, the sale must have been on credit, but the giving of a note is not payment unless so agreed (13 Me. 103), the buyer must be insolvent, and such insolvency must have been unknown at the time of the sale (102 N. C. 390; 27 Barb. [N. Y.] 663), and the goods must be in transit, *i. e.*, they must not have come into the actual or constructive possession of the buyer (16 Neb. 614; 40 Iowa, 627).

STORES. The victuals and provisions collected together for the subsistence of a ship's company; of a camp; or any like body of men.

Store, as commonly used, is equivalent of the English "shop," when indicating a place where merchandise is sold, but in the broader sense it means a place of deposit; a storehouse. 53 Ala. 481; 25 Am. Rep. 643; Ann. Cas. 1913E 1126 note.

A restaurant and bakery may be carried on in a building insured for use as a store. 60 Mich. 425.

A shop is a place where goods are sold by retail. 15 Gray (Mass.) 197.

STOUTHRIEFF. In Scotch law. Formerly this word included in its signification every species of theft accompanied with violence to the person; but of late years it has become the *vox signata* for forcible and masterful depredation within or near the dwelling house; while "robbery" has been more particularly applied to violent depredation on the highway or accompanied by house breaking. Alis. Sc. Law, 227.

STOWAGE. In maritime law. The proper arrangement in a ship of the different articles of which a cargo consists, so that they may not injure each other by friction, or be damaged by the leakage of the ship.

STRADDLE. A privilege in the holder to demand of the seller at a certain price within a certain time certain property, or to require him to take, at the same price within the same time, the same property. 83 N. Y. 95. See "Gambling Contract."

STRAMINEUS HOMO. A man of straw.

STRANDING. In maritime law. The running of a ship or other vessel on shore. It is either accidental or voluntary.

Accidental stranding takes place where the ship is driven on shore by the winds and waves.

Voluntary stranding takes place where the ship is run on shore either to preserve her from a worse fate, or for some fraudulent purpose. Marsh. Ins. bk. 1, c. 12, § 1.

In a Marine Insurance, "a touch and go" is not a stranding; in order to constitute a stranding, the ship must be stationary. 1 Starkie, 130; 4 M. & S. 503.

STRANGER. A person born out of the United States; but in this sense the term "alien" is more properly applied until he becomes naturalized.

A person who is not privy to an act or contract. Example, he who is a stranger to the issue shall not take advantage of the verdict. Brooke, Abr. "Record," pl. 3; Viner, Abr. 1. And see Comyn, Dig. "Abatement" (H 54).

When a man undertakes to do a thing, and a stranger interrupts him, this is no excuse. Comyn, Dig. "Condition" (L 14). When a party undertakes that a stranger shall do a certain thing, he becomes liable as soon as the stranger refuses to perform it. Bac. Abr. "Conditions" (Q 4).

STRATAGEM. A deception, either by words or actions, in times of war, in order to obtain an advantage over an enemy.

Stratagems, though contrary to morality, have been justified unless they have been accompanied by perfidy, injurious to the rights of humanity, as in the example given by Vattel of an English frigate, which, during a war between France and England, appeared off Calais and made signals of distress in order to allure some vessel to come to its relief, and seized a shallop and its crew who had generously gone out to render it assistance. Vattel, Droit des Gens, liv. 3, c. 9, § 178.

Sometimes stratagems are employed in making contracts. This is unlawful and fraudulent, and avoids the contract. See "Fraud."

STRATOCRACY. A military government; government by military chiefs of an army.

STRAW BAIL. Nominal or worthless bail. Professional sureties, so called, it is said, from an ancient custom of such persons of wearing a straw about their clothing, that they might be known to one in search of bail.

Common bail (*q. v.*)

STRAW MEN. Men who used in former days to ply about courts of law, so called from their manner of making known their occupation (*i. e.*, by a straw in one of their shoes), recognized by the name of "straw shoes." An advocate or lawyer who wanted a convenient witness knew by these signs where to find one, and the colloquy between the parties was brief. "Don't you remember?" said the advocate. The party looked at the fee, and gave no sign; but the fee increased, and the powers of memory increased with it. "To be sure I do." "Then come into court and swear it!" And straw shoes went into court and swore it. Athens abounded in straw shoes. Quart. Rev. xxxiii, 344.

STRAY. See "Estray."

STREET. A public thoroughfare or highway in a city or village. 4 Serg. & R. (Pa.) 106; 11 Barb. (N. Y.) 399; 39 Ill. App. 474. See "Highway."

STREET RAILROAD. A railroad constructed on a street for the purpose of conveying passengers and to accommodate street travel, making frequent stops to take on and let off passengers and without regular stations; it conforms to the grade of the street and its fundamental purpose is to accommodate local street travel. 228 Ill. 273.

STREIGHTEN. In the old books. To narrow or restrict. "The *habendum* should not streighten the devise." 1 Leon. 58.

STREPITUS (Law Lat.) In old records. Estrepement or strip; a species of waste or destruction of property. Spelman.

STRICT CONSTRUCTION. A rule of judicial interpretation or exposition which follows closely the letter of the statute or instrument construed disfavoring any extension or relaxation of it by implication, favor, or equity; a close and conservative adherence to the literal or textual interpretation. It is not the exact converse of "liberal construction," for it does not consist in giving words the narrowest meaning of which they are susceptible. 267 Ill. 86.

STRICT FORECLOSURE. See "Foreclosure."

STRICT SETTLEMENT. A settlement of lands to the parent for life, and after his death to his first and other sons in tail, with an interposition of trustees to preserve the contingent remainders.

STRICTISSIMI JURIS (Lat. the most strict right or law). In general, when a person receives an advantage, as the grant of a license, he is bound to conform strictly to the exercise of the rights given him by it, and in case of a dispute it will be strictly construed. See 3 Story (U. S.) 159.

STRICTO JURE (Lat.) In strict law. 1 Kent, Comm. 65.

STRICTUM JUS (Lat.) The rigor of law, strict law, in contradistinction to equity.

STRIKE. Used as an abbreviated form of "strike out" or "strike off," as a motion "to strike" evidence.

The combined act or effort of workmen to obtain some concession by stopping work altogether at a preconcerted time, and refusing to continue until the concession is granted. 255 Ill. 222.

STRIKING A DOCKET. In English practice. Entering the creditor's affidavit and bond in bankruptcy. 1 Deac. Bankr. 106.

STRIKING A JURY. In English practice. Where, for nicety of the matter in dispute, or other cause, a special jury is necessary, upon motion and rule granted thereon, the sheriff is to attend the prothonotary or proper officer with the book of freeholders, and to take indifferently forty-eight of the principal freeholders, when the attorneys on each side, being present, are to strike off twelve respectively, and the remaining twenty-four are returned. 3 Bl. Comm. 357. Essentially the same practice prevails in some of the states.

STRIKING OFF THE ROLL. Disbarment.

STRONG HAND. The words "with strong hand" imply a degree of criminal force, whereas the words *vi et armis* ("with force and arms") are mere formal words in the action of trespass, and the plaintiff is not bound to prove any force. The statutes relating to forcible entries use the words "with a strong hand," as describing that degree of force which makes an entry or detainer of lands criminal. See "Forcible Entry or Detainer."

STRUCK. In pleading. A word essential in an indictment for murder, when the death arises from any wounding, beating, or bruising. 1 Bulst. 184; 5 Coke, 122; 3 Mod. 202; Cro. Jac. 655; Palmer, 282; 2 Hale, P. C. 184, 186, 187; Hawk. P. C. bk. 2, c. 23, § 82; 1 Chit. Crim. Law, *243; 6 Bin. (Pa.) 179.

STRUCK JURY. A special jury obtained by striking. See "Striking a Jury."

STRUCK OFF. A term applied to a case which the court, having no jurisdiction over, and not being able to give judgment, order to be taken off the record. This is done by an entry to that effect.

STRUCK OFF, or KNOCKED DOWN. Property is understood to be "struck off" or "knocked down" when the auctioneer, by the fall of his hammer, or by any other audible or visible announcement, signifies to the bidder that he is entitled to the property on paying the amount of his bid, according to the terms of the sale. 7 Hill (N. Y.) 431, 439.

STRUMPET. A harlot, or courtesan. The word was formerly used as an addition. Jacob.

STUFF GOWN. The robe of barristers who have not been made queen's or king's counsel. See "Silk Gown."

STULTIFY (Lat. *stultus*, stupid). To make one out mentally incapacitated for the performance of an act.

It has been laid down by old authorities (Litt. § 405; 4 Coke, 122; Cro. Eliz. 898) that no man should be allowed to stultify himself, *i. e.*, plead disability through mental unsoundness. This maxim was soon doubted as law (1 Hagg. Ecc. 414; 2 Bl. Comm. 292), and has been completely overturned (4 Kent, Comm. 451).

STULTILOQUIUM. In old English law. Vicious or disorderly pleading, for which a fine was imposed by King John, supposed to be the origin of the fines for *beaupleader* (*q. v.*) Crabb, Hist. Eng. Law, 135.

STUMPTAIL. Depreciated currency. 35 Ill. 163.

STUPIDITY. In medical jurisprudence. That state of the mind which cannot perceive and embrace the data presented to it by the senses, and therefore the stupid person can, in general, form no correct judgment. It is a want of the perceptive powers. Ray, Med. Jur. c. 3, § 40. See "Imbecility."

STUPRUM (Lat.) In Roman law. The criminal sexual intercourse which took place between a man and a single woman, maid, or widow, who before lived honestly. Inst. 4. 18. 4; Dig. 48. 5. 6; Id. 50. 16. 101; 1 Bouv. Inst. Theolo. ps. 3, quaest. 2, art. 2, p. 252.

STYLE. As a verb, to call, name, or entitle one; as a noun, the title or appellation of a person.

The names in which a cause is entitled.

SUA SPONTE (Lat.) Of his or its own motion.

SUAPTE NATURA (Lat.) In its own nature. *Suapte natura sterilis*, barren in its own nature and quality; intrinsically barren. 5 Maule & S. 170.

SUB (Lat.) Under; upon.

SUB CONDITIONE. Upon condition; under condition.

SUB DISJUNCTIONE (Law Lat.) In the alternative. Fleta, lib. 2, c. 60, § 21.

SUB JUDICE (Lat.) Under or before a judge or court; under judicial consideration; undetermined. 12 East, 409.

SUB MODO (Lat.) Under a qualification. A legacy may be given *sub modo*, that is, subject to a condition or qualification.

SUB PEDE SIGILLI (Lat.) Under the foot of the seal; under seal. This expression is used when it is required that a record should be certified under the seal of the court.

SUB POTESTATE (Lat.) Under or subject to the power of another; as, a wife is under the power of her husband; a child is subject to that of his father; a slave to that of his master.

SUB SALVO ET SECURO CONDUCTU. Under safe and secure conduct. 1 Strange, 430. Words in the old writ of *habeas corpus*.

SUB SILENTIO (Lat.) Under silence; without any notice being taken. Sometimes passing a thing *sub silentio* is evidence of consent.

SUB SPE RECONCILIATIONIS (Lat.) Under the hope of reconcilement. 2 Kent, Comm. 127.

SUB SUO PERICULO (Law Lat.) At his own risk. Fleta, lib. 2, c. 5, § 5.

SUBAGENT. A person appointed by an agent to perform some duty, or the whole of the business relating to his agency. See "Agent."

SUB-BALLIVUS (Law Lat.) In old English law. An under bailiff; a sheriff's deputy. Fleta, lib. 2, c. 68, § 2.

SUBCONTRACT. A contract by one who has contracted for the performance of labor or service with a third party for the whole or part performance of that labor or service. 9 Mees. & W. 710; 3 Gray (Mass.) 362; 17 Wend. (N. Y.) 550; 22 Wend. (N. Y.) 395; 1 E. D. Smith (N. Y.) 716; 2 E. D. Smith (N. Y.) 558. See 'Contract."

SUBDELEGARE (Law Lat.) In old English law. To sub-delegate; to appoint a delegate of a delegate; to delegate power already delegated.

SUBDITUS (Lat.) In old English law. A vassal; a dependent; any one under the power of another. Spelman; Bracton, fol. 412.

SUBDIVIDE. To divide a part of a thing which has already been divided. For example, when a person dies leaving children, and grandchildren, the children of one of his own who is dead, his property is divided into as many shares as he had children, including the deceased, and the share of the deceased is subdivided into as many shares as he had children.

SUBDUCT. In English probate practice, to subduct a *caveat* is to withdraw it.

SUBHASTARE (Lat.) In the civil law. To sell at public auction, which was done *sub hasta*, under a spear; to put or sell under the spear. Calv. Lex.

SUBHASTATIO (Lat.) In the civil law. A sale by public auction, which was done under a spear, fixed up at the place of sale as a public sign of it. Calv. Lex. The Roman custom of setting up a spear at an auction seems to have been derived from the circumstance that at first only those things which were taken in war were sold in that manner. Adams, Rom. Ant. 59.

SUBINFEUDATION. The act of an inferior lord by which he carved out a part of an estate which he held of a superior, and granted it to an inferior tenant to be held of himself.

It was an indirect mode of transferring the fief, and resorted to as an artifice to elude the feudal restraint upon alienation. This was forbidden by the statute of *Quia Emptores*. 18 Edw. I.; 2 Bl. Comm. 91; 3 Kent, Comm. 406.

SUBJACENT SUPPORT. An easement of support of the soil as against an adjoining tract of land, so that the dominant tract shall not fall in by reason of undermining or withdrawal of support from beneath. Tiedeman, Real Prop. § 618; 66 Pa. St. 429.

SUBJECT.

——**In Scotch Law.** The thing which is the object of an agreement.

——**In Governmental Law.** An individual member of a nation, who is subject to the laws. This term is used in contradistinction to "citizen," which is applied to the same individual when considering his political rights.

In monarchical governments, by "subject" is meant one who owes permanent allegiance to the monarch. See "Body Politic;" Greenl. Ev. § 286; Phil. Ev. 732, note 1.

SUBJECT MATTER. The right which one party claims as against the other, and claims the judgment of the court upon. 41 Mich. 93. The cause of action. 15 N. Y. 509.

SUBJECTION (Lat. *sub*, under, *jacio*, to put, throw). The obligation of one or more persons to act at the discretion or according to the judgment and will of others. Private subjection is subjection to the authority of private persons. Public subjection is subjection to the authority of public persons.

SUBLATA CAUSA TOLLITUR EFFECtus. Remove the cause and the effect will cease. 2 Bl. Comm. 203.

SUBLATA VENERATIONE MAGISTRAtuum, respublica ruit. The commonwealth perishes, if respect for magistrates be taken away. Jenk. Cent. Cas. 48.

SUBLATO FUNDAMENTO CADIT OPUS. Remove the foundation, the structure or work falls. Jenk. Cent. Cas. 106.

SUBLATO PRINCIPALI TOLLITUR ADjunctum. If the principal be taken away, the adjunct is also taken away. Co. Litt. 389.

SUBLEASE. A lease by a tenant to another person of a part of the premises held by him, or a part of his term; an under lease. If the whole premises be let by the tenant for his entire term, so that there is no reversion in him, it is not a subletting, but an assignment of his lease.

SUBMERGENCE. The sudden disappearance of riparian lands under the water, whereby they are lost to the owner. See 100 N. Y. 424.

SUBMISSION (Lat. *submissio,—sub,* under, *mittere,* to put,—a putting under). Used of persons or things. A putting one's person or property under the control of another; a yielding to authority. A citizen is bound to submit to the laws, a child to his parents, a guardian to his ward. A victor may enforce the submission of his enemy.

—**In Trial Practice.** The leaving of a cause with the court or jury for decision.

—**To Arbitration.** An agreement by which parties submit a matter of difference to the decision of one or more arbitrators. 4 N. Y. 157.

—**To Court.** This, usually known as "submission of controversy," is the submission of an agreed statement of facts to the court, without trial of the issues, for a decision thereon.

SUBNERVARE. To hamstring by cutting the sinews of the legs and thighs.

It was an old custom *meretrices et impudicas mulieres subnervare.* Wharton.

SUBNOTATIONS (Lat.) In civil law. The answers of the prince to questions which had been put to him respecting some obscure or doubtful point of law. See "Rescript."

SUBORN (Lat. *subornare,* from *sub,* under, and *ornare,* to prepare). In criminal law. To procure another to commit perjury. Steph. Crim. Law, 74. Literally, to instruct one privily, or in an underhanded manner, what to say; to prepare secretly, or underhand; to procure unlawfully. Sayer, 292. *Subornare est quasi subtus in aure ipsum male ornare,* to suborn is to instruct one privily, as by whispering in his ear, with a bad design. 3 Inst. 167.

SUBORNATION OF PERJURY. In criminal law. The procuring another to commit legal perjury, who, in consequence of the persuasion, takes the oath to which he has been incited. Hawk. P. C. bk. 1, c. 69, § 10.

SUBPOENA (Lat. *sub,* under, *poena,* penalty).

—**In Practice.** A process to cause a witness to appear and give testimony, commanding him to lay aside all pretenses and excuses, and appear before a court or magistrate therein named, at a time therein mentioned, to testify for the party named, under a penalty therein mentioned. This is called distinctively a *subpoena ad testificandum.*

A subpoena *duces tecum* is one whereby the witness is commanded to bring with him books or papers in his possession or under his control, to produce the same in evidence.

—**In Chancery Practice.** A mandatory writ or process directed to and requiring one or more persons to appear at a time to come and answer the matters charged against him or them. The writ of subpoena was originally a process in the courts of common law to enforce the attendance of a witness to give evidence; but this writ was used in the court of chancery for the same purpose as a citation in the courts of civil and canon law, to compel the appearance of a defendant, and to oblige him to answer upon oath the allegations of the plaintiff.

It was invented by John Waltham, bishop of Salisbury, and chancellor to Richard II., under the authority of the statutes of Westminster II. and 13 Edw. I. c. 34, which enabled him to devise new writs. Cruise, Dig. tit. 11, c. 1, §§ 12-17. See Viner, Abr.; 1 Swanst. 209.

SUBREPTIO (Lat.) In civil law. Obtaining gifts to escheat, etc., from the king by concealing the truth. Bell, Dict.; Calv. Lex. "Subripere."

SUBREPTION. In French law. The fraud committed to obtain a pardon, title, or grant, by alleging facts contrary to truth.

SUBROGATIO EST TRANSFUSIO UNIUS creditoris in alium, eadem vel mitiori conditione. Subrogation is the substituting one creditor in the place of another on the same or a better condition. Merlin, Quest. de Droit. "Subrogation."

SUBROGATION. The substitution of another person in the place of a claimant, to whose rights he succeeds in relation to the claim. That change which puts another person in the place of the creditor, and which makes the right, the mortgage, or the security which the creditor has, pass to the person who is subrogated to him,—that is to say, who enters into his right. Domat, Civ. Law, pt. i. lib. iii. tit. i. § vi.

It is a legal fiction by force of which an obligation extinguished by payment made by a third party is considered as continuing to subsist for the benefit of this third person, who makes but one and the same person with the creditor in the view of the law. Subrogation is the act of putting one thing in place of another, or one person in place of another. Guyot, Rep. Univ. "Subrogation," § ii.

Subrogation gives to the substitute all the rights of the party for whom he is substituted. 4 Md. Ch. 253. Among the earlier civil-law writers, the term seems to have been used synonymously with "substitution;" or, rather, "substitution" included "subrogation," as well as its present more limited signification. See Domat, Civ. Law, passim; Poth. Obl. passim. The term "substitution" is now almost altogether confined to the law of devises and chancery practice. See "Substitution."

The word "subrogation" is originally found only in the civil law, and has been adopted, with the doctrine itself, thence into equity. It is an equitable doctrine (3 Ired. Eq. [N. C.] 386), but in the law, as distinguished from equity, it hardly appears as a term, except perhaps in those states where, as in Pennsylvania, equity is administered through the forms of law, and those where the distinction between legal and equitable remedies has been abolished. There the term "subrogation," adopted from the Roman law, has of late years come into quite general use. 6 Pa. St. 504. The equitable doctrine of marshalling assets is plainly derived from the Roman law of subrogation or substitution; and although the word is, or, rather, has been, used sparingly in the common law, many of the doctrines of subrogation are familiar to the courts of common law.

Subrogation differs from cession in this, that while cession only substitutes the one to whom the debt is ceded in place of the ceder, in subrogation the debt would have become extinguished but for the effect of the subrogation; and also because, although subrogation supposes a change in the person of the creditor, it does not imply novation; but, through the fiction of the law, the party who is subrogated is considered as making only one and the same person with the creditor, whom he succeeds. Masse, Dr. Comm. "Payment in Subrogation."

It is one thing to decide that a surety is entitled, on payment, to have an assignment of the debt, and quite another to decide that he is entitled to be subrogated or substituted as to the equities and securities to the place of the creditor, as against the debtor and his cosureties. Story, Eq. Jur. § 493, note; 2 McLean (U. S.) 451; 1 Dev. (N. C.) 137.

The legal subrogation of the civilians is generally intended by the term "subrogation." Some original interest is essential to entitle one to subrogation. Thus, a surety paying the debt is subrogated to the rights of the creditor against the principal (23 Minn. 74; 28 N. Y. 271), and the holder of a lien who pays a prior lien is subrogated to the rights of the lienholder whom he pays (2 Allen [Mass.] 111); but a mere stranger or volunteer paying a debt has no right to subrogation (93 N. Y. 235; 76 Va. 262).

——**In the Civil Law.** Subrogation of persons is of three sorts:

First, the canonists understand by subrogation the succession of a priest to the rights of action of the occupant of a benefice who has died during a suit. Guyot, Rep. Univ. "Subrogation of Persons," § i.

Second, the second sort arose from a local custom of the Bourbonnais, and had for its object the protection of the debtor from the effects of collusion on the part of the attaching creditor.

Third, subrogation in fact to aliens and pledgees, which is only the change of one creditor for another. See Guyot, ut supra, and, also, Masse Dr. Comm.

Nearly all the instances in which the common law has adopted the doctrines of subrogation have arisen under this latter class.

Subrogation is either legal or conventional.

Legal subrogation is that resulting by operation of law from the satisfying of a claim as to which the person making payment has some original privilege. 14 Cal. 565.

Conventional subrogation results as its name indicates, from the agreement of the parties, and can take effect only by agreement. This agreement is, of course, with the party to be subrogated, and may be either by the debtor or creditor. Civ. Code La. 1249.

Thus, it may happen when the creditor receiving payment from the third person subrogates the payor to his right against the debtor. This must happen by express agreement; but no formal words are required. This sort of subrogation only takes place where there is a payment of the debt by a third party,—not where there is an assignment, in which case, subrogation results from the assignment.

This principle is recognized by the common law in cases where, upon payment, the securities are transferred to a party having an interest in the payment. Or, in case the debtor borrows money from a third party to pay a debt, he may subrogate the lender to the rights of the creditor; for by this change the rights of the other creditors are not injuriously affected. To make this mode of subrogation valid, the borrowing and discharge must take place before a notary. In the borrowing, it must be declared that the money has been borrowed to make payment, and in the discharge, that it has been made with money furnished by the creditor. Masse, Dr. Comm. lib. 5, tit. 1, c. 5, §§ 1, 2.

SUBROGEE. A person who is subrogated; one who succeeds to the rights of another by subrogation.

SUBROGUER, *Surroguer.* L. Fr. To make a deputy or surrogate; to substitute. Kelham.

SUBSCRIBE. To write under, 54 L. J. Q. B. 213; 14 Q. B. D. 667; to give assent to; to attest; 24 L. J. Q. B. 171; 4 E. & B. 450; placing a signature at the end of an instrument, 4 Colo. 282.

While the idea of a written signature is involved, yet by common usage it is often employed to include an agreement, written or oral, to some purpose for the promotion of which numerous persons are uniting their means and effort. 143 Iowa 13, 19; 136 Am. St. Rep. 731n. See "Sign; Signature; Subscription."

SUBSCRIBING WITNESS. One who subscribes his name to a writing in order to be able at a future time to prove its due execution; an attesting witness.

In order to make a good subscribing witness, it is requisite he should sign his name to the instrument himself, at the time of its execution, and at the request or with the assent of the party. 6 Hill (N. Y.) 303; 11 Mees. & W. 168; 1 Greenl. Ev. (4th Ed.) § 569a; 5 Watts (Pa.) 399.

SUBSCRIPTIO (Lat. from *subscribere*). In the civil law. A writing under, or underwriting; a writing of the name under or at the bottom of an instrument by way of attestation or ratification; subscription. The *subscriptio testium* (subscription of witnesses) was one of the formalities in the execution of wills, being required by the imperial constitutions in addition to the seals of the witnesses. Inst. 2. 10. 3.

That kind of imperial constitution which was granted in answer to the prayer of a petitioner who was present. Calv. Lex.

SUBSCRIPTION (Lat. *sub*, under, *scribo*, to write). The placing a signature at the bottom of a written or printed engagement, or it is the attestation of a witness by so writing his name; but it has been holden that the attestation of an illiterate witness by making his mark is a sufficient subscription. 7 Bing. 457; 2 Ves. Sr. 454; 1 Atk. 177; 1 Ves. Jr. 11; 3 P. Wms. 253; 1 Ves. & B. 392.

"Subscribe," according to both its popular and literal signification, requires a signature at the end of a document. 4 Colo. 282. See "Signature; Subscribe."

The act by which a person contracts, in writing, to furnish a sum of money for a particular purpose; as, a subscription to a charitable institution, a subscription for a book, for a newspaper, and the like.

SUBSCRIPTION LIST. A list of subscribers to some agreement with each other or a third person.

SUBSELLIA (Lat. from *sub*, under, and *sella*, a seat). In the Roman law. Lower seats or benches, occupied by the *judices* (judges or jurors), and by inferior magistrates when they sat in judgment, as distinguished from the tribunal of the *praetor*. Calv. Lex.; Budaeus.

SUBSEQUENS MATRIMONIUM TOLLIT peccatum praecedens. A subsequent marriage (of the parties) removes a previous fault, *i. e.*, previous illicit intercourse, and legitimates the offspring. A rule of Roman law.

SUBSIDY. A legislative grant of money in aid of a private enterprise deemed to promote the public welfare.

——**In English Law.** An aid, tax, or tribute granted by parliament to the king for the urgent occasions of the kingdom, to be levied on every subject of ability, according to the value of his lands or goods. Jacob.

——**In International Law.** The assistance given in money by one nation to another to enable it the better to carry on a war, when such nation does not join directly in the war. Vattel, liv. 3, § 82. See "Neutrality."

SUBSIGNARE (Lat. from *sub*, under, and *signare*, to seal or sign). In the civil law. To undersign; to subscribe. According to the strict etymology, to seal under, or seal. But the word is said, in the Digests, to have been used among the ancient Romans in the sense of "writing." *Subsignatum dicitur quod ab aliquo subscriptum est, nam veteres subsignationis verbo pro adscriptione uti solebant*, that is said to be undersigned which is underwritten by any one, for the ancients were accustomed to use the word *subsignatio* for *adscriptio*. Dig. 50. 16. 39. Some copies of the Digests have *subscriptione* in place of *adscriptione*.

SUBSTANCE (Lat. *sub*, under, *stare*, to stand). That which is essential. It is used in opposition to form.

It is a general rule that on any issue it is sufficient to prove the substance of the issue. For example, in a case where the defendant pleaded payment of the principal sum and all interest due, and it appeared in evidence that a gross sum was paid, not amounting to the full interest, but accepted by the plaintiff as full payment, the proof was held to be sufficient. 2 Strange, 690; 1 Phil. Ev. 161.

It is also used in the sense of "property." Cowp. 307.

SUBSTANTIVE LAW. That portion of the body of the law which contains the rights and duties and the regulations of government, as opposed to that part which contains the rules and remedies by which the substantive law is administered. The latter is called, in opposition to "substantive law," the "adjective law," or the "remedial law." The exact boundary between the two is difficult of definition, and has been the cause of much learned discussion.

SUBSTITUTE (Lat. *substitutus*). One placed under another to transact business for him. In letters of attorney, power is generally given to the attorney to nominate and appoint a substitute.

Without such power, the authority given to one person cannot, in general, be delegated to another, because it is a personal trust and confidence, and is not, therefore, transmissible. The authority is given to him to exercise his judgment and discretion, and it cannot be said that the trust and confidence reposed in him shall be exercised at the discretion of another. 2 Atk. 88; 2 Ves. Jr. 645. But an authority may be delegated to another when the attorney has express power to do so. Bunb. 166; T. Jones, 110. See Story, Ag. §§ 13, 14. When a man is drawn into the militia, he may in some cases hire a substitute.

SUBSTITUTED SERVICE. See "Service."

SUBSTITUTES. In Scotch law. Where an estate is settled on a long series of heirs, substituted one after another, in tailzie, the person first called in the tailzies is the institute; the rest the heirs of tailzie, or the substitutes. Ersk. Inst. 3. 8. 8. See "Tailzie."

SUBSTITUTIO (Lat. from *substituere, to* substitute). A putting of one person in the place of another.

——**In the Civil Law.** The appointment of one person as heir in place of another, in the event of the first not taking the inheritance. As, *si ille haeres non erit, ille haeres esto*, if such a one will not be heir, let such a one be heir. Inst. 2. 15. pr. And a testator might appoint one heir after another in this way, to what extent he pleased (*in quantum velit testator substituere potest*), which was called making several grades of heirs (*plures gradus haeredum*), the person last named, without further alternative, being termed "necessary heir" (*necessarius haeres*), or heir at all events. Id.

SUBSTITUTIO HAEREDIS (Lat.) In Roman law, it was competent for a testator, after instituting a *haeres* (called the "*haeres institutus*"), to substitute another (called the "*haeres substitutus*") in his place in a certain event. If the event upon which the substitution was to take effect was the refusal of the instituted heir to accept the inheritance at all, then the substitution was called "*vulgaris*" (or common); but if the event was the death of the infant (*pupillus*) after acceptance, and before attaining his majority (of fourteen years if a male, and of twelve years if a female), then the substitution was called "*pupillaris*" (or for minors). Brown.

SUBSTITUTION (Lat. *substitutio*). In civil law. The putting of one person in the place of another, so that he may, in default of ability in the former, or after him, have the benefit of a devise or legacy.

Direct substitution is merely the institution of a second legatee in case the first should be either incapable or unwilling to accept the legacy; for example, if a testator should give to A. his estate, but provides that, in case he cannot legally receive it, or he willfully refuses it, it shall go to B.

Fidei commissary substitution is that which takes place when the person substituted is not to receive the legacy until after the first legatee, and, consequently, must receive the thing bequeathed from the hands of the latter; for example, I institute A. my heir, and I request that at his death he shall deliver my succession to B. Merlin, Repert.; 5 Toullier, Dr. Civ. 14. See "Subrogation."

SUBSTITUTIONAL, or SUBSTITUTIONARY. Where a will contains a gift of property to a class of persons, with a clause providing that, on the death of a member of the class before the period of distribution, his share is to go to his issue, if any, so as to substitute them for him, the gift to the issue is said to be substitutional or substitutionary. A bequest to such of the children of A. as shall be living at the testator's death, with a direction that the issue of such as shall have died shall take the shares which their parents would have taken, if living at the testator's death, is an example. Under such a gift, the issue of children dead at the date of the will cannot take anything. 2 Jarm. Wills, 771 et seq.

SUBSTITUTIONARY EXECUTOR. A person nominated by the testator to be executor in the event that the person primarily nominated shall fail to qualify or cease to act.

SUBTENANT. An under tenant.

SUBTRACTION (Lat. *sub*, away, *traho*, to draw). The act of withholding or detaining anything unlawfully.

In French law. The act of taking something fraudulently. It is generally applied to the taking of the goods of the estate of a deceased person fraudulently. See "Expilation."

SUBTRACTION OF CONJUGAL RIGHTS. The act of a husband or wife living separately from the other without a lawful cause. 3 Bl. Comm. 94.

SUBVASSORES (Law Lat.) In old Scotch law. Base holders; inferior holders; they who held their lands of knights. Skene de Verb. Sign.

SUCCESSIO (Lat.) In the civil law. A coming in place of another, on his decease; a coming into the estate which a deceased person had at the time of his death. This was either by virtue of an express appointment of the deceased person by his will (*ex testamento*), or by the general appointment of law in case of intestacy (*ab intestato*). Inst. 2. 9. 7; Heinec. Elem. Jur. Civ. lib. 2, tit. 10; Id. lib. 3, tit. 13.

SUCCESSION.

——**In Louisiana.** The right and transmission of the rights and obligations of the deceased to his heirs. The estate, rights, and charges which a person leaves after his death, whether the property exceed the charges, or the charges exceed the property, or whether he has left only charges without property. The succession not only includes the rights and obligations of the deceased as they exist at the time of his death, but all that has accrued thereto since the opening of the succession, as also of the new charges to which it becomes subject. That right by which the heir can take possession of the estate of the deceased, such as it may be.

(1) Irregular succession is that which is established by law in favor of certain persons, or of the estate in default of heirs, either legal or instituted by testament.

(2) Legal succession is that which is established in favor of the nearest relations of the deceased.

(3) Testamentary succession is that which results from the constitution of the heir, contained in a testament executed in the form prescribed by law. See "Heir;"

"Descent;" Poth. des Success.; Toullier, Dr. Civ. lib. 3, tit. 1.

——**In Common Law.** The mode by which one set of persons, members of a corporation aggregate, acquire the rights of another set which preceded them. This term in strictness is to be applied only to such corporations. 2 Bl. Comm. 430.

——**In Stirpes.** The lineal descendants, infinitum, of any person deceased, shall represent their ancestor who stand in the same place as the person himself would have done had he been living. These representatives take neither more nor less, but just so much as their principals would have done. 114 Ill. 605. See "Per Stirpes; Stirpes."

SUCCESSION TAXES. Taxes levied on the sucessions due or inheritance of a decedent's estate. They are variously called "inheritance taxes," "collateral inheritance taxes," "transfer taxes," and perhaps other names. The local statutes imposing them determine the modes for their collection, and the persons or properties liable.

SUCCESSOR. One who follows or comes into the place of another.

This term is applied more particularly to a sole corporation, or to any corporation. The word "heir" is more correctly applicable to a common person who takes an estate by descent. 12 Pick. (Mass.) 322; Co. Litt. 8b.

A person who has been appointed or elected to some office after another person.

SUCCURRITUR MINORI; FACILIS EST lapsus juventutis. A minor is to be aided; youth is liable to err. Jenk. Cent. Cas. 47.

SUCH. The word such is descriptive, and is a relative word, and as such must be referred to the last antecedent, unless the meaning of the sentence would thereby be impaired. 190 Mich. 313, 324.

SUCKEN, or **SUCHEN.** In Scotch law. The whole lands restricted to a mill,—that is, whose tenants are bound to grind there. The possessors of these lands are called "suckeners." Bell, Dict.

SUE. To commence or continue legal proceedings for the recovery of a right. See "Action;" "Suit."

SUE OUT. In practice. To obtain judicially; to issue. Applied only to process; particularly such as is granted specially. To sue out a writ is to obtain and issue it; to issue it on leave obtained for the purpose.

SUERTE. In Spanish law. A small lot of ground. 5 Tex. 83.

SUFFER. To suffer an act to be done, by a person who can prevent it, is to permit or consent to it; to approve of it, and not to hinder it. It implies a willingness of the mind. 19 Conn. 505.

SUFFERANCE, TENANCY AT. See "Tenancy."

SUFFERANCE WHARVES. Wharves on which goods may be landed before any duty is paid. They are appointed for the purpose by the commissioners of the customs. 16 & 17 Vict. c. 107, § 13; 2 Steph. Comm. 500, note.

SUFFERING A RECOVERY. A recovery was effected by the party wishing to convey the land suffering a fictitious action to be brought against him by the party to whom the land was to be conveyed (the demandant), and allowing the demandant to recover a judgment against him for the land in question. The vendor, or conveying party, in thus assisting or permitting the demandant so to recover a judgment against him, was thence technically said to "suffer a recovery." Brown.

SUFFRAGAN (Law Lat. *suffraganeus*). A titular bishop ordained to assist the bishop of the diocese in his spiritual functions, or to take his place. The number was limited to two to each bishop by 26 Hen. VIII. c. 14. So called because by his suffrage ecclesiastical causes were to be judged. Termes de la Ley.

SUFFRAGE. Vote; the act of voting; the right to vote.

SUGGESTIO FALSI (Lat.) A statement of a falsehood. This amounts to a fraud whenever the party making it was bound to disclose the truth.

The following is an example of a case where chancery will interfere and set aside a contract as fraudulent, on account of the *suggestio falsi:* A purchaser applied to the seller to purchase a lot of wild land, and represented to him it was worth nothing, except for a sheep pasture, when he knew there was a valuable mine on the lot, of which the seller was ignorant. The sale was set aside. 2 Paige, Ch. (N. Y.) 390; 4 Bouv. Inst. note 3837 et seq. See "Concealment;" "Misrepresentation;" "Representation;" "Suppressio Veri."

SUGGESTION. In practice. Information. It is applied to those cases where, during the pendency of a suit, some matter of fact or circumstance which will materially affect or put a stop to the suit in its existing form, which for some reason cannot be pleaded, 186 Mich. 617, 625; such as death or insolvency of a party. The counsel of the other party announces the fact in court, or enters it upon the record. The fact is usually admitted, if true, and the court issues the proper order thereupon. See 2 Sellon, Prac. 191.

In wills, when suggestions are made to a testator for the purpose of procuring a devise of his property in a particular way, and when such suggestions are false, they generally amount to a fraud. Bac. Abr.

"Wills" (G 3); 5 Toullier, Dr. Civ. note 706.

SUGGESTIVE INTERROGATION. A phrase which has been used by some writers to signify the same thing as "leading question." 2 Benth. Ev. bk. 3, c. 3. It is used in the French law.

SUI GENERIS (Lat.) Of its own kind; the only one of its kind.

SUI HAEREDES (Lat.) In the civil law. One's own heirs; proper heirs. Inst. 2. 19. 2; Dig. 38. 16.

SUI JURIS (Lat. of his own right). Possessing all the rights to which a freeman is entitled; not being under the power of another, as a slave, a minor, and the like.

To make a valid contract, a person must, in general, be *sui juris*. Every one of full age is presumed to be *sui juris*. Story, Ag. 10.

SUICIDE. Self-destruction and suicide are synonymous and mean the voluntary destruction of one's self. 29 Ill. App. 439. If a person who is incapable, by reason of unsoundness of mind, of resisting an insane impulse to take his own life, or to understand the general nature or consequences and effects of his act, kills himself, it is not suicide. 209 Ill. 33. At common law, suicide was a felony entailing forfeiture of estate. 1 Hale, P. C. c. 27.

Since the abolition of forfeitures, punishment of suicide is, of course, impossible, but an attempt to commit suicide is indictable (9 Cox, C. C. 247); and one who persuades another to suicide is guilty of murder (4 Bl. Comm. 189; 123 Mass. 422), though, if he be not present at the commission of the suicide, it is held that he cannot be punished, because he is an accessory before the fact, and the prior conviction of the principal is impossible (9 Car. & P. 79).

SUING AND LABORING CLAUSE. A clause in an English policy of marine insurance, generally in the following form: "In case of any loss or misfortune, it shall be lawful for the assured, their factors, servants, and assigns, to sue, labor, and travel for, in, and about the defense, safeguard, and recovery of the" property insured, "without prejudice to this insurance; to the charges whereof we, the assurers, will contribute." The object of the clause is to encourage the assured to exert themselves in preserving the property from loss. 15 C. B. (N. S.) 291; 2 Q. B. Div. 501; 4 App. Cas. 755.

SUIT. In its broadest sense, any proceeding in a court of justice by which a party pursues a remedy which the law affords him. In this sense, it is a broader term than "action," including proceedings in petition. 2 Pet. (U. S.) 449; 14 Pet. (U. S.) 540.

"Suit" applies to criminal proceedings (143 Mass. 136), and proceedings both in equity and at law (20 How. Pr. [N. Y.] 381).

In a narrower sense, "suit" has been held synonymous with "action." 4 Wall. (U. S.) 112. And "suit" is commonly applied to proceedings in equity, and "action" to proceedings at law. 9 Barb. (N. Y.) 300.

——**In Louisiana.** A suit is a real, personal, or mixed demand made before a competent judge, by which the parties pray to obtain their rights and a decision of their disputes. Code Prac. art. 96. In that acceptation, the words "suit," "process," and "cause" are in that state almost synonymous.

——**At Common Law.** The term had several meanings, not included in the idea of proceedings in court, as:

(1) Suit of court, an attendance which a tenant owes to his lord's court. Cowell; Jacob, 4.

(2) Suit covenant, where one has covenanted to do suit and service in his lord's court.

(3) Suit custom, where service is owed time out of mind.

(4) The following one in chase; as, fresh suit.

(5) A petition to a king, or a great person, or a court.

SUIT SILVER, or **SUTER SILVER.** A small rent or sum of money paid in some manors to excuse the freeholders' appearance at the courts of their lord. Cowell.

SUITAS (Law Lat.) In the civil law. The condition or quality of a *suus haeres*, or proper heir. Halifax, Anal. bk. 2, c. 9, No. 11; Calv. Lex. This term seems to have been framed by the later civilians.

SUITE (French.) Those persons who, by his authority, follow or attend an ambassador or other public minister.

In general, the suite of a minister are protected from arrest, and the inviolability of his person is communicated to those who form his suite. Vattel, lib. 4, c. 9, § 120; 1 Dall. (Pa.) 177; Baldw. (U. S.) 240. See "Ambassador."

SUITOR. One who is a party to a suit or action in court; one who is a party to an action. In its ancient sense, "suitor" meant one who was bound to attend the county court; also, one who formed part of the *secta*.

SUITORS' DEPOSIT ACCOUNT. Formerly suitors in the English court of chancery derived no income from their cash paid into court unless it was invested at their request and risk. Now, however, it is provided by the Court of Chancery (Funds) Act 1872, that all money paid into court, and not required by the suitor to be invested, shall be placed on deposit, and shall bear interest at two per cent. per annum for the benefit of the suitor entitled to it. The sum required for the payment of this interest is produced by placing all money in court not required for meeting current demands in the hands of the commissioners for the reduction of the national debt, who invest it in government securities. This arrangement is called the "suitors' deposit account." See Chancery Funds Consolidated Rules, 1874; Report of Chancery Funds Commissioners (1864) lvii.

SUITORS' FEE FUND. A fund arising partly from the fees of the English court of chancery, and partly from the surplus income of the suitors' fund (*q. v.*) Out of it the salaries and other expenses of the court of chancery were paid. By the Courts of Justice (Salaries and Funds) Act 1866, the suitors' fee fund was transferred to the commissioners for the reduction of the national debt, and the salaries and expenses formerly paid out of it were charged on the consolidated fund. Rep. Chanc. Fund Comm. 1864.

SUITORS' FUND. A fund belonging to the English court of chancery, and consisting of two parts. Fund A consisted of government stocks resulting from the investment of so much of the money in court belonging to the suitors as was not required for current purposes. Part of the income arising from these investments was employed in paying certain expenses of the court, and the balance was invested in government stocks, which formed fund B. Subsequently the surplus income of both funds was annually added to the suitors' fee fund (*q. v.*) By the Courts of Justice, etc., Act 1869, the suitors' fund was transferred to the commissioners for the reduction of the national debt, and the consolidated fund was made liable for the due payment of the money which belonged to the suitors, and had been invested as above stated. Chanc. Funds Comm. Rep. 1864.

SULCUS. A small brook or stream of water. Cowell.

SUM. A summary or abstract; a compendium; a collection.

SUM IN GROSS. An entire sum, as distinguished from one composed of separate or specified parts. 16 Wend. (N. Y.) 61, 262.

SUMMA CARITAS EST FACERE JUSTItiam singulis et omni tempore quando necesse fuerit. The greatest charity is to do justice to every one, and at any time whenever it may be necessary. 11 Coke, 70.

SUMMA EST LEX QUAE PRO RELIGIone facit. That is the highest law which favors religion. 10 Mod. 117, 119; 2 Chanc. Cas. 18.

SUMMA RATIO EST QUAE PRO RELIGIone facit. That is the highest law which which determines in favor of religion. Co. Litt. 341a; Broom, Leg. Max. (3d London Ed.) 18; 5 Coke, 14b; 10 Coke, 55a; 2 Chanc. Cas. 18.

SUMMAM ESSE RATIONEM QUAE PRO religione facit. That consideration is strongest which determines in favor of religion. Dig. 11. 7. 43, cited in Grotius de Jure Belli, lib. 3, c. 12, § 7. See 10 Mod. 117, 119.

SUMMARY PROCEDURE ON BILLS OF exchange. This phrase refers to St. 18 & 19 Vict. c. 67, passed in 1855, for the purpose of facilitating the remedies on bills and notes by the prevention of frivolous or fictitious defenses. By this statute, a defendant in an action on a bill or note, brought within six months after it has become payable, is prohibited from defending the action without the leave of the court or a judge. See 2 Steph. Comm. 118, note; Lush, Prac. 1027.

SUMMARY PROCEEDING. A form of trial in which the ancient established course of legal proceedings is disregarded, especially in the matter of trial by jury, and, in the case of the heavier crimes, presentment by a grand jury. See 8 Gray (Mass.) 329.

In no case can the party be tried summarily unless when such proceedings are authorized by legislative authority, except perhaps in cases of contempts; for the common law is a stranger to such a mode of trial. 4 Bl. Comm. 280. See 2 Kent, Comm. (6th Ed.) 73; 2 Conn. 819; 4 Conn. 535; 37 Me. 172; 4 Hill (N. Y.) 145; 8 Gray (Mass.) 329; 4 Dev. (N. C.) 15; 10 Yerg. (Tenn.) 59.

SUMMARY TRIALS. A modern term employed to designate criminal trials before magistrates, justices of the peace, or other inferior judicial officers or courts, which trials are not according to the common-law trial by jury on indictment, but are conducted in a less formal and cautious manner. Only the minor offenses are tried thus. It seems that the term should include a trial on indictment if it lacks the element of trial by a common-law jury.

SUMMER-HUS SILVER. A payment to the lords of the wood on the Wealds of Kent, who used to visit those places in summer, when their under tenants were bound to prepare little summer houses for their reception, or else pay a composition in money. Custumale de Newington juxta Sittingburn, M. S.; Cowell.

SUMMING UP. In practice. The act of making a speech before a court and jury, after all the evidence has been heard, in favor of one of the parties in the cause, is called "summing up." When the judge delivers his charge to the jury, he usually sums up the evidence in the case. 6 Harg. St. Tr. 832; 1 Chit. Crim. Law, 632. See "Charge."

SUMMON. In practice. To notify the defendant that an action has been instituted against him, and that he is required to answer to it at a time and place named. This is done by a proper officer's either giving the defendant a copy of the summons, or having it at his house, or by reading the summons to him.

SUMMONERS. Petty officers who cite men to appear in any court.

SUMMONITIO (Law Lat.) In old English practice. A summoning or summons; a writ by which a party was summoned to appear in court, of which there were various kinds. Spelman; Fleta, lib. 6, c. 6.

A command or precept of the king that one be before him to answer or do something, or that one be and have such a one to answer or to do something. Bracton, fol. 333.

SUMMONITIONES AUT CITATIONES nullae liceant fieri intra palatium regis. Let no summonses or citations be served within the king's palace. 3 Inst. 141.

SUMMONITORES SCACCARII. Officers who assisted in collecting the revenues by citing the defaulters therein into the court of exchequer.

SUMMONS.

——**In Common-Law Practice.** The name of a writ commanding the sheriff, or other authorized officer, to notify a party to appear in court to answer a complaint made against him, and in the said writ specified, on a day therein mentioned. Viner, Abr.; 2 Sellon, Prac. 356; 3 Bl. Comm. 279.

The writ of summons was substituted by St. 2 Wm. IV. c. 39, for the original writs by which actions were formerly commenced.

——**In Code Practice.** The proceeding to commence an action in many of the code states consists of a notice to defendant, requiring him to serve an answer to the complaint. It is ordinarily signed by the plaintiff or his attorney, bears no teste, and is not process. It may be served by any disinterested person or by the attorney.

In other code states the summons runs in the name of the state or people, is issued by the clerk under seal, and is served by the sheriff.

Some of the states permit the use of either of these two modes of summons. See "Process."

SUMMONS AND SEVERANCE. See "Severance."

SUMMUM JUS (Lat.) Strict right; extreme right. 3 Bl. Comm. 392; 1 Burrows, 54. The extremity or rigor of the law. Burr. Sett. Cas. 588. Lord Bacon applies the phrase to strict law, untempered by equity. Works, IV. 274.

SUMMUM JUS, SUMMA INJURIA. The rigor or height of law is the height of of wrong. Hob. 125.

SUMPTUARY LAWS. Laws relating to the expenses of the people, and made to restrain excess in apparel, food, drink, furniture, etc.

They originated in the view that luxury is, in some of its degrees, opposed to public policy, and that the state is bound to interfere against it. Montesq. Esprit des Lois, bk. 7, c. 2, 4, and Tacitus, Ann. bk. 2, c. 33; Id. bk. 3, c. 52.

In England, in 1336, it was enacted (10 Edw. III. c. 3), that, inasmuch as many mischiefs had happened to the people of the realm by excessive and costly meats, by which, among other things, many who aspired in this respect beyond their means were impoverished and unable to aid themselves or their liege lord in time of need, all men were forbidden to have served more than two courses at a meal, each of but two sorts of victual, except on the principal feasts of the year, and then only three courses were allowed. Blackstone states that this is still unrepealed. 4 Bl. Comm. 170. Subsequent statutes—that of 1363, and those of 1463 and 1482—regulated the dress, and to some extent the diet, of the people, with careful regard to their rank. The substance of these statutes will be found in Knight's History of England, vol. 2, pp. 272-274. They were repealed by 1 Jac. I. c. 25.

SUNDAY. The first day of the week. In some of the New England states it begins at sunsetting on Saturday, and ends at the same time the next day; but in other parts of the United States it generally commences at twelve o'clock on the night between Saturday and Sunday, and ends in twenty-four hours thereafter. 6 Gill & J. (Md.) 268. And see Bac. Abr. "Heresy, etc." (D), "Sheriff" (N 4); 1 Salk. 78; 1 Sellon, Prac. 12. The "Sabbath," the "Lord's Day," and "Sunday" all mean the same thing. 6 Gill & J. (Md.) 268. See 3 Watts (Pa.) 56, 59; 6 Watts (Pa.) 231.

SUN SET. A definite period of time at any given locality. What that time is can only be known from scientific calculations. It is not precisely the same on any two days in succession, nor is it exactly the same at any two points distant apart on the same day. It is later at a point west than one further east, and of this fact the court may take judicial notice. 111 Ill. 135.

SUNSTROKE. An acute prostration from excessive heat of weather; and the same effects may be produced by heat which is not of solar origin. 100 Ill. App. 195.

SUO NOMINE (Lat.) In his own name.

SUO PERICULO (Lat.) At his own peril or risk.

SUPELLEX (Lat.) In the Roman law. Household furniture. Dig. 33. 10.

SUPER ALTUM MARE (Lat.) Upon the high sea. See "High Seas."

SUPER FIDEM CHARTARUM, MORTUIS testibus, erit ad patriam de necessitate recurrendum. The truth of charters is necessarily to be referred to a jury when the witnesses are dead. Co. Litt. 6.

SUPER JURARE. A term anciently used when a criminal endeavored to excuse himself by his own oath, or the oath of one or two witnesses, and the crime objected against him was so plain and notorious that he was convicted on the oaths of many more witnesses. Wharton.

SUPER PRAEROGATIVA REGIS. A writ which formerly lay against the king's tenant's widow for marrying without the royal license. Fitzh. Nat. Brev. 174.

SUPER STATUTO. 1 Edw. III. c. 12. A writ that lay against the king's tenant holding in chief, who aliened the king's land without his license.

SUPER STATUTO DE ARTICULIS CLERI. A writ which lay against a sheriff or other officer who distrained in the king's highway, or on lands anciently belonging to the church.

SUPER STATUTO FACTO POUR SENESCHAL et marshal de roy, etc. A writ which lay against a steward or marshal for holding plea in his court, or for trespass or contracts not made or arising within the king's household.

SUPER STATUTO VERSUS SERVANTES et laboratores. A writ which lay against him who kept any servants who had left the service of another, contrary to law.

SUPER VISUM CORPORE (Lat.) Upon view of the body. When an inquest is held over a body found dead, it must be *super visum corpore*. See "Coroner."

SUPERCARGO. In maritime law. A person specially employed by the owner of a cargo to take charge of and sell to the best advantage merchandise which has been shipped, and to purchase returning cargoes and to receive freight, as he may be authorized.

Supercargoes have complete control over the cargo and everything which immediately concerns it, unless their authority is either expressly or impliedly restrained. 12 East, 381. Under certain circumstances, they are responsible for the cargo (4 Mass. 115. See 1 Gill & J. [Md.] 1), but the supercargo has no power to interfere with the government of the ship (3 Pardessus, note 646; 1 Boul. P. Dr. Com. 421).

SUPERDEMANDA (Law Lat.) In old English practice. An over demand; a demand of more than was just or due. *Cadit in misericordiam pro superdemanda,* becomes subject to amercement for his over demand. Bacton, fol. 179b.

SUPERFICIARIUS (Lat.) In civil law. He who has built upon the soil of another, which he has hired for a number of years or forever, yielding a yearly rent. This is not very different from the owner of a lot on ground rent in Pennsylvania. Dig. 43. 18. 1.

SUPERFICIES (Lat.) In civil law. Whatever has been erected on the soil.

SUPERFLUA NON NOCENT. Superfluities do no injury. Jenk. Cent. Cas. 184.

SUPERFLUOUS LANDS. In English law. Lands acquired by a railway company under its statutory powers, and not required for the purposes of its undertaking. The company is bound, within a certain time, to sell such lands, and, if it does not, they vest in and become the property of the owners of the adjoining lands. 13 Ch. Div. 607.

SUPERINDUCTIO (Lat.) In the civil law. A species of obliteration. Dig. 28. 4. 1.

SUPERINSTITUTION. Where a church is full by institution, and a second institution is granted to the same church, this is a superinstitution, and necessarily raises the question who is entitled to the benefice. It is said that the party who obtains a superinstitution may try his title by ejectment, but that, in consequence of its inconveniences, this method is discouraged, and the more usual remedy of a *quare impedit* adopted. Phillim. Ecc. Law, 476.

SUPERIOR. One who has a right to command; one who holds a superior rank; as, a soldier is bound to obey his superior.

In estates, some are superior to others. An estate entitled to a servitude or easement over another estate is called the "superior" or "dominant," and the other the "inferior" or "servient" estate. 1 Bouv. Inst. note 1612.

SUPERIOR AND VASSAL. In Scotch law. A feudal relation corresponding with the English "lord and tenant." Bell, Dict.

SUPERIOR COURT.

——**In English Law.** A term applied collectively to the three courts of common law at Westminster, namely, the king's bench, the common pleas, the exchequer.

It denotes a court of intermediate jurisdiction between the courts of inferior or limited jurisdiction and the courts of last resort.

——**In American Law.** A court of intermediate jurisdiction between the inferior courts and those of last resort.

In Delaware it is the court of last resort; and in some of the states there is a superior court for cities.

SUPERIORITY. In Scotch law. The *dominium directum* of lands, without the profit. 1 Forbes, Inst. pt. 2, p. 97; Bell, Dict.

SUPERNUMERARII (Lat.) In Roman law. Those advocates who were not *statuti* (*q. v.*)

The *statuti* were inscribed in the matriculation books, and formed a part of the college of advocates in each jurisdiction. The supernumeraries were not attached to any bar in particular, and could reside where they pleased. They took the place of advocates by title as vacancies occurred in that body.

SUPERONERATIO (Law Lat. *superonenare*). Surcharging a common, *i. e.*, putting in beasts of a number or kind other than the right of common allows. It can only be of a common appendant or appurtenant. Bracton, fol. 229, and Fleta, lib. 4, c. 23, § 4, give two remedies, novel dissesin and writ of admeasurement, by which latter remedy no damages are recovered till the second offense. Now, distraining, trespass, and case are used as remedies. 3 Bl. Comm. 238*.

SUPERONERATIONE PASTURAE. A judicial writ that lay against him who was impleaded in the county court for the surcharge of a common with his cattle, in a case where he was formerly impleaded for it in the same court, and the cause was removed into one of the superior courts. Obsolete.

SUPERPLUSAGIUM. Overplus; surplus; residue or balance. Spelman.

SUPERSEDE. To stay, stop, interfere with, or annul; *e. g.*, to supersede the proceedings in outlawry, or in bankruptcy, or in lunacy, etc.

SUPERSEDEAS (Lat. that you set aside). A stay of proceedings. The name of a writ containing a command to stay the proceedings at law. It is either express, by the issuance of a writ of supersedeas, or implied, by the issuance of a writ, as of *certiorari*, a writ of error when bail is given, etc., which operate as supersedeas.

SUPERSTITIOUS USE. In English law. When lands, tenements, rents, goods, or chattels are given, secured, or appointed for and towards the maintenance of a priest or chaplain to say mass; for the maintenance of a priest or other man to pray for the soul of any dead man in such church or elsewhere; to have and maintain perpetual obits, lamps, torches, etc., to be used at certain times to help to save the souls of men out of purgatory,—in such cases the king, by force of several statutes, is authorized to direct and appoint all such uses *cy pres* under the sign manual. Bac. Abr. "Charitable Uses and Mortmain" (D); Duke, Char. Uses, 105; 6 Ves. 567; 4 Coke, 104.

In the United States, where all religious opinions are free, and the right to exercise them is secured to the people, the English doctrine of superstitious uses does not prevail. In Alabama and Wisconsin gifts for prayer or masses for the departed are invalid chiefly on the ground of want of living beneficiaries. 6 Cyc. 920.

SUPPLEMENT, LETTERS OF. In Scotch practice. A process by which a party not residing within the jurisdiction of an inferior court may be cited to appear before it. Bell, Dict.

SUPPLEMENTAL. That which is added to a thing to complete it; as, a supplemental affidavit, which is an additional affidavit to make out a case; a supplemental bill.

SUPPLEMENTAL AFFIDAVIT. In practice. An affidavit made in addition to a previous affidavit, for the purpose of supplying some deficiency in it.

SUPPLEMENTAL ANSWER. One which was filed in chancery for the purpose of correcting, adding to, and explaining an answer already filed. Smith, Ch. Prac. 334.

SUPPLEMENTAL BILL. In equity practice. A bill brought as an addition to an original bill to supply some defect in its original frame or structure which cannot be supplied by amendment. See 1 Paige Ch. (N. Y.) 200; 15 Miss. 456; 22 Barb. (N. Y.) 161; 14 Ala. (N. S.) 147; 18 Ala. (N. S.) 771. It may be brought by a plaintiff or defendant (2 Atk. 533; 2 Ball & B. 140; 1 Story, C. C. [U. S.] 218), and as well after as before a decree (3 Md. Ch. 306; 1 Macn. & G. 405; Story, Eq. Pl. § 338; Hinde, Chanc. Prac. 43), but must be within a reasonable time (2 Halst. [N. J.] 465). See "Original Bill."

SUPPLEMENTAL BILL, BILL IN THE nature of a. See "Bill in the Nature, etc."

SUPPLEMENTAL CLAIM. A further claim which was filed when further relief was sought after the bringing of a claim. Smith, Ch. Prac. 655.

SUPPLEMENTAL COMPLAINT. In code practice. A complaint supplying some defect or omission in the original complaint, not curable by amendment.

SUPPLETORY OATH. In ecclesiastical law. An oath given by the judge to the plaintiff or defendant upon half proof, as by one witness, already made. The oath, added to the half proof, enables the judge to decide. It is discretionary with the judge. Strange, 80; 3 Bl. Comm. 370*.

SUPPLICATIO (Lat.) In civil law. A petition for pardon of a first offense; also, a petition for reversal of judgment; also, equivalent to *duplicatio*, which is our "rejoinder." Calv. Lex.

SUPPLICAVIT (Lat.) In English law. The name of a writ issuing out of the king's bench or chancery for taking sureties of the peace. It is commonly directed to the justices of the peace, when they are averse to acting in the affair in their judicial capacity. 4 Bl. Comm. 233. See Viner, Abr.; Comyn, Dig. "Chancery" (4 R), "Forcible Entry" (D 16, 17).

SUPPLICIUM (Lat.) In civil law. A corporal punishment ordained by law; the punishment of death; so called because it was customary to accompany the guilty man to the place of execution, and there offer supplications for him.

SUPPLIES. In English law. Extraordinary grants to the king by parliament to supply the exigencies of the state. Jacob.

SUPPONERE (Lat.) In old English law. To put under; to put in place of another; to substitute fraudulently; to put a false thing in place of the true or genuine; to put a strange child in place of the true heir.

SUPPORT. In the law of easements. The right to rest the beams or framework of a building into a wall of an adjoining building. Also rights of lateral and subjacent support which pertain to owners of adjoining lands. See "Party Walls;" "Lateral Support."

In the law of decedents' estates the term "support" is sometimes used as a synonym for the allowance of articles or money set apart for the survivor and children.

SUPPRESS. To put a stop to anything when actually existing. Does not extend to prevention by suppressing what may lead to it. 34 L. J. M. C. 9; 17 C. P. N. S. 625.

SUPPRESSIO VERI (Lat.) Concealment of truth. See "Fraud."

SUPPRESSIO VERI, EXPRESSIO FALSI. Suppression of the truth is (equivalent to) the expression of what is false. 11 Wend. (N. Y.) 374, 417.

SUPPRESSIO VERI, SUGGESTIO FALSI. Suppression of the truth is equivalent to the suggestion of what is false. 23 Barb. (N. Y.) 521, 525.

SUPRA (Lat.) Above; upon.

SUPRA PROTEST (over protest). In mercantile law. A term applied to an acceptance of a bill by a third person, after protest for nonacceptance by the drawee. 3 Kent, Comm. 87.

SUPREMA VOLUNTAS (Lat.) The last will. *Et suprema voluntas quod mandat fierique jubet, parere necesse est,* and what a last will commands and orders to be done must be obeyed. Doderidge, J., Latch, 137.

SUPREMACY. Sovereign dominion, authority, and pre-eminence; the highest state. In the United States, the supremacy resides in the people, and is exercised by their constitutional representative,—the president and congress. See "Sovereignty."

SUPREMACY, ACT OF. See "Act of Supremacy."

SUPREMACY, OATH OF. In English law. An oath to uphold the supreme power of the kingdom in the person of the reigning sovereign.

SUPREME. That which is superior to all other things; as, the supreme power of the state, which is an authority over all others; the supreme court, which is superior to all other courts.

SUPREME COURT. A court of superior jurisdiction in many of the states of the United States and the federal court of last resort.

The name is properly applied to the court of last resort, and is so used in most of the states. In nearly all the states there is a supreme court, but in one or two there is a court of appellate jurisdiction from the supreme court.

SUPREME COURT OF ERRORS. In American law. An appellate tribunal, and the court of last resort, in the state of Connecticut.

SUPEME COURT OF JUDICATURE. The court formed by the English judicature act of 1873, as modified by the judicature act of 1875, the appellate jurisdiction act of 1876, and the judicature acts of 1877, 1879, and 1881, in substitution for the various superior courts of law, equity, admiralty, probate, and divorce, existing when the act was passed, including the court of appeal in chancery and bankruptcy, and the exchequer chamber. It consists of two permanent divisions, viz., a court of original jurisdiction, called the "high court of justice," and a court of appellate jurisdiction, called the "court of appeal." Its title of "supreme" is now a misnomer, as the superior appellate jurisdiction of the house of lords and privy council, which was originally intended to be transferred to it, has been allowed to remain.

SUPREME JUDICIAL COURT. In American law. An appellate tribunal, and the court of last resort, in the states of Maine, Massachusetts, and New Hampshire.

SUPREMUS (Lat.) In the civil law. Last; the last.

SUPREMUS EST, QUEM NEMO SEQUITUR. He is last whom no one follows. Dig. 50. 16. 92.

SUR (French). Upon. In the titles of real actions, "*sur*" was used to point out what the writ was founded upon. Thus, a real action brought by the owner of a reversion or seigniory, in certain cases where his tenant repudiated his tenure, was called "a writ of right *sur disclaimer*." So, a writ of entry *sur disseisin* was a real action to recover the possession of land from a disseisor.

SUR CUI IN VITA. A writ that lay for the heir of a woman whose husband had aliened her land in fee, and she had omitted to bring the writ of *cui in vita* for the recovery thereof, in which case, her heir might have this writ against the tenant after her decease. Cowell. See "Cui in Vita."

SURCHARGE. To put more cattle upon a common than the herbage will sustain, or than the party hath a right to do. 3 Bl. Comm. 237.

In case of common without stint, it could only happen when insufficient herbage was left for the lord's own cattle. 1 Rolle, Abr. 399.

The remedy was by distraining the beasts beyond the proper number; an action of trespass which must have been brought by the lord of the manor; an action on the case, or a writ of admeasurement of pasture. 2 Bl. Comm. 238, note.

——**In Equity Practice.** To prove the omission of an item from an account which is before the court as complete, which should be inserted to the credit of the party surcharging. Story, Eq. Jur. § 526; 2 Ves. Jr. 565; 11 Wheat. (U. S.) 237; 8 Rich. Eq. (S. C.) 248. It is opposed to "falsify" (*q. v.*) Leave to surcharge and falsify is granted in preference to opening an account, in case of an account stated by the parties or reported by an auditor, where the party obtaining the liberty would be concluded by the account were it not granted. See "Account;" "Auditor."

SURDUS (Lat.) In the civil law. Deaf; a deaf person. Inst. 2. 12. 3. *Surdus et mutus*, a deaf and dumb person. Id.; Dig. 28. 1. 6. 1; Id. 28. 1. 7; Id. 50. 17. 124; Fleta, lib. 6, c. 38, § 1; Id. c. 40, § 2.

SURETY. A person who binds himself for the payment of a sum of money, or for the performance of something else, for another, who is already bound for the same. See "Suretyship."

SURETY COMPANY. An association or corporation engaged in the business of offering itself, in consideration of a premium paid, as a surety for the fidelity of persons in positions of trust, or for the responsibility of persons bound to the performance of any act.

SURETY OF THE PEACE. Surety of the peace is a species of preventive justice, and consists in obliging those persons whom there is a probable ground to suspect of future misbehavior, to stipulate with, and to give full assurance to the public that such offense as is apprehended shall not take place, by finding pledges or securities for keeping the peace, or for their good behavior. Brown.

SURETYSHIP. An undertaking to answer for the debt, default, or miscarriage of another by which the surety becomes bound as the principal or original debtor is bound.

It differs from "guaranty" in this, that suretyship is a primary obligation to see that the debt is paid, while guaranty is a collateral undertaking, essentially in the alternative, to pay the debt if the debtor does not pay it. 24 Pick. (Mass.) 252. And, accordingly, a surety may be sued as a promisor to pay the debt, while a guarantor must be sued specially on his contract. 8 Pick. (Mass.) 423.

While guaranty applies only to contracts not under seal, and principally to mercantile obligations, suretyship may apply to all obligations under seal or by parol. The subjects are, however, nearly related, and many of the principles are common to both. There must be a principal debtor liable, otherwise the promise becomes an original contract; and, the promise being collateral, the surety must be bound to no greater extent than the principal. Suretyship is one of the contracts included in the statute of frauds (29 Car. II. c. 3.)

Kent, C. J., divides secondary undertakings into three classes: (1) Cases in which the guaranty or promise is collateral to the principal contract, but is made at the same time, and becomes an essential ground of the credit given to the principal or direct debtor. Here there is not, and need not be, any other consideration than that moving between the creditor and original debtor. (2) Cases in which the collateral undertaking is subsequent to the creation of the debt, and was not the inducement to it, though the subsisting liability is the ground of the promise, without any distinct and unconnected inducement. Here there must be some further consideration shown, having an immediate respect to such liability; for the consideration for the original debt will not attach to this subsequent promise. (3) When the promise to pay the debt of another arises out of some new and original consideration of benefit or harm moving between the newly-contracting parties. 8 Johns. (N. Y.) 29; 21 Y. 415; 21 Me. 459; 15 Pick. (Mass.) 159.

A simpler division is into two classes: (1) Where the principal obligation exists before the collateral undertaking is made. (2) Where there is no principal obligation prior in time to the collateral undertaking. In the last class, the principal obligation may be contemporaneous with or after the collateral undertaking. The first class includes Kent's second and third, the second includes Kent's first, to which must be added cases where the guaranty referring to a present or future principal obligation does not share the consideration thereof, but proceeds on a distinct consideration. Moreover, there are other original undertakings out of the statute of frauds, and valid, though by parol, besides his third class. These are where the credit is given exclusively to the promissor, though the goods or consideration pass to another.

Under this division, undertakings of the first class are original, (1) when the principal obligation is thereby abrogated; (2) when, without such abrogation, the promisor, for his own advantage, apparent on the bargain, undertakes for some new consideration moving to him from the promisee; (3) where the promise is in consideration of some loss or disadvantage to the promisee; (4) where the promise is made to the principal debtor on a consideration moving from the debtor to the promissor. Theobald, Sur. 37 et seq., 49 et seq.

SURFACE WATER. Water which spreads over the surface of the ground, or stands in swamps, or percolates through or under the soil. It has its origin most commonly in rains and melted snow. 84 Wis. 438, 20 L. R. A. 40.

SURGEON. A surgeon, formerly, was a mere operator, who joined his practice to that of a barber. At the present time the profession has risen into great and deserved eminence, and surgery is now, properly speaking, treatment of bodily injuries and ills by manual operations and the use of surgical instruments and appliances.

SURMISE (Law Fr. and Eng.) In old practice. Suggestion. "The plaintiff, upon a surmise of goods come to the hands of the executors, shall have a *sci. fa.*" 1 Leon. 68, 286; Hardr. 82, 311.

SURNAME. A name which is added to the Christian name. In modern times, these have become family names. The family name is that which is continued from parent to child. 149 Iowa 672; 31 L. R. A. (N. S.) 1112.

They are called "surnames," because originally they were written over (*sur*) the name in judicial writings and contracts. They were and are still used for the purpose of distinguishing persons of the same name. They were taken from something attached to the persons assuming them; as, John Carpenter, Joseph Black, Samuel Little, etc. See "Name."

SURPLUS. That which is left from a fund which has been appropriated for a particular purpose; the remainder of a thing; the overplus; the residue. See 18 Ves. 466.

SURPLUSAGE.

——**In Accounts.** A greater disbursement than the charges amount to; a balance over. 1 Lew. 219.

——**In Pleading.** Allegations of matter wholly foreign and impertinent to the cause. All matter beyond the circumstances necessary to constitute the action is surplusage. Cowp. 683; 5 East, 275; 10 East, 205; 2 Johns. Cas. (N. Y.) 52; 1 Mason (U. S.) 57; 16 Tex. 656.

SURPLUSAGIUM NON NOCET. Surplusage does no harm. 3 Bouv. Inst. note 2949; Broom, Leg. Max. (3d London Ed.) 559.

SURPRISE. In equity practice. The act by which a party who is entering into a contract is taken unawares, by which sudden confusion or perplexity is created, which renders it proper that a court of equity should relieve the party so surprised. 2 Brown, Ch. 150; 1 Story, Eq. Jur. § 120, note.

The situation in which a party is placed, without any default of his own, which will be injurious to his interests. 8 Mart. (La.; N. S.) 407.

Mr. Jeremy (Eq. Jur. 366, 383, note) seems to think that the word "surprise" is a technical expression, and nearly synonymous with "fraud." It is sometimes used in this sense when it is deemed presumptive of, or approaching to, fraud. 1 Fonbl. Eq. 123; 3 Chanc. Cas. 56, 74, 103, 114. See 6 Ves. 327, 338; 16 Ves. 81, 86, 87; 2 Brown, Ch. 326; 1 Cox 340.

SURREBUTTER. In pleading. The plaintiff's answer to the defendant's rebutter. It is governed by the same rules as the replication. See 6 Comyn, Dig. 185; 7 Comyn, Dig. 389.

SURREJOINDER. In pleading. The plaintiff's answer to the defendant's rejoinder. It is governed in every respect by the same rules as the replication. Steph. Pl. 77; Archb. Civ. Pl. 284; 7 Comyn, Dig. 389.

SURRENDER. A yielding up of an estate for life or years to him who has an immediate estate in reversion or remainder, by which the lesser estate is merged in the greater by mutual agreement. Co. Litt. 337b.

The deed by which the surrender is made.

A surrender is of a nature directly opposite to a release; for, as the latter operates by the greater estate descending upon the less, the former is the falling of a less estate into a greater, by deed. A surrender immediately divests the estate of the surrenderor, and vests it in the surrenderee, even without the assent of the latter. Shep. Touch. 300, 301.

The technical and proper words of this conveyance are, surrender and yield up; but any form of words by which the intention of the parties is sufficiently manifested will operate as a surrender. Perk. § 607; 1 Term R. 441; Comyn, Dig. "Surrender" (A).

The surrender may be express or implied. The latter is when an estate incompatible with the existing estate is accepted, or the lessee takes a new lease of the same lands. 16 Johns. (N. Y.) 28; 2 Wils. 26; 1 Barn. & Ald. 50; 2 Barn. & Ald. 119; 5 Taunt. 518. And see 6 East, 86; 9 Barn. & C. 288; 7 Watts (Pa.) 123; Cruise, Dig. tit. 32, c. 7; Comyn, Dig.; 4 Kent, Comm. 102; Rolle, Abr.; 11 East, 317, note.

SURRENDER BY BAIL. The delivery, by his bail, of the accused person, or principal again into custody, or to a person or court having authority to re-commit or re-bail him. 220 Ill. 354.

SURRENDER OF COPYHOLD. The yielding of a copyhold into the hands of the lord. The usual method of transferring copyholds was by a surrender of the copyhold to the lord, to the use of the intended transferee, and the acceptance of him by the lord.

SURRENDER OF CRIMINALS. The act by which the public authorities deliver a person accused of a crime, and who is found in their jurisdiction, to the authorities within whose jurisdiction it is alleged the crime has been committed. See "Extradition."

SURRENDER TO USES OF WILL. A right of copyholders in some manors to devise their copyholds by surrendering them to the uses of their wills during their lives.

SURRENDEREE. One to whom a surrender has been made.

SURRENDEROR. One who makes a surrender; as, when the tenant gives up the estate and cancels his lease before the expiration of the term. One who yields up a freehold estate for the purpose of conveying it.

SURREPTITIOUS. That which is done in a fraudulent, stealthy manner.

SURROGATE (Lat. *surrogatus*, from *subrogare*, or *surrogare*, to substitute).

——**In English Law.** A deputy or substitute of the chancellor, bishop, ecclesiastical or admiralty judge, appointed by him. He must take an oath of office. He can grant licenses, hold courts, and adjudicate cases to the same extent and with the same authority as his principal, provided his grant of powers has been coextensive with those possessed by his principal. The office has arisen by usage, but it is sanctioned by canon 128, and recognized by St. 26 Geo. II. c. 33, 56 Geo. III. c. 82, and 10 Geo. IV. c. 53, by which latter act it was provided that the surrogates of the arches and consistory of London are to continue after the death of the judges of those courts till new appointments are made. 1 Phillim. Ecc. Law, 205; 3 Burn, Ecc. Law, 667.

——**In American Law.** A term used in some states to denote the judge to whom jurisdiction of the probate of wills, the grant of administration, and of guardianship is confided. In some states, he is called "surrogate," in others, "judge of probate," "register," "judge of the orphans' court," etc. He is ordinarily a county officer, with a local jurisdiction limited to his county.

——**Court.** In the United States. A state tribunal, with similar jurisdiction to the court of ordinary, court of probate, etc. (*q. v.*) relating to matters of probate, etc. 2 Kent, Comm. 409, note (b).

SURSISA (Law Lat. from Law Fr. *sursise, q. v.*) In old English law. Neglect; default. *Potest defendere summonitionem et sursisam*, he may defend [deny] the summons and the default. Bracton, fol. 356.

SURSISE (Law Fr. from *sursiser, q. v.*) In old English law. Neglect; omission; default; a ceasing or cessation. *De somounses, et de sursises, et de essoines.* Britt. c. 120. *E ki le cri orat e sursera, la sursise li Rei amend*, and whoever hears the cry [hue and cry], and neglects to pursue it, shall make amends for the neglect to the king. LL. Gul. Conq. lib. 48.

SURSISER, or SURCESSER (Law Fr.) To neglect; to omit doing a thing; to surcease; to fail to obey process. *Si levesque sursist nostre somounse, si soit attache de vener par destresse*, if the bishop fail to obey our summons, he shall be attached to appear by distress. Britt. c. 26. See "Sursise."

SURSUM REDDERE (Law Lat.) In old conveyancing. To render up; to surrender. See "Sursum Redditio."

SURSUM REDDITIO (Law Lat.) In old conveyancing. A surrender. The yielding up of an estate for life or years to him that hath an immediate estate in reversion or remainder, wherein the estate for life or years may drown by mutual agreement between them. A surrender must be by mutual agreement of the parties. 91 Ill. App. 520.

SURVEY. The act by which the quantity of a piece of land is ascertained. An instrument *sui generis*, in the nature of a partition; a customary mode in which a proprietor has set off to himself, in severalty a part of the common estate. 56 N. J. Law 237. The paper containing a statement of the courses, distances, and quantity of land is also called a "survey."

By "survey" is also understood an examination; as, a survey has been made of your house, and now the insurance company will insure it.

A plan and description of the present existence, state, condition, and mode of use of the insured property. 179 Mich. 443, 453.

SURVEY OF A VESSEL. An examination of a vessel to determine her condition. It is frequently had where some disaster has befallen the ship before proceeding to make repairs, or take measures for saving her.

SURVIVE. Ordinarily means to live longer than some other individual, but it may mean to continue to live beyond a specified period, event or condition. 220 Ill. 511.

It imports that the person who is to survive must be living at the death of the person whom, or at the happening of the event which, he is to survive. To outlive. "To live after" is somewhat ambiguous. See "Survivor." 35 L. J. Ch. 640; L. R. 2 Eq. 341.

SURVIVOR. One who survives another; one who outlives another; one of two or more persons who lives after the other or others have deceased; the longest liver of two or more joint tenants, or of any two or more persons who have a joint interest in anything. See 2 Bl. Comm. 183, 184.

One or more of certain individuals named or referred to, who are living when any other or others of them happen to die. See 1 Cush. (Mass.) 118; 11 Grat. (Va.) 67.

This is the natural and proper meaning of the term, which is usually given to it by the courts, in the construction of wills. 2 Jarm. Wills, 609-616 (435-439, Perkins' Ed. 1849). In some cases, however, "survivor" has been construed to mean "other," where it has appeared necessary in order to give effect to the apparent intention of the testator. See Id. 616-619 (440-442, Perkins' Ed.); 2 Williams, Ex'rs, 1256. See "Survive."

SURVIVORSHIP. The living of one of two or more persons after the death of the other or others.

Survivorship is where a person becomes entitled to property by reason of his having survived another person who had an interest in it. The most familiar example is in the case of joint tenants, the rule being that, on the death of one of two joint tenants, the whole property passes to the survivor.

SURVIVORSHIP, CLAUSE OF. An express clause in a devise or deed of gift to tenants in common that the property is to go to the survivor. Sometimes called the "clause of accruer."

SUS' PER COLL'. In English law. In the English practice, a calendar is made out of attainted criminals, and the judge signs the calendar with their separate judgments in the margin. In the case of a capital felony, it is written opposite the prisoner's name, "Let him be hanged by the neck," which, when the proceedings were in Latin, was "*suspendatur per collum*," or, in the abbreviated form, "*Sus' per coll'*." 4 Bl. Comm. 403.

SUSPEND. The word "suspend" in its natural significance rather imports something which may not be permanent, than that which necessarily is so; but which, while it ordinarily implies a temporary cessation, may, in certain connections, imply a termination. 167 Mich. 123, 131.

SUSPENDER. In Scotch law. He in whose favor a suspension is made.

In general, a suspender is required to give caution to pay the debt in the event it shall be found due. Where the suspender cannot, from his low or suspected circumstances, procure unquestionable security, the lords admit juratory caution; but the reasons of suspension are in that case to be considered with particular accuracy at passing the bill. Act 8 Nov. 1682; Ersk. Inst. 4. 3. 6.

SUSPENDERE (Law Lat.) In old English law. To hang; to execute by hanging. *Suspensus*, hanged. See "Sus' per Coll'."

SUSPENSE. When a rent, profit *a prendre*, and the like, are, in consequence of the unity of possession of the rent, etc., of the land out of which they issue, not *in esse* for a time, they are said to be in suspense, *tunc dormiunt;* but they may be revived or awakened. Co. Litt. 313a.

SUSPENSION. A temporary stop of a right, of a law, and the like.

In times of war, the *habeas corpus* act may be suspended by lawful authority.

There may be a suspension of an officer's duties or powers when he is charged with crimes. Wood, Inst. 510.

Suspension of a right in an estate is a partial extinguishment, or an extinguishment for a time. It differs from an extinguishment in this, a suspended right may be revived; one extinguished is absolutely dead. Bac. Abr. "Extinguishment" (A).

The suspension of a statute for a limited time operates so as to prevent its operation for the time; but it has not the effect of a repeal. 3 Dall. (Pa.) 365.

——**In Scotch Law.** That form of law by which the effect of a sentence condemnatory, that has not yet received execution, is stayed or postponed till the cause be again considered. Ersk. Inst. 4. 3. 5. Suspension is competent, also, even where there is no decree, for putting a stop to any illegal act whatsoever. Ersk. Inst. 4. 3. 7.

Letters of suspension bear the form of a summons, which contains a warrant to cite the charter.

——**In Ecclesiastical Law.** An ecclesiastical censure, by which a spiritual person is either interdicted the exercise of his ecclesiastical function, or hindered from receiving the profits of his benefice. It may be partial or total; for a limited time, or forever, when it is called "deprivation" or "amotion." Ayliffe, Par. 501.

SUSPENSION OF A RIGHT. The act by which a party is deprived of the exercise of his right for a time.

When a right is suspended by operation of law, the right is revived the moment the bar is removed; but when the right is suspended by the act of the party, it is gone forever.

SUSPENSION OF ARMS. An agreement between belligerents, made for a short time, or for a particular place, to cease hostilities between them.

SUSPENSION, PLEAS IN. Those alleging matter of temporary incapacity to proceed with the action. Steph. Pl. 45.

SUSPENSIVE CONDITION. One which prevents a contract from going into operation until it has been fulfilled; as, if I promise to pay you one thousand dollars on condition that the ship Thomas Jefferson shall arrive from Havre, the contract is suspended until the arrival of the ship. 1 Bouv. Inst. note 731.

SUSPICION. That state of mind which in a reasonable man would lead to inquiry. 137 Wis. 66, 73.

SUSUM. In old European records. A form of the Lat. *sursum*, up, upwards.

SUUM CUIQUE TRIBUERE (Lat.) To render unto every man that which belongs to him. One of the three precepts to which Justinian said that the law might be reduced. Inst. 1. 1. 3. The others are *alterum non laedere* and *honeste vivere* (*q. v.*)

SUUS HAERES (Lat.) In civil law. The proper heir, as it were, not called in from outside.

Those descendants who were under the power of the deceased at the time of his death, and who are most nearly related to him. Calv. Lex.

SUUS JUDEX (Lat.) In old English law. A proper judge; a judge having cognizance of a cause. Literally, one's own judge. Bracton, fol. 401.

SUZEREIGN (Norman Fr. *suz*, under, and *re* or *rey*, king). A lord who possesses a fief whence other fiefs issue. Dict. de l' Academie Française. A tenant *in capite* or immediately under the king. Note 77 of Butler & Hargrave's notes, Co. Litt. lib. 3.

SWAIN MOTE, SWEIN MOTE, or SWAIN gemote (from Saxon *swang*, an attendant, or boclandman, or freeholder, and *mote*, or *gemote*, a meeting). In forest law. A court holden before the verderors, as judges, by the steward of the swein mote, thrice in every year, the sweins or freeholders within the forest composing the jury. Its principal jurisdiction is, first, to inquire into the oppressions and grievances committed by the officers of the forest, and, secondly, to receive and try presentments certified from the court of attachments against offenses in vert and venison. 3 Bl. Comm. 71, 72; Cowell.

SWEAR. To take an oath administered by some officer duly empowered. See "Affirmation;" "Oath."

To use such profane language as is forbidden by law. This is generally punished by statutory provinces in the several states. See "Profaneness."

SWEARING THE PEACE. Showing to a magistrate that one has just cause to be afraid of another in consequence of his menaces, in order to have him bound over to keep the peace. See "Surety of the Peace."

SWEATING. The questioning of a person in custody charged with crime in an attempt to obtain from him information concerning his connection with crime or knowledge thereof, after he has been arrested and in custody, by plying him with questions or by threats or other wrongful means, extorting from him information to be used against him as testimony upon his trial for such alleged crime. 153 Ky. 412, 155 S. W. 1131, Ann. Cas. 1915C 134.

SWINDLER. A cheat; one guilty of defrauding divers persons. 1 Term R. 748; 2 H. Bl. 531; Starkie, Sland. & L. 135. See 10 How. Pr. (N. Y.) 128.

Swindling is usually applied to a transaction where the guilty party procures the delivery to him, under a pretended contract, of the personal property of another, with the felonious design of appropriating it to his own use. 2 Russ. Crimes, 130; Alis. Crim. Law Sc. 250; 2 Mass. 406.

SWORN BROTHERS. Persons who, by mutual oaths, covenant to share in each other's fortunes. See Sedg. Edw. Conf. c. 35.

SYB AND SOM (Saxon). Peace and security. Words occurring in the laws of Canute. *Eallum Cristenum mannum syb and som gemene*, to all Christian men let there be common peace and security. LL. Ecc. Canuti R. c. 17.

SYLLABUS. A headnote of a reported decision, briefly stating a conclusion on a point of law presented in the case.

SYLVA CAEDUA (Lat.) In ecclesiastical law. Wood of any kind which was kept on purpose to be cut, and which, being cut, grew again from the stump or root. Lyndw. Prov. 190; 4 Reeve, Hist. Eng. Law, 90.

SYMBOLAEOGRAPHY. The art or cunning rightly to form and make written instruments. It is either judicial or extrajudicial; the latter being wholly occupied with such instruments as concern matters not yet judicially in controversy, such as instruments of agreements or contracts, and testaments or last wills. Wharton.

SYMBOLIC DELIVERY. The delivery of some thing as a representation or sign of the delivery of some other.

Where an actual delivery of goods cannot be made, a symbolical delivery of some particular thing, as a halfpenny, will vest the property equally with an actual delivery. Long, Sales, 162; 8 How. (U. S.) 399; 6 Md. 10; 19 N. H. 419; 39 Me. 496; 11 Cush. (Mass.) 282; 3 Cal. 140.

SYMBOLUM ANIMAE. A mortuary, or soul scot.

SYMOND'S INN. Formerly an inn of chancery.

SYNALLAGMATIC CONTRACT. In the civil law. A bilateral or reciprocal contract, in which the parties expressly enter into mutual engagements, each binding himself to the other. Such are the contracts of sale, hiring, etc. Pothier Obl. part 1, c. 1, sect. 1, art. 2. Civil Code of Louis. Art. 1758.

SYNCOPARE. To cut short, or pronounce things so as not to be understood. Cowell.

SYNDIC. In French law. The assignee of a bankrupt.

One who is chosen to conduct the affairs and attend to the concerns of a body corporate or community. In this sense, the word corresponds to director or manager. Rodman, Notes to Code de Com. p. 351; Civ. Code La. art. 429; Dalloz.

SYNDICATE. Persons united for the purpose of an enterprise too large for individuals to undertake.

A group of financiers who buy up the shares of a company in order to sell them at a profit by creating a scarcity. See 108 Pa. St. 162.

SYNDICUS (Greek). One chosen by a college, municipality, etc., to defend its cause. Calv. Lex. See "Syndic."

SYNGRAPH (Greek). A deed, bond, or other instrument of writing, under the hand and seal of all the parties. It was so called because the parties "wrote together."

Formerly such writings were attested by the subscription and crosses of the witnesses; afterwards, to prevent frauds and concealments, they made deeds of mutual covenant in a script and rescript, or in a part and counterpart, and in the middle between the two copies they wrote the word *syngraphus* in large letters, which, being cut through the parchment, and one being delivered to each party, on being afterwards put together, proved their authenticity.

Deeds thus made were denominated *syngraphs* by the canonists, and by the common lawyers, *chirographs*. 2 Bl. Comm. 296.

SYNOD. An ecclesiastical assembly.

SYR (Law Fr.) Sir. A word used by counsel in addressing a court. Keilw. 170b. Year Books, passim.

T

T. An abbreviation of *Termino*, or *Term*, in the old reports.

An abbreviation of *Teste*, in old writs. 1 Inst. Cler. 13.

T. Every person who was convicted of felony, short of murder, and admitted to the benefit of clergy, was at one time marked with this letter upon the brawn of the thumb. The practice is abolished. 7 & 8 Geo. IV. c. 27.

T. R. E. In old records, *tempore Regis Edwardi*, in the time of King Edward. Of common occurrence in Domesday Book, where the valuation of manors as it was in the time of Edward the Confessor is recounted.

TABARD. A short gown; a herald's coat; a sur coat.

TABARDER. One who wears a tabard or short gown. The name is still used as the title of certain bachelors of arts on the old foundation of Queen's College, Oxford. Enc. Lond.

TABELLA (Lat.) In civil law. A small table on which votes were often written. Cicero, in Rull. 2. 2. Three tablets were given to the judges; one with the letter "A" for *absolutio*, one with "C" for *condemnatio*, and one with "N L" for *non liquet*, not proven. Calv. Lex.

TABELLIO (Lat.) In Roman Law. An officer among the Romans, who reduced to writing, and into proper form, agreements, contracts, wills, and other instruments, and witnessed their execution.

The term *tabellio* is derived from the Latin *tabula, seu tabella*, which, in this sense, signified those tablets or plates covered with wax which were then used instead of paper. 8 Toullier, Dr. Civ. note 53; Delauriere, sur Ragneau, Notaire.

Tabelliones differed from notaries in many respects. They had judicial jurisdiction in some cases, and from their judgments there were no appeals. Notaries were then the clerks or aiders of the *tabelliones;* they received the agreements of the parties, which they reduced to short notes; and these contracts were not binding until they were written *in extenso*, which was done by the *tabelliones*. Enc. de M. D'Alembert, "Tabellion;" Jacob, "Tabellion;" Merlin, Repert. "Notaire," § 1; 3 Giannone, Istoria di Napoli, p. 86.

TABERNA (Lat. from *tabula*, a board).

——**In the Civil Law.** A shop, as being inclosed with boards (*quod tabulis clauditur*). Dig. 14. 3. 3; Id. 14. 3. 5. 10. 13; Id. 14. 3. 8; Id. 14. 3. 13. 2; Id. 14. 3. 18.

Any building fit for habitation (*omne utile ad habitandum aedificium*). Dig. 50. 16. 183.

A wine shop. Calv. Lex.

——**In Old English Law.** A drinking house; a tavern. Taverns and wakes (*tabernae vigiliaeque*) are spoken of in Fleta as places of nocturnal resort by servants, to the neglect of their duties. Fleta, lib. 2, c. 72, § 9. And see Id. c. 82, § 3.

TABERNACULUM (Law Lat.) In old records. A public inn or house of entertainment. Consuet. Dom. de Farendon, MS. fol. 48; Cowell.

TABERNARIUS (Lat. from *taberna*, a shop).

——**In the Civil Law.** A shop keeper. Dig. 14. 3. 5. 7.

——**In Old English Law.** A taverner or tavern keeper. Fleta, lib. 2, c. 12, § 17.

TABLE DE MARBRE (Fr.) In old French law. Table of Marble; a principal seat of the admiralty, so called. These Tables de Marbre are frequently mentioned in the Ordonnance of the Marine. Ord. Mar. liv. 1, tit. 1, art. 10; Id. tit. 2, art. 13; Id. tit. 3, art. 3.

TABLE RENTS. Rents paid to bishops and other ecclesiastics, appropriated to their table or housekeeping. Jacob.

TABLES. A synopsis in which many particulars are brought together in a general view, as, genealogical tables, which are composed of the names of persons belonging to a family. 2 Bouv. Inst. notes 1963, 1964.

TABLEAU OF DISTRIBUTION. In Louisiana. A list of creditors of an insolvent estate, stating what each is entitled to. 4 Mart. (La.; N. S.) 535.

TABULA IN NAUFRAGIO (Lat. a plank in a wreck). In English law. A figurative term used to denote the power of a third mortgagee, who, having obtained his mortgage without any knowledge of a second mortgage, may acquire the first incumbrance, and squeeze out and have satisfaction before the second. 2 Ves. Jr. 573; 2 Fonbl. Eq. bk. 3, c. 2, § 2; 2 Vent. 337; 1 Chanc. Cas. 162; 1 Story, Eq. Jur. §§ 414, 415. See "Tacking."

TABULAE. In civil law. Contracts and written instruments of all kinds, especially wills. So called because originally written on tablets and with wax. Calv. Lex.

TABULAE NUPTIALES. In the civil law. A written record of a marriage; or the agreement as to the *dos*.

TABULARIUS. In the civil law. A notary.

TAC. A kind of customary payment by a tenant. Blount, Ten. 155.

TAC FREE. Free from payments, etc.; *e. g., "tac free de omnibus propriis porcis suis infra metas de C," i. e.*, paying nothing for his hogs running within that limit. Jacob.

TACIT (from Lat. *taceo*, to be silent). That which, although not expressed, is understood from the nature of the thing, or from the provision of the law; implied.

TACIT LAW. A law which derives its authority from the common consent of the people without any legislative enactment. 1 Bouv. Inst. 120.

TACIT RELOCATION. In Scotch law. The tacit or implied renewal of a lease when the landlord, instead of warning a tenant, has allowed him to continue without making a new agreement. Bell, Dict. "Relocation."

TACIT TACK. See "Tacit Relocation."

TACITA QUAEDAM HABENTUR PRO expressis. Certain things, though unexpressed, are considered as expressed. 8 Coke, 40.

TACITE (Lat.) Silently; impliedly; tacitly.

TACK. In Scotch law. A contract of location by which the use of land or any other immovable subject is let to the lessee or tacksman for a certain yearly rent, either in money, the fruits of the ground, or services. Ersk. Inst. 2. 6. 8. This word is nearly synonymous with "lease."

TACK DUTY. Rent reserved upon a lease.

TACKING.

——**Of Securities.** The union of securities given at different times, so as to prevent any intermediate purchaser's claiming title to redeem or otherwise discharge one lien, which is prior, without redeeming or discharging other liens, also which are subsequent, to his own title. Jeremy, Eq. Jur. bk. 1, c. 2, § 1, pp. 188-191; 1 Story, Eq. Jur. § 412.

The doctrine is not recognized in the United States. 37 Vt. 345.

——**Of Possession.** The connecting of successive possessions by persons in privity, so as to make a continuous adverse possession. 80 Hun (N. Y.) 287.

TACKSMAN. In Scotch law. A tenant.

TACTIS SACROSANCTIS (Law Lat.) In old English law. Touching the holy (evangelists). Fleta, lib. 3, c. 16, § 21. "A bishop may swear *visis evangeliis* (looking at the Gospels), and not *tactis*, and it is good enough." Vaughan, C. J., Freem. 133.

TACTIS SACROSANCTIS SCRIPTURIS (Lat.) In old European law. Touching the holy Scriptures. Feud. lib. 2, tit. 2, pr. *Sacrosanctis evangeliis tactis.* Code, 3. 1. 14. 1.

TACTO PER SE SANCTO EVANGELIO (Law Lat.) Having personally touched the holy Gospel. Cro. Eliz. 105. The description of a corporal oath.

TAIL. See "Estates."

TAIL AFTER POSSIBILITY OF ISSUE extinct. The estate of a surviving tenant in special tail after the death, without surviving issue, of the person from whose body the issue to inherit was to spring. 2 Bl. Comm. 124.

TAIL FEMALE. An estate tail limited to the female heirs of the donee.

TAIL GENERAL. An estate tail granted to one and the heirs of his body in general. 2 Bl. Comm. 113.

TAIL MALE. An estate tail limited to the male heirs of the donee.

TAIL SPECIAL. An estate tail granted to one and certain only of the heirs of his body, as those to be begotten on his then wife. 2 Bl. Comm. 113.

TAILLE (French).

——**In Old French Law.** A tax or assessment levied by the king, or by any great lord, upon his subjects. Brande.

——**In Old English Law.** The fee which is opposed to fee simple, because it is so minced or pared that it is not in the owner's free power to dispose of it, but it is, by the first giver, cut or divided from all other, and tied to the issue of the donee,—in short, an estate tail.

TAILZIE. In the Scotch law, an arbitrary line of succession laid down by a proprietor, in substitution of a legal line of succession. A deed of tailzie creates a Scotch entail by which, until 11 & 12 Vict. c. 36, 16 & 17 Vict. c. 94, and 31 & 32 Vict. c. 84, an estate might be tied up forever. See, also, 38 & 39 Vict. c. 61.

TAINT. Attainder (*q. v.*)

TAKE. A technical expression which signifies to receive; as, a devisee will take under the will. The devisee takes only when the possession of the testator has ceased. 41 N. J. Law, 70.

To seize; as, to take and carry away, either lawfully or unlawfully.

To choose; *e. g., ad capiendas assisas*, to choose a jury.

To obtain; *e. g.*, to take a verdict in court, to get a verdict.

TAKER. One to whom an estate comes. The "first taker" is he who holds the immediate estate, with expectant estates following, or the first of a line of grantees.

TAKING. An element of "larceny" (*q. v.*)

TALE. In English law. The ancient name of the declaration or count. 3 Bl. Comm. 293.

TALES (Lat. *talis*, such, like). In practice. A number of jurors added to a deficient panel sufficient to supply the deficiency.

A list of such jurymen as were of the tales, kept in the king's bench office in England.

TALES DE CIRCUMSTANTIBUS (Lat. a like number of the bystanders). A sufficient number of jurors selected from the bystanders to supply a deficiency in the panel.

The order of the judge for taking such bystanders as jurors.

Whenever, from any cause, the panel of jurors is insufficient, the judge may issue the above order, and the officer immediately executes it. See 2 Hill (S. C.) 381; 2 Pa. St. 412; Coxe (N. J.) 283; 1 Blackf. (Ind.) 63; 2 Har. & J. (Md.) 426; 1 Pick. (Mass.) 43, note. The number to be drawn on successive panels is in the discretion of the court. 17 Ga. 497.

TALESMAN. A person summoned to act as a juror from among the bystanders in the court.

TALIO (Lat. from *talis*, such, like). In the civil law. Like for like; punishment in the same kind; the punishment of an injury by an act of the same kind, as an eye for an eye, a limb for a limb, etc. Called *similitudo supplicii*, likeness of punishment; *reciproca poena*, reciprocal punishment. Calv. Lex.; Adams, Rom. Ant. 291.

TALIS INTERPRETATIO SEMPER FIenda est, ut evitetur absurdum, et inconveniens, et ne judicium sit illusorium. Interpretation is always to be made in such a manner that what is absurd and inconvenient is to be avoided, and so that the judgment be not nugatory. 1 Coke, 52.

TALIS NON EST EADEM, NAM NULlum simile est idem. What is like is not the same, for nothing similar is the same. 4 Coke, 18.

TALIS RES, VEL TALE RECTUM, QUAE vel quod non est in homine adtunc superstite sed tantummodo est et consistit in consideratione et intelligentia legis, et quod alii dixerunt talem rem vel tale rectum fore in nubibus. Such a thing or such a right as is not vested in a person then living, but merely exists in the consideration and contemplation of law, is said to be in abeyance, and others have said that such a thing or such a right is in the clouds. Co. Litt. 342.

TALITER PROCESSUM EST. Upon pleading the judgment of an inferior court, the proceedings themselves, and this general judgment, and on which the same was founded, must, to some extent, appear in the pleading, but the rule is that they may be alleged with a general allegation that "such proceedings were had," instead of a detailed account of the proceedings themselves, and this general allegation is called the "*taliter processum est.*" A like concise mode of stating former proceedings in a suit is adopted at the present day in chancery proceedings upon petitions, and in actions in the nature of bills of revivor and supplement. Brown.

TALLAGE (Fr. *tailler*, to cut). In English law. A term used to denote subsidies, taxes, customs, and, indeed, any imposition whatever by the government for the purpose of raising a revenue. Bac. Abr. "Smuggling, etc." (B); Fortescue de Laud. 26; Madd. c. 17; 2 Inst. 531, 532; Spelman.

TALLAGERS. Tax or toll gatherers; mentioned by Chaucer.

TALLAGIUM (perhaps from French *taille*, cut off). A term including all taxes. 2 Inst. 532; Stat. de tal. non Concedendo, temp. Edw. I.; Stow, Annals, 445; 1 Bl. Comm. 311*. Chaucer has *talaigiers* for "tax gatherers."

TALLAGIUM FACERE. To give up accounts in the exchequer, where the method of accounting was by tallies.

TALLATIO. A keeping account by tallies. Cowell.

TALLIA. Commons in meat or drink; tax or tribute.

TALLY (Fr. *tailler;* Ital. *tagliare, i. e., scindere*, to cut off). A stick cut into two parts, on each whereof is marked, with notches or otherwise, what is due between debtor and creditor. Hence the *tallier* of the exchequer is now called the "teller." Lex. Const. 205; Cowell. One party must have one part, and the other the other, and they must match. *Tallies* in the exchequer are abolished by 2 Geo. III. c. 82. There was the same usage in France. Dict. de l'Acad. Franc.; Poth. Obl. pt. 4, c. 1, art. 2, § 8.

TALLY TRADE. A system of dealing, by which dealers furnish certain articles on credit, upon an agreement for the payment of the stipulated price by certain weekly or monthly installments. McCulloch, Dict. A tally was a common security for money in the day of Edw. I. 2 Reeve, Hist. Eng. Law, c. xi. p. 253.

TALTARUM'S CASE. A case reported in Y. B. 12 Edw. IV. 19-21, which is said to have established the foundation of common recoveries, and their efficacy to bar an entail.

TALZIE. See "Tailzie."

TAM QUAM. A phrase used where a proceeding is applied or referred to two things or persons.

A writ of error from inferior courts, when the error is supposed to be as well in giving the judgment as in awarding execution upon it. *Tam in redditione judicii, quam in adjudicatione executionis.*

A *venire tam quam* was one by which a jury was summoned, as well to try an issue as to inquire of the damages on a default. 2 Tidd, Prac. 722, 895.

TAMEN (Lat.) Notwithstanding; nevertheless; yet.

TANGIBLE PROPERTY. That which may be felt or touched. It must necessarily be corporeal, but it may be real or personal.

TANISTRY (*a thanis*). In Irish law. A species of tenure founded on immemorial usage, by which lands, etc., descended *seniori et dignissimo viri sanguinis et cognominis, i. e.*, to the oldest and worthiest man of the blood and name. Jacob.

TANTEO (Spanish). In Spanish law. Preemption. White, New Recop. bk. 2, tit. 2, c. 3.

TANTUM BONA VALENT, QUANTUM vendi possunt. Things are worth what they will sell for. 3 Inst. 305.

TARDE VENIT (Lat.) In practice. The name of a return made by the sheriff to a writ, when it came into his hands too late to be executed before the return day.

The sheriff is required to show that he has yielded obedience to the writ, or give a good excuse for his omission; and he may say, *quod breve adeo tarde venit quod exequi non possunt.* It is usual to return the writ with an indorsement of *tarde venit.* Comyn, Dig. "Retorn" (D 1).

TARE. An allowance in the purchase and sale of merchandise for the weight of the box, bag, or cask, or other thing, in which the goods are packed. It is also an allowance made for any defect, waste, or diminution in the weight, quality, or quantity of goods. It differs from "tret" (*q. v.*)

TARIFF. Customs, duties, toll, or tribute payable upon merchandise to the general government are called "tariff." The rate of customs, etc., also bears this name, and the list of articles liable to duties is also called the "tariff."

TASSARE (Law Lat.) In old English law. To stack; to heap up.

TASSUM (*Tassa.* L. Lat.) In old English law. A heap; a hay-mow, or hay-stack.

TAURI LIBERI LIBERTAS. A common bull, because he was free to all the tenants within such a manor, liberty, etc.

TAVERN. A place of entertainment; a house kept up for the accommodation of strangers. Webster. Originally, a house for the retailing of liquors to be drunk on the spot. Webster.

In almost all the states, the word has come to mean the same as "inn," with no particular reference to the sale of liquors. See 2 Kent, Comm. (9th Ed.) 597*, note (a); 5 N. H. 258.

Tavern, hotel, inn and public house are in this country used synonymously; and while they entertain the traveling public, and keep guests, and receive compensation therefor, they do not lose their character, though they may not have the privilege of selling liquors. The distinction, as respects inn and tavern keepers, observed in England under the common law, does not exist with us, and different names are applied to them, though "hotel" and "house" are usually and commonly used to denote a higher order of public houses than the ordinary tavern or inn. The word "tavern" includes all hotels and houses that entertain and accommodate the public for compensation. 46 Mo. 593, Ann. Cas. 1914B 874, note.

TAVERN KEEPER. An innkeeper (*q. v.*)

TAVERNER. (Law Fr. and Eng.; Fr. *tavernier*, from *taverne*). In old English law. A seller of wine; one who kept a house or shop for the sale of wine. *Et puis soit enquis de taverners que ount vendu vyns encontre la droit assise*, and afterwards it shall be inquired of taverners who have sold wines against the right assize. Britt. c. 30. A retailer of wines. Hardr. 338. "Taverner" is used as the addition of a person in a writ in the Register. Reg. Orig. 195. But "tavern keeper" has now, for the most part, taken its place.

TAX. A contribution imposed by government on individuals for the service of the state. 13 Pa. St. 104; 115 Ill. 109. It is distinguished from a subsidy, as being certain and orderly. Jacob.

A sum of money assessed under the authority of the state on the personal property of an individual for the use of the state. 60 Me. 124.

It is distinguished from a local assessment, as being imposed without reference to peculiar benefits to particular individuals or property. 84 N. Y. 108; 22 Minn. 494. See "Special Assessment."

"Excise" and "impost" are sometimes used as synonymous with "tax," but in strictness apply only to taxes upon production or consumption, and upon imports, respectively.

Taxes are either:

(1) Direct or indirect, direct being those assessed on the property, person, business, etc., of those who are to pay them, and indirect being a tax levied on commodities before they reach the consumer. Cooley, Tax'n, 6.

(2) *Ad valorem* or specific, *ad valorem* being those imposed in proportion to value,

and specific those consisting of a fixed sum imposed upon an article or thing by name.

(3) General or local, general being those imposed on property throughout the state, and local being those imposed on the locality specially benefitted.

Taxes are also classified according to the nature of the property on which they are imposed, as income taxes, inheritance taxes, personal property taxes, etc.

TAX DEED. An instrument whereby the officer of the law undertakes to convey the title of the rightful proprietor to the purchaser at the tax sale, or sale of the land for nonpayment of taxes.

TAX FERRETS. Persons who engage in the business of searching for property omitted from taxation. 218 Ill. 477.

TAX LEVY. The amount of tax to be raised, or the official act by which the amount is determined upon.

TAX LIEN. A statutory lien on lands to secure the payment of taxes, which exists in favor of the public.

TAX LISTS. The assessment roll; the list of persons or property against whom or which taxes are levied.

TAX SALE. A sale of lands for the nonpayment of taxes assessed thereon. A sale made in a proceeding in rem. 108 Ill. 334.

TAX TITLE. A title to land derived through the sale of it for delinquent taxes, or through the foreclosure of a tax lien.

TAXATI. Soldiers of a garrison or fleet, assigned to a certain station. Spelman.

TAXATIO (Lat.) In the civil law. The modification by a judge of the amount of damages claimed or sworn to by the plaintiff.

TAXATIO ECCLESIASTICA. The valuation of ecclesiastical benefits made through every diocese in England, on occasion of Pope Innocent IV. granting to King Henry III. the tenth of all spirituals for three years. This taxation was first made by Walter, bishop of Norwich, delegated by the pope to this office in 38 Hen. III., and hence called "*Taxatio Norwicencis.*" It is also called "Pope Innocent's Valor." Wharton.

TAXATIO EXPENSARUM (Law Lat.) In old English practice. Taxation of costs.

TAXATIO NORWICENCIS. See "Taxatio Ecclesiastica."

TAXATION. The process of taxing or imposing a tax. Webster.

——**In Practice.** Adjustment. Fixing the amount; *e. g.*, taxation of costs. 3 Chit. Gen. Prac. 602.

TAXATION OF COSTS. In practice. Fixing the amount of costs to which a party is entitled.

It is a rule that the jury must assess the damages and costs separately, so that it may appear to the court that the costs were not considered in the damages; and when the jury give costs in an amount insufficient to answer the costs of the suit, the plaintiff may pray that the officer may tax the costs, and such taxation is inserted in the judgment. This is said to be done *ex assensu* of the plaintiff, because at his prayer. Bac. Abr. "Costs" (K). The costs are taxed in the first instance by the prothonotary or clerk of the court. See 2 Wend. (N. Y.) 244; 1 Cow. (N. Y.) 591; 7 Cow. (N. Y.) 412; 2 Yerg. (Tenn.) 245, 310; 6 Yerg. (Tenn.) 412; Harper (S. C.) 326; 1 Pick. (Mass.) 211; 10 Mass. 26; 16 Mass. 370. A bill of costs, having been once submitted to such an officer for taxation, cannot be withdrawn from him and referred to another. 2 Wend. (N. Y.) 252.

TAXERS. Two officers yearly chosen in Cambridge, England, to see the true gauge of all the weights and measures.

TAXING MASTERS. Officers of the English supreme court, who examine and allow or disallow items in bills of costs. See 1 Chit. Archb. Prac. (12th Ed.) 507; Smith, Ch. Prac. 12, 62, 829; 2 Daniell, Ch. Prac. (5th Ed.) 1308.

TAXING OFFICER. Each house of parliament has a taxing officer, whose duty it is to tax the costs incurred by the promoters or opponents of private bills. May, Parl. Prac. 843.

TAXT WARD. An annual payment made to a superior in Scotland, instead of the duties due to him under the tenure of wardholding. Abolished.

TEAM, or THEAME. A royalty or privilege granted, by royal charter, to a lord of a manor, for the having, restraining, and judging of bondmen and villeins, with their children, goods, chattels, etc. Glanv. 1, 5, c. ii.

TEAMSTER. One who drives horses in a wagon for the purpose of carrying goods for hire. He is liable as a common carrier. Story, Bailm. § 496. See "Carrier."

TECHNICAL. That which properly belongs to an art.

In the construction of contracts it is a general rule that technical words are to be taken according to their approved and known use in the trade in which the contract is entered into, or to which it relates, unless they have manifestly been understood in another sense by the parties. 2 Bos. & P. 164; 6 Term R. 320; 3 Starkie, Ev. 1036.

TEIND COURT. In Scotch law. A court which has jurisdiction of matters relating to the augmentation of stipends, and the valuation and sale of tithes.

It is held before justices of the court of sessions organized as a separate court, with distinct clerks and ministerial officers. Bell, Dict.

TEINDS. In Scotch law. That liquidated proportion of the rents or goods of the people which is due to churchmen for performing divine service, or exercising the other spiritual functions proper to their several offices. Ersk. Inst. 2. 10. 2.

TEINLAND. Thainland (*q. v.*)

TELEGRAPHIAE. Written evidence of things past. Blount.

TELLER (*tallier*, one who keeps a tally). An officer in a bank or other institution; a person appointed to receive votes; a name given to certain officers in the English exchequer.

TELLERS IN PARLIAMENT. In the language of parliament, the "tellers" are the members of the house selected to count the members when a division takes place. In the house of lords, a division is effected by the "noncontents" remaining within the bar, and the "contents" going below it, a teller being appointed for each party. In the commons, the "ayes" go into the lobby at one end of the house, and the "noes" into the lobby at the other end, the house itself being perfectly empty, and two tellers being appointed for each party. May, Parl. Prac.

TELLIGRAPHUM. An Anglo-Saxon charter of land. 1 Reeve, Hist. Eng. Law, c. 1, p. 10.

TELLWORC. That labor which a tenant was bound to do for his lord for a certain number of days.

TEMENTALE, or **TENEMENTALE.** A tax of two shillings upon every ploughland; a decennary (*q. v.*)

TEMERE (Lat.) In the civil law. Rashly; inconsiderately; without sufficient cause. A plaintiff was said *temere litigare*, who demanded a thing out of malice, or sued without just cause, and who could show no ground or cause of action. Brissonius.

TEMPLARS. A religious order of knighthood, instituted about the year 1119, and so called because the members dwelt in a part of the temple of Jerusalem, and not far from the sepulchre of our Lord. They entertained Christian strangers and pilgrims charitably, and their profession was at first to defend travellers from highwaymen and robbers. The order was suppressed A. D. 1307, and their substance given partly to the knights of St. John of Jerusalem, and partly to other religious orders. Brown.

TEMPLE. Two English inns of court, thus called because anciently the dwelling place of the Knights Templar. On the suppression of the order, they were purchased by some professors of the common law, and converted into *hospitia*, or inns of court. They are called the "Inner" and "Middle Temple," in relation to Essex House, which was also a part of the house of the Templars, and called the "Outer Temple," because situated without Temple Bar. Enc. Lond.

TEMPORAL AFFAIRS. The temporal affairs of a church are understood to be the revenues, lands and tenements, in other words, secular possessions, with which it is endowed. The hiring of a sexton to perform the duties incident to his office has nothing to do with the management of the temporalities of the church. 76 Ill. 253.

TEMPORAL LORDS. The peers of England; the bishops are not in strictness held to be peers, but merely lords of parliament. 2 Steph. Comm. 330, 345.

TEMPORALIS ACTIO (Lat.) An action which could only be brought within a certain period.

TEMPORALIS EXCEPTIO (Lat.) A temporary exception which barred an action for a time only.

TEMPORALITIES (Law Lat. *temporalia*). Revenues, lands, tenements, and lay fees which bishops have from livery of the king, and in virtue of which they sit in parliament. 1 Rolle, Abr. 881.

TEMPORARY. Which is to last for a limited time.

A temporary statute, or one which is limited in its operation for a particular period of time after its enactment; the opposite of perpetual. 70 Ill. 399. See Statute.

TEMPORIS EXCEPTIO (Lat.) In civil law. A plea of lapse of time in bar of an action, like our statute of limitations. Dig. "De Diversis Temporalibus Actionibus."

TEMPUS (Lat.) In civil and old English law. Time in general. A time limited; a season; *e. g.*, *tempus pessonis*, mast time in the forest.

TEMPUS CONTINUUM (Lat.) In civil law. A period of time which runs continually having once begun, feast days being counted as well as ordinary days, and it making no difference whether the person against whom it runs is present or absent. Calv. Lex.

TEMPUS ENIM MODUS TOLLENDI OBligationes et actiones, quia tempus currit contra desides et sui juris contemptores. For a time is a means of destroying obligations and actions, because time runs against the slothful and contemners of their own rights. Fleta, lib. 4, c. 5, § 12.

TEMPUS SEMESTRE. Half a year, and not six lunar months. Westminster II. c. 5.

TEMPUS UTILE (Lat.) In civil law. A period of time which runs beneficially; *i. e.*, feast days are not included, nor does it run against one absent in a foreign country, or on business of the republic, or detained by stress of weather. But one detained by sickness is not protected from its running; for it runs where there is powers to act by an agent, as well as where there is power to act personally; and the sick man might have deputed his agent. Calv. Lex.

TENANCY. The state or condition of a tenant; the estate held by a tenant.

TENANT (Lat. *eneo*, *tenere*, to hold). One who holds or possesses lands or tenements by any kind of title, either in fee, for life, for years, or at will. In a popular sense, he is one who has the temporary use and occupation of lands or tenements which belong to another, the duration and other terms of whose occupation are usually defined by an agreement called a "lease," while the parties thereto are placed in the relation of landlord and tenant. 5 Man. & G. 54; Bouv. Inst. Index.

——**Tenants in Common.** Such as hold lands and tenements by several and distinct titles, and not by a joint title, but occupy in common, the only unity recognized between them being that of possession. They are accountable to each other for the profits of the estate; and if one of them turns another out of possession, an action of ejectment will lie against him. They may also have reciprocal actions of waste against each other. 2 Bl. Comm. 191. See "Estate in Common;" 7 Cruise, Dig.; Bac. Abr. "Joint Tenants, and Tenants in Common;" Comyn, Dig. "Abatement" (E 10, F 6), "Chancery" (3 V 4), "Devise" (N 8), "Estates" (K 8, R 2); 1 Vern. 353; Archb. Civ. Pl. 53, 73.

——**Tenant by the Curtesy.** A species of life tenant who, on the death of his wife seised of an estate of inheritance, after having issue by her which is capable of inheriting her estate, holds her lands for the period of his own life. After the birth of such a child, the tenant is called "tenant by the curtesy initiate" (Co. Litt. 29a; 2 Bl. Comm. 126); but to consummate the tenancy four things are requisite: lawful marriage, actual seizin of the wife, issue capable of inheriting, and death of the wife. The first three without the last constitute tenancy by the curtesy initiate. The husband's estate is initiate on issue had, and consummate on the death of the wife. 142 Ill. 393; 4 Kent's Com. pp. 28-30; 44 Ill. 58; 128 Ill. 102. See "Curtesy."

——**Tenant in Dower.** Another species of life tenant, occurring where the husband of a woman is seised of an estate of inheritance, and dies, and the wife thereby becomes entitled to hold the third part of all the lands and tenements of which he was seised at any time during the coverture to her own use, for the term of her natural life. See "Dower;" 2 Bl. Comm. 129; Comyn, Dig. "Dower" (A).

——**Tenant of the Demesne.** One who is tenant of a mesne lord; as, where A. is tenant of B. and C. of A.; B. is the lord, A. the mesne lord, and C. the tenant of the demesne. Hammond, N. P. 392, 393.

——**Tenant in Fee.** Under the feudal law, one who held his lands either immediately or derivatively from the sovereign, in consideration of the military or other services he was bound to perform. If he held directly from the king, he was called a "tenant in fee," *in capite*. With us, the highest estate which a man can have in land has direct reference to his duty to the state, 108 Ill. App. 10. From it he ultimately holds his title, to it he owes fealty and service, and if he fails in his allegiance to it, or dies without heirs upon whom this duty may devolve, his lands revert to the state under which he held. Subject to this qualification, however, a tenant in fee has an absolute unconditional ownership in land, which, upon his death, vests in his heirs, 122 Ill. 328; and hence he enjoys what is called an "estate of inheritance." See "Estates"; 2 Bl. Comm. 81; Litt. § 1; Plowd. 555.

——**Joint Tenants.** Two or more persons to whom lands or tenements have been granted to hold in fee simple, for life, for years, or at will. In order to constitute an estate in joint tenancy, the tenants thereof must have one and the same interest, arising by the same conveyance, commencing at the same time, and held by one and the same undivided possession. 2 Bl. Comm. 180. The principal incident to this estate is the right of survivorship, by which, upon the death of one joint tenant, the entire tenancy remains to the surviving cotenant, and not to the heirs or other representatives of the deceased, the last survivor taking the whole estate. It is an estate which can only be created by the acts of the parties, and never by operation of law. Co. Litt. 184b; 2 Cruise, Dig. 43; 4 Kent. Comm. 358; 2 Bl. Comm. 179; 7 Cruise, Dig. "Joint Tenancy;" Prest. Est.

——**Tenant for Life.** One who has a freehold interest in lands, the duration of which is confined to the life or lives of some particular person or persons, or to the happening or not happening of some uncertain event. 1 Cruise, Dig. 76. When he holds the estate by the life of another, he is usually called tenant *pur autre vie*. 2 Bl. Comm. 120; Comyn, Dig. "Estates" (F 1). See "Estate for Life;" "Emblements."

——**Tenant by the Manner.** One who has a less estate than a fee in land, which remains in the reversioner. He is so called because in avowries and other pleadings it is specially shown in what manner he is tenant of the land, in contradistinction to the veray tenant, who is called simply "tenant." See "Veray."

——**Tenant by the Marital Right.** At common law, by virtue of the marriage alone, and without the birth of issue, the husband was seized of an estate, during coverture, in the lands held by his wife in fee. He is said to have been seized of the freehold jure uxoris. He took the rents and profits during the joint lives of himself and his wife. This estate was ended by the death of the wife or the death of the husband. It is a freehold estate in the husband, since it must continue during their joint lives, and it may by possibility last during his life. It was liable to be sold on execution against the husband. 142 Ill. 393; 2 Kent, Comm. 130.

——**Tenant paravail.** The tenant of a tenant. He is so called because he has the avails or profits of the land.

——**Tenant in Severalty.** He who holds lands and tenements in his own right only, without any other person being joined or connected with him in point of interest during his estate therein. 2 Bl. Comm. 179.

——**Tenant at Sufferance.** He who comes into possession by a lawful demise, but after his term is ended continues the possession wrongfully by holding over. He has only a naked possession, stands in no privity to the landlord, and may, consequently, be removed without notice to quit. Co. Litt. 57b; 2 Leon. 46; 3 Leon. 153; 1 Johns. Cas. (N. Y.) 123; 4 Johns. (N. Y.) 150, 312; 5 Johns. (N. Y.) 128.

——**Tenant in Tail.** One who holds an estate in fee, which by the instrument creating it is limited to some particular heirs, exclusive of others; as, to the heirs of "his body," or to the heirs, "male or female," of his body. The whole system of entailment, rendering estates unalienable, is so directly opposed to the spirit of our republican institutions as to have become very nearly extinct in the United States. Most of the states, at an early period of our independence, passed laws declaring such estates to be estates in fee simple, or provided that the tenant and the remainderman might join in conveying the land in fee simple. In New Hampshire, Chancellor Kent says, entails may still be created; while in some of the states they have not been expressly abolished by statute, but in practice they are now almost unknown. See "Entail;" 2 Bl. Comm. 113.

——**Tenant at Will.** One who holds rent free by permission of the owner, or where he enters under an agreement to purchase, or for a lease, but has not paid rent; or one who is placed on land without a term prescribed, or without any terms or rent reserved, but as a mere occupier. 184 Ill. 337. Formerly all leases for uncertain periods were considered to be tenancies at will merely; but in modern times they are construed into tenancies from year to year; and, in fact, the general language of the books now is that the former species of tenancy cannot exist without an express agreement to that effect. 8 Cow. (N. Y.) 75; 4 Ired. (N. C.) 291; 3 Dana (Ky.) 66; 12 Mass. 325; 23 Wend. (N. Y.) 616; 12 N. Y. 346. The great criterion by which to distinguish between tenancies from year to year and at will is the payment or reservation of rent. 5 Bing. 361; 2 Esp. 718.

A tenancy at will must always be at the will of either party, and such a tenant may be ejected at any time, and without notice; but as soon as he once pays rent, he becomes tenant from year to year. 1 Watts & S. (Pa.) 90; Tayl. Landl. & Ten. § 56; Co. Litt. 55; 2 Lilly, Reg. 555; 2 Bl. Comm. 145. See Comyn. Dig. "Estates" (H 1); 12 Mass. 325; 17 Mass. 282; 1 Johns. Cas. (N. Y.) 33; 2 Caines Cas. (N. Y.) 314; 2 Caines (N. Y.) 169; 9 Johns. (N. Y.) 13, 235, 331.

A tenant holding over is not a tenant at will unless he holds over by the express or implied consent of his landlord. 40 Mich. 283.

——**Tenant for Years.** He to whom another has let lands, tenements, or hereditaments for a certain number of years, agreed upon between them, and the tenant enters thereon. Before entry, he has only an inchoate right, which is called an *interesse termini;* and it is of the essence of this estate that its commencement as well as its termination be fixed and determined, so that the lapse of time limited for its duration will, *ipso facto,* determine the tenancy; if otherwise, the occupant will be tenant from year to year, or at will, according to circumstances. See "Lease;" Tayl. Landl. & Ten. § 54; 2 Bl. Comm. 140.

——**Tenant from Year to Year.** Where lands or tenements have been let without any particular limitation for the duration of the tenancy; hence any general occupation with permission, whether a tenant is holding over after the expiration of a lease for years, or otherwise, becomes a tenancy from year to year. 3 Burrows, 1609; 1 Term R. 163; 3 East, 451; 3 Barn. & C. 478; 9 Johns. (N. Y.) 330; 3 Zab. (N. J.) 311. The principal feature of this tenancy is that it is not determinable even at the end of the current year, unless a reasonable notice to quit is served by the party intending to dissolve the tenancy upon the other. 4 Cow. (N. Y.) 349; 3 Hill (N. Y.) 547; 11 Wend. (N. Y.) 616; 8 Term R. 3; 5 Bing. 185.

TENANT A VOLUNTE (Law Fr.) Tenant at will. Litt. § 68. See "Tenant."

TENANT BY COPY OF COURT ROLL (shortly, "tenant by copy"). The old fashioned name for a copyholder. Litt. § 73.

TENANT RIGHT. In leases from the crown, corporations, or the church, it is usual to grant a further term to the old tenants in preference to strangers; and, as this expectation is seldom disappointed, such tenants are considered as having an ulterior interest beyond their subsisting term; and this interest is called the "tenant right."

Bac. Abr. "Leases and Terms for Years" (U).

TENANT TO THE PRAECIPE. Before the English fines and recoveries act, if land was conveyed to a person for life, with remainder to another in tail, the tenant in tail in remainder was unable to bar the entail without the concurrence of the tenant for life, because a common recovery could only be suffered by the person seised of the land. In such a case, if the tenant for life wished to concur in barring the entail, he usually conveyed his life estate to some other person in order that the *praecipe* in the recovery might be issued against the latter, who was therefore called the "tenant to the *praecipe*." Williams, Seisin, 169.

TENANTS BY THE VERGE. These "are in the same nature as tenants by copy of court roll [*i. e.*, copyholders]. But the reason why they be called 'tenants by the verge' is, for that when they will surrender their tenements into the hands of their lord to the use of another, they shall have a little rod (by the custome) in their hand, the which they shall deliver to the steward or to the bailife, * * * and the steward or bailife, according to the custome, shall deliver to him that taketh the land the same rod, or another rod, in the name of seisin; and for this cause they are called 'tenants by the verge;' but they have no other evidence [title deed] but by copy of court roll." Litt. § 78; Co. Litt. 61a.

TENAUNT (Law Fr. from *tener*, to hold). In old English law. Tenant; a tenant.

TENDE. To tender or offer. Old Nat. Brev. 123.

TENDER (Lat. *tendere*, to extend, to offer). An offer to deliver something, made in pursuance of some contract or obligation, under such circumstances as to require no further act from the party making it to complete the transfer.

As applied to cases of mutual and concurrent promises, means readiness to perform, provided the other party is ready and willing to perform. 143 Ill. 502.

To constitute a valid tender, there must be an actual production (46 Barb. [N. Y.] 227), at the time (90 N. Y. 442) and place (6 Barb. [N. Y.] 258) where the obligation was due, of the full amount (41 Vt. 66), in current funds (34 N. Y. 649) by the person who is under obligation, or his agent (11 Ga. 570), and an offer to the creditor or his agent (46 Barb. [N. Y.] 227) absolutely and without condition, to which the creditor may rightfully object (39 N. Y. 481), of the exact amount due, but tender of an excessive amount is good if no change is asked in return (25 Ind. 261), and the tender must be kept good by continued readiness to pay or deliver the amount or property tendered (24 Vt. 536; 86 Ill. 431).

TENDER OF AMENDS. An offer by a person who has been guilty of any wrong or breach of contract to pay a sum of money by way of amends. If a defendant in an action make tender of amends, and the plaintiff decline to accept it, the defendant may pay the money into court, and plead the payment into court as a satisfaction of the plaintiff's claim. Mozley & W.

TENDER OF ISSUE. The conclusion of a pleading whereby the pleader offers to refer the averments thereof to a trial. The common tender of an issue of fact is, "and of this he puts himself upon the country." Steph. Pl. 54, 230.

TENEMENT (from Lat. *teneo*, to hold). Everything of a permanent nature which may be holden.

Its original meaning, according to some, was house or homestead. Jacob. In modern use, it also signifies rooms let in houses. 10 Wheat. (U. S.) 204.

In its most extensive signification, "tenement" comprehends everything which may be holden, provided it be of a permanent nature; and not only lands and inheritances which are holden, but also rents and profits *a prendre* of which a man has any frank tenement, and of which he may be seised *ut de libero tenemento*, are included under this term. Co. Litt. 6a; 2 Bl. Comm. 17; 1 Washb. Real Prop. 10; 17 Pick. (Mass.) 105. But the word "tenement" simply, without other circumstances, has never been construed to pass a fee. 10 Wheat. (U. S.) 204. See 4 Bing. 293; 1 Term R. 358; 3 Term R. 772; 3 East, 113 5 East, 239; 1 Barn. & Adol. 161; Comyn, Dig. "Grant" (E 2), "Trespass" (A 2); 1 Washb. Real Prop. 10.

Bracton says that tenements acquired by a villein were as to the lord in the same condition as chattels, because bought with the chattels which rightfully belong to the lord. Bracton, 26.

TENEMENTAL LAND. Land distributed by a lord among his tenants, as opposed to the demesnes which were occupied by himself and his servants. 2 Bl. Comm. 90.

TENEMENTIS LEGATIS. An ancient writ, lying to the city of London, or any other corporation (where the old custom was that men might devise by will lands and tenements, as well as goods and chattels), for the hearing and determining any controversy touching the same. Reg. Orig. 244.

TENEMENTUM (Law Lat. from *tenere*, to hold). In old English law. A tenement; a thing held by service; a fee, fief, or feudal estate; an estate which a tenant holds of a lord. Spelman. *Devenio homo vester, de tenemento quod de vobis teneo*, I become your man, of the tenement which I hold of you. Bracton, fol. 80. *Liberum tenementum*, a free tenement, or freehold, as distinguished from *villenagium*.

TENENDAS (Lat.) In Scotch law. The name of a clause in charters of heritable rights, which derives its name from its first words, *tenendas praedictas terras*, and expresses the particular tenure by which the lands are to be holden. Ersk. Inst. bk. 2, tit. 3, note 0.

TENENDUM (Lat.) That part of a deed which was formerly used in expressing the tenure by which the estate granted was holden; but since all freehold tenures were converted into socage, the *tenendum* is of no further use, even in England, and is therefore joined to the *habendum* in this manner,—to have and to hold. The words "to hold" have now no meaning in our deeds. 2 Bl. Comm. 298. See "Habendum."

TENENS. A tenant; the defendant in a real action.

TENENTIBUS IN ASSISA NON ONERandis. A writ that formerly lay for him to whom a disseisor had alienated the land whereof he disseised another, that he should not be molested in assize for damages, if the disseisor had wherewith to satisfy them. Reg. Orig. 214.

TENEO (Lat. I hold). Said by Lord Coke to have the following significations:

To have, as an estate. Co. Litt. 1b.

To hold of some superior. Id.

To keep, as a covenant. Id.

To bind, as an obligation. Id.

To judge or deem. Id.

See these senses applied to the word "tenant." Id. See "Tenere."

TENER (Law Fr.) In old English law. To hold. *A aver et tener a luy et a ses heires*, to have and to hold to him and his heirs. Litt. § 625.

To keep. *Tener hors de droit heire*, to keep out the right heir. Britt. c. 65.

TENERE (Lat.)

——**In the Civil Law.** To hold. A term expressive of mere fact, without reference to right; or expressive of what was termed corporeal and natural possession. *Habere* (to have) and *possidere* (to possess), on the other hand, were terms expressive of right, or what was termed "civil" possession. Calv. Lex. See "Habere."

To observe or keep. Calv. Lex.

To bind. Id.

To be of force or validity. Id.

——**In Old English Law.** To hold by service, in the feudal sense. *De tenemento quod de vobis teneo*, of the tenement which I hold of you. Bracton, fol. 80; Co. Litt. 1b.

To hold judicially. *Tenere placitum*, to hold plea; to take cognizance of an action; to exercise or entertain jurisdiction. *Prohibemus vobis ne teneatis placitum*, we prohibit you that you do not hold plea. Reg. Orig. 34. *Tenere placita*, to hold pleas; to have a court of one's own. Finch, Law, bk. 2, c. 14.

To hold, or be seised of; to have. Co. Litt. 1b.

TENERI (Lat.) In contracts. That part of a bond where the obligor declares himself to be held and firmly bound to the obligee, his heirs, executors, administrators, and assigns, is called the *teneri.* 3 Call (Va.) 350.

TENET (Lat. he holds). In pleading. A term used in stating the tenure in an action for waste done during tenancy.

When the averment is in the *tenet*, the plaintiff, on obtaining a verdict, will recover the place wasted, namely, that part of the premises in which the waste was exclusively done, if it were done in a part only, together with treble damages. But when the averment is in the *tenuit*, the tenancy being at an end, he will have judgment for his damages only. 2 Greenl. Ev. § 652.

TENHEDED, or **TIENHEOFED.** A dean.

TENHEVED (Saxon *tienheofod*, from *tien*, ten, and *heofod*, head). In old English law. The head of a tithing, or decennary; a tithingman, chief pledge, head borough or borsholder. Spelman.

TENMENTALE, or **TENMANTALE.** The number of ten men, which number, in the time of the Saxons, was called a "decennary;" and ten decennaries made what was called a "hundred." Also a duty or tribute paid to the crown, consisting of two shillings for each ploughland. Enc. Lond.

TENNE. A term of heraldy, meaning orange color. In engravings it should be represented by lines in bend sinister crossed by others bar-ways. Heralds who blazon by the names of the heavenly bodies call it "dragon's head," and those who employ jewels, "jacinth." It is one of the colors called "stainand." Wharton.

TENOR.

——**In Pleading.** A term used to denote that an exact copy is set out, 5 Wend. (N. Y.) 273; 14 Ohio St. 61; 1 Mass. 203; 1 East, 180, and the cases cited in the notes; and binds the pleader to the strictest accuracy. And an indictment for forgery of an instrument, professing to set it out according to its tenor, should give the names, in describing the instrument, spelled as they appear spelled in the original. 66 Ill. 346.

——**In Chancery Pleading.** A certified copy of records of other courts removed into chancery by *certiorari*. Gresl. Ev. 309.

TENOR EST QUI LEGEM DAT FEUDO. It is the tenor of the feudal grant which regulates its effect and extent. Craig, Jus Feud. (3d Ed.) 66. See Co. Litt. 19a; 2 Bl. Comm. 310; 2 Coke. 71; Broom, Leg. Max. (3d London Ed.) 410; Wright, Ten. 21, 52, 152.

TENORE INDICTAMENTI MITTENDO. A writ whereby the record of an indictment, and the process thereupon, was called out of another court into the Queen's (or king's) Bench. Reg. Orig. 69.

TENORE PRAESENTIUM. By the tenor of these presents, *i. e.*, the matter contained therein, or rather the intent and meaning thereof. Cowell.

TENSERIAE. A sort of ancient tax or military contribution. Wharton.

TENTERDEN'S ACT. St. 9 Geo. IV. c. 14, extending the statutes of frauds to certain other contracts.

TENTHS.

——**In English Law.** A temporary aid issuing out of personal property, and granted to the king by parliament; formerly the real tenth part of all the movables belonging to the subject. 1 Bl. Comm. 308.

——**In English Ecclesiastical Law.** The tenth part of the annual profit of every living in the kingdom, formerly paid to the pope, but by St. 26 Hen. VIII. c. 3, transferred to the crown, and afterwards made a part of the fund called "Queen Anne's Bounty." 1 Bl. Comm. 284-286.

TENUIT (Lat. he held). In pleading. A term used in stating the tenure in an action for waste done after the termination of the tenancy. See "Tenet."

TENURA EST PACTIO CONTRA COMmunem feudi naturam ac rationem, in contractu interposita. Tenure is a compact contrary to the common nature and reason of the fee, put into a contract. Wright, Ten. 21.

TENURE (from Lat. *tenere*, to hold). A term of extensive signification. While it means the mode by which one holds an estate in land, it imports any kind of holding from mere possession to the owning of the inheritance. 153 Cal. 718; 96 Pac. 500; Ann. Cas. 1914D 636.

In the most general sense, the mode or right of holding, as "tenure of office." More specifically, the mode by which a man holds an estate in lands.

Such a holding as is coupled with some service, which the holder is bound to perform so long as he continues to hold.

The thing held is called a "tenement;" the occupant, a "tenant;" and the manner of his holding constitutes the "tenure."

Classification of feudal tenures.

(1) The principal species of tenure which grew out of the feudal system was the tenure by knight's service. This was essentially military in its character, and required the possession of a certain quantity of land, called a "knight's fee," the measure of which, in the time of Edward I., was estimated at twelve ploughlands, of the value of twenty pounds per annum. He who held this portion of land was bound to attend his lord to the wars forty days in every year, if called upon. It seems, however, that if he held but half a knight's fee, he was only bound to attend twenty days. Many arbitrary and tyrannical incidents or lordly privileges were attached to this tenure, which at length became so odious and oppressive that the whole system was destroyed at a blow by St. Charles II. c. 24, which declared that all such lands should thenceforth be held in free and common socage,—a statute, says Blackstone, which was a greater acquisition to the civil property of this kingdom than even *Magna Charta* itself; since that only pruned the luxuriances which had grown out of military tenures, and thereby preserved them in vigor, but the statute of King Charles extirpated the whole, and demolished both root and branches. See "Feudal Law;" Co. Litt. 69; St. Westminster I., c. 36.

(2) Tenure in socage seems to have been a relic of Saxon liberty which, up to the time of the abolition of military tenures, had been evidently struggling with the innovations of the Normans. Its great redeeming quality was its certainty; and in this sense it is by the old law writers put in opposition to the tenure by knight's service, where the tenure was altogether precarious and uncertain. Littleton defines it to be where a tenant holds his tenement by any certain service, in lieu of all other services, so that they be not services of chivalry or knight's services; as, to hold by fealty and twenty shillings rent, or by homage, fealty, and twenty shillings rent, or by homage and fealty without any rent, or by fealty and a certain specified service, as, to plough the lord's land for three days. Litt. 117; 2 Bl. Comm. 79. See "Socage."

(3) Other tenures have grown out of the two last-mentioned species of tenure, and are still extant in England, although some of them are fast becoming obsolete. Of these is the tenure by grand serjeanty, which consists in some service immediately respecting the person or dignity of the sovereign; as, to carry the king's standard, or to be his constable or marshal, his butler or chamberlain, or to perform some similar service. While the tenure by petit serjeanty requires some inferior service, not strictly military or personal, to the king; as, the annual render of a bow or sword. The late duke of Wellington annually presented his sovereign with a banner, in acknowledgment of his tenure. There are also tenures by copyhold and in frankalmoigne, in burgage and of gavelkind; but their nature, origin, and history are explained in the several articles appropriated to those terms. 2 Bl. Comm. 66; 2 Inst. 233.

(4) Tenures were distinguished by the old common-law writers, according to the quality of the service, into free or base. The former were such as were not unbecoming a soldier or a freeman to perform, as, to serve the lord in the wars; while the latter were only considered fit for a peasant, as, to

plough the land, and the like. They were further distinguished with reference to the person from whom the land was held; as, a tenure *in capite*, where the holding was of the person of the king, and tenure *in gross*, where the holding was of a subject. Before the statute of *Quia Emptores* (18 Edw. I), any person might, by a grant of land, have created an estate as a tenure of his person, or of his house or manor; and although by *Magna Charta* a man could not alienate so much of his land as not to leave enough to answer the services due to the superior lord, yet, as that statute did not remedy the evil then complained of, it was provided by the statute above referred to, that if any tenant should alien any part of his land in fee, the alienee should hold immediately of the lord of the fee, and should be charged with a proportional part of the service due in respect to the quantity of land held by him. The consequence of which was that, upon every such alienation, the services upon which the estate was originally granted became due to the superior lord, and not to the immediate grantee. 4 Term R. 443; 4 East, 271; Crabb, Real Prop. § 735.

Wharton's classification is as follows:

(A) Lay tenures.

- I. Frank tenement, or freehold.
  - (1) The military tenures (abolished, except grand serjeanty, and reduced to free socage tenures) were: Knight service proper, or tenure in chivalry; grand serjeanty; cornage.
  - (2) Free socage, or plough service; either petit serjeanty tenure in burgage, or gavelkind.
- II. Villeinage.
  - (1) Pure villeinage (whence copyholds at the lord's [nominal] will, which is regulated according to custom).
  - (2) Privileged villeinage, sometimes called "villein socage" (whence tenure in ancient demesne, which is an exalted species of copyhold, held according to custom, and not according to the lord's will), and is of three kinds: Tenure in ancient demesne; privileged copyholds, customary freeholds, or free copyholds; copyholds of base tenure.

(B) Spiritual tenures.

- I. Frankalmoigne, or free alms.
- II. Tenure by divine service.

TENURE BY DIVINE SERVICE. See "Divine Service."

TENURE OF OFFICE. See "Tenure;" "Term of Office."

TERCE. In Scotch law. A life rent competent by law to widows who have not accepted of special provisions in the third part of the heritable subjects in which the husband died infeft.

The terce takes place only where the marriage has subsisted for a year and a day, or where a child has been born alive of it. No terce is due out of lands in which the husband was not infeft, unless in case of a fraudulent omission. Craig, Inst. 423, § 28. The terce is not limited to lands, but extends to teinds, and to servitudes and other burdens affecting lands. Ersk. Inst. 2. 9. 26; Burge, Confl. Laws, 429-435.

TERCER. In the Scotch law, a widow that possesses the third part of her husband's land, as her legal jointure. 1 Kames, Eq. pref.

TERM.

——**In Construction.** Word; expression; speech.

Terms are words or characters by which we announce our sentiments, and make known to others things with which we are acquainted. These must be properly construed or interpreted in order to under stand the parties using them.

——**In Contracts.** The space of time granted to a debtor for discharging his obligation. These are express terms, resulting from the positive stipulations of the agreement, as, where one undertakes to pay a certain sum on a certain day, and also terms which tacitly result from the nature of the things which are the object of the engagement, or from the place where the act is agreed to be done. For instance, if a builder engage to construct a house for me, I must allow a reasonable time for fulfilling his engagement. 1 Wis. 314.

——**In Estates.** The limitation of an estate; as, a term for years, for life, and the like. The word "term" does not merely signify the time specified in the lease, but the estate, also, and interest that passes by that lease, and therefore the term may expire during the continuance of the time; as, by surrender, forfeiture, and the like. 2 Bl. Comm. 145; 8 Pick. (Mass.) 339.

——**Of Court.** The space of time during which a court holds a session. The stated periods during which courts sit for the dispatch of business. Sometimes the term is a monthly, at others it is a quarterly, period, according to the constitution of the court.

TERM ATTENDANT ON THE INHERITANCE. See "Attendant Terms."

TERM FOR YEARS. An estate for years, and the time during which such estate is to be held, is each called a "term"; hence the term may expire before the time, as, by a surrender. Co. Litt. 45. See "Estate for Years."

TERM IN GROSS. A term of years is said to be either in gross (outstanding) or attendant upon the inheritance. It is outstanding, or in gross, when it is unattached or disconnected from the estate or inheritance, as where it is in the hands of some third party having no interest in the inheritance. It is attendant when vested in some trustee in trust for the owner of the inheritance. Brown.

TERM OF OFFICE. The term of office as fixed by law is sometimes used interchangeably with the term or time of occupancy of the incumbent of such office, but it must be distinctly borne in mind that the term of office as fixed by law is entirely different from the period of time such office is held by the incumbent thereof, some times referred to as the term. The general rule seems to be that the term of office, when not fixed as to the date of its beginning and ending by a constitution or statute, begins in the case of elective offices on the date of election. 280 Ill. 444.

TERM PROBATORY. The time during which evidence may be taken in a cause.

TERM TO CONCLUDE. In English ecclesiastical practice. An appointment by the judge of a time at which both parties are understood to renounce all further exhibits and allegations.

TERM TO PROPOUND ALL THINGS. In English ecclesiastical practice. An appointment by the judge of a time at which both parties are to exhibit all the acts and instruments which make for their respective causes.

TERMS AND CONDITIONS. The words as used in contracts generally mean the propositions, limitations, and exactions which comprise in whole or in part the agreement, and govern the contracting parties, defining what they obligate themselves to do or not to do. 173 Mich. 314.

TERMINABLE PROPERTY. Such property (*e. g.*, leaseholds, terminable annuities, etc.), as has no permanent duration, but must and will end at a certain time, usually determined beforehand.

TERMINARE (Lat.) In old English law. To end or determine; to dispose of judicially; to decide.

TERMINATING BUILDING SOCIETIES. Societies, in England, where the members commence their monthly contributions on a particular day, and continue to pay them until the realization of shares to a given amount for each member, by the advance of the capital of the society to such members as required it, and the payment of interest as well as principal by them, so as to insure such realization within a given period of years. They have been almost superseded by permanent building societies.

TERMINER (Law Fr.; from Lat. *terminare q. v.*). To determine. *A oyer et terminer toutes quereles*, to hear and determine all complaints. Britt. fol. 1.

TERMINO. In Spanish law. A common; common land. Common because of vicinage. White, New Recop. bk. 2, tit. 1, c. 6, § 1, note.

TERMINUM (Lat.) In civil law. A day set to the defendant. Spelman. In this sense, Bracton, Glanville, and some others sometimes use it. Reliquiae Spelmanianae, p. 71; Beames, Glanv. 27, note.

TERMINUM QUI PRETERIIT, WRIT OF entry ad. A writ which lay for the reversioner, when the possession was withheld by the lessee, or a stranger, after the determination of a lease for years. Brown.

TERMINUS (Lat.) A boundary or limit, either of space or time. A bound, goal, or borders parting one man's land from another's. *Est inter eos non de terminis, sed tota possessione contentio.* Cic. Acad. 4, 43. It is used also for an estate for a term of years; *e. g.*, *"interesse termini."* 2 Bl. Comm. 143.

Terminus a quo. The starting point of a private way is so called. Hammond, N. P. 196. The point or place from which the grantee is to set out in order to use the way. 19 Ill. 563.

Terminus ad quem. The point of termination of a private way is so called. 19 Ill. 564.

TERMINUS ANNORUM CERTUS DEBET esse et determinatus. A term of years ought to be certain and determinate. Co. Litt. 45.

TERMINUS ET (AC) FEODUM NON possunt constare simul in una eademque persona. A term and the fee cannot both be in one and the same person at the same time. Plowd. 29; 3 Mass. 141.

TERMINUS JURIS (Law Lat.) In English ecclesiastical practice. The time of one or two years, allowed by law for the determination of appeals. Halifax, Anl. bk. 3, c. 11, No. 38.

TERMOR. One who holds lands and tenements for a term of years, or life. Litt. § 100; 4 Tyrwh. 561.

TERRA. Earth; land.

——**Terra Affirmata.** Land let to farm.

——**Terra Boscalis.** Woody land.

——**Terra Culta.** Cultivated land.

——**Terra Debilis.** Weak or barren land.

——**Terra Dominica (or Indominicata).** The demesne land of a manor. Cowell.

——**Terra Excultabilis.** Land which may be plowed. Mon. Angl. i. 426.

——**Terra Extendenda.** A writ addressed to an escheator, etc., that he inquire and find out the true yearly value of any land, etc., by the oath of twelve men, and to certify the extent into the chancery. Reg. Writs, 293.

——**Terra Frusca** (or **Frisca**). Fresh land, not lately plowed. Cowell.

——**Terra Hydata.** Land subject to the payment of hydage. Selden.

——**Terra Lucrabilis.** Land gained from the sea, or inclosed out of a waste. Cowell.

——**Terra Manens Vacua Occupanti Conceditur.** Land lying unoccupied is given to the first occupant. 1 Sid. 347.

——**Terra Normanorum.** Land held by a Norman. Par. Ant. 197.

——**Terra Nova.** Land newly converted from wood ground or arable. Cowell.

——**Terra Putura.** Land in forests, held by the tenure of furnishing food to the keepers therein. 4 Inst. 307.

——**Terra Sabulosa.** Gravelly or sandy ground.

——**Terra Testamentalis.** Gavelkind land, being disposable by will. Spelman.

——**Terra Transit cum Onere.** Land passes with the incumbrances. Co. Litt. 231; Broom, Leg. Max (3d London Ed.) 437, 630.

——**Terra Vestita.** Land sown with corn. Cowell.

——**Terra Wainabilis.** Tillable land. Cowell.

——**Terra Warrenata.** Land that has the liberty of free warren.

TERRAE DOMINCALES REGIS. The demesne lands of the crown.

TERRAGES. An exemption from all uncertain services. Cowell.

TERRARIUS. In old English law. A landholder.

TERRE TENANT (improperly spelled *ter tenant*). One who has the actual possession of land; but, in a more technical sense, he who is seised of the land; and in the latter sense, the owner of the land, or the person seised, is the terre tenant, and not the lessee. 4 Watts & S. (Pa.) 256; Bac. Abr. "Uses and Trusts." It has been holden that mere occupiers of the land are not terre tenants. See 16 Serg. & R. (Pa.) 432; 3 Pa. 229; 2 Saund. 7, note 4; 2 Bl. Comm. 91, 328.

TERRIER. In English law. A roll, catalogue, or survey of lands, belonging either to a single person or a town, in which are stated the quantity of acres, the names of the tenants, and the like.

By the ecclesiastical law, an inquiry is directed to be made from time to time of the temporal rights of the clergyman of every parish, and to be returned into the registry of the bishop. This return is denominated a "terrier." 1 Phil. Ev. 602, 603.

TERRIS BONIS ET CATALLIS REHAbendis post purgationem. A writ for a clerk to recover his lands, goods, and chattels, formerly seized, after he had cleared himself of the felony of which he was accused, and delivered to his ordinary to be purged. Reg. Orig.

TERRIS ET CATALLIS TENTIS ULTRA debitum levatum. A judicial writ for the restoring of lands or goods to a debtor who is distrained above the amount of the debt. Reg. Jud.

TERRIS LIBERANDIS. A writ that lay for a man convicted by attaint, to bring the record and process before the king, and take a fine for his imprisonment, and then to deliver to him his lands and tenements again, and release him of the strip and waste. Reg. Orig. 232. Also it was a writ for the delivery of lands to the heir, after homage and relief performed, or upon security taken that he should perform them. Id. 293.

TERRITORIAL COURTS. The courts established in the territories of the United States.

TERRITORIUM (Lat. from *terra*, land). A territory, or district; the territorial limits of a government; the extent or limits of the jurisdiction of a court.

TERRITORY. A part of a country separated from the rest, and subject to a particular jurisdiction. The extent or compass of land and the waters thereof within the bounds of or belonging to the jurisdiction of any sovereign state, or city or other body. 110 Ill. App. 370.

The word is derived from *terreo*, and is said to be so called because the magistrate within his jurisdiction has the power of inspiring a salutary fear. *Dictum est ab eo quod magistratus intra fines ejus terrendi jus habet.* Henrion de Pansy, Auth, Judiciaire, 98. In speaking of the ecclesiastical jurisdictions, Francis Duaren observes that the ecclesiastics are said not to have territory, nor the power of arrest or removal, and are not unlike the Roman magistrates of whom Gellius says *vocationem habebant non prehensionem.* De Sacris Eccles. Minist. lib. 1, c. 4.

——**In American Law.** A portion of the country subject to and belonging to the United States which is not within the boundary of any of the states.

TERROR (Lat.) That state of the mind which arises from the event or phenomenon that may serve as a prognostic of some catastrophe; affright from apparent danger.

One of the constituents of the offense of riot is that the acts of the persons engaged in it should be to the terror of the people, as a show of arms, threatening speeches, or turbulent gestures; but it is not requisite, in order to constitute this crime, that personal violence should be committed. 3 Campb. 369; 1 Hawk. P. C. c. 65, § 5; 4 Car. & P. 373, 538. See Rolle, 109; Dalton, Just. c. 186; Viner, Abr. "Riots" (A 8).

TERTIA DENUNCIATIO (Lat.) In old English law. Third publication or proclamation of intended marriage. *Cum bannum et tertia denunciatio fiat,* when the banns and third publication are made. Bracton, fol. 307b.

TERTIUS INTERVENIENS (Lat.) In civil law. One who, claiming an interest in the subject or thing in dispute in action between other parties, asserts his right to act with the plaintiff, to be joined with him, and to recover the matter in dispute, because he has an interest in it, or to join the defendant, and with him oppose the interest of the plaintiff, which it is his interest to defeat. He differs from the intervener, or he who interpleads in equity. 4 Bouv. Inst. n. 3819, note.

TEST. Something by which to ascertain the truth respecting another thing. 7 Pa. St. 428; 6 Whart. (Pa.) 284. See Test Act.

TEST ACT. Act 25 Car. II. c. 2, by which it was enacted that all persons holding any office, civil or military (excepting some very inferior ones), or receiving pay from the crown, or holding a place of trust under it, should take the oath of allegiance and supremacy, and subscribe a declaration against transubstantiation, and receive the sacrament according to the usage of the Church of England, under a penalty of £500 and disability to the office. 4 Bl. Comm. 59. From this act the word "test" originally acquired its signification in connection with the word "oath." 116 Ill. 606. An odious act now abolished, 9 Geo. IV, c. 17, so far as taking sacrament is concerned, and a new form of declaration substituted. Enc. Brit.

TEST ACTION. An action brought to determine a doubtful right affecting many persons. It may be an action selected from a number of pending actions brought to enforce such a right, the parties agreeing that all actions shall follow the decision in the test action, or a single action may be brought by one person at the instance of all to determine the right. Test cases are sometimes had in criminal practice where the validity of a statute or ordinance is questioned, and a prosecution is lodged against one person, with the tacit understanding that further prosecutions will be postponed, or will be determined according to the result of that one.

TEST OATH. An oath required as a condition precedent to the right to fill a public office. Generally, an oath of present allegiance, or of denial of connection with some past insurrection.

TEST PAPER. A paper submitted to the jury as a test or standard by which to determine the genuineness of other writings. 7 Pa. St. 428; 6 Whart. (Pa.) 284. Only admissible when no collateral issue can be raised concerning it. See 14 N. Y. 439; 1 Greenl. Ev. § 581.

TESTABLE. A person is said to be testable when he has capacity to make a will. A man of twenty-one years of age and of sane mind is testable. The capacity to make a will must be distinguished from a special power to dispose of property by will. Thus, a power given to a married woman by a settlement to dispose of property by will does not make her testable. L. R. 7 H. L. 593. But if property is settled on a married woman for her separate use, she is testable so far as that property is concerned.

TESTACY. The condition of one dying having made a will. Opposed to "intestacy" (*q. v.*) It may exist as to all property, or may be but "partial," as to such only as is disposed of.

TESTAMENT. In civil law. The appointment of an executor or testamentary heir, according to the formalities prescribed by law. Domat, liv. 1, tit. 1, § 1.

At first there were only two sorts of testaments among the Romans,—that called *calatis comitiis,* and another called *in procinctu.* In the course of time, these two sorts of testament having become obsolete, a third form was introduced, called *per aes et libram,* which was a fictitious sale of the inheritance to the heir apparent. The inconveniences which were experienced from these fictitious sales again changed the form of testaments, and the praetor introduced another, which required the seal of seven witnesses. The emperors having increased the solemnity of these testaments, they were called "written" or "solemn" testaments, to distinguish them from "nuncupative" testaments, which could be made without writing. Afterwards military testaments were introduced in favor of soldiers actually engaged in military service.

(1) A testament *calatis comitiis,* or made in the *comitia,*—that is, the assembly of the Roman people,—was an ancient manner of making wills, used in times of peace among the Romans. The *comitia* met twice a year for this purpose. Those who wished to make such testaments caused to be convoked the assembly of the people by these words, *calatis comitiis.* None could make such wills that were not entitled to be at the assemblies of the people. This form of testament was repealed by the law of the Twelve Tables.

(2) A civil testament is one made according to all the forms prescribed by law, in contradistinction to a military testament, in making which some of the forms may be dispensed with. Civil testaments are more ancient than military ones; the former were in use during the time of Romulus, the latter were introduced during the time of Coriolanus. See Hist. de la Jur. Rom. de M. Terrason, p. 119.

(3) A common testament is one which is made jointly by several persons. Such testaments are forbidden in Louisiana (Civ. Code La. art. 1565), and by the laws of France (Civ. Code 968), in the same words, namely: "A testament cannot be made by the same act, by two or more persons, either for the benefit of a third person, or under the title of a reciprocal or mutual disposition."

(4) A testament *ab irato* is one made in a gust of passion or hatred against the presumptive heir, rather than from a desire to benefit the devisee. When the facts of unreasonable anger are proved, the will is annulled as unjust, and as not having been freely made. See "Ab Irato."

(5) A mystic testament (called a "solemn testament," because it requires more formality than a nuncupative testament) is a form of making a will which consists principally in enclosing it in an envelope and sealing it in the presence of witnesses.

This kind of testament is used in Louisiana. The following are the provisions of the Civil Code of that state on the subject, namely: The mystic or secret testament, otherwise called the "close testament," is made in the following manner: The testator must sign his dispositions, whether he has written them himself, or has caused them to be written by another person. The paper containing these dispositions, or the paper serving as their envelope, must be closed and sealed. The testator shall present it thus closed and sealed to the notary and to seven witnesses, or he shall cause it be closed and sealed in their presence; then he shall declare to the notary, in the presence of the witnesses, that that paper contains his testament written by himself, or by another by his direction, and signed by him, the testator. The notary shall then draw up the act of superscription, which shall be written on that paper, or on the sheet that serves as its envelope, and that act shall be signed by the testator and by the notary and the witnesses. 5 Mart. (La.) 182. All that is above prescribed shall be done without interruption or turning aside to other acts; and in case the testator, by reason of any hindrance that has happened since the signing of the testament, cannot sign the act of superscription, mention shall be made of the declaration made by him thereof, without its being necessary in that case to increase the number of witnesses. Those who know not how or are not able to write, and those who know not how or are not able to sign their names, cannot make dispositions in the form of the mystic will. If any one of the witnesses to the act of superscription knows not how to sign, express mention shall be made thereof. In all cases the act must be signed by at least two witnesses. Civ. Code La. arts. 1577-1580.

(6) A nuncupative testament was one made verbally, in the presence of seven witnesses. It was not necessary that it should have been in writing; the proof of it was by parol evidence. See "Nuncupative Will."

In Louisiana, testaments, whether nuncupative or mystic, must be drawn up in writing, either by the testator himself, or by some other person under his dictation. The custom of making verbal statements, that is to say, resulting from the mere deposition of witnesses who were present when the testator made known to them his will, without his having committed it or caused it to be committed to writing, is abrogated. Nuncupative testaments may be made by public act, or by act under private signature. Civ. Code La. arts. 1568-1570.

(7) An olographic testament is one which is written wholly by the testator himself. In order to be valid, it must be entirely written, dated, and signed by the hand of the testator. It is subject to no other form. See Civ. Code La. art. 1581.

See "Will."

TESTAMENTA LATISSIMAM INTERpretationem habere debent. Wills ought to have the broadest interpretation. Jenk. Cent. Cas. 81.

TESTAMENTARY. Belonging to a testament; as, a testamentary gift; a testamentary guardian, or one appointed by will or testament; letters testamentary, or a writing under seal, given by an officer lawfully authorized, granting power to one named as executor to execute a last will or testament.

TESTAMENTARY CAPACITY. Mental capacity sufficient to make a valid will.

TESTAMENTARY CAUSES. In English law. Causes relating to probate of testaments and administration, and accounts upon the same. They are enumerated among ecclesiastical causes by Lord Coke. 5 Coke, 1, and tables of cases at the end of the part. Over these causes the probate court has now exclusive jurisdiction, by 20 & 21 Vict. c. 77, amended by 21 & 22 Vict. c. 95.

TESTAMENTARY DISPOSITION. A gift which does not take effect as an executed and completed transfer to the donee, either legal or equitable, during the lifetime of the donor. 136 Ill. 398.

TESTAMENTARY GUARDIAN. A guardian appointed by last will of a father to have custody of his child and his real and personal estate till he attains the age of twenty-one. In England, the power to appoint such guardian was given by 12 Car. II. c. 24. The principles of this statute have been generally adopted in the United States (12 N. H. 437), but not in Connecticut (1 Swift, Dig. 48).

TESTAMENTUM (Lat.)

——**In the Civil Law.** A testament; a will, or last will.

——**In Old English Law.** A testament or will; a disposition of property made in contemplation of death. Bracton, fol. 60.

A general name for any instrument of conveyance, including deeds and charters, and so called either because it furnished written testimony of the conveyance, or because it was authenticated by witnesses (*testes*). Spelman.

TESTAMENTUM EST VOLUNTATIS nostrae justa sententia, de eo quod quis post mortem suam fieri velit. A testament is the just expression of our will concerning that which any one wishes done after his death; or, as Blackstone translates, "the legal declaration of a man's intentions which he wills to be performed after his death." 2 Bl. Comm. 499; Dig. 28. 1. 1; Id. 29. 3. 2. 1.

TESTAMENTUM, I. E., TESTATIO MENtis, facta nullo praesente metu periculi, sed *cogitatione mortalitatis.* A testament, *i. e.*, the witnessing of one's intention, made under no present fear of danger, but in expectancy of death. Co. Litt. 322.

TESTAMENTUM INOFFICIOSUM (Lat.) In the civil law. An unofficious testament.

TESTAMENTUM OMNE MORTE CONsummatum. Every will is completed by death. Co. Litt. 232.

TESTATE. The condition of one who leaves a valid will at his death.

TESTATION. Witness; evidence.

TESTATOR (Lat.) One who has made a testament or will.

TESTATORIS ULTIMA VOLUNTAS EST perimplenda secundum veram intentionem suam. The last will of a testator is to be fulfilled according to his real intention. Co. Litt. 322.

TESTATRIX (Lat.) A woman who makes a will or testament.

TESTATUM (Lat.)

——**In Practice.** The name of a writ which is issued by the court of one county to the sheriff of another county in the same state, when the defendant cannot be found in the county where the court is located; for example, after a judgment has been obtained, and a *ca. sa.* has been issued, which has been returned *non est inventus*, a *testatum ca. sa.* may be issued to the sheriff of the county where the defendant is. See Viner, Abr. "Testatum," 259.

——**In conveyancing.** That part of a deed which commences with the words "this indenture witnesseth."

TESTATUS (Lat.) In the civil law. Testate; one who has made a will. *Testatus et intestatus*, testate and intestate. Dig. 50. 17. 7.

TESTE MEIPSO (Lat.) In old English law and practice. A solemn formula of attestation by the sovereign, used at the conclusion of charters, and other public instruments, and also of original writs out of chancery. Spelman.

TESTE OF A WRIT (Lat.) In practice. The concluding clause, commencing with the word "witness," etc. A signature in attestation of the fact that a writ is issued by authority.

The act of Congress of May 8, 1792 (1 Story, U. S. Laws, 227), directs that all writs and process issuing from the supreme or a circuit court shall bear *teste* of the chief justice of the supreme court, or, if that office be vacant, of the associate justice next in precedence; and that all writs or process issuing from a district court shall bear *teste* of the judge of such court, or, if the said office be vacant, of the clerk thereof. See Serg. Const. Law, Index; 20 Viner, Abr. 262; Steph. Pl. 25.

TESTED. Bearing *teste*.

TESTES (Lat.) Witnesses.

TESTES QUI POSTULAT DEBET DARE eis sumptus competentes. Whosoever demands witnesses must find them in competent provision.

TESTES, TRIAL PER. A trial had before a judge without the intervention of a jury, in which the judge is left to form in his own breast his sentence upon the credit of the witnesses examined; but this mode of trial, although it was common in the civil law, was seldom resorted to in the practice of the common law, but it is now becoming common when each party waives his right to a trial by jury. Brown. See "Trial."

TESTIBUS DEPONENTIBUS IN PARI numero dignioribus est credendum. When the number of witnesses is equal on both sides, the more worthy are to be believed. 4 Inst. 279.

TESTIFY. To give evidence according to law; the examination of a witness who declares his knowledge of facts.

TESTIMONIA PONDERANDA SUNT, non numeranda. Evidence is to be weighed, not enumerated.

TESTIMONIAL. A certificate under the hands of a justice of the peace testifying the place and time when and where a soldier or mariner landed, and the place of his dwelling and birth, whither he is to pass. Cowell; 3 Inst. 85. The document holds a kind of doubtful position midway between a certificate and a permit, or pass. Brown.

TESTIMONIAL PROOF. In civil law. A term used in the same sense as "parol evidence" is used at common law, and in contradistinction to "literal proof," which is written evidence.

TESTIMONIES. In Spanish law. An attested copy of an instrument by a notary. Newman & Barretti; Tex. Dig.

TESTIMONIUM CLAUSE. In conveyancing. That clause of a deed or instrument with which it concludes: "In witness whereof, the parties to these presents have hereunto set their hands and seals."

TESTIMONY. The statement made by a witness under oath or affirmation.

For distinction between "testimony" and "evidence," see "Evidence."

TESTIS (Lat.) A witness.

TESTIS DE VISU PRAEPONDERAT aliis. An eye witness outweighs others. 4 Inst. 470.

TESTIS LUPANARIS SUFFICIT AD FACtum in lupanari. A lewd person is a sufficient witness to an act committed in a brothel. Moore, 817.

TESTIS NEMO IN SUA CAUSA ESSE potest. No one can be a witness in his own cause. Otherwise in England, by St. 14 & 15 Vict. 99, and many of the states of the United States.

TESTIS OCULATUS UNUS PLUS VALET quam auriti decem. One eye witness is worth ten ear witnesses. 4 Inst. 279. See 3 Bouv. Inst. note 3154.

TESTMOIGNE. This is an old and barbarous French word, signifying, in the old books, evidence. Comyn, Dig.

TESTMOIGNES NE POENT TESTIFIE le negative, mes l'affirmative. Witnesses cannot witness to a negative; they must witness to an affirmative. 4 Inst. 279.

TEXTUS ROFFENSIS (Law Lat.) In old English law. The Rochester text. An ancient manuscript containing many of the Saxon laws, and the rights, customs, tenures, etc., of the church of Rochester, drawn up by Ernulph, bishop of that see from A. D. 1114 to 1124. Cowell. Blount gives it a greater antiquity.

THAINLAND, or **THANELAND.** In old English law. The land which was granted by the Saxon kings to their thains or thanes was so called. Crabb, Com. Law, 10.

THALER. A silver coin of Germany. The composition and value of this piece formerly varied considerably in different portions of the country,—the value ranging from ninety-five to one hundred and five cents. But the convention of the German states in 1838 fixed the weight of the thaler at 343.8 grains troy, and the fineness at 750 thousandths, which is the only standard now in use. The value, at this rate, is seventy-two cents. The name (thaler) is supposed to have originated from the German word *thal*, a dale, or valley,—the first thalers having been coined in the valley of Joachim, from which it obtained the name of "Joachim's thaler." From this coin the word "dollar," as applied to Spanish and American coins, is derived.

THALWEG. A line following the lowest part of a valley whether under water or not. Webster. Where a navigable river forms the boundary of coterminous states, the thalweg, or middle of the navigable channel is generally taken as the line of separation between them. 145 Ill. 603.

THANE (Saxon *thenian*, to serve). In Saxon law. A word which sometimes signifies a nobleman; at others, a freeman, a magistrate, an officer, or minister. A tenant of the part of the king's lands called the king's "thaneage." Termes de la Ley.

THANEAGE OF THE KING. In old English law. A certain part of the king's land or property, of which the ruler or governor was called "thane." Cowell; Blount.

THANESHIP. The office and dignity of a thane; the seigniory of a thane.

THAVIES INN. An inn of chancery. See "Inns of Chancery."

THE. A demonstrative word which particularizes the noun before which it stands and limits its meaning more definitely and particularly than the indefinite article "a". 261 Ill. 417.

THEFT. A popular term for larceny, adopted in lieu of the latter term by the Penal Code of Texas.

——**In Scotch Law.** The secret and felonious abstraction of the property of another for sake of lucre, without his consent. Alis. Crim. Law, 250.

THEFT BOTE. The act of receiving a man's goods from the thief, after they had been stolen by him, with the intent that he shall escape punishment.

This is an offense punishable at common law by fine and imprisonment. Hale, P. C. 130. See "Compounding a Felony."

THEFT BOTE EST EMENDA FURTI capta, sine consideratione curiae domini regis. Theft bote is the paying money to have goods stolen returned, without having any respect for the court of the king. 3 Inst. 134.

THELONIO IRRATIONABILI HABENDO. A writ that formerly lay for him that had any part of the king's demesne in fee farm, to recover reasonable toll of the king's tenants there, if his demesne had been accustomed to be tolled. Reg. Orig. 87.

THELONIUM. An abolished writ for citizens or burgesses to assert their right to exemption from toll. Fitzh. Nat. Brev. 226.

THELUSSON ACT. An English statute (39 & 40 Geo. III. c. 98), forbidding the holding of property for the purpose of accumulation beyond a period of twenty-one years from the death of the testator. It was so called because its necessity and passage were suggested by the curious will of one Thelusson, who provided that his estate should be accumulated until the body of it should constitute the largest estate, as the testator designed, in the world.

THEM, or **THEME.** The power or right of having jurisdiction over villeins, their offspring, and cattle.

THEMMAGIUM. A duty or acknowledgment paid by inferior tenants in respect of theme. Cowell.

THEN. In the grammatical sense is an adverb of time. In such case the context should plainly show that it was so used before effect is thus given to it. 233 Pa. St. 35; Ann. Cas. 1913B 321; 2 Atk. 308; 19 N. Mex. 477. It is often used for the purpose of denoting an event or contingency, and is equivalent to the words "in that event" or "in that case." Frequently used in legal instruments to designate limitations of estates, or future contingencies on which they are made to depend. When thus used it becomes a word of reference, and does not indicate any particular point of time. 6 Gray (Mass.) 24; 16 Ga. 557; Ann. Cas. 1913B 321. See "Then and There."

THEN AND THERE. Refers to the time and place last specified, unless some phrase is used in connection therewith which shows that a different reference was intended. 263 Ill. 476, 477; 138 Ill. 556. In an indictment it means at the time and place charged, and refers to a single transaction only. 19 N. Mex. 477; Ann. Cas. 1917D 825; 153 Ind. 93.

THEOCRACY. A species of government which claims to be immediately directed by God.

La religion, qui, dans l'antiquite, s'associa souvent au despotisme, pour regner par son bras ou a son ombrage, a quelquefois tente de regner seule. C'est ce qu'elle appelait le regne de Dieu, la theocratie. Religion, which in former times frequently associated itself with despotism, to reign by its power or under its shadow, has sometimes attempted to reign alone; and this she has called the "reign of God,"—theocracy. Matter, de l'Influence des Moeurs sur les Lois, et de l'Influence des Lois sur les Moeurs, 189.

THEODOSIAN CODE. See "Code."

THEOF. In Saxon law. Offenders who joined in a body of seven to commit depredations. Wharton.

THEREBY. By that; by that means; in consequence of that; through the agency or in consequence of that. 113 Ill. App. 556.

THEREUPON. An adverb signifying immediately, at once, without delay, and it is in that sense that it would ordinarily be understood. 23 Ill. App. 618.

THESAURUS, or **THESAURIUM.** The treasury; a treasure.

THESAURUS ABSCONDITUS. Treasure hidden, or buried. Spelman.

THESAURUS COMPETIT DOMINO REGI, et non domino libertatis, nisi sit per verba specialia. A treasure belongs to the king, and not to the lord of a liberty, unless it be through special words. Fitz. Coron. 281.

THESAURUS INVENTUS. Treasure trove (*q. v.*)

THESAURUS INVENTUS EST VETUS dispositio pecuniae, etc., cujus non extat modo memoria, adeo ut jam dominum non habeat. Treasure trove is an ancient hiding of money, etc., of which no recollection exists, so that it now has no owner. 3 Inst. 132.

THESAURUS NON COMPETIT REGI, nisi quando nemo scit qui abscondit thesaurum. Treasure does not belong to the king unless no one knows who hid it. 3 Inst. 132.

THESAURUS REGIS EST VINCULUM pacis et bellorum nervus. The king's treasure is the bond of peace and the sinews of war. Godb. 293.

THESE. The plural of "this" and opposed to "those," relates to the persons or things nearest or last mentioned, and "those" to the most remote or first mentioned. 69 Ill. App. 386.

THESMOTHETE. A law maker; a law giver.

THIEF. One who has been guilty of larceny or theft. 113 Ill. App. 450.

THIEVES. The term "thieves" is broad enough in law to cover both compound and simple larceny, and, in common parlance to include the latter; and when used in a policy of insurance upon the cargo of a vessel, it is not restricted in its application to external or assailing thieves, as pirates, rovers, etc., but covers a simple larceny committed by a stranger to the ship. 1 Hill (N. Y.) 25, affirmed in 26 Wend. (N. Y.) 563. And see 5 Paige (N. Y.) 285.

THINGS. By this word is understood every object, except man, which may become an active subject of right. Code du Canton de Berne, art. 332.

Any object that may be possessed; all matters of substance in contradiction to persons; whatever may be possessed or owned; subjects of property and dominion; synonymous with "effects" or "goods" or "assets" or "property." 240 Pa. St. 261, 87 Atl. 590. Ann. Cas. 1915A 24.

In this sense it is opposed, in the language of the law, to the word "persons." See Property; Res.

THINGS IN ACTION. A chose in action. Civ. Code Cal. § 953. See "Chose."

THINGS PERSONAL. Goods, money, and all other movables which may attend the owner's person wherever he thinks proper to go. 2 Bl. Comm. 16. Things personal consist of goods, money, and all other movables, and of such rights and profits as relate to movables. 1 Steph. Comm. 156.

THINGS REAL, or REALTY. Such things as are permanent, fixed, and immovable, which cannot be carried out of their place, as lands and tenements. 2 Bl. Comm. 16. This definition has been objected to, as not embracing incorporeal rights. Mr. Stephen defines things real to "consist of things substantial and immovable, and of the rights and profits annexed to or issuing out of these." 1 Steph. Comm. 156. Things real are otherwise described to consist of lands, tenements, and hereditaments. See "Real."

THINGUS. A thane or nobleman; knight or freeman. Cowell.

THINK. To believe. When a witness prefaces his testimony with "I think," he is to be taken as testifying to what he remembers. 288 Ill. 97; 43 S. W. Rep. (Tex.) 536.

THIRD BOROW. In old English law. A constable. Lambard, Duty of Const. 6; 28 Hen. VII. c. 10.

THIRD-NIGHT-AWN-HINDE. By the laws of St. Edward the Confessor, if any man lay a third night in an inn, he was called a "third-night-awn-hinde," and his host was answerable for him if he committed any offense. The first night, forman-night, or uncuth (unknown), he was reckoned a stranger; the second night, twa-night, a guest; and the third night, an awn-hinde, a domestic. Bracton, lib. 3.

THIRD PARTIES. A term used to include all persons who are not parties to the contract, agreement, or instrument of writing by which their interest in the thing conveyed is sought to be affected. 1 Mart. (La.; N. S.) 384. See, also, 2 La. 425; 6 Mart. (La.) 528.

But it is difficult to give a very definite idea of "third persons;" for sometimes those who are not parties to the contract, but who represent the rights of the original parties, as executors, are not to be considered third persons. See 1 Bouv. Inst. note 1335 et seq.

THIRD PENNY. In old English law. Of the fines and other profits of the county courts (originally, when those courts had superior jurisdiction, before other courts were created) two parts were reserved to the king, and a third part, or penny, to the earl of the county. See "Denarius Tertius Comitatus;" Kennett, Par. Ant. 418; Cowell.

THIRDINGS. The third part of the corn growing on the land, due to the lord for a heriot on the death of his tenant, within the manor of Turfat, in Hereford. Blount.

THIRDS. Occurring in a will, construed to mean the same thing as dower. 2 Keyes (N. Y.) 558; 2 Abb. Pr. (N. S.; N. Y.) 418, affirming 46 Barb. (N. Y.) 609.

THIRLAGE. In Scotch law. A servitude by which lands are astricted or thirled to a particular mill, and the possessors bound to grind their grain there, for the payment of certain multures and sequels as the agreed price of grinding. Ersk. Inst. 2. 9. 18.

THIS. A demonstrative word referring particularly to what is present or near in place, time, or thought, or to something just mentioned or about to be mentioned. 248 Ill. 144.

THIS DAY SIX MONTHS (or THREE months). Fixing "this day six months or three months" for the next stage of a bill is one of the modes in which the house of lords and the house of commons reject bills of which they disapprove. A bill rejected in this manner cannot be reintroduced in the same session.

THISTLE TAKE. It was a custom within the manor of Halton, in Chester, that if, in driving beasts over a common, the driver permit them to graze or take but a thistle, he shall pay a halfpenny apiece to the lord of the fee. And at Fiskerton, in Nottinghamshire, by ancient custom, if a native or a cottager killed a swine above a year old, he paid to the lord a penny, which purchase of leave to kill a hog was also called "thistle take." Cowell.

THOROUGHFARE. A street or way opening at both ends into another street or public highway, so that one can go through and get out of it without returning. It differs from a *cul de sac*, which is open only at one end.

Whether a street which is not a thoroughfare is a highway seems not fully settled. 1 Vent. 189; 1 Hawk. P. C. c. 76, § 1. In a case tried in 1790, where the *locus in quo* had been used as a common street for fifty years, but was no thoroughfare, Lord Kenyon held that it would make no difference; for otherwise the street would be a trap to make people trespassers. 11 East, 375. This decision in several subsequent cases was much criticised, though not directly overruled. 5 Taunt. 126; 5 Barn. & Ald. 456; 3 Bing. 447; 1 Campb. 260; 4 Adol. & E. 698. But in a later English case the decision of Lord Kenyon was affirmed by the unanimous opinion of the court of queen's bench. The doctrine established in the latter case is that it is a question for the jury, on the evidence, whether a place which is not a thoroughfare is a highway or not. 14 Eng. Law & Eq. 69. And see 28 Eng. Law & Eq. 30. In the United States there are but few cases in which this question has been discussed; though in Rhode Island it has been determined that a street terminating upon private land, and extending neither to another way, a mill, a market, nor other public place, is incapable of dedication to the public as a highway. 2 R. I. 172. And a similar decision has been made in New York. 23 N. Y. 103. And see 23 N. H. 331; 7 Johns. (N. Y.) 106.

THOSE. See "These."

THOUGHT. The operation of the mind. No one can be punished for his mere thoughts, however wicked they may be. Human laws cannot reach them,—first, because they are unknown; and secondly, unless made manifest by some action, they are not injurious to any one; but when they manifest themselves, then the act which is the consequence may be punished. Dig. 50. 16. 225.

THRAVE, THREAVE (Sax.) L. Lat. *trabes, trava.* In old English law. A measure of corn or grain, consisting of twenty-four sheaves of four shocks, six sheaves to every shock. Stat. 2 Hen. VI. c. 2. Cowell.

THREAD. A figurative expression used to signify the central line of a stream or watercourse. Harg. Law Tr. 5; 4 Mason (U. S.) 397; Holt, 490. See "Filum Aquae."

THREAT. A menace brought to the knowledge of the one sought to be affected thereby. 84 Iowa 473; 51 N. W. 25. It may affect the life, character, or property of the person against whom it is made. It need not be in any particular form or phrase, but must be directly made. Any language which conveys with sufficient clearness to be understood the proposition that a charge will be made is enough. The threat may be bluntly spoken, or it may be thinly veiled in suggestive terms. 69 Ill. App. 399.

Threats in themselves are not indictable or actionable, but if a threat is accompanied by appearance of present ability and intention to carry out the threat, it is an assault (1 Ired. [N. C.] 125); and, if made with the purpose of extorting money it is a misdemeanor at common law (1 Hawk. [P. C.] c. 53, § 1). If business is interrupted, or freedom of locomotion is restrained, it is actionable. 27 Mich. 267.

THRENGES. Vassals, but not of the lowest degree; those who held lands of the chief lord.

THRITHING. A division consisting of three or four hundreds.

THUDE WEALD. A woodward, or person that looks after a wood.

THURINGIAN CODE. One of the "barbarian codes," as they are termed; supposed by Montesquieu to have been given by Theodoric, king of Austrasia, to the Thuringians, who were his subjects. Esprit des Lois, lib. 28, c. 1.

THWERTNICK. The custom of giving entertainments to a sheriff, etc., for three nights.

TICKET. A mere receipt, token or voucher adopted for convenience to show that the passenger has paid his fare from one place to another. It does not constitute the contract of carriage. Parol evidence of the contract is admissible. 161 Ill. 195; 149 Ill. 607; 162 Ill. 531.

TICKETS OF LEAVE. In English criminal law, licenses to be at large, which are granted to convicts for good conduct, but are recallable upon subsequent misconduct. See 6 & 7 Vict. c. 7; 16 & 17 Vict. c. 99, § 9; 20 & 21 Vict. c. 3, § 5; 27 & 28 Vict. c. 47, §§ 4-10; 34 & 35 Vict. c. 112; 4 Steph. Comm. (7th Ed.) 451, note.

TIDE. The ebb and flow of the sea.

The law takes notice of three kinds of tides, viz., the high spring tides, which are the fluxes of the sea at those tides which happen at the two equinoctials; the spring tides, which happen twice every month, at the full and change of the moon; the neap or ordinary tides, which happen between the full and change of the moon, twice in twenty-four hours. Angell, Tide Waters, 68. The changeable condition of the tides produces, of course, corresponding changes in the line of high-water mark. Now, inasmuch as the soil of all tidal waters up to the limit of high-water mark, at common law, is in the crown, or, in this country, in the state, it is important to ascertain what is high-water mark, in legal contemplation, considered as the boundary of the royal or public ownership. In an English case this ownership has been held to be limited by the average of the medium high tides between the spring and the neap in each quarter of a lunar revolution during the year, excluding only extraordinary catastrophes or overflows. 4 De Gex, M. & G. 206; 3 Barn. & Ald. 967; 5 Barn. & Ald. 268; 2 Doug. 629; 7 Pet. (U. S.) 324; 1 Pick. (Mass.) 180; 2 Johns. (N. Y.) 357. See "River."

TIDE WATER. Water which flows and reflows with the tide. All arms of the sea, bays, creeks, coves, or rivers, in which the tide ebbs and flows, are properly denominated "tide waters."

The term "tide water" is not limited to water which is salt, but embraces, also, so much of the water of fresh rivers as is propelled backwards by the ingress and pressure of the tide. 5 Coke, 107; 2 Doug. 441; 6 Clark & F. 628; 7 Pet. (U. S.) 324. The supreme court of the United States has decided that, although the current of the river Mississippi at New Orleans may be so strong as not to be turned backwards by the tide, yet if the effect of the tide upon the current is so great as to occasion a regular rise and fall of the water, it might properly be said to be within the ebb and flow of the tide. 7 Pet. (U. S.) 324. The flowing, however, of the waters of a lake into a river, and their reflowing, being caused by the occasional swell and subsidence of the lake, and not by the ebb and flow of regular tides, do not constitute such a river a tidal, or, technically, navigable, river. 20 Johns. (N. Y.) 98. And see 17 Johns. (N. Y.) 195; 2 Conn. 481; Woolr. Waters, c. ii.; Angell, Tide Waters, c. iii.

TIDESMAN. In English law, a tidewaiter or custom-house officer, who watches on board of merchant ships till the duty on goods be paid, and the ships unladen.

TIEL. An old manner of spelling *tel*; such as *nul tiel* record, no such record.

TIEMPO INHABIL (Spanish). In Louisiana. A time when a man is not able to pay his debts.

A man cannot dispose of his property, at such a time, to the prejudice of his creditors. 4 Mart. (La.; N. S.); 292; 3 Mart. (La.) 270; 10 Mart. (La.) 70.

TIERCE (Law Fr.; from Lat. *tertius*). Third. *Tierce mien,* third hand. Britt. c. 120.

TIGNI IMMITTENDI (Lat.) In civil law. A servitude which confers the right of inserting a beam or timber from the wall of one house into that of a neighboring house, in order that it may rest on the latter, and that the wall of the latter may bear this weight. Dig. 8. 2. 36; Dig. 8. 5. 14.

TIGNUM. In the civil law, any material for building.

TIHLER. In old Saxon law, an accusation.

TIMBER. As a generic term, it properly signifies only such trees as are used in building either ships or dwellings. 160 Mich. 186, 189. See "Timber Trees."

TIMBER TREES. Oak, ash, elm, and such other trees as are commonly used for building. 2 Bl. Comm. 28. But it has been contended, *arguendo,* that to make it timber, the trees must be felled and severed from the stock. 6 Mod. 23; Starkie, Slander, 79; 12 Johns. (N. Y.) 239. See "Waste."

TIMBERLODE. A service by which tenants were bound to carry timber felled from the woods to the lord's house. Cowell.

TIME DEPOSIT. A deposit for a fixed time, which is not usually subject to check. 271 Ill. 348.

TIME IMMEMORIAL. Time out of mind.

In England this is said to be before the beginning of the reign of Richard I. 2 Bl. Comm. 31.

TIME OUT OF MEMORY. See "Time Immemorial."

TIMORES VANI SUNT AESTIMANDI qui non cadunt in constantem virum. Fears which do not affect a brave man are vain. 7 Coke, 17.

TINBOUNDING. A custom regulating the manner in which tin is obtained from waste land, or land which has formerly been waste land, within certain districts in Cornwall and Devon. Bain. M. & M. 146 et seq. The custom is described in the leading case on the subject as follows: "Any person may enter on the waste land of another, and may mark out by four corner boundaries a certain area; a written description of the plot of land so marked out with metes and bounds, and the name of the person, is recorded in the local Stannaries court, and is proclaimed on three successive court days. If no objection is sustained by any other person, the court awards a writ to the bailiff to deliver possession of the said 'bounds of tinwork' to the 'bounder,' who thereupon has the exclusive right to search for, dig, and take for his own use all tin and tin ore within the enclosed limits, paying as a royalty to the owner of the waste a certain proportion of the produce under the name of 'toll tin.'" 10 Q. B. 26, cited in Elt. Comm. 113. The right of tinbounding is not a right of common (see "Common"), but is an interest in land, and, in Devonshire, a corporeal hereditament (Elt. Comm. 114). In Cornwall, tin bounds are personal estate. Bain. M. & M. 150. See "Stannary Courts."

TINEL LE ROY. The king's hall, wherein his servants used to dine and sup. 13 Rich. II. st. 1, c. 3.

TINEMAN, or **TIENMAN.** A petty officer in the forest, who had the care of vert and venison at night, and other servile duties. Cowell.

TINEWALD. The ancient parliament or annual convention of the people in the Isle of Man.

TINKERMEN. Fishermen who destroyed the young fry on the river Thames, by nets and unlawful engines. Cowell.

TINSEL OF THE FEU. The loss of an estate held in feu in Scotland, from allowing two years' feu duty to remain unpaid. Bell, Dict.

TIPPLING HOUSE. A place where spirituous liquors are sold and drunk in violation of law. Sometimes the mere selling is considered as evidence of keeping a tippling house.

TIPSTAFF. An officer appointed by the marshal of the court of king's bench to attend upon the judges with a kind of rod or staff tipped with silver.

In the United States, the courts sometimes appoint an officer who is known by this name, whose duty it is to wait on the court and serve its process.

TITHES. In English law. A right to the tenth part of the produce of lands, the stocks upon lands, and the personal industry of the inhabitants. These tithes are raised for the support of the clergy.

TITHING. In English law. Formerly, a district containing ten men, with their families. In each tithing there was a tithing-man, whose duty it was to keep the peace, as a constable now is bound to do. St. Armand, in his Historical Essay on the Legislative Power of England (page 70), expresses an opinion that the tithing was composed not of ten common families, but of ten families of lords of a manor.

TITHINGMAN. In Saxon law. The head or chief of a decennary of ten families. He was to decide all lesser causes between neighbors. Now tithingmen and constables are the same thing. Jacob.

In New England, a parish officer to keep good order in church. Webster.

TITIUS. A Roman name commonly used in the civil law in illustrating rules of example, or to designate a fictitious person, like the John Doe of English law.

TITLE. The means whereby the owner of lands hath the just possession of his property. Co. Litt. 345; 2 Bl. Comm. 195. See 1 Ohio, 349. This is the definition of title to lands only.

(1) A bad title is one which conveys no property to the purchaser of an estate.

(2) A doubtful title is one which the court does not consider to be so clear that it will enforce its acceptance by a purchaser, nor so defective as to declare it a bad title, but only subject to so much doubt that a purchaser ought not to be compelled to accept it. 1 Jac. & W. 568; 9 Cow. (N. Y.) 344.

(3) A good title is that which entitles a man by right to a property or estate, and to the lawful possession of the same.

(4) A marketable title is one which a court of equity considers to be so clear that it will enforce its acceptance by a purchaser.

The doctrine of marketable titles is purely equitable and of modern origin. Atkins, Titles, 26. At law every title not bad is marketable. 5 Taunt. 625; 6 Taunt. 263; 1 Marsh. 258. See 2 Pa. Law J. 17.

There are several stages or degrees requisite to form a complete title to lands and tenements. The lowest and most imperfect degree of title is the mere possession, or actual occupation of the estate, without any apparent right to hold or continue such possession. This happens when one man disseises another. The next step to a good and perfect title is the right of possession, which may reside in one man while the actual possession is not in himself, but in another. This right of possession is of two sorts,—an apparent right of possession, which may be defeated by proving a better, and an actual right of possession, which will stand the test against all opponents. The mere right of property, the *jus proprietatis*, without either possession or the right of possession. 2 Bl. Comm. 195.

Title to real estate is acquired by descent, by purchase, and by adverse possession.

Title to personal property may accrue in three different ways,—by original acquisition, by transfer by act of law, by transfer by act of the parties.

Title by original acquisition is acquired by occupancy (see "Occupancy"); by accession (see "Accession"); by intellectual labor (see "Literary Property").

The title to personal property is acquired and lost by transfer by act of law, in various ways,—by forfeiture, succession, marriage, judgment, insolvency, intestacy (*q. v.*)

Title is acquired and lost by transfer by the act of the party by gift, by contract, or sale.

——**In Legislation.** That part of an act of the legislature by which it is known and distinguished from other acts; the name of the act.

——**In Literature.** The particular division of a subject, as a law, a book, and the like; for example, Digest, book 1, title 2. The name of a newspaper, book, etc.

——**Personal Relations.** A distinctive appellation denoting the rank to which the individual belongs in society.

The constitution of the United States forbids the grant by the United States or any state of any title of nobility. Titles are bestowed by courtesy on certain officers. The president of the United States sometimes receives the title of "Excellency;" judges and members of congress, that of "Honorable;" and members of the bar and justices of the peace are called "Esquires." Cooper, Just. Inst. 416; Brackenridge, Law Misc.

Titles are assumed by foreign princes, and among their subjects they may exact these marks of honor; but in their intercourse with foreign nations they are not entitled to them as a matter of right. Wheaton, Int. Law, pt. 2, c. 3, § 6.

——**In Pleading.** The right of action which the plaintiff has. The declaration must show the plaintiff's title, and if such title be not shown in that instrument, the defect cannot be cured by any of the future pleadings. Bac. Abr. "Pleas, etc." (B 1).

——**In Practice.** That part of a pleading or other paper in a cause that states the names of the parties plaintiff and defendant thereto.

TITLE, COVENANTS FOR. They comprise "covenants for seisin, for right to convey, against incumbrances, for quiet enjoyment, sometimes for further assurance, and almost always of warranty." Rawle, Cov. § 21.

TITLE DEEDS. Those deeds which are evidences of the title of the owner of an estate.

The person who is entitled to the inheritance has a right to the possession of the title deeds. 1 Car. & M. 653.

TITULADA. In Spanish law. Title. White New Recop. bk. 1, tit. 5, c. 3, § 2.

TITULARS OF ERECTION. See "Lords of Erection."

TITULUS (Lat.)

—**IN the Civil Law.** Title; the source or ground of possession; the means whereby possession of a thing is acquired, whether such possession be lawful or not.

—**In Old Ecclesiastical Law.** A temple or church; the material edifice. So called because the priest in charge of it derived therefrom his name and title. Spelman.

TITULUS EST JUSTA CAUSA POSSIdendi id quod nostrum est. Title is a just cause of possessing that which is ours. 8 Coke, 153 (305); Co. Litt. 345b.

TITULUS EST JUSTA CAUSA POSSIdendi id quod nostrum est; dicitur a tuendo. A title is the just right of possessing that which is our own; it is so called from "*tuendo*," defending. 8 Coke, 153.

TO. "To" often has a meaning nearly synonymous with "towards," although its ordinary meaning is not satisfied unless the point or object is actually attained. 54 Mich. 87; 6 Ex. 205; 20 L. J. Ex. 146.

In expressing a boundary, is a term of exclusion, unless, by necessary implication, manifestly used in a different sense. Sumner's R. 178.

TO HAVE AND TO HOLD. The words in a conveyance which show the estate intended to be conveyed. 132 Ill. 605. Thus, in a conveyance of land in fee simple, the grant is to "A. and his heirs, to have and to hold the said (land) unto and to the use of the said A., his heirs and assigns, forever." See Williams, Real Prop. 198.

Strictly speaking, however, the words "to have" denote the estate to be taken, while the words "to hold" signify that it is to be held of some superior lord, *i. e.*, by way of tenure (*q. v.*) The former clause is called the "*habendum*," the latter, the "*tenendum*." Co. Litt. 6a.

TO WIT. That is to say, 99 Ill. 560; namely; *scilicet*; *videlicet*.

—**In Pleading.** In describing various articles in general terms, "to wit" is used to avoid a variance and a positive averment which must be strictly proved. 47 Ill. 177.

TOALIA. A towel. There is a tenure of lands by the service of waiting with a towel at the king's coronation. Cowell.

TOFT. A place or piece of ground on which a house formerly stood, which has been destroyed by accident or decay. It also signifies a messuage.

TOGATI (Lat.) In Roman law. Under the empire, when the *toga* had ceased to be the usual costume of the Romans, advocates were nevertheless obliged to wear it whenever they pleaded a cause. Hence they were called *togati*. This denomination received an official or legal sense in the imperial constitutions of the fifth and sixth centuries; and the words *togati*, *consortium* (*corpus*, *ordo*, *collegium*) *togatorum*, frequently occur in those acts.

TOKEN. A document or sign of the existence of a fact.

Tokens are either public or general, or privy tokens. They are either true or false. When a token is false, and indicates a general intent to defraud, and is used for that purpose, it will render the offender guilty of the crime of cheating (12 Johns. [N. Y.] 292); but if it is mere privy token, as, counterfeiting a letter in another man's name, in order to cheat but one individual, it would not be indictable (9 Wend. [N. Y.] 182; 1 Dall. [Pa.] 47; 2 Const. [S. C.] 139; 2 Va. Cas. 65; 4 Hawks [N. C.] 348; 6 Mass. 72; 12 Johns. [N. Y.] 293; 2 Dev. [N. C.] 199; 1 Rich. [S. C.] 244).

—**In Common Law.** In England, this name is given to pieces of metal, made in the shape of money, passing among private persons by consent at a certain value. 2 Chit. Com. Law, 182.

TOLERATION (Lat.) In some countries, where religion is established by law, certain sects who do not agree with the established religion are nevertheless permitted to exist; and this permission is called "toleration." They are permitted and allowed to remain rather as a matter of favor than a matter of right.

In the United States there is no such thing as toleration; all men have an equal right to worship God according to the dictates of their consciences.

"We sometimes hear it said that all religions are tolerated in Ohio, but the expression is not strictly accurate. It is not by mere toleration that every individual here is protected in his belief or disbelief. He reposes not on the leniency of government, or the liberality of any class or sect of men, but upon his natural indefeasible rights of conscience, which are beyond the the control or interference of any human authority." 2 Ohio St. 392.

TOLERATION ACT. St. 1 Wm. & Mary, st. 1, c. 18, confirmed by 10 Anne, c. 2, by which all persons dissenting from the Church of England (except Roman Catholics and persons denying the Trinity) were relieved from such of the acts against Nonconformists as prevented their assembling for religious worship according to their own forms, or otherwise restrained their religious liberty, on condition of their taking the oaths of allegiance and supremacy, and subscribing a declaration against transubstantiation; and in case of dissenting ministers, subscribing also to certain of the Thirty-nine Articles. The clause of this act which excepted persons denying the Trinity from the benefits of its enactments was repealed by 53 Geo. III. c. 160. 4 Broom & H. Comm. 67. The disqualifications of Roman Catholics have been since, for the most part, removed.

TOLL. Toll at common law includes a large class of dues and exactions that are in the nature of fixed rights, and cannot be lawfully exceeded, and are generally, if not universally, connected with some franchise which involves duties as well as privileges of a general or public nature, such as those which belong to fairs, markets, mills, turnpikes, ferries and bridges. 41 Mich. 279.

A sum of money for the use of something generally applied to the consideration which is paid for the use of a road, bridge, or the like, of a public nature.

The compensation paid to a miller for grinding another person's grain.

The rate of taking toll for grinding is regulated by statute in most of the states. See 2 Washb. Real Prop.; 6 Q. B. 31.

A Saxon word originally signifying a payment in towns, markets, or fairs for goods and cattle bought and sold there. It is now also popularly applied to the charges which canal and railroad companies require for the transportation of goods; but it does not necessarily import an immediate payment. The word means nothing more than a compensation for the privilege or service granted; and the period of payment depends, as in other cases, on the understanding of the parties.

Various definitions of the term collected, and the nature of tolls, considered. 29 Barb. (N. Y.) 589; 3 Abb. Ct. App. Dec. (N. Y.) 1 Keys (N. Y.) 72.

To bar, defeat, or take away; as, to toll an entry into lands is to deny or take away the right of entry. To toll the statute of limitations is to interrupt its running. See "Tolls."

TOLL BOOTH. A prison; a custom house; an exchange; also the place where goods are weighed.

TOLL DISH. A vessel by which the toll of corn for grinding is measure.

TOLL THOROUGH. In English law. A toll for passing through a public highway, or over a ferry or bridge. Cowell.

TOLL TRAVERSE. In English law. A toll for passing over private grounds. Cowell.

TOLL TURN. In English law. A toll on beasts returning from a market. 1 Crabb, Real Prop. p. 101, § 102. A toll paid at the return of beasts from fair or market, though they were not sold. Cowell.

TOLLS. In a general sense, tolls signify any manner of customs, subsidy, prestation, imposition, or sum of money demanded for exporting or importing of any wares or merchandise, to be taken of the buyer. 2 Inst. 58.

TOLLAGE. Payment of toll; money charged or paid as toll; the liberty or franchise of charging toll.

TOLLE VOLUNTATEM ET ERIT OMNIS actus indifferens. Take away the will, and every action will be indifferent. Bracton, fol. 2.

TOLLER, or TOLER (Law Fr. from Lat. *tollere, q. v.*) To take away; to bar or defeat. *Discents que tollent entries,* descents which toll or bar entries. Litt. § 385.

TOLLERE (Lat.) In the civil law. To lift up or raise; to elevate; to build up. See "Servitus Altius non Tollendi."

To take away; to dissolve or destroy. *Tollitur omnis obligatio solutione ejus quod debetur,* every obligation is dissolved by the payment of that which is due. Inst. 3. 30, pr. See Fleta, lib. 2, c. 60, § 5.

To put an end to an action. Calv. Lex. To quash, or annul a judgment. Id.; Spiegelius.

To bring up, or educate. Calv. Lex.; Adams, Rom. Ant. 51.

TOLNETUM, *Theolnetum.* Law Lat. In old English law. Toll.

A tax, charge or imposition.

TOLSESTER. An old excise; a duty paid by tenants of some manors to the lord for liberty to brew and sell ale. Cowell.

TOLSEY. The same as toll booth (*q. v.*) Also, a place where merchants meet; a local tribunal for small civil causes held at the Guildhall, Bristol.

TOLT. A writ whereby a cause depending in a court baron was taken and removed into a county court. Old Nat. Brev. 4.

TOLTA. Wrong; rapine; extortion. Cowell.

TONNAGE. The capacity of a ship or vessel; the duties paid on the tonnage of a ship.

This term is most usually applied to the capacity of a vessel in tons, as determined by the legal mode of measurement; and, as a general rule, in the United States, the official tonnage of a vessel is considerably below the actual capacity of the vessel to carry freight.

For the rule for determining the tonnage of British vessels under the law of England, see McCulloch, "Tonnage;" Eng. Merch. Shipp. Act 1854, §§ 20-29.

In the United States it is provided that the tonnage of a vessel shall be her entire internal cubic capacity in tons of one hundred cubic feet each, to be ascertained in the manner prescribed by the statute. Rev. St. U. S. § 4153.

TONNAGE RENT. When the rent reserved by a mining lease or the like consists of a royalty on every ton of minerals gotten in the mine, it is often called a "tonnage rent." There is generally a dead rent in addition. See "Rent."

TONNAGIUM (Law Lat.) In old English law. A custom or impost upon wines and other merchandise exported or imported, according to a certain rate per ton. Spelman; Cowell.

TONNETIGHT. In old English law. The quantity of a ton or tun, in a ship's freight or bulk, for which tonnage or tunnage was paid to the king. Pat. 2 Rich. II; Cowell.

TONODERACH. In old Scotch law. A thief taker (*qui fures exquirit*). LL. Ken. Reg. § 5; Spelman.

TONSURA (Lat. from *tondere,* to shave or clip). In old English law. A shaving or polling; the having the crown of the head shaven; tonsure. One of the peculiar badges of a clerk or clergyman. *Habitus et tonsura clericalis,* the clerical habit and tonsure without which no man originally could be admitted to the privilege of clergy. 2 Hale, P. C. 372; 4 Bl. Comm. 366; Nov. 5, c. 2.

TONTINE. In French law. The name of a partnership composed of creditors or recipients of perpetual or life rents or annuities, formed on the condition that the rents of those who may die shall accrue to the survivors, either in whole or in part.

This kind of partnership took its name from Tonti, an Italian, who first conceived the idea and put it in practice. Merlin, Repert.; Dalloz; 5 Watts (Pa.) 351.

TONTINE INSURANCE. A system of life insurance whereby the surplus funds of the insurer are accumulated during a period called the "tontine period," and then distributed to such of the policy holders as then survive. See 38 Hun (N. Y.) 309.

TOOK AND CARRIED AWAY. In criminal pleading. Technical words necessary in an indictment for simple larceny. Bac. Abr. "Indictment" (G 1); Comyn, Dig. "Indictment" (G 6); Cro. Car. 37; 1 Chit. Crim. Law, 244. See "Asportation."

TOOLS. Those implements which are commonly used by the hand of one man in some physical operation when applied or directed by hand, and are movable to accomplish such operation as distinguished from a machine operated by some motive power other than that of the hand. 156 Wis. 78. It has been held to include also the implements of a professional man. 17 Mich. 342.

The apparatus of a printing office, such as types, presses, etc., are not, therefore, included under the term "tools." 13 Mass. 82; 10 Pick. (Mass.) 423; 3 Vt. 133. And see 2 Pick. (Mass.) 80; 5 Mass. 313.

TORNADO. Tornado is synonymous with "hurricane" and means a violent storm.

A violent gust of wind or a tempest distinguished by the vehemence of the wind and by a whirling, progressive motion, usually accompanied by thunder, lightning, and torrents of rain, and commonly of short duration and small breadth. 151 Ia. 73, 77, Ann. Cas. 1913A, 266n.

TORT. (Fr. *tort;* from Lat. *torquere,* to twist, *tortus,* twisted, wrested aside). A private or civil wrong or injury; a wrong independent of contract. 1 Hilliard, Torts, 1.

The commission or omission of an act by one without right, whereby another receives some injury, directly or indirectly, in person, property, or reputation.

"The word 'tort' means nearly the same thing as the expression 'civil wrong.' It denotes an injury inflicted otherwise than by mere breach of contract; or, to be more nicely accurate, a tort is a disturbance of another in rights which the law has created, either in the absence of contract, or in consequence of a relation which a contract had established between the parties." Bish. Non-Cont. Law, § 4.

(1) Distinguished from breach of contract. As recognized by the law for the enforcement of rights and redress of injuries, torts may be distinguished from breach of contracts by these qualities: That parties jointly committing torts are severally liable without right to contribution from each other; that the death of either party destroys the right of action; that persons under personal disabilities to contract are liable for their torts; that attachment, arrest, and imprisonment are allowed on claims arising under contracts. 1 Hilliard, Torts, 3. A tort, however, may grow out of, or make part of, or be coincident with, a contract; as in the familiar case of a fraudulent sale or fraudulent recommendation of a third person. Indeed, the wrong of fraud almost necessarily implies an accompanying contract. In these cases, the law often allows the party injured an election of remedies; that is, he may proceed against the other party either as a debtor or contractor, or as a wrongdoer. 10 Hilliard, Torts, 28; 10 C. B. 83; 24 Conn. 392.

(2) Distinguished from crime. The distinction of public wrongs from private crimes, and misdemeanors from civil injuries, seems principally to consist in this, that private wrongs or civil injuries are

an infringement or privation of the civil rights which belong to individuals merely as individuals. "Public wrongs or crimes and misdemeanors are a breach and violation of the public rights and duties due to the whole community in its social aggregate capacity." 4 Bl. Comm. 5.

TORTFEASOR. A wrongdoer; one who commits or is guilty of a tort.

TORTURA LEGUM PESSIMA. The torture or wresting of laws is the worst kind of torture. 4 Bac. Works, 434.

TORTURE. Bodily pain or hurt inflicted with the object of compelling a disclosure of guilt or of knowledge in respect of a crime or its perpetrator. It was imposed by various means, and under sanction of law.

TOT. In old English practice. A word written by the foreign opposer or other officer opposite to a debt due the king, to denote that it was a good debt, which was hence said to be "totted." St. 42 Edw. III. c. 9.

TOTA CURIA (Law Lat.) In the old reports. The whole court.

TOTAL LOSS. In insurance. A total loss in marine insurance is either the absolute destruction of the insured subject by the direct action of the perils insured against, or a constructive—sometimes called "technical"—total loss, in which the assured is deprived of the possession of the subject, still subsisting *in specie*, or where there may be remnants of it or claims subsisting on account of it, and the assured, by the express terms or legal construction of the policy, has the right to recover its value from the underwriters, so far as, and at the rate at which, it is insured, on abandonment and assignment of the still subsisting subject or remnants or claims arising out of it. 2 Phil. Ins. c. xvii.; 2 Johns. (N. Y.) 286.

A constructive total loss may be by capture; seizure by unlawful violence; as, piracy (1 Phil. Ins. § 1106; 2 Eng. Law & Eq. 85); or damage to ship or goods over half of the value at the time and place of loss (2 Phil. Ins. § 1608; 1 Curt. [U. S.] 148; 9 Cush. [Mass.] 415; 5 Denio [N. Y.] 342; 6 Denio [N. Y.] 282; 19 Ala. [N. S.] 108; 1 Johns. Cas. [N. Y.] 141; 6 Johns. [N. Y.] 219); or loss of the voyage (2 Phil. Ins. §§ 1601, 1606, 1619; 4 Me. 431; 24 Miss. 461; 19 N. Y. 272; 1 Mart. [La.] 221); though the ship or goods may survive *in specie*, but so as not to be fit for use in the same character for the same service or purpose (2 Phil. Ins. § 1605; 2 Caines, Cas. [N. Y.] 324; Valin, tom. 2 tit. Ass. a. 46); or by jettison (2 Phil. Ins. §§ 1616, 1617; 1 Caines [N. Y.] 196); or by necessity to sell on account of the action and effect of the peril insured against (2 Phil. Ins. § 1623; 5 Gray [Mass.] 154; 1 Cranch [U. S.] 202); or by loss of insured freight consequent on the loss of cargo or ship (2 Phil. Ins. §§ 1642, 1645; 18 Johns. [N. Y.] 208).

There may be a claim for a total loss in addition to a partial loss. 2 Phil. Ins. § 1743; 17 How. (U. S.) 595. A total loss of the ship is not necessarily such of cargo (2 Phil. Ins. §§ 1601 et seq., 1622; 3 Bin. [Pa.] 287); nor is submersion necessarily a total loss (2 Phil. Ins. § 1607; 7 East, 38); nor is temporary delay of the voyage (2 Phil. Ins. §§ 1618, 1619; 5 Barn. & Ald. 597).

A constructive total loss, and an abandonment thereupon of the ship, is a constructive total loss of freight; and a constructive total loss and abandonment of cargo has a like effect as to commissions or profits thereon; and the validity of the abandonment will depend upon the actual facts at the time of the abandonment, as the same may subsequently prove to have been. 2 Phil. Ins. § 1630 et seq.; 3 Johns. Cas. (N. Y.) 93.

TOTIDEM VERBIS (Lat.) In so many words.

TOTIES QUOTIES (Lat.) As often as the thing shall happen.

TOTIS VIRIBUS (Lat.) With all one's might or power; with all his might; very strenuously.

TOTUM PRAEFERTUR UNICUIQUE parte. The whole is preferable to any single part. 3 Coke, 41a.

TOUCH AND STAY. Words frequently introduced in policies of insurance, giving the party insured the right to stop and stay at certain designated points in the course of the voyage. A vessel which has the power to touch and stay at a place in the course of the voyage must confine herself strictly to the terms of the liberty so given; for any attempt to trade at such a port during such a stay, as, by shipping or landing goods, will amount to a species of deviation which will discharge the underwriters, unless the ship have also liberty to trade as well as to touch and stay at such a place. 1 Marsh. Ins. 275; 1 Esp. 610; 5 Esp. 96.

TOUJOURS ET UNCORE PRIST (Law Fr. always and still ready). This is the name of a plea of tender; as, where a man is indebted to another, and he tenders the amount due, and afterwards the creditor brings a suit, the defendant may plead the tender, and add that he has always been and is still ready to pay what he owes, which may be done by the formula *toujours et uncore prist*. He must then pay the money into court; and if the issue be found for him, the defendant will be exonerated from costs, and the plaintiff made justly liable for them. 3 Bouv. Inst. note 2923. See "Tout Temps Prist."

TOUR D'ECHELLE. In French law. A right which the owner of an estate has of placing ladders on his neighbor's property to facilitate the reparation of a party wall, or of buildings which are supported by that wall. It is a species of servitude. Lois des Bat. pt. 1, c. 3, sec. 2, art. 9, § 1.

The space of ground left unoccupied around a building for the purpose of enabling the owner to repair it with convenience. This is not a servitude, but an actual corporeal property.

TOURN. In old English law. A court of record, having criminal jurisdiction, in each county, held before the sheriff twice a year, in one place after another, following a certain circuit or rotation.

TOUT (Fr.) All.

TOUT CE QUE LA LOI NE DEFEND pas est permis. Everything is permitted which is not forbidden by law.

TOUT TEMPS PRIST (Law Fr. always ready). In pleading. A plea by which the defendant signifies that he has always been ready to perform what is required of him. The object of the plea is to save costs; as, for example, where there has been a tender and refusal. 3 Bl. Comm. 303; Comyn, Dig. "Pleader" (2 Y 5). So, in a writ of dower, where the plea is detinue of charters, the demandant might reply, "Always ready." Rast. Entr. 229b; Stearns, Real Actions, 310. See "Uncore Prist."

TOUT UN SOUND (Law Fr.) All one sound; *idem sonans*.

TOUTE EXCEPTION NON SURVEILLEE tend a prendre la place du principe. Every exception not watched tends to assume the place of the principle.

TOWARDS. In a course of line leading to or in the direction of. 180 Mich. 654.

TOWN.

——In General. The word "town" sometimes indicates a division of the county next smaller in extent than the county itself. It is also often used to denote a small city or village. 125 Ga. 559; 54 S. E. 539. The word may be and frequently is used as meaning "township" and vice versa. 244 Ill. 554; 82 Ill. 121. See "Township."

——Organization, Purpose and Government. In the New England states, the town is for many purposes the unit of civil government. In other states, the county is the unit, and the town has local government in only a few matters. Generally they are mere political organizations created wholly by statute for certain purposes of local government. They are vested with no franchises or special privileges for their own benefit, have only such powers as the statute confers, and are subject to no obligations, except such as are derived from statutory provisions. 161 Mich. 571, 576.

——In English Law. The term "town" or "vill" comprehends under it the several species of cities, boroughs, and common towns. 1 Bl. Comm. 114.

TOWN CLERK. An officer who manages the public business of a town.

TOWN COLLECTOR. An officer of a town charged with collecting the township taxes.

TOWN COMMISSIONER. One of the board of officers in whom, under the laws of some of the states, the management of the business of a town is vested. Abbott.

TOWN CRIER. An officer in a town whose business it is to make proclamations.

TOWN MEETING. An assemblage of the voters of a town to select town officers and discuss other business of the town.

TOWN PLAT. The acknowledgment and recording of a town plat vests the legal title to the ground embraced in the streets and alleys in the corporation of the town. Therefore it is held that the proprietor who has thus dedicated the streets and alleys to the public cannot maintain trespass for an injury to the soil or freehold. The corporation alone can seek redress for such injury. 11 Ill. 554; 13 Ill. 54, 308. This is not so, however, with a highway. The original owner of the fee must bring his action for an injury to the soil. 13 Ill. 54. See "Highway." If the streets or alleys of a town are dedicated by a different mode from that pointed out by the statute, the fee remains in the proprietor, burdened with the public easement. 13 Ill. 312.

TOWN REEVE. The reeve or chief officer of a town.

TOWN TAX. One levied to meet the separate expenses of a town. Opposed to "state tax," "county tax."

TOWNS IMPROVEMENT. The English Towns Improvement Clauses Act of 1847 was passed to consolidate in one act certain provisions usually contained in acts for paving, draining, cleansing, lighting, and improving towns. Local acts appointing commissioners for the improvement of towns generally incorporate the provisions of this act, but such acts are now rarely passed, as the provisions of the general health acts, the local government acts, the sanitary acts, and the public health acts have practically superseded them.

TOWNSHIP. The public lands of the United States are surveyed first into tracts called "townships," being in extent six miles square. The subdivisions of a township are called "sections," each a mile square, and containing six hundred and forty acres. These are subdivided into quarter sections, and from that into lots of forty acres each. This plan of subdividing the public lands was adopted by Act Cong. May 18, 1796. See Brightly, Dig. U. S. Laws, 493.

In some states the largest subdivision of a county. See "Town."

TRA. In old practice. The caret mark made to show where a clause or word left out, and interlined in writing, should come in. 1 Instr. Cler. 20.

TRABES (Lat.) In the civil law. A beam or rafter of a house. Calv. Lex.

In old English law. A measure of grain, containing twenty-four sheaves, a thrave. Spelman.

TRACEA. In old English law. The track or trace of a felon, by which he was pursued with the hue and cry; a footstep, hoof print, or wheel track. Bracton, fols. 116, 121b.

TRACT. An area, or a region of land or water of indefinite extent. 70 Ill. App. 44.

TRACTENT FABRILIA FABRI. Let smiths perform the work of smiths. 3 Coke, Epist.

TRADAS IN BALLIUM. You deliver to bail. In old English practice. The name of a writ which might be issued in behalf of a party who, upon the writ *de odio et atia*, had been found to have been maliciously accused of a crime, commanding the sheriff that, if the prisoner found twelve good and lawful men of the county who would be mainpernors for him, he should deliver him in bail to those twelve, until the next assize. Bracton, fol. 123; 1 Reeve, Hist. Eng. Law, 252.

TRADE. The original meaning of the word "trade" was "track" or "course," hence "trade-wind." In modern use it is employed in three different senses: (1) An occupation; a handicraft by which one earns a livelihood; mechanical employment in contradistinction to agriculture and the liberal arts. Ann. Cas. 1916A 1197; 86 Tex. 250; 22 L. R. A. 490; (2) Sale or exchange of merchandise or other property; a mercantile business, as opposed to the liberal arts or professions, 230 Ill. 236; and (3) a broader and more extended meaning synonymous with "commerce." 142 Ga. 267; Ann. Cas. 1916A 1197.

TRADE-MARK. A symbol, emblem, or mark used by a person to indicate that the article to which it is affixed is manufactured or sold by him, or that he carries on business at a particular place. 35 L. J. Ch. 61.

Its original use was by manufacturers, but its use has been extended to other than tradesmen, to indicate the nature of their business, their identity, or the place where their business is carried on. Slater, Trade-Marks, 232; 55 Barb. (N. Y.) 151; 7 Cush. (Mass.) 322; 2 Barb. Ch. (N. Y.) 101.

The office of a trade-mark is to indicate the origin, ownership, nature, etc., of goods manufactured or sold, or the person by whom, or the place where, they are so manufactured or sold. The essentials, therefore, of a good trade-mark, are that it be truthful in its express or implied statements, and that it be incapable of truthful application to other goods. 57 How. Pr. (N. Y.) 1; 39 Conn. 450.

Descriptive words, or words indicating quality or attributes, which may be truthfully applied by others to the same class of goods, cannot constitute a valid trade-mark. 136 Ill. 215; 67 Ga. 562.

Arbitrary or fanciful names, constituting the majority of trade-marks, derive their value from the fact that they have come to identify the goods of the user, and cannot, therefore, be truthfully used by others. 51 Fed. 829; 63 Hun (N. Y.) 330.

TRADE-MARKS REGISTRATION ACT 1875. St. 38 & 39 Vict. c. 91, amended by the acts of 1876 and 1877. It provides for the establishment of a register of trade-marks under the superintendence of the commissioners of patents, and for the registration of trade-marks as belonging to particular classes of goods, and for their assignment in connection with the good-will of the business in which they are used. Registration is substituted for public use as the mode of acquiring the right to a trade-mark, so that now no one can enforce his right to a trade-mark until it is registered. For the purposes of the act, a trade-mark consists (1) of a name of an individual or firm printed, impressed, or woven in some particular and distinctive manner; (2) of a written signature or copy of a written signature of an individual or firm; or (3) of a distinctive device, mark, heading, label or ticket. See 3 Ch. Div. 659. There may be added to any one or more of these essential particulars any letters, words, or figures. Certain kinds of marks used as trade-marks before the passing of the act may be registered under the act, although not coming within the statutory definition. See generally, as to the act, Sebastian, Trade-Marks; 4 App. Cas. 479; 15 Ch. Div. 181.

TRADE-NAME. A trade-name is a name which by user and reputation has acquired the property of indicating that a certain trade or occupation is carried on by a particular person. The name may be that of a person, place, or thing, or it may be what is called a "fancy name" (*i. e.*, a name having no sense, as applied to the particular trade), or word invented for the occasion, and having no sense at all. Seb. Trade-Marks, 37.

TRADE UNION. An association of workmen, usually, but not necessarily, employed in the same trade, for the purpose of combined action in securing the most favorable wages and conditions of labor. Popularly abbreviated to "union."

TRADE USAGE. A usage connected with the practice of a particular trade.

TRADER. One who makes it his business to buy merchandise, or goods and chattels, and to sell the same for the purpose of making a profit. The quantum of dealing is immaterial, when an intention to deal generally exists. 3 Starkie, 56; 2 Car. & P. 135; 1 Term R. 572.

A farmer who, in addition to his usual business, occasionally buys a horse not calculated for his usual occupation, and sells him again to make a profit, and who, in the course of two years, had so bought and sold five or six horses, two of which had been sold, after he had bought them, for the sake of a guinea profit, was held to be a trader. 1 Term R. 537, note; 1 Price, 20. Another farmer, who bought a large quantity of potatoes, not to be used on his farm, but merely to sell again for a profit, was also declared to be a trader. 1 Strange, 513. See 7 Taunt. 409; 5 Bos. & P. 78; 11 East, 274.

A butcher who kills only such cattle as he has reared himself is not a trader; but if he buy them and kill and sell them with a view to profit, he is a trader. 4 Burrows, 21, 47. See 2 Rose, 38; 3 Campb. 233; Cooke, Bankr. Law, 48, 73; 2 Wils. 169; 1 Atk. 128; Cowp. 745.

A brickmaker who follows the business for the purpose of enjoying the profits of his real estate merely is not a trader; but when he buys the earth by the load or otherwise, and manufactures it into bricks, and sells them with a view to profit, he is a trader. Cooke, Bankr. Law, 52, 63; 7 East, 442; 3 Car. & P. 500; Moody & M. 263; 2 Rose, 422; 2 Glyn & J. 183; 1 Brown, Ch. 173.

For further examples the reader is referred to 4 Man. & R. 486; 9 Barn. & C. 577; 1 Term R. 34; 1 Rose, 316; 2 Taunt. 178; 2 Marsh. 236; 3 Moore & S. 761; 10 Bing. 292; Peake, 76; 1 Vent. 270; 3 Brod. & B. 2; 6 Moore, 56.

TRADICION (Spanish). In Spanish law. Delivery. White, New Recop. bk. 2, tit. 2, c. 9.

TRADING CORPORATIONS. Such corporations as are engaged in trading or trading and commerce, including all corporations engaged in a business which properly falls within the definition of trading. Fletcher Cyclopedia Corporations 121. See Trade.

TRADING VALUE. A rather vague and variable standard, meaning such value as an ingenious and energetic puffing would lead the buyer to believe he could realize from the stuff in his next deal. 233 Ill. 453.

TRADITIO (Lat.)

——**In the Civil Law.** Delivery; transfer of possession; a giving possession of a corporeal thing; a derivative mode of acquiring, by which the owner of a corporeal thing, having the right and the will of aliening it, transfers it for a lawful consideration to the receiver. Heinec. Elem. Jur. Civ. lib. 2, tit. 1, § 380.

——**In Old English Law.** Delivery or livery.

TRADITIO BREVIS MANUS (Lat.) In civil law. The delivery of a thing by the mere consent of the parties; as, when Peter holds the property of Paul as bailee, and afterwards he buys it, it is not necessary that Paul should deliver the property to Peter, and he should redeliver it to Paul. The mere consent of the parties transfers the title to Paul. 1 Duv. note 252; 21 Me. 231; Poth. ad Pand. lib. 50, cdlxxiv.; 1 Bouv. Inst. note 944.

TRADITIO CLAVIUM (Lat.) In the civil law. Delivery of keys; a symbolical kind of delivery, by which the ownership of merchandise in a warehouse might be transferred to a buyer. Inst. 2. 1. 44.

TRADITIO LOQUI FACIT CHARTAM. Delivery makes the deed speak. 5 Coke, 1.

TRADITIO NIHIL AMPLIUS TRANSferre debet vel potest, ad eum qui accipit, quam est apud eum qui tradit. Delivery cannot and ought not to transfer to him who receives more than was in possession of him who made the delivery. Dig. 41. 1. 20.

TRADITIO REI (Lat.) Delivery of the thing. See 5 Maule & S. 82.

TRADITION (Lat. *trans*, over, *do*, *dare*, to give). In civil law. The act by which a thing is delivered by one or more persons to one or more others.

The delivery of possession by the proprietor with an intention to transfer the property to the receiver. Two things are, therefore, requisite in order to transmit property in this way,—the intention or consent of the former owner to transfer it, and the actual delivery in pursuance of that intention.

Tradition is either real or symbolical. Real tradition takes place where the *ipsa corpora* of movables are put into the hands of the receiver. Symbolical tradition is used where the thing is incapable of real delivery, as, in immovable subjects, such as lands and houses, or such as consist *in jure* (things incorporeal), as, things of fishing, and the like. The property of certain movables, though they are capable of real delivery, may be transferred by symbol. Thus, if the subject be under lock and key, the delivery of the key is considered as a legal tradition of all that is contained in the repository. Cujas, Observations, liv. 11, c. 10; Inst. 2. 1. 40; Dig.

41. 1. 9; Ersk. Inst. 2. 1. 10. 11; Civ. Code La. art. 2452 et seq. See "Delivery"

TRADITOR (Law Lat.) In old English law. A traitor; one guilty of high treason. Fleta, lib. 1, c. 21, § 8.

TRADITOR IN BALLIUM (Law Lat.) In old practice. Is delivered to bail. Emphatic words of the old Latin bail piece. 1 Salk. 105.

TRAFFIC. Commerce; trade; sale or exchange of merchandise, bills, money, and the like.

TRAINBANDS. The militia; the part of a company trained to martial exercises.

TRAISTIS. In old Scotch law. A roll containing the particular dittay taken up upon malefactors, which, with the porteous, is delivered by the justice clerk to the coroner, to the effect that the persons whose names are contained in the porteous may be attached, conform to the dittay contained in the traistis. So called because committed to the traist [trust], faith, and credit of the clerks and coroner. Skene de Verb. Sign.

TRAITOR. One guilty of treason. See charge of Judge Sprague, District Court of Massachusetts, 1682; Bish. Crimes.

The punishment of a traitor is death.

TRAITOROUSLY. In pleading. A technical word, which is essential in an indictment for treason in order to charge the crime, and which cannot be supplied by any other word or any kind of circumlocution. Having been well laid in the statement of the treason itself, it is not necessary to state every overt act to have been traitorously committed. See Bac. Abr. "Indictment" (G 1); Comyn, Dig. "Indictment" (G 6); Hawk. P. C. bk. 2, c. 25, § 55; 1 East, P. C. 115; 2 Hale, P. C. 172, 184; 4 Bl. Comm. 307; 3 Inst. 15; Cro. Car. 37; Carth. 319; 2 Salk. 683; 4 Harg. St. Tr. 701; 2 Ld. Raym. 870; Comb. 259; 2 Chit. Crim. Law, 104 note (b).

TRANSACTIO (Lat.) In the civil law. The settlement of a suit or matter in controversy, by the litigating parties, between themselves, without referring it to arbitration. Halifax, Civ. Law, bk. 3, c. 8, No. 14. An agreement by which a suit, either pending or about to be commenced, was forborne, or discontinued on certain terms. Calv. Lex. See Dig. 2. 15; Fleta, lib. 4, c. 17, § 2.

TRANSACTION (from Lat. *trans* and *ago*, to carry over). Whatever may be done by one person which affects another's rights and out of which cause of action may arise. 151 Wis. 266, 271; 143 Wis. 564, 572, 128 N. W. 445; the doing or the performing of any affair, management of any matter; as the transaction of business; that which is done or in the process of being done; an affair. 149 Ia. 645, 650.

——**In civil law.** An agreement between two or more persons, who, for the purpose of preventing or putting an end to a lawsuit, adjust their difference, by mutual consent, in the manner which they agree on. In Louisiana this contract must be reduced to writing. Civ. Code La. art. 3038.

Transactions regulate only the differences which appear to be clearly comprehended in them by the intentions of the parties, whether they be explained in a general or particular manner, unless it be the necessary consequence of what is expressed; and they do not extend to differences which the parties never intended to include in them. Civ. Code La. art. 3040.

To transact, a man must have the capacity to dispose of the things included in the transaction. 1 Domit, Lois Civ. 1. 13. 1; Dig. 2. 15. 1; Code, 2. 4. 41. In the common law, this is called a compromise. See "Compromise."

TRANSCRIPT (Lat.) A copy of an original writing, deed, or record.

——**In Appellate Practice.** The copy of the record transmitted to the appellate court.

TRANSCRIPTIO PEDIS FINIS LEVATI mittendo in cancellarium. A writ which certified the foot of a fine levied before justices in eyre, etc., into the chancery. Reg. Orig. 669.

TRANSCRIPTIO RECOGNITIONIS FACTAE coram justiciariis itinerantibus, etc. An old writ to certify a cognizance taken by justices in eyre. Reg. Orig. 152.

TRANSFER (Lat. *trans*, over, *fero*, to bear or carry). The act by which the owner of a thing delivers it to another person, with the intent of passing the rights which he has in it to the latter. 1 Ala. 669; 36 Conn. 426.

TRANSFER OF A CAUSE. Removal of it to another court.

TRANSFERABLE. Capable of being passed to another. Railway passage tickets and personal privileges or licenses are often made "Not Transferable," *i. e.*, valid only in the purchaser's hands.

TRANSFEREE. He to whom a transfer is made.

TRANSFERENCE. In Scotch law. The name of an action by which a suit which was pending at the time the party died is transferred from the deceased to his representatives, in the condition in which it stood formerly. If it be the pursuer who is dead, the action is called a transference active; if the defender, it is a transference passive. Ersk. Inst. 4. 1. 32.

TRANSFEROR. One who makes a transfer.

TRANSFERUNTUR DOMINIA SINE TITulo et traditione, per usucaptionem, scil, per longam continuam et pacificam possessionem. Rights of dominion are transferred without title or delivery, by usucaption, to wit, long and quiet possession. Co. Litt. 113.

TRANSFRETATIO. (Lat.) In old English law. A crossing of the Strait (of Dover); a passing or sailing over from England to France.

TRANSGRESSIO EST CUM MODUS NON servatur nec mensura, debit enim quilibet in suo facto modum habere et mensuram. Transgression is when neither mode nor measure is preserved, for every one in his act ought to have a mode and measure. Co. Litt. 37.

TRANSGRESSION (Lat. *trans*, over, *gressio*, a step). The violation of a law.

TRANSGRESSIONE MULTIPLICATA, crescat poena inflictio. When transgression is multiplied, let the infliction of punishment be increased. 2 Inst. 479.

TRANSHIPMENT. In maritime law. The act of taking the cargo out of one ship, and loading it in another.

When this is done from necessity, it does not affect the liability of an insurer on the goods. 1 Marsh. Ins. 166; Abb. Shipp. 240. But when the master tranships goods without necessity, he is answerable for the loss of them by capture by public enemies. 1 Gall. (U. S.) 443.

TRANSIENT MERCHANT. The term has reference rather to the character of the business than to the residence of the merchant. 151 Iowa 221, 226.

In an ordinance exacting a license from that class of persons, a transient merchant, trader, dealer, or vendor is one who, for a short space of time locates at a place, 119 Wis. 224; or who carries or transports his goods from house to house or place to place, and makes sales and deliveries of his wares as do other merchants or salesmen. 38 Ill. App. 361; or one who conducts a mercantile business from a fixed place of business temporarily maintained in a community; 171 Iowa 678, Ann. Cas. 1917E, 505; 159 Ill. 295, as distinguished from hawkers, peddlers, or salesmen or agents who merely solicit orders for the goods of their principals. 119 Wis. 244; 159 Ill. 295.

TRANSIRE. In English law. A warrant for the custom house to let goods pass; a permit. See, for a form of a transire, Harg. Law Tr. 104.

TRANSIT IN REM JUDICATAM. It passes into a judgment. Broom, Leg. Max. (3d London Ed.) 298; 11 Pet. (U. S.) 100. See, also, 18 Johns. (N. Y.) 463; 2 Sumn. (U. S.) 436; 6 East, 251.

TRANSIT TERRA CUM ONERE. The land passes with its burden. Co. Litt. 231a; Shep. Touch. 178; 5 Barn. & C. 607; 7 Mees. & W. 530; 3 Barn. & Ald. 587; 18 C. B. 845; 24 Barb. (N. Y.) 365; Broom, Leg. Max. (3d London Ed.) 437, 630.

TRANSITIVE COVENANT. One binding the representatives of the covenantor.

TRANSITORY ACTION. In practice. An action the cause of which might have arisen in one place or county as well as another.

In general, all personal actions, whether *ex contractu* (5 Taunt. 25; 6 East, 352; 2 Johns. Cas. [N. Y.] 335; 3 Caines [N. Y.] 374; 3 Serg. & R. [Pa.] 500; 1 Chit. Pl. 243), or *ex delicto* (1 Chit. Pl. 243), are transitory.

Such action might, at common law, be brought in any county, but in the United States statutes have been passed prescribing in what counties the suit may be brought.

TRANSITUS (Lat.) A transit. See "Stoppage in Transitu."

TRANSLADO (Spanish). A transcript.

TRANSLATION. The reproduction in one language of what has been written or spoken in another.

In pleading, when a libel or an agreement written in a foreign language must be averred, it is necessary that a translation of it should also be given.

In evidence, when a witness is unable to speak the English language so as to convey his ideas, a translation of his testimony must be made. In that case, an interpreter should be sworn to translate to him, on oath, the questions propounded to him, and to translate to the court and jury.

The bestowing of a legacy which had been given to one, on another. This is a species of ademption; but it differs from it in this, that there may be an ademption without a translation, but there can be no translation without an ademption. Bac. Abr. "Legacies" (C).

The transfer of property; but in this sense it is seldom used. 2 Bl. Comm. 294. See "Interpreter."

——**In Ecclesiastical Law.** The removal from one place to another; as, the bishop was translated from the diocese of A. to that of B. in the civil law, "translation" signifies the transfer of property. Clef des Lois Rom.

TRANSLATITIUM EDICTUM. So much of the edict promulgated by the former praetor as was retained and republished by his successor.

TRANSLATIVE FACT. A fact by means of which a right is transferred or passes from one person to another.

TRANSMISSION (from Lat. *trans*, over, *mitto*, to send). In civil law. The right which heirs or legatees may have of passing to their successors the inheritance or legacy to which they were entitled, if they happen to die without having exercised their rights. Domat. liv. 3, tit. 1, § 10; 4 Toullier, Dr. Civ. note 186; Dig. 50. 17. 54; Code, 6. 51.

TRANSPORTATION (from Lat. *trans*, over, beyond, *porto* to carry). In English law. A punishment inflicted by virtue of sundry statutes. It was unknown to the common law. 2 H. Bl. 223. It is a part of the judgment or sentence of the court that the party shall be transported or sent into exile. 1 Chit. Crim. Law, 789-796; Princ. Pen. Law, a. 4, § 2.

TRANSUMPTS. In the Scotch law, an action of transumpt is an action competent to any one having a partial interest in a writing, or immediate use for it, to support his title or defenses in other actions. It is directed against the custodier of the writing, calling upon him to exhibit it, in order that a transumpt, *i. e.*, a copy, may be judicially made and delivered to the pursuer. Bell, Dict.

TRASSATUS. One who is drawn, or drawn upon. The drawee of a bill of exchange. Heinec. de Camb. c. 6, §§ 5, 6.

TRAVAIL. The act of child bearing.

A woman is said to be in her travail from the time the pains of child bearing commence, until her delivery. 5 Pick. (Mass.) 63; 6 Me. 460.

TRAVERSE (Law Fr. *traverser*, to turn over, to deny). To deny; to put off.

——**In Civil Pleading.** To deny or controvert anything which is alleged in the previous pleading. Lawes, Pl. 116. A denial. Willes, 224. A direct denial in formal words: "Without this, that, etc." (*absque hoc*). 1 Chit. Pl. 523, note (a). A traverse may deny all the facts alleged (1 Chit. Pl. 525), or any particular material fact (20 Johns. [N. Y.] 406).

(1) A common traverse is a direct denial, in common language, of the adverse allegations, without the *absque hoc*, and concluding to the country. It is not preceded by an inducement, and hence cannot be used where an inducement is requisite. 1 Saund. 103b, note 1.

(2) A general traverse is one preceded by a general inducement, and denying all that is last before alleged on the opposite side, in general terms, instead of pursuing the words of the allegation which it denies. Gould, Pl. vii. 5, 6. Of this sort of traverse the replication *de injuria sua propria absque tali causa*, in answer to a justification, is a familiar example. Bac. Abr. "Pleas" (H 1); Steph. Pl. 171; Gould, Pl. c. 7, § 5; Archb. Civ. Pl. 194.

(3) A special traverse is one which commences with the words *absque hoc*, and pursues the material portion of the words of the allegation which it denies. Lawes, Pl. 116-120. It is regularly preceded by an inducement consisting of new matter. Gould, Pl. c. 7, §§ 6, 7; Steph. Pl. 188. A special traverse does not complete an issue, as does a common traverse. 20 Viner, Abr. 339; Yelv. 147, 148; 1 Saund. 22, note 2.

(4) A traverse upon a traverse is one growing out of the same point or subject matter as is embraced in a preceding traverse on the other side. Gould, Pl. c. 7, § 42, note. It is a general rule that a traverse well intended on one side must be accepted on the other. And hence it follows, as a general rule, that there cannot be a traverse upon a traverse if the first traverse is material. The meaning of the rule is that, when one party has tendered a material traverse, the other cannot leave it and tender another of his own to the same point upon the inducement of the first traverse, but must join in that first tendered; otherwise the parties might alternately tender traverses to each other in unlimited succession, without coming to an issue. Gould, Pl. c. 7, § 42. The rule, however, does not apply where the first traverse is immaterial, nor where it is material if the plaintiff would thereby be ousted of some right or liberty which the law allows. Poph. 101; F. Moore, 350; Hob. 104; Cro. Eliz. 99, 418; Comyn, Dig. "Pleader" (G 18); Bac. Abr. "Pleas" (H 4); Bouv. Inst. Index.

——**In Criminal Practice.** To put off or delay the trial of an indictment till a succeeding term. More properly, to deny or take issue upon an indictment. Dick. Sess. 151; 4 Bl. Comm. 351.

TRAVERSE JURY. A petit or trial jury.

TRAVERSE OF AN OFFICE. Proof that an inquisition made of lands or goods by the escheator is defective and untruly made.

TRAVERSER. One who traverses or denies.

TRAVERSING ANSWER or **TRAVERSING NOTE.** In suits under the old English practice in chancery, where the defendant refused or neglected to file an answer to the bill, the plaintiff might file either a traversing answer or a traversing note, which produced the same effect as if the defendant had filed an answer traversing the case made by the bill. Daniell, Ch. Prac. 436. The modern practice dispenses with these fictions. See Rules of Court xxix. passim. See, also, "Pro Confesso."

TREACHER, TRECHETOUR, or **treachour.** A traitor.

TREADMILL. An instrument of prison discipline in England. It is composed of a large revolving cylinder, having ledges or steps fixed around its circumference. The prisoners walk up these ledges, and their weight moves the cylinder around.

TREASON.

——**At Common Law.** This word imports a betraying, treachery, or breach of allegiance. 4 Bl. Comm. 75.

Treason was either:

(1) High treason, which was the compassing of the king's death, the aiding and comforting of his enemies, the forging or counterfeiting of his coin, the counterfeiting of the privy seal, or the killing of the chancellor, or either of the king's justices.

(2) Petit treason, which was where a wife murdered her husband, a servant his master, or an ecclesiastic his lord or ordinary. 4 Bl. Comm. 73.

——**In the United States.** The constitution of the United States (article 3, § 3) defines treason against the United States to consist only in levying war against them, or in adhering to their enemies, giving them aid or comfort. This offense is punished with death. Act April 30, 1790 (1 Story, U. S. Laws, 83). By the same article of the constitution, no person shall be convicted of treason unless on the testimony of two witnesses to the same overt act, or on confession in open court. See, generally, 3 Story, Const. 39, p. 667; 1 Bl. Comm. Append. 275, 276; 3 Wilson, Law Lect. 96-99; Foster, Disc. (I); Fed. Cas. No. 14, 692; 4 Cranch (U. S.) 126; 469-508; 1 Dall. (U. S.) 35; 2 Dall. (U. S.) 246, 355; 3 Wash. C. C. (U. S.) 234; 1 Johns. (N. Y.) 553; 11 Johns. (N. Y.) 549; Comyn, Dig. "Justices" (K); 1 East, P. C. 37-158; 2 Chit. Crim. Law, 60-102; Archb. Crim. Pl. 378-387.

TREASON FELONY. An offense under 11 & 12 Vict. c. 12, consisting of compassing, etc., to depose her majesty, or to levy war to intimidate parliament, etc. Mozley & W.

TREASONABLE. Having the nature or guilt of treason.

TREASURE TROVE. Found treasure. This name is given to such money or coin, gold, silver, plate, or bullion, which, having been hidden or concealed in the earth or other private place so long that its owner is unknown, has been discovered by accident. Should the owner be found, it must be restored to him; and in case of not finding him, the property, according to the English law, belongs to the king. In the latter case, by the civil law, when the treasure was found by the owner of the soil, he was considered as entitled to it by the double title of owner and finder; when found on another's property, one-half belonged to the owner of the estate and the other to the finder; when found on public property, it belonged one-half to the public treasury and the other to the finder. Lecon. du Dr. Rom. §§ 350-352. This includes not only gold and silver, but whatever may constitute riches; as, vases, urns, statues, etc.

The Roman definition includes the same things under the word *pecunia;* but the thing found must have a commercial value; for ancient tombs would not be considered a treasure. The thing must have been hidden or concealed in the earth, and no one must be able to establish his right to it. It must be found by a pure accident, and not in consequence of search. Dalloz, "Propriete," art. 3, § 3.

According to the French law, *le tresor est toute chose cachee ou enfouie, sur laquelle personne ne peut justifier sa propriete, et quie est decouverte par le pur effet du hasard.* Code Civ. 716. See 4 Toullier, Dr. Civ. note 34. See, generally, 20 Viner, Abr. 414; 7 Comyn, Dig. 649; 1 Brown, Civ. Law, 237; 1 Bl. Comm. 295; Poth. Traite du Droit de Propriete, art. 4.

TREASURER'S REMEMBRANCER. He whose charge was to put the lord treasurer and the rest of the judges of the exchequer in remembrance of such things as were called on and dealt in for the sovereign's behoof. There is still one in Scotland.

TREASURY. That fiscal department of the government which controls the payments of the public money in accordance with the votes of the legislature.

TREASURY BENCH. In the English house of commons, the first row of seats on the right hand of the speaker is so called, because occupied by the first lord of the treasury, or principal minister of the crown. Brown.

TREASURY CHEST FUND. A fund, in England, originating in the unusual balances of certain grants of public money, and which is used for banking and loan purposes by the commissioners of the treasury. Its amount was limited by St. 24 & 25 Vict. c. 127, and has been further reduced to one million pounds, the residue being transferred to the consolidated fund by St. 36 & 37 Vict. c. 56. Wharton.

TREASURY STOCK. Stock reserved at the time of organization as assets of the corporation and the stockholders to be used in furtherance of corporate purposes. In respect to mining stock it has been held to mean "such stock as is set aside for the actual development of the property." Stock which has been issued as full paid to certain stockholders and has by them been subsequently donated to the corporation to be used by it in furtherance of its purposes is often spoken of as treasury stock. Strictly speaking it is not treasury stock, however, but occupies rather the status of any other property that it may own and which it may sell or barter at any time as it would sell or barter other personal property. 5 Fletcher Cyclopedia of Corporations, 5601.

TREATY. Treaties are agreements made and entered into by one independent state with another, in conformity with law, by which it places itself under an obligation.

The following are not considered treaties:

(1) Agreements entered into by a state with private individuals.

(2) Agreements between a state and the church, and especially concordats of the different states with the pope.

(3) Agreements by sovereigns or sovereign dynasties, whether among themselves or with foreign states, relative to their personal or dynastic pretensions to the government of a country. Glenn, Int. Law, 139; Hall, Int. Law, 323, note 1.

——**Treaty of Alliance.** One entered into by two or more states with a view of securing concerted action for the purpose designated in the treaty. Alliances may be either equal or unequal, and either offensive or defensive, or both. Davis, Int. Law, 82, note.

——**Treaty of Guaranty.** One entered into for the purpose of securing the observance of a treaty already existing, or the permanence of an existing state of affairs. The treaty of London of 1832, by which France, Great Britain, and Russia guarantied the sovereignty and independence of Greece, is an example.

——**Treaty of Peace.** A treaty of peace is an agreement or contract made by belligerent powers, in which they agree to lay down their arms, and by which they stipulate the conditions of peace and regulate the manner in which it is to be restored and supported. Vattel, bk. 4, c. 2, § 9.

TREATY OF PARIS. An agreement, more properly, perhaps, termed a "declaration," signed at Paris April 16, 1856, by representatives of Great Britain, Austria, France, Prussia, Russia, Sardinia, and Turkey.

The points agreed on relate to maritime law in time of war and are:

(1) Privateering is abolished.

(2) The neutral flag covers enemy's goods except contraband of war.

(3) Neutral goods, except contraband of war, are not subject to capture under the enemy's flag.

(4) Blockade, to be effective, must be maintained by a force sufficient to prevent access to the coast of the enemy.

TREATY OF VERSAILLES. The treaty of peace between Germany and the Allied Powers which concluded the World War. It was signed at Versailles on June 28, 1919, and ratifications were exchanged at Paris on Jan. 10, 1920. The treaty was not ratified by the United States.

TREATY OF WASHINGTON. A treaty signed on May 8, 1871, between Great Britain and the United States of America, with reference to certain differences arising out of the war between the northern and southern states of the Union, the Canadian fisheries, and other matters. Wharton.

TREBLE COSTS.

——**In English Practice.** The taxed costs and three-fourths the same added thereto. It is computed by adding one-half for double costs, and, in addition, one-half of one-half for treble costs. 1 Chit. 137; 1 Chit. Prac. 27.

——**In American Law.** In Pennsylvania the rule is different. When an act of assembly gives treble costs, the party is allowed three times the usual costs, with the exception that the fees of the officers are not to be trebled when they are not regularly or usually payable by the defendant. 2 Rawle (Pa.) 201.

In New York, the English method is followed. 9 Wend. (N. Y.) 443.

TREBLE DAMAGES. In actions arising *ex contractu*, some statutes give treble damages, and these statutes have been liberally construed to mean actually treble damages; for example, if the jury give twenty dollars damages for a forcible entry, the court will award forty dollars more, so as to make the total amount of damages sixty dollars. 4 Barn. & C. 154; McClel. 567.

The construction on the words "treble damages" is different from that which has been put on the words "treble costs." See 6 Serg. & R. (Pa.) 288; 1 Browne (Pa.) 9; 1 Cow. (N. Y.) 160, 175, 176, 584; 8 Cow. (N. Y.) 115.

TREBUCKET. The name of an engine of punishment, said to be synonymous with "tumbrel."

TREMAGIUM, TREMESIUM, or **TERMISSIUM.** The reason or time of sowing summer corn, being about March, the third month, to which the word may allude. Cowell.

TRES FACIUNT COLLEGIUM. Three form a corporation. Dig. 50. 16. 85; 1 Bl. Comm. 469.

TRESAYLE. An abolished writ sued on ouster by abatement on the death of the grandfather's grandfather.

TRESPASS. Any misfeasance or act of one man, whereby another is injuriously treated or damnified. 3 Bl. Comm. 208; 7 Conn. 125.

Any unlawful act committed with violence, actual or implied, to the person, property, or rights of another.

Any unauthorized entry upon the realty of another, to the damage thereof.

The word is used oftener in the last two somewhat restricted significations than in the first sense here given. In determining the nature of the act, neither the amount of violence or the intent with which it is offered, nor the extent of the damage accomplished or the purpose for which the act was committed, are of any importance; since a person who enters upon the land of another without leave, to lead off his own runaway horse, and who breaks a blade of grass in so doing, commits a trespass. 2 Humph. (Tenn.) 325; 6 Johns. (N. Y.) 5.

It is said that "some" damage must be committed to make an act a trespass. It is undoubtedly true that damage is required to constitute a trespass for which an action will lie; but, so far as the tort itself is concerned, it seems more than doubtful if the mere commission of an act affecting another, without legal authority, does not constitute trespass, though, until damage is done, the law will not regard it, inasmuch as the law does not regard trifles.

The distinction between the different classes of trespass is of importance in determining the nature of the remedy.

A trespass committed with force is said to be done *"vi et armis;"* one committed by entry upon the realty, "by breaking the close."

——**In Practice.** A form of action which lies to recover damages for the injury sustained by the plaintiff, as the immediate consequence of some wrong done forcibly to his person or property, against the person committing the same. Force is the essential of the action, and distinguishes it from "trespass on the case."

TRESPASS DE BONIS ASPORTATIS (Lat. *de bonis asportatis*, for goods which have been carried away). In practice. A form of action brought by the owner of goods to recover damages for unlawfully taking and carrying them away. 1 Me. 117.

It is no answer to the action that the defendant has returned the goods. 1 Bouv. Inst. note 36 (H).

TRESPASS FOR MESNE PROFITS. A form of action, supplemental to an action of ejectment, brought against the tenant in possession to recover the profits which he has unlawfully received during the time of his occupation. 3 Bl. Comm. 205; 4 Burrows, 1668. The person who actually received the profits is to be made defendant, whether defendant to the ejectment or not. 11 Wheat. (U. S.) 280. It lies after a recovery in ejectment (5 Cow. [N. Y.] 33; 11 Serg. & R. [Pa.] 55), or entry (6 N. H. 391), but not trespass to try title (Const. [S. C.] 102; 1 McCord [S. C.] 264); and the judgment in ejectment is conclusive evidence against the defendant for all profits which have accrued since the date of the demise stated in the declaration in ejectment (1 Blackf. [Ind.] 56; 2 Rawle [Pa.] 49); but suit for any antecedent profits is open to a new defense, and the tenant may plead the statute of limitations as to all profits accruing beyond the period fixed by law (3 Bl. Comm. 205, note; 2 Root [Conn.] 440).

TRESPASS ON THE CASE. In practice. The form of action by which a person seeks to recover damages caused by an injury unaccompanied with force, or which results indirectly from the act of the defendant. It is more generally called simply "case." See "Case;" 3 Bouv. Inst. notes 3482-3509.

TRESPASS QUARE CLAUSUM FREGIT (Lat. *quare clausum fregit*, because he has broken the close). In practice. The form of action which lies to recover damages for injuries to the realty consequent upon entry without right, but not by force, upon the plaintiff's land.

TRESPASS TO TRY TITLE. An action authorized in a few states by statutes allowing title to be tried in trespass *q. c. f.* The nature and scope of the action differs with the various statutes. In South Carolina, the action is in the nature of ejectment, while in Texas it is an action to quiet title.

TRESPASS VI ET ARMIS (Lat. *vi et armis*, with force and arms). In practice. The form of action which lies to recover damages for an injury which is the immediate consequence of a forcible wrongful act done to the person or personal property. 2 Const. (S. C.) 294. It is distinguished from case in this, that the injury in case is the indirect result of the act done. See "Case;" 4 Bouv. Inst. note 3583.

TRESPASSER. One who does an unlawful act, or a lawful act in an unlawful manner, to the injury of the person or property of another.

TRESPASSER AB INITIO. A term applied to denote that one who has commenced a lawful act in a proper manner has performed some unlawful act, or some lawful act in an unlawful manner, so connected with the previous act that he is to be regarded as having acted unlawfully from the beginning. See 8 Coke, 146; 5 Taunt. 198; 7 Adol. & E. 176; 11 Mees. & W. 740; 15 Johns. (N. Y.) 401. See "Ab Initio."

TRESTONARE. To turn or divert another way. Cowell.

TRET. An allowance made for the water or dust that may be mixed with any commodity. It differs from "tare."

TREYNE. (L. Fr.) In old English law. Drawn; dragged to the scaffold.

TREYT. Withdrawn, as a juror. Written also "treat." Cowell.

TRIA CAPITA. In the Roman law, were *civitas, libertas, and familia, i. e.*, citizenship, freedom, and family rights. See "Caput;" "Status."

TRIAL. The examination before a competent tribunal, according to the law of the land, of the facts put in issue in a cause for the purpose of determining such issue. 4 Mason (U. S.) 232.

The methods of trial at common law were:

(1) By certificate, where the evidence of the person certifying is the only proper criterion of the point in dispute. 3 Bl. Comm. 333.

(2) By inspection or examination, where the judges upon the testimony of their

senses decide the point in dispute.

(3) By witnesses, without the intervention of a jury (3 Bl. Comm. 336).

(4) By jury, which is that form of trial in which the facts are determined by twelve men impartially selected from the body of the county. See "Jury."

(5) By the record, where an issue of *nul tiel* record is joined in any action.

(6) By grand assize, a peculiar method of trial allowed in writs of right. See "Grand Assize."

(7) By wager of battel, which, in the old English law, was a barbarous mode of trying facts, among a rude people, founded on the supposition that heaven would always interpose and give the victory to the champions of truth and innocence. This mode of trial was abolished in England as late as St. 59 Geo. III. c. 46, A. D. 1818. It never was in force in the United States. See 3 Bl. Comm. 337; 1 Hale, Hist. Com. Law, 188. See a modern case, 1 Barn. & Ald. 405.

(8) By wager of law, which mode of trial has fallen into complete disuse; but, in point of law, it seems in England to be still competent in most cases to which it anciently applied. The most important and best-established of these cases is the issue of *nil debet*, arising in action of debt on simple contract, or the issue of *non detinet*, in an action of detinue. In the declaration in these actions, as in almost all others, the plaintiff concludes by offering his suit (of which the ancient meaning was followers or witnesses, though the words are now retained as mere form) to prove the truth of his claim. On the other hand, if the defendant, by a plea of *nil debet* or *non detinet*, deny the debt or detention, he may conclude by offering to establish the truth of such plea "against the plaintiff and his suit, in such manner as the court shall direct." Upon this, the court awards the wager of law (Co. Entr. 119a; Lilly, Entr. 467; 3 Chit. Pl. 479), and the form of this proceeding, when so awarded is that the defendant brings into court with him eleven of his neighbors, and for himself makes oath that he does not owe the debt or detain the property.

TRIAL AT BAR. Trial before all the judges at the bar of the court in which the suit is brought. Steph. Pl. 84. Seldom used except in cases of great importance.

TRIAL AT NISI PRIUS. Trial before a justice of assize; the usual method of trial. 3 Bl. Comm. 353.

TRIAL LIST. A list of cases marked down for trial for any one term.

TRIATIO IBI SEMPER DEBET FIERI, ubi juratores meliorem possunt habere notitiam. Trial ought always to be had where the jurors can have the best information. 7 Coke, 1.

TRIBUERE (Lat.) In the civil law. To give. Calv. Lex. To distribute.

TRIBUNAL. The seat of a judge; the place where he administers justice. The whole body of judges who compose a jurisdiction. 155 Ill. App. 405. The jurisdiction which the judges exercise.

The term is Latin, and derives its origin from the elevated seat where the tribunes administered justice.

TRIBUNAUX DE COMMERCE. In the French law, courts consisting of a president, judges, and substitutes elected in an assembly of the principal traders. No person under thirty years is eligible as a member of the tribunal, and the president must be forty years of age, at the least. The tribunal takes cognizance of all cases arising between merchants, and also of all disagreements arising among partners. The course of procedure is as in civil cases, and with an appeal to the regular courts. Brown.

TRIBUTE. A contribution which is sometimes raised by the sovereign from his subjects to sustain the expenses of the state. It is also a sum of money paid by one nation to another under some pretended right. Wolff. § 1145.

TRICESIMA. An ancient custom in a borough in the county of Hereford, so called, because thirty burgesses paid 1d. rent for their houses to the bishop, who was lord of the manor.

TRIDING MOTE. The court held for a triding or trithing. Cowell.

TRIENNIAL ACT. An act limiting the duration of every parliament to three years, unless sooner dissolved. It was passed by the long parliament in 1640, and afterwards repealed, and the term was fixed at seven years by the septennial act (St. 1 Geo. I. st. 2, c. 38).

TRIENS (Lat.) In the Roman law. A subdivision of the *as*, containing four *unciae;* the proportion of four-twelfths or one-third. Tayl. Civ. Law, 492; 2 Bl. Comm. 462, note (m).

TRIGAMUS. In old English law. One who has been thrice married; one who, at different times and successively, has had three wives; a trigamist. 3 Inst. 88.

TRIGILD. In Saxon law. A triple gild, geld, or payment; three times the value of a thing, paid as a composition or satisfaction. Spelman, voc. "Geldum."

TRINITY HOUSE. In English law. The short name usually given to a society incorporated in the reign of Henry VIII., and charged by successive acts of parliament with duties relating to the marine, especially in relation to pilotage, and the erection and maintenance of lighthouses, beacons, and sea marks.

TRINITY MASTERS. Elder brethren of the Trinity House. If a question arising in an admiralty action depends upon technical skill and experience in navigation, the judge or court is usually assisted at the hearing by two trinity masters, who sit as assessors, and advise the court on questions of a nautical character. Williams & B. Adm. Jur. 271; Sweet.

TRINITY SITTINGS. Sittings of the English court of appeal and of the high court of justice in London and Middlesex, commencing on the Tuesday after Whitsun week, and terminating on the 8th of August.

TRINITY TERM. In English law. One of the four terms of the court. It begins on the 22d day of May, and ends on the 12th of June. St. 11 Geo. IV., and Wm. IV., c. 70. It was formerly a movable term.

TRINOBANTES, TRINONANTES, or **TRInovantes.** In habitants of Britain, situated next to the Cantii, northward, who occupied, according to Camden and Baxter, that country which now comprises the counties of Essex and Middlesex, and some part of Surrey. But if Ptolemy be not mistaken, their territories were not so extensive in his time, as London did not then belong to them. The name seems to be derived from the three following British words: *Tri, now, hant, i. e.*, inhabitants of the new city (London). Enc. Lond.

TRINODA NECESSITAS (Lat.) The threefold necessary public duties to which all lands were liable by Saxon law, viz., for repairing bridges, for maintaining castles or garrisons, and for expeditions to repel invasions. In the immunities enumerated in king's grants, these words were inserted, "*exceptis his tribus, expeditione, pontis et arcis constructione.*" Kennett, Par. Ant. 46; 1 Bl. Comm. 263.

TRIORS. In practice. Persons appointed according to law to try whether a person challenged to the favor is or is not qualified to serve on the jury. They do not exceed two in number, without the consent of the prosecutor and defendant, or unless some special case is alleged by one of them, or when only one juror has been sworn and two triors are appointed with him. Co. Litt. 158a; Bac. Abr. "Juries" (E 12).

TRIPARTITE. Consisting of three parts; as, a deed tripartite, between A. of the first part, B. of the second part, and C. of the third part.

TRIPLICACION (Law Fr.) In old pleading. A rejoinder in pleading; the defendant's answer to the plaintiff's replication. Britt. c. 77.

TRIPLICATIO (Lat.) In civil law. The reply of the plaintiff (*actor*) to the rejoinder (*duplicatio*) of the defendant (*reus*). It corresponds to the surrejoinder of common law. Inst. 4. 14; Bracton, lib. 5, tit. 5, c. 1.

TRIPLUM (Lat.) In the civil law. The triple value of a thing. *Actio in triplum*, an action for the triple value. Inst. 4. 6. 21. 24.

TRISTIS. A forest immunity. Manw. For. Law, 1, 86.

TRITHING (Saxon, *trithinga*). The third part of a county, consisting of three or four hundreds.

A court within the circuit of the trithing, in the nature of a court leet, but inferior to the county court. Camd. 102. The ridings of Yorkshire are only a corruption of trythings. 1 Bl. Comm. 116; Spelman, 52; Cowell.

TRITHING MOTE. The court held for a trithing or riding.

TRITHING REEVE. A governor of a trithing.

TRIUMVIR. A trithing man or constable of three hundred. Cowell.

TRIUMVIRI (or **TREVIRI**, or **TRESVIRI**) **capitales** (Lat.) In Roman law. Officers who had charge of the prison, through whose intervention punishments were inflicted. Sallust, in Catilin. They had eight lictors to execute their orders. Vicat.

TRIVERBIAL DAYS. In the civil law. Juridical days; days allowed to the praetor for deciding causes; days on which the praetor might speak the three characteristic words of his office, viz., *do, dico, addico*. Calv. Lex. Otherwise called "*dies fasti.*" 3 Bl. Comm. 424, and note (w).

TRIVIAL. Of small importance. It is a rule in equity that a demurrer will lie to a bill on the ground of the triviality of the matter in dispute, as being below the dignity of the court. 4 Bouv. Inst. note 4237. See Hopk. 112; 4 Johns. Ch. (N. Y.) 183; 4 Paige, Ch. (N. Y.) 364.

TRONAGE. In English law. A customary duty or toll for weighing wool; so called because it was weighed by a common trona, or beam. Fleta, lib. 2, c. 12.

TRONATOR. A weigher of wool. Cowell.

TROPHY MONEY. Money formerly collected and raised in London, and the several counties of England, towards providing harness and maintenance for the militia, etc.

TROVER (Fr. *trouver*, to find). In practice. A form of action which lies to recover damages against one who has, without right, converted to his own use goods or personal chattels in which the plaintiff has a general or special property.

The action was originally an action of trespass on the case where goods were found by the defendant and retained against the plaintiff's rightful claim. The manner of gaining possession soon came to be disregarded, as the substantial part of the action is the conversion to the defendant's use; so that the action lies whether the goods came into the defendant's possession by finding or otherwise, if he fails to deliver them up on the rightful claim of the plaintiff. It differs from detinue and replevin in this, that it is brought for damages, and not for the specific articles; and from trespass in this, that the injury is not necessarily a forcible one, as trover may be brought in any case where trespass for injury to personal property will lie; but the converse is not true. In case possession was gained by a trespass, the plaintiff, by bringing his action in this form, waives his right to damages for the taking, and is confined to the injury resulting from the conversion. 17 Pick. (Mass.) 1; 21 Pick. (Mass.) 559; 17 Me. 434; 7 T. B. Mon. (Ky.) 209.

TRUCE. In international law. An agreement between belligerent parties by which they mutually engage to forbear all acts of hostility against each other for some time, the war still continuing. Burlam. Nat. Law, pt. 4, c. 11, § 1.

Truces are of several kinds,—general, extending to all the territories and dominions of both parties, and particular, restrained to particular places, as, for example, by sea, and not by land, etc. Burlam. Nat. Law, pt. 4, c. 11, § 5. They are also absolute, indeterminate, and general; or limited and determined to certain things; for example, to bury the dead. Id. See 1 Kent, Comm. 159; Halleck, Int. Law, 654; Wheaton, Int. Law, 682.

TRUCE OF GOD (Law Lat. *treuza Dei*; Saxon *treuge* or *trewa*, from German *treu*; Fr. *treve de Dieu*). In the middle ages, a limitation of the right of private warfare introduced by the church. This truce provided that hostilities should cease on holidays, from Thursday evening to Sunday evening of each week, the whole season of Advent and Lent, and the octaves of great festivals. The penalty for breach of the truce was excommunication. The protection of this truce was also extended constantly to certain places, as, churches, convents, hospitals, etc., and certain persons, as, clergymen, peasants in the field, crusaders (Clermont, 1095), and, in general, all defenseless persons. It was first introduced into Acquitaine in 1077, and into England under William the Conqueror. Enc. Am.

TRUCK ACT. St. 1 & 2 Wm. IV. c. 37, passed to abolish what is commonly called the "truck system," under which employers were in the practice of paying the wages of their work people in goods, or of requiring them to purchase goods at certain shops. This led to laborers being compelled to take goods of inferior quality at a high price. The act applies to all artificers, workmen, and laborers, except those engaged in certain trades, especially iron and metal works, quarries, cloth, silk, and glass manufactories. It does not apply to domestic or agricultural servants. Smith, Mast. & S. 166; St. 23 & 24 Vict. c. 151, § 28. Acts similar in purpose have been passed in some of the United States.

TRUE BILL. In practice. Words indorsed on a bill of indictment when a grand jury, after having heard the witnesses for the government, are of opinion that there is sufficient cause to put the defendant on his trial. Formerly the indorsement was *Billa vera* when legal proceedings were in Latin. It is still the practice to write on the back of the bill *Ignoramus*. When the jury do not find it to be a true bill, the better opinion is that the omission of the words "a true bill" does not vitiate an indictment. 11 Cush. (Mass.) 473; 13 N. H. 488. See 5 Me. 432, and Bennett's note.

TRUE, PUBLIC, and NOTORIOUS. These three qualities used to be formally predicated in the libel in the ecclesiastical courts of the charges which it contained, at the end of each article severally.

TRUST. A right of property, real or personal, held by one party for the benefit of another.

The party holding is called the "trustee," and the party for whose benefit the right is held is called the *cestui que trust*, or, using a better term, the "beneficiary."

Sometimes the equitable title of the beneficiary, sometimes the obligation of the trustee, and, again, the right held, is called the "trust." But the right of the beneficiary is in the trust, the obligation of the trustee results from the trust, and the right held is the subject matter of the trust. Neither of them is the trust itself. All together they constitute the trust.

An equitable right, title, or interest in property, real or personal, distinct from its legal ownership.

A personal obligation for paying, delivering, or performing anything where the person trusting has no real right or security, for by that act he confides altogether to the faithfulness of those intrusted.

An obligation upon a person, arising out of a confidence reposed in him, to apply property faithfully and according to such confidence. Willis, Trust, 1; 4 Kent, Comm. 295; 2 Fonbl. Eq. 1; 1 Saunders, Uses, 6; Cooper, Eq. Pl. Introd. 27; 3 Bl. Comm. 431.

The Roman *fidei commissa* were, under the name of "uses," first introduced by the clergy into England in the reign of Richard II. or Edward III., and, while perseveringly prohibited by the clergy, and wholly discountenanced by the courts of common law, they grew into public favor, and gradually developed into something like a regular branch of law, as the court of chancery rose into importance and power. For a long time the beneficiary, or *cestui que trust,* was without adequate protection; but the statute of uses, passed in 27 Henry VIII., gave adequate protection to the interests of the *cestui que trust.* Prior to this statute, the terms "use" and "trust" were used, if not indiscriminately, at least without accurate distinction between them. The distinction, so far as there was one, was between passive uses, where the feoffee had no active duties imposed on him, and active trusts, where the feoffee had something to do in connection with the estate. The statute of uses sought to unite the seisin with the use, making no distinction between uses and trusts, the result being that, by a strict construction, both uses and trusts were finally taken out of its intended operation, and were both included under the term "trust." The statute was passed in 1538; but trusts did not become settled on their present basis till Lord Nottingham's time, in 1676. 2 Washb. Real Prop. Index, "Trust;" 1 Greenl. Cruise, Dig. 338.

(1) Trusts are either active, being those in which the trustee has some duty to perform, or passive (sometimes called "dry"), which require the performance of no duty by the trustee, but by force of which the legal title merely rests in the trustee.

(2) Trusts are either executed or executory, executed trusts being those fully declared by the person creating it, so that nothing need be done to make it complete, while an executory trust is one requiring some further act to complete the intention of the creator, as a conveyance to B. in trust to convey to C.

(3) Trusts are either for value or voluntary, accordingly as they are or are not based on a valuable consideration.

(4) Trusts are public or private, accordingly as their object is for the general public good, or for the benefit of certain individuals.

(5) Trusts are, as to the manner of their creation, either express or implied.

Express trusts are those which are created in express terms in the deed, writing, or will. The terms to create an express trust will be sufficient if it can be fairly collected upon the face of the instrument that a trust was intended. Express trusts are usually found in preliminary sealed agreements, such as marriage articles, or articles for the purchase of land; in formal conveyances, such as marriage settlements, terms for years, mortgages, assignments for the payment of debts, raising portions, or other purposes; and in wills and testaments, when the bequests involve fiduciary interests for private benefit or public charity. They may be created even by parol. 6 Watts & S. (Pa.) 97.

Implied trusts are those which, without being expressed, are deducible from the nature of the transaction as matters of intent, or which are superinduced upon the transaction by operation of law, as matters of equity, independently of the particular intention of the parties. The term is used in this general sense, including constructive and resulting trusts, and also in a more restricted sense, excluding those classes.

TRUST DEED. A form of mortgage in use in Missouri and some other states, and in the District of Columbia. A deed is made in trust with a power of sale, and the power is exercised for the mortgagee's benefit. Similar deeds are frequently made by railroad companies or other corporations to secure bond issues where of necessity the creditors secured are very numerous.

TRUSTEE. A person in whom some estate, interest, or power in or affecting property of any description is vested for the benefit of another.

One to whom property has been conveyed to be held or managed for another.

——**In Scotch Law.** He who creates a trust.

TRUSTEE ACTS. Sts. 13 & 14 Vict. c. 60, and 15 & 16 Vict. c. 55, passed to enable the court of chancery (now the high court of justice, on petition presented in the chancery division) to appoint new trustees of a settlement, will, or other instrument creating a trust, whenever a trustee's death, lunacy, absence or refusal to act, or other reason, makes it necessary to apply to the court. In other words, when the power of appointing new trustees contained in the instrument, or provided by statute, cannot be exercised. They also empower the court, where property is held upon trust or mortgage by a lunatic or person of unsound mind, or out of the jurisdiction of the court, to transfer it by a vesting order (*q. v.*) to some other person, or to make an order appointing some person to execute a deed in the place of a trustee or mortgagee, so as to give it the same effect as if the trustee or mortgagee had executed it. Lewin, Trusts; Shelf. R. P. St. 647; Daniell, Ch. Prac. 1798; Pope, Lun. 263. See "Petition."

TRUSTEE DE SON TORT. Sometimes called constructive trustee. One who without authority undertakes to execute a trust, or assumes the management of trust property, or otherwise intermeddling with the trust affairs. Such persons are subject to the same rules and the same liability as other trustees. 182 Ill. 96.

TRUSTEE EX MALEFICIO. One who, by reason of his own wrong or fraud in acquiring property, is regarded as holding it as a trustee for the purpose of rectifying the wrong.

TRUSTEE IN BANKRUPTCY. A trustee in bankruptcy is a person in whom the property of a bankrupt is vested in trust for the creditors, not for the bankrupt. 10 Ch. Div. 388, 434. His duty is to discover, realize, and distribute it among the creditors, and for that purpose to examine the bankrupt's property, accounts, etc., to investigate proofs made by creditors, and to admit, reject, expunge, or reduce them, according to circumstances. He also has to keep various accounts of his dealings with the property, and of the course of the bankruptcy, which are audited by the committee of inspection and the comptroller in bankruptcy. Robson, 488.

TRUSTEE PROCESS. In practice. A means of reaching goods, property, and creditors of a debtor in the hands of third persons, for the benefit of an attaching creditor.

It is a process, so called, in the New England states, and similar to the garnishee process of others. It is a process given by statute 15 of the statutes of Massachusetts. All goods, effects, and credits so intrusted or deposited in the hands of others that the same cannot be attached by ordinary process of law may by an original writ of process, the form of which is given by the statute, be attached in whose hands or possession soever they may be found, and they shall, from the service of the writ, stand bound and be held to satisfy such judgment as the plaintiff may recover against the principal defendant. Cushing, Trustee Process 2.

The trustees, on suing out and service of the process, according to statute, and its entry in court, may come into court and be examined on oath as to property of the principal in their hands. If the plaintiff recovers against the principal, and there are any trustees who have not discharged themselves under oath, he shall have execution against them. Cushing, Trustee Process, 4; 2 Kent, Comm. (8th Ed.) 497, note.

TRUSTEE RELIEF ACTS. In England, if a person has in his hands a sum of money subject to a trust, and he does not know who is beneficially entitled to it, he may, instead of incurring the responsibility of paying it to the wrong person, or of instituting an action for the execution of the trust, pay it into court under the trustee relief acts (10 & 11 Vict. c. 96, and 12 & 13 Vict. c. 74).

TRUSTOR. A word occasionally, though rarely, used as a designation of the creator, donor, or founder of a trust.

TRY. To examine by judicial modes in order to determine.

TUAS RES TIBI HABETO (Lat.) Have or take your things to yourself. The form of words by which, according to the old Roman law, a man divorced his wife. Dig. 24. 2. 21. Otherwise expressed, "*Tuas res tibi agito.*"

TUB MAN. In English law. A barrister who has a preaudience in the exchequer, and also one who has a particular place in court, is so called.

TUCHAS. In Spanish law. Objections or exceptions to witnesses. White, New Recop. bk. 3, tit. 7, c. 10.

TUERTO. In Spanish law. Tort. Las Partidas, pt. 7, tit. 6, lib. 5.

TUICION. Law Fr. (from Lat. *tuitio*). Protection.

TUITISCUS. (L. Lat.) In old European law. Of the people, or native population; the language of a country. *Tuitiscè;* in the vernacular. Spelman.

TUMBREL. An instrument of punishment made use of by the Saxons, chiefly for the correction of scolding women by ducking them in water, consisting of a stool or chair fixed to the end of a long pole.

TUMULTUOUS PETITIONING. By St. 13 Car. II. st. 1, c. 5, signing of more than twenty names to any petition to the crown or either house of parliament for the alteration of matters established by law in church or state, unless the contents thereof had been approved by three justices, or the majority of the grand jury at assizes or quarter sessions, or the delivery of a petition by more than ten persons. 4 Steph. Comm. 255.

TUN. A measure of wine or oil, containing four hogsheads.

TUNGREVE (Saxon *tungaraeva, i. e., villae praepositus*). A reeve or bailiff. Spelman; Cowell.

One who in estates, which we call "manors," sustains the character of master, and in his stead disposes and arranges everything. *Qui in villis (quae dicimus maneriis) domini personam sustinet, ejusque vice omnia disponit atque moderatur.*

TURBA (Lat.) In the civil law. A multitude; a crowd or mob; a tumultuous assembly of persons. Said to consist of ten or fifteen at the least. Dig. 47. 8. 4. 2. 3.; Calv. Lex.

TURBARY. In English law. A right to dig turf; an easement.

TURN, or TOURN. The great court leet of the county, as the old county court was the court baron. Of this the sheriff is judge, and the court is incident to his office; wherefore it is called the "sheriff's tourn," and it had its name originally from the sheriff making a turn or circuit about his shire, and holding this court in each respective hundred. 2 Hawk. P. C. c. 10.

TURNKEY. A person under the superintendence of a jailer, whose employment is to open and fasten the prison doors, and to prevent the prisoners from escaping.

It is his duty to use due diligence; and he may be punished for gross neglect or willful misconduct in permitting prisoners to escape.

TURNPIKE. A gate set across a road, to stop travelers and carriages until toll is paid for passage thereon. In the United States, turnpike roads are often called "turnpikes," just as mail coach, hackney coach, stage coach, are shortened to mail, hack, and stage. Enc. Am.

TURNPIKE ROAD. A road or highway over which the public have the right to travel upon payment of toll, and on which the parties entitled to such toll have the right to erect gates and bars to insure its payment. 6 Mees. & W. 428; 1 Ry. Cas. 665; 22 Eng. Law & Eq. 113; 16 Pick. (Mass.) 175; 8 Barb. (N. Y.) 492.

TURPIS CAUSA (Lat.) A base or vile consideration, forbidden by law, which makes the contract void; as, a contract the consideration of which is the future illegal cohabitation of the obligee with the obligor.

TURPIS EST PARS QUAE NON CONVEnit cum suo toto. That part is bad which accords not with its whole. Plowd. 161.

TURPITUDE (Lat. *turpitudo*, from *turpis*, base). Everything done contrary to justice, honesty, modesty, or good morals is said to be done with turpitude.

TURPITUDO (Lat.) Turpitude.

TURRIS. (Lat.) In old English law. A tower; the tower; the Tower of London. Fleta, lib. 6, c. 11, §§ 6, 7.

TUT (L. Fr.) All; a corruption of *tout.*

TUTA EST CUSTODIA QUAE SIBIMET creditur. That guardianship is secure which trusts to itself alone. Hob. 340.

TUTELA (Lat.) A power given by the civil law over a free person to defend him, when, by reason of his age, he is unable to defend himself. Women, by the civil law, could only be tutors of their own children. A child under the power of his father was not subject to tutelage, because not a free person, *caput liberum.* D. lib. 26, tit. 1, ff. *de tutelis;* Inst. lib. 1, tit. 13, *de tutelis;* Inst. lib. 3, tit. 28, *de obligationibus quae ex quasi cont. nascunter.* Nov. 72, 94. 155. 118.

Tutela legitima was where the tutor was appointed by the magistrate. Leg. 1, D. ff. *de leg. tut.*

Tutela testamentaria was where the tutor was appointed by will. D. lib. 26, tit. 2, ff. *de testament, tut.;* C. lib. 5, tit. 28, *de testament. tut.;* Inst. lib. 1, tit. 14, *qui testamento tutores dari possunt.*

TUTELA LEGITIMA (Lat.) In the civil law. Legal tutelage; tutelage created by act of law, as where none had been created by testament. Inst. 1. 15. pr.

TUTELA TESTAMENTARIA (Lat.) In the civil law. Testamentary tutelage or guardianship; that kind of tutelage which was created by will. Calv. Lex.

TUTELAE ACTIO (Lat.) In the civil law. An action of tutelage; an action which lay for a ward or pupil, on the termination of tutelage, against the tutor or guardian, to compel an account. Calv. Lex.

TUTELAGE. Guardianship; state of being under a guardian.

TUTELAM REDDERE (Lat.) In the civil law. To render an account of tutelage. Calv. Lex. *Tutelam reposcere,* to demand an account of tutelage.

TUTEUR OFFICIEUX. In French law, a person over fifty years of age may be appointed a tutor of this sort to a child over fifteen years of age, with the consent of the parents of such child, or (in their default) the *conseil de famille.* The duties which such a tutor becomes subject to are analogous to those in English law of a person who puts himself *in loco parentis* to any one. Brown. See "In Loco Parentis."

TUTEUR SUBROGE. In French law, in the case of an infant under guardianship, a second guardian is appointed to him, the duties of the latter (who is called the "*subroge tuteur*") only arising where the interests of the infant and his principal guardian are in conflict. Code Nap. 420; Brown.

TUTIUS ERRATUR EX PARTE MITIORI. It is safer to err on the side of mercy. 3 Inst. 220.

TUTIUS SEMPER EST ERRARE ACquietando, quam in puniendo; ex parte misericordia quam ex parte justitia. It is always safer to err in acquitting than punishing; on the side of mercy than on the side of justice. Branch, Princ.; 2 Hale, P. C. 290.

TUTOR. In civil law. One who has been lawfully appointed to the care of the person and property of a minor.

By the laws of Louisiana, minors under the age of fourteen years, if males, and under the age of twelve years, if females, are, both as to their persons and their estates, placed under the authority of a tutor. Civ. Code La. art. 263. Above that age, and until their majority or emancipation, they are placed under the authority of a curator. Id.

TUTOR ALIENUS (Lat.) In English law. The name given to a stranger who enters into the lands of an infant within the age of fourteen and takes the profits.

He may be called to an account by the infant, and be charged as guardian in socage. Litt. § 124; Co. Litt. 89b, 90a; Harg. Law Tr. note 1.

TUTOR PROPRIUS (Lat.) The name given to one who is rightly a guardian in socage, in contradistinction to a *tutor alienus.*

TUTORSHIP. The power which an individual, *sui juris*, has to take care of the person of one who is unable to take care of himself. Tutorship differs from curatorship.

TUTRIX (Lat.) A woman who is appointed to the office of a tutor.

TUZ (L. F.) All; a corruption of touts.

TWA NIGHT GEST (Sax.) On the second night, a guest. Spelman. See "Guest."

TWELFHINDI. The highest rank of men in the Saxon government, who were valued at 1,200s. If any injury were done to such persons, satisfaction was to be made according to their worth. Cowell.

TWELVE-DAY WRIT. A writ issued under St. 18 & 19 Vict. c. 67, for summary procedure on bills of exchange and promissory notes, abolished by rule of court in 1880. Wharton.

TWELVEMONTH. In the singular, includes the whole year, but in the plural twelve months of twenty-eight days each. 6 Coke, 62; 2 Bl. Comm. 140, note.

TWELVE TABLES. Laws of ancient Rome, composed in part from those of Solon and other Greek legislators, and in part from the unwritten laws and customs of the Romans.

These laws first appeared in the year of Rome 303, inscribed on ten plates of brass. The following year two others were added, and the entire code bore the name of the "Laws of the Twelve Tables." The principles they contained were the germ of all the Roman law, the original source of the jurisprudence of the greatest part of Europe.

See a fragment of the Law of the Twelve Tables in Cooper, Just. 656; Gibb. Hist. Rom. Emp. c. 44; Code, § 27.

TWICE IN JEOPARDY. See "Jeopardy."

TWYHINDI. The lower order of Saxons, valued at 200s. in the scale of pecuniary mulcts inflicted for crimes. Cowell.

TYBURN TICKET. In English law. A certificate given to the prosecutor of a felon to conviction.

By 10 & 11 Wm. III. c. 23, the original proprietor or first assignee of such certificate is exempted from all and all manner of parish and ward offices within the parish or ward where the felony shall have been committed. Bac. Abr. "Constable" (C).

TYHTLAN (Saxon). In Saxon law. An accusation, impeachment, or charge of any offense. *Nex componat aliquis pro ulla tyhtlan, si non intersit testimonium praepositi regis*, nor shall any one compound for any accusation, unless there be present evidence on behalf of the king. LL. Ethelr. c. 2; Cowell.

TYLWITH (Brit. from *tyle*, the site of a house, or *tylath*, a beam in a building). A tribe or family branching or issuing out of another. Cowell.

U

U. R. *Ut rogas,* as you desire. In Roman law, a vote in favor of a proposed law or a candidate. See "Rogare."

UBERRIMA FIDES (Lat. most perfect good faith). A phrase used to express the perfect good faith, concealing nothing, with which a contract must be made; for example, in the case of insurance, the insured must observe the most perfect good faith towards the insurer. 1 Story, Eq. Jur. § 317; 3 Kent, Comm. (4th Ed.) 283.

UBI ALIQUID CONCEDITUR, CONCEDItur et id sine quo res ipsa esse non potest. When anything is granted, that also is granted without which the thing granted cannot exist. Broom, Leg. Max. (3d London Ed.) 429; 13 Mees. & W. 706.

UBI ALIQUID IMPEDITUR PROPTER unum, eo remoto, tollitur impedimentum. When anything is impeded by one single cause, if that be removed, the impediment is removed. 5 Coke, 77a.

UBI CESSAT REMEDIUM ORDINARIUM ibi decurritur ad extraordinarium. When a common remedy ceases to be of service, recourse must be had to an extraordinary one. 4 Coke, 93.

UBI CULPA EST, IBI POENA SUBESSE debet. Where the crime is committed, there the punishment should be inflicted. Jenk. Cent. Cas. 325.

UBI DAMNA DANTUR, VICTUS VICTOri in expensis condemnari debet. Where damages are given, the losing party should be adjudged to pay the costs of the victor. 2 Inst. 289; 3 Bl. Comm. 399.

UBI EADEM RATIO, IBI IDEM JUS. Where there is the same reason, there is the same law. 7 Coke, 18; Broom, Leg. Max. (3d London Ed.) 145.

UBI ET DANTIS ET ACCIPIENTIS TURpitudo versatur, non posse repeti dicimus; quotiens autem accipientis turpitudo versatur, repeti posse. Where there is turpitude on the part of both giver and receiver, we say it cannot be recovered back, but as often as the turpitude is on the side of the receiver alone, it can be recovered back. 17 Mass. 562.

UBI FACTUM NULLUM, IBI FORTIA nulla. Where there is no act, there can be no force. 4 Coke, 43.

UBI JUS, IBI REMEDIUM. Where there is a right, there is a remedy. 1 Term R. 512; Co. Litt. 197b; 3 Bouv. Inst. note 2411; 4 Bouv. Inst. 3726.

UBI JUS INCERTUM, IBI JUS NULLUM. Where the law is uncertain, there is no law.

UBI LEX ALIQUEM COGIT OSTENDERE causam, necesse est quod causa sit justa et legitima. Where the law compels a man to show cause, it is necessary that the cause be just and legal. 2 Inst. 269.

UBI LEX EST SPECIALIS, ET RATIO ejus generalis, generaliter accipienda est. Where the law is special, and the reason of it is general, it ought to be taken as being general. 2 Inst. 43.

UBI LEX NON DISTINGUIT, NEC NOS distinguere debemus. Where the law does not distinguish, we ought not to distinguish. 7 Coke, 5.

UBI MAJOR PARS EST, IBI TOTUM. Where is the greater part, there is the whole. F. Moore, 578.

UBI MATRIMONIUM, IBI DOS. Where there is marriage, there is dower. Bracton, 92.

UBI NON ADEST NORMA LEGIS, OMnia quasi pro suspectis habenda sunt. When the law fails to serve as a rule, almost everything ought to be suspected. Bac. Aph. 25.

UBI NON EST ANNUA RENOVATIO, IBI decimae non debent solvi. Where there is no annual renovation, there tithes ought not to be paid.

UBI NON EST CONDENDI AUCTORItas, ibi non est parendi necessitas. Where there is no authority to establish, there is no necessity to obey. Dav. 69.

UBI NON EST DIRECTA LEX, STANDum est arbitrio judicis, vel procedendum ad similia. Where there is no direct law, the judgment of the judge must be depended upon, or reference made to similar cases.

UBI NON EST LEX, IBI NON EST transgressio quoad mundum. Where there is no law, there is no transgression, as it regards the world. 4 Coke, 1b.

UBI NON EST MANIFESTA INJUSTItia, judices habentur pro bonis viris, et judicatum pro veritate. Where there is no manifest injustice, the judges are to be regarded as honest men, and their judgment as truth. 1 Johns. Cas. (N. Y.) 341, 345.

UBI NON EST PRINCIPALIS, NON POtest esse accessorius. Where there is no principal, there can be no accessory. 4 Coke, 43.

UBI NULLA EST CONJECTURA QUAE ducat alio, verba intelligenda sunt ex proprietate non grammatica sed populari ex usu. Where there is no inference which would lead in any other direction, words are to be understood according to their proper meaning, nongrammatical, but according to popular usage. Grotius de Jure Belli, lib. 2, c. 16, § 2.

UBI NULLUM MATRIMONIUM, IBI NULlum dos. Where there is no marriage there is no dower. Co. Litt. 32a.

UBI PERICULUM, IBI ET LUCRUM COLlocatur. He at whose risk a thing is, should receive the profits arising from it.

UBI PUGNANTIA INTER SE IN TESTAmento juberentur, neutrum ratum est. When two directions conflicting with each other are given in a will, neither is held valid. Dig. 50. 17. 188, pr.

UBI QUID GENERALITER CONCEDItur, in est haec exceptio, si non aliquid sit contra jus fasque. Where a thing is conceded generally, this exception arises, that there shall be nothing contrary to law and right. 10 Coke, 78.

UBI QUIS DELINQUIT IBI PUNIETUR. Let a man be punished where he commits the offense. 6 Coke, 47.

UBI REVERA (Lat.) Where in reality; where in truth, or in point of fact. Cro. Eliz. 645; Cro. Jac. 4.

UBI VERBA CONJUNCTA NON SUNT, sufficit alteratum esse factum. Where words are used disjunctively, it is sufficient that either one of the things enumerated be performed. Dig. 50. 17. 110. 3.

UBICUNQUE EST INJURIA, IBI DAMnum sequitur. Wherever there is a wrong, there damage follows. 10 Coke, 116.

UBICUNQUE FUERIMUS IN ANGLIA (Law Lat. Wheresoever we shall be in England). The style of the return of writs in the court of king's or queen's bench; it being in theory a movable court, attendant upon the sovereign's person. 3 Bl. Comm. 41, 284. See Fleta, lib. 2, c. 2, § 5; Id. lib. 2, c. 64, § 19.

UDAL. A term mentioned by Blackstone, as used in Finland to denote that kind of right in real property which is called in English law "allodial." 2 Bl. Comm. 45, note (f). The term is used in Orkney and Zetland. 1 Forbes, Inst. pt. 3, pp. 6, 82.

UKAAS, or UKASE. The name of a law or ordinance emanating from the czar of Russia.

ULLAGE. In commercial law. The amount wanting when a cask, on being gauged, is found only partly full.

ULNA FERREA. The standard ell of iron, which was kept in the exchequer for the rule of measure. Mon. Angl. ii. 383.

ULNAGE. Alnage; a duty for measuring cloth.

ULTERIUS CONCILIUM. (L. Lat.) Further argument. A common term in the older reports. 1 Burr. 1020; 2 Wils. 243.

ULTIMA RATIO. The last resort.

ULTIMA VOLUNTAS (Lat.) In old English law. Last will; the last will. *In testamento suo, in ultima voluntate sua,* in his testament, in his last will. Reg. Orig. 244b.

ULTIMA VOLUNTAS TESTATORIS EST perimplenda secundum veram intentionem suam. The last will of a testator is to be fulfilled according to his true intention. Co. Litt. 322; Broom, Leg. Max. (3d London Ed.) 505.

ULTIMATE FACTS. The main or primary facts in an issue. The logical results of the proofs. 175 Ill. 482. The facts which prove the ultimate facts are evidentiary facts or probative facts. The ultimate facts are to be pleaded, while the others are not, being "evidence."

ULTIMATUM (Lat.) The last proposition made in making a contract, a treaty, and the like; as, the government of the United States has given its *ultimatum,*—has made the last proposition it will make to complete the proposed treaty. The word also means the result of a negotiation, and it comprises the final determination of the parties concerned in the object in dispute.

ULTIMUM SUPPLICIUM (Lat.) The last or extreme punishment; the penalty of death.

ULTIMUM SUPPLICIUM ESSE MORtem solam interpretamur. The extremest punishment we consider to be death alone. Dig. 48. 19. 21.

ULTIMUM TEMPUS PARIENDI (Lat.) The extreme period of bearing; the extreme period between the conception and the birth of a child. 2 Steph. Comm. 317.

ULTIMUS HAERES (Lat.) The last or remote heir; the lord. So called in contradistinction to the *haeres proximus* and the *haeres remotior.* Dalr. Feud. Prop. 110.

ULTRA. In Latin phrases. Beyond; outside of.

ULTRA MARE (Lat. beyond sea). One of the old essoins or excuses for not appearing in court at the return of process. Bracton, fol. 338.

ULTRA POSSE NON POTEST ESSE, ET vice versa. What is beyond possibility cannot exist, and the reverse, what cannot exist is not possible. Wingate, Max. 100.

ULTRA REPRISES. After deductions.

ULTRA VIRES (Lat.) The modern technical designation, in the law of corporations, of acts beyond the scope of their powers, as defined by their charters or acts of incorporation; as distinguished from acts which are authorized.

It was early contended that a corporation could not exceed its powers; that the acts of its agents beyond the charter powers of the corporation were not the acts of the corporation; but it is now well settled that "corporations, like natural persons, have power and capacity to do wrong. They may, in their dealings and contracts, break over the liability imposed upon them by their charters, and when they do so, their exemption from liability cannot be claimed on the mere ground that they have no attributes or faculties which render it possible for them to thus act." 119 Ind. 324. The act need not necessarily be expressly prohibited by the charter or by statute. Nor need it be in any sense immoral or injurious to others. It may be an act which could be lawfully done by a natural person. It may be even praiseworthy, as in the case of a gift by a corporation for charitable or religious purpose. Yet, if it is not authorized by the charter of the corporation, or is not an implied or incidental power, it is ultra vires. 3 Fletcher Cyclopedia Corporations, 2571.

There is much conflict in the cases as to the validity of an *ultra vires* contract. In some states, it is held that, if the corporation had no authority to make the contract, it is void, but if it was within the general scope of the corporate power, and the want of power in that case was because of particular facts, it is valid (43 Wis. 420; 8 Ohio 257); while in several states it is held that "the plea of *ultra vires* should not prevail, whether it is imposed for or against the corporation, when it would not advance justice, but, on the contrary, would accomplish a legal wrong (63 N. Y. 62; 151 Ill. 531).

ULTRONEUS WITNESS. In Scotch law. A witness who offers his testimony without being regularly cited. The objection only goes to his credibility, and may be removed by a citation at any time before the witness is sworn. See Bell, Dict. "Evidence."

UMBILICUS. (Lat.) Literally, the navel; the center of any thing. The name given to the fourth and middle part of the Digests, consisting of eight books, from the twentieth to the twenty-seventh, both inclusive.

UMPIRAGE. The decision of an umpire. This word is used for the judgment of an umpire, as the word "award" is employed to designate that of arbitrators.

UMPIRE. A person selected by arbitrators who cannot agree as to the subject matter referred to them for the purpose of deciding the matter in dispute.

His province is to determine the issue submitted to the arbitrators on which they have failed to agree and to make an award thereon, which is his sole award. Neither of the original arbitrators is required to join in the award in order to make it valid and binding on the parties. In the absence of any agreement or assent by the parties to the controversy, dispensing with a full hearing by the umpire, it is his duty to hear the whole case, and to make a distinct award thereon as the result of his judgment. He stands, in fact, in the same situation as a sole arbitrator, and he is bound to hear and determine the case in like manner as if it had been originally submitted to his determination. 75 Ill. 30.

Sometimes the term is applied to a single arbitrator selected by the parties themselves. Kyd, Awards, 6, 75, 77; Caldwell, Abr. 38; Dane, Abr. Index; 3 Viner, Abr. 93; Comyn, Dig. "Arbitrament" (F); 4 Dall. (U. S.) 271, 432; 4 Scott, N. S. 378; Bouv. Inst. Index.

UN NE DOIT PRISE ADVANTAGE DE son tort demesne. One ought not to take advantage of his own wrong. 2 And. 38. 40.

UNA CUM OMNIBUS ALIIS (Lat. together with all other things). A phrase in old conveyancing. Hob. 175.

UNA PERSONA VIX POTEST SUPplere vices duarum. One person can scarcely supply the place of two. 4 Coke, 118.

UNA VOCE (Lat.) With one voice; unanimously.

UNALIENABLE. In capable of being sold. Things which are not incommerce, as public roads, are in their nature unalienable. Some things are unalienable in consequence of particular provisions in the law forbidding their sale or transfer; as, pensions granted by the government. The natural rights of life and liberty are unalienable.

UNANIMITY (Lat. *unus*, one, *animus*, mind). The agreement of all the persons concerned in a thing, in design and opinion.

Generally, a simple majority of any number of persons is sufficient to do such acts as the whole number can do,—for example, a majority of the legislature can pass a law; but there are some cases in which unanimity is required,—for example, a traverse jury composed of twelve individuals cannot decide an issue submitted to them unless they are unanimous.

UNAVOIDABLE ACCIDENT. An unavoidable accident is necessarily one occurring not because of negligence. 243 Ill. 460.

UNCEASESATH. An oath by relations not to avenge a relation's death. Blount.

UNCERTAINTY. Vagueness or obscurity of language in written instruments.

UNCIA. The twelfth part of the Roman *as*. Dess. Dict. du Dig. "As." The *as* was used to express an integral sum; hence *uncia* for one-twelfth of anything, commonly one-twelfth of a pound, *i. e.*, an ounce. Id.; 2 Bl. Comm. 462, note (m).

UNCIA TERRAE (Lat.) This phrase often occurs in charters of the British kings, and denotes some quantity of land. It was twelve *modii*, each *modius* possibly one hundred feet square. Mon. Angl. tom. 3, pp. 198, 205.

UNCIARIUS HAERES. In the Roman law, an heir to one-twelfth of an estate or inheritance. Calv. Lex.

UNCLAIMED DIVIDENDS. In English bankruptcy practice, dividends remaining unclaimed for five years are forfeited to the government (Bankruptcy Act 1869, § 116), but may, upon satisfactory proof of right thereto, be paid over to the creditors entitled (38 & 39 Vict. c. 77, § 32). And in chancery, the lord chancellor may, under St. 16 & 17 Vict. c. 98, § 3, order dividends unclaimed for fifteen years to be carried to "the suitors' unclaimed dividend account;" and these, under 32 & 33 Vict. c. 91, are transferred to the public on their indemnity. Dividends not being claimed for ten years on stock in the Bank of England, the stock is forthwith transferred to the government on the like indemnity. Brown.

UNCONSCIONABLE BARGAIN. A contract which no man in his senses, not under delusion, would make, on the one hand, and which no fair and honest man would accept, on the other. 4 Bouv. Inst. note 3848.

UNCONSTITUTIONAL. That which is contrary to the constitution.

UNCORE PRIST (Law Fr. still ready). In pleading. A plea or replication that the party pleading is still ready to do what is required. Used in connection with the words *tout temps prist*, the whole denotes that the party always has been and still is ready to do what is required, thus saving costs where the whole cause is admitted, or preventing delay where it is a replication, if the allegation is made out. 3 Bl. Comm. 303.

UNCUTH. In Saxon law. Unknown; a stranger. A person entertained in the house of another was, on the first night of his entertainment, so called. Bracton, fol. 124b.

UNDE COGNATI (Lat.) In the civil law. A species of the *bonorum possessio* granted to *cognates*, or relations on the part of the mother. Inst. 3. 10. 1. 2; Dig. 38. 8; Heinec. Elem. Jur. Civ. lib. 3, tit. 10, § 724; Halifax, Anal. bk. 2, c. 11, No. 5.

UNDE LEGITIMI (Lat.) In the civil law. A species of the *bonorum possessio* granted to *agnates*, or the lawful heirs. Inst. 3. 10. 1. 2; Dig. 38. 7; Heinec. Elem. Jur. Civ. lib. 3, tit. 10, § 723; Halifax, Anal. bk. 2, c. 11, No. 5.

UNDE LIBERI (Lat.) In the civil law. A species of the *bonorum possessio* granted to emancipated children, or the proper heirs of the deceased. Heinec. Elem. Jur. Civ. lib. 3, tit. 10, § 722; Halifax, Anal. bk. 2, c. 11, No. 5; Inst. 3. 10. 1. 2; Dig. 38. 6.

UNDE NIHIL HABET. See "Dower."

UNDE VI (Lat. wherefrom by force). In the civil law. The technical name of that species of interdict which was granted to recover the possession of an immovable thing wherefrom a person had been ejected by force. Inst. 4. 15. 6; Heinec. Elem. Jur. Civ. lib. 4, tit. 15, § 1303; 1 Mackeld. Civ. Law, 250, § 253.

UNDE VIR ET UXOR (Lat.) In the civil law. A species of the *bonorum possessio* granted to a husband or wife, and by which they succeeded each other, on failure of the *cognati*. Inst. 3. 10. 1. 2; Dig. 38. 11; Heinec. Elem. Jur. Civ. lib. 3, tit. 10, § 725; Halifax, Anal. bk. 2, c. 11, No. 5.

UNDEFENDED. In pleading. Without defense or denial. Where judgment passes by default against a defendant, the language in which the default is recorded is that the defendant "says nothing in bar or preclusion of the action, whereby the plaintiff remains therein undefended against the said defendant." Archb. Forms, 336.

UNDER-CHAMBERLAINS OF THE EXchequer. Two officers who cleaved the tallies written by the clerk of the tallies, and read the same, that the clerk of the pell and comptrollers thereof might see their entries were true. They also made searches for records in the treasury, and had the custody of Domesday Book. Abolished.

UNDER LEASE. An alienation by a tenant of a part of his lease, reserving to himself a reversion. It differs from an "assignment," which is a transfer of all the tenant's interest in the lease. 3 Wils. 234; W. Bl. 766. And even a conveyance of the whole estate by the lessee, reserving to himself the rent, with a power of re-entry for nonpayment, was held to be not an assignment, but an under lease. Strange, 405. In Ohio it has been decided that the transfer of a part only of the lands, though for the whole term, is an under lease. 2 Ohio, 216. In Kentucky, such a transfer, on the contrary, is considered as an assignment. 4 Bibb (Ky.) 538. See "Lease."

UNDER SHERIFF. In English law. A person appointed by the sheriff of a county to perform all his ordinary duties in his behalf. Sometimes confounded with a deputy sheriff, but the latter term is properly applicable to those whom the sheriff appoints to execute process in his behalf, and who have no other powers than such as appertain to that particular duty. 1 Bl. Comm. 345, note.

UNDERTAKING. In the primary sense of the word, an undertaking is a promise.

In the old books, "undertaker" means a promisor. 1 Salk. 27.

"Undertaking" is frequently used in the special sense of a promise given in the course of legal proceedings by a party or his counsel, generally as a condition to obtaining some concession from the court or the opposite party.

UNDER TENANT. One who holds by virtue of an underlease.

UNDER TUTOR. In Louisiana. In every tutorship there shall be an under tutor, whom it shall be the duty of the judge to appoint at the time letters of tutorship are certified for the tutor.

It is the duty of the under tutor to act for the minor whenever the interest of the minor is in opposition to the interest of the tutor. Civ. Code La. arts. 300, 301; 1 Mart. (La.; N. S.) 462; 9 Mart. (La.) 643; 11 La. 189; Poth. des Personnes, partie prem. tit. 6, § 5, art. 2. See "Procurator;" "Protutor."

UNDERTOOK. Assumed; promised. This is a technical word, which ought to be inserted in every declaration of *assumpsit* charging that the defendant undertook to perform the promise which is the foundation of the suit; and this, though the promise be founded on a legal liability, or would be implied in evidence. Bac. Abr. "Assumpsit" (F); 1 Chit. Pl. 88, note (p).

UNDERWRITER. In insurance. The party who agrees to insure another on life or property, in a policy of insurance. He is also called the "insurer."

UNDERWRITING. As applied to corporate stock, an underwriting agreement is an agreement made before such stock is offered to the public whereby the signer, or "underwriter" agrees for a certain compensation to take a stipulated number of shares of stock, or a portion thereof, if the public does not subscribe for or take all of such stock. The same definition applies to the underwriting of corporate bonds, and it is an agreement by the subscribers, based on a consideration, to insure the sale of the bonds subscribed at a stipulated price, and, if they are not sold to others, that the subscribers will purchase and pay for them at the price fixed therein. It has been held that an underwriting in this sense is a purchase together with a guaranty of a sale of the bonds. Fletcher Cyclopedia Corporations 950.

UNDIQUE. (Lat.) On all sides; from every quarter. 1 Curtis R. 350.

UNDIVIDED. Held by the same title by two or more persons, whether their rights are equal as to value or quantity, or unequal.

Tenants in common, joint tenants, and partners hold an undivided right in their respective properties until partition has been made. The rights of each owner of an undivided thing extend over the whole and every part of it, *totum in toto, et totum in qualibet parte.* See "Per My et Per Tout."

UNDRES (Saxon). In old English law. Minors or persons under age.

UNDUE INFLUENCE. Any improper constraint, machination or urgency of persuasion whereby the will of a person is overpowered, and he is induced to act otherwise than he would have done. It has been said to imply more subtle influence than "duress" (see Story, Eq. Jur. § 239), but has been held to include threats and violence, in which use it is synonymous with "duress" (33 N. J. Eq. 494). As used in respect to wills, it includes duress.

UNEQUIVOCALLY. Without doubt; without room to doubt. 83 Ill. 89; 2 Ill. App. 51.

UNFAIR COMPETITION. Unfair competition consists in conducting a trade or business in such a manner that there is an express or implied representation that the goods or business of one man are the goods or business of another. 167 Iowa 202.

UNG. Law Fr. One; an old form of *un.* Kelham.

UNGELD. In Saxon law. An outlaw; a person whose murder required no composition to be made, or *weregeld* to be paid, by his slayer.

UNIARE. (L. Lat.) To unite; to make one; to join in a body.

UNICA TAXATIO (Lat.) In practice. The ancient language of a special award of *venire,* where of several defendants one pleads, and one lets judgment go by default, whereby the jury who are to try and assess damages on the issue are also to assess damages against the defendant suffering judgment by default. Lee.

UNIFORM. Conforming to one rule, mode, or unvarying standard; agreeing with each other; substantially one and the same; not different at different times or places; applicable to all places or divisions of a country. A law is uniform when all persons brought within the relation and circumstances provided for are affected alike; when it has uniform operation upon all within the class upon which it purports to operate. 266 Ill. 387.

UNIFORMITY, ACT OF. St. 13 & 14 Car. II. c. 4, which regulates the terms of membership in the Church of England and the colleges of Oxford and Cambridge. See St. 9 & 10 Vict. c. 59. The act of uniformity has been amended by St. 35 & 36 Vict. c. 35, which *inter alia* provides a shortened form of morning and evening prayer. Wharton.

UNIFORMITY OF PROCESS. In English law. An act providing for uniformity of process in personal actions in his majesty's courts of law at Westminster. 2 Wm. IV. c. 39 (23d May, 1832); 3 Chit. St. 494.

UNIFORMITY OF TAXATION. Equality in the burden of taxation, 373 Ill. 247; taxation which acts alike on all persons similarly situated. 139 Wis. 544, 557; 121 N. W. 347. See "Uniform."

UNILATERAL CONTRACT. A contract lacking in mutuality of obligation.

—**In the Civil Law.** When the party to whom an engagement is made makes no express agreement on his part, the contract is called "unilateral," even in cases where the law attaches certain obligations to his acceptance. Civ. Code La. art. 1758; Code Nap. 1103. A loan of money and a loan for use are of this kind. Poth. Obl. pt. 1, c. 1, § 1, art. 2; Lec. Elm. § 781.

UNINTELLIGIBLE. That which cannot be understood.

When a law, a contract, or will is unintelligible, it has no effect whatever.

UNIO (Lat.) In canon law. A consolidation of two churches into one. Cowell.

UNIO PROLIUM (Lat. union of offspring). A species of adoption used among the Germans, which takes place when a widower having children marries a widow who also has children. These parents then agree that the children of both marriages shall have the rights to their succession, as those which may be the fruits of their marriage. Lec. Elm. § 187.

UNION.

—**In the English Poor Law.** Two or more parishes which have been consolidated for the better administration of the poor law therein.

—**In Ecclesiastical Law.** Two or more benefices which have been united into one benefice. Such a union may be made under St. 1 & 2 Vict. c. 106, passed "to abridge the holding of benefices in plurality," and amended by St. 13 & 14 Vict. c. 98; and under St. 23 & 24 Vict. c. 142, passed "to make better provision for the union of contiguous benefices in cities, towns and boroughs" (in substitution for St. 18 & 19 Vict. c. 127), amended by St. 34 & 35 Vict. c. 90.

UNITAS PERSONARUM. The unity of persons, as that between husband and wife, or ancestor and heir.

UNITED STATES COURT COMMISSIONers. Officers, more properly "Commissioners of the Circuit Courts of the United States," authorized by Rev. St. U. S. § 627, to be appointed by the circuit court in each district to exercise such powers as may be expressly conferred on them by statute. They have the powers of committing magistrates in respect to federal offenses (Rev. St. § 1014), and other *quasi* judicial powers.

UNITY. In the law of estates. The agreement or coincidence of certain qualities in the title of a joint estate or an estate in common. It is the peculiar characteristic of an estate in joint tenancy and is fourfold, unity of interest, unity of title, unity of time, and unity of possession. In other words, joint tenants have one and the same interest accruing by one and the same conveyance, commencing at one and the same time, and held by one and the same undivided possession. 2 Bl. Comm. 180.

UNITY OF INTEREST. One of the properties of a joint estate; all the joint tenants being entitled to one period of duration or quantity of interest in the lands. 2 Bl. Comm. 181.

UNITY OF POSSESSION. This term is used to designate the possession by one person of several estates or rights. For example, a right to an estate to which an easement is attached, or the dominant estate, and to an estate which an easement incumbers, or the servient estate may become the property of one person, in which case the easement is extinguished. 3 Mason (U. S.) 172; Poph. 166; Latch, 153. And see Cro. Jac. 121. But a distinction has been made between a thing that has being by prescription, and one that has its being *ex jure naturae*. In the former case, unity of possession will extinguish the easement; in the latter,—for example, the case of a watercourse,—the unity will not extinguish it. Poth. Contr. 166.

By the Civil Code of Louisiana (article 801), every servitude is extinguished when the estate to which it is due and the estate owing it are united in the same hands. But it is necessary that the whole of the two estates should belong to the same proprietor; for if the owner of one estate only acquires the other in part or in common with another person, confusion does not take effect. See "Merger."

UNITY OF SEISIN. The condition which exists where a person seised of land which is subject to an easement, *profit a prendre*, or similar right, also becomes seised of the land to which the easement or other right is annexed. The term is usually applied to cases where the seisin is that of a tenant in fee simple, and is equally high or predurable in both pieces of land, so that the easement or other right is extinguished by the unity of seisin.

UNITY OF TIME. One of the essential properties of a joint estate; the estates of the tenants being vested at one and the same period. 2 Bl. Comm. 181.

UNITY OF TITLE. One of the essentials of a joint estate; the estate of all the tenants being created by one and the same act.

UNIUS OMNINO TESTIS RESPONSIO non audiatur. Let not the evidence of one witness be heard at all. Code, 4. 20. 9; 3 Bl. Comm. 370.

UNIUSCUJUSQUE CONTRACTUS INITIum spectandum est, et causa. The beginning and cause of every contract must be considered. Dig. 17. 1. 8; Story, Bailm. § 56.

UNIVERSAL AGENT. One who is appointed to do all the acts which the principal can personally do, and which he may lawfully delegate the power to another to do. Such an agency may potentially exist, but it must be of the rarest occurrence. Story, Ag. 18.

UNIVERSAL LEGACY. In civil law. A testamentary disposition by which the testator gives to one or several persons the whole of the property which he leaves at his decease. Civ. Code La. art. 1599; Civ. Code art. 1003; Poth. Donations Testamentaires, c. 2, sec. 1, § 1.

UNIVERSAL PARTNERSHIP. The name of a species of partnership by which all the partners agree to put in common all their property, *universorum bonorum,* not only what they then have, but also what they shall acquire. Poth. du Contr. de Societe, note 29.

UNIVERSAL REPRESENTATION. In Scotch law. The heir universally represents his ancestor, *i. e.,* is responsible for his debts. Originally, this responsibility extended only to the amount of the property to which he succeeded; but afterwards certain acts on part of the heir were held sufficient to make him liable for all the debts of the ancestor. Bell, Dict. "Passive Titles."

UNIVERSALIA SUNT NOTIORA SINGUlaribus. Things universal are better known than things particular. 2 Rolle, 294; 2 C. Rob. Adm. 294.

UNIVERSATIS (Lat.) In the civil law. A corporation aggregate. Dig. 3. 4. 7. Literally, a whole formed out of many individuals. 1 Bl. Comm. 469.

UNIVERSITAS FACTI (Lat.) In the civil law. A plurality of corporeal things of the same kind, which are regarded as a whole; *e. g.,* a herd of cattle, a stock of goods. 1 Mackeld. Civ. Law, 154, § 149; Inst. 2. 20. 18.

UNIVERSITAS JURIS (Lat.) In civil law. A quantity of things of various kinds, corporeal and incorporeal, taken together as a whole, *e. g.,* an estate. It is used in contradistinction to *universitas facti,* which is a whole made up of corporeal units. Mackeld. Civ. Law, § 149.

UNIVERSITAS RERUM (Lat.) In civil law. Several things not mechanically united, but which, taken together, in some legal respects are regarded as one whole. Mackeld. Civ. Law, § 149.

UNIVERSITAS VEL CORPORATIO NON dicitur aliquid facere nisi id sit collegialiter deliberatum, etiamsi major pars id faciat. A university or corporation is not said to do anything unless it be deliberated upon collegiately, although the majority should do it. Dav. 48.

UNIVERSITY. The name given to certain societies or corporations which are seminaries of learning where youth are sent to finish their education. Among the civilians, by this term is understood a corporation.

UNIVERSITY COURT. See "Chancellors' Courts in the Two Universities."

UNIVERSUS (Lat.) The whole; all together. Calv. Lex.

——**In Old English Law.** The whole; all *Universitatem vestram scire volumus,* we will that all of you know. Cart. Conf. 49 Hen. III.

UNJUST. That which is done against the perfect rights of another; that which is against the established law; that which is opposed to a law which is the test of right and wrong. 1 Toullier, Dr. Civ. tit. prel. note 5; Aust. Jur. 276, note; Lec. Elm. § 1080.

UNKOUTH. Unknown. The law French form of the Saxon "uncouth," or "uncuth." Britt. c. 12.

UNLAGE (Saxon, from *un,* without, and *lag,* law). An unjust law. LL. Hen. I. c. 34, 84; Cowell.

UNLARICH. In old Scotch law. That which is done without law or against law. Spelman.

UNLAW. In Scotch law. A witness was formerly inadmissible who was not worth the king's unlaw, *i. e.,* the sum of £10 Scots, then the common fine for absence from court and for small delinquencies. Bell, Dict.

UNLAWFUL. That to which the law is opposed. It is not strictly synonymous with "illegal," though so used quite often. "Illegal" means positively forbidden, while "unlawful" may include things which are immoral, or against public policy. Sweet.

UNLAWFUL ASSEMBLY. In criminal law. A disturbance of the public peace by three or more persons who meet together with an intent mutually to assist each other in the execution of some unlawful enterprise of a private nature, with force and violence. If they move forward towards its execution, it is then a rout; and if they actually execute their design, it amounts to a riot. 4 Bl. Comm. 140; 1 Russ. Crimes, 254; Hawk. P. C. c. 65, § 9; Comyn, Dig. "Forcible Entry" (D 10); Viner, Abr. "Riots, etc." (A).

UNLAWFULLY. In pleading. This word is frequently used in indictments in the description of the offense. It is necessary when the crime did not exist at common law, and when a statute, in describing an offense which it creates, uses the word (1 Moody, Cr. Cas. 339); but it is unnecessary whenever the crime existed at common law and is manifestly illegal (1 Chit. Crim Law, *241; Hawk. bk. 2, c. 25, § 96; 2 Rolle, Abr. 82; Bac. Abr. "Indictment" (G 1); 1 Ill. 199; 2 Ill. 120.

UNLIQUIDATED DAMAGES. Such damages as are unascertained; as those arising out of torts, as well as those following breaches of contract, where the amount of damages has not, by agreement, been determined. 95 Ill. App. 101; 176 Ill. App. 523; 208 Ill. App. 187. In general, such damages cannot be set off. No interest will be allowed on unliquidated damages. 1 Bouv. Inst. note 1108.

UNLIQUIDATED DEBT. A debt which one of the parties cannot alone render certain. 69 Ill. 523; 48 Ill. 409.

UNLIQUIDATED DEMAND. When any part of a demand is, in good faith, disputed, it is unliquidated. A demand is not liquidated, even if it appears that something is due, unless it appears how much is due, and when it is admitted that one of two specific sums is due, but there is a genuine dispute as to which is the proper amount, the demand is regarded as unliquidated, within the meaning of that term as applied to the subject of accord and satisfaction. 97 Ill. App. 455; 183 Ill. 183; 161 Ill. 345; 138 N. Y. 231.

UNMARRIED. Generally signifies never having been married, but sometimes used in the sense of not having a husband or wife living. 187 Ill. 315. The word is of flexible meaning to be construed with reference to the context. 170 Ill. 312.

UNNATURAL OFFENSE. Sodomy or buggery.

UNO ABSURDO DATO, INFINITA SEquuntur. One absurdity being allowed, an infinity follow. 1 Coke, 102.

UNO ACTU (Lat.) In a single act; by one and the same act.

UNO FLATU (Lat.) In one breath. 3 Man. & G. 45. *Uno fiatu, et uno intuitu,* at one breath, and in one view. 3 Story (U. S.) 504.

UNOCCUPIED. Unoccupied means no one has the actual use or possession. 153 Ill. App. 33.

Unoccupied and vacant are words of the same import. 87 Mich. 138; 49 N. W. 480.

UNQUES (Law Fr.) Still; yet. This barbarous word is frequently used in pleas, as *ne unques* executor, *ne unques* guardian; *ne unques* accouple; and the like.

UNQUES PRIST (Law Fr.) Always ready. The same as *"uncore prist."*

UNSEATED LAND. Wild or unoccupied land. See "Seated Lands."

UNSEAWORTHY. See "Seaworthiness."

UNSOLEMN WAR. That war which is not carried on by the highest power in the states between which it exists, and which lacks the formality of a declaration. Grotius de Jure Belli, et Pac. lib. 1, c. 3, § 4. A formal declaration to enemy is now disused, but there must be a formal, public act proceeding from the competent source. With us, it has been said, it must be an act of congress. 1 Kent, Comm. 55; 1 Hill (N. Y.) 409. See "War."

UNSOUND MIND, or UNSOUND MEMory. These words have been adopted in several statutes, and sometimes indiscriminately used, to signify not only "lunacy," which is periodical madness, but also a permanent adventitious insanity, as distinguished from idiocy. 1 Ridg. Parl. Cas. 518; 3 Atk. 171.

The term "unsound mind" seems to have been used in those statutes in the same sense as "insane;" but they have been said to import that the party was in some such state as was contradistinguished from idiocy and from lunacy, and yet such as made him a proper subject of a commission to inquire of idiocy and lunacy. Shelf. Lun. 5; Ray, Med. Jur. prel. § 8; 8 Ves. 66; 12 Ves. 447; 19 Ves. 286; 1 Beck, Med. Jur. 573; Cooper, Ch. Cas. 108; 2 Madd. Chanc. Prac. 731, 732.

UNTHRIFT. A person of outrageous prodigality.

UNTIL. Usually a word of limitation, unless there are other controlling expressions in the connection, showing that a different meaning is intended. 12 Ill. 304.

When time is given to file a pleading until a day named, "until" is ordinarily exclusive. 126 Iowa 669.

The word may, either in a contract or a law, have an exclusive or an inclusive meaning according to the subject to which it is applied, the nature of the transaction which it specifies, and the connection in which it is used. 12 Ill. 304; 87 Ill. 347.

UNTRUE. A statement is untrue which not express things exactly as they are. 188 Ill. 138.

UNUMQUODQUE EODEM MODO QUO colligatum est dissolvitur. In the same manner in which anything is bound, it is loosened. 2 Rolle, 39.

UNUMQUODQUE EST ID QUOD EST principalius in ipso. That which is the principal part of a thing is the thing itself. Hob. 123.

UNUMQUODQUE LIGAMEN DISSOLVItur eodem ligamine quod ligatur. Every obligation is dissolved in the same manner in which it is contracted. 12 Barb. (N. Y.) 366, 375.

UNUMQUODQUE PRINCIPORUM EST sibimetipse fides; et perspicua vera non sunt probanda. Every principle is its own evidence, and plain truths are not to be proved. Co. Litt. 11; Branch, Princ.

UPLIFTED HAND. When a man accused of a crime is arraigned, he is required to raise his hand, probably in order to identify the person who pleads. Perhaps for the same reason, when a witness adopts a particular mode of taking an oath, as, when he does not swear upon the gospel, but upon Almighty God, he is requested to hold up his hand.

UPPER BENCH. The king's bench was so called during Cromwell's protectorate, when Rolle was chief justice. 3 Bl. Comm. 202.

UPSET PRICE. In sales by auctions, an amount for which property to be sold is put up, so that the first bidder at that price is declared the buyer. Wharton.

UPSUN. In Scotch law. Between the hours of sunrise and sunset. Poinding must be executed with "upsun" (*i. e.*, while the sun is up). 1 Forbes, Inst. pt. 3, p. 32.

URBAN. Relating to a city; relating to houses.

URBAN SERVITUDES. Servitudes attached to an urban estate, such as the right of support, of drip, of drain, etc. 3 Kent, Comm. 436.

URBS (Lat.) In civil law. A walled city. Often used for *civitas*. Ainsworth. It is the same as *oppidum*, only larger. *Urbs*, or *urbs aurea*, meant Rome. Du Cange. In the case of Rome, *urbs* included the suburbs. Dig. 50. 16. 2. pr. It is derived from *urbum*, a part of the plough by which the walls of a city are first marked out. Ainsworth.

URE (Norman-French; from Lat. *opera*, a work). "Operation" or "effect." To put in ure, therefore, is to put in operation. See St. 13 Eliz. c. 2, § 1.

USAGE. Long and uniform practice. In its most extensive meaning, this term includes "custom" and "prescription," though it differs from them. In the narrower sense, it is applied to the habits, modes, and course of dealing which are observed in trade generally, as to all mercantile transactions, or to some particular branches of trade. See 9 Wend. (N. Y.) 349.

A usage must be generally known and established, and so well settled and so uniformly acted upon, as to raise a fair presumption that it was known to both parties, and that they contracted with reference to and in conformity with it. 207 Ill. App. 325.

USANCE. In commercial law. The time which, by usage or custom, is allowed in certain countries for the payment of a bill of exchange. Poth. Contr. du Change, note 15.

USE. Use is not the thing itself or any part thereof, but is that which the thing will produce, 163 Mich. 353; that which the user is to enjoy, hold, occupy, and have the fruit thereof. 163 Mich. 556, 562.

——In Lands. A confidence reposed in another, who was made tenant of the land, or terre tenant, that he would dispose of the land according to the intention of the *cestui que use*, or him to whose use it was granted, and suffer him to take the profits. Plowd. 352; Gilb. Uses, 1; Bac. Law Tr. 150, 306; Cornish, Uses, 13; 1 Fonbl. Eq. 363; 2 Fonbl. Eq. 7; Saunders, Uses, 2; Co. Litt. 272b; 1 Coke, 121; 2 Bl. Comm. 328; 2 Bouv. Inst. note 1885 et seq.

A right in one person, called the *cestui que use*, to take the profits of land which another has the legal title and possession, together with the duty of defending the same, and of making estates thereof according to the direction of the *cestui que use*.

Uses were derived from the *fidei commissa* of the Roman law. It was the duty of a Roman magistrate, the praetor *fidei commissarius*, whom Bacon terms the particular chancellor for uses, to enforce the observance of this confidence. Inst. 2. 23. 2. They were introduced into England by the ecclesiastics in the reign of Edward III., before 1377, for the purpose of avoiding the statutes of mortmain, and the clerical chancellors of those times held them to the *fidei commissa*, and binding in conscience. To obviate many inconveniences and difficulties which had arisen out of the doctrine and introduction of uses, the statute of 27 Henry VIII. c. 10, commonly called the "Statute of Uses," or, in conveyances and pleadings, the statute for transferring uses into possession, was passed. It enacts that, "when any person shall be seised of lands, etc., to the use, confidence, or trust of any other person or body politic, the person or corporation entitled to the use in fee simple, fee tail, for life, or years, or otherwise, shall from thenceforth stand and be seised or possessed of the land, etc., of and in the like estate as they have in the use, trust, or confidence, and that the estates of the persons so seised to the uses shall be deemed to be in him or them that have the use, in such quality, manner, form, and condition as they had before in the use." The statute thus executes the use,—that is, it conveys the possession to the use, and transfers the use to the possession, and, in this manner, making the *cestui que use* complete owner of the lands and tenements, as well at law as in equity. 2 Bl. Comm. 333; 1 Saund. 254, note 6.

A modern use has, therefore, been defined to be an estate of right which is acquired through the operation of the statute of 27 Henry VIII. c. 10; and which, when it may take effect according to the rules of the common law, is called the "legal estate," and, when it may not, is denominated a "use," with a term descriptive of its modification. Cornish, Uses, 35.

The common-law judges decided, in the construction of this statute, that a use could not be raised upon a use (Dyer, 155 [A]), and that, on a feoffment to A. and his heirs to the use of B. and his heirs in trust for C. and his heirs, the statute executed only the first use, and that the second was a mere nullity. The judges also held that, as the statute mentioned only such persons as were seised to the use of others, it did not extend to a term of years, or other chattel interests, of which a termor is not seised, but only possessed. Bac. Law Tr. 335; Poph. 76; Dyer, 369; 2 Bl. Comm. 336. The rigid literal construction of the statute by the courts of law again opened the doors of the chancery courts. 1 Madd. Chanc. Prac. 448, 450.

Uses and trusts are often spoken of together by the older and some modern writers; the distinction being those trusts which were of a permanent nature, and required no active duty of the trustee, being called "uses;" those in which the trustee had an active duty to perform, as, the payment of debts, raising portions, and the like, being called "special" or "active" trusts, or simply "trusts." 1 Spence, Eq. Jur. 448.

For the creation of a use, a consideration either valuable, as money, or good, as relationship in certain degrees, was necessary. Crompt. 49b; 3 Swanst. 591; 7 Coke, 40; Plowd. 298; 17 Mass. 257; 4 N. H. 229, 397; 14 Johns. (N. Y.) 210. See "Resulting Use." The property must have been *in esse*, and such that seisin could be given. Crabb, Real Prop. §§ 1610-1612; Cro. Eliz. 401. Uses were alienable, although in many respects resembling choses in action, which were not assignable at common law. Cornish, Uses, 19; 2 Bl. Comm. 331. When once raised, it might be granted or devised in fee, in tail, for life, or for years. 1 Spence, Eq. Jur. 455.

The effect of the statute of uses was much restricted by the construction adopted by the courts. It practically resulted, it has been said, in the addition of these words, "to the use," to every conveyance. Williams, Real Prop. 133. The intention of the statute was to destroy the estate of the feoffee to use, and to transfer it by the very act which created it to the *cestui que use*, as if the seisin or estate of the feoffee, together with the use, had, *uno flatu*, passed from the feoffer to the *cestui que use*. A very full and clear account of the history and present condition of the law of uses is given by Professor Washburn (2 Real Prop. 91-156), which is of particular value to the American student. Consult, also, Spence, Eq. Jur.; Cornish, Uses; Bac. Law Tracts; Greenl. Cruise, Dig.

Classification:

(1) A springing use is one limited to arise on a future event, where no preceding estate is limited, and which does not take effect in derogation of any other interest than that of the grantor.

(2) A shifting use is one which takes effect in derogation of some other estate, and is either limited by the deed by which it is created, or authorized to be created by some one named in the deed.

(3) A contingent use is one limited to take effect as a remainder.

(4) Resulting use. Where the use returns to the person who raised it because of impossibility of execution or by expiration, it is sometimes called a "resulting use." 2 Bl. Comm. 335.

——**In Civil Law.** A right of receiving so so much of the natural profits of a thing as is necessary to daily sustenance. It differs from "usufruct," which is a right not only to use, but to enjoy. 1 Browne, Civ. Law, 184; Lec. Elm. §§ 414, 416.

USE AND OCCUPATION. The character of the holding of another's land where there is no lease; also the name of an action of *assumpsit* by which a recovery is had for use and occupation.

USEE. A person for whose use a suit is brought. See 24 Miss. 77.

USER. The actual exercise of a franchise or incorporeal hereditament. User of a corporate franchise is an acceptance thereof; or nonuser may be a cause for dissolution. An easement may be prescribed upon user continued for the required time adverse to the owner of the land. Nonuser with intent to abandon extinguishes a prescriptive easement.

USER DE ACTION (Law Fr.) In old practice. The pursuing or bringing an action. Cowell.

USES TO BAR DOWER. When a conveyance of land is made in England to a person who was married to his present wife on or before the first of January, 1834, and he wishes to prevent her right to dower from attaching to the land, it is conveyed to the following uses: (1) To such uses as the purchaser shall appoint; (2) in default of appointment, to the use of him and his assigns during his life; (3) in the event of the determination of that estate, by forfeiture or otherwise, in his lifetime, to the use of a trustee during the life of the purchaser, in trust for him; with (4) an ultimate limitation to his heirs and assigns forever. By this means, the purchaser has a full power of alienation, without having a greater estate in possession than an estate for life, to which the wife's dower does not attach, and the intermediate estate of the trustee prevents the remainder in fee simple from vesting in the purchaser in possession, and so becoming liable to dower, by any accidental merger of the life estate. See Williams, Real Prop. 305, and Append. (D). See, also, "Dower."

USHER. This word is said to be derived from *huissier*, and is the name of an inferior officer in some English courts of law. Archb. Prac. 25.

USHER OF THE BLACK ROD. The gentleman usher of the black rod is an officer of the house of lords appointed by letters patent from the crown. His duties are, by himself or deputy, to desire the attendance of the commons in the house of peers when the royal assent is given to bills, either by the queen or king in person or by commission, to execute orders for the commitment of persons guilty of breach of privilege, and also to assist in the introduction of peers when they take the oaths and their seats. May, Parl. Law; Brown.

USO. In Spanish law. Usage; that which arises from certain things which men say and do and practice uninterruptedly for a great length of time, without any hindrance whatever. Las Partidas, pt. 1, tit. 2, lib. 1.

USQUE (Lat.) Up to; until.

USQUE AD MEDIUM FILUM VIAE (Lat.) To the middle thread of the way. See "Ad Medium Filum;" 7 Gray (Mass.) 22, 24.

UST. L. Fr. Had. *Ust este;* had been. *Usses, ussomus;* should or would have. Yearb. M. 8 Edw. III. 2.

USUAL. Common, frequent, ordinary, customary, general. 71 Ill. App. 153; 172 Ill. 605; 182 Ill. 541.

USUAL COVENANTS. The usual covenants expressed in a deed are "seisin" or "right to convey," "quiet enjoyment," "further assurance," "warranty," and "against incumbrances." In a lease, the covenant of quiet enjoyment is the only one that is always usual, the question being determined by circumstances and the custom of a locality. Rawle, Cov.; Tayl. Landl. & Ten. § 45.

USUAL TERMS. A phrase in the common-law practice, which meant pleading issuably, rejoining *gratis*, and taking short notice of trial. When a defendant obtained further time to plead, these were the terms usually imposed.

USUARIUS (Lat.) In the civil law. One who had the mere use of a thing belonging to another for the purpose of supplying his daily wants; a usuary. Dig. 7. 8. 10. pr.; Calv. Lex.

USUCAPIO CONSTITUTA EST UT ALIquis litium finis esset. Prescription was instituted that there might be an end to litigation. Dig. 41. 10. 5; Broom, Leg. Max. (3d London Ed.) 801, note; Wood, Civ. Law (3d Ed.) 123.

USUCAPTION. In civil law. The manner of acquiring property in things by the lapse of time required by law.

It differs from "prescription," which has the same sense, and means, in addition, the manner of acquiring and losing, by the effect of time regulated by law, all sorts of rights and actions. Merlin, Repert. "Prescription;" Aylife, Pand. 320; Wood, Inst. 165; Lec. Elm. § 437; 1 Browne, Civ. Law, 264, note; Vattel, bk. 2, c. 2, § 140.

USUFRUCT. In civil law. The right of enjoying a thing the property of which is vested in another, and to draw from the same all the profit, utility, and advantage which it may produce, provided it be without altering the substance of the thing.

Perfect usufruct is of things which the usufructuary can enjoy without altering their substance, though their substance may be diminished or deteriorated naturally by time or by the use to which they are applied; as, a house, a piece of land, animals, furniture, and other movable effects.

Imperfect or *quasi* usufruct is of things which would be useless to the usufructuary if he did not consume and expend them or change the substance of them; as, money, grain, liquors. In this case, the alteration may take place. Civ. Code La. art. 525 et seq.; 1 Browne, Civ. Law, 184; Poth. Tr. du Douaire, note 194; Ayliffe, Pand. 319; Poth. ad Pand. tom. 6, p. 91; Lec. Elm. § 414; Inst. lib. 2, tit. 4; Dig. lib. 7, tit. 1, lib. 1; Code, lib. 3, tit. 33.

USUFRUCTUARY. In civil law. One who has the right and enjoyment of a usufruct.

Domat, with his usual clearness, points out the duties of the usufructuary, which are to make an inventory of the things subject to the usufruct, in the presence of those having an interest in them; to give security for their restitution when the usufruct shall be at an end; to take good care of the things subject to the usufruct; to pay all taxes and claims which arise while the thing is in his possession as a ground rent, and to keep the thing in repair at his own expense. Lois Civ. liv. 1, tit. 11, § 4. See "Estate for Life."

USUFRUIT. In the French law, the same as the usufruct of the English and Roman law.

USURA (Lat. from *usus*, use). In the civil law. Money given for the use of money; interest. Dig. 50. 16. 121. Commonly used in the plural, *usurae*. Dig. 22. 1.

Usura centesima, usurae centesimae or *usurae asses*, twelve per cent. per annum, or one per cent. monthly. The highest rate of interest allowed before the time of Justinian. 2 Bl. Comm. 462, and note (m); Halifax, Anal. bk. 2, c. 15, No. 6; Calv. Lex.

Usurae deunces, eleven per cent. 2 Bl. Comm. ubi supra.

Usurae dextances, ten per cent. Id.

Usurae dodrantes, nine per cent. Id.

Usurae besses, eight per cent. Id.

Usurae septunces, seven per cent. Id.

Usurae semisses, six per cent. Id.

Usurae quincunces, five per cent. Id.

Usurae quadrantes, four per cent. This was the rate established by Justinian. Id.

Usurae trientes, three per cent. Id.

Usurae sextances, two per cent. Id.

Usurae unciae, one per cent. Id.

USURA EST COMMODUM CERTUM quod propter usum rei mutuatae recipitur. Sed secundario spirare de aliqua retributione, ad voluntatem ejus qui mutuatus est, hoc non est vitiosum. Usury is a certain benefit which is received for the use of a thing lent. But to have an understanding (literally, to breathe or whisper), in an incidental way, about some compensation to be made at the pleasure of the borrower, is not unlawful. Branch, Princ.; 5 Coke, 70b; Glanv. lib. 7, c. 16.

USURA MARITIMA. Interest taken on bottomry or respondentia bonds, which is proportioned to the risk, and is not affected by the usury laws.

USURAE or **USURA** (Lat.) In the civil law. Interest on money. Di. 22. 1. See "Usura."

USURARE (Law Lat.) In old English law. To pay interest; to carry or be chargeable with interest. Artic. Magna Cart. Johan. c. 34; Fleta, lib. 2, c. 57, § 7.

USURARIUS (Law Lat.) In old English law. An usurer. Fleta, lib. 2, c. 52, § 14.

USURPATIO (Lat. from *usurpare*). In the civil law. The interruption of a usucaption by some act on the part of the real owner. Dig. 41. 3. 2; Calv. Lex.

USURPATION. The unlawful assumption of the use of property which belongs to another; an interruption or the disturbing a man in his right and possession. Tomlins.

According to Lord Coke, there are two kinds of usurpation,—first, when a stranger, without right, presents to a church, and his clerk is admitted; and, second, when a subject uses a franchise of the king without lawful authority. Co. Litt. 277b.

——**In Governmental Law.** The tyrannical assumption of the government by force, contrary to and in violation of the constitution of the country.

USURPATION OF ADVOWSON. An injury which consists in the absolute ouster or dispossession of the patron from the advowson or right of presentation, and which happens when a stranger who has no right presents a clerk, and the latter is thereupon admitted and instituted.

USURPER. One who assumes the right of government by force, contrary to and in violation of the constitution of the country. Toullier, Dr. Civ. note 32.

USURY. An illegal profit required and received by a lender of a sum of money from the borrower; something exacted for the use of money in excess of and in addition to the interest allowed by law; a loan or forbearance of money for a greater rate of interest than that allowed by law. 234 Ill. 229.

Originally, the word was applied to all interest reserved for the use of money, and in the early ages, taking such interest was not allowed.

USUS (Lat.) In Roman law. A precarious enjoyment of land, corresponding with the right of *habitatio* of houses, and being closely analogous to the tenancy at sufferance or at will of English law. The *usuarius* (*i. e.*, tenant by *usus*) could only hold on so long as the owner found him convenient, and had to go so soon as ever he was in the owner's way (*molestus*). The *usuarius* could not have a friend to share the produce. It was scarcely permitted to him (Justinian says) to have even his wife with him on the land; and he could not let or sell, the right being strictly personal to himself. Brown.

USUS BELLICI (Lat.) In international law. Warlike uses or objects. It is the *usus bellici* which determine an article to be contraband. 1 Kent, Comm. 141.

USUS EST DOMINIUM FIDUCIARIUM. A use is a fiduciary ownership. Bac. Uses.

USUS ET STATUS SIVE POSSESSIO potius differunt secundum rationem fori, quam secundum rationem rei. Use and estate, or possession, differ more in the rule of the court than in the rule of the matter. Bac. Uses.

USUS FRUCTUS. In the civil law. Usufruct; the right of using and enjoying the profits of a thing belonging to another, without impairing its substance.

UT (Lat.) In old English law. That. A particle particularly appropriated to express a *modus*, or qualification, as *si* was used to express a condition. Bracton, fol. 18b. Co. Litt. 204a. This shows that *modus* and *conditio* had essentially a different import. The use of *ut* in this peculiar application was taken from the civil law.

UT AUDIVI (Lat.) As I heard. Freem. 5, 19; Bunb. 165; Dyer, 30b. A reporter's note.

UT CREDO (Lat.) As I believe. Dyer, 76b. A reporter's note.

UT CURRERE SOLEBAT (Lat.) As it was wont to run; applied to a watercourse.

UT DE FEODO (Law Lat.) As of fee.

UT POENA AD PAUCOS, METUS AD omnes preveniat. That punishment may happen to a few; the fear of it affects all. 4 Inst. 63.

UT RES MAGIS VALEAT QUAM PEREat. That the thing may rather have effect than be destroyed.

If a will is capable of a construction which will support a charitable bequest therein, the court is bound to give it that construction. 46 Wis. 70.

UT ROGAS. See "Rogare."

UT SUMMAE POTESTATIS REGIS EST posse quantum velit, sic magnitudinus est velle quantum possit. As the highest power of a king is to be able to do all he wishes, so the highest greatness of him is to wish all he is able to do. 3 Inst. 236.

UTAS (Law Lat.; Law Fr. *utave*). In old English practice. Octave; the octave (*octava*); the eighth day following any term or feast; as the *Utas* of St. Michael, the *Utas* of St. Hilary. Cowell; Y. B. H. 9 Edw. III. 4; Dyer, 78 (Fr. Ed.)

UTERINE (Lat. *uterinus*). Born of the same mother (*ex eodem utero*). A uterine brother or sister is one born of the same mother, but by a different father.

UTERO GESTATION. Pregnancy.

UTERQUE (Lat.) Both; each. "The justices, being in doubt as to the meaning of this word in an indictment, demanded the opinions of grammarians, who delivered their opinions that this word doth aptly signify 'one of them'." 1 Leon. 241.

UTFANGETHEF. Literally, an out-taken thief. The privilege of the lord of a manor to punish a thief dwelling outside his liberty for crimes committed therein.

UTI (Lat.) In the civil law. To use. Strictly, to use for necessary purposes; as distinguished from "*frui*," to enjoy. Heinec. Elem. Jur. Civ. lib. 2, tit. 4, § 415.

UTI FRUI (Lat.) In the civil law. To have the full use and enjoyment of a thing, without damage to its substance. Calv. Lex. Hence "*usus fructus*" (*q. v.*)

UTI POSSIDETIS. Lat. as you possess. In international law. A phrase used to signify that the parties to a treaty are to retain possession of what they have acquired by force during the war.

UTI ROGAS (Lat.) As you ask. In Roman law. The form of words by which a vote in favor of a proposed law was orally expressed. The letters U. R. on a ballot, expressed the same sentiment. Adam's Rom. Ant. 98, 100.

UTILE PER INUTILE NON VITIATUR. What is useful is not vitiated by the useless. 3 Bouv. Inst. notes 2949, 3293; 2 Wheat. (U. S.) 221; 2 Serg. & R. (Pa.) 298; 17 Serg. & R. (Pa.) 297; 6 Mass. 303; 12 Mass. 438; 9 Ired. (N. C.) 254. See 18 Johns. (N. Y.) 93, 94.

UTILIDAD (Spanish). In Spanish law. The profit of a thing. White, New Recop. bk. 2, tit. 2, c. 1.

UTILIS (Lat.) In the civil law. Useful; beneficial; equitable; available. *Actio utilis*, an equitable action. Calv. Lex. *Dies utilis*, an available day.

UTLAGATUS. In old English law. An outlaw.

UTLAGATUS EST QUASI EXTRA LEGem positus. Caput gerit lupinum. An outlaw is, as it were, put out of the protection of law. He bears the head of a wolf. 7 Coke, 14.

UTLAGATUS PRO CONTUMACIA ET fuga, non propter hoc convictus est de facto principali. One who is outlawed for contumacy and flight is not on that account convicted of the principal fact. Fleta.

UTLAGE (Law Fr.) An outlaw. Britt. c. 12.

UTLEP, or UTLEPE (Saxon). In old English law. Escape; the escape of a robber or robbers (*escapium latronum*). Fleta, lib. 1, c. 47, § 14.

UTRUBI. In Scotch law. An interdict as to movables, by which the colorable possession of a *bona fide* holder is continued until the final settlement of a contested right. Corresponding to *uti possidetis* as to heritable property. Bell, Dict.

UTTER. To publish; to pass or give currency to.

——**In Criminal Law.** The presentation or passing as genuine of a forgery or counterfeit.

To constitute the crime of uttering a forged instrument, the instrument must, with knowledge of its forged character, be asserted to be good, either directly or indirectly, by words or actions. 1 Whart. Crim. Law, § 703; 2 Bin. (Pa.) 332.

The instrument need not be passed; it is enough if it is presented or offered as genuine. 25 Mich. 388; 48 Mo. 520.

UTTER BAR. See "Outer Bar."

UTTER (or OUTER) BARRISTER. In English law. Those barristers who plead without the bar, and are distinguished from "benchers," or those who have been readers, and who are allowed to plead within the bar, as the king's counsel are. The same as "ouster barrister."

UTYME. (L. Fr.) An eighth. Mem. in Scacc. 25 Edw. I.

UX'. An abbreviation of *uxor.* 1 Instr. Cler. 13.

UXOR (Lat.) In civil law. A woman lawfully married.

UXOR ET FILIUS SUNT NOMINA NAturae. Wife and son are names of nature. 4 Brac. Works, 350.

UXOR NON EST SUI JURIS, SED SUB potestate viri. A wife is not her own mistress, but is under the power of her husband. 3 Inst. 108.

UXOR SEQUITUR DOMICILIUM VIRI. A wife follows the domicile of her husband. Tray. Lat. Max. 606.

UXORCIDE. A wife murderer; the killing of a wife. It is regarded in law and punished as homicide (*q. v.*)

V

V. A common abbreviation of *versus*, in the titles of causes, and reported cases.

V. F. An abbreviation of *verba fecit* (spoke). Tayl. Civ. Law, 564.

V. G. *Verbi gratia*, for the sake of example.

VS. In practice. A very common contraction of *versus* (against), used in entitling papers. Britt. c. 123.

V. V. B. C. An abbreviation of *vous voies bein coment*, you see well how. Common in the Year Book. See Y. B. M. 2 Hen. VI. 1.

VACANCY. A place which is empty. As applied to official position, has reference to an office that is unoccupied, one without an incumbent; an office not filled. 107 Ark. 386; 155 S. W. 502; Ann. Cas. 1915A 573.

It has been held to include an office newly created, and not yet filled. 108 Mo. 153. As used in statutes, it has been held to include temporary vacancies. 38 Ohio St. 23; and sometimes an office temporarily filled when it is evident from the context that such meaning was intended. 107 Ark. 386; 155 S. W. 502; Ann. Cas. 1915A 573.

By the constitution of the United States, the president has the power to fill vacancies that may happen during the recess of the senate. Whether the president can create an office and fill it during the recess of the senate seems to have been much questioned. Story, Const. § 1553. See Sergeant, Const. Law, c. 31; 1 Ill. 70.

There has been much discussion whether a failure to elect constitutes a vacancy, the question generally arising where the governor has power to fill vacancies between the sessions of the legislature, and seeks to appoint after adjournment of the legislature, without agreeing on a selection. The better reason is to the effect that a vacancy exists, and it has been so held (15 R. I. 621; 91 N. Y. 634); but the United States senate, construing section 3, art. 1, Const. U. S., providing, "if vacancies [in the senate] happen by resignation or otherwise during the recess of the legislature," the governor may appoint, has uniformly held that there was no power of appointment in the governor where the legislature had adjourned after a failure to elect.

VACANT. Vacant means empty of everything but air, wherefore a house full of furniture, clothing, etc., left in charge of servants, is not vacant. 153 Ill. App. 33, § 249a.

VACANT POSSESSION. A term applied to an estate which has been abandoned by the tenant. The abandonment must be complete in order to make the possession vacant, and therefore, if the tenant have goods on the premises, it will not be so considered. 2 Chit. 177; 2 Strange, 1064; Buller, N. P. 97; Comyn, Landl. & Ten. 507, 517.

VACANT SUCCESSION. An inheritance for which the heirs are unknown.

VACANTIA BONA (Lat.) In civil law. Goods without an owner. Such goods escheat.

VACATE. To annul; to render an act void; as, to vacate an entry which has been made on a record when the court has been imposed upon by fraud, or taken by surprise.

VACATIO (Lat.) In the civil law. Exemption; immunity; privilege; dispensation; exemption from the burden of office. Calv. Lex.

VACATION. That period of time between the end of one term and beginning of another. During vacation, rules and orders are made in such cases as are urgent, by a judge at his chambers.

VACATUR (Law Lat. it is vacated). In practice. A rule or order by which a proceeding is vacated; a vacating.

VACQUER (L. Fr.) To be at leisure. Kelham.

VACUA POSSESSIO. The vacant possession, *i. e.*, free and unburdened possession, which (*e. g.*) a vendor had and has to give to a purchaser of lands.

VADELECT. In old English law. A servant; a ministerial officer. Cowell.

VADES. In the civil law, pledges; sureties; bail; security for the appearance of a defendant or accused person in court. Calv. Lex.

VADIARE DUELLUM. To wage combat. Where two contending parties, on a challenge, give and take a mutual pledge of fighting. Cowell.

VADIARE LEGEM (L. Lat.) In old English law. To wage law; to give gage or security to make one's law at a day assigned. Spelman.

VADIATIO. L. Lat. (L. Fr. *gager*). In old English law. Wager.

VADIMONIUM (Lat.) In the Roman law. Bail or security; the giving of bail for appearance in court; a recognizance. Calv. Lex.

VADIUM. In the civil law. Pledge or security.

VADIUM MORTUUM (Lat.) A mortgage or dead pledge. It is a security given by the borrower of a sum of money, by which he grants to the lender an estate in fee, on condition that, if the money be not repaid at the time appointed, the estate so put in pledge shall continue to the lender as dead or gone from the mortgagor. 2 Bl. Comm. 257; 1 Powell, Mortg. 4.

VADIUM PONERE. To take bail or pledges for a defendant's appearance.

VADIUM VIVUM (Lat.) A species of security by which the borrower of a sum of money made over his estate to the lender until he had received that sum out of the issues and profits of the land. It was so called because neither the money nor the lands were lost, and were not left in dead pledge, but this was a living pledge, for the profits of the land were constantly paying off the debt. Litt. § 206; 1 Powell, Mortg. 3; Termes de la Ley.

VADLET. In old English law. The king's eldest son; hence the valet or knave follows the king and queen in a pack of cards. Barr. Obs. St. 344.

VAGABOND (Fr. and Eng.; from Lat. *vagabundus*, from *vagari*, to wander). A wandering person; one who habitually goes about from place to place; one who has no settled residence or domicile. *Les vagabonds sont les gens sans domicile*, vagabonds are people without a domicile. Vattel, liv. 1, c. 19, s. 219. A vagabond is said to be a person who, without traveling in quest of a domicile, has really and truly no certain domicile at all. Phillim. Dom. 23.

In English and American law, "vagabond" is always used in a bad sense, denoting one who is without a home; a strolling, idle, worthless person. Vagabonds are described in old English statutes as "such as wake on the night and sleep on the day, and haunt customable taverns and ale houses, and routs about; and no man wot from whence they came, nor whither they go." 4 Bl. Comm. 169. Rogues and vagabonds are classed together by St. 17 Geo. II. c. 5; 5 Geo. IV. c. 83; 1 & 2 Vict. c. 38; 4 Steph. Comm. 309. In American law, the term "vagrant" is employed in the same sense. See "Vagrant."

VAGABUNDUM NUNCUPAMUS EUM qui nullibi domicilium contraxit habitationis. We call him a vagabond who has acquired nowhere a domicile or residence. Phillim. Dom. 23, note.

VAGRANCY. Vagrancy is distinguished from disorderly conduct and breaches of the peace, and includes only such cases of vagabondage as are known to the common law; and its statutory definition cannot be enlarged by municipal ordinance. 41 Mich. 299.

VAGRANT. A person who lives idly, without any settled home. A person who refuses to work, or goes about begging. This latter meaning is the common one in statutes punishing vagrancy. See 1 Wils. 331; 5 East, 339; 8 Term R. 26.

VAGRANT ACT. In English law. St 5 Geo. IV. c. 83, which is an act for the punishment of idle and disorderly persons. 2 Chit. St. 145.

VAGUENESS. Uncertainty.

Certainty is required in contracts, wills, pleadings, judgments, and, indeed, in all the acts on which courts have to give a judgment, and if they be vague so as not to be understood, they are, in general, invalid. 5 Barn. & C. 583; 1 Russ. & M. 116; 1 Chit. Prac. 123. A charge of frequent intemperance and habitual indolence is vague and too general. 2 Mart. (La.; N. S.) 530. See "Certainty."

VAILLER (L. Fr.) To be worth; to be of the value.

VALE. In Spanish law. A promissory note. White, New Recop. bk. 3, tit. 7, c. 5, § 3.

VALEAT QUANTUM VALERE POTEST. It shall have effect as far as it can have effect. Cowp. 600; 4 Kent, Comm. 493; Shep. Touch. 87.

VALEC, VALECT, or **VADELET.** A young gentleman; also a servitor or gentleman of the chamber. Cowell.

VALECTA (L. Lat.) In old English law. A body-servant, or attendant; a valet; a ward of the crown. Spelman.

VALESHERIA. In old English law. The proving by the kindred of the slain, one on the father's side, and another on that of the mother, that a man was a Welshman.

VALID (Lat. *validus*). Strong; effectual; of binding force. An act, deed, will, and the like, which has received all the formalities required by law, is said to be valid or good in law.

VALIDITY. Freedom from vices of substance; effectiveness in point of law. It is broader than "form" or "requisites," as they are often applied; "form" signifying only regularity or technical phraseology, while "requisites" imports only positive requirements or essentials, and not matters extraneous to the act or instrument itself.

VALOR BENEFICIORUM (Lat.) In ecclesiastical law. The value of every ecclesiastical benefice and preferment, according to which the first fruits and tenths are collected and paid. The valuation by which the clergy are at present rated was made 26 Hen. VIII., and is commonly called the "King's Books." 1 Bl. Comm. 284*, note 5.

VALOR MARITAGII (Lat.) The amount forfeited under the ancient tenures by a ward to a guardian who had offered her a marriage without disparagement, which she refused. It was so much as a jury would assess, or as any one would give *bona fide*, for the value of the marriage. Litt. 110.

A writ which lay against the ward, on coming of full age, for that he was not married by his guardian, for the value of the marriage, and this, though no convenient marriage had been offered. Termes de la Ley.

VALUABLE CONSIDERATION. An equivalent in money or value for a thing purchased. See "Consideration."

VALUATION. The act of ascertaining the worth of a thing. The estimated worth of a thing.

It differs from "price," which does not always afford a true criterion of value; for a thing may be bought very dear or very cheap. In some contracts, as in the case of bailments or insurances, the thing bailed or insured is sometimes valued at the time of making the contract, so that, if lost, no dispute may arise as to the amount of the loss. 2 Marsh. Ins. 620; 1 Caines (N. Y.) 80; 2 Caines (N. Y.) 30; Story, Bailm. §§ 253, 254; Park, Ins. 98; Weskett, Ins.; Phil. Ins. See "Policy."

VALUATION ASSESSORS. In Pennsylvania, the assessors who estimate the value of property for taxation.

VALUE. The utility of an object. The price demanded or accepted as equivalent to the utility of anything. 161 Ill. 251; 154 Ill. 662. The worth of an object in purchasing other goods. The value of a thing is what it will produce. The first may be called "value in use;" the latter, "value in exchange." It is a relative term, depending upon different circumstances, 235 Ill. 435, and has no fixed criteria. 21 Minn. 322.

"Value" differs from "price." The latter is applied to live cattle and animals. In a declaration, therefore, for taking cattle, they ought to be said to be of such a price; and in a declaration for taking dead chattels, or those which never had life, it ought to lay them to be of such a value. 2 Lilly, Abr. 629.

VALUE RECEIVED. A phrase usually employed in a bill of exchange or promissory note, to denote that a consideration has been given for it.

The expression value received, when put in a bill of exchange, will bear two interpretations,—the drawer of the bill may be presumed to acknowledge the fact that he has received value of the payee (3 Maule & S. 351), or when the bill has been made payable to the order of the drawer, it implies that value has been received by the acceptor (5 Maule & S. 65). In a promissory note, the expression imports value received from the payee. 5 Barn. & C. 360. See 5 Wheat. (U. S.) 282.

VALUED POLICY. A valued policy is one where the value has been set on the ship or goods insured, and this value has been inserted in the policy in the nature of liquidated damages, to save the necessity of proving it in case of loss. 1 Bouv. Inst. note 1230. See "Policy."

VALVASORS, or VIDAMES. An obsolete title of dignity next to a peer. 2 Inst. 667; 2 Steph. Comm. (7th Ed.) 612.

VANA EST ILLA POTENTIA QUAE nunquam venit in actum. Vain is that power which is never brought into action. 2 Coke, 51.

VANI TIMORES SUNT AESTIMANDI, qui non cadunt in constantem virum. Vain are those fears which affect not a firm man. 7 Coke, 27.

VANI TIMORIS JUSTA EXCUSATIO non est. A frivolous fear is not a legal excuse. Dig. 50. 17. 184; 2 Inst. 483; Broom, Leg. Max. (3d London Ed.) 256, note.

VANTARIUS (Law Lat.) In old records. A fore footman. Spelman; Cowell.

VARDA. In old Scotch law. Ward; custody; guardianship. Answering to "warda," in old English law. Spelman. It had also the sense of "award." Skene de Verb. Sign.

VARIANCE. In pleading and practice. A disagreement or difference between two parts of the same legal proceeding which ought to agree together. Variances are between the writ and the declaration, and between the declaration, or bill in equity, and the evidence.

VARRANTIZATIO (Law Lat.) In old Scotch law. Warranty. Craig. de Jur. Feud. 152.

VAS (Lat.) In the civil law. A pledge; a surety; one who became bail or surety for another in a criminal proceeding or civil action. Calv. Lex. The plural, *vades* (*q. v.*), was more commonly used.

VASALLUS (Law Lat.) In feudal law. A vassal; the grantee of a fief; a feudatory. Feud. lib. 1, tit. 26; Id. lib. 2, tit. 2 et passim. Skene writes the word *vassallus.*

VASLETTUS (Law Lat.) A valet or ward. Cowell; Spelman.

VASSAL. In feudal law. The name given to the holder of a fief bound to perform feudal service. This word was then always correlative to that of "lord," entitled to such service.

The vassal himself might be lord of some other vassal.

In after times, this word was used to signify a species of slave who owed servitude, and was in a state of dependency on a superior lord. 2 Bl. Comm. 53; Merlin, Repert.

VASSELERIA. The tenure or holding of a vassal. Cowell.

VASTITAS (Law Lat. from *vastum, q. v.*) In old English law. A waste. Fleta, lib. 4, c. 22, § 6.

VASTUM (Law Lat.) Waste; a waste or common lying open to the cattle of all tenants who have a right of commoning. Par. Ant. 351; Cowell.

VASTUM FORESTAE VEL BOSCI (Law Lat.) In old records. Waste of a forest or wood. That part of a forest or wood wherein the trees and underwood were so destroyed that it lay in a manner waste and barren. Par. Ant. 351, 497; Cowell.

VAUDERIE. Sorcery; witchcraft; the profession of the Vaudois. 3 Hallam, Mid. Ages, c. ix., pt. 2, p. 386, note.

VAVASOR or **VAVASOUR** (Law Lat.) In old English law. The vassal or tenant of a baron; one who held under a baron, and who had also tenants under him.

One who in dignity was next to a baron; a title of dignity next to a baron. Camd. Brit. 109. See "Valvasors." Bracton, in enumerating the various ranks of persons under the king, mentions them in the following order: Dukes, counts or earls, barons, magnates or *vavasors*, and knights (*duces, comites, barones, magnates sive vavasores, et milites*). Bracton, fol. 5b. And again, immediately after describing barons, as powerful men under the king (*potentes sub rege*), he proceeds to a description of *vavasors* as men of great dignity (*viri magnae dignitatis*), adding the following etymology of the word: *Vavasor enim nihil melius dici poterit quam vas sortitus ad valetudinem*, for a *vavasor* cannot be better described than a vessel or pledge (*vas*) chosen for strength. Id.

The term *vavasor* first came into use in England after the Conquest, being another form of *valvasor*, which was employed in the feudal law of the continent. LL. Gul. Conq. l. 24. As a title of dignity, it occurs as late as the time of Chaucer, but afterwards fell into disuse, and is now wholly antiquated. 1 Bl. Comm. 403. The etymology of the word given by Bracton seems to present *vas* (a vessel), *validus* (strong), and *sortitus* (chosen), as its constituent elements, which is very different from that given of *valvasor* (*q. v.*)

VAVASORY. The lands that a *vavasour* held. Cowell.

VECTIGAL (Lat. from *vehere*, to carry). In the civil law. A custom or impost upon goods brought into or carried out of a state (*quod pro rebus civitati invectis vel evectis publico solvitur*). Calv. Lex.

In a general sense, a tax or tribute of any kind, paid for the use of the state. Id. See Dig. 50. 16. 17. 1; Id. 6. 3; Id. 39. 4. See a list or tariff of articles subject to this imposition. Id. 39. 4. 16. 7.

VECTIGAL JUDICIARIUM. Fines paid to the crown to defray the expenses of maintaining courts of justice. 3 Salk. 33.

VECTIGAL, ORIGINE IPSA, JUS CAESArum et regum patrimoniale est. Tribute, in its origin, is the patrimonial right of emperors and kings. Dav. 12.

VECTIAGALIA (Lat.) In Roman law. Duties which were paid to the prince for the importation and exportation of certain merchandise. They differed from "tribute," which was a tax paid by each individual. Code, 4. 61. 5. 13.

VECTURA (Law Lat. from *vehere*, to carry). In maritime law. Freight. Locc. de Jur. Mar. lib. 3, c. 6, § 7 et seq.

VEE (Law Fr. from *veer*, to forbid). In old English law. Refusal; refusal to deliver or return a thing. *Defende tort et force, et la torcenôuse detenue, et le vee des bestes avaunditz*, defends the wrong and the force, and the wrongful taking, and the wrongful detention, and the refusal of the beasts aforesaid. Britt. c. 2. *Respoyne al vee*, answer to the refusal. Id.

VEE DE NAME (Law Fr.; Law Lat. *vetitum namium*). In old English law. Refusal of a thing distrained; refusal to deliver or return a thing taken as a distress; sometimes translated "withernam" (*q. v.*) *Plees de vee de name.* Britt. cc. 19, 20, 103.

VEER (L. Fr.) In old English law. To see.

VEHMGERICHT. See "Fehmgerichte."

VEIES (Law Fr.) Distresses forbidden to be replevied; the refusing to let the owner have his cattle which were distrained. Kelham.

VEJOURS. An obsolete word, which signified viewers or experts.

VELABRUM. In old English law, a toll booth. Cro. Jac. 122.

VELITIS JUBEATIS QUIRITES? (Lat.) Is it your will and pleasure, Romans? The form of proposing a law to the Roman people. Tayl. Civ. Law, 155.

VELLE (Lat.) In the civil law. To will; to be willing; to consent. Calv. Lex.

VELLE NON CREDITUR QUI OBSEQUItur imperio patris vel domini. He is not presumed to consent who obeys the orders of his father or his master. Dig. 50. 17. 4.

VELTRARIA. The office of dog leader or courser. Cowell.

VELTRARIUS. One who leads greyhounds. Blount.

VENAL. Something that is bought. The term is generally applied in a bad sense; as, a venal office is an office which has been purchased.

VENARIA. Beasts caught in the woods by hunting.

VENATIO (Law Lat. from *venari*, to hunt). In old English law. The chase or hunt. Cowell.

VEND. To sell a chattel. As commonly used, it suggests an offering for sale to any buyer.

VENDEE. A purchaser; a buyer.

VENDENS EANDEM REM DUOBUS fallarius est. He is fraudulent who sells the same thing twice. Jenk. Cent. Cas. 107.

VENDIBLE. Capable of being sold; salaable.

VENDICARE (Lat.) In the civil and old English law. To claim a thing as one's own; to assert a right to a thing. To take a thing as one's own. Calv. Lex.

VENDITAE. In old European law. A tax on things sold in markets and fairs. Spelman.

VENDITIO (Lat.) In the civil law. In a strict sense, sale; the act of selling; the contract of sale, otherwise called "*emptio venditio.*" Inst. 3. 24; Dig. 18. 1; Calv. Lex.

In a large sense, any mode or species of alienation; any contract by which the property or ownership of a thing may be transferred. Id.

VENDITION. A sale; the act of selling.

VENDITIONI EXPONAS (Lat. that you expose to sale). In practice. The name of a writ of execution, directed to the sheriff, commanding him to sell goods or chattels, and in some states lands, which he has taken in execution by virtue of a *fieri facias*, and which remain unsold.

Under this writ, the sheriff is bound to sell the property in his hands, and he cannot return a second time that he can get no buyers. Cowp. 406. And see 2 Saund. 47. 1; 2 Chit. 390; Comyn, Dig. "Execution" (C 8); Graham, Prac. 359; 3 Bouv. Inst. note 3395.

VENDITOR (Lat.) In civil and old English law. A seller; a vendor. Inst. 3. 24; Code, 4. 54; Bracton, fol. 41.

VENDITOR REGIS (Lat.) In old English law. The king's salesman, or person who exposed to sale goods or chattels seized or distrained to answer any debt due to the king. Cowell. This office was granted by Edw. I. to Philip de Lordiner, but was seized into king's hands for abuse thereof. 2 Edw. II.

VENDOR. The seller; one who disposes of a thing in consideration of money. Generally applied only to the seller of realty.

VENDOR'S LIEN. An equitable lien or implied agreement in favor of the vendor of land sold for the purchase money, 175 Ill. 441, where the deed expresses, contrary to the fact, that the purchase money is paid. Unless waived, the lien remains till the whole purchase money is paid. 16 Ves. 329; 4 Russ. 336; 1 W. Bl. 123; 2 P. Wms. 291; 1 Jac. & W. 234; 1 Vern. 267.

VENDUE. A public auction.

VENDUE MASTER. An auctioneer.

VENIA AETATIS. In the civil law. The privilege of age. A privilege granted by a prince or sovereign, in virtue of which a person is entitled to act, *sui juris*, as if he were of full age. Calv. Lex.; Story, Confl. Laws, § 60, note.

VENIAE FACILITAS INCENTIVUM EST delinquendi. Facility of pardon is an incentive to crime. 3 Inst. 236.

VENIRE (Lat. to come). The name of a writ (more commonly called *venire facias*) by which a jury is summoned.

VENIRE FACIAS (Lat. that you cause to come). In practice. According to the English law, the proper process to be issued on an indictment for any petit misdemeanor, on a penal statute, is a writ called *venire facias*.

It is in the nature of a summons to cause the party to appear. 4 Bl. Comm. 18; 1 Chit. Crim. Law, 351.

VENIRE FACIAS AD RESPONDENDUM. A writ to summon a person, against whom an indictment for a misdemeanor has been found, to appear and be arraigned for the offense. A justice's warrant is now more commonly used. Archb. Crim. Pl. 81.

VENIRE FACIAS DE NOVO (Lat.) In practice. The name of a new writ of *venire facias*. This is awarded when, by reason of some irregularity or defect in the proceeding on the first *venire*, or the trial, the proper effect of the *venire* has been frustrated, or the verdict become void in law; as, for example, when the jury has been improperly chosen, or an uncertain, ambiguous, or defective verdict has been rendered. Steph. Pl. 120; 1 Sellon, Prac. 150.

VENIRE FACIAS JURATORES (Lat.; frequently called *venire* simply). In practice. The name of a writ directed to the sheriff, commanding him to cause to come from the body of the county, before the court from which it issued, on some day certain and therein specified, a certain number of qualified citizens who are to act as jurors in the said court. Steph. Pl. 104; 2 Graydon, Forms. 314. And see 6 Serg. & R. (Pa.) 414; Comyn, Dig. "Enquest" (C 1), etc.,

"Pleader" (2 S 12, 3 O 20). "Process" (D 8); 3 Chit. Prac. 797. See "Jury."

VENIRE FACIAS TOT MATRONAS. A writ to summon a jury of matrons to execute the writ *de ventre inspiciendo* (*q. v.*)

VENIREMAN. A juror summoned by *venire.*

VENIT ET DEFENDIT (Law Lat.) In old pleading. Comes and defends. The proper words of appearance and defense in an action. 1 Ld. Raym. 177.

Venit et defendit vim et injuriam, comes and says. Y. B. M. 1 Edw. II. 2; 2 Salk. 443.

VENIT ET DICIT. In old pleading. Comes and says. Y. B. M. 1 Edw. II. 2. 2 Salk. 544.

VENKU (L. Fr.) In old English law. Vanquished; overcome in judicial combat.

VENTE A REMERE. In French law. A sale made, reserving a right to the seller to repurchase the property sold by returning the price paid for it.

The term is used in Canada and Louisiana. The time during which a repurchase may be made cannot exceed ten years, and, if by the agreement it so exceed, it shall be reduced to ten years. The time fixed for redemption must be strictly adhered to, and cannot be enlarged by the judge, nor exercised afterwards. Civ. Code La. arts. 1545-1549.

The following is an instance of a *vente a remere.* A. sells to B. for the purpose of securing B. against indorsements, with a clause that "whenever A. should relieve B. from such indorsements, without B.'s having recourse on the land, then B. would reconvey the same to A. for A.'s own use." This is a *vente a remere,* and until A. releases B. from his indorsements, the property is B.'s, and forms no part of A.'s estate. 7 Mart. (La.; N. S.) 278. See 1 Mart. (La.; N. S.) 528; 3 La. 153; 4 La. 142; Tropl. Vente, c. 6; 6 Toullier, Dr. Civ. p. 257.

VENTER, or **VENTRE** (Lat. the belly). The wife (so applied in matters relating to child bearing). For example, a man has three children by the first and one by the second *venter.* A child is said to be *in ventre sa mere* before it is born; while it is a foetus.

VENTRE INSPICIENDO (Lat.) In English law. A writ directed to the sheriff, commanding him that, in the presence of twelve men, and as many women, he cause examination to be made whether a woman therein named is with child or not, and if with child, then about what time it will be born, and that he certify the same. It is granted in a case when a widow, whose husband had lands in fee simple, marries again soon after her husband's death, and declares herself pregnant by her first husband, and, under that pretext, withholds the lands from the next heir. Cro. Eliz. 506; Fleta, lib. 1, c. 15.

VENUE (Law Lat. *visnetum,* neighborhood. The word was formerly spelled *visne.* Co. Litt. 125a). In practice. The county in which the facts are alleged to have occurred, and from which the jury are to come to try the issue. Gould, Pl. c. 3, § 102; Archb. Civ. Pl. 86; Cowp. 176; 1 How. (U. S.) 241; 86 Mich. 7. In modern practice, it is used as synonymous with "place of trial." See 7 How. Pr. (N. Y.) 462.

The designation of the county in which the cause is to be tried in pleadings and writs. Comyn, Dig. "Pleader" (C 20); 86 Mich. 7. Generally, in modern pleading, in civil practice, no special allegation is needed in the body of the declaration, the venue in the margin being understood to be the place of occurrence till the contrary is shown. 1 Hempst. 236. See statutes and rules of court of the various states, and Reg. Gen. Hilary Term, 4 Hen. IV.

VERAY. An ancient manner of spelling *vrai,* true.

In the English law there are three kinds of tenants,—veray, or true tenant, who is one who holds in fee simple; tenant by the manner (*q. v.*), who is one who has a less estate than a fee which remains in the reversioner; veray tenant by the manner, who is the same as tenant by the manner, with this difference only, that the fee simple, instead of remaining in the lord, is given by him or by the law to another. Hammond, N. P. 394.

VERBA ACCIPIENDA SUNT SECUNDum subjectum materiam. Words are to be interpreted according to the subject matter. 6 Coke, 6, note.

VERBA ACCIPIENDA UT SORTIENTUR effectum. Words are to be taken so that they may have some effect. 4 Bac. Works, 258.

VERBA AEQUIVOCA AC IN DUBIO SENsu posita, intelliguntur digniori et potentiori sensu. Equivocal words, and those in a doubtful sense, are to be taken in their best and most effective sense. 6 Coke, 20.

VERBA ALIQUID OPERARI DEBENT—debent intelligi ut aliquid operentur. Words ought to have some effect; words ought to be interpreted so as to give them some effect. 8 Coke, 94.

VERBA ALIQUID OPERARI DEBENT, verba cum effectu sunt accipienda. Words are to be taken so as to have effect. Bac. Max. reg. 3, p. 47. See 1 Duer, Ins. 210, 211, 216.

VERBA ARTIS EX ARTE. Terms of art should be explained from the art. 2 Kent, Comm. 556, note.

VERBA CANCELLARIAE. Words of the chancery. The technical style of writs framed in the office of chancery. Fleta, lib. 4, c. 10, § 3.

VERBA CHARTARUM FORTIUS ACCIPIuntur contra proferentem. The words of deeds are to be taken most strongly against the person offering them. Co. Litt. 36a; Bac. Max. reg. 3; Noy, Max. (9th Ed.) p. 48; 3 Bos. & P. 399, 403; 1 Cromp. & M. 657; 8 Term R. 605; 15 East, 546; 1 Ball & B. 335; 2 Pars. Cont. 22; Broom, Leg. Max. (3d London Ed.) 72, note, 529.

VERBA CUM EFFECTU ACCIPIENDA sunt. Words are to be interpreted so as to give them effect. Bac. Max. reg. 3.

VERBA CURRENTIS MONETAE, TEMPus solutionis designant. The words "current money" refer to the time of payment. Dav. 20.

VERBA DEBENT INTELLIGI CUM EFfectu. Words should be understood effectively. 2 Johns. Cas. (N. Y.) 97, 101.

VERBA DEBENT INTELLIGI UT ALIquid operantur. Words ought to be so understood that they may have some effect. 8 Coke, 94a.

VERBA DICTA DE PERSONA, INTELLIgi debent de conditione personae. Words spoken of the person are to be understood of the condition of the person. 2 Rolle, 72.

VERBA FORTIUS ACCIPIUNTUR CONtra proferentem. Words are to be taken most strongly against him who uses them. Bac. Max. 11, reg. 3.

VERBA GENERALIA GENERALITER sunt intelligenda. General words are to be generally understood. 3 Inst. 76.

VERBA GENERALIA RESTRINGUNTUR ad habilitatem rei vel aptitudinem personae. General words must be restricted to the nature of the subject matter, or the aptitude of the person. Bacon, Max. reg. 10; 11 C. B. 254, 356.

VERBA ILLATA (RELATA) INESSE VIdentur. Words referred to are to be considered as if incorporated. Broom, Max. (3d London Ed.) 600, 603; 11 Mees. & W. 183, 188; 10 C. B. 261, 263, 266.

VERBA IN DIFFERENTI MATERIA PER prius, non per posterius, intelligenda sunt. Words referring to a different subject are to be interpreted by what goes before, not by what follows. Calv. Lex.

VERBA INTELLIGENDA SUNT IN CASU possibili. Words are to be understood in reference to a possible case. Calv. Lex.

VERBA INTENTIONI, ET NON E CONtra, debent inservire. Words ought to wait upon the intention, not the reverse. 8 Coke, 94; 2 Bl. Comm. 379.

VERBA ITA SUNT INTELLIGENDA, UT res magis valeat quam pereat. Words are to be so understood that the subject matter may be preserved rather than destroyed. Bac. Max. reg. 3; Plowd. 156; 2 Bl. Comm. 380; 2 Kent, Comm. 555.

VERBA MERE AEQUIVOCA, SI PER communem usum loquendi in intellectu certo sumuntur, talis intellectus praeferendus est. When words are merely equivocal, if by common usage of speech they acquire a certain meaning, such meaning is to be preferred. Calv. Lex.

VERBA NIHIL OPERARI MELIUS EST quam absurde. It is better that words should have no operation than to operate absurdly. Calv. Lex.

VERBA NON TAM INTUENDA, QUAM causa et natura rei, ut mens contrahentium ex eis potius quam ex verbis appareat. Words are not to be looked at so much as the cause and nature of the thing, since the intention of the contracting parties may appear from those rather than from the words. Calv. Lex.

VERBA OFFENDI POSSUNT, IMO AB eis recedere licet, ut verba ad sanum intellectum reducantur. You may disagree with words, nay, you may recede from them, in order that they may be reduced to a sensible meaning. Calv. Lex.

VERBA ORDINATIONIS QUANDO VERIficari possunt in sua vera significatione, trahi ad extraneum intellectum non debent. When the words of an ordinance can be made true in their true signification, they ought not to be warped to a foreign meaning. Calv. Lex.

VERBA POSTERIORA PROPTER CERTItudinem addita, ad priora quae certitudine indigent, sunt referenda. Subsequent words added for the purpose of certainty are to be referred to preceding words in which certainty is wanting. Wingate, Max. 167; 6 Coke, 236.

VERBA PRAESENTI (Lat.) Present words; words instantly operative.

VERBA PRECARIA (Lat.) In the civil law. Precatory words (*q. v.*), such as *peto* (I beg), *rogo* (I ask), *volo* (I will), *cupio* (I desire), etc.

VERBA PRO RE ET SUBJECTA MATEria accipi debent. Words should be received most favorably to the thing and the subject matter. Calv. Lex.

VERBA QUAE ALIQUID OPERARI POSsunt non debent esse superflua. Words which can have any effect ought not to be treated as surplusage. Calv. Lex.

VERBA QUANTUMVIS GENERALIA, AD aptitudinem restringuntur, etiamsi nullam aliam paterentur restrictionem. Words, howsoever general, are restrained to fitness (*i.*

e., to harmonize with the subject matter), though they would bear no other restriction. Spiegelius.

VERBA RELATA HOC MAXIME OPERantur per referentiam ut in eis inesse videntur. Words to which reference is made in an instrument have the same effect and operation as if they were inserted in the clause referring to them. Co. Litt. 359; Broom, Leg. Max. (3d London Ed.) 599; 14 East, 568.

VERBA SECUNDUM MATERIAM SUBjectam intelligi nemo est qui nescit. There is no one who is ignorant that words should be understood according to the subject matter. Calv. Lex.

VERBA SEMPER ACCIPIENDA SUNT IN mitiori sensu. Words are always to be taken in their milder sense. 4 Coke, 17.

VERBA STRICTAE SIGNIFICATIONIS ad latam extendi possunt, si subsit ratio. Words of a strict signification can be given a wide signification if reason require. Calv. Lex.; Spiegelius.

VERBA SUNT INDICES ANIMI. Words are indications of the intention. Latch, 106.

VERBAL. Parol; by word of mouth; as, verbal agreement; verbal evidence. Sometimes incorrectly used for "oral."

VERBAL NOTE. In diplomatic language, a memorandum or note not signed, sent when an affair has continued a long time without any reply, in order to avoid the appearance of an urgency which perhaps the affair does not require, and, on the other hand, not to afford any ground for supposing that it is forgotten, or that there is no intention of prosecuting it any further, is called a "verbal note."

VERBAL PROCESS. In Louisiana. A written account of any proceeding or operation required by law, signed by the person commissioned to perform the duty, and attested by the signature of witnesses. See "Proces Verbal."

VERBERA. (Lat.) In old English law. Blows; beatings. Fleta, lib. 2, c. 53, § 1.

VERBIS STANDUM UBI NULLA AMBIguitas. One must abide by the words where there is no ambiguity. Tray. Lat. Max. 612.

VERBUM IMPERFECTI TEMPORIS rem adhuc imperfectam significat. The imperfect tense of the verb indicates an incomplete matter. 6 Wend. (N. Y.) 103, 120.

VERDEROR (from Fr. *verdeur*, from *vert* or *verd*, green; Law Lat. *viridarius*). An officer in king's forest, whose office is properly to look after the *vert*, for food and shelter for the deer. He is also sworn to keep the assizes of the forest, and receive and enroll the attachments and presentments of trespasses within the forest, and certify them to the swain mote or justice seat. Cowell; Burn, Ecc. Law; Manw. For. Law, pt. 1, p. 332.

VERDICT. The expression of the concurrence of individual judgments, rather than the product of mixed thoughts. 17 Kan. 462; 20 Ann. Cas. 880.

——**In practice.** The unanimous decision made by a jury and reported to the court on the matters lawfully submitted to them in the course of a trial of a cause.

It is the theory of jury trials that, from the testimony each individual juror should be led to the same conclusion; and this unanimous conclusion is the certainty of fact sought in the law. 17 Kan. 462; 20 Ann. Cas. 880.

Under comparatively recent statutory provisions in some states a verdict or special finding in a civil case, concurred in by three-fourths of the jurors only, is valid. 171 Mo. 84; 70 S. W. 891; 7 Ohio App. 99; 100 Ohio St. 315; 125 N. E. 875.

(1) A general verdict is one by which the jury pronounce at the same time on the fact and the law, either in favor of the plaintiff or defendant. Co. Litt. 228; 4 Bl. Comm. 461. The jury may find such a verdict whenever they think fit to do so.

(2) A partial verdict in a criminal case is one by which the jury acquit the defendant of a part of the accusation against him, and find him guilty of the residue.

The following are examples of this kind of a verdict, namely: When they acquit the defendant on one count, and find him guilty on another, which is indeed a species of general verdict, as he is generally acquitted on one charge, and generally convicted on another; when the charge is of an offense of a higher, and includes one of an inferior, degree, the jury may convict of the less atrocious by finding a partial verdict. Thus, upon an indictment for burglary, the defendant may be convicted of larceny, and acquitted of the nocturnal entry; upon an indictment for murder, he may be convicted of manslaughter; robbery may be softened to simple larceny; a battery into a common assault. 1 Chit. Crim. Law, 638, and the cases there cited.

(3) A privy verdict is one delivered privily to a judge out of court. A verdict of this kind is delivered to the judge after the jury have agreed, for the convenience of the jury, who, after having given it, separate. This verdict is of no force whatever, and this practice, being exceedingly liable to abuse, is seldom if ever allowed in the United States. The jury, however, are allowed in some states, in certain cases, to seal their verdict and return it into court, as, for example, where a verdict is agreed upon during the adjournment of the court for the day.

(4) A public verdict is one delivered in open court. This verdict has its full effect, and, unless set aside, is conclusive on the facts, and, when judgment is rendered upon it, bars all future controversy, in personal actions. A private verdict must afterwards be given publicly in order to give it any effect.

(5) A special verdict is one by which the facts of the case are put on the record, and the law is submitted to the judges. 1 Litt. (Ky.) 376; 4 Rand. (Va.) 504; 1 Hen. & M. (Va.) 235; 1 Wash. C. C. (U. S.) 499; 2 Mason (U. S.) 31.

The jury have an option, instead of finding the negative or affirmative of the issue, as in a general verdict, to find all the facts of the case as disclosed by the evidence before them, and, after so setting them forth, to conclude to the following effect: "That they are ignorant, in point of law, on which side they ought upon those facts to find the issue; that if, upon the whole matter, the court shall be of opinion that the issue is proved for the plaintiff, they find for the plaintiff accordingly, and assess the damages at such a sum, etc.; but if the court are of an opposite opinion, then they find *vice versa*." This form of finding is called a "special verdict." In practice they have nothing to do with the formal preparation of the special verdict. When it is agreed that a verdict of that kind is to be given, the jury merely declare their opinion as to any fact remaining in doubt, and then the verdict is adjusted without their further interference. It is settled, under the correction of the judge, by the counsel and attorneys on either side, according to the state of the facts as found by the jury, with respect to all particulars on which they have delivered an opinion, and, with respect to other particulars, according to the state of facts which it is agreed that they ought to find upon the evidence before them. The special verdict, when its form is thus settled, is together with the whole proceedings on the trial, then entered on record; and the question of law, arising on the facts found, is argued before the court in banc, and decided by that court as in case of a demurrer. If either party be dissatisfied with their decision, he may afterwards resort to a court of error. Steph. Pl. 113; 1 Archb. Prac. 189; 3 Bl. Comm. 377; Bac. Abr. "Verdict" (D, E).

There is another method of finding a special verdict. This is when the jury find a verdict generally for the plaintiff, but subject, nevertheless, to the opinion of the judges or the court above on a special case, stated by the counsel on both sides, with regard to a matter of law. 3 Bl. Comm. 378. And see 10 Mass. 64; 11 Mass. 358. See, generally, Bouv. Inst. Index.

(6) A sealed verdict is one arrived at and delivered, to be returned to the court when it shall again convene after a recess or adjournment for the day, during which the agreement of the jurors is reached. It is inclosed in a sealed packet, and is opened and read at the ensuing sitting of the court, in the presence of the jury. It is permitted by special direction of the court in order to avoid confining the jury for a long period after agreeing, and enables them to separate subject to the duty to attend the opening of the verdict.

VERDICT SUBJECT TO OPINION OF court. A verdict returned by the jury, the entry of judgment upon which is subject to the determination of points of law reserved by the court upon the trial.

VERDIT (Law Fr. from *ver*, true, and *dit*, a saying). In old English law. Verdict; a declaration by a jury of the truth of a matter in issue, submitted to them for trial.

VEREBOT (Saxon). In old records. A packet boat, or transport vessel. Cowell.

VEREDICTUM (Law Lat. from *vere*, truly, or *verus*, true, and *dictum*, a saying). In old English law. A verdict; a declaration of the truth of a matter in issue, submitted to a jury for trial.

VEREDICTUM, QUASI DICTUM VERItatis; ut judicium, quasi juris dictum. A verdict is, as it were, the saying of the truth, in the same manner that a judgment is the saying of the law. Co. Litt. 226.

VERGE. "At common law, the coroner of the county had no jurisdiction within the compass of the king's court, which bounds the jurisdiction of the lord high steward of the household, and comprehends a circuit of twelve miles round the residence of the court (wherever held). This jurisdiction is usually called the 'verge,' within which the coroner of the king's household, or, as commonly called, the 'coroner of the verge,' had jurisdiction over all matters within the duty of a coroner, exclusive of the coroner of the county. A jurisdiction so exclusive, particularly as the king's court was movable, was found to be attended with many inconveniences, * * * and therefore it was found expedient to impart, in some cases, to the coroner of the county, a jurisdiction concurrent with that of the coroner of the verge." Jervis, Cor. 5, 59; Sts. 28 Edw. I. c. 3, and 33 Hen. VIII. c. 12, § 3.

VERGELT. In Saxon law. A mulct or fine for a crime. See "Wergild."

VERGENS AD INOPIAM (Law Lat.) In Scotch law. Verging towards poverty; in declining circumstances. 2 Kames, Eq. 8.

VERGERS. In English law. Officers who carry white wands before the justices of either bench. Cowell. Mentioned in Fleta as officers of the king's court, who oppressed the people by demanding exorbitant fees. Fleta, lib. 2, c. 38.

VERIFICATION (Lat. *verum*, true, *facio*, to make).

——**In Common-Law Pleading.** An averment by the party making a pleading that he is prepared to establish the truth of the facts which he has pleaded.

The usual form of verification of a plea containing matter of fact is, "And this he is ready to verify," etc. See 1 Chit. Pl. 537, 616; Lawes, Civ. Pl. 144; 1 Saund. 103, note 1; Willes, 5; 3 Bl. Comm. 309.

——**In Code Pleading.** The affidavit of the party, or his agent or attorney, to the truth of a pleading.

——**In Practice.** The examination of the truth of a writing; the certificate that the writing is true. See "Authentication."

VERITAS (Lat. from *verus*, true). Truth; verity.

VERITAS, A QUOCUNQUE DICITUR, A Deo est. Truth, by whomsoever pronounced, is from God. 4 Inst. 153.

VERITAS DEMONSTRATIONIS TOLLIT errorem nominis. The truth of the description removes the error of the name. 1 Ld. Raym. 303. See "Legatee."

VERITAS HABENDA EST IN JURATOre; justitia et judicium in judice. Truth is the desideratum in a juror; justice and judgment in a judge. Bracton, 185b.

VERITAS NIHIL VERETUR NISI ABscondi. Truth fears nothing but concealment. 9 Coke, 20.

VERITAS NIMIUM ALTERCANDO AMITtitur. By too much altercation truth is lost. Hob. 344.

VERITAS NOMINIS TOLLIT ERROREM demonstrationis. The truth of the name takes away the error of description. Bac. Max. reg. 25; Broom, Leg. Max. (3d London Ed.) 571; 8 Taunt. 313; 2 Jones, Eq. (N. C.) 72.

VERITAS, QUAE MINIME DEFENSAtur opprimitur; et qui non improbat, approbat. Truth which is not sufficiently defended is overpowered; and he who does not disapprove, approves. 3 Inst. 27.

VERITATEM QUI NON LIBERE PROnunciat, proditor est veritatis. He who does not speak the truth freely is a traitor to the truth. 4 Inst. Epil.

VERITY. The quality of being very true or real. Webster. Complete and absolute truth. The record of a court of record is said to import verity.

VERS (Law Fr.; from Law Lat. *versus*, *q. v.*) In old practice. Against. *Excepcions vers le juge, ou vers le pleyntyfe, vers qui il purra dire*, exceptions against the judge, or against the plaintiff, against whom he may say. Britt. c. 57.

VERSARI (Lat.) In the civil law. To be employed; to be exercised; to be continually engaged; to be conversant. *Versari male in tutela*, to misconduct one's self in a guardianship. Calv. Lex. *Versari in lucro*, to be in gain, or a gainer. Id.

VERSUS (Law Lat.) In practice. Against; an abbreviation of the Latin *adversus*. Used by Bracton indifferently with *contra* (*q. v.*) *Actio competit contra eum*, an action lies against him. Bracton, fol. 103b. *Actio datur versus eum*, an action is given against him. Id. Retained in modern practice, in the titles of causes, but commonly in its contracted forms, *vs.* and *v.* The French form, *vers*, frequently occurs in Britton.

VERT. Everything bearing green leaves in a forest. Bac. Abr. "Courts of the Forest;" Manw. For. Law, 146.

VERY LORD AND VERY TENANT. An immediate lord and tenant. Blount.

VEST. To give an immediate fixed right of present or future enjoyment; to give a legal or an equitable seisin. 246 Pa. St. 348; Ann. Cas. 1916D 573. An estate is vested in possession when there exists a right of present enjoyment; and an estate is vested in interest when there is a present fixed right of future enjoyment. Fearne, Cont. Rem. 2. See Rop. Leg. 757; Comyn, Dig.; Vern. 323, note; 5 Ves. 511.

VESTED IN INTEREST. A legal term applied to a present fixed right of future enjoyment; as reversions, vested remainders, such executory devises, future uses, conditional limitations, and other future interests as are not referred to, or made to depend on, a period or event that is uncertain. Wharton.

VESTED IN POSSESSION. An existing right of present enjoyment.

VESTED LEGACY. A legacy is said to be vested when the words of the testator making the bequest convey a transmissible interest, whether present or future, to the legatee in the legacy. Thus, a legacy to one to be paid when he attains the age of twenty-one years is a vested legacy, because it is given unconditionally and absolutely, and therefore vests an immediate interest in the legatee, of which the enjoyment only is deferred or postponed. Brown.

VESTED REMAINDER. The accepted definition of a vested remainder is, that it is one that throughout its continuance gives to the remainderman or his heirs the right to the immediate possession, whenever and however the preceding estate may determine. There must be some certain defined person in being and ascertained who answers the description of remainderman at some time during the continuance of the particular estate and not merely at the time fixed for its termination. 270 Ill. 228; 266 Ill. 17. See "Remainder."

VESTED RIGHT. A right resting on a perfect obligation. 1 Hill (N. Y.) 324. A fixed immediate right of present or future enjoyment. 24 Miss. 90.

An expectancy (8 N. Y. 110), *e. g.*, an inchoate right of dower (104 Ill. 403), is not a vested right.

There is no vested right in a remedy. 58 Wis. 621; 57 Pa. St. 433; 1 Neb. 419.

VESTER, *Vestre.* L. Fr. In old English law. To vest; to enure. Kelham.

VESTIGIUM (Law Lat.) In the law of evidence. A trace, or track; a mark left by a physical object. *Vestigia carectae,* the tracks of a cart. Fleta, lib. 1, c. 25, § 6.

VESTIMENTUM (Law Lat. from *vestire,* to clothe). In old English law. Clothing. A figurative expression denoting the character, quality, or circumstance of right, as opposed to the negation or destitution of right, which was compared to a state of nakedness. *Possessio est nuda donec ex tempore et seysina pacifica acquiratur vestimentum,* the possession is naked until a clothing [*i. e.*, of right] be acquired by time and peaceable seisin. Bracton, fol. 160.

——**In Feudal Law.** Investiture; seisin. Lord Mansfield, C. J., 1 Burrows, 109, quoting Bracton, fol. 160.

——**In Old English Law.** The technical form of a contract, requisite to give it effect. Fleta, lib. 2, c. 56, §§ 3, 4.

VESTING ORDER. In English law. A decree passing title in lieu of a conveyance for that purpose. Wharton.

VESTRY.

——**In England.** A parochial assembly.

——**In the United States.** A body of men, chosen by the parish of an Episcopal church, to have the care and management, in conjunction with the wardens, of the church's temporal affairs. Webster.

VESTRY CESS. A rate levied in Ireland for parochial purposes, abolished by 27 Vict. c. 17.

VESTRY CLERK. An officer appointed to attend vestries, and take an account of their proceedings, etc. 1 Steph. Comm. (7th Ed.) 122, note; 2 Steph. Comm. 699, note; 13 & 14 Vict. c. 57, §§ 6-8.

VESTRYMEN. A select number of parishioners elected in large and populous parishes to take care of the concerns of the parish; so called because they used ordinarily to meet in the vestry of the church. Cowell.

VESTUE. Clothed. *Contract vestue,* a clothed contract. The opposite of *nue,* naked or nude. Britt. c. 28.

VESTURA. A crop of grass or corn. Cowell. Also a garment; metaphorically applied to a possession or seisin.

VESTURA TERRAE. See "Vesture of Land."

VESTURE. In old English law. Profit of land. "How much the vesture of an acre is worth." Cowell.

VESTURE OF LAND. A phrase including all things, trees excepted, which grow upon the surface of the land and clothe it externally.

He who has the vesture of land has a right, generally, to exclude others from entering upon the superficies of the soil. Co. Litt. 4b; Hammond, N. P. 151. See 7 East, 200; 1 Vent. 393; 2 Rolle, Abr. 2.

VETERA STATUTA (Lat.) The name of *vetera statuta*—ancient statutes—has been given to the statutes commencing with *Magna Charta,* and ending with those of Edward II. Crabb, Hist. Eng. Law, 222.

VETITUM NAMIUM (Law Lat. *vetitum,* forbidden, *namium,* taking). Where the bailiff of a lord distrains beasts or goods of another, and the lord forbids the bailiff to deliver them when the sheriff comes to make replevin, the owner of the cattle may demand satisfaction *in placitum de vetito namio.* 2 Inst. 140; Rec. in Thesaur. Scacc.; 2 Bl. Comm. 148.

VETO (Lat. I forbid). A term including the refusal of the executive officer whose assent is necessary to perfect a law which has been passed by the legislative body, and the message which is usually sent, stating such refusal, and the reasons therefor.

By the constitution of the United States government, the president has a power to prevent the enactment of any law, by refusing to sign the same after its passage, unless it be subsequently enacted by a vote of two-thirds of each house. Const. U. S. art. 1, § 7. When a bill is engrossed, and has received the sanction of both houses, it is transmitted to the president for his approbation. If he approves of it, he signs it. If he does not, he sends it, with his objections, to the house in which it originated, and that house enter the objections on their journal, and proceed to reconsider the bill. See Story, Const. § 878; 1 Kent, Comm. 239. Similar powers are possessed by the governors of many of the states.

The veto power of the British sovereign has not been exercised for more than a century. It was exercised once during the reign of Queen Anne. 10 Edinb. Rev. 411; Parke, Lect. 126. But anciently the king frequently replied, *Le roy s'avisera,* which was in effect withholding his assent. In France the king had the initiative of all laws, but not the veto. See 1 Toullier, Dr. Civ. nn. 39, 42, 52, note 3.

VETUS JUS (Lat.) The old law; old law. A term used in the civil law, sometimes to designate the law of the Twelve Tables, and sometimes merely a law which was in force previous to the passage of a subsequent law.

Calv. Lex. A law principle or doctrine of long standing.

VETUSTAS (Lat. from *vetus*, old). In the civil law. Antiquity; ancient or former law or practice; the same with *antiquitas*. Inst. 3. 1. 15.

VEXATA QUAESTIO. A vexed question; a point often discussed, but undertermined.

VEXATIOUS SUIT. A suit which has been instituted maliciously, and without probable cause, whereby a damage has ensued to the defendant.

VI AUT CLAM. In the civil law. By force or covertly. Dig. 43. 24.

VI BONORUM RAPTORUM (Lat.) In the civil law. Of goods taken away by force. The name of an action given by the praetor as a remedy for the violent taking of another's property. Inst. 4. 2; Dig. 47. 8; Heinec. Elem. Jur. Civ. lib. 4. tit. 2.

VI ET ARMIS (Lat.) With force and arms. With actual or implied force. 18 Ill. 203; 147 Ill. 340. See Trespass.

VIA (Lat.) A cart way, which also includes a foot way and a horse way. See "Way."

VIA ANTIQUA VIA EST TUTA. The old way is the safe way. 1 Johns. Ch. (N. Y.) 527, 530.

VIA PUBLICA (Lat.) In the civil law. A public way or road, the land itself belonging to the public. Dig. 43. 8. 2. 21.

VIA REGIA (Lat.) In English law. The king's highway for all men. Co. Litt. 56a. The highway or common road, called "the king's" highway, because authorized by him, and under his protection. Cowell. Called also *via regalis*. Fleta, lib. 1. c. 24, § 8.

VIA TRITA EST TUTISSIMA. The beaten road is the safest. 10 Coke, 142; 4 Maule & S. 168.

VIA TRITA, VIA TUTA. The old way is the safe way. 5 Pet. (U. S.) 223.

VIABILITY (from the French *vie*). Capability of living. A term used to denote the power a new-born child possesses of continuing its independent existence.

That a child may be viable, it is necessary that not only the organs should be in a normal state, but likewise all the physiological and pathological causes which are capable of opposing the establishment or prolongation of its life be absent.

Although a child may be born with every appearance of health, yet, from some malformation, it may not possess the physical power to maintain life, but which must cease from necessity. Under these circumstances, it cannot be said to exist more than temporarily,—no longer, indeed, than is necessary to prove that a continued existence is impossible.

It is important to make a distinction between a viable and a nonviable child, although the latter may outlive the former. The viable child may die of some disease on the day of its birth, while a nonviable child may live a fortnight. The former possesses the organs essential to life, in their integrity; while the latter has some imperfection which prevents the complete establishment of life.

As it is no evidence of nonviability that a child dies within a few hours of its birth, neither is it a proof of viability if a child appears to be well, and the function of respiration be fully established.

There are many affections which a child may have at birth that are not necessarily mortal, such as transposition of some of the organs, and other malformations. There are also many diseases which, without being necessarily mortal, are an impediment to the establishment of independent life, affecting different parts of the system, such as inflammation, in addition to many malformations. There is a third class, in which are many affections that are necessarily mortal, such as a general softening of the mucous membrane of the stomach and intestines, developed before birth, or the absence of the stomach, and a number of other malformations. These distinctions are of great importance; for children affected by peculiarities of the first order must be considered as viable; affections of the second may constitute extenuating circumstances in questions of infanticide; while those of the third admit of no discussion on the subject of their viability.

The question of viability presents itself to the medical jurist, under two aspects,—first, with respect to infanticide, and, second, with respect to testamentary grants and inheritances. Billard, Infants (Translation by James Stewart, M. D.) Appendix; Briand, Med. Leg. 1ere Partie, c. 6, art. 2. See 2 Savignay, Dr. Rom. Append. III., for a learned discussion of this subject.

VIABLE (Lat. *vitae habilis*, capable of living). A term applied to a child who is born alive in such an advanced state of formation as to be capable of living. Unless he is born viable, he acquires no rights, and cannot transmit them to his heirs, and is considered as if he had never been born.

VIAE SERVITUS (Lat.) A right of way over another's land.

VIANDER. In old English law. A returning officer. 7 Mod. 13.

VICARAGE. In ecclesiastical law. The living or benefice of a vicar, usually consisting of the small tithes. 1 Burn, Ecc. Law, 75, 79.

VICARIUS NON HABET VICARIUM. A deputy cannot appoint a deputy. Branch,

Max. 38; Broom, Leg. Max. (3d London Ed.) 758; 2 Bouv. Inst. note 1300.

VICE (Lat.; ablative of *vicis*, place). In the place or stead. *Vice mea*, in my place. Used in the composition of words denoting a delegated or deputed authority.

A term used in the civil law and in Louisiana, by which is meant a defect in a thing; an imperfection. For example, epilepsy in a slave, roaring and crib biting in a horse, are vices. Redhibitory vices are those for which the seller will be compelled to annul a sale and take back the thing sold. Poth. Vente, 203; Civ. Code La. arts. 2498-2507.

VICE-ADMIRALTY COURTS. In English law. Courts established in the queen's possessions beyond the seas, with jurisdiction over maritime causes, including those relating to prize. 3 Steph. Comm. 435; 3 Bl. Comm. 69.

VICE CHAMBERLAIN. A great officer under the lord chamberlain, who, in the absence of the lord chamberlain, has the control and command of the offices appertaining to that part of the royal household which is called the "chamber." Cowell.

VICE CHANCELLOR. An equity judge who acts as assistant to the chancellor, holding a separate court, from which an appeal lies to the chancellor.

VICE CHANCELLOR OF THE UNIVERsities. See "Chancellors' Courts in the Universities."

VICE COMES (Lat.) The sheriff.

VICE COMES DICITUR QUOD VICEM comitis suppleat. "*Vice comes*" (sheriff) is so called because he supplies the place of the "*comes*" (earl). Co. Litt. 168.

VICE COMES NON MISIT BREVE (Lat. the sheriff did not send the writ). An entry made on the record when nothing has been done by virtue of a writ which has been directed to the sheriff.

VICE COMITISSA (Law Lat.) In old English law. A viscountess. Spelman. *Vice comitissa dotissa*, viscountess dowager. Com. 185.

VICE CONSTABLE OF ENGLAND. An ancient officer in the time of Edward IV.

VICE CONSUL. An officer who performs the duties of a consul within a part of the district of a consul, or who acts in the place of a consul. See 1 Phil. Ev. 306.

VICE DOMINUS. In Saxon law. A governor of a province.

VICE GERENT. A deputy or lieutenant.

VICE MARSHAL. An officer who was appointed to assist the earl marshal.

VICE-PRINCIPAL. One who performs personal duties of the master which cannot be delegated, as distinguished from a foreman or superior servant. 216 Ill. 628.

VICE VERSA (Lat.) On the contrary; on opposite sides.

VICEROY. One empowered to act in place of the king; as a colonial governor.

VICINAGE. The neighborhood; the venue.

VICINETUM (Lat.) The neighborhood; vicinage; the venue. Co. Litt. 158b.

VICINI VICINIORA PRAESUMUNTUR scire. Neighbors are presumed to know things of the neighborhood. 4 Inst. 173.

VICINIA (Lat. from *vicinus*, near). In the civil law. Nearness of dwelling; neighborhood; a neighborhood; a neighboring place. Distinguished from *confinium*, as being applied to urban estates. Calv. Lex.

VICINITY. The term does not denote so close a connection as "neighborhood." 190 Ill. 625.

VICIOUS INTROMISSION. In Scotch law. A meddling with the movables of a deceased, without confirmation or probate of his will or other title. Wharton.

VICIS ET VENELLIS MUNDANDIS. An ancient writ against the mayor or bailiff of a town, etc., for the clean keeping of their streets and lanes. Reg. Orig. 267.

VICOUNTIEL. Belonging to the sheriff.

VICOUNTIEL JURISDICTION. That jurisdiction which belongs to the officers of a county; as sheriffs, coroners, etc.

VICTUS (Lat.) In the civil law. Sustenance; support; the means of living. The word included everything necessary to the support of human life (*quae ad vivendum homini necessaria sunt*). Dig. 50. 16. 43.

VIDAME. In French feudal law. Originally, an officer who represented the bishop, as the viscount did the count. In process of time, these dignitaries erected their offices into fiefs, and became feudal nobles, such as the *vidame* of Chartres, Rheims, etc.; continuing to take their titles from the seat of the bishop whom they represented, although the lands held by virtue of their fiefs might be situated elsewhere. Brande.

A chief in the neighborhood of a church or abbey, who acted as its protector. Steph. Lect. 236.

Blackstone, quoting Camden, makes *vidame* to be a title in old English law, synonymous with that of *valvasor*. 1 Bl. Comm. 403.

VIDE (Lat.) A word of reference. *Vide ante*, or *vide supra*, refers to a previous passage, *vide post*, or *vide infra*, to a subsequent passage, in a book.

VIDEBIS EA SAEPE COMMITTI, QUAE saepe vindicantur. You will see those things frequently committed which are frequently punished. 3 Inst. Epilog.

VIDELICET (Lat.) A Latin adverb, signifying to wit, that is to say, namely; *scilicet.* This word is usually abbreviated *viz.*

The office of the *videlicet* is to mark that the party does not undertake to prove the precise circumstances alleged; and in such cases he is not required to prove them. Steph. Pl. 309; 7 Cow. (N. Y.) 42; 4 Johns. (N. Y.) 450; 3 Term R. 67, 643; 8 Taunt. 107; Greenl. Ev. § 60; 1 Litt. (Ky.) 209. See Yelv. 94; 3 Saund. 291a, note; 4 Bos. & P. 465; Dane, Abr. Index; 2 Pick. (Mass.) 214, 222; 16 Mass. 129.

VIDETUR QUI SURDUS ET MUTUS NE poet faire alienation. It seems that a deaf and dumb man cannot alienate. 4 Johns. Ch. (N. Y.) 441, 444.

VIDIMUS. We have seen. A species of exemplification of the enrollment of charters, etc. An *inspeximus (q. v.)*

VIDUA REGIS. In old English law. A king's widow. The widow of a tenant *in capite.* So called because she was not allowed to marry a second time without the king's permission; obtaining her dower also from the assignment of the king, and having the king for her patron and defender. Spelman.

VIDUITY. Widowhood.

VIE (Fr.) Life. See "Pur Autre Vie."

VIEW. Inspection; a prospect.

Every one is entitled to a view from his premises; but he thereby acquires no right over the property of his neighbors. The erection of buildings which obstruct a man's view, therefore, is not unlawful, and such buildings cannot be considered a nuisance. 9 Coke, 58b. See "Ancient Lights;" "Nuisance."

——**In Practice.** In most real and mixed actions, in order to ascertain the identity of land claimed with that in the tenant's possession, the tenant is allowed, after the demandant has counted, to demand a view of the land in question, or, if the subject of claim be rent, or the like, a view of the land out of which it issues. Viner, Abr.; Comyn, Dig.; Booth, 37; 2 Saund. 45b; 1 Reeve, Hist. Eng. Law, 435. The term is also sometimes applied to the practice of sending the jury, in the custody of an officer, to the scene of the transaction involved in the action, that they may be the better able to understand the evidence. It may also be ordered in a criminal trial to instruct the jury in respect to the place.

VIEW AND DELIVERY. When a right of common is exercisable not over the whole waste, but only in convenient places indicated from time to time by the lord of the manor or his bailiff, it is said to be exercisable after "view and delivery." Elton, Commons, 233.

VIEW, DEMAND OF. In real actions, the defendant was entitled to demand a view, that is, a sight of the thing, in order to ascertain its identity and other circumstances; as, if a real action were brought against a tenant, and such tenant did not exactly know what land it was that the demandant asked, then he might pray the view, which was that he might see the land which the demandant claimed. Brown.

VIEW OF AN INQUEST. A view or inspection taken by a jury, summoned upon an inquisition or inquest, of the place or property to which the inquisition or inquiry refers. Brown.

VIEW OF FRANK PLEDGE. In English law. An examination to see if every freeman within the district had taken the oath of allegiance, and found nine freemen pledges for his peaceable demeanor. 1 Reeve, Hist. Eng. Law, 7. It took place, originally, once in each year, after Michaelmas, and subsequently twice, after Easter and Michaelmas, at the sheriff's tourn or court leet at that season held. See "Court Leet;" "Sheriff's Tourn."

VIEWERS. Persons appointed by the courts to see and examine certain matters, and make a report of the facts, together with their opinion, to the court. In practice, they are usually appointed to lay out roads, and the like.

VIGILANTIBUS ET NON DORMIENTIbus jura subserviunt. The laws serve the vigilant, not those who sleep. 2 Bouv. Inst. note 2327. See "Laches;" Broom, Leg. Max. (3d London Ed.) 799.

VIGORE CUJUS (Law Lat.) By force whereof. 1 Ld. Raym. 412.

VIIS ET MODIS (Lat.) In the ecclesiastical courts, service of a decree or citation *viis et modis, i. e.*, by all "ways and means" likely to affect the party with knowledge of its contents, is equivalent to substituted service in the temporal courts, and is opposed to personal service. Phillim. Ecc. Law, 1258, 1283.

VILL. In England, this word was used to signify the parts into which a hundred or wapentake was divided. Fortesc. c. 24. See Co. Litt. 115b. It also signifies a town or city. Barr. Obs. St. 133.

VILLA EST EX PLURIBUS MANSIONIbus vicinata, et collata ex pluribus vicinis, et sub appellatione villarum continentur burgi et civitates. Vill is a neighborhood of many mansions, a collection of many neighbors, and under the term of "vills," boroughs and cities are contained. Co. Litt. 115.

VILLAGE. Any small assemblage of houses for dwelling or business, or both whether incorporated or not, 76 Minn. 469; 79 N. W. 510, or whether situated upon regularly laid out streets or not. 71 Ill. 569; 27 Ill. 49.

The word "village" has different meanings, and the sense in which it is employed must be determined from the context. 273 Ill. 180.

"Towns" will include "villages," 125 Ga. 559; 54 S. E. 539, but the terms are not synonymous within the meaning of the law. 197 Ill. 452.

Villages are auxiliaries of the government in the important business of municipal rule, 17 Wall. 328; agencies in the administration of civil government; public corporations partaking of the nature of municipal corporations in their incidents. 77 Me. 530; 1 Atl. 689, 690.

VILLAIN. An epithet used to cast contempt and contumely on the person to whom it is applied.

To call a man a villain in a letter written to a third person will entitle him to an action without proof of special damages. 1 Bos. & P. 331.

VILLANIS REGIS SUBTRACTIS REDUcendis. A writ that lay for the bringing back of the king's bondmen that had been carried away by others out of his manors whereto they belonged. Reg. Orig. 87.

VILLANUM SERVITIUM (Law Lat.) In old English law. Villein service. Fleta, lib. 3, c. 13, § 1.

VILLEIN (*vilis*, base or *villa*, estate). A person attached to a manor, who was substantially in the condition of a slave, who performed the base and menial work upon the manor for the lord, and was generally a subject of property, and belonging to him. 1 Washb. Real Prop. 26.

The feudal villein of the lowest order, unprotected as to property, and subject to the most ignoble services. But his circumstances were very different from the slave of the Southern states, for no person was, in the eye of the law, a villein, except as to his master; in relation to all other persons he was a freeman. Litt. Ten. §§ 189, 190; Hallam, View Mid. Ages, vol. 1, 122, 124; Id. vol. 2, 199.

VILLEIN IN GROSS. A villein annexed to the person of the lord, and transferable by deed from one person to another. Litt. § 181.

VILLEIN REGARDANT. A villein annexed to the manor or land; a serf.

VILLEIN SERVICES. Base, but certain and determined, services. 1 Steph. Comm. (7th Ed.) 187.

VILLEIN SOCAGE (Saxon, *soc*, free, or Lat. *soca*, a plough). The villeins, from living on one piece of land, came at last to be allowed to hold it by tenure of villeinage, *e. g.*, uncertain menial services. These services at last became fixed; the tenure was then called "villein socage." 1 Washb. Real Prop. 26.

VILLENAGIUM (Law Lat.) In old English law. Villenage; the condition or tenure of a villein; bondage. Glanv. lib. 5, c. 1.

VILLENOUS JUDGMENT. In old English law. A judgment given by the common law in attaint, or in cases of conspiracy.

Its effects were to make the object of it lose his *liberam legem*, and become infamous. He forfeited his goods and chattels, and his lands during life; and this barbarous judgment further required that his lands should be wasted, his houses razed, his trees rooted up, and that his body should be cast into prison. He could not be a juror or witness. Burrows, 996, 1027; 4 Bl. Comm. 136.

VIM VI REPELLERE LICET, MODO fiat moderamine inculpatae tutelae, non ad sumendam vindictam, sed ad repulsandam injuriam. It is lawful to repel force by force; but let it be done with the self-control of blameless defense,—not to take revenge, but to repel injury. Co. Litt. 162.

VINCULACION. In Spanish law. An entail. Schmidt, Civ. Law, 308.

VINCULO. In Spanish law. The bond, chain, or tie of marriage. White, New Recop. bk. 1, tit. 6, c. 1, § 2.

VINCULO MATRIMONII. See "Divorce."

VINCULUM (Lat.) A chain; a connected series; a connection or relation. See "Consanguinity."

A bond; a band; a tie. *Vinculum matrimonii*, the bond or tie of marriage; the matrimonial obligation.

The binding force of law. *Obligatio est juris vinculum*, obligation is a bond of law, or legal tie. Bracton, fol. 99.

VINDEX. In the civil law, a defender.

VINDICARE (Lat.) In the civil law. To claim, or challenge; to demand one's own; to assert a right in or to a thing; to assert or claim a property in a thing; to claim a thing as one's own. Calv. Lex. To avenge; to punish.

VINDICATIO (Lat.) In the civil law. The claiming a thing as one's own; the asserting of a right or title in or to a thing.

The name of an action *in rem*, by which a right or thing was claimed. Inst. 4. 6. 15.

VINDICATION. In civil law. The claim made to property by the owner of it. 1 Bell, Comm. (5th Ed.) 281. See "Revendication."

VINDICATORY PARTS OF LAWS. The sanction of the laws, whereby it is signified what evil or penalty shall be incurred by such as commit any public wrongs, and transgress or neglect their duty. 1 Steph. Comm. 37; 1 Brown & H. Comm. 50-1.

VINDICTA. In Roman law. A rod or wand, and, from the use of that instrument in their course, various legal acts came to be distinguished by the term; *e. g.*, one of the three ancient modes of manumission was by the *vindicta;* also the rod or wand intervened in the progress of the old action of *vindicatio*, whence the name of that action. Brown.

VINDICTIVE DAMAGES. Exemplary or punitive damages.

VIOL (Fr.) In French law. Rape. Barr. Obs. St. 139.

VIOLENCE. The abuse of force. Theorie des Lois Criminelles, 32. That force which is employed against common right, against the laws, and against public liberty. Merlin, Repert. The term is synonymous with "physical force." 31 Conn. 212. See "Force."

VIOLENT PRESUMPTION. A strong or necessary presumption. 3 Bl. Comm. 371; Burr. Circ. Ev. 60.

VIOLENT PROFITS. In Scotch law. The gains made by a tenant holding over are so called. Ersk. Inst. 2. 6. 54.

VIOLENTA PRAESUMPTIO ALIQUANdo est plena probatio. Violent presumption is sometimes full proof. Co. Litt. 6b.

VIPERINA EST EXPOSITIO QUAE CORrodit viscera textus. That is a viperous exposition which gnaws or eats out the bowels of the text. 11 Coke, 34.

VIR ET UXOR CENSENTUR IN LEGE una persona. Husband and wife are considered one person in law. Co. Litt. 112; Jenk. Cent. Cas. 27.

VIR ET UXOR SUNT QUASI UNICA persona, quia caro et sanguis unus; res licet sit propria uxoris, vir tamen ejus custos, cum sit caput mulieris. Man and wife are, as it were, one person, because only one flesh and blood; although the property may be the wife's, the husband is keeper of it, since he is the head of the wife. Co. Litt. 112.

VIR MILITANS DEO NON IMPLICETUR secularibus negotiis. A man fighting for God must not be involved in secular business. Co. Litt. 70.

VIRES ACQUIRIT EUNDO. It gains strength by continuance. 1 Johns. Ch. (N. Y.) 231, 237.

VIRGA. An obsolete word, which signifies a rod of staff, such as sheriffs, bailiffs, and constables carry as a badge or ensign of their office.

VIRGATA REGIA (Law Lat.) In old English law. The royal verge; the verge; the bounds of the king's household, within which the court of the steward had jurisdiction. Crabb, Hist. Eng. Law, 185. A space of twelve leagues in circuit around the king's palace or residence. Fleta, lib. 2, c. 2, § 2; Id. c. 4, § 2.

VIRGE, TENANT BY. A species of copyholder, who holds by the virge or rod.

VIRGO INTACTA. A pure virgin.

VIRIDARIO ELIGENDO. A writ for choice of a verderer in the forest. Reg. Orig. 177.

VIRILÍA (Lat.) The privy members of a man. Bracton, lib. 3, p. 144.

VIRTUS. (Lat.) In old English practice. The substance or tenor.

VIRTUTE CUJUS. By virtue whereof. This was the clause in a pleading justifying an entry upon land, by which the party alleged that it was in virtue of an order from one entitled that he entered.

VIRTUTE OFFICII (Lat.) By virtue of his office. A sheriff, a constable, and some other officers may *virtute officii* apprehend a man who has been guilty of a crime in their presence.

VIS (Lat. force). Any kind of force, violence, or disturbance relating to a man's person or his property.

VIS ABLATIVE (Lat.) In the civil law. Ablative force; force which is exerted in taking away (*auprendo*) a thing from another. Calv. Lex.

VIS ARMATA. In the civil and old English law. Armed force; force exerted by means of arms, weapons, or anything that can hurt or injure.

VIS CLANDESTINA (Lat.) In old English law. Clandestine force; such as is used by night. Bracton, fol. 162.

VIS COMPULSIVA. In civil and old English law. Compulsive force; that which is exerted to compel another to do an act against his will; force exerted by menaces or terror. Bracton, fol. 162.

VIS DIVINA (Lat.) In the civil law. Divine or superhuman force; the act of God, Dig. 19. 2. 25. 6.

VIS EXPULSIVA (Lat.) In old English law. Expulsive force; force used to expel another, or put him out of his possession. Bracton contrasts it with *vis simplex*, and divides it into expulsive force with arms, and expulsive force without arms. Bracton, fol. 162.

VIS EXTURBATIVA (Lat.) In the civil law. Exturbative force; force used to thrust out (*exturbare*) another. Force used between two contending claimants of possession, the one endeavoring to thrust out the other. Calv. Lex.

VIS FLUMINIS (Lat.) In the civil law. The force of a river or stream; the force exerted by the rapidity or magnitude of a current of water.

VIS IMPRESSA (Lat.) Immediate force; original force. This phrase is applied to cases of trespass when a question arises whether an injury has been caused by a direct force, or one which is indirect. When the original force, or *vis impressa*, had ceased to act before the injury commenced, then there is no force, the effect is mediate, and the proper remedy is trespass on the case.

When the injury is the immediate consequence of the force, or *vis proxima*, trespass, *vi et armis* lies. 3 Bouv. Inst. note 3483; 4 Bouv. Inst. note 3583.

VIS INERMIS. In old English law. Unarmed force; the opposite of *"vis armata."* Bracton, fol. 162.

VIS INJURIOSA. In old English law. Wrongful force; otherwise called *"illicita"* (unlawful). Bracton, fol. 162.

VIS INQUIETATIVA. In the civil law. Disquieting force. Calv. Lex. Bracton defines it to be where one does not permit another to use his possession quietly and in peace. Bracton, fol. 162.

VIS LAICA. In old English law. Lay force; an armed force used to hold possession of a church. Reg. Orig. 59, 60.

VIS LEGIBUS EST INIMICA. Force is inimicial to the laws. 3 Inst. 176.

VIS LICITA. In old English law. Lawful force. Bracton, fol. 162.

VIS MAJOR (Lat.) A superior force. In law it signifies inevitable accident.

This term is used in the civil law in nearly the same way that the words "act of God" (*q. v.*) are used in the common law. Generally, no one is responsible for an accident which arises from the *vis major;* but a man may be so where he has stipulated that he would, and when he has been guilty of a fraud or deceit. 2 Kent, Comm. 448; Poth. Pret a Usage, notes 48, 60; Story, Bailm. § 25.

VIS PERTURBATIVA (Lat.) In old English law. Perturbative force. Force used between parties contending for a possession; or, as Bracton explains it, where one contends that he possesses the thing, though he has not the right, and the other asserts that he is in possession, since he has the right (*ubi quis contendit se possidere cum jus non habeat, et alius dicat se esse in possessione, cum jus habeat*). Bracton, fol. 162.

VIS PROXIMA (Lat.) Immediate force. See "Vis Impressa."

VIS SIMPLEX. In old English law. Simple or mere force. Distinguished by Bracton from *"vis armata,"* and also from *"vis expulsiva."* Bracton, fol. 162.

VISA. In civil law. The formula put upon an act; a register; a commercial book, in order to approve of it and authenticate it.

VISCOUNT (Lat. *vice comes*). This name was made use of as an arbitrary title of honor, without any office pertaining to it, by Henry VI. for the first time. The sheriff or earl's deputy holds the office of *vice comes*, of which viscount is a translation, but used, as we have just seen, in a different sense. The dignity of a viscount is next to an earl. 1 Bl. Comm. 397.

VISE. An indorsement on a passport by the authorities, denoting that it has been examined, and that the person who bears it is permitted to proceed on his journey. Webster.

VISINETUS (L. Lat.) In old English law. Venue.

VISITATION. The act of examining into the affairs of a corporation.

The power of visitation is applicable only to ecclesiastical and eleemosynary corporations. 1 Bl. Comm. 480; 2 Kyd, Corp. 174. The visitation of civil corporations is by the government itself, through the medium of the courts of justice. See 2 Kent, Comm. 240.

VISITATION AND SEARCH. In international law. The right of a belligerent to board neutral private vessels on the high seas, or in the waters of either belligerent, and examine their papers and cargo. See Wheaton, Int. Law, § 525; Hall, Int. Law, p. 724.

VISITATION BOOKS. Compilations made out or collected by the heralds in the circuits which their commissions authorized them to make, for the purpose of inquiring into the state of families and registering marriages and descents which were verified to them by oath. They are good evidence of pedigree. 3 Bl. Comm. 105.

VISITER. An inspector of the government, of corporations, or bodies politic. 1 Bl. Comm. 482. See Dane, Abr. Index; 7 Pick. (Mass.) 303; 12 Pick. (Mass.) 244.

VISNE. The neighborhood; a neighboring place; a place near at hand; the venue.

Formerly the visne was confined to the immediate neghborhood where the cause of action arose, and many verdicts were disturbed because the visne was too large, which becoming a great grievance, several statutes were passed to remedy the evil. 21 Jac. I. c. 13, gives aid after verdict, where the visne is partly wrong,—that is, where it is warded out of too many or too few places in the county named. 16 & 17

Car. II. c. 8, goes further, and cures defects of the visne wholly, so that the cause is tried by a jury of the proper county. See "Venue."

VISUS (Lat.) In old English practice. View; inspection, either of a place or person.

Examination or inspection by jurors of the subject of an action. Fleta, lib. 4, c. 6, § 1 et seq. See "Vew."

VISUS TERRAE (L. Lat.) In old English practice. View of land. Stat. Westm. 2, c. 48.

VITILITIGATION. Cavilous litigation. Obsolete. Webster.

VITIOUS INTROMISSION. See "Vicious Intromission."

VITIUM CLERICI NOCERE NON DEBET. Clerical errors ought not to prejudice. Jenk. Cent. Cas. 23; Dig. 34. 5. 3.

VITIUM EST QUOD FUGI DEBET, NE, si rationem non invenias, mox legem sine ratione esse clames. It is a fault which ought to be avoided, that if you cannot discover the reason, you should presently exclaim that the law is without reason. Ellesmere, Postn. 86.

VITIUM SCRIPTORIS. In old English law. The fault or mistake of a writer or copyist; a clerical error. Gilb. For. Rom. 185.

VIVA AQUA. In the civil law. Living water; running water; that which issues from a spring or fountain (*quae fonte exit*). Calv. Lex.

VIVA PECUNIA (Law Lat.) In old English law. Live cattle. See "Pecunia."

VIVA VOCE (Lat. with the living voice). Verbally. It is said a witness delivers his evidence *viva voce* when he does so in open court. The term is opposed to "deposition." It is sometimes opposed to "ballot;" as, the people vote by ballot, but their representatives in the legislature vote *viva voce*.

VIVA VOX (Lat.) The living voice; oral utterance, as distinguished from written words. Hence the common phrase, *viva voce*, by word of mouth.

VIVARIUM, or VIVARY (Lat. from *vivus*, alive).

——**In the Civil Law.** An inclosed place, where live wild animals are kept. Calv. Lex.; Spelman; A. Gell. Noct. Att. ii. 20.

——**In Old English Law.** A place in land or water where living things are kept; a vivary. Most commonly in law it signifies a park, warren, or fishery. In the statute of Merton (c. 11) it is taken for a warren and fishery. 2 Inst. 100; Fleta, lib. 2, c. 41, § 2.

VIVUM VADIUM. See "Vadium Vivum."

VIX (Lat.) Scarcely; hardly; rarely.

VIX ULLA LEX FIERI POTEST QUAE omnibus commoda sit, sed si majori parti, prospiciat, utilis est. Scarcely any law can be made which is beneficial to all; but if it benefit the majority, it is useful. Plowd. 369.

VOCABULA ARTIS (Lat.) Words of art; "vocables" of art; technical terms. Co. Litt. pref.; 5 Coke, 121b.

VOCABULA ARTIUM EXPLICANDA sunt secundum definitiones prudentium. Terms of art should be explained according to the definitions of those who are most experienced in that art. Puffendorff, de Off. Hom. lib. 1, c. 17, § 3; Grotius de Jure Belli, lib. 2, c. 16, § 3.

VOCARE AD CURIAM. In feudal law. To summon to court. Feud. lib. 2, tit. 22.

VOCATIO IN JUS (Lat.) In Roman law. According to the practice in the *legis actiones* of the Roman law, a person having demand against another verbally cited him to go with him to the praetor; *in jus eamus; in jus te voco.* This was denominated *vocatio in jus.* If a person thus summoned refused to go, he could be compelled by force to do so, unless he found a *vindex*,—that is, a procurator, or a person to undertake his cause. When the parties appeared before the praetor, they went through the particular formalities required by the action applicable to the cause. If the cause was not ended the same day, the parties promised to appear again at another day, which was called *vadimonium*. See Matt. v. 25.

VOCIFERATIO (Lat.) In old English law. Outcry; hue and cry. Cowell.

VOCO (Lat.) In civil and old English law. I call; I summon; I vouch. *In jus voco te*, I summon you to court; I summon you before the praetor. The formula by which a Roman action was anciently commenced. Adams, Rom. Ant. 242. *Voco talem*, I call or vouch such a one. The old formula of vouching to warranty. Bracton, fol. 382b.

VOID. That which has no force or effect. "Void" is often loosely used in varied meanings, and applied indifferently to a thing which has no force or effect, and is an absolute nullity, or to that which by reason of some inherent vice or defect, may be adjudged void by a court when the question is presented to it; 214 Ill. 395; often used in the sense of "voidable" (*q. v.*) 44 Pa. St. 15.

VOIDABLE. That which has some force or effect, but which, in consequence of some inherent quality, may be legally annulled or avoided.

The steps to avoid it must be taken by the proper party and by means of a direct attack upon it. 156 Ill. 544; 181 Ill. App. 53; 252 Ill. 42.

VOILOIR, *Voillour*. L. Fr. In old English law. A will; a testament. Kelham.

VOIR DIRE. A preliminary examination of a witness or venireman to ascertain whether he is competent.

VOLENTI NON FIT INJURIA. He who consents cannot receive an injury. 2 Bouv. Inst. notes 2279, 2327; Broom, Leg. Max. (3d London Ed.) 245; Shelf. Mar. & Div. 449; Wingate, Max. 482; 4 Term R. 657; Plowd. 501.

VOLO (Lat.) I will; I wish or desire. One of the appropriate words used in Roman testaments to create a trust. Inst. 2. 24. 3. Bracton uses it as a term of conveyance. Bract. fol. 18b.

VOLUIT SED NON DIXIT. He willed, but did not say. 4 Kent, Comm. 538.

VOLUMEN (Lat. from *volvere*, to roll.) In the civil law. A volume; so called from its form, being rolled up.

VOLUMUS. We will. The first word of a clause in the royal writs of protection and letters patent.

VOLUNTARIUS DAEMON. A drunkard. Co. Litt. 247a.

VOLUNTARY. Willingly; done with one's consent; negligently. Wolff. § 5.

VOLUNTARY ANSWER. In chancery practice. An answer put in by a defendant, when the plaintiff had filed no interrogatories which required an answer.

VOLUNTARY ASSIGNMENT. An assignment made by a debtor in trust for the benefit of his creditors. So called in contradistinction from "compulsory assignments," or such as are made under statutes of bankruptcy and insolvency, or by order of some competent court. Burrill, Assignm. p. 4; 10 Paige (N. Y.) 445; 1 Comst. (N. Y.) 201.

VOLUNTARY CONVEYANCE. The transfer of an estate made without any adequate consideration of value.

VOLUNTARY DEPOSIT. In civil law. A deposit which is made by the mere consent or agreement of the parties. 1 Bouv. Inst. note 1054. See "Deposit."

VOLUNTARY ESCAPE. The giving to a prisoner voluntarily any liberty not authorized by law. 5 Mass. 310; 2 Chipm. (Vt.) 11; 3 Har. & J. (Md.) 559; 2 Har. & G. (Md.) 106; 2 Bouv. Inst. note 2332. See "Escape."

VOLUNTARY IGNORANCE. A willing omission to learn or know.

VOLUNTARY JURISDICTION. In ecclesiastical law. That kind of jurisdiction which requires no judicial proceedings; as, the granting letters of administration and receiving the probate of wills.

VOLUNTARY MANSLAUGHTER. See "Manslaughter."

VOLUNTARY NONSUIT. In practice. The abandonment of his cause by a plaintiff, and an agreement that a judgment for costs be entered against him. 3 Bouv. Inst. note 3306.

VOLUNTARY OATH. An oath taken in some extrajudicial matter, or before some magistrate or officer who cannot compel it to be taken.

VOLUNTARY PAYMENT. That made by free will and choice. Not compelled by process or force.

VOLUNTARY REDEMPTION. In Scotch law. Where a mortgagee receives the sum due into his own hands, and discharges the mortgage, without any consignation. Bell, Dict.

VOLUNTARY SALE. One made freely, without constraint, by the owner of the thing sold. 1 Bouv. Inst. note 974.

VOLUNTARY SETTLEMENT. A transaction whereby a grantor makes and executes a deed which he does not deliver to the grantee, but leaves it with a notary with instructions to record the deed after the death of the grantor is a voluntary settlement. 216 Ill. 164.

VOLUNTARY WASTE. That which is either active or willful, in contradistinction to that which arises from mere negligence, which is called "permissive" waste. 2 Bouv. Inst. 2394 et seq. See "Waste."

VOLUNTAS DONATORIS, IN CHARTA doni sui manifeste expressa observetur. The will of the donor, clearly expressed in the deed, should be observed. Co. Litt. 21a.

VOLUNTAS EST JUSTA SENTENTIA de eo quod quis post mortem suam fieri velit. A will is an exact opinion or determination concerning that which each one wishes to be done after his death.

VOLUNTAS ET PROPOSITUM DISTINguunt maleficia. The will and the proposed end distinguish crimes. Bracton, 2b, 136b.

VOLUNTAS FACIT QUOD IN TESTAmento scriptum valeat. The will of the testator gives validity to what is written in the will. Dig. 30. 1. 12. 3.

VOLUNTAS IN DELICTIS NON EXITUS spectatur. In offenses, the will, and not the consequences, are to be looked to. 2 Inst. 57.

VOLUNTAS REPUTABATUR PRO FACto. The will is to be taken for the deed. 3 Inst. 69.

VOLUNTAS TESTATORIS AMBULATOria est usque ad mortem. The will of a testator is ambulatory until his death; that is, he may change it at any time. See 1 Bouv. Inst. note 83; 4 Coke, 61.

VOLUNTAS TESTATORIS HABET INterpretationem latam et benignam. The will of a testator has a broad and liberal interpretation. Jenk. Cent. Cas. 260; Dig. 50. 17. 12.

VOLUNTAS ULTIMA TESTATORIS EST perimplenda secundum veram intentionem suam. The last will of a testator is to be fulfilled according to his true intention. Co. Litt. 322.

VOLUNTEER.

——**In Conveyances.**

Persons who receive a voluntary conveyance.

It is a general rule of the courts of equity, that they will not assist a mere volunteer who has a defective conveyance. Fonbl. Eq. bk. 1, c. 5, § 2. And see the note there for some exceptions to this rule. See, generally, 1 Madd. 271; 1 Supp. Ves. Jr. 320; 2 Supp. Ves. Jr. 321; Powell, Mortg. Index; 4 Bouv. Inst. notes 3968-3973.

——**Rendition of Services.** One who introduces himself into matters which do not concern him, and does, or undertakes to do, something which he is not bound to do or which it is not in pursuance or protection of any interest of the master, and which is undertaken in the absence of any peril requiring him to act as on an emergency. 279 Ill. 17.

One who has no interest in the work being done; a person who gives his services without any express or implied promise of remuneration in return. 82 Ill. App. 674.

——**In Military Law.** Persons who, in time of war, voluntarily enlist in the military service.

Their rights and duties are prescribed by the municipal laws of the different states, but when in actual service, they are subject to the laws of the United States and the articles of war.

VOTE. Suffrage; the voice of an individual in making a choice by many. The total number of voices given at an election; as, the presidential vote.

VOTING TRUST. A voting trust may be comprehensively defined as one created by an agreement between a group of the stockholders of a corporation and the trustee, or by a group of identical agreements between individual stockholders and a common trustee, whereby upon certain contingencies or under certain circumstances, it is provided that control over the stock owned by such stockholders shall be lodged in the trustee, either with or without a reservation to the owners or persons designated by them of the power to direct how such control shall be used. 3 Fletcher Cyclopedia Corporations 2871.

VOTUM. A vow or promise. *Dies votorum,* the wedding day. Fleta, 1, 4.

VOUCHEE. In common recoveries, the person who is called to warrant or defend the title is called the "vouchee." 2 Bouv. Inst. note 2093.

——**In Accounts.** An account book in which are entered the acquittances or warrants for the accountant's discharge. Any acquittance or receipt which is evidence of payment, or of the debtor's being discharged. See 3 Halst. (N. J.) 299; 1 Metc. (Mass.) 218.

VOUCHER. The ordinary meaning of "voucher" is a document which shows that services have been performed or expenses incurred. It covers any acquittance or receipt discharging the person or evidencing payment by him. When used in connection with the disbursement of moneys it implies some instrument that shows on what account or by what authority a particular payment has been made, or that services have been performed which entitle the party to whom it is issued to payment. It vouches for the truth of accounts or estimates. 136 Ill. App. 465.

——**In Old Conveyancing.** The person on whom the tenant to the *praecipe* calls to defend the title to the land, because he is supposed to have warranted the title to him at the time of the original purchase.

The person usually employed for this purpose is the crier of the court, who is therefore called the "common voucher." Cruise, Dig. tit. 36, c. 3, § 1; 22 Viner, Abr. 26; Dane, Index. See "Recovery."

VOUCHER TO WARRANTY. The calling one who has warranted lands, by the party warranted, to come and defend the suit for him. Co. Litt. 101b.

VOUS VEIES (VOIES, or VEITZ) BIEN coment (Law Fr. you see well how). Formal words anciently used by counsel in addressing the court. Y. B. T. 1 Edw. III. 9; Y. B. H. 2 Edw. III. 9; Y. B. P. 8 Edw. III. 23; Y. B. M. 4 Hen. VI. 1.

VOX (L. Lat.) In old practice. Speech; saying; statement. Fleta, lib. 2, c. 61, § 1; c. 63, § 9.

VOX EMISSA VOLAT; LITERA SCRIPta manet. Words spoken vanish; words written remain. A written contract cannot be varied by parol proof. Broom, Leg. Max. (3d London Ed.) 594; 1 Johns. (N. Y.) 571, 572.

VULGARIS OPINIO EST DUPLEX, VIZ., orta inter graves et discretos, quae multum veritatis habet, et opinio orta inter leves et vulgares homines absque specie veritatis.

Common opinion is of two kinds, viz., that which arises among grave and discreet men, which has much truth in it, and that which arises among light and common men, without any appearance of truth. 4 Coke, 107.

VULGARIS PURGATIO (Law Lat.) In old English law. Common purgation; a name given to the trial by ordeal, to distinguish it from the canonical purgation, which was by the oath of the party. 4 Bl. Comm. 342.

VULGO CONCEPTI (Lat.) In the civil law. Spurious children; bastards; those who cannot point out their father, or, if they can, have him for a father whom it is not lawful to have (*qui patrem demonstrare non possunt, vel qui possunt quidem, sed eum habent quem habere non licet*). Dig. 1. 5. 23.

VULGO QUAESITI (Lat.) In the civil law. Spurious children; literally, gotten from the people; the offspring of promiscuous cohabitation, who are considered as having no father. Inst. 3. 4. 3; Id. 3. 5. 4.

VYCINE (Law Fr.; Lat. *vicinus*). A neighbor. Dyer, 36b (Fr. Ed.)

W

WACREOUR (Law Fr.) In old English law. A vagabond or vagrant. *De wacreours per pays.* Britt. c. 29.

WADIUS, *Wadium.* L. Lat. In old European law. A pledge. Spelman.

WADSET. In Scotch law. A right by which lands or other heritable subjects are impignorated by the proprietor to his creditor in security of his debt. Like other heritable rights, it is protected by seisin.

Wadsets, by the present practice, are commonly made out in the form of mutual contracts, in which one party sells the land, and the other grants the right of reversion. Ersk. Inst. 2. 8. 1. 2.

Wadsets are proper where the use of the land shall go for the use of the money; improper where the reverser agrees to make up the deficiency; and where it amounts to more, the surplus profit of the land is applied to the extinction of the principal. Ersk. Inst. 2. 8. 12. 13.

WADSETTER. In Scotch law. A creditor to whom a wadset is made.

WAFTORS. Conductors of vessels at sea. Cowell.

WAGE. To give a pledge or security for the performance of anything; as to wage or gage deliverance to wage law, etc. Co. Litt. 294. This word is but little used.

WAGER. A wager is a contract by which two or more parties agree that a certain sum of money or other thing shall be paid or delivered to one of them on the happening of an uncertain event. 75 Ill. 560; 78 Ill. App. 241; 113 Ill. 239.

A bet (*q. v.*)

WAGER OF BATTEL. A superstitious mode of trial which formerly disgraced the English law.

The last case of this kind was commenced in the year 1817 but not proceeded in to judgment; and at the next session of the British parliament an act was passed to abolish appeals of murder, treason, felony, or other offenses, and wager of battel, or joining issue or trial by battel, in writs of right. 59 Geo. III. c. 46. For the history of this species of trial, see 3 Bl. Comm. 337; 4 Bl. Comm. 347; Enc. "Gage de Bataille;" Steph. Pl. 122, and Append. note 35.

WAGER OF LAW. In old practice. An oath taken by a defendant in an action of debt that he does not owe the claim, supported by the oaths of eleven neighbors.

When an action of debt is brought against a man upon a simple contract, and the defendant pleads *nil debet,* and concludes his plea with this plea, with this formula, "And this he is ready to defend against him the said A. B. and his suit, as the court of our lord the king here shall consider," etc., he is then put in sureties (*vadios*) to wage his law on a day appointed by the judge. The wager of law consists in an oath taken by the defendant on the appointed day, and confirmed by the oaths of eleven neighbors or compurgators. This oath had the effect of a verdict in favor of the defendant, and was only allowed in the actions of debt on simple contract and detinue; nor was it allowed to any one not of good character. In consequence of this privilege of the defendant, *assumpsit* displaces debt as a form of action on simple contracts, and, instead of detinue, trover was used. But in England, wager of law was abolished by 3 & 4 Wm. IV. c. 42, § 13. And even before its abolition it had fallen into disuse. It was last used as a method of defense in 2 Barn. & C. 538, where the defendant offered to wage his law, but the plaintiff abandoned the case. This was in 1824. If it ever had any existence in the United States, it is now completely abolished. 8 Wheat. (U. S.) 642.

The name (in law Latin, *vadiatio legis*) comes from the defendant's being put in pledges (*vadios*) to make his oath on the appointed day. There was a similar oath in the Roman law, and in the laws of most of the nations that conquered Rome. It was very early in use in England, as Glanville distinctly describes it. Glanv. lib. 1, c. 9, 12. See Steph. Pl. 124, 250, and note xxxix.; 2 Inst. 119; Mod. Entr. 179; Lilly, Entr. 467; 3 Chit. Pl. 497; 13 Viner, Abr. 58; Bac. Abr.; Dane, Abr. Index. For the origin of this form of trial, see Steph. Pl. note xxxix.; Co. Litt. 394, 395; 3 Bl. Comm. 341.

WAGER POLICY. In insurance law. A policy without any real interest to support it; a policy in which the insured has no interest, being in fact nothing more than a wager or bet between the parties, whether such a voyage would be performed, or such a ship arrive safe. 3 Kent, Comm. 277, 278. A mere hope or expectation, without some interest in the subject matter, is a wager policy. Id. 275. Mr. Arnould defines a wager policy to be "one in which the parties, by express terms, disclaim, on the face of it, the intention of making a contract of indemnity." 1 Arnould, Ins. 276 (281, Perkins Ed.) Policies of this kind are now generally held to be illegal. Id. 285 (289); 1 Duer, Ins. 93-95, 154, 155.

WAGERING CONTRACTS. See "Gambling Contract."

WAGES. A compensation given to a hired person for manual or other inferior services.

The term "wages" does not include "salary," and the term "wages earned" is an apt expression in regard to laborers who are only entitled to pay for services actually rendered, but is entirely inappropriate when used concerning public officers or clerks who receive annual salaries, which are not due until the end of the year, and who are entitled to be paid so long as they hold their offices, without regard to the services rendered. 25 Abb. N. C. (N. Y.) 368. See "Salary."

WAIFS. Stolen goods waived or scattered by a thief in his flight in order to effect his escape.

Such goods, by the English common law, belong to the king. 1 Bl. Comm. 296; 5 Coke, 109; Cro. Eliz. 694. This prerogative has never been adopted here against the true owner, and never put in practice against the finder, though against him there would be better reason for adopting it. 2 Kent, Comm. 292. See Comyn, Dig.; 1 Brown, Civ. Law, 239, note.

WAINABLE. In old records. That may be plowed or manured; tillable. Cowell; Blount.

WAINAGE. In old English law. The team and instruments of husbandry belonging to a countryman, and especially to a villein who was required to perform agricultural services.

WAINAGIUM (Saxon *woeg;* Lat. *vagina*). What is necessary to the farmer for the cultivation of his land. Barr. Obs. St. p. 12; Magna Charta, c. 14. According to Selden and Lord Bacon, it is not the same as *contenementum,* used in the same chapter of *Magna Charta,* meaning the power of entertaining guests, or countenance, as common people say.

WAITING CLERKS. Officers whose duty it formerly was to wait in attendance upon the court of chancery. The office was abolished in 1842 by St. 5 & 6 Vict. c. 103. Mozley & W.

WAIVE. A term applied to a woman as "outlaw" is applied to a man. A man is an outlaw; a woman is a waive. Crabb.

To abandon or forsake a right.

To abandon without right; as, "if the felon waives,—that is, leaves any goods in his flight from those who either pursue him, or are apprehended by him so to do,—he forfeits them, whether they be his own goods, or goods stolen by him." Bac. Abr. "Forfeiture" (B).

WAIVER. The voluntary surrender and relinquishment of a right. 29 Minn. 191. The intentional relinquishment of a known right. 153 Ill. 468.

It is a somewhat narrower term than "abandonment" (*q. v.*) and is applied to rights, not to property.

To constitute a waiver proper, there must ordinarily be a valuable consideration (75 N. Y. 453), a full knowledge of the right to be waived (48 N. Y. 399), and an actual intent to waive (15 Gray [Mass.] 229); but where there are circumstances of estoppel, *i. e.,* where a party has misled another to his prejudice as to intent to insist on a right, it amounts to a waiver, irrespective of intent (7 Lea [Tenn.] 467), or consideration (30 N. Y. 164); and there are certain acts to which the law imputes the character of a waiver, irrespective of intent, as the right to a dilatory plea is waived by pleading to the merits (29 Conn. 82).

Unless affected by the statute of frauds (9 Wend. [N. Y.] 79), no special formalities are required, and even a writing under seal may be waived by parol (101 U. S. 527).

WAIVIARE. (L. Lat.) In old English law. To waive; to throw away; to forsake, or abandon. Spelman.

WAKEMAN. The chief magistrate of Ripon, in Yorkshire. Camd. Brit.

WAKENING. In Scotch law. The revival of an action.

An action is said to sleep when it lies over, not insisted on for a year, in which case it is suspended. Ersk. Inst. 4. 1. 33. With us a revival is by *scire facias.*

WALAPAUZ (Lomb.) In old Lombardic law. The disguising the head or face, with the intent of committing a theft. LL. Longobard, tit. 15, cap. ult.

WALESCHERY. The being a Welshman. Spelman.

WALISCUS. In Saxon law. A servant or any ministerial officer. Cowell.

WALKERS. Foresters who have the care of a certain space of ground assigned to them. Cowell.

WALLA, or WALLIA (Law Lat.; from Saxon *wal;* Lat. *vallum*). In old English law. A bank of earth cast up for a mound, or boundary; a wall; a sea wall. 2 Mon. Angl. 920; Cowell; Spelman, voc. Wallia.

WAND OF PEACE. In Scotch law. The wand which the messenger carries along with his blazon, in executing a caption, and with which he touches the prisoner. A sliding along this staff of a movable ring, or the breaking of the staff, is a protest that the officer has been resisted or deforced. Burton, Law Scot. p. 572; Bell, Dict. "Imprisonment."

WANG (Saxon). In old English law. A field. Blount.

The cheek or jaw wherein the teeth are set. "Hence, with Chaucer," says Blount, "we call the cheek teeth or grinders 'wangs' and 'wang teeth,' which is also notified in that old way of sealing writings:

'And in witness that this is sooth,
I bite the wax with my wang tooth.' "

WANLASS. An ancient customary tenure of lands; *i. e.*, to drive deer to a stand, that the lord may have a shot. Blount, Ten. 140.

WANTON. Reckless; disregarding the rights of others; without reasonable excuse See 14 Tex. App. 201. The act must be intentional, with design, and under circumstances evincing a reckless destructive spirit. 147 Wis. 70, 75. It is not synonymous with "wilful." 28 Ind. 290.

WAPENTAKE (from Saxon, *wapen, i. e., armatura*, and *tac, i. e., tactus*). A Saxon court, held monthly by the alderman for the benefit of the hundred.

It was called a "wapentake" from "wapen," arms, and "tac," to touch; because, when the chief of the hundred entered upon his office, he appeared in the field on a certain day, on horseback, with a pike in his hand, and all the principal men met him with lances. Upon this he alighted, and they all touched his pike with their lances, in token of their submission to his authority. In this court, causes of great moment were heard and determined, as Mr. Dugdale has shown from several records. Besides which, it took cognizance of theft, trials by ordeal, view of frank pledge, and the like; whence after the Conquest it was called the sheriff's tourn, and, as regarded the examination of the pledges, the court of the view of frank pledge. These pledges were no other than the freemen within the liberty, who, according to an institution of King Alfred, were mutually pledged for the good behavior of each other. Fortesc. de Laud. c. 24; Dugd. Orig. Jur. 27; 4 Bl. Comm. 273. Sir Thomas Smith derives it from the custom of taking away the arms, at the muster of each hundred, from those who could not find sureties for good behavior. Rep. Angl. lib. 2, c. 16.

WAR. War is a hostile contest with arms between two or more states or communities claiming sovereign rights. Field, Int. Code, p. 467.

Classification:

(1) War is either offensive, defensive, or auxiliary. The distinction between offensive and defensive war has been based on the provocation leading to the war, but this test is difficult of application. The most practical test is as to the belligerent in whose territory the war is waged. See Glenn, Int. Law, 169.

An auxiliary war is one undertaken by a third nation in support of a belligerent.

(2) War is either public or private, accordingly as it has or has not the sanction of the sovereign power of the state.

A insurrectionary war in which one party is a government, and the other is not, has been called "mixed war."

(3) War is either perfect (sometimes called "solemn"), or imperfect (sometimes called "unsolemn"), accordingly as it has been declared in due form by the sovereign power, or is limited as respects places or persons. 25 Wend. (N. Y.) 483.

(4) War is either foreign or civil, according as it is between independent states, or between a state, as such, and a party or section of its own subjects. Civil war is distinguished from a mere treasonable insurrection only by degree, "by the number, power, and organization of the persons who originate and carry it on." 2 Black (U. S.) 635.

WAR, ARTICLES OF. See "Articles of War."

WARACTUM (Law Lat.) In old English law. Fallow; fallow ground. *Quando tenementum jacet incultum et ad waractum*, when the tenement lies untilled, and at fallow. Bracton, fol. 228b.

WARD. An infant placed by authority of law under the care of a guardian.

While under the care of a guardian, a ward can make no contract whatever binding upon him, except for necessaries. When the relation of guardian and ward ceases, the latter is entitled to have an account of the administration of his estate from the former. During the existence of this relation, the ward is under the subjection of his guardian, who stands *in loco parentis*. See "Guardian."

A subdivision of a city to watch in the daytime, for the purpose of preventing violations of the law. It is the duty of all police officers and constables to keep ward in their respective districts.

WARD FEGH. (Saxon.) In old records. Ward fee; the value of a ward, or the money paid to the lord for his redemption from wardship. Blount.

WARD HOLDING.. In old Scotch law. Military tenure by which lands were held. It was so called from the yearly tax in commutation of the right to hold vassals' lands during minority. It was abolished in 1747. Burton, Law Scot. p. 375; Bell, Dict.

WARD IN CHANCERY. An infant who is under the superintendence of the chancellor.

WARDS AND LIVERIES. In English law. The title of a court of record established in the reign of Henry VIII. See "Court of Wards and Liveries."

WARDA (Law Lat.)

——**In Old English Law.** Ward; guard; protection; keeping; custody. Spelman.

A ward; an infant under wardship. Spelman.

——**In Old Scotch Law.** An award; the judgment of a court.

WARDEN. A guardian; a keeper. This is the name given to various officers; as, the warden of the prison, the wardens of the port of Philadelphia, church wardens.

WARDEN OF THE CINQUE PORTS. Governor of the ports of England lying next France, with the authority of admiral, and power of sending out writs in his own name, etc. The constable of Dover Castle is the warden of the Cinque Ports, and was first appointed by William the Conqueror; but John I. granted to the wardens their privileges on condition that they should provide a certain number of vesesls for forty days as often as the king should require them. See "Cinque Ports."

WARDMOTE (from *ward,* and Saxon *mote,* or *gemote,* a meeting). In English law. A court held in every ward in London.

The wardmote inquest has power to inquire into and present all defaults concerning the watch and police doing their duty, that engines, etc., are provided against fire, that persons selling ale and beer be honest and suffer no disorders, nor permit gaming, etc., that they sell in lawful measures, and searches are to be made for beggars, vagrants, and idle persons, etc., who shall be punished. Chart. Hen. II.; Enc. Lond. 185; Cunningham; Wharton. See Cowell; 4 Inst. 249; 2 Show. 525; Enc. Lond. 185; Chart. Hen. II.

WARDPENNY. Wardage.

WARDSHIP.

——**In English Law.** The right of the lord over the person and estate of the tenant, when the latter was under a certain age.

——**In Modern Law.** The status of a ward (*q. v.*)

WARDSHIP IN CHIVALRY. An incident to the tenure of knight service.

WARDSHIP IN COPYHOLDS. The lord is guardian of his infant tenant by special custom.

WARDWIT, WARDWYTE, or **WARDwite.** In old English law. Immunity or exemption from the duty or service of ward, or from contributing to such service. Spelman. Exemption from amercement for not finding a man to do ward. Fleta, lib. 1, c. 47, § 16; Co. Litt. 83.

WARDWRIT. The being quit of giving money for the keeping of wards. Spelman.

WARECTARE. To plough up land designed for wheat in the spring, in order to let it lie fallow for better improvement, which in Kent is called "summer land."

WAREHOUSE. A place used for the reception and storage of goods and merchandise. 23 Me. 47.

WAREHOUSE RECEIPT. A receipt by a warehouseman for chattels placed in his custody. Its return is usually required in order to obtain the property. By custom of trade it has come to be virtually negotiable in many instances. Grain, provisions, and many other staple commodities are largely transferred by delivery or indorsement of warehouse receipts.

WAREHOUSEMAN. A person who receives goods and merchandise to be stored in his warehouse for hire.

WARENTIZARE. L. Lat. In old English law. To warrant; to save one harmless. Spelman.

WARGUS. (L. Lat.) In old European law. an outcast; an exile; a banished person.

WARNING. In old English probate practice. A notice to one who had entered a caveat to appear and set forth his interest. Sweet.

WARNOTH. In old English law. An ancient custom, whereby, if any tenant holding of the Castle of Dover failed in paying his rent at the day, he should forfeit double and for the second failure, treble, etc. Cowell.

WARRANDICE. In Scotch law. A clause in a charter of heritable rights, by which the grantor obliges himself that the right conveyed shall be effectual to the receiver. It is either personal or real. A warranty. Ersk. Inst. 2. 3. 11.

WARRANT. In its broadest sense, "a writing from a competent authority, in pursuance of law, directing the doing of an act, and addressed to an officer or person competent to do the act, and affording him protection from damage if he does it." 71 N. Y. 376.

In practice, it is largely confined to process of a criminal or *quasi* criminal nature, the more important being:

(1) Warrant of arrest, which is a writ issued by a justice of the peace or other authorized officer, directed to a constable or other proper person, requiring him to arrest a person therein named, charged with committing some offense, and to bring him before that or some other justice of the peace.

(2) Bench warrant, which is a process granted by a court, authorizing a proper officer to apprehend and bring before it some one charged with some contempt, crime, or misdemeanor.

(3) Search warrant, which is a process issued by a competent court or officer, authorizing an officer therein named or described to examine a house or other place for the purpose of finding illicit or contraband goods or goods which it is alleged have been stolen.

——**Municipal Warrants.** The name "warrant" is also given to a class of municipal securities, in the nature of a bill of exchange, drawn by an officer of a municipality upon the treasurer thereof. 19 Wall. (U. S.) 468.

WARRANT OF ATTORNEY. An instrument in writing, addressed to one or more attorneys therein named, authorizing them, generally, to appear in any court, or in some specified court, on behalf of the person giving it, and to confess judgment in favor of some particular person therein named, in an action of debt, and usually containing a stipulation not to bring any writ of error, or file a bill in equity, so as to delay him.

WARRANT OF COMMITMENT. The written authority by which a court empowers a jailer to commit a person to custody.

WARRANT TO SUE AND DEFEND. In old practice. A special warrant from the crown, authorizing a party to appoint an attorney to sue or defend for him. Gilb. C. P. 32; 3 Bl. Comm. 25.

A special authority, given by a party to his attorney, to commence a suit, or to appear and defend a suit, in his behalf. These warrants are now disused, though formal entries of them upon the record were long retained in practice. 1 Burrill, Prac. 39.

WARRANTEE. One to whom a warranty is made. Shep. Touch. 181.

WARRANTIA CHARTAE. An ancient and now obsolete writ, which was issued when a man was enfeoffed of land with warranty, and then he was sued or impleaded in assize or other action, in which he could not vouch or call to warranty.

It was brought by the feoffor pending the first suit against him, and had this valuable incident, that when the warrantor was vouched, and judgment passed against the tenant, the latter obtained judgment simultaneously against the warrantor, to recover other lands of equal value. Termes de la Ley; Fitzh. Nat. Brev. 134; Dane, Abr. Index; 2 Rand. (Va.) 141, 148, 156; 4 Leigh (Va.) 132; 11 Serg. & R. (Pa.) 115; Viner, Abr.; Co. Litt. 100; Hob. 22, 217.

WARRANTIZARE EST DEFENDERE ET acquietare tenentem, qui warrantum vocavit, in seisina sua; et tenens de re warranti excambium habebit ad valentiam. To warrant is to defend and insure in peace the tenant, who calls for warranty, in his seisin; and the tenant in warranty will have an exchange in proportion to its value. Co. Litt. 365.

WARRANTOR. One who makes a warranty. Shep. Touch. 181.

WARRANTOR POTEST EXCIPERE quod querens non tenet terram de qua petit warrantiam, et quod donum fuit insufficiens. A warrantor may object that the complainant does not hold the land of which he seeks the warranty, and that the gift was insufficient. Hob. 21.

WARRANTY.

——**In Insurance.** A statement or agreement by the insured, which is part of the contract of insurance, and the truth of which is essential to the validity of the policy.

For the distinction between "warranty" and "representation," see "Representation."

——**In Sales of Personal Property.** An undertaking, express or implied, by which the seller insures the existence of certain facts as to the thing sold. It is an express or implied statement of something which the party undertakes shall be a part of the contract, and, though part of the contract, yet collateral to the express object of it. 4 Mees. & W. 404.

It is express when the undertaking is by express words of the seller; it is implied when it results by inference of law from the nature of the transaction.

——**In Sales of Real Property.** In old law, a real covenant, whereby the grantor of an estate of freehold and his heirs were bound to warrant the title, and, either upon voucher or by judgment in a writ of *warrantia chartae*, to yield other lands to the value of those from which there had been an eviction by a paramount title. Co. Litt. 365a.

Collateral warranty existed when the heir's title was not derived from the warranting ancestor, and yet it barred the heir from claiming the land by any collateral title, upon the presumption that he might thereafter have assets by descent from or through the ancestor; and it imposed upon him the obligation of giving the warrantee other lands in case of eviction, provided he had assets. 2 Bl. Comm. 301, 302.

Lineal warranty existed when the heir derived title to the land warranted, either from or through the ancestor who made the warranty.

St. 4 Anne, c. 16, annulled these collateral warranties, which had become a great grievance.

In the United States, warranty in its original form, it is presumed, has never been known. The more plain and pliable form of a covenant has been adopted in its place; and this covenant, like all other covenants, has always been held to sound in damages, which, after judgment, may be recovered out of the personal or real estate, as in other cases. And in England the matter has become one of curious learning, and of little or no practical importance. See 4 Kent, Comm. 469; 3 Rawle (Pa.) 67, note; 2 Wheat. (U. S.) 45; 9 Serg. & R. (Pa.) 268; 11 Serg. & R. (Pa.) 109; 4 Dall. (Pa.) 442; 1 Sumn. (U. S.) 358; 17 Pick. (Mass.) 14; 1 Ired. (N. C.) 509; 2 Saund. 38, note 5.

WARRANTY DEED. One which contains covenants of warranty.

WARRANTY, VOUCHER TO. In old practice. The calling a warrantor into court by the party warranted (when tenant in a real action brought for recovery of such lands), to defend the suit for him (Co. Litt. 101b; Comyn, Dig. "Voucher" [A 1]; Booth, Real Actions, 43; 2 Saund. 32, note 1), and the time of such voucher is after the demandant has counted.

It lies in most real and mixed actions, but not in personal. Where the voucher has been made and allowed by the court, the vouchee either voluntarily appears, or there issues a judicial writ (called a *summons ad warrantizandum*), commanding the sheriff to summon him. Where he, either voluntarily or in obedience to this writ, appears and offers to warrant the land to the tenant, it is called entering into the warranty; after which he is considered as tenant in the action, in the place of the original tenant. The demandant then counts against him *de novo*, the vouchee pleads to the new count, and the cause proceeds to issue.

WARREN (Ger. *wahren;* Fr. *garenne*). A place privileged by prescription or grant of the king for the preservation of hares, conies, partridges, and pheasants, or any of them. Termes de la Ley. An action lies for killing beasts of warren inside the warren; but they may be killed *damage feasant* on another's land. 5 Coke, 104. It need not be inclosed. 4 Inst. 318.

WARSCOT. A contribution usually made towards armor in the time of the Saxons.

WARTH. A customary payment for castle guard. Cowell.

WASH TRADES. See "Gambling Contract."

WASHING HORN. The sounding of a horn for washing before dinner. The custom is still observed in the. Temple.

WASTE. Lasting and wrongful injury by the holder of a particular estate to the detriment of the holder of the reversion or remainder.

To constitute waste, the injury must be wrongful (3 Sup. Ct. N. Y. 60), by the tenant, or through his fault (2 Minor, Inst. p. 529), and must occasion lasting injury to the inheritance (1 Washb. Real Prop. 147).

What constitutes waste in a particular case is a question of fact. 22 N. J. Law, 521.

Waste is distinguished from "trespass" in that the latter is the act of a stranger, while waste is the act of a tenant.

It is distinguished from *"devastavit,"* which is waste by an executor or administrator.

(1) Permissive waste consists in the mere neglect or omission to do what will prevent injury (69 Mich. 259), as, to suffer a house to go to decay for the want of repair. And it may be incurred in respect to the soil, as well as to the buildings, trees, fences, or live stock on the premises. See "Permissive Waste."

(2) Voluntary waste consists in the commission of some destructive act; as, in pulling down a house, or ploughing up a flower garden. 1 Paige, Ch. (N. Y.) 573.

(3) Equitable waste is such injury to the inheritance as is within the legal right of the tenant, but which a man of ordinary prudence would not commit in the management of his own property. 29 Law J. Ch. 598.

(4) Meliorating waste is that which increases the present value of the estate, but damages the inheritance by charging it with added burden, as by improvement, the unpaid cost whereof is a lien.

WASTORS. Thieves. Cowell.

WATCH AND WARD. A phrase used in the English law to denote the superintendence and care of certain officers whose duties are to protect the public from harm.

WATCHMAN. An officer in many cities and towns, whose duty it is to watch during the night and take care of the property of the inhabitants.

He possesses, generally, the common-law authority of a constable to make arrests, where there is reasonable ground to suspect a felony, though there is no proof of a felony having been committed. 1 Chit. Crim. Law, 24; 2 Hale, P. C. 96; Hawk. P. C. bk. 2, c. 13, § 1, etc.; 1 East, P. C. 303; 2 Inst. 52; Comyn, Dig. "Imprisonment" (H 4); Dane, Abr. Index; 3 Taunt. 14; 1 Barn. & Ald. 227; Peake, 89; 1 Moody, C. C. 334; 1 Esp. 294.

WATER BAILIFF. In English law. An officer appointed to search ships in ports. 10 Hen. VII. 30.

WATER BAYLEY. In American law. An officer mentioned in the colony laws of New Plymouth (A. D. 1671), whose duty was to collect dues to the colony for fish taken in their waters. Colony Laws (Ed. 1836) 164, 166. Probably another form of water bailiff (*q. v.*)

WATERCOURSE. This term is applied to the flow or movement of the water in rivers, creeks, and other streams.

Surface water flowing from one tract to another having a fixed and determinate course, so as to uniformly discharge it upon the servient tract at a fixed and definite point, the course thus uniformly followed by the water in its flow is a watercourse. 177 Ill. 140.

WATER MEASURE. A greater measure than the Winchester, formerly used for selling coals in the pool, etc. 22 Car. II. c. 11.

WATER ORDEAL. In Saxon and old English law. The ordeal or trial by water.

which was of two kinds,—by hot water and by cold water. The hot-water ordeal was performed by plunging the bare arm up to the elbow in boiling water, and escaping unhurt thereby. 4 Bl. Comm. 343; Spelman. The cold-water ordeal was performed by casting the person suspected into a river or pond of cold water, when, if he floated therein, without any action of swimming, it was deemed an evidence of his guilt, but, if he sank, he was acquitted. Id.

WATERED STOCK. Stock which is issued as fully paid up, when in fact the whole amount of the par value thereof has not been paid in. If any amount less than the whole face value of the stock has not been paid, and the stock has been issued as fully paid, then the stock is watered to the extent of the deficit. Watered stock is, accordingly stock which purports to represent, but does not represent, in good faith, money paid into the treasury of the company, or money's worth actually contributed to the working capital of the concern. 188 Mich. 7, 13; Cook on Corporations. See Watering Stock.

WATERGANG (Law Lat. *watergangium*). A Saxon word for a trench or course to carry a stream of water, such as are commonly made to drain water out of marshes. Ord. Mar. de Rom. Chart. Hen. III.

WATERGAVEL. A rent paid for fishing in, or other benefit from, some river. Chart. 15 Hen. III.

WATERING STOCK. Fictitiously increasing the capital stock of a corporation. It is commonly done when the ordinary profits exceed an ordinary return on the investment, and as much new stock is then issued as will reduce the rate of earnings to normal. See Watered Stock.

WATERSCAPE. An aqueduct or passage for water.

WATLING (or WETLING) STREET. One of the four great Roman ways or roads in Britain. Cowell; Blount; LL. Gul. Conq. lib. 30; Fleta, lib. 2, c. 61, § 21. Otherwise called "Verlam Street," from its passing through Verulam. Spelman, voc. "Ikenild Street."

WAVESON. Such goods as appear upon the waves after shipwreck. Jacob.

WAX SCOT. Duty anciently paid twice a year towards the charge of wax candles in churches. Spelman.

WAY. A passage, street, or road.

In its most general sense, it includes both public highways and private ways (Co. Litt. 56a; but it is generally used as synonymous with "private way" (*q. v.*) See "Way from Necessity."

WAY BILL. A writing in which are set down the names of passengers who are carried in a public conveyance, or the description of goods sent with a common carrier by land. When the goods are carried by water, the instrument is called a "bill of lading," and this term is now commonly applied to carriage by land as well.

WAY FROM NECESSITY. A way which is necessarily incident to a grant and without which the grant would be useless. 194 Ill. 250. It arises by implication where the only manner of enjoying the benefit of the grant would be to pass over other lands of the grantor. 222 Ill. 540; 221 Ill. 638; 77 Ill. 574.

WAY-GOING CROP. In Pennsylvania. By the custom of the country, a tenant for a term certain is entitled, after the expiration of his lease, to enter and take away the crop of grain which he had put into the ground the preceding fall. This is called the "way-going crop." 5 Bin. (Pa.) 289; 2 Serg. & R. (Pa.) 14; 1 Pa. St. 224. See "Away-Going Crop."

WAYLEAVE. A right of way over or through land for the carriage of minerals from a mine or quarry. It is an easement (*q. v.*), being a species of the class called "rights of way," and is generally created by express grant or reservation. A wayleave rent may be a fixed annual sum, or a sum payable according to the quantity of minerals drawn over the way, or a combination of the two. Bainb. Mines (4th Ed.) 211 et seq.; Elph. Conv. 264.

WAYNAGIUM. Implements of husbandry. 1 Reeve, Hist. Eng. Law, c. 5, 268.

WAYWARDENS. The English highway acts provide that in every parish forming part of a highway district there shall annually be elected one or more waywardens. The waywardens so elected, and the justices for the county residing within the district, form the highway board for the district. Each waywarden also represents his parish in regard to the levying of the highway rates, and in questions arising concerning the liability of his parish to repairs, etc. Highway Acts 1862, 1863, 1864, 1878.

WEALD (Sax.) A wood; the woody part of a country, as the *weald* of Kent. Camd. Brit. 247. 4 Mod. 343, arg.

WEALREAF. The robbing of a dead man in his grave.

WEAPON. An instrument of offensive or defensive combat; something to fight with. 81 Wis. 243.

WEAR or WEIR. A great dam made across a river, accommodated for the taking of fish, or to convey a stream to a mill. Jacob. See "Dam."

WEAR AND TEAR. Deterioration by use.

WED. A covenant or agreement; whence a wedded husband.

WEDBEDRIP (Saxon). In old English law. A customary service which tenants paid to their lords, in cutting down their corn, or doing other harvest duties; as if a covenant to reap for the lord at the time of his bidding or commanding. Cowell.

WEEK. A period of time commencing on Sunday morning and ending on Saturday night. 60 Neb. 260.

Though it usually means any consecutive seven days, it will sometimes be interpreted to mean the ordinary notion of a week reckoning from Sunday to Sunday. 24 L. J. 368, 416.

WEIGHAGE. In English law. A duty or toll paid for weighing merchandise. It is called "tronage" for weighing wool at the king's beam, or "pesage" for weighing other avoirdupois goods. 2 Chit. Com. Law, 16.

WEIGHTS OF AUNCEL. See "Auncel Weight."

WEIR. See "Wear."

WELL KNOWING. The technical words to plead *scienter.*

WELSH MORTGAGE. In English law. A species of security which partakes of the nature of a mortgage, as there is a debt due, and an estate is given as a security for the repayment, but differs from it in the circumstances that the rents and profits are to be received without account till the principal money is paid off, and there is no remedy to enforce payment, while the mortgagor has a perpetual power of redemption.

It is a species of *vivum vadium.* Strictly, however, there is this distinction between a Welsh mortgage and a *vivum vadium,*—in the latter, the rents and profits of the estate are applied to the discharge of the principal after paying the interest; while in the former, the rents and profits are received in satisfaction of his interest only. 1 Powell, Mortg. 373a.

WEND. A certain quantity or circuit of land. Cowell.

WERE, or **WERA.** The name of a fine among the Saxons imposed upon a murderer.

The life of every man, not excepting that of the king himself, was estimated at a certain price, which was called the "were," or *aestimatio capitis.* The amount varied according to the dignity of the person murdered. The price of wounds was also varied according to the nature of the wound, or the member injured.

WEREGELT THEF (Saxon). In old English law. A robber who might be ransomed. Fleta, lib. 1, c. 47, § 13.

WERELADA. A purging from a crime by the oaths of several persons, according to the degree and quality of the accused. Cowell.

WERGILD, or **WEREGILD.** In old English law. The price which, in a barbarous age, a person guilty of homicide or other enormous offense was required to pay, instead of receiving other punishment. 4 Bl. Comm. 188.

See, for the etymology of this word, and a tariff which was paid for the murder of the different classes of men, Guizot, Essais sur l'Histoire de France, Essai, 4eme, c. 2, § 2.

WERPIRE (Law Lat.) In old European law. To throw; to throw away; to waive. Spelman.

WERRA (Law Lat.) In old English law. War; private war, as well as public. Spelman.

WERVAGIUM (Law Lat.) In old records. Wharfage; money paid at a wharf for lading or unlading goods. 1 Mon. Angl. 550. Cowell.

WEST SAXON LAGE. The law of the West Saxons, which was observed in the counties in the south and west of England, from Kent to Devonshire, in the beginning of the eleventh century. Supposed by Blackstone to have been much the same with the laws of Alfred. 1 Bl. Comm. 65.

WESTMINSTER. A city by express creation of Henry VIII. It was dissolved as a see and restored to the bishopric of London by Edward VI. and turned into a collegiate church, subject to a dean, by Queen Elizabeth. The superior courts sat here, and the common-law courts have continued to do so, as do still the divisions of the high court of justice which represent them. The chancery division, except upon the first day of certain sittings, sits at Lincoln's Inn. Wharton.

WESTMINSTER THE FIRST. St. 3 Edw. I., A. D. 1275. This statute, which deserves the name of a code rather than an act, is divided into fifty-one chapters. Without extending the exemption of churchmen from civil jurisdiction, it protects the property of the church from the violence and spoliation of the king and the nobles, provides for freedom of popular elections, because sheriffs, coroners, and conservators of the peace were still chosen by the freeholders in the county court, and attempts had been made to influence the election of knights of the shire, from the time when they were instituted. It contains a declaration to enforce the enactment of *Magna Charta* against excessive fines, which might operate as perpetual imprisonment; enumerates and corrects the abuses of tenures, particularly as to marriage of wards; regulates the levying of tolls, which were imposed arbitrarily by the barons and by cities and boroughs; corrects and restrains the powers of the king's escheator and other officers; amends the criminal law, putting the crime of rape on the footing to which it has been lately restored, as a most grievous, but not capital, offense; and embraces the subject of procedure in civil and criminal matters, introducing many regulations to render it cheap, simple, and expeditious. 1 Campb. Lives, L. Ch. p. 167; 2 Reeve, Hist. Eng. Law, c. 9, p. 107. Certain parts of this act are repealed by St. 26 & 27 Vict. c. 125. Wharton.

WESTMINSTER THE SECOND. St. 13 Edw. I. st. 1, A. D. 1285, otherwise called the *Statute de Donis Conditionalibus*. See "De Donis, the Statute." See 2 Reeve, Hist. Eng. Law, c. 10, p. 163. Certain parts of this act are repealed by St. 19 & 20 Vict. c. 64, and St. 26 & 27 Vict. c. 125. Wharton.

WESTMINSTER THE THIRD. St. 18 Edw. I. st. 1, A. D. 1290. Otherwise called the *Statute Quia Emptores*. See "Quia Emptores."

WHACK. A slang word meaning to divide into shares; apportion; parcel out; make a division settlement; square accounts; pay. 188 Mich. 617, 632.

WHARF. A space of ground artificially prepared for the reception of merchandise from a ship or vessel, so as to promote the convenient loading and discharging of such vessel.

A structure on the margin of navigable waters, alongside of which vessels can be brought for the sake of being conveniently loaded or unloaded. 62 Conn. 138; 93 N. Y. 151.

WHARFAGE. The money paid for landing goods upon, or loading them from, a wharf. Dane, Abr. Index; 4 Cal. 41, 45.

WHARFINGER. One who owns or keeps a wharf for the purpose of receiving and shipping merchandise to or from it for hire.

WHATSOEVER. "Whatsoever," as a rule, excludes any limitation or qualification, and implies that the genus to which it relates is to be understood in its utmost generality. 53 L. J. Q. B. 344; 13 Q. B. D. 843; 50 L. T. 778; 32 W. R. 813; 48 J. P. 501.

WHEEL. The punishment of the wheel was formerly to tie a criminal on a wheel, and then to break his bones until he expired. This barbarous punishment was never used in the United States, and it has been abolished in almost every civilized country.

WHEN. At which time.

In wills, standing by itself unqualified and unexplained, this is a word of condition, denoting the time at which the gift is to commence. 6 Ves. 243; 2 Mer. 286. The context of a will may show that the word "when" is to be applied to the possession only, not to the vesting of a legacy; but to justify this construction, there must be circumstances, or other expressions in the will, showing such to have been the testator's intent. 7 Ves. 422; 9 Ves. 230; 11 Ves. 489; Cooper, 145; 3 Brown, Ch. 471. For the effect of the word "when" in contracts and in wills in the French law, see 6 Toullier, Dr. Civ. note 520.

WHEREAS. This word implies a recital, and, in general, cannot be used in the direct and positive averment of a fact in a declaration or plea. Those facts which are directly denied by the terms of the general issue, or which may, by the established usage of pleading, be specially traversed, must be averred in positive and direct terms; but facts, however material, which are not directly denied by the terms of the general issue, though liable to be contested under it, and which, according to the usage of pleading, cannot be specially traversed, may be alleged in the declaration by way of recital, under a whereas. Gould, Pl. c. 43, § 42; Id. c. 3, § 47; Bac. Abr. "Pleas, etc." (B 5, 4); 2 Chit. Pl. 151, 178, 191.

WHILE. An adverb expressing duration. 246 Ill. 580.

During the time that. It seems to necessarily imply some degree of continuance. 101 Ill. App. 12; 141 Ill. 625.

WHIPPING POST. A post to which criminals are tied to inflict the punishment of whipping, which is in use in Delaware, and perhaps one or two other states.

WHITE ACRE. A fictitious name given to a piece of land, in the English books, for purposes of illustration. See "Black Acre."

WHITE BONNET. In Scotch law. A fictitious bidder at an auction. Where there is no upset price, and the auction is not stated to be without reserve, there is no authority for saying that employment of such person is illegal. Burton, Law Scot. 362.

WHITE FRIARS. A place in London, between the Temple and Blackfriars, which was formerly a sanctuary, and therefore privileged from arrest.

WHITE PERSONS. Persons of the Caucasian race. It excludes Indians, Mongolians, etc. 5 Sawy. (U. S.) 115. The general rule is that a person having three-fourths or more of Caucasian blood is regarded as white. See 3 Dana (Ky.) 382.

WHITE RENTS. In English law. Rents paid in silver, and called "white rents," or *redditus albi*, to distinguish them from other rents which were not paid in money. 2 Inst. 19. See "Alba Firma."

WHITE SPURS. A kind of esquires, Cowell.

WHITEHART SILVER. A mulct on certain lands in or near to the forest of Whitehart, paid into the exchequer, imposed by Henry III. upon Thomas de la Linda for killing a beautiful white hart which that king before had spared in hunting. Camd. Brit. 150.

WHITTANWARII (Law Lat.) In old English law. A class of offenders who whitened stolen oxhides and horsehides so that they could not be known and identified. Barr. Obs. St. 124, note (f).

WHOLE BLOOD. Being related by both the father and mother's side. This phrase is used in contradistinction to "half blood," which is relation only on one side. See "Blood."

WHOLESALE. To sell by wholesale is to sell by large parcels, generally in original packages, and not by retail.

WHORE. A woman who practices unlawful commerce with men, particularly one that does so for hire; a prostitute. While a woman may acquire that character without being generally accessible to men, as where she is the mistress of one man, yet the term implies the idea that the offenses against chastity on the part of the person to whom it is applied are public and notorious, and it is not proper to apply it to a woman who has yielded only to her affianced. 43 Iowa 183.

WHOREDOM. Any act of sexual intercourse between a married female and a male person not her husband, or between an unmarried female and a male person, is whoredom. 6 Ind. 343.

WICK, or WIC. A town or village. A termination denoting territorial limits of authority. Thus, "bailiwick" is the territory to which the authority of a bailiff extends.

WIDOW. A woman whose husband is dead, and who has not remarried. 164 Iowa 208; 145 N. W. 467.

As used in statute of distributions, this does not include a divorced woman, though it may in the law of dower. 37 Hun (N. Y.) 152; 103 N. Y. 284, 288.

WIDOW'S BENCH. The share of her husband's estate which a widow is allowed besides her jointure.

WIDOW'S CHAMBER. In English law. In London, the apparel of a widow and the furniture of her chamber, left by her deceased husband, is so called, and the widow is entitled to it. 2 Bl. Comm. 518.

WIDOW'S QUARANTINE. See "Quarantine."

WIDOW'S TERCE. The right which a wife has after her husband's death to a third of the rents of lands in which her husband died infeft; dower. Bell, Dict.

WIDOWER. A man whose wife is dead. A widower has a right to administer on his wife's separate estate, and, as her administrator, to collect debts due to her, generally for his own use.

WIDOWHOOD. The state of a man whose wife is dead, or of a woman whose husband is dead. In general, there is no law to regulate the time during which a man must remain a widower, or a woman a widow, before they marry a second time. The term widowhood is mostly applied to the state or condition of a widow.

WIFE'S EQUITY. See "Equity to a Settlement."

WILD ANIMALS. Animals in a state of nature; animals *ferae naturae.* See "Animal."

WILD LAND. Unimproved and uncultivated; land left in a state of nature, uninhabited, unoccupied and uncultivated, and not in use by the owner, his agent or lessee, for any artificial purpose. 156 Wis. 257, 259.

WILD'S CASE, RULE IN. A devise to B. and his children or issue, B. having no issue at the time of the devise, gives him an estate tail, which would become a life estate in the first taker under our statute. 194 Ill. 400; 221 Ill. 64. But if he have issue at the time, B. and his children take joint estates for life. 6 Coke, 16b; White & T. Lead. Cas. Real Prop. 542, 581. The rule was intended to enlarge the estate, and not to cut it down. 221 Ill. 64.

WILL. The legal declaration of a man's intention respecting the disposition of his property, which he wills to be performed after his death. See 2 Bl. Comm. 309. See Joint Will.

The word is of common-law origin, the corresponding civil-law term being "testament" (*q. v.*) "Will," "testament," and "last will and testament" are now said to be synonymous. Schouler, Wills, § 2.

In general, any instrument executed with the required formalities, conferring no present rights, but intended to take effect on the death of the maker, will be considered to be a will. 4 Wend. (N. Y.) 168; 104 Pa. St. 240.

(1) Holographic (or olographic) wills are those written and signed entirely with the testator's own hand. By reason of this, certain formalities in execution are in some jurisdictions dispensed with.

(2) Nuncupative wills are those made by oral declaration in the presence of witnesses. They are not in use in the United States, and in England are confined to seamen and soldiers in active service.

(3) Mystic wills, in Louisiana, are wills sealed in the presence of witnesses. See "Mystic Testament."

"WILL." See "May."

WILL, ESTATE AT. See "Estates."

WILLFUL. In the common sense, voluntary or intentional. In criminal law, the term generally means more than "voluntary," and implies an evil mind or intent. 96 U. S. 699; 140 Ind. 246; 20 Pick. [Mass.] 206; 14 Tex. App. 200. Thus, one who acts in good faith, believing that no highway existed at that place, is not guilty of "willfully" obstructing a highway. 34 Wis. 675.

WILLFUL ACT. A "willful" differs essentially from a "negligent" act. The one is positive, and the other negative. Intention is always separated from negligence by a precise line of demarcation. 38 Jones & S. (N. Y.) 281, 317, affirmed in 63 N. Y. 77.

WILLFULLY. Intentionally.

In charging certain offenses, it is required that they should be stated to be willfully done. Archb. Crim. Pl. 51, 58; Leach, C. C. 556.

In Pennsylvania, it has been decided that the word "maliciously" was an equivalent for the word "willfully," in an indictment for arson. 5 Whart. (Pa.) 427. See "Willful."

WILLS ACT. See "Statute of Wills."

WINCHESTER MEASURE. The standard measure which was originally kept at Winchester. It is abolished by 5 & 6 Wm. IV. c. 63.

WINCHESTER, STATUTE OF. A statute passed in the 13th year of the reign of Edward I., by which the old Saxon law of police was enforced, with many additional provisions. 2 Reeve, Hist. Eng. Law, 163; Crabb, Hist. Eng. Law, 189. It was repealed by St. 7 & 8 Geo. IV. c. 27. See "Constable."

WINDING UP. The term used in England to denote the dissolution of a corporation or partnership, and the settlement of its affairs.

WINDOW TAX. A tax on windows, levied on houses which contained more than six windows, and were worth more than £5 per annum; established by St. 7 Wm. III. c. 18. St. 14 & 15 Vict. c. 36, substituted for this tax a tax on inhabited houses.

WINDSOR FOREST. A royal forest founded by Henry VIII.

WINDSTORM. A tumultuous outburst of wind. 151 Ia. 73, 77, Ann. Cas. 1913A 266n. See Tornado.

WINTER CIRCUIT. An occasional circuit appointed for the trial of prisoners, in England, and in some cases of civil causes, between Michaelmas and Hilary terms.

WINTER HEYNING. The season between 11th November and 23d April, which is excepted from the liberty of commoning in certain forests. St. 23 Car. II. c. 3.

WISBUY, LAWS OF. A code of maritime laws, compiled at Wisbuy, the ancient capital of Gothland in Sweden, towards the close of the thirteenth century, and which, soon after their promulgation, were adopted as laws of the sea by all the nations of modern Europe. Even in the time of Cleirac (who published them, with a commentary, in his work entitled *Les Us et Coutumes de la Mer*), they were still observed in Sweden, Denmark, Flanders, and in the north of Germany. These laws resemble in many respects the laws of Oleron, to which, indeed, according to Cleirac, they were but a supplement, and they were adopted as the basis of the later collection known as the "Laws of the Hanseatic League." 3 Kent, Comm. 13, and note; 1 Duer, Ins. 40, 41; Intród. Disc. Lect. ii. They have been published in the United States, in the appendix to the first volume of Peters' Admiralty Decisions.

WISTA. A measure of land among the Saxons, containing sixty acres.

WITAM. The purgation from an offense by the oath of the requisite number of witnesses.

WITE. In Saxon law. A punishment, pain, penalty, mulct, or criminal fine. Cowell. It was the fine paid to the magistrate, as distinguished from "were," the compensation paid to the injured persons.

WITEKDEN. A taxation of the West Saxons, imposed by the public council of the kingdom.

WITENA DOM. In Saxon law. The judgment of the county court, or other court of competent jurisdiction, on the title to property, real or personal. 1 Spence, Eq. Jur. 22.

WITENA GEMOTE (spelled, also *witena gemot, gewitena gemote,* from the Saxon *wita,* a wise man, *gemote,* assembly,—the assembly of wise men). An assembly of the great men of the kingdom in the time of the Saxons, to advise and assist in the government of the realm.

It was the grand council of the kingdom, and was held, generally, in the open air, by public notice or particular summons, in or near some city or populous town. These notices or summonses were issued upon determination by the king's select council, or the body met without notice, when the throne was vacant, to elect a new king. Subsequently to the Norman Conquest it was called *commune concilium regni, curia magna,* and, finally "parliament;" but its character had become considerably changed. It was a court of last resort more especially for determining disputes between the king and his thanes, and, ultimately, from all inferior tribunals. Great offenders, particularly those who were members of or might be summoned to the king's court, were here tried. The casual loss of title deeds was supplied, and a very extensive equity jurisdiction exercised. 1 Spence, Eq. Jur. 73-76; 1 Bl. Comm. 147, 148; 1 Reeve, Hist. Eng. Law, 7; 9 Coke, pref.

The principal duties of the witena gemote, besides acting as high court of judicature, was to elect the sovereign, assist at his coronation, and co-operate in the enactment and administration of the laws. It made treaties jointly with the king, and aided him in directing the military affairs of the kingdom. Examinations into the state of churches, monasteries, their possessions, discipline, and morals, were made before this tribunal. It appointed magistrates, and regulated the coin of the kingdom. It also provided for levying upon the people all such sums as the public necessities required; and no property of a freeman was, in fact, taxable without the consent of the gemote. Bede, lib. 2, c. 5; 3 Turner, Ang. Sax. 209; 1 Dugd. Mon. 20; Saxon, Chron. 126, 140.

WITENS. The chiefs of the Saxon lords or thanes, their nobles, and wise men.

WITH. A word used to denote association in respect of situation or environment, and not simultaneous happening. 54 Ill. App. 436.

WITH STRONG HAND. In pleading. A technical phrase indispensable in describing a forcible entry in an indictment. No other word or circumlocution will answer the same purpose. 8 Term R. 357.

WITHDRAWING A JUROR. In practice. An agreement made between the parties in a suit to require one of the twelve jurors impanelled to try a cause to leave the jury box; the act of leaving the box by such a juror is also called the withdrawing a juror.

This arrangement usually takes place at the recommendation of the judge, when it is obviously improper the case should proceed any further.

The effect of withdrawing a juror puts an end to that particular trial, and each party must pay his own costs. 3 Term R. 657; 2 Dowl. 721; 1 Cromp., M. & R. 64. But the plaintiff may bring a new suit for the same cause of action. Ryan & M. 402; 3 Barn. & Adol. 349. See 3 Chit. Prac. 916.

WITHDRAWING RECORD. The withdrawing by plaintiff's attorney of the *nisi prius* record filed in a cause, before jury is sworn, has the same effect as a motion to postpone. 2 Car. & P. 185; 3 Campb. 333; Paine & D. Prac. 465.

WITHERNAM. In practice. The name of a writ which issues on the return of *elongata* to an *alias* or *pluries* writ of replevin, by which the sheriff is commanded to take the defendant's own goods which may be found in his bailiwick, and keep them safely, not to deliver them to the plaintiff until such time as the defendant chooses to submit himself and allow the distress, and the whole of it to be replevied, and he is thereby further commanded that he do return to the court in what manner he shall have executed the writ. Hammond, N. P. 453; 2 Inst. 140; Fitzh. Nat. Brev. 68, 69; Grotius de Jure Belli, 3. 2. 4. note 1.

WITHHOLD. To hold back; to restrain; to keep from action; to retain; to keep back; not to grant. 146 Iowa 360, 374, 140 Am. St. Rep. 282.

WITHIN. In the limits or compass of; not further in length than; not exceeding in quantity; inside the limits of; not going outside of; not beyond or exceeding. 150 Ill. 634.

WITHOUT DAY. This signifies that the cause or thing to which it relates is indefinitely adjourned; as, when a case is adjourned without day, it is not again to be inquired into. When the legislature adjourn without day, they are not to meet again. This is usually expressed in Latin, *sine die*.

WITHOUT IMPEACHMENT OF WASTE. When a tenant for life holds the land without impeachment of waste, he is, of course, dispunishable for waste, whether willful or otherwise. But still this right must not be wantonly abused, so as to destroy the estate; and he will be enjoined from committing malicious waste. Dane, Abr. c. 78, a. 14, § 7; Bac. Abr. "Waste" (N); 2 Eq. Cas. Abr. "Waste" (A, pl. 8); 2 Bouv. Inst. note 2402. See "Impeachment of Waste."

WITHOUT ISSUE. This phrase has been construed to mean "without having had issue," irrespective of whether they survive or not. 215 Ill. 110.

WITHOUT PREJUDICE. A phrase frequently used in connection with admissions, orders, etc. Its general effect is to reserve certain rights which would otherwise be indirectly or impliedly affected. See 20 Wall. (U. S.) 12; 58 Vt. 414.

WITHOUT RECOURSE. An indorsement of a negotiable instrument, whereby the indorser relieves himself of any liability to subsequent holders. The usual form is by prefixing the words "Without recourse" to the indorser's signature.

WITHOUT RESERVE. These words are frequently used in conditions of sale at public auction, that the property offered, or to be offered, for sale, will be sold without reserve.

When a property is advertised to be sold without reserve, if a puffer be employed to bid, and actually bid at the sale, the courts will not enforce a contract against a purchaser, into which he may have been drawn by the vendor's want of faith. 5 Madd. 34. See "Puffer."

WITHOUT STINT. Without limit. Applied to common, it is the same as common *sans nombre.*

WITHOUT THIS, THAT. In pleading. These are technical words used in a traverse (*q. v.*) for the purpose of denying a material fact in the preceding pleadings, whether declaration, plea, replication, etc. In Latin it is called *absque hoe* (*q. v.*) Lawes, Pl. 119; Comyn, Dig. "Pleader" (G 1); Summary of Pleading, 75; 1 Saund. 103, note; Ld. Raym. 641; 1 Burrows, 320; 1 Chit. Pl. 576, note (a).

WITNESS. One who gives oral testimony in a judicial proceeding. If his testimony be given by deposition, he is known as a "deponent;" if by affidavit, as an "affiant."

One who is present at any transaction, particularly persons required by law to be present, by way of preappointed evidence. If the witness signs an instrument to denote that same was executed in his presence, he is called a "subscribing" or "attesting" witness.

WITNESSING PART. In a deed or other formal instrument, that part which comes after the recitals, or, where there are no recitals, after the parties. It usually commences with a reference to the agreement or intention to be effectuated, then states or refers to the consideration, and concludes with the operative words and parcels, if any. Where a deed effectuates two distinct objects, there are two witnessing parts. 1 Dav. Prec. Conv. 63 et seq.

WOLF'S HEAD. In old English law. A term applied to outlaws. They who were outlawed in old English law were said to carry a wolf's head; for, if caught alive, they were to be brought to the king, and if they defended themselves, they might be slain and their heads carried to the king, for they were no more to be accounted of than wolves. Termes de la Ley, "Woolforthfod."

WOMEN. All the females of the human species. All such females who have arrived at the age of puberty. *Mulieris appellatione etiam virgo viri potens continetur.* Dig. 50. 16. 13. See 84 Ill. 11.

WOOD CORN. A certain quantity of grain paid by the tenants of some manors to the lord for the liberty to pick up dried or broken wood. Cowell.

WOOD GELD. The cutting of wood within the forest, or rather the money paid for the same. Cowell.

WOOD PLEA COURT. A court held twice in the year in the forest of Clun, in Shropshire, for determining all matters of wood and agistments. Cowell.

WOOD STREET COMPTER. The name ot an old prison in London.

WOODGELD. In old English law. To be free from the payment of money for taking of wood in any forest. Co. Litt. 233a.

The same as "pudzeld."

WOODMOTE. The court of attachment. Cowell.

WOODWARDS. Officers of the forest, whose duty consists in looking after the wood and vert and venison, and preventing offenses relating to the same. Manw. For. Laws, 189.

WOOLSACK. The seat of the lord chancellor of England in the house of lords, being a large square bag of wool, without back or arms, covered with red cloth. Webster. The judges, king's counsel-at-law, and masters in chancery sit also on woolsacks. The custom arose from wool being a staple of Great Britain from early times. Enc. Am.

WORD. One or more syllables which, when united, convey an idea; a single part of speech.

Words will be construed according to their strict and primary acceptation, unless from the context of the writing, and the intention of the parties collected from it, they appear to have been used in a different sense, or unless in their strict sense they are incapable of being carried into effect. 109 Ill. 416. This is equally true of words having a technical meaning unless the very nature of the subject indicates or the context suggests their use in a technical sense. 283 Ill. 503.

The natural import of words is that which their utterance promptly and uniformly suggests to the mind, that which common use has affixed to them; the technical is that which is suggested by their use in reference to a science or profession, that which particular use has affixed to them, and when the natural and technical import unite upon a word, both rules combine to control its construction. 1 Col. 359.

The omission of a letter will not ordinarily affect the meaning of a word unless such omission makes a word of another signification. 3 Salkeld 225.

WORDS OF LIMITATION. In a conveyance or will, words which have the effect of marking the duration of an estate are termed "words of limitation." Fearne, Cont. Rem. 78.

WORDS OF NEGOTIABILITY. Those words in an instrument which render it negotiable. The words "to the order of" before the name of the payee, or the words "or order," or "or bearer," after the name, are the usual words of negotiability. See "Negotiable Instrument."

WORDS OF PROCREATION. To create an estate tail by deed, it is necessary that words of procreation should be used in order to confine the estate to the descendants of the first grantee, as in the usual form of limitation,—"to A. and the heirs of his body."

WORDS OF PURCHASE. Words of purchase are words which denote the person who is to take the estate. Thus, if I grant land to A. for twenty-one years, and after the determination of that term to A.'s heirs, the word "heirs" does not denote the duration of A.'s estate, but the person who is to take the remainder on the expiration of the term, and is, therefore, called a "word of purchase." Williams, Real Prop.; Fearne, Cont. Rem. 76 et seq. Hence, "words of purchase" and "words of limitation" are opposed to each other.

WORK AND LABOR. One of the common counts in *assumpsit,* used to declare on work and labor done and materials furnished.

WORK BEAST, or **WORK HORSE.** These terms mean an animal of the horse kind, which can be rendered fit for service, as well as one of maturer age and in actual use. 8 Bush (Ky.) 587.

WORKHOUSE. A prison where prisoners are kept in employment; a penitentiary. A house provided where the poor are taken care of and kept in employment.

WORKING DAYS. In settling lay days, or days of demurrage, sometimes the contract specifies "working days;" in the computation, Sundays and custom-house holidays are excluded. 1 Bell, Comm. (5th Ed.) 577.

WORKSHOP. The place where the work of making, altering, etc., is done upon a product; a shop where any manufacture or handiwork is carried on, whether for the purpose of repair or manufacture; a building in which an artisan carries on his business, or laborers, workmen, or mechanics, by the use of tools or machinery manufacture, alter or repair articles of trade. 188 Ill. App. 501.

WORLD. This term sometimes denotes all persons whatsoever who may have, claim, or acquire an interest in the subject matter; as in saying that a judgment *in rem* binds "all the world."

WORSHIP. The act of paying divine honors to the Supreme Being; religious reverence and homage; adoration paid to God or a being viewed as God; adoration; a religious act of reverence; honor paid to the Supreme Being or by heathen nations to their deities; the performance of those external acts and the observance of all those rites and ceremonies in which men engage with the professed and sole view of honoring God. 245 Ill. 338; 200 Ill. 572; 132 Ill. 285.

In the United States, this is free, every one being at liberty to worship God according to the dictates of his conscience. See "Public Worship."

——**In English Law.** A title or addition given to certain persons. 2 Inst. 666; Bac. Abr. "Misnomer" (A 2).

WORT, or **WORTH.** A curtilage or country farm.

WORTHIEST OF BLOOD. An expression used to designate that in descent the sons are to be preferred to daughters, which is the law of England. See some singular reasons given for this in Plowd. 305.

WORTHINE, or **WORTHING OF LAND.** A certain quantity of land so called in the manor of Kingsland, in Hereford. The tenants are called "worthies."

WOUND. An injury to the person, whereby the skin is broken. Steph. Crim. Law, 171.

——**In Medical Parlance.** Injuries of every description that affect either the hard or soft parts of the body, and it comprehends bruises, contusions, fractures, luxations, etc. 167 Mich. 31. Breaking of a bone has been held not to be a wounding. 4 Car. & P. 381.

——**In Law.** Any lesion of the body. 167 Mich. 31.

WOUNDING. An aggravated species of assault and battery, consisting in one person giving another some dangerous hurt. 3 Bl. Comm. 121.

WRECCUM MARIS SIGNIFICAT ILLA bona quae naufragio ad terram pelluntur. A wreck of the sea signifies those goods which are driven to shore from a shipwreck.

WRECK (called in Law Lat. *wreccum maris,* and in Law Fr. *wrec de mer*). In a popular sense, a ship which has received injuries rendering her incapable of navigation.

——**In Maritime Law.** Such goods as, after a shipwreck, are cast upon the land by the sea, and left there within some country, so as not to belong to the jurisdiction of the admiralty, but to the common law. 2 Inst. 167; 1 Bl. Comm. 290-293.

WRECK COMMISSIONERS. Persons appointed by the English lord chancellor under Merch. Shipp. Act 1876, § 29, to hold investigations at the request of the board of trade into losses, abandonments, damages, and casualties of or to ships on or near the coast of the United Kingdom, whereby loss of life is caused.

WRECKFREE. Exempt from the forfeiture of shipwrecked goods and vessels to the king. Cowell.

WRIT.* In practice. A mandatory precept, issued by the authority and in the name of the sovereign or the state, for the purpose of compelling the defendant to do something therein mentioned.

*The common-law writs, of which there were a multitude, generally bore specific Latin names, from their purpose, or from their emphatic words. The aim in the present work has been to place these according to their customary form. The great majority of them, being customarily introduced by the prefix "De," or "Pro," will be found so placed. Those not customarily so introduced will be found under the first word of their names. Writs having English names are placed under the name without the prefix "Writ of" (*e. g.*, "Habeas Corpus") except where such short form is never used, in which case the prefix is used, and the phrase placed under "W" (*e. g.*, "Writ of Right").

It is issued by a court or other competent jurisdiction, and is returnable to the same. It is to be under seal and tested by the proper officer, and is directed to the sheriff or other officer lawfully authorized to execute the same. Writs are divided into original, by which actions or proceedings are begun, of mesne process, by which interlocutory proceedings are initiated, of execution, by which the judgment or decree is carried into effect. See 3 Bl. Comm. 273; 1 Tidd, Prac. 93; Gould, Pl. c. 2, § 1.

WRIT OF ASSISTANCE. In English practice, a chancery writ issued in aid of commissioners of sequestration, who were unable to obtain possession of the property. In early English practice, the writ had more extensive use, being used generally to eject persons from land wrongfully held; but it has been to a great extent superseded by statutory writs of possession and delivery. In the United States, the writ issues out of chancery to aid the sheriff in giving possession of land pursuant to a sale by him.

WRIT OF ASSOCIATION. In English practice. A writ whereby certain persons (usually the clerk of assize and his subordinate officers) are directed to associate themselves with the justices and sergeants; and they are required to admit the said persons into their society in order to take the assizes. 3 Bl. Comm. 59.

WRIT OF ATTACHMENT. A writ employed to enforce obedience to an order or judgment of the court. It commands the sheriff to attach the disobedient party, and to have him before the court to answer his contempt. Smith, Actions, 176. It is used not only as a writ of execution (*e. g.*, to enforce a judgment for the recovery of chattels), but also to enforce obedience to interlocutory orders, injunctions, etc.

WRIT OF CERTIORARI. A writ whose object is to bring up the record of a proceeding from an inferior to a superior tribunal. 196 Ill. 323. See "Certiorari."

WRIT OF CONSPIRACY. The name of an ancient writ, now superseded by the more convenient remedy of an action on the case, which might have been sued against parties guilty of a conspiracy. Fitzh. Nat. Brev. 260. See "Conspiracy."

WRIT OF COVENANT. In practice. A writ which lies where a party claims damages for breach of covenant, *i. e.*, of a promise under seal.

WRIT OF DEBT. In practice. A writ which lies where the party claims the recovery of a debt, *i. e.*, a liquidated or certain sum of money alleged to be due to him.

This is debt "in the *debet*," which is the principal and only common form. There is another species mentioned in the books, called the debt "in the *detinet*," which lies for the specific recovery of goods under a contract to deliver them. 1 Chit. Pl. 101.

WRIT OF DECEIT. The name of a writ which lies where one man has done anything in the name of another, by which the latter is damnified and deceived. Fitzh. Nat. Brev. 217.

The modern practice is to sue a writ of trespass on the case to remedy the injury.

WRIT OF DELIVERY. A writ of execution employed to enforce a judgment for the delivery of chattels. It commands the sheriff to cause the chattels mentioned in the writ to be returned to the person who has obtained the judgment, and, if the chattels cannot be found, to distrain the person against whom the judgment was given until he returns them. Smith, Actions, 175.

WRIT OF DETINUE. In practice. A writ which lies where a party claims the specific recovery of goods and chattels, or deeds and writings, detained from him. This is seldom used. Trover is the more frequent remedy, in cases where it may be brought.

WRIT OF DOWER. In practice. A writ which lies for a widow claiming the specific recovery of her dower, no part having been yet assigned to her. It is usually called a writ of dower *unde nihil habet.* 3 Chit. Pl. 393; Booth, 166.

There is another species, called a "writ of right of dower," which applies to the particular case where the widow has received a part of her dower from the tenant himself, and of land lying in the same town in which she claims the residue. Booth, 166; Glanv. lib. 6, c. 4. 5. This latter writ is seldom used in practice.

WRIT OF EJECTMENT. In practice. The name of a process issued by a party claiming land or other real estate, against one who is alleged to be unlawfully in possession. See "Ejectment."

WRIT OF ENTRY. A real action to recover the possession of land where the tenant (or owner) has been disseised or otherwise wrongfully dispossessed. If the disseisor has aliened the land, or if it has descended to his heir, the writ of entry is said to be in the *per*, because it alleges that the defendant (the alienee or heir) obtained possession "through" the original disseisor. If two alienations (or descents) have taken place, the writ is in the *per* and *cui*, because it alleges that the defendant (the second alienee) obtained possession "through" the first alienee, to whom the original disseisor had aliened it. If more than two alienations (or descents) have taken place, the writ is in the *post*, because it simply alleges that the defendant acquired possession "after" the original disseisin. Co. Litt. 238b; 3 Bl. Comm. 180. The writ of entry was abolished, with other real actions, in England, by St. 3 & 4 Wm. IV. c. 27, § 36, but is still in use in a few of the states of the Union.

WRIT OF ERROR. A writ by which a superior court commands an inferior to send up the record of a proceeding for review. A writ of error lay only to a court of record (88 Pa. St. 291) after final judgment (2 Mass. 445), and lies only to errors of law (141 Mass. 194) apparent of record (72 N. Y. 393).

Error was the appropriate remedy at common law to review proceedings at law, while an appeal (*q. v.*) lay in equity.

——**Writ of Error Coram Nobis.** The ordinary writ of error which issued from a superior to an inferior court.

——**Writ of Error Coram Vobis.** A writ which issued to review proceedings previously had in the court issuing it. See "Coram Vobis."

It was called at length in the old books, *breve de errore corrigendo*, a writ about correcting error; the abbreviation of which (*breve de errore*) has been literally translated, "writ of error." Sometimes simply termed "error." Defined by Lord Coke to be a writ which "lieth where a man is grieved by any error in the foundation, proceeding, judgment, or execution [of a suit], and thereupon it is called *breve de errore corrigendo*." Co. Litt. 288b.

WRIT OF FALSE JUDGMENT. A writ which appears to be still in use to bring appeals to the English high court from inferior courts not of record proceeding according to the course of the common law. Archb. Prac. 1427.

WRIT OF MAINPRIZE. In English law. A writ directed to the sheriff (either generally, when any man is imprisoned for a bailable offense and bail has been refused, or specially, when the offense or cause of commitment is not properly bailable below) commanding him to take sureties for the prisoner's appearance, commonly called "mainpernors," and to set him at large. 3 Bl. Comm. 128.

WRIT OF MESNE. In old English law. A writ which was so called by reason of the words used in the writ, namely, *Unde idem A., qui medius est inter C. et praefatum B.;* that is, A., who is mesne between C., the lord paramount, and B., the tenant paravail. Co. Litt. 100a.

WRIT OF POSSESSION. This is the writ of execution employed to enforce a judgment to recover the possession of land. It commands the sheriff to enter the land and give possession of it to the person entitled under the judgment. Smith, Actions, 175.

WRIT OF PRAECIPE. This writ is also called a writ of covenant, and is sued out by the party to whom lands are to be conveyed by fine, the foundation of which is a supposed agreement or covenant that the one shall convey the land to the other. 2 Bl. Comm. 349, 350.

WRIT OF PREVENTION. This name is given to certain writs which may be issued in anticipation of suits which may arise. Co. Litt. 100.

WRIT OF PROCLAMATION. In English practice. A writ which issues at the same time with the *exigi facias*, by virtue of St. 31 Eliz. c. 3, § 1, by which the sheriff is commanded to make proclamations in the statute prescribed.

When it is not directed to the same sheriff as the writ of *exigi facias* is, it is called a "foreign writ of proclamation." Lee; 4 Reeve, Hist. Eng. Law, 261.

WRIT OF PROTECTION. In England, the sovereign may, by his writ of protection, privilege any person in his service from arrest in civil proceedings during a year and a day; but this prerogative is seldom, if ever, exercised. Archb. Prac. 687. See Co. Litt. 130a.

WRIT OF RECAPTION. In practice. A writ which lies where, pending an action of replevin, the same distrainer takes, for the same supposed cause, the cattle or goods of the same distrainee. See Fitzh. Nat. Brev. 169.

This writ is nearly obsolete, as trespass, which is found to be a preferable remedy, lies for the second taking; and, as the defendant cannot justify, the plaintiff must necessarily recover damages proportioned to the injury.

WRIT OF RESTITUTION. A writ which is issued on the reversal of a judgment commanding the sheriff to restore to the defendant below the thing levied upon, if it has not been sold, and, if it has been sold, the proceeds. Bac. Abr. "Execution" (Q).

WRIT OF RIGHT. In practice. The remedy appropriate to the case where a party claims the specific recovery of corporeal hereditaments in fee simple, founding his title on the right of property, or mere right, arising either from his own seisin or the seisin of his ancestor or predecessor. Fitzh. Nat. Brev. 1 (B); 3 Bl. Comm. 391.

At common law, a writ of right lies only against the tenant of the freehold demanded. 8 Cranch (U. S.) 239.

This writ brings into controversy only the rights of the parties in the suit; and a defense that a third person has better title will not avail. 7 Wheat. (U. S.) 27; 3 Pet. (U. S.) 133; 3 Bing. (N. S.) 434; 4 Bing. (N. S.) 711; 5 Bing. (N. S.) 161; 4 Scott, 209; 6 Scott, 435, 738; 6 Adol. & E. 103; 1 H. Bl. 1; 3 Taunt. 167; 5 Taunt. 326; 1 Marsh. 68; 2 Bos. & P. 570; 4 Bos. & P. 64; 4 Taunt. 572; 2 W. Bl. 1261; 2 Car. & P. 187; 271; 8 Cranch (U. S.) 229; 2 Wheat. (U. S.) 306; 11 Me. 312; 7 Wend. (N. Y.) 250; 3 Bibb (Ky.) 57; 3 Rand. (Va.) 563; 2 J. J. Marsh. (Ky.) 104; 2 A. K. Marsh. (Ky.) 396; 1 Dana (Ky.) 410; 2 Leigh (Va.) 1; 4 Mass. 64; 17 Mass. 74.

WRIT OF SUMMONS. In ordinary actions in the English high court, the writ of summons is a writ issued at the instance of the plaintiff for the purpose of giving the defendant notice of the claim made against him, and of compelling him to appear and answer it if he does not admit it. It is the first step in the action.

The court of probate had power to cause questions of fact, arising in suits or proceedings, to be tried by a jury by means of an issue directed to one of the superior courts of law. The issues were contained in a document called a "writ of summons." Browne, Prob. Prac. 314; Court of Probate Act 1857; § 35. This practice seems no longer applicable. Rules of Court, xxxvi. 29.

WRIT OF TOLL. In English law. The name of a writ to remove proceedings on a writ of right patent from the court baron into the county court. 3 Bl. Comm. Append. No. 1, § 2.

WRIT OF WASTE. The name of a writ to be issued against a tenant who has committed waste of the premises. There are several forms of this writ. That against a tenant in dower differs from the others. Fitzh. Nat. Brev. 125. See "Waste."

WRITER OF THE TALLIES. In England. An officer of the exchequer whose duty it was to write upon the tallies the letters of tellers' bills.

WRITERS TO THE SIGNET. In Scotch law. Anciently, clerks in office of the secretary of state, by whom writs passing the king's signet were prepared. Their duty now is to prepare the warrants of all lands flowing from the crown, and to sign almost all diligencies of the law affecting the person or estate of a debtor, or for compelling implement of decree of superior court. They may act as attorney or agent before court of sessions, and have various privileges. Bell, Dict. "Clerk to Signet."

WRITING. In the most general sense of the word, "writing" denotes a document, whether manuscript or printed, as opposed to mere spoken words. Writing is essential to the validity of certain contracts and other transactions. Sweet.

WRITING OBLIGATORY. A bond; an agreement reduced to writing, by which the party becomes bound to perform something, or suffer it to be done.

A contract under seal. 7 Yerg. (Tenn.) 350.

WRITTEN. The words "written" or in writing" may be construed to include printing, except where the written signature is required by law. 52 Mich. 520.

Words traced with a pen, stamped, printed, engraved or made legible by any other device, are written. 287 Ill. 493; 35 Ind. App. 94; 103 Ind. 98.

WRITTEN LAW. One of the two leading divisions of the Roman law, comprising the *leges, plebiscita, senatus consulta, principum placita, magistratuum edicta,* and *responsa prudentum.* Inst. 1. 2. 3.

Statute law; law deriving its force from express legislative enactment. 1 Bl. Comm. 62, 85.

WRONG. An injury; a tort; a violation of right.

In its most usual sense, wrong signifies an injury committed to the person or property of another, or to his relative rights, unconnected with contract; and these wrongs are committed with or without force. But in a more extended signification, wrong includes the violation of a contract. A failure by a man to perform his undertaking or promise is a wrong or injury to him to whom it was made. 3 Bl. Comm. 158.

A public wrong is an act which is injurious to the public generally, commonly known by the name of "crime," "misdemeanor," or "offense;" and it is punishable in various ways, such as indictments, summary proceedings, and, upon conviction, by death, imprisonment, fine, etc.

Private wrongs which are injurious to individuals, unaffecting the public. These are redressed by actions for damages, etc. See "Tort."

WRONGDOER. One who commits an injury; a tort feasor. See Dane, Abr. Index.

WRONGFULLY INTENDING. In pleading. Words used in a declaration when, in an action for an injury, the motive of the defendant in committing it can be proved, for then his malicious intent ought to be averred. This is sufficiently done if it be substantially alleged, in general terms, as wrongfully intending. 3 Bouv. Inst. note 2871.

WRONGOUS, or **WRANGOUS.** In Scotch law. Wrongful; unlawful; as wrongous imprisonment. Ersk. Princ. 4. 4. 25.

WULTAVA, or **WULITAVA** (Law Lat.) In old European law. A disfiguring of the face. Addit. ad L. Frison, tit. 3, § 16; Spelman.

WULVESHEVED, or **WULFESHEOFOD** (Saxon, from *wulfe,* wolf, and *heofod,* head). In Saxon law. Wolf's head; a term applied to an outlaw.

WURTH (Saxon). In Saxon law. Worthy; competent; capable. *Atheswurthe,* worthy of oath; admissible or competent to be sworn. Spelman. See "Othesworthe."

WYTE. In old English law. Acquittance or immunity from amercement. Fleta, lib. 1, c. 47, §§ 15-17.

X-Y-Z

X. A contraction of the word *extra*, used in citing that part of the canon law called Gregory's Decretals.

XENODOCHIUM. In the civil and old English law. An inn allowed by public license for the entertainment of strangers and other guests. Calv. Lex.; Cowell.

A hospital; a place where sick and infirm persons are taken care of. Cowell.

XENODOCHY. Reception of strangers; hospitality. Enc. Lond.

XYLON. A punishment among the Greeks answering to our stocks. Wharton.

YA ET NAY. In old records. Mere assertion and denial, without oath. Cowell; Blount.

YARD. An enclosed space or area, generally attached to a dwelling-house. A common term in deeds. 1 Chit. Gen. Pr. 176.

YARDLAND. In old English law. A quantity of land containing twenty acres. Co. Litt. 69a.

YCEL (Law Fr.) It; this; the same. Kelham.

YCEMENT (Law Fr.) Thus; in like manner. Kelham.

YCESTES (Law Fr.) These. Kelham.

YCEUX, *Yceaux.* L. Fr. Those; them. Kelham.

YCONOMUS, or OECONOMUS (Law Lat.) In old records. An advocate or defender; a patron. Cowell.

YEAR. The period in which the revolution of the earth around the sun, and the accompanying changes in the order of nature, are completed.

The civil year differs from the astronomical, the latter being composed of three hundred and sixty-five days, five hours, forty-eight seconds and a fraction, while the former consists sometimes of three hundred and sixty-five days, and at others, in leap years, of three hundred and sixty-six days.

The year is divided into half-year, which consists, according to Coke (Litt. 135b), of one hundred and eighty-two days; and quarter of a year, which consists of ninety-one days (Id.; 2 Rolle, Abr. 521, lib. 40). It is further divided into twelve months.

The civil year commences immediately after 12 o'clock at night of the thirty-first day of December,—that is the first moment of the first day of January,—and ends at midnight of the thirty-first day of December twelve months thereafter. See Comyn, Dig. Annus; 2 Bl. Comm. 140, note; Chit. Prac. Index. "Time."

In computing time by the calendar year, days are not counted, but the calendar is examined and the day numerically corresponding to that day in the following year is ascertained, and the calendar year expires on that day less one. 209 Ill. App. 320. 279 Ill. 408.

Unless from the context or otherwise a different intent is gathered, the word "year" when used in a statute is construed to mean a calendar year. 104 Iowa 204; 104 Iowa 293.

In New York it is enacted that whenever the term "year" or "years" is or shall be used in any statute, deed, verbal or written contract, or any public or private instrument whatever, the year intended shall be taken to consist of three hundred and sixty-five days; half a year, of a hundred and eighty-two days; and a quarter of a year, of ninety-two days; and the day of a leap year, and the day immediately preceding, if they shall occur in any period so to be computed, shall be reckoned together as one day. Rev. St. pt. 1, c. 19, tit. 1, § 3.

YEAR AND DAY. A period of time much recognized in law.

It is not in all cases limited to a precise calendar year. In Scotland, in computing the term, the year and day is to be reckoned, not by the number of days which go to make up a year, but by the return of the day of the next year that bears the same denomination. 1 Bell, Comm. (5th Ed.) 721; 2 Stair, Inst. 842. See Bac. Abr. Descent (I 3); Ersk. Inst. 1. 6. 22. In the law of all the Gothic nations, it meant a year and six weeks.

It is a term frequently occurring; for example, in case of an estray, if the owner challenged it not within a year and a day, it belonged to the lord. 5 Coke, 108. So of a wreck. 2 Inst. 168. This time is given to prosecute appeals and for actions in a writ of right, and, after entry or claim, to avoid a fine. Plowd. 357a. And if a person wounded die in that time, it is murder 3 Inst. 53; 6 Coke, 107. So, when a judgment is reversed, a party, notwithstanding the lapse of time mentioned in the statute of limitations pending that action, may commence a fresh action within a year and a day of such reversal. 3 Chit. Prac. 107. Again, after a year and a day have elapsed from the day of signing a judgment, no execution can be issued till the judgment be revived by *scire facias*. Bac. Abr. "Execution" (H); Tidd. Prac. 1108.

Protection lasted a year and a day; and if a villein remain from his master a year and a day in an ancient demesne, he is free.

Cunningham. If a person is afraid to enter on his land, he may make claim as near as possible, which is force for a year and a day. 3 Bl. Comm. 175. In case of prize, if no claim is made within a year and a day, the condemnation is to captors as of course. 2 Gall. (U. S.) 388. So, in case of goods saved, the court retains them till claim, if made within a year and a day, but not after that time. 8 Pet. (U. S.) 4.

The same period occurs in the civil law, in Book of Feuds, the Laws of the Lombards, etc.

YEAR BOOKS. Books of reports of cases in a regular series from the reign of the English King Edward II., inclusive, to the time of Henry VIII., which were taken by the prothonotaries or chief scribes of the courts, at the expense of the crown, and published annually, whence their name "Year Books." They consist of eleven parts, namely: Part 1. Maynard's Reports *temp.* Edw. II.; also divers Memoranda of the Exchequer *temp.* Edw. I. Part 2. Reports in the first ten years of Edw. III. Part 3. Reports from 17 to 39 Edw. III. Part 4. Reports from 40 to 50 Edw. III. Part 5. Liber Assisarum; or, Pleas of the Crown *temp.* Edw. III. Part 6. Reports *temp.* Hen. IV. and Hen. V. Parts 7 and 8. Annals; or Reports of Hen. VI. during his reign, in two vols. Part 9. Annals of Edw. IV. Part 10. Long Quinto; or, Reports in 5 Edw. IV. Part 11. Cases in the reigns of Edward V., Rich. III., Hen. VII., and Hen. VIII.

YEAR, DAY, AND WASTE (Lat. *annus, dies, et vastum*). A part of king's prerogative, whereby he takes the profits of the lands and tenements of those attainted of petty treason or felony, for a year and a day, but, in the end, may waste the tenements, destroy the houses, root up the woods, gardens, and pasture, and plough up the meadows (except the lord of the fee agree with him for redemption of such waste); after which the lands are to be restored to the lord of the fee. Staundf. Prerog. c. 16, fol. 44. By *Magna Charta*, it would appear that the profits for a year and a day were given in lieu of the waste. 9 Hen. III, c. 22. But 17 Edw. II. declares the king's right to both.

YEARS, ESTATE FOR. See "Estates."

YEOMAN. In the United States, this word does not appear to have any very exact meaning. It is usually put as an addition to the names of parties in declarations and indictments. In England it signifies a free man who has land of the value of forty shillings a year. 2 Inst. 668; 2 Dall. (Pa.) 92.

YEOVEN, or YEVEN. Given (dated).

YIELD. In the law of real property, to perform a service due by a tenant to his lord. Hence the usual form of reservation of a rent in a lease begins with the words "yielding and paying."

YIELDING AND PAYING. These words, when used in a lease, constitute a covenant on the part of the lessee to pay the rent (Platt, Cov. 50; 3 Pa. St. 464; 1 Sid. 447, pl. 9; 2 Lev. 206; 3 Term R. 402; 1 Barn. & C. 416; 2 Dowl. & R. 670), but whether it be an express covenant or not seems not to be settled (Styles, 387, 406, 451; Sid. 240, 266; 2 Lev. 206; T. Jones, 102; 3 Term R. 402).

In Pennsylvania, it has been decided to be a covenant running with the land. 3 Pa. St. 464. See 1 Saund. 233, note 1; 9 Vt. 191.

YINGEMAN. A word occurring in the laws of Henry I. (c. 16), which Spelman thinks might be a mistake for Ynglishman, or Englishman.

YORK, CUSTOM OF. Recognized by 22 & 23 Car. II. c. 10, and 1 Jac. II. c. 17. By this custom, the effects of an intestate are divided according to the anciently universal rule of *pars rationabilis.* 4 Burn, Ecc. Law, 342.

YORK, STATUTE OF. The name of an English statute, passed 12 Edw. II., A. D. 1318, and so called because it was enacted at York. It contains many wise provisions and explanations of former statutes. Barr. Obs. St. 174. There were other statutes made at York in the reign of Edward III., but they do not bear this name.

YORKSHIRE LAND REGISTRIES. These are regulated by Sts. 2 & 3 Anne, c. 4, 5 Anne, c. 18 (6 Anne, c. 20, in the statutes of the realm), as to the West Riding; 6 Anne, c. 35 (or 62), as to the East Riding, and 8 Geo. II. c. 6.

YOUNGER CHILDREN. This phrase, when used in English conveyancing with reference to settlements of land, signifies all such children as are not entitled to the rights of an eldest son. It therefore includes daughters, even those who are older than the eldest son. Mozley & W.

Z is frequently used for *y*, in old English and Scotch records.

ZABULUM (Law Lat.) In old records. Coarse sand or gravel. Blount.

ZE (Old Scotch). Ye. Skene de Verb. Sign. voc. "Homagium."

ZEIR (Old Scotch). Year. "*Zeir* and day." Bell, Dict.

ZELDE (Old Scotch.) A gift or donation. Skene de Verb. Sign. voc. "Herezelda."

ZETETICK. Proceeding by inquiry. Enc. Lond.

ZOLLVEREIN. A union of German states for uniformity of customs, established in

1819. It continued until the unification of the German empire, including Prussia, Saxony, Bavaria, Wurtemberg, Baden, Hasse-Cassel, Brunswick, and Mecklenburg-Strelitz, and all intermediate principalities. It has now been superseded by the German empire; and the federal council of the empire has taken the place of that of the Zoll Verein. Wharton.

ZONE RATES. Application of specific rates between certain specific points in one territory to certain specific points in another territory, without special regard to the actual distance.

ZONING OF CITIES. Statutory provisions adopted in some states regulating, or authorizing municipal authorities to regulate, the districts of a city in which certain trades, factories, etc., may be operated.

ZUCARIUM (Law Lat.) In old English law. Sugar. Fleta, lib. 2, c. 12, § 4.

ZYGOCEPHALUM. In the civil law. A measure or quantity of land. Nov. 17, c. 8. As much land as a yoke of oxen could plow in a day. Calv. Lex.

ZYGOSTATES. In the civil law. A weigher; an officer who held or looked to the balance in weighing money between buyer and seller; an officer appointed to determine controversies about the weight of money. Spelman.

TABLE OF ABBREVIATIONS

Of Reports and Standard Text Books

A. B. Anonymous Reports at the end of Benloe.
A'B. R. J. N. S. W. A'Beckett's Reserved (Equity) Judgments, New South Wales.
A'B. R. J. P. P. A'Beckett's Reserved Judgments. Port Philip.
A. C. R. American Criminal Reports, edited by Hawley.
A. D. American Decisions (Select Cases), San Francisco.
A. K. Marsh. A. K. Marshall's Kentucky Reports.
A. L. R. American Law Reports Annotated.
A. L. Reg. American Law Register, Philadelphia.
A. Moo. A. Moore's Reports, in 1 Bosanquet & Puller.
A. P. B. Ashurst's Paper Books, in Lincoln's Inn Library.
A. R. C. American Ruling Cases.
A. & A. Corp. Angell & Ames on Corporations.
A. & E. Adolphus & Ellis' English Queen's Bench Reports;—Admiralty and Ecclesiastical.
A. & E. A. C. American and English Annotated Cases.
A. & E. Encyc. of L. American and English Encyclopedia of Law.
A. & E. N. S. Adolphus & Ellis' English Queen's Bench Reports, New Series.
A. & F. Fix. Amos & Ferard on Fixtures.
A. & H. Arnold & Hodges' English Queen's Bench Reports.
Ab. Eq. Cas. Equity Cases Abridged, English.
Abb. Abbott's United States Circuit and District Court Reports.
Abb. Adm. Abbott's Admiralty Reports.
Abb. App. Dec. Abbott's New York Court of Appeals Decisions.
Abb. Cl. Ass. Abbott's Clerks and Conveyancers' Assistant.
Abb. Ct. App. Abbott's New York Court of Appeals Decisions.
Abb. Dig. Corp. Abbott's Digest of the Law of Corporations.
Abb. F. Abbott's Forms of Pleading.
Abb. F. Sup. Abbott's Forms of Pleading, Supplement.
Abb. Int. Abbott's Introduction to Practice under the Codes.
Abb. L. Dic. Abbott's Law Dictionary.
Abb. Leg. Rem. Abbott's Legal Remembrancer.
Abb. N. Cas. Abbott's New Cases, New York.
Abb. N. Y. App. Abbott's New York Court of Appeals Decisions.
Abb. Pl. Abbott's Pleadings under the Code.
Abb. Pr. Abbott's New York Practice Reports.
Abb. Pr. N. S. Abbott's New York Practice Reports, New Series.
Abb. Sh. Abbott on Shipping.
Abb. Tr. Ev. Abbott's Trial Evidence.
Abb. U. S. Abbott's United States Circuit Court Reports.
Abdy R. Pr. Abdy's Roman Civil Procedure.
Abdy & W. Gai. Abdy & Walker's Gaius & Ulpian.
Abdy & W. Just. Abdy & Walker's Justinian.
Abr. Cas. Crawford & Dix's Abridged Cases, Ireland.
Abr. Cas. Eq. (or **Eq. Cas.**) (English) Equity Cases Abridged.
Act. Acton's English Privy Council Reports.
Act. Can. Acta Cancellariae, by Monro.
Act. Reg. Acta Regia, an Abstract of Rymer's Foedera.
Act of Sed. Act of Sederunt.
Ad. Con. Addison's Contracts.
Ad. Eq. Adams' Equity.
Ad. & E. Adolphus & Ellis' English King's Bench Reports.
Adams. Adams' Reports (41, 42 Maine);—Adams' Reports (1 N. H.).
Add. Addison's Reports, Pennsylvania;—Addams' English Ecclesiastical Reports.
Add. Con. Addison on Contracts.
Add. Ecc. (or **E. R.**) Addams' Ecclesiastical Reports.
Add. Pa. Addison's Pennsylvania Reports.
Add. Tor. Addison on Torts.
Adm. & Ecc. English Law Reports, Admiralty and Ecclesiastical.
Adolph & E. Adolphus & Ellis' English King's Bench Reports.
Adye C. M. Adye on Courts-Martial.
Aelf. C. Canons of Aelfric.
Agn. Fr. Agnew on the Statute of Fraud.
Agn. Pat. Agnew on Patents.
Agra H. C. Agra High Court Reports, India
Aik. Aiken's Vermont Reports.
Aik. Stat. (or **Dig.**) Aiken's Digest of Alabama Statutes.
Aird Civ. Law. Aird's Civil Laws of France.
Al. Aleyn's Select Cases, King's Bench.
Al. & N. Alcock & Napier's Irish King's Bench Reports.
Ala. Alabama Reports;—Minor's Alabama Reports.
Ala. App. Alabama Appellate.
Ala. N. S. Alabama Reports, New Series (Alabama Reports, proper).
Ala. Sel. Cas. Alabama Select Cases, by Shepherd.
Alb. L. J. Albany Law Journal.
Alc. Alcock's Irish Registry Cases.

Alc. & N. Alcock & Napier's Irish King's Bench Reports.
Ald. Alden's Condensed Reports, Pennsylvania.
Alex. Br. Stat. Alexander's British Statutes in Force in Maryland.
Aleyn. Aleyn's Select Cases, English King's Bench.
All. Allen (see Allen, below).
All. N. B. Allen's New Brunswick Reports.
All. Ser. Allahabad Series, Indian Law Reports.
Allen. Allen's Massachusetts Reports;—Allen's Reports, New Brunswick;—Aleyn's English King's Bench Reports.
Am. American;—Amended;—Amendment.
Am. Bankr. R. American Bankruptcy Reports.
Am. Cr. Rep. American Criminal Reports, edited by Hawley.
Am. Cr. Tr. Chandler's American Criminal Trials.
Am. Dec. American Decisions (Select Cases), San Francisco.
Am. Dig. American Digest.
Am. Jur. American Jurist, Boston.
Am. L. J. American Law Journal (Hall's), Philadelphia.
Am. L. J. N. S. American Law Journal, New Series, Philadelphia.
Am. L. Reg. American Law Register, Philadelphia.
Am. L. Rev. American Law Review, Boston.
Am. L. T. American Law Times, Washington and New York.
Am. L. T. Bankr. American Law Times Bankruptcy Reports.
Am. L. T. R. American Law Times Reports.
Am. Lead. Cas. American Leading Cases (Hare & Wallace's).
Am. Neg. Cas. American Negligence Cases.
Am. Neg. Dig. American Negligence Digest.
Am. Neg. Rep. American Negligence Reports.
Am. Rep. American Reports.
Am. St. Rep. American State Reporter.
Amb. (or **Ambl.**) Ambler's English Chancery Reports.
Ames. Ames' Reports (4-7 Rhode Island);—Ames' Reports (1 Minn.).
Ames Cas. B. & N. Ames' Cases on Bills and Notes.
Ames, K & B. Ames, Knowles & Bradley's Reports (8 Rhode Island).
And. Andrew's English King's Bench Reports; — Anderson's English Common Pleas Reports.
And. Cr. Law. Andrews on Criminal Law.
And. & Ston. J. A. Andrews & Stoney's Supreme Court of Judicature Acts.
Ang. Angell & Durfee's Reports (1 Rhode Island).
Ang. Car. Angell on Carriers.
Ang. & A. Corp. Angell & Ames on Corporations.
Ang. & Dur. Angell & Durfee's Reports (1 Rhode Island).
Ann. Cas. Annotated Cases, American.
Annaly. Annaly's edition of Lee t. Hardwicke.
Anon. Anonymous.
Ans. Con. Anson on Contracts.
Anst. Anstruther's English Exchequer Reports.
Anth. Anthon's New York Nisi Prius Reports.
Anth. N. P. Anthon's New York Nisi Prius Reports.
Anth. Shep. Anthon's edition of Sheppard's Touchstone.
Ap. Just. Apud Justinianum (or Justinian's Institutes).
App. Appleton's Reports (19, 20 Maine).
App. Cas. Appeal Cases, English Law Reports.
App. Cas. Beng. Sevestre & Marshall's Bengal Reports.
App. Ct. Rep. Bradwell's Illinois Appeal Court Reports.
App. Div. Appellate Division (N. Y.).
App. Rep. Appeal Reports, Ontario.
Appleton. Appleton's Reports (19, 20 main).
Arbuth. Arbuthnot's Select Criminal Cases, Madras.
Arch. Court of Arches, England.
Arch. Civ. Pl. Archbold's Civil Pleading and Evidence.
Arch. C. L. Pr. Archbold's New Common Law Practice.
Arch. C. P. Archbold's Practice in the Common Pleas.
Arch. Cr. L. Archbold's Criminal Law.
Arch. Cr. Pl. Archbold's Criminal Pleading.
Arch. Cr. Prac. Archbold's Criminal Practice.
Arch. Cr. Proc. Archbold's Criminal Procedure.
Arch. J. C. Pr. Archibald on Practice of Judges' Chambers.
Arch. K. B. Forms. Archbold's Forms in King's Bench and Common Pleas.
Arch. K. B. Pr. Archbold's King's Bench Practice.
Arch. N. P. Archbold's Nisi Prius.
Arch. P. C. Archbold's Pleas of the Crown.
Arch. P. (or **Pr.**) **Ch.** Archbold's Practice by Chitty.
Arch. P. K. B. (or **Q. B.**) Archbold's Practice in the King's (or Queen's) Bench.
Arch. Part. Archbold's Law of Partnership.
Arch. Pr. Q. S. Archbold's Practice in Quarter Sessions.
Archer & Hogue. Archer & Hogue's Reports (2 Florida).
Arg. Bills Ex. Argles' French Law of Bills of Exchange.
Arg. Inst. Institution au Droit Français, par M. Argon.
Ariz. Arizona.
Ark. Arkansas Reports;—Arkley's Scotch Justiciary Reports.
Arkl. Arkley's Justiciary Reports, Scotland.
Arms. M & O. Armstrong, Macartney & Ogle's Irish Nisi Prius Reports.

Arms. Tr. Armstrong's Limerick Trials, Ireland.
Arn. Arnold's English Common Pleas Reports;—Arnot's Criminal Trials, Scotland.
Arn. Ins. Arnold's Marine Insurance.
Arn. Mun. Cor. Arnold's Municipal Corporations.
Arn. & Hod. Arnold and Hodges' English Queen's Bench Reports.
Arnot Cr. C. Arnot's Criminal Cases, Scotland.
Arun. Mines. Arundell on the law of Mines.
Ash. (or **Ashm.**) Ashmead's Pennsylvania Reports.
Ashe. Ashe's Tables to the Year Books (or to Coke's Reports; or to Dyer's Reports).
Ashurst MS. Ashurst's Paper Books, Lincoln's Inn Library;—Ashurst's Manuscript Reports, printed in 2 Chitty.
Asp. Cas. (or **Rep.**) English Maritime Law Cases, New Series, by Aspinall.
Ass. Liber Assisarum,—Book of Assizes.
Ass. Jerus. Assizes of Jerusalem.
Ass. Reg. Da. Assisa Regis David.
Asso & Man. Asso & Manuel's Institutes of Spanish Civil Law.
Ast. Ent. Aston's Entries.
Atch. Atchison's English Navigation and Trade Reports.
Ath. Mar. Set. Atherley on Marriage Settlements.
Atl. Atlantic Reporter.
Atwater. Atwater's Reports (in 1 Minnesota).
Auch. Auchinleck's Manuscript Cases, Scotch Court of Session.
Aust. Austin's English County Court Cases;—Australia.
Aust. Jur. Austin's Lectures on Jurisprudence;—Australian Jurist.
Aust. L. T. Australian Law Times.
Austin C. C. Austin's English County Court Reports.
Ayl. Pand. Ayliffe's Pandect of the Roman Civil Law.
Ayl. Par. Ayliffe's Parergon Juris Canonici Anglicani.
Az. Mar. Law. Azuni's Maritime Law.

B. Barbour's Session Laws, New York.
B. C. C. Brown's Chancery Cases;—Bail Court Cases (Lowndes & Maxwell).
B. D. & O. Blackham, Dundas, & Osborne's Nisi Prius Reports, Ireland.
B. M. Burrow's Reports *temp.* Mansfield.
B. Mon. Ben Monroe's Reports, Kentucky.
B. R. Bancus Regis, or King's Bench;—Bankruptcy Reports;—Bankruptcy Register, New York.
B. R. C. British Ruling Cases.
B. W. C. C. Butterworth's Workmen's Compensation Cases.
B. & A. Barnewall & Adolphus' English King's Bench Reports;—Barnewall & Alderson's English King's Bench Reports;—Barron & Arnold's English Election Cases;—Baron & Austin's English Election Cases;—Banning & Arden's Patent Reports.
B. & Ad. Barnewall & Adolphus' English King's Bench Reports.
B. & Ald. Barnewall & Alderson's King's Bench Reports.
B. & Arn. Barron & Arnold's English Election Cases.
B. & Aust. Barron & Austin's English Election Cases.
B. & B. Broderip & Bingham's English Common Pleas Reports;—Ball & Beatty's Irish Chancery Reports;—Bench & Bar (periodical), Chicago, New York.
B. & C. Barnewall & Cresswell's English King's Bench Reports.
B. & H. Blatchford & Howland's United States District Court Reports.
B. & H. Lead. Ca. Bennett & Heard's Leading Criminal Cases.
B. & L. Browning & Lushington's English Admiralty Reports.
B. & L. Pr. Bullen & Leake's Precedents of Pleading.
B. & P. Bosanquet & Puller's English Common Pleas Reports.
B. & P. N. R. Bosanquet & Puller's New Reports.
B. & S. Best & Smith's English Queen's Bench Reports.
Ba. & Be. Ball & Beatty's Irish Chancery Reports.
Bab. Auc. Babington's Law of Auctions.
Bab. Set-off. Babington's Law of Set-off.
Bac. Abr. Bacon's Abridgment.
Bac. Ca. Bacon's Case of Treason, 1641.
Bac. Comp. Arb. Bacon's Complete Arbitration.
Bac. Gov. Bacon on Government.
Bac. Law Tr. Bacon's Law Tracts.
Bac. Lease. Bacon on Leases and Terms of Years.
Bav. Lib. Reg. (or **T. E.**) Bacon's Liber Regis, vel Thesaurus Rerum Ecclesiasticarum.
Bac. Max. Bacon's Maxims of the Law.
Bac. Uses. Bacon's Essay on Uses.
Bagl. Bagley's Reports (16 California).
Bagl. & Har. Bagley & Harman's Reports (17-19 California).
Bai. (or **Bail.**) Bailey's Law Reports, South Carolina.
Bai. (or **Bail.**) **Eq.** Bailey's Equity Reports, South Carolina.
Bail. Ct. Rep. Saunders & Cole's English Bail Court Reports;—Lowndes & Maxwell's English Bail Court Cases.
Bald. Baldwin's United States Circuit Court Reports.
Balf. Pr. Balfour's Practicks of the Law of Scotland.
Ball. Lim. Ballantine on Limitations.
Ball & B. Ball & Beatty's Irish Chancery Reports.
Bank. Bankruptcy;—Bankruptcy Court.
Bank. Reg. Bankruptcy Register.
Bank. Rep. American Law Times Bankruptcy Reports.
Bank. & Ins. R. Bankruptcy and Insolvency Reports, English.
Banks. Banks' Reports (1-5 Kansas).
Bann. & Ard. Banning & Arden's Patent Cases.

Bar. Barnardiston's English King's Bench Reports;—Bar Reports in all the Courts, English;—Barbour (see Barb.).
Bar. Chy. Barnardiston's English Chancery Reports.
Bar. Eq. Barton's Suit in Equity.
Bar Int. Pr. R. Bar, Das Internationale Privat-und-Strafrecht.
Bar. & Ad. Barnewall & Adolphus, English King's Bench Reports.
Bar. & Al. Barnewall & Alderson's English King's Bench Reports.
Bar. & Arn. Barron & Arnold's English Election Cases.
Bar. & Aust. Barron & Austin's English Election Cases.
Bar. & Cr. Barnewall & Cresswell's English King's Bench Reports.
Barb. Barbour's Supreme Court Reports, New York;—Barber's Reports (14-24 Arkansas).
Barb. Ch. Barbour's New York Chancery Reports.
Barb. Ch. Pr. Barbour's Chancery Practice.
Barb. Cr. L. Barbour's Criminal Law.
Barb. Cr. P. Barbour's Criminal Pleadings.
Barc. Dig. Law Sc. Barclay's Digest of the Law of Scotland.
Barn. Barnardiston's English King's Bench Reports;—Barnes' English Common Pleas Reports.
Barn. Ch. Barnardiston's English Chancery Reports.
Barn. & Ad. Barnewall & Adolphus' English King's Bench Reports.
Barn. & Ald. Barnewall & Alderson's English King's Bench Reports.
Barn. & Cr. Barnewall & Cresswell's English King's Bench Reports.
Barnes. Barnes' Notes of Cases in Common Pleas.
Barr. Barr's Reports (1-10 Pennsylvania State);—Barry (see Barry).
Barr. & Arn. Barron & Arnold's English Election Cases.
Barr. & Aus. Barron & Austin's English Election Cases.
Barron Mir. Barron's Mirror of Parliament.
Bart. Eq. Barton's Suit in Equity.
Bart. L. Pr. Barton's Law Practice.
Bat. Stat. Battle's Revised Statutes of North Carolina, 1873.
Bates. Bates' Delaware Chancery Reports.
Batt. Batty's Irish King's Bench Reports.
Bax. Baxter's Reports, Tennessee.
Bay. Bay's South Carolina Reports;—Bay's Reports (1-3 and 5-8 Missouri).
Bea. Costs (or **C. E.**) Beames' Costs in Equity.
Bea. Eq. Pl. Beames' Equity Pleading.
Bea. Ne Ex. Beames on the Writ of Ne Exeat Regno.
Bea. Ord. Beames' Orders in Chancery.
Bea. Pl. Eq. Beames' Pleas in Equity.
Beas. Beasley's New Jersey Chancery Reports.
Beat. Beatty's Irish Chancery Reports.
Beav. Beavan's English Rolls Court Reports.
Beav. O. C. Beavan's Ordines Cancellariae.
Beaw. Lex. Mer. Beawes' Lex Mercatoria.
Bec. Cr. Beccaria on Crimes and Punishments.
Bee (or **Bee Adm.**) Bee's United States District Court Reports.
Bel. Bellewe's English King's Bench Reports;—Bellasis' Bombay Reports;—Bering's Ceylon Reports.
Bel. Ca. *t.* H. VIII. Bellewe's Cases, Henry VIII (Brook's New Cases).
Bel. Prob. Belknap's Probate Law of California.
Beling. Beling's Ceylon Reports.
Beling & Van. Beling & Vanderstraaten's Ceylon Reports.
Bell. Bell's English Crown Cases Reserved;—Bell's Scotch Appeal Cases;—Bell's Scotch Session Cases;—Bell's Calcutta Reports;—Bellewe's English King's Bench Reports;—Brooke's New Cases, by Bellewe;—Bellinger's Reports (4-8 Oregon);—Bellasis' Bombay Reports.
Bell App. Cas. Bell's Scotch House of Lords (Appeal) Cases.
Bell Arb. Bell's Law of Arbitration in Scotland.
Bell C. C. Bell's English Crown Cases Reserved;—Bellasis' Civil Cases, Bombay;—Bellasis' Criminal Cases, Bombay.
Bell C. H. C. Bell's Reports, Calcutta High Court.
Bell Cas. Bell's Cases, Scotch Court of Session.
Bell. Cas. *t.* H. VIII. Brooke's New Cases (collected by Bellewe).
Bell. Cas. *t.* R. II. Bellewe's English King's Bench Reports (time of Richard II.).
Bell Cr. Ca. Bell's Engish Crown Cases Reserved;—Bellasis' Criminal Cases, Bombay.
Bell. Del. Beller's Delineations of Universal Law.
Bell Dict. Bell's Dictionary and Digest of the Laws of Scotland.
Bell fol. Bell's folio Reports, Scotch Court of Session.
Bell H. L. Bell's House of Lords Cases, Scotch Appeals.
Bell oct. (or **8vo.**) Bell's octavo Reports, Scotch Court of Session.
Bell P. C. Bell's Cases in Parliament, Scotch Appeals.
Bell Ses. Cas. Bell's Cases in the Scotch Court of Session.
Bellas. Bellasis' Criminal (or Civil) Cases, Bombay.
Bellewe. Bellewe's English King's Bench Reports.
Bellewe *t.* H. VIII. Brooke's New Cases (collected by Bellewe).
Belt Bro. Belt's edition of Brown's Chancery Reports.
Belt Sup. Belt's Supplement to Vesey Senior's English Chancery Reports.
Belt Ves. Sen. Belt's edition of Vesey Senior's English Chancery Reports.
Ben. Benedict's United States District Court Reports.
Ben. Adm. Benedict's American Admiralty Practice.
Ben. & Dal. Benloe & Dalison's English Common Pleas Reports.

Ben. & H. L. C. Bennett & Heard's Leading Criminal Cases.
Bendl. Bendloe (see Benl.).
Bened. Benedict's United States District Court Reports.
Benet Ct.-M. Benet on Military Law and Courts-Martial.
Beng. L. R. Bengal Law Reports, India.
Beng. S. D. A. Bengal Sudder Dewanny Adawlut Reports.
Benj. Sa. Benjamin on Sales.
Benl. Benloe's or Bendloe's English King's Bench Reports.
Benl. in Ashe. Benloe at the end of Ashe's Tables.
Benl. in Keil. Benloe or Bendloe in Keilway's Reports.
Benl. New. Benloe's Reports, English King's Bench.
Benl. Old. Benloe of Benloe & Dalison, English Common Pleas Reports.
Benl. & Dal. Benloe & Dalison's Common Pleas Reports.
Benn. See Bennett, below.
Benn. & H. Cr. Cas. Bennett & Heard's Leading Criminal Cases.
Benn. & H. Dig. Bennett and Heard's Massachusetts Digest.
Benne. Reporter of Vol. 7 Modern Reports.
Bennett. Bennett's Reports (1 California);—Bennett's Reports (1 Dakota);—Bennett's Reports (16-21 Missouri).
Bent. Cod. Bentham's Codification.
Bent. Const. Code. Bentham's Constitutional Code for all Nations.
Bent. Ev. (or **Jud. Ev.**) Bentham's Judicial Evidence.
Bent. Mor. & Leg. Bentham's Principles of Morals and Legislation.
Bent. Pun. Bentham's Rationale of Punishment.
Bent. The. Leg. Bentham's Theory of Legislation.
Ber. Berton's New Brunswick Reports.
Berry. Berry's Reports (1-9 Missouri Court of Appeals).
Bert. Berton's New Brunswick Reports.
Best Beg. & Rep. Best on the Right to Begin and Reply.
Best Ev. Best on Evidence.
Best Jur. Tr. Best on Trial by Jury.
Best & Sm. Best and Smith's English Queen's Bench Reports.
Betts' Adm. Pr. Betts' Admiralty Practice.
Betts' Dec. Blatchford & Howland's United States District Court Reports;—Olcott's United States District Court Reports.
Bev. Emp. L. Bevin on Employer's Liability for Negligence of Servants.
Bew. & N. Pr. Bewley & Naish on Common Law Procedure.
Bibb. Bibb's Reports, Kentucky.
Bick. & Hawl. Bicknell & Hawley's Reports (10 Nevada).
Big. Bignell's Reports, India.
Big. Cas. Bigelow's Cases, William I. to Richard I.
Big. Cas. B. & N. Bigelow's Cases on Bills & Notes.
Big. Cas. Torts. Bigelow's Leading Cases in Torts.
Big. Eng. Proc. Bigelow's English Procedure.
Big. Eq. Bigelow on Equity.
Big. Est. Bigelow on Estoppel.
Big. Fr. Bigelow on Frauds.
Big. Jarm. Wills. Bigelow's edition of Jarman on Wills.
Big. Lead. Cas. Bigelow's Leading Cases in Bills and Notes; Torts; or Wills.
Big. Plac. Bigelow's Placita Anglo-Normannica.
Big. Proc. Bigelow's English Procedures.
Big. Torts. Bigelow on Torts.
Bign. Bignell's Indian Reports.
Bilb. Ord. Ordinances of Bilboa.
Billot Extrad. Billot, Traité de l'Extradition.
Bin. Binney's Pennsylvania Reports.
Bing. Bingham's English Common Pleas Reports.
Bing. Act. & Def. Bingham's Actions and Defences in Real Property.
Bing. N. C. Bingham's New Cases, English Common Pleas.
Bing. R. P. Bingham on the Law of Real Property.
Binm. Ind. Binmore's Index-Digest of Michigan Reports.
Binn. Binney's Pennsylvania Reports.
Bird Supp. Bird's Supplement to Barton's Conveyancing.
Bish. Burr. Bishop's edition of Burrill on Assignments.
Bish. Con. Bishop on Contracts.
Bish. Cr. L. Bishop on Criminal Law.
Bish. Cr. Proc. Bishop on Criminal Procedure.
Bish. Mar. & Div. Bishop on Marriage and Divorce.
Bishop Mar. Wom. Bishop on Married Women.
Bish. Noll. Pros. Bishop's Law of Nolle Prosequi.
Bish. Stat. Cr. Bishop on Statutory Crimes.
Bisp. Eq. Bispham's Principles of Equity.
Biss. Bissell's United States Circuit Court Reports.
Biss. Stat. Bissell's Minnesota Statutes.
Bitt. Pr. Case. Bittleston's Practice Cases, Judicature Act.
Bitt. W. & P. Bittleson, Wise, & Parnell's Reports (2, 3 New Practice Cases).
Bl. Black's United States Supreme Court Reports;—Blatchford's United States Circuit Court Reports;—Blackford's Indiana Reports;—Blount's Law Dictionary;—Henry Blackstone's English Common Pleas Reports;—W. Blackstone's English King's Bench Reports;—Blackstone's Commentaries.
Bl. Com. Blackstone's Commentaries.
Bl. D. & O. Blackham, Dundas, & Osborne's Irish Nisi Prius Reports.
Bl. H. Henry Blackstone's English Common Pleas Reports.
Bl. L. T. Blackstone's Law Tracts.
Bl. Pr. Cas. Blatchford's Prize Cases.
Bl. R. (or **Bl. W.**) Sir William Blackstone's English King's Bench Reports.

Bl. & H. Blatchford & Howland's United States District Court Reports.

Bl. & W. Mines. Blanchard & Weeks' Leading Cases on Mines.

Bla. Black (see Bl.);—Blackstone (see Black.).

Bla. Ch. Bland's Maryland Chancery Reports.

Bla. Com. Blackstone's Commentaries.

Bla. H. Henry Blackstone's English Common Pleas Reports.

Bla. W. Sir William Blackstone's Reports, English King's Bench.

Black. Black's United States Supreme Court Reports;— Black's Reports (30-53 Indiana);—H. Blackstone's English Common Pleas Reports;—W. Blackstone's English King's Bench Reports;—Blackford's Indiana Reports.

Black. Anal. Blackstone's Analysis of the Laws of England.

Black. Com. Blackstone's Commentaries on the Laws of England.

Black. D. & O. Blackham, Dundas, & Osborne's Irish Nisi Prius Reports.

Black. H. Henry Blackstone's English Common Pleas Reports.

Black. Mag. Ch. Blackstone on Magna Charta.

Black R. Black's United States Supreme Court Reports;—W. Blackstone's English King's Bench Reports.

Black. W. William Blackstone's English King's Bench Reports.

Blackf. Blackford's Indiana Reports.

Blackst. Blackstone (see Black).

Blackw. Sc. Atc. Blackwell's Scotch Acts.

Blake. Blake's Reports (1 Montana).

Blake Ch. Pa. Blake's Chancery Practice, New York.

Blan. Lim. Blanshard on Statute of Limitations.

Bland. Bland's Maryland Chancery Reports.

Bland's Ch. See Bland.

Blash. Juries. Blashfield, Instructions to Juries.

Blatchf. Blatchford's United States Circuit Court Reports.

Blatchf. Pr. Cas. Blatchford's Prize Cases.

Blatchf. & H. Blatchford & Howland's United States District Court Reports.

Blax. Eng. Co. Blaxland's Codex Legum Angelicanum.

Bleckley. Bleckley's Reports (34, 35 Georgia).

Bli. Bligh's English House of Lords Reports.

Bli. N. S. Bligh's English House of Lords Reports, New Series.

Bliss Co. Pl. Bliss on Code Pleading.

Bliss Ins. Bliss on Life Insurance.

Blunt. Mod. Völk. Bluntschli, Das Moderne Völkerrecht.

Boh. Dec. Bohun's Declarations and Pleadings.

Bomb. H. Ct. Bombay High Court Reports.

Bomb. Sel. Cas. Bombay Select Cases.

Bomb. Ser. Bombay Series, Indian Law Re-Reports.

Bond. Bond's United States Circuit Court Reports.

Booraem. Booraem's Reports (6-8 California).

Borr. Borradaile's Reports, Bombay.

Bos. Bosworth's New York Superior Court Reports.

Bos. Pl. Bosanquet's Rules of Pleading.

Bos. & D. Lim. Bosanquet & Darby's Limitations.

Bos. & Pul. Bosanquet & Puller's English Common Pleas Reports.

Bos. & Pul. N. R. Bosanquet & Puller's New Reports, English Common Pleas.

Bosw. Bosworth's New York Superior Court Reports.

Bou. Inst. Bouvier's Institutes of American Law.

Bouln. Boulnois' Reports, Bengal.

Bourke. Bourke's Reports, Calcutta High Court.

Bousq. Dict. de Dr. Bousquet, Dictionnaire de Droit.

Bouv. Inst. Bouvier's Institutes of American Law.

Boyd Adm. Boyd's Admiralty Law, Ireland.

Boyle Act. Boyle's Précis of an Action at Common Law.

Br. Bracton; — Bradford; — Bradwell; — Brayton; — Breese; — Brevard; — Brewster; — Bridgman; — Brightly; — British; — Britton; — Brockenbrough; — Brooke; — Broom; — Brown; — Brownlow;—Bruce;—see below, especially under Bro.

Br. Abr. Brooke's Abridgment.

Br. Brev. Jud. Brownlow's Brevia Judicialia, etc.

Br. C. C. British (or English) Crown Cases (American Reprint);—Brown's Chancery Cases, English.

Br. Cr. Ca. British (or English) Crown Cases (American reprint).

Br. Leg. Max. Broom's Legal Maxims.

Br. Not. Brooke's Office of a Notary.

Br. N. C. Brooke's New Cases, English King's Bench.

Br. P. C. Brown's English Parliamentary Cases.

Br. Syn. Brown's Synopsis of Decisions, Scotch Court of Session.

Br. & Fr. Broderick & Fremantle's Ecclesiastical Cases, English.

Br. & Gold. Brownlow & Goldborough's English Common Pleas Reportes.

Br. & L. Browning & Lushington's English Admiralty Reports.

Bra. Bracton de Legibus, etc., Angliae.

Brac. Bracton de Legibus, etc., Angliae.

Brad. Bradford's Surrogate Reports, New York; Bradford's Kentucky Statutes;—Bradford's Iowa Reports;—Bradwell's Illinois Reports.

Bradf. Bradford's New York Surrogate Reports;—Bradford's Reports, Iowa.

Bradw. Bradwell's Appellate Reports, Illinois.

Branch. Branch's Reports (1 Florida).

Branch Pr. Branch's Principia Legis et Equitatis (Maxims).

Brandenburg Bankr. Brandenburg's Bankruptcy.
Brandenburg Dig. Brandenburg's Bankruptcy Digest.
Brandt Sur. Brandt on Suretyship and Guaranty.
Bray. Brayton's Vermont Reports.
Breese. Breese's Reports (1 Illinois).
Brev. Brevard's South Carolina Reports.
Brev. Sel. Brevia Selecta, or Choice Writs.
Brewer. Brewer's Reports (19-26 Maryland).
Brewst. Brewster's Pennsylvania Reports.
Brice Ult. V. Brice's Ultra Vires.
Bridg. J. Sir J. Bridgman's English Common Pleas Reports.
Bridg. O. Sir Orlando Bridgman's English Common Pleas Reports.
Bright. Brightly's Nisi Prius Reports.
Bright. N. P. Brightly's Pennsylvania Nisi Prius Reports.
Bright. Pur. Dig. Brightly's edition of Purdon's Digest of Pennsylvania Laws.
Brisbin. Brisbin's Reports (in 1 Minnesota).
Brit. (or **Britt.**) Britton's Ancient Pleas of the Crown.
Brit. Cr. Cas. British (or English) Crown Cases.
Brit. Rul. Cas. British Ruling Cases.
Bro. Browne's Pennsylvania Reports;—Brown's Michigan Nisi Prius Reports;—Brown's English Chancery Reports;—Brown's Parliamentary Cases.
Bro. A. & R. Brown's United States District Court Reports (Admiralty and Revenue Cases).
Bro. Abr. Brooke's Abridgment.
Bro. Adm. Brown's United States Admiralty Reports.
Bro. C. C. (or **C. R.**) Brown's English Chancery Cases, or Reports.
Bro. Ch. Brown's English Chancery Reports.
Bro. Ch. Pr. Browne's Practice of the High Court of Chancery.
Bro. Div. Pr. Browne's Divorce Court Practice.
Bro. Ecc. Brooke's Six Judgments in Ecclesiastical Cases (English).
Bro. Fr. Browne on the Statute of Frauds.
Bro. Leg. Max. (or **Bro. Max.**) Brooms' Legal Maxims.
Bro. N. C. Brooke's New Cases, English King's Bench.
Bro. N. P. Brown's Michigan Nisi Prius Reports.
Bro. P. C. Brown's English Parliamentary Cases.
Bro. Pa. Browne's Pennsylvania Reports.
Bro. Prac. (or **Prax.**) Brown's Practice (Praxis), or Precedents in Chancery.
Bro. Prob. Pr. Browne's Probate Practice.
Bro. St. Fr. Browne on the Statute of Frauds.
Bro. Tr. M. Browne on Trade Marks.
Bro. Us. & Cus. Browne's Law of Usages and Customs.
Bro. & Fr. Broderick & Fremantle's English Ecclesiastical Cases.
Bro. & G. Brownlow & Goldesborough's lish Common Pleas Reports.
Bro. & Lush. Browning & Lushington's English Admiralty Reports.
Brock. Brockenbrough's Marshall's Decisions, U. S. Circuit Court.
Brock. Cas. Brockenbrough's Virginia Cases.
Brock. & Hol. Brockenbrough & Holmes' "Virginia Cases."
Brod. & Bing. Broderip & Bingham's English Common Pleas Reports.
Brod. & Fr. Broderick & Fremantle's Ecclesiastical Cases.
Brooke. Brooke's New Cases. English King's Bench.
Brooke Abr. Brooke's "La Graunde Abridgment."
Brooke N. C. Brooke's New Cases, English King's Bench Reports.
Brooke Not. Brooke on the Office and Practice of a Notary.
Brooke (Petit) Brooke's New Cases.
Brooke Six Judg. Brooke's Six Ecclesiastical Judgments (or Reports).
Broom Leg. Max. Broom's Legal Maxims.
Brough. Civ. Pro. Broughton's Indian Civil Procedure.
Broun. Broun's Justiciary Reports, Scotland.
Brown. Brown's English Parliamentary Cases;—Brown's English Chancery Reports;—Brown's United States District Court Reports;—Brown's Michigan Nisi Prius Reports;—Brown's Reports (4-10 Nebraska);—Brownlow (& Goldesborough's) English C. P. Reports;—see also Bro., above.
Brown A. & R. Brown's United States District Court Reports (Admiralty and Revenue Cases).
Brown N. P. Brown's Michigan Nisi Prius Reports.
Brown. & Gold. Brownlow & Goldesborough's English Common Pleas Reports.
Brown & Hemingway. Brown & Hemingway's Reports (53-58 Mississippi).
Brown. & Lush. Browning & Lushington's English Admiralty Reports.
Brown. & Lush. M. & D. Browning & Lushington on Marriage and Divorce.
Browne. Browne's Pennsylvania Reports;—Browne's Reports (97-107 Massachusetts);—see also Bro.
Browne St. Fr. Browne on the Statute of Frauds.
Browne Us. Browne on Usages and Customs.
Browne & Gray. Browne & Gray's Reports 110-114 Massachusetts).
Brownl. & Gold. Brownlow & Goldesborough, English Common Pleas Reports.
Bru. (or **Bruce**) Bruce's Scotch Court of Session Reports.
Bryce Civ. L. Bryce's Study of the Civil Law.
Buch. Buchanan's (Eben J. or James) Reports, Cape of Good Hope.
Buch. Cas. (or **Tr.**) Buchanan's Remarkable Criminal Cases, Scotland.
Buck. Cooke. Bucknill's Cooke's Cases of Practice, Common Pleas.

Buck. Dec. Buckner's Decisions (in Freeman's Mississippi Chancery Reports).
Buff. Super. Ct. Sheldon's Buffalo (N. Y.) Superior Court Reports.
Bull N. P. Buller's Law of Nisi Prius.
Bulst. Bulstrode's English King's Bench Reports.
Bump Fr. Conv. Bump on Fraudulent Conveyances.
Bunb. Bunbury's English Exchequer Reports.
Burr. Burrows' English King's Bench Reports;—Burnett's Wisconsin Reports.
Bur. M. Burrows' Reports *temp.* Mansfield.
Bur. & Gres. Eq. Pl. Burroughs & Gresson's Irish Equity Pleader.
Burke Cel. Tr. Burke's Celebrated Trials.
Burl. Nat. Burlamaqui's Natural and Politic Law.
Burm. L. R. Burmah Law Reports.
Burn. Burnett's Wisconsin Reports.
Burn Eccl. Burn's Ecclesiastical Law.
Burnet. Burnet's Manuscript Decisions, Scotch Court of Session.
Burnett. Burnett's Wisconsin Reports.
Burr. Burrow's English King's Bench Reports.
Burr. Ass. Burrill on Assignments.
Burr. S. C. Burrows' English Settlement Cases.
Burr Tr. Rob. Burr's Trial, reported by Robertson.
Burr. & Gr. Eq. Pl. Burroughs & Gresson, Irish Equity Pleader.
Burt. Cas. Burton's Collection of Cases and Opinions.
Burt. Parl. Burton's Parliamentary Diary.
Burt. Sc. Tr. Burton's Scotch Trials.
Busb. Busbee's Law Reports, North Carolina.
Busb. Eq. Busbee's Equity Reports, North
Bush. Bush's Kentucky Reports.
Bush Dig. Bush's Digest Florida Laws.
Butts Sh. Butts' edition of Shower's English King's Bench Reports.
Byl. Bills. Byles on Bills of Exchange.
Byl. Exch. Byles' Law of Exchange.
Byl. Us. L. Byles on the Usury Laws.
Byn. War. Bynkershoek's Law of War.
Bynk. Bynkershoek's Quaestionum Juris Publici.

C. Cowen (New York);—Connecticut;—California;—Colorado;—Canada.
C. B. Common Bench Reports (Manning, Granger, & Scott).
C. B. N. S. Common Bench Reports, New Series.
C. C. Circuit Court;—Crown Cases;—Chancery Cases;—County Court;—City Court;—Civil Code;—Cepi Corpus;—Coleman's Cases (New York);—Cases in Chancery; — Causes Célèbres; — Civil Code;—Code Civil Français, or Code Napoléon.
C. C. B. Code de Commerce Belge.
C. C. E. Caines' Cases in Error, N. Y.;—Cases of Contested Elections.
C. C. P. Code of Civil Procedure.
C. C. Q. Civil Code of Quebec.
C. C. R. Crown Cases Reserved;—City Courts Reports; County Court Reports;—Circuit Court Reports.
C. Com. Code de Commerce.
C. Cr. Pr. Code of Criminal Procedure.
C. D. Comyn's Digest;—Commissioner's Decisions, United States Patent Office.
C. E. Gr. C. E. Greene's New Jersey Equity Reports.
C. F. Code Forestier Français.
C. H. & A. Carrow, Hamerton, & Allen's New Sessions Cases, English.
C. H. Rep. City Hall Reporter (Lomas'), New York City.
C. Instr. Cr. Code d'Instruction Criminelle.
C. J. Corpus Juris.
C. J. C. Corpus Juris Civilis;—Couper's Judiciary Cases, Scotland.
C. J. Can. Corpus Juris Canonici.
C. J. Civ. Corpus Juris Civilis.
C. L. J. Central Law Journal, St. Louis;—Chicago Law Journal;—Canada Law Journal, Toronto.
C. L. J. N. S. Canada Law Journal, New Series.
C. L. N. Chicago Legal News.
C. L. R. Common Law Reports, printed by Spottiswoode; —"English Common Law Reports," American reprint;—Cleveland Law Record, Cleveland, Ohio.
C. M. & R. Compton, Meeson, & Roscoe's English Exchequer Reports.
C. N. Code Napoleon (or Civil Code).
C. N. Conf. Cameron & Norwood's North Carolina Conference Reports.
C. N. P. C. Campbell's Nisi Prius Cases.
C. P. C. (or Coop.) C. P. Cooper's English Chancery Practice Cases;—Code de Procédure Civile.
C. P. C. *t.* Br. C. P. Cooper's English Chancery Reports *temp.* Brougham.
C. P. C. *t.* Cott. C. P. Cooper's English Chancery Reports *temp.* Cottenham.
C. P. Div. Common Pleas Division, English Law Reports.
C. P. U. C. Common Pleas Reports, Upper Canada.
C. R. Chancery Reports;—Code Reporter, New York.
C. R. N. S. Code Reports, New Series, New York.
C. S. C. Canada Supreme Court;—Consolidated Statutes of Canada.
C. S. L. C. Consolidated Statutes of Lower Canada.
C. S. U. C. Consolidated Statutes of Upper Canada.
C. S. & P. Craigie, Stewart, & Paton's Scotch Appeal Cases.
C. T. Constitutiones Tiberii.
C. Theod. Codex Theodosiani.
C. *t.* K. Cases *temp.* King (Macnaghten's Select Chancery Cases, English).
C. *t.* N. Cases *temp.* Northington (Eden's English Chancery Reports).
C. *t.* T. Cases *temp.* Talbot, English Chancery.
C. Vict. Dominion of Canada Statutes in the Reign of Victoria.
C. W. Dud. C. W. Dudley's Law or Equity Reports, South Carolina.

C. & A. Cooke & Alcock's Irish King's Bench Reports.
C. & C. Coleman & Caines' Cases, New York.
C. & D. Corbett and Daniell's English Election Cases;—Crawford & Dix's Irish Circuit Cases.
C. & D. A. C. Crawford & Dix's Abridged Cases, Irish.
C. & D. C. C. Crawford & Dix's Irish Circuit Cases.
C. & F. Clark & Finnelly's English House of Lords Reports.
C. & J. Crompton & Jervis' English Exchequer Reports.
C. & K. Carrington & Kirwan's English Nisi Prius Reports.
C. & L. Connor & Lawson's Irish Chancery Reports.
C. & M. Crompton & Meeson's English Exchequer Reports; — Carrington & Marshman's English Nisi Prius Reports.
C. & Marsh. Carrington & Marshman's English Nisi Prius Reports.
C. & N. Cameron & Norwood's North Carolina Conference Reports.
C. & P. Carrington & Payne's English Nisi Prius Reports;—Craig & Phillips' Chancery Reports.
C. & R. Cockburn & Rowe's English Election Cases.
Cahill's Ill. St. Cahill's Illinois Statutes.
Cai. Caines' New York Term Reports;—Caius (or Gaius) (see Gaius).
Cai. Cas. (or **Cas Err.**) Caines' New York Cases in Error.
Cai. Pr. Caines' Practice.
Cai. T. R. Caines' (Term) Reports, New York.
Caii. Caii or Gaii Institutiones (see Gaius).
Cain. Caines (see Cai.).
Cairn's Dec. Cairn's Decisions in the Albert Arbitration.
Cal. California Reports;—Calcutta;— Calthrop's English King's Bench Reports;—Caldecott's English Settlement Cases;—Calendae.
Cal. App. California Appellate.
Cal. L. J. California Law Journal, San Francisco.
Cal. Leg. Adv. Calcutta Legal Adviser, India.
Cal. Leg. Obs. Calcutta Legal Observer.
Cal. Rep. California Reports;—Calthrop's English King's Bench Reports.
Cal. S. D. A. Calcutta Sudder Dewanny Adawlut Reports.
Cal. Ser. Calcutta Series Indian Law Reports.
Cal. W. R. Calcutta Weekly Reporter, India.
Cald. (J. P. or **Set. Cas.)** Caldecott's English Magistrate's (Justice of the Peace) and Settlement Cases.
Call. Call's Virginia Reports.
Calth. Calthrop's English King's Bench Reports.
Cam. Cameron's Reports, Upper Canada, Queen's Bench.
Cam. Duc. Camera Ducata (Duchy Chamber).
Cam. Op. Cameron's Legal Opinions, Toronto.
Cam. & Nor. Cameron & Norwood's North Carolina Conference Reports.
Camp. Campbell's English Nisi Prius Reports;—see also Campbell.
Camp. Ch. Jus. Campbell's Lives of the Chief Justices.
Camp. Ld. Ch. Campbell's Lives of the Lord Chancellors.
Camp. N. P. Campbell's English Nisi Prius Reports.
Camp. Rom. L. (or **Comp.**) Campbell's Compendium of Roman Law.
Campbell. Campbell's English Nisi Prius Reports;— Campbell's Reports of Taney's United States Circuit Court Decisions;—Campbell's Legal Gazette Reports, Pennsylvania.
Can. Cr. Acts. Canada Criminal Acts, Taschereau's edition.
Can. L. J. Canada Law Journal, Toronto;—(Lower) Canada Law Journal, Montreal.
Can. L. T. Canadian Law Times.
Can. S. C. Rep. Canada Supreme Court Reports.
Car. H. & A. Carrow, Hamerton, and Allen's New Sessions Cases, English.
Car. Laws. Caruther's History of a Lawsuit. Cases in Chancery.
Car. & Kir. Carrington & Kirwan's English Nisi Prius Reports.
Car. & Mar. Carrington & Marshman's English Nisi Prius Reports.
Car. & P. Carrington & Payne's English Nisi Prius Reports.
Carp. P. C. Carpmael's English Patent Cases.
Carpenter. Carpenter's Reports (53 California).
Carr. Ham. & Al. Carrow, Hamerton, & Allen's New Sessions Cases, English.
Carrau. Carrau's edition of "Summary Cases," Bengal.
Cart. de For. Carta de Foresta (the Charter of the Forest).
Carter. Carter's English Common Pleas Reports;—Carter's Reports (1 & 2 Indiana).
Carth. Carthew's English King's Bench Reports.
Cary. Cary's English Chancery Reports.
Cary Lit. Cary's Commentary on Littleton's Tenures.
Cas. Casey's Reports (25-36 Pennsylvania State).
Cas. B. R. Cases Banco Regis *temp.* William III. (12 Modern Reports).
Cas. B. R. Holt. Cases and Resolutions (of Settlements; *not* Holt's King's Bench Reports).
Cas. C. L. Cases in Crown Law.
Cas. Ch. Cases in Chancery, English;—Select Cases in Chancery;—Cases in Chancery (9 Modern Reports).
Cas. Eq. Cases in Equity, Gilbert's Reports;—Cases and Opinions in Law, Equity, and Conveyancing.
Cas. Eq. Abr. Cases in Equity, Abridged, English.

Cas. F. T. Cases *tempore* Talbot, by Forrester, English Chancery.
Cas. in C. Cases in Chancery;—Select Cases in Chancery.
Cas. K. B. Cases in King's Bench (8 Modern Reports).
Cas. K. B. *t.* H. Cases *tempore* Hardwicke (W. Kelynge's English King's Bench Reports).
Cas. L. & Eq. Cases in Law and Equity (10 Modern Reports);—(Gilbert's) Cases in Law and Equity, English.
Cas. Pr. C. P. Cases of Practice, English Common Pleas (Cooke's Reports).
Cas. Pr. K. B. Cases of Practice in the King's Bench.
Cas. R. Casey's Reports (25-36 Pennsylvania State).
Cas. S. C. (Cape G. H.) Cases in the Supreme Court, Cape of Good Hope.
Cas. Sett. Cases of Settlement, King's Bench.
Cas. Six Cir. Cases on the Six Circuits, Ireland.
Cas. *t.* Ch. II. Cases *tempore* Charles II., in Vol. 3 of Reports in Chancery.
Cas. *t.* F. Cases *tempore* Finch, English Chancery.
Cas. *t.* Geo. I. Cases *tempore* George I., English Chancery (8, 9 Modern Reports).
Cas. *t.* H. Cases *tempore* Hardwicke, English King's Bench (Ridgway, Lee, or Annaly);—Cases *tempore* Holt, English King's Bench (Holt's Reports);—West's Chancery Reports, *tempore* Hardwicke.
Cas. *t.* K. Select Cases *tempore* King, English Chancery (edited by Macnaghten);—Moseley's Chancery Reports, *tempore* King.
Cas. *t.* Lee. (Phillimore's) Cases *tempore* Lee, English Ecclesiastical.
Cas. *t.* Mac. Cases *tempore* Macclesfield (10 Modern Reports).
Cas. *t.* Nap. Cases *tempore* Napier, by Drury, Irish Chancery.
Cas. *t.* North. Cases *tempore* Northington (Eden's English Chancery Reports).
Cas. *t.* Plunk. Cases *tempore* Plunkett, by Lloyd & Gould, Irish Chancery.
Cas. *t.* Q. A. Cases *tempore* Queen Anne (11 Modern Reports).
Cas. *t.* Sugd. Cases *tempore* Sugden, Irish Chancery.
Cas. *t.* Tal. Cases *tempore* Talbot, English Chancery.
Cas. *t.* Wm. III. Cases *tempore* William III. (12 Modern Reports).
Cas. Tak. & Adj. Cases Taken and Adjudged (first edition of Reports in Chancery; see n. 5, p. 76).
Cas. Wm. I. Bigelow's Cases, William I. to Richard I.
Casey. Casey's Reports (25-36 Pennsylvania State).
Cay Abr. Cay's Abridgment of the English Statutes.
Cel. Tr. Celebrated Trials;—Burke's Celebrated Trials.
Cent. Dig. Century Digest.
Cent. L. J. Central Law Journal, St. Louis, Mo.
Ch. App. Cas. Chancery Appeal Cases, English Law Reports.
Ch. Bills. Chitty on Bills.
Ch. Black. Chitty's Blackstone;—Chase's Blackstone.
Ch. Cas. Ch. Choyce Cases in Chancery.
Ch. Cham. Chancery Chambers' Reports, Ontario.
Ch. Col. Op. Chalmers' Colonial Opinions.
Ch. Cr. L. Chitty's Criminal Law.
Ch. Div. Chancery Division, English Law Reports.
Ch. Pl. Chitty on Pleading.
Ch. Rep. Reports in Chancery;—Irish Chancery Reports.
Ch. R. M. R. M. Charlton's Georgia Reports.
Ch. T. U. P. T. U. P. Charlton's Georgia Reports.
Ch. & Cl. Cas. Cripp's Church and Clergy Cases.
Chal. Op. Chalmers' Colonial Opinions.
Chamb. Rep. Chancery Chambers Reports, Ontario.
Chan. Chaney's Reports (37-44 Michigan).
Chand. Chandler's Reports, Wisconsin;—Chandler's Reports (20 and 38-44 New Hampshire).
Chand. Cr. Tr. Chandler's American Criminal Trials.
Chaney. Chaney's Reports (37-44 Michigan).
Char. Merc. Charta Mercatoria.
Charl. Pr. Cas. Charley's English Practice Cases.
Charl. R. M. R. M. Charlton's Georgia Reports.
Charl. T. U. P. T. U. P. Charlton's Georgia Reports.
Chart. (or **Rot. Chart.**) Rotulus Chartarum (The Charter Roll).
Chart. Antiq. Chartae Antiquae.
Chart. Forest. Charta de Foresta.
Chase. Chase's United States Circuit Court Decisions.
Chase's Bl. Chase's edition of Blackstone.
Chase Tr. Chase's Trial (Impeachment) by the United States Senate.
Chev. Cheve's South Carolina Law Reports.
Chev. Ch. (or **Eq.**) Cheve's South Carolina Equity Reports.
Chic. L. B. Chicago Law Bulletin, Illinois.
Chic. Leg. N. Chicago Legal News, Illinois.
Chip. Chipman's Reports, New Brunswick.
Chip. D. D. Chipman's Vermont Reports.
Chip. MS. Reports printed from Chipman's Manuscript, New Brunswick.
Chip. N. N. Chipman's Vermont Reports.
Chit. Chitty's English Bail Court Reports.
Chit. Arch. Pr. Chitty's Edition of Archbold's Practice.
Chit. B. C. Chitty's English Bail Court Reports.
Chit. Bills (or **B. & N.**) Chitty on Bills.
Chit. Bl. Chitty's edition of Blackstone's Commentaries.
Chit. Burn's J. Chitty's edition of Burn's Justice.
Chit. Con. Chitty on Contracts.
Chit. Cr. L. Chitty's Criminal Law.
Chit. Des. Chitty on the Law of Descents.
Chit. Gen. Pr. Chitty's General Practice.

Chit. Pl. Chitty on Pleading.
Chit. Pr. Chitty's General Practice.
Chit. Prec. Chitty's Precedents in Pleading.
Chit. Prer. Chitty's Prerogatives of the Crown.
Chit. R. Chitty's English Bail Court Reports.
Chit. & H. Bills. Chitty & Hulme on Bills of Exchange.
Chitt. Chitty's English Bail Court Reports; —see also Chit.
Cho. Ca. Ch. Choyce Cases in Chancery.
Chr. Rep. Chambers Reports, Upper Canada.
Chr. Rob. Christopher Robinson's English Admiralty Reports.
Chron. Div. Cts. Chronicles of the Divorce Courts.
Chron. Jur. Chronica Juridicalia.
Cin. Law Bul. Cincinnati Law Bulletin, Cincinnati, Ohio.
Cin. S. C. Rep. Cincinnati Superior Court Reporter.
City Ct. Rep. City Courts Reports, New York City.
City H. Rec. City Hall Recorder (Rogers'), New York.
City H. Rep. Lomas' City Hall Reporter, New York.
City Rec. City Record, New York.
Civ. Pr. Rep. Civil Procedure Reports, New York.
Cl. (or **Rot. Cd.**) Rotulus Clausarum (The Close Roll);—Clark (see Clark and Clarke).
Cl. App. Clark's Appeal Cases, House of Lords.
Cl. Can. Ins. Clarke's Canada Insolvent Acts.
Cl. Ch. Clarke's Chancery Reports, New York.
Cl. Home. Clerk Home, Scotch Session Cases.
Cl. & Fin. Clark & Finnelly's House of Lords Cases.
Cl. & Fin. N. S. House of Lords' Cases, by Clark (see n. 12, p. 73).
Cl. & H. Clarke's & Hall's Contested Elections in Congress.
Clar. Parl. Chr. Clarendon's Parliamentary Chronicle.
Clark. English House of Lords Cases, by Clark;—Pennsylvania Law Journal Reports, edited by Clark;—Clark's Reports (58 Alabama);—see also Clarke.
Clark & Fin. Clark & Finnelly's House of Lords Reports.
Clark & Fin. N. S. Clark & Finnelly's Reports, New Series (Clark, see n. 12, p. 73).
Clarke. Clarke's New York Chancery Reports;—Clarke's edition of 1-8 Iowa;—Clarke's Reports (19-22 Michigan);—Clarke's Notes of Cases, Bengal;—see also Clark.
Clarke Ch. Clarke's New York Chancery Reports.
Clayt. Clayton's English Reports, York Assizes.
Clerk Home. Clerk Home's Decisions, Scotch Court of Session.
Clerke Pr. Clerke's (or Clarke's) Praxis Admiralitatis.
Clif. Clifford's United States Circuit Court Reports.
Clif. & Rick. Clifford & Rickard's English Locus Standi Reports.
Clif. & St. Clifford & Stephens' English Locus Standi Reports.
Clow L. C. on Torts. Clow's Leading Cases on Torts.
Co. County;—Company;—Coke's English King's Bench Reports.
Co. Cop. Coke's Copyholder.
Co. Ct. Chr. County Courts Chronicle, London.
Co. Ct. Rep. County Court Reports, English.
Co. Cts. Coke on Courts (4th Institute).
Co. Ent. Coke's Book of Entries.
Co. G. Reports and Cases of Practice in C. P. *temp.* Anne, Geo. I., and Geo. II., by Sir G. Coke. (Same as Cooke's Practice Reports.)
Co. Lit. Coke on Littleton (1st Institute).
Co. M. C. Coke's Magna Charta (2d Institute).
Co. P. C. Coke's Pleas of the Crown (3d Institute).
Co. Pl. Coke's Pleadings (sometimes published separately).
Co. Rep. Coke's Reports, King's Bench.
Cobb. Cobb's Reports (6-20 Georgia).
Cobb. Parl. Hist. Cobbett's Parliamentary History.
Cobb. St. Tr. Cobbett's (afterwards Howell's) State Trials.
Cochr. Cochran's Nova Scotia Reports.
Cock. & Rowe. Cockburn & Rowe's Election Cases.
Cocke. Cocke's Reports (16-18 Alabama);—Cocke's Reports (14, 15 Florida).
Cod. Jur. Civ. Codex Juris Civilis.
Code Civ. Code Civile Française (*or* Code Napolèon.)
Code Com. B. Code de Commerce, Belge.
Code Com. I. Code de Commerce, Italien.
Code For. Code Forestier Français.
Code I. Code d' Instruction Criminelle.
Code La. Civil Code of Louisiana.
Code M. Code Municipal, Quebec.
Code N. (or **Nap.**) Code Napolèon (*or* Code Civil).
Code P. Code Pénal.
Code P. C. Code de Procédure Civile.
Code Pro. Code of Procedure.
Code Rep. New York Code Reporter.
Code Rep. N. S. New York Code Reports, New Series.
Codes Fr. Les Codes Françaises.
Cogh. Epit. Coghlan's Epitome of Hindu Law Cases.
Coke. Coke's English King's Bench Reports.
Coke Ent. Coke's Book of Entries.
Coke Inst. Coke's Institutes.
Coke Lit. Coke on Littleton.
Col. Colorado Reports.
Col. C. C. Collyer's English Chancery Cases.

Col. Cas. Coleman's Cases (of Practice), New York.
Col. L. Rep. Colorado Law Reporter.
Col. & Cai. Coleman and Caines' Cases, New York.
Cold. Coldwell's Tennessee Reports.
Colds. Pr. Coldstream's Scotch Court of Session Procedure.
Cole. Cole's edition of Iowa Reports.
Coll. Collyer's English Chancery Cases;—Colles' Parliamentary Cases.
Coll. Caus. Cél. Collection des Causes Célèbres, Paris.
Coll. Jurid. Collectanea Juridica.
Coll. L. D. et O. Collection des Lois, Décrets et Ordonnances.
Coll. P. C. Colles' English Parliamentary (House of Lords) Cases.
Colles. Colles' English Parliamentary Cases.
Colly. Collyer's English Vice Chancellors' Reports.
Colly. Part. Collyer on Partnership.
Colo. Colorado Reports.
Colo App. Colorado Appeals.
Colo. L. Rep. Colorado Law Reporter.
Colq. Colquit's Reports (1 Modern).
Columbia L. Rev. Columbia Law Review.
Colvil. Colvil's Manuscript Decisions, Scotch Court of Session.
Coly. Guar. (De) Colyar on Guarantees.
Com. Comyn's Reports, English King's Bench;—Comberbach's English King's Bench Reports;—Comstock's Reports (1-4 New York Court of Appeals).
Com. B. Common Bench;—(English) Common Bench Reports (Manning, Granger, and Scott).
Com. B. N. S. (English) Common Bench Reports, New Series.
Com. Jour. Journals of the House of Commons.
Com. Law Rep. English Common Law Reports (American Reprint);—Common Law Reports, published by Spottiswoode.
Com. Pl. Common Pleas, English Law Reports.
Com. Pl. Div. Common Pleas Division, English Law Reports.
Com. Pl. Reptr. Common Pleas Reporter, Scranton, Pa.
Comb. Comberbach's English King's Bench Reports.
Comm. Commentaries;—Blackstone's Commentaries.
Comst. Comstock's Reports (1-4 New York Court of Appeals).
Comyns. Comyns' English King's Bench Reports.
Con. Conover's Reports (16-52 Wisconsin); Continuation of Rolle's Reports (2 Rolle).
Con. Cus. Conroy's Custodiam Reports.
Con. & Law. Connor & Lawson's Irish Chancery Reports.
Con. & Sim. Connor and Simonton's South Carolina Equity Digest.
Cond. Ch. R. (or **Eng. Ch.**) Condensed English Chancery Reports (American Reprint).
Cond. Eccl. Condensed Ecclesiastical Reports (American reprint).
Cond. Ex. R. Condensed Exchequer Reports (Price, &c., American reprint).
Cond. Rep. U. S. Peters' Condensed United States Reports.
Conf. Conference Reports (by Cameron and Norwood), North Carolina.
Conf. Chart. Confirmatio Chartarum.
Cong. Gl. Congressional Globe, Washington.
Cong. Rec. Congressional Record, Washington.
Conn. Connecticut;—Connecticut Reports.
Conover. Conover's Reports (16-52 Wisconsin.)
Conr. Conroy's Custodiam Reports.
Cons. del M. Consolato del Mare.
Cons. Ord. in Ch. Consolidated General Orders in Chancery.
Consist. Rep. English Consistorial Reports, by Haggard.
Const. Constitutional Reports, South Carolina, by Mills;—Constitutional Reports, South Carolina, by Treadway;—Constitutional Reports, Vol. 1, South Carolina, by Harper.
Const. N. S. Constitutional Reports (Mill), South Carolina, New Series.
Const. Oth. Constitutiones Othoni (found at the end of Lyndewood's Provinciale).
Const. S. C. Constitutional Reports, South Carolina, printed by Treadway.
Const. S. C. N. S. S. C. Constitutional Reports, New Series, printed by Mills.
Const. U. S. Constitution of the United States.
Consuet. Feud. Consuetudines Feudorum; or, the Book of Feuds.
Conv. Est. Convention of the Estates of Scotland.
Coo. & H. Tr. Cooke & Harwood's Charitable Trusts Acts.
Cooke. Cooke's Cases of Practice, English Common Pleas;—Cooke's Reports, Tennessee.
Cooke Pr. Cas. Cooke's Practice Reports, English Common Pleas.
Cooke & Al. Cooke's & Alcock's Reports, Irish King's Bench.
Cooke & H. Ch. Tr. Cooke & Harwood's Charitable Trust Acts.
Cool. Black. Cooley's edition of Blackstone.
Cool. Con. Law. Cooley's Constitutional Law.
Cool. Con. Lim. Cooley's Constitutional Limitations.
Cool. Tax. Cooley on Taxation.
Cool. Torts. Cooley on Torts.
Cooley. Cooley's Reports (5-12 Michigan).
Coop. Cooper's Tennessee Chancery Reports;—Cooper's English Chancery Reports *temp.* Eldon;—Cooper's English Chancery Reports *temp.* Cottenham;—Cooper's English Chancery Reports *temp.* Brougham;—Cooper's English Practice Cases, Chancery.
Coop. C. C. (or **Cas.**) Cooper's Chancery cases *temp.* Cottenham.
Coop. C. & P. R. Cooper's Chancery and Practice Reporter, Upper Canada.

Coop. Ch. Cooper's Tennessee Chancery Reports.
Coop. Inst. (or **Just.**) Cooper's Institutes of Justinian.
Coop. Pr. Cas. Cooper's Practice Cases, English Chancery.
Coop. Rec. Cooper's Public Records of Great Britain.
Coop. Sel. Ca. Cooper's Select Cases *temp.* Eldon, English Chancery.
Coop. ***t.*** **Br.** Cooper's Cases *temp.* Brougham, English Chancery.
Coop. ***t.*** **Cott.** Cooper's Cases *temp.* Cottenham, English Chancery.
Coop. ***t.*** **Eld.** Cooper's Cases *temp.* Eldon, English Chancery.
Coop. Ten. Chy. Cooper's Tennessee Chancery Reports.
Cooper. Cooper (see Coop., above).
Copp Min. Dec. Copp's United States Mining Decisions.
Cor. Coryton's Bengal Reports.
Corp. Jur. Corpus Juris.
Corp. Jur. Can. Corpus Juris Canonici.
Corp. Jur. Civ. Corpus Juris Civilis.
Corp. Jur. Germ. Corpus Juris Germanici.
Corvin. El. Corvinus' Elementa Juris Civilis.
Coryton. Coryton's Reports, Calcutta High Court.
Cot. Abr. Cotton's Abridgment of the Records.
Cou. Couper's Justiciary Reports, Scotland.
Count. Cts. Ch. County Courts Chronicle, London.
Court. & Macl. Courtenay & Maclean's Scotch Appeals (6 and 7 Wilson & Shaw).
Cout. de N. Coutumes de Normandie.
Cout. de P. Coutumes de Paris.
Cow. Cowen's New York Reports;—Cowper's English K. B. Reports.
Cow. N. Y. Cowen's New York Reports.
Cowp. Cowper's English King's Bench Reports.
Cowp. Cas. Cowper's Cases, in the third volume of Reports in Chancery.
Cox. Cox's English Chancery Reports;—Cox's English Criminal Cases;—Cox's Reports (25-27 Arkansas).
Cox C. C. Cox's English Criminal Cases.
Cox Ch. Cox's English Chancery Cases.
Cox Ch. Pr. Cox's Chancery Practice.
Cox Cr. Ca. Cox's English Criminal Cases.
Cox Mc. & H. Cox, McCrae, & Hertslet's English County Court Reports.
Cox Tr. M. Ca. Cox's American Trade Mark Cases.
Cox & Atk. Cox & Atkinson, English Registration Appeal Reports.
Coxe. Coxe's Reports, New Jersey.
Coxe Bract. Coxe's translation of Güterbach's Bracton.
Cr. Cranch's Reports, United States Supreme Court;—Cranch's United States Circuit Court Reports.
Cr. C. C. Cranch's United States Circuit Court Cases (Reports).
Cr. Cas. Res. Crown Cases Reserved.
Cr. M. & R. Crompton, Meeson, & Roscoe's English Exchequer Reports.
Cr. Pat. Dec. Cranch's Decisions on Patent Appeals.
Cr. S. & P. (or **Cr. & St.**) Craigie, Stewart, & Paton's Scotch Appeal Cases.
Cr. & Dix. Crawford & Dix's Irish Circuit Court Cases.
Cr. & Dix Ab. Cas. Crawford & Dix's (Irish) Abridged Cases.
Cr. & M. Crompton & Meeson's English Exchequer Reports.
Cr. & Ph. Craig & Phillips' English Chancery Reports.
Crabb Conv. Crabb's Treatise on Conveyancing.
Crabb Eng. L. Crabb's History of the English Law.
Crabb R. P. Crabb on Real Property.
Crabbe. Crabbe's United States District Court Reports.
Craig & Ph. Craig and Phillips' English Chancery Reports.
Craig. & St. (or **Craig. St. & Pat.**). Craigie, Stewart, and Paton's Scotch Appeal Cases.
Craik C. C. Craik's English Causes Célèbres.
Cranch. Cranch's United States Supreme Court Reports.
Cranch C. C. (or **D. C.**) Cranch's U. S. Circuit Court Reports, District of Columbia.
Cranch Pat. Dec. Cranch's Patent Decisions.
Craw. & D. Crawford & Dix's Circuit Court Cases, Ireland.
Craw. & D. Ab. Cas. Crawford & Dix's Abridged Cases, Ireland.
Creas. Col. Const. Creasy's Colonial Constitutions.
Creas. Eng. Cons. Creasy's Rise and Progress of the English Constitution.
Creas. Int. L. Creasy on International Law.
Creasy. Creasy's Ceylon Reports.
Cress. Ins. Cas. Cresswell's English Insolvency Cases.
Crim. L. Mag. Criminal Law Magazine, Jersey City, N. J.
Cripp Ch. Cas. Cripp's Church and Clergy Cases.
Critch. Critchfield's Reports (5-21 Ohio State).
Cro. (Croke's English King's Bench Reports;—Keilway's English King's Bench Reports.
Cro. Car. Croke's English King's Bench Reports *temp.* Charles I. (3 Cro.).
Cro. Eliz. Croke's English King's Bench Reports *temp.* Elizabeth (1 Cro.).
Cro. Jac. Croke's English King's Bench Reports *temp.* James (Jacobus) (I) (2 Cro.).
Crockford. English Maritime Law Reports, published by Crockford.
Croke. See Cro., above.
Cromp. Star Chamber Cases by Crompton.
Cromp. M. & R. Crompton, Meeson, and Roscoe's English Exchequer Reports.
Cromp. R. & C. Pr. Crompton's Rules and Cases of Practice.
Cromp. & F. Fitzherbert's Justice, enlarged by Crompton.
Cromp. & Jerv. Crompton & Jervis's English Exchequer Reports.
Cromp. & Mees. Crompton & Meeson's English Exchequer Reports.

Crounse. Crounse's Reports (3 Nebraska).
Crowther. Crowther's Ceylon Reports.
Cru. Dig. Cruise's Digest of Law of Real Property.
Cru. Fin. Cruise's Fines and Recoveries.
Cru. Us. Cruise on Uses.
Crumrine. Pittsburgh Reports, edited by Crumrine.
Cummins. Cummins' Idaho Reports.
Cun. (or **Cunn.**) Cunningham's English King's Bench Reports.
Cur. Curtis' United States Circuit Court Reports.
Cur. Dec. Curtis' Decisions, United States Supreme Court.
Curry. Curry's Reports (6-19 Louisiana).
Curt. Curtis United States Circuit Court Reports;—Curteis' English Ecclesiastical Reports.
Curt. Adm. Dig. Curtis' Admiralty Digest.
Curt. C. C. Curtis' United States Circuit Court Decisions.
Curt. Dec. Curtis' United States Supreme Court Decisions.
Curt. Ecc. Curteis' English Ecclesiastical Reports.
Curtis. Curtis' United States Circuit Court Reports.
Curw. Ov. Cas. Curwen's Overruled Cases, Ohio.
Cush. Cushing's Massachusetts Reports;—Cushman's Mississippi Reports.
Cush. Elec. Cas. Cushing's Election Cases in Massachusetts.
Cush. Man. Cushing's Manual of Parliamentary Law.
Cush. Parl. Law. Cushing's Law and Practice of Legislative Assemblies.
Cushing. Cushing's Massachusetts Reports.
Cushman. Cushman's Mississippi Reports.
Cyc. Cyclopedia of Law and Procedure.
Cyc. Corp. Fletcher's Cyclopedia of Corporations.
Cyc. Dict. Cyclopedic Law Dictionary.

D. Digest (particularly the Digest of Justinian); Dallas' United States and Pennsylvania Reports;—Denio's Reports, New York;—Dunlop, Bell, & Murray's Reports, Scotch Session Cases (second series).
D. Abr. D'Anvers' Abridgment.
D'Agu. Œuv. D'Aguesseau, Œuvres.
D. B. Domesday Book.
D. Chip. D. Chipman's Reports, Vermont.
D. F. & J. De Gex, Fisher, & Jones' English Chancery Reports.
D. F. & J. B. De Gex, Fisher, & Jones' English Bankruptcy Reports.
D. G. De Gex;—De Gex's English Bankruptcy Reports.
D. J. & S. De Gex, Jones, & Smith's English Chancery Reports.
D. J. & S. B. De Gex, Jones, & Smith's English Bankruptcy Reports.
D. M. & G. De Gex, Macnaghten, & Gordon's English Chancery Reports.
D. M. & G. B. De Gex, Macnaghten, & Gordon's English Bankruptcy Reports.
D. N. S. Dowling's Reports, New Series, English Bail Court;—Dow, New Series (Dow & Clark, English House of Lords Cases).
D. P. Domus Procerum (House of Lords).
D. P. B. Dampier Paper Book, in Lincoln's Inn Library.
D. P. C. Dowling's English Practice Cases.
D. & B. Dearsly & Bell's English Crown Cases.
D. & C. Dow & Clark's English House of Lords (Parliamentary) Cases.
D. & Ch. Deacon and Chitty's English Bankruptcy Reports.
D. & E. Durnford & East's (Term) Reports, English King's Bench.
D. & J. De Gex & Jones' English Chancery Reports.
D. & J. B. De Gex & Jones' English Bankruptcy Reports.
D. & L. Dowling & Lowndes' English Bail Court Reports.
D. & M. Davison & Merivale's English Queen's Bench Reports.
D. & R. Dowling & Ryland's English King's Bench Reports.
D. & R. M. C. Dowling & Ryland's English Magistrates' Cases.
D. & R. N. P. Dowling & Ryland's English Nisi Prius Cases.
D. & S. Doctor and Student;—Drewry & Smale's Chancery Reports.
D. & W. Drury & Walsh's Irish Chancery Reports;—Drury & Warren's Irish Chancery Reports.
Da. Dakota;—Dakota Territory Reports.
Dak. Dakota Territory Reports.
Dal. Dallas' United States Reports;—Dalison's English Common Pleas Reports (bound with Benloe);—Dalrymple's Scotch Session Cases.
Dall. Dallas' Pennsylvania and United States Reports;—Dallas' Styles, Scotland;—Dallas, Laws of Pennsylvania.
Dall. Dec. (or **Dall. Dig.**) Dallam's Texas Decisions, printed originally in Dallam's Digest.
Dall. in Keil. Dallison in Keilway's Reports, English King's Bench.
Dall. L. Dallas' Laws of Pennsylvania.
Dall. S. C. Dallas' United States Supreme Court Reports.
Dallas. Dallas' Pennsylvania and United States Reports.
Dalr. Dalrymple's Decisions, Scotch Court of Session;—(Dalrymple of) Stair's Decisions, Scotch Court of Session;—Dalrymple of) Hailes' Scotch Session Cases.
Dalrymple. (Sir Hew) Dalrymple's Scotch Session Cases;—(Sir David Dalrymple of) Hailes' Scotch Session Cases;—(Sir James Dalrymple of) Stair's Scotch Session Cases;—see also Dal.
Daly. Daly's New York Common Pleas Reports.
Dan. Daniell's Exchequer and Equity Reports;—Dana's Kentucky Reports;—Danner's Reports (42 Alabama).
Dan. Ch. Daniell's Chancery Practice.
Dan. Neg. Ins. Daniel's Negotiable Instruments.
Dan. Ord. Danish Ordinances.
Dan. & Ll. Danson & Lloyd's Mercantile Cases.
Dana. Dana's Kentucky Reports.

Dana Wh. Dana's edition of Wheaton's International Law.
Dane Abr. Dane's Abridgment of American Law.
Danner. Danner's Reports (42 Alabama).
Dans. & L. Danson & Lloyd's English Mercantile Cases.
Danv. Abr. D'Anvers' Abridgment of Law.
Dart. Col. Ca. Dartmouth College Case.
Das. Dasent's Bankruptcy and Insolvency Reports;—also Common Law Reports, Vol. 3.
Dass. Stat. Dassler's Kansas Statutes.
Dav. Davies' United States District Court Reports (now republished as 2 Ware);—Davy's or Davies' Irish King's Bench and Exchequer Reports;—Davies' English Patent Cases;—Davis' Reports (Abridgment of Sir Ed. Coke's Reports);—Davis' Hawaiian Reports.
Dav. Coke. Davis' Abridgment of Coke's Reports.
Dav. Pat. Cas. Davies' English Patent Cases.
Dav. & Mer. Davison & Merivale's Reports, Queen's Bench.
Daveis. Daveis' United States District Court Reports (Ware, Vol. 2).
Davies. Davies' or Davis', or Davys') Irish King's Bench Reports.
Davis. Davis' Hawaiian Reports;—Davies' (or Davys') Irish King's Bench Reports.
Day. Days' Connecticut Reports;—Connecticut Reports, proper, reported by Day.
De B. Mar. Int. L. De Burgh's Maritime International Laws.
De Gex. De Gex's English Bankruptcy Reports.
De G. F. & J. De Gex, Fisher, & Jones' English Chancery Reports.
De G. F. & J. By. De Gex, Fisher, & Jones' English Bankruptcy Appeals.
De G. J. & S. De Gex, Jones & Smith's English Chancery Reports.
De G. J. & S. By. De Gex, Jones & Smith's English Bankruptcy Appeals.
De G. M. & G. De Gex, Macnaghten, & Gordon's English Chancery Reports.
De G. M. & G. By. De Gex, Macnaghten, & Gordon's English Bankruptcy Appeals.
De G. & J. De Gex & Jones' English Chancery Reports.
De G. & J. By. De Gex & Jones' English Bankruptcy Appeals.
De G. & Sm. De Gex & Smale's English Chancery Reports.
De Jure Mar. Malloy's De Jure Maritimo.
De Witt. DeWitt's Reports (24-36 Ohio State).
Dea. Deady's United States District Court Reports.
Dea. & Sw. Deane & Swabey's Reports, Probate and Divorce.
Deac. Deacon's English Bankruptcy Reports.
Deac. Dig. Deacon's Digest of the Criminal Law.
Deac. & Chit. Deacon & Chitty's English Bankruptcy Reports.
Dead. Or. Laws. Deady & Lane's Oregon General Laws.
Deady. Deady's United States Circuit Court Reports.
Deane. Deane (& Swabey's) English Probate & Divorce Reports;—Deane's Reports (24-26 Vermont).
Deane Ecc. Rep. Deane & Swabey's English Ecclesiastical Reports.
Deane & Sw. Deane & Swabey's English Ecclesiastical Reports.
Dears. C. C. Dearsly's English Crown Cases.
Dears. & B. C. C. Dearsly and Bell's English Crown Cases.
Deas. & And. Deas & Anderson's Reports, Scotch Court of Session.
Dec. Col. Coleccion de los Decretos.
Dec. Com. Pat. Decisions of the Commissioner of Patents.
Dec. Fern. Decretos del Fernando, Mexico.
Dec. *t.* H. & M. Decisions in Admiralty *temp.* Hay and Marriott.
Decretal. The *Decretalia* of the Canon Law.
Del. Delaware Reports;—Delane's English Revision Cases.
Del. Ch. Delaware Chancery Reports, by Bates.
Del. Cr. Cas. Delaware Criminal Cases, by Houston.
Dem. Cond. Étran. Demangeat's Condition Civile, Étrangers en France.
Demol. C. N. Demolombe's Code Napoléon.
Den. Denio's New York Reports;—Denis' Reports (32 Louisiana Annual).
Den. C. C. Denison's English Crown Cases.
Den. & P. Denison & Pearce's English Crown Cases (2 Denison).
Den. & Sc. Pr. Denison & Scott's House of Lords Appeal Practice.
Denio. Denio's New York Reports.
Desaus. Eq. Desaussure's South Carolina Equity Reports.
Dest. Sh. & Adm. Desty on Shipping and Admiralty.
Detroit Leg. N. Detroit Legal News.
Dev. Devereux's North Carolina Law Reports;—Devereux's Reports, United States Court of Claims.
Dev. C. C. Devereux's Reports, United States Court of Claims.
Dev. Deeds. Devlin, Deeds and Real Estate.
Dev. Eq. Devereux's North Carolina Equity Reports.
Dev. L. (or **Dev. N. B.**) Devereux's North Carolina Law Reports.
Dev. & Bat. Devereux & Battle's North Carolina Law Reports.
Dev. & Bat. Eq. Devereux & Battle's North Carolina Equity Reports.
DeWitt. DeWitt's Reports (24-36 Ohio State).
Di. (or **Dy.**) Dyer's English Reports, King's Bench.
Dial. Sc. Dialogue de Scaccario.
Dic. Dom. Dicey on Domicil.
Dic. Par. Dicey on Parties to Actions.
Dice. Dice's Reports (71-73 Indiana).
Dick. Dickens' English Chancery Reports.
Dict. C. F. Dictionnaire des Codes Français.
Dict. de Jur. Dictionnaire de Jurisprudence.

Dict. Dr. Com. Dictionnaire Droit Commercial.
Dict. Nat. Dictionnaire du Notariat.
Dig. The Pandects, or Justinian's Digest of the Civil Law.
Dig. R. Pr. Digby's Introduction to the History of Real Property.
Dill. Dillon's United States Circuit Court Reports.
Dill. Mun. Cor. Dillon on Municipal Corporations.
Dill. Mun. Bonds. Dillon on Municipal Bonds.
Dill. Rem. Caus. Dillon on the Removal of Causes.
Dirl. Dirleton's Decisions, Court of Session.
Disn. Disney's Ohio Superior Court Reports.
Diss. ad Flet. Selden's Dissertatio ad Fletam.
Doct. & St. Doctor and Student.
Dod. (or **Dods.**) Dodson's English Admiralty Reports.
Dom. Boc. Domesday Book.
Dom. Civ. Law. Domat's Civil Law.
Domes. Domesday Book.
Donn. Donnelly's Reports, English Chancery;—Donnell's Irish Land Cases.
Dor. Md. Laws. Dorsey's Maryland Laws.
Dorion. Dorion's Quebec Queen's Bench Reports.
Doug. Douglas' Michigan Reports;—Douglas' English King's Bench Reports;—Douglas' English Election Cases.
Doug. El. Ca. Douglas' English Election Cases.
Dow (or **Dow P. C.**) Dow's House of Lords (Parliamentary) Cases;—Dowling's English Practice Cases.
Dow & C. Dow & Clark's English House of Lords Cases.
Dow. & L. Dowling & Lowndes' English Bail Court Reports.
Dow. & Ry. Dowling & Ryland's English King's Bench Reports;—Dowling & Ryland's English Nisi Prius Cases.
Dow. & Ry. M. C. Dowling & Ryland's English Magistrates' Cases.
Dow. & Ry. N. P. Dowling & Ryland's English Nisi Prius Cases. (Often bound at end of Vol. I., Dowl. & Ryl. K. B. Rep.)
Dow N. S. Dow & Clark's English House of Lords Cases.
Dowl. (or **Dowl. P. C.**) Dowling's English Bail Court (Practice) Cases.
Dowl. N. S. Dowling's English Bail Court Reports, New Series.
Dowl. Pr. Dowling's Common Law Practice.
Dowl. & Lownd. Dowling & Lowndes' English Practice Cases.
Dowl. & Ryl. Dowling & Ryland's English King's Bench Reports.
Dowl. & Ryl. M. C. Dowling & Ryland's English Magistrates' Cases.
Dowl. & Ryl. N. P. Dowling & Ryland's English Nisi Prius Cases.
Dr. Drewry's English Vice Chancellors' Reports;—Drury's Irish Chancery Reports *temp.* Sugden;—Drury's Irish Chancery Reports *temp.* Napier.
Dr. & Sm. Drewry & Smale's English Vice Chancellors' Reports.
Dru. & Wal. Drury & Walsh's Irish Chancery Reports.
Dru. & War. Drury & Warren's Irish Chancery Reports.
Drake Att. Drake on Attachment.
Draper. Draper's Upper Canada King's Bench Reports.
Drew. Drewry's English Vice Chancellors' Reports;—Drew's Reports (13 Florida).
Drew. Eq. Pl. Drewry's Equity Pleading.
Drew. & Sm. Drewry & Smale's English Vice Chancellors' Reports.
Drink. Drinkwater's English Common Pleas Reports.
Drone Cop. Drone on Copyrights.
Dru. Drury's Irish Chancery Reports *temp.* Sugden.
Dru. *t.* Nap. Drury's Irish Chancery Reports *temp.* Napier.
Dru. & Wal. Drury & Walsh's Irish Chancery Reports.
Dru. & War. Drury & Warren's Irish Chancery Reports.
Dud. (Geo.) Dudley's Georgia Reports.
Dud. Ch. (or **Eq.**) Dudley's South Carolina Equity Reports.
Dud. L. (or S. C.) Dudley's South Carolina Law Reports.
Duer. Duer's New York Superior Court Reports.
Dun. & Cum. Dunphy & Cummins' Remarkable Trials.
Dunc. Eccl. L. Duncan's Scotch Parochial Ecclesiastical Law.
Dunc. Ent. Cas. Duncan's Scotch Entail Cases.
Dunl. Abr. Dunlap's Abridgment of Elementary Law;—Dunlap's Abridgment of Coke's Reports.
Dunlop (or **Dunl. B. & M.**) Dunlop, Bell, & Murray's Reports, Second Series, Scotch Session Cases.
Durand. Spec. Jur. Durandi Speculum Juris.
Durfee. Durfee's Reports (2 Rhode Island).
Durie. Durie's Scottish Court of Session Cases.
Durn. & E. Durnford & East's English King's Bench Reports (Term Reports).
Dutch. Dutcher's New Jersey Reports.
Duv. Duvall's Kentucky Reports.
Dw. Stat. Dwarris on Statutes.
Dy. Dyer's English King's Bench Reports.

E. B. & E. Ellis, Blackburn, & Ellis' English Queen's Bench Reports.
E. B. & S. (Ellis) Best & Smith's English Queen's Bench Reports.
E. C. L. English Common Law Reports (American reprint).
E. D. S. E. D. Smith's New York Common Pleas Reports.
E. E. English Exchequer Reports (Amer. reprint).
E. E. R. English Ecclesiastical Reports.
E. L. & Eq. English Law and Equity Reports (American reprint).
E. P. C. East's Pleas of the Crown.

E. R. East's King's Bench Reports.
E. & A. Spink's Ecclesiastical and Admiralty Reports.
E. & A. R. Error and Appeal Reports, Ontario.
E. & B. Ellis & Blackburn's Queen's Bench Reports.
E. & E. Ellis & Ellis' English Queen's Bench Reports.
E. & Y. Eagle & Younge's English Tithe Cases.
Ea. East's English King's Bench Reports.
Eag. & Yo. Eagle & Young's English Tithe Cases.
East. East's King's Bench Reports;—East's Notes of Cases in Morley's East Indian
East N. of C. East's Notes of Cases (in Morley's East Indian Digest).
East P. C. East's Pleas of the Crown.
Eccl. R. English Ecclesiastical Reports (American reprint).
Eccl. & Ad. Spink's Ecclesiastical and Admiralty Reports.
Ed. Eden's English Chancery Reports.
Ed. Bro. Eden's edition of Brown's English Chancery Reports.
Ed. C. R. Edwards' New York Chancery Reports.
Eden. Eden's English Chancery Reports.
Edg. Edgar's Reports. Court of Session, Scotland.
Edg. C. Canons enacted under King Edgar.
Edict. (or **Edicta**) Edicts of Justinian.
Edinb. L. J. Edinburgh Law Journal.
Edm. Sel. Ca. Edmonds' New York Select Cases.
Edw. Edwards' New York Chancery Reports;—Edwards' English Admiralty Reports;—Edwards' Reports (2, 3 Missouri).
Edw. Abr. Edwards' Abridgment of Prerogative Court Cases.
Edw. Adm. Edwards' English Admiralty Reports.
Edw. Ch. Edwards' New York Chancery Reports.
Edw. Lead. Dec. Edwards' Leading Decisions in Admiralty (Edwards' Admiralty Reports).
Edw. Pr. Cas. Edwards' Prize Cases (English Admiralty Reports).
Edw. Pr. Ct. Cas. Edwards' Abridgment of Prerogative Court Cases.
Edw. (Tho.) Edwards' English Admiralty Reports.
Eir. Lambard's Eirenarcha.
El. Elchies' Decisions, Scotch Court of Session.
El. B. & E. Ellis, Blackburn, & Ellis' English Queen's Bench Reports.
Elect. Cas. N. Y. New York Election Cases (Armstrong's).
El. & Bl. Ellis & Blackburn's English Queen's Bench Reports.
El. & El. Ellis & Ellis' English Queen's Bench Reports.
Ell. Bl. & Ell. Ellis, Blackburn, & Ellis' English Queen's Bench Reports.
Ell. & Bl. Ellis & Blackburn's English Queen's Bench Reports.
Ell. & Ell. Ellis & Ellis' English Queen's Bench Reports.
Elph. Conv. Elphinstone's Introduction to Conveyancing.
Els. W. Bl. Elsley's edition of Wm. Blackstone's English K. B. Reports.
Elw. Mal. (or **Med. Jur.**) Elwell on Malpractice and Medical Jurisprudence.
Emer. Ins. Emerigon on Insurance.
Emer. Mar. Lo. Emerigon on Maritime Loans.
Ency. of Ev. Encyclopedia of Evidence.
Ency. of L. & Pr. Encyclopedia of Law and Practice.
Ency. of Pl. & Pr. Encyclopedia of Pleading and Practice.
End. Bdg. Ass. Endlich on Building Associations.
Eng. English's Reports (6-13 Arkansas);—"English Reports" (American reprint, edited by Moak).
Eng. Ad. English Admiralty Reports (Amer. reprint).
Eng. C. C. (or **Cr. Cas.**) English Crown Cases (American reprint).
Eng. Ch. English Chancery;—"English Chancery Reports" (American reprint).
Eng. C. L. English Common Law Reports (American reprint).
Eng. Eccl. English Ecclesiastical Reports (American reprint).
Eng. Exch. English Exchequer Reports (American reprint).
Eng. Judg. Scotch Court of Session Cases, decided by the "English Judges."
Eng. L. & Eq. English Law and Equity Reports (American reprint).
Eng. Rep. Moak's English Reports (American reprint);—English's Reports (6-13 Arkansas).
Eng. Rul. Cas. English Ruling Cases.
Eng. Sc. Ecc. English and Scotch Ecclesiastical Reports.
Eng. & Ir. App. Law Reports, English and Irish Appeal Cases.
English. English's Reports (6-13 Arkansas).
Ent. Coke's Entries;—Rastell's Entries.
Entries, Antient. Rastell's Entries (so cited in Rolle Abr.).
Entries, Old Book of. Liber Intrationum.
Entries, New Book of. Rastell's Entries, to distinguish from Liber Intrationum;—Coke's Entries, to distinguish from Rastell's Entries.
Eq. Cas. Equity Cases in 9 Modern Reports.
Eq. Cas. Abr. Equity Cases Abridged (English).
Eq. Draft. Equity Draftsman (Van Heythuysen's, edited by Hughes).
Eq. Judg. Equity Judgments (by A'Beckett), New South Wales.
Eq. Rep. Gilbert's Equity Reports;—Harper's South Carolina Equity Reports;—The Equity Reports, published by Spottiswoode.
Err. & App. Error and Appeals Reports, Upper Canada.
Ersk. Dec. Erskine's U. S. Circuit Court, &c., Decisions, in 35 Georgia.

Ersk. Inst. Erskine's Institutes of the Law of Scotland.
Ersk. Prin. Erskine's Principles of the Law of Scotland.
Esp. Espinasse's English Nisi Prius Reports.
Esp. Dig. Espinasse's Digest of the Law of Actions and Trials.
Esp. N. P. Espinasse's Digest of the Law of Nisi Prius.
Esprit des Lois. Montesquieu's Spirit of Laws.
Est. Prac. (or **Pl.**) Estee's Code Pleading. Practice and Forms.
Euer. Euer's Doctrina Placitandi.
Eun. Wynne's Eunomus.
Evans. Evans' Reports, Washington Territory (announced, but never published).
Ewell Bl. Ewell's edition of Blackstone.
Ewell Cas. Inf. (or **L. C.**) Ewell's Leading Cases on Infancy, &c.
Ewell Fix. Ewell on the Law of Fixtures.
Exch. Exchequer Reports (Welsby, Hurlstone, & Gordon;—English Law Reports, Exchequer.
Exch. Cas. Exchequer Cases (Legacy Duties, &c.), Scotland.
Exch. Div. Exchequer Division, English Law Reports.
Exch. Rep. Exchequer Reports (Welsby, Hurlstone, & Gordon);—English Exchequer Reports (American reprint).
Eyre, MS. Eyre, Manuscript Notes of Cases, King's Bench (in Library of the New York Law Institute).

F. Faculty Collection of Court of Sessions Decisions; — Fitzherbert's Abridgment, octavo edition.
F. Abr. Fitzherbert's Abridgment.
F. C. Faculty Collection of Decisions, Scotch Court of Session, folio edition.
F. C. R. Fearne on Contingent Remainders.
F. N. B. Fitzherbert's Natura Brevium.
F. & F. Foster & Finlason's English Nisi Prius Reports.
F. & Fitz. Falconer & Fitzherbert's English Election Cases.
F. & S. Fox & Smith's Irish King's Bench Reports.
Fac. Coll. (or **Fac. Dec.**) Faculty Collection of Decisions, Court of Sessions.
Fairfield. Fairfield's Reports (10-12 Maine).
Falc. Falconer's Scotch Court of Session Cases.
Farresley. Farresley Reports (7 Modern Reports);—Farresley's Cases in Holt's King's Bench Reports.
Fear. Rem. Fearne on Contingent Remainders.
Fed. The Federalist, by Hamilton.
Fed. Cas. Federal Cases.
Fed. Rep. The Federal Reporter.
Fed. St. Ann. Federal Statutes Annotated.
Fergusson. (Fergusson of) Kilkerran's Scotch Session Cases.
Fern. Dec. Decretos del Fernando, Mexico.
Fin. Finch's English Chancery Reports;—Finlason (see Finl.).
Finch. English Chancery Reports *temp.* Finch.
Finch Nomot. Finch's Nomotechnia.
Finch Prec. Precedents in Chancery, edited by Finch.
Finl. L. C. Finlason's Leading Cases on Pleading.
First pt. Edw. III. Part II. of the Year Books.
First pt. H. VI. Part VII. of the Year Books.
Fish. Fisher's U. S. Patent Cases;—Fisher's U. S. Prize Cases.
Fish. C. L. Dig. Fisher's Digest of English Common Law Reports.
Fish. Crim. Dig. Fisher's Digest of English Criminal Law.
Fish. Pat. Cas. Fisher's United States Patent Cases.
Fish. Pat. Rep. Fisher's United States Patent Reports.
Fish. Pr. Cas. Fisher's United States Prize Cases.
Fitzg. Fitzgibbon's English King's Bench Reports.
Fitzh. Abr. Fitzherbert's Abridgment.
Fitzh. N. B. Fitzherbert's New Natura Brevium.
Fl. Fleta;—Flanders (see Fland.).
Fl. & K. Flanagan & Kelly's Irish Rolls Court Reports.
Fla. Florida;—Florida Reports.
Flan. & Kel. Flanagan & Kelly's Irish Rolls Court Reports.
Fland. Ch. J. Flanders' Lives of the Chief Justices of the United States.
Fletcher Cyc. Corp. Fletcher, Cyclopedia Corporations.
Flip. Flippin's United States Circuit Court Reports.
Fogg. Fogg's Reports (32-35 New Hampshire).
Fol. P. L. Cas. Foley's English Poor Law Cases.
Fonbl. (or **Fonbl. N. R.**) Fonblanque's English Cases (or New Reports) in Bankruptcy.
Fonbl. Eq. Fonblanque on Equity.
For. Forrest's Exchequer Reports;—Forrester's Chancery Reports (Cases *temp.* Talbot);—Fortescue de Laudibus Legum Angliae.
For. de Laud. Fortescue de Laudibus Legum Angliae.
Forb. Forbes' Decisions in the Scotch Court of Session.
Forman. Forman's Reports, Illinois.
Forr. Forrest's English Exchequer Reports;—Forrester's English Chancery Cases (commonly cited, Cases *temp.* Talbot).
Fors. Cas. & Op. Forsyth's Cases and Opinions on Constitutional Law.
Fort. Fortescue's English King's Bench, &c., Reports.
Fort. de Laud. Fortescue de Laudibus Legum Angliae.
Fost. Foster's English Crown Law or Crown Cases;—Foster's N. H. Reports;—Foster's Legal Chronicle Reports, Pennsylvania.

Fost. & Fin. Foster & Finlason's English Nisi Prius Reports.
Foster. Foster's English Crown Law;—Legal Chronicle Reports (Pa.), edited by Foster;—Foster's N. H. Reports.
Foster Fed. Pr. Foster on Federal Practice.
Fox & Sm. Fox & Smith's Irish King's Bench Reports.
Fr. Freeman's English King's Bench and Chancery Reports.
Fr. Chy. Freeman's English Chancery Reports;—Freeman's Mississippi Chancery Reports.
France. France's Reports (3-4 Colorado).
Franc. Judg. Francillon's Judgments, County Courts.
Fraz. Frazer's Admiralty Cases, &c., Scotland.
Fred. Code. Frederician Code, Prussia.
Free. Freeman's English King's Bench Reports (1 Free., Freeman's King's Bench Reports;—2 Free., Freeman's Chancery Reports);—see also Freem.
Free. Ch. Freeman's English Chancery Reports;—Freeman's Mississippi Chancery Reports.
Freem. C. C. Freeman's English Chancery Cases.
Freem. Ch. See Free. Ch.
Freem. (Ill.) Freeman's Reports (31-96 Illinois).
French. French's Reports (6 New Hampshire).
Fry Lun. Fry on Lunacy.
Fry Sp. Per. Fry on Specific Performance of Contracts.
Full B. R. Full Bench Rulings, Bengal (or Northwestern Provinces).
Fulton. Fulton's Reports, Bengal.

G. Gale's English Exchequer Reports.
G. Gr. G. Green's Iowa Reports.
G. M. Dudl. G. M. Dudley's Georgia Reports.
G. & D. Gale & Davison's English Queen's Bench Reports.
G. & H. Gavin & Hord's Indiana Statutes.
G. & J. Gill & Johnson's Maryland Reports;—Glyn & Jameson's English Bankruptcy Reports.
Ga. Georgia;—Georgia Reports.
Ga. App. Georgia Appeals.
Ga. Dec. Georgia Decisions.
Gaius (or Gaii) Gaius' Institutes (Gaii Institutionum Commentarii).
Galbraith. Galbraith's Reports (9-11 Florida).
Galb. & M. Galbraith & Meek's Reports (12 Florida).
Gale. Gale's English Exchequer Reports.
Gale & Dav. Gale & Davison's Queen's Bench.
Gall. Gallison's Reports, United States Circuit Courts.
Gardenhire. Gardenhire's Reports (14, 15 Missouri).
Gaspar. Gaspar's Small Cause Court Reports, Bengal.
Gayarré. Gayarré's Reports (25-28 Louisiana Annual).
Geld. & Ox. Nova Scotia Decisons, by Geldert & Oxley.
Geo. Coop. George Cooper's English Chancery Cases, time of Eldon.
Geo. Dec. Georgia Decisions.
George. George's Reports (30-39 Mississippi).
Gib. Dec. Gibson's Scottish Decisions.
Gibbs. Gibbs' Reports (2-4 Michigan).
Gif. (or Giff.) Giffard's English Vice-Chancellors' Reports.
Gil. Gilman's Reports (6-10 Illinois);—Gilmer's Virginia Reports;—Gilbert's English Chancery Reports;—Gilbert's English Cases in Law and Equity.
Gil. & Fal. Gilmour & Falconer's Scotch Session Cases.
Gilb. Cas. Gilbert's English Cases in Law and Equity.
Gilb. Ch. Gilbert's English Chancery Reports.
Gilb. Eq. Gilbert's English Equity or Chancery Reports.
Gilb. K. B. Gilbert's Cases in Law and Equity, English.
Gildersleeve. Gildersleeve's Reports (1 New Mexico).
Gilfillan. Gilfillan's edition of Minnesota Reports.
Gill. Gill's Maryland Reports.
Gill & Johns. Gill & Johnson's Maryland Reports.
Gilm. Gilman's Reports (6-10 Illinois);—Gilmer's Reports, Virginia; Gilmour's Reports, Scotch Court of Session.
Gilm. & Falc. Gilmour & Falconer's Reports, Scotch Court of Session.
Gilp. Gilpin's United States District Court Reports.
Glanv. Glanville de Legibus et Consuetudinibus Angliae.
Glas. Glascock's Reports in all the Courts of Ireland.
Glenn. Glenn's Reports (16-18 Louisiana Annual).
Glyn & Jam. Glyn & Jameson's Reports. English Bankruptcy.
Godb. Godbolt's English King's Bench Reports.
Gold. (or Goldes.) Goldesborough's or Gouldsborough's English K. B. Reports.
Good. & Wood. Full Bench Rulings, Bengal, edited by Goodeve & Woodman.
Gould. Gouldsborough's English King's Bench Reports.
Gould Pl. Gould's Principles of Pleading in Civil Actions.
Gow. Gow's English Nisi Prius Cases.
Gow Part. Gow on Partnership.
Gr. Grant's Cases, Pennsylvania;—Green's New Jersey Reports;—Greenleaf's Laws of N. Y.;—Greenleaf's Maine Reports.
Gr. Brice. Green's edition of Brice on Ultra Vires.
Gr. Eq. (or Ch.) (H. W.) Green's New Jersey Equity Reports;—Gresley's Equity Evidence.
Gr. Ev. Greenleaf on Evidence.
Grand Cout. Grand Coutumier de Normandie.
Granger. Granger's Reports (22, 23 Ohio State).

Grant. Grant's Upper Canada Chancery Reports;—Grant's Pennsylvania Cases;—(Grant of) Elchies' Scotch Session Cases;—Grant's Jamaica Reports.
Grant Cas. Grant's Pennsylvania Cases.
Grant Ch. Grant's Upper Canada Chancery Reports.
Grant E. & A. Grant's Error and Appeal Reports, Ontario.
Grant Pa. Grant's Pennsylvania Cases.
Grant U. C. Grant's Upper Canada Chancery Reports.
Grat. (or **Gratt.**) Grattan's Virginia Reports.
Gray. Gray's Massachusetts Reports.
Green. Green's New Jersey Law or Equity Reports;—Green's Reports (11 Rhode Island);—G. Greene's Iowa Reports;—Greenleaf's Maine Reports.
Green Bri. Green's edition of Brice's Ultra Vires.
Green. C. E. C. E. Greene's Chancery Reports, New Jersey.
Green Ch. H. W. Green's New Jersey Chancery Reports.
Green Cr. L. Rep. Green's Criminal Law Reports.
Green L. (or N. J.) J. S. Green's Law Reports (13-15 New Jersey).
Greene. G. Greene's Iowa Reports;—C. E. Greene's N. J. Equity Reports.
Greenl. Greenleaf's Reports (1-9 Maine).
Greenl. Ev. Greenleaf on Evidence.
Grenier. Grenier's Ceylon Reports.
Griswold. Griswold's Reports (14-19 Ohio).
Gro. B. P. Grotius, De Jure Belli ac Pacis.
Gro. Dr. Grotius, Le Droit de la Guerre.
Gro. Ges. & Verord. Grotofend's Gesetze und Verordnungen.
Gut. Brac. Guterbock's Bracton.
Gwil. Ti. Cas. Gwillim's Tithe Cases.
Gwill. Bac. Abr. Gwillim's edition of Bacon's Abridgment.
H. Howard's United States Supreme Court Reports;—Hill's New York Reports.
H. Bl. Henry Blackstone's English Common Pleas Reports.
H. C. R. High Court Reports, India.
H. C. R. N. W. P. High Court Reports, Northwest Provinces, India.
H. I. Rep. Hawaiian Islands Reports.
H. L. (or **H. L. Cas.**) House of Lords Cases.
H. L. Rep. English House of Lords Reports.
H. W. Gr. H. W. Green's New Jersey Equity Reports.
H. & B. Hudson & Brooke's Irish King's Bench Reports.
H. & C. Hurlstone & Coltman's English Exchequer Reports.
H. & D. Lalor's Supplement to Hill & Denio's New York Reports.
H. & G. Harris & Gill's Maryland Reports.
H. & H. Horn & Hurlstone's English Exchequer Reports;—Harrison & Hodgin's Municipal Reports, Upper Canada.
H. & J. Harris & Johnson's Maryland Reports;—Hayes & Jones' Exchequer Reports, Ireland.
H. & M. Hening & Munford's Virginia Reports;—Hemming & Miller's English Vice-Chancellors' Report.
H. & McH. Harris & McHenry's Maryland Reports.
H. & N. Hurlstone & Norman's English Exchequer Reports.
H. & P. Hopwood & Philbrick's English Election Cases.
H. & R. Harrison & Rutherfurd's English Common Pleas Reports.
H. & T. Hall & Twell's English Chancery Reports.
H. & W. Harrison & Wollaston's English King's Bench Reports;—Hurlstone & Walmsley's English Echequer Reports.
Ha. Hare's Chancery Reports.
Ha. & Tw. Hall & Twell's English Chancery Reports.
Haddington. Haddington's Manuscript Reports, Scotch Court of Session.
Hadley. Hadley's Reports (45-48 New Hampshire).
Hag. (or **Hagg.**) **Adm.** Haggard's English Admiralty Reports.
Hag. (or **Hagg.**) **Con.** Haggard's English Consistory Reports.
Hag. (or **Hagg.**) **Ecc.** Haggard's English Ecclesiastical Reports.
Hagan. Hagan's Utah Reports.
Hagans. Hagans' Reports (1-5 West Virginia).
Hagn. & Mill. Hagner & Miller's Reports (2 Maryland Chancery).
Hailes. Hailes' Decisions, Scotch Court of Session.
Hal. Int. Law. Halleck's International Law.
Hal. Law. Halsted's New Jersey Law Reports.
Halc. Min. Cas. Halcomb's Mining Cases, London, 1826.
Hale. Hale's Reports (33-37 California).
Hale Anal. Hale's Analysis of the Law.
Hale Com. Law. Hale's History of the Common Law.
Hale Cr. Prec. Hale's Precedents in Criminal Cases.
Hale P. C. Hale's Pleas of the Crown.
Hale Prec. Hale's Precedents in (Ecclesiastical) Criminal Cases.
Hall. Hall's New York Superior Court Reports;—Hall's Reports (56, 57 New Hampshire).
Hall Jour. Jur. Journal of Jurisprudence (Hall's).
Hall Int. Law. Hall on International Law;—Halleck's International Law.
Hall. Law of W. Halleck's Law of War.
Hall & Tw. Hall & Twell's Reports, English Chancery.
Hallam. Hallam's Constitutional History of England.
Hallett. Hallett's Reports (1, 2 Colorado).
Hals. Halsted's New Jersey Law Reports.
Hals. Ch. (or **Eq.**) Halsted's New Jersey Equity Reports, 1845-1853.
Hammond. Hammond's Reports (1-9 Ohio);—Hammond's Reports (36-44 Georgia).
Hammond & Jackson. Hammond & Jackson's Reports (45 Georgia).

Han. Hannay's Reports, New Brunswick.
Hand. Hand's Reports (40-45 New York).
Handy. Handy's Ohio Reports.
Hann. Hannay's New Brunswick Reports.
Har. St. Tr. Hargrave's State Trials.
Har. & Gill. Harris & Gill's Maryland Reports.
Har. & John. Harris & Johnson's Maryland Reports.
Har. & McH. Harris & McHenry's Maryland Reports.
Har. & Ruth. Harrison & Rutherfurd's English Common Pleas Reports.
Har. & Woll. Harrison & Wollaston's English King's Bench Reports.
Harc. Harcarse's Decisions, Scotch Court of Session.
Hard. Hardin's Kentucky Reports;—Hardres' English Exchequer Reports.
Hardw. Cases *temp.* Hardwicke, by Ridgway;—Cases *temp.* Hardwicke, by Lee.
Hare. Hare's English Vice-Chancellors' Reports.
Hare & Wal. L. C. American Leading Cases, edited by Hare & Wallace.
Harg. Hargrave's State Trials;—Hargrove's Reports (68-75 N. C.).
Harg. St. Tr. Hargrave's State Trials.
Hargrove. Hargrove's Reports (68-75 North Carolina).
Harm. Harmon's Reports (13-15 California);—Harmon's Upper Canada Common Pleas Reports.
Harp. Harper's South Carolina Law Reports.
Harp. Con. Cas. Harper's Conspiracy Cases, Maryland.
Harp. Eq. Harper's Equity Reports, South Carolina.
Harp. L. (or S. C.) Harper's South Carolina Law Reports.
Harr. Harrison's Reports, New Jersey;—Harrington's Reports, Delaware;—Harrington's Chancery Reports, Michigan;—Harris' Reports (13-24 Pennsylvania State);—Harrison's Reports (15-17 & 23-29 Indiana).
Harr. & G. Harris & Gill's Maryland Reports.
Harr. & Hodg. Harrison & Hodgin's Upper Canada Municipal Reports.
Harr. & J. Harris & Johnson's Maryland Reports.
Harr. & M'H. Harris & M'Henry's Maryland Reports.
Harr. & Ruth. Harrison & Rutherfurd's English Common Pleas Reports.
Harr. & Sim. Harris & Simrall's Reports (49-52 Mississippi).
Harr. & Woll. Harrison & Wollaston's English King's Bench Reports.
Harring. Harrington's Delaware Reports;—Harrington's Michigan Chancery Reports, 1842.
Harris. Harris' Pennsylvania Reports (13-24 Pennsylvania State).
Harris & Simrall. Harris & Simrall's Reports (49-52 Mississippi).
Harrison. Harrison's Reports (15-17 & 23-29 Indiana).
Hart. Dig. Hartley's Digest of Laws, Texas.
Hartley. Hartley's Reports (4-10 Texas).
Hartley & Hartley. Hartley & Hartley's Reports (11-21 Texas).
Harv. L. Rev. Harvard Law Review.
Hast. Hasting's Reports (69, 70 Maine).
Hast. Tr. Trial of Warren Hastings.
Hav. Ch. Rep. Haviland's Chancery Reports, Prince Edward Island.
Hawk. P. C. Hawkins' Pleas of the Crown.
Hawk. Pl. Cr. See Hawk. P. C.
Hawkins. Hawkins' Reports (19-24 Louisiana Annual.)
Hawks. Hawks' North Carolina Reports.
Hawl. Cr. R. Hawley's American Criminal Reports.
Hay. Haywood's North Carolina Reports;—Haywood's Tennessee Reports;—Hayes' Irish Exchequer Reports.
Hay & M. (or **Marr.**) Hay & Marriott's Admiralty Reports (usually cited Marriott's Reports).
Hayes Exch. Hayes' Irish Exchequer Reports.
Hayes & Jo. Hayes & Jones' Irish Exchequer Reports.
Hayw. Haywood's North Carolina Reports;—Haywood's Tennessee Reports.
Haz. Pa. Reg. Hazard's Pennsylvania Register, 16 vols.
Head. Head's Tennessee Reports.
Heath. Heath's Reports (36-40 Maine).
Hein. Heineccius, Elementa Juris Naturae et Gentium.
Heisk. Heiskell's Tennessee Reports.
Helm. Helm's Reports (2-9 Nevada).
Hem. & Mill. Hemming & Miller's English Vice-Chancellors' Reports.
Hemp. (or **Hempst.**) Hempstead's United States Circuit Court Reports.
Hen. St. Hening's Virginia Statutes.
Hen. & Mun. Hening & Munford's Virginia Reports.
Hepb. Hepburn's Reports (3, 4 California).
Her. Est. Herman's Law of Estoppel.
High Ct. High Court Reports, Northwest Provinces of India.
High Ex. Rem. High on Extraordinary Legal Remedies.
High Inj. High on Injunctions.
High Rec. High on the Law of Receivers.
Hill. Hill's N. Y. Reports;—Hill's Law Reports, South Carolina.
Hill & Den. Lalor's Supplement to Hill & Denio's Reports, New York.
Hill Eq. (or **Ch.**) Hill's Equity South Carolina Reports, 1833-1837.
Hill N. Y. Hill's New York Reports.
Hill S. C. Hill's South Carolina Reports (Law or Equity).
Hillyer. Hillyer's Reports (20-22 California).
Hilt. Hilton's New York Common Pleas Reports.
Hob. Hobart's English King's Bench Reports.
Hodg. Hodges' English Common Pleas Reports.

Hoff. Hoffman's Land Cases. United States District Court;—Hoffman's New York Chancery Reports.

Hoff. Ch. Hoffman's New York Chancery Reports.

Hoff. N. Y. Hoffman's New York Chancery Reports.

Hoffm. Ch. Hoffman's New York Chancery Reports.

Hog. Hogan's Irish Rolls Court Reports; (Hog. of) Harcarse's Scotch Session Cases.

Hog. St. Tr. Hogan's State Trials, Pennsylvania.

Hogue. Hogue's Reports (1-4 Florida).

Hollinshead. Hollinshead's Minnesota Reports (see n. 3, p. 31).

Holm. Holmes' United States Circuit Court Reports.

Holm. Com. Law. Holmes on the Common Law.

Holt. Holt's English King's Bench Reports;—Holt's English Nisi Prius Reports;—Holt's English Equity Reports.

Holt Adm. Ca. Holt's English Admiralty Cases (Rule of the Road).

Holt Eq. Holt's English Equity Reports.

Holt N. P. Holt's English Nisi Prius Reports.

Home. Home's Manuscript Decisions, Scotch Court of Session;—see also Kames.

Home (Cl.) Clerk Home, Scotch Session Cases.

Hooker. Hooker's Reports (26 Connecticut).

Hoonahan. Hoonahan's Sind Reports, India.

Hopk. Adm. (or Judg.) Hopkinson's Pennsylvania Admiralty Judgments.

Hopk. Adm. Dec. Admiralty Decisions of Hopkinson, in Gilpin's Reports.

Hopk. Ch. Hopkins' New York Chancery Reports.

Hopw. & Colt. Hopwood & Coltman's English Registration Appeal Cases.

Hopw. & Phil. Hopwood & Philbrick's English Registration Appeal Cases.

Hor. & Th. Cas. Horrigan & Thompson's Cases on Self-Defence.

Horn & H. Horn & Hurlstone's English Exchequer Reports.

Horne Mir. Horne's Mirrour of Justices.

Horr. & Th. Horrigan & Thompson's Cases on Self-Defence.

Horw. Y. B. (Horwood's) Year Book of Edward I.

Houst. Houston's Delaware Reports.

Houst. Cr. Cas. Houston's Delaware Criminal Cases.

Hov. Sup. Hovenden's Supplement to Vesey, Jr.'s English Chancery Reports.

How. Howard's United States Supreme Court Reports;—Howard's Mississippi Reports;—Howard's N. Y. Practice Reports.

How. App. Howard's New York Court of Appeals Cases.

How. Cas. Howard's New York Court of Appeals Cases;—Howard's Popery Cases.

How. Ch. Pr. Howard's Chancery Practice.

How. Cr. Tr. Howison's Criminal Trials (Virginia).

How. Pr. Howard's New York Practice Reports.

How. S. C. (or U. S.) Howard's United States Supreme Court Reports.

How. St. Howell's Michigan Statutes.

How. St. Tr. Howell's English State Trials.

Hubbard. Hubbard's Reports (45-51 Maine).

Hud. & Br. Hudson & Brooke's Irish King's Bench Reports.

Hugh. Hughes' United States Circuit Court Reports;—Hughes' Kentucky Reports;—Hughes' Entries.

Humph. Humphreys' Tennessee Reports.

Hun. Hun's New York Supreme Court Reports.

Hurd St. Hurd's Illinois Statutes.

Hurl. & Colt. Hurlstone & Coltman's English Exchequer Reports.

Hurl. & Gord. Hurlstone & Gordon's Reports (10, 11 Exchequer Reports, English).

Hurl. & Nor. Hurlstone & Norman's English Exchequer Reports.

Hurl. & Walm. Hurlstone & Walmsley's English Exchequer Reports.

Hut. (or Hutt.) Hutton's English Common Pleas Reports.

Hutch. Car. Hutchinson on Carriers.

Hux. Judg. Huxley's Book of Judgments (see Townsend).

Hyde. Hyde's Reports, Bengal.

I. Institutes (of Justinian).

Ia. Iowa Reports.

Ida. Idaho;—Idaho Reports.

Il Cons. Mar. Il Consolato del Mare.

Ill. Illinois;—Illinois Reports.

Ill. App. Illinois Appellate.

Ind. Indiana;—Indiana Reports;—India;—(East) Indian;—Index.

Ind. App. Indiana Appellate;—Law Reports, Indian Appeals.

Ind. L. C. Eq. Indermaur's Leading Cases in Conveyancing and Equity.

Ind. L. R. (East) Indian Law Reports.

Ind. L. Reg. Indiana Legal Register, Lafayette.

Ind. Rep. Indiana Reports.

Ind. Super. Indiana Superior Court Reports (Wilson's).

Ind. T. Indian Territory.

Ins. L. J. Insurance Law Journal, New York and St. Louis.

Ins. Mon. Insurance Monitor, New York.

Ins. Rep. Insurance Reporter, Philadelphia.

Inst. Institutes; Coke's Institutes;—Institutes of Justinian.[1]

Interstate Com. R. Interstate Commerce Reports.

Iowa. Iowa Reports.

Ir. Irish;—Ireland;—Iredell's N. C. Law or Equity Reports.

[1] When preceded by a number (thus, 2 Inst.), this abbreviation refers to Coke's Institutes. When followed by a number, it refers to Justinian; thus, Inst. I. 2, 3, means Book I., title 2, section 3, of the Institutes of Justinian.

Ir. C. L. Irish Common Law Reports.
Ir. Ch. Irish Chancery Reports.
Ir. Cir. Irish Circuit Reports.
Ir. Eccl. Irish Ecclesiastical Reports, by Milward.
Ir. Eq. Irish Equity Reports.
Ir. Jur. Irish Jurist, Dublin.
Ir. L. Irish Law Reports.
Ir. L. N. S. Irish Common Law Reports.
Ir. L. R. Irish Law Reports (1838-1850);—The Law Reports, Ireland.
Ir. L. T. Irish Law Times, Dublin.
Ir. L. T. Rep. Irish Law Times Reports.
Ir. Law & Ch. Irish Common Law and Chancery Reports (New Series).
Ir. Law & Eq. Irish Law and Equity Reports (Old Series).
Ir. Law Rec. Irish Law Recorder.
Ir. Law Rep. Irish Law Reports (1838-1850).
Ir. Law Rep. N. S. Irish Common Law Reports.
Ir. R. C. L. Irish Reports, Common Law Series.
Ir. R. Eq. Irish Reports, Equity Series.
Ir. R. Reg. App. Irish Reports, Registration Appeals.
Ir. R. Reg. & L. Irish Reports, Registry and Land Cases.
Ir. St. Tr. Irish State Trials (Ridgeway's).
Ir. Stat. Irish Statutes.
Ir. T. R. Irish Term Reports (by Ridgeway, Lapp, & Schoales).
Ired. Iredell's North Carolina Law Reports.
Ired. Eq. Iredell's North Carolina Equity Reports.

J. Institutes of Justinian;—Johnson's New York Reports.
J. J. Mar. J. J. Marshall's Kentucky Reports.
J. Kel. Sir John Kelyng's English Crown Cases.
J. P. Sm. J. P. Smith's English King's Bench Reports.
J. S. Gr. J. S. Green's New Jersey Reports.
J. & La. T. Jones & La Touche's Irish Chancery Reports.
J. & S. Jones & Spencer's New York Superior Court Reports.
J. & W. Jacob & Walker's English Chancery Reports.
Jac. Jacob's English Chancery Reports.
Jac. Fish. Dig. Jacob's American edition of Fisher's English Digest.
Jac. & Walk. Jacob & Walker's English Chancery Reports.
Jackson. Jackson's Reports (46-58 Georgia).
Jackson & Lumpkin. Jackson & Lumpkin's Reports (59-64 Georgia).
James. James' Nova Scotia Reports;—King James.
James Sel. Cas. James' Select Cases, Nova Scotia.
James. & Mont. Jameson & Montagu's English Bankruptcy Reports (in 2 Glyn & Jameson).
Jar. Chy. Pr. Jarman's Chancery Practice.
Jar. Wills. Jarman on Wills.
Jebb (or Jebb C. C.) Jebb's Irish Crown Cases.
Jebb & B. Jebb & Bourke's Irish Queen's Bench Reports.
Jebb & S. Jebb & Symes' Irish Queen's Bench Reports.
Jeff. Jefferson's Virginia Reports.
Jeff. Man. Jefferson's Manual of Parliamentary Practice.
Jenn. Jennison's Reports (14-18 Michigan).
Jenn. Sug. A. Jennett's Sugden Acts.
John. (or Johns.) Johnson's New York Reports;—Johnson's Reports of Chase's Decisions;—Johnson's Reports, Chancery, Maryland;—Johnson's English Vice-Chancellors' Reports.
John. Am. Not. John's American Notaries.
Johns. Cas. Johnson's New York Cases.
Johns. Ch. Johnson's New York Chancery Reports;—Johnson's English Vice-Chancellors' Reports;—Johnson's Maryland Chancery Decisions.
Johns. Ct. Err. Johnson's Reports, New York Court of Errors.
Johns. Dec. Johnson's Maryland Chancery Decisions.
Johns. Rep. Johnson's Reports, New York Supreme Court.
Johns. U. S. Johnson's Reports of Chase's U. S. Circuit Court Decisions.
Johns. V. C. Johnson, English Vice-Chancellors' Reports.
Johns. & Hem. Johnson & Hemming's English Chancery Reports.
Johnst. (N. Z.) Johnston's Reports, New Zealand.

Jones 1. Sir. William Jones' English King's Bench Reports.
Jones 2. Sir Thomas Jones' English King's Bench Reports.
Jones. Jones' Reports (43-48, 52-57, 61, 62 Alabama;—Jones' Reports (11, 12 Pennsylvania State);—Jones' Reports (22-30 Missouri);—Jones' Law or Equity Reports, North Carolina;—Jones' Irish Exchequer Reports;—Jones' Upper Canada Common Pleas Reports.
Jones B. Jones' Law of Bailments.
Jones, Barclay & Whittlesey. Jones, Barclay, & Whittlesey's Reports (31 Missouri).
Jones Ch. Mort. Jones on Chattel Mortgages.
Jones Mort. Jones on Mortgages.
Jones N. C. Jones' North Carolina Law Reports.
Jones (Pa.) Jones' Reports (11, 12 Pennsylvania State).
Jones T. Sir Thomas Jones' English King's Bench Reports.
Jones U. C. Jones' Reports, Upper Canada.
Jones W. Sir William Jones' English King's Bench Reports.
Jones & C. Jones & Cary's Irish Exchequer Reports.
Jones & La T. Jones & La Touche's Irish Chancery Reports.
Jones & Sp. Jones & Spencer's New York Superior Court Reports.

Jud. & Sw. Judah & Swan's Reports, Jamaica.
Jur. The Jurist, London, 1854 [or, the Jurist or Quarterly Journal of Jurisprudence, 1827;—or the Jurist, Washington;—or the Jurist, New York].
Jur. N. S. The Jurist, New Series, London.
Jur. N. Y. The Jurist, or Law and Equity Reporter, New York.
Jur. (Sc.) The Scottish Jurist, Edinburgh.
Juta. Juta's Cape of Good Hope Reports.

K. Keyes' New York Court of Appeals Reports;—Kenyon's English King's Bench Reports.
K. C. R. Reports in the time of Chancellor King.
K. & J. Kay & Johnson's English Vice-Chancellors' Reports.
Kam. Kames' Decisions of the Scottish Court of Session.
Kam. Sel. Dec. Kames' Select Decisons, Scotch Court of Session.
Kan. (or Kans.) Kansas;—Kansas Reports.
Kan. App. Kansas Appeals.
Kay. Kay's English Vice-Chancellors' Reports.
Kay & Johns. Kay & Johnson's English Vice-Chancellors' Reports.
Ke. Keen's English Rolls Court Reports.
Keane & Gr. Keane & Grant's English Registration Appeal Cases.
Keb. Keble's English King's Bench Reports.
Keen. Keen's English Rolls Court Reports.
Keil. (or Keilw.) Keilway's English King's Bench Reports.
Kel. 1. Sir John Kelyng's English Crown Cases.
Kel. 2. Wm. Kelynge's English Chancery Reports.
Kel. Ga. Kelly's Georgia Reports (1-3 Georgia).
Kel. J. Sir John Kelyng's English Crown Cases.
Kel. W. Wm. Kelynge's English Chancery Reports.
Kelly. Kelly's Reports (1-3 Georgia).
Kelly & Cobb. Kelly & Cobb's Reports (4, 5 Georgia).
Ken. Dec. Kentucky Decisions, by Sneed.
Kenan. Kenan's Reports (76-85 North Carolina).
Kent. Kent's Commentaries on American Law;—Kentucky (see Ky.).
Keny. Kenyon's English King's Bench Reports.
Keny. Ch. (or 3 Keny.) Chancery Reports at the end of 2 Kenyon.
Kern. Kernan's Reports (11-14 New York Court of Appeals).
Kerr. Kerr's New Brunswick Reports;—Kerr's Reports (18-22 Indiana).
Kerr Inj. Kerr on Injunctions.
Kerr Rec. Kerr on Receivers.
Key. Keye's New York Court of Appeals Reports.
Kilk. Kilkerran's Decisions, Scotch Court of Session.
King. King's Reports (5, 6 Louisiana Annual.
King, Cas. *temp.* Select Cases *temp.* King, English Chancery.
Kir. (or Kirb.) Kirby's Connecticut Reports.
Kn. (or Kn. A. C.) Knapp's Appeal Cases (English Privy Council).
Kn. N. S. W. Knox, New South Wales Reports.
Kn. & Moo. Knapp & Moore's Reports (3 Knapp's Privy Council Reports).
Kn. & O. Knapp & Ombler's English Election Reports.
Knowles. Knowles' Reports (3 Rhode Island).
Ky. Kentucky;—Kentucky Reports.
Ky. Dec. Sneed's Kentucky Decisions.
Kyd. Aw. Kyd on Awards.
Kyd Bills. Kyd on Bills of Exchange.
Kyd Corp. Kyd on Corporations.

L. Lansing's Supreme Court Reports, New York.
L. Abr. Lilly's Abridgment.
L. All. Leges Allemanni.
L. Bai. Leges Baiarum.
L. C. Eq. White & Tudor's Leading Cases in Equity.
L. C. J. Lower Canada Jurist, Montreal.
L. C. L. J. Lower Canada Law Journal, Montreal.
L. C. R. Lower Canada Reports.
L. Ed. Lawyers' Edition Supreme Court Reports.
L. I. Legal Intelligencer, Philadelphia.
L. J. The Law Journal, London.
L. J. Adm. Law Journal, New Series, Admiralty.
L. J. App. Law Journal, New Series, Appeals.
L. J. Bank. Law Journal, New Series, Bankruptcy.
L. J. C. C. R. Law Journal, New Series, Crown Cases Reserved.
L. J. C. P. Law Journal, New Series, Common Pleas.
L. J. Ch. Law Journal, New Series, Chancery.
L. J. C. P. D. Law Journal, New Series, Common Pleas Decisions.
L. J. D. & M. Law Journal, New Series, Divorce and Matrimonial.
L. J. Ecc. Law Journal, New Series, Ecclesiastical Cases.
L. J. Exch. Law Journal, New Series, Exchequer.
L. J. Ex. D. Law Journal, New Series, Exchequer Division.
L. J. H. L. Law Journal, New Series, House of Lords.
L. J. M. C. Law Journal, New Series, Magistrates' Cases.
L. J. M. & W. Morgan & Williams' Law Journal, London.
L. J. Mat. Cas. Law Journal, New Series, Divorce and Matrimonial.
L. J. N. C. Law Journal, Notes of Cases.
L. J. N. S. The Law Journal, New Series, London.
L. J. O. S. The Law Journal, Old Series, London.

L. J. P. (or **P. C.**) Law Journal, New Series, Privy Council.
L. J. P. D. & A. Law Journal, New Series, Probate, Divorce, and Admiralty.
L. J. Prob. Law Journal, New Series, Probate.
L. J. Q. B. Law Journal, New Series, Queen's Bench.
L. J. Q. B. D. Law Journal, New Series, Queen's Bench Division.
L. J. Rep. Law Journal Reports.
L. J. Rep. N. S. Law Journal Reports, New Series.
L. J. Sm. Smith's Law Journal, London.
L. M. (or **Mag.**) **& L. R.** Law Magazine and Law Review, London.
L. M. & P. Lowndes, Maxwell, & Pollock's English Bail Court Reports.
L. Mag. & Rev. Law Magazine and Review, London.
L. N. Liber Niger, or the Black Book.
L. O. Legal Observer, London.
L. R. A. Lawyers' Reports Annotated.
L. R. A. (N. S.) Lawyers' Reports Annotated, New Series.
L. R. A. & E. English Law Reports, Admiralty and Ecclesiastical.
L. R. App. English Law Reports, Appeal Cases, House of Lords.
L. R. Burm. Law Reports, British Burmah.
L. R. C. C. English Law Reports, Crown Cases Reserved.
L. R. C. P. English Law Reports, Common Pleas.
L. R. C. P. D. English Law Reports, Common Pleas Division.
L. R. Ch. English Law Reports, Chancery, Appeal Cases.
L. R. Ch. D. English Law Reports, Chancery Division.
L. R. Eq. English Law Reports, Equity.
L. R. Ex. English Law Reports, Exchequer.
L. R. Ex. Div. English Law Reports, Exchequer Division.
L. R. H. L. English Law Reports, English and Irish Appeal Cases.
L. R. H. L. Sc. English Law Reports, Scotch and Divorce Appeal Cases.
L. R. Ind. App. English Law Reports, Indian Appeals.
L. R. Ir. Law Reports, Ireland.
L. R. N. S. Irish Law Recorder, New Series.
L. R. N. S. W. Law Reports, New South Wales.
L. R. P. C. English Law Reports, Privy Council, Appeal Cases.
L. R. P. Div. English Law Reports, Probate, Divorce, and Admiralty Division.
L. R. P. & D. English Law Reports, Probate and Divorce.
L. R. Q. B. English Law Reports, Queen's Bench.
L. R. Q. B. Div. English Law Reports, Queen's Bench Division.
L. R. S. A. Law Reports, South Australia.
L. R. Sc. & D. English Law Reports, Scotch and Divorce Cases, before the House of Lords.
L. R. Sess. Cas. English Law Reports, Sessions Cases.
L. R. Stat. English Law Reports, Statutes.
L. Repos. Law Repository.
L. Rev. Law Review.
L. T. Law Times Journal, London;—Law Times, Scranton, Pa.
L. T. B. Law Times Bankruptcy Reports (American).
L. T. N. S. (or **L. T. R. N. S.**) Law Times (New Series) Reports, London, 1843.
L. T. R. The Law Times Reports in all the Courts.
L. & B. Prec. Leake & Bullen's Precedents of Pleading.
L. & C. Leigh & Cave's English Crown Cases Reserved.
L. & C. C. C. Leigh & Cave's Crown Cases.
L. & E. English Law & Equity Reports (American reprint).
L. & E. Rep. Law and Equity Reporter, New York.
L. & G. *t.* Plunk. Lloyd & Goold's Irish Chancery Reports *temp.* Plunkett.
L. & G. *t* Sug. Lloyd & Goold's Irish Chancery Reports *temp.* Sugden.
L. & M. Lowndes & Maxwell's English Practice Cases.
L. & T. Longfield & Townsend's Irish Exchequer Reports.
L. & W. Lloyd & Welsby's English Mercantile Cases.
La. Louisiana;—Louisiana Reports;—Lane's English Exchequer Reports.
La. An. Louisiana Annual Reports.
La. L. J. Louisiana Law Journal, New Orleans; — Louisiana Law Journal (Schmidt's), New Orleans, 1842.
La. T. R. Louisiana Term Reports (3-12 Martin's Louisiana).
Lab. Labatt's California District Court Reports;—Labatt, Master and Servant;—Labuan.
Lack. Leg. R. Lackawanna Legal Record.
Lalor. Lalor's Supplement to Hill & Denio's New York Reports.
Lanc. Bar. The Lancaster Bar (periodical).
Lane. Lane's English Exchequer Reports.
Lang. Ca. (or **L. C.**) **Cont.** Langdell's Cases on the Law of Contracts.
Lang. Ca. (or **L. C.**) **Sales.** Langdell's Cases on the Law of Sales.
Lang. Cont. Langdell's Cases on Contracts;—Langdell's Summary of the Law of Contracts.
Lang. Eq. Pl. Langdell's Summary of Equity Pleading;—Langdell's Cases in Equity Pleading.
Lang. Sales. Langdell's Cases on the Law of Sales.
Lang. Sum. Cont. Langdell's Summary of the Law of Contracts.
Lans. Lansing's New York Supreme Court Reports.
Lans. Ch. Lansing's Chancery Decisions, New York.
Latch. Latch's English King's Bench Reports.
Lathrop. Lathrop's Reports (115-131 Massachusetts).
Lauder. (Lauder of) Fountainhall's Scotch Session Cases.
Law Cas. Wm. I. Law Cases, William I. to Richard I.

Law Chr. Law Chronicle, London (or Edinburgh).
Law Chr. & Jour. Jur. Law Chronicle and Journal of Jurisprudence.
Law. Con. Lawson on Contracts.
Law Mag. Law Magazine, London.
Law Mag. & Rev. Law Magazine and Review.
Law Notes. Law Notes, London;—Law Notes, Northport, N. Y.
Law Rep. Law Reports (see L. R.);—Law Reporter, Boston [or London;—or Toronto;—or Montreal].
Law Rev. Law Review, London;—American Law Review, Boston.
Law Rev. & Qu. J. Law Review and Quarterly Journal, London.
Law T. Law Times, London;—Law Times, Scranton, Pa.
Law T. Rep. N. S. Law Times Reports, New Series.
Law. Wheat. Lawrence's Edition of Wheaton on International Law.
Lawrence. Lawrence's Reports (20 Ohio).
Ld. Ken. Lord Kenyon's English King's Bench Reports.
Ld. Raym. Lord Raymond's English King's Bench Reports.
Lea. Lea's Tennessee Reports;—Leach.
Leach. Leach's English Crown Cases.
Leach Cl. Cas. Leach's Club Cases, London.
Lead. Cas. Am. American Leading Cases, by Hare & Wallace.
Lead. Cas. Eq. Leading Cases in Equity, by White & Tudor.
Leake Cont. Leake on the Law of Contracts.
Lee. Lee's English Ecclesiastical Reports;—Lee's Reports (9-12 California).
Lee G. Sir George Lee's English Ecclesiastical Reports.
Lee *t.* Hard. Lee's Cases *temp.* Hardwicke, English K. B. and Ch.
Leg. Int. Legal Intelligencer, Philadelphia.
Leg. News. Legal News, Chicago;—Legal News, Montreal.
Leg. Oler. Laws of Oleron.
Leg. Rev. Legal Review, London.
Leg. Wisb. Laws of Wisbury.
Legg. Leggett's Reports, Sind, India.
Leigh. Leigh's Virginia Reports.
Leigh & C. Leigh & Cave's English Crown Cases.
Lest. L. L. Lester's Decisions in Public Land Cases.
Lester. Lester's Reports (31-33 Georgia).
Lester Supp. (or **Lest. & But.**) Lester & Butler's Supplement to Lester's Georgia Reports.
Lev. Levinz's English King's Bench Re-Reports.
Lev. Ent. Levinz's Entries.
Lew. C. C. Lewin's English Crown Cases.
Lewis. Lewis' Reports (1 Nevada).
Lex Cust. Lex Custumaria.
Lex Man. Lex Maneriorum.
Lex Mer. Am. Lex Mercatoria Americana.
Lex Merc. Red. Lex Mercatoria Rediviva, by Beawes.
Lex Parl. Lex Parliamentaria.
Ley. Ley's English King's Bench Reports.
Lib. Ass. Liber Assisarum (Year Books, Part V.).
Lib. Ent. Old Books of Entries.
Lib. Feud. Liber Feudorum, at the end of the Corpus Juris Civilis.
Lib. Intr. Liber Intrationum, Old Book of Entries.
Lib. Nig. Liber Niger, the Black Book.
Lib. Pl. Liber Placitandi, Book of Pleading.
Lib. Reg. Register Books.
Lib. Rub. Liber Rubens, the Red Book.
Lieb. Herm. Lieber's Hermeneutics.
Lil. Lilly's English Assize Reports.
Lind. Part. Lindley's Laws of Partnership.
Lit. (or **Litt.**) Littell's Kentucky Reports;—Littleton's English Common Pleas Reports;—Littleton's Tenures.
Lit. (or **Litt.**) **Sel. Ca.** Littell's Select Kentucky Cases.
Lit. (or **Litt.**) **Ten.** Littleton's Tenures.
Littel. Littell's Kentucky Reports.
Liv. Livington's Mayor's Court Reports, New York.
Ll. & G. *t* P. Lloyd & Goold's Irish Chancery Reports *temp.* Plunkett.
Ll. & G. *t* S. Lloyd & Goold's Irish Chancery Reports *temp.* Sugden.
Ll. & W. Lloyd & Welsby's Mercantile Cases.
Lock. Rev. Ca. Lockwood's New York Reversed Cases.
Lofft. Lofft's English King's Bench Reports.
Lom. Dig. Lomax's Digest of Real Property.
Lom. Ex. Lomax on the Law of Executors.
Longf. & T. Longfield & Townsend's Irish Exchequer Reports.
Lorenz. Lorenz's Ceylon Reports.
Low. Lowell's United States District Court Reports.
Low. Can. Jur. Lower Canada Jurist, Montreal.
Low. Can. L. J. Lower Canada Law Journal.
Low. Can. R. Lower Canada Reports.
Lownd. M. & P. Lowndes, Maxwell, & Pollock's English Bail Court Reports.
Lownd. & M. Lowndes & Maxwell's English Bail Court Reports.
Luc. (or **Lucas**) Lucas' Reports (Modern Reports, Part X.).
Ludden. Ludden's Reports (43, 44 Maine).
Lush. Lushington's English Admiralty Reports.
Lush. Pr. L. Lushington on Prize Law.
Lut. (or **Lutw.**) Lutwyche's English Common Pleas Reports.
Lut. Ent. Lutwyche's Entries.
Lut. R. C. Lutwyche's English Registration Appeal Cases.
Luz. Leg. Obs. Luzerne Legal Observer, Carbondale, Pa.
Luz. Leg. Reg. Luzerne Legal Register, Wilkesbarre, Pa.
Lyne (Wal.) Lyne's Irish Chancery Cases., from Wallis' Notes.

M. Miles, Pennsylvania Reports;—Morison's Dictionary of Decisions, Scotch Court of Session;—Session Cases, 3d Series, Scotland (Macpherson, &c.).

M. C. C. Moody's English Crown Cases, Reserved.

M. D. & D. (or **De G.**) Montagu, Deacon, & De Gex's English Bankruptcy Reports.

M. G. & S. Manning, Granger, & Scott's English Common Pleas Reports.

M. & A. Montagu & Ayrton's English Bankruptcy Reports.

M. & B. Montagu & Bligh's English Bankruptcy Reports.

M. & C. Mylne & Craig's English Chancery Reports;—Montagu & Chitty's English Bankruptcy Reports.

M. & G. Manning & Granger's English Common Pleas Reports;—Maddock & Geldart's English Chancery Reports.

M. & Gel. Maddock & Geldart's English Chancery Reports (6 Maddock).

M. & Gord. Macnaghten & Gordon's English Chancery Reports.

M. & K. Mylne & Keen's English Chancery Reports.

M. & M. Moody & Malkin's English Nisi Prius Reports.

M. & M'A. Montagu & M'Arthur's English Bankruptcy Reports.

M. & P. Moore & Payne's English Common Pleas Reports.

M. & R. Manning & Ryland's English King's Bench Reports;—Moody & Robinson's English Nisi Prius Reports;—Maclean & Robinson's Scotch Appeal Cases.

M. & R. M. C. Manning & Ryland's English Magistrate Cases.

M. & S. Maule & Selwyn's English King's Bench Reports;—Moore & Scott's English Common Pleas Reports.

M. & W. Meeson & Welsby's English Exchequer Reports.

M. & Y. Martin & Yerger's Tennessee Reports.

Mac. & G. Macnaghten & Gordon's Chancery Reports.

Mac. P. C. Macrory's Patent Cases.

Mac. & Rob. Maclean & Robinson's Appeal Cases.

Macal. McAllister's United States Circuit Court Reports.

MacArth. MacArthur's District of Columbia Reports.

Macas. Macassey's Reports, New Zealand.

Maccl. Macclesfield's Reports (Modern Reports, Part X.).

Macd. Jam. Macdougall's Jamaica Reports.

Macf. Macfarlane's Reports, Jury Courts, Scotland.

Mack. Inst. Mackenzie's Institutes of the Law of Scotland.

Macl. McLean's United States Circuit Court Reports;—Maclaurin's Scotch Criminal Decisions.

Macl. & R. Maclean & Robinson's Scotch Appeal Cases.

Macn. Macnaghten's Select Cases in Chancery *temp.* King (see n. 15, p. 78);—W. H. Macnaghten's Reports, India.

Macn. (Fr.) Sir Francis Macnaghten's Bengal Reports.

Macn. N. A. Beng. Macnaghten's Nizamut Adawlut Reports, Bengal.

Macn. S. D. A. Beng. (W. H.) Macnaghten's Sudder Dewanny Adawlut Reports, Bengal.

Macn. Sel. Cas. Select Cases in Chancery *tempore* King, edited by Macnaghten.

Macn. & G. Macnaghten & Gordon's English Chancery Reports.

Macph. Macpherson, Lee, & Bell's (Third Series) Scotch Court of Session Cases.

Macq. Macqueen's Scotch Appeal Cases.

Macq. H. L. Cas. Macqueen's Scotch Appeal Cases (House of Lords).

Mad. H. C. Madras High Court Reports.

Mad. S. D. A. R. Madras Sudder Dewanny Adawlut Reports.

Mad. Sel. Dec. Madras Select Decrees.

Mad. Ser. Madras Series (East) Indian Law Reports.

Mad. & Gel. Maddock & Geldart's English Chancery Reports (6 Maddock).

Madd. Maddock's Reports, English Chancery.

Mag. Cas. Magistrate's Cases (especially the series edited by Bittleston, Wise, & Parnell).

Mag. Char. Magna Charta.

Mag. Rot. Magnus Rotulus (the great Roll of the Exchequer).

Magruder. Magruder's Reports (1, 2 Maryland).

Mai. Maine;—Maine Reports.

Mai. Anc. L. Maine's Ancient Law.

Mai. Inst. Maine's History of Institutions.

Mai. Vil. Com. Maine's Village Communities.

Maitland. Maitland's Manuscript Scotch Session Cases.

Man. Manning's Reports (English Court of Revision);—Manning's Reports (1 Michigan;—See also Mann.

Man. Cas. Manumission Cases in New Jersey, by Bloomfield.

Man. Gr. & S. Manning, Granger, & Scott, English Common Pleas Reports.

Man. & G. Manning & Granger's English Common Pleas Reports.

Man. & Ry. Manning & Ryland's English King's Bench Reports.

Man. & Ry. Mag. Cas. Manning & Ryland's English Magistrates' Cases.

Manb. Coke. Manby's Abridgment of Coke's Reports.

Manning. Manning's Reports (1 Michigan).

Mar. March's English King's Bench Reports;—Marshall's United States Circuit Court Reports;—Marshall's Kentucky Reports;—Martin's Louisiana Reports;—Martin's North Carolina Reports;—Marshall's Reports, Bengal.

Mar. L. C. English Maritime Law Cases (Crockford).

Mar. L. C. N. S. English Maritime Law Cases, New Series (Aspinall).

Mar. La. Martin's Louisiana Reports.

Mar. N. C. Martin's North Carolina Reports.

Mar. N. S. Martin's Louisiana Reports, New Series.

Mar. R. English Maritime Law Reports.

March N. C. March's New Cases, English King's Bench.

Marr. Marriott's English Admiralty Decisions;—Marrack's European Assurance Cases.

Marsh. Marshall's United States Circuit Court Decisions;—Marshall's English Common Pleas Reports;—Marshall's Bengal Reports.

Marsh. (A. K.) A. K. Marshall's Kentucky Reports.

Marsh. Beng. (or Calc.) Marshall's Reports, Bengal.

Marsh. Dec. Marshall's United States Circuit Court Decisions (or Marshall on the Federal Constitution).

Marsh. (J. J.) J. J. Marshall's Kentucky Reports.

Marsh. Op. Marshall's Constitutional Opinions.

Mart. Dec. United States Decisions in Martin's North Carolina Reports.

Mart. (N. C.) Martin's North Carolina Reports.

Mart. N. S. Martin's Louisiana Reports, New Series.

Mart. U. S. C. C. Martin's United States Circuit Court Reports.

Mart. & Yerg. Martin & Yerger's Tennessee Reports.

Martin. Martin's Louisiana Reports;—Martin's North Carolina Reports;—Martin's Reports (21-30 Georgia);—Martin's Reports (54-62 Indiana).

Mas. Mason's United States Circuit Court Reports.

Mass. Massachusetts;— Massachusetts Reports.

Matson. Matson's Reports (22-24 Connecticut).

Matthews. Matthews' Reports (6 West Virginia).

Mau. & Sel. Maule & Selwyn's English King's Bench Reports.

Maur. Dec. Mauritius Decisions.

Mayn. Maynard's Reports, Edward II. (Year Books, Part I.).

McA. L. & Ten. McAdam on Landlord and Tenant.

McAll. McAllister's United States Circuit Court Reports.

McAr. McArthur's District of Columbia Reports.

McBride. McBride's Reports (1 Missouri).

McCah. McCahon's Kansas Reports.

McCar. McCarter's New Jersey Equity Reports.

McCl. McClelland's English Exchequer Reports.

McCl. & Y. McClelland & Younge's Exchequer Reports.

McCook. McCook's Reports (1 Ohio State).

McCord. McCord's South Carolina Law Reports.

McCord Eq. (or Ch.) McCord's South Carolina Equity Reports.

McCorkle. McCorkle's Reports (65 North Carolina).

McCr. McCrary's United States Circuit Court Reports.

McFar. McFarlane's Reports (Scotch Jury Court).

McGill. McGill's Manuscript Scotch Session Cases.

McGl. McGloin's Louisiana Reports.

McL. McLean's United States Circuit Court Reports.

McL. & R. McLean & Robinson's Scotch Appeal Cases.

McMul. McMullan's South Carolina Law Reports.

McMul. Eq. McMullan's South Carolina Equity Reports.

McPherson. McPherson, Lee, & Bell's (Third Series) Scotch Session Cases.

McQ. MacQueen's Scotch Appeal (House of Lords) Cases.

McQuillin Mun. Corp. McQuillin on Municipal Corporations.

Md. Maryland Reports;—Harris & McHenry's Maryland Reports.

Md. Ch. Maryland Chancery Reports.

Me. Maine;—Maine Reports.

Means. Means' Kansas Reports.

Mechem. Mechem on Agency,—on Partnership.

Meddaugh. Meddaugh's Reports (13 Michigan).

Mees. & Ros. Meeson & Roscoe's English Exchequer Reports.

Mees. & Wels. Meeson & Welsby's English Exchequer Reports.

Meigs. Meigs' Tennessee Reports.

Menz. Menzies' Reports, Cape of Good Hope.

Merc. Cas. Mercantile Cases.

Merl. Quest. Merlin, Questions de Droit.

Merl. Repert. Merlin, Répertoire de Jurisprudence.

Met. (or Metc.) Metcalf's Mass. Reports;—Metcalfe's Kentucky Reports.

Metc. Ky. Metcalfe's Kentucky Reports.

Mich. Michigan Reports.

Mich. N. P. Michigan Nisi Prius Reports.

Mil. Miles' Pennsylvania Reports;—Miller (see Mill.).

Mill. Mills' South Carolina Constitutional Reports;—Miller's Reports (1-5 Louisiana);—Miller's Reports (3-18 Maryland).

Mill. Dec. Miller's Decisions (Woolworth's Reports), United States Circuit Court;—Miller's Decisions, United States Supreme Court.

Mill. La. Miller's Reports (1-5 Louisiana).

Mill. Md. Miller's Reports (3-18 Maryland).

Miller. Miller's Reports (1-5 La.);—Miller's Reports (3-18 Md.).

Milw. Milward's Irish Ecclesiastical Reports.

Min. Minor's Alabama Reports.

Min. Inst. Minor's Institutes of Common and Statute Law.

Minn. Minnesota Reports.

Mir. (or Mir. Just.) Horne's Mirror of Justices.

Miss. Mississippi Reports.

Mit. Ch. Pl. Mitford's Equity Pleading.

Mitf. Eq. Pl. Mitford's Equity Pleading.

Mo. Missouri Reports;—Moore's English King's Bench Reports;—Moore's English Common Pleas Reports;—Moore's English Privy Council Reports;—Modern Reports, English King's Bench, &c. (see Mod.).

Mo. App. Missouri Appeals Reports.
Mo. (F.) Sir Francis Moore's English King's Bench Reports.
Mo. I. A. Moore's Indian Appeals.
Mo. (J. B.) J. B. Moore's English Common Pleas Reports.
Moak Eng. Rep. Moak's English Reports.
Moak Und. Moak's edition of Underhill on Torts.
Mod. Modern Reports, English King's Bench, &c.
Mod. Cas. Modern Cases (6th Modern Reports).
Mod. Cas. L. & Eq. Modern Cases at Law and Equity (8 and 9 Modern Reports).
Mod. Cas. per Far. (or *t* **Holt**) Modern Cases *temp.* Holt, by Farresby (7 Modern Reports).
Mod. Rep. The Modern Reports, English King's Bench, Ec.;—Modern Reports by Style (Style's King's Bench Reports).
Mol. (or **Moll.**) Molloy's Irish Chancery Reports.
Mon. Montana Reports;—T. B. Monroe's Kentucky Reports.
Mon. (B.) B. Monroe's Kentucky Reports.
Mon. (T. B.) T. B. Monroe's Kentucky Reports.
Mont. Montana Reports;—Montagu's English Bankruptcy Reports;—Montesquieu;—Montriou's Bengal Reports.
Mont. Cas. Montriou's Cases in Hindoo Law.
Mont. Cond. Rep. Montreal Condensed Reports.
Mont. D. & DeG. Montagu, Deacon, & De Gex's English Bankruptcy Reports.
Mont. Dig. (or **Eq. Pl.**) Montagu's Digest of Pleadings in Equity.
Mont. Sp. L. Montesquieu's Spirit of Laws.
Mont. & Ayr. Montagu & Ayrton's English Bankruptcy Reports.
Mont. & Ayr. B. L. Montagu & Ayrton on the Bankrupt Laws.
Mont. & Bl. Montagu & Bligh's English Bankruptcy Reports.
Mont. & C. Montagu & Chitty's English Bankruptcy Reports.
Mont. & MacA. Montagu & MacArthur's English Bankruptcy Reports.
Montr. Montriou's Reports, Bengal;—Montriou's Supplement to Morton's Reports (see n. 6, p. 145).
Moo. Francis Moore's English King's Bench Reports;—J. M. Moore's English Common Pleas Reports;—Moody's English Crown Cases.
Moo. A. Moore's Reports (1 Bosanquet & Puller, after page 470).
Moo. C. C. Moody's English Crown Cases Reserved.
Moo. Cr. C. Moody's Crown Cases, English Courts.
Moo. Ind. App. Moore's Reports, Privy Council, Indian Appeals.
Moo. P. C. Moore's Privy Council Cases.
Moo. Tr. Moore's Divorce Trials.
Moo. & Mal. Moody & Malkin's English Nisi Prius Reports.
Moo. & Pay. Moore & Payne's English Common Pleas Reports.
Moo. & Rob. Moody & Robinson's English Nisi Prius Reports.
Moo. & Sc. Moore & Scott's English Common Pleas Reports.
Mood. Moody's English Crown Cases Reserved.
Mood. & Malk. Moody & Malkin's English Nisi Prius Reports.
Moore. Moore's English King's Bench Reports;—Moore's English Common Pleas Reports;—Moore's English Privy Council Reports;—Moore's Reports (28-33 Arkansas).
Moore Int. L. Moore's Digest of International Law.
Moore K. B. Sir F. Moore's English King's Bench Reports.
Moore P. C. Moore's Privy Council Reports.
Moore & P. Moore & Payne's English Common Pleas Reports.
Moore & S. Moore & Scott's English Common Pleas Reports.
Moore & Walker. Moore & Walker's Reports (22-24 Texas).
Mor. Corp. Morawetz on Private Corporations.
Mor. Ia. Morris' Iowa Reports.
Morr. Morris' Reports, Iowa;—See also Morris.
Morr. Dict. (or **M. Dict.**) Morison's Dictionary of Decisions, Scotch Court of Session.
Morr. St. Cas. Morris' State Cases, Mississippi.
Morr. Supp. Supplement to Morison's Dictionary, Scotch Court of Session.
Morris. Morris' Iowa Reports;—Morris' Reports (5 California);—Morris' Reports (43-48 Mississippi);—Morris' Jamaica Reports;—Morris' Bombay Reports.
Morris & Har. Morris & Harrington's S. D. A. Reports, Bombay.
Morton. Morton's Reports, Bengal.
Mos. Mosely's English Chancery Reports.
Mumf. Mumford's Jamaica Reports.
Munf. Munford's Virginia Reports.
Mur. Murphey's North Carolina Reports;—Murray's Jury Court Reports (Scotland);—Murray's Ceylon Reports;—Murray's New South Wales Reports.
Mur. & Hurl. Murphy & Hurlstone's English Exchequer Reports.
Murph. Murphey's North Carolina Reports.
Murr. Murray's Scotch Jury Trials;—Murray's Laws and Acts of Parliament (Scotch);—Murray's Ceylon Reports;—Murray's New South Wales Reports.
Mutukisna. Mutukisna's Ceylon Reports.
Myl. & Cr. Mylne & Craig's English Chancery Reports.
Myl. & K. Mylne & Keen's English Chancery Reports.
Myr. Myrick's California Probate Court Reports.

N. B. R. National Bankruptcy Register, New York;—New Brunswick Reports.
N. Benl. New Benloe, English King's Bench Reports.

N. C. North Carolina Reports;—Notes of Cases (English Ecclesiastical and Maritime).
N. C. C. New Chancery Cases (Younge & Collyer).
N. C. C. A. Negligence and Compensation Cases Annotated.
N. C. Conf. North Carolina Conference Reports.
N. C. Ecc. Notes of Cases in the Ecclesiastical and Maritime Courts.
N. C. T. Rep. North Carolina Term Reports.
N. Chip. N. Chipman's Vermont Reports.
N. D. North Dakota.
N. E. Northeastern Reporter.
N. F. Newfoundland Reports
N. H. New Hampshire Reports.
N. H. & C. English Railway and Canal Cases, by Nichol, Hare, Carrow, &c.
N. J. New Jersey;—New Jersey Reports;—Novellae Justiniani.
N. J. Eq. (or Ch.) New Jersey Equity Reports.
N. J. Law. New Jersey Law Reports.
N. J. L. J. New Jersey Law Journal, Somerville, N. J.
N. L. Nelson's Lutwyche, English Common Pleas Reports.
N. M. New Mexico Reports.
N. of Cas. Notes of Cases, English Ecclesiastical and Maritime Courts);—Notes to Cases at Madras (by Strange).
N. P. Nisi Prius;—New Practice;—Nova Placita;—Notary Public.
N. P. C. Nisi Prius Cases.
N. P. R. Nisi Prius Reports.
N. R. The New Reports (English);—Bosanquet & Puller's New Reports;—Novissima Recopilacion.
N. R. B. P. New Reports of Bosanquet & Puller.
N. S. L. R. Nova Scotia Law Reports.
N. S. W. L. R. New South Wales Law Reports.
N. Sc. Dec. Nova Scotia Decisions.
N. W. P. H. C. Northwest Provinces, High Court Reports, India.
N. W. Rep. Northwestern Reporter, St. Paul, Minn.
N. Y. New York Court of Appeals Reports.
N. Y. App. Dec. New York Court of Appeals Decisions.
N. Y. App. Div. New York Appellate Division.
N. Y. Cas. Err. New York Cases in Error (Caines' Cases).
N. Y. Ch. Sent. New York Chancery Sentinel.
N. Y. City H. Rec. New York City Hall Recorder.
N. Y. Code Rep. N. S. New York Code Reports, New Series.
N. Y. Code Reptr. New York Code Reporter.
N. Y. Cr. R. New York Criminal Reports.
N. Y. Leg. N. New York Legal News.
N. Y. Leg. Obs. New York Legal Observer (Owen's).
N. Y. Op. Att. Gen. Sickel's Opinions of the Attorneys-General of New York.
N. Y. Pr. New York Practice Reports.
N. Y. Rep. New York Court of Appeals Reports.
N. Y. Reptr. New York Reporter (Gardenier's).
N. Y. St. Rep. New York State Reporter.
N. Y. Super. Ct. New York Superior Court Reports.
N. Y. Supp. New York Supplement.
N. Y. Suprm. Ct. New York Supreme Court Reports.
N. Y. T. R. New York Term Reports (Caines' Reports).
N. & H. Nott & Huntington's Reports (1-7 U. S. Court of Claims).
N. & Hop. Nott & Hopkins' Reports (8-15 U. S. Court of Claims).
N. & M. Nevile & Manning's English King's Bench Reports.
N. & Mc. Nott & McCord's South Carolina Reports.
N. & P. Nevile & Perry's English King's Bench Reports.
Napton. Napton's Reports (4 Missouri).
Narr. Mod. Narrationes Modernae, or Style's King's Bench Reports.
Nat. B. R. National Bankruptcy Register.
Nat. Brev. Natura Brevium.
Nd. Newfoundland Reports.
Neb. Nebraska Reports.
Neb. Unoff. Nebraska Unofficial.
Nel. (Nels. or Nels. 8vo) Nelson's English Chancery Reports.
Nell. Nell's Ceylon Reports.
Nels. Fol. Rep. Finch's Chancery Reports, edited by Nelson.
Nev. Nevada Reports.
Nev. & Man. Nevile & Manning's English King's Bench Reports.
Nev. & Man. Mag. Cas. Nevill & Manning's English Magistrates' Cases.
Nev. & McN. Neville & McNamara's Railway and Canal Cases.
Nev. & P. Nevile & Perry's English King's Bench Reports.
Nev. & P. Mag. Cas. Nevile & Perry's English Magistrates' Cases.
New Ann. Reg. New Annual Register, London.
New Benl. New Benloe's Reports, English King's Bench.
New Br. New Brunswick Reports.
New Cas. Eq. New Cases in Equity (8, 9 Modern Reports).
New Mag. Cas. New Magistrates' Cases (Bittleston, Wise, & Parnell).
New Pr. Cases. New Practice Cases (English).
New Rep. New Reports in all the Courts, London;—Bosanquet & Puller's New Reports (4, 5 Bos. & Pul.).
New Sess. Cas. Carrow, Hamerton, & Allen's New Sessions Cases (English).
New Term Rep. New Term Reports (see n. 7, p. 49);—Dowling & Ryland's King's Bench Reports.
New York. See N. Y.

Newb. Newberry's United States Admiralty Reports.
Newbyth. Newbyth's Manuscript Decisions, Scotch Session Cases.
Newell. Newell on Libel and Slander.
Newf. Sel. Cas. Newfoundland Select Cases.
Norris. Norris' Reports (82-96 Pennsylvania).
Nort. L. C. Norton's Leading Cases on Inheritance, India.
North. Reports *temp.* Northington (Eden's English Chancery Reports).
Northw. Rep. Northwestern Reporter, St. Paul, Minn.
Not. Cas. Notes of Cases in the English Ecclesiastical and Maritime Courts;—Notes of Cases at Madras (Strange).
Not. Dec. Notes of Decisions (Martin's North Carolina Reports).
Nott & Hop. Nott & Hopkins' Reports (8-15 United States Court of Claims).
Nott & Hunt. Nott & Huntington's Reports (1-7 U. S. Court of Claims).
Nott & McC. Nott & McCord's South Carolina Reports.
Nov. Novellae.
Nov. Rec. Novissimi Recopilacion de las Leyes de España.
Noy. Noy's English King's Bench Reports.

O. Ohio Reports;—Oregon Reports;—Otto's United States Supreme Court Reports.
O. Ben. Old Benloe's Reports, English Common Pleas.
O. Bridg. Orlando Bridgman's Reports, English Common Pleas;—Carter's Reports, *temp.* Bridgman, English Common Pleas.
O. C. A. Ohio Courts of Appeal.
O. S. Ohio State Reports.
O. St. Ohio State Reports.
O'Mal. & H. O'Malley & Hardcastle's English Election Cases.
Odg. Lib. Odger on Libel and Slander.
Off. Gaz. Pat. Off. Official Gazette, United States Patent Office, Washington, D. C.
Officer. Officer's Reports (1-9 Minnesota).
Ogden. Ogden's Reports (12-15 Louisiana).
Ohio. Ohio Reports.
Ohio App. Ohio Appellate.
Ohio C. C. Ohio Circuit Court.
Ohio Dec. Ohio Decisions.
Ohio L. J. Ohio Law Journal.
Ohio N. P. Ohio Nisi Prius.
Ohio N. P. (N. S.) Ohio Nisi Prius, New Series.
Ohio R. Cond. Ohio Reports, Condensed.
Ohio St. Ohio State Reports.
Okla. Oklahoma.
Okla. Cr. Oklahoma Criminal.
Olc. (or **Olc. Adm.**). Olcott's United States District Court (Admiralty) Reports.
Old Ben. Benloe in Benloe & Dalison, English Common Pleas Reports.
Oldr. Oldright's Reports, Nova Scotia.
Oliv. B. & L. English Railway and Canal Cases, Vols. 5-7, by Oliver, Beavan, & Lefroy.
Oll. B. & F. Olliver, Bell, & Fitzgerald's New Zealand Reports.
Ont. Ontario;—Ontario Reports.
Ont. App. Ontario Appeal Reports.
Ont. Pr. Rep. Ontario Practice Reports.
Op. Att. Gen. Opinions of the United States Attorneys-General.
Op. N. Y. Atty. Gen. Sickel's Opinions of Attorneys-General of New York.
Or. Oregon Reports.
Or. T. Rep. Orleans Term Reports (1, 2 Martin's Louisiana).
Ord. de la Mar. Ordonnance de la Marine de Louis XIV.
Oreg. Oregon Reports.
Orl. Bridgman. Orlando Bridgman's English Common Pleas Reports.
Orl. T. R. Orleans Term Reports (1, 2 Martin's Louisiana Reports).
Ormond. Ormond's Reports (12-15 Alabama).
Ott. Otto's United States Supreme Court Reports.
Out. Outerbridge's Reports (97, 98 Pennsylvania State).
Over. Overton's Tennessee Reports.
Ow. Owen's English K. B. Reports;—New South Wales Reports.
Oxley. Young's Vice-Admiralty Decisions, Nova Scotia, edited by Oxley.

P. Partidas;—Peters;—Pickering's Massachusetts Reports.
P. A. D. Peters' Admiralty Decisions.
P. C. Pleas of the Crown;—Parliamentary Cases;—Practice Cases;—Prize Cases;—Patent Cases;—Privy Council;—Political Code;—Penal Code;—Prize Court;—Probate Court;—Precedents in Chancery—Procédure Civile.
P. C. C. Privy Council Cases;—Peters' Circuit Court Reports.
P. C. R. Parker's Criminal Reports, New York.
P. E. I. Rep. Prince Edward Island Reports (Haviland's).
P. F. S. P. F. Smith's Reports (51-81½ Pennsylvania State).
P. I. Rep. Philippine Islands Reports.
P. Jr. & H. (or **P. & H.**) Patton, Jr., & Heath's Virginia Reports.
P. N. P. Peake's English Nisi Prius Cases.
P. O. Cas. Perry's Oriental Cases, Bombay.
P. R. Parliamentary Reports;—Pennsylvania Reports, by Penrose & Watts.
P. R. U. C. Practice Reports, Upper Canada.
P. R. & D. Power, Rodwell, & Dew's English Election Cases.
P. S. C. U. S. Peters' Supreme Court, United States.
P. S. R. Pennsylvania State Reports.
P. U. R. Public Utilities Reports.
P. W. (or **P. Wms.**) Peere Williams' English Chancery Reports.
P. & C. Prideaux & Cole's Reports, English Courts (New Session Cases, Vol. 4).
P. & D. Perry & Davison's English Queen's Bench Reports.
P. & H. Patton (Jr.) & Heath's Virginia Reports.

P. & K. Perry & Knapp's English Election Cases.
P. & W. Penrose & Watts' Pennsylvania Reports.
Pa. Pennsylvania Reports, by Penrose & Watts;—Pennsylvania State Reports.
Pa. L. G. Legal Gazette Reports (Campbell's), Pennsylvania.
Pa. L. J. Pennsylvania Law Journal Reports (Clark's);—Pennsylvania Law Journal, Philadelphia.
Pa. L. Rec. Pennsylvania Law Record, Philadelphia.
Pa. St. Pennsylvania State Reports.
Pa. St. Tr. Pennsylvania State Trials (Hogan's).
Pac. Pacific Report.
Page Contr. Page on Contracts.
Pai. Paine's United States Circuit Court Reports;—Paige's New York Chancery Reports.
Pai. Ch. Paige's New York Chancery Reports.
Paine C. C. Paine's United States Circuit Court Reports.
Pal. (or **Palm.**) Palmer's English King's Bench Reports.
Palm. Palmer's English King's Bench Reports.
Pand. The Pandects.
Papy. Papy's Rep. (5, 6 Florida).
Par. Parker's English Exchequer Reports.
Par. Adm. Parsons on the Law of Shipping and Admiralty.
Par. Am. Law (or **Comm.**) Parson's Commentaries on American Law.
Par. Bills & N. Parsons on Notes and Bills.
Par. Cont. Parsons on Contracts.
Par. Dec. Parsons' Decisions, Massachusetts (see n. 7, p. 30).
Par. Eq. Cas. Parsons' Select Equity Cases, Pennsylvania.
Park. Parker's New York Criminal Reports;—Parker's English Exchequer Reports.
Park. Cr. Cas. Parker's New York Criminal Cases.
Park. Exch. Parker's English Exchequer Reports.
Park. Rev. Cas. Parker's English Exchequer Reports (Revenue Cases).
Parker. Parker's English Exchequer Reports;—Parker's New York Criminal Reports;—Parker, N. H. Reports.
Parl. Cas. Parliamentary Cases (House of Lords Reports).
Pars. Eq. Cas. Parsons' Select Equity Cases, Pennsylvania.
Part. Las Siete Partidas (see Moreau).
Paschal. Paschal's Reports (28-31 Texas).
Pat. Paton's Scotch Appeal Cases;—Paterson's Scotch Appeal Cases.
Pat. App. Cas. Paton's Scotch Appeal Cases (Craigie, Stewart, & Paton);—Paterson's Scotch Appeal Cases.
Pat. & Mur. Paterson & Murray's reports, New South Wales.
Pater. Paterson's Scotch Appeal Cases;—Paterson's New South Wales Reports.
Paton. (Craigie, Stewart, &) Paton's Scotch Appeal Cases (see p. 133).
Patr. Elect. Cas.—Patrick's Election Cases, Upper Canada.
Patt. & H. Patton & Heath's Virginia Reports.
Pea. Peake's English Nisi Prius Reports.
Peake Add. Cas. Peake's Additional Cases (Vol. 2 of Peake).
Peake Ev. Peake on the Law of Evidence.
Peake N. P. Peake's English Nisi Prius Cases.
Pears. Pearson's Reports, Pennsylvania.
Pearce C. C. Pearce's Reports, in Dearsly's Crown Cases, English.
Peck. Peck's Tennessee Reports;—Peck's Reports (11-30 Illinois); Peckwell's English Election Reports.
Peere Wms. Peere Williams' Reports, English Chancery.
Pen. Pennington's Reports, New Jersey.
Pen. & W. Penrose & Watts' Pennsylvania Reports.
Penn. Pennsylvania State Reports;—Pennypacker's Pennsylvania Reports;—Pennington's New Jersey Reports;—Penrose & Watts' Pennsylvania Reports.
Penn. Rep. Pennsylvania State Reports;—Penrose & Watts' Penn. Reports.
Penn. St. (or **St. R.**) Pennsylvania State Reports.
Penning. Pennington's New Jersey Reports.
Penr. & W. Penrose & Watts' Pennsylvania Reports.
Per. Tr. Perry on Trusts.
Per. & Dav. Perry & Davison's English King's Bench Reports.
Per. & Kn. Perry & Knapp's English Election Reports.
Perk. Pr. Bk. Perkins' Profitable Book (Conveyancing).
Perry. Sir Erskine Perry's Reports, in Morley's (East) Indian Digest;—Perry's Oriental Cases.
Perry & Kn. Perry & Knapp's English Election Cases.
Pet. Peters' United States Supreme Court Reports;—Peters' United States Circuit Court Reports;—Peters' Admiralty Reports;—Peters' Prince Edward Island Reports.
Pet. Adm. Peters' U. S District Court Reports (Admiralty Decisions).
Pet. Br. Petit Brooke, or Brooke's New Cases, English King's Bench.
Pet. C. C. Peters' United States Circuit Court Reports.
Pet. Cond. Peters' Condensed Reports United States Supreme Court.
Pet. S. C. Peters' United States Supreme Court Reports.
Peters Adm. Peters' U. S. District Court Reports (Admiralty Decisions).
Petersd. Abr. Petersdorff's Abridgment.
Petit Br. Petit Brooke, or Brooke's New Cases, English King's Bench.
Ph. Phillips' English Chancery Reports;—Phillimore's English Ecclesiastical Reports (see Phil.).
Ph. St. Tr. Phillipp's State Trials.

Pheney Rep. Pheney's New Term Reports (see n. 87, p. 100).
Phil. Phillips' English Chancery Reports; —Phillips' North Carolina Reports;— Phillips' English Election Cases;—Phillimore's Ecclesiastical Reports.
Phil. Civ. & Can. Law. Phillimore's Civil and Canon Law.
Phil. Cop. Phillips' Law of Copyright Designs.
Phil. Dom. Phillimore's Law of Domicil.
Phil. Ecc. Judg. Phillimore's Ecclesiastical Judgments.
Phil. Ecc. Law. Phillimore's Ecclesiastical Law.
Phil. Ecc. R. Phillimore's English Ecclesiastical Reports.
Phil. Eq. Phillips' North Carolina Equity Reports.
Phil. Int. Law. Phillimore's International Law.
Phil. Int. Rom. Law. Phillimore's Introduction to the Roman Law.
Phil. Law. Phillips' North Carolina Law Reports.
Phil. N. C. Phillips' North Carolina Law Reports.
Phil. Rom. Law. Phillimore's Private Law among the Romans.
Phil. St. Tr. Phillipp's State Trials.
Phila. Philadelphia Reports.
Phillips. Phillips' English Chancery Reports;—Phillips' North Carolina Reports, Law or Equity.
Pick. Pickering's Massachusetts Reports.
Pike. Pike's Reports (1-5 Arkansas).
Pin. (or **Pinn.**) Pinney's Wisconsin Reports.
Piston. Piston's Mauritius Reports.
Pitc. Tr. Pitcairn's Criminal Trials, Scotland.
Pitts. L. J. Pittsburgh Legal Journal.
Pitts. Rep. Pittsburgh (Pennsylvania) Reports.
Pl. (or **Pl. Com.**) Plowden's Commentaries or Reports, English King's Bench, &c.
Pl. C. Placita Coronæ (Pleas of the Crown).
Pl. Par. Placita Parliamentaria.
Plac. Abbrev. Placitorum Abbreviatio.
Plac. Ang. Nor. Bigelow's Placita Anglo-Normanica.
Plac. Gen. Placita Generalia.
Plow. Plowden's English King's Bench Reports.
Pol. Cont. Pollock on Principles of Contract at Law and Equity.
Pol. (or **Pollex.**) Pollexfen's Reports, English King's Bench, &c.;—Police.
Pol. Dig. Part. Pollock's Digest of the Laws of Partnership.
Pollock & Maitl. Pollock and Maitland's History of English Common Law.
Pom. Eq. Juris. Pomeroy's Equity Jurisprudence.
Pop. (or **Poph.**) Popham's English King's Bench Reports.
Poph. (2). Cases at the end of Popham's Reports.
Porter. Porter's Alabama Reports;—Porter's Reports (3-7 Indiana).
Post. Post's Reports (23, 24 Michigan);— Post's Reports (42-44 Missouri).
Poth. Cont. Pothier on Contracts.
Poth. Cont. Sale. Pothier on the Contract of Sale.
Poth. Mar. Cont. Pothier's Treatise on Maritime Contracts.
Poth. Ob. Pothier on the Law of Obligations.
Poth. Œuv. Œuvres de Pothier.
Poth. Part. Pothier on Partnership.
Poth. Proc. Civ. Pothier de la Procédure Civile.
Pott. Corp. Potter on Corporations.
Pott. Dwarris. Potter's Edition of Dwarris on Statutes.
Pr. Price's English Exchequer Reports;— Principium (the beginning of a title, law, or section).
Pr. C. K. B. Practice Cases in the King's Bench.
Pr. Ch. Precedents in Chancery, by Finch; —Practice in the High Court of Chancery.
Pr. Dec. Printed Decisions (Sneed's Kentucky Decisions).
Pr. Div. Probate Division, Law Reports;— Pritchard's Divorce and Matrimonial Cases.
Pr. Exch. Price's English Exchequer Reports.
Pr. & Div. Probate and Divorce, English Law Reports.
Pres. Conv. Preston's Conveyancing.
Pres. Est. Preston on Estates.
Pri. (or **Price**) Price's English Exchequer Reports.
Prickett. Prickett's Reports (Idaho).
Prid. & C. Prideaux & Cole's Reports (English), New Sessions Cases, Vol. 4.
Prin. Dec. Printed Decisions (Sneed's), Kentucky.
Priv. Counc. App. Privy Council Appeals.
Prob. Div. Probate Division, English Law Reports.
Prob. & Adm. Div. Probate and Admiralty Division, Law Reports.
Prob. & Div. Probate and Divorce, English Law Reports.
Prob. & Mat. Probate and Matrimonial Cases.
Pugs. Pugsley's Reports, New Brunswick.
Pugs. & Bur. Pugsley & Burbridge's Reports, New Brunswick.
Pulsifer. Pulsifer's Reports (65-68 Maine).
Purd. Dig. Purdon's Digest of Pennsylvania Laws.
Pyke. Pyke's Lower Canada King's Bench Reports.

Q. Quadragesms (Year Books, Part IV.).
Q. B. Queen's Bench Reports (Adolphus & Ellis, New Series);—English Law Reports, Queen's Bench;—Queen's Bench Reports, Upper Canada;—Queen's Bench Reports, Quebec.
Q. B. Div. Queen's Bench Division, English Law Reports.

Q. B. R. Queen's Bench Reports, by Adolphus & Ellis (New Series).
Q. B. U. C. Queen's Bench Reports, Upper Canada.
Q. L. R. Quebec Law Reports.
Quadr. Quadragesms (Year Books, Part IV.).
Quin. Quincy's Massachusetts Reports.
Quinti, Quinto. Year Book, 5 Henry V.
R. Rawle's Pennsylvania Reports;—Rettie, Crawford, & Melville's (Fourth Series) Scotch Session Cases.
R. C. L. Ruling Case Law.
R. I. Rhode Island Reports.
R. L. & S. Ridgeway, Lapp, & Schoales' Irish King's Bench Reports.
R. L. & W. Robert, Leaming, and Wallis' English County Court Reports.
R. M. Ch. R. M. Charlton's Georgia Reports.
R. *t.* F. (Reports *temp.*) Finch, English Chancery.
R. *t.* H. Reports *temp.* Hardwicke (Lee), English King's Bench;—Reports *temp.* Holt (Cases concerning Settlements).
R. *t.* Q. A. Reports *temp.* Queen Anne (11 Modern).
R. & M. Russell & Mylne's English Chancery Reports;— Ryan & Moody's English Nisi Prius Reports.
Ram F. Ram on Facts.
Rand. Randolph's Virginia Reports;—Randolph's Reports (21-24 Kansas);—Randolph's Reports (7-11 Louisiana Annual).
Raney. Raney's Reports (16 Florida).
Rawle. Rawle's Pennsylvania Reports;—see also Raw., above.
Rawle Pen. & W. (Rawle) Penrose & Watts' Pennsylvania Reports.
Raym. Lord Raymond's English King's Bench Reports.
Raym. Ld. Lord Raymond's English King's Bench Reports.
Raym. Sir T. Sir Thomas Raymond's English King's Bench Reports.
Rec. Dec. Vaux's Recorder's Decisions, Philadelphia.
Red. Redfield's New York Surrogate Reports.
Red. Wills. Redfield on the Law of Wills.
Redf. Redfield's New York Surrogate Reports;—see also Red.
Redington. Redingtons' Reports (31-35 Maine).
Reeve Eng. Law. Reeve's History of the English Law.
Rep. (1, 2, &c.) 1, 2, &c., Coke's English King's Bench Reports.
Rep. Report, or Reports;—Repealed;—Répertoire;—Wallace's "The Reporters";—The Reporter, Boston, Mass.;—The Reporter, Washington and New York.
Rep. Ass. Y. (Clayton's) Reports of Assises at Yorke.
Rep. Cas. Eq. Gilbert's Chancery Reports.
Rep. Cas. Madr. Reports of Cases, Dewanny Adawlut, Madras.
Rep. Cas. Pr. Reports of Cases of Practice (Cooke's).
Rep. Ch. Reports in Chancery, English.
Rep. Ch. Pr. Reports on Chancery Practice.
Rep. Com. Cas. Reports of Commercial Cases, Bengal.
Rep. Const. Ct. Reports of the Constitutional Court, South Carolina (Treadway, Mill, or Harper).
Rep. Eq. Gilbert's English Reports in Equity.
Rep. in Can. Reports in Chancery, English.
Rep. Jur. Repertorium Juridicum.
Rep. Q. A. Reports *temp.* Queen Anne (11 Modern).
Rep. Sel. Cas. Ch. Kelynge's (W.) Reports, English Chancery.
Rep. *t.* Finch. (Reports *temp.*) Finch, English Chancery.
Rep. *t.* Hard. Lee's Reports *temp.* Hardwicke, English King's Bench.
Rep. *t.* Holt. Reports *temp.* Holt (English Cases of Settlement).
Rep. *t.* O. Br. Carter's English Common Pleas Reports *temp.* O. Bridgman.
Rep. *t.* Q. A. Reports *temp.* Queen Anne (11 Modern Reports).
Rep. *t.* Talb. Reports *temp.* Talbot, English Chancery.
Rep. Yorke Ass. Reports of Assises at Yorke (Clayton's Reports).
Reports. Coke's English King's Bench Reports.
Rettie. Rettie, Crawford, & Melville's Scotch Session Cases (4th series).
Reynolds. Reynolds' Reports (40, 41 Mississippi).
Rice. Rice's South Carolina Law Reports.
Rice Eq. (or **Ch.**) Rice's South Carolina Equity Reports.
Rich. Richardson's South Carolina Law Reports;—Richardson's Reports (3-5 New Hampshire).
Rich. Ch. (or **Eq.**) Richardson's South Carolina Equity Reports.
Rich. Eq. (or Ch.) Cas. Richardson's South Carolina Equity Cases.
Rich. N. S. Richardson's Reports, South Carolina, New Series.
Rich. & W. Richardson & Woodbury's Reports (2 New Hampshire).
Ridg. (or **Ridg. *t.* Hard.**, or **Ridg. Cas.**, or **Ridg. & Hard.**) Ridgeway's Reports *temp.* Hardwicke, Chancery and K. B.
Ridg. Ap. (or **P. C.**) Ridgeway's Irish Appeal (or Parliamentary) Cases.
Ridg. L. & S. Ridgeway, Lapp, & Schoales' Irish Term Reports.
Ridg. Rep. (or **St. Tr.**) Ridgeway's (individual) Reports of State Trials in Ireland.
Ril. (or **Riley**). Riley's South Carolina Law Reports.
Ril. (or **Riley**) **Eq.** (or **Ch.**) Riley's South Carolina Chancery Reports.
Rob. Robinson's Virginia Reports; —Robinson's Louisiana Reports;—Robertson's New York Superior Court Reports;—Robertson's English Ecclesiastical Reports;—Chr. Robinson's English Admiralty Reports;—W. Robinson's English Admiralty Reports:—Robinson's Scotch Appeal Cases;—Robertson's Scotch Ap-

peal Cases;—Robinson's Reports (38 California);—Robinson's Reports (1-4 Louisiana Annual);—Roberts' Reports (29-31 Louisiana Annual);—Robards' Reports (12, 13 Missouri);—Robards' Conscript Cases, Texas;—Chr. Robinson's Upper Canada Reports;—J. L. Robinson's Upper Canada Reports;—Robertson's Reports (1 Hawaiian).

Rob. App. Robinson's Scotch Appeal Cases.

Rob. Cas. Robertson's Scotch Appeal Cases.

Rob. Chr. Chr. Robinson's English Admiralty Reports.

Rob. Consc. Cas. Robards' Conscript Cases, Texas (see n. 1, p. 58).

Rob. Jun. William Robinson's English Admiralty Reports.

Rob. L. & W. Roberts, Leaming, & Wallis' County Court Reports.

Rob. La. Robinson's Louisiana Reports.

Rob. S. I. Robertson's Sandwich Islands (Hawaiian) Reports.

Rob. Sc. App. Robinson's Scotch Appeals, English House of Lords.

Rob. Sr. Ct. Robertson's New York Superior Court Reports.

Rob. U. C. Robinson's Reports, Upper Canada.

Rob. Va. Robinson's Virginia Reports.

Rob. Wm. Adm. Wm. Robinson's English Admiralty Reports.

Robards. Robards' Reports (1, 2, and 13 Missouri);—Robards' Texas Conscript Cases.

Robards & Jackson. Robards and Jackson's Reports (26, 27 Texas).

Robb Pat. Cas. Robb's United States Patent Cases.

Roberts. Roberts' Reports (29-31 Louisiana Annual).

Roberts Emp. Liab. Roberts on Federal Liabilities of Carriers.

Robertson. Robertson's Scotch Appeal Cases;—Robertson's New York Superior Court Reports;—Robertson's New York Marine Court Reports;—Robertson's English Ecclesiastical Reports;—Robertson's Hawaiian Reports;—see also Rob., above.

Robin. App. Robinson's Scottish Appeal Cases.

Robinson. Chr. Robinson's English Admiralty Reports;—W. Robinson's English Admiralty Reports;—Robinson's Virginia Reports;—Robinson's Louisiana Reports;—Robinson's Scotch Appeal Cases;—Robinson's Reports (38 California);—Chr. Robinson's Reports, Upper Canada;—J. L. Robinson's Reports, Upper Canada.

Rodman. Rodman's Reports (78 Kentucky).

Rolle. Rolle's English King's Bench Reports.

Rolle Abr. Rolle's Abridgment of the Common Law.

Rolls Ct. Rep. Rolls Court Reports.

Root. Root's Connecticut Reports.

Rose (or **Rose B. C.**) Rose's Reports, English Bankruptcy.

Rot. Cur. Reg. Rotuli Curiae Regis.

Rot. Flor. Rotae Florentinae (Reports of the Supreme Court, or Rota, of Florence).

Rot. Parl. Rotulae Parliamentariae.

Rot. Pat. Rotuli Patentes (Patent Rolls).

Rot. Plac. Rotulus Placitorum (the Plea Roll).

Rowell. Rowell's Reports (45-52 Vermont).

Ruff. (or **Ruff. & H.**) Ruffin's (& Hawks') North Carolina Reports (see n. **11**, p. 47).

Runnell. Runnell's Reports (38, 39 Iowa).

Russ. *t.* Eld. Russell's English Chancery Reports *temp.* Eldon.

Russ. & Ches. Russell & Chesley's Reports, Nova Scotia.

Russ. & Ches. Eq. Russell & Chesley's Equity Reports, Nova Scotia.

Russ. & Geld. Russell & Geldert's Reports, Nova Scotia.

Russ. & M. Russell & Mylne's English Chancery Reports.

Russ. & Ry. Russell & Ryan's English Crown Cases Reserved.

S. Shaw, Dunlop, & Bell's Scotch Court of Session Reports (1st Series);—Shaw's Appeal Cases, House of Lords, Scotland.

S. A. L. R. South Australian Law Reports.

S. App. Shaw's Scotch House of Lords (Appeal) Cases.

S. C. South Carolina Reports, New Series.

S. C. R. South Carolina Reports, New Series;—Harper's South Carolina Reports.

S. Car. South Carolina Reports, New Series.

S. D. South Dakota.

S. D. A. Sudder Dewanny Adawlut Reports, India.

S. D. & B. Shaw, Dunlop, & Bell's Scotch Court of Session Reports (1st Series).

S. D. & B. Sup. Shaw, Dunlop, & Bell's Supplement, containing House of Lords Decisions.

S. E. Southeastern Reporter.

S. F. A. Sudder Foujdaree Adawlut Reports, India.

S. L. C. App. Stuart's Lower Canada Appeal Cases.

S. V. A. R. Stuart's Vice-Admiralty Reports, Quebec.

S. W. Southwestern Reporter.

S. & B. Smith & Batty's Irish King's Bench Reports.

S. & C. Saunders & Cole's English Bail Court Reports.

S. & D. Shaw, Dunlop, & Bell's Scotch Court of Session Reports (1st Series).

S. & L. Schoales & Lefroy's Irish Chancery Reports.

S. & M. Shaw & Maclean's Appeal Cases, House of Lords;—Smedes & Marshall's Mississippi Reports.

S. & M. Chy. Smedes & Marshall's Mississippi Chancery Reports.

S. & R. Sergeant & Rawle's Pennsylvania Reports.

S. & R. Neg. Shearman & Redfield on the Law of Negligence.

S. & S. Sausse & Scully's Irish Rolls Court Reports;—Simons & Stuart, English Vice-Chancellors' Reports.

S. & Sm. Searle & Smith's English Probate and Divorce Reports.

S. & T. Swabey & Tristram's English Probate and Divorce Reports.

Salk. Salkeld's English King's Bench Reports.

Sand. Sandford's New York Superior Court Reports.

Sand. Chy. Sandford's New York Chancery Reports.

Sand. I. Rep. Sandwich Island (Hawaiian) Reports.

Sandf. Sandford's New York Superior Court Reports;—Sandford's Reports (59 Alabama).

Sandf. Ch. Sandford's New York Chancery Reports.

Sau. & Sc. Sausse & Scully's Irish Rolls Court Reports.

Saund. Saunders' English King's Bench Reports.

Saund. & C. Saunders & Cole's English Bail Court Reports.

Saund. & Mac. Saunders & Macrae's English County Court Cases.

Sausse & Sc. Sausse & Scully's Irish Rolls Court Reports.

Sav. Savile's English Common Pleas Reports.

Saw. (or **Sawy.**) Sawyer's United States Circuit Court Reports.

Sax (or **Saxt.**) Saxton's New Jersey Chancery Reports.

Say. Sayer's English King's Bench Reports.

Sc. Scott's Reports, English Common Pleas;—Scammon's Illinois Reports.

Sc. Sess. Cas. Scotch Court of Session Cases.

Sc. & Div. App. Scotch and Divorce Appeals (Law Reports).

Scam. Scammon's Reports (2-5 Illinois).

Sch. Bailm. Schouler on Bailment.

Sch. Dom. Rel. Schouler on Domestic Relations.

Sch. H. & W. Schouler on Husband and Wife.

Sch. Per. Prop. Schouler on the Law of Personal Property.

Sch. & Lef. Schoales & Lefroy's Irish Chancery Reports.

Schalk. Schalk's Jamaica Reports.

Schoul. Schouler (see Sch.).

Sco. Scott's English Common Pleas Reports.

Sco. N. R. Scott's New Reports, English Common Pleas.

Scrib. Dow. Scribner on the Law of Dower.

Searle Sm. Searle & Smith's English Probate and Divorce Reports.

Secd. pt. Edw. III. Part 3 of the Year Books.

Secd. pt. H. VI. Part 8 of the Year Books.

Sedg. Dam. Sedgwick on the Measure of Damage.

Sedg. L. Cas. Sedgwick's Leading Cases on Damages.

Seign. Rep. Seigniorial Reports, Lower Canada.

Sel. Cas. Ch. Select Cases in Chancery (Part 3 of Cases in Chancery).

Sel. Cas. D. A. Select Cases (Sudder), Dewanny Adawlut, India.

Sel. Cas. Ev. Select Cases in Evidence (Strange).

Sel. Cas. N. F. Select Cases, Newfoundland.

Sel. Cas. N. W. P. Selected Cases, Northwest Provinces, India.

Sel. Cas. N. Y. Yates' Select Cases, New York.

Sel. Cas. *t.* Br. (Cooper's) Select Cases *temp.* Brougham.

Sel. Cas. *t.* King. Select Cases in Chancery *temp.* King.

Sel. Cas. *t.* Nap. (Drury's) Select Cases *temp.* Napier, Irish Chancery.

Sel. Cas. with Opin. Select Cases with Opinions, by a Solicitor.

Sel. Dec. Bomb. Selected Decisions, Sudder Dewanny Adawlut, Bombay.

Sel. Dec. Madr. Select Decrees, Sudr Udawlut, Madras.

Sel. N. P. Selwyn's Law of Nisi Prius.

Seld. Selden's Reports (5-10 New York Court of Appeals).

Selw. & Barn. The First part of Barnewall & Alderson's English K. B. Reports.

Serg. & Lowb. Rep. English Common Law Reports, American reprint edited by Sergeant & Lowber.

Serg. & Raw. Sergeant & Rawle's Pennsylvania Reports.

Sess. Cas. Sessions Cases (English King's Bench Reports);—Scotch Court of Session Cases.

Sett. (or **Sett. & Rem.**) **Cas.** English Settlement and Removal Cases (Burrow's Settlement Cases).

Sev. H. C. Sevestre's High Court Reports, Bengal.

Sev. S. D. A. Sevestre's Sudder Dewanny Adawlut Reports, Bengal.

Sh. Shower's English Parliamentary Cases;—Shower's English King's Bench Reports;—Shepley's Reports (13-18 and 21-30 Maine);—Shaw's Scotch Appeal Cases;—Shaw, &c., First Series Scotch Court of Session Cases;—Shaw's Scotch Justiciary Cases;—Shaw's Scotch Teind Court Reports;—G. B. Shaw's Reports (10-11 Vermont);—W. G. Shaw's Reports (30-35 Vermont);—Shirley's Reports (49-55 New Hampshire);—Sheldon's Buffalo (N. Y.) Superior Court Reports;—Shepherd's Reports (19-21, 24-41, 49-51, 60, 63, 64 Alabama);—Shipp's Reports (66, 67 North Carolina);—Shand's Reports (11-14 South Carolina);—Shadforth's Reserved Judgments, Victoria.

Sh. App. Shaw's Scotch Appeal Cases.

Sh. Crim. Cas. Shaw's Criminal Cases (Justiciary Court).

Sh. Jus. Shaw's Justiciary Cases, Scotland.

Sh. W. & C. Shaw, Wilson, & Courtenay's Scotch Appeals Reports (Wilson & Shaw's Reports).

Sh. & Dunl. Shaw & Dunlop's Scotch Court of Session Reports (1st series).

Sh & Macl. Shaw & Maclean's Scotch Appeal Cases.
Shand. Shand's Reports (11-14 South Carolina, N. S.).
Shars. Black. Sharswood's edition of Blackstone's Commentaries.
Shars. Comm. L. Sharswood's Commercial Law.
Shars. Law Lec. Sharswood's Lectures on the Profession of the Law.
Shars. Leg. Eth. Sharswood's Legal Ethics.
Shaw. Shaw, Scotch Appeal Cases;—Shaw, &c., 1st Series Scotch Court of Session Cases;—Shaw's Scotch Justiciary Cases; —Shaw's Scotch Teind Reports;—G. B. Shaw's Reports (10, 11 Vermont);—W. G. Shaw's Reports (30-35 Vermont).
Shaw Dec. Shaw's (&c.) Decisions in the Scotch Court of Session (1st series).
Shaw, Dunl. & B. Shaw, Dunlop, & Bell's (1st Series) Scotch Session Cases.
Shaw (G. B.) G. B. Shaw's Reports (10, 11 Vermont).
Shaw H. L. Shaw's Scotch Appeal Cases, House of Lords.
Shaw Jus. Shaw's (John) Scotch Justiciary Cases.
Shaw T. Cas. Shaw's Scotch Teind Cases.
Shaw (W. G.) W. G. Shaw's Reports (30-35 Vermont).
Shearm. & Red. Neg. Shearman & Redfield on Negligence.
Sheld. Sheldon's Reports, Superior Court of Buffalo, N. Y.
Shep. Shepley's Reports (13-18 and 21-30 Maine);—Shepherd's Reports (19-21, 24-41, 60, 63, 64 Alabama).
Shepherd. Shepherd's Reports (19-21, 24-41, 60, 63, 64 Alabama).
Shepley. Shepley's Reports (13-18 and 21-30 Maine).
Shipp. Shipp's Reports (66, 67 North Carolina).
Shirley. Shirley's Reports (49-55 New Hampshire).
Show. Shower's Parliamentary Cases;—Shower's K. B. Reports.
Show. K. B. Shower's English King's Bench Reports.
Show. P. C. Shower's English Parliamentary Cases.
Sick. Sickles' Reports (46-85 New York Court of Appeals).
Sid. Siderfin's English King's Bench Reports.
Sim. Simons' English Vice-Chancery Reports.
Sim. N. S. Simons' English Vice-Chancery Reports, New Series.
Sim. & Stu. (or **Sim. & S.**) Simons & Stuart's English Vice-Chancery Reports.
Sinclair. Sinclair's Manuscript Decisions, Scotch Session Cases.
Skin. Skinner's English King's Bench Reports.
Skinker. Skinker's Reports (65-72 Missouri).
Slade. Slade's Reports (15 Vermont).
Sm. & Bat. Smith & Batty's Irish King's Bench Reports.
Sm. & G. Smale & Giffard's English Vice-Chancery Reports.
Sm. & M. Smedes & Marshall's Mississippi Reports.
Sm. & M. Ch. Smedes & Marshall's Mississippi Chancery Reports.
Sma. & Giff. Smale & Giffard's English Vice-Chancellors' Reports.
Smed. & M. Smedes & Marshall's Mississippi Reports.
Smed. & M. Ch. Smedes & Marshall's Mississippi Chancery Reports.
Smi. & Bat. Smith & Batty's Irish King's Bench Reports.
Smith. Smith's New Hampshire Reports; —J. P. Smith's English King's Bench Reports;—P. F. Smith's Pennsylvania State Reports;—E. P. Smith's Reports (15-27 New York Court of Appeals);—E. D. Smith's New York Common Pleas Reports;—Smith's Reports (54, 55 California);—Smith's Reports, Indiana;—Smith's Reports (61-64 Maine);—Smith's Reports (1-11 Wisconsin);—Smith's volume of Heiskell's Tennessee Reports;—see also Sm.
Smith C. P. (or **E. D.**) E. D. Smith's Common Pleas Reports, New York.
Smith, E. P. (or **Ct. App.**) E. P. Smith's Reports (15-27 New York Court of Appeals).
Smith Ind. Smith's Indiana Reports.
Smith, J. P. J. P. Smith's English King's Bench Reports.
Smith Lead. Cas. Smith's Leading Cases.
Smith Me. Smith's Reports (61-64 Maine).
Smith N. H. Smith's New Hampshire Reports.
Smith N. Y. Smith's Reports (15-27 New York Court of Appeals).
Smith, P. F. (or **Pa.**) P. F. Smith's Pennsylvania State Reports.
Smith Wis. Smith's Reports (1-11 Wisconsin).
Smith & B. R. R. C. Smith & Bates' American Railway Cases.
Smith & Bat. Smith & Batty's Irish King's Bench Reports.
Smoult. Notes of Cases in Smoult's Collection of Orders, Calcutta.
Smy. Smythe's Irish Common Pleas Reports.
Sneed. Sneed's Tennessee Reports;—Sneed's Kentucky Decisions.
Sneed Dec. Sneed's Kentucky Decisions.
So. Southern Reporter.
So. Aus. L. R. South Australia Law Reports.
So. Car. South Carolina;—South Carolina Reports.
So. Car. Const. South Carolina Constitutional Reports (by Treadway, by Mill, or by Harper).
South Aus. L. R. South Australia Law Reports.
Southard. Southard's New Jersey Reports.
Sp. Spinks' English Ecclesiastical and Admiralty Reports;—Spear's South Carolina Law Reports.

Sp. Eq. (or **Ch.**) Spear's South Carolina Equity Reports.
Sp. Glos. Spelman's Glossary.
Sp. Laws. Spirit of the Laws, Montesquieu.
Sp. Pr. Cas. Spinks' Prize Cases.
Sparks. Sparks' Reports, British Burmah.
Spaulding. Spaulding's Reports (71-73 Maine).
Spear (or **Speer**) Spear's (or Speer's) South Carolina Law Reports.
Spear (or **Speer**) **Eq.** Spear's (or Speer's) South Carolina Equity Reports.
Spel. Feuds. Spelman on Feuds.
Spel. Gl. Spelman's Glossary.
Spel. L. T. Spelman's Law Tracts.
Spel. Rep. Spelman's Reports, Manuscript English King's Bench.
Spencer. Spencer's New Jersey Reports;—Spencer's Reports (10-20 Minnesota).
Spinks. Spinks' English Ecclesiastical and Admiralty Reports.
Spinks P. C. Spinks' English Prize Cases.
Spooner. Spooner's Reports (12-15 Wisconsin).
Spottis. Sir R. Spottiswoode's Reports, Scotch Court of Session.
Spottis. C. L. & Eq. Rep. Common Law & Equity Reports, published by Spottiswoode.
Spr. Sprague's United States District Court (Admiralty) Decisions.
St. Story's United States Circuit Court Reports (see Sto.);—Stair's Scotch Court of Session Reports;—Stuart (Milne & Peddie), Scotch Session Cases.
St. M. & P. Stuart, Milne, & Peddie's Scotch Session Cases.
St. Tr. The State Trials (English).
Stair. Stair's Reports, Scotch Court of Sessions.
Stanton. Stanton's Reports (11-13 Ohio).
Star. Starkie's English Nisi Prius Reports;—see also Stark.
Stark. Starkie's English Nisi Prius Reports.
Stark. C. L. Starkie's Criminal Law.
Stark. Cr. Pl. Starkie's Criminal Pleading.
Stark. Ev. Starkie on Evidence.
Stark. Jury Tr. Starkie on Trial by Jury.
Stark. Lib. Starkie on Libel.
Stark. N. P. Starkie's English Nisi Prius Reports.
Stark. Sl. & L. Starkie on Slander & Libel.
Stat. Glo. Statute of Gloucester.
Stat. Marl. Statute of Marlbridge.
Stat. Mert. Statute of Merton.
Stat. Mod. Lev. Fin. Statute Modus Levandi Fines.
Stat. Westm. Statute of Westminster.
Stat. Winch. Statute of Winchester.
State Tr. The State Trials, English.
Steph. Com. Stephen's Commentaries on the Laws of England.
Steph. Const. Stephens on the English Constitution.
Steph. Cr. L. Stephen's General View of the Criminal Law.
Steph. Dig. Stephen's Digest, New Brunswick Reports.
Steph. Dig. Cr. L. Stephen's Digest of the Criminal Law.
Steph. Dig. Ev. Stephen's Digest of the Law of Evidence.
Steph. N. P. Stephen's Law of Nisi Pruis.
Steph. Pl. Stephen on Pleading.
Stew. Stewart's Alabama Reports;—Stewart's N. J. Equity Reports.
Stew. Adm. (or **V. A.**) Stewart's Vice-Admiralty Reports, Nova Scotia.
Stew. Eq. Stewart's Reports (28-33 New Jersey Equity).
Stew. & P. Stewart & Porter's Alabama Reports.
Stiles. Stiles' Reports (22-29 Iowa).
Sto. Story's United States Circuit Court Reports.
Sto. Ag. Story on Agency.
Sto. Bailm. Story on Bailment.
Sto. Bills. Story on Bills.
Sto. C. C. Story's United States Circuit Court Reports.
Sto. Comm. Story's Commentaries.
Sto. Con. Story on Contracts.
Sto. Conf. Law. Story on Conflict of Laws.
Sto. Const. Story on the United States Constitution.
Sto. Const. Cl. B. Story's Constitutional Class Book.
Sto. Cont. Story on Contracts.
Sto. Eq. Jur. Story on Equity Jurisprudence.
Sto. Eq. Pl. Story on Equity Pleadings.
Sto. Part. Story on Partnership.
Sto. Pl. Story's Civil Pleading.
Sto. Sales. Story on Sales of Personal Property.
Stock. Stockton's New Jersey Equity Reports.
Stockett. Stockett's Reports (27-53 Maryland).
Stockt. Ch. Stockton's New Jersey Chancery Reports.
Str. Strange's English King's Bench Reports.
Stra. Cas. Ev. (or **Str. 8vo.**) Strange's Cases of Evidence ("Octavo Strange").
Stra. Strange (see Str.).
Stringfellow. Stringfellow's Reports (9-11 Missouri).
Strob. Strobhart's South Carolina Law Reports.
Strob. Eq. (or **Ch.**) Strobhart's South Carolina Equity Reports.
Stu. Adm. (or **V. A**) Stuart's Vice-Admiralty Reports, Lower Canada.
Stu. Ap. Stuart's Appeal Cases (Lower Canada King's Bench Reports).
Stu. K. B. (or **L. C.**) Stuart's Lower Canada Reports.
Stu. Mil. & Ped. Stuart, Milne, & Peddie's Scotch Court of Session Reports.
Stuart. Stuart's Lower Canada Reports;—Stuart's Vice-Admiralty Reports;—Stuart, Milne, & Peddie's Scotch Session Cases.
Sty. Style's English King's Bench Reports.
Sug. Est. Sugden on the Law of Estates.
Sug. Hd. Bk. Sugden's Hand-Book of Property Law.
Sug. Pow. Sugden on Powers.

Sug. Pr. Sugden on the Law of Property.
Sug. Pr. St. Sugden on Property Statutes.
Sug. Vend. Sugden on Vendors and Purchasers.
Sugd. Sugden (see Sug.).
Sum. *Sumner's United States Circuit Court* Reports.
Sumn. Sumner's United States Circuit Court Reports.
***Sumn.* Ves.** (or ***Sum.* Ves.**) Sumner's edition of Vesey's Reports.
Sup. Ct. Supreme Court Reporter.
Supp. Ves. Jun. Supplement to Vesey, Jr.'s, Reports.
Suth. Sutherland's Reports.
Suth. Dam. Sutherland's Damages.
Suth. F. B. R. Sutherland's Full Bench Rulings, Bengal.
Suth. P. C. J. (or **A.**) Sutherland's Privy Council Judgments (or Appeals).
Suth. Stat. Const. Sutherland's Statutory Construction.
Sw. Swanston's English Chancery Reports;—Swabey's English Admiralty Reports;—Sweeney's New York Superior Court Reports;—Swan's Tennessee Reports;—Swinton's Scotch Justiciary Cases.
Sw. (or **Swab.**) **& Tr.** Swabey & Tristram's English Probate and Divorce Reports.
Swab. Swabey's English Admiralty Reports.
Swan. Swan's Tennessee Reports;—Swanston's English Chancery Reports.
Swan. Ch. *Swanston's English* Chancery Reports.
Swans. (or **Swanst.**) Swanston's English Chancery Reports.
Sween. *Sweeney's New York Superior* Court Reports.

T. B. Mon. T. B. Monroe's Kentucky Re*ports.*
T. Jones (or **2 Jones**) T. Jones' English King's Bench Reports.
T. L. Termes de la Ley.
T. R. *Term Reports (Durnford & East)*;—Teste Rege.
T. R. N. S. Term Reports New Series (East's Reports).
T. R. (N. Y.) Caines' (Term) Reports, New York.
T. Raym. Sir T. Raymond's English King's Bench Reports.
T. U. P. Charlt. T. U. P. Charlton's Reports, Georgia.
T. & C. Thompson & Cook's New York Supreme Court Reports.
T. & G. Tyrwhitt & Granger's English Exchequer Reports.
T. & M. Temple & Mew's Crown Cases, English.
T. & P. Turner & Phillips' Reports, English Chancery.
T. & R. Turner & Russell's English Chancery Reports.
Tal. (or **Talb.**) Cases *tempore* Talbot, English Chancery.
Tan. Taney's United States Circuit Court Reports.
Tanner. Tanner's Reports (8-14 Indiana).
Tap. Tappan's *Ohio Reports.*
Taun. (or **Taunt.**) Taunton's English Common Pleas Reports.
Tay. (J. L.) J. L. Taylor's North Carolina *Reports.*
Tay. L. & T. Taylor's Landlord and Tenant.
Tay. N. C. Taylor's North Carolina Reports.
Tay. U. C. Taylor's Upper Canada Reports.
Tay. & B. Taylor & Bell's Bengal Reports.
Taylor. Taylor's North Carolina Reports;—*Taylor's Upper* Canada *Reports*;—Taylor's Bengal Reports.
Temp. Geo. II. Cases in Chancery *tempore* George II.
Temp. & M. *Temple & Mew's English* Crown Cases.
Tenn. Tennessee Reports (Overton's).
Tenn. Ch. Cooper's Tennessee Chancery *Reports.*
Term. Term Reports, King's Bench (Durnford & East's Reports).
Term N. C. Term Reports, North Carolina, by Taylor.
Term. de la L. Les Termes de la Ley.
Terr. Terrell's Reports (52 Texas).
Terr. & Walk. Terrell & Walker's Reports (38-51 Texas).
Tex. Texas Reports.
Tex. App. Texas Court of Appeals Reports
Tex. Civ. App. Texas Court of Civil Appeals.
Tex. Cr. Texas Criminal Court.
Tex. Cr. App. Texas Criminal Court of Appeals.
Tex. Supp. Texas Supplement.
Th. & C. Thompson & Cook's New York Supreme Court Reports.
Theo. Wills. Theobald on Wills.
Thes. Brev. Thesaurus Brevium.
Thom. Thomson's Reports, Nova Scotia.
Thom. Dec. 1 Thomson, Nova Scotia Reports.
Thom. Rep. 2 Thomson, Nova Scotia Reports.
Thom. & Fr. Thomas & Franklin's Reports (1 Maryland Chancery).
Thomas. Thomas' Reports, Wyoming Territory.
Thomp. Cal. Thompson's Reports (39, 40 California).
Thomp. Neg. Thompson on Negligence.
Thomp. Tenn. Cas. Thompson's "Unreported" Tennessee Cases.
Thomp. & C. Thompson & Cook's New York Supreme Court Reports.
Thompson. Thompson's Reports (39, 40 California).
Thomson. Thomson's Nova Scotia Reports.
Tichb. Tr. Report of the Tichborne Trial, London.
Tidd App. Appendix to Tidd's Practice.
Tidd Pr. Tidd's Practice.
Tiffany. Tiffany's Reports (28-39 New York Court of Appeals).
Tiffany Landl. & T. Tiffany on Landlord and Tenant.

Tiffany Real Prop. Tiffany on Real Property.
Tobey. Tobey's Reports (9, 10 Rhode Island).
Tot. (or **Toth.**) Tothill's English Chancery *Reports.*
Touch. Sheppard's Touchstone.
Town. Sl. & Lib. Townshend on Slander and Libel.
Town. St. Tr. Townsend's Modern State Trials.
Tr. App. New York Transcript Appeals.
Tr. Ch. Transactions of the High Court of Chancery (Tothill's Reports).
Trans. App. Transcript Appeals, New York.
Tread. Treadway's South Carolina Constitutional Reports.
Tristram. Tristram's Supplement to 4 Swabey & Tristram.
Tuck. Tucker's New York Surrogate Reports;—Tucker's Select Cases, Newfoundland.
Tud. Cas. Merc. Law. Tudor's Leading Cases on Mercantile Law.
Tud. Cas. R. P. Tudor's Leading Cases on Real Property.
Tupper. Tupper's Reports, Ontario Appeals;—Tupper's Upper Canada Practice Reports.
Tur. (or **Turn.**) **& Rus.** Turner & Russell's English Chancery Reports.
Turner. Turner's Reports (35 Arkansas).
Tuttle. Tuttle's Reports (23-32 and 41-51 California).
Tuttle & Carpenter. Tuttle & Carpenter's Reports (52 California).
Tyler. Tyler's Vermont Reports.
Tyng. Tyng's Reports (2-17 Massachusetts).
Tyr. (or **Tyrw.**) Tyrwhitt's English Exchequer Reports.
Tyr. & Gr. Tyrwhitt & Granger's English Exchequer Reports.

U. Utah;—Utah Reports.
U. B. Pr. Upper Bench Precedents *temp.* Car. I.
U. C. C. P. Upper Canada Common Pleas Reports.
U. C. Ch. Upper Canada Chancery Reports.
U. C. Cham. Upper Canada Chambers Reports.
U. C. E. & A. Upper Canada Error and Appeal Reports.
U. C. K. B. Upper Canada King's Bench Reports, Old Series.
U. C. L. J. Upper Canada Law Journal, Toronto.
U. C. O. S. Upper Canada King's Bench Reports, Old Series.
U. C. Pr. (or **P. R.**) Upper Canada Practice Reports.
U. C. Q. B. Upper Canada Queen's Bench Reports.
U. C. Q. B. O. S. Upper Canada Queen's (King's) Bench Reports, Old Series.
U. S. United States;—United States Reports.
U. S. App. United States Appeals.
U. S. Ct. Cl. Reports of the United States *Court of Claims.*
U. S. E. Encyclopedia of United States Reports.
U. S. R. S. United States Revised Statutes.
U. S. Stat. *United States Statutes at Large.*
U. S. Sup. Ct. United States Supreme Court Reporter.
Ulp. Ulpiani Fragmenta.
Und. Torts. *Underhill on Torts.*
Und. Tr. Underhill on Trusts and Trustees.
Up. Ben. Pr. Upper Bench Precedents, *temp.* Car. I.
Utah. Utah Reports.

V. L. R. Victorian Law Reports, Australia.
V. & B. Vesey & Beames' English Chancery Reports.
V. & S. Vernon & Scriven's Irish King's Bench Reports.
Va. Virginia Reports;—Gilmer's Virginia Reports.
Va. Cas. Virginia Cases (by Brockenbrough & Holmes).
Va. R. Virginia Reports;—Gilmer's Virginia Reports.
Vanderstr. Vanderstraaten's Ceylon Reports.
Van K. Van Koughnet's Reports (15-21 Upper Canada C. P.).
Vatt. Vattel's Law of Nations.
Vaug. (or **Vaugh.**) Vaughan's English Common Pleas Reports.
Vaux. Vaux's Recorder's Decisions, Philadelphia.
Ve. (or **Vea.**) Vesey (see Ves.).
Ve. (or **Vea.**) **& B.** Vesey & Beames' English Chancery Reports.
Veazey. Veazey's Reports (36-46 Vermont).
Vent. Ventris' English Common Pleas Reports.
Ver. (or **Verm.**) Vermont Reports.
Vern. Vernon's English Chancery Reports.
Vern. & Scr. Vernon & Scriven's Irish King's Bench Reports.
Ves. Vesey, Senior's, English Chancery Reports.
Ves. Jr. Vesey, Junior's, English Chancery Reports.
Ves. Jun. Supp. Supplement to Vesey, Jr.'s, Reports, by Hovenden.
Ves. Sen. Vesey, Senior's, Chancery Reports.
Ves. & Bea. Vesey & Beames' English Chancery Reports.
Vez. Vezey's (Vesey's) English Chancery Reports (see Ves.).
Vict. L. R. Victorian Law Reports, Australia.
Vict. Rep. Victorian Reports.
Vil. & Br. Vilas & Bryant's edition of the Wisconsin Reports.
Vin. Abr. Viner's Abridgment.
Vin. Supp. Supplement to Viner's Abridgment.
Virgin. Virgin's Reports (52-60 Maine);—Virginia (see Va.).
Von H. Const. Hist. Von Holst's Constitutional History of the United States.

Von Ihr. Str. for L. Von Ihring's Struggle for Law.
Vr. Vroom's New Jersey Reports.
Vt. Vermont;—Vermont Reports.

W. Wheaton's United States Supreme Court Reports;—Wendell's New York Reports;—Watts' Reports, Pennsylvania;—Statute of Westminster.
W. Bl. Sir William Blackstone's English King's Bench Reports.
W. C. & Ins. Rep. Workmen's Compensation and Insurance Reports.
W. C. C. Washington's United States Circuit Court Reports.
W. H. & G. Welsby, Hurlstone, & Gordon's English Exchequer Reports.
W. Jo. Sir William Jones' English King's Bench Reports.
W. Kel. William Kelynge's English Chancery Reports.
W. N. Weekly Notes, London.
W. N. Cas. Weekly Notes of Cases, Philadelphia.
W. P. Cas. Wollaston's English Bail Court (Practice) Cases.
W. R. Weekly Reporter, London;—Weekly Reporter, Bengal;—Wendell's Reports;—Wisconsin Reports;—West's Reports (English Chancery).
W. Rep. West's Reports *temp.* Hardwicke, English Chancery.
W. Rob. W. Robinson's English Admiralty Reports.
W. Va. West Virginia Reports.
W. W. & D. Willmore, Wollaston, & Davison's English Q. B. Reports.
W. W. & H. Willmore, Wollaston, & Hodges' English Q. B. Reports.
W. & M. Woodbury & Minot's United States Circuit Court Reports;—William & Mary.
W. & S. Watts & Sergeant's Pennsylvania Reports;—Wilson & Shaw's Scotch Appeal Cases.
W. & T. Eq. Ca. (or **L. C.**) White & Tudor's Leading Cases in Equity.
Wait Act. & Def. Wait's Actions and Defences.
Walk. Ch. Walker's Michigan Chancery Reports.
Walk. Mich. Walker's Michigan Chancery Reports.
Walk. Miss. Walker's Mississippi Reports.
Walker. Walker's Mississippi Reports;—Walker's Michigan Chancery Reports;—Walker's Reports (25 Texas).
Wall. Wallace's United States Supreme Court Reports;—Wallace (Senior), United States Circuit Court Reports;—(Wallace's) Philadelphia Reports;—Wallis, Irish Chancery Reports.
Wall. Jr. Wallace's (J. W.) United States Circuit Court Reports.
Wall. Rep. Wallace on The Reporters;—Wallace's United States Supreme Court Reports.
Wall. S. C. Wallace's United States Superior Court Reports
Wall. Sen. Wallace's (J. B.) United States Circuit Court Reports.
Wallis by L. Wallis' Irish Chancery Reports, by Lyne.
Walp. Rub. Walpole's Rubric of Common Law.
Warden. Warden's Reports (2, 4 Ohio State).
Warden & Smith. Warden & Smith's Reports (3 Ohio State).
Ware. Ware's United States District Court Reports.
Warv. Abst. Warvelle's Abstracts.
Warv. El. R. P. Warvelle's Elements of Real Property.
Warv. V. & P. Warvelle's Vendors and Purchasers of Real Property.
Wash. Washington Reports;—Washington's United States Circuit Court Reports;—Washington's Virginia Reports;—Washburn on Real Property;—Washburn's Reports (16-23 Vermont).
Wash. C. C. Washington's United States Circuit Court Reports.
Wash. Cr. L. Washburn on Criminal Law
Wash. R. P. Washburn on Real Property.
Wash. Ter. Washington Territory Reports.
Wash. Va. Washington's Virginia Reports.
Washburn. Washburn's Reports (16-23 Vermont).
Wat. C. G. H. Watermeyer's Cape of Good Hope Reports.
Watermeyer. Watermeyer's Cape of Good Hope Reports.
Watk. Con. Watkins on Conveyancing.
Watk. Cop. Watkins on Copyholds.
Watk. Des. Watkins on Descents.
Watts. Watts' Penn. Reports;—Watts' Reports (16, 17 West Virginia).
Watts & Serg. Watts & Sergeant's Pennsylvania Reports.
We. West's English House of Lords Cases;—West's Chancery Reports.
Webb. Webb's Reports (6-20 Kansas).
Webb, A'B. & W. Webb, A'Beckett, & Williams' Victorian Reports, Australia.
Webb, A'B. & W. Eq. Webb, A'Beckett, & Williams' Equity Reports, Victoria.
Webb, A'B. & W. I. P. & M. Webb, A'Beckett, & Williams' Insolvency, Probate, and Matrimonial Reports, Victoria.
Webb, A'B. & W. Min. Webb, A'Beckett, & Williams' Mining Cases, Victoria.
Webb & Duval. Webb & Duval's Reports (1-3 Texas).
Wells Res. Ad. Wells' Res Adjudicata and Stare Decisis.
Welsb. H. & G. Welsby, Hurlstone & Gordon, English Exchequer Reports.
Welsh. Welsh's Registry Cases, Ireland;—Welsh's Irish Cases at Sligo, 1838;—Welsh's (Irish) Case of James Feighny, 1838.
Wend. Wendell's New York Reports.
West. West's Reports, English House of Lords;—West's Reports, English Chancery;—Western's Tithe Cases;—Weston's Reports (11-14 Vermont).
West Chy. West's English Chancery Reports.

West t. H. West's English Chancery Reports *temp.* Hardwicke.
West H. L. West's Reports, English House of Lords.
West Va. West Virginia Reports.
Westm. Statute of Westminster.
Weston. Weston's Reports (12-14 Vermont).
Wh. Wheaton's United States Supreme Court Reports;—Wheaton's International Law;—Wharton's Pennsylvania Reports;—Wheeler's New York Criminal Reports.
Wh. Cr. Cas. Wheeler's New York Criminal Cases.
Wh. & T. L. C. White & Tudor's Leading Cases in Equity.
Whar. Wharton's Pennsylvania Reports.
Whar. Ag. Wharton on Agency.
Whar. Am. Cr. L. Wharton's American Criminal Law.
Whar. Con. Law. Wharton's Conflict of Laws.
Whar. Cr. Ev. Wharton on Criminal Evidence.
Whar. Cr. Law. Wharton's American Criminal Law.
Whar. Cri. Pl. Wharton's Criminal Pleading and Practice.
Whar. Hom. Wharton's Law of Homicide.
Whar. Neg. Wharton's Law of Negligence.
Whar. St. Tr. Wharton's United States State Trials.
Whar. & St. Med. Jur. Wharton & Stillé's Medical Jurisprudence.
Whart. Wharton (see Whar.).
Wheat. Wheaton's United States Supreme Court Reports.
Wheat. Int. Law. Wheaton's International Law.
Wheel. Wheeler's New York Criminal Cases;—Wheelock's Reports (32-37) Texas).
Wheel. Cr. C. Wheeler's New York Criminal Cases.
Wheel. Cr. Rec. Wheeler's Criminal Recorder, New York (1 Wheeler's Criminal Cases).
White. White's Reports (10-15 West Virginia).
White & T. L. Cas. White & Tudor's Leading Cases in Equity.
Whittlesey. Whittlesey's Reports (32-41 Missouri).
Wigm. Ev. Wigmore on Evidence.
Wight. (or **Wightw.**) Wightwick's English Exchequer Reports.
Wilc. Cond. Rep. Wilcox's Condensed Reports, Ohio.
Wilcox. Wilcox's Reports (10 Ohio).
Wilk. & Ow. Wilkinson, Owen, Patterson, & Murray's "New South Wales Reports."
Will. Willes' English Common Pleas Reports.
Will. Mass. Williams' Reports (1 Massachusetts).
Will. Woll. & Dav. Willmore, Wollaston, & Davison's English Q. B. Reports.
Will. Woll. & Hodg. Willmore, Wollaston, & Hodges' English Q. B. Reports.
Will. Vt. Williams' Reports (27-29 Vermont).
Willes. Willes' English Common Pleas Reports.
Williams. Williams' (Peere) English Chancery Reports;—Williams' Reports 27-29 Vermont);—Williams' Reports (1 Mass.).
Williams P. Peere Williams' English Chancery Reports.
Williston. Williston on Contracts;—Williston on Sales.
Willm. W. & D. Willmore, Wollaston, & Davison's English Q. B. Reports.
Willm. W. & H. Willmore, Wollaston, & Hodges' English Q. B. Reports.
Wils. Wilson's English Common Pleas Reports.
Wils. Ch. Wilson's English Chancery Reports.
Wils. Ent. Wilson's Entries and Pleadings (same as 3 Lord Raymond).
Wils. Exch. Wilson's English Exchequer Reports.
Wils. (Ind.) Wilson's Indiana Superior Court Reports.
Wils. & Court. Wilson & Courtenay's Scotch Appeals Cases (see Wilson & Shaw).
Wils. & Sh. Wilson & Shaw's Scotch Appeals Cases.
Wilson. Wilson's English Common Pleas Reports;—Wilson's English Chancery Reports;—Wilson's English Exchequer Equity Reports;—Wilson's Indiana Superior Court Reports;—Wilson's Reports (1, 2 Oregon).
Win. Winston's Law Reports, North Carolina;—Winch's English Common Pleas Reports.
Win. Eq. Winston's Equity Reports, North Carolina.
Winch. Winch's English Common Pleas Reports.
Winst. Winston's Law or Equity Reports, North Carolina.
Wis. Wisconsin Reports.
Wisb. Laws of Wisbuy.
Withrow. Withrow's Reports (9-21 Iowa).
Wm. Bl. William Blackstone's English King's Bench Reports.
Wm. Rob. William Robinson's English Admiralty Reports.
Wms. Mass. Williams' Reports (1 Massachusetts).
Wms. Vt. Williams' Reports (27-29 Vermont).
Wol. Wollaston's English Bail Court Reports.
Wolf. & B. Wolferstan & Bristow's English Election Cases.
Wolf. & D. Wolferstan & Dew's English Election Cases.
Woll. (or **Woll. P. C.**) Wollaston's English Bail Court Reports (Practice Cases).
Wood. Woods' United States Circuit Court Reports;—Wood's English Tithe Cases.
Wood Land. & T. Wood on Landlord and Tenant.

Wood. & M. (or **Woodb. & M.**) Woodbury & Minot's United States Circuit Court Reports.
Woods (or **Woods C. C.**) Woods' United States Circuit Court Reports.
Woolw. Woolworth's United States Circuit Court Reports;—Woolworth's Reports (1 Nebraska).
Wright. Wright's Reports (37-50 Pennsylvania State);—Wright's Ohio Reports.
Wy. Wyoming Reports;—Wythe's Virginia Chancery Reports.
Wy. Dick. Wyatt's Dickens' Chancery Reports.
Wyatt, W. & A'B. Wyatt, Webb, & A'Beckett's Reports, Victoria.
Wyatt, W. & A'B. Eq. Wyatt, Webb & A'Beckett's Equity Reports, Victoria.
Wyatt, W. & A'B. I. P. & M. Wyatt, Webb, & A'Beckett's Insolvency, Probate, and Matrimonial Reports, Victoria.
Wyatt, W. & A'B Ew. Wyatt, Webb & A'Beckett's Equity Reports, Victoria.
Wyatt & Webb. Wyatt & Webb's Reports, Victoria.
Wyatt & W. Eq. Wyatt & Webb's Equity Reports, Victoria.
Wyatt & W. I. P. & M. Wyatt & Webb's Insolvency, Probate, and Matrimonial Reports, Victoria.
Wyatt & W. Min. Wyatt & Webb's Mining Cases, Victoria.
Wyman. Wyman's Reports, India.
Wythe. Wythe's Virginia Chancery Reports.

X. 1, 9, 6, 4. Book I., Title 9, Chapter 6, Paragraph 4, of the Decretals of Pope Gregory 9.

Y. Yeates' Pennsylvania Reports.
Y. B. Year Books, English King's Bench, &c.
Part 1 cited as 1[1] E. 2. Reports in the reign of Edward II. Maynard's Edward II. Parts 2, 3, 4 cited as 1 E. 3. Reports in the reign of Edward III. (3 parts). First part of Edw. III. Second part of Edw. III. Third part of Edw. III. (or Quadragesms). Part 5 cited as 1 Ass. Book of Assizes in the reign of Edward III. Liber Assissorum. Part 6 cited as 1 H. 4, 1 H. 5. Reports in the reigns of Henry IV. and V. Year Book of H. IV. Parts 7 and 8 cited as 1 H. 6. Reports in the reign of Henry VI. (2 vols.). First part of H. VI. Second part of H. VI. Part 9 cited as 1 E. 4. Reports in the reign of Edward IV. Year Book of Edw. IV. Part 10 cited as 5 E. 4. Reports in the 5th year of Edward IV. Longo Quinto. Part 11 cited as 1 E. 5, 1 R. 3, 1 H. 7, 1 H. 8. Reports in the reigns of Edward V., Richard III, and Henry VII. and VIII. Year Books of Edw. V., Richard III, Henry VII and Henry VIII.
Y. B. Ed. I. Year Books of Edward I.
Y. B. S. C. Year Book, Selected Cases, 1.
Y. & C. Younge & Collyer's English Chancery Reports.
Y. & J. Younge & Jervis' English Exchequer Reports.
Yale L. J. Yale Law Journal.
Yates Sel. Cas. Yates' New York Select Cases.
Yea. (or **Yeates**) Yeates Pennsylvania Reports.
Yel. (or **Yelv.**) Yelverton's English King's Bench Reports.
Yerg. Yerger's Tennessee Reports.
Yorke Ass. Clayton's Reports (Yorke Assises).
You. Younge's English Exchequer Equity Reports.
You. & Coll. Ch. Younge & Collyer's English Chancery Reports.
You. & Coll. Ex. Younge & Collyer's English Exchequer Equity Reports.
You. & Jerv. Younge & Jervis' English Exchequer Reports.
Young. Young's Reports (21-26 Minnesota).
Young Adm. Young's Nova Scotia Admiralty Cases.
Younge. Younge's English Exchequer Equity Reports.
Younge & Coll. Ch. Younge & Collyer's English Chancery Cases.
Younge & Coll. Ex. Younge & Collyer's English Exchequer Equity Reports.
Younge & Jerv. Younge & Jervis' English Exchequer Reports.

Zab. Zabriskie's New Jersey Reports.

[1] Or the number denoting the year of the reign in which the case was reported.

www.ingramcontent.com/pod-product-compliance
Lightning Source LLC
LaVergne TN
LVHW081055220926
848484LV00022B/2507